Random House
FRENCH-ENGLISH
ENGLISH-FRENCH
DICTIONARY

English–French
Dictionary

Random House
FRENCH-ENGLISH
ENGLISH-FRENCH
DICTIONARY

Hélène Gutman

BALLANTINE BOOKS • NEW YORK

http://www.randomhouse.com

Library of Congress Catalog Card Number: 97-93537

ISBN 0-345-41438-1

Manufactured in the United States of America

First Ballantine Books Edition: August 1997

10 9 8 7 6 5 4 3 2

Explanatory Notes

In both sections of the dictionary, all terms (including geographical and other proper nouns) are entered in a single A to Z alphabetical listing.

Many main entries contain phrases and expressions that appear as boldface subentries. If a main entry term is repeated in a subentry in exactly the same form, it is replaced by a long boldface dash. For instance, at the main entry **abaisser** the user will find the phrase **-la voix**, which stands for **abaisser la voix.**

In the translations given after a main entry, nearly synonymous terms are separated by a comma, whereas terms different in meaning are separated by a semicolon. For instance, at the main entry **chambarder,** the translations are: to turn upside down, to upset; to clear out, to throw out.

The feminine forms of French adjectives are shown at the main entry, following the masculine form: **heureux, euse** *adj.* If a feminine form is unchanged from the masculine, only one form is shown: **atomique** *adj.* If a masculine French noun can be used in the feminine gender, the feminine form is shown at the main entry, the gender to be chosen depending on the gender of the person or animal in question: **chien, ne** *n.m.f.* Common feminine nouns have their own main entry, such as **actrice.** The plural forms of certain French nouns are also shown at the main entry: **cheval** *n.m., pl. chevaux.*

In written French, capital letters do not usually show an accent: (capitalized) Etats-Unis versus (lowercase) état.

If an English word is translated as a French phrase, the gender indication is often placed after the French noun rather than after the entire French phrase: **bias** *n.* parti *m.* pris.

Pronunciation of French

The following concise guide describes the approximate pronunciation of the letters and frequent combinations of letters occurring in the French language. A study of it will enable the reader to pronounce French adequately most of the time. While the guide cannot list all the exceptions to the established pronunciations, or cover the manner in which adjacent words affect each other in speech, such exceptions and variations will readily be learned as one develops facility in the language.

French Letter	Description of Pronunciation
a, à	Between *a* in *calm* and *a* in *hat.*
â	Like *a* in *calm.*
ai	Like *e* in *bed.*
au	Like *oa* in *coat.*
b	As in English. At the end of words, usually silent.
c	Before *e, i, y,* like *s.* Elsewhere, like *k.* When *c* occurs at the end of a word and is preceded by a consonant, it is usually silent.
ç	Like *s.*

French Description of
Letter Pronunciation

cc Before *e, i,* like *x.*
Elsewhere, like *k.*

ch Usually like *sh* in *short.*
ch is pronounced like *k* in
words of Greek origin before *a,*
o, and *u* and before consonants.

d At beginning and in middle of
words, as in English.
At end of words, usually silent.

e At end of words, normally
silent; indicates that preceding
consonant letter is pronounced.
Between two single consonant
sounds, usually silent.
Elsewhere, like English *a* in
sofa.

é Approximately like *a* in *hate.*

è, ê, ei Like *e* in *bed.*

eau Like *au.*

ent Silent when it is the third person plural ending.

er (end of words) At end of words
of more than one syllable, usually like *a* in *hate,* the *r* being
silent; otherwise like *air* in
chair. See below under *r.*

es Silent at end of words.

eu A vowel sound not found in
English; like French *e,* but pronounced with the lips rounded
as for *o.*

ez At end of words, almost always
like English *a* in *hate,* the *z*
being silent.

f As in English; silent at the end
of a few words.

g Before *e, i, y,* like *z* in *azure.*
Elsewhere, like *g* in *get.*
At end of words, usually silent.

gn Like *ni* in *onion.*

gu Before *e, i, y,* like *g* in *get.*
Elsewhere, like *g* in *get* plus

French Description of
Letter Pronunciation

French *u* (see below).

h In some words, represents a
slight tightening of the throat
muscles (in French, called
"aspiration")
In most words, silent.

i, î Like *i* in *machine.*

ill (-il at end of words) like *y* in
yes, in many but not all words.

j Like *z* in *azure.*

k As in English.

l As in English, but always pronounced "bright," with tongue
in front of mouth.

m, n When double, and when single
between two vowel letters or at
beginning of word, like English
m and *n* respectively. When single at end of syllable (at end of
word or before another consonant), indicates nasalization of
preceding vowel.

o Usually like *u* in English *mud,*
but rounder.
When final sound in word, and
often before *s* and *z,* like *ô.*

ô Approximately like *oa* in *coat.*

oe, oeu Like *eu.*

oi Approximately like a combination of the consonant *w* and the
a of *calm.*

ou,
oû, où Like *ou* in *tour.*

p At end of words, usually silent.
Between *m* and *t, m* and *s, r*
and *s,* usually silent.
Elsewhere, as in English.

ph Like *f.*

pn, ps Unlike English, when *pn* and *ps*
occur at the beginning of the
words the *p* is usually sounded.

qu Usually like *k.*

French Letter	Description of Pronunciation
r	A vibration either of the uvula, or of the tip of the tongue against the upper front teeth. See above under *er*.
s	Generally, like *s* in *sea*. Single *s* between vowels, like *z* in *zone*. At end of words, normally silent.
sc	Before *e* or *i*, like *s*. Elsewhere, like *sk*.
t	Approximately like English *t*, but pronounced with tongue tip against teeth. At end of words, normally silent. When followed by *ie, ion, ium, ius,* and other diphthongs beginning with a vowel, *t* generally is like English *s* in *sea* (unless the *t* itself is preceded by an *s* or an *x*).

French Letter	Description of Pronunciation
th	Like *t*.
u, û	A vowel sound not found in English; like the *i* in *machine* but with lips rounded as for *ou*.
ue	After *e* or *g* and before *il*, like *eu*.
v	As in English.
w	Usually like *v*; in some people's pronunciation, like English *w*.
x	Generally sounds like *ks*; but when the syllable *ex* begins a word and is followed by a vowel, *x* sounds like *gz*. At end of words, usually silent.
y	Generally like *i* in *machine*; but when between two vowels, like *y* in *yes*.
z	Like *z* in *zone*. At end of words, often silent (see above under *ez*).

Prononciation de l'Anglais

Ce guide reproduit approximativement les sons de l'anglais.

	Français	Anglais

Voyelles

a	*comme cheval*	cat
a	*comme gaz*	father, calm
e	*comme bec*	red, said
e	*comme décrire*	mate, say
e	*comme tristement* ("e" muet)	seven, garden, mission
i	*comme fixe*	ravine, me
i	*comme bistro*	kit, chin
o	*comme chaud*	rose, toad, fellow
o	*comme forme*	paw, taught, thought
u	*comme moulin*	bull, took, wool
u	*comme soupe*	room, rule, flew
u	*comme soeur*	sum, brother

Diphtongues

ai	*comme ailleurs*	tight, sky
au	*comme caoutchouc*	round, tower
oi	*comme boycotter*	toy, choice

Consonnes

b	*comme boîte*	best, tub
d	*comme donner*	darling, rudder
f	*comme falloir*	fact, pharmacy
g	*comme gamine*	game, gift
h	*(aspiré, comme la consonne espagnole "j" de junta)*	hotel, host
j	*comme djinn*	jewel, gesture
k	*comme kilo*	kite, can, chorus
l	*comme lent*	lark, pillow
m	*comme mélange*	mellow, camel
n	*comme net*	north, winner
ng	*comme parking*	ring, tanker
p	*comme pied*	pear, top
r	*comme retour* ("r" rétroflexe)	roar, tar

	Français	Anglais
s	comme masse	safe, cit, class
t	comme tasse	tight, stopped, market
sh	comme chasse	shell, fashion, machine
tch	comme caoutchouc	choose, mature, such
th	comme la consonne castillane "d" de pedir	then, other
th	comme la consonne castillane "c" de círculo	thing, tooth
v	comme vive	very, love, of
w	comme foi, week-end	water, swept, quest
y	comme fier, yeux	yellow, unite
z	comme rose, zeste	zero, his
zh	comme jour	leisure, azure

Abbreviations Used in the Dictionary

abbr.	abbreviation	Diplom.	diplomacy
adj.	adjective	Distil.	distilling
adv.	adverb	Eccl.	ecclesiastic
Adm.	administration	Electr.	electricity
Agr., Agric.	agriculture	Eng.	engineering
Alg.	algebra	Engl.	English
Anat.	anatomy	Engrav.	engraving
Anc.	ancient	Entom.	entomology
Antiq.	antiquity	Equit.	equitation
Arch.	archaic	excl.	exclamation
Archaeol.	archaeology	f., fem.	feminine
Architect	architecture	Fenc.	fencing
Arith.	arithmetic	Feud.	feudalism
art.	article	Fig.	figurative
Artill.	artillery	Fin.	finance
Astrol.	astrology	Fortif.	fortification
Astron.	astronomy	Found.	foundry
Auto.	automotive	Fr.	French
aux.	auxiliary	fut.	future
Aviat.	aviation	Gard.	gardening
Bank.	banking	Geneal	genealogy
Bill.	billiards	Geog.	geography
Bot.	botany	Geol.	geology
Brew.	brewing	Geom.	geometry
Build.	building	Gr.	Greek
Callig.	calligraphy	Gramm.	grammar
Carp.	carpentry	Herald.	heraldry
Chem.	chemistry	Hist.	history
Cine.	cinema	Horol.	horology
collect	collectively	Horsem.	horsemanship
Comm.	commerce	Hort.	horticulture
compar.	comparative	Hunt.	hunting
condit.	conditional	i.	intransitive
conj.	conjunction	Ichth.	ichthyology
Culin.	culinary arts	Idiomat.	idiomatic
Danc	dancing	imper.	imperative mood
def.	definite	imp.,	impersonal
defect.	defective	impers.	
dem.,	demonstrative	indef.	indefinite
demonst.		indic.	indicative mood
Dent.	dentistry	infin.	infinitive mood
dimin.	diminutive	Insur.	insurance

Infml.	informal	Philos.	philosophy
interj.	interjection	Phot.	photography
invar.	invariable	phr.	phrase
iron., ironic.	ironically	Phys.	physics
irreg.	irregular	Physiol.	physiology
jewel.	jewelry	pl., plur.	plural
Join.	joinery	poet.	poetry, poetically
lang.	language	Pol. econ.	political economy
Lat.	Latin	Polit.	politics
Lit.	literature	poss.	possessive
Log.	logic	p.p.	past participle
m., masc.	masculine	prep.	preposition
Mach.	machinery	pres.	present tense
Magn.	magnetism	pret.	preterit
Man.	manage	Print.	printing
Mason.	masonry	pron.	pronoun
Math.	mathematics	Pros.	prosody
Metall.	metallurgy	pr.p.	present participle
Metaphys.	metaphysics	Psychol.	psychology
Meteor.	meteorology	Railw.	railways
Med.	medicine	refl.	reflexive
Mil.	military	rel.	relative
Min.	mineralogy, mining	Rhet.	rhetoric
mod.	modern	Rom.	Roman
Mus.	music	Script.	scripture
Mythol.	mythology	Sculpt.	sculpture
n.	noun, neuter	sing.	singular
Naut.	nautical	Statist.	statistics
n.f.	feminine noun	Subj.	subjunctive mood
n.f.pl.	feminine plural noun	superl.	superlative degree
n.m.	masculine noun	Surg.	surgery
n.m.pl.	masculine plural noun	Surv.	surveying
nom.,		t.	transitive, term
nomin.	nominative case	Technol.	technology
Numis.	numismatics	Theat.	theater
obj., objec.	objective case	v	verb
Opt.	optics	V.	voyez (see)
Ornith.	ornithology	Vet., Veter.	veterinary
Pathol.	pathology	v.auxil.	auxiliary verb
Parliam.	parliamentary procedure	v.i.	intransitive verb
Pej.	pejorative	v.refl.	reflexive verb
pers.	person, personal	v.t.	transitive verb
Pharm.	pharmacy	Vulg.	vulgar
Philol.	philology	Zool.	zoology

French Irregular Verbs

Infinitive	*Pres. Part.*	*Past Part.*	*Pres. Indic.*	*Future*
aller	allant	allé	vais	irai
asseoir	asseyant	assis	assieds	assiérai
atteindre	atteignant	atteint	atteins	atteindrai
avoir	ayant	eu	ai	aurai
battre	battant	battu	bats	battrai
boire	buvant	bu	bois	boirai
conduire	conduisant	conduit	conduis	conduirai
connaître	connaissant	connu	connais	connaîtrai
courir	courant	couru	cours	courrai
craindre	craignant	craint	crains	craindrai
croire	croyant	cru	crois	croirai
devoir	devant	dû	dois	devrai
dire	disant	dit	dis	dirai
dormir	dormant	dormi	dors	dormirai
écrire	écrivant	écrit	écris	écrirai
envoyer	envoyant	envoyé	envoie	enverrai
être	étant	été	suis	serai
faire	faisant	fait	fais	ferai
falloir	—	fallu	(il) faut	(il) faudra
joindre	joignant	joint	joins	joindrai
lire	lisant	lu	lis	lirai
mettre	mettant	mis	mets	mettrai
mourir	mourant	mort	meurs	mourrai
naître	naissant	né	nais	naîtrai
ouvrir	ouvrant	ouvert	ouvre	ouvrirai
plaire	plaisant	plu	plais	plairai
pleuvoir	pleuvant	plu	(il) pleut	(il) pleuvra
pouvoir	pouvant	pu	peux	pourrai
prendre	prenant	pris	prends	prendrai
recevoir	recevant	reçu	reçois	recevrai

Verbes Irréguliers Anglais

Infinitif	Prétérit	Participe Passé	Infinitif	Prétérit	Participe Passé
arise	arose	arisen	eat	ate	eaten
awake	awoke	awoken	fall	fell	fallen
be	was	been	feed	fed	fed
bear	bore	borne	feel	felt	felt
beat	beat	beaten, beat	fight	fought	fought
become	became	become	find	found	found
begin	began	begun	flee	fled	fled
bend	bent	bent	fling	flung	flung
bet	bet, betted	bet, betted	fly	flew	flown
bid	bade, bid	bidden, bid	forget	forgot	forgotten
bind	bound	bound	forgive	forgave	forgiven
bite	bit	bitten	forsake	forsook	forsaken
bleed	bled	bled	freeze	froze	frozen
blow	blew	blown	get	got	gotten
break	broke	broken	give	gave	given
breed	bred	bred	go	went	gone
bring	brought	brought	grind	ground	ground
build	built	built	grow	grew	grown
burn	burned, burnt	burned, burnt	hang	hung, hanged	hung, hanged
burst	burst	burst	have	had	had
buy	bought	bought	hear	heard	heard
cast	cast	cast	hide	hid	hidden, hid
catch	caught	caught	hit	hit	hit
choose	chose	chosen	hold	held	held
cling	clung	clung	hurt	hurt	hurt
come	came	come	keep	kept	kept
cost	cost	cost	kneel	knelt, kneeled	knelt, kneeled
creep	crept	crept	know	knew	known
cut	cut	cut	lay	laid	laid
deal	dealt	dealt	lead	led	led
dig	dug	dug	leap	leaped, leapt	leaped, leapt
dive	dived, dove	dived	leave	left	left
do	did	done	lend	lent	lent
draw	drew	drawn	let	let	let
dream	dream, dreamt	dreamed, dreamt	lie	lay	lain
drink	drank	drunk	light	lighted, lit	lighted, lit
drive	drove	driven	lose	lost	lost
dwell	dwelt, dwelled	dwelt, dwelled	make	made	made

Infinitif	Prétérit	Participe Passé	Infinitif	Prétérit	Participe Passé
mean	meant	meant	spend	spent	spent
meet	met	met	spill	spilled, spilt	spilled, spilt
pay	paid	paid	spin	spun	spun
prove	proved	proved, proven	spit	spit, spat	spit, spat
put	put	put	split	split	split
read	read	read	spoil	spoiled, spoilt	spoiled, spoilt
rid	rid, ridded	rid, ridded	spread	spread	spread
ride	rode	ridden	spring	sprang, sprung	sprung
ring	rang	rung	stand	stood	stood
rise	rose	risen	steal	stole	stolen
run	ran	run	stick	stuck	stuck
say	said	said	sting	stung	stung
see	saw	seen	stink	stank, stunk	stunk
seek	sought	sought	stride	strode	stridden
sell	sold	sold	strike	struck	struck, stricken
send	sent	sent	string	strung	strung
set	set	set	strive	strove, strived	striven, strived
sew	sewed	sewn, sewed	swear	swore	sworn
shake	shook	shaken	sweep	swept	swept
shave	shaved	shaved, shaven	swell	swelled	swollen, swelled
shed	shed	shed	swim	swam	swum
shine	shone	shone	swing	swung	swung
shoot	shot	shot	take	took	taken
show	showed	shown, showed	teach	taught	taught
shrink	shrank, shrunk	shrunk, shrunken	tear	tore	torn
shut	shut	shut	tell	told	told
sing	sang	sung	think	thought	thought
sink	sank, sunk	sunk, sunken	throw	threw	thrown
sit	sat	sat	thrust	thrust	thrust
sleep	slept	slept	tread	trod	trodden, trod
slide	slid	slid	wake	woke	woken
sling	slung	slung	wear	wore	worn
slink	slunk	slunk	weave	wove, weaved	woven, wove
slit	slit	slit	win	won	won
smell	smelled, smelt	smelt	wind	wound	wound
sow	sowed	sown, sowed	wring	wrung	wrung
speak	spoke	spoken	write	wrote	written
speed	sped, speeded	sped, speeded			

French–English
Dictionary

A

A *n.m.* the first letter of the alphabet. A, a. **un grande A**, un **A majuscule**, a capital A. **un petit a**, un **a minuscule**, a small a, a little **a**. **une panse d'a**, the first stroke of a small a. **ne savoir ni A ni B**, to know nothing, to be an ignoramus.

a 3rd pers. sing. pres. indic. of AVOIR.

à *prep.* The preposition **à** combines with the masculine definite article **le** when followed by a word beginning with a consonant, and with its plural **les**; **au**, instead of **à le**; and **aux**, instead of **à les**. This preposition is rendered into English in many different manners, as will be seen by the following examples:

at. **à six heures**, at six o'clock. **vendre à perte**, to sell at a loss.

to. **aller à Rome**, to go to Rome. **écrire à son ami**, to write to one's friend.

in. **à Londres, à Paris**, in London, in Paris. **au faubourg Saint-Germain**, in the faubourg St. Germain. **une blessure à l'épaule**, a wound in the shoulder. **à mon avis**, in my opinion. **cuit à l'eau**, boiled in water. **à la hâte**, in haste, hastily. **jeter au feu**, to throw into the fire.

by. **vendre à la livre, à la douzaine**, to sell by the pound, by the dozen. **payer au mois**, to pay by the month. **un à un**, one by one. **pas à pas**, step by step.

of. **pensez à moi**, think of me. **emprunter à un ami**, to borrow from a friend.

with. **à bras ouverts**, with open arms. **un livre à la main**, with a book in one's hand.

on. **à pied, à cheval**, on foot, on horseback. **à genoux**, on one's knees. **à cette occasion**, on that occasion. **à la télévision**, on television.

from. **ôtez le bâton à cet enfant**, take the stick from that child. **à ce que je vois**, from what I see.

for. **traduire mot à mot**, to translate word for word. **c'est à vous de parler**, it is for you (it is your turn, your duty) to speak. **à jamais**, forever. **quant à moi**, as for me.

under. **être à couvert**, to be undercover. **fouler aux pieds**, to tread underfoot.

within. **à dix pas de chez nous**, within ten steps of our house. **à portée de voix**, within speaking distance.

When used with **de**, expressed or understood, to indicate a number approximately, **à** may be rendered in several manners: **de cinq à six cents hommes**, from five to six hundred men. **de dix à douze francs**, from ten to twelve francs.

In phrases indicating ownership **à** is suppressed and the word following it takes the possessive form. **ce cheval est à moi, à lui, à nous, à vous, à eux, à Jean**, this horse is mine, his, ours, yours, theirs, John's. **un ami à moi**, a friend of mine.

When placed between two nouns or a noun and a verb, and the last word, or an adjective of similar meaning, is put first: **arbre à fruit**, fruit tree. **armes à feu**, firearms. **moulin à eau, à vent**, watermill, windmill. **chapeau à larges bords**, broad-brimmed hat. **chambre à coucher**, bedroom. **canne à sucre**, sugarcane.

In many idiomatic phrases, **à** is entirely suppressed or replaced by a totally different word: **au secours!** help! **à l'assassin!** murder! **une voiture à quatre chevaux**, a carriage and four, a four-in-hand.

Used before an infinitive denotes generally what is to be done: **la femme est à plaindre**, the woman is to be pitied. **c'est une chose à souhaiter**, it is a thing to be wished for.

abaissant, e *adj.* degrading.

abaisse *n.f.* thin sheet of pie paste; thin crust (of a pie or tart).

abaissé, e *p.p.* lowered, etc. **les yeux abaissés**, with downcast eyes.

abaissement *n.m.* lowering; taking down, putting down, subsiding; fall, going down (barometer); abatement, reduction (of price, etc.); humbling (of persons or states); abasement. **l'~ des eaux**, the abatement of the waters. **~ volontaire**, self abasement, self humiliation.

abaisser *v.t.* to lower; to reduce, to let down, put down, bring down, cast down (as the eyes); to abase, to humble; to degrade (persons); **~ la voix**, to lower the voice. **s'~**, *v.refl.* to lower, to get lower; to stoop; to fall; to sink; to subside (as floods); to abase, to humble oneself. **je ne me abaisserai point à me justifier**, I will not condescend (or stoop) to justify myself.

abaisseur *n.m. Anat.* depressor.

abandon *n.m.* abandonment; act of abandoning; state of being abandoned; renunciation of rights; desertion; act of forsaking; ease, freedom. **faire ~ de**, to abandon, to give up. **laisser à l'~**, to leave to rack and ruin. **à l'~**, at random, in confusion. **dans un ~ universel**, forsaken by everybody.

abandonné, e *adj.* forsaken, deserted; given up, given over (as a patient, by a physician); profligate, reckless. *n.m.* waif.

abandonnement *n.m.* abandonment; relinquishment (of claims or rights); resignation; profligacy.

abandonner *v.i.* to abandon; to leave; to give up; to forsake. **~ son parti**, to give up one's party.

~ **la partie**, to give it up, ~ **son pays**, to leave one's country. **les médecins l'ont complètement abandonné,** the doctors have completely given him up. **s'~,** *v.refl.* to entrust, to resign, to commit oneself to; to give way to one's passions; to be addicted to; to be disheartened; to be slovenly. **il s'abandonne à la colère,** he gives way to anger.

abaque *n.m.* abacus.

abasourdir *v.t.* to deafen, to stun, to astound.

abasourdissant, e *adj.* deafening.

abâtardir *v.t.* to debase, to deteriorate; to corrupt (languages, doctrines). **plantes abâtardies,** degenerate plants. **s'~,** *v.refl.* to degenerate, to deteriorate; to become corrupt.

abâtardissement *n.m.* degeneracy, deterioration.

abat-jour *n.m., pl.* **des abat-jour** skylight; reflector; lampshade; blind.

abattage *n.m.* felling (of timber); slaughtering (of oxen, etc., for food).

abattant *n.m.* flap (of a table, of an envelope); shutter.

abattis *n.m.* felling (of timber); pulling down (of buildings); felled wood; *Sport.* slaughter (of game); giblets.

abattement *n.m.* prostration; lowness of spirits; dejection; *Herald.* abatement. **tomber dans l'~,** to get low-spirited.

abatteur *n.m.* lumberjack. **grand ~ de besogne,** a hard worker.

abattoir *n.m.* slaughterhouse.

abattre *v.t.* to fell (trees); to lay low; to beat down; to slaughter; to prostrate; to fell; to knock down; to slay; *Naut.* to heave down; to throw down. **~ une maison,** to pull down a house. **~ des idoles,** to throw down idols. **~ des arbres,** to fell trees. **~ un homme,** to knock down a man. **~ les moissons,** to cut down the harvest. **petite pluie abat grand vent,** a little rain will still a great wind. **se laisser ~,** to give way to discouragement. **s'~,** *v.refl.* to fall down; to fall upon, to abate; to become low-spirited. **le vent s'abat,** the wind falls. **l'orage va s'~ sur nous,** the storm will soon burst upon us.

abattu, e *adj.* depressed, prostrated; downcast, dejected, downhearted. **il dit qu'il se sent tout ~,** he says he feels quite low-spirited.

abat-vent *n.m.* screen; louver board; mat to protect plants.

abbaye *n.f.* abbey, monastery.

abbé *n.m.* abbot, abbé: a title given to Catholic ecclesiastics in general.

abbesse *n.f.* abbess.

ABC *n.m.* ABC; alphabet, ABC-book, primer, spelling-book.

abcès *n.m.* abscess.

abdication *n.f.* abdication; renunciation (of rights); disinheriting (of a monarch, child). **faire ~,** to abdicate.

abdiquer *v.t.* to abdicate (sovereignty); to

resign. **s'~,** *v.refl.* to be abdicated, to neglect.

abdomen *n.m.* abdomen.

abdominal, e *adj.* abdominal.

abducteur *adj. Anat.* abductor. *n.m.* abductor.

abduction *n.f.* abduction.

abécédaire *adj.* alphabetical. *n.m.* ABC-book, primer.

abeille *n.f.* bee. **~ domestique, ~ de ruche,** honeybee. **~ mâle,** drone. **~ femelle ou reine,** female or queen bee. **~ neutre,** working bee, worker. **essaim d'~s,** swarm of bees. **éleveur d'~s,** beekeeper.

aberration *n.f.* aberration; vagary. **~ de la lumière, des étoiles,** aberration of light, of the stars. **~ des sens,** aberration of the senses.

abêtir *v.t.* to render dull or stupid. **s'~,** *v.refl.* to grow more and more stupid.

abêtissant, e *adj.* stupefying.

abhorrer *v.t.* to abhor, to loathe, to detest. **se faire ~ de ses voisins,** to incur the abhorrence of one's neighbors.

abîme *n.m.* abyss, the deep; the unfathomable depth. **les profonds ~s de la mer,** the great depths of the ocean.

abîmer *v.t.* to ruin, to spoil, to injure, to vanquish (in discussion). **s'~,** *v.refl.* to fall into an abyss, to sink, to get spoiled.

abject, e *adj.* abject, mean, low.

abjectement *adv.* abjectly, despicably, vilely.

abjection *n.f.* abjection; vileness.

abjuration *n.f.* abjuration; solemn renunciation.

abjurer *v.t. and i.* to abjure, to renounce. **s'~,** *v.refl.* to be abjured, to be renounced.

ablatif *n.m. Gram.* ablative.

ablette *n.f.* bleak; whitebait.

ablution *n.f.* ablution, washing. **faire ses ~s,** to wash oneself.

abnégation *n.f.* abnegation, self-denial. **faire ~ de,** to renounce.

aboi *n.m.* barking, baying (of dogs); last extremity. **aux abois,** at bay, hard up. **jusqu'aux derniers abois,** till death. **être aux abois,** to be hard pressed, to be in desperate straits.

aboiement, *n.m.* bark, barking (of dogs).

abolir *v.t.* to abolish; to do away with.

abolissable *adj.* abolishable; repealable.

abolissement *n.m.* abolishment.

abolition *n.f.* abolition; suppression, repeal.

abolitionniste *n.m.f.* abolitionist.

abominable *adj.* abominable. **une odeur ~,** an intolerable stench. **il fait un temps ~,** the weather is wretched.

abominablement *adv.* abominably.

abomination *n.f.* abomination. **avoir en ~,** to loathe.

abominer *v.t.* to loathe, to abominate.

à-bon-compte *n.m., pl.* **des à-bon-compte** cash advance (to meet current expenditure).

abondamment *adv.* abundantly, plentifully.

abondance *n.f.* abundance; plenty; copiousness. **parler d'~** to extemporize, to speak off the cuff.

parler d'~ de coeur, to speak from the fullness of the heart. corne d'~, horn of plenty, cornucopia.

abondant, e adj. abounding in (or with); abundant, copious; prolific; voluble (in speech); prolix (in speaking or writing); luxuriant. pays ~ en blé, a countryside abounding in corn.

abonder v.i. to abound; to be abundant. ~ de biens, to have abundant wealth. ~ dans son sens, to be of the same opinion; to be in full agreement.

abonné, e n.m.f. subscriber (to a journal, a theater, etc.); holder of a season ticket (for a railway, concert, etc.).

abonnement n.m. subscription (to a journal, a theater, etc.); season ticket. on n'entre aujourd'hui que par ~, only season tickets admitted today. l'~ part du premier du mois, subscriptions run from the 1st of the month.

abonner v.t. to subscribe (to a journal); to contract for. s'~, v.refl. to subscribe (to a journal, etc.), to become a subscriber (to). on s'abonne à, subscriptions received at.

abord n.m. access (of a port, etc.); arrival, landing. à l'~, au premier ~, at first meeting, at first view. d'~, at first. tout d'~, first of all.

abordable adj. approachable, accessible. homme très ~, a very approachable man.

abordage n.m. boarding (ship). prendre à l'~, boarding.

aborder v.i. to arrive; to land (at or on). v.i. to approach; to accost (a person); to come to, to broach a subject of discussion; Naut. to run foul of, to come into collision with. ~ un vaisseau, to board a ship. s'~, v.refl. to accost each other. Naut. to run foul of, to join battle.

aborigène adj. aboriginal, indigenous.

aborner v.t. to place landmarks.

abortif, ve adj. abortive.

abot n.m. hobble; a fetter to prevent horses from straying.

aboucher v.t. to arrange an interview between. s'~, v.refl. to come together, to confer together.

about n.m. butt (of a plank).

abouter v.t. to join end to end.

aboutir v.i. to end, to meet in or at; to result in. n'~ à rien, to lead to nothing, to come to nothing.

aboutissants n.m.pl. details, particulars (of things). savoir tous les tenants et aboutissants d'une affaire, to know the long and short of an affair.

aboutissement n.m. result, outcome.

aboyant, e adj. barking, baying.

aboyer v.i. to bark, to bay, to raise an outcry after or against; to hunt after. chien qui aboie ne mord pas, barking dogs never bite. ~ à la lune, to bay at the moon.

aboyeur n.m. barker, snarler

abracadabra n.m. abracadabra.

abrasion n.f. Med. abrasion (of the skin).

abrégé n.m. abridgment (of a book); abstract. en ~, briefly, in few words. écrire un mot en ~, to abbreviate a word.

abrègement n.m. summary; abridgment; curtailment.

abréger v.t. to abridge (a book); to abbreviate (a word); to shorten. les excès abrègent la vie, excesses shorten life. abrégez! be short! prenez ce chemin, il abrège, take this road, it is shorter. s'~, v.refl. to be shortened.

abreuvage n.m. watering (of horses); irrigating (of land).

abreuver v.c. to water (horses, etc.); to irrigate (meadows); to soak (with water); to overwhelm (with grief, etc.). s'~, v.refl. to be watered; to drink. s'~ de larmes, to be bathed in tears.

abreuvoir n.m. watering place, horse trough.

abréviation n.f. abbreviation.

abri n.m. shelter, refuge. ~ contre la pluie, shelter from rain. trouver un ~, to find shelter, to get undercover. se tenir à l'~, to keep safe. se mettre à l'~, to get under shelter. sans ~, homeless.

abricot n.m. apricot. confiture d'abricots, apricot jam.

abricotier n.m. apricot tree.

abriter v.t. to shelter; to screen, to protect. s'~, v.refl. to shelter oneself; to find protection.

abrivent n.m. shelter (from wind).

abrogation n.f. abrogation, repeal (of law, etc.).

abroger v.t. to abrogate, to repeal (laws). s'~, v.refl. to be abrogated.

abrupt, e adj. abrupt; rugged, precipitous. style ~, abrupt style.

abruptement adv. abruptly, steeply.

abruti, e adj. and n.m.f. stupid. c'est un ~, he is an idiot.

abrutir v.t. to exhaust; to stupefy. s'~, v.refl. to become exhausted, stupefied.

abrutissant, e adj. exhausting, stupefying.

abrutissement n.m. physical and/or mental exhaustion.

absence n.f. absence. ~ d'esprit, absence of mind. s'apercevoir de l'~ de quelqu'un, ou quelque chose, to miss a person or something; to feel the want of.

absent, e adj. absent; missing; ~ par congé, absent on leave. être ~ de chez soi, to be absent (or away) from home. n.m.f. person absent. les absents ont toujours tort, the absent are always in the wrong.

absentéisme n.m. absenteeism.

absenter (s') v.refl. to absent oneself; to be absent. to keep out of the way.

absinthe n.f. absinthe; wormwood; bitters.

absolu, e adj. absolute; complete; peremptory. pouvoir ~, absolute power. d'un ton ~, in a peremptory tone.

absolument adv. absolutely, definitely.

absolution n.f. absolution; discharge (of a prisoner).

absolutisme *n.m.* absolutism.

absorbant, e *adj.* engrossing; absorbent.

absorber *v.t.* to absorb; to imbibe; to swallow up; *Fig.* to engross (attention). **s'~,** *v.refl.* to be absorbed.

absorption *n.f.* absorption.

absoudre *v.t.* to absolve; to exonerate; to acquit.

abstenir (s') *v.refl.* to abstain (from eating, drinking, etc.); to refrain. **elle s'est abstenue d'écrire,** she refrained from writing. **dans le doute, abstiens-toi,** when in doubt, abstain.

abstention *n.f.* abstention; withdrawal.

abstentionnisme *n.m.* refusal to vote.

abstentionniste *adj.* nonvoter.

abstinence *n.f.* abstinence; fasting. **jours d'~,** fast days.

abstinent *adj.* abstemious.

abstraction *n.f.* abstraction; abstract idea. **faire ~ de,** to abstract. **~ faite des inconvénients,** to say nothing of the inconveniences.

abstraire *v.t.* to abstract.

abstrait, e *adj.* abstract, abstruse, absent (in mind).

abstraitement *adv.* abstractedly, in the abstract.

abstrus, e *adj.* abstruse.

absurde *adj.* absurd, preposterous. **il est ~ de croire que . . . .,** it is absurd to believe that . . . *n.m.* the absurd; absurdity. **tomber dans l'~,** to fall into the absurd.

absurdement *adv.* absurdly; nonsensically.

absurdité *n.f.* absurdity, absurdness. **dire des ~s,** to talk nonsense. **cet homme est d'une ~ sans égale,** that man has no equal for absurdity.

abus *n.m.* abuse, misuse, wrongful use. **~ d'autorité,** abuse of authority. **~ de confiance,** breach of trust.

abuser *v.i.* to abuse; to misuse, to waste; to put upon. **usez, n'abusez pas,** use, but do not abuse. **~ de son temps,** to misuse one's leisure or time. **vous abusez de ma bonté,** you take advantage of my kindness. **s'~,** *v.refl.* to be mistaken.

abuseur *n.m.* deceiver, cheat.

abusif, ive *adj.* abusive, improper.

abusivement *adv.* abusively; improperly.

acabit *n.m.* taste, quality (of fruit, etc.). **poires d'un bon ~,** fine-flavored pears. **gens du même ~,** people of the same type.

acacia *n.m.* acacia.

académicien *n.m.* academic, academician; member of an academy.

académie *n.f.* academy; riding school, fencing school; casino. **Académie française,** the French Academy.

académique *adj.* academic, academical; speculative, theoretical.

académisme *n.m.* conventionalism, lack of originality.

acajou *n.m.* mahogany. **bois d'~,** mahogany.

acanthe *n.f.* acanthus. **feuille d'~,** acanthus leaf.

acariâtre *adj.* bad-tempered, cantankerous.

accablant, e *adj.* overwhelming, crushing; tiresome, annoying. **témoignage accablant,** overwhelming evidence.

accablé *p.p.* overpowered. **~ de dettes,** head over heels in debt.

accablement *n.m.* prostration, extreme depression; despondency, dejection. **être dans l'~,** to be miserable.

accabler *v.t.* to overwhelm (with blows, misfortunes, honors, favors, etc.); to crush. **les affaires l'accablent,** he is overwhelmed with business. **~ de reproches,** to load with reproaches. **s'~,** *v.refl.* to overburden oneself.

accalmie *n.f. Naut.* lull (during a storm).

accaparement *n.m.* monopolizing, forestalling, cornering.

accaparer *v.t.* to monopolize, to engross; to forestall, to buy up.

accapareur, se *n.m.f.* monopolizer, forestaller.

accastillage *n.m.* superstructure (of a ship).

accastiller *v.t.* to add the superstructure (to a ship).

accéder *v.i.* to accede (to); to acquiesce (in).

accélérateur, trice *adj.* accelerating. **force accélératrice,** accelerating power.

accélération *n.f.* acceleration (of motion), hastening, dispatch (of business).

accéléré, e *p.p.* accelerated, quickened. **pas ~,** double-quick time.

accélérer *v.t.* to accelerate; to quicken.

accent *n.m.* accent, stress of the voice. **~ tonique,** tonic accent. **n'avoir pas d'~,** to speak without any accent. **en francais en emploie trois accents, l'~ aigu (´), l'~ grave (`) et l'~ circonflexe (ˆ),** in French there are three accents, the acute, the grave, and the circumflex. **~ nasillard,** twang.

accentuation *n.f.* accentuation.

accentué, e *p.p.* accented, accentuated.

accentuer *v.t.* to accent, to accentuate, to emphasize.

acceptable *adj.* acceptable.

acceptant, e *n.f.* acceptor (of a donation or legacy).

acceptation *n.f.* acceptance. **l'~ d'une lettre de change,** the acceptance of a bill of exchange.

accepter *v.t.* to accept. **~ une lettre de change,** to accept a bill of exchange.

accepteur *n.m.* accepter (in a general sense).

acception *n.f.* acceptance, favor, preference; acceptation, meaning. **ce mot a plusieurs ~s,** this word has several acceptations.

accès *n.m.* access (to something (with à)); (with **auprès de**) access to (a person); fit, paroxysm (of passion); attack. **donner ~ à la pitié,** to give way to compassion. **par ~,** by fits.

accessibilité *n.f.* accessibility, access.

accessible *adj.* accessible, easy of access.

accession *n.f.* accession, adhesion; increase, addition.

accessit *n.m.* certificate of merit. **il a eu un prix et deux accessits,** he obtained one prize and two certificates of merit.

accessoire *adj.* accessory. *n.m.* accessory, dependency; prop. (in theatrical lang.) **garantie accessoire** *n.f.* collateral security.

accessoirement *adv.* accessorily; over and above.

accident *n.m.* accident; casualty. **par ~,** by accident, accidentally. **accident d'auto,** car accident; **accident d'avion,** airplane crash. **accident mortel,** fatality.

accidenté, e *adj.* rough, undulating, uneven. **pays ~,** hilly countryside.

accidentel, le *adj.* accidental, fortuitous. **une mort accidentelle,** accidental death.

accidentellement *adv.* accidentally, by accident.

accise *n.f.* excise.

acclamation *n.f.* acclamatization.

acclamer *v.i.* to cheer, to acclaim.

acclimatation *n.f.* acclimatization.

acclimaté, e *p.p.* acclimatized.

acclimatement *n.m.* acclimation, acclimating.

acclimater *v.t.* to acclimate, to acclimatize. **s'~,** to become acclimatized.

accointance *n.f.* acquaintance; *(pejorative)* intimacy.

accolade *n.f.* accolade; embrace; *Print.* brackets ({}); brace. **une ~ de lapereaux,** a brace of rabbits. **donner l'~ à,** to dub a knight; to embrace, to hug.

accolage *n.m.* fastening (grape vines, etc., to an arbor).

accoler *v.t.* to embrace; to fasten (vines, etc.); to prop; to join together.

accommodable *adj.* accommodating.

accommodage *n.m.* cooking (of food); dressing.

accommodant, e *adj.* accommodating; easygoing. **peu ~,** hard to deal with.

accommodation *n.f.* accommodation.

accommodement *n.m.* accommodation; settlement; agreement. **homme d'~,** an accommodating man. **entrer en voie d'~,** to take steps toward an arrangement.

accommoder *v.t.* to accommodate; to suit; to arrange, to cook. **cet aubergiste accommode bien ses pratiques,** that innkeeper treats his customers well. **le voilà bien accommodé,** what a pretty pickle he is in! **s'~,** *v.refl.* to make oneself comfortable; to make one's way; to come to terms; to agree to; to put up with. **bien s'~,** to make one's way in the world. **s'~ de tout,** to take things easily. **accommodez-vous,** make yourself quite at home.

accompagnateur, trice, *n.m.f.* accompanist.

accompagnement *n.m.* accompanying; attendance; accompaniment.

accompagner *v.t.* to accompany; to attend; to be in harmony with. **il accompagne bien,** he is a good accompanist. **s'~,** *v.refl.* to join with; to accompany oneself.

accompli, e *p.p.* accomplished; completed. **trente ans ~s,** full thirty years. *adj.* accomplished; perfect; complete. **un scélérat ~,** a thorough scoundrel. **un homme ~,** a perfect gentleman.

accomplir *v.t.* to accomplish; to complete; to fulfill; to carry out. **s'~,** *v.refl.* to be accomplished, fulfilled.

accomplissement *n.m.* accomplishment; completion; fulfillment.

accord *n.m.* accord; understanding; agreement; chord; pitch. **d'un commun ~,** by mutual agreement. **d'~,** agreed. **d'accord avec,** in harmony with. **l'~ conclu entre la France et l'Allemagne,** the agreement concluded between France and Germany. **ce piano ne tient pas l'~,** this piano does not stay in tune.

accordable *adj.* agreeable; reconciliable. *Mus.* tunable.

accordéon *n.m.* accordion.

accorder *v.t.* to reconcile; to bring into accord; to conciliate; to admit; to accord; to tune; to harmonize (colors); *Gram.* (with **avec**) to make an agreement with. **s'~,** *v.refl.* to agree; to be in accord with; to consent to; to coincide with; to be granted; to be in unison. **elle ne s'accorde pas avec elle-même,** she is inconsistent with herself.

accordeur *n.m.* reconciler; tuner.

accordoir *n.m.* tuning key.

accort, e *adv.* easy-tempered; engaging.

accostable *adj.* accostable; approachable.

accoster *v.t.* to accost; to come alongside (a boat). **s'~,** *v.refl.* to berth.

accotement *n.m.* footpath; shoulder (of road).

accoter *v.t.* to prop up; to lean to one side. **s'~,** *v.refl.* to lean against.

accotoir *n.m.* prop; armrest.

accouchée *n.f.* a woman in childbirth.

accouchement *n.m.* childbirth; delivery; a painful or difficult task. **l'art des ~s,** midwifery. **c'était un ~ pour lui,** it was a difficult task for him.

accoucher *v.i.* to be delivered of; to give birth to, to speak out. **~ avant terme,** to miscarry. **elle a accouché heureusement,** she has been safely delivered. **accouchez,** out with it!

accoucheur *n.m.* obstetrician.

accoucheuse *n.f.* midwife.

accoudé, e *p.p.* leaning on one's elbow.

accouder (s') *v.refl.* to lean on one's elbow.

accoudoir *n.m.* arm *or* elbow (of a chair); rail (across a window).

accouple *n.f.* leash.

accouplé, e *p.p.* coupled; yoked (as oxen); paired (as birds).

accouplement *n.m.* coupling; yoking (of oxen); pairing (of birds); union.

accoupler *v.t.* to couple; to put together; to pair; to yoke. **s'~,** *v.refl.* to copulate.

accourir *v.i.* to run; to flock together; to hasten.

~ **de toutes parts,** to come running from all directions.

accoutrement *n.m.* attire.

accoutrer *v.t.* to accouter, to dress up.

accoutumance *n.f.* custom, habit.

accoutumé, e *adj.* accustomed; used to, habituated. **à l'heure** ~, at the usual hour.

accoutumer *v.t.* to accustom, to habituate. **s'~,** *v.refl.* (with **à** or **avec**) to accustom oneself to; to get used to.

accrédité, e *p.p.* and *adj.* of high repute, influential. **le chef le plus** ~, the most influential chief.

accréditer *v.t.* to sanction, to countenance, to accredit (an envoy, an agent). **s'~,** *v.refl.* to get into credit, to gain credit.

accroc *n.m.* tear (in a dress, etc.), hitch, impediment, hindrance. **faire un** ~ **à,** to tear.

accroche-coeur *n.m.* heartbreaker.

accrocher *v.t.* to hang on a hook; to hang up; to tear (a coat, etc.). **on lui a accroché de l'argent,** he has been done out of some money. **s'~,** *v.refl.* to catch on, to lay hold of each other; to hold on to; to grapple with.

accroire *v.t.* to believe, used in the infinitive only. **faire** ~, to make (a person) believe (a falsehood). **en faire** ~, to deceive.

accroissement *n.m.* growth (of animals or plants); aggrandizement, enlargement, extension.

accroître *v.t.* to increase (wealth, power). *v.i.* to grow; to increase; to extend. **s'~,** *v.refl.* to increase; to grow.

accroupi, e *adj.* squatting.

accroupir (s') *v.refl.* to squat, to crouch.

accroupissement *n.m.* squatting, crouching.

accru, e *adj.* increased. *n.f.* spreading, extension (of a forest).

accueil *n.m.* reception; welcome. **bon** ~, a hearty welcome. **mauvais** ~, a bad reception. **faire bon** ~ **à,** to welcome; to honor (a bill or draft).

accueillant, e *adj.* (of persons) easy of access; hospitable, welcoming.

accueillir *v.t.* to receive, to welcome. ~ **bien ou mal,** to receive well or ill. **être accueilli par une tempête,** to be assailed by a storm.

accul *n.m.* cul-de-sac, place without exit, blind alley.

acculer *v.t.* to drive into a corner; to bring (an animal) to bay. **s'~,** *v.refl.* (with **à**) to back against (a wall, tree, etc.).

acculturation *n.f.* acculturation.

accumulateur, trice *n.m.f.* accumulator (goods or money). *adj.* accumulative, acquisitive.

accumulation *n.f.* accumulation.

accumuler *v.t.* to accumulate, to hoard. ~ **faute sur faute,** to add fault to fault. **s'~,** *v.refl.* to accumulate.

accusable *adj.* accusable, chargeable.

accusateur, trice *n.m.f* accuser, impeacher.

accusatif *n.m.* accusative case, accusative.

accusation *n.f.* accusation; impeachment; charge; indictment.

accusé, e *n.m.f.* accused person; (in a criminal court) prisoner. ~ **de réception,** acknowledgment of receipt (of a letter, parcel, etc.).

accuser *v.t.* to accuse; (with **de**) to charge with; to arraign, to bring to trial; to impeach; to acknowledge (receipt of a letter, etc.). **vous m'en accuserez réception,** you will acknowledge receipt of it. **s'~,** *v.refl.* to admit; to confess.

acéphale *adj.* and *n.* acephalous; headless. **les huîtres sont des** ~s, oysters are acephala, acephalans.

acerbe *adj.* acerbic; harsh.

acéré, e *adj.* sharp.

acérer *v.t.* to sharpen.

acétate *n.m.* acetate. ~ **de plomb,** acetate of lead.

acétylène *n.f.* acetylene.

achalandage *n.m.* customers, clientele.

achalandé, e *adj.* having customers. **boutique bien** ~e, much frequented shop.

achalander *v.t.* to attract customers, to draw trade. **s'~,** *v.refl.* to get customers.

acharné, e *p.p.* and *adj.* desperate; implacable. **un animal** ~ **sur sa proie,** an animal in hot pursuit. **une lutte** ~e, a desperate struggle.

acharnement *n.m.* rage, ravenousness, relentlessness; passion. **avec** ~, desperately.

acharner (s') *v.refl.* to be excited, fierce; to be implacable. ~ **au travail,** to stay hard at work.

achat *n.m.* purchase; ~ **d'or et d'argent,** gold and silver bought here. **prix d'**~, purchase price. **faire des** ~s, to go shopping. **pouvoir d'**~, purchasing power.

achée *n.f.* red earthworms (used as bait in angling).

acheminement *n.m.* first step, preparation. **un** ~ **à la paix,** a first step toward peace.

acheminer *v.t.* to forward, to go forward. **s'~,** *v.refl.* to set out, to make for, to advance, to progress.

acheter *v.t.* to purchase, to buy; to bribe (a functionary, a voter, etc.). ~ **en gros, en détail,** to buy wholesale, to buy retail. ~ **à crédit,** to buy on credit. ~ **chat en poche,** to buy a pig in a poke. **s'~,** *v.refl.* to buy for oneself; to be purchasable. **je me suis acheté une maison,** I have bought myself a house.

acheteur *n.m.* buyer, purchaser.

achevé, e *adj.* perfect, out-and-out; downright; egregious. **orateur** ~, a perfect orator. **fou** ~, a perfect madman. **scélérat** ~, downright rascal.

achèvement *n.m.* finishing, completion, conclusion.

achever *v.t.* to finish; to complete, to kill, to dispatch. ~ **une entreprise,** to complete an undertaking. ~ **ses jours,** to end one's days. **s'~,** *v.refl.* to come to an end. **sa vie s'acheva en paix,** his life ended in peace.

achoppement *n.m.* stumbling. **pierre d'~**, stumbling block.

achopper *v.i.* to stumble. **c'est là où tous ont achoppé**, that is where all have stumbled.

achromatique *adj.* achromatic.

achromatisme *n.m.* achromatism.

aciculaire *adj.* acicular; needle-shaped: said of crystals and leaves.

acide *adj.* acid. *n.m.* acid.

acidification *n.f.* acidification.

acidifier *v.t.* to acidify; to make sour. **s'~**, *v.refl.* to become acid.

acidité *n.f.* acidity, sourness.

acidulé *adj.* slightly acid. **bonbon acidulé**, sour candy drops.

aciduler *v.t.* to acidulate.

acier *n.m.* steel. **~ fondu**, cast steel. **~ en poule**, blistered steel. **fil d'~**, steel wire.

aciérie *n.f.* steelworks, steel factory.

acmé *n.m.* acme; summit.

acné *n.f.* acne

acolyte *n.m.* acolyte, accomplice.

acompte *n.m.* payment on account, installment. **par ~**, by installments.

acoquinant, e *adj.* captivating, enthralling.

acoquiner *v.t.* to captivate, to become habitual to. **s'~**, *v.refl.* (with **à**) to become habituated to, to develop a strong liking for.

à-coup *n.m.* jerk; sudden stop. **travailler par ~s**, to work in fits.

acoustique *adj.* acoustic. **cordon ~**, speaking tube. **cornet ~**, ear trumpet. **voûte ~**, whispering gallery. *n.f.* acoustics.

acquéreur *n.m.* purchaser, buyer.

acquérir *v.t.* to purchase, to obtain. **s'~**, *v.refl.* to be acquired.

acquêt *n.m.* acquisition.

acquiescement *n.m.* (with **à**) to acquiescence in; compliance with.

acquiescer *v.i.* (with **à**) to acquiesce in; to comply (with).

acquis, e *p.p.* acquired, won over. **bien mal ~**, ill-gotten wealth. *n.m.* acquisition; acquired knowledge. **il a beaucoup d'~**, he has great assets.

acquisition *n.f.* purchase, acquisition, acquirement. **faire l'~ de**, to make the purchase of.

acquit *n.m.* discharge (of a debt, an obligation); receipt (of a bill); lead (at billiards). **pour ~**, received, paid, settled. **à l'~ de**, for the account of. **par manière d'~**, for form's sake. **par acquit de conscience**, as a matter of duty.

acquit-à-caution *n.m.* permit; bond note.

acquittement *n.m.* discharge (of debts); acquittal.

acquitter *v.t.* to clear, to pay off (debts); to receipt (a store bill, etc.); to acquit. **s'~**, *v.refl.* (with **de**) to free oneself from (debts), to pay off; to acquit oneself of (an obligation); to fulfill (a duty); to lead off (at billiards).

acre *n.f.* acre (of land). *adj.* acrid; acrimonious. **saveur ~**, an acrid taste.

acreté *n.f.* acridity, aridness; acrimony, bitterness.

acrimonie *n.f.* acrimony.

acrimonieux, se *adj.* acrimonious.

acrobate *n.m.f.* acrobat.

aeronyme *n.m.* acronym.

acropole *n.f.* acropolis.

acrostiche *n.m.* acrostic. *adj.* acrostic, acrostical.

acte *n.m.* action, act; decree. **~ glorieux**, glorious act. **~ criminel**, criminal act. **~ de foi**, act of faith. **faire ~ d'autorité**, to show, to exert one's authority. **faire ~ de bonne volonté**, to show one's good will. **faire ~ de complaisance**, to show one's readiness to oblige. **faire ~ de présence**, to make one's appearance, to be present. **~ du parlement**, act of parliament. **tragédie en cinq ~s**, tragedy in five acts. **~ faux**, forged deed. **rédiger un ~**, to draw up a deed. **~ de société**, deed of partnership. **~ de naissance, de marriage, de décès**, certificate of birth, marriage, death.

acteur *n.m.* actor, player, performer.

actif, ve *adj.* active, quick, nimble. **homme ~**, active man. **vie active**, active life. **verbe ~**, active verb. **voix active**, active voice. *n.m.* assets. **l'~ et le passif**, assets and liabilities.

action *n.f.* action, deed, motion; effect; lawsuit; battle; series of events; share (of a bank, etc.). **l'~ du feu sur les mêtaux**, the action of fire on metals. **mauvaise ~**, evil deed, bad action. **~s de grâce**, thanksgiving. **l'~ du poison**, the action of the poison. **entrer en ~**, to begin operations. **mettre en ~**, to carry into effect. **~ nominative**, personal action. **~ au porteur**, share to bearer. **~ privilégiée**, preference share.

actionnaire *n.m.* shareholder, stockholder.

actionner *v.t.* to bring an action against, to sue.

activant, e *adj.* stimulating.

activement *adv.* actively.

activer *v.t.* to push forward, to urge on; to stir up.

activisme, *n.m.* militancy, activism.

activiste, *n.m.* activist.

activité *n.f.* activity; activeness, action. **l'~ des travaux**, the active progress of the works. **en ~**, in activity. **les fabriques sont en pleine ~**, the factories are in full production.

actrice *n.f.* actress.

actualisation *n.f.* actualization, updating.

actualiser, *v.t.* to actualize, to update.

actualité *n.f.* reality; actuality, passing event; novelty, fashion of the day. **un ouvrage plein d'~**, a very contemporary work.

actuel, le *adj.* real, actual; effective, of the day. **le président ~ est**, the current president is.

actuellement *adv.* at present. **on joue ~**, they are now playing.

acuité *n.f.* acuteness, sharpness.

acuponcture *n.f.* acupuncture.

adage *n.m.* adage. **un vieil adage**, an old saying, proverb.

adaptation *n.f.* adaptation.
adapté, e *p.p.* adapted; suitable.
adapter *v.t.* to adapt; to adjust; to suit. **s'~,** *v.refl.* to fit; to suit. **s'~ mal,** to fit badly.
addition *n.f.* addition; anything added, reckoning, bill, check.
additionnel, le *adj.* additional.
additionner *v.t.* to add; to add up.
adducteur *adj. m. Anat.* adducent. *n.m.* adductor; adducent muscle.
adduction d'eau, *m.f.* water supply.
adepte *n.m.f.* adept.
adéquat, e *adj.* adequate.
adhérence *n.f.* adhesion, adherence.
adhérent, e *adj.* adherent, adhering. *n.m.* adherent.
adhérer *v.i.* (with à) to adhere to; to join.
adhésif, ve *adj.* adhesive.
adhésion *n.f.* adhesion. **donner son ~ à un projet,** to agree to participate in a project.
adieu *adv.* adieu, farewell, good-bye. **dire ~,** to bid adieu, to take leave. **visite d'~,** farewell visit. **je ne vous dis pas ~, sans ~,** I won't say good-bye. **sans plus d'~x,** without further leave-taking. *n.m.* adieu. **un dernier ~,** a last farewell.
adipeux, se *adj.* adipose, fatty, fleshy.
adjacent, e *adj.* adjacent, contiguous.
adjectif, ve *adj.* adjective, adjectival. *n.m.* adjective.
adjectivement *adv.* adjectively.
adjoindre *v.t.* to adjoin. **on lui adjoignit un aide,** an assistant was given to him. **s'~,** *v.refl.* to take on (an aide or assistant). **adjoignez-vous un aide,** get an assistant.
adjoint, e *adj.* adjunct; assistant. **professeur ~,** adjunct professor, *or* assistant professor. *n.m.* associate, deputy (of a mayor, or other functionary); *Gram.* adjunct.
adjonction *n.f.* adjunction; addition. **l'~ d'une lettre à un mot,** the addition of a letter to a word.
adjudant *n.m. Milit.* adjutant.
adjudicataire *n.m.f.* purchaser, buyer (at sales); contractor.
adjudicateur *n.m.* auctioneer; awarder.
adjudication *n.f.* sale by auction; award, awarding. **~ aux enchères,** selling by auction. **par ~,** by contract. **mettre en ~,** to contract for.
adjugé, e *p.p.* adjudged; knocked down, adjudged. **adjugé!** (at sales by auction), gone!
adjuger *v.t.* to adjudge, to knock down to (at auction). **s'~,** *v.refl.* to claim for oneself.
adjuration *n.f.* adjuration, plea.
adjurer *v.t.* to adjure; to implore.
adjuteur *n.m.* adjutor, assistant.
adjuvant, e *adj.* adjuvant. *n.m. Med.* adjuvant.
admettre *v.t.* to give admittance into; to admit; to allow, to permit. **~ dans sa maison,** to admit into one's house. **ses excuses furent admises,** his excuses were received. **je n'ad-**

mets pas qu'il en soit ainsi, I do not admit that it is so. **admettons que cela soit vrai,** let us suppose that to be true.
administrant, e *adj.* administering, managing.
administrateur *n.m.* administrator; manager, trustee.
administratif, ve *adj.* administrative.
administration *n.f.* administration, managing body; trusteeship; management. **mauvaise ~,** mismanagement.
administrativement *adv.* administratively.
administré, e *n.m.* person under one's jurisdiction, citizen. **le maire et ses administrés,** the mayor and his fellow citizens.
administrer *v.t.* to administer; to distribute (justice). **~ des coups de poing,** to cuff, to strike with the fists. **~ des coups de bâton,** to thrash with a stick, to cudgel. **s'~,** *v.refl.* to be administered; to administer to oneself.
admirable *adj.* admirable, excellent.
admirablement *adv.* admirably.
admirateur, trice *n.m.f. n.* admirer; (used adjectively) admiring.
admiratif, ive *adj.* inclined to admire; expressing admiration.
admiration *n.f.* admiration. **être en ~ de, dans l'~ de,** to admire.
admirer *v.t.* to admire; to wonder at, to be astonished at. **s'~** *v.refl.* to admire oneself. **se faire ~,** to make oneself admired.
admis, e *p.p.* admitted. **c'est un fait admis,** it is an acknowledged fact.
admissibilité *n.f.* admissibility.
admissible *adj.* admissible.
admission *n.f.* admission, admittance.
admonestation *n.f.* admonition; caution.
admonester *v.t.* to admonish; to reprimand.
admoniteur *n.m.* admonisher.
admonition *n.f.* admonition; reprimand.
adolescence *n.f.* adolescence, youth.
adolescent, e *n.m.f.* adolescent, youth, teenager.
adoniser *v.t.* to dress up, to overdress. **s'~,** *v.refl.* to overdress oneself.
adonner (s'), *v.refl.* to devote oneself to; to become addicted to. **s'~ à l'étude,** to apply oneself to study. **s'~ à boire,** to take to drinking.
adoptant *n.m.* adopter.
adopté, e *p.p.* adopted, carried, agreed to. **proposition adoptée à l'unanimité,** motion carried unanimously.
adopter *v.t.* to adopt; to carry; to pass (a bill).
adoptif, ive *adj.* adoptive. **fils ~,** adoptive son.
adoption *n.f.* adoption; carrying (of a motion, a resolution). **pays d'~,** adopted country.
adorable *adj.* adorable, divine.
adorateur, trice *s.* adorer, worshiper. **~ du feu,** fire-worshiper.
adoration *n.f.* worship; adoration.
adorer *v.t.* to adore; to worship, to be very fond of.
ados *n.m.* sloping bed (backed against a wall).

adossé, e *p.p.* backed (against a wall, etc.); set back to back.

adossement *n.m.* being set back to back; backing.

adosser *v.t.* (with **à** or **contre**) to lean against; to rest, to support. **s'~,** *v.refl.* to lean back (against); to be backed (by). **il s'adossa contre un arbre,** he leaned back against a tree.

adouber *v.i.* to adjust (a chess piece) without moving it. *Naut.* to repair.

adoucir *v.t.* to sweeten; to soften; to relieve, to allay (pain); to soothe, appease (anger, fury), to diminish (a punishment); to smooth down; to temper, to modify. **s'~,** *v.refl.* to grow softer or milder; to be relieved, to be mitigated. **le temps s'est adouci,** the weather has grown mild.

adoucissage *n.m.* first polish (given to metals, etc.).

adoucissant, e *adj.* and *n.m.* soothing; emollient.

adoucissement *n.m.* sweetening; softening; rendering, growing milder (as the weather); alleviation (of pain); soothing (of grief, etc.); extenuation (of a fault); mitigation (of a punishment).

ad patres *Lat.* **aller ad patres,** to go to kingdom come, to die.

adresse *n.f.* address; cleverness, adroitness. **l'~ d'une lettre,** the address of a letter. **à l'~ de,** addressed to. **cela va à l'~ d'un tel,** that is intended for so-and-so. **bureau d'adresses,** inquiry office. **~ de félicitations,** congratulatory address. **tour d'~,** sleight of hand trick.

adresser *v.t.* to address a letter; to speak to. **je vous ai adressé à l'homme qui pouvait le mieux vous renseigner,** I sent you to the man best able to inform you. **s'~,** *v.refl.* to apply to; to address, to speak to. **adressez-vous à M. un tel,** apply to Mr. so-and-so. **s'~ ici,** apply within.

adroit, e *adj.* adroit, dexterous, clever, shrewd. **adroit tireur,** clever marksman. **~ mensonge,** artful lie.

adroitement *adv.* adroitly, cleverly, expertly; artfully.

adulateur, trice *n.m.f.* adulator, flatterer; sycophant. **~,** *adj.* adulatory, flattering.

adulation *n.f.* adulation, flattery.

aduler *v.t.* to adulate, to flatter.

adulte *adj.* adult, grown up. *n.m.f.* adult.

adultération *n.f.* adulteration; falsification.

adultère *n.m.f.* adulterer; *f.* adulteress, *adj.* adulterous, impure. *n.m.* adultery.

adulterer *v.t.* to adulterate.

adultérin, e *adj.* adulterine, adulterous; born of adultery.

advenant *adj.* in the event of. **~ le décès,** in case of death.

advenir *v.i.* to happen, to come to pass. **advienne que pourra,** come what may.

adventice *adj.* adventitious; self-propagating.

adverbe *n.m.* adverb.

adverbial, e *adj. Gram.* adverbial.

adverbialement *adv.* adverbially.

adversaire *n.f.* adversary, opponent.

adversatif, ive *adj. Gram.* adversative.

adverse *adj.* adverse, opposite. **fortune ~,** adverse fortune.

adversité *n.f.* adversity, adverse fortune; *pl.* misfortunes, troubles.

aérage *n.m.* ventilation (of rooms, mines, etc.). **puits d'~,** airshaft (of a mine).

aération *n.f.* aeration; ventilation.

aéré *p.p.* ventilated; aerated.

aérer *v.t.* to ventilate; to aerate, to air. **une chambre bien aérée,** a well-aired room.

aérien, ne *adj.* airy, of or in the air.

aérifère *adj.* air-conducting.

aériforme *adj.* aeriform.

aérobique *n.f.* aerobics.

aéro-club *n.m.* flying club.

aérodrome *n.m.* airfield.

aérodynamique *n.f.* aerodynamics.

aérofrein *n.m.* air brake.

aérogare *n.f.* airport, air terminal.

aérogramme *n.m.* airmail letter.

aérographe *n.f.* airbrush.

aérolithe *n.m.* aerolite, aerolith.

aérologie *n.f.* aerology.

aéromancie *n.f.* aeromancy.

aéromètre *n.m.* aerometer.

aérométrie *n.f.* aerometry.

aéronaute *n.m.f.* aeronaut.

aéronautique *adj.* aeronautic. *n.f.* aeronautics.

aérophobe *n.m.f.* person afflicted with aerophobia.

aérophobie *n.f.* aerophobia; dread of air.

aéroplane *n.m.* airplane.

aéroport *n.m.* airport.

aérostat *n.m.* balloon, air balloon.

aérostatique *adj.* aerostatic. *n.f.* aerostatics.

afatonier *n.m.* sloe tree; the common blackthorn.

affabilité *n.f.* affability.

affable *adj.* affable.

affablement *adv.* affably.

affabulation *n.f.* moral of a fable.

affadir *v.t.* to render insipid; to pall on (on the stomach); to disgust. **~ le coeur,** to cause nausea. **s'~,** *v.refl.* to lose taste; to become insipid.

affadissant, e *adj.* vapid, insipid; mawkish, sickening.

affadissement *n.m.* insipidity.

affaiblir *v.t.* to weaken; to enfeeble; to grow feeble. **~ le courage,** to dampen the courage. **s'~,** *v.refl.* to become, to grow weak *or* feeble; to grow faint.

affaiblissant, e *adj.* weakening, enfeebling.

affaiblissement *n.m.* weakness; debility, enfeeblement; relaxation (of discipline).

affaire *n.f.* affair, matter, thing, concern, question; *pl.* business; affairs; speculation, operation; fortune; difficulty, scrape, mess; case, lawsuit.

~ agréable, agreeable affair. une ~ d'intirêt, a money matter, a question of property. c'est une étrange ~, it is a strange affair, matter, business. c'est bien une autre ~, that is quite another affair, a very different matter. une mauvaise ~, a bad piece of business. ne rien faire à l'~, not to affect the matter. pour ~s, on business. en ~s, in business. parler d'affaires, to talk business. nous avons fait ~ ensemble, we have done business together. faire de grandes ~s, to do business on a large scale. les ~s vont bien, business is thriving. un marchand a ~ à toutes sortes de gens, a merchant does business with all sorts of people. je lui ferai son ~, I will get even with him. se mettre dans les ~s, to go into business, to set up in trade. il s'est retiré des ~s, he has retired from business. ~s d'Etat, affairs of state. il est au-dessus de ses ~s, he is well off, he has capital enough and to spare. homme d'~s, agent; steward. cabinet, bureau d'~s, agency office, agent's office. une ~ d'or, a profitable speculation. j'ai fait hier une excellente ~, I made a good speculation yesterday. il se fait peu d'~s à la Bourse, there is but little business going on at the Stock Exchange. son ~ est faite, his fortune is made. s'attirer une ~, to get into a scrape. se tirer d'~, to get out of a scrape, out of a predicament. vous avez une belle ~ là, you are in a pretty mess now. ~ civile, civil suit, cause. ~ criminelle, criminal case, prosecution, trial.

affairé, e adj. busy, occupied, bustling. **trop ~,** overwhelmed with business.

affaissement n.m. sinking, subsidence (as of the soil); giving way.

affaisser v.t. to weigh down; to sink; to settle. **s'~,** v.refl. to sink down; to settle (as the soil); to subside; to give way; to collapse.

affalé, e p.p. slumped, collapsed.

affaler v.t. to lower (a boat, etc.); to drive toward the coast. **s'~,** v.refl. to slide down a rope; to be driving toward a lee shore.

affamé, e p.p. famishing, famished, hungry; starving; thirsting for.

affamer v.t. to famish, to starve.

affectation n.f. affectation; appropriation (of funds to a certain purpose). **quelle ~!** what sham!

affecté, e p.p. affected.

affecter v.t. to affect, to have a preference for; to feign, to assume; to set apart funds. **s'~,** v.refl. to be affected, to be moved; to be distressed or afflicted.

affectif, ve adj. affective; emotional.

affection n.f. affection; fondness; Med. affection, disease. **il me prit en ~,** he took a liking to me.

affectionné, e p.p. beloved. **~ par toute la maison,** beloved by all the household. adj. attached; affectionate. **votre très ~ serviteur,** your most devoted servant. **votre ami très ~,** your most affectionate friend.

affectionner v.t. to like, to have a liking for; to interest. **s'~,** v.refl. (with à) to become attached to; to be fond of, to delight in; to love each other.

affectueusement adv. affectionately, lovingly.

affectueux, se adj. affectionate, loving.

afférent, e adj. belonging to, pertaining to.

affermer v.t. to rent (as a landlord); to farm out; to take on lease.

affermir v.t. to make firm; to strengthen; to establish; to harden. **s'~,** v.refl. to become firm; to grow stronger; to harden.

affermissement n.m. consolidation; strengthening.

affété, e adj. affected; mannered.

afféterie n.f. affectation. **avec ~,** with mannerisms.

affichage n.m. putting up posters.

affiche n.f. poster. **tenir l'affiche,** to have a long run. **la pièce a tenu l'affiche pendant un an,** the play ran for one year. **~ à la main,** handbill. **faire ~ de,** to make a show.

affiché, e p.p. posted; advertised. **dévotion affichée,** ostentatious piety.

afficher v.t. to put up (bills); to publish; to expose. **défense d'~,** post no bills. **s'~,** v.refl. to court notoriety; to be stuck up. **s'~ pour homme sans moeurs,** to proclaim one's own immorality.

afficheur n.m. billposter.

affidé, e adj. trustworthy; m. faithful adherent; confederate, accomplice, henchman.

affilage n.m. sharpening.

affilé, e adj. sharp; (of the tongue) glib.

affiler v.t. to sharpen, to give keenness to.

affileur n.m. sharpener.

affiliation n.f. affiliation.

affilié, e p.p. affiliated. n.f. associate.

affilier v.t. to affiliate; to associate. **s'~,** v.refl. to join.

affiloir n.m. knife sharpener.

affinage n.m. refining.

affiner v.t. to refine; to point (nails, etc.); to trick. **s'~,** v.refl. to become purer; to mature.

affinerie n.f. refinery.

affineur n.m. refiner.

affinité n.f. affinity; connection, congeniality.

affins n.m.pl. affines.

affiquet n.m. knickknack; knitting sheath.

affirmatif, ve adj. affirmative.

affirmation n.f. affirmation; Log. predication.

affirmative n.f. affirmative. **à l'~,** in the affirmative.

affirmativement adv. affirmatively.

affirmer v.t. to affirm; Log. to predicate.

affixe n.m. affix.

affleuré, e p.p. made level or flush. adj. flush.

affleurement n.m. leveling; outcrop.

affleurer v.t. to make level or flush; to rise to the level of; to crop out.

afflictif, ve *adj.* afflicting the person. **peines afflictives,** corporal punishments.

affliction *n.f.* affliction; misfortune.

affligé *adj.* afflicted; grieved; affected by disease. **je suis ~ de vous voir si malade,** I am grieved to see you so ill. **les affligés,** the mourners.

affligeant, e *adj.* afflicting, distressing.

affliger *v.t.* to afflict; to distress, to grieve. **~ la chair,** to mortify the flesh. **s'~,** *v.refl.* to afflict oneself; to be grieved; to grieve.

afflouer *v.t. Naut.* to float.

affluence *n.f.* afflux; (of people) affluence, throng; (of things) abundance.

affluent, e *adj.* tributary (as streams); *Med.* affluent. *n.m.* tributary. **Le Rhin et ses ~s,** the Rhine and its tributaries.

affluer *v.i.* to flow; (of people) to flock, (of things) to abound; *Med.* to rush.

afflux *n.m.* afflux, rush.

affolé, e *p.p.* dotingly fond of; distracted. **être ~ de,** to be infatuated with.

affolement *n.m.* madness; distraction.

affoler *v.t.* to drive mad. **s'~,** *v.refl.* to be infatuated with.

affourcher *v.t.* to place astride; to moor with two anchors set at an angle. **s'~,** *v.refl.* to be so moored.

affranchi, e *p.p.* emancipated; freed; exempt; postpaid. **les lettres non affranchies seront refusées,** unpaid letters will be refused. *n.m.f.* freed man, freed woman.

affranchir *v.t.* to enfranchise; to release, to discharge (a prisoner); to pay the postage. **s'~,** *v.refl.* to free oneself; to shake off.

affranchissement *n.m.* enfranchisement; release; prepayment (of postage).

affranchisseur *n.m.* deliverer, liberator.

affre *n.f.* terror. **les ~s de la mort,** the terrors or pangs of death.

affrètement *n.m.* chartering, freighting. **contrat d'~,** charter party.

affréter *v.t.* to freight.

affréteur *n.m.* freighter.

affreusement *adv.* frightfully, dreadfully, shockingly. **~pâle,** ghastly pale.

affreux, se *adj.* frightful, dreadful, shocking; sad; hideous; abominable. **un spectacle ~,** a frightful spectacle. **temps ~,** horrible weather.

affriandé, e *p.p.* enticed; tempted. **~ par les promesses,** allured by promises. **~ de butin,** eager for booty.

affriander *v.t.* to entice, to tempt.

affriolant *adj.* appetizing, alluring.

affrioler *v.t.* to entice.

affront *n.m.* affront; dishonor; insult. **avaler un ~,** to swallow an insult. **essuyer un ~,** to receive an affront. **ne pouvoir digérer un ~,** to be unable to ignore an affront. **faire ~ à,** to disgrace. **il fait ~ à toute sa famille,** he is a disgrace to his whole family.

affronté, e *p.p.* braved; deceived.

affronter *v.t.* to confront, to face; to brave, to cheat. **s'~,** *v.refl.* to confront each other, to stand face to face.

affronteur, euse *n.m.f.* deceiver, cheat.

affublé, e *p.p.* **plaisamment ~,** dressed ludicrously.

affublement *n.m.* ridiculous clothing.

affubler *v.t.* to wrap up, to dress up ridiculously. **s'~,** *v.refl.* to muffle or dress oneself in a ridiculous manner.

affût *n.m.* carriage (of a cannon). *Sport.* hiding place; watch, lookout. **choisir un bon ~,** to choose a good hiding place. **être à l'~,** to lie in wait.

affûtage *n.m.* sharpening, toolchest; redressing (of an old hat); place of a cannon in battery.

affûter *v.t.* to sharpen, to set.

afin *conj.* in order to; (with **que** followed by the subjunctive) in order that. **~ d'aller à son but,** to attain his end. **~ que cela soit plus facile,** in order that it may be easier.

africain, e *adj.* African. *n.m.f.* African.

Afrique *n.f.* Africa.

agaçant, e *adj.* provoking; tantalizing.

agacement *n.m.* setting on edge (of the teeth); *Fig.* irritation.

agacer *v.t.* to set on edge. **ce bruit agace les dents,** that noise sets one's teeth on edge; to irritate (the nerves); to annoy; to provoke; to excite. **s'~,** *v.refl.* to be set on edge (as the teeth); to be irritated; to tease one another.

agacerie *n.f.* enticement. **elle lui fait des agaceries continuelles,** she is always trying to attract his attention.

agape *n.f.* love feast (of the early Christians); feast.

âge *n.m.* age, years, old age, period, epoch, years. **bas ~,** infancy. **~ de raison,** years of discretion. **~ nubile,** marriageable age. **~ viril,** manhood. **~ d'homme,** manhood, man's estate. **il ne paraît pas son ~,** he does not look his age. **sur l'~,** elderly. **retour de l'~,** the downhill of life. **être d'un certain ~,** to be an older person. **être entre deux ~s,** to be of middle age. **quel ~ a-t-elle?** how old is she? what is her age? **l'~ de la chevalerie,** the age, the days of chivalry. **le moyen ~,** the Middle Ages. **l'~ d'or,** the golden age. **l'~ d'airain, de fer,** the bronze age, the iron age.

âgé, e *adj.* aged, old. **un homme ~,** an aged man.

agence *n.f.* agency.

agencé, e *p.p.* arranged, fitted; dressed up extravagantly.

agencement *n.m.* arrangement; *Paint.* arrangement, composition; *pl.* fittings.

agencer *v.t.* to set up, arrange an office.

agenda *n.m.* datebook; ritual of a church.

agenouiller (s') *v.refl.* to kneel down.

agent *n.m.* agent; steward. **~ comptable,** an

accountant. ~ **d'affaires**, agent. ~ **de change**, stockbroker. ~ **de police**, police agent.

agglomération *n.f.* agglomeration.

agglomérer *v.t.* to agglomerate.

agglutination *n.f.* agglutination.

agglutiner *v.t.* to agglutinate; to join together. **s'~**, *v.refl.* to be agglutinated.

aggravant, e *adj.* aggravating.

aggravation *n.f.* aggravation. **l'~ du mal,** aggravation of the disease.

aggraver *v.t.* to aggravate; to increase. **s'~**, *v.refl.* to become aggravated, to get worse; to grow heavier.

agile *adj.* agile; nimble.

agilement *adv.* with agility, nimbly.

agilité *n.f.* agility; nimbleness.

agir *v.i.* to act, to behave. **le moment d'~ est venu,** the time to act is come. ~ **bien,** to act right, to do right. ~ **mal,** to do wrong. **faire ~,** to cause. **vous avez agi en ami,** you have acted as a friend. **s'~,** *v.refl.* to be the question, the point in question. **voici ce dont il s'agit,** this is the point in question. **de quoi s'agit-il?** what is the point in question? what's up? **il s'agit de vous dans cette affaire,** you are concerned in this business. **il s'agit de vos intérêts,** your interests are at stake. **il ne s'agit point que vous écriviez, il faut que vous y alliez vous-même,** this is no case for writing, you must go in person.

agissant, e *adj.* active; stirring; efficacious. **homme ~,** an active man. **remède ~,** an active remedy.

agitateur *n.m.* agitator.

agitation *n.f.* agitation, commotion; disturbance; emotion; unrest. **l'~ des vagues,** the turbulence of the waves.

agiter *v.t.* to agitate; to shake; to move, to stir; to disturb; to discuss; to toss (as the waves do a ship); to jolt (as a carriage). **s'~,** *v.refl.* to be agitated; to agitate oneself; to move; to toss about.

agneau *n.m.* lamb. **côtelette d'~,** lamb cutlet.

agnelage *n.m.* lambing.

agneler *v.i.* to lamb.

agnelet *n.m.* lambkin.

agneline *adj.f.* **laine ~,** lamb's wool.

agnelle *n.f.* ewe lamb.

agnosticisme *n.m.* agnosticism.

agnostique *n.m.f.* agnostic.

agonie *n.f.* agony; anguish; pangs of death. **il a été à l'~,** he has been at death's door.

agonir *v.t. Vulg.* to abuse.

agonisant, e *adj.* dying, expiring. *n.m.f.* a dying person. **les morts et les agonisants,** the dead and the dying.

agoniser *v.i.* to be expiring; to be at the point of death.

agrafe *n.f.* hook; clasp, snap (of cloak, necklace, bracelet, etc.); hook and staple (to fasten window shutters). ~ **et porte,** hook-and-eye.

agrafer *v.t.* to hook, to clasp.

agraire *adj.* agrarian. **la loi ~,** the agrarian law.

agrandir *v.t.* to enlarge, to extend, to increase, to exaggerate. ~ **une maison,** to enlarge a house, to extend. ~ **ses vues,** to enlarge one's views. **ce prince a agrandi sa nation,** that prince has aggrandized his nation. **s'~,** *v.refl.* to be enlarged, to enlarge, to grow larger. **cette ville s'agrandit rapidement,** this town is rapidly enlarging.

agrandissement *n.m.* enlargement; aggrandizement; exaltation. ~ **d'une ville,** the growth of a town.

agréable *adj.* agreeable; pleasant; pleasing; welcome. **lieu ~,** pleasant place. **compagnon ~,** agreeable, pleasant companion. **une femme ~,** a charming woman. **une sensation ~,** a pleasurable sensation. **un bon feu est ~ en hiver,** a good fire is nice in winter. **mêler l'utile à l'~,** to blend the useful with the agreeable.

agréablement *adv.* agreeably; pleasantly; acceptably.

agréé, e *n.m.* lawyer, attorney *adj.* approved.

agréer *v.t.* to accept; to approve; to receive favorably. **le roi agréa la démission du ministre,** the king accepted the minister's resignation. ~ **un vaisseau,** to rig out a ship. *v.i.* to be acceptable to. **ce mariage aurait agréé à toute la famille,** that marriage would have been acceptable to all the family.

agrégatif, ive *adj.* aggregative.

agrégation *n.f.* aggregation; assemblage; corporation; *Univ.* fellowship; competitive examination qualifying successful candidates, to hold teaching posts in lycées or universities.

agrégé *n.m. Univ.* fellow; professor.

agréger *v.t.* to admit. **s'~,** *v.refl.* to be aggregated with.

agrément *n.m.* consent, favor, charm, approbation, approval. **avec mon ~,** with my consent. **l'~ des lieux,** the charm of the place. **arts d'~,** accomplishments. **agrémenter** *v.t.* to ornament, to adorn.

agresseur *n.m.* aggressor. **il était l'~,** he was the aggressor.

agressif, ve *adj.* aggressive.

agression *n.f.* aggression.

agressivement *adv.* aggressively.

agreste *adj.* rustic, wild; (of persons) rude, savage. **manières agrestes,** boorish manners.

agricole *adj.* agricultural. **travail ~,** field labor. **industrie ~,** farming.

agriculteur *n.m.* agriculturist. *adj.* agricultural.

agriculture *n.f.* agriculture; farming.

agriffer (s') *v.refl.* to cling.

agripper *v.t.* to snatch up.

agronome *n.m.* scientific agriculturist.

agronomie *n.f.* agronomy.

agronomique *adj.* agronomic.

agrouper *v.t.* to group.

aguerri, e *adj.* inured to war; inured, hardened.

aguerrir *v.t.* to inure to war; to harden. **s'~,**

v.refl. to become inured to war; to get inured, hardened. **tâchez de vous ~ contre les voluptés,** strive to harden yourself against voluptuousness.

aguets *n.m.pl.* lying in wait; *sing.* ambush. **être aux ~,** to be lying in wait. **mettre aux ~,** to set (persons) on the watch.

aguimpé, *e adj.* wimpled.

ah *int.* ah!

ahan *n.m.* laborious effort.

ahaner *v.i.* to labor hard.

aheurtement *n.m.* stubbornness.

aheurter (s') *v.refl.* to be stubborn in.

ahuri, *e p.p., adj.* dumbfounded; flurried.

ahurir *v.t.* to dumbfound; to bewilder.

ahurissement *n.m.* dumbfounding, bewilderment.

aidant, *e p.p.* and *adj.* aiding. *n.m.f.* helper.

aide *n.f.* aid; help, assistance; relief. **leur ~ nous fut très utile,** their assistance was very useful to us. *n.m.f.* assistant, helper. **aide-de-camp,** aide-de-camp. **~ des cérémonies,** assistant master of ceremonies. **~ de cuisine,** sous chef.

aider *v.t.* to aid, to help; to relieve (the poor); to promote; to abet. **~ quelqu'un de ses conseils,** to help someone with one's advice. **aidez-moi à descendre,** help me down. **aide-toi, le ciel t'aidera,** heaven helps those who help themselves. **s'~,** *v.refl.* to help oneself; to assist one another *or* each other; to exert oneself. **aidez-vous les uns les autres,** help one another. *v.i.* (with **à**) to help, to assist. **~ au succès,** to contribute to the success. **ils lui aidaient à tromper le roi,** they helped him to deceive (*or* in deceiving) the king.

aïe *interj.* oh! ouch! ow!

aïeul *n.m.* grandfather; ancestor. **~ paternel,** paternal grandfather.

aïeule *n.f.* grandmother.

aïeux *n.m.pl.* ancestors, forefathers.

aigle *n.m.* eagle. **~ impérial,** imperial eagle. **~ royal,** golden eagle. **crier comme un ~,** to shriek. **avoir des yeux d'~,** to be eagle-eyed. *Fig.* **c'est un ~,** he is a genius. *n.f.* eagle. **les aigles romaines,** the Roman eagles.

aiglette *n.f. Herald.* eaglet.

aiglon *n.m.* eaglet; young eagle.

aigre *adj.* acid, sour; sharp, piercing (as sounds); harsh; brittle; crabbed (of persons). *n.m.* acidity, sourness (in taste or smell); sharpness. **sentir l'~,** to smell sour *or* stale.

aigre-doux, douce *adj.* sourish. **des oranges aigres-douces,** sourish oranges.

aigrefin *n.m.* swindler.

aigrelet, *te adj.* sourish, tartish. **paroles aigrelettes,** sharp words.

aigrement *adv.* sourly, harshly.

aigrette *n.f.* eagret; topknot of feathers; tuft of feathers.

aigretté, *e adj.* having a topknot of feathers.

aigreur *n.f.* acidity, sourness; acrimony, sharpness; ill feeling; *pl.* acidity of stomach; brittleness (of metals). **ce vin a de l'~,** this wine is sour. **l'~ de la discussion,** the acrimony of the discussion.

aigri, *e p.p.* soured; irritated. **~ par le malheur,** soured by misfortune.

aigrir *v.t.* to turn sour; to irritate; to aggravate. *v.i.* to become or turn sour. **le lait a aigri,** the milk has gone sour. **s'~,** *v.refl.* to become or turn sour; to become irritated.

aigrissement *n.m.* souring; exasperation.

aigu, *ë adj.* sharp-pointed; acute; shrill; violent; *Gram.* opposed to **grave,** said of accents. **épigramme aiguë,** stinging epigram. **voix aiguë,** shrill voice. **maladie aiguë,** acute disease.

aiguayer *v.t.* to bathe; to rinse.

aigue-marine *n.f.* aquamarine; beryl.

aiguière *n.f.* ewer; water-jug.

aiguillage *n.m. Railw.* switching.

aiguille *n.f.* needle. **~ de montre,** etc., hand (clock). **~ de clocher,** spire. **~ à coudre,** sewing needle. **~ à passer,** bodkin. **~ à repriser,** darning needle. **~ à tricoter,** knitting needle. **ouvrage à l'~,** needle-work. **de fil en ~,** from one thing to another. **~ aimantée,** magnetic needle. **~ d'inclinaison,** dipping needle. **~ de chemin de fer,** switches.

aiguillée *n.f.* needleful.

aiguiller *v.t.* to switch (of railroads).

aiguillette *n.f.* tagged lace. strip of beef (culinary).

aiguilleur *n.m.* switchman (of railroads).

aiguillier *n.m.* needle maker; needle case.

aiguillon *n.m.* goad; spur; sting (of bees, etc.); prickle.

aiguillonnement *n.m.* goading; pricking; incitement.

aiguillonner *v.t.* to goad; to spur on. **~ les boeufs,** to goad oxen. **Aiguillonné par la faim,** impelled by hunger.

aiguisage, aiguisement *n.m.* sharpening (of blade tools).

aiguiser *v.t.* to sharpen. **pierre à ~,** whetstone. **une promenade vous aiguisera l'appétit,** a walk will stimulate your appetite. **~ une épigramme,** to sharpen an epigram.

aiguiseur *n.m.* grinder.

ail *n.m.,pl.* **ails** or **aulx** garlic. **ail d'Espagne,** rocambole. **gousse d'~,** clove of garlic.

aile *n.f.* wing, pinion; aisle of a church. **à tire d'~,** at a single flight. **l'oiseau bat ses ~s,** the bird flaps its wings. **être sur l'~,** to be on the wing. **bouts d'ailes,** pinions. **sur les ~s du temps,** on the wings of time. **voler à tire d'~,** to wing a rapid flight. **battre les ~s,** to flap wings. **ne battre que d'une ~,** to be crippled. **rogner les ~s à quelqu'un,** to clip someone's wings. **voler de ses propres ~s,** to stand on one's own legs.

ailé, *e adj.* winged. **vis ailée,** wingnut (of a screw).

aileron *n.m.* pinion; end of a bird's wing; fin; float (of a water wheel).

aillade *n.f.* garlic sauce.

ailleurs *adv.* elsewhere; somewhere else. **nulle part ~,** nowhere else. **partout ~,** in any other place. **d'~,** *adv.* moreover, besides; otherwise.

aimable *adj.* lovely; lovable; amiable; agreeable. **un caractère ~,** an amiable disposition. **manières ~s,** pleasing manners. **vous seriez bien ~ de me rendre ce service,** it would be very kind of you to do me this service. *n.m.* **faire l'~,** to affect kindness.

aimablement *adv.* amiably.

aimant, e *adj.* loving. **naturel ~,** a loving disposition.

aimant *n.m.* magnet. **les pôles d'un ~,** the poles of a magnet.

aimantation *n.f.* magnetization.

aimanté, e *adj.* magnetic.

aimanter *v.t.* to magnetize. **s'~,** *v.refl.* to be magnetized.

aimé, e *adj.,p.p.* loved, beloved; *n.* beloved one. **~ de Dieu,** beloved of God. **~ de tous,** loved by all. **bien-aimé,** well beloved.

aimer *v.t.* to love, to like, to be partial to, to be fond of. **~ son père,** to love one's father. **il aime les enfants,** he is fond of children. **j'aime le fruit,** I like fruit. **le saule aime l'humidité,** the willow flourishes in moist ground. **qui aime bien, châtie bien,** who loves well, chastens well. **se faire ~ de,** to win the affection of. **j'aime à voir comme vous l'instruisez,** I am pleased to see how you teach him. **~ mieux,** to like better, to prefer. **il aime mieux son argent que ses amis,** he prefers his money to his friends. *v.i.* to love, to be in love. **s'~,** *v.refl.* to love; to like each other. **aimez-vous les uns les autres,** love one another.

aine *n.m.* groin.

aîné, e *adj.* eldest; senior. **mon frère ~,** my eldest brother. *n.m.f.* eldest, senior.

aînesse *n.f.* priority of birth. **droit d'~,** birthright.

ainsi *adv.* so, thus. **il s'exprima ~,** he expressed himself thus. **~ va le monde,** so goes the world. **s'il en est ~,** if such be the case. *conj.* so, thus; therefore. **~ il est évident que,** thus, it is evident that. **~ que,** just as. **~ que je l'espère,** as I hope.

air *n.m.* air; look, appearance, mien, bearing; tune, air, melody. **~ pur,** pure air. **prendre l'~,** to take the air. **fendre l'~,** to cleave the air. **battre l'~,** to beat the air. **un courant d'~,** a draft. **en plein ~,** in the open air. **il n'y a pas un souffle d'~,** there is not a breath of air. **en l'~,** in the air. **fortune en l'~,** imaginary wealth. **contes en l'~,** idle stories. **être en l'~,** to be in a flutter. **son ~ froid et réservé,** his cold reserved air. **~ timide,** bashful air. **~ de simplicité,** air of simplicity. **avoir l'~,** to look, to appear. **il a l'~ mauvais,** he looks ill tempered.

il a bon ~, he has a gentlemanly appearance. **il a l'~ bon,** he has a good-natured look. **elle a l'~ bien étourdi,** she looks very giddy. **se donner de grands ~s,** to give oneself lofty airs. **l'~ va bien aux paroles,** the tune is well suited to the words.

airain *n.m.* brass; impudence. **l'~ sonne,** the bell rings. **cœur d'~,** unfeeling heart. **front d'~,** brazen face.

aire *n.f.* threshing floor; *Geom.* area; surface; eyrie (of an eagle, etc.). **~ de vent,** point of the compass. **~ d'un vaisseau,** speed of a ship.

airée *n.f.* flour (of wheat, etc.) **airelle** *n.f.* whortleberry, huckleberry.

ais *n.m.* thin plank of wood; stave (of a cask); pressboard.

aisance *n.f.* ease; facility; easy circumstances. **il est dans l'~,** he is well off. **fosse d'aisances,** cesspool.

aise *n.f.* joy, gladness, ease. **sauter d'~,** to jump for joy. **ne pas se sentir d'~,** to be beside oneself with joy. **être à son ~,** to be at ease. **être mal à son ~,** to be ill at ease. **mettre quelqu'un à son ~,** to put someone at ease. **se mettre à son ~,** to make oneself at home. **en prendre à son ~,** to talk lightly. **aimer ses ~s,** to indulge oneself. **à l'~,** at ease. *adj.* glad; delighted. **j'en suis bien ~,** I am very glad of it. **je suis ~ de mon sort,** I am content with my lot.

aisé, e *adj.* easy; well-to-do; commodious. **cela est bien ~,** that is very easy. **manières aisées,** easy manners. **une famille aisée,** a well-to-do family.

aisément *adv.* easily.

aisselle *n.f.* armpit.

ajonc *n.m.* furze, gorse.

ajourer *v.t.* to pierce, to perforate; to hemstitch (linen).

ajournement *n.m.* summons; adjournment, postponement.

ajourner *v.t.* to summon; to adjourn (a debate, etc.); to postpone. **s'~,** *v.refl.* to adjourn; to be postponed, adjourned.

ajoutage *n.m.* piece added, addition.

ajouté, e *p.p.,n.m.* addition; words added.

ajouter *v.t.* to add (to). **~ une aile à une maison,** to add a wing to a house. **~ foi à,** to believe, to put faith in. **s'~,** *v.refl.* to be added.

ajustage *n.m.* adjusting.

ajustement *n.m.* adjustment, adjusting, arrangement (of disputes); fitting parts of machines; dress, attire. **l'~ d'un poids,** the adjustment of a weight.

ajuster *v.t.* to adjust, to settle, to arrange (disputes); to fit (one thing to another); to fit up (a house, etc.); to lay out (a garden); to dress, to adorn. **~ une balance,** to adjust a scale. **~ un différend,** to settle a dispute. **elle est en train d'~ ses cheveux,** she is just fixing her hair. **vous voilà bien ajusté,** you are in a pretty pickle. **s'~**, *v.refl.* to be adjusted; to adapt oneself; to fix oneself up. **ces deux pièces s'ajustent bien,** those two pieces fit well together.

ajusteur *n.m.* sizer; fitter.

alambiqué, e *p.p.* distilled; (*adj.*) convoluted, tortuous.

alambiquer *v.t.* and *n.* to overrefine.

alanguir *v.t.* to droop, to weaken.

alanguissement *n.m.* languidness, languishment.

alarmant, e *adj.* alarming.

alarme *n.f.* alarm, terror. **cloche d'~,** alarm bell. **sonner l'~,** to sound the alarm.

alarmer *v.t.* to alarm, to give a signal of danger. **s'~,** *v.refl.* to be alarmed.

alarmiste *n.m.f.* alarmist.

albâtre *n.m.* alabaster; whiteness. **blanc comme ~,** white as alabaster, white as snow.

albatros *n.m.* albatross.

albinos *n.m.* albino.

albumine *n.f.* albumen; the white of eggs.

alcaïque *adj.* and *n.m.* alcaic; **vers ~,** alcaic verse.

alchimie *n.f.* alchemy.

alchimique *adj.* alchemical.

alchimiste *n.m.* alchemist.

alcool *n.m.* alcohol.

alcoolat *n.m.* aromatized spirit.

alcoolique *adj.* alcoholic.

alcoolisation *n.f.* alcoholization.

alcooliser *v.t.* to alcoholize.

alcoolisme *n.m.* alcoholism.

alcoolomètre *n.m.* alcoholometer.

alcootest *n.m.* breathalyser, breath test.

alcôve *n.f.* alcove, recess.

aléatoire *adj.* aleatory, eventual, contingent.

alêne *n.f.* awl. **en ~,** awl-shaped (leaves).

alénier *n.m.* awl maker.

alénois *n.m.* common garden cress.

alentir *v.t.* to slow down. **s'~,** *v.refl.* to slow down, to cool down.

alentour *adv.* around, about. **les villages d'~,** the surrounding villages.

alentours *n.m.pl.* neighborhood, vicinity; persons about. **les ~ du château,** the environs of the mansion.

alerte *interj.* look out! *n.f.* alert, alarm. **donner une ~,** to give an alarm. **en ~,** on the lookout. *adj.* alert, wide awake, smart, shrewd; quick, nimble.

alésage *n.m.* boring, drilling.

aléser *v.t.* to bore smooth.

alésoir *n.m.* boring machine, borer.

alevin, alvin *n.m.* fry, young fish.

alevinage *n.m.* fish breeding; young fish.

aleviner *v.t.* to stock (a pond, etc.) with fry.

alevinier *n.m.* breeding pond (for fish).

alexandrin *adj.* and *n.m.* Alexandrine.

alezan, e *adj.* chestnut color (of a horse). **~ clair,** light chestnut.

alganon *n.m.* chain (of a galley slave).

algarade *n.f.* military incursion; upbraiding, quarrel, prank. **faire une ~,** to give an insult.

algèbre *n.f.* algebra; treatise on algebra.

algébrique *adj.* algebraical, algebraic.

algébriquement *adv.* algebraically.

algébriste *n.m.* algebraist.

algue *n.f. Bot.* alga. **~ marine,** seaweed.

alibi *n.m.* (*pl.* **alibis**) alibi.

alibilité *n.f.* nutritive quality.

aliboron *n.m.* stupid person. **maître ~,** ignoramus.

alidade *n.f.* alidade; index with sight vanes, with a telescope.

aliénabilité *n.f.* alienability.

aliénable *adj.* alienable, transferable.

aliénataire *n.m.f.* alienee.

aliénateur, trice *n.m.f. s.* alienator, transferrer.

aliénation *n.f.* alienation; change of affection; madness. **~ mentale,** insanity.

aliéné, e *p.p., adj.* alienated (of property); insane, deranged, mad. *n.m.f.* lunatic. **hôpital d'~s,** lunatic asylum, madhouse.

aliéner *v.t.* to alienate (estates or rights). **~ son bien,** to alienate, to sell one's property. **~ l'esprit,** to derange, to deprive of reason. **s'~,** *v.refl.* to be alienated; to lose one's reason, to become insane.

aliforme *adj.* wing-shaped.

aligné, e *p.p.* set in lines.

alignement *n.m.* setting in a straight line; *Print.* lining, ranging (of letters). **être d'~,** to be in line. **prendre un ~,** to trace out. **perdre l'~,** to get out of line.

aligner *v.t.* to arrange in a line; to put into precise order (as words, figures, etc.); *Milit.* to dress; to put troops in line; *Print.* to range (letters). **~ ses phrases,** to polish one's sentences. **s'~,** *v.refl.* to be in line; *Milit.* to fall into line; *Print.* to line.

aliment *n.m.* aliment, food, nourishment; supply; allowance for maintenance. **le boeuf est un ~ substantiel,** beef is substantial food.

alimentaire *adj.* alimentary; nourishing. **régime ~,** diet. **pension ~,** alimony.

alimentation *n.f.* alimentation; diet, food; supply (of a market, etc.); feeding (of a fire).

alimenté, e *p.p.* fed, nourished; provisioned; kept alive.

alimenter *v.i.* to feed; to nourish, to nurture; to supply (rivers, engines, etc.). **s'~,** *v.refl.* to be fed, supplied, kept alive, etc.

alimenteux, teuse *adj.* nutritive, nourishing.

aliments *n.m.pl. Leg.* alimony, allowance.

alinéa *n.m.* paragraph; *Print.* break.

alise *n.f.* service tree.

alisier *n.m.* service tree.

alité, e *p.p.* confined to one's bed, laid up; bed ridden. **il est ~ depuis huit jours,** he has been in bed for the last week.

aliter *v.t.* to confine to one's bed, to lay up. **s'~,** *v.refl.* to lay up (through illness).

allaitante adj.f. nursing, breast-feeding.

allaitement n.m. nursing.

allaiter v.t. to suckle, to nurse; to bring up.

allant adj. stirring, bustling.

allant n.m. goer. **allants et venants**, people coming and going.

alléchant, e adj. alluring, enticing.

allèchement n.m. allurement, enticement.

allécher v.t. to allure, to entice.

allée n.f. going; passage, walk, path (in parks, gardens). l'**~ est facile, le retour est très difficile**, going is easy, getting back again is very difficult. **allées et venues**, comings and goings. **~ couverte**, a shady walk.

allégation n.f. allegation; assertion, quotation.

allège n.f. sill (of window).

allégeance n.f. allegiance, loyalty.

allégement n.f. lightening, easing; alleviation, mitigation (of grief, pain, etc.).

alléger v.t. to lighten, to relieve; to relieve (from pain); to alleviate, to allay (suffering); to soothe (grief). Naut. to buoy up; to slacken (a rope). **~ les charges publiques**, to lighten the public burdens; s'**~**, v.refl. to ease oneself (of a burden); to find relief.

allégir v.t. to reduce the size, the volume, to lighten.

allégorie n.f. allegory.

allégorique adj. allegorical.

allégoriquement adv. allegorically.

allégoriser v.t. to allegorize.

allégoriste n.m. allegorist.

allègre adj. active, brisk, lively.

allègrement adv. briskly, gaily, joyfully.

allégresse n.f. activity, sprightliness; cheerfulness, glee. **avec ~**, blithely. **cris d'~**, shouts of joy.

allegretto n.m. and adv. alegretto.

allégro n.m and adv. allegro.

alléguer v.t. to cite, to quote; to allege.

alleluia n.m. alleluia, hallelujah.

Allemagne n.f. Germany.

allemand, e adj. German. n.m.f. German. **une querelle d'Allemand**, a groundless quarrel. **une jeune ~e**, a German girl.

aller v.i. to go; to move, to work (as machinery); to grow, to get, to become, to be; to travel; to fit, to suit; to amount to, to stand. **~ et venir**, to come and go, to go to and fro. **~ de Paris à Rome**, to go from Paris to Rome. **~ en Italie**, to go to Italy. **~ à l'église**, to go to church. **~ au marché**, to go to market. **~ au bal, au concert, au spectacle**, to go to the ball, the concert, the theater. **~ vite, à pied, à cheval, en voiture**, to go on foot, on horseback, by car. **ce chien va à l'eau**, this dog takes to the water. **~ aux renseignements**, to make inquiries. **~ aux bois, à l'eau**, to go for wood, water. **~ son chemin**, to attend to one's business. **cela va sans dire**, that is a matter of course. **les fleuves vont à la mer**, rivers run (flow) to the sea. **ce chemin va droit à la ville**, this road runs, leads straight to the town. **son nom ira à la postérité**, his name will go down to posterity. **cette machine ne va pas bien**, that machine does not work well. **ma montre va mal**, my watch is off. **ma pendule va quinze jours**, my clock runs for two weeks. **~ en justice**, to go to court. **ses accents vont au coeur**, his words are very affecting. **ce travail va rapidement**, this work advances rapidly. **~ mieux**, to feel better; **~ de mieux en mieux**, to get better and better. **le commerce va mal, va bien**, business is bad, is good. **cela vous va bien**, that suits you. **comment allez vous?** how are you? how do you do? **je vais très bien**, I am quite well. **~ par mer, par le chemin de fer**, to travel by sea, by rail. **cet habit ne vous va pas**, that outfit does not fit you; **votre chapeau va bien mal**, your hat is a very bad fit. **~ comme un gant**, to fit like a glove. **cette dentelle va bien à votre robe**, that lace goes well with your dress. **les dépenses vont jusqu'à mille francs**, the expenses amount (come) to a thousand francs. **~ le droit chemin**, to act honourably. **il va selon son caprice**, he acts according to his fancy. **ce vase va au feu**, that pot will stand the fire. **je vais travailler**, I am going to work. **on va diner**, they are going to dine. **il va venir**, he is coming. **nous allons voir ce qu'il dira**, we shall soon see what he will say. **cela ne va pas**, that will not do. **ses goûts ne peuvent pas aller avec les miens**, his tastes cannot agree with mine. **il va criant par la ville**, he goes shouting about the town. **je n'irai pas faire cette sottise**, I will be sure not to do something foolish like that. **faire ~**, to purge. **~ au-devant de**, to go to meet (a person). **ces deux bas vont ensemble**, those two stockings make a pair. **~ grand train**, to walk fast, to keep a large establishment. **cela va trop loin**, that is going too far. **la dépense ira plus loin qu'on ne pense**, the expense will be greater than we thought. **~ sur**, to be about. **cette dame va sur quarante ans**, that lady is nearly forty years of age. **faire ~**, to set in motion; to drive; to catch, to take in. **faire ~ un cheval**, to make a horse go. **faire ~ une machine**, etc., to start a machine, etc. **laisser ~**, to let go, to let loose. **je le laisse ~ où il veut**, I let him go wherever he pleases. **se laisser ~**, to give way to, to yield to. **il se laisse ~ à la douleur**, he gives himself up to grief. **ne vous laissez pas ~ comme cela**, don't give way like that. **en ~**, to turn out. **il en va de cette entreprise comme de l'autre**, that business turns out like the other. **y ~**, to stake, to play. **allez-y doucement**, go gently, take it easy. **il y va de votre fortune**, your fortune is at stake. **il y va de la vie**, life is at stake. **s'en ~**, v.refl. to go away, to be off. **va-t'en, allez-vous-en!** get out of here! **il s'en est allé au galop**, he galloped off. **mon habit s'en va,** my coat is wearing out. *n.m.* going. **~ et retour,** the journey there and back. **billet d'~ et de retour,** round trip ticket.

alliage *n.f.* alloy, mixture. **le bronze est un ~,** bronze is an alloy.

alliance *n.f.* alliance, marriage; wedding ring.

allié, e *p.p.* allied. *n.m.f.* ally.

allier *v.t.* to alloy, to mix, to marry. **s'~,** *v.refl.* to combine (as metals); to intermarry.

alligator *n.m.* alligator.

allitération *n.f.* alliteration.

allocation *n.f.* allocation.

allocution *n.f.* allocution.

allodial, e *adj.* freehold.

allonge *n.f.* leaf (of a table); rider (of a bill of exchange).

allongé, e *p.p.* lengthened; elongated.

allongement *n.m.* lengthening.

allonger *v.t.* to lengthen; to spin out. **~ le visage,** to pull a long face. **s'~,** *v.refl.* to lengthen, to grow longer. **les jours s'allongent,** the days are lengthening.

allouer *v.t.* to allow, to admit.

alluchon *n.m.* cog, tooth (of a wheel).

allumage *n.m.* lighting (of lamps, etc.).

allumer *v.t.* to light (a fire, a lamp); to kindle, to excite. **~ la guerre,** to start a war. **s'~,** *v.refl.* to light, to take fire; to be inflamed.

allumette *n.f.* match (for starting fire). **boîte d'~s,** box of matches.

allumeur, euse *n.m.f.* igniter; *Auto.* distributor.

allure *n.f.* gait, bearing. **cette affaire prend une mauvaise ~,** that affair is taking a bad turn.

allusif, ive *adj.* allusive.

allusion *n.f.* allusion. **faire ~ à,** to allude to, to refer to. **~ peu voilée,** a broad hint.

alluvial, e, **alluvien,** enne *adj.* alluvial.

alluvion *n.m.* alluvion.

almanach *n.m.* almanac, calendar.

aloi *n.m.* standard, alloy. **or de bon ~,** gold of a high standard. *Fig.* **homme de bas ~,** cad.

alors *adv.* then. **jusqu'alors,** until then. **alors comme alors,** we'll cross that bridge when we come to it.

alose *n.f.* shad, alose.

alouette *n.f.* lark, skylark. **~ des bois,** woodlark. **pied d'~,** larkspur. **il attend que les ~s lui tombent toutes rôties,** he expects things to come to him without any trouble.

alourdir *v.t.* to make dull, heavy. **je me sens tout alourdi,** I feel quite heavy. **s'~,** *v.refl.* to grow or become heavy, dull.

alourdissement *n.m.* heaviness, dulness.

aloyau *n.m.* sirloin (of beef).

alpaga *n.m.* alpaca.

alpestre *adj.* Alpine.

alpha *n.m.* alpha; the beginning.

alphabet *n.m.* alphabet.

alphabétique *adj.* alphabetic, alphabetical. **par ordre ~,** in alphabetical order.

alphabétiquement *adv.* alphabetically.

alpin, e *adj.* Alpine.

alpiste *n.m.* canary grass.

alsacien, enne *adj.* Alsatian.

alsine *n.m.f.* chickweed.

altérabilité *n.f.* alterability, alterableness.

altérable *adj.* alterable.

altérant, e *adj.* causing thirst.

altératif, ive *adj.* alterative.

altération *n.f.* alteration. **sans ~,** unaltered. **l'~ de sa voix,** the change, the faltering of his voice.

altercation *n.f.* altercation; wrangling, dispute.

altéré, e *p.p., adj.* altered, changed; injured; thirsty, dry.

altérer *v.t.* to alter, to change, to impair, to misrepresent, to cause thirst. **le soleil altère ces couleurs,** the sun fades those colors. **~ la viande,** to taint meat. **~ un texte,** to corrupt a texte. **~ l'amitié,** to weaken friendship. **quel sujet inconnu vous altère?** what unknown cause disturbs you? **les salaisons altèrent,** salty foods make one thirsty. **s'~,** *v.refl.* to alter, to be altered, to be spoiled. **là-dessus sa voix s'altéra,** thereupon his voice faltered.

alternance *n.f.* alternance; rotation.

alternant, e *adj.* alternating, alternate.

alternat *n.m.* alternity, alternation.

alternatif, ive *adj.* alternative; choice, option (between two possible actions).

alternation *n.f.* alternation.

alternative *n.f.* alternation, alternative, choice, option. **il n'y a pas d'~,** there is no alternative.

alternativement *adv.* alternately.

alterne *adj.* alternate.

alterné, e *p.p.* alternated.

alterner *v.i.* to alternate.

altesse *n.f.* highness. **son ~ royale,** his Royal Highness.

altier, ère *adj.* proud; lofty. **un caractère ~,** a haughty temper.

altimètre *n.m.* altimeter.

altitude *n.f.* altitude.

alto *n.m.* tenor violin; alto.

altruisme *n.m.* unselfishness; altruism.

altruiste *adj.* unselfish.

alude *n.f.* aluta, colored sheepskin.

alumelle *n.f.* long thin blade (of a sword or knife).

alumine *n.f.* alumina.

aluminer *v.t.* to mix with alumina.

alumineux, euse *adj.* aluminous.

aluminium *n.m.* aluminium.

alun *n.m.* alum.

alunir *v.i.* to land on the moon.

alvéolaire *adj.* alveolar, cellular.

alvéole *n.m.* cell (of a honeycomb).

alvéolé, e *adj.* honeycombed.

amabilité *n.f.* amability; **il m'a fait l'~ de,** he did me the favor of.

amadou *n.m.* amadou, tinder (wood).

amadouer *v.t.* to coax, to wheedle.

amadoueur, euse *n.m.* coaxer, wheedler.

amaigri, e *adj.* emaciated, thin.

amaigrir *v.t.* to make thin, to emaciate. **s'~,** *v.refl.* to grow thin, to waste away.

amaigrissement *n.f.* growing thin or spare, emaciation.

amalgamation *n.f.* amalgamation.

amalgame *n.m.* amalgam.

amalgamer *v.t.* to amalgamate. **s'~,** *v.refl.* to amalgamate, to combine.

amande *n.f.* almond; kernel (of stone fruit). **~ lisse,** almond candy. **huile d'~,** oil of almonds.

amandé *n.m.* milk of almonds.

amandier *n.m.* almond tree.

amant *n.m.* lover, sweetheart; admirer.

amante *n.f.* lover, sweetheart; mistress.

amarante *n.f.* amaranth; amaranth-colored.

amarinage *n.m.* process of getting sealegs.

amariner *v.i.* to grow accustomed to the sea; develop sealegs.

amarque *n.f.* buoy.

amarrage *n.m.* anchorage, lashing (of a ship).

amarre *n.f.* mooring; hawser.

amarrer *v.t.* to moor (a vessel); to lash (a gun, etc.); to make fast.

amaryllis *n.f.* amaryllis, daffodil.

amas *n.m.* heap; mass; store; accumulation. **un ~ de sable,** a heap of sand.

amasser *v.t.* to amass, to heap up, to hoard up; to hoard money. **cet avare amasse toujours,** that miser goes on hoarding. **s'~,** *v.refl.* to be amassed; to collect.

amassette *n.f.* pallette knife.

amasseur, euse *n.m.f.* hoarder.

amateur *n.m.* amateur; lover; (adjectively) fond of (the arts, etc.). **ce n'est qu'un ~,** he is only a dabbler.

amatir *v.t.* to deaden, to dull (gold).

amazone *n.f.* Amazon; riding habit.

ambages *n.f.pl.* ambages, circumlocution. **sans ambages,** plainly, without beating around the bush.

ambassade *n.m.* embassy.

ambassadeur *n.m.* ambassador.

ambassadrice *n.f.* ambassadress.

ambiant, e *adj.* ambient, surrounding.

ambidextre *adj.* ambidextrous.

ambigu, ë *adj.* ambiguous.

ambiguïté *n.f.* ambiguity.

ambigument *adv.* ambiguously.

ambitieusement *adv.* ambitiously.

ambitieux, euse *adj.* ambitious.

ambition *n.f.* ambition.

ambitionner *v.t.* to be ambitious.

amble *n.m.* amble. **aller l'~,** to amble.

ambler *v.i.* to amble.

ambre *n.m.* amber. **il est fin comme l'~,** he is a shrewd fellow. **~ gris,** ambergris.

ambré, e *p.p.* amber; amber-colored.

ambrette *n.f.* ambrette; musk-seed.

Ambroise *n.m.* Ambrose; Ambrosius.

ambroisie *n.f.* ambrosia. **d'~,** ambrosial.

ambrosien, ne *adj.* Ambrosian, of St. Ambrose.

ambulance *n.f.* ambulance; field hospital.

ambulant, e *adj.* itinerant, strolling. **comédiens ambulants,** strolling players. **marchand ~,** peddler.

ambulatoire *adj.* ambulatory; itinerant.

âme *n.f.* soul; a person; breath; spirit; motto; sound post (of a violin); small wood (in the middle of a faggot); core (of a plaster model); chamber (of a cannon). **l'immortalité de l'~,** the immortality of the soul. **grandeur d'~,** greatness of soul, magnanimity. **sans ~,** unfeeling. **une ~ noble, généreuse,** a noble, a generous mind. **tranquillité d'~,** peace of mind. **ville de dix mille ~s,** a town of ten thousand souls. **pauvre ~!** poor soul, poor creature. **rendre l'~,** to give up the ghost. **sur mon ~,** on my soul. **la bonne foi est l'~ du commerce,** good faith is the very soul of business. **du fond de l'~,** from the bottom of the soul.

amélioration *n.f.* amelioration, improvement.

améliorer *v.t.* to mend, to improve; to make better. **s'~,** *v.refl.* to get better, to improve.

amen *n.m.* amen.

aménagement *n.m.* arrangement, disposition.

aménager *v.t.* to dispose, to arrange, to lay out.

amendable *adj.* improvable (as land).

amende *n.f.* fine, penalty. **dix mille francs d'~,** ten thousand francs fine, a fine of ten thousand francs. **~ honorable,** an apology.

amendé, e *p.p.* amended. **projet de loi ~,** an amended bill.

amendement *n.m.* amendment, improvement.

amender *v.t.* to amend, to improve, to mend. **~ le sol,** to improve land.

amener *v.t.* to bring (a person); to draw; to bring over; to strike, to lower (flag, sail). **~ une affaire à bonne fin,** to bring a thing to a happy conclusion. **je l'ai amené à le faire,** I induced him to do it. **~ un accident,** to cause an accident. **~ son pavillon,** to strike one's colors.

aménité *n.f.* amenity; urbanity.

amenorrhée *n.f.* amenorrhea.

amenuiser *v.t.* to thin.

amer, ère *adj.* bitter, painful, sharp. **douleur amère,** poignant grief. *n.m.* bitterness, *pl.* bitters; gall. *Naut.* landmark.

amèrement *adv.* bitterly.

américain, e *adj.* and *n.m.f.* American.

américaniser *v.t.* to Americanize.

amertume *n.f.* bitterness, sorrow, affliction. **dans l'~ de son âme,** in the bitterness of his soul.

améthyste *n.m.* amethyst.

ameublement *n.m.* furniture.

ameublir *v.t.* to break up soil; to convert realty into personal property.

ameublissement *n.m.* mellowing, pulverizing (of soil).

ameulonner *v.t.* to stack (hay, in the field).

ameuter *v.t.* to train (hounds); to excite. **s'~**, *v.refl.* to rebel, to riot.

ami, e *n.m.f.* friend. **~ de collège**, college friend. **bonne ~e**, sweetheart. **un de mes ~s**, a friend of mine. **chambre d'~**, spare bedroom. **agir en ~**, to act as a friend. **l'~ de tout le monde n'est l'~ de personne**, everybody's friend is nobody's friend. **mon cher ami**, my dear friend. *adj.* friendly. **sentiments amis**, friendly feelings.

amiable *adj.* amicable; friendly. **accueil ~**, a kind reception. **à l'~**, amicably. **vente à l'~**, sale by private contract.

amiablement *adv.* amicably.

amiante *n.m.* amianthus, asbestos.

amical, e *adj.* amicable, friendly. **peu ~**, unfriendly.

amicalement *adv.* amicably.

amidon *n.m.* starch.

amidonner *v.t.* to starch.

aminci, e *p.p.* made thin; slender.

amincir *v.t.* to make thin. **s'~**, *v.refl.* to become or grow thinner.

amincissement *n.m.* thinning.

amiral *n.m.* admiral. **grand ~**, lord high admiral. **vice-~**, vice admiral. **contre-~**, rear admiral. **vaisseau ~**, admiralship, flagship.

amirauté *n.f.* admiralship; admiralty.

amitié *n.f.* friendship; affection, respect, friendly feeling. **les liens d'une ~**, the bonds of a friendship. **mon ~ pour vous**, my friendship for you. **par ~**, out of friendship. **prendre en ~**, to take a liking to. **faites-moi l'~ de m'écrire**, do me the kindness of writing to me. **présentez mes ~s à madame votre mère**, remember me kindly to your mother.

ammoniac, aque *adj.* **sel ~**, sal ammoniac.

ammoniacal, e *adj.* ammoniacal.

ammoniaque *n.f.* ammonia.

ammonium *n.m.* ammonium.

amnistie *n.f.* amnesty.

amnistié, e *p.p.* pardoned *n.* person amnestied.

amnistier *v.t.* to pardon by amnesty.

amodiateur *n.m.* leaseholder.

amodiation *n.f.* leasing.

amodier *v.t.* to lease out.

amoindrir *v.t.* to lessen, to diminish; to decrease. **s'~**, *v.refl.* to grow less, to diminish.

amoindrissement *n.m.* diminution.

amolli, e *p.p.* softened; mollified; enervated.

amollir *v.t.* to soften; to mollify; to enervate. **la chaleur amollit la cire**, heat softens wax. **s'~**, *v.refl.* to soften, to be mollified; to become effeminate.

amollissant, e *adj.* enervating.

amollissement *n.m.* softening; mollification; enervation.

amonceler *v.t.* to heap up, to pile up; to amass;

to drift, to drive into heaps. **le vent amoncelle la neige**, the wind drifts the snow. **s'~**, *v.refl.* to be heaped *or* piled up. **les nuages s'amoncellent**, the clouds are gathering.

amoncellement *n.m.* accumulation; piling up.

amont *n.m.* water upstream. **en ~**, upstream. **en ~ du pont**, above the bridge.

amorce *n.f.* bait, allurement; cap (of powder). **mettre l'~ à l'hameçon**, to bait the hook. **sans brûler une ~**, without firing a shot.

amorcer *v.t.* to bait (a hook); to decoy; to prime (firearms). **~ un hameçon**, to bait a hook.

amorphe *adj.* amorphous.

amortir *v.t.* to deaden; to weaken; to assuage (the passions); to abate; to liquidate (a debt); to sink (money). **~ ses dettes**, to pay off one's debts. **~ un coup**, to deaden a blow. **s'~**, *v.refl.* to be deadened; to be paid off.

amortissable *adj.* redeemable (of annuities, etc.).

amortissement *n.m.* liquidation, paying off (of a debt); sinking. **caisse d'~**, sinking fund.

amour *n.m.* love. **mourir d'~**, to die of love. **languir d'~**, to be lovesick. **~ paternel**, **maternel, filial**, paternal, maternal, filial love. **l'~ des sciences**, the love of the sciences. **~ du plaisir, du jeu**, love of pleasure, love of gaining. **pour l'~ de Dieu**, for God's sake. **~-propre**, self-esteem. **l'~-propre est le père des illusions**, self-love is the source of self-deception. **cet enfant est l'~ de sa mère**, this child is his mother's darling. **mon ~**, my love, my darling. **l'~ est aveugle**, love is blind. **quel ~ d'enfant!** what a lovely child! **beau comme un ~**, strikingly handsome.

amouraché *e p.p.* (**de**, with) enamoured.

amouracher *v.t.* to inflame with love. **s'~**, *v.refl.* (**de**, with) to be enamoured, to be smitten.

amourette *n.f.* love affair, intrigue.

amoureusement *adv.* lovingly, amorously.

amoureux, euse *adj.* amorous, in love. **il est ~ de cette femme**, he is in love with that woman. **lettres ~ses**, love letters. **chanson ~se**, love song.

amoureux, se *n.m.f.* lover, sweetheart.

amours *n.f.pl.* love, loves, amours; cupids. **premières ~**, first love. **de folles ~**, foolish, illicit love. **une porte surmontée d'~**, a door surmounted by cupids.

amovibilité *n.f.* liability to removal or dismissal.

amovible *adj.* removable; liable to dismissal.

amphibie *adj. and n.m.* amphibious; amphibian *pl.* amphibians *or* amphibia.

amphibologie *n.f.* amphibology.

amphigouri *n.m.* a burlesque composition; rigmarole.

amphigourique *adj.* unintelligible, ludicrous.

amphigouriquement *adv.* unintelligibly, nonsensically.

amphithéâtral, e *adj.* amphitheatrical.

amphithéâtre *n.m.* amphitheater.

amphitryon *n.m.* amphytryon; host, entertainer.

amphore *n.f.* amphora.

ample *adj.* ample, wide, spacious; plenteous.

amplement *adv.* amply, widely, abundantly, copiously, fully.

ampleur *n.f.* ampleness, fulness.

ampliatif, ive *adj.* additional.

ampliation *n.f.* duplicate (of a deed, etc.). **par ~,** as a duplicate.

amplificateur *n.m.* amplifier.

amplification *n.f.* amplification; development; enlarger (photographic).

amplifier *v.t.* to amplify, to enlarge upon.

amplitude *n.f.* amplitude.

ampoule *n.f.* vial; blister on the feet or hands; bulb.

ampoulé, e *adj.* bombastic, inflated. **style ~,** high-flown style.

ampouler *v.t.* to blister.

ampoulette *n.f.* half-minute glass.

amputation *n.f.* amputation.

amputé, e *p.p.* amputated. *n.m.f.* person amputated.

amputer *v.t.* to amputate.

amulette *n.f.* amulet.

amure *n.f.* tack of sail.

amurer *v.t.* to haul aboard a tack.

amusable *adj.* capable of being amused.

amusant, e *adj.* amusing, entertaining, pleasing.

amusement *n.m.* amusement, entertainment, pastime; sham, trick.

amuser *v.t.* to amuse; to divert. **cette aventure a amusé tout Paris,** this adventure has amused all Paris. **~ l'ennemi,** to deceive the enemy. **s'~,** *v.refl.* to amuse oneself; to be amused; to enjoy oneself; to waste time. **ne vous amusez pas en chemin,** don't dawdle. **amusez-vous bien,** enjoy yourself, have fun.

amusette *n.f.* toy; petty amusement, child's play. **ce n'est pour lui qu'une ~,** it's only child's play to him.

amuseur, euse *n.m.f.* amuser.

amygdale *n.f.* tonsil.

amygdalite *n.f.* tonsillitis.

amylacé, e *adj.* amylaceous, starchy.

an *n.m.* year. **il y a un ~,** a year ago. **il reviendra dans un ~,** he will return in a year. **avoir soixante ~s,** to be sixty (years of age). **agé d'un ~,** a year old; (of horses, etc.) yearling. **tous les ~s,** every year. **tous les deux ~s,** every two years. **le jour de l'~,** New Year's Day. **bon ~, mal ~,** year in, year out. **une fois, deux fois par ~,** once, twice a year. **bout de l'~,** anniversary mass (celebrated a year after a person's death). **l'~ de grâce, l'~ de Notre-Seigneur,** year of grace, year of our Lord. **l'~ mil neuf cent trois,** the year one thousand nine hundred and three.

ana an affix added to names with the sense of *belonging to.*

anabaptisme *n.m.* anabaptism.

anabaptiste *n.m.* anabaptist.

anacarde *n.m.* cashew nut.

anacardier *n.m.* anacardium, cashew tree.

anachorète *n.m.* anchorite, hermit.

anachronisme *n.m.* anachronism.

anacréontique *adj.* anacreontic.

anagogique *adj.* anagogical.

anagramme *n.f.* anagram.

analogie *n.f.* analogy.

analogique *adj.* analogical.

analogiquement *adv.* analogically.

analogue *adj.* analogous.

analyse *n.f.* analysis, digest; parsing. **faire l'~ de,** to analyse; to parse.

analyser *v.t.* to analyze, to parse. **~ une phrase,** to parse a sentence.

analyste *n.m.* analyst.

analytique *adj.* analytical.

analytiquement *adv.* analytically.

anamorphose *n.f.* anamorphosis.

ananas *n.m.* pineapple.

anaphore *n.f.* anaphora.

anaphorisme *n.m.* excessive use of anaphora.

anaphrodisiaque *adj.* and *n.m.* anaphrodisiac.

anaphrodite *adj.* anaphroditic; impotent.

anarchie *n.f.* anarchy.

anarchiste *n.m.* anarchist.

anarrhique *n.m.* wolf fish.

anastrophe *n.f.* anastrophe.

anathématiser *v.t.* to anathematize.

anathème *n.m.* anathema, curse. **frapper d'~,** to anathematize.

anatife *n.m.* barnacle; small mollusk.

anatomie *n.f.* anatomy; dissection.

anatomique *adj.* anatomical.

anatomiquement *adv.* anatomically.

anatomiser *v.t.* to dissect.

anatomiste *n.m.* anatomist.

ancêtres *n.m.pl.* ancestors, forefathers. **un de ses ~,** one of his ancestors.

anche *n.f.* reed (of a clarinet, etc.); reed pipe (of an organ).

anchois *n.m.* anchovy.

ancien, ne *adj.* ancient, old former, late. **les anciens Grecs,** the ancient Greeks. **l'~ président,** the former, the late president. **mon ~ maître,** my old master. *n.m.f.* elder, senior.

anciennement *adv.* anciently, of old.

ancienneté *n.f.* ancientness; seniority. **par ~,** by seniority.

ancillaire *adj.* ancillary.

ancolie *n.f.* columbine.

ancrage *n.m.* anchorage.

ancre *n.f.* anchor; anchor (of a clock); lever (of a watch.) **maîtresse ~,** sheet anchor. **~ d'affourche,** small bower anchor. **~ de flot, de jusant, de terre, du large,** flood, ebb, shore anchor. **~ à jet,** stream anchor, kedge. **jeter l'~,** to cast anchor, to anchor. **lever l'~,** to weigh anchor. **être à l'~,** to ride at anchor.

ancré, e *p.p.* anchored.

ancrer *v.i.* to cast anchor, to anchor.

andain *n.m.* swath (in mowing).

andalous, ouse, andalousien, enne *adj.* and *n.m.f.* Andalusian.

andante *adv.* and *n.m.* andante.

andouille *n.f.* chitterling (sausage); roll, twist (of tobacco leaves); *Infml.* imbecile, duffer. **bougre d'andouille**, blithering idiot.

andouiller *n.m.* antler.

andouillette *n.f.* small pork sausage.

androgyne *n.m., adj.* androgynous.

âne *n.m.* ass, donkey; *Fig.* dolt, blockhead. **têtu comme un ~**, as stubborn as a mule. **pont aux ~s, pons asinorum** (math.). **c'est le pont aux ~s**, every fool knows that. **coq-à-l'~**, cock and bull story. **promenade à l'~**, donkey ride. **faute d'un point, Martin perdit son ~**, it is foolish to make false economies. **on ne saurait faire boire un ~ qui n'a pas soif**, you can lead a horse to water but you can't make him drink.

anéantir *v.t.* to annihilate; to reduce to nothing, to crush; to suppress. **s'~**, *v.refl.* to be annihilated; to come to nothing.

anéantissement *n.m.* annihilation; reducing to nothing, to ruin.

anecdote *n.f.* anecdote.

anémie *n.f.* anemia.

anémique *adj.* affected with anemia.

anémomètre *n.m.* anemometer.

anémone *n.f.* anemone.

anémoscope *n.m.* anemoscope.

ânerie *n.f.* gross stupidity, gross ignorance; gross blunder.

ânesse *n.f.* female donkey.

anesthésie *n.f.* anesthesia.

anesthésique *adj.* anesthetic.

anévrismal *adj.* aneurysmal.

anévrisme *n.m.* aneurysm.

anfractueux, euse *adj.* anfractuous.

anfractuosité *n.f.* anfractuosity.

ange *n.m.* angel. **~ déchu**, fallen angel. **~ gardien**, guardian angel. **être aux ~s**, to be in raptures.

angélique *adj.* angelic. *n.f.* angelica.

angéliquement *adv.* angelically.

angelot *n.m.* angel (coin); cheese made in Normandy.

angélus *n.m.* angelus.

angine *n.f.* angina, quinsy.

angineux, euse *adj.* anginal, anginose.

angiologie *n.f.* angiology.

anglais, e *adj.* English, British. *n.m.* Englishman; *n.f.* English woman; a dance; cursive (writing); ringlet, curl.

angle *n.m.* angle. **~ droit, aigu, obtus**, right, acute, obtuse angle.

angleux, euse *adj.* many-cornered, as the kernel of a walnut.

anglican, e *adj.* Anglican. **l'Eglise ~e**, the Church of England.

anglicanisme *n.m.* Anglicanism.

angliciser *v.t.* to anglicize.

anglicisme *n.m.* anglicism.

anglomane *adj.* and *n.m.f.* crazy about English things.

anglomanie *n.f.* anglomania.

anglophobe *adj.* anglophobe.

anglo-saxon, onne *adj.* and *n.m.f.* Anglo-Saxon.

angoisse *n.f.* anguish, pang. **les ~s de la mort**, the pangs of death.

angon *n.m.* javelin; fishhook.

angora *n.m.* Angora.

anguillade *n.m.* lash, stroke or cut.

anguille *n.f.* eel. **~ argentée**, silver eel. **~ de mer**, conger eel. **il y a quelque ~ sous roche**, there is a snake in the grass.

angulaire *adj.* angular. **pierre ~**, cornerstone.

angulé, e *adj.* angulated.

anguleux, euse *adj.* angular.

anicroche *n.f.* obstacle, hindrance; hitch.

ânier, ère *n.m.f.* donkey driver.

animadversion *n.f.* animadversion.

animal *n.m.* animal, beast, brute. **~ domestique**, domestic animal. **quel vilain ~**, what a nasty brute!

animal, e *adj.* animal; sensual. **vie animale**, animal life. **règne ~**, animal kingdom.

animalcule *n.m.* animalcule.

animalier, animaliste *n.m.* painter, sculptor of animals.

animalisation *n.f.* animalization.

animaliser *v.t.* to animalize.

animalité *n.f.* animality.

animation *n.f.* animation.

animé, e *adj.* animated, lively. **scène animée**, an animated scene. **ville animée**, bustling town. *n.f.* anime, gum animi.

animer *v.t.* to animate; to enliven; to stimulate; to inspire. **~ la conversation**, to enliven conversation. **~ les passions**, to excite the passions. **~ le teint**, to heighten the color, the complexion. **s'~**, *v.refl.* to become animated, to cheer up, to take courage.

animosité *n.f.* animosity; passion, heat.

anis *n.m.* anise, anisum. **graine d'~**, anise seed.

aniser *v.t.* to flavor with aniseed.

anisette *n.f.* anisette.

Anjou *n.m.* Anjou.

ankylose *n.f.* ankylosis.

ankyloser *v.t.* to ankylose. **s'~**, *v.refl.* to become ankylosed.

annal, e *adj.* for a year.

annales *n.f.pl.* annals.

annaliste *n.m.* annalist.

annate *n.f.* annates; *pl.* first fruits.

anneau *n.m.* ring; link (of a chain), curl, ringlet. **~ brisé**, split ring. **anneaux de Saturne**, Saturn's rings.

année *n.f.* year. **les quatre saisons de l'~**, the

four seasons of the year. **~ bissextile,** leap year. **~ scolaire,** school year. **ses belles ~s,** the prime of life. **chargé d'~s,** stricken in years. **une ~ dans l'autre,** year after year. **l'~ prochaine,** next year. **à l'~,** by the year. **je vous souhaite la bonne ~,** I wish you a happy new year. **année-lumière ou ~ de lumière,** *n.f.* light year.

annelé, e *p.p.* annulated; ring streaked.

anneler *v.t.* to curl (hair); to ring (pigs).

annelet *n.m.* small ring.

annélides *n.m.pl.* earthworms.

annelure *n.f.* curling (of hair).

annexe *n.f.* annex; district church; schedule; addition.

annexer *v.t.* to annex.

annexion *n.f.* annexation.

annihilation *n.f.* annihilation.

annihiler *v.t.* to annihilate, to annul.

anniversaire *adj.* anniversary. **fête ~,** anniversary festival. *n.m.* anniversary; birthday.

annonce *n.f.* announcement; notice; advertisement. **faire une ~,** to advertise.

annoncer *v.t.* to advertise, to inform, to announce, to give notice of, to predict; to be the precursor, the harbinger. **annoncez-vous,** introduce yourself. **ce vent annonce la tempête,** this wind forebodes a storm. **on a annoncé la vente dans les journaux,** the sale has been advertised in the papers. **s'~,** *v.refl.* to announce oneself, to make oneself known. **l'affaire s'annonce bien,** it's a promising thing.

annonceur *n.m.* announcer.

annonciateur *n.m.* **~trice,** *n.f.* forerunner; announcer (person).

annoncier *n.m.* **~cière,** *n.f.* publicity manager.

annotateur *n.m.* **~trice,** *n.f.* annotator.

annotation *n.f.* annotation.

annoter *v.t.* to annotate.

annuaire *n.m.* yearbook. **~ du commerce,** trade directory. **~ militaire,** army list. **annuaire du téléphone,** telephone directory.

annualité *n.f.* yearly recurrence.

annuel, le *adj.* annual.

annuellement *adv.* annually, yearly.

annuité *n.f.* annuity.

annulaire *adj.* annular. **doigt ~,** ring finger.

annulation *n.f.* annulment; canceling (of a deed).

annuler *v.t.* to annul, to render null and void; to cancel.

anobli, e *adj.* ennobled. *n.m.f.* person ennobled.

anoblir *v.t.* to ennoble.

anoblissement *n.m.* ennoblement.

anodin, e *adj.* anodyne; palliative; insignificant.

anomal, e *adj.* anomalous.

anomalie *n.f.* anomaly.

ânon *n.m.* donkey's foal, young donkey.

ânonnement *n.m.* stuttering, hemming and hawing.

ânonner *v.i.* to hem and haw; to hesitate in reading.

anonymat *n.m.* anonymity.

anonyme *adj.* anonymous.

anonymement *adv.* anonymously.

anorak *n.m.* winter jacket.

anorexie *n.f.* loss of appetite, anorexia.

anse *n.f.* handle (of a basket, pot, etc.); creek, inlet, small bay. **faire danser l'anse du panier,** to pocket profits in marketing. **faire le pot à deux anses,** to set one's arms akimbo.

ansière *n.f.* fishing net; trawl.

antagonisme *n.m.* antagonism.

antagoniste *n.m.* antagonist. *adj.* antagonist.

antan *n.m.* last year; of yore. **les neiges d'~,** the snows of yesteryear.

ante *n.f.* handle (of a painter's pencil); *pl. Arch.* facings of a doorway.

antécédemment *adv.* antecedently, previously.

antécédence *n.f.* antecedence, precedence.

antécédent, e *adj.* antecedent, previous, anterior. *n.m.* antecedent; antecedents; previous conduct. **il a de bons ~s,** his past conduct has been good.

antéchrist *n.m.* Antichrist.

antédiluvien, ne *adj.* antediluvian.

antéfixe *n.f. Arch.* antefixa.

antenne *n.f.* antenna, aerial. **antenne de radar,** radar scanner; feeler (of insects).

antépénultième *adj.* antepenultimate. *n.f.* antepenult.

antérieur, e *adj.* anterior, fore. **un fait ~,** a previous fact. **la partie antérieure d'une maison,** the front of a house.

antérieurement *adv.* anteriorly, previously.

antériorité *n.f.* anteriority.

anthère *n.f.* anther, tip.

anthologie *n.f.* anthology.

anthracite *n.m.* anthracite.

anthropographie *n.f.* anthropography.

anthropologie *n.f.* anthropology.

anthropologique *adj.* anthropological.

anthropométrie *n.f.* anthropometry.

anthropomorphe *adj.* anthropomorphous.

anthropomorphisme *n.m.* anthropomorphism.

anthropomorphite *n.m.* anthropomorphite.

anthropophage *adj.* anthropophagous. *n.m.f.* cannibal.

anthropophagie *n.f.* anthropophagy, cannibalism.

anti against, before (prefix).

antiacide *adj.* and *n.m.* antacid.

antiaérien, enne *adj.* antiaircraft.

antialcoolique *adj.* teetotaling, antialcohol.

antiatomique *adj.* antiatomic.

antibiotique *adj.* antibiotic.

antibrouillard *n.m.* foglight.

antibruit *n.m.* soundproofing.

anticancéreux, euse *adj.* tending to prevent cancer.

antichambre *n.f.* anteroom. **faire ~,** to dance attendance.

antichar *adj.* antitank. **un appareil antichar,** an antitank weapon.

antichrétien, enne *adj.* antichristian.

anticipation *n.f.* anticipation. **par ~,** beforehand.

anticiper *v.t.* to anticipate; to forestall. *v.i.* (with *sur*) to anticipate; to encroach on; to antedate.

anticivique *adj.* anticivic.

anticivisme *n.m.* anticivism.

anticlérical *adj.* anticlerical.

anticléricalisme *n.m.* anticlericalism.

anticommunisme *n.m.* anticommunism.

anticonceptionnel *adj.* contraceptive.

anticonformisme *n.m.* nonconformism.

anticonstitutionnel *adj.* anticonstitutional.

anticonstitutionnellement *adv.* (the longest French word) anticonstitutionally.

anticorps *n.m.* antibody.

antidartreux, euse *adj.* antidartrous.

antidate *n.f.* antedate.

antidater *v.t.* to antedate.

antidémocratique *adj.* antidemocratic.

antidotaire *n.m.* antidotary; book of antidotes.

antidote *n.m.* antidote.

antienne *n.f.* anthem. **entonner une ~,** to strike up an anthem. **chanter toujours la même ~,** to be always harping on the same thing.

antiépileptique *adj.* and *n.m.* antiepileptic.

antiesclavagisme *n.m.* antislavery.

antigel *n.m.* antifreeze.

antigivre *n.m.* deicer.

antigouvernemental *adj.* antigovernment.

antigréviste *adj.* antistrike.

antiheros *n.m.* antihero.

antihygiénique *adj.* unsanitary.

antilibéral *adj.* antiliberal.

antilogie *n.f.* antilogy.

antilope *n.f.* antelope.

antimilitarisme *n.m.* antimilitarism.

antimite *adj.* mothproof.

antimoine *n.m.* antimony.

antimonarchique *adj.* antimonarchical.

antimonial, é *adj.* and *n.m.* antimonial.

antimonié, e, antimonifère *adj.* antimonial.

antinational, e *adj.* antinational.

antinomie *n.f.* antinomy.

antinucléaire *adj.* antinuclear.

antipathie *n.f.* antipathy, aversion. **une ~ naturelle,** a natural antipathy.

antipathique *adj.* antipathetic, repugnant. **cet homme m'est ~,** I can't stand that man.

antipatriotique *adj.* antipatriotic.

antipestilentiel, elle *adj.* antipestilential.

antiphilosophique *adj.* antiphilosophical.

antiphrase *n.f.* antiphrasis.

antipode *n.m.* antipode.

antiputride *adj.* and *n.m.* antiputrefactive, antiseptic.

antiquaille *n.f.* worthless piece of antiquity, rubbish.

antiquaire *n.m.* antiquary.

antique *adj.* antique, old-fashioned, quaint. **meubles antiques,** old-fashioned furniture. **vase ~,** antique vase. *n.f.* antique. **le cabinet des antiques,** the museum of antiquities. **à l'~,** in an antique style.

antiquité *n.f.* antiquity; days of yore; old age. **l'~ d'une ville,** the ancientness of a town. **les héros de l'~,** the heroes of antiquity. **de toute ~,** from the remotest times.

antiraciste *adj.* antiracist.

antirationnel *adj.* antirational.

antiréligieux, euse *adj.* antireligious.

antirépublicain, e *adj.* and *n.m.f.* antirepublican.

antirévolutionnaire *adj.* antirevolutionary.

antirides *adj.* antiwrinkle.

antirouille *adj.* antirust.

antisémite *adj.* antisemitic.

antisémitisme *n.m.* antisemitism.

antiseptique *adj.* and *n.m.* antiseptic.

antisocial, e *adj.* antisocial.

antisportif *adj.* unsportsmanlike.

antistrophe *n.f.* antistrophe.

antisyphilitique *adj.* and *n.m.* antisyphilitic.

antithèse *n.f.* antithesis.

antithétique *adj.* antithetic, antithetical.

antivénérien, enne *adj.* and *n.m.* antivenereal.

antonomase *n.f.* antonomasia.

antre *n.m.* cave, cavern, den.

anuité, e *p.p.* benighted.

anuiter (s') *v.refl.* to be benighted; to be overtaken by the night.

anus *n.m.* anus.

anxiété *n.f.* anxiety, anxiousness.

anxieux, se *adj.* anxious.

aoriste *n.m.* aorist.

aorte *n.f.* aorta.

aortique *adj.* aortic.

août *n.m.* August. **la mi-~,** the middle of August.

aoûté, e *p.p.* ripened (by the heat of August).

aoûter *v.t.* and *v.i.* to ripen.

aoûteron *n.m.* harvester.

aoûtien, ienne *adj.* person taking vacation in August.

apache *n.m.* (formerly) Paris street hooligan.

apagogie *n.f.* apagogy.

apaisant *adj.* soothing, consoling.

apaisement *n.m.* appeasement.

apaiser *v.t.* to appease, to allay, to soothe, to still; to lull; to stay (hunger); to quench (thirst); to quell (a revolt, rebellion, etc.). **~ le peuple,** to appease the people. **la pluie a apaisé le vent,** the rain has made the wind stop. **apaise ta douleur,** moderate your grief. **s'~,** *v.refl.* to be appeased, calmed, etc. **il s'apaisera bientôt,** he will soon calm down. **cette grande colère s'apaisera,** this violent anger will subside.

l'incendie s'apaisa peu à peu, the conflagration gradually subsided.

apanage n.m. appanage; prerogative.

apanager v.t. to endow with an appanage.

apanagiste adj. and n.m. apanagist.

aparté adv. Theat. aside. n.m. words aside.

apathie n.f. apathy.

apathique adj. apathetic.

apathiquement adv. apathetically.

apatride adj. stateless.

apercevable adj. perceivable, perceptible.

apercevance n.f. perception.

apercevoir v.t. to perceive, to discern; to remark, to observe. **j'aperçois bien son intention,** I clearly perceive his intention. **s'~,** v.refl. to perceive; to see; to observe. **elle s'est aperçue de son erreur,** she perceived her mistake.

aperçu n.m. rapid view, glance; list. **un ~ des prix,** a list of prices.

apéritif, ive adj. laxative. n.m. laxative medicine, liqueur.

apesanteur n.f. weightlessness.

apetissement n.m. lessening, diminution.

apetisser v.t. to lessen, to reduce (in size). v.i. to diminish.

à peu près adv. nearly, about.

aphélie n.f. aphelion.

aphérèse n.f. aphaeresis.

aphone adj. aphonous, voiceless.

aphorisme n.m. aphorism.

aphoristique adj. aphoristic.

aphrodisiaque adj. aphrodisiac.

aphte n.m. aphta, thrush.

aphteux, euse adj. aphthous.

aphylle adj. leafless.

api n.m. api (apple).

apiculteur n.m. beekeeper.

apiculture n.f. apiculture, beekeeping.

apitoiement n.m. compassion.

apitoyant adj. pitiful.

apitoyer v.t. to excite pity. **s'~,** v.refl. to feel pity.

aplanir v.t. to even, to smooth, to level. **s'~,** v.refl. to grow smooth, easy.

aplanissement n.m. making even, smoothing.

aplatir v.t. to flatten, to make flat. **s'~,** v.refl. to flatten, to become flat.

aplatissement n.m. flattening, flatness.

aplatisseur n.m. flattener.

aplatissoire n.f. rolling mill.

aplomb n.m. perpendicular, plumb, assurance, self-command. **ce balcon est hors d'~,** this balcony is out of plumb. **il répondit avec ~,** he replied with self-possession. **d'~,** straight, perpendicularly, in plumb. **être d'~,** to be straight.

apocalypse n.f. apocalypse. **l'~,** the Revelation, catastrophe that suggests the end of the world.

apocalyptique adj. apocalyptic, obscure.

apocope n.f. apocope.

apocryphe adj. apocryphal.

apode n.m. apode, apodon. adj. apodal.

apodictique adj. apodictic.

apogée n.f. apogee, zenith; Fig. height, climax.

apologétique adj. apologetic.

apologie n.f. apology. **écrire une ~,** to write an apology.

apologue n.m. apologist.

apoplectique adj. and e n.m.f. apopléctic.

apoplexie n.f. apoplexy. **attaque d'~,** apoplectic stroke. **il fut frappé d'~,** he was struck with apoplexy. **tomber en ~,** to have an apoplectic fit.

apostat adj. and n.m. apostate.

aposter v.t. to set on the watch. **~ des témoins,** to suborn (false) witnesses.

a posteriori adv. phr. a posteriori.

apostille n.f. marginal note. **en ~,** in the margin.

apostiller v.t. to add a note (to a petition, etc.).

apostolat n.m. apostleship.

apostolique adj. apostolic.

apostrophe n.f. apostrophe, reproach.

apostropher v.t. to apostrophize; to address.

apothéose n.f. apotheosis.

apothicaire n.m. apothecary. **mémoire d'~,** an extravagant bill.

apôtre n.m. apostle. **faire le bon ~,** to pretend to be well intentioned.

apparâitre v.i. to appear. **il lui apparut un spectre,** a spectre appeared to him.

apparat n.m. pomp, state, display; syllabus. **discours d'~,** a studied speech. **avec grand ~,** with great pomp.

appareil n.m. preparation, pomp; apparel, attire; apparatus, dressing (surg.). **on fait de grands ~s pour son entrée,** great preparations are being made for his entry. **~ de guerre,** warlike preparations. **~ de chimie,** chemical apparatus. **faire un premier ~,** to apply a first dressing.

appareillage n.m. getting under sail; preparing to set sail.

appareillement n.m. pairing, yoking.

appareiller v.t. to match. Arch. to mark stones. v.i. to sail, to get under sail. **s'~,** v.refl. to join oneself to; to pair (as birds).

appareilleur n.m. dresser, trimmer.

apparemment adv. apparently.

apparence n.f. appearance, outward show, probability. **avoir l'~,** to have the appearance. **en ~,** apparently, in appearance. **pour les ~s,** for appearances' sake. **selon les ~s,** according to appearances.

apparent, e adj. apparent, plain, seeming, not real.

apparenté, e p.p. related, connected.

apparenter v.t. to marry, to marry one's children into good families. **s'~,** v.refl. with à to marry into.

appariement, apparîment n.m. matching, pairing.

apparier v.t. to match in pairs. **~ les chevaux**

de carrosse, to match carriage horses. s'~, v.refl. to pair, to couple.

appariteur n.m. mace bearer, beadle.

apparition n.f. appearing, appearance; apparition, phantom.

apparoir v.t. to appear.

appartement n.m. apartment. ~ à louer meublé ou non meublé, apartment to rent, furnished or unfurnished.

appartenance n.f. appurtenance.

appartenant, e adj. appertaining, belonging.

appartenir v.i. belong to; to be the duty of. v.imp. il appartient, it becomes, it is meet, it is fit. il appartient à un bon juge de ..., it is the duty of an upright judge to ....

appas n.m.pl. attractions, charms.

appât n.m. bait; allurement, enticement.

appâter v.i. to bait, to allure; to feed.

appauvrir v.t. to impoverish, to make poor. s'~, v.refl. to impoverish oneself; to become impoverished.

appauvrissement n.m. impoverishment.

appeau n.m. bird call; decoy bird.

appel n.m. call, appeal. la cloche sonne l'~ au dîner, the bell is ringing for dinner. faire l'~, to call the roll. manquer à l'~, to be absent. cour d'~, court of appeal. interjeter ~, to give notice of appeal. sans ~, without appeal. battre l'~, to summon by beating a drum.

appelant, e adj. appellant. n.m.f. appelant; decoy, decoy bird.

appelé, e p.p. called, named, etc. beaucoup d'~s et peu d'élus, many are called, but few are chosen.

appeler v.t. to call; to call on; to summon, to name; to invoke. ~ le garçon, to call the waiter. ~ au secours, to call for help. ~ un médecin, to call in a doctor. v.t. to call, to appeal. en ~, to appeal (against). il en a apelé, he has given notice of appeal. j'en appelle à votre honneur, I appeal to your honor. s'~, v.refl. to be called or named. comment vous appelez-vouz? what is your name?

appellatif, ve adj. appellative.

appellation n.f. calling; appellation; appeal. ~ controlée, government guarantee of quality (esp. of wine).

appendice n.m. appendix; appendage.

appendicite n.f. appendicitis.

appendre v.t. to append; to hang up.

appentis n.m. lean-to, shed.

appesanti, e p.p. made heavy; dull.

appesantir v.t. to make heavy; to weigh down, to impair. le sommeil appesantit ses yeux, sleep made his eyes heavy. s'~, v.refl. to become heavy; to be weighed down, to get dull; to dwell upon.

appesantissement n.m. heaviness; dulness; chastisement.

appétence n.f. appetence; appetency, craving, longing.

appéter v.t. to crave.

appétissant, e adj. appetizing; tempting; relishing. mets ~s, an appetizing dish.

appétit n.m. appetite; longing; craving. exciter l'~, to excite the appetite. gagner de l'~, to get an appetite. ôter l'~, to spoil one's appetite. l'~ vient en mangeant, the more one has, the more one wants. bon ~! I wish you a good appetite, enjoy your meal. de bon ~, heartily.

appiècement n.m. piecing.

applaudi, e p.p. applauded.

applaudir v.t. to applaud; to praise, to approve. ~ une pièce, un acteur, to applaud a play, an actor. s'~, v.refl. (with de), to applaud oneself; to admire oneself. les sots s'applaudissent sans cesse, fools are always praising themselves.

applaudissement n.m. applause; clapping of hands; praise. un tonnerre d'~s, a thunder of applause. salve d'~s, round of applause.

applaudisseur n.m. applauder.

applicable adj. applicable; suitable; appliable. argent ~ à cette dépense, money applicable to that expense. cette loi n'est pas ~ aux mineurs, that law does not apply to minors.

application n.f. application; appropriation of funds, etc.; industry. l'~ d'une fable, the application (the moral) of a fable. cette étude demande une grande ~, that study requires intense application.

applique n.f. charging; bracket; inlaid work, decoration, trimmings.

appliqué, e p.p. applied; careful; studious. soufflet bien ~, a well-applied blow. science ~e aux arts, science applied to the arts.

appliquer v.t. to apply; to put, place on, to appropriate, to employ; to attribute, to award (a punishment); to devote (one's attention, etc.). ~ un cataplasme sur une plaie, to apply a poultice to a sore. ~ une somme d'argent, to employ a sum of money. s'~, v.refl. to be applied; to be put, laid, set, placed on, to, or against; to devote oneself to. je me suis appliqué à, I made a point of.

appoint n.m. exact change. faire l'~, to make up a sum with small change.

appointé, e p.p. having a salary; appointed. n.m. Milit. soldier or officer receiving extra pay.

appointement n.m.,pl. salary. recevoir de gros ~s, to receive a high salary. c'est lui qui fournit aux ~s, it is he who supplies what is necessary.

appointer v.t. to refer; to give a salary to; Milit. to punish; to point, to sharpen.

appointement n.m. wooden stage or bridge; landing stage.

apport n.m. market; dowry; chattels; share; deposit (of documents). acte d'~, deposit receipt, shareholder's contribution.

apporter v.t. to bring; to carry; to bring forward. ~ de Lyon à Paris, to bring from Lyons to Paris. la guerre apporte bien des calamités, war brings or causes many calamities. ~ de bonnes raisons, to offer good reasons.

apposer *v.t.* to affix; to insert; to set. ~ un sceau sur un acte, to affix a seal to a document. ~ les scellés, to put under seal. ~ sa signature à, to sign.

apposition *n.f.* affixing; appending (of a signature, etc.); insertion; apposition. faire l'apposition des scellés, to affix the seals.

appréciabilité *n.f.* appreciability.

appréciable *adj.* appreciable.

appréciateur, trice *n.m.f.* appreciator; valuer. il trouva des ~s de son talent, he found appreciators of his talent.

appréciatif, ve *adj.* appreciative.

appréciation *n.f.* estimate; appreciation. ~ d'une propriété, the valuation of an estate.

apprécier *v.t.* to value, to esteem; to estimate. ce diamant a été apprécié à cent mille francs, this diamond has been valued at one hundred thousand francs. s'~, *v.refl.* to appreciate oneself; to set a value on oneself.

appréhender *v.t.* to apprehend; to take into custody. *Fig.* to be apprehensive, to fear.

appréhensible *adj.* apprehensible.

appréhensif, ve *adj.* apprehensive, anxious, timid.

appréhension *n.f.* apprehension; perception; fear. il avait l'~ vive, he was a man of quick apprehension. j'en prends peu d'~, I have little fear of it.

apprendre *v.t.* to learn; to be informed of, to hear, to teach, to inform. j'apprendrai l'allemand, I shall learn German. ~ par coeur, to learn by heart. ~ à fond, to learn thoroughly. j'ai tout appris de lui et par lui, I have heard everything about him and from himself. il vient d'~ la mort de son fils, he has just heard of his son's death. il apprendra qui je suis, he shall know who I am. ~ la grammaire à un enfant, to teach a child grammar. j'ai appris à lire à mon fils, I have taught my son to read. on m'a appris la mort de votre oncle, I have been informed of your uncle's death. s'~, *v.refl.* to teach oneself; to teach each other; to know, to come to one's knowledge. cette dame s'est apprise à filer, that lady has taught herself to spin. les arts s'apprennent par la pratique, the arts are learned by practice.

apprenti, e *n.m.f.* apprentice. un ~ menuisier, an apprentice to a carpenter. *adj.* apprenticed.

apprentissage *n.m.* apprenticeship. faire son ~, to serve one's apprenticeship. contrat d'~, indentures of apprenticeship. mettre en ~, to make an apprentice of.

apprêt *n.m.* preparation; dressing; cooking; affectation. les ~s d'un voyage, the preparations for a voyage. faire de grands ~s, to make great preparations.

apprêtage *n.m.* dressing; glazing.

apprêté, e *p.p.* prepared; dressed (as food); studied. *Fig.* affected. un ragoût bien ~, a well-made stew. des manières apprêtées, affected manners.

apprêter *v.t.* to prepare, to get ready; to cook, to dress. ~ le dîner, to prepare the dinner. comment faut-il ~ ce lièvre? how must this hare be dressed? ~ un chapeau, to trim a hat. *v.i.* ~ à rire, to set people laughing. s'~, *v.refl.* to prepare oneself, to prepare, to get ready; to be preparing. le dîner s'apprête, the dinner is being prepared.

apprêteur, euse *n.m.f.* dresser, finisher.

appris, e *p.p.* learned; taught; trained. mal ~, ill-bred.

apprivoisable *adj.* tamable.

apprivoisement *n.m.* taming.

apprivoiser *v.t.* to tame; to make familiar or sociable. ~ un lion, to tame a lion. s'~, *v.refl.* to be tamed, to get tame, to become sociable, to lose one's shyness (of persons). s'~ avec, to become familiar with.

approbateur, trice *n.m.f.* approver. *adj.* approving. regard ~, an approving look.

approbatif, ve *adj.* approving. geste ~, an approving gesture. arrêté ~, approbatory decision.

approbation *n.f.* approbation, approval. donner son ~, to give one's approbation. incliner la tête en signe d'~, to nod assent.

approbativement *adv.* approvingly.

approchable *adj.* approachable; accessible.

approchant, e *adj.* like, not unlike. *prep.* near, about.

approche *n.f.* approach, coming, access. être d'~ difficile, to be unapproachable.

approcher *v.t.* to bring; put, or draw near, nearer or close to. approchez cette table, draw the table near *or* nearer. *v.i.* to approach, to draw, come, go near; to resemble, to be like. l'heure approche, the hour is approaching. le bruit approche, the noise is getting nearer. s'~, *v.refl.* to approach, to draw, go, come, or get near (or nearer). il s'approcha d'elle avec respect, he approached her with respect. approchez-vous du feu, come closer to the fire.

approfondir *v.t.* to deepen; to make deeper; to delve deep into; to fathom; to examine (or search) thoroughly, to make a profound (or an exhaustive) study of. ~ un puits, to deepen a well. ~ une question, to delve deep into a question. sans ~, superficially.

approfondissement *n.m.* deepening; profound investigation.

appropriation *n.f.* appropriation; embezzlement.

approprier *v.t.* to appropriate; to adapt, to suit, to clean. ~ son langage aux circonstances, to adapt one's language to circumstances. s'~, *v.refl.* to adapt or accommodate oneself (to); to appropriate to one's use.

approuvé, e *p.p.* approved; approved of. ~ **l'écriture ci-dessus,** approved the above. **lu et ~,** read and approved.

approuver *v.t.* to approve; to consent to; to commend. **je n'approuve pas cette clause,** I do not approve of that clause.

approvisionnement *n.m.* stock, supply, provisioning.

approvisionner *v.t.* to supply. **s'~,** *v.refl.* to provide oneself (with); to lay in a stock.

approximatif, ive *adj.* approximative.

approximation *n.f.* approximation; rough guess. **par ~,** approximately.

approximativement *adv.* approximately.

approximer *v.t.* to approximate.

appui *n.m.* support, stay, protection, prop. **il faut un ~ à cet arbre,** that tree requires a prop. **ce bâton me sert d'~,** this stick serves me as a support. **l'~ de cette croisée est dangereux,** the handrail of that window is dangerous. **à hauteur d'~,** chest-high. **donnez-lui votre ~,** give him your support. **l'argent est un puissant ~,** money is a powerful support. **point d'~,** fulcrum, point of support. **à l'~,** in support. **à l'~ de mon dire,** to support my assertion. **sans ~,** unsupported; friendless.

appui-aérien *n.m.* air support.

appui-bras, *n.m.* armrest.

appui-main *n.m. Paint.* mahlstick.

appui-tête *n.m.* headrest.

appuyé, e *p.p.* supported; seconded. **je la vis ~e contre la muraille,** I saw her leaning against the wall.

appuyer *v.t* to support, to stay, to lean, to base, to aid, to help; to back. ~ **un arbre,** to prop up a tree. ~ **une échelle contre un mur,** to set a ladder against a wall. ~ **une demande,** to support an application. ~ **ses coudes sur une table,** to lean one's elbows on a table. **sur quoi appuyez-vous ces assertions?** on what do you base these assertions? *v.t.* to rest on, to dwell upon; to be supported by. **la poutre appuie sur ce mur,** the beam is supported by this wall. ~ **sur un mot,** to lay stress (or emphasis) on a word. **s'~** *v.refl.* to be supported or sustained. **une maison qui s'appuie contre une colline,** a house backed (or built) against a hill. ~ **sur un bâton,** to lean on a stick. **appuyez-vous sur moi,** lean on me.

âpre *adj.* harsh; tart, sharp; rugged, rough, stern; greedy. **une voix ~,** a harsh or gruff voice. **fruit ~,** sour fruit. **chemin ~,** a rough road. ~ **au gain,** greedy of gain. **homme ~,** a greedy or grasping man. **âprement** *adv.* harshly; roughly; fiercely. **le froid a commencé bien ~,** the cold has set in with great severity.

après *prep.* after, next to. ~ **lui,** after him. **six mois ~ le siège,** six months after the siege. ~ **le dîner il est sorti,** after dinner he went out. **marcher ~ quelqu'un,** to tread in a person's steps. ~ **coup,** too late. ~ **tout,** after all.

être ~ une chose, to be about or after a thing. **attendre ~ quelqu'un,** to wait for a person. **d'~,** from, after. **peindre d'~ nature,** to paint from nature. **tableau d'~ Raphaël,** a painting in the style of Raphael. *adv.* after, or afterward. **cinquante ans ~,** fifty years afterward. **peu de temps ~,** shortly after, not long after or afterward. **ci-~,** further on, below; hereafter.

après-demain *adv.* the day after tomorrow.

après-dîner *n.f.* after-dinner; afternoon, evening.

après-midi *n.f.* or *n.m.* afternoon.

après-souper *n.m.* after supper.

âpreté *n.f.* harshness, roughness; tartness; unevenness, ruggedness; severity; asperity. **l'~ des chemins,** the roughness of the roads. **l'~ de la saison,** the inclemency of the season.

a priori *adv.* at first sight.

à propos *adv.* by the way. **à-propos** *n.m.* suitability.

apside *n.f.* apsis; apogee (of the moon).

apte *adj.* capable. ~ **à succéder,** capable of inheriting; qualified. **il est ~ à remplir cet emploi,** he is qualified for filling that office.

aptitude *n.f.* aptitude; fitness; disposition. **il n'a guère d'~ aux mathématiques,** he has little aptitude for mathematics.

apurement *n.m.* auditing; closing.

apurer *v.t.* to audit; to verify and pass (an account).

aquarelle *n.f.* aquarelle; *pl.* watercolors.

aquarelliste *n.m.* watercolorist.

aquarium *n.m* aquarium.

aquatinte *n.f.* aquatinte.

aquatique *adj.* aquatic; watery, marshy. **oiseau ~,** waterfowl.

aqueduc *n.m* aqueduct; conduit. ~ **souterrain,** culvert, sewer.

aqueux, euse *adj.* aqueous, watery. **la partie aqueuse du sang,** the aqueous portion of the blood.

aquifère *adj.* water-bearing.

aquilant, aquilain *adj.* eagle-colored. *n.m.* eagle-colored horse.

aquilin *adj.* Aquiline. **nez ~,** aquiline (or Roman) nose.

aquilon *n.m.* aquilon; the north wind.

aquosité *n.f.* aquosity.

arabe *adj.* Arabian; Arabic. *n.m.f.* Arab, Arabian.

arabesque *adj. and n.m.* arabesque; tracery (*s.*)

arabine *n.f.* arabine.

arabique *adj.* Arabic, Arabian. **Golfe ~,** the Arabian Gulf.

arable *adj.* arable; plowed.

arachide *n.f.* peanut.

arachnide *n.f.* arachnidan.

arachnoïde *n.f.* arachnoid.

arack *n.m.* arrack.

araignée *n.f.* spider *Naut.* crowfoot. **toile d'~,** spider web. **pattes d'~,** spidery handwriting.

araire *n.m.* swingplow.

aranéiforme *adj.* araneiform.

arasement *n.m.* leveling; flush shoulder (of a tenon).

araser *v.t. Arch.* to level.

aratoire *adj.* agricultural, farming. **travaux ~s,** farm work; husbandry.

arbalète *n.f.* crossbow; trap (for moles, etc.).

arbalétrier *n.m.* crossbow-man; principal rafter.

arbitrage *n.m.* arbitrage. **~ de change,** arbitrage of exchange.

arbitraire *adj.* arbitrary, despotic.

arbitrairement *adv.* arbitrarily.

arbitral, e *adj.* arbitral. **jugement ~,** judgment by arbitrators.

arbitralement *adv.* by arbitration.

arbitration *n.f.* arbitration.

arbitre *n.m.* arbitrator; umpire. **libre ~,** free will.

arbitrer *v.t.* to arbitrate; to estimate.

arboré, e *p.p.* and *adj.* arboreous.

arborer *v.t.* to erect; to set up. **~ un étendard,** to raise a standard.

arborescence *n.f.* arborescence.

arborescent, e *adj.* arborescent.

arboriculteur *n.m.* arboriculturist.

arboriculture *n.f.* arboriculture.

arboriste *n.m.* arborist; nurseryman.

arbouse *n.f.* arbutus berry.

arbousier *n.m.* arbutus strawberry tree. **~ traînant,** trailing arbutus.

arbre *n.m.* tree. *Machin.* shaft. **~ fruitier,** fruit tree. **jeune ~,** sapling. **~ en espalier,** wall tree. **~ de haute futaie,** timber tree. **tel ~ tel fruit,** the fruit never falls far from the tree. **entre l'~ et l'écorce il ne faut pas mettre le doigt,** never interfere in a family quarrel. **~ généalogique,** genealogical tree. **~ de couche,** horizontal shaft. **~ moteur,** driving shaft.

arbrisseau *n.m.* shrub. **lieu planté d'arbrisseaux,** shrubbery.

arbuste *n.m.* bush, shrub.

arc *n.m.* bow, longbow; arch. **tirer de l'~,** to shoot with the bow. **bander un ~,** to bend a bow. **avoir plusieurs cordes à son ~,** to have several strings to one's bow. **~ de triomphe,** triumphal arch.

arcade *n.f.* arcade; piazza.

arcane *n.m.* arcanum.

arcanson *n.m.* black colophony, black rosin or resin.

arcasse *n.f.* stern frame, cheek (of a block or pulley).

arc-boutant *n.m.* flying buttress *Fig.* buttress. **ce ministre a été longtemps l'~ de l'état,** that minister has long been the mainstay of the State.

arc-bouter *v.t.* to buttress; to prop or set against.

arc-doubleau *n.m.* projecting arch.

arceau *n.m.* arch, vault.

arc-en-ciel *n.m.* rainbow.

archaïque *adj.* archaic.

archaïsme *n.m.* archaism.

archal *n.m.* used only in **fil d'archal,** brass wire.

archange *n.m.* archangel.

archangélique *adj.* archangelic.

arche *n.f.* arch (of a bridge); ark. **l'~ de Noé,** Noah's ark. **l'~ d'alliance,** the ark of the covenant. **c'est l'~ sainte,** that is a forbidden subject. **l'~ du témoignage,** the ark of the testimony.

archée *n.f.* span (of an arch).

archelet *n.m.* small drill bow.

archéologie *n.f.* archeology.

archéologique *adj.* archeological.

archéologue *n.m.* archeologist.

archer *n.m.* archer.

archet *n.m.* bow (of a violin); drill bow; wire saw.

archétype *n.m.* archetype. *adj.* archetypal.

archevêché *n.m.* archbishopric; archbishop's palace.

archevêque *n.m.* archbishop.

archi arch (prefix).

archidiacre *n.m.* archdeacon.

archiduc *n.m.* archduke.

archiducal, e *adj.* archducal.

archiduchesse *n.f.* archduchess.

archipel *n.m.* archipelago.

architecte *n.m.* architect.

architectonique *adj.* architectonic.

architectonographe *n.m.* architectonographer.

architectonographie *n.f.* architectonography.

architectural, e *adj.* architectural.

architecture *n.f.* architecture.

architrave *n.f.* architrave.

archives *n.m.pl.* archives, records, record office.

archiviste *n.m.* archivist, keeper of records.

archivolte *n.f.* archivolt.

archure *n.f.* casing (of millstones).

arçon *n.m.* saddle bow. **pistolet d'~,** horse pistol. **~ de devant,** pummel. **perdre les ~s,** to lose one's seat (horse), to lose one's presence of mind.

arctique *adj.* arctic. **pôle ~,** the arctic (or north) pole.

ardélion *n.m.* busybody.

ardemment *adv.* ardently, fervently, passionately, earnestly.

ardent, e *adj.* ardent, intense, burning, fiery, glowing; mettlesome. **charbon ~,** live coal, burning coal. **fièvre ~e,** burning fever. **chapelle ~e,** chapelle ardente (a place fitted up with numerous lighted tapers as a repository for a corpse). **passion ~e,** ardent passion. **cheveux d'un blond ~,** sandy hair.

ardent, *n.m.* ignis fatuus, will-o'-the-wisp.

ardeur *n.f.* ardor, heat, fervor, passion, flame; mettle, spirit. **l'~ de son zèle,** the ardor of his zeal. **l'~ de la jeunesse,** the ardor of youth.

ardoise *n.f.* slate; slate color. **crayon d'~,** slate pencil. **couvreur en ~,** person who installs slate roofs.

ardoisé, e *p.p., adj.* slated; slate-colored.

ardoiser *v.t.* to slate.

ardoisier, ère *adj.* slatelike, slaty. *n.m.* slate-digger, slate quarryman.

ardoisière *n.f.* slate quarry.

ardu, e *adj.* arduous, difficult.

are *n.m.* are: 100 square meters.

aréfaction *n.f.* arefaction, desiccation.

areligieux, ieuse, *adj.* areligious.

arénation *n.f.* arenation.

arène *n.f.* sand; arena.

aréneux, euse *adj.* arenose, sandy.

aréole *n.f.* areola.

aréomètre *n.m.* areometer.

aréométrie *n.f.* areometry.

aréopage *n.m.* Areopagus.

aréopagite *n.m.* Areopagite.

arête *n.f.* fish bone; skeleton (of a fish); awn, beard, edge; arris. **~ de voûte,** groin of an arch.

argent *n.m.* silver; money, coin, cash. **~ en lingot,** silver in ingots. **~ monnayé,** coined silver. **blanc comme l'~,** white as silver. **~ vierge ou natif,** virgin or native silver. **~ de bon aloi,** standard silver. **vif ~,** quicksilver, mercury. **un ~ fou,** no end of money. **avoir beaucoup d'~,** to have a great deal of money. **être en ~,** to have plenty of money. **~ comptant,** cash, ready money. **être à court d'~,** to be short of money. **toucher de l'~,** to receive money. **faire ~ de tout,** to turn everything into money. **une affaire d'~,** a money matter. **jeter son ~ par la fenêtre,** to squander money. **mettre de bon ~ contre du mauvais,** to throw good money after bad. **point d'~ point de Suisse,** nothing for nothing.

argenté, e *p.p.* silvered. *adj.* silver-white, silvery.

argenter *v.t.* to silver.

argenterie *n.f.* silverplate, plate.

argenteur *n.m.* silverer, silver plater.

argenteux, euse *adj.* moneyed, wealthy.

argentier *n.m.* treasurer; minister of finance.

argentifère *adj.* argentiferous.

argentin, e *adj.* silvery; silver-toned, silvery; argentine. **gris argenté,** silver-gray.

argenture *n.f.* silvering.

argile *n.f.* clay, argil, potter's clay.

argileux, euse *adj.* argillaceous, clayey.

argilière *n.f.* clay pit.

argilifère *adj.* argiliferous.

argon *n.m.* argon.

argonaute *n.m.* argonaut.

argot *n.m.* slang; *Hortic.* stub.

argoter *v.t.* and *v.i.* to cut off the stubs left in pruning.

argousin *n.m.* prison guard.

arguer *v.t.* to accuse. *v.i.* to infer, to conclude.

argument *n.m.* argument, reason, plea; proof. **~ en forme,** formal argument.

argumentateur *n.m.* arguer, argumentizer.

argumentation *n.f.* argumentation, reasoning.

argumenter *v.i.* to argue.

argutie *n.f.* quibble, quirk.

aria *n.m.* bother, mess. **quel ~!** what a bother!

arianisme *n.m.* Arianism.

aride *adj.* arid, dry, barren, sterile. **terre ~,** arid soil.

aridité *n.f.* aridity, dryness; barrenness.

arien, ne *adj.* and *n.m.f.* Arian.

ariette *n.f. Mus.* arietta.

aristarque *n.m.* Aristarchus; aristarch.

aristocrate *n.m.f.* aristocrat. *adj.* aristocratic.

aristocratie *n.f.* aristocracy.

aristocratique *adj.* aristocratic.

aristocratiquement *adv.* aristocratically.

arithméticien *n.m.* arithmetician.

arithmétique *n.f.* arithmetic. *adj.* arithmetical.

arithmétiquement *adv.* arithmetically.

arlequin *n.m.* harlequin; spotted redshank. **habit d'~,** patchwork, motley.

arlequinade *n.m.* harlequinade.

armada *n.f.* armada. *Fig.* hordes of, heaps of.

armateur *n.m.* shipowner, fleetowner, shipper.

armature *n.f.* ironwork, braces.

arme *n.f.* arm, weapon. **~s offensives, défensives,** offensive, defensive weapons. **~ à feu,** firearm. **~s blanches,** swords, sabers, bayonets; sidearms. **maître d'~s,** fencing master. **faire les ~s,** to fence. **un fait d'~s,** an exploit in war. **place d'~s,** parade ground. **salle d'~,** armory; a place in which arms are kept. **assaut d'~s,** fencing match. **porter les ~s,** to be a soldier. **être sous les ~s,** to be under arms or in arms. **rendre les ~s,** to lay down arms. **passer par les ~s,** to put to the sword; to shoot.

armé, e *p.p.* **~ à la légère,** light-armed. **la force ~e,** the troops, the military. **~ jusqu'aux dents,** armed to the teeth. **à main ~e,** by force of arms, by force.

armée *n.f.* army, host, multitude. **~ navale,** fleet. **les ~s de terre et de mer,** the land and sea forces. **~ permanente,** standing army. **~ d'occupation,** army of occupation.

armement *n.m.* arming, accouterments; armament; fitting out (of ships).

armer *v.t.* to arm, to supply with arms; to excite to arms; to cock (a gun), to equip (a ship); to man (a boat). **s'~,** *v.refl.* to arm oneself, to take up arms. **il s'arma d'une épée,** he armed himself with a sword. **~ de courage,** to take courage. **~ contre la pluie,** to take precautions against rain.

armet *n.m.* headpiece.

armillaire *adj.* armillary. **sphère ~,** armillary sphere.

armille *n.f.* annulet.

armistice *n.m.* armistice.

armoire *n.f.* cupboard; clothes closet.

armoiries *n.f.pl.* arms, coat of arms, armorial bearings; hatchment.

armorial *adj.* armorial. *n.m.* book of heraldry.

armorier *v.t.* to emblazon, to put a coat of arms on (a carriage, etc.).

armoriste *n.m.* armorist.

armurier *n.m.* gunsmith, armorer.

arnaque *n.f.* ripoff, sting.

arnaquer *v.t.* to rip off, to con.

arnaquer *n.m.* con man, ripoff artist.

aromate *n.m.* aromatic.

aromatique *adj.* aromatic.

aromatisation *n.f.* aromatization.

aromatiser *v.t.* to aromatize; to flavor.

arome *n.m.* aroma, flavor.

aronde *n.f.* swallow. **queue d'~,** dovetail.

arpège *n.m.* arpeggio.

arpéger *v.i.* to play in arpeggio.

arpent *n.m.* arpent (old French measure of an acre).

arpentage *n.m.* land measuring, surveying.

arpenter *v.t.* to measure, to survey (land); to stride along.

arpenteur *n.m.* surveyor.

arpenteuse *n.f.* citigrade spider.

arpon *n.m.* crosscut saw.

arqué, e *p.p.* arched; bent, crooked.

arquebuse *n.f.* arquebuse.

arquer *v.t.* and *v.i.* to arch; to curve, to bend.

arrache-bouchon *n.m.* corkscrew.

arrache-clous *n.m.* nail puller.

arrachement *n.m.* pulling up; tearing off, down, or away; digging up (potatoes, etc.). **~ des mauvaises herbes,** weeding.

arrache-pied (d') *adv.* without intermission, uninterruptedly.

arracher *v.t.* to pull up by the roots; to pull or draw out (a nail); to extract (a tooth); to tear or pull out (the hair), to tear or pluck out (the eyes); to snatch; to wrest. **~ quelqu'un de sa retraite,** to tear a person from his retreat. **il arracha le livre de ma main,** he snatched the book from my hand. **on lui arrachera le pouvoir,** they will wrest power from him. **on ne peut lui ~ un mot,** one cannot get a word out of him. **~ de l'argent à une personne,** to get money out of a person. **arrachez-lui son secret,** wring his secret from him. **~ la peau à un animal, l'écorce à un arbre,** to strip off the skin of an animal, the bark of a tree. **s'~,** *v.refl.* to tear or force oneself away. **je me suis arraché à mes livres,** I have torn myself from my books. **arrachez-vous de ce lieu funeste,** fly from this fatal spot.

arracheur *n.m.* extirpator, extractor. **~ de dents,** tooth puller. **mentir comme un ~,** to lie like a carpet.

arraisonner *v.t.* to reason with (a person); to hail (a vessel).

arrangé, e *p.p.* arranged; affected.

arrangeant, e *adj.* accommodating, obliging.

arrangement *n.m.* arrangement; adjustment, settlement; order; furnishing (of rooms, etc.); laying out (of gardens, etc.). **il s'est chargé de l'~ de mes livres,** he has undertaken the arrangement of my books. **l'~ des mots, des idées,** the proper order of words, of ideas. **prendre des ~s avec ses créanciers,** to come to terms with one's creditors.

arranger *v.t.* to arrange, to put in order; to adjust, to settle (differences, etc.); to make arrangements for; to contrive; to repair, to clean. **~ des livres,** to arrange books. **~ une maison, une chambre,** to arrange a house, a room. **~ ses affaires,** to arrange one's affairs. **~ une montre,** to repair or clean a watch. **cela ne m'arrange pas,** that will not suit me. **comme l'orage vous a arrangé,** what mess the storm has put you in. **s'~,** *v.refl.* ro arrange oneself; to be arranged. **tout s'arrangea parfaitement,** everything was perfectly arranged. **arrangez-vous autour de la table,** place yourselves around the table. **je m'arrangerai pour vous payer dans un mois,** I will arrange matters so as to pay you in a month. **arrangez-vous!,** do as you like. **ils n'ont pas voulu ~, ils plaideront,** they have refused to negotiate, they will go to court. **je m'arrangerai de peu,** I shall make do, or be content with little.

arrentement *n.m.* renting out.

arrenter *v.t.* to rent out.

arrérager *v.t.* to get in arrears.

arrérages *n.m.pl.* arrears.

arrestation *n.f.* arrest; apprehension; custody. **on a fait de nombreuses ~s,** numerous arrests have been made.

arrêt *n.m.* judgment, decree, arrest; prison; sentence (of a criminal court); stoppage. **rendre un ~,** to give judgment. **prononcer un ~ de mort,** to pass sentence of death. **l'~ des affaires commerciales,** the stoppage or interruption of business transactions. **temps d'~,** temporary interruption. **mandat d'~,** warrant. **maison d'~,** jail. **mettre aux ~s,** to lock up. *Sport.* pointing. **chien d'~,** pointer, setter. **tenir le gibier en ~,** to remain on the point.

arrêté, e *p.p.* stopped, arrested, checked, hindered, fastened, fixed. **dessein ~,** fixed purpose. *n.m.* resolution; decision, order. **~ de compte,** the final statement of an account.

arrête-porte *n.m.* doorstop.

arrêter *v.t.* to stop; to stay, to detain, to hinder, to arrest; to check; to obstruct; to come to terms. **~ un cheval,** to stop a horse. **~ une pendule,** to stop a clock. **aucune considération ne peut l'~,** no consideration can restrain him. **rien ne peut ~ le temps,** nothing can arrest (stop or stay) the flight of time. **~ un homme pour dettes,** to arrest a man for debt. **~ un voleur,** to catch a thief. **~ un volet que le vent agite,** to fasten a shutter being banged by the wind. **~ un marché,** to conclude a bargain. *v.i.* to stop; to stand still; to tarry; to conclude; to dwell upon. **nous arrêtâmes quelques jours**

à Bordeaux, we stayed a few days at Bordeaux. **s'~,** *v.refl.* to stop, to come to a standstill; to remain, to stay; to pause. **il s'arrêta un instant et puis il reprit,** he stopped (or paused) a moment, and then he resumed. **ma montre vient de ~,** my watch has just stopped. **~ en beau chemin,** to stop in the midst of success. **il s'arrête à tous les coins de rue,** he loiters at the corner of every street. **~ à des bagatelles,** to limit one's attention to trifles. **ne vous arrêtez pas à ce qu'il dit,** pay no attention to what he says. **il s'arrêta longtemps sur les services qu'il vous avait rendus,** he dwelt long on the services he had rendered you.

arrhes *n.f.pl.* earnest money; deposit.

arrière *adv.* away with, have done with; astern. **avoir vent ~,** to have the wind astern. *n.m.* rear, back part, hind part (of anything); stern. **les voiles de l'~,** the aftersails. **en ~,** backward, behind. **il fit un pas en ~,** he made a step backward, he stepped back. **être en ~,** to be behind. **en ~ de,** behind. **ces gens-là sont en ~ de leur siècle,** those people, are behind the times. **feux arrière,** rear lights.

arriéré, e *adj.* backward, behind in progress; in arrears; overdue. **province ~e,** backward province. **payment ~,** payment overdue. *n.m.* arrears (of payments, work, etc.).

arrière-bouche *n.f.* pharynx, back of the mouth.

arrière-boutique *n.f.* room at the back of a shop.

arrière-change *n.m.* compound interest.

arrière-corps *n.m.* recess; back of a building.

arrière-cour *n.f.* backyard.

arrière-faix *n.m.* afterbirth.

arrière-garant *n.m.* surety of a surety.

arrière-garde *n.f.* rearguard.

arrière-goût *n.m.* aftertaste.

arrière-grand-mère *n.f.* great-grandmother.

arrière-grands-parents *n.m.pl.* great-grand-parents.

arrière-grand-père *n.m.* great-grandfather.

arrière-main *n.m.* backstroke; hindquarters (of a horse).

arrière-pays *n.m.* hinterland.

arrière-pensée *n.f.* mental reservation; hidden motive.

arrière-petite-fille *n.f.* great-granddaughter.

arrière-petit-fils *n.m.* great-grandson.

arrière-petits-enfants *n.m.pl.* great-grandchildren.

arrière-plan *n.m.* background.

arriérer *v.t.* to delay, to defer, to put off. **s'~,** *v.refl.* to stay behind, to lag behind.

arrière-saison *n.f.* latter end of autumn; the latter years of life.

arrière-train *n.m.* the part of a vehicle supported by the back wheels; hindquarters (animal).

arrière-voussure *n.f.* back arch.

arrimer *v.t.* to stow; to trim the hold.

arrivage *n.m.* arrival.

arrivée *n.f.* arrival; coming, advent. **à mon ~ en Angleterre,** on my arrival in England.

arriver *v.t.* to arrive, to arrive at, to come to shore; to approach, to reach, to attain; to succeed; *Naut.* to veer, to bear up. **la flotte arriva devant Alger,** the fleet arrived at (or off) Algiers. **le paquebot vient d'~,** the steamer has just arrived. **~ à bon port,** to arrive safely. **il n'était pas encore arrivé,** he had not yet arrived. **j'arrive au point le plus difficile,** I now come to the most difficult point. **la lettre n'est pas arrivée à son adresse,** the letter did not reach its address. **la vieillesse arrive,** old age is coming on. **la nuit arrivait,** night was coming on. **voulant ~ à la vérité,** wishing to get at the truth. **il arriva à ses fins,** he attained his ends. **cela peut ~ à tout le monde,** that may happen to anybody. **les malheurs n'arrivent jamais seuls,** misfortunes never come single. *v.impers.* to happen, to chance. **il est arrivé des nouvelles d'Espagne,** news has arrived from Spain or, **il arriva que le pauvre homme mourut,** now it came to pass that the poor man died. **quoi qu'il arrive,** whatever may happen. **arrive qui plante,** happen what may.

arrivisme *n.m.* unscrupulous ambition.

arriviste *n.m.f.* go-getter, careerist.

arrogamment *adv.* arrogantly.

arrogance *n.f.* arrogance.

arrogant, e *adj.* arrogant, overbearing.

arroger (s') *v.refl.* to arrogate to oneself, to arrogate.

arrondi, e *adj.* rounded, round, roundish.

arrondir *v.t.* to round; to enlarge; to round off. **~ ses phrases,** to round one's phrases. **~ un cap,** to double a cape. **s'~,** *v.refl.* to become round. **sa taille s'arrondit,** she is getting stout.

arrondissement *n.m.* rounding; roundness; ward, arrondissement (of Paris).

arrosage *n.m.* watering, irrigation.

arrosement *n.m.* watering; sprinkling.

arroser *v.t.* to water. **~ une plante,** to water a plant. **j'ai été bien arrosé,** I got thoroughly soaked (by the rain). **il arrosa le tout d'une bouteille de vin,** he washed down the whole with a bottle of wine.

arrosoir *n.m.* watering can.

arrugie *n.f.* *Min.* drain.

arsenal *n.m.* arsenal.

arsenic *n.m.* arsenic.

art *n.m.* art. **l'~ de la peinture,** the art of painting. **l'~ de l'éloquence,** the art of eloquence. **les ~s libéraux,** the liberal arts. **les ~s mécaniques,** the mechanical arts. **les ~s industriels,** the industrial arts. **les ~s d'agrément,** accomplishments.

artefact *n.m.* artifact.

artère *n.f.* artery.

artériel, le *adj.* arterial.

artériole *n.f.* small artery.

artérite *n.f.* arteritis.

arthralgie *n.f.* arthralgia.

arthrite *n.f.* arthritis.

arthritique *adj.* arthritic.

arthrose *n.f. Anat.* arthrosis.

artichaut *n.m.* artichoke.

article *n.m.* article, clause, item of an account; *Gram.* article. ~ **de fond,** leading article. **beaucoup d'~s de toilette,** many toilet articles. **faire bien l'~,** to be a good salesman (i.e. to puff up). **c'est un autre ~,** that is another thing, a different matter.

articulaire *adj.* articular; belonging to or affecting the joints.

articulation *n.f.* articulation, joint.

articuler *v.t.* to articulate. **s'~,** *v.refl.* to be articulated, distinct.

artifice *n.m.* artifice, contrivance; stratagem; shuffling. **feu d'~,** fireworks.

artificiel, le *adj.* artificial. **des fleurs ~s,** artificial flowers.

artificiellement *adv.* artificially.

artificier *n.m.* firework maker, pyrotechnist.

artificieusement *adv.* artfully; cunningly, craftily.

artificieux, se *adj.* artful; wily, cunning, crafty.

artillerie *n.f.* artillery; ordnance. **pièce d'~,** piece of ordnance. **grosse ~,** heavy artillery. **~ à cheval,** horse artillery. **~ de siège,** siege artillery. **soldat d'~,** gunner.

artilleur *n.m.* artilleryman; gunner.

artisan *n.m.* artisan, mechanic, operative, workman.

artiste *n.m.f.* artist, performer, player.

artistement *adv.* artistically; skillfully.

artistique *adj.* artistic.

aryen, ne *adj.* Aryan.

as *n.m.* ace (of cards). **~ de pique,** ace of spades.

asbeste *n.m.* asbestos.

ascendance *n.f.* ascendency.

ascendant, e *adj.* ascending; ascendant. *n.m.* ascendant, ascendancy, influence.

ascenseur *n.m.* elevator.

ascension *n.f.* ascension; ascent; Ascension Day.

ascensionnel, le *adj.* ascensional.

ascète *n.m.f.* ascetic; hermit.

ascétique *adj.* ascetic. *n.m.f.* ascetic.

ascétisme *n.m.* asceticism.

ascité *n.f.* ascites, dropsy.

asclépiade *n.m.* asclepiad.

asiatique *adj.* Asiatic.

asile *n.m.* asylum, refuge, shelter; **être sans ~,** to be homeless.

asine *adj.* of the ass. **race ~,** the ass breed.

aspect *n.m.* aspect, look, sight.

asperge *n.f.* asparagus. **botte d'~s,** bundle of asparagus.

asperger *v.t.* to sprinkle.

aspergès *n.m.* sprinkler, aspergillum.

aspérité *n.f.* asperity, roughness, harshness.

aspersion *n.f.* aspersion, sprinkling.

aspersoir *n.m.* holy-water brush.

asphalte *n.m.* asphalt.

asphyxiant, e *adj.* suffocating.

asphyxie *n.f.* asphyxia, suffocation.

asphyxié, e *p.p.* asphyxiated, suffocated.

asphyxier *v.t.* to asphyxiate, to suffocate. **s'~,** *v.refl.* to asphyxiate oneself.

aspic *n.m.* aspic; backbiter; spike lavender.

aspirail *n.m.* airhole.

aspirant, e *adj.* sucking, suction. *n.m.f.* aspirant (to); candidate. **~ de marine,** a midshipman.

aspirateur, trice *adj.* inhaling (of pumps). *n.m.* aspirator, vacuum cleaner.

aspiration *n.f.* inspiration; inhaling; exhaustion, suction; *Gram.* rough breathing.

aspiré, e *p.p.* inspired; aspirated.

aspirée *n.f.* aspirate.

aspirer *v.t.* to inhale; to exhaust. **~ l'air,** to inhale the air. *Gram.* to aspirate. **s'~,** *v.refl.* to be aspirated. *v.i.* to breathe; to aspire.

assagir *v.t.* to render wise. *v.i.* to become wise.

assaillant *n.m.* assailant; aggressor.

assaillir *v.t.* to assail, to attack, to assault.

assainir *v.t.* to make or render healthy. **~ une ville,** to improve the sanitary condition of a town.

assainissement *n.m.* improving the sanitary condition; cleansing; salubrity.

assaisonnement *n.m.* seasoning, condiment.

assaisonner *v.t.* to season, to spice; to give a relish to.

assassin *n.m.* assassin; murderer. **à l'~!** murder! *adj.* murderous, murdering, killing.

assassinant, e *adj.* tiresome, annoying, boring, killing.

assassinat *n.m.* assassination, murder.

assassiner *v.t.* to assassinate, to murder, to kill; to bore, to pester.

assaut *n.m.* assault; attack, shock, onslaught. **donner l'~ à une ville,** to storm a town. **emporter d'~,** to take by storm. **~ d'armes,** assault of arms, fencing match.

asséhement *n.m.* draining (of mines, etc.).

assécher *v.t.* to drain.

assemblage *n.m.* assemblage, union; (printing) gathering; (carpentry) joining.

assemblé, e *p.p.* assembled; joined.

assemblée *n.f.* assembly, meeting, company.

assembler *v.t.* to collect, to gather, to bring together. **s'~,** *v.refl.* to assemble, to meet, to come together; to congregate. **qui se ressemble s'assemble,** birds of a feather flock together.

assembleur, euse *n.m.f.* gatherer (bookbinding); collector.

asséner *v.t.* to strike, to apply. **il lui asséna un coup de bâton sur la tête,** he gave him a blow on the head with a stick.

assentiment *n.m.* assent, approbation.

assentir *v.i.* to assent.

asseoir *v.t.* to seat; to place, to set, to lay. **faire ~,** to cause to be seated. **il les fit ~,** he made them sit down. **~ une statue sur son piédestal,** to set a statue on a pedestal. **~ un trône,** to establish a throne. **~ les fondements d'une maison,** to lay the foundation of a house. **s'~,** *v.refl.* to seat oneself, to sit down. **asseyez-vous,** please be seated. **il s'assit à droite,** he took his seat on the right.

assermenté, e *p.p.* sworn.

assermenter *v.t.* to swear. **~ un fonctionnaire public,** to swear in a public servant.

assertif, ive *adj.* assertive.

assertion *n.f.* assertion.

asservir *v.t.* to reduce to servitude; to enslave, to subjugate, to conquer. **s'~,** *v.refl.* to be the slave (of).

asservissant, e *adj.* enslaving.

asservissement *n.m.* enslavement, servitude, slavery, subjection.

assesseur *n.m.* assessor.

assez *adv.* enough; sufficiently; rather, pretty. **l'avare n'a jamais ~,** the miser never has enough. **~ bon,** good enough. **il est ~ riche pour acheter ce domaine,** he is rich enough to purchase that property. **~ souvent,** often enough. **on ne peut ~ estimer un tel avantage,** we cannot sufficiently prize such an advantage. **cette femme est ~ jolie,** that woman is rather pretty. **cet ouvrage est ~ bien fait,** this work is pretty well done. **~ bien,** pretty well. *n.m.* enough. **~ vaut festin,** enough is as good as a feast.

assidu, e *adj.* assiduous, painstaking, diligent, steady.

assiduité *n.f.* assiduity, application, diligence.

assidûment *adj.* assiduously, diligently.

assiégé, e *p.p.* besieged *n.m.* person besieged. **les assiégés,** the besieged.

assiégeant, e *adj.* besieging. *n.m.* besieger.

assiéger *v.t.* to besiege, to lay siege to, to beset. **les créanciers l'assiégent à toute heure,** his creditors dunned him at all hours.

assiette *n.f.* plate, position, situation, seat; state (of mind). **~s blanches,** clean plates. **~ d'argent,** silverplate. **~ à soupe,** soup plate. **piqueur d'~** or **pique-~,** sponger. **perdre son ~,** to lose one's seat (or balance). **l'~ de cette maison,** the site of that house. **si votre esprit demeure dans la même ~,** if your mind remains in the same state. **n'être point dans son ~ ordinaire,** not to be in one's usual temper.

assiettée *n.f.* plateful.

assignant, e *n.m.f.* plaintiff (in a lawsuit).

assignation *n.f.* summons, writ, assignment. **donner une ~** to serve a summons, a subpoena (of a witness).

assigné, e *p.p.* summoned. *n.m.f.* defendant.

assigner *v.t.* to assign, to summon, to appoint; to attribute.

assimilable *adj.* assimilable.

assimilation *n.f.* assimilation.

assimiler *v.t.* to assimilate, to liken, to compare. **s'~,** *v.refl.* to assimilate oneself, to compare oneself.

assis, e *p.p.* seated, sitting. **~ dans un bon fauteuil,** seated in a good armchair. *n.m.* sitting.

assise *n.f.* row, stratum, layer.

assises *n.f.pl.* assizes, court of assize.

assistance *n.f.* attendance, audience; help; congregation (of a church). **~ publique,** public assistance, welfare.

assistant, e *adj.* assistant. *n.m.f.* assistant; *pl.* bystanders. **un des ~,** a bystander.

assister *v.i.* to attend, to be present. **tout Paris assista à ses funérailles,** all Paris was present at (or attended) his funeral. *v.t.* to assist, to help; to attend. **~ les pauvres,** to help the poor.

association *n.f.* association, partnership, society. **~ commerciale,** trading company. **~ en participation,** joint venture. **~ de secours mutuels,** mutual benefit society.

associé, e *n.m.* associate, partner, copartner. **~ commanditaire,** silent partner. **~ principal,** senior partner.

associer *v.t.* to associate, to take into partnership. **s'~,** *v.refl.* to become partner, to associate together. **nous nous sommes associés pour cette entreprise,** we have entered into partnership for that enterprise.

assoiffé *adj.* thirsty; eager.

assolement *n.m.* rotation of crops.

assoler *v.t.* to rotate crops.

assombrir *v.t.* to make somber, to obscure. **s'~,** *v.refl.* to become gloomy. **le ciel s'assombrit,** the sky is overcast.

assommant, e *adj.* tiresome, tedious, boring. **bavard ~,** crashing bore.

assommer *v.t.* to fell to the ground, to knock on the head, to stun, to bore. **~ un boeuf,** to knock down an ox. **la chaleur m'assomme,** the heat overpowers me.

assommeur *n.m.* slaughterer (of animals).

assommoir *n.m.* bludgeon; knock-down blow.

assomption *n.f.* assumption; Assumption.

assonance *n.f.* assonance.

assonant, e *adj.* assonant.

assorti, e *p.p.* assorted, matched, paired; stocked. **mariage bien ~,** a well-matched marriage. **un attelage bien ~,** a well-matched team (of horses, etc.) **magasin bien ~,** well-stocked shop.

assortiment *n.m.* assortment, matching, stock. **livres d'~,** books purchased for sale.

assortir *v.t.* to sort, to match; to pair; to stock a shop. **~ des couleurs,** to match colors. *v.i.* to match, to suit. **s'~,** *v.refl.* to be assorted, to match, to suit.

assortissant, e *adj.* suitable, becoming.

assoté, e *p.p.* infatuated.

assoter *v.t.* to infatuate. **s'~,** *v.refl.* to be (or become) infatuated.

assoupi, e *adj.* sleepy, drowsy. **être ~,** to doze.

assoupir *v.t.* to make drowsy; to send to sleep; to lull, to appease. **on cherchait à ~ cette affaire,** they tried to hush up that affair. **s'~,** *v.refl.* to become drowsy; to doze, to slumber, to take a nap; to be lulled. **il s'assoupit chaque jour après son dîner,** he takes a nap every day after dinner.

assoupissant, e *adj.* causing sleep. **potion assoupissante,** sleeping potion.

assoupissement *n.m.* drowsiness, sleepiness. **je tombai dans un profond ~,** I fell into a deep slumber.

assouplir *v.t.* to make supple; to make flexible; to break (or break in) horses. **~ une étoffe,** to soften a textile fabric. **s'~,** *v.refl.* to become supple.

assourdir *v.t.* to deafen, to make deaf, to stun, to muffle (sound); to tone down. **trop de bruit nous assourdit,** too much noise deafens us.

assourdissant, e *adj.* deafening.

assourdissement *n.m.* deafening noise; din.

assouvir *v.t.* to sate, to glut, to satiate, to gorge; to gratify, to satisfy. **il ne peut ~ sa faim,** he cannot satisfy his hunger. **s'~,** *v.refl.* to satiate oneself; to be satiated.

assouvissement *n.m.* satiating, glutting, gratification.

assujettir *v.t.* to subject, to subdue, to bind, to fasten. **~ une province,** to subject (or subdue) a province. **~ les passions,** to subdue the passions. **s'~,** *v.refl.* to subject oneself, to submit.

assujettissement *n.m.* subjection; slavery.

assumer *v.t.* to assume.

assurance *n.f.* assurance, certainty, reliance, trust; boldness, spirit; insurance. **j'ai la ferme ~ qu'il vous aidera,** I have full confidence that he will help you. **il parle avec ~,** he speaks boldly. **~ maritime,** marine insurance. **~ mutuelle,** mutual insurance. **~ contre l'incendie,** fire insurance. **~ sur la vie,** life insurance. **compagnie d'~,** insurance company. **police d'~,** policy of insurance. **avec ~,** safely.

assuré, e *p.p.* assured, insured, secured. **maison ~e contre l'incendie,** house insured against fire. **son revenu est bien ~,** his income is well secured. *adj.* secure, sure, certain, steady. **une retraite ~e,** a safe retreat. **tenez-le pour ~,** consider it certain. **des pas mal ~s,** tottering steps. *n.m.f.* insured, person insured.

assurément *adv.* assuredly, surely. **oui ~,** yes, certainly. **~ non,** certainly not.

assurer *v.t.* to secure, to assure, to affirm, to guarantee, to assert, to insure. **~ un plancher,** to secure a floor. **cette femme assure qu'elle n'a que vingt ans,** that woman declares that she is only twenty. **nous sommes assurés du succès,** we are assured of success. **je vous en assure,** I assure you of it. **j'ai assuré ma maison contre l'incendie,** I have insured my house against fire. **~ la bouche d'un cheval,**

to accustom a horse to the bit. **s'~,** *v.refl.* to secure, to make sure of, to be certain of. **il s'assura contre cet événement,** he secured himself against that event. **assurez-vous que je viendrai,** be sure that I will come.

assureur *n.m.* insurer; underwriter.

astérie *n.f.* starfish.

astérisme *n.m.* constellation.

astérisque *n.m.* asterisk (*).

astéroïde *n.m.* asteroid.

asthénie *n.f.* asthenia, debility.

asthmatique *adj.* asthmatic.

asticot *n.m.* maggot. **quel drôle d'asticot!** what a peculiar person!

asticoter *v.t.* to tease, to bother, to annoy.

astiquer *v.t.* to smooth, to polish; to fix up (one's person).

astracan or **astrakan** *n.m.* Astracan; lamb's fur.

astragale *n.m. Arch.* astragal; *Anat.* astragalus, the anklebone; *Bot.* the sweet milk vetch.

astral, e *adj.* astral, starry.

astre *n.m.* heavenly body; star. **l'~ du jour,** the orb of day, the sun. **~ de la nuit,** the orb of night, the moon.

astreignant *adj.* exacting, absorbing.

astreindre *v.t.* to bind, to force, to compel; to restrict, to limit. **s'~,** *v.refl.* to bind oneself; to force oneself.

astreint *adj.* bound, compelled, subjected, liable.

astringent, e *adj.* astringent. *n.m.* astringent.

astrolabe *n.m.* astrolabe.

astrolâtrie *n.f.* astrolatry; star worship.

astrologie *n.f.* astrology.

astrologique *adj.* astrologic, astrological.

astrologiquement *adv.* astrologically.

astrologue *n.m.* astrologer.

astronaute *n.m.f.* astronaut.

astronautique *n.f.* astronautics.

astronef *n.m.* spaceship.

astronome *n.m.* astronomer.

astronomie *n.f.* astronomy.

astronomique *adj.* astronomical.

astronomiquement *adv.* astronomically.

astrophysicien *n.m.* astrophysicist.

astrophysique *n.f.* astrophysics.

astuce *n.f.* artfulness, low cunning, craft, craftiness.

astucieusement *adv.* artfully, cunningly, craftily.

astucieux, euse *adj.* artful, cunning, crafty, wily.

asymetrie *n.f.* asymmetry.

atavisme *n.m.* atavism.

atelier *n.m.* workshop, workroom; studio (artist's); factory. **l'~ d'un menuisier,** a cabinetmaker's workshop. **un chef d'~,** a foreman.

atermoiement *n.m.* delay (for negotiating with creditors); putting off.

atermoyer *v.t.* to delay, to put off (the payment of a debt).

athée *n.m.* atheist. *adj.* atheist.

athéisme *n.m.* atheism.

athlète *n.m.* athlete; wrestler; champion.

athlétique *adj.* athletic; stalwart, lusty, robust. *n.f.* wrestling, etc.

atlantique *adj.* Atlantic. *n.f.* the Atlantic ocean.

atlas *n.m.* atlas.

atmosphère *n.f.* atmosphere.

atmosphérique *adj.* atmospheric, atmospherical.

atome *n.m.* atom, tiny bit.

atomique *adj.* atomic, atomical. **théorie ~,** atomic theory.

atomisation *n.f.* destruction, pulverisation, splitting.

atomiser *v.t.* to atomize, to pulverize.

atomiste *n.m.* atomist.

atomistique *adj.* atomic, atomical. **théorie ~,** atomic theory.

atone *adj.* dull, debilitated, not accented.

atour *n.m.* (chiefly used in the plural) attire. **elle avait ses plus beaux ~s,** she was dressed in her best, in all her finery. **dame d'~,** lady of the bedchamber.

atourner *v.t.* to dress up, to deck out.

atout *n.m.* trump, trump card, advantage. **jouer ~,** to play a trump.

âtre *n.m.* hearth, fireplace, hearthstone.

atroce *adj.* atrocious; outrageous, heinous.

atrocement *adv.* atrociously.

atrocité *n.f.* atrocity, atrociousness, wickedness.

atrophie *n.f.* atrophy.

atrophier *v.t.* to cause atrophy. **s'~,** *v.refl.* to be atrophied, to waste away.

attabler *v.t.* to set at table (for eating, drinking or playing). **s'~,** *v.refl.* to seat oneself at table, to sit down to table.

attachant, e *adj.* attaching, interesting, engaging.

attache *n.f.* tie; tether, leash, cord, bond. **mettre un chien à l'~,** to tie up a dog. **chien d'~,** yard dog. **être toujours à l'~,** to be tied down to business.

attaché, e *p.p.* attached, fastened, joined; bent on, bound. *n.m.* attaché (of an embassy); follower, adherent. **~-case** *n.m.* briefcase.

attachement *n.m.* attachment; affection, tie, bond.

attacher *v.t.* to attach, to fasten, to tie, to bind, to chain. **~ un cheval à un poteau,** to fasten (or tie) a horse to a post. **~ avec des clous,** to fasten together with nails. **~ un ruban avec une épingle,** to pin on a ribbon. **~ de l'importance à quelque chose,** to attach importance to a thing. **~ un sens, une idée à un mot,** to attach a meaning, an idea to a word. **attacher du prix à,** to set value on. **s'~,** *v.refl.* to attach oneself, to be attached to, to stick to. **le chien s'attache à son maître,** the dog is attached to his master. **je m'attachais à lui, et il s'attachait à moi,** I became attached to him and he to me.

attaquable *adj.* attackable, assailable; liable to attack.

attaquant *n.m.* aggressor, assailant.

attaque *n.f.* attack, onset, onslaught, charge, aggression. **~ de goutte, d'apoplexie,** an attack (or fit) of gout, of apoplexy.

attaquer *v.t.* to attack, to assail, to assault, to fall on or upon; to impugn, to contest (the validity of). **~ l'ennemi,** to attack the enemy. **~ un gigot,** to attack a leg of mutton. **cet ouvrage attaque la religion,** that work attacks religion. **~ en justice,** to sue, to prosecute. **bien attaqué, bien défendu,** he gave as good as he got. **s'~,** *v.refl.* to attack, to challenge, to fall upon, to fall foul of. **~ à plus fort que soi,** to attack a person stronger than oneself. **un valet qui s'attaque à son maître,** a valet who argues with his master.

attarder *v.t.* to delay. **s'~,** *v.refl.* to be belated; to linger behind. **ne vous attardez pas,** do not be late.

atteindre *v.t.* to attain, to reach, to arrive at, to get at, to get to. **vous n'avez pas encore atteint l'âge exigé,** you have not yet attained the age required. **il atteindra son but,** he will attain (or gain) his end. **~ le but,** to hit the mark. **ce danger ne peut m'~,** that danger cannot touch me. **nous ne pûmes ~ le bâtiment anglais,** we could not overtake the English vessel. **il fut atteint d'une maladie dangereuse,** he was attacked by a dangerous disease. *v.i.* to attain; to reach, to get at. **~ à la perfection,** to attain (or attain to) perfection. **~ au but,** to reach the goal, to succeed.

atteint, e *p.p.* attained; struck; bit. **le but ayant été ~,** the end (or object) having been attained.

atteinte *n.f.* blow, stroke, attach, fit, touch; harm, injury, wrong, offense. **hors d'~,** beyond reach, out of reach; **~ mortelle,** mortal wound. **une légère ~ de goutte,** a touch (twinge) of the gout. **porter ~,** to injure.

attelage *n.m.* team. **~ de boeufs,** a yoke of oxen.

atteler *v.t.* to hitch horses to. **~ des chevaux à un carrosse, ~ une voiture,** to hitch horses to a carriage.

attelle *n.f.* splint.

attenant, e *adj.* adjoining; contiguous, next. **la maison ~e,** the adjoining (or next) house. *adv.* close by. **je demeure tout ~,** live close by.

attendant *adv.* **en ~ mieux,** till something better turns up. **en ~,** in the meantime, meanwhile, meantime. **en ~ que,** till, until. **en ~ qu'il vienne,** till he comes.

attendre *v.t.* to wait for, to expect, to look forward to. **il y a plus d'une heure que je vous attends ici,** I have been waiting for you here over an hour. **le dîner vous attend,** dinner is waiting for you. **~ sous l'orme,** to dance attendance. **se faire ~,** to keep people waiting. **voilà le sort qui vous attend,** such is the fate that awaits you. *v.i.* to wait; to stay, to stop. **attendez ici un moment,** wait here a moment. **je suis**

las d'~, I am tired of waiting. **vous ne perdrez rien pour ~,** you will lose nothing by waiting. **tout vient à point à qui sait ~,** all things come to him who waits. **il ennuie à qui attend,** waiting is tiresome. **il fait ~ ses créanciers,** he makes his creditors wait. **s'~,** v.refl. to expect; to look for; to hope, to apprehend. **je m'attends à vous voir demain,** I expect to see you tomorrow. **ne vous attendez pas que je le fasse,** do not expect me to do it. **je ne m'attendais pas à cela,** I did not expect that. **attendez-vous-y,** I hope you get it!

attendrir v.t. to make tender, to move, to touch. **la vertu souffrante attendrit tous les cœurs,** suffering virtue moves every heart. **s'~,** v.refl. to become tender, to be moved. **la viande s'attendrit à la cuisson,** meat becomes tender when cooked. **l'art d'~,** the art of evoking pity. **~ sur le sort des malheureux,** to feel compassion for the unfortunate.

attendrissant, e adj. touching, moving.

attendrissement n.m. tenderness, feeling compassion.

attendu, prep. considering, on account of. **~ que,** considering that, seeing that; whereas.

attentat n.m. attempt, attack or assault. **~ à la pudeur,** indecent assault.

attentatoire adj. derogatory, prejudicial, damaging.

attente n.f. waiting; expectation, hope. **être dans l'~ de,** to be waiting for. **salle d'~,** waiting-room. **tromper, frustrer l'~,** to deceive, to disappoint expectations. **contre toute ~,** against all expectation.

attenter v.t. to attempt, to make an attempt. **~ à la vie de quelqu'un,** to make an attempt on a person's life. **~ à ses jours,** to attempt suicide.

attentif, ive adj. attentive, heedful, mindful; watchful.

attention n.f. attention, heed, care; regard, consideration. **cette étude exige une grande ~,** that study requires great attention. **faire ~ à,** to mind, to pay attention to. **~!** attention! mind, be attentive! look out! **faute d'~,** for want of attention, inadvertently.

attentionné, e adj. attentive.

attentisme n.m. wait-and-see policy.

attentiste adj. and n.m.f. in favor of a wait-and-see policy.

attentivement adv. attentively, with attention, intently.

atténuant, e adj. attenuant, extenuating. n.m. attenuant, diluent.

atténuation n.f. attenuation; extenuation.

atténuer v.t. to attenuate; to make thin **or** weak; to debilitate, to extenuate, to subdue, to soften.

atterrage n.m. making land; landing.

atterrand adj. astounding, overwhelming.

atterré adj. horror-stricken, dumbfounded.

atterrer v.t. to throw to the ground, to overthrow, to strike down; to overwhelm. **ce**

derniermalheur l'atterra, this last misfortune overwhelmed him. **cette nouvelle m'atterra,** this news overwhelmed me. v.i. to make for land.

atterrir v.i. to make land, to land.

atterrissage n.m. landfall, making land.

atterrissement n.m. alluvium; deposit of soil.

attestation n.f. attestation; testimonial, certificate.

attester v.t. to attest, to certify; to witness to.

attiédir v.i. to make tepid **or** lukewarm. **s'~,** v.refl. to become lukewarm, to cool, to get cool.

attiédissement n.m. lukewarmness, coolness.

attifer v.t. to dress up. **s'~,** v.refl. to dress oneself up.

attique adj. attic. n.m. attic, attic story.

attirail n.m. apparatus, appliances, acoutrements, luggage, utensils, instruments, tackle. **~ de chasse,** hunting equipment. **~ de cuisine,** kitchen utensils. **~ de guerre,** war matériel.

attirant, e adj. attractive, engaging, alluring.

attirer v.t. to attract; to allure, to win over. **l'aimant attire le fer,** the magnet attracts iron. **un malheur en attire un autre,** one misfortune brings on another. **~ l'attention du public,** to attract the attention of the public. **s'~,** v.refl. to draw upon oneself; to attract one another. **il s'attire toujours des affaires,** he is always getting into scrapes.

attiser v.t. to mend or make up (a wood fire), to stir up, to excite.

attiseur n.m. fire builder; *Fig.* meddler.

attisoir n.m. poker.

attitré, e adj. regularly appointed; hired.

attitude n.f. attitude, posture.

attouchement n.m. touch, feeling; contact.

attracteur, trice adj. attracting, attractile.

attractif, ive adj. attractive.

attraction adj. attraction. **parc des attractions,** amusement park.

attraire v.t. to attract, to allure, to draw.

attrait n.m. attraction, allurement, charm. **l'~ de la gloire,** the attractions of glory. **elle était parée de tous les ~s de la jeunesse et de la beauté,** she was adorned with all the charms of youth and beauty.

attrapade n.f. quarrel, rebuke.

attrape n.f. trap; catch, trick; take-in.

attrape-lourdaud, attrape-nigaud n.m. booby trap.

attrape-mouche n.m. Venus flytrap.

attraper v.t. to trap, to catch; to cheat, to dupe. **~ des oiseaux avec de la glu,** to catch birds with lime twigs. **~ un rhume,** to catch a cold. **~ la ressemblance,** to catch the likeness (drawing). **~ quelqu'un sur le fait,** to catch someone in the act. **~ la fièvre,** to catch a fever. **ce charlatan a attrapé bien du monde,** that impostor has taken in a great many people. **être attrapé,** to be taken in. **j'ai attrapé la plus**

mauvaise place, I got the very worst place.

attrapé! caught! you are in for it. **s'~,** *v.refl.* to overreach one another; to quarrel with. **je me suis attrapé à une porte,** I ran against a door.

attrapeur, euse *n.m.f.* deceiver, deluder.

attrapoire *n.f.* trap, trick, pitfall.

attrayant, e *adj.* attractive, engaging, enticing, charming.

attribuable *adj.* attributable; owing to.

attribuer *v.t.* to ascribe to, to attribute to, to impute, to assign to, to invest with. **s'~,** *v.pron.* to attribute to oneself, to arrogate, to claim. **~ des droits,** to arrogate (or claim) rights.

attribut *n.m.* attribute; *Log.* predicate.

attributif, ive *adj.* attributive.

attribution *n.f.* conferring; prerogative, powers, functions. **ceci entre dans les ~s du préfet,** this is comprised in the prefect's functions.

attristant, e *adj.* sad, sorrowful, melancholy, afflicting.

attrister *v.t.* to sadden; to make sad, to grieve, to afflict, to cast down. **s'~,** *v.refl.* to grieve; to give way to sorrow; to distress oneself; to be grieved.

attrition *n.f.* attrition.

attroupement *n.m.* mob, rabble.

attrouper *v.t.* to assemble; to draw together. **s'~,** *v.refl.* to troop or collect together to form a mob.

atypique *adj.* atypical.

au, aux *art.* (for **à le, à les**) to the.

aubade *n.f.* morning serenade; reproof, lecture.

aubaine *n.f.* godsend, windfall, stroke of good luck, bargain.

aube *n.f.* dawn, daybreak; alb (priest's garment); *Naut.* paddle-board.

aubépine *n.f.* hawthorn.

aubère *adj.* and *n.m.* dappled, dapple-gray.

auberge *n.f.* inn.

aubergine *n.f.* eggplant.

aubergiste *n.m.f.* innkeeper.

aubier *n.m.* sapwood, alburnum.

auburn *adj.* auburn.

aucun, e *adj.* and *pron.* any, none; no, not any. **je n'ai jamais fait ~ mal,** I have never done any harm. **~ philosophe n'ignore que ...,** no philosopher is ignorant that .... **je doute qu'~ de vous le fasse,** I doubt that any of you will do it. **~ n'est prophète chez soi,** no one is a prophet in his own country.

aucunement *adv.* any way, in any way, by any means, at all. **je ne le connais ~,** I do not know him at all. **est-ce que je vous incommode? ~, monsieur,** do I inconvenience you? Not in the least, sir.

audace *n.f.* audacity, daring, boldness, impudence. **être plein d'~,** to be full of daring. **avec ~,** insolently.

audacieusement *adv.* audaciously, daringly, boldly.

audacieux, euse *adj.* audacious, daring.

au-deça *adv.* on this side.

au-dedans *adv.* within, inside.

au-dehors *adv.* outside.

au-delà de *adv.* beyond.

au-dessous *adv.* below.

au-dessus *adv.* above.

au-devant *adv.* toward. **aller ~ d'un danger,** to anticipate danger.

audibilité *n.f.* audibility.

audible *adj.* audible.

audience *n.f.* audience, hearing; sitting, auditory. **demander, accorder une ~,** to request, to grant an audience. **salle d'~,** audience chamber. **~ particulière,** private audience. **~ publique,** public audience. **~ à huis clos,** closed-door session. **cette affaire occupera trois ~s,** that affair will occupy three sessions.

audiencier *n.m.* **huissier ~,** crier (of a court of law).

audiovisuel *adj.* audio-visual.

auditeur *n.m.* hearer, auditor.

auditif, ive *adj.* auditory.

audition *n.f.* hearing; audition; auditing (of an account). **~ des témoins,** the hearing (or examination) of witnesses.

auditionner *v.t.* to audition.

auditoire *n.m.* audience; congregation; auditory.

auditorium *n.m.* auditorium.

auge *n.f.* trough; horse trough, hod.

augée *n.f.* trayful, hodful.

auget *n.m.* small trough; seed trough, drawer (of birdcage); spout (of a millhopper).

augment *n.m.* *Gram.* augment; *Med.* augmentation, augment.

augmentateur, trice *n.m.f.* augmenter.

augmentatif, ive *adj.* augmentative.

augmentation *n.f.* augmentation; increase.

augmenté, e *p.p.* augmented, enlarged (in size).

augmenter *v.t.* to augment, to increase, to enlarge. **chaque jour il augmente sa fortune,** he increases his fortune every day. **~ le prix des denrées,** to raise the price of food. *v.i.* to augment, to grow, to increase. **le froid va en augmentant,** it keeps getting colder. **s'~,** *v.refl.* to augment, to be increased.

augural, e *adj.* augural.

augure *n.m.* augur, soothsayer; augury, omen: **de bon ~,** of good augury or omen. **de mauvais ~,** ill-omened, ominous.

augurer *v.t.* to augur. **~ mieux de l'avenir,** to augur better of the future.

auguste *adj.* august, majestic, grand.

augustement *adj.* augustly, majestically.

aujourd'hui *adv.* today, this day; nowadays, at present. **il fait bien chaud ~,** it is very hot today. **le jour d'~,** this day. **d'~ en huit, en quinze,** a week from now, two weeks from now. **il y a ~ huit jours, quinze jours,** a week, two weeks ago today. **les hommes d'~,** the men of the present day; the men of the day, of the period.

aulx *pl.* V. **ail.** of ail, which see.

aumône *n.f.* alms, charity, almsgiving. **faire l'~,**

to give alms. **demander l'~,** to beg. **donner l'~ à,** to give alms to. **vivre d'~,** to live on charity.

aumônerie *n.f.* chaplaincy.

aumônier *n.m.* chaplain (of a college, hospital, etc.). **aumônière** *n.f.* almoner (of a convent, etc.); alms-bag, alms-purse.

aumuce, aumusse *n.f.* amice, amess; a fur cap.

aunaie *n.f.* alder plot, alder grove.

aune *n.f.* ell (a former measure of length). **une ~ de soie,** an ell of silk. **mésurer les autres à son ~,** to judge others by one's own standards. *n.m. Bot.* alder.

auner *v.t.* to measure; to judge.

auparavant *adv.* before, previously; first. **quelques mois ~,** some months before.

auprès *adv.* near, close by; at hand, near or close at hand. **tout ~ coule une petite rivière,** close by runs a rivulet.

auprès de, *prep.* near, near to, close to, by; about, with. **venez ~ de moi,** come near or close to me. **avoir libre accès ~ de quelqu'un,** to have free access to a person. **trouver grâce ~ de,** to find favor with. **il est heureux ~ de nous,** he is happy compared with us.

auréole *n.f.* aureola; halo; *Med.* areola.

auriculaire *adj.* auricular. **témoin ~, confession ~,** auricular confession. **doigt ~,** *n.m.* the little finger.

auricule *n.f.* auricle, the outer ear.

aurifère *adj.* auriferous.

aurification *n.f. Dent.* filling with gold.

aurifier *v.t.* to fill (decayed teeth) with gold.

aurore *n.f.* dawn; daybreak, break of day, morning; East, dawning. **l'~ commençait à paraître,** the morning began to break. **l'~ aux doigts de roses,** rosy-fingered dawn. **l'~ de la vie,** the dawn of life. **avant l'~,** before dawn. **~ boréale,** aurora borealis, northern lights.

auscultation *n.f.* auscultation.

ausculter *v.t.* to sound with a stethoscope.

auspice *n.m.* auspice, omen. **heureux ~,** a happy omen.

aussi *adv.* also, too, likewise, besides; therefore, so, as. **lui et les autres ~,** him (or he) and the others also. **si le soleil est ~ grand qu'il paraît,** if the sun is as large as it looks. **vous le croyez? et moi ~,** you think so? so do I. **avec une sagesse ~ rare,** with wisdom so rare, so unusual. *conj.* so, and so, therefore. **ces étoffes sont belles, ~ coûtent-elles cher,** this fabric is handsome, and therefore expensive. **~ bien,** likewise. **je le sais ~ bien que lui,** I know that as well as he.

aussitôt *adv.* immediately, at once. **j'irai ~,** I will go at once. **~ dit, ~ fait,** no sooner said than done. **votre père y sera ~ que vous,** your father will be there as soon as you are.

austère *adj.* austere, harsh, rough, sharp, strict, severe.

austèrement *adv.* austerely, strictly.

austérité *n.f.* austerity, severity; strictness.

austral, e *adj.* austral, southern.

autan *n.m.* south wind.

autant *adv.* as much, as many, so much, so many. **je vous en rendrai mille fois ~,** I will repay you a thousand times as much. **c'est un homme mort ou ~ vaut,** he is a dead man or as good as dead. **~ vaudrait parler à un sourd,** you might as well talk to a deaf person. **deux fois ~,** twice as much. **~ de têtes, ~ d'opinions,** as many opinions as there are people. **~ qu'il est en moi,** as far as is in my power. **~ que je puis me rappeler,** as far (or as well) as I can remember. **augmenter ~ la somme,** to increase the sum by so much. **~ que je sache,** as far as I know, for all I know. **d'autant plus, d'autant moins, d'autant mieux,** all the more, all the less, all the better. **il fut d'~ plus facile à le repousser,** it was all the easier to repulse him. **je suis d'~ moins disposé à le servir,** I am so much less disposed to serve him. **il est d'~ moins formidable qu'il est sans armes,** he is all the less formidable as (or because) he has no arms.

autel *n.m.* altar; *Astron.* Ara. **dresser un ~,** to set up an altar. **respectez les ~s,** respect religion.

auteur *n.m.* author, inventor, maker, contriver, founder, discoverer. **l'~ de cette guerre,** the originator of that war. **il est l'~ de sa fortune,** he is the maker of his own fortune. **l'~ d'un faux bruit,** the originator of a false report. **l'~ d'un livre,** the author of a book. **l'~ d'un procède,** the inventor of a process.

authenticité *n.f.* authenticity.

authentifier *v.t.* to authenticate.

authentique *adj.* authentic; original. *n.f.* original, original text.

authentiquer *v.t.* to authenticate.

autisme *n.m.* autism.

autiste ou autistique *adj.* autistic.

auto *n.f.* car. *pref.* auto-, self-.

autobiographe *n.m.* autobiographer.

autobiographie *n.f.* autobiography.

autobus *n.m.* bus.

autocar *n.m.* motor coach, tour bus.

autocensure *n.f.* practice of criticizing oneself.

autochtone *n.m.* autochthon. *adj.* autochthonal, aboriginal.

autocrate *n.m.* autocrat.

autocratie *n.f.* autocracy.

autocratique *adj.* autocratic.

autocritique *n.f.* self-criticism.

autodafé *n.m.* auto-da-fé.

autodéfense *n.f.* self-defense.

autodidacte *adj.* self-taught, self-educated.

autodrome *n.m.* a autorace track; speedway.

autogestion *n.f.* worker management, control of business by workers.

auto-école *n.f.* driving/school.

autographier *v.t.* to autograph.

automate *n.m.* automaton.

automatique adj. automatic. **distributeur ~**, coin machine.

automnal, e adj. autumnal, autumn.

automne n.m.f. autumn, the fall. **l'~ de la vie,** the autumn of life.

automobile n.f. automobile.

automateur, trice adj. self-starting, self-motivating.

autonome adj. autonomous.

autonomie n.m. autonomy; self-government, independence.

autoportrait n.m. self-portrait.

autopsie n.f. autopsy.

autorisation n.f. authorization; license.

autoriser v.t. to authorize, to license, to empower, to sanction. **s'~,** v.refl. to acquire authority; to be authorized.

autorité n.f. authority, legal power, sway; consideration, weight, credit. **l'~ des lois, des magistrats,** the authority of the laws, of the judges. **être en ~,** to be in authority. **avoir de l'~,** to have power.

auto-stop n.m. hitchhiking.

auto-stoppeur, euse n.m.f. hitchhiker.

autour adv. around, round about. **tout ~,** all around. **autour de,** prep. around, about. **il y a de très belles promenades ~ de la ville,** there are fine walks around the town.

autre adj. other. **il m'a invité avec deux ~s personnes,** he invited me with two other persons. **entre ~s choses il exigea que...,** among other things he required that ... **l'une et l'~ saison est favorable,** both seasons are favorable. **d'~s temps, d'~s moeurs,** other times, other customs. **de temps à ~,** from time to time. **~ part,** elsewhere. **c'est bien un ~ homme,** he is a completely different man. indef.pron. other. **je prends celui-ci, et je vous laisse l'~,** I will take this, and leave the other to you. **ils s'aiment l'un l'~,** they love each other (or one another). **l'un ou l'~,** either. **ni l'un ni l'~,** neither. **l'un et l'~,** both. **l'un vaut l'~,** one is as good as the other. **l'un dans l'~,** one with another. **d'~s vous diront,** others will tell you. **à d'~s!** I tell it to the marines! **il en sait bien d'~s,** he knows many other tricks.

autrefois adv. formerly, in the old days.

autrement adv. otherwise, else, or else. **je pense ~,** I think otherwise. **il écrit ~ qu'il ne pense,** he thinks one thing and writes another. **tout ~,** very differently. **c'est un homme qui n'est pas ~ riche,** he is not a very rich man.

autruche n.f. ostrich. **plumes d'~,** ostrich feathers. **il a un estomac d'~,** he can eat anything.

autrui n.m. others, other people. **souffrir des maux d'~,** to feel for others' woes. **mal d'~ n'est que songe,** other people's misfortunes are easily borne.

auvent n.m. porch roof.

auvergnat, e adj. and n.m.f. Auvergnat, (native) of Auvergne.

Auvergne n.f. Auvergne.

aux contraction of à les.

auxiliaire adj. auxiliary. **verbes ~s,** auxiliary verbs. n.m. auxiliary; aid.

auxiliairement adv. accessorily, secondarily.

avachi adj. shapeless, flabby, sloppy (person).

avachir v.t. to distort, to get out of form, to impair. **s'~,** v.refl. to get or wear out of shape (as shoes, clothes, etc.); to get or become flabby.

aval n.m. the lower part of a river; guarantee, surety. adv. downstream, down the river, downward. **un des bateaux allait amont, l'autre ~,** one of the boats was going upstream, the other downstream. **en ~ de,** below.

avalage n.m. navigating downstream.

avalanche n.f. avalanche.

avalant, e adj. going downstream. **bateaux montants ou ~s,** boats going up or down stream, up or down the river.

avalé, e p.p. swallowed; adj. hanging down, flabby. **joues ~es,** flabby cheeks.

avaler v.t. to swallow, to endure (an affront); to guarantee. **~ une tasse de bouillon,** to swallow a bowl of broth. **on lui fera ~ cela,** they will make him swallow that. **~ un affront,** to swallow an insult. **s'~,** v.refl. to be swallowed; to go downstream.

avaleur n.m. swallower, glutton.

à-valoir n.m. installment.

avance n.f. projection, advance, start, advances, advance money. **il a deux kilomètres d'~ sur nous,** he is two kilometers ahead of us. **prendre l'~ sur quelqu'un,** to get a head start on a person. **faire une ~ de mille francs,** to make an advance of a thousand francs. **être en ~,** to be early. **faire des ~s,** to make advances to. adv. in advance, beforehand. **payer d'~, par ~, une année de son loyer,** to pay a year's rent in advance.

avancé p.p. and adj. advanced, early. **poste ~,** forward post, outpost (military). **je n'en suis pas plus ~,** I am not a bit better off. **un jeune ~,** a precocious youth. **viande ~e,** tainted meat. **poisson ~,** stale fish.

avancement n.m. advancement, progress, improvement, promotion.

avancer v.t. to move, push, bring, or draw forward; to hold out; to promote, to forward; to hasten; to move forward (as a watch or clock); to pay beforehand. **~ la main,** to hold out one's hand. **~ un ouvrage,** make progress in a project. **la chaleur avance la végétation,** heat hastens vegetation. **votre montre retarde, avancez-la dix minutes,** your watch is too slow, move it up ten minutes. **j'ai avancé trois mois de gages à mon domestique,** I have advanced my servant three months' wages. v.i. to advance, to go forward, to make progress, to proceed, to keep on; to gain (as watches, etc.). **l'ennemi avançait,** the enemy was advancing. **ce travail avance lentement,** this work goes slowly. **le balcon n'avance pas assez,** the balcony does not project enough. **cette horloge avance de dix minutes,** this clock is ten minutes fast. **ma montre avance d'une minute par jour,** my watch gains a minute a day. **s'~,** *v.refl.* to advance, to move forward, to make progress, to progress; to get on, to draw near. **~ sur la scène,** to come forward on the stage. **je reconnais que je me suis trop avancé,** I acknowledge that I have gone too far. **l'hiver s'avance,** the winter is far advanced.

avanie *n.f.* insult; outrage. **une sanglante ~,** an atrocious outrage.

avant *prep.* before, forward. **il marchait ~ moi,** he walked before me. **il faudrait mettre ce chapitre ~ l'autre,** this chapter must be placed before the other. **~ la fin de l'année,** before the end of the year. **bien ~ l'heure,** long before the hour. **~ tout il faut prendre nos précautions,** above all, we must take our precautions. **avant de, avant que de,** before. **~ de** or **~ que de partir, ~,** before starting. **avant que,** *conj.* before. **venez me voir ~ que je parte,** come and see me before I leave. **avant,** *adv.* far; before. **n'allez pas si ~,** do not go so far. **bien ~ en mer,** far out at sea. **bien ~ dans l'hiver,** far into the winter, in the depth of winter. **quelques jours ~,** some days before. **elle est plus libre qu'~,** she is freer than before. **en ~,** on, ahead. **aller en ~,** to go ahead. **se pencher en ~,** to lean forward. *n.m.* front, forepart (of a vehicle, etc.); *Naut.* forepart, head. **gagner l'~ de,** to get ahead of.

avantage *n.m.* advantage, superiority; upper hand; success. **les ~s de la paix,** the advantages of peace. **tirer ~ de,** to turn to account, to get some good out of. **tirer ~ de tout,** to make the best of everything. **avoir l'~ sur quelqu'un,** to have the advantage (the upperhand) of a person. **poursuivre ses ~s,** to follow up one's advantage, one's successes.

avantager *v.t.* to give an advantage; to favor. **s'~,** *v.refl.* to give each other mutual advantages; to turn to one's own advantage.

avantageusement *adv.* advantageously. **se marier ~,** to marry well. **s'habiller ~,** to dress to the best advantage.

avantageux, euse *adj.* advantageous, profitable, beneficial. **proposition ~,** an advantageous proposal. **l'issue ~ de votre affaire,** the favorable outcome of your affair. **prendre un ton, un air ~,** to assume a pretentious tone.

avant-bec *n.m.* upstream cutwater.

avant-bouche *n.f.* front of the mouth.

avant-bras *n.m.* forearm.

avant-corps *n.m.* forepart (of a building).

avant-cour *n.m.* front yard.

avant-coureur *n.m.* forerunner, precursor. *adj.* precursory.

avant-courrier, ière *n.m.f.* forerunner, harbinger.

avant-dernier, ière *n.m.f.* the next to last. *adj.* next to last. **il est l'~,** he is the next to last.

avant-garde *n.f.* vanguard; avant-garde.

avant-goût *n.m.* foretaste, anticipation. **un ~ de la béatitude du ciel,** a foretaste of heavenly bliss.

avant-hier *adv.* and *n.m.* the day before yesterday.

avant-jeu *n.m.* prelude, preliminary.

avant-main *n.m.* forehand stroke; forehanded blow; forequarters (of a horse).

avant-mur *n.m.* outer or outmost wall.

avant-pied *n.m.* metatarsus; the front of the foot; outer vamp.

avant-poignet *n.m.* forewrist.

avant-port *n.m.* outer harbor.

avant-poste *n.m.* outpost.

avant-première *n.f.* dress rehearsal.

avant-projet *n.m.* rough draft; proposed legislation.

avant-propos *n.m.* preface; preamble.

avant-quart *n.m.* warning strokes (clock).

avant-scène *n.f.* stage box; proscenium.

avant-toit *n.m.* projecting roof.

avant-veille *n.f.* the day before the eve (of a holiday). **l'~ de Noël,** the day before Christmas Eve.

avare *adj.* avaricious, miserly, stingy. **être ~ de son temps,** to be ungenerous with one's time. *n.m.f.* miser. **un ~ parfait,** a thorough miser.

avarement *adv.* avariciously.

avarice *n.f.* avarice; stinginess.

avaricieux, euse *adj.* avaricious; stingy.

avarie *n.f.* damage (to any goods during conveyance). **sans ~,** undamaged. **~s simples,** ordinary damage, wear and tear. **régler les ~s,** to state the damages.

avarier *v.t.* to damage. **la pluie a avarié les foins,** the rain has damaged the hay. **s'~,** *v.refl.* to spoil, to become spoiled.

avatar *n.m.* misadventure.

à vau-de-route *adv.phr.* helter-skelter.

à vau-l'eau *adv.phr.* downstream. **le corps du noyé s'en allait ~,** the body of the drowned man was carried away by the current.

avec *prep.* with; in respect to. **s'entretenir ~ quelqu'un,** to converse with a person. **le soldat marche ~ son sac et ses armes,** the soldier marches with his knapsack and arms. **~ cela,** in spite of that. **il a pris mon manteau et s'en est allé ~,** he has taken my coat and gone off with it. **d'~,** from. **séparer l'or d'~ l'argent,** to separate gold from silver.

aveinière *n.f.* oat field, field of oats.

aveline *n.f.* filbert.

avelinier *n.m.* filbert tree.

avénacé, e *adj.* avenaceous.

avenamment *adv.* engagingly.

avenant, e *adj.* comely, good-looking; prepossessing, pleasing. **une femme très ~e,** a very engaging woman. **à l'~,** in keeping, in conformity. à l'~ de, in keeping with. être à l'~ de, to match. le dessert fut à l'~ du repas, the dessert was in keeping with the meal.

avènement *n.m.* accession, arrival, approach; advent. l'~ de la Réforme au seizième siècle, the advent of the Reformation in the sixteenth century. Charles XII à son ~, Charles XII, on his accession.

avenir *v.i.* to happen, to occur, to befall. à l'~, in the future, henceforth. il en adviendra ce qu'il pourra, come what may of it. *n.m.* future, fate, destiny, or prosperity. dans un ~ prochain, in the near future, at no distant day. lire dans l'~, to read the future. assurer l'~ de ses enfants, to secure the future of one's children. un jeune homme d'~, a promising young man. que dira l'~? what will posterity say?

à-venir *n.m.* writ of summons addressed to a defendant in a civil suit.

Avent *n.m.* Advent.

aventure *n.f.* adventure. raconter ses ~s, to tell one's adventures. ~ amusante, amusing adventure. dire la bonne ~, to tell fortunes. diseur, diseuse de bonne ~, fortune teller. d'~, par ~, by chance.

aventurer *v.t.* to venture, to risk. s'~, *v.refl.* to venture oneself, to risk, to hazard.

aventureux, euse *adj.* adventurous, venturous; venturesome.

aventurier, ère *n.m.f.* adventurer, adventuress; rover, freebooter.

aventurisme *n.m.* foolhardiness, venturesomeness.

avenu, e *p.p.* happened, occurred. nul et non ~, null and void.

avenue *n.m.* avenue, walk.

avérer *v.t.* to prove, to aver.

avéron *n.m.* wild oats.

averse *n.f.* shower of rain.

aversion *n.f.* aversion, dislike, antipathy. avoir de l'~ pour, to have an aversion for. prendre quelqu'un en ~, to take a dislike to a person. c'est ma bête d'~, I can't stand him.

averti, e *p.p.* informed, warned, cautioned.

avertir *v.t.* to warn, to caution, to give notice of. ~ une personne de quelque chose, to inform a person of a thing.

avertissement *n.m.* foreword (of books); warning, caution. c'est un ~ au lecteur, it is a hint to the reader.

avertisseur *n.m.* callboy (of a theater); alarm bell.

aveu *n.m.* avowal, confession, approbation. l'~ d'une dette, the acknowledgment of a debt. homme sans ~, a vagabond, a vagrant.

aveuglant *adj.* dazzling, overpowering.

aveugle *adj.* blind, ignorant, unenlightened. devenir ~, to become blind. soumission ~, blind submission. passion ~, blind passion. *n.m.f.* blind man, blind woman. un pauvre ~, a poor blind man. une vieille ~, a blind old

woman. au royaume des ~s les borgnes sont rois, in the kingdom of the blind, one-eyed men are kings. crier comme un ~, to make a great outcry.

aveuglement *n.m.* blindness.

aveuglément *adv.* blindly.

aveugler *v.t.* to blind, to dazzle; to obscure; *Naut.* to stop a leak. l'éclat du soleil m'aveugle, the brightness of the sun blinds me. la prospérité aveugle l'homme, man is blinded by prosperity. deux voies d'eau qu'on s'efforça vainement d'~, two leaks which we vainly attempted to stop. s'~, *v.refl.* to blind oneself; to be blinded.

aveuglette *n.f.* used only in the adverbial phrase: à l'~, groping about (as in the dark).

aveulir *v.t.* to weaken, to enervate. s'aveulir, *v. refl.* to sink into sloth.

aveulissant *adj.* enfeebling, enervating.

aveulissement *n.m.* limpness, enervation.

aviateur *n.m.* aviator.

aviation *n.f.* aviation.

avide *adj.* greedy, eager; avid; covetous, grasping. être ~ de gloire, to seek glory.

avidement *adv.* greedily, eagerly, covetously.

avidité *n.f.* avidity greediness, eagerness; covetousness.

avilir *v.t.* to debase, to degrade, to dishonor, to disgrace, to disparage, to corner. s'~, *v.refl.* to debase, to degrade, to disgrace oneself.

avilissant, e *adj.* debasing, degrading. conduite ~e, degrading conduct.

avilissement *n.m.* debasement, degradation; depreciation (of goods, etc.); disparagement, discredit.

aviné, e *p.p.* seasoned with wine (as casks).

aviner *v.t.* to season with wine. ~ une cuve, to season a vat.

avion *n.m.* airplane, aircraft. avion-cargo, freight plane.

aviron *n.m.* oar.

avis *n.m.* opinion, mind; advice, counsel, notice, warning, information, news. donner son ~, to give one's opinion. il lui est ~ que, he is of the opinion that. à mon ~, to my mind, in my opinion. autant de têtes, autant d'~, as many opinions as there are people. prendre les ~, to take the votes. donner des ~, to give advice (*or* counsel). ~ important, important notice. ~ au public, notice to the public. ~ au lecteur, notice to the reader. on a reçu ~ de Rome, *news has been received from Rome.* lettre d'~, letter of advice.

avisé, e *adj.* prudent, circumspect, cautious. c'est un homme sage et ~, he is a wise and prudent (or cautious) man. il est fort ~, he is very circumspect.

aviser *v.t.* to advise, to perceive. *v.i.* to think of, to consider, to reflect on, to see to. ~ à un moyen, to think of a means. avisez-y, see to it. s'~, *v.refl.* to consider, to take it into one's head. ~ d'un bon expédient, to think of a good solution. **on ne s'avise jamais de tout,** we cannot think of everything.

aviso *n.m.* dispatch boat, gunboat.

avitaillement *n.m.* store of provisions.

avitailler *v.t.* to supply a ship or fortress with provisions.

avivage *n.m.* polishing (of metals); brightening, reviving (colors).

aviver *v.t.* to brighten; to color, to polish. **s'~,** *v.refl.* to become brighter, to brighten. **une couleur qui s'avive,** a color that becomes brighter.

avocaillon *n.m.* unethical lawyer.

avocasser *v.i.* to be an unethical lawyer.

avocasserie *n.f.* unethical practice of law; ineffectual quibbling.

avocassier, ère *adj.* quibbling.

avocat, e *n.m.* lawyer, advocate. **~ général,** attorney general.

avoine *n.f.* oats. **les ~s sont belles cette année,** the oat crop is good this year.

avoir *v.t.* to have, to get, to possess. **~ du bien,** to have property. **~ de la fortune,** to have a fortune. **n'~ rien,** to have nothing. **~ de quoi vivre,** to have enough to live on. **ils ont pour eux la justice,** they have justice on their side. **~ mal à la tête,** mal aux yeux, mal au doigt, to have a headache, bad eyes, a bad (or sore) finger. **il avait ce jour-là un habit bleu,** he wore a blue coat that day. **~ une bague au doigt,** to wear a ring on one's finger. **vous n'avez qu'à dire un mot,** et la chose sera faite, you have but to say the word and the thing will be done. **avoir** is often rendered by **to be** and the noun by an adjective: **~ faim, soif, chaud, froid,** to be hungry, thirsty, hot, cold. **~ quinze ans,** to be fifteen years old. **cette planche a six pieds de long et dix pouces de large,** this plank is six feet long and ten inches wide. **to be the matter with. qu'avez-vous que vous ne mangez plus? je n'ai rien,** what is the matter with you, that you do not eat? Nothing ails me, or there is nothing the matter with me. **en ~,** to catch it, to be in trouble. **il en a,** he has caught it. **vous en aurez,** you're going to get it. **~ beau,** to be in vain. **il a beau se remuer, il ne réussira pas,** it is useless for him to exert himself, he will not succeed. **ils ont beau se cacher,** it is useless for them to hide themselves.

y avoir. il y a, etc. *v.t. impers.* **il y a,** there is, there are. **il y avait, il y eut,** there was, there were. **il y a un an,** a year ago. **il y a longtemps que je suis ici,** I have been here a long time. **il y en a qui disent,** there are those who say. **combien y a-t-il de Paris à Orléans?**

How far is it from Paris to Orléans?

avoir *n.m.* fortune, property, possessions. **tout son ~ était chez ce banquier,** his whole fortune was in the hands of that banker. credit side. **doit et ~,** debit and credit.

avoisinant, e *adj.* neighboring, adjoining, adjacent.

avoisiné, e *p.p.* **être bien ~,** to have good neighbors.

avoisiner *v.t.* to border on; to be contiguous.

avorté, e *adj.* abortive.

avortement *n.m.* abortion; miscarriage.

avorter *v.i.* to miscarry. **faire ~,** to cause abortion; *Fig.* to fail, to come to nothing. **l'entreprise avorta faute de fonds,** the undertaking failed, for want of money.

avorton *n.m.* abortion.

avouable *adj.* avowable.

avoué *n.m.* attorney. **étude d'~,** an attorney's office.

avouer *v.t.* to avow; to confess, to acknowledge; to admit. **~ une dette,** to acknowledge a debt. **s'~,** *v.refl.* to confess or acknowledge oneself; to be avowed, confessed, or acknowledged. **~ coupable,** to confess one's guilt. **cela ne peut ~,** that cannot be acknowledged.

avril *n.m.* April. **poisson d'~,** April fool. **recevoir un poison d'~,** to be made an April fool.

avulsion *n.f.* avulsion.

axe *n.m.* axis; axle. **~ coudé,** cranked axle.

axer *v.t.* to center, to guide. **axer sa vie sur,** to concentrate upon, to be guided by.

axillaire *adj.* axillary. **fleurs ~,** axillary flowers.

axiome *n.m.* axiom.

axonge *n.f. Pharm.* hog's lard.

ayant cause *n.m.* trustee, executor, assign.

ayant droit *n.m.* interested party, claimant.

azalea, azalée *n.f.* azalea.

azimut *n.m.* azimuth.

azimutal, e *adj.* azimuthal; azimuth.

azotate *n.m.* nitrate.

azote *n.m.* nitrogen.

azoté, e *adj.* nitrogenized.

azotique *adj.* nitric.

azotite *n.m.* nitrite.

azur *n.m.* azure, sky blue. **le soleil se couchait dans une nuée d'or et d'~,** the sun was setting in a cloud of gold and azure.

azuré, e *adj.* azure, azured. **la voûte ~e,** the blue sky.

azurer *v.t.* to azure; to tint with blue.

azurin, e *adj.* pale azure, pale blue.

azyme *adj.* unleavened, azyme. **pain ~,** unleavened bread. **la fête des ~s,** the Feast of Unleavened Bread.

B

b *n.m.* b: the second letter of the alphabet. **un B majuscule,** a capital B. **un B minuscule,** a small B. **ne savoir ni A ni B,** to be an ignoramus.

baba *n.m.* bun, soft cake. *adj.* surprised, astonished.

babeurre *n.m.* buttermilk.

babiche *n.f.* Babichon *n.m.* a lapdog.

babil *n.m.* prattle, chatter; prating.

babillage *n.m.* babbling, prattling, chatter.

babillard, e *adj.* babbling, chattering; talkative. **enfant ~,** a prattling child. *n.m.f.* babbler, prater, chatterer. **c'est un franc ~,** he is a great babbler.

babillement *n.m.* babbling; loquacity, talkativeness.

babiller *v.i.* to chatter; to babble, to prate; to babble.

babine, babouine *n.f.* lip (of certain animals); *pl.* chops. **il s'en lèche les babines,** he licks his lips (or chops) over it.

babiole *n.f.* plaything, toy; knickknack.

babord *n.m.* port side. *adv.* to port.

bâbordais *n.m.* port watch.

babouche *n.f.* babouche; Turkish slipper.

babouin *n.m.* baboon.

bac *n.m.* ferryboat, tank, vat. *Infml.* the baccalauréat.

baccalauréat *n.m.* baccalaureate; bachelor's degree, high-school diploma.

baccara *n.m.* baccara: a game at cards.

bacchanale *n.f.* bacchanal; noisy revel; bacchanalia.

bacchantes *n.f.pl.Infml.* moustache, whiskers.

bâche *n.f. Gard.* hotbed frame; cistern; awning (of wagon); tarpaulin.

bachelier, ère *n.m.f.* student who has passed his/her baccalauréat. *n.m.* squire. **~ ès lettres,** bachelor of letters.

bâcher *v.t.* to cover with a tarpaulin.

bachique *adj.* bacchic, bacchical; jovial, drunken.

bâchot *n.m.* wherry. *Infml.* the baccalauréat.

bachoter *v.t.Infml.* to cram for a test, usually the baccalauréat.

bachoteur *n.m.* ferryman, boatman.

bacille *n.m.* bacillus.

bâclage *n.m.* barring of a door or window; patching up.

bâcle *n.f.* wooden or metal bar for a door or window.

bâclé, e *p.p.* patched up. **c'est une affaire ~e,** it is a hastily done job.

bâcler *v.t.* to bar; to patch up.

badaud, e *n.m.f.* onlooker, gaper, rubbernecker.

badauderie *n.f.* gaping, rubbernecking.

baderne *n.f.,Infml.* old man (usually a soldier) who is narrow-minded or stubborn.

badigeon *n.m.* whitewash, limewash.

badigeonnage *n.m.* whitewashing, limewashing (of walls).

badigeonner *v.t.* to limewash, to whitewash.

badigeonneur *n.m.* whitewasher, limewasher; *Pej.* painter who lacks skill or talent.

badin, e *adj.* merry, playful, jocose, jesting. **elle est fort ~,** she is very playful. **esprit ~,** a playful wit.

badinage *n.m.* playfulness, sportiveness; jesting, joking, foolery. **un innocent ~,** an innocent jest. **ceci n'est point un ~,** this is no joke.

badine *n.f.* switch, light cane.

badiner *v.i.* to play, to trifle, to toy, to jest. **c'est assez ~,** enough of joking. **c'est un homme qui ne badine pas,** he is a man that never jokes.

badinerie *n.f.* joke, jest.

bafouer *v.t.* to scoff at, to ridicule, to scorn. **on l'a bafoué,** they scoffed at him.

bafouiller *v.i.* to mutter, to speak indistinctly.

bâfrer *v.i.* to eat like a glutton, to stuff oneself, to pig out.

bâfreur *n.m.* glutton, gourmand.

bagage *n.m.* baggage; luggage. **plier ~,** to pack off.

bagarre *n.f.* fight, row; brawl, squabble.

bagasse *n.f.* cane trash; slut, a loose woman.

bagatelle *n.f.* trifle, knickknack, bauble, trinket. **il se fâcha pour une ~,** he took offense about nothing. **~! nonsense!**

bagne *n.m.* prison.

bagou, bagout *n.m.* gab, gift of the gab. **il a du ~,** he has the gift of the gab.

bague *n.f.* ring. **-s et joyaux,** rings and jewels.

baguenaude *n.f.* bladder nut. *Infml.* jaunt, wandering along, loitering about.

baguenauder *v.i.* to trifle away one's time, to fiddle-faddle; to wander along, to loiter about.

baguenaudier *n.m.* bladder nut tree.

baguer *v.t.* to put a ring on. **~ un oiseau,** to put a band on a bird's leg.

baguette *n.f.* switch; rod, wand; ramrod. **~ de tambour,** drumstick. **~ magique,** magic wand.

baguier *n.m.* ring case, ring stand.

bah *interj.* bah! nonsense!

bahut *n.m.* trunk, chest.

bai, e *adj.* bay. **un cheval ~,** a bay horse.

baie *n.f.* bay; berry; a gulf. *Arch.* bay.

baignade *n.f.* bathe, dip; watering place for horses.

baigné, e *p.p.* bathed, washed. **ses beaux yeux étaient baignés de larmes,** her beautiful eyes were suffused with tears.

baigner *v.t.* to bathe; to wet, to bedew; to wash. **~ un enfant,** to bathe a child. **se ~ les yeux, les pieds,** etc., to bathe one's eyes, one's feet, etc. **se ~,** *v.refl.* to bathe, to bathe oneself, to take a bath. se ~ dans la rivière, to bathe in the river.

baigneur, euse *n.m.f.* bathing attendant; bather.

baignoire *n.f.* bath; bathtub; *Theat.* box on a level with the pit.

bail *n.m.* baux *pl.* lease. ~ à vie, lease for life. ~ à terme, lease for years. rompre ou résilier un ~, to cancel a lease.

baille *n.f. Naut.* bucket, small tub.

bâillement *n.m.* yawning, a yawn, a gap, fissure. un long ~, a long yawn.

bailler *v.t.* to give. ~ des coups, to give (or deal) blows. vous me la baillez belle, you are pulling my leg.

bâiller *v.i.* to yawn; to gape, to be open, to be ajar.

bailleur, bailleresse *n.m.f.* lessor. le ~ et le preneur, the lessor and the lessee. ~ de fonds, capitalist, moneylender.

bailli *n.m.* bailiff.

bailliage *n.m.* bailiwick.

bâillon *n.m.* gag; anything put into the mouth to prevent speech; muzzle (to keep a horse, etc., from biting). mettre un ~ à, to gag; to silence.

bâillonné, ee *p.p.* gagged. il fut ~ par les voleurs, he was gagged by the thieves. la presse ~e par des lois rigoureuses, the press gagged (silenced) by severe laws.

bâillonner *v.t.* to gag. ~ la presse, to gag (or silence) the press.

bain *n.m.* bath; bathing. ~ de pieds, foot bath. ~ de vapeur, steam bath. salle de ~, bathroom.

bain-marie *n.m.* double boiler.

baïonnette *n.f.* bayonet.

baisemain *n.m.* kissing of hands.

baisement *n.m.* kissing of something that is holy. le ~ de la croix, the kissing of the cross.

baiser *v.t.* to kiss. ~ la main d'une femme, to kiss a lady's hand. *n.m.* kissing, kiss. ~ d'amitié, friendly kiss.

baisoter *v.t.* to give very many little kisses.

baisse *n.f.* fall, decline (in price), abatement. être en ~, to be falling.

baissé, e *p.p.* lowered, etc., downcast; broken, declining. l'œil morne et la tête ~e, with eye and drooping head.

baisser *v.t.* to lower, to let down, to drop, to humble. ~ un tableau, une glace, to lower a painting, a mirror. ~ un store, to lower a blind; *Theat.* ~ le rideau, to lower the curtain. ~ la voix, to lower one's voice. les boulangers ont baissé le prix du pain, the bakers have lowered the price of bread. la modestie fait ~ les yeux, modesty makes one look down. *v.i.* to fall; to subside, to go down, to get low. la rivière a baissé de trois pieds, the river has fallen three feet. la Bourse baisse, stocks are falling. sa vue baisse, his sight is failing. le jour baisse, the day is on the wane. se ~, *v.refl.* to stoop; to bow down. baissez-vous davantage, stoop lower.

baissier *n.m. Stock-Ex.* bear; person expecting a drop in the stock market.

bal *n.m.* ball, ~ public, public dance. ~ costumé ou travesti, costume ball. ~ paré, fancy dress ball. ~ de charité, charity ball.

balade *n.f.* ramble. faire une ~, to take a stroll.

baladeuse *n.f.* pushcart; trailer.

baladin, e mountebank, juggler, buffoon.

baladinage *n.m.* coarse joking.

balafre *n.f.* gash, scar.

balafrer *v.t.* to gash; to wound (on the face).

balai *n.m.* broom, ~ de plume, feather duster. il fait ~ neuf, a new broom sweeps clean.

balance *n.f.* balance, pair of scales, weighing machine; *Fig.* balance. la ~ commerciale, trade balance. la ~ des paiements, the balance of payments. la ~ des forces, the balance of power.

balancelle *n.f.* felucca.

balancement *n.m.* balancing or swaying, swinging, rocking.

balancer *v.t.* to balance; to poise; to swing, to weigh, to counterbalance. ~ un javelot, une épée, to poise a javelin, to brandish a sword. ~ un compte, to balance an account. ~ ses bras, to swing one's arms. *v.i.* to oscillate, to hesitate, to waver. voilà ce qui me fait ~, that is what makes me hesitate. il n'y avait plus à ~, there was no longer room for hesitation. ~ une pierre par la fenêtre, to throw a stone out the window; to get rid of something or someone. ~ un employé, to fire an employee. se ~, *v.refl.* to swing or sway. cette femme se balance trop en marchant, that woman swings too much in walking. nos comptes se balancent, our accounts are square.

balancier *n.m.* pendulum (of a clock); balance wheel (of a watch); balancing pole.

balançoire *n.f.* swing; seesaw.

balayage *n.m.* sweeping.

balayer *v.t.* to sweep. ~ la poussière, to sweep up the dust. sa robe balaye la terre, her dress sweeps along the ground; *Fig.* to sweep away, to push aside. ~ les obstacles, to sweep away obstacles. ~ les soucis, to push aside worries.

balayette *n.f.* small broom.

balayeur, euse sweeper; *n.f.* mechanical street sweeper.

balayures sweepings; refuse. les ~ des rues, the sweepings of the streets.

balbutiement *n.m.* stammering, stuttering, lisping.

balbutier *v.t.* and *v.i.* to stammer, to stutter; to lisp. ~ un compliment, to stammer out a compliment.

balcon balcony.

baldaquin *n.m.* church canopy.

baleine *n.f.* whale. pêche à la ~, whaling. fanon de ~, whale bone; plastic or metal ribs or stays. ~s d'un parapluie, ribs of an umbrella.

baleiné *adj.* whale-boned.

baleinier, ère *adj.* whaling. *n.m.* whaling ship, whaler.

balisage *n.m.* buoying.

balise *n.f.* sea mark, buoy; ~ **de sauvetage,** signaling buoy.

baliser *v.t.* to put up beacons or buoys; to mark out (an airstrip) with ground lights.

balistique *n.f.* ballistics.

baliverne *n.f.* trifle, nonsense. **il me conte des ~s,** he tells me nonsense.

ballade *n.f.* ballad.

ballant, e *adj.* swinging. **aller les bras ~s,** to swing one's arms in walking.

ballast *n.m.* ballast.

balle *n.f.* ball, bullet; bale, pack. **lancer la ~,** to throw the ball. **renvoyer la ~,** to return the ball, to give tit for tat. **prendre la ~ au bond,** to catch the ball on the bounce. **à vous la ~,** it is your turn to play. ~ **de coton,** bale of cotton. ~ **d'avoine,** husks of oats.

baller *v.i.* to dance, to jig.

ballerine *n.f.* ballerina; ballet shoe.

ballet *n.m.* ballet.

ballon *n.m.* balloon; football.

ballonné, e *p.p.* swelled out, distended.

ballonnement *n.m.* distension, swelling.

ballonner *v.t.* to swell, to distend.

ballot *n.m.* bale; pack, package. *Pej.* nitwit, clod, imbecile.

ballotin *n.m.* small bale, parcel.

ballottage *n.m.* balloting, ballot.

ballottement *n.m.* tossing (or shaking) about.

ballotter *v.t.* to toss, to knock about. *v.i.* to shake about; to shuffle about.

balluchon, baluchun *n.m.* bundle (of clothes).

balnéaire *adj.* relating to bathing. V. STATION

balourd, e *n.m.f.* dolt, dunce.

balourdise *n.f.* stupid blunder; stupidity.

balsamine *n.f.* Bot. balsam.

balsamique *adj.* balsamic, balsamical.

balustrade *n.f.* balustrade.

balustre *n.m.* baluster; spoke in the back of a chair.

bambin, e *n.m.f.* little boy, little girl; brat.

bambochade *n.f.* low-life, sketch from low life.

bamboche *n.f.* large marionette or puppet; spree, lark.

bambocher *v.i.* to go (or be) on a spree.

bambocheur, euse *n.m.f.* dissolute person; rake.

bambou *n.m.* bamboo.

ban *n.m.* ban, proclamation. ~ **de mariage,** banns of marriage. **dispense de ~s,** marriage license. **publier les ~s,** to publish the banns; drum roll preceding the proclamation of an order; round of rhythmical applause.

banal, e *adj.* belonging to a manor; common, hackneyed, commonplace. **expression ~,** a hackneyed (or commonplace) expression.

banalité *n.f.* banality; commonplace.

banane *n.f.* banana.

bananier *n.m.* banana tree.

banc *n.m.* bench, pew. ~ **de bois,** wooden bench, seat, bench. **les ~s des avocats,** the lawyers' benches. **être encore sur les ~s,** to be still at school. **ce navire a échoué sur un ~ de sable,** that ship has stranded on a sand bank. **un ~ de corail,** a coral reef. ~ **de harengs,** a shoal of herrings.

bancaire *adj.* banking.

bancal, e *adj.* bandy-legged, bowlegged; wobbly (furniture).

banche *n.f.* a bank of marl visible at low water.

bancroche *adj.* bandy-legged, bowlegged.

bandage *n.m.* bandage; truss; tire (of wheels); hoop.

bande *n.f.* band, strip, reel of film; band, gang, crew, set; troop. ~ **de papier,** strip of paper. ~ **de journal,** newspaper wrapper. ~ **dessinée,** comics. **une ~ de terre,** a strip of ground. **une ~ joyeuse,** a merry crew. ~ **de voleurs,** gang of thieves. **faire ~ à part,** to form a separate.

bandeau *n.m.* band, group, bandage. **mettre un ~ sur les yeux de quelqu'un,** to blindfold a person.

bandelette *n.f.* narrow band. ~ **de momie,** wrappings of a mummy.

bander *v.t.* to bind up, to bandage; to bend (a bow); to tighten (a cord). ~ **une blessure,** to bind up a wound. ~ **les yeux à quelqu'un,** to blindfold (or hoodwink) someone; to stretch tightly, to strain. ~ **ses muscles,** to tighten one's muscles. **se ~,** *v.refl.* to bind up; to resist. **se ~ les yeux,** to blindfold oneself.

banderole *n.f.* pennant; streamer; shoulder belt.

bandit *n.m.* bandit; ruffian, robber.

bandoulière *n.f.* shoulder belt. **porter en ~,** to carry in a sling.

banlieue *n.f.* suburb(s), outskirts; environs.

banlieusard, e *n.m.f.* *n.f.* suburbanite.

banne *n.f.* hamper; tarpaulin, awning.

banni, e *p.p.* banished.

bannière *n.f.* banner, standard, flag, colors, streamer.

bannir *v.t.* to banish; to exile.

bannissement *n.m.* banishment.

banque *n.f.* bank, banking business. **avoir un compte en ~,** to have an account open at a bank. ~ **d'escompte,** discount bank. **billet de ~,** banknote.

banqueroute *n.f.* bankruptcy. **faire ~,** to go bankrupt. ~ **frauduleuse,** fraudulent bankruptcy.

banqueroutier, ère bankrupt *n.m.f.* person.

banquet banquet, feast. **salle de ~,** banquet hall.

banqueter *v.i.* to banquet; to feast.

banqueteur *n.m.* banqueter.

banquette *n.f.* bench; seat in a car, bus,

train, etc. on the top of a coach, etc.; footpath; windowsill.

banquier *n.m.* banker.

banquise *n.f.* ice floe, ice field, ice pack.

baobab *n.m.* baobab.

baptême *n.m.* baptism; christening; ducking. **nom de ~,** Christian name. **extrait de ~,** certificate of baptism.

baptisé, e *p.p.* baptized, christened; nicknamed.

baptiser *v.t.* to baptize; to christen; to nickname.

baptismal, e *adj.* baptismal. **fonts baptismaux,** the baptismal font.

baptistaire *adj.* of baptism.

baptiste Baptist. **Saint Jean ~,** St. John the Baptist.

baptistère *n.m.* baptistery.

baquet *n.m.* tub; tray (for mixing plaster).

bar *n.m.* bar, pub. *Ichth.* bass. **~ rayé,** striped bass.

baragouin *n.m.* gibberish; jabber.

baragouinage *n.m.* gibberish, jabbering.

baragouiner *v.i.* to talk gibberish. *v.t.* to jabber. **il baragouine le français,** he murders the French language.

baragouineur, euse *n.m.f.* jabberer.

baraque *n.f.* hut; field barracks. *pl.* booth; hovel; cupboard, locker. **sa maison n'est qu'une ~,** his house is but a wretched hole.

baraquement *n.m.* camp of huts.

baraquer *v.t.* to house in a hut.

barattage *n.m.* churning (milk or cream).

baratte *n.f.* churn.

baratter *v.t.* to churn.

barbare *adj.* barbarian; barbarous, savage; cruel, brutal. *n.m.* barbarian.

barbarie *n.f.* barbarism; barbarity; inhumanity, lack of taste, boorishness. **les siècles de ~,** the ages of barbarism, the barbarous ages. **faire un acte de ~,** to commit a barbarous act.

barbarisme *n.m. Gram.* barbarism.

barbe *n.f.* beard; (of goats, monkeys, etc) whiskers; vane, web (of a feather); awn (of barley, wheat, etc.); barb (on certain plants); wattle (of fowls). **porter la ~,** to wear a beard. **rire dans sa ~,** to laugh in one's sleeve.

barbeau *n.m. Ichth.* barbel; *Bot.* blue-bottle.

barbelé, e *adj.* barbed. *n.m.* barbed wire. *n.m.pl.* barbed wire fencing.

barbet *n.m.* water spaniel.

barbiche *n.f.* a small beard (on the chin).

barbier *n.m.* barber; shaver.

barbifier *v.t.* to shave. **se faire ~,** to get shaved. **se ~,** *v.refl.* to be bored.

barbillon *n.m.* barb; fishhook.

barbon *n.m.* graybeard, dotard.

barbotage *n.m.* paddling.

barboté, e *p.p.* spluttered.

barbotement *n.m.* paddling; spluttering.

barboter *v.i.* to dabble. **les canards aiment à ~,** ducks like to dabble in mud. **on barbote**

dans les rues, one has to wade in the streets. *v.t. Infml.* to filch.

barboteur, euse *n.m.f.* paddler; flounderer; thief, pilferer.

barboteuse *n.f.* rompers (of a child).

barbotière *n.f.* duck pond.

barbouillage *n.m.* daubing; daub; scrawl.

barbouillé, e *p.p.* daubed, smeared; grimy.

barbouiller *v.t.* to smear; to daub; to scribble; to blot (esp. with ink). **se ~ le visage de confiture,** to smear jam on one's face. **~ un slogan sur un mur,** to daub a slogan on a wall. **~ des toiles en amateur,** to mess around with paint and canvas. **à nauseate, to upset. ~ l'estomac,** to upset one's stomach.

barbouilleur *n.m.* dauber; scribbler.

barbu, e *adj.* bearded. **homme ~,** bearded man.

barbue *n.f.* brill.

barcarolle *n.f.* barcarolle (boat song).

barde *n.f.* bard; armor for a horse; slice of bacon. *n.m.* bard; a poet.

bardé, e *p.p.* barded; larded, covered with a thin broad slice of bacon. **~ de cordons,** covered with knightly orders; caparisoned.

bardeau *n.m.* shingle.

barder *v.t.* to bard; to put armor on a horse; to lard.

barème *n.m.* scale, schedule; price list. **~ des impôts,** tax schedule.

barge *n.f.* barge.

barguigner *v.i.* to hesitate; to hem and haw.

baril *n.m.* barrel, cask.

barillet *n.m.* middle ear.

bariolage *n.m.* mixture (of various colors); variegation.

bariolé, e *p.p.* motley; many-colored; variegated, checkered. **habit ~,** a motley coat.

barioler *v.t.* to paint with many colors; to variegate.

barmaid *n.f.* barmaid.

barman *n.m.* bartender.

baromètre *n.m.* barometer. **le ~ est à la pluie, au beau fixe,** the barometer is at rain, at fair.

barométrique *adj.* barometric.

baron *n.m.* baron.

baronnage *n.m.* baronage.

baronne *n.f.* baroness.

baronnet *n.m.* baronet.

baronnie *n.f.* barony.

baroque *adj.* irregular; rough; *Fig.* odd, uncouth; whimsical, fantastic. **perle ~,** an ill-shaped pearl. **un costume ~,** an uncouth costume. **expression ~,** strange expression.

baroscope *n.m.* baroscope.

baroud *n.m. Infml.* fight, scrap, combat. **~ d'honneur,** last-ditch stand.

baroudeur *n.m. Infml.* scrapper, fighter.

barque *n.f.* boat; barge; bark. **~ de pêcheur,** fishingboat. **conduire la ~,** to steer the boat; to manage an enterprise.

barquée *n.f.* boatload.

barrage *n.m.* barrier; barricade; dam. **~ de police,** police roadblock.

barre *n.f.* bar; barrier, hindrance; helm, tiller; *Hydrog.* bore. **~ d'appui,** a handrail. **se présenter à la ~ d'un tribunal,** to appear at the bar of a tribunal.

barreau *n.m.* bar; rail. **les ~x d'une prison,** prison bars. **fenêtre garnie de ~x,** a window secured by bars, by a grating. **fréquenter le ~,** to practice at the bar.

barrette *n.f.* cardinal's cap; biretta; small bar; pin, brooch.

barricade *n.f.* barricade.

barricader *v.t.* to barricade. **~ une rue,** to barricade a street **se ~,** *v.refl.* to barricade oneself; to go into seclusion.

barrière *n.f.* barrier, bar, toll gate; hindrance, obstacle.

barrique *n.f.* barrel, cask. **descendre une ~ à la cave,** to let down a barrel into the winecellar.

baryton *n.m.* baritone.

baryum *n.m.* barium.

bas, basse *adj.* low, lower; flat, mean, abject, base, vile, contemptible, common. **siège ~,** low seat. **plafond ~,** low ceiling. **~se mer, ~se marée,** low water, low tide, ebb tide. **tout le pays ~ est inondé,** all the low country is flooded. **~ prix,** low price. **acheter à ~ prix,** to buy cheap. **les fonds publics sont ~,** the public funds are low. **le ~ peuple,** the populace, the mob. **à voix ~se,** in a low voice, in a whisper. **avoir l'âme ~se,** to have a mean soul. **le ~ latin,** low Latin. **le ~allemand,** low German. **la ~se Egypte,** lower Egypt. **le ~ Rhin,** the lower Rhine. **avoir la vue ~se,** to be short-sighted. **faire main ~ sur,** to lay violent hands on, to seize. **au ~ mot,** at the lowest estimate, at least.

bas *n.m.* bottom, lower part; foot, bottom (of a mountain; ladder; page, list, etc.); small (of the leg). **il y avait au ~ de la lettre,** there was at the bottom (or end) of the letter. **son nom se trouvait au ~ de la liste,** his name was at the bottom of the list. **il y a des hauts et des ~ dans la vie,** there are ups and downs in life.

bas *adv.* low. **cet oiseau vole ~,** that bird flies low. **trois étages plus ~,** three stories lower. **il demeure trois portes plus ~,** he lives three doors lower down. **ses pertes multipliées l'ont mis bien ~,** his repeated losses have brought him very low. **parlez plus ~,** speak lower. **couler ~,** *Naut.* to sink. **mettre ~ les armes,** to lay down one's arms. **mettre chapeau ~,** to take off one's hat. **mettre ~,** (of animals) to bring forth young. **tenir ~,** keep down or under. **à bas,** down. **tous mes arbres sont à ~,** all my trees are down. **à ~ les chapeaux!**

off with your hats! hats off! **à ~ les ministres!** down with the ministers! **en bas,** below. **où est votre père? il est en ~.** Where is your father? He is below (or downstairs). **rouler de haut en ~,** to roll downward, to roll from top to bottom.

bas *n.m.* stocking **~ de nylon,** nylon stocking. **~ de soie,** silk stocking. **~ sans couture,** seamless stocking. **~ culotte, tights. ~ culotte,** pantyhose. *Infml.* **~ de laine,** savings, nest egg.

basalte *n.m.* basalt.

basaltique *adj.* basaltic.

basane *n.f.* tanned sheepskin. **relié en ~,** bound in sheepskin.

basané, e *p.p.* tanned, sunburned. *adj.* swarthy, tawny.

basaner *v.t.* to tan.

bas-bleu *n.m.* bluestocking

bascule *n.f.* weighing machine; seesaw. **faire la ~,** to sway up and down. **fauteuil à ~,** rocking chair.

basculer *v.i.* to seesaw.

base *n.f.* base, bottom, foot, basis, foundation, fundamental principle, groundwork, grounds. **la ~ d'une colonne, d'un piédestal,** base of a column, of a pedestal. **~ d'opérations,** base of operations. **~ navale,** naval base.

baser *v.t.* to base; to ground, to found. (*Milit.*) to base, to have as a base. **~ des avions sur un porte-avions,** to base airplanes on an aircraft carrier. **se ~,** *v.refl.* to be based, grounded, fixed.

bas-fond *n.m.* bottom; shoal, shallow water

basilic *n.m.* sweet basil; basilisk; cockatrice.

basilique *n.f.* basilica, *adj.* basilical.

basin *n.m.* dimity.

basique *adj. Chem.* basic.

basket (-ball) *n.m.* basketball.

bas-mât *n.m. Naut.* lower mast.

basque *n.f.* skirt, flap. *n.m.* Basque, *adj.* Basque. **la langue ~,** the Basque language.

bas-relief *n.m.* low-relief, bas-relief.

basse *n.f. Mus.* bass, bass voice. *Naut.* ridge or reef.

basse-cour *n.f.* farm yard; backyard.

basse-fosse *n.f.* dungeon.

bassement *adv.* basely, meanly, vilely, lowly. **il a agi ~,** he has acted basely.

bassesse *n.f.* lowness, baseness, meanness, vileness, servility. **commettre une ~,** to commit a mean action.

basset *n.m.* basset, fox terrier.

bassin *n.m.* basin, reservoir; dock; pelvis. **~ de la Seine,** the basin of the Seine. **~ d'échouage,** drydock. **droits de ~,** dock fees.

bassine *n.f.* pan. **~ à confitures,** preserving pan.

bassiner *v.t.* to warm (as a bed), to bathe (as the eyes); to sprinkle. *Infml.* to bore someone.

bassinet *n.m. Eccl.* collection plate.

bassinoire *n.f.* warming pan. *Infml.* boring person.

basson *n.m.* bassoon; bassoonist.

baste *Interj.* who cares! never mind!

bastide *n.f.* country house; small fortress.

bastille *n.f.* fortress.

bastingage *n.m. Naut.* side rails, railing.

bastion *n.m.* bastion. *Fig.* stronghold, bulwark.

bastonnade *n.f.* bastinado. **recevoir la ~**, to be beaten.

bastringue *n.m. Infml.* dance hall, honky-tonk joint; loud musical band; din, racket. stuff, junk.

bas-ventre *n.m.* abdomen.

bât *n.m.* pack saddle. **cheval de ~**, a packhorse. **chacun sait où le ~ le blesse**, everyone knows his own weak points.

bataclan *n.m.* stuff, junk. V. BASTRINGUE

bataille *n.f.* battle; fight, engagement, action. **donner (ou livrer) ~**, to give battle. **~ rangée**, pitched battle. **cheval de ~**, charger, war-horse. **champ de ~**, battlefield. **ranger une armée en ~**, to draw up an army in battle array, in order of battle.

batailler *v.i.* to battle; to struggle hard.

batailleur, euse *n.m.f.* person fond of fighting; disputer. *adj.* disputatious, combative.

bataillon *n.m.* battalion. **chef de ~**, major.

bâtard, e *adj.* bastard, illegitimate; mongrel. **un enfant ~**, a bastard child. **lévrier ~**, mongrel greyhound. *n.m.f.* bastard (male or female); illegitimate child.

bâtardeau *n.m.* embankment; cofferdam.

bâté, e *p.p.* saddled.

bateau *n.m.* boat. **~ à voiles**, sailboat. **~ à vapeur**, steamboat, steamer. **~ de sauvetage**, lifeboat.

batelée *n.f.* boatload.

bateleur, euse *n.m.f.* juggler, mountebank, clown.

batelier, ère *n.m.f.* boatman, boatwoman; waterman.

batellerie *n.f.* transport of goods by riverboat; river craft (collective sense).

bâter *v.t.* to saddle (a beast of burden).

bathymétrie *n.f.* bathymetry.

bâti, e *p.p.* built. **un homme bien ~**, a well-built man. *n.m.* framework, support, stand. **~ de fenêtre**, window frame.

batifolage *n.m.* frolicking.

batifoler *v.i.* to frolic, to romp.

batifoleur *n.m.* rollicker.

bâtiment *n.m.* building, structure, edifice; vessel. **~ de guerre**, warship, man of war. **~ marchand**, merchant ship, merchantman.

bâtir *v.t.* to build, to erect; to establish; to tack together. **~ une maison**, to build a house. **~ des châteaux en Espagne**, to build castles in the air.

bâtisse *n.f.* the masonry (of a building), the shell (of a house).

bâtisseur *n.m.* builder, developer. **~ d'empires**, empire builder. **c'est un grand ~**, he is always building.

batiste *n.f.* cambric. **toile de ~**, cambric. **~ d'Ecosse**, Scotch cambric.

bâton *n.m.* stick, walking stick, staff; truncheon, club; wand. **à ~s rompus**, by fits and starts, desultorily, off and on. **coup de ~**, blow with a stick. **mener le ~ haut**, to rule with a high hand. **~ à deux bouts**, quarter-staff. **~ pastoral**, bishop's crosier. **~ de mesure**, the baton of the conductor of an orchestra. **~ de ski**, ski pole.

bâtonner *v.t.* to beat with a stick, to cane.

battage *n.m.* beating of a rug or carpet; threshing (of corn); churning (of butter).

battant, e *adj.* fighting, inclined to fight; beating, pelting. **porte ~e**, swinging door. **une pluie ~e**, a pelting rain. *n.m.* clapper (of a bell); leaf (of a folding door).

batte *n.f.* bat; wooden sword (of a harlequin); churn staff.

battement *n.m.* beating; clapping; stamping; banging (of doors); flapping (of wings); shuffling (of cards); ticking; beating (of the heart); interval. **les ~s du cœur**, the beating of the heart. **il est sujet aux ~s de cœur**, he is subject to palpitations of the heart. **un ~ de trente minutes pour changer d'avion**, a thirty-minute interval, to change planes.

batterie *n.f.* fight, fighting; scuffle, beating (of drums); battery (guns); car battery; set of percussion instruments in a jazz band. **~ flottante**, floating battery. **~ de campagne**, field battery. **~ de cuisine**, kitchen utensils.

batteur *n.m.* beater; percussionist in a jazz band. **~ en grange**, thresher (of corn). **~ d'or**, goldbeater. **~ de pavé**, rambler. **~ à oeufs**, egg-beater.

batteuse *n.f.* beater; thresher (of corn). **~ mécanique**, threshing machine.

battoir *n.m.* beater; bat. **des mains comme des ~s**, large hands.

battre *v.t.* to beat, to strike, to flog, to thrash; to vanquish, to defeat; to break (a record); to hammer, to beat (a metal); to shuffle (cards). **~ quelqu'un à coups de poings**, to beat someone with one's fists. **~ quelqu'un comme plâtre**, to beat someone to a pulp. **~ quelqu'un à mort**, to beat someone to death. **~ l'ennemi**, to beat, to defeat the enemy. **~ tous les records**, to break all the records. **~ le fer pendant qu'il est chaud**, to strike while the iron is hot. **~ le rappel**, to sound the roll call. **~ la retraite**, to sound the retreat. **~ la campagne**, to scour the countryside. **~ monnaie**, to coin money. **~ froid à quelqu'un**, to give someone the cold shoulder. **~ les ailes**, to flap wings. *Naut.* **~ un pavillon**, to fly a flag.

battre (se) *v.refl.* to beat oneself; to fight each other. **se ~ à coups de poing**, to fight with fists. **se ~ en duel**, to fight a duel.

battu, e *p.p.* beaten; thrashed. **chemin ~**, beaten path or track. **autant vaut bien ~ que mal ~**, in for a penny, in for a pound.

batture *n.f.* gold lacquering; coral reef.

bau *n.m. Naut.* beam. **maître ~,** midship beam.

baudet *n.m.* ass, donkey; trestle.

baudrier *n.m.* cross belt, shoulder belt. **~ d'Orion,** Orion's belt.

bauge *n.f.* lair (of a wild boar); *Fig.* a pigsty.

baume *n.m.* balsam, balm. *Fig.* balm.

bavard, e *adj.* talkative, chattering, tale-telling, gossiping. *n.m.f.* chatterer, chatter/tattle box; tale.

bavardage *n.m.* talkativeness, loquacity; gossip.

bave *n.f.* slobber, foam; slime.

baver *v.i.* to slobber; to foam (at the mouth); to dribble.

bavette *n.f.* bib (of an apron).

baveux, se *adj.* dribbling; slobbering.

bavoir *n.m.* baby's bib.

bavure *n.f.* smudge, smear; *Fig.* slip-up, screw-up.

bayer *v.i.* to gape. **~ aux corneilles,** to stand gaping like a simpleton.

bazar *n.m.* bazaar.

bazarder *v.t. Infml.* to get rid of something quickly; to sell at any price.

béant, e *adj.* gaping; yawning. **demeurer bouche ~e,** to stand gaping.

béat, e *adj.* sanctimonious, smug; blissful.

béatement *adv.* sanctimoniously, smugly; blissfully.

béatification *n.f.* beatification.

béatifier *v.t.* to beatify.

béatifique *adj.* beatific.

béatitude *n.f.* beatitude; bliss.

beau or **bel, belle,** *pl.* **beaux** *adj.* **bel** is used instead of **beau** before a vowel or mute **h**), beautiful, fine; lofty; noble, handsome, lovely; smart; nice, fair. **un bel enfant,** a beautiful child. **avoir l'air ~,** to look beautiful. **de belles couleurs,** beautiful (or fine) colors. **un bel oiseau,** a beautiful bird. **une belle vue,** a beautiful view. **un ~ discours,** a fine speech. **une belle pensée,** a fine thought. **les ~x-arts,** the fine arts. **un ~ jour pour lui,** a glorious day for him. **un ~ nom,** a glorious (or honorable) name. **un ~ parleur,** a smooth, glib talker. **un bel homme,** a handsome man. **un ~ monsieur,** a fashionable gentleman. **une belle dame,** an elegant lady. **le ~ monde,** the fashionable world. **une belle somme,** a large amount (of money). **comme vous voilà ~ aujourd'hui!** how smart you look today! **me voilà dans un bel état,** here am I in a fine mess. **vous avez fait un ~ coup,** you have made a nice job of it. **en dire de belles,** to say foolish things. **l'échapper belle,** to have a narrow escape. **une belle mer,** a smooth sea. **le ~ sexe,** the fair sex. **beau,** *n.m.* the best; beauty, **voilà le ~ de l'affaire,** that is the beauty (the best) of the affair. **inspirer le goût du ~,** to instill a taste for the beautiful. **le baromètre se tient au ~ fixe,** the barometer stands at set fair. **beau, bel, belle,** *adv.* **voir tout en ~,** to see the bright side of every thing. **bel et bien,**

thoroughly, roundly. **j'ai ~ dire,** I have spoken in vain.

beaucoup *adv.* much, many, a great deal, a good deal. **~ d'argent,** a great deal of money. **~ de livres,** many books. **il reste ~ à faire,** much remains to be done. **c'est ~ qu'il daigne de vous parler,** it is a big thing if he deigns to speak to you. **un chemin ~ plus facile,** a much easier road. **je suis son aîné à ~ près,** I am his elder by a great deal (or by far). **de ~ le plus riche,** by far the richest. **il s'en faut de ~,** far from it.

beau-fils *n.m.* son-in-law; stepson.

beau-frère *n.m.* brother-in-law; stepbrother.

beau-père *n.m.* father-in-law; stepfather.

beaupré *n.m.* bowsprit.

beauté *n.f.* beauty, loveliness. **la ~ idéale,** ideal beauty. **la ~ d'un paysage,** the beauty of a landscape. **grain de ~,** beauty spot. **une ~,** a beautiful woman, *Infml.* a real looker.

bébé *n.m.* baby.

bec *n.m.* beak, bill (of birds); snout (of certain animals); nib (of pen); burner (of a gas light). **avoir ~ et ongles,** to be able to look after, defend oneself, **coup de ~,** stinging remark, taunt. **blanc ~,** a beardless boy. **tenir quelqu'un le ~ dans l'eau,** to keep one in suspense. **~ à ~,** face to face. **~ sucré,** sweet tooth. **caquet bon ~,** *Fig.* chatterbox.

bécane *n.f.* bike, bicycle, motorbike; *Infml.* microcomputer.

bécarre *n.m.* and *adj. Mus.* natural.

bécasse *n.f.* woodcock; *Infml.* stupid woman.

bécassine *n.f. Ornith.* snipe.

bec-de-cane *n.m.* slide bolt; lever handle of a door.

bec-de-corbin *n.m.* flat-nosed pliers.

bec-de-lièvre *n.m.* harelip.

béchamel *n.f.* cream sauce.

bêche *n.f.* spade.

bêcher *v.t.* to dig, *Infml.* to show arrogance or contempt.

bêcheur, euse *n.m.f. Infml.* arrogant or haughty person.

becquée *n.f.* beakful, billful.

becqueter *v.t.* to peck.

bedaine *n.f. Infml.* paunch, belly.

bédane *n.m.* chisel.

bedon *n.m. Infml.* potbelly.

Bédouin, e *adj.* and *n.m.f.* Bedouin.

bée *adj.* open (mouth) to express shock or astonishment.

béer *v.i.* to be open (esp. the mouth).

beffroi *n.m.* bell tower, belfry; alarm bell.

bégaiement *n.m.* stammering, stuttering.

bégayer *v.i.* to stammer, to stutter, to lisp. *v.t.* to stammer out. **~ une excuse,** to stammer out an excuse.

bègue *adj.* stammering, stuttering *n.m.f.* stammerer, stutterer.

bégueule *n.f.* haughty prude. **faire la ~,** to play

the prude. *adj.* haughtily prudish.

bégueulerie *n.f.* prudery.

béguin *n.m.* child's bonnet; infatuation; boyfriend, girlfriend.

beige *adj.* raw, not dyed; beige. *n.f.* serge of raw wool.

beignet *n.m.* fritter; eggroll; doughnut.

bel *adj. n.m.* V. BEAU

bêlant, e *adj.* bleating.

bêlement *n.m.* bleating (of sheep).

bêler *v.i.* to bleat, to baa (said of sheep).

belette *n.f.* weasel.

Belge *adj.* Belgian. **Belge** *n.m.f.* Belgian.

Belgique *n.f. Geog.* Belgium *adj.* Belgic.

bélier *n.m.* ram, battering ram; the Ram, Ariès.

bélière *n.f.* clapper (of a bell).

bélître *n.m.* beggar; knave, scoundrel.

belladone *n.f.* belladonna, deadly nightshade.

bellâtre *n.m.f.* faded beau, faded belle.

belle *adj.* V. BEAU *n.f.* beauty. **la ~ et la Bête,** Beauty and the Beast.

belle-de-jour *n.f.* bindweed.

belle-de-nuit *n.f.* marvel of Peru.

belle-fille *n.f.* daughter-in-law, stepdaughter.

belle-mère *n.f.* mother-in-law, stepmother.

belle-soeur *n.f.* sister-in-law; stepsister.

bellicisme *n.m.* warmongering.

belliciste *n.m.* warmonger.

belligérant, e *adj.* belligerent.

belliqueux, euse *adj.* warlike, quarrelsome.

bellot, otte *adj. Infml.* pretty, cute.

belvédère *n.m.* belvedere, terrace.

bémol *n.m. Mus.* flat.

bénédicité *n.m.* grace (before meal). **dire le ~,** to say grace.

bénédictin, e *s. and adj.* Benedictine (monk or nun).

bénédiction *n.f.* benediction, blessing, consecration. **la ~ d'une église,** the consecration of a church.

bénéfice *n.m.* benefit, advantage; profit; benefice, privilege. *Fin.* **~ brut,** gross profit. **~ net, net** profit. *Jurispr.* **~ du doute,** benefit of the doubt. **représentation à ~,** benefit night (or performance).

bénéficiaire *adj.* showing a profit. *n.m.* beneficiary; *Fin.* recipient, payee. **~ d'un chèque,** payee on a check.

bénéficier(de) *v.i.* to benefit from, to profit by. *Jurispr.* **~ d'un non-lieu,** to be unconditionally discharged.

bénéfique *adj.* beneficent, beneficial.

benêt *adj. and n.m.* foolish, silly; a simpleton, fool.

bénévole *adj.* benevolent, kind, gentle; voluntary, unpaid, of a charitable nature. *n.m.f.* volunteer.

bénévolement *adv.* benevolently; voluntarily; from pure goodwill.

béni, e *p.p.* blessed.

bénignement *adv.* benignly, benignantly.

bénignité *n.f.* benignity; kindness, graciousness; mildness of an (illness).

bénin, igne *adj.* benign, kind, easygoing, tame; mild. **remède ~,** a benign, mild remedy.

bénir *v.t.* to bless, to praise, to consecrate, to give one's blessing to. **Dieu vous benisse!** God bless you!

bénit, e *p.p.* blessed, consecrated, hallowed. **pain ~,** consecrated bread. **eau ~e,** holy water.

bénitier *n.m.* holy-water basin, fount.

benjamin, e *n.m.f.* (youngest son, youngest daughter.

benne *n.f.* hamper, bin. **(camion à) ~ basculante,** dump truck.

benoît, e *adj. Pej.* ingratiating, mealy-mouthed.

benoîtement *adv. Pej.* in an ingratiating, mealy-mouthed way.

benzine *n.f.* benzine.

benzoate *n.f.* benzoate.

benzoïque *adj.* benzoic.

béquille *n.f.* crutch; stand (of a bicycle), prop.

béquiller *v.i.* to walk with a crutch; *Naut.* to shore up (a boat).

bercail *n.m.* sheepfold, fold. **ramener au ~,** to bring back to the fold.

berceau *n.m.* cradle; *Fig.* birth; infancy; childhood; beginning, origin; birth place; *Mech.*) **~ d'un moteur,** engine mounting.

bercer *v.t.* to rock; to lull, to deceive, to delude. **se ~,** *v.refl.* to delude (oneself.)

berceuse *n.f.* lullaby.

béret *n.m.* beret.

berge *n.f.* bank of a river.

berger *n.m.* shepherd.

bergère *n.f.* shepherdess; easy chair.

bergerie *n.f.* sheepfold; pastorals, pastoral poems.

berline *n.f.* four-door car.

berlingot *n.m.* caramel candy; carton (esp. milk).

berlue *n.f.* dimness of sight. **avoir la ~,** to have hallucinations; to delude oneself.

bermuda *n.m.* Bermuda shorts.

bernacle *n.f. Zool.* barnacle.

berne *adj. and n.f.* **drapeaux en ~,** flags at half-mast.

berner *v.t.* to dupe, to hoodwink.

bernique *n.f. Infml.* limpet.

béryl *n.m.* beryl.

besogne *n.f.* work, labor.

besogner *v.i.* to labor, to work at a boring or difficult task.

besogneux, euse *adj.* needy, necessitous.

besoin *n.m.* want, need, necessity, indigence, poverty. **le ~ d'argent,** the want of money. **être dans le ~,** to be in want. **subvenir aux ~ s de quelqu'un,** to supply a person's wants or needs. **au ~,** if necessary, when needed. **avoir besoin de,** to need, to be in want of. **j'ai ~ de vous,** I need you. **je n'ai plus ~ de rien,** I no longer want for anything. **il est besoin,** *verb. phr.* (+

subj.) it is necessary or needful. **il est ~ que je parte bientôt,** it is necessary for me to leave soon. *plur.* **faire ses ~s,** to relieve oneself.

bestiaire *n.m.* bestiarius, beast-fighter. *Lit.* bestiary, book of fables.

bestial, e *adj.* bestial, beastly, brutish.

bestialement *adv.* bestially, in a beastlike manner.

bestialité *n.f.* bestiality.

bestiaux *n.m. pl.* cattle, livestock.

bestiole *n.f.* small animal, insect.

bêta-asse *n.m.* numbskull, stupid person.

bêtail *n.m.* cattle, livestock.

bête *n.f.* beast, brute, dumb creature, fool **~s à corne,** horned cattle. **~s à laine,** sheep **~s de somme,** beasts of burden **~ à bon Dieu,** ladybug. **morte la ~, mort le venin,** dead men tell no tales. **faire la ~,** to play the fool. **~ noire,** personal aversion. *adj.* foolish, silly, stupid. **avoir un air ~,** to have a stupid look, to look like a fool.

bétel *n.m.* betel.

bêtement *adv.* foolishly, like a fool, stupidly.

bêtifier *v.i.* to speak in a foolish or childish manner.

bêtise *n.f.* folly, foolishness, stupidity; foolery, nonsense. **quelle ~!** what nonsense!

béton *n.m.* concrete.

bétonner *v.t.* to build with concrete.

bette *n.f.* beet, leaf-beet.

betterave *n.f.* beet, beetroot.

beuglement *n.m.* bellowing, lowing of cows and oxen.

bougler *v.i.* to bellow, to low; to roar, to shout.

beurre *n.m.* butter. **~ frais,** fresh butter. **au ~ noir,** with butter sauce browned in a pan.

beurré, e *p.p.* buttered. *n.m.* butter-pear *n.f.* slice of bread and butter.

beurrer *v.t.* to butter.

beurrier *n.m.* butter dish.

bévue *n.f.* blunder.

biais *n.m.* slant; *Fig.* expedient, means. **en ~,** slantwise; askew; indirectly. **par le ~ de,** by means (indirectly) of.

biaiser *v.i.* to slant, to skew; *Fig.* to prevaricate, to sidestep (an issue).

bibelot *n.m.* knickknack.

biberon *n.m.* baby bottle.

Bible *n.f.* Bible.

bibliographe *n.m.* bibliographer.

bibliographie *n.f.* bibliography.

bibliographique *adj.* bibliographic, bibliographical.

bibliophile *n.m.* bibliophile, booklover.

bibliothécaire *n.m.* librarian.

bibliothèque *n.f.* library, bookcase, bookshelves.

biblique *adj.* biblical.

bicarbonate *n.m.* bicarbonate.

biceps *adj.* and *n.m.* biceps; the biceps muscle.

biche *n.f.* hind, doe.

bichon, onne *n.m.f.* lap dog; little dear, darling.

bichonner to pamper, to cosset. **se ~,** to dress oneself up, to prettify oneself.

bicolore *adj.* bicolored, two-colored.

biconcave *adj.* biconcave.

biconvexe *adj.* biconvex.

bicoque *n.f.* shanty, hovel.

bicorne *n.m.* cocked hat.

bicot *n.m.* kid (goat).

bicyclette *n.f.* bicycle, bike.

bidasse *n.m. Infml.* simple soldier, buck private.

bide *n.m. Infml.* belly, paunch. **faire un ~,** to fail, to flop.

bidet *n.m.* pony, nag; bidet.

bidon *n.m.* can; jerrycan.

bidonville *n.f.* shantytown.

bief *n.m.* mill course; reach.

bielle *n.f.* connecting rod, side rod.

bien *n.m.* good, benefit, blessing, welfare, wellbeing, prosperity. **le ~ et le mal,** good and evil. **faire du ~,** to do good. **grand ~ vous fasse,** much good may it do you. **homme de ~,** a good (or virtuous) man. **lorsqu'on a des ~s,** when one has property. **~s fonciers,** lands, real estate. **le ~ public,** public good. **à ~,** successfully. **mener une entreprise à ~,** to conduct an undertaking successfully. **en ~,** honestly. **prendre en ~,** to take in good part. *adv.* well; indeed; rightly, justly; accurately, perfectly, thoroughly; right, proper; fully; comfortable; good-looking, handsome (before an adj. or adv.) very, much, far. **il se conduit ~,** he behaves well. **champ ~ cultivé,** a well-cultivated field. **aller ~,** to be well, in good health; (of things) to go well. **ses affaires vont ~,** his business is prospering, is going well. **il parle ~,** he speaks well. **je comprends ~ que …,** I perfectly understand that … **il est ~ entendu que …,** it is well (clearly) understood that … **le voilà ~!** he is in a pretty pickle! **elle est ~ malheureuse,** she is very unhappy. **il est ~ malade,** he is very ill. **il fut ~ surpris,** he was much surprised. **nous sommes très ~ ici,** we are very comfortable here. **cette femme est ~,** that woman is good-looking. **~ de l'argent,** a great deal of money. **~ des gens,** many people. **il y a ~ deux kilomètres d'ici là,** it is a full two kilometers from here to there. **vous avez ~ raison,** you are quite right. *conj.* **~ que,** though, although.

bien-aimé, e *adj.* well-beloved, beloved; darling.

bien-être *n.m.* welfare, well-being; comfort; comforts.

bienfaisance *n.f.* beneficence; charity.

bienfaisant, e *adj.* beneficent, charitable, kind.

bienfait *n.m.* benefit, favor, kind act; profit, advantage. **un ~ n'est jamais perdu,** a kindness is never lost.

bienfaiteur, trice *m.f.* benefactor, benefactress.

bien-fonds *n.m.* real estate.

bienheureux, euse *adj.* blessed; blissful.

biennal, e *adj.* biennial.

bienséance *n.f.* decorum, decency, manners.

bienséant, e *adj.* proper, becoming, decorous, decent.

bientôt *adv.* soon, shortly. **je reviendrai ~,** I will soon come back.

bienveillance *n.f.* kindness, benevolence, good will.

bienveillant, e *adj.* kind, benevolent.

bienvenu, e *adj.* welcome. **il est ~ partout,** he is welcome everywhere. *n.m.f.* welcome person. **soyez le ~, la ~e,** you are welcome here.

bienvenue *n.f.* welcome.

bière *n.f.* beer; coffin.

biffer *v.t.* to erase, to cross out; to cancel.

bifteck *n.m.* steak.

bifurcation *n.f.* bifurcation, branching off.

bifurquer *v.t.* to bifurcate, to fork.

bigame *adj.* bigamous. *n.m.* bigamist.

bigamie *n.f.* bigamy.

bigarade *n.f.* Seville orange.

bigarré, e *adj.* variegated, motley, streaked.

bigarreau *n.m.* red-and-white-heart cherry.

bigarrer *v.t.* to make motley, to variegate, to checker, to speckle.

bigarrure *n.f.* medley, mixture.

bigler *v.i.* to squint.

bigleux, euse *adj.* and *mf.* cross-eyed; *Infml.* as blind as a bat.

bigorneau *n.m.* periwinkle.

bigot, e *adj.* sanctimonious.

bigoterie *n.f.* sanctimoniousness.

bigoudi *n.m.* hair curler.

bigre, *Interj. Infml.* gosh!, golly!

bigrement *adv. Infml.* a lot, awfully.

bijou *n.m.* jewel, trinket; love, darling.

bijouterie *n.f.* jewelry.

bijoutier, ière *n.m.f.* jeweller.

bilan *n.m.* balance sheet; **déposer son ~,** to file for bankruptcy.

bilatéral, e *adj.* bilateral; (jur.) reciprocal.

bile *n.f.* bile; *Infml.* anger, worry. **se faire de la ~,** to worry, to fret.

biler (se) *v. Infml.* to fret, to get worked up.

bilieux, euse *adj. Infml.* easily upset (person).

bilingue *adj.* bilingual.

billard *n.m.* billiards; billiard table; billiard room.

bille *n.f.* billiard ball; marble (to play with); block, log (of timber).

billet *n.m.* note, bill, ticket; circular; **~ d'invitation pour un dîner,** an invitation to dinner. **~ d'entrée,** admission ticket. **~ d'aller et de retour,** round-trip ticket. **~ de loterie,** lottery ticket. **~ de banque,** banknote. **~ à ordre,** promissory note.

billetterie *n.f.* automatic teller machine (ATM).

billevesée *n.f.* silly stuff, trash, nonsense.

billion *n.m.* trillion, a thousand billions.

billot *n.m.* block of wood (for use by butchers or executioners); support for an anvil.

bimbeloterie *n.f* manufacture of or trade in novelty items or trinkets.

bimensuel, le *adj.* twice per month.

bimestriel, le *adj.* once every two months.

bimoteur *adj.* and *n.m.* twin-engine or bimotored airplane.

binage *n.m.* hoeing, second tillage.

binaire *adj.* binary.

biner *v.t.* to hoe.

binette *n.f.* hoe, weeder; *Infml.* head; facial expression.

binocle *n.m.* lorgnette, pince-nez.

binoculaire *adj.* binocular.

binôme *n.m.* binomial.

biographe *n.m.* biographer.

biographie *n.f.* biography.

biographique *adj.* biographical, biographic.

biologie *n.f.* biology.

biologique *adj.* biological.

biopsie *n.f.* biopsy.

biparti, e, *adj.* divided in two; bilateral; *Polit.* bipartisan.

bipartite *adj.* V. BIPARTI.

bipédal, e *adj.* bipedal.

bipède *adj.* bipedal; two-legged. *n.m.* biped.

biplace *adj.* and *n.m. Aviat., Mech.* two-seater.

biplan *n.m.* biplane.

bipolaire *adj.* bipolar.

bique *n.f. Infml.* nanny-goat.

biquet, te *n.m.f. Zool.* kid; *Infml.* term of affection.

bis, e *adj.* brown; swarthy. **pain ~,** brown bread.

bis *Interj.* encore! **crier ~,** to cry encore.

bisaïeul, e *n.m.f.* great-grandfather, great-grandmother.

bisannuel, elle *adj.* biennial.

bisbille *n.f.* wrangling, bickering.

biscornu, e *adj.* ill-shaped; odd, bizarre, outlandish.

biscotte *n.f* melba toast.

biscuit *n.m.* biscuit, cracker; unglazed porcelain. **s'embarquer sans ~,** to commence an enterprise without due preparations.

bise *n.f.* north wind; *Infml.* kiss.

biseau *n.m.* bevel. **taillé en ~,** beveled.

biseautage *n.m.* beveling.

biseauter *v.t.* to bevel; to mark cards (for cheating).

biset *n.m.* rock dove.

bisexué, e *adj. Bot.* bisexual.

bisexuel, elle *adj.* and *n.m.f.* bisexual.

bismuth *n.m.* bismuth.

bison *n.m.* bison.

bisque *n.f.* kind of cream soup.

bisquer *v.i.* to be riled.

bisser *v.t.* to encore.

bissextil, e *adj.* **année ~e,** leap year.

bissexué, e *adj. Bot.* V. BISEXUEL.

bissexuel, elle *adj.* V. BISEXUEL.

bistouri *n.m. Surg.* lancet.

bistre *n.m.* bistre, blackish-brown.

bistré, e *p.p.* colored with bistre; tanned, swarthy, tawny.

bistrot, bistro *n.m.* café, pub, small bar. **bit** *n.m. Comp.* bit.

bitte *n.f. Naut.* bit, bitt — **d'amarrage,** mooring post. *Vulg.* penis.

bitume *n.m.* bitumen.

bitumineux, euse *adj.* bituminous.

bivalve *adj.* bivalvular. *n.m.* bivalve.

bivouac *n.m.* bivouac.

bivouaquer *v.i.* to bivouac.

bizarre *adj.* bizarre, odd, strange.

bizarrement *adv.* in a bizarre, odd manner.

bizarrerie *n.f.* oddness, strangeness; *pl.* peculiarities.

bla-bla *n.m. Infml.* claptrap, nonsense; gibberish.

blafard, e *adj.* palish, dim, dull; wan.

blague *n.f.* tobacco pouch. *Infml.* hoax, joke, fib.

blaguer *v.i.* to hoax, to kid, to joke, to tease, to fool.

blagueur, euse *adj.* and *n.m.f.* joker, tease, leg-puller, fibber.

blaireau *n.m.* badger.

blâmable *adj.* blamable.

blâme *n.m.* blame, reproach; reprimand. **il ne mérite pas le ~,** he does not deserve blame. **sans ~,** blameless.

blâmer *v.t.* to blame, to find fault with, to censure.

blanc, blanche *adj.* and *mf.* white, pale; blank, clean. **blanche comme neige,** innocent, pure. **~ d'oeuf,** egg white. **~ de l'oeil,** the white of the eye. **papier ~,** blank paper. **chèque en ~,** blank check. *Typog.* white line, blank space.

blanc-bec *n.m.* greenhorn; beardless boy; inexperienced youth.

blanchaille *n.f.* small fry, whitebait.

blanchâtre *adj.* whitish.

blanchement *adv.* cleanly, clean.

blancheur *n.f.* whiteness.

blanchiment *n.m.* bleaching; blanching; washing.

blanchir *v.t.* to whiten; to white, to make white; to wash, to clean. **~ les dents,** to whiten the teeth. **~ des draps, des serviettes, des chemises,** to wash sheets, napkins, shirts. **~ une planche,** to plane a board. *v.i.* to whiten, to bleach (as textile fabrics); to fade (as colors); to wash. **cet homme commence à ~,** that man is beginning to turn gray. **se ~** *v.refl.* to be bleached; to become white.

blanchissage *n.m.* washing.

blanchissant, e *adj.* whitening; foaming.

blanchisserie *n.f.* laundry, washhouse.

blanchisseur, euse *n.m.f.* washerman, *n.m.;* washerwoman, *n.f.;* bleacher.

blanquette *n.f.* blanquette, a white wine of Languedoc. **~ de veau,** stewed veal.

blasé, adj. indifferent, sick of everything, blasé.

blaser *v.t.* to pall, to blunt, to cloy, to sicken; to harden. **les excès blasent le goût,** excesses pall the taste. **se ~,** *v.refl.* to be palled, cloyed, or surfeited. **~ sur les vrais plaisirs,** to have no relish for true pleasures.

blason *n.m.* coat of arms; heraldry, blazon, blazonry.

blasonner *v.t.* to blazon, to explain or paint armorial bearings; to criticize, to censure.

blasphémateur, trice *n.m.f.* blasphemer.

blasphématoire *adj.* blasphemous.

blasphème *n.m.* blasphemy.

blasphémer *v.i.* to blaspheme. *v.t.* to blaspheme; to curse.

blatte *n.f.* cockroach.

blé *n.m.* corn, wheat, grain. **~ froment,** wheat. **grands ~s,** wheat and rye. **petits ~s,** oats and barley. **~ noir,** buckwheat. **~ de Turquie,** maize, Indian corn. **la halle au ~,** the grain exchange, the grain market. **manger son ~ en herbe,** to spend one's money before receiving it.

blême *adj.* wan, pale, pallid.

blémir *v.i.* to turn pale.

blèsement *n.m.* lisping.

bléser *v.t.* to lisp.

blessant, e *adj.* offensive.

blessé, e *p.p.* and *n.m.f.* wounded; hurt, injured. **les morts et les ~s,** the killed and the wounded.

blesser *v.t.* to wound, to hurt, to cut, to gall, to injure; to offend. **il fut blessé au bras,** he was wounded in the arm. **son orgueil en fut blessé,** his pride was hurt by it. **ces souliers me blessent,** these shoes hurt (pinch) me. **cela ne blesse personne,** that offends nobody. **~ l'oreille,** to offend the ear. **se ~,** *v.refl.* wound, hurt oneself; to wound each another (or one another).

blessure *n.f.* wound, hurt, injury. **vos regards vont rouvrir mes ~s,** your looks will reopen my wounds.

blet, te *adj.* soft. **poire ~ te,** overripe pear.

blette *n.f.* strawberry spinach, blitum virgatum.

bleu, e *adj.* blue **des yeux ~s,** blue eyes. **conte ~,** fairy tale. *n.m.* blue. *n.m.* new conscript, novice. **~ de ciel,** sky blue. **~ de Prusse,** Prussian blue. **corden ~,** first-rate cook. **couvert de ~s,** all black and blue. **être dans une colere ~e,** to be in a towering rage. **il n'y a vu que du ~,** he was unaware of what was going on. **en rester ~,** to be flabbergasted. **l'argent a passé au ~,** the money has vanished.

bleuâtre *adj.* bluish.

bleuir *v.t.* to blue.

blindage *n.m.* armor plating.

bloc *n.m.* block; log (of wood), stock; lump. **en ~,** as a whole. *Econ.* freeze. *Psych.* mental block. **~ des prix,** price freeze.

blocaille *n.f.* rubblestones, rubblework.

blockhaus *n.m.* blockhouse.

bloc-notes, *n.m.pl.* writing pad.

blocus *n.m.* blockade; investment.

blond, e *adj.* blond, fair, light, flaxen. **cheveux**

~s, blond, fair (light or flaxen) hair. *n.m.*
blondness. ses cheveux étaient d'un ~ cin-
dré, her hair was ash blond. ~ ardent, fiery
red, carroty (hair).

blondasse, *adj.* flaxen-haired; washed out.

blondeur, *n.f.* fairness, blondness.

blondir *v.i.* to whiten, to grow light or fair.

blondissant, e *adj.* yellowish, golden.

bloqué, e *p.p.* blockaded; pocketed (billiards).

bloquer *v.t.* to steady, to wedge, to stop wob-
bling; to block, stop up, get stuck.

blottir (se) *v.refl.* nestle, cuddle.

blouse *n.f.* blouse; (child's) pinafore; overalls;
smock.

blouser *v.t.* to hole, to pocket (at billiards); to
mislead, con. se ~, *v.refl.* to hole one's own ball;
to mistake, to go wrong.

blouson *n.m.* sports jacket.

blue jeans *n.m.pl.* blue jeans.

blues *n.m.* blues; a blues song.

bluette *n.f.* spark, sparkle; flash (of wit or
humor).

bluff *n.m.* bluff.

bluffer *v.i., v.t.* to bluff.

bluffeur *n.m.* bluffer.

blush *n.m.* blusher (makeup).

boa *n.m.* boa (snake); drape of feathers or fur.

bobard, *n.m.* tall story, lie.

bobèche *n.f.* sconce; socket.

bobine *n.f.* bobbin; spool.

bobiner *v.t.* to reel.

bobinette *n.f.* wooden latch.

bobineur, euse *n.m.f.* reeler, winder.

bobo *n.m.* sore, boo-boo.

bocage *n.m.* grove.

bocager, ère *adj.* woodland, wood, of groves.

bocal *n.m.* wide-mouthed bottle, glass jar; *Mus.*
mouthpiece.

boeuf *n.m.* ox; beef. un troupeau de ~s, a herd
of oxen, a drove. mettre la charrue devant
les ~s, to put the cart before the horse. c'est un
~, he is as big, as strong as an ox.

bof! exclamation expressing lack of enthusiasm.

boghei *n.m.* buggy; light carriage.

bogue *n.f.* husk.

Bohême *n.m.f.* Bohemian; gypsy; wanderer.

bohémien, enne *adj.* Bohemian. *n.m.f. Pej.*
gypsy.

boire *v.t.* to drink; to swallow, to pocket (an
affront). buvez un verre d'eau, drink a glass of
water. c'est la mer à ~, that is no easy matter.
l'éponge boit l'eau, the sponge sucks up water.
v.i. to drink, to tipple. ~ à longs traits, to drink
deep. faire ~ un cheval, to water a horse. qui a
bu boira, once a drunkard, always a drunkard
n.m. drink, drinking. le ~ et le manger, food
and drink.

bois *n.m.* wood; forest; timber; horns (of deer);
Mus. woodwinds. ~ de chêne, de sapin, de
châtaignier, d'acajou, oak, pine, chestnut,
mahogany. meubles de ~, wooden furniture.

faire flèche de tout ~, to leave no stone
unturned. il est du ~ dont on fait les flûtes,
he is of an easy temper. ~ de construction,
timber. ~ gisant ou abattu, felled timber ~ à
brûler (or de chauffage), firewood. ~ vert,
green wood. une voie de ~, a load of wood. on
verra de quel ~ je me chauffe, they shall see
what sort of person I am. un ~ de lit, a bedstead (of wood).

boisage *n.m.* woodwork.

boisé, e *p.p.* wainscoted, panelled. pays ~, woodland country.

boisement *n.m.* afforestation.

boiser *v.t.* to wainscot; to plant.

boiserie *n.f.* wainscot, wainscoting.

boisseau *n.m.* bushel.

boisson *n.f.* drink, beverage, drinking. être
adonné à la ~, to be given to drinking. être
pris de ~, to be high, three sheets to the wind.

boite *n.f.* box; case. ~ aux lettres, mailbox.
mettre une lettre à la ~, to mail a letter. ~ à
thé, tea caddy. ~ de nuit, night club, cabaret.
mettre en ~, to pull somebody's leg. *Aer.*
~ noire, black box.

boitement *n.m.* halting, limping.

boiter *v.i.* to halt, to halt, to limp. un cheval
qui boite, a lame horse.

boiterie *n.f.* lameness, halting, limping.

boiteux, euse *adj.* lame, limping, halting. *n.m.f.*
lame person, a cripple.

boitier *n.m.* box of surgical instruments.

boitillement *n.m.* slight limping.

boitiller *v.t.* to hobble slightly

bol *n.m.* bowl, basin. en avoir ras le ~, to be fed
up.

bolide *n.m.* racing car.

bombance *n.f.* feasting, good cheer. faire ~, to
feast.

bombarde *n.f. Mus.* bombarde (organ stop).

bombardement *n.m.* bombardment.

bombarder *v.t.* to bombard.

bombardier *n.m.* bombardier.

bombe *n.f.* bomb, bombshell. tomber comme
une ~, to fall like a bomb.

bombé, e *adj.* bulged, barreled; convex.

bombement *n.m.* bulging, swelling out, convexity; barrelling.

bomber *v.t.* to bulge, to swell out. *v.i.* to become
convex, to bulge, to jut out. ce mur bombe, this
wall bulges out.

bomberie *n.f.* bomb (or shell) foundry.

bombyx *n.m.* silkworm.

bon, bonne *adj.* good, advantageous, profitable,
lucrative; wholesome, beneficial, suitable, fit,
proper, right, favorable, fortunate, happy;
clement, benevolent, humane, kind; good-
natured, affectionate; valid, safe, available, nice,
palatable. c'est une bonne affaire pour vous,
it is a good thing for you. à quoi ~? what is the
use (or the good)? trouver ~, to think right,
good or proper. j'ai fait quatre bonnes kilo-

mètres, I have done a good four kilometers. **un ~ quart d'heure**, a good quarter of an hour. **une bonne fois pour toutes**, once and for all. **une bonne maison de commerce**, respectable company. **~ pour mille francs**, good for a thousand francs. **un ~ mot**, a witty remark, a witticism. **bonne odeur**, nice (or pleasant) smell. **sentir ~**, to smell nice. *Typog.* **~ à tirer**, ready for press. *n.m.* good, good quality; the best; ticket, coupon, voucher; good points. **il a préféré le ~ à l'utile**, he preferred the good to the useful. **cet homme a du ~**, that man has good qualities. **le ~ de l'affaire**, the best of the business, the fun of the thing. **~ de caisse**, cash voucher. **~ de pain**, ticket for bread. **~ marché**, cheap. **bonne année**, Happy New Year. **~ sens**, common sense. **c'est ~**, all right, very good.

bonasse *adj.* soft, silly, simple, easy, simpleminded.

bon-bec *n.m.* chatterbox, gossip.

bonbon *n.m.* candy.

bonbonnière *n.f.* box for candy; neat little house.

bon-chrétien *n.m.* William's pear.

bond *n.m.* bound, leap, spring, skip, bounce (of a ball, etc.). **par sauts et par ~s**, by fits and starts, desultorily. **prendre la balle au ~**, to strike the ball on the rebound; to seize an opportunity. **faire faux ~**, to play foul, to disappoint.

bonde *n.f.* sluice; bung, bunghole.

bonde *adj.* crammed, packed.

bondieuserie *n.f.* bigotry. *pl.* religious trappings.

bondir *v.i.* to bound, to leap, to jump, to skip; to bounce. **~ de rage**, to leap with rage. **le coeur me bondit de joie**, my heart leaped for joy.

bondissant, e *adj.* bounding; skipping; frisking.

bondissement *n.m.* bounding, skipping, bouncing.

bonheur *n.m.* happiness, blessing, welfare, good fortune, good luck; fortune, luck. **avoir du ~**, to be lucky. **porter ~ à**, to bring good luck to. **le ~ de l'Etat**, the prosperity (or welfare) of the state. **véritable ~**, true happiness. **~ éternel**, eternal happiness. **par ~**, luckily, fortunately.

bonhomie *n.f.* good nature, easy temper, simplicity, credulity.

bonhomme *n.m.* good-natured, worthy, simple man; old man, old codger; man, fellow. **faux ~**, one who affects to be a good man, a hypocrite. **ce petit ~ travaille bien**, this little fellow works well.

boni *n.m.* surplus, bonus.

bonification *n.f.* improvement (of land, wine, etc.); allowance.

bonifier *v.t.* to improve; to get better. **se ~**, *v.refl.* to improve, to get better. **plusieurs choses se bonifient lorsqu'on les garde**, many things improve by keeping.

boniment *n.m.* sweet talk, a line; sales pitch.

bonjour *n.m.* hello, good morning. **je vous souhaite le ~**, I wish you good day.

bonne *n.f.* cleaning woman, maid. **~ à tout faire**, maid of all work. **~ d'enfants**, nanny.

bonnement *adv.* simply, sincerely, really.

bonnet *n.m.* cap. **~ de coton, de laine**, cotton, woollen cap. **~ de nuit**, nightcap. **~ d'âne**, dunce's cap. **les gros ~s**, the bigwigs. **être triste comme un ~ de nuit**, to be down in the dumps. **avoir la tête près du ~**, to be hotheaded. **ce sont deux têtes dans un ~**, they are hand and glove together. **c'est ~ blanc et blanc ~**, there are six of one and half a dozen of the other. **opiner du ~**, to nod assent. **jeter son ~ par-dessus les moulins**, to throw off all sense of propriety.

bonneterie *n.f.* hosiery; hosiery business.

bonneteur *n.m.* card sharp, three-card monte player.

bonsoir *n.m.* good evening, good night.

bonté *n.f.* goodness; excellence; kindness.

bonze *n.m.* bonze.

borborygme *n.m.* stomach rumbling.

bord *n.m.* border, edge, brim; shore, bank, side, brink; hem (of garments). **les deux vaisseaux étant à ~**, the two vessels being alongside each other. **aller à ~**, to go on board. **jeter par-dessus le ~**, to heave overboard. **mouiller le ~ de ses lèvres**, to wet the edge of one's lips. **chapeau à larges ~s**, broad-brimmed hat. **aller au ~ de la mer**, to go to the seashore. **les ~s du Rhin**, the banks of the Rhine. **le ~ d'an précipice**, the brink of a precipice.

bordé, e *p.p.* bordered, trimmed, tucked in.

bordée *n.f.* broadside, volley. **une ~ d'injures**, a volley of abuse.

bordel *n.m.* brothel.

border *v.t.* to plank, to border, to line; to hem, to edge; to tuck in (bedcovers). **le quai qui borde la rivière**, the quay that borders the river. **~ un rideau de bleu**, to border a curtain with blue. **on borda toutes les rues de soldats**, they lined all the streets with soldiers. **~ une voile**, to haul aft a sail.

bordereau *n.m.* note, memorandum; **~ de vente**, sales slip.

bordure *n.f.* border, edging; curb; frame.

boréal, e *adj.* boreal, northern.

borée *n.m.* Boreas; north wind.

borgne *adj.* one-eyed; obstructed; unsavory. **changer son cheval ~ contre un aveugle**, to have the worst of a bargain. **compte ~**, muddled account. *n.m.* one-eyed person. **au royaume des aveugles les ~s sont rois**, the one-eyed are kings among the blind.

bornage *n.m.* boundary line.

borne *n.f.* landmark, limit, boundary, bounds; milestone. **rester dans de justes ~s**, to remain within bounds. **~ postale**, pillar letter-box. **routière**, milestone. **~ fontaine**, public fountain.

borné, e *p.p.* limited, bounded, confined, restricted; narrow, shallow; mean. **~ par mon sujet,** confined, restricted by my subject. **intelligence ~e,** stunted, narrow intellect.

borner *v.t.* to mark the bounds, to bound, to limit, to confine. **se ~,** *v.refl.* to limit, to confine, to content, *or* restrict oneself, each other. **je me suis borné à demander,** I contented myself with asking.

Bosnie *n.f.* Bosnia.

Bosphore *n.m.* Bosphorus.

bosquet *n.m.* grove, thicket.

bossage *n.m.* embossment.

bosse *n.f.* bump, hump; dent, bruise; *Paint.* relief. **avoir la ~ de la musique,** to have a talent for music. **le chameau a deux ~s,** the camel has two humps. **ouvrages de demi-~,** sculptures in half-relief.

bosselage *n.m.* embossing.

bosselé, e *p.p.* embossed; bruised, dented.

bosseler *v.t.* to emboss, to dent.

bosselure *n.f.* embossment.

bosser *v.t.* to work hard, to keep one's nose to the grindstone.

bosseur, euse, *adj.* hardworking. **~** *n.m.f.* hard worker.

bossu, e *adj.* hump-backed, hunch-backed

bossuer *v.t.* to dent *or* bruise. **se ~,** *v.refl.* to be bruised.

bot *adj. m.* **pied ~,** clubfoot.

botanique *n.f.* botany *adj.* botanical.

botaniser *v.i.* to botanize, to herborize.

botaniste *n.m.* botanist.

botte *n.f.* boot; bundle, bunch, truss, hank. **une paire de ~s,** a pair of boots. **~ à caoutchou,** rubber boots. **mettre du foin dans ses ~s,** to feather one's nest. **a propos de ~s,** without rhyme or reason. **une ~ de foin,** a truss of hay. **une ~ de navets,** a bunch of turnips.

botté, e *adj.* booted; in boots.

botteler *v.t.* to sheaf.

botter *v.t.* to supply with boots; to make boots. **ce cordonnier botte bien,** that shoemaker makes good boots. **se ~,** *v.refl.* to put on one's boots. **se ~ bien,** to wear good boots.

bottier *n.m.* bootmaker.

bottillon *n.m.* bootee.

bottin *n.m.* phone directory.

bottine *n.f.* ankle boot.

bouc *n.m.* he-goat, goat. **~ émissaire,** scape-goat.

boucan *n.m.* smokehouse for meat; uproar, row.

boucaner *v.t.* and *n.* to smoke-dry meat; to hunt the wild ox.

boucanier *n.m.* buccaneer; pirate.

bouchage *n.m.* stopping, corking.

bouche *n.f.* mouth; opening; muzzle (of a firearm). **ouvrir, fermer la ~,** to open, to shut one's mouth. **faire venir l'eau à la ~,** to make one's mouth water. **bonne ~,** a pleasant

taste in one's mouth. **faire la petite ~,** to screw up one's mouth; to be hard to please. **avoir la ~ sur le coeur,** to speak from one's heart. **à pleine ~,** fully, roundly, in plain terms. **~ close,** mum's the word. **la ~ d'un canon,** the mouth of a cannon. **~ à feu,** a piece of ordnance. **les ~s du Nil,** the mouths of the Nile. **~ d'aération,** hot-air vent. **~ d'égout,** manhole. **~ d'incendie,** fire hydrant. **~ à ~,** mouth-to-mouth resuscitation.

bouchée *n.f.* mouthful. **il n'en ferait qu'une ~,** he would eat it in one gulp.

boucher *v.t.* to stop; to block up; to obstruct a passage, a road, a view; to cork. **on boucha les fenêtres,** they stopped up the windows. **~ la vue,** to block the view. **~ un trou,** to stop up a hole; to pay a debt. **se ~ le nez,** to hold one's nose.

boucher *n.m.* butcher.

bouchère *n.f.* butcher's wife, butcher woman.

boucherie *n.f.* butcher's shop; shambles; butcher's meat; butchery, carnage.

bouche-trou *n.m.* stop-gap.

bouchoir *n.m.* iron door of an oven or furnace.

bouchon *n.m.* stopper; cork; float (of a fishing line); wisp (of straw). **~ de cristal,** glass stopper. **~ à l'émeri,** ground glass stopper. **mettre un ~ à,** to cork. **faire sauter le ~,** to let the cork fly. **frotter un cheval avec un ~ de paille,** to rub down a horse with a wisp of straw.

bouchonner *v.t.* to roll, twist up; to rub down (a horse); to form a traffic jam.

bouchonnier *n.m.* cork cutter; dealer in corks.

boucle *n.f.* buckle; ring; curl (of hair). **~s d'oreilles,** earrings.

bouclé, e *p.p.* buckled; curled.

boucler *v.t.* to buckle; to curl (hair).

bouclier *n.m.* buckler, shield; protection, defense; limpet.

Bouddha *n.m.* Buddha.

bouddhique *adj.* Buddhist.

bouddhisme *n.m.* Buddhism.

bouddhiste *n.m.* Buddhist.

bouder *v.i.* to pout, to sulk; *Gard.* to be stunted in growth.

bouderie *n.f.* pouting; sulking.

boudeur, euse *adj.* and *n.* pouting; sulky; sulky person.

boudin *n.m.* pudding; large curl; *Arch.* torus. **~ noir,** black pudding.

boudiné, *adj.* sausage-shaped. **~ dans,** squeezed into, bursting out of.

boudiner *v.t.* to dress in close-fitting garments.

boudoir *n.m.* boudoir.

boue *n.f.* mud, dirt, mire. **traîner dans la ~,** to drag through the dirt. **une âme de ~,** a despicable mind. **tirer quelqu'un de la ~,** to raise one from an abject state.

bouée *n.f.* buoy. **~ de sauvetage,** life buoy.

boueur *n.m.* scavenger.

boueux, euse *adj.* dirty, muddy, foul.

bouffant, e *adj.* puffing; puffed, ample, full.

bouffarde *n.f.* short thick tobacco pipe.

bouffe *adj.* comic. *n.m.* comic opera singer; food.

bouffée *n.f.* puff, a whiff, a gust of wind. **une ~ de fumée,** a puff of smoke.

bouffer *v.i.* to puff, to swell, to rise (as bread); to bulge out. *Infml.* to eat, to guzzle.

bouffi, e *p.p.* puffed, swelled, puffy; bloated. **chair ~e,** puffy flesh. **être ~ de colère, de rage,** to be bursting with anger. **style ~,** inflated or turgid style.

bouffir *v.t.* to puff or swell.

bouffissure *n.f.* swelling, bloatedness, puffiness.

bouffon *n.m.* buffoon; fool, jester; **servir de ~,** to be the butt of a joke.

bouffon, onne *adj.* droll, funny, ludicrous, farcical.

buffonner *v.i.* to play the buffoon.

bouffonnerie *n.f.* buffoonery; practical joke.

bouge *n.m.* run-down place; sleazy bar.

bougeoir *n.m.* flat candlestick

bougeotte *n.f.* **avoir la ~,** to have the fidgets

bouger *v.i.* to move, to budge. **ne bougez pas de là,** do not move from there.

bougie *n.f.* candle; sparkplugs, *Surg.* probe.

bougonner *v.i.* to grumble; to scold.

bougre *n.m.* chap, fellow. **pauvre ~,** poor fellow. *Interj.* by Jove!

boui-boui *n.m.* greasy spoon.

bouillabaisse *n.f.* highly seasoned fish soup, bouillabaisse.

bouillant, e *adj.* boiling; scalding; impetuous, hotheaded. **eau ~e,** boiling water. **caractère ~,** fiery, impetuous temper.

bouille *n.f. fam.* face, mug.

bouillerie *n.f.* brandy distillery.

bouilleur *n.m.* distiller.

bouilli *p.p.* boiled. *n.m.* boiled beef.

bouillie *n.f.* baby food; hasty pudding; pulp (to make paper). **faire de la ~ pour les chats,** to waste one's efforts.

bouillir *v.i.* to boil. **faire ~,** to cause to boil, to boil. **cela fait ~ le pot,** that keeps the pot boiling.

bouilloire *n.f.* kettle, teakettle.

bouillon *n.m.* broth, stock. **~ de veau, de poulet,** veal broth, chicken broth. **une tasse de ~,** a cup of broth. **boire un ~,** to experience a heavy loss.

bouillonnant, e *adj.* bubbling, boiling.

bouillonnement *n.m.* ebullition; bubbling.

bouillonner *v.i.* to bubble up; to gush out; to boil over, to boil.

bouillotte *n.f.* kettle; (game at cards) bouillotte.

boulaie *n.f.* birch plantation.

boulangerère *n.m.f.* baker.

boulanger *v.t.* to bake, to make bread.

boulangerie *n.f.* bakery.

boule *n.f.* billiard ball, bowl. **cette ~ terrestre,** this earthly orb. **une ~ de neige,** a snowball. **~ de cristal,** crystal ball.

bouleau *h.m.* birch tree.

bouledogue *n.m.* bulldog.

boulet *n.m.* cannonball; fetlock joint (of horses). **être condamné au ~,** to be condemned to penal servitude with a ball and chain.

boulette *n.f.* croquette; meatball; blunder, mistake. **faire une ~,** to make a blunder.

boulevard *n.m.* boulevard.

bouleversant, e *adj.* overwhelming, astonishing.

bouleversement *n.m.* overthrow, wreck; turmoil, disorder; panic.

bouleverser *v.t.* to throw down, to overturn, to agitate, to upset, to destroy. **cela m'a tout bouleversé,** that has quite unbinged me. **se ~,** *v.refl.* to be turned upside down.

boulier *n.m.* a kind of fishing net.

boulimie *n.f.* bulimia.

boulimique *adj.* bulimic.

boulingrin *n.m.* bowling green; grass plot.

boulon *n.m.* bolt.

boulonner *v.t.* to bolt, to fasten together with bolts.

boulot *n.m.* job. **quel boulot!** what a tough job!

boulot, otte *adj.* dumpy. *n.* a dumpy person.

boulotten *v.t.* to stuff in, to tuck in (food).

bouquet *n.m.* cluster, bunch, bouquet; tuft. **un ~ de violettes,** a bouquet of violets. **ce vin a un ~ délicieux,** this wine has a delicious bouquet (or flavor). **voilà le ~,** to top it all off. **~ garni,** bouquet garni, herbal bouquet.

bouquetier *n.m.* flower vase.

bouquetière *n.f.* flower girl.

bouquetin *n.m.* wild goat, ibex.

bouquin *n.m.* secondhand book. **ce n'est qu'un ~,** it is a worthless old book. *Infml.* book.

bouquiner *v.i.* to hunt for old books.

bouquinerie *n.f.* old-book trade.

bouquineur *n.m.* book-hunter.

bouquiniste *n.m.* dealer in old books, esp. in stalls along the Seine in Paris.

bourbe *n.f.* mire, mud.

bourbeux, euse *adj.* muddy, miry.

bourbier *n.m.* slough, quagmire; scrape, mess. **tomber dans un ~,** to get into a scrape.

bourde *n.f.* fib; lie, falsehood.

bourder *v.i.* to fib, to hoax.

bourdeur *n.m.* fibber, liar.

bourdon *n.m.* bumblebee; drone; big bell; walking staff; *Typ.* omission, out.

bourdonnant, e *adj.* humming, buzzing.

bourdonnement *n.m.* humming, buzzing, buzz, hum.

bourdonner *v.i.* to hum, to buzz; to drone; to murmur; to ring (ears). *v.t.* to hum, to bore, to pester.

bourg *n.m.* market town.

bourgade *n.f.* small town.

bourgeois, e *n.m.f.* bourgeois, middle-class person. **un bon ~,** a worthy citizen. **les ~s et les ouvriers,** masters and men, the employers and the employed. *adj.* of or belonging to a citizen; substantial, valid; private; vulgar, unrefined. **maison ~e,** private house or residence. **cuisine ~e,** good plain cooking. **avoir l'air ~,** to look like a common person.

bourgeoisement *adv.* in a citizenlike manner, simply.

bourgeoisie *n.f.* middle class. **droits de ~,** freedom of a city.

bourgeon *n.m.* bud, shoot; pimple.

bourgeonné, e *adj.* pimpled, pimply; covered with pimples.

bourgeonnement *n.m.* budding time.

bourgeonner *v.i.* to bud, to shoot forth.

bourgeonnier *n.m.* bullfinch.

Bourgogne *n.f.* Burgundy. *n.m.* Burgundy wine.

bourlinguer *v.i.* to work hard, to drudge.

bournous *n.m.* burnous.

bourrache *n.f.* borage.

bourrade *n.f.* shove, push.

bourras *n.m.* coarse hemp cloth.

bourrasque *n.f.* squall; fit, outburst.

bourratif *adj. Infml.* stodgy.

bourre *n.f.* wad, stuffing.

bourreau *n.m.* executioner; hangman, brute, butcher.

bourreler *v.t.* to torment, to torture, to rack.

bourrelet *n.m.* weatherstripping; padding.

bourrelier *n.m.* saddler.

bourrellerie *n.f.* saddlery.

bourrer *v.t.* to fill, to stuff; to thrash, to abuse. **~ un enfant de grec et de latin,** to cram a boy with Greek and Latin. **se ~,** *v.refl.* to stuff oneself (with food, etc.).

bourriche *n.f.* basket, picnic basket.

bourrique *n.f.* donkey, stubborn person.

bourru, e *adj.* churlish, boorish, morose, surly; peevish, testy, waspish; raw, unfermented (as wine).

bourse *n.f.* purse, small bag; scholarship; stock exchange; *pl.* scrotum. **coupeur de ~,** thief. **tenir la ~,** to hold the pursestrings. **sans ~ delier,** without spending a penny. **la ~ ou la vie,** your money or your life. **le cours de la ~,** stock list. **une ~ entière,** full scholarship. **faire ~ à part,** each paying his own expenses. **faire ~ commune,** to share expenses.

boursicotage *n.m.* stock-market dabbling.

boursicoter *v.t.* to save little by little; to dabble in stocks.

boursier, ère *n.m.f.* pursemaker; speculator on the stock exchange; scholarship student. *adj.* pertaining to the stock exchange.

boursiller *v.i.* to collect money in common, to contribute.

boursouflage *n.m.* bombast, fustian.

boursouflé, e *adj.* inflated, swollen, swelled; turgid, bombastic. **ce gros ~,** that great bloated fellow.

boursoufler *v.t.* to swell; to puff up, to blister.

boursouflure *n.f.* swelling, puffiness, turgidness.

bousculade *n.m.* crush, jostling (as in a crowd).

bousculer *v.t.* to turn upside down, to tumble; to hustle, to jostle.

bouse *n.f.* cow dung.

bousillage *n.m.* mud wall; botched, bungled work.

bousiller *v.i.* to build with mud; to botch, to bungle.

bousilleur, euse *n.m.f.* botcher, bungler.

bousin *n.m.* noise, rumpus.

boussole *n.f.* compass, mariner's compass; guide, director.

bout *n.m.* end, tip; bit, scrap. **le mot qui est au ~ de la ligne,** the word at the end of the line. **je le sais sur le ~ des doigts,** I know it perfectly well. **c'est le ~ du monde,** it is the end of the world. **au ~ de huit jours,** in a week's time. **joindre les deux ~s,** to make ends meet. **le ~ de la langue,** the tip of the tongue. **montrer le ~ de l'oreille,** to show one's true colors. **brûler la chandelle par les deux ~s,** to be uneconomical. **une économie de ~ de chandelle,** paltry savings. **un ~ d'homme,** a bit of a man. **on ne sait par quel ~ le prendre,** one does not know how to take him. **a ~ portant,** point blank. **à bout,** at an end, exhausted. **être à ~,** to be worn out. **ma patience est à ~,** my patience is exhausted. **il met ma patience à ~,** he puts me out of patience. **venir à ~ de,** to overcome, to manage. **en viendrez-vous à ~?** will you be able to manage it? **bout à bout,** end to end. **d'un ~ à l'autre,** from beginning to end.

boutade *n.f.* sally; whim, caprice. **par ~,** by fits and starts.

boute-en-train *n.m.* lively person, life of the party.

bouteille *n.f.* bottle; bottleful. **~ de verre,** a glass bottle. **boucher, déboucher une ~,** to cork, uncork a bottle. **mettre en ~,** to bottle. **n'avoir rien vu que par le trou d'une ~,** to be ignorant of the world. **c'est la ~ à l'encre,** it is a very obscure affair.

bouter *v.t.* to put. *v.i.* to get ropy (as wine); to oust, to cast out.

boutique *n.f.* shop, stall. **~ bien garnie,** well-stocked shop. **tenir ~,** to have a shop.

boutiquier, ère *n.m.f.* shopkeeper, dealer.

boutoir *n.m.* snout (of a wild boar). **coup de ~,** cutting remark.

bouton *n.m.* bud, pimple, nipple, button, stud; knob (of door). **~ de rose,** rosebud. **~ d'or,** buttercup. **~ de chemise,** shirt button, stud.

boutonné, e *p.p.* pimpled; buttoned up; reserved.

boutonner *v.i.* to bud *v.t.* and *n.* to button. **se ~,** *v.refl.* to button one's coat; to button.

boutonnet *n.m.* small bud.

boutonnière *n.f.* buttonhole.

bouture *n.f.* Hort. cutting.
bouvier *n.m.* cow herd, ox driver.
bouvillon *n.m.* young steer.
bouvreuil *n.m.* bullfinch.
bovin, e *adj.* bovine.
boxe *n.f.* boxing.
boxer *v.t.* and *n.* to box.
boxeur *n.m.* boxer; pugilist.
boyau *n.m.* gut, bowel, hose, branch. **corde à ~,** catgut.
boycottage *n.m.* boycott.
boycotter *v.t.* to boycott.
bracelet *n.m.* bracelet.
brachial, e *adj.* brachial.
braconnage *n.m.* poaching.
braconner *v.i.* to poach.
braconnier *n.m.* poacher.
brader *v.t.* to undersell.
braderie *n.f.* clearance sale.
braguette *n.f.* fly (trousers).
brahmane *n.m.* Brahmin.
brahmanique *adj.* brahminical.
brahmanisme *n.m.* brahminism.
braillard, e *adj.* brawling, bawling, squalling. *n.* brawler.
brailler *v.i.* to bawl, to shout; to brawl.
brailleur, euse *adj.* bawling; squalling; brawling. *n.m.f.* bawler; squaller; brawler.
braiement *n.m.* braying (of an ass).
braire *v.i.* to bray.
braise *n.f.* smoldering embers, live coals.
braiser *v.t.* to braise.
braisière *n.f.* braising pan
bran *n.m.* bran; excrement.
brancard *n.m.* stretcher, litter; shafts (of a cart).
brancardier *n.m.* litter bearer.
branchage *n.m.* branches, boughs.
branche *n.f.* branch, arm. **à ~,** branched. **~s gourmandes,** shoot rising from an underground stem or root. **s'accrocher à toutes les ~s,** to have recourse to all sorts of expedients.
brancher *v.i.* to branch off; to plug in.
branchial, e *adj.* branchial.
branchies *n.f.pl.* branchiae; gills of fishes.
brandade *n.f.* brandade, a Provençal dish of cod.
brande *n.f.* heath.
brandebourg *n.m.* braid on a uniform.
brandillement *n.m.* swinging, swaying or shaking about.
brandiller *v.t.* and *v.i.* to swing or shake about.
brandir *v.t.* to brandish; to flourish.
brandon *n.m.* wisp; firebrand. **~ de discorde,** firebrand, mischiefmaker.
branlant, e *adj.* shaking, tottering.
branle *n.m.* swinging, swing; swinging, swaying or rocking motion. **le ~ d'une cloche,** the ringing of a bell. **être en ~,** to be in motion.
branle-bas *n.m.* pandemonium. *Naut.* clearing (for action); **~!** clear the decks!
branler *v.t.* and *v.i.* to swing; to shake, to wag; to

brandish. **~ dans le manche,** to fit loosely in the handle; to be shaky.
branloire *n.m.* seesaw.
braque *n.m.* Zool. French pointer; mad-cap. *adj.* giddy, harebrained, crazy.
braquement *n.m.* pointing, leveling, aiming (of guns, etc.).
braquer *v.t.* to point (a gun or telescope); to level.
bras *n.m.* arm; power, hand. **à ~ tendu,** with outstretched arm, at arm's length. **frapper à ~ raccourci,** to strike or hit with all one's might. **donner, offrir le ~,** to give, to offer one's arm. **recevoir à ~ ouverts,** to receive with open arms. **avoir les ~ longs,** to have extensive influence. **siège à ~,** armchair. **être le ~ droit de quelqu'un,** to be a person's right hand. **des ~ inutiles,** useless hands. **les ~ manquent,** there is a labor shortage. **avoir beaucoup d'affaires sur les ~,** to have many things going on. **moulin à ~,** handmill. **voiture à ~,** handcart. **à tour de ~,** with all one's strength. **à ~ le-corps,** around the waist. **il le prit à ~ le-corps,** he seized him around the waist. **~-dessus, ~-dessous,** arm-in-arm.
braser *v.t.* to braze.
brasero *n.m.* brazier.
brasier *n.m.* clear bright fire; passion, flame; chafing dish.
brasillement *n.m.* glittering of the sea.
brasiler *v.t.* to braize. *v.i.* to sparkle (as the sea); to grill or broil.
brassage *n.m.* mixing, mashing (of malt); brewing.
brassard *n.m.* armband.
brasse *n.f.* the French fathom, six feet; breaststroke (in swimming).
brassée *n.f.* armful; breaststroke (in swimming).
brasser *v.t.* to mix, to stir up; to mash, to brew. **se ~,** *v.refl.* to be brewing
brasserie *n.f.* brewery; tavern.
brasseur, euse *n.m.f.* brewer.
brassière *n.f.* shoulder strap. **~ de sauvetage,** life jacket.
brasure *n.f.* brazing; soldering.
bravache *n.m.* hector, bully.
bravacherie *n.f.* bullying, blustering.
bravade *n.f.* bravado, bragging, blustering.
brave *adj.* brave, bold, valiant; showy, smart; kind, obliging. **il est ~ comme l'épée qu'il porte,** he is brave as the sword he wears. **il n'est ~ qu'en paroles,** he is brave only in words. **c'est un homme ~,** he is a brave man. **c'est un ~ homme,** he is a worthy man, an honest fellow.
bravement *adj.* bravely, gallantly, courageously; ably, finely.
braver *v.t.* to brave, to defy, to face, to encounter fearlessly. **il alla le ~ jusque chez lui,** he went and defied him even in his own house. **~ l'autorité,** to brave authority, or the authorities.
bravo *Interj.* bravo!

bravoure n.f. bravery; valor, gallantry, courage.

brebis n.f. ewe; sheep. ~ **galeuse**, black sheep. **la ~ du bon Dieu**, the faithful. **faire un repas de ~**, to make a dry meal, to eat without drinking.

brèche n.f. gap, breach. **battre en ~**, to batter in, to breach. **cela fait ~ à sa fortune**, that makes a hole in his fortune.

brèche-dent adj. gap-toothed.

brechet n.m. breastbone, brisket.

bredi-breda adv. hastily.

brédissure n.f. Med. lockjaw.

bredouillage n.m. sputtering, spluttering.

bredouille n.f. lurch. **revenir ~**, to return sheepish.

bredouillement n.m. spluttering, stammering.

bredouiller v.i. to splutter, to stutter.

bredouilleur, euse n.m.f. splutterer, stammerer.

bref, brève adj. brief, short, curt, quick, concise. **à ~ délai**, at short notice. **être ~**, to be brief. adv. in short, briefly. n.m. brief (Pope's pastoral letter); church calendar.

brelan n.m. brelan (a game played with three cards); gambling house.

breloque n.f. trinket; charm.

Brésil n.m. Geog. Brazil; Brazil.

Bretagne n.f. Geog. Brittany. **La Grande ~**, Great Britain.

bretelle n.f. strap, suspender. **une paire de ~s**, a pair of suspenders. **il en a jusqu'aux ~s**, he is in great difficulties, in a terrible scrape.

bretteler v.t. to cut stones with toothed instruments; to chase (gold or silver plate).

bretteur n.m. fighter, fighting man, bully.

breuvage n.m. beverage; drink.

brève n.f. short syllable; Mus. breve, double whole note.

brevet n.m. patent; certificate, diploma. **~ d'invention**, patent for an invention.

brevetable adj. patentable, liable to be patented.

breveté, e p.p. patented; appointed by letters patent. n.m.f. patentee.

breveter v.t. to patent, to license.

bréviaire n.m. breviary.

bribe n.f. pl. scraps, leavings (of meals).

bric-à-brac n.m. odds and ends, curiosities.

bricolage n.m. pottering, do-it-yourself repairs.

bricole n.f. ~s, this and that, things. **de ~, par ~**, indirectly, unexpectedly.

bricoler v.i. to do odd jobs.

bride n.f. bridle; reins; curb. check; restraint; string (of bonnet); loop (for a button). **mettre une ~ à un cheval**, to put a bridle on a horse. **serrer la ~**, to hold in (or rein in). **lâcher la ~**, to loose the rein. **tourner la ~**, to turn back. **courir à ~ abattue**, to run full speed.

brider v.t. to bridle; to fasten, to curb, to keep under, to restrain.

brie n.m. Brie cheese.

brief, ève adj. curt, brief, short.

brièvement adv. briefly.

brièveté n.f. brevity, shortness, briefness; conciseness, succinctness.

brigade n.f. brigade; gang (of workmen).

brigadier n.m. corporal (of cavalry); Naut. bowman.

brigand n.m. ruffian, brigand, bandit.

brigandage n.m. brigandage; robbery, plunder.

brigander v.i. to rob, to plunder.

brigue n.f. intrigue; faction.

briguer v.t. to intrigue, to solicit ~ **les honneurs**, to aspire to for honors.

brigueur, euse n.m.f. petitioner, solicitor, suitor; candidate.

brillamment adv. brilliantly, glitteringly; splendidly.

brillance n.f. brightness, brilliance.

brillant, e adj. brilliant, shining, glittering, sparkling; beaming, showy; dazzling. **tout ~ d'or**, all glittering with gold. **des yeux ~s**, sparkling eyes. **un ~ avenir**, a brilliant future. n.m. brilliance, brightness; luster, splendor, brilliant (diamond). **faux ~s**, imitation diamonds.

brillanté, e p.p. dimity.

brillanter v.t. to cut (a diamond) as a brilliant.

brifler v.i. to shine, to beam, to radiate; to glitter, to glisten, to sparkle. **le soleil brille**, the sun shines.

brimade n.m. hazing; victimization.

brimer v.t. to play tricks on, to haze.

brin n.m. blade, slip; sprig, spray, shoot; bit, jot. **c'est un beau ~ d'homme**, he is a tall well-made man. **un ~ d'herbe**, a blade of grass. **un ~ de romarin**, a sprig of rosemary.

brinde n.f. toast, health. **porter des ~s**, to propose toasts.

brindille n.f. sprig, twig.

brio n.m. pep, spirit, brio.

brioche n.f. brioche (sort of bun); blunder, mistake. **quelle ~!** what a blunder!

briquaillons n.m. pl. brickbats, broken bricks.

brique n.f. brick. ~ **réfractaire**, fire brick.

briquet n.m. lighter. **battre le ~**, to strike a light.

briquetage n.m. brickwork; imitation brickwork.

briqueter v.t. to brick.

briqueterie n.f. brickmaking; brickyard.

briquetier n.m. brickmaker.

briquette n.f. charcoal briquette.

bris n.m. breaking; breaking open (a door, etc.).

brisant n.m. sandbank, reef, shoal; pl. breakers (waves).

brise n.f. breeze.

brisé, e p.p. broken, shattered. **voix ~e**, tremulous voice. ~ **par les souffrances**, bowed down by suffering. **porte ~e**, folding doors. **chaise ~e**, folding chair.

brise-cou n.m. daredevil.

brisées n.f. pl. scattered boughs; traces, footsteps. **suivre les ~s de quelqu'un**, to follow in a person's track. **revenir sur ses ~s**, to retrace one's steps.

brise-glace n.m. icebreaker (boat).

brise-lames *n.m.* breakwater.

brisement *n.m.* breaking. **~ de coeur** contrition of heart.

brise-mottes *n.m.* harrow.

briser *v.t.* to break, to shatter, to smash, to crush, to ruin, to destroy. **~ son avenir**, to ruin one's prospects. **je suis brisé**, I am sore all over. *v.i.* to break (as waves against rocks). **se ~**, *v.refl.* to break to pieces, to be smashed, to snap.

brise-tout *n.m.* person who breaks everything, clumsy person.

briseur *n.m.* breaker. **les ~s d'images**, the iconoclasts.

brise-vent *n.m.* windbreak.

brisoir *n.m.* brake (for flax and hemp).

brisure *n.f.* break; fold.

broc *n.m.* jug, pitcher, jugful. **de bric et de ~**, by hook or by crook.

brocantage *n.m.* broker's trade; dealing in secondhand goods, etc.

brocanter *v.i.* to buy and sell secondhand goods.

brocanteur, euse *n.m.f.* broker, dealer in secondhand goods.

brocard *n.m.* scoff, sneer, taunt.

brocarder *v.t.* and *n.* to to scoff, to sneer, to taunt.

brocardeur, euse *n.m.f.* scoffer, sneerer, taunter.

brocart *n.m.* brocade.

brocatelle *n.f.* brocade fabric.

brochage *n.m.* sewing, stitching (of books).

broche *n.f.* spit (for roasting); knitting needle; spindle, spigot; skewer; broch. **à la ~**, spit-roasted.

broché, e *p.p.* brocaded; paperback.

brochée *n.f.* spitful (of meat).

brocher *v.t.* to stitch; to brocade.

brochet *n.m.* pike (fish).

brochette *n.f.* skewer, spit for roasting.

brochure *n.f.* pamphlet, brochure.

brocoli *n.m.* broccoli.

brodé, e *p.p.* embroidered.

broder *v.t.* to embroider; to embellish, to exaggerate (a narrative).

broderie *n.f.* embroidery; embellishment, exaggeration.

brodeur, euse *n.m.f.* embroiderer; embellisher (of a story), etc.).

broncher *v.i.* to react, respond.

bronches *n.f. pl.* bronchia, bronchial tubes.

bronchique *adj.* bronchial.

bronze *n.m.* bronze; *Fig.* iron, steel.

bronzé, e *p.p.* bronzed, suntanned.

bronzer *v.t.* to bronze, to brown, to suntan.

brosse *n.f.* brush. **~ à habits**, clothes brush. **~ à cheveux**, hairbrush. **~ à dents**, toothbrush.

brossé, e *p.p.* brushed; thrashed, drubbed. *n.f.* brushing; beating, drubbing.

brosser *v.t.* to brush; to thrash, to drub. **se ~**, *v.refl.* to brush oneself.

brou *n.m.* walnut shell; husk.

brouée *n.f.* mist, fog.

brouet *n.m.* broth.

brouette *n.f.* wheelbarrow, barrow.

brouettée *n.f.* barrowful.

brouetter *v.t.* to wheel in a barrow.

brouhaha *n.m.* cheers; uproar hullabaloo. **quel ~!** what an uproar!

brouillage *n.m.* interference, jamming (radio).

brouillamini *n.m.* muddle, confusion.

brouillard *n.m.* fog, mist, haze

brouillasser *v.i.* to be misty or foggy.

brouille *n.f.* disagreement, discord, variance.

brouillé, e *p.p.* mingled, mixed; embroiled, confused. **des oeufs ~s**, scrambled eggs. **être ~ avec quelqu'un**, to have quarreled with a person.

brouillement *n.m.* mixing, mingling.

brouiller *v.t.* to mix, to beat (as eggs); to jumble, to throw into confusion; to embroil; to shuffle **~ les cartes**, to shuffle the cards. *v.i.* to blunder, to bungle, to fumble; to make mischief, to cause trouble. **se ~**, *v.refl.* to become confused, perplexed, embroiled; to quarrel. **ma mémoire se brouille**, my memory gets confused.

brouillerie *n.f.* disagreement, misunderstanding, quarrel, falling out.

brouillon, onne *adj.* meddlesome, meddling, mischief-making; bungling. *n.m.f.* meddler, mischief-maker, busybody, blunderer. *n.m.* first (or rough) draft (of a writing); scratch paper.

brouir *v.t.* to blast, to blight.

brouissure *n.f.* blight.

broussaille *n.f.* brushwood, underwood; briars.

broutant, e *adj.* browsing.

brouter *v.t.* and *n.* to browse, to nibble grass or the shoots of trees.

broutilles *n.f. pl.* young shoots (of trees, etc.); knickknacks, trifles.

broyer *v.t.* to pound, to grind, to pulverize, to crush, to bray (ink).

broyeur *n.m.* pounder, grinder; hemp dresser. **un broyeur de noir**, a sad sack.

bru *n.f.* daughter-in-law.

bruant *n.m.* yellow-hammer; *Ornith.* bunting.

brucelles *n.f. pl.* pliers, tweezers.

brugnon *n.m.* nectarine.

bruine *n.f.* drizzle, drizzling, rain.

bruiner *v.i. impers.* **Il bruine**, it's drizzling.

bruire *v.i. defect.* to rustle; to sigh (wind); to murmur; to rattle.

bruissement *n.m.* rustling noise; roaring; buzzing, humming.

bruit *n.m.* noise; din, rattle, clatter, report (of a gun); slam (of a door); crack (of a whip); riot, commotion. **faire du ~**, to make a noise. **sans ~**, quietly. **vivre loin du ~**, to live in peace and quiet. **faire plus de ~ que de besogne**, to make more noise than work. **~s de Bourse**, stock-exchange rumors. **un faux ~**, a false rumor. **beaucoup de ~ pour rien,** much ado about nothing. **à grand ~,** noisily, loudly.

bruitage *n.m.* sound effects.

bruiter *v.t.* to make sound effects.

brûlant, e *adj.* burning, scorching, fervent, ardent, glowing.

brûlé, e *p.p.* burned, burnt; burning; sunburned, tanned. *n.m.* burn, burning. **cela sent le ~,** it smells like something burning.

brûle-gueule *n.m.* short pipe.

brûle-pourpoint *adv.* in the face, straight out.

brûler *v.t.* to burn; to inflame, to consume; to cauterize; to scorch; to dry up. **~ l'encens devant,** to burn incense before, to flatter. **~ de fond en comble,** to burn to the ground. **~ du café,** to roast coffee. **~ la cervelle à quelqu'un,** to blow out a person's brains. *v.i.* to burn, to be on fire, to be inflamed. **la tête lui brûle,** his head is burning hot. **se ~,** *v.refl.* to burn oneself; to be burnt *or* scorched.

brûlerie *n.f.* distillery.

brûle-tout *n.m.* save-all.

brûleur, euse *n.m.f.* arsonist.

brûlot *n.m.* flare; fireship; burnt brandy.

brûlure *n.f.* burn; scald.

brumaire *n.m.* Brumaire; the second month of the French Republican calendar (from Oct. 23rd to Nov. 21st).

brumasser *v.t.* to be hazy or misty.

brume *n.f.* mist, fog.

brumeux, euse *adj.* foggy, misty.

brun *adj. n.m.f.* brown, dark. *n.m.* brown (the color); dark man. **~ foncé,** dark brown.

brunâtre *adj.* brownish.

brune, *n.f.* dusk. **une petite ~,** a little dark-haired woman.

brunet, te *n.m.f.* brown-haired boy or girl.

brunir *v.t.* to brown, to bronze, to darken; to burnish; to polish (gold, etc.). *v.i.* to become brown *or* tanned. **se ~,** *v.refl.* to become dark, to be burnished.

brunissage *n.m.* burnishing, polishing.

brunisseur, euse *n.m.f.* burnisher.

brunissoir *n.m.* burnisher.

brunissure *n.f.* burnishing (of metals).

brusque *adj.* blunt, abrupt, unexpected.

brusquement *adv.* bluntly, roughly, harshly; abruptly.

brusquer *v.t.* to treat rudely, harshly; to offend.

brusquerie *n.f.* abruptness, bluntness, rudeness.

brut, e *adj.* brute, brutish, rough, rude; raw, crude, uncultivated; *Comm.* gross. **un diamant ~,** a rough (*or* uncut) diamond. **matière ~e,** raw material. **fer ~,** crude iron. **produit ~,** gross proceeds (of a farm, business, etc.). **recette ~e,** gross receipts. **poids ~,** gross weight.

brutal, e *adj.* brutal; surly, bearish. *n.m.* brute, brutal person.

brutalement *adv.* brutishly; brutally; cruelly.

brutaliser *v.t.* to treat brutally, to maltreat, to ill-treat.

brutalité *n.f.* brutishness, brutality; ill-treatment. **faire une ~,** to do a brutal action.

brute *n.f.* brute; stupid person.

bruyamment *adv.* noisily, clamorously, obstreperously.

bruyant, e *adj.* noisy; clamorous; boisterous, blustering.

bruyère *n.f.* heath, heather, moor. **coq de ~,** grouse.

buanderie *n.f.* laundry, laundromat.

buandier, ère *n.m.f.* washerman, launderer, bleacher.

bube *n.f.* pimple.

buccal, e *adj.* buccal, mouth.

bûche *n.f.* log, blockhead, thickhead, dolt. **~ de Noël,** Yule log; rich log-shaped pastry Christmas Eve. **cet homme est une vraie ~,** that man is a thorough blockhead.

bûcher *n.m.* funeral pyre, stake. *v.t.* to hew; to cut away. *v.i.* to cram (for an exam); to hammer away.

bûcheron *n.m.* woodcutter, lumberjack.

bûchette *n.f.* twig.

bucolique *adj.* bucolic. *n.f.* bucolic or pastoral poetry.

budget *n.m.* budget. **~ de l'Etat,** State budget. **~ d'un ménage,** household expenses.

budgétaire *adj.* budgetary.

buée *n.f.* steam on windowpanes, condensation.

buffet *n.m.* cupboard, sideboard; refreshment room.

buffle *n.m.* buffalo.

bugle *n.f. Bot.* bugle.

buis *n.m.* boxwood. **le ~ nain,** dwarf box. **~ piquant,** butcher's broom.

buisson *n.m.* bush; thicket.

buissonneux, euse *adj.* bushy.

bulbe *n.m. Bot.* bulb.

bulbeux, euse *adj.* bulbous.

bulbifère *adj.* bulbiferous.

bulbiforme *adj.* bulbiform.

Bulgarie *n.f.* Bulgaria.

bulle *n.f.* bubble; *Med.* blister; bead (of glass); bull (pope's). **~ de savon,** soap bubble. *adj.* and *n.m.* **papier ~,** brown wrapping paper.

bulletin *n.m.* bulletin; report card (school).

bure *n.f.* homespun, cowl.

bureau *n.m.* desk, bureau; office; board. **aller au ~,** to go to work, to the office. **~ de placement,** unemployment office.

bureaucrate *n.m.* bureaucrat.

bureaucratie *n.f.* bureaucracy.

burette *n.f.* cruet; oilcan (for machines).

burgau *n.m.* mother-of-pearl oyster.

burin *n.m.* graver; dentist's drill.

buriner *v.t.* to engrave.

burlesque *adj.* burlesque. *n.m.* burlesque.

burlesquement *adv.* in a burlesque manner, ludicrously.

burnous *n.m.* burnous.

bursal, e *adj.* fiscal.

bus *n.m.* abbreviation of **autobus**, bus.

buse *n.f.* buzzard; dunce, dolt.

busqué, e *p.p.* hooked.

buste *n.m.* bust. **un ~ de plâtre**, a plaster bust.

bustier *n.m.* strapless brassiere or blouse.

but *n.m.* goal, mark, aim, object, purpose, design; base (baseball). **frapper le ~**, to hit the mark. **manquer son ~**, to miss one's mark. **pour parvenir à ce ~**, to attain this end. **~ à ~**, upon a par, evenly. **nous sommes ~ à ~**, we are even. **de ~ en blanc**, point-blank. **tirer de ~ en blanc**, to fire point-blank.

buté, ~e *adj.* stubborn, dead set.

butée *n.f.* abutment, pier.

buter *v.i.* to hit (the mark); to stumble at; to aim at. *v.t.* to butt; to push, to run against; to prop up; to buttress (a wall). **se ~**, *v.refl.* to

butin *n.m.* booty; prey; pillage, plunder.

butiner *v.t.* to spoil, to plunder. *v.t.* to despoil.

butoir *n.m.* buffer (railway); doorstop.

butorde *n.f.* stupid girl or woman.

butte *n.f.* knoll, hillock, rising ground; butt. **être en ~ à**, to be the butt of.

buttée *n.f.* V. BUTÉE.

butter *v.t.* to bank, to raise up earth in a mound around (a tree, etc.); to stumble.

butyrique *adj.* butyric. **acide ~**, butyric acid.

buvable *adj.* drinkable.

buvant, e *adj.* drinking.

buvard *n.m.* blotting paper.

buvetier *n.m.* tavern keeper.

buvette *n.f.* refreshment room (train station).

buveur, euse *n.m.f.* drinker.

buvoter *v.i.* to sip; to tipple.

Byzantin, e *adj.* Byzantine.

C

c *n.m.* C; the third letter of the alphabet.

çà *adv.* here. **~ et là**, here and there.

ça *pron.* (contraction of **cela**) that. **c'est ~**, that is it. **comme ~**, like that. **comment ~?** how is that?

cabale *n.f.* cabala, cabal.

cabaliste *n.m.* cabalist.

cabalistique *adj.* cabalistics.

caban *n.m.* car coat, pea jacket.

cabane *n.f.* cabin, shack, shed. **en ~**, behind bars. *Infml.* **~ à lapins**, rabbit hutch.

cabanon *n.m.* small cabin.

cabaret *n.m.* tavern.

cabaretier, ère *n.m.f.* landlord, landlady of a tavern.

cabas *n.m.* basket, drum (for fruit); shopping bag.

cabestan *n.m.* capstan.

cabillaud *n.m.* codfish, cod.

cabine *n.f. Naut.* cabin; airplane cockpit. **~ téléphonique**, phone booth.

cabinet *n.m.* closet; study, cabinet, office. **~ de toilette**, toilet. **~ d'étude, de travail**, study room.

câblage *n.m.* cable TV installation; wiring; twisting together, cabling.

câble *n.m.* cable; **~ d'amarrage**, mooring line. **télévision par ~**, cable TV.

câbler *v.t.* to link up with cable network, to wire for cable.

caboche *n.f. Infml.* noggin, head; hobnail (for shoes).

cabochon *n.m.* stud nail. **~ à carafe**, stopper. *Infml.* noggin, head.

cabosser *v.t.* to dent.

cabot *n.m.* dog, mutt. *Ichth.* bullhead. *Infml.* ham actor.

cabotage *n.m. Naut.* coasting. **vaisseau de ~**, coast vessel.

caboter *v.i.* to coast.

caboteur *n.m. Naut.* coaster, tramp steamer.

cabotin *n.m.* ham actor.

cabotinage *n.m.* playacting, showing off.

cabrer (se) *v.refl.* to rear, to revolt, to rebel.

cabri *n.m.* kid; young goat.

cabriole *n.f.* caper; somersaults.

cabrioler *v.i.* to caper.

cabriolet *n.m.* cabriolet.

cabus *adj. m.* headed (cabbage).

caca *n.m. Infml.* **faire ~**, to excrete.

cacao *n.m.* cocoa, chocolate.

cacahouète *n.f.* peanut.

cacaoté, ée *adj.* cocoa-flavored.

cacaotier *n.m.* cocoa tree (or plant).

cacatoès *n.m.* cockatoo.

cachalot *n.m.* sperm whale.

cache *n.f.* hiding place; *Phot.* mask.

caché, e *p.p.* hidden; secret. **douleurs ~es**, secret griefs.

cache-cache *n.m.* hide-and-seek (a game).

cachemire *n.m.* cashmere (scarf).

cache-nez *n.m.* muffler, scarf.

cache-pot *n.m.* ornamental flowerpot.

cacher *v.t.* to hide, to secrete. **~ son jeu**, not to show one's cards. **il ne cache rien**, he has no secrets. **se ~**, *v.refl.* to hide oneself.

cacher, ère *adj.* kosher.

cachet *n.m.* seal; stamp; ticket. **~ de la poste**, postmark, stamp; *Pharm.* tablet.

cacheter *v.t.* to seal; to close.

cachette *n.f.* hiding place. **en ~**, in secret, secretly.

cachot *n.m.* dungeon, cell.

cachotterie *n.f.* secrecy.

cachottier, ère *n.m.f.* secretive person.

cacique *n.m.* big shot.

cacochyme *adj.* doddering.

cacophonie *n.f.* cacophony.

cactus *n.m.* cactus.

cadastrer *v.t.* to survey, to register.

cadavéreux, euse *adj.* cadaverous; corpselike.

cadavre *n.m.* corpse, cadaver.

cadeau *n.m.* present, gift.

cadenas *n.m.* padlock.

cadenasser *v.t.* to padlock.

cadence *n.f.* cadence, rate, rhythm.

cadencé, e *adj.* rhythmical.

cadencer *v.t.* to cadence, to give rhythm to.

cadet, ette *adj.* younger, youngest. *Infml.* **le ~ de mes soucis,** the least of my worries; *Mil.* student officer.

cadrage *n.m. Cinem. Phot.* centering.

cadran *n.m.* dial; face (of a clock or watch). **~ solaire,** sundial.

cadrature *n.m.f. Clock.* dial train, dial work.

cadre *n.m.* frame (of a picture); setting, surrounding; manager, executive. **~ d'emballage,** packing case; space, box. **n'écrivez pas dans ce ~,** do not write in this space. **quel ~ magnifique!** what a magnificent setting! **être dans le ~ d'un accord,** to be within the scope of an agreement.

cadrer *v.i.* to square; *Cinem. Phot.* to center.

cadreur *n.m.* cameraman.

caduc, caduque *adj.* decaying, null and void, obsolete.

caducée *n.m.* caduceus; wand.

caecum *n.m.* caecum.

cafard, e *n.m.* cockroach; hypocrite; sneak, squealer. *Infml.* **avoir le ~,** to have the blues.

cafardage *n.m. Infml.* gossiping, sneaking.

cafarder *v.t. Infml.* to tell tales on.

cafardeur, ~euse *n.m. Infml.* sneak.

cafardeux, ~euse *adj. Infml.* feeling blue, dejected.

café *n.m.* coffee; café.

caféier *n.m.* coffee tree.

caféière *n.f.* coffee plantation.

caféine *n.f.* caffeine.

cafetan *n.m.* caftan.

cafétéria *n.m.* cafeteria.

cafetier *n.m.* café owner.

cafetière *n.f.* coffeepot.

cafre *adj.* and *n.m.f.* kafir.

cafouillage *n.m. Infml.* muddle, bungle.

cafouiller *v.t. Infml.* to flounder, to go wrong, to be in shambles.

cafouilleur, euse, cafouilleux, ~euse *n.m.* muddler, botcher.

cage *n.f.* cage; coop, for poultry; case. **~ d'escalier,** staircase. **~ d'ascenseur,** elevator shaft.

cageot *n.m.* crate, hamper (fruits, vegetables).

cagibi *n.m.* storage room.

cagneux, euse *adj.* knock-kneed.

cagnotte *n.f.* kitty, nest egg.

cagot, ote *n.m.f.* bigot.

cagoule *n.f.* hood.

cahier *n.m.* exercise book, copybook; notebook.

cahin-caha *adv.* so-so, poorly.

cahot *n.m.* jolt; *Fig.* ups and downs.

cahotant, e *adj.* jolting bumpy.

cahotement *n.m.* jolting, bumping.

cahoter *v.t.* to jolt; to toss.

cahoteux, euse *adj.* bumpy.

cahute *n.f.* hut, shack.

caïd *n.m.* big shot.

caillasse *n.f.* gravel, pebbles.

caille *n.f. Orn.* quail.

caillement *n.m.* curdling; clotting.

cailler *v.t.* to curdle, to clot.

caillette *n.f.* rennet; abomasum.

caillot *n.m.* clot.

caillou *n.m.* flint, pebble.

cailloutage *n.m.* pebblework.

caillouter *v.t.* to gravel.

caillouteux, euse *adj.* pebbly, flinty.

cailloutis *n.m.* **en ~,** macadamized.

caïman *n.m.* cayman; American crocodile.

Caire, Le *n.m.* Cairo.

caisse *n.f.* case (of wine); box; a drum; crate (for glass, earthenware, etc.); cash box; till, coffer, safe; fund. **allez à la ~, et vous serez payé,** go to the cashier (or the cashier's office), and you will be paid. **livre de ~,** cash book. **~ d'amortissement,** sinking fund. **~ d'épargne** savings bank. **grosse ~,** big drum, body (of coach, etc.).

caissette *n.f.* small box.

caissier *n.m.f.* cashier, teller, bank clerk.

caisson *n.m.* caisson, ammunition wagon; box, crate, case.

cajoler *v.t.* to cajole, to wheedle, to coax, to baby.

cajolerie *n.f.* cajolery.

cajoleur, euse *n.m.f.* cajoler, wheedler.

cajou *n.m.* cashew nut.

cake *n.m.* fruitcake.

cal *n.m.* callosity; callus.

calage *n.m.* wedging, steadying, choking, locking, keying.

calamar *n.m.* squid.

calamine *n.f.* calamine; carbon deposit.

calaminer (se) *v.t.* to carbon up.

calamité *n.f.* calamity.

calamiteux, euse *adj.* calamitous.

calandre *n.f. Auto.* radiator grill.

calandrer *v.t.* to calender; to mangle (laundry).

calangue *n.f.* creek.

calcaire *adj.* calcareous. *n.m.* limestone.

calcanéum *n.m.* calcaneum; heel bone.

calcification *n.f.* calcification.

calcifier *v.t.* to calcify.

calcination *n.f.* calcination, calcining.

calciner *v.t.* to calcine **se ~,** *v.refl.* to calcine.

calcium *n.m.* calcium.

calcul *n.m.* calculation, computation, estimate, calculus (stone).

calculable *adj.* calculable.

calculateur, trice *adj.* calculating.

calculatrice n.f. calculator, pocket calculator.
calculer v.t. to calculate.
cale n.f. wedge. ~ **de quai,** slip.
calé adj. steady; jammed; Infml. bright, clever.
calebasse n.f. calabash; gourd.
calèche n.f. barouche, open carriage.
caleçon n.m. undershorts (men's), trunks, drawers.
calembour n.m. play on words, pun.
calembredaine n.f. silly joke, nonsense.
calendrier n.m. calendar.
calepin n.m. notebook.
caler v.t. Naut. to draw; to steady with a wedge; to stall (vehicle.) ~ **sa tête sur l'oreiller,** to prop up one's head on a pillow; ~ **son estomac,** to fill oneself up; **se** ~, to prop oneself.
calfat n.m. caulker.
calfatage n.m. caulking.
calfater v.t. to caulk.
calfeutrage n.m. stopping up (of cracks), listing (of doors).
calfeutrer v.t. to stop up (doors or windows). **se** ~, to keep oneself warm.
calibrage n.m. calibrating, measuring; gauging, grading.
calibre n.m. caliber; size, diameter; grade (eggs, fruits).
calibrer v.t. to measure the caliber of, to gauge.
calice n.m. chalice; calyx, cup (of flower). **boire le** ~, to drink the cup; to swallow the pill.
calicot n.m. calico.
califat n.m. caliphate.
calife n.m. caliph.
califourchon n.m. **à** ~, astride, astraddle.
câlin, e adj. cuddly, cuddlesome. n.m. cuddle.
câliner v.t. to cuddle. **se faire** ~, to be petted.
câlinerie n.f. tenderness.
calleux, euse adj. callous, hard, indurated, horny.
calligraphe n.m. calligrapher.
calligraphie n.f. calligraphy, penmanship.
calligraphier v.t. to write beautifully.
calligraphique adj. calligraphic.
callosité n.f. callosity, callousness.
calmant, e adj. sedating, tranquilizing, painkilling. n.m. sedative, tranquilizer, painkiller.
calmar n.m. squid.
calme adj. calm, quiet, tranquil; dull. **les affaires sont** ~**s,** business is slow. n.m. calm, quietness, stillness; calmness, ~ **plat,** dead calm. **le** ~ **de la nuit,** the stillness of night.
calmement adv. calmly, quietly.
calmer v.t. to calm, to cool. to appease, to pacify, to quiet; to soothe, to allay. **se** ~, v.refl. to calm oneself, to become calm, quiet, or composed. **calmez-vous,** calm down. **la douleur s'est calmée,** the pain has been eased.
calomel n.m. calomel.
calomniateur, trice n.m.f. calumniator; slanderer.

calomnie n.f. calumny, slander.
calomnier v.t. to calumniate, to slander.
calomnieusement adv. calumniously, slanderously.
calomnieux, euse adj. calumnious, slanderous, libellous.
calorie n.f. calorie.
calorifique adj. calorific.
calorifuge adj. heat-insulating, heat-retaining; fireproof.
calorifugeage n.m. lagging, insulating (pipes).
calorifuger v.t. to lag, to insulate (pipes).
calorimètre n.m. calorimeter.
calorimétrie n.f. calorimetry.
calorique n.m. caloric, heat.
calot n.m. garrison cap; large marble.
calotin n.m. Infml. churchgoer.
calotte n.f. calotte (priest's); skullcap. **l'influence de la** ~, priestly influence; the skull; Infml. box on the ear. **donner une** ~, to clout on the ear.
calotter v.t. to box the ears.
calquage n.m. tracing.
calque n.m. tracing.
calquer v.t. to trace (a drawing), to copy by tracing.
calter v.t. to scram, to clear out.
calumet n.m. calumet, pipe.
calvaire n.m. Calvary; Mount Calvary, crucifix; suffering, sore burden.
calvinisme n.m. Calvinism.
calviniste n.m.f. Calvinist.
calvitie n.f. baldness.
camaïeu n.m. cameo; Paint. monochrome.
camail n.m. camail.
camarade n.m.f. comrade; companion; mate, fellow; chum. ~ **de classe,** classmate. ~ **d'école,** schoolmate. ~ **de voyage,** traveling companion.
camaraderie n.f. companionship, intimacy.
camard, e n.m.f. a snubnosed person. adj. flat, snub; flat-nosed, snubnosed.
cambiste n.m. cambist; money changer.
cambouis n.m. dirty oil or grease.
cambrage n.m. curving, bending, arching.
cambré, e adj. curved, bent, arched.
cambrer v.t. to bend; to curve. **se** ~, v.refl. to camber; to become curved or bent.
cambriolage n.m. break-in, burglary.
cambrioler v.t. to break into, to burglarize.
cambrioleur n.m. burglar.
cambrousse n.f. Infml. country. **en pleine** ~, in the middle of nowhere.
cambrure n.f. curve.
cambuse n.f. Naut. steward's room; dump.
came n.m. cam, dope, drugs, stuff, junk.
camée n.f. cameo.
camé, e adj. Infml. doped, drugged. n.m.f. junkie.
caméléon n.m. chameleon; Fig. turncoat.
camélia n.m. camelia.

camelot *n.m.* street peddler, vendor; newspaper deliverer.

camelote *n.f.* trash, rubbish, junk.

camembert *n.m.* Camembert (cheese).

caméra *n.f.* movie camera.

cameraman *n.m.* cameraman.

camériste *n.f.* chambermaid.

camion *n.m.* truck.

camionnage *n.m.* trucking.

camionnette *n.f.* van.

camionneur *n.m.* truck driver.

camisole *n.f.* short nightgown. ~ de force, strait jacket.

camomille *n.f.* camomile.

camouflage *n.m.* camouflage, cover-up.

camoufler *v.t.* to camouflage, to hide, to conceal, to cover up, to disguise.

camouflet *n.m.* snub.

camp *n.m.* camp; faction, party. *Infml.* **ficher le ~**, to scram, to clear off.

campagnard, e *adj.* country. *n.m.f.* country man, country woman.

campagne *n.f.* country, fields; countryside; political campaign. **partir en ~**, to launch a campaign. **battre la ~**, to scour the country. **ouvrir la ~**, to open the campaign. **dans cette première ~**, in this first campaign. **canons de ~**, field guns. **en ~**, in the field.

campagnol *n.m.* vole.

campanile *n.m.f.* campanile; bell tower.

campanule *n.f.* campanula; bell flower; Canterbury bell.

campement *n.m.* camping, encampment, camp. **effets de ~**, camp equipment.

camper *v.i.* to camp, to encamp. **se ~**, *v.refl.* to encamp, to pitch one's camp; to plop oneself down. **il se campa dans un fauteuil**, he plopped himself down in an armchair.

campeur, euse *n.m.f.* camper.

camphre *n.m.* camphor.

camphré, e *adj.* camphorated, camphorate.

camphrier *n.m.* camphor tree.

camping *n.m.* camping. **faire du ~**, to go camping.

campos *n.m.* holiday, day off.

camus, e *adj.* snub, pug, pug-nosed, flat-nosed; disappointed; dumbfounded. *n.m.f.* snub-nosed person. **un vilain ~**, an ugly, flat-nosed fellow.

Canada (le), Canada.

canaille *n.f.* rabble, riffraff, rascal, scamp; *pl.* (of children) brats. **c'est une ~**, he is a scamp.

canaillerie *n.f.* lowness, rascality; low trick.

canal *n.m.* canal, conduit, drain; channel, strait; *Anat.* duct. **un pays coupé de canaux**, a country intersected by canals. **~ alimentaire**, the stomach and intestines; via, through. **par le ~ d'un ami**, through or via a friend. **le ~ de la Manche**, the English Channel.

canalisation *n.f.* canalization pipes.

canaliser *v.t.* to canalize; to channel; to make a canal.

canapé *n.m.* sofa, couch; open sandwich.

canard *n.m.* duck, drake; hoax; false report; *Infml.* newspaper. **~ sauvage**, wild duck.

canardeau *n.m.* duckling.

canarder *v.t.* to fire on, to shoot from under shelter. *v.i.* to quack (on a musical instrument); *Naut.* to pitch, to plunge.

canardière *n.f.* duck pond; punt gun.

canari *n.m.* canary.

canasson *n.m.* *Infml.* nag (horse). *Pej.* ~ **jade**, hack.

canasta *n.f.* canasta (game).

cancan *n.m.* cancan (a dance). **dire des ~**, to spread gossip.

cancaner *v.i.* to gossip; to quack (duck).

cancanier, ère *adj.* addicted to gossip. *n.m.f.* scandalmonger, gossipy person.

cancer *n.m.* cancer. *Astron.* Cancer, the Crab.

cancéreux, euse *adj.* cancerous. *n.m.f.* person with cancer.

cancérigène *adj.* carcinogenic, cancer-producing.

cancérologue *n.m.f.* oncologist.

cancre *n.m.* miser; (in schools) dunce.

cancrelat *n.m.* cockroach.

candélabre *n.m.* candelabrum; chandelier.

candeur *n.f.* ingenuousness, guilelessness; innocence, naiveté.

candi, e *p.p.* candied. *n.m.* candy, sugar candy.

candidat *n.m.* candidate, applicant.

candidature *n.f.* candidacy.

candide *adj.* candid, ingenuous, guileless; innocent, naive.

candidement *adv.* candidly; sincerely.

candir (se) *v.refl.* to candy. **faire candir**, to candy.

cane *n.f.* duck.

canéphore *n.f.* canephora.

canepin *n.m.* split lambskin.

caner *v.i.* to chicken out.

caneton *n.m.* duckling.

canevas *n.m.* canvas; sketch, outline.

caniche *n.m.f.* poodle.

caniculaire *adj.* canicular. **jours ~s**, dog days.

canicule *n.f.* hot days; the dog days.

canif *n.m.* penknife, pocket knife.

canin, e *adj.* canine. **dents ~es**, the canine (or eye) teeth.

caniveau *n.m.* gutter.

cannage *n.m.* caning, cane-bottoming (of chairs, etc.).

canne *n.f.* cane; walking stick. **~ à sucre**, sugar-cane.

canne à pêche *n.f.* fishing rod.

canneler *v.t.* to channel, to flute (as a column, etc.).

cannelier *n.m.* cinnamon tree.

cannelle *n.f.* cinnamon; tap; spigot.

cannelure *n.f.* fluting (of a column); groove, fluting.

canner *v.t.* to cane-bottom, to cane (chairs, etc.).

Cannes *n.f.* Cannes (in France).

canneur, euse *n.m.f.* cane worker.

cannibale *n.m.* cannibal, man eater.

cannibalisme *n.m.* cannibalism.

canoë *n.m.* canoe.

canoéiste *n.m.f.* canoeist.

canon *n.m.* cannon; guns; barrel (of a gun); round, canon (in music). **~ de campagne**, field gun. **un coup de ~**, a cannon shot. **les ~ de l'Eglise**, the canons of the Church. **à trois voix**, canon for three voices; model, perfect example.

cañon *n.m.* canyon.

canonisation *n.f.* canonization.

canoniser *v.t.* to canonize.

canonnade *n.m.* cannonade, cannonading.

canonner *v.t.* to cannonade. **se ~**, *v.refl.* to cannonade each other.

canonnier *n.m.* gunner.

canonnière *n.f.* gunboat.

canot *n.m.* boat, dinghy. **~ de sauvetage**, lifeboat.

canotage *n.m.* boating, rowing.

canoter *v.i.* to boat, to row.

canotier *n.m.* rower, boatman.

cantaloup *n.m.* cantaloupe.

cantate *n.f.* cantata.

cantatrice *n.f.* singer.

cantilène *n.f.* cantilena.

cantine *n.f.* canteen. **school ~**, lunchroom (at school).

cantinier, ière *n.m.f.* canteen keeper.

cantique *n.m.* canticle, song of praise; psalm.

canton *n.m.* canton; district, township.

cantonade *n.f.* *Theat.* side scenes. **parler à la ~**, to speak to a person behind the scenes. **crier à la ~**, to tell the whole world.

cantonal *adj.* cantonal.

cantonnement *n.m.* cantonment; quartering, billeting.

cantonner *v.t.* *Milit.* to canton, to lodge troops in villages. **se ~**, to confine oneself.

cantonnier *n.m.* road man, road mender.

cantonnière *n.f.* valance (of a bed or window).

canular *n.m.* *Infml.* hoax, joke, trick.

canule *n.f.* cannula.

canuler *v.t.* *Infml.* to bore, to plague.

caoutchouc *n.m.* rubber.

caoutchouter *v.t.* to rubberize, to coat with rubber.

caoutchouteux, euse *adj.* rubbery.

cap *n.m.* cape, headland; ship's bow. **doubler un ~**, to double a cape. **le ~ de Bonne Espérance**, the Cape of Good Hope. **~ dépasser ou franchir le ~ des 50 ans**, to turn 50. **mettre le ~ sur**, to head for.

capable *adj.* capable, able; fit, likely. **être ~ de tout**, to be capable of everything. **ce sont des livres capables de vous amuser**, they are books likely to amuse you. **faire le ~**, to pretend to ability.

capacité *n.f.* capacity, capability, ability. **~ du cerveau**, the capacity (volume) of the brain. **mesures de ~**, measures of capacity.

caparaçon *n.m.* caparison.

caparaçonner *v.t.* to caparison.

cape *n.f.* cape. **de ~ et d'épée**, cloak-and-dagger (novel, film). **rire sous ~**, to laugh up one's sleeve.

capeline *n.f.* wide-brimmed sun hat.

capharnaüm *n.m.* pigsty, disorderly place.

capillaire *adj.* capillary. *n.m.* maiden-hair.

capillarité *n.f.* capillarity.

capilotade *n.m.* **mettre en ~**, to beat to a pulp; to slander.

capitaine *n.m.* captain; instructor, leader. **~ de pavillon**, flag captain. **~ de vais-seau**, post-captain; instructor, leader.

capital, e *adj.* capital, chief, principal, essential. **peine ~**, capital punishment. **les sept péchés capitaux**, the seven deadly or mortal sins. *n.m.* capital, funds, stock. **capitale** *n.f.* capital of a country.

capitalisation *n.f.* capitalization.

capitalisable *adj.* which can be capitalized.

capitaliser *v.t.* to capitalize; to realize.

capitalisme *n.m.* capitalism.

capitaliste *n.m.* capitalist.

capitation *n.f.* capitation, head tax.

capiteux, euse *adj.* heady, intoxicating.

capiton *n.m.* padding, wadding.

capitonnage *n.m.* padding, upholstering.

capitonner *v.t.* to pad.

capitulaire *adj.* capitulary. *n.m.* capitulary.

capitulard, e *adj.* defeatist.

capitulation *n.f.* capitulation, surrender; *Fig.* abandonment.

capituler *v.t.* to capitulate, to surrender; to come to terms.

capon *n.m.* coward.

caporal *n.m.* *Mil.* corporal.

caporalisme *n.m.* authoritarianism, militarism.

capot *n.m.* cover; capot (game).

capotage *n.m.* overturning.

capote *n.f.* top (car); *Mil.* overcoat. **~ anglaise**, condom.

capoter *v.t.* to overturn.

câpre *n.f.* caper.

caprice *n.m.* caprice, whim; fit, sudden impulse. **les ~s de la fortune**, the whims of fortune.

capricieusement *adv.* capriciously, whimsically.

capricieux, euse *adj.* capricious, freakish, moody, fanciful, uncertain.

capricorne *n.m.* *Astron.* Capricorn; capricorn beetle.

câprier *n.m.* caper bush.

caprin, ine *adj.* goatlike.

capsulage *n.m.* capsuling, capping.

capsulaire *adj.* capsular.

capsule *n.f.* capsule.

capsuler *v.t.* to put a capsule or cap on.

captage *n.m.* harnessing (flow of water); picking up (message).

captateur, trice *n.m.f.* inveigler; person seeking to gain an inheritance.

captation *n.f.* captation, inveigling.

capter *v.t.* to catch; to intercept (message); to tune in to (broadcast); to pick up (mail); *Fig.* to win by insidious means; to rivet (attention).

capteur *n.m.* sensor, detector.

captieusement *adv.* captiously.

captieux, euse *adj.* captious; deceptive, insidious.

captif, ive *adj.* captive. **ballon ~,** a captive balloon. *n.m.* captive, prisoner.

captivant, e *adj.* fascinating, captivating, bewitching, gripping, enthralling.

captiver *v.t.* to captivate, to fascinate, to bewitch, to enthrall.

captivité *n.f.* captivity, bondage.

capture *n.f.* capture.

capturer *v.t.* to capture.

capuche *n.f.* hood.

capuchon *n.m.* hood; top, cap (pen).

capuchonné, e *adj.* hooded.

capucin *n.m.* Capuchin, Capuchin friar.

capucine *n.f.* nasturtium; slide of a musket.

caque *n.f.* barrel, keg. **la ~ sent toujours le hareng,** what is bred in the bone will come out in the flesh.

caquelon *n.m.* earthenware fondue dish.

caquet *n.m.* cackle, cackling; chatter, gossip. **rabattre le ~ à quelqu'un,** to stop a person's babble.

caquetage *n.m.* cackling, babbling; gossip.

caqueter *v.i.* to cackle; to prate; to gossip.

car *conj.* because, for. *n.m.* bus.

carabin *n.m.* medical student.

carabine *n.f.* rifle, gun.

carabiné, e *p.p.* stiff; raging, violent, heavy. **fièvre ~,** raging fever.

carabinier *n.m.* carbineer; rifleman.

caraco *n.m.* loose blouse.

caractère *n.m.* temper, disposition, expression, originality. **il est sans ~ officiel,** be is without official authority. **avoir du ~,** to have character or backbone. **le ~ de cette visite,** the nature of this visit. **petits ~s,** small print.

caratériel, elle *adj.* disturbed. **une personne ~,** a disturbed person.

caractérisation *n.f.* caracterization.

caractérisé, e *adj.* marked, blatant, pointed.

caractériser *v.t.* to characterize.

caractéristique *adj.* characteristic. *n.f.* characteristic.

carafe *n.f.* decanter, water bottle.

carafon *n.m.* small decanter (usually a quarter of a bottle of wine).

carambolage *n.m.* multiple crash, collision (car); cannon (billiards).

caramboler *v.i.* to collide with.

caramel *n.m.* caramel; burnt sugar.

caramélisation *n.f.* caramelization.

caraméliser *v.t.* to caramelize.

carapace *n.f.* carapace, shell.

carapater (se) *v.t.* to run off, to clear off.

carat *n.f.* carat.

caravane *n.f.* trailer. **une ~ de voitures,** a procession of cars.

caravanier *n.m.* caravaneer.

caravaning *n.m.* campsite in a trailer camp.

caravansérail *n.m.* caravanserai.

caravelle *n.f.* caravel.

carbochimie *n.f.* organic chemistry.

carbonate *n.m.* carbonate, washing soda.

carbone *n.m.* carbon.

carbonifère *adj.* carboniferous; containing coal.

carbonique *adj.* carbonic. **acide ~,** carbonic acid.

carbonisation *n.f.* carbonization.

carboniser *v.t.* to carbonize.

carbonnade *n.f.* meat grilled on charcoal.

carburant *adj.* motor fuel.

carburateur *n.m.* carburetor.

carburation *n.f.* carburation; *Techn.* carburization.

carbure *n.m.* carbide.

carburé, e *adj.* carburetted.

carburer *v.t.* to carburet; *Techn.* to carburize; *Infml.* **ça carbure ici!** it's going strong over here!

carcan *n.m.* carcan, iron collar; pillory.

carcasse *n.f.* carcass; *Arch.* shell, skeleton.

carcéral, e *(pl.)* **aux** *adj.* pertaining to prison or jail.

cardage *n.m.* carding.

cardan *n.m.* universal joint.

carder *v.t.* to card.

cardeur, euse *n.m.f.* carder. **cardeuse** *n.f.* carding machine.

cardiaque *adj.* cardiac. **crise cardiaque,** heart attack.

cardinal *adj.* cardinal; principal, chief. **les points cardinaux,** the cardinal points. *n.m.* cardinal.

cardinalat *n.m.* cardinalate, cardinalship.

cardiogramme *n.m.* cardiogram.

cardiographe *n.m.* cardiograph.

cardiographie *n.f.* cardiography.

cardiologie *n.f.* cardiology.

cardiologue *n.m.* cardiologist, heart specialist.

cardio-vasculaire *adj.* cardiovascular.

cardite *n.f.* carditis.

carême *n.m.* Lent. **faire ~, faire le ~,** to keep Lent. **provisions de ~,** Lenten food. **la mi-~,** mid-Lent.

carême-prenant *n.m.* Shrove Tuesday; Mardi Gras time; Mardi Gras reveler. *Fig.* a regular guy.

carénage *n.m.* careening.

carence *n.f.* total absence of assets, insolvency, deficiency, shortage; shortcoming, incompetence.

carène *n.f.* keel; bottom, careen; carina.

caréner *v.t.* to careen, to streamline.

caressant, e *adj.* caressing, affectionate; tender.

caresse *n.f.* caress, endearment; fawning. **faire des ~s à,** to caress.

caresser *v.t.* to caress, to fondle; to stroke, to pat (a dog).

cargaison *n.f.* cargo; freight, shipload.

cargo *n.m.* cargo boat, freighter, tramp steamer.

cargue *n.f.* brail.

carguer *v.t.* to brail.

cari *n.m.* curry.

cariatide *n.f.* caryatid.

caribou *n.m. Zool.* caribou.

caricatural, e *(pl.)* **aux** *adj.* caricatural.

caricature *n.f.* caricature.

caricaturer *v.t.* to caricature.

caricaturiste *n.m.* caricaturist.

carie *n.f.* caries, decay, cavity (tooth).

carier *v.t.* to decay, to rot; **se ~,** to decay.

carillon *n.m.* chimes, peal (of church bells). **sonner le ~,** to chime, to ring the bells.

carillonnement *n.m.* chiming.

carillonner *v.t.* to chime, to ring a peal.

carillonneur *n.m.* chimer, bell ringer.

carlin *n.m.* pug dog.

carlingue *n.f.* cockpit, cabin.

carme *n.m.* Carmelite.

carmélite *n.f.* Carmelite nun.

carmin *n.m.* carmine.

carminé, e *adj.* carmine, purplish red, crimson.

carnage *n.m.* carnage, slaughter, massacre, butchery.

carnassier, ère *adj.* flesh-eating, carnivorous. *n.m.* flesh eater, carnivorous animal.

carnassière *n.f.* game bag.

carnation *n.f.* carnation; flesh tints.

carnaval *n.m.* carnival.

carne *n.f.* tough or leathery meat; *Pej.* nag.

carné, e *adj.* flesh-colored.

carnet *n.m.* notebook. **~ d'adresses,** address book. **~ de chèques,** checkbook. **~ de notes,** report card (school). **~ de timbres,** book of stamps.

carnier *n.m.* gamebag.

carnivore *adj.* carnivorous. *n.m. pl.* the carnivora.

carolingien, ienne *adj.* Carolingian.

carotide *adj.* and *n.f.* carotid.

carottage *n.m. Infml.* cadging; swiping.

carotte *n.f.* carrot; roll (of leaf tobacco); cheating trick.

carotter *v.i. v.t.* to swindle (*or* dupe).

carotteur, euse *n.m.f.* swindler, cheat.

caroube *n.f.* carob.

caroubier *n.m.* carob tree.

carpe *n.f.* carp. **muet comme une ~,** as dumb as a post; *Anat.* carpus; the wrist.

carpeau *n.m.* young carp.

carpelle *n.f.* carpel.

carpette *n.f.* carpet, rug, doormat.

carpien, enne *adj.* carpal.

carquois *n.m.* quiver.

carrare *n.m.* Carrara marble.

carre *n.f.* edge.

carré, e *adj.* square; square-shouldered. **un mètre ~,** a square meter. **un nombre ~,** a square number. **racine ~e,** square root. **réponse ~e,** a straightforward answer. *n.m.* square; landing (of staircase). **~ d'as,** four aces. **~ d'agneau,** loin of lamb. **~ des officers,** the officers' wardroom.

carreau *n.m.* tile; floor; pane (of glass); diamond (cards); cushion. **coucher sur le ~,** to lie on the floor. **as de ~,** ace of diamonds. **se tenir à ~,** to lie low, to beware.

carrefour *n.m.* crossroad.

carrelage *n.m.* tiles.

carreler *v.t.* to tile.

carreleur *n.m.* paver (for brick or tile floors), tiler.

carrément *adv.* squarely; flatly; straight out, bluntly, firmly. **il me refusa ~,** he refused me flatly.

carrer *v.t.* to square. **se ~,** to settle comfortably.

carrier *n.m.* quarryman, quarrier.

carrière *n.f.* career; quarry, stone pit. **le bout de la ~,** the end of the race, the wire, finish line. **la ~ militaire,** the military career. **~ de marbre, d'ardoise,** marble quarry, slate quarry.

carriériste *n.m.f.* careerist.

carriole *n.f.* a carryall, jalopy.

carrossable *adj.* fit for carriages. **route ~,** carriage road.

carrosse *n.m.* coach. **rouler ~,** to live in style.

carosser *v.t.* to fit a body to (autom.).

carrosserie *n.f.* panel body.

carrousel *n.m.* merry-go-round.

carrure *n.f.* build (person); squareness; caliber, stature.

cartable *n.m.* schoolbag.

carte *n.f.* card; cardboard, ticket; map, chart. **~ blanche,** carte blanche, unlimited powers. **~ de visite,** calling card. **~ d'électeur,** voter's card. **un jeu de ~s,** a pack of cards. **battre, mêler les ~s,** to shuffle the cards. **tirer les ~s,** to tell fortunes by cards. **~ à payer,** reckoning. **~ des vins,** wine list. **mettre ~s sur table,** to tell the truth.

cartel *n.m.* challenge, defiance, cartel; wall clock.

cartésianisme *n.m.* **cartesianism;** the philosophy of Descartes.

cartésien, enne *adj.* Cartesian.

cartilage *n.m.* cartilage; gristle.

cartilagineux, euse *adj.* cartilaginous; gristly.

cartographe *n.m.* cartographer.

cartographie *n.f.* cartography, mapmaking.

cartographique *adj.* cartographic(al).

cartomancie *n.f.* fortune-telling by cards.

cartomancien, enne *n.m.f.* fortune-teller by cards.

carton *n.m.* cardboard, paste board; bandbox, hat box; cartoon, sketch (paint.). *Print.* cancel.

reliure en ~, binding in boards. faire un ~, to make a good score. ~ de bureau, cartoon.

cartonnier, ère n.m.f. nest of cardboard boxes or drawers.

cartouche n.f. cartridge, refill (pen).

cartouchière n.f. cartridge belt; cartridge pouch.

caryatide n.f. V. CARLATIDE.

cas n.m. case, event, cause, suit, state, situation; matter, affair. en ce ~, je n'irai pas, in that case I shall not go. le ~ échéant, if need be. en ~ de besoin, in case of need. il est dans un vilain ~, he is in an awkward position. faire ~ de to set a value on, to think much of. en ~ qu'il vienne, in case he should come. en tout ~, comptez sur moi, in any case, rely on me. elle ne fait jamais aucun ~ de nos conseils, she always ignores our advice. en aucun ~ il ne viendra, he will come under no circumstances. ~ de conscience, moral dilemma.

casanier, ère adj. stay-at-home; homebody.

cascade n.f. cascade; waterfall; Fig. (events) stream, torrent, spate; peal (laughter).

cascadeur, euse n.m.f. stuntman, stuntwoman.

case n.f. cabin, compartment; square (of a chess-board).

caséine n.f. casein.

caser v.t. to place, to find a place, to install. casez bien tout cela dans votre tête, bear that well in mind. il est bien casé, he has a good situation v.i. to make or secure a point (at backgammon). se ~ v.refl. to find a place for oneself, to be placed.

caserne n.f. barracks (for soldiers), ~ de pompièrs, firehouse.

casernement n.m. lodging, quartering in barracks.

caserner v.t. to lodge in barracks. v.i. to live in barracks.

cash adv. cash down.

cash-flow n.m. cash flow.

casier n.m. set of pigeon holes; compartment; drawer. ~ à bouteille, bottle rack. ~ judiciaire, police record. ~ vierge, clean record.

casino n.m. casino.

casoar n.m. cassowary.

casque n.m. helmet.

casqué, e adj. helmeted.

casquer v.t. and v.i. Infml. to fork out, to foot the bill.

casquette n.f. cap. ~ de chasse, hunting cap.

cassable adj. breakable.

cassade n.f. fib; sham.

cassage n.m. breaking.

cassant, e adj. brittle; hard. Fig. curt, abrupt (tone of voice).

cassation n.f. cassation. cour de ~, Supreme Court of Appeal; Mil. reduction to the ranks.

cassave n.f. cassava.

casse n.f. Typog. case; breakage, breaking; cassia; ~-cou, stuntman. ~-croûte, snack, lunch.

~-noisettes, ~-noix, nutcracker. ~-pieds, bore. ~-tête, puzzle; headache (problem).

cassé, e adj. broken, cracked.

cassement n.m. breaking. ~ de tête, head-splitting anxiety.

casser v.t. to break; to shatter, crack, rend, split or cleave; Mil. to discharge; to annul. se ~ la tête, to rack one's brain. qui casse les verres les paie, he that does the damage must pay for it. ~ un officier, to dismiss an officer. ~ un testament, to declare a will null and void. se ~, v.refl. to break; to be broken to pieces, to wear out.

casserole n.f. saucepan, stewpan; jalopy.

cassette n.f. casket; cash box; privy purse; a little box; cassette.

casseur, euse n.m.f. breaker; scrapmetal dealer.

cassis n.m. black currant bush or tree; black currants.

cassonade n.f. brown sugar.

cassure n.f. break; fracture.

castagnette n.f. castanet.

caste n.f. caste. esprit de ~, class consciousness. hors ~, outcast.

castel n.m. castle, manor.

castor n.m. beaver.

castrat n.m. castrato; a male soprano; eunuch, castrated man.

castration n.f. castration, spaying.

castrer v.t. to castrate, to neuter, to spay; to emasculate.

casuel, elle adj. casual; precarious; incidental. n.m. casual income; fees, perquisites.

catabolisme n.m. catabolism.

catacombes n.f. pl. catacombs.

catadiopre n.m. Auto. reflector.

catafalque n.m. catafalque.

catalectes n.m. pl. catalects.

catalepsie n.f. catalepsy.

cataleptique adj. cataleptic. n.m.f. cataleptic patient.

Catalogne n.f. Catalonia.

catalogue n.m. catalog; list.

cataloguer v.t. to catalog; to categorize; Infml. to size up, to label.

catalyse n.f. catalysis.

catalyseur n.m. catalyst.

catalytique adj. catalytic.

catamaran n.m. catamaran.

cataplasme n.m. cataplasm, poultice.

catapultage n.m. catapulting, catapult-launching.

catapulte n.f. catapult.

catapulter v.t. to catapult.

cataracte n.f. cataract. Fig. flood, deluge.

catarrhal, e adj. catarrhal.

catarrhe n.m. catarrh. ~ pulmonaire, bronchitis.

catarrheux, euse adj. catarrhous; catarrhal.

catastrophe n.f. catastrophe, calamity.

catastrophé, e *adj.* wrecked, shattered, stunned.

catastropher *v.t.* to shatter, to stun.

catastrophique *adj.* catastrophic, disastrous.

catch *n.m.* wrestling.

catcheur, euse *n.m.f.* wrestler.

catéchiser *v.t.* to catechize; to lecture, to scold.

catéchisme *n.m.* catechism.

catéchiste *n.m.* catechist.

catéchuménat *n.m.* catechumenate.

catéchumène *n.m.f.* catechumen.

catégorie *n.f.* category; class; kind. **morceaux de première ~,** prime cut.

catégorique *adj.* categorical, explicit.

catégoriquement *adv.* categorically.

catégoriser *v.t.* to categorize.

cathédrale *adj.* and *n.f.* cathedral.

cathéter *n.m.* catheter.

cathode *n.f.* cathode.

catholicisme *n.m.* Catholicism.

catholicité *n.f.* catholicity.

catholique *adj.* Catholic, Orthodox. *n.m.f.* Catholic. **pas ~,** doubtful, suspicious.

catimini, en ~ *adv.* by stealth, secretly.

catin *n.f. Infml.* whore.

cauchemar *n.m.* nightmare.

cauchemardesque *adj.* nightmarish.

caudal, e *adj.* caudal.

causal, e *adj.* causal.

causalité *n.f.* causality.

causant, e *adj.* talkative, chatty.

causatif, ive *adj.* causative.

cause *n.f.* cause, reason, motive ground; suit, action, legal process. **point d'effet sans ~,** no effect without a cause. **et pour ~,** and for good reasons. **cela est hors de ~,** that is out of the question. **mettre hors de ~,** to clear, to exonerate. **prendre fait et ~ pour quelqu'un,** to take a person's part. **à ~ de son ami,** for his friend's sake. **à ~ de cela,** on account of that. **cela est hors de ~,** that is out of the question. **mettre hors de ~,** to clear, to exonerate.

causer *v.t.* to cause, to be the cause of, to give (pleasure, pain, etc). *v.i.* to chat, to talk, to converse familiarly; to chatter, to blab, to babble. **~ de choses et d'autres,** to talk of this and that.

causerie *n.f.* chat, chatting, gossip.

causette *n.f.* a short chat.

causeur, euse *adj.* chatty, talkative. *n.m.f.* talker, conversationist; gossip, tattler.

causeuse *n.f.* love seat.

causticité *n.f.* causticity.

caustique *adj.* caustic.

caustiquement *adv.* caustically.

cautèle *n.f.* cunning, guile.

cauteleux, euse *adj.* crafty; cautious; cunning, sly.

cautérisation *n.f.* cauterization.

cautériser *v.t.* to cauterize.

caution *n.f.* security deposit, surety, bail. **être ~ de quelqu'un,** to bail someone out. **un**

homme sujet à ~, a man not to be trusted. **mettre en liberté sous ~,** to release on bail; deposit.

cautionnement *n.m.* security; bail.

cautionner *v.t.* to give security for; to be responsible for; to guarantee.

cavalcade *n.f.* cavalcade; ride; equestrian exercise.

cavalcader *v.i.* to cavalcade; to ride.

cavale *n.f.* mare. **être en ~,** to be on the run.

cavaler *v.i.* to run; *Infml.* to annoy. **il commence à nous ~,** we are beginning to get fed up with him. *v.refl.* **se ~,** to rush.

cavalerie *n.f.* cavalry. **grosse ~,** heavy cavalry. **~ légère,** light cavalry.

cavaleur *n.m. Infml.* womanizer.

cavaleuse *n.f. Infml.* nympho, woman who chases men.

cavalier, ère *n.m.f.* rider; horseman. *n.m.* horsewoman. *n.m.f.* horse soldier, trooper; cavalier; partner (in dancing); (at chess) knight; *adj.* cavalier; free and easy; haughty.

cavalièrement *adv.* cavalierly.

cavatine *n.f.* cavatina.

cave *n.f.* cellar, case of liqueurs for the table. *n.m.* sucker, dupe. *adj.* hollow, sunken (eyes, cheeks).

caveau *n.m.* a small cellar, singing club; burial vault.

caverne *n.f.* cavern; cave; den.

caverneux, euse *adj.* cavernous, hollow, sepulchral. **voix caverneuse,** sepulchral (hollow) voice.

caviar *n.m.* caviar.

caviste *n.m.* cellarman.

cavité *n.f.* cavity; hollow.

CD-ROM *n.m.* CD-ROM.

ce, cet *n.m.,* **cette** *n.f.,* **ces** *pl.m.f. demonstr. adj.* this, *pl.* these. **ce** *demonstr. adj.* this, *pl.* these. **ce** this hero. **cet homme, cet homme-ci,** this man. That, these; *pl.* those. **ce livre, ce livre-là,** that book. **ces livres-là,** those books. **ces gens,** these people.

ce, c', ç' *demonstr. pron.* this, these; that those; it, they. **c'est vrai,** it (or that) is true. **c'est un malheur,** it (this or that) is a misfortune. **ce sont des malheurs,** they (these or those) are misfortunes. **c'est vous que je cherche,** it is you whom I seek. **c'est moi qui le dis,** it is I who say it. **est-ce vous?** is it you? **étaient-ce nos amis?** was it our friends? **à ce qu'il m'a dit,** from what he told me. **faites ce dont je vous ai parlé,** do what I told you about. **c'est ce dont je voulais vous parler,** that is what I wanted to speak with you about. **c'est ce à quoi j'ai fait allusion,** that is what I alluded to. **ce à quoi je pense,** what I am thinking of. **ce qu'il demande, c'est une pension,** what he asks for is a pension. **c'est à vous de parler,** it is your turn to speak. **c'est à lui de décider,** it is for him to decide. **c'est pourquoi,** that is why. **c'est-à-dire,** that is to say, that is.

céans *adv.* within, in this house. **la dame de ~,** the lady of the house.

ceci *pron.* this. **~ est à moi, cela est à vous,** this is mine, that is yours. **que veut dire ~?** what does this mean? **à ~ près que,** except that.

cécité *n.f.* blindness.

cédant, e *adj. Law.* transferring, assigning, granting. *n.m.f.* transferrer.

céder *v.t.* to cede, to yield up; to transfer, to give up. **~ le pas à,** to give precedence to. *v.i.* to yield; to give way; to give in. **la porte céda à nos efforts,** the door yielded to our efforts. **~ par faiblesse,** to give in out of weakness. to dispose of, to let, to part with, to sell. **~ un bail,** to sell a lease.

cédille *n.f.* cedilla.

cedrat *n.m.* citron.

cèdre *n.m.* cedar, cedar tree.

cédulaire *adj.* pertaining to income tax schedules. **impôts ~s,** scheduled taxes.

ceindre *v.t.* to surround; to enclose, to fence, to bind, to gird, to encircle. **une corde lui ceint les reins,** a cord girds his loins. **se ~,** *v.refl.* to gird oneself with, to gird on.

ceinture *n.f.* girdle, belt, sash, waistband, waist; fence, zone. **~ de sauvetage,** life jacket. **nu jusqu'à la ~,** stripped to the waist. **Petite, Grande ~,** Inner, Outer Circle (Paris transport). **~ de sécurité,** seat belt. *Infml.* **se serrer la ~,** to tighten one's belt, to do without.

ceinturer *v.t.* to belt, to surround, to encircle; *Sport.* to tackle, to grip around the waist.

ceinturon *n.m.* belt.

cela, ça *demonstr. pron.* that. **~ est fort beau,** that is very fine. **~ ne fait rien,** that makes no difference. **point de ~,** none of that. **c'est ~,** that is it. **comment ~?** how so? **avec ~?** what next?

célébrant *n.m. and adj.* the officiating priest.

célébration *n.f.* celebration.

célèbre *adj.* celebrated, renowned.

célébrer *v.t.* to celebrate, to solemnize, to extol, to glorify, to praise; to sing.

célébrité *n.f.* celebrity, renown; distinguished person.

celer *v.t.* to conceal, to hide, to keep secret. **se faire ~,** not to receive visitors.

céleri *n.m.* celery.

célérité *n.f.* celerity, promptness, speed.

célesta *n.m. Mus.* celesta.

céleste *adj.* celestial, heavenly.

célibat *n.m.* celibacy, bachelorhood.

célibataire *adj.* single, unmarried. *n.m.f.* unmarried person.

celle *pr. dem.* V. CELUI.

cellier *n.m.* cellar, storeroom.

cellulaire *adj.* cellular. **téléphone ~,** cellular phone. **tissu ~,** cellular tissue. **voiture ~,** police van.

cellule *n.f.* cellule, *Mil.* cell; *Aviat.* airframe.

celluleux, euse *adj.* cellular.

cellulite *n.f.* cellulite.

celluloïd *n.m.* celluloid.

cellulose *n.f.* cellulose.

celui *n.m. sing.* **celle** *n.f. sing.* **ceux** *n.m. pl.* **celles** *n.f. pl. demonstr. pron.* he, him, she, her; they, them, those, **celui à qui je parlais,** he to whom I was speaking. **ceux qui ont vecu avant nous,** those who lived before us. **celui-ci, celle-ci, ceux-ci, celles-ci,** this, these. **celui-là, celle-là, ceux-là, celles-là,** that, those. **entre tous ces tableaux, celui-ci seul me plaît,** of all these paintings, this one alone pleases me. **celui-là n'est pas beau,** that one is not fine.

cément *n.m.* cement.

cénacle *n.m. Rel.* cinacle; literary group.

cendre *n.f.* ashes, embers. **jour** (or **mercredi**) **des Cendres,** Ash Wednesday. **renaître de ses ~s,** to rise from one's ashes.

cendré, e *adj.* ash-colored, ashen.

cendrer *v.t.* to mix ashes with; to make ash-colored.

cendreux, euse *adj.* covered with ashes.

cendrier *n.m.* ashpan; ashtray.

cendrillon *n.f.* Cinderella.

Cène *n.f.* Last Supper (of Christ); communion, Lord's Supper (Protestants).

cénobite *n.m.* cenobite, hermit.

cénotaphe *n.m.* cenotaph.

cens *n.m.* census, poll tax.

censé, e *adj.* considered, supposed. **vous êtes ~ d'avoir fait,** you are supposed to have done it.

censément *adv.* supposedly; practically.

censeur *n.m.* censor, critic, censurer, deputy, headmaster (school).

censitaire *n.m. and adj.* vassal. **électeur ~,** duly qualified elector, voter based on property qualification.

censurable *adj.* censurable.

censure *n.f.* censorship; censure; blame, condemnation; *Fin.* audit.

censurer *v.t.* to censure; to blame.

cent *adj.* hundred. **~ ans,** a hundred years. **cinq pour ~,** five per cent. (Cent takes the plural except when followed by another number.) **deux ~s hommes,** two hundred men. **deux ~ vingt hommes,** two hundred and twenty men. **trois ~s,** three hundred. **faire les ~ pas,** to pace up and down. **elle ne va pas attendre ~ septans,** she can't wait forever.

centaine *n.f.* hundred; **une ~ d'années,** a hundred years.

centaure *n.m.* centaur.

centenaire *adj. and n.m.f.* centenary, centenarian; centennial.

centésimal, e *adj.* centesimal.

centiare *n.m.* centiare; a square meter.

centième *adj.* hundredth. *n.m.* hundredth, hundredth part.

centigrade *adj.* centigrade.

centigramme *n.m.* centigram.

centilitre *n.m.* centilitre.

centime *n.m.* centime, one-hundredth of a franc.

centimètre *n.m.* centimeter.

centrage *n.m.* centering.

central, e *adj.* central. **centrale électrique,** power station.

centralisation *n.f.* centralization, centralizing.

centraliser *v.t.* to centralize.

centre *n.m.* center, heart. **le ~ de Paris,** the heart of Paris. office, center. **~ commercial,** shopping center, mall. **~ aéré,** day camp. **~ hospitalier,** hospital complex.

centrer *v.t.* to center, to focus (up) on.

centrifuge *adj.* centrifugal.

centripète *adj.* centripetal.

centrisme *n.m.* centrism.

centriste *adj. n.m.f.* centrist.

centuple *adj. and n.m.* centuple; hundredfold.

centupler *v.t.* to centuple, to increase a hundredfold.

cep *n.m.* vine-stock.

cèpe, ceps *n.m.* an edible fungus.

cependant *adv.* **~ que,** while. *conj.* still, yet, nevertheless; however, for all that.

céphalique *adj.* cephalic.

céramique *adj. and n.f.* ceramic; ceramics.

céramiste *n.m.f.* ceramist.

Cerbère *n.m.* Cerberus; a surly doorkeeper.

cerceau *n.m.* hoop; **faire courir un ~,** to roll a hoop.

cerclage *n.m.* hooping (of barrels).

cercle *n.m.* circle; sphere. hoop, ring (of a cask); round; club, party, company. **étendre le ~ du devoir,** to enlarge the circle (or sphere) of duty. **quart de ~,** quadrant. **~ politique,** political club.

cercler *v.t.* to hoop, to ring.

cerueil *n.m.* coffin; *Fig.* grave.

céréale *adj. f.* cereal. *n.f.* cereal. **le prix des ~s,** the price of grain. **~s,** cereal (breakfast).

céréalier, ière *n.m.f.* cereal grower; grain-carrier or ship.

cérébelleux, euse *adj.* cerebellar.

cérébral, e *adj.* cerebral.

cérébro-spinal, e *n.m., pl.* **-aux** *adj.* cerebro-spinal.

cérémonial, e *adj.* ceremonial.

cérémonie *n.f.* ceremony; forms of civility. **tenue ou habit de ~,** formal dress. **faire des ~s,** to make a fuss. **sans ~,** informally.

cérémonieusement *adv.* ceremoniously, formally.

cérémonieux, euse *adj.* ceremonious, formal.

cerf *n.m.* stag, deer.

cerfeuil *n.m.* chervil.

cerf-volant *n.m.* stag beetle; kite.

cerisaie *n.f.* cherry orchard.

cerise *n.f.* cherry.

cerisier *n.m.* cherry tree.

cerne *n.f.* ring. **un arbre a autant d'années que de ~s,** a tree is as many years old as it has rings. ring, mark, shadow. **les ~s sous ses yeux,** the rings under his eyes.

cerneau *n.m.* green walnut.

cerner *v.t.* to encircle, to surround, to make a circle or ring around, to dig around. **des yeux cernés,** eyes with rings under them. **la ville fut cernée,** the town was surrounded.

certain, e *adj.* certain, assured, positive; stated, fixed, sure, undoubted, definite, without doubt, determined, undisputed, legal (date), clear, convinced, confident. **il en est ~,** he is positive (about it). **dans une ~e mesure,** to some extent. **personne d'un ~ âge,** an older person. **tenir pour ~,** to hold for certain. **cet homme jouit d'une ~e réputation,** that man enjoys a certain reputation. *n.m.* the certain, some. **quitter le ~ pour l'incertain,** to leave the certain for the uncertain. **~s prétendent que,** some people claim that.

certainement *adv.* certainly, surely, to be sure, for certain.

certes *adv.* certainly, indeed.

certificat *n.m.* certificate; diploma; *Fig.* guarantee.

certification *n.f.* certification; guarantee; attestation.

certifié, e *adj.* certified.

certifier *v.t.* to certify, to attest, to assure, to guarantee; *(Law)* to authenticate, to witness.

certitude *n.f.* certainty, certitude, assurance.

cérumen *n.m.* ear wax, cerumen.

cerveau *n.m.* brain, mind intellect. **rhume de ~,** head cold, coryza. **~ vide,** a brainless (or empty-headed) man. **~ brûlé,** a hot-headed person.

cervelet *n.m.* cerebellum.

cervelle *n.f.* brains; head, mind, sense.

cervical, e *adj.* cervical.

cervoise *n.f.* barley beer.

ces *pr. dem.* V. CE.

césar *n.m.* Caesar; *Fig.* great captain, emperor.

césarien, enne *adj.* Caesarean.

cessant, e *adj.* ceasing. **tous empêchements ~s,** if there be no obstacle.

cessation *n.f.* cessation, suspension (of payments).

cesse *n.f.* ceasing. **sans ~,** without ceasing, incessantly, constantly.

cesser *v.i.* to cease, to stop, to desist, to abstain from. **il a cessé de pleuvoir,** it has stopped raining. *v.t.* to cease, to discontinue.

cessez-le-feu *n.m.* ceasefire.

cessible *adj. Law* transferable, assignable.

cession *n.f.* transfer assignment (of property to creditors).

cessionnaire *n.m.f.* transferee, assignee.

c'est-à-dire *conj.* that is. **~ que,** which means that.

cesure *n.f.* caesura.

cet, cette *adj. dem.* V. CE.

cétacé, e *adj.* and *n.m.* cetaceous; cetaceous animal.

ceux *adj. dem* V. CELUI.

chablis *n.m.* Chablis wine; deadwood.

chacal *n.m.* jackal.

chaconne *n.f.* chacone (a kind of dance).

chacun, e *pron.* each, each one, every one.
~ **d'eux a refusé,** each of them has refused. **on se retira ~ chez soi,** each person went back to his own home. **nous avons pris ~ notre chapeau,** we each took our hat. ~ **pour soi** every man for himself.

chafouin, e *n.m.f.* and *adj.* mean-looking person; sorry, weasel-faced.

chagrin *n.m.* grief, sorrow, affliction, trouble, uneasiness; vexation; shagreen. **peau de ~,** shagreen leather.

chagrin, e *adj.* sorrowful, sad, downhearted, melancholy, morose, surly.

chagrinant, e *adj.* distressing, melancholy.

chagriner *v.t.* to grieve, to afflict, to distress, to chagrin, to vex. **se ~,** *v.refl.* to grieve, to afflict, to fret; to torment oneself.

chah *n.m.* shah.

chahut *n.m.* uproar, rowdyism, rumpus.

chahuter *v.i.* to make an uproar, to make a commotion, to be rowdy.

chai *n.m.* wine and spirits store.

chaine *n.f.* chain, shackle; manacle, fetter, bond; bondage, ~ **de montre,** watch chain. ~ **d'arpenteur,** surveyor's chain, land chain. ~ **de montagnes,** chain of mountains. ~ **de fabrication,** production line. ~ **alimentaire,** food chain. ~ **de montage,** assembly line. (television) **premierè ~,** channel one.

chainette *n.f.* small chain.

chainon *n.m.* link (of a chain).

chair *n.f.* flesh; meat. ~ **vive,** live flesh; living flesh. **en ~ et en os,** in flesh and bone, in person. **il n'est ni ~, ni poisson,** he is neither fish nor fowl. **mortifier sa ~,** to mortify one's flesh. **cela fait venir la ~ de poule,** that gives goose bumps, goose flesh, goose pimples.

chaire *n.f.* pulpit; chair; professorship; desk; throne (of a bishop). **l'éloquence de la ~,** pulpit eloquence.

chaise *n.f.* chair. ~ **rembourrée,** a stuffed chair. ~ **à porteurs,** sedan chair. ~ **roulante,** wheelchair. ~ **à bascule,** rocking chair.

chaland *n.m.* lighter; barge.

chaland, e *n.m.f.* customer.

châle *n.m.* shawl.

chalet *n.m.* chalet; Swiss cottage.

chaleur *n.f.* heat; fire, zeal, vehemence. ~ **animale,** animal heat. **durant les grandes ~s,** during the hot weather (of summer). **dans la ~ d'un premier mouvement,** in the ardor of a first impulse. *Fig.* warmth (greeting); heat, fervor (combat, discussion). **craint la ~,** keep in a cool place.

chaleureusement *adv.* warmly.

chaleureux, euse *adj.* warm.

chalît *n.m.* bedstead.

challenge *n.m.* contest, tournament, trophy.

chaloir *v. imp.* to matter, to signify. **il ne me chaut de cela,** it does not matter to me.

chaloupe *n.f.* launch or longboat. ~ **de sauvetage,** lifeboat.

chalumeau *n.m.* blowtorch.

chalut *n.m.* trawl net, trawl.

chalutier *n.m.* trawler.

chamade *n.f. Fig.* **battre la ~,** to beat wildly (heart).

chamailler *v.i.* to squabble. **se ~,** *v.refl.* to squabble, to wrangle.

chamaillerie *n.f.* wrangling, bickering.

chamailleur, euse *adj.* quarrelsome, wrangling. *n.m.f.* bickerer, squabbler.

chamarrer *v.t.* to adorn, to bedeck.

chamarrure *n.f.* rich pattern, rich trimming.

chambard *n.m.* row, racket, rumpus.

chambardement *n.m.* upheaval.

chambarder *v.t.* to turn upside down, to upset; to clear out, to throw out.

chambellan *n.m.* chamberlain.

chambouler *v.t.* to turn upside down, to cause chaos, to upset.

chambranle *n.m.* casing; mantelpiece; window case.

chambre *n.f.* chamber, room, court or assembly; the part of a cannon containing the charge; *Opt.* camera. ~ **à coucher,** bedroom. ~ **des députés,** house of representatives. ~ **de commerce,** chamber of commerce. ~ **civile,** court for civil causes. *Opt.* ~ **noire,** camera obscura. ~ **haute,** house of peers (or lords). ~ **basse,** lower house.

chambrée *n.f.* chamberful (of persons, etc.); mess (soldiers); barracks. **comme j'étais de ~ avec lui,** as I slept in the same room with him.

chambrer *v.i.* to lodge, to sleep in the same room. *v.t.* to seclude (a person) by force or craft; to take aside (a person); to bring to room temperature.

chambrette *n.f.* small room (or chamber).

chambrière *n.f.* chambermaid; long horsewhip; prop for the shaft of a cart.

chameau *n.m.* camel.

chamelier *n.m.* camel driver.

chamelle *n.f.* female camel.

chamois *n.m.* chamois; chamois leather.

champ *n.m.* field, country fields; ground; scope, opportunity, theme, subject, space; *Paint.* ground, background. ~ **de course,** racetrack. **en plein ~,** in the open country. ~ **de bataille,** battlefield. ~ **labouré,** a plowed field. **prendre la clef des ~s,** to run away. **avoir du ~ devant soi,** to have time at one's disposal. **sur-le-~,** immediately, directly. **tomber, mourir au ~ d'honneur,** to be killed in action.

Champagne *n.f.* Champagne (province of France). *n.m.* champagne. ~ **mousseux,**

sparkling champagne. ~ **frappé,** iced champagne.

champêtre *adj.* rural, country. **garde ~,** fieldkeeper.

champignon *n.m.* mushroom; fungus, toadstool. **conche de ~s,** mushroom bed. *Infml.* **appuyer sur le ~,** to put one's foot down, to hurry.

champignonnière *n.f.* mushroom bed.

champion *n.m.* champion.

championnat *n.m.* championship.

chançard, e *adj.* lucky. *n.m.f.* lucky devil, lucky dog.

chance *n.f.* chance, hazard, luck, risk. **je n'ai pas de ~,** I have no luck. **avoir toutes les ~s contre soi,** to have all the odds against oneself.

chancelant, e *adj.* tottering, staggering, wavering, hesitating, unsteady, unsettled.

chanceler *v.i.* to totter, to stagger, to waver, to hesitate, to be unsteady.

chancelier *n.m.* chancellor.

chancellerie *n.f.* chancellor's office.

chanceux, euse *adj.* hazardous, uncertain, doubtful, risky; lucky (person).

chancre *n.m.* canker; chancre.

chandail *n.m.* sweater, pullover.

chandelier *n.m.* candlestick, candelabra.

chandelle *n.f.* candle. **économie de bouts de ~,** penny wise and pound foolish. **le jeu n'en vaut pas la ~,** the game is not worth the effort.

change *n.m.* change, exchange. **~ de monnaies,** money changing. **agent de ~,** stockbroker. **~ extérieur,** foreign exchange. **lettre de ~,** bill of exchange. **taux de ~,** exchange, rate of exchange.

changeant, e *adj.* changeable, unsteady, fickle, wavering, unsettled, variable. **humeur ~e,** change of mood.

changement *n.m.* change; *Mil.* transfer. **~ de propriétaire,** under new management.

changer *v.t.* to change, to exchange, to alter, to transform, to turn. *v.i.* to change, to alter. **~ de couleur,** to change color. **le vent venant à ~,** the wind happening to change. **~ de place avec,** to switch, trade places with. **~ de domicile,** to move. **une promenade lui changera les idées,** a walk will take her mind off things. **cela ne change rien à l'affaire,** it doesn't make the slightest difference. **se ~,** *v.refl.* to change, to change one's clothes. **il n'a pas de quoi se ~,** he doesn't even have a change of clothes. **se ~ en,** to turn into, to change into.

changeur, euse *n.m.f.* money changer.

chanoine *n.m.* canon.

chanoinesse *n.f.* canoness.

chanson *n.f.* song, story, nonsense. **~ à boire,** drinking song. **toujours la même ~,** always the same old story. **~ que tout cela!** that is all nonsense!

chansonnette *n.f.* short song.

chansonnier, ère *n.m.f.* songwriter, ballad maker. *n.m.* songbook.

chant *n.m.* singing, song, air, chant, melody, chirp (bird); canto, book. **leçon de ~,** singing lesson. **~ mélodieux,** melodious song. **le ~ du rossignol,** the song of the nightingale. **le ~ du cygne,** swan song. **le ~ du coq,** cockcrow. **~ de Noël,** Christmas carol. **~s d'église,** church music, chanting. **dans le deuxième ~ de Don Juan,** in the second canto of *Don Juan.*

chantable *adj.* fit or worthy to be sung.

chantage *n.m.* blackmail, blackmailing.

chantant, e *adj.* lyrical; easily sung; tuneful.

chanteau *n.m.* piece of a loaf, chunk of bread. **passez-moi le ~,** hand me the loaf.

chanter *v.i.* to sing, to chant; to say too much; to crow (as the cock). **~ juste,** to sing in tune. **~ faux,** to sing out of tune. **je le ferai ~ sur un autre ton,** I will make him sing a different tune. **faire ~ quelqu'un,** to extort money, to blackmail. *v.t.* to sing; to chant, to praise; to talk nonsense. **que chantez-vous là?** what are you saying there; what nonsense is that?

chanterelle *n.f.* E-string (*Mus.*) (of a violin, etc.); musical bottle; decoy bird.

chanteur, euse *n.m.f.* singer, vocalist; songbird. V. MAITRE.

chantier *n.m.* construction site; depot, yard; roadworks (*pl.*), men at work; *Naut.* yard. **~ de construction navale,** shipyard. *Fig.* mess, shambles. **ta chambre est un vrai ~,** your bedroom is a mess.

chantonnement *n.m.* humming.

chantonner *v.i.* to hum (a song). *v.t.* to hum.

chantoung *n.m.* shantung (silk).

chantourner *v.t.* to jigsaw, to whipsaw.

chantre *n.m.* singer; songster; chanter; precentor (of a cathedral).

chânvre *n.m.* hemp.

chanvreux, euse *adj.* hempen.

chanvrier, ère *n.m.f.* hemp grower, hemp seller.

chaos *n.m.* chaos, confusion.

chaotique *adj.* chaotic.

chapardage *n.m.* petty theft, scrounging.

chaparder *v.t.* to pilfer, to scrounge, to sneak, to filch.

chapardeur, euse *adj.* petty thief.

chape *n.f.* cope (priest's); cape, cope (of a vault).

chapeau *n.m.* hat. **~ de soie, de feutre, de paille,** silk hat, felt hat, straw hat. **porter la main au ~,** to touch one's hat (in saluting). **~ bas,** hats off! **~ chinois,** Chinese bells.

chapelain *n.m.* chaplain.

chapelet *n.m.* rosary, beads. *Arch.* chaplet; chain pump; string (of onions). **dire son ~,** to pray the rosary. **défiler son ~,** to tell one's story.

chapelier, ère *n.m.f.* hatter, hat manufacturer.

chapelle *n.f.* chapel, altar vessels. **maître de ~,** chapel master, precentor. **~ ardente,** place with candles burning around a coffin.

chapellerie *n.f.* hatmaking; hat trade; hatter's shop.

chapelure *n.f.* breadcrumbs.

chaperon *n.m.* hood; chaperone; *Arch.* coping (of a wall); holster cap. **le petit ~ rouge**, Little Red Riding Hood.

chaperonner *v.t.* to hood (a hawk); *Arch.* to cope (a wall); to chaperone (a young lady).

chapiteau *n.m.* head; top of a still, etc.; *Arch.* capital; *Mach.* dome, crest; big top (circus).

chapitre *n.m.* chapter; head, subject, matter; **avoir voix au ~**, to have a voice in the matter.

chapitrer *v.t.* to reprimand, to admonish, to lecture.

chapon *n.m.* capon; piece of bread boiled in the soup; crust rubbed with garlic.

chaque *adj.* each, every. **~ pays a ses coutumes**, every country has its customs. **à ~ jour suffit sa peine**, sufficient unto the day is the evil thereof.

char *n.m.* chariot; cart, wagon.

charabia *n.m.* gibberish, gabble.

charade *n.f.* charade, riddle, puzzle.

charançon *n.m.* weevil.

charançonné, e *adj.* weevilly, weeviled.

charbon *n.m.* charcoal, coal. **~ de bois**, charcoal. **~ animal**, animal charcoal. **~ ardent**, hot embers, burning coal. **être sur des ~s ardents**, to be on pins and needles; anthrax, carbuncle; *Agr.* smut, black rust.

charbonnage *n.m.* coal pit, coal mine.

charbonnée *n.f.* grilled, deviled rib of pork or beef; layer of coal (in a brick- or limekiln).

charbonner *v.t.* to char, to blacken, **se ~ le visage**, to blacken one's face. *v.i.* to char, to become charred carbonized.

charbonnier, ière *n.m.f.* charcoal burner; charcoal dealer. **~ est maître chez lui**, a man's house is his castle.

charcuter *v.t.* to chop up (meat); to mangle, to hack to pieces. *Infml.* to knife, to butcher (a surgical patient).

charcuterie *n.f.* pork butcher's meat; pork butcher's shop, delicatessen of pork specialties and other prepared foods.

charcutier, ère *n.m.f.* pork butcher; *Fig.* butcher (surgeon).

chardon *n.m.* thistle; spike placed on walls, etc.

chardonneret *n.m.* goldfinch.

charge *n.f.* load, cargo, load, lading; maintenance fee; burden; tax; expense; accusation; indictment, trust, care, charge; caricature. **il a sa ~**, *Fig.* he has drunk a bit too much. **à ~**, dependent (child). **avoir ~ d'âmes**, to have the care of souls (priest). **les ~s publiques**, public functions. **~ de notaire**, office of a notary. **témoin à ~**, witness for the prosecution. **une ~ de cavalerie**, a cavalry charge. **revenir à la ~**, to return to the charge. **mettre double ~**, to double-load. **faire la ~ d'une personne**, to caricature a person. **à la ~ de**, on condition of.

se démettre de sa ~, to resign one's functions. **enfants confiés à la ~ de**, children in the care of.

chargé, e *p.p.* charged; loaded, laden, burdened; *Med.* furred (as the tongue, etc.); *n.m.* **~ d'affaires**, chargé d'affaires. **mot ~ de sens**, word full of meaning. **regard ~ de menaces**, threatening look. **horaire ~**, busy schedule. **il a la conscience ~e**, his conscience is burdened or troubled. **cet homme a un passé ~**, this is a man with a past. **~ de mission** *n.m.* (official) representative.

chargeant, e *adj.* heavy, clogging.

chargement *n.m.* lading, shipping; freight.

charger *v.t.* to load. to charge; to burden, to encumber; to fill; to impute; to entrust, to overdraw. **~ de chaînes**, to load with chains. **~ une lettre**, to register a letter **~ à balle**, to load with bullets. **~ un compte**, to overcharge an account. **se ~ de faire quelque chose**, to take something upon oneself. **il s'en charge**, he'll see to it. **il va ~ la voiture**, he is going to load the car. **on l'a chargé d'une mission importante**, he was assigned an important mission. **il m'a chargé de vous transmettre ses amitiés**, he sends you his regards. **se ~**, *v.refl.* to load oneself; to undertake; to become overcast (as the sky). **se ~ d'une dette**, to take on a debt. **le ciel se chargea peu à peu**, the sky gradually became overcast.

chargeur *n.m.* loader, shipper, freighter.

chariot *n.m.* wagon, cart.

charitable *adj.* charitable.

charitablement *adv.* charitably.

charité *n.f.* charity; kindness, benevolence; alms. **demander la ~**, to beg. **sœur de ~**, Sister of Charity. **~ bien ordonnée commence par soi-même**, charity begins at home.

charivari *n.m.* charivari, discordant music, clatter, noise, hubbub.

charlatan *n.m.* quack, mountebank, charlatan.

charlatanerie *n.f.* charlatanry; quackery.

charlatanesque *adj.* charlatanical, quackish.

charlatanisme *n.m.* charlatanism.

charleston *n.m.* charleston.

charmant, e *adj.* charming, delightful, pleasant.

charme *n.m.* charm, magic spell, delight; hornbeam, yoke elm. **rompre un ~**, to break a spell. *Fig.* fascination, seduction.

charmé, e *adj.* bewitched, fascinated.

charmer *v.t.* to charm, to bewitch, to delight, to fascinate, to captivate. **je suis charmé de vous voir**, I am delighted to see you.

charmeur, euse *n.m.f.* charmer.

charnel, elle *adj.* carnal; sensual.

charnellement *adv.* carnally, sensually.

charnier *n.m.* charnel house.

charnière *n.f.* hinge.

charnu, e *adj.* fleshy; plump; brawny.

charognard *n.m.* vulture.

charogne *n.f.* carrion.

charpente *n.f.* timberwork, carpenter's work; frame, framework. **bois de ~**, building timber.

charpenterie *n.f.* carpentry.

charpentier *n.m.* carpenter; shipwright.

charpie *n.f.* shred. **mettre en charpie**, to shred.

charretier, ère *n.m.f.* carter, wagon driver, *Pej.* **jurer comme un ~**, to swear like a trooper.

charrette *n.f.* cart. **~ à bras**, handcart.

charriage *n.m.* cartage.

charrier *v.t.* to cart, to carry in a cart. **~ quel-qu'un**, to take someone for a ride, to poke fun at someone.

charroi *n.m.* cartage.

charron *n.m.* wheelwright.

charroyer *v.t.* to cart.

charrue *n.f.* plow. **mettre la ~ devant les boeufs**, to put the cart before the horse. **passer la ~ sur**, to plow.

charte *n.f.* charter. **la Grande ~**, Magna Carta.

charter *n.m. Aviat.* flight, plane.

chartreuse *n.f.* Carthusian convent; Carthusian nun; a liqueur distilled by the monks of the Grande Chartreuse near Grenoble.

chartreux *n.m.* Carthusian friar.

Charybde *n.m.* Charybdis. **tomber de ~ en Scylla**, to fall out of the frying pan into the fire.

chas *n.m.* eye (of a needle).

chasse *n.f.* chase; hunting; shooting; game; play (of a machine). **~ à courre**, hunting with hounds. **~ á l'homme**, manhunt. **~ aux sor-cières**, witch hunt. **~ du renard**, fox hunting. **maison de ~**, hunting lodge. **donner la ~**, to chase, to pursue. **donner la ~ à**, to chase. **tirer la ~ d'eau**, to flush the toilet. **~-neige**, snow-plow.

châsse *n.f.* reliquary.

chassé *n.m. Danc.* chassé.

chassé-croisé *n.m. Danc.* chassé-croisé; change (of situation, places, etc.).

chasser *v.t.* to chase; to hunt; to drive away; to expel, to discharge; to pursue. **~ les mouches**, to shoo flies. *v.i.* to hunt. **~ à cor et à cri**, to hunt with horn and hound. **bon chien chasse de race**, to be a chip off the old block. **ce bâti-ment chasse sur ses ancres**, that ship is dragging her anchors.

chasseresse *n.f.* and *adj.* huntress.

chasseur, euse *n.m.f.* hunter; sportsman, hunts-man, shooter; **~ de têtes**, headhunter, bellboy.

chassie *n.f.* rheum.

chassieux, euse *adj.* bleary eyed.

châssis *n.m.* frame.

chaste *adj.* chaste, pure, uncorrupt, refined.

chastement *adv.* chastely, purely.

chasteté *n.f.* chastity, chasteness, purity.

chat, chatte *n.m.f.* cat, (of the male) tomcat. *Infml.* puss, pussy; sweetie. **petit ~**, a kitten. **appeler un ~ un ~**, to call a spade a spade; not to mince words. **à bon ~ bon rat**, tit for tat. **il n'y a pas de quoi fouetter un ~**, it is a mere trifle. **acheter ~ en poche**, to buy a pig in a poke. **~ échaudé craint l'eau froide**, once bit-ten, twice shy. **quand le ~s n'y sont pas les souris dansent sous la table**, when the cat's away the mice will play. *Bot.* **pieds de ~**, cat's foot, cotton rose. **oeil de ~**, snapdragon.

châtaigne *n.f.* chestnut. **~ d'eau**, water chest-nut. **~ de mer**, sea urchin. **flanquer une ~ (à quelqu'un)**, to punch someone.

châtaigneraie *n.f.* chestnut grove.

châtaignier *n.m.* chestnut tree.

châtain *adj. n.m.* chestnut, auburn, nut-brown. **~ clair**, light auburn (hair).

château *n.m.* castle, palace, mansion, country house. **le ~ de Fontainebleau**, the palace of Fontainebleau. **faire des ~x en Espagne**, to build castles in the air.

châtelain, e *n.m.f.* and *adj.* owner of a manor. *n.f.* chatelaine, a jewel suspended from the waistband.

chat-huant *n.m.* screech owl, brown owl.

châtier *v.t.* to chastise, to correct, to punish; to castigate, to chasten. **qui aime bien, châtie bien** spare the rod and spoil the child. **~ son style**, to polish one's style.

chatière *n.f.* cat's hole, cat trap.

châtiment *n.m.* chastisement, castigation, cor-rection, corporal punishment.

chatoiement *n.m.* play of colors, shimmering.

chaton *n.m.* kitten; *Bot.* catkin; setting of a gem.

chatouille, *n.f.* tickle. **craindre les ~s**, to be ticklish.

chatouillement *n.m.* tickling.

chatouiller *v.t.* to tickle.

chatouilleux, euse *adj.* ticklish, touchy.

chatoyant, e *adj.* shimmering, iridescent, glis-tening.

chatoyer *v.i.* to shimmer, to sparkle, to glisten.

châtrer *v.t.* to castrate, to emasculate; to muti-late (books); to geld (male animals), to spay (female animals). **~ un cheval**, to geld a horse.

chatte *n.f.* she-cat.

chatterie *n.f.* daintiness; dainty foods; wheedling caress.

chaud, e *adj.* hot, warm, hasty, hotheaded, vio-lent, furious, animated. **tout ~**, burning hot. **tempérament ~**, hot temper. **un ami ~**, a warm friend. **cela est encore tout ~**, that is still quite recent. *adv.* hot, warm. **servir ~**, **boire ~, manger ~**, to serve, drink, eat hot. *Fig.* **elle a eu ~**, she had a narrow escape. **ça ne lui fait ni ~ ni froid**, he/she couldn't care less. **pleurer à ~es larmes**, to cry one's eyes out.

chaud *n.m.* heat. **avoir ~**, to be hot. **il fait ~**, it is hot.

chaudement *adv.* hotly, warmly, briskly, actively

chaudière *n.f.* boiler (of an engine).

chaudron *n.m.* caldron.

chauffage *n.m.* fuel, firing, **~ central**, central heating.

chauffant *adj.* heating; electric (blanket).

chauffard *n.m.* reckless driver, hit-and-run driver.

chauffe-assiettes *n.m.* plate-warmer.

chauffe-pieds *n.m.* foot-warmer.

chauffer *v.t.* to heat; to warm; *v.i.* to heat up, to warm up, to get hot. **le bain chauffe**, the bath is being heated. **se ~**, *v.refl.* to warm oneself; *Infml.* **ca va ~!** things are getting hot. **il va voir de quel bois je me chauffe**, he is going to find out what stuff I am made of.

chaufferette *n.f.* foot warmer.

chaufferie *n.f.* boiler room (factory).

chauffeur *n.m.* chauffeur, driver.

chaulage *n.m. Agr.* liming; lime washing (of trees).

chauler *v.t. Agr.* to lime; to lime-wash (trees).

chaume *n.m.* thatch.

chaumière *n.f.* thatched cottage.

chaussant, e *adj.* well-fitting.

chaussé, e *p.p.* booted, shod. **bien ~**, well-shod, well-fitted.

chaussée *n.f.* bank; causeway; road, roadway. **rez-de-~**, ground floor.

chausse-pied *n.m.* shoehorn.

chausser *v.t.* to put on (boots, shoes, stockings, etc.); to fit. *v.i.* **se ~**, *v.refl.* to put on one's stockings, shoes, etc.

chaussette *n.f.* sock.

chausseur *n.m.* shoemaker, footwear specialist.

chausson *n.m.* slipper; bootee (baby); pump (dancer). **~ aux pommes**, apple turnover.

chaussure *n.f.* shoe; footwear; *Infml.* **trouver ~ à son pied**, to find one's match.

chauve *adj.* bald.

chauve-souris *n.f.* bat.

chauvin, e *adj.* chauvinistic. *n.m.f.* chauvinist.

chauvinisme *n.m.* chauvinism.

chaux *n.f.* lime. **pierre à ~**, limestone. **~ vive, éteinte**, quicklime, slaked lime. **blanc de ~**, limewash.

chavirer *v.i.* to capsize, to upset. *v.t.* to capsize, to turn upside down; to turn inside out.

chéchia *n.f.* tarboosh, fez.

chef *n.m.* head; leader, principal, chief; *Law.* count, right. **de son ~**, on one's own authority. **~ de parti**, leader of a party. **~ de bureau**, head or chief clerk. **~ d'orchestre**, conductor of an orchestra. **~ de rayon**, supervisor. **~ de cuisine**, chef, head cook. **au premier ~**, in the highest degree.

chef-d'oeuvre *n.m.* masterpiece.

chef-lieu *n.m.* county seat.

cheftaine *n.f.* scoutmistress, den mother.

cheik *n.m.* sheik.

chelem *n.m.* slam (at cards.)

chemin *n.m.* way; road, passage, path, course, means, method. **se mettre en ~**, to set off. **passer son ~**, to go one's way. **s'arrêter en beam ~**, to stop short in the midst of success. **aller son petit bonhomme de ~**, to go plodding on. **tout les ~s mènent à Rome**, all

roads lead to Rome. **~ faisant**, on the way. **~ de traverse**, side road. **~ vicinal**, village road. **par ~ de fer**, by rail.

cheminée *n.f.* chimney, fireplace; lamp globe; mantelpiece. **manteau de ~**, mantelpiece.

cheminement *n.m.* walking, progress.

cheminer *v.i.* to go on, to walk, to make one's way; to advance, to progress. **~ lentement**, to trudge on slowly.

chemise *n.f.* shirt, file folder; case, casing. **~ de nuit**, nightgown. **vendre jusqu'à sa ~**, to sell one's shirt off one's back.

chemisette *n.f.* short-sleeved shirt or blouse.

chemisier, ère *n.m.f.* shirtmaker; shirt waist.

chênaie *n.f.* oak grove.

chenal *n.m.* channel, mill race, gutter (of a roof).

chenapan *n.m.* scamp, rascal, scoundrel.

chêne *n.m.* oak, evergreen oak.

chéneau *n.m.* gutter (of a roof).

chenil *n.m.* kennel.

chenille *n.f.* caterpillar, grub; chenille (silk trimming).

chenu, e *adj.* hoary, gray-headed.

cheptel *n.m.* livestock; **~ mort**, farm implement. **~ vif**, livestock.

chèque *n.m.* check (bank).

chéquier *n.m.* checkbook.

cher, chère *adj.* dear, beloved; cherished; valuable, precious, costly, expensive. *adv.* dear, dearly. **être ~**, to be expensive.

chercher *v.t.* to seek, to search for, to look for, to fetch, to try. **que cherchez-vous?** what are you looking for? **~ midi à quatorze heures**, to look for difficulties where there are none. **~ querelle**, to pick a quarrel. **il ne cherchait pas à dissimuler sa joie**, he did not seek to hide his joy.

chercheur, euse *n.m.f.* seeker; researcher, research worker; *Techn.* finder (telescope); *Radio.* cat's whisker; **~ d'or**, gold digger. **~ de trésor**, treasure hunter. *adj.* inquiring (mind); searching (look).

chèrement *adv.* dearly, tenderly; at a high price.

chéri, e *p.p.* cherished, beloved, dear, darling.

chérif *n.m.* sheriff, sharif.

chérir *v.t.* to cherish, to love dearly, to idolize, to hug. **se ~** *v.refl.* to cherish each other, to be cherished.

cherry *n.m.* cherry brandy.

cherté *n.f.* high price.

chérubin *n.m.* cherub.

chétif, ive *adj.* puny, sickly (child, plant); stunted (plant); poor (mine, harvest); paltry, puny (person); weak (body, memory, health); paltry (reason).

chétivement *adv.* poorly; punily; weakly.

cheval *n.m. pl.* chevaux, horse, cavalry. **~ de bataille**, war horse, charger. **~ de carrosse**, carriage horse. **~ de selle, de trait**, saddle horse, draft horse. **~ pur-sang**, thoroughbred horse. **~ à bascule**, rocking horse. **monter sur**

ses grands chevaux, to get on one's high horse. brider son ~ par la queue, to go about something the wrong way. à ~ donné on ne regarde pas à la bride, one must not look a gift horse in the mouth. une machine de 200 chevaux, an engine of 200 horsepower. ~ marin, seahorse, walrus. faire du ~, to ride on horseback.

chevalement n.m. shoring, scaffolding (construction); frame.

chevaler v.i. to shore up.

chevaleresque adj. knightly, chivalrous; gentlemanly.

chevalerie n.f. chivalry, knighthood.

chevalet n.m. easel, wooden horse (an instrument of torture); bridge (of a stringed instrument); trestle; clothes horse.

chevalier n.m. knight, cavalier, sandpiper. armer ~, to knight a person. ~ errant, knight-errant. ~ de la Légion d'Honneur, knight of the Legion of Honor. ~ d'industrie, wheeler-dealer.

chevalière n.f. a signet ring.

chevaline adj. f. equine.

chevauchant, e adj. overlapping.

chevauchée n.f. horseback ride.

chevauchement n.m. overlapping; riding; Geol. thrust fault.

chevaucher v.i. to ride horseback, to ride along; to sit astride; to overlap. se chevaucher, v. refl. to overlap.

chevelu, e adj. long haired, hairy, bearded. le cuir ~, the scalp (of the head). n.m. Bot. beard (of a root).

chevelure n.f. head of hair, hair.

chevet n.m. bedhead; bedside (sick person). lampe, table, livre de ~, bedside lamp, table, book. Arch. chevet.

cheveu n.m. hair. fendre, couper un ~ en quatre, to split a hair; to quibble. se prendre aux ~x, to come to blows. tiré par les ~x, farfetched.

cheville n.f. peg, pin, bolt (metal). ficher une ~, to drive in a peg. la ~ du pied, the ankle. Fig. aucun ne lui arrive à la ~, he is head and shoulders above the others.

cheviller v.i. to peg, to pin, to bolt.

chèvre n.f. goat. ménager la ~ et le chou, to have it both ways. sawhorse; gin (machine).

chevreau n.m. kid, kid leather.

chèvrefeuille n.m. honeysuckle.

chevrette n.f. young she-goat; shrimp.

chevreuil n.m. roebuck.

chevrier, ère n.m.f. goatherd; white kidney bean.

chevron n.m. rafter; Arch. chevron; Mil. stripe.

chevronné p.p. experienced, practiced, veteran.

chevrotant, e adj. tremulous, quavering, shaking.

chevrotement n.m. tremulousness, quavering of the voice.

chevroter v.i. to kid (goats); to speak or sing in a tremulous voice.

chevrotine n.f. buckshot.

chewing-gum n.m. chewing gum.

chez prep. at the house of; at, to, in, with, at home. il est allé ~ lui, he has gone home. vous êtes ~ vous, you are at home. il est ~ le libraire, he is at the bookseller's. ~ les anciens, among (or with) the ancients. c'est une habitude ~ moi, it is a habit with me. n.m. un ~ moi, a home of my own. son ~ lui, his own home. elle revient de ~ son frère, she is returning from her brother's house.

chialer v.i. Infml. to blubber, to cry.

chialeur, euse n.m.f. crybaby, blubberer.

chiant, e adj. Infml. draggy, boring.

chiasse n.f. fly speck, runs.

chic n.m. chic, style. adj. fine, smart. c'est très ~, it is awfully nice.

chicane n.f. chicanery, cavilling, quibbling, quibble. chercher ~, to pick a quarrel.

chicaner v.i. to quibble. v.t. to wrangle over; to pester, to dispute. ~ le vent, Naut. to hug the wind. se ~, v.refl. to go to court with one another; to wrangle with one another.

chicaneries n.f. pl. chicanery; quibbling.

chicaneur, euse n.m.f. quibbler. adj. quibbling.

chicanier, ère n.m.f. quibbler. adj. quibbling.

chiche adj. scanty; stingy, sparing. qu'il est ~! how stingy he is! être ~ de ses paroles, to be sparing of one's words.

chichement adv. stingily.

chichi n.m. airs, fuss.

chicorée n.f. chicory, wild endive.

chicot n.m. stump; stub.

chicotin n.m. extract of aloe.

chié adj. il est ~ ce type, damn guy.

chiée n.f. Infml. a lot of.

chien, ne n.m.f. dog n.m. bitch n.f. grand ~, dog star, Sirius, cock (of fire-arms). ~ de berger, sheepdog. ~ de garde, watch dog, house dog. ~ de chasse, hunting dog. ~ d'arrêt, pointer. ~ couchant, setter. ~ de mer, dogfish. entre ~ et loup, at dusk. leurs ~s ne chassent point ensemble, they cannot agree. mener une vie de ~, to lead a dog's life. ils s'accordent comme ~s et chats, they get along like cats and dogs. il n'est pas trop ~ avec ses ouvriers, he is not a bad master. temps de ~, miserable weather. V. ABOYER, CHASSER.

chiendent n.m. couch grass.

chiffe n.f. old rag; flimsy stuff.

chiffon n.m. rag.

chiffonner v.t. to crumple, to rumple, to tumble; to ruffle.

chiffonnier, ère n.m.f. ragpicker; chiffonnier.

chiffrage n.m. coding; ciphering; stamping (stationery); marking; calculating.

chiffre n.m. figure, number, total amount; monogram. ~s romains, Roman numerals. la clef d'un ~, the key of a code. écrire en ~s, to write in code.

chiffrer v.i. to calculate. v.t. to number; to value in figures; Mus. to figure (a bass). se ~, to amount to.

chiffreur n.m. coder.

chignole n.f. drill.

chignon n.m. chignon; bun (hair).

Chili n.m. Chile.

chimère n.f. chimera, idle fancy.

chimerique adj. chimerical, wild, fanciful.

chimie n.f. chemistry.

chimiothérapie n.f. chemotherapy.

chimique adj. chemical.

chimiquement adv. chemically.

chimiste n.m. chemist.

chimpanzé n.m. chimpanzee; chimp.

chinchilla n.m. chinchilla.

Chine n.f. China.

chiner v.t. to color, to dye.

chinois, e adj. Chinese.

chinoiserie n.f. Chinese knickknacks; nonsense.

chiot n.m. pup(py).

chiottes n.f.pl., Vulg. restroom.

chiper v.t. Infml. to pinch, to swipe.

chipeur, euse n.m.f. petty thief.

chipie n.f. Infml. proud disagreeable woman.

chipolata n.f. chipolata (kind of stew).

chipotage n.m. Infml. quibbling; picking, nib-bling (food).

chipoter v.i. to quibble, to pick, to nibble; to be finicky.

chips n.m.pl. potato chips.

chique n.f. chigger; quid (of tobacco).

chiqué n.m. Infml. make-believe, pretense, bluff; fuss, showing off.

chiquement adv. stylishly, smartly.

chiquenaude n.f. flick.

chiquer v.i. to chew tobacco.

chiromancie n.f. chiromancy, palmistry.

chiromancien, ienne n.m.f. chiromancer.

chiropracteur n.m. chiropractor.

chiropractie n.f. chiropractic.

chirurgical, e adj. surgical.

chirurgie n.f. surgery.

chirurgien n.m. surgeon.

chiure n.f. fly speck, fly dirt.

chlorate n.m. chlorate.

chlore n.m. chlorine.

chloré, e adj. chlorinated.

chlorhydrique adj. hydrochloric.

chlorique adj. chloric.

chloroforme n.m. chloroform.

chloroformer v.t. to chloroform.

chlorophylle n.f. chlorophyll.

chlorure n.m. chloride, chloruret.

choc n.m. shock, collision; conflict, onset; blow, disaster. soutenir le ~, to stand the shock.

chocolat n.m. chocolate.

chocolaté, e adj. chocolate flavored.

chocolaterie n.f. chocolate factory; chocolate shop.

chocolatier, ière n.m. chocolate dealer, maker or manufacturer.

chocottes n.f.pl. Infml. avoir les ~, to have the jitters.

choeur n.m. chorus, choir; chancel (in a church). chanter en ~, to sing in chorus.

choir v.i. to fall.

choisir v.t. to choose; to make choice of; to select, to pick out, to single out.

choix n.m. choice, selection, option. sans ~, indiscriminately. n'avoir pas de ~, to have no alternative.

choléra n.m. cholera.

cholérique adj. choleric; affected with cholera.

cholestérol n.m. cholesterol.

chômage n.m. unemployment.

chômer v.i. to be out of work; to be unemployed.

chômeur, euse n.m.f. unemployed person.

chope n.f. beer glass; glass of beer, mug.

choper v.t. to nab; se faire ~, to get nabbed.

chopine n.f. nearly an English pint.

choquant, e adj. shocking.

choquer v.t. to shock, to strike against; to collide with to run against, to wound, to hurt: Naut. to surge. ~ l'oreille, to shock (or offend) the ear. v.i. to be offensive, to hurt one's feelings; to touch glasses. se ~, v.refl. to collide with; to be shocked or offended.

choral, e adj. choral. n.m. chorale.

chorégraphe n.m. choreographer.

chorégraphie n.f. choreography.

chorégraphique adj. choreographic.

choriste n.m. chorister.

chorus n.m. chorus. faire ~, to sing in chorus, to chime in.

chose n.f. thing, matter, affair, business. dire bien des ~s à quelqu'un, to present one's compliments to a person. autre ~, another thing; anything else. monsieur ~, Mr. What's-His-Name. peu de ~, a trifle. ce n'est pas grand ~, it is no great matter. adj. bizarre, peculiar; après avoir entendu la nouvelle, il s'est senti tout ~, after hearing the news, he felt somewhat peculiar.

chou n.m. cabbage. ~ frise, kale. ~ rouge, red cabbage. -x de Bruxelles, Brussels sprouts. bête comme ~, dull as dishwater, stupid. aller planter ses ~x, Fig. to go and live in the country. V. CHEVRE. faire ~ blanc, to fail, to miss one's aim. mon petit ~, my little darling.

choucas n.m. jackdaw.

chou-chou n.m. favorite; pet.

chouchouter v.t. to pet, to pamper, to coddle.

choucroute n.f. sauerkraut.

chouette n.f. owl; adj. nice. sois ~, prête-moi ta voiture, be nice/a sport, lend me your car.

chow-chow n.m. chow (dog).

choyer v.i. to fondle, to pet, to pamper, to coddle, to cherish. se ~, v.i. refl. to pamper oneself.

chrême *n.m.* chrism; consecrated oil.

chrétien, ienne *adj.* Christian.

chrétiennement *adv.* Christianly, like a Christian.

Chrétienté *n.f.* Christendom.

Christ *n.m.* Christ. *n.m.* crucifix.

Christianiser *v.t.* to Christianize.

Christianisme *n.m.* Christianity.

chromage *n.m.* chromium plating.

chromate *n.m.* chromate.

chromatique *adj.* chromatic. *n.m.* chromatic.

chromatisme *n.m.* chromatism.

chrome *n.m.* chrome, chrominum.

chromo *n.m.* chromo.

chromosome *n.m.* chromosome.

chronicité *n.f.* chronic character (of a disease).

chronique *n.f.* chronicle, ~ **politique**, political chronicle. *adj.* chronic.

chroniqueur *n.m.* chronicler.

chrono *n.m. (abbr.* **chronomètre**) stopwatch.

chronologie *n.f.* chronology.

chronologique *adj.* chronologic, chronological.

chronomètre *n.m.* chronometer; stopwatch.

chronomérique *adj.* chronometric, chronometrical.

chrysalide *n.f.* chrysalis, grub.

chrysanthème *n.m.* chrysanthemum.

chuchotement *n.m.* whispering, whisper.

chuchoter *v.i.* to whisper.

chuchoteur, euse *n.m.f.* whisperer.

chuintant *adj.* whispering.

chut *interj.* hush! be still!

chute *n.f.* fall; tumble; falling; falling off; cascade, cataract; slope, declivity; downfall; ruin; overthrow. **la ~ des feuilles**, the fall of the leaves. **~ d'eau**, waterfall. **la ~ du jour**, nightfall. **la ~ d'une voile**, the depth of a sail.

chuter *v.i. Theat.* to fail.

Chypre *n.f.* Cyprus.

ci *adv.* here; opposed to **là. ci-git un tel**, here lies so-and-so. **ci-inclus**, enclosed. **ci-joint**, attached. **cet homme-ci**, this man. **-ci-après**, below. **ci-contre**, on the other side. **ci-dessus**, above. **ci-dessous**, below, hereafter. **ci-devant**, formerly, before; late. **par-ci, par-là**, here and there, now and then.

cible *n.f.* target.

ciboire *n.m.* ciborium, pyx.

ciboulette *n.f.* chives.

ciboulot *n.m. Infml.* head, bean.

cicatrice *n.f.* scar.

cicatrisant, e *adj.* scarring, healing.

cicatrisation *n.f.* healing; cicatrization.

cicatriser *v.t.* to cicatrize, to mark with a scar or scars; to seam. **s'~**, *v.refl.* to scar, to be skinning over.

cidre *n.m.* cider.

ciel (*pl.* **cieux**) *n.m.* heaven, weather; firmament, sky, paradise. **sous le ~**, beneath the sky. **remuer ~ et terre**, to leave no stone unturned. **que le ~ m'en préserve!** God forbid! **~ cou-**vert, cloudy sky. **le ~ de l'Italie**, the climate of Italy.

cierge *n.m.* wax candle, taper. **~ du Pérou**, torch thistle.

cigale *n.f.* cicada, grasshopper.

cigare *n.m.* cigar.

cigarette *n.f.* cigarette.

cigogne *n.f.* stork.

ciguë *n.f.* hemlock.

cil *n.m.* eyelash; (*pl.*) **cilia. Bot.** hairs, lash.

cillement *n.m.* twinkling, winking (of the eyes).

ciller *v.t.* to wink.

cime *n.f.* top, summit.

ciment *n.m.* cement. **~ armé**, reinforced concrete. **lait de ~**, thin mortar.

cimenter *v.t.* to cement; to unite firmly; to strengthen.

cimetière *n.m.* cemetery, burial ground, graveyard.

ciné *n.m. abbr.* **cinéma**, movies.

cinéaste *n.m.f.* filmmaker.

cinéma *n.m.* cinema; movie theater; screen; pictures. **faire un ~**, to make a fuss or a big deal of; to film.

cinémascope *n.m.* cinemascope.

cinémathèque *n.f.* film library, film archives.

cinématique *n.f.* kinematics.

cinématographe *n.m.* cinematograph.

cinématographie *n.f.* filmmaking; cinematography.

cinématographier *v.t.* to film.

cinéphile *n.m.f.* moviegoer, film fan.

cinéraire *adj.* cinerary. *n.f.* cineraria.

cinétique *adj.* kinetic. *n.f.* kinetics.

cinglant *adj.* biting, keen, bitter (cold); driving, lashing (rain); cutting, stinging, scathing (irony).

cinglé, e *adj.* nutty; screwy; loco.

cingler *v.i.* to sail, to steer. *v.t.* to lash, to switch; to shingle. **le vent leur cinglait le visage**, the wind cut their faces.

cinq *adj.* five. *n.m.* five.

cinquantaine *n.f.* about fifty. **il a passé la ~**, he is over fifty.

cinquante *adj.* fifty.

cinquantenaire *n.m.* fiftieth anniversary. *adj.* fifty-year-old.

cinquantiéme *adj.* fiftieth.

cinquième *adj.* fifth. *n.m.* fifth.

cinquièmement *adv.* fifthly.

cintrage *n.m.* bending; centering.

cintre *n.m.* semicircle; center; a vaulted roof; hanger (clothes). **en plein ~**, semicircular.

cintré, e *adj.* arched, curved.

cintrer *v.t.* to arch.

cirage *n.m.* shoe polish; waxing. **être dans le ~**, to be dazed, to be out.

circoncire *v.t.* to circumcise.

circoncision *n.f.* circumcision.

circonférence *n.f.* circumference.

circonflexe *adj.* circumflex.

circonlocution *n.f.* circumlocution.

circonscription *n.f.* circumscription.

circonscrire *v.t.* to encircle, to enclose; to limit.

circonspect, ecte *adj. m.f.* circumspect, prudent, wary, vigilant; cautious.

circonspection *n.f.* circumspection; caution, watchfulness, wariness, cautiousness.

circonstance *n.f.* circumstance; occurrence, event; occasion. **~s atténuantes,** extenuating circumstances.

circonstancié, e *adj.* detailed.

circonstanciel, elle *adj.* circumstantial.

circonvenir *v.t.* to circumvent, to deceive.

circonvoisin, ine *adj.* adjacent, adjoining.

circonvolution *n.f.* circumvolution.

circuit *n.m.* circuit; circumference, circumlocution; tour; trip; circulation. **mettre quelqu'un hors de ~,** to get rid of someone.

circulaire *adj.* circular; round. *n.f.* circular (letter).

circulation *n.f.* circulation, traffic. **mettre en ~,** to put in circulation.

circulatoire *adj.* circulatory.

circuler *v.i.* to circulate, to have currency; to spread. **circulez, messieurs!** move on, gentlemen!

circumnavigation *n.f.* circumnavigation.

cire *n.f.* wax; earwax. **~ à cacheter,** sealing wax.

ciré, e *adj.* waxed; polished.

cirer *v.t.* to wax; to black, to clean (shoes, boots, etc.).

cireur, euse *n.m.f.* polisher (floor); shoeshiner (shoes); **cireuse** *n.f.* floor polisher, waxer.

cireux, euse *adj.* waxy, waxen.

ciron *n.m. Entom.* mite.

cirque *n.m.* circus. **il nous fait son ~ à chaque fois que nous sortons,** he makes a scene every time we go out. **quel ~!** what chaos! what a mess!

cirrhose *n.f.* cirrhosis.

cirrus *n.m.* cirrus.

cisaille *n.f.* clippings, parings (of coin); *pl.* shears.

cisailler *v.t.* to clip, to cut off (base coin).

ciseau *n.m.* chisel. **~ à froid,** cold chisel.

ciseaux *n.m.pl.* scissors *pl.* **une paire de ~,** a pair of scissors.

ciseler *v.t.* to chase; to chisel.

ciseleur *n.m.* engraver.

ciselure *n.f.* chasing; sculpture; chased work.

cistercien, enne *adj.* Cistercian. *n.m.* Cistercian; a monk.

citadelle *n.m.* citadel.

citadin, ine *n.m.f.* townsperson.

citation *n.f.* citation; summons; subpoena; quotation.

cité *n.f.* city housing development. **~ dortoir,** bedroom community. **~-jardin,** garden city.

citer *v.t.* to cite; to quote; to mention. **~ un témoin,** to cite, to summon a witness.

citerne *n.f.* cistern, tank.

cithare *n.f.* cithara, cither.

citoyen, enne *n.m.f.* citizen. **un grand ~,** a great patriot.

citrique *adj.* citric.

citron *n.m.* citron, lemon. *adj.* lemon-colored.

citronnade *n.f.* lemonade.

citronnelle *n.f.* citronella.

citronnier *n.m.* citron tree, lemon tree.

citrouille *n.f.* pumpkin; noggin (head).

cive *n.f.* chives.

civet *n.m.* jugged hare.

civette *n.f.* civet, civet cat; chive(s).

civière *n.f.* litter, stretcher.

civil, e *adj.* civil, courteous, polite. **la vie ~e,** civil life. **droits ~s,** civil rights. **tribunal ~,** civil court. **génie ~,** civil engineering. **guerre ~e,** civil war.

civilement *adv.* civilly, politely.

civilisable *adj.* civilizable, that can be civilized.

civilisateur, trice *adj.* civilizing. *n.m.f.* civilizer.

civilisation *n.f.* civilization.

civiliser *v.t.* to render a criminal process civil; to civilize. **se ~,** *v.refl.* to become civilized.

civilité *n.f.* civility, courtesy, politeness, compliments.

civique *adj.* civic.

civisme *n.m.* good citizenship.

clabaud *n.m.* noisy hound; babbler, bawler.

clabaudage *n.m.* barking (of dogs); brawling, clamor.

clabauder *v.i. Hunt.* to open false; to bawl out, to brawl.

clac *Interj.* slam (door); snap! crack! (whip).

clafoutis *n.m.* tart, fruit flan.

claie *n.f.* hurdle.

clair, e *adj.* bright, light, clear, luminous, shining, sparkling, transparent, fair; limpid, distinct, shrill; plain, obvious. **cette chambre est fort ~e,** this room is very light. **~ comme du cristal,** as clear as crystal. **un ~ ruisseau,** a limpid stream. **teint ~,** clear complexion. **avoir l'esprit ~,** to have a lucid mind. **sauce ~e,** thin sauce. *n.m.* light. **~ de lune,** moonlight. *adv.* clearly, distinctly, plainly, clear. **voir ~,** to see clearly. **tirer à ~, tirer au ~,** to drawn off; to clear up, to elucidate.

clairement *adv.* clearly.

clairet *adj., n.m* (of wine) pale, pale-colored, light. *n.m.* pale wine, infusion of aromatic plants with wine, honey and sugar.

clairière *n.f.* glade; thin place (in cloth).

clair-obscur *n.m.* chiaroscuro.

clairon *n.m.* bugle.

claironnant, ante *adj.* brassy; strident.

claironner *v.i./v.t.* to shout, to proclaim.

clairsemé, e *adj.* thinly sown; thin, rare.

clairvoyance *n.f.* clear-sightedness, perspicacity; acute discernment; clairvoyance.

clairvoyant, e *adj.* clear-sighted, clear-seeing; perspicacious, discerning.

clam *n.m.* clam.

clamer *v.t.* to proclaim, to shout out.

clamser *v.i. Infml.* to kick the bucket; to croak.

clameur *n.f.* clamor, outcry.

clan *n.m.* clan.

clandestin, ine *adj.* clandestine, underhanded.

clandestinement *adv.* clandestinely.

clandestinité *n.f.* clandestineness; secrecy.

clapet *n.m.* valve, clack valve. *Infml.* **ferme ton ~!** shut up!

clapier *n.m.* rabbit burrow; rabbit hutch.

clapoter *v.i.* to ripple.

clappement *n.m.* clacking; smacking (of the tongue).

clapper *v.i.* to smack, to clap (with the tongue).

claquage *n.m.* (muscle) pulling, straining.

claquante, e *adj. Infml.* breaking, exhausting, killing.

claque *n.f.* slap, smack; *Theat.* claque, clappers, hired applauders. *n.m.* opera hat; house of prostitution.

claqué, e *adj.* strained; dead beat, exhausted; fed up.

claquement *n.m.* clap; clapping (of hands); chattering (of the teeth); cracking (of a whip).

claquemurer *v.t.* to immure, to shut up. **se ~,** *v.refl.* to shut oneself up.

claquer *v.i.* to crack, to clap, to smack. **~ des mains,** to clap hands, to clap. **faire ~ ses doigts,** to snap one's fingers. **faire ~ un fouet,** to crack a whip. **faire ~ son fouet,** to affect authority. *v.t.* to slap, to smack, to clap. *Infml.* to buy the farm (die); to blow (money); **se ~,** to overwork oneself.

claquette *n.f.* **~s,** tap dancing.

clarification *n.f.* clarification.

clarifier *v.t.* to clarify, to clear. **se ~** *v.refl.* to clarify, to clear up, to grow clear; to settle.

clarine *n.f.* cattle bell; cowbell.

clarinette *n.f.* clarinet.

clarinettiste *n.m.f.* clarinetist.

clarté *n.f.* light, clearness, brightness; transparency; enlightenment.

classe *n.f.* class, rank, order; kind; form. **la ~ ouvrière,** the working class. **la rentrée des ~s,** the first day of school. **aller en ~,** to go to school.

classement *n.m.* classing; classification; ranking; grading; sorting; sizing; closing (court case).

classer *v.t.* to class; to classify; to sort; to grade; to rank; to close (court case); **se ~,** to rank as.

classeur *n.m.* file; filing cabinet.

classification *n.f.* classification.

classifier *v.t.* to classify.

classique *adj.* classic, classical; standard. **livre ~,** classic book.

claudication *n.f.* claudication, lameness.

claudiquer *v.i.* to limp.

clause *n.f.* clause, condition.

claustral, e *adj.* cloistral; monastic.

claustration *n.f.* confinement.

claustrer *v.t.* to confine, to immure. **se ~,** to confine oneself.

claustrophobie *n.f.* claustrophobia.

clavecin *n.m.* harpsichord.

clavicule *n.f.* clavicle, collar bone.

clavier *n.m.* keyboard.

clef *n.f.* key; clue; plug (of taps); *Mus.* key; wrench; the highest stone of an arch; keystone. **mettre la ~ sous la porte,** to remove secretly. **prendre la ~ des champs,** to scamper away. **~ anglaise,** monkey wrench.

clématite *n.f.* clematis.

clémence *n.f.* clemency, mercy.

clément, e *adj.* clement, merciful.

clémentine *n.f.* tangerine, clementine orange.

clenche *n.f.* latch.

cleptomane *n.m.f.* kleptomaniac.

cleptomanie *n.f.* kleptomania.

clerc *n.m.* clerk; clergyman, scholar.

clergé *n.m.* clergy.

clérical, e *adj.* clerical.

clic *n.m.* click, clip-clop (horse).

cliché *n.m.* stereotype; stereotype plate; *Photo.* negative.

client, e *n.m.f.* client; customer; guest (hotel); patron; patient.

clientèle *n.f.* clientele, clients, practice; business, customers (of a trader).

clignement *n.m.* wink, winking, twinkling, blinking.

cligner *v.t.* to wink. **~ les yeux,** to wink.

clignotant, e *adj.* winking, blinking; winker; blinker; direction light.

clignotement *n.m.* winking, twinkling, blinking.

clignoter *v.i.* to wink, to twinkle, to blink.

climat *n.m.* climate; *Fig.* mood; atmosphere.

climatique *adj.* climatic. **station ~,** health resort.

climatisation *n.f.* air conditioning.

climatiseur *v.t.* to air-condition.

climatiser *n.m.* air conditioner.

climatologie *n.f.* climatology.

climatologique *adj.* climatological.

clin *n.m.* wink; hint; reference to. **en un ~ d'œil,** in the twinkling of an eye, in an instant.

clinique *n.f.* clinic. *adj.* clinical.

clinquant *n.m.* tinsel, false glitter.

clip *n.m.* clip (jewelry).

clique *n.f.* clique, set, gang. **prendre ses ~s et ses claques,** to pack up, to clear off.

cliquet *n.m.* click; catch.

cliqueter *v.i.* to clash, to click; to make a sharp noise by striking.

cliquetis *n.m.* clang; clash, clashing; jingle.

clisse *n.f.* cheese drainer, wicker (round a bottle).

clisser *v.t.* to cover with wickers; to splint.

clitoridien, ne *adj.* clitoral.

clitoris *n.m.* clitoris.

clivage *n.m.* cleavage.

cliver *v.t.* to cleave (a diamond).

cloaque *n.m.* cloaca, sewer; cesspool.

clochard, e *n.m.f. Infml.* Parisian tramp, hobo.

cloche *n.f.* bell; diving bell; dish cover. **sonner les ~s,** to ring the bells. **qui n'entend qu'une ~, n'entend qu'un son,** one should hear both sides of a story. **quelle ~,** what an idiot.

cloche-pied *n.m.* hopping. **sauter à ~,** to hop. **aller à ~,** to hobble.

clocher *n.m.* steeple, bell tower.

clocher *v.i.* to limp, to hobble; *to clash; Fig.* to go wrong somewhere. **raisonnement qui cloche,** lame argument.

clocheton *n.m.* bell turret.

clochette *n.f.* little bell, hand bell; bell flower.

cloison *n.f.* partition; bulkhead. **~ étanche,** watertight bulkhead; barrier.

cloisonnage *n.m.* partition work.

cloisonné, e *adj.* chambered, having compartments; cloisonné.

cloisonnement *n.m.* partitioning; compartmentalization.

cloisonner *v.t.* to divide up; to partition off.

cloître *n.m.* cloister.

cloîtrer *n.m.* to cloister, to close up, to wall in.

cloîtrier *n.m.* cloistered monk.

clope *n.f.* cigarette.

clopin-clopant *adv.* haltingly, limpingly.

clopiner *v.i.* to hobble along, to limp.

cloque *n.f.* blister.

clore *v.t.* to close; to shut up; to finish, to conclude. **~ un compte,** to close an account.

clos, e *p.p.* of clore, closed, shut, shut up. **à huis ~,** behind closed doors. **ce sont lettres ~es,** it is a secret. **bouche ~e!** mum's the word! *n.m.* close, enclosure.

clôture *n.f.* enclosure, fence; seclusion, retirement; settling up. **faire une ~ autour d'un bois,** to fence in a wood. **la ~ de la discussion,** the end of the discussion.

clôturer *v.t.* to close (an account, a discussion).

clou *n.m.* nail; stud; boil, carbuncle; *Fig.* to go wrong somewhere. **à vis,** screw. **mettre quelque chose au ~,** *Infml.* to pawn something. *Infml.* **des ~,** no way; **river son ~ à quelqu'un,** to shut someone up; *Infml.* jug, stir (prison). **~ de girofle,** clove.

clouage *n.m.* nailing.

clouer *v.t.* to nail; to fix; to confine. **être cloué à son bureau,** to be riveted to one's desk.

clown *n.m.* clown.

clownerie *n.f.* clowning.

club *n.m.* club.

coaccusé, e *n.m.* codefendant.

coacquéreur *n.m.* joint purchaser.

coadjuteur *n.m.* coadjutor.

coadministrateur *n.m.* codirector; *Law.* co-trustee.

coagulable *adj.* coagulable.

coagulant, e *adj.* coagulative.

coagulation *n.f.* coagulation.

coaguler *v.t.* to coagulate, to curdle. **se ~,** *v.refl.* to coagulate, to curdle.

coaliser *v.t.* to unite. **se ~,** *v.refl.* to form a coalition; to league.

coalition *n.f.* coalition.

coassement *n.m.* croak, croaking.

coasser *v.i.* to croak (as a frog).

coassocié *n.m.* copartner, joint partner.

coassurance *n.f.* coinsurance.

coauteur *n.m.* coauthor, joint author; *Law.* accomplice.

cobalt *n.m.* cobalt.

cobaye *n.m.* cavy, guinea pig.

cobelligérant, e *adj.* cobelligerent.

cobra *n.m.* cobra.

coca *n.m.* coca; Coca-Cola.

cocagne *n.f.* feast. **pays de ~,** land of plenty.

cocaïne *n.f.* cocaine.

cocarde *n.f.* cockade.

cocasse *adj.* odd, funny, comical, laughable.

cocasserie *n.f.* drollness, funniness.

coccinelle *n.f.* cocinella; ladybug.

coccyx *n.m.* coccyx.

coche *n.m.* passage boat, barge. **faire la mouche du ~,** to make a useless bustle.

cochenille *n.f.* cochineal.

cocher *n.m.* coachman, driver. *v.t.* to notch; to check off (as on a list).

cochère *adj., n.f.* **porte ~,** carriage entrance.

cochon *n.m.* swine, hog, pig. **~ de lait,** suckling pig. **c'est un ~,** *Vulg.* he is a dirty fellow, a dirty pig. *adj.* dirty.

cochonnaille *n.f.* delicatessen pork-products with.

cochonner *v.t.* to farrow. *Vulg.* to bungle, to botch.

cochonnerie *n.f.* dirtiness, filthiness, nastiness; obscenity, smuttiness; trash, rubbish.

cochonnet *n.m.* piglet.

cocktail *n.m.* cocktail; cocktail party.

coco *n.m.* cocoa; *(childish)* sweetie, darling; *Pej.* commie (communist); *Drug.* snow, coke. **lait de ~,** coconut milk.

cocon *n.m.* cocoon.

cocorico *n.m. Excl.* cock-a-doodle-do.

cocotier *n.m.* coconut tree.

cocotte *or* **cocote** *n.f. Infml.* chicken; sweetie, darling; saucepan.

cocu *n.m. Vulg.* cuckold.

cocufier *v.t.* to cuckold, to be unfaithful to.

codage *n.m.* coding, encoding.

code *n.m.* code. **~ civil,** civil law; code (standard of behavior). *Infml.* **les ~s,** antiglare headlights.

codébiteur, trice *n.m.f.* joint debtor.

coder *v.t.* to code.

codétenu, e *n.m.f.* fellow prisoner, inmate.

codex *n.m.* pharmacopeia; codex.

codicillaire *adj.* codicillary.

codicille *n.m.* codicil.

codification *n.f.* codification.

codifier *v.t.* to codify.

codirecteur, trice *n.m.f.* codirector; joint manager.

coefficient *n.m.* coefficient.

coéquipier, ière *n.m.f.* teammate.

coercitif, ive *adj.* coercive.

coercition *n.f.* coercion.

coéternel, elle *adj.* coeternal.

coeur *n.m.* heart; mind, soul; affection, love; spirit; courage, firmness; mettle; generosity; depth, core, middle. **les maladies du ~,** heart diseases. **avoir le ~ gros,** to have one's heart full. **aller au ~,** to go to the heart. **de ~,** hearty; sincerely. **affaire de ~,** love affair. **loin des yeux, loin du ~,** out of sight, out of mind. **avoir quelque chose sur le ~,** to have a weight on the mind. **apprendre par ~,** to learn by heart. **c'est un ~ d'or,** he has a kind heart. **de tout ~,** heartily. **à contre-~,** against one's will. **du fond du ~,** from the bottom of one's heart. **prendre une chose à ~,** to take to heart. **être sans ~,** to be heartless, low-minded. **avoir mal au ~,** to be sick, to be queasy. **le ~ de la ville,** the heart of the city. **au ~ de l'été,** in the height of summer.

coexistant, ante *adj.* coexisting, coexistent.

coexistence *n.f.* coexistence.

coexister *v.i.* coexist.

coffrage *n.m.* boxing; framing; coffering.

coffre *n.m.* chest; coffer; drum (of a mill); box; trunk; thorax; trunk (auto.). **avoir le ~ bon,** to have a sound chest.

coffre-fort *n.m.* safe, strongbox.

coffrer *v.t. Infml.* to lock up, to imprison.

coffret *n.m.* (small) box.

cogérant, e *n.m.f.* joint manager.

cogestion *n.f.* comanagement.

cogiter *v.i.* to cogitate; to ponder.

cognac *n.* cognac.

cognassier *n.m.* quince, quince tree.

cogne *n.m.* cop (police).

cognée *n.f.* felling axe.

cognement *n.m.* banging; hammering; striking.

cogner *v.t.* to knock in, to thump, to strike; to knock. *v.i.* to knock, to strike against. **se ~,** *v.refl.* to knock, to strike (against).

cognitif, ive *adj.* capable of knowing.

cognition *n.f.* cognition.

cohabitation *n.f.* cohabitation.

cohabiter *v.i.* to cohabit.

cohérence *n.f.* coherence.

cohérent, e *adj.* coherent.

cohéritier, e *n.m.f.* coheir, joint heir.

cohésif, ive *adj.* cohesive.

cohésion *n.f.* cohesion.

cohorte *n.f.* cohort; band, troop, gang.

cohue *n.f.* crowd.

coi, coite *adj. n.f.* quiet, still; calm, snug.

coiffe *n.f.* headdress, cap, lining (of hats); caul.

coiffer *v.i.* to put on one's head; to dress the hair of; to cap (bottles); to infatuate. **enfant coiffé,** child born with a caul on its head. **être né coif-** fé, to be born lucky. **elle le coiffa d'un seau d'eau,** she threw a pail of water over his head. *v.i.* to dress hair; to become, to fit, to suit. **se ~,** *v.refl.* to do one's hair. **elle se coiffe avec beaucoup de goût,** she dresses her hair very becomingly. *Fig.* to be infatuated (with).

coiffeur, euse *n.m.*, *n.m.f.* hairdresser; (**coiffeuse**) dressing table, coiffeuse (furniture).

coiffure *n.f.* hairstyle, hairdo.

coin *n.m.* corner, angle, nook; stamp; quoin; clock (of stockings); wedge. **le ~ d'une maison,** the corner of a house. **les quatre ~s du monde,** the four corners of the world. **enfoncer le ~,** to drive in the wedge.

coinçage *n.m.* wedging.

coincement *n.m.* jamming.

coincer *v.t.* to wedge; to jam. **se ~,** to get jammed, stuck.

coïncidence *n.f.* coincidence.

coïncident, e *adj.* coincident.

coïncider *v.i.* to coincide.

coin-coin *n.m.* (duck) quack; (auto.) honk honk.

coinculpé, e *n.m.f.* codefendant.

coing *n.m.* quince.

coït *n.m.* coition.

coke *n.m.* coke.

cokéfaction *n.f.* coking.

col *n.m.* neck (of the body, a bottle, etc.); pass, defile; collar; shirt collar. **faux ~,** detachable collar.

cola *n.m.* cola.

colchique *n.m.* colchicum; crocus.

colégataire *n.m.f.* colegatee; joint legatee.

coléoptère *n.m.* coleopteran, beetle.

colère *n.f.* anger, passion, wrath, ire; fury, rage. *adj.* choleric, passionate, hotheaded.

coléreux, euse *adj.* quick-tempered; irascible.

colérique *adj.* choleric, passionate, irascible.

colibacille *n.m.* colon bacillus.

colibri *n.m.* hummingbird.

colifichet *n.m.* toy, trinket, bauble, knickknack.

colimaçon *n.m.* snail. **escalier en ~,** spiral staircase.

colin *n.m.* colin; hake.

colin-maillard *n.m.* blindman's bluff.

colique *n.f.* colic, diarrhea; stomach pain.

colis *n.m.* package, parcel.

colisée *n.m.* coliseum.

colite *n.f.* colitis.

collaborateur, trice *n.m.f.* joint author; coauthor; contributor (in a newspaper); collaborator, associate.

collaboration *n.f.* collaboration; contribution.

collaborer *v.i.* to work jointly; to collaborate; to cooperate.

collage *n.m.* sizing; pasting; paper-hanging.

collant, e *adj.* tight, close-fitting *n.m.pl.* **bas ~s,** tights.

collatéral, e *adj.* collateral.

collation *n.f.* collation; lunch, luncheon; snack.

collationner *v.t.* to collate; to compare. *v.i.* to give a snack.

colle *n.f.* paste, glue; teaser; puzzler; **vivre à la ~,** to live together.

collecte *n.f.* collection; contribution; collect (a short prayer).

collecter *v.t.* to collect.

collecteur *n.m.* collector. *adj.* principal. **égout ~,** main sewer (in Paris).

collectif, ive *adj.* collective.

collection *n.f.* collection; set; assortment.

collectionner *v.t.* to collect (books, plants, insects, medals, etc.).

collectionneur, euse *n.m.f.* collector.

collectivement *adv.* collectively.

collectivisation *n.f.* collectivization.

collectiviser *v.t.* to collectivize.

collectivisme *n.m.* collectivism.

collectiviste *n.m.f.* collectivist.

collectivité *n.f.* collectivity; group; community.

collège *n.m.* high school. **~ électoral,** constituency (of electors).

collégial, e *adj.* collegial, collegiate.

collégialité *n.f.* collegiality.

collégien, ienne *n.m.f.* high-school student.

collègue *n.m.* colleague.

coller *v.t.* to stick, to paste, to glue; to size; to clarify; to stump by questioning. **~ du papier,** to hang wallpaper. **se ~,** *v.refl.* to paste, to glue; to stick, to be closely applied.

collerette *n.f.* collar; frill.

collet *n.m.* collar (of a gown, a coat); cape; neck (of mutton); band for the neck. **prendre quelqu'un au ~,** to take a person by the collar. **tendre un ~,** to set a snare. **~ d'une ancre,** crown of an anchor. **~ montant,** stand-up collar. **~ rabattu,** turned-down collar.

colleter *v.t.* to collar; to seize by the collar. *v.i.* to set, to lay snares (for catching game). **se ~,** *v.refl.* to collar each other, to seize each other by the collar.

colleur *n.m.* paster, gluer; paperhanger; poster hanger.

collier *n.m.* necklace; collar; chain. **un ~ de chien,** a dog's collar. **donner un coup de ~,** to make an effort, to give a good pull. **~ de misère,** drudgery, toil.

collimateur *n.m.* collimator; *Infml.* **avoir quelqu'un dans le ~,** to have someone in one's sight.

colline *n.f.* hill. **une petite ~,** a hillock.

collision *n.f.* collision.

collocation *n.f.* classing (of creditors).

collodion *n.m.* collodion.

colloque *n.m.* colloquy, conference.

collusion *n.f.* collusion.

collutoire *n.m.* mouthwash, gargle.

collyre *n.m.* collyrium, eyewash.

colmatage *n.m.* warping; sealing; filling in.

colmater *v.t.* to seal; to fill in; **se ~,** to become clogged.

colocataire *n.m.f.* joint tenant.

colombage *n.m.* half-timbering.

colombe *n.f.* dove; joist.

Colombie *n.f.* Colombia.

colombier *n.m.* dovecote, pigeon house.

colombin, ine *adj.* columbine; dove-colored.

colon *n.m.* colonist, planter, cultivator.

côlon *n.m. Anat.* colon.

colonel *n.m.* colonel.

colonial, e *adj.* colonial. **produits coloniaux,** colonial produce.

colonialisme *n.m.* colonialism.

colonialiste *adj. n.m.f.* colonialist.

colonie *n.f.* colony, settlement. **~ de vacances,** summer camp.

colonisateur, trice *adj.* colonizing. *n.m.f.* colonizer.

colonisation *n.f.* colonization.

coloniser *v.t.* to colonize; to settle.

collonade *n.f.* colonnade.

colonne *n.f.* column; pillar; bed post; row. **~ vertébrale,** spine. **une ~ de chiffres,** a row of figures.

colonnette *n.f.* little column.

colophane *n.f.* colophony, rosin.

coloquinte *n.f.* colocynth, bitter apple.

colorant, e *adj.* coloring.

coloration *n.f.* coloration.

coloré, e *p.p.* colored; ruddy. **teint ~,** ruddy complexion.

colorer *v.t.* to color; to tinge. **se ~,** *v.refl.* to color. **l'orient se colore,** the sun is rising.

coloriage *n.m.* coloring.

colorier *v.t.* to color. **~ un dessin, une carte,** to color a drawing, a card.

coloris *n.m.* coloring. **ce tableau pèche par le ~,** the coloring of that painting is not good.

coloriste *n.m.* colorist.

colossal, e *adj.* colossal, huge, gigantic.

colosse *n.m.* colossus.

colportage *n.m.* hawking, peddling.

colporter *v.t.* to hawk, to peddle; to hawk about.

colporteur *n.m.* hawker, peddler.

colt *n.m.* gun, pistol.

coltiner *v.t.* to take on; to carry. **se ~,** to put up with.

columbarium *n.m.* columbarium.

colza *n.m.* colza.

coma *n.m.* coma.

comateux, euse *adj.* comatose.

combat *n.m.* combat, fight, fighting, conflict, battle, engagement; duel; struggle, strife. **~ à outrance,** desperate, mortal combat. **~ simulé,** sham fight. **au fort du ~,** in the thick of the fight. **être hors de ~,** to be disabled. **~ de taureaux,** bullfight.

combatif, ive *adj.* combative, ready to fight.

combativité *n.f.* combativeness.

combattant *n.m.* combatant; fighter; champion.

combattre *v.t.* to fight, to combat, to fight with; to contest. **~ les préjugés,** to combat prejudice. **~ la nature,** to contend with nature. **~ ses passions,** to oppose one's passions. *v.i.* to combat, to fight, to contend, to war; to contend, to strive. ~ **à l'épée**, to fight with swords. ~ **corps à corps**, to grapple, to fight hand to hand. se ~, *v.refl.* to combat, to fight.

combien *adv.* how much; how (with much, many; far, long, etc.) ~ **est faux ce que vous avancez!** how far what you say is from the truth! ~ **y avait-il de personnes?** how many persons were there? ~ **y a-t-il de Paris à Versailles?** how far is it from Paris to Versailles? ~ **de temps resterez-vous?** how long will you stay? ~ **cela vous a-t-il coûté?** how much did that cost you?

combinaison *n.f.* combination; scheme (color); slip (underwear); overall. *Chem.* compound.

combinard, e *adj.* scheming *n.m.f.* schemer.

combinat *n.m.* industrial complex.

combinatoire *adj.* combinative; combinatory.

combine *n.f.* scheme.

combiné *n.m. Chem.* compound; (telephone) receiver.

combiner *v.t.* to combine; to contrive, to concert. se ~, to combine, to unite, to scheme.

comble *adj.* heaped; full. *n.m.* top, height, highest pitch, acme, utmost; roof. le ~ **de la félicité**, the height of happiness. **de fond en ~**, from top to bottom, down to the ground; utterly.

comblement *n.m.* filling up.

combler *v.t.* to heap, to heap up; to load; to fill up. ~ **un fossé**, to fill up a ditch. ~ **une lacune**, to fill in a blank. ~ **de bienfaits**, to load with benefits.

combustibilité *n.f.* combustibility, combustibleness.

combustible *adj.* combustible; inflammable. *n.m.* fuel, combustible substance.

combustion *n.f.* combustion; burning.

comédie *n.f.* comedy, play; theater. **jouer, représenter une ~**, to act, to put on a comedy. **jouer la ~**, to act a farce. **quelle ~!** what a farce!

comédien, ienne *n.m.f.* comedian, actor. *Fig.* showoff. ~**s ambulants**, strolling players. **il est bon ~**, he is a clever dissembler.

comestible *adj.* edible, eatable. *n.m.* victuals, provisions.

comète *n.f.* comet.

comique *adj.* comic, comical; ludicrous, laughable, funny. *n.m.* comedy, comic art; comic character; comic author, comic writer, comic actor, comedian.

comiquement *adv.* comically.

comité *n.m.* committee; board; council; a group of persons. **petit ~**, small party.

commandant *adj.* commanding. **officier ~**, commanding officer. *n.m.* commander; commanding officer, commandant. ~ **d'une escadre**, commodore.

commande *n.f. Com.* order. **de ~**, ordered, bespoken; pretended. **maladie de ~**, feigned illness; *Aviat.* control, controlling. **prendre les ~s**, to take control.

commandement *n.m.* command; order given; injunction, mandate; precept, law; commandment; authority, power; summons. **avoir quelque chose à ~**, to have a thing in one's command.

commander *v.t.* to command, to order, to direct, to bid; to have the command of; to govern, to rule; to order, to bespeak. ~ **l'estime, le respect**, to command esteem, respect. ~ **un diner**, to order a dinner. *v.i.* to command; to rule, to sway; to bid, to order; to master. ~ **à ses passions**, to govern one's passions. se ~, *v.refl.* to command oneself; to be master of oneself.

commandeur *n.m.* commander (of knighthood).

commanditaire *n.m.* silent partner.

commandite *n.f.* limited partnership; share.

commanditer *v.t.* to finance as a silent partner.

commando *n.m.* commando.

comme *adv.* as; like; as well as; so much as; as much as; as it were; how. **rire** ~ **un bossu**, to laugh heartily. **un véritable ami est** ~ **un autre soi-même**, a true friend is a second self. ~ **l'on dit**, as we say. ~ **on fait son lit, on se couche**, we must reap what we sow. **un homme** ~ **lui**, a man like him. **il est** ~ **mort**, he is as if he were dead. **je lui demandai** ~ **il se portait**, I asked him how he was. ~ **il est changé!** how he has changed!

comme *conj.* as; as . . . so; whereas; since, because.

commémoratif, ive *adj.* commemorative.

commémoration *n.f.* commemoration.

commémorer *v.t.* to commemorate, to remember.

commençant, e *n.m.f.* beginner, novice.

commencement *n.m.* beginning, commencement.

commencer *v.t.* to begin, to commence, to start. *v.i.* to begin, to commence, to take the first step. **il commence à pleuvoir**, it is beginning to rain.

commensal, e *n.m.f.* messmate; fellow boarder. **être commensaux**, to board together.

commensalisme *n.m.* commensalism.

commensurable *adj.* commensurable.

comment *adv.* how, in what manner, in what way; why, wherefore. ~ **cela?** how is that? how so? *interj.* what! indeed! ~**!** **c'est lui?** what! is that he? *n.m.* wherefore. **savoir le pourquoi et le** ~, to know the why and wherefore.

commentaire *n.m.* comment; commentary; remark, observation. **pas de** ~**!** make no remarks!

commentateur, trice *n.m.f.* commentator; annotator; correspondent.

commenter *v.t.* to comment, to comment on, to commentate, to annotate. *v.i.* to comment on; to criticize.

commérage *n.m.* idle gossip, gossiping.

commerçant, e *adj.* commercial, trading,

mercantile. n.m. merchant, trader, dealer.

commerce n.m. commerce, trade, traffic; interchange, communication; acquaintance, correspondence; conversation. ~ **en gros**, wholesale trade. ~ **de détail**, retail trade. **fonds de** ~, business. **maison de** ~, business firm. **une personne d'un** ~ **agréable**, a very pleasant acquaintance.

commercer v.i. to trade, to traffic, to deal.

commercial, e adj. commercial. n.m. van, utility vehicle.

commercialement adv. commercially.

commercialisation n.f. marketing; commercialization.

commercialiser v.t. to market; to commercialize.

commère n.f. gossip (person); godmother.

commettre v.t. to commit, to entrust; to commend, to confide; to compromise; to expose; to perpetrate; to embroil, to make mischief. ~ **sa réputation**, to expose one's reputation. ~ **un péché**, to commit a sin. **se** ~, v.refl. to confide, to entrust oneself; to compromise oneself.

comminatoire adj. comminatory.

commis n.m. clerk; salesman. **premier** ~, head clerk. **petit** ~, junior clerk. ~ **aux vivres**, steward (of a ship). ~ **voyageur**, commercial traveler.

commisération n.f. commiseration.

commissaire n.m. commissioner. ~ **des guerres**, commissary. ~ **des vivres**, commissary. ~ **de police**, commissioner of police. ~-**priseur**, auctioneer; appraiser.

commissariat n.m. police station.

commission n.f. commission, charge, errand, message; committee; shopping. **charger quelqu'un d'une** ~, to charge a person with a commission. **faire la** ~, to carry on the business of a commission agent. **faire les** ~**s**, to run errands. ~ **permanente**, standing committee.

commissionnaire n.m. commission agent, agent; errand boy, porter. ~ **chargeur**, freight commissioner.

commissionner v.t. to commission; to empower.

commissure n.f. commissure.

commode adj. commodious, convenient; comfortable, easy. **une maison** ~, a commodious house. n.f. chest of drawers, drawers.

commodément adv. commodiously, conveniently.

commodité n.f. convenience, accommodation.

commotion n.f. shock; concussion; Fig. commotion, disturbance.

commotionner v.t. to shock; to shake; to concuss.

commuable adj. Law. commutable.

commuer v.t. Law. to commute.

commun, e adj. common; usual; general, public; vulgar, mean. **faire bourse** ~**e**, to hold funds in common. **n'avoir rien de** ~ **avec**, to have nothing in common with. **d'un** ~ **accord**, with one accord. **le sens** ~, common sense. **cette femme a des manières** ~**es**, that woman's manners are very low class. n.m. common stock. **travailler en** ~, to work together. **le** ~ **des hommes**, the generality of mankind.

communal, e adj. communal; parish, of the parish. **chemin** ~, by-road, back road.

communautaire adj. of the community. **center** ~, community center.

communauté n.f. community, society. ~ **de biens**, goods held in common (between husband and wife).

commune n.f. commune, parish; parishioners; town hall, township; district; borough.

communément adv. commonly.

communiant, e n.m.f. communicant, person who is making his/her communion.

communicable adj. communicable.

communicateur, trice adj. connecting.

communicatif, ive adj. communicative.

communication n.f. communication; contact (with); transmission; message; call (telephone). **mettre en** ~, to connect. **avoir la** ~, to be put through (phone call). **porte de** ~, door of communication.

communier v.i. to communicate, to receive the sacrament. v.t. to administer the communion.

communion n.f. communion; fellowship; rite of receiving the sacrament of holy communion. **faire sa première** ~, make one's first communion. ~ **d'esprit**, same intellectual outlook.

communiquant, e adj. communicating.

communiqué n.m. communiqué; report; statement; press release; bulletin.

communiquer v.t. to communicate, to impart; to transmit; to deliver. v.t. to communicate, to be in communication. **le défenseur peut** ~ **avec l'accusé**, the counsel can communicate with the prisoner. **se** ~, v.refl. to be communicated; to communicate itself.

communisant, e adj. communistic; n.m.f. communist sympathizer, fellow traveler.

communisme n.m. communism.

communiste n.m. communist.

commutateur n.m. switch; commutator.

commutatif, ive adj. commutative.

commutation n.f. commutation.

commuter v.t. to commute; to substitute.

compacité n.f. compactness.

compact, e adj. compact, solid, dense.

compagne n.f. female companion; playmate; helpmate, consort; wife.

compagnie n.f. company; society; covey (of partridges). **fausser** ~, to quit company. **être en** ~, to be in company. **être de bonne** ~, good company. **être de mauvaise** ~, to be bad company. ~ **d'assurances**, insurance company.

compagnon n.m. companion; fellow; consort; associate, partner. ~ **de voyage**, traveling companion. **joyeux** ~, jolly fellow. **bon** ~, good fellow. **un dangereux** ~, a dangerous fellow.

comparable *adj.* comparable, that may be compared.

comparaison *n.f.* comparison; simile, similitude. **au delà de toute ~,** beyond all comparison. **~ n'est pas raison,** to compare is not to prove. **en ~ de,** in comparison with. **par ~,** comparatively.

comparaître *v.i.* to appear. **~ en justice,** to appear in a court of law.

comparatif, ive *adj.* comparative. *n.m. Gram.* comparative degree, comparative.

comparativement *adv.* comparatively.

comparer *v.t.* to compare.

comparoir *v.i.* to appear (in a court of justice).

comparse *n.m.f.* extra (theater).

compartiment *n.m.* compartment, a division.

comparution *n.f. Law.* appearance.

compas *n.m.* compass. **~ à trois branches,** triangular compass.

compassé, e *adj.* formal, starched.

compasser *v.t.* to measure with a compass.

compassion *n.f.* compassion, pity, mercy.

compatibilité *n.f.* compatibility.

compatible *adj.* compatible, congruous, consistent, suitable. **cette loi n'est pas ~ avec nos moeurs,** this law is not consistent with our customs.

compatir *v.i.* to sympathize with. **il compatit aux maux des autres,** he feels for the trouble of others.

compatissant, e *adj.* compassionate, tender. **une âme ~e,** a tender heart.

compatriote *n.m.f.* compatriot; fellow countryman; fellow countrywoman.

compensateur, trice *adj.* compensating. *n.m.* compensating balance.

compensation *n.f.* compensation, amends.

compensatoire *adj.* compensatory.

compenser *v.t.* to compensate, to counterbalance, to make amends for, to make up for; to set off; to offset. **se ~, v.refl.** to compensate.

compère *n.m.* crony; accomplice. **un rusé ~,** a crafty fellow.

compère-loriot *n.m.* stye (on the eye).

compétence *n.f.* competence, competency. **cela n'est pas de sa ~,** he is not competent to judge that.

compétent, e *adj.* competent; capable; suitable, proper. **vous n'êtes pas ~ pour cela,** you are not fit for that.

compétiteur *n.m.* competitor.

compétitif, ive *adj.* competitive.

compétition *n.f.* competition, rivalry.

compilateur *n.m.* compiler.

compilation *n.f.* compilation.

compiler *v.t.* to compile.

complainte *n.f.* complaint; lamentation; lament.

complaire *v.i.* to please, to gratify. **se ~, v.refl.** to take delight (in).

complaisamment *adv.* complaisantly, obligingly.

complaisance *n.f.* complaisance; kindness, favor. **abuser de la ~ de quelqu'un,** to take an unfair advantage of a person's good nature.

complaisant, e *adj.* complaisant, complacent, obliging. **un homme ~,** an obliging man.

complément *n.m.* complement; *Gram.* object.

complémentaire *adj.* complementary, complemental.

complet, ète *adj.* complete; whole, full, entire; perfect. **un habillement ~,** a complete suit of clothes. *n.m.* full complement. **être au ~,** to be full, booked up.

complètement *adv.* completely, wholly, fully, entirely. *n.m.* completion.

compléter *v.t.* to complete, to perfect. **se ~,** to complement one another, to match.

complétif, ive *adj. Gram.* completive; objective.

complexe *adj.* complex, complicated, intricate.

complexer *v.t.* to give a complex.

complexion *n.f.* constitution (body); mood, disposition.

complexité *n.f.* complexity.

complication *n.f.* complication; intracacy.

complice *adj.* accessory (to). *n.m.f.* accomplice.

complicité *n.f.* complicity.

complies *n.f.pl.* compline.

compliment *n.m.* compliment; congratulation. **faire ~ à quelqu'un de,** to compliment a person upon. **je vous en fais mon ~,** I wish you joy.

complimenter *v.t.* to compliment.

complimenteur, euse *adj.* complimentary. *n.m.f.* complimenter; flatterer.

compliqué, e *adj.* complicated; intricate.

compliquer *v.t.* to complicate; to entangle. **se ~, v.refl.** to become complicated, to get intricate.

complot *n.m.* plot; conspiracy.

comploter *v.t.* to plot.

comploteur *n.m.* plotter.

componction *n.f.* compunction; contrition, repentance.

comportement *n.m.* behavior.

comporter *v.t.* to include; imply. **se ~, v.refl.** to behave oneself, to demean oneself, to comport oneself. **se ~ mal,** to misbehave.

composant, e *adj.* component. *n.m. Chem.* component.

composé, e *adj.* mixed; composite; stiff, formal. **une société bien ~e,** a select society. **intérêt ~,** compound interest.

composer *v.t.* to compose; to compound. **~ son visage,** to compose one's looks. *v.i.* to compose; to compound; to come to an arrangement; to compromise; to agree. **se ~,** to be composed.

composite *adj.* heterogenous; *Arch.* composite. *n.m.* composite order.

compositeur, trice *n.m.f. Print.* compositor; *Mus.* composer.

composition *n.f.* composition, composing; theme; agreement, settlement. **venir à une ~,**

to come to terms. **c'est un homme de bonne ~**, he is a good sort of man.

compost *n.m.* compost.

compostage *n.m.* stamping; dating; punching (ticket).

composter *v.t.* to compost.

compote *n.f.* stewed fruit. **~ de pommes**, applesauce. **faire une ~ de fruits**, to make stewed fruit. **avoir les yeux en ~**, to have a pair of black eyes.

compréhensibilité *n.f.* comprehensibleness.

compréhensible *adj.* comprehensible; understandable.

compréhensif, ive *adj.* comprehensive; understanding.

compréhension *n.f.* comprehension; apprehension, understanding.

comprendre *v.t.* to comprehend, to include; to take into; to conceive, to apprehend; to understand, to make out. **je comprends fort bien ce que vous me dites**, I perfectly understand what you tell me. **se ~**, to be understood.

compresse *n.f.* compress.

compresseur *n.m.* compressor; steamroller.

compressibilité *n.f.* compressibility.

compressible *adj.* compressible.

compressif, ive *adj.* compressive.

compression *n.f.* compression; squeezing.

comprimé, e *adj.* compressed; checked, repressed; *Med.* tablet.

comprimer *v.t.* to compress; to condense; to check, to restrain, to repress, to keep down.

compris, e *adj.* inclusive; included; contained; agreed; understood. **service ~**, service included; **le pâté de maisons qui est ~ entre ces deux rues**, the block contained between these two streets. **c'est ~**, it's agreed. **as-tu ~ ce que j'ai dit?** did you understand what I said?

compromettant, e *adj.* compromising; implicating; dangerous.

compromettre *v.i.* to make a compromise, to compromise. *v.t.* to commit, to compromise; to expose. **~ sa dignité**, to compromise one's dignity. **se ~**, *v.refl.* to commit oneself, to compromise oneself; to be involved.

compromis *n.m.* compromise; an adjustment of differences by mutual concession; arrangement.

compromission *n.f.* compromising act.

comptabiliser *v.t.* to post.

comptabilité *n.f.* bookkeeping, accounts *pl.* accounting.

comptable *adj.* accountable, responsible. **agent ~**, accountant *n.m.* accountant, bookkeeper.

comptant *adj.* ready; in cash. **argent ~**, cash. *n.m.* **au ~**, in cash.

compte *n.m.* account, reckoning, calculation; computation, score, profit, advantage; consideration, regard; reason. **faire un ~**, to make a calculation. **~ rond**, round number. **être loin de son ~**, to have made a calculation error. **les bons ~s font les bons amis**, short reckonings make long friends. **à bon ~**, cheap, on advantageous terms. **~ courant**, **~-chèques**, checking account. **~ de dépôt**, savings account. **~-joint**, joint account. **solde de ~**, payment in full. **pour solde de tout ~**, in full payment. **régler un ~**, to settle an account. **prendre sur son ~**, to take upon oneself. **à ce ~-là**, upon that score; if that is so. **tenir ~ de**, to take into account. **rendre ~ de**, to account for. **j'ai reçu mille francs à ~**, I have received a thousand francs on account. **au bout du ~**, after all, when all is said and done. **~-gouttes**, dropper. **au ~-gouttes**, drop by drop, sparingly. **~-rendu**, transaction; report. **en fin de ~**, at last.

compter *v.t.* to count, to reckon; to number; to add up; to comprise; to pay. **~ ses pas**, to walk slowly. *v.i.* to calculate, to reckon, to make a computation; to count; to add up accounts; to calculate, to mean, to intend, to rely upon; to settle accounts. **il compte partir demain**, he intends to go tomorrow. **nous comptons sur vous**, we rely on you. **à ~ de demain**, beginning tomorrow.

compteur *n.m.* reckoner; indicator; meter.

comptoir *n.m.* counter, bar (of taverns); bank branch office.

compulser *v.t.* to inspect, to search; to examine (books, papers).

compulsif, ve *adj.* compulsive.

compulsion *n.f.* compulsion.

computation *n.f.* computation.

comte *n.m.* count, earl.

comté *n.m.* earldom; county, shire.

comtesse *n.f.* countess.

con, ne *adj.* stupid, idiotic.

concassage *n.m.* crushing; grinding.

concasser *v.t.* to pound, to crush; to grind.

concasseur *adj.* crushing; breaking. *n.m.* crusher; grinder.

concaténation *n.f.* concatenation.

concave *adj.* concave.

concavité *n.f.* concavity, hollowness.

concéder *v.t.* to concede, to grant.

concentration *n.f.* concentration.

concentrer *v.t.* to concentrate; to free from extraneous matter; to condense; to focus. **être concentrer en soi-même**, to be wrapped up in oneself. **se ~**, *v.refl.* to be concentrated.

concentrique *adj.* concentric.

concept *n.m.* concept.

conception *n.f.* conception; apprehension, understanding, notion, thought.

conceptualisation *n.f.* conceptualization.

conceptualiser *v.t.* to conceptualize.

conceptuel, le *adj.* conceptual.

concernant *prep.* concerning, relating to, with respect to

concerner *v.t.* to concern; to relate to, to belong to. **cela ne vous concerne pas**, that does not concern you.

concert *n.m.* concert; concord, harmony. **de ~**,

in concert. **marcher de ~,** to go hand in hand.

concertant, e *n.m.f.* performer in a concert. *adj.* in concert.

concertation *n.f.* dialog; meeting.

concerté, e concerted.

concerter *v.t.* to concert, to contrive, to plan, to devise. **se ~,** *v.refl.* to plan with others, to lay (their) heads together.

concertiste *n.m.f.* concert artist; performer.

concerto *n.m.* concerto.

concession *n.f.* concession; grant.

concessionnaire *n.m.f.* agent; dealer.

concevable *adj.* conceivable.

concevoir *v.t.* to conceive; to imagine; to apprehend, to comprehend, to understand. **je n'y conçois rien,** I cannot conceive it. *v.i.* to conceive, to become pregnant; to comprehend, to understand. **se ~,** *v.refl.* to be conceived, imagined.

concierge *n.m.f.* concierge, doorkeeper, porter; janitor; gossip.

conciergerie *n.f.* porter's lodge; janitor's post, *(cap.)* famous prison in Paris.

concile *n.m.* council (of prelates); decree of a council.

conciliable *adj.* reconcilable.

conciliabule *n.m.* confabulation, secret meeting.

conciliaire *adj.* relating to a council.

conciliant, e *adj.* conciliating, reconciling.

conciliateur, trice *n.m.f.* conciliator. *adj.* conciliatory, conciliating.

conciliation *n.f.* arbitration; reconciliation.

conciliatoire *adj.* conciliatory.

concilier *v.t.* to arbitrate; to reconcile. **se ~,** *v.refl.* to be conciliated, to be reconciled.

concis, e *adj.* concise, brief, short.

concision *n.f.* conciseness; brevity.

concitoyen, enne *n.m.f.* fellow citizen.

conclave *n.m.* conclave; the assembly of cardinals.

concluant, e *adj.* conclusive.

conclure *v.t.* to conclude, to settle; to close, to infer. *v.i.* to conclude, to infer, to decide.

conclusion *n.f.* conclusion; inference. **tirer une ~,** to draw a conclusion, an inference. *Law.* **prendre des ~s,** to make a motion.

concocter *v.t.* to concoct; to brew up.

concombre *n.m.* cucumber.

concomitance *n.f.* concomitance, concomitancy.

concomitant, e *adj.* concomitant; concurrent with.

concordance *n.f.* concordance; agreement.

concordant, e *adj.* concordant.

concordat *n.m.* concordat, agreement; bankrupt's certificate.

concorde *n.f.* concord, union; harmony.

concorder *v.i.* to agree; to concur; to coincide; to match.

concourant, e *adj.* concurrent.

concourir *v.i.* to concur, to contribute; to cooperate, to contribute, to compete. **tout semblait**

~ à le sauver, everything seemed to conspire to save him. **être admis à ~,** to be allowed to compete.

concours *n.m.* concurrence, cooperation; competition; help; assistance. **son ~ m'a été fort utile,** his assistance was very useful to me. **~ de circonstances,** combination of circumstances.

concret, ète *adj.* concrete.

concrétion *n.f.* concretion. **concrétiser,** *v.t.* to put in concrete form (a plan, etc.).

concubinage *n.m.* concubinage.

concubine *n.f.* concubine.

concupiscence *n.f.* concupiscence.

concupiscent, e *adj.* concupiscent.

concurremment *adv.* in concurrence, concurrently.

concurrence *n.f.* competition, opposition. **soutenir la ~,** to keep up a competition. **jusqu'à la ~ de,** to the extent of.

concurrencer *v.t.* to compete with.

concurrent, e *n.m.f.* competitor, rival. *adj.* concurrent.

concurrentiel, le *adj.* competitive.

concussion *n.f.* extortion; bribery.

condamnable *adj.* condemnable, blamable.

condamnation *n.f.* condemnation; conviction; judgment, sentence. **subir sa ~,** to undergo one's sentence. **passer ~,** to pass sentence; to confess oneself to be in the wrong.

condamné, e *p.p.* condemned, doomed; walled up (as a door, a window). *n.m.f.* convict.

condamner *v.t.* to condemn, to sentence, to doom; to censure, to blame; to give up on (a sick person); to wall up. **~ à une amende,** to fine. **se ~,** to condemn oneself.

condensable *adj.* condensable.

condensateur *n.m.* condenser.

condensation *n.f.* condensation.

condenser *v.t.* to condense. **se ~,** *v.refl.* to condense, to become condensed.

condenseur *n.m.* condenser.

condescendance *n.f.* condescension.

condescendant, e *adj.* condescending.

condescendre *v.i.* to condescend, to yield; to comply.

condiment *n.m.* condiment; seasoning.

condisciple *n.m.* schoolmate.

condition *n.f.* condition; fortune; state, situation; circumstances; quality, rank, station; clause; article, terms, offer. **des gens de ~,** people of rank. **en quelque ~ qu'on soit,** whatever one's station may be. **un homme de ~,** a man of rank. **quelles sont ses ~s?** what are his terms? **vendre à ~,** to sell upon condition. **entrer en ~,** to go into service. **sans ~,** unconditionally. **à ~ de,** upon condition of. **à ~ que,** provided that; on condition that.

conditionnel, elle *adj.* conditional. *n.m. Gram.* conditional mood.

conditionnement *n.m.* packaging; wrapping; conditioning.

conditionner *v.t.* to condition; to package, to wrap up, to prepack.

condoléances, *n.f.* condolence, sympathy. **lettre de ~,** letter of condolence.

condominium *n.m.* condominium.

condor *n.m.* condor.

conductance *n.f.* electrical conductance.

conducteur, trice *n.m.f.* conductor; leader, guide; driver. *adj.* conducting, leading. **fil ~,** conducting wire.

conductibilité *n.f.* conductibility.

conductible *adj.* that conducts electricity or heat.

conduction *n.f.* conduction, transmission by a conductor.

conduire *v.t.* to conduct, to lead, to guide, to accompany, to take; to drive; to lead the way to; to convey; to escort; to show; to prevail on; to be at the head of; to command; to sway; to manage, to transmit (electricity). **~ un aveugle,** to lead a blind man. **~ un enfant à l'école,** to take a child to school. **~ la barque,** to be at the head of an affair. **je vous conduirai au théâtre,** I will take you to the theater. **~ un orchestre,** to lead an orchestra. **vous ne savez pas ~,** you cannot drive. *v.i.* to lead. **permis de ~,** driver's license. **se ~,** *v.refl.* to find one's way; to be led, conducted, to behave. **se ~ bien,** to behave well.

conduit *n.m.* duct, pipe, tube. **~ d'eau,** water pipe.

conduite *n.f.* conducting, leading, guidance; management, direction, charge; behavior; driving (of cars); conveyance; superintendence, administration. **prendre la ~ d'une entreprise,** to manage an enterprise. **bonne ~,** good behavior. **avoir de la ~,** to be steady. **tuyau de ~,** delivery pipe.

cône *n.m.* cone.

confection *n.f.* execution, construction, making; drawing out; *Com.* making, making up; ready-made clothes. **magasin de ~s,** ready-made clothes warehouse.

confectionner *v.t.* to make, to execute; to make out; to make up (clothes). **se ~,** *v.refl.* to be made.

confédération *n.f.* confederation, confederacy.

confédéré, e *adj.* confederate. *n.m.* confederate, associate.

confédérer se, ~ *v.refl.* to confederate.

conférence *n.f.* lecture.

conférencier *n.m.* lecturer.

conférer *v.t.* to confer, to bestow, to give, to grant; to collate; to compare. *v.i.* to converse.

confesse *n.f.* confession. **aller à ~,** to go to confession.

confesser *v.t.* to confess; to acknowledge, to avow. **~ ses péchés,** to confess one's sins. **péché confessé est à moitié pardonné,** a fault confessed is half forgiven. **se ~,** *v.refl.* to confess. **il est allé se ~,** he is gone to confess.

confesseur *n.m.* confessor.

confession *n.f.* confession; acknowledgment; avowal. **on lui donnerait le bon Dieu sans ~,** he looks as if butter would not melt in his mouth. **~ de foi,** confession of faith.

confessionnal *n.m.* confessional.

confiance *n.f.* confidence, trust, reliance, dependence; reliance upon; assurance, boldness. **homme de ~,** person entrusted with confidential matters. **digne de ~,** trustworthy.

confiant, e *adj.* confident, trusting.

confidence *n.f.* confidence; secret, secrecy. **faire une ~ à quelqu'un,** to trust a person with a secret.

confident, e *n.m.f.* confidant, confidante.

confidentiel, elle *adj.* confidential.

confidentiellement *adv.* confidentially.

confier *v.t.* to confide (to), to trust, to entrust (to, with); to tell in confidence. **se ~,** *v.refl.* to confide (in), trust (in), to trust (to).

configuration *n.f.* configuration.

confiner *v.i.* to confine. **se ~,** *v.refl.* to confine oneself.

confins *n.m.pl.* confines, borders, frontiers. **aux ~ de la terre,** to the remotest parts of the earth.

confire *v.t.* to preserve; to pickle.

confirmation *n.f.* confirmation.

confirmer *v.t.* to confirm; to ratify. **~ quelqu'un,** to confirm a person; *Fig.* to give a person a slap in the face. **se ~,** *v.refl.* to be confirmed. **la nouvelle ne s'est pas confirmée,** the news proved to be unfounded.

confiscable *adj.* confiscable; liable to forfeiture.

confiscation *n.f.* confiscation; forfeiture.

confiserie *n.f.* candy store; sweet; candy.

confiseur, euse *n.m.f.* confectioner.

confisquer *v.t.* to confiscate.

confit, e *p.p.* preserved; pickled.

confiture *n.f.* preserve, jam.

conflagration *n.f.* conflagration.

conflit *n.m.* conflict, strife, clash; fight.

confluent, e *adj.* confluent.

confluer *v.i.* to join, to meet; to be confluent.

confondre *v.t.* to confound; to mistake for; to overwhelm; to astound; to blend; to confuse, to disorder. **se ~,** *v.refl.* to be confounded; to be lost (in apologies).

conformation *n.f.* conformation, structure.

conforme *adj.* conformable; like, resembling; consistent; certified. **pour copie ~,** certified copy.

conformé, e *adj.* formed, shaped, made.

conformément *adv.* conforming to; in accordance with.

conformer *v.t.* to conform. **se ~,** *v.refl.* to conform (to), to comply (with). **se ~ à la loi,** to submit to law.

conformisme *n.m.* conformity.

conformiste *n.m.f.* conformist.

conformité *n.f.* conformity, agreement, submission. **en ~ de,** in conformity with, according to.

confort *n.m.* comfort; aid; ease.

confortable *adj.* comfortable.

confortablement *adj.* comfortably.

conforter *v.t.* to comfort, to strengthen; to console.

confraternel, le *adj.* brotherly, fraternal.

confraternité *n.f.* confraternity.

confrère *n.m.* fellow member; colleague.

confrérie *n.f.* confraternity, brotherhood; sisterhood.

confrontation *n.f.* confrontation.

confronter *v.t.* to confront. ~ **les témoins avec l'accusé,** to confront the witnesses with the accused.

confucianisme *n.m.* Confucianism.

confus, e *adj.* confounded; confused; ashamed; obscure; indistinct; foggy.

confusément *adv.* confusedly.

confusion *n.f.* confusion; disorder; shame. **il a mis tout en ~,** he has made a mess of things. **je le dis à ma ~,** I'm ashamed to say so.

congé *n.m.* leave, discharge; dismissal; warning, notice; holiday (in schools). *Naut.* pass, clearance. **prendre ~,** to take leave. **recevoir ~,** to receive notice to quit.

congédier *v.t.* to discharge, to dismiss; to disband; to turn away, to turn off; to lay off.

congélable *adj.* freezable.

congélateur *n.m.* freezer.

congélation *n.f.* congelation; freezing.

congeler *v.t.* to congeal, to freeze. **se ~,** *v.refl.* to congeal.

congénital, e *adj.* congenital.

congère *n.f.* snowdrift.

congestion *n.f.* congestion; stroke. ~ **cérébrale,** stroke.

congestionner *v.t.* to cause a congestion.

conglomérat *n.m.* conglomerate.

conglomération *n.f.* conglomeration.

conglomérer *v.t.* to conglomerate.

congratulation *n.f.* congratulation.

congratuler *v.t.* to congratulate.

congre *n.m.* conger eel.

congrégation *n.f.* congregation.

congrès *n.m.* congress, assembly of representatives or deputies; convention (meeting).

congressiste *n.m.f.* congress member.

congru, e *adj.* congruous, proper, suitable.

congruence *n.f.* congruence.

congruent *adj.* congruent.

conifère *adj.* coniferous. *n.m.* coniferous.

conique *adj.* conic, conical.

conjectural, e *adj.* conjectural.

conjecture *n.f.* conjecture; surmise, guess. **fausse ~,** misconjecture.

conjecturer *v.t.* to conjecture.

conjoint, e *adj.* conjoined; united, wedded. *n.m.f.* spouse. **les ~s,** the husband and wife.

conjointement *adv.* cojointly, jointly.

conjonctif, ive *adj.* conjunctive.

conjonction *n.f.* conjunction.

conjonctivite *n.f.* conjunctivitis.

conjoncture *n.f.* conjuncture; crisis, critical time.

conjoncturel, le *adj.* relating to an economic crisis.

conjugable *adj.* that can be conjugated.

conjugaison *n.f.* conjugation.

conjugal, e *adj.* conjugal.

conjugalement *adv.* conjugally.

conjuguer *v.t.* to conjugate. **se ~,** *v.refl.* to be conjugated.

conjuration *n.f.* conspiracy, plot; *pl.* supplications, entreaties.

conjuré, e *n.m.* conspirator.

conjurer *v.t.* to conspire, to plot; to implore, to entreat. ~ **la colère céleste,** to avert divine wrath.

connaissable *adj.* easily known.

connaissance *n.f.* knowledge; acquaintance; learning; skill; notice, information; consciousness. **perdre ~,** to lose consciousness. **reprendre ~,** to come to oneself. **conserver toute sa ~,** to retain one's faculties. **avoir ~ de,** to be aware of, to be acquainted with. **donner ~ de,** to give notice of. **prendre ~ de,** to examine, to look into, to study. **parler en ~ de cause,** to speak of a thing with knowledge of the matter; to be well informed. **faire la ~ de quelqu'un,** to get acquainted with a person.

connaissement *n.m.* bill of lading.

connaisseur, euse *n.m.f.* connoisseur, good judge (of).

connaître *v.t.* to know, to perceive, to understand; to be informed of; to learn; to be versed in; to be acquainted with; to be aware of; to recognize. ~ **quelqu'un de nom, de vue,** to know a person by name, by sight. **se faire ~,** to make oneself known. **il connaît tout le monde,** he is acquainted with everybody. *v.i.* to know, to have knowledge; to take cognizance of. **se ~,** *v.refl.* to know oneself; to know something about. **connais toi toi-même,** know thyself. **il se connaît en livres,** he is a good judge of books.

connecter *v.t.* to connect.

connerie *n.f.* extreme stupidity.

connexe *adj.* connected.

connexion *n.f.* connection; link.

connivence *n.f.* connivance.

connotation *n.f.* connotation.

connu, e *p.p.* known. *n.m.* what is known. **il est ~ comme le loup blanc,** he is known by everyone. **le ~ et l'inconnu,** the known and the unknown.

conque *n.f.* conch; marine shell; concha, cavity of the external ear.

conquérant, e *adj.* conquering. *n.m.* conqueror.

conquérir *v.t.* to conquer; to subdue; to gain, to win.

conquête *n.f.* conquest. **pays de ~,** conquered country.

conquistador *n.m.* conquistador.

consacrer *v.t.* to consecrate, to dedicate, to devote; to hallow; to perpetuate. se ~, *v.refl.* to devote oneself.

consanguin, ine *adj.* on the father's side. frère ~, half-brother on the father's side.

consanguinité *n.f.* consanguinity.

consciemment *adv.* consciously, knowingly.

conscience *n.f.* consciousness; perception, consci.entiousness, honesty; awareeness. avoir la ~ large, to have an accommodating conscience. n'avoir point de ~, to have no sense of justice. la main sur la ~, sincerely.

consciencieusement *adv.* conscientiously.

consciencieux, euse *adj.* conscientious.

conscient, e *adj.* conscious.

conscription *n.f.* conscription; draft.

conscrit *n.m.* conscript, recruit.

consécration *n.f.* consecration.

consécutif, ive *adj.* consecutive; in a row.

consécutivement *adv.* consecutively.

conseil *n.m.* counsel, advice, council; board; adviser, counselor. la nuit porte ~, sleep on it. prendre ~ de quelqu'un, to seek advice from a person. assembler un ~, to assemble a council. ~ municipal, town council. ~ des ministres, cabinet council. ~ d'administration, board of administration.

conseiller *v.t.* to counsel, to advise; to recommend.

conseiller, ère *n.m.f.* counselor, adviser. *n.m.* councilor; member of a council; counselor.

conseilleur, *n.m.* officious adviser.

consensus *n.m.* consensus.

consentant, ante *adj.* consenting, willing.

consentement *n.m.* consent, assent.

consentir *v.i.* to consent, to agree, to assent; to acquiesce, to accede. qui ne dit mot consent, silence implies consent. *v.t. Law.* to consent to.

conséquemment *adv.* consistently, consequently in consequence.

conséquence *n.f.* consequence; inference; result, issue; importance, weight. cela ne tire pas à ~, that proves nothing. ces faits sont de la dernière ~, these facts are of the greatest importance. en ~ de vos ordres, in consequence of, in conformity with your orders.

conséquent, e *adj.* consistent; just. *n.m.* consequent. par ~, consequently, in consequence, therefore.

conservateur, trice *n.m.f.* preserver, guardian; keeper; *Polit.* conservative. *adj.* conservative.

conservation *n.f.* preservation, conservation; registration (of mortgages).

conservatisme *n.m.* conservatism.

conservatoire *adj.* conservative. *n.m.* conservatory (music).

conserve *n.f.* preserve. ~ de viande, preserved meat; canned meat. *Naut.* consort. naviguer de ~, to sail in convoy.

conserver *v.t.* to preserve, to keep; to conserve;

to pickle (in vinegar); to can; to retain; to bottle. se ~, *v.refl.* to keep, to be preserved; to take care of one's health; to preserve oneself.

considérable *adj.* eminent, notable, illustrious, distinguished; considerable. peu ~, of little consequence.

considérablement *adv.* considerable; substantially.

considérant *n.m.* preamble (of a law); grounds; *conj.* ~ que, considering that.

considération *n.f.* consideration; reflection, meditation; deliberation; reason; importance; *pl.* remarks; reflections. prendre en ~, to take into consideration. en ~ de, in consideration of, for the sake of. par ~ pour, out of consideration for.

considérer *v.t.* to consider; to behold, to look on (or at); to weigh; to regard; to examine. tout bien considéré, all things considered. se ~, *v.refl.* to regard oneself; to esteem oneself.

consignation *n.f.* consignment; consignation; deposit. caisse des dépôts et ~s, government deposit and consignment office.

consigne *n.f.* orders, instructions; confinement; baggage room, check room; custom; deposit. donner une ~, to give orders. lever la ~, to revoke orders.

consigner *v.t.* to deposit; *Com.* to put in consignment, to record; to confine to quarters; to refuse admittance to.

consistance *n.f.* consistency; stability; credit, firmness. un esprit sans ~, a person of no steadiness. c'est un homme sans ~, he is a man of no credit. cette nouvelle prend de la ~, this news is gaining credit.

consistant, e *adj.* consistent; having consistency.

consister *v.i.* to consist, to be composed, to be made up.

consistoire *n.m.* consistory.

consolable *adj.* consolable.

consolant, e *adj.* consoling, comforting.

consolateur, trice *n.m.f.* consoler, comforter. *adj.* consoling, comforting.

consolation *n.f.* consolation, comfort.

console *n.f.* console.

consoler *v.t.* to console; to comfort, to solace, to soothe. se ~, *v.refl.* to console oneself, to be consoled, to be comforted.

consolidation *n.f.* consolidation; reinforcement; strengthening.

consolider *v.t.* to consolidate, to strengthen; to fund. se ~, *v.refl.* to consolidate.

consommable *adj.* consumable; edible; drinkable.

consommateur *n.m.* consumer; customer.

consommation *n.f.* consummation; consumption; drink.

consommé, e *p.p.* consumed. *adj.* consummate; complete; *n.m. Culin.* consommé.

consommer v.t. to consummate; to complete, to accomplish, to finish; to consume.

consomption n.f. consumption; destruction; *Med.* consumption.

consonance n.f. consonance.

consonant, e adj. consonant.

consonne n.f. *Gram.* consonant.

consortium n.m. consortium.

consorts n.m., pl. consorts, partners; company.

conspirateur n.m. conspirator.

conspiration n.f. conspiracy, plot. **tramer une ~,** to conspire, to plot a conspiracy.

conspirer v.i. to conspire; to plot. **tout conspire à me nuire,** everything is against me.

conspuer v.t. to shout down; to boo.

constamment adv. constantly, invariably.

constance n.f. constancy; steadfastness, firmness, steadiness, persistence.

constant, e adj. constant, steadfast; persevering; steady, stable; certain, undoubted.

constat n.m. report, record.

constatation n.f. ascertaining, establishment; statement; findings; inquiry; certification; observation.

constater v.t. to ascertain, to establish; to prove, to verify; to state.

constellation n.f. constellation.

constellé, e adj. constellated, starry.

consteller v.t. to constellate.

consternant adj. dismaying.

consternation n.f. consternation; dismay.

consterner v.t. to astound, to dismay, to strike with consternation.

constipation n.f. constipation.

constipé, e adj. constipated.

constiper v.t. to constipate, to bind. **se ~,** v.refl. to become constipated.

constituant, e adj. constituent; component.

constituer v.t. to constitute, to compose; to make up; to set up; to make; to settle; to empower. **~ un gouvernement,** to constitute a government. **qui vous a constitué juge?** who made you a judge? **~ une rente à quelqu'un,** to provide an annuity to a person. **se ~,** v.refl. to constitute, to be made up of; to amass, to form.

constitutif, ive adj. constitutive.

constitution n.f. constitution; composition; peculiar structure; temperament; *Law.* appointment; settlement (of annuities, of pensions, etc.).

constitutionnaliser v.t. to constitutionalize, to include in a constitution.

constitutionnalité n.f. constitutionality.

constitutionnel, elle adj. constitutional.

constitutionnellement adv. constitutionally.

constricteur n.m. constrictor.

constriction n.f. constriction.

constructeur n.m. builder, constructor; shipbuilder; manufacturer.

construction n.f. construction, building; edifice, structure. **~ de navires,** shipbuilding. **vais-**

seau de ~ française, French-built ship.

construire v.t. to construct; to build, to erect, to frame; *Gram.* to construe. **~ une machine,** to construct a machine. **~ un navire,** to build a ship. **~ une phrase,** to construe a sentence. **se ~,** v.refl. to be constructed.

consubstantiation n.f. consubstantiation.

consubstantiel, elle adj. consubstantial.

consul n.m. consul.

consulaire adj. consular.

consulat n.m. consulate.

consultant, e adj.m. consulting. **médecin ~,** consulting physician. n.m.f. person consulted; consultant.

consultatif, ive adj. consultative; advisory.

consultation n.f. consultation; opinion (legal).

consulter v.t. and v.i. to consult, to deliberate; to refer to; to consider; to confer about. **~ un avocat,** to consult a lawyer. **~ son chevet,** sleep on a matter. **~ ses intérêts,** to consider one's interest. **se ~,** v.refl. to consider, to reflect.

consumer v.t. to consume; to destroy, to burn, to eat up; to devour; to squander; to waste; to waste away. **le temps consume toutes choses,** time consumes everything. **se ~,** v.refl. to be consumed; to be wasted; to ruin one's health; to waste one's strength. **se ~ de douleur,** to pine away with grief.

contact n.m. contact; touch, connection. *Elect.* switch. **mettre en ~,** to bring into contact. **~ de terre,** ground connection; **clef de ~,** ignition key. **lentille de ~ or verre de ~,** contact lens.

contacter v.t. to contact.

contagieux, euse adj. contagious; infectious; catching.

contagion n.f. contagion, infection; contagiousness.

container n.m. container.

contamination n.f. contamination.

contaminer v.t. to contaminate.

conte n.m. tale, story. **~ de fées,** fairy tale. **c'est un ~ extravagant, ridicule,** it is a most extravagant or ridiculous story. **faire des ~s,** to tell stories, to fib. **~ en l'air,** idle story. **~ de bonne femme,** old wives' tale.

contemplateur, trice n.m.f. contemplator.

contemplatif, ive adj. contemplative.

contemplation n.f. contemplation.

contempler v.t. to contemplate; to behold, to survey, to gaze on; to ponder. v.i. to contemplate, to meditate, to muse, to think.

contemporain, aine adj. contemporaneous; contemporary. n.m.f. contemporary.

contempteur, trice n.m.f despiser, scorner.

contenance n.f. capacity, contents; *Naut.* capacity; extent; countenance, look, bearing. **cette propriété est de la ~ de dix hectares,** that estate extends ten hectares. **une humble ~,** a humble look. **perdre ~,** to lose face. **faire bonne ~,** to put a good face on the matter, to show spirit.

contenant *n.m.* container.

contenir *v.t.* to contain; to hold; to hold within certain limits; to include; to comprehend, to comprise; to confine, to curb. **la troupe avait peine à ~ la foule,** the soldiers could hardly keep the crowd back. **elle a peine à ~ sa joie,** she can scarcely contain her joy. **se ~,** *v.refl.* to contain oneself, to restrain oneself. **il ne put pas se ~,** he could not contain himself.

content, e *adj.* content, contented, satisfied; pleased; glad, happy. **~ de peu,** easily satisfied. **être ~ de quelqu'un,** to be pleased with a person. **il est ~ de vous voir,** he is pleased to see you.

contentement *n.m.* content, contentedness, satisfaction. **~ passe richesse,** enough is as good as a feast.

contenter *v.t.* to content, to satisfy; to please, to gratify. **on ne saurait ~ tout le monde,** it is impossible to please everyone. **se ~,** *v.refl.* to be contented, to be satisfied; to be content. **contentez-vous de cela,** be satisfied with that.

contentieux, euse *adj.* disputed; contested; contentious; in litigation. **affaire contentieuse,** litigious affair. *n.m.* affairs in litigation. **bureau ~,** disputed claims office.

contenu *n.m.* contents; *adj.* (anger) restrained, suppressed.

conter *v.t.* to tell, to relate; to report. **on conte que,** it is reported that.... **~ fleurettes,** to say sweet nothings to a woman. *v.i.* to tell stories.

contestataire *adj.* rebellious.

contestation *n.f.* contest, contestation, strife, dispute, debate.

conteste *n.f.* contestation, dispute. **sans ~,** indisputably.

contester *v.t.* to contest, to dispute, to call in question, to controvert. **~ à quelqu'un sa qualité,** to call a person's rank in to question. **~ une créance,** to dispute a debt. *v.i.* to dispute, to wrangle. **se ~,** *v.refl.* to be contested.

conteur, euse *n.m.f.* storyteller, narrator; fibber.

contexte *n.m.* context.

contexture *n.f.* contexture, texture.

contigu, guë *adj.* contiguous, touching, adjacent, adjoining. **sa maison est contiguë à la mienne,** his house adjoins mine.

contiguïté *n.f.* contiguity, contiguousness.

continence *n.f.* continence.

continent, e *adj.* continent. *Med.* continual. *n.m.* continent, mainland.

continental, e *adj.* continental.

contingence *n.f.* contingence, contingency; occurrence; eventuality.

contingent, e *adj.* contingent; casual, accidental. *n.m.* contingent, share, quota.

contingentement *n.m.* quota system.

continu, e *adj.* continuous; uninterrupted. *n.m.* continuous matter; space.

continuateur, trice *n.m.f.* continuator.

continuation *n.f.* continuation.

continuel, elle *adj.* continual; uninterrupted.

continuellement *adv.* continually, unceasingly, uninterruptedly.

continuer *v.t.* to continue, to proceed with; to persevere in; to prolong; to protract; to carry on; to hold, to keep. *v.i.* to continue; to hold on; to extend, to prolong. **continuez à bien faire,** continue to do well. **se ~,** *v.refl.* to be continued.

continuité *n.f.* continuity; duration.

contondant, e *adj.* blunt, bruising.

contorsion *n.f.* contortion, twisting, writhing.

contorsionner *v.t.* to contort, to distort.

contorsionniste *n.m.f.* contortionist.

contour *n.m.* contour, circuit, circumference; outlines.

contourné, e *adj.* distorted, crooked.

contourner *v.t.* to give the proper contour to; to wind around; to distort, to twist, to deform; to bypass; to go round. **se ~,** *v.refl.* to get out of shape; to grow crooked, distorted.

contraceptif, ive *adj.* contraceptive.

contraception *n.f.* contraception.

contractant, e *adj.* contracting. *n.m.* contractor, contracting party.

contracte, e *adj.* contracted; tense (person).

contracter *v.t.* to contract, to stipulate; to enter into; to draw to; to make; to get; to catch; to tense up. **~ des dettes,** to contract debts. **~ une maladie,** to catch a disease. **se ~,** *v.refl.* to be contracted; to contract, to shrink.

contractile *adj.* contractile.

contraction *n.f.* contraction.

contractuel, elle *adj.* stipulated by contract. *n.m.f.* traffic manager.

contracture *n.f.* diminution; contraction.

contradicteur *n.m.* contradicter, opponent.

contradiction *n.f.* contradiction; opposition; discrepancy; inconsistency. **esprit de ~,** spirit of contradiction.

contradictoire *adj.* contradictory; inconsistent.

contradictoirement *adv.* contradictorily; *Law.* in the presence of both parties.

contraignant, e *adj.* constraining.

contraindre *v.t.* to impose, to put a restraint upon; to constrain, to force, to coerce, to oblige. **se ~,** *v.refl.* to constrain oneself, to restrain oneself, to refrain (from).

contraint, e *adj.* constrained, forced, obliged.

contrainte *n.f.* constraint, compulsion, force, coercion; necessity, restraint. **sans ~,** freely; unconstrainedly.

contraire *adj.* contrary, opposite, adverse; hostile, repugnant, unfavorable; contradictory, inconsistent; hurtful. **en sens ~,** in the opposite direction. **le café vous est ~,** coffee is not good for you. **au ~,** on the contrary. **bien au ~,** quite the contrary. **au ~ de,** against, contrary to.

contrairement *adv.* contrarily; unlike.

contralto *n.m.* contralto.

contrariant, e *adj.* provoking; annoying, vexatious.

contrarier *v.t.* to contradict, to gainsay; to thwart, to be contrary to; to provoke.

contrariété *n.f.* opposition, hindrance; annoyance; vexation.

contrastant, e *adj.* contrasting.

contraste *n.m.* contrast.

contraster *v.i.* to contrast. *v.t.* to contrast, to set off by opposition.

contrat *n.m.* contract, instrument; agreement; bargain; compact; deed. **~ de vente**, deed of sale. **~ de mariage**, marriage contract. **passer un ~**, to enter into a contract. **signer un ~**, to sign a contract.

contravention *n.f.* Infraction, contravention; fine; parking ticket.

contre *prep.* against; versus; contrary to; near, near to, close to, close by; in exchange for; in spite (of). **le pour et le ~**, the pros and cons. **~-attaque**, counterattack. **~-espionnage**, counterespionage, counterintelligence. **~-examiner**, to cross-examine. **fâché ~**, angry with. **aller ~ vent et marée**, to sail against wind and tide. **sa maison est ~ la mienne**, his house is close to mine. *adv.* against it, against. **parler pour et ~**, to speak for and against. *n.m.* the opposite side.

contre-accusation *n.f.* countercharge.

contre-allée *n.f.* sidewalk, path.

contrebalancer *v.t.* to counterbalance. **se ~**, *v.refl.* to counterbalance one another.

contrebande *n.f.* contraband, smuggled goods; smuggling. **faire la ~**, to smuggle. **de ~**, smuggled, contraband.

contrebandier, ière *n.m.f.* smuggler.

contrebasse *n.f.* double bass.

contrebassiste *n.m.* double base player.

contrebasson *n.m.* double bassoon.

contrecarrer *v.t.* to counteract.

contrechamp *n.m.* (film) reverse shot.

contrecœur *n.m.* back (of a chimney). **à ~**, reluctantly.

contrecoup *n.m.* rebound, counterstroke.

contre-courant *n.m.* countercurrent. **à ~**, upstream.

contredanse *n.f.* quadrille; country dance.

contredire *v.t.* to contradict, to gainsay, to deny, to be inconsistent with; to disprove, to refute. *v.i.* to contradict. **il aime à ~**, he is fond of contradicting. **se ~**, *v.refl.* to contradict oneself; to contradict each other.

contredit, e *n.m.* Law. reply; contradiction. **sans ~**, beyond doubt, without contradiction.

contrée *n.f.* country; region.

contre-expertise *n.f.* cross-examination.

contrefaçon *n.f.* counterfeiting; counterfeit; pirating; forgery; imitation.

contrefacteur *n.m.* counterfeiter, forger.

contrefaire *v.t.* to counterfeit; to imitate; to copy; to disguise; to forge; to ape, to mimic.

~ son écriture, to disguise one's writing.

contrefait, e *p.p.* counterfeit, imitated, forged; deformed.

contrefort *n.m.* Arch. buttress; spur (of a mountain chain).

contre-indication *n.f.* contraindication.

contre-indiquer *v.t.* to contraindicate.

contremaitre *n.m.* foreman; boatswain's mate.

contremaîtresse *n.f.* forewoman.

contremarche *n.f.* countermarch; stair, riser.

contrepartie *n.f.* counterpart; contrary, reverse.

contrepèterie *n.f.* spoonerism.

contrepoids *n.m.* counterpoise; counterbalance, balancing pole, **à ~**, off balance.

contrepoint *n.m.* counterpoint.

contrepoison *n.m.* antidote.

contrer *v.t.* to counter; to double; to cross; to thwart; to interfere.

contreseing *n.m.* countersignature, countersign.

contresens *n.m.* opposite meaning, wrong sense, misconstruction, misinterpretation; wrong reading; mistranslation. **cette traduction est pleine de ~**, that translation is full of misinterpretations.

contresigner *v.t.* to countersign.

contretemps *n.m.* mischance, mishap, disappointment, untoward accident; syncopation. **à ~**, unseasonably, at a wrong time.

contrevenant, e *n.f.* offender, transgressor.

contrevenir *v.i.* to counteract; to infringe, ringe, to transgress, to violate.

contrevent *n.m.* shutter.

contribuable *n.m.* contributor; taxpayer.

contribuer *v.i.* to contribute; to promote, to forward. **~ au succès d'une affaire**, to contribute to the success of an affair.

contributif, ive *adj.* contributive, contributing.

contribution *n.f.* contribution, tax; Com. average. **~s directes**, assessed taxes. **receveur des ~s**, tax collector.

contrister *v.t.* to sadden, to grieve, to afflict.

contrit, e *adj.* contrite, penitent.

contrition *n.f.* contrition.

contrôlable *adj.* verifiable; controllable.

contrôle *n.m.* control; Milit. lists, rolls; stamp; mint mark; check, checking. **rayer des ~s**, to cross off.

contrôler *v.t.* to control, to register; to check; to censure; to find fault with; to stamp, to mark (gold and silver).

contrôleur, euse *n.m.f.* ticket taker, controller; superintendent; fault-finder; inspector; regulator; time clock. **~ aérien**, air traffic controller. **~ des impôts**, assessor. **~ douanes**, customs inspector.

contrordre *n.m.* countermand.

controuver *v.t.* to invent, to fabricate, to forge.

controversable *adj.* controvertible, disputable; controversial.

controverse *n.f.* controversy; debate, disputation.

controversé, e *p.p.* controverted, debated, disputed.

controverser *v.t.* to controvert, to debate, to dispute.

contumace *n.f.* refusal to appear in court, default. *n.m.f.* defaulter.

contusion *n.f.* contusion, bruise.

contusionner *v.t.* to bruise.

conurbation *n.f.* conurbation.

convaincant, e *adj.* convincing.

convaincre *v.t.* to convince, to persuade; to convict. **se ~,** *v.refl.* to convince oneself; to be convinced.

convaincu, e *p.p.* convinced; convicted.

convalescence *n.f.* convalescence.

convalescent, e *adj.* convalescent. *n.m.f.* person in a state of convalescence.

convection *n.f.* convection.

convenable *adj.* suitable, proper, fit; appropriate, adapted; apposite; convenient, meet, right, expedient, advisable; congruous, consistent; according with; becoming; seemly; decorous. **un mariage ~,** a suitable marriage. **j'ai jugé ~ de le faire,** I thought it advisable to do it. **une personne ~,** a well-bred person.

convenablement *adv.* suitably, fitly, conveniently, becomingly, decorously.

convenance *n.f.* agreement; relation, conformity; suitableness, fitness, propriety; congruity; decency, decorum; good breeding. **mariage de ~,** a suitable match. **observer les ~s,** to observe the rules of decorum. **il a été d'une ~ parfaite,** he behaved most decorously.

convenir *v.i.* to admit, to acknowledge, to grant, to allow; to avow, to agree. **il est convenu lui-même de son erreur,** he has admitted his error. **cette maison m'a convenu,** that house suited me. **tout le monde lui convient,** everybody pleases him. **il convient de se taire,** it is advisable to be silent. **se ~,** *v.refl.* to suit each other; to agree.

convention *n.f.* convention, agreement; covenant, contract, compact. **~ verbale,** verbal agreement. **tenir une ~,** to keep an agreement. **langage de ~,** conventional language.

conventionnel, elle *adj.* conventional.

conventionnellement *adv.* conventionally.

conventualité *n.f.* convent life.

conventuel, elle *adj.* conventual.

convenue, e *adj.* agreed; admitted; stipulated.

convergence *n.f.* convergence.

convergent, e *adj.* converging, convergent.

converger *v.i.* to converge; to tend to one point.

convers, erse *adj.* lay.

conversation *n.f.* conversation, talk. **entrer en ~, lier ~,** to enter into conversation.

converser *v.i.* to converse.

conversion *n.f.* conversion, change, changing.

converti, e *n.m.f.* convert.

convertibilité *n.f.* convertibility.

convertible *adj.* convertible.

convertir *v.t.* to convert, to change, to transform, to turn; to bring over to an opinion. **se ~,** *v.refl.* to be converted, to be changed, to be turned; to convert.

convertissage *n.m.* conversion.

convertisseur *n.m.* converter.

convexe *adj.* convex.

convexité *n.f.* convexity.

conviction *n.f.* conviction, belief. **par ~,** from conviction. *Law.* **pièce à conviction,** exhibit (evidence).

convier *v.t.* to invite, to beg, to request; to prompt. **~ à un banquet,** to invite to a banquet.

convive *n.m.f.* guest. **un bon ~,** a good companion at table.

convivialité *n.f.* conviviality.

convocation *n.f.* convocation; summons.

convoi *n.m.* convoy; cortege; funeral train. **~ de grande vitesse,** fast train. V. TRAIN.

convoiement *n.m.* escorting; convoying.

convoiter *v.t.* to covet.

convoitise *n.f.* covetousness; cupidity; lust.

convoquer *v.t.* to convoke, to convene, to summon, to assemble.

convoyer *v.t.* to convoy; to escort.

convoyeur *n.m.* convoy, convoy ship; conveyor. **~ de fonds,** security guard (transferring bank-notes).

convulser *v.t.* to convulse, to contract by spasms.

convulsif, ive *adj.* convulsive.

convulsion *n.f.* convulsion, fit; spasm.

convulsionnaire *n.m.f.* convulsionary.

convulsionner *v.t.* to convulse; to upset.

convulsivement *adv.* convulsively.

coobligé *n.m.* cosigner (of a loan).

coopérateur, trice *n.m.f.* co-operator; joint operator; fellow worker. *adj.* cooperating, cooperative.

coopératif, ive *adj.* cooperative.

coopération *n.f.* cooperation; support.

coopératisme *n.m.* cooperation, cooperative movement.

coopérative *n.f.* cooperative; coop.

coopérer *v.i.* to cooperate; to contribute.

cooptation *n.f.* cooptation.

coopter *v.t.* to coopt.

coordination *n.f.* coordination; arrangement.

coordonnateur, trice *adj.* coordinating, *n.m.f.* coordinator.

coordonné, e *adj.* coordinated. *n.f.pl.* **~es,** coordinates; name, address, and telephone number.

coordonner *v.t.* to dispose, to arrange.

copain (ou copin), copine *n.m.f.* friend, pal; buddy; mate; boyfriend or girlfriend.

coparticipant, e *adj.* in copartnership; *n.m.f.* copartner.

coparticipation *n.f.* copartnership; profit-sharing.

copeau *n.m.* wood chip; shaving.

copiage *n.m.* copying; reproducing.

copie *n.f.* copy, transcript; imitation, likeness; *Print.* copy, manuscript; task.

copier *v.t.* to copy; to transcribe; to imitate, to mimic.

copieur, euse *n.m.f.* copier, copy cat.

copieusement *adv.* copiously; abundantly, heartily.

copieux, euse *adj.* copious, abundant, hearty.

copilote *n.m.f.* copilot.

copinage *n.m. Infml.* favoritism.

copine *n.f.* girlfriend V. COPAIN.

copiner *v.t.* to make friends with.

copiste *n.m.* copier, copyist, imitator.

coposséder *v.t.* to co-own; to own jointly.

copossession *n.f.* cotenancy, joint ownership.

copra(h) *n.m.* copra.

coproduction *n.f.* coproduction.

copropriétaire *n.m.f.* joint proprietor, joint owner.

copropriété *n.f.* co-ownership; joint ownership.

copte *n.m.* Copt; Coptic.

copulation *n.f.* copulation.

copyright *n.m.* copyright.

coq *n.m.* cock; rooster; *Naut.* cook. **~ de combat,** game cock. **~ de bruyère,** grouse. **être comme un ~ en pâte,** to live in clover. **sauter du coq-à-l'âne,** to jump from one subject to another. **il est le ~ de son village,** he rules the roost.

coquard *n.m.Infml.* black eye, shiner.

coque *n.f.* shell, cockle; *Naut.* bull. **des oeufs à la ~,** soft-boiled eggs. **~ de perle,** pearl shell.

coquelet *n.m.* cockerel.

coquelicot *n.m.* wild poppy, corn poppy.

coqueluche *n.f.* favorite, darling; whooping cough.

coquerie *n.f.* cook's galley (ship).

coquet, ette *adj.* coquettish, flirting; smart. *n.m.* flirt.

coquetier *n.m.* eggcup. **gagner le ~,** to win the jackpot.

coquetterie *n.f.* flirtation; affectation.

coquillage *n.m.* shellfish; shell.

coquille *n.f.* shell (of eggs, fruits), goods of no value, *Print.* misprint. **rentrer dans sa ~,** to draw in one's horns. **à qui vendez vous vos ~s?** do not expect to cheat me!

coquillette *n.f.* shell-shaped pasta.

coquin, ine *n.m.f.* rascal. **petit ~,** little rascal. *adj.* roguish; debauched; lazy.

coquinerie *n.f.* trick; knavery, roguery, rascality.

cor *n.m.* horn, French horn; corn (on the feet). **~ de chasse,** hunting horn. **donner, sonner du ~,** to blow, to wind the horn. **à ~ et à cri,** with hue and cry.

corail, *pl.* **coraux** *n.m.* coral. **pêche du ~,** coral fishing.

corallien, ienne *adj.* coral; coralline; coral reef.

coran *n.m.* Koran.

coranique *adj.* Koranic.

corbeau *n.m.* raven, crow; *Arch.* corbel, *Naut.* grappling iron.

corbeille *n.f.* basket; its contents. stock-market trading floor; *Arch.* corbel, *Gard.* flower bed. **une ~ de fleurs,** a basket of flowers. **~ de mariage,** wedding presents.

corbillard *n.m.* hearse.

cordage *n.m.* rope, cord; cordage, measuring (of wood) by the cord.

corde *n.f. Mus.* string, line; skipping rope; halter tone; chord. **la grosse ~,** the main point. **~ d'emballage,** package string. **~ de violon,** violin string. **sauter à la ~,** to skip. **friser la ~,** to be in a perilous situation. **tenir la ~,** to have the best chance. **tendre la ~,** to stretch the bow. **avoir deux ~s à son arc,** to have two strings to one's bow. **avoir la ~ de pendu,** to have rotten luck. **habit usé jusqu'à la ~,** threadbare coat. **pleuvoir des ~s,** to rain cats and dogs.

cordeau *n.m.* line, cord; tow line.

cordelière *n.f.* Franciscan nun; tie, belt (robe); *Arch.* cable moulding; *Print.* border.

cordelle *n.f.* tow line, tow rope.

cordial, e *adj.* cordial; hearty, sincere. *n.m.* cordial.

cordialement *adv.* cordially, heartily, sincerely.

cordialité *n.f.* cordiality; heartiness, sincerity.

cordier *n.m.* ropemaker, cordmaker.

cordillères *n.f.pl. Geog.* Cordilleras.

cordon *n.m.* yarn; string, cord, line, thread; ribbon; tape; hand; edge, milled edge (of coins); **~ de sonnette,** bell rope, bell pull. **le grand ~ de la Légion d'Honneur,** the broad ribbon of the Legion of Honor. **~ ombilical,** umbilical cord. **~ dorsale,** spinal cord. *(Mus.)* **instruments à ~s,** string instruments. **~-bleu** *pl. Culin. (pl.)* **~s-bleu,** cordon-bleu cook.

cordonner *v.t.* to twist; to braid, to plait.

cordonnerie *n.f.* shoe repair.

cordonnet *n.m.* twist, string; braid.

cordonnier, ière *n.m.f.* shoe repairer.

cordouan *n.m.* cordovan; Spanish leather.

coreligionnaire *n.m.f.* fellow believer.

coriace *adj.* tough; hard, stiff as leathers; *Infml.* close-fisted, miserly; *Bot.* cartilaginous.

coriandre *n.f.* coriander.

coricide *n.m.* remedy for corns.

corindon *n.m.* corundum, adamantine spar.

cormier *n.m.* service tree.

cormoran *n.m.* cormorant, sea raven.

cornac *n.m.* elephant driver; guide, mentor.

cornard *n.m. Vulg.* cuckold.

corne *n.f.* horn; shoehorn; corner (of a hat); hoof; dog's ear (of a book); *Naut.* gaff, throat; a feeler of a snail; lunar crescent. **bêtes à ~s,** horned cattle. **montrer les ~s,** to show one's teeth. **~ d'abondance,** cornucopia, horn of plenty. **avoir, porter des ~s,** to be a cuckold. **faire une ~ à un feuillet,** to turn down the corner of a page. **~ de cerf,** hartshorn.

cornée *n.f* cornea.

cornéenne *n.f. Geol.* aphanitté.

corneille *n.f.* crow. **une bande de ~s,** a flock of crows. **bayer aux ~s,** stare vacantly.

cornélien, ne *adj.* cornelia; impossible choice.

cornemuse *n.f.* bagpipe.

corner *v.i.* to blow, to tingle, to ring, to sing. *v.t.* to trumpet abroad; to gore (of a bull).

cornet *n.m.* horn, cornet; cone; paperbag; dice box. **~ à piston,** cornet. **un ~ de dragées,** a bag of sugared almonds. **~ de glace,** ice cream cone.

cornettiste *n.m.f.* cornet player. *n.f.* cornet (kind of a hat).

corniaud *n.m.* (dog) mongrel, mixed breed; fool.

corniche *n.f.* ledge, road. **La Grande Corniche,** famous seaside road on French Riviera.

cornichon *n.m.* pickle.

Cornouailles *n.* Cornwall.

cornu, e *adj.* horned; angular, cornered; extravagant; whimsical; retort.

corollaire *n.m.* corollary; consequence.

corolle *n.f.* corolla.

coronaire *adj.* coronary.

corporatif, ive *adj.* corporative; corporate.

corporation *n.f.* corporation, corporate body.

corporatisme *n.m.* corporation.

corporel, elle *adj.* corporal, bodily.

corps *n.m.* body, person; substance; frame; corpse; creature; bodice; system; corporation; company; corps, volume; barrel (of a pump). **il a le diable au ~,** he's got the devil in him. **un ~ de fer,** an iron frame. **prendre du ~,** to get stout. **faire ~ neuf,** to take a new lease on life. **exposer un ~,** to lay a corpse in state. **separation de ~ et de biens.** *Law.* legal separation. **contrainte par ~,** arrest for debt. **les ~s célestes,** heavenly bodies. **~ de logis,** detached building. **les ~ de métiers,** the trade companies; *Print.* the size of a letter. **~ diplomatique,** the diplomatic corps. **~ d'armée,** body of troops. **à ~ perdu,** headlong. **à son ~ défendant,** in self-defense; reluctantly. **~ à ~,** hand-to-hand (fight).

corpulence *n.f.* corpulence, stoutness.

corpulent, e *adj.* corpulent, stout.

corpus *n.m.* corpus, collected writings.

corpusculaire *adj.* corpuscular.

corpuscule *n.m.* corpuscle.

correct, e *adj.* correct, accurate; right; proper; adequate.

correctement *adv.* correctly, accurately.

correcteur, trice *n.m.f.* corrector, *Print.* proofreader.

correctif, ive *adj.* corrective.

correction *n.f.* correction, correctness; accuracy; reproof; punishment, discipline. *Print.* reading. **sauf ~,** errors excepted. **maison de ~,** reformatory.

correctionnel, elle *adj. Law.* relative to misdemeanors. **tribunal ~,** criminal court.

corrélatif, ive *adj.* correlative. *n.m.* correlative.

corrélation *n.f.* correlation.

correspondance *n.f.* correspondence; connections; relation; communication. **service de ~,** connecting service (travel).

correspondant, e *adj.* corresponding, correspondent. *n.m.* correspondent; pen pal.

correspondre *v.i.* to correspond; to communicate; to suit, to fit. **se ~,** *v.refl.* to correspond with each other; to communicate with each other.

corrida *n.f.* bullfight; *Infml.* mess, battle.

corridor *n.m.* corridor, gallery, lobby.

corrigé *n.m.* corrected copy; key (to a book).

corriger *v.t.* to correct; to amend, to reclaim, to reform; to repair, to redress; to rectify; *Print.* to read; to soften; to punish, to chastise. **~ des épreuves,** to correct, to proofread. **se ~,** *v.refl.* to correct oneself; to amend; to be corrected.

corroborant, e *adj.* corroborant. *n.m. Med.* corroborant.

corroboratif, ive *adj.* corroborating, corroborative. *n.m. Med.* corroborant.

corroboration *n.f.* corroboration, strengthening.

corroborer *v.t.* to corroborate, to strengthen.

corrodant, e *adj.* corroding. *n.m.* corrosive.

corroder *v.t.* to corrode.

corroirie *n.f.* currying.

corrompre *v.t.* to corrupt; to spoil, to mar, to taint; to alter, to putrify; to deprave; to bribe, to suborn. **~ les moeurs,** to corrupt the morals. **il s'est laissé ~ par des présents,** he was bribed with presents. **se ~,** *v.refl.* to be corrupted, spoiled, tainted. **les moeurs se corrompent,** morals are becoming corrupted.

corrompu, e *p.p.* and *adj.* corrupt, corrupted; spoiled, tainted, depraved. **un coeur ~,** a dissolute heart.

corrosif, ive *adj.* corrosive. *n.m.* corrosive.

corrosion *n.f.* corrosion.

corroyer *v.t.* to curry (skins, leather); to puddle; to hammer (iron); to plane (wood).

corrupteur, trice *adj.* corrupting. *n.m.f.* corrupter; briber; suborner.

corruptible *adj.* corruptible.

corruption *n.f.* corruption; decay; putrefaction; corruptness; depravity; bribery.

corsage *n.m.* trunk, bust, bodice (of a dress). **un ~ étroit,** a narrow bodice. **un ~ décolleté,** a low bodice.

corsaire *n.m.* corsair; pirate.

Corse *n.f.* Corsica.

corsé, e *adj.* full-bodied (wine); strong; racy (story).

corset *n.m.* bodice; corset; *Surg.* bandage.

cortège *n.m.* retinue, train; escort; procession; attendants.

cortex *n.m.* cortex.

cortical, e *adj.* cortical.

cortisone *n.f.* cortisone.

corvée *n.f.* forced labor; chore.

corvette *n.f.* corvette, sloop of war.

cosaque *n.m.* Cossack.

cosécante *n.f.* cosecant.

cosignataire *adj.*, *n.m.f.* cosignatory.

cosinus *n.m.* cosine.

cosmétique *adj.* cosmetic. *n.f.* art of using cosmetics.

cosmétologie *n.f.* beauty care, cosmetology.

cosmétologue *n.m.f.* cosmetician, cosmetologist.

cosmique *adj.* cosmic.

cosmogonie *n.f.* cosmogony.

cosmographie *n.f.* cosmography.

cosmologie *n.f.* cosmology.

cosmonaute *n.m.f.* cosmonaut, astronaut.

cosmopolite *n.m.* cosmopolite. *adj.* cosmopolitan.

cosmopolitisme *n.m.* cosmopolitanism.

cosmos *n.m.* cosmos.

cosse *n.f.* pod, cod, shell, husk, hull.

cossu, e *adj.* podded, husked, *Fig.* rich, wealthy.

costal, e *adj.* costal.

costard *n.m. Infml.* suit.

costaud, e *adj. Infml.* strong, hefty.

costume *n.m.* costume; dress; suit. **grand ~**, full dress.

costumer *v.t.* to dress; to dress up. **se ~**, *v.refl.* to get dressed up.

costumier *n.m.* dresser.

cozy *n.m.* corner divan with shelves attached.

cotangente *n.f.* cotangent.

cotation *n.f.* quotation; valuation; quoting; marketing.

cote *n.f.* quota, share; letter, figure, number; quotation. **payer sa ~**, to pay one's quota. **faire une ~ mal taillée**, to make a rough compromise.

côte *n.f.* rib; hill, slope; shore, coast; *Bot.* midrib. **se casser une ~**, to break a rib. **au bas de la ~**, at the bottom of the hill. **raser la ~**, to sail close along shore. **ils marchaient ~ à ~**, they were walking side by side.

coté, e *adj. Fin.* listed; *Fig.* esteemed, respected.

côté *n.m.* side, border, margin; flank; broadside, beam ends. **il a mal au ~**, he has a pain in his side. **il regarde tout par le mauvais ~**, he looks at everything in the wrong light. **d'un ~ à l'autre**, from side to side. **je vais de votre ~**, I am going your way. **de tous ~s**, in all directions. **le ~ maternel**, the mother's side. **de mon ~**, for my part. **donner à ~**, to miss the mark. **tournez-vous un peu plus de ~**, turn yourself a little more on one side.

coteau *n.m.* slope, declivity; hill, hillock.

cotelé, e *adj.* ribbed. **velours ~**, corduroy.

côtelette *n.f.* chop (of lamb, mutton, or pork); cutlet (of veal).

coter *v.t.* to quote; to mark; *Fin.* to assess; to number, to letter.

coterie *n.f.* coterie, club, society, circle; set, clique.

cothurne *n.m.* buskin; *Fig.* tragedy.

côtier, ière *adj.* coasting. **bâtiment ~**, coasting vessel.

côtière *n.f.* line of coasts; *Gard.* border; shelving bed.

cotillon *n.m.* petticoat; cotillion. **régime du ~**, petticoat government.

cotisant, e *n.m.f.* subscriber.

cotisation *n.f.* contribution; subscription; dues; collection.

cotiser *v.t.* to assess, to rate. **se ~**, *v.refl.* to contribute, to subscribe.

coton *n.m.* cotton. **~ uni**, plain cotton. **filature de ~**, cotton spinning; cotton mill. **élever un enfant dans du ~**, coddle a child. **il file un mauvais ~**, he is going to the dogs. **~-tige**, swab.

cotonnade *n.f.* cottons, cotton fabrics.

cotonné, e *p.p.* (of hair) woolly.

cotonner *v.i.* to cotton, to pad. **se ~**, *v.refl.* to become downy.

cotonneux, euse *adj.* cottony, downy, nappy; soft.

cotonnier *n.m.* cotton plant. *adj.* cotton; cottony.

côtoyer *v.t.* to go by the side of; to coast, to skirt, to run along the coast; to frequent; to rub elbows with.

cotre *n.m. Naut.* cutter.

cottage *n.m.* cottage.

cotte *n.f.* petticoat; coat. **~ de maille**, coat of mail.

cotutelle *n.f.* joint guardianship.

cotuteur, trice *n.m.f. Law.* joint guardian.

cou or **col** *n.m.* neck, collar (of a shirt). **avoir un ~ de cygne**, to have a white neck. **se jeter, sauter au ~ de quelqu'un**, to throw one's arms around a person's neck. **prendre ses jambes à son ~**, to take to one's heels. **jusqu'au ~**, up to the elbows.

couac *n.m. Mus.* false note.

couard *n.m.* and *adj.* coward; cowardly.

couardise *n.f.* cowardice.

couchant, e *adj.* setting. **soleil ~**, setting sun. **chien ~**, setter. **faire le chien ~**, to cringe, to fawn. *n.m.* west; sunset; wane, decline.

couche *n.f.* bed, couch; bedstead; confinement, childbed; baby's diaper; *Gard.* hotbed, frame, layer, coat, coating; seam, stratum; class (social). **la ~ nuptiale**, the nuptial bed. **être en ~**, to give birth; to be recovering from childbirth. **elle est morte en ~**, she died in childbirth. **fausse ~**, miscarriage. **une ~ de peinture**, a coat of paint.

couché, e *p.p.* in bed; gone to bed; lying down; recumbent; set. **à soleil ~**, at sunset.

coucher *v.t.* to put to bed, to lay, to lay down flat; to sleep; to knock down; to incline. **~ un enfant**, to put a child to bed. **~ en joue**, to aim at, to take aim. **~ avec**, to sleep with, to make love. *v.i.* to lie, to lie down. **~ à l'hôtel**, to sleep at a hotel. **~ à la belle étoile**, to sleep in the open air. **se ~**, *v.refl.* to go to bed. **se ~ comme les poules**, to go to bed with the chickens. **allez vous ~**, go to bed. **comme on fait son lit, on se couche**, as you make your bed, so you must lie in it. **le soleil se couche**, the sun is setting. *n.m.* going to bed; bedtime. **au ~ du soleil**, at sunset.

couchette *n.f.* bedstead; bed; sleeping car.

coucheur, euse *n.m.f.* bedfellow. **un mauvais ~**, a difficult person to deal with, a tough customer.

couci-couça *adv.phr.* so-so, indifferently.

coucou *n.m.* cuckoo; cuckoo clock; *Interj.* peek-aboo.

coude *n.m.* elbow; bend, angle; sudden turn; winding. **~ d'un tuyau**, elbow of a pipe. **se serrer les ~s**, to stick together, to show solidarity.

coudé, e *adj.* bent; cranked.

coudée *n.f.* cubit; arm's length. **avoir ses ~s franches**, to have elbow room.

cou-de-pied *n.m.* instep.

couder *v.t.* to bend. **se ~**, *v.refl.* to form an elbow.

coudoiement *n.m.* close contact; elbowing.

coudoyer *v.t.* to elbow; to jostle. **se ~**, *v.refl.* to elbow each other, to jostle.

coudre *v.t.* to sew; to stitch; to seam; to tack. **~ la peau du renard à celle du lion**, to be strong and crafty.

coudrier *n.m.* hazel, hazel tree.

couenne *n.f.* rind; porpoise skin; *Med.* buffy coat.

couenneux, euse *adj. Med.* buffy. **angine couenneuse**, diphtheria.

couette *n.f.* (bed) comforter; little tail.

couffe *n.m.* bale; basket.

couguar *n.m.* cougar.

couic *n.m. Exclam.* squeak.

couille *n.f. Vulg.* testicle. **~ molle**, gutless person.

couillonnade *n.f. Infml.* rot; baloney.

couillon *n.m.* idiot, twerp, jerk.

couillonner *v.t.* to swindle; to take for a ride.

couinement *n.m.* squealing; whining.

couiner *v.i.* to squeal, to whine.

coulage *n.m.* leakage; leaking.

coulant, e *adj.* flowing, fluent, running, gliding; smooth; easy; accommodating. **noeud ~**, slipknot. **être ~ en affaires**, to be accommodating in business matters. *n.m.* neck jewel; slide, slider; runner.

coule *n.f.* cowl. **être à la ~**, to know the ropes. **avoir à la ~**, to have it easy.

coulé, e *n.m. Mus.* slur; slide, step; casting (metal).

coulée *n.f.* running hand; *Metall.* casting; cast; spray, tapping, running off.

couler *v.i.* to flow; to run; to move along, as a fluid; to stream; to circulate; to proceed, to issue, to emanate; to glide along; to sink a ship; to run down; to leak; to slip off; to glide; to trickle down. **faire ~ le sang**, to shed blood. **la**

chandelle coule, the candle gutters. **ce tonneau coule**, that cask leaks. **~ à fond**, to sink (ship). *v.t.* to strain; to cast, to run, to sink, *Mus.* to slur; *Danc.* to glide over. **~ une glace**, to cast a plate of glass. **~ quelqu'un à fond**, to ruin a person. **se ~**, *v.refl.* to glide, to slip, to steal.

couleur *n.f.* color; coloring; paint; flag; colors; suit (at cards); complexion; appearance.
~ claire, light color. **~ voyante**, gaudy, showy color. **~ tranchante**, glaring color. **~ sombre, foncée**, dark color. **~ à l'huile**, oil color. **vous change de ~**, your color is changing. **les gens de ~**, (people) of color. **prendre ~**, to look well. **sous ~ de**, on the pretext of. **prendre des ~s**, to blush.

couleuvre *n.f.* adder, snake. **~ à collier**, grass snake.

coulis *n.m.* a purée *adj.* **vent ~**, sharp draft.

coulissant, e *adj.* sliding.

coulisse *n.f.* groove; sliding shutter; *Theat.* wings; green room; *Fin.* outside brokers. **à ~**, sliding. **propos de ~s**, green room talk.

coulisseau *n.m.* runner.

coulisser *v.i.* to slide, run.

coulissier *n.m. Fin.* outside broker.

couloir *n.m.* strainer, colander; lobby; slope (for running wood).

coup *n.m.* blow, stroke; hit; knock; (with the fist) blow, punch; (with the elbow) push, nudge, jab; (with the foot) kick; (with a whip) lash; (with a pointed weapon) stab, thrust; (with a sword) cut, slash, gash; (with the open hand) slap, smack; beat (of drum); clap (of thunder); gust (of wind); shot, report (of firearms), move (at chess). **il me donne un petit ~ sur l'épaule**, he pats my shoulder. **~ de revers**, backhanded blow. **mauvais ~**, unlucky blow. **assommer, rouer de ~s**, to beat unmercifully. **asséner un ~**, to strike a blow. **détourner un ~**, to ward off a blow. **amortir un ~**, to deaden a blow. **~ de griffe**, scratch. **~ d'ongles**, nip, scratch. **~ de poignard**, stab. **~ de couteau**, cut, stab. **un ~ de bec**, a piece of slander. **faire d'une pierre deux ~s**, to kill two birds with one stone. **donner un ~ d'épée dans l'eau**, to beat the air. **flanquer des ~s à quelqu'un**, to give someone a licking. **~ de grâce**, the deathblow stroke. **tirer un ~**, to fire a shot. **~ perdu**, random shot. **~ de sifflet**, whistle, whistling. **~ de Jarnac**, unfair blow; secret pass. **frapper de grands ~s**, to employ decisive measures. **~ de peigne**, combing, a touch of the comb. **donner un ~ de chapeau**, to take off one's hat. **~ de main**, a helping blow; *Milit.* a sudden attack. **donner un ~ d'épaule**, to give a helping hand. **il jeta un ~ d'oeil sur le document**, he glanced over the document. **un ~ de vent**, a gust of wind. **~ d'état**, coup, violent measure. **voilà un beau ~**, that is a good stroke. **faire un ~ de tête**, to do a rash deed. **~ de maître**, masterly stroke. **~ d'essai**, first attempt. **man-**

quer son ~, to miss one's aim. **boire un ~,** to drink a glass. **le ~ de l'étrier,** the parting cup. **j'ai encore deux ~s à jouer,** I still have two turns to play. **nous réussirons à ~ sur,** we shall certainly succeed. **votre lettre est arrivée après ~,** your letter came too late. **pour le ~, je vous tiens,** this time, I have you! **tout à ~,** suddenly. **tout d'un ~,** all at once.

coupable *adj.* guilty. **une négligence ~,** criminal negligence. *n.m.f.* guilty person; culprit.

coupage *n.m.* cutting; mixing (as wine with water).

coupant, e *adj.* cutting, sharp. *n.m.* sharp edge.

coupe *n.f.* cutting; cut; *Arch.* section; chalice, bowl; cut, fit, fashion. **la ~ des cheveux,** hairstyle. **la ~ des bois,** felling of trees. **la ~ des pierres,** stonecutting; **la ~ d'un habit,** the cut, the fit of a coat. **être sous la ~ de quelqu'un,** to be under a person's thumb. **boire la ~ jusqu'à la lie,** to drink to the last dregs. **faire la ~,** to swim hand over hand.

coupé *n.m.* brougham; coupé. *adj.* short, laconic. **un style ~,** broken style.

coupe-gorge *n.m.* den of thieves.

coupe-jarret *n.m.* cutthroat, ruffian.

coupe-légumes *n.m.* vegetable knife.

coupe-papier *n.m.* paper knife, paper cutter.

couper *v.t.* to cut, to carve; to cut up, off, into, out, down, up, across, away; to clip, to pare; to intersect; to dilute, to water; to geld, to castrate; to shape, to cleave. **~ en deux,** to cut in two. **~ l'herbe sous le pied à quelqu'un,** to supplant someone. **~ dans le vif,** to cut to the quick. **il me coupe les bras et les jambes,** he dumbfounds me. **~ un habit,** to cut out a coat. **~ le chemin à quelqu'un,** to stop a person. **~ la fièvre,** to stop the fever. **la parole à quelqu'un,** to cut a person short. **~ court,** to cut short. **~ le vin,** to dilute wine. **~ à travers champs,** to cut across the field. **j'ai mêlé les cartes, coupez,** I have shuffled, cut. **se ~,** *v.refl.* to cut oneself; to cut. **elle s'est coupé la main,** she has cut her hand. **ces deux routes se coupent,** those two roads cross.

couperet *n.m.* cleaver, chopper.

couperosé, e *adj.* blotched.

coupeur, euse *n.m.f.* cutter.

couple *n.f.* couple (two things of the same kind); pair, brace. **une ~ de serviettes,** a couple of napkins. *n.m.* couple, pair (male and female); two persons united together. **un jeune ~,** a young couple. **un ~ bien assorti,** a well-matched pair.

coupler *v.t.* to couple, to link.

couplet *n.m.* couplet, verse; *Theat.* tirade.

coupole *n.f.* cupola, dome.

coupon *n.m.* coupon, remnant (of tissue); (theater) ticket.

coupure *n.f.* cut, incision, ditch, trench; *Fortif.* entrenchment; suppression; cutting; small banknote. **~ de courant,** power cut, power outage.

cour *n.f.* court, court of law; yard, courtyard; courtship. **~ d'entrée,** entrance court, front yard. **basse-~,** farmyard, poultry yard. **eau bénite de ~,** vain promises. **faire la ~ à une femme,** to make advances to a woman. **la ~ du roi Pétaud,** chaos, bedlam. **~ d'appel,** court of appeal.

courage *n.m.* courage, daring; spirit, mettle; bravery; cheer; heart; temper. **prendre ~,** to take courage. **manque de ~,** faintheartedness. **je n'ai pas le ~ de lui refuser cela,** I have not the heart to refuse him that.

courageusement *adv.* courageously, gallantly; spiritedly.

courageux, euse *adj.* courageous; gallant; spirited. **une ame ~se,** a noble mind. **un trait ~,** a gallant deed.

courailler *v.t. Pej.* to chase. **~ après les femmes,** to chase after women.

couramment *adv.* currently; fluently.

courant, e *adj.* running, flowing, current, present; ordinary, usual. **écriture ~e,** cursive writing. **le mois ~,** the current, the present month. *n.m.* current, stream, tide; wave (opinion); course, run, routine; present month, instant; in the course of. **aller contre le ~,** to go against the stream. **le ~ du affaires,** business as usual. **mettre, tenir quelqu'un au ~ d'une affaire,** to keep someone posted. **être au ~,** to be acquainted with.

courante *n.f.* courant (dance); runs (diarrhea).

courbatu, e *adj.* foundered (as a horse); aching.

courbaturé, e *adj.* stiff; aching.

courbe *adj.* curved, bent. *n.f.* curve; turn, bend, *Veter.* curb.

courber *v.t.* to bend, to bow, to curve, to stoop, to weigh down. **courbé de vieillesse,** bent with age. *v.i.* to bend, to bend down, to bow, to bow down, to stoop. **se ~,** *v.refl.* to bend; to be bent, to bow oneself down.

courbette *n.f.* curvet; servile bow. **faire des ~s,** to bow and scrape.

courbetter *v.i.* to curvet.

courbure *n.f.* curvature, curve; bending.

courette *n.f.* small yard.

coureur *n.m.* runner; racer, errand boy, messenger; porter; rover; rambler, stroller; womanizer; frequenter, goer. **~ de spectacles,** theatergoer. **~ de nuit,** one who keeps late hours.

coureuse *n.f. Infml.* slut; manhunter.

courge *n.f.* squash, gourd.

courir *v.i.* to run, to run away; to flee, to hasten away, to run after; to flow; to circulate, to be current; to spread; to flow on, to go on, to extend, to stretch; to sail. **~ à toutes jambes,** to run as fast as possible. **~ devant le vent,** to scud. **~ des bordées,** to tack, to beat to windward. **manger en courant,** to eat in a hurry. **laisser ~ sa plume,** to write whatever comes to mind. **faire ~ des bruits,** to spread gossip. **faire ~ une santé,** to propose a toast. **par le temps**

qui court, as times go. les maladies qui courent, the diseases going around. *v.t.* to run after, to pursue; to chase, to hunt; to search for; to hunt, to seek after, to follow; to frequent. ~ les rues, to run about the streets. il ne faut pas ~ deux lièvres à fois, we must not have too many irons in the fire. ~ les bals, les théâtres, to frequent balls and theaters. ~ les risques, to run risks. ~ le monde, to travel over the world. cette nouvelle court les rues, this news is the talk of the place.

couronne *n.f.* crown, wreath, garland, coronet, halo, crown (of the teeth); corona. la ~ du martyre, the crown of martyrdom. les diamants de la ~, the crown jewels.

couronnement *n.m.* coronation, crowning, finishing, completion, perfection. c'est le ~ de l'oeuvre, this crowns the work.

couronner *v.t.* to crown, to wreath, to honor, to dignify, to adorn; to complete; to surmount. la fin couronne l'oeuvre, all's well that ends well. se ~, *v.refl.* to crown oneself; to be crowned.

courrier *n.m.* courier, messenger; mail, letters, correspondence. faire son ~, to write one's letters.

courriériste *n.m.f.* columnist.

courroie *n.f.* leather strap, strap, belt. allonger la ~, to strain the rope (*fig.*).

courroucé, e *adj.* angry, wrathful; raging. regarder d'un oeil ~, to cast angry looks.

courroucer *v.t.* to incense, to provoke, to anger. se ~, *v.refl.* to grow angry.

courroux *n.m.* wrath, rage, anger. un juste ~, a just anger.

cours *n.m.* course; current; currency; stream, flow; route, way; vent; scope; circulation, path, track; treatise. remonter le ~ d'un fleuve, to go against the stream of a river. donner libre ~ à sa colère, to give full vent to one's rage. le ~ de notre existence, the course of our existence. ~ public, public course of lectures. ce jeune homme a fini ses ~, this young man has finished his studies. cette monnaie n'a plus ~, this money is no longer current. ~ du change, rate of exchange. voyage de long ~, long sea voyage.

course *n.f.* course, race, run, running; flight; errand; journey, drive, fare; length (of a piston stroke). achever sa ~, to run out one's race. ~ de chevaux, horse race; horse racing. faire une ~ à pied, to race (on foot). il y a une longue ~ d'ici là, it is a long way from here to there.

coursier *n.m.* courser; messenger.

coursive *n.f.* gangway.

court *n.m.* (tennis) court.

court, e *adj.* short, brief; limited; scanty; succinct. être ~ d'argent, to be short of money. être ~, to be brief. à ~ échéance, *Com.* short-dated. avoir la vue ~e, to be shortsighted. *n.m.*

short. savoir le ~ et le long d'une chose, to know the long and the short of a thing. *adv.* short; suddenly. couper ~, to cut short. s'arrêter tout ~, to stop short.

courtage *n.m.* brokerage.

courtaud, aude *n.m.f.* thick-set, dumpy person; (of dogs, horses) docked and cropped. *adj.* thick-set, dumpy, docked, cropped.

court-bouillon *n.m.* court bouillon, a preparation for cooking fish.

court-circuit *n.m.* short circuit.

courtier *n.m.* broker. ~ d'assurances, insurance broker. ~ marron, unlicensed broker. ~ maritime, ship broker. ~ de change, stockbroker; money broker, bill broker.

courtilière *n.f.* mole cricket.

courtisan *n.m.* courtier. *adj.* courtly, of a courtier.

courtisane *n.f.* courtesan.

courtiser *v.t.* to court; to try to please; to woo. ~ le peuple, to flatter the people. ~ une femme, to court a woman.

courtois, e *adj.* courteous.

courtoisement *adv.* courteously.

courtoisie *n.f.* courtesy; courteousness.

couscous *n.m.* couscous.

cousette *n.f.* dressmaker's assistant.

couseuse *n.f.* stitcher; sewing machine.

cousin, ine *n.m.f.* cousin. ~ germain, first cousin.

cousin *n.m.* gnat.

coussin *n.m.* cushion; pillow.

coussinet *n.m.* pad, small cushion.

cousu, e *p.p.* sewed. bouche ~e, mum's the word. être tout ~ d'or, to be rolling in money.

coût *n.m. Law.* cost, charge; expense.

coûtant *adj.* prix ~, cost, price.

couteau *n.m.* knife; dagger. ~ à découper, carving knife. ~ à deux lames, double-bladed knife. ~ de cuisine, kitchen knife. ~ de poche, pocketknife. jouer des ~x, to fight with swords. être à ~x tirés, to be mortal enemies.

coutelas *n.m.* cutlass.

coutelier, ière *n.m.f.* cutler. *n.f.* knife case.

coutellerie *n.f.* cutlery; cutler's shop.

coûter *v.i.* to cost, to be expensive, to be costly, to require, to be painful; to pain. ça coûte chèr, that's expensive. l'argent ne lui coûtre guère, he spends money freely. rien ne lui coûte, he spares no pains. tout lui coûte, everything is an effort to him. coûte que coûte, cost what it may. il vous en coûtera la vie, it will cost you your life.

coûteusement *adv.* expensively.

coûteux, euse *adj.* expensive. peu ~, inexpensive.

coutil *n.m.* ticking.

coutume *n.f.* custom, usage, habit, practice. une fois n'est pas ~, once does not mean always. avoir ~ de, to be accustomed to. il se porte mieux que de ~, he is better than usual.

coutumier, ière *adj.* accustomed, customary; habitual, common. **il est ~ du fait,** he is an old offender. **droit ~,** common law. *n.m.* collection of customs.

couture *n.f.* sewing, stitching, seam; needlework; couture. **haute ~,** high fashion, designer's wear.

couturé, e *p.p.* seamed; scarred.

couturier *n.m.* couturier, fashion designer.

couturière *n.f.* seamstress, dressmaker.

couvée *n.f.* brood; hatch.

couvent *n.m.* convent, monastery.

couver *v.t.* to brood on, to sit on; to incubate; to brood over. **~ des yeux,** to devour with one's eyes. *v.i.* to brood, to sit; to smolder. **le feu couve sous la cendre,** the fire is smoldering. **se ~,** *v.refl.* to be brooding; to lurk, to hatch.

couvercle *n.m.* cover. **~ de marmite,** pot lid.

couvert, erte *p.p.* and *adj.* covered, clothed, clad; obscure, dark; cloudy, overcast; secret, hid, veiled. **mots ~s,** ambiguous words. **allée ~e,** shady walk. **temps ~,** cloudy weather.

couvert *n.m.* table setting; shelter; covered spot. **~s,** silverware. **mettre le ~,** to set the table. **ôter le ~,** to clear the table. **des ~s d'argent,** silver forks and spoons. **mettre à ~,** to shelter. **être à ~,** to be under shelter, to have security. **à ~ de l'orage,** sheltered from the storm.

couverte *n.f.* glaze; covering; *Naut.* deck.

couverture *n.f.* cover, covering; quilt, comforter; blanket; roof; guarantee. **~ de cheval,** horse blanket. **~ en tuile,** tile roof.

couveuse *n.f.* brooding hen incumbator.

couvre-chef *n.m.* headgear.

couvre-feu *n.m.* curfew.

couvre-lit *n.m.* bedspread.

couvre-pieds *n.m.* counterpane, quilt.

couvre-plat *n.m.* dish cover.

couvreur *n.m.* tiler, thatcher. **~ en ardoises,** slater.

couvrir *v.t.* to cover; to lay over, to set over; to cover up, to wrap up, to envelop; to clothe; to spread over, to overwhelm, to load; to protect, to shelter; to hide; to plaster; to palliate; to excuse; to defray; to tile. **~ de chaume,** to thatch. **~ les pauvres,** to clothe the poor. **~ de honte,** to cover with shame. **~ une enchère,** to outbid. **se ~,** *v.refl.* to cover oneself; to put on; to be cloudy, to be overcast. **l'horizon se couvre,** things are beginning to look dark.

coxalgie *n.f.* coxalgia.

coyote *n.m.* coyote.

crabe *n.m.* crab.

crac *n.m.* crack, cracking. *interj.* pop!

crachat *n.m.* spit, spittle.

craché, e *adj.* **c'est son père tout craché,** he's the spitting image of his father.

crachement *n.m.* spitting; *Infml.* crackle (loudspeaker). **~ de sang,** spitting up blood, hemoptysis.

cracher *v.t.* to spit; to sputter (as a pen). **~ au nez, au visage de quelqu'un,** to spit in a person's face. **~ au bassin,** to contribute. *v.t.* to spit, to spit out; to sputter out, to throw out, to utter; to shower down. **~ des proverbes,** to utter proverbs.

crachin *n.m.* drizzle.

crachoir *n.m.* spittoon.

crack *n.m.* crack horse; *Infml.* wizard, ace, champion.

Cracovie *n.f.* Krakow.

craie *n.f.* chalk. **carrière de ~,** chalk pit.

craindre *v.t.* to fear; to be afraid of; to dread; to stand in awe of: **je ne crains pas de le dire,** I do not hesitate to say so. **il craint que je ne vienne,** he is afraid of my coming. **se faire ~,** to make oneself feared (*or* dreaded). **ces plantes craignent la gelée,** those plants cannot stand frost.

crainte *n.f.* fear, apprehension, dread; awe. **dans la ~ de tomber,** fearful of falling. **il parle peu, de ~ de se méprendre,** for fear of being mistaken he speaks but little. **de ~ que l'on ne vous trompe,** for fear you should be deceived.

craintif, ive *adj.* fearful.

craintivement *adv.* fearfully, timidly.

cramer *v.t. Infml.* to burn.

cramoisi, e *adj.* crimson, red, scarlet. *n.m.* crimson.

crampe *n.f.* cramp.

crampon *n.m. Sports.* iron plate (for shoes), crampon.

cramponner *v.t.* to cramp. **se ~,** *v.refl.* to cling.

cran *n.m.* notch; indentation; *Print.* nick (of a letter). **monter d'un ~,** to rise a notch higher. **baisser d'un ~,** to take down a notch.

crâne *n.m.* skull, cranium.

crânement *adv.* boldly; pluckily.

crâner *v.t. Infml.* to show off.

crânerie *n.f.* pluck; daring.

crâneur, euse *n.m.f.* showoff.

crânien, ienne *adj.* cranial.

cranter *v.t.* to notch.

crapaud *n.m.* toad. **laid comme un ~,** as ugly as a toad.

crapouillot *n.m. Mil.* trench mortar.

crapule *n.f.* scum; scoundrel.

crapuleux, euse *adj.* crapulous; grossly debauched.

craque *n.f.* fib.

craqueler *v.t.* to crack; to crackle.

craquement *n.m.* cracking; chattering.

craquer *v.i.* to creak; to crack; to crackle; to brag. **faire ~ ses doigts,** to crack one's fingers.

craqueter *v.i.* to gabble; to crackle.

crasse *adj.n.f.* gross, thick, coarse, crass. **ignorance ~,** gross ignorance. *n.f.* dirt, filth, squalor; dross.

crasseux, euse *adj.* dirty, foul; miserly. *n.m.f.* filthy person; miser.

cratère *n.m.* crater; mouth of a volcano.

cravache *n.f.* riding crop. **coups de ~,** horsewhipping.

cravacher *v.t.* to flog; to horsewhip.

cravate *n.m.* necktie.

cravater *v.t.* to put on a tie. **se ~,** *v.refl.* to put on one's tie.

crawl *n.m.* crawl (swimming).

crayeux, euse *adj.* chalky.

crayon *n.m.* crayon; pencil; sketch, picture. **~ à cils, à lèvres,** eyebrow pencil, lipstick. **~ de pastel,** crayon.

crayonner *v.t.* to pencil, to sketch; to scribble.

créance *n.f.* credence; belief, credit; debt, money owing; trust. **lettres de ~,** credentials, letters of credence. **lettre de ~,** letter of credit.

créancier, ière *n.m.f.* creditor.

créateur, trice *adj.* creative. **un esprit ~,** a creative mind. *n.m.* creator, maker.

création *n.f.* creation, work, production.

créativité *n.f.* creativity.

créature *n.f.* creature.

crécelle *n.f.* rattle.

crèche *n.f.* crib; nursery, day nursery; **~ de Noël,** Christ Child's crib.

crécher *v.i. Infml.* to live, to hang out; to crash.

crédence *n.f.* sideboard, credenza.

crédibilité *n.f.* credibility.

crédit *n.m.* credit; trust, influence, interest, power, name; credit side; **faire ~,** to give credit. **acheter à ~,** to buy on credit. **~ à court/long terme,** short/long term credit.

créditer *v.t.* to credit; to set to the credit of.

créditeur *n.m.* creditor. *adj.* credit.

credo *n.m.* creed.

crédule *adj.* credulous; gullible.

crédulité *n.f.* credulity.

créer *v.t.* to create; to make, to invent, to form; to produce; to give rise to, to give birth to. **~ un rôle,** *Theat.* to create a part. **~ des emplois,** to create jobs.

crémation *n.f.* cremation.

crématoire *adj.* crematorium.

crème *n.f.* cream; the best part of a thing; the best. **~ anglaise,** custard. **~ fouettée,** whipped cream. **fromage à la ~,** cream cheese. **~ de tartre,** cream of tartar.

crémerie *n.f.* milk shop; dairy.

crémeux, euse *adj.* creamy.

crémier, iére *n.m.* dairyman. *n.f.* dairywoman.

Crémone *n.m.* Cremona.

créneau *n.m.* loophole; battlement; pinnacle.

crénelé, e *adj.* loopholed; *Herald.* embattled; *Bot.* crenelated.

créneler *v.t.* to indent; to crenelate.

crénelure *n.f.* indentation; crenalation.

créole *n.m.f.* and *adj.* creole.

créosote *n.f.* creosote.

crêpe *n.m.* crêpe; crape; veil. *n.f.* crepe, thin pancake.

crêper *v.t.* to crape, to crisp. **se ~,** *v.refl.* to become craped.

crêperie *n.f.* crêperie, pancake shop.

crépi *adj.* roughcast.

crépir *v.t. Arch.* to roughcast.

crépiter *v.i.* to crepitate, to crackle.

crépu, e *adj.* frizzy (as hair), woolly; crisped.

crépusculaire *adj.* crepuscular; twilight.

crépuscule *n.m.* crepuscule, twilight; dawn.

crescendo *adv.* crescendo. *n.m.* crescendo.

cresson *n.m.* cress; cresses, watercress.

Crésus *n.m.* Croesus. *n.m.* extremely rich.

crétacé, e *adj.* cretaceous.

crête *n.f.* crest; cock's comb; top edge.

Crête *n.f.* Crete.

crétin *n.m.* cretin; moron.

crétinerie *n.f.* stupidity; idiocy.

crétinisme *n.m.* cretinism; idiocy.

cretonne *n.f.* cretonne.

creusage *n.m. Engrav.* deepening; sinking (of a well).

creuser *v.t.* to hollow, to dig, to excavate; to deepen; to delve, to sink, to hollow out, to scoop; to examine, to sift. **~ un puits,** to sink a well. **se ~ le cerveau, la tête,** to rack one's brains. *v.i.* to dig. **~ en terre,** to dig into the ground. **se ~,** *v.refl.* to become hollow. **ce vieil arbre commence à se ~,** that old tree is beginning to get hollow.

creuset *n.m.* crucible; test.

creux, creuse *adj.* hollow; excavated; concave; sunken; deep; empty; light; vain; shallow. **des yeux ~,** hollow eyes. **un chemin ~,** a sunken road. **avoir le ventre ~,** to have an empty stomach. **esprit ~,** shallow mind. **idées ~s,** vain fancies. *n.m.* hollow, cavity, excavation; hole, pit, depression; depth (of a ship). **faire un ~ en terre,** to make a hole in the ground. **le ~ de la main,** the hollow of the hand.

crevaison *n.f.* puncture, blowout (tire).

crevant, e *adj.* (tiring) killing; (funny) priceless, funny.

crevasse *n.f.* crevice, crack, chap. **avoir des ~s aux mains,** to have chapped hands.

crevasser *v.t.* to crevice, to crack, to chap. **se ~,** *v.refl.* to crack, to chap.

crevé, e *adj.* burst; dead; dead beat, exhausted.

crève-coeur *n.m.* heartbreak.

crever *v.i.* to burst, to break, to fly open; to break away; to die. **l'orage crevera bientôt,** the storm will soon break out. **~ de rire,** to burst with laughing. **~ de faim,** to be dying with hunger. *v.t.* to burst, to break, to break open; to kill (with fatigue), to work to death; to tear; to cram, to stuff. **~ les yeux à quelqu'un,** to put out a person's eyes. **se ~,** *v.refl.* to burst; to kill oneself.

crevette *n.f.* shrimp, prawn.

crevettier *n.m.* shrimp net; shrimp boat.

cri *n.m.* cry; clamor, shout; crying; squeak; screaming; acclamation; outcry, shriek, scream, squawk, yelling, howling; roar. **~ aigu, perçant,** shrill cry, scream, screaming; shriek, squeak. **pousser un ~,** to cry, to cry out; to shout out; to give a squeak. **hauts ~s,** outcry. **demander**

à grands ~s, to clamor for. ~ de guerre, war cry. ~ plaintif, plaintive cry; whine. à cor et à ~, with hue and cry. dernier ~, latest fashion.

criaillement *n.m.* squawking; screeching; squalling.

criailler *v.i.* to bawl, to squawk; to scold.

criant, e *adj.* crying, glaring. un abus ~, a glaring abuse.

criard, e *adj.* clamorous, noisy, squawking; screaming; shrill, harsh, scolding. humeur ~e, scolding temper. une femme ~e, a scolding woman. *n.m.f.* bawler, squawker, scolder.

crible *n.m.* sieve.

cribler *v.t.* to sift; to riddle, to screen (coal, earth); to pierce all over, to riddle, to pepper. criblé de coups de couteau, riddled with stabs. criblé de dettes, overwhelmed with debt.

cribleur, euse *n.m.f.* sifter.

cric *n.m.* screw jack, (car) lifting jack.

cricket *n.m.* (sport) cricket.

cricri *n.m.* chirping.

criée *n.f.* fish-market auction. vente à la ~, sale by auction.

crier *v.i.* to cry out, to cry, to shout, to bawl, to squawk; to exclaim, to utter censure or reproach; to blame, to complain loudly, to proclaim; to screech, to hoot (as nocturnal birds); to gabble; to squeak, to squeal (as pigs); to howl (as a dog), to bark, to yelp (as a dog); to chirp (as insects); to rumble (as the bowels); to creak (as a door). ~ au voleur, au feu, to cry out "thieves!", "fire!" ~ à l'injustice, to speak out against injustice. ~ misère, to complain of poverty. ~ famine, to cry famine. il ne fait que ~, he does nothing but scold. cette porte crie, that door creaks. *v.t.* to cry, to utter loud cries; to proclaim. il va criant cela partout, he is proclaiming it everywhere.

crieur, euse *n.m.f.* crier; bawler, hawker.

crime *n.m.* crime; offense, guilt, felony. ~ capital, capital offense. ce n'est pas un si grand ~, it is not such a great crime.

Crimée *n.m.f.* Crimea.

criminaliser *v.t.* to remove from a civil to a criminal court.

criminaliste *n.m.* criminalist.

criminalité *n.f.* criminality.

criminel, elle *adj.* criminal; guilty. une main ~le, a guilty hand. un procès ~, a criminal trial. *n.m.f.* criminal; culprit, offender, transgressor.

criminologie *n.f.* criminology.

criminologiste *n.m.f.* criminologist.

crin *n.m.* hair (from the mane or tail of horses, etc.); horsehair. cheval à tous ~s, horse with flowing mane and tail. prendre aux ~s, to seize by the hair.

crincrin *n.m.* screeching fiddle.

crinière *n.f.* mane; coarse hair (of a person); wig.

crinoline *n.f.* crinoline.

crique *n.f.* creek, cove.

criquet *n.m.* locust; cricket.

crise *n.f.* crisis; fit; attack; burst; outburst; tantrum; shortage; slump. piquer une ~, to throw a tantrum. ~ de rage, a fit.
~ économique, economic crisis, slump.

crispant, e *adj.* irritating, annoying.

crispation *n.f.* shrivelling; contraction; fidgets.

crisper *v.t.* to shrivel, to contract, to give the fidgets. se ~, *v.refl.* to shrivel, to contract.

crispin *n.m.* gant à ~, gauntlet.

crissement *n.m.* grating, grinding (of the teeth).

crisser *v.i.* to grate; to grind.

cristal *n.m.* crystal; crystal glass; cut glass; spar. ~ de roche, rock crystals. porcelaines et cristaux, china and glassware.

cristallerie *n.f.* art of making crystal; glassworks, glass house.

cristallin, ine *adj.* crystalline; clear, pellucid. lentille ~e, crystalline lens. *n.m.* crystalline.

cristallisation *n.f.* crystallization.

cristalliser *v.t.* and *v.i.* to crystallize; to assume the form of crystals. se ~, *v.refl.* to crystallize.

cristallisoir *n.m.* crystallizing pan.

cristallographie *n.f.* crystallography.

cristallomancie *n.f.* crystal-gazing, crystallomancy.

critère *n.m.* criterion; measure.

critiquable *adj.* open to criticism.

critique *adj.* critical; censorious. humeur ~, a critical or censorious temper. *n.f.* criticism; critique; censure; critics. ~ littéraire, literary criticism. faire la ~ de, to criticize. *n.m.* critic; fault-finder. *n.f.* (movie or theatre) review.

critiquer *v.t.* to criticize; to censure, to reflect upon.

croassement *n.m.* croak, croaking, cawing.

croasser *v.i.* to croak, to caw.

Croatie *n.f.* Croatia.

croc *n.m.* hook; boathook; fang, canine tooth.

croc-en-jambe *n.m.* trip, tripping up. donner un ~ à, to trip up, to supplant.

croche *adj.n.f.* eighth note. double ~, sixteenth note. triple ~, thirty-second note.

crochet *n.m.* hook, little hook; crochet. broder au ~, to crochet. ~ de serrurier, picklock; canine tooth; fang (of a snake, of certain insects) *Print.* brackets. la route fait un ~ en cet endroit, the road makes a bend at that place. vivre aux ~s de quelqu'un, to live off someone.

crochetage *n.m.* lockpicking.

crocheter *v.t.* to pick (a lock); to penetrate.

crocheteur *n.m.* ~ de serrures, de portes, burglar; housebreaker.

crochu, e *adj.* hooked, crooked; clawlike. avoir les mains ~es, to be light-fingered.

crocodile *n.m.* crocodile. larmes de ~, crocodile tears.

crocus *n.m.* crocus.

croire *v.t.* to believe; to credit, to put confidence in, to trust; to put trust in; to believe in; to think. **je le crois bien,** I believe it. **je n'en crois rien,** I do not believe it at all. **à l'en ~,** if we are to believe him. **je ne crois pas qu'il vienne,** I do not believe he will come. *v.i.* to believe; to trust; to believe in, to hold as the object of faith. **~ aux songes,** to believe in dreams. **~ en dieu,** to believe in God. **se ~,** *v.refl.* to believe oneself to be, to think oneself to be, to look upon oneself as. **cet homme se croit habile,** that man thinks he is clever. **s'en ~,** to think much of oneself.

croisade *n.f.* crusade.

croisé *n.m.* crusader; twill; twilled tissue. *adj.* crossed; twilled (as a tissue); *adj.* double-breasted (as a coat).

croisée *n.f.* window; sash, casement; transept (of a church); cross (of an anchor).

croisement *n.m.* crossing; cross-breeding; crossroad; junction; intersection; folding (arms).

croiser *v.t.* to cross; to intersect, to thwart; to erase, to cancel; to twill (fabric). **se ~ les bras,** to fold one's arms. **~ la baïonnette,** to charge bayonets. *v.i.* to cross; to lap over; *Naut.* to cruise. **~ à vue de terre,** to cruise along the coast. **se ~,** *v.refl.* to cross; to be crossed, to cross each other, to thwart each other.

croiseur *n.m. Naut.* cruiser.

croisière *n.f.* cruise.

croisillon *n.m.* crossbar, horizontal bar of a cross.

croissance *n.f.* growth, increase; *Econ.* development. **~ économique,** economic development.

croissant, e *adj.* growing, increasing. *n.m.* crescent; crescent moon; croissant (pastry); pruning hook. **en forme de ~,** crescent-shaped.

croître *v.i.* to grow; to shoot up, to sprout; to thrive, to increase, to lengthen; to rise, to swell. **~ à vue d'oeil,** to grow very fast. **ne faire que ~ et embellir,** to grow handsomer every day. **les jours commencent à ~,** the days are lengthening.

croix *n.f.* cross; affliction; badge, or insignia, of an order of knighthood. **mettre en ~,** to crucify. **élever une ~,** to set up a cross. **le signe de la ~,** the sign of the cross. **il faut faire une ~ à la cheminée,** we must chalk that up. **~ de la Légion d'honneur,** cross of the Legion of Honor. **~ de Malte,** Maltese cross.

croquant *n.m.* peasant, boor; poor wretch, *Fr. Hist.* countrymen, peasantry.

croquant, e *adj.* crackling, crunchy, crisp.

croque-au-sel *adv.* à la, with a bit of salt only.

croque-madame *n.m.* toasted ham and cheese sandwich with a fried egg on top.

croque-mitaine *n.m.* bogeyman.

croque-monsieur *n.m.* toasted ham and cheese sandwich.

croque-mort *n.m.* mortician.

croquer *v.i.* to be crisp, to crackle. *v.t.* to crunch; to devour; to gobble up, to sketch. **un enfant gentil à ~,** a darling child. **~ le marmot,** to dance attendance.

croquet *n.m. Sport.* croquet.

croquette *n.f.* croquette.

croqueur, euse *n.m.f.* gourmandizer; big eater, devourer. **~ de diamants,** gold digger.

croquis *n.m.* sketch, outline, rough draft. **faire le ~ d'une figure,** to sketch a face.

crosne *n.m.* Chinese artichoke.

cross (-country) *n.m. Sport.* cross-country.

crosse *n.f.* crosier; pastoral staff; hook (of a stick), butt end (of a gun); lacrosse (game). **jouer à la ~,** to play lacrosse. **à coups de ~,** with the butt ends of their muskets. **chercher des ~s,** to pick a quarrel, to look for trouble.

crotale *n.m.* crotalum; rattlesnake.

crotte *n.f.* dirt, mud, mire (in the streets); dung; droppings; manure. **~ de bique,** it's rubbish. **(Cul.) ~ au chocolat,** chocolate. **il fait bien de la ~,** it is very dirty. **être dans la ~,** to be in filth and misery.

crotté, e *p.p.* and *adj.* dirty; foul; squalid; wretched, sorry. **un habit ~,** a coat covered with dirt. **être ~ jusqu'aux oreilles,** to be up to one's neck in dirt.

crotter *v.t.* to dirt, to dirty; to bemire; to bespatter with mud. **se ~,** *v.refl.* to dirty oneself, to get dirty.

crottin *n.m.* dung (of horses, sheep, etc.); manure.

croulant, e *adj.* crumbling; falling apart; tottering. **vieux ~,** old fossil.

crouler *v.i.* to be tumbledown; to crumble, to go to ruin; to fall in, to sink down. **la maison croule,** the house is falling.

croup *n.m.* croup.

croupe *n.f.* croup, rump, buttocks; top. **monter en ~,** to get up behind (on a horse).

croupeton (à) *adv.phr.* squatting.

croupi, e *p.p.* stagnant.

croupier *n.m.* croupier.

croupion *n.m.* rump.

croupir *v.i.* to lie (in filth); to remain inactive; to lie; to stagnate, to lie stagnant; to rot, to corrupt.

croupissant, e *adj.* stagnant, standing.

croustade *n.f.* croustade.

croustillant, e *adj.* crisp, crusty, crunchy.

croustiller *v.i.* to crunch.

croûte *n.f.* crust (cheese) rind; pie crust; scab. **casser la ~,** to have a snack.

croûton *n.m.* crust (of bread) bit of crust; toasted crust; crouton; old fool.

croyable *adj.* credible.

croyance *n.f.* belief; faith; credit; persuasion, conviction. **cela passe toute ~,** that is beyond belief.

croyant, e *adj.* faithful. *n.m.f.* believer, faithful. **les vrais ~s,** the true believers, the faithful.

cru *n.m.* growth; vineyard. **boire du vin de son**

~, to drink wine from one's own vineyard.

cru, crue *adj.* crude, raw; hard; blunt; free, indecent, smutty; unripe. **eau ~e,** hard water. **lait ~,** unpasteurized milk. **de la viande ~e,** raw, uncooked meat. **une réponse ~e,** a harsh answer. **à ~,** on the bare skin.

cruauté *n.f.* cruelty, cruelness, barbarity.

cruche *n.f.* pitcher, jug; blockhead.

cruchon *n.m.* small jug.

crucial, e *adj.* cross-shaped, decisive, crucial.

crucifère *adj.* cruciferous.

crucifier *v.t.* to crucify.

crucifix *n.m.* crucifix, cross.

crucifixion *n.f.* crucifixion.

cruciforme *adj.* cruciform, cross-shaped.

crudité *n.f.* crudeness; crudity, rawness; hardness (of water); coarseness of expression. **~s,** raw vegetable snacks.

crue *n.f.* rise, rising, swelling; growth. **la ~ d'une rivière,** the rise of a river.

cruel, elle *adj.* cruel; ruthless, merciless, unmerciful; inhuman; barbarous, ferocious; hard; inflexible; hard-hearted; grievous, painful.

cruellement *adv.* cruelly; barbarously; painfully; very, extremely.

crûment *adv.* crudely, bluntly, roughly; harshly, coarsely.

crustacé, e *adj.* crustaceous. *n.m.* crustacea, crustaceans.

crypte *n.f.* crypt.

cryptogramme *n.m.* cryptogram.

cryptographie *n.f.* cryptography.

crypton *n.m.* Krypton.

cubage *n.m.* cubature; cubage; cubic content.

cube *n.m.* cube; building block; bouillon cube. *adj.* cubic, cubical.

cuber *v.t.* to find the solid or cubic contents of, to cube.

cubique *adj.* cubic.

cubital, e *adj.* cubital.

cubitus *n.m.* ulna, cubit.

cucul *adj.* **~ (la praline),** *Infml.* silly, goofy.

cueillette *n.f.* gathering crop; harvest; charitable collection; mixed cargo.

cueillir *v.i.* to gather, to pick out, to pluck; to win. **~ des fleurs,** to gather flowers. **~ des lauriers,** to win a victory.

cuiller, cuillère *n.f.* spoon. **~ à bouche, ~ à table,** tablespoon. **~ à café, ~ à thé,** teaspoon.

cuillerée *n.f.* spoonful.

cuir *n.m.* skin; hide; leather. **~ chevelu,** scalp. **tanner le ~ à quelqu'un,** to tan someone's hide. **~ de Russie,** Russian leather.

cuirasse *n.f.* cuirass, breastplate; armor. **le défaut de la ~,** the edge, the extremity of the cuirass; the vulnerable point.

cuire *v.t.* to cook; to boil, to bake, to roast, to broil, to grill. **~ du pain,** to bake bread. **~ des briques,** to burn bricks. **faire ~,** to cook. *v.i.* to bake, to be cooked , to be done; to smart, to burn. **la main me cuit,** my hand smarts.

il vous en cuira, you shall suffer for it.

cuisant, e *adj.* smarting, smart; sharp, keen, biting; exquisite, poignant. **un froid ~,** a bitter cold.

cuisine *n.f.* kitchen; cooking; galley (ship). **~ bourgeoise,** plain cooking. **faire la ~,** to cook. **la ~ française,** French cooking. **chef de ~,** head cook, chef.

cuisiner *v.i.* to cook.

cuisinier *n.m.* cook.

cuisinière *n.f.* cook; stove.

cuissardes *n.f.pl.* waders; thigh boots.

cuisse *n.f.* thigh, leg (of a fowl); drumstick.

cuisson *n.f.* cooking; boiling, baking, roasting, broiling; smarting.

cuissot *n.m.* haunch (of venison).

cuistot *n.m. Infml.* cook.

cuistre *n.m.* pedant; prig.

cuistrerie *n.f.* pedantry.

cuit, e *p.p.* cooked, dressed, done, baked, etc. **trop ~,** overdone. **~ au four,** baked.

cuite *n.f.* baking (of porcelain, pottery, etc.); burning (of bricks, lime, etc.); batch. *Infml.* **prendre une ~,** to have too much to drink.

cuivre *n.m.* copper. **~ battu,** wrought copper. **~ jaune,** brass.

cuivré, e *adj.* copper-colored; copper; auburn; bronzed; (voice) metallic.

cuivrer *v.t.* to copper; to cover with sheets of copper.

cuivreux, euse *adj.* coppery; cuprous.

cul *n.m. Vulg.* bottom, posterior, breech, backside; rump; ass. **~-sec,** bottoms up. **avoir dans le ~,** to be screwed. **en rester sur le ~,** to be astonished.

culasse *n.f.* breech (of a gun, musket, etc.); *Auto.* cylinder head.

culbute *n.f.* somersault, fall, tumble.

culbuter *v.t.* to send head over heels; to upset; to overthrow; to throw down. *v.i.* to turn head over heels; to fall; to fall, to come to ruin; to be ruined.

cul-de-lampe *n.m. Arch.* bracket; *Print.* tailpiece.

cul-de-sac *n.m.* cul-de-sac, dead end.

culer *Naut. v.i.* to go aback, to fall astern.

culinaire *adj.* culinary.

culminant, e *adj.* culminating.

culminer *v.i.* to culminate.

culot *n.m. Infml.* **avoir du ~,** to have a lot of nerve.

culotte *n.f.* breeches; panties.

culotter se ~, *v.refl.* to put one's pants on.

culpabilité *n.f.* culpability, guilt, guiltiness.

culte *n.m.* worship; cult.

cultivable *adj.* cultivable.

cultivateur, trice *adj.* agricultural. *n.m.* cultivator, agriculturist, farmer.

cultivé, e *adj.* cultured; cultivated; well-educated.

cultiver *v.t.* to cultivate; to improve; to cherish; to farm; to grow.

cultuel, le *adj.* pertaining to worship.

culture *n.f.* cultivation; culture.

cumin *n.m.* cumin, caraway seeds.

cumul *n.m. Law.* accumulation; plurality (of offices).

cumulable *adj.* that can be held simultaneously; that can be received simultaneously.

cumulard *n.m.* pluralist, person holding more than one political office at a time.

cumulatif, ive *adj.* cumulative.

cumulativement *adv.* by accumulation.

cumuler *v.t.* to accumulate, to cumulate; to hold more than one office.

cumulo-nimbus *n.m.* cumulonimbus.

cumulus *n.m.* cumulus.

cunéiforme *adj.* cuneiform.

cupide *adj.* covetous, greedy.

cupidement *adv.* covetously, greedily.

cupidité *n.f.* cupidity, covetousness; ardent longing.

cupidon *n.m.* cupid, love.

cupule *n.f.* cupula, cupule.

curabilité *n.f.* curability, curableness.

curable *adj.* curable.

curage *n.m.* cleansing, cleaning out (of canals, rivers, wells, etc.).

curare *n.m.* curare.

curatelle *n.f.* guardianship; trusteeship (of a property).

curateur *n.m.* guardian, curator; trustee.

curatif, ive *adj.* curative.

cure *n.f.* care, healing; *Eccl.* living, benefice; vicarage. **il n'en a ~,** he cares nothing about it.

curé *n.m.* parish priest, parson, rector, vicar.

cure-dent *n.m.* toothpick.

curée *n.f. Hunt.* quarry.

cure-oreille *n.m.* cotton swab.

cure-pied *n.m.* hoof pick (horse).

cure-pipe *n.m.* pipecleaner.

curer *v.t.* cleanse, to clean out (a well, a ditch, a sewer, etc.). **se ~ les dents,** to pick one's teeth.

curetage *n.m.* curettage, curetting.

curette *n.f.* scraper.

curieusement *adv.* curiously, inquisitively.

curieux, euse *adj.* curious; inquisitive. *n.m.* curious, inquisitive person; sightseer.

curiosité *n.f.* curiosity, inquisitiveness, rarity; odd, peculiar, strange; nosy.

curiste *n.m.f.* person who takes a water cure.

curling *n.m. Sport.* curling.

curriculum vitae *n.m.* curriculum vitae; résumé.

curry *n.m.* curry.

curseur *n.m.* cursor.

cursif, ive *adj.* cursive, running. *n.f.* cursive writing.

curviligne *adj.* curvilinear, curvilineal.

cutané, e *adj.* cutaneous.

cuticule *n.m.f.* cuticle.

cuvage *n.m.* fermentation (of wine).

cuve *n.f.* vat, tub; tank.

cuvée *n.f.* vintage.

cuver *v.i.* to ferment. *v.t.* ~ **son vin,** to sleep it off.

cuvette *n.f.* basin; cistern (of a barometer); cap (of a watch).

cyanose *n.f.* cyanosis.

cyanure *n.m.* cyanide.

cybernéticien, ne *n.m.f.* cyberneticist. *adj.* cybernetic.

cybernétique *n.f.* cybernetics.

cyclable *adj.* **piste ~,** bicycle track.

cyclamen *n.m.* cyclamen, sowbread.

cycle *n.m.* cycle.

cyclique *adj.* cyclic, cyclical.

cycliste *n.m.f.* cyclist.

cycloïdal, ale *adj.* cycloid, cycloidal.

cycloïde *n.f.* cycloid.

cyclomateur *n.m.* moped.

cyclomotoriste *n.m.f.* moped rider.

cyclonal, e *n.m.pl.* ~**aux** *adj.* cyclonic.

cyclone *n.m.* cyclone.

cyclope *n.m.* Cyclops.

cyclopéen, enne *adj.* cyclopean, cyclopic.

cygne *n.m.* swan. **jeune ~,** cygnet.

cylindrage *n.m.* mangling (linen); rolling (roads).

cylindre *n.m.* cylinder; roller, barrel (of an organ).

cylindrée *n.f.* capacity. **petite ~,** small car engine.

cylindrer *v.t.* to shape like a cylinder; to roll (a walk, etc.); to mangle (cloth).

cylindrique *adj.* cylindric, cylindrical.

cymbale *n.f.* cymbal.

cymbalier *n.m.* cymbal player.

cynique *adj.* cynic, cynical. *n.m.* cynic.

cyniquement *adv.* cynically.

cynisme *n.m.* cynicism.

cynocéphale *n.m.* cynocephalus, baboon.

cynodrome *n.m.* greyhound track.

cyprès *n.m.* cypress, cypress tree; cypress wood.

cystite *n.f.* cystitis, bladder infection.

czar *n.m.* czar, tzar.

czarine *n.f.* tsarina.

D

D *n.m.* the fourth letter of the alphabet; **D',** contraction of **de.**

Da (da) added to the adverbs **oui, non** or **nenni,** truly, certainly. **oui-da,** yes indeed. **non-da, nenni-da,** no indeed.

dactyle *n.m. Poet.* dactyl; *Bot.* dactylis.

dactylique *adj.* dactylic.

dactylographe *n.f.* typist.

dactylographie *n.f.* typing, typewriting.

dactylographier *v.t.* to type.

dactylographique adj. typing.

dada n.m. horse, hobbyhorse.

dadais n.m. booby, ninny, goof.

dague n.f. dagger, dirk; tusks (of a wild boar); Naut. rope's end, cat-o'-nine-tails.

daguerréotype n.m. daguerreotype.

dahlia n.m. dahlia.

daigner v.i. to deign, to condescend, to vouchsafe; to be pleased.

daim n.m. deer, fallow deer, buck.

daine n.f. doe.

dais n.m. canopy; dais.

dallage n.m. pavement of flagstones; flagging.

dalle n.f. flagstone, flag; slab; slice (of large fish).

daller v.t. to pave with flags.

dalmatien, ne n.m.f. (dog) dalmatian.

daltonien, ne adj. colorblind.

daltonisme n.m. colorblindness.

dam n.m. damage, injury.

damas n.m. Damascus; damask; damascus steel; Damson plum.

damassé n.m. damask linen, damask.

damasser v.t. to damask.

dame n.f. Lady; Poet. lady; a married woman; king, queen, man (at checkers, cards, backgammon, chess). **faire la grande ~,** to act like a grand lady. **Notre-Dame,** Our Lady. **les ~s de France,** the princesses of the royal family. **~ d'honneur,** maid of honor. **~ de compagnie,** lady's companion. **jouer aux ~s,** to play checkers. **interj.** indeed, nay, why. **mais, ~,** why, to be sure.

dame-jeanne n.f. demijohn (large round glass bottle).

damer v.t. (at checkers) to crown. **~ le pion à quelqu'un,** to outwit someone.

damier n.m. checkerboard.

damnable adj. damnable.

damnation n.f. damnation.

damné, e adj. damned; hateful, abominable; confounded; cursed. **être l'âme ~e de quelqu'un,** to be the tool of a person. n.m. **souffrir comme un ~,** to suffer infernally.

damner v.t. to damn. **se ~,** v.refl. to damn oneself.

damoiselle n.f. damsel.

dan n.m. (judo) dan.

dancing n.m. dance hall, public ballroom.

dandin n.m. booby, ninny.

dandinement n.m. swinging, waddling, slouching.

dandiner v.i. to swing one's body about; to slouch. **se ~,** v.refl. to waddle along.

dandy n.m. dandy.

Danemark n.m. Denmark.

danger n.m. danger; peril; risk; harm. **mettre en ~,** to endanger.

dangereusement adv. dangerously.

dangereux, euse adj. dangerous.

danois, e adj. Danish. n.m.f. Dane; Danish, the language of the Danes.

dans prep. in; within; into; about; out of, from; inside; according to. **il entra ~ la chambre,** he went into the room. **cela va couter ~ les 1,000F,** it's going to cost about 1000 Francs. **il a mangé dans le plat,** he ate from the dish. **sa sera fait ~ une semaine,** it will be done within a week.

dansant, e adj. dancing. **soirée ~e,** dancing party.

danse n.f. dance; dancing. **~ macabre,** dance of Death.

danser v.i. to dance. **apprendre à ~,** to learn dancing. **ne savoir sur quel pied ~,** not to know which way to turn. **faire ~ quelqu'un,** to make someone suffer for something. v.t. to dance.

danseur, euse n.m.f. dancer.

dard n.m. dart, sting; Hort. pistil (of a flower); arrowhead.

darder v.t. to shoot with a dart; to harpoon; to dart. **le soleil darde ses rayons,** the sun darts forth its rays.

dare-dare adv. Infml. very quickly.

darne n.f. slice (of salmon, etc.).

dartre n.f. Med. tetter, blotch, eruption, disease of the skin.

darwinien, ne adj. Darwinian.

darwinisme n.m. Darwinism.

datable adj. datable.

datation n.f. dating.

date n.f. date. **à cette ~-là, nous avions déjà déménagé,** we had already moved at that time. **~ limite,** deadline. **de fraîche ~,** recently. **nous nous connaissons de longue ~,** we've known each other for a long time.

dater v.t. to date. v.i. to date, to reckon, to count. **cela date de loin,** that dates from a long way back. **à ~ de ce jour,** from today.

dateur n.m. date stamp.

datif n.m. dative, dative case.

datif, ive adj. Law. dative.

datte n.f. Bot. date.

dattier n.m. date tree.

daube n.f. stew with spices. **boeuf en ~,** beef casserole with wine and vegetables.

dauber v.t. to stew.

dauphin n.m. dolphin. n.m. dauphin.

dauphine n.f. dauphine.

daurade n.f. sea bream, gilthead (fish).

davantage adv. more; longer; farther. **pas ~,** no more. **sans crier ~,** without crying any longer. **reculer ~,** to back up farther.

davier n.m. Surg. forceps; Naut. davit.

de prep. of, 's; about; from; to, for; with, in, on, upon; out of, some, any. **le livre ~ Jean.** John's book. **la haine ~s méchants,** the hatred of the wicked. **avoir pitié ~ quelqu'un,** to have pity for a person, to pity a person. **~ la tragédie grecque,** on Greek tragedy. **natif ~ Rouen,** native of Rouen. **le vent du nord,** the north wind. **les vins ~ Bourgogne,** Burgundy wines.

un mal ~ tête, a headache. un chapeau d'homme, a man's hat. une bouteille ~ vin, a bottle of wine. désireux ~, desirous of. digne ~, worthy of. s'éloigner d'un lieu, to go away from a place. sortir ~ la ville, to go out of the town. ~ la tête aux pieds, from top to toe. ~ jour en jour, from day to day. sauter ~ joie, to leap for joy. mourir ~ faim, to die of hunger. faire entrer quelqu'un ~ force, to force a person to enter. coup ~ fusil, gunshot. un signe ~ tête, a nod. jouer du violon, ~ la harpe, to play the violin, the harp. vivre ~ légumes, to live on vegetables. prendre ~ la nourriture, to take some food. donnez-moi du pain, give me some bread. n'avez-vous point d'enfants? have you no children? l'art ~ bien dire, the art of speaking well. il est temps ~ partir, it is time to leave. négliger d'écrire, to neglect writing. dites-lui ~ venir, tell him to come. plus ~ cent hommes, more than a hundred men. plus grand ~ toute la tête, a whole head taller. vous n'aurez rien ~ plus, you shall have nothing else. ~ par le roi, in the king's name.

dé n.m. die; thimble. **jouer aux ~s,** to play at dice.

déambulatoire n.m. ambulatory.

déambuler v.i. to stroll about.

débâcle n.f. clearing (of a port); breaking up (of the ice); overthrow, ruin, downfall.

déballage n.m. unpacking; display, layout.

déballer v.t. to unpack.

débandade n.f. disbanding. **à la ~,** in confusion, helter-skelter. **mettre tout à la ~,** to turn every thing upside down.

débandement n.m. disbanding (of troops).

débander v.t. to take off a band, a bandage (from the eyes); to unbend; to relax. **se ~,** v.refl. to remove a bandage; to slacken; (of the weather) to get milder. v.i. to disband; to leave the ranks.

débaptiser v.t. to change the name of (a person).

débarbouillage n.m. (face) washing.

débarbouiller v.t. to wash, to clean the face of. **se ~,** v.refl. to wash one's face.

débarcadère n.m. landing place (on a quay); platform (of a railway station).

débarder v.t. to unload (floated wood); to clear of the wood felled.

débardeur n.m. docker, stevedore; (clothing) tank top.

débarquement n.m. landing, disembarkment.

débarquer v.t. to land, to disembark, to unship. v.i. to land, to disembark, to go on shore. **tu débarques?** where have you been?

débarras n.m. Infml. riddance, disencumbrance. **bon ~,** good riddance!

débarrasser v.t. to clear, to clear away, to clear up, to disencumber; to rid; to free; to deliver. **se ~,** v.refl. to get clear (of), to get rid (of), to rid oneself (of), to get free (from), to shake off. il se débarrassa de son manteau, he got rid of his coat.

débat n.m. debate, contest, dispute, controversy.

débâtir v.t. to demolish, to pull down.

debattre v.t. to debate, to discuss, to contend for. **~ le prix d'un objet,** to dispute the price of a thing. **se ~,** v.refl. to struggle, to strive; to writhe.

débauchage n.m. firing, laying off, dismissal.

débauche n.f. debauch; debauchery; lewdness; dissoluteness.

débauché, e p.p. debauched; dissolute, lewd. n.m. debauchee, rake.

débaucher v.t. to debauch; to seduce; to entice away, to lead away. **se ~,** v.refl. to become debauched; to be led away (from one's duties).

débaucheur, euse n.m.f. debaucher, corrupter.

débecter v.t. to disgust, to make sick.

débile adj. feeble, weak. n.m.f. Pej. moron.

débilitant, e adj. debilitating.

débilité n.f. debility, weakness, feebleness; mental deficiency.

débiliter v.t. to debilitate, to weaken, to enfeeble.

débine n.f. straits, needy circumstances, difficulties.

débiner v.t. Infml. to abuse, to slander. **se ~,** to scram, to run away.

débit n.m. sale, traffic, market, demand, shop; cutting (of wood); delivery, utterance; debit, debit side (of an account). **~ de vin,** wine shop. **porter au ~ de quelqu'un,** to carry to a person's debit.

débitage n.m. cutting up (of wood).

débitant, e n.m.f. retailer, retail dealer.

débiter v.t. to retail, to sell; to saw, to cut up (wood, stone, etc.); to debit; to utter; to deliver. **se ~,** v.refl. to sell, to be sold. **cette marchandise se débite très bien,** these goods sell very well. Infml. **~ des salades,** to utter rubbish.

débiteur, trice n.m.f. debtor. **être ~ de,** to be in debt to. adj.n.m. debtor. **compte ~,** debit.

déblai n.m. excavation, digging, cutting; earthwork, earth (from a cutting); rubbish.

déblaiement n.m. cutting, digging, clearing.

déblatérer v.t. to utter; to bluster about.

déblayer v.t. to clear away.

déblocage n.m. unblocking; releasing.

débloquer v.i. to unlock; to unjam.

déboire n.m. aftertaste; disappointment, vexation.

déboisement n.m. clearing of woods, deforestation.

déboiser v.t. to clear of woods, to deforest.

déboîtement n.m. dislocation.

déboiter v.t. to dislocate, to put out of joint (a bone). **se ~,** v.refl. to be dislocated.

débonnaire adj. gentle, meek, easy, complaisant.

débordant, e adj. exuberant, overflowing.

débordement n.m. overflow, overflowing, invasion, eruption, flood; outburst.

déborder v.i. to overflow, to run over; to burst

forth, to project, to jut out, *Naut.* to get clear, to shear off. *v.t.* to project, extend, jut out beyond; to outflank; to edge (plate of lead). se ~, *v.refl.* to overflow (as rivers), to break out, to burst forth, to break forth.

débotter *v.t.* to pull off the boots of, to unboot. se ~, *v.refl.* to pull one's boots off.

débouchage *n.m.* uncorking, opening.

débouché *n.m.* outlet, issue, end; *Com.* opening, market.

déboucher *v.t.* to uncork (a bottle), to open, to clear (a passage). *v.i. Milit.* to debouch, to pass out; (of roads or streets) to run.

déboucler *v.t.* to unbuckle; *Naut.* to free, to clear off (a harbor); to uncurl (hair). se ~, *v.refl.* to come unbuckled; (of hair), to uncurl.

débouler *v.i.* to bolt, to run off suddenly; to tumble down.

déboulonnage *n.m.* bolt removal.

déboulonner *v.t.* to unbolt, to take out the rivets.

débourber *v.t.* to cleanse, to clean out (mud), *Metall.* to trunk; to extricate (a carriage) from mud.

déboursement *n.m.* disbursement.

débourser *v.t.* to disburse, to expand, to lay out.

debout *adv.* upright, standing on end, erect. mettre un tonneau ~, to set a cask on end. se tenir ~, to stand upright, to stand.

débouter *v.t.* to dismiss (lawsuit).

déboutonner *v.t.* to unbutton; to take off the button of. se ~, *v.refl.* to unbutton one's clothes.

débraille, e *p.p.* loose; half-dressed; untidy, sloppy, slovenly.

débrailler (se) *v.refl.* to loosen one's clothes.

débranchement *n.m.* unplugging; disconnecting.

débrancher *v.t.* to unplug; to disconnect; to cut off.

débrayage *n.m. Auto.* clutch.

débrayer *v.t.* to disengage; to declutch; *Tech.* to release.

debridement *n.m.* unbridling (of a horse).

débrider *v.t.* to unbridle (a horse). *v.i.* to unbridle one's horse; to stop, to halt. sans ~, at a stretch, without stopping.

débris *n.m.* remains; fragments, wreck, ruins; waste.

débrouillard, e *adj. Infml.* smart; resourceful.

débrouillardise, débrouille *n.f.* resourcefulness.

débrouiller *v.t.* to unravel, to disentangle; to clear up; to explain, to solve. se ~, *v.refl.* to get disentangled, to be unraveled; to clear up; to work one's way out of a situation.

débrouissailler *v.t.* to clear off (brushwood).

débusquer *v.t.* to drive out; to oust, to turn out; to dislodge.

début *n.m.* (at play), first throw, first cast, first play; beginning, lead; start; opening. faire un

beau ~, to begin well. au ~ de, at the beginning of.

débutant, e *n.m.f.* debutant, new performer, beginner.

débuter *v.i.* to play first, to lead; to begin, to commence; to come out; to make one's first appearance. ~ dans le monde, to set out in the world.

deçà *prep.* on this side of; within. *adv.* on this side. ~ delà, here and there. par ~, on this side of. il demeure en ~ du pont, he lives on this side of the bridge.

décachetage *n.m.* unsealing, opening.

décacheter *v.t.* to unseal; to break the seal of; to open.

décade *n.f.* decade.

décadence *n.f.* decay, decline, downfall.

décadent, e *adj.* decadent. *n.m.f.* decadent.

decaèdre *adj.* decahedral. *n.m.* decahedron.

décaféiné, e *adj.* decaffeinated, caffeine-free.

décagone *n.m.* decagon. *adj.* decangular.

décagramme *n.m.* decagram.

décaisser *v.t.* to take out of its box; to unpack; *Fin.* to pay out; to disburse.

décalage *n.m.* gap, interval; time difference.

décalaminer *v.i.* to decarbonize.

décalcification *n.f.* decalcification.

décalcifier *v.i.* to decalcify. se ~, to become decalcified.

décalcomanie *n.f.* decal.

décaler *v.t.* to unwedge; to shift; to move forward/backward.

décalitre *n.m.* decaliter.

décalogue *n.m.* Decalogue, the Ten Commandments.

décalotter *v.t.* to take the top off.

décalquer *v.t.* to counter-draw.

décamètre *n.m.* decameter.

décamper *v.i.* to decamp; to make off, to march off, to move off.

décanat *n.m.* deanship.

décantation *n.f.* decantation, decanting.

décanter *v.t.* to decant, to pour off gently.

décapage *n.m.* cleaning (of metals), scouring, pickling.

décapant, e *n.m.* paint remover; acid solution; abrasive.

décaper *v.t.* to clean (metals). *v.i. Naut.* to sail beyond a cape.

décapitation *n.f.* decapitation, beheading.

décapiter *v.t.* to behead, to decapitate.

décapodes *n.m.pl.* decapoda.

décapotable *adj. Auto.* convertible.

décapsuler *v.t.* to remove the cap or cork of a bottle.

décapsuleur *n.m.* bottle opener.

décarcasser (se) *v.i. Infml.* to go to a hell of a lot of trouble.

décarreler *v.t.* to unfloor, to unpave.

décasyllabe *adj.* decasyllabic.

décathlon *n.m.* decathlon.

décavé, e *adj. Infml.* broke, cleaned out; ruined.

décaver *v.t.* (at play) to win the stake of, to sweep the stake of.

décédé, e *p.p.* deceased. *n.f.* deceased.

décéder *v.i.* to die, to expire.

décelable *adj.* discernible, noticeable.

déceler *v.t.* to disclose, to reveal, to betray. **se ~,** *v.refl.* to betray oneself.

décélération *n.f.* deceleration.

décembre *n.m.* December.

décemment *adv.* decently, in a decent manner.

décence *n.f.* decency, propriety.

décennal, e *adj.* decennial.

décent, e *adj.* decent.

décentrage *n.m.* throwing off center.

décentralisation *n.f.* decentralization.

décentraliser *v.t.* to decentralize.

décentrer *v.i.* to throw off center.

déception *n.f.* deception.

décerner *v.t.* to award, to decree; to issue out.

décès *n.m.* decease, death; demise.

décevant, e *adj.* deceitful, deceptive.

décevoir *v.t.* to deceive; to disappoint.

déchaînement *n.m.* unbridling; fury, wildness, outburst, rage.

déchaîner *v.t.* to unchain, to let loose, to unbridle, to unbind, to unfetter; to incense, to exasperate. **se ~,** *v.refl.* to break loose, to get loose from one's chains, to rage, to run riot, to run wild.

déchanter *v.i.* to become disillusioned.

décharge *n.f.* discharge; unloading; explosion, report, sound; release (from an obligation); relief, storage room. **pièce de ~,** storage room. **des témoins à ~,** witnesses for the accused.

déchargement *n.m.* discharge, unloading.

décharger *v.t.* to discharge; to unload, to unburden; to ease, to relieve; to exonerate; to release, to free, to give vent to, to let off, to fire, to fire off, to deal (a blow). **~ un navire,** to unload a ship. **~ une voiture,** to unload a car. **~ sa conscience,** to ease one's conscience. **~ son coeur,** to unburden one's mind. **~ un accusé,** to exculpate a prisoner. **~ son fusil sur quelqu'un,** to fire at a person. *v.i.* to unload; *Print.* to come off. **se ~,** *v.refl.* to unburden oneself. **~ d'une faute sur quelqu'un,** to shift the blame to someone else.

décharné, e *p.p.* or *adj.* fleshless; emaciated, lean, thin. **un visage ~,** an emaciated face. **un style ~,** an impoverished style.

décharner *v.t.* to strip the flesh off; to emaciate, to make lean, to make thin.

déchaussé, e *adj.* barefooted, barefoot.

déchaussement *n.m.* pulling off (shoes, boots); *Surg.* lancing (the gums); *Agr.* baring (the root of a tree).

déchausser *v.t.* to pull off the shoes of; *Surg.* to lance the gum of; *Agr.* to bare, to lay bare, to dig about (the root of a tree). **se ~,** *v.refl.* to pull off one's shoes, (of teeth) to become, to get bare.

dèche *n.f. Infml.* flat broke, dead broke.

déchéance *n.f.* decadence, decay, falling off.

déchet *n.m.* waste; scum (person); scrap; bit. *pl.* garbage, trash.

déchiffrable *adj.* decipherable; legible.

déchiffrement *n.m.* deciphering.

déchiffrer *v.t.* to decipher, to figure out; *Mus.* to sight-read. **se ~,** *v.refl.* to be deciphered; to be made out.

déchiffreur *n.m.* decipherer; decoder; scanner.

déchiqueter *v.t.* to cut up, to cut to pieces, to slash; to pink (border of fabric).

déchiqueture *n.f.* slashing, pinking.

déchirant, e *adj.* heart-rending, harrowing; heartbreaking; (pain) excruciating.

déchirement *n.m.* laceration, tearing, rending; anguish, pain. **~ de coeur,** anguish, heart-rending anguish. **~ d'entrailles,** excruciating pain in the bowels.

déchirer *v.t.* to tear, to rend; to lacerate; to rip up; to tear to pieces; to divide; to distress with anguish; to harrow, to torment; to sting; to backbite, to slander. **~ une lettre,** to tear a letter. **~ la société en partis opposés,** to divide society into opposed parties. **~ quelqu'un à belles dents,** to slander a person outrageously. **se ~,** *v.refl.* to be torn, to tear each other; to slander, to defame, to revile, to abuse each other.

déchirure *n.f.* tear, rent; *Surg.* laceration.

déchoir *v.i.* to fall, to fall; to decline; to lose rank; *Law.* to forfeit. **~ de son rang,** to lose one's rank. **~ de son droit,** to forfeit one's right.

déchristianiser *v.t.* to unchristianize.

déchu, e *p.p.* fallen; lost. **les anges ~s,** the fallen angels.

décibel *n.m.* decibel.

décidé, e *adj.* decided; clear, unequivocal; settled; decisive. **c'est un homme ~,** he is a resolute man.

décidément *adv.* decidedly.

décider *v.t.* to decide, to determine; to settle, to conclude; to fix; to persuade, to resolve. **qu'avez-vous décidé?** what have you decided upon? *v.i.* to decide; to judge; to determine. **se ~,** *v.refl.* to be decided, to be determined; to make up one's mind.

décigramme *n.m.* decigram.

décilitre *n.m.* deciliter.

décimal, e *adj.n.f.* decimal. **fractions ~es,** decimal fractions.

décimation *n.f.* decimation.

décimer *v.t.* to decimate; to destroy, to carry off, to sweep off.

décimètre *n.m.* decimeter.

décisif, ive *adj.* decisive; critical; crucial.

décision *n.f.* decision, resolution.

déclamateur *n.m.* declaimer; haranguer; spouter. *adj.* declamatory. **un style ~,** a declamatory style.

déclamation *n.f.* declamation, harangue; elocution; bombastic speech. **tomber dans la ~**, to degenerate into a declamatory style.

déclamatoire *adj.* declamatory.

déclamer *v.t.* to declaim; to recite, to deliver; to spout. *v.i.* to declaim; to speak in an inflated style; to exclaim, to inveigh.

déclarable *adj.* dutiable; declarable.

déclarant, e *n.m.f.* informant; declarant.

déclaratif, ive *adj.* declaratory, declarative.

déclaration *n.f.* declaration; proclamation, statement; disclosure; statue (of bankruptcy); schedule; verdict; (birth, death, etc.) notification, registration.

déclaratoire *adj.* declaratory, declarative.

déclaré, e *p.p. and adj.* declared, avowed, open. **un ennemi ~**, an open enemy.

déclarer *v.t.* to declare; to proclaim, to publish; to state; to assert; to reveal, to discover. **se ~**, *v.refl.* to declare oneself; to speak one's mind; to profess, to pronounce oneself; to declare; to show in favor of; to decide in favor of; (fire) to break out. **la peste se déclara**, the plague broke out.

déclassé, e *n.m.f.* lowered; downgraded.

declassement *n.m.* change of class; downgrading.

déclasser *v.t.* to change the class of, to unclass.

déclenchement *n.m.* launching; triggering off; release.

déclencher *v.t.* to launch; to trigger off; to release; to start; to set off. **se ~**, to go off; to release itself; to begin, to start; to be triggered off.

déclencheur *n.m.* release mechanism.

déclin *n.m.* decline, decay; wane, waning. **le ~ de la lune**, the wane of the moon.

déclinable *adj. Gram.* declinable.

déclinaison *n.f.* declination; *Gram.* declension. **~ de la boussole**, variation of the compass.

déclinant, e *adj.* declining, deviating.

décliner *v.i.* to decline, to deviate; to be on the wane, to fall off, to sink. **il décline tous les jours**, he is getting sicker every day. *v.t.* to decline; to avoid; to shun. **~ une fonction**, to decline a function. **une invitation**, to decline an invitation. **~ son nom**, to state one's name.

déclivité *n.f.* declivity.

déclouer *v.t.* to unnail.

décocher *v.t.* to discharge, to shoot, to let fly. **~ une flèche**, to let fly an arrow.

décoction *n.f. Pharm.* decoction.

décodage *n.m.* decoding; deciphering.

décoder *v.t.* to decode; to decipher.

décodeur *n.m.* decoder; decipherer.

décoiffer *v.t.* to disarrange the hair of; to mess up. **se ~**, *v.refl.* to undo one's hair.

décoincer *v.t.* to unjam; to unwedge; to loosen.

décollage *n.m.* unsticking, ungluing; *Aviat.* take-off, taking off.

décollation *n.f.* beheading; decapitation.

décollement *n.m.* ungluing, unpasting.

décoller *v.t.* to behead, to decapitate; to unglue, to unpaste, to unstick; (at billiards) to disengage. **se ~**, *v.refl.* to come unglued, to come off.

décolleté, e *adj.* low-cut, low; open. **une robe ~e**, a low-cut dress. **une femme ~e**, a woman in a low-cut dress. *n.m.* cleavage.

décolleter *v.t.* to cut low (a dress); (of persons) to bare the neck and shoulders of. *v.i.* to leave bare the neck and shoulders. **se ~**, *v.refl.* **cette femme se décollette trop**, that woman wears her dresses too low.

décolonisation *n.f.* decolonization.

décoloniser *v.t.* to decolonize.

décolorant, e *adj.* bleaching, decolorizing, decolorant. *n.m.* bleaching agent; decolorant.

décoloration *n.f.* decolorization, decoloration.

décoloré, e *adj.* colorless, faded, pale; bleached.

décolorer *v.t.* to discolor. **se ~**, *v.refl.* to lose one's color, to fade. **son teint se décolore**, her complexion is fading.

décombres *n.m.pl.* rubbish.

décommander *v.t.* to countermand; to cancel.

décomposable *adj.* decomposable.

décomposer *v.t.* to decompose; to analyze; to alter. **visage décomposé**, distorted countenance. **se ~**, *v.refl.* to decompose, to be decomposed.

décomposition *n.f.* decomposition; analysis; resolution; dissolution; corruption.

décompression *n.f.* decompression.

décomprimer *v.t.* to decompress; to depressurize.

décompte *n.m.* discount, abatement; disappointment.

décompter *v.t.* to deduct, to write off. *v.i.* to make deductions; to be disappointed.

déconcentrer *v.t.* to decentralize; to distract. **se ~**, to lose concentration; to be distracted.

déconcertant, e *adj.* disconcerting, perplexing.

déconcerter *v.t.* to disconcert; to baffle, to foil; to confuse. **se ~**, *v.refl.* to be disconcerted.

déconfiture *n.f.* discomfiture; defeat; havoc; failure, insolvency.

décongélation *n.f.* defrosting.

décongeler *v.t.* to defrost.

décongestionner *v.i. Med.* to decongest, to relieve congestion; *Fig.* to clear (blockage).

déconnecter *v.i.* to disconnect.

déconner *v.i Vulg.* to fool around.

déconseiller *v.t.* to dissuade from; to advise against.

déconsidération *n.f.* discredit, disfavor.

déconsidérer *v.t.* to discredit; to bring into disrepute.

déconsigner *v.t.* to refund the deposit on (bottle); to claim (as a suitcase from a baggage counter), to release.

décontenancer *v.t.* to embarrass, to confuse. **se ~**, *v.refl.* to be embarrassed, confused.

décontracté, e *adj.* relaxed, cod, laid back.

décontracter *v.t.* to relax.

décontraction n.f. relaxation.

déconvenue n.f. mishap; disappointment.

décor n.m. decoration; scene, scenery, decor; set; setting. **entrer dans le ~**, to drive off the road. **envoyer dans le ~**, to force (someone) off the road.

décorateur n.m. decorator; interior decorator; set designer; set artist; scene painter.

décoratif, ive adj. decorative, ornamental.

décoration n.f. decoration; ornament; insignia (of knighthood).

décorer v.t. to decorate; to adorn, to embellish. **il fut décoré sur le champ de bataille**, he was knighted on the field of battle.

décorticage n.m. peeling; shelling; hulling, husking; dissection.

décortication n.f. decortication, husking.

décortiquer v.t. to decorticate, to husk, to peel off the bark.

décorum n.m. decorum, propriety.

décote n.f. rebate; tax relief.

découcher v.i. to sleep away from home.

découdre v.t. to unsew, to unstitch. **se ~**, v.refl. to come unsewn, to come unstitched.

découler v.i. to trickle; to ensue.

découpage n.m. cutting out; carving.

découper v.t. to cut, to cut off; (at table) to carve. **~ une broderie**, to cut embroidery.

découpeur, euse n.m.f. carver; one that cuts out.

découpeuse n.f. cutting machine; jigsaw.

découplé, e p.p. strapping, well built, strong-limbed.

découpure n.f. indentation; cutting out; cut-paper work.

décourageant, e adj. discouraging, disheartening.

découragement n.m. discouragement; dejection, despondency.

décourager v.t. to discourage, to dishearten, to dispirit; to dissuade. **se ~**, v.refl. to lose courage, to be discouraged.

découronner v.t. to discrown; Milit. sweep the top of a hill.

décousu, e adj. unsewn, unstitched; desultory, unconnected, incoherent. **un style ~**, an incoherent style. n.m. unconnectedness, incoherence.

découvert, e adj. uncovered; bare; open. n.m. Com. uncovered balance; deficit. **se montrer à ~**, to show oneself in one's true colors. **être à ~**, to be unprotected.

découverte n.f. discovery; invention; detection; lookout; reconnoitering.

découvreur n.m. discoverer.

découvrir v.t. to uncover, to expose; to discover, to disclose. **~ un plat**, to uncover a dish. **~ les racines d'un arbre**, to lay bare the roots of a tree. **~ un trésor**, to discover a treasure. **~ une fraude**, to expose a fraud. **se ~**, v.refl. to uncover oneself, to show oneself; to unbosom oneself.

la mer se découvre dans le lointain, the sea is visible in the distance; (sky) to clear up.

décrassage n.m. scouring; scrubbing; cleaning; cleansing.

décrasser v.t. to clean, to take the dirt off; to wash; to scour (linen). **se ~**, v.refl. to clean oneself, to get the dirt off; to polish.

décréditer v.t. to discredit; to bring into discredit. **se ~**, v.refl. to lose one's credit, to become discredited; to fall into discredit.

décrépir v.t. to remove the roughcast from. **se ~**, to peel.

décrépit, e adj. decrepit.

décrépitude n.f. decrepitude.

décret n.m. decree; enactment; executive order; edict.

décréter v.t. to decree; to enact; to order; to announce.

décrier v.t. to decry; to disparage. **se ~**, v.refl. to bring oneself into disrepute.

décrire v.t. to describe, to relate, to narrate. **se ~**, v.refl. to be described; to follow, to trace; to curve.

décrochage n.m. unhooking; unhanging; taking down; dropping out (school).

décrocher v.t. to unhook, to take down; to pick up (telephone); to free; to land (contract, job); to drop out (school). **se ~**, to come unhooked; to get unhooked; to dislocate (jaw).

décroiser v.t. to uncross.

décroissance n.f. decrease.

décroissant, e adj. decreasing, diminishing; Math. descending.

décroît n.m. Agr. diminution; Astron. wane.

décroître v.i. to decrease, to diminish. **les jours décroissent**, the days are getting shorter.

décrotter v.t. to clean, to brush. **se ~**, v.refl. to clean, to brush oneself off.

décrue n.f. decrease, fall.

décryptage n.m. deciphering.

décrypter v.t. to decipher.

déçu, e adj. disappointed.

décuple adj. tenfold.

décupler v.i. to increase tenfold. **~ ses forces**, to strengthen ten times.

dédaigner v.t. to disdain, to despise, to scorn, to look down upon; to slight; to disregard.

dédaigneusement adv. disdainfully, scornfully.

dédaigneux, euse adj. disdainful, scornful.

dédain n.m. disdain, scorn.

dédale n.m. labyrinth, maze; confusion.

dedans adv. in, within, inside; indoors; in it. **être resté ~**, to stay inside. **la situation au ~ du pays**, the situation inside the country. **le vélo lui est rentré ~**, the bicycle ran into him/her. n.m. inside, interior; home.

dédicace n.f. dedication; autograph.

dédicacer v.t. to autograph.

dédicatoire adj. dedicatory.

dédier v.t. to dedicate.

dédire v.t. to contradict, to gainsay; to disavow.

se ~, *v.refl.* to recant, to recall, to retract, to go back on one's word.

dédit *n.m.* unsaying, retraction, recanting; forfeiture, penalty. **payer le ~,** to pay the penalty.

dédommagement *n.m.* indemnification, indemnity, damages; amends, compensation.

dédommager *v.t.* to indemnify; to make amends (for), to make up, to compensate. **se ~,** *v.refl.* to indemnify oneself, to make up.

dédorer *v.t.* to ungild. **se ~,** *v.refl.* to lose the gilding.

dédouanement *n.m.* customs clearance.

dédouaner *v.t.* to clear through customs.

dédoublement *n.m.* reduction by half; division into two.

dédoubler *v.t.* to remove the lining; to unfold; to divide in two. **se ~,** to split (personality); to unfold.

déductible *adj.* deductible.

déductif, ive *adj.* deductive.

déduction *n.f.* deduction; abatement; diminution.

déduire *v.t.* to deduct; to enumerate, to state; to deduce, to infer.

déesse *n.f.* goddess, female deity.

de facto *adv.* de facto.

défaillance *n.f.* fainting fit; weakness, falling; faintness; fault; breakdown. **tomber en ~,** to faint away.

défaillant, e *adj.* failing; perishing, weak, feeble, faint; faltering. *n.m.f.* defaulter.

défaillir *v.i.* to fail, to fall short, to be wanting; to grow weak; to decay; to faint, to sink. **son courage défaillit,** his courage failed him. **j'ai senti ~ ma force et mes esprits,** I felt my strength and courage fail me.

défaire *v.t.* to unmake, to undo, to annul; to rid (of), to deliver, to untie, to unbind; to unknot; to unrivet; to unravel; to bring down; to unpack. **~ une malle, un paquet,** to unpack a trunk, a parcel. **~ son habit,** to take off one's coat. **se ~,** *v.refl.* to come undone; to loose, to loosen, to rid oneself of; to get rid of; to spoil (as wine). **sa cravate s'est défait** his tie is untied. **on se défait des idées tristes le plus tôt qu'on peut,** we get rid of sad thoughts as soon as we can. **je cherche à me ~ de ma maison,** I am trying to sell my house. **se ~ d'un domestique,** to get rid of a servant.

défait, e *adj.* ravaged, haggard (face); disheveled (hair); disarranged.

défaite *n.f.* defeat, rout, overthrow; shift, evasion. **après la ~ des ennemis,** after the defeat of the enemy.

défaitisme *n.m.* defeatism.

défaitiste *n.m.f.* defeatist.

défalcation *n.f.* defalcation, deduction.

défalquer *v.t.* to defalcate, to deduct, to take off.

défaut *n.m.* defect, flaw, fault, blemish; weak side; want, deficiency, default; drawback; shortage. **~ de courage,** lack of courage. **trouver**

quelqu'un en ~, to catch a person in fault. **les ~s d'un diamant,** the flaws of a diamond. **à ~ de vin, nous boirons de l'eau,** we must drink water for lack of wine.

défaveur *n.f.* disfavor, disgrace, discredit.

défavorable *adj.* unfavorable, disadvantageous.

défavorablement *adv.* unfavorably.

défavoriser *v.t.* to disadvantage; to penalize; to underprivilege; to be unfair/less fair.

défécation *n.f.* defecation.

défectif, ive *adj.* defective.

défection *n.f.* defection; falling off, falling away.

défectueux, euse *adj.* defective, imperfect.

défectuosité *n.f.* defect, imperfection; flaw.

défendable *adj.* defensible, defendable.

défendant *p.p.* defending. **à son corps ~,** in self-defense; reluctantly, unwillingly, under coercion.

défendeur, eresse *n.m.f.* defendant.

défendre *v.t.* to defend, to protect; to stand by, to stand up for, to repel a claim; to shelter, to screen, to shield, to forbid, to prohibit. **~ sa patrie,** to defend one's country. **je vous défends d'y aller,** I forbid you to go there. **se ~,** *v.refl.* to defend oneself; to excuse oneself, to deny; to forbear. **se ~ du froid,** to protect oneself from cold.

défenestration *n.f.* defenestration.

défenestrer *v.t.* to defenestrate.

défense *n.f.* defense, protection; fortification; prohibition; apology, justification; tusk (of boar, elephant), fang; *Naut.* fender. **se mettre en ~,** to stand on one's guard. **être hors de ~,** not to be in a condition to defend oneself. **~ d'entrer,** no admittance.

défenseur *n.m.* defender, vindicator, champion; advocate; supporter; counsel.

défensif, ive *adj.* defensive.

défensive *n.f.* defensive, safeguard. **être sur la ~,** to be on the defensive.

déféquer *v.t.* to defecate.

déférence *n.f.* deference, regard, respect.

déférent *adj.n.m. Astron.* **cercle ~,** deferent. *Anat.* **canal ~,** deferent canal, deferent. *n.m. Astron.* deferent. **~e,** *adj.n.f.* deferential.

déférer *v.t.* to defer. *v.i.* to defer; to yield to another's opinion, to comply.

déferlement *n.m.* breaking; outpourings.

déferler *v.t. Naut.* to unfurl; to break.

défi *n.m.* defiance, challenge. **accepter un ~,** to accept a challenge. **mettre au ~,** to defy.

défiance *n.f.* distrust, mistrust; diffidence, suspicion; distrustfulness.

défiant, e *adj.* distrustful, mistrustful, diffident.

déficeler *v.t.* to untie. **se ~,** to come untied.

déficience *n.f.* deficiency.

déficient, e *adj.* deficient.

déficit *n.m.* deficit, deficiency. **être en ~,** to have a deficit.

défier *v.t.* to defy; to challenge, to dare; *Naut.* to fend, to bear off. **je vous défie de deviner**

cette énigme, I defy you to guess that enigma.
se ~, v.refl. to defy each other; to mistrust one
another, to suspect; to be on one's guard against.

défigurer v.t. to disfigure; to distort; to spoil the
face of; to deface, to deform; to mar, to alter. se
~, v.refl. to disfigure oneself; to become disfig-
ured, to be altered.

défilé n.m. filing off (of soldiers); defile; pass,
strait; parade; procession; march.

défiler v.t. to unthread, to unstring; to parade; to
march. ~ des perles, to unstring pearls. se ~,
v.refl. to come unstrung. v.i. to march off; to
sneak off.

défini, e adj. definite; determinate, precise,
exact.

définir v.t. to define, to determine with precision, to ascertain; to describe; to explain. se ~,
v.refl. to be defined.

définissable adj. definable.

définitif, ive adj. definitive. en ~, definitively;
finally.

définition n.f. definition; (crossword) clue;
(television) resolution.

définitivement adv. definitively, positively,
finally.

déflagration n.f. deflagration.

déflation n.f. deflation.

défleurir v.i. to shed its blossoms. v.t. to nip the
blossom of, to strip of blossom; to rub off the
bloom of (ripe fruit); to destroy the charm of.

déflexion n.f. deflection.

défloration n.f. defloration.

déflorer v.t. to deflower; to seduce; to take off
the freshness of.

défonçage n.m. Agr. digging up; deep plowing;
smashing; breaking down.

défoncement n.m. staving (of a cask); cutting
up, breaking up (of roads); digging in.

défoncer v.t. to stave; to break the bottom of a
cask; to bash in; to cut up (roads); to dig up (a
piece of ground); Milit. to break through; to
break down se ~, v.refl. (drugs) to get high, to
be high.

déformant, e adj. deforming, distorting.

déformation n.f. deformation; distortion; twist.

déformer v.t. to deform, to put out of shape; to
distort. se ~, v.refl. to grow deformed; to get out
of shape.

défoulement n.m. release; letting off steam.

défouler(se) v.i. to let off steam.

défraichir v.t. to take off the freshness of. se ~,
v.refl. to fade.

defrayer v.t. to defray, to support; to amuse, to
divert ~ la chronique, to be the talk of the
town.

défrichement n.m. clearing (land).

défricher v.t. to clear; to cultivate; to unravel, to
clear up ~ des terres, to clear lands.

défricheur n.m. clearer of land.

défriser v.t. to uncurl (hair), Infml. to disappoint. se ~, v.refl. to uncurl.

défroisser v.t. to smooth out.

défroquer v.t. to unfrock. se ~, v.refl. (of a
monk) to give up monastic life.

défunt, e adj. deceased, defunct; late.

dégagé, e adj. redeemed, taken out of pawn,
free; easy; unconstrained, flippant; open, casual,
clear (sky). manières ~es, casual manners.
chambre ~e, room with a private entrance.
une taille ~e, a graceful shape.

dégagement n.m. redeeming, disengagement;
release.

dégager v.t. to redeem; to free, to disengage; to
set free; to ease, to relieve ~ une porte, to clear
a doorway ~ la tête, to relieve the head of congestion. se ~, v.refl. to disengage oneself; to
extricate oneself; to get clear, to get away; to
break away; to be disengaged, to be relieved,
eased, set free; Chem. to be emitted. se ~ de ses
liens, to break one's bonds.

dégaine n.f. awkwardness.

dégainer v.t. to unsheath, to draw; to lug out.
n.m. unsheathing.

déganter v.t. to unglove, to take off the gloves of.
se ~, v.refl. to take off one's gloves.

dégarnir v.t. to strip; to untrim; ~ un appartement, to strip an apartment of its furniture. se
~, v.refl. to strip oneself (of); to part (with); to
become thin or empty (as a room). vous avez
eu tort de vous ~, you were wrong to part
with your ready money. sa tête se dégarnit, he
is getting bald.

dégât n.m. damage; devastation.

dégel n.m. thaw.

dégelée n.f. Vulg. shower of blows; beating.

dégeler v.t. to thaw. v.i. to warm up; to melt.

dégénéré, e adj. n.m. degenerate; defective.

dégénérer v.i. to degenerate; to deteriorate, to
become worse, to decline.

dégénérescence n.f. degeneration, degeneracy.

dégirrage n.m. de-icing; defrosting.

dégivrer v.t. to de-ice; to defrost.

dégivreur n.m. de-icer; defroster.

déglaçage n.m. déglacement n.m. de-icing;
Culin. deglazing.

déglacer v.t. to de-ice; Culin. to deglaze.

déglinguer v.i. Infml. to fall to pieces.

déglutir v.t. to swallow.

déglutition n.f. swallowing.

dégobiller v.t. to vomit; to throw up.

dégonflé, e adj. flat (tire); Infml. chicken, afraid.

dégonflémént n.m. reduction; going down;
emptying; deflation.

dégonfler v.t. to reduce (a swelling); to reduce
the volume of, to empty (a balloon). se ~, v.refl.
to be reduced; to diminish (in volume), to go
down; to relieve (one's heart).

dégorgement n.m. outflow, outfall; overflowing,
unstopping (of a pipe, of a spout).

dégorgeoir n.m. spout, place where waters are
discharged.

dégorger v.t. to vomit; to unstop, to clear (a

pipe, a spout); to clean, to scour. *v.i.* to overflow; to disgorge, to discharge; to empty; to purge (fish); to cleanse, to scour. se ~, *v.refl.* to get clear, to get unstopped; to disgorge itself.

dégot(t)er *v.t. Infml.* to dig up, to find.

dégouliner *v.i.* to drip; to trickle.

dégourdi, e *adj.* acute, sharp, shrewd; lively.

dégourdir *v.t.* to take the numbness from, to sharpen, to make shrewd; to polish ~ ses jambes, to take the stiffness out of one's legs. se ~ *v.refl.* to remove numbness from, to revive, to become sharp; to brighten up.

dégoût *n.m.* disgust; aversion; *pl.* vexation, mortifications, dislike, aversion. surmonter son ~ to overcome one's dislike.

dégoûtant, e *adj.* disgusting, loathsome, nauseous, odious, hateful, offensive; distasteful. un vieux ~, a dirty old man.

dégoûté, e *adj.* disgusted, squeamish, fastidious. fatre le ~ to be squeamish.

dégoûter *v.t.* to disgust. se ~, *v.refl.* to be disgusted, to loathe, to be sick, to be weary, tired.

dégouttant, e *adj.* dripping, dropping.

dégoutter *v.i.* to drip; to trickle down. la sueur lui dégoutte du front, the sweat is trickling from his brow.

dégradant, e *adj.* degrading.

dégradation *n.f.* degradation, abasement, baseness; damage, deterioration.

dégradé *n.m.* gradation; range of colors; moderation.

dégrader *v.t.* to degrade, to lower, to debase, to dishonor, to disgrace; to damage, to dilapidate; *Paint.* to degrade (light or color). se ~, *v.refl.* to degrade, to debase, to disgrace oneself, to become defaced; to be dilapidated.

dégrafer *v.t.* to unhook, to unclasp. se ~, *v.refl.* to come unhooked.

dégraissage *n.m.* cleaning, scouring (fabric).

dégraisser *v.t.* to take off grease; to skim off the fat of; to impoverish; to clean; to thin. ~ un bouillon, to skim broth.

degré *n.m.* degree; grade; extent, point; pitch, height; step, stair; flight of steps, steps (of a monument); remove. par ~s, gradually. au suprême ~, in the highest degree.

dégressif, ive *adj.* regressive; degressive.

dégrèvement *n.m.* reduction, diminution (of taxes).

dégrever *v.t.* to free (a property) from encumbrance; to reduce a tax.

dégringolade *n.f.* tumbling down, tumble, fall.

dégringoler *v.i.* to tumble down, to roll over; to fall.

dégrisement *n.m.* sobering up.

dégriser *v.t.* to sober; to cool, to bring to one's senses. se ~, *v.refl.* to sober up.

dégrossir *v.t.* to rough out; to shape out, to form; to make a rough sketch of; to trim.

dégrossissage *n.f.* roughing out; *Build.* trimming.

dégrouiller(se) *v.i. Infml.* dégrouilles-toi, move it!

déguenillé, e *adj.* ragged, tattered, in tatters. tout ~, all in rags. *n.m.f.* ragged person.

dégueniller *v.t.* to tear in tatters.

déguerpir *v.t.* to yield up. *v.i.* to pack off; to beat it; to scram, to decamp; to be off.

dégueulasse *adj. Infml.* disgusting. il est ~, he is a dirty pig.

dégueuler *v.i. Infml.* to vomit.

déguisé, e *p.p.* disguised; in disguise. *n.m.f.* disguised person.

déguisement *n.m.* costume, disguise; pretext; dissimulation.

déguiser *v.t.* to disguise, to conceal; to cloak. se ~, *v.refl.* to disguise oneself; to be disguised. se ~ en, to dress up as (as for Halloween).

dégustateur *n.m.* taster.

dégustation *n.f.* tasting (of wines and liquors).

déguster *v.t.* to taste, to sample; to enjoy. il a dégusté avec cette affaire, he had a rough time with this deal.

déhanché *p.p.* or *adj.* ungainly, waddling.

déhanchement *n.m.* swaying; waddling gait.

déhancher(se) *v.i.* to become dislocated; to sway one's hips, to wiggle.

dehors *adv.* out; without, on the outside; out of doors; abroad. au ~, outside. mettre quelqu'un ~, to kick someone out, to throw someone out. en ~ de, outside of. toutes voiles ~, all sails spread. *n.m.* outside, exterior; the outbuildings of a house; outworks (of a place). garder les ~, to keep up appearances.

déification *n.f.* deification.

déifier *v.t.* to deify.

déisme *n.m.* deism.

déiste *n.m.f.* deist.

déité *n.f.* deity, divinity.

déjà *adv.* already; previously; again. ça coûte combien ~? how much is it again?

déjection *n.f.* excrements.

déjeuner *v.i.* to lunch. *n.m.* lunch.

déjouer *v.i.* to outsmart; to baffle, to thwart.

delà *prep.* beyond au ~, farther; beyond au ~ des mers, beyond the sea.

délabré, e *adj.* shattered, dilapidated; tattered. une maison ~e, a dilapidated house.

délabrement *n.m.* decay, dilapidation; ruin.

délabrer *v.t.* to tear to tatters; to dilapidate, to decay; to shatter se ~, *v.refl.* to get dilapidated; to be impaired.

délacer *v.t.* to unlace. se ~, *v.refl.* to come unlaced.

délai *n.m.* delay; time limit; extension of time; deadline; waiting period. prolonger un ~, to extend a deadline. dans les plus brefs ~s, as quickly as possible.

délaissé, e *adj.* abandoned, forsaken; neglected.

délaissement *n.m.* abandonment, relinquishment; destitution; forlornness.

délaisser *v.t.* to abandon, to forsake, to cast off, to desert, to relinquish.

délassant, e *adj.* relaxing; diverting.

délassement *n.m.* relaxation; recreation, diversion, entertainment.

délasser *v.t.* to refresh, to repose, to relax. **se ~**, *v.refl.* to refresh oneself; to relax.

délateur, trice *n.m.f.* informer, accuser.

délation *n.f.* act of informing.

délavage *n.m.* fading; watering down.

délavé, e *adj.* dilute, diluted; faded; washed-out. **des couleurs ~es**, diluted colors; weak, dim.

délaver *v.t.* to dilute (colors); to water down; to wash out.

délayage *n.m.* diluting; thinning down.

délayer *v.t.* to dilute, to mix with water.

délectable *adj.* delectable; delicious; delightful.

délectation *n.f.* delectation, delight.

délecter *v.t.* to delight. **se ~**, *v.refl.* to delight, to take delight. **se ~ d l'étude**, to take delight in study.

délégation *n.f.* delegation; commission; *Law.* assignment.

délégué, e *p.p.* delegated. *n.m.f.* delegate.

déléguer *v.t.* to delegate; to instruct, to commit; to assign (a debt).

délétère *adj.* deleterious; injurious, pernicious.

délibératif, ive *adj.* deliberative.

délibération *n.f.* deliberation; resolution. **mettre en ~**, to bring under deliberation.

délibéré, e *adj.* deliberate, decided, resolute. **de propos ~**, deliberately; with set purpose. *n.m.* deliberation.

délibérément *adv.* deliberately; resolutely, boldly; intentionally.

délibérer *v.i.* to deliberate; to debate; to resolve. **le temps de ~ était passé**, it was too late to deliberate.

délicat, e *adj.* delicate; weak, tender, soft; dainty; touchy; scrupulous. **une santé ~e**, a delicate health. **une expression ~e**, a refined expression. **situation ~e**, tricky situation.

délicatement *adv.* delicately; gently; daintily.

délicatesse *n.f.* delicacy; tenderness; daintiness; refinement. **la ~ du langage**, the delicacy of the language. **les ~s de la table**, the delicacies of the table.

délice *n.m.* **~s** *n.f.pl.* delight. **il est les ~s de ceux qui vivent avec lui**, he delights all those he lives with.

délicieusement *adv.* delightfully; deliciously.

délicieux, euse *adj.* delicious; delightful.

délictueux, euse *adj. Law.* guilty; offensive; relating to a misdemeanor.

délié, e *adj.* loose, untied; thin; slender; shrewd, sharp; subtle. *n.m.* thin stroke, upstroke (in writing).

délier *v.t.* to untie; to loosen; to unbind; to release, to absolve. **~ la langue de quelqu'un**, to make someone talk. **se ~**, *v.refl.* to come untied, undone; to get loose.

délimitation *n.f.* settling boundaries, marking limits.

délimiter *v.t.* to settle boundaries, to mark limits.

délinquance *n.f.* delinquency.

délinquant, e *n.m.f.* delinquent, offender.

délirant, e *adj.* delirious; *Fig.* frenzied.

délire *n.m.* delirium; deliriousness; lightheadedness; frenzy. **avoir le ~**, to be delirious.

délirer *v.i.* to be delirious, to rave.

délirium tremens *n.m.* delirium tremens.

délit *n.m.* offense, delinquency; misdemeanor; mason, wrong bed (of stones). **prendre en flagrant ~**, to catch in the act.

délivrance *n.f.* delivery, deliverance; release; relief; issue (passport); childbirth.

délivrer *v.t.* to deliver; to release, to set free, to liberate, to rescue; to hand over, to give. **~ des marchandises**, to deliver goods. **se ~**, *v.refl.* to deliver oneself, to shake off; to get rid.

déloger *v.i.* to move; *Infml.* to decamp; to scamper away. *v.t.* to throw out; to expel.

déloyal, e *adj.* disloyal, treacherous, false; unfair.

déloyalement *adv.* disloyally, treacherously, falsely.

déloyauté *n.f.* disloyalty, treachery.

delta *n.m.* delta; deltaplane (trademark).

deltoïde *adj.* deltoid.

déluge *n.m.* deluge, flood. **un ~ d'injures**, a deluge of abuse.

déluré, e *adj.* sharp, shrewd.

délurer *v.i.* to smarten up. **se ~**, to become smart; *Pej.* to smart off, to be a wise guy.

démagnétisation *n.f.* demagnetization.

démagogie *n.f.* demagogy.

démagogique *adj.* demagogic.

démagogue *n.m.* demagogue.

demain *adv.* tomorrow; **après ~**, the day after tomorrow; **~ en huit**, a week from tomorrow. *n.m.* tomorrow.

demande *n.f.* demand; request, application; petition. **faire une ~**, to make an application. **faire une ~ en mariage**, to make an offer of marriage. **à sotte ~ point de réponse**, a silly question needs no answer.

demander *v.t.* to ask, to ask for, to beg, to request, to petition, to solicit, to beseech; to inquire, to question, to interrogate, to demand; to order, to require. **~ instamment**, to entreat, to implore. **je ne demande pas mieux**, I am quite willing. **ne ~ qu'amour et simplesse**, to wish only for a quiet life. **cette affaire demande beaucoup de soin**, this affair needs great care. **on est venu vous ~**, someone asked to see you. **se ~**, *v.refl.* to be asked for; to be requested; to wonder; to think. **je me demande ce qu'il a dit**, I wonder what he said. **cela ne se demande pas**, that is a matter of course.

demandeur, euse *n.m.f.* asker, demander; plaintiff.

démangeaison *n.f.* itching, itch; longing.

démanger *v.i.* to itch; to have a longing (for); to long.

démantèlement *n.m.* dismantling.

démanteler *v.t.* to dismantle.

démantibuler *v.t.* to break (the jaw), to put out of joint.

démaquillage *n.m.* removal of makeup.

démaquillant, e *adj.* used for removing make-up. *n.m.* makeup remover.

démaquiller *v.i.* to take makeup off. **se ~,** to take off one's makeup.

démarcation *n.f.* demarcation. **ligne de ~,** line of demarcation.

démarche *n.f.* gait, walk, step; bearing, port; act, measure; procedure; approach. **faire une ~,** to take steps.

démarquage *n.m.* removing labels. *Fig.* pirating.

démarque *n.f.* marking down.

démarquer *v.t.* to unmark.

démarquer *v.t.* to unmark. **se ~,** *v.refl.* to lose its mark; to dissociate oneself; to stick out.

démarrage *n.m.* unmooring; *Auto.* start; pulling away.

démarrer *v.t.* to unmoor; *Auto.* to start; to pull away; to get moving; to get off the ground.

démarreur *n.m. Auto.* starter.

démasquer *v.t.* to unmask; to divulge. **se ~,** *v.refl.* to take off one's mask; to show oneself in one's true colors.

démêlage *n.m.* combing, sorting (of wool, etc.).

démêlé *n.m.* dispute, strife, contest, quarrel.

démêler *v.t.* to untangle; to unravel; to comb out (hair); to clear up; to figure out; to distinguish; to contest; to quarrel. **~ le vrai du faux,** to distinguish truth from falsehood. **il n'est pas aisé à ~,** he is not easy to figure out. **se ~,** *v.refl.* to be unraveled; to extricate, to free oneself; to be unraveled; to get clear of.

démêloir *n.m.* large-toothed comb.

démembrement *n.m.* dismemberment; dismembered part.

démembrer *v.t.* to dismember; to separate. **se ~,** *v.refl.* to be dismembered.

déménagement *n.m.* move; moving out (household).

déménager *v.t.* to move; to carry (possessions) to a different residence. *v.i.* to move; to change residence, to get away; *Fig.* to get silly or childish.

déménageur *n.m.* mover, moving man; moving company.

démence *n.f.* madness, insanity; dementia. **tomber en ~,** to become insane.

démener (se) *v.refl.* to struggle; to strive hard.

dément, e *adj.* mad, insane, lunatic.

démenti *n.m.* lie, contradiction; disappointment; denial; refutation. **donner un ~ à,** to give the lie to, to expose as a lie.

démentiel, le *adj.* insane.

démentir *v.t.* to belie; to give the lie to; to contradict. **voudriez-vous me ~?** do you mean to contradict me? **se ~,** *v.refl.* to contradict oneself; to contradict each other; to break one's promise; to cease, to fall off. **ses bontés pour moi ne se sont jamais démenties,** he has never been anything else but kind to me.

démerder (se) *v.i. Infml.* to look after oneself, to get around.

démérite *n.m.* demerit.

démériter *v.i.* to do amiss, wrong; to forfeit the esteem; to be unworthy (**de,** of).

démesure *n.f.* excessiveness, immoderation.

démesuré, e *adj.* immoderate; excessive, inordinate; disproportionate.

démesurément *adv.* immoderately, excessively, inordinately.

démettre *v.t.* to dislocate; to put out of joint; to dismiss. **il s'est démis le pied,** he has dislocated his foot. **se ~,** *v.refl.* to be dislocated, to be out of joint; to resign a position. **il s'est demis de ses fonctions,** he has resigned his post.

demeurant, e *adj.* dwelling, residing, living. *n.m.* remainder, rest. **au ~,** besides, after all; in other respects.

demeure *n.f.* abode, dwelling; residence; *Law.* delay. **une sombre ~,** a gloomy abode. **changer sa ~,** to change one's residence. **être en ~ avec,** to be behind with (creditors). **mettre quelqu'un en ~,** to summon to court, to subpoena. **à ~,** resident, immovable, as a fixture.

demeuré, e *adj. Infml.* retarded.

demeurer *v.t.* to live, to dwell, to reside; to take a long time, to stop, to be left; to remain. **~ à la campagne,** to live in the country. **~ d'accord,** to agree, to be agreed. **~ à ne rien faire,** to stand idle. **~ en chemin,** to stop halfway. **~ court,** to stop short.

demi, e *adj.* half, demi, semi. **une heure et ~e,** an hour and a half. **une ~ heure,** half an hour. **deux heures et ~e,** half past two. **à fourbe, fourbe et ~,** set a thief to catch a thief. *adv.* half; in part; by half. **faire les choses à ~,** to do things by halves. *n.m. Arith.* half.

demie *n.f.* half; half-hour. **cette pendule sonne les ~s,** that clock strikes the half-hours.

demi-bas *n.m.* knee-high stocking; knee sock.

demi-cercle *n.m.* semicircle; protractor.

demi-dieu *n.m.* demigod.

demi-douzaine *n.f.* half a dozen.

demi-finale *n.f.* semifinal.

demi-finaliste *n.m.f.* semifinalist.

demi-fond *n.m.* medium-distance running.

demi-frère *n.m.* half-brother.

demi-gros *n.m.* retail wholesale.

demi-jour *n.m.* dim light; twilight.

demi-journée *n.f.* half day; (work) part-time.

demi-litre *n.m.* half liter.

demi-longueur *n.f.* (sport) a half-length.

demi-lune *n.f.* half moon.

demi-mesure *n.f.* half-measure.

demi-mot *n.m.* understanding without having to say it all.

demi-pause *n.f.* (*Mus.*) half rest.

demi-pension *n.f.* boarding house; (school) day boarding; half-board.

demi-place *n.f.* (transport) half-fare.

demi-saison *n.f.* midseason.

demi-sel *adj.* slightly salted.

demi-soeur *n.f.* half-sister.

demi-solde *n.f.* half-pay.

demi-sommeil *n.m.* somnolence, half-sleep, drowsing.

demi-tarif *n.m.* half-price; (transport) half-fare.

demi-teinte *n.f.* half-tone (color).

demi-tour *n.m.* about-face; *Auto.* U-turn. **faire ~,** to turn back.

démilitarisation *n.f.* demilitarization.

démilitariser *v.t.* to demilitarize.

déminage *n.m.* mine clearance.

déminer *v.i.* to clear of mines.

démineur *n.m.* mine clearer.

démis, e *adj.* dislocated.

démission *n.f.* resignation. **donner sa ~,** to give in one's resignation, to resign.

démissioner *v.i.* to resign.

démiurge *n.m.* demiurge.

démobilisation *n.f.* demobilization.

démobiliser *v.t.* to demobilize.

démocrate *adj.* democratic; *n.m.f.* democrat.

démocratie *n.f.* democracy.

démocratique *adj.* democratic.

démocratiquement *adv.* democratically.

démocratisation *n.f.* democratization.

démocratiser *v.t.* to democratize.

démodé, e *adj.* old-fashioned, out of date, outdated.

démoder(se) *v.i.* to go out of fashion.

démographe *n.m.f.* demographer.

démographie *n.f.* demography.

démographique *adj.* demographic.

demoiselle *n.f.* young girl, young lady; miss; dragonfly. **une ~ de cinquante ans,** a maiden lady of fifty. **~ d'honneur,** maid of honor. **rester ~,** to remain single.

démolir *v.t.* to demolish; to pull down; to break up; *Fig.* to overthrow, to ruin.

démolissage *n.m.* slating.

démolisseur *n.m.* demolisher; overthrower.

démolition *n.f.* demolition; pulling down; *pl.* old building materials, rubbish.

démon *n.m.* demon; devil; fiend; imp. **c'est un petit ~,** he is a little devil.

démonétisation *n.f.* demonetization (withdrawal of currency from circulation).

démonétiser *v.t.* to demonetize.

démoniaque *adj.* demoniac, demoniacal. *n.m.f.* demoniac; madman.

démonologie *n.f.* demonology.

démonstrateur *n.m.* demonstrator.

démonstratif, ive *adj.* demonstrative, demonstrating.

démonstration *n.f.* demonstration.

démontable *adj.* that can be dismantled.

démontage *n.m.* taking down, taking to pieces.

démonte-pneu *n.m.* **démonte-pneus** *n.m.pl.* tire iron.

démonter *v.t.* to dismount, to take to pieces; to undo; to confound, to baffle, to alter. **~ une machine,** to take a machine to pieces. **se ~,** *v.refl.* to come to pieces; to dislocate; to get out of order; to break up; to be confounded.

démontrable *adj.* demonstrable.

démontrer *v.t.* to demonstrate; to make evident; to show, to prove.

démoralisant, e *adj.* demoralizing.

démoralisateur, trice *adj.* demoralizing; *n.m.f.* demoralizer.

démoralisation *n.f.* demoralization.

démoraliser *v.t.* to demoralize.

démordre *v.i.* to let go, to loose one's hold; to depart (from), to give up. **elle ne veut pas en ~,** she won't budge, she is sticking to her guns.

démouler *v.t.* to remove from a mold.

démultiplier *v.t. Tech.* to gear down, to reduce.

démuni, e *adj.* lacking, without. **~ de tout,** destitute. **~ de talent,** untalented.

démunir *v.t.* to deprive of ammunition (a place); to leave unprovided with necessities. **se ~,** *v.refl.* to deprive oneself (of), to part (with).

démystification *n.f.* demystification.

démystifier *v.t.* to demystify, to enlighten.

démythifier *v.t.* to demythologize.

dénasalisation *n.f.* denasalization.

dénasaliser *v.i.* to denasalize.

dénatalite *n.f.* decrease in the birth rate.

dénaturation *n.f.* denaturation.

dénaturé, e *adj.* unnatural.

dénaturer *v.t.* to alter, to change the nature of; to misapply; to misconstrue; to denaturalize. **~ un fait,** to misrepresent a fact.

dénégation *n.f.* denial.

déneigement *n.m.* snow removal.

déneiger *v.t.* to clear of snow.

déni *n.m.* denial; refusal. **~ de justice,** refusal of justice.

déniaiser *v.t.* to sharpen up, to sharpen the wits (of); to dupe, to cheat, to take in; to take away somebody's innocence. **se ~,** *v.refl.* to get sharper; to learn wit.

dénicher *v.t.* to dislodge; to turn out; to ferret out. *v.i.* to fly (from the nest), to fly off; to be off; to get away.

dénicheur *n.m.* one who unearths or digs up something.

dénicotiniser *v.t.* to remove nicotine from.

dénier *v.t.* to deny; to disown; to refuse.

dénigrement *n.m.* disparagement; detraction.

dénigrer *v.t.* to disparage; to decry.

déniveler *v.t.* to make uneven; to lower.

dénivellation *n.f.* **dénivellement** *n.m.* lowering; making uneven.

dénombrable *adj.* countable.

dénombrement *n.m.* numbering; census; enumeration list.

dénombrer *v.t.* to number, to count, to enumerate.

dénominateur *n.m.* denominator.

dénominatif, ive *adj.* denominative.

dénomination *n.f.* denomination, name.

dénommé, e *adj.* named. **un ~ Paul,** a man called Paul.

dénommer *v.t.* to denominate; to name.

dénoncer *v.t.* to denounce, to declare; to accuse, to inform against. **se ~,** *v.refl.* to be denounced; to denounce oneself, each other.

dénonciateur, trice *n.m.f.* denunciator, informer; *adj.* accusatory, denunciatory.

dénonciation *n.f.* denouncement, denunciation; information, accusation.

dénotation *n.f.* denotation.

dénoter *v.t.* to denote, to indicate.

dénouement *n.m.* outcome, ending, conclusion.

dénouer *v.t.* to untie, to undo (a rope); to unravel, to clear up. **se ~,** *v.refl.* to come untied; to come undone; *Fig.* to be unraveled.

dénoyauter *v.t.* to stone, to pit (fruit).

denrée *n.f.* commodity; foodstuffs; perishable food.

dense *adj.* dense, compact.

densité *n.f.* density, compactness.

dent *n.f.* tooth; cog, tine, prong, spike. **faire ses ~s,** to teethe. **~s de sagesse,** wisdom teeth. **arme jusqu'aux ~s,** armed to the teeth. **n'avoir pas de quoi mettre sous la ~,** not to have anything to eat; not to have enough to live upon. **mordre à belles ~s,** to bite as hard as possible. **avoir une ~ contre quelqu'un,** to have a grudge against a person. **déchirer à belles ~s,** to slander outrageously. **montrer les ~s,** to show one's teeth; to threaten. **prendre le mors aux ~s,** (of a horse), to bolt; to set about a thing with haste. **être sur les ~s,** to be worn out.

dent-de-lion *n.m.* dandelion.

dentaire *adj.* dental.

dental, e *adj.* dental. *n.f. Gram.* dental.

denté, e *adj.* toothed, cogged. **roue ~e,** cogwheel, toothed wheel.

dentelé, e *adj.* jagged, notched; denticulated; dentate.

denteler *v.t.* to notch, to indent.

dentelle *n.f.* lace.

dentellière *n.f.* lacemaker.

dentelure *n.f.* indentation.

dentier *n.m.* denture.

dentifrice *n.m.* dentifrice, toothpaste.

dentiste *n.m.* dentist.

dentition *n.f.* dentition.

denture *n.f.* set of teeth; teeth of a wheel (clock).

dénudé, e *adj.* bare; bold; naked.

dénuder *v.t.* to denude, to lay bare.

dénué, e *adj.* destitute; devoid, void; stripped.

dénuement *n.m.* destitution, want, poverty, indigence.

dénuer *v.t.* to deprive, to strip. **se ~,** *v.refl.* to deprive oneself, to strip oneself; to leave oneself destitute.

dénutrition *n.f.* malnutrition.

déodorant *adj.*, *n.m.* deodorant.

déontologie *n.f.* deontology, medical code of ethics.

déontologique *n.f.* deontological, ethical.

dépannage *n.m.* repairing; *Auto.* breakdown service.

dépanner *v.t.* to repair, to fix; to help out.

dépanneur *n.m.* repairman; breakdown mechanic.

dépanneuse *n.f.* breakdown truck, wrecker.

dépaqueter *v.t.* to unpack.

dépareillé, e *adj.* lacking a match (of a pair), imperfect. **un volume ~,** an odd lot.

dépareiller *v.t.* to render incomplete; to break a set of.

déparer *v.t.* to strip, to disfigure; to spoil, to mar, to disparage.

déparié, e *adj.* odd, lacking a match, not part of a pair.

déparier *v.t.* to take away (one of a pair); to part, to separate.

départ *n.m.* parting; departure, leaving, division.

départager *v.t.* **~ les voix,** to decide between; to cast the deciding vote.

département *n.m.* department; province. **chaque ~ de France est administré par un préfet,** each department of France is administered by a prefect.

départemental, e *adj.* departmental; *n.m.* secondary road.

départir *v.t.* to dispense, to distribute, to divide, to allot. **se ~,** *v.refl.* (with **de**) to desist (from); to give up, to depart, to deviate, to swerve (from). **ce n'est pas une règle dont on ne puisse se ~,** it is not a rule from which we may not depart.

dépasser *v.t.* to pass, to go beyond, to exceed; to surpass, to overreach. **~ les limites,** to go beyond the limits. **~ le but,** to overshoot the mark. **se ~,** *v.refl.* to surpass oneself.

dépassionner *v.t.* to take the heat out of.

dépatouiller(se) *v.i. Infml.* to get out of a mess.

dépaver *v.t.* to unpave.

dépaysé, e *adj.* homesick, strange; uprooted.

dépaysement *n.m.* homesickness; disorientation.

dépayser *v.t.* to send from home, to send abroad. **se ~,** *v.refl.* to leave one's home, one's country.

dépeçage *n.m.* cutting up; carving up.

dépecer *v.t.* to cut up; to carve; to take to pieces. **~ de la viande,** to cut up meat. **se ~,** *v.refl.* to be cut up; to be carved.

dépêche *n.f.* dispatch; telegram; wire.

dépêcher *v.t.* to dispatch; to expedite, to hasten;

to send away hastily; to forward. se ~, v.refl. to hasten, to make haste, to look sharp, to hurry.

dépeindre v.t. to describe, to depict, to portray, to paint, to picture, to delineate.

dépenaillé, e adj. ragged, tattered, in rags, in tatters.

dépendance n.f. dependency; dependence.

dépendant, e adj. n.m.f. dependent.

dépendre v.i. (with de) to depend (on); to be subject to, to be under; to belong to. **mon sort dépend de lui**, my fate depends on him.

dépens n.m.pl. expense, cost, charge. **aux ~ de**, at the expense of. *Law.* costs.

dépense n.f. expense, expenditure; outlay, cost, charge. **faire de grandes ~s**, to be extravagant.

dépenser v.t. to spend, to expend; to disburse; to waste. se ~, to exert oneself. **il se dépense pour rien**, he is wasting his time.

dépensier, ière adj. and s. extravagant; wasteful; prodigal; spendthrift. n.m. bursar.

déperdition n.f. loss, waste.

dépérir v.i. to perish, to decay, to decline, to pine away; to lose strength; to wither.

dépérissement n.m. perishing, decay, decline, dwindling, pining away; withering; waste.

dépersonnalisation n.f. depersonalization.

dépersonnaliser v.t. to depersonalize.

dépêtrer v.t. to disengage, to disentangle, to extricate, to free. se ~, v.refl. to get out; to extricate, to clear oneself.

dépeuplement n.m. depopulation.

dépeupler v.t. to depopulate; to thin. se ~, v.refl. to depopulate.

déphasage n.m. emotional disconnectedness. ~ **horaire**, time difference.

déphasé, e adj. out of touch; disoriented.

dépiauter v.t. *Infml.* to skin.

depilation n.f. depilation.

dépilatoire n.m. depilatory.

dépiler v.t. to cause the hair to fall. se ~, v.refl. to lose the hair (as an animal).

dépiquer v.t. to unquilt; to unstitch; to pick out the stitches of; *Gard.* to transplant. se ~, v.refl. to get better humored, to recover one's good humor.

dépister v.t. *Hunt.* to track; to hunt out, to ferret out; to throw off the scent; to screen for (disease).

dépit n.m. despite, spite; vexation. **en ~ de**, in spite of.

dépiter v.t. to vex, to spite, to thwart, to provoke. se ~, v.refl. to be annoyed.

déplacé, e adj. removed; displaced, out of place; uncalled for, improper, misplaced.

déplacement n.m. displacement; displacing; change of place. **frais de ~**, traveling expenses.

déplacer v.t. to displace, to move; to change; to shift. se ~, v.refl. to change one's place, one's residence; to leave one's residence.

déplaire v.i. to displease; to be disagreeable; to offend. **ne vous en déplaise**, by (with) your

leave. se ~, v.refl. to be displeasing to oneself; to find no pleasure; to dislike; to wither.

déplaisant, e adj. unpleasant, unpleasing, disagreeable, annoying.

déplaisir n.m. displeasure; dislike, distaste, offense, vexation, grief, sorrow.

déplantage n.m. **déplantation** n.f. digging up (plant).

déplâtrer v.t. to unplaster.

déplier v.t. to unfold, to open; to show (goods).

déplisser v.t. to unpleat. se ~, v.refl. to lose its pleats.

déploiement n.m. unfolding; unfurling (of a flag); deploy, deployment; display; show.

déplorable adj. deplorable; lamentable.

déplorablement adv. deplorably, lamentably.

déplorer v.t. to deplore, to lament; to regret.

déployé, e adj. displayed; unfolded, unfurled; flying.

déployer v.t. to display; to spread; to unfold, to unfurl; to deploy. ~ **les voiles**, to unfurl the sails. se ~, v.refl. to be unfolded; to be unfurled; to spread; to be displayed.

déplumer v.t. to pluck. se ~, v.refl. to molt, to shed feathers; *Infml.* to grow bald.

dépolariser v.t. to depolarize.

dépolir v.t. to take the polish off. se ~, v.refl. to lose its polish; to tarnish.

dépoliser v.t. to depoliticize.

déponent adj. *Gram.* deponent. n.m. *Gram.* deponent.

dépopulation n.f. depopulation.

déportation n.f. deportation.

déporté, e p.p. and n.m.f. person condemned to deportation; convict.

déportement n.m. behavior, misconduct; *Auto.* swerve; lurch.

déporter v.t. to transport; to deport; to send to a concentration camp.

déposant, e adj. deposing; testifying, bearing witness. n.m.f. *Law.* deponent; depositer.

déposer v.t. to lay, to set, to put down; to lay aside, to deposit, to settle; to file (a complaint). v.i. (of a liquor) to leave a deposit; to settle; to depose; to give testimony; to bear witness; to copyright. se ~, to settle (dust, sediment).

dépositaire n.m.f. depositary; guardian, trustee.

déposition n.f. deposition, deposing; evidence. **faire une ~**, to give evidence.

déposséder v.t. to dispossess; to oust; to deprive of.

dépossession n.f. dispossession.

dépôt n.m. depositing, deposit; trust; depository; depot; warehouse; store; sediment. **faire un ~**, to make a deposit.

dépoter v.t. to decant (wine, liquors); to unpot (a plant).

dépotoir n.m. dump; garbage dump, dumping ground.

dépouille n.f. skin, hide; remains, mortal remains; effects (of deceased persons); crop (of grain, fruit, etc.), spoil, plunder, booty, prey. **la ~ d'un serpent**, the shed skin of a serpent. **la ~ mortelle**, mortal remains.

dépouillé, e *adj.* bare; stripped (of); unadorned; lacking in, without.

dépouillement *n.m.* despoiling; privation; relinquishment, renouncement; abstract (of accounts, etc.); summing up (of votes by ballot).

dépouiller *v.t.* to skin; to strip off; to lay bare; to pull off the clothes of, to throw off; to despoil, to rob; to gather, to reap (crops, etc.); to make an abstract (of accounts); to count up (votes). **on l'a dépouille de tous ses vêtements**, they pulled all his clothes off. **se ~,** *v.refl.* to cast, to shed its skin; to molt; to strip oneself.

dépourvu, e *adj.* unprovided (with); destitute, devoid, void (of). **au ~,** unawares.

dépravation *n.f.* depravation.

dépraver *v.t.* to deprave; to corrupt; to vitiate. **se ~,** *v.refl.* to become depraved.

dépréciation *n.f.* depreciation.

déprécier *v.t.* to depreciate; to undervalue, to underrate; to disparage. **~ une marchandise**, to depreciate goods. **se ~,** *v.refl.* to depreciate, to fall in value; to disparage one another.

déprédateur, trice *n.m.f.* depredator. *adj.* depredatory.

déprédation *n.f.* depredation; plunder.

déprendre *v.t.* to part, to separate. **se ~,** *v.refl.* to disengage oneself; to get free.

dépressif, ve *adj.* depressive.

dépression *n.f.* depression; dip; breakdown; slump. **~ nerveuse**, nervous breakdown. **~ économique**, slump.

déprimant, e *adj.* depressing.

déprime *n.f. Infml.* the blues.

déprimé, e *adj.* depressed, flattened, flat; low.

déprimer *v.t.* to depress, to abase; to humble; to disparage, to underrate. **se ~,** *v.refl.* to disparage each other; to be flattened.

dépuceler *v.t. Vulg.* to deflower.

depuis *prep.* from; since; after. **~ ce temps-là**, ever after. **~ peu**, recently. **~ quand?** how long? since when? *adv.* since; since then; ever since. **~ que**, since. **~ qu'elle est venue**, since she came.

députation *n.f.* deputation; deputyship.

député *n.m.* deputy, delegate, representative.

députer *v.t.* to depute; to delegate. *v.i.* to send a deputation.

déracinement *n.m.* uprooting, extirpation.

déraciner *v.t.* to uproot; to extirpate. **se ~,** *v.refl.* to be uprooted; to be eradicated.

déraillement *n.m.* derailment.

dérailler *v.i.* to run off the rails.

déraison *n.f.* unreason, unreasonableness, nonsense; folly.

déraisonnable *adj.* unreasonable, irrational; preposterous.

déraisonnablement *adv.* unreasonably, irrationally, preposterously.

déraisonner *v.i.* to talk nonsense, to wander, to rave.

dérangé, e *adj.* disordered; disturbed.

dérangement *n.m.* disorder, confusion; disturbance, indisposition.

déranger *v.t.* to bother; to displace; to put out of place; to disorder, to confuse; to unsettle, to disturb; to indispose. **je ne veux pas ~ ces personnes,** I do not wish to disturb these people. **se ~,** *v.refl.* to inconvenience oneself; to be embarrassed. **ne vous dérangez pas,** do not disturb yourself.

dératé, e *adj.* **courir comme un ~,** to run like the wind.

derechef *adv.* once more.

déréglé, e *adj.* irregular, out of order; inordinate, intemperate, dissolute, wild. **une machine ~e,** a machine out of order. **une vie ~e,** a dissolute life.

dérèglement *n.m.* disorder, dissoluteness, licentiousness, wildness. **vivre dans le ~,** to lead a disorderly life.

déréglément *adv.* disorderly, irregularly, wildly, dissolutely.

dérégler *v.t.* to put out of order, to disorder. **se ~,** *v.refl.* to get out of order; to become licentious; to go astray. **cette horloge s'est déréglée,** this clock is out of order.

dérider *v.t.* to unwrinkle, to smooth (the brow), to cheer up. **se ~,** *v.refl.* to cheer up.

dérision *n.f.* derision, mockery. **tourner en ~,** to ridicule.

dérisoire *adj.* mocking, laughable.

dérivatif, ive *adj.* derivative. *n.m.* derivative.

dérivation *n.f.* derivation.

dérive *n.f.* leeway, drift. **en ~,** adrift. **aller en ~,** to drift.

dérivé, e *adj.* and *n.m. Gram.* derivative.

dériver *v.i.* to leave the shore; to drift, to go adrift, to be derived; to originate. *v.t.* to derive.

dériveur *n.m.* storm sail; sailing dinghy.

dermatologie *n.f.* dermatology.

dermatologiste *n.m.f.* **dermatologue** *n.m.f.* dermatologist.

dermatose *n.f.* dermatosis.

derme *n.m.* skin, derma.

derne *n.m.* magpie.

dernier, iere *adj.* last; latest; (of two) latter; lowest; meanest; youngest; utmost; utter. **avant-~,** next to last. **on l'a traité avec le ~ mépris,** he was treated with the greatest scorn. **mettre la ~e main à,** to give the finishing stroke to. **rendre le ~ soupir,** to breathe one's last. **dimanche ~,** last Sunday. **arriver au ~ degré,** to attain the highest degree. *n.m.f.* last. **il est arrivé le ~,** he was the last to come. **jusqu'au ~,** to the last.

dernièrement *adv.* lately, recently.

dérobé, e *p.p.* stolen, spare; private, secret. **escalier ~,** backstairs, private staircase. **à la ~e,** stealthily, by stealth. **s'en aller à la ~e,** to steal away, to slink off.

dérober v.t. to steal, to rob, to filch, to pilfer, to purloin; to conceal; to screen, to shelter. se ~, v.refl. to steal away, to slink off, to shun. le vaisseau se déroba bientôt à la vue, we soon lost sight of the ship.

dérogation n.f. derogation.

dérogatoire adj. derogatory.

déroger v.i. to derogate; to detract from, to disparage, to condescend, to stoop.

dérouillée n.f. Infml. thrashing, belting.

dérouiller v.t. to rub off the rust of, to polish, to furbish; to brighten up. se ~, v.refl. to lose rust; to grow polished; to brighten up, to polish up, to freshen up one's memory.

déroulement n.m. unrolling; development; unfolding. pendant le ~, during the development of the case.

dérouler v.t. to unroll; to unfold, to display; Print. to run out (on a press); se ~, v.refl. to unroll; to be unrolled, to be unfolded; to spread out; to unfold itself; to occur, to happen, to take place; to uncoil; to unwind; to proceed. le film se déroule dans les années 50, the movie takes place in the 50s.

déroutant, e adj. disconcerting.

déroute n.f. rout; defeat, overthrow of an army; confusion; failure.

dérouter v.t. to lead astray; to confuse, to embarrass, to baffle. cette réponse le dérouta, this answer disconcerted him.

derrière Prep. and adv. behind; at the back of. regarder ~ soi, to look behind. n.m. back (of an object); backside, behind (anat.); Milit. rear. chambre de ~, back room. porte de ~, backdoor. couvrir, assurer ses ~s, to cover one's rear. par ~, from behind.

derviche n.m. dervish.

des, de les, of the; from the; some.

des Prep. from, since; as early as; as far back as; ever since; consequently; as long ago as. ~ le moyen âge, as far back as the Middle Ages. ~ qu'elle part, the minute she goes. ~ à present, immediately. ~ lors, from then, from now. ~ lors que, since, as. ~ que, as soon as, when.

désabusement n.m. disabusing, undeceiving; disillusionment.

désabuser v.t. to disabuse, to undeceive; to disillusion; to disappoint. se ~, v.refl. to be undeceived; to be disabused.

désaccord n.m. disagreement; discord; dissent; dissension, variance. être en ~, to be at variance. le ~ de deux instruments, two instruments out of tune with each other.

désaccorder v.t. to untune, to put out of tune. se ~, v.refl. to get out of tune.

désaccoupler v.t. to uncouple. se ~, v.refl. to get uncoupled.

désaccoutumer v.t. to break (of a habit). se ~, v.refl. to lose the habit; to get out of the habit (of).

désagréable adj. disagreeable, unpleasant.

désagréablement adv. disagreeably, unpleasantly.

désagrégation n.f. disaggregation.

désagréger v.t. to break up, to separate.

désagrément n.m. disagreeableness, unpleasantness; annoyance; inconvenience, discomfort. les ~s de notre état, the annoyances of our trade. s'attirer des ~s, to get into trouble.

désaimanter v.t. to demagnetize.

désaltérant, e adj. thirst-quenching; refreshing.

désaltérer v.t. to quench the thirst of. se ~, v.refl. to quench one's thirst.

désamorcer v.t. to defuse; to uncap; to unprime (gun).

désappointement n.m. disappointment.

désappointer v.t. to disappoint.

désapprendre v.t. to unlearn; to forget.

désapprobateur, trice adj. disapproving. n.m.f. disapprover; censor.

désapprobation n.f. disapprobation, disapproval.

désapprouver v.t. to disapprove, to disapprove of; to censure, to condemn.

désarçonner v.t. to dismount, to unhorse; to throw; to disconcert, to baffle, to foil, to run down.

désarmant, e adj. disarming.

désarmement n.m. disarming; unrigging.

désarmer v.t. to unarm; to disarm; to quell; to appease; to uncock (a gun); v.i. to disarm, to lay down arms. ~ la colère céleste, to appease divine wrath. se ~, v.refl. to unarm; to be disarmed.

désarroi n.m. disarray, disorder, confusion; overthrow.

désarticuler v.t. to disarticulate; to disjoint.

désassembler v.t. to take to pieces; to disjoint; to dismantle; to take apart.

désassorti, e adj. odd, not matched.

désassortir v.t. to unmatch, to break the set of, to spoil a collection of.

désastre n.m. disaster.

désastreusement adv. disastrously.

désastreux, euse adj. disastrous.

désattrister v.t. to cheer up.

désavantage n.m. disadvantage; prejudice, detriment, injury, damage. à son ~, to his disadvantage.

désavantager v.t. to disadvantage, to prejudice; to wrong.

désavantageusement adv. disadvantageously.

désavantageux, euse adj. disadvantageous, inconvenient; injurious, hurtful; detrimental.

désaveu n.m. disavowal; denial; disowning; disclaiming; recanting; retraction.

désavouer v.t. to disavow, to deny, to disown; to disclaim; to recant, to retract. ~ sa signature, to repudiate one's signature.

descellement n.m. unsealing, unfastening.

desceller v.t. to unseal; to unfasten.

descendance *n.f.* descent; lineage.

descendant, e *adj.* descending; descendant. **la marée ~e**, the ebb tide, the ebb; *Milit.* coming off, relieved. **garde ~e**, guard coming off duty, relieved guard. *n.m.f.* descendant; offspring.

descendre *v.i.* to descend; to move, come, go downward; to go down, to come down; to alight; to stay (at a hotel); to make a descent; to invade; to proceed from; to get off (bus, etc.). **~ de cheval**, to descend, to alight from horseback. **~ d'une famille illustre**, to descend from an illustrious family. **~ chez un ami**, to stay at a friend's house. *v.t.* to take down; to reach down; to bring down; to lower. **~ un tableau**, to take a picture down. **~ du vin à la cave**, to lower wine into the cellar. **l'omnibus me descend à ma porte**, the bus lets me out at my door.

descente *n.f.* descent, going down, coming down, getting down; alighting; declivity, slope; landing, disembarking; search raid (of the police). **la ~ des Goths en Italie**, the descent of the Goths into Italy. **~ de lit**, bedside carpet, rug.

descriptif, ive *adj.* descriptive.

description *n.f.* description.

désembarquement *n.m.* disembarkment; landing.

désembarquer *v.t.* to disembark; to put on shore.

désembourber *v.t.* to drag out, to get out of the mud. **se ~**, *v.refl.* to drag oneself out of the mud.

désemparer *v.t.* to leave, to quit. **s'occuper d'une chose sane ~**, to keep at a thing; not to rest. *v.t.* to leave, to quit.

désemplir *v.t.* to diminish the contents of, to make less full. *v.i.* to get empty. **se ~**, *v.refl.* to get empty, to get low.

désenchainer *v.t.* to unchain.

désenchantement *n.m.* disenchantment; disillusion.

désenchanter *v.t.* to disenchant; to disillusion.

désencombrer *v.t.* to clear, to free from rubbish; to disencumber.

désenfler *v.t.* to reduce the swelling of; to empty (a balloon). *v.i.* to become less swollen. **se ~**, *v.refl.* to become less swollen.

désengager *v.t.* to release from an obligation.

désenivrer *v.t.* to sober, to make sober. *v.i.* to get sober. **se ~**, *v.refl.* to get sober; to sober up.

désensabler *v.t.* to dig out of the sand; to dredge.

désensibiliser *v.t.* to desensitize.

désensorceler *v.t.* to disenchant.

désentraver *v.t.* to unfetter; to unshackle.

déséquilibre *n.m.* disequilibrium, imbalance; unbalance.

déséquilibré, e *adj.* unbalanced. *n.m.f.* unbalanced person.

déséquilibrer *v.t.* to unbalance.

désert, e *adj.* desert, wild, waste; unfrequented. *n.m.* desert; wilderness, waste; solitude, a lonely place. **prêcher dans le ~**, to preach to deaf ears.

déserter *v.t.* to desert, to leave; to abandon, to forsake. *v.i.* to desert; to quit, to leave; to fly off; to run away.

déserteur *n.m.* deserter.

désertion *n.f.* desertion.

désertique *adj.* barren, desert.

désespérance *n.f.* despair; hopelessness.

désespérant, e *adj.* disheartening, discouraging, dispiriting.

désespére, e *p.p. or adj.* desperate; hopeless; in despair; desponding; disheartened. *n.m.f.* desperate person, desperate. **courir, crier comme un ~**, to run, to shout like a madman.

désespérément *adv.* desperately, despairingly.

désespérer *v.i.* to despair; to lose all hope. **~ d'un malade**, to give up on a patient. *v.t.* to drive to despair; to cause to despair; to despair. **se ~**, *v.refl.* to despair, to be in despair; to give way to despair, to give oneself up to despair.

désespoir *n.m.* despair; hopelessness, desperation; despondency; vexation. **en ~ de cause**, as a last shift. **mettre au ~**, to vex, to concern, to grieve.

déshabillé *n.m.* state of undress; négligée.

déshabiller *v.t.* to undress; to disrobe; to strip. **~ saint Pierre pour habiller saint Paul**, to rob Peter to pay Paul. **se ~**, *v.refl.* to get undressed; to take off one's clothes; to strip.

déshabituer *v.t.* to unaccustom; to break (of a habit). **se ~**, *v.refl.* to get out of the habit (of).

désherbage *n.m.* weeding.

désherbant *n.m.* weed killer.

désherber *v.t.* to weed.

déshériter *v.t.* to disinherit.

déshonnète *adj.* immodest; dishonest.

déshonnètement *adv.* indecently, immodestly.

déshonnèteté *n.f.* indecency, immodesty.

déshonneur *n.m.* dishonor, disgrace, discredit.

déshonorant, e *adj.* dishonorable, disgraceful, discreditable.

déshonorer *v.t.* to dishonor; to disgrace, to bring shame upon; to seduce. **~ sa famille**, to disgrace one's family. **se ~**, *v.refl.* to dishonor, to disgrace oneself.

déshydratation *n.f.* dehydration.

déshydrater *v.t.* to dehydrate.

design *n.m.* design.

désignation *n.f.* designation, choice.

désigner *v.t.* to designate, to indicate; to point out; to mark out; to appoint; to choose. **~ le jour d'une vente**, to set the day for a sale.

désillusion *n.f.* disillusion.

désillusionner *v.t.* to free from illusions, to undeceive. **se ~**, *v.refl.* to lose one's illusions.

désincarner(se) *v.i.* to become disembodied, to leave the body.

désinence *n.f. Gram.* termination, ending.

désinfectant, e *adj.* disinfecting. *n.m.* disinfectant, deodorizer.

désinfecter *v.i.* to disinfect, to deodorize; to purify.

désinfection *n.f.* disinfection.

désintégrer *v.t.* to disintegrate. se ~, to split up, to disintegrate.

désintéressé, e *adj.* disinterested; unselfish; unbiased, impartial.

désintéressement *n.m.* disinterestedness; indifference.

désintéresser *v.t.* to disengage; to buy out (a person's interest); to indemnify. se ~, *v.refl.* to lose one's interest, to take no further interest; to become indifferent.

désintoxication *n.f.* detoxification.

désintoxiquer *v.t.* to detoxify.

désinvolte *adj.* casual, relaxed, free.

désinvolture *n.f.* unconstraint; ease.

désir *n.m.* desire; wish.

désirable *adj.* desirable.

désirer *v.i.* to desire; to wish for; to covet. **elle désire avec ardeur connaître la vérité,** she is longing to know the truth. **je désire que vous parliez,** I wish you to speak. **ne rien laisser à ~,** to leave nothing to be desired. **sa faire ~,** to play hard-to-get.

désireux, euse *adj.* desirous, anxious, eager.

désistement *n.m.* desistance; *Law.* nonsuit.

désister (se) *v.refl.* (with de) to desist (from), to give up, to abandon; to waive.

désobéir *v.i.* to disobey.

désobéissance *n.f.* disobedience.

désobéissant, e *adj.* disobedient; unsubmissive. *n.m.f.* disobedient person.

désobligeamment *adv.* disobligingly, unpleasantly.

désobligeance *n.f.* offensiveness.

désobligeant, e *adj.* disobliging; unkind, offensive; ungracious, unfriendly.

désobliger *v.t.* to disoblige; to offend; to displease.

désodorisant, e *adj. n.m.* deodorant.

désodoriser *v.t.* to deodorize.

désoeuvré, e *adj.* unoccupied, unemployed, idle. *n.m.f.* idler; a lazy person.

désoeuvrement *n.m.* inactivity, idleness.

désolant, e *adj.* distressing; discouraging; grievous; annoying; tiresome; provoking.

désolation *n.f.* desolation; devastation, destruction; disconsolateness; sadness; vexation, grief.

désolé, e *p.p. or adj.* desolate; solitary; disconsolate, grieved; annoyed; sorry.

désoler *v.t.* to desolate; to lay waste, to ravage; to distress, to afflict, to grieve; to vex, to annoy; to torment, to tease. se ~, *v.refl.* to grieve, to lament, to be disconsolate, to be distressed.

désolidariser (se) *v.t.* to disunite, separate.

désopilant, e *adj.* funny, comical, hilarious.

désordonné, e *adj.* disorderly; confused; dissolute, loose; wild. **mener une vie ~e,** to lead a disorderly life.

désordre *n.m.* disorder; confusion; disturbance,

uproar; dissension, discord; devastation; dissoluteness, licentiousness.

désorganisation *n.f.* disorganization.

désorganiser *v.t.* to disorganize. se ~, *v.refl.* to become disorganized.

désorienter *v.t.* to disorientate; to confuse; to bewilder, to disconcert, to puzzle. se ~, *v.refl.* to lose one's way; to be disconcerted.

désormais *adv.* henceforth, henceforward, hereafter, in the future; from now on.

désossement *n.m.* boning.

désosser *v.t.* to bone.

désoxydation *n.f.* deoxidation.

désoxyder *v.t.* to deoxidate.

despote *n.m.* despot. *adj.* despotic.

despotique *adj.* despotic.

despotiquement *adv.* despotically.

despotisme *n.m.* despotism.

desquels, desquelles contraction of de lesquels, de lesquelles.

dessaisir *v.t.* to dispossess of. se ~, *v.refl.* (with de) to relinquish; to part (with); to give up the possession (of).

dessaisissement *n.m.* parting with, relinquishment.

dessalé, e *p.p.* freshened, soaked; sharp, deep; unsalted, salt free. *n.m.f.* sharp fellow, sharp woman.

dessaler *v.t.* to freshen; to soak, to unsalt. se ~, *v.refl.* to freshen, to unsalt.

dessangler *v.t.* to ungirth.

desséchant, e *adj.* drying; withering; parching.

desséché, e *p.p.* dried; dried up; dessicated; dry; drained, withered.

dessèchement *n.m.* drying; drainage; draining; drying up.

dessécher *v.t.* to dry, to dry up; to drain, to exhaust; to parch; to wither; to emaciate, to waste. ~ **un marais,** to drain a marsh. ~ **le coeur,** to harden the heart. se ~, *v.refl.* to dry up, to wither; to become insensible. **son âme s'est desséchée,** he has become hard-hearted.

dessein *n.m.* design; project; scheme; purpose, aim, object, view; termination, resolution. **je suis venu à bout de mon ~,** I have accomplished my goal. **faire ~ de,** to intend, to design. **à ~,** on purpose. **dire quelque chose à ~,** to say a thing on purpose, intentionally. **à ~ de,** with the intent of, in order to. **à ~ que,** in order that. **j'aime assez ce ~,** I like that pattern.

desseller *v.t.* to unsaddle (a horse).

desserrer *v.t.* to loosen; to open; *Print.* to unlock (a form). ~ **les dents,** to open one's mouth; to speak. se ~, *v.refl.* to loosen, to come loose; to come undone.

dessert *n.m.* dessert.

desserte *n.f.* sideboard table.

desservir *v.t.* to remove, to take away (from a table); to clear the table; to serve poorly, to serve, to officiate; to stop; to run. **il m'a**

desservi auprès du ministre, he has spoken against me to the minister. **ce village n'est desservi que par une ligne d'autobus,** there is only one bus line in this village.

dessicatif, ive *adj.* desiccative.

dessiccation *n.f.* desiccation, drying.

dessiller *v.t.* to open, to unseal (the eyelids). **se ~,** *v.refl.* to open one's eyes.

dessin *n.m.* drawing; design; draft, sketch; outline; pattern; arrangement. **~ à main levée,** freehand drawing. **~ lavé,** washed (or shaded) drawing. **le ~ d'un châle,** the pattern of a shawl.

dessinateur, trice *n.m.f.* person who draws; cartoonist; draftsperson.

dessiner *v.t.* to draw; to design; to delineate, to sketch; to set off (a shape, figure). **se ~,** *v.refl.* to be delineated; to appear; to be visible; to loom. **les Alpes se dessinent à l'horizon,** the Alps are visible on the horizon.

dessouder *v.t.* to unsolder. **se ~,** *v.refl.* to come unsoldered.

dessoûler *v.t. Vulg.* to sober up, to make sober. *v.i. Vulg.* to get sober. **se ~,** *v.refl. Vulg.* to get sober.

dessous *adv.* under, underneath, below, beneath. **au-dessous de,** below; under. **au-dessous, en ~,** underneath. **par ~,** under. **ci-dessous,** beneath, below. **là-dessous,** beneath that, under there, below, underneath. *Prep.* under, underneath, beneath. **je l'ai cherché sur la table et il était ~,** I looked on the table for it and it was under it. *n.m.* under part, underside; bottom. **le ~ d'une table,** the under part of a table. **avoir le ~,** to get the worst of it.

dessus *adv.* above, on, upon, over. **sens ~-dessous,** upside down. **ci-dessus,** above. **au-dessus,** above, overhead. **au-dessus de,** above, over. **en ~,** on the top. **par-dessus,** over, upon. **par-dessus le marché,** on top of it all, into the bargain. *Prep.* on, upon, above, over. *n.m.* upper part, upper side, top. **le ~ de la tête,** the top (or crown) of the head. **le ~ d'un panier,** the upper crust, the best of the bunch. **avoir le ~,** to have the best of it. **prendre le ~,** to get the upper hand.

destin *n.m.* destiny, fate; lot, doom, fortune.

destinataire *n.m.f.* addressee; payee; consignee.

destination *n.f.* destination. **à ~ de,** bound for; (of a letter) addressed to.

destiné, e *p.p.* destined, appointed; bound for; (of a letter) addressed to.

destinée *n.f.* destiny, fate; lot, doom; career.

destiner *v.t.* to destine, to doom, to fate; to design, to appoint; to intend, to purpose; to reserve. **se ~,** *v.refl.* to be destined, to be intended. **il se destine à l'Eglise,** he is destined to the church.

destituer *v.t.* to dismiss.

destitution *n.f.* dismissal.

destrier *n.m.* steed, charger.

destroyer *n.m. Naut.* destroyer.

destructeur, trice *n.m.f.* destroyer. *adj.* destroying, destructive.

destructible *adj.* destructible.

destructif, ive. *adj.* destructive.

destruction *n.f.* destruction, destroying.

désuet, ète *adj.* outdated; old-fashioned; obsolete.

désuétude *n.f.* desuetude; discontinuance. **tomber en ~,** to grow obsolete.

désunion *n.f.* disunion; disjunction; *Fig.* discord.

désunir *v.t.* to disconnect; to disunite; to disjoin. **se ~,** *v.refl.* to be disjointed; to disunite.

détachable *adj.* detachable.

détachant *n.m.* stain remover.

détachement *n.m.* disengagement; indifference; detachment, group.

détacher *v.t.* to detach; to loose, to untie, to unbind; to undo; to separate, to disengage; to play staccato; to clean, to take the spots out of. **~ un chien,** to untie a dog, to let a dog loose. **se ~,** *v.refl.* to get loose; to get free; to come undone, untied, unfastened; to be detached, to detach oneself. **se ~ d'un parti,** to be separated from a group.

détail *n.m.* detail; particular; circumstance; retail, item. **le ~ d'un compte,** the items of an account. **donner le ~ exact d'une affaire,** to give a detailed account of an affair. **vendre en ~,** to sell retail.

détaillant, e *adj.* retail. *n.m.f.* retailer, retail dealer.

détailler *v.t.* to retail; to detail. **~ une histoire,** to relate a story in detail.

détaler *v.t.* to scamper away, to run off.

détartrage *n.m.* scaling.

détartrer *v.t.* to scale.

détaxe *n.f.* reduction of a tax.

détaxer *v.t.* to reduce (a tax).

détecter *v.t.* to detect.

détecteur, trice *adj.* detecting; *n.m.* detector.

détection *n.f.* detection.

détective *n.m.* detective.

déteindre *v.t.* to take out the color of. *v.i.* to lose its color, to fade. **se ~,** *v.refl.* to lose its color; to change color.

dételage *n.m.* unyoking; unharnessing; uncoupling.

dételer *v.t.* to unyoke (oxen); to ease off, to give up (doing something).

détendre *v.t.* to unbend; to unstring; to loosen, to slacken; to relax; to ease; to expand. **~ un arc,** to unbend a bow. **~ son esprit,** to relax one's mind. **se ~,** *v.refl.* to unbend, to relax; to loosen; to be slackened; to become milder.

détendu, e *adj.* relaxed; unbent.

détenir *v.t.* to detain; to withhold, to keep back.

détente *n.f.* trigger (of a gun); détente; easing; recreation; spring; improvement. **une ~ inter-**

nationale s'est produite, there has been an international easing of tension; relaxation.

détenteur, trice n.m.f. holder; detainer.

détention n.f. Law. detention; confinement, imprisonment. ~ **préventive**, custody (suspect). ~ **arbitraire**, false imprisonment. **maison de** ~, prison.

détenu, e p.p. detained; withheld; confined. n.m.f. prisoner.

détergent, e adj. detergent; cleansing. n.m. detergent.

détérioration n.f. deterioration; damage.

détériorer v.t. to deteriorate; to impair; to damage; to spoil; to deface. **se** ~, v.refl. to deteriorate; to get spoiled.

déterminable adj. determinable.

déterminant, e adj. determinative; decisive.

détermination n.f. determination, resolution. **prendre une** ~, to come to a determination.

déterminé, e adj. definite, fixed; determined, positive; resolved on; resolute; bold.

déterminer v.t. to determine; to settle; to decide; to rule; to cause, to occasion. **se** ~, v.refl. to determine, to resolve; to make up one's mind.

déterré, e p.p. unearthed; disinterred. n.m. disinterred corpse. **avoir l'air d'un** ~, to look like a corpse.

déterrer v.t. to dig up; to unearth; to disinter, to exhume; to find out; to bring to light.

détestable adj. detestable; wretched; hateful; vile; execrable; odious; foul.

détester v.t. to detest; to abhor; to hate, to dislike. **elle déteste cet homme,** she can't stand this man.

détonant, e adj. detonating. n.m. explosive.

détonation n.f. detonation; report.

détoner v.i. to detonate.

détonner v.i. to sing out of tune; to jar.

détordre v.t. to untwist; to undo. **se** ~, v.refl. to come untwisted.

détortiller v.t. to untwist (a string, a lace, etc.); to unravel. **se** ~, v.refl. to come untwisted.

détour n.m. circuit; turn; detour, deviation; roundabout way. **parler sans** ~, to speak straightforwardly. **faire un** ~, to go the long way around.

détourné, e adj. unfrequented, indirect; roundabout.

détournement n.m. turning aside; embezzlement. ~ **de mineur,** abduction of a minor. ~ **d'avion,** hijacking.

détourner v.t. to turn aside; to change (the conversation); to ward off; to embezzle. ~ **quelqu'un du droit chemin,** to lead a person astray. **il détourna la tête pour ne pas me voir,** he turned his head away so as not to see me. ~ **des fonds,** to embezzle funds. v.t. to turn off, to turn; to hijack (plane); to distract. **il a détourné attention,** he has distracted their attention. ~ **la conversation,** to change the subject. **se** ~, v.refl. to go out of one's

way; to deviate, to turn off; to turn aside.

détracteur n.m. detractor; defamer. adj. n.m. detractive, disparaging.

détraqué, e adj. out of order; mad.

détraquement n.m. derangement; disorder.

détraquer v.t. to disorder, to derange; to put out of order; to throw into confusion; to upset. **se** ~, v.refl. to get out of order; to break up; to get disordered; to fall into confusion. **ma montre s'est détraquée,** my watch has gone out of order.

détremper v.t. to dilute; to render liquid or thin; to soak. **la pluie a détrempé les chemins,** the rain has soaked the roads. **se** ~, v.refl. to be diluted; to soak; to be weakened; to soften.

détresse n.f. distress; misery.

détriment n.m. detriment; prejudice, damage. **au** ~ **de,** to the detriment of.

détritus n.m. detritus; debris.

détroit n.m. strait, straits.

détromper v.t. to undeceive. **se** ~, v.refl. to be undeceived.

détrôner v.t. to dethrone.

détruire v.t. to destroy; to pull down, to demolish, to overthrow; to subvert; to ruin; to impair. **la ville a été détruite de fond en comble,** the town was razed to the ground. **la vérité détruit l'erreur,** truth annihilates error. **se** ~, v.refl. to destroy oneself; to kill each other; to fall to decay, to fall to ruin.

dette n.f. debt; duty; obligation.

deuil n.m. mourning; grief, sorrow. **prendre le** ~, to go into mourning. **faire son** ~ **d'une chose,** to give up a thing for lost.

deux adj. two. ~ **fois,** twice. ~ **à,** two by two. **tous les** ~, both. **tous les** ~ **jours,** every other day. **c'est à** ~ **pas d'ici,** it's a couple of steps from here. **j'ai** ~ **mots à lui dire,** I want to have a word with him/her. n.m. two; second; **deuce** (at cards). **double-**~, two deuces.

deuxième adj. second. **le** ~ **étage,** the second floor; U.S. third floor.

deuxièmement adv. secondly.

deux-mâts n.m. Naut. two-master.

deux-points n.m.pl. Gram. colon.

dévaler v.t. to go down. v.i. to go down; to run down.

dévaliser v.t. to rob, to strip.

dévalorisation n.f. loss in value, depreciation.

dévaloriser v.t. to depreciate; **se** ~, to depreciate, to lose value.

dévaluation n.f. devaluation.

dévaluer v.t. to devaluate.

devancer v.t. to precede; to go before; to outrun; to outstrip; to be ahead of, to forestall. ~ **quelqu'un à la course,** to outrun a person. ~ **son époque,** to be ahead of one's time.

devancier, ère n.m.f. predecessor. pl. predecessors, forefathers.

devant prep. before; in front of, opposite to, over against; near to the front of; Naut. ahead

of. **assis ~ le feu,** sitting in front of the fire.
aller ~ soi, to go straight ahead. *adv.* before;
ahead. *n.m.* front, forepart. **le ~ d'un edifice,**
the front of a building. *Infml.* **batir sur le ~,** to
grow stout. **prendre les ~s,** to go before; to
forestall. **aller au-~ de quelqu'un,** to go meet
a person.

devanture *n.f.* front. **~ de boutique,** shopfront.

dévastateur, trice *adj.* devastating; destructive.
~trice. *n.m.f.* desolator, destroyer.

dévastation *n.f.* devastation; destruction.

dévaster *v.t.* to devastate; to lay waste.

déveine *n.f.* run of bad luck.

développement *n.m.* development, growth,
expansion; unfolding; unwrapping; developing
(photo); *Geol.* evolution.

développer *v.t.* to unwrap, to uncover; to unfold;
to develop; to explain; to unravel. **se ~,** *v.refl.* to
be unwrapped; to be unfolded; to develop oneself; to grow; to expand, to enlarge; to spread
out. **cet enfant se developpe,** that child is
growing.

devenir *v.i.* to become, to get, to grow, to turn, to
be. **~ pouvre,** to become poor. **~ pâle,** to turn
pale. **que deviendrai-je?** what will become of
me?

dévergondage *n.m.* shamelessness; licentiousness; eccentricity.

dévergondé, e *adj.* shameless; licentious. *n.m.f.*
shameless person.

dévergonder *v.t.* to render shameless. **se ~,**
v.refl. to become shameless, to lose all sense of
shame.

déverrouiller *v.t.* to unbolt (a door).

devers *prep.* toward, to; near, by. **par ~ soi,** in
one's possession; for oneself.

déversement *n.m.* pouring.

déverser *v.t.* to pour. *v.i.* to pour, to flow, to run
over; to discharge; to dump. **~ sa colère,** to
pour out one's anger. **se ~,** *v.refl.* to flow, to run.
les eaux se deversèrent dans le canal, the
waters flowed into the canal.

déversoir *n.m. Hydraul.* overflow.

dévêtir *v.t.* to undress. **se ~,** *v.refl.* to get
undressed.

déviation *n.f.* deviation.

dévidoir *n.m.* winder; reel.

dévier *v.i.* to deviate; to swerve, to stray. **se ~,**
v.refl. to deviate, to swerve.

devin, devineresse *n.m.f.* seer, diviner,
soothsayer.

deviner *v.t.* to divine; to foretell, to predict; to
conjecture; to guess. **~ une énigme, une charade,** to guess a riddle, a charade.

devinette *n.f.* riddle, puzzle.

devis *n.m. Infml.* talk; estimate (of costs, etc.).
~ approximatif, rough estimate.

dévisager *v.t.* to disfigure; to stare at rudely. **se
~,** *v.refl.* to stare rudely at each other.

devise *n.f.* device; emblem; motto; *Fin.* currency.
~ étrangère, foreign currency.

deviser *v.t.* to chat; to converse.

dévisser *v.t.* to unscrew.

de visu *adv.* witnessed with one's own eyes.

dévitaliser *v.t.* to devitalize; to kill the nerve of
(tooth, etc.).

dévoilement *n.m.* unveiling; disclosure;
revelation.

dévoiler *v.t.* to unveil; to disclose, to discover, to
unravel; to reveal. **se ~,** *v.refl.* to unveil oneself;
to be discovered, to be disclosed.

devoir *v.t.* to owe; to be in debt; to be obliged; to
be indebted, (followed by an infinitive) must,
ought, should; to be. **je lui dois cent francs,** I
owe him a hundred francs. **qui doit a tort,** a
debtor is always in the wrong. **il aurait dû
venir,** he should have come. **nous devons dire
la vérité,** we ought to speak the truth. **tous les
hommes doivent mourir,** all men must die. **le
devais le voir hier,** I was supposed to see him
yesterday. **se ~,** *v.refl.* to owe to oneself. **se ~ à
sa patrie,** to have a duty to one's country. *n.m.*
duty; obligation; task, exercise, homework,
assignment. **faire son ~,** to do one's duty. **se
mettre en ~ de,** to set about, to prepare for, to
prepare to. **les derniers ~s,** funeral rites. **un ~
difficile,** a difficult task.

dévolu, e *adj.* vested; devolved, transferred.
procès ~ à la cour, a cause belonging to the
court. **jeter son ~ sur,** to fix one's mind upon.

dévolution *n.f. Law.* devolution.

dévorant, e *adj.* devouring; ravenous; consum-
ing; destroying; wasting. **soif ~e,** burning
thirst.

dévorer *v.t.* to devour; to eat up, to swallow
down; to consume, to destroy; to squander, to
run through, to waste; to enjoy with avidity; to
pore over, to gaze at. **l'orgueil dévore cet
homme,** that man is consumed with pride.

dévoreur, euse *n.m.f.* devourer.

dévot, e *adj.* devout; godly. *n.m.f.* devout person,
religious person.

dévotement *adv.* devoutly.

dévotion *n.f.* devotion. **pratiques de ~,** performance of religious duties. **faire ses ~s,** to perform one's devotions.

dévoué, e *adj.* devoted, faithful, dedicated.

dévouement *n.m.* devotion, devotedness; self-
sacrifice.

dévouer *v.t.* to devote; to dedicate. **se ~,** *v.refl.* to
devote oneself; to give oneself up. **se ~ à son
pays,** to devote oneself to one's country.

dévoyer *v.t.* to mislead, to lead astray. **se ~,** *v.refl.*
to lose one's way; to go astray; to swerve.

dextérité, *n.f.* dexterity, dexterousness, adroitness, skill.

diabète *n.m.* diabetes.

diabètique *adj.* diabetic.

diable *n.m.* devil; wretch; fellow. **tirer le ~ par
la queue,** to be hard up. **un bon ~,** a good sort
of fellow. **un pauvre ~,** a poor devil. **avoir le ~
au corps,** to be full of the devil. **envoyer à**

tous les ~s, to send to the devil. que le ~ vous emporte! the devil take you! cela ne vaut pas le ~, that is not worth a thing. une affaire du ~, a most troublesome affair. *Interj.* rats! darn! que ~ avez-vous? what on earth is the matter with you?

diablement *adv.* devilishly, excessively.

diablerie *n.f.* witchcraft; devilry; mischief.

diablesse *n.f.* she-devil.

diablotin *n.m.* imp, young devil; cracker (party favor); jack-in-the-box.

diabolique *adj.* diabolical, devilish.

diaboliquement *adv.* diabolically.

diadème *n.m.* diadem.

diagnostic *n.m.* diagnostic.

diagnostique *adj.* diagnostic; characteristic.

diagnostiquer *v.t.* to diagnose.

diagonal *adj.* diagonal. *n.f.* diagonal.

diagonalement *adv.* diagonally.

diagramme *n.m.* diagram.

dialecte *n.m.* dialect.

dialectique *adj.* dialectic, dialectical; logical. *n.f.* dialectic, dialectics.

dialectiquement *adv.* dialectically.

dialogue *n.m.* dialogue.

dialoguer *v.i.* to converse.

dialyse *n.f.* dialysis.

diamant *n.m.* diamond.

diamantaire *n.m.* diamond cutter; diamond merchant.

diamétral, e *adj.* diametrical.

diamétralement *adv.* diametrically.

diamètre *n.m.* diameter.

diapason *n.m. Mus.* diapason; tuning fork; pitch. se mettre au ~, to be in tune.

diaphane *adj.* diaphanous, transparent, translucent.

diaphragme *n.m.* diaphragm; midriff.

diapositive, diapo *n.f.* slide (photo), transparency.

diapré, e *p.p.* dappled, variegated.

diaprer *v.t.* to dapple, to variegate, to diversify. se ~, *v.refl.* to become variegated.

diaprure *n.f.* variegation.

diarrhée *n.f.* diarrhea.

diaspora *n.f.* diaspora.

diastase *n.f.* diastasis.

diastole *n.f.* diastole.

diastyle *n.m.* diastyle.

diathermie *n.f.* diathermy, diathermia.

diatomique *adj.* diatomic.

diatonique *adj.* diatonic.

diatribe *n.f.* diatribe.

dichotomie *n.f.* dichotomy.

dichromatique *adj.* dichromatic.

dico *n.m. Infml.* dictionary.

dicotyledone *adj.* dicotyledonous.

dictaphone *n.m.* dictaphone.

dictateur *n.m.* dictator.

dictatorial, e *adj.* dictatorial.

dictature *n.f.* dictatorship.

dictée *n.f.* dictation. écrire sous la ~, to write from dictation.

dicter *v.t.* to dictate, to suggest, to prompt; to prescribe, to command.

diction *n.f.* diction; style; elocution, delivery, utterance.

dictionnaire *n.m.* dictionary.

dicton *n.m.* saying, maxim, proverb.

didactique *adj.* didactic. *n.m.* didactic language, didactic style. *n.f.* didactics.

dièdre *adj.* dihedral. *n.m.* dihedron.

dierèse *n.f.* dieresis.

dièse *n.f. Mus.* sharp.

diesel *n.m.* diesel.

dièser *v.t. Mus.* to sharp, to make higher by a semitone.

diète *n.f.* diet; regimen; abstinence.

diététicien, ne *n.m.f.* dietician.

diététique *adj.* dietetical. *n.f.* dietetics *pl.*

dieu *n.m.* God. le bon ~, God Almighty, the good Lord. porter le bon ~, to carry the Holy Sacrament. plaise à ~! please God! à ~ ne plaise! God forbid! pour l'amour de ~, for God's sake.

diffamant, e *adj.* defamatory; slanderous, libelous.

diffamateur, trice *n.m.f.* defamer; slanderer, libeler.

diffamation *n.f.* defamation, slander.

diffamatoire *adj.* defamatory; slanderous, libelous.

diffamer *v.t.* to defame, to slander, to libel.

différé, e *adj.* delayed; deferred; (pre-) recorded.

différemment *adv.* differently.

différence *n.f.* difference; distinction, discrepancy, disparity.

différenciation *n.f.* differentiation.

différencier *v.t.* to distinguish; to make a difference between.

différend *n.m.* difference, quarrel, dispute, debate; disagreement.

différent, e *adj.* different; unlike, dissimilar; various, contrary.

différentiel, elle *adj.* differential. *n.f.* differential.

différer *v.t.* to defer, to delay, to put off, to postpone. *v.i.* to defer, to delay, to put off, to procrastinate; to differ; to be different, to be unlike.

difficile *adj.* difficult; hard; arduous; particular, fastidious. un problème ~, a difficult problem. un chemin ~, a heavy road. un homme ~, a man hard to please.

difficilement *adv.* with difficulty.

difficulté *n.f.* difficulty; obstacle, impediment, hindrance. faire des ~s, to raise objections.

difforme *adj.* deformed; ugly; distorted.

difformité *n.f.* deformity; disfigurement.

diffraction *n.f.* diffraction.

diffus, e *adj.* diffuse; prolix; verbose, wordy.

diffusément *adv.* diffusely; verbosely; wordily.

diffuser *v.t.* to diffuse; to spread; to circulate; to broadcast.

diffusion *n.f.* diffusion.

digérer *v.t.* to digest; to think over, to reflect upon; to endure. *v.i.* to digest. **se ~,** *v.refl.* to be digested.

digestible *adj.* digestible.

digestif, ive *adj.* digestive. *n.m.* digestive.

digestion *n.f.* digestion.

digital, e *adj.* digital.

digitale *n.f.* digitalis, foxglove.

digitaline *n.f.* digitaline.

digne *adj.* worthy; deserving, meritorious; dignified. **une conduite ~ d'éloges,** conduct worthy of praise.

dignement *adv.* worthily; deservedly; suitably; with dignity.

dignitaire *n.m.* dignitary.

dignité *n.f.* dignity; importance. **monter en ~,** to rise in rank. **un air de ~,** a dignified look.

digression *n.f.* digression.

digue *n.f.* dike, dam; mound, embankment; barrier, obstacle.

diktat *n.m.* dictate.

dilapidateur, trice *adj.* dilapidating, wasteful, extravagant. *n.m.f.* dilapidator; waster, squanderer.

dilapidation *n.f.* dilapidation, waste.

dilapider *v.t.* to dilapidate, to waste, to squander.

dilatabilite *n.f.* dilatability.

dilatable *adj.* dilatable.

dilatant, e *adj.* dilating, dilative.

dilatation *n.f.* dilatation, expansion; distention; *Surg.* enlargement.

dilater *v.t.* to dilate; to enlarge, to distend. **se ~,** *v.refl.* to dilate, to expand; to swell.

dilatoire *adj.* dilatory.

dilemme *n.m.* dilemma.

dilettante *n.m.* dilettante.

dilettantisme *n.m.* dilettantism.

diligemment *adv.* diligently; carefully, expeditiously, speedily, promptly.

diligence *n.f.* diligence; assiduity, care; *Jurisp.* suit; proceedings; promptness; stagecoach.

diligent, e *adj.* diligent; careful, assiduous, industrious, quick.

diluer *v.t.* to dilute. **se ~,** *v.refl.* to become diluted.

dilution *n.f.* dilution.

diluvien, enne *adj.* diluvian, diluvial.

diluvium *n.m. Geol.* diluvium.

Dimanche *n.m.* Sunday. **~ de Pâques,** Easter Sunday. **~ des Rameaux,** Palm Sunday.

dimension *n.f.* dimension; measurement.

diminuer *v.t.* to diminish, to lessen, to abate; to decrease; to shorten. *v.i.* to diminish; to lessen, to shorten; to decrease. **se ~,** to lower oneself.

diminutif, ive *adj.* diminutive. *n.m.* diminutive.

diminution *n.f.* diminution; lessening; decrease; abatement; deduction; reduction.

dimorphe *adj.* dimorphous.

dinde *n.f.* turkey, ninny.

dindon *n.m.* turkey; ninny.

dindonneau *n.m.* young turkey.

diner *v.i.* to dine. **~ en ville,** to dine out. *n.m.* dinner.

dingue *adj.* nuts, crazy, loony. *n.m.f.* nutcase, nut.

dinosaure *n.m.* dinosaur.

diocésain, aine *adj. n.m.f.* diocesan.

diocèse *n.m.* diocese.

diode *n.f.* diode.

dioptrie *n.f.* diopter.

dioptrique *n.f.* dioptrics. *adj.* dioptric.

diorama *n.m.* diorama.

dioxyde *n.m.* dioxide.

diphasé, e *adj.* diphase.

diphtérie *n.f.* diphtheria.

diphtongue *n.f. Gram.* diphthong.

diplodocus *n.m.* diplodocus.

diplomate *n.m.* diplomat. *adj.* diplomatic.

diplomatie *n.f.* diplomacy; diplomatic service.

diplomatique *adj.* diplomatic. **le corps ~,** the diplomatic corps. *n.f.* diplomacy.

diplomatiquement *adv.* diplomatically.

diplôme *n.m.* diploma.

diplômé, e *adj.* certified. *n.m.f.* holder of a diploma or certificate.

diplômer *v.i.* to grant a diploma, to award a certificate.

diplopie *n.f.* diplopia.

dipsomane *adj.* dipsomaniacal. *n.m.f.* dipsomaniac.

diptyques *n.m.pl.* diptych.

dire *v.t.* to say; to tell, to speak; to state; to express; to write; to recite; to name; to utter. **~ un mot,** to say a word. **sans mot ~,** without saying a word. **~ la vérité,** to speak the truth, to tell the truth. **~ du bien de,** to speak well of. **~ des injures à quelqu'un,** to call a person names. **on m'a dit que,** I have been told that. **comme on dit,** as the saying goes. **on dirait qu'il va pleuvoir,** it looks as if it were going to rain. **que voulez-vous ~?** what do you mean? **si le coeur vous en dit,** if you feel like it. **cela va sans ~,** that goes without saying. **voilà qui est dit,** that's settled. **pour ainsi ~,** so to say; as it were. **qui ne dit mot consent,** silence implies consent. **se ~,** *v.refl.* to be spoken; to be said; to profess to be, to call oneself. *n.m.* say, saying; declaration, statement; report; allegation. **au ~ de tout le monde,** by everybody's account. **au ~ des chercheurs,** according to researchers.

direct, e *adj.* direct; straight, private (link, connection). **ligne ~e,** private line. **il y a un rapport ~ entre ces deux meurtres,** there is a link between these two murders.

directement *adv.* directly; straight; exactly.

directeur, trice *adj.* managing; leading; guiding. *n.m.f.* director; manager; guide; governor (of a prison); principal (school).

direction *n.f.* direction, directorship; guidance; management, way. **dans quelle ~ va-t-elle?**, where is she heading? **la bonne ~**, the right way. **elle est en charge de la ~ de la compagnie**, she is in charge of the management of the company. **se plaindre à la direction**, to make a complaint to the management.

directive *n.f.* directive; instruction, order.

directorial, e *adj.* directorial.

dirigeable that can be directed. **ballon ~**, navigable balloon, dirigible.

dirigéant, e *adj.* directing, leading. *n.m.f.* leader, ruler, manager; director.

diriger *v.t.* to direct; to lead, to guide; to manage. **se ~**, *v.refl.* to direct one's steps (toward), to proceed (to), to direct or guide oneself.

discal, e *adj., m.pl.* **hernie discale**, *Med.* slipped disk.

discernement *n.m.* discernment; judgment, discerning. **L'age de ~**, years of discretion.

discerner *v.t.* to discern; to distinguish; to see, to perceive, to distinguish, to discriminate.

disciple *n.m.* disciple; pupil, scholar; follower.

disciplinable *adj.* disciplinable.

disciplinaire *adj.* disciplinary.

discipline *n.f.* discipline, order; correction, punishment.

discipliner *v.t.* to discipline; to train; to punish. **se ~**, *v.refl.* to become disciplined.

discontinu, e *adj.* discontinuous.

discontinuer *v.t.* to discontinue; to interrupt, to leave off; to break off. *v.i.* to discontinue, to interrupt, to cease.

discontinuité *n.f.* discontinuity, discontinuation.

disconvenir *v.i.* to deny, to disown; not to admit.

discordance *n.f.* discordance; disagreement; *Mus.* discord, dissonance.

discordant, e *adj.* discordant; dissonant, unharmonious, jarring; harsh, unmusical; not in tune.

discorde *n.f.* discord; dissension, strife.

discorder *v.i.* to disagree; to be dissonant, to be discordant.

discothèque *n.f.* record collection; record library; disco(thèque).

discourir *v.i.* to discourse, to converse.

discours *n.m.* discourse, conversation; speech. **pronouncer un ~**, to make a speech. **les parties de ~**, the parts of speech.

discourtois, e *adj.* discourteous; unmannerly; uncivil.

discourtoisement *adv.* discourteously.

discourtoisie *n.f.* discourtesy.

discredit *n.m.* discredit, disrepute; disfavor, disgrace.

discréditer *v.t.* to discredit; to bring into disrepute; to disgrace.

discret, ète *adj.* discreet; reserved; modest; silent; quiet; plain; simple.

discrètement *adv.* discreetly; quietly; gently.

discrètion *n.f.* discretion, tact. **s'en remettre à la ~ de quelqu'un**, to trust to a person's discretion. **à ~**, unlimited. **le garçon nous apporte du vin à ~**, the waiter is bringing us as much wine as we want.

discrimination *n.f.* discrimination.

discriminatoire *adj.* discriminatory, discriminating.

discriminer *v.t.* to discriminate, to distinguish.

disculpation *n.f.* exculpation.

disculper *v.t.* to exculpate, to justify, to clear. **se ~**, *v.refl.* to exonerate oneself, to clear oneself.

discursif, ive *adj.* discursive.

discussion *n.f.* discussion, argument.

discutable *adj.* disputable, questionable.

discuter *v.t.* to discuss, to debate, to argue. **~ un projet de loi**, to debate a bill.

disert, e *adj.* voluble, fluent; eloquent.

disette *n.f.* dearth; scarcity; want, need, penury.

diseur, euse *n.m.f.* teller, talker. **diseuse de bonne aventure**, fortuneteller.

disgrâce *n.f.* disgrace, disfavor.

disgracié, e *p.p.* disgraced; out of favor; in disgrace.

disgracier *v.t.* to disgrace.

disgracieusement *adv.* ungracefully; awkwardly.

disgracieux, euse *adj.* awkward, ungraceful.

disjoindre *v.t.* to disjoin, to separate; *Law.* to sever. **se ~**, *v.refl.* to become separated.

disjonctif, ive *adj.* *Gram.* disjunctive.

disjonction *n.f.* separation.

dislocation *n.f.* dislocation.

disloquer *v.t.* to dislocate; to put out of joint. **se ~**, *v.refl.* to be dislocated, to be put out of joint.

disparaître *v.i.* to disappear; to vanish; to pass away; to die; to be lost; to eliminate. **il l'a fait ~**, he got rid of him/her, he eliminated him/her.

disparate *n.f.* incongruity. *adj.* disparate; unlike; incongruous.

disparité *n.f.* disparity; unlikeness; inequality.

disparition *n.f.* disappearance, disappearing.

disparu, e *adj.* vanished, lost, departed; dead; deceased, extinct. **porté ~**, reported missing. *n.m.f.* deceased, dead, departed; missing soldier.

dispendieusement *adv.* expensively.

dispendieux, euse *adj.* expensive, costly.

dispensaire *n.m.* dispensary; welfare center.

dispensateur, trice *n.m.f.* dispenser, distributor.

dispense *n.f.* dispensation; exemption; permission; license.

dispenser *v.t.* to dispense; to deal out, to distribute; to bestow. **se ~**, *v.refl.* to be dispensed, to be distributed; to exempt oneself (from).

disperser *v.t.* to disperse; to spread, to scatter. **se ~**, *v.refl.* to disperse; to be dispersed, to be scattered.

dispersion *n.f.* dispersion; scattering.

disponibilité *n.f.* availability; available funds; liquid assets. **en ~**, unattached (as an officer).

disponible *adj.* available. *n.m.* disposable funds; cash in hand.

dispos *adj. n.m.* refreshed.

disposer *v.i.* to dispose; to arrange; to order, to lay out; to prepare, to make ready; to make fit; to incline, to induce. **~ un jardin avec art,** to arrange a garden tastefully. *v.i.* to dispose; to settle, to ordain. **se ~,** *v.refl.* to be disposed, arranged, ordered, placed; to arrange oneself; to prepare oneself.

dispositif *n.m.* device, mechanism. **~ de défense,** defense system. **un ~ policier,** a police operation.

disposition *n.f.* disposition; disposal, arrangement; order; plan of a work; arrangement of troops; frame of mind, temper. **être en bonne ~,** to be in a right state of mind, to be well. **tout est à votre ~,** everything is at your disposal.

disproportion *n.f.* disproportion.

disproportionné, e *adj.* disproportionate; out of proportion; inadequate.

dispute *n.f.* dispute, discussion; quarrel.

disputer *v.i.* to dispute; to argue, to debate; to quarrel, to wrangle. *v.t.* to dispute. **~ la victoire,** to dispute the victory. **se ~,** *v.refl.* to quarrel, to wrangle.

disquaire *n.m.* record dealer.

disqualification *n.f.* disqualification.

disqualifier *v.t.* to disqualify; to discredit.

disque *n.m.* disc; discus; *Mus.* record. **~ laser,** compact disc, CD.

dissection *n.f.* dissection.

dissemblable *adj.* dissimilar, unlike, different.

dissemblance *n.f.* dissimilitude, dissimilarity, unlikeness.

dissémination *n.f.* dissemination, dispersion; diffusion.

disséminer *v.t.* to desseminate; to scatter; to spread.

dissension *n.f.* dissension; discord.

dissentiment *n.m.* disagreement.

disséquer *v.t.* to dissect.

dissertation *n.f.* dissertation, essay.

disserter *v.i.* to discourse; to write an essay.

dissidence *n.f.* dissent, disagreement, dissidence.

dissident, e *adj.* dissenting, dissident. *n.m.f.* dissident, dissenter.

dissimilitude *n.f.* dissimilitude, unlikeness, dissimilarity.

dissimulateur, trice *n.m.f.* dissembler.

dissimulation *n.f.* dissimulation; concealment.

dissimulé, e *adj.* dissembling; secretive; hidden.

dissimuler *v.t.* to dissemble; to conceal; to disguise. *v.i.* to dissemble, to feign. **se ~,** *v.refl.* to be concealed, to be hidden.

dissipateur, trice *n.m.f.* spendthrift; squanderer, waster. *adj.* wasteful, extravagant.

dissipation *n.f.* dissipation, squandering; waste, wastefulness; recreation; inattention. **vivre dans la ~,** to lead a dissolute life.

dissiper *v.t.* to dissipate; to scatter; to disperse, to dispel; to squander, to waste; to run through.

le soleil dissipe les ténèbres, the sun dispels darkness. **~ sa jeunesse,** to waste one's youth. **se ~,** *v.refl.* to be dissipated, to be dispersed; to be squandered, to waste away; to divert oneself.

dissociable *adj.* dissociable.

dissociation *n.f.* dissociation, separation.

dissocier *v.t.* to dissociate. **se ~,** to dissociate oneself.

dissolu, e *adj.* dissolute.

dissoluble *adj.* dissolvable, dissoluble, (substance) soluble.

dissolument *adv.* dissolutely.

dissolution *n.f.* dissolution; breaking-up; decomposition.

dissolvant, e *adj.* solvent. *n.m.* solvent; nail-polish remover.

dissonance *n.f.* dissonance, discord.

dissonant, e *adj.* dissonant, discordant, unharmonious.

dissoudre *v.t.* to dissolve; to melt, to liquify; to ruin; to destroy; to annul. **se ~,** *v.refl.* to dissolve; to melt; to be dissolved.

dissuader *v.t.* to dissuade.

dissuasif, ive *adj.* dissuasive.

dissuasion *n.f.* dissuasion.

dissyllabe *adj.* dissyllabic. *n.m.* dissyllable.

dissyllabique *adj.* dissyllabic.

dissymétrie *n.f.* dissymmetry.

distance *n.f.* distance; respect, reserve; gap. **la ~ séparant deux générations,** the gap separating two generations. **tenir à ~,** to keep at a distance.

distancer *v.t.* to distance; to outrun.

distant, e *adj.* distant, far.

distendre *v.t.* to distend, to stretch out; to enlarge, to swell. **se ~,** *v.refl.* to be distended.

distension *n.f.* distention; stretching; enlargement.

distillateur *n.m.* distiller.

distillation *n.m.* distillation.

distiller *v.t.* to distil; to vent, to discharge. **se ~,** *v.refl.* to be distilled.

distillerie *n.f.* distillery.

distinct, te *adj.* distinct; clear, plain.

distinctement *adv.* distinctly; clearly.

distinctif, ive *adj.* distinctive; distinguishing. **caractère ~,** distinctive character.

distinction *n.f.* distinction; separation; difference. **une personne de ~,** a person of rank. **avoir de la ~,** to be distinguished (person).

distinguable *adj.* distinguishable.

distingué, e *adj.* distinguished; eminent; illustrious, celebrated. **des manières ~es,** gentlemanly, ladylike manners.

distinguer *v.t.* to distinguish; to discriminate; to discern, to perceive; to honor. **~ les sons,** to distinguish sounds. **se ~,** *v.refl.* to be distinguished; to be eminent; to be different; to appear; to distinguish oneself.

distinguo *n.m. Infml.* distinction.

distordre *v.t.* to distort.

distorsion *n.f.* distortion.

distraction *n.f.* distraction; absentmindedness; inattention, diversion, recreation, relaxation.

distraire *v.t.* to distract, to divert; to take away; to disturb; to entertain, to amuse. **se ~**, *v.refl.* to divert one's attention; to divert oneself, to amuse oneself.

distrait, e *adj.* absorbed; diverted, absent; inattentive, heedless.

distraitement *adv.* absentmindedly, inattentively.

distrayant *p.p. and adj.* diverting, entertaining.

distribuer *v.t.* to distribute; to apportion, to dispense; to allot; to arrange; to lay out. **se ~**, *v.refl.* to be distributed.

distributeur, trice *n.m.f.* distributer, dispenser. **~ automatique**, coin-operated machine.

distributif, ive *adj.* distributive.

distribution *n.f.* distribution; division; disposition; delivery (of letters); cast (of characters).

district *n.m.* district.

dit, dite aforesaid, said; told; spoken, uttered. **la dite maison**, the said house. **susdit**, abovementioned.

dithyrambe *n.m.* dithyramb.

dithyrambique *adj.* dithyrambic.

dito, ditto *adv.* ditto.

diurétique *adj. and n.m.* diuretic.

diurne *adj.* diurnal, daily.

diva *n.f.* diva, prima donna.

divagation *n.f.* wandering, rambling.

divaguer *v.i.* to wander, to ramble, to talk wildly. **tu divagues complètement!** you are completely out of your mind.

divan *n.m.* divan (council of state, among the Turks); sofa, couch.

divergence *n.f.* divergence, difference, disagreement, discordance.

divergent, e *adj.* divergent; different, contrary.

diverger *v.i.* to diverge.

divers, erse *adj.* diverse; different, various.

diversifier *v.t.* to diversify, to vary.

diversion *n.f.* diversion. **faire une ~**, to create a diversion; to divert.

diversité *n.f.* diversity, difference, dissimilitude; variety.

divertir *v.t.* to divert; to entertain, to distract. **se ~**, *v.refl.* to divert oneself, to amuse oneself.

divertissant, e *adj.* diverting, amusing, entertaining, pleasing.

divertissement *n.m.* diversion, entertainment, recreation; *Theat.* interlude.

dividende *n.m.* dividend.

divin, ine *adj.* divine; heavenly; sublime.

divinateur, trice *n.m.f.* diviner.

divination *n.f.* divination.

divinatoire *adj.* divinatory.

divinement *adv.* divinely; heavenly.

diviniser *v.t.* to deify.

divinité *n.f.* divinity; Godhead, deity.

diviser *v.t.* to divide, to separate. **se ~**, *v.refl.* to

divide; to be divided, to be separated, to be severed, to part, to separate.

diviseur *n.m.* divisor. *adj.* dividing.

divisibilité *n.f.* divisibility.

divisible *adj.* divisible; separable.

division *n.f.* division; separation; partition; discord, difference.

divisionnaire *adj.* divisional, divisionary.

divorce *n.m.* divorce.

divorcer *v.i.* to divorce; to be divorced. **se ~**, *v.refl.* to be divorced.

divulgation *n.f.* disclosure, divulgence, making public.

divulger *v.t.* to divulge, to make public.

dix *adj.* ten, tenth. **chapitre ~**, chapter ten. *n.m.* **le ~ du mois**, the tenth of the month.

dix-huit *adj.* eighteen; eighteenth.

dix-huitième *adj.* eighteenth.

dixième *adj. n.m.f.* tenth.

dix-neuf *adj.* nineteen, nineteenth. **page ~**, nineteenth page. *n.m.* nineteen.

dix-neuvième *adj.* nineteenth. *n.m.f.* nineteenth, nineteenth part.

dix-sept *adj.* seventeen, seventeenth. *n.m.* seventeen; seventeenth.

dix-septième *adj.* seventeenth. *n.m.f.* seventeenth; seventeenth part.

dizaine *n.f.* ten, about ten.

do *n.m. Mus.* do.

docile *adj.* docile, tractable, manageable.

docilement *adv.* with docility.

docilité *n.f.* docility.

dock *n.m.* dock.

docte *adj.* learned, erudite.

docteur *n.m.* doctor, physician. **~ en droit**, doctor of laws. **~ en médecine**, doctor of medicine.

doctoral, e *adj.* doctoral.

doctorat *n.m.* doctorate, Ph.D.

doctrinaire *n.m.* doctrinaire person. *adj.* pedantic, schoolmasterly, doctrinaire.

doctrinal, e *adj.* doctrinal.

doctrine *n.f.* doctrine, principle, teaching.

document *n.m.* document; title deed.

documentaire *n.m.* documentary.

documentaliste *n.m.f.* archivist; researcher.

documentation *n.f.* documentation.

documenter *v.t.* to document. **se ~**, to gather material.

dodécaèdre *n.m.* dodecahedron.

dodécagone *n.m.* dodecagon.

dodelinement *n.m.* nodding.

dodeliner *v.i.* to nod.

dodo *interj.* **faire ~**, to go to sleep, to go nightnight.

dodu, e *adj.* plump, chubby.

dogmatique *adj.* dogmatic.

dogmatiquement *adv.* dogmatically.

dogmatiser *v.i.* to dogmatize.

dogmatisme *n.m.* dogmatism.

dogme *n.m.* dogma, tenet.

dogue *n.m.* mastiff.

doigt *n.m.* finger (of the hand); toe (foot). **le ~ du milieu**, the middle finger. **à deux ~s à/de**, on the brink of. **montrer du ~**, to point at. **mon petit ~ me l'a dit**, a little bird told me. **ils sont comme les deux ~s de la main**, they are hand in glove. **mettre le ~ sur la plaie**, to hit the nail on the head. **se mordre les ~s**, to repent of something. **un ~ de vin**, just a drop of wine.

doigté *n.m.* touch; tact; savoir-faire.

doigter *v.t. Mus.* to finger.

doit *n.m.* debit side. **doit et avoir**, debit and credit.

doléance *n.f.* complaint; lament; grief.

dolent, e *adj.* doleful; mournful, sorrowful, sad.

dollar *n.m.* dollar; U.S. *Infml.* buck.

dolmen *n.m.* dolmen.

dolomie, dolomite *n.f.* dolomite.

D.O.M. *n.m.* French overseas department (Département d'outre-mer).

domaine *n.m.* domain, property estate.

dôme *n.m.* dome; cupola.

domestication *n.f.* domestication.

domesticité *n.f.* domesticity; domestics.

domestique *adj.* domestic; household; private. *n.m.* domestic servant; household. *n.f.* domestic servant, housemaid.

domicile *n.m.* domicile; abode; residence; dwelling.

domicilier (se) *v.refl.* to settle, to be domiciled.

dominance *n.f.* dominance.

dominant, e *adj.* dominant; predominant, prevailing, ruling.

dominateur, trice *n.m.f.* dominator, ruler. *adj.* dominative, dominating, ruling.

domination *n.f.* domination, dominion; power.

dominer *v.i.* to have dominion (over); to govern; to rise above, to tower. **il faut que la raison domine sur les passions**, reason must predominate over passion. **se tête domine au-dessus de la foule**, his head rises above the crowd. *v.t.* to dominate, to rule, to govern, to command; to overlook. **une colline qui domine la plaine**, a hill that rises above the plain. **se ~**, *v.refl.* to master one's passions, to restrain oneself.

dominion *n.m.* dominion.

domino *n.m.* domino. **une partie de ~s**, a game of dominoes.

dommage *n.m.* damage, wrong, injury, harm, loss. **c'est ~**, it is a pity. *Law.* **~s et intérêts**, damages.

dommageable *adj.* prejudicial, injurious, detrimental, hurtful.

domptable *adj.* tamable.

dompter *v.t.* to subdue; to vanquish; to quell; to master; to tame. **~ se passions**, to control one's passions. **~ un cheval**, to break in a horse. **se ~**, *v.refl.* to master, to govern, to subdue one's passions.

dompteur *n.m.* subduer; conqueror; tamer (of beasts).

don *n.m.* gift, present; donation; endowment, power, faculty; knack; Don (a Spanish title). **les ~s de la nature**, natural gifts. **le ~ de la parole**, the gift of speech.

donataire *n.m.f.* donee.

donateur, trice *n.m.f.* donor, giver.

donation *n.f.* donation, gift.

donc therefore; then; consequently. **je pense, ~ je suis**, I think, therefore I am; so; thus. **tiens ~!** yeah right! **dis donc, Paul, ou étais-tu hier?** say Paul, where were you yesterday? **faites ~ attention où vous allez!** watch where you go!

donjon *n.m.* dungeon.

don Juan *n.m.* Don Juan, womanizer.

donnant *adj.* giving. **donnant donnant**, fifty-fifty; cash and carry.

donne *n.f.* deal (at cards).

donée *n.f.* opinion, idea; datum, (*pl.*) data.

donner *v.t.* to give; to bestow, to impart; to present with; to give away; to supply. **~ la bénédiction**, to pronounce the benediction. **~ un délai**, to grant an extension. **~ à entendre**, to hint, to give a hint. **~ sa parole**, to give one's word. **~ le bon exemple**, to set a good example. **~ congé**, to fire (from a job). **quel âge donnez-vous à cette personne?** how old do you think that person is? **s'en ~ à cœur joie**, to take one's fill of it. *v.i.* to give, to give away, to bestow; to produce; to hit, to knock; to run; to fall. **~ à rire**, to excite laughter. **qui donne aux pauvres prête à Dieu**, he who gives to the poor lends unto the Lord. **qui donne tôt donne deux fois**, he that gives soon gives twice. **les blés ont plus donné cette année**, the harvest was more plentiful this year. **~ dans un piée, ~ dedans**, to fall into a snare. **la maison donne sur la rue**, the house looks onto the street. **mes fenêtres donnent sur le jardin**, my windows look onto the garden. **se ~**, *v.refl.* to give oneself, to be given; to be performed; to be fought.

donneur, euse *n.m.f.* giver; donor, bestower.

dont *pron.* whose, of whom, of which, that of. **l'ennui est une maladie ~ le travail est le remède**, weariness is an illness, the remedy of which is work. **l'ami ~ je parle**, the friend of whom I am speaking.

donzelle *n.f.* damsel, wench.

dopage *n.m.* doping.

dopant *n.m.* dope, drug. *adj.* stimulant.

doper *v.t.* to dope. **se ~**, to take dope.

doré, e *p.p. or adj.* gilt; gilded, golden, gold. *n.m.* gilding. **jeunesse dorée**, gilded youth.

dorénavant *adv.* from now on, in the future, henceforth, from this time on, for the future.

dorer *v.t.* to gild, to gild over. **se ~**, *v.refl.* to be gilded, to be gilt; to become yellow. **on va se faire dorer la pilule**, we are going to get tan, to sunbathe.

doreur, euse *n.m.f.* gilder.

dorioter v.t. to coddle, to pamper. **se ~**, v.refl. to indulge oneself; to take one's ease.

dormant, e adj. sleeping, dormant; stagnant; Naut. standing. n.m. sleeper.

dormeur, euse n.m.f. sleeper.

dormir v.i. to sleep; to be asleep; to slumber; to be inactive, to lie dormant. **~ sur les deux oreilles**, to sleep soundly; to have nothing to fear. **qui dort dîne**, sleeping is as good as eating. **laisser ~ une affaire**, to let an affair lie dormant. **il n'y a pire eau que l'eau qui dort**, still waters run deep. n.m. sleep.

dormitif, ive adj. n.m. dormitive, sleeping potion.

dorsal, e adj. dorsal. **épine ~e**, spine.

dortoir n.m. dormitory.

dorure n.f. gilding; glazing pastry with the yolk of eggs.

dos n.m. back. **en avoir plein le ~**, to be fed up. **être sur le ~ de quelqu'un**, to be on someone's back. **elle a bon ~ avec son histoire!**, she looks good in her story! **il s'est mis un sacré problème sur le ~**, he has got himself into a mess. **sac à ~**, backpack.

dosage n.m. mixture; precise dosing.

dose n.f. dose; portion, quantity.

doser v.t. to dose.

dossard n.m. number (on an athlete's uniform).

dossier n.m. back (of a seat), headboard (of a bed); file, folder.

dot n.f. dowry, portion.

dotal, e adj. pertaining to a dowry.

dotation n.f. endowment.

doter v.t. to endow; to equip; to give; to bestow.

douane n.f. customs, duties; customs office. **droits de ~**, custom duties, customs. **exempt de douane**, duty-free.

douanier n.m. customs officer. adj. customs.

doublage n.m. lining (of a sail); sheathing (of a ship), doubling; folding; Film. dubbing. **~ en cuivre**, copper-sheathing.

double adj. double, twofold, duplicate, deceitful, two-faced. **acte ~**, duplicate. **tenue des livres en partie ~**, double-entry bookkeeping. n.m. double; duplicate. **payer le ~**, to pay double. **c'est le ~ du prix**, the price is twice as much.

doublé, e p.p. or adj. doubled; lined. n.m. plated work. Film. dubbed.

doublement adv. doubly. n.m. doubling.

doubler v.t. to double, repeat, to line; Film. to dub; Auto. to overtake, to pass. **~ un manteau**, to line a cloak. v.i. to double. **la population de cette ville a presque doublé**, the population of this town has nearly doubled. **~ le pas**, to speed up. **il double un acteur connu**, he stands in for a well-known actor.

doublet n.m. doublet (at backgammon), doublets.

doublon n.m. dubloon; a Spanish gold coin.

doublure n.f. lining. Theat. substitute. Film. stand-in; stuntman, stuntwoman.

douce adj. V. DOUX.

douce-amère n.f. bitter sweet, woody nightshade.

douceâtre adj. sweetish.

doucement adv. softly, gently, quietly, calmly, peacefully, smoothly; sweetly, mildly, tenderly, slowly, leisurely. **parler doucement**, to speak slowly.

doucereux, euse adj. sweetish; mawkish, mealy-mouthed.

doucettement adv. gently, softly.

douceur n.f. sweetness; smoothness, softness, mildness, gentleness; suavity. **la ~ de la température**, the mildness of the temperature. **prendre quelqu'un par la ~**, to deal kindly or gently with a person. **prendre les choses en ~**, to take things easy.

douche n.f. shower. **écossaise**, ups and downs, succession of good and bad news.

doucher v.t. to give a shower to.

doué, e adj. gifted, talented; blessed with.

douer v.t. to endow.

douille n.f. socket; cartridge.

douillet, ette adj. downy, soft; delicate, tender; sensitive. n.m.f. overly-delicate person.

douillettement adv. softly; delicately.

douleur n.f. pain, ache; pangs; grief, sorrow, affliction.

douloureuse n.f. Infml. bill, check. **apportez-vous la ~**, bring us the check.

douloureusement adv. painfully, sorrowfully, mournfully.

douloureux, euse adj. painful, sorrowful, afflicting, grievous.

doute n.m. doubt; doubting, hesitation, indecision; scepticism; misgiving, distrust, mistrust; scruple. **dans le ~, abstiens-toi**, when in doubt, don't do it. **hors de ~**, beyond doubt. **sans ~**, undoubtedly, without doubt, doubtless.

douter v.i. to doubt; to hesitate; to distrust; to suspect. **je doute qu'il vienne**, I do not believe he will come. **se ~**, v.refl. to suspect, to surmise, to conjecture. **elle s'est doutée de ce qui se faisait**, she suspected what was being done. **il y avait des choses dont il ne se doutait pas**, there were things he had not the least idea of.

douteux adj. doubtful; dubious, uncertain, questionable; suspicious, ambiguous; hazardous; wavering, undecided.

Douvres n. Dover.

doux, douce adj. sweet; mild, soft; fragrant, melodious, mellow; gentle, smooth. **un mets trop ~**, too sweet a dish. **eau douce**, fresh water; soft water. **les ~s paroles n'écorchent point la bouche**, soft words break no bones. **billet ~**, love letter. **il fait ~**, the weather is mild. **une douce pente**, an easy slope. adv. sweetly; softly, gently; slowly. **tout ~**, gently, not so fast.

douzaine n.f. dozen. **une demi-~**, half a dozen.

douze adj. twelve. n.m. twelve.

douzième *adj.* twelfth. **le ~ siècle,** the twelfth century. *n.m.* twelfth.

doyen, ne *n.m.f.* dean; oldest member, senior member. **le ~ d'âge,** the oldest member.

doyenné *n.m.* deanship.

draconien, enne *adj.* draconian, severe, cruel.

dragage *n.m.* dredging; dragging.

dragée *n.f.* sugared almond.

drageifié, e *adj.* sugar-coated.

dragon *n.m.* dragon; dragoon.

drague *n.f.* dredge, dragnet; dredger.

draguer *v.t.* to dredge; *Naut.* to drag. **~ une ancre,** to drag an anchor; *Infml.* to chase (after girls/boys), to cruise.

dragueur *n.m.* dredger.

dragueur, euse *n.m.f.* cruiser, flirt.

drain *n.m.* drain.

drainage *n.m.* draining, drainage.

dramatique *adj.* dramatic. **auteur ~,** dramatist, playwright. *n.m.* drama, dramatic style.

dramatiquement *adv.* dramatically.

dramatisation *n.f.* dramatization.

dramatiser *v.t.* to dramatize.

dramaturge *n.m.* dramatist, playwright.

dramaturgie *n.f.* dramaturgy; treatise on dramatic art.

drame *n.m.* drama; play.

drap *n.m.* cloth, sheet. **être dans de beaux ~,** to be in a mess. **~-housse,** fitted sheet.

drapeau *n.m.* flag; colors. *Milit.* **être sous les ~ de,** to serve under.

draper *v.t.* to drape. **se ~,** *v.refl.* to cover, to wrap oneself.

Dresde *n.m.* Dresden.

dressage *n.m.* straightening; breaking; training (of horses, etc.).

dresser *v.t.* to erect; to set up, to prick up; to raise; to pitch; to fix; to lay, to arrange; to trim, to draw up; to train; to straighten. **le cheval dresse les oreilles,** the horse pricks up its ears. **~ une tente,** to pitch a tent. **~ un piè,** to lay a snare. **~ un cheval,** to train a horse. *v.i.* **cela fait ~ les cheveux sur la tête,** that makes one's hair stand on end. **se ~,** *v.refl.* to stand up, to stand erect, to rise. **se ~ sur la pointe du pied,** to stand on tiptoe.

dresseur, euse *n.m.f.* (animal) trainer.

dressoir *n.m.* dresser; sideboard; straightening.

dribbler *v.i. Sport.* to dribble.

drogue *n.f.* drug.

drogué, e *n.m.f.* drug addict, junkie.

droghuer *v.t.* to drug. **se ~,** *v.refl.* to take/use drugs.

droguerie *n.f.* hardware store.

droguiste *n.m.* hardware store owner.

droit, droite *adj.* right; straight, direct, upright, honest, just, straightforward. **le ~ chemin,** the straight road, the right way. **un angle ~,** a right angle. **la rive ~ d'une rivière,** the right bank of a river. *adv.* right; straightly, directly, straightforwardly; uprightly; honestly, justly. **viser ~,** to aim right. **aller ~ au but,** to go straight to the point.

droit *n.m.* right; equity; law, justice; legal title; privilege, prerogative, duty; tax, due. **~s civils,** civil rights. **les ~s de l'hospitalité,** the rules of hospitality. **~ écrit,** statute law. **~ coutumier,** common law. **~ d'ainesse** birthright. **~s de douane,** customs duties. **à qui de ~,** to whom it may concern. **~s de l'homme,** human rights.

droite *n.f.* straight; right hand; (politics) right wing. **à ~,** on the right.

droitement *adv.* rightly, uprightly, righteously, justly, honestly.

droitier, ière *adj.* right-handed.

droiture *n.f.* rectitude; uprightness, integrity, honesty, righteousness. **agir avec ~,** to act honestly.

drolatique *adj.* comical, droll.

drôle *adj.* droll; comical, funny, humorous; odd, strange. *n.m.* scoundrel. **un drôle de type.**

drôlement *adv.* comically; oddly; awfully, terribly. **il fait ~ froid aujourd'hui,** it's awfully cold today.

drôlerie *n.f.* drollery; droll thing.

dromadaire *n.m.* dromedary.

dru *adj.* thick, thick-set, close-set; (of birds) fledged. *adv.* thick; thick-set, fast, quickly. **les coups tombaient ~ comme grêle,** the blows followed each other in quick succession.

druide *n.m.* druid.

dryade *n.f.* dryad, wood nymph.

du *art. n.m. sing.* of the; some, any.

dû, due *p.p.* of **devoir,** owed; due; owing. *n.m.* due; that which is owed.

dualisme *n.m.* dualism.

dualiste *adj.* dualistic. *n.m.* dualist.

dualité *n.f.* duality.

dubitatif, ive *adj.* dubitative.

duc *n.m.* duke; eagle owl.

duché *n.m.* dukedom; duchy.

duchesse *n.f.* duchess.

ductile *adj.* ductile.

ductilité *n.f.* ductility.

duègne *n.f.* duenna, governess.

duel *n.m.* duel, duelling; *Gram.* dual.

dûment *adv.* duly.

dumping *n.m.* (trade) dumping. **faire du ~,** to dump.

dune *n.f.* dune.

dunette *n.f. Naut.* poop.

duo *n.m.* duo; duet.

duodécimal, e *adj.* duodecimal.

duodénum *n.m.* duodenum.

dupe *n.f.* dupe; sucker.

duper *v.t.* to dupe, to deceive, to trick, to cheat.

duperie *n.f.* dupery, trick.

duplex *adj. Telecom.* duplex, transmission, link-up. *n.m.* duplex (apartment).

duplicate *n.m.* duplicate.

duplication *n.f.* duplication.

duplicité *n.f.* duplicity.

duquel *pron. n.m. sing.* of whom, of which, from which.

dur, e *adj.* hard; touch; avaricious; difficult; rough, austere; dull, stupid; severe, rigorous; cruel, obdurate. **un oeuf ~**, a hard-boiled egg. **cela est ~ à digérer**, that is hard to digest. **des manières ~s**, rough manners. **~ au travail**, hard-working. *adv.* hard; diligently, laboriously. **travailler ~**, to work hard. *n.m.f.* **c'est un vrai ~**, he is a real tough guy. *Infml.* **être ~ d'oreille/ de la feuille**, to be hard of hearing.

durabilité *n.f.* durability.

durable *adj.* durable; lasting; continuing, permanent, stable.

durablement *adv.* durably, lastingly.

durant *prep.* during; lasting; for.

durcir *v.t.* to harden; to toughen. *v.i.* to harden; to grow hard, to get hard; to toughen. **se ~**, *v.refl.* to harden; to grow hard, to get hard, to toughen.

durcissement *n.m.* hardening; induration.

durée *n.f.* duration; continuance.

durement *adv.* hardly; hard, severely, rigorously; harshly, rudely.

durer *v.i.* to last, to endure, to continue, to hold out. **certaines fleurs ne durent qu'un jour**, some flowers do not last more than a day. **ce**

drap dure beaucoup, this cloth wears very well.

dureté *n.f.* hardness; toughness; thickness; unkindness, cruelty; obduracy; hard-heartedness; harshness; rigor. **la ~ de la viande**, the toughness of meat. **la ~ d'un climat**, the inclemency of a climate.

durillon *n.m.* callosity; corn.

duvet *n.m.* down; *Infml.* feather bed; down quilt.

duveté, e *adj.* downy.

duveteux, euse *adj.* downy, resembling down.

dynamique *adj.* dynamic. *n.f. Mech.* dynamics.

dynamisme *n.m.* dynamism.

dynamite *n.f.* dynamite.

dynamiter *v.t.* to dynamite, to blow up with dynamite.

dynamo *n.f.* dynamo, generator.

dynamogène *adj.* **dynamogénique** *adj.* dynamogenic.

dynamomètre *n.m.* dynamometer.

dynastie *n.f.* dynasty.

dynastique *adj.* dynastic.

dysenterie *n.f.* dysentery.

dyslexie *n.f.* dyslexia.

dyslexique *adj. n.m.f.* dyslexic.

dyspepsie *n.f.* dyspepsia.

dystrophie *n.f.* dystrophy.

dytique *n.m.* water beetle.

E

E initial, used as an abbreviation of **est**, east.

eau *n.f.* water; rain; sweat; urine. **~ de source**, spring water. **~ de pluie**, rainwater. **~ de puits**, well water. **~ gazeuse**, sparkling water. **~ régale**, aqua regia. **~ de Seltz**, Seltzer water. **~ douce**, soft water; fresh water. **~ de mer**, sea water. **~ croupie**, ditch water. **~ distillée**, distilled water. **~ bénite**, holy water. **porter de l'~ à la rivière, à la mer**, to carry coals to Newcastle. **mettre de l'~ dans son vin**, to lower one's pretensions. **faire venir l'~ au moulin**, to bring grist to the mill. **pêcher en ~ troublé**, to fish in rough waters. **cette affaire est tombée dans l'~**, this affair has fallen apart. **revenir sur l'~**, to get afloat again, to land on one's feet. **les ~x sont basses**, the river is low; *Fig.* (he) is hard up. **à fleur d'~**, level with the water; between wind and water. **faire ~**, *Naut.* to leak. **faire de l'~**, to take in fresh water. **suer sang et ~**, to make tremendous efforts. **être tout en ~**, to be all sweaty. **l'~ m'en vient à la bouche**, it makes my mouth water. **aller à l'~**, to take to the water (of a dog).

eau-de-vie *n.f.* brandy, eau-de-vie. **~ de Cognac**, cognac.

eau-forte *n.f.* etching.

ébahi, e *adj.* amazed, astounded.

ébahir *v.refl.* to wonder, to be amazed, to be astounded.

ébarber *v.t.* to pare, to clip; to strip (quills); to scrape.

ébat *n.m.* frolic, sport, pastime, diversion, play. **prendre ses ~s**, to sport, to play.

ébattre *v.refl.* to frolic, to skip about; to play, to sport.

ébaubi, e *adj. Infml.* amazed, astounded.

ébauche *n.f.* sketch, outline, rough draft.

ébaucher *v.t.* to rough out; to sketch; to make a rough draft of; to outline. **~ un sourire**, to give a faint smile.

ébène *n.f.* ebony. **bois d'~**, ebony. **des cheveux d'~**, jet black hair.

ébénier *n.m.* ebony. **faux ~**, laburnum.

ébéniste *n.m.* cabinetmaker.

ébénisterie *n.f.* cabinetmaking; cabinetry.

éberluer *v.t.* to astound, to dumbfound.

éblouir *v.t.* to dazzle; to astonish; to surprise. **s'~**, *v.refl.* to be dazzled.

éblouissant, e *adj.* dazzling; splendid.

éblouissement *n.m.* dazzling, dazzle, dazzling light; dizziness; giddiness; dimness of sight.

ébonite *n.f.* ebonite.

éborgner *v.t.* to blind in one eye; *Gard.* to nip off buds. **s'~**, *v.refl.* to blind oneself in one eye; to put out each other's eyes.

éboueur *n.m.* garbageman; garbage collector.

ébouillanter *v.t.* to scald. **s'~**, to scald oneself.

éboulement *n.m.* falling in, falling down; landslide.

ébouler *v.t.* to cause to fall. *v.i.* to fall in. s'~, *v.refl.* to fall in, to fall down, to crumble; to slip.

éboulis *n.m.* rubbish.

ébouriffant, e *adj.* astounding, stunning.

ébouriffé, e *adj.* in disorder, disordered; agitated; in a flurry. **des cheveux ~s,** dishevelled hair.

ébouriffer *v.t.* to mess up (one's hair), to throw into disorder. s'~, *v.refl.* to mess up one's hair; to be amazed.

ébrancher *v.t.* to lop, to prune; to trim.

ébranlement *n.m.* shake, shaking, concussion; agitation; perturbation, disturbance; trouble.

ébranler *v.t.* to shake; to agitate; to move; to stagger. **la tempète ébranlait la maison,** the storm shook the house. **~ le crédit public,** to weaken public faith. **~ la santé,** to weaken the health. s'~, *v.refl.* to shake, to be shaken; to tremble, to totter.

ébrécher *v.t.* to notch; to chip off; to impair. **~ un couteau,** to notch a knife. **cela a ébréché sa réputation,** that has damaged his reputation. s'~, *v.refl.* to be notched.

ébriété *n.f.* intoxication, inebriation.

ébrouement *n.m.* snorting.

ébrouer *v.t.* s'~, *v.refl.* to snort.

ébruitement *n.m.* spreading, disclosure, divulsion.

ébruiter *v.t.* to make public, to divulge; to spread, to report. s'~, *v.refl.* to be rumored.

ébullition *n.f.* ebullition; boiling. **être en ~,** to be boiling over with excitement.

écaille *n.f.* scale; shell. **~ de tortue,** tortoise shell.

écailler *v.t.* to scale; to peel off; to flake, to chip. s'~, *v.refl.* to scale; to peel off in scales; to shell.

écailleux, euse *adj.* scaly, squamous.

écale *n.f.* shell (of nuts, peas, etc.); hull; husk.

écaler *v.t.* to shell; to hull, to husk. s'~, *v.refl.* to be hulled, to be husked.

écarlate *n.f. adj.* scarlet.

écarquiller *v.t.* to open wide. **~ les yeux,** to open one's eyes very wide.

écart *n.m.* step aside; digression; deviation; fault, error; *Veter.* strain; (at cards) cards discarded. **à l'~,** in a lonely place; aside, apart. **il se tenait à l'~,** he stood aside. **se mettre à l'~,** to step aside. **~ de langage,** strong/bad language.

écarté, e *adj.* wide apart; lonely; isolated; remote, secluded; apart. **les bras ~s,** arms apart. *n.m.* écarté (at cards).

écarteler *v.t.* to quarter.

écartement *n.m.* separation; opening; spreading; space, distance, gap.

écarter *v.t.* to turn aside, to lead astray; to keep away; to remove from; to set aside; to scatter; to spread, to widen; to discard (cards). **~ les soupçons,** to remove suspicion. **~ les jambes,** to spread one's legs. **~ la foule,** to disperse the crowd. s'~, *v.refl.* to deviate; to turn aside; to swerve, to go astray; to widen, to open. s'~ **de la**

route, to go out of the way. **ne vous écartez pas,** do not go out of the way. **la foule s'écarte pour lui laisser passage,** the crowd makes way for her/him to pass.

écarteur *n.m. Med.* retractor.

ecchymose *n.f. Surg.* echymosis.

ecclésiastique *adj.* ecclesiastic, ecclesiastical; church, clerical. *n.m.* clergyman.

écervelé, e *adj.* hare-brained, boneheaded. *n.m.f.* bonehead, birdbrain.

échafaud *n.m.* scaffold; stage.

échafaudage *n.m.* scaffolding; display.

échafauder *v.i.* to scaffold; to erect scaffolding. *v.t.* to prepare, to make a great display of. s'~, *v.refl.* to scaffold; to erect a scaffold, a stage; to make preparations; to support, to help, to advance oneself; to be supported, to be upheld.

échalas *n.m.* stake, pole.

échalote *n.f.* shallot.

échancré, e *adj.* with a plunging neckline; indented, jagged.

échancrer *v.t.* to hollow out, to scoop out; to cut low; to scallop, to indent, to notch.

échancrure *n.f.* hollow, hollowing out; indentation.

échange *n.m.* exchange; barter; interchange. **commerce d'~,** trade by barter. **libre ~,** free trade.

échangeable *adj.* exchangeable.

échanger *v.t.* to exchange; to change; to barter. **~ des coups,** to exchange blows.

échantillon *n.m.* sample, pattern, specimen.

échantillonnage *n.m.* sampling.

échantillonner *v.t.* to take samples; to sort; to test; to gauge.

échappatoire *n.f.* subterfuge, shift, evasion, excuse.

échappé, e *n.m.f.* one who has escaped; a fugitive.

échappée *n.f.* vista; glimpse; gleam (sunlight).

échappement *n.m.* escape, flight; escapement. **pot d'~,** muffler. **tuyau d'~,** exhaust pipe.

échapper *v.i.* (with **de**) to escape, to escape from, to flee, to fly; to break loose; to make one's escape; to break out of; to leak. **~ d'un danger,** to escape from a danger. **~ d'un naufrage,** to escape from a shipwreck. **il sera bien heureux s'il échappe,** he will be very lucky if he recovers from it. **~ à la poursuite de l'ennemi,** to elude the pursuit of the enemy. **j'ai beau chercher dans mon ésprit, son nom m'échappe,** I search in vain, his name escapes me. **laisser ~,** to let slip, to lose, to miss. *v.t.* to escape; to avoid. **j'ai échappé la mort,** I have escaped death. **il ne l'échappera pas,** he'll catch it. **l'~ belle,** to have a narrow escape. s'~, *v.refl.* to escape; to flee, to get away, to slip away, to make one's escape; to steal away; to run out; to spread; (of water) to ooze, to make its way. s'~ **de prison,** to escape from prison. **le cheval s'est échappé,** the horse has broken loose. **il**

s'échappait jusqu'à dire ...**, he forgot himself so far as to say ...

écharde *n.f.* splinter.

écharpe *n.f.* scarf, sash; sling; pulley beam. **porter le bras en ~,** to carry one's arm in a sling.

écharper *v.t.* to cut, to slash, to gash; to cut to pieces. **ce régiment s'est fait ~,** that regiment was cut to pieces. **s'~,** *v.refl.* to cut each other to pieces.

échasse *n.f.* stilt. **marcher avec d'~,** to walk on stilts.

échassier *n.m.* wader.

échauder *v.t.* to scald. **s'~,** *v.refl.* to scald oneself; to burn one's fingers.

échauffé, e *adj.* heated; excited, overexcited; inflamed. *n.m.* heat, hot smell. **sentir l'~,** to have a hot smell.

échauffement *n.m.* heating; overheating.

échauffer *v.i.* to heat; to overheat; to excite; to inflame; to vex. **~ les oreilles à quelqu'un,** to provoke a person. **s'~,** *v.refl.* to grow warm; to become heated; to become animated, to fly into a passion. **cette pièce s'échauffe vite,** this room warms up fast. **la dispute s'échauffe,** the quarrel is getting hot. **la conversation commençait à s'~,** the conversation started to heat up.

échauffourée *n.f. Milit.* affray, fray, skirmish.

échéable *adj.* falling due (bill, debt).

échéance *n.f.* expiration; term; *Com.* maturity; falling due (of a bill). **à longue ~,** long-dated. **à courte ~,** short-dated. **jusqu'à l'~,** till due.

échéant, e *adj.* due, **le cas ~,** should the occasion arise.

échec *n.m.* check; blow; rebuff; defeat. **son travail a été un vrai ~,** his business has been a failure. **voué à l'~,** bound to fail, doomed to failure. **être ~ et mat,** to be checkmated.

échecs *n.m.pl.* chess; chessmen. **faire une partie d'~s,** to play a game of chess.

échelle *n.f.* ladder; scale. **~ de corde,** rope ladder. **~ sociale,** social ladder. **après lui il faut tirer l'~,** no one could do better; he has left nothing undone. **faire la courte ~,** to climb upon each other's shoulders.

échelon *n.m.* round; step, grade, echelon.

échelonnement *n.m.* spreading out; staggering.

échelonner *v.t.* to place in echelons; to place at intervals. **s'~,** *v.refl.* to be placed in echelons; to proceed gradually.

écheveau *n.m.* skein; hank. **démêler l'~ d'une intrigue,** to untangle a plot.

échevelé, e *adj.* disheveled; with disheveled hair.

écheveler *v.t.* to dishevel the hair of. **s'~,** *v.refl.* to dishevel, to be disheveled.

échine *n.f.* spine, backbone, back, chine. **courber l'~,** to submit, to obey.

échiner *v.t.* to break the back of. **s'~,** *v.refl.* to break one's back; to overexert oneself; to wear oneself out.

échiquier *n.m.* chessboard; checkered pattern; government treasury.

écho *n.m.* echo.

échographie *n.f.* ultrasonography.

échoir *v.i. defect.* to fall to the lot of, to fall, to come; to be due. **cela m'est échu en partage,** that fell to my lot. **la lettre de change est échue,** the bill of exchange is due.

échouer *v.i.* to strand; to run aground; to founder; to fail; to ruin; to end up. **elle a fait ~ tous leurs plans,** she has ruined all their plans. **il a échoué dans un blé perdue,** he ended up in the middle of nowhere. **le navire échoue sur un écueil,** the ship grounds on a reef. *v.t. Naut.* to strand; to run aground. **s'~,** *v.refl.* to run aground.

éclaboussement *n.m.* splashing.

éclabousser *v.t.* to splash; (reputation) to smear, to tarnish.

éclaboussure *n.f.* splash; splash of mud; (reputation) smear, stain.

éclair *n.m.* lightning; flash of lightning; flash; gleam; glitter.

éclairage *n.m.* lighting.

éclairagiste *n.m. Theater.* electrician; *Film.* lighting engineer.

éclaircie *n.f.* clearing; clear spot (in a cloudy sky); glade.

éclaircir *v.t.* to clear; to clear up; to brighten up; to explain; to unravel, to solve, to eludicate, to illustrate. **~ un mystère,** to clear up a mystery. **le temps éclaircit la vérité,** time brings truth to light. **s'~,** *v.refl.* to clear, to clear up; to get bright, to become bright, to brighten. **le temps s'éclaircit,** the weather is clearing up. **tous vos doutes bientôt s'éclairciront,** all your doubts will soon be cleared up.

éclaircissement *n.m.* clearing up; explanation; elucidation; solution. **donner des ~s,** to give explanations.

éclairement *n.m.* illumination.

éclairer *v.t.* to light; to light up, to enlighten; to illuminate; to shed light upon; to watch, to observe. *v.i.* to give light; to shine, to glitter, to gleam. **s'~,** *v.refl.* to be lighted, to be lighted up; to become enlightened.

éclat *n.m.* fragment, piece; chip, splinter, burst, explosion; clap of thunder; noise, crash; splendor. **un ~ de pierre,** a chip of stone. **un ~ de bois,** a splinter. **un ~ de rire,** a burst of laughter. **rire aux ~,** to burst with laughter. **l'~ du soleil,** the brightness of the sun. **l'~ des yeux,** the brightness of the eyes. **voler en ~s,** to shatter in pieces.

éclatant, e *adj.* bright; brilliant, shining, dazzling, radiant, resplendent; splendid, gorgeous; loud sound. **une lumière ~e,** a bright, a brilliant light. **une ~e blancheur,** dazzling whiteness. **une robe ~e,** a splendid dress.

éclatement *n.m.* burst, explosion; *Med.* rupture; (tire) blowout.

éclater *v.i.* to split; to splinter; to fly into pieces; to explode; to break suddenly, to fly open; to burst out. **la bombe éclata en tombant,** the shell burst as it fell. **~ de rire,** to burst out laughing. **le tonnerre éclata,** the thunder broke forth. **elle éclata en pleurs et en cris,** she burst out crying and sobbing. **une soudaine joie éclatant sur son front,** her face expressing a sudden joy. **faire ~,** to splinter; to burst, to cause to break out, to cause to explode. **s'~,** *v.refl.* to splinter, to split; to fly into pieces; to burst out.

éclectique *adj. n.m.* eclectic.

éclectisme *n.m.* eclecticism.

éclipse *n.f.* eclipse.

éclipser *v.t.* to eclipse, to obscure, to darken; to cloud. **s'~,** *v.refl.* to eclipse; to be eclipsed, to be obscured; to be thrown into the shade; to disappear. **après s'être éclipsé pendant cinq mois,** after disappearing for five months.

écliptique *n.f. adj.* ecliptic.

éclisser *v.t.* to splint.

écloppé, e *adj.* lame, limping.

éclore *v.i. defect.* to hatch, to be hatched; to open; to dawn, to break. **faire ~,** to hatch. **les oeufs sont éclos ce matin,** the eggs hatched this morning. **une fleur qui commence à ~,** a flower which is beginning to blossom. **le jour est près d'~,** the day is about to dawn.

éclosion *n.f.* hatching, hatch; opening, blowing, blossoming.

éclusée *n.f.* lock of water; lockful; lockage.

écluser *v.t.* to lock; to pass (a vessel) through a lock.

écoeurant, e *adj.* sickening, disgusting.

écoeurement *n.m.* disgust, nausea; *Fig.* disgust, discouragement.

écoeurer *v.t.* to sicken, to disgust. **s'~,** *v.refl.* to become disgusted, to get sick.

école *n.f.* school. **~ du soir,** evening school. **~ de médecine,** school of medicine. **~ de droit,** law school. **~ de danse,** dancing school. **~ hôtelière,** hotel management school. **~ maternelle,** kindergarten, nursery school. **faire l'~ buissonnière,** to play hooky, to play truant.

écolier, ière *n.m.f.* schoolchild, pupil.

écologie *n.f.* ecology.

écologique *adj.* ecological.

écologiste *n.m.f.* ecologist.

éconduire *v.t.* to show out, to show the door; to dismiss.

économat *n.m.* bursarship; bursar's office.

économe *n.m.f.* bursar (of a college). *adj.* thrifty, economical.

économétrie *n.f.* econometrics.

économie *n.f.* economy; thrift, frugality, thriftiness. **~ de bouts de chandelle,** paltry savings. **faire des ~s,** to save money.

économique *adj.* economic, economical. *n.f.* economics.

économiquement *adv.* economically.

économiser *v.t.* to economize; to save.

économiste *n.m.* economist.

écorce *n.f.* bark; rind; peel; outside. **il ne faut pas juger du bois par l'~,** one must not judge a book by its cover. **l'~ terrestre,** the earth's crust.

écorcement *n.m.* barking (of trees), stripping.

écorcer *v.t.* to strip off; to peel.

écorché, e *adj.* flayed, skinned; excoriated.

écorcher *v.t.* to flay, to skin; to strip; to gall; to fret; to grate on; to overcharge; to fleece. **~ l'anguille par la queue,** to begin at the wrong end. **vous m'avez écorché la jambe,** you have scratched my leg. **~ une langue,** to murder a language. **s'~,** *v.refl.* to scratch oneself.

écorchure *n.f.* scratch, excoriation.

écorner *v.t.* to cut down, to curtail, to diminish; to dog-ear (a book). **~ son revenu,** to curtail, to diminish one's income.

écossais, e *adj.* Scottish. *n.m.f.* plaid fabric; Scotsman, Scotswoman.

Écosse *n.f.* Scotland. **Nouvelle ~,** Nova Scotia.

écosser *v.t.* to husk, to shell.

écosystème *n.m.* ecosystem.

écot *n.m.* quota, share. **payez votre ~,** pay your share.

écoulement *n.m.* flowing, flow; issue; sale. **il ~ de la marchandise,** the sale of the goods.

écouler *v.i.* to run, to flow; to let off; to sell; to dispose of. **s'~,** *v.refl.* to run away; to flow away, to flow; to be discharged, to glide away; to pass away. **le vin s'écoulait du tonneau,** the wine was running out of the barrel. **le temps s'écoule bien vite,** time passes quickly.

écourter *v.t.* to shorten; to dock; to cut too short; to curtail.

écoute *n.f.* listening; ear (boar). (radio) **être à l'~ de,** to be tuned in to. **être aux ~s,** to eavesdrop. **table d'~,** wiretapping set. **cester à l'~,** to stay tuned. *Naut.* sheet, sail.

écouter *v.t.* to listen to, to hear; to overhear, to mind, to heed, to give heed to. **n'~ que d'une oreille,** to pay little attention to what is being said. **~ aux portes,** to listen at the door, to eavesdrop. **~ sa conscience,** to listen to one's conscience. **elle sait se faire ~ de ses enfants,** she knows how to make her children listen to her. **s'~,** *v.refl.* to listen to one's own voice; to be overly-careful of oneself.

écouteur *n.m.* (telephone) receiver, earpiece; *pl.* headphones; listener, eavesdropper.

écrabouiller *v.t. Infml.* to crush, to squash.

écran *n.m.* screen; filter; shield. **~ solaire,** sunscreen.

écrasant, e *adj.* crushing, overwhelming; oppressive; humiliating.

écrase *adj.* flat; crushed; squashed. **un nez ~,** a flat nose.

écrasement *n.m.* crushing; bruising, quashing; overwhelming.

écraser *v.t.* to crush; to run over; to overbear, to overpower; to overwhelm, to oppress, to grind down. **cette femme a été écrasée par une voiture,** that woman was run over by a car. **être écrasé de travail,** to be overwhelmed with work. **il est écrasé par son rival,** his rival overshadows him. *Infml.* **~!** shut up, enough. **s'~,** *v.refl.* to be crushed.

écrémage *n.m.* skimming.

écrémer *v.t.* to cream; to cream off; to skim; to take the best part of.

écrevisse *n.f.* crawfish, crayfish.

écrier *v.refl.* to exclaim, to cry out.

écrin *n.m.* jewel case, casket of jewels.

écrire *v.t.* to write; to write down, to set down; to spell. **~ fin,** to write small. **~ une lettre,** to write a letter. **comment écrivez-vous ce mot?** how do you spell that word? **s'~,** *v.refl.* to be written; to be spelled. **ce mot ne s'écrit pas comme il se pronounce,** that word is not spelled (or written) as it is pronounced.

écrit *n.m.* writing; an instrument or document; written agreement; work, book. **signer un ~,** to sign a deed.

écriteau *n.m.* billboard.

écriture *n.f.* writing; handwriting; accounts; Scripture. **une belle ~,** beautiful handwriting. **une mauvaise,** poor handwriting. **passer les ~s de,** to make an entry of. **l'Écriture sainte,** the Holy Scriptures, Holy Writ.

écrivain *n.m.* writer; author.

écrou *n.m.* screw nut.

écrouer *v.t.* to lock up, to jail.

écroulement *n.m.* collapse, caving in, falling down, falling; fall.

écrouler *v.i.* to fall in (by sinking). **faire ~,** to pull down. **s'~,** *v.refl.* to fall in, to fall down, to sink down; to fall to pieces, to crumble away; to break up. **l'empire s'écroula de toutes parts,** the empire was utterly destroyed.

écru, e *adj.* unwashed; unbleached. **fil ~,** unbleached thread. **toile ~,** unbleached cloth, brown holland.

écu *n.m.* shield; crown; an old French coin.

écueil *n.m.* rock, shelf, reef, sandbank; danger. **donner sur un ~,** to strike against a rock.

écuelle *n.f.* porringer; ladle; saucer.

éculé, e *adj.* down-at-the-heel.

écumage *n.m.* skimming, scumming.

écume *n.f.* foam, froth, spume; scum; froth. **l'~ des flots,** the foam of the waves. **l'~ de la bière,** the froth of beer. **l'~ du pot au feu,** the skimming of the broth. **~ de mer,** meerschaum (for pipes).

écumer *v.i.* to foam, to froth, to spume. **la mer écume,** the sea foams. **~ de rage,** to foam with rage. *v.t.* to scum, to skim. **~ le pot,** to skim the pot.

écumeux, euse *adj.* foamy, frothy; foaming; spumy.

écumoire *n.f.* skimmer.

écureuil *n.m.* squirrel.

écurie *n.f.* stable.

écusson *n.m.* escutcheon, scutcheon; coat of arms; *Agr.* escutcheon; *Arch.* knob.

écuyer *n.m.* squire, riding master.

eczéma *n.m.* eczema.

edelweiss *n.m.* edelweiss.

Éden *n.m.* Eden.

édicter *v.t.* to enact, to order (by edict), to impose (a fine).

édifice *n.m.* edifice; building; structure.

édifier *v.t.* to build, to erect; to edify; to inform.

Édimbourg *n.m.* Edinburgh.

édit *n.m.* edict, decree. **faire un ~,** to issue a decree.

éditer *v.t.* to publish (a book); to edit.

éditeur *n.m.* publisher; editor.

édition *n.f.* edition, original edition.

éditorial *adj.* editorial.

éditorialiste *n.m.f.* editorial writer.

édredon *n.m.* eiderdown, comforter.

éducateur, trice *n.m.f.* educator; instructor. *adj.* educational.

éducatif, ive *adj.* educational, educative.

education *n.f.* education; breeding, rearing; training; upbringing. **recevoir une bonne ~,** to have a good education.

édulcorer *v.t.* to sweeten.

éduquer *v.t.* to educate, to bring up, to breed.

effaçable *adj.* effaceable; erasable.

effacé, e *adj.* (color) faded; (person) unobtrusive; (life) retired, secluded.

effacement *n.m.* effacement, effacing, obliterating; blotting out.

effacer *v.t.* to efface; to obliterate, to erase; to strike out; to rub out, to rub off; to erase (by rubbing); to scratch out, to wipe out. **s'~,** *v.refl.* to be, or to become effaced or obliterated, to come out; to blot out; to wash out; to wear out; to disappear.

effarant, e *adj.* bewildering; alarming.

effaré, e *adj.* alarmed, startled, shaken; aghast.

effarement *n.m.* alarm, bewilderment.

effarer *v.t.* to bewilder, to alarm. **s'~,** to become bewildered; to become scared.

effaroucher *v.t.* to scare, to frighten; to scare away, to frighten away. **s'~,** *v.refl.* to be scared away; to be scared, to be startled; to take alarm. **mon cheval s'est effarouché,** my horse was startled.

effectif, ive *adj.* effective, real. *n.m.*

effectivement *adv.* effectively; in reality, in effect, really, indeed.

effectuer *v.t.* to effect, to perform, to execute, to realize, to fulfil. **s'~,** *v.refl.* to be effected, to be carried into effect, to be accomplished.

efféminer *v.t.* to effeminate, to make effeminate, to soften.

effervescence *n.f.* effervescence.

effervescent, e *adj.* effervescent; in a turmoil, agitated, overexcited.

effet *n.m.* effect; act, deed; execution, accomplishment; bill of exchange; goods; property, belonging, result, consequence. **ca ne lui a fait aucun ~,** it did nothing to her/him, it was totally ineffective. **~s visuels,** visual effects. **la loi n'a point d'~ rétroactif,** the law is not retroactive. **à cet ~,** to this effect. **à l'~ de,** with the intent to. **~ de commerce,** bill. **~s mobiliers,** (law) personal property. **en ~,** in effect, in reality, indeed.

effeuiller *v.t.* to strip the leaves of. **s'~,** *v.refl.* to shed its leaves.

efficace *adj.* efficient, effective.

efficacement *adv.* efficiently, efficaciously, effectually.

efficacité, *n.f.* efficacy, efficaciousness; efficiency, efficience. *n.f.* efficiency.

efficient, e *adj.* efficient.

effigie *n.f.* effigy; figure, representation.

effile, e *adj.* slender, slim; thin. *n.m.* fringe, trimming.

effiler *v.t.* to unravel; to thin (the hair); to taper; (knife) to sharpen. **s'~,** *v.refl.* to come unraveled, to fray; to taper.

effilocher *v.t.* to undo; to pick to pieces.

efflanquer *v.t.* to make lean; to reduce in flesh.

effleurement *n.m.* grazing, touching slightly.

effleurer *v.t.* to strip the flowers off; to graze, to skin; to skim along; to touch lightly upon. **ne faire qu'~ la terre en laborant,** to plow the soil very superficially. **l'idée ne m'en avait pas effleuré l'esprit,** the idea never crossed my mind. **s'~,** *v.refl.* to fade, to wither; to be touched lightly.

effluve *n.m.* effluvium; emanation.

effondrement *n.m.* deep digging; ruin, overthrow.

effondrer *v.t.* to collapse; to cave in, to give way; *Fin.* to slump; to break open. **s'~,** *v.refl.* to give way, to sink down, to fall in.

efforcer *v.refl.* to make an effort; to strain oneself; to exert oneself; to strive, to endeavor, to try.

effort *n.m.* effort; strain; endeavor; force, strength; pressure. **faire des ~s pour courir,** to make efforts to run.

effraction *n.f. Law.* breaking, breaking open. **vol avec ~,** housebreaking; burglary.

effraie *n.f.* barn owl, white owl, screech owl.

effrayant, e *adj.* frightful, dreadful, fearful; terrible.

effrayer *v.t.* to frighten; to scare; to terrify. **s'~,** *v.refl.* to be frightened; to be alarmed, to take fright, to be scared. **il ne s'effraye de rien,** nothing scares him.

effréné, e *adj.* unbridled, unbounded, unrestrained, rampant, immoderate, ungovernable. **une passion ~e,** an unrestrained passion.

effriter *v.t.* to crumble. **s'~,** to crumble away; to be eroded.

effroi *n.m.* fright, dread, dismay. **pâlir d'~,** to turn pale with fright.

effronté, e *adj.* fresh; insolent; brazen, impudent, shameless, bold, saucy. **une femme ~,** a bold, an unblushing woman. *n.m.f.* an impudent person, a saucy person.

effrontément *adv.* impudently, boldly, saucily.

effronterie *n.f.* effrontery, shamelessness, impudence. **quelle ~,** what impudence! **il faut payer d'~,** we must tough it out.

effroyable *adj.* frightful; horrible; tremendous, dreadful.

effroyablement *adv.* frightfully, horribly.

effusion *n.f.* effusion; outpouring. **~ de tendresse,** a burst of tenderness. **~ de sang,** bloodshed.

égal, e *adj.* equal; alike; even, uniform, regular, equable, steady; fair; indifferent. **marcher d'un pas ~,** to keep pace with. **un caractère ~,** an even temper. **tout lui est ~,** he doesn't care about anything. *n.m.f.* equal. **à l'~ de,** equal to; as much as, like.

également *adv.* equally; alike; likewise, too, also; in like manner; both.

égaler *v.t.* to equal; to equalize; to match; to compare. **s'~,** *v.refl.* to make oneself equal, to equal.

égalisation *n.f.* equalization.

égaliser *v.t.* to equalize, to equal; to level. **~ un terrain,** to level a piece of ground.

égalitaire *adj.* egalitarian.

égalité *n.f.* equality; evenness; levelness; smoothness; equanimity. **l'~ du sol,** the evenness of the ground. **~ d'humeur,** equanimity of mind.

égard *n.m.* regard, respect; esteem; consideration; attentions. **là l'égard de votre fils,** regarding your son. **il lui a manqué d'~s,** he was disrespectful to him/her, he was inconsiderate towards him/her. **à cet ~,** regarding, concerning, in this respect. **à tous ~,** in every respect, in all respects. **à mon ~,** toward me, to me.

égaré, e *p.p. or adj.* strayed, stray, lost; going astray. **des sentiers ~s,** devious paths. **les yeux ~s,** staring eyes.

égarement *n.m.* wandering; error; aberration. **égarement d'esprit,** mental aberration.

égarer *v.t.* to mislead; to lead astray; to bewilder; to mislay; to unsettle. **j'avais égaré ce livre,** I had mislaid this book. **s'~,** *v.refl.* to lose one's way, to lose oneself, to go astray, to go wrong, to stray. **il est facile de s'~ dans les rues de Paris,** it is easy to get lost in the streets of Paris. **la lettre s'est égarée,** the letter has been lost.

égayer *v.t.* to enliven; to cheer, to divert; to gladden; to rejoice; to cheer up, to amuse; *Hort.* to thin, to lop off. **~ la conversation,** to enliven the conversation. **s'~,** *v.refl.* to cheer up, to be (or become) cheerful, to brighten up; to divert oneself. **il faut vous ~ un peu,** you must divert yourself a little.

Égée *n.m.* Ageus. **la mer ~,** the Aegean Sea.

églantier *n.m.* ~ **sauvage,** wild rosebush.

églantine *n.f. Bot.* eglantine, dogrose.

église *n.f.* church. l'~ **anglicane,** the Church of England. **un homme d'~,** a churchman, a clergyman.

égo *n.m.* self, ego.

égoïne *n.f.* handsaw.

égoïsme *n.m.* egoism; selfishness.

égoïste *n.m.f.* selfish person. *adj.* selfish; egotistic.

égorger *v.t.* to cut the throat of; to kill, to slaughter, to slay, to butcher, to murder. **s'~,** *v.refl.* to cut one's own throat; to cut each other's throats, to murder each other.

égosiller *v.refl.* to shout one's head off, to get hoarse; (of birds) to sing loud.

égotisme *n.m.* egotism.

égotiste *adj.* egotistic, egotistical; vain; conceited. *n.m.f.* egotist.

égout *n.m.* dripping; drip; sewer, drain, sink. ~ **collecteur de Paris,** main sewer of Paris.

égouttage *n.m.* draining, drainage.

égoutter *v.t.* to drain; to let drip. *v.i.* to drain dry; to drip. **faire ~,** to drain dry; to let drip. **s'~,** *v.refl.* to drain.

égouttoir *n.m.* drainer; dishrack.

égratigner *v.t.* to scratch; to claw. **s'~,** *v.refl.* to scratch oneself; to scratch each other.

égratignure *n.f.* scratch. **s'en sortir sans une ~,** to come out of it without a scratch, unhurt.

égrenage *n.m.* shelling (of grains); picking off (grapes) from the bunch.

égrener *v.t.* to shell (grains), to take out the seed of. **s'~,** *v.refl.* to shell (as corn or grain); (of grapes) to fall from the stalk.

égrillard, e *adj. Infml.* sprightly, brisk. *n.m.* sprightly young fellow. *n.f.* lively girl.

Égypte *n.m.* Egypt.

Égyptien, enne *n.m.f.* Egyptian. *adj.* Egyptian.

égyptologie *n.f.* egyptology.

égyptologue *n.m.f.* egyptologist.

eh *interj.* ah, ha. **eh bien!** well! well now!

éhonté, e *adj.* shameless, brazen.

eider *n.m.* eider.

éjaculation *n.f.* ejaculation.

éjaculatoire *adj.* ejactulatory.

éjaculer *v.t.* to ejaculate.

éjectable *adj.* ejector (seat).

éjecter *v.t. to eject.* **se faire ~,** to get kicked out.

éjection *n.f.* ejection.

élaboration *n.f.* elaboration.

élaborer *v.t.* to elaborate; to work out. **s'~,** *v.refl.* to be elaborated; to be worked out.

élan *n.m.* spring, bound, jump; flight; burst, outburst, outbreak; transport, rapture; elk, moose-deer.

élancé, e *adj.* slender; slim.

élancement *n.m.* starting; twinge, twitch; longing, desire, aspiration. **un ~ douloureux,** a shooting pain.

élancer *v.t.* to shoot, to shoot out, to throw out, to dart forth. *v.i.* to shoot, to twinge, to twitch. **s'~,** *v.refl.* to spring; to start up; to shoot forth; to burst forth; to dash.

élargir *v.t.* to enlarge; to widen; to extend, to dilate; to release, to set free. ~ **ses idées,** to expand one's ideas. ~ **un prisonnier,** to release a prisoner. **s'~,** *v.refl.* to enlarge, to widen, to grow wider; to stretch; to let out; to spread out.

élargissement *n.m.* enlargement; widening, enlarging, increase. l'~ **d'une rue,** the widening of a street.

élasticité *n.f.* elasticity.

élastique *adj.* elastic; buoyant. *n.m.* elastic, rubber band.

électeur, trice *n.m.f.* voter, constituent, elector.

électif, ive *adj.* elective.

élection *n.f.* election; choice. l'~ **d'un président,** the election of a president.

électoral, e *adj.* electoral, elective. **droit ~,** right to vote.

électoralisme *n.m.* electioneering.

électorat *n.m.* electorate.

électricien, ienne *n.m.f.* electrician.

électricité *n.f.* electricity.

électrification *n.f.* electrification.

électrifier *v.t.* to electrify.

électrique *adj.* electric, electrical. **courant ~,** electric current.

électrisable *adj.* electrifiable.

électrisant, e *adj.* electrifying, thrilling, charming, enchanting.

électrisation *n.f.* electrification, electrization.

électriser *v.t.* to electrify. **s'~,** *v.refl.* to electrify, to become electric; to be electrified.

électroacoustique *adj.* electroacoustic(al); *n.f.* electroacoustics.

électro-aimant *n.m.* electromagnet.

électrocardiogramme *n.m.* electrocardiogram.

électrocardiographe *n.m.* electrocardiograph.

électrocardiographie *n.f.* electrocardiography.

électrochimie *n.f.* electrochemistry.

électrochimique *adj.* electrochemical.

électrochoc *n.m.* electric shock treatment.

électrocuter *v.t.* to electrocute.

électrocution *n.f.* electrocution.

électrode *n.f.* electrode.

électrodynamique *adj.* electrodynamic. *n.f.* electrodynamics.

électro-encéphalogramme *n.m.* electro-encephalogram.

électrogène *adj.* generating. **groupe ~,** power plant.

électrolyse *n.f.* electrolysis.

électromagnétique *adj.* electromagnetic.

électromagnétisme *n.m.* electromagnetism.

électromécanique *adj.* elecromechanical. *n.f.* electromechanics.

électroménager *adj.* domestic, household. *n.m.* ~**s,** household appliances.

électrométallurgie *n.f.* electrometallurgy.

électromètre *n.m.* electrometer.

électromoteur, trice adj. Phys. electromotive. n.m. electrometer.

électron n.m. electron.

électronégatif, ive adj. electronegative.

électronicien, ne n.m.f. electronics engineer.

électronique adj. electronic; n.f. electronics.

électrostatique adj. electrostatic; n.f. electrostatics.

électrothérapie n.f. electrotherapy.

élégamment adv. elegantly.

élégance n.f. elegance.

élégant, e adj. elegant; stylish; fashionable. **un style ~,** an elegant style. n.m. dandy, fashionable gentleman. n.f. fashionable lady.

élégiaque adj. elegiac; plaintive, sorrowful, mournful. n.m. elegist.

élégie n.f. elegy.

élément n.m. element, component; ingredient; cell; fact; pupil. **nous avons tous les ~s qu'il nous faut,** we have all the facts we need. **c'est le meilleur ~ de la classe,** he/she is the best pupil of the class. **être dans son ~,** to be in one's element. **les premiers ~s,** the rudiments.

élémentaire adj. elementary; primary; rudimentary.

éléphant n.m. elephant.

éléphantesque adj. enormous, gigantic.

éléphantiasis n.f. elephantiasis.

éléphantin, ine adj. elephantine.

élevage n.m. breeding, rearing (of cattle).

élévateur, trice adj. lifting; n.m. elevator.

élévation n.f. elevation, erection (building); raising; altitude; eminence, rise; exaltation; dignity. **l'~ de sa voix,** the raising of his voice. **quelle ~ de sentiment!** what noble sentiments! **l'~ du caractère,** nobleness of mind.

élève n.m.f. pupil, schoolchild (in elementary school).

élevé, e p.p. and adj. elevated; raised high, tall, towering; eminent. **bien/mal ~,** well/ill mannered, well/badly brought up.

élever v.t. to raise; to elevate, to raise up, to uplift; to heighen; to set up; to increase; to build up, to erect; to breed, to rear; to educate. **ses services l'ont élevé au plus haut rang,** his services have raised him to the highest rank. **~ le prix d'une chose,** to raise the price of a thing. **~ des difficultés,** to raise difficulties. **c'est le devoir des parents d'~ leurs enfants,** it is the parents' duty to raise their children. **~ des chevaux,** to breed horses. **s'~,** v.refl. to rise, to arise, to mount; to amount; to raise oneself; to be elevated; to stand up; to be started. **nous vîmes s'~ un nuage de poussière,** we saw a cloud of dust rise. **s'~ au-dessus des passions,** to rise above passion.

éleceur, euse n.m.f. breeder (animals).

elfe n.m. elf.

éligibilité n.f. eligibility.

éligible adj. eligible. n.m. eligible person.

élimer v.t. to wear out. **s'~,** v.refl. to wear out, to be worn out.

élimination n.f. elimination; extermination.

éliminatoire adj. eliminatory; disqualifying.

éliminer v.t. to eliminate, to get rid of; to exterminate; to strike out, to remove.

élire v.t. to elect. Law. to appoint.

élision n.f. elision.

élite n.f. choice, pick, elite, best, prime.

élixir n.m. elixir.

elle pers. pron. n.f. she; her; it. **~-même,** herself; itself. **~s-mêmes,** themselves.

ellipse n.f. ellipsis; Geom. ellipse.

élocution n.f. elocution.

éloge n.m. eulogy, praise, commendation. **faire l'~ de quelqu'un,** to praise a person. **digne d'~s,** praiseworthy, commendable.

élogieux, euse adj. commendary, full of praise.

éloigné, e adj. distant, remote; far. **un pays ~,** a distant country. **des parents ~s,** distant relatives.

éloignement n.m. removal; removing; departure; withdrawal; neglect; absence; distance, remoteness. **ceux qui demandaient son ~ faisaient eux-mêmes son éloge,** even those who asked for his removal praised him.

éloigner v.t. to remove, to put away; to dismiss; to put off, to send away, to alienate, to indispose. **éloignez cette table,** remove that table. **~ des soupçons,** to avert suspicion. **s'~,** v.refl. to go away, to go far; to go off, to move away. **éloignez-vous un peu,** move away a little. **s'~ de son sujet,** to wander from one's subject.

élongation n.f. elongation.

éloquence n.f. eloquence.

éloquent, e adj. eloquent.

élu, e p.p. elected, chosen; elect; appointed. n.m. elected person; chosen; elect.

élucidation n.f. elucidation.

élucider v.t. to elucidate.

éluder v.t. to elude, to evade; to escape, to shun. **~ une question,** to evade a question.

émaciation n.f. emaciation.

émacié, e adj. emaciated, lean, thin.

émail n.m. enamel; enamelwork.

émailler v.t. to enamel. **s'~,** v.refl. to be enameled.

émanation n.f. emanation.

émancipation n.f. emancipation.

émanciper v.t. to emancipate; to liberate. **s'~,** v.refl. to become emancipated.

émaner v.i. to emanate; Fig. to proceed from.

émasculation n.f. emasculation; castration.

émasculer v.t. to emasculate, to castrate.

emballage n.m. packing; wrapping.

emballer v.t. to pack, to pack up; to send off. **~ des marchandises,** to pack up goods. **s'~,** v.refl. to set off, to depart in haste; to go off; to get overexcited.

embarcadère n.m. wharf (of port); pier; departure platform.

embarcation *n.f.* boat, small craft.

embardée *n.f. Naut.* yaw, lurch, skid; swerve; wild steering.

embargo *n.m.* embargo.

embarquement *n.m.* embarkation; loading; boarding; shipping; shipment (of goods).

embarquer *v.t.* to embark; to ship, to put on shipboard, to put on board; to take on board. **~ des marchandises**, to ship goods. **~ quelqu'un dans une intrigue**, to draw a person into an intrigue. **s'~**, *v.refl.* to embark; to go on shipboard; to take shipping.

embarras *n.m.* obstruction; obstacle, hindrance; encumbrance; embarrassment; derangement. **causer de l'~ à**, to embarrass; to inconvenience. **faire de l'~**, to make a fuss. **eprouver de l'~**, to feel embarrassment.

embarrassant, e *adj.* embarrassing; troublesome; perplexing.

embarrasser *v.t.* to obstruct; to block up; to be in the way off; to hinder, to retard; to encumber; to clog; to hamper; to embarrass, to puzzle. **un air embarrassé**, an embarrassed look. **s'~**, *v.refl.* to be entangled, to become entangled; to become embarrassed; to be perplexed. **s'~ dans ses discours**, to lose track of what one is saying.

embaucher *v.t.* to hire.

embaucheur *n.m.* recruiter.

embaumer *v.t.* to embalm; to perfume, to scent.

embellir *v.t.* to embellish; to beautify, to adorn, to set off. **~ une histoire**, to embellish a story. *v.i.* to grow beautiful or handsome; to grow handsomer; to improve. **s'~**, *v.refl.* to become beautiful; to adorn oneself.

embellissement *n.m.* embellishment; decoration; ornament.

emberlificoter *v.t. Infml.* to mix up; to entangle.

embêtant, e *adj.* annoying, boring, tiresome.

embêtement *n.m.* annoyance, bother; nuisance, aggravation.

embêter *v.t.* to annoy, to bore, to bother, to tease.

emblée *adv. phr.* right away, at once, with the greatest ease, without difficulty; without opposition. **être nommé d'~**, to be elected without opposition.

emblème *n.m.* emblem, device; symbol.

embobiner *v.t.* to wheedle; to mix up.

emboitement *n.m.* fitting in, joint, insertion.

emboiter *v.t.* to fit in, to joint; to set in; to clamp. **s'~**, *v.refl.* to fit into each other, to fit in. **~ le pas à quelqu'un**, to follow in someone's footsteps.

embonpoint *n.m.* plumpness, stoutness, lustiness. **avoir de l'~**, to be stout.

embouchée, e *p.p.* mouthed; entered into a narrow passage. **mal ~**, foul-mouthed.

emboucher *v.t.* to put to the mouth; to blow (a trumpet, etc.), to tongue (a flute) or to bit (a horse). **~ la trompette**, to sound the trumpet, to trumpet. **s'~**, *v.refl.* to fall, to discharge, to empty itself (into).

embouchure *n.f.* mouthpiece (of a wind instrument); tonguing, blowing (of the horn); bridle bit (of a horse); mouth. **l'~ de la Seine**, the mouth of the Seine.

embourber *v.t.* to stick in the mud; to involve. **~ quelqu'un dans une mauvaise affaire**, to involve a person in a troublesome affair. **s'~**, *v.refl.* to stick, to sink in the mud; to be involved.

embouteillage *n.m.* traffic jam; bottleneck.

embouteiller *v.t.* to jam, to block.

emboutir *v.t.* to crash into, to stamp. **s'~**, to crash (against).

embranchement *n.m.* branching, branching off; junction (of roads); branch; *Railw.* branch line.

embrancher *v.t.* to branch, to join. **s'~**, *v.refl.* to join each other, to join; *Railw.* to branch off.

embrasement *n.m.* conflagration; burning; fire.

embraser *v.t.* to fire, to set on fire, to inflame. **s'~**, *v.refl.* to catch fire, to be inflamed, to be aglow.

embrassade *n.f.* embrace; kissing; hugging

embrassement *n.m.* embrace.

embrasser *v.t.* to embrace; to hug; to kiss, to comprise, to take in. **il embrassa sa femme et ses enfants**, he kissed his wife and children. **~ une cause**, to embrace, to adopt a cause. **s'~**, *v.refl.* to embrace each other.

embrayer *v.t. Mech.* to engage, to put in gear.

embrocher *v.t.* to put food on a spit; to skewer; to run through.

embrouillé, e *adj.* perplexed, embroiled; intricate.

embrouillement *n.m.* confusion, perplexity; intricacy.

embrouiller *v.t.* to embroil; to involve in troubles; to confound, to confuse, to perplex, to entangle. **~ une affaire**, to complicate a situation. **s'~**, *v.refl.* to become confused, intricate; to become embroiled, to become perplexed.

embroussaillé, e *adj.* bushy; overgrown; intricate.

embrumé, e *adj.* foggy, hazy, misty, dark.

embrumer *v.t.* to cover with fog, haze, mist; to overcast; to darken. **s'~**, *v.refl.* to get foggy, hazy, misty, to haze.

embryon *n.m.* embryo.

embûche *n.f.* ambush; snares, trap. **dresser des ~s**, to lay an ambush, to lay snares.

embué, e *adj.* misty.

embuscade *n.f.* ambush. **être en ~**, to lie in wait, to ambush.

embusquer *v.t.* to ambush, to place in ambush. **s'~**, *v.refl.* to ambush, to lie in ambush, to lie in wait.

émeraude *n.f.* emerald.

émergence *n.f.* emergence.

émerger *v.i.* to emerge.

émeri *n.m.* emery. **papier ~**, sandpaper.

émerite *adj.* retired; perfect, skilled.

émersion *n.f.* emersion.

émerveillement *n.m.* astonishment, amazement, wonder.

émerveiller *v.t.* to astonish, to amaze. **s'~**, *v.refl.* to wonder, to be astonished, to be amazed, to be wonderstruck.

émétique *n.m.* emetic. *adj.* emetic, inducing vomiting.

émetteur, trice *adj.* transmitting, transmitter; *n.m.* transmitter, transceiver.

émettre *v.t.* to emit; to give out, to throw out, to issue; to utter (sounds); to express.

émeute *n.f.* riot, disturbance.

émietter *v.t.* to crumble, to crumb, to fritter away. **s'~**, *v.refl.* to crumble.

émigrant, e *n.m.f.* emigrant. *adj.* emigrant, emigrating.

émigration *n.f.* emigration; (of birds) migration.

émigré, e *n.m.f.* emigrant.

émigrer *v.i.* to emigrate; (of birds) to migrate.

émincer *v.t.* to mince.

éminemment *adv.* eminently.

éminence *n.f.* eminence, eminency, height, hill.

éminent, e *adj.* eminent; distinguished, high, elevated.

émir *n.m.* emir.

émirat *n.m.* emirate.

émissaire *n.m.* emissary. *adj.* **bouc ~**, scapegoat.

émission *n.f.* emission, utterance; issue; program; broadcast.

emmagasinage *n.m.* warehousing, storing.

emmagasiner *v.t.* to warehouse; to store up; to accumulate.

emmaillotter *v.t.* to swaddle, to wrap up.

emmanchement *n.m.* putting a handle.

emmancher *v.t.* to haft, to put a handle to; to helve (an axe, a hatchet). *Fig.* to begin, to set about. **~ une affaire**, to set about an affair. **s'~**, *v.refl.* to fit on; to be done, to be easy. **cela ne s'emmanche pas ainsi**, that cannot be done so easily.

emmanchure *n.f.* sleeve hole, armhole.

emmêler *v.t.* to entangle, to complicate. **s'~**, *v.refl.* to get entangled.

emménagement *n.m.* moving in.

emménager *v.i.* to move in.

emmener *v.t.* to take away; to carry away; to drive away.

emment(h)al *n.m.* Emmenthal, Swiss cheese.

emmerdant, e *adj. Vulg.* annoying or boring.

emmerdement *n.m. Vulg.* nuisance; trouble. **avoir des ~s**, to be in deep trouble.

emmerder *v.t.* to bother; to annoy; to bore. **s'~**, to be extremely bored or annoyed.

emmerdeur, euse *n.m.f. Vulg.* nuisance.

emmitoufler *v.t.* to wrap up, to muffle up. **s'~**, *v.refl.* to muffle or wrap oneself up.

emmurer *v.t.* to wall in, to immure.

émoi *n.m.* emotion, anxiety, flutter, flurry, alarm. **mettre en ~**, to stir up.

émonder *v.t. Hort.* to prune, to lop, to trim.

émotif, ive *adj.* emotional; emotive; *n.m.f.* emotional person.

émotion *n.f.* emotion; excitement; feeling; tremor. **les ~s de l'âme**, the agitations of the mind.

émotionel, le *adj.* emotional.

émotionner *v.t.* to cause emotion.

émoulu, e *adj.* sharp, sharpened. **être frais ~ du collège**, to be right out of high school.

émousser *v.t.* to blunt, to take off the edge of; to dull; to clear moss from. **s'~**, *v.refl.* to become blunt or dull.

émoustiller *v.t.* to exhilarate, to rouse, to stir up, to titillate.

émouvant, e *adj.* moving, touching.

émouvoir *v.t.* to move; to disturb, to rouse, to raise; to excite, to stir, to stir up. **s'~**, *v.refl.* to be moved; to be touched, to be affected.

empaillage *n.m.* stuffing (of animals), taxidermy.

empailler *v.t.* to stuff (animals); to upholster (of chairs).

empailleur, euse *n.m.f.* (chair) upholsterer; (animal) taxidermist.

empalement *n.m.* impalement.

empaler *v.t.* to impale.

empaqueter *v.t.* to pack, to pack up, to bundle up, to wrap up. **s'~**, *v.refl.* to wrap oneself up. *Infml.* to be packed together, to be huddled together.

emparer *v.refl.* (with **de**) to take possession of; to seize upon; to lay hold of, to secure. **s'~ d'un héritage**, to seize upon an inheritance.

empâté, e *p.p.* clammy, sticky; fattened; *Paint.* impasted.

empâter *v.t.* to make clammy, sticky; to fatten, to stuff (poultry).

empattement *n.m.* base, basement; (of foundations) footing.

empêchement *n.m.* impediment; hindrance, obstruction. **sans ~**, unimpeded.

empêcher *v.t.* to hinder; to prevent; to forbid; to impede; to embarrass. **cela empêche de voir**, that blocks the view. **~ un mariage**, to prevent a marriage. **l'un n'empêche pas l'autre**, one does not preclude the other. **s'~**, *v.refl.* to keep oneself (from); to keep (from); to help, to forbear, to refrain (from). **il n'a pu s'~ de palir**, he could not help turning pale.

empereur *n.m.* emperor.

empester *v.t.* to infect; to taint; to stink.

empêtrer *v.t.* to entangle, to hamper; to shackle. **s'~**, *v.refl.* to get hampered; to get entangled; to be embarrassed.

emphase *n.f.* emphasis; pomposity, bombast, grandiloquence.

emphatique *adj.* emphatic, striking; pompous, bombastic.

emphatiquement *adj.* emphatically; pompously.

emphysème *n.m.* emphysema.

empiéter *v.t.* to encroach upon; to infringe upon; to invade. *v.i.* (with **sur**) to encroach (upon), to invade. ~ **sur les droits de quelqu'un,** to encroach upon a person's rights.

empiffrer (s') *v.refl.* to stuff oneself.

empilement *n.m.* piling, piling up, stacking.

empiler *v.t.* to pile, to pile up; to stack. **s'~,** *v.refl.* to be piled up.

empire *n.m.* empire; sway, rule; dominion; power over, control over; influence. **elle est sous son ~,** she is under his/her control.

empirer *v.t.* to make worse; to worsen, to aggravate. *v.i.* to get worse.

emplacement *n.m.* site, spot, ground; location; campsite.

emplâtre *n.m. Pharm.* patch; salve, ointment.

emplette *n.f.* purchase. **faire des ~,** to go shopping.

emplir *v.t.* to fill, to fill up. **s'~,** *v.refl.* to fill.

emploi *n.m.* employment; use; job, trade. **l'~ du temps,** schedule. **chercher de l'~,** to look for work. **être sans ~,** to be unemployed.

employé, ée *n.m.f.* employee.

employer *v.t.* to employ; use, to make use of; to appreciate, to devote. **bien ~ son temps,** to make good use of one's time. **s'~,** *v.refl.* to be employed, to be used; to occupy oneself. **ce mot ne s'emploie pas dans ce sens,** that word is not used in that sense.

employeur, euse *n.m.f.* employer.

empocher *v.t. Infml.* to pocket.

empoigner *v.t.* to seize; to grasp, to lay hold of. **~ quelqu'un par les bras,** to grasp a person by the arms. **s'~,** *v.refl.* to be seized, to be grasped.

empois *n.m.* starch.

empoisonnant, e *adj. Infml.* irritating; annoying, bothersome.

empoisonnement *n.m.* poisoning.

empoisonner *v.t.* to poison; to infect; to corrupt, to taint; to embitter. **s'~,** *v.refl.* to poison oneself, to take poison.

empoisonneur, euse *n.m.f.* poisoner. *adj.* poisonous.

emporté, e *adj.* passionate, hasty, fiery, hotheaded. **un caractère ~,** hasty temper.

emportement *n.m.* passion; fit; burst, outburst, violence. **un ~ de colère,** a fit of anger.

emporter *v.t.* to carry away; to take away; to carry off; to run away with; to carry off with violence; to surpass. **emportez vos meubles,** take your furniture away. **~ un blessé,** to carry away a wounded man. **la colère l'a emporté à la vengeance,** anger excited him to revenge. **un boulet lui emporta la tête,** a cannonball carried off his head. **l'~ sur,** to prevail, to get the better of. **la sagesse l'emporte toujours sur la folie,** wisdom always prevails over folly. **s'~,** *v.refl.* to be carried away, to be carried off; to fly into a passion; to take fright; to run away (as a

horse). **(plats) à ~,** take-out food, food to go. **~ la bouche,** to be too spicy, to burn the mouth. **se laisser ~,** to get carried away.

empoté, e *adj.* awkward, clumsy; *n.m.f.* awkward person.

empourprer *v.t.* to purple, to tinge with purple. **s'~,** *v.refl.* to be purpled; to flush, to blush.

empoussiéré, e *adj.* dusty.

empreindre *v.t.* to imprint; to stamp. **s'~,** *v.refl.* to leave a print.

empreint, e *p.p.* imprinted, stamped.

empreinte *n.f.* impress, impression, stamp, mark; print, footprint.

empressé, e *adj.* bustling; stirring; prompt; willing; earnest; zealous.

empressement *n.m.* earnestness, eagerness, readiness, promptness; alacrity. **avec ~,** earnestly, with haste.

empresser *v.refl.* to hasten; to be eager, to be earnest; to be anxious; to be in a hurry. **je m'empressai de l'avertir,** I hastened to warn him.

emprise *n.f.* hold; influence; grip. **elle a de l'~ sur lui,** she has a grip on him.

emprisonnement *n.m.* imprisonment; confinement.

emprisonner *v.t.* to imprison; to confine.

emprunt *n.m.* borrowing; loan. **faire un ~,** to borrow.

emprunter *v.t.* to borrow; to assume, to imitate, to counterfeit. **un mot emprunté au latin,** a word borrowed from Latin.

emprunteur, euse *n.m.f.* borrower. *adj.* borrowing, that borrows.

empuantir *v.t.* to infect; to make stink. **s'~,** *v.refl.* to become putrid; to begin to stink.

ému, e *adj.* moved; touched; filled with emotion.

emulation *n.f.* emulation.

emulsion *n.f.* emulsion.

en *prep.* in. **vivre ~ Angleterre,** to live in England. **un officer ~ retraite,** a retired officer. **être ~ bonne santé,** to be in good health. **être ~ paix, ~ guerre,** to be at peace, at war. **vivre ~ repos,** to live peacefully. **une femme ~ deuil,** a woman in mourning. **~ peu de temps,** in a short time. **aller ~ France,** to go to France. **vous remettez de jour ~ jour,** you put off from day to day. **traduire ~ anglais,** to translate into English. **parler ~ ami,** to speak like a friend.

en *pron.* of (from, about, with, by, for, etc.). him *n.m.* her *n.f.* them *n.f.pl.* **je connais ces gens-là, vous ~ serez satisfait,** I know those people, you will be pleased with them. (In a partitive sense) some, any. **j'ai des pommes; ~ voulez-vous?** I have some apples; would you like some? **vous ~ aurez,** you'll have some.

encadrement *n.m.* framing, frame.

encadrer *v.t.* to frame; to encircle; to insert. **~ gravure,** to frame an engraving. **ils ne peuvent pas s'~,** they can't stand each other.

encager v.t. to encage, to cage; Fig. to confine, to imprison.

encaisse n.f. cash in hand.

encaissement n.m. packing, packing up; collection, receipt (of bills); embankment.

encaisser v.t. to pack in a case or box, to collect, to receive (bills, money); to embank (a river).

encapuchonner v.t. to put a hood on. s'~, v.refl. to wear a hood; to cover one's head.

encarter v.t. Print. to insert. s'~, v.refl. to be inserted.

en-cas n.m. snack.

encastrement n.m. fitting in.

encastrer v.t. to fit in, to let in; to set into a groove. s'~, v.refl. to fit together.

enceinte adj. pregnant. n.f. enclosure; fence; wall; precinct; hall (of a tribunal).

encens n.m. incense; praise, flattery.

encercler v.t. to surround, to encircle.

enchaînement n.m. chaining; chain, succession.

enchaîner v.t. to chain; to bind, to restrain; to link, to enslave, to fetter, to chain down; to connect. s'~, v.refl. to be linked, to be connected together.

enchanté, e adj. delighted; enchanted. je suis ~ de faire votre connaissance, I'm pleased to meet you. la fée habite dans la forêt ~, the fairy lives in the enchanted forest.

enchantement n.m. enchantment; spell, charm; wonder; fascination; delight. comme par ~, as if by magic.

enchanter v.t. to enchant; to charm; to enrapture; to delight. cette musique m'a enchanté, that music delighted me.

enchâsser v.t. to enshrine; to enchase; to set; to preserve. ~ un diamant, to set a diamond.

enchère n.f. bid, bidding; outbidding; auction. folle ~, resale at any price of overstock merchandise. mettre aux ~s, to sell by auction.

enchérir v.t. to bid for; to outbid; to become more expensive.

enchevêtrer v.t. to entangle, to confuse, to embroil. ~ une affaire, to complicate an affair. s'~, v.refl. to get entangled.

enclaver v.t. to enclose; to surround, to confine on all sides; to frame together. s'~, v.refl. to be locked, to be enclosed.

enclencher v.t. to interlock; to engage, to set in motion.

enclin, ine adj. inclined, prone, disposed.

enclore v.t. defect. to enclose; to fence in.

enclos, e p.p. and n.m. enclosure.

enclume n.f. anvil; Anat. incus. être entre l'~ et le marteau, to be between the devil and the deep blue sea.

encoche n.f. notch.

encoignure n.f. corner.

encollage n.m. pasting.

encoller v.t. to paste.

encolure n.f. neck and shoulders (of a horse); neck (of a coat).

encombrant, e adj. cumbersome, bulky, large-sized; in the way.

encombre n.m. impediment, hindrance, obstacle; accident. sans ~, without problems.

encombrement n.m. traffic, traffic-jam; congestion.

encombrer v.t. to obstruct, to stop up, to block up, to fill, to stuff up. s'~, v.refl. to burden oneself.

encontre adv. against. je ne vais pas à l'~ de ce que vous dites, I'm not contradicting what you are saying.

encore adv. still; yet; again, once again, once more, still more; as yet; at all; even; also, as well. il vit ~, he is still alive. j'en veux ~, I want some more. ~ une fois, once more. ceci nous fournit ~ une autre raison, this furnishes us with yet one more reason. aviez-vous ~ quelque chose à faire? had you anything else to do? ~ que, though, although. ~ un mot et tu seras puni! another word and you'll be punished. il est ~ plus petit que moi, he is even smaller than I am. non seulment il ne part pas aujourd'hui, mais ~, il reste dix jours de plus, not only is he not leaving today, he is staying for another ten days. interj. again!

encorné, e adj. horned.

encornet n.m. squid.

encourageant, e adj. encouraging.

encouragement n.m. encouragement; support.

encourager v.t. to encourage, to cheer; to incite; to support. s'~, v.refl. to encourage one another.

encourir v.t. to incur; to bring upon.

encrasser v.t. to soil, to dirt; to grease, to make greasy. s'~, v.refl. to soil, to get dirty.

encre n.f. ink. ~ de Chine, India ink. ~ d'imprimerie, printing ink.

encroûter v.t. to encrust. s'~, v.refl. to crust, to stagnate.

encyclique adj. encyclical. n.f. encyclical letter.

encyclopédie n.f. encyclopaedia.

endetté, e adj. in debt; indebted.

endettement n.m. getting into debt.

endetter v.t. to get into debt. s'~, v.refl. to run into debt, to incur debts.

endive n.f. endive.

endoctriner v.t. to indoctrinate.

endolori, e adj. painful, aching.

endolorir v.t. to hurt, to be aching; to cause pain.

endommagement n.m. damage, injury.

endommager v.t. to damage, to injure, to harm, to impair.

endormant, e adj. soporific, soporiferous, sleepy; Fig. tiresome.

endormi, e adj. asleep, sleeping; drowsy; sleepy. j'ai le pied tout ~, my foot is asleep. n.m.f. sleepyhead.

endormir v.t. to lull; to lull asleep; to rock to sleep, to wheedle; to benumb; to quiet; to soothe. bercer un enfant pour l'~, to soothe pain. s'~, v.refl. to fall asleep, to go to sleep. il ne peut s'~, he cannot go to sleep.

endos *n.m.* endorsement.

endossement *n.m.* endorsement.

endosser *v.t.* to put on; to saddle; to endorse.

endroit *n.m.* place, spot, passage; side; right side (of a fabric etc.). **je vais à tel ~,** I am going to such-and-such a place. **à (or en) son ~,** toward him; respecting him.

enduire *v.t.* to do over, to lay on a coat, to coat. **~ de goudron,** to tar.

enduit *n.m.* coat, coating; layer; plaster; glaze, glazing.

endurance *n.f.* endurance; stamina.

endurant, e *adj.* enduring; bearing, supporting with patience; patient.

endurci, e *adj.* hardened, callous, insensible.

endurcir *v.t.* to harden; to make hard; to make hardy, firm or strong. **~ le corps,** to harden the body. **s'~,** *v.refl.* to harden; to grow hardened.

endurcissement *n.m.* hardening; toughness; *Fig.* hardness.

endurer *v.t.* to endure; to bear, to suffer; to bear with patience, to support, to put up with. **~ de la douleur,** to bear pain.

énergétique *adj.* energetic.

énergie *n.f.* energy; force, vigour. **agir avec ~,** to act energetically.

énergique *adj.* energetic.

énergiquement *adv.* energetically.

énervant, e *adj.* irritating, annoying.

énervé, e *adj.* irritated; annoyed.

énervement *n.m.* irritation, annoyance; excitement; nervousness.

énerver *v.t.* to irritate; to annoy; to get on someone's nerves. **s'~,** to get excited. **tu m'énerves au plus haut point,** you are getting on my nerves.

enfance *n.f.* childhood; infancy. **tomber en ~,** enter one's second childhood.

enfant *n.m.f.* child; offspring, issue. **sans ~,** childless. **faire l'~,** to behave like a child. **c'est un jeu d'~,** that's child's play. **un ~ terrible,** an incorrigible child. **c'est bien l'~ de sa mère,** he (she) is his (her) mother's own child. **un bon ~,** a good fellow, a simpleton. **un ~ de Paris,** a native of Paris.

enfanter *v.t.* to bring forth, to give birth to; to engender.

enfantillage *n.m.* child's play, childishness, puerility.

enfantin, ine *adj.* infantile, childish.

enfariner *v.t.* to sprinkle with flour, to flour, to dust.

enfer *n.m.* hell. **un feu d'~,** a blazing fire.

enfermer *v.t.* to shut up, to shut in; to confine; to lock up; to enclose; to hem in; to include. **~ quelqu'un dans sa chambre,** to shut a person up in his room. **~ à clef,** to lock up. **s'~,** *v.refl.* to shut oneself up. *Fig.* **s'~ sur soi-même,** to retreat into oneself.

enficeler *v.t.* to tie up, to tie with a twine.

enfiévré, e *adj.* feverish, hot, fervid, ardent, passionate.

enfiévrer *v.t.* to fever, to fire, to inflame. **s'~,** to become feverish; to become nervous; to become excited.

enfiler *v.t.* to thread, to string, to file, to run through; to put on. **~ le pas,** to follow; to go along. **s'~,** *v.refl.* to be threaded; to be strung, to be run through.

enfin *adv.* at last, finally; in short, in a word; at length. **~, je vous rencontre,** I meet you at last.

enflammé, e *p.p.* burning; in flames, in a blaze; inflamed.

enflammer *v.t.* to set on fire, to kindle, to fire; to ignite. **s'~,** *v.refl.* to kindle, to take fire, to be kindled, to blaze, to become excited; to become inflamed.

enflé, e *p.p.* swollen, blown up, inflated.

enfler *v.t.* to swell, to puff, to inflate, to puff up, to elate. **le vent enfle les voiles,** the wind swells the sails. *v.i.* to swell, to rise. **s'~,** *v.refl.* to swell, to be swollen, to puff (with air or wind). **son pied commence à s'~,** his foot is beginning to swell.

enflure *n.f.* swelling; *Infml.* jerk.

enfoncement *n.m.* sinking, sinking down; driving; forcing in; breaking in, breaking open, bursting open; hollow. **un ~ de terrain,** a hollow place.

enfoncer *v.t.* to sink; to drive down, to thrust down; to force in; to break in. **~ un clou dans le mur,** to drive a nail into the wall; **~ son chapeau sur la tête,** to pull one's hat over one's eyes. **~ une porte,** to break a door in. *v.i.* to sink, to sink down, to go to the bottom. **s'~,** *v.refl.* to sink; to sink down, to subside, to plunge, to sink in; to take in (to deceive); to get into a mess. **s'~ dans le bois,** to get away into the wood. **à ces mots il s'enfonça dans son lit,** at these words he buried himself in his bed. **s'~ dans l'ignorance,** to be immersed in ignorance.

enfouir *v.t.* to bury; to conceal. **s'~,** *v.refl.* to go into a hole, as a fox, to bury oneself.

enfouissement *n.m.* burying, hiding.

enfourcher *v.t.* to bestride, to straddle.

enfourner *v.t.* to put in the oven. **s'~,** *v.refl.* to embark, to get into.

enfreindre *v.t.* to infringe, to violate, to break, to transgress. **~ les lois,** to transgress the laws.

enfuir (s') *v.refl.* to flee, to run away, to get away, to escape, to elope. **ils se sont enfuis de tous côtés,** they ran away on all sides.

enfumer *v.t.* to smoke; to fill with smoke; to smoke out.

engagé, e *adj.* committed; enlisted. *n.m.* soldier enlisted; volunteer.

engageant, e *adj.* engaging, winning, attractive.

engagement *n.m.* pledging, pawning; engagement; contract; promise; pledge; obligation; beginning; start. **l'~ des négociations,** the beginning of the negotiations.

engager *v.t.* to pledge; to pawn, to engage; to

unite; to hire; to get into. *Milit.* to enlist. **j'engage ma parole d'honneur,** I give you my word. **s'~,** *v.refl.* to engage oneself; to pledge oneself, to bind oneself; *Milit.* to enlist; to hire oneself; to penetrate. **s'~ dans les liens du mariage,** to bind oneself by marriage. **ne vous engagez pas dans cette affaire,** do not embark in that business. **son pied s'engagea dans l'étrier,** his foot got tangled in the stirrup. **le combat s'engagea vers la fin du jour,** the fight began toward the end of the day.

engelure *n.f.* chilblain.

engendrer *v.t.* to engender, to breed; to generate; to produce. **le jeu engendre les querelles,** gambling causes quarrels.

engin *n.m.* engine, machine, instrument, tool.

englober *v.t.* to blend together; to put together; to unite.

engloutir *v.t.* to swallow up; to engulf; to absorb, to overwhelm (as waves). **s'~,** *v.refl.* to be swallowed up, to be engulfed.

engloutissement *n.m.* swallowing up.

engluer *v.t.* to lime; to ensnare, to take in. **s'~,** *v.refl.* to be caught, to be taken in.

engorgement *n.m.* obstruction, stoppage; *Med.* congestion, engorgement.

engorger *v.t.* to obstruct, to stop up, to choke up. **s'~,** *v.refl.* to be choked up, to be stopped up.

engouement *n.m.* obstruction (in the throat, etc.); *Fig.* infatuation.

engouffrer *v.t.* to engulf, to swallow up. **s'~,** *v.refl.* to be engulfed, to be swallowed up; (of the wind); to rush (into). **le vent s'engouffre dans la cheminée,** the wind blows down the chimney.

engourdi, e *adj.* numb; torpid; dull.

engourdir *v.t.* to numb; *Fig.* to dull, to stupefy, to deaden. **le froid engourdit les membres,** cold numbs the limbs. **s'~,** *v.refl.* to get numbed, to become torpid, to be dull.

engourdissement *n.m.* torpor; numbness, torpidness.

engrais *n.m.* manure; compost, fertilizer.

engraissement *n.m.* fattening; corpulence; manure.

engraisser *v.t.* to fatten; to feed well; to manure; to enrich. *v.i.* to fatten; to grow fat. **s'~,** *v.refl.* to fatten; to grow fat; to become ccorpulent, stout; to thrive; to get rich.

engranger *v.t. Agr.* to house, to get in (grain), to store in a barn.

engraver *v.t. Naut.* to strand; to run aground. *v.i. Naut.* to strand, to run on a sandbank. **s'~,** *v.refl.* to become stranded.

engrenage *n.m.* gear. **il a été pris dans l'~,** he got caught in the system.

engrener *v.t.* to put in gear; *Agr.* to put grain into (the mill); to feed with grain. **~ une affaire,** to begin a business.

engrosser *v.t. Vulg.* to knock up; to get pregnant.

engueulade *n.f. Infml.* trading insults, telling off, bawling out; blast. **engueuler** *v.t. Infml.* to blast. **s'~,** to blast at each other.

enguirlander *v.t.* to encircle with a garland; to scold. **se faire ~,** to get scolded.

enhardir *v.t.* to make bold; to encourage. **s'~,** *v.refl.* to get bold.

en-haut *adv.* upstairs.

énième *adj. Infml.* **pour la ~ fois, je te répète,** for the thousandth time, I'm telling you.

énigmatique *adj.* enigmatic, enigmatical.

énigme *n.f.* enigma; riddle.

énivrant, e *adj.* intoxicating; elating.

énivrement *n.m.* intoxication; inebriation; infatuation.

énivrer *v.t.* to intoxicate, to inebriate, to make drunk; to enrapture; to elate. **s'~,** *v.refl.* to become intoxicated, to get drunk, to be elated.

enjambée *n.f.* stride. **faire de grandes ~s,** to take long strides.

enjamber *v.t.* to stride; to stride over. **~ un fossé,** to stride over a ditch. *v.i.* to stride; to take a stride.

enjeu *n.m.* stake. **retirer son ~,** to remove one's stake from a game.

enjoindre *v.t.* to enjoin; to order to charge. **on lui enjoint de répondre,** he is ordered to answer.

enjôler *v.t.* to inveigle, to cajole; to wheedle.

enjôleur, euse *n.m.f.* inveigler, cajoler, wheedler.

enjoliver *v.t.* to embellish, to ornament, to adorn.

enjoliveur *n.m. Auto.* hub cap.

enjoué, e *adj.* playful, sprightly, merry, cheerful. **une jeune fille ~e,** a merry young girl.

enjouement *n.m.* playfulness, sprightliness, cheerfulness.

enlacer *v.t.* to hug; to interlace; to interweave; to intertwine, to entwine. **~ quelqu'un dans ses bras,** to hug a person in one's arms. **s'~,** *v.refl.* to be interlaced, interwoven; to be entwined.

enlaidir *v.t.* to make ugly. *v.i.* to grow, to become ugly. **s'~,** *v.refl.* to become ugly.

enlèvement *n.m.* carrying away; removal; carrying off; kidnapping, abduction.

enlever *v.t.* to raise, to lift, to lift up, to take up; to sweep away; to carry off; to kidnap; to abduct; to buy up; to enrapture. **~ un corps,** to remove a body. **le vent enlève la poussière,** the wind blows the dust up. **~ l'écorce d'un arbre,** to strip the bark from a tree. **la benzine enlève les taches de graisse,** benzine takes out grease stains. **s'~,** *v.refl.* to rise; to be lifted up, to be raised; to be taken off; to strip off, to peel off; to go off; to come out. **cet ouvrage s'est enlevé en quelques jours,** this work was sold in a few days.

enliser *v.t.* to suck in. **s'~,** to sink in quicksand.

enluminer *v.t.* to color; to illuminate. **~ un livre,** to illuminate a book.

enneigé, e *adj.* covered with snow, snowed up.

ennemi, e *n.m.f.* enemy; foe. **passer à l'~,** to the enemy. *adj.* hostile; inimical, unfriendly, opposite.

ennuager (s') *v.i.* to cloud over.

ennui *n.m.* boredom; tedium, tediousness, weariness; *(pl.)* troubles. **il se cherche des ~s,** he is looking for trouble. **quel ~!** what a bore!

ennuyant, e *adj.* annoying, bothersome, tiresome, wearisome, irksome, tedious.

ennuyé, e *adj.* annoyed, worried, bothered, troubled.

ennuyer *v.t.* to weary; to tire; to annoy, to bore, to tease, to bother. **tout cela m'ennuie,** all that bores me. **s'~,** *v.refl.* to weary oneself, to become weary; to grow tired; to feel dull. **s'~ de tout,** to be weary of (or disgusted with) everything.

ennuyeusement *adv.* tediously, irksomely.

ennuyeux, euse *adj.* tedious, wearisome, irksome, tiresome, dull; annoying, troublesome, boring. **un livre ~,** boring book. **que c'est ~!** how boring!

énoncé, e *n.m.* enunciation; statement, declaration.

énoncer *v.t.* to enunciate; to declare, to state, to set forth; to express, to word. **~ son opinion,** to state one's opinion. **s'~,** *v.refl.* to be expressed; to express oneself, to speak. **il s'énonce avec facilité,** he expresses himself with ease.

énonciation *n.f.* enunciation; utterance, expression; statement.

énorgueillir *v.t.* to make proud. **s'~,** *v.refl.* to pride oneself, to be proud.

énorme *adj.* enormous; huge. **les vacances, ça fait un bien ~,** vacations do you a world of good.

énormément *adv.* tremendously, enormously; hugely.

énormité *n.f.* enormity; enormousness; hugeness; absurdity.

enquérir (s') *v.refl.* to inquire, to make inquiries.

enquête *n.f.* inquiry; investigation; survey. **ordonner une ~,** to order an investigation to be made.

enquêter *v.t.* to investigate.

enquêteur, euse, trice *n.m.f.* police officer in charge of an investigation.

enquiquinant, e *adj. Infml.* bothersome, irritating, annoying.

enquiquiner *v.t. Infml.* to bother, to irritate, to annoy.

enquiquineur, euse *n.m.f. Infml.* pain in the neck, nuisance, pest.

enraciner *v.t.* to root. **s'~,** *v.refl.* to root, to take root.

enragé, e *adj.* enraged, desperate; (of animals) mad, rabid; to be crazy about. **un chien ~,** a mad dog. **manger de la vache ~e,** to suffer great hardships and privations. *n.m.f.* insane person; furious person. **se battre comme un ~,** to fight like a madman.

enrageant *adj.* maddening, provoking, vexing.

enrager *v.i.* to go mad, to become mad; to be enraged, exasperated, vexed; to be in a rage. **il enrage de se voir humilié,** he is vexed at being humiliated. **faire ~,** to drive mad, to exasperate.

enrayage *n.m.* jamming.

enrayer *v.t.* to jam. **~ une maladie,** to stamp out a disease. **s'~,** to jam.

enregistrement *n.m.* registration; recording; entry. **bureau d'~,** registrar office.

enregistrer *v.t.* to register; to enroll; to enter on a register; to record; to make a note of; to check. **s'~,** *v.refl.* to be registered; to be recorded; to be enrolled.

enrhumer *v.t.* to give a cold to (a person). **s'~,** *v.refl.* to catch a cold.

enrichi, e *Pej.* enriched; nouveau riche.

enrichir *v.t.* to enrich; to make rich; to adorn; to embellish. **~ une langue,** to enrich a language. **s'~,** *v.refl.* to enrich a language. **s'~,** *v.refl.* to enrich oneself; to grow rich. **il s'est enrichi par le commerce,** he has grown rich in business.

enrichissement *n.m.* enriching.

enrober *v.t.* to coat; to cover with. **des noisettes enrobées de chocolat,** hazelnuts covered with chocolate.

enrôlé, e *n.m.f.* recruit.

enrôlement *n.m.* enlistment; enrollment.

enrôler *v.t.* to enroll; to enlist. **s'~,** *v.refl.* to enroll oneself; to enlist.

enroué, e *adj.* hoarse.

enrouer *v.t.* to make hoarse. **s'~,** *v.refl.* to become hoarse.

enrouler *v.t.* to roll, to roll up; to wrap round. **s'~,** *v.refl.* to roll oneself up, to roll.

ensabler *v.t.* to run aground, to strand; to cover with sand. **s'~,** *v.refl.* to run on a sandbank, to run aground, to strand.

ensanglanté, e *adj.* bloody; bloodstained.

ensanglanter *v.t.* to stain with blood; to bloodstain.

enseignant, e *n.f.* teaching. *n.m.f.* teacher.

enseigne *n.f.* sign; signboard, emblem. **à bonnes ~s,** on sure grounds, justly. **nous sommes tous deux logés à la même ~,** we both are in the same boat. **les ~s romaines étaient des aigles,** eagles were the emblem of the Romans. *n.m.* ensign; midshipman.

enseignement *n.m.* education; teaching profession; teaching.

enseigner *v.t.* to teach; to instruct; to inform; to educate; to show. **~ la jeunesse,** to teach, to instruct youth. **~ une langue,** to teach a language.

ensemble *adv.* together; both at the same time; at once. **ils sont sortis ~,** they went out together. *n.m.* couple, pair; unity; whole; overall; set, collection; group, body; development; suit, outfit. **il a un superbe ~,** he is wearing an astonishing suit. **les grands ~s de la banlieue,** the suburb's developments. **j'ai un ~ à thé,** I have a tea set; ensemble; harmony; uniformity.

ensemencer *v.t.* to sow (a field).

enserrer *v.t.* to clasp, to hug, to embrace.

ensevelir *v.t.* to shroud, to lay out (a corpse); to bury. **s'~,** *v.refl.* to bury oneself, to be buried.

ensevelissement *n.m.* shrouding, burying.

ensoleillé, e *adj.* sunny.

ensommeillé, e *adj.* sleepy, drowsy.

ensorceler *v.t.* to bewitch, *Fig.* to charm, to enchant, to fascinate, to captivate, to win.

ensorceleur, euse *n.m.f.* bewitcher; sorcerer, sorceress; enchanter, enchantress; charmer.

ensorcellement *n.m.* bewitchment, enchantment, fascinating, charm.

ensuite *adv.* afterward, then, next; later; in the end; after. **elle lui a dit ~ que,** then she told him/her. **il est venu d'abord et elle est arrivée ~,** he came first and she arrived afterward.

ensuivre (s') *v.refl.* defect, to follow, to ensue; to result; to proceed, to spring.

entacher *v.t.* to taint; to stain, to sully, to tarnish.

entaille *n.f.* cut; notch, jag; nick; groove; gash, slash.

entailler *v.t.* to cut, to notch, to jag; to gash.

entame *n.f.* first cut.

entamer *v.t.* to make the first cut into, to cut; to attack; to injure, to impair; to open (as a can or bottle). **~ un sujet,** to begin a subject. **~ la peau,** to cut the skin. **~ la réputation de quelqu'un,** to attack a person's reputation.

entartrer *v.t.* to scale (a fish).

entassement *n.m.* heaping up, piling up; accumulation.

entasser *v.t.* to heap, to heap up; to amass, to hoard up; to pile up, to accumulate. **~ des sacs de blé,** to pile up sacks of grain. **s'~,** *v.refl.* to be piled up, to accumulate.

entendant, e *adj.* **mal ~,** hard of hearing.

entendement *n.m.* understanding; intellect; mind; intelligence.

entendeur *n.m.* **à bon ~ salut,** a word to the wise is sufficient.

entendre *v.i.* to hear of; to understand; to mean; to expect. **il n'entend pas de cette oreille-la,** he is deaf on that matter, he does not want to hear anything on that subject. **il entend de travers,** he hears wrong. **elle ne veut entendre à nulle proposition,** she will not listen to any proposal. **j'entends qu'on m'obéisse,** I intend to be obeyed. *v.t.* to hear; to listen to; to heed; to understand. **~ du bruit,** to hear a noise. **j'entends parler à côté,** I hear talking, close by. **~ des témoins,** to take witnesses' depositions. **donner à ~,** to give to understand. **~ à demi-mot,** to take a hint. **chacun fait comme il entend,** everyone does as he thinks proper. **s'~,** *v.refl.* to be heard; to understand one another; to hear oneself; to agree; to come to an understanding. **sa voix ne s'entend pas,** his voice is not heard. **ce passage ne s'entend pas facilement,** that passage is difficult to understand. **nous nous entendons bien,** we are on good terms. **ils s'entendent comme larrons en foire,** they are hand and glove together; they are as thick as thieves. **il s'entend aux affaires,** he understands business. **on ne s'entend plus ici,** you can't hear yourself think in here.

entendu, e *adj.* agreed; settled; understood; granted. **nous nous sommes tous ~s sur le sujet,** we have all agreed on the matter. **d'accord, c'est ~,** O.K., that's understood. **bien ~,** certainly, of course, to be sure. **bien ~ que,** on condition that, provided that.

entente *n.f.* meaning, sense; judgment; understanding. **mots à double ~,** ambiguous words.

entériner *v.t.* *Law.* to ratify, to confirm.

enterrement *n.m.* burial; funeral. **faire une mine d'~,** to have a funeral look.

enterrer *v.t.* to bury, to inter, to hide, to conceal. **il nous enterrera tous,** he will outlive us all. **il a enterré son secret,** he has concealed his secret. **s'~,** *v.refl.* to be buried, to be interred.

en-tête *n.m.* heading, head.

entêté, e *adj.* obstinate, stubborn, pigheaded. **un enfant ~,** an obstinate child.

entêtement *n.m.* obstinacy, stubborness.

entêter *v.t.* to go to the head of; to make giddy; to intoxicate, to elate. **sa grandeur l'entête,** his grandeur makes him conceited. **il s'était laissé ~ de je ne sais quelles prédictions,** he went out on a limb with predictions of some kind or other. **s'~,** *v.refl.* to become obstinate, to get stubborn; to take a fancy to. **il s'~ à vouloir sortir sous cette pluie,** he is persisting in going out in this rain.

enthousiasme *n.m.* enthusiasm; rapture, ecstasy. **avec ~,** with enthusiasm, enthusiastically.

enthousiasmer *v.t.* to enrapture, to throw into raptures. **s'~,** *v.refl.* to become enthusiastic.

enthousiaste *n.m.f.* enthusiast; *adj.* enthusiastic.

enticher *v.refl.* to be infatuated with.

entier, ière *adj.* entire; whole, integral; perfect; singleminded. **l'année entière,** the whole year. **j'ai attendu une heure tout entière,** I waited a whole hour. **un nombre ~,** a whole number. *n.m.* whole, total, totality; entirely, wholeness. **lait ~,** whole milk. **en ~,** wholly, entirely, fully, in full.

entièrement *adv.* entirely, wholly, fully, completely.

entité *n.f.* entity.

entomologie *n.f.* entomology.

entomologique *adj.* entomologic, entomological.

entomologiste *n.m.* entomologist.

entonner *v.t.* to put into casks; to drink. **s'~,** *v.refl.* (of the wind) to rush, to blow (into). *v.t.*

Mus. to intone; to strike up (an air), to begin; to sing, to intone. **~ des cantiques,** to strike up hymns.

entonnoir *n.m.* funnel.

entorse *n.f.* strain, sprain; twist, wrench. **se donner une ~ au pied,** to sprain one's foot. **donner une ~ à la vérité,** to pervert, to twist, the truth.

entortiller *v.t.* to twist, to entwine, to wind; to wrap up, to wrap; to entangle, to circumvent. **entortillez cela dans un linge,** wrap that up in linen. **on vous a bien entortillé,** they have completely gotten around you. **s'~,** *v.refl.* to twist, to twine; to get entangled. **le lierre s'entortille autour de l'orme,** ivy twines itself around elm trees.

entour *n.m.* **à l'entour,** around, surrounding. *(pl.)* environs.

entourage *n.m.* entourage; surroundings; circle; connections, acquaintances. **son ~ nuit à sa réputation,** his connections damage his reputation.

entourer *v.t.* to surround; to enclose on all sides, to encompass; to hem in, to beset. **~ un champ de haies,** to hedge in a field. **~ de soins,** to take great care of. **s'~,** *v.refl.* to surround oneself.

entourloupette *n.f.* dirty trick. **faire une ~,** to play a dirty trick.

entournure *n.f.* armhole.

entracte *n.m.* interlude, intermission, break. **pendant l'~,** during the intermission.

entraide *n.f.* mutual help.

entraider (s') *v.refl.* to aid, to help, to assist each other.

entrailles *n.f.pl.* bowels; entrails; guts, pity, compassion; feeling; yearning; womb. **sans ~,** unfeeling. **il a fouillé les ~ de la terre,** he has dug into the bowels of the earth.

entrain *n.m.* spirits, high spirits; animation, life, spirit.

entraînant, e *adj.* captivating, winning. **un style ~,** a captivating style.

entraînement *n.m.* training, coaching; enthusiasm; fire, ardor, allurement. **l'~ d'un cheval de course,** the training of a racehorse.

entraîner *v.t.* to carry away, to force away; to hurry away; to induce; to persuade; to win over; to entail; to train, to coach (as a runner, a horse, etc.). **le mauvais exemple nous entraîne,** we are led astray by bad example. **cet orateur entraîne tous les esprits,** that orator captivates all his hearers. **s'~,** *v.refl.* to lead each other; to go in for training.

entraîneur, euse *n.m.f.* coach.

entraîneuse *n.f. Infml.* bar or dance hostess.

entr'apercevoir *v.t.* to get a glimpse of.

entrave *n.f.* shackle, fetter, trammel.

entraver *v.t.* to shackle, to clog, to hinder, to embarrass. **ces bruits de guerre entravent les affaires,** these rumors of war hinder business.

entre *prep.* between, among; in. **Tours est ~ Paris et Bordeaux,** Tours is between Paris and Bordeaux. **~ la poire et le fromage,** at dessert. **ils parlaient ~ eux,** they were talking among themselves. **cela soit dit ~ nous,** that is between ourselves. **~ autre avis,** among other opinions. **~ quatre yeux,** in private. **passer ~ les mailles du filet,** to slip through the net. **certains d'~ nous,** some among us.

entrebâillé *adj.* ajar.

entrebâiller *v.t.* to set ajar.

entrebâilleur *n.m.* door chain.

entrechat *n.m.* caper, entrechat (dance step).

entrechoquer (s') *v.refl.* to knock (or to strike) against each other.

entrecôte *n.m.* sirloin steak.

entrecouper *v.t.* to intersect, to cross; to intersperse; to interrupt; to break. **s'~,** *v.refl.* to interfere; to cut; to cross each other.

entrecroiser *v.t.* to intertwine, to cross. **s'~,** *v.refl.* to cross each other.

entre-déchirer (s') *v.refl.* to tear one another to pieces; to slander one another.

entre-détruire (s') *v.refl.* to destroy each other.

entre-deux *n.m.* interval; middle; insertion.

entre-dévorer (s') *v.refl.* to devour each other.

entrée *n.f.* entrance; entry, entrance of an actor; admittance, admission; avenue; commencement; opening; customs, duty; *Cook.* entrée. **faire son ~,** to make one's entry. **l'~ au collège,** the admission to college. **l'~ de la maison,** the entrance of the house. **l'~ du mois,** the beginning of the month. **droit d'~ et de sortie,** import and export duty. **~ libre,** free admission.

entrefaite *n.f.* interval, meantime, meanwhile. **sur ces ~s, il arriva,** meanwhile he arrived.

entr'égorger (s') *v.refl.* to cut each other's throats; to kill each other.

entre-jambes *n.m.* crotch.

entrelacer *v.t.* to interlace, to interweave, to intertwine. **s'~,** *v.refl.* to be interlaced, entwined, intertwisted.

entremêler *v.t.* to intermix, to intermingle. **s'~,** *v.refl.* to intermix, to intermingle.

entremets *n.m.* sweet, dessert.

entremetteur, euse *n.m.f.* intermediate agent, go-between; procurer/pimp.

entremettre (s') *v.refl.* to intervene, to interfere, to interpose, to go between, to meddle.

entremise *n.f.* intervention, interference, mediation, medium, agency. **par l'~ d'un ami,** by the intervention of a friend.

entreposer *v.t.* to warehouse, to store.

entrepôt *n.m.* warehouse. **mettre en ~,** to put in storage.

entreprenant, e *adj.* enterprising; bold, daring, venturesome.

entreprendre *v.t.* to undertake; to engage in, to enter upon, to set about; to attempt, to try; to contract for, to contract; to endeavour. **ce n'est**

pas tout à ~, il faut exécuter, it is not enough to undertake a thing, one must execute it.

entrepreneur, euse *n.m.f.* entrepreneur; contractor. ~ **de pompes funèbres,** undertaker, funeral director.

entreprise *n.f.* firm; undertaking, enterprise; attempt; contract; concern; encroachment. **former une ~,** to form a project.

entrer *v.i.* to enter, to enter into; to go in, into; to come in, to get in; to walk in, to step in; to drop in; to commence; to engage in, to enlist in. ~ **dans une maison,** to enter a house. **ne laissez pas ~,** do not let anyone come in. **les racines des plantes entrent dans la terre,** the roots of plants go down into the soil. **cela n'est jamais entré dans la tête de personne,** it never entered anybody's mind. ~ **dans les détails,** to go into details. ~ **dans le fond d'une affaire,** to get to the bottom of an affair. ~ **dans le commerce,** to go into business. ~ **en fonctions,** to take up one's duties (of a job). ~ **en conversation,** to enter into conversation. ~ **en matière,** to enter upon a subject. ~ **dans une dépense,** to share an expense. **faire entrer,** to take in; to show in, to usher in, to introduce; to let in; to have in; to cause to enter; to set an account in a book; to introduce. ~ **en fraude,** to smuggle in. **il faudra ~ ce piano par la fenêtre,** this piano must be brought in by the window.

entresol *n.m.* entresol, mezzanine.

entre-temps *adv.* meanwhile, in the meantime. *n.m.* interval, meantime.

entretènement *n.m.* maintenance, keeping up; preservation.

entretenir *v.t.* to hold together; to keep up, to provide for; to maintain, to preserve; to entertain. ~ **une maison,** to take care of a house. ~ **une correspondance,** to keep up a correspondence. ~ **une nombreuse famille,** to support a large family. **je cherche l'occasion de l' ~ de ma demande,** I am trying to find an opportunity to talk with him about my request. **s'~,** *v.refl.* to support each other; to be maintained; to keep oneself; to subsist; to converse. **s'~ de propos frivoles,** to talk about frivolous things.

entretien *n.m.* preservation; maintenance; conversation, talk. **pourvoir à l'~ de sa famille,** to provide for the support of his family. **mon père m'a rapporté l'~ qu'il eut avec vous,** my father told me about the conversation he had with you.

entre-tuer (s') *v.refl.* to kill each other.

entrevoir *v.t.* to catch a glimpse of, to see imperfectly; to foresee. ~ **les intentions de quelqu'un,** to find out a person's intentions. ~ **des malheurs,** to foresee misfortunes.

entrevue interview; meeting.

entrouvert, e *p.p.* opened; gaping; half-open; (of a door) ajar.

entrouvrir *v.t.* to half-open, to open a little. ~ **la porte,** to set the door ajar. **s'~,** *v.refl.* to open, to stand ajar.

entuber *v.t. Infml.* to do, to con. **se faire ~,** to be conned.

énumération *n.f.* enumeration; numbering.

énumérer *v.t.* to enumerate, to count up.

envahir *v.t.* to invade; to overrun, to encroach upon.

envahissant, e *adj.* invading.

envahissement *n.m.* invasion; overrunning; infringement, encroachment.

envahisseur *n.m.* invader. *adj.n.m.* invading.

envasement *n.m.* silting up.

envaser *v.t.* to silt up; to sink in mud. **s'~,** *v.refl.* to get filled with silt; to sink and stick in mud.

enveloppe *n.f.* envelope; wrapper, cover, covering; coat. **mettre une lettre sous ~,** to put a letter in an envelope.

enveloppement *n.m.* envelopment, wrapping.

envelopper *v.t.* to envelop; to wrap up, to fold up; to cover; to involve; to surround; to hide; to shroud, to darken, to obscure, to blind; to encircle. ~ **l'ennemi,** to surround the enemy. *v.refl.* to wrap oneself up; to hide oneself; to be involved.

envenimer *v.t.* to inflame; to envenom; to poison; to exasperate, to irritate. **s'~,** *v.refl.* to fester; to grow virulent; to become inflamed; to be envenomed.

envergure *n.f.* (of birds) spread of the wings; scale, scope; range.

envers *prep.* toward, to. ~ **et contre tous,** against the whole world. *n.m.* reverse; verso; back. **l'~ du décor,** the seamy side of life. **l'~ de la médaille,** the other side of the issue. **à l'~,** inside out; upside down, wrong side up; the wrong way. **avoir la tête à l'~,** to be out of one's senses.

envi (à l') *adv.* in emulation, competing with each other. **à l'~ de,** competing with. **nos fabricants travaillent tous à l'~ les uns des autres,** our manufacturers are all competing with each other.

enviable *adj.* enviable.

envie *n.f.* envy, enviousness; longing, desire; craving; hangnail; mark. **il vaut mieux faire ~ que pitié,** better to be envied than pitied. **avoir ~ de,** to want, to feel like, to be in the mood for.

envier *v.t.* to envy; to be envious of; to long for, to covet. **il a toujours envié le succès de son frère,** he has always been envious of his brother's success. **s'~,** *v.refl.* to be envious of each other.

envieux, euse *adj.* envious.

enviné, e *adj.* seasoned with wine.

environ *adv.* and *prep.* about; nearly. **il est ~ deux heures,** it is about two o'clock. **il y a ~ vingt ans,** about twenty years ago.

environnant, e *adj.* surrounding; neighboring.

environnement *n.m.* environment.

environner *v.t.* to surround, to encompass. **l'océan environne les Iles Britanniques de toutes parts,** the ocean surrounds the British Isles on all sides.

envisager *v.t.* to view, to contemplate; to face; to consider. **j'envisage l'avenir avec terreur,** I am frightened to think of the future. **s'~,** *v.refl.* to look at each other, to be looked at.

envoi *n.m.* sending; dispatch, shipping; parcel; package; goods sent; envoy. **faire un ~ de marchandises,** to ship goods. **votre ~ est arrivé,** your parcel arrived.

envol *n.m.* taking off; takeoff; flight.

envoler (s') *v.refl.* to fly away, to take flight, to take wing; to disappear, to vanish.

envoûtement *n.m.* bewitching; magical charm.

envoûter *v.t.* to bewitch; to cast a spell upon.

envoyé, e *n.m.* messenger; envoy. *adj. Infml.* **ça, c'est bien ~!** well said! got you!

envoyer *v.t.* to send; to dispatch; to forward, to send on; to send off; to throw. **~ quelqu'un à la campagne,** to send a person to the country. **~ chercher quelqu'un,** to send for a person. **~ promener, ~ balader, ~ sur les roses,** to send packing, to send to hell. **~ de la fumée,** to blow smoke. **~ un coup de pied à quelqu'un,** to give a person a kick. **s'~,** *Infml.* to gulp down. **s'~ en l'air,** *Vulg.* to have sex.

envoyeur *n.m.* sender.

épagneul, e *n.m.f.* spaniel.

épais, aisse *adj.* thick; dense, gross, heavy, stupid. **papier ~,** thick paper. **être ~,** to be dull. **un brouillard ~,** a dense fog. **que son intelligence est épaisse!** how dullwitted he is! *n.m.* thickness. *adv.* thick, thickly; densely.

épaisseur *n.f.* thickness; depth; denseness, density; dullness.

épaissir *v.t.* to thicken; to make thick or thicker. **s'~,** *v.refl.* to thicken; to be crowded. **l'ombre s'est épaissie,** the shadow has grown darker.

épaississement *n.m.* thickening.

épanchement *n.m.* effusion, outpouring; overflowing; shedding. **des ~s de coeur,** effusions of the heart. **un ~ de sang dans le cerveau,** an effusion of blood in the brain.

épancher *v.t.* to pour out; to effuse; to shed; to open one's heart. **s'~,** *v.refl.* to overflow; to be poured out, to be effused.

épandre *v.t.* to spread; to expand; to extend over, to disseminate; to spill; to shed. **s'~,** *v.refl.* to spread; to spread itself, to be spread; to be scattered.

épanouir *v.t.* to cause to; to open; to cheer; to brighten. **s'~,** *v.refl.* to blossom, to bloom, to open; to brighten up. **des fleurs qui s'épanouissent,** flowers that bloom. **son visage s'épanouit,** his face brightened up.

épanouissement *n.m.* blossoming; brightening (of the countenance); blossoming (out).

épargnant, e *adj.* saving, sparing, thrifty. *n.m.f.* saver, investor.

épargne *n.f.* saving, economy; savings. **caisse d'~,** savings bank.

épargner *v.t.* to spare; to economize, to save. **~ son argent,** to save one's money. **épargnez-vous ce soin,** spare yourself this worry. **la mort n'épargne personne,** death spares nobody. **s'~,** *v.refl.* to spare oneself; to spare each other.

éparpillement *n.m.* scattering, dispersion.

éparpiller *v.t.* to scatter, to disperse, to spread about, to disseminate.

épars, e *adj.* scattered, dispersed.

épatant *adj.* great, fantastic, stunning, terrific.

épaté, e *p.p.* flat, flattened. **un nez ~,** a flat nose; thunderstruck, amazed.

épater *v.t.* to amaze; to stun. **s'~,** *v.refl.* to be stunned, to be amazed.

épaule *n.f.* shoulder. **hausser les ~s,** to shrug one's shoulders.

épauler *v.t.* to shoulder (a gun); to back, to help, to support.

épaulette *n.f.* shoulder strap, shoulder pad; epaulet.

épave *adj.* stray. *n.f.* stray animal, stray. **~s maritimes,** wreck.

épée *n.f.* sword. **se battre à l'~,** to fight with swords. **un coup d'~ dans l'eau,** a useless effort. **rendre son ~,** to surrender.

épeler *v.t.* to spell.

éperdu, e *adj.* distracted; bewildered, desperate, frantic. **~ d'amour,** desperately in love.

éperdument *adv.* distractedly, passionately; desperately.

éperlan *n.m.* smelt, sparling.

éperon *n.m.* spur.

éperonner *v.t.* to spur.

épervier *n.m.* sparrow hawk; *Fish.* cast net.

éphémère *adj.* ephemeral. *n.m.* mayfly.

épi *n.m.* ear, spike or head of grain; tuft (of hair). **fleurs en ~,** spiked flowers.

épice *n.f.* spice. **pain d'~,** gingerbread.

épicé, e *adj.* spiced, spicy, seasoned.

épicer *v.t.* to spice, to season.

épicerie *n.f.* grocery, grocery store, grocery business.

épicier, ière *n.m.f.* grocer.

épicurien, enne *adj.* epicurean, given to luxury. *n.m.* epicurean, epicure, sensualist, voluptuary.

épidémie *n.f.* epidemic.

épidémique *adj.* epidemic.

épiderme *n.m.* epidermis; cuticle; skin.

épidermique *adj.* epidermic, epidermal.

épier *v.t.* to watch, to spy, to be on the watch for; to wait for. **~ quelqu'un,** to watch a person. **s'~,** *v.refl.* to watch, to spy on one another.

épieu *n.m.* spike.

épigramme *n.f.* epigram; witty remark.

épigraphe *n.f.* epigraph; motto.

épilation *n.f.* hair removal, depilation.

épilatoire *adj.* depilatory, hair removing.

épilepsie *n.f.* epilepsy.

épileptique *adj.* epileptic. *n.m.f.* epileptic.

épiler *v.t.* to depilate, to remove hair, to pluck. **crème à ~**, depilatory cream, hair removing cream. **pince à ~**, tweezers.

épilogue *n.m.* epilogue.

épiloguer *v.t.* to find fault (with), to carp (at), to criticize.

épinard *n.m.* spinach.

épine *n.f.* thorn; spine, prickle; difficulty. **être sur les ~s**, to be on tenterhooks. **il n'y a pas de roses sans ~s**, every rose has its thorns. **~ dorsale**, spine, backbone.

épineux, euse *adj.* thorny; prickly, perplexing; intricate, knotty.

épingle *n.f.* pin. **~ à cheveux**, hairpin. **tirer son ~ du jeu**, to get out of a scrape. **il est tiré à quatre ~s**, he looks spiffy.

épingler *v.t.* to pin. *Infml.* **se faire ~**, to get caught.

Epiphanie *n.f.* Epiphany.

épique *adj.* epic.

épiscopal, e *adj.* episcopal; Episcopal (church); Episcopalian. *n.m.f.* Episcopalian (person).

épiscopat *n.m.* episcopate, bishopric; episcopacy.

épisode *n.m.* episode; incident.

épisodique *adj.* episodic, occasional.

épistémologie *n.f.* epistemology.

épitaphe *n.f.* epitaph.

épître *n.f.* epistle, letter. **les ~s d'Horace**, the epistles of Horace. **les ~s de saint Paul**, the Epistles of Saint Paul. **le côté de l'~**, the right-hand side of the altar.

éploré, e *adj.* weeping; in tears; mournful. **tout ~**, all in tears.

épluchage *n.m.* peeling.

épluche-légume, *pl.* **épluche-légumes** *n.m.* vegetable peeler.

éplucher *v.t.* to peel, to clean; to examine, to sift out. **~ de la salade**, to clean salad ingredients. **~ un livre**, pick a book to pieces.

épluchure *n.f.* peelings.

épointer *v.t.* to break the point of. **s'~**, *v.refl.* to be broken, to break at the point.

éponge *n.f.* sponge. *Infml.* **boire comme une ~**, to drink like a fish. **passer l'~**, to draw a veil, to forget (a fault).

éponger *v.t.* to sponge; to sponge up. **s'~**, *v.refl.* to wipe one's face.

épopée *n.f.* epic.

époque *n.f.* epoch; period, time; date. **à cette ~**, at that time, in those days.

époumoner *v.t.* to shout, to scream at the top of one's lungs.

épouse *n.f.* wife, spouse.

épouser *v.t.* to marry, to wed, to adopt, to embrace. **~ la fortune**, to marry into money. **s'~**, *v.refl.* to marry each other, to marry. **épousseter** *v.t.* to dust, to brush. **s'~**, *v.refl.* to dust oneself off.

époustouflant, e *adj. Infml.* staggering, amazing.

épouvantable *adj.* frightful, dreadful, horrible, appalling, tremendous.

épouvantablement *adv.* frightfully, dreadfully; tremendously.

épouvantail *n.m.* scarecrow.

épouvante *n.f.* fright, terror, dread, dismay, alarm. **prendre l'~**, to take fright. **frapper d'~**, to strike with terror.

épouvanter *v.t.* to frighten, to terrify, to appall, to scare. **s'~**, *v.refl.* to take fright; to be frightened, terrified.

époux *n.m.* husband, spouse; *pl.* husband and wife, married couple.

éprendre (s') *v.refl.* to fall in love (with). **ils se sont épris l'un de l'autre**, they have fallen in love with each other.

épreuve *n.f.* trial; test, proof; ordeal, affliction, suffering. **mettre à l'~ la patience de quelqu'un**, to try someone's patience. **à l'~ du feu**, fireproof. **corriger une ~**, to correct an exam.

épris, e *adj.* in love, taken (with).

éprouver *v.t.* to try; to feel, to experience, to suffer, to afflict, to distress; to experiment with, to prove, to test. **~ de la douleur**, to feel grief or pain.

éprouvette *n.f.* test tube.

épuisant, e *adj.* exhausting.

épuisé, e *p.p.* exhausted; drained, spent, worn out; out of print.

épuisement *n.m.* exhaustion; lassitude, weariness. **jusqu'à l'~ des stocks**, while supplies last.

épuiser *v.t.* to exhaust; to drain, to empty; to draw out; to spend, to use; to waste; to wear out, to weary, to tire out; overtire. **~ un sujet**, to exhaust a subject. **cela m'épuise**, that exhausts me. **s'~**, *v.refl.* to be exhausted; to be drained off, to be emptied; to exhaust oneself. **après s'être épuisé en vain à lui explique**, after having exhausted himself in vain in explaining.

épurateur *n.m.* filter; purifier.

épuration *n.f.* purifying, purification; refinement, refining.

épure *n.f.* working draft, diagram.

épurer *v.t.* to purify; to refine; to purge. **~ de l'eau en la filtrant**, to purify water by filtering it. **s'~**, *v.refl.* to be purified.

équateur *n.m.* equator; Ecuador.

équation *n.f.* equation.

équatorial, e *adj.* equatorial.

équerre *n.f.* square (tool).

équestre *adj.* equestrian.

équidistant, e *adj.* equidistant.

équilatéral, e *adj.* equilateral.

équilibre *n.m.* equilibrium; balance.

équilibrer *v.t.* to balance.

équinoxe *n.m.* equinox.

équipage *n.m.* equipage; equipment; outfit; carriage; crew; dress, attire apparel, garb; plight.

équipe *n.f.* crew; team; set, gang, squad.

équipement *n.m.* equipment; outfit.

équiper *v.t.* to equip; to provide with. **s'~,** *v.refl.* to equip oneself.

équipier, ière *n.m.f.* team, crew member; partner.

équitable *adj.* equitable; just, upright; fair, impartial; reasonable.

équitablement *adv.* equitably, justly, uprightly, impartially, fairly.

équitation *n.f.* equitation; horsemanship; riding.

équité *n.f.* equity; justice.

équivalence *n.f.* equivalence, equivalency.

équivalent, e *adj.* equivalent. *n.m.* equivalent.

équivaloir *v.i.* to be equivalent; to amount.

équivoque *adj.* equivocal; ambiguous; dubious. *n.f.* equivocalness; ambiguity, double meaning.

érable *n.m.* maple tree. **sirop d'~,** maple syrup.

éraflure *n.f.* scratch.

éraillé, e *adj.* frayed; bloodshot.

ère *n.f.* era.

érectile *adj.* erectile.

érection *n.f.* erection; establishment, institution.

éreintant, e *adj. Infml.* exhausting, backbreaking, killing.

éreinté e *adj.* beat, worn out, bushed.

ergot *n.m.* ergot. **monter sur ses ~s,** to ride one's high horse.

ergoter *v.i.* to quibble.

ériger *v.t.* to erect, to raise, to found; to set up. **s'~,** *v.refl.* to be erected, to be raised, to be built.

ermitage *n.m.* hermitage.

ermite *n.m.* hermit, solitary, recluse.

éroder *v.t.* to erode.

érosif, ve *adj.* erosive.

érosion *n.f.* erosion.

érotique *adj.* erotic.

érotisme *n.m.* eroticism.

érotomanie *n.f. Med.* erotomania, erotomany.

errant, e *adj.* wandering; rambling, errant, unsettled, vagrant. **la vie ~e que je mène depuis quarante ans,** the wandering life I have led these forty years. **le juif ~,** the Wandering Jew. **chevalier ~,** knight-errant.

erratique *adj.* erratic.

errer *v.i.* to err; to wander, to stroll, to roam, to range; to stray. **~ çà et là,** to roam around.

erreur *n.f.* error; mistake, fault; fallacy, blunder. **sauf ~,** errors excepted. **faire, commettre une ~,** to make a mistake. **faire ~,** to mistake, to be mistaken.

erroné, e *adj.* erroneous; false, wrong, mistaken; untrue, unsound.

éructation *n.f.* belch.

éructer *v.t.* to belch.

érudit, e *adj.* erudite, learned. *n.m.f.* scholar.

érudition *n.f.* erudition; learning, scholarship.

éruptif, ive *adj.* eruptive.

éruption *n.f.* eruption; outburst.

ès *prop.* **bachelier ~ sciences,** bachelor of sciences.

escabeau *n.m.* stool, stepladder.

escadre *n.f.* squadron, fleet. **chef d'~,** commodore; rear-admiral.

escadrille *n.f.* fleet; flotilla.

escadron *n.m.* squadron (of cavalry). **chef d'~,** major.

escalade *n.f.* scaling, climbing, climb; escalade.

escalader *v.t.* to scale, to climb over; to escalade.

escale *n.f.* stop, stopover (travel). **vol sans ~,** nonstop flight.

escalier *n.m.* staircase; stairs, stairway. **~ de service,** back stairs. **~ roulant,** escalator. **~ de secours,** fire escape. **~ en limaçon,** winding staircase.

escamotable *adj.* retractable.

escamoter *v.t.* to juggle; to pilfer, to filch.

escampette *n.f.* **prendre la poudre d'~,** to take to one's heels.

escapade *n.f.* running away, running off.

escargot *n.m.* snail, escargot; spiral staircase.

escarmouche *n.f.* skirmish.

escarole *n.f.* endive; escarole.

escarpé, e *adj.* steep; precipitous, abrupt; bluffy; craggy, rocky. **une colline ~e,** a steep hill.

escarpement *n.m.* escarpment; steepness; slope.

escarpin *n.m.* pump (shoe).

escient *n.m.* knowledge. **à bon ~,** knowingly, willingly, in good earnest.

esclaffer (s') *v.i. Infml.* to burst out laughing.

esclandre *n.m.* scandal; scene. **faire ~,** to make a scene.

esclavage *n.m.* slavery; servitude, bondage.

esclavagisme *n.m.* slave system.

esclavagiste *adj.* proslavery. *n.m.f.* person in favor of slavery.

esclave *n.m.f.* slave.

escogriffe *n.m.* tall, ungainly fellow.

escompte *n.m.* discount.

escompter *v.t.* to discount; *Fig.* to anticipate. **s'~,** *v.refl.* to be discounted.

escorte *n.f.* escort, convoy; attendants; train, retinue.

escorter *v.t.* to escort, to attend, to accompany; to convoy.

escouade *n.f.* squad.

escrime *n.f.* fencing.

escrimer *v.i.* to fence. **s'~,** *v.refl.* to do one's best, to strive hard; to try, to apply oneself.

escrimeur, euse *n.m.f.* fencer.

escroc *n.m.* con man, swindler.

escroquer *v.t.* to con, to swindle; to cheat; to swindle out of.

escroquerie *n.f.* racket, fraud, swindling, swindle.

ésotérique *adj.* esoteric, secret, private.

espace *n.m.* space; room, volume. **un grand ~,** a large space. **laisser de l'~,** to leave space (*or* room).

espacement *n.m.* spacing, interval.

espacer *v.t.* to place, to set some distance apart;

to leave a space between; *Print.* to space. **s'~,** *v.refl.* to spread.

espadon *n.m.* swordfish.

espadrille *n.f.* sandal.

Espagne *n.f.* Spain.

Espagnol, e *adj.* Spanish. *n.m.f.* Spaniard. *n.m.* Spanish (language).

espèce *n.f.* species; kind, sort; ready cash. **des gens de toute ~,** people of all kinds. **~ humaine,** mankind. **payer en ~s,** to pay in cash.

espérance *n.f.* hope; expectation; trust, anticipation. **je suis venu dans l'~ de vous trouver,** I have come expecting to see you.

espérer *v.t.* to hope, to hope for, to expect; to trust. **j'espère le voir aujourd'hui,** I expect to see him today. **espérez et prenez courage,** hope and take courage. **je n'espère plus,** I have no further hopes.

espiègle *adj.* frolicsome; waggish; mischievous. *n.m.f.* frolicsome child; roguish trick.

espièglerie *n.f.* frolic; roguish trick.

espion, onne *n.m.f.* spy.

espionnage *n.m.* espionage, spying.

espionner *v.t.* to spy.

esplanade *n.f.* esplanade.

espoir *n.m.* hope; expectation, expectance, expectancy. **sans ~,** hopeless.

esprit *n.m.* spirit; soul; mind; wit; sense; intellect. **le saint ~,** the Holy Spirit. **chasser les ~s,** to drive away the spirits. **un ~ fort,** a freethinker. **l'~ de parti,** partisan enthusiasm. **~ de corps,** team spirit. **l'~ d'invention,** an inventive mind. **former le coeur et l'~,** to form the heart and mind. **reprendre ses ~s,** to recover one's senses. **avoir un ~ vif,** to be quick-witted. **il a beaucoup d'~,** he has a great deal of humor. **une femme d'~,** a smart woman.

esquif *n.m.* skiff.

esquimau, de, *adj.* eskimo. **chien ~,** husky (dog).

esquintant, e *adj.* tiring, exhausting.

esquinter *v.t.* to mess up, to ruin. **s'~,** to work oneself to death, to overwork oneself.

esquisse *n.f.* sketch, outline; rough draft; plan; rough cast.

esquisser *v.t.* to sketch; to outline, to delineate; to plan; to dash off.

esquiver *v.t.* to dodge, to evade, to elude, to avoid, to shun. *v.i.* to slip aside. **s'~,** *v.refl.* to escape, to slip away, to slip off, to slip out, to slink away.

essai *n.m.* essay; trial, experiment, test; attempt.

essaim *n.m.* swarm; multitude.

essayage *n.m.* trying on, fitting. **salon d'~,** fitting room.

essayer *v.t.* to try; to attempt, to endeavour; to test drive. **~ un vêtement,** to try on clothes, to make an effort. **s'~,** *v.refl.* to test oneself.

essence *n.f.* gas, gasoline; essence; spirits, substance; essential oil; perfume; species (of trees). **l'~ divine,** the divine essence. **~ de térében-**

thine, oil of turpentine. **~ de lavande,** oil of lavender.

essentiel, elle *adj.* essential; necessary, indispensable. *n.m.* essential; main point. **c'est là l'~,** that is the main point.

essentiellement *adv.* essentially; greatly.

esseulé, e *adj.* lonesome.

essieu *n.m.* axle.

essor *n.m.* flight; soaring; free scope, free play. **un sublime ~,** a towering flight. **l'~ du génie,** the flight of genius.

essorage *n.m.* spin drying.

essorer *v.t.* to wring out; to spin dry.

essoufflé, e *p.p.* out of breath, breathless.

essoufflement *n.m.* breathlessness.

essouffler *v.t.* to put out of breath. **s'~,** *v.refl.* to get out of breath.

essuie-glace *n.m.* windshield wiper.

essuie-main *n.m.* handtowel.

essuie-tout *n.m.inv.* paper towel.

essuyer *v.t.* to wipe; to wipe off; to wipe dry; to dry; to endure. **~ ses mains avec une serviette,** to wipe one's hands on a napkin. **~ les larmes de quelqu'un,** to dry a person's tears; to give comfort. **~ des pertes,** to undergo losses. **~ le feu de l'ennemi,** to stand the enemy's fire. **s'~,** *v.refl.* to dry oneself.

est *n.m.* east.

estampe *n.f.* stamp; engraving, print.

estampille *n.f.* stamp; impression; trade mark.

esthète *n.m.f.* esthete.

esthéticien, ne beautician, cosmetologist, beauty specialist.

esthétique *adj.* asthetic, attracture. *n.f.* aesthetic; attractiveness. **chirurge ~,** plastic surgery.

estimable *adj.* estimable.

estimation *n.f.* estimation, valuation, estimate, appraisal. **faire l'~ de,** to estimate, to appraise.

estime *n.f.* esteem; great regard, high value; reckoning. **être en grande ~,** to be held in high esteem.

estimer *v.t.* to estimate; to esteem; to value, to rate, to appraise, to set a price on. **~ des meubles,** to appraise furniture. **~ trop,** to overrate. **~ trop peu,** to undervalue. **s'~,** *v.refl.* to esteem, to value, to prize oneself; to esteem one another.

estival, e *adj.* estival.

estivant, e *n.m.f.* vacationer.

estomac *n.m.* stomach. **se emplir l'~,** to fill one's stomach. **avoir l'~ creux, vide,** to have an empty stomach.

estomaquer *v.t.* to astound, to flabbergast.

estompe *n.f.* stump (drawing).

estomper *v.t.* to stump, to shadow with a stump (drawing).

estrade *n.f.* platform, stage.

estragon *n.m.* tarragon.

estropié, e *adj.* crippled, maimed, mutilated. *n.m.f.* cripple.

estropier *v.t.* to cripple; to lame, to maim; to mangle, to murder.

estuaire *n.m.* estuary.

esturgeon *n.m.* sturgeon.

et *conj.* and; both. ~ **vous** ~ **moi,** both you and I.

étable *n.f.* stable; stall; cattle shed. ~ **à boeufs,** ox stall; sty, pigsty.

établi, e *p.p.* fixed, set; established.

établi *n.m.* workbench.

établir *v.t.* to establish; to fix; to set; to set up, to settle; to prove. ~ **une manufacture,** to set up a factory. ~ **une vérité,** to prove a truth. ~ **des principes,** to lay down principles. **s'~,** *v.refl.* to settle; to establish a residence. **ils se sont établis en province,** they have settled in the country. **s'~ pour son compte,** to set up for oneself.

établissement *n.m.* establishment; building; settlement, setting up, foundation. **l'~ d un tribunal,** the establishment of a court. **l'~ d'un fait,** the stating of a fact.

étage *n.m.* story, floor, row, tier; degree, rank. **maison à sept ~s,** house seven stories high. **le premier ~,** the first (American second) floor. **des gens de bas ~,** people of low class, vulgar people.

étager *v.t.* to place in rows one above the other.

étagère *n.f.* shelf; set of shelves, whatnot, étagère.

étain *n.m.* tin; pewter.

étalage *n.m.* shop window, display, show; stand. **faire ~ de,** to show off, to parade.

étaler *v.t.* to show (goods, etc.), to display; to apply; to spread out, to lay out; to show. ~ **des livres sur une table,** to spread books upon a table. ~ **un grand luxe,** to display great luxury. **s'~,** *v.refl.* to show oneself off; to spread oneself out; to sprawl, to lie sprawling/to fall flat. **s'~ sur l'herbe,** to stretch oneself out on the grass.

étalon *n.m.* stallion. ~ **de haras,** studhorse; standard. **d'~,** standard, flag.

étalonnage, étalonnement *n.m.* standardization; calibration; stamping, sealing (weights, etc.).

étalonner *v.t.* to calibrate; to standardize; to stamp, to seal (weights and measures).

étamage *n.m.* tinning; silvering (of glass), plating.

étanche *adj.* waterproof; tight; watertight.

étanchéité *n.f.* waterproofness; watertightness.

étancher *v.t.* to stop; to stanch; to quench; to slake. ~ **une voie d'eau,** to stop a leak. **s'~,** *v.refl.* to be stopped; to be stanched; to be quenched.

étang *n.m.* pond.

étape *n.f.* stage; step; stopping place. **cette ~ est longue,** this stage is long.

état *n.m.* state; condition, position, predicament, case; plight; rank; calling, trade. ~ **civil,** marital status. **en bon ~,** in good condition, sound; (of a building) in good repair. ~ **de frais,** account of expenses. ~ **des lieux,** condition of the premises. **en tout ~ de cause,** however it may be. **faire ~ de,** to think highly of. **affaire d'~,** state affair. **mettre en ~ d'arrestation,** to put under arrest. **mettre quelqu'un hors d'~ de nuire,** to make somebody harmless, to disarm somebody.

état-major *n.m.* staff. ~ **général,** general staff.

États-Unis *n.m.pl.* the United States.

étau *n.m.* vice; *Fig.* stranglehold.

étayer *v.t.* to prop, to shore up, to support. **s'~,** *v.refl.* to support each other; to be proposed up.

etc. abbreviation of **et cetera,** etc.

été summer, summertime. **au milieu de l'~,** in the middle of summer. **fleur d'~,** summer flower.

éteindre *v.t.* to extinguish; to put out, to quench; to smother, to blow out; to damp; to appease, to still, to calm; to extirpate, to exterminate; to root out. ~ **le feu,** to put out the fire. ~ **les sentiments,** to cool the feelings. **s'~,** *v.refl.* to go out, to be extinguished, to be quenched, to be put out; to be dim; to die away. **le feu s'éteint,** the fire is going out. **un malade qui s'éteint,** a sick person who is dying.

éteint, e *adj.* out; dead; dying; extinct.

étendard *n.m.* standard; flag, colors, banner.

étendre *v.t.* to extend; to lengthen, to prolong, to draw out; to spread; to stretch; to lay. ~ **une ligne,** to extend a line. ~ **les bras, les jambes,** to stretch out one's arms, one's legs. ~ **un tapis,** to spread out a carpet. ~ **ses ailes,** to spread out its wings. ~ **un homme sur le carreau,** to send a man sprawling. ~ **du linge sur une corde,** to hang up laundry on a line. **s'~,** *v.refl.* to spread, to stretch, to reach; to stretch oneself. **s'~ sur le gazon,** to stretch out upon the grass.

étendu, e *adj.* extensive; large; wide; stretched. **une forêt fort ~e,** a very extensive forest.

éternel, elle *adj.* eternal, endless, everlasting. *n.m.* the Eternal, God, the Everlasting.

éternellement *adv.* eternally, everlastingly.

éterniser *v.t.* to perpetuate; to immortalize. **s'~,** to drag on, to overstay.

éternité *n.f.* eternity. **cet entretien a duré une ~,** this meeting lasted forever. **ça faisait une ~ qu'ils ne s'étaient pas vus,** it was ages since they'd last seen each other.

éternuement *n.m.* sneeze; sneezing.

éternuer *v.i.* to sneeze.

éther *n.m.* ether.

Éthiopie *n.f.* Ethiopia.

éthique *n.f.* ethics. *adj.* ethic, ethical.

ethnie *n.f.* ethnic group.

ethnique *adj.* ethnic.

ethnocentrisme *n.m.* ethnocentrism.

ethnographe *n.m.* ethnographer.

ethnographie *n.f.* ethnography.

ethnographique *adj.* ethnographic, ethnographical.

ethnologie *n.f.* ethnology.

ethnologique *adj.* ethnologic, ethnological.

ethnologue *n.m.* ethnologist.

étincelant, e *adj.* sparkling; glittering, brilliant, shining, glistening; twinkling. **une étoile ~e, a** twinkling star.

étinceler *v.i.* to sparkle; to shine, to glitter, to glisten, to glare; to flash; to twinkle. **ses yeux étincelaient de mille feux,** his/her eyes were sparkling with a thousand lights.

étincelle *n.f.* spark, sparkle.

étincellement *n.m.* sparkling; twinkling.

étiolé, e *adj.* etiolated; whitened; weakened.

étioler *v.t.* to etiolate, to blanch. **s'~,** *v.refl.* to etiolate; to become white; to wither; to fade away.

étique *adj.* consumptive; emaciated; lean.

étiqueter *v.t.* to label; to ticket.

étiquette *n.f.* label; ticket.

étirer *v.t.* to draw, to draw out, to stretch out, to lengthen. **s'~,** *v.refl.* to be drawn out; to stretch oneself.

étoffe *n.f.* stuff; tissue, fabric. **avoir l'~ de,** to be cut out for, to have the makings of.

étoile *n.f.* star; asterisk. **~ polaire,** pole star. **~ du soir,** evening star, Venus. **être né sous une heureuse ~,** to be born under a lucky star. **coucher à la belle ~,** to sleep in the open air.

étoilé, e *adj.* starry; spangled; starred. **le ciel est ~,** the sky is studded with stars. **la voûte ~e,** the starry heavens.

étole *n.f.* stole.

étonnemment *adv.* astonishingly, wonderfully.

étonnant, e *adj.* astonishing, wonderful, amazing, surprising.

étonnement *n.m.* astonishment, wonder, amazement, surprise. **il fut saisi d'~ à cette vue,** he was struck with astonishment at this sight.

étonner *v.t.* to astonish; to amaze, to surprise; to astound, to strike with amazement. **cela m'étonne bien un peu,** indeed that surprises me. **s'~,** *v.refl.* to be astonished; to be amazed, to be surprised; to wonder, to marvel. **je m'étonne de vos manières,** your proceedings surprise me. **il ne faut pas s'en ~,** you must not be astonished at it.

étouffant, e *adj.* suffocating, stifling; sultry.

étouffée *n.f.* stew. **à l'~,** stewed.

étouffement *n.m.* suffocation; stifling; hushing up.

étouffer *v.t.* to suffocate, to stifle, to smother, to choke, to strangle. **~ la révolte,** to suppress rebellion. **~ une affaire,** to hush up an affair. **le temps est lourd, on étouffe,** the weather is sultry, we are suffocating. **s'~,** *v.refl.* to be suffocating, to be stifling, to be suffocated, to be stifled, to be choked, to choke. **s'~ de rire,** to choke with laughter.

étourderie *n.f.* giddiness, thoughtlessness, heedlessness; thoughtless act. **faire des ~s,** to act thoughtlessly.

étourdi, e *adj.* stunned; benumbed; giddy, thoughtless, heedless. **un enfant ~** a giddy child. *n.m.f.* heedless person, giddy person. **agir en ~,** to act thoughtlessly.

étourdiment *adv.* giddily, thoughtlessly.

étourdir *v.t.* to stun; to confound or make dizzy; to stupefy; to flash; to astound; to numb. **c'est un bruit qui étourdit les oreilles,** this noise is deafening. **s'~,** *v.refl.* to forget one's troubles; to shake off one's thoughts.

étourdissant, e *adj.* stunning, deafening; astounding, amazing.

étourdissement *n.m.* state of being stunned; giddiness, dizziness.

étourneau *n.m.* starling.

étrange *adj.* strange; unusual, uncommon, odd, queer; weird.

étrangement *adv.* strangely; oddly.

étranger, ère *adj.* foreign; strange; unknown; irrelevant. **une langue étrangère,** a foreign language. **ministère des affaires etrangères,** foreign office. **un corps ~,** a foreign body. **ce fait est ~ à la cause,** this fact is irrelevant to the cause. **cette science lui est tout à fait étrangère,** this science is quite unknown to him. *n.m.* foreign people; foreign country, foreign land; foreign parts. **à l'~,** abroad. *n.m.f.* foreigner; stranger; alien.

étrangeté *n.f.* strangeness; oddness, uncouthness.

étranglement *n.m.* strangulation.

étrangler *v.t.* to strangle; to throttle, to suffocate, to make too narrow, to compress. **~ une affaire,** to gloss over an affair. **s'~,** *v.refl.* to strangle oneself.

étrangleur, euse *n.m.f.* strangler.

être *v.i.* to be, to exist, to belong to; to lie, to stand, to be situated. **~ ou ne pas ~,** to be or not to be. **ce livre est à moi,** this book is mine. **je suis à vous dans un moment,** I will be with you in a moment. **je suis de Paris,** I am a native of Paris. **c'est à vous de parler,** it's your turn to speak. **où en êtes-vous de votre ouvrage?** how far have you gotten in your work? **où en est l'affaire?** how is the affair getting on? **il en est ainsi,** so it is, so it stands.

être *n.m.* being; existence; soul; creature. **l'Etre Suprême,** the Supreme Being. **un pauvre petit ~,** a poor little creature.

étreindre *v.t.* clasp; to hug, to press in one's arms, to grasp. **s'~,** *v.refl.* to clasp, to grasp one another.

étreinte *n.f.* tie, embrace; clasp, hug.

étrenne *n.f.* New Year's gift.

étrier *n.m.* stirrup.

étrille *n.f.* currycomb.

étriper *v.t.* to gut; to disembowel. **s'~,** *v.refl.* to unwind oneself (as a rope), to fight.

étriqué, e *adj.* scanty, curtailed; narrow.

étroit, e *adj.* narrow; close; limited, of small

extent; shallow. **esprit ~**, narrow mind. **des vues ~es**, narrow views. **un habit ~**, a tight coat.

étude *n.f.* study; office. **faire ses ~**, to study, to go to school. **~ de marché**, market research. **salle d'~**, study hall.

étudiant, e *n.m.f.* student. **~ en droit**, law student. **~ en médecine**, medical student.

étudier *v.i.* to study; to learn; to examine; to scrutinize; to observe; to calculate; to practice (music). **~ les mathématiques**, to study mathematics. **s'~**, *v.refl.* to study oneself; to introspect.

étui *n.m.* case, box.

étuve *n.f.* steamroom.

étuvée *n.f.* à l'~, steamed.

étuvement *n.m.* formenting.

étymologie *n.f.* etymology.

étymologique *adj.* etymological.

étymologiquement *adv.* etymologically.

eucalyptus *n.m.* eucalyptus.

eucharistie *n.f.* Eucharist.

eucharistique *adj.* eucharistic.

euh *interj.* er!

eunuque *n.m.* eunuch.

euphémique *adj.* euphemistic.

euphémisme *n.m.* euphemism.

euphorie *n.f.* euphoria.

euphorique *adj.* euphorie.

euphorisant, e *adj.* euphoriant. *n.m. Infml.* pep pill.

Europe *n.f.* Europe.

Européen, enne *adj.* European. *n.m.f.* European.

euthanasie *n.f.* euthanasia.

eux *pron. n.m.pl.* them; they.

évacuation *n.f.* evacuation.

évacuer *v.t.* to evacuate; to withdraw from a place; to eject, to throw out; to discharge. **le public a évacué la salle**, the public evacuated the room. **faire ~**, to clear. **s'~**, *v.refl.* to be evacuated; to be cleared.

évadé, e *adj.* escaped. *n.m.f.* fugitive.

évader (s') *v.refl.* to evade, to escape, to make one's escape (from), to slip away; to break loose.

évaluable *adj.* appraisable, assessable.

évaluation *n.f.* valuation, estimate; appraisal.

évaluer *v.t.* to value, to appraise. **s'~**, *v.refl.* to be worth; to be valued, estimated, *or* rated.

évanescent, e *adj.* evanescent.

évangélique *adj.* evangelic, evangelical.

évangéliquement *adv.* according to the Gospel.

évangéliser *v.t.* to evangelize.

évangélisme *n.m.* evangelism, evangelicalism.

évangéliste *n.m.* evangelist.

Evangile *n.m.* Gospel. **prêcher l'~**, to preach the Gospel. **c'est parole d'~**, it's Gospel truth.

évanoui, e *adj.* unconscious.

évanouir (s') *v.refl.* to pass out, to faint; to vanish. **elle s'est évanouie**, she fainted.

évanouissement *n.m.* fainting.

évaporation *n.f.* evaporation.

évaporé, e *p.p.* evaporated; heedless, giddy. *n.m.f.* giddy person.

évaporer *v.t.* to evaporate; to give vent to, to let out. **s'~**, *v.refl.* to evaporate; to be dissipated, to disappear.

évasé, e *adj.* wide, wide-open; bell-mouthed.

évasement *n.m.* widening, width (of the opening).

évasif, ive *adj.* evasive.

évasion *n.f.* escape, breaking loose; evasion.

évasivement *adv.* evasively.

évêché *n.m.* bishopric; episcopate; bishop's palace.

éveil *n.m.* awakening; warning, hint; alert, alarm. **donner l'~**, to give the alert. **être en ~**, to be on the watch.

éveillé, e *adj.* awake, wakeful; watchful; attentive; lively, brisk, sharp. **tenir ~**, to keep awake. **une jeune fille ~e**, a sharp girl.

éveiller *v.t.* to awake; to awaken, to wake, to stir up; to arouse. **~ les soupçons**, to arouse suspicion. **s'~**, *v.refl.* to awake; to wake, to wake up; to be awakened.

évènement *n.m.* event; occurence. **comme l'~ l'a justifié**, as justified by the event.

éventail *n.m.* fan (handheld). *Arch.* fanlight. **en ~**, fan-shaped.

éventer *v.t.* to fan; to air; to ventilate; to deaden (wine, etc.), to make flat; to find out; to divulge, to make known. **~ un secret**, to divulge a secret. **s'~**, *v.refl.* to fan oneself; to go flat (as wine); to get injured (by exposure to the air); to get wind of, to be divulged. **le secret s'est éventé**, the secret is divulged.

éventration *n.f.* rupture.

éventrer *v.t.* to rip up, open; to disembowel; to gut; to break open. **s'~**, *v.refl.* to rip oneself up; to rip up each other.

éventualité *n.f.* possibility; eventuality; contingency.

éventuel, elle *adj.* eventual; contingent; possible.

éventuellement *adv.* eventually.

évêque *n.m.* bishop.

évertuer (s') *v.refl.* to struggle hard.

éviction *n.f.* eviction.

evidemment *adv.* evidently; obviously, clearly; of course; apparently.

évidence *n.f.* evidence, obviousness, clearness. **mettre en ~**, to make evident.

évident, e *adj.* evident; obvious, clear.

évier *n.m.* sink.

évincer *v.t.* to evict.

éviter *v.t.* to avoid, to shun; to keep clear of; to evade. **elle m'évite**, she shuns me. **~ une querelle**, to avoid a quarrel. **s'~**, *v.refl.* to avoid, to shun each other.

évolué, e *adj.* developed, advanced.

évoluer *v.i.* to evolve; to progress; to develop; to advance.

évolution *n.f.* evolution; development; movement.

évoquer *v.t.* to evoke; to call up; to raise.

ex *adv. prep.* ex.

exacerbation *n.f.* exacerbation.

exacerber *v.t.* to exacerbate, to aggravate, to make worse.

exact, e *adj.* exact; punctual, accurate; correct; true. **soyez ~ au rendez-vous,** be on time to the appointment. **un compte ~,** an accurate, account.

exactement *adv.* exactly; strictly; punctually; accurately, precisely.

exactitude *n.f.* punctuality; accuracy.

ex aequo *adv.* even; tied for first place.

exagération *n.f.* exaggeration.

exagérer *v.t.* to exaggerate; to go too far; to take too far.

exaltant, e *adj.* exalting, exhilarating.

exaltation *n.f.* exaltation; enthusiasm.

exalté, e *p.p.* exalted, extolled; overexcited, enthusiastic; hotheaded. *n.m.f.* wild enthusiast.

exalter *v.t.* to exalt; to praise, to extol, to magnify, to glorify; to excite; to work up. **s'~,** *v.refl.* to be exalted, extolled, magnified; to exalt, to praise each other; to become excited.

examen *n.m.* examination, scrutiny; exam, test, quiz; investigation; **faire l'~ de,** to examine. **~ de conscience,** self-examination. **subir un ~,** to undergo an examination.

examinateur, trice *n.m.f.* examiner.

examiner *v.t.* to examine; to scrutinize, to investigate, to weigh, to consider. **~ à fond,** to examine thoroughly. **s'~,** *v.refl.* to examine oneself, to examine each other, to look at each other.

exaspérant, e *adj.* exasperating.

exaspération *n.f.* exasperation.

exaspérer *v.t.* to exasperate; to enrage. **s'~,** *v.refl.* to become exasperated.

exaucer *v.t.* to hear favorably, to hear, to hearken to, to grant.

excavation *n.f.* excavation.

excaver *v.t.* to excavate; to cut through.

excédant, e *adj.* exceeding; wearisome, tiring.

excédent *n.m.* surplus; excess.

excéder *v.t.* to exceed; to go beyond, to surpass, to transcend; to tire out; to maltreat. **une dette qui excède cent francs,** a debt exceeding a hundred francs. **s'~,** *v.refl.* to tire oneself out, to wear oneself out. **s'~ de travail,** to overwork oneself.

excellemment *adv.* excellently.

excellence *n.f.* excellence, excellency. **par ~,** excellently, preeminently. **son Excellence,** his Excellency.

excellent, e *adj.* excellent.

exceller *v.i.* to excel; to be eminent; to be superior; to surpass, to outdo.

excentrique *adj.* eccentric; odd, strange; distant from the center. *n.m.* eccentric.

excepter *v.t.* to except; to exclude; to exempt.

exception *n.f.* exception.

exceptionnel, elle *adj.* exceptional.

exceptionnellement *adv.* exceptionally, by exception.

excès *n.m.* excess, outrage. **l'~ du froid,** the excessive cold. **~ de travail,** overload of work.

excessif, ive *adj.* excessive; extreme; immoderate, intemperate.

excessivement *adv.* excessively, to excess; exceedingly, greatly, immoderately.

excitant, e *adj.* exciting. *n.m.* excitant, stimulant.

excitation *n.f.* excitement, excitation.

exciter *v.t.* to excite, to prompt, to drive on, to set on; to stimulate, to animate, to stir up, to rouse, to raise. **s'~,** *v.refl.* to rouse oneself, to get excited; to excite each other, to be excited.

exclamatif, ive *adj.* exclamatory.

exclamation *n.f.* exclamation; outcry, cry, clamor. **point d'~,** exclamation point.

exclamer (s') *v.refl.* to exclaim; to cry out, to shout.

exclure *v.t.* to exclude; to expel; to shut out; to deny admission to; to debar; to rule out.

exclusif, ive *adj.* exclusive.

exclusion *n.f.* exclusion; expulsion. **à l'~,** to the exclusion of.

exclusivité *n.f.* exclusiveness; exclusive rights.

excommunication *n.f.* excommunication.

excommunier *v.t.* to excommunicate.

excrément *n.m.* excrement; *Fig.* scum, dregs, outcast.

excréter *v.t.* to excrete.

excrétion *n.f.* excretion.

excroissance *n.f.* excrescence, outgrowth.

excursion *n.f.* excursion; trip; tour, inroad, incursion.

excusable *adj.* excusable; pardonable.

excuse *n.f.* excuse; apology, pretext.

excuser *v.t.* to excuse; to apologize, to pardon. **excusez-moi,** excuse me, pardon me. **s'~,** *v.refl.* to excuse oneself, to make an excuse; to apologize.

exécrable *adj.* execrable; abominable, hateful, detestable.

exécuter *v.t.* to execute; to perform, to do, to effect, to fulfil, to carry into effect, to carry out, to achieve. **~ des ordres,** to execute orders. **~ un criminel,** to execute a criminal. **s'~,** *v.refl.* to comply; to be performed, to be done. **ses ordres s'exécutèrent ponctuellement,** his orders were punctually executed.

exécution *n.f.* execution; performance, fulfilment, achievement. **mettre à ~,** to carry out, execute. **en ~ de,** in pursuance of. **~ militaire,** military execution.

exemplaire *adj.* exemplary, model; perfect. **punition ~,** punishment as an example. *n.m.* exemplar; model or pattern; copy. **il n'y a que deux ~s de ce livre dans Paris,** there are only two copies of that book in Paris.

exemple *n.m.* example; pattern, model; instance. **suivre l'~ de quelqu'un,** to follow a person's example. **faire un ~ de quelqu'un,** to make an example of a person. **sans ~,** unprecedented. **par ~,** for instance. **par ~!** indeed! really!

exempt, e *adj.* exempt, exempted, free. **être ~ du service militaire,** to be exempt from military service.

exempter *v.t.* to exempt; to free from; to privilege; to dispense with. **s'~,** *v.refl.* to exempt oneself.

exemption *n.f.* exemption; privilege.

exercer *v.t.* to exercise: to train; to drill; to practice; to perform the duties of; to perform. **~ des soldats,** to drill, to instruct soldiers. **~ la mémoire,** to exercise the memory. **~ une profession,** to practice a profession. **s'~,** *v.refl.* to exercise oneself, to exercise, to practice. **s'~ à la course,** to practice running.

exercice *n.m.* exercise; training; drill; exertion; practice, performance. **l'~ militaire,** the military exercise. **faire de l'~,** exercise. **l'~ d'une religion,** the practice of a religion. **l'~ d'une profession,** the practice of a profession. **entrer en ~,** to take up one's duties.

exhaler *v.t.* to exhale; to send out, to emit, to breathe out, to vent, to give vent to. **~ sa colère,** to vent one's anger. **s'~,** *v.refl.* to be exhaled; to exhale, to emanate. **l'éther s'exhale rapidement,** ether evaporates rapidly.

exhausser *v.t.* to raise, to raise up; to raise higher. **s'~,** *v.refl.* to be raised.

exhaustion *n.f.* exhaustion.

exhiber *v.t.* to exhibit; to display; to parade; to present. **s'~,** *v.refl.* to show oneself.

exhibition *n.f.* exhibition; public show, public display.

exhorter *v.t.* to exhort; to encourage, to incite. **s'~,** *v.refl.* to exhort, to work oneself up; to exhort one another.

exhumation *n.f.* exhumation; disinterment.

exhumer *v.t.* to disinter; to exhume; to bring to light.

exigeant, e *adj.* demanding; finicky; hard to please; fastidious; particular; difficult.

exigence *n.f.* unreasonableness; exigence, exigency; pressing necessity, urgency; demand; requirement. **les ~s de notre position,** the exigencies of our station.

exiger *v.t.* to demand; to require; to extort; to claim; to want. **il exige des intérêts exorbitants,** he demands an exorbitant interest rate.

exil *n.m.* exile; banishment.

exilé, e *n.m.f.* exile *adj.* exiled.

exiler *v.t* to exile, to banish. **s'~,** *v.refl.* go into exile; to withdraw, to seclude oneself.

existant, e *adj.* existing, existent.

existence *n.f.* existence; being, life.

exister *v.i.* to exist, to be extant, to live, to have life.

exode *n.m.* exodus.

exonération *n.f.* exoneration; discharge; exemption.

exonérer *v.t.* to exonerate; to discharge; to exempt.

exorbitant, e *adj.* exorbitant; excessive.

exorciser *v.t.* to exorcise; to conjure.

exorcisme *n.m.* exorcism.

exorciste *n.m.* exorcist.

exorde *n.m.* exordium; *Fig.* beginning.

exotique *adj.* exotic. **une plante ~,** an exotic plant.

expansible *adj.* expansible.

expansif, ive *adj.* expansive; diffusive; unreserved. **force expansive,** expansive power. **un homme peu ~,** a reserved man.

expansion *n.f.* expansion.

expatriation *n.f.* expatriation.

expatrier *v.t.* to expatriate. **s'~,** *v.refl.* to expatriate oneself; to leave one's country.

expectation *n.f.* expectation.

expectative *n.f.* expectation; expectancy. **être dans l'~,** to live in hope.

expectorer *v.t.* to expectorate, spit. **faire ~,** to spit.

expédient *adj.m.* expedient; fit, suitable, proper; profitable, advantageous. *n.m.* expedient; contrivance, device, way. **proposer un ~,** to suggest an expedient. **en être aux ~s,** to be casting about for a way to do it.

expédier *v.t.* to dispatch, to send off; (of goods) to forward, to ship; to perform quickly. **~ des marchandises par le chemin de fer,** to ship goods by railway. **~ une affaire,** to settle an affair. **s'~,** *v.refl.* to hasten; to be dispatched.

expéditeur *n.m.* sender; shipper.

expéditif, ive *adj.* expeditious; quick, prompt.

expédition *n.f.* expedition; dispatch; sending, forwarding; shipment; *pl.* copy (of a deed). **l'~ des affaires,** taking care of business. **~ maritime, naval,** naval expedition. **faire l'~ de,** to forward, to send off.

expéditionnaire *n.m.* sender, shipper; expeditionary.

expéditivement *adv.* expeditiously.

expérience *n.f.* experience; experiment. **par ~,** by *or* from experience. **faire des ~s de physiologie,** to make experiments in physiology.

expérimental, e *adj.* experimental.

expérimentation *n.f.* experimentation.

expérimenté, e *p.p.* tried, tested. *adj.* experienced; expert; practiced.

expérimenter *v.t.* to experiment, to try, to test.

expert, e *adj.* expert; skillful; skilled. *n.m. Law.* expert; surveyor; appraiser. **~-comptable,** certified public accountant (C.P.A.).

expertise *n.f.* examination; evaluation; appraisal; survey; report of survey.

expertiser *v.t.* to value, to appraise, to evaluate.

expiation *n.f.* expiation, atonement.

expiatoire *adj.* expiatory.

expier *v.t.* to expiate, to atone for; to make reparation for.

expirant, e *adj.* expiring, dying.

expiration *n.f.* expiration; deadline.

expirer *v.t.* to expire, to breathe out, to die. **il expira entre les bras de son ami,** he expired in the arms of his friend. **le bail expire le premier mai,** the lease will expire May first.

explicable *adj.* explainable, explicable.

explication *n.f.* explanation, explication; interpretation; discussion; argument. **~ de texte,** critical analysis.

explicite *adj.* explicit.

explicitement *adv.* explicitly.

expliquer *v.t.* to explain; to analyse, to elucidate; to expound; to interpret; to account for; to construe; to translate (an author). **~ un passage,** to analyse a passage. **je ne peux m'~ votre conduite,** I cannot understand your conduct. **s'~,** *v.refl.* to explain oneself, to speak plainly; to be explained.

exploit *n.m.* exploit, deed, achievement; *Law.* writ.

exploitable *adj.* exploitable; marketable; distrainable.

exploitant ~, e *n.m.f.* farmer, cultivator (of lands), improver, grower (of woods). *adj.* farming.

exploitation *n.f.* exploitation; improving, farming, cultivation (of lands, estates, etc.); growing (of woods); working (of mines); execution of works. **en pleine ~,** in full activity, in operation.

exploiter *v.t.* to improve; to cultivate (a farm, an estate), to farm; to grow (a wood or forest); to work (a mine, a road, etc.); to take advantage of. **~ la curiosité publique,** to play upon public curiosity. *v.i. Law.* to serve writs.

exploiteur, euse *n.m.f.* farmer, improver; grower; worker; manager; one who profits unfairly from the labor of others.

explorateur, trice *n.m.f.* explorer. *adj.* exploratory.

exploration *n.f.* exploration.

explorer *v.t.* to explore.

exploser *v.t.* to blow up, to explode, to burst.

explosif, ive *adj.* explosive. *n.m.f.* explosive substance.

explosion *n.f.* explosion; blowing up; *Fig.* bursting.

exportateur *n.m.* exporter.

exportation *n.f.* export.

exporter *v.t.* to export.

exposant, e *n.m.f.* petitioner; exhibiter; *Alg.* exponent, index.

exposé, e *n.m.* statement; account. *adj.* exposed, displayed, exhibited.

exposer *v.t.* to expose; to exhibit; to endanger, to risk; to lay open; to expound; to explain. **~ un tableau,** to exhibit a painting. **~ en vente,** to exhibit for sale. **~ au danger,** to expose to danger. **~ une doctrine,** to expound a doctrine. **s'~,** *v.refl.* to expose oneself, to make oneself liable; to run the risk. **s'~ aux insultes,** to

expose oneself to insults. **s'~ à un refus,** to risk a refusal.

exposition *n.f.* exposition; exposure; exhibition; show. **~ au nord,** northern exposure. **~ de peinture,** exhibition of paintings.

exprès *adv.* on purpose, purposely, intentionally, deliberately. **il a fait ~ de venir en retard,** he has come late on purpose.

exprès, esse *adj.* express; positive; explicit. *n.m.* express; messenger.

express *adj. n.m.* express train; espresso (coffee).

expressément *adv.* expressly.

expressiv, ive *adj.* expressive.

expression *n.f.* expression; expressiveness. **l'~ d'un voeu,** the expression of a wish. **force d'~,** expressiveness. **l'~ de la voix,** the expression of the voice. **réduire à la plus simple ~,** to reduce to the lowest terms.

expressionisme *n.m.* expressionism.

expressioniste *n.m.f.* expressionist. *adj.* expressionistic.

expressivement *adv.* expressively.

exprimer *v.t.* to express; to voice; to press out, to squeeze out; to utter. **~ le jus d'un fruit,** to press out the juice of a fruit. **s'~,** *v.refl.* to be expressed, to be pressed out; to express oneself; to be expressed; to be uttered.

expropriation *n.f.* dispossession, dispossessing.

exproprier *v.t.* to take possession of the property of (a debtor); to dispossess.

expulser *v.t.* to expel, to drive out of; to expulse, to evict; to eject, to throw out; to dispossess of property.

expulsif, ive *adj.* expulsive.

expulsion *n.f.* expulsion; *Law.* ejection; *Med.* evacuation.

expurger *v.t.* to expurgate.

exquis, e *adj.* exquisite, delightful. **des vins ~,** exquisite wines.

extase *n.f.* ecstasy; trance. **tomber en ~,** to fall into ecstasy.

extasier (s') *v.refl.* to be in ecstasies, to be enraptured.

extatique *adj.* ecstatic.

extensible *adj.* extensible, extensile.

extensif, ive *adj.* extensive, expansive.

extension *n.f.* extent; extension; stretching; enlargement, increase.

exténuer *v.t.* to exhaust.

extérieur, eure *adj.* exterior, external, outer, outside; foreign. *n.m.* exterior; outside, outer appearance. **à l'~,** on the outside, outdoors.

extérieurement *adv.* externally, outwardly; on the surface; in appearance.

extérioriser *v.t.* to express; to exteriorize; to externalize.

exterminateur, trice *adj.* exterminating, destroying. *n.m.* exterminator.

extermination *n.f.* extermination, eradication.

exterminer *v.t.* to exterminate; to destroy

utterly; to eradicate, to root out. **s'~**, *v.refl.* to exterminate each other.

externe *adj.* external, outer; outward. *n.m.* medical intern.

extincteur, trice *adj.* extinguishing. *n.m.* fire extinguisher.

extinction *n.f.* extinction; extinguishment; (voice) loss, aphonia. **l'~ des feux**, lights out.

extirper *v.t.* to extirpate; to root out; to cut out, to cut off.

extorquer *v.t.* to extort.

extorsion *n.f.* extortion.

extra *n.m.adj.* prime, first rate; great, terrific. **cette fille est ~**, she is a terrific girl. *n.m.* extra; temporary job; treat.

extracteur *n.m.* extracter.

extraction *n.f.* extraction; descent; birth, origin. **l'~ d'une dent**, the pulling of a tooth.

extrader *v.t.* to extradite.

extradition *n.f.* extradition.

extraire *v.t.* to extract; to draw out; to take out, to make extracts from. **~ une dent**, to extract a tooth.

extrait *n.m.* extract; abstract; certificate (of birth, death, or marriage).

extraordinaire *adj.* extraordinary; unusual, special; odd, strange. **un évènement ~**, an extraordinary event. **des manières ~s**, odd manners. *n.m.* extraordinariness.

extraterrestre *adj.* extraterrestrial.

extravagance *n.f.* extravagance, wildness, folly. **l'~ de sa conduite**, the wildness of his conduct. **dire des ~**, to talk extravagantly.

extravagant, e *adj.* extravagant; unreasonable. **un homme ~**, an extravagant man. *n.m.f.* extravagant person.

extrême *adj.* extreme; utmost, outermost, furthest; excessive, greatest; most violent. **à l'~ frontière**, at the extreme boundary. **~ dans ses idées**, with extravagant thoughts. *n.m.* extreme; furthest degree; extremity. **évitez les ~s**, avoid extremes. **les ~s se touchent**, extremes meet.

extrêmement *adv.* extremely, excessively.

extrémiste *adj. n.m.f.* extremist.

extrémité *n.f.* end; tip; extremity; limit. **les ~s supérieures**, the upper extremities. **pousser les choses à l'~**, to carry things to extremes.

exubérance *n.f.* exuberance.

exubérant, e *adj.* exuberant.

exultation *n.f.* exultation; rapture.

exulter *v.i.* to exult; to triumph.

eye liner *n.m.* eye-liner.

F

F FR., abbreviation of **franc**, franc.

fa *n.m. Mus.* fa, F. **clef de ~**, bass clef.

fable *n.f.* fable, tale.

fabricant *n.m.* manufacturer.

fabricateur, trice *n.m.f.* fabricator; forger; coiner.

fabrication *n.f.* fabrication; manufacture; making; forgery. **~ de la toile**, manufacture of linen.

fabrique *n.f.* manufacture; factory; fabrication. **la ~ des étoffes de soie**, the manufacture of silks. **monter une ~**, to set up a factory.

fabriquer *v.t.* to manufacture, to make; to fabricate; to coin, to forge. *Infml.* to be up to. **~ des draps**, to manufacture cloth. **~ de la fausse monnaie**, to counterfeit money. **se ~**, *v.refl.* to be fabricated, to be manufactured.

fabulateur, trice *adj.* pathological lying. *n.m.f.* pathological liar.

fabulation *n.f.* fabrication.

fabuler *v.t.* to fabricate; to make up stories.

fabuleusement *adv.* fabulously.

fabuleux, euse *adj.* fabulous.

fabuliste *n.m.* fabulist.

fac *n.f.* abbrev. of **faculté**.

façade *n.f.* front, face, facade, frontage.

face *n.f.* face; front, facade, frontage; aspect, appearance. **faire ~ à**, to face, to meet; to front, to stand opposite to. **la ~ de la terre**, the face of the earth. **à la ~ de**, in the face of, before. **regarder quelqu'un en ~**, to look a person in the face. **nous voilà ~ à ~ avec la verité**, we are now face to face with truth.

facétie *n.f.* joke.

facette *n.f.* facet.

fâché, e *adj.* angry, displeased, offended; sorry. **avoir l'air ~**, to look angry. **je suis ~ qu'il ait dit cela**, I am sorry that he said so.

fâcher *v.t.* to make angry, to offend, to anger, to irritate, to grieve. **il ne faut ~ personne**, we must offend nobody. **se ~**, *v.refl.* to be angry, to be offended; to get angry; to take offense. **ne vous fâchez pas**, don't get angry.

fâcheux, euse *adj.* sad, unpleasant, displeasing; cross, unfortunate, regrettable, deplorable. **un ~ accident**, an unfortunate accident. **cela est ~**, that is unpleasant. **c'est ~**, it's a pity. *n.m.f.* troublesome person; bore.

facial, e *adj.* facial.

facile *adj.* easy. **c'est plus ~ à dire qu'à faire**, it's easier said than done. **il est ~ à vivre**, he is easy-going.

facilement *adv.* easily.

facilité *n.f.* facility; easiness, ease; quickness; aptitude; easy terms. **marcher avec ~**, to walk with ease, easily. **parler avec ~**, to speak fluently. **ses créanciers lui donnèrent des ~**, his creditors gave him easy terms, (or) an installment plan.

faciliter *v.t.* to facilitate; to ease.

façon *n.f.* fashion; make, making; shape; cut; workmanship; manner, way, method; fuss; manners, ceremony; plowing. **en quelque ~**, in some manner. **en aucune ~**, by no means. **de cette ~**, in this manner, this way. **de quelque ~ que ce soit**, anyhow. **~ de parler**, manner of speech. **faire des ~s**, to make a fuss. **sans ~**, without ceremony. **un homme sans ~**, a plain man. **de ~ à plaire à tout le monde**, so as to please everybody.

façonner *v.t.* to make, to make up; to work; to figure, to shape, to mold; plow (a field). **se ~**, *v.refl.* to be shaped.

facteur *n.m.* postman, letter carrier, mailman.

factice *adj.* artificial, imitation; false; phony.

faction *n.f.* faction. **être en ~**, to be on guard, to be on duty.

facture *n.f.* invoice, bill of parcels; composition (of music, verse). **faire une ~**, to write out an invoice.

facturer *v.t.* to invoice, to make an invoice of.

facultatif, ive *adj.* optional.

faculté *n.f.* faculty, ability, virtue, property; talent, means, property, department or division of a university. **les ~s intellectuelles**, the intellectual faculties. **la ~ de droit**, the law school. **chacun suivant ses ~s**, everyone according to his means.

fada *n.m.f.* crackpot.

fadaise *n.f.* trifle, nonsense, twaddle.

fadasse *adj.* insipid, faint, pale.

fade *adj.* insipid; tasteless, dull, flat; colorless. **une couleur ~**, a dull color.

fagot *n.m.* bundle, idle story. **conter des ~s**, to tell idle stories.

fagoter *v.t.* to bundle up; to dress frightfully; to tell (idle stories). **se ~**, *v.refl.* to be tied in bundles; to dress oneself frightfully.

faible *adj.* weak; feeble, faint; poor. **un esprit ~**, a weak mind. *n.m.* weak person; *pl.* the weak, the feeble. **son ~, c'est le chocolat**, he has a weakness for chocolate.

faiblement *adv.* weakly, feebly, faintly, slightly.

faiblesse *n.f.* weakness; feebleness, faintness; frailty, frailness; fainting, swoon. **~ d'un argument**, the weakness of an argument. **la ~ de ses ressources**, the slenderness of his resources. **tomber en ~**, to faint, to swoon away. **la ~ d'une mère pour ses enfants**, a mother's partiality for her children.

faiblir *v.i.* to faint; to grow weak; to give way; to relent; to relax; to fail.

faïence *n.f.* faïence, earthenware, crockery.

faille *n.f.* fault; flaw, weakness.

faillir *v.i.* to fail; to miss; to fall short; to decline; to become bankrupt. **le jour commençait à ~**, the day was almost spent. **j'ai failli en cette occasion**, I did wrong on that occasion. **j'ai failli mourir**, I was near dying.

faillite *n.f.* bankruptcy. **faire ~**, to go bankrupt. **être en ~**, to be bankrupt.

faim *n.f.* hunger; craving, appetite; thirst. **avoir ~**, to be hungry. **mourir de ~**, to die of hunger,

to die of starvation. **un meurt-de-~**, one who died of starvation. **avoir une ~ de loup**, as hungry as a bear.

fainéant, e *adj.* idle, lazy, sluggish, sluggard. *n.m.f.* lazy person, idler; sluggard, lounger, lazybones; do-nothing.

fainéantise *n.f.* idleness, laziness.

faire *v.t.* to make; to do, to form, to perform; to effect; to create; to cause; to obtain, to get; to make up; to be; to render. **~ du pain**, to make bread. **~ un habit**, to make a coat. **l'oiseau fait son nid**, the bird builds its nest. **~ des vers**, to compose verses. **~ un discours**, to make a speech. **~ une description**, to give a description. **~ la guerre**, to make war. **~ un crime**, to perpetrate a crime. **~ du bruit**, to make noise. **~ la pluie et le beau temps**, to be all-powerful. **cela ne lui fait ni chaud ni froid**, it is all the same to him. **~ fortune**, to make a fortune. **~ cas de**, to make much of, to value. **~ un lit**, to make a bed. **~ une chambre**, to clean a room. **~ la cuisine**, to cook. **~ le dîner**, to cook dinner. **~ la barbe**, to shave. **~ du progrès**, to make progress. **deux et deux font quatre**, two and two make (or) are four. **~ le bien**, to do good. **~ justice**, to do justice. **la nature a tout fait pour lui**, nature has bestowed all its gifts on him. **je ne sais que ~**, I don't know what to do. **faites votre devoir**, do your duty. **il ne sait pas ~ son métier**, he does not know his trade. **~ la médecine**, to practice medicine. **~ de bonnes études**, to have a sound education. **~ le fou**, to play the fool. **~ la sourde oreille**, to turn a deaf ear. **~ des visites**, to pay visits. **j'ai fait ~ un habit**, I have had a coat made. **~ les vivres**, to take in a fresh supply of provisions. **~ route**, to sail, to be bound (to). **~ voile**, to sail, to set sail. **~ horreur**, to strike with horror. **~ de la peine**, to grieve, to pain. **~ peur**, to frighten. **~ savoir**, to inform. *v.i.* to do; to act; to suit, to contrive; to manage; to succeed. **laissez-moi ~**, leave it to me. **en ~ de même**, to do likewise. **ce tableau ne fait pas bien où il est**, that picture does not look good where it is. **il ne fait que dormir**, he is always asleep. **il fait sec aujourd'hui**, it is dry today. **il fait cher vivre à Paris**, it is expensive living in Paris. **se ~**, *v.refl.* to make oneself; to become, to turn; to be formed. **se ~ des amis**, to make friends. **elle s'est faite religieuse**, she has become a nun. **se ~ belle**, to make oneself pretty. **Paris ne s'est pas fait en un jour**, Paris was not built in a day. **se ~ à la fatigue**, to get used to hardships. **elle s'est fait connaître**, she made herself known. **le mariage se fera bientôt**, the wedding will soon take place. **comment cela se fait-il?** how's that? **il se fit un grand silence**, there was a great silence. *n.m.* making, execution; (in the fine arts) manner, style (of an artist); execution.

faire-part *n.m.* notice; announcement. **~ de mariage,** wedding invitation.

fair-play *n.m.* fair play.

faisable *adj.* feasible.

faisan *n.m.* pheasant.

faisceau *n.m.* bundle; beam; *Anat.* fasciculus. **~ lumineux,** beam of light.

fait, e *p.p.* made, done; fit; finished; used, accustomed; made for. **tenez cela pour ~,** consider it as done. **aussitôt dit, aussitôt ~,** no sooner said than done. **avoir la taille bien ~e,** to be well shaped. **~ à la fatigue,** used to fatigue. **c'est une affaire ~e,** it is a done deal. **c'est ~, c'en est ~ de moi,** it is all over with me.

fait *n.m.* fact; deed, act, exploit; event; reality; matter, case. **citer un ~,** to quote a fact. **le ~ est que,** the fact is that. **au ~,** in fact, indeed. **voici le ~ en deux mots,** this is a brief statement of the affair. **être au ~ de,** to be acquainted with. **tout à ~,** totally, entirely.

falaise *n.f.* cliff.

fallacieux, euse *adj.* fallacious.

falloir *v.i. impers.* to be necessary; to want, to require, to need; must, should, ought. **il me faut de l'argent,** I need money. **il faut le faire,** it must be done. **il faudra le satisfaire,** you must satisfy him. **il faut que je voyage,** I must travel. **il faut qu'il m'écoute,** he must listen to me. **il fallait venir plus tôt,** you should have come sooner. **faites cela comme il faut,** do that as it should be done. **il ne se conduit pas comme il faut,** he does not behave properly. **s'en ~,** *v.refl.* to want, to be wanting; to be nearly. **il s'en fallut de peu de voix,** it was close by a few votes. **il s'en est fallu de peu qu'il ne fût tué,** he came close to being killed. **encore faut-il que,** but at least; I must, however.

falsification *n.f.* falsification; adulteration (of goods); debasement (of coin).

falsifier *v.t.* to falsify; to forge; to alter; to adulterate; to debase (coin).

falzar *n.m. Infml.* pants, trousers.

famé, e *adj.* famed. **mal ~,** (of) bad reputation.

famélique *adj.* starving, famished. *n.m.* starving person.

fameux, euse *adj.* famous; renowned; celebrated; noted, notorious; *Infml.* precious; great.

familial, e *adj.* domestic, family. **entreprise ~e,** family-owned business. **placement ~,** foster home.

familiariser *v.t.* to familiarize; to accustom, to habituate. **se ~,** *v.refl.* to grow familiar; to get accustomed, to get used (to).

familiarité *n.f.* familiarity; intimacy, close acquaintance.

familier, ière *adj.* familiar; intimate, close; affable. *n.m.f.* familiar.

familièrement *adv.* informally; colloquially.

famille *n.f.* family. **avoir un air de ~,** to have a family resemblance.

famine *n.f.* famine, starvation. **crier ~ sur un**

tas de blé, to complain of poverty, when one has enough and to spare.

fan *n.m.* (sports) fan.

fana *adj. Infml.* nuts, crazy, wild about.

fanatique *adj.* fanatic, fanatical. *n.m.f.* fanatic, enthusiast, zealot.

fanatisme *n.m.* fanaticism.

fané, e *p.p.* faded; withered.

faner *v.t.* to fade, to wither, to tarnish (a color). **se ~,** *v.refl.* to fade, to fade away, to wither.

fanfare *n.f.* flourish (of trumpets); fanfare.

fanfaron, onne *adj.* boastful, swaggering, bragging. *n.m.f.* boaster, braggart.

fanfreluche *n.f.* bauble, frills.

fantaisie *n.f.* imagination, fancy; whim, caprice; liking; fantasy. **avoir en ~,** to fancy. **avoir des ~s,** to be fanciful. **il lui a pris une ~ de,** he took a fancy to.

fantasmagorie *n.f.* phantasmagoria.

fantasmagorique *adj.* phantasmagoric.

fantasme *n.m.* fantasy.

fantasque *adj.* fantastic, fanciful, whimsical, capricious; odd.

fantassin *n.m.* foot-soldier, infantryman.

fantastique *adj.* fantastic, fanciful; chimerical.

fantôme *n.m.* phantom, ghost, specter.

faon *n.m.* fawn.

farce *n.f. Cook.* stuffing; low comedy, trick, practical joke, prank. **faire une ~ à quelqu'un,** to play a trick on someone.

farceur, euse *n.m.f.* buffoon; joker, comic fellow.

farcir *v.t.* to stuff; to cram. *v.refl.* to be stuffed.

fardeau *n.m.* burden, load, weight.

farder *v.t.* make up (the face), to gloss, to varnish, to dress up (goods). **se ~,** *v.refl.* to put on makeup. *v.i.* to sink down, to sink in, to sink, to settle down. **se ~ le visage,** to make up one's face.

farfadet *n.m.* hobgoblin, elf.

farfouiller *v.t.* to rummage.

farine *n.f.* flour, farina. **~ de froment,** whole-wheat flour. **~ de maïs,** cornstarch.

fariner *v.t.* to flour.

farineux, euse *adj.* farinaceous, starchy.

farouche *adj.* fierce; wild; shy, skittish, timid, unsociable; surly. **un air ~,** a grim look.

fascicule *n.m.* volume (book); fascicle.

fascinant, e *adj.* fascinating.

fascination *n.f.* fascination.

fasciner *v.t.* to fascinate, to charm, to enchant, to captivate.

fascisme *n.m.* fascism.

fasciste *adj. n.m.f.* fascist.

faste *n.m.* pomp, splendour, magnificence, gorgeousness; ostentation; display; show. **sans ~,** without pomp.

fastidieux, euse *adj.* tedious, tiresome, dull.

fastueux, euse *adj.* pompous, magnificent, gorgeous, ostentatious.

fatal, e *adj.* fatal, inevitable; deadly. **un coup ~,** a mortal blow.

fatalement adv. fatally; inevitably.

fatalisme n.m. fatalism.

fataliste n.m. fatalist.

fatalité n.f. fatality; mischance; fate.

fatidique adj. fateful, fatal.

fatigant, e adj. tiring, tiresome, tedious.

fatigue n.f. fatigue; weariness. **tomber de ~,** to collapse with fatigue.

fatiguer v.t. to fatigue, to tire, to weary; to harass. **la lecture fatigue la vue,** reading tires one's eyes. **se ~,** v.refl. to fatigue oneself, to tire oneself; to be fatigued, to be tired.

faubourg n.m. suburb; outskirt.

fauché, e n.m.f. Infml. broke, flat broke.

faucher v.t. to mow, to mow down. **~ l'herbe,** to mow the grass.

faucon n.m. falcon, hawk.

faufiler v.t. to baste, to tack. **se ~,** v.refl. to be basted, to be tacked; to slip in, into or through.

faune n.m. faun; fauna, wildlife.

faussaire n.m. forger.

faussement adv. falsely, wrongfully.

fausser v.t. to distort. **~ compagnie,** to give somebody the slip.

faute n.f. fault; error, mistake, blunder, defect; scarcity, dearth; lack. **prendre en ~,** to find at fault. **il est mort ~ de secours,** he died for lack of help. **sans ~,** without a fault; without fail.

fauteuil n.m. armchair.

fautif, ive adj. faulty; imperfect, bad; erroneous, incorrect. n.m.f. culprit.

fauve adj. fawn-colored, tawny. n.m. fawn-color. **bêtes ~s,** wild beasts.

faux, fausse adj. false; untrue, discordant; erroneous; out of tune; untuned; sham. **un ~ bruit,** a false report. **il est ~ que,** it is false that. **fausse note,** false note. **note fausse,** note out of tune. **un ~ pas,** a false step. **fausse conche,** miscarriage. **fausse monnaie,** counterfeit coin. **diamants ~,** fake diamonds. **~ frais,** incidental expenses. **fausse piste,** wrong track. **~ témoignage,** perjury. n.m. falsehood; error; forgery; alteration of any deed. **être dans le ~,** to be wrong. **commettre, faire un ~,** to commit forgery. adv. falsely, wrongfully, erroneously. **raisonner ~,** to argue falsely. **chanter ~,** to sing out of tune. **accuser à ~,** to accuse wrongfully.

faux n.f. scythe.

faveur n.f. favor; kindness, grace. **faites-moi la ~ de lui parler,** do me the favor of speaking to him. **s'approcher à la ~ de la nuit,** to approach under cover of darkness.

favorable adj. favorable, propitious.

favorablement adv. favorably.

favori, ite adj. favorite. n.m.f. favorite.

favoriser v.t. to favor, to befriend, to encourage; to aid, to assist. **le temps nous favorise,** the weather is on our side.

favoritisme n.m. favoritism.

fax n.m. fax.

faxer v.t. to fax.

fayot n.m. Infml. kidney bean; Infml. toady.

fayotter v.t. Infml. to toady, to suck up.

fébrile adj. febrile, feverish.

fécal, e adj. fecal. **matières ~s,** feces.

fécond, e adj. fecund, prolific; fruitful, fertile; rich; pregnant. **avoir l'esprit ~,** to have a fertile imagination. **des pluies ~es,** gentle rains.

fécondation n.f. fertilization. **~ artificielle,** artificial insemination.

féconder v.t. to impregnate; to fertilize.

fécondité n.f. fecundity, fruitfulness; fertility, copiousness; richness.

fecule n.f. starch.

féculent, e adj. starchy. n.m. starchy food.

fédéral, e adj. federal.

fédération n.f. federation.

fédéré, e adj. federate.

fée n.f. fairy.

féerie n.f. enchantment; fairyland.

féerique adj. like fairyland; delicately fanciful.

feindre v.t. to feign; to sham, to simulate, to pretend. **~ de la joie,** to feign joy. **se ~,** v.refl. to feign, to pretend to be.

feint, e p.p. feigned; sham, counterfeit, false.

feinte n.f. dissimulation; feint; pretense.

feinter v.t. Sport. to feint, to fake.

félé, e p.p. or adj. cracked (of glass); crazy.

féler v.t. to crack. **se ~,** v.refl. to crack; Fig. to be cracked.

félicitation n.f. congratulation.

féliciter v.t. to congratulate. **se ~,** v.refl. to congratulate oneself, to congratulate each other; to rejoice.

félin, e adj. feline.

félir v.i. to spit (as the cat).

félon, onne adj. felonious; traitorous, treacherous, false. n.m.f. traitor.

félonie n.f. felony, treason.

fêlure n.f. crack; chink.

femelle n.f. female (animal). adj. female; she; (of birds) hen; (of rabbits etc.) doe. **un renard ~,** a she-fox.

féminin, e adj. feminine; female; tender; womanly; womanish. **une voix ~e,** a feminine voice. **genre ~,** feminine gender.

féminiser v.t. to make feminine.

féminisme n.m. feminism.

féministe adj.n.m.f. feminist.

féminité n.f. femininity.

femme n.f. woman; wife; female. **une ~ mariée,** a married woman. **~ de chambre,** maid. **~ de charge,** housekeeper. **~ de ménage,** cleaning lady. **~ d'affaires,** businesswoman. **avoir ~ et enfants,** to have a wife and children.

femmelette n.f. weak woman; effeminate man.

fémoral, e adj. femoral.

fémur n.m. femur, thighbone.

fenaison n.f. haymaking; hay time, hay harvest.

fendre v.t. to split; to slit; to cleave; to splinter, to break. ~ **du bois,** to split wood. ~ **l'âme, le coeur,** to break the heart. ~ **un cheveu en quatre,** to split hairs. **se ~,** *v.refl.* to split; to cleave; to be split, to crack, to chap; to burst. **le bois blanc se fend facilement,** white wood is easily split.

fendu, e *p.p.* split, slit, cleft, cut, cracked; chapped; (of the mouth) wide open.

fenêtre *n.f.* window; casement. **condamner une ~,** to block up a window. **jeter par la ~,** to throw out of the window. **enveloppe à ~,** window envelope.

fenil *n.m.* hayloft.

fenouil *n.m.* fennel.

fente *n.f.* split, crack, cleft, cranny, crevice; slit.

féodal, e *adj.* feudal.

fer *n.m.* iron; sword; shoe (of a horse); head (of a lance); tag (of a lace). **~s,** irons, chains, captivity. **~ fondu,** cast iron. **~ forgé,** wrought iron. **avoir un ~ qui cloche,** to have a screw loose. **il faut battre le ~ pendant qu'il est chaud,** we must strike while the iron is hot. **~s à friser,** curling irons. **mettre les ~s au feu,** to put the irons in the fire. **mettre un ~ à un cheval,** to shoe a horse. **tomber les quatre ~s en l'air,** to go sprawling. **en ~ à cheval,** in the form of a horseshoe. **mettre les ~ à,** to chain, to shackle, to fetter, to manacle, to handcuff. **rompre, briser ses ~,** to break one's chains. **avoir une santé de ~,** to have a strong constitution.

ferblanc *n.m.* tinned iron; tin plate, tin.

férié, e *adj.* celebrated as a holiday, of holidays. **jour ~,** holiday.

ferme *adj.* firm, steady; strong, vigorous, bold; steadfast, resolute. **un pas ~,** a firm step. **rester ~,** to stand firm. *adv.* firmly; compactly, closely; strongly; steadily, steadfastly. **frapper ~,** to strike hard. **se tenir ~,** to stand firm.

ferme *n.f.* farm; farmhouse. **cour d'une ~,** farmyard. *Excl.* **~ la bouche! ~la! la!** shut up!

fermé, e *adj.* closed, shut; exclusive; impassive, impenetrable; unresponsive, uncommunicative; inaccessible.

fermement *adv.* firmly; strongly, steadily.

ferment *n.m.* ferment, leaven; yeast.

fermentation *n.f.* fermentation; agitation.

fermenter *v.i.* to ferment; to effervesce.

fermentescible *adj.* fermentable.

fermer *v.t.* to close, to shut; to shut up; to fasten; **~ une fenêtre,** to close, to shut a window. **~ à clef,** to lock. **~ au verrou,** to bolt. **~ en attachant,** to fasten. **~ la bouche à quelqu'un,** to silence a person. **~ la marche,** to bring up the rear, to go last. *v.i.* to shut, to close; to be shut; to be closed. **se ~,** *v.refl.* to shut, to close, to close itself; to shut up, to close up; to be shut, to be closed. **cette porte se ferme d'elle-même,** this door shuts by itself.

fermeté *n.f.* firmness; stability; strength, vigor; constancy. **~ d'esprit,** strength of mind.

fermeture *n.f.* fastening; shutting; closing; shutting off; closing off; closing down. **Fermeture Éclair,** (trademark) zipper.

fermier *n.m.* farmer.

fermière *n.f.* (woman) farmer.

fermoir *n.m.* clasp.

féroce *adj.* ferocious, fierce; wild, savage.

férocité *n.f.* ferocity; ferociousness, wildness, cruelty.

ferraille *n.f.* old iron, scrap iron.

ferrer *v.t.* to shoe (horses).

ferreux, euse *adj.* ferrous.

ferroviaire *adj.* rail, railway.

ferry-boat *n.m.* ferry.

fertile *adj.* fertile; fruitful; prolific, productive; inventive. **une année ~,** a productive year.

fertilisant, e *adj.* fertilizing, enriching.

fertilisation *n.f.* fertilization.

fertiliser *v.t.* to fertilize; to make fruitful; to manure.

fertilité *n.f.* fertility, fruitfulness.

fervent, e *adj.* fervent; ardent, zealous.

ferveur *n.f.* fervor, fervency, ferventness; earnestness. **avec ~,** fervently, with fervor.

fesse *n.f.* buttock; (pl.) bottom, backside.

fessée *n.f.* spanking.

fesse-mathieu *n.m. Infml.* skinflint, miser.

fesser *v.t.* to spank.

fessier, ière *adj.* gluteal; *Infml.* rump, buttocks.

festin *n.m.* feast, banquet. **faire un ~,** to banquet.

festival *n.m.* festival.

festivités *n.f.pl.* festivities.

festoyer *v.t.* to feast.

fête *n.f.* holiday; feast; festival; faire; party; show. **jour de ~,** holiday. **la ~ Dieu,** Corpus Christi day. **ce n'est pas tous les jours ~,** every day is not Sunday; Christmas comes but once a year. **je vous souhaite une bonne ~,** I wish you many happy returns of the day.

fêter *v.t.* to keep as a holiday, to observe; to celebrate; to feast, to entertain (a person).

fétiche *n.m.* fetich; mascot.

fétichisme *n.m.* fetishism.

fétichiste *n.m.f.* fetishist.

fétide *adj.* fetid.

feu *n.m.* fire; light; gunfire; heat, inflammation; ardor; mettle; passion; beacon, signal light; lantern; hearth, home. **prendre ~,** to catch fire. **mettre de l'huile sur le ~,** to add fuel to the fire. **n'y voir que du ~,** to be dazzled by something. **crier au ~,** to yell fire. **faire du ~,** to make a fire. **il n'y a pas de ~ sans fumée, il n'y a pas de fumée sans ~,** where there is smoke, there is fire. **brûler à petit ~,** to burn by a slow fire; to kill by inches. **j'en mettrais ma main au ~,** I would stake my life on it. **cesser le ~,** to cease fire. **faire ~,** to fire. **~ d'artifice,** fireworks. **~ de joie,** bonfire. **le ~ des regards,** fiery looks. **les ~x de l'été,** the heat of summer. **le ~ de la jeunesse,** the fire of youth. **plein de ~**, spirited, full of ardor. **tout est en ~**, all is in flame. **~x de pierre précieuse**, sparkles/lights of a precious stone. **avoir le visage en ~**, to be red in the face. **~x de bord/de position**, navigation lights. **le ~ des projecteurs**, the glare of the spotlights. **~ arrière**, rear light. **~ rouge**, traffic light. **~x de croisement**, low beams. **avez-vous du ~?** do you have a match/a light? **faire ~ de tout bois**, to be resourceful, to make the most of what is available. *adj.* flame-colored.

feu, e *adj.* late, deceased, defunct. **~ mon père, mon ~ père**, my deceased father. **~ la reine, la ~e reine**, the late queen.

feuillage *n.m.* foliage.

feuille *n.f.* leaf; sheet (of paper); newspaper; foil (of mirrors); bill, list. **sans ~s**, leafless. **chute des ~s**, fall of the leaves. **trembler comme une ~**, to tremble like a leaf. **~ d'or**, gold leaf. **~ d'étain**, tin foil. **~ blanche**, blank sheet of paper. **~ volante**, looseleaf paper. **~ hebdomadaire**, weekly paper. **~ du matin**, morning paper. **~ de route**, itinerary. **~ de paye**, pay slip; payroll.

feuilleter *v.t.* to peruse, to leaf through (book).

feuilleton *n.m.* soap opera.

feuillu, e *adj.* leafy; full of leaves.

feutrage *n.m.* felting.

feutre *n.m.* felt; old hat; felt-tipped pen, felt pen.

feutrer *v.t.* to felt; to pad.

fève *n.f.* bean. **~ de haricot**, kidney bean.

février *n.m.* February.

fiabilité *n.f.* reliability.

fiable *adj.* reliable, trustworthy.

fiacre *n.m.* hackney carriage.

fiançailles *n.f.pl.* engagement. **bague de ~**, engagement ring.

fiancé, e *p.p.* fiancé, fiancée.

fiancer *v.t.* to engage; to betroth. **se ~**, *v.refl.* to become engaged.

fiasco *n.m.* fiasco. **faire ~**, to fail.

fiber *n.f.* fiber; filament. **les ~s du coeur**, the heartstrings.

fibreux, euse *adj.* fibrous.

ficeler *v.t.* to tie with string, to tie up. **se ~**, *v.refl. Infml.* to dress up, to dress out.

ficelle *n.f.* string, twine. **tirer les ~s**, to pull the strings. **connaître les ~s**, to know the ropes. *adj.* given to trickery.

fiche *n.f.* card, index card, slip, form; pin (of hinges), peg. **~ de paye**, pay slip.

ficher *v.t.* to drive in, to thrust in; to stick in; to file; to have a file/record on; to fix (one's eyes); *Vulg.* to give. **~ des coups**, to deal blows; *Infml.* to do. **fiche-moi la paix!** leave me alone! **qu'est-ce qu'il fiche?** what is he doing? what is he up to? **fichez le camp!** get out! **je m'en fiche comme de l'an quarante**, I don't give a darn, I couldn't care less. **il se fiche de toi**, he is pulling your leg. **fiche tout ça par terre**, put everything on the floor. **il s'est fiché dans la**

tête que, he's got it into his head that, he's made up his mind that. **se ~ en l'air**, to smash oneself up.

fichier *n.m.* card index, card file, file.

fichtre *interj. Infml.* gosh!

fichtrement *adv. Infml.* darned, awfully.

fichu, e *adj. Infml.* rotten, lousy; lost, busted, done; dressed, rigged out; shaped, built; hopeless; able, capable. **~ temps**, rotten weather. **elle est mal ~e aujourd'hui**, she feels lousy today. **s'ils sont partis en mer, ils sont ~s**, if they went to sea, they are done for. **être bien/mal ~**, to be good/bad looking. **c'est ~**, it's hopeless. **ils sont bien ~s d'y aller!** they'd have the guts to go there! *n.m.* neckerchief, kerchief.

fictif, ive *adj.* fictitious; imaginary, not real.

fiction *n.f.* fiction; fabrication.

fictivement *adv.* fictitiously.

fidèle *adj.* faithful, true, loyal, trusty. **une traduction ~**, a faithful translation. *n.m.f.* faithful friend; trusty follower, true believer.

fidèlement *adv.* faithfully; truly; honestly.

fidélité *n.f.* fidelity; faithfulness, loyalty; trustiness. **prêter serment de ~**, to take an oath of allegiance.

fiduciaire *adj.* fiduciary.

fief *n.m.* fief.

fieffé, e *adj. Infml.* arrant, regular, downright. **un ~ fripon**, a shameless scoundrel.

fiel *n.m.* gall; bile; spleen.

fiente *n.f.* droppings (bird).

fier *v.t.* to trust, to entrust. **se ~**, *v.refl.* to trust, to confide (in), to rely (on), to depend (on). **je me fie à vous**, I trust to you. **fiez-vous-y**, have confidence in.

fier, ière *adj.* proud; haughty; puffed up. **un homme ~ et hautain**, a proud and haughty man. **faire le ~**, to carry one's head high.

fier-à-bras *n.m. Infml.* bully.

fièrement *adv.* proudly.

fierté *n.f.* pride; dignity.

fièvre *n.f.* fever; frenzy. **accès de ~**, fit of fever. **~ de cheval**, violent fever. **avoir la ~**, to have a fever.

fiévreusement *adj.* feverishly, excitedly, with frenzy, frenetically.

fiévreux, euse *adj.* feverish; having fever; *Fig.* restless. *n.m.f.* person sick with a fever.

figer *v.t.* to congeal, to coagulate; to freeze, to stiffen. **se ~**, *v.refl.* to be congealed, to be coagulated, to harden.

figue *n.f.* fig. **moitié ~ et moitié raisin**, half willingly, half by force.

figuier *n.m.* fig tree.

figurant, e *adj.* figuring, figurative. *n.m.f. Theat.* extra.

figuration *n.f.* figuration; extras.

figurativement *adv.* figuratively, symbolically.

figure *n.f.* figure; face; figurehead; figured passage/(music); face card; shape, form; diagram; symbol. **faire une triste ~**, to show a sad face.

~ **de rhétorique,** rhetorical figure. **être bien de ~,** to have a handsome face.

figurer *v.t.* to figure; to represent; to show as; to be an extra; to dance in figures; to appear; to make a figure. **se ~,** *v.refl.* to fancy, to imagine. **vous ne pouvez pas vous ~ ce que c'est,** you cannot imagine what it is.

figurine *n.f.* figurine.

fil *n.m.* thread; yarn; wire; edge (of a knife); vein (in marble); string (of pearls). **~ blanc,** white thread; white yarn. **~ d'emballage,** string for tying packages. **~ de laine,** woolen thread. **~ de coton,** cotton yarn. **~ de soie,** silk thread. **ne tenir qu'à un ~,** to hang by a thread. **donner du ~ à retordre à quelqu'un,** to give a person a great deal of trouble. **je crois que je tiens le bout du ~,** I think I hold the clue. **~s de la vierge,** gossamers. **le ~ de la vie,** the thread of life. **rompre le ~ d'un discours,** to break off the thread of a talk. **~ à plomb,** plumb line. **~ d'Ariane,** Ariadne's thread. **dans le sens du ~,** with the grain. **contre le ~,** against the grain. **donner le ~ à un couteau,** to sharpen, to give an edge to a knife. **passer un coup de ~,** to make a phone call. **être mince comme un ~,** to be as thin as a rail. **au ~ des jours,** with each passing day.

filage *n.m.* spinning.

filament *n.m.* filament; fine thread.

filamenteux, euse *adj.* filamentous; thready.

filandreux, euse *adj.* stringy, fibrous; dull, prosy.

filant, e *adj.* flowing, (of stars) shooting, falling.

filasse *n.f.* tow. *adj.* flaxen, tow-colored.

filature *n.f.* spinning; shadowing; tailing.

file *n.f.* line; row. **à la ~,** one after another. **prendre la ~,** to fall into line.

filer *v.t.* to spin; to twist into threads; to give; to fly; to fly off; to go off; to run. **il m'a filé 100 Francs,** he slipped me 100 Francs. **que le temps file!** time flies! **il a filé vite fait,** he has taken off very fast. **mon collant a filé,** my stocking has a run; *Naut.* **~ du cable,** to pay out more cable. **~ dix noeuds à l'heure,** to run ten knots an hour. **faire ~ des troupes,** to send off troops. **~ doux,** to lower one's tone.

filet *n.m.* thread; string; filament; fillet; stream; dash (of vinegar); net. **un ~ d'eau,** a thread of water, a streamlet. **un coup de ~,** a haul (fishing). **tendre des ~s,** to lay a net. **prendre au ~,** to ensnare.

filial, e *adj.n.m.* branch office.

filiation *n.f.* filiation; connection, relation.

filière *n.f.* rope, screw plate; channels; procedures; network. **passer par la ~ habituelle,** to follow/go through the usual channels.

filiforme *adj.* filiform, threadlike.

fille *n.f.* daughter; girl. **belle-~,** daughter-in-law; stepdaughter. **petite-~,** granddaughter. **petite ~,** little girl. **jeune ~,** young girl, young lady.

une vieille ~, an old maid. **~ d'honneur,** maid of honour.

fillette *n.f.* little girl.

filleul *n.m.* godson.

filleule *n.f.* goddaughter.

film *n.m.* movie, motion picture; film.

filmage *n.m.* shooting, filming.

filmer *v.t.* to film, to shoot.

filon *n.m.* vein; source; bonanza. **remonter le ~,** to go to the source.

filou *n.m.* pickpocket, thief, petty thief; cheat, swindler.

filouter *v.t.* to pick pockets; to cheat.

fils *n.m.* sons, offspring. **le ~ aîné,** the eldest son. **~ unique,** only son. **petit-~,** grandson. **il est ~ de son père,** he is a chip off the old block.

filtrage *n.m.* filtering.

filtrant, e *adj.* filtering, straining.

filtration *n.f.* filtration.

filtre *n.m.* filter, strainer.

filtrer *v.t.* to filter, to strain.

fin *n.f.* end; extremity, last part, limit; aim, object, view. **à la ~ du mois,** at the end of the month. **la ~ couronne l'oeuvre,** all's well that ends well. **à ces ~s,** to this end. **mener à bonne ~,** to bring to a successful conclusion. **à la ~,** at last. **en ~ de compte,** finally.

fin, e *adj.* fine; delicate; small, thin; keen, acute, subtle, sly, cunning, shrewd, sharp. *or* **~,** fine gold. **pierres fines,** precious stones. **un ~ connoisseur en vins,** a good judge of wine. **fines herbes,** herbes. **une taille ~e,** a slender waist. **une pluie ~e,** fine rain. **un ~ matois,** a sharp blade, a cunning fellow. **du ~ fond de l'Écosse,** from the farthest part of Scotland. **avoir l'oreille ~e,** to have sharp hearing. **~ matois,** cunning fellow, sharp fellow; bottom; gist. **faire le ~,** to look shrewd. **savoir le fort et le ~,** to be thoroughly acquainted with something.

final, e *adj.* final; ultimate, ending; lasting. **finale** *n.f.* final syllable, last syllable. *n.m. Mus.* finale.

finalement *adv.* finally; lastly, at last, ultimately.

finaliste *adj.* finalist; *n.m.f.* finalist.

finance *n.f.* ready money, çash; finance; bankers.

financer *v.i.* to advance money, to finance.

financier, ière *adj.* financial. *n.m.* financier.

financièrement *adv.* financially.

finasser *v.i. Infml.* to finesse; to maneuver.

fine *n.f.* fine Champagne. **une fine à l'eau,** brandy and water.

finement *adv.* finely, delicately; skillfully, artfully; ingeniously.

finesse *n.f.* fineness; delicacy, thinness, smallness; acuteness, sharpness; nicety; cunning; artifice. **la ~ de l'ouïe,** the acuteness of hearing. **user de ~,** to display cunning.

fini, e *p.p.* or *adj.* finished; perfect; polished; accomplished; over. **c'est un homme ~,** he is a broken man. *n.m.* finish; finishing, perfection, last polish.

finir *v.t.* to finish; to complete, to accomplish; to end, to terminate; to conclude; to finish off; to stop, to quit, to terminate; to expire; to conclude; to die. **son bail finit bientôt,** her lease expires soon.

finissage *n.m.* finishing.

finissant, e *adj.* finishing, ending, coming to its end. *n.m.f.* person graduating from grade school.

finlandais, e *adj.* Finnish. *n.m.f.* Finn.

Finlande *n.f.* Finland.

finnois, e *adj.* Finnish. *n.m.f.* Finn. *n.m.* Finnish language.

firmament *n.m.* firmament; the sky, the heavens.

firme *n.f. Bus.* firm.

fisc *n.m.* treasury, Internal Revenue.

fiscal, e *adj.* fiscal. **fraude ~e,** tax evasion. **année ~e,** fiscal year.

fiscalisation *n.f.* funding through taxation, making subject to tax.

fiscalité *n.f.* fiscal laws.

fission *n.f.* fission.

fissure *n.f.* fissure; crevice, crack, slit; split.

fissurer *v.t.* to crack, to split.

fiston *n.m. Infml.* son, sonny, junior.

fistulaire *adj.* fistular.

fistule *n.f.* fistula.

fixateur *n.m. Photo.* fixative; fixing bath, hairspray.

fixation *n.f.* fixation; stability, steadiness; settling, appointing, determining.

fixe *adj.* fixed; stable; firm; steady; settled, set; determined; appointed; regular. **étoiles ~s,** stars set in the sky. **prix ~,** fixed price. *n.m.* fixed salary.

fixement *adv.* fixedly; steadily, steadfastly, firmly.

fixer *v.t.* to fix; to fasten, to attach firmly; to stick; to set down; to appoint; to establish, to settle. **~ avec une épingle,** to pin. **~ ses yeux sur quelqu'un,** to fix one's eyes upon a person. **~ l'attention,** to fix one's attention. **se ~,** *v.refl.* to fix; to fasten; to stick; to be fixed; to rest, to settle; to concentrate. **tous les yeux se fixèrent sur lui,** all looks were riveted on him.

fixité *n.f.* steadiness, firmness; steadfastness; stability.

flac *n.m. Excl.* plop, splash.

flacon *n.m.* bottle, small bottle; flask, flagon; perfume bottle.

flagellation *n.f.* flagellation.

flageller *v.t.* to flagellate, to whip, to lash, to thrash. **se ~,** *v.refl.* to flagellate oneself; to scourge one another.

flageoler *v.i.* to tremble, to shake.

flageolet *n.m.* flageolet; kidney bean.

flagrant, e *adj.* flagrant. **en ~ délit,** in the very act.

flair *n.m.* scent, smell, smelling.

flairer *v.t.* to scent, to smell, to smell out.

flamand, e *adj.* Flemish. **langue ~e,** Flemish language. *n.m.f* Fleming; Flemish language.

flamant *n.m.* flamingo.

flambant, e *adj.* flaming, blazing. **tout ~ neuf,** brand-new, spanking new.

flambeau *n.m.* torch; candlestick.

flamber *v.i.* to flame, to blaze, to blaze up. *Cook.* to singe.

flamboyant, e *adj.* flaming, blazing; bright, shining; flamboyant.

flamboyer *v.i.* to blaze, to flame, to flash; to sparkle; to shine, to glitter.

flamme *n.f.* flame; blaze, flash, fire; passion; fervency. **la ~ d'une bougie,** the flame of a candle. **jeter feu et ~,** to burst out in anger, to breathe fire.

flan *n.m.* custard.

flanc *n.m.* flank; side; womb, entrails; bosom. **se battre les ~s,** to exert oneself to no purpose.

flanelle *n.f.* flannel.

flâner *v.i.* to lounge, to saunter, to loiter, to stroll.

flânerie *n.f.* lounging, sauntering, loitering, stroll.

flâneur, euse *n.m.f.* stroller, saunterer, loiterer.

flanquer *v.t.* to flank; to be at the sides of a building; to secure, to guard on the side; to fling; to hit (a blow). **se ~,** *v.refl.* to throw oneself; to fall. **se ~ par terre,** to fall down on the ground.

flaque *n.f.* puddle of water.

flash *n.m. Photo.* flash.

flasque *adj.* flabby, flaccid. *n.m. n.f.* hub cap.

flatter *v.t.* to flatter; to coax; to caress; to stroke, to soothe, to calm; to humor. **la musique flatte l'oreille,** music pleases the ear. **~ une personne,** to flatter a person. **il se flatte de réussir,** he flatters himself he will succeed.

flatterie *n.f.* flattery; adulation, cajolery, wheedling; caress; fawning (of a dog).

flatteur, euse *adj.* flattering; wheedling; coaxing; complimentary; fawning. *n.m.f.* flatterer; fawner; wheedler.

flatteusement *adv.* flatteringly.

fléau *n.m.* flail; scourge, plague; beam (of a balance); bar (of a door).

flèche *n.f.* arrow; bolt, shaft; spire. **sa carrière est montée en ~,** his/her career has really taken off.

fléchette *n.f.* dart.

fléchir *v.t.* to bend; to bow; to move; to soften. **~ le genou,** to bend the knee, genuflect. **rien ne peut le ~,** nothing can move him; *v.i.* to bend; to incline; to deflect, to swerve; to bow down; to yield, to submit; to be on the decline.

fléchissement *n.m.* bending; giving way.

fléchisseur *n.m.* flexor muscle .

flegmatique *adj.* phlegmatic; cold, unfeeling; sluggish. *n.m.* a dull phlegmatic man.

flegmatiquement *adv.* phlegmatically; coldly.

flegme *n.m.* phlegm; coldness.

flemmard, e *adj. Infml.* lazy. *n.m.f.* lazybones, idler.

flemmarder *v.i. Infml.* to laze, to lounge about.

flemmardise *n.f. Infml.* laziness.

flemme *n.f. Infml.* laziness.

flet *n.m. Ichth.* flounder, fluke.

flétan *n.m.* halibut.

flétrir *v.t.* to wither, to fade, to blight; to blast; to stigmatize; to stain, to tarnish. **l'âge flétrit la beauté,** age destroys beauty. **se ~,** *v.refl.* to wither; to fade away; to shrivel; to be blighted; to pine away, to waste, to decay, to be sullied; to be dishonored. **les fleurs se flétrissent du matin au soir,** flowers fade away from morning to night. **sa beauté commence à se ~,** her beauty is on the wane.

flétrissure *n.f.* withering, fading; stigma of shame, mark of infamy; blemish.

fleur *n.f.* flower bloom, blossom; prime; youth; choice, best; essence. **un bouquet de ~s,** a bouquet of flowers. **être en ~,** to be in the prime of life. **~ de farine,** fine flour. **à ~ de terre,** even with the ground. **à ~ d'eau,** on a level with the water.

fleurir *v.i.* to flower, to blossom, to bloom, to blow; to flourish; to thrive; to adorn, to deck, to embellish with flowers.

fleuriste *n.m.f.* florist.

fleuron *n.m.* flower, *Print.* jewel, ornament.

fleuve *n.m.* river, a large stream. **l'embouchure d'un ~,** the mouth of a river. **un ~ d'éloquence,** a stream of eloquence.

flexibilité *n.f.* flexibility.

flexible *adj.* flexible, pliable, pliant, supple.

flexion *n.f.* flection; *Gram.* inflection.

flibustier *n.m.* freebooter, buccaneer.

flic *n.m. Infml.* cop.

flic flac *adv.* splash.

flingue *n.m. Infml.* gun.

flinguer *v.t. Infml.* to gun down, to put a bullet in.

flint, flint-glass *n.m.* flint glass.

flipper *n.m.* pinball machine; flipper.

flipper *v.i. Infml.* to freak out, to flip.

flirt *n.m.* flirting.

flirter *v.i.* to flirt.

floc *n.m. Interj.* flop, plop, splash.

flocon *n.m.* flake; flock (fabric).

floconneux, euse *adj.* flaky; woolly.

flopée *n.f. Infml.* mass, load, huge amount.

floraison *n.f.* flowering, bloom.

floral, e *adj.* floral.

Florence *n.f.* Florence.

florissant, e *adj.* flourishing; blooming; thriving, prosperous.

flot *n.m.* wave, billow; flood, surge; tide; stream; crowd (of persons). **être à la merci des ~s,** to be at the mercy of the waves. **versant des ~s de larmes,** shedding floods of tears. **à ~,** afloat. **mettre à ~,** to set afloat; *Fig.* to set up.

flottable *adj.* navigable for rafts.

flottaison *n.f.* floating. **ligne de ~,** water line.

flottant, e *adj.* floating; wavering, waving, undulating, flowing; baggy. **une robe ~e,** flowing dress.

flotte *n.f.* fleet; float. *Infml.* heavy rain.

flottement *n.m.* undulation; wavering, irresolution.

flotter *v.i.* to float; to flow, to waft; to flutter; to waver, to hesitate. **faire ~ du bois,** to float wood. **~ entre deux partis,** to waver between two parties.

flotteur *n.m.* raftsman; float.

flottille *n.f.* flotilla; squadron.

flou *adj.* blurred; fuzzy. *n.m.* fuzziness; softness.

flouer *v.t. Vulg.* to cheat, to bilk, to dupe.

fluctuant, e *adj.* fluctuating.

fluctuation *n.f.* fluctuation; variation.

fluctuer *v.i.* to fluctuate.

fluide *adj.* fluid. *n.m.* fluid.

fluidifier *v.t.* to fluidify.

fluidité *n.f.* fluidity, fluency (of speech).

fluor *n.m.* fluorine.

fluorescent, e *adj.* fluorescent.

fluorine *n.f.* fluorspar, calcium fluoride.

fluorure *n.m.* fluoride.

flûte *n.f.* flute; small French roll; **~ à bec,** recorder. **petite ~,** piccolo. **accorder ses ~s,** to come to an arrangement together. **ce qui vient de la ~ s'en retourne au tambour,** easy come, easy go. *Interj.* darn, damn.

flûté, e *adj.* reedy.

flûtiste *n.m.* flutist, flautist, flute player.

fluvial, e *adj.* fluvial.

flux *n.m.* flux; flow, flood; tide. **le ~ et le reflux,** the ebb and flow.

fluxion *n.f.* inflammation; swelling; fluxion. **~ de poitrine,** inflammation of the lungs.

focal, e *adj.* focal.

foetus *n.m.* fetus.

foi *n.f.* faith; faithfulness, fidelity; trust, confidence, credit. **engager sa ~,** to pledge one's faith. **en bonne ~, de bonne ~,** with good faith, sincerely, candidly, fairly. **mauvaise ~,** dishonesty, unfairness. **digne de ~,** trustworthy. **profession de ~,** profession of faith.

foie *n.m.* liver. **avoir les ~s,** to be scared to death.

foin *n.m.* hay. **une meule de ~,** a haystack.

foire *n.f.* fair. **ils s'entendent comme larrons en ~,** they are hand and glove together. *Infml.* mess.

foirer *v.i. Infml.* to fail. **faire ~,** to cause to fail. **il a tout fait foiré!** everything has failed because of him!

foireux, euse *adj. Vulg.* yellow; coward.

fois *n.f.* time. **une ~,** once. **deux ~,** twice. **trois ~,** three times. **une ~ par an,** once a year. **combien de ~?** how often? **une ~ n'est pas coutume,** once is not always. **toutes les ~ que,** whenever. **pour la dernière ~,** for the last time. **trois ~ deux font six,** three times two are six. **à la ~**, at once, at the same time, together.

foison *n.f.* plenty, abundance. **à ~**, plentifully, abundantly.

foisonner *v.i.* to abound; to swarm; to swell; to increase, to multiply.

folie *n.f.* madness, insanity; folly; passion; fatuity; extravagance; mirth. **faire une ~**, to commit a foolish act. **aimer à la ~**, to love to distraction. **les Folies Bergères**, the Folies Bergères.

folklore *n.m.* folklore.

folle *adj.f.* crazy. *n.f.* crazy woman.

follement *adv.* madly.

fomentateur, trice *n.m.f.* fomenter, trouble maker.

fomentation *n.f.* fomentation; *Fig.* excitation, instigation.

fomenter *v.t.* to foment; to encourage, to abet.

foncé, e *adj.* deep, dark.

foncer *v.t.* to bottom (a cask); to sink (a well); to charge, to rush, to dash; to darken. **il a foncé dans le tas**, he charged into the crowd.

foncier, ière *adj.* land, landed; deep, skilled. **propriétaire ~**, landholder, landowner.

foncièrement *adv.* thoroughly, completely; fundamentally.

fonction *n.f.* function; duty; office; charge. **entrer en ~**, to come into office.

fonctionnaire *n.m.f.* official; state employee; bureaucrat.

fonctionnel, elle *adj.* functional.

fonctionnement *n.m.* working; functioning.

fonctionner *v.t.* (of machinery) to work, to go; to act, to operate.

fond *n.m.* bottom; depth; ground; end; background; groundwork; foundation; main point; basis; crown (of a bat); seat (of trousers). **le ~ d'un puits**, the bottom of a well. **un abîme sans ~**, a bottomless pit. **il y a un ~ de vérité dans ces plaintes**, there is some foundation to those complaints. **au ~ de la Russie**, in the remotest part of Russia. **le ~ est occupé par des arbres**, the background is filled with trees. **de ~ en comble**, from top to bottom. **examiner les choses à ~**, to get to the bottom of things. **au ~**, in reality, in the main. **~ de teint**, make-up foundation. **aller à ~ de train**, to go at full speed.

fondamental, e *adj.* basic. **idées ~es**, basic ideas.

fondamentalement *adv.* fundamentally; radically; completely.

fondant, e *adj.* melting.

fondateur, trice *n.m.f.* founder.

fondation *n.f.* foundation; groundwork; founding; endowment.

fondé, e *adj.* founded; well-founded; authorized, justified; funded, consolidated. *n.m.* person authorized to act for another. **~ de pouvoir**, attorney, legal representative.

fondement *n.m.* foundation; groundwork; basis, cause, reason; grounds. **les ~s d'une ville**, the foundation of a town. **ce bruit est sans ~**, this rumor is unfounded.

fonder *v.t.* to found; to lay the foundation of; to establish, to institute, to create, to set up; to endow. **~ une famille**, to start a family. **se ~**, *v.refl.* to be founded, to rely (upon).

fonderie *n.f.* foundry; founding; smelter.

fondre *v.t.* to melt, to dissolve, to melt down, to dissipate; to cast (in a mold); to smelt (ores); to vanish. **~ de la cire**, to melt wax. **~ une cloche**, to cast a bell. **faire ~**, to melt. **le sucre fond dans l'eau**, sugar melts in water. **~ en larmes**, to dissolve into tears. **~ sur l'ennemi**, to rush upon the enemy. **se ~**, *v.refl.* to melt; to blend; to be melted; to dissolve; to become mild, to be subdued. **l'armée se fondait peu à peu**, the army was gradually diminishing. **ces teintes se fondent bien ensemble**, those dyes blend well.

fondrière *n.f.* bog, quagmire, slough; pit (of snow).

fonds *n.m.* ground, soil, land, landed property; funds; cash; capital, business, stock in trade. **avoir des ~ considérables**, to have plenty of cash. **~ social**, capital, capital stock. **être en ~**, to be in cash. **placer son argent à ~ perdu**, to sink one's capital. **~ de commerce**, a business.

fondu, e *adj.* melted, blended, lost. **fondue** *n.f.* **~ savoyarde**, melted Swiss cheese.

fontaine *n.f.* fountain, spring, cistern; urn (for tea, etc.). **eau de ~**, spring water.

fonte *n.f.* melting (of metals); casting (in a mold); cast iron.

football, foot *n.m.* soccer. **terrain de ~**, soccer field.

footballeur *n.m.* soccer player.

footing *n.m.* jogging. **faire du ~**, to go jogging.

for *n.m.* **le ~ intérieur**, one's conscience.

forage *n.m.* boring, drilling; sinking.

forain, e *adj.* itinerant. **marchand ~**, hawker. **théâtre ~**, traveling show. *n.m.f.* stallkeeper.

forban *n.m.* pirate, bandit, crook.

forçat *n.m.* galley slave; convict (condemned to hard labor). **travailler comme un ~**, to work like a slave.

force *n.f.* strength; force, power, might, vigor; violence, constraint; moral energy; fortitude. **avoir de la ~**, to have strength. **de tout ses ~s**, with all his might. **tour de ~**, feat of strength mastery. **la ~ de l'âge**, prime of life. **~ motrice**, moving power. **céder à la ~ majeure**, to yield to what cannot be resisted, to circumstances. **la ~ publique**, the police. **maison de ~**, house of correction. **à ~ de**, because of. **à ~ de pleurer**, by the power of tears. **être de ~ à**, to be equal to, a match for. **by the power of tears.** *adv.* much, a great deal of. **~ compliments**, many (compliments). **de gré ou de ~**, by fair means or foul, willing or not.

forcé, e *adj.* forced; broken open; strained. **à**

marches forcées, by forced marches.

forcément *adv.* evidently, inevitably; forcibly, necessarily.

forcené, e *adj.* mad, furious. *n.m.f.* madman, madwoman.

forceps *n.m.* forceps.

forcer *v.t.* to force; to break open; to strain, to overdo; to increase; to constrain, to oblige, to make; to assault and take; to violate; *Hort.* to bring forward and ripen prematurely. ~ **une porte,** to break a door open. ~ **la main à quelqu'un,** to compel a person to do a thing. ~ **la voix,** to strain the voice. **se ~,** *v.refl.* **le pas,** to increase one's speed; to force oneself, to strain oneself; to do violence to one's feelings (or inclinations).

forclore *v.t. Law.* to foreclose.

forclusion *n.f. Law.* foreclosure.

forer *v.t.* to bore, to drill.

forestier, ière *adj.* forest, of forests, relating to forests. **garde-~,** forester, forest ranger. *n.m.* forester; ranger, keeper.

forêt *n.f.* forest.

forfaire *v.i.* to forfeit, to lose.

forfait, e *p.p.* forfeited. *n.m.* crime, heinous crime; contract. **prendre à ~,** to contract for. **travailler à ~,** to work on contract.

forger *v.t.* to forge; to make, to fabricate; to counterfeit; to coin. ~ **des mots,** to coin words. ~ **des nouvelles,** to invent news. **se ~,** *v.refl.* to be forged; to imagine, to produce.

forgeron *n.m.* smith, blacksmith. **en forgeant on devient ~,** practice makes perfect.

formaliser *v.t.* to formalize. *v.refl.* **se ~ de,** to take offense at.

formalité *n.f.* formality, procedure.

format *n.m.* format; size. **grand ~,** large size.

formation *n.f.* formation; training.

forme *n.f.* form; shape; figure, mold; appearance, aspect; *pl.* conventions. **la matière et la ~,** matter and form. **les ~s de la justice,** the forms of judicial proceedings. **sans ~ de procès,** without formality, without ceremony. **faire quelque chose dans les ~s,** to do something the conventional way.

formel, elle *adj.* positive, categorical; absolute; definite.

formellement *adv.* positively, absolutely, explicitly, expressly.

former *v.t.* to form; to shape, to fashion, to mold; to make; to make up; to train, to discipline. ~ **un parti,** to form a party. ~ **des soldats,** to train soldiers. ~ **une objection,** to raise an objection. **se ~,** *v.refl.* to form; to take a form; to be formed; *Milit.* to draw up. **il s'était formé une ligue,** a league had been formed. **le goût se forme par la lecture des bons auteurs,** reading good authors improves one's taste.

formica *n.m.* (trademark) Formica.

formidable *adj.* great, fantastic, terrific, formidable; tremendous.

formulaire *n.m.* form (papers); formulary.

formule *n.f.* formula; sentence, expression; system, way. **il a trouvé la ~,** he has found the system, he has figured out how to go about it. ~ **de politesse,** polite way, polite manners.

formuler *v.t.* to draw up in due form; to formulate.

fornicateur, trice *n.m.f.* fornicator.

fornication *n.f.* fornication.

forniquer *v.i.* to fornicate.

fort, e *adj.* strong; vigorous, mighty, robust; lusty, stout, sturdy; sound; powerful, able; capable; potent; firm, solid; loud; compact; thick, dense. **être ~ comme un Turc,** to be as strong as a horse. **ville ~e,** fortified town. **une ~e somme,** a large sum. **une ~e pluie,** a heavy rain. **une ~e douleur,** a violent pain. **il est ~ aux échecs,** he is a good chess player. **un élève fort en maths,** a good math student. **c'est un peu ~,** that is going too far. **il n'est pas très ~ en maths,** he is not very good at math. **c'est plus ~ que moi,** It's too much for me, I can't help it. *n.m.* strong man; strongest part of a thing; thickest part; strength; heat, heart; depth; skill; fort, stronghold. **le ~ d'une poutre,** the strongest part of a beam. **voilà le ~ de l'objection,** that is the main point of the objection. **le plus ~ en est fait,** the major part of it is done. **au ~ du combat,** in the midst of the fight. **la critique est son ~,** he is an excellent critic. *adv.* strongly, hard, vigorously, with strength. **frapper ~,** to strike hard. **de plus en plus ~,** louder and louder. **il pleut ~,** it's raining hard. **il gèle ~,** it's freezing.

fortement *adv.* strongly; forcibly; hard; very much.

forteresse *n.f.* fortress, stronghold.

fortifiant, e *adj.* strengthening, invigorating. *n.m.* tonic.

fortification *n.f.* fortification.

fortifier *v.t.* to strengthen; to fortify; to invigorate. **l'exercice fortifie le corps,** exercise strengthens the body. **cela fortifie les soupçons,** that strengthens our suspicions. **se ~,** *v.refl.* to grow strong, to acquire strength; to strengthen; to be strengthened.

fortiori (à) *adv.* a fortiori, all the more so.

fortuit, e *adj.* fortuitous; accidental, incidental.

fortuitement *adv.* fortuitously, by chance.

fortune *n.f.* fortune, wealth; chance, luck. **tenter la ~,** to try one's luck. **chercher ~,** to seek one's fortune. **chacun est artisan de sa ~,** everyone is the architect of his own fortune. **faire contre ~ bon cœur,** to make the best of one's bad fortune. **faire ~,** to make a fortune, to get rich.

fortuné, e *adj.* fortunate, happy, lucky.

forum *n.m.* forum.

forure *n.f.* drilled hole, hole.

fosse *n.f.* pit; hole; den; grave; trench. **la ~ aux lions,** the lions' den. ~ **commune,** common grave. ~ **septique,** septic tank.

fossé *n.m.* ditch; drain; moat. ~ **d'écoulement,** ditch, drain.

fossette *n.f.* dimple.

fossile *adj.* fossil. *n.m.* fossil.

fossoyeur *n.m.* gravedigger.

fou (**fol** before a vowel or a mute h, *f.* **folle**) *adj.* mad; insane, enraged, furious; extravagant, wild; playful; doting on. **devenir** ~, to become mad. **il est** ~ **de joie,** he is mad with joy. **folle ambition,** foolish ambition. ~ **rire,** giggles. **il me rend** ~! he's driving me insane! *n.m.f.* madman, madwoman; a lunatic; jester. **plus on est de** ~**s, plus on rit,** the more the merrier. **à chaque** ~ **sa marotte,** every man has his hobby. **faire le** ~, to play the fool.

foudre *n.f.* lightning; thunderbolt. **il a été frappé par la** ~, he was struck by lightning. **coup de** ~, love at first sight.

foudroiement *n.m.* striking of thunder.

foudroyant, e *adj.* thundering; flashing; overwhelming, crushing. **des regards** ~**s,** withering looks.

foudroyer *v.t.* to strike with thunder. ~ **du regard,** to look daggers at somebody.

fouet *n.m.* whip; lash; whipping. **faire claquer son** ~, to crack one's whip; to blow one's own horn.

fouetter *v.t.* to whip, to lash; to flog; to cut, to be cutting (as the wind); to beat. ~ **des oeufs,** to beat eggs. **le vent me fouette le visage,** the wind cuts my face. **la grêle fouettait contre la fenêtre,** hail pattered against the window.

fougère *n.f.* fern.

fougue *n.f.* passion; ardor; fire; spirit, heat. **apaiser sa** ~, to calm his fury. **la** ~ **des passions,** the heat of passion. **être plein de** ~, to be fiery.

fougueux, euse *adj.* fiery; passionate, impetuous, fierce; hotheaded; mettlesome, spirited. **un caractère** ~, a fiery temper. **cheval** ~, a spirited horse.

fouille *n.f.* excavation, digging.

fouiller *v.t.* to dig, to excavate, to search; to ransack; to scan; to rummage; to comb; to seek. ~ **la terre,** to dig the earth. ~ **des ruines,** to excavate ruins; *Sculpt.* to sink, to hollow. ~ **un voleur,** to frisk a thief. ~ **dans une armoire,** to ransack a cupboard. ~ **dans les poches de quelqu'un,** to feel in a person's pockets. **se** ~, *v.refl.* to search one's pockets; to search each other.

fouillis *n.m. Infml.* mess; confusion.

fouine *n.f.* marten; ferreter; *Infml.* snoop, weasel (animal or person); pitchfork.

fouiner *v.i. Infml.* to nose around, to ferret. ~ **dans les affaires des autres,** to be nosy.

fouineur, euse *adj.* nosy. *n.m.f.* snoop.

fouir *v.t.* to dig.

foulard *n.m.* scarf, foulard.

foule *n.f.* crowd; throng; the mob, the mass, the populace, the rabble. **se perdre dans la** ~,

to be lost in a crowd. **une** ~ **de raisons,** a host of reasons. **de tous côtés le peuple vient en** ~, people come in crowds from all sides.

foulé, e *adj.* trodden; sprained. **avoir le pied** ~, to have a sprained foot.

foulée *n.f. pl.* tracks (of deer); tread (of a step); pile; stride.

fouler *v.t* to tread; to sprain. **il s'est foulé le pied en tombant,** he fell down and sprained his foot. **se** ~, *v.refl.* to sprain one's ankle/wrist. *Derog.* **ça va! tu ne te foule pas trop?** I can see you're not killing yourself!

foulure *n.f.* sprain, strain.

four *n.m.* oven; furnace, kiln (for bricks); hearth (metals). **chauffer le** ~, to heat the oven, to bake. **on ne peut être à la fois au** ~ **et au moulin,** one cannot be in two places at once. *Theat.* **faire** ~, to fail, to flop.

fourbe *adj.* knavish, cheating, crafty, false. *n.m.f.* knave, rogue, cheat; hypocrite.

fourberie *n.f.* cheating, knavish trick; knavery.

fourbi *n.m.* mess.

fourbu, e *adj.* dead tired.

fourche *n.f.* fork; pitchfork. **en** ~, forked.

fourcher *v.i.* to fork. **la langue lui a fourché,** he has made a slip of the tongue.

fourchette *n.f.* fork, table fork. **c'est une bonne** ~, he is a great eater.

fourgon *n.m.* van; baggage cart, wagon.

fourgonnette *n.f.* van, small van; delivery van.

fourguer *v.t. Infml.* to unload (sell).

fourmi *n.f.* ant. **avoir des** ~**s dans les jambes,** to have pins and needles in one's leg.

fourmilier *n.m.* anteater.

fourmilière *n.f.* anthill; swarm of ants; swarm.

fourmillant, e *adj.* swarming; full (of).

fourmillement *n.m.* swarming; tingling, pins and needles.

fourmiller *v.i.* to swarm; to throng, to be crowded.

fournaise *n.f.* furnace.

fourneau *n.m.* furnace. ~ **de verrerie,** glass furnace. **haut** ~, blast furnace.

fournée *n.f.* batch.

fourni, e *p.p.* furnished, supplied, stocked. *adj.* thick.

fournil *n.m.* bakehouse.

fournir *v.t.* to furnish (**de,** with); to supply with, to provide; to store; to procure, to give. **se** ~, *v.refl.* to be furnished; to supply oneself (with).

fournisseur *n.m.* supplier; tradesman; purveyor; contractor (for the army).

fourniture *n.f.* furnishing; supply, provision; remittance. ~**s de bureau,** stationery.

fourré, e *adj.* furred; filled, stuffed; covered with fur. **coup** ~, underhand blow. **manteau** ~, heavy coat. *n.m.* thicket, cover.

fourrer *v.t.* to stuff; to stick; to shove. ~ **son nez partout où l'on n'a que faire,** to stick one's nose where one has no business. **se** ~, *v.refl.* to get, to hide, to push oneself in. **se** ~ **sous un**

lit, to hide under a bed. **ces gens-là se four-rent partout,** those people intrude themselves everywhere. **~ quelque chose dans sa poche,** to stick something in one's pocket. **il est tout le temps fourré chez elle,** he is always at her place.

fourreur n.m. furrier.

fourrière n.f. pound (stray animals).

fourrure n.f. fur.

fourvoiement n.m. going the wrong way, going astray.

fourvoyer v.t. to mislead, to lead astray. **se ~,** v.refl. to go wrong, to go astray; to be grossly mistaken.

foutaise n.f. Infml. poppy cock.

foutoir n.m. Infml. mess, shambles.

foutre v.t. Infml. V. FICHER.

foutu, e adj. Infml. V. FICHU.

fox n.m. Abbrev. (-terrier), fox terrier.

foyer n.m. hearth, fireplace; hearthstone; fire-side; home, homestead; Theat. green room; focus. **un ~ de marbre,** a marble hearthstone. **~ de lumière,** focus of light. **lunettes à double ~,** bifocals.

frac n.m. dress coat, tails.

fracas n.m. crash, sudden noise; tumult, bustle, fuss. **le ~ du tonnerre,** the crash of thunder. **quel ~ dans cette maison!** what a bustle there is in that house! **faire du ~,** to make a noise.

fracasser v.t. to shatter, to break. **se ~,** v.refl. to shatter, to be shattered.

fraction n.f. fraction; breaking. **~ décimale,** decimal.

fractionnement n.m. division into fractions.

fractionner v.t. to divide into fractions.

fracture n.f. breaking, breaking open; fracture.

fracturer v.t. to fracture; to break. **se ~,** v.refl. to be fractured, to be broken.

fragile adj. fragile, brittle; weak, frail.

fragilité n.f. fragility, frailty, frailness, weakness.

fragment n.m. fragment; scrap, extract.

fragmentaire adj. fragmentary.

fragmentation n.f. division into fragments.

fragmenter v.t. to divide into fragments.

frai n.m. spawning; spawn; fry; wear (of coins).

fraîche n.f. adj. V. FRAIS.

fraîchement adv. coolly; freshly.

fraîcheur n.f. coolness, freshness, cool; bloom; ruddiness; chill. **la ~ du matin,** the cool of the morning.

fraîchir v.i. to freshen (breeze).

frais, fraîche adj. fresh; cool, brisk; new, recent; flourishing. **le temps est ~,** the weather is cool. **les matinées sont fraîches en automne,** in autumn, mornings are cool. **du beurre ~,** fresh butter. **le teint ~,** a fresh complexion. n.m. cool-ness, freshness; fresh air; cool place. **prendre, respirer le ~,** to breathe the fresh air.

frais n.m.pl. expenses, costs, charges, outlay. **des ~ immenses,** great expenses. **faux ~,** inciden-tal expenses. **~ de transport,** shipping expens-es. **faire les ~,** to pay the expenses. **se mettre en ~,** to go to expenses; to take a lot of trouble.

fraise n.f. strawberry; ruff, frill; countersink; dentist's drill.

fraisier n.m. strawberry plant.

framboise n.f. raspberry.

framboisier n.m. raspberry bush.

franc, franche adj. free; exempt of charges, clear, open, frank, straightforward, straight, sin-cere. **un homme ~,** a frank man. **~ de port,** postage paid. adv. frankly, freely, openly, sincere-ly, plainly, undisguisedly. **je vous dirai tout ~ que . . . ,** I'll tell you plainly that . . . .

franc n.m. franc (money). **ça vaut bien 20 ~s,** it's worth 20 francs.

français, aise adj. French. n.m.f. Frenchman, Frenchwoman. n.m. French, French language. **apprendre le ~,** to learn French. **en bon ~,** in plain French; plainly.

France n.f. France.

Francfort n.m. Frankfurt. **~ sur le Mein,** Frankfurt-am-Main.

franchement adv. frankly; freely, openly, sin-cerely, ingenuously, plainly, readily; resolutely.

franchir v.t. to clear, to leap over, to jump over, to surmount. **~ une haie,** to clear a hedge. **~ des obstacles,** to overcome obstacles.

franchise n.f. liberty, freedom; franchise; exemption; frankness, sincerity, unreservedness. **un homme plein de ~,** a plain-spoken man.

franchissement n.m. crossing, jumping.

franciser v.t. to gallicize, to Frenchify, to make French. **se ~,** v.refl. to become French; to become Frenchified.

franc-maçon n.m. freemason.

franc-maçonnerie n.f. freemasonry.

franco adv. free of expense; (of a letter) postage paid; (of a parcel) shipping paid.

francophone adj. French-speaking. n.f. French speaker, Francophone.

frange n.f. fringe. pl. bangs (hair).

frangin n.m. Infml. brother, bro.

frangine n.f. Infml. sister, sis.

frangipane n.f. frangipane.

franquette n.f. **à la bonne ~,** simply, without any fuss.

frappant, e adj. striking; impressive.

frappe n.f. Coin. stamp; Print. set of matrices.

frappé, e adj. struck; iced. **du champagne ~,** iced champagne.

frapper v.t. to strike; to hit, to knock; to stamp; to coin, to mint; to ice (liquids); to beat. **~ de la monnaie,** to stamp money. **~ fort,** to strike hard. **~ du pied,** to stamp with the foot. **~ des mains,** to clap one's hands. **se ~,** v.refl. to hit oneself; to knock one's head (against).

fraternel, elle adj. fraternal, brotherly.

fraternité n.f. brotherhood, fraternity.

fratricide n.m. fratricide. adj. fratricidal.

fraude n.f. fraud; deception, deceit, cheat,

imposition; smuggling. **en ~,** fraudulently.

frauder *v.t.* to defraud; to cheat.

fraudeur, euse *n.m.f.* smuggler.

frauduleusement *adv.* fraudulently, by hand.

frauduleux, euse *adj.* fraudulent; dishonest.

frayer *v.t.* to trace out, to clear, to open (a way).

frayeur *n.f.* fright, dread, fear.

fredonner *v.i.* to hum.

freezer *n.m.* freezer.

frégate *n.f.* frigate; frigate bird.

frein *n.m.* brake, bit (of a bridle), bridle; check. **ronger son ~,** to champ the bit; to fret oneself. **mettre un ~ à son ambition,** to rein in one's ambition. **mettre le ~,** to put on the brake.

freiner *v.t.* to brake.

frêle *adj.* frail; weak; feeble, fragile.

frelon *n.m.* hornet.

frémir *v.i.* to rustle; to shudder; to shake; to quaver; to roar. **le feuillage frémit,** the leaves rustle. **faire ~ les cordes d'un instrument,** to make the cords of an instrument vibrate. **il nous a raconté une histoire à faire ~,** he told us a thrilling story.

frémissant, e *adj.* vibrating, quivering, trembling; shuddering, shivering.

frémissement *n.m.* rustling (as of leaves); simmering (of boiling water), vibration; quivering, trembling; shuddering.

frêne *n.m.* ash, ash tree.

frénésie *n.f.* frenzy.

frénétique *adj.* frenetic, frantic.

fréquemment *adv.* frequently, often.

fréquence *n.f.* frequency.

fréquent, e *adj.* frequent.

fréquentable *adj.* respectable. **ces gens ne sont pas ~s,** you can't associate with these people.

fréquentation *n.f.* frequentation, frequenting.

fréquenter *v.t.* to frequent; to resort to, to associate with. **nous les fréquentons peu,** we don't associate much with them.

frère *n.m.* brother; friar. **~ aîné,** elder brother. **~ cadet,** younger brother. **demi-~,** half brother. **beau-~,** brother-in-law.

fresque *n.f.* fresco.

fret *n.m.* freight; cargo, load.

fréter *v.t.* to charter, to freight; to load with goods.

frétillant, e *adj.* frisky, lively, brisk.

frétillement *n.m.* frisking, friskiness; wriggling.

frétiller *v.i.* to wriggle; to fidget; to frisk, to wag.

friable *adj.* friable, crumbly.

friand, e *adj.* fond (of). *n.m.* meat roll.

friandise *n.f.* daintiness; sweet.

fric *n.m.* *Infml.* dough, cash.

fricassée *n.f.* fricassee.

friction *n.f.* friction, rub, rubbing.

frictionner *v.t.* to rub, to rub down. **se ~,** *v.refl.* to rub oneself.

frigidaire *n.m.* fridge, refrigerator.

frigide *adj.* frigid.

frigo *n.m.* fridge.

frigorifier *v.t.* to freeze; to petrify. **être frigorifié,** to be frozen.

frigorifique *adj.* frigorific.

frileux, euse *adj.* chilly; feeling cold. *n.m.f.* chilly person.

frime *n.f.* *Infml.* sham, pretense.

frimer *v.t.* to show off.

frimeur, euse *n.m.f.* showoff.

fringant, e *adj.* frisky; brisk, lively, smart; dashing.

fringuer (se) *v.refl.* to dress, to get dressed.

fringues *n.f.pl.* *Infml.* clothes.

friper *v.t.* to wrinkle, to rumple, to crumple. **cet homme a fripé tout son bien,** that man has squandered all his property. **se ~,** *v.refl.* to get rumpled; to be worn out.

friperie *n.f.* old clothes; used-clothing shop.

frire *v.t.* to fry; to cook in a frying pan. **faire ~,** to fry.

friser *v.t.* to graze lightly. **se friser la moustache,** to curl one's moustache. **se faire ~,** to have one's hair curled. **~ la cinquantaine,** to be getting on for fifty. **se ~,** *v.refl.* to curl one's hair.

frisotter *v.t.* to curl, to frizz.

frisquet, ette *adj.* chilly, cool.

frisson *n.m.* shiver; chill, shudder; thrill. **cela donne le ~,** it makes one shudder.

frissonnant, e *adj.* shivering.

frissonnement *n.m.* shivering; shiver; shuddering.

frissonner *v.i.* to shiver, to shudder.

frit, e *p.p.* fried; ruined, lost, done for.

frites *n.f.* French fries.

friture *n.f.* frying; frying butter, oil or grease; fried fish.

frivole *adj.* frivolous.

frivolement *adv.* frivolously.

frivolité *n.f.* frivolity; frivolousness. *pl.* trifles.

froc *n.m.* hood; frock; *Infml.* pants.

froid, e *adj.* cold; cool. **avoir l'air ~,** to look cold. *n.m.* cold; coldness; cold weather; chilliness. **avoir ~,** to be cold. **avoir ~ aux mains,** to have cold hands. **ça ne me fait ni chaud ni ~,** I couldn't care less. **avoir ~ dans le dos,** to have chills. **faire un ~ de canard,** to be freezing cold.

froidement *adv.* coldly; calmly; indifferently.

froideur *n.f.* coldness; chilliness, chill; frigidity, coolness, unfriendliness.

froissement *n.m.* bruising; clashing; crumpling; straining.

froisser *v.t.* to crush; to rumple, to ruffle; to offend. **~ du papier,** to crease paper. **il m'a froissé,** he hurt my feelings. **se ~,** *v.refl.* to be rumpled; to take offense.

froissure *n.f.* bruise, hurt, injury; rumple.

frôlement *n.m.* grazing; contact; rustling.

frôler *v.t.* to graze; to brush.

fromage *n.m.* cheese. **~ à la crème,** cream

cheese. ~ de Hollande, Dutch cheese. **entre la poire et le ~,** at dessert.

fromager, ère *n.m.f.* cheesemaker. *n.m.* cheese mold.

fromagerie *n.f.* cheese dairy; cheese store.

froment *n.m.* wheat.

froncer *v.t.* to knit; to gather, to lay in plaits. **~ les sourcils,** to frown. **se ~,** *v.refl.* to gather; to knit.

front *n.m.* front; forehead, brow; face; boldness, assurance. **un ~ élevé,** a high forehead. **avoir le ~ de,** to have the nerve to. **faire ~,** to face. **mener deux affaires de ~,** to manage two things at once.

frontal, e *adj.* frontal, head-on. **collision ~e,** head-on collision. *n.m.* frontal bone; frontal.

frontière *n.f.* frontier, border.

frottement *n.m.* friction, rubbing.

frotter *v.t.* to rub; to scour, to clean, to anoint; to wax and polish; to scrub; to thrash. **se ~ les mains,** to rub one's hands. **se ~,** *v.refl.* to rub oneself; to rub each other; to associate with; to come into contact with. **qui s'y frotte s'y pique,** don't you dare touch it.

frottis *n.m.* smear.

froussard, e *adj.* chicken. *n.m.f.* coward.

frousse *n.f.* fright. **avoir la ~,** to be scared.

fructifier *v.i.* to fructify; to be fruitful; to thrive, to prosper; to profit.

fructueusement *adv.* fruitfully, profitably, successfully.

fructueux, euse *adj.* fruitful, useful, beneficial; salutary; profitable, lucrative.

frugal, e *adj.* frugal.

frugalement *adv.* frugally.

frugalité *n.f.* frugality.

fruit *n.m.* fruit; product; produce; offspring; advantage, profit, benefit; consequence. **une corbeille de ~s,** a fruit basket. **les ~s du travail,** the fruits of labor.

fruité, e *adj.* fruity (wine).

fruitier, ière *adj.* fruit, fruit-bearing. **arbre ~,** fruit tree. *n.m.f.* fruit seller, greengrocer.

frusques *n.f.pl. Infml.* rags, clothes.

frustration *n.f.* frustration.

frustrer *v.t.* to frustrate; to disappoint.

fuchsia *n.m.* fuchsia.

fuel, fuel-oil *n.m.* heating oil, fuel oil.

fugace *adj.* fugacious; flying, fleeing away, fleeting, fugitive.

fugitif, ive *adj.* fugitive; fleeing, running away, runaway; transient, fleeting, short-lived. *n.m.f.* fugitive; deserter.

fugue *n.f.* running away; *Mus.* fugue.

fugueur, euse *adj.n.m.f.* runaway.

fuir *v.i.* to fly; to flee; to run away, to escape, to take flight; to leave; to pass away, to glide away; to avoid, to shun. **le temps fuit,** time flies. **le tonneau fuit,** the barrel leaks. **tout le monde fuit cet homme,** everybody avoids that man. **se ~,** *v.refl.* to avoid, to shun each other.

fuite *n.f.* flight; evasion, shift; leak; subterfuge. **prendre la ~,** to take flight.

fulgurant, e *adj.* flashing.

fulminant, e *adj.* thundering; fulminating.

fulminer *v.i.* to fulminate; to hurl thunder; to detonate, to explode with noise; to storm, to rage, to fume.

fumant, e *adj.* smoking; fuming, reeking, steaming.

fumé, e *p.p.* smoked.

fumée *n.f.* smoke; fume; reek. **il n'y a pas de ~ sans feu,** where there is smoke there is fire.

fumer *v.i.* to smoke; to reek, to fume, to evaporate; to be enraged. **~ des jambons,** to smoke hams.

fumeur, euse *n.m.f* smoker.

fumeux, euse *adj.* smoky.

fumier *n.m.* dung, manure; *Infml.* bastard, piece of shit. **un tas de ~,** a heap of dung.

fumiste *n.m.* chimney sweep. *Infml.* phony, fake, fraud.

funambule *n.m.f.* funambulist, tightrope walker.

funèbre *adj.* funeral; funeral; dismal, mournful, gloomy; dark.

funérailles *n.f.pl.* funeral, obsequies, burial.

funéraire *adj.* funeral; funerary. **salon ~,** funeral home, funeral parlor.

funeste *adj.* fatal; baleful; disastrous; mortal; gloomy.

funiculaire *adj.* funicular. *n.m.* funicular railway.

fur *n.m.* price; rate. **au ~ et à mesure,** in proportion; as you go along.

furax *adj. inv.* mad, fuming, pissed off, raging.

furet *n.m.* ferret; snoop.

fureter *v.i.* to rummage; to nose around.

fureteur, euse *n.m.f.* snooping person.

fureur *n.f.* fury; rage; wrath; enthusiasm; mania. **entrer en ~,** to get into a fury, to get into a rage. **faire ~,** to be in vogue.

furie *n.f.* fury, rage, wrath, madness, passion. **comme une ~,** furious, furiously.

furieusement *adv.* furiously.

furieux, euse *adj.* furious; raging, frantic, fierce, violent, impetuous. **des cris ~,** furious cries. **un combat ~,** a furious fight.

furin *n.m.* high seas.

furoncle *n.m.* furuncle, boil.

furtif, ive *adj.* furtive.

furtivement *adv.* furtively.

fusain *n.m.* spindletree; charcoal (for drawing).

fusée *n.f.* rocket; fuse (of a bomb).

fuselage *n.m.* fuselage.

fusible *adj.* fusible. *n.m.* fuse.

fusil *n.m.* steel (to sharpen knives); rifle; gun, shotgun; gas lighter. **~ de chasse,** hunting gun. **~ mitrailleur,** machine gun.

fusillade *n.f.* gunfire, shooting, firing.

fusiller *v.t.* to shoot. **se ~,** *v.refl.* to fire at each other.

fusion *n.f.* fusion, melting; merger.

fusionnement *n.m.* fusion, blending; merging.

fusionner *v.t.* to merge, to blend; to unite.

futaie *n.f.* timber trees, forest for logging.

futé, e *adj.* sly, sharp, crafty, cunning.

futile *adj.* futile, frivolous, idle, vain, worthless.

futilement *adv.* futilely, triflingly, frivolously.

futilité *n.f.* futility, frivolity; vanity, trifle.

futur, e *adj.* future. *n.m. Gramm.* future.

fuyant, e *adj.* flying, fleeting, fleeing; vanishing; (of colors) fading; (of forehead) receding.

fuyard, e *n.m.* fugitive, runaway.

G

gabardine *n.f.* raincoat.

gâcher *v.t.* to mix, to temper (mortar, plaster); to mess up, to spoil; to ruin, to waste. **il a gâché la fête,** he ruined the party. **gâchette** *n.f.* trigger; tumbler.

gâcheur, euse *adj.* wasteful. *n.f.* bungler; botcher.

gâcheux, euse *adj.* splashy, sloppy, muddy.

gâchis *n.m.* mortar; mess, waste. **quel ~,** what a waste, what a mess.

gadget *n.m.* gadget.

gadoue *n.f.* sludge, mud; night soil.

gaffe *n.f.* boathook, blunder; idiot. *Infml.* **fais ~ à toi!** take care of yourself; watch out! **fais ~!** be careful!

gaffer *v.t.* to hook (with a boathook); to mess up. **il a vraiment gaffé cette fois-ci!** he really messed up this time.

gag *n.m.* gag, joke.

gaga *adj.* doddering, senile.

gage *n.m.* pledge; pawn, deposit, gage, forfeit; security, token; promise; *pl.* wages. **mettre en ~,** to pledge, to pawn, to put in pawn. **retirer un ~,** to redeem a pledge. **payer les ~s,** to pay the wages.

gager *v.t.* to wager, to bet; to hire; to pledge. **je gagerais ma vie,** I would bet my life on it.

gagnant, e *adj.* winning, gaining. *n.m.f.* winner.

gagne-pain *n.m.* livelihood, means of subsistence.

gagner *v.t.* to gain; to earn, to get; to win; to deserve; to acquire, to win over, to bring over, to arrive at. **~ dix francs,** to earn ten francs. **~ de l'argent au jeu,** to win money at gambling. **~ du temps,** to gain time. **j'ai gagné doucement la porte sans rien dire,** I gently made my way to the door without saying a word. **~ le dessus,** to get the better of. **~ de vitesse,** to outstrip (a person); to overtake. **il gagne à être connu,** he improves upon acquaintance. **son poème y gagnerait beaucoup,** it would improve his poem very much.

gai, e *adj.* gay; cheerful, lively, merry, jovial, jolly; homosexual. **~ comme un pinson,** as happy as a lark. **une chanson ~e,** a lively song. *adv.* gaily, merrily, cheerily.

gaiement *adv.* gaily, cheerily, cheerfully, merrily.

gaieté *n.f.* gaiety, cheerfulness, liveliness, mirth, jovialness, jollity, good spirits. **avoir de la ~,** to be merry. **de ~ de coeur,** wantonly.

gaillard, e *adj.* licentious, smutty; spirited; gay, joyous; jovial, jolly, sprightly; tipsy. *n.m.* jolly fellow. **un gros ~,** a great big fellow.

gaillarde *n.f.* strapping girl; wench.

gaillardement *adv.* gaily, merrily, cheerfully, sprightly; wantonly; boldly, spiritedly.

gain *n.m.* gain; profit, benefit; lucre; gaining, winning. **l'espérance du ~,** the hope of gaining. **c'est un ~ tout clair,** it is clear profit. **il a eu ~ de cause,** he gained his cause. **~ de temps,** time saver.

gaine *n.f.* sheath; case; girdle. **la ~ d'un couteau,** the sheath of a knife.

gala *n.m.* gala, show; festivity; feast, banquet.

galactique *adj.* galactic.

galamment *adv.* gallantly, courteously, politely; gracefully; handsomely, with good grace, gracefully.

galant, e *adj.* gallant; courteous, polite, civil, courtly; fine, gentlemanly; polite. **un homme ~,** a gallant man (toward ladies). *n.m.* gallantry, civility; gallant.

galanterie *n.f.* gallantry; politeness; compliment. **dire des ~s,** to pay compliments.

galaxie *n.f.* galaxy.

galbe *n.m.* sweep, curve; contour (of the face).

gale *n.f.* itch; scab (in sheep); mange (in dogs); scurf (in plants).

galère *n.f.* galley; drudgery. **vogue la ~,** come what may. **qu'allait-il faire dans cette ~?** what business had he there? **c'est une vraie ~,** it's a real drag.

galerie *n.f.* gallery; corridor, lobby; balcony; audience. **~ de tableaux,** art gallery. **la ~ est nombreuse,** there are many spectators. **faire rire la ~,** to make the audience laugh.

galérien *n.m.* galley slave; convict.

galet *n.m.* pebble; boulder; stone beach, shingly beach, strand. **jeu de ~s,** shuffleboard.

galetas *n.m.* garret.

galette *n.f.* frangipane. **~ des rois,** puff pastry (eaten in France during Christmastime).

galeux, euse *adj.* itchy; mangy; (of sheep) scabby, scabbed; (of trees) scurfy. *n.m.f.* person infected with the itch.

galimatias *n.m.* nonsense, gibberish.

galion *n.m.* galleon.

galipette *n.f.* somersault.

Galles *n.f.* **pays de ~,** Wales.

gallois, e *adj.* Welsh. *n.m.f.* Welshman, Welshwoman; Welsh.

gallon *n.m.* gallon.

gallo-romain, e *adj.* Gallo-Roman.

galonner *v.t.* to lace.

galop *n.m.* gallop. **petit ~,** canter. **grand ~,** full gallop.

galopade *n.f.* galloping.

galoper *v.i.* to gallop; to run fast. **faire ~ un cheval,** to make a horse gallop. **il a galopé toute la matinée,** he has been running about all the morning.

galopin *n.m.* little rogue, imp.

galvaniser *v.t.* to galvanize; to electrify.

galvauder *v.t. Infml.* to put into disorder, to disturb, to tumble.

gambade *n.f.* gambol.

gambader *v.t.* to gambol, to frisk about.

gamberger *v.i. Infml.* to think.

gambette *n.f. Infml.* leg.

gambit *n.m.* gambit.

gamelle *n.f.* tin container; mess kit; *Infml.* hit, blow.

gamin, e *n.m.f.* kid, urchin.

gaminerie *n.f.* childish tricks.

gamme *n.f.* gamut, scale. **changer de ~,** to alter one's tone, one's behavior.

gammé, e *adj.* **croix ~e,** swastika.

ganglion *n.m.* ganglion.

gangrène *n.f.* gangrene. *Fig.* corruption.

gangster *n.m.* gangster, gang member.

gangstérisme *n.m.* gangsterism.

gant *n.m.* glove. **des ~s blancs,** white gloves. **une paire de ~s,** a pair of gloves. **cela vous va comme un ~,** that fits you like a glove. **il va falloir prendre des ~s avec elle,** we'll have to be gentle with her.

ganter *v.t.* to glove; to fit with gloves; to fit. **se ~,** *v.refl.* to put on one's gloves.

garage *n.m.* garage; docking; boathouse.

garagiste *n.m.* garage owner; garage mechanic.

garant, e *n.m.f.* guarantee, voucher; warrantor; surety, security. **tout homme est ~ de ses actions,** every man is responsible for his actions.

garanti, e *n.m.f.* person guaranteed.

garantie *n.f.* guarantee, warranty; warrantying, guaranteeing. **~ de droit,** implied warranty. **sans ~,** not guaranteed.

garantir *v.t.* to guarantee; to warrant, to be security for, to protect. **je garantis cette montre pour un an,** I guarantee this watch for a year. **se ~,** *v.refl.* to preserve, to shelter, to shield oneself.

garce *n.f. Vulg.* bitch.

garçon *n.m.* boy, bachelor, single man, porter, waiter, messenger. **faire vie de ~,** to lead a bachelor's life. **~ manqué,** tomboy.

garde *n.f.* guard, ward, protection; keeping, custody, care, trust; watch; caution, duty, service; flyleaf (of books); hilt (of a sword); *Fenc.* a posture of defense. **donner en ~,** to trust to a person's care. **ce chien est de bonne ~,** that is a good housedog. **prendre ~,** to take care, to be careful, to mind, to beware; to take notice. **être de ~,** to be on duty. **être de ~,** to be on guard,

to be on duty. **~ d'honneur,** honor guard. *n.m.* guard, warden, keeper, guardian. **~ forestier,** forest ranger.

garde-barrière *n.m.f.* gatekeeper.

garde-chasse *n.m.* gamekeeper.

garde-chiourme *n.m.* prison guard.

garde-côte *n.m. pl.* coast guard.

garde du corps *n.m.* bodyguard.

garde-fou *n.m.* handrail; (of a bridge, etc.); parapet (of a terrace); lifeline.

garde-malade *n.m.f.* nurse.

garde-manger *n.m.* pantry.

garde-meuble *n.m.* furniture storage.

garder *v.t.* to keep, to save; to look after, to attend, to mind, to babysit, to attend to, to guard, to defend; to preserve; to nurse, to assist, to watch; to protect, to keep guard, to uphold, to maintain, to sustain; to observe. **veuillez me ~ ma place,** kindly save my seat. **chien qui garde la maison,** dog guarding the house. **~ les malades,** to nurse the sick. **~ la chambre,** to stay in one's room. **Dieu m'en garde!** God forbid! **c'est un homme qui ne peut rien ~,** that man can't keep anything. **~ rancune à quelqu'un,** to have a grudge against someone. **~ son sérieux,** to keep a straight face. **~ le silence,** to keep silent. **~ un secret,** to keep a secret. **se ~,** *v.refl.* to guard oneself; to take care not to, to beware of, to mind, to keep; to be preserved. **gardez-vous bien de le croire,** don't believe a word he says.

garde-robe *n.f.* wardrobe.

garderie *n.f.* nursery school, day-care center.

gardeur, euse *n.m.f.* keeper, herder.

gardien, ienne *n.m.f.* guardian, keeper, warden, keeper; caretaker; attendant; babysitter.

gare *interj.* look out! beware! watch out! make way!

gare *n.f.* (train) station.

garer *v.t.* to park; to moor (at a dock). **se ~,** *v.refl.* to park; to make room; to get out of the way; to keep out of the way; to guard (against), to mind. **garez-vous de cet homme,** watch out for that man.

gargariser *v.t.* **se ~,** *v.refl.* to gargle.

gargouille *n.f.* spout (of a gutter); waterspout; drainpipe.

gargouillement *n.m.* gurgling, rumbling (in the stomach).

gargouiller *v.i.* to cause a rumbling; to gurgle.

garnement *n.m.* worthless fellow, scamp, rascal.

garni, e *adj.* furnished; garnished; provided (de, with). **bouquet ~,** herbs in a cheesecloth pouch to add to soup or sauce. **chambre ~e,** furnished room. **pizza toute garnie,** pizza with everything on it.

garnir *v.t.* to furnish; to provide, to stock, to supply, to fit out; to adorn; to trim (with lace, flowers, etc.); to mount (with jewels). **~ une boutique,** to stock a shop. **se ~,** *v.refl.* to deck oneself out. **la salle commence à se ~,** the house is beginning to fill.

garnison *n.f.* garrison.

garnissage *n.m.* garnishing; trimming.

garniture *n.f.* ornament; trimming, garnish (of a dish).

garrot *n.m.* withers (horse); garrot; tourniquet.

garrotter *v.t.* to bind (strongly); to tie down.

gars *n.m.* guy.

gaspillage *n.m.* spoiling, wasting; squandering; waste.

gaspiller *v.t.* to spoil; to waste; to squander, to run through; to fritter away.

gaspilleur, euse *n.m.f.* waster, squanderer; spendthrift.

gastralgie *n.f.* gastralgia.

gastrique *adj.* gastric.

gastrite *n.f.* gastritis.

gastronome *n.m.* gastronome(r), gastronomist, epicure.

gastronomie *n.f.* gastronomy.

gastronomique *adj.* gastronomic.

gâté, e *p.p.* spoiled, marred; tainted.

gâteau *n.m.* cake.

gâter *v.t.* to waste, to spoil; to taint. **se ~,** *v.refl.* to spoil; to be spoiled; to go bad; to taint; to decay. **ces fruits se sont gâtés,** those fruits are spoiled.

gâterie *n.f.* treat; spoiling (of children).

gâteux, euse *adj.* senile; doddering. *n.m.f.* dotard, dodderer.

gauche *adj.* left; clumsy; awkward, gawky. **la rive ~ d'un fleuve,** the left bank of a river. **une tournure ~,** an awkward figure. *n.f.* left hand, left side, left-hand side, left; *Milit.* left wing; left flank. **prendre sur la ~,** to turn to the left. **à droite et à ~,** to the right and left.

gauchement *adv.* awkwardly, clumsily.

gaucher, ère *adj.* left-handed.

gaucherie *n.f.* awkwardness; blunder.

gauchiste *adj. n.m.f.* leftist.

gaufre *n.f.* waffle.

gauler *v.t.* to beat (trees) with a pole; to knock down (fruit).

gaulois, oise *adj.* Gallic, Gaulish; *Fig.* primitive, antique. *n.m.f.* Gaul. *n.m.* Gallic tongue, Gallic language; (improperly) old French. *n.f.* popular brand of French cigarettes.

gaver *v.t.* to fatten poultry; *Infml.* to stuff. **se ~,** to stuff oneself.

gaz *n.m.* gas. **bec de ~,** gas burner. **tuyau de ~,** gas pipe. **compteur à ~,** gas meter.

gaze *n.f.* gauze; veil.

gazelle *n.f.* gazelle.

gazer *v.t.* to gas. *Infml.* **ça ~?** what's up?

gazette *n.f.* newspaper, blabbermouth.

gazeux, euse *adj.* gaseous, carbonated. **boisson gazeuse,** soft drink.

gazoduc *n.m.* pipeline.

gazoline *n.f.* gasoline.

gazon *n.m.* grass, lawn.

gazouillement, gazouillis *n.m.* warbling, twitter, twittering, chirp; prattle, babbling, babble, prattle.

gazouiller *v.i.* to warble, to twitter, to chirp; to babble, to prattle, to lisp.

geai *n.m.* jay.

géant, e *n.m.f.* giant *n.m.,* giantess *n.f. adj.* giant, gigantic.

geignement *n.m.* moaning.

geindre *v.i. Infml.* to moan, to whine.

gel *n.m.* frost, freezing.

gélatine *n.f.* gelatine.

gelé, e *adj.* frostbitten, frozen. *n.f.* frost; jelly. **une forte ~,** a hard frost. **~ blanche,** hoarfrost. **~ de veau,** calf's-foot jelly.

geler *v.t.* to freeze; to congeal; to blast with cold; to kill by cold; to be frostbitten; to be chilled. **la rivière a gelé,** the river has frozen. **se ~,** *v.refl.* to freeze, to be frozen.

gélule *n.f.* capsule.

Gémeaux *n.m.pl.* Gemini, the Twins.

gémir *v.i.* to groan; to moan; to wail, to bewail, to lament; to mourn.

gémissant, e *adj.* groaning, moaning, wailing.

gémissement *n.m.* groan, groaning; moaning, wail, wailing. **pousser des ~s,** to groan.

gemme *n.f.* gem. **pierres ~s,** precious stones, gems.

gênant, e *adj.* troublesome, embarrassing; inconvenient; tedious, irksome, bothersome, annoying.

gencive *n.f.* gum (mouth).

gendarme *n.m.* armed policeman. *pl.* flaws, spots (in diamonds).

gendarmerie *n.f.* police force.

gendre *n.m.* son-in-law.

gêne *n.f* annoyance; uneasiness, difficulty; embarrassment. **sans ~,** without ceremony; free and easy, at home. **cet homme est tout à fait sans ~,** that man makes himself quite at home. **il est sans ~!** he has some nerve! **être dans la ~,** to be in straitened circumstances.

généalogie *n.f.* genealogy; pedigree.

généalogique *adj.* genealogical.

généalogiste *n.m.* genealogist.

gêner *v.t.* to bother, to annoy; to impede; to embarrass; to be in the way of; to put restraint on; to disturb; to inconvenience. **~ quelqu'un dans ses projets,** to be in a person's way. **je crains de vous ~,** I am afraid of disturbing you. **se ~,** *v.refl.* to inconvenience oneself; to be inconvenienced. **on ne doit pas se ~ entre amis,** friends must not stand on ceremony. **ne vous gênez pas,** make yourself at home.

général, e *adj.* general. **en ~,** in general, generally. *n.m.* general. **~ en chef,** general in chief. **avocat ~,** attorney-general.

généralement *adv.* generally, in general.

généralisation *n.f.* generalization.

généraliser *v.t.* to generalize.

généraliste *n.m.* general practitioner.

générateur, trice *adj.* generative. *n.m.* generator; boiler.

génération *n.f.* generation; descent. **de ~ en ~,** from generation to generation.

générer *v.t.* to generate.

généreusement *adv.* generously; nobly.

généreux, euse *adj.* generous; noble; bountiful; liberal.

générique *adj.* generic, generical. *n.m.* production credits.

générosité *n.f.* generosity; liberality; bounteousness.

Gênes *n.f.* Genoa.

Genèse *n.f.* Genesis.

génétique *adj.* genetic. *n.f.* genetics.

génétiquement *adv.* genetically.

Genève *n.f.* Geneva.

génial, e *adj.* ingenious, inspired, terrific, fantastic. **un type ~,** a great guy.

génie *n.m.* genius; engineering; spirit. **être dépourvu de ~,** to lack brilliance. **un homme de ~,** a man of genius. **~ militaire,** military engineering. **~ civil,** civil engineering. **officier du ~,** engineer officer.

genièvre *n.m.* juniper, juniper tree; juniper berry; gin.

génital, e *adj.* genital.

géniteur *n.m.* generator.

génocide *n.m.* genocide.

genou *n.m.* knee; ball and socket joint. **se mettre à ~x,** to kneel down. **tenir un enfant sur les ~x,** to hold a child on one's lap.

genouillère *n.f.* knee pad; boot top; kneecap.

genre *n.m.* genus; kind, type, sort; species, class, order; fashion, style; gender, genre. **le ~ humain,** mankind. **c'est le ~ de personne qui . . . ,** that's the kind of people who . . . **ça n'est pas son ~,** that's not his/her style, that's not like him/her. **des affaires en tout ~,** all kinds of deals.

gens *n.m.pl.* people, persons, folks. **les vieilles ~,** old people. **ce sont des ~ résolus,** they are resolute people. **tous les honnêtes ~,** all honest people. **de bonnes ~,** good people. **tous ces gens-là,** all those people. **le droit des ~,** the law of nations. **des ~ d'esprit,** intelligent people. **les ~ d'Église,** clergy.

gent *n.f. pl.* **gens** nation, race, tribe.

gentiane *n.f.* gentian.

gentil, ille *adj.* gentle, noble; pretty, nice, kind, pleasing, graceful. **c'est une gentille fille,** she is a nice girl. **comme c'est ~ à vous de . . . ,** how nice of you to . . .

gentillesse *n.f.* kindness, graciousness, favor; prettiness.

gentiment *adv.* kindly, prettily, gracefully.

génuflexion *n.f.* genuflection; kneeling.

géocentrique *adj.* geocentric.

géographie *n.f.* geography.

géographique *adj.* geographic, geographical. **carte ~,** map.

géologie *n.f.* geology.

géologique *adj.* geological.

géologue *n.m.* geologist.

géométrie *n.f.* geometry.

géométrique *adj.* geometric, geometrical.

géométriquement *adv.* geometrically.

géophysique *n.f.* geophysics.

gérance *n.f.* management.

géranium *n.m.* geranium.

gérant, e *n.m.f.* manager, director; acting partner. *adj.* managing.

gerbe *n.f.* sheaf. **lier des ~s,** to bind sheaves.

gerber *v.t.* to bind in sheaves; to pile.

gercer *v.t.* to chap; to crack (the earth, etc.). *v.i.* to chap; to crack. **se ~,** *v.refl.* to chap.

gerçure *n.f.* chap; crack, crevice, cleft, chink.

gérer *v.t.* to manage, to run, to administer.

gériatrie *n.f.* geriatrics.

germain, aine *adj.* German. **cousins ~s,** first cousins.

germe *n.m.* germ, shoot, sprout; treadle (of an egg); origin, bud, seed. **en ~,** in the bud.

germer *v.i.* to germinate, to sprout, to bud, to shoot, to spring up.

germination *n.f.* germination.

germoir *n.m.* hotbed.

gésier *n.m.* gizzard.

gésir *v.i.* to lie. **ci-gît un tel,** here lies so and so.

gestapo *n.f.* gestapo.

gestation *n.f.* gestation.

geste *n.m.* gesture; sign, action. **un ~ naturel,** a natural gesture. **faire des ~s,** to gesticulate.

gesticulation *n.f.* gesticulation.

gesticuler *v.i.* to gesticulate.

gestion *n.f.* management, administration.

geyser *n.m.* geyser.

ghetto *n.m.* ghetto.

gibet *n.m.* gibbet.

gibier *n.m.* game. *Fig.* **~ de potence,** gallows bird, person deserving to be hanged.

giboulée *n.f.* shower, hail shower. **les ~s de mars,** April showers.

giclée *n.f.* squirt, spurt.

gicler *v.i.* to squirt, to spurt, to splash.

gideur *n.m.* jet; spray nozzle, sprinkler.

gifle *n.f.* smack, slap in the face, box on the ear.

gifler *v.t.* to smack, to slap the face of.

gigantesque *adj.* gigantic.

gigolo *n.m.* gigolo.

gigot *n.m.* leg of mutton. *pl. Infml.* legs, shanks; leg-of-mutton sleeve.

gigoter *v.i. Infml.* to kick about, to wriggle, to shake one's leg, to move around.

gilet *n.m.* vest; jacket. **~ de sauvetage,** life jacket. **~ pare-balles,** bulletproof vest.

gin *n.m.* gin.

gingembre *n.m.* ginger.

girafe *n.f.* giraffe.

giration *n.f.* gyration.

giratoire *adj.* gyratory; rotatory.

girl *n.f.* chorus girl.

girofle *n.m.* clove. **clou de ~,** whole clove.

girolle *n.f.* edible mushroom, chanterelle.

girouette *n.f.* weathervane.

gisant,e *adj.* lying down.

gisement *n.m. Geol.* deposit. *Miner.* position of minerals in the earth.

gît V. GÉSIR.

gitan,e *adj. n.m.f.* gypsy. *n.f.* brand of French cigarettes.

gîte *n.m.* abode; lodging; resting place; leg of beef. **revenir au ~,** to return home. **chercher un ~,** to look for lodgings.

givre *n.m.* hoarfrost, rime.

givré,e *adj.* rimy, frosty; *Infml.* nuts, crazy.

glaçage *n.m.* glazing, icing, frosting, glossing.

glaçant,e *adj.* freezing, chilling.

glace *n.f.* ice, freezing point, coldness, ice cream. **glazing** (for pastry). **froid comme la ~,** as cold as ice.

glacé,e *adj.* iced, frozen, icy; frosted; frigid; glazed; candied. **de l'eau ~e,** ice water. **de papier ~,** glossy paper.

glacer *v.t.* to ice; to freeze; to chill; to depress, to cast down; to dampen; to glaze. **~ le sang dans les veines,** to make one's blood run cold. **se ~,** *v.refl.* to freeze; to become congealed; to run cold; to chill, to be chilled.

glaciaire *adj.* glacial, icy, ice. **époque ~,** ice age.

glacial,e *adj.* glacial, icy, frozen; freezing, cold. *Fig.* cold, frigid, cool, chilly.

glacier *n.m.* glacier.

glacière *n.f.* glacier; ice box.

glacis *n.m.* glacis, sloping bank; glazing, varnish.

glaçon *n.m.* ice cube.

glaïeul *n.m.* gladiolus.

glaire *n.f.* mucus, phlegm, glair, egg white.

glaise *n.f.* clay; loam. **terre ~,** clay, potter's earth.

glaisière *n.f.* clay pit; loam pit.

glaive *n.m.* sword. **le ~ de la justice,** the sword of justice.

gland *n.m.* acorn; tassel; glans, moocher. **des ~s de rideaux,** curtain tassels.

glande *n.f.* gland; kernel.

glander *v.i. Infml.* to hang around, to mooch.

glandeur,euse *n.m.f.* moocher.

glaner *v.t.* to glean; to pick up.

glapir *v.i.* to yelp; to squeak, to scream.

glapissement *n.m.* yelp, yelping; squeaking.

glas *n.m.* knell; toll, tolling. **~ funèbre,** funeral knell, death knell.

glaucome *n.m.* glaucoma.

glissade *n.m.* slip, slopping; slide, glide.

glissant,e *adj.* slippery; sliding.

glissement *n.m.* sliding, slipping. **~ de terrain,** landslide.

glisser *v.i.* to slide; to slip, to glide, to graze, to skid; to escape from; to slide off. **la barque glissit sur l'eau tranquille,** the boat glided through the still water. **le pied lui a glissé,** his foot slipped. **~ sa main dans la poche,** to slip one's hand into one's pocket. **glissez-lui un mot à l'oreille,** whisper a word in his ear. **se ~,** *v.refl.* to slip, to glide, to steal, to creep, to insinuate oneself.

global,e *adj.* total, global.

globe *n.m.* globe; sphere, orb, ball; eyeball. **~ de feu,** ball of fire. **~ terrestre,** the earth.

globulaire *adj.* globular.

globule *n.m.* globule, cell.

globuleux,euse *adj.* globulous, globular.

gloire *n.f.* glory; honor, fame, renown, splendor, magnificence; glorification; halo. **se couvrir de ~,** to cover oneself with glory. **vains ~,** vainglory. **Newton fut la ~ de son siècle,** Newton was the glory of his age. **faire quelque chose pour la ~,** to do something for nothing.

glorieusement *adv.* gloriously.

glorieux,euse *adj.* glorious; vainglorious; glorified; blessed. *n.m.f.* boaster, vaunter, conceited person.

glorification *n.f.* glorification.

glorifier *v.t.* to glorify, to praise; to laud. to extol; to make glorious. **se ~,** *v.refl.* to glory (in), to be proud (of), to boast (of).

glossaire *n.m.* glossary, vocabulary.

glotte *n.f.* glottis.

glouglou *n.m.* gurgle, gurgling. **faire ~,** to gurgle; gobbling (of turkey).

glouglouter *v.i.* to gobble.

gloussement *n.m.* cluck, clucking.

glousser *v.i.* to cluck.

glouton,onne *adj.* gluttonous, greedy, voracious *n.m.f.* glutton.

gloutonnerie *n.f.* gluttony, greediness; voracity.

glu *n.f.* line, birdlime. **prendre à la ~,** to line, to catch with lime.

gluant,e *adj.* glutinous, viscous, gluey, slimy, tenacious, adhesive, sticky.

glucose *n.f.* glucose.

gluten *n.m.* gluten.

glutineux,euse *adj.* glutinous; viscous, viscid, adhesive, sticky.

glycérine *n.f.* glycerine.

gnan gnan *adj. Infml.* namby-pamby.

gnognotte *n.f.* trifle, trash.

gnôle *n.f. Infml.* booze.

gnon *n.m. Infml.* punch (usu. to the head).

go (tout de) *adv. Infml.* straight out, right away.

goal *n.m.* goal, goal keeper.

gobelet *n.m.* goblet; cup, beaker.

gobe-mouches *n.m.* flycatcher (bird); fly trap (plant).

gober *v.t.* to swallow down, to gobble up; to believe credulously.

godasse *n.f. Infml.* shoe.

godillot *n.m.* boot; army boot.

goéland *n.m.* gull, seagull.

goélette *n.f.* schooner.

goémon *n.m.* seaweed.

gogo *adv.* plentifully, in plenty.

goguenard,e *adj. Infml.* mocking, jeering, bantering; jovial, merry. *n.m.f.* jeerer, banterer, joker, scoffer.

goinfre *n.m. Infml.* pig.

goinfrer *v.i.* to gormandize, to guzzle. **se ~,** to make a pig of oneself.

golf *n.m.* golf; golf course.

golfe *n.m.* gulf. **courant das ~,** Gulf Stream.

golfeur, euse *n.m.f.* golfer.

gomina *n.f.* brilliantine.

gominé, e *adj.* plastered down, slicked down.

gommage *n.m.* gumming, erasing, rubbing out.

gomme *n.f.* gum. **~ à effacer,** erase. **~ à môcher,** chewing gum.

gommé, e *p.p. or adj.* gummed; gummy.

gommer *v.t.* to gum.

gond *n.m.* hinge. *Infml.* **il m'a fait sortir hors de mes ~,** he put me in a rage.

gondole *n.f.* gondola.

gondoler *v.i.* to warp; to crinkle, to wrinkle.

gondolier *n.m.* gondolier.

gonflé, e *p.p.* swollen, inflated, distended; (of sails) full-blowing, *Fig.* puffed up. **il est vraiment ~!** he has some nerve.

gonflement *n.m.* swelling, inflation, distended.

gonfler *v.t.* to swell; to swell out, to inflate, to distend; to blow up, to fill with air; *Fig.* to puff up, to elate. **se ~,** *v.refl.* to swell, to swell out, to swell up; to be puffed up, to be swollen.

gong *n.m.* gong.

gonorrhée *n.f.* gonorrhea.

gonzesse *n.f. Infml.* chick; woman.

gorge *n.f.* throat; bosom, neck (of women), gorge; entrance; groove (of a pulley). **se couper la ~ l'un l'autre,** to cut each other's throats, to kill each other. **mal de ~,** sore throat. **rire à ~ déployée,** to split one's sides with laughing. **rire sous ~,** to laugh up one's sleeve. **il en a menti dans sa ~,** he has lied in his teeth. **faire des ~s chaudes de quelqu'un,** or **quelque chose,** to jeer at a person or thing. **avoir une belle ~,** to have a fine neck and shoulders.

gorgée *n.f.* mouthful. **boire à petites ~s,** to sip.

gorger *v.t.* to gorge, to glut, to cloy, to satiate, to fill. **se ~,** *v.refl.* to gorge oneself, to glut oneself, to satiate.

gorille *n.m.* gorilla.

gosier *n.m.* throat; windpipe; *Fig.* voice; gullet. **ça lui est resté en travers du ~,** he found it hard to take, it stuck in his craw.

gosse *n.m.f. Infml.* kid. **sale ~,** brat. **~ de niches,** rich little brat. **beau ~,** cute, nice-looking young man.

gothique *adj.* Gothic; barbarous; old, ancient; old-fashioned. *n.m.* Gothic, Gothic style. *n.f.* black letter, Gothic letter.

goudron *n.m.* tar.

goudronnage *n.m.* tarring.

goudronner *v.t.* tar.

goudronneux, euse *adj.* tarry.

gouffre *n.m.* gulf; abyss, whirlpool, ruin.

gouge *n.m.* gouge, a semicircular chisel.

gouine *n.f. Infml.* dyke, lesbian.

goulée *n.f.* gulp, large mouthful.

goulet *n.m.* narrow channel (of a port, etc.); bottleneck.

goulot *n.m.* neck (of a bottle).

goulu, e *adj.* gluttonous, greedy, voracious. *n.m.f.* glutton, great eater.

goulûment *adv.* gluttonously, greedily.

goupille *n.f.* pin, peg, bolt.

goupiller *v.t.* to pin, to key, to fix up, to rig.

goupillon *n.m.* holy-water sprinkler, bottle brush.

goupillonner *v.t.* to cleanse with a bottle brush.

gourde *n.f.* gourd.

gourdin *n.m.* club, cudgel. **donner des coups de ~,** to cudgel.

gourer (se) *v.i. Infml.* to screw up, to make a mistake, to make a blooper.

gourmand, e *adj.* gluttonous, greedy. *n.m.f.* glutton, a greedy eater; gourmand, gastronomist, epicure; *Hort.* sucker.

gourmander *v.t.* to chide, to scold, to rate, to rebuke sharply, to reprimand, to reprove, to control, to subdue; *Cook.* to lard, to stuff.

gourmandise *n.f.* gluttony, greediness; *pl.* delicacies.

gourmet *n.m.* connoisseur; epicure.

gourou *n.m.* guru.

gousse *n.f.* pod; husk. **~ d'ail,** clove of garlic.

goût *n.m.* taste; relish; flavor, savor; appetite, relish, delight; liking; fashion. **avoir le ~ fin,** to have a delicate taste. **cela plait au ~,** that pleases the palate. **~ piquant,** spicy taste. **manquer de ~,** to lack taste. **trouver une chose à son ~,** to find a thing to one's liking. **une plaisonterie de mauvais ~,** a bad joke, a vulgar joke.

goûter *v.t.* to taste; to relish; to like; to enjoy; to try; to smell; to experience; to snack. **~ le vin,** to taste the wine. **~ de tous les plaisirs,** to try all kinds of pleasure. **se ~,** *v.refl.* to be tasted, to be relished. **une sauce doit toujours se ~,** a sauce should always be tasted.

goutte *n.f.* drop; gout (disease). **~ d'eau,** a drop of water. **prendre une ~ de vin,** to have a drop of wine. **accès de ~,** attack of gout. *adv.* at all, in the least, a jot, a bit. **la nuit était noire, on n'y voyait ~,** it was a dark night we could not see a bit. **n'entendre ~ à ce que dit quelqu'un,** not to understand a word of what a person is saying.

gouttelette *n.f.* droplet, little drop.

goutter *v.i.* to drop, to drip.

gouttière *n.f.* eaves; roof; gutter; rainspout; furrow. **creusé en ~,** grooved, channeled, furrowed.

gouvernable *adj.* governable.

gouvernail *n.m.* rudder; helm, tiller. **tenir le ~,** to be at the helm.

gouvernant, e *adj.* governing, ruling.

gouvernante *n.f.* governor's wife; governess; housekeeper.

gouverne *n.f.* guidance, guide, rule. **pour votre ~,** for your guidance.

gouvernement *n.m.* government; rule; administration, management; governorship; government house. *Naut.* steering. **le ~ d'une banque,** the management of a bank.

gouvernemental, e *adj.* governmental.

gouverner *v.t.* to govern, to rule, to command, to control, to conduct, to manage. **bien ~ sa barque,** to manage one's business well. **cette femme gouverne son mari,** that woman rules her husband. *v.i. Naut.* to steer; to govern. **~ à la voile,** to steer with the sails. **se ~,** *v.refl.* to govern, to rule oneself; to be governed, to be ruled; to behave, to conduct oneself.

gouverneur *n.m.* governor; helmsman.

goyave *n.f.* guava.

grabuge *n.m.* squabble, scuffle, brawl, quarrel, wrangling.

grâce *n.f.* grace; favor; pardon; indulgence; gracefulness; charm, elegance; thanks; mercy. **danser avec ~,** to dance gracefully. **de bonne ~,** with a good grace, cheerfully. **les trois grâces,** the three graces. **être dans les bonnes ~s de quelqu'un,** to be in the good graces of a person. **obtenir sa ~,** to obtain one's pardon. **faites-moi ~ de vos observations,** do not make any remarks. **droit de ~,** pardoning power. **dire les ~s,** to say grace. **je vous rends ~s,** I thank you. **~ à Dieu, ~ au ciel,** thank God, thank Heaven. **~ à vous,** thanks to you.

gracier *v.t. Law.* to pardon.

gracieusement *adv.* graciously; kindly, gracefully; free of charge.

gracieux, euse *adj.* graceful; agreeable; gracious; benevolent; engaging; free.

gracilité *n.f.* slenderness.

grade *n.m.* rank, grade.

gradé, e *adj. n.m.* **militaire ~,** noncommissioned officer.

gradin *n.m.* step, bench, raised seat.

graduation *n.f.* graduation.

gradué, e *adj.* graduated, graded, progressive.

graduel, elle *adj.* gradual; progressive.

graduellement *adj.* gradually, by degrees.

gradeur *v.t.* to graduate; to increase gradually.

graffiti *n.m.pl.* graffiti.

graillement *n.m.* hoarseness (of the voice).

grain *n.m.* grain, kernel, berry; seed; bean; bead; speck. **un ~ de blé,** a grain of wheat. **~ de café,** coffee bean. **~ de moutarde,** grain of mustard seed. **~ de poivre,** peppercorn. **~ de poussière,** speck of dust. **avoir un ~,** to be crazy. **un ~ de chapelet,** a bead of a rosary. **~ de beauté,** mole, beauty spot.

graine *n.f.* seed (of plants). **c'est une mauvaise ~,** he is a bad seed. **prends-en de la ~,** learn from it.

graissage *n.m.* greasing; lubricating, oiling, lubrication.

graisse *n.f.* grease, fat. **~ de mouton,** mutton suet; *Cook.* dripping; suet.

graisser *v.t.* to grease; to make greasy; to dirty, to bribe. **~ une roue,** to grease a wheel. **~ la patte à quelqu'un,** to grease someone's palm, to bribe a person.

graisseux, euse *adj.* greasy, oily, smeared with grease; dirty.

grammaire *n.f.* grammar.

gramme *n.m.* gram.

grand, e *adj.* big, large, great, tall, broad, lofty, full, grand; sublime; main, essential. **une ~ ville,** a large town, a great city. **un ~ homme,** a great man. **un homme ~,** a tall man. **une ~e fortune,** a large fortune. **de ~s biens,** great wealth. **le ~ point est d'obtenir son consentement,** the main point is to obtain his consent. **une ~e dame,** a great lady. **le ~ jour,** broad daylight. **le ~ air,** the open air. **le ~ mat,** the mainmast. **le ~ monde,** high life, high society. **quand vous serez ~,** when you are grown up. **les ~es personnes,** grown ups. **ce n'est pas grand-chose,** it's no big deal. **grand-mère,** grandmother; granny, grandma. *n.m.* great man, *pl.* grown-ups; the great. **du petit au ~,** by comparing great things with small ones. **travailler en ~,** to work on a large scale. **agir en ~,** to act nobly.

grand-duc *n.m.* grand duke; eagle owl.

Grande-Bretagne *n.f.* Great Britain.

grandement *adv.* grandly, nobly, handsomely; highly; greatly, much. **il a fait les choses ~,** he did things handsomely. **avoir ~ raison,** to be quite right.

grandeur *n.f.* greatness; height, tallness; size; largeness, magnitude, importance; dignity, power; grandeur, magnificence, pomp. **la ~ d'une province,** the extent of a province. **une étoile de première ~,** a star of the first magnitude. **~ d'âme,** greatness of soul, magnanimity. **de moyenne,** middle-sized.

grandiloquent, e *adj.* grandiloquent; bombastic, pompous.

grandiose *adj.* grand, majestic.

grandir *v.i.* and *v.t.* to grow; to spring up; to get tall; to increase, to grow greater. *v.refl.* to make oneself taller; to make oneself greater.

grandissant, e *adj.* increasing; growing.

grand-oncle *n.m.* great-uncle.

grand-père *n.m.* grandfather, grandpa.

grand-tante *n.f.* great-aunt.

grange *n.f.* barn.

granit(e) *n.m.* granite.

granuleux, euse *adj.* granulous, granular, granulated; rough, rugged.

graphique *adj.* graphic, graphical. *n.m.* drawing.

grappe *n.f.* bunch, cluster; grapeshot. **~ de raisin,** bunch of grapes. **mordre à la ~,** to indulge one's desires.

grappin *n.m. Naut.* grapnel, grappling irons. **mettre le ~ sur quelqu'un,** to grab someone by the collar.

gras, grasse *adj.* fat, fatty, plump, fleshy; rich; coarse, smutty; oily. **l'huile est une substance ~ se,** oil is a greasy substance. **un homme ~,** a fat man. **tuer le veau ~,** to kill the fatted calf. **faire la ~se matinée,** to sleep in. *n.m.* fat, flesh, meat; calf (of the leg). **aimer le ~,** to like fat.

grassement *adv.* at ease, comfortably, generously, liberally, handsomely. **vivre ~,** to live comfortably.

grassouillet, ette *adj.* plump, fattish.

gratification *n.f.* gratification, gratuity, reward; favor.

gratifier *v.t.* to favor, to oblige, to bestow, to confer, to grant; to attribute. **se ~,** *v.refl.* to grant, to bestow to each other.

gratin *n.m.* crust; dish with toasted cheese topping. *Infml.* **le ~ da la société,** the elite, the upper crust.

gratiné, é *adj.* crusty. *Infml.* spicy, juicy; tough, hard. **il nous a donné un examen ~,** he gave us a hard test. *n.f.* onion soup au gratin.

gratis *adv.* gratis, gratuitously, for nothing, freely, free of cost.

gratitude *n.f.* gratitude.

gratte-ciel *n.m.* skyscraper.

gratte-cul *n.m.* rose hip.

gratte-papier *n.m.* scribbler, pen-pusher.

grattement *n.m.* scratching.

gratter *v.t.* to scrape, to scratch, to rate; to scribble. **~ le papier,** to write on paper. **~ l'endroit qui demange,** to scratch where it itches. **~ l'épaule à quelqu'un,** to curry favor with a person. **se ~,** *v.refl.* to scratch oneself; to scratch each other.

gratuit, e *adj.* gratuitous; voluntary, for nothing. **école ~e,** free school. **à titre ~,** for free.

gratuité *n.f.* gratuitousness, gratuity, free gift.

gratuitement *adv.* gratuitously; gratis, for nothing.

grave *adj.* heavy; ponderous, grave, serious, thoughtful, solemn, weighty. *Mus.* low, deep. **une contenance ~,** a serious, a solemn look. **un air ~,** a grave look. **une maladie ~,** a serious illness. **une voix ~,** a deep, low-pitched voice. *n.m. Mus.* low tone, from grave to gay.

gravé, e *p.p.* engraved; pitted; carved.

graveler *v.t.* to gravel.

gravement *adv.* gravely; seriously; grievously, severely.

graver *v.t.* to engrave, to imprint.

graveur *n.m.* engraver. **~ sur bois,** wood engraver, woodcut artist.

gravier *n.m.* gravel.

gravillon *n.m.* fine gravel.

gravir *v.t.* and *v.i.* to climb, to clamber up, to mount, to ascend. **~ une montagne,** to climb a mountain.

gravitation *n.f.* gravitation.

gravité *n.f.* gravity, heaviness, weight; seriousness, graveness, demureness; importance; griev- ousness; serious nature; *Mus.* lowness of sound. **center de la ~,** center of gravity. **avoir de la ~,** to be serious, grave. **la ~ d'une maladie,** the serious nature of an illness.

graviter *v.i.* to gravitate.

gravure *n.f.* engraving, print cut. **~ sur bois,** woodcut. **~ sur acier,** steel engraving. **~ en taille-douce,** copperplate engraving. **~ à l'eau-forte,** etching. **~ au trait,** line engraving. **~ avant la lettre,** proof engraving.

gré *n.m.* will, pleasure; inclination; mind. **agir de plein ~,** to act willingly. **de ~ ou de force,** by fair means or foul. **de bon ~,** willingly. **bon ~ mal ~,** willing or unwilling. **se laisser aller au ~ des flots,** to commit oneself to the mercy of the waves. **au ~ du vent,** in the wind. **au ~ de son désir,** to one's heart's content. **savoir ~ à,** to thank.

grec, grecque *adj.* Greek, Grecian. **c'est du ~ pour lui;** it is Greek to him.

Grèce *n.f.* Greece.

greffe *n.m.* clerk's office (at a court); record office, registry; transplant, graft. **~ du coeur,** heart transplant.

greffer *v.t.* to graft; to transplant.

greffier *n.m.* court clerk, registrar.

grège *adj.* raw. **soie ~,** raw silk.

grêle *adj.* slender, slim, thin, shrill; small. **intestins ~s,** small intestines. **voix ~,** shrill voice.

grêle *n.f.* hail, hailstorm.

grêlon *n.m.* hailstone.

grelot *n.m.* small bell (for horses, etc.). **attacher le ~,** to bell the cat.

grelottant, e *adj.* shivering.

grelotter *v.i.* to shiver with cold, to shiver, to quake.

grenade *n.f.* pomegranate; grenade. *n.f.* Granada.

grenadier *n.m.* pomegranate tree; *Milit.* grenadier.

grenadine *n.f.* grenadine (silk or syrup).

grenaison *n.f.* seeding, producing seed (of growing crops).

grenat *n.m.* garnet.

greneler *v.t.* to grain (leather).

grenier *n.m.* hay loft; granary; storehouse, attic, garret. **~ à blé,** granary. **la Sicile était le ~ de l'Italie,** Sicily was the breadbasket of Italy. **aller du ~ à la cave, de la cave au ~,** to talk nonsense. **charger en ~,** to load in bulk.

grenouille *n.f.* frog.

grès *n.m.* sandstone; grit, gritstone.

grésil *n.m.* sleet.

grésillement *n.m.* shriveling, shrinking; chirping (of crickets).

grésiller *v.i.* to sleet; to shrivel.

grève *n.f.* strand, beach, sandy shore; strike. **~ de la faim,** hunger strike.

grevé, e *p.p.* wronged, injured, aggrieved; encumbered, burdened.

gréviste *n.m.f.* striker.

gribouillage *n.m. Infml.* scrawl, scribble.

gribouiller *v.i. Infml.* to scrawl; to scribble, to daub.

grief, ève *adj.* grievous, enormous. *n.m.* grievance, wrong suffered, injury. **faire ~,** to hold (something) against (someone).

grièvement *adv.* grievously, greatly, badly, enormously, dangerously.

griffe *n.f.* claw, talon, fang, stamped signature.

griffer *v.t.* to claw, to scratch. **se ~,** *v.refl.* to scratch one another.

griffon *n.m.* griffin, griffon.

griffonnage *n.m.* scrawl, scribble.

griffonner *v.t.* to scrawl, to scribble.

griffu, e *adj.* equipped with claws.

griffure *n.f.* scratch.

grignoter *v.t.* to nibble.

gri-gri *n.m.* grigri.

gril *n.m.* grill. **être sur le ~,** to be on tenter-hooks.

grillade *n.f.* boiled meat.

grillage *n.m.* latticework (for windows), framework (in wood). *Metall.* roasting.

grillager *v.i.* to lattice, to grate.

grille *n.f.* to fence, to enclose, grating, railing. **séparer par une ~,** to rail off.

griller *v.t.* to broil, to grill, to scorch; to enclose with a grille; to grate, to toast, to burn; to roast. **~ des côtelettes,** to broil chops. **~ un feu rouge,** to jump a red light. **~ un fusible,** to blow a fuse. **se faire ~ au soleil,** to get a tan.

grille-pain, toaster.

grillon *n.m.* cricket.

grimace *n.f.* grimace, grin; affection, sham. **faire la ~ à quelqu'un,** to make faces, to grin at a person. **faire la ~,** to make faces.

grimacer *v.i.* to grin to make faces; to grimace.

grime *n.m.* stage makeup.

grimoire *n.m.* incomprehensible nonsense.

grimpant, e *adj.* climbing. **plante ~e,** climbing plant, climber, creeper.

grimper *v.i.* to mount, to ascend, to climb, to climb up, to clamber; to creep (of plants). **~ sur un toit,** to climb on a roof.

grimpeur, euse *n.m.f.* climber.

grinçant, e *adj.* grating. *Infml.* biting, caustic.

grincement *n.m.* gnashing, grinding (of the teeth).

grincer *v.t.* to grind, to gnash, to grate.

grincheux, euse *adj.* grumpy, cranky, peevish, cross.

gringalet *n.m. Infml.* puny person, shrimp.

griotte *n.f.* black cherry; speckled marble.

grippage *n.m.* jamming; rubbing, friction.

grippe *n.f.* flu; aversion, antipathy.

gripper *v.t.* to seize, to catch hold of, to lay hold of, to snatch up; to nab.

grippe-sou *n.m.* money grabber, skinflint.

gris, e *adj.* gray, grey; gray-headed; tipsy, drunk; cloudy, dull. **des yeux ~,** gray eyes. **faire ~e**

mine à quelqu'un, to give a person black looks. **un temps ~,** dull weather.

grisantie *adj.* exhilarating, intoxicating.

grisâtre *adj.* grayish, dull.

grisbi *n.m. Infml.* dough, green, moolah (money).

gris-gris *n.m.* grigri, charm, amulet.

grisonnant, e *adj.* grizzled, growing gray.

grisonner *v.i.* to turn gray, to grow gray.

grive *n.f.* thrush. **faute de ~s, on mange des merles,** beggars can't be choosers.

grivois, e *n.m. adj.* gross, broad, obscene, smutty.

grizzli *n.m.* grizzly bear.

Groenland *n.m.* Greenland.

grog *n.m.* grog.

groggy *adj.* dazed, groggy.

grognement *n.m.* grunt, grunting; growl, growling; snort, snorting.

grogner *v.i.* to grunt; to grumble, to growl.

grognon *adj. Infml.* grouchy, grumpy, grumbling, growling, peevish. *n.m.f.* grumbler, growler, moaner.

groin *n.m.* snout.

grol(l)e *n.f. Infml.* shoe.

grommeler *v.i. Infml.* to grumble, to murmur, to mutter.

grondement *n.m.* growing, rumbling, roaring.

gronder *v.i.* to growl, to snarl; to grumble; to scold.

groom *n.m.* bellboy.

gros, osse *adj.* big, large, bulky, stout, important; heavy; coarse, thick. **grosse femme,** big woman. **~ bétail,** large cattle. **avoir le coeur ~ de soupirs,** to have a bursting heart. **la mer est grosse,** the sea is rough. **jouer ~ jeu,** to play high. **faire la grosse voix,** to speak gruffly. **des ~ mots,** foul language, bad words. **un ~ marchand,** a wealthy merchant. **~ temps,** foul weather; stormy weather. *n.m.* bulk; main part, body; mass, generality. **il fait le ~ de la besogne,** he does the main part of the work. **marchand en ~,** wholesale dealer. **prix de ~,** wholesale price. *adv.* largely; much, a good deal, a great deal. **cela coûte ~,** that costs a great deal. **il y a ~ à parier que . . . ,** it's a safe bet that . . . .

groseille *n.f.* currant. **~ rouge,** red currant. **~ blanche,** white currant, **~ verte, à maquereau,** gooseberry.

groseillier *n.m.* currant, currant bush, currant tree.

grossesse *n.f.* pregnancy.

grosseur *n.f.* size, bulk, largeness, thickness; stoutness; swelling.

grossier, ière *adj.* coarse, gross, thick, rude, uncouth, boorish; rough, vulgar, low, mean; foulmouthed. **des dehors ~s,** a vulgar exterior. **ignorance grossière,** gross ignorance.

grossièrement *adv.* coarsely, rudely, grossly, imperfectly.

grossièreté *n.f.* coarseness, grossness, rudeness; roughness; boorishness. **dire des grossièretés,** use crude language.

grossir *v.i.* to grow larger, to grow bigger; to grow stouter, to swell out, to make larger, to make bigger; to make stouter; to swell; to swell up, to enlarge, to magnify. **les pluies ont grossi la rivière,** the river is swelled with rain. **des verres qui grossissent les objets,** glasses which magnify objects. **se ~,** *v.refl.* to grow larger, to grow bigger, to increase, to swell.

grossissant, e *adj.* magnifying, enlarging, increasing, swelling; growing bigger. **verre ~,** magnifying glass.

grossiste *n.m.f.* wholesaler, wholesale dealer.

grosso-modo *adv. phr.* summarily, briefly, in few words.

grotesque *adj.* grotesque; extravagant.

grotte *n.f.* cave, grotto.

grouillant, e *adj.* crawling with, stirring; swarming with, full of.

grouillement *n.m.* grumbling, rumbling (as of intestines).

grouiller *v.i.* to stir, to move; to grumble, to swarm.

groupe *n.m.* group, cluster, clump (of trees).

groupement *n.m.* grouping.

grouper *v.t.* to group, to form an assemblage. **se ~,** *v.refl.* to group, to group together, to crowd, to form a group.

gruau *n.m.* meal; oatmeal.

grue *n.f.* crane (bird and machine); streetwalker, whore. **manoeuvrer une ~,** to work a crane. **faire le pied de ~,** to be kept waiting.

gruger *v.t.* to crunch; to dupe.

grumeau *n.m.* clot, clod, lump.

grumeler (se), *v.refl.* to clot.

gruyère *n.m.* gruyere cheese, Swiss cheese.

guenille *n.f.* rag; *pl.* old clothes, rags, tatters. **en ~s,** in tatters, ragged.

guenon *n.f.* monkey, she-monkey; fright, ugly woman.

guêpe *n.f.* wasp. **une taille de ~,** a very slender waist, wasp-waist.

guêpier *n.m.* wasps' nest, hornets' nest; **tomber dans un ~,** to fall into a trap.

guère *adv.* little, not much; few. **ce mot ne s'emploie plus ~,** that word is seldom used now. **il n'a plus ~ à vivre,** he will not live long. **est-il mort? il ne s'en faut ~,** is he dead? almost.

guéret *n.m.* plowed land left unsown.

guéridon *n.m.* small round table; stand.

guérilla *n.f.* guerilla.

guérir *v.t.* to cure, to heal, to recover, to get well. **~ quelqu'un,** to cure a person. **cette blessure guérira bientôt,** that wound will soon heal. **se ~,** *v.refl.* to recover one's health, to recover, to get well again, to cure oneself; to get cured.

guérison *n.f.* cure; healing.

guérissable *adj.* curable, healable.

guérisseur *n.m.* healer; quack (charlatan); medicine man.

guérite *n.f.* sentry box; watchtower.

guerre *n.f.* war; strife, warfare. **faire la ~,** to make war. **~ civile,** civil war. **~ de religion,** religious war. **de ~ lasse,** war weary, reluctantly. **en ~,** at war. **à la ~ comme à la ~,** we must take things as they come.

guerrier, ière *adj.* warlike, martial. *n.m.f.* warrior.

guet *n.m.* watch; guard. **faire le ~,** keep watch. **être au ~,** to be on the watch; patrol. **~-apens,** ambush, trap, ambuscade.

guetter *v.t.* to watch, to be on the watch for; to lie in wait for, to wait for. **se ~,** *v.refl.* to watch one another.

guetteur *n.m.* watchman, watcher; lookout.

gueulante *n.f.* yell. **pousser une ~,** to shout and yell.

gueulard *adj. n.m.* loudmouthed, noisy, loud. *n.m.f. Vulg.* bawler.

gueule *n.f.* mouth (of animals); jaws, chops; opening; muzzle (of a gun). **la ~ d'un lion,** the mouth of a lion. *Vulg.* **être fort en ~** to have the gift of the gab. **ça a de la ~,** it has some style. **avoir la ~ de bois,** to have a hangover. **ferme ta ~,** shut up! shut your mouth! **faire la ~,** to make a face, to be upset.

gueule-de-loup *n.f.* snap dragon.

gueuler *v.i. Vulg.* to brawl, to yell, to blast out.

gueuleton *n.m. Vulg.* feast, banquet.

gueuse *n.m. Metall.* pig iron.

gueux, euse *adj.* beggarly, poor, needy. **~ comme un rat d'église,** as poor as a church mouse. *n.m.f.* beggar, ragamuffin; rascal, knave, scoundrel.

gui *n.m.* mistletoe.

guibolle *n.f. Infml.* leg.

guichet *n.m.* box office, window; counter; booking office; ticket office.

guichetier *n.m.* clerk, teller.

guide *n.m.* guide, leader; guidebook. *n.f.* rein (of a bridle).

guider *v.t.* to guide, to lead, to direct, to govern; to drive; to steer.

guidon *n.m.* handlebars; field colors.

guigne *n.f.* bad luck, jinx. **quelle ~!** what rotten luck!

guigner *v.i.* to leer, to peep, to glance, to have in view, to have an eye on.

guignol *n.m.* puppet. **spectacle de ~,** puppet show. **arrête de faire ton ~,** stop acting like a fool.

guillemet *n.m.* quotation marks. **entre ~s,** quote, unquote; in quotes.

guillotine *n.f.* guillotine.

guillotiner *v.t.* to guillotine.

guimauve *n.f.* marsh.

guimbarde *n.f.* jew's harp, old junk, old crock.

guindé, e *p.p.* hoisted; strained, forced, unnatural, stiff.

guinder *v.t.* to hoist, to raise, to lift; to strain, to

force. se ~, v.refl. to climb up; to be strained, to
be forced.

Guinée n.f. Guinea.

guirlande n.f. garland; ornament; wreath.

guise n.f. way, wise, guise, manner; liking,
humor, fancy. **en ~ de**, by the way; instead of.
n'en faire qu'à sa ~, to do as one pleases.

guitare n.f. guitar.

guitarist n.m. guitar player.

Gulf-stream n.m. Gulf Stream.

gustation n.f. gustation.

guttural, e adj. gutteral. n.f. Gram. gutteral.

Guyane n.f. Guiana.

gymnase n.m. gymnasium.

gymnaste n.m. gymnast.

gymnastique adj. gymnastics, physical education.

gynécologie n.f. gynecology.

gynécologique adj. gynecological.

gynécologue n.m.f. gynecologist.

gyroscope n.m. gyroscope.

H

H hydrogen. **bombe H**, hydrogen bomb. **l'heure
h**, zero hour.

ha interj. ha! ah!

habile adj. able, clever, skillful, expert; knowing,
cunning; quick, expeditious, active. **un copiste
~**, a quick copyist. **un ~ hologer**, a skillful
watchmaker. n.m. clever man; cunning fellow.

habilement adv. quickly, readily; cleverly,
skillfully.

habileté n.f. ability; cleverness, skill, skillfulness;
sharpness.

habilité n.f. competency; qualification.

habiliter v.t. to qualify, to render competent, to
enable.

habillage n.m. trussing (poultry); dressing.

habillé, e p.p. dressing, clothed.

habillement n.m. clothing; clothes; dress.
~ complet, a complete suit of clothes.

habiller v.t. to dress; to clothe; to attire; to fit
(clothes), to adorn; to cover, to wrap up; Cook. to
prepare; to truss (for the spit). **~ un enfant**, to
dress a child. **~ les pauvres**, to clothe the poor.
ce tailleur m'habille depuis longtemps, that
tailor has worked for me a long time. **ce costume vous habille très bien**, that suit fits you
very well. **s'~**, v.refl. to dress oneself, to dress, to
be clothed. **il s'habille très bien**, he dresses
very well.

habilleur, euse n.m.f. dresser.

habit n.m. garment, apparel, clothes; coat, dress
coat. **~s d'homme**, men's clothes. **l'~ ne fait
pas le moine**, the cowl does not make the
monk, clothes don't make the man.

habitable adj. habitable, inhabitable.

habitacle n.m. abode, habitation, mansion;
Aviat. cockpit.

habitant, e n.m.f. inhabitant, dweller, resident;
inmate. **les ~s des forêts**, the denizens of the
forests.

habitat n.m. habitat.

habitation n.f. habitation; dwelling, residence;
house; abode, stay; haunt; settlement (in a
colony). **une charmante ~**, a charming residence. **maison d'~**, dwelling house. **~ à loyer
modéré (H.L.M.)**, housing project, low cost
housing.

habiter v.t. to inhabit, to live; to dwell, to reside;
to abide (in); (of animals) to haunt, to frequent.

~ un pays, to live in a country. Law. cohabit.
~ à la compagne, to live in the country. **~ sous
des tentes**, to live in tents.

habituation n.f. habituation.

habitude n.f. habit, custom, use, practice, wont.
une mauvaise ~, a bad habit. **par ~**, out of
habit, by habit. **comme d'~**, as usual.

habitué, e p.p. habituated, accustomed, used to.
n.m.f. regular customer.

habituel, elle adj. habitual; customary, usual.

habituellement adv. habitually, usually,
regularly.

habituer v.t. to accustom, to use, to inure. **s'~**,
v.refl. to get accustomed, to accustom oneself,
s'~ au travail, to accustom oneself to work.

hâblerie n.f. bragging, boasting.

hâbleur, euse n.m. bragger, braggart, boaster.

hache n.f. axe, hatchet. **~ d' armes**, battle-axe.
enterrer la ~ de guerre, to bury the hatchet.

haché, e adj. chopped, minced, ground, jerky; **de
la viande ~ e**, ground meat.

hacher v.t. to chop, to hew, to hack, to hash, to
mince. **~de la viande**, to mince meat.

hachette n.f. hatchet.

hachis n.m. mincemeat, hash. **~ par mentier**,
shepherd's, cottage pie.

hachisch n.m. hashish.

hachoir n.m. chopping-board, chopping block,
chopping knife.

hachure n.m. hatching.

hachurer v.t. to hatch, to hachure.

haddock n.m. haddock.

hagard, e adj. haggard, wild, fierce.

haie n.f. hedge. **~ vive**, living hedge. **entourer
d'une ~**, to hedge in; line, row. **former la ~**, to
stand on a line.

haillon n.m. rag, tatter.

haine n.f. hatred, hate, spite, destination. **avoir
de la ~ pour quelqu'un**, to hate a person. **la ~
est aveugle**, hatred is blind.

haineusement adv. hatefully, spitefully.

haineux, euse adj. hateful; spiteful, malignant,
malevolent.

haïr v.t. to detest, to abhor, to dislike, to loathe.
~ à la mort, to hate mortally. **se ~**, v.refl. to
hate oneself; to hate each other.

haïssable adj. hateful, odious, detestable.

halage n.m. towing, hauling, drawing. **chemin**

de ~, towpath, towing path, track road. **corde de ~**, tow line.

hâle, e *p.p.* sunburnt, tanned.

haleine *n.f.* breath; wind. **retenir son ~**, to hold one's breath. **perdre ~**, to get out of breath. **un ouvrage de longue ~**, a long work. **mauvaise ~**, bad breath. **tenir en ~**, to keep (someone) in suspense.

haler *v.t.* to haul; to drag, to tow, to heave. **~ à bord**, to haul in. **~ un bâtiment**, to tow a ship.

hâler *v.t.* to burn, to brown, to tan. **se ~**, *v.refl.* to be sunburned, to be tanned.

haletant, e *adj.* panting, puffing, out of breath, breathless.

haleter *v.i.* to pant, to breathe quickly, to puff, to blow, to be breathless.

haleur *n.m.* hauler, tracker.

hall *n.m.* lobby, lounge; hall.

halle *n.f.* market, market place.

hallebarde *n.f.* halberd. **tomber des ~s**, to rain cats and dogs.

hallucinant, e *adj.* hallucinating; incredible, unbelievable.

hallucination *n.f.* hallucination.

halluciner *v.t.* to hallucinate, to delude.

hallucinogène *adj.* hallucinogenic. *n.m.* hallucinogen.

halo *n.m.* halo.

halogène *adj.* halogenous. *n.m.* halogen.

halte *n.f.* halt, stopping; stopping-place; stop, stand. **faire ~**, to stop; to halt. *interj.* halt! stand! **halte là!** halt! stop! there! hold it!

haltères *n.m.pl.* dumbbells, weights.

haltérophile *n.m.* weightlifter.

haltérophilie *n.f.* weightlifting.

hamac *n.m.* hammock.

hamburger *n.m.* hamburger.

hameau *n.m.* hamlet.

hameçon *n.m.* hook, fishhook; bait. **mordre à l'~**, to bite at the hook, to take the bait.

hampe *n.f.* staff; stem, stalk; scape.

hamster *n.m.* hamster.

hanche *n.f.* hip, haunch.

handball *n.m.* handball.

handicap *n.m.* handicap; disadvantage.

handicapé, e *adj.* handicapped, disabled; *n.m.f.* handicapped, disabled person.

handicaper *v.t.* to handicap.

hangar *n.m.* shed, warehouse.

hanter *v.t.* to haunt.

hantise *n.f.* obsession, obsessive fear.

happer *v.t.* to snap, to snap up, to snatch; to catch, to nab, to gather.

harakiri *n.m.* harakiri.

harangue *n.f.* harange, speech, oration, address. *Infml.* lecture.

haranguer *v.t.* to harangue; to make a speech. *Infml.* to lecture.

haras *n.m.* stud farm.

harassant, e *adj.* exhausting.

harassement *n.m.* exhaustion, extreme fatigue.

harasser *v.t.* to exhaust, to weary, to tire out.

harcèlement *n.m.* harassing, torment, teasing.

harceler *v.t.* to harass, to torment, to tease, to plague, to worry, to annoy.

harde *n.f.* herd (of deer); flock (of birds).

hardi, e *adj.* bold; daring, hardy, fearless, undaunted, dauntless, firm, intrepid.

hardiesse *n.f.* boldness, courage, intrepidity; assurance; impudence, forwardness. **excuses si je prends la ~ de**, excuse the liberty I take of. **la ~ des expressions**, the boldness of expression. **une grande ~ de style**, a great boldness of style.

hardiment *adv.* boldly, daringly, hardily, fearlessly, impudently. **marcher ~ au combat**, to go boldly to fight.

harem *n.m.* harem.

hareng *n.m.* fresh herring. **~ saur**, red herring. **~ fumé**, kipper, smoked herring.

hargne *n.f.* aggressiveness, irritation.

hargneusement *adv.* aggressively, nastily.

hargneux, euse *adj.* morose, churlish, peevish, cross; (of horses) vicious; (of dogs) snarling.

haricot *n.m. Bot.* bean. **~ de mouton**, lamb stew. *Infml.* **c'est la fin des ~s**, that takes the cake, that's the limit.

harmonica *n.m.* harmonica.

harmonie *n.f.* harmony, unison, concord, agreement. **être en ~ avec**, to be in harmony with.

harmonieusement *adv.* harmoniously.

harmonieux, euse *adj.* harmonious.

harmonique *adj.* harmonic, harmonical, harmonious, concordant.

harmoniser *v.t.* to harmonize. **se ~**, *v.refl.* to harmonize, to correspond.

harmonium *n.m.* harmonium.

harnacher *v.t.* to harness. **se ~**, *v.refl.* to rig oneself out.

harnais *n.m.* harness.

harpe *n.f.* harp.

harpie *n.f.* harpy, vixen, shrew.

harpiste *n.m.f.* harpist.

harpon *n.m.* harpoon, fish spear.

harponner *v.t.* to harpoon.

hasard *n.m.* hazard; chance, accident, risk, danger, jeopardy. **un coup de ~**, a stroke of fortune. **parler au ~**, to talk at random. **dire quelque chose à tout ~**, to say a thing, just in case; **aller au ~**, to walk aimlessly; **comme par ~**, what a coincidence; **aurais-tu un stylo à me prêter par ~?** would you lend me a pen by any chance?

hasarder *v.t.* to hazard, to jeopardize; to venture, to risk. **~ sa vie**, to hazard one's life. **se ~**, *v.refl.* to hazard, to venture, to risk, to risk oneself, to run the risk.

hasardeux, euse *adj.* hazardous, bold, venturesome; dangerous.

hasch, haschich *n.m.* grass, pot, hash.

hase *n.f.* doe.

hâte *n.f.* haste, hastiness, hurry. **j'avais ~ de**

partir, I was in a hurry to go. **s'habiller à la ~,** to dress in haste. **en toute ~,** in a rush.

hâter *v.t.* to hasten, to hurry, to get on, to urge on, to urge forward, to push on, to push forward. **~ le pas,** to quicken one's pace. **il faut ~ ces ouvriers,** these workmen must be pushed on. **se ~,** *v.refl.* to hasten, to make haste. **hâtons-nous,** let's hurry.

hâtif, ive *adj.* forward, premature; hurried.

hâtivement *adv.* early; hastily, in haste.

hauban *n.m.* shroud.

hausse *n.f.* lift, block; support, rise. **les fonds sont en ~,** stocks are rising.

haussement *n.m.* raising, lifting; shrugging, shrug (of the shoulders). *Fig.* rising (of the prices).

hausser *v.t.* to raise, to raise up; to lift up; to shrug (the shoulders), to increase, to get higher; to be higher. **~ les épaules,** to shrug one's shoulders, to shrug. **~ le prix du pain,** to raise the price of bread. **les prix ont haussé,** the prices have risen. **faire ~ le prix du grain,** to make the price of corn rise. **se ~,** *v.refl.* to rise, to raise oneself. **se ~ sur la pointe des pieds,** to stand on tiptoe.

haussier *n.m.* *Fin.* bull, speculator.

haut, e *adj.* high; lofty; tall, upper; *Mus.* sharp, acute; loud, aloud. **un homme de ~e taille,** a very tall man. **lire à ~e voix,** to read aloud. **pousser de ~s cris,** to raise an outcry. **avoir la parole ~e, le verbe ~,** to talk very loudly. **le ~ Rhin,** the Upper Rhin. *n.m.* height, hill, mountain, elevated ground; summit, top; upper part. **tomber de son ~,** to fall full length. **le ~ d'une page,** the top of a page. **il y a des ~s et des bas dans la vie,** there are ups and downs in life. *adv.* high, highly; up, high up, aloft, on high; above; loud, loudly. **il mène ses gens ~ la main,** he rules his people with a high hand. **parler ~,** to speak aloud. **il est en ~,** he is upstairs. **la lumière vient d'en ~,** the light comes from above.

hautain, e *adj.* haughty, supercilious, lofty, arrogant. **un homme ~,** a haughty man.

hautbois *n.m.* oboe.

haut-de-chausse or **haut-de-chausses** *n.m.* breeches.

haute-contre *n.f.* counter tenor.

hautement *adv.* proudly; boldly; highly; plainly.

hauteur *n.f.* height; altitude; eminence, hill; hautiness. **la ~ d'un arbre,** the height of a tree. **la ~ des pensées,** the elevation of ideas. **parler avec ~,** to speak haughtily.

haut-fond *n.m.* shoal.

haut-le-corps *n.m.* bound, start.

haut-parleur *n.m.* amplifier, loudspeaker.

havane *n.f.* Havana. *n.m.* Havana cigar.

hâve *adj.* pale, wan.

havresac *n.m.* haversack, knapsack.

hé *interj.* (for calling) eh! oh! **eh bien!** well! **eh quoi! vous n'être pas encore parti!** what! are you not gone yet?

hebdomadaire *adj.* weekly.

hébergement *n.m.* lodging, harbor.

héberger *v.t.* to accommodate, to lodge; to harbor.

hébété, e *p.p.* dulled, stupefied.

hébéter *v.t.* to stupefy, to stulify. **s'~,** *v.refl.* to grow stupid, to become dull.

hébétude *n.f.* dulness, stupidity.

hébraïque *adj.* Hebrew, Hebraic.

hébraïsant *n.m.* hebraïstic, hebraïstical.

hébraïser *v.i.* hebraize; to conform to the Hebrews.

hébraïsme *n.m.* hebraism.

hébreu *n.m.* Hebrew; the Hebrew language. *adj.* *n.m.* Hebrew, Hebraic.

hécatombe *n.f.* hecatomb; slaughter.

hectare *n.m.* hectare.

hecto *n.m.* abbreviation of **hectogramme.**

hectogramme *n.m.* hectogram.

hectolitre *n.m.* hectoliter.

hectomètre *n.m.* hectometer.

hédonisme *n.m.* hedonism.

hédoniste *adj.* hedonist, hedonistic; *n.m.f.* hedonist.

hégémonie *n.f.* supremacy, predominance.

hein *interj.* oh? hey? what?

hélas *interj.* alas!

héler *v.t.* to bail, to speak; to call **se ~,** *v.refl.* to greet each other.

hélice *n.f.* helix; screw, propeller.

hélicoïde *adj.* helicoïd.

hélicon *n.m.* helicon.

hélicoptère *n.m.* helicopter.

héliport *n.m.* heliport.

helix *n.m.* *Anat.* helix.

hellène *n.m.* Greek.

hellénique *adj.* hellenic, Grecian, Greek.

hellénisme *n.f.* Hellenism, Grecism.

helléniste *n.m.* Hellenist.

helvétie *n.f.* Helvetia.

helvétique *adj.* Swiss, helvetic.

hem *interj.* hem.

hématologie *n.f.* hematology.

hématome *n.m.* hematoma.

hémicycle *n.m.* hemicycle.

hémiplégie *n.f.* hemiplegia.

hémiplégique *adj.* hemiplegic.

hémisphère *n.m.* hemisphere.

hémisphérique *adj.* hemispheric, hemispherical.

hémoglobine *n.f.* hemoglobin.

hémophile *n.f.* hemophilia, *n.m.f.* hemophiliac.

hémophilie *n.f.* hemophilia.

hémorragie *n.f.* hemorrhage.

hémoragique *adj.* hemorrhagic.

hémorroïde *n.f.pl.* hemorrhoids, piles.

hémostatique *adj.* hemostatic.

henné *n.m.* henna.

hennir *v.i.* to neigh.

hennissement *n.m.* neigh, neighing.

hépatique *adj.* hepatic; hepatical. *n.f.* liverwort.

hépatite *n.f.* hepatitis.

heptagone *adj.* heptagonal, heptangular. *n.m.* heptagon.

héraldique *adj.* heraldic.

herbacé, e *adj.* herbaceous.

herbage *n.m.* herbage; herbs; pasture; meadow.

herbe *n.f.* herbs; grass. ~**s médicinales**, medicinal herbs. **mauvaise** ~, weed. ~**s potagères**, pot herbs. **mauvaise** ~ **croît toujours**, bad weeds grow apace. **fines** ~**s**, mixed herbs. **un brin d'**~, a blade of grass. **mettre un cheval à l'**~, to put a horse to pasture. **couper l'**~ **sous le pied à quelqu'un**, to cut the grass under a person's feet, pull the rug out from under someone.

herbicide *adj.* herbicidal; *n.m.* herbicide, weed killer.

herbier *n.m.* herbal, herbarium.

herbivore *adj.* herbivorous. *n.m.* herbivorous animal.

herboriser *v.i.* to herborize.

herboriste *n.m.f.* herbalist, herborist.

herboristerie *n.f.* herbalist's shop.

herbu, e *adj.* grass-covered, grassy.

Hercule *n.m.* Hercules. *Fig.* Hercules, athlete, strong man.

herculéen, enne *adj.* Herculean.

hère *n.m.* poor wretch.

héréditaire *adj.* hereditary.

hérédité *n.f.* heredity, right, inheritance.

hérésie *n.f.* heresy.

hérétique *adj.* heretical; *n.f.* heretic.

hérissé, e *adj.* erect, standing on end; bristling; hairy, prickly. **un pays** ~ **de montagnes**, a country covered with mountains.

hérisser *v.t.* to bristle, to bristle up, to set up. **le lion hérisse sa crinière**, the lion bristles up his mane. **se** ~, *v.refl.* to bristle; to bristle up; to stand erect, to stand on end; to be covered. **ses cheveux se hérissent**, his hair stood on end.

hérisson *n.m.* hedgehog, sea urchin.

héritage *n.m.* inheritance, heritage.

hériter *v.i.* to inherit.

héritier, ière *n.m.* heir, inheritor, heiress. ~ **légitime**, legitimate heir. ~ **universel**, sole heir. ~ **présomptif**, heir presumptive; heir apparent.

hermaphrodisme *n.m.* hermaphrodism, hermaphroditism.

hermaphrodisme *n.m.* hermaphrodite. *adj.* hermaphroditic.

hermétique *adj.* hermetic.

hermétiquement *adv.* hermetically, closely.

hermine *n.f.* ermine.

hernie *n.f.* hernia, rupture. ~ **étranglée**, strangulated hernia.

héroïne *n.f.* heroine.

héroïque *ad.* heroic.

héroïquement *adj.* heroically.

héroïsme *n.m.* heroism.

héron *n.m.* heron.

héronneau *n.m.* young heron.

héros *n.m.* hero.

herpès *n.m.* herpes, cold sores.

hésitant, e *adj.* hesitating; wavering, undecided, faltering; stammering.

hésitation *n.f.* hesitation, doubt, uncertainty, stammering, faltering.

hésiter *v.i.* to hesitate, to doubt, to be doubtful, to waver, to demur, to pause, to falter, to stammer, **sans** ~, without hesitation.

hétéroclite *adj.* heteroclite, heteroclitic, heteroclitical; anomalous; whimsical, ridiculous, uncouth. **des manières** ~**s**, uncouth manner.

hétérosexualité *n.f.* heterosexuality.

hétérosexuel, le *adj.* heterosexual.

hêtre *n.m.* beech, beech tree.

heu *interj.* hum, ha.

heure *n.f.* hour, time, duration, o'clock. **une demi** ~, half an hour. **deux** ~**s**, two hours. **il est parti à quatre** ~**s du matin**, he left at four o'clock in the morning. **quelle** ~ **est-il?** what time is it? **deux heures un quart**, a quarter past two. **a l'**~, by the hour later; **à tout à l'**~, see you later. ~ **de pointe**, peak time, rush hour; **de bonne** ~, early; on time. **à la bonne** ~, well and good, that's right. **à toute** ~, at all hours, always. **sur l'**~, at once, directly. **tout à l'**~, (future) presently, directly, (past) just now, a moment ago. **livre d'**~**s**, prayer book. **la dernière** ~, the last moments, the last hour.

heureusement *adv.* happily; luckily; fortunately; successfully. ~ **qu'il n'a rien vu**, luckily, he did not see a thing.

heureux, euse *adj.* happy; fortunate; successful; prosperous; lucky; propitious, favorable. ~ **hasard**, lucky chance. **c'est fort** ~ **pour vous**, it is very fortunate for you, good for you. **une heureuse vieillesse**, a happy old age.

heurt *n.m.* shock, collision, knock, clash. **cette collaboration ne va pas sans quelques** ~**s**, this collaboration isn't going along without a few disagreements.

heurter *v.t.* to hit, to strike hard, to knock, to run (against). ~ **quelqu'un**, to run into a person. ~ **contre une pierre**, to strike against a stone. **se** ~, *v.refl.* to knock oneself, to knock, to strike, to hit. **il s'est heurté contre la table**, he knocked himself against the table.

heurtoir *n.m.* knocker (of a door).

hexagonal, e *adj.* hexagonal.

hexagone *n.m.* hexagon; l'~, France.

hexamètre *n.m.* hexameter.

hiatus *n.m.* hiatus.

hibernal, e *adj.* hibernal.

hibernant, e *adj.* hibernating.

hibernation *n.f.* hibernation.

hiberner *v.i.* to hibernate, to winter.

hibiscus *n.m.* hibiscus.

hibou *n.m.* owl.

hic *n.m.* rub, difficulty. **voilà le** ~, there's the rub.

hideux, euse *adj.* hideous.

hier *adv.* yesterday. ~ **matin,** yesterday morning. **avant-~,** the day before yesterday.

hiérarchie *n.f.* hierarchy.

hiérarchique *adj.* hierarchical, hierarchic.

hiérarchiquement *adv.* hierarchically.

hiératique *adv.* hieratic, hieratical.

hiéroglyphe *n.m.* hieroglyphic, hieroglyph.

hiéroglyphique *adj.* hieroglyphic, hieroglyphical.

hi-fi *n.f.* hi-fi, high fidelity.

hi-hi *Excl.* ha ha!

hilarant, e *adj.* hilarious, laughing, exhilarating, laughing gas.

hilare *adj.* hilarious.

hilarité *n.f.* hilarity; exhilaration, cheerfulness, glee, mirth.

hile *n.m.* hilum.

hindi *n.m.* hindi.

hindou, e *n.m.* Hindu, Hindoo.

hindouisme *n.m.* Hinduism.

hippie *adj.* hippie.

hippique *adj.* horse, of horses, relating to horses.

hippocampe *n.m.* hippocampus, seahorse.

hippodrome *n.m.* racetrack.

hippopotame *n.m.* hippopotamus, hippo.

hirondelle *n.f.* swallow. **une ~ ne fait pas le printemps,** one swallow does not make a summer.

hirsute *adj.* hirsute; hairy, shaggy.

hispanique *adj.* Hispanic.

hispano-américain, e *adj. n.m.f.* Hispanic-American.

hispano-moresque *adj.* Hispano-Moresque.

hisser *v.t.* to hoist, to raise. **se ~,** *v.refl.* to raise oneself, to hoist oneself, to get up.

histoire *n.f.* history; tale, narration story. **~ sainte,** sacred history. **il me raconta son ~,** he hold me his story. **le plus beau de l'~,** the best of the story. **voilà bien des ~s!** what a fuss!

histologie *n.f.* histology.

historien *n.m.* historian.

historique *adj.* historical, historic. *n.m.* history, narration, recital (of facts).

historiquement *adv.* historically; according to history.

hitlérien, ne *adj.* Hitlerite, nazi.

hit-parade *n.m.* top of the charts, top of the pops.

hiver *n.m.* winter. **un ~ doux,** a mild winter.

hivernal, e *adj.* hibernal, wintry.

hiverner *n.m.* to winter, to hibernate.

ho *interj.* ho, hey!

hochement *n.m.* nod, shake.

hocher *v.t.* to nod, to shake, to wag, to toss. **~ la tête,** to toss one's head.

hochet *n.m.* rattle; toy.

hockey *n.m.* hockey.

hockeyeux, euse *n.m.f.* hockey player.

holà *interj.* ho! *n.m. Infml.* stop, end. **mettre le ~,** to put a stop to (a quarrel).

hold-up *n.m.* hold-up.

hollandais, e *adj.* Dutch. *n.m.f.* Dutchman, Dutchwoman, *pl.* Dutch.

Hollande *n.f.* Holland. **fromage de ~,** Dutch cheese.

holocauste *n.m.* holocaust; sacrifice.

homard *n.m.* lobster.

homélie *n.f.* homily, sermon.

homéopathe *n.m.* homeopath(ist).

homéopathie *n.f.* homeopathy.

homéopathique *adj.* homeopathic.

Homère *n.m.* Homer.

Homerique *adj.* Homeric.

homicide *n.m.* homicide; murder; manslaughter. *n.m.f.* homicide; murderer. *adj.* homicidal, murderous.

hommage homage, tribute, respects, regards. **rendre ~,** to do homage. **présenter, offrir, rendre ses ~s à quelqu'un,** to pay one's respects to a person.

homme *n.m.* man, mankind, husband. **les ~s du nord,** the men of the north. **un pauvre ~,** a poor spirited fellow. **un ~ pauvre,** a poor man. **~ bon, ~ de bien,** good, right-minded man. **un ~ grand,** a tall man. **un brave ~,** an worthy man, a honest fellow. **un ~ brave,** a brave, daring man. **~ d'épée,** a soldier. **~ d'église,** a churchman, an ecclesiastic. **~ de lettres,** man of letters. **~ d'état,** statesman. **~ de loi,** lawyer. **~ d'affaires,** businessman, **~grenouille,** frogman. **c'est mon ~,** he is is my man. **il a trouvé son ~,** he has found his match.

homogène *adj.* homogenous.

homogénéité *n.f.* homogenousness, homogeneity.

homologuer *v.t.* to be homologate, to confirm, to ratify.

homonyme *adj.* homonymous. *n.m.* homonymous word; (of persons) namesake, homonym.

homosexualité *n.f.* homosexuality.

homosexuel, le *adj. n.m.f.* homosexual.

hongre *adj.* gelded, gelt. **cheval ~,** gelding.

Hongrie *n.f.* Hungary.

Hongrois, e *adj.* and *n.m.f.* Hungarian.

honnête *adj.* honest; upright, virtuous; honorable, proper, decent; polite, kind, courteous. **un ~ homme,** an honest man. **un homme ~,** a gentleman. **une famille ~,** a respectable family.

honnêtement *adv.* honestly; uprightly, honorably, modestly, respectably; decently; politely, civilly. **il lui a parlé fort ~,** he spoke very politely to him.

honnêteté *n.f.* honesty, integrity, uprightness, probity, attention, regards; kindness; modesty, decency; politeness. **il a eu l'~ de venir nous voir,** he had the courtesy to come to see us.

honneur *n.m.* honor; credit, glory; reputation. **faire ~ à son pays,** to be an honor to one's country. **faire ~ à une lettre de change,** to pay a draft when it is due. **affaire d'~,** matter of honor. **être en ~,** to be in favor, in request.

honnir *v.t.* to disgrace, to dishonor. **honni soit qui mal y pense!** evil be to him who evil thinks.

honorabilité *n.f.* honorableness.

honorable *adv.* honorable; creditable, reputable; respectable, honest.

honorablement *adv.* honorably; reputably, fairly; respectably.

honoraire *adj.* honorary. *n.m.* fee. **les ~s d'un avocat,** a lawyer's fees.

honorer *v.t.* to honor, to respect; to exalt, to dignify, to be an honor to. **honore ton père et ta mère,** honor thy father and thy mother. **cette conduite vous honore,** your conduct does you credit. **~ une traite,** to honor a draft. **s'~,** *v.refl.* to do oneself honor; to honor, to respect each other; to glory (in); to think, to deem it an honor, to hold it as an honor. **je m'honore de son estime,** I am proud of his esteem.

honorifique *adj.* honorary.

honte *n.f.* shame; disgrace, dishonor, discredit; reproach, scandal. **effacer la ~ d'une mauvaise action,** to efface the shame of a bad action. **être la ~, faire la ~ de sa famille,** to be the disgrace of one's family. **avoir ~ d'avoir fait un mauvaise action,** to be ashamed of having done a bad thing. **faire ~ à quelqu'un,** to make someone ashamed. **mauvaise ~, fausse ~,** bashfulness; false shame.

honteusement *adv.* shamefully, disgracefully, scandalously.

honteux, euse *adj.* shameful, disgraceful, disreputable, scandalous, ignominious, bashful, shy, ashamed, sheepish, shamefaced. **une conduite honteuse,** a shameful behavior. **être ~ d'avoir manque de parole,** to be ashamed at not having kept one's word. **avoir l'air ~,** to look bashful.

hop *Excl.* **~-là!** off you go!

hôpital *n.m.* hospital.

hoquet *n.m.* hiccough, hiccup. **avoir le ~,** (to) have the hiccups.

horaire *adj.* timetable, schedule.

horde *n.f.* horde; gang.

horizon *n.m.* horizon, extent, space, scene, scenery, view; **changer d'~,** to change scenery.

horizontal, e *adj.* horizontal.

horizontalement *adv.* horizontally.

horloge *n.f.* clock. **~ d'église,** church clock. **l'~ sonne midi,** the clock is striking twelve. **l'~ avance,** the clock is too fast. **monter, remonter une ~,** to wind up a clock.

horloger, ère *adj.* watchmaking, clockmaking; *n.m.f.* clockmaker, watchmaker.

horlogerie *n.f.* clockmaking, watchmaking; **bijouterie-~,** jewelry store.

hormis *prep.* but, save, saving, except, excepting, with the exception of.

hormonal, e *adj.* hormonal.

hormone *n.f.* hormone.

horoscope *n.m.* horoscope. **tirer l'~ de quelqu'un,** to cast a person's horoscope.

horreur *n.f.* horror, dreadfulness; dread; horrid thing, fright, ugly person. **frémir d'~,** to shud-der with horror. **cela fait ~ à penser,** it makes one shudder to think of it. **cela fait ~,** it's frightening. **ce chapeau est une ~,** that hat is horrible. **on m'a dit des ~s de cet homme-là,** I was told horrid things about that man. **faire ~,** to disgust.

horrible *adj.* horrible, horrid, frightful, shocking, frightful. **cela est ~ à voir,** it is horrible to look at.

horriblement *adv.* horribly, horridly; dreadfully, frightfully, shockingly; extremely, exceedingly.

horrifier *v.i.* to horrify.

horrifique *adj.* horrific.

horripiler *v.t.* to exasperate, to irritate.

hors *adv.* out, except, but, save. *prep.* out of, without, at the outside of, beyond. **~ de la ville,** outside of town. **être ~ de soi,** to be beside oneself. **~ de danger,** out of danger. **~ d'haleine,** out of breath. **~ de prix,** exorbitant price. **~ de combat,** disabled, **~ d'atteinte,** out of reach. **~bord,** speedboat; **~-d'oeuvre,** hors-d'oeuvre, appetizer; **~ la loi,** outlaw. **~-taxe,** duty-free.

hortensia *n.m.* hydrangea.

horticole *adj.* horticultural.

horticulteur, trice *n.m.f.* horticulturist.

horticulture *n.f.* horiculture; gardening.

hospice *n.m.* hospice.

hospitalier, ière *adj.* hospitable. *n.m.* hospitaller.

hospitalisation *n.f.* hospitalization.

hospitaliser *v.i.* hospitalize.

hospitalité *n.f.* hospitality.

hostie *n.f.* victim, offering; host, consecrated wafer.

hostile *adj.* hostile.

hostilité *n.f.* hostility.

hôte *n.m.* host; guest, visitor. **regaler ses ~s,** to treat one's guests. **les ~s des bois, des forêts,** the denizens of the forests. **table d'~,** set menu.

hôtel *n.m.* hotel, mansion, large house. **avoir un ~,** to have a mansion. **~ de ville,** town hall.

hôtelier, ière *n.m.f.* hotelkeeper; **école ~ière,** hotel management school.

hôtellerie *n.f.* hotel trade, hotel business.

hôtesse *n.f.* hostess, guest, landlady, **~ d'accueil,** receptionist; **~ de l'air,** stewardess, flight attendant.

hou *Excl.* boo!

houblon *n.m.* hops (in beer-making).

houe *n.f.* hoe.

houille *n.f.* coal.

houiller, ère *adj.* coal. **terrain ~,** coal field. **dépôt ~,** coal deposit.

houillère *n.f.* coal pit.

houle *n.f.* swell (of the sea).

houlette *n.f.* shepherd's crook. **être sous la ~ de,** to be under the control of.

houleux, euse *adj.* swelling, rough.

houppe *n.f.* tuft. **en ~,** tufted. **~ à poudrer,** powder puff.

houppelande *n.f.* great coat.

houppette *n.f.* powder puff.

hourra *n.m.* hurrah; **pousser des ~s**, to cheer.

houspiller *v.t.* to scold.

housse *n.f.* dust sheet, cover.

houx *n.m.* holly.

hublot *n.m.* scuttle, porthole.

huche *n.f.* hutch, bin, chest.

huée *n.f.* hooting, shouting, hoot, shout, boo.

huer *v.t.* to boo.

huguenot, e *n.m.f.* Huguenot, *adj.* Huguenot.

huilage *n.m.* oiling, lubrication.

huile *n.f.* oil. **~ d'olive**, olive oil. **~ de foie de morue**, cod liver oil. **jeter de l'~ sur le feu**, to add fuel to the fire.

huiler *v.t.* to oil; to lubricate with oil; to anoint with oil.

huileux, euse *adj.* oily, greasy, fatty.

huilier *n.m.* oil cruet, cruet stand.

huis *n.m.* door. **à ~ clos**, with closed doors, privately. **juger une affaire à ~ clos**, to hear a case in private.

huissier *n.m.* usher; process server, sheriff's officer, bailiff.

huit *adj.* eight. *n.m.* eight, eighth. **le ~ du mois**, the eighth of the month.

huitaine *n.f.* eight days, eight; week. **dans la ~**, in the course of the week, within the week.

huitième *adj.* eighth. **le ~ siècle**, the eighth century. *n.m.* eighth.

huître *n.f.* oyster. **~ perlière**, pearl oyster.

hululer *v.i.* to screech.

hum *Excl.* hem.

hulotte *n.m.* owlet, tawny owl, brown owl.

humain, e *adj.* humble, modest. **votre très ~ serviteur**, your very humble servant. *n.m.* mortal, human being.

humainement *adv.* humanly; humanely, with kindness.

humanisation *n.f.* humanization.

humaniser *v.t.* to humanize, to civilize, to soften, to soften down. **se ~**, *v.refl.* to become humanized, to grow humane, to grow gentle.

humaniste *n.m.* humanist.

humanitaire *adj.* humanitarian.

humanité *n.f.* humanity, human nature; mankind, *pl.* humanities.

humble *adj.* humble, modest. **votre très ~ serviteur**, your very humble servant.

humblement *adv.* humbly.

humectation *n.f.* wetting, moistening.

humecter *v.t.* to wet, to moisten, to damp. **s'~ le gosier**, to wet one's whistle. **s'~** *v.refl.* to be moistened, to become moist. **ses yeux s'humectaient**, his eyes were wet (with tears).

humer *v.t.* to inhale. **~ l'air**, to inhale air.

humérus *n.m.* humerus.

humeur *n.f.* humor; disposition, mood, whim, fancy, caprice. **être d'~ à**, to be in a mood; to be disposed to. **être de bonne ~**, to be

in a good mood. **avoir de l'~**, to be moody.

humide *adj.* humid, wet, damp, moist. **une chambre ~** a damp room. **la saison est ~**, the season is wet.

humidificateur *n.m.* humidifier.

humidification *n.f.* humidification.

humidifier *v.t.* to humidify.

humidité *n.f.* humidity, moisture, dampness; damp weather; wetness.

humiliant, e *adj.* humiliating.

humiliation *n.f.* humiliation.

humilier *v.t.* to humiliate. **s'~**, *v.refl.* to abase oneself; to stoop.

humoriste *n.m.* humorist.

humoristique *adj.* humoristic.

humour *n.m.* humor.

humus *n.m.* humus.

hunier *n.m.* top sail.

huppe *n.f.* tuft, crest.

huppé, e *adj.* tufted topping; cunning, clever. **les plus ~s y sont pris**, the sharpest are taken in.

hure *n.f.* head; jowl. **~ de sanglier**, boar's head.

hurlement *n.m.* howl, howling; outcry, roar, shriek, scream.

hurler *v.i.* to howl; to yell, to shriek, to scream; to roar; to bellow.

hutte *n.f.* hut.

hyacinthe *n.f.* hyacinth; jacinthe.

hybride *adj.* hybrid.

hydratant, e *adj.* moisterizing; *n.m.* moisterizer.

hydratation *n.f.* hydration.

hydrate *n.m.* hydrate. **~s de carbone**, carbohydrate.

hydrater *v.refl.* to hydrate, moisturize. **s'~**, to become moisturized.

hydraulique *adj.* hydraulic. *n.f.* hydraulics.

hydravion *n.m.* seaplane, hydroplane.

hydre *n.f.* hydra.

hydrocarbure *n.m.* hydrocarbon.

hydrodynamique *n.f. pl.* hydrodynamics.

hydroelectricité *n.f.* hydroelectricity.

hydroelectrique *adj.* hydroelectric.

hydrogène *n.m.* hydrogen.

hydrogénér *v.t.* to hydrogenate, to hydrogenize.

hydroglisseur *n.m.* hydroplane.

hyène *n.f.* hyena.

hygiène *n.f.* hygiene.

hygiènique *adj.* hygienic, **papier ~**, toilet paper.

hymen *n.m.* hymen. *Poet.* union, marriage.

hyménée *n.m.* union.

hymne *n.m.* hymn; **chanter des ~s**, to sing hymns *n.f.* hymn (as sung in churches).

hyperbole *n.f.* hyperbole.

hyperglycémie *n.f.* hyperglycemia.

hypermétrope *adj.* hypermetropic; far-sighted.

hypermétropie *n.f.* hypermetropia.

hypernerveux, euse *adj.* overly excitable, high strung.

hypernervosité *n.f.* overexcitability.

hypersensibilité *n.f.* hypersensitiveness, hyper-sensitivity.

hypersensible *adj.* hypersensitive.
hypersonic *adj.* hypersonic.
hypertendu, e *adj.* hypertensive.
hypertension *n.f.* high blood pressure, hypertension.
hypertrophie *n.f. Med.* hypertrophy.
hypertrophier *v.t.* to enlarge; to cause hypertrophy to.
hypnose *n.f.* hypnosis.
hypnotique *adj.* hypnotic.
hypnotiser *v.t.* to hypnotize.
hypnotisme *n.m.* hypnotism.
hypocondriaque *adj.* hypocondriac.
hypocrisie *n.f.* hypocrisy.

hypocrite *adj.* hypocritical.
hypocritement *adv.* hypocritically; falsely.
hypodermique *adj.* hypodermic.
hypoglycémie *n.f.* hypoglycemia.
hypothécaire *adj.* mortgager.
hypothèque *n.f.* mortgage.
hypothequer *v.t.* to mortgage.
hypothermie *n.f.* hypothermia.
hypothèse *n.f.* hypothesis, speculation.
hypothétique *adj.* hypothetic, hypothetical.
hypothétiquement *adv.* hypothetically.
hystérectomie *n.f.* hysterectomy.
hystérie *n.f.* hysteria.
hystérique *adj.* hysteric, hysterical.

I

iambe *n.m.* iambic foot. *adj.* iambic.
iambique *adj.* iambic.
ibère *n.m. pl.* Iberia, Spain.
ibérie *n.f.* Iberia.
iberien, enne *adj.* Iberian.
ibérique *adj.* Iberian.
ibidem *adv.* ibidem.
ibis *n.m. Ornith.* ibis.
ici *adv.* here. **venez ~**, come here. **loin d'~**, far from here. **par ~**, this way, through here. **jusqu'~**, so far, until now, till now, **~-bas**, here below, in this world.
iconoclaste *n.m.* iconoclast. *adj.* iconoclastic.
iconographe *n.m.* iconographer.
ictère *n.m.* icterus, jaundice.
ictérique *adj.* jaundiced.
idéal, e *adj.* ideal; imaginary, unreal. *n.m.* ideal. **l'~ de la beauté**, the ideal of beauty.
idéaliser *v.t.* to idealize, to make ideal.
idéalisme *n.m.* idealism.
idéaliste *n.m.* idealist *adj.* idealistic.
idée *n.f.* idea, conception, notion; thought. **donner une ~ d'une chose**, to give an idea of something. **on n'a pas d'~ de cela**, no one has any idea of it. **cet auteur a des ~s**, that author has imagination. **en ~**, in idea, ideally. **je n'ai aucune ~ de ce fait**, I have no recollection of that fact. **il n'a pas la moindre ~ de ce qui s'est passé**, he doesn't have the slightest clue, any recollection of what happened. **se faire de ~s**, to imagine. **ça lui est complètement sorti de l'~**, he totally forgot about it. **~ fixe**, obsession. **~ lumineuse**, brainstorm.
idem *adv.* idem, ditto.
identification *n.f.* identification.
identifier *v.t.* to identify. **s'~**, *v.refl.* to be identified, to become identical; to identify oneself (with).
identique *adj.* identical, the same.
identité *n.f.* identity.
idéographie *n.f.* ideography, ideographics.
idéologie *n.f.* ideology.
idéologique *adj.* ideological.
idéologue *n.m.* ideologist.

idiomatique *adj.* idiomatic.
idiome *n.m.* idiom; dialect; language.
idiosyncrasie *n.f.* idiosyncrasy.
idiot, e *adj.* idiotic, idiotical, foolish, stupid, senseless, *n.m.f.* idiot; a foolish person, fool.
idiotie *n.f.* idiocy, imbecility.
idiotisme *n.m.* idiom, idiotism, idiocy, imbecility.
idolâtre *adj.* idolatrous; idolizing. *n.m.f.* idolater; pagan; idolizer.
idolâtrer *v.i.* to idolize; to worship.
idolâtrie *n.f.* idolatry.
idole *n.f.* idol.
idylle *n.f.* idyll.
idyllique *adj.* idyllic.
igloo *n.m.* igloo.
igname *n.f.* yam.
ignare *adj.* ignorant, illiterate. *n.m.* ignoramus, dunce, ignorant man.
ignifuge *adj.* fireproof.
ignition *n.f.* ignition.
ignoble *adj.* ignoble, mean, base, vile, worthless.
ignoblement *adv.* ignobly.
ignominie *n.f.* ignominy.
ignominieusement *adv.* ignominiously.
ignominieux, euse *adj.* ignominious, ignominiously.
ignorance *n.f.* ignorance, blunder, mistake, errors. **profonde ~**, great ignorance. **croupir dans l'~**, to wallow in ignorance. **il la tient en ~**, he is keeping her in the dark.
ignorant, e *adj.* ignorant, unlearned, unlettered, illiterate; unaware of. *n.m.f.* ignorant person; *Infml.* ignoramus, dunce.
ignoré, e *adj.* unknown, ignored.
ignorer *v.t.* to be ignorant of, not to know, to be unacquainted with. **s'~**, *v.refl.* not to know oneself, to be ignorant of one's own powers.
iguane *n.m.* iguana.
il *pers pron. n.m.* he; it, there. **~ fait beau**, it's nice weather. **~ pleut**, it's raining. **~ est vrai**, it is true. **~ y a des gens qui**, there are people who.
île *n.f.* island, isle.

illégal, e *adj.* illegal; unlawful.

illégalement *adv.* illegally, unlawfully.

illégalité *n.f.* illegality; unlawfulness; unlawful act.

illégitime *adj.* illegitimate; unlawful.

illégitimement *adv.* illegitimately, unlawfully.

illettré, e *adj.* illiterate.

illicite *adj.* illicite; prohibited by law or morals, unlawful.

illicitement *adv.* illicitly, unlawfully.

illico *adv.* immediately, at once.

illimité, e *adj.* unlimited, unbounded, boundless.

illisible *adj.* illegible, unreadable.

illisiblement *adv.* illegibly.

illogique *adj.* illogical.

illogiquement *adv.* illogically.

illogisme *n.m.* illogicality.

illumination *n.f.* illumination.

illuminé, e *n.m.* illuminate; visionary. *adj.* illuminated, lighted.

illuminer *v.t.* to illuminate; to illumine, to enlighten. **s'~**, *v.refl.* to be illuminated.

illusion *n.f.* illusion; self-deception, self-delusion; chimera, hallucination. **se faire ~ à soi-même**, to delude, to deceive oneself.

illusionner *v.t.* to delude, to deceive. **s'~**, *v.refl.* to delude, to deceive oneself.

illusionniste *n.m.f.* illusionist.

illusoire *adj.* illusive, illusory, delusive; fallacious; imaginary.

illusoirement *adv.* illusively, delusively, deceitfully, fallaciously.

illustrateur, trice *n.m.f.* illustrator.

illustration *n.f.* illustration.

illustre *adj.* famous, illustrious; eminent. *n.m.* illustrious.

illustré *adj.* illustrated; *n.m.* comic book.

illustrer *v.t.* to illustrate; to do honor, to explain, to elucidate; to make clear. **s'~**, *v.refl.* to render oneself illustrious.

illustrissime *adj.* most illustrious.

image *n.f.* image, semblance, likeness; picture. **voir son ~ dans l'eau,** to see one's reflection in the water. **être sage comme une ~,** to be very quiet, as good as can be.

imager *v.t.* to picture, to embellish with imagery.

imaginable *adj.* imaginable.

imaginaire *adj.* imaginary, visionary; **malade ~,** hypochondriac.

imaginatif, ive *adj.* imaginative, imagining.

imagination *n.f.* imagination; fancy, invention, conception, thought.

imaginer *v.t.* to imagine; to conceive, to image, to fancy; to contrive; to surmise, to believe. **s'~**, *v.refl.* to imagine, to fancy oneself; to be imagined.

iman *n.m.* imam; a muslim priest.

imbécile *adj.* imbecile; weak, foolish, silly. *n.m.f.* idiot, fool, simpleton, ninny. **c'est un ~,** he is a fool.

imbécillité *n.f.* imbecility; idiocy.

imberbe *adj.* beardless, unbearded, raw, unexperienced.

imbiber *v.t.* to soak, to imbue. **s'~**, *v.refl.* to imbibe, to soak, to drink in.

imbrication *n.f.* overlapping, interweaving.

imbroglio *n.m.* imbroglio, intricacy, confusion.

imbu, e *p.p. Infml.* imbued, full of.

imbuvable *adj.* undrinkable, unbearable.

imitable *adj.* imitable.

imitateur, trice *adj.* imitative; imitating. *n.m.f.* imitator, impersonator.

imitatif, ive *adj.* imitative.

imitation *n.f.* imitation, forging, counterfeiting; copy.

imiter *v.t.* to imitate; to copy; to mimic, to impersonate. **s'~**, *v.refl.* imitate one another; to be imitated.

immaculé, e *adj.* immaculate; spotless, undefiled; **~ Conception,** Immaculate Conception.

immanent, e *adj.* immanent, constant.

immangeable *adj.* uneatable; inedible.

immanquable *adj.* infallible, certain, sure.

immanquablement *adv.* infallibly, without fail.

immatériel, elle *adj.* immaterial.

immatriculation *n.f.* matriculation, registration, enrollment.

immatricule *n.f.* matriculation; enrollment.

immatriculer *v.t.* to register, to enroll, to matriculate.

immature *adj.* immature.

immaturité *n.f.* immaturity.

immédiat, e *adj.* immediate; instant.

immédiatement *adv.* immediately.

immense *adj.* immense; infinite; huge; boundless.

immensément *adv.* immensely.

immensité *n.f.* immensity, unbounded, greatness, unlimited extent, infinity, boundlessness.

immensurable *adj.* immensurable, immeasurable.

immerger *v.t.* to immerge, to immerse. **s'~**, *v.refl.* immerged, to be immersed, to be plunged.

immérité, e *adj.* unmerited, undeserved.

immersion *n.f.* immersion.

immésurable *adj.* immeasurable, immensurable.

immettable *adj.* unwearable.

immeuble *adj.* immovable, not movable; real. *n.m.* landed estate; real estate; building.

immigrant, e *adj.* immigrating. *n.m.f.* immigrant.

immigration *n.f.* immigration.

immigrer *v.i.* to immigrate.

imminence *n.f.* imminence.

imminent, e *adj.* imminent, impending; near.

immiscer *v.t.* to mix up (with), **s'~**, *v.refl.* (with **dans**) to interfere (in); to meddle (with); to intermeddle (with).

immission *n.f.* immission, injection.

immobile *adj.* immovable; fixed, motionless.

immobilier, ère *adj. Jurisp.* immovable; real, of real estate. *n.m.* landed property, real estate.

immobilisation *n.f.* immobilization, standstill, stop; *Jurisp.* realization; conversion into real property; fixed assets.

immobiliser *v.t.* to immobilize, to stand still, to stop; *Jurisp.* to realize; to fix, to lock up, **s'~**, *v.refl.* to come to a stop.

immobilité *n.f.* immobility, inaction, inactivity.

immodération *n.f.* immoderation, excess.

immoderé, e *adj.* immoderate, intemperate, excessive, extravagant, unreasonable.

immodérément *adv.* immoderately.

immodeste *adj.* immodest; indecent.

immodestement *adv.* immodestly, indecently.

immodestie *n.f.* immodesty.

immolation *n.f.* immolation.

immoler *v.t.* to immolate, to sacrifice, to slay, to slaughter; to make sport of, to ridicule.

immonde *adj.* unclean, filthy, foul, dirty; impure.

immondices *n.f.* trash.

immondicité *n.f.* uncleanness, impurity.

immoral, e *adj.* immoral.

immoralement *adv.* immorally.

immoralité *n.f.* immorality.

immortaliser *v.t.* to immortalize. **s'~**, *v.refl.* to immortalize oneself.

immortalité *n.f.* immortality.

immortel, elle *adj.* immortal; imperishable. *n.m.f.* immortal.

immortelle *n.f.* everlasting flower.

immortellement *adv.* immortally.

immuable *adj.* immutable, unchangeable, invariable, unalterable; immovable.

immuablement *adv.* immutably, unchangeably.

immunisation *n.f.* immunization.

immuniser *v.t.* to immunize.

immunité *n.f.* immunity.

immutabilité *n.f.* immutability, immutableness.

impact *n.m.* impact.

impair, e *adj.* uneven, odd.

imparable *adj.* unstoppable.

impardonnable *adj.* unforgivable, unpardonable.

imparfait, e *adj.* imperfect; incomplete; defective. *n.m.* imperfect tense, imperfect.

imparfaitement *adv.* imperfectly.

imparité *n.f.* imparity, oddness.

impartable *adj.* impartible, indivisible.

impartageable *adj.* indivisible.

impartial, e *adj.* impartial.

impartialement *adv.* impartially.

impartialité *n.f.* impartiality, impartialness.

impartir *v.t.* to allow; to invest, to grant, to bestow.

impasse *n.f.* cul-de-sac, dead end, inextricable difficulty, deadlock; **~ budgétaire,** budget deficit.

impassibilité *n.f.* impassibility, impassibleness.

impassible *adj.* impassible, impassive;

unmoved, undisturbed; unaffected.

impassiblement *adv.* impassively.

impatiemment *adv.* impatiently.

impatience *n.f.* impatience, eagerness; hastiness; fidgets.

impatient, e *adj.* impatient; eager; anxious; longing. **~ de partir,** impatient to go.

impatienter *v.t.* to put out of patience, to provoke. **s'~**, *v.refl.* to grow impatient, to lose all patience.

impayable *adj.* invaluable, matchless, priceless; odd, queer; capital, admirable; funny.

impayé, e *adj.* unpaid, outstanding.

impeccable *adj.* impeccable.

impeccablement *adv.* impeccably, spotlessly.

impénétrabilité *n.f.* impenetrability.

impénétrable *adj.* impenetrable; impervious; inscrutable, unfathomable. **un secret ~,** an impenetrable secret.

impénitence *n.f.* lack of remorse, unrepentance.

impénitent, e *adj.* unpenitent.

impensable *adj.* unthinkable, unbelievable.

imper *n.m.* V. IMPERMEABLE.

impératif, ive *adj.* imperative. *n.m.* imperative mood.

impérativement *adv.* imperatively.

impératrice *n.f.* empress.

imperceptibilité *n.f.* imperceptibility.

imperceptible *n.f.* imperceptible; subtle.

imperceptiblement *adv.* imperceptibly.

imperdable *adj.* that cannot be lost.

imperfectible *adj.* not perfectible.

imperfection *n.f.* imperfection; fault, defect.

impérial, e *adj.* imperial.

impériale *n.f.* deck, top.

impérialement *adv.* imperially.

impérialisme *n.m.* imperialism.

impérialiste *n.m.* imperialist.

impérieusement *adv.* imperiously; with urgency.

impérieux, euse *adj.* imperious; haughty; pressing, urgent.

impérissable *adj.* imperishable, unperishing; indestructible, everlasting, undying.

impéritie *n.f.* unskilfulness, incapacity, ignorance.

imperméabilisation *n.f.* waterproofing.

imperméabiliser *v.t.* to waterproof.

imperméable *adj.* impermeable; impervious, waterproof. **~ à l'air,** airtight. *n.m.* mackintosh, raincoat.

impersonalité *n.f.* impersonality.

impersonnel, elle *adj.* impersonal.

impersonnellement *adv.* impersonally.

impertinemment *adv.* impertinently, insolently; improperly, saucily.

impertinence *n.f.* impertinence, irrelevance; nonsense, extravagance.

impertinent, e *adj.* impertinent, irrelevant, senseless, insolent, saucy.

imperturbable *adj.* imperturbable; un-

shaken, unmoved, immovable, composed.
imperturbablement *adv.* imperturbably.
impétigo *n.m.* impetigo.
impétrant, e *n.m.f.* recipient.
impétueusement *adv.* impetuously, violently, forcibly.
impétueux, euse *adj.* impetuous, boisterous, violent, raging, fierce, wild; passionate, hasty, violent.
impétuosité *n.f.* impetuosity, impetuousness; violence, fury; vehemence.
impie *adj.* impious, ungodly, godless, irreligious. *n.m.f.* impious person, infidel.
impiété *n.f.* impiety, impiousness, ungodliness.
impitoyable *adj.* pitiless, merciless, unmerciful, hard-hearted.
impitoyablement *adv.* pitilessly, mercilessly, unmercifully, without mercy.
implacabilité *n.f.* implacability.
implacablement *adv.* implacable.
implant *n.m.* implant.
implantation *n.f.* implantation, planting; establishment, introduction.
implanter *v.t.* to implant. **s'~,** *v.refl.* to be planted, to take root.
implication *n.f.* implication.
implicite *adj.* implicit.
implicitement *adv.* implicitly.
impliquer *v.t.* to implicate, to involve; to imply.
imploration *n.f.* imploration, supplication.
implorer *v.t.* to implore, to supplicate; to invoke, to cry to, to beseech, to beg.
imploser *v.i.* to implode.
implosion *n.f.* implosion.
impoli, e *adj.* impolite, uncivil, rude.
impoliment *adv.* impolitely, uncivilly, rudely.
impolitesse *n.f.* impoliteness, incivility.
impondérabilité *n.f.* imponderability.
impondérable *adj.* imponderable.
impopulaire *adj.* unpopular.
impopularité *n.f.* unpopularity.
importable *adj.* importable; unwearable.
importance *n.f.* importance, consequence; moment, weight. **cette place lui donne beaucoup d'~,** this post make him a man of importance. **se donner des airs d'~,** to look consequential. **d'~,** extremely, very; heartily, soundly.
important, e *adj.* important; weighty, of importance, of consequence; consequential; conceited. **dans les occasions ~s,** on important occasions; **c'est un homme ~,** he is an important man. *n.m.* main point, important part, essential part. **l'~ est de savoir ce qu'on veut,** the main point is to know what is wanted.
importateur *n.m.* importer.
importation *n.f.* importation; importing; imports, import.
importer *v.t.* to import; to introduce, to be of importance or consequence; to signify, to matter, to concern. **cela ne m'importe pas,** I don't mind; I don't care. **n'importe comment,** no

matter how, anyhow. **n'importe lequel,** no matter which. **n'importe quoi,** no matter what. **n'importe qui,** no matter who, anyone. **n'importe où,** no matter where, anywhere. **n'importe,** never mind.
import-export *n.m.* import-export business.
importun, e *adj.* importunate; troublesome; obtrusive. **un visiteur ~,** an unwelcome visitor. *n.m.f.* importunate person; troublesome person; intruder, bore.
importunément *adv.* importunately.
importuner *v.t.* to importune; to tease, to plague, to trouble, to pester, to molest, to bore. **je crains de vous ~,** I am afraid to annoy you.
importunité *n.f.* importunity.
imposable *adj.* taxable.
imposant, e *adj.* imposing, impressive, commanding. **une cérémonie ~e,** an imposing ceremony.
imposer *v.t.* to impose; to lay on; to obtrude, to thrust, to force, to inflict, to set, to fix; to tax; to assess. **~ aux autres ses opinions,** to obtrude one's opinions upon others. **~ silence,** to inflict or to order silence on; to silence. **~ de nouvelles contributions,** to assess new taxes. **~ le respect,** to command respect, to awe, to overawe; to fill with respect, to keep in awe. **s'~,** *v.refl.* to impose oneself.
imposition *n.f.* imposition; taxation; the laying on of hands; assessment of a tax; tax, duty, impost.
impossibilité *n.f.* impossibility.
impossible *adj.* impossible. **il lui est ~ de rester tranquille,** it is impossible for him to keep quiet. *n.m.* impossibility. **c'est tenter l'~,** that is attempting the impossible. **à l'~ nul n'est tenu,** what cannot be helped must be endured. **faire l'~,** to do one's best.
imposte *n.f.* impost, transom.
imposteur *n.m.* imposter; deceiver.
imposture *n.f.* imposture, deception, deceit, cheat; delusion.
impôt *n.m.* tax.
impotence *n.f.* impotence, impotency.
impotent, e *adj.* impotent.
impraticable *adj.* impracticable; impassable.
imprécation *n.f.* imprecation.
imprécatoire *adj.* imprecatory.
imprécis, e *adj.* inaccurate.
imprécision *n.f.* inaccuracy.
imprégnation *n.f.* impregnation.
imprégner *v.t.* to impregnate; to imbue. **s'~,** *v.refl.* to be impregnated; to be imbued, to become saturated.
imprenable *adj.* impregnable.
impresario *n.m.* impresario, manager.
imprescriptibilité *n.f.* imprescriptibility.
imprescriptible *adj.* imprescriptible.
impression *n.f.* impression; pression, pressure; influence; impulse, stamp, print, impress; printing; edition; mark, trace. **ça lui a fait une**

drôle d'~, he/she got a strange impression from it. une belle ~, a good print.

impressionabilité *n.f.* impressionability.

impressionnable *adj.* impressionable.

impressionnant, e *adj.* impressive.

impressionner *v.t.* to impress, to make an impression on; *Fig.* to affect, to move. s'~, *v.refl.* to be affected.

impressionniste *adj.* impressionistic; *n.m.f.* impressionist.

imprévisible *adj.* unforeseeable, unpredictable

impressionnisme *n.m.* impressionism.

imprévoyance *n.f.* improvidence, lack of fore-sight.

imprévoyant, e *adj.* improvident; unforeseeing.

imprévu, e *adj.* unforeseen, unexpected.

imprimante *n.f.* printer.

imprimé *n.m.* print, printed paper; printed book.

imprimer *v.t.* to impress, to imprint, to print, to stamp, to mark. ~ **des étoffes,** to print fabrics, ~ **un livre,** to print a book. s'~, *v.refl.* to be stamped, to be imprinted.

imprimerie *n.f.* printing, typography; printer's, print shop.

imprimeur *n.m.* printer, printing press.

improbabilité *n.f.* improbability.

improbable *adj.* improbable, unlikely.

improbablement *adv.* improbably.

improbité *n.f.* improbity, dishonesty.

improductif, ive *adj.* unproductive.

improductivité *n.f.* unproductiveness.

impromptu *n.m.* impromptu. *adj.* impromptu, off-hand; *adv.* impromptu; out of the blue.

impropre *adj.* improper; unsuitable, unfit.

improprement *adv.* improperly, inaccurately.

impropriété *n.f.* impropriety; unfitness; inaptitude.

improvisateur, trice *n.m.* improviser.

improvisation *n.f.* improvisation, extemporane-ous speaking; impromptu.

improviser *v.i.* to improvise; to extemporize. s'~, *v.refl.* to be improvised; to be produced.

improviste (à l') *adv.* unexpectedly, by surprise, out of the blue, without warning.

imprudemment *adv.* imprudently.

imprudence *n.f.* imprudence.

imprudent, e *adj.* imprudent.

impubère *adj.* below the age of puberty.

impudemment *adv.* impudently, shamelessly.

impudence *n.f.* impudence; shamelessness, brazenness, effrontery.

impudent, e *adj.* impudent, shameless, brazen, bold-faced. *n.m.f.* impudent person.

impudeur *n.f.* immodest, unchaste, lewd.

impudicité *n.f.* impudicity; unchastity, lewdness.

impudique *adj.* unmodest, unchaste, lewd.

impudiquement *adv.* immodestly.

impuissance *n.f.* impotence, helplessness, impotency, powerlessness, inability, helpless.

impulsif, ive *adj.* impulsive.

impulsion *n.f.* impulse, impulsion; impetus, incentive, incitement, instigation.

impunément *adv.* with impunity; without inconvenience.

impuni, e *adj.* unpunished.

impunité *n.f.* impunity.

impur, e *adj.* impure, foul, unchaste, lewd, obscene.

impurement *adv.* impurely.

impureté *n.f.* impurity, impureness; foulness.

imputabilité *n.f.* imputability.

imputable *adj.* imputable; attributable, chargeable.

imputation *n.f.* imputation; charge. une ~ **calomnieuse,** slanderous charge.

imputer *v.t.* to impute; to ascribe, to set to the account of; to deduct (from). ~ **à crime,** to accuse of a crime.

imputrescible *adj.* incorruptible.

inabordable *adj.* inaccessible, unapproachable.

inacceptable *adj.* unacceptable.

inaccessibilité *n.f.* inaccessibility, inaccessibleness.

inaccessible *adj.* inaccessible; unattainable; unapproachable, out of reach.

inaccomplissement *n.m.* inexecution, nonper-formance.

inaccoutumé, e *adj.* unaccustomed, unusual.

inacheté, e *adj.* unbought.

inachevé, e *adj.* unachieved, unfinished, incomplete.

inactif, ive *adj.* inactive, indolent, inert, dull (of funds), unemployed.

inaction *n.f.* inaction. dans l'~, in inaction, inactive; unemployed.

inactivité *n.f.* inactivity; inertness; sluggishness.

inadaptation *n.f.* maladjustment.

inadéquat, e *adj.* inadequate.

inadmissible *adj.* inadmissible.

inadvertance *n.f.* inadverterence, inadvertency, heedlessness, inattention; oversight, mistake. par ~, inadvertently.

inaltérable *adj.* unalterable, immutable, unchanging, invariable, unspoilable.

inaltéré, e *adj.* unaltered.

inamical, e *adj.* unfriendly, unkind, inimical.

inamovible *adj.* irremovable, unremovable; for life.

inanimé, e *adj.* inanimate; lifeless, dull; inert.

inanité *n.f.* inanity, vacuity, frivolousness, vanity.

inanition *n.f.* starvation. tomber d'~, to faint from lack of food.

inapaisé, e *adj.* unappeased, unpacified, unquenched.

inaperçu, e *adj.* unperceived, unseen; unno-ticed, unobserved, unheeded.

inapplicable *adj.* inapplicable.

inapplication *n.f.* inapplication; inattention.

inappliqué, e *adj.* inattentive, unapplied.

inappréciable *adj.* inappreciable, invaluable, inestimable.

inapte *adj.* inapt, unfit.

inaptitude *n.f.* inaptitude, unfitness.

inarticulé, e *adj.* inarticulate.

inassouvi, e *adj.* unsatiated, unglutted, unquenched.

inattaquable *adj.* unassailable, irreproachable, upright; unobjectionable.

inattendu, e *adj.* unexpected, unforeseen, unlooked for.

inattentif, ive *adj.* inattentive, unmindful.

inattention *n.f.* inattention.

inaudible *adj.* inaudible.

inaugural, e *adj.* inaugural, opening.

inauguration *n.f.* inauguration, opening.

inaugurer *v.t.* to inaugurate; to open.

inavouable *adj.* unavowable, shameful, not to be acknowledged.

inavoué, e *adj.* unavowed, unconfessed.

incalculable *adj.* incalculable, countless, innumerable, numberless.

incandescence *n.f.* incandescence.

incandescent, e *adj.* incandescent.

incantation *n.f.* incantation; enchantment, conjuration.

incapable *adj.* incapable, incompetent, unable; unfit; unskilful; disqualified, incapacitated. **il est ~ de courir,** he is unable to run.

incapacité *n.f.* incapacity, incapability, inability, incompetency, unfitness; disqualification, disability. **frapper d'~,** to incapacitate; to disqualify.

incarcération *n.f.* incarceration.

incarcérer *v.t.* to incarcerate.

incarnat, e *adj.* crimson, incarnate. *n.m.* crimson.

incarnation *n.f.* incarnation, embodiment.

incarné, e *adj.* incarnate, (nail) ingrowing, ingrown.

incarner *v.t.* to incarnate, to embody, to personify; **s'~,** *v.refl.* to become incarnate, to be embodied; (nail) to become ingrown.

incartade *n.f.* prank.

incassable *adj.* unbreakable.

incendiaire *adj.* incendiary, inflammatory; *n.m.f.* incendiary, arsonist.

incendie *n.m.* fire; conflagration. **~ par malveillance,** arson.

incendié, e *adj.* burnt down; *n.m.f.* victim of a fire.

incendier *v.t.* to set fire in, to burn down.

incertain, e *adj.* uncertain, doubtful; unsettled, unsteady, undecided, undetermined. *n.m.* uncertain, uncertainty.

incertitude *n.f.* uncertainty; doubt; indecision, irresolution, hesitation; fickleness, instability, unsteadiness.

incessamment *adv.* immediately, directly, forthwith. **il doit partir ~,** he must go immediately.

incessant, e *adj.* incessant, unceasing, uninterrupted.

inceste *n.m.* incest. *n.m.f.* incestuous person. *n.m.f.* incestuous.

incestueux, euse *adj.* incestuous. *n.m.f.* incestuous person.

inchangé, e *adj.* unchanged, unaltered.

inchangeable *adj.* unchangeable.

incidemment *adv.* incidentally.

incidence *n.f.* incidence.

incident *n.m.* incident, incidental, accidental, occasional.

incinérateur *n.m* incinerator.

incinération *n.f.* incineration, cremation.

incinérer *v.t.* incinerate, to cremate.

incise *n.f.* incidental phrase.

inciser *v.t.* to incise; to make an incision, to tap (a tree).

incisif, ive *adj.* incisive; cutting, sharp, keen; *n.f.* incisor.

incision *n.f.* incision.

incitation *n.f.* incitement, instigation; impulse.

inciter *v.t.* to incite, to push on, to stir up, to urge.

incivil, e *adj.* uncivil, impolite; rude.

incivilement *adv.* uncivilly, impoliteness.

incivilité *n.f.* incivility; rudeness, impoliteness.

inclinaison *n.f.* inclination; obliquity.

inclination *n.f.* inclination; leaning; bow, bending; stooping; propensity; proneness; attachment. **suivre son ~,** to follow one's inclination.

incliner *v.t.* to incline; to lean; to bow; to bend; to cause to stoop or bow; to stoop. **~ le corps,** to bend one's body. **s'~,** *v.refl.* to incline, to lean; to bend, to bow; to hang down; to stoop.

inclure *v.t.* to include, to enclose, to insert.

inclus, e *adj.* enclosed. **ci-inclus,** herein enclosed.

inclusif, ive *adj.* inclusive; comprehending.

incoercible *adj.* irrepressible.

incognito *adv.* incognito. *n.m.* incognito. **garder l'~,** to preserve the incognito.

incohérence *n.f.* incoherence; inconsistency, incongruity.

incohérent, e *adj.* incoherent.

incolore *adj.* colorless.

incomber *v.i.* to be incumbent (on); to be somebody's responsibility.

incombustibilité *n.f.* incombustibility.

incombustible *adj.* incombustible.

incommensurable *adj.* incommensurable; immeasurable.

incommodant, e *adj.* unpleasant, annoying.

incommode *adj.* inconvenient; uncomfortable.

incommodé, e *p.p.* or *adj.* indisposed, unwell.

incommodément *adv.* inconveniently, uncomfortably.

incommoder *v.t.* to inconvenience, to disturb, to annoy.

incommodité *n.f.* inconvenience, inconveniency; indisposition.

incommunicable *adj.* incommunicable.

incommutabilité *n.f.* incommutability.

incommutable *adj.* incommutable; nontransferable; indisputable.

incommutablement *adv.* indisputably.

incomparable *adj.* incomparable, peerless, matchless, unmatched; unrivaled.

incomparablement *adv.* incomparably.

incompatibilité *n.f.* incompatibility.

incompatible *adj.* incompatible; incongruous, unsuitable; disagreeing.

incompétence *n.f.* incompetence, inefficiency.

incompétent, e *adj.* incompetent; disqualified; unable, incapacitated.

incomplet, ète *adj.* incomplete, imperfect, defective.

incompréhensible *adj.* incomprehensible.

incompréhensiblement *adv.* incomprehensibly, inconceivably.

incompressible *adj.* incompressible.

incompris, e *adj.* misunderstood, not understood, not appreciated.

inconcevable *adj.* inconceivable.

inconcevablement *adv.* inconceivably.

inconciliabilité *n.f.* irreconcilability, incompatibility.

inconciliable *adj.* irreconcilable, incompatible.

inconditionnel, le *adj.* unconditional. *n.m.f.* unconditional supporter, fan.

inconditionnellement *adv.* unconditionally, unquestioningly.

inconduite *n.f.* misconduct, misbehavior.

incongélable *adj.* uncongealable.

inconfort *n.m.* lack of comfort, discomfort.

inconfortable *adj.* uncomfortable.

inconfortablement *adv.* uncomfortably.

incongru, e *adj.* incongruous, unfit, improper, unsuitable.

incongruité *n.f.* incongruity, indecency.

incongrûment *adv.* incongruously, improperly.

inconnu, e *adj.* unknown. *n.m.f.* unknown, stranger. *n.f.* unknown quantity.

inconsciemment *adv.* unconsciously, unknowingly.

inconscience *n.f.* unconsciousness; madness.

inconscient, e *adj.* unconscious; thoughtless; mad, crazy.

inconséquence *adj.* inconsequence, inconsistency; imprudence, inconsiderateness.

inconséquent, e *adj.* inconsistent; thoughtless, inconsiderate.

inconsidération *n.f.* inconsiderateness; thoughtlessness, inconsiderate.

inconsidéré, e *adj.* unconsidered, unexamined; inconsiderate; thoughtless, heedless.

inconsidérément *adv.* inconsiderately.

inconsistance *n.f.* lack of consistency; inconsistency; softness, looseness.

inconsistant, e *adj.* lacking in consistency; inconsistent; loose, weak.

inconsolable *adj.* inconsolable, disconsolate.

inconsommable *adj.* unfit for consumption; unconsumable, unable to be consummated.

inconstance *n.f.* inconstancy, unsteadiness; uncertainty; changeableness. **l'~ des modes,** the fickleness of fashion.

inconstant, e *adj.* inconstant; wavering, unstable, fickle, changeable, variable; uncertain, unsettled *n.m.f.* inconstant, fickle person.

inconstitutionnalité *n.f.* unconstitutionality.

inconstitutionnel, elle *adj.* unconstitutional.

inconstitutionnellement *adv.* unconstitutionally.

incontestabilité *n.f.* incontestability.

incontestable *adj.* incontestable, indisputable, unquestionable.

incontestablement *adv.* incontestably, indisputably, incontrovertibly.

incontesté, e *adj.* uncongested, undisputed, unquestioned.

incontinence *n.f.* incontinence.

incontinent, e *adv.* incontinent.

incontrôlable *adj.* unverifiable.

incontrôlé, e *adj.* unverified.

inconvenable *adj.* unbecoming, unseemly.

inconvenance *n.f.* impropriety, unsuitableness.

inconvenant, e *adj.* improper, unsuitable, unbecoming, unseemly.

inconvénient *n.m.* inconvenience, disadvantage; drawback. **il n'y a pas d'~ à cela,** there is no inconvenience in that.

inconvertible *adj.* inconvertible.

incoordination *n.f.* lack of coordination.

incorporation *n.f.* incorporation.

incorporel, elle *adj.* incorporeal.

incorporer *v.t.* to incorporate; to embody. **s'~,** *v.refl.* to incorporate, to be embodied.

incorrect, e *adj.* incorrect.

incorrectement *adv.* incorrectly, inaccurately.

incorrection *n.f.* incorrectness; inaccuracy.

incorrigibilité *n.f.* incorrigibleness, incorrigibility.

incorrigible *adj.* incorrigible.

incorrigiblement *adv.* incorrigibly.

incorruptibilité *n.f.* incorruptibility.

incorruptible *adj.* incorruptible.

incrédibilité *n.f.* incredibility.

incrédule *adj.* incredulous; unbelieving, sceptical. *n.m.f.* unbeliever, infidel, disbeliever; incredulous person.

incrédulité *n.f.* incredulity; disbelief, unbelief, scepticism.

increvable *adj.* puncture proof; tireless.

incrimination *n.f.* accusation, charge.

incriminer *v.t.* to incriminate, to accuse, to impeach.

incrochetable *adj.* unpickable (as a lock).

incroyable *adj.* incredible.

incroyablement *adv.* incredibly.

incroyance *n.f.* unbelief.

incroyant *n.m.* unbeliever.

incrustation *n.f.* incrustation.

incruster *v.t.* to incrust; to inlay. **s'~,** *v.refl.* to become incrusted; to be inlaid.

incubateur, trice *adj.* incubating. *n.f.* incubator.

incubation *n.f.* incubation.

incuber *v.t.* to incubate.

inculpation *n.f.* indictment, charge.

inculpé, e *p.p.* accused. *n.m.f.* the accused, the defendant.

inculper *v.t.* to indict, to charge.

inculquer *v.t.* to inculcate, to instil.

inculte *adj.* uncultivated, unplowed; waste; rude, uneducated.

incultivable *adj.* that cannot be cultivated.

inculture *n.f.* ignorance, lack of education; lack of cultivation.

incurable *adj. and n.m.* incurable.

incurie *n.f.* carelessness, heedlessness, negligence.

incursion *n.f.* incursion; inroad, irruption; excursion, expedition, trip.

incurvation *n.f.* incurvation; crookedness.

indatable *adj.* undatable.

Inde *n.f.* India. **les ~s**, the Indies. **~s occidentales**, West Indies.

indécemment *adv.* indecently.

indécence *n.f.* indecency; immodesty.

indécent, e *adj.* indecent; unseemly, immodest, shameful; obscene.

indéchiffrable *adj.* undecipherable, illegible; unintelligible, obscure, intricate; incomprehensible, impenetrable.

indécis, e *adj.* undecided, doubtful; undefined.

indécision *n.f.* indecision, hesitation, doubt.

indécomposable *adj.* indecomposable.

indécrottable *adj.* rude, untractable; hopeless.

indéfendable *adj.* indefensible.

indéfini, e *adj.* indefinite, unlimited, unbounded.

indéfiniment *adv.* indefinitely.

indéfinissable *adj.* indefinable; undefinable.

indélébile *adj.* indelible.

indélébilité *n.f.* indelibility.

indélicat, e *adj.* indelicate; unbecoming, impolite, rude, tactless.

indélicatement *adv.* indelicately.

indélicatesse *n.f.* indelicacy.

indemne *adj.* unharmed.

indemnisation *n.f.* indemnification.

indemniser *v.t.* to indemnify; to make good. **s'~**, *v.refl.* to indemnify oneself.

indemnité *n.f.* indemnity, compensation, allowance.

indémontable *adj.* that cannot be dismantled.

indéniable *adj.* undeniable, indisputable, unquestionable, indubitable.

indentation *n.f.* indentation.

indépendamment *adv.* independently; freely; without connection; beyond, in addition (to).

indépendance *n.f.* independence.

indépendant, e *adj.* independent; free. *n.m.* independent.

indéracinable *adj.* that cannot be eradicated.

indescriptible *adj.* indescribable.

indésirable *adj.* undesirable. *n.f.* indestructibility.

indestructibilité *n.f.* indestructibility.

indestructible *adj.* indestructible; imperishable.

indéterminable *adj.* indeterminable.

indétermination *n.f.* indetermination; indecision.

indéterminé, e *adj.* indeterminate, unlimited; vague.

index *n.m.* index; table of contents; forefinger; **être à l'~** to be blacklisted.

indexation *n.f.* indexing.

indic *n.f. Infml.* grass.

indicateur, trice *n.m.f.* indicator; informer. *n.m.* guide, gauge. *adj.m.* indicatory, indicating.

indicatif, ive *adj.* indicative; indicatory, showing *n.m.* area code.

indication *n.f.* indication, information; mark, sign. **donner des ~s**, to give information.

indice *n.m.* indication, sign, mark; index.

indicible *adj.* unspeakable, unutterable, ineffable, indescribable, inexpressible.

indiciblement *adv.* unspeakably, unutterably, ineffably.

indiction *n.f.* convocation; indiction.

indien, enne *n.m.f.* Indian. *adj.* Indian. **océan ~**, Indian Ocean.

indifféremment *adv.* indifferently; with indifference.

indifférence *n.f.* indifference; unconcern.

indifférent, e *adj.* indifferent; immaterial, unimportant; immaterial, unimportant, unconcerned. **cela m'est tout à fait ~**, it doesn't matter to me at all. *n.m.f.* indifferent person.

indigence *n.f.* indigence, poverty, penury, want, destitution.

indigène *adj.* indigenous, native. *n.m.f.* native.

indigent, e *adj.* indigent, poor, needy, destitute *n.m.f.* indigent person, poor person; pauper.

indigeste *adj.* indigestible, undigested; crude.

indigestion *n.f.* indigestion.

indignation *n.f.* indignation. **contenir son ~**, to contain one's indignation.

indigne *adj.* unworthy; undeserving, worthless, shameful, contemptible. **~ de vivre**, unworthy of living. **cela est ~**, that is shameful.

indigné, e *adj.* indignant.

indignement *adv.* unworthily; shamefully.

indigner *v.t.* to make indignant; to rouse the indignation of. **s'~**, *v.refl.* to be indignant, to be angry.

indignité *n.f.* unworthiness, worthlessness; baseness; indignity, insult. **c'est une ~**, it is an indignity.

indigo *n.m.* indigo.

indiquer *v.t.* to indicate; to point out; to direct; to be indicative of; to disclose.

indirect, e *adj.* indirect.

indirectement *adv.* indirectly.

indiscernable *adj.* indiscernible.

indiscipline *n.f.* indiscipline.

indiscipliné, e *adj.* undisciplined; indocile, unruly.

indiscret, ète *adj.* indiscreet; tactless; prying. **une visite indiscrète,** an indiscreet visit.

indiscrètement *adv.* indiscreetly, tactlessly.

indiscrètion *n.f.* indiscretion; indiscreetness, imprudence, inconsiderateness.

indiscutable *adj.* indisputable, unquestionable.

indispensable *adj.* indispensable; requisite.

indisponibilité *n.f.* unavailability.

indisponible *adj.* unavailable.

indisposé, e *adj.* indisposed; unwell.

indisposer *v.t.* to indispose.

indisposition *n.f.* indisposition; disinclination; unwillingness, unfavorableness, dislike.

indisputable *adj.* indisputable; incontestable, unquestionable.

indisputablement *adv.* indisputably.

indissociable *adj.* inseparable.

indissolubilité *n.f.* indissolubility.

indissoluble *adj.* indissoluble.

indistinct, e *adj.* indistinct.

indistinctement *adv.* indistinctly.

indistinction *n.f.* indistinctness.

individu *n.m.* individual; *Infml.* fellow. **quel est cet ~?** who is that fellow?

individualisation *n.f.* individualization.

individualiser *v.t.* to individualize.

individualisme *n.m.* individualism.

individualiste *n.m.* individualist.

individualité *n.f.* individuality.

individuel, elle *adj.* individual.

individuellement *adv.* individually.

indivis, e *adj.* undivided.

indivisibilité *n.f.* indivisibility, indivisibleness.

indivisible *adj.* indivisible; inseparable.

indivisiblement *adv.* indivisibly.

indivision *n.f.* joint possession.

Indo-Chine *n.f.* Indo-China.

Indo-Chinois, e *adj., n.m.f.* Indo-Chinese.

indocile *adj.* indocile; unmanageable; disobedient.

indocilité *n.f.* indocility, intractableness.

indolemment *adv.* indolently, lazily.

indolence *n.f.* indolence, sluggishness.

indolent, e *adj.* indolent, sluggish, lazy.

indomptable *adj.* unconquerable, indomitable.

indompté, e *adj.* unconquered, untamed, wild; unsubdued, uncontrolled, unmanaged.

indu, e *adj.* undue, unseasonable. **heure ~e,** unseasonable hour.

indubitable *adj.* indubitable, certain, evident.

indubitablement *adv.* indubitably, undoubtedly.

inducteur *n.m.* inductor *adj.m.* inductive.

inductif, ive *adj.* inductive.

induction *n.f.* induction.

induire *v.t.* to induce, to lead, to influence, to infer, to conclude. **~ en erreur,** to mislead.

indulgemment *adv.* indulgently.

indulgence *n.f.* indulgence, fondness, tenderness. **avoir l'~ pour quelqu'un,** to show indulgence, to make an allowance for a person.

indulgent, e *adj.* indulgent, lenient.

indûment *adv.* unduly.

industrialisation *n.f.* industrialization.

industrialiser *v.t.* to industrialize; **s'~,** to become industrialized.

industrie *n.f.* trade; industry. **produits de l'~,** products of industry.

industriel, elle *adj.* industrial, manufacturing. *n.m.* manufacturer.

industriellement *adv.* industriously.

industrieux, euse *adj.* ingenious, industrious.

inébranlable *adj.* immovable; unshaken, unmoved; steady, steadfast, fixed; resolute.

inébranlablement *adv.* immovably.

inédit, e *adj.* published, unprecedented.

ineffabilité *n.f.* ineffability, ineffableness, unspeakableness.

ineffable *adj.* ineffable, unspeakable, unutterable, inexpressible.

ineffablement *adv.* ineffably unspeakably.

inefficace *adj.* inefficient, ineffectual, ineffective.

inefficacement *adv.* inefficaciously, inefficiently, ineffectually, ineffectively.

inefficacité *n.f.* inefficacy, inefficaciousness.

inégal, e *adj.* unequal, uneven, rough; irregular. **un caractère ~,** an uneven temper.

inégalable *adj.* incomparable, matchless.

inégalé, e *adj.* unmatched.

inégalement *adv.* unequally; unevenly.

inégalité *n.f.* inequality, unevenness, inequality.

inélégance *n.f.* inelegance.

inélégant, e *adj.* inelegant.

inéligibilité *n.f.* ineligibility.

inéligible *adj.* ineligible.

inéluctable *adj.* ineluctable; irresistible.

inepte *adj.* inept, unfit, unsuitable; silly, absurd.

ineptie *n.f.* ineptitude.

inépuisable *adj.* inexhaustible.

inéquation *n.f.* inequation.

inerte *adj.* inert; inactive; sluggish.

inertie *n.f.* inertia; sluggishness; passivity. **force d'~,** force of inertia.

inescompté, e *adj.* unexpected, unhoped for.

inespéré, e *adj.* unhoped for; unexpected; unlooked for.

inesthétique *adj.* unaesthetic.

inestimable *adj.* inestimable; invaluable; priceless.

inévitable *adj.* inevitable, unavoidable.

inévitablement *adv.* inevitably, unavoidably.

inexact, e *adj.* inexact, inaccurate, incorrect.

inexactement *adv.* inaccurately, incorrectly.

inexactitude *n.f.* inexactness, inaccuracy, incorrectness.

inexcusable *adj.* inexcusable; unpardonable, unjustifiable.

inexcusablement *adv.* inexcusably.

inexercé, e *adj.* untrained.

inexistence *n.f.* not existent.

inexorable *adj.* inexorable, inflexible, unrelenting, relentless, implacable.

inexorablement *adv.* inexorably.

inexpérience *n.f.* inexperience.

inexpérimenté, e *adj.* inexperienced; untried.

inexpiable *adj.* inexpiable, unatonable.

inexpié, e *adj.* unexpiated.

inexplicable *adj.* inexplicable; unaccountable.

inexplicablement *adv.* inexplicably.

inexpliqué, e *adj.* unexplained.

inexploitable *adj.* unexploitable, unworkable.

inexplorable *adj.* unexplorable.

inexploité, e *adj.* unexploited.

inexploré, e *adj.* unexplored.

inexplosible *adj.* unexplosive.

inexpressif, ive *adj.* inexpressive.

inexprimable *adj.* inexpressible; unutterable.

inexpugnable *adj.* inexpugnable, impregnable.

in extremis *adv.* at the last minute.

inextinguible *adj.* unextinguishable, unquenchable.

inextricable *adj.* inextricable.

infaillibilité *n.f.* infallibility.

infaillible *adj.* infallible.

infailliblement *adv.* infallibly.

infaisable *adj.* impracticable.

infamant, e *adj.* infamous; ignominious.

infâme *adj.* infamous; ignominious; base; filthy.

infamie *n.f.* infamy, ignominy; disrepute, disgrace, shame; shameful action.

infant *n.m.* infante, infant prince.

infante *n.f.* infanta (in Spain and Portugal), infant princess.

infanterie *n.f.* infantry; foot soldiers.

infanticide *n.m.* infanticide.

infarctus *n.m.* heart attack, coronary thrombosis.

infatigable *adj.* indefatigable; untiring.

infatigablement *adv.* indefatigably.

infatuation *n.f.* infatuation.

infatuer *v.t.* to infatuate.

infécond, e *adj.* unfruitful, infertile, sterile, barren.

infécondité *n.f.* unfruitfulness, sterility, barrenness.

infect, e *adj.* foul, stinking; unwholesome, noisome.

infecter *v.t.* to infect; to taint; to corrupt.

infectieux, euse *adj.* infectious.

infection *n.f.* infection; stink, stench.

inférence *n.f.* inference, deduction, conclusion.

inférer *v.t.* to infer, to deduce, to conclude.

inférieur, e *adj.* inferior; lower; below, beneath.

inférieurement *adv.* in a lower position; in a inferior way.

infériorité *n.f.* inferiority.

infernal, e *adj.* infernal; diabolical, devilish.

infertile *adj.* inferile, unfruitful, sterile, barren.

infertilisable *adj.* incapable of fertilization.

infertilité *n.f.* infertility, barrenness.

infestation *n.f.* infestation.

infester *v.t.* to infest; to harass; (of spirits) to haunt.

infidèle *adj.* unfaithful; faithless, false; untrue; unbelieving. *n.m.f.* infidel.

infidèlement *adv.* unfaithfully, faithlessly.

infidélité *n.f.* unfaithfulness, faithlessness, infidelity; inaccuracy, disloyalty. **faire commettre une ~,** to commit an infidelity.

infiltration *n.f.* infiltration.

infiltrer s'~ *v.t.* to infiltrate; to seep, to percolate, to filter (into); *Fig.* to creep, to glide.

infime *adj.* tiny, minuscule; lowest, meanest.

infini, e *adj.* infinite, boundless, unlimited, endless, numberless. *n.m.* infinite **a l'~,** infinitely, ad infinitum.

infiniment *adv.* infinitely, boundlessly.

infinité *n.f.* infinity; **une ~ de gens,** any number of people.

infinitésimal, e *adj.* infinitesimal.

infinitif *n.m.* infinitive.

infirmation *n.f.* invalidation.

infirme *adj.* disabled, infirm, weak, crippled. *n.m.f.* disabled person, infirm person, invalid.

infirmer *v.t.* to invalidate, to reverse; to annul.

infirmerie *n.f.* infirmary.

infirmier, ière *n.m.f.* nurse. **~ diplômé(e)** registered nurse.

infirmité *n.f.* disability, infirmity.

inflammable *adj.* inflammable.

inflammatoire *adj.* inflammatory.

inflammation *n.f.* inflammation.

inflation *n.f.* inflation.

inflationniste *adj.* inflationary.

infléchir *v.t.* to inflect, to bond. **s'~,** *v.refl.* to be inflected, to bend.

inflexibilité *n.f.* inflexibility.

inflexible *adj.* inflexible, unbending.

inflexiblement *adv.* inflexibly.

inflexion *n.f.* inflexion, inclination, modulation.

infliger *v.t.* to inflict. **s'~,** *v.refl.* to be inflicted.

influence *n.f.* influence; sway.

influençable *adj.* easily influenced.

influencer *v.t.* to influence, to sway, to bias.

influent, e *adj.* influential.

influenza *n.f.* influenza.

influer *v.i.* to have influence. **~ sur,** to influence, to have an influence on or over, to sway.

influx *n.m.* impulse.

informateur, trice *n.m.f.* computer informant, informer.

informaticien, ne *n.m.f.* computer scientist.

informatif, ive *adj.* informative.

information *n.f.* inquiry, information, news. **prendre des ~s,** to make inquiries.

informatique *n.f.* computer science, data processing.

informatisation *n.f.* computerization.

informatiser *v.i.* to computerize.

informe *adj.* shapeless, misshapen.

informé *n.m.* inquiry.

informel, le *adj.* informal.

informer *v.t.* to inform, to apprise. *v.i.* to investigate; to inform (against). **s'~,** *v.refl.* to inquire, to make inquiries; to ask.

infortune *n.f.* misfortune.

infortuné, e *adj.* unfortunate, unhappy, unlucky.
infraction *n.f.* infraction, infringement, breach. **une ~ à la loi,** a violation of the law.
infranchissable *adj.* insuperable, impassable.
infrangible *adj.* infrangible.
infrarouge *adj.* infrared.
infrason *n.m.* infrasound, infrasonic vibrations.
infrastructure *n.f.* infrastructure; ground system.
infréquenté, e *adj.* unfrequented.
infroissable *adj.* wrinkleproof, crease-resistant.
infructueux, euse *adj.* unsuccessful, fruitless.
infus, e *adj.* innate, inborn.
infuser *v.t.* to infuse; to brew; to steep. **s'~,** *v.refl.* to be infused, to steep, to draw (as tea).
infusion *n.f.* infusion, herb tea.
ingambe *adj.* active, brisk, nimble.
ingénier (s') *v.refl.* to exercise one's wits; to contrive, to try hard, to rack one's brain.
ingénierie *n.f.* engineering.
ingénieur *n.m.* engineer. **~ civil,** civil engineer.
ingénieusement *adv.* ingeniously.
ingénieux, euse *adj.* ingenious; clever.
ingéniosité *n.f.* ingeniousness, ingenuity.
ingénu, e *adj.* ingenuous; artless, frank.
ingénuité *n.f.* ingenuousness; frankness, candidness, artlessness, innocence.
ingénument *adv.* ingenuously; openly, artlessly; frankly.
ingérence *n.f.* meddling, interference.
ingérer *v.t.* to ingest. **s'~,** *v.refl.* to meddle, to interfere (with). **s'~ dans les affaires de quelqu'un,** to meddle in someone's affairs.
ingestion *n.f.* ingestion.
inglorieux, euse *adj.* inglorious.
ingouvernable *adj.* ungovernable, unruly.
ingrat, e *adj.* ungrateful; thankless; unfruitful; unprofitable. **un sujet ~,** an unpromising subject. *n.m.f.* ingrate.
ingratitude *n.f.* ingratitude, ungratefulness, thanklessness.
ingrédient *n.m.* ingredient.
inguérissable *adj.* incurable; inconsolable.
ingurgiter *v.t.* to ingurgitate; to swallow greedily.
inhabileté *n.f.* unskilfulness, inability, inexpertness.
inhabilité *n.f.* incapacity, disability, inability.
inhabitable *adj.* uninhabitable.
inhabité, e *adj.* uninhabited.
inhabitué, e *adj.* unaccustomed, unused to.
inhabituel, elle *adj.* unaccustomed, unusual, unfamiliar.
inhalateur, trice *adj.* inhaling. *n.m.* inhaler.
inhalation *n.f.* inhalation.
inhaler *v.t.* to inhale.
inharmonieux, euse *adj.* inharmonious, discordant.
inhérence *n.f.* inherence, inherency.
inhérent, e *adj.* inherent.

inhiber *v.t.* to inhibit, to forbid, to prohibit, to interdict.
inhibition *n.f.* inhibition, restraint.
inhospitalier, ère *adj.* inhospitable.
inhumain, e *adj.* inhuman.
inhumainement *adv.* inhumanly; cruelly.
inhumanité *n.f.* inhumanity, cruelty.
inhumation *n.f.* inhumation, interment, burial.
inhumer *v.t.* to inhume, to inter, to bury.
inimaginable *adj.* unimaginable, inconceivable.
inimitable *adj.* inimitable.
inimitie *n.f.* enmity, hostility; feud; hatred.
ininflammable *adj.* nonflammable, uninflammable.
inintelligemment *adv.* unintelligently.
inintelligence *n.f.* unintelligence.
inintelligent, e *adj.* unintelligent.
inintelligibilité *n.f.* unintelligibility.
inintelligible *adj.* unintelligible.
inintelligiblement *adv.* unintelligibly.
inintéressant *adj.* uninteresting.
ininterrompu, e *adj.* uninterrupted.
inique *adj.* iniquitous; unrighteous, unjust, wicked.
iniquité *n.f.* iniquity, injustice; unrighteousness.
initial, e *adj.f.* initial.
initialement *adv.* initially.
initiateur, trice *n.m.f.* initiator, originator.
initiation *n.f.* initiation.
initiative *n.f.* initiative.
initier *v.t.* to initiate. **s'~,** *v.refl.* to become initiated; to get acquainted (with).
injecter *v.t.* to inject. **s'~,** *v.refl.* to be injected.
injection *n.f.* injection.
injonction *n.f.* injunction, order.
injure *n.f.* insult, affront, abuse. **dire des ~s à quelqu'un,** to insult a person, to abuse a person.
inurier *v.t.* to insult, to abuse, to revile.
injurieusement *adv.* injuriously; wrongfully, hurtfully, insultingly; abusively.
injurieux, euse *adj.* injurious, wrongful, hurtful; insulting, abusive, offensive.
injuste *adj.* unfair, unjust; wrongful, wrong. *n.m.* wrong, unjust.
injustement *adv.* unjustly.
injustice *n.f.* injustice.
injustifiable *adj.* unjustifiable, wrong.
injustifié, e *adj.* unjustified.
inlassable *adj.* tireless, untiring.
inné, e *adj.* innate, inborn, natural.
innervation *n.f.* innervation.
innocemment *adv.* innocently; guiltlessly.
innocence *n.f.* innocence, harmlessness, simplicity.
innocent, e *adj.* innocent; harmless; guiltless; simple, credulous. *n.m.f.* innocent, innocent person. **naux ~s les mains pleines,** fortune favors the innocent, beginner's luck.
innocenter *v.t.* to declare innocent, to acquit, to discharge.

innocuité *n.f.* innocuousness, innoxiousness, harmlessness.

innombrable *adj.* innumerable, countless.

innovateur, trice *adj.* innovative; *n.m.f.* innovator.

innovation *n.f.* innovation.

innover *v.t.* to innovate.

inobservable *adj.* inobservable, unobservable.

inoccupé, e *adj.* unoccupied, vacant; unemployed, idle.

inoculable *adj.* inoculable.

inoculation *n.f.* inoculation.

inoculer *v.t.* to inoculate.

inodore *adj.* inodorous, odorless, scentless.

inoffensif, ive *adj.* inoffensive, harmless.

inondation *n.f.* inundation; flood; deluge; overflow.

inonder *v.t.* to inundate, to overflow, to flood, to deluge, to submerge; to overwhelm; to overrun. **la sueur l'inondait,** he was covered with perspiration. **la pluie nous inondait,** we were drenched with the rain.

inopérable *adj.* inoperable.

inopiné, e *adj.* unexpected, unforeseen, unlooked for.

inopinément *adv.* unexpectedly, suddenly.

inopportun, e *adj.* untimely, inconvenient.

inopportunément *adv.* inopportunely.

inoubliable *adj.* unforgettable.

inouï, e *adj.* unheard of; unprecedented.

inoxydable *adj.* stainless. *n.m.* stainless steel.

inqualifiable *adj.* inqualifiable, incongruous, unspeakable, scandalous.

inquiet, ète *adj.* worried, uneasy; anxious. **des regards ~s,** anxious looks.

inquiétant, e *adj.* disturbing, upsetting.

inquiéter *v.t.* to disquiet; to disturb, to trouble, to upset, to annoy, to harass. **cette nouvelle m'inquiète,** this news makes me uneasy. **s'~,** *v.refl.* to be disquieted, to be disturbed, to be uneasy; to fret; to make oneself uneasy; to be anxious. **il ne s'inquiète de rien,** he doesn't worry about anything.

inquiétude *n.f.* concern, agitation; uneasiness, anxiety. **~ d'esprit,** uneasiness of mind.

inquisiteur, trice *n.m.f.* inquisitor; *adj.* inquisitive.

inquisition *n.f.* inquisition; inquiry, search.

insaisissable *adj.* not seizable; *Fig.* imperceptible, indiscernible.

insalubre *adj.* insalubrious.

insalubrité *n.f.* insalubrity, unhealthiness, unhealthy.

insanité *n.f.* insanity, madness.

insatiable *adj.* insatiable.

insatiablement *adv.* insatiably.

insatisfaction *n.f.* dissatisfaction.

insatisfait, e *adj.* unsatisfied; dissatisfied.

inscription *n.f.* inscription; registration.

inscrire *v.t.* to inscribe; to set down, to put down, to enter; to register, to record (in a book).

s'~, *v.refl.* to register, to enter one's name.

insécable *adj.* indivisible.

insecte *n.m.* insect.

insecticide *adj.* insecticide. *n.m.* insect spray.

insécurité *n.f.* insecurity.

insémination *n.f.* insemination.

inséminer *v.t.* to inseminate.

insensé, e *adj.* insane; mad, deranged; senseless, unwise, stupid, foolish. **des propos ~s,** foolish talk. *n.m.f.* insane person.

insensibilité *n.f.* insensitivity; numbness.

insensible *adj.* insensitive; unfeeling, imperceptible. **il est ~ au froid,** he is impervious to cold.

insensiblement *adv.* imperceptibly, insensibly.

inséparable *adj.* inseparable. *n.m.f.pl.* lovebirds.

insérer *v.t.* to insert, to put in, to set in. **s'~,** *v.refl.* to be inserted.

insertion *n.f.* insertion.

insidieusement *adv.* insidiously.

insidieux, euse *adj.* insidious.

insigne *adj.* signal, notorious; egregious. *n.m.* badge, token; insignia *pl.*

insignifiance *n.f.* insignificance.

insignifiant, e *adj.* insignificant.

insinuant, e *adj.* insinuating.

insinuation *n.f.* insinuation; hint, innuendo.

insinuer *v.t.* to insinuate, to imply, to hint, to suggest. **s'~,** *v.refl.* to insinuate; to creep in; to find one's way; to insinuate oneself; to worm oneself.

insipide *adj.* insipid, tasteless, unsavory, flat, dull, spiritless.

insipidité *n.f.* insipidity, insipidness; tastelessness, flatness, dullness.

insistance *n.f.* insistence, insisting, persistence.

insister *v.i.* to insist, to persist; to dwell on; to lay a stress on.

insociable *adj.* unsociable.

insolation *n.f.* insolation; sunstroke.

insolemment *adv.* insolently, impertinently.

insolence *n.f.* insolence, disrespect, rudeness, impudence, arrogance. **dire des ~s,** to say insolent remarks.

insolent, e *adj.* and *n.m.f.* insolent; impudent, overbearing.

insolite *adj.* unusual, unwonted, unprecedented.

insoluble *adj.* insoluble; unsolvable.

insolvable *adj.* insolvent.

insomniaque *adj.* and *n.m.f.* insomniac.

insomnie *n.f.* sleeplessness, insomnia.

insondable *adj.* unfathomable, unsoundable.

insonore *adj.* soundproof.

insonorisation *n.f.* soundproofing.

insonoriser *v.t.* to soundproof.

insouciamment *adv.* carelessly, thoughtlessly.

insouciance *n.f.* carelessness, thoughtlessness, heedlessness.

insouciant, e *adj.* careless, thoughtless, heedless.

insoucieux, euse *adj.* careless, free from anxiety.
insoumis, e *adj.* unsubmissive, insubordinate, rebellious; unsubmissive. *n.m. Mil.* absentee.
insoumission *n.f.* insubordination.
insoupçonnable *adj.* above suspicion.
insoupçonné, e *adj.* unsuspected.
insoutenable *adj.* untenable, intolerable, unbearable.
inspecter *v.t.* to inspect; to examine, to oversee, to survey.
inspecteur, trice *n.m.f.* inspector; overseer, surveyor.
inspection *n.f.* inspection; view, sight; watch. **faire l'~ de**, to inspect, to examine, to survey.
inspiration *n.f.* inspiration, breathing; inhaling; suggestion.
inspirer *v.t.* to inspire, to breathe into, to inhale, to instill, to suggest, to prompt. **s'~**, to draw one's inspiration from, to be inspired (by).
instabilité *n.f.* instability; unsteadiness.
instable *adj.* unstable, unsteady.
installation *n.f.* installation, setting up; installment, fitting up; *pl.* fixtures.
installer *v.t.* to install, to set up, to induct. **s'~**, *v.refl.* to install oneself, to settle down.
instamment *adv.* earnestly, urgently.
instance *n.f.* earnest entreaty, solicitation, urgency; process, suit. **en première ~**, before the inferior court. **ils sont en ~ de divorce**, their divorce proceedings are under way.
instant, e *adj.* urgent, pressing. *n.m.* instant; moment. **attendez-moi un ~**, wait for me a moment. **à l'~, dans l'~**, instantly, immediately.
instantané, é *adj.* instantaneous.
instantanéité *n.f.* instantaneity, instantaneousness.
instantanément *adv.* instantaneously.
instar de (à l') *adv.* like, as, after, in imitation of.
instauration *n.f.* founding, establishment; building.
instaurer *v.t.* to institute, to establish.
instigateur, trice *n.m.f* instigator.
instigation *n.f.* instigation.
instiguer *v.t.* to instigate, to cite, to spur.
instinct *n.m.* instinct.
instinctif, ive *adj.* instinctive.
instinctivement *adv.* instinctively.
instituer *v.t.* to institute, to establish; to found; to appoint.
institut *n.m.* institute, institution.
instituteur, trice *n.m.f.* institutor, founder; (elementary school) teacher.
institution *n.f.* institution.
instructeur *n.m.* instructor. *adj.* **sergent ~**, drill sergeant. **juge ~**, examining magistrate.
instructif, ive *adj.* instructive.
instruction *n.f.* instruction; teaching; education; learning. knowledge, attainments; information; lesson; advice, counsel; information, direction, order. **un homme d'une grande ~**, a well-educated man. **recevoir des ~s**,

to be given instructions. **juge d'~**, examining magistrate.
instruire *v.t.* to instruct; to teach, to inform; to educate. **~ la jeunesse**, to instruct youth. **s'~**, *v.refl* to educate oneself, to instruct oneself; to inform one another; to be under examination.
instruit, e *adj.* learned, well-informed, well-educated; instructed.
instrument *n.m.* instrument; implement; means; deed. **~ de chirurgie**, surgical instrument.
instrumental, e *adj.* instrumental.
instrumentation *n.f.* instrumentation.
instrumenter *v.i.* to draw up a document, deeds, etc.; to score, to orchestrate.
instrumentiste *n.m.* instrumentalist.
insu *n.m.* **à l'~ de**, unknown to. **à mon ~**, unknown to me, without my knowing it.
insubmersible *adj.* unsinkable.
insubordination *n.f.* insubordination.
insubordonné, e *adj.* insubordinate.
insuffisamment *adv.* insufficiently.
insuffisance *n.f.* insufficiency, deficiency; incompetency.
insuffisant, e *adj.* insufficient; inadequate; incompetent.
insulaire *adj.* insular. *n.m.f.* islander, insular.
insuline *n.f.* insulin.
insultant, e *adj.* insulting; abusive.
insulte *n.f.* insult; affront. **faire une ~**, to insult.
insulter *v.t.* to insult; to outrage, to affront; to be an insult to.
insupportable *adj.* unbearable.
insurgé, e *adj.* revolted; *n.m.* insurgent, rebel.
insurgence *n.f.* insurgence.
insurger (s') *v.i.* to rise, to rebel, to revolt.
insurmontable *adj.* insurmountable, insuperable.
insurrection *n.f.* insurrection, rebellion.
intact, e *adj.* intact, untouched; uninjured, unharmed, whole, entire, sound.
intangible *adj.* intangible.
intarissable *adj.* endless, inexhaustible.
intégral, e *adj.* integral, whole, entire. *n.f.* integral.
intégralement *adv.* integrally, wholly, completely.
intégralité *n.f.* wholeness, entireness, integrality.
intégrant, e *adj.* integrant, integral.
intégration *n.f.* integration.
intègre *adj.* righteous, upright, just, honest, of integrity.
intègrement *adv.* uprightly, justly, honestly.
intégrer *v.t.* to integrate.
intégrité *n.f.* integrity; entireness; soundness, uprightness, probity.
intellect *n.m.* intellect.
intellectuel, elle *adj.*, *n.m.f.* intellectual.
intellectuellement *adv.* intellectually.
intelligemment *adv.* intelligently.
intelligence *n.f.* intelligence; intellect; under-

standing, mind; knowledge, skill, ability; harmony; commerce, correspondence. **~ bornée**, narrow understanding.

intelligent, e *adj.* intelligent; bright; sharp.

intelligible *adj.* intelligible; audible, clear, plain, comprehensible.

intelligiblement *adv.* intelligibly, clearly, audibly, distinctly.

intempérance *n.f.* intemperance.

intempérant, e *adj.* intemperate; immoderate.

intempérie *n.f.* inclemency. **~s**, bad weather.

intempestif, ve *adj.* untimely.

intenable *adj.* unbearable, intolerable, untenable, indefensible.

intendance *n.f.* direction, superintendence. *Milit.* supply services.

intendant *n.m* attendant; steward; manager; surveyor; commissary.

intense *adj.* intense; violent; severe.

intensément *adv.* intensely.

intensif, ive *adj.* intensive.

intensifier *v.t.* to intensify.

intensité *n.f.* intensity, intenseness, extreme degree; violence.

intensivement *adv.* intensively, intensely.

intenter *v.t.* to bring (an action, a charge), to enter.

intention *n.f.* intention; intent, thought; intenseness, intensity; purpose, design. **il a l'~ de partir,** he intends to leave. **à l'~ de,** on account of, for the sake of, for the benefit of.

intentionné, e *adj.* intentioned. **bien ~,** well-intentioned; well-meaning.

intentionnel, elle *adj.* intention, intended, deliberate.

intentionnellement *adv.* intentionally, deliberately, on purpose.

interactif *adj.* interactive.

interaction *n.f.* interaction.

intercalaire *adj.* divider.

intercaler *v.t.* to intercalate; to insert, to interpolate. **s'~,** to come in between.

intercéder *v.i.* to intercede.

intercepter *v.t.* to intercept.

interception *n.f.* interception.

interclasse *n.m.* (class) break.

interdiction *n.f.* interdiction; ban; prohibition; interdict; privation (of civil rights). **~ de fumer,** no smoking. **~ de ... non ....**

interdire *v.t.* to interdict; to forbid; to ban; to prohibit; to deprive; to suspend; to confound, to astonish, to astound. **tout lui est interdit,** he is forbidden everything.

interdisciplinaire *adj.* interdisciplinary.

interdit, e forbidden, prohibited; dumbfounded, amazed. *n.m.* interdict.

intéressant, e *adj.* interesting; attractive, worthwhile. **il lui a fait une offre très ~e,** he gave him/her an extremely attractive offer.

intéressé, e *adj.* interested; selfish. *n.m.* interested party.

intéresser *v.t.* to interest; to concern. **on l'a intéressé dans cette affaire,** they have given him an interest in that affair. **s'~,** *v.refl.* to be interested, to take an interest; to interest oneself. **il a ~ à l'écouter sinon ...,** he'd better listen to him/her, or else ...

intérêt *n.m.* interest; advantage, profit; concern; self interest, selfishness. **l'~ public,** public interest. **avoir ~ à,** to have an interest in. **prendre les ~s de quelqu'un,** to defend a person's interests.

interférence *n.f.* interference.

interférer *v.t.* to interfere; to interact.

intérieur, e *adj.* interior; internal, inner, inward. *n.m.* interior; inside.

intérieurement *adv.* internally, interiorly, inwardly.

intérim *n.m.* interim, temp. **elle a été employée par ~,** she has been employed as a temp.

intérimaire *adj.* interim, temporary. *n.m.f.* temporary worker, temp.

intérioriser *v.t.* to internalize, to interiorize.

intérioriser *v.t.* to internalize.

interligne *n.m.* interval, space between two lines; interlineation.

interlocuteur, trice *n.m.f.* interlocutor, speaker.

interlocution *n.f.* interlocution.

interlope *n.m.* interloper, interloping vessel. *adj.* intrusive, contraband, illegal, illicit.

interloquer *v.t.* to disconcert, to dumbfound.

intermède *n.m.* interlude, intermediate.

intermédiaire *adj.* intermediary, intermediate, intervening; between. *n.m.* intermediate; go-between, middle-man; medium, interposition, mediation, agency. **par l'~ d'un tel,** by the interposition of such.

interminable *adj.* interminable, endless.

intermission *n.f.* mission.

intermittence *n.f.* on and off, sporadically, intermittently.

intermittent, e *adj.* intermittent. **fièvre ~e,** intermittent fever.

internat *n.m.* boarding school; internship.

international, e *adj.* international.

internationalement *adv.* internationally.

internationalisation *n.f.* internationalization.

interne *adj.* internal; interior, inward, inner. *n.m.* boarder (in schools); intern, resident medical student.

internement *n.m.* internment; confinement.

interner *v.t.* to send into, to confine, to intern.

interpellation *n.f.* interpellation, summons, question.

interpeller *v.t.* to call upon; to question, to hail, to call out.

interphone *n.m.* intercom; 3-way line.

interplanétaire *adj.* interplanetary.

interposer *v.t.* to interpose; to place between. **s'~,** *v.refl.* to be interposed; to interpose.

interposition *n.f.* interposition; intervention.

interprétation *n.f.* interpretation.

interprète *n.m.f.* interpreter; translator, expounder; spokesperson.

interpréter *v.t.* to expound; to interpret.

interrogateur, trice *n.m.f.* interrogator; examiner. *adj.* interrogatory.

interrogatif, ive *adj.* interrogative.

interrogation *n.f.* interrogation; examination. **point d'~,** question mark.

interrogatoire *n.m.* interrogatory, examination questioning; cross-examination.

interroger *v.t.* to interrogate, to question. **s'~,** *v.refl.* to question each other, to examine oneself.

interrompre *v.t.* to interrupt; to break off, to cut off. **s'~,** *v.refl.* to be interrupted; to interrupt oneself, to leave off.

interrupteur, trice *adj.* of interrupting. *n.m.* switch interrupter.

interruption *n.f.* interruption, break; termination. **~ de grossesse,** abortion.

intersection *n.f.* intersection.

interstellaire *adj.* interstellar.

interstice *n.m.* interstice.

intervalle *n.m.* gap; lapse, interval. **par ~s,** on and off.

intervenir *v.i.* to intervene; to interpose; to interfere, to occur.

intervention *n.f.* intervention, interference.

interview *n.f.* interview.

interviewé, e *n.m.f.* interviewee.

interviewer *v.t.* to interview.

interviewe(u)r *n.m.* interviewer.

intestin, e *adj.* intestine; internal. *n.m.* intestine.

intestinal, e *adj.* intestinal.

intimation *n.f.* notice, notification, summons.

intime *adj.* intimate, inmost, inward, internal; close; familiar. *n.m.* intimate friend.

intimement *adv.* intimately, closely.

intimidant, e *adj.* intimidating.

intimidation *n.f.* intimidation.

intimider *v.t.* to intimidate, to frighten, to abash, to dishearten. **s'~,** *v.refl.* to feel intimidated, to get frightened.

intimité *n.f.* intimacy, privacy.

intitulé, e *p.p.* entitled.

intituler *v.t.* to entitle, to call, to name. **s'~,** *v.refl.* to entitle oneself, to call oneself.

intolérable *adj.* intolerable, unbearable.

intolérance *n.f.* intolerance.

intolérant, e *adj.* intolerant.

intonation *n.f.* intonation.

intoxication *n.f.* poisoning.

intoxiquer *v.t.* to poison, to intoxicate.

intraduisible *adj.* untranslatable.

intraitable *adj.* intractable, ungovernable, unmanageable; stubborn, unreasonable.

intra-muros *adv. phr.* intramural, in town.

intransigeant *n.m.* intransigent.

intra-utérin, e *adj.* intrauterine.

intraveineux, euse *adj.* intravenous; *n.f.* intravenous injection.

intrépide *adj.* intrepid; fearless.

intrigant, e *adj.* intriguing.

intrigue *n.f.* intrigue, scrape; plot scheme. **sortir d'~,** to get out of a scrape.

intrigué, e *adj.* perplexed, puzzled.

intriguer *v.i.* to intrigue. *v.t.* to perplex, to puzzle. to lay the plot.

intrinsèque *adj.* intrinsic.

introduction *n.f.* introduction; presentation, preliminary; first process.

introduire *v.t.* to introduce, to bring in, to usher in, to show in; to present, to put in; to let in. **~ quelqu'un,** to present a person. **~ des marchandises dans un pays,** to import goods into a country. **s'~,** *v.refl.* to be introduced, to enter, to penetrate; to get in; to gain admittance.

introuvable *adj.* undiscoverable, not to be found.

introverti, e *adj.* introverted, introvert. *n.m.f.* introvert.

intrus, e *p.p.* intruded. *n.m.f.* intruder.

intrusion *n.f.* intrusion.

intuitif, ive *adj.* intuitive.

intuition *n.f.* intuition.

inusable *adj.* that cannot be worn out; durable.

inusité, e *adj.* unused, not in use; obsolete, out of use.

inutile *adj.* useless; worthless, fruitless, unprofitable; needless.

inutilement *adv.* uselessly, to no purpose, needlessly.

inutilisé, e *adj.* not utilized, unused.

invaincu, e *adj.* unconquered.

invalidation *n.f.* invalidation.

invalide *adj.* invalid, infirm, disabled; void, null. *n.m.f.* disabled person, invalid.

invalider *v.t.* to invalidate.

invalidité *n.f.* invalidity; nullity.

invariable *adj.* unchangeable, immutable, unalterable, constant.

invariablement *adv.* invariably, unchangeably, unalterably.

invasif, ive *adj.* invasive.

invasion *n.f.* invasion; irruption.

invective *n.f.* invective; abuse.

invendable *adj.* unsaleable.

invendu, e *adj.* unsold.

inventaire *n.m.* inventory. **faire l'~ de,** to take an inventory of. **faire son ~,** to take stock.

inventer *v.t.* to invent; to find out; to contrive; to imagine; to fabricate, to feign.

inventeur, trice *n.m.f.* inventor.

inventif, ive *adj.* inventive.

invention *n.f.* invention, discovery, inventiveness.

inventorier *v.t.* to make an inventory.

inverse *adj.* inverse, inverted. *n.m.* reverse, contrary, opposite. **faire l'~,** to do the reverse.

inversement *adv.* inversely, vice versa.

inversion *n.f.* inversion.

invertébré, e *adj.* invertebrate.
investigateur, trice *n.m.f.* investigator. *adj.* searching, scrutinizing, investigating, investigatory.
investigation *n.f.* investigation. **faire des ~s sur**, to investigate, to make inquiries into or about.
investir *v.t.* to invest.
investissement *n.m.* investment.
investiture *n.f.* investiture.
invétéré, e *adj.* inveterate; obstinate.
invincible *adj.* invincible; unconquerable.
inviolable *adj.* inviolable.
invisibilité *n.f.* invisibility.
invisible *adj.* invisible.
invisiblement *adv.* invisibly.
invitation *n.f.* invitation.
invité, e *n.m.* guest.
inviter *v.t.* to invite; to request; to beg. **s'~**, *v.refl.* to invite oneself.
invivable *adj.* unbearable.
invocation *n.f.* invocation.
invocatoire *adj.* invocatory.
involontaire *adj.* involuntary.
involontairement *adj.* involuntarily.
invoquer *v.t.* to invoke; to call upon; to plead.
invraisemblable *adj.* unlikely, implausible.
invraisemblablement *adv.* unlikely.
invraisemblance *n.f.* unlikelihood.
invulnérabilité *n.f.* invulnerability.
invulnérable *adj.* invulnerable.
ion *n.m.* ion.
ioniser *v.t.* to ionize.
Irak *n.m.* Iraq.
Iran *n.m.* Iran.
Iranien, enne *adj.* Iranian.
Irascible *adj.* irascible, short-tempered.
iridescent, e *adj.* iridescent.
iridium *n.m.* iridium.
iris *n.m.* iris.
irisation *n.f.* iridescence.
irisé *adj.* iridescent.
iriser *v.t.* to make iridescent.
Irlandais, e *adj.* Irish. *n.m.* Irishman. *n.f.* Irish woman.
Irlande *n.f.* Ireland.
ironie *n.f.* irony.
ironique *adj.* ironic, ironical.
ironiquement *adv.* ironically.
ironiser *v.i.* to be ironic(al) about, to speak with irony.
irradier *v.i.* to irradiate, to shine.
irrationnel, elle *adj.* irrational, unreasonable, absurd, foolish, preposterous, unwise.
irrationnellement *adv.* irrationally, absurdly.
irréalisable *adj.* infeasible, impracticable; unattainable.
irréconciliable *adj.* irreconcilable; incongruous, incompatible.
irréductible *adj.* irreductible.
irréel, le *adj.* unreal.

irréfléchi, e *adj.* thoughtless, heedless, inconsiderate.
irréfutable *adj.* irrefutable.
irréfutablement *adv.* irrefutably.
irréfuté, e *adj.* unrefuted.
irrégularité *n.f.* irregularity.
irrégulier, ière *adj.* irregular, disorderly, inordinate.
irrégulièrement *adv.* irregularly.
irrémédiable *adj.* irremediable, irretrievable.
irrémédiablement *adv.* irremediably.
irremplaçable *adj.* irreplaceable.
irréparabilité *n.f.* irreparability.
irréparable *adj.* irrepairable; irretrievable.
irréparablement *adv.* irreparably, irretrievably.
irréprochable *adj.* irreproachable, irreprehensible.
irréprochablement *adv.* irreproachably. *adj.* irresistible.
irrésistible *adj.* irresistible.
irrésistiblement *adv.* irresistibly.
irrésolu, e *adj.* irresolute, unsolved, unresolved.
irrespirable *adj.* irrespirable, unbreathable.
irresponsable *adj.* irresponsible.
irrévérence *n.f.* irreverence; disrespect.
irrévérencieux, euse *adj.* irreverent.
irrévérent, e *adj.* irreverent.
irréversible *adj.* irreversible.
irrévocabilité *n.f.* irrevocability.
irrévocable *adj.* irrevocable; irreversible, unalterable, unchangeable.
irrévocablement *adv.* irrevocably, irreversibly.
irrigation *n.f.* irrigation.
irriguer *v.t.* to irrigate.
irritabilité *n.f.* irritability.
irritable *adj.* irritable.
irritant, e *adj.* irritating; irritative, irritant. *n.m.* irritant.
irritation *n.f.* irritation; annoyance, exasperation, anger.
irriter *v.t.* to irritate; to inflame, to exasperate; to excite; to tease. **s'~**, *v.refl.* to become irritated.
irruption *n.f.* irruption; invasion.
isard *n.m. Zool.* izard.
islam *n.m.* Islam.
islamique *adj.* Islamic.
islamisme *n.m.* Islamism.
isolant, e *adj.* insulating.
isolation *n.f.* isolation.
isolé, e *adj.* insulated, isolated, alone; lone, lonely.
isolement *n.m.* insulation, isolation.
isoler *v.t.* to insulate, to isolate; to detach; to separate.
Israël *n.m.* Israel.
Israélien, ienne *adj.* Israeli.
israélite *n.m.f.* Israelite, Hebrew; Jew. *adj.* Jewish.
issu, e *p.p.* issued, sprung, born, descended.
issue *n.f.* exit, outlet; end, way out. **à l'~ de**, at the end of; on leaving.
Italie *n.f.* Italy.

Italien, enne adj. Italian, n.m.f. Italian. n.m. Italian, Italian language.

italique n.m. italic.

item adv. item, also, likewise, ditto.

itinéraire adj. itinerary.

ivoire n.m. ivory. **la Côte d'~**, the Ivory Coast.

ivoirerie n.f. ivory trade, ivory sculpture.

ivre adj. inebriated, drunk, intoxicated; tipsy. **~ mort**, dead drunk. **~ de joie**, overjoyed.

ivresse n.f. inebriety, inebriation, drunkenness, intoxication.

ivrogne adj. drunk, drunken, n.m. drunkard, tippler.

ivrognerie n.f. drunkenness, ebriety, tippling.

J

j' contraction of **je**.

jabot n.m. crop (of a bird); frill (of a shirt).

jacasser v.i. to chatter, to yak, to gossip.

jachère n.f. Agr. fallowness. **terre en ~**, fallow land. **être en ~**, to lie fallow.

jacinthe n.f. hyacinth.

jack n.m. (phone) jack.

jacquet n.m. backgammon.

jacter v.refl. to jabber.

jaculatoire adj. jaculatory.

jade n.m. jade.

jadis adv. of old, of yore, in times of old. adj. of yore. **au temps ~**, in days of yore.

jaguar n.m. jaguar, American tiger.

jaillir v.i. to gush out, to spurt out, to spring up; to burst; to flash.

jaillissement n.m. gushing, spouting, spirting.

jais n.m. jet. **noir comme du ~**, jet-black.

jalonner v.t. to stake out.

jalousé, e adj. regarded with jealousy.

jalousement adv. jealously.

jalouser v.t. to be jealous of, to envy.

jalousie n.f. jealousy; envy; Venetian blind. **mort de ~**, sick with jealousy.

jaloux, ouse adj. jealous; envious.

Jamaïque, la n.f. Jamaica.

jamais adv. ever; (with **ne**) never. **je ne lui parle ~**, I never speak to him. **pour ~**, forever. n.m. never, time without end. **au grand ~**, never.

jambe n.f. leg; shank. **courir à toutes ~s**, to run as fast as one can. **faire la belle ~**, to strut about. **cela ne lui rend pas la ~ mieux faite**, he is none the better for that. **prendre ses ~s à son cou**, to take to one's heels. **ça me fait une belle ~!** do I look like I care?

jambé, e adj. legged. **bien ~**, nice pair of legs.

jambon n.m. ham; Infml. thigh.

jambonneau n.m. small ham; knuckle of ham.

jante n.f. rim.

janvier n.m. January.

japonaiserie n.f. Japanese curio.

jappement n.m. yelping, yelp, yapping, yap.

japper v.i. to yelp, to yap.

jaquette n.f. jacket, coat.

jardin n.m. garden. **~ potager**, vegetable garden. **~ d'agrément**, pleasure garden, flower garden. **~ botanique**, **~ des plantes**, botanical garden. **~ d'enfants**, kindergarten.

jardinage n.m. gardening.

jardiner v.i. to garden.

jardinier, ière n.m.f. gardener. n.f. flower stand. dish of mixed vegetables.

jargon n.m. jargon; gibberish; cant.

jarre n.f. jar.

jarret n.m. ham; knuckle of veal; shin of beef. **couper les ~s à**, to hamstring.

jarretelle n.f. a suspender, garter.

jarretière n.f. garter. **il ne lui va pas à la ~**, he cannot be compared to him. **chevalier de la ~**, Knight of the Garter.

jars n.m. gander.

jas n.m. stock (of an anchor).

jaser v.i. to chatter, to prate, to gossip, to yak.

jasmin n.m. jasmine.

jaspe n.m. jasper.

jasper v.t. to marble, to vein.

jaspure n.f. marbling.

jatte n.f. bowl, saucer.

jauge n.f. gauge; gauging rod; burden, tonnage.

jaugeage n.m. gauging.

jauger v.t. to gauge, to measure; to size up. **~ du regard**, to inspect (someone).

jaunâtre adj. yellowish.

jaune adj. yellow; (of the complexion) sallow. n.m. yellow; yolk (of an egg). **rire ~**, forces laugh.

jaunir v.i. to grow yellow, to turn yellow. v.t. to yellow, to make yellow.

jaunissant, e adj. turning yellow, golden, ripening.

jaunisse n.f. jaundice. **faire une ~**, to be green with envy.

jaunissement n.m yellowing.

Java n.f. Java. Infml. **faire la ~**, to live it up, to have a wild party.

javel n.f. **eau de ~**, bleach.

javelot n.m. javelin, spear.

jazz n.m. jazz.

je pron. pers. I. **je m'en-foutisme,** Infml. couldn't-care-less attitude. **je ne sais quoi**, indefinable touch.

jean n.m. jeans.

jeep n.f. jeep.

Jéhova n.m. Jehovah, Yahveh.

jérémiade n.f. jeremiad, whining.

jersey n.f. jersey; sweater.

jésuite n.m. Jesuit.

jésuitique adj. Jesuitic, Jesuitical.

Jésus n.m. Jesus, Jesus Christ.

jet n.m. throw; throwing, hurl, shoot, sprout; casting (of metals); cast; gush, spirt, jet; flash, stream; sketch, outline; throwing overboard, jetsam, jetson. **~ de pierre**, stone's throw. **fondre une**

statue d'un seul ~, to make a statue at one cast. ~ d'eau, jet. ~ de lumière, flash of light.

jeté, e *n.m.* jeté ballet.

jetée *n.f.* jetty, pier.

jeter *v.t.* to throw, to throw away, down; to cast, to fling, to hurl, to toss; to let go, to let fall, to drop. ~ à la mer, to throw overboard. ~ de la poudre aux yeux de quelqu'un, to flash, to show off in someone's face. ~ par terre, ~ à terre, to throw on the ground. ~ un pont sur une rivière, to throw a bridge over a river. ~ l'ancre, to cast anchor. ~ l'argent, to throw away money. ~ les hauts cris, to raise an outcry. se ~, *v.refl.* to be thrown, to be hurled, to throw oneself. se ~ à genoux, to throw oneself on one's knees. se ~ au cou de quelqu'un, to fall upon a person's neck. se ~ dans une entreprise, to rush into an undertaking. ce fleuve se jette dans la mer, that river flows into the sea.

jeton *n.m.* token. avoir les ~s, to have the jitters, to be scared. faux ~, hypocrite.

jeu *n.m.* play; game, sport, acting; execution. ~ d'enfant, child's play. les ~x de la fortune, the tricks of fortune. ~ de mots, play on words, pun. ~x de bourse, stock exchange speculations. avoir un beau ~, to have a good hand; to have fine cards. à beau ~ beau retour, one good turn deserves another. jouer gros ~, to play high. un ~ de cartes, a pack of cards.

jeudi *n.m.* Thursday. ~ saint, Maundy-Thursday.

jeun *adv.* fasting; sober.

jeune *adj.* young; youthful, younger; junior. une ~ fille, a young girl. un ~ chien, a puppy. *n.m.* youth; *pl.* young people.

jeûne *n.m.* fast; fasting. faire ~, to fast.

jeûner *v.i.* to fast.

jeunesse *n.f.* youth, youthfulness, young people. la première ~, early youth. élever la ~, to train youth.

jeunet, ette *adj.* very young.

jiu-jitsu *n.m. Sport* jiu-jitsu.

joaillerie *n.f.* jeweler's trade; jewelry.

joaillier, ère *n.m.f.* jeweler.

Job *n.m.* Job.

jobard *n.m.* simpleton, ninny; nuts.

jockey *n.m.* jockey.

Joconde *n.f.* la ~, the Mona Lisa.

joie *n.f.* joy, youthfulness, mirth, delight, gladness, cheerfulness. être ivre de ~, to be overjoyed. être dans la ~, to be overjoyed. s'en donner à coeur ~, to thoroughly enjoy a thing.

joindre *v.t.* to join, to unite together; to connect, to couple; to combine, to overtake; to meet. ~ l'utile à l'agréable, to combine the useful with the agreeable. ~ les mains, to clasp hands. ~ le geste à la parole, to suit the action to the word, to put one's money where one's mouth is. ~ au téléphone, to contact by phone. se ~, *v.refl.* to join; to be joined, to be united; to combine; to couple (as animals).

joint, e *p.p.* joined, united, added. ci-~, enclosed, herewith.

joint *n.m* joint; articulation; seam.

jointure *n.f.* joint, joining, articulation.

joker *n.m.* joker.

joli, e *adj.* pretty; nice; handsome; fine, neat. une ~e main, a pretty hand. être dans un ~ état, to be in a fine state.

joliment *adv.* prettily; nicely; finely. cela est ~ travaillé, that is prettily done.

jonc *n.m.* rush; cane.

joncher *v.t.* to strew, to scatter; to cover.

jonction *n.f.* junction, joining; meeting.

jongler *v.i.* to juggle.

jonglerie *n.f.* juggling, trickery, deceit.

jongleur *n.m.* juggler, trickster, deceiver, cheat.

jonque *n.f.* junk.

jonquille *n.f.* jonquil.

joue *n.f.* cheek. aux ~s creusés, hollow-cheeked. coucher, mettre en ~ to take aim at. en ~! *Milit.* present!

jouer *v.i.* to play; to act; to sport; to play upon; to ply; to handle, to represent; to sham, to feign, to counterfeit; to gamble, to speculate. ~ avec les mots, ~ sur les mots, to play upon words, to quibble, to pun. ~ à colin-maillard, to play blindman's-buff. ~ au billard, to play pool. ~ au plus sûr, to play the safest game. ~ du violon, to play the violin. ~ une carte, to play a card. ~ gros jeu, to run great risks. ~ sa vie, to risk one's life. ~ la comédie, to take a part in a comedy. ~ un personnage, to play a character. se ~, *v.refl.* to play; to amuse oneself, to be played; to laugh at, to mock; to baffle. ceci se joue à quatre mains, this is composed for four hands.

jouet *n.m.* plaything, toy; sport, laughing stock. être le ~ de la fortune, to be the sport of fortune.

joueur, euse *n.m.f.* player; gambler; speculator. ~ à la baisse, bear. ~ à la hausse, bull.

joufflu, e *adj.* chubby, chubby-cheeked. *n.m.f.* chubby-cheeked person.

jouir *v.i.* (with de) to enjoy; (sexual) to have an orgasm. cet homme jouit du présent, that man enjoys the present. ~ d'une terre, to possess an estate.

jouissance *n.f.* enjoyment; pleasure; possession; (sexual) orgasm, climax.

joujou *n.m.* plaything, toy.

jour *n.m.* day, daytime; light, opening; passage, means. pendant le ~, in the daytime. toute la journée, all day long. de ~ en ~, from day to day. tous les ~s, every day. huit ~s, a week. ~ de fête, holiday. a chaque ~ suffit sa peine, sufficient unto the day is the evil thereof. vivre au ~ le ~, to live from day to day. le ~ baisse, it is getting dark. en plein ~, in broad daylight. mettre au ~, to bring to light. mettre quelque chose dans son ~, to put a thing in a proper light. dans un faux ~, in a bad light. il

y a du ~ entre ces planches, there are openings between these boards. **ses livres sont à ~,** his/her books are in order.

journal *n.m.* newspaper, paper; journal; diary; logbook. **~ quotidien,** daily newspaper. **~ hebdomadaire,** weekly paper, weekly journal.

journalier, ière *adj.* daily; diurnal, quotidian. *n.m.* day laborer, journeyman.

journalisme *n.m.* journalism.

journaliste *n.m.* journalist.

journée *n.f.* day, daytime; day's work; day's journey. **une belle ~,** a fine day. **toute la ~,** all day long. **à petites ~s,** by easy stages. **il a bien gagné sa ~,** he deserves his day's earnings.

journellement *adv.* daily, every day.

joute *n.f.* joust, tilt.

jouvence *n.f.* youth. **Fontaine de ~,** Fountain of Youth.

jovial, e *adj.* jovial, merry.

jovialement *adv.* jovially, merrily, joyfully.

jovialité *n.f.* joviality, jovialness, merriment.

joyau *n.m.* jewel, gem.

joyeusement *adv.* joyously, joyfully.

joyeux, euse *adj.* cheerful, joyous; joyful, gay, glad.

jubilation *n.f.* jubilation, rejoicing, merriment.

jubilé *n.m.* jubilee.

jucher *v.i.* to roost, to perch. *v.t.* to perch. **se ~,** *v.refl. Fig.* to perch oneself.

judaïque *adj.* Judaic, Judaical, Jewish.

judaïsme *n.m.* Judaism.

judas *n.m.* Judas, traitor; peephole.

judiciaire *adj.* judicial; judiciary.

judiciairement *adv.* judicially.

judicieusement *adv.* judiciously; discreetly, wisely.

judicieux, euse *adj.* judicious; discreet, prudent.

judo *n.m.* judo.

judoka *n.m.f.* judoka.

juge *n.m.* judge; magistrate, justice; your Honor. **~ de paix,** justice of the peace. **oui, Monsieur/Madame le Juge,** yes, your Honor.

jugeable *adj.* amenable.

jugement *n.m.* judgment; trial; sentence; verdict; decision; opinion, view. **passer en ~** to be brought up for trial, to stand trial. **je me rends à votre ~,** I'll go with your opinion.

jugeote *n.f.* common sense.

juger *v.t.* to judge; to sentence; to determine; to estimate; to pass sentence. **~ un procès,** to judge, to try a cause. **~ à propos,** to think fit. **~ de,** to judge, to give one's opinion on. **vous pouvez ~ de ma surprise,** you can imagine how surprised I was. **se ~,** *v.refl.* to judge oneself; to judge one another; to be tried.

jugulaire *adj.* jugular. *n.f.* jugular; *pl.* chin straps.

juguler *v.t.* to suppress, to halt; to strangle.

juif, ive *adj.* Jewish. *n.m.f.* Jew, Jewish person.

juillet *n.m.* July.

juin *n.m.* June.

juiverie *n.f. Pej.* Jewry; Jewish quarter, ghetto.

jujube *n.f.* jujube.

juke-box *n.m.* jukebox.

julep *n.m.* julep.

julien, enne *adj.* **potage à la ~,** julienne soup, vegetable soup.

jumbo (jet) *n.m.* jumbo (jet).

jumeau, elle *adj.* twin; semidetached (house); double (as certain fruits). *n.m.f.* twin. **vrais/faux jumeaux/jumelles,** identical/fraternal twins.

jumelée *adj.* coupled.

jumelles *n.f.pl.* cheeks (of a press, etc.); sidepieces; opera glasses, binoculars.

jument *n.f.* mare.

jungle *n.f.* jungle.

junior *adj. inv.* junior.

Junon *n.f.* Juno.

junte *n.f.* junta.

jupe *n.f.* skirt. **il est toujours dans les ~s de sa mère,** he is still tied to his mother's apron strings. **~ culotte** *n.f.* culottes.

Jupiter *n.m.* Jupiter.

jupon *n.m.* petticoat, slip.

jurassique *adj. Geol.* Jurassic. **terrain ~,** Jurassic group, oolitic series.

juré, e *adj.* sworn. *n.m.* juror; of the jury.

jurer *v.t.* to swear; to blaspheme, to curse, to take an oath, to promise upon oath; to contrast; to clash. **il à juré de dire la verité,** he has sworn to tell the truth. **~ la perte de quelqu'un,** to swear to ruin a person. **il ne faut ~ de rien,** you can never tell. **ne ~ que par quelqu'un,** to swear by someone. **à tout propos,** to be always swearing. **ces couleurs jurent ensemble,** those colors clash together. **se ~,** to swear, to vow to oneself; to pledge to each other.

juridiction *n.f.* jurisdiction.

juridique *adj.* juridical, legal.

juridiquement *adv.* juridically, according to the law, legally.

jurisconsulte *n.m.* jurisconsult, lawyer, legal expert.

jurisprudence *n.f.* jurisprudence. **~ des arrêts,** law of precedents.

juriste *n.m.* jurist.

juron *n.m.* oath, curse.

jury *n.m.* jury; committee board, board of examination. **former la liste du ~,** to impanel. **chef du ~,** foreperson.

jus *n.m.* juice; gravy.

jusque *prep.* to, till, until; as far as. **jusqu'à présent,** till now. **jusqu'à nouvel ordre,** till further orders. **depuis Paris jusqu'à Rouen,** from Paris to Rouen. **jusqu'où,** how far. **jusqu'ici,** up to here, so far; hitherto, till now. **jusque-là,** so far. **jusqu'au ciel,** up to the skies. **il vendrait jusqu'à sa chemise,** he would sell even the shirt on his back. **je resterai jusqu'à ce que vous ayez fini,** I'll stay until you finish.

juste *adj.* just; right, upright, honest, fair,

virtuous; true; exact, accurate; tight, just barely enough. **une ~ punition,** a just punishment. **un homme ~,** a just man. **de ~s soupçons,** justifiable doubts. **ma montre est ~,** my watch is right. *n.m.* upright man; what is just. *adv.* just; exactly, accurately; merely. **tout ~,** just, exactly. **chanter ~,** to sing in tune.

justement *adv.* justly; uprightly; properly; exactly.

justesse *n.f.* barely; accuracy, exactness; precision, propriety; fitness, appropriateness. **il est arrivé de ~,** he barely made it.

justice *n.f.* justice; equity, integrity, uprightness. **rendre la ~,** to administer justice. **poursuivre en justice,** to take legal action. **faire ~ à quelqu'un,** to do justice to a person. **se faire ~ à soi-même,** to do oneself justice.

justifiable *adj.* justifiable.

justificatif, ive *adj.* justificative, justificatory. **pièce justificative,** proof, voucher.

justification *n.f.* justification; proof.

justifier *v.t.* to justify, to vindicate; to excuse, to clear; to substantiate. **se ~,** *v.refl.* to justify, to vindicate, to clear oneself.

jute *n.m.* jute.

juteux, euse *adj.* juicy.

juvénile *adj.* juvenile, youthful.

juvénilité *n.f.* juvenility; youthfulness, freshness.

juxtaposer *v.t.* to juxtapose, to place side by side. **se ~,** *v.refl.* to be juxtaposed, to be in juxtaposition.

juxtaposition *n.f.* juxtaposition.

K

kakatoès *n.m.* cockatoo.

kaki *adj.,n.m.* khaki, olive-drab.

kaleidoscope *n.m.* kaleidoscope.

kangourou *n.m.* kangaroo.

kaolin *n.m.* kaolin, porcelain.

karaté *n.m.* karate.

karma *n.m.* karma.

kart *n.m.* kart, go-cart.

kasbah *n.f.* kasba, casba.

kasher *adj.* kosher.

kayak *n.m.* kayak, canoe.

kermesse *n.f.* church, charity fair.

kerosène *n.m.* kerosene, fuel.

ketchup *n.m.* ketchup.

khôl *n.m.* eyeliner.

kibboutz *n.m.* kibbutz.

kidnapper *v.t.* to kidnap, to abduct.

kidnappeur, euse *n.m.f.* kidnapper.

kidnapping *n.m.* abduction.

kif *n.m.* kif, kef (marijuana).

kif-kif *adj.inv. Infml.* all the same.

kilo *n.m.* abbreviation of kilogramme.

kilogramme *n.m.* kilogram.

kilolitre *n.m.* kiloliter.

kilométrage *n.m.* mileage.

kilomètre *n.m.* kilometer.

kilométrique *adj.* in kilometers.

kilotonne *n.f.* kiloton.

kilowatt *n.m.* kilowatt.

kilowatt-heure *n.m.* kilowatt-hour.

kimono *n.m.* kimono.

kinésithérapeute *n.m.f.* physiotherapist.

kinésithérapie *n.f.* physiotherapy.

kiosque *n.m.* kiosk; newsstand.

kirsch *n.m.* kirsch.

kitchenette *n.f.* kitchenette.

kiwi *n.m.* kiwi.

klaxon *n.m.* horn.

klaxonner *v.i.* to honk.

kleptomane *adj.,n.m.f.* kleptomaniac.

kleptomanie *n.f.* kleptomania.

knock-out, k.o. *n.m.* knockout. *adj.* knocked out.

knout *n.m.* knout.

koala *n.m.* koala, koala bear.

krach *n.m.* financial crash.

kyrielle *n.f.* litany; string, list.

kyste *n.m.* cyst.

kystique *adj.* cystic.

L

L *n.f.* or *n.m.* L the twelfth letter of the alphabet. **l'** contraction of LE or LA.

la *art. f.* the; *pron. f.* her, it. **la voici,** here she is. *Mus.* A. **donner le/la,** to give an A, to set the pitch.

là *adv.* there. **là-bas,** over there. **là-dedans,** in there. **là-dessous,** under there, underneath, beneath that, below. **là-dessus,** thereupon, upon which, then. **là-haut,** above, up there. **de ~ je conclus que,** from that I conclude that. **l'oiseau s'est enfui par ~,** the bird flew that way.

label *n.m.* stamp; seal.

labeur *n.m.* labor, toil; pains, work; cultivation; plowing. **en ~,** under cultivation.

labial, e *adj. n.f.* labial.

labo *n.m.* lab.

laborantin, e *n.m.f.* lab assistant.

laboratoire *n.m.* laboratory.

laborieusement *adv.* laboriously; painfully.

laborieux, euse *adj.* laborious, diligent; hard-working; difficult.

labour *n.m.* tillage, plowing.

labourable *adj.* arable.

labourage *n.m.* tillage, plowing, plow.

labourer *v.t.* and *v.i.* to plow, to till; to plow up; to tear up; to drudge; to toil and moil.

laboureur *n.m.* agricultural laborer; plowman; husbandman.

labrador *n.m.* Labrador.

labyrinthe n.m. labyrinth; maze, entanglement.

lac n.m. lake.

lacet v.t. to tie, to lace.

lacération n.f. laceration.

lacérer v.t. to lacerate, to tear, to maul, to rip up.

lacet n.m. lace; snare; zigzag (of a road).

lâche adj. loose; slack, lax; indolent; faint-hearted, cowardly. **une corde ~,** a slack rope. n.m. coward.

lâchement adv. loosely; weakly; indolently, slothfully; cowardly.

lâcher v.t. to loosen; to slacken, to unloose, to let out; to relax; to release, to let out, to get loose; to slip; to escape; (of a gun) to go off. **~ une corde,** to loosen a rope. **~ pied,** to give way, to lose ground. **~ sa proie,** to let one's prey go. **~ les chiens,** to let the dogs loose. **~ le mot,** to let out the word. **se ~,** v.refl. to slacken, to loosen, to grow loose, to get loose; to give way.

lâcheté n.f. cowardice, cowardliness; faint-heartedness. **la ~ de sa conduite,** his cowardly conduct.

lacis n.m. network.

laconique adj. short, brief, concise.

lacrymal, e adj. lachrymal.

lacrymagène adj. lachrymatory. **gaz-~,** tear-gas.

lactation n.f. lactation.

lacté, e adj. lactescent; milky. **voie ~e,** Milky Way, (galaxy).

lactescence n.f. milkiness.

lactique adj. lactic.

lactose n.f. lactose, sugar of milk.

lacune n.f. lacuna, air cell; hollow cavity, hiatus, gap, blank.

lad n.m. stable boy.

ladite adj. Jur. the aforesaid.

ladre adj. leprous; measly; stingy, avaricious, sordid, mean. n.m. leper, curmudgeon.

lagon n.m. lagoon.

lagune n.f. lagoon; morass, shallow pond.

La Haye n.f. the Hague.

lai, e adj. laical. n.m.pl. laymen. n.m. lay; short poem or song.

laïcité n.f. secularity.

laid, e adj. ugly. **~ comme le péché,** as ugly as sin.

laideur n.f. ugliness; unsightliness. **la ~ d'une action,** the ugliness of an action.

laie n.f. wild sow; forest path; stonecutter's hammer.

lainage n.f. woolen goods, woolen stuffs, woolens.

laine n.f. wool; worsted.

laineux, euse adj. woolly.

laïque adj. laic, laical, lay. n.m. layperson, laic. pl. laity.

laisse n.f. leash. **en ~,** leashed.

laisser v.t. to leave; to depart; to bequeath; to let alone; to give up; to leave off; to omit; to let. **à prendre ou à ~,** take it or leave it. **~ des biens**

à ses enfants, to leave wealth to one's children. **~ quelqu'un tranquille,** to leave a person alone. **laissons cela,** leave that out. **laissez-moi parler,** let me speak. **se ~,** v.refl. to allow, to let oneself. **se ~ aller à ses passions,** to give way to one's passions. **se ~ aller,** to slip; to let oneself go. **cela se laisse manger,** that is eatable.

laisser-aller n.m. freedom, unconstraint, ease.

laisser-faire n.m. laissez-faire, noninterference.

laissez-passer n.m. pass; permit for transit.

lait n.m. milk. **~ de vache,** cow's milk. **petit ~,** whey. **~ de poule,** eggnog.

laitage n.m. dairy, dairy product.

laiteux, euse adj. milky; lacteal; milk-colored.

laiton n.m. brass.

laitue n.f. lettuce.

laïus n.m. Infml. long speech; verbiage; lecture.

lama n.m. llama.

lambeau n.m. rag, tatter; shred; strip; scrap. **en ~x,** in rags, in tatters.

lambiner v.i. to dawdle; to waste time, to loiter.

lambris n.m. paneling, panelwork; wainscot, (of marble) lining; roof, ceiling.

lambrissage n.m. paneling.

lambrisser v.t. to wainscot; to panel; to line.

lame n.f. wainscoting, plate (of metal); strip; blade; wave, surge; wire (of gold or silver). **couteau à deux ~s,** double-bladed knife.

lamé, e adj. worked with (gold or silver) wire.

lamelle n.f. lamella, thin plate.

lamentable adj. lamentable; awful, pitiful.

lamentablement adv. lamentably.

lamentation n.f. lamentation; wailing, moan. **lamenter (se)** v.t. to lament; to bewail; to moan, to bemoan.

laminage n.m. laminating, rolling.

laminer v.t. to laminate; to roll, to roll out.

lampadaire n.m. streetlamp, lamppost, floor lamp.

lampant, e adj. refined (oil).

lampe n.f. lamp. **~ à luile,** oil lamp. **~ de bureau,** desk lamp. **~ de chevet,** bedside lamp. **~ de poche,** flashlight. **~ à souder,** blowtorch.

lampée n.f. gulp.

lampion n.m. Chinese lantern; illumination lamp.

lance n.f. lance; spear; hose; nozzle. **~ d'incendie,** firehose.

lancement n.m. launch, launching.

lancer v.t. to lance, to throw, to dart, to let fly; to fling, to hurl; to launch. **~ un coup de pied,** to kick. **~ des regards,** to cast looks. **~ quelqu'un dans le monde,** to set a person up in the world. **~ un vaisseau,** to launch a ship. **se ~,** v.refl. to dart, to rush, to fly, to spring, to launch. **se ~ dans les affaires,** to launch out into business.

lancette n.f. lancet.

lancinant, e adj. shooting, twinging.

landau n.m. baby carriage.

langage *n.m.* language; speech. ~ **des fleurs,** the language of flowers. ~ **de programmation,** programming language. ~ **interactif,** interactive language.

lange *n.m.* diaper.

langoureusement *adv.* languishingly.

langoureux, euse *adv.* languishingly; languid.

langouste *n.f.* crawfish, crayfish.

langoustine *n.f.* prawn.

langue *n.f.* tongue; language, speech. **avoir la ~ bien pendue,** to have the gift of the gab. **tenir sa ~,** to hold one's tongue. **donner sa ~ au chat,** to give up guessing. **c'est une mauvaise ~,** he or she is a backbiter. ~ **morte,** dead language. ~ **maternalle,** mother tongue. **la ~ des mathématiques,** the language of mathematics. **~-de-chat,** ladyfinger.

langueur *n.f.* languor, languidness; slowness. **un regard plein de ~,** a languishing look.

languir *v.i.* to languish; to decay; to pine away; to droop, to pine, to pine away; to flag; to wither. ~ **d'amour,** to be lovesick. **la conversation languissait,** the conversation flagged.

languissant, e *adj.* languishing, languid; drooping, pining; feeble, weak.

lanière *n.f.* thong, strap; strip; lash.

lanterne *n.f.* lantern, lamppost, ~ **sourde,** Chinese lantern. **il veut faire croire que des vessies sont des ~s,** he wants to make us believe the moon is made of green cheese.

lapalissade *n.f.* truism.

laper *v.i.* to lap.

lapidation *n.f.* stoning, lapidation.

lapin *n.m.* rabbit.

laps *n.m.* lapse. ~ **de temps,** lapse of time.

lapsur *n.m.* slip.

laque *adj.* lacquer, gum lac. *n.f.* lac. *n.m.* lacquered ware, Japan ware; hair spray.

laquelle *pron. f.* who, which, that.

laquer *v.t.* to lacquer.

larbin *n.m. Pej.* servant, maid, flunky, **je ne suis pas ton ~!** I'm not your maid!

larcin *n.m.* larceny, theft, pilfering.

lard *n.m.* bacon, lard. **c'est du ~ ou du cochon?** is it true or not?

larder *v.t.* to lard; to stab; to pierce; to assail.

lardon *n.m.* slice of bacon.

largage *n.m.* letting go.

large *adj.* broad, wide; extensive, ample; lax, loose, large. **une ~ concession,** a great concession. **des idées ~s,** liberal ideas. *adv.* largely; grandly. *n.m.* breadth, width; open sea. **cette étoffe a un mètre de ~,** this fabric is a meter wide. **gagner, prendre le ~,** to clear off; to get to the open sea. **se promener de long en ~,** to walk back and forth.

largement *adv.* largely; liberally, bountifully.

largesse *n.f.* largess, bounty, present, liberality.

largeur *n.f.* breadth, width; broadness, largeness, wideness.

larguer *v.t. Naut.* to loose, to slacken, to slack off,

to ease, to let go, to let fly, to cast off; to let run. ~ **une voile,** to loose a sail.

larme *n.f.* tear. **avoir les ~s aux yeux,** to have tears in one's eyes. **verser, répandre des ~s,** to shed tears. **pleurer à chaudes ~s,** to shed bitter tears. **donnez-moi une ~ de vin,** give me a drop of wine.

larmoiement *n.m.* weeping.

larmoyant, e *adj.* weeping, in tears.

larmoyer *v.i.* to sweep, to shed tears, to cry.

laron, onnesse *n.m.f.* thief. **ils s'entendent comme ~s en foire,** they are thick as thieves. **l'occasion fait le ~,** opportunity makes the thief.

larve *n.f.* larva.

laryngite *n.f.* laringitis.

laryngologiste *n.m.f.* laryngologist, throat specialist.

laryngotomie *n.f.* laryngotomy.

larynx *n.m.* larynx.

las, lasse *adj.* tired, weary; disgusted.

lasagne *n.f.pl.* lasagna.

lascar *n.m* streetwise person.

laser *n.m.* laser. ~ **rayon,** laser beam.

lassant, e *adj.* tiring, fatiguing, wearing; wearisome, tedious, tiresome.

laser *v.t.* to tire, to weary, to fatigue. **se ~,** *v.refl.* to get tired, to get weary, to grow weary.

lassitude *n.f.* lassitude, weariness.

lasso *n.m.* lasso.

latent, e *adj.* latent, hid, concealed, secret, not seen. **chaleur ~e,** latent heat.

latéral, e *adj.* lateral, side.

latéralement *adv.* laterally, sideways.

latex *n.m.* latex.

latin, e *adj.* Latin. **il en perd son ~,** he is getting confused.

latitude *n.f.* latitude; extent; scope.

latrines *n.f.pl.* latrines, privies.

latte *n.f.* lath, board.

latter *v.t.* to lath.

laudatif, ive *adj.* laudatory.

lauréat *adj. m.* laureate. *n.m.* laureate, prizewinner.

laurier *n.m.* laurel, bay leaves; bay, baytree. **se reposer sur ses ~s,** to rest on one's laurels.

lavable *adj.* washable.

lavabo *n.m.* bathroom sink; washroom; lavatory.

lavage *n.m.* washing.

lavande *n.f.* lavender.

lave *n.f.* lava. ~**glace** *n.m.* windshield washer. ~ **vaisselle** *n.m.* dishwasher.

lavé, e *adj.* washed, (of colors) faint, pale; light.

lavement *n.m.* washing; injection.

laver *v.t.* to wash, to clean, to cleanse; to wash off, out, away, up; to bathe. ~ **la vaisselle,** to wash the dishes. ~ **son linge sale en famille,** to wash one's dirty laundry in public. **se ~,** *v.refl.* to wash oneself.

laverie *n.f.* laundromat.

lavette *n.f.* dishmop; *Infml.* puny.

lavis *n.m.* wash, wash drawing.

laxatif, ive *adj.* and *n.m.* laxative.

laxisme *n.m.* laxity.

layette *n.f.* baby clothes, layette.

le *art.m.s.* the. *pron.m.s.* him, it; so. **je le vois,** I see him or it. **le voici,** here he is.

lé *n.m.* breadth, width (of fabric). **un demi-lé,** a half breadth.

leader *n.m.* leader.

leadership *n.m.* leadership.

lèche *n.f. Vulg.* **~-cul,** bootlicker, **faire de la ~,** to suck up. **~-vitrine,** window-shopping.

lécher *v.t.* to lick; to lick up; to flatter, to fawn. **se ~,** *v.refl.* to lick oneself.

leçon *n.f.* lesson; lecture, reading. **donner des ~s d'anglais,** to give English lessons. **~ particulière,** private lesson, tutoring.

lecteur, trice *n.m.f.* reader, (church) lecteur; lecturer.

lecture *n.f.* reading. **faire la ~ d'un contrat,** to read a contract.

ledit *n.m.* the aforesaid.

légal, e *adj.* legal; lawful.

légalement *adv.* legally, lawfully.

légalisation *n.f.* authentication, legalization.

légaliser *v.t.* to legalize.

légalité *n.f.* legality, lawfulness. **sortir de la ~,** to go beyond the law.

légat *n.m.* legate.

légataire *n.m.f.* legatee. **~ universel,** sole legatee.

légation *n.f.* legation.

légendaire *adj.* legendary.

légende *n.f.* legend; myth.

léger, ère, *adj.* light; slight; trilling; gently, soft; slender; nimble, agile, active, swift; easy; airy, unsubstantial; fickle; giddy; inconsiderate, thoughtless, frivolous. **au coeur ~,** lighthearted. **un ~ soupçon,** a slight doubt. **infanterie légère,** light infantry. **une tête légère,** a thoughtless person. **des paroles légères,** inconsiderate words.

légèrement *adv.* lightly; nimbly; slightly, thoughtlessly, heedlessly.

légèreté *n.f.* lightness; nimbleness; swiftness; ease, facility; giddiness, frivolity; carelessness. **la ~ de l'air,** the lightness of the air. **la ~ de sa conduite,** his thoughtless conduct.

légiférer *v.i.* to legislate.

légion *n.f.* legion.

légionnaire *n.m.* legionary; legionnaire.

législateur, trice *n.m.* and *adj.* legislator, law-maker.

législatif, ive *adj.* legislative.

législation *n.f.* legislation.

législature *n.f.* legislature.

légiste *n.m.* **médecin ~,** medical expert, pathologist.

légitimation *n.f.* legitimation; recognition (of deputies).

légitime *adj.* legitimate; lawful, legal. **~ défense,** self-defense.

légitimement *adv.* legitimately; lawfully, rightfully, justly; justifiably.

légitimer *v.t.* to legitimate, to legitimize; to recognize (powers, titles); to justify, to warrant.

légitimité *n.f.* legitimacy, lawfulness, legality.

legs *n.m.* legacy, bequest.

léguer *v.t.* to bequeath; to hand down to posterity; to leave.

légume *n.m.* vegetable. **grosse ~,** big shot.

légumineux, euse *adj.* leguminous.

leitmotiv *n.m.* leitmotif.

lendemain *n.m* following day, next day, day after.

lénifier *v.t.* to soothe, to calm, to soften.

lent, e *adj.* slow.

lente *n.f.* nit, the egg of a louse.

lentement *adv.* slowly.

lenteur *n.f.* slowness; tardiness; sluggishness; dullness.

lentille *n.f.* lentil; lens. **~ de contact,** contact lense, bob (of a pendulum).

léopard *n.m.* leopard.

lépidoptère *n.m.* lepidopter. *adj.* lepidopteral.

lèpre *n.f.* leprosy.

lépreux, euse *adj.* leprous. *n.m.f.* leper.

lequel *pron.m.* who, that; whom, that, which, that. **laquelle me donnes-tu?** which one will you give me? **te souviens-tu du sujet duquel je t'ai parlé?** do you remember the matter I spoke to you about?

lesbienne *adj.* lesbian.

lèse *adj.f.* offended. **~ majesté,** high treason.

léser *v.t.* to injure, to hurt, to wrong.

lésiner *v.i.* to be stingy, to haggle.

lésinerie *n.f.* stinginess, meanness.

lésion *n.f.* injury, hurt, wrong; damage; lesion.

lessive *n.f.* wash. **faire la ~,** to wash.

lessivé, e *adj. Infml.* washed out, exhausted, dead beat.

lessiver *v.t.* to wash.

lest *n.m.* ballast.

leste *adj.* light; nimble, brisk, active; lively, smart; indecorous; free.

lestement *adv.* lightly, nimbly, briskly, actively, smartly; unhesitatingly; freely; indecorously.

lester *v.t.* to ballast. **se ~,** *v.refl.* to take in ballast; to stuff oneself.

léthargie *n.f.* lethargy.

léthargique *adj.* lethargic.

lettre *n.f.* letter; type, character. **~ majuscule,** capital letter. **à la ~, au pied de la ~,** to the letter, literally. **~ de change,** bill of exchange. **~ de crédit,** letter of credit. **~ chargée,** registered letter.

lettré, e *adj.* literate.

leu *n.m.* **à la queue ~,** in Indian file.

leucémie *n.f.* leukemia.

leur *pron. m.f. pl.* to them, them. **je leur ai dit,** I told them. *adj. poss. m.f.* their. **~ mère,** their mother. **leurs jardins,** their gardens. *pron. poss. m.* theirs. **mes amis sont aussi les leurs,** my friends are also theirs. *n.m.* **ils y ont mis du ~,** they did their share, they helped.

leurre *n.m.* lure, decoy, bait; delusion, deception. **cela lui sert de ~ pour les attirer,** he entices them by this allurement.

leurrer *v.t.* to lure, to entice, to allure, to decoy. **se ~,** *v.refl.* to delude oneself.

levage *n.m.* raising.

levain *n.m.* leaven; yeast. **sans ~,** unleavened.

levant *adj.m.* and *n.m.* rising. east; Levant. **du ~ au couchant,** from east to west.

levé, e *p.p.* raised, lifted, uplifted, erect, up (out of bed). *n.m.* Mus. rise (of the foot or hand).

levée *n.f.* raising; pick up, collection (of letters). **faire des ~s de troupes,** to raise troops.

lever *v.t.* to raise, to lift, to lift up, to uplift; to heave up, to hold up, to uphold; to haul up, to weigh (anchor); to levy, to collect, to raise (taxes). **~ les mains au ciel,** to raise one's hands toward Heaven. **~ les yeux,** to look up. **~ le pied,** to lift one's foot. **~ le siège,** to raise the siege. **~ le camp,** to break up camp. **~ un plan,** to draw a plan. **~ les fruits d'une terre,** to gather the fruit of an estate. *v.i.* to rise; to come up, to grow. **se ~,** *v.refl.* to rise; to be raised, to move upward, to arise; to get up; to stand up; to spring; to clear up (of the weather). **se ~ de table,** to leave the table. **se ~ de bon matin,** to get up early. **le vent se lève,** the wind is rising. *n.m.* rising; getting up. **le ~ du rideau,** the rise of the curtain. **le ~ du soleil,** sunrise.

levier *n.m.* lever. **~ de fer,** crowbar. **~ de vitesse,** gearshift.

lévitation *n.f.* levitation.

lévite *n.m.* levite.

levraut *n.m.* leveret.

lèvre *n.f.* lip. **rire du bout des ~s,** to give a faint laugh. **le rouge à lèvres,** lipstick.

levrette *n.f.* greyhound bitch.

lèvrier *n.m.* greyhound.

levure *n.f.* yeast, baking powder.

lexical *adj.* lexical.

lexique *n.m.* lexicon, small dictionary, vocabulary.

lézard *n.m.* lizard.

lézarde *n.f.* crevice, crack (in a wall).

lézardé, e *adj.* full of cracks, chinky.

lézarder *v.t.* to crack, to chink, to rend. **se ~,** *v.refl.* to crack, to chink, to crevice.

liaison *n.f.* joining, junction, joint, upstroke (in writing); Mus. slur; tie, bond. *(Ling.)* sounding of final consonant before initial vowel sound. **~ amoureuse,** (love) affair. **~ d'affaires,** business connection.

liane *n.f.* liana; creeper.

liant, e *adj.* supple; flexible; compliant; courteous. *n.m.* flexibility; affability.

liasse *n.f.* file, bundle (of papers).

liban *n.m.* Lebanon.

libanais *adj.* Lebanese.

libeller *v.t.* to word, to draw up (a request, etc.). Fin. to specify the object of.

libellule *n.f.* libellula, dragonfly.

libérable *adj.* that may be liberated, discharged.

libéral, e *adj.* liberal; generous, broadminded. **il exerce une profession libérale,** he's a professional man.

libéralement *adv.* liberally; freely; generously.

libéralisme *n.m.* liberalism.

libéralité *n.f.* liberality; generosity; donation.

libérateur, trice *n.m.f.* liberator. *adj.* liberating, delivering.

libération *n.f.* liberation; deliverance; discharge, release.

libérer *v.t.* to liberate, to deliver, to free; to discharge. **se ~,** *v.refl.* to free oneself, to be liberated, to be discharged (from), to get rid (of).

liberté *n.f.* liberty; freedom; free will. **~ politique,** political liberty. **prendre trop de libertés,** to take too many liberties. **~ sous caution,** release on bail. **~ de parole,** freedom of speech.

libertin, e *adj.* libertine, licentious. *n.m.f.* libertine.

libertinage *n.m.* libertism, debauchery, licentiousness; waywardness, wildness.

libidineux, euse *adj.* libidinous.

libraire *n.m.* bookseller. **~ éditeur,** bookseller and publisher.

librairie *n.f.* book shop; bookstore. **~-papeterie,** stationery store.

libre *adj.* free, at liberty, exempt; bold; unrestrained; licentious. **presse ~,** free press. **~ arbitre,** free will. **il n'est pas ~,** he is busy. **elle est ~,** she is single.

libre-échange *n.m.* free trade.

libre-échangiste *n.m.* free trader.

librement *adv.* freely, without restraint; boldly.

libre-service *n.m.* self-service. **restaurant ~,** self-service restaurant. **station-essence ~,** gas station.

librettiste *n.m.* librettiste.

license *n.f.* license; permit; Univ. bachelor's degree.

licencié, e *p.p.* disbanded. *n.m.f.* **~ès,** Bachelor of. *adj.* laid off.

licenciement *n.m.* disbanding; redundancy; lay off.

licencier *v.t.* Mil. to disband (troops); to make redundant; to lay off.

lichette *n.f.* Infml. a tiny bit, a drop of.

licite *adj.* lawful, legal.

licitement *adv.* licitly, lawfully.

licorne *n.f.* unicorn.

lie *n.f.* sediment, dregs; grounds (of beer).

lié, e *p.p.* bound, fastened, tied; united, connected, joined.

liège *n.m.* Bot. cork oak. *n.f.* Liege.

liègeois, e *adj.* of Liege. **chocolat ~,** chocolate ice cream topped with whipped cream. *n.m.* inhabitant of Liege.

lien *n.m.* bond, chains; tie, link. ~ **conjugal,** marriage bond.

lier *v.t.* to bind; to tie, to tie up, to tie down; to bind fast, to connect, to link. ~ **les mains à quelqu'un,** to bind a person's hands. **il est fou à ~,** he is completely crazy. ~ **conversation avec quelqu'un,** to strike a conversation with a person. **se ~,** *v.refl.* to bind oneself; to be bound, to be fastened, to be tied; (of a sauce) to thicken; combine. **ils se sont liés d'amitié,** they have become closely acquainted.

lièrre *n.m.* ivy.

liesse *n.f.* mirth, jollity.

lieu *n.m.* place, space, spot, ground; site; lieu, room; cause; *pl.* premises. ~ **humide,** damp place. **un ~ charmant,** a charming place. **être sur le ~x du crime/d'un accident,** to be at the scene of the crime/of an accident. **en tout ~,** everywhere. **état des ~x,** inventory of fixtures. **en premier ~,** in the first place. **donner ~ à,** to give rise to. **les ~x d'aisances,** privy, lavatory. **au ~ de,** instead of. **au ~ que,** whereas.

lieue *n.f.* league.

lieutenant *n.m.* lieutenant.

lièvre *n.m.* hare. **il ne faut pas courir deux ~s à la fois,** one thing at a time.

lifting *n.m.* face lift.

ligament *n.m.* ligament.

ligamenteux, euse *adj.* ligamentous.

ligature *n.f.* ligature.

lignage *n.m.* lineage.

lignager *n.m.* person of the same lineage.

ligne *n.f.* line; rank; path of duty; equator, equinoctial circle. **décrire une ~,** to describe a line. **hors ~,** beyond comparison. ~ **de bataille,** line of battle. **pêcher à la ~,** to angle fish. **garder la ~,** to keep one's figure.

lignée *n.f.* lineage, line, progeny, issue, offspring.

lignite *n.m.* lignite.

ligoter *v.t.* to tie up, to bind hand and foot.

ligue *n.f.* league, confederacy, confederation.

lilas *n.m.* lilac.

limace *n.f.* slug, naked snail.

limande *n.f.* dab.

limbe *n.m.* limb, boarder, edge of a leaf.

limbes *n.m.pl.* limbo, limbus.

lime *n.f.* file, sweet lemon. ~ **douce,** smooth file. ~ **à ongles,** nail file.

limer *v.t.* to file; to smooth, to polish, to finish off; to drain (a marsh).

limier *n.m.* bloodhound. *Infml.* sleuth, dick, detective.

limitatif, ive *adj.* limiting.

limitation *n.f.* limitation.

limitativement *adv.* limitedly.

limite *n.f.* limit; boundary, landmark.

limiter *v.t.* to limit, to bound, to set bounds to; to confine. **se ~,** to limit oneself, to restrict oneself.

limitrophe *adj.* bordering (upon), adjacent (to); frontier.

limogeage *n.m.* dismissal, lay off, shelving.

limoger *v.t.* to dismiss, to lay off, to shelve.

limon *n.m.* mud, slime, ooze; dust, clay, earth.

limonade *n.f.* (fizzy) lemonade.

limoneux, euse *adj.* muddy, shiny, oozy, limose.

limousine *n.f.* limousine.

limpide *adj.* limpid, clear, transparent, pure.

limpidité *n.f.* limpidity, clearness; transparency.

lin *n.m.* flax. **graine de ~,** flaxseed, linseed. **tissu de ~,** linen.

linceul *n.m.* shroud.

linéaire *adj.* linear; lineal.

linéal, e *adj.* lineal.

linge *n.m.* linen; cloth. ~ **fin,** fine linen. ~ **de table,** table linen.

lingère *n.f.* linen maid; seamstress; linen cupboard.

lingerie *n.f.* linen; laundry room, mud room.

lingot *n.m.* ingot. **or, argent en ~,** bullion.

lingual, e *adj.* lingual.

linguiste *n.m.* linguist.

linguistique *n.f.* linguistics. *adj.* linguistic.

linoléum *n.m.* linoleum.

linot *n.m.* **linotte** *n.f.* linnet. **c'est une tête de linotte,** he is a hare-brain.

lion *n.m.* lion, Leo. **part du ~,** lion's share. **Richard Coeur-de-~,** Richard the lion-hearted.

lionceau *n.m.* lion cub.

lionne *n.f.* lioness.

lipide *n.m.* lipid.

liquéfaction *n.f.* liquefaction.

liquéfiable *adj.* liquefiable.

liquéfier *v.t.* to liquefy; to melt. **se ~,** *v.refl.* to liquefy, to be melted.

liqueur *n.f.* liquor; liquid.

liquidateur *adj.m.* liquidating. *n.m.* liquidator.

liquidation *n.f.* liquidation; settlement; winding up; selling off; clearance.

liquide *adj.* liquid; watery; flowing. **du ~,** liquid assets, available cash. *n.m.* liquid; fluid.

liquider *v.t.* to liquidate; to wind up; to settle, to pay off. ~ **des marchandises,** to sell off. **se ~,** *v.refl.* to pay off, to clear off one's debts; to settle.

liquidité *n.f.* liquidity. ~**s,** liquid assets.

liquoreux, euse *adj.* sweet, luscious.

lire *v.t.* to read. **savoir ~,** to know how to read. **dans l'attente de vous ~,** looking forward to hearing from you.

lis *n.m.* lily. **fleurs de ~,** fleur-de-lis.

liseré *n.m.* border (of ribbons); stripe.

lisibilité *n.f.* legibility.

lisible *adj.* legible; readable.

lisiblement *adv.* legibly.

lisière *n.f.* selvage; border, skirt, outskirt, extremity, verge. **la ~ d'un bois,** the outskirts of a wood.

lissage *n.m.* smoothing, glossing.

lisse *adj.* smooth, soft, sleek, glossy. *n.f.* handrail; warp (of tapestry); rail, riband, ribband.

lisser *v.t.* to smooth, to gloss, to polish, to glaze.

liste *n.f.* list; roll, catalog. **~ du jury,** panel of the jury.

lit *n.m.* bed, bedstead; channel, way; stratum, layer. **~ de mort,** death bed. **garder le ~,** to stay in bed. **~ de plume,** feather bed. **des enfants du premier ~,** children from the first marriage.

litanie *n.f.* litany.

literie *n.f.* bedding.

lithographe *n.m.* lithographer.

lithographie *n.f.* lithography.

lithographier *v.t.* to lithograph.

lithographique *adj.* lithographic.

litière *n.f.* litter; stable litter.

litigant, e *adj.* contending in a lawsuit.

litige *n.m.* litigation.

litigieux, euse *adj.* litigious; contested.

litre *n.m.* liter.

littéraire *adj. n.f.* literary.

littérairement *adv.* literally, in a literary point of view.

littéral, e *adj.* literal.

littéralement *adv.* literally.

littérature *n.f.* literature.

littoral, e *adj.* littoral, coastal. *n.m.* seashore, coastline.

liturgie *n.f.* liturgy.

liturgique *adj.* liturgical.

liturgiste *n.m.* liturgist.

livide *adj.* livid.

lividité *n.f.* lividness, lividity.

living (~room) *n.m.* living room.

livrable *adj.* deliverable; ready.

livraison *n.f.* delivery. **~ à domicile,** we deliver. **~ gratuite,** free delivery.

livre *n.m.* book. **~s classiques,** classical books, schoolbooks. **~ de compte,** account book. **~ de vaisse,** cash book. **grand-~,** ledger. **tenir les ~s en partie double,** to keep the books by double entry. **~ de bord,** log book. **~ de cuisine,** cook book, cookery book.

livre *n.f.* pound (in weight); pound (sterling).

livrée *n.f.* livery; livery servants.

livrer *v.t.* to deliver; to give over; to hand over; to surrender. **~ de la marchandise,** to deliver goods. **se ~,** *v.refl.* to deliver oneself up, to indulge in; to give way to; to confide. **se ~ à la douleur, au désespoir,** to yield, to give way to grief, to despair. **se ~ à l'étude,** to apply oneself to study.

livret *n.m.* small book, booklet. **~ de caisse d'épargne,** depositor's book.

livreur, euse *n.m.f.* delivery boy/girl.

lobby *n.m.* lobby.

lobe *n.m.* lobe.

lobotomie *n.f.* lobotomy.

local, e *adj.* local. *n.m.* premises; house.

localement *adv.* locally.

localisation *n.f.* localization.

localiser *v.t.* to localize, to locate. **se ~,** *v.refl.* to be localized, to be located.

localité *n.f.* locality.

locataire *n.m.f.* tenant; lodger.

locatif, ive *adj.* belonging to, incumbent on the tenant; renting, in tent. **valeur locative,** renting value.

location *n.f.* renting, rental, letting, location. **bureau de ~,** box office. **location-vente** *n.f.* rent with option to buy.

loch *n.m.* log. **livre de ~,** log.

locomoteur, trice *adj.* locomotive, locomotor.

locomotion *n.f.* locomotion.

locomotive *n.f.* locomotive, engine.

locomotrice *n.f.* electric engine, motor unit.

locuste *n.f.* locust.

locuteur, trice *n.m.f.* speaker.

locution *n.f.* locution, phrase.

logarithme *n.m.* logarithm.

logarithmique *adj.* logarithmic, logarithmical.

loge *n.f.* lodge; hut; booth (at fairs); box. **être aux premières loges,** to have the best seat(s).

logeable *adj.* habitable, roomy.

logement *n.m.* housing, lodging, lodgings; apartment, quarters.

loger *v.i.* to lodge; to stay, to give a lodging; to house; to put up (at). **se ~,** *v.refl.* to lodge, to take a lodging, to take lodgings; to fit.

logeur, euse *n.m.f.* landlord.

loggia *n.f.* loggia.

logiciel *n.m.* software.

logicien, ienne *n.m.f.* logician.

logique *n.f.* logic. *adj.* logical.

logiquement *adv.* logically.

logis *n.m.* house, habitation, home. **rentrer au ~,** to return home. **corps de ~,** main building.

logistique *adj.* logistic *n.f.* logistics.

loi *n.f.* law; rule, power, authority, dominion, sway. **faire des ~s,** to enact, to make laws. **~ écrite,** written law, statute law. **la ~ du plus fort,** might is right.

loin *adv.* far, afar, far off, far away, distant, remote. **~ de sa patrie,** far from one's country. **~ des yeux ~ du coeur,** out of sight out of mind. **s'en aller au ~,** to go far off. **de ~,** from far, afar. **du plus ~ qu'elle s'en souvienne,** as far as she can remember.

lointain, e *adj.* far, remote, distant. *n.m.* distance.

loir *n.m.* dormouse. **dormir comme un ~,** to sleep like a log.

loisir *n.m.* leisure; leisure time; spare time, at leisure.

lombaire *adj.* lumbar.

lombric *n.m.* earthworm.

Londres *n.f.* London.

long, longue *adj.* long; slow; tedious. **une longue vie,** a long life. **un ~ discours,** a long speech. *n.m.* length. **cette maison a douze mètres de ~,** that house is twelve meters long. **de ~ en large,** backward and forward, up and

down. **le ~ de**, along. **tout le ~ de la semaine**,
all through the week. **tout de son ~**, at his full
length. **en dir ~, bien ~**, to have a great deal to
say. *n.f.* long syllable. **à la ~**, in the long run.

longanimité *n.f.* forbearance, long-suffering.

longe *n.f.* tether; longe, loin (meat).

longer *v.t.* to go along; to coast along; to run
along.

longévité *n.f.* longevity.

longitude *n.f.* longitude.

longitudinal, e *adj.* longitudinal.

longitudinalement *adv.* longitudinally.

longtemps *adv.* a long time, a great while, long.
aussi ~ qu'il le faudra, as long as necessary.

longuement *adv.* long, a long time; lengthily; at
length.

longuet, ette *adj.* longish, rather long.

longueur *n.f.* length; slowness; prolixity. **en ~**,
lengthwise; to a great length; slowly. **traîner
une affaire en ~**, to get on very slowly with a
thing.

longue-vue *n.f.* spy glass, small telescope.

looping *n.m.* loop. **faire des ~s**, to loop the
loop.

lopin *n.m.* plot, bit, morsel, piece, snack; portion,
share, patch.

loquace *adj.* loquacious, talkative.

loquacité *n.f.* loquaciousness, loquacity,
talkativeness.

loque *n.f.* rag, tatter.

loquet *n.m.* latch (of a door).

lorgner *v.i.* to eye, to ogle; to quiz.

lorgnette *n.f.* spy glass, opera glass.

lorgnon *n.m.* pince-nez.

loriot *n.m.* golden oriole.

lors *adv.* then, that time, at that time. **dès ~**,
since then, from that time.

lorsque *conj.* when.

losange *n.m.* lozenge. **en ~**, diamond-shaped.

lot *n.m.* lot; share; parcel, portion; prize (at
lottery).

loterie *n.f.* lottery; raffle.

loti, e *p.p.* **bien ~**, well off. **mal ~**, badly off.

lotion *n.f.* lotion.

lotir *v.t.* to lot, to allot, to assign; to portion, to
share, to sort.

lotissement *n.m.* housing development; sale (by
lots).

loto *n.m.* loto (game).

lotte *n.f.* lote, eelpout.

lotus *n.m.* lotus.

louable *adj.* laudable, commendable, praiseworthy; rentable.

louablement *adv.* laudably, commendably,
praiseworthily.

louange *n.f.* praise; commendation.

louanger *v.t.* to praise; to commend, to laud. **se
~**, *v.refl.* to praise each other.

louangeur, euse *n.m.f.* praiser. *adj.* laudatory.

loubard(e) *n.m.f.* hoodlum.

louche *adj.* suspicious, shady, fishy; squinting;
squint-eyed. *n.m.* ambiguity; something suspicious. *n.f.* (soup) ladle.

loucher *v.i.* to squint.

louer *v.t.* to hire; to rent; to praise, to commend,
to laud. **~ une maison à quelqu'un**, to rent a
house. **je viens de ~ un appartement,** I have
just rented an apartment. **~ une voiture,** to
rent a car. **se ~**, *v.refl.* (of things) to be hired; to
praise oneself, each other; to be pleased with.

loufoque *adj.* goofy, crazy; *n.m.f.* screwball,
crackpot.

loulou *n.m.* spitz. **~ de Poméranie,**
Pomeranian.

loulou *n.m.f.* darling. *n.m. Infml.* fishy person,
hooligan.

loup *n.m.* wolf; black velvet mask. **il est connu
comme le ~ blanc,** everybody knows him. **les
~s ne se mangent pas entre eux,** dog doesn't
eat dog, there's honor among thieves. **quand on
parle du ~, on en voit la queue,** speak of the
devil. **mon petit ~,** honey, sweetheart.

loup-cervier *n.m.* lynx.

loupe *n.f.* magnifying glass, lens.

louper *v.t. Infml.* to miss; to mess up, to make a
mess of.

loup-garou *n.m.* werewolf.

lourd, e *adj.* heavy, weighty, ponderous; dull,
sluggish, indolent, drowsy; clumsy, heavy-
handed. **une ~e tâche,** a heavy task. **le temps
est ~,** the weather is sultry.

lourdaud, e *n.m.f* clumsy, blockhead, dunce,
dolt, dullard.

lourdement *adv.* heavily; awkwardly, clumsily;
grossly.

lourdeur *n.f.* heaviness; sluggishness; clumsiness.

loustic *n.m.* joker, rascal.

loutre *n.f.* otter; otterskin.

louve *n.f.* she-wolf.

louveteau *n.m.* young wolf, wolf's cub.

louvoyer *v.i. Naut.* to tack, to tack about; to beat,
to ply to windward; *Fig.* to be evasive, to beat
around the bush.

lover *v.t.* to coil.

loyal, e *adj.* honest; true, faithful; loyal.

loyalement *adv.* honestly, uprightly, fairly;
faithfully.

loyauté *n.f.* honesty, probity, integrity, fairness,
loyalty.

loyer *n.m.* rent.

lubie *n.f.* whim, caprice, fancy.

lubricité *n.f.* lechery, lasciviousness, lewdness,
lust.

lubrifier *v.t.* to lubricate.

lubrique *adj.* lecherous, lewd, lubric, wanton.

lucarne *n.f.* dormer window, garret window.

lucide *adj.* lucid; clear; sane.

lucidement *adv.* lucidly; clearly.

lucidité *n.f.* lucidness, clearness.

luciole *n.f.* firefly.

lucratif, ive *adj.* lucrative, profitable, gainful.

lucre *n.m.* gain, profit.

lueur *n.f.* glimpse, glimmering; gleam, glimmer, light. **une ~ blafarde,** a dim light.

luge *n.f.* sledge, sled, toboggan.

lugubre *adj.* lugubrious, mournful, sorrowful, dismal, doleful, melancholy.

lugubrement *adj.* lugubriously, dismally, dolefully.

lui *pers. pron. m.* he, him; it; to him, to her, to it. **c'est de lui que je parle,** I'm talking about him. **je lui ai fait peur,** I scared him/her.

lui-même *pron. m.* himself.

luire *v.i.* to shine; to gleam; to glitter.

luisant, e *adj.* shining; glittering; glossy. *n.m.* gloss.

lumbago *n.m.* lumbago.

lumière *n.f.* light; enlightenment, knowledge, luminary. **mettre une vérité en ~,** to illustrate a truth. **éteindre une ~,** to put out a light, to turn off a light, to switch off a light.

luminaire *n.m.* lights, lighting.

lumineux, euse *adj.* luminous.

luminosité *n.f.* radiance, brightness, luminosity.

lunaire *adj.* lunar, lunary. *n.f.* moonwort.

lunatique *adj.* whimsical, moody.

lunch, luncheon *n.m.* lunch, luncheon.

lundi *n.m.* Monday.

lune *n.f.* moon. **pleine ~,** full moon. **nouvelle ~,** new moon. **~ de miel,** honeymoon. *Infml.* buttocks.

luné, e *adj.* **être bien/mal,** to be in a good/bad mood.

lunetier *n.m.* optical-lens maker.

lunette *n.f.* telescope; *pl.* glasses. **porter des ~s,** to wear glasses.

lupanar *n.m.* brothel.

lupin *n.m.* lupine.

lupus *n.m.* lupus.

lurette *n.f.* **il y a belle lurette qu'on ne s'est vu,** we haven't seen each other for a long time.

luron *n.m.* jolly person.

lustre *n.m.* luster; gloss; chandelier.

lustré, e *p.p.* having a lustre; glossy.

lustrer *v.t.* to give a luster to, to give a gloss to, to shine, to glaze.

luthérien, enne *adj.* Lutheran.

luthier *n.m.* musical instrument maker.

lutin *n.m.* goblin, hobgoblin, elf, spirit, sprite.

lutrin *n.m.* lettern, lectern, reading stand, music stand. **chanter au ~,** to sing at the choir stall.

lutte *n.f.* wrestling, struggle; strife, contest, fight. **~ contre la faim,** fight against hunger.

lutter *v.i.* to wrestle; to strive; to fight; to struggle, to contend. **~ contre la tempête,** to strive against the storm.

lutteur *n.m.* wrestler; fighter.

luxation *n.f.* luxation; dislocation.

luxe *n.f.* luxury; sumptuousness; luxuriance; profusion.

Luxembourg *n.m.* Luxembourg.

luxer *v.t.* to dislocate, to put out of joint.

luxueusement *adv.* luxuriously, sumptuously.

luxueux, euse *adj.* luxurious; sumptuous; rich.

luxure *n.f.* lust, lewdness, lechery.

luxuriance *n.f.* luxuriance, luxuriancy, exuberance.

luxuriant, e *adj.* luxuriant, exuberant.

luxurieusement *adv.* lustfully, lewdly.

luxurieux, euse *adj.* lustful, lewd, lecherous.

luzerne *n.f.* lucern, alfalfa.

lycée *n.m.* high school.

lycéen, ne *n.m.f.* high school student.

lynchage *n.m.* lynching.

lyncher *v.t.* to lynch.

lynx *n.m.* lynx.

lyre *n.f.* lyre, dulcimer; *Fig.* poetry; *Astron.* Lyra; lyre bird.

lyrique *adj.* lyric, lyrical.

lyrisme *n.m.* lyricism; enthusiasm.

M

m *n.f.* or *m.* M. m; the thirteenth letter of the alphabet .

M. monsieur.

m' contraction of **me.**

ma *adj. poss. fs.* my.

maboul, e *adj.* crazy, nuts.

macabre *adj.* ghastly, gruesome. **danse ~,** dance of death.

macadam *n.m.* macadam, (macadamized) road.

macadamiser *v.t.* to macadamize.

macaque macaque.

macareux *n.m.* puffin.

macaron *n.m.* macaroon.

macaroni *n.m.* macaroni.

macchabée *n.m. Infml.* corpse, stiff.

macédoine *n.f.* medley, hodgepodge; miscellany. **~ de légumes,** mixed vegetables.

macération *n.f.* maceration; *Fig.* mortification; pickling; soaking.

macérer *v.t.* to macerate; to pickle. **se ~,** *v.refl.* to be macerated; to mortify oneself.

mâche *n.f.* corn salad, lamb's lettuce.

mâcher *v.t.* to chew, to masticate; to champ. **~ de la besogne,** to cut out work (for a person).

machette *n.f.* machete.

machiavélique *adj.* Machiavellian.

machiavélisme *n.m.* Machiavellism.

machin, e *n.m.f. Infml.* thing, thingamajig. **c'est quoi ce ~ là?** what's this thing? **hé! ~!** hey! you!

machinal, e *adj.* mechanical, automatic, unconscious.

machinalement *adv.* mechanically, automatically, unconsciously.

machination *n.f.* machination; plot, plotting.

machine *n.f.* machine; engine; machinery; intrigue, plot. **~ électrique,** electrical machine.

~ à vapeur, steam engine. **~ à coudre,** sewing machine. **~ à laver,** washing machine. **langage machine,** machine language.

machiner *v.t.* to scheme, to plot, to plan, to contrive.

machinerie *n.f.* machinery, machine room, engine room; plant. **machinisme** *n.m.* mechanization.

machiniste *n.m.* machinist, stagehand.

mâchoire *n.f.* jaw, jawbone.

mâchonner *v.t.* to mumble; to munch.

mâchouiller *v.t. Infml.* to chew, to munch.

mâchurer *v.t.* to soil, to dirty, to smudge.

maçon *n.m.* mason; builder; bricklayer.

maçonnage *n.m.* mason's work, masonry.

maçonner *v.t.* to build (with stone, etc.); to wall up, to block up (a door).

maçonnerie *n.f.* masonry, mason's work.

maçonnique *adj.* masonic.

maculer *v.t.* to stain, to blur.

madame *n.f.* madam, *pl.* **mesdames.** *Infml.* ma'am; (before the name) Mrs. **je vous demande pardon ~,** I beg your pardon, madam. **Mme. D,** Mrs. D. **faire la ~,** to play the grand lady. **comment va madame votre mère?** how is your mother?

mademoiselle *n.f., pl.* **mesdemoiselles,** miss. **Mlle X,** Miss X; young lady, young girl.

Madère *n.f.* Madeira. *n.m.* madeira, Madeira wine.

madone *n.f.* madonna.

Madras *n.m.* Madras. *n.m.* scarf; madras (cotton).

maestro *n.m. Mus.* maestro.

maf(f)ia *n.f.* mafia; gang.

magasin *n.m.* shop; store; warehouse; magazine (of rifle). **~ d'armes,** armory. **grand ~,** department store. **marchandises en ~,** stock. **Londres, le ~ du monde,** London, the emporium of the world. **courir les ~s,** to shop, to go shopping.

magasinage *n.m.* storage; warehousing.

magazine *n.m.* magazine. *Infml.* mag.

mage *n.m.* magus. **les Rois ~s,** the magi, the Wise Men.

magicien, enne *n.m. f.* magician.

magie *n.f.* magic. **~ noire,** black magic.

magique *adj.* magic, magical.

magistral, e *adj.* magistral; principal; authoritative; colossal.

magistralement *adv.* magisterially, authoritatively; thoroughly.

magistrat *n.m.* magistrate.

magistrature *n.f.* magistracy. **~ assise,** the judges, the Bench. **~ debout,** body of public prosecutors.

magnanime *adj.* magnanimous.

magnanimement *adj.* magnanimously.

magnanimité *n.f.* magnanimity.

magnat *n.m.* magnate, tycoon.

magner (se) *v.t. Infml.* to hurry up, to move it.

magne-toi, on est déjà en retard! move it! we are late already!

magnésium *n.m.* magnesium.

magnétique *adj.* magnetic. **champ ~,** magnetic field. **une bande ~,** magnetic tape. **piste ~,** magnetic strip. **monnaie ~,** plastic money.

magnétiser *v.t.* to mesmerize, to magnetize.

magnétiseur, euse *n.m.f.* mesmerizer, magnetizer.

magnétisme *n.m.* magnetism.

magnéto *n.m.* tape recorder; video recorder.

magnéto-électrique *adj.* magneto-electric.

magnétophone *n.m.* tape recorder.

magnétoscope *n.m.* video (tape) recorder, V.C.R. (video cassette recorder).

magnificat *n.m.* Magnificat.

magnificence *n.f.* magnificence.

magnifier *v.t.* to magnify, to extol, to exalt.

magnifique *adj.* magnificent; grand; splendid.

magnifiquement *adj.* magnificently.

magnitude *n.f.* magnitude.

magnum *n.m.* magnum.

magot *n.m.* magot; Barbary ape; hoard (of money).

magouille *n.f. Infml.* graft, scheme; shady dealing.

magouiller *v.i.* to graft, to scheme.

mahométan, e *n.m. f.* Muslim.

mai *n.m.* May; maypole.

maigre *adj.* lean, thin, meager, spare, poor, sorry. **long et ~,** tall and thin. **~ comme un clou,** as thin as a rake. **de la viande ~,** lean meat. **jour ~,** day of abstinence. **soupe ~,** vegetable soup. **un ~ repas,** poor meal. **~ lean.** **faire ~,** to eat fish and vegetables.

maigrelet, ette *adj.* skinny, scrawny.

maigrement *adv.* meagerly, sparely, poorly, badly.

maigreur *n.f.* leanness, thinness, slenderness.

maigrir *v.i.* to get thin, to lose weight.

maille *n.f.* stitch; mesh. **avoir ~ à partir avec quelqu'un,** to have an argument with a person, to have a bone to pick with someone.

maillon *n.m.* link.

maillot *n.m.* leotard; top, jersey. **~ de bain,** bathing suit, swimsuit.

main *n.f.* hand. **la ~ droite,** the right hand. **n'y pas aller de ~ morte,** not to pull one's punches. **se donner la ~,** to shake hands. **faire sa ~,** to have one's hand in; to get accustomed. **forcer la ~ à quelqu'un,** to compel a person to do a thing. **lever la ~ sur quelqu'un,** to lift one's hand to strike a person. **j'en mettrais la ~ au feu,** I swear to that. **mettre la ~ à l'ouvrage,** to set to work. **faire ~ basse sur,** to lay violent hands on; to pillage. **à deux ~s,** with both hands. **en venir aux ~s,** to come to blows. **de première ~,** firsthand. **de la ~ à la ~,** from hand to hand. **de bonne ~,** on good authority. **de longue ~,** of long standing. **la dernière ~,** the finishing touch. **en ~,** in hand. **en bonne ~,**

en ~ sûre, in good hands. sous la ~, at hand, ready at hand. s'il me tombe jamais sous la ~! if ever he falls into my hands! en un tour de ~, in a twinkling. avoir la ~, to open (at cards). ~ de justice, hand of justice; prêter ~ forte, to give assistance.

main-d'oeuvre n.f. manpower, labor, workforce.

mainlevée n.f. withdrawal.

mainmise n.f. seizure.

maint, e adj. many a, many. ~e fois, ~es fois, many a time.

maintenance n.f. maintenance unit.

maintenant adv. now, at present, at this time.

maintenir v.t. to maintain, to support, to sustain, to keep up, to abide by. se ~, v.refl. to keep up, to remain; to be maintained; to hold one's own; to stand one's ground.

maintien n.m. maintaining, maintenance, keeping up; deportment.

maire n.m. mayor.

mairie n.f. mayoralty, city hall.

mais conj. but; why. ~, qu'ai-je dit? why, what have I said? ~ oui, why yes.

maïs n.m. maize, Indian corn.

maison n.f. house, habitation, home, household; establishment; firm. ~ de campagne, country house. être à la ~, to be at home. ~ de santé, nursing home. ~ de jeu, gambling house. ~ d'arrêt, prison, jail. tenir la ~, to manage the house. il est de la ~, he belongs to the family. la ~ royale, the royal household. ~ de commerce, commercial house; firm. ~ de commission, commission agency.

maisonnée n.f. whole house, family, household.

maisonnette n.f. small house, cottage.

maître n.m. master; owner; instructor; teacher; être son ~, to be one's own master. nul ne peut servir deux ~s, no one can serve two masters. trouver son ~, to find one's match. ~ de danse, dancing master. ~ des cérémonies, master of ceremonies. ~ d'hôtel, majordomo, maître d', headwaiter. en ~, in a masterly manner.

maîtresse n.f. mistress; owner; teacher. ~ d'école, schoolteacher. en ~, authoritatively. une ~ femme, a superior woman.

maîtrise n.f. mastery; control.

maîtriser v.t. to master; to subdue, to overcome. ~ ses passions, to master one's passions. se ~, v.refl. to control oneself.

majesté n.f. majesty.

majestueux, euse adj. majestic.

majeur, e adj. major, greater; important; of age; force ~e, unforeseen accidents.

major n.m. major. état-~, staff, staff officers.

majordome n.m. majordomo, maître d'.

majorer v.t., to raise, to increase.

majorité n.f. majority.

majuscule adj. (of letters) capital. n.f. capital letter.

mal n.m. evil; ill, wrong; harm, injury, wrong,

mischief; wickedness; pain, ache, soreness. faire le ~, to do wrong. vous me faites ~, you are hurting me. il se donne beaucoup de ~, he works very hard. ~ de tête, headache. ~ de coeur, sickness, nausea. ~ de dents, toothache. ~ de gorge, sore throat. ~ de mer, seasickness. adv. ill, badly, amiss. ~ à l'aise, uncomfortable. prendre ~ une chose, to take offence at a thing. se trouver ~, to faint. être ~ avec quelqu'un, to be on bad terms with a person. il n'est pas mal, he isn't bad looking. il a mal fait de dire, he shouldn't have said.

malade adj. ill; sick, unwell; sore. avoir l'esprit ~, to have a disordered mind. n.m.f. sick person, patient.

maladie n.f. illness, sickness, malady, complaint; (of animals) distemper, disease. contracter une ~, to catch a disease. ~ du pays, homesickness, nostalgia.

maladif, ive adj. sickly, ailing, unhealthy.

maladivement adv. unhealthily, morbidly.

maladresse n.f. awkwardness, clumsiness, awkward thing, blunder.

maladroit, e adj. awkward, clumsy, gauche; unhandy, bungling.

maladroitement adv. awkwardly.

malaise n.m. uncomfortableness, discomfort; uneasiness.

malaisé, e adj. hard, difficult, inconvenient; embarrassed.

malaria n.f. malaria.

malavisé, e adj. ill-advised, imprudent.

malaxer v.t. to knead, to beat, to work up.

malchance n.f. bad luck. avoir de la ~, to be unlucky. malchanceux, euse adj. unlucky.

maldonne n.f. (at cards) bad deal, misdeal.

mâle n.m. male. adj. male; he (animals), cock (birds); manly, masculine; vigorous. voix ~, manly voice.

malédiction n.f. curse.

maléfice n.m. evil spell.

maléfique adj. malefic, evil; unlucky.

malencontreusement adv. unluckily.

malencontreux, euse adj. unlucky, untoward.

mal-en-point adv. in bad shape. il est ~, he is not feeling well.

malentendant, e adj. hearing impaired, hard of hearing.

malentendu n.m. misunderstanding, mistake.

malfaçon n.f. bad work; defect.

malfaisant, e adj. malevolent, mischievous; wicked; injurious, noxious, hurtful.

malfaiteur, trice n.m.f. crook, thief.

malfamé, e adj. ill-famed, disreputable.

malformation n.f. malformation.

malfrat m. crook.

malgracieusement adv. rudely, ungraciously.

malgré prep. in spite of, despite; notwithstanding. ~ cela, for all that, nevertheless. ~ que, although.

malhabile adj. clumsy, awkward.

malheur *n.m.* unhappiness; misfortune; bad luck, unluckiness, mishap. **tomber dans le ~**, to fall into misfortune. **avoir du ~**, to have bad luck. **par ~**, unluckily, unfortunately; unhappily.

malheureusement *adv.* unhappily; miserably, wretchedly; unfortunately; unluckily.

malheureux, euse *adj.* unhappy; unfortunate, unlucky; wretched.

malhonnête *adj.* dishonest; impolite, unmannerly, rude. **un homme ~**, a rude man. **une conduite ~**, rude behavior.

malhonnêtement *adv.* dishonestly, impolitely, rudely.

malhonnêteté *n.f.* dishonesty; impoliteness, rudeness; rude thing.

malice *n.f.* spite, malice, maliciousness, malignity; mischievousness, prank, trick. **faire une ~ à quelqu'un**, to play a trick on someone.

malicieusement *adv.* maliciously, mischievously.

malicieux, euse *adj.* malicious, mischievous, spiteful; sly, roguish.

malin, igne *adj.* malignant; shrewd, cunning, sharp, mischievous. **un enfant ~**, a mischievous child. **un regard ~**, a roguish look. **l'esprit ~**, the evil spirit.

malingre *adj.* puny, sickly, ailing; weakly.

malintentionné, e *adj.* ill-intentioned, spiteful.

malle *n.f.* trunk; mail-boat. **faire sa ~**, to pack.

malléable *adj.* malleable; *Fig.* supple, docile, pliant, compliant.

mallette *n.f.* attaché-case, small trunk.

malmener *v.t.* to maltreat; to abuse; to scold.

malnutrition *n.f.* malnutrition.

malodorant, e *adj.* foul-smelling, smelly.

malotru, e *n.m.f.* rude boor.

Malouines *adj.* **Iles Malouines**, Falkland Islands.

malpoli, e *adj.* impolite, rude, fresh.

malpropre *adj.* unfit; dirty, unclean, untidy.

malsain, e *adj.* unhealthy; unwholesome; insalubrious.

malséant, e *adj.* unseemly, unbecoming, unsuitable, improper, indecorous.

malt *n.m.* malt.

maltraiter *v.t.* to maltreat; to use roughly; to injure, to wrong.

malveillance *n.f.* malevolence, ill will.

malveillant, e *adj.* malevolent, malicious.

malversation *n.f.* malpractice.

maman *n.f.* mama, mommy, mother. **grand' ~, bonne ~**, grandma, grandmother.

mamelle *n.f.* teat, breast, udder.

mamelon *n.m.* nipple; (of beasts) teat; eminence, hillock.

mamie *n.f.* grandma, gran, granny.

mammifère *n.m.* mammal.

mamours *n.m.pl.* caresses. **faire des mamours à quelqu'un**, to fondle s.o.

management *n.m.* management.

manager *n.m.* manager, agent.

manche *n.m.* handle; haft, helve (of an axe), stick. **jeter le ~ après la cognée**, to throw the helve after the hatchet. **~ à balai**, broomstick. *n.f.* sleeve. **`~s courtes**, short sleeves. **c'est une autre paire de ~s**, that is quite another thing. **être dans la ~ de quelqu'un**, to be in favor with a person. **~ à vent**, windsail. **La Manche**, the English Channel, the Channel.

manchot, e *adj.* and *n.m.f.* one-armed, one-handed person.

mandarin *n.m.* mandarin.

mandarine *n.f.* mandarin, tangerine.

mandat *n.m.* mandate, warrant, writ, order, commission; money order (to pay); check; draft. **~ de poste**, post-office order; money order. **~ d'arrêt**, warrant.

mandataire *n.m.f.* mandatory, proxy, agent.

mandater *v.t.* to deliver an order for the payment of.

mandibule *n.f.* mandible.

mandoline *n.f.* mandoline.

mandrill *n.m.* mandrill, ribbed-nosed baboon.

manège *n.m.* training of horses; riding school; merry-go-round, carousel.

manette *n.f.* handle, small handle.

manganèse *n.m.* manganese.

mangeable *adj.* edible, eatable.

mangeaille *n.f.* food (of some domestic animals); victuals; feed, grub.

mangeoire *n.f.* manger, trough.

manger *v.t.* to eat; to wear away, to consume, to corrode; to squander, to run through. **la rouille mange le fer**, rust eats iron. **~ tout son bien**, to squander one's fortune. **~ comme quatre**, to eat very heartily. **l'appétit vient en mangeant**, eating whets the appetite. **donner à ~**, to give food, to serve food, to feed. (of animals) to feed. **se ~**, *v.refl.* to be eaten; to prey upon each other; to eat each other up. *n.m.* eating; food; victuals.

mange-tout *n.m.* spendthrift.

mangeur, euse *n.m. f.* eater.

mangouste *n.f.* mongoose, mangosteen.

mangue *n.f.* mango.

maniable *adj.* easy to handle; workable, easy to be worked.

maniaque *adj.* finicky, picky, fussy; mad; *n.m.f.* maniac, fusspot.

manie *n.f.* habit; mania; madness, obsession.

maniement *n.m.* touch; handling; management, conduct.

manier *v.t.* to handle, to finger, to feel; to manage, to treat; to conduct, to govern. **~ la plume**, to write. **~ un cheval**, to manage a horse.

manière *n.f.* manner, way, mode, method; style; fashion; custom; mannerism. **la ~ dont**, the manner in which. **à la ~ de**, in the manner of, in the way of; in the style of, in the fashion of. **d'aucune ~, en aucune ~**, by no means, not at all. **n'avoir pas de ~s, manquer de ~s**, to have no pretentions. **par ~ de,** by way of. **il parla de ~ à convaincre les juges,** he spoke so as to convince the judges.

maniéré, e *adj.* affected, pretentious.

manif *n.f.* (abbrev. of **manifestation),** demonstration.

manifestant, e *n.m.f.,* demonstrator.

manifestation *n.f.* manifestation, demonstration; appearance, revelation; event.

manifeste *adj.* manifest, evident, plain, conspicuous, obvious, clear, apparent. *n.m.* manifesto.

manifestement *adv.* manifestly, clearly, obviously.

manifester *v.t.* to manifest, to display, to show, to evince. **se ~,** *v.refl.* to manifest oneself; to appear.

manigance *n.f.* scheme, maneuver, intrigue.

manigancer *v.t.* to plot, to contrive.

manipulateur, trice *n.m.f.* manipulator; technician; key; transmitter.

manipulation *n.f.* manipulation; handling.

manipuler *v.t.* to manipulate.

manitou *n.m.* manitou; big shot.

manivelle *n.f.* crank; tiller.

manne *n.f.* manna.

mannequin *n.m.* mannequin, model, dummy.

manoeuvre *n.f.* manual labor; maneuver, movement, evolution of troops; evolution of a ship or a fleet; *pl.* rigging; drill, drilling. *n.m.* workman; mason's laborer; journeyman; bungler cobbler. **travail de ~,** drudgery.

manoeuvrer *v.t.* and *v.i.* (of a ship) to work; to maneuver; to contrive, to plot. **il a bien manoeuvré dans cette affaire,** he worked that affair cleverly.

manquant, e *adj.* wanting, missing.

manque *n.m.* lack of, want; deficiency, miss; failure; omission. **~ d'argent,** lack of money.

manqué, e *adj.* missed, failed, unsuccessful. **un projet ~,** a failure.

manquement *n.m.* fault, omission; oversight; want.

manquer *v.t.* to miss; to lose; to fail; **~ son coup,** to miss one's aim. **~ le but,** to miss the mark. **~ l'occasion,** to miss the opportunity. **les forces lui manquent,** his strength fails him. **c'est l'argent qui lui manque,** it is money he wants. **il manque deux personnes,** two persons are missing. **~ de tout,** not to have anything. **~ de parole,** to fail in one's promise. **je vous attends demain, n'y manquez pas,** I expect you tomorrow, be there. **je n'y manquerai pas,** I will not fail. **il a manqué d'être tué,** he was very near to being killed.

mansarde *n.f.* mansard-roofed, attic.

mansardé, e *adj.* with sloping ceilings.

mansuétude *n.f.* leniency, mildness, gentleness.

mante *n.f.* mantis, *Fig.* man-eater.

manteau *n.m.* coat, cover. **sous le ~,** underhand, secretly.

manucure *n.f.* manicure.

manuel, elle *adj.* manual *n.m.* manual, handbook.

manuellement *adj.* manually.

manufacture *n.f.* factory.

manufacturer *v.t.* to manufacture.

manuscrit, e *adj.* manuscript. *n.m.* manuscript.

manutention *n.f.* maintenance, handling of goods.

manutentionnaire *n.m.f.* warehouse man, packer.

manutentionner *v.t.* to handle (goods).

mappemonde *n.f.* map of the world.

maquereau *n.m.* mackerel; pimp.

maquerelle *n.f. Infml.* madame.

maquette *n.f.* rough sketch; rough model.

maquignon *n.m.* horse-dealer; jockey; jobber.

maquillage *n.m.* makeup.

maquiller *v.t.* to make up; to disguise, to fake. **se ~,** *v.refl.* to put on makeup.

maquilleur, euse *n.m.f.* makeup artist.

maquis *n.m.* bush; **prendre le ~,** to take to the bush, to go underground.

maraîcher *n.m.* market gardener, truck farmer; *adj.* market gardening, truck farming.

marais *n.m.* swamp.

marasme *n.m.* marasmus, consumption; atrophy, emaciation; stagnation, paralysis.

marathon *n.m.* marathon.

maraudeur *n.m.* marauder, pilferer.

marbre *n.m.* marble, grindstone, pounding stone; marbled color.

marbrer *v.t.* to marble; to stain or vein like marble.

marbrerie *n.f.* marble-cutting; marble mason's yard.

marbrier, ière *n.m.f.* marble cutter, marble polisher.

marbrière *n.f.* marble quarry.

marbrure *n.f.* marbling.

marc *n.m.* mark, marc, residuum; grounds (of coffee). **~ d'or,** gold mark.

marcassin *n.m.* young wild boar.

marchand, e *n.m.f.* merchant, dealer, trader; shopkeeper, tradesman, storekeeper. **~ en gros,** wholesale dealer; (at auctions) bidder. **~ en détail,** retail dealer, retailer; shopkeeper. *adj.* marketable, saleable. **prix ~,** trade price, wholesale price. **ville ~e,** trading town. **navire ~,** merchant ship, freighter. **marine ~e,** merchant marine.

marchandage *n.m.* bargaining, haggling.

marchander *v.t.* to bargain, to haggle.

marchandeur, euse *n.m. f.* haggler.

marchandise *n.f.* merchandise, goods. **~ en magasin,** stock in hand.

marche *n.f.* **marches** *pl.* border, military frontier; walk; gait, pace, step; march, distance; procession; progress. **en ~,** on the march, marching. **~ forcée,** forced march. **sonner la ~,** to strike up a march. **~ militaire,** march. **~ funèbre,** funeral march. **ordre de ~,** order of

sailing. **la ~ de la nature,** the course of nature.
les ~ s d'un escalier, the steps of a staircase.
marché *n.m.* market; marketplace; bargain, contract. **aller au ~,** to go to the market. **~ au poisson,** fish market. **~ aux fleurs,** flower market. **bon ~,** cheap. **faire un bon ~,** to make a good bargain. *Infml.* **par-dessus le ~,** on top of that, to top that. **le ~ des valeurs,** the stockmarket. **~ noir,** black market. **~ aux puces,** flea market. **étude de ~,** market study. **Marché commun,** Common Market.
marchepied *n.m.* step, running board (car); stepladder.
marcher *v.i.* to walk; to tread, to step; to go; to advance; to march; to sail (boat). **~ à grands pas,** to take long steps. **~ à quatre pattes,** to crawl. **~ en ordre de bataille,** to march in battle array. **~ en ligne,** to sail in line. **ma montre marche très bien,** my watch works very well. **cette affaire ne ~pas,** that deal isn't working. **je le ferai ~ droit,** I shall make him behave well. *n.m.* walk, gait.
marcheur, euse *n.m. f.* walker, sailer (boat).
mardi *n.m.* Tuesday. **~ gras,** Shrove Tuesday.
mare *n.f.* pond, pool.
marécage *n.m.* swamp, bog.
marécageux, euse *adj.* swampy, boggy.
maréchal *n.m.* marshal. **~ ferrant,** blacksmith. **~ de France,** marshal, fieldmarshal. **~ des logis,** quartermaster.
maréchaussée *n.f.* a corps of mounted police.
marée *n.f.* tide. **basse ~,** low tide, low water. **haute ~,** high tide, high water. **la ~ monte,** the tide is coming in. **~ humaine,** flood of people.
marelle *n.f.* hopscotch.
margarine *n.f.* margarine.
marge *n.f.* margin; time; space; means.
margeur *n.m.* margin stop, feeder.
marginal, e *adj.* marginal.
marguerite *n.f.* daisy.
mari *n.m.* husband, spouse.
mariage *n.m.* marriage; matrimony, wedlock; wedding, nuptials. **assister à un ~,** to be present at a wedding.
marié *n.m.* bridegroom. **nouveaux ~s,** newlyweds; newly married couple.
mariée *n.f.* married woman; bride. **se plaindre que la ~ est trop belle,** to complain of a thing being too good.
marier *v.t.* to marry; to wed, to espouse; to match (to *or* with); to unite, to join. **le maire les a mariés,** the mayor married them. **~ des couleurs,** to blend colors. **se ~,** *v.refl.* to marry; to be married; to get married; to blend; to suit.
marie-salope *n.f. Vulg.* slut; (mud) barge.
marieur, euse *n.m. f.* matchmaker.
marihuana, marijuana *n.f.* marijuana, pot, hemp.
marin, e *adj.* marine, sea, *n.m.* seaman, sailor, mariner.
marina *n.f.* marina.

marinade *n.f.* marinade; pickled meat.
marine *n.f.* navigation; marine shipping; naval service; navy, marine. **la ~ anglaise,** the British navy. **~ marchande,** merchant marine. **bleu ~,** navy blue.
mariner *v.t.* to pickle, to marinate.
mariole *n.m. Infml.* **faire le ~,** to show off, to goof off.
marionnette *n.f.* puppet; *pl.* puppet show.
marital, e *adj.* marital.
maritalement *adv.* maritally; as a spouse; like married persons.
maritime *adj.* maritime, naval.
marjolaine *n.f.* marjoram.
marketing *n.m.* marketing.
marmaille *n.f. Infml.* brats *pl.* set of brats.
marmelade *n.f.* marmalade. **en ~,** *Fig.* in a stew, torn up.
marmite *n.f.* pot; boiler.
marmiton *n.m.* scullion, kitchen boy.
marmonner *v.t. Infml.* to mumble, to mutter.
marmoréen, enne *adj.* marmorean, marmoreal.
marmot *n.m.* brat, little boy.
marmotte *n.f.* marmot; woodchuck. **dormir comme une ~,** to sleep like a log.
marmotter *v.t.* to mumble, to mutter.
maroquin *n.m.* morocco leather.
maroquinerie *n.f.* leather goods store; leather trade.
maroquinier *n.m.* leather goods storeowner.
marotte *n.f.* hobby. **chacun a sa ~,** everybody has his hobby.
marquage *n.m.* marking.
marquant, e *adj.* conspicuous; striking. remarkable.
marque *n.f.* scar, mark; note, sign; stamp, brand, stigma; token; proof, evidence. **~ de fabrique,** trademark. **un homme de ~,** a man of importance. **il en a encore la ~,** he still bears a scar.
marqué, e *pa. p. or adj.* marked, evident; striking. **être ~ au front,** to have a mark on one's forehead.
marquer *v.t.* to mark; to stamp; to brand, to burn; to stigmatize as infamous; to mark out; to indicate; to accentuate; to score. **le thermomètre marque vingt-cinq degrés,** the thermometer indicates twenty-five degrees. **j'ai marqué cela dans mon agenda,** I have written that in my notebook. **cette robe lui marque bien la taille,** this dress accentuates her waistline nicely.
marqueur, euse *n.m. f.* marker; scorer.
marraine *n.f.* godmother.
marrant, e *adj. Infml.* funny; odd.
marre *n.f. Infml.* **j'en ai ~,** I'm fed up.
marrer (se) *v.refl.* to laugh, to have a good laugh, to crack up.
marri, e *adj.* sorry, grieved, concerned.
marron *n.m.* chestnut, sweet chestnut; chestnut

color; marron. ~ **glacé,** glazed chestnut *adj. m.* marron; chestnut color.

marron, onne *adj.* fugitive, runaway; (of animals) running wild; unlicensed, clandestine.

courtier ~, unlicensed broker. *n.m. f.* marroon; a runaway slave.

marronnier *n.m.* chestnut-tree.

Mars *n.m.* Mars.

marteau *n.m.* hammer; knocker (on a door).

pilon, steam-hammer. ~ **à deux mains,** sledgehammer. **il est** ~, he is nuts.

martel *n.m.* hammer; *Fig.* uneasiness. **se mettre** ~ **en tête,** to be worried sick; to get worked up.

martèlement *n.m.* pounding, hammering.

marteler *v.t.* to hammer.

martial, e *adj.* martial; warlike.

martien, ne *adj. m.f.* Martian.

martin-pêcheur *n.m. Ornith.* kingfisher.

martyr, e *n.m. f.* martyr.

martyre *n.m.* martyrdom.

martyriser *v.t.* to martyr; *Fig.* to torment, to persecute, to torture.

marxisme *n.m.* Marxism. **marxiste** *adj., n.m.f.* marxist.

mascara *n.m.* mascara.

mascarade *n.f.* marquerade.

mascotte *n.f.* mascot.

masculin, e *adj.* masculine.

masculinité *n.f.* masculinity.

masochisme *n.m.* masochism. **masochiste,** *n.m.f.* masochist.

masque *n.m.* mask; pretence. ~ **à oxygène,** oxygen mask. ~ **de plongée,** diving mask.

masqué, e *adj.* masked, disguised.

masquer *v.t.* to mask; to hide. **se** ~, *v.refl.* to mask, to disguise oneself; to put on a mask.

massacrante *adj.* cross, peevish, unbearable.

massacre *n.m.* massacre, slaughter, butchery.

massacrer *v.t.* to massacre, to slaughter, to slay; to murder.

massage *n.m.* massage.

masse *n.f.* mass; lump; heap; bulk, body, stock; estate (of bankrupt or deceased person); the whole; the multitude; magnitude. **c'est une** ~ **de chair,** he is a mass of flesh. **soulever les** ~**s,** to stir up the people. **en** ~, in a body; in a mass.

masser *v.t.* to massage.

masseur, euse *n.m.f.* masseur; masseuse.

massif, ive *adj.* massive; weighty; solid; heavy. *n.m.* solid mass (of masonry).

massivement *adv.* massively.

mass media *n.m.pl.* mass media(s).

massue *n.f.* club. **coup de** ~, stunning blow.

mastic *n.m.* mastic; putty; cement.

masticage *n.m.* puttying; cementing.

mastication *n.f.* mastication.

mastiquer *v.t.* to putty; to cement; to masticate.

mastoc *n.m. Infml.* heavy, clumsy fellow.

masturbation *n.f.* masturbation.

masturber (se) *v.refl.* to masturbate.

mat *n.m.* (at chess) mate. *adj. m.* (at chess) mated, checkmated.

mat, e *adj.* matt, unburnished; unpolished.

argent ~, matt-finished silver. **un son** ~, a dull sound.

mât *n.m.* mast (of a ship); pole. **grand** ~, main mast. **grand** ~ **de hune,** main topmast. ~**de misaine,** foremast. ~ **d'artimon,** mizzenmast.

matador *n.m.* matador.

match *n.m.* match, game. ~ **de football,** soccer game. ~ **nul,** tie game.

matelas *n.m.* mattress.

matelasser *v.t.* to stuff, to pad, to line.

matelot *n.m.* sailor, seaman.

mater *v.t.* to checkmate (at chess); to enervate, to subdue; to conquer; to mortify, to humble, to bring down.

mâter *v.t.* to mast.

materialiser *v.t.* to materialize.

materialiste *adj.* materialistic. *n.m.f.* materialist.

materiaux *n.m.pl.* materials.

materiel, elle *adj.* material. *n.m.* material; stock, hardware.

matériellement *adv.* materially; grossly.

maternel, elle *adj.* maternal, motherly. **langue** ~, mother tongue, *n.f.* **la** ~**le,** kindergarten.

maternellement *adv.* maternally, motherly.

materner *v.t.* to mother (s.o.).

maternité *n.f.* maternity, motherhood.

math(s) *n.m.f. Infml.* math.

mathématicien, enne *n.m. f.* mathematician.

mathématique *adj.* mathematic, mathematical *n.f.* mathematics *pl.*

mathématiquement *adv.* mathematically.

matheux, euse *n.m.f. Infml.* math expert.

matière *n.f.* matter, material, stuff; subject, topic; contents (of a book); cause, reason. ~**s d'or et d'argent,** bullion. ~**s premières,** raw materials. **entrer en** ~, to enter into the subject. ~ **grasse,** fat content.

matin *n.m.* morning. **du** ~ **au soir,** from morning till night. **de grand** ~, early in the morning. *adv.* early, early in the morning.

matinal, e *adj.* morning; early, rising early.

matinalement *adv.* early, early in the morning.

matinée *n.f.* morning, forenoon; morning party.

matou *n.m.* tomcat.

matraque *n.f.* bludgeon, billy.

matraquer *v.t.* to beat up, to bludgeon; to sting; (media) to bombard.

matriarcal, e *adj.* matriarcal.

matrice *n.f.* matrix, matrice, womb; mold; standard weight, measure *adj. f.* mother, primitive.

matricide *n.m.f.* matricide.

matriculaire *n.m.* registration.

matricule *n.f.* register; registration; certificate; registration certificate.

matrone *n.f.* matron.

mâture *n.f.* masts, masting.

maturité *n.f.* maturity, ripeness. **manquer de ~**, to be immature.

maudire *v.t.* to curse.

maudit, e *pa. p.* cursed; damned.

maugréer *v.i.* to grumble; to grouse.

maussade *adj.* gloomy; grumpy, disgruntled; (weather) cloudy; depressing.

mauvais, e *adj.* bad; evil, ill; wicked, ill-natured; mischievous; naughty. **~e excuse,** bad excuse. **~e tête,** bad temper. **~ sujet,** bad student/ pupil. *n.m.* bad. **il y a du bon et du ~ dans cet ouvrage,** there is good and bad in that work. *adv.* bad, badly, ill. **sentir ~,** to smell bad.

mauve *n.f.* mauve, purple; mallow.

mauviette *n.f.* lark, skylark; weakling.

maxillaire *adj.* maxillar, maxillary.

maxima *adj.* maximum.

maximal *adj.* maximal.

maxime *n.f.* maxim, saying. **avoir pour ~,** to hold as a maxim.

maximum *n.m.* maximum; *Fig.* acme, height; the most.

mayonnaise *n.f.* mayo, mayonnaise.

mazout *n.m.* fuel oil.

me, m', *pron. pers.* me. **me voici,** here I am. **on ~ l'a dit,** I was told. **elle ~ l'a dit,** she told me.

mea-culpa *n.m.* (Latin) it's my fault, I'm to blame.

méandre *n.m.* meander, maze, winding.

mec *n.m. Infml.* guy, bloke.

mécanicien *n.m.* mechanic. **~ dentiste,** dental technician; engineer.

mécanique *n.f.* mechanics, machinery, mechanism; machine. *adj.* mechanic, mechanical.

mécaniquement *adv.* mechanically.

mécaniser *v.t.* to mechanize, to render mechanical.

mécanisme *n.m.* mechanism, structure.

mécano *n.m. Infml.* mechanic.

Mécène *n.m.* Maecenas; *Fig.* patron, sponsor.

méchamment *adv.* wickedly, spitefully, maliciously.

méchanceté *n.f.* meanness, malice, maliciousness, spite, spitefulness, naughtiness.

méchant, e *adj.* nasty, mean, bad, wicked, perverse; malicious, spiteful, evil. **un homme ~,** a nasty man, a bad man. **une ~e langue,** an evil tongue. *n.m. f.* wicked man *or* woman; evil-doer, wrong-doer; naughty child.

mèche *n.f.* wick (of lamps, etc.); match, tinder; lock (of hair). **être de ~ avec,** to be hand in glove with. **vendre la ~,** to let the cat out of the bag.

mécompte *n.m.* miscalculation.

méconnaissable *adj.* unrecognizable.

méconnaitre *v.t.* not to recognize, not to know again, to deny; to slight, to disregard.

méconnu, e *pa. p.* unrecognized; forgotten; disowned, denied; disregarded, ignored, slighted, unappreciated.

mécontent, e *adj.* discontented, dissatisfied, displeased. *n.m. f.* malcontent.

mécontentement *n.m.* discontent, dissatisfaction, displeasure.

mécontenter *v.t.* to discontent, to dissatisfy, to displease.

Mecque *n.f.* **la ~,** Mecca.

médaille *n.f.* medal. *Fig.* **le revers de la ~,** the dark side of the picture.

médaillé, e *adj.* rewarded; (substantively) medallist.

medaillon *n.m.* medallion, locket.

médecin *n.m.* physician, doctor.

médecine *n.f.* medicine, physic. **~ légale,** forensic *or* legal medicine.

média *n.m.* media.

médial, e *adj.* median.

médiat, e *adj.* mediate.

médiateur, trice *n.m. f.* mediator. *n.f.* **servir de ~,** to mediate, to be a mediator. *adj.* mediating.

médiathèque *n.f.* media library.

médiation *n.f.* mediation, intervention.

médiatisation *n.f.* mediatization.

médiatiser *v.t.* to give media coverage to (sth), to turn (sth) into a media event.

médi(cal), e *adj.* medical.

médicament *n.m.* drug, medicine.

médicamenteux, euse *adj.* medicinal.

médication *n.f.* treatment, medication.

médicinal, e *adj.* medicinal.

médico- préf. medico-. **médico-légal,** medico-legal, forensic.

médiéval, e *adj.* medieval.

médiocre *adj.* middling, mean; mediocre; ordinary. *n.m.* mediocrity.

médiocrement *adv.* middlingly, passably; indifferently; poorly, hardly.

médiocrité *n.f.* mediocrity; poorness; medium.

médire *v.i.* to speak ill; (with **de**) to speak ill of, to backstab, to slander, to backbite, to traduce.

médisance, *n.f.* backstabbing, slander, backbiting.

médisant, e *adj.* slanderous; scandalous. *n.m. f.* slanderer, backbiter, traducer, backstabber.

méditatif, ive *adj.* meditative. *n.m.* meditative man.

méditation *n.f.* meditation.

méditer *v.t.* to meditate; to think over; to contemplate, to plan, to project, to muse, to ponder.

Méditerrané, e *adj.* mediterranean. **Mer ~e,** Mediterranean Sea, Mediterranean. *n.f.* Mediterranean Sea, Mediterranean.

méditerranéen, enne *adj., n.m.f.* Mediterranean.

médium *n.m.* medium.

méduse *n.f.* jellyfish, Medusa.

méduser *v.t.* to petrify, to astound.

meeting *n.m.* meeting.

méfait *n.m.* misdeed, misdoing.

méfiance *n.f.* mistrust, distrust.

méfiant, e *adj.* mistrustful, distrustful, suspicious.

méfier (se) *v.refl.* (with **de**) to mistrust, to distrust, to suspect.

mégarde *n.f.* inadvertence, inadvertency. **par ~**, inadvertently.

mégère *n.f.* shrew.

mégot *n.m.* cigarette butt.

meilleur, e *adj.* better; best. **la ~ partie**, the best part. *n.m.* best. **le ~ de l'affaire**, the best of the affair. **boire du ~**, to drink the best wine.

méjuger *v.i.* to misjudge. **se ~** *v.refl.* to underestimate oneself.

mélancolie *n.f.* melancholy.

mélancolique *adj.* melancholy, melancholic; sad, dismal; gloomy.

mélange *n.m.* mixture. medley; mixing, mingling; blending; crossing (of breeds); mash (for brewing).

mélanger *v.t.* to mix, to mingle, to blend; to confuse, to mix up. **se ~,** *v.refl.* to mix, to mingle, to blend.

mélasse *n.f.* molasses; treacle.

mêlé, e *pa. p. adj.* mixed; entangled. *n.f.* melee, scuffle, fray; free-for-all.

mêler *v.t.* to mix; to mingle, to blend; to intermingle; to entangle; to shuffle (cards). **~ des couleurs,** to blend colors. **~ les cheveux,** to entangle one's hair. **se ~,** *v.refl.* to mix, to mingle, to be mixed; to take in hand; to interfere in; to meddle (with). **se ~ des affaires de quelqu'un,** to meddle with a person's business. **de quoi vous mêlez-vous?** none of your business!

méli-mélo *n.m. Infml.* jumble, medley.

mélo *n.m.* melodrama, tear-jerker.

mélodie *n.f.* melody, tune.

mélodieusement *adv.* melodiously, musically, sweetly.

mélodieux, euse *adj.* melodious, musical, sweet; harmonious; tuneful.

mélodramatique *adj.* melodramatic.

mélodrame *n.m.* melodrama.

mélomane *n.m.f.* music-lover.

mélomanie *n.f.* melomania.

melon *n.m.* melon.

membrane *n.f.* membrane.

membre *n.m.* member; limb; rib, timber (ship).

membré, e *adj.* limbed.

même *adj.* same, self. **ce sont les ~s gens,** they are the same people. **la chose ~,** the very thing. **moi-~,** myself. *n.m.* same, same thing. **cela revient au ~,** that comes to the same thing. *adv.* even; likewise, also. **les goûts sont différents, souvent ~ opposés,** tastes are different and often even opposite. **a ~ de,** able to, enabled to. **de ~,** likewise, even so. **faites de ~,** do the same. **de ~ que,** as, so as, just as. **de ~ que vous, j'ai été voir,** I went to see, just as you did. **tout de ~,** in the same way; all the same though. **il a quand ~ fait ça!** he did it anyway!

mémento *n.m.* memento, notebook; summary.

mémoire *n.f.* memory; remembrance, recollection, record, memorial, name. **perdre la ~,** to lose one's memory. **rafraîchir la ~,** to call to mind. **de ~ d'homme,** from time immemorial, in the memory of man. **je n'ai pas de ~ de cela,** I have no recollection of that. *n.m.* memorandum, note, account; memoir; bill; dissertation (univ). **~ tampon,** buffer store. **~ morte,** read-only memory, ROM. **~ vive,** random access memory, RAM.

mémorable *adj.* memorable.

mémorablement *adv.* memorably.

mémorandum *n.m.* memorandum; notebook.

mémorial *n.m.* memorial.

mémorialiste *n.m.* memorialist.

mémorisation *n.f.* memorization, memorizing.

mémoriser *v.* to memorize, to store.

menaçant, e *adj.* menacing; threatening.

menace *n.f.* threat, menace. **~ en l'air,** empty threat.

menacer *v.t.* to threaten, to menace. **une maison qui menace ruine,** a tottering house. **le cholera menaçait de gagner Paris,** Paris was threatened with cholera.

ménage *n.m.* housekeeping; household; family life. **faire bon ~,** to agree together; to get along together. **femme de ~,** cleaning woman, daily help. **jeune ~** newly married couple. **se mettre en ~,** to live with someone. **faire le ~,** to do the housework.

ménagement *n.m.* deference, regard; caution, discretion.

ménager *v.t.* to husband; to use with economy; to spare; to be careful of; to take care of; to treat with prudence, caution; to contrive; to manage. **~ ses paroles,** to mind what one says. **~ son temps,** to make the most of one's time. **~ son crédit,** to spare one's credit. **~ sa santé,** to take care of one's health. **~ les expressions,** to weigh the terms, the expressions. **~ l'occasion,** to improve the opportunity. **se ~,** *v.refl.* to take care of oneself, of one's health, to conduct oneself carefully. **se ~ bien avec tout le monde,** to keep on good terms with everybody.

ménager, ère *adj.* careful, saving, economical, sparing, thrifty. *n.m. f.* economizer; housekeeper.

ménagerie *n.f.* menagerie.

mendiant, e *adj.* begging, mendicant. *n.m. f.* beggar, mendicant. **les quatre ~s,** the four orders of mendicant friars (Jacobins, Franciscans, Augustins and Carmelites); dessert of nuts, raisins, figs and almonds.

mendicité *n.f.* mendicity, begging.

mendier *v.t.* to beg; to implore. to solicit.

mener *v.t.* to lead; to take; to guide, to direct, to conduct; to command; to influence; to drive (cattle); to carry on, to direct. *v.i.* to lead, to go. **~ la danse,** to lead the dance. **~ quelqu'un par le nez,** to lead a person by the nose. **~ les bêtes aux champs,** to drive cattle to graze. **~ à bonne fin,** to terminate (a thing) happily. **cela ne mène à rien,** that is going nowhere.

ménestrel *n.m.* minstrel.

meneur *n.m.* conductor, leader; driver (of animals); *Fig.* ringleader, leader.

menhir *n.m.* menhir.

méninge *n.f.* meninges; **se creuser les ~s,** to rack one's brain.

méningite *n.f.* meningitis.

ménisque *n.m.* meniscus.

ménopause *n.f.* menopause.

ménorrhée *n.f.* menorrhoea.

menotte *n.f.* little hand; tiny hand; *pl.* handcuffs. **mettre les ~s à quelqu'un,** to handcuff a person.

mensonge *n.m.* lie, falsehood, fib.

mensonger, ère *adj.* lying, untrue, false; deceitful, delusive; illusory.

mensongèrement *adv.* untruly, falsely.

menstruation *n.f. Med.* menstruation.

menstruel, elle *adj.* menstrual.

menstrues *n.f.pl.* menses.

mensualisation *n.f.* monthly salary.

mensualiser *v.t.* to pay on a monthly basis.

mensualité *n.f.* monthly payment, installment, salary.

mensuel, elle *adj.* monthly.

mensuellement *adv.* monthly.

mensuration *n.f.* measurement.

mental, e *adj.* mental; intellectual. **alienation ~,** mental alienation, insanity.

mentalement *adv.* mentally.

mentalité *n.f.* mentality.

menteur, euse *adj.* lying; (of things) deceitful, false; delusive. *n.m.f.* liar.

menthe *n.f.* mint. **~ anglaise,** peppermint.

menthol *n.m.* menthol.

mention *n.f.* mention. **reçu avec ~,** graduated with honors.

mentionner *v.t.* to mention, to make mention of.

mentir *v.i.* to lie, to tell lies; to deceive. **il a menti,** he lied.

menton *n.m.* chin.

mentor *n.m.* mentor, guide.

menu, e *adj.* slender, thin, slim, small. **les ~s plaisirs de la vie,** life's small pleasures. *n.m.* detailed account, minute detail; particulars *pl.*; menu, bill of fare. *adv.* small. **écrire ~,** to write small.

menuet *n.m.* minuet.

menuiserie *n.f.* carpentry, woodwork.

menuisier *n.m.* carpenter, cabinet maker.

méprendre (se) *v.refl.* to be mistaken; (with *à*) to mistake. **vous vous méprenez,** you are mistaken.

mépris *n.m.* contempt, scorn, disregard, disdain. **avoir du ~ pour quelqu'un,** to feel contempt for a person. **tomber dans le ~,** to fall into contempt.

méprisable *adj.* contemptible, despicable.

méprisant, e *adj.* contemptuous, scornful.

méprise *n.f.* mistake; oversight, error, blunder.

mépriser *v.t.* to despise, to condemn; to slight.

mer *n.f.* sea; the deep. **en pleine ~,** on the open sea. **haute ~,** high sea. **sur ~,** at sea. **tomber à la ~,** to fall overboard. **ce n'est pas la ~ à boire!** (it's) no big deal.

mercantile *adj.* mercantile, commercial.

mercenaire *adj.* mercenary.

mercerie *n.f.* haberdashery, notions store.

merci *n.f.* mercy. **demander ~,** to beg for mercy. **crier ~,** to cry mercy. *n.m.* thanks. **dire ~,** to say thank you. **Dieu ~,** thank God!.

mercredi *n.m.* Wednesday. **~ des cendres,** Ash Wednesday.

Mercure *n.m.* Mercury. *n.m.* mercury; quicksilver.

merde *n.f. Vulg.* shit. **il est dans la ~,** he is in a mess. **elle ne se prend pas pour de la ~,** she has a high opinion of herself.

merdeux, euse *adj. Infml.* shitty.

merdier *n.m. Infml.* mess, pigsty.

merdique *adj. Infml.,* shitty, crappy.

mère *n.f.* mother; cause, source. **grand-~,** grandmother. **belle-~,** mother-in-law; stepmother. *adj.* stepmother. **la reine ~,** the queen mother. **la ~patrie,** the mother country.

méridien *n.m.* meridian.

méridien, ienne *adj.* meridian. *n.f.* meridian line; midday nap. **faire la ~,** to take one's afternoon nap.

méridional, e *adj.* meridional; southern. *n.m.* southerner.

meringue *n.f.* meringue.

merise *n.f.* wild cherry.

merisier *n.m.* wild cherry tree.

méritant, e *adj.* deserving.

mérite *n.m.* merit; worth, due; value, excellence.

mériter *v.t.* to merit, to deserve; to earn; to be worthy of; to be worth. **cette nouvelle mérite confirmation,** this news needs confirmation.

méritoire *adj.* meritorious, praiseworthy.

merlan *n.m.* whiting.

merle *n.m.* blackbird.

merluche *n.f.* stockfish, dried cod.

merveille *n.f.* wonder, marvel; prodigy, miracle. **c'était ~ de le voir,** it was astonishing to see him. **faire des ~s,** to perform wonders. **promettre monts et ~s,** to promise wonders. **à ~,** excellently.

merveilleusement *adv.* wonderfully, marvelously.

merveilleux, euse *adj.* marvelous, wonderful; superior, wonderfully good.

mes *adj. poss. m.f. pl.* my.

mésange *n.f.* tit, titmouse, tomtit.

mésaventure *n.f.* misfortune, misadventure, mischance, mishap.

mesdames *f.pl.* v. MADAME.

mésentente *n.f.* disagreement, dissension, misunderstanding.

mésestimer *v.t.* to underestimate, to think little of; to undervalue.

mésintelligence *n.f.* disagreement, dissension, misunderstanding, variance.

mesquin, e *adj.* mean, petty, paltry; stingy, niggardly.

mesquinement *adv.* meanly, shabbily; stingily.

mesquinerie *n.f.* meanness, shabbiness, pettiness; stinginess.

mess *n.m.* mess (officers').

message *n.m.* message.

messager, ère *n.m.f.* messenger; harbinger. **les hirondelles sont les ~ères du printemps,** swallows are the harbingers of spring.

messagerie *n.f.* messenger service.

messe *n.f.* mass. **dire la ~,** to say mass.

messianique *adj.* messianic.

Messie *n.m.* Messiah.

mesurable *adj.* measurable.

mesure *n.f.* measure; standard; measurement; dimension, size; *Mus.* time, bar. **~ de longueur,** measure of length. **chanter en ~,** to sing in time. **manquer de ~,** to be lacking in moderation. **la ~ du possible,** the best of one's possibilities. **à ~,** in proportion, accordingly. **au fur et à ~ que,** gradually, as. **sur ~,** custom-made, (suit) to order.

mesuré, e *adj.* measured; circumspect, cautious; guarded.

mesurer *v.t.* to measure; to proportion, to adjust; to consider, to weigh. **~ ses paroles, ses expressions,** to weigh one's words, one's expressions. **se ~,** *v.refl.* to be measured; to measure oneself.

mesureur *n.m.* measurer.

métabolisme *m.* metabolism.

métal *n.m.* metal.

métallique *adj.* metallic.

métallisation *n.f.* metallization.

métalliser *v.t.* to metallize.

métallurgie *n.f.* metallurgy.

métallurgique *adj.* metallurgic.

métallurgiste *n.m.* metallurgist, metal-worker.

métamorphose *n.f.* metamorphosis.

métamorphoser *v.t.* to metamorphose, to transform, to change. **se ~,** *v.refl.* to metamorphose oneself; to be metamorphosed, changed.

métaphore *n.f.* metaphor.

métaphorique *adj.* metaphoric, metaphorical.

métaphoriquement *adv.* metaphorically.

métaphysique *n.f.* metaphysics *pl. adj.* metaphysic, metaphysical; to abstract.

métastase *n.f.* metastasis.

météo *n.f.* (abbrev. of **météorologie**), weather report, weather forecast.

météore *n.m.* meteor.

météorique *adj.* meteoric.

météorite *n.f.* meteorite.

météorologie *n.f.* meteorology.

météorologique *adj.* meteorologic, meteorological.

météorologue *n.m.* meteorologist, weather person.

méthane *n.m.* methane.

méthode *n.f.* method, way, custom, habit. **avec ~,** methodically.

méthodique *adj.* methodic, methodical, precise, formal.

méthodiquement *adv.* methodically.

méthodisme *n.m.* Methodism.

méthodiste *n.m.f.* Methodist.

méticuleusement *adv.* scrupulously, meticulously.

méticuleux, euse *adj.* meticulous, fastidious, overly-scrupulous.

méticulosité *n.f.* meticutousness.

métier *n.m.* job, occupation, trade, handicraft, business, calling, profession. **exercer un ~,** to follow a trade. **le ~ des armes,** the military profession. **avoir le coeur au ~,** to be fond of one's work. **être du ~,** to be of the craft.

métis, se *adj.* mixed, half-breed; (of animals) mongrel, crossbreed; (of plants) hybrid *n.m.f.* person of a mixed breed, half-breed, mestizo; (of animals) mongrel.

métissage *n.m.* crossbreeding.

métrage *n.m.* measurement, measuring.

mètre *n.m.* meter.

métrer *v.t.* to measure by the meter.

métreur *n.m.* quantity surveyor.

métrique *adj.* metrical, metric.

métro *n.m.* subway.

métronome *n.m.* metronome.

métropole *n.f.* metropolis; capital of a country; mother country.

métropolitain, e *adj.* metropolitan.

mets *n.m.* dish of food.

mettable *adj.* wearable, fit to be worn.

metteur, euse *n.m.f.* **~ en œuvre,** mounter, setter (of pearls, etc.). **~ en scène,** director; producer, stage manager.

mettre *v.t.* to put, to set, to place, to lay; to put on (clothes); to employ; to range, to rank, to rate; to put (in, out); to bring; to use. **~ sous les yeux,** to set before the eyes. **~ la nappe,** to lay the tablecloth. **~ de côté,** to set, to lay aside. **~ son chapeau,** to put on one's hat. **~ quelqu'un dans son tort,** to prove someone wrong. **~ en état de,** to enable. **~ en liberté,** to set free. **~ en ordre,** to set in order. **~ en évidence,** to show; to prove. **~ à l'aise,** to set at ease. **~ à bout,** to put out of patience. **~ ses gants, son habit,** to put on one's gloves, one's coat. **~ des paroles en musique,** to set words to music. **~ de l'esprit dans ses écrits,** to show wit in one's writings. **~ du temps à faire quelque chose,** to take a long time to do a thing. **~ quelqu'un à la raison,** to bring someone to his senses. **~ à la retraite,** to pension off; to discharge. **~ en pièces,** to tear to pieces; to break to pieces. *Print.* **~ en pages,** to make up. *Naut.* **~ à la mer,** to put to sea. **~ la voile,** to set sail. **~ à terre,** to put ashore, to land. **se ~,** *v.refl.* to place, to put oneself; to begin, to set about, to stand; to sit down. **se ~ à la fenêtre,**

to go to the window. **se ~ au lit**, to go to bed. **se ~ dedans**, to get in, to get oneself into a scrape. **se ~ en route**, to set out, to start. **se ~ en colère**, to get angry. **se ~ dans les affaires**, to go into business. **se ~ mal avec quelqu'un**, to have a quarrel with someone. **se ~debout**, to stand up. **se ~ à table**, to sit down at the table. **se ~ à rire**, to start laughing. **se ~ à pleuvoir**, to start raining. **se ~ à travailler**, to begin to work.

meublant, e *adj.* decorative.

meuble *n.m.* piece of furniture; furniture, household furniture.

meublé, e *adj.* furnished; **appartement ~**, furnished apartment.

meubler *v.t.* to furnish (a house); to stock (a farm); to store, to stock; to enrich. **se ~** *v.refl.* to furnish one's lodgings, to get one's furniture; to be stocked; **~ la conversation**, to keep a conversation going.

meuglement *n.m.* mooing, lowing.

meugler *v.i.* to low, to moo.

meule *n.f.* millstone, grindstone; cock, rick, stack (of hay etc.), mow. **mettre en ~**, to cock, to stack, to mow. **~ de fromage**, round, flat cheese.

meunier *n.m.* miller.

meunière *n.f.* miller's wife; miller (woman).

meurt-de-faim *n.m.* half-starved wretch.

meurtre *n.m.* murder, manslaughter, homicide.

meurtri, e *adj.* bruised.

meurtrier, ière *n.m.f.* murderer *m.* murderess *f.* *adj.* murderous; murdering; bloody, deadly.

meurtrière *n.f.* loophole, murderess.

meurtrir *v.t.* to bruise, to contuse. **~ le visage**, to bruise the face.

meurtrissure *n.f.* bruise, contusion.

meute *n.f.* pack (of hounds).

mexicain, e *adj.* Mexican. *n.m.f.* Mexican.

Mexique *n.m.* Mexico.

mezzanine *n.f.* mezzanine.

mi *adv.* equally. *adj.* (invariable) half, mid; middle. **a ~ chemin**, halfway. **la ~ août**, the middle of August. *n.m. Mus.* mi, E.

miaou *n.m.* miaow.

miaulement *n.m.* mewing (of cats); caterwauling.

miauler *v.i.* to meow, to mew; to caterwaul.

miche *n.f.* loaf (of bread).

micmac *n.m.* underhand work, intrigue, foul play.

micro *n.m. Infml.* mike, microphone.

microbe *n.m.* microbe.

micro-onde *n.f.* microwave. **four à ~,** microwave oven.

micro-ondes *n.m.* microwave (oven).

micro-ordinateur *n.m.* micro (computer).

micro-organisme *n.m.* microorganism.

microphone *n.m.* microphone.

microplaquette *n.f.* microchip.

microprocesseur *n.m.* microprocessor.

microscope *n.m.* microscope.

microscopie *n.f.* microscopy.

microscopique *adj.* microscopic.

midi *n.m.* noon; midday; the middle of the day; south. **~ et demi**, half past twelve. **à ~**, at noon. **chercher ~ à quatorze heures**, to look for difficulties where there are none. **cet homme est du ~**, that man is from the south.

mie *n.f.* soft bread, the white inside of bread.

miel *n.m.* honey. **lune de ~**, honeymoon.

miellé, e *adj.* honeyed.

mielleusement *adv.* sweetly, lusciously.

mielleux, euse *adj.* honey, honeyed; luscious.

mien, mienne *pron poss.* mine. **c'est le ~**, it is mine. **vos affaires sont les miennes**, your business is also mine.

miette *n.f.* crumb; little bit. **mettre en ~s**, to crumble, to break into crumbs.

mieux *adv.* better. **Il chante ~ qu'avant**, he sings better than before. **aimer ~**, to like better, to prefer. **vous feriez ~ de rester**, you had better stay. **tant ~**, so much the better. *adj.* better; best. **voici ce que j'ai de ~**, this is the best thing I have. **n.m.** best. **le ~ est de se taire**, it is best to say nothing. **faire de son ~**, to do one's best. **ça devient de ~ en ~**, it's getting better and better. **~ vaut tard que jamais**, better late than never.

mièvre *adj.* delicate; finicky.

mignardise *n.f.* delicacy.

mignon, onne *adj.* cute. *n.m.f.* cutie.

migraine *n.f.* migraine, headache.

migration *n.f.* migration.

migratoire *adj.* migratory.

mijaurée *n.f.* affected woman.

mijoter *v.t.* to simmer.

milice *n.f.* war, warfare; troops; militia.

milieu *n.m.* middle, midst; center; heart. **au ~ de la foule**, in the midst of the crowd. **au beau ~**, in the very middle. **juste ~**, true middle; milieu, environment, circle, golden mean. **dans le ~ où il vit**, in the society he belongs to. *Infml.* **le ~**, the underworld.

militaire *adj.* military. *n.m.* soldier; military.

militairement *adv.* militarily.

militant, e *adj.* militant, activist.

militariser *v.t.* to militarize.

militarisme *n.m.* militarism.

militariste *mf.* militarist.

militer *v.i.* to militate.

mille *adj.* (invariable) thousand, a thousand, many. **dix ~ francs**, ten thousand francs. **il y ~ et ~ choses à dire là-dessus**, there are a great many things to be said about that. *n.m.* thousand, a thousand, one thousand. *n.m.* mile.

mille-feuille *n.f.* mille-feuille pastry, napoléon, milfoil, yarrow.

millénaire *adj.* millennial.

millésime *n.m.* date (of coins, medals, etc.); vintage.

millet *n.m.* millet, birdseed.

milliard *n.m.* a thousand millions, billion.

milliardaire *adj. m.f.* multimillionaire, billionaire.

millième *adj.* thousandth. *n.m.* thousandth part.

millier *n.m.* thousand; thousand weight.

milligramme *n.m.* milligram.

millilitre *n.m.* milliliter.

millimètre *n.m.* millimeter.

million *n.m.* million.

millionnaire *adj.* worth millions. *n.m.f.* millionaire.

mime *n.m.* mime; mimic.

mimer *v.i.* to mime.

mimétisme *n.m.* mimesis, mimicry.

mimique *adj.* mimic. *n.f.* mimic art, mimicry.

mimosa *n.f.* mimosa.

minable *adj.* pitiful, pathetic, miserable, sorry, shabby.

minaret *n.m.* minaret.

minauder *v.i.* to simper, to mince.

minauderie *n.f.* simpering, smirking, mincing manners.

mince *adj.* thin; slim, slender.

minceur *n.f.* thinness, slenderness.

mincir *v.i.* to get thinner, slimmer.

mine *n.f.* look, mien, appearance, aspect; countenance. **avoir bonne ~,** to look well. **faire bonne ~ à quelqu'un,** to receive a person well. **~ d'or,** gold mine. **~ de charbon de terre,** coal mine. **exploiter une ~,** to work a mine. **~ de crayon,** (pencil) lead.

miner *v.t.* to undermine, to mine.

minerai *n.m.* ore.

minéral *n.m.* mineral. *adj.* mineral.

minéralisation *n.f.* mineralization.

minéraliser *v.t.* to mineralize.

minéralogie *n.f.* mineralogy.

minéralogique *adj.* mineralogical.

minéralogiste *n.m.* mineralogist.

Minerve *n.f.* Minerva; surgical collar.

minet, ette *n.m.f.* pussy, kitty.

mineur *n.m.* miner, pitman, minor mode.

mineur, e *adj.* minor, smaller, less, lesser. *Mus.* minor. **l'Asie Mineure,** Asia Minor. **une fille mineure,** a girl under age *n.m.f.* minor; a person under age.

miniature *n.f.* miniature.

minier, ière *adj.* mining.

minimal, e *adj.* minimal.

minime *adj.* very small, trifling. *n.m.* minim.

minimum *n.m.* minimum.

ministère *n.m.* ministry, agency, service; administration, board, cabinet. **le ~ public,** the public prosecutor. **~ de l'économie,** department of finance, treasury.

ministériel, elle *adj.* ministerial.

ministre *n.m.* minister, Secretary of State, priest, pastor, parson, a Protestant clergyman. **premier ~,** prime minister.

minoritaire *adj.* minority; *n.m.f.* the minority.

minorité *n.f.* minority.

minuit *n.m.* midnight, twelve o'clock at night.

minuscule *adj.* small, minuscule, little, tiny. *n.f.* Print. lowercase.

minute *n.f.* minute (of time); moment, instant.

minuter *v.t.* to time.

minuterie *n.f.* timer, (automatic) time switch.

minutie *n.f.* trifle, trifling matter; minutiae.

minutieusement *adv.* minutely, meticulously.

minutieux, euse *adj.* minute, particular, meticulous, circumstantial.

mioche *n.m.* kid, brat.

mirabelle *n.f.* mirabelle, plum.

miracle *n.m.* miracle.

miraculeusement *adv.* miraculously.

miraculeux, euse *adj.* miraculous.

mirador *n.m.* watchtower, mirador, observation post.

mirage *n.m.* mirage; looming.

mire *n.f.* sight (of a gun or firearm), aim. **prendre sa ~,** to take sight, to take aim. **point de ~,** aim, object aimed at. **ligne de ~,** line of sight.

mirer *v.t.* to aim at, to take aim at, to aim; to examine. **se ~,** *v.refl.* to look at oneself; to admire oneself.

mirette(s) *n.f. Infml.* peepers.

mirifique *adj.* wonderful, marvelous.

mirobolant, e *adj.* fabulous, terrific, staggering.

miroir *n.m.* mirror.

miroitant, e *adj.* glittering.

miroitement *n.m.* glittering, reflection (of light); flashing.

miroiter *v.t.* to polish up. *v.i.* to glitter, to shine, to be reflected.

mise *n.f.* share; stake; bid, bidding; offer; currency, circulation (of coins); dress; admissibility. **~ en possession,** putting into possession. **~ en accusation,** indictment; impeachment. **~ en liberté,** release (from jail). **~ à prix,** reserve price. **~ en vente,** putting up for sale. **~ en scène,** production. **~ en pages,** page makeup, layout. **~ en train,** making ready. **~ à l'eau,** launch, launching (of a ship). **~ au point,** clarification. **de ~,** admissible.

miser *v.t.* to stake (sur, on), to count (sur, on).

misérable *adj.* wretched; destitute, poor; pitiable; miserable. *n.m.f.* wretch, wretched person; rogue, knave, villain.

misérablement *adv.* miserably, wretchedly.

misère *n.f.* poverty, want, destitution; misery, distress; annoyance, plague; trifle, mere nothing. **tomber dans la ~,** to fall into poverty. **faire des ~s à quelqu'un,** to plague someone.

miséricorde *n.f.* mercy, compassion, pity; forgiveness, pardon. **crier ~,** to plead for mercy. **à tout péché ~,** one ought to forgive all offenses.

miséricordieusement *adv.* mercifully.

miséricordieux, euse *adj.* merciful, compassionate.

misogyne *adj.* misogynous; *m.f.* misogynist.

miss *n.f.* beauty queen. **~ France,** Miss France.

missel *n.m.* missal.

missile *n.m.* missile.

mission *n.f.* mission. **envoyer en ~,** to send on a mission. **remplir une ~,** to fulfil a mission.

missionnaire *n.m.* missionary.

missive *adj. n.f.* missive.

mistral *n.m.* mistral.

mite *n.f.* mite; moth.

mité, e *adj.* moth-eaten.

miteux, euse *adj.* dingy, shabby.

mitigation *n.f.* mitigation.

mitiger *v.t.* to mitigate, to soften; to abate, to moderate, to assuage.

mitonner *v.t.* to simmer, to cook with care; to humor (a person), to coddle, to fondle. **se ~,** *v.refl.* to simmer, to soak; to coddle oneself; to be prepared.

mitoyen, enne *adj.* middle, intermediate.

mitoyenneté *n.f.* joint ownership.

mitraillade *n.f.* (volley of) shots, machine-gun fire.

mitrailler *v.t.* to machine gun.

mitrailleuse *n.f.* machine gun.

mixage *n.m.* mixing.

mixer *v.t.* to mix.

mixeur *n.m.* blender.

mixte *adj.* mixed *n.m.* mixed body.

mixture *n.f.* mixture.

mobile *adj.* movable, changeable, variable; fickle, unsteady. *n.m.* moving body, body in motion, mover, motive, spring, cause. **l'argent est son unique ~,** money is his only motive.

mobilier, ière *adj.* personal, movable (of personal property). **les biens ~s,** the personal estate or property; movables, chattels. *n.m.* furniture, set of furniture.

mobilisation *n.f.* mobilization; raising (of capital).

mobiliser *v.t.* to mobilize; to rally; to convert into movables.

mobilité *n.f.* mobility, movableness, fickleness, inconstancy, versatility.

mobylette *n.f.* moped.

mocassin *n.m.* moccasin.

moche *adj. Infml.* ugly.

mocheté *n.f. Infml.* ugliness.

modalité *n.f.* modality; form, mode, method. **~ de paiement,** method of payment, installment plan.

mode *n.m.* mode; form, method. *n.f.* mode; fashion, vogue, manner, way, custom. **une vieille ~,** an old style. **à la ~,** fashionable. **c'est la dernière ~,** it is the latest style.

modelage *n.m.* modelling.

modèle *n.m.* model; copy, pattern; example.

modelé *n.m.* relief; contours.

modeler *v.t.* to model; to mold; to form, to shape. *v.i.* to model. **se ~,** *v.refl.* (with **sur**) to copy, to imitate, to take for one's model.

modéliste *n.m.* dress-designer.

moderateur, trice *n.m.f.* moderator.

modération *n.f.* moderation; abatement, diminution, mitigation (of a penalty).

modéré, e *adj.* moderate.

modérément *adv.* moderately; temperately.

modérer *v.t.* to moderate; to slacken; to restrain, to subdue. **~ ses passions,** to moderate one's passions. **~ sa dépense,** to reduce one's expenses. **se ~,** *v.refl.* to restrain, to moderate oneself; to keep one's temper.

moderne *adj.* modern. *n.m.* modern.

modernisation *n.f.* modernization.

moderniser *v.t.* to modernize.

modern style *adj. n.m.* art nouveau.

modeste *adj.* modest; reserved, unassuming; moderate; humble.

modestement *adv.* modestly; decently; moderately.

modestie *n.f.* modesty; decency; moderation.

modifiable *adj.* modifiable.

modificateur, trice *adj.* modifying. *n.m.* modifier.

modification *n.f.* modification, change.

modifier *v.t.* to modify. **se ~,** *v.refl.* to become modified.

modique *adj.* moderate, small.

modiste *n.f.* milliner.

modulation *n.f.* modulation.

module *n.m.* module; diameter (of a medal); modulus.

moduler *v.i.* to modulate, to sing; (of birds) to warble.

moelle *n.f.* marrow (of bones); pith (of plants); medulla. **jusqu'à la ~,** to the bone.

moelleusement *adv.* softly; luxuriously; mellowly, with mellowness.

moelleux, euse *adj.* soft; marrowy, pithy; mellow.

moeurs *n.f.pl.* manners; morals; habits, customs. **sans ~,** without morals. **autres temps, autres ~,** manners change with the times.

moi *pron.pers.* me. **regardez ~,** look at me. **venez avec ~,** come with me. **selon ~,** in my opinion. **donnez-le ~,** give it to me. **~, trahir le meilleur de mes amis!** I, betraying my best friend!

moignon *n.m.* stump (of amputated limbs, branches, etc.).

moindre *adj.* less, lesser, inferior (to). **le ~ inconvénient,** the least inconvenience. **la ~ chose que je lui doive,** the least thing I owe him.

moindrement *adv.* the least.

moine *n.m.* monk, friar; bed-warmer, heater.

moineau *n.m.* sparrow.

moins *adv.* less, fewer (than), under; minus. **encore ~,** still less. **de ~ en ~,** less and less. **~ que rien,** less than nothing, next to nothing. **~ je travaille, ~ je gagne,** the less I work, the less I earn. **il est midi ~ quart,** it is a quarter to twelve. *n.m.* the least, the least thing; the least quantity; the fewest. **c'est le ~ que vous puissiez faire,** it is the least you can do. **a ~**

de, unless. a ~ qu'elle ne m'écrive, unless she writes to me. au ~, at least. du ~, at least, however; still, nevertheless. pour le ~, at the least.

moirer v.t. to water (textile fabrics).

mois n.m. month. le cinq de ce ~, the fifth of the month. le ~ prochain, next month.

moisi, e adj. moldy, musty. n.m. mildew, moldiness.

moisir v.i. to mildew, to mold, to become moldy, to grow moldy. se ~, v.refl. to grow moldy.

moisissure n.f. mildew, moldiness, mustiness, moldy.

moisson n.f. harvest, crop.

moissonner v.t. to harvest, to gather in, to reap.

moissonneur, euse n.m.f. reaper; harvester. ~ batteuse, combine harvester.

moite adj. moist, damp, humid.

moiteur n.f. moistness, moisture, dampness.

moitié n.f. half. adv. half. à ~ prix, at half price.

moka n.m. mocha.

molaire adj. molar. n.f. molar tooth.

môle n.m. mole, pier, jetty.

moléculaire adj. molecular.

molécule n.f. molecule.

molestation n.f. molestation.

molester v.t. to molest, to annoy, to harass.

mollasse adj. flabby; (of a stuff) flimsy; molasse, limestone.

mollement adv. softly; slackly; flabbily. résister ~, to resist weakly. travailler ~, to work without spirit.

mollesse n.f. softness, mildness; weakness, feebleness, indolence.

mollet, n.m. calf (of the leg).

molleton n.m. soft flannel, swanskin.

moletonner v.t. to line with fleece.

mollo adv. Infml. easy. vas-y ~! take it easy, relax.

mollusque n.m. mollusc.

molosse n.m. mastiff; huge.

môme n.m.f. Infml. kid.

moment n.m. moment, instant; opportunity, occasion; momentum. le ~ est mal choisi pour faire cela, it is not the right time to do that. saisir le bon ~, to seize the right time. attendez un ~, wait a moment. à tout ~, à tous ~s, at every moment, at every turn. au ~ où, just as.

momentané, e adj. momentary.

momentanément adv. momentarily, for a moment.

momie n.f. mummy.

momification n.f. mummification.

momifier v.t. to mummify.

mon adv. poss. m.f. ma; n.f.pl. mes my. ~ père et ma mère, my father and mother. mes amis, my friends. ~ âme, my soul.

monacal, e adj. monachal; monastic.

monarchie n.f. monarchy.

monarchique adj. monarchic, monarchical.

monarchisme n.m. monarchism.

monarchiste n.m. monarchist.

monarque n.m. monarch.

monastère n.m. monastery.

monastique adj. monastic.

monceau n.m. heap, pile, stack.

mondain, aine adj. fashionable; worldly; mundane. n.m.f. socialite.

mondanité n.f. worldliness, worldly vanities; society.

monde n.m. world, society, civilization; countries; mankind; people; multitude. faire le tour du ~, to go (or to sail) round the world. pas le moins du ~, not in the least. tout le ~, everybody. aller dans le ~, to go into society. le grand ~, the upper circles, great people. le beau ~, fashionable society. il y avait beaucoup de ~, there were many people. recevoir du ~, to see company at home; mettre un enfant au ~, to give birth; c'est la fin du ~! that's the end of the world! il connaît bien son ~, he knows his people well. le tiers ~, the Third World.

monder v.t. to hull; to peel (barley).

mondial, e adj. worldwide.

mondialement adv. throughout the world.

mondialisation n.f. worldwide expansion.

mondovision n.f. television broadcast through satellite.

monétaire adj. monetary.

monétisation n.f. giving currency (to paper), transformation into coin; coining, coinage.

monétiser v.t. to give currency to (paper money).

moniteur, trice n.m.f. instructor, coach, counselor; monitor.

monition n.f. monition.

monnaie n.f. money; coin; coinage; cash; mint. fausse ~, counterfeit coin. battre ~, to coin money, to coin; to raise money. de la petite ~, small change. je n'ai pas de ~, I have no change. payer en même ~, to return evil for evil. payer en ~ de singe, to make fun of a person instead of paying him.

monnayage n.m. coinage, mintage.

monnayer v.t. to coin; to mint.

monnayeur n.m. coiner, moneyer. faux ~, counterfeiter.

mono adv. mono.

monocle n.m. monocle.

monocorde n.m. monochord.

monogame adv. monogamous. n.m. monogamist.

monogamie n.f. monogamy, monogamia.

monogramme n.m. monogram.

monographe n.m. monographer, monographist.

monographie n.f. monograph, monography.

monographique adj. monographic, monographical.

monologue n.m. monologue, soliloquy.

monologuer v.i. soliloquize.

monomoteur, trice *adj.* single-engined. *n.m.* single-engined aircraft.

mononucléaire *adj.*, *n.m.* mononuclear.

monopole *n.m.* monopoly.

monopoliser *v.t.* to monopolize; to obtain a monopoly of.

monorail *adj. m.* monorail.

monosyllabe *n.m.* monosyllable *adj.* monosyllabic.

monosyllabique *adj.* monosyllabic.

monothéisme *n.m.* monotheism.

monothéiste *n.m.* monotheist. *adj.* monotheistic.

monotone *adj.* monotonous.

monotonie *n.f.* monotony.

monseigneur *n.m.* Your Highness, Your Eminence, lord.

monsieur *n.m.* sir, gentleman, Mister. **faire le ~,** to play the fine gentleman. **un vilain ~,** a despicable fellow. **mon cher ~,** my dear sir. **~ un tel,** Mr. so and so.

monstre *n.m.* monster *adj.* monster, monstrous, enormous, extraordinary; very large.

monstrueusement *adv.* monstrously.

monstrueux, euse *adj.* monstrous; prodigious; enormous, huge.

monstruosité *n.f.* monstrosity; monstrousness, enormity; monster.

mont *n.m.* mount, mountain le **~ Blanc,** Mont Blanc. **par ~s et par vaux,** up hill and down dale.

montage *n.m.* carrying up; taking up; mounting, setting, editing; montage.

montagnard, e *adj.* mountain, mountainous. *n.m.f.* mountaineer; highlander.

montagne *n.f.* mountain.

montagneux, euse *adj.* mountainous, hilly.

montant, e *adj.* ascending, rising; uphill, *n.m.* upright; post; amount, total, sum total. **le ~ de la note,** the amount of the bill.

montée *n.f.* ascent, rising, rise, acclivity, rise of a hill; staircase. **la ~ est douce,** the ascent is easy.

monter *v.i.* to ascend; to mount; to rise, to arise, to go up; to climb, to clamber up, to walk up, to ride, to set (jewels). **~ et descendre,** to go up and down. **~ au haut d'un arbre,** to climb up a tree. **~ dans sa chambre,** to go up to one's room. **~ à cheval,** to ride, to mount a horse, to ride horseback. **~ une côte,** to ascend a hill. **~ un coup,** to premeditate a job. **~ une affaire,** to set up a business. **~ la tête à quelqu'un,** to work a person up. **le baromètre monte,** the barometer is going up. **la marée monte,** the tide is rising. **se ~,** *v.refl.* to be mounted; to provide onself; to get excited; to amount to, to furnish oneself with.

monteur *n.m.* mounter, setter (of gems); framer; editor (of films).

montgolfière *n.f.* air balloon.

monticule *n.m.* hillock.

montre *n.f.* watch; show; display; appearance.

faire ~ d'(esprit), to show off one's wit. **~ d'or,** gold watch. **~-bracelet,** wristwatch.

montrer *v.t.* to show; to exhibit, to point out; to manifest, to evince; to teach. **montrez-moi cette lettre,** show me that letter. **~ quelqu'un au doigt,** to point at a person. **se ~,** *v.refl.* to show oneself, to make one's appearance; to prove oneself.

monture *n.f.* animal (for the saddle), nag; mounting, setting; stock (of a gun, a pistol).

monument *n.m.* monument; edifice; tomb.

monumental, e *adj.* monumental.

moquer (se) *v.refl.* (with de) to laugh at; to deride, to mock; to make fun of, to scoff at. **se ~ de quelqu'un,** to laugh at a person. **c'est se ~ du monde,** it is making fun of people. **se faire ~ de soi,** to get laughed at.

moquerie *n.f.* mockery, derision, jeer, jeering, scoffing.

moquette *n.f.* carpet, carpeting; decoy bird.

moqueur, euse *adj.* mocking, deriding, jeering, scoffing; scornful.

moral, e *adj.* moral. *n.m.* morale, spirit, mind, moral faculties, mental faculties.

morale *n.f.* morals, morality; moral, code, ethic; reprimand, lecture, **faire la ~ à quelqu'un,** to lecture someone.

moralement *adv.* morally.

moralisateur, trice *adj.* moralizing; good, sound.

moralisation *n.f.* moralization.

moraliser *v.i.* to moralize, to lecture.

moraliste *n.m.* moralist, philosopher.

moralité *n.f.* moral reflection, moral (of a fable); morality; morals. **il est d'une ~ irréprochable,** he is a man of irreproachable character.

moratoire *n.m.* moratorium.

morbide *adj.* morbid; mellow, soft and delicate.

morbidité *n.f.* morbidity.

morceau *n.m.* bit, morsel; piece, passage, text. **un ~ de pain,** a piece of bread. **un ~ sur le pouce,** a snack. **~x choisis,** select pieces. **un ~ à quatre mains,** a piece of music for four hands.

morceler *v.t.* to parcel out, subdivide. **se ~,** *v.refl.* to be parcelled out.

morcellement *n.m.* parcelling out, subdividing.

mordant, e *adj.* biting; mordant; corrosive; caustic, sarcastic. **un homme ~,** a sarcastic man. *n.m.* mordant; keenness, poignancy.

mordicus *adv. Infml.* obstinately, stoutly, tenaciously.

mordillage *n.m.* nibbling.

mordiller *v.t.* to nibble; to gnaw.

mordoré, e *adj.* reddish brown.

mordre *v.t.* to bite, to nibble, to gnaw; to bite off, to nip, to nip off; to snap at a bait; to eat away, to corrode; to hold fast on; to catch on. **se ~ la langue,** to bit one's tongue. **~ la poussière, la terre,** to bite the dust. **~ à l'hameçon,** to snap

at the bait. **il n'y mordra pas,** he won't buy it.
se ~, *v.refl.* to bite oneself; to bite each other.
mordu, e *pa. p.* bitten, bit. **c'est un ~ de la musique,** he is crazy about music.

morfondre (se) *v.t.* to mope.

morgue *n.f.* haughtiness, arrogance; morgue, mortuary.

moribond, e *adj.* dying. *n.m. f.* dying person.

morille *n.f.* morel.

mormon *n.m.* Mormon.

morne *adj.* dejected, sad, dull, gloomy, dismal.

morose *adj.* morose, surly, peevish, churlish, sour.

morosité *n.f.* moroseness, morosity, surliness, peevishness.

morphème *n.m.* morpheme.

morphine *n.f.* morphine, morphia.

morphologie *n.f.* morphology.

morpion *n.m.* crablouse; child, kid, brat.

mors *n.m.* bit (of a bridle). **prendre le ~ aux dents,** to bolt; to buckle down (to), to work earnestly; to fly into a passion.

morse *n.m.* walrus, seahorse; Morse code.

morsure *n.f.* bite, biting; sting.

mort *n.f.* death; decease, demise; ruin, destruction. **~ subite,** sudden, death. **mettre à ~,** to put to death. **souffrir mille ~s,** to be in a predicament. **affronter la ~,** to face death. **la peine de ~,** capital punishment. **blessé à ~,** mortally wounded.

mort, e *adj.* dead, inanimate, lifeless; deathlike; **à demi ~,** half-dead. **langue ~e,** dead language. **nature ~e,** still life. *Naut.* upper works. *n.m.f.* dead person; dead; dead body. **le jour des ~s,** All Souls' Day. **office des ~s,** burial service.

mortadelle *n.f.* mortadella, Bologna sausage.

mortalité *n.f.* mortality.

mortel, elle *adj.* mortal; deadly, fatal, excessive, tedious, harassing. **la dépouille ~e,** the mortal remains. *n.m. f.* mortal. **un heureux ~,** a happy mortal.

mortellement *adv.* mortally, deadly, fatally, irrecoverably, excessively, extremely, intensely.

mortier *n.m.* mortar.

mortification *n.f.* mortification.

mortifier *v.t.* to mortify.

mort-né *adj. m.* stillborn child.

mortuaire *adj.* mortuary; burial.

morue *n.f.* cod, cod fish.

morve *n.f.* glanders (of horses); snot.

morveux, euse *adj.* (of horses) glandered; snotty, snot-nosed.

mosaïque *adj.* Mosaic. *n.f.* mosaic-work, mosaic.

mosquée *n.f.* mosque.

mot *n.m.* word; expression, term; saying, motto, sentence; a line; message. **~ dérivé,** derivative word. **bon ~,** jest, witticism. **gros ~s,** vulgar words. **dire un ~ à l'oreille,** to whisper a word in a person's ear. **lâcher le ~,** to let out the word. **quel est votre dernier ~?** what is your lowest price? **se donner le ~,** to plan a thing

together. **en un ~,** in a word, in short. **en deux ~,** in a word. **~ à ~,** word for word, verbatim, literally. **sans ~ dire,** without a word, **~s croisés,** crosswords. **~ de passe,** password. **il n'a pas mâché ses ~s,** he didn't mince his words.

motard *n.m,* motorcycle cop; biker.

motel *n.m.* motel.

motet *n.m.* motet.

moteur, trice *n.m. f.,* engine; **~ à reaction,** jet engine, motor *adj.* moving; motive.

motif *n.m.* motive; incitement, incentive, cause, reason, grounds. *Mus.* subject of a composition.

motion *n.f.* motion, movement.

motivation *n.f.* motivation.

motiver *v.t.* to justify, to cause, to motivate, to stimulate; to allege the motive or the grounds of; to bring about.

moto *n.f. Infml.* (motor) bike.

motocross *n.m.* motorcross.

motoculteur *n.m.* cultivator.

motocycle *n.m.* motorcycle.

motocyclette *n.f.* motorcycle.

motocyclisme *n.m.* motorcycle racing.

motocycliste *n.m.f.* motorcyclist.

motonautique *adj.* motor boat, speedboat.

motorisation *n.f.* motorization.

motoriser *v.* to motorize.

motrice *n.f.* motor unit.

motte *n.f.,* block (butter); clod, lump.

motus *interj.* hush! mum! **~ et bouche cousue,** not a word to anyone.

mou, mol, molle *adj.* soft; weak, feeble; slack; tame. **une vie molle et oisive,** an idle, luxurious life. *n.m.* lights (of an animal); *Naut.* slack.

mouchard *n.m.* snitch, spy, stool pigeon; informer.

moucharder *v.i. Infml.* to snitch, to squeal on; to spy on.

mouche *n.f.* fly; patch, beauty spot; tuft (of beard). **grosse ~,** blow fly. **quelle ~ l'a piqué?** what is the matter with him? what has gotten into him? **faire la ~ du coche,** to make a useless scene. **faire d'une ~ un éléphant,** to make a mountain of a mole hill. **une fine ~,** a sly cunning person.

moucher *v.t.* to wipe the nose of (a child); to snuff (a candle). **se ~,** *v.refl.* to blow one's nose. **il ne se mouche pas du pied,** he is no fool.

moucheron *n.m.* gnat, small fly; snuff (of a candle).

moucheté, e *adj.* spotted, speckled; blunted, tipped with a button (as a foil).

moucheter *v.t.* to spot, to speckle.

mouchoir *n.m.* handkerchief.

moudre *v.t.* to grind.

moue *n.f.* pouting; wry face, grimace.

mouette *n.f.* gull, seagull, mew, seamew.

moufle *n.f.* mitten; tackle, block and fall. *n.m. Chem.* muffle.

mouillage *n.m.* wetting, soaking, watering; anchorage, anchoring.

mouillé, e *adj.* wet, moist. **des yeux ~s de larmes,** eyes wet with tears.

mouiller *v.t.* to wet, to moisten; to soak, to drench; to steep; to water, to bathe, to cast, to let go (the anchor); to anchor, to moor. **se ~,** *v.refl.* to get wet, to be drenched. **mes yeux se mouillèrent,** my eyes filled with tears.

mouillette *n.f.* sippet.

moulage *n.m.* molding, casting.

moule *n.m.* mold, cast form. **jeter au ~,** to cast. **une personne faite au ~,** a well-shaped person. *n.f.* mussel; simpleton.

mouler *v.t.* to model, to cast. **se ~,** *v.refl.* (with sur) to fit exactly; to be modelled; (with sur) to imitate, to take as a model, to pattern on. **se ~ sur quelqu'un,** to model oneself on someone.

moulin *n.m.* mill. **~ à eau,** watermill **~ à vent,** windmill. **~ à café,** coffee mill. **faire venir l'eau au ~,** to bring grist to the mill. **un ~ à paroles,** chatterbox, babbler.

moulu, e *pa. p.* ground; divided; *Fig.* beaten; bruised.

moulure *n.f.* molding.

mourant, e *adj.* dying, expiring; deathlike; languishing. **des regards ~s,** languishing looks *n.m. f.* dying person; *pl.* the dying.

mourir *v.i.* to die; to decease, to perish, to lose life; to drop off; to go off; to go out (of a fire); to come to an end. **~ de vieillesse,** to die of old age. **~ de faim,** to starve, to die of hunger. **je suis triste à ~,** I am grieved to death. **faire ~,** to put to death, to kill; to be the death of. **elle nous a fait ~ de rire,** she was killing us, we were dying of laughter. **être mort d'enquiétude,** to be worried sick. **être mort d'ennui,** to be bored to tears. **se ~,** *v.refl.* to be dying; to die away, to come to an end; to go out. **se faire du ~,** *fig.* to be worried sick.

mouron *n.m.* pimpernel; chickweed.

mousquet *n.m.* musket.

mousquetaire *n.m.* musketeer.

mousse *adj.* blunt. *n.m.* cabin boy, ship's boy. *n.f.* moss; foam, froth; lather (of soap).

mousseline *n.f.* muslin.

mousser *v.i.* to froth, to foam; to lather (as soap); to sparkle (as wine). **faire ~,** to froth; to puff.

mousseron *n.m.* button-mushroom.

mousseux, euse *adj.* mossy, moss; foaming, frothy.

mousson *n.f.* monsoon.

moussu, e *adj.* mossy; moss-clad, moss-grown; moss.

moustache *n.f.* mustache; whiskers (of animals).

moustiquaire *n.m.* mosquito net.

moustique *n.m.* mosquito.

moût *n.m.* must; sweet wort.

moutard *n.m.* little boy, brat, urchin.

moutarde *n.f.* mustard, **la ~ lui est montée au nez,** he lost it, he flew off the handle.

mouton *n.m.* sheep, mutton, sheep's wool, mild person, prison spy. **troupeau de ~s,** flock of sheep. **revenons à nos ~s,** let us resume our subject.

moutonner *v.t.* to frizzle, to render fleecy, to foam, to froth.

moutonneux, euse *adj.* foamy, frothy.

mouvement *n.m.* motion, movement, bustle, stir. maneuver, evolution. *Mus.* movement, time, measure. **~ accéléré,** accelerated motion. **faire un ~,** to move. **mettre en ~,** to set in motion. **le ~ de la population,** the fluctuation of the population. **changer de ~,** to play faster or slower. **les ~s de l'âme,** the impulses of the soul; **faire un ~ de tête,** to nod. **le ~ d'une pendule,** the movement of a clock. **les ~s populaires,** disturbances among the people.

mouvementé, e *adj.* agitated, stormy.

mouvoir *v.t.* to move, to stir. **se ~,** *v.refl.* to move; to stir.

moyen, enne *adj.* middle, mean, average; middling; middle-sized, moderate. **Moyen Aêge,** Middle Ages. **température ~e,** mean temperature. **de taille ~e,** middle-sized. **de ~e grandeur,** middle-sized *n.m.* mean, means; medium, way, power, parts. **trouver le ~ de faire quelque chose,** to find the means of doing something. **par tous les ~,** by all means. **il n'y a pas ~ de faire cela,** there is no way to do that. **c'est un homme sans ~s,** he has no abilities. **au ~ de,** by means of. **il n'a pas les ~s de s'acheter une voiture,** he can't afford to buy himself a car.

moyennant *prep.* by means of, for. **~ que,** on condition that.

moyenne *n.f.* mean, average; **avoir la ~,** to get the passing grade.

moyennement *adv.* moderately, middlingly.

moyenner *v.t.* to mediate, to procure.

muable *adj.* mutable, changeable.

mucus *n.m.* mucus.

mue *n.f.* moulting, moult; mewing; moulting time; slough, cast skin (of animals); mew; breaking (of the voice).

muer *v.t.* to change; to moult, to mew, to break (as the voice).

muet, ette *adj.* mute dumb, speechless; silent. **sourd et ~,** deaf and dumb.

mufle *n.m.* muffle; muzzle, snout; *Fig.* skunk.

mugir *v.i.* to bellow, to low, to roar, to bawl out, to vociferate.

mugissement *n.m.* bellowing, bellow (of bulls); lowing (of oxen); roaring.

muguet *n.m.* lily of the valley.

mulâtre, esse *n.m.f.,* mulatto.

mule *n.f.* slipper; mule, she-mule. **~ Jenny,** mule, mule-jenny.

mulet *n.m.* mule, he-mule; mullet.

mulot *n.m.* field mouse.

multicolore *adj.* multicolor, many-colored.

multiculturalisme *m.* multiculturalism.

multiculturel *adj.* multicultural.

multidisciplinaire *adj.* multidisciplinary.

multifide *adj. Zool.* multifid.

multiflore *adj.* multiflorous, many-flowered.

multiforme *adj.* multiform.

multilatéral, e *adj.* multilateral, many-sided.

multipare *adj.* multiparous.

multiple *adj.* multiple.

multiplicateur *n.m.* multiplier.

multiplication *n.f.* multiplication.

multiplier *v.t.* to multiply. **se ~,** *v.refl.* to multiply.

multiprocesseur *n.m.* multiprocessor.

multiprogrammation *n.f.* multiprogramming.

multiracial *adj.* multiracial.

multirisque *adj.* **assurance ~,** comprehensive insurance.

multitude *n.f.* multitude.

municipal, e *adj.* municipal *n.m.* municipal officer, municipal guard.

municipalité *n.f.* municipality; town council; town hall.

munir *v.t.* to supply, to provide (with). **se ~,** *v.refl.* to provide oneself (with); *Fig.* to arm oneself (with).

munition *n.f.* ammunition, munition. **pain de ~,** soldier's bread; *pl.* provisions, stores; munitions.

munitionnaire *n.m.* commissary of provisions.

munitionner *v.t.* to supply with munitions.

muqueux, euse *adj.* mucous.

mur *n.m.* wall. **entourer de ~s,** to wall in. **mettre quelqu'un au pied du ~,** to put someone up against a wall. **le Mur des Lamentations,** the Wailing Wall. **~ du son,** sound barrier.

mûr, e *adj.* ripe, mature; **des fruits ~s,** ripe fruits.

murage *n.m.* walling up.

muraille *n.f.* wall, rampart. **sans ~s,** unwalled. **la Grande Muraille de Chine,** the Great Wall of China.

mural, e *adj.* mural.

mûre *n.f.* mulberry. **~ sauvage,** blackberry.

mûrement *adv.* maturely.

murer *v.t.* to wall, to wall in; to enclose or surround with walls; to wall up.

mûrier *n.m.* mulberry tree, mulberry.

mûrir *v.i.* to ripen, to mature; to come to maturity; to bring to completeness or perfection. **se ~,** *v.refl.* to ripen, to mature, to grow ripe.

mûrissant, e *adj.* ripening.

murmure *n.m.* murmur; (of winds) breath, whispering; hum (of bees). **le ~ des eaux,** the purling of water. **~ d'approbation,** murmur of approbation.

murmurer *v.i.* to murmur; to mutter; (of bees) to hum. **je ne sais ce qu'il murmure entre ses dents,** I do not know what he is muttering between his teeth. **se ~,** *v.refl.* to be whispered, to be whispered about.

musaraigne *n.f.* shrew (mouse).

musarder *v.i.* to loiter, to trifle, to dawdle.

musc *n.m.* musk.

muscade *n.f.* nutmeg. **noix ~,** nutmeg.

muscadet *n.m.* muscadel, muscatel.

muscat *adj.* musk, muscadel, muscatel *n.m.* muscatel grape; musk-pear.

muscle *n.m.* muscle.

musclé, e *adj.* muscled.

muscler *v.t.* to develop the muscles of. **se ~,** to develop one's muscles.

musculaire *adj.* muscular.

musculation *n.f.* bodybuilding.

musculature *n.f.* musculature.

muse *n.f.* Muse.

museau *n.m.* muzzle, snout.

musée *n.m.* museum.

museler *v.t.* to muzzle; to silence, to gag.

muselière *n.f.* muzzle; gag.

muséum *n.m.* natural history museum.

musical, e *adj.* musical.

musicalement *adv.* musically.

music-hall *n.m.* music hall; show business.

musicien, ienne *n.m. f.* musician.

musicographe *n.m.* musicgrapher.

musique *n.f.* music; band, musicians. **~ vocale,** vocal music. **~ instrumentale,** instrumental music.

musqué, e *adj.* musked, musk, musky. **boeuf ~,** musk ox. **style ~,** affected style. **paroles ~es,** flattering words.

musulman, e *n.m. f.,* Muslim, Moslem.

mutabilité *n.f.* mutability.

mutation *n.f.* mutation; change.

muter *v.t.* to transfer, to mute, to change; to mutate.

mutilateur, trice *n.m. f.* mutilator.

mutilation *n.f.* mutilation; maiming.

mutiler *v.t.* to mutilate; to maim.

mutin, e *adj.* seditious; mutinous. *n.m. f.* rebel, rioter, mutineer.

mutiné, e *adj.* mutinous.

mutiner *v.t.* to raise, to excite; to rise up; *Fig.* to excite, to stir up. **se ~,** *v.refl.* to mutiny, to rise up, to rebel, to revolt; to grow angry.

mutinerie *n.f.* revolt; mutiny.

mutisme *n.m.* speechlessness, muteness; silence.

mutualité *n.f.* mutuality; mutual insurance.

mutuel, elle *adj.* mutual; reciprocal, interchanged.

mutuellement *adv.* mutually, reciprocally.

mycose *n.f.* mycosis, athlete's foot.

myocarde *n.m.* myocardum.

myope *n.m.f.* myope, short-sighted person. *adj.* myopic, short-sighted.

myopie *n.f.* myopy.

myosotis *n.m.* myosotis, forget-me-not.

myriade *n.f.* myriad.

myrtille *n.f.* bilberry, black wortleberry.

mystère *n.m.* mystery, secret; enigma. **faire**

~ de, faire un ~ de, to make a mystery of.
mystérieusement *adv.* mysteriously.
mystérieux, euse *adj.* mysterious, obscure, secret, hidden. *n.m.* mysteriousness.
mysticisme *n.m.* mysticism.
mystificateur *adj.* hoax, deceptive. *n.m.* hoaxer, deceiver.

mystification *n.f.* hoax, mystification.
mystifier *v.t.* to hoax, to mystify.
mystique *adj. n.m.f.* mystic, mystical.
mystiquement *adv.* mystically.
mythe *n.m.* myth; fable.
mythique *adj.* mythic, mythical.
mythologie *n.f.* mythology.

N

n *n.m.* the fourteenth letter of the alphabet. N, contraction of NE, (abbrev.) north.
n' V. NE.
na *Interj.* so there. **je ne dirais rien, ~!** I won't say a thing, so there!
nabot, e *n.m.f.* dwarf.
nacelle *n.f.* skiff, bark; nacelle; basket.
nacre *n.f.* nacre, mother of pearl.
nacré, e *adj.* nacreous, pearly.
nacrer *v.t.* to give a nacreous luster to.
nage *n.f.* swimming, swim. **à la ~,** swimming, by swimming. **se jeter à la ~,** to jump into the water. **être en ~, tout en ~,** to be covered in perspiration, in sweat.
nageoire *n.f.* fin, flipper; float.
nager *v.i.* to swim; to row, to pull. **~ entre deux eaux,** to swim under water; *Fig.* to waver between two parties. **~ dans le sang,** to be bathed in blood.
nageur, euse *n.m.f.* swimmer; rower.
naguère *adj.* lately, not long since, not long ago.
naïf, ïve *adj.* simple, ingenuous, green; naive. *n.m.* naive style; that which is natural.
nain, e *n.m.f.* dwarf. **de ~,** dwarfish. *adj.* dwarf, dwarfish.
naissance *n.f.* birth; beginning, rise, spring; springing (of an arch). **jour de ~,** birthday. **lieu de ~,** birthplace. **la ~ d'une ville,** the origin of a town. **donner ~ à,** to give birth to.
naître *v.i.* to be born; to come into the world; to spring up, to come up; to arise, to originate; to take its rise, to rise. **ce ruisseau naît près d'ici,** this stream begins near here. **cela me fit ~ l'idée de voyager,** that gave me the idea of traveling. **encore à ~,** yet unborn.
naïvement *adv.* ingenuously, naively, innocently.
naïveté *n.f.* ingenuousness, artlessness, naiveté, simplicity, naturalness.
nana *n.f. Infml.* girlfriend.
nantir *v.t.* to provide oneself with; to secure, to make sure of.
naphtaline *n.f.* mothballs.
nappe *n.f.* cloth, tablecloth, sheet (of water); layer (**brouillard**). **mettre la ~,** to lay the cloth.
napper *v.t.* to coat.
napperon *n.m.* tablemat.
narcisse *n.m.* Narcissus. *n.m.* narcissus.
narcissique *adj.* narcissistic.
narcissisme *n.m.* narcissism.
narcotique *adj.* narcotic. *n.m.* narcotic.

narguer *v.t.* to taunt, to nag, to defy, to set in defiance; to snap one's fingers at.
narine *n.f.* nostril.
narquois, e *adj.* mocking, satirical; sly; deep, cunning.
narrateur, trice *n.m.f.* narrator, relater.
narratif, ive *adj.* narrative.
narration *n.f.* narration; narrative.
narrer *v.t.* to narrate, to relate, to recite, to tell, to state.
nasal, e *adj.* nasal. **sons nasaux,** nasal sounds.
nasale *n.f. Gram.* nasal.
naseau *n.m.* nostril.
nasillard, e *adj.* snuffling; having a nasal twang.
nasillement *n.m.* snuffling.
nasiller *v.i.* to snuffle; to speak through the nose.
natal, e *adj.* natal; native.
natalité *n.f.* birth rate.
natation *n.f.* swimming.
natif, ive *adj.* native; natural. *n.m.* native.
nation *n.f.* nation; people.
national, e *adj.* national.
nationalement *adv.* nationally.
nationalisation *n.f.* nationalization.
nationaliser *v.t.* to nationalize.
nationalité *n.f.* nationality.
nativité *n.f.* nativity.
natte *n.f.* mat, matting; braid.
natter *v.t.* to mat; to braid.
naturalisation *n.f.* naturalization.
naturaliser *v.t.* to naturalize; to acclimate.
naturalité *n.f.* naturalness; citizenship.
nature *n.f.* nature, kind, sort, species, description. **la ~ humaine,** human nature. **paysage fait d'après ~,** a landscape drawn from nature. **tableau de ~ morte,** a painting of still life. **payer en ~,** to pay in kind. **contre ~,** unnaturally.
naturel, elle *adj.* natural; nature, free, easy. *n.m.* native; nature; disposition, temper. **c'est le ~ du poisson de vivre dans l'eau,** it is the nature of fish to live in water. **un bon ~,** a good-natured man. **au ~,** from nature, to the life. *Culin.* simply cooked.
naturellement *adv.* naturally.
naufrage *n.m.* wreck; shipwreck. **faire ~,** to be shipwrecked; to be wrecked.
naufragé, e *adj.* shipwrecked, wrecked.
nauséabond, e *adj.* nauseous, loathsome, sickening.

nausée *n.f.* nausea, disgust, loathing.

nautile *n.m.* nautilus.

nautique *adj.* nautic, nautical; naval, sea. **carte ~,** (sea) chart.

naval, e *adj.* naval. **combat ~,** sea fight.

navet *n.m.* turnip, flop. **ce film était un vrai ~,** this film was a turkey.

navette *n.f.* shuttle (transport).

navigabilité *adj.* navigability; seaworthiness; airworthiness.

navigable *adj.* navigable.

navigateur *n.m.* navigator; sailor. *adj.* seafaring.

navigation *n.f.* navigation; voyage.

naviguer *v.i.* to navigate, to sail.

navire *n.m.* ship, vessel. **~ marchand,** merchant ship.

navrant, e *adj.* heartrending, distressing.

navrer *v.t.* to wound; to break the heart of, to wring, to distress.

nazi *adj. n.m.f.* nazi.

nazisme *n.m.* nazism.

ne *adv.* (with **pas** or **point**) no, not. **il ~ veut pas,** he doesn't want. **je ~ sais pas,** I don't know. **il ~ cesse de se plaindre,** he complains all the time. **vous ~ sauriez le refuser,** you could not refuse it. **~ que,** but, only. **~ plus,** no more, no longer. **~ ... rien,** nothing. **~ personne,** nobody.

né, e *p.p.* of **naître,** born; by birth. **mort ~,** still-born. **nouveau ~,** newborn. **être né(e) sous une bonne étoile,** to be born under a lucky star.

néanmoins *adv.* nevertheless, however, notwithstanding.

néant *n.m.* nothing; nullity; nought, naught, nothingness.

nébuleuse *n.f.* nebula.

nébuleux, euse *adj.* nebulous, cloudy, unclear.

nécessaire *adj.* necessary, requisite. **c'est un mal ~,** it is a necessary evil. *n.m.pl.* necessities. **faire le ~,** to do what is necessary.

nécessairement *adv.* necessarily; needs, indispensably.

nécessité *n.f.* necessity; unavoidableness, need. **faire de ~ vertu,** to make a virtue of necessity. **tomber dans la ~,** to fall into poverty. **la ~ n'a pas de loi,** necessity knows no law. **de ~,** necessarily. **par ~,** through want, from necessity.

nécessiter *v.t.* to necessitate; to compel, to force, to oblige.

nécessiteux, euse *adj.* needy, indigent, in need.

nec plus ultra *n.m. Lat.* ne plus ultra.

nécrologie *n.f.* necrology.

nécromancie *n.f.* necromancy.

nectar *n.m.* nectar.

néfaste *adj.* ill-omened, inauspicious, unlucky, fatal.

nèfle *n.f.* medlar. **ça lui a coûté des ~s,** it cost him almost nothing.

négatif, ive *adj.* negative; denying. *Photo.* negative.

négation *n.f.* negation; denial, disavowal.

négative *n.f.* negative; refusal.

négativement *adv.* negatively, in the negative.

négligé, e *adj.* neglected; offhand; (of persons) negligent, slovenly, regardless, neglectful. *n.m.* undress, negligee, dishabille.

négligeable *adj.* that may be neglected or omitted, insignificant.

négligemment *adv.* casually, neglectfully, negligently.

négligence *n.f.* negligence; neglect.

négligent, e *adj.* negligent, neglectful.

négliger *v.t.* to neglect, to slight, to slight over, to be negligent of; to disregard. **se ~,** *v.refl.* to neglect oneself.

négoce *n.m.* trade, business.

négociable *adj.* negotiable.

négociant *n.m.* wholesaler, dealer, merchant.

négociateur, trice *n.m.f.* negotiator.

négociation *n.f.* negotiation.

négocier *v.i.* to negociate.

nègre *n.m. Pej.* negro. **la traite des ~s,** to work like a slave.

négresse *n.f. Pej.* negress.

négrier *n.m.* slave ship; slave trader.

neige *n.f.* snow. **devenir blanc comme ~,** to become as white as snow. **bonhomme de ~,** snow man.

neiger *v.i. impers.* to snow.

neigeux, euse *adj.* snowy.

nénuphar *n.m.* nenuphar, water lily.

néon *n.m.* neon, neon light.

nerf *n.m.* nerve, sinew, tendon, ligament; strength, force, power; sinews. **il me porte sur les ~s,** he is getting on my nerves. **avoir les ~s à fleur de peau,** to be on the edge.

nerveusement *adv.* nervously.

nerveux, euse *adj.* nervous, sinewy, wiry, vigorous; forcible, spirited. **dépression ~,** nervous breakdown.

nervosité *n.f.* nervousness.

n'est-ce-pas *adj.* isn't it, doesn't he/she/it? **elle est gentille, ~?** she is a nice girl, isn't she?

net, nette *adj.* clean; neat, tidy; sound; pure, clear, unspotted; legible; net. **avoir les mains nettes,** to have clean hands. **avoir la conscience nette,** to have a clear conscience. **bénefice ~,** net profits. *n.m.* fair copy. **mettre au ~ un écrit,** to make a fair copy of a writing. *adv.* at once, short, clean off, right off. **pour vous parler ~,** to be frank with you. **je vais lui dire tout ~,** I'm going to tell him/her right out. **s'arrêter ~,** to stop short.

nettement *adv.* cleanly, neatly; clearly; distinctly; plainly, explicitly; frankly.

netteté *n.f.* cleanness, cleanliness, neatness, clearness; brilliancy; plainness. **il a beaucoup de ~ dans les idées,** his ideas are very clear.

nettoiement, nettoyage *n.m.* cleansing, cleaning; clearing; scouring; sweeping. **~ à sec,** dry cleaning.

nettoyer *v.t.* to clean, to clear, to rid of, to sweep; to wipe; to wash up. ~ **la cuisine,** to clean the kitchen. **il s'est fait ~,** he got cleaned out, robbed.

nettoyeur, euse *adj.* cleaning. *n.m.f.* cleaner.

neuf *adj.* nine; ninth. **ils sont ~,** they are nine. **cent ~,** one hundred and nine. **~ fois,** nine times. **le ~ juillet,** the 9th of July. *n.m.* nine. **le ~ de coeur,** the nine of hearts.

neuf, neuve *adj.* new; fresh, novel, inexperienced, green, novice, raw. **une maison neuve,** a new house. **il est tout ~ dans ce métier-là,** he is quite a novice in that trade. **des pensées neuves,** new thoughts. *n.m.* new; what is new; something new. **à ~,** like new, anew, new again. **mettre à ~,** to renovate.

neurasthénie *n.f.* depression, neurosis.

neurologie *n.f.* neurology.

neutralisation *n.f.* neutralization.

neutraliser *v.t.* to neutralize. **se ~,** *v.refl.* to neutralize each other.

neutralité *n.f.* neutrality.

neutre *adj.* and *n.m.* neuter; neutral. **le genre ~,** the neuter gender. **verbe ~,** neuter verb. **le droit des ~s,** the rights of neuters.

neutron *n.m.* neutron.

neuvième *adj.* ninth. *n.m.* ninth; ninth part.

neuvièmement *adv.* ninthly.

neveu *n.m.* nephew.

névalgie *n.f.* neuralgia.

névralgique *adj.* neuralgic.

névrite *n.f.* neuritis.

névritique *adj.* neurotic.

névrose *n.f.* neurosis.

névrosé, e *adj. n.m.f.* neurotic (person).

névrotique *adj.* neurotic (thing).

nez *n.m.* nose; face, visage; scent; smell. **un ~ aquilin,** an aquiline nose. **un ~ camus,** a snub nose. **un ~ retroussé,** a turned-up nose. **ne pas voir plus loin que son ~,** not to see beyond one's nose. **tirer les vers du ~ à quelqu'un,** to pump a person. **mettre le ~ dans les affaires d'autrui,** to meddle in other people's business. **se casser le ~,** to be disappointed. **regarder quelqu'un au ~,** to stare at a person. **mettre le ~ dehors,** to look out. **fermer à quelqu'un la porte au ~,** to shut the door in a person's face. **rire au ~ de quelqu'un,** to laugh at a person's face. **ce chien a bon ~,** that dog has scent. **avoir bon ~,** to be sagacious.

ni *conj* nor; (repeated) neither . . . nor. **n'être ~ bon ~ mauvais,** to be neither good nor bad.

niable *adj.* deniable.

niais, e *adj.* silly, simple, foolish. *n.m.f.* simpleton, ninny.

niaisement *adv.* foolishly.

niaiserie *n.f.* silly thing, foolery, nonsense, trifle.

niche *n.f.* niche; recess; (for a dog), kennel; prank, trick. **faire des ~s à quelqu'un,** to play tricks on a person.

nichée *n.f.* nestlings; nest; brood; lot, set, crew.

nicher *v.t.* to nestle, to nest; to build a nest; to lodge, to put, to place. **se ~,** *v.refl.* to nestle; to lie, to hide oneself; to creep (into).

nichon *n.m. Infml.* breast.

nickel *n.m.* nickel. **sa maison est ~,** her house is spick and span.

nicotine *n.f.* nicotine.

nid *n.m.* nest; home. **petit à petit l'oiseau fait son ~,** little strokes fell great oaks. **trouver la pie au ~,** to find a mare's nest.

nièce *n.f.* niece.

nier *v.t.* to deny; to disown. **~ une dette,** to deny a debt.

nigaud, e *adj.* silly. *n.m.f.* simpleton.

nihilisme *n.m.* nihilism; nothingness, nihility; reduction to nothing.

nihiliste *n.m.f.* nihilist. *adj.* nihilistic.

nitouche *n.f.* **Sainte ~,** sanctimonious person, demure-looking person, demure hypocrite.

nitrate *n.m.* nitrate.

nitrification *n.f.* nitrification.

nitrifier (se) *v.refl.* to nitrify.

nitrique *adj.* nitric.

nitrite *n.m.* nitrite, azotite.

nitrogène *n.m.* nitrogen, azote.

nitroglycérine *n.f.* nitroglycerine.

niveau *n.m.* level. **~ d'eau,** water level. **~ des eaux,** watermark. **être au ~ de,** to be level with, to be on a level with. **l'eau lui arrivait au ~ des genoux,** the water was up to his knees.

niveler *v.t.* to level, to bring to equality of condition, rank or degree.

nivellement *n.m.* leveling.

nobiliaire *adj.* noble of the nobility. *n.m.* peerage, list of the nobility.

noble *adj.* noble, generous. **~ de naissance,** of noble birth. *n.m.* noble, nobleman.

noblement *adv.* nobly, generously.

noblesse *n.f.* nobility, nobleness. **la haute ~,** high nobility. **petite ~,** lesser nobility, gentry. **la ~ de ses sentiments,** the nobleness of his feelings. **~ du style,** loftiness of style.

noce *n.f.pl.* wedding, nuptials, marriage. **épouser une femme en premières ~s,** to take as a first wife. **~s d'argent,** silver wedding. **faire la ~,** *Infml.* to live it up; to enjoy oneself. **n'être pas à la ~,** to be in no pleasant situation.

nocif, ive *adj.* harmful.

noctambule *n.m.f.* noctambulist, sleepwalker. *adj.* night-walking.

noctune *adj.* nocturnal; nightly. *n.m. Mus.* serenade.

Noël *n.m.* Christmas, Yule. **Noël** Christmas carol. **à la fête de ~,** at Christmas. **arbre de ~,** Christmas tree. **le père Noël,** Santa Claus.

noeud *n.m.* knot; bow (or ribbons); tie; hitch, difficulty; bond; snare, noose; knob, knuckle; nautical distance. *Astron.* node. **un ~ serré,** a hard knot. **double ~,** doubleknot. **~ coulant,**

noose, slip knot. **filer six** ~**s à l'heure,** to run six knots an hour. **voici le** ~ **de cet événement,** this is the knotty point of this event. **bois plein de** ~**s,** knotty wood.

noir, e *adj.* black, dark; sable; obscure; gloomy, mournful, low-spirited; wicked, heinous, foul. **des cheveu** ~**s,** black hair. **manière** ~**e,** ~ **comme jais,** jet-black. **la nuit** ~**e,** dark night. **chambre** ~**e,** darkroom. **rendre** ~, to blacken, to defame. **magie** ~**e,** black magic. **pain** ~, brown bread. **teint** ~, dark complexion. *n.m.* black; mourning. ~ **d'ivoire,** ivory-black. **broyer du** ~, to be sad, to have the blues. **quitter le** ~, to go out of mourning. **voir tout en** ~, to see the dark side of things.

noirâtre *adj.* blackish; dusky.

noiraud, e *adj.* dark; swarthy. *n.m.f.* dark person.

noirceur *n.f.* blackness, darkness, obscurity; black spot; baseness, foulness, heinousness.

noircir *v.i.* to blacken, to grow black, to darken, to obscure; to throw a gloom over; to sadden. **se** ~ **les cheveux,** to darken one's hair. **se** ~, *v.refl.* to blacken, to grow black; to get cloudy. **le temps se noircit,** it is getting cloudy.

noise *n.f.* quarrel, strife. **chercher des** ~**s à quelqu'un,** to pick a fight with somebody.

noisetier *n.m.* hazel, hazel (tree).

noisette *n.f.* hazelnut, hazel color, nut-brown color.

noix *n.f.* walnut, nut. ~ **verte,** green walnut. ~ **d'acajou,** cashew. ~ **de coco,** coconut. ~ **muscade,** nutmeg. **à la** ~, lousy.

nom *n.m.* name; fame, reputation; noun. ~ **de famille,** family name, last name. **un** ~ **de baptême,** a Christian name. **petit** ~, Christian name. ~ **de demoiselle,** maiden name. ~ **propre,** proper noun. ~ **commun,** common noun. **au** ~ **de,** in the name of, in behalf of. **de** ~, by name.

nomade *adj.* nomadic. *n.m.* nomad.

nombrable *adj.* numerable.

nombre *n.m.* number; multitude, great many; harmony. ~ **cardinal,** cardinal number. ~ **ordinal,** ~ **entier,** whole number, integer. ~ **pair,** even number. ~ **impair,** odd number. **être en** ~ **suffisant,** to be in sufficient number. **au** ~ **de,** in the number of, among. **dans le** ~, among. **en** ~, in great numbers.

nombrer *v.t.* to count.

nombreux, euse *adj.* numerous; harmonious.

nombril *n.m.* navel; bellybutton. **elle se prend pour le** ~ **du monde,** she thinks she is the center of the world.

nomenclature *n.f.* nomenclature.

nominal, e *adj.* nominal.

nominalement *adv.* nominally, in name.

nominateur *n.m.* nominator.

nominatif, ive *adj.* nomination, appointment.

nommé, e *adj.* named, called. **une femme** ~ **Catherine,** a woman named Catherine. **a jour** ~, on the appointed day. **à point** ~, in the nick of time.

nommément *adj.* nominally, by name; particularly, namely.

nommer *v.t.* to name; to call; to nominate, to mention. ~ **un enfant,** to name a child. ~ **ses complices,** to give the names of one's accomplices. **le roi le nomma capitaine de ses gardes,** the king appointed him captain of his guards. **se** ~, *v.refl.* to give or to tell one's name; to be named. **comment se nomme-t-il?** what is his name?

non *adj.* no; not. **il est en peine,** ~ **sans raisons,** he is in trouble and not without reason. ~ **que je sache,** not that I know of. ~ **loin de la ville se trouve le château,** not far from the town is the castle.

nonagénaire *adj.* of ninety, ninety years old. *n.m.f.* nonagenarian.

non-agression *n.f.* nonaggression.

non-alcoolisé *adj.* nonalcoholic.

non-assistance *n.f.* failure to help a person in danger.

nonchalamment *adv.* carelessly, heedlessly; listlessly.

nonchalance *n.f.* carelessness, heedlessness, indifference, coolness; listlessness.

nonchalant, e *adj.* careless, heedless; listless; indifferent, cool.

non-conformiste *n.m.f.* nonconformist.

non-conformité *n.f.* nonconformity.

non-être *n.m.* non entity, non existence.

non-fumeur *n.m., adj.* nonsmoker.

non-intervention *n.f.* nonintervention.

non-lieu *n.m.* no bill; no ground for prosecution.

non-moi *n.m.* non ego.

nonne *n.f.* nun, sister.

nonobstant *prep.* notwithstanding, in spite of.

non-paiment *n.f.* nonpayment.

non-sens *n.m.* nonsense.

nord *n.m.* north. *adj.* north, northern, northerly, towards the north. **pole** ~, north pole.

nord-est *n.m.* north east. *adj.* north east, north eastern, north easterly.

nord-ouest *n.m.* north west. *adj.* north west, north western, north westerly.

normal, e *adj.* normal.

normalement *adv.* normally.

normalisation *n.f.* normalization.

normaliser *v.t.* to normalize, to standardize.

normalité *n.f.* normality.

norme *n.f.* norm, rule, standard.

nos *adj. poss. pl.* of **notre,** our.

Norvège *n.f.* Norway.

Norvègien, enne *adj.* Norwegian. *n.m.f.* Norwegian.

nostalgie *n.f.* nostalgia, homesickness.

nostalgique *adj.* nostalgic, homesick.

nota *n.m.* note, remark.

notabilité *n.f.* notability, respectability, notable, notable person.

notable *adj.* notable, remarkable, signal,

considerable, principal, leading. *n.m.* notable, leading man, noteworthy man. **assemblée des ~s**, assembly of the notables.

notablement *adv.* notably, remarkably, considerably.

notaire *n.m.* notary, notary public.

notamment *adv.* especially, particularly.

notariat *n.m.* functions of a notary; profession of a notary.

notarié, e *adj.* notarized.

notation *n.f.* notation.

note *n.f.* note; mark, grade; annotation; record, minute, bill, account. **prendre des ~s**, to take notes. **~ fausse**, wrong note. **payer la ~**, to pay the bill.

noter *v.t.* to note, to note down; to mark, to notice, to observe.

notice *n.f.* notice, account; list; short catalog.

notification *n.f.* notification, notice.

notifier *v.t.* to notify, to make known.

notion *n.f.* knowledge, information, notion; idea.

notoire *adj.* notorious; manifest, evident, publicly known.

notoirement *adv.* notoriously.

notoriété *n.f.* notoriety, notoriousness.

notre *adj. poss. m.f.* our.

notre *pron. poss.* our. **pour votre bien et pour le ~**, for your good and ours. *n.m.* our own, ours. **nous défendons le ~**, we defend our own. **il est des ~s**, he is one of us.

Notre-Dame *n.f.* Our Lady, the Virgin Mary.

nouba *n.f. Infml.* party. **ils ont fait la ~ toute la nuit**, they partied all night long.

nouer *v.t.* to tie, to knot; to form. **~ amitié**, to form a friendship. **se ~**, *v.refl.* to be tied, to form knots, to set (as fruit blossoms), to grow rickety.

noueux, euse *adj.* knotty, knotted.

nougat *n.m.* nougat, almond cake.

nouille *n.f.* noodle.

nounou *n.f. Infml.* nanny.

nounours *n.m.* teddy bear.

nourri, e *adj.* fed, nourished.

nourrice *n.f.* nurse, wet nurse. **mettre un enfant en ~**, to put a child out to nurse.

nourricier, ère *adj.* nourishing, nutritive, nutritious, foster. *n.m.* **parents nourriciers**, foster parents.

nourrir *v.t.* to nourish, to feed, to maintain, to board; to nurture, to nurse, to bring up; to maintain; to cherish; to promote; to keep up, to keep alive. **le bois nourrit le feu**, wood feeds the fire. **~ son imagination**, to feed one's imagination. **se ~**, *v.refl.* to feed; to live. **se ~ de pain**, to live on bread.

nourrissant, e *adj.* nourishing, nutritive, nutritious.

nourrisson *n.m. Infml.* infant; foster-child.

nourriture *n.f.* food, nourishment; nutriment, nutrition, aliment; diet; board; maintenance, support, sustenance. **prendre de la ~**, to take

something to eat. **une ~ saine**, wholesome food.

nous *pers. pr. n.m.f.pl.* we; us; to us. **où sommes ~?** where are we? **il ~ voit**, he sees us. **il ~ a parlé**, he spoke to us. **c'est à ~**, it's ours. **~ voici**, here we are. **~-aimons**, we love each other. **~ mêmes**, ourselves.

nouveau, nouvel *adj. m.*, **nouvelle** *adj. f.* new; fresh, recent; novel. **vin ~**, new wine. **le ~ monde**, the new world. **le nouvel an**, the new year. **la nouvelle lune**, the new moon. **un homme ~**, an upstart. *n.m.* new, something new, novel; novelty, newness. **il nous faut du ~**, we want something new. **à ~**, anew, newly, again. **de ~**, anew, newly, again, afresh, once more. **~-né**, newborn (baby).

nouveauté *n.f.* newness, novelty; innovation. **c'est une ~ que de vous voir**, it is quite a novelty to see you.

nouvelle *n.f.* news; intelligence, short story. **avoir des ~s de quelqu'un**, to hear from a person. **vous aurez de mes ~s**, you shall hear from me. **recevoir des ~s de**, to hear from. **point de ~s, bonne ~s**, no news is good news. **il a écrit une charmante ~**, he has written a pretty tale.

nouvellement *adv.* newly, recently, lately, freshly.

nouvelliste *n.m.* short-story writer.

novale *n.f.* newly cleared land, new land; *pl.* tithes on new lands. *adj. f.* new.

novembre *n.m.* November.

novice *n.m.f.* novice; apprentice. *adj.* new, novice, inexperienced, raw, green; unskilful.

noviciat *n.m.* novitiate; *Fig.* apprenticeship.

noyade *n.f.* drowning.

noyau *n.m.* stone, pit (of fruit), nucleus; core (of statues); newel (of stairs). **fruits à ~**, pitted fruit. **le ~ d'une colonie**, the origin of a colony.

noyé, e *p.p.* drowned. *n.m.f.* drowned person.

noyer *v.t.* to drown; to flood, to deluge, to swamp; to overpower, to overwhelm. **~ son chagrin dans le vin**, to drown one's sorrow in wine. **se ~**, *v.refl.* to drown oneself; to be drowned. **se ~ dans les larmes**, to be drowned in tears.

noyer *n.m.* walnut (tree).

nu, e *adj.* naked; bare, nude, uncovered, poor; simple, plain; open. **il était tout ~**, he was stark naked. **avoir la tête ~e, être nu-tête**, to be bareheaded. **aller nu-pieds**, to go barefooted. **~e propriété**, bare ownership, reversion, reversionary interest. *n.m.pl.* naked, destitute. **vêtir les ~s**, to clothe the naked; nudity, naked figure; naked (of a wall). **à ~**, nakedly; open. **monter un cheval à ~**, to ride a horse bare-back.

nuage *n.m.* cloud, mist, darkness, doubt, gloom, sadness. **un ciel sans ~**, a cloudless sky. **un ~ de sauterelles**, a cloud of locusts. **un ~ de poussière**, a cloud of dust.

nuageux, euse *adj.* cloudy.

nuance *n.f.* shade, tint; difference. **il y a une**

certain ~ entre ces deux couleurs, there is a slight difference between these two colors.

nuancer *v.t.* to shade, to shadow, to tint. se ~, *v.refl.* to be blended.

nubile *adj.* nubile.

nubilité *n.f.* nubility.

nucléaire *adj.* nuclear.

nudisme *n.m.* nudism.

nudiste *adj. n.m.* nudist.

nudité *n.f.* nudity; nakedness; bareness.

nuée *n.f.* cloud, swarm (of insects), shower (of arrows); host, multitude (of enemies).

nuire *v.i.* to injure, to harm, to hurt. il ne cherche qu'à ~, he only seeks to injure people. le froid a nuï à la vigne, the cold has been hurtful to the wine. se ~, *v.refl.* to injure oneself; to injure each other.

nuisance *n.f.* nuisance.

nuisible *adj.* noxious, injurious, hurtful, harmful, prejudicial.

nuit *n.f.* night; nighttime; darkness. il fait ~, it is dark. il se fait ~, it is getting dark. à ~ tombante, at nightfall. bonne ~, goodnight. ~ blanche, sleepless night. passer la ~, to spend the night.

nuitamment *adv.* nightly, by night, in the night.

nuitée *n.f.* night, night's work, night's lodging.

nul, nulle *adj.* no, not any, null. ce mariage est ~, that marriage is null. *pron. m.* none, nobody, no one, no man. ~ n'est content de sa for-

tune, no man is satisfied with what he has. *n.f.* nullity, syllable or phrase of no meaning.

nullement *adv.* in no way, not at all, by no means.

nullité *n.f.* nullity; incapacity.

nûment *adv.* nakedly, plainly.

numéraire *adj.* counting, legal. valeur ~, legal value (of coin). *n.m.* coin, hard cash.

numérel, e *adj.* numeral.

numérateur *n.m.* numerator.

numération *n.f.* numeration.

numérique *adj.* numerical.

numériquement *adv.* numerically.

numéro *n.m.* number. nous habitons au ~ douze, we live at number twelve. il a fait le mauvais ~, he dialed the wrong number. ~ d'immatriculation, license number, registration.

numérotage *n.m.* numbering.

numéroter *v.t.* to number.

nuptial, e *adj.* nuptial. robe ~e, wedding dress.

nuque *n.f.* nape (of the neck).

nutritif, ive *adj.* nutritive; nutritious, nourishing. substance nutritive, nutritive substance, nutritive matter.

nutrition *n.f.* nutrition.

nylon *n.m.* nylon.

nymphe *n.f.* nymph.

nymphomane *adj. n.f.* nymphomaniac.

nymphomanie *n.f.* nymphomania.

O

O *n.m.* O, o: the 15th letter of the alphabet. o, abbreviation of ouest, west.

ô *interj.* oh; oh, ah, ha.

oasis *n.f.* oasis.

obédience *n.f.* obedience; token of obedience towards the pope; *Infml.* submission.

obéir *v.i.* (with à) to obey; to submit to; to yield to. se faire ~, to make oneself obeyed. le chien obéit à son maître, the dog obeys his master.

obéissance *n.f.* obedience; submissiveness.

obéissant, e *adj.* obedient, submissive, supple, dutiful.

obélisque *n.m.* obelisk.

obéerer *v.t.* to run into debt, to involve in debt. s'~, *v.refl.* to get into debt.

obèse *adj.* obese.

obésité *n.f.* obesity.

objecter *v.t.* to object, to oppose; to reproach. s'~, *v.refl.* to be objected.

objectif, ive *adj.* objective. *n.m.* object glass, lens; objective; aim, object, end.

objection *n.f.* objection; adverse argument.

objectivement *adv.* objectively.

objectivité *n.f.* objectivity, objectiveness.

objet *n.m.* object; subject, matter; aim, intent, purpose; article; goods. vous étiez l'~ de notre entretien, you were the subject of our

conversation. c'est un ~ de première nécessité, it is an object of the first necessity.

objurgation *n.f.* objurgation.

obligation *n.f.* obligation; bond; contract. avoir des ~s à quelqu'un, to be under an obligation to a person. être dans l'~ de, to be under an obligation to. ~ au porteur, bearer bond.

obligatoire *adj.* mandatory, obligatory, binding, compulsory.

obligatoirement *adv.* obligatorily.

obligé, e *adj.* obliged; bound; indispensable. *n.m.f.* person obliged, person under obligation. je suis votre ~, I am obliged to you. il m'a ~ à le faire, he forced me to do it; debtor; indenture (of apprenticeship).

obligeamment *adv.* obligingly.

obligeance *n.f.* obligingness.

obligeant, e *adj.* obliging; courteous, kind.

obliger *v.t.* to oblige; to bind; to compel; to constrain; to gratify. l'envie de parvenir l'a obligé d'étudier, the wish to succeed made him study. s'~, *v.refl.* to bind oneself, to force oneself (to do something), to oblige one another.

oblique *adj.* oblique; slanting; sloping; indirect, crooked. ligne ~, oblique line.

obliquement *adv.* obliquely; indirectly.

obliquer *v.i.* to bear left/right.

obliquité *n.f.* obliqueness; insincerity.

oblitération *n.f.* obliteration; stopping.

oblitérer *v.t.* to obliterate, to efface, to wipe out; to stop. **s'~,** *v.refl.* to be obliterated, to be effaced; to disappear; to be stopped.

oblong, gue *adj.* oblong.

obnubiler *v.i.* to obsess, to be obsessed by.

obole *n.f.* offering; farthing, mite; a very small sum.

obscène *adj.* obscene.

obscénité *n.f.* obscenity.

obscur, e *adj.* obscure; dark, dim, unknown; humble. **une nuit ~,** a dark night. **l'~ avenir,** the unknown future. *n.m.* obscurity, darkness.

obscurantisme *n.m.* obscurantism.

obscurcir *v.t.* to obscure; to darken, to sully, to dim; to cloud. **s'~,** *v.refl.* to get obscure, to darken; to grow dim. **le temps s'obscurcit,** the weather is growing dark. **la vue s'obscurcit,** the sight grows dim.

obscurcissement *n.m.* darkening; dimness; darkness, obscurity.

obscurément *adv.* obscurely, darkly, dimly.

obscurité *n.f.* obscurity; darkness. **dissiper l'~,** to dispel darkness. **l'~ du discours,** obscurity of language. **être dans l'~,** to be in the dark.

obsédante, e *adj.* obsessing, haunting, obsessive.

obséder *v.t.* to best; to obsess; to possess (of evil spirits).

obsèques *n.m.f.pl.* funeral.

obséquieusement *adv.* obsequiously.

obséquieux, euse *adj.* obsequious.

obséquiosité *n.f.* obsequiousness.

observable *adj.* observable.

observance *n.f.* observance.

observateur, trice *n.m.f.* observer. *adj.* observing, observant.

observation *n.f.* observation; observance, keeping, remark, note, notice. **l'~ des lois,** the observance of laws.

observatoir *n.m.* observatory.

observer *v.t.* to observe, to keep; to notice, to mind; to watch. **observez la nature,** study nature. **faire ~ quelque chose à quelqu'un,** to make a person observe a thing, to call a person's attention to a thing. **s'~,** *v.refl.* to be observed, to be kept; to be circumspect, to be upon one's guard.

obsession *n.f.* obsession, haunting.

obstacle *n.m.* obstacle.

obstetrical, e *adj.* obstetric.

obstétrique *n.f.* obstetrics.

obstination *n.f.* obstinacy; obstinateness, stubbornness, wilfulness.

obstiné, e *adj.* obstinate; stubborn, headstrong; perstitent. *n.m.f.* obstinate person.

obstinément *adv.* obstinately, stubbornly, wilfully.

obstiner *v.t.* to render obstinate; to gainsay, to contradict. **s'~,** *v.refl.* to be obstinate (in), to persist (in), to be firmly bent (on).

obstruction *n.f.* obstruction.

obstruer *v.t.* to obstruct, to block up, to stop up, to bar, to close. **s'~,** *v.refl.* to get obstructed, to get blocked up.

obtempérer *v.i.* to obey, to comply (with); to submit to.

obtenir *v.t.* to obtain; to get; to acquire; to come by. **s'~,** *v.refl.* to be obtained.

obtention *n.f.* obtaining, obtainment.

obturateur, trice *adj.* stopping, blocking up. *n.m.* stopper.

obturation *n.f.* closing up, sealing, stopping.

obtus, e *adj.* obtuse; dull; blunt. **avoir l'esprit ~,** to be dimwitted.

obus *n.m.* Artill. shell.

obusier *n.m.* Artill. howitzer.

occase *adj. Infml.* bargain, good deal.

occasion *n.f.* occasion; opportunity; second hand; cause, reason. **à la première ~,** on the first occasion. **à l'~,** should an opportunity arise. **d'~,** second hand.

occasionnel, elle *adj.* occasional.

ocasionnellement *adv.* occasionally.

occasionner *v.t.* to occasion, to cause.

occident *n.m.* occident, west; western countries.

occidental, e *adj.* occidental; western, west, westerly. **Les Indes ~es,** the West Indies.

occipit *n.m. Infml.* occiput, back of the head.

occlusion *n.f.* occlusion, shutting up.

occultation *n.f.* occultation.

occulte *adj.* occult, secret, hidden.

occulter *v.t.* to hide, to conceal.

occupant, e *adj.* occupying; in occupation. *n.m.* tenant, occupier.

occupation *n.f.* occupation; occupancy; business, trade. **être sans ~,** to be without employment.

occupé, e *adj.* occupied; engaged, employed; busy.

occuper *v.t.* to occupy; to possess, to hold; to use, to employ; to take up, to hold possession. **il occupe le premier étage de cette maison,** he lives on the first floor of that house. **il occupe cent ouvriers,** he employs a hundred workmen. **s'~,** *v.refl.* to occupy oneself, to keep oneself busy; to be engaged in; to apply oneself; to be occupied with. **vous vous ennuyez, il faut vous ~,** you are bored, so do something. **il m'a promis de s'~ de moi,** he has promised to do something for me. **s'~ de ses affaires,** to mind one's own business.

occurrence *n.f.* occurrence, emergency; occasion. **en l'~,** in these circumstances.

occurrent, e *adj.* occurring.

océan *n.m.* ocean; sea. **l'~ Atlantique,** the Atlantic Ocean.

océanique *adj.* oceanic.

océanographie *n.f.* oceanography.

octave *adj.* octave.

octobre *n.m.* October.

octogénaire *n.m.f.* octogenarian, octogenary. *adj.* octogenary.

octroi *n.m.* grant, granting, concession.

octroyer *v.t.* to grant; to afford.

oculaire *adj.* ocular, eyeglass. **témoin ~,** eye witness.

oculiste *n.m.* oculist.

odeur *n.f.* odor; smell, scent, fragrance; perfume.

odieusement *adv.* odiously; hatefully, detestably.

odieux, euse *adj.* odious; hateful, detestable.

odorant, e *adj.* odorant, odorous, fragrant, smelling.

odorat *n.m.* smell, smelling, the sense of smell, olfaction.

oecuménique *adj.* ecumenic, ecumenical.

oedème *n.f.* edema.

oeil *n.m.* (yeux *pl.*) eye, sight, look; aspect; lustre (of precious stones); soft corn (on the foot), bubble (of soup), hole (in bread). **de bons yeux,** good eyes. **cligner les yeux,** to wink. **avoir mal aux yeux,** to have sore eyes. **baisser les yeux,** to look down. **lever les yeux au ciel,** to look up. **manger, dévorer quelqu'un des yeux,** to look intently at a person. **cela coûte les yeux de la tête,** that is exceedingly expensive. **fermer les yeux,** to close one's eyes. **ne dormir que d'un ~,** to sleep with one eye open. **ne pas en croire ses yeux,** not to believe one's eyes. **à l'~ nu,** with the naked eye. **~ de verre,** glass eye. **avoir les yeux tendres,** to have loving eyes. **voir quelque chose d'un bon ~,** to look favorably on a thing. **avoir bon pied bon ~,** to be strong and healthy, to be alert. **faire les yeux doux à,** to look lovingly at. **à l'~,** for nothing. **à vue d'~,** visibly. **entre les deux yeux,** full in the face. **~ pour ~, dent pour dent,** eye for eye, tooth for tooth. **loin des yeux, loin du coeur,** out of sight, out of mind. **blesser les yeux,** to offend the sight. **être tout yeux,** to be all eyes. **avoir l'~ sur quelqu'un,** to be watching a person. **pour les beaux yeux de quelqu'un,** for a person's sake; gratuitously. **~ d'aiguille,** eye of a needle. **~-de-boeuf,** bull's eye (glass). **~-de-chat,** cat's eye (mineralogy).

oeillade *n.f.* look, glance; wink.

oeuillet *n.m.* eyelet; carnation.

oesophage *n.m.* esophagus.

oeuf *n.m.* egg, roe (of fish). **des ~s frais,** fresh eggs. **un ~dur,** a hard-boiled egg. **~ à la coque,** soft-boiled egg. **des ~s sur le plat,** fried eggs. **marcher sur des ~s,** to walk on thin ice. **mettre tous ses ~s dans le même panier,** to put all one's eggs in one basket. **tête/crane d'~,** *Infml.* bonehead. **qu'il aille se faire cuire un ~,** he'd better not count on it, he can keep dreaming.

oeuvre *n.f.* work; deed; body of work. **~ d'art,** work of art. **chef d'~,** masterpiece. **mettre en ~,** to work up. **bonnes ~s,** good deeds. **~ pies,** acts of piety. **à l'~ on connais l'ouvrier,** the

workman is known by his work. *n.m. Arch.* building. **le grand ~,** the great work, the philosopher's stone. **hors d'~,** appetizer.

offesant, e *adj.* offensive.

offence *n.f.* offence, wrong, affront.

offense, e *n.m.f.* offended person, offended party.

offenser *v.t.* to offend, to injure, to insult; to hurt; to transgress. **~ quelqu'un,** to offend a person. **s'~,** *v.refl.* to take offence; to be offended.

offenseur *n.m.* offender; insulter.

offensif, ive *adj.* offensive. *n.f.* offensive. **prendre l'~,** to assume the offensive.

offensivement *adv.* offensively.

office *n.m.* office; duty; employment, business, function; service, act of worship; prayer. **d'~,** systematically, automatically. **un avocat nommé d'~ pour défendre un accusé,** a counselor appointed by the judge to plead for the accused. **il vous offre ses bons ~s auprès du ministre,** he offers to speak in your favor to the minister. **le saint ~,** the Holy Office. **~ des morts,** prayers for the dead. *n.f.* pantry; *pl.* offices.

official *n.m.* official.

officialisation *n.f.* officialization, made official.

officialiser *v.t.* to make official.

officiant, e *adj.* officiating. *n.m.* officiating minister.

officiel, elle *adj.* official.

officiellement *adv.* officially.

officier *v.i.* to officiate (as a priest).

officier *n.m.* officer. **~ de police,** police officer. **~ en retraite,** retired officer. **sous ~,** noncommissioned officer.

officieusement *adv.* officiously.

officieux, euse *adj.* officious. *n.m.f.* officious person, busybody.

officinal, e *adj.* officinal.

offrande *n.f.* offering, oblation; offer.

offrant *n.m.* bidder. **au plus ~,** to the highest bidder.

offre *n.f.* offer, bid, proposal. **~ d'emploi,** employment ad. *Pol. Econ.* supply.

offrir *v.t.* to offer; to present (in worship); to bid. **~ la main à une dame,** to offer one's hand to a lady. **~ un sacrifice,** to offer up a sacrifice. **s'~,** *v.refl.* to offer oneself, to propose onself; to offer; to present itself.

offset *n.m.* offset.

ofusquer *v.t.* to obscure, to cloud, to darken, to dazzle; to offend. **le soleil m'offusque les yeux,** the sun dazzles my eyes. **il a été offusqué par sa remarque,** he was offended by his/her comment.

ogive, e *n.f.* ogive, pointed arch. *adj.* ogive.

ogre *n.m.* ogre.

ogresse *n.f.* ogress.

oh *interj.* oh! O! ah!

ohé *interj.* Hi! Hello! **~ du navire!** ship ahoy!

oïdium *n.m.* odium.

oie *n.f.* goose (*pl.* geese); ninny, simpleton. **petite ~**, little goose. **jeu de l'oie**, snakes and ladders.

oignon *n.m.* onion; bulb, bulbous root; *Med.* bunion; callosity. **qu'il s'occupe de ses ~s**, (tell him) to mind his own business.

oindre *v.t.* to anoint.

oint, e *p.p.* anointed.

oiseau *n.m.* bird, fowl. **~ de proie**, bird of prey. **~ de passage**, bird of passage. **~-mouche**, hummingbird. **la belle plume fait le bel ~**, fine feathers make fine birds. **à vol d'~**, in a straight line. **plan à vue d'~**, bird's-eye view. *Infml.* fellow. **un drôle d'~**, a strange duck, a weird person.

oiseux, euse *adj.* idle; trifling, frivolous.

oisif, ive *adj.* idle; unoccupied, not busy; (of funds) unemployed. *n.m.* idler.

oisillon *n.m.* little bird.

oisivement *adv.* idly.

oisiveté *n.f.* idleness.

o.k. *interj.*, o.k. **c'est ~**, that's cool.

oléagineux, euse *adj.* oleaginous, oily.

oléoduc *n.m.* oil pipeline.

olfactif, ive *adj.* olfactory, olfactive. **nerf ~**, olfactory nerve.

olfaction *n.f.* olfaction; smelling.

olibrius *n.m.* pretender, braggart, boaster.

oligarchie *n.f.* oligarchy.

olivâtre *adj.* olive-colored.

olive *n.f.* olive; olive-color. **huile d'~**, olive oil.

olivier *n.m.* olive tree.

olympique *adj.* Olympic.

ombilic *n.m.* umbilicus; navel.

ombilical, e *adj.* umbilical.

ombrage *n.m.* shade, umbrage; offence.

ombrager *v.t.* to shade; to obscure, to darken; to cover, to offend, to take offense. **s'~**, *v.refl.* to get shady.

ombrageux, euse *adj.* touchy, overly sensitive, shy, skittish.

ombre *n.f.* shade, shadow, gloom, shelter, cover, background, umbrage, distrust; umber (earth). **passer comme une ~**, to vanish like a shadow. **l'~ de la nuit**, the shadow of the night. **se reposer à l'~ d'un arbre**, to rest under the shade of a tree. **avoir peur de son ~**, to be afraid of one's shadow. **cet artiste est resté dans l'~ toute sa vie**, this artist has remained unknown all his/her life. **terre d'~**, umber. *n.m. Ichth.* umber, grayling; ombre (a game at cards).

ombrelle *n.f.* parasol, sunshade.

ombrer *v.t.* to shade.

ombreux, euse *adj.* shady, shadowy.

omelette *n.f.* omelet. **on ne fait pas d'~ sans casser des oeufs**, you can't make an omelet without breaking eggs.

ometire *v.t.* to omit; to pass by, to neglect; to leave out, not to mention; to pass over.

omission *n.f.* omission; neglect; oversight, fault, error. **sauf erreur ou ~**, errors excepted.

omnibus *n.m.* omnibus.

omnipotence *n.f.* omnipotence; almighty power.

omnipotent, e *adj.* omnipotent, almighty.

omniprésence *n.f.* omnipresence.

omniprésent, e *adj.* omnipresent.

omniscience *n.f.* omniscience.

omniscient, e *adj.* omniscient.

omnivore *adj.* omnivorous.

omoplate *n.f.* shoulder blade, scapula.

on *indef. pron. n.s.* people, we, they, one. **~ dit**, people say, they say. **~ frappe à la porte**, somebody is knocking at the door. **~ y va**, let's go. **ce n'est qu'un ~ dit**, it is a mere rumor.

onagre *n.m.* onager, wild ass. *n.f.* evening primrose.

once *n.f.* ounce. **il n'y a pas une ~ de vérité dans ce qu'il a dit**, there isn't an ounce of truth in what he said.

oncle *n.m.* uncle.

onction *n.f.* unction, anointment; earnestness.

onctueusement *adv.* unctuously; earnestly.

onctueux, euse *adj.* unctuous, oily; *Fig.* impressive; earnest.

onctuosité *n.f.* unctuousness.

onde *n.f.* wave; surge, billow; undulation. **~s sonores**, sound waves.

ondé *adj.* wavy; waved.

ondée *n.f.* shower. **une forte ~**, a heavy shower.

ondoiement *n.m.* undulation, waving motion; private baptism.

ondoyant, e *adj.* undulating, waving, wavy.

ondoyer *v.i.* to wave, to undulate; to baptize privately.

ondulant, e *adj.* undulating.

ondulation *n.f.* undulation.

ondulatoire *adj.* undulatory.

ondulé, e *adj.* undulated.

onduler *v.i.* to undulate, to wave.

onéreux, euse *adj.* costly, onerous.

ongle *n.m.* nail; claw (of birds); hoof (of horses). **se couper les ~s**, to cut one's nails. **manger, ronger ses ~s**, to bite one's nails.

onguent *n.m.* ointment, salve.

onomatopée *n.f.* onomatopoeia.

ontologie *n.f.* ontology, metaphysics.

ontologique *adj.* ontological.

ontologiste *n.m.* ontologist, metaphysician.

O.N.U. *n.f. abbrev* of **Organisation des Nations Unies**, U.N. (United Nations).

onyx *n.m.* onyx.

onze *adj.* eleven; eleventh. **page ~**, the eleventh page. *n.m.* eleven; the eleventh. **le ~ du mois**, the eleventh of the month.

onzième *adj.* eleventh. *n.m.* eleventh part. *n.f. Mus.* eleventh.

opacité *n.f.* opacity, opaqueness.

opale *n.f.* opal.

opalescence *n.f.* opalescence.

opalin, e *adj.* opaline.

opaque *adj.* opaque.

opéra *n.m.* opera; opera house. **~ comique,** comic opera.

opérant, e *adj.* operating, operative, active.

opérateur, trice *n.m.f.* operator; cameraman.

opération *n.f.* operation, performance; transaction. **subir une ~,** to undergo an operation. **~ de la Bourse,** stock exchange business.

opératoire *adj.* operative.

opérer *v.t.* to operate; to effect, to produce, to work out; to perform. **se faire ~,** to undergo an operation. **s'~,** *v.refl.* to be effected, to be operated.

opérette *n.f.* operetta.

ophtalmologie *n.f.* ophthalmology.

ophtalmologiste *n.m.* ophthalmologist.

ophtalmoscope *n.m.* ophthalmoscope.

opiacé, e *adj.* opiated.

opiat *n.m.* opiate.

opiner *v.i.* to give one's opinion, to speak; to vote, to be of opinion. **~ du bonnet,** to nod.

opiniâtre *adj.* opinionated; obstinate, stubborn, headstrong. **aversion ~,** obstinate aversion. **combat ~,** stubborn fight.

opiniâtrement *adv.* obstinately, stubbornly; firmly, steadily.

opiniâtreté *n.f.* obstinacy, stubbornness, resolution, steadiness.

opinion *n.f.* opinion; estimate; vote; doctrine. **les ~s sont partagées,** opinions are divided. **l'~ publique,** public opinion.

opium *n.m.* opium.

opportun, e *adj.* opportune, seasonable, timely, well-timed; convenient, expedient.

opportunément *adv.* opportunely, seasonably, in proper time.

opportuniste *adj., n.m.f.* opportunist.

opportunité *n.f.* opportunity.

opposant, e *adj.* opposing, opposite, opponent, adverse. *n.m.* opponent, adversary.

opposé, e *adj.* opposite; adverse, opposed; contrary. **des partis ~s,** adverse, opposite parties. *n.m.* opposite, reverse, contrary. **l'un est l'~ de l'autre,** one is the opposite of the other.

opposer *v.t.* to oppose, to face, to place in front, to put in opposition. **~ le vice à la vertu,** to oppose vice to virtue. **s'~,** *v.refl.* to be opposed, to be contrary, to object, to oppose, to combat.

opposite *n.m.* opposite, reverse, contrary. **à l'~ de,** opposite, facing, in front of.

opposition *n.f.* opposition, obstacle, difference. **je n'y mets aucune ~,** I offer no opposition to it. **~ de sentiments,** difference of feeling. **être de l'~,** to be a member of the opposition.

oppresser *v.t.* to oppress; to depress.

oppresseur *n.m.* oppressor.

oppressif, ive *adj.* oppressive.

oppression *n.f.* oppression, tyranny, hardship, misery.

opprimant, e *adj.* oppressing.

opprimé, e *p.p.* oppressed. **les ~s,** the oppressed.

opprimer *v.t.* to oppress.

opter *v.i.* to choose, to opt.

opticien, ne *n.m.f.* optician.

optimal, e *adj.* optimal, optimum.

optimisme *n.m.* optimism.

optimiste *n.m.f.* optimist.

option *n.f.* option, choice.

optique *adj.* optic, optical. *n.f.sg.pl.* optics; optical illusion.

opulence *n.f.* opulence, wealth, riches, affluence.

opulent, e *adj.* opulent, wealthy, rich, affluent.

or *conf.* now, presently.

or *n.m.* gold. **feuille d'~,** goldleaf. **être cousu d'~,** to be rolling in riches. **il vaut son pesant d'~,** he is worth his weight in gold.

oracle *n.m.* oracle.

orage *n.m.* storm, thunderstorm. **un ~ se prépare,** a storm is brewing. **le temps est à l'~,** the weather is stormy. **il y a de l'~ dans l'air,** there's going to be trouble.

orageusement *adv.* stormily.

orageux, euse *adj.* stormy; tempestuous. **le malade a passé une nuit fort orageuse,** the patient has had a restless night.

oraison *n.f.* speech, oration, discourse, prayer, orison. **~ funèbre,** a funeral oration.

oral, e *adj.* oral; verbal. **examen ~,** oral examination.

oralement *adv.* orally; by word of mouth.

orange *n.f.* orangy; orange-color.

orangé, e *adj.* orange, orange-colored.

orangeade *n.f.* orangeade.

oranger *n.m.* orange, orange tree. **eau de fleur d'~,** orange-flower water.

orang-outang *n.m.* orang-outang.

orateur, trice *n.m.f.* orator, speaker.

oratoire *adj.* oratorial, oratorical. *n.m.* oratory.

orbe *n.m.* orb; orbit. *adj.* bruising, dead (as a wall).

orbital, e *adj.* orbital.

orbite *n.f.* orbit.

orchestral, e *adj.* orchestral.

orchestration *n.f. Mus.* orchestration, organization; scoring.

orchestre *n.m.* orchestra, band.

orchestrer *v.t. Mus.* to score, to orchestrate, to organize.

orchidée *n.f.pl.* orchids.

ordinaire *adj.* ordinary; accustomed; usual, common. **sa nourriture ~,** his ordinary food. *n.m.* usual practice; ordinary fare; ordinary; ordinary allowance. **à l'~,** as usual. **d'~, pour l'~,** usually, ordinarily.

ordinairement *adv.* ordinarily, usually.

ordinateur, trice *n.m.* computer. **mettre sur ~,** to computerize, to insert data. **mise sur ~,** computerization.

ordination *n.f.* ordination.

ordonnance *n.f.* ordering; order; disposition; array; mandate, injunction, precept; ordinance, statute, law; orderly; prescription (of a doctor).

~ de police, police order. **officier d'~,** orderly officer.

ordonnancement *n.m.* passing order for payment.

ordonnancer *v.t.* to pass for payment.

ordannateur, trice *n.m.f.* orderer; regulator, disposer.

ordonné, e *adj.* in order, orderly; well-ordered. *n.f.* ordinate.

ordonner *v.t.* to order; to regulate; to appoint, to ordain; to prescribe (of a physician). **il m'ordonne de partir,** he orders me to go.

ordre *n.m.* order; array; regularity; discipline; society, class; *pl.* holy orders; command, injunction. **mettre en ~,** to put, to set in order. **mettre ~ à quelque chose,** to see to a thing. **~ de succession,** the order of succession. **rappeler à l'~,** to call to order. **~ du jour,** order of the day. **en bon ~,** in good order. **de premier ~,** first rate, first class. **l'~ de Saint Benoît,** the order of Benedictines. **entres dans le ~s,** to enter into orders. **jusqu'à nouvel ~,** till further notice. **à l'~ de,** payable to.

ordure *n.f.* filth, dirt; rubbish; filthiness. *Infml.* **sale ~!** dirty bastard!

ordurier, ière *adj.* filthy, obscene.

orée *n.f.* border, verge, outskirts (of a wood).

oreille *n.f.* ear; hearing. **entendre des deux ~s,** to listen with both ears. **être tout ~s,** to be all ears. **prêter l'~,** to lend an ear, to give ear. **parler à l'~,** to whisper in the ear. **être dur d'~,** to be hard of hearing. **faire la sourde ~,** to turn a deaf ear. **cela écorche l'~,** that hurts the ear. **laisser passer le bout de l'~,** to let the cat out of the bag. **dormir sur les deux ~s,** to feel no uneasiness about a thing. **avoir l'~ basse,** to hang one's ears; to be down in the mouth. **se faire tirer l'~,** to be reluctant. **avoir la puce à l'~,** to get someone suspicious. **jusqu'aux ~s,** up to the ears; up to one's neck. **par dessus les ~s,** head over heels.

oreiller *n.m.* pillow. **taie d'~,** pillowcase.

oreillette *n.f.* auricle; ear flap.

oreillon *n.m.pl.* mumps.

ores *adv.* now. **d'~ est déjà,** from now on.

orfèvre *n.m.* goldsmith, silversmith.

orfèvrerie *n.f.* goldsmith's art; gold and silver goods.

organe *n.m.* organ, voice; agent, agency; medium.

organique *adj.* organic.

organiquement *adv.* organically.

organisateur, trice *adj.* organizing. *n.m.f.* organizer.

organisation *n.f.* organization.

organisé, e *adj.* organized.

organiser *v.t.* to organize. **s'~,** *v.refl.* to get organized.

organisme *n.m.* organism.

organiste *n.m.f.* organist.

orgasme *n.m.* orgasm.

orge *n.f.* barley. **pain d'~,** barley bread. **~ mondé,** pot barley, Scotch barley. **~ perlé,** pearl barley (orge is masculine in these examples).

orgeat *n.m.* orgeat.

orgie *n.f.pl.* orgy.

orgue *n.m. Mus.* organ.

orgueil *n.m.* pride; arrogance; boast; ostentation, splendor. **faire l'~ de, être l'~ de,** to be the pride of.

orgeuilleusement *adv.* proudly.

orgueilleux, euse *adj.* proud; conceited; arrogant, haughty, supercilious. *n.m.f.* proud person.

orient *n.m.* Orient; the East. **l'empire d'~,** the Eastern Empire.

oriental, e *adj.* east, eastern, orient, oriental.

orientalisme *n.m.* orientalism.

orientaliste *n.m.* orientalist.

orientation *n.f.* orientation, adjustment; direction. **~ professionnelle,** career advising.

orientaux *n.m.pl.* Orientals, Asiatics.

orienter *v.t.* to give the right aspect, the right direction to; to set rightly; to set toward the east; to trim (the sails). **s'~,** *v.refl.* to ascertain one's position; to find one's way.

orifice *n.m.* orifice, opening, aperture, mouth.

origan *n.m.* marjoram.

orginaire *adj.* native (of), proceeding (from); originating from.

originairement *adv.* originally, in the beginning, at first.

original, e *adj.* original; eccentric, odd, queer. **l'édition ~e d'un livre,** the first edition of a book. **on n'est pas plus ~ que lai,** you can't be more eccentric than he is. *n.m.* original; first copy. **une copie conforme à l'~,** an exact copy. *n.m.f.* eccentric person; humorist.

originalement *adv.* originally.

originalité *n.f.* originality; eccentricity, oddness.

origine *n.f.* origin; rise, source, spring, cause; fountain; derivation, etymology; original. **vous êtes Grec d'~,** you are of Greek extraction. **dès l'~,** originally; from the beginning. **dans l'~,** originally, at first, at the origin.

originel, elle *adj.* original.

originellement *adv.* originally.

Orion *n.m.* Orion.

orme *n.m.* elm.

ormeau *n.m.* young elm, abalone.

orné *p.p.* adorned, ornamented.

ornement *n.m.* ornament.

ornamental, e *adj.* ornamental.

ornementer *v.t.* to ornament, to decorate.

orner *v.t.* to adorn, to ornament, to embellish, to decorate. **les vertus ornent l'âme,** virtues adorn the soul. **s'~,** *v.refl.* to be adorned.

ornière *n.f.* rut.

ornithologie *n.f.* ornithology.

ornithologique *adj.* ornithological.

ornithologiste, ornithologue *n.m.* ornithologist.

orphelin, e *n.m.f.* orphan. ~ **de père,** fatherless child. ~ **de mère,** motherless child.

orphelinat *n.m.* orphanage.

orteil *n.m.* toe. **le gros ~,** the big toe.

orthodontie *n.f.* orthodontics.

orthodontiste *n.m.f.* orthodontist.

orthodoxe *adj.* orthodox.

orthogénie *n.f.* birth control, family planning.

orthogonal, e *adj.* orthogonal.

ortographe *n.f.* ortography; spelling. **faute d'~,** misspelling, wrong spelling.

orthographie *n.f.* orthography; orthographic projection.

ortographier *v.t.* to spell.

orthographique *adj.* orthographic, orthographical.

ortographiquement *adv.* orthographically.

orthopédie *n.f.* orthopedics.

orthopédique *adj.* orthopedic.

orthopédiste *n.m.* orthopedist.

orthophonie *n.f.* speech therapy.

orthophoniste *n.m.f.* speech therapist.

ortie *n.f.* nettle.

os *n.m.* bone. **ronger un ~,** to pick, to gnaw a bone. **en chair et en ~,** in person. **jusqu'à la moelle des ~,** to the backbone. **être trempé jusqu'aux ~,** to be soaking wet. **tomber sur un ~,** to find a problem.

oscillant, e *adj.* oscillating.

oscillation *n.f.* oscillation.

oscillatoire *adj.* oscillatory.

osciller *v.i.* to oscillate.

osculation *n.f.* osculation.

osé, e *adj.* bold, daring.

oseille *n.f.* sorrel; dough.

oser *v.t.* to dare, to venture, to risk, to be so bold as.

osier *n.m.* osier. **d'~,** wicker.

ossature *n.f.* animal or human frame, skeleton, skeletal structure; frame.

osselet *n.m.* knucklebones.

ossements *n.m.pl.* bones.

osseux, euse *adj.* osseous, bony.

ossification *n.f.* ossification.

ossifier *v.t.* to ossify; to change into bones. **s'~,** *v.refl.* to ossify.

ossuaire *n.m.* ossuary.

ostensible *adj.* ostensible; visible, apparent.

ostensiblement *adv.* visibly, obviously, evidently, ostensibly.

ostensoir *n.m.* monstrance.

ostentation *n.f.* ostentation, vain display, show, parade.

ostracisme *n.m.* ostracism; banishment. **frapper d'~,** to ostracize.

ostréiculture *n.f.* oyster culturing.

otage *n.m.* hostage. **en ~,** as a hostage.

otarie *n.f.* otary, sea lion, sea otter.

oter *v.t.* to take away, to remove; to take out, off, to put off, out; to deprive; to displace. **otez cette table de là,** take that table away from there.

~ **son chapeau,** to take off one's hat. ~ **la vie à quelqu'un,** to take a person's life. ~ **une tache,** to take out a stain. **s'~,** *v.refl.* to get away, out, off; to be carried, taken away; to deprive oneself of.

otite *n.f.* ear infection, otitis.

oto-rhino-laryngologie, O.R.L. *n.f.* otorhinolaryngologie, ear, nose and throat.

oto-rhino-laryngologiste *n.m.f.* ear, nose and throat specialist, otologist.

ottoman, e *adj.* Ottoman. *n.m.pl.* Ottomans, Turks.

ou *conj.* or. **oui ~ non,** yes or no. ~ ... ~, either ... or.

où *adv.* where; at in, to what place; to which, in which; when. ~ **allez-vous?** where are you going? ~ **est-il?** where is he? **l'état ~ nous sommes,** the state in which we are. **d'~ venezvous?** where do you come from? ~ **irezvous?** which way will you go?

ouais *interj.* yeah.

ouate *n.f.* wadding; padding; cotton wool.

ouater *v.t.* to wad, to wad, to stuff with padding.

oubli *n.m.* forgetting; forgetfulness; oblivion, neglect; omission. **tomber dans l'~,** to fall into oblivion.

oublier *v.t.* to forget; to neglect; to be unmindful of. **n'oubliez pas que je vous attends,** do not forget that I expect you. ~ **l'heure,** to forget the time. **s'~,** *v.refl.* to forget oneself; to be forgotten.

oubliettes *n.f.pl.* oubliettes, trap dungeon.

ouest *n.m.* West.

ouf *interj.* Whew! **sans avoir le temps de dire ~,** without having the time to take a breath.

oui *adv.* yes. **ne dire ni ~ ni non,** to give no positive answer. ~ **da,** yes, indeed. *n.m.* yes. *Infml.* **pour un ~ et pour un non,** for the hell of it.

oui-dire *n.m.* hearsay.

oui, e *p.p.* hear, having heard.

ouïe *n.f.* hearing. *pl.* gills (of fish). *Mus.* soundhole (of a violin, etc.).

ouie! ouille! *Interj.* ouch!

ouir *v.t.* to hear.

ouistiti *n.m.* marmoset, monkey.

ouragan *n.m.* hurricane.

ourlet *n.m.* hem.

ours *n.m.* bear. ~ **blanc,** white bear. **un ~ mal léché,** an uncouth person, a bear. **il ne faut pas vendre la peau de l'~ avant de l'avoir tué,** you must not count your chickens before they are hatched.

ourse *n.f.* she-bear; Bear, Ursa. **la grande ~,** the Big Dipper. **la petite ~,** the Little Dipper, Ursa Minor.

oursin *n.m.* sea urchin.

ourson *n.m.* bear cub.

oust(e) *Interj.* out! scram!

outil *n.m.* tool, implement.

outillage *n.m.* set of tools, implements.

outiller *v.t.* to supply with tools, to equip.

outrage *n.m.* outrage; insult.

outrageant, e *adj.* (of things) insulting, outrageous.

outrager *v.i.* to outrage, to insult; to offend.

outrageusement *adv.* outrageously.

outrageux, euse *adj.* outrageous.

outrance *n.f.* excess. **à ~,** to excess; to the utmost; to the death. **combat à ~,** mortal fight.

outre *n.f.* leather bottle.

outre *prep.* beyond; besides; above. **d'~ mer,** overseas; from beyond the seas. **~ mésure,** beyond all measure. *adv.* beyond, farther, further. **passer ~,** to go on, to take no notice (of a thing). **~ que,** besides that. **en ~,** besides, in addition, moreover, furthermore.

outré, e *adj.* outraged, furious.

outremer *n.m.* ultramarine.

outrepasser *v.t.* to go beyond, to exceed; to overstep, to transgress.

outrer *v.t.* to carry too far, to exaggerate; to provoke.

outsider *n.m. Sports.* outsider.

ouvert, e *adj.* open; uncovered; unsealed; unfastened; unfortified. **la porte est ~e,** the door is open. **lire à livre ~,** to read at sight. **à bras ~s,** with open arms. **parler à coeur ~,** to speak frankly. **compte ~,** running account.

ouvertement *adv.* openly; plainly; frankly.

ouverture *n.f.* opening; gap, width (of a door); overture (of an opera). **l'~ de la chasse,** the opening of the shooting season. **~ de coeur,** openness of heart. **séance d'~,** inaugural meeting.

ouvrable *adj.* working.

ouvrage *n.m.* work; labor, workmanship; artistic production; literary production. **se mettre à l'~,** to set to work. **~ à l'aiguille,** needlework.

ouvragé, e *adj.* worked, wrought.

ouvrant, e *adj.* opening. **toit ~,** sunroof.

ouvré, e *adj.* worked, wrought.

ouvrier, ière *adj.* operative, working. **cheville ouvrière,** main bolt. *n.m.f.* worker, operative, mechanic, artisan. **la classe ~,** working class. **~ en dentelles,** lace-worker.

ouvrir *v.t.* to open, to unclose, to unlock (with a key); to broach, to sharpen (the appetite); to give access; to begin, to commence. **~ une fenêtre,** to open a window. **~ les rideaux,** to draw the curtains. **s'~ un passage,** to force one's way through. **~ boutique,** to open a shop. **s'~,** *v.refl.* to open; to be opened. **les boutiques s'ouvrent,** the shops are being opened. **s'~ à quelqu'un,** to open up to someone.

ovaire *n.m.* ovary.

ovale *adj.* oval. *n.m.* oval.

ovarien, ne *adj.* ovarian.

ovation *n.f.* ovation.

ove *n.m.* ovum.

ové, e *adj.* egg-shaped.

ovine *adj. f.* ovine.

ovni *n.m.* (abbrev. of) **objet volant non identifié,** UFO, unidentified flying object.

ovulation *n.f.* ovulation.

ovule *n.m.* ovule.

oxydation *n.f.* oxidation, oxidization.

oxyde *n.m.* oxide.

oxyder *v.t.* to oxidize, to oxidate. **s'~,** *v.refl.* to oxidate.

oxygénation *n.f.* oxygenation.

oxygène *n.m.* oxygen. *adj.* oxygen.

oxygéner *v.t.* to oxygenize, to oxygenate. **s'~,** *v.refl.* to be oxigenized or oxygenated.

ozone *n.m.* ozone.

P

pacage *n.m.* pasture, grazing land.

pacemaker *n.m.* pacemaker.

pacha *n.m.* pacha, pasha.

pachyderme *adj.* pachydermatous. *n.m.* pachyderm; *pl.* pachydermata.

pacificateur, trice *n.m.f.* pacifier, peacemaker. *adj.* pacifying.

pacification *n.f.* pacification.

pacifier *v.t.* to pacify; to appease, to calm, to still.

pacifique *adj.* pacific, peaceful, peaceable. **l'océan Pacific,** the Pacific Ocean, the Pacific.

pacifiquement *adv.* peaceably, quietly, gently.

pacifiste *adj.* pacifist, pacifistic. *n.m.f.* pacifist.

pacotille *n.f.* cheap goods.

pacte *n.m.* pact, agreement, contract.

paddock *n.m.* paddock. *Infml.* bed. **aller au ~,** to hit the sack.

paf *Interj.* bang, bam, wham. *Infml.* tipsy.

pagaie *n.f.* paddle.

pagaille *n.f. Infml.* mess, chaos.

paganisme *n.m.* paganism, heathenism.

pagayer *v.i.* to paddle.

pagayeur *n.m.* paddler.

page *n.f.* page (of a book). **la mise en ~,** page setting. **être à la ~,** to be up to date.

pagination *n.f.* pagination, paging (of a book).

paginer *v.t.* to page; to folio.

pagode *n.f.* pagoda.

paie *n.f.* pay, wages. **jour de ~,** payday.

paiement *n.m.* payment.

païen, enne *adj.* and *n.m.f.* pagan; heathen, heathonish. **la religion païenne,** the pagan religion.

paillard, e *n.m.f.* lewd person, rake. *adj.* dissolute, lewd, libidinous, lecherous, wanton.

paillasse *n.f.* straw mattress. *n.m.* clown.

paillasson *n.m.* straw mat, mat; doormat.

paille *n.f.* straw, chaff, flaw, defect (in coins, gems, glass, etc.), chip, mote. **menue ~,** chaff. **voir une ~ dans l'oeil de son prochain,** to see the mote in a neighbor's eye. **rompre la ~,**

to annul a bargain, to fall out. **tirer à la courte ~**, to draw lots. *adj.* straw-colored.

pailler *v.t.* to straw.

pailleté, e *adj.* spangled, sequined.

paillette *n.f.* spangle, gold dust (found in rivers), flaw (in diamonds).

pain *n.m.* bread. **~ rassis**, stale bread. **~ bis**, brown bread. **petit ~**, roll. **~ de munition**, ammunition bread. **~ d'épice**, gingerbread. **~ quotidien**, daily bread. **~ azyme**, unleavened bread. **un ~ de quatre livres**, a four pound loaf. **manger son ~ blanc le premier**, to have the best first. **avoir du ~ sur la planche**, to have a lot of work to do. **gagner son ~**, to earn one's living.

pair, e *adj.* even, equal, like. **nombre ~**, even number. *n.m.* peer; an equal; fellow, mate; par. **au ~**, au pair. **de ~**, on an equal footing, on a par.

paire *n.f.* pair, couple, brace. **une ~ de perdrix, de faisans**, a brace of partridges, of pheasants. **une ~ de boeufs**, a pair (or yoke) of oxen. **les deux font la ~**, they are well matched. **une ~ de gants**, a pair of gloves.

paisible *adj.* peaceable, peaceful; pacific, placid, quiet, tranquil. **une retraite ~**, a peaceful retreat. **mener une vie ~**, to lead a peaceful life.

paisiblement *adv.* peacefully, peaceably, quietly.

paître *v.t.* and *v.i.* to graze, to pasture, to feed (cattle), to take to pasture. **~ l'herbe nouvelle**, to graze new grass. **envoyer ~ quelqu'un**, to send a person about his business.

paix *n.f.* peace; quiet; rest; silence. **être en ~**, to be at peace. **laisser quelqu'un en ~**, to let a person alone. **faire la ~**, to make peace. *interj.* peace! hush! silence!

pal *n.m.* pale; empalement.

palace *n.m.* palace.

palais *n.m.* palace; court (of justice); palate.

pâle *adj.* pale, pallid, wan. **un visage ~**, a pale face. **un peu ~**, palish, somewhat pale. **le soleil est bien ~**, the sun is very pale.

paléontologie *n.f.* paleontology.

palet *n.m.* quoit, (hockey) puck. **jouer au ~**, to play at quoits.

paletot *n.m.* coat, overcoat. **tomber sur le ~**, to jump on someone with anger.

palette *n.f.* pallet, palette; paddle (of wheels); *Print.* slice, spatula.

pâleur *n.f.* paleness, pallor.

palichon, ne *adj. Infml.* pale.

palier *n.m.* landing (on stairs). **voisin de ~**, same floor neighbors.

pâlir *v.i.* to turn pale; to grow pale. **~ de colère**, to turn pale with anger.

palissade *n.f.* fence, palisade, stockade; paling.

palissandre *n.m.* rosewood.

pâlissant, e *adj.* growing pale, turning pale; declining.

pallier *v.t.* to palliate; to mitigate, to alleviate.

palmarès *n.m.* prize list.

palme *n.f.* palm; *Fig.* victory, triumph. **remporter la ~**, to win.

palmé, e *adj.* palmate, palmated; webbed. **pieds ~s**, web-footed.

palmier *n.m.* palm tree.

palombe *n.f.* ringdove.

pâlot, otte *adj.* palish, rather pale, wannish.

palourde *n.f.* clam.

palpabilité *n.f.* palpability, palpableness.

palpable *adj.* palpable.

palpation *n.f.* palpation.

palper *v.t.* to feel, to palpate, to examine, to handle, to finger; *Fig.* to pocket (money).

palpitant, e *adj.* palpitating; thrilling. **un coeur ~**, a palpitating heart.

palpitation *n.f.* palpitation; throbbing.

palpiter *v.i.* to pound, to palpitate, to throb, to beat.

paludisme *n.m.* malaria.

pamphlet *n.m.* pamphlet.

pamplemousse *n.m.* grapefruit.

pampre *n.m.* wine branch (with foliage and fruit).

pan *n.m.* piece; part; side face. **un ~ de mur**, a side of a wall. **~ d'un habit**, flap, tail of a coat. *n.m.* Pan. **flûte de ~**, Pan's pipes. *Interj.* bang! crack!

panacée *n.f.* panacea.

panache *n.m.* plume, panache.

panaméricain *adj.* Pan-American.

panarabe *adj.* Pan-Arab.

panard *adj. m.* knock-kneed. *Infml.* foot.

pancarte *n.f.* placard; bill, placard.

pancréas *n.m.* pancreas.

panda *n.m.* panda.

pané, e *adj.* breaded.

panel *n.m.* panel.

paner *v.t.* to cover with breadcrumbs.

panier *n.m.* basket. **~ d'osier**, wicker basket. **~ au pain**, bread basket. **un ~ percé**, a spendthrift. **il ne faut pas mettre tous ses oeufs dans un même ~**, don't put all your eggs in the same basket.

panique *adj.* and *n.f.* panic.

panne *n.f.* head (of a hammer). *Auto.* breakdown. **être en ~ d'essence**, to run out of gas; lard.

panneau *n.m.* panel; bulletin board, billboard; sign, snare, trap. **tomber, donner dans le ~**, to fall into the snare.

panoplie *n.f.* panoply.

panorama *n.m.* panorama.

panoramique *adj.* panoramic.

pansage *n.m.* dressing, grooming, care of a horse.

panse *n.f. Infml.* belly, paunch; belly (of a bottle, of a retort).

pansement *n.m.* dressing (of wounds), bandage; grooming (of horses).

panser *v.t.* to dress (wounds); to bandage; to dress, to groom (horses).

pantalon *n.m.* pants, slacks, trousers.

pantelant, e *adj.* puffing, gasping; palpitating; panting.

panthère *n.f.* panther.

pantin *n.m.* dancing puppet, jumping Jack.

pantois, e *adj.* flabbergasted; panting. *Fig.* astounded, amazed.

pantomime *n.m.* pantomime. *n.f.* pantomime.

pantoufle *n.f.* slipper.

paon *n.m.* peacock.

paonne *n.f.* peahen.

papa *n.m.* papa, pa, dad, daddy. **grand-~, bon-~**, grandpa(pa).

papal, e *adj.* papal.

papauté *n.f.* papacy.

papaye *n.f.* papaya.

pape *n.m.* pope.

papelard, e *n.m.* paper.

papérasse *n.f.* waste paper, old paper; red tape.

paperasserie *n.f. Infml.* forms; red tape.

papéterie *n.f.* paper mill, paper manufacturing; stationery, stationery shop.

papétier *n.m.* paper maker, paper manufacturer; stationer. *adj.* paper making; stationery.

papier *n.m.* paper, writing, document. **~ à dessin**, drawing paper. **~ bavard**, blotting paper. **~ à musique**, music paper. **~ glacé**, glazed paper. **~ d'emballage**, packing paper, wrapping paper. **~ peint**, wallpaper. **~ de verre**, sandpaper. **~-monnaie**, paper money. **~s d'identité**, driver's license, identification papers. **~ aluminium**, aluminum foil.

papille *n.f.* papilla. **~s gustatives**, tastebuds.

papillon *n.m.* butterfly. **~ de nuit**, moth. **~s noirs**, blue devils, blues.

papillonner *v.i.* to flutter about, to flutter.

papillote *n.f.* twist of paper; candy wrapped in paper.

papilloter *v.t.* to twinkle, to blink; to dazzle.

papoter *v.i.* to chatter.

papule *n.f.* pimple.

papyrus *n.m.* papyrus.

pâque *n.f.* Passover.

pâques *n.m.* Easter. *n.m.pl.* **~ fleuries**, Palm Sunday.

pâquebot *n.m.* liner. **~ à vapeur**, (steam) ship, steamer.

pâquerette *n.f.* daisy.

paquet *n.m.* packet, package, parcel, bundle; lumpish person, lump; **faire ses ~s**, to pack off. **hasarder, risquer le ~**, to run the risk, to run it. **~ de nerfs**, nervous wreck.

paquetage *n.m.* packing up.

paqueter *v.t.* to pack.

par *prep.* by, through; in, about; from, out of; during, on, with; by means of. **il est passé ~ Lyon**, he went through Lyons. **je me promenais un matin ~ un beau soleil**, I was taking a walk one fine sunny morning. **je le pris ~ le bras**, I took him by the arm. **cet édifice a été consumé ~ le feu**, this building was destroyed by fire. **~ ambition**, out of, by ambition. **~ pitié**, for pity, for pity's sake. **obtenir un emploi ~ faveur**, to obtain a job through favor. **il débuta ~ dire**, he began by saying. **diviser un livre ~ chapitres**, to divide a book into chapters. **on paye tant ~ tête**, you pay so much a head. **tant ~ an**, so much a year. **de ~ le roi**, in the king's name. **de ~ le monde**, in the world, somewhere. **j'ai entendu dire quelques mots, par-ci, par-là**, I have heard a few words here and there. **~ derrière**, behind, from behind. **par-devant**, before, in front. **~ en bas**, downward; at the bottom; from below. **~ en haut**, upward; at the top. **venez ~ ici**, come this way.

parabole *n.f.* parable; parabola.

parachever *v.t.* to finish, to carry through, to complete. **se ~**, *v.refl.* to be finished, to be completed.

parachute *n.m.* parachute.

parade *n.m.* parade; pageant, show, pageantry, pomp.

parader *v.i.* to show off; to parade; to make a show.

paradigme *n.m.* paradigm, example, model.

paradis *n.m.* paradise; balcony (of theater).

paradisiaque *adj.* paradisiacal.

paradisier *n.m.* bird of paradise.

paradoxal, e *adj.* paradoxical.

paradoxalement *adv.* paradoxically.

paradoxe *n.m.* paradox.

paraffine *n.f.* parafin.

parages *n.m.pl.* area, around. **il est toujours dans les ~**, he is always around; latitude.

paragraphe *n.m.* paragraph.

paraître *v.i.* to appear; to come out; to show oneself; to make an appearance; to be seen; to seem, to look. **il n'ose plus ~ devant elle**, he is afraid to appear before her. **~ en public**, to appear in public. **ce livre vient de ~**, this book has just been published. **pour ~ honnête homme, il faut l'être**, one must be an honest man to appear so. **cela me paraît beau**, it seems fine to me. **faire ~**, to show, to display, to make appear; to bring to light, to bring forth, to bring out; to set forth. **faire ~ une brochure**, to publish a pamphlet. *v.impers.* to appear; to be; to seem. **il paraît qui oui**, it appears so.

parallèle *adj.* parallel. *n.f.* parallel; parallel line. *n.m.* parallel; comparison.

parallèlement *adv.* parallel, in the same way.

parallélisme *n.m.* parallelism; resemblance, comparison.

parallélogramme *n.m.* parallelogram.

paralyser *v.t.* to paralyze, to cripple. *Fig.* to destroy.

paralysie *n.f.* paralysis.

paralytique *adj.* paralyzed, palsied, paralytic. *n.m.f.* paralytic.

paramètre *n.m.* parameter.

paramilitaire *adj.* paramilitary.

paragon *n.m.* paragon, model, pattern. *adj.* Jewel. perfect, without a flaw.

paranoïa *n.f.* paranoia.

paranoïaque *adj.* paranoiac, *n.m.f.* paranoid.

paranoïde *adj.* paranoid.

paranormal, e *adj.* paranormal.

parapente *n.f.* hang gliding.

parapet *n.m.* parapet.

parapher *v.t.* to initial.

paraphrase *n.f.* paraphrase.

paraphraser *v.t.* to paraphrase; to amplify.

paraplégie *n.f.* paraplegia.

parapluie *n.m.* umbrella.

parapsychologie *n.m.* parapsychology.

parasite *n.m.* parasite; hanger-on, sycophant, spunger; inteference. *adj.* parasitic, parasitical.

parasiter *v.t.* to interfere, to cause interference; to live as a parasite on, to live off.

parasol *n.m.* parasol.

paratonnerre *n.m.* lightning conductor; lightning rod.

paravent *n.m.* screen, folding screen.

parbleu *Interj.* zounds! forsooth! egad!

parc *n.m.* park. ~ **d'attraction**, amusement park. ~ **de stationnement**, parking lot; pen (for cows, etc.); fold (for sheep); sheepfold; bed (of oysters), oysterbed.

parcelle *n.f.* small part, particle, parcel, portion, patch (of land).

parcellement *n.m.* parcelling, portioning out.

parceller *v.t.* to parcel, to portion out; to subdivide.

parce que *conj.* because.

parchemin *n.m.* parchment; *pl.* parchments, titles.

parcimonie *n.f.* stinginess, parsimony.

parcimonieusement *adv.* parsimoniously, sparingly.

parcimonieux, euse *adj.* parsimonious.

parcmètre *n.m.* parking meter.

parcourir *v.t.* to go over, to go through; to wander over; to travel over; to walk over, to drive over, to ride over; to look over, to run over. ~ **la ville**, to wander around town. ~ **un livre**, to skim a book.

parcours *n.m.* distance, trip, journey; course (of a river), length; line.

pardessus *n.m.* overcoat.

pardi *Interj.* of course.

pardon *n.m.* pardon, forgiveness; *pl.* indulgences. **je vous demande** ~, I beg your pardon.

pardonnable *adj.* pardonable.

pardonner *v.t.* to pardon; to forgive, to excuse; to overlook.~ **une offense**, to forgive an offence. **je lui pardonne de m'avoir offensé**, I forgive him for having offended me.

paré, e *adj.* dressed, adorned; ready, all set; *Fenc.* parried, warded off.

pareil, eille *adj.* and *n.m.f.* like, similar, the same, equal; such. **toutes choses pareilles,**
everything equal. **c'est un homme sans** ~, that man has not his equal. **un ~ ouvrage annonce du génie,** such a work shows genius.

pareille *n.f.* the like, tit for tat. **rendre la** ~, to give tit for tat.

pareillement *adv.* similarly, in like manner; too, also, likewise.

parent, e *n.m.f.* relative, relation; kinsman, kinswoman. **elles ne sont nullement** ~**es,** they are no relations whatever. **un ~ éloigné,** a distant relative. **un enfant doit obéir à ses** ~**s,** a child must obey his parents.

parental, e *adj.* parental.

parenté *n.f.* consanguinity, affinity, relationship, kin, kindred; kinsfolk.

parenthèse *n.f.* parenthesis. **entre** ~**s,** by the way.

parer *v.t.* to dress, to set off; to adorn, to ornament, to deck; to trim; to parry, to ward off; to shelter; to guard against, to defend oneself from; to find a remedy for. **pour** ~ **cet inconvénient,** to avoid this inconvenience. **il faut** ~ **à cet inconvenient,** we must find a remedy for this inconvenience. **se** ~, *v.refl.* **ils se sont parés de leurs habits de fête,** they dressed themselves in their best. **porter un manteau pour se** ~ **de la pluie,** to wear a coat to shelter oneself from the rain.

pare-balles *n.m.* bulletproof. **pare-brise** *n.m.* windshield. **pare-chocs** *n.m.* bumper. **pare-feu** *n.m.* fire guard.

paresse *n.f.* idleness, laziness, sloth; sluggishness; indolence, inactivity.

paresser *v.i.* to laze, to idle, to be idle.

paresseusement *adv.* idly, lazily, slothfully, sluggishly.

paresseux, euse *adj.* idle, lazy, slothful; sluggish. *n.m.f.* idler, lazy person; sluggard. *Zool.* sloth.

parfaire *v.t.* to complete, to perfect, to finish; to make up. **se** ~, *v.refl.* to be finished, to be completed.

parfait, e *adj.* perfect, complete, finished, accomplished. **nul homme n'est** ~, no man is perfect. *n.m.* perfection; *Gram.* perfect tense, preterite tense.

parfaitement *adv.* perfectly; completely, thoroughly.

parfois *adv.* sometimes, at times, occasionally, now and then.

parfum *n.m.* perfume, scent, fragrance.

parfumer *v.t.* to perfume, to scent. **se** ~, *v.refl.* to use perfumes; to perfume oneself.

parfumerie *n.f.* perfumery.

parfumeur, euse *n.m.f.* perfumer.

pari *n.m.* wager, bet.

paria *n.m.* outcast.

parier *v.t.* to bet, to wager. ~ **vingt contre un,** to bet twenty to one.

pariétal, e *adj.* parietal. *n.m.* parietal bone.

parieur *n.m.* better, wagerer, punter.

Paris *n.m.* Paris.

parité *n.f.* parity, likeness, parallel instance; comparison.

parjure *n.m.* perjury; *n.m.f.* perjurer. *adj.* perjured; forsworn.

parjurer (se) *v.refl.* to perjure onself, to forswear oneself.

parking *n.m.* parking lot.

parlant, e *adj.* speaking; expressive; lifelike, living.

parlement *n.m.* parliament, congress.

parlementaire *adj.* parliamentary. *n.m.* parliamentarian.

parlementer *v.i.* to parley.

parler *v.i.* to speak; to talk; to converse. ~ **da nez**, to speak through the nose. ~ **en public**, to speak in public. ~ **à tort et à travers**, to talk foolishly. ~ **en l'air**, to talk at random. ~ **de la pluie et du beau temps**, to speak about various things. **faire** ~ **de soi**, to be talked about, to be spoken of, to get a bad name. ~ **plusieurs langues**, to speak several languages. ~ **français**, to speak French. ~ **musique**, to speak about music. ~ **affaires**, to talk about business. **se** ~, *v.refl.* to be spoken; to speak to each other. **la langue anglaise se parle partout**, English is spoken everywhere. *n.m.* speaking, speech; to speak; way, manner of speaking.

parleur, euse *n.m.f.* talker; speechmaker; speaker, orator. *adj.* talkative; fond of conversation.

parloir *n.m.* parlor, visiting room.

parmesan *adj.* Parmesan. *n.m.* Parmesan cheese.

parmi *prep.* amid; among.

parodie *n.f.* parody.

parodier *v.t.* to parody.

parodiste *n.m.* parodist.

paroi *n.f.* wall; partition; *Mason.* face, facing; inner side, side.

paroisse *n.f.* parish; parish church.

paroissial, e *adj.* parish, parochial.

paroissien, ienne *n.m.f.* parishioner. *Infml.* **un drole de** ~, a funny fellow; (in the masc.) prayer-book.

parole *n.f.* word, language, speech; saying, sentence, permission; eloquence; affirmation. **de bonnes** ~**s**, good, kind words. **prendre la** ~, to take the floor; to begin to speak. **demander la** ~, to ask permission to speak. **couper la** ~ **à quelqu'un**, to cut a person short. **porte-**~, spokesman. **donner sa** ~, to give one's word. **tenir sa** ~ **garder sa** ~, to keep one's word, to be as good as one's word. **manquer à sa** ~, **manquer de**, not to keep one's word. **ma** ~ **d'honneur**, I give you my word. **les organes de la** ~, the organs of speech. **avoir le don de la** ~, to have the gift of eloquence. **il la** ~ **lente**, he speaks slowly.

parolier, ière *n.m.f.* lyric writer.

paronyme *n.m.* paronyme, paronymous word.

paroxisme *n.m.* paroxysm, climax.

parquer *v.t.* to pen (cattle), to pen up; to fold (sheep); to bed (oysters). *Milit.* to park. **se** ~, *v.refl.* to set, to establish a park, to park (car).

parquet *n.m.* bar (of a tribunal), public prosecutor's offices; pit (of stock exchange, and theater); pew (in a chapel); *Theat.* orchestra; patch of land; parquet floor.

parrain *n.m.* godfather, sponsor.

parrainage *n.m.* sponsorship.

parrainer *v.t.* to sponsor.

parricide *n.m.f.* and *adj.* parricide, parricidal.

parsemer *v.t.* to strew, to sprinkle, to scatter.

part *n.f.* part; portion, share; interest, concern, participation. **la plus forte** ~, the greatest share. **la** ~ **du lion**, the lion's share. **avoir une** ~ **du gâteau**, to have a share in the profits. **je prends** ~ **à tout ce qui le touche**, I take an interest in all that concerns him. **pour ma** ~, for my part. **faire** ~ **de quelque chose à quelqu'un**, to let someone know of something, to inform someone of something. **dites-lui de ma** ~, tell him from me. **autre** ~, elsewhere. **nulle** ~, nowhere. **quelque** ~, somewhere. **mettez cela à** ~, put that aside. **il le prit à** ~ **et lui dit**, he took him aside and told him. **c'est un fait à** ~, that is a particular case, that is quite another thing. **raillerie à** ~, joking aside. **un coup lui peça le bras de** ~ **en** ~, a stroke went right through his arm. **j'ai couru de** ~ **et d'autre**, I have been everywhere. **il arrive des soldats de toutes** ~**s**, soldiers are coming from all directions.

partage *n.m.* division, distribution; partition; part, lot, share, portion.

partager *v.t.* to share, to have a share, to partake, to divide; to separate into parts; to take part in, to distribute, to allot. ~ **un gâteau**, to divide a cake. **se** ~ **quelque chose**, to share something. ~ **les peines de quelqu'un**, to share in a person's troubles. **je partage ses soupçons**, I share his suspicions. **se** ~, *v.refl.* to be divided.

partageur, euse *n.m.f.* sharer.

partance *n.f.* sailing, departure, bound, outbound. **en** ~, on the point of sailing. **point de** ~, point of departure.

partant, e *adj.* **être** ~, to be in favor of something, to go for something. *n.m.* one that sets out.

partant *adv.* therefore, consequently, in consequence.

parténaire *n.m.f.* partner.

parterre *n.m.* flower bed, flower plot; flower garden; *Theat.* pit.

parti *n.m.* party, side, part; decision, resolve; choice, means, measure; offer, profit; profession, calling; match, marriage; *Milit.* small detachment. **un** ~ **politique**, a political party. **prendre** ~ **contre quelqu'un**, to take part against a person. **prendre son** ~, to make up one's mind, to resolve. **de** ~ **pris**, designedly, intentionally. **il**

prit le ~ de ne plus m'en parler, he made up his mind to not speak to me about it any more.

tirer ~ de tout, to turn everything to account.

un bon ~, a good match.

parti, e *adj.* tipsy. il est bien ~, he is well under way. il est mal ~, he had a bad start. *n.f.* party.

partial, e *adj.* partial.

partialement *adv.* partially, with partiality.

partialité *n.f.* partiality, bias, favor; *pl.* divisions, factions.

participant, e *adj.* participating. *n.m.f.* participant.

participation *n.f.* participation; involvement.

participe *n.m.* participle.

participer *v.i.* (with à) to participate in, to partake of; to share in, to take part in.

particulariser *v.t.* to particularize, to specify. se ~, *v.refl.* to particularize; to distinguish oneself from others.

particularité *n.f.* peculiarity, characteristic.

particule *n.f.* particle.

particulier, ière *adj.* particular; peculiar; private, singular; odd, strange. leçons ~s, private lessons. j'en fais en cas ~, I take a particular interest in it. *n.m.* particular; detail; particular circumstances; privacy; private person, individual. en ~, privately, in private.

particulièrement *adv.* particularly, in particular; especially.

partie *n.f.* part; match (in play), game; party (of pleasure); account entry; line (of business). première ~ d'un livre, the first part of a book. les cinq ~s du monde, the five parts of the world. les ~s du discours, the parts of speech. ~ double, double entry. ~ simple, simple entry. perdre la ~, to lose the game. une ~ d'échecs, a game of chess. une ~ de pêche, a fishing party. c'est ~ remise, it is only put off. se porter ~ contre quelqu'un, to appear against a person. ~s belligérantes, belligerent parties. en ~, partly, in part. ~ par menaces, ~ par surprise, partly by threats and partly by surprise.

partiel, elle *adj.* partial.

partiellement *adv.* partially; by parts; *Fin.* by instalments.

partir *v.i.* to set out, to set off, to start; to depart; to leave; to set sail; to proceed; to spring (of birds). ~ pour la campagne, to go to the countryside. ~ de Paris, to leave Paris. ~ d'un grand éclat de rire, to burst out laughing. j'ai vu ~ le coup, I saw where the shot came from. cela part du bon coeur, that comes from the heart. à ~ d'aujourd'hui, from this day forth. avoir maille à ~, to have a bone to pick with a person. ils ont maille à ~, they cannot agree. *n.m.* leaving, departure.

partisan, e *n.m.f.* partisan; advocate, supporter.

partition *n.f.* partition; score.

partouse *n.f.* *Infml.* orgy.

partout *adv.* everywhere. ~ où, wherever.

de ~, on all sides, from all sides; all over.

parturition *n.f.* parturition.

parure *n.f.* ornament, attire, dress; set (of jewels, etc.).

parution *n.f.* publication.

parvenir *v.i.* to reach; to arrive at, to attain, to get at; to succeed. il y est parvenu, he succeeded.

parvis *n.m.* parvis, court.

pas *n.m.* step, pace; footstep; footprint; tread; gait; progress, proceeding. doubler le ~, to quicken one's pace. sur les ~ de quelqu'un, at a person's heels. à chaque ~, at every step, at every movement. revenir sur ses ~, to retrace one's steps. tout dépend du premier ~, everything depends on the first step. il n'y a que le premier ~ qui coûte, the difficulty is in the outset. faux ~, false step, trip. à petits ~, with short steps. à grands ~, with long steps. ~ accéléré, quick step. aller au ~, to pace, to walk. tirer quelqu'un d'un mauvais ~, to get a person out of a scrape. *Naut.* straits. le ~ de Calais, the Straits of Dover. ~ à ~, step by step. de ce ~, directly, immediately.

pas *adv.* not; no, not any.

passable *adj.* passable, tolerable, middling, so-so, not so good. mention passable, pass, passing grade.

passablement *adv.* passably, tolerably, middingly; so-so.

passage *n.m.* passage; passing; migration (of birds); pass, way, path; thoroughfare; voyage; fare. son ~ fut court, his stay was a short one. fermer, boucher le ~, to stop the passage. se frayer un ~, to cut one's way through. payer son ~, to pay one's passage. le ~ du jour à la nuit, the transition from day to night. ~ interdit, no entry. ~ souterrain, underpass, passage. ~ à tabac, beating up.

passager, ère *adj.* migratory, of passage; passing; transient, fleeting. *n.m.f.* passenger.

passagèrement *adv.* transiently, momentarily.

passant, e *adj.* passing. rue ~e, busy street. *n.m.f.* passer-by. en ~, on the way.

passation *n.f.* executing (a deed); transfer of power.

passe *n.f.* situation, state; pass; narrow passage; (at billiards and tennis) port; (at play) stake; odd money. être dans une mauvaise ~, to be going through bad times. ~-temps, spare time, leisure time; hobby.

passé, e *adj.* past; ended; over. le temps ~, past times. la semaine ~e, last week. *n.m.* past; past time. j'ai oublié tout le ~, I have forgotten the past. *prep.* beyond; over.

passe-partout *n.m.* master key; latch key. l'argent est un bon ~, a golden key opens every lock.

passe-passe *n.m.* sleight of hand. tour de ~, sleight of hand trick.

passeport *n.m.* passport.

passer *v.i.* to pass; to go; to run, to proceed, to flow; to move through; to strain, to percolate; to thrust; to die, to expire; to go down, to pass for; to go across, to cross, to pass over; to hand, to transmit; to utter; to strain, to filter; to run; to thrust. ~ **au salon**, to go into the dining room. ~ **par Paris**, to go by way of Paris. ~ **devant quelqu'un**, to pass before a person. ~ **à l'ennemi**, to pass over to the enemy. ~ **outre**, to go farther, to go on, to proceed. **la Seine passe à Paris**, the Seine runs through Paris. **il vient de** ~ **entre mes bras**, he just died in my arms. **ce vin peut** ~, this wine is tolerable. ~ **de génération en génération**, to pass from generation to generation. **les années passent**, years go by. **avec des livres, le temps passe**, with books, time flies. ~ **là-dessus**, to pass over, to forgive a thing. **tout lui passe par les mains**, everything passes through his hands. **je suis passé par là, je sais ce qui en est**, I have gone through that, I know what it is. **il faut en** ~ **par là**, one must submit to that, one must go through that. ~ **sur les défauts d'une personne**, to overlook a person's faults. **faire** ~ **sous les yeux de quelqu'un**, to lay before the eyes of a person. ~ **le pont**, to cross the bridge. ~ **son chemin**, to go along; to go about one's business; to go one's way. ~ **des marchandises en fraude**, to smuggle goods. ~ **une pièce de monnaie fausse**, to put a false coin into circulation. ~ **de la farine au tamis**, to sift flour through a sieve. ~ **les bras dans les manches de sa robe**, to slip one's arms into the sleeves of a dress. ~ **le jour à ne rien faire**, to spend the day in idleness. ~ **deux jours sans manger**, to go two days without eating. ~ **un fait sous silence**, to omit a fact. **la dépense passe la racette**, the expenditure is beyond the receipt. ~ **au fil de l'épée**, to put to the sword. ~ **un soldat par les armes**, to execute a soldier. **se** ~, *v.refl.* to happen, take place; to be content with, to do without. **le temps passe**, time passes by. **il faut que jeunesse se passe**, you cannot put old heads on young shoulders. **cette mode se passera bientôt**, that style will not last long. **que s'est-il passé?** what happened? **ne pouvoir se** ~ **de vin**, not to be able to do without wine.

passereau *n.m.* sparrow.

passerelle *n.f.* overpass, footbridge, gangway, catwalk.

passeur *n.m.* ferryman, smuggler.

passible *adj.* liable, subject to, punishable.

passif, ive *adj.* passive. **verbe** ~, passive verb. *n.m.* debts, liabilities.

passion *n.f.* passion; anger; love; affection. **suivre ses** ~**s**, to give way to one's passions.

passionnant, e *adj.* fascinating, thrilling, exciting.

passionné, è *adj.* passionate, vehement.

passionnel, elle *adj.* passion, passionate. **crime** ~, crime of passion.

passionnément *adv.* passionately; ardently.

passionner *v.t.* to impassion; to move with passion, to affect strongly. **se** ~, *v.refl.* to become impassioned; to be enamoured (of), to be smitten (with); to be excited.

passivement *adv.* passively.

passoire *n.f.* passiveness, passivity.

passoire *n.f.* strainer.

pastel *n.m.* pastel.

pastèque *n.f.* watermelon.

pasteur *n.m.* pastor; shepherd.

pastiche *n.m.* imitation.

pastille *n.f.* drops, pastille; lozenge.

pastoral, e *adj.* pastoral. *n.m.* pastoral (a liturgical book).

pat *n.m.* (at chess) stalemate.

patapouf *n.m. Infml.* fatty, humpty-dumpty, stout man.

pataquès *n.m. Infml.* slip, mistake, fault (in pronunciation).

patata *Interj.* **et patati et** ~, and so on; blah, blah, blah.

patate *n.f.* sweet potato; *Infml.* idiot.

patatras *Interj.* slapbang, crash!

pataud, e *adj.* clumsy, awkward. *n.m.f.* awkward person. *n.m.* large-pawed dog.

patauger *v.i.* to splash, to plunge about; to flounder; to flounce; to dabble, to paddle.

patchouli *n.m.* patchouli.

pâte *n.f.* paste; dough (for bread); pulp *pl.* pasta; *Print.* pie; sort, kind; temper, disposition. ~ **levée**, raised dough. **avoir la main à la** ~, to be at work. ~**s d'Italie**, Genoise. ~ **d'amandes**, almond paste. ~ **feuilletée**, puff, flaky pastry. ~ **à fritte**, batter.

pâté *n.m.* pâté, pie; blot (of ink); *Print.* pie; block (of houses). **faire un** ~, to make a blot. ~ **de maison**, block (houses).

pâtée *n.f.* meat (for dogs, etc.).

patelin *n.m. Infml.* small town, village.

patelle *n.f.* patella; limpet.

paent, e *adj.* patent, manifest, obvious, evident. **lettres** ~**s**, letters patent.

patentable *adj.* licensable.

patente *n.f.* patent, letters of patent; bill of health, bill; license. **prendre une** ~, to take out a license.

patente, e *adj.* licensed. *n.m.f.* licensed, dealer.

patenter *v.t.* to license.

pater *n.m.* paternoster, Lord's prayer; large bead (of a rosary).

paternel, elle *adj.* paternal; fatherly. **l'amour** ~, fatherly love.

paternellement *adv.* paternally.

paternité *n.f.* paternity, fatherhood.

pâteux, euse *adj.* pasty; sticky, clammy, mealy; viscous, adhesive; doughy; thick.

pathétique *adj.* pathetic; affecting; touching. *n.m.* pathetic, pathos.

pathétiquement *adv.* pathetically, touchingly, movingly.

pathologie n.f. pathology.

pathologique adj. pathologic, pathological.

patibulaire adj. patibulary. n.m. gallows.

patiemment adv. patiently, with patience.

patience n.f. patience; endurance, forbearance; perseverance. **pousser à bout la ~ de quelqu'un,** to try someone's patience. **prendre ~,** to take patience, to be patient.

patient, e adj. patient, enduring; long-suffering, constant; forbearing. n.m. patient; sufferer.

patienter v.t. to have patience.

patin n.m. skate; brake block; French kiss.

patinage n.m. skating.

patiner v.i. to skate.

patineur, euse n.m.f. skater.

patinoire n.f. skating rink.

patio n.m. patio.

pâtir v.i. to suffer.

pâtisserie n.f. pastry; pastrymaking; pastry business; pastry shop.

pâtissier, ière n.m.f. pastry chef.

patois n.m. patois, dialect.

patriarcal, e adj. patriarchal.

patriarcat n.m. patriarchate, patriarchy.

patriarche n.m. patriarch.

patrie n.f. native country, fatherland.

patrimoine n.m. patrimony; inheritance, heritage.

patriote n.m.f. patriot. adj. patriot, patriotic.

patriotique adj. patriotic, patriot.

patriotisme n.m. patriotism.

patron n.m. employer, boss, patron, master; protector; defender; patron saint; skipper, cockswain; pattern, model; templet, template; stencil plate. **~ d'une robe,** pattern of a dress. **avoir un bon ~,** to have a good boss, employer.

patronage n.m. patronage; protection, support.

patronal, e adj. patronal.

patronat n.m., **le ~,** employers.

patronne n.f. female employer, boss, patroness; protectress, patron; Milit. cartridge box.

patronner v.t. to patronize, to sponsor.

patronnesse n.f. patroness (of a charity festival).

patronyme n.m. surname.

patrouille n.f. patrol.

patrouiller v.i. to patrol.

patte n.f. paw, foot. **~ de lion,** a lion paw. **un chien qui donne la ~,** a dog that gives its paw. **marcher à quatre ~s,** to walk on all fours, to crawl. **des ~s de mouche,** scrawls (in writing). **être entre les ~s de quelqu'un,** to be in a person's clutches. **faire ~ de velours,** to be all smirks and smiles. **graisser la ~ à quelqu'un,** to bribe a person.

patte-d'oie n.f. crossing; crow's foot.

pâturage n.m. pasture, grazing.

pâture n.f. food; pasture; grazing ground.

paume n.f. palm; tennis. **jeu de ~,** game of tennis.

paumé, e adj. Infml. lost; clueless.

paumer (se) v.t. to lose oneself, to get lost.

paupérisme n.m. pauperism.

paupière n.f. eyelid.

pause n.f. pause; stop; rest, break.

pauser v.i. to pause; Mus. to make a rest.

pauvre adj. poor; needy, indigent, in want; sorry, pitiful. **un esprit ~,** a poor mind. **un pays ~,** a barren country. n.m. poor person (pl. the poor, poor people). Infml. **~ de moi!** poor me! **le ~, il a dû en baver,** poor guy, he must have gone through hell.

pauvrement adv. poorly; wretchedly.

pauvet, ette n.m.f. poor creature, poor little thing.

pauvreté n.f. poverty; poorness, destitution, need, want, penury, indigence.

pavage n.m. paving.

pavane n.f. pavane.

pavaner (se) v.refl. to peacock, to strut.

pavé n.m. paving stone; pavement, paving. **se promener sur le ~ de Paris,** to walk about the streets of Paris. **brûler le ~,** to go, walk or ride very fast; to tear along (the road, etc). **être sur le ~,** to be homeless. **battre le ~,** to idle about town. **le haut du ~,** the wall. **tenir le haut du ~,** to be on the side of the wall; Fig. to hold the first rank.

pavement n.m. paving; pavement.

paver v.t. to pave.

pavillon n.m. villa, pavilion; bell (of a trumpet); Naut. flag, colors; standard, ensign.

pavoiser v.t. to dress, to deck, to adorn with flags.

pavot n.m. poppy. **graine de ~,** poppyseed.

payable adj. payable; due.

payant, e adj. paying; that pays; paid.

paye n.f. pay, salary; wages; payment.

payement, paiement n.m. payment. **faire un ~,** to make a payment.

payer v.t. to pay, to pay for; to pay off; to reward, to recompense. **~ ses dettes,** to pay one's debts. **se faire ~,** to obtain payment, to get paid. **~ des marchandises,** to pay for goods. **~ comptant,** to pay cash. **il me le payera,** he shall pay for it. **il refuse de ~,** he refuses to pay. **~ de sa personne,** to sacrifice oneself. **se ~,** v.refl. to pay oneself; to be paid; to be satisfied, to indulge in. **je vais me ~ ce plaisir-là,** I will indulge in that pleasure.

payeur, euse n.m.f. payer; paymaster.

pays n.m. country; land; native land, native country, fatherland; birthplace; home. **un beau ~,** a beautiful country. **~ plot, ~ de plaine,** flat, open country. **Pays-Bas,** Netherlands. **battre du ~,** to roam about the country, to ramble about. **battre le ~,** to scour the countryside; to wander. **en ~ étranger,** in a foreign country, abroad. **~ natal,** native country, native land. **nul n'est prophète en son ~,** no man is a prophet in his own country.

paysage n.m. landscape; scenery.

paysagiste *n.m.* landscape painter.

paysan, anne *n.m.f.* peasant; countryman, countrywoman. **les ~s,** the peasants, the peasantry.

paysannerie *n.f.* peasantry; country manners, country fashions.

P.C.V. *n.m.* abbrev. of **Per Ce Voir,** reverse charges, collect call.

P.D.G. *n.m.* abbrev. of **président directeur général,** chairman and managing director (CEO).

péage *n.m.* toll; toll booth.

peau *n.f.* skin; hide (of large animals); leather; rind. **n'avoir que les os et la ~,** to be nothing but skin and bone. **~ de vache,** cowhide. *Infml.* **j'aurai sa ~,** I'll have his hide!

pécari *n.m.* peccary.

peccadille *n.f.* peccadillo, slight offence, petty fault.

pêche *n.f.* peach.

pêche *n.f.* fishing; fishery; fish (caught); picking up. **~ à la ligne,** angling. **aller à la ~,** to go fishing. **faire une bonne ~,** to get a good catch.

péché *n.m.* sin, transgression. **faire, commettre un ~,** to commit a sin. **les sept ~s capitaux,** the seven deadly sins. **~ originel,** original sin. **à tout ~ miséricorde,** we must not desire the death of the sinner.

pécher *v.i.* to sin, to trespass, to transgress, to offend.

pêcher *n.m.* peachtree.

pêcher *v.t.* to fish; to catch; to find. **où a-t-il péché cela?** where did he get that from? **~ en eau troublé,** to fish in troubled waters.

pêcherie *n.f.* fishery, fishing place.

pécheur, pécheresse *n.m.f.* sinner, transgressor. *adj.* sinning, transgressing; sinful, wicked.

pêcheur, euse *n.m.f.* fisher; fisherman. **~ à la ligne,** angler. *adj.* fishing. **bateau ~,** fishing boat.

pécore *n.f.* silly and stuck-up girl/woman.

pectoral, e *adj.* pectoral. **sirup ~,** cough syrup, expectorant. *n.m.* pectoral muscle; pectoral breast plate.

pécule *n.m.* savings, stock of money; cash.

pécuniaire *adj.* pecuniary.

pédagogie *n.f.* pedagogy, educational method.

pédagogique *adj.* educational, pedagogical.

pédale *n.f.* pedal; treadle. **~ d'embrayage,** clutch. *Infml.* **perdre les ~,** to lose it. *n.m. Vulg.* homosexual.

pédaler *v.t.* to pedal.

pédaleur, euse *n.m.f.* cyclist, pedalist.

pédalo *n.m.* pedal boat.

pédant, e *n.m.f.* pendant.

pédanterie *n.f.* pedantry.

pédantesque *adj.* pedantic.

pédé *n.m.* homo, gay.

pédéraste *n.m.* pederast.

pédérastie *n.f.* pederasty.

pédiatre *n.m.f.* pediatrician.

pédiatrie *n.f.* pediatrics.

pédicure *n.m.* pedicure.

pedigree *n.m.* pedigree.

peeling *n.m.* facial.

pègre *n.f.* underworld.

peigne *n.m.* comb. **~ fin,** fine-toothed comb. **se donner un coup de ~,** to run a comb through one's hair. **passer au ~ fin,** to go through something with a fine-toothed comb.

peigner *v.t.* to comb. **se ~,** *v.refl.* to comb one's hair.

peignoir *n.m.* peignoir, light bathrobe.

peinard, e *adj. Infml.* cool. **c'est ~, ici,** it's cool here, it's quiet here. **qu'il se tienne ~,** he should keep his nose clean.

peindre *v.t.* to paint; to portray; to depict, to describe, to picture. **~ un paysage,** to paint a landscape. **se faire ~,** to have one's picture drawn. **~ tout en beau,** to show the bright side of everything. **apprendre à ~,** to learn painting. **se ~,** *v.refl.* to paint oneself, to be painted.

peine *n.f.* pain; punishment, penalty; suffering, torment; anguish, sorrow, grief, affliction; trouble; pains. **infliger une ~,** to inflict a punishment. **sous ~ d'amende,** under penalty of a fine. **partager les ~s de quelqu'un,** to share in a person's sorrow. **faire de la ~ à quelqu'un,** to pain a person. **se donner de la ~,** to take trouble. **c'est ~ perdue,** it is all of no use. **en être pour sa ~,** to have one's trouble for nothing. **cela n'en vaut pas la ~, ce n'est pas la ~,** that is not worth while. **toute ~ mérite salaire,** every laborer is worthy of his hire. **à ~,** hardly, scarcely. **à ~ étions-nous entrés,** we had hardly got in. **faire quelque chose à grand-~,** to do something with much difficulty. **~ capitale,** capital punishment. **~ de mort,** death sentence. **défense d'entrer sous ~ de poursuite,** trespassers will be prosecuted.

peiné, e *adj.* grieved, afflicted, sorry, concerned.

peiner *v.t.* to fatigue; to give (a person) trouble; to pain, to give pain to, to distress.

peint, e *p.p.* painted; colored. **toiles ~es,** prints. **papiers ~s,** wallpapers.

peintre *n.m.* painter; portrayer. **~ en bâtiments,** house painter.

peinture *n.f.* painting; picture, paint. **~ à l'huile,** oil painting. **~ sur verre,** glass staining. **en ~,** painted; in painting.

peinturlurer *v.t.* to paint roughly; to daub.

péjoratif, ive *adj.* derogatory, perjorative. **sens ~,** disparaging sense, derogatory way.

Pékinois, e *adj., m.f.* Pekinese.

pélage *n.m.* coat, fur.

pelé *p.p.* peeled. *Infml.* **trois tendus et deux ~s,** hardly nobody.

pêle-mêle *adv.* pell-mell, confusedly, disorderly, helter-skelter. *n.m.* confusion.

peler *v.t.* to peel; to take off the bark, to strip off;

to pare (a fruit); to come off. **se ~**, *v.refl.* to come off; to peel. *Infml.* to be cold.

pélerin, e *n.m.f.* pilgrim.

pèlerinage *n.m.* pilgrimage.

pélican *n.m.* pelican.

pelisse *n.f.* pelisse.

pelle *n.f.* shovel. *Infml.* **ramasser une ~,** to have a fall.

pelleter *v.t.* to shovel.

pellicule *n.f.* thin skin or membrane; *Photo.* film; dandruff.

pelote *n.f.* ball (of thread, silk, etc.); pin cushion.

peloter *v.t.* to wind (thread, etc.); to make up into a ball. *Infml.* to pet, to fondle, to cajole. **se ~,** to be necking.

peloton *n.m.* group, cluster; platoon, squad. **~ d'exécution,** firing squad.

pelotonner *v.t.* to wind (thread). **se ~,** *v.refl.* to snuggle (up); to be rolled up; to roll itself up; to double oneself up; to gather in groups, to form a cluster.

pelouse *n.f.* lawn.

peluche *n.f.* plush, shag. **jouet en ~,** stuffed toy.

pelucher *v.i.* to wear rough, to become shaggy.

pelure *n.f.* paring, peel. **~ d'oignon,** onion peel. *Infml.* thin coat.

pelvien, enne *adj.* pelvic.

pelvis *n.m.* pelvis.

pénal, e *adj.* penal. **code ~,** penal code.

pénalisation *n.f.* penalization.

pénaliser *v.t.* to penalize.

pénalité *n.f.* penalty.

penalty *n.m.* penalty.

penaud, e *adj.* abashed, sheepish.

penchant, e *adj.* inclining; inclined; prone, inclined (to). *n.m.* declivity, slope, side; decline; inclination; propensity; proneness. **suivre son ~,** to follow one's inclination. **avoir un ~ pour quelqu'un,** to be fond of a person.

penché, e *adj.* leaning; stooping; bending. **la tour ~ de Pise,** the leaning tower of Pisa.

pencher *v.t.* to incline; to lean, to bend, to bow down, to be inclined, to slope, to stoop. **~ la tête,** to bend one's head. **~ vers la clémence,** to lean towards mercy. **se ~,** *v.refl.* to lean, to bend; to bend down; to stoop. **se ~ à la fenêtre,** to lean out of the window.

pendable *adj.* hanging, abominable, atrocious. **un tour ~,** an abominable trick.

pendaison *n.f.* hanging.

pendant, e *adj.* hanging; hanging down, pendent. *n.m.* pendant. **~s d'oreilles,** pendants, drop earrings. *prep.* pending, during, for. **~ la nuit,** during the night. **~ que,** *conj.* while.

pendentif *n.m.* pendant; pendentive.

penderie *n.f.* wardrobe; walk-in closet.

pendiller *v.i.* to dangle, to swing; to flutter about.

pendre *v.t.* to hang, to hang up, to suspend, to be suspended; to dangle, to hang down. **les traîtres furent pendus,** the traitors were

hanged. **des fruits pendaient des arbres,** fruit hung from the trees. **se ~,** *v.refl.* to hang oneself; to hang. **se ~ à la sonnette,** to ring the bell with all one's might. **se ~ au cou de quelqu'un,** to hang around a person's neck. **se ~ à un arbre,** to hang oneself to a tree.

pendu, e *p.p.* hanged; hung, hung up; suspended; hanging; dangling. **avoir la langue bien ~e,** to have the gift of gab. **être ~ aux oreilles de quelqu'un,** to keep talking to a person. *n.m.* hanged man.

pendule *n.m.* pendulum. *n.f.* timepiece; clock.

pêne *n.m.* bolt (of a lock).

pénétrabilité *n.f.* penetrability.

pénétrable *adj.* penetrable.

pénétrant, e *adj.* penetrating; piercing, acute, keen, sharp, discerning.

pénétration *n.f.* penetration; *Fig.* insight, activeness (of mind).

pénétrer *v.t.* to penetrate; to enter; to pass through; to pierce; to penetrate into; to understand; to fathom, to dive into; to break (into); to pierce; to dive (into), to fathom. **~ dans l'intérieur d'un pays,** to penetrate into the interior of a country. **ces paroles ont pénétré jusqu'au fond de mon coeur,** these words went to my heart. **se ~,** *v.refl.* (of things) penetrate into each other; to convince oneself, to impress one's mind.

pénible *adj.* painful; difficult, laborious; distressing. **un travail ~,** a laborious piece of work.

péniblement *adv.* painfully, laboriously.

péniche *n.f.* barge.

pénicilline *n.f.* penicillin.

péninsulaire *adj.* peninsular.

péninsule *n.f.* peninsula.

pénis *n.m.* penis.

pénitence *n.f.* penitence; repentance, contrition; penance. **faire ~,** to do penance. **mettre en ~,** to punish.

pénitencier *n.m.* penitentiary.

pénitent, e *adj.* penitent; repentant, contrite. *n.m.f.* penitent.

pénitentiaire *adj.* penitentiary.

pénombre *n.f.* penumbra; darkness; shadowy light.

pensable *adj.* conceivable. **pas ~,** unthinkable, inconceivable.

pensant, e *adj.* thinking. **bien ~,** right thinking.

pense-bête *n.m. Infml.* memory jogger.

pensée *n.f.* thought; idea, conception; mind; design, intention; meaning; sketch. **les grandes ~s viennent du coeur,** noble thoughts come from the heart. **parler contra sa ~,** to speak against one's mind. **être présent à la ~ de quelqu'un,** to be in a person's mind. **lire dans la ~ de quelqu'un,** to read a person's thoughts. **entrer dans la ~ d'un auteur,** to enter into the spirit of an author.

penser *v.t.* to think; to conceive; to think about;

to cogitate, to think of, to judge, to believe, to estimate; to be of opinion; to muse on, to intend, to mean. **je pense que mes raisons sont meilleures que les vôtres**, I think my reasons are better than yours. **à ce que je pense**, according to my idea. **quiconque pense fait ~**, whoever thinks makes others think. **façon de ~**, way of thinking. **~ mal d'autrui**, to think badly of others. **cela donne à ~**, that makes one consider. **je pensais à toi**, I was thinking of you. **nous pensions partir aujourd'hui**, we were thinking of leaving today. *n.m.* way of thinking; mind; thought.

penseur, euse *n.m.f.* thinker. **libre ~**, free thinker.

pensif, ive *adj.* pensive; thoughtful.

pension *n.f.* pension; board; board and lodging; boarding house, boarding school; schooling (price). **~ de retraite**, retirement pension. **demi~**, half-board. **~ complète**, American plan. **aller en ~**, to go to boarding school.

pensionnaire *n.m.f.* pensioner; boarder (of a boardinghouse, school, etc.). **demi ~**, half-boarder.

pensionnat *n.m.* school, boarding school.

pensionner *v.t.* give a pension.

pentagonal, e *adj.* pentagonal.

pentagone *n.m.* pentagon. (US) **le ~**, the Pentagon.

pentateuque *n.m.* pentateuch.

pente *n.f.* declivity, slope; incline; descent; ascent, accilivity.

pentacôte *n.f.* Pentecost. **dimanche de la ~**, Pentecost Sunday.

pénurie *n.f.* shortage, penury; scarcity, dearth, poverty.

pépé *n.m. Infml.* grandad, grandpa; old man.

pépée, e *n.f. Infml.* chick, broad.

pépère *n.m. Infml.* **un vieux ~**, an old man. *adj.* comfy.

pépettes *n.f.pl. Infml.* cash, dough.

pépie *n.f.* pip. **avoir la ~**, *Fig.* to be thirsty.

pépiement *n.m.* chirping, chirp.

pépin *n.m.* pip (of fruit); grape stone. **avoir un ~**, to have a small problem. umbrella.

pépinière *n.f.* nursery (trees).

pépiniériste *n.m.* nursery gardener.

pépite *n.f.* nugget (of gold).

péquenaud, e *adj. Infml.* peasant. *n.m.f.* country bumpkin.

péquiste *adj.* (of the) Parti Québécois, P.Q.

perçant, e *adj.* piercing, sharp; pointed; quick, shrill, acute; keen; biting; penetrating. **vue ~e**, a keen sight. **yeux perçants**, piercing eyes.

percé, e *p.p.* pierced; perforated; tapped; opened. **un panier ~**, *Fig.* a spendthrift. **~ à jour**, pierced through.

percée *n.f.* opening; riding (in a wood); breach.

percement *n.m.* piercing, boring; cutting; opening.

perce-neige *n.f.* snowdrop.

percepteur *adj.* perceptive. *n.m.* tax collector.

perceptibilité *n.f.* perceptibility.

perceptif, ive *adj.* perceptive.

perceptible *adj.* perceptible, perceivable; collectible.

perception *n.f.* perception; gathering; collection (of taxes, rent, etc.).

percer *v.t.* to pierce; to bore, to drill; to perforate; to broach, to break, to burst. **l'abscès a percé**, the abscess has burst. **le soleil perce la nuage**, the sun breaks through the clouds. **ses cris percent l'air**, his cries rend the air. **cet affreux spectacle perce le coeur**, it is a heart-rending sight. **~ un mystère**, to solve a mystery. **~ une porte dans un mur**, to make a door in a wall. **finir par ~**, to get along at last. **se ~**, *v.refl.* to be bored, to be pierced.

perceuse *n.f.* drill.

percevable *adj.* (of a tax) collectible; perceivable.

percevoir *v.t.* to gather in; to collect (rents, taxes); to perceive; to feel; to discern.

perche *n.f.* perch; pole.

percher *v.i.* to perch, to roost. **se ~**, *v.i.* to perch, to roost; *Fig.* to perch oneself.

perchiste *n.m.f.* pole vaulter; boom operator.

perchoir *n.m.* perch, roost.

perclus, e *adj.* crippled, paralyzed.

perolateur *n.m.* percolator.

percussion *n.f.* percussion.

percuter *v.t.* to percuss, to strike.

perdant, e *n.m.f.* loser. *adj.* losing.

perdition *n.f.* perdition. **en ~**, in distress.

perdre *v.t.* to lose; to mislay; to miss; to waste; to ruin, to spoil. **n'avoir rien à ~**, to have nothing to lose. **~ ses forces**, to lose one's strength. **~ la tête**, to lose one's head. **le jeu l'a perdu**, gambling ruined him. **vous avez bien perdu de n'être pas à notre soirée**, you missed out by not coming to our party. **se ~**, *v.refl.* to be lost; to lose onself; to get bewildered. **cet usage se perd de jour en jour**, this custom is gradually falling into disuse. **se ~ dans la foule**, to get lost in the crowd. **je me perds dans cette pensée**, this thought bewilders me.

perdreau *n.m.* young partridge.

perdrix *n.f.* partridge.

perdu, e *p.p.* lost; mislaid; wasted, bewildered, perplexed; ruined; done for, undone. **c'est de l'argent perdu**, it's money wasted. **c'est du temps perdu**, it's a waste of time. **coup ~**, random shot. **à corps ~**, headlong, desperately. **heures ~es, moments ~s**, leisure hours. **nous sommes ~s**, we are lost.

père *n.m.* father. **~ adoptif**, adoptive father. **~ nourricier**, foster father. **beau ~**, father-in-law; stepfather. **grand ~**, grandfather. **les ~s de l'Eglise**, the Fathers of the Church.

pérégrination *n.f.* peregrination.

péremption *n.f.* limitation, extinction, peremption.

péremptoire *adj.* peremptory; decisive, positive.

pérennité *n.f.* perennity, perpetuity.

péréquation *n.f.* equalization.

perfectibilité *n.f.* perfectibility.

perfectible *adj.* perfectible.

perfection *n.f.* perfection. **en ~, dans la ~**, to perfection, perfectly.

perfectionnement *n.m.* improvement, improving.

perfectionner *v.t.* to perfect; to improve; to improve on. **se ~**, *v.refl.* to improve; to improve oneself.

perfectionisme *n.m.* perfectionism.

perfectionniste *n.m.f.* perfectionist.

perfide *adj.* perfidious, treacherous, faithless; deceitful, insidious. *n.m.f.* traitor.

perfidement *adv.* perfidiously, treacherously.

perfidie *n.f.* perfidy, perfidiousness; treachery, faithlessness; act of perfidy.

perforant, e *adj.* perforating.

perforateur, trice *adj.* perforating. *n.f.* drilling machine; card punch.

perforation *n.f.* perforation.

perforer *v.t.* to perforate.

performance *n.f.* performance.

perfusion *n.f.* perfusion.

péril *n.m.* peril, danger, hazard, risk, jeopardy. **mettre en ~**, to endanger, to imperil. **faire une chose à ses risques et ~s**, to undertake a thing at one's peril.

périlleusement *adv.* perilously, dangerously.

périlleux, euse *adj.* perilous, dangerous, hazardous.

périmer *v.i.* to lapse, to expire.

périmètre *n.m.* perimeter.

périnatal *adj.* perinatal.

périnatologie *n.f.* perinatal medicine.

période *n.f.* period; cycle. *n.m.* pitch, acme, height; stage, degree. **le plus haut ~ de la gloire**, the height of glory.

périodicité *n.f.* periodicity.

périodique *adj.* periodic, periodical; recurring. **ouvrage ~**, periodical. *n.m.* periodical.

périodiquement *adv.* periodically.

péripatéticien, enne *adj.* peripatetic. *n.m.f.* peripatetic; streetwalker, prostitute.

péripétie *n.f.* catastrophe; sudden change of fortune; vicissitude.

périphérie *n.m.* periphery; outskirts.

périphérique *adj.* peripheral. **boulevard ~**, ring road.

périple *n.m.* long journey.

périr *v.i.* to perish; to die; to be lost (at sea). **son nom ne périra pas**, his name cannot perish. **~ corps et biens**, to perish crew and cargo.

périscopique *adj.* periscopic.

périssable *adj.* perishable.

péritonite *n.f.* peritonitis.

perle *n.f.* pearl; bead. **~ fine**, real pearl. **nacre de ~s**, mother-of-pearl. **~ de Venise**, glass bead, bugle. **c'est la ~ des hommes**, he is the best of men.

perlé, e *adj.* pearled; pearly.

perler *v.t.* to pearl; to thicken (sugar); to give a finish to.

perlier, ière *adj.* pearl-bearing, pearl. **huître ~e**, pearl oyster.

perlimpinpin *n.m.* **pudre de ~**, fake cure.

perime *n.m.* *Infml. Milit.* leave.

permanence *n.f.* permanence, permanency. **en ~**, permanent; permanently. **être de permanence**, to be on duty.

permanent, e *adj.* permanent, durable, lasting; standing. *n.f.* perm, permanent wave.

perméabilité *n.f.* permeability; perviousness.

perméable *adj.* permeable, pervious.

permettre *v.t.* to permit; to allow; to authorize; to let; to admit. **s'il m'est permis de parler ainsi**, if I may express myself. **je me permettrai de vous dire**, allow me to tell you. **si je peux me permettre**, if I may say. **permettez-moi de vous dire**, allow me to tell you. **se ~**, *v.refl.* to be tolerated. **ils ne peuvent se ~ d'y aller en avion**, they can't afford to take the plane to go (there).

permis, e *p.p.* permitted, allowed; lawful; allowable. *n.m.* permit, permission, license. **~ de conduire**, driver's license.

permissif, ive *adj.* permissive; allowing.

permission *n.f.* permission, leave, permit; allowance. **avec votre ~**, with your permission.

permissionnaire *n.m.* soldier on leave.

permutabilité *n.f.* permutability.

permutable *adj.* permutable, exchangeable, commutable.

permutation *n.f.* permutation, exchange, change, commutation.

permuter *v.t.* to exchange, to change, to permute; to exchange one's employment. **se ~**, *v.refl.* to be permuted, to be exchanged.

pernicieux, euse *adj.* pernicious; deadly, fatal, noxious; hurtful, ruinous, destructive; malignant.

péroné *n.m.* fibula.

peroxyde *n.m.* peroxide.

perpendiculaire *adj.* perpendicular.

perpendiculairement *adv.* perpendicularly.

perpétration *n.f.* perpetration.

perpétrer *v.t.* to perpetrate; to commit; to do, to perform.

perpette *n.f.* *Infml.* **à ~**, miles away, in the boonies. **il est prisonnier à ~**, he got life.

perpétuation *n.f.* perpetuation.

perpétuel, elle *adj.* perpetual; lasting; everlasting.

perpétuellement *adv.* perpetually, continually.

perpétuer *v.t.* to perpetuate. **se ~**, *v.refl.* to be perpetuated; to last.

perpétuité *n.f.* perpetuity. **à ~**, *adj.* for ever; for life.

perplexe *adj.* confused, perplexed; puzzled.

perplexité *n.f.* confusion, perplexity.

perquisition *n.f.* perquisition; search. **mandat de ~,** search warrant.

perquisitionner *v.i.* to make a search.

perron *n.m.* perron, stoop.

perroquet *n.m.* parrot; top-gallant sail.

perruche *n.f.* female parrot; paroquet; mizzen-top-gallant sail.

perruque *n.f.* wig.

perruquier, ière *n.m.f.* wigmaker.

pers *adj.* bluish, blue; bluish-green; dark blue.

persécuter *v.t.* to persecute; to torment, to annoy. **se ~,** *v.refl.* to persecute each other.

persécuteur, trice *n.m.f.* and *adj.* persecutor, tormentor; importunate person, troublesome person; persecuting.

persécution *n.f.* persecution.

persévérance *n.f.* perseverance.

persévérant, e *adj.* persevering.

persévérer *v.i.* to persevere, to pursue steadfastly, to go on, to hold on.

persienne *n.f.* Venetian shutter (slatted).

persiflage *n.m.* mockery, quizzing, banter.

persifler *v.t.* to mock, to quiz, to banter.

persifleur *n.m.* mocker, quiz, banterer. *adj.* mocking.

persil *n.m.* parsley.

persillade *n.f.* cold beef and parsley.

persillé, e *adj.* sprinkled with parsley.

persistance *n.f.* persistence, persistency.

persistant, e *adj.* persistent; persevering, steady, constant.

persister *v.i.* to persist.

personnage *n.m.* personage; person, character, part; figure.

personnalisation *n.f.* personalization, impersonation.

perisonnaliser *v.t.* to personalize, to impersonate, to give something a personalized touch.

personalité *n.f.* personality.

personne *n.f.* person; body, life; self. **aimer sa ~,** to be fond of oneself. **j'y étais en ~,** I was there myself, I was there in person. **il est bien de sa ~,** he is a fine-looking man. *n.m.* anybody, anyone; no one, nobody. **~ n'est parfait,** nobody is perfect. **je n'ai trouvé ~,** I did not find anyone. **quelqu'un est-il venu? ~,** did anybody come? Nobody.

personnel, elle *adj.* personal. **l'intérêt ~,** personal interest. *n.m.* personal qualities; persons; clerks, officials, officers; staff. **cette compagnie a beaucoup de ~,** this company has a large staff.

personnellement *adv.* personally; in person.

personnification *n.f.* personification.

personnifier *v.t.* to personify. **se ~,** *v.refl.* to be personified.

perspectif, ive *adj.* perspective; prospect.

perspective *n.f.* perspective; vista, view, prospect. **avoir la ~ d'une grande fortune,** to have the prospect of having a large fortune. **en ~,** in perspective, in prospect, in view.

perspicace *adj.* perspicacious, acute, keen, discerning.

perspicacité *n.f.* perspicacity; insight.

persuader *v.t.* to persuade, to induce; to convince. **se ~,** *v.refl.* to persuade oneself, to think, to imagine; to be persuaded.

persuasif, ive *adj.* persuasive.

persuasion *n.f.* persuasion; conviction, opinion, belief.

perte *n.f.* loss, waste; ruin; overthrow; leakage. **la ~ du sommeil,** the privation of sleep. **la ~ d'une bataille,** the loss of a battle. **courir à sa ~,** to hasten to one's ruin. **vendre à ~,** to sell at a loss. **à ~ de vue,** out of sight. **en pure ~,** in vain, to no purpose.

pertinemment *adv.* pertinently, to the purpose.

pertinence *n.f.* pertinence, pertinency, relevancy.

pertinent, e *adj.* pertinent, relevant.

pertubateur, trice *n.m.f.* troublemaker, disturber, perturber. *adj.* disturbing, perturbing.

perturbation *n.f.* perturbation; trouble, uneasiness; disturbance, perturbance, commotion, disorder.

perturber *v.t.* to disturb, to disrupt, to perturb.

pervenche *n.f.* periwinkle.

pervers, e *adj.* perverse; depraved, wicked. *n.m.* pervert.

perversion *n.f.* perversion; corruption; trouble, disorder.

perversité *n.f.* perverseness, perversity; depravity, corruption.

pervertir *v.t.* to pervert; to lead astray, to corrupt, to deprave. **~ l'ordre des choses,** to pervert the order of things. **se ~,** *v.refl.* to be perverted, to become perverse.

pesage *n.m.* weighing.

pesamment *adv.* heavily; clumsily.

pesant, e *adj.* heavy; weighty, ponderous; clumsy, awkward; slow, sluggish; dull, drowsy. **un sommeil ~,** a heavy sleep. **un style ~,** a heavy style. *n.m.* weight. **valoir son ~ d'or,** to be worth one's weight in gold.

pesanteur *n.f.* gravity; heaviness; ponderousness; weight; slowness, sluggishness. **il fit sentir la ~ de son bras,** he made them feel the weight of his arm. **la ~ d'esprit,** dullness of mind.

pesée *n.f.* weighing; lift.

pèse-lettre *n.m.* postal scale.

peser *v.t.* to weigh; to poise; to ponder, consider; to compare, to balance. **~ du pain,** to weigh bread. **~ les raisons,** to weigh one's reasons. **tous les corps pèsent,** all bodies weigh. **cette viande pèse sur l'estomac,** that meat is heavy to digest. **se ~,** *v.refl.* to be weighed; to weigh oneself.

pessimisme *n.m.* pessimism.

pessimiste *n.m.* pessimist.

peste *n.f.* pest, pestilence, plague; scourge.

pester *v.i. Infml.* to curse, to inveigh against; to rail at.

pesticide *adj.* pesticidal. *n.f.* pesticide.

pestiféré, e *adj.* infected with the plague; pestiferous. *n.m.f.* plague victim.

pestilence *n.f.* pestilence; plague; *Fig.* corruption.

pestilentiel, elle *adj.* pestilential, pestilent, foul.

pet *n.m. Vulg.* fart.

pétale *n.m.* petal.

pétant, e *adj. Infml.* on the dot, sharp.

pétarade *n.f.* crackling; backfire.

pétard *n.m.* firecracker.

péter *v.i. Vulg.* to break wind; to crackle; to crack; to burst. **~ la santé,** to be bursting with health.

péteux, euse *n.m.f.* crestfallen person; coward.

pétillant, e *adj.* sparkling; crackling.

pétillement *n.m.* crackling; sparkling.

pétiller *v.i.* to crackle; to crepitate; to sparkle. **le sel pétille dans le feu,** salt crackles in the fire. **~ d'esprit,** to sparkle with wit. **le sang lui pétille dans les veines,** his blood boils in his veins.

pétoile *n.m.* petiole.

petiot, e *adj. Infml.* tiny.

petit, e *adj.* little, small, diminutive, short; unimportant, petty, trifling, trivial, slight, nice; mean, of little value, ungenerous, selfish. **une ~e ville,** a small town. **une ~e somme d'argent,** a small sum of money. **un ~ esprit,** a narrow-minded man. **se faire ~,** to make oneself small. **cela est bien ~,** that is very mean. **~ marchand,** small tradesman. **ma ~ femme,** my darling wife. *n.m.f.* little boy, little girl; little child, little one; darling, dear; young one. **en ~,** in miniature. **~ à ~,** little by little, gradually, by degrees. **~ ami,** boyfriend. **~e amie,** girlfriend. **~ cousin,** little cousin. **~ déjeuner,** breakfast.

petite-fille *n.f.* granddaughter.

petitement *adv.* little, meanly; poorly, slenderly; sparingly; shabbily, pettily.

petitesse *n.f.* littleness, smallness; diminutiveness; minuteness. **~ d'esprit,** narrow-mindedness.

petit-fils *n.m.* grandson.

petit-gris *n.m.* gray squirrel; snail.

pétition *n.f.* petition.

pétitionnaire *n.m.f.* petitioner.

pétitionner *v.i.* to petition; to present a petition.

petits-enfants *n.m.pl.* grandchildren.

pétoche *n.f. Infml.* scare, fear. **flanquer la ~,** to scare the hell out of somebody.

pétoire *n.f. Infml.* popgun.

peton *n.m. Infml.* tiny foot, foot (of children), tootsy.

pétoncle *n.f.* scallop.

pétrel *n.m.* petrel.

pétri, e *p.p.* kneaded; formed, made, made up; full. **il était ~ d'honneur,** he was a most honorable man.

pétrifiant, e *adj.* petrifying, petrifactive.

pétrification *n.f.* petrification, petrifaction.

pétrifier *v.t.* to petrify. **se ~,** *v.refl.* to petrify, to be petrified.

pétrin *n.m.* kneading trough, dough trough; *Fig.* scrape, jam, mess. **se mettre dans le ~,** to get into a scrape.

pétrir *v.t.* to knead; to mold; *Fig.* to form, to make, to make up.

pétrissage *n.m.* kneading.

pétrochimie *n.f.* petrochemistry.

pétrochimique *adj.* petrochemical.

pétrodollar *n.m. Fin.* petrodollar.

pétrolifère *adj.* petroliferous. **gisement ~,** oil-field. **région ~,** oil-bearing region.

pétrole *n.m.* petroleum, oil.

pétulance *n.f.* vivacity, liveliness.

pétulant, e *adj.* vivacious, lively.

peu *n.m.* little, a little; *pl.* few, a few. **je vous recommande un ~ de repos,** I recommend that you rest a little. **vivre de ~,** to live on little. **attendez un ~,** wait a moment. *adv.* little; few. **bien ~, fort ~, très ~,** very little. **~ ou point,** little or none. **nous étions ~ à cette fête,** there were only a few of us at this festival. **il a ~ de livres,** he has few books. **~ de paroles suffiront,** a few words will do. **~ sage,** unwise. **~ soigneux,** careless. **~ à ~,** little by little; by degrees, gradually. **à ~ près, à ~ de chose près,** nearly, about, thereabout. **dans ~, sous ~,** soon, shortly. **depuis ~,** not long ago; a short time since, a little while since. **pour ~ que vous preniez soin,** if you only take care of it. **quelque ~,** somewhat, rather, a little. **tant soit ~,** ever so little. **de ~,** just, hardly, barely. **il a réussi son examen de ~,** be barely passed his test.

peuplade *n.f.* tribe; people, population.

peuple *n.m.* people; nation; the common people; multitude; crowd. **~s du Nord,** the people of the North. **le petit ~, le bas ~,** the common people, the rabble. *adj.* vulgar, common.

peuplement *n.m.* peopling; population; stocking (with fish).

peupler *v.t.* to people, to populate; to stock (with animals); to breed. **se ~,** *v.refl.* to be peopled; to become populous.

peuplier *n.m.* poplar.

peur *n.f.* fear, fright, dread. **mourir de ~,** to die of fright. **avoir ~ de son ombre,** to be afraid of one's shadow. **faire ~ à quelqu'un,** to frighten a person. **de ~ de,** for fear of. **de ~ que,** for fear. **faire une ~ bleue,** to give someone a bad scare.

peureusement *adv.* fearfully, timorously.

peureux, euse *adj.* fearful, timorous, timid. *n.m.f.* coward, chicken.

peut-être *adv.* perhaps, maybe. **~ ira-t-il quand même,** he might go anyway, perhaps he will go anyway. **~ pas,** maybe not.

pèze *n.m. Infml.* dough.

phalange *n.f.* phalanx; bone joint.

phallocrate *n.m.* male chauvinist.

phantasme *n.m.* phantasm.

pharamineux, euse *adj.* phenomenal, prodigious.

pharaon *n.m.* Pharaoh; faro.

pharaonique *adj.* Pharaonic.

phare *n.m.* lighthouse; beacon; headlight, beam.

pharmaceutique *adj.* pharmaceutic, pharmaceutical.

pharmacie *n.f.* pharmacy; drugstore; dispensary (in a hospital); medicine chest.

pharmacien, ne *n.m.f.* pharmacist; chemist and druggist.

pharmacologie *n.f.* pharmacology.

pharyngite *n.f.* pharyngitis.

pharinx *n.m.* pharinx.

phase *n.f.* phase, phasis; *Fig.* turn, aspect, stage.

phénoménal, e *adj.* phenomenal; *Infml.* wonderful, amazing.

phénomène *n.m.* phenomenon; wonder; prodigious, extraordinary person; freak, character.

philanthrope *n.m.* philanthropist.

philanthropie *n.f.* philanthropy.

philanthropique *adj.* philanthropic, philanthropical.

philatélie *n.f.* philately, stamp collecting.

philatéliste *n.m.f.* stamp collector, philatelist.

philharmonique *adj.* philharmonic.

philologie *n.f.* philology.

philologique *adj.* philologic, philological.

philosophale *adv. f.* pierre ~, philosopher's stone.

philosophe *n.m.* philosopher. *adj.* philosophic, philosophical.

philosopher *v.i.* to philosophize.

philosophie *n.f.* philosophy.

philosophique *adj.* philosophic, philosophical.

philosophiquement *adv.* philosophically.

philosophisme *n.m.* philosophism.

philtre *n.m.* philter; love potion; love charm.

phobie *n.f.* phobia.

phobique *adj.* phobic.

phonème *n.m.* phoneme.

phonétique *adj.* phonetic. écriture ~, phonetic writing. *n.f.* phonetics.

phonographe *n.m.* phonograph.

phonologie *n.f.* phonology.

phonothèque *n.f.* sound archives.

phoque *n.m.* seal; sealskin.

phosphate *n.m.* phosphate.

phosphore *n.m.* phosphorus, phosphor.

phosphorescent, e *adj.* phosphorescent.

photo *n.f.* photo, picture, snap, shot. prendre en ~, to take a picture. appareil ~, camera.

photocopie *n.f.* photocopy, photostat.

photocopier *v.t.* to photocopy, to photostat, to xerox.

photocopieur, ieuse *n.m.f.* photocopier, xerox.

photogénique *adj.* photogenic.

photographe *n.m.* photographer.

photographie *n.f.* photography; photograph.

photographier *v.t.* to photograph, to take a picture (of).

photographique *adj.* photographic, photographical.

photogravure *n.f.* photoengraving.

photométrie *n.f.* photometry.

photomontage *n.m.* photomontage.

photophobie *n.f.* photophobia.

photosphère *n.f.* photosphere.

photosynthèse *n.f.* photosynthesis.

phrase *n.f.* phrase, sentence.

phraséologie *n.f.* phraseology.

phraser *v.i.* to phrase; to form phrases.

phréatique *adj.* nappe ~, ground water.

physicien, ne *n.m.f.* physicist.

physico-mathématique *adj.* relating to mathematical physics.

physiologie *n.f.* physiology.

physiologique *adj.* physiologic.

physiologiste *n.m.* physiologist.

physionomie *n.f.* physiognomy, look; expression.

physionomiste *n.m.* physiognomist.

physique *adj.* physical, external. force ~, physical strength. *n.f.* physics. *n.m.* constitution; body; figure.

physiquement *adv.* physically, materially.

piaf *n.f. Infml.* sparrow.

piaffer *v.i.* to make a show, to be ostentatious; (of horses) to paw the ground.

piaillement *n.m.* chirping, cheeping.

piailler *v.i.* to chirp, to cheep. *Infml.* to bawl, to squeal.

piaillerie *n.f.* chirping, cheeping, bawling.

piailleur, euse *n.m.f. Infml.* bawler.

pianiste *n.m.* pianist.

piano *n.m.* piano. ~ droit, upright piano. ~ à queue, grand piano. jouer du ~, to play the piano. *adv.* piano, softly.

pianoter *v.i.* to tinkle (away); to drum, to strum (finger).

piaule *n.f. Infml.* room, place.

piaulement *n.m.* cheeping, peeping; whining.

piauler *v.i.* to whine, to whimper.

pic *n.m.* pickaxe, pick; peak. ~ vert, woodpecker. le ~ de Ténériffe, the Peak of Tenerife. à ~, perpendicularly; apeak. *Infml.* just in time.

picaresque *adj.* picaresque.

pichet *n.m.* pot, jug.

pickpocket *n.m.* pickpocket.

picoler *v.i. Infml.* to booze.

picorer *v.i.* to peck, to pick.

picotement *n.m.* pricking, tingling.

picoter *v.t.* to pock, to strike with the beak; to pick up food with the beak; to prick, to cause to tingle; to irritate.

pictural, e *adj.* pictorial.

pie *n.f.* pius. *n.f.* magpie, pie. *adj.* oeuvres ~s, charitable deeds. être aussi bavard(e) qu'une ~, to be a chatterbox.

pièce *n.f.* piece; portion, bit; patch; room; barrel; cask (of wine); gun, cannon; coin (of money); head (of cattle); documents, papers; performance, play. **mettre en ~s**, to cut to pieces; to break to pieces. **~ de résistance**, main dish. **cela vaut tant la ~**, it is so much a piece. **donner la ~ à quelqu'un**, to give a person a gratuity. **~ justificative**, voucher. **tout d'une ~**, all of one piece, all of a lump.

piècette *n.f.* small coin.

pied *n.m.* foot; *Fig.* support leg (of a table, etc.); root (of a plant). **~ droit**, right foot. **~ plat**, flat foot. **des ~s de cochon**, pig's feet. **marcher ~s nus**, or **nu ~s**, to walk barefooted. **frapper du ~**, to stamp. **chausser à coups de ~**, to kick out. **ne savoir sur quel ~ danser**, not to know which way to turn. **ne pas se moucher du ~**, to be no fool. **perdre ~**, to be out of one's depth. **lever le ~**, *Fig.* to scamper away, to run away. **lâcher ~**, to give up; to lose ground, to yield. **portrait en ~**, full-length portrait. **grâce à son médecin, le voilà enfin sur ~**, thanks to his doctor, he is back on his feet. **prendre ~**, to get a footing, to establish a footing. **être sur un bon ~**, to be well off; to be in a good position. **le ~ d'un arbre**, the foot of a tree. **le ~ d'une montagne**, the foot of a mountain. **mettre quelqu'un au ~ du mur**, to put a person's back to the wall. **au ~ de la lettre**, literally. **être à ~**, to be on foot. **de ~ ferme**, unflinchingly; resolutely.

pied-à-terre *n.m.* pied-à-terre.

piédestal *n.m.* pedestal.

piège *n.m.* snare, trap. **tendre un ~**, to set a trap. **tomber dans un ~**, to be caught in a trap.

piéger *v.t.* to trap, to snare.

pie-grièche *n.f.* shrike. *Fig.* shrew.

pierraille *n.f.* rubble, broken stones.

pierre *n.f.* stone; gem; rock, foundation; pebble; calculus; **~ angulaire**, cornerstone. **~ à aiguiser**, whetstone. **~ à chaux**, limestone. **~ à fusil**, gun-flint, flint. **~ ponce**, pumice. **~ à bâtir**, building stone. **~ philosophale**, philosopher's stone. **poser la première ~**, to lay the first stone. **geler à ~ fendre**, to freeze hard. **faire d'une ~ deux coups**, to kill two birds with one stone. **~ qui roule n'amasse pas mousse**, a rolling stone gathers no moss. **coeur de ~**, heart of stone.

pierreries *n.f.pl.* precious stones, gems.

pierreux, euse *adj.* stony; full of stones.

piété *n.f.* piety, devotion.

piétinement *n.m.* trampling, stamping.

piétiner *v.i.* to trample; to stamp.

piétisme *n.m.* pietism.

piétiste *n.m.f.* pietist.

piéton, onne *n.m.f.* pedestrian.

piètre *adj.* poor, miserable, wretched, sorry, paltry, shabby. **faire ~ figure**, to have a wretched appearance.

piètrement *adv.* miserably, poorly, wretchedly, sorrily.

pieu *n.m.* stake; pile; post. *Infml.* **aller au ~**, to hit the sack.

pieusement *adv.* piously, godly, devoutly.

pieuter (se) *v.t.* to hit the sack.

pieuvre *n.f.* octopus.

pieux, euse *adj.* pious; godly, devout.

pif *n.m.* *Infml.* (nose) beak, schnazz, schnozzle; paf! smack!

pifomètre *n.m.* *Infml.* **au ~**, by rule of thumb.

pigeon *n.m.* pigeon, dove; *Fig.* dupe. **~ ramier**, wood pigeon. **~ domestique**, domestic pigeon. **~ voyageur**, carrier pigeon.

pigeonner *v.t. Infml.* to con, to swindle.

pigeonnier *n.m.* pigeon house, dovecot.

piger *v.i. Infml.* to get it.

pigiste *n.m.f.* freelancer.

pigment *n.m.* pigment.

pigmentaire *adj.* pigmentary.

pigmentation *n.f.* pigmentation.

pignocher *v.i. Infml.* to nibble, to eat squeamishly.

pignon *n.m.* gable (of a house). **avoir ~ sur rue**, to have a house of one's own; to be an important person; pinion; pine.

pile *n.f.* pile, heap, mass; pier (of a bridge); reverse (of coins); beating; battery. *Infml.* thrashing, beating. **en ~**, in a pile, in a heap. **il s'est arrêté ~**, he stopped short. **elle est arrivée à deux heures ~**, she arrived at two o'clock sharp.

piler *v.t.* to pound; to bruise; *Infml.* to slam on the brake.

pilier *n.m.* pillar; *Fig.* supporter.

pillage *n.m.* looting, pillage, plunder.

pillard, e *adj.* pillaging, plundering. *n.m.f.* looting, pillaging, plundering. *n.m.f.* looter, pillager, plunderer, robber.

piller *v.t.* to loot, to pillage, to plunder, to steal; to ransack, to rifle.

pilleur *n.m.* looter.

pilonnage *n.m.* beating, pounding.

pilonner *v.t.* to beat, to pound.

pilori *n.m.* pillory.

pilotage *n.m.* piloting. **poste de ~**, cockpit.

pilote *n.m.* pilot; driver.

piloter *v.t.* to pilot, to fly.

pilotin *n.m.* pilot's apprentice.

pilotis *n.m.* piling.

pilule *n.f.* pill.

pimbêche *n.f. Infml.* stuck up, girl or woman who is full of herself. **c'est une vraie ~**, she is so full of herself.

piment *n.m.* pimento; hot red pepper.

pimenter *v.t.* to spice, to give spice to.

pimpant, e *adj.* spruce, smart. **une toilette ~e**, a smart dress.

pimprenelle *n.f.* burnet; pimpernel.

pin *n.m.* pine, fir; Scotch fir.

pinacle *n.m.* pinnacle; top, summit. **être sur le ~**, *Fig.* to have reached the pinnacle.

pinailler *v.t. Infml.* to quibble, to split hairs.

pinacothèque *n.f.* picture gallery.

pinard *n.m. Infml.* wine, booze.

pince *n.f.* pinch, pinching, gripe; hold; tongs; pincers, pinchers, pliers; crowbar, claw (of a lobster). **~ à sucre,** sugar tongs. **~ à épiler,** tweezers. **~ à ongles,** nail clippers. **avoir la ~ forte,** to have a strong hand.

pincé, e *adj.* pursed; affected, stiff.

pinceau *n.m.* brush (of a painter).

pincée *n.f.* pinch.

pincement *n.m.* pinching. **avoir un ~ au coeur,** to have a lump in one's throat.

pincer *v.i.* to pinch; to nip; to gripe; to catch, to clip; to lay hold of. **~ le doigt de quelqu'un,** to pinch a person's finger. **~ les lèvres,** to compress one's lips. **on a pincé le voleur,** the thief has been caught. **se ~,** *v.refl.* to pinch oneself.

pince-sans-rire *n.m.* person of dry humor.

pincette *n.f.* pinching; tongs (for the fire), pincers.

pinçon *n.m.* pinch. **se faire un ~,** to give oneself a pinch, to pinch oneself.

pinède *n.f.* pine forest.

pingouin *n.m.* penguin.

ping-pong *n.m.* Ping-Pong.

pingre *adj.* stingy. *n.m.f.* skinflint.

pinson *n.m.* chaffinch. **gai comme un ~,** as merry as a lark.

pintade *n.f.* Guinea hen; Guinea fowl.

pinte *n.f.* pint, quart.

pin-up *n.f.* pin-up girl.

pioche *n.f.* pickax.

piocher *v.t.* to dig; to toil, to work hard, to study hard.

piocheur *n.m.* digger, delver, hard worker.

pion *n.m.* (at chess) pawn; checker.

pioncer *v.i. Infml.* to snooze.

pionnier *n.m.* pioneer.

pipe *n.f.* pipe. **casser sa ~,** to die, to pass away.

pipeline *n.m.* pipeline.

pipi *n.m. slang* urine.

piquant, e *adj.* prickly; stinging; sharp, tart; pungent, keen, pointed, biting, nipping. **de la moutarde trop ~e,** very strong mustard. **le froid est ~,** the cold is piercing.

pique *n.f.* pike; spear (of a pike). *n.m.* spade (at cards). **envoyer des ~s à quelqu'un,** to make cutting remarks.

piqué, e *p.p.* pricked; stung; stitched; quilted; larded; acid; piqued, nettled, irritated. *n.m.* quilting.

pique-assiette *n.m.* parasite, freeloader.

pique-nique *n.m.* picnic.

piquer *v.t.* to prick; to puncture; to interest; to bite, to sting, to nettle; to excite; to spur (a horse); to quilt, to stitch. **cette épingle m'a piqué,** that pin pricked me. **quelle mouche vous a piqué?** what is the matter with you? **cette réponse l'a piqué au vif,** that answer stung him to the quick. **~ une tête,** to dive into

the water. **se ~,** *v.refl.* to prick oneself; (of wine) to get sour; to spot (of paper).

piquet *n.m.* picket, pointed stake. **être droit comme un ~,** to be as upright as a post. *School.* **aller au ~,** to stand in the corner.

piqueter *v.t.* to spot; to mark with spots; to stake out.

piquette *n.f.* cheap wine.

piqûre *n.f.* prick, puncture; pricking; (of serpents and insects) sting; warbles; sting; pain; injection, shot.

pirate *n.m.* pirate. **~ de l'air,** air hijacker.

pirater *v.i.* to pirate.

piraterie *n.f.* piracy; hijacking; robbery; extortion.

pire *adj.* worse. **le remède est ~ que le mal,** the remedy is worse than the evil. *n.m.* worst. **pour le meilleur et pour le ~,** for better or for worse.

pirogue *n.f.* pirogue.

pis *adv.* worse. **de mal en ~, de ~ en ~,** from bad to worse, worse and worse. **tant ~,** so much the worse; too bad. **et qui ~ est,** and what is worse. *n.m.* worst. **mettre les choses au ~,** to look at the worst side of things. **~ aller,** worst; makeshift. *n.m.* breast; udder (of a cow, a she-goat, etc.); dug, teat, pap.

piscine *n.f.* swimming pool.

pisse *n.f. Infml.* urine.

pissement *n.m. Infml.* urination.

pissenlit *n.m.* dandelion.

pisser *v.i.* to pee. *Infml.* to piss. **~ dans un violon,** to hit one's head against a brick wall.

pissoir *n.m.* urinal.

pissotière *n.f.* public urinal.

pistache *n.f.* pistachio, pistachio nut.

piste *n.f.* track, trace, trail; strip. **~ d'envol,** runway. **~ d'atérrissage,** landing strip. **suivre à la ~,** to track (an animal); to trail.

pister *v.t.* to track, to trail; to tail.

pistil *n.m.* pistil.

pistolet *n.m.* gun, pistol. **~ mitrailleur,** automatic pistol. **tirer un coup de ~,** to fire a pistol.

piston *n.m.* piston; sucker; (of a pump). **fusil à ~,** percussion gun. **il a eu ce travail par ~,** someone pulled strings to get him this job.

pistonner *v.t.* to pull strings for.

piteusement *adv.* piteously.

piteux, euse *adj.* piteous; pitiful, pathetic. **parler d'un ton ~,** to speak in a pitiful tone.

pitié *n.f.* pity; compassion, commiseration; pitifulness. **digne de.~,** pitiable, deserving pity. **par ~,** for pity's sake; out of pity. **sans ~,** pitiless, ruthless. **prendre ~,** to take, to have pity on; to pity. **avoir ~,** to have pity; to pity. **il vaut mieux faire envie que ~,** it is better to excite envy than pity.

piton *n.m.* eyebolt; piton, peg; peak (of a mountain).

pitoyable *adj.* pitiful; compassionate, full of

piety; piteous, pitiable; lamentable. **cela est ~,** that is pathetic.

pitoyablement *adv.* piteously, pitiably.

pitre *n.m.* clown; fool.

pittoresque *adj.* picturesque. *n.m.* picturesque, picturesqueness.

pivert *n.m.* green woodpecker.

pivoine *n.f.* peony.

pivot *n.m.* pivot; taproot.

pivoter *v.i.* to pivot. **faire ~,** to turn; *Naut.* to slue.

pizza *n.f.* pizza. **une tranche de ~,** a slice of pizza.

placage *n.m.* veneering (of wood); plating (of metals); *Fig.* patchwork.

placard *n.m.* cupboard (in a wall); placard; advertisement, bill, libel.

placarder *v.t.* to lay; to placard, to post (a placard); to satirize (a person).

place *n.f.* place, spot, ground; stand; seat; room; condition, post; town, market town. **si vous étiez à sa ~,** if you were in his place, if you were in his shoes. **faire ~ à quelqu'un,** to make room for a person. **à la ~ de,** instead of. **se tenir à sa ~,** to keep still. **un homme en ~,** a man in office. **sur la ~,** in the market; on change. **100 francs la ~,** a 100-francs seat.

placement *n.m.* placing, investment. **bureau de ~,** employment agency.

placenta *n.m.* placenta.

placentaire *adj.* placental.

placer *v.t.* to place; to put; to set in a place; to lay; to invest, to put out. **~ des spectateurs,** to seat spectators. **se ~,** *v.refl.* to place; to seat oneself; to get a place, a situation.

placide *adj.* placid.

placidement *adv.* placidly.

placidité *n.f.* placidness, placidity; mildness, gentleness.

plafond *n.m.* ceiling.

plafonner *v.t.* to reach a maximum.

plage *n.f.* shore, seashore, beach.

plagiaire *n.m.* plagiarist. *adj.* plagiary.

plagiat *n.m.* plagiarism.

plaider *v.i.* to litigate; to plead; to discuss, to vindicate. **~ une affaire,** to plead a cause. **~ coupable,** to plead guilty.

plaideur, euse *n.m.f.* litigant.

plaidoirie *n.f.* pleading; speech (of a counsel).

plaidoyer *n.m.* defense counsel's plea.

plaie *n.f.* wound; sore, injury, damage; evil. **rouvrir une ~,** to reopen a wound. **mettre le doigt sur la ~,** to point out the evil.

plaignant, e *adj.* complaining. *n.m.f.* complainer; plaintiff, complainant.

plaindre *v.t.* to pity, to feel sorry for, to commiserate. **~ les malheureux,** to pity the poor. **vous êtes bien à ~,** you are much to be pitied. **se ~,** *v.refl.* to complain; to lament. **se ~ de,** to complain of.

plaine *n.f.* plain; open, level field.

plain-pied *n.m.* on the same level as.

plainte *n.f.* complaint, wailing, accusation, charge. **porter ~,** to sue.

plaintif, ive *adj.* plaintive; lamenting, complaining.

plaintivement *adv.* plaintively, mournfully, moanfully.

plaire *v.i.* to please; to gratify; to be pleasant to, to give pleasure to. **~ à tout le monde,** to please everybody. **tout ce qu'il vous plaira,** anything you please. **s'il vous plaît,** if you please, please. **plaise à Dieu qu'il en soit ainsi!** Please God it were so. **à Dieu ne plaisé,** God forbid. **se ~,** *v.refl.* to please oneself; to please each other; to be fond of; to be delighted; to delight; (of plants) to thrive. **elle ne se plaît pas dans cette maison,** she is not happy in that house. **c'est une plante qui se plaît dans les lieux humides,** this plant thrives in damp places. **se ~ à etudier,** to like studying.

plaisamment *adv.* pleasantly; agreeably; humorously, merrily; ludicrously, comically; ridiculously.

plaisance *n.f.* pleasure. **bateau de ~,** pleasure boat. **port de ~,** marina.

plaisancier, ière *n.m.f.* yachtman, yachtwoman.

plaisant, e *adj.* pleasant; pleasing, agreeable; humorous, amusing.

plaisanter *v.i.* to joke; to trifle. **c'est un homme qui ne plaisante pas,** he is not a man to be trifled with.

plaisanterie *n.f.* joke, jest; joking, jesting. **~ à part,** joking aside, no kidding.

plaisantin *n.m.* joker.

plaisir *n.m.* pleasure; delight, enjoyment. **prendre ~ à,** to take pleasure in. **se faire un ~ de,** to be pleased to. **les ~s de la campagne,** the pleasures, the sports of the country. **avec ~,** with pleasure. **faire ~,** to please. **tel est son ~,** such is her/his wish. **à ~,** wantonly, gratuitously.

plan, e *adj.* plane, plain, level, even, flat. *n.m.* plane; plan; draught; map; design. **~ d'une ville,** map of a town. **gros ~,** close-up. **arrière ~,** background. **lever un ~,** to take a plan. **lever des ~s,** surveying.

plan *n.m.* map; framework.

planche *n.f.* board, plank; stage. **faire la ~,** to float, to swim on one's back; *Engrav.* plate; bed (in a garden). **monter sur les ~s,** to go on stage. **~ de salut,** last hope.

plancher *n.m.* floor, flooring. **mettre le pied au ~,** to step on the gas.

plancton *n.m.* plankton.

planer *v.i.* to glide; to hang over; to hover; to soar. **l'aigle plane,** the eagle soars. **un silence planait dans la pièce,** silence was hanging over the room. **il plane complètement,** he is always day-dreaming.

planétaire *adj.* planetary.

planétarium *n.m.* planetarium.

planète *n.f.* planet.

planeur *n.m.* glider.

plannificateur, trice *adj.* planning; *n.m.f.* planner.

planification *n.f.* planning.

planifier *v.t.* to plan.

planisphere *n.m.* planisphere.

planque *n.f. Infml.* hideout, hiding place; cushy job.

planquer *v.t.* to hide. **se ~,** *v.refl.* to hide oneself.

plant *n.m.* sapling; *Hort.* plant; plantation of young trees; bed.

plantage *n.m.* planting, plantation.

plantaire *adj.* plantar, of the sole (of the foot).

plantation *n.f.* planting; plantation; settlement; colony.

plante *n.f.* plant; herb; shrub. **jardin des ~s,** botanical garden; sole (of the foot).

planter *v.t.* to plant; to set; to sow; to fix. **~ des fleurs,** to plant flowers. **il veut tout ~,** he wants to give it all up. **~ quelqu'un,** to let someone stand. **~ un couteau dans,** to stick a knife into. **se ~,** *v.refl.* to be planted; to place, to put, to station; to set oneself.

planteur *n.m.* planter, grower.

planton *n.m.* orderly (soldier); orderly duty.

plantureux, euse *adj.* abundant, luxuriant, copious, plentiful.

plaque *n.f.* plate; badge. **~ de cuivre,** copper plate. **~ d'immatriculation,** license plate.

plaqué, e *adj.* plated; veneered. *n.m.* plated goods; plated metal.

plaquer *v.t.* to plate; to veneer (wood); to lay down (turf); to plaster; to lay; *Infml.* to get rid of, to ditch, to chuck. **elle l'a plaqué,** she ditched him. **il l'a plaqué contre,** he pinned him against.

plaquette *n.f.* small plate, tablet.

plasma *n.m.* plasma.

plastic *n.m.* plastic explosive.

plasticité *n.f.* plasticity.

plastifier *v.t.* to coat with plastic.

plastiquage *n.m.* planting of a plastic bomb.

plastique *adj.* plastic. *n.f.* modeling, molding.

plat, e *adj.* flat; level; tasteless, dead; spiritless; dull, depressed; lank (as the hair). **un pays ~,** a flat country. **assiette ~e,** a flat plate. **un vin ~,** flat wine. **style ~,** dull style. **calme ~,** dead calm. **le ~ de la main,** the back of the hand. **coucher à ~,** to lay flat. *n.m.* plate; dish; *Naut.* mess; scale (of a balance); sheet (of glass). **un ~ creux,** a deep dish. **un ~ de viande,** a dish of meat.

platane *n.m.* plane tree.

plateau *n.m.* tray, plateau. *Milit.* platform; *Naut.* shoal, shallow; scale (of a balance).

plate-bande *n.f.* flower bed. **marcher sur les ~ de quelqu'un,** to trespass on someone's preserve.

plate-forme *n.f.* platform.

platement *adv.* flatly, insipidly, dully; frankly, openly.

platine *n.f.* plate, plate (of a lock); lock (of firearms); *Print.* platen. *n.m.* platinum, platina.

platise *n.f.* nonsense; flat, senseless thing.

platitude *n.f.* flatness, dullness, vapidness; platitude.

platonique *adj.* Platonic.

plâtrage *n.m.* plaster work; plastering.

plâtras *n.m.* rubbish; old plaster.

plâtre *n.m.* plaster, cast. **~ de Paris,** plaster of Paris. **mouler en ~,** to cast in plaster.

piâtrer *v.t.* to plaster; to smooth over; to patch up.

plausibilité *n.f.* plausibility, plausibleness.

plausible *adj.* plausible.

plausiblement *adv.* plausibly.

plein, e *adj.* full, filled; replete; compact; solid; abounding; (of animals) with young, big. **~ comme un oeuf,** as full as an egg. **la chambre était ~e de monde,** the room was full of people. **ce tableau est ~ de vie,** that picture is full of life. **~ de soi-même,** conceited. **avoir de visage ~,** to have a full face. **~e lune,** full moon. **en ~ air,** in the open air. **en ~ jour,** in broad daylight. **en ~ hiver,** in the middle of winter. **en ~ champ,** in the open field. **en ~ full,** plenitude. **avoir de l'argent ~ ses poches,** to have one's pockets full of money. **en ~,** completely, quite; directly. **tout ~,** much, many; a great many; a great deal. **il y a tout ~ de monde sur la place,** the place is crowded with people. **parler la bouche ~e,** to speak with one's mouth full. **travail à ~ temps,** full-time job. **faites-le plein, s'il vous plaît,** fill it up, please.

pleinement *adv.* fully, entirely, completely; quite; thoroughly.

plénipotentiaire *n.m.* plenipotentiary.

plénitude *n.f.* plenitude; fullness; repletion; abundance; completeness.

pléonasme *n.m.* pleonasm.

pleur *n.m.* weeping, crying; wailing, tears. **verser des ~s,** to shed tears. **essuyer les ~s de quelqu'un,** to dry a person's tears.

pleurer *v.i.* to weep, to cry; to shed tears. **~ à chaudes larmes,** to weep bitterly. **~ comme un enfant,** to cry like a child. **~ quelqu'un,** to mourn for a person. **~ la mort d'un fils,** to mourn for the loss of a son. **~ de rire,** to die of laughter. **les coups pleuvaient de tous les côtés,** blows were coming from all over the place.

pleurnicher *v.i.* to whimper, to whine, to snivel.

pleurnicheur, euse *n.m.f.* whimperer, whiner, sniveller.

pleutre *n.m.* coward.

pleuvoir *v.i. impers.* to rain. **il pleut à verse,** it's pouring. **quand il pleuvrait des hallebardes,** even if it were to rain cats and dogs.

plexiglas *n.m.* Lucite, Plexiglas.

plexus *n.m.* plexus.

pli *n.m.* fold, plait, double; wrinkle; cover, envelop. **faire un ~ à une feuille de papier,** to fold a sheet of paper. **les plis d'une robe,** the folds of a dress. **cet habit ne fait pas un ~,** that coat fits well, is without a crease. **je vous envoie cent francs sous ce ~,** I send you a hundred francs herein inclosed. **faux ~,** crease, pucker. **ça ne fait pas un ~,** no doubt.

pliable *adj.* folding, supple, yielding, docile.

pliage *n.m.* folding.

pliant, e *adj.* pliant, pliable; flexible; supple, yielding, tractable. **table ~e,** a folding table. *n.m.* folding chair, camp stool.

plier *v.t.* to fold, to fold up; to tuck; to bend, to bow, to gather up, to pack. **~ une lettre,** to fold a letter. **~ une serviette,** to fold a napkin. **~ bagage,** to pack up. **~ le coude,** to bend one's elbow. **~ les genoux,** to bend one's knees. **un roseau qui plie,** a reed that bends. **faire ~ un arc,** to bend a bow. **~ sous le poids des années,** to sink under the weight of years. **~ sous le joug,** to bend under the yoke. **se ~,** *v.refl.* to be folded; to stoop; to bow; to be bent. **le bois se plie peu à peu,** wood gradually bends. **se ~ aux désirs de quelqu'un,** to yield to a person's desires.

plisser *v.t.* to plait, to form plaits; to take creases. **se ~,** *v.refl.* to be plaited; to take creases; to wrinkle, to screw up (eyes); to be wrinkled, to pucker.

pliure *n.f.* folding.

plomb *n.m.* lead; shot; plumb line, plummet. **il a du ~ dans la tête,** he is a wise man. **avoir du ~ dans l'aile,** to be in a bad way. **avoir des jambes de ~,** to feel heaviness in the legs. **à ~,** plumb, perpendicularly, vertically.

plombage *n.m.* plumbing, leading, sealing; filling (of a tooth).

plomber *v.t.* to lead; to fit with lead; to plumb; to fill (tooth). **se ~,** *v.refl.* to take a leaden hue.

plomberie *n.f.* plumbing, plumber's store.

plombeur *n.m.* plumber.

plombier *n.m.* plumber.

plonge *n.f. restaurant.* washing up, dishwashing.

plongeant, e *adj.* plunging; downward.

plongée *n.f.* diving, submersion; dive.

plongeoir *n.m.* diving board.

plongeon *n.m.* **faire le ~,** to plunge in, to dive; to duck.

plonger *v.t.* to plunge; to duck, to dive, to dip. **~ dans la mer,** to plunge into the sea. **se ~,** *v.refl.* to plunge oneself, to plunge; to dive.

plongeur *n.m.* diver, plunger. *adj.* plunging, diving.

plot *n.m.* contact (stud).

plouc *n.f. Infml.* clodhopper, yokel.

plouf *Interj.* splash.

ployer *v.t.* to bend, to bow; to give way; to yield. *Fig.* to subdue, to curb. **~ les genoux,** to bend one's knees. **se ~,** *v.refl.* to be bent; to bend, to bow, to give way; to yield.

pluie *n.f.* rain. **petite ~ fine,** drizzle. **~ bat-** tante, pelting rain. **parler de la ~ et du beau temps,** to talk of indifferent matters. **faire la ~ et le beau temps,** to rule the roost. **après la ~ le beau temps,** after a storm comes a calm. **une ~ de pierres,** a shower of stones.

plumage *n.m.* plumage, feathers.

plumard *n.f. Infml.* sack, bed.

plume *n.f.* feather. **mettre de la ~ dans un oreiller,** to stuff a pillow with feathers. **~ d'oie,** *adj.* quill (pen). **écrire au courant de la ~,** to write off hand. **une bell ~,** a good writer. **laisser des ~s,** to get one's fingers burnt.

plumeau *n.m.* feather duster.

plumer *v.t.* to fleece, to pluck.

plupart *n.f.* most part, most, greatest part, majority. **la ~ des hommes,** most men. **pour la ~,** for the most part, mostly. **la ~ du temps,** most of the time, mostly, generally.

puriel, elle *adj.* plural.

plus *n.m.* most; more; besides; plus. **le ~ que je puisse faire,** the most I can do, all I can do. *adv.* (noting comparison) more. **~ tôt,** sooner, earlier. **~ tard,** later. **~ loin,** further, farther. **le ~ tôt, le ~ tard,** the sooner, the later. **au ~ tôt,** as soon as possible. **au ~ tard,** at the latest. **je suis ~ que content,** I am more than satisfied. **il n'est pas ~ riche que moi,** he is not richer than I am. **~ d'un,** more than one. **il a une tête de ~ que moi,** he is a head taller than I am. **~ on a, ~ on veut avoir,** the more people have, the more they want. **~ on travaille, moins on s'ennuie,** the more we work, the shorter the time seems. **je n'espère ~,** I am not hoping anymore. **il n'est ~ que l'ombre de lui-même,** he is but a shadow of himself. **le ~ vertueux,** the most virtuous. **les livres les ~ utiles,** the most useful books. **au ~, tout au ~,** at most, at the most; at the best. V. AUTANT. **de ~ en ~,** more, and more. **ni ~ ni moins,** neither more nor less; just the same. **non ~,** neither, not either; nor. **vous ne l'aimez pas, moi non ~,** you do not like him, neither do I.

plusieurs *adj. pl.* several, many. *n.m.pl.* several people, several, many.

plus-que-parfait *adj.* pluperfect. *n.m.* pluperfect tense.

plus-value *n.f.* superior value, increase in value, appreciation (goods, land); surplus.

plutonique *adj.* plutonic, plutonian.

plutonium *n.m.* plutonium.

plutôt *adv.* rather; sooner. **choisir une chose ~ qu'une autre,** to choose one thing rather than another.

pluvial, e *adj.* pluvial, rainy.

pluvieux, euse *adj.* pluvious, rainy.

pneu *n.m.* tire.

pneumatique ~ *adj.* pneumatic, inflatable. *n.f.* pneumatics.

pneumonie *n.f.* pneumonia.

pochard, e *n.m.f.* drunkard.

poche *n.f.* pocket; pouch; sack, bag. **payer de sa**

~, to pay out of one's pocket. **n'avoir pas sa langue dans sa** ~, to be a great talker. **c'est dans la** ~, it's in the bag.

poché, e adj. poached; (of the eyes) black and blue, black.

pochée n.f. pocketful.

pocher v.t. to bag; to poach (eggs); Infml. to blacken (the eyes) of anyone.

pocheter v.t. to keep in one's pocket. v.i. to be kept in one's pocket.

pochette n.f. pocket handkerchief; small pocket.

podium n.m. podium.

poêle n.m. skillet.

poêlon n.m. earthen saucepan; skillet.

poème n.m. poem.

poésie n.f. poetry.

poète n.m. poet.

poétique adj. poetic, poetical.

poétiser v.i. to poetize.

pognon n.m. Infml. dough, bread.

poids n.m. weight; burden; importance, power, moment, consequence. **faire bon** ~, to give good weight. **c'est une affaire de** ~, it is a weighty matter. **un homme de** ~, a man of importance.

poignant, e adj. pointed, sharp, acute; poignant, heart-rending, keen, bitter; severe.

poignard n.m. dagger.

poignarder v.t. to stab.

poigne n.f. grip; hand.

poignée n.f. handful; handle. **une** ~ **de riz**, a handful of rice. **à** ~, by the handful; by handfuls. **une** ~ **de gens**, a few people. **une** ~ **de main**, a handshake.

poignet n.m. wrist; wristband.

poil n.m. hair, wool (of certain animals); beard; nap (of cloth), pile. **un chien à long** ~, a long-haired dog. **c'est au** ~, that's great, that's perfect. **à** ~, bare, naked. **être de mauvais** ~, to be in a bad mood. **reprendre du** ~ **de la bête**, to get back on one's feet.

poilu, e adj. hairy; shagged, shaggy.

poinçon n.m. point; punch; stamp, mark on plate, etc.

poinçonner v.t. to stamp, to punch (ticket), to mark (plate).

poing n.m. fist; hand. **fermer le** ~, to clench one's fist. **coup de** ~, punch, blow with a fist. **se battre à coups de** ~, to box.

point n.m. stitch; point, spot, speck, full stop; mark (in examinations); aim, purpose, question, difficulty; size (of shoes). **avoir un** ~ **de côté**, to have a stich in one's side. **faire un** ~, to do a stitch. ~ **de départ**, point of departure, starting point. ~ **d'appui**, fulcrum; Build. prop; Milit. base of operations. ~ **de vue**, viewpoint, point of view. **deux** ~, colon. ~ **et virgule**, semicolon. ~ **d'interrogation**, question mark. ~ **d'exclamation**, exclamation point. **donner un bon** ~ **à un élève**, to give a good mark to a pupil. **un** ~ **d'histoire**, an historical question.

sur ce ~, in this respect. **le** ~ **capital, le** ~ **essentiel**, the main point. **venir au** ~, to come to the point. **à un tel** ~, to such a degree. ~ **du jour**, the break of day. **à** ~, in the nick of time; medium (rare).

point adv. not, not at all; none; not any. ~ **du tout**, not at all.

pointage n.m. pointing, aiming; timekeeping.

pointe n.f. point (sharp end); prick, puncture; sting; nail, touch. **marcher sur la** ~ **du pied**, to walk on tiptoe.

pointer v.t. to prick; to stick; to point, to aim, to level; to rise, to shoot, to sprout; to appear, to peep, to dawn. **se** ~, to show up.

pointiller v.t. to dot; to stipple.

pointilleux, euse adj. particular, fastidious; touchy.

pointu, e adj. pointed; sharp; peaked.

pointure n.f. size.

poire n.f. pear. **garder une** ~ **pour la soif**, to save somethng for a rainy day.

poireau n.m. leek.

poireauter v.t. Infml. **faire** ~ **quelqu'un**, to make someone wait for a long time.

poirier n.m. pear tree.

pois n.m. pea. **petits** ~, green peas. ~ **chiche**, chickpea.

poison n.m. poison.

poisse n.f. jinx.

poisser v.t. to make sticky, to soil.

poisseux, euse adj. sticky.

poisson n.m. fish; pisces. ~ **de mer**, saltwater fish. ~ **d'avril**, April fool.

poissonnerie n.f. fishmarket.

poissonnier n.m. fishmonger.

poissonnière n.f. fishmonger (woman); fish kettle.

poitrine n.f. chest, breast; brisket (of beef).

poivre n.m. pepper. ~ **noir**, pepper, black pepper. ~ **de la Jamaïque**, Jamaican pepper, pimento, allspice. ~ **en grains**, whole pepper, peppercorns.

poivrier n.m. pepper plant.

poivrière n.f. pepper; spice; pepper plantation.

poivron n.m. green/red pepper.

poivrot, e n.m.f. boozer, drunkard.

poker n.m. poker.

poix n.f. pitch; shoemaker's wax.

polaire adj. polar. **étoile** ~, polar star.

polariser v.t. to polarize.

pôle n.m. pole. ~ **arctique**, North pole. ~ **magnétique**, magnetic pole.

polémique adj. polemic. **écrivain** ~, polemic.

poli, e adj. polished; bright, refined; polite. **des manières** ~**es**, polite manners. n.m. polish, gloss; polishing.

police n.f. police; policy. **agent de** ~, police officer. ~ **d'assurance**, insurance policy. **faire la** ~ **de**, to maintain order in.

polichinelle n.m. Punchinello, punch; buffoon; Fig. buffoon.

policier, ière *n.m.f.* police officer.

poliment *adv.* politely, civilly.

polir *v.t.* to polish; to refine; to make elegant and polite. **~ le marbre,** to polish marble. **~ son style,** to polish one's style. **se ~,** *v.refl.* to be polished.

polissage *n.m.* polishing.

politesse *n.f.* politeness, refinement; good breeding; civility, compliment. **la ~ des moeurs,** the refinement of manners. **faire une ~ à quelqu'un,** to do a person a kindness.

politicien, ne *n.m.f.* politician, politico.

politique *adj.* political. *n.m.* politician. *n.f.* politics; policy. **parler ~,** to talk politics.

politiquement *adv.* politically.

polluant, e *adj.* polluting; *n.m.* pollutant.

polluer *v.t.* to pollute.

pollution *n.f.* pollution.

polo *n.m.* polo; shirt.

poltron, onne *adj.* cowardly. *n.m.f.* coward.

polycopier *v.t.* to duplicate.

polygame *n.m.f.* polygamist. *adj.* polygamous.

polygamie *n.f.* polygamy; polygamia.

polyglotte *adj.* polyglot.

polymère *n.m.* polymer.

polythéisme *n.m.* polytheism.

polythéiste *n.m.* polytheist. *adj.* polytheistic, polytheistical.

pommade *n.f.* ointment, cream. **passer de la ~ à quelqu'un,** to butter someone up.

pomme *n.f.* apple; knob, ball. **~ cuite,** baked apple. **~ de pin,** fir cone. **~ de terre,** potato. **~ d'Adam,** Adam's apple. **~ d'arrosoir,** sprinkling rose. **~ de chou,** head of a cabbage.

pommette *n.f.* cheekbone.

pommier *n.m.* apple tree.

pompe *n.f.* pomp, show, pageantry, state; pump. **la ~ du style,** the loftiness of the style. **entrepreneur de ~ funèbres,** undertaker, mortician. **~ à main,** hand pump. **~ à incendie,** fire engine.

pomper *v.t.* to pump; to suck up.

pompette *adj.* tipsy.

pompeusement *adv.* pompously.

pompeux, euse *adj.* pompous.

pompier *n.m.* fireman.

poncer *v.t.* to sand (paper), to pumice.

ponceuse *n.f.* sander.

ponction *n.f.* puncture.

pontualité *n.f.* punctuality.

pontuation *n.f.* punctuation.

ponctuel, elle *adj.* punctual; exact.

ponderation *n.f.* ponderation, equilibration; poising, balancing.

ponderer *adj.* to balance, to poise.

pondre *v.t.* to lay (eggs).

poney *n.m.* pony.

pont *n.m.* bridge; deck (of a ship); flap (of trousers). **~ de bateaux,** bridge of boats. **faire le ~,** to take a day off between two holidays or take a long weekend.

pontage *n.m.* bypass operation.

ponte *n.f.* laying eggs, laying; laying time; eggs.

pontife *n.m.* pontiff.

pontifical *adj.* pontifical. *n.m.* pontifical.

pop *adj. n.m.f.* pop (music, art).

pope *n.m.* pope.

populace *n.f.* populace, mob, rabble.

populaire *adj.* popular; vulgar. **les classes ~,** the working classes.

popularité *n.f.* popularity.

population *n.f.* population.

populo *n.m.* riffraff, rabble.

porc *n.m.* hog, pig, porker; pork, swine. **jeune ~,** porker. **troupeau de ~s,** herd of swine. **~ frais,** fresh pork. **côte de ~,** sparerib. *Infml.* pig.

porcelaine *n.f.* porcelain, china(ware).

porc-épic *n.m.* porcupine.

porche *n.m.* porch.

porcherie *n.f.* pigsty.

pore *n.m.* pore.

poreux, euse *adj.* porous.

porno *adj. Infml.* porno. **film ~,** porno movie.

pornographie *n.f.* pornography.

pornographique *adj.* pornographic.

porosité *n.f.* porosity.

port *n.m.* port; harbor, haven; wharf, quay; postage; deportment; burden (of a ship). **~ de mer,** seaport. **arriver à bon ~,** to arrive safely. **le ~ est payé,** postage paid. **permis de ~ d'armes,** license to carry guns. **d'un ~ distingué,** of gentlemanly bearing.

portable *adj.* portable; fit to wear.

portail *n.m.* portal, gate.

portatif, ive *adj.* portable; hand; pocket.

porte *n.f.* gate; gateway; door; doorway; entrance; portal. **la ~ d'une maison,** the door of a house. **les ~s d'une ville,** the gates of a town. **de derrière,** back door. **~ à deux battants,** folding doors. **frapper à la ~,** to knock at the door. **fermer la ~ à clef,** to lock the door. **enfoncer une ~,** to break down a door. **mettre à la ~,** to throw out. **prendre, gagner la ~,** to take to the door. **de ~ en ~,** from door to door.

porté, e *adj.* inclined, disposed, prone, ready. *n.m.* wear (of clothes).

porte-aiguille *n.m.* needlecase.

porte-avions *n.m.* aircraft carrier.

porte-bagages *n.m.* luggage carrier.

porte-bonheur *n.m.* lucky charm.

porte-clefs *n.m.* key ring.

porte-documents *n.m.* briefcase, attaché case.

porte-drapeau *n.m.* standard bearer.

portée *n.f.* brood (of animals); bearing, shot, range; reach; call (of the voice); hearing. **cela n'est pas à ma ~,** that is not within my reach. **cela est hors de la ~ de son esprit,** that is quite beyond his capacity.

portefeuille *n.m.* wallet; portfolio; billfold, bonds.

portemanteau *n.m.* coat hanger; coat rack.

porte-monnaie *n.m.* purse, wallet.

porte-parole *n.m.* mouthpiece, spokesperson.

porter *v.t.* to bear, to support; to yield; to carry; to wear, to utter. ~ **du bois,** to carry wood.

~ **tout le poids des affaires,** to bear the whole weight of business. **cette somme porte intérêt,** that sum bears (or yields) interest.

~ **respect,** to have respect. ~ **au nom,** bear a name. **ce monument porte cette inscription,** this monument bears that inscription.

~ **témoignage,** to bear witness *or* testimony. ~ **la parole,** to be the spokesperson. ~ **une lettre à la poste,** to take a letter to the post office. ~ **une canne,** to carry a cane. ~ **de mauvaises nouvelles,** to be the bearer of bad news. **la nuit porte conseil,** sleep on it. ~ **le bras en écharpe,** to carry one's arm in a sling. ~ **la tête haute,** to carry one's head high. ~ **bien son âge,** not to look one's age. ~ **tout à l'extrême,** to always carry things to extremes. ~ **aux nues,** to praise to the skies. ~ **une bague,** to wear a ring. ~ **les cheveux longs,** to wear one's hair long. ~ **la barbe,** to wear a beard. ~ **des lunettes,** to wear glasses. ~ **le deuil,** to go into mourning. ~ **ombrage,** to give umbrage.

~ **bonheur,** to bring good luck. ~ **malheur,** to bring bad luck. **être porté à la verta,** to be inclined to virtue. ~ **un jugement sur une chose,** to pass judgment upon something.

~ **des articles sur une facture,** to put down items on a bill. ~ **à faux,** not to bear steady. **son objection porte sur ce point,** that is what he objects to. **sa tête a porté contre une pierre,** his head struck against a stone. ~ **au nord,** to stand off to the north. ~ **au large,** to stand off, to bear off from the land (boat). ~ **sur les nerfs,** to get (on someone's) nerves. **ce vin porte à la tête,** this wine goes to the head. **se ~,** *v.refl.* to be borne, supported, sustained; to be carried. **se ~ bien,** to be well. **comment vous portez-vous?** how are you doing? **se ~ héritier,** to assume the character of an heir. **se ~ partie contre quelqu'un,** to appear against a person.

porter *n.m.* wear; **prêt-à-~,** ready-to-wear.

porteur, euse *n.m.f.* bearer; carrier, porter; holder. ~ **d'une lettre de recommandation,** the bearer of a letter of recommendation.

~ **d'une lettre de change,** holder of a bill. ~ **d'actions,** shareholder.

porte-savon *n.m.* soapdish.

porte-serviette *n.f.* towel rack.

porte-voix *n.m.* megaphone.

portier *n.m.* doorman, porter.

portière *n.f.* door.

portion *n.f.* portion, part, share, lot; allowance.

portique *n.m.* portico; porch.

porto *n.m.* port wine, port.

portrait *n.m.* portrait; likeness, picture. **faire le ~ de quelqu'un,** to do a portrait of someone. ~ **en pied,** full-length portrait. ~ **en buste,** half-length portrait. **faire faire son ~,** to have one's portrait done.

portuaire *adj.* harbor.

pose *n.f.* laying, setting, putting up, putting down; pose, posture; exposure. ~ **de la première pierre,** the laying of the first stone. *Photo.* **24 ~s,** 24 exposures.

posé, e *adj.* steady, composed, staid, sedate.

posément *adv.* staidly, sedately.

poser *v.t.* to place; to set, to put, to lay, to lay down; to admit, to grant; to lie, to bear, to rest; to sit (for a portrait). *Mus.* to pitch. ~ **le pied,** to step, to set one's foot. ~ **les armes,** to lay down one's arms. ~ **un principe,** to lay down a principle. ~ **une question,** to ask a question. **se ~,** *v.refl.* (of birds) to alight, to perch; to settle; to play the part (of); to set up (for).

poseur *n.m.* layer, placer. *Infml.* actor; affected person, snob.

positif, ive *adj.* positive; certain; real; explicit. **les sciences positives,** positive sciences. **esprit ~,** matter-of-fact mind. **un homme ~,** a practical man. *n.m.* positiveness; reality.

position *n.f.* position; site, situation; place; attitude, posture; circumstances. **la ~ du corps,** the position of the body. **être dans une ~ critique,** to be in a difficult position. **feux de ~,** navigation lights.

positivement *adv.* positively; precisely, expressly, explicitly.

posséder *v.t.* to possess; to own, to have the ownership of, to be in possession of, to be possessed of; enjoy; to be worth; to rule over. ~ **une maison,** to own a house. ~ **parfaitement sa langue maternelle,** to know one's own language thoroughly. **se ~,** *v.refl.* to be possessed.

possesseur *n.m.* possessor; owner; holder.

possessif, ive *adj.* possessive.

possession *n.f.* possession; occupation. **prendre ~ de,** to take possession of.

possibilité *n.f.* possibility.

possible *adj.* possible; feasible. **venez le plus tôt ~,** come as soon as possible. *n.m.* possibility; what is possible; utmost, best. **je ferai mon ~, tout mon ~,** I'll do my best. **ignorant et présomptueux au ~,** as ignorant and conceited as can be.

postal, e *adj.* postal.

postdater *v.t.* to postdate.

poste *n.f.* post office; post; mail. *n.m.* post; place, situation; a military station; guardhouse; berth; station of a ship. **conduire quelqu'un au ~,** to take a person to the police station. ~ **123,** extension 123. ~ **de contrôle,** control tower.

poster *v.t.* to post, to mail; to place, to station. **se ~,** *v.refl.* to post oneself, to place oneself.

postérieur, e *adj.* posterior; subsequent in time; coming after; hinder; hind. *n.m.* posterior, behind.

postérieurement *adv.* posteriorly, subsequently, afterward, after.

postériori (à) *adv.* a posteriori.

postérité *n.f.* posterity, descendants; issue.

posthume *adj.* posthumous.

postiche *adj.* false, artificial. **cheveux ~s**, false hair.

postillon *n.m.* postillion

postillonner *v.i.* to splutter, to sputter.

postnatale *adj.* postnatal.

postopérative *adj.* postoperative.

post-scriptum *n.m.* postscript.

postulant, e *n.m.f.* candidate, applicant, postulant.

postuler *v.t.* to solicit, to apply for, to postulate. *v.i.* to conduct a suit.

posture *n.f.* posture; attitude; situation, state, position, condition.

pot *n.m.* pot; **~ de terre**, earthen pot. **~-au-feu**, beef and vegetable stew. **~-de-vin**, bribe. **~ pourri**, hodge-podge; medley. **découvrir le ~ aux roses**, to find out what's been going on. **il n'a vraiment pas de ~**, he really has no luck. **coup de ~**, stroke of luck.

potable *adj.* potable, drinkable.

potage *n.m.* soup.

potager, ère *adj.* vegetable. *n.m.* vegetable garden.

potassium *n.m.* potassium.

pote *n.m. Infml.* pal, buddy.

poteau *n.m.* post; stake.

potelé, *adj.* plump, chubby.

potence *n.f.* gallows.

potentiel, elle *adj.* potential.

potentiellement *adv.* potentially.

poterie *n.f.* pottery, earthenware.

potiche *n.f.* Chinese vase.

potin *n.m. Infml.* noise, prattle.

potion *n.f.* potion, draft.

potiron *n.m.* pumpkin.

pou *n.m.* louse; *pl.* lice.

pouah *Interj.* ugh! yuck!

poubelle *n.f.* garbage, trash; garbage can.

pouce *n.m.* thumb; inch. **mettre les ~s**, to give in. **manger sur le ~**, to have a snack. **donner un coup de ~ à**, to help out, to lend a hand.

poucet *n.m.* Tom Thumb.

poudre *n.f.* powder, dust. **~ à canon**, gunpowder. **jeter de la ~ aux yeux de quelqu'un**, to throw dust into the eyes of a person; to impose on. **mettre le feu aux ~s**, to fan the flame.

poudrer *v.t.* to powder. **se ~**, to powder one's face.

poudreux, euse *adj.* dusty, powdery.

poudreuse *n.f.* powder snow.

poudrier *n.m.* compact.

poudrière *n.f.* powder horn; powder magazine; *Fig.* powder keg.

pouf *Interj.* plump! thump! *n.m.* puff. **faire ~**, to puff; powder puff; large cushion, stool.

pouffer *v.i.* to burst out. **~ de rire**, to burst out laughing.

pouffiasse *n.f. Pej.* floozey.

pouilles *n.f.pl.* quarrel. **chercher des ~ à quelqu'un**, to look for trouble (with a person).

pouilleux, euse *adj.* lousy, crummy.

poulailler *n.m.* hen roost; poultry house, balcony (in a theater).

poulain *n.m.* colt; foal; promising young athlete.

poule *n.f.* hen; fowl; pool (at play). **la ~ aux oeufs d'or**, the hen that laid the golden eggs. **une ~ mouillée**, a coward. *adj.* (of steel) blistered.

poulet *n.m.* chicken; cop; love.

poulette *n.f.* hen chicken; pullet. *Fig.* dame, broad. **à la ~**, with melted butter.

pouliche *n.f.* filly.

poulie *n.f.* pulley; *Naut.* block.

poulpe *n.m.* octopus.

pouls *n.m.* pulse. **tâter le ~ à quelqu'un**, to feel a person's pulse.

poumon *n.m.* lung.

poupe *n.f.* stern. **avoir le vent en ~**, to sail before the wind; to be in luck, to be in favor.

poupée *n.f.* doll.

pouponner *v.t.* to coddle, to mother.

pour *prep.* for; in order to; on account of; in the interest of, toward; with respect to, with regard to. **ceci est ~ vous**, that is for you. **traduire mot ~ mot**, to translate word for word. **jour ~ jour**, to a day. **oeil ~ oeil, dent ~ dent**, an eye for an eye, a tooth for a tooth. **il n'y est ~ rien**, he has nothing to do with it. **~ ainsi dire**, so to speak. **~ peu que vous en preniez soin**, if you only take care of it. *n.m.* pro, for. **le ~ et le contre**, pros and cons.

pourboire *n.m.* tip, gratuity.

pourcentage *n.m.* percentage. **travailler au ~**, to work on commission.

pourchasser *v.t.* to pursue, to chase, to hunt after, to hunt down, to hound.

pourfendre *v.t.* to cleave in two, to cleave.

pourlécher *v.t.* to lick. **se ~**, *v.refl.* to lick one's chops.

pourparlers *n.m.* negotiations, parley, conference.

pourpier *n.m.* purslain.

pourpoint *n.m.* doublet. **à brûle ~**, within arm's length, point-blank.

pourpre *n.f.* purple, crimson.

pourquoi *conj.* why; for what reason; wherefore. **s'en aller sans dire ~**, to go away without giving a reason. **c'est ~**, therefore, that's why. **~ êtes-vous venu?** why did you come? *n.m.* why, wherefore.

pourri, e *p.p.* rotten. **~ de fric**, filthy rich. *n.m.* rotten part; rottenness.

pourrir *v.i.* to rot; to grow rotten; to decay. **se ~**, *v.refl.* to rot; to grow rotten; to corrupt.

pourrissement *n.m.* decaying, deterioration.

pourriture *n.f.* rottenness, rot.

poursuite *n.f.* pursuit; chase; suit, proceedings; prosecution. **~s**, legal action.

poursuivant, e *adj.* pursuing; suing. *n.m.* plaintiff, prosecutor.

poursuivre *v.t.* to pursue; to go after, to chase; to

torment; to prosecute, to sue; to keep up, to go on, to proceed, to continue. ~ l'ennemi, to pursue the enemy. le malheur le poursuit, he always meets with misfortune. ~ sa route, to pursue one's way. il faut ~ à garder le silence, you must continue to be silent. se ~, v.refl. to pursue one another; to be pursued.

pourtant conj. nevertheless, however; still, yet.

pourtour n.m. circumference, surround.

pourvoi n.m. appeal, petition (for mercy).

pourvoir v.i. to provide; to purvey, to appoint; to furnish, to supply; to look to, to see to, to attend to. ~ aux besoins de quelqu'un, to provide for a person's needs. ~ quelqu'un de tout ce qu'il lui faut, to provide a person with all that is necessary. se ~, v.refl. to provide oneself (with); to appeal (in a court); to petition.

pourvoyeur, euse n.m.f. purveyor; (in a negative sense) supplier.

pourvu adj. provided, supplied, endowed.

pourvu que conj. provided that, if.

pousse n.f. shoot, sprout; growth (of teeth).

poussée n.f. push, pushing; shoving. donner une ~ à quelqu'un, to give a person a push.

pousser v.t. to push; to thrust, to shove, to drive; to set up; to drive on, in, to; to set forth, to carry on, to extend, to grow, to sprout, to shoot up. ~ un fauteuil, to push an armchair. ~ des soupirs, to heave sighs. ~ des travaux, to push on with work. ~ quelqu'un à, to incite a person. se ~, v.refl. to be pushed; to push one another; to go on, to proceed. se ~ dans le monde, to make one's way in the world.

poussette n.f. stroller.

poussière n.f. dust; powder; remains, ashes; pollen; spray (of water). couvert de ~, covered with dust. morder la ~, to bite the dust.

poussiérieux, euse adj. dusty.

poussin n.m. chick. mon petit ~, my little darling.

poutre n.f. beam; girder (of a floor).

poutrelle n.f. small beam; girder.

pouvoir v.i. to be able, to have power to. ~ venir, to be able to come. il pouvait parler, he could speak. sauve qui peut! help! vous pouvez aller le voir, you may go and see him. le projet pourrait bien réussir, the plan might succeed. puisse-t-il réussir, may he succeed. nous n'y pouvons rien, we cannot help it. sachant ce que vous pouvez faire, knowing what you can do. vous pouvez beaucoup sur son esprit, you have great influence over him. n'en ~ plus, to be exhausted. se ~, v.refl. to be possible, can be, may be, done. je ne sais pas si cela se peut, I do not know if it can be done. il se peut qu'il vienne, he may come. cela se peut, that may be, that is possible.

pouvoir n.m. power; strength, force, means; authority, sway, influence, control. autant qu'il est en notre ~, as much as it lies in our power. au ~ de, in the power of. pleins ~s, full pow-

ers. ~ suprême, supreme power. s'emparer du ~, to usurp power.

pragmatique adj. pragmatic.

praire n.f. clam.

prairie n.f. meadow, mead; (in the western states of America) prairie.

praline n.f. praline.

practicable adj. practicable, feasible, that may be done. cela n'est pas ~, that is impracticable. un chemin ~, a practicable road.

practicien n.m. practitioner, practician.

pratiquant, e adj. practising, observant, churchgoer.

pratique n.f. practice, observance; method; use; conduct, dealing; commerce. mettre en ~, to put in practice. la ~ de la médecine, the practice of medicine. avoir la ~ des affaires, to have experience in business. adj. practical; feasible, practicable; experienced.

pratiquement adv. practically.

pratiquer v.t. to practice; to exercise; to frequent; to tamper with; to exercise a profession. ~ la médecine, to practice medicine. ~ un trou, to make a hole.

pré n.m. meadow, mead.

préalable adj. beforehand, previous, preliminary. question ~, previous question. n.m. preliminary.

préalablement adv. previously.

préambule n.m. preamble.

préau n.m. covered playground (school); courtyard (prison, convent).

préavis n.m. forewarning, previous advice.

précaire adj. precarious; uncertain, unsettled, unsteady.

précairement adv. precariously.

précaution n.f. precaution; caution, wariness.

précautionneux, euse adj. cautious, wary.

précédemment adv. before, above, previously, already.

précédence n.f. precedence, priority.

précédent, e adj. preceding, precedent, anterior, antecedent, previous. n.m. precedent.

précéder v.t. to precede, to go before.

précepte n.m. precept; rule, maxim.

précepteur n.m. tutor.

prêcher v.t. to preach; to lecture. ~ toujours la même chose, to be always harping on the same thing. ~ dans le désert, to preach in the desert.

prêcheur n.m. preacher; lecturer, sermonizer. adj. preaching.

précieusement adv. preciously.

précieux, euse adj. precious; valuable, costly; affected. pierres ~es, precious stones. un souvenir ~, a sweet recollection. se donner un air ~, to look affected.

précipice n.m. precipice, abyss, chasm. tomber dans un ~, to fall into a precipice.

précipitamment adv. precipitately, hastily, hurriedly.

précipitation n.f. precipitation, hurry, hastiness. **marcher avec ~**, to hurry along.

précipiter v.t. to precipitate; to cast, to throw down; to hasten, to hurry. **~ ses pas**, to hasten along. **~ sa faite**, to hasten one's flight. **se ~**, v.refl. to precipitate oneself; to rush down, to dash, to spring forth. **se ~ par une fenêtre**, to throw oneself out a window. **se ~ dans le danger**, to rush into danger.

précis, e adj. precise, exact, accurate. **à deux heures ~es**, at two o'clock precisely. n.m. abstract, summary.

précisément adv. precisely, exactly.

préciser v.t. to state precisely, to specify.

précision n.f. precision, preciseness, exactness, accuracy.

précité, e adj. aforesaid, abovementioned.

précoce adj. precocious. **enfant ~**, precocious child. **une mort ~**, a premature death.

précocement adv. precociously.

précocité n.f. precociousness, precocity.

préconcevoir v.t. to preconceive.

préconçu, e p.p. or adj. preconceived.

préconiser v.t. to recommend, to praise.

précurseur n.m. precursor, forerunner; harbinger. adj.m. precursory.

prédateur, trice adj. predatory. n.m. predator.

prédécesseur n.m. predecessor.

prédestination n.f. predestination.

prédétermination n.f. predetermination.

prédéterminer v.t. to predetermine.

prédiction n.f. prediction; foretelling, foreboding, prophecy.

prédilection n.f. predilection, preference.

prédire v.t. to predict, to foretell, to prophesy.

prédisposer v.t. to predispose.

prédisposition n.f. predisposition.

prédominance n.f. predominance.

prédominant, e adj. predominant, prevalent.

prédominer v.i. to predominate, to prevail.

prééminence n.f. preeminence, superiority.

prééminent, e adj. preeminent; surpassing.

préemption n.f. preemption.

préétablir v.t. to preestablish; to establish beforehand.

préexistence n.f. preexistence, previous existence.

préexister v.i. to preexist, to exist beforehand.

préface n.f. preface, prelude, preamble.

préfectoral, e adj. of a prefecture; of a prefect.

préfecture n.f. prefecture.

préférable adj. preferable.

préférablement adv. preferably, in preference.

préférence n.f. preference; choice. **de ~**, in preference.

préférer v.t. to prefer, to choose. **lequel des deux préfères-tu?** which one do you like better?

préfet n.m. prefect. **~ de police**, prefect of police.

préhistoire n.f. prehistory.

préhistorique adj. prehistoric.

préjudice n.m. prejudice, injury, wrong, detriment, harm. **causer un ~ à quelqu'un**, to do any injury, a prejudice to a person, to wrong a person. **au ~ de**, to the prejudice of. **sans ~ de**, without prejudice to.

préjudiciable adj. prejudicial, injurious, detrimental.

préjugé n.m. bias, precedent; presumption; prejudice. **il est exempt de ~s**, he is free from prejudice.

préjuger v.t. to prejudge.

prélasser (se) v.refl. to sprawl, to lounge.

pré-laver v.t. to prewash.

prélèvement n.m. deduction; withdrawal; sample. **~ bancaire**, bank withdrawal. **~ de sang**, blood sample.

prélever v.t. to deduct; to withdraw; to remove; to draw out.

préliminaire adj. preliminary. n.m.pl. preliminaries.

prélude n.m. prelude.

prématuré, e adj. premature; precocious; untimely. n.m.f. premature baby, premmie.

prématurément adv. prematurely.

préméditation n.f. premeditation.

préméditer v.t. to premeditate; to intend.

prémices n.f.pl. first fruits.

premier, ière adj. first; former; early; old, ancient; primitive, primary; prime, premier. **le ~ jour de la semaine**, the first day of the week. **~ ministre**, prime minister. n.m.f. first; foremost, former; first. n.m. leader, chief. **le ~ du mois**, the first day of the month. **demeurer au ~**, to live on the first floor. n.f. first performance (of a play), first proof (of a book).

premièrement adv. first, firstly, in the first place.

premier-né n.m. first born.

prémisses n.f.pl. premises.

prémonition n.f. premonition.

prémonitoire adj. premonitory.

prémunir v.t. to forewarn, to warn; to caution; to forearm, to prepare. **se ~**, v.refl. to provide; to be provided.

prénatal, e adj. prenatal.

prendre v.t. to take; to pick up, to get, to fetch; to grasp; to lay hold of, to seize, to catch; take up, to surprise; to have, to book; to let in; to put on, to assume; to gain; to charge; to receive; to kindle, to deceive, to tackle; to conquer, to strike; to break out. **~ quelqu'un par la main**, to take a person by the hand. **se laisser ~ au piège, à l'hameçon**, to fall into the snare, to be caught with the bait; to be taken in. **quand la colère me prend**, when I am overcome by anger. **~ l'air**, to take a breath. **~ le frais**, to breathe the fresh air. **~ de l'embonpoint**, to get stout. **~ de l'âge**, to grow old. **~ des forces**, to take strength. **il prend le vol de 15h00**, he takes the 3:00 p.m. flight. **~ goût à**, to take a liking to.

~ peur, to get scared. ~ plaisir à, to take pleasure in, to delight in. ~ quelqu'un en amitié, to conceive a friendship for a person. ~ connaissance de, to get acquainted with. ~ le dessus, to get the upper hand, the best of. ~ fait et cause de quelqu'un, to undertake a person's defense. ce professeur prend vingt francs par leçon, that professor charges twenty francs a lesson. ~ congé de quelqu'un, to take leave of a person. ~ des leçons, to take lessons. ~ des airs, to assume airs. le ~ mal, to take it badly. ~ son parti, to resign oneself. ~ à gauche, to turn to the left. ~ à travers champs. to go through the fields. ~ le large, to bear, to stand off. ~ la mer, to go out to sea. ~ patience, to take patience. ~ garde, to beware. ~ l'habitude, to get into the habit of; to become accustomed. le feu a pris à la maison, the fire broke out in the house. l'envie lui prit de sortir, he felt like going out. se ~, v.refl. to be taken, to be seized; to take, to catch. se ~ par la main, to take each other by the hand. Ils se sont pris aux cheveux, they came to blows. sa robe s'était prise aux ronces, her dress had got caught in the brambles. le renard s'est pris au piège, the fox was caught in the trap. se ~ d'amitié pour quelqu'un, to conceive friendship for a person. s'en ~ à tout le monde, to lay the blame on everybody. s'y ~ mal, to go the wrong way about (doing something).

preneur, euse n.m.f. taker; catcher; buyer; lessee.

prénom n.m. first name.

prénommer v.t. to name, to call, to give a name to.

prénuptial, e adj. premarital.

préoccupation n.f. preoccupation, concern, anxiety.

préoccuper v.t. to preoccupy; to disturb. se ~, v.refl. to be preoccupied.

préparateur, trice n.m.f. assistant.

préparatifs n.m. pl. preparation.

préparation n.f. preparation.

préparatoire adj. preparatory; preparative; preparing; previous; preliminary. n.m. preparative.

préparer v.t. to prepare; to get ready. -un dîner, to prepare a dinner se ~, v.refl. to prepare oneself, to get ready se ~ à partir, to get ready to go. un orage se prepare, a storm is coming.

prépondérance n.f. preponderance.

prépondérant, e adj. preponderant; casting (vote).

préposé, ée n.m.f. officer.

préposer v.t. to appoint.

préposition n.f. preposition.

préretraite n.f. early retirement.

prérogative n.f. perogative.

près adv and prep near, close. il demeure tout ~, he lives close by. il demeure ~ de l'église, he lives near the church. s'asseoir ~ de quelqu'un, to sit by a person. il est ~ de deux heures, it is nearly two o'clock. vous avez gagné ~ de dix mille francs, you have won about ten thousand francs. à cela ~, with exception, nearly. j'ai été payé à cent francs ~, they paid me all except a hundred francs. à peu de chose ~, nearly, within a trifle. à peu. ~, nearly, pretty much. c'est la même chose à peu ~, that is nearly the same thing. de ~ et de loin, far and wide. de trop ~, to closely. ne pas y regarder de si ~, not to be too particular.

présage n.m. presage, omen.

présager v.t. to presage, to augur, to forebode, to foretell.

presbyte adj. far-sighted, long-sighted, presbyopic.

presbytère n.m. presbytery.

prescience n.f. prescience, foreknowledge, foresight.

préscolaire adj. preschool.

prescriptible adj. prescriptable.

prescription n.f. prescription.

prescrire v.t. to prescribe, to direct, to order, to command, to recommend. se ~, v.refl. to be prescribed, ordered.

préséance n.f. precedence.

présence n.f. presence, ~ d'esprit, presence of mind.

présent, e adj. present. avoir l'esprit ~, to be alert. le temps ~, the present time. n.m. present time, present; gift. à ~, at present, now. pour le ~, for the time being. dès, á ~, from now, henceforth.

présentable adj. presentable.

présentateur, trice n.m.f. (show) host, announcer, presenter.

présentation n.f. presentation.

présentement adv. at present, now.

présenter v.t. to present, to introduce; to offer; to give; to exhibit, to show; bring forward; to explain. j'aimerais vous ~ ma fille, I would like to introduce my daughter to you, I would like you to meet my daughter. cela présente des inconvénients, that presents difficulties. ~ à quelqu'un ses respects, to pay one's respects to a person. se ~, v.refl. to present oneself; to come forward; to call (on). il ne sait pas se ~, he does not know how to behave. se ~ bien, to look good. se ~ pour une place, to apply for a position. se ~ chez quelqu'un, to call on someone, at their home. cette affaire se présente bien, this affair has promise.

préservateur, trice adj. preserving, preservatory, preservative.

préservatif, ive adj. preservative, n.m. condom.

préservation n.f. preservation.

préserver v.t. to preserve; to save. se ~, v.refl. to preserve oneself; to keep off.

présidence n.f. presidency.

président, e n.m.f. president, chairperson.

présidentiel, elle *adj.* presidential.

présider *v.i.* to preside, to take the chair; (with à or sur) to preside over, to watch over, to direct.

présomption *n.f.* presumption, presumptuousness, confidence.

présomptueux, euse *adj.* presumptuous, too confident, conceited.

presque *adv.* almost, nearly, all but; scarcely. ~ **rien**, almost nothing.

presqu'île *n.f.* peninsula.

pressant, e *adj.* pressing, urgent; important.

presse *n.f.* press; printing press; throng. **mettre sous ~**, to put in press. **~-citron**, *n.m.* lemon squeezer. **~-papier**, *n.m.* paperweight. **~-purée**, *n.m.* potato masher. **~-livres**, bookends.

pressentiment *n.m.* presentiment, hunch; foreboding.

pressentir *v.t.* to have a presentiment of, to foresee; to sound out.

presser *v.t.* to press; to squeeze; to hug; to crowd, to throng; to urge on, to hurry. ~ **une éponge**, to squeeze a sponge. ~ **quelqu'un de questions**, to bombard a person with questions. ~ **le départ d'une personne**, to hasten a person's departure. ~ **une affaire**, to hurry an affair. **se ~**, *v.refl.* to press; to squeeze; to crowd, to make haste, to hurry. **se ~ de faire une chose**, to hurry to do a thing.

pressing *n.m.* dry cleaning.

pression *n.f.* pressure. **haute ~**, high pressure. **à basse ~**, low pressure. **bière à la ~**, draft beer.

pressurisation *n.f.* pressurization.

prestance *n.f.* presence, port, deportment, bearing.

prestation *n.f.* service, benefit; performance.

preste *adj.* quick, agile; sharp. *adv.* quickly, quick.

prestement *adv.* quickly, nimbly, readily.

prestidigitateur *n.m.* juggler, conjuror, prestidigitator.

prestidigitation *n.f.* juggling, sleight of hand, prestidigitation.

prestige *n.m.* prestige; influence.

prestigieux, euse *adj.* fascinating, prestigious, marvelous.

présumer *v.t.* to presume, to suppose, to conjecture, to anticipate. **se ~**, *v.refl.* to be presumed.

prêt, e *adj.* ready, in readiness; willing. **le dîner est ~**, the dinner is ready. *n.m.* loan.

prêt-à-porter *n.m.* ready-to-wear, ready made.

prétendant, e *n.m.f.* pretender, claimant, candidate; suitor.

prétendre *v.t.* to claim, to lay claim to; to maintain; to contend, to intend, to pretend to. **il prétend être**, he claims to be. **veux-tu prétendre que c'est vrai?** do you mean to tell me that this is true?

prétendu, e *adj.* pretended, feigned, false; supposed; so called. *n.m.f.* intended, future husband or wife.

prête-nom *n.m.* agent; man of straw, figurehead.

prétentieux, euse *adj.* conceited; pretentious.

prétention *n.f.* pretension, claim. **sans ~s**, unpretending, unassuming.

prêter *v.t.* to lend; to grant; to attribute, to ascribe. ~ **main-forte**, to lend assistance. ~ **l'oreille**, to listen carefully. **se ~**, *v.refl.* to be lent; (of persons) to indulge (in); to yield, to give way (to). **elle n'a pas voulu se ~ au jeu**, she refused to be part of the game.

prêteur, euse *adj.* lending, lender. *n.m.f.* lender. ~ **sur gages**, pawnbroker.

prétexte *n.m.* pretext, pretence.

prétexter *v.t.* to allege; to pretend, to feign; to sham.

prêtre *n.m.* priest.

prêtre-ouvrier *n.m.* worker priest.

prêtresse *n.f.* priestess.

prêtrise *n.f.* priesthood.

preuve *n.f.* proof evidence, mark, token, testimony. **en venir à la ~**, to come to the proof. **faire ~ de courage**, to prove one's courage. **faire ~ de**, to show proof of; to prove. **donner une ~ de son amitié**, to prove one's friendship.

prévaloir *v.i.* to prevail; to get the better. **l'erreur prévalait partout**, *v.refl.* (with **de**) to avail oneself (of); to be proud (of).

prévaricateur, trice *n.m.f.* prevaricator. *adj.* prevaricating.

prévarication *n.f.* prevarication; betrayal of trust.

prévenance *n.f.* consideration, kindness.

prévenant, e *adj.* considerate; kind; obliging.

prévenir *v.t.* to warn, to inform; to precede; to arrive before; to anticipate, to forestall; to get a head start on; to prevent, to hinder. ~ **quelqu'un d'un danger**, to warn a person of a danger. **il m'a fait ~ de son retour**, he informed me of his return. **se ~**, *v.refl.* to anticipate each other's wishes.

préventif, ive *adj.* preventive; (of imprisonment) before trial.

prévention *n.f.* prevention; prepossession; bias, prejudice; accusation. **juger sans ~**, to judge without prejudice.

prévenu, e *n.m.f.* accused person, prisoner.

prévisible *adj.* foreseeable.

prévision *n.f.* prevision; forecast; anticipation.

prévoir *v.t.* to foresee, to anticipate.

prévoyance *n.f.* forecast, foresight; prevision.

prévoyant, e *adj.* provident, prudent, cautious, careful.

prier *v.t.* to pray (to), to beseech; to entreat; to beg, to request; to desire. ~ **quelqu'un d'une chose**, to request something of a person. ~ **quelqu'un à dîner**, to desire a person to come to dinner.

prière *n.f.* prayer; entreaty; supplication, request. **être en ~**, to be praying. **faire la ~**, to say one's prayers.

primaire *adj.* primary; elementary.

primate *n.m.* primate.

primauté *n.f.* primacy, supremacy, priority.

prime *adj.* first. **de ~abord**, at first sight, at first. *n.f.* prime; premium; prize, reward. **~ d'assurance**, insurance premium. **réponse des ~s**, option. **à ~**, at a premium.

primitif, ive *adj. and n.m.* primitive; primary, first, original, primeval.

primitivement *adv* primitively.

primo *adv.* first, in the first place.

primordial, e *adj.* primordial; first.

prince *n.m.* prince.

princesse *n.f.* princess.

princier, ière *adj.* princely, of a prince.

principal *adj.* principal; chief, head; main, essential; fundamental. *n.m.* principal, principal thing, essential part, main point. **rembourser le ~**, to pay off the principal.

principalement *adv.* principally, chiefly.

principauté *n.f.* princedom; principality.

principe *n.m.* principle, source; beginning, rule, precept. **dans le ~**, in the beginning. **établir un ~**, to establish a principle. **partir d'un ~**, to proceed from a principle. **de bons ~s**, good principles. **avoir comme ~**, to have as a policy.

printanier, ière *adj.* spring, early.

printemps *n.m.* spring, springtime; prime, blown **au ~**, in the spring, in springtime. **au ~ de la vie**, in the bloom of youth.

priori (à) *adv.* a priori.

prioritaire *adj.* priority holder. *n.m.f.* person who has right of way (car).

priorité *n.f.* priority.

pris, e *p.p.* taken; caught; taken in; shaped.

prise *n.f.* taking, capture, seizure; hold, influence, pinch (of snuff); dose (of medicine); source, tap (of water). **~ de possession**, taking possession of. **lâcher ~**, to loose one's hold. **être aux ~s**, to come to words. **~ de courant**, plug. **en ~**, in gear.

priser *v.t.* to appraise, to value, to estimate; to put a price on; to esteem, to value, to snuff. **se ~**, *v.refl.* to prize oneself; to be prized, to be valued. *v.i.* to take snuff.

priseur, euse *n.m.f.* appraiser; snuff-taker. *adj.* appraising. **commissaire ~**, auctioneer and appraiser.

prison *n.f.* prison, jail.

prisonnier, ière *n.m.f.* prisoner.

privation *n.f.* privation; deprivation; hardship; want.

privatisation *n.f.* privatization.

privatiser *v.t.* privatize.

privé, e *adj.* private, personal. **la vie ~e**, private life.

priver *v.t.* to deprive. **~ quelqu'un de ses biens**, to deprive a person of his property. **se ~**, *v.refl.* to deprive oneself.

privilège *n.m.* privilege.

privilégié, e *n.m.* privileged person; favored.

privilégier *v.t.* to privilege, to grant a privilege to.

prix *n.m.* price; value, cost; cost price; charge; worth; prize; reward. **le ~ du blé est augmenté**, the price of corn has risen. **~ élevé**, high price **bas ~**, low price. **~ fixe**, set price. **~ coûtant**, cost price. **à tout ~**, at any price; at any cost. **sans ~**, invaluable, inestimable, priceless. **le ~ du temps**, the value of time. **gagner, remporter le ~**, to obtain the prize. **décerner le ~**, to award the prize. **au ~ de**, at the expense of, in comparison with.

probabilité *n.f.* probability.

probable *adj.* probable, likely, credible.

probablement *adv.* probably, likely.

probation *n.f.* probation.

probe *adj.* upright, honest, of integrity.

probité *n.f.* probity, uprightness, honesty, integrity.

problématique *adj.* problematic.

problème *n.m.* problem; question; puzzle. **résoudre un ~**, to solve a problem.

procède *n.m.* proceeding, behavior, conduct; procedure; process, operation. **se servir d'un ~ nouveau**, to make use of a new process.

procéder *v.i.* to proceed, to go on, to go forward; to behave; to act. **~ avec mesure**, to act cautiously. **~ criminellement contre quelqu'un**, to prosecute a person.

procédure *n.f.* procedure; practice; proceedings.

procès *n.m.* lawsuit, process, suit, action; trial. **~ criminel**, criminal suit. **~ civil**, civil suit. **gagner son ~**, to win a case. **être en ~**, to be involved in a lawsuit. **faire un ~ à quelqu'un**, to bring an action against a person. **sans autre forme de ~**, without further ceremony.

procession *n.f.* procession.

procès-verbal *n.m.* minutes (of proceedings); official report; proceedings.

prochain, e *adj.* next, nearest (in place); approaching, coming. **le mois ~**, next month. *n.m.* neighbor, fellow-being.

prochainement *adv.* shortly, soon, in a short time, *film* coming soon.

proche *adj.* near, nearby, closeby. **la ville la plus ~**, the nearest town. **il sont très ~s parents**, they are very close relatives. *prep.* near. **~ de**, near, **ils étaient ~ de la ville**, they were near the town. *adv.* near; close by; at hand. **tout ~**, close by.

proches *n.m.pl.* relations, relatives.

proclamation *n.f.* proclamation; publication.

proclamer *v.t.* to proclaim, to publish, to promulgate; to trumpet forth.

procréation *n.f.* procreation, generation.

procuration *n.f.* procuration; power; proxy.

procurer *v.t.* to procure; to get, to obtain; to furnish; to forward. **se ~**, *v.refl.* to be procured; to get; to procure oneself. **se ~ de l'argent**, to obtain money.

procureur *n.m.* proxy; attorney, public prosecu-

tor, district attorney. **agir par ~,** to act by proxy.
~général, attorney general.

prodige *n.m.* prodigy, wonder, marvel.

prodigieux, euse *adj.* prodigious, wonderful, wondrous; amazing.

prodigue *adj.* prodigal, lavish, profuse, wasteful, unsparing. *n.m.f.* prodigal, spendthrift.

prodiguer *v.t.* to lavish, to be lavish with, prodigal of, unsparing of, to squander, to waste. **~ des compliments,** to pour out compliments. **se ~,** *v.refl.* to lavish one's services.

producteur, trice *adj.* productive, breeding. *n.m.* producer.

productif, ive *adj.* productive.

production *n.f.* production; the act of producing, bringing forth, product, produce.

productivité *n.f.* productivity.

produire *v.t.* to produce; to bring forward; to show, to set forth. **~ des témoins,** to produce witnesses. **ce pays produit de l'or,** this country produces gold. *v.i.* to reproduce; to deliver particulars. **se ~,** *v.refl.* to go forth, to come forward; to make oneself known.

produit *n.m.* proceeds; product, produce; production. **il vit du ~ de ses terres,** he lives on the produce of his land. **~ net,** net proceeds. **~s chimiques,** chemicals.

proéminence *n.f.* prominence, prominency; protuberance.

proéminent, e *adj.* prominent, protuberant, jutting out.

prof *n.m.f.* teacher.

profanateur, trice *n.m.f.* profaner. *adj.* profaning.

profanation *n.f.* profanation.

profane *adj.* profane. *n.m.f.* uninitiated person, lay person.

profaner *v.t.* to profane, to desecrate; to debase, to defile. **~ un temple,** to desecrate a temple.

proférer *v.t.* to utter, to give utterance to.

professer *v.t.* to profess; to acknowledge. **~ une doctrine,** to profess a doctrine.

professeur *n.m.* professor, teacher.

profession *n.f.* profession, declaration; occupation, trade. **les ~s libérales,** liberal professions. **un tailleur de ~,** a tailor by trade.

professionnel, elle *adj.* professional.

profil *n.m.* profile; side view.

profit *n.m.* profit; gain, advantage, benefit, utility, avail. **~s et pertes,** profit and loss. **mettre à ~,** to profit, by, to avail oneself of, to turn to account. **il a tiré ~ de cette situation,** he benefited from the situation.

profitable *adj.* profitable, advantageous.

profiter *v.i.* to profit; to gain, to derive profit, to benefit, to avail oneself (of); to take advantage (of). **~ des avis qu'on vous donne,** to profit from the advice that is given you. **~ des circonstances,** to make the best of circumstances. **cela ne lui a pas profité,** it was of no use to him.

profond, e *adj.* deep; profound; thorough, consummate. **un puits ~,** a deep well. **une ~ ignorance,** profound ignorance. **un ~ soupir,** a deep sigh. *n.m.* depth, abyss.

profondément *adv.* deeply, profoundly.

profondeur *n.f.* depth; profundity, length; profoundness.

profus, e *adj.* profuse, lavish.

profusément *adv.* profusely; lavishly, prodigally.

profusion *n.f.* profusion, profuseness, prodigality, extravagant expenditures; great abundance.

progéniture *n.f.* progeny, offspring.

prognostique *adj.* prognostic.

programmateur, trice *n.m.f.* programmer.

programmation *n.f.* programming.

programme *n.m.* programme. **~ de spectacle,** playbill.

programmer *v.t.* to program, to plan, to schedule. **programmeur, euse** *n.m.f.* programmer.

progrès *n.m.* progress; advancement; proficiency; improvement. **faire des ~ dans ses études,** to make progress in one's studies.

progresser *v.i.* to progress, to make progress, to improve.

progressif, ive *adj.* progressive.

progression *n.f.* progression, advancement; course.

prohiber *v.t.* to prohibit, to forbid.

prohibitif, ive *adj.* prohibitive, prohibitory.

prohibition *n.f.* prohibition.

proie *n.f.* prey. **oiseau de ~,** bird of prey. **elle était en ~ au déséspoir,** despair preyed upon her.

projecteur *n.m.* projector; spotlight; searchlight; floodlight.

projectif, ive *adj.* projective.

projectile *n.m.* projectile, missile.

projection *n.f.* projection; casting, throwing.

projet *n.m.* project, scheme, plan, design. **faire de ~s,** to make plans. **projet de loi,** bill.

projeter *v.t.* to project; to scheme, to contrive, to plan; to contemplate. **un corps qui projette son ombre,** a body that projects its shadow. **~ un long voyage,** to play a long journey. **se ~,** *v.refl.* to project.

prolétaire *n.m.* proletarian, laborer.

prolétariat *n.m.* proletariat, working class.

prologue *n.m.* prologue.

prolongation *n.f.* prolongation.

prolongement *n.m.* prolongation.

prolonger *v.t.* to prolong; to lengthen in time, to protract; to draw out; to put off, to delay. **~ un mur,** to lengthen a wall. **se ~,** *v.refl.* to be prolonged; to be protracted; to continue.

promenade *n.f.* walking, walk, promenade, ride, drive, excurson. **faire une ~,** to take a walk, ride, drive, etc.

promener *v.t.* to take out (for a walk, ride, or drive); to lead, to take about; to walk; to take out. **~ sa vue, ses regards,** to let one's eyes wander. **se ~,** *v.refl.* to walk, to promenade, to take a walk; to take a ride, a drive, etc. **se ~ de long en large dans sa chambre,** to walk back and forth. **se ~ à cheval,** to ride.

promeneur, euse *n.m.f.* walker.

promenoir *n.m.* covered walk.

promesse *n.f.* promise; word. **faire une ~,** to make a promise, to give one's word.

prometteur, euse *adj.* promising.

promettre *v.t.* to promise; to forebode. **~ et tenir sont deux,** it is one thing to promise and another to perform. **se ~,** *v.refl.* to promise oneself; to promise each other; to be promised.

promiscuité *n.f.* promiscuousness.

promontoire *n.m.* promontory, headland, high cape.

promoteur *n.m.* promoter, developer. *adj.* promoting.

promotion *n.f.* promotion; raise, advancement.

promouvoir *v.t.* to promote; to advance; to prefer.

prompt, e *adj.* prompt; quick; hasty; speedy. **~e répose,** quick reply.

promptement *adv.* promptly, rapidly, quickly.

promptitude *n.f.* promptness; quickness, rapidity; readiness; hastiness.

promulgation *n.f.* promulgation.

promulguer *v.t.* to enact, to publish, to promulgate.

prôner *v.t.* to preach to; to lecture; to praise, to extol, to preach up.

pronom *n.m.* pronoun.

pronominal, e *adj.* pronominal.

prononcer *v.t.* to pronounce; to utter; to declare; to speak. **~ un jugement,** to pronounce a judgment. **~ un discours,** to deliver a speech. **l'Église a prononcé,** the Church has decided. **se ~,** *v.refl.* to be pronounced; to pronounce oneself; to declare one's intention, to speak out.

prononciation *n.f.* pronunciation; utterance.

pronostic *n.m.* forecast, prediction, prognostication, presage, token; prognosis.

pronostiquer *v.t.* to prognosticate, to foretell.

pronostiqueur *n.m.* forecaster, foreteller.

propagande *n.f.* propaganda.

propagateur, trice *adj.* propagating. *n.m.f.* propagator.

propagation *n.f.* propagation, extension; increase; diffusion, spreading. **la ~ des lumières,** the diffusion of light.

propager *v.t.* to propagate; to spread abroad, to diffuse, to disseminate. **se ~,** *v.refl.* to propagate; to be propagated; to spread.

propension *n.f.* propensity, propension; bent of mind; inclination.

prophète *n.m.* prophet, foreteller, seer. **nul n'est ~ dans son pays,** no one is a prophet in his own country.

prophétesse *n.f.* prophetess.

prophétie *n.f.* prophecy.

prophétique *adj.* prophetic.

prophétiser *v.t.* to prophesy; to predict, to foretell.

propice *adj.* propitious, favorable. **une occasion ~,** a favorable opportunity.

proportion *n.f.* proportion; symmetry; ratio. **compas de ~,** sector. **à ~ de, en ~ de,** in proportion to.

proportionnel, elle *adj.* proportional; proportionate.

proportionner *v.t.* to proportion, to adjust relatively; to accommodate, to regulate. **se ~,** *v.refl.,* to be in proportion; to be proportioned; to adapt oneself.

propos *n.m.* purpose, resolution; object, view; subject, matter; discourse, talk, chat. **dans le moment qu'il tenait ces ~,** while he was holding this conversation. **~ de table,** table talk. **à ~,** timely, seasonably, opportunely. **vous être venu à ~,** you came at the proper time. **mal à ~,** unseasonably. **il ne jugea pas à ~ de venir,** he did not think it was appropriate to come. **à ~ de,** with respect to, with regard to. **à ~ de la lettre que vous m'avez écrite,** about the letter you wrote me. **à ~ de rien,** for nothing at all. **à ~, pouvez-vous me dire pourquoi,** by the way, can you tell me why. **à tout ~,** at every turn. **de ~ délibéré,** deliberately, purposely, on purpose. **hors de ~,** unseasonably; without a cause.

proposable *adj.* that may be proposed; suitable.

proposer *v.t.* to propose; to move (a resolution); to offer; to bid (a price). **~ quelqu'un pour un emploi,** to designate a person for an office. *v.i.* **l'homme propose et Dieu dispose,** man proposes and God disposes. **se ~,** *v.refl.* to be proposed; to propose oneself, to offer oneself; to intend, to design.

proposition *n.f.* proposition; proposal; motion. **faire une ~,** to make a proposal.

propre *adj.* own, one's own; same; very; proper; appropriate; fit; apt, able, qualified; clean, neat, tidy; nice, becoming. **son ~ fils,** his own son. **le mouvement ~specific d'un astre,** the motion of a star. **le sens ~ d'un mot,** the proper meaning of a word. **il n'y a pas d'homme qui ne soit ~ à quelque chose,** every man is able to do something. **un enfant ~,** a clean child. **cet escalier n'est pas ~,** those stairs are not clean. *n.m.* characteristic; nature, property; real property. **le ~ de l'oiseau, c'est de voler,** it is inherent that birds fly. **avoir en ~,** possess, to own.

proprement *adv.* properly; correctly, rightly; strictly. **~ dit,** properly, so called. **à parler ~,** properly speaking. **s'habiller ~,** to dress nicely, neatly.

propreté *n.f.* cleanliness, cleanness; neatness, niceness, tidiness.

propriétaire *n.m.f.* proprietor, proprietress; owner; (of houses) landlord, landlady.

propriété *n.f.* property; virtue; nature; peculiarity; propriety, fitness. **~ industrielle**, patent rights. **~ littéraire**, copyright. **une grande ~**, a large estate.

propulser *v.t.* propel.

propulseur *adj.* propelling; propulsive, propulsory. *n.m.* propeller.

propulsion *n.f.* propulsion.

prorogation *n.f.* prorogation; prolongation.

proroger *v.t.* to prorogue; to adjourn; to prolong.

proscrire *v.t.* to prescribe; to outlaw, to banish, to exile; to exclude; to forbid. **~ un usage**, to forbid a practice.

proscrit, e *p.p.* proscribed; banished. *n.m.* person proscribed, proscript, outlaw, exile.

prose *n.f.* prose.

prospectus *n.m.* prospectus leaflet; bill, handbill.

prospère *adj.* prosperous; thriving, flourishing, successful.

prospérer *v.i.* to prosper, to succeed, to be prosperous; to thrive, to flourish.

prospérité *n.f.* prosperity.

prostate *n.f.* prostate.

prosternation *n.f.* prostration.

prosternement *n.m.* prosternation, prostration.

prosterner *v.t.* to prostrate; to lay flat, to overthrow. **se ~**, *v.refl.* to prostrate oneself.

prostitué *n.f.* prostitute.

prostituer *v.t.* to prostitute. **se ~**, *v.refl.* to prostitute oneself.

prostitution *n.f.* prostitution.

prostration *n.f.* prostration.

protagoniste *n.m.* protagonist.

protecteur, trice *n.m.f.* protector, protectress; patron, patroness; supporter. *adj.* protecting, sheltering. **un air ~**, a patronizing air.

protection *n.f.* protection, shelter, help.

protéger *v.t.* to protect; to defend; to support; to favor, to patronize; to foster; to shelter. **se ~**, *v.refl.* to be protected; to protect oneself.

protéine *n.f.* protein.

protestant, e *n.m.f.* protestant.

protestantisme *n.m.* protestantism.

protestation *n.f.* protestation; protest.

protester *v.t.* to protest; to affirm; to assure. **~ de son innocence**, to protest one's innocence. **~ une lettre de change**, to protest a bill of exchange.

prothèse *n.f.* prosthesis.

protocole *n.m.* protocol; etiquette.

prototype *n.m.* prototype.

protubérance *n.m.* protuberance.

protubérant, e *adj.* protuberant, prominent.

prouesse *n.f.* prowess, exploit.

prouvable *adj.* provable.

prouver *v.t.* to prove; to make good, to make out, to substantiate; to give a proof of; to be a proof of.

provenance *n.f.* origin, place of export; source. **de toutes ~s**, from any place.

provenir *v.i.* to come from; to originate; to proceed, to arise, to spring.

proverbe *n.m.* proverb. **passer en ~**, to become proverbial.

proverbial, e *adj.* proverbial.

providence *n.f.* providence.

providentiel, elle *adj.* providential.

province *n.f.* province; country. **vivre en ~**, to live in the country.

provincial, e *adj.* provincial; country, countrified. *n.m.f.* provincial; country person; *pl.* country people. *n.m.* provincial (a religious order's superior).

proviseur *n.m.* headmaster, principal.

provision *n.f.* provision; stock, supply; *pl.* victuals, food. **des ~s de bouche**, provisions. **faire des ~s**, to go food shopping; *Fin.* cover, fund, deposit, fee. **verser une ~**, to pay a retaining fee, a commission.

provisionnel, elle *adj.* provisional.

provisoire *adj.* provisional, provisory, temporary. **gouvernement ~**, provisional government.

provisoirement *adv.* provisionally.

provocant, e *adj.* provocative, provoking.

provocateur, trice *adj.* provocative, instigating; irritating. *n.m.f.* provoker; instigator, abettor.

provocation *n.f.* provocation; instigation; challenge; stimulus, incitement.

provoquer *v.t.* to provoke; to incite, to stimulate; to challenge, to irritate, to incense.

proxénète *n.m.* pimp, procurer.

proximité *n.f.* proximity, vicinity, nearness.

prude *adj.* prudish; demure. *n.m.* prude.

prudemment *adv.* prudently.

prudence *n.f.* prudence; discretion.

prudent, e *adj.* prudent, careful; discreet; circumspect.

prud'homme *n.m.* good and wise man; skilled hand. **conseil de ~s**, trade council.

prune *n.f.* plum. **pour des ~s**, for nothing.

prunelle *n.f.* sloe; apple (of the eye); pupil.

prunier *n.m.* plum tree.

psalmodie *n.f.* psalmody; droning; plainsong.

psalmodier *v.i.* to psalmodize; to sing psalms; to sing plainsong. *v.t.* to drone out.

psaulme *n.m.* psalm.

pseudo *n.m.* pseudo.

pseudonyme *adj.* pseudonymous. *n.m.* pseudonym, assumed name.

psychanalyse *n.f.* psychoanalysis.

psychiatre *n.m.f.* psychiatrist.

psychiaty *n.f.* psychiatric.

psychique *adj.* psychic, psychical, psychological.

psychologie *n.f.* psychology.

psychologique *adj.* psychologic, psychological.

psychologue *n.m.* psychologist.

psychopathe *n.m.f.* psychopath.

psychose *n.f.* psychosis.

psychothérapie *n.f.* psychotherapy.

psychotique *adj. n.m.f.* psychotic.

puant, e *adj.* stinking, offensive, foul, disgusting.

puanteur *n.f.* stink, offensive smell, stench.

pub *n.f. Infml. abbrev. of* **publicité** ad, advertising.

puberté *n.f.* puberty.

pubis *n.m.* pubis.

public, ique *adj.* public, notorious. *n.m.* public. **en ~,** in public.

publication *n.f.* publication; proclamation; promulgation.

publiciste *n.m.* publicist.

publicité *n.f.* publicity, notoriety; ad, advertising, advertisement.

public relations *n.f.* public relations.

publier *v.t.* publish. **~ un livre,** to publish a book.

publiquement *adv.* publicly; openly.

puce *n.f.* flea. **mettre la ~ à l'oreille de quelqu'un,** to alert someone about something. **marché aux ~s,** flea market. **mettre à quelqu'un la ~ à l'oreille,** to make a person uneasy. *adj.* puce, puce-colored.

puceau *adj. n.m.* virgin.

pucelage *n.m.* virginity.

pucelle *n.f.* virgin.

pudeur *n.f.* modesty, decency. **avoir de la ~,** to have modesty. **être sans ~,** to be shameless, **attentat à la ~,** indecent exposure.

pudibond, e *adj.* prudish, modest.

pudique *adj.* chaste, modest.

puer *v.i.* to stink.

puéril, e *adj.* juvenile, puerile, childish.

puérilité *n.f.* puerility, childishness.

puis *adv.* then, next, afterward.

puiser *v.t.* to draw, to fetch; to let in. **~ de l'eau à une fontaine,** to draw water from a spring.

puisque *conj.* since, as, seeing that. **pourquoi le demander, ~ vous le savez?** since you know it, why do you ask?

puissamment *adv.* powerfully, mightily; forceably; extremely.

puissance *n.f.* power, might, sway, dominion; influence; authority; strength, muscular force. **toute ~,** omnipotence. **les grandes ~s de l'Europe,** the great powers of Europe. **la ~ de la parole,** the power of the spoken word.

puissant, e *adj.* powerful; mighty, potent; cogent, forcible, strong. **tout-~,** all-powerful, omnipotent.

puits *n.m.* well; pit, shaft (of a mine) **la vérité est au fond d'un ~,** truth lies at the bottom of a well.

pull *n.m.* sweater, pullover.

pull-over *n.m.* sweater, pullover.

pulluler *v.i.* to multiply, to go on increasing; to grow fast; to swarm.

pulmonaire *adj.* pulmonary.

pulpe *n.f.* pulp.

pulpeux, euse *adj.* pulpous, pulpy, fleshy, sexy.

pulsation *n.f.* pulsation, beat, pulse, throbbing.

pulsion *n.f.* pulsion, urge, drive, impetus.

pulvérisateur *n.m.* vaporizer, atomizer; pulverizer spray.

pulvérisation *n.f.* pulverization.

pulvériser *v.t.* to pulverize, to crush, to knock.

puma *n.m.* puma, cougar, mountain lion.

punaise *n.f.* bug; thumbtack.

punch *n.m.* punch. **~ au rhum,** rum punch.

punching-ball *n.m.* punching ball, punching bag.

punir *v.t.* punish. **se faire ~,** to get punished. **se ~,** *v.refl.* to punish oneself.

punissable *adj.* punishable, liable to punishment.

punitif, ive *adj.* punitive.

punition *n.f.* punishment.

pupille *n.m.f.* ward, pupil. *n.f.* pupil (of eye).

pupitre *n.m.* desk, music stand.

pur, e *adj.* pure, genuine, unadulterated; uncorrupted, unblemished, stainless; neat (of spirits, wine etc.). **de l'eau ~e,** pure water. **un ciel ~,** a clear sky. **mathématiques ~es,** pure mathematics. **c'est un ~ caprice,** it is a mere whim. **un verre de rhum ~,** a glass of neat rum. **c'est la ~e verité,** it is the simple truth. **en ~e perte,** to no purpose. **~-sang,** thoroughbred (horse).

purée *n.f.* mashed potato(es).

purement *adv.* purely; innocently; merely, solely, simply.

pureté *n.f.* purity, pureness; genuineness; clearness; innocence, chastity. **la ~ de l'eau,** the purity of the water. **la ~ du coeur,** the purity of the heart.

purgatif, ive *adj.* purgative, purging, cathartic. *n.m.* purgative, cathartic.

purgation *n.f.* purgation; purge, purgative, cathartic.

purgatoire *n.m.* purgatory.

purge *n.f.* cleansing, purge, purgative, cathartic.

purger *v.t.* to purge, to cleanse, to purify, to purge away, to clear. **se ~,** *v.refl.* to purge oneself, to purify oneself.

purifiant, e *adj.* purifying.

purificateur *n.m.* purifier.

purification *n.f.* purification.

purifier *v.t.* to purify; to cleanse, to refine. **~ l'eau,** to purify water. **se ~,** *v.refl.* to purify oneself; to become pure.

puritain, e *n.m.f.* puritan. *adj.* puritan, rigid.

putain *n.f. Vulg.* whore, hustler, hooker, tramp. **oh ~!** *exclam. Vulg.* oh darn!

putatif, ive *adj.* putative, reputed, supposed.

pute *n.f.* whore; *Vulg.* hustler, hooker.

putois *n.m. Zool.* polecat.

putréfaction *n.f.* putrefaction.

putride *adj.* putrid, putrified.

puy *n.m.* mount.

puzzle *n.m.* puzzle, jigsaw puzzle.

pygargue *n.m.* pygarg, pygargus.

pygmée *n.m.* pygmy; dwarf.

pyjama *n.m.* pyjamas, pajamas.

pyramide *n.f.* pyramid. **en ~,** pyramidically.

pyromane *n.m.f.* pyromaniac, arsonist.

pyrotechie *n.f.* pyrotechnics.

pyrotechnique *adj.* pyrotechnic(al).

Q

quadrangle *n.m.* quadrangle.

quadrangulaire *adj.* quadrangular; four-cornered, four-angled.

quadrant *n.m.* quadrant.

quadrillage *n.m.* partitioning, grid.

quadriller *v.t.* to checker, to cover, to criss-cross.

quadrimoteur *adj.* four-engined. *n.m.* four-engined plane.

quadripartite *adj.* quadripartite, four-party conference.

quadriphonie *n.f.* quadrophonics, four-channel sound.

quadriréacteur *n.m.* four-engined jet plane.

quadrisyllabe *n.m.* quadrisyllabe.

quadrupède *adj.* quadruped, four-footed. *n.m.* quadruped.

quadruple *adj.* and *n.m.* quadruple, fourfold.

quadrupler *v.t.* to quadruple, to increase four-fold.

quai *n.m.* quay, wharf, pier. **à ~,** (of a vessel) alongside of a wharf.

qualificatif, ive *adj.* qualifying; qualificative.

qualitatif, ive *adj.* qualitative.

qualification *n.m.* title, epithet; designation, qualification.

qualifier *v.t.* to qualify; to entitle, to give the title of; to style, to call. **se ~,** *v.refl.* to call, to style oneself.

qualitatif, ive *adj.* qualitative.

qualité *n.f.* quality; fitness, capability.

~ requise, qualification. **un homme de ~,** a man of quality. of high rank. **en ~ de,** in the character of, in the capacity of.

quand *adj.* when; whenever. *conj.* though, although, even. **~ même,** even though, even if, although. **je pense qu'il viendra ~ même,** I believe he'll come anyway.

quant *adv.* (always followed by à) as for, as to. **~ à present,** as to the present.

quantifiable *adj.* quantifiable.

quantification *n.f.* quantification.

quantifier *v.t.* to quantify.

quanitatif, ive *adj.* quantitative.

quantité *n.f.* quantity, amount; deal; number, multitude. **en ~,** in great numbers, many in number.

quantum *n.m.* quantum.

quarantaine *n.f.* forty; Lent; age of forty; quarantine. **mettre en ~,** to put into quarantine; *Infml.* to give the silent treatment.

quarante *adj.* and *n.m.* forty.

quarantenaire *adj.* forty-year, fortieth anniversary.

quarantième *adj.* fortieth.

quart *adj.* fourth. *n.m.* quarter; fourth; point (of the compass); *naut.* watch. **un ~ d'heure,** a quarter of an hour. **~ de cercle,** quadrant. **être de ~,** to keep the watch. **le ~ monde,** the Fourth World.

quartier *n.m.* quarter; fourth part; district, ward, neighborhood; lodgings; barracks; mercy. **le premier ~ de la lune,** the first quarter of the moon. **tout le ~ était en émoi,** the whole quarter was in an uproar. **~ général,** headquarters. **~ d'hiver,** winter quarters. **point de ~,** no mercy. **c'est un ~ tranquille,** it's a quiet neighborhood.

quartz *n.m.* quartz.

quasi *adv.* almost; scarcely; hardly.

quasiment *adv.* almost, nearly, just about.

quatorze *adj.* fourteen; fourteenth. *n.m.* fourteen; fourteenth day.

quatorzième *adj.* fourteenth.

quatrain *n.m.* quatrain.

quatre *adj.* four; fourth. **être tiré à ~ épingles,** to be dressed-up. **marcher à ~ pattes,** to walk on all fours. **un de ces ~ matins,** one of these days. *n.m.* four; fourth. **cela est clair comme deux et deux font ~,** that is as clear as can be. **sa lettre est datée du ~,** his letter is dated the fourth. **~-épices** *n.f.pl.* allspice.

quatre-temps *n.m.pl.* ember days.

quatre-vingtième *adj.* eightieth.

quatre-vingts *adj.* eighty. **quatre-vingt un,** eighty-one. **quatre-vingt-dixième,** ninetieth.

quatrième *adj.* fourth. *Fig.* **en ~ vitesse,** at the speed of light, very fast. *n.m.* fourth day, fourth; fourth part; fourth floor; fourth story; fourth person, fourth.

quatrièmement *adv.* fourthly.

quatuor *n.m.* quartet.

que *rel. pron.* whom, that; which, what. **le fils qu'il aimait,** the son whom he loved. **voici le livre ~ j'ai acheté,** this is the book that I bought. **je ne sais ~ dire,** I do not know what to say. **je n'ai ~ faire,** I have nothing to do. **~ sais-je?** what do I know? **qu'est-ce c'est ~ cela?** what is that? *adv.* how much, how many; how. **~ de fois je suis venu ici!** how many times have I been here! **qu'il fait beau!** what beautiful weather! *conj.* that; whether; as, when; unless; till, until; yet, but; lest; in order. **je crois qu'il est honnête,** I believe that he is an honest man. **vois dites qu'il viendra,** you say that he will come. **qu'il écrive ou non,** c'est la même chose, whether he writes or not, it is the same thing. **approchez, ~ je vous parle,** come nearer, so I may speak to you. **~ Dieu vous bénisse,** God bless you. **attendez qu'il ne pleuve plus,** wait till the rain is over. **ce vin-là est pire ~ le premier,** this wine is worse than the first. **autant d'hommes ~ de femmes,** as many men as women. **tout riches qu'ils sont,** as rich as they are. **nous n'avons ~ peu de temps à vivre,** we have but a short time to live. **je n'ai ~ quinze ans,** I am but fifteen years of age. **je ne sors ~ deux fois par semaine,** I go out only twice a week. **il ne fait ~ boire et manger,** he does nothing but eat and drink. **c'est ~ je ne savais pas,** it is because I did not know.

quel, quelle *adj.* what. **quelle heure est-il?** what time is it? **~ qu'il soit,** whoever he may be. **~s que soient ses talents,** whatever his talents may be.

quelconque *adj.* whatever, whatsoever, any. **une raison ~,** any reason whatever.

quelque *adj.* some; any; a few; whatever. **~s écrivains ont traité ce sujet,** some authors have treated this subject. **~ chose,** something; anything. **~ part,** somewhere. **~s amis,** a few friends. **~ peu,** a little. *adv.* about, nearly; some. **il y a ~ soixante ans,** some sixty years ago. **~s ennemis que vous ayez,** whatever enemies you may have.

quelque chose *pron. indéf.* something, anything. **elle lui a dit ~,** she told him/her something, she said something to her/him. **dis-lui n'importe quoi mais dis-lui ~,** tell him/her anything but him/her something. **vous prendrez bien ~?** what will you have?

quelquefois *adv.* sometimes; now and then, on occasion, once in a while.

quelque part *adv.* somewhere, anywhere. **il doit bien être ~!** he must be somewhere.

quelqu'un, une *n.m.f.* somebody, someone; some; anybody. **~ m'a dit cela,** somebody told it to me. **~s vous diront que ...,** some will tell you that ...

quémander *v.i.* to beg.

quémandeur, euse *n.m.f.* beggar.

qu'en-dira-t-on *n.m.* gossip.

querelle *n.f.* quarrel; dispute, altercation; wrangling; strife, brawling, quarreling. **chercher ~ à quelqu'un,** to pick a fight with a person.

quereller *v.i.* to quarrel with, to quarrel; to wrangle. **se ~,** *v.refl.* to quarrel, to have a quarrel.

question *n.f.* question; query; controversy; rack; matter. **poser une ~,** to ask a question. **mettre à la ~,** to torture; to put on the rack. **~ de vie ou de mort,** matter of life or death.

questionnaire *n.m.* questionnaire.

questionner *v.t.* to question, to interrogate.

quête *n.f.* quest, search, collection (for the poor, etc.) **se mettre en ~ de,** to search, to seek for. **faire la ~ à l'église,** to make the collection at church.

quêter *v.t.* to search, to beg (alms); to collect (money); to gather; to seek for.

queue *n.f.* tail; queue, line. *Bot.* stem; stalk (of fruit); handle. cue (of billiards). **tirer le diable par la ~,** to live from hand to mouth. **cela n'a**

ni ~ ni tête, that has neither head nor tail. **~ de cerise,** cherry stalk. **à la ~ leu leu,** one after another in a row. **faire la ~,** to wait on line. **piano à ~,** grand piano. **~ de cheval,** ponytail.

qui *rel. pron.* who; whoever, whom; that, which; what. **l'homme ~ parle,** the man who is speaking. **le chien ~ aboie,** to dog that barks. **la femme à ~ vois venez de parler,** the woman to whom you have just spoken. **qui demandez-vous?** whom do you want? **~ que ce soit,** whoever (it may be). **~ que vous sayez,** whoever you are. **sur le ~-vive,** on the alert.

quiche *n.f.* quiche.

quiconque *indef. pron.* whoever, whichever, anyone. **~ y touche et ...,** anyone touches this and ...

quiétude *n.f.* quietude, quietness, tranquility.

quignon *n.m.* chunk, hunk (of bread).

quincaillerie *n.f.* hardware store; hardware.

quincaillier *n.m.* hardware dealer.

quinine *n.f.* quinine.

quinquagénaire *n.m.f.* and *adj.* quinquagenarian, fifty years old.

quinte *n.f. Mus.* fifth. fit (of coughing).

quintessence *n.f.* quintessence; essential part; pith.

quintuple *adj.* quintuple, fivefold.

quintupler *v.t.* to quintuple.

quinzaine *n.f.* fifteen, about fifteen, two weeks.

quinze *adj.* fifteen; fifteenth. **~ jours,** fortnight. **tout les ~ jours,** every two weeks.

quinzième *adj.* fifteenth.

quiproquo *n.m.* mistake, blunder; mistaken identity.

quittance *n.f.* receipt, bill; discharge.

quitte *adj.* discharged, out of debt; quit; free, clear. **être ~ envers quelqu'un,** to be quits with a person. **il le fera ~ à être punit,** he will do it even if he knows he'll be punished for it.

quitter *v.t.* to leave, to quit; to leave off; to give up; to lay aside; to part from. **~ ses livres, ses études,** to leave one's books, one's studies. **~ la partie,** to give up the game. **~ son pays,** to leave one's country. **~ ses mauvaises habitudes,** to leave off one's bad habits. **~ le deuil,** to go out of mourning. **se ~,** *v.refl.* to part from each other, to part.

quitus *n.m.* discharge, release; receipt in full.

qui-vive *n.m. Milit.* challenge; who goes there? **le ~ de la sentinelle,** the challenge of the sentry. **être sur le ~,** to be on the alert.

quoi *pron.* what, which, that. **à ~ pensez-vous?** what are you thinking about? **ce à ~ nous pensions,** what we are thinking of. **dites-moi en ~ je peux vous servir,** tell me what I can do for you. **avoir de ~,** to have the wherewithal, to have the means. **il n'y a pas de ~,** *n.m.* don't mention it. **je ne sais ~,** I do not know what. **sur ~,** whereupon. **~ qu'il arrive,** whatever happens.

interj. what! how! ~ **donc!** what! what then!
quoique *conj.* though, although. **quoiqu'il fût notre ami,** though he was our friend.
quorum *n.m.* quorum.
quota *n.m.* quota.

quote-part *n.f.* quota, share, portion.
quotidien, ienne *adj.* daily.
quotidiennement *adv.* daily, every day.
quotient *n.m.* quotient.
quotité *n.f.* quota, part, share.

R

rebâchage *n.m.* endless repetition.
rabâcher *v.i.* to say the same thing over and over again, *v.t.* to say over and over.
rabâcheur, euse *n.m.f.* endless repeater of the same thing.
rabais *n.m* diminution (of price); abatement, reduction, discount.
rabaisser *v.t.* to lower, to take down; to reduce, to diminish, to abate; to put down; to humble; to depreciate; to disparage. **il l'a rabaissé devant tout le monde,** he put him down in front of everybody. ~ **le mérite de quelqu'un,** to disparage a person's merit.
rabat *n.m.* band; flap.
rabat-joie *n.m.* killjoy.
rabattre *v.t.* to lower, to put down; to beat down; to diminish; to soften; to humble; to beat up (game, fugitives). ~ **son prix,** to lower one's price. **se ~,** *v.refl.* to be beat down; to turn down.
rabbin *n.m.* rabbi.
rabbinat *n.m.* rabinate.
rabbinique *adj.* rabbinic, rabbinical.
rabbiniste *n.m.* rabbinist.
rabiole, rabioule *n.f.* turnip, kohlrabi.
raboter *v.t.* to plane; to polish.
raboteur *n.m.* planer.
raboteux, euse *adj.* (of wood) knotty; rough, uneven; rugged. **chemin ~,** uneven road.
rabougri, e *adj.* shriveled, stunted.
rabougrir *v.t.* to shrivel up, to stunt, to be stunted. **se ~,** *v.refl.* to become stunted.
rabrouer *v.t.* to brush off, to snub, to check, to rebuke, to snap at.
racaille *n.f.* rabble; trash, rubbish.
raccommodage *n.m.* mending, repairing; darning.
raccommoder *v.t.* to mend, to repair; to patch; to put to rights, to reconcile. ~ **du linge,** to mend linen. ~ **deux amis,** to reconcile two friends. **se ~,** *v.refl.* to mend one's clothes; to be reconciled, to make up.
raccompagner *v.t.* to take back (home); to accompany, to see to.
raccord *n.m.* joining, union; addition; accord.
raccordement *n.m.* joining, union; leveling.
raccorder *v.t.* to join, to unite; to harmonize.
raccourci, e *n.m.* short cut. **prendre un ~,** to take a short cut.
raccourcir *v.t.* to shorten; to curtail, to abridge. ~ **un manteau,** to shorten a coat. **se ~,** *v.refl.* to get shorter, to shorten; to contract oneself, to draw up; to shrink.

raccordissement *n.m.* shortening; contracting, contraction.
raccoutumer (se) *v.refl.* to reaccustom oneself.
raccroc *n.m.* (at play) lucky hit.
raccrocher *v.t.* to hook on again; to hang up. **raccrochez ce tableau,** hang up that painting again. **ne raccrochez pas,** don't hang up. **se ~,** *v.refl.* to cling (to), to hold on to.
race *n.f.* race; (of animals) breed. **la ~ humaine,** the human race. **c'est un chien de ~,** this dog has a pedigree, this dog is a purebred.
racé, e *adj.* purebred, pedigree, thoroughbred.
rachat *n.m.* redemption; repurchase; buying back.
racheter *v.t.* to redeem, to buy back, to buy again, to repurchase; to buy up, to ransom. ~ **un cheval,** to buy a horse back. ~ **un ôtage,** to ransom a hostage. **se ~,** *v.refl.* to redeem oneself; to free oneself, to make up for.
rachitique *adj.* rickety, rachitic.
racial, e *adj.* racial.
racine *n.f.* root. **prendre ~,** take root. ~ **carrée,** square root.
racisme *n.m.* racism.
raciste *adj., n.m.f.* racist.
racket *n.m. Infml.* racket, racketeering, extorsion.
racketteur *n.m.* racketeer, extorsionist, extortioner.
raclée *n.f.* hiding, drubbing, thrashing.
raclement *n.m.* scraping. ~ **de gorge,** clearing of the throat.
racier *v.t.* to scrape, to scrape off; to grate; to scrape on.
racolage *n.m.* soliciting, enlisting, touting, recruiting.
racoler *v.t.* to enlist; to solicit; to tout; to recruit; to pick up.
racoleuse *n.f.* streetwalker.
racontar *n.m.* gossip.
raconter *v.t.* to relate, to tell, to narrate, to recite. ~ **un fait,** to relate, to tell a fact. ~ **une histoire,** to relate a story.
raconteur, euse *n.m.f.* relator, narrator, teller.
racornir *v.t.* to harden; to shrivel up. **se ~,** *v.refl.* to harden, to grow hard, to get hard; to shrivel up.
radar *n.m.* radar.
radeau *n.m.* raft; float.
radial, e *adj.* radial.
radiant, e *adj.* radiant.
radiateur *n.m.* heater; radiator.

radiation *n.f.* radiation; canceling; striking out.

radical, e *adj.* radical.

radicalement *adv.* radically; fundamentally.

radier *v.i.* to radiate, to shine; to beam, to obliterate; to strike off.

radieux, euse *adj.* radiant; beaming with joy, beaming.

radin, e *adj. Infml.* stingy.

radinerie *n.f. Infml.* stinginess.

radio *n.f.* radio; x-ray.

radioactif, ive *adj.* radioactive.

radioactivité *n.f.* radioactivity.

radiodiffuser *v.t.* to broadcast.

radiodiffusion *n.f.* broadcasting.

radiogramme *n.m.* wireless message.

radiographie *n.f.* x-ray.

radis *n.m.* radish. ~ **noir,** horseradish. *Infml.* il n'a jamais un ~ sur lui, he is always broke.

radium *n.m.* radium.

radius *n.m.* radius.

radotage *n.m.* dotage, second childhood, senility, nonsense.

radoter *v.i.* to be in his/her dotage, to drivel; to rave, to talk nonsense, to wander.

radoteur, euse *n.m.* to repeat oneself all the time, dotard.

radoucir *v.t.* to soften, to make soft or mild, to allay, to calm down, to soothe, to pacify a person. se ~, *v.refl.* to soften, to become, to grow milder. le temps commence à se ~, the weather is growing milder.

radoucissement *n.m.* getting milder; softening, calming down; mitigation, assuagement, abatement.

rafale *n.f.* squall; gust, blast, burst, storm. ~ **de vent,** storm. une ~ **de mitraillette,** a hail of bullets.

raffermir *v.t.* to harden, to make firm, to strengthen. ~ **le courage des soldats,** to give the soldiers more courage. se ~, *v.refl.* to harden, to grow harder, to gain strength; to improve.

raffermissement *n.m.* hardening; strengthening; consolidation, improvement.

raffinage *n.m.* refining.

raffiné, e *adj.* refined; subtle.

raffinement *n.m.* refinement, refining.

raffiner *v.t.* and *v.i.* to refine, to purify; to polish. se ~, *v.refl.* to refine, to become more refined, more subtle.

raffinerie *n.f.* refinery.

raffoler *v.i.* to be crazy about, to be nuts about, to be wild about.

rafistoler *v.t.* to patch up.

rafraîchir *v.t.* to refresh; to cool; to freshen; to refresh, to become cool. la plaie rafraîchît l'air, rain cools the air. ~ la mémoire à quelqu'un, to refresh someone's memory, to remind a person of something. se ~, *v.refl.* to cool. to become cool; to refresh oneself; to be refreshed. le temps se reafraîchit, the weather is getting cool.

rafraîchissant, e *adj.* cooling, refreshing.

rafraîchissement *n.m.* cooling drink; refreshment.

ragaillardir *v.t.* to cheer up, to make happy.

rage *n.f.* rage; rabies; frenzy, fury, madness; passion, mania.

rager *v.i.* to fume, to be fuming, to be furious, to be enraged; to fret, to be in a rage.

ragot *adj.* gossip, twaddle, silly talk.

ragoût *n.m.* stew. faire un ~, to make a stew.

ragoûtant, e *adj.* relishing, savory; inviting, tempting; pleasing, agreeable.

ragrafer *v.t.* to clasp, to hook again.

raid *n.m.* raid.

raide *adj.* stiff; rigid; inflexible, unyielding, steep, precipitous; hardy; tight; swift. avoir le bras ~ de froid, to have one's arm numbed with cold. ~ comme une barre de fer, as stiff as a poker. c'est un homme raide, he is a rigid man. des contours ~s et secs, stiff outlines. une corde ~, a tight rope. *adv.* vigorously; quickly; swiftly, rapidly.

raideur *n.f.* stiffness; rigidity; inflexibility; stubborness; harshness.

raidir *v.t.* to stiffen; to tighten. se ~, *v.refl.* to stiffen; to get stiff.

raidissement *n.m.* straightening; stiffening.

raie *n.f.* line, stroke (made with a pen, a pencil, etc.); part (of the hair); furrow; *Ichth.* skate, ray-fish, streak; a mark.

raifort *n.m.* horseradish.

rail *n.m.* rail. ~s, tracks.

railler *v.t.* to banter, to joke, to laugh at, to jeer at. se ~, *v.refl.* to mock; to make fun (of), to laugh (at).

raillerie *n.f.* raillery, banter, jest, jesting. tourner quelque chose en ~, to turn a thing to ridicule.

raisin *n.m.* grapes. ~ sec, raisin.

raison *n.f.* reason; sense; judgment; reasoning; right; proof, argument; cause, motive, ground. parler avec ~, to talk sensibly. avoir ~, to be right. donner ~, à quelqu'un, to side with a person. entendre ~, to listen to reason. il a ses ~s pour agir ainsi, he has his reasons for doing so. à plus forte ~, with still more reason. demander ~, to demand satisfaction. se faire ~ à soi-même, to do oneself justice. avoir ~ de, to have the upper hand of. à ~ de, *prep.* at the rate of. en ~ de, by reason of, in consideration of.

raisonnable *adj.* reasonable; rational; judicious; right; moderate. une personne ~, a reasonable person. cette demande est ~, that is a reasonable request.

raisonnablement *adv.* reasonably; rationally; justly, rightly; tolerably, moderately.

raisonnement *n.m.* reasoning; argument.

raisonner *v.t.* to reason; to argue; to debate.

rajeunir *v.t.* to make young again; to rejuvenate; to revive; to prune, to trim (a tree).

se ~, *v.refl.* to make oneself look younger.

rajeunissement *n.m.* rejuvenation, growing young again.

rajouter *v.t.* to add again; to add more.

rajustement *n.m.* readjustment.

rajuster *v.t.* to readjust, to arrange, to put in order. se ~, *v.refl.* to straighten oneself up.

râle *n.m.* rail; rattling; death, rattle.

râlement *n.m.* rattling.

ralentir *v.t.* to slow down, to slacken. se ~, *v.refl.* to slow oneself down; to become less intense; to lessen.

ralentissement *n.m.* slowing down, slowing up.

râler *v.i.* to growl, to moan, to grumble, to have the death rattle.

râleur, euse *n.m.f.* moaner. **quel ~,** what a pain.

ralliement *n.m.* rallying, rally.

rallier *v.t.* to rally.

rallonge *n.f.* extension; extension leaf.

rallongement *n.m.* lengthing, extension.

rallonger *v.t.* to lengthen; to let out, to extend. se ~, *v.refl.* to lengthen; to become longer.

rallumer *v.t.* to light again; to rekindle, to revive. se ~, *v.refl.* to be lighted again; to burst out again; to rekindle, to revive.

rallye *n.m.* rally.

Ramadan *n.m.* Ramadan.

ramassage *n.m.* gathering; picking up.

ramasse-miettes *n.m.* crumb tray.

ramasser *v.t.* to pick up, to take up; to gather, to collect. ~ **les cartes,** to pick up the cards. se ~, *v.refl.* to assemble, to muster; to collect, to get together. **il s'est ramassé une fessée,** *Infml.* he got a spanking. *n.m.* picking up; taking up.

ramassis *n.m.* heap, collection; bunch; pile.

rame *n.f.* stick (for growing peas etc.); oar (of a boat); ream of paper. **aller à la ~,** to row. ~ **de métro,** subway, underground.

rameau *n.m.* bough, small branch, offshoot, offset. **dimanche des ~x,** Palm Sunday.

ramener *v.t.* to bring back, to take back. **cette mesure a ramené l'ordre,** this measure restored order. **elle l'a ramené chez lui,** she brought him back home. *Infml.* **et ne la ramène pas!** and not another word! se ~, *v.refl.* to be brought back.

ramequin *n.m.* ramekin.

ramer *v.i.* to row, to work hard, to prop (peas etc.).

rameur, euse *n.m.f.* rower, oarsman, oarswoman.

rameuter *v.t.* to round up, to gather.

ramification *n.f.* ramification.

ramifier (se) *v.refl.* to branch out, to branch.

ramollir *v.t.* to soften; to make soft; to enervate. se ~, *v.refl.* to soften, to relent; to become soft, to feel compassion; to be enervated.

ramollissement *n.m.* softening.

rampe *n.f.* ramp, slope, incline; gradient, banisters; footlights; floats.

rampement *n.m.* creeping, crawling.

ramper *v.i.* to creep, to crawl; to grovel.

rancart *n.m.* *Infml.* tip, meeting, date. **mettre au ~,** to put by, to lay aside.

rance *adj.* rancid, rank. **sentir le ~,** to smell rancid, rank.

ranch *n.m.* ranch.

rancir *v.i.* to grow, to become rancid or rank.

rancoeur *n.f.* resentment.

rançon *n.f.* ransom. **mettre à ~,** to set a ransom on.

rançonnement *n.m.* ransoming; extortion, fleecing.

rançonner *v.t.* to ransom.

rançonneur, euse *n.m.f.* extortioner.

rancune *n.f.* grudge, rancour, spite, malice.

rancunier, ière *adj.* vindictive, rancorous, spiteful, malicious.

randonnée *n.f.* drive, outing, hike; circuit, round.

rang *n.m.* range, row, rank; tier (of boxes). **dernier ~,** last row. **se ~ s serrés,** to leave, to quit, the ranks; to rise from the ranks. **être au premier ~,** to be in the first rank.

rangé *n.f.* range, row, line.

rangement *n.m.* arranging, putting in order.

ranger *v.t.* to clean, to put in order, to rank, to classify; to class. ~ **des livres,** to put books in order. se ~, *v.refl.* to place oneself; to draw up; to stand back; to go over. se ~ **autour d'une table,** to draw round a table. se ~ **à l'avis de quelqu'un,** to adopt a person's opinion.

ranimer *v.t.* to revive, to reanimate, to restore to life, to rekindle, to recover. **cette nouvelle a ranimé son espoir,** this news made him hopeful again. se ~, *v.refl.* to revive; to recover life, to be restored to health, to be reanimated; to cheer up, to be enlivened.

rapace *adj.* rapacious, ravenous; voracious; *n.m.pl.* rapacious birds, birds of prey.

rapacité *n.f.* rapacity, rapaciousness, ravenousness.

rapatriement *n.m.* repatriation.

rapatrier *v.t.* to repatriate, to bring back to one's country.

râpe *n.f.* rasp, grater.

râper *v.t.* rasp, to grate.

rapetisser *v.t.* to lessen, to make little; to shorten. ~ **un habit,** to shorten a coat. se ~, *v.refl.* to lessen, to shorten, to get shorter; to make oneself small.

rapide *adj.* rapid; swift, speedy, fleet; fast, quick, *n.m.* rapid, torrent.

rapidement *adv.* rapidly, swiftly.

rapidité *n.f.* rapidity, swiftness, speed.

rapiècer *v.t.* to piece, to patch, to patch up, to repair.

raplatir *v.t.* to flatten.

rappel *n.m.* recall, calling back; reminder; booster. ~ **à l'ordre,** to call to order.

rappeler *v.t.* to call again; to call back; to recall; to remind. ~ **un ambassadeur,** to recall an ambassador. ~ **quelqu'un à la vie,** to restore a person to life. **~ à l'ordre,** to call to order. **se ~ quelque chose,** to recollect, to remember, to recall a thing to mind. **vous rappelez-vous?** do you remember? **je ne me la rappelle pas,** I do not remember it. *v.i. Milit.* to call up.

rappliquer *v.i. Infml.* to come back.

rapport *n.m.* bearing; yield; produce; report, account, statement; affinity, connection; harmony, agreement; intercourse. **le ~ de mes terres,** the produce of my land. **le ~ du docteur,** doctor's report. **faire un ~,** to make a report. **ça n'a aucun ~ avec ce que je te dis,** that has nothing to do with what I am telling you. **avoir des ~ avec quelqu'un,** to have intercourse with a person. **mettre une personne en ~ avec une autre,** to introduce a person to another. **par ~ à,** in, with respect to. **sous le ~ de,** with regard to. **sous tous les ~s,** in every respect.

rapporter *v.t.* to bring back; to take back; to add; to report, to produce; to bring in; to tell tales, to relate; to tell; to yield; to produce; to fetch (of a dog). **l'argent ne lui rapporte que 3%,** the money brings him in only 3 percent. **~ tout ce qui s'est passé,** to relate all that happened. **il rapporte tout,** he tells, repeats everything. **se ~,** *v.refl.* to agree; to correspond, to be in accordance; to relate, to refer; to be connected (with). **ce passage se rapporte à,** this passage refers to. **s'en ~ à,** to refer the matter to; to leave it to. **je m'en rapporte à votre témoignage,** I rely on your testimony.

rapporteur, euse *n.m.f.* telltale; gossiper; reporter *n.m.* reporter.

rapprochement *n.m.* bringing nearer, drawing close; joining; reconciliation.

rapprocher *v.t.* to draw near again; to bring nearer, to draw closer; to draw up; to reconcile; to bring together. **se ~,** *v.refl.* to draw near again; to draw nearer; to approach each other; to be reconciled. **les nuages se rapprochent l'un de l'autre,** the clouds are drawing nearer to each other. **se ~ de quelqu'un,** to go nearer to a person.

rapt *n.m.* abduction, rape, kidnapping.

raquette *n.f.* racket, snowshoe.

rare *adj.* rare, uncommon; scarce; odd; thin, scanty. **un livre ~,** a rare book. **l'argent est fort ~,** money is very scarce.

raréfaction *n.f.* scarcity, rarefaction.

rarement *adv.* rarely, seldom, infrequently.

rarissime *adj.* very rare, extremely rare.

ras, e *adj.* close-shaven, short-haired; short; bare. **à poil ~,** short-haired. **~e campagne,** open country, flat country. **faire table ~e,** to sweep away everything. *n.m.* short-nap cloth. **à ~ de,** up to. **au ~ de l'eau,** to the water's edge. **~-lebol,** to be fed up. **j'en ai ~-le-bol de vos disputes,** I've have it with your arguments.

raser *v.t.* to shave; to raze, to raze to the ground; to graze; to skim, to touch lightly. **se faire ~,** to

get shaved. **~ une maison,** to pull down a house. **une balle lui rasa le visage,** a shot passed close to his face. **se ~,** *v.refl.* to shave oneself, to shave; to get shaved.

raseur, euse *n.m.f.* bore.

rasoir *n.m.* razer, shaver.

rassasier *v.t.* to satiate, to safe, to satisfy. **~ sa curiosité,** to satisfy one's curiosity. **se ~,** *v.refl.* to be satiated; to be satisfied.

rassemblement *n.m.* rounding up, assembling, collecting, gathering, crowd.

rassembler *v.t.* to reassemble; to gather together again; to bring together again; to assemble, to put together. **~ ses forces,** to muster up one's strength. **~ ses idées,** to collect one's thoughts. **se ~,** *v.refl.* to reassemble, to meet again, to meet, to collect.

rasseoir *v.t.* to reseat, to seat again. **se ~,** *v.refl.* to sit down again; to settle down, to calm down.

rasséréner *v.t.* to make serene, to clear up; to calm, to quiet. **se ~,** *v.refl.* to become serene, to clear up.

rassurant, e *adj.* reassuring, tranquilizing.

rassurer *v.t.* to reassure, to tranquilize, to encourage; to strengthen, to make firm. **il n'était pas rassuré,** he wasn't at ease. **se ~,** *v.refl.* to be reassured, tranquilized, relieved; to tranquilize oneself; to clear up, to settle, to become settled. **rassurez-vous,** don't worry.

rat *n.m.* rat. **mort aux ~s,** rat poison. **prendre un ~,** to catch a rat. **~ de cave,** small taper. **~ d'église,** regular church goer, church mouse. **petit ~ de l'Opéra,** young ballet dancer of the Opéra de Paris. **~ d'hôtel,** hotel thief.

ratatiner (se) *v.refl.* to shrivel, to shrivel up.

ratatouille *n.f.* stew, ratatouille.

rate *n.f.* spleen.

rater *v.i.* to miss fire, to miss; to fail.

ratification *n.f.* ratification.

ratifier *v.t.* to ratify; to confirm; to approve and sanction; to make valid.

ration *n.f.* ration. **mettre à la ~,** to give allowance to.

rationnel, elle *adj.* rational; reasonable.

rationnellement *adv.* rationally.

rationner *v.t.* to ration, to put on short allowance.

raton *n.m.* raccoon; small rat.

rattacher *v.t.* to tie again, to fasten up again; to connect. **rattachez ce chien,** tie this dog up again. **se ~,** *v.refl.* to be tied, fastened, attached. **ces causes se rattachent les unes aux autres,** these causes are connected.

rattraper *v.t.* to catch again, to take again, to retake; to catch up, to overtake. **on ne m'y rattrapera plus,** I won't be caught again. **je vous rattraperai,** I will catch up with you. **~ le temps perdu,** to make up for lost time. **se ~,** *v.refl.* to seize hold of; to be caught again, to recover, to get back; to make up for.

rature *n.f.* scrapings; erasure, suppression.

raturer *n.f.* to scrape, to erase, to cross out, to scratch out, to efface, to suppress.

rauque *adj.* hoarse, harsh.

ravage *n.m.* ravage, destruction.

ravager *v.t.* to ravage; to lay waste, to devastate.

ravalement *n.m.* rough casting, restoration.

ravaler *v.t.* to swallow again, to put down, to lower; to debase, to cut back (tree), to dress (a wall). **~ se paroles**, to eat one's words. **se ~,** *v.refl.* to debase, to degrade oneself.

ravir *v.t.* to delight; to carry away; to deprive of, to despoil, to strip, to rob; to enrapture, to charm, to delight, to transport, to overjoy. **à ~,** to admiration, delightfully. **chanter à ~,** to sing wonderfully well. **une femme belle à ~,** a ravishing woman.

raviser (se) *v.refl.* to change one's mind.

ravissant, e *adj.* ravishing; delightful, enchanting, charming, bewitching, lovely. **une beauté ~e,** a bewitching beauty. **un spectacle ~,** a delightful show.

ravissement *n.m.* ravishment, ravishing; rape; ecstasy, trasport, rapture, delight.

ravisseur, euse *n.m.f.* abductor, kidnapper.

ravitaillement *v.t.* provision, supply.

ravitailler *v.t.* to provide with supplies. **se ~,** *v.refl.* to take fresh supplies, to get fresh provisions.

raviver *v.t.* to restore; to brighten up, to reanimate; to make burn (fire). **~ une douleur,** to revive grief. **~ un tableau,** to restore a painting. **se ~,** *v.refl.* to lighten up again; to revive.

revoir *v.t.* to have again, to get again.

rayer *v.t.* to scratch (engraving); to stripe, to streak; to groove, to scratch out, to erase; to strike out. **~ un mot,** to scratch, to cross out a word.

rayon *n.m.* ray; beam; radius; spoke (of a wheel); shelf. **un ~ de lumière,** a ray of light. **dans un ~ d'un mille,** in the radius of a mile.

rayonnant, e *adj.* radiant; radiating; beaming; shining, effulgent.

rayonner *v.i.* to radiate; to beam, to shine.

rayure *n.f.* stripe, streak.

raz *n.m.* race. **~ de marée,** tidal wave.

réacteur *n.m.* reactor; jet engine.

réactif, ive *adj.* reactive. *n.m.* reagent, test.

réaction *n.f.* reaction.

réactiver *v.t.* to reactivate.

réadaptation *n.f.* readjustment, rehab, rehabilitation.

réadapter *v.t.* to readapt.

réadmission *n.f.* readmission, readmittance.

réffirmer *v.t.* to reaffirm.

réagir *v.i.* to react.

réalisateur, trice *n.m.f.* director, producer (of films).

réalisation *n.f.* realization; fulfilment.

réaliser *v.t.* to realize; to fulfill, to achieve; to produce; to convert into money. **se ~,** *v.refl.* to be realized.

réalisme *n.m.* realism.

réaliste *n.m.* realist.

réalité *n.f.* reality. **en ~,** in reality, really, indeed, in fact.

réanimation *n.f.* resuscitation.

réanimer *v.t.* to resuscitate.

réapparition *n.f.* reappearance; return.

réapprovisionner *v.t.* to restock.

réarmement *n.m.* rearming.

réarmer *v.t.* rearm.

réassurer *v.t.* to reinsure, to reassure.

rebaisser *v.t.* to lower again.

rebelle *adj.* rebellious, rebel; stubborn; obstinate. *n.m.f.* rebel.

rebeller (se) *v.refl.* to rebel, to revolt.

rébellion *n.f.* rebellion, revolt.

rebiffer *v.t.* to turn up (one's nose). *v.i.* to resist. **se ~,** *v.refl.* to resist.

reboisement *n.m.* reforestation, replanting (woods).

reboiser *v.t.* to reforest, to replant (with forest trees).

rebondir *v.i.* to rebound, to bounce back; to spring back, to start back.

rebord *n.m.* edge, rim. **le ~ d'une table,** the edge of a table. **le ~ d'un fossé,** to edge of a ditch.

rebours *n.m.* wrong way (of the grain, of nap, etc.). **à ~,** against the grain; the wrong way; backward. **compte à ~,** countdown.

rebrousser *v.t.* to turn up, to turn back (the hair); to brush up; to retrace. **~ chemin,** to retrace one's steps.

rebutant, e *adj.* repulsive, disagreeable. **une besogne ~e,** tedious work.

récalcitrant, e *adj.* refractory, stubborn, obstinate; uncomplying; reluctant *n.m.* refractory.

récapitulation *n.f.* recapitulation.

récapituler *v.t.* to recapitulate; to sum up.

recaser *v.t. Infml.* to rehouse; to find oneself a new job/relationship.

recel *n.m.* receiving (of stolen goods).

receler *v.t.* to conceal, to hide; to receive stolen goods; to harbour. **la terre recele des trésors dans son sein,** the earth contains hidden treasures.

receleur, euse *n.m.f.* receiver (of stolen goods).

récemment *adv.* recently, lately, of late.

recensement *n.m.* census; numbering; statement; verification.

recenser *v.t.* to take the census; to verify (goods).

récent, e *adj.* recent, new, fresh, late.

récépissé *n.m.* receipt, written acknowledgment of receipt.

réceptacle *n.m.* receptacle.

réception *n.f.* reception; receipt; welcome; entertainment. **accuser ~ d'une lettre,** to acknowledge the receipt of a letter. **accusé de ~,** acknowledgment of receipt.

réceptioniste *n.m.f.* receptionist.

récession *n.f.* recession.

recevabilité *n.f.* receivableness, receivability.

recette *n.f.* receipt; reception; receivership; recipe. **la dépense excède la ~**, the expenditure exceeds the receipts. **il a fait une bonne ~**, he made good money.

receveur, euse *n.m.f.* receiver; recipient. **~ des contributions**, tax collector. **~ des postes**, postmaster (postmistress).

recevoir *v.t.* to receive; to accept; to admit; to entertain; to take. **~ un cadeau**, to receive a present. **~ l'aumône**, to receive alms. **~ un ordre**, to receive an order. **~ les excuses de quelqu'un**, to accept a person's excuses.

rechange *n.m.* change, replacement. **vêtements de ~**, change of clothes. **pièces de ~**, spare parts.

rechanger *v.t.* to change again, to rechange. **se ~**, *v.refl.* to change one's clothes.

réchapper *v.i.* to escape; to recover (from an illness).

recharge *n.f.* refill, reload, recharging.

rechargement *n.m.* refilling; recharging, reloading.

recharger *v.t.* to load again, to reload, to recharge. **se ~**, *v.refl.* to load again; to reload.

réchaud *n.m.* gas stove; plate warmer, hot plate.

réchauffage *n.m.* warming again; reheating.

réchauffement *n.m.* warming up.

réchauffer *v.t.* to heat again; to warm up (food); to make warm again; to rekindle, to revive; to give new spirit to. **se ~**, *v.refl.* to warm oneself up; to get warm again; to rekindle, to revive; to grow warm again.

rêche *adj.* rough, harsh. **cette étoffe est ~**, this stuff is rough.

recherche *n.f.* search; seeking; pursuit; inquiry, investigation; examination; suit, research. **la ~ de la vérité**, the search for truth. **il est vêtu avec une extrême ~**, he is dressed with studied elegance.

recherché, e *adj.* sought after; in great request, in demand; choice; of studied refinement; refined; affected. **une personne ~e dans sa toilette**, a person carefully and tastefully dressed.

rechercher *v.t.* to research, to seek again, to look again for; to seek after, to seek for. **il est recherché pour meurtre**, he is wanted for murder.

rechute *n.f.* relapse.

récidive *n.f.* reapparition (of a former illness); relapse; second offence. **en cas de ~**, in case of a second offence.

récidiver *v.i.* to reappear; to repeat an offence; to relapse.

récidiviste *n.m.* repeat offender.

récif *n.m.* reef.

récipient *n.m.* container, receptacle.

réciprocité *n.f.* reciprocity.

réciproque *adj.* reciprocal; mutual. *n.m.* like, the same thing. **rendre le ~ à**, to return the same.

réciproquement *adv.* reciprocally; conversely.

récit *n.m.* story, narrative, account. **faire le ~ de ce qui s'est passé**, to give an account of what happened.

récitation *n.f.* recitation, reciting.

réciter *v.t.* to recite, to perform a recitative.

réclamant, e *n.m.f.* claimant.

réclamation *n.f.* claim, demand; complaint.

réclame *n.f.* advertisement.

réclamer *v.i.* to object, to make an objection, to implore, to beseech, to entreat, to crave, to call upon; to claim, to lay claim to, to ask for. **~ de l'aide**, to ask for help. **se ~**, *v.refl.* (with de) to declare oneself connected with, known to; to make use of the name of, to be reclaimed.

reclus, e *adj.* cloistered. *n.m.f.* recluse.

réclusion *n.f.* reclusion, confinement, imprisonment.

recoiffer *v.t.* to fix (a person's) hair again. **se ~**, *v.refl.* to fix one's own hair again.

recoller *v.t.* to paste, to glue again.

récolte *n.f.* harvest, crop, gathering. **faire la ~**, to gather in the harvest.

récolter *v.t.* to harvest, to gather in, to reap.

recommandable *adj.* recommendable; commendable; (of person) respectable.

recommandation *n.f.* recommendation, registration (of letter); detainer.

recommandé, e *adj.* recorded, certified, registered. *n.m.* certified mail, registered mail.

recommander *v.t.* to recommend; to charge, to enjoin; to exhort, to advise. **se ~**, *v.refl.* to recommend, to command oneself. **se ~ à Dieu**, to commend oneself to God.

recommencement *n.m.* beginning again, recommencement.

recommencer *v.t.* to start again, recommence, to begin again.

récompense *n.f.* recompense, reward; award, compensation.

récompenser *v.t.* to recompense, to reward, to make amends, to compensate. **se ~**, *v.refl.* to be rewarded, to be recompensed, to make amends.

recomposer *v.t.* to recompose.

recomposition *n.f.* recomposition.

recompter *v.t.* to count, to count over, to reckon again.

réconciliation *n.f.* reconciliation.

réconcilier *v.t.* to reconcile. **se ~**, *v.refl.* to reconcile oneself with; to be reconciled; to make up (with).

reconduire *v.t.* to take back, to go back with; to escort; to accompany home.

réconfort *n.m.* comfort, consolation.

réconforter *v.t.* to strengthen; to comfort, to console; to cheer. **se ~**, *v.refl.* to be strengthened, revived; to be comforted, consoled.

reconnaissable *adj.* recognizable.

reconnaissance *n.f.* recognition; acknowledgment; verification; lookout; discovery; gratitude, thankfulness. **avoir de la ~ pour,** to be grateful for. **montrer sa ~,** to show one's gratitude. **~ d'une dette,** acknowledgment of a debt. **aller en ~,** to reconnoiter.

reconnaissant, e *adj.* thankful, grateful.

reconnaître *v.t.* to recognize; to acknowledge; to admit. *Naut.* to make out, to overhaul. **le ~ à sa demarche,** to know him by his walk. **~ un gouvernement,** to recognize a government. **sa signature,** to own one's signature. **~ les bienfaits qu'on a reçus,** to be thankful for benefits received. **se ~,** *v.refl.* to be recognized; to recognize oneself, each other; to know where one is.

reconnu, e *p.p.* recognized.

reconquérir *v.t.* to reconquer, to recover.

reconsidérer *v.t.* to reconsider.

reconstituer *v.t.* to reconstitute, to constitute again.

reconstitution *n.f.* reconstitution, reconstruction.

reconstruction *n.f.* reconstruction, rebuilding.

reconstruire *v.t.* to rebuild, to reconstruct.

recopier *v.t.* copy again.

record *n.m.* record.

recoucher *v.t.* to lay down again; to put (a person) to bed again. **se ~,** *v.refl.* to go back to bed.

recoudre *v.t.* to sew again.

recouper *v.t.* to cut again.

recourber *v.t.* to curve, to bend round. **se ~,** *v.refl.* to curve; to be curved, to be bent.

recourir *v.t.* to run again; to have recourse, to turn, to apply; to resort; to appeal. **~ aux armes,** to resort to arms.

recours *n.m.* recourse; resort; appeal. **~ en cassation,** appeal to the supreme court. **~ en grâce,** petition for mercy.

recouvrer *v.t.* to recover; to regain, to get back; to collect, to gather. **~ la santé,** to recover one's health. **~ les contributions,** to collect the taxes.

recouvrir *v.t.* to cover again; to cover up again; to cover over. **la neige recouvre l'herbe,** the snow covers the grass. **se ~,** *v.refl.* to be covered again; to get cloudy, overcast again. **le temps se recouvre,** it is getting cloudy again.

recracher *v.t.* to spit (out) again.

récréation *n.f.* recreation; diversion, amusement; (of children) play. **heure de ~,** recess time. **en ~,** at play.

recréer *v.t.* to recreate; to create anew; to enliven; to relieve; to divert; to amuse. **se ~,** *v.refl.* to divert; to amuse oneself.

recrier *v.i.* **se ~,** *v.refl.* to exclaim, to cry out, to protest.

récrimination *n.f.* recrimination.

récriminatoire *adj.* recriminatory.

récriminer *v.i.* to recriminate (against).

récrire *v.t.* to write again, to rewrite, to write back, to answer.

recroqueviller (se) *v.refl.* to shrivel up, to shrink.

recrudescence *n.f.* outburst, increase, recrudescence.

recrue *n.f.* recruit.

recrutement *n.m.* recruiting, recruitment.

recruter *v.t.* to recruit. **se ~,** *v.refl.* to be recruited.

rectangle *n.m.* rectangle. *adj.* rectangular, right angled.

rectangulaire *adj.* rectangular, right-angled.

rectification *n.f.* rectification, correction.

rectifier *v.t.* to rectify.

recto *n.m.* first page (of a leaf); right side; right-hand page (of a book).

reçu, e *adj.* accepted, admitted. *n.m* receipt. **au ~de,** on receipt of.

recueil *n.m* collection; selection. **un ~ de chansons,** a collection of songs.

recueillement *n.m.* composure, meditation, comtemplation.

recueillir *v.t.* to reap, to gather, to get; to collect, to receive, to take in (home). **~ les suffrages,** to collect the votes. **~ ses idées,** to collect one's ideas. **se ~,** *v.refl.* to be collected; to collect one's thoughts; to mediate, to reflect; to commune with oneself.

recuire *v.t.* to cook again; to reheat; (of glass and metals) to anneal.

recul *n.m.* recoil, recoiling; retreat.

reculer *v.t.* to move back, to draw back; to put back; to back up, to recede, to fall back; to recoil. **la voiture a reculé,** the car moved backward. **~ d'un pas,** to move back a step. **c'est un homme qui ne recule jamais,** he never flinches. **~ pour mieux sauter,** to go back to take a better leap. **se ~,** *v.refl.* to move back, to go back; to go farther back.

reculons á *adv.* backward, backwards.

récupérable *adj.* recoverable; retrievable.

récupération *n.f.* recovery; retrieval; reprocessing; recycling. **~ des matières plastiques,** recycling plastic material.

récupérer *v.t.* to recover, to retrieve. **se ~,** *v.refl.* to recover; to retrieve one's losses.

récurer *v.t.* to scour; to clean out.

récusation *n.f.* challenge (of judges, jurors, witnesses, etc.); exception.

récuser *v.t.* to challenge; to object to, to impugn. **se ~,** *v.refl.* (of a judge) to excuse oneself (judging, voting, etc.).

récyclage *n.m.* retraining, reorientation; recycling.

recycler *v.t.* to retrain; to reorient; to recycle.

rédacteur, trice *n.f.* editor (of a letter, a newspaper); clerk (in a public office).

rédaction *n.f.* drawing up (of a deed, etc.); wording (of any writing); editing (of periodicals); body of editors or writers (of a newspaper); editor's office.

reddition *n.f.* surrender (of a town); giving in (of accounts), rendering.

redécouverte *n.f.* rediscover.

redescendre *v.i.* to descend again; to go down again; to bring down again, to take down again.

redevable *adj.* indebted; beholden, obliged. **il vous est ~ de sa fortune,** he owes his fortune to you.

redevance *n.f.* rent; license, fee. **~ d'auteur,** author's royalties.

redevenir *v.t.* to become again.

redevoir *v.t.* to owe still.

rediffusion *n.f.* repeat, rerun.

rédiger *v.t.* to draw up, to write, to word; to edit (a newspaper).

redire *v.t.* to say again; to repeat; to find fault with. **il n'y a rien à ~ à sa conduite,** there is nothing to say about his conduct. **trouver à ~ à tout,** to find fault with everything.

redistribuer *v.t.* to redistribute; to deal back again.

redistribution *n.f.* redistribution; new distribution.

redondance *n.f.* redundance, redundancy.

redondant, e *adj.* redundant; superfluous.

redonner *v.t.* to give again; to give back again; to return, to indulge again; *Milit.* to charge again. **se ~,** *v.refl.* to indulge again (in); to return.

redoublement *n.m.* redoubling; reduplication; increase.

redoubler *v.t.* double; to increase; to line again, to repeat (a grade in school). **~ de soins,** to be more careful than ever. **se ~,** *v.refl.* to be increased; to be redoubled.

redoutable *adj.* fearsome, frightening; formidable, dreadful.

redouter *v.t.* to dread, to fear.

redressement *n.m.* straightening; redress, redressing; relief; reparation.

redresser *v.t.* to straighten, to make straight; to erect again; to put right, to set right, to amend; to relieve. **~ les torts,** to right the wrongs. **~ la têtes,** to hold up one's head. **se ~,** *v.refl.* to get straight again; to get upright, to stand erect; to be assuming.

réduction *n.f.* reduction, reducing; decrease; abatement.

réduire *v.t.* to reduce; to diminish; to shorten; to bring down; to abate; to subdue, to compel. **~ en poudre,** to reduce to powder. **~ en cendres,** to reduce to ashes. **~ quelqu'un au désespoir,** to drive a person to despair. **se ~,** *v.refl.* to be reduced; to reduce oneself; to be brought under.

réduit *n.m.* small habitation, retreat; hovel, hole.

réédification *n.f.* reedification, rebuilding.

réédifier *v.t.* to rebuild, to re-edify.

rééditer *v.t.* to edit a second time.

réel, elle *adj.* real, actual, true, genuine. *n.m.* reality, what is real.

réélection *n.f.* re-election.

réélire *v.t.* to re-elect.

réellement *adv.* really, in reality, truly, in fact.

réévaluation *n.f.* re-evaluation.

réévaluer *v.t.* to re-evaluate.

réexpédier *v.t.* to forward again, to send back.

refaire *v.t.* to make again; to do again; to do over again, to repair; to restore. **se ~,** *v.refl.* to be made again; to recover one's health; to be refreshed.

refait, e *p.p.* done again, duped.

réfectoire *n.m.* refectory.

référence *n.f.* reference; relation; information.

référendum *n.m.* referendum.

référer *v.t.* to refer; to attribute; to ascribe; to report, to make a report. **se ~,** *v.refl.* to refer; to leave to the decision of. **s'en ~ à quelqu'un,** to leave a matter to the decision of another person.

refermer *v.t.* to shut again. **se ~,** *v.refl.* to shut again, to close again.

refiler *v.t. Infml.* to pass, to give.

réfléchi, e *adj.* reflected, reflecting; deliberate. **peu ~,** unreflecting.

réfléchir *v.t.* to reflect; to throw back, to reverberate (sound); to echo; to think, to ponder. **réfléchissez-y bien,** reflect well upon it. **se ~,** *v.refl.* to reflect, to be reflected.

réfléchissant, e *adj.* reflecting, reflective.

réfléchissement *n.m.* reflection, reverberation (of sound).

réflecteur *adj. n.m.* reflecting. *n.m.* reflector.

reflet *n.m.* reflection, glint.

refléter *v.t.* to reflect. **se ~,** *v.refl.* to reflect, to be reflected.

refleurir *v.i.* to blossom again, to bloom again, to reflourish.

réflexe *adj.* reflex.

réflexion *n.f.* reflection; thought. **faite des ~s,** to make remarks. **toute ~ faire,** all things considered.

refluer *v.i.* to flow back, to ebb.

reflux *n.m.* reflux; (of the tide) ebb, ebbing.

réformation *n.f.* reform, reformation; amendment.

réforme *n.f.* reform, reformation, amendment; *Milit.* discharge.

réformé, e *p.p.* reformed; amended. *adj.* reformed. **église ~e,** reformed church. *n.m.* reformer, protestant.

réformer *v.t.* to reform; to form again. **se ~,** *v.refl.* to form again; to be formed again.

réformer *v.t.* to reform; to restore; to improve; to amend. **~ les lois,** to reform laws. **~ des troupes,** to discharge troops. **se ~,** *v.refl.* to reform, to amend.

réformiste *n.m.* reformer.

refoulement *n.m.* driving back, forcing back; holding back; flowing back (of water); ebbing (of the tide); compression, repression.

refouler *v.t.* to drive back, to force back, to go against (the tide), to flow back; (of the tide) to ebb; to compress, to repress.

refractaire *adj.* refractory; rebellious;

fireproof; stubborn. *n.m.* rebel, defaulter.

réfracter *v.t.* to refract. **se ~,** *v.refl.* to be refracted.

réfractif, ive *adj.* refractive.

réfraction *n.f.* refraction. **double ~,** double refraction.

refrain *n.m.* refrain (of a song); *Fig.* theme, constant theme; tune.

réfrigérateur *n.m.* refrigerator, fridge.

réfrigération *n.f.* refrigeration.

réfrigérer *v.t.* to refrigerate, to cool.

refroidir *v.t.* to cool; to chill; to lessen; to damp. **se ~,** *v.refl.* to cool, to grow cool.

refroidissement *n.m.* cooling; coolness; chilliness.

refuge *n.m.* refuge; shelter, retreat.

réfugié, e *n.m.f.* refugee.

réfugier (se) *v.refl.* to take refuge, to take shelter.

refus *n.m.* refusal, denial. **cela n'est pas de ~,** I won't say no willingly.

refuser *v.t.* to refuse; to decline; to deny. **~ une offre,** to refuse an offer. **~ la porte à quelqu'un,** not to let a person in. **se ~,** *v.refl.* to be refused, to be declined; (with **à**) to refuse, to deny; to deny oneself. **il se refuse à travailler,** he refuses to work. **se ~ à l'évidence,** to refuse to accept the obvious. **il ne se refuse rien,** he denies himself nothing.

réfutable *adj.* refutable.

réfuter *v.t.* to refute, to disprove.

regagner *v.t.* to regain; to win back, to recover. **~ le temps perdu,** to make up for lost time. **~ le port,** to reach the port. **~ du terrain,** to gain ground.

régal *n.m.* treat, entertainment, feast.

régaler *v.t.* to treat, to entertain; to amuse. **se ~,** *v.refl.* to feast, to treat oneself; to treat one another.

regard *n.m.* eyes; look, glance, gaze; notice, regard, attention. **elle lançait des ~s furieux,** she cast angry looks. **fixer ses ~s sur quelqu'un,** to look fixedly at a person. **au ~ de,** with regard to, respecting. **en ~,** opposite.

regardant e *adj.* stingy.

regarder *v.t.* to look at, to consider; to look upon, to mind, to heed. **~ quelqu'un en face,** to look a person in the face. **~ de haut en bas,** to look from top to bottom. **cette maison regarde le couchant,** this house faces the west. *v.i.* to mind, to pay attention, to attend (to); to look (to), to care. **cela ne vous regarde pas,** that doesn't concern you. **~ devant soi,** to look before one. **~ de près,** to be particular. **il n'y regarde pas de si près,** he is not so particular. **se ~,** *v.refl.* to look at oneself; to look at each other, to gaze at one another.

regarnir *v.t.* to furnish again, to garnish again.

régénérer *v.t.* to regenerate, to revive, to uplift.

régie *n.f.* administration, management, production management (of film), control room.

régime *n.m.* rule, command; regimen, diet; form

of government. **se mettre au ~,** to go on a diet.

région *n.f.* region; country; land.

régional, e *adj.* regional.

régir *v.t.* to rule, to govern; to manage, to administer.

régisseur *n.m.* manager, stage manager; director.

registre *n.m.* register; record; account book.

réglage *n.m.* adjustment.

règle *n.f.* rule; ruler (for paper, etc.); model, pattern; period. *pl.* **cela est de ~,** it is the rule. **~ être en ~,** to be in order, straight. **avoir ses ~s,** to have one's period.

réglé, e *adj.* regular; steady; settled; methodical. **une vie ~e,** a regular life. **à des heures ~es,** at fixed hours.

règlement *n.m.* settlement; regulation; rule.

réglementaire *adj.* relating to regulations; regular.

réglementation *n.f.* regulation.

réglementer *v.i.* to make regulations; to regulate.

régler *v.t.* to rule; to regulate, to order; to settle. **~ ses affaires,** to put one's affairs in order. **j'ai réglé cette note,** I have paid that bill. **se ~,** *v.refl.* to be regulated; to regulate oneself; to be settled; to be ruled, to go (by).

réglisse *n.f.* liquorice.

règne *n.m.* reign; power, influence, rule, sway; prevalence; kingdom. **le ~ de la justice,** the reign of justice. **le ~ animal,** the animal kingdom.

régner *v.i.* to reign; to rule. **le silence régnait dans l'assemblée,** the assembly was silent.

regonfler *v.t.* to reinflate, to pump up, to put air (in tires); to swell again, to fill again.

regorgement *n.m.* overflowing, overflow.

regorger *v.i.* to overflow; to abound; to be full. **~ de biens,** to abound with wealth. **se ~,** *v.refl.* to gorge, to cram oneself.

régresser *v.i.* to regress, to recede.

régressif, ive *adj.* regressive, returning, going back.

régression *n.f.* regression.

regret *n.m.* regret. **avoir du ~,** to feel sorry, to regret. **à ~,** with regret, reluctantly.

regrettable *adj.* regrettable, unfortunate.

regretter *v.t.* to regret, to be sorry for.

regrossir *v.t.* to regain weight.

regrouper *v.i.* to bring together, to round up, to regroup.

régularisation *n.f.* straightening out, putting into order.

régulariser *v.i.* to regularize; to set right.

régularité *n.f.* regularity; regular course; steadiness.

régulier, ière *adj.* regular; exact, punctual. *n.m.* regular; monk; soldier.

régulièrement *adv.* regularly; exactly, punctually.

régurgiter *v.t.* to regurgitate.

réhabilitation *n.f.* rehabilitation.

réhabiliter *v.t.* to rehabilitate; to reinstate. **se ~,** *v.refl.* to be rehabilitated; to be reinstated; to rise again.

réhabituer *v.t.* to accustom, to habituate again.

réhausser *v.t.* to raise higher, to raise; to heighten; to enhance; to increase; to set off. **~ un mur,** to raise a wall higher. **~ le prix d'une marchandise,** to raise the price of goods. **~ l'éclat, le mérite d'une action,** to enhance the merit of an action. **se ~,** *v.refl.* to be raised higher; to raise oneself in public esteem.

réimpression *n.f.* reprinting; reprint.

réimprimer *v.t.* to reprint.

rein *n.m.* kidney; *pl.* loins. **douleur aux ~s,** back pain. **avoir les ~s solides,** to be strong in the back.

réincarnation *n.f.* reincarnation.

réincarrier (se) *v.i.* to be reincarnated.

réincorporer *v.t.* to reincorporate.

reine *n.f.* queen. **la ~ mère,** the queen mother.

réinfecter *v.t.* to reinfect.

réintégration *n.f.* reintegration, reinstatement.

réintégrer *v.t.* to reintegrate; to reinstate.

réitération *n.f.* reiteration; repetition.

réitérer *v.t.* reiterate. **se ~,** *v.refl.* to be reiterated.

réjaillir *v.i.* to gush out; to spurt out; to flash, to reflect; to spring, to rise; to bound; to fly back. **faire ~ de l'eau,** to make water gush out.

rejet *n.m.* rejection; refusal; denial; young shoot; cast.

rejeter *v.t.* to throw again, to throw back; to reject, to cast off; to vomit; to carry (accounts). **~ une balle,** to throw back a ball. **~ une faute sur quelqu'un,** to lay the blame on someone. **se ~,** *v.refl.* to fall back (onto).

rejeton *n.m.* shoot (of a plant); offspring; scion.

réjoindre *v.t.* to rejoin; to join again; to overtake. **se ~,** *v.refl.* to join again, to reunite; to rejoin each other; to meet again.

réjouer *v.t.* to play again.

réjouir *v.t.* to rejoice, to make joyful; to gladden, to cheer, to delight. **cette nouvelle doit vous ~,** this news must please you. **se ~,** *v.refl.* to rejoice; to delight oneself; to be delighted, to be glad.

réjouissance *n.f.* rejoicing. **~s,** festivities.

réjouissant, e *adj.* joyous, merry; amusing.

relâche *n.m.* respite; discontinuace; relaxation; rest; *Theat.* no performance. **travailler sans ~,** not to cease working. **il y a ~ aujourd'hui à l'Opera,** there is no performance at the Opera tonight.

relâchement *n.m.* relaxation; loosening; looseness; laxity, decline. **~ des moeurs,** looseness of morals.

relâcher *v.t.* to relax; to slacken; to loose, to loosen; to unbend; to remit, to abate, to release. **~ des cordes,** to slacken, to loosen ropes. **~ la discipline,** to relax the discipline. **~ un prisonnier,** to release a prisoner; to put into port.

se ~, *v.refl.* to slacken, to loosen, to get slack. **le temps se relâche,** the weather is getting milder.

relais *n.m.* shift; inn.

relater *v.t.* to relate, to state.

relatif, ive *adj.* relative.

relation *n.f.* relation; reference, respect; connection, intercourse, correspondence, commerce. **nous sommes en ~ d'affaires avec sa maison,** we are on business terms with his house. **il a de belles ~s,** he is very well connected.

relativement *adv.* relatively.

relativité *n.f.* relativity.

relaver *v.t.* to wash again.

relax *adj.* laid back; relaxed.

relaxant *adj.* relaxing.

relaxation *n.f.* relaxation.

relaxer *v.t.* to relax.

relever *v.t.* to raise up again, to set up again; to take up; to pick up; to elevate, to heighten; to set off; to enhance; to revive; to extol, to exhalt. **~ une chaise,** to pick up a chair. **~ le défi,** to accept the challenge. **~ la tête,** to hold up one's head. **~ les fautes,** to point out mistakes. **~ la sentinelle,** to relieve the guard. *v.i.* to recover (from illness). **~ de maladie,** to recover from illness. **se ~,** *v.refl.* to rise again; to get up again; to stand up; to rise (from one's bed).

relief *n.m.* relief, relieve. **carte en ~,** relief map.

relier *v.t.* to bind (again); to unite, to join.

religieusement *adv.* religiously, scrupulously.

religieux, euse *adj.* religious; devout. *n.m.f.* monk, friar; nun.

religion *n.f.* religion; piety, devoutness. **se faire une ~ d'une chose,** to make a point of a thing. **entrer en ~,** to become a monk, a nun.

relire *v.t.* to read again, to read over.

reliure *n.f.* binding, book binding.

reloger *v.t.* to rehouse.

reluire *v.i.* to shine, to glitter, to gleam. **tout ce qui reluit n'est pas or,** all is not gold that glitters.

reluisant, e *adj.* shining, glittering; glossy.

remâcher *v.t.* to chew again, to ruminate; to turn over in one's mind.

remarier *v.t.* to remarry. **se ~,** *v.refl.* to remarry, to marry again.

remarquable *adj.* remarkable, outstanding, observable, noticeable.

remarquablement *adv.* remarkably.

remarque *n.f.* remark; notice; observation.

remarquer *v.t.* to remark; to notice, to note, to observe, to take notice of. **se ~,** *v.refl.* to be noticed, to attract attention.

remblayer *v.t.* to fill up; to embank.

remboîtement *n.m.* putting together again; resetting.

remboîter *v.t.* to put together again; to reset, to set.

rembourrer *v.t.* to stuff, to pad; to cram, to stuff. **se ~,** *v.refl.* to be stuffed; to stuff oneself.

remboursement *n.m.* reimbursement, repayment; redeeming.

rembourser *v.t.* to reimburse, to repay; to redeem. **se ~,** *v.refl.* to reimburse oneself, to repay oneself.

rembrunir *v.t.* to make darker, *Fig.* to sadden; to afflict. **se ~,** *v.refl.* to get dark; *Fig.* to become gloomy, sombre; to sadden; to darken.

remède *n.m.* remedy, cure.

remédiable *adj.* remediable; curable.

remédier *v.t.* to remedy.

remémoration *n.f.* remembrance, recollection.

remémorer *v.t.* to remind, to put in mind; to remember. **se ~,** *v.refl.* to remember, to recollect.

remerciement *n.m.* thanks; acknowledgment.

remercier *v.t.* to thank, to give thanks to; to decline; to be excused; to dismiss. **je vous remercie,** I thank you.

remettre *v.t.* to put back again; to lay again; to call back, to recollect; to deliver, to remit; to entrust; to put off; to delay; to set to rights; to reconcile, to forgive. **~ son chapeau,** to put on one's hat again. **~ une lettre à quelqu'un,** to deliver a letter to a person. **~ de l'argent,** to hand over money. **il ne faut jamais ~ au lendemain ce qu'on peut faire le jour même,** we must not put off till tomorrow what can be done today. **le voilà tout-à-fait remis,** he is back on his feet. **~ les péchés,** to forgive sins. **~ en question,** to challenge. **se ~,** *v.refl.* to go again, to begin again; to set again; to be deferred; to resume; to call to mind; to recover. **se ~ au travail,** to start working. **se ~ en route, en chemin,** to resume one's journey. **se ~ d'une frayeur,** to recover from a fright.

remeubler *v.t.* to refurnish.

réminiscence *n.f.* reminiscence, recollection.

remise *n.f.* delivery; the act of delivering, giving; remittance; commission, allowance; discount; forgiveness; pardon; abatement, moderation; delay, putting off.

rémission *n.f.* indulgence, mercy; remission; pardon.

remonter *v.t.* to climb (up); to go up again, to reascend; to remount; to rise again; to ascend; to fit up again; to take up again; to wind up (as clocks, watches). **~ à cheval,** to mount a horse. **la baromètre remonte,** the barometer is rising. **~ au déluge,** to go back to the flood. **~ un escalier,** to go upstairs again. **~ le fleuve,** to go up the river. **~ une machine,** to put a machine together again. **~ une montre,** to wind up a watch. **~ le courage, le moral de quelqu'un,** to rouse a person's courage. **se ~,** *v.refl.* to be remounted; to stock oneself again; to wind up (a clock, etc.).

remontrance *n.f.* reprimand, reproof.

remords *n.m.* remorse. **avoir des ~,** to feel remorse.

remorque *n.f.* trailer; towing.

remorquer *v.t.* to tow, to tug, to drag.

remorqueur *n.m.* tugboat.

rempart *n.m.* rampart, bulwark, fortification; safeguard.

remplaçant, e *n.m.f.* substitute.

remplacement *n.m.* replacing, replacement; substitution.

remplacer *v.t.* to take the place of; to replace. **se ~,** *v.refl.* to replace one another; to be replaced.

remplir *v.t.* to refill, to fill again; to fill, to fill up, to cram, to stuff; to store; to complete, to occupy; to discharge, to effect. **se ~ le ventre,** to cram oneself. **~ un poste,** to hold an office. **~ son devoir,** to fulfil, to do one's duty. **se ~,** to fill; to be filled; to get filled; to cram oneself. **se ~ de monde,** to be crowded.

remplissage *n.m.* filling, filling in; padding.

remporter *v.t.* to carry back; to carry away; to win, to gain. **~ prix,** to win the prize. **~ la victoire,** to win the victory.

remue-ménage *n.m.* commotion.

remue-méninges *n.m.* brainstorming.

remuer *v.t.* to move; to agitate, to disturb; to flick, to wag. **~ une table,** to move a table. **~ ciel et terre,** to move heaven and earth, **se ~,** *v.refl.* to move oneself, to move, to stir.

rémunérateur, trice *adj.* rewarding; remunerative. **un travail ~,** profitable work. *n.m.f.* rewarder.

rémunération *n.f.* remuneration; compensation; reward.

rémunérer *v.t.* to remunerate; to reward.

renâcler *v.i.* to snuff up, to snort; to demur, to grumble.

renaissance *n.f.* new birth, second birth; regeneration, revival, renewal; Renaissance.

renaissant, e *adj.* springing up again, renascent; reviving, recurring.

renaître *v.i.* to be born again; to spring up again, to rise again. **~ à la vie,** to revive. **mes forces renaissent,** my strength is returning. **~ à l'espérance,** to feel hope again.

renard *n.m.* fox. **chasse au ~,** foxhunting. **c'est un fin ~, un vrai ~,** he is a sly fox.

renarde *n.f.* vixen.

renardeau *n.m.* fox's cub, cub, vixen.

renchérir *v.t.* to raise the price of. (with **sur**) to outdo, to improve on, to add.

rencontre *n.f.* meeting; encounter. **aller à la ~ de quelqu'un,** to go to meet a person.

rencontrer *v.t.* to meet, to meet with, to encounter. **~ quelqu'un,** to meet a person. **se ~,** *v.refl.* to meet each other; to meet. **nos idées se rencontrent,** our ideas agree.

rendement *n.m.* produce, yield.

rendez-vous *n.m.* rendez-vous; meeting, appointment.

rendormir *v.t.* to put to sleep again. **se ~,** *v.refl.* to fall asleep again, to go to sleep again.

rendre *v.t.* to return; to give back; to render, to restore; to repay; to surrender; to give up; to yield, to produce; to cast up; to translate; to express. *v.i.* to give back, to pay back; (of wounds) to run; to vomit; to lead, to go. ~ à César ce qui est à César, to give to someone what belongs to him/her. ~ hommage, to render homage. ~ visite à quelqu'un, to pay a person a visit. ~ service à quelqu'un, to do a favor for a person. ~ la pareille, to give tit for tat. ~ la santé à quelqu'un, to restore a person to health. ces grains rendent soixante pour cent, this corn yields sixty percent. ~ l'âme, to give up the ghost. ~ un arrêt, to pass a sentence. ~ la justice, to administer justice. ~ justice à quelqu'un, to do a person justice. ~ ses comptes, to be accountable (for something). se ~, *v.refl.* to be returned, to be rendered, to be repaid; to render oneself; to go, to repair, to betake oneself to; to surrender. je me rendrai chez vous à neuf heures, I'll go to your house at 9 a.m. se ~ ridicule, to make oneself ridiculous. se ~ prisonnier, to surrender oneself. se ~ à la raison, to yield to reason.

rendu, e *p.p.* returned, repaid; delivered; arrived; conveyed; done, rendered; tired. compte ~, report, return; account. ~ à la liberté, restored to freedom. *n.m.* return; tit for tat.

rêne *n.f.* rein. tenir les ~s de l'empire, to hold the reins of the empire.

renégat, e *n.m.f.* renegade.

renfermer *v.t.* to shut up again; to shut up, to confine; to conceal; to hide; to be close. se ~, *v.refl.* to shut oneself up; to retire; to be shut.

renflement *n.m.* swelling; enlargement.

renfler *v.i.* to swell; to rise; to enlarge, to puff up, to inflate. se ~, *v.refl.* to swell; to rise.

renfoncement *n.m.* hollow, cavity, recess, corner.

renfoncer *v.t.* to pull down. ~ son chapeau, to pull down one's hat.

renforcement *n.m.* strengthening; reinforcement.

renforcer *v.t.* to strengthen; to make, to render stronger; to reinforce; to increase, to augment. se ~, *v.refl.* to get stronger, to gather strength, to strengthen; to be reinforced.

renfort *n.m.* reinforcement; supply; aid.

renier *v.t.* to deny, to disown; to disavow; to abjure.

renifler *v.i.* to sniff.

renne *n.m.* reindeer.

renom *n.m.* renown, fame; reputation; celebrity.

renommé, e *adj.* renowned, famed, famous.

renommée *n.f.* renown, fame; celebrity, reputation.

renommer *v.t.* to name again; to mention again; to re-appoint; to re-elect; to talk of. se ~, *v.refl.* to become renowned.

renoncer *v.t.* to renounce; to give up, to relinquish, to forsake; to resign, to disown, to disclaim, to deny. ~ à la couronne, to give up the crown. ~ à sa religion, to abjure one's religion.

renonciation *n.f.* renunciation; relinquishment.

renouer *v.t.* to tie again; to knot again; to tie up; to renew. ~ une alliance, to renew a vow. ~ amitié, to renew friendship. se ~, *v.refl.* to be tied again; to be resumed; to be renewed.

renouveau *n.m.* springtide, revival, renewal.

renouvelable *adj.* renewable.

renouveler *v.t.* to renew; to renovate, to revive, to refresh, to restore; to increase, to recommence, to begin again. se ~, *v.refl.* to renew, to begin again; to be renewed; to be revived.

renouvellement *n.m.* renewal; renovation, renewing; revival; reiteration, repetition, repeating. ~ d'un traité, renewal of a treaty.

rénovateur, trice *n.m.f.* renovator.

rénovation *n.f.* renovation, renewal; restoration.

rénover *v.t.* to renew, to renovate, to restore.

renseignement *n.m.* information, indication; hint, intelligence; *pl.* reference.

renseigner *v.t.* to inform; to direct. se ~, *v.refl.* to obtain information; to make inquiries.

rentabiliser *v.t.* to make profitable.

rentable *adj.* profitable.

rente *n.f.* yearly income, revenue; rent, annuity; funds, stock. ~ sur l'État, government annuity. acheter des ~s, to buy stock.

rentier, ière *n.m.f.* person of independent means.

rentrée *n.f.* reentering, reentrance; reopening, start of term/year (schools, etc.); (of crops) gathering in; housing (of plants); warehousing (of goods); receipt (of taxes).

rentrer *v.i.* to reenter; to go in again, to come in again; to come home again, to return; to go back; to get again; to reopen (as schools, etc.), to recover (money, debts). ~ dans sa maison, to go home again. ~ dans son bien, to recover one's property. ~ en possession, to gain possession. ~ en fonctions, to resume one's functions, to take in, to carry in, to get in; to gather in, to house.

renversant, e *adj. Infml.* stunning, stupefying.

renverse (à la) *adv.* on one's back, backward.

renversement *n.m.* overthrow; upsetting; throwing over; subversion; confusion; turning; ruin. le ~ du gouvernement, the overthrow of the government.

renverser *v.t.* to reverse; to turn upside down; to invert; to disorder, to derange; to upset; to spill; to overthrow. ~ l'esprit, la tête, to turn a person's head. se faire ~ par une voiture, to be run over by a car. ~ une table, to throw down a table. ~ un gouvernement, to overthrow a government. se ~, *v.refl.* to upset, to be overturned; to fall back; to throw oneself back, to be thrown down, to be overthrown, to be upset.

renvoi *n.m.* return; returning, sending back; reverberation (of sound); dismissal, discharge; adjournment; reference (in a book, etc.). le ~ de la discussion, the adjournment of the discussion.

renvoyer *v.t.* to send again; to return; to send

back; to dismiss, to discharge; to postpone, to delay; to reflect (light, heat, etc.); to refer (to a note). **~ la balle à quelqu'un,** to throw back the ball. **~ un employé,** to fire an employee.

réouverture *n.f.* reopening.

repaire *n.m.* haunt, den. **~ de voleurs,** den, haunt of thieves.

répandre *v.t.* to shed; to pour out; to spill; to spread; to diffuse, to expand; to exhale; to propagate, to scatter. **~ des larmes,** to shed tears. **le soleil répand la lumière,** the sun diffuses light. **se ~,** *v.refl.* to be shed, to flow; to be poured out; to be spread; to be exhaled; to be propagated, diffused, spread abroad. **se ~ dans le monde,** to spread all over the world.

réparable *adj.* reparable; retrievable.

reparaître *v.i.* to reappear; to show oneself again.

réparateur, trice *n.m.f.* repairer, mender; redresser (of wrongs). *adj.* reparative; repairing, restoring; invigorating.

réparation *n.f.* reparation; repair; *pl.* repairs; amends, relief.

réparer *v.t.* to repair; to mend; to retrieve; to recover; to make up for, to make amends for, to make reparation for. **~ une route,** to repair a road. **~ ses forces,** to recover one's strength. **se ~,** *v.refl.* to be repaired."

reparler *v.i.* to speak again.

repartir *v.t.* to reply, to answer; to set off again, to start again, to leave again.

répartir *v.t.* to divide, to portion out, to share, to distribute; to assess (taxes).

répartition *n.f.* division; apportionment, allotment; assessment (of taxes).

repas *n.m.* meal.

repassage *n.m.* ironing.

repasser *v.i.* to pass back, to go back, to return; to read over again, to go over again; to iron. **je repasserai demain,** I will come back tomorrow. **~ quelque chose dans son esprit,** to turn a thing over in one's mind.

repayer *v.t.* to repay, to pay again.

repêcher *v.t.* to fish up again.

repeindre *v.t.* to repaint; to retouch.

repentir (se) *v.refl.* to repent; to rue.

repentir *n.m.* repentance, penitence; alteration, correction.

répercussion *n.f.* repercussion; reverberation.

répercuter *v.t.* to echo, to reverberate, to reflect. **se ~,** *v.refl.* to reverberate.

repère *n.m.* benchmark (in leveling); mark; landmark, reference point.

repérer *v.t.* to mark, to put a mark on; to spot, to locate.

répertoire *n.m.* repertory; index; alphabetical index; repertory. **~ d'adresses,** address book.

répéter *v.t.* to repeat; to say again; to rehearse. **~ une leçon,** to recite a lesson. **~ une tragédie,** to rehearse a tragedy. **se ~,** *v.refl.* to repeat oneself; to be repeated; to be renewed.

répétition *n.f.* repetition; reiteration; recital; rehearsal; private lesson.

repeuplement *n.m.* repeopling; restocking.

repeupler *v.t.* to repeople; to restock (a pond, a forest). **se ~,** *v.refl.* to be repeopled; to be restocked.

répit *n.m.* break, rest, respite, reprieve. **prendre un moment de ~,** to take a break.

replacement *n.m.* replacement, replacing; reinvestment (of funds).

replacer *v.t.* to replace. **se ~,** *v.refl.* to replace oneself; to get a new place.

replanter *v.t.* to replant.

replier *v.t.* to fold again; to fold up, to coil up; to force back. **se ~,** *v.refl.* to fold up; to coil up; to wind; to fall back; to retreat.

réplique *n.f.* reply, answer. **donner à quelqu'un la ~,** to give a person his cue.

répliquer *v.t.* to retort; to reply.

replonger *v.t.* to plunge again; to dip again; to immerse again. **se ~,** *v.refl.* to plunge again, to dive again; to be plunged again; to be immersed again.

répondeur *n.m.* answering machine.

répondre *v.t.* to answer; to reply; to refute; to respond; to come up (to); to realize; to be responsible, accountable; to correspond. **je ne réponds plus de rien,** I will not be answerable for anything. **ses forces ne répondent pas à son zèle,** his strength is not equal to his zeal. **se ~,** *v.refl.* to answer oneself; to answer each other; to respond to each other; to correspond; to agree, to suit.

réponse *n.f.* answer; reply. **avoir ~ à tout,** to have an answer for everything.

report *n.m.* postponement, transfer.

reportage *n.m.* report, article, coverage.

reporter *v.t.* to carry back; to reconvey, to transport back; to convey; to carry forward; (in accounts) to carry over. **se ~,** *v.refl.* to be carried back; to transport oneself, to go back (in imagination).

reporter *n.m.* (newspaper) reporter.

repos *n.m.* rest; tranquility; pause. **prendre du ~,** to take a rest.

reposer *v.t.* to replace, to put again, to lay again; to rest; to lay at rest; to quiet; to relieve; to ground (arms). **~ la tête sur un oreiller,** to lay one's head on a pillow. **cela repose la vue,** that rests the eyes; to lie; to settle. **laisser ~ du vin,** to let wine settle. **se ~,** *v.refl.* to put, to lay, to place oneself again; to be at rest, to repose; to confide in. **il faut les laisser se ~,** let them rest. **se ~ sur ses lauriers,** to take it easy, to remain idle.

repoussant, e *adj.* repulsive, repugnant.

repoussement *n.m.* driving back; recoil (of a gun).

repousser *v.t.* to push, to thrust, to throw back; to repel; to repulse; to reject; to rebuff; to spurn; (of plants) to shoot forth again; **~ l'ennemi,** to drive the enemy back. ~ **une demande,** to reject a proposal. *v.i.* to spring; (of guns) to recoil, to kick; to spring again, to sprout again.

répréhensible *adj.* reprehensible.

reprendre *v.t.* to take again; to take back; to retake; to resume, to recover; to take up (a stitch); to reprove, to flame. ~ **sa place,** to take one's place again. ~ **du courage,** to take courage again. ~ **ses esprits,** ~ **ses sens,** to come back to one's senses. ~ **ses forces,** to recover one's strength. ~ **une lecture,** to resume one's reading. **on ne m'y reprendra plus,** I shall not be caught at it again; to reply, to answer; to return; to take root again; to recover, to get better; to revive; to begin again; to freeze again. **le froid a repris,** the cold has set in again. **cette mode reprend,** this fashion is coming back. **se ~,** *v.refl.* to be taken again; to close up again; to correct oneself.

représailles *n.f.pl.* retaliation.

représentant, e *n.m.* rep, traveling salesperson; representative.

représentatif, ive *adj.* representative.

représentation *n.f.* exhibition; production; representation; spectacle; performance; appearance. **la première ~ d'un pièce,** the first performance of a show.

représenter *v.t.* to present again; to show, to produce; to bring forth; to represent; to perform. ~ **une tragédie,** to act a tragedy. **se ~,** *v.refl.* to present oneself again; to make one's appearance again, to reappear; to be represented, to be performed.

répression *n.f.* repression.

réprimable *adj.* repressible.

réprimande *n.f.* reprimand; reproof, rebuke.

réprimer *v.t.* to repress; to check; to restrain. **se ~,** *v.refl.* to be repressed.

repris, e *p.p.* retaken. *n.m.* ~ **de justice,** habitual offender.

reprise *n.f.* retaking; recovery; resumption; revival; burden (of a song); darning, repetition; reperformance (of a play); underpinning (of a wall). **à plusieurs ~s,** several times, repeatedly.

réprobation *n.f.* reprobation; blame.

reproche *n.m.* reproach, blame, objection. **accabler quelqu'un de ~s,** to load a person with reproaches. **sans ~,** blameless.

reprocher *v.t.* to reproach, to blame, to grudge, to take exception to; to object to. **elle nous reproche de n'avoir rien fait,** she blames us for not doing anything. **se ~,** *v.refl.* to be reproached; to grudge oneself.

reproducteur, trice *adj.* reproductive; breeding.

reproductif, ive *adj.* reproductive.

reproduction *n.f.* reproduction; breeding (of stock); reprinting.

reproduire *v.t.* to reproduce; to raise, to breed (stock); to reprint, to republish. **se ~,** *v.refl.* to be reproduced; to reappear; to show oneself again; to occur again.

réprouver *v.t.* to condemn; to disapprove of.

reptile *n.m.* reptile.

repu, e *adj.* well filled, satiated.

républicain, e *n.m.f.* and *adj.* republican.

république *n.f.* commonwealth; republic.

répudier *v.t.* to repudiate.

répugnance *n.f.* repugnance; dislike. **avoir de la ~,** to dislike.

répugnant, e *adj.* repugnant; loathsome, disgusting.

répugner *v.i.* to be repugnant, to feel reluctant, to be unwilling, to be loath; to be loathsome. **cet homme me répugne,** I cannot bear that man.

répulsif, ive *adj.* repulsive, repelling.

répulsion *n.f.* repulsion; repugnance, aversion, dislike.

réputation *n.f.* reputation; character, fame, name. **perdre sa ~,** to lose one's good name.

réputé, e *adj.* well known, reputable.

requérir *v.t.* to require; to demand, to call in, to claim.

requête *n.f.* request; petition; demand. **présenter une ~,** to present a petition. **faire une ~,** to make a request.

requin *n.m.* shark.

réquisition *n.f.* requisition; summons; call.

réquisitoire *n.m.* closing argument.

rescousse *n.f.* rescue.

réseau *n.m.* network; system; plexus; *Arch.* tracery.

réservation *n.f.* reservation.

réserve *n.f.* stock; reserve; coyness; shyness. **se tenir sur la ~,** to be reserved. **à la ~ de,** with reservation of; excepting. **en ~,** in reserve, in stock. **sans ~,** without any reserve, unreserved.

réservé, e *adj.* reserved; cautious, guarded, circumspect; shy.

réserver *v.t.* to reserve; to keep back; to lay by, to put by. **se ~,** *v.refl.* to reserve oneself; to wait for an opportunity; to intend, to mean.

réservoir *n.m.* reservoir; tank, cistern; well; receptacle; gas tank.

résidant, e *adj.* resident.

résidence *n.f.* residence.

résident *n.m.* resident.

résider *v.i.* to reside, to dwell, to live, to abide.

résidu *n.m.* residue; remainder; residuum.

résiduel, elle *adj.* residual.

résignation *n.f.* resignation.

résigner *v.t.* to resign; to give up; to abdicate. **se ~,** *v.refl.* to resign oneself; to submit.

résiliation *n.f.* canceling, annuling.

résilier *v.t.* to cancel, to annul (a lease, a contract).

résistance *n.f.* resistance; obstacle; opposition; stamina, endurance.

résistant, e *adj.* resisting; withstanding, opposing.

résister *v.i.* to resist; to oppose, to withstand; to endure; to hold out. ~ **à la douleur,** to resist pain.

résolu, e *p.p.* resolved; solved; decided. *adj.* resolute; bold.

résolument *adv.* resolutely, boldly, stoutly, courageously.

résolution *n.f.* resolution; solution; canceling (of a lease, bond, etc.). **prendre une ~,** to come to a resolution.

résonner *v.i.* to resound; to echo; to reverberate.

résorber *v.t.* to resorb, to reabsorb.

résoudre *v.t.* to resolve, to dissolve, to solve, to explain; to cancel, to annul. **~ une difficulté,** to solve a difficulty. **~ un problème,** to resolve, to solve a problem. **se ~,** *v.refl.* to resolve; to dissolve, to be dissolved; to decide, to make up one's mind.

respect *n.m.* respect; reverence. **perdre le ~,** to lose respect. **sauf votre ~,** with all due respect. **tenir en ~,** to keep in check.

respectabilité *n.f.* respectability.

respectable *adj.* respectable, honorable.

respecter *v.t.* to respect, to esteem, to honor. **se ~,** *v.refl.* to respect oneself; to respect each other.

respectif, ive *adj.* respective.

respectivement *adv.* respectively.

respectueusement *adv.* respectfully.

respectueux, euse *adj.* respectful; deferential, courteous.

respirable *adj.* breathable.

respiration *n.f.* respiration, breathing.

respiratoire *adj.* respiratory.

respirer *v.i.* to breathe; to respire; to rest, to take breath. **l'air que nous respirons,** the air we breathe.

resplendir *v.i.* to be resplendent; to shine bright.

resplendissant, e *adj.* resplendent; very bright.

responsabilité *n.f.* responsibility.

responsable *adj.* responsible; accountable, answerable.

ressemblance *n.f.* resemblance; similarity; likeness.

ressemblant, e *adj.* resembling, similar, like, alike.

ressembler *v.i.* to be like; to resemble. **ce portrait vous ressemble beaucoup,** this portrait is very like you. **se ~,** *v.refl.* to resemble each other, to be like each other; to be alike. **qui se ressemble s'assemble,** birds of a feather flock together.

ressentir *v.t.* to resent, to feel, to experience. **~ du bien-être,** to feel comfortable. **se ~,** *v.refl.* to feel; to feel the effects of, to feel the influence of.

resserrement *n.m.* tightening; closing; constriction; contraction.

resserrer *v.t.* to tie again; to narrow; to confine more closely; to bind. **resserrez ce noeud,** tie this knot tighter. **~ l'amitié,** to strengthen the bonds of friendship. **se ~,** *v.refl.* to be contracted; to become narrower; to shrink.

resservir *v.i.* to serve again; to avail again. **se ~,** *v.refl.* (with **de**) to use again.

ressort *n.m.* spring; elasticity; activity, energy,

force, strength; means; jurisdiction, resort, department. **cette affaire est du ~ de la cour de Paris,** this matter is under the jurisdiction of the Paris courts. **en dernier ~,** in last resort. **cela n'est pas de mon ~,** that is not within my competence.

ressortir *v.i.* to go out again, to come out again. **les ombres font ~ les lumières,** shades set off the light parts, to be in the jurisdiction (of); to be amenable (to).

ressortissant, e *adj.* subject. *n.m.f.* subject, national, citizen.

ressource *n.f.* resource; resort, means. **il est sans ~,** he is without means. **c'est un homme de ~,** he is a resourceful man.

ressouvenir (se) *v.refl.* to remember; to recollect, to call back to mind.

ressusciter *v.t.* to resuscitate; to raise from the dead; to revivify; to come to life again; to revive. **se ~,** *v.refl.* to revive; to return to life, to recover life.

restant, e *adj.* remaining, left. **adresser une lettre poste ~e,** to address a letter to be kept till called for. *n.m.* rest, remainder, residue.

restaurant *n.m.* restaurant.

restaurateur, trice *n.m.f.* restorer; restorator; restaurant owner.

restauration *n.f.* restoration; catering.

restaurer *v.t.* to restore; to repair; to revive; to renew. **~ un tableau,** to restore a painting. **se ~,** *v.refl.* to refresh oneself, to take refreshment.

reste *n.m.* rest, residue, remainder, remnant; *pl.* leavings, scraps, remains. **le ~ de la journée,** the rest of the day. **les ~s d'un repas,** the leftovers of a meal. **et le ~,** and so forth, and so on. **ce tombeau contient ses ~s,** his remains lie in this grave. **être en ~,** to be indebted. **au ~, du ~,** also, besides; nevertheless, yet.

rester *v.i.* to remain; to be left, to be left remaining. **restez à votre place,** remain in your place. **il est resté stupéfait,** he stood astounded. **voici ce qui me reste de l'argent,** this is all that is left of the money. **il me reste à vous dire,** I have still to tell you.

restituer *v.t.* to restore, to make restitution of, to give back.

restitution *n.f.* restitution; restoration.

restreindre *v.t.* to restrict, to limit, to confine. **se ~,** *v.refl.* to restrict oneself, to limit oneself.

restrictif, ive *adj.* restrictive.

restriction *n.f.* restriction; reserve, reservation.

résultat *n.m.* result, outcome.

résulter *v.i.* to result; to ensue.

résumé *n.m.* recapitulation, summary; résumé; abstract.

résumer *v.t.* to recapitulate, to sum up, to make a summary of, to summarize. **se ~,** *v.refl.* to recapitulate, to sum up; to be summed up; to be condensed.

résurrection *n.f.* resurrection, rising (from the dead); revival; resuscitation.

rétablir *v.t.* to reestablish; to restore; to reinstate; to set up again; to recruit. ~ **la réputation de quelqu'un,** to restore a person's reputation. ~ **sa santé,** to recover one's health. **se ~,** *v.refl.* to be reestablished; to be restored, to improve; to recover one's health.

rétablissement *n.m.* reestablishment; restoration; recovery.

retaper *v.t.* to fix up; to retype.

retard *n.m.* delay; slowness (of watches); backwardness.

retardataire *adj.* backward; latecomer; loiterer.

retardement *n.m.* delay; deferment.

retarder *v.t.* to delay, to defer, to put off; to postpone. ~ **son départ,** to put off one's departure; to be too slow; (with **de**) to be slow, to lose. **cette pendule retarde,** that clock is slow. **ma montre retarde de cinq minutes par jour,** my watch loses five minutes a day.

retenir *v.t.* to have again, to hold again, to get again, to get back; to detain; to withhold; to retain, to keep, to keep back; to deduct; to hire; to carry. ~ **une leçon,** to remember a lesson. **retenez bien ceci,** remember this. ~ **une loge au théâtre,** to take a box at the theater. ~ **son haleine,** to hold one's breath. ~ **sa langue,** to hold one's tongue. ~ **quelqu'un à dîner,** to keep a person at dinner. **un rhume l'a retenu dans sa chambre,** a cold confined him to his room. ~ **la main, le bras de quelqu'un,** to hold back a person's hand, arm. ~ **sa colère,** to restrain one's anger. **se ~,** *v.refl.* to seize hold, to seize; to check oneself, to keep back, to hold back; to restrain oneself; to be retained, to refrain, to forbear. **cet homme ne sait pas se ~,** that man cannot restrain himself.

rétention *n.f.* retention, retaining.

retentir *v.i.* to resound, to echo, to re-echo, to ring.

retentissant, e *adj.* resounding, ringing; sonorous.

retentissement *n.m.* resounding, resound; noise, outburst.

retenu, e *adj.* reserved, cautious, wary, circumspect, prudent; discreet; timid, coy; modest.

retenue *n.f.* reserve, caution, prudence, discretion; modesty; stoppage (of money); (in schools) detention. **ne garder aucune ~ dans sa conduite,** to be unreserved in one's way of behaving. **être en ~,** to be in detention.

réticence *n.f.* reticence; reluctance.

retirer *v.t.* to withdraw; to draw back, to take back; to derive from; to recall. ~ **son bras,** to draw one's arm back. ~ **sa parole,** to retract one's word; (of the tide) to be ebbing. **se ~,** *v.refl.* to retire; to withdraw; to go off; to draw back; to retreat. **retirez-vous d'ici,** go away from here. **il s'est retiré dans son appartement,** he has retired to his apartment. **se ~ du commerce,** to retire from business. **se ~ en province,** to go into the country. **la mer se retire,** the tide ebbs.

retombée *n.f.* springing (of arches); fallout.

retomber *v.i.* to fall again, to relapse. **ses longs cheveux retombant sur son visage,** her long hair falling over her face. ~ **dans la misère,** to fall back into poverty. ~ **sur ses pieds,** to land one's feet.

rétorquer *v.t.* to retort.

retors, e *adj.* twisted; wrung; *Fig.* deep, crafty, sly. *n.m.* crafty, cunning person.

retouche *n.f.* retouching, touch up.

retour *n.m.* return. **par ~ du courier,** by return post. **le ~ du printemps,** the return of spring. **billet de ~,** return ticket. **être de ~,** to be back. **il sera de ~ bientôt,** he will be back soon.

retourner *v.t.* to turn; to turn over, up, down, round, back; to revolve, to agitate; to send back, to return; to go again; to come back, to go back. ~ **une carte,** to turn a card. ~ **le sol,** to turn up the soil. **j'ai retourné ces marchandises,** I returned those articles. ~ **en arrière,** to turn back. ~ **chez soi,** to return home, to go back home. **se ~,** *v.refl.* to turn oneself; to turn; to turn round. **se ~ dans son lit,** to turn in one's bed. **s'en ~,** to turn back; to return, to go back.

retracer *v.t.* to trace; to trace again. **se ~,** *v.refl.* to be retraced; to recall, to recollect.

rétractation *n.f.* recantation, retractation; disavowal.

rétracter *v.t.* to recant, to retract, to recall; to unsay; to withdraw. **se ~,** *v.refl.* to recant, to retract, to make a recantation, to eat one's words; to retract, to be drawn back.

retrait *n.m.* redeeming; repurchase; withdrawal (of a bill); ebb.

retraite *n.f.* retreat; retiring; retirement; pension; refuge, shelter. **battre en ~,** to retreat, to draw off. **donner ~ à,** to shelter, to harbor. ~ **de voleurs,** a den of thieves. **caisse des ~s,** retirement fund. **mettre à la ~,** to pension off. **prendre sa ~,** to retire.

retraité, e *adj.* and *n.m.f.* retired.

retransmission *n.f.* broadcasting.

retravailler *v.i.* to work again. *Fig.* to finish, to polish.

rétrécir *v.t.* to narrow, to shrink; to take in (clothes). **se ~,** *v.refl.* to narrow, to get narrower, to shrink.

rétrécissement *n.m.* narrowing; narrowness; shrinking (of cloth); contracting.

rétribuer *v.t.* to remunerate, to pay, to reward.

rétribution *n.f.* rumuneration, retribution, reward, payment; salary, fee.

rétroactif, ive *adj.* retroactive, retrospective.

rétrograde *adj.* retrograde; retrogressive.

rétrograder *v.i.* to retrograde; to go back; to retreat.

rétroprojecteur *n.m.* overhead projector.

rétropropulsion *n.f.* reverse thrust.

rétrospectif, ive *adj.* retrospective.

retrouvailles *n.f.pl.* reunion.

retrouver *v.t.* to find again; to recover; to meet

again. se ~, *v.refl.* to be found again; to be one-self again, to meet again.

rétroviseur *n.m.* rearview mirror.

réunion *n.f.* meeting.

réunir *v.t.* to reunite, to bring together again; assemble; to collect; to get together. se ~, *v.refl.* to reunite; to be united again; to join, to meet; to assemble, to gather together.

réussir *v.i.* to succeed, to be successful; to prosper, to thrive; to execute well, to carry out well.

rétissite *n.f.* success, issue, end result.

revanche *n.f.* revenge, return, retaliation. **avoir sa ~,** to have one's revenge. **prendre sa ~,** to take one's revenge.

rêvasser *v.i.* to daydream.

rêvasserie *n.f.* daydreaming.

rêve *n.m.* dream.

réveil *n.m.* awaking, waking, wakening; reveille.

réveille-matin *n.m.* alarm clock.

réveiller *v.t.* to awake, to rouse; to wake, to wak-en; to stir up. ~ **l'attention,** to rouse attention. se ~, *v.refl.* to awake, to wake up; to rouse one-self up, to be roused. se ~ **en sursaut,** to wake up suddenly.

réveillon *n.m.* Christmas Eve or New Year's Eve party.

réveillonner *v.i.* to celebrate Christmas or New Year's Eve.

révélateur, trice *n.m.f.* revealer; approver. *n.m. Photo.* developer. *adj.* revealing, disclosing.

révélation *n.f.* revelation; disclosure, discovery.

révéler *v.t.* to reveal, to disclose, to divulge, to discover. *Infml.* to tell. se ~, *v.refl.* to reveal one-self, to be revealed.

revenant *n.m.* ghost, apparition. **tiens, un ~!** hello stranger.

revendeur, euse *n.m.f.* retailer; retail dealer.

revendication *n.f.* claim, claiming.

revendiquer *v.t.* to claim, to reclaim (responsibility).

revendre *v.t.* to sell again, to resell.

revenir *v.i.* to return; to come back, to go back; to recur, to revive, to recover; to come to, to cost. **je reviens pour vous dire,** I came back to tell you. ~ **à la charge,** to begin again; to get over. ~ **à ses moutons,** ~ **à son sujet,** to return to one's subject. **cela me revient à l'esprit,** that recurs to my mind. ~ **d'une maladie,** to recov-er from an illness. **je n'en reviens pas,** I can't believe it, I can't get over my surprise. **cela revient au même,** that amounts to the same thing. ~ **sur son opinion,** to change one's opinion. ~ **sur ses pas,** to retrace one's steps. ~ **sur une affaire,** to reconsider a matter. ~ **sur ses engagements,** not to keep one's engagements. **faire revenir,** to recall (a per-son), to call back; to recover (from fainting); to get back; to bring back, to restore, to revive; to brown.

revente *n.f.* resale.

revenu, e *p.p.* returned, come back, back. *n.m.* revenue, income.

rêver *v.i.* to dream, to have dreams; to be dream-ing; to muse. ~ **de quelqu'un,** to dream of a person. ~ **toute la nuit,** to dream all night. **cela donne à ~,** that makes one consider.

réverbération *n.f.* reverberation, reflection.

réverbère *n.m.* reflector; streetlamp (with a reflector).

révérend, e *adj.* reverend.

révérer *v.t.* to revere, to honor.

rêverie *n.f.* reverie, musing, dreaming.

revers *n.m.* back, reverse; back of the hand; fac-ing (of clothes). ~ **de la médaille,** the other side of the coin. **éprouver des ~,** to have revers-es, misfortunes.

reverser *v.t.* to pour out again.

revêtement *n.m.* facing, lining, casing; covering.

revêtir *v.t.* to clothe, to invest with, to dress (in), to array (with); to put on; to endow with; to line, to coat with. ~ **les pauvres,** to clothe the poor. **l'autorité dont il est revêtu,** the authority he is invested with. se ~, *v.refl.* (with **de**) to clothe oneself (in), to put on; to invest oneself (in); to assume.

rêveur, euse *adj.* dreaming, musing, dreamy. *n.m.f.* dreamer.

revient *n.m.* cost. **prix de ~,** cost price.

revirement *n.m.* sudden change; *Naut.* tacking.

réviser *v.t.* to revise; to review.

revision *n.f.* revision, revisal, reexamination; revise.

révisionnisme *n.m.* revisionism.

révisionniste *n.m.f.* revisionist.

revivre *v.i.* to revive; to come to life again. **faire ~,** to bring to life again.

révocation *n.f.* revocation; repeal, reversal; dismissal.

revoici *adv.* back again, here ... is again, here ... are again.

revoilà *adv.* back again, there ... is again, there ... are again.

revoir *v.t.* to see again; to revise, to look over again. ~ **un manuscrit,** to revise a manuscript. *n.m.* seeing again. **au ~,** bye. se ~, *v.refl.* to see each other again; to meet again.

révoltant, e *adj.* revolting.

révolte *n.f.* revolt; rebellion.

révolter *v.t.* to revolt, to rebel, to excite, to insti-gate; to stir up, to rouse. se ~, *v.refl.* to revolt; to rebel; to mutiny, to rise, to be indignant (at).

révolution *n.f.* revolution.

révolutionnaire *adj.* revolutionary.

révolutionner *v.t.* to revolutionize.

revolver *n.m.* gun, revolver.

révoquer *v.t.* to revoke; to annul; to dismiss (a clerk). ~ **une loi,** to repeal a law. se ~, *v.refl.* to be recalled; to be called back.

revu, e *p.p.* seen again; revised, examined, corrected.

revue *n.f.* review; retrospect; survey; magazine;

periodical publication. **faire la ~ de**, to examine. **passer en ~**, to review.

révulser (se) *v.t.* to contort, to distort, to revolt, to disgust.

révulsif, ive *adj. n.m.* revolting.

révulsion *n.f.* revulsion.

rez-de-chaussée *n.m.* ground level; ground floor, (U.S.) first floor.

rehabiller *v.t.* to dress again. **se ~**, *v.refl.* to dress oneself again.

rhapsodie *n.f.* rhapsody.

rhapsodique *adj.* rhapsodic, rhapsodical.

rhétorique *n.f.* rhetoric.

Rhin *n.m.* Rhine. **vin du ~**, Rhenish wine, Rhine wine, Rhenish.

rhinocéros *n.m.* rhinoceros, rhino.

rhododendron *n.m.* rhododendron.

rhubarbe *n.f.* rhubarb.

rhum *n.m.* rum.

rhumatisme *n.m.* rheumatism, arthritis.

rhume *n.m.* cold. **~ de cerveau**, head cold.

ribambelle *n.f. Infml.* string; host, swarm, lot, herd, crowd, flock.

ricanement *n.m.* sneer, sneering, smirking, giggle, giggling.

ricaner *v.i.* to sneer, to chuckle, to smirk, to snigger.

ricaneur, euse *n.m.f.* sneerer, titterer, giggler. *adj.* sneering, chuckling, giggling.

riche *adj.* rich, wealthy, fertile, fruitful, abundant; copious. **un pays ~**, a wealthy country. *n.m.* rich man.

richement *adv.* richly; amply, abundantly, copiously.

richesse *n.f.* riches; wealth; richness. **la ~ du sol**, the richness of the soil.

richissime *adj.* extremely, enormously, excessively rich.

ricin *n.m.* ricinus, castor-oil plant. **huile de ~**, castor oil.

ricocher *v.i.* to ricochet, to rebound.

ricochet *n.m.* rebound (on the water); chain, succession, ricochet. **tir à ~s**, ricochet firing. **par ~**, indirectly, by chance.

rictus *n.m.* grin, grimace.

ride *n.f.* wrinkle; ripple (on water); *Naut.* laniard (of sails).

ridé *adj.* wrinkled, shriveled.

rideau *n.m.* curtain; screen. **~ de lit**, bed curtain. **tirer le ~**, to draw the curtain. **tirer le ~ sur quelque chose**, to draw the curtain over something. **baisser le ~**, to close the curtain.

rider *v.t.* to wrinkle; to shrivel; to ripple. **se ~**, *v.refl.* to be wrinkled, to shrivel; (of water) to ripple.

ridicule *adj.* ridiculous. **il est ~**, he is ridiculous. *n.m.* the ridiculous, ridiculousness. **tourner en ~**, to ridicule, to turn into ridicule.

ridiculement *adv.* ridiculously.

ridiculiser *v.t.* to ridicule. **se ~**, *v.refl.* to make oneself ridiculous.

rien *n.m.* nothing, anything. **~ n'est plus admirable**, nothing is more admirable. **cela vaut ~ du tout**, that is worth nothing at all. **ne ~ faire**, to do nothing. **cela ne fait ~**, it doesn't matter. **ne savoir ~ du tout**, to know nothing at all. **tout ou ~**, all or nothing. **réduire à ~**, to reduce to nothing. **~ que cela?** is that all? **en un ~ du temps**, in no time. **comme si de ~ n'était**, as if nothing had happened.

rieur, euse *n.m.f.* laugher. *adj.* laughing.

rigide *adj.* rigid; stiff; strict, exact; severe.

rigidité *n.f.* rigidity, rigidness; severity; strictness.

rigolade *n.f.* fun, laugh, laughter. **une partie de ~**, a lot of fun.

rigoler *v.i.* to laugh, to have fun, to be laughing.

rigolo, ette *adj.* funny, comical. *n.m.f.* joker; phoney; comic.

rigoureusement *adv.* rigorously.

rigoureux, euse *adj.* rigorous; rigid; severe; harsh, cruel. **un hiver ~**, a rigorous winter.

rigueur *n.f.* rigor; severity, harshness, strictness; rigorousness. **user de ~**, to show severity. **la ~ de l'hiver**, the severity of the winter. **à la ~**, rigorously; strictly; strictly speaking.

rilletes *n.f.pl.* potted pork.

rime *n.f.* rhyme; verse.

rimer *v.i.* to rhyme.

rinçage *n.m.* rinsing.

rincer *v.t.* to rinse; to wash; to drench (with rain). **~ des verres, des bouteilles**, to rinse glasses, bottles. **il a été bien rincé**, he was drenched.

ring *n.m. Sports.* ring.

riposte *n.f.* retort, reply. **prompt à la ~**, to be quick at repartee, to be quick with a comeback.

riposter *v.i.* to reply; to answer (back).

riquiqui *adj. Infml.* tiny, weeny, stingy.

rire *v.i.* to laugh; to joke, to make a game of. **éclater de ~, ~ aux éclats**, to burst out laughing. **~ aux larmes**, to laugh until one cries. **~ à gorge déployée**, to roar with laughter, to laugh one's head off. **~ du bout des lèvres**, to give a forced laugh, to titter. **mourir de ~**, to die laughing. **n'avoir pas envie de ~**, to be in no laughing mood. **vous voulez ~**, you must be joking. **~ de quelqu'un**, to laugh at a person. **~ au nez de quelqu'un**, to laugh in a person's face. **se ~**, *v.refl.* to laugh (at), to make fun (of). *n.m.* laughing, laugh, laughter. **fou ~**, giggles, uncontrollable laughter. **un gros ~**, loud laugh. **~ moqueur**, sneer. **partir d'un éclat de ~**, to burst out laughing.

ris *n.m.* laugh, laughter; *Naut.* reef; sweetbread. **~ de veau**, calf's sweetbread. defense battery (of a port).

risée *n.f.* laughter; laugh; mockery; derision; laughing stock; butt of jokes, gust of wind, blast. **devenir la ~ du public**, to become the laughing stock of the public.

risque *n.m.* risk; hazard, peril, danger. **au ~ de,** at the risk of.

risquer *v.t.* to risk; to hazard, to venture. **~ sa vie,** to risk one's life. **~ le tout pour le tout,** to risk all to win all. **qui ne risque rien, n'a rien,** nothing ventured, nothing gained. **se ~,** *v.refl.* to run the risk; to risk.

rituel, le *n.m. adj.* ritual.

rivage *n.m.* shore; seashore, coast.

rival, e *n.m.f.* rival; competitor. *adj.* rival; competing.

rivaliser *v.i.* to compete, to vie (with), to rival.

rivalité *n.f.* rivalry, competition, strife.

rive *n.f.* bank, shore, riverside. **sur la ~ gauche,** on the left bank (of the river).

riverain *n.m.* riverside resident; owner of a riverside property.

rivière *n.f.* river. **des ~s de sang,** streams of blood. **~ de diamants,** diamond necklace.

riz *n.m.* rice.

rizière *n.f.* rice plantation, rice paddy.

robe *n.f.* robe; gown, dress. **porter la ~,** to be a magistrate. **une ~ de femme,** a woman's dress. **~ de mariée,** a wedding dress. **~ de chambre,** robe, gown, dressing gown.

robinet *n.m.* faucet.

robot *n.m.* robot.

robuste *adj.* robust; strong, sturdy, hardy, hearty.

robustesse *n.f.* robustness.

roc *n.m.* rock.

rocaille *n.f.* pebbles; rock work; stones.

roche *n.f.* rock; stone. **~ sous l'eau,** sunken rock.

rocher *n.m.* rock; cliff. **~ escarpé,** steep rock, cliff, crag.

rocheux, euse *adj.* rocky. **les montagnes Rocheux,** the Rocky Mountains.

rock *n.m.* rock; rock and roll.

rocker *n.m.f.* rock musician; rock fan.

roder *v.t.* to polish, to grind in (valve); to get into stride.

rôder *v.i.* to roam, to ramble, to rove, to wander; *Pej.* to prowl.

rôdeur, euse *n.m.f.* rover, wanderer; stroller; prowler.

rogne *n.f.* anger. **être en ~,** to be angry.

rogner *v.t.* to curtail; to clip (coin); to cut off; to pare.

rognon *n.m.* kidney.

roi *n.m.* king. **de** or **par le ~,** in the king's name. **vive le ~!** long live the king. **le jour des Rois,** Epiphany.

rôle *n.m.* roll; scroll; list; part, character. **le ~ de Phèdre,** the part of Phaedra. **jouer un ~, faire un ~,** to play a part. **à tour de ~,** in turn, by rotation.

roman, e *adj. n.m.* novel. **faire un ~,** to write a novel. **cela tient du ~,** that is like a romance. **~ policier,** detective novel.

romance *adj. n.f.* romance. *n.f.* ballad, song; romance.

romancier, ière *n.m.* novelist.

romanesque *adj.* and *n.m.* romantic. **une histoire ~,** a romantic story. *n.m.* romance.

romantique *adj.* romantic. *n.m.* romanticist.

romantisme *n.m.* romanticism.

romarin *n.m.* rosemary.

rompre *v.t.* to break; to shatter, to dash to pieces; to snap; to break off; to burst, to open by force; to break up; to infringe; to break in, to inure, to part, to divide; to rupture; to fall out; to have done. **~ un bâton,** to break a stick. **~ le pain,** to break bread. **~ ses chaînes,** to break one's chains. **~ la glace,** to break the ice. **~ une conversation,** to interrupt a conversation. **~ le sommeil de quelqu'un,** to disturb a person's sleep. **~ le silence,** to break the silence. **~ un traité,** to break a treaty. **~ un mariage,** to end a marriage. **~ un cheval,** to break in a horse. **il vaut mieux plier que ~,** it is better to bend than to break. **~ avec quelqu'un,** to break up with a person. **se ~,** *v.refl.* to be broken; to break; to divide; to break off; to be refracted; to lose one's order; to break up; to discontinue.

rompu, e *adj.* broken; broken off; broken up; broken; interrupted; inured.

ronchonner *v.i.* to grumble, to grouch, to grouse.

rond, e *adj.* round, rounded; plain; chubby, plump, full. **table ~e,** round table. **cela fait, en nombre ~, mille francs,** it is a round sum of a thousand francs. *n.m.* round; circle; ring. **en ~,** round, roundly; in a round; in a ring. **tourner en ~,** to turn round and round. **~ de serviette,** a napkin ring.

ronde *n.f.* round; *Milit.* beat; patrol. *Mus.* roundelay. **faire la ~,** to go on the beat, on patrol, to keep watch. **à la ~,** around, all around, roundabout. **boire à la ~,** to drink in turn.

rond-de-cuir *n.m. Infml.* office clerk, bureaucrat.

rondelet, ette *adj.* roundish, stoutish, plump.

rondelle *n.f.* slice, disc; washer (of a wheel, etc.).

rondement *adv.* roundly; fast, swiftly, briskly, with speed, openly, boldly, frankly, plainly.

rondeur *n.f.* roundness; rotundity; bluntness, plainness. **la ~ de la terre,** the roundness of the earth.

rond-point *n.m.* crossroads, traffic circle.

ronflement *n.m.* snoring, snore; snorting (of horses); roaring, roar (of thunder, cannon); rumbling (of wind); pealing, peal (of an organ); humming (of a top).

ronfler *v.i.* to snore; (of a horse) to snort; to roar (as thunder, cannon etc.); to rumble (as wind); (of an organ) to peal; (of tops) to hum.

ronfleur, euse *n.m.f.* snorer. *adj.* snoring.

ronger *v.i.* to gnaw; to nibble, to eat, to bite (one's nails), (of a horse) to champ; to corrode, to consume, to eat up. **~ un os,** to gnaw a bone. **~ son frein,** to champ one's bit. *Fig.* to fret. **se ~,** *v.refl.* to fret; to be consumed, to be corroded. **se ~ les ongles,** to bite one's nails.

rongeur, euse *adj.* gnawing; rodent. *n.m.* rodent.

ronron *n.m.* purring.

ronronner *v.i.* to purr.

roquefort *n.m.* Roquefort cheese.

roquette *n.f.* rocket.

rosace *n.f.* rose, rosette; rose window.

rosbif *n.m.* roast beef. *Pej.* English person.

rose *n.f.* rose; rose diamond; rosette, rose window. **être sur des ~s,** to lie on a bed of roses. *adj.* rose, rose-colored; rose-hued, rosy. *n.m.* rose color, rosiness.

rosé, e *adj.* rosy; pink; (wine) rosé.

roseau *n.m.* reed.

rosée *n.f.* dew.

roseraie *n.f.* rose garden.

rosier *n.m.* rose bush, rose tree.

rossignol *n.m.* nightingale.

rot *n.m.* burp, belch.

rotatif, ive *adj.* rotative, rotatory.

rotation *n.f.* rotation.

rotatoire *adj.* rotary.

roter *v.i.* to burp, to belch.

rôti, e *adj.* roasted, roast. *n.m.* roast meat, roast.

rôtir *v.t.* to roast. **~ de la viande,** to roast meat. **se ~,** *v.refl.* to roast, to be roasted. **faire ~,** to roast; to broil.

rôtisserie *n.f.* grill, steakhouse, rotisserie.

rôtissoire *n.f.* Dutch oven, rotisserie.

rotonde *n.f.* rotunda, roundhouse.

rotule *n.f.* patella, kneecap. **être sur les ~,** to be beat, to be exhausted.

roturier, ière *adj.* plebeian, common. *n.m.f.* plebeian, commoner.

rouage *n.m.* wheelwork (of a machine); machinery; movement; wheel; *Fig.* wheels, machinery; means.

roue *n.f.* wheel. **faire la ~,** to do a cartwheel. **~ dentée,** cog wheel.

rouer *v.t.* to coil (a rope). **~ de coups,** to thrash, to beat up.

rouge *adj.* red; crimson; (of the eyes) bloodshot, bloody. **devenir ~,** to turn red. **fer ~,** red-hot iron. *n.m.* red, red color; redness.

rougeâtre *adj.* reddish.

rouge-gorge *n.m.* robin.

rougeole *n.f.* measles.

rougeur *n.f.* goodness, red; blushing, flush. **la ~ des lèvres,** the redness of the lips.

rougir *v.t.* to redden; to make red, to blush. **~ de colère,** to blush with anger.

rougissant, e *adj.* reddening; blushing.

rouille *n.f.* rust; rustiness.

rouiller *v.t.* to rust; to impair, to weaken. **se ~,** *v.refl.* to rust; to get rusty; *Fig.* to weaken, to decline; to impair.

rouleau *n.m.* roll, scroll, roller; curler. **un ~ de papier,** a roll of paper.

roulement *n.m.* rolling, roll; *Milit.* roll; circulation (of money). **fondes de ~,** cash in hand. **~ des yeux,** rolling of the eyes.

rouler *v.t.* to drive, to roll; to wheel; to roll up, to beat, to hoax, to take in, to be rolled, to run on wheels; to revolve, to rumble. **~ les yeux,** to roll one's eyes. **pierre qui roule n'amass pas mousse,** a rolling stone gathers no moss. **~ sur l'or,** to roll in money. **il s'est fait ~,** he was conned. **se ~,** *v.refl.* to roll, to be rolled; to wind, to roll oneself. **se ~ sur le gazon,** to roll on the grass.

roulette *n.f.* small wheel; castor, roller; roulette (a game). **les ~s d'un fauteuil,** the castors of an armchair. **cela va comme sur des ~s,** it's going very smoothly.

roulis *n.m.* Naut. rolling; roll, rolling.

roulotte *n.f.* trailer, caravan.

roupiller *v.i.* Infml. to sleep, to snooze, to doze, to slumber.

rouquin, e *adj.* red-haired. *n.m.f.* redhead.

rouspéter *v.i.* Infml. to grouse, to grumble (at).

route *n.f.* road, way; highway; route; direction; highway. **se mettre en ~,** to start, to set out. **être sur la ~ de quelqu'un,** to be in a person's way.

routier, ière *adj.* of roads, road. **carte routière,** road map. *n.m.* truck driver, long distance driver; sailing directions; chart; roadster (bicycle). **un vieux ~,** an old timer.

routine *n.f.* routine; habit; practice; custom.

routinier, ière *n.m.f.* person acting by routine. *adj.* of routine.

rouvrir *v.t.* to reopen, to open again. **se ~,** *v.refl.* to open again.

roux, ousse *adj.* auburn, russet; reddish-brown; red. **lune rouse,** April moon. *n.m.f.* red-haired person. *n.m.* russet; red. **~ ardent,** fiery red.

royal, e *adj.* royal; regal; kingly.

royalement *adv.* royally.

royaume *n.m.* kingdom; realm.

royauté *n.f.* royalty, sovereignty.

ruban *n.m.* ribbon; tape.

rubéole *n.f.* German measles, rubella.

rubescent, e *adj.* rubescent.

rubis *n.m.* ruby. **faire ~ sur l'ongle,** to drink to the last drop. **payer ~ sur l'ongle,** to pay in cash.

rubrique *n.f.* column, heading, red chalk, head, title.

ruche *n.f.* hive; beehive; ruche.

rude *adj.* rugged, rough, coarse; hard, severe; difficult. **~s manières,** coarse manners. **un ~ choc,** a terrible shock. **avoir le peau ~,** to have a rough skin. **une tâche ~,** a hard task. **un ~ homme,** a tough, firm man.

rudement *adv.* roughly, harshly, coarsely, severely, hardly. **frapper ~ à une porte,** to knock violently at a door. **parler ~ à quelqu'un,** to speak harshly to a person.

rudesse *n.f.* roughness; coarseness; ruggedness; harshness; unkindness, severity. **la ~ des moeurs,** the coarseness of manners. **la ~ de sa voix,** the harshness of the voice.

rudiment *n.m.* rudiment, element.

rudimentaire *adj.* rudimentary.
rudoyer *v.t.* to bully, to maltreat.
rue *n.f.* street; rue.
ruée *n.f.* rush. **la ~ vers l'or,** the gold rush.
ruelle *n.f.* alley, lane.
ruer *v.t.* to kick. **se ~,** *v.refl.* to rush (upon).
rugby *n.m.* rugby.
rugir *v.i.* to roar; to bellow.
rugissement *n.m.* roar, bellowing.
rugissant, e *adj.* roaring.
rugosité *n.f.* roughness, ruggedness.
rugueux, euse *adj.* rough.
ruine *n.f.* ruin; fall, decay, wreck. **ce palais menace ~,** that palace is falling to ruin. **tomber en ~s,** to fall into ruins.
ruiner *v.t.* to ruin; to destroy; to overthrow, to ravage, to waste, to undo; to spoil. **le jeu l'a ruiné,** gambling ruined him. **~ sa santé,** to ruin one's health. **se ~,** *v.refl.* to ruin, to fall into decay, to decay; to be ruined, to be spoiled, to ruin oneself; to ruin each other.
ruineusement *adv.* ruinously.
ruineux, euse *adj.* tottering, *Fig.* costly, ruinous, wasteful.
ruisseau *n.m.* small stream, brook, rivulet, rill, gutter. **tomber dans le ~,** to fall into the gutter.

ruisselant, e *adj.* streaming; dripping.
ruisseler *v.i.* to stream, to trickle, to drip.
rumeur *n.f.* rumor, murmur, grumbling; hum, uproar. **les ~s de la foule,** the clamor of the crowd.
ruminant, e *adj. n.m.* ruminant.
ruminer *v.t.* to ruminate; to chew the cud; to chew over again, to muse on, to ruminate on.
rupture *n.f.* rupture; fracture, breach; breaking off. **la ~ de la paix,** the rupture of peace. **~ d'un mariage,** breaking up of a marriage.
rural, e *adj.* rural.
ruse *n.f.* artifice, wile, trick, ruse, dodge, craft. **~ de guerre,** stratagem of war.
rusé, e *adj.* artful, crafty, sly, cunning, deep. **avoir l'air ~,** to look cunning.
ruser *v.i.* to double, to use artifice, craft, to dodge.
rustique *adj.* rustic; rural; coarse, rough, unpolished. **un repas ~,** a rustic meal. *n.m.* rustic countryman.
rut *n.m.* rut, rutting, rutting-time, heat.
rutabaga *n.m.* rutabaga.
rutilant, e *adj.* bright red, shining, rutilant.
rythme *n.m.* rhythm.
rythmique *adj.* rhythmical.

S

S *n.f.* sud, south.
sa *adj. poss. n.f.* her, its. V. SON.
sabbat *n.m.* sabbat; sabbath; nocturnal revels (of witches); *Infml.* uproar, row, racket.
sabbatique *adj.* sabbatical.
sable *n.m.* sand. **~ de rivière,** gravel. **~ mouvant,** quicksand. **banc de ~,** sandbank.
sablé, e *adj.* sanded, speckled; shortbread, cookie. **allée ~e,** gravel walk.
sabler *v.t.* to sand, to gravel, *Infml.* to drink off, to toss off, to gulp down.
sablière *n.f.* sand pit; gravel pit.
sablonner *v.t.* to scour with sand.
sablonneux, euse *adj.* sandy.
sabot *n.m.* wooden shoe, sabot, hoof; skid.
sabotage *n.m.* sabotage.
saboter *v.i.* to sabotage.
sabrer *v.t.* to sabre; *Fig.* to hurry over, to patch up.
sac *n.m.* sack; bag; knapsack; sack cloth; pouch, belly; plunder, sacking. **un ~ de cuir,** a leather bag. **un ~ de dame,** a lady's bag. **~ de voyage,** overnight bag. **vider son ~,** to get something off one's chest. **l'affaire est dans le ~,** the deal is in the bag. **mettre une ville à ~,** to sack a town.
saccade *n.f.* jerk; jolt; fit, start.
saccader *v.t.* to jerk.
saccager *v.t.* to ransack, to sack, to pillage, to plunder.
sacerdoce *n.m.* priesthood.
sachet *n.m.* sachet, scent bag, perfume cushion. **thé en ~s,** teabags.

sacoche *n.f.* bag; saddlebag.
sacre *n.m.* consecration (of a bishop), coronation (of a king).
sacré, e *adj.* sacred; consecrated; holy; religious. *Infml.* cursed, damned.
sacrement *n.m.* sacrament. **le saint ~,** the holy sacrament, the sacrament.
sacrément *adv.* terribly. **j'ai eu ~ peur!** I was scared to death!
sacrer *v.t.* to consecrate (a bishop); to crown (a king). *Infml.* to curse, to swear.
sacrifice *n.m.* sacrifice, offering, victim.
sacrifier *v.t.* to sacrifice, to immolate.
sacrilège *n.m.* sacrilege. *adj.* sacrilegious; sacrilegious person.
sacrum *n.m.* sacrum.
sadique *adj.* sadistic. *n.m.f.* sadist.
sadisme *n.m.* sadism.
safari *n.m.* safari.
safran *n.m.* saffron.
saga *n.f.* saga.
sagacité *n.f.* sagacity, acuteness, shrewdness.
sage *adj.* wise; sage; sagacious; judicious, sober, cool, modest, well-behaved, good (of children). **de ~s mesures,** wise measures. **cet enfant est ~,** that child is good. *n.m.* wiseman, sage.
sage-femme *n.f.* midwife.
sagement *adv.* wisely, judiciously, sensibly.
sagesse *n.f.* wisdom, prudence, moderation; good behavior, goodness (of children).
sagittaire *n.m.* archer, Sagittarius.

saignant, e adj. bleeding, bloody, underdone, rare (meat).

saignement n.m. bleeding.

saigner v.i. to bleed, to lose blood, to kill (an animal), to drain; to exhaust, to extort. **~ du nez**, to have a nosebleed. **~ à blanc**, to bleed to death. **se ~**, v.refl. to bleed oneself; to drain oneself.

saillant, e adj. salient; projecting, prominent, striking.

saillie n.f. gush, spurt, projection, prominence.

saillir v.i. to break forth, to gush, to leap, to project, to jut out, to stand out.

sain, e adj. sound, healthy, uninjured, wholesome, sane. Naut. clear. **~ de corps**, healthy in body. **~ et sauf**, safe and sound. **l'exercice est ~**, exercise is healthy. **côte ~e**, clear coast.

saindoux n.m. lard.

sainement adv. soundly, healthily, wholesomely.

saint, e adj. holy; sacred, pious, godly, saintly, saint. **la ~e Bible**, the holy Bible. **la Terre Sante**, the Holy Land. **semaine ~e**, Holy Week, Passion Week. **jeudi ~**, Maundy Thursday. **vendredi ~**, Good Friday. **~ Pierre et ~ Paul**, St. Peter and St. Paul. n.m.f. saint. **il ne sait à quel ~ se vouer**, he does not know which way to turn. **la ~ Jean**, midsummer. **la ~ Michel**, Michaelmas. **il vaut mieux s'adresser à Dieu qu'à ses ~s**, it is better to go straight to headquarters. **script ~ des saints**, holy of holies.

saintement adv. piously.

sainte-nitouche n.f. hypocrite.

sainteté n.f. holiness, sanctity, saintliness, sacredness. **Sa Sainteté** (the pope), His Holiness.

saisir v.t. to seize; to lay hold of, to catch; to grasp; to seize upon; to come upon; to startle; to restrain, to attach; to vest in. **~ l'occasion**, to seize the opportunity. **la peur l'a saisie**, she was struck with fear. **se ~**, v.refl. to grasp each other; to lay hold of, to take possession of; to apprehend, to arrest; to prey upon; to be struck.

saisissable adj. seizable; (of rents).

saisissant, e adj. piercing, chilling; striking, startling.

saisissement n.m. chill; startle; shock.

saison n.f. season; time. **la belle ~**, summer. **morte-~**, dead season. **cela n'est plus de ~**, that is out of season.

salade n.f. salad. **panier à ~**, salad bowl.

saladier n.m. salad bowl.

salaire n.m. salary; pay, wages, hire; reward, recompense.

salarié, e p.p. salaried, hired; paid. n.m.f. employee, wages earner.

salaud, e adj. Infml. bastard.

sale adj. dirty; nasty, filthy, obscene, indent. **avoir les mains ~s**, to have dirty hands. **du linge ~**, dirty laundry.

salé, e adj. salted, salt. **eau ~e**, salt water. **un propos ~**, a coarse remark. **à ce prix, c'est ~**, at that price, it is overcharging. n.m. salt pork. **petit ~**, pickled pork.

salement adv. dirtily, nastily, filthily.

saler v.t. to salt; to season with salt; to cure; to overcharge.

saleté n.f. dirtiness, dirt, nastiness, filthiness.

salière n.f. salt cellar.

saligaud, e n.m.f. filthy pig.

salir v.t. to dirty, to soil; to make filthy, to stain, to tarnish, to sully. **~ ses habits**, to dirty one's clothes. **~ la réputation de quelqu'un**, to sully a person's reputation. **se ~**, v.refl. to dirty oneself; to get soiled.

salissant, e adj. soiling; apt to soil.

salive n.f. saliva, spittle.

saliver v.i. to salivate.

salle n.f. room, hall, ward (in hospitals). **~ à manger**, dining room. **~ d'attente**, waiting room. **~ de bain**, bathroom. **~ de cinéma**, movie theater, cinema. **~ de séjour**, living room. **~ de concert**, concert hall. **~ de spectacle**, auditorium, theater, audience.

salon n.m. living room, lounge, show, exhibition. **~ de coiffure**, hairdressing salon. **~ du prêt-à-porter**, fashion show.

salop, e adj. n.m.f. V. SALAUD.

saloperie n.f. rubbish, trash, junk, dirt, mess. **vous avez fait des ~s partout!** you've trashed the place!

salopette n.f. overalls, coveralls.

salubre adj. healthy.

saluer v.t. to salute, to greet, to wave. **il nous a salués**, he waved at us. **se ~**, v.refl. to salute each other.

salut n.m. salutation, salute, greeting, benediction. **il me rendit mon ~**, he returned my greeting. **~ militaire**, military salute. n.m. safety; salvation. **faire son ~**, to work out one's salvation.

salutaire adj. salutary; wholesome; beneficial, useful.

salutation n.f. salutation; salute; bow; pl. compliments, respects.

samedi n.m. Saturday.

sanctification n.f. sanctification.

sanctifier v.t. to sanctify; to hallow; to consecrate; to keep holy. **se ~**, v.refl. to become pure or holy.

sanction n.f. punishment, sanction; assent; support.

sanctionner v.t. to sanction; to confirm, to penalize.

sanctuaire n.m. sanctuary; refuge.

sandale n.f. sandal.

sandwich n.f. sandwich.

sang n.m. blood; family, kindred; race, breed. **perdre son ~**, to lose one's blood. **suer ~ et eau**, to work hard. **cela glace le ~**, it makes one's blood run cold. **un cheval de pur ~, un pur ~**, a thoroughbred horse.

sang-froid n.m. cool(ness); composure,

temper. **de ~**, cold-blooded, in cold blood.

sanglant, e *adj.* bleeding; bloody; blood-stained.

sangle *n.f.* band, strap; girth (of a saddle).

sangler *v.t.* to bind, to strap, to girth; to lash. **se ~**, *v.refl.* to lash oneself.

sanglier *n.m.* boar, wild boar.

sanglot *n.m.* sob, sobbing. **éclater en ~s**, to burst into tears.

sangloter *v.i.* to sob.

sangsue *n.f.* leech, *Fig.* bloodsucker.

sanguin, e *adj.* blood, blood-red, sanguine.

sanitaire *adj.* sanitary.

sans *prep.* without; but, unless, except; but for, had it not been for, were it not for. **mourir ~ enfants**, to die childless. **~ cet obstacle, nous aurions réussi**, had it not been for that obstacle, we would have succeeded. **~ façon**, without ceremony. **~ faute**, faultless; without fail. **~ crainte**, fearlessly. **~ que personne s'en aperçoive**, without anybody noticing. **~ abri**, *n.m.f.* homeless person.

sans-coeur *n.m.* heartless person.

sans-gêne *n.m.* inconsiderate person.

sans-le-sou *n.m.f.* penniless person, poor person.

sans-souci *n.m.* easy going, carefree person.

santé *n.f.* health, toast. **bonne ~**, good health. **boire à la ~ de quelqu'un**, to drink to a person's health.

saper *v.t.* to sap; to undermine; to subvert.

sapeur *n.m.* **~ pompier**, firefighter.

saphir *n.m.* sapphire.

sapide *adj.* palatable.

sapin *n.m.* fir, fir tree. **~ de Noël**, Christmas tree.

sarcasme *n.m.* sarcasm.

sarcastique *adj.* sarcastic.

sardine *n.f.* sardine.

satanique *adj.* satanic, satanical; diabolical, infernal.

satellite *n.m.* satellite.

satiété *n.f.* satiety; satiation, repletion; fulness.

satin *n.m.* satin. **robe de ~**, satin dress.

satiné, e *adj.* satiny, glossy; soft. *n.m.* gloss.

satire *n.f.* satire.

satirique *adj.* satiric, satirical. *n.m.* satirist.

satisfaction *n.f.* satisfaction; contentment; atonement.

satisfaire *v.t.* to satisfy; to gratify, to please, to content; to indulge, to give satisfaction; to fullfil; to make amends. **~ sa curiosité**, to satisfy one's curiosity. **~ sa vengeance**, to indulge in revenge. **~ aux désirs de quelqu'un**, to gratify a person's desires. **~ à ses obligations**, to fulfill one's obligations. **se ~**, *v.refl.* to satisfy, to gratify oneself; to be satisfied, to be appeased.

satisfaisant, e *adj.* satisfactory.

satisfait, e *p.p.* satisfied; gratified. *adj.* pleased, gratified.

saturation *n.f.* saturation.

saturer *v.t.* to saturate; to satiate. **se ~**, *v.refl.* to get saturated.

saturne *n.m.* Saturn.

satyre *n.m.* lecher.

sauce *n.f.* sauce, gravy. **~ piquante**, spicy sauce.

saucisse *n.f.* sausage.

saucisson *n.m.* dry sausage.

sauf, sauve *adj.* safe, unhurt; secure, except, excepting; excepted; but. **~ erreurs**, errors excepted.

sauf-conduit *n.m.* safe conduct.

sauge *n.f.* sage.

saugrenu, e *adj.* absurd, preposterous, ridiculous.

saule *n.m.* willow. **~ pleureur**, weeping willow.

saumon *n.m.* salmon; salmon color.

saupoudrer *v.t.* to dredge; to sprinkle, to powder.

saut *n.m.* leap, jump, skip. **~ périlleux**, somersault. **au ~ du lit**, on first getting up, on leaving one's bed.

sauter *v.i.* to leap, to jump; to spring; to vault; to bound; to skip, to hop, to pop out, to fly out, to blow up, to explode. **~ sur un pied**, to hop. **~ de joie**, to jump for joy. **~ en selle**, to spring into the saddle. **~ aux yeux**, to be very evident. **faire ~**, to make (a person) jump; to blow up, to blow out. **faire ~ la banque**, to break the bank. **~ un fossé**, to clear a ditch.

sauterelle *n.f.* grasshopper, locust.

sauteur, euse *n.m.f.* leaper, jumper. *n.f.* **sauteuse**, *Culin.* fryer.

sautillant, e *adj.* skipping, hopping.

sautillement *n.m.* skipping, hopping.

sautiller *v.i.* to skip; to hop.

sauvage *adj.* wild, savage; fierce, barbarous; rude; shy. **des animaux ~s**, wild beasts. **un site ~**, a wild area. **un enfant ~**, an unsociable child. *n.m.f.* savage; unsociable person.

sauvagement *adv.* wildly; unsociably.

sauvagerie *n.f.* savagery, brutality, savageness, unsociableness, shyness.

sauvegarde *n.f.* safeguard, safe-keeping, protection; shield.

sauvegarder *v.t.* to safeguard; to shield.

sauve-qui-peut *n.m.* run-for-your-life!

sauver *v.t.* to save, to rescue; to keep, to spare; to conceal. **~ la vie à quelqu'un**, to save a person's life. **~ les apparances**, to save face. **se ~**, *v.refl.* to save oneself; to escape; to be saved; to flee. **se ~ de prison**, to get out of prison. **se ~ à toutes jambes**, to run away as fast as one can.

sauvetage *n.m.* saving; salvage; rescuing, rescue. **bateau de ~**, lifeboat. **bouée de ~**, life preserver.

sauveteur *n.m.* rescuer.

sauvette (à la) *n.f.* hastily, quickly, hurriedly.

sauveur *n.m.* saver; deliverer; Saviour.

savant, e *adj.* learned; erudite. *n.m.f.* scientist; scholar.

saveur *n.f.* savor; taste, flavor, zest. **sans ~**, tasteless.

savoir *v.t.* to know; to be aware of; to have a knowledge of; to know how. **il ne sait rien,** he knows nothing. **qu'en sait-on?** what do we know about it? **reste à ~ si ...,** it remains to be seen if ... **~ la grammaire,** to know grammar. **~ jouer de violon,** to know how to play the violin. **sait-il écrire?** can he write? **je ne sais que faire,** I don't know what to do. **que je sache,** as far as I know, for all I know. **se ~,** *v.refl.* to be known. **tout se sait tôt ou tard,** the truth is sure to come out. *n.m.* knowledge, learning. **acquérir un grand ~,** to acquire great knowledge.

savoir-faire *n.m.* skill, tact, dexterity; management; wits.

savoir-vivre *n.m.* polished manners.

savon *n.m.* soap, lecture. **passer un ~ à quelqu'un,** to lecture, to scold a person.

savonner *v.t.* to soap, to wash (with soap); to lather (for shaving); *Infml.* to lecture, to reprimand, to rebuke, to scold. **se ~,** *v.refl.* to wash.

savonneux, euse *adj.* soapy.

savourer *v.t.* to savor, to relish, to enjoy; to take delight in.

savoureux, euse *adj.* savory; pleasing to the taste; relishing.

saxophone *n.m.* saxophone.

scabreux, euse *adj.* indecent, shocking.

scalp *n.m.* scalp.

scalpel *n.m.* scalpel.

scalper *v.t.* to scalp.

scandale *n.m.* scandal; disgrace; shame; exposure; slander.

scandaleusement *adv.* scandalously; shamefully.

scandaleux, euse *adj.* scandalous; shameful; disgraceful.

scandaliser *v.t.* to scandalize; to offend, to give offence, to shock. **se ~,** *v.refl.* to be scandalized; to be shocked.

sceau *n.m.* seal, *pl.* seals of the State; stamp, impress. **apposer son ~,** to affix one's seal.

sceller *v.t.* to seal; to seal up, to ratify.

scénario *n.m.* scenario, script, screenplay.

scénariste *n.m.f.* screenwriter, scriptwriter.

scène *n.f.* scene; *Theat.* stage; scenery. **faire une ~ à quelqu'un,** to have a scene with a person. **mettre sur la ~,** to represent on the stage.

scénique *adj.* scenic, theatrical, dramatic.

scepticisme *n.m.* scepticism.

sceptique *adj.* sceptic, sceptical. *n.m.* sceptic.

sceptre *n.m.* sceptre; ensign of royalty; royal power; sovereign authority; sway, dominion, superiority.

schéma *n.m.* outline, diagram, scheme, sketch.

schizophrène *n.m.f.* schizophrenic.

schizophrénie *n.f.* schizophrenia.

schnaps *n.m. Infml.* booze, schnapps.

scie *n.f.* saw, buzz saw; sawfish; *Infml.* bore, tiresome thing. **~ circulaire,** circular. **~ à main,** band saw.

sciemment *adv.* knowingly, wittingly.

science *n.f.* science, knowledge, learning.
~-fiction, science fiction, sci-fi.

scientifique *adj.* scientific. *n.m.f.* scientist.

scientifiquement *adv.* scientifically.

scientiste *adj.* Christian Scientist.

scier *v.t.* to saw, to cut down, to reap (corn); to take one's breath away, to stagger, to astonish. **~ le dos à quelqu'un,** to bore a person.

scierie *n.f.* sawmill.

scintillant, e *adj.* scintillating, sparkling.

scintillement *n.m.* sparkling, twinkling, glittering, scintillation.

scintiller *v.i.* to twinkle, to scintillate, to sparkle, to glitter.

sclérose *n.f.* sclerosis.

scolaire *adj.* school; academic. **année ~,** academic year.

scolarité *n.f.* schooling, school attendance.

scolastique *adj.* scholastic, school. *n.f.* scholasticism. *n.m.* scholastic.

scoop *n.m.* scoop.

score *n.m.* score.

scorpion *n.m.* scorpion.

scotch *n.m.* Scotch whiskey.

scotcher *v.t.* to tape.

scout *n.m.* scout, Boy Scout.

script *n.m.* movie script; printing; *n.m.f.* continuity person.

scrupule *n.m.* scruple; scrupulousness; doubt, difficulty.

scrupuleusement *adv.* scrupulously.

scrupuleux, euse *adj.* scrupulous.

scruter *v.t.* to scrutinize; to search closely, to pry into.

scrutin *n.m.* ballot, balloting, poll.

sculpter *v.t.* to sculpt, to sculpture, to carve, to engrave.

sculpteur *n.m.* sculptor. **femme ~,** sculptress.

sculpture *n.f.* sculpture, carving.

se *pers. pron.* oneself; himself, herself, itself; themselves, one another. **il s'est fait mal,** he hurt himself. **elles ~ sont embrassées,** they kissed each other.

séance *n.f.* seat; sitting; meeting; session. **~ tenante,** forthwith. **la ~ est ouverte,** the meeting is open. **suspendre la ~,** to adjourn the meeting.

séant, e *adj.* becoming, seemly, proper, fitting.

séau *n.m.* pail, bucket.

sec, sèche *adj.* dry; dried; severe; sharp; cold unfeeling; straight. **la terre est sèche,** the earth is dry. **du bois ~,** dry wood. **avoir une toux sèche,** to have a dry cough. **d'un oeil ~,** with tearless eyes. **vin ~,** dry wine. **répondre d'un ton ~,** to answer coldly. **perte sèche,** dead loss. **un coup ~,** a hard blow. *adv.* sharply, harshly; hard. **boire ~,** to drink wine straight; to drink hard. **faire cul sec,** to drink straight up. **net voyage à ~,** dry cleaning. **à ~,** dry; without water. **la rivière est à ~,** the river is

dried up. **être à ~,** to be hard up; to want money.
séchage *n.m.* drying.
séché, e *p.p.* dried.
sèchement *adv.* dryly; coldly, frigidly; sharply, harshly, severely; plainly, barrenly. **je lui ai écrit fort ~,** I wrote a very cold letter to him/her.
sécher *v.t.* to dry, to dry up, to wither. **se ~,** *v.refl.* to dry oneself; to dry, to dry up; to become dry.
sèche-cheveux, hair drier. **sèche-linge,** drier.
sécheresse *n.f.* dryness; drought; bluntness, abruptness; harshness.
second, e *adj.* second. *n.m.* second; assistant; backer; second floor; *Naut.* mate. **il demeure au ~,** he lives on the second floor.
secondaire *adj.* secondary. **enseignement ~,** high school education.
seconde *n.f.* eleventh grade.
seconder *v.t.* to second, to support, to back up.
secouer *v.t.* to shake, to agitate; to toss; to throw off. **~ la tête,** to shake one's head. **cette maladie l'a bien secoué,** that illness has weakened him very much. **~ la poussière,** to shake off the dust. **~ sa paresse,** to shake of one's idleness. **se ~,** *v.refl.* to shake, to rouse oneself.
secourable *adj.* helpful, helping.
secourir *v.t.* to help, to aid, to assist, to relieve.
secourisme *n.m.* first aid.
secouriste *n.m.f.* first-aid worker.
secours *n.m.* help, aid; relief, spare. **demander du ~,** to ask for help. **au ~!** help! help! **roue de ~,** spare tire.
secousse *n.f.* tremor, shake, shaking, agitation, concussion; shock; jerk; toss, tossing.
secret, ète *adj.* secret; hidden, concealed; occult; private. **sciences ~s,** occult sciences. **un escalier ~,** private staircase. *n.m.* secret; secrecy, privacy. **garder un ~,** to keep a secret. **c'est mon ~,** that is my secret. **en ~,** in secret, in secrecy.
secrétaire *n.m.* secretary; clerk; writing desk, bureau. **~ d'ambassade,** secretary to an embassy. **~ particulier,** private secretary.
secrétariat *n.m.* secretaryship; secretary's office.
secrètement *adv.* secretly, in secret, privately, in private.
sécréter *v.t.* to secrete.
sécrétion *n.f.* secretion; the matter secreted.
sectaire *n.m.* sectarian. *adj.* sectarian.
secte *n.f.* sect.
secteur *n.m.* sector; area, zone.
section *n.f.* section; platoon.
sectionnement *n.m.* division.
sectionner *v.t.* to cut, to divide; to form into sections.
séculaire *adj.* secular, centenarian (of a century).
sécurisant *adj.* reassuring.
sécurité *n.f.* security, secureness; confidence. **~ sociale,** social security.
sédatif, ive *adj. n.m.* sedative.
sédentaire *adj.* sedentary; stationary.

sédentariser *v.t.* to settle; to make a thing settle.
sédiment *n.m.* sediment, settlings, deposit.
sédimentaire *adj.* sedimentary.
séditieux, euse *adj.* seditious; mutinous, rebellious, riotous. *n.m.* rebel.
sédition *n.f.* sedition; mutiny, riot.
séducteur, trice *n.m.f.* seducer; enticer, deluder. *n.m.* seducer; womanizer. *adj.* seducing, seductive, enticing.
séduction *n.f.* seduction, seducement; enticement, appeal.
séduire *v.t.* to seduce, to charm, to attract, to captivate, to fascinate.
séduisant, e *adj.* seductive; alluring, tempting; charming.
segment *n.m.* segment.
ségrégation *n.f.* segregation.
seigle *n.m.* rye.
seigneur *n.m.* lord. **Notre Seigneur,** Our Lord. **à tout ~, tout honneur,** honor to whom honor is due.
sein *n.m.* bosom; breast; womb; midst, heart. **le ~ de l'Église,** the bosom of the Church. **le ~ de la terre,** the bosom of the earth. **donner le ~ à un enfant,** to breastfeed a child. **porter en son ~,** to carry in the womb.
seize *adj.* and *n.m.* sixteen, sixteenth. **le ~ juillet,** the sixteenth of July.
seizième *adj.* and *n.m.* sixteenth; sixteenth day.
séjour *n.m.* stay, sojourn; abode, dwelling, habitation. **salle de ~,** living room.
séjourner *v.i.* to sojourn; to abide; to stay; to remain, to continue.
sel *n.m.* salt; *Fig.* wit, piquancy, smartness.
sélect *adj. Infml.* high class, exclusive.
sélection *n.f.* selection.
sélectionner *v.t.* to choose, to select.
self *n.m.* **~-service,** self-service restaurant, cafeteria.
selle *n.f.* saddle; stool (of the bowels). **être bien en ~,** to sit well in one's saddle; to be firmly seated. **aller à la ~,** to move one's bowels.
seller *v.t.* to saddle.
selon *prep.* according to. **~ moi,** in my opinion. **c'est ~,** that all depends. **~ que,** *conj.* as.
semaine *n.f.* week; week's time. **la ~ prochaine,** next week.
semblable *adj.* like, resembling, similar, alike; such. *n.m.* similar thing; fellow creature; fellow, like.
semblablement *adv.* likewise, too; similarly.
semblance *n.f.* resemblance, likeness, semblance.
semblant, e *n.m.* appearance, semblance; show; pretence, mask. **un ~ d'amitié,** an appearance of friendship. **faire ~,** to pretend, to feign. **ne faire ~ de rien,** to appear to take no notice.
sembler *v.i.* to appear, to seem; to look. **il me semble qu'il n'y a rien de mieux à faire,** I don't think there is anything better to do. **faites comme bon vous semblera,**

do just as you think proper, do as you wish.

semelle *n.f.* sole (of shoes). **battre la ~,** to beat the hoof, to tramp. **ne pas reculer d'une ~,** not to move an inch.

semence *n.f.* seed; semen.

semer *v.t.* to show, to scatter, to strew, to spread, to spread abroad, to disseminate. **~ du blé,** to sow wheat. **~ la terreur,** to spread terror. **~ la discorde,** to sow discord. **il faut ~ pour recueillir,** we must sow to reap.

semestre *n.m.* semester, half-year, six months.

semestriel, elle *adj.* half-yearly, semiannual.

semi *prefix.* semi, half, demi.

semi-automatique *adj.* semiautomatic.

semi-circulaire *adj.* semicircular.

séminaire *n.m.* seminary; seminar, training center.

sémiologie *n.f.* semiology.

sémiologique *adj.* semiological.

semiotique *adj.* semiotic.

semi-remorque *n.f.* trailer.

sénat *n.m.* senate.

sénateur *n.m.* senator.

sénatorial, e *adj.* senatorial.

sénile *adj.* senile.

sénilité *n.f.* senility.

sens *n.m.* sense; meaning; direction. **les cinq ~,** the five senses. **le bon ~,** good sense. **perdre le ~,** to lose one's wits. **~ commun,** common sense. **~ propre,** proper meaning. **~ figuré,** figurative sense. **à mon ~,** in my opinion. **aller en ~ contraire,** to go in the opposite direction. **~ desus dessous,** upside-down. **~ interdit,** no entry. **~ unique,** one-way.

sensation *n.f.* sensation. **faire ~,** to create excitement, a sensation.

sensationnel, le *adj.* terrific, fantastic.

sensé, e *adj.* sensible, judicious.

sensément *adv.* sensibly.

sensibilisation *n.f.* sensitization, sensitizing.

sensibiliser *v.t.* to sensitize.

sensibilité *n.f.* oversensitivity; sensitiveness; tenderness, feeling.

sensible *adj.* sensitive; feeling, painful, acute, perceptible. **une oreille ~,** a quick ear. **c'est son endroit ~,** it is his sensitive part.

sensiblement *adv.* perceptibly; feelingly; greatly, much; approximately.

sensitif, ive *adj.* sensitive; sensory.

sensualité *n.f.* sensuality.

sensuel, elle *adj.* sensual.

sensuellement *adv.* sensually.

sentence *n.f.* sentence; maxim; judgment; decision. **prononcer une ~,** to pass sentence, to sentence.

senteur *n.f.* scent; odor; perfume. **pois de ~,** sweet pea.

sentier *n.m.* path, footpath.

sentiment *n.m.* feeling, perception; sensation; sense; sensiblity; opinion. **un ~ douloureux,** a painful sensation. **juger par ~,** to judge from

the heart. **au ~ de beaucoup de gens,** according to many people's opinion. **veuillez agréer, Monsieur, Madame, l'expression de mes ~s distingués,** yours faithfully, sincerely. **mes meilleurs ~s,** best wishes.

sentimental, e *adj.* sentimental.

sentimentalement *adv.* sentimentally.

sentimentalité *n.f.* sentimentality.

sentinelle *n.f.* guard, sentry; sentinel. *Infml.* **faire la ~,** to be on the lookout.

sentir *v.t.* to feel; to perceive, to smell; to taste; to have a taste of. **~ le froid,** to feel the cold. **~ la soif,** to feel, to be thirsty. **~ une rose,** to smell a rose. **~ de loin,** to perceive, to smell out. **ça sent la pluie,** it looks/feels like rain. **cela sent bon,** that smells good. **cette viande commence à ~,** that meat begins to smell. **se ~,** *v.refl.* to be felt; to feel oneself, to feel.

séparable *adj.* separable.

séparation *n.f.* separation; parting; severing; partition. **~ de corps,** judicial separation.

séparément *adv.* separately; apart; distinctly.

séparer *v.t.* to separate; to set apart; to part, to sever. **le mur qui sépare ces deux maisons,** the wall that divides these two houses. **se ~,** *v.refl.* to separate; to be separated, to be divided; to part; to break up.

sept *adj., n.m.* seven; seventh.

septembre *n.m.* september.

septième *adj., n.m.* seventh. **le ~ du mois,** the seventh of the month.

septièmement *adv.* seventhly.

septique *adj.* septic.

sépulcre *n.m.* sepulcher, grave, tomb; monument.

sépulture *n.f.* sepulture, burial; tomb, vault.

séquelle *n.f.* aftermath, consequences.

séquence *n.f.* sequence.

séquestration *n.f.* sequestration.

séquestre *n.m.* sequestration; confinement, detention, deposit. **mettre en ~,** to sequester.

séquestrer *v.t.* to sequester; to sequestrate; to put away. **se ~,** *v.refl.* to sequester oneself.

serein, e *adj.* serene. *n.m.* evening dew.

sereinement *adv.* calmly, serenely.

sérénade *n.f.* serenade. **donner une ~,** to serenade.

sérénité *n.f.* serenity.

sergent *n.m.* sergeant. **~ major,** sergeantmajor.

série *n.f.* series, succession. **~ noire,** a succession of disasters, one disaster after another, crime thriller book.

sérieusement *adv.* seriously.

sérieux, euse *adj.* serious; grave, solemn, earnest; important. **une maladie sérieuse,** a serious illness. **un poste ~,** an important post. *n.m.* seriousness, earnestness. **garder son ~,** to keep a straight face. **prendre au ~,** to take a thing seriously.

serin, e *n.m.f.* canary.

seriner *v.t. Infml.* to repeat over and over again to.

seringue *n.f.* syringe.

serment *n.m.* oath, swearing. **prêter ~,** to take oath, to be sworn.

sermon *n.m.* sermon, lecture.

sermonner *v.t. Infml.* to lecture.

serpent *n.m.* serpent; snake. **~ à sonnettes,** rattlesnake.

serpenter *v.i.* to wind, to meander.

serre *n.f.* greenhouse; pressure, pressing; *Infml.* grasp, grip; (of birds of prey) talon.

serrement *n.m.* pressing, pressure; squeezing, squeeze. **~ de main,** handshake. **~ de coeur,** anguish of heart.

serrer *v.t.* to tighten; to tie; to fasten; to press; to squeeze; to hug, to embrace; to clasp; to clench (the fist). **~ de près quelqu'un,** to be at a person's heels. **cela serre le coeur,** that is heartrending. **~ les rangs,** to close ranks. **se ~,** *v.refl.* to crowd one another, to press close; to sit close; to lace in (the waist); to grow tighter. **se ~ la ceinture,** to tighten one's belt. **se ~ les coudes,** to stick together, to back each other up.

serre-tête *n.m.* headband.

serrure *n.f.* lock. **~ de sûreté,** safety lock.

serrurier *n.m.* locksmith.

sertir *v.t.* to set (jewelry).

sérum *n.m.* serum.

servant *adj., n.m.* serving; in waiting. **frère ~,** lay brother. *n.m.* gunner.

servante *n.f.* servant, maid; *Fig.* handmaid.

serveur, euse *n.f.* bartender; server; waiter/waitress.

serviable *adj.* helpful; obliging.

service *n.m.* service; charge, tip; set; office; duty; operation. **tout à votre ~,** at your service. **rendre un ~ à quelqu'un,** to return a favor. **~ à thé,** tea set. *Mil.* military service. **~ après vente,** after-sale service.

serviette *n.f.* napkin; towel. **~ d'avocat,** briefcase.

servile *adj.* servile; slavish.

servir *v.t.* to serve; to attend, to wait (on), to assist the priest at; to aid, to help; to contribute to, to conduce; to be of use. **se faire ~,** to be waited upon. **~ un gigot,** to serve a leg of mutton. **~ de jouet à quelqu'un,** to serve as a person's plaything. **à quoi lui sert-il de pleurer?** what is the use of crying? **à quoi sert-il de vous écouter?** what use is it listening to you? **se ~,** *v.refl.* to serve oneself; to help oneself; to be served; to avail oneself of, to profit by; to have. **servez-vous,** help yourself. **se ~ de béguilles,** to use crutches.

serviteur *n.m.* servant.

servitude *n.f.* servitude.

ses *adj. poss. pl.* of son, sa. V. son.

session *n.f.* session; sitting.

seuil *n.m.* threshold; doorstep.

seul, e *adj.* alone; single; by oneself, lonely. **~ dans sa chambre,** alone in one's room. **pas une ~e maison,** not a single house. **la seule raison qu'un puisse donner,** the only reason one can give. **il l'a fait tout ~,** he did it on his own.

seulement *adv.* only; solely, simply, merely. **je vais au spectacle ~ pour la musique,** I only go to the theater for the sake of the music. **non ~,** not only.

sève *n.f.* sap, strength (of wine); *Fig.* vigor, strength, pith.

sévère *adj.* severe; rigid, harsh, stern, strict, grave. **une panition ~,** a severe punishment.

sévèrement *adv.* severely; harshly, sternly; gravely.

sévérité *n.f.* severity; sternness; austerity; strictness; inclemency; extremity.

sévices *n.m.pl.* cruelty.

sévir *v.i.* to proceed with rigor; to act ruthlessly; to rage.

sevrage *n.m.* weaning.

sevrer *v.t.* to wean (a child), to sever. **se ~,** *v.refl.* to wean oneself; to withdraw (from).

sexe *n.m.* sex; sex organ; genitals. **le beau ~, le ~,** fair sex, the sex.

sexualité *n.f.* sexuality.

sexuel, elle *adj.* sexual.

sexy *adj.* sexy.

shampooing *n.m.* shampoo.

shampouiner *v.t.* to shampoo.

shérif *n.m.* sheriff.

shoot *n.m.* shot.

shooter *v.t.* to shoot. **se ~,** *Infml.* to fix, to shoot up drugs.

short *n.m.* shorts.

show *n.m.* show. **~-business,** show business, showbiz.

si *conj.* if; allowing that; provided; whether. **s'il venait, il me ferait plaisir,** I'd be pleased if he came. **~ ce n'est,** if not; except; but; but for. *adv.* so, in such a manner; so much; such; however; yes, truly. **un homme ~ honnête,** such an honest man. **je ne suis pas ~ riche,** I am not so rich. **vous dites que non, je dis que ~,** you say no, I say yes. *n.m. Mus.* si, B.

siamois, e *adj., n.m.f.* Siamese.

sidérant, e *adj.* stunning, amazing.

sidérer *v.t.* to stun, to amaze.

siècle *n.m.* century; age; period; epoch, era. **au dernier ~,** in the last century. **de ~ en ~,** from age to age.

siège *n.m.* seat; bench; central office; siege. **~ rustique,** rustic seat. **le ~ du gouvernement,** the government's headquarters. **~ épiscopal,** episcopal see. **lever le ~,** to raise the siege. **état de ~,** martial law.

siéger *v.i.* (of a bishop) to hold one's see; (of courts of justice, assemblies, etc.) to sit, to be seated.

sien, ienne *adj. poss.* his, hers, its, one's own. *n.m.* one's own, his own, her own. **mettre du ~,** to contribute. *n.m.pl.* one's, his, her family, relations, kindred; one's friends; one's people. **il a soin des ~s,** he takes care of his family. **on n'est jamais trahi que par les ~s,** it is always our best friends who betray us. *n.f.pl. Infml.* pranks, tricks. **faire des siennes,** to play tricks.

sieste *n.f.* nap, siesta.

sifflement *n.m.* whistling, whistle; hissing, hiss, wheezing; (of arrows) whiz, hissing.

siffler *v.i.* to whistle; to hiss; to boo. **~ un chien,** to whistle to a dog. **~ une pièce,** to boo a play.

sifflet *n.m.* whistle; hiss; catcall. **donner un coup de ~,** to whistle. **couper le ~ à quelqu'un,** to confound a person.

signal *n.m.* signal; sign.

signalement *n.m.* description.

signaler *v.t.* to describe (a person); to point out, to mark out; to bring to notice; to signal, to post (computer). **se ~,** *v.refl.* to stand out.

signataire *n.m.f.* signer, subscriber.

signature *n.f.* signing; signature.

signe *n.m.* sign; token, mark; indication; omen. **ceci est un mauvais ~,** this is a bad sign. **un ~ de tête,** a nod.

signer *v.i.* to sign; to mark. **~ son nom,** to sign one's name. **se ~,** *v.refl.* to cross oneself, to make the sign of the cross.

signification *n.f.* signification; import, sense, significance, legal notice.

signifier *v.t.* to signify; to denote; to mean, to notify, to intimate; to bring to serve (a notice).

silence *n.m.* silence, stillness. **rompre le ~,** to break the silence. **garder le ~,** to remain silent. **passer une chose sous ~,** to pass a thing over in silence.

silencieusement *adv.* silently.

silencieux, euse *adj.* silent.

silhouette *n.f.* silhouette, outline; figure.

sillage *n.m.* speed; wake of ship, track, trail.

sillon *n.m.* furrow; ridge; track, trail; wake. **tracer un ~,** to plow a furrow.

sillonner *v.t.* to furrow; to ridge; to cut; to groove.

simagrée *n.f.* grimace; *pl.* affectation.

similaire *adj.* similar.

similarité *n.f.* similarity.

similitude *n.f.* similitude, likeness, resemblance, similarity; simile, comparison.

simple *adj.* simple; single; only; mere, bare; plain; easy; silly, credulous. **une allée simple, s'il vous plaît,** a one-way ticket, please. **c'est tout ~,** it is quite simple. *n.m.* silly person, simpleton.

simplement *adv.* simply, only, solely, merely.

simplicité *n.f.* simplicity, naturalness; simpleness.

simplification *n.f.* simplification.

simplifier *v.t.* to simplify. **se ~,** *v.refl.* to become simplified, to be simplified.

simulation *n.f.* simulation, feigning, feint.

simuler *v.t.* to simulate, to feign.

simultané, e *adj.* simultaneous.

simultanément *adv.* simultaneously; together.

sincère *adj.* sincere; candid, open.

sincèrement *adv.* sincerely, unfeignedly.

sincérité *n.f.* sincerity.

singe *n.m.* monkey; ape, baboon; imitator. **payer en monnaie de ~,** to sweet talk a person instead of paying him/her. *adj.* apish, aping, mimicking.

singer *v.t.* to ape, to mimic.

singerie *n.f.* antics; monkey business; mimicry. **faire des ~s,** to play silly tricks.

singularité *n.f.* singularity; peculiarity; oddity, oddness.

singulier, ière *adj.* singular; particular, odd, strange. *n.m.* singular number.

singulièrement *adv.* singularly; particularly; strangely.

sinistre *adj.* sinister; inauspicious; unfavorable. *n.m.* disaster, catastrophe, damage; loss (by fire, shipwreck, etc.).

sinistrement *adv.* sinisterly, perversely.

sinon *conj.* otherwise, else, or else, if not; except, but, unless. **je ne sais rien, ~ qu'il a été tué,** I know nothing, except that he was killed.

sinueux, euse *adj.* sinuous, winding; meandering.

sinuosité *n.f.* sinuosity; winding.

sinus *n.m.* sine; sinus.

siphonné, e *adj.* loony, nuts.

sirène *n.f.* siren, mermaid.

sirop *n.m.* syrup.

siroter *v.i.* to sip.

site *n.m.* site, situation, spot, setting, landscape.

sitôt *adv.* so soon; as soon. **~ que,** as soon as.

situation *n.f.* situation; position, state.

situer *v.t.* to seat; to place.

six *adj.* six; sixth. *n.m.* six; sixth day, sixth. **le ~ janvier,** the sixth of January.

sixième *adj.* sixth. *n.m.* sixth; the sixth part. *n.f.* sixth grade; sequence of six cards.

ski *n.m.* ski, skiing. **~ nautique,** water skiing.

skier *v.i.* to ski.

skieur, ieuse *n.m.f.* skier.

slalom *n.m.* slalom.

slip *n.m.* briefs, underwear, underpants, trunks.

smic *n.m.* minimum (legal) wage.

smoking *n.m.* tuxedo, dinner jacket.

snob *n.m.f.* snob.

sobre *adj.* temperate; sober, abstemious; sparing.

sobrement *adv.* temperately; soberly; abstemiously; frugally; moderately; sparingly.

sobriété *n.f.* temperance; sobriety, soberness; abstemiousness; moderation.

sobriquet *n.m.* nickname.

sociable *adj.* sociable, social.

social, e *adj.* social.

socialement *adv.* socially.

société *n.f.* society; company; partnership; fellowship. **~ par actions,** incorporated company. **dissoudre une ~,** to dissolve partnership. **~ anonyme,** public company.

sociologie *n.f.* sociology.

socle *n.m.* socle; plinth; pedestal.

soda *n.m.* soda.

sodium *n.m.* sodium.

soeur *n.f.* sister, nun. **~s jumelles,** twin sisters.

sofa *n.m.* sofa.

soi *pers. pron. n.f.* self, oneself, himself, herself, it, itself. **chez ~,** at one's own house; in one's own country. **on n'est bien que chez ~,** there is no place like home. **n'avoir pas d'argent sur ~,** to be carrying no money (on oneself). **soi-même,** oneself, self. **se louer ~,** to praise oneself. **un ami est un autre ~,** a friend is a second self.

soi-disant *adv.* so called.

soie *n.f.* silk; bristle (of swine); tang (of a knife). **~ grège,** raw silk. **~ torse,** twisted silk.

soif *n.f.* thirst. **avoir ~,** to be thirsty. **il faut garder une poire pour la ~,** we must put something away for a rainy day.

soigner *v.t.* to take care of; to look after; to do, to execute with care; to nurse, to tend (a child, a patient); (of a doctor) to attend. **c'est ce médecin qui l'a soigné,** that is the doctor who attended him. **se ~,** *v.refl.* to take care of oneself.

soigneusement *adv.* carefully, with care.

soigneux, euse *adj.* careful; attentive; mindful.

soin *n.m.* care; attention; attendance (to the sick). **prendre ~ de sa santé,** to take care of one's health. **avoir ~ de quelqu'un,** to take care of a person. **~ paternel,** paternal care. **donner des soins à malade,** to attend a patient.

soir *n.m.* evening; afternoon; eve. **depuis le matin jusqu'au ~,** from morning till night. **hier au ~, hier ~,** yesterday evening. **le ~ de la vie,** the decline of life.

soirée *n.f.* evening; evening party, soirée. **une belle ~,** a beautiful evening. **aller en ~,** to go to an evening party.

soit *adv.* be it so, so let it be, let it be so. *conj.* say; supposing; namely; either; whether. **~ que l'on parle, ~ que l'on écoute,** whether speaking or listening.

soixantaine *n.f.* about sixty; threescore; sixty years of age.

soixante *adj.* sixty. **~ dix,** seventy. **page ~,** sixtieth page. *n.m.* sixty.

sol *n.m.* ground; soil. *Mus.* G, sol. **la clef de ~,** the G clef.

solaire *adj.* solar. **système ~,** solar system.

soldat *n.m.* soldier. **simple ~,** private.

solde *n.f.* pay (of soldiers), payment. **demi-~,** half pay. *n.m.* sale, final settling; balance; discharge; job lot (of goods). **pour ~ de compte,** in full settlement.

solder *v.t.* to pay; to settle, to liquidate (an account); to pay; to balance. **se ~,** *v.refl.* to be settled; to be balanced.

sole *n.f.* sole; groundplate.

soleil *n.m.* sun; sunshine; sunflower; monstrance. **le ~ se lève,** the sun rises. **le ~ levant,** the rising sun; sunrise. **coucher du ~,** sunset. **avoir place au ~,** to live. **se chauffer au ~,** to warm oneself in the sun.

solennel, elle *adj.* solemn; pompous; important.

solennité *n.f.* solemnity; seriousness, solemness.

solidaire *adj.* liable, responsible; interdependent.

soldiarement *adv.* jointly.

solidarité *n.f.* joint responsibility or liability; solidarity; joint interest; fellowship.

solide *adj.* solid; firm; robust; weighty; substantial. **corps ~,** solid body. **un terrain ~,** firm ground. *n.m.* solid; reality.

solidement *adv.* solidly, densely, firmly.

solidifier *v.t.* to solidify. **se ~,** *v.refl.* to become solid.

solidité *n.f.* solidity; firmness, soundness, strength, reality.

solitaire *adj.* solitary; lonely, lonesome. *n.m.* solitary; solitaire, recluse. *Jewel.* a diamond.

solitude *n.f.* loneliness.

sollicitation *n.f.* solicitation; excitement; earnest request; entreaty.

solliciter *v.t.* to solicit; to entreat, to implore; to beseech. **~ les bons offices de quelqu'un,** to solicit a person's help.

soluble *adj.* solvable; soluble.

solution *n.f.* solution; dissolution; discharge, release.

sombre *adj.* dark; somber; obscure, dim, gloomy; dull. **le temps est ~,** the weather is dull. **des reflexions ~s,** gloomy thoughts. *n.m.* darkness, obscurity; sadness, gloominess.

sombrement *adv.* gloomily, somberly, sadly.

sombrer *v.i.* to founder, to sink.

sommaire *adj.* summary, brief. *n.m.* summary, abstract, epitome.

sommation *n.f.* summons; writ; process; summation.

somme *n.f.* sum; amount. **la ~ totale est,** the total amount is. **~ toute, en ~,** on the whole, after all; in short. *n.m.* sleep; nap. **faire un ~,** to take a nap.

sommeil *n.m.* sleep; sleeping; inactivity. **durant le ~,** while sleeping. **~ léger,** light sleep. **un ~ de mort,** a sound sleep. **avoir ~,** to be sleepy. **tomber de ~,** to be ready to drop. **accablé de ~,** overcome with sleep.

sommeiller *v.i.* to nap, to doze.

sommer *v.t.* to summon; to call upon; to demand the surrender of; *Math.* to sum up, to sum.

sommet *n.m.* summit; top, apex, height; zenith; acme; crown (of the head).

sommier *n.m.* boxspring.

somnambule *n.m.f.* somnambulist, sleepwalker. *adj.* somnambulic, sleepwalking.

somnifère *adj.* narcotic, soporific, soporiferous. *n.m.* sleeping pill.

somnolence *n.f.* sleepiness, drowsiness; inertia.

somnolent, e *adj.* somnolent, sleepy.

somptueusement *adv.* sumptuously.

somptueux, euse *adj.* sumptuous; splendid.

son *adj. poss. n.m.* his, her, its; one's. ~ **père**, his, her father. *n.m.* bran (of wheat, etc.); sound. **le ~ des cloches**, the sound, ringing of bells.

sondage *n.m.* survey, poll, sounding; *Min.* boring.

sonder *v.t.* to sound; to fathom; to probe; to bore (the ground); to taste (cheese, etc.). **~ quelqu'un**, to sound a person. **~ le terrain**, *Fig.* to feel one's way.

songe *n.m.* dream; illusion.

songer *v.i.* to dream; to have dreams; to think idly; to muse; to reflect, to think, to imagine. **je songeais que j'étais riche**, I dreamt I was rich. **~ à son salut**, to think of one's salvation. **~ à tout**, to think of everything. **songez-y**, bear it in mind. **j'avais songé une comédie**, I had thought of a comedy.

songeur *n.m.* dreamer. *adj.n.m.* dreaming.

sonnant, e *adj.* sounding, resounding; ringing; sonorous. **espèces ~es**, hard cash, ready money. **à l'heure ~e**, punctual to the hour.

sonner *v.i.* to sound; to ring; to tinkle; to toll; to strike. **les cloches sonnent**, the bells are ringing. **~ du cor**, to blow the horn. **midi est sonné**, twelve noon has struck. **~ les cloches**, to ring the bells. **~ la charge**, *Milit.* to sound the charge. **se faire ~ les cloches**, to be reprimanded.

sonnerie *n.f.* ringing, ring (of bells); set of bells; bells; sound (of the trumpets); the striking part (of clocks).

sonnette *n.f.* bell. **agiter la ~**, to ring the bell.

sonore *adj.* sonorous, resonant.

sonorité *n.f.* tone, resonance, acoustics of hall; sonorousness.

sophistication *n.f.* sophistication.

soporifique *adj.* soporiferous, soporific. *n.m.* soporific, narcotic.

soprano *n.m.* soprano.

sorbet *n.m.* sherbet, sorbet.

sorcellerie *n.f.* sorcery, witchcraft, magic, enchantment.

sorcier, ière *n.m.f.* sorcerer, sorceress, enchanter, enchantress; magician, wizard, witch.

sordide *adj.* sordid; filthy, dirty; mean, miserly, niggardly, stingy.

sort fate; destiny; lot. **améliorer son ~**, to improve one's condition. **le ~ en est jeté**, the die is cast. **tirer au sort**, to draw lots. **jeter un ~ à, sur quelqu'un**, to put a spell on someone.

sortable *adj.* suitable, acceptable.

sortant, e *adj.* winning, retiring, outgoing, going out. **numéro ~**, number drawn.

sorte *n.f.* sort; kind, species; class; rank; condition; manner, way. **de telle ~**, in such a manner. **de la ~**, so, thus, in that manner, in this way. **de ~ que**, so that; so as. **en quelque ~**, in a way.

sortie *n.f.* exit, going out; coming out; leaving; outlet; way out, output (computer); egress; *Milit.* sally, sortie; outburst. **cette maison a deux ~s**, that house has two exits. **à la ~ du spectacle**, at the end of the play.

sortilège *n.m.* sortilege, spell, charm, sorcery, witchcraft.

sortir *v.i.* to go out, to walk out, to step out; to come out, to come forth; to leave, to issue; to retire, to leave; to spring from; to emerge; to bring out, to take out, to get out; to deviate from. **~ de la chambre**, to go out of the room. **les yeux lui sortent de la tête**, *Fig.* his eyes are popping out of his head. **~ de table**, to rise from table. **il vient de ~**, he just went out, he has just gone out. **~ du lit**, to get out of bed. **~ de son devoir**, to swerve from duty. **~ du sujet**, to wander from the subject. **~ des papiers d'un tiroir**, to take papers out of a drawer. **~ quelqu'un d'embarras**, to get a person out of trouble. **au ~ de**, on leaving, on coming out of; on leaving. *Law.* to have. **cette sentence sortira son plein et entier effet**, that sentence will have its full effect.

sosie *n.m.* double.

sot, otte *adj.* stupid; silly, foolish. *n.m.f.* fool.

sottise *n.f.* foolishness, silliness, nonsense, foolish thing, silly thing.

sou *n.m.* penny, cent. **être sans le ~**, to be penniless. **machine à ~s**, slot machine.

souche *n.f.* stump, stock (of a tree); chump, stub, *Fig.* blockhead, dolt.

souci *n.m.* care, anxiety, concern; marigold. **se faire du ~**, to worry.

soucier *v.t.* to disturb, to trouble. **se ~**, *v.refl.* to care, to concern oneself, to be concerned, to be anxious. **ne se ~ de rien**, to care about nothing. **je me soucie peu de cela**, I don't care much about/for that.

soucieux, euse *adj.* concerned; anxious, worried.

soucoupe *n.f.* saucer. **~ volante**, flying saucer.

soudain, e *adj.* sudden, unexpected. *adv.* of a sudden, suddenly, all of a sudden.

soudainement *adv.* suddenly.

souder *v.t.* to solder, to weld (iron, etc.); to joint, to unite. **se ~**, *v.refl.* to be soldered, to unite, to join.

souffle *n.m.* breath; puff, blast, respiration, breathing, gasp; inspiration, influence. **à bout de ~** breathless.

soufflement *n.m.* blowing.

souffler *v.i.* to blow; to puff; to pant; to whisper, to breathe, to swell, to blow out; to whisper. **le vent souffle**, the wind blows. **~ quelque chose à l'oreille de quelqu'un**, to whisper something in a person's ear. **ne pas ~ mot**, not to say a word.

souffrance *n.f.* suffering, pain. *Law.* sufferance.

souffrant, e *adj.* suffering, in pain; ailing; diseased; patient.

souffre-douleur *n.m.* scapegoat, drudge.
souffrir *v.t.* to suffer; to bear, to support, to abide, to undergo; to stand; to tolerate, to allow, to endure a pain; to suffer pain; to be grieved. ~ **la faim, la soif,** to suffer from hunger, from thirst. **je ne puis pas ~ cet homme,** I cannot bear that man.
souhait *n.m.* wish, desire. **à vos ~s,** God bless you. **à ~,** according to one's wishes, at one's heart's desire or content.
souhaitable *adj.* desirable.
souhaiter *v.t.* to wish; to desire, to wish for. ~ **le bonjour à quelqu'un,** to wish a person good morning.
soûl, e *adj.* drunk, satiated. *n.m.* fill; belly full. **il a mangé tout son ~,** he has eaten his fill.
soulagement *n.m.* alleviation, relief.
soulager *v.t.* to ease, to relieve; to lighten; to alleviate. **se ~,** *v.refl.* to relieve oneself; to be relieved.
soûler *v.t.* to intoxicate, to make drunk. **se ~,** *v.refl.* to get drunk.
soulèvement *n.m.* rising; heaving; agitation; revolt; indignation. ~ **de coeur,** nausea. **le ~ des flots,** the swelling of the waves.
soulever *v.t.* to raise, to lift, to lift up, to rouse, to revolt, to rise, to turn (in the stomach). ~ **un fardeau,** to lift up a burden. **se ~,** *v.refl.* to raise oneself, to rise, to be lifted up; to heave; to swell, to rise up with indignation, in revolt.
soulier *n.m.* shoe.
souligner *v.t.* to underline, to accentuate.
soulte, soute *n.f.* balance; settlement. ~ **d'échange,** balance of exchange.
soumettre *v.t.* to subdue, to subjugate; to subject, to overcome. ~ **un peuple,** to subdue a people. **se ~,** *v.refl.* to submit, to yield; to give in; to consent, to engage. **se ~ à la raison,** to submit to reason.
soumis, e *adj.* subject; submissive, obedient, dutiful.
soumission *n.f.* submission; obedience, yielding; compliance.
soupape *n.f.* valve; plug. ~ **de sûreté,** safety valve.
soupçon *n.m.* suspicion; conjecture; *Fig.* dash (small amount).
soupçonner *v.t.* to suspect; to surmise. **se ~,** *v.refl.* to suspect each other.
soupçonneux, euse *adj.* suspicious, distrustful.
soupe *n.f.* soup. **être ~ au lait,** to be quick tempered.
souper *n.m.* supper, dinner. *v.i.* to have supper, to dine.
soupeser *v.t.* to try the weight of by lifting; to weigh.
soupir *n.m.* sigh, breath, gasp, *Mus.* crotchet, rest. **pousser des ~s,** to heave sighs. **rendre le dernier ~,** to breathe one's last.
soupirer *v.i.* to sigh, to breathe; to heave sighs; to long, to wish.

souple *adj.* supple; pliant; lithe; flexible.
souplesse *n.f.* suppleness; flexibility. **la ~ de la voix,** the flexibility of the voice.
source *n.f.* spring, source, origin, rise. **les ~s du Nil,** the sources of the Nile. **cela coule de ~,** it flows naturally. **tenir une nouvelle de bonne ~,** to have news from good authority.
sourcil *n.m.* eyebrow, brow.
sourciller *v.i.* to frown. **sans ~,** without batting an eyelid.
sourd, e *adj.* deaf; hearing-impaired; (of sound) hollow, muffled, dull, dead. ~ **et muet,** deaf-mute. ~ **comme un pot,** as deaf as a post. **faire la ~ oreille,** to turn a deaf ear. **une voix ~,** a hollow voice. **un bruit ~,** a dull noise. **douleur ~e,** dull pain. **lanterne ~e,** dark lantern. *n.m.f.* deaf person. **crier comme un ~,** to shout as one deaf. **il n'est point de pire ~ que celui qui ne vent pas entendre,** none is so deaf as those who will not hear.
sourdement *adv.* low, without noise, rumblingly; *Fig.* secretly.
sourdine *n.f. Mus.* mute. **en ~,** secretly, on the sly.
souriant, e *adj.* smiling.
souricière *n.f.* mousetrap. *Fig.* trap, snare, noose.
sourire *v.i.* to smile, to please, to favor. ~ **à quelqu'un,** to smile at a person. *n.m.* smile.
souris *n.f.* mouse, knuckle-joint (of a leg of mutton).
sournois, e *adj.* sly, deep, cunning. *n.m.f.* sly person.
sournoisement *adv.* slyly.
sous *prep.* under, below, beneath; in, during. ~ **le ciel,** under the sky. **être ~ clef,** to be locked up. ~ **peu,** shortly. ~ **le prétexte,** under pretence. **affirmer ~ serment,** to affirm under oath.
souscripteur *n.m.* subscriber.
souscription *n.f.* subscription; signature.
souscrire *v.t.* to sign, to subscribe (to); to sign one's name; to consent, to assent. **se ~,** *v.refl.* to be subscribed.
sous-développé *adj.* underdeveloped.
sous-développement *n.m.* underdevelopment.
sous-entendre *v.t.* to imply. **se ~,** *v.refl.* to be understood.
sous-entendu, e *p.p.* understood; unexpressed. *n.m.* thing understood.
sous-louer *v.t.* to sublet.
sous-main en ~, secretly.
sous-marin, e *adj.* submarine; submerged; under.
sous-officier *n.m.* noncommissioned officer.
soussigné, e *p.p.* undersigned, underwritten. *n.m.f.* the undersigned.
sous-sol *n.m.* basement.
sous-titre *n.m.* subtitle.
soustraction *n.f.* subtraction; deduction.
soustraire *v.t.* to take away, to abstract, to remove; to purloin; to subtract. ~ **des pièces**

d'un dossier, to abstract documents from a brief, to subtract. **se ~,** *v.refl.* to escape (from), to flee (from). **se ~ aux recherches de la justice,** to abscond.

soute *n.f.* storeroom, magazine, oil tank.

soutenable *adj.* bearable, tenable.

soutener *n.m.* supporter, pimp.

soutenir *v.t.* to sustain, to support, to bear, to bear up, to prop, to prop up; to assist, to second; to maintain; to keep up, to uphold; to favor, to stand up against. **~ une famille,** to maintain a family. **~ le courage de quelqu'un,** to keep up a person's courage. **~ son rang, sa dignité,** to keep up one's rank, one's dignity. **~ sa réputation,** to keep up one's reputation. **~ la conversation,** to keep up the conversation. **~ une discussion,** to keep up a discussion. **~ une doctrine,** to defend a doctrine. **je soutiens que ...,** I maintain that ... **se ~,** *v.refl.* to stand, to stand upright; to support oneself, to sustain oneself; to keep up; to continue one's success. **on ne peux pas supporter cette opinion,** that opinion cannot be supported.

soutenu, e *adj.* constant, steady.

souterrain, e *adj.* subterranean, underground. *n.m.* subterranean place, cave, cavern, vault, tunnel.

soutien *n.m.* support, prop; protection; supporter, maintainer. **~-gorge,** *n.m.* bra, brassiere.

soutirer *v.t.* to draw off, to rack, to rack off (wine, etc.), to get out of.

souvenir (se) *v.refl.* to remember, to recollect, to call to mind, to bear in mind. **je m'en souviens,** I remember it. *n.m.* remembrance, recollection; memento, souvenir, memorandum, keepsake; memory. **en ~ de moi,** in remembrance of me. **un ~ d'amitié,** a token of friendship. **rappeler une chose au ~ de quelqu'un,** to remind a person of something.

souvent *adv.* often.

souverain, e *adj.* sovereign, supreme. *n.m.f.* sovereign.

soyeux, euse *adj.* silken, silky.

spacieusement *adv.* spaciously; roomily.

spacieux, euse *adj.* spacious; large, wide, ample, roomy.

spaghetti *n.m.* spaghetti.

spasme *n.m.* spasm.

spatule *n.f.* spatula, spoonbill bird.

speaker, ine *n.m.f.* news announcer.

spécial, e *adj.* special, peculiar, particular; professional.

spécialement *adv.* specially, especially, particularly.

spécialisation *n.f.* specialization.

spécialiser *v.t.* to specialize, to mention specifically.

spécialiste *n.m.* specialist.

spécialité *n.f.* specialty, particularity.

spécieusement *adv.* speciously.

spécieux, euse *adj.* specious.

spécification *n.f.* specification.

spécifier *v.t.* to specify; to particularize.

spécifique *adj.n.m.* specific.

spécifiquement *adv.* specifically.

spécimen *n.m.* specimen, sample.

spectacle *n.m.* spectacle; sight; play; performance; theater. **se donner en ~,** to expose oneself to public view. **aller au ~,** to go to the theater.

spectaculaire *adj.* spectacular.

spectateur, trice *n.m.f.* spectator; onlooker; *pl.* audience.

specter *n.m.* spectre; apparition; phantom, ghost, spectrum. **~ solaire,** solar spectrum.

spectral, e *adv.* spectral; ghostly.

spéculation *n.f.* speculation.

spéculer *v.t.* to observe, to speculate.

speech *n.m.* speech.

sperme *n.m.* sperm.

sphère *n.f.* sphere; celestial globe; orb.

spirale *n.f.* spiral, spiral curve.

spirite *n.m.* spiritist, spiritualist.

spiritisme *n.m.* spiritism, spiritualism.

spiritualisation *n.f.* spiritualization.

spiritualiser *v.t.* to spiritualize.

spiritualisme *n.m.* *Philos.* spiritualism.

spiritualiste *n.m.f.* spiritualist.

spiritualité *n.f.* spirituality.

spirituel, elle *adj.* spiritual; witty. **le pouvoir ~,** the spiritual power. **une femme ~le,** a witty, a clever woman. *n.m.* spirituality.

spirituellement *adv.* spiritually; in spirit, wittily, cleverly, ingeniously.

splendour *n.f.* splendor, brilliancy.

splendide *adj.* splendid, magnificent.

spontané, e *adj.* spontaneous.

spontanéité *n.f.* spontaneity.

spontanément *adv.* spontaneously.

sporadique *adj.* sporadic.

sport *n.m.* sport.

sportif, ive *adj.* sporting; athletic. *n.m.f.* athlete.

spot *n.m.* spot, spotlight; commercial, ad.

squelette *n.m.* skeleton.

squelettique *adj.* scrawny, skeletal.

stabilisation *n.f.* stabilization.

stabiliser *v.t.* to stabilize.

stabilité *n.f.* stability, solidity; stableness, firmness, constancy.

stable *adj.* stable, solid, durable, lasting; steady, steadfast, firm.

stade *n.m.* stadium, arena.

stage *n.m.* training, internship, residence; term of probation.

stagiaire *adj. n.m.* trainee, intern.

stagnant, e *adj.* stagnant, still, standing.

stagnation *n.f.* stagnation.

stalactite *n.f.* stalactite.

stalagmite *n.f.* stalagmite.

stand *n.m.* stand; stall; shooting range.

standard *n.m.* standard, switchboard. *adj.* standard.

star *n.f.* movie star.

starter *n.m.* starter, choke of car.

station *n.f.* station; standing; stay; stop; resort. **faire une ~,** to make a halt. **~ de ski,** ski resort.

stationnement *n.m.* parking. **~ interdit,** no parking.

stationner *v.i.* to park.

statique *adj.* static. *n.f.* statics.

statistique *n.f.* statistics. *adj.* statistic, statistical.

statue *n.f.* statue.

statuer *v.t.* to ordain, to enact, to decree; to decide, to resolve.

statuette *n.f.* statuette.

statu quo *n.m.* status quo.

stature *n.f.* stature.

statut *n.m.* statute; written law.

steak *n.m.* steak.

sténo(graphe) *n.m.* stenographer, shorthand typist.

sténographie *n.f.* stenography, shorthand.

stéréo *adj., n.f.* stereo.

stéréotype *adj.* stereotype.

stéréotyper *v.t.* to stereotype.

stérile *adj.* sterile; barren, unfruitful; unproductive. **année ~,** unfruitful year.

stérilet *n.m.* contraceptive loop, coil, IUD.

stériliser *v.t.* to sterilize.

stérilité *n.f.* sterility, barrenness, unfruitfulness.

sternum *n.m.* sternum, breastbone.

stéthoscope *n.m.* stethoscope.

steward, esse *n.m.f.* steward, stewardess, flight attendant.

stigmate *n.m.* mark; scar (of a wound); stigma.

stigmatiser *v.t.* to stigmatize, to brand.

stimulant, e *adj.* stimulating, stimulant. *n.m.* stimulus, stimulative, incitement, spur.

stimulation *n.f.* stimulation.

stimuler *v.t.* to stimulate, to excite, to incite, to rouse, to urge, to spur on.

stipulation *n.f.* stipulation.

stipuler *v.t.* to stipulate, to contract.

stock *n.m.* stock.

stocker *v.t.* to stock.

stoïque *adj.* stoic. *n.m.* stoic.

stoïquement *adv.* stoically.

stop *Interj.* stop! *n.m.* stop sign; brake light. **faire du ~,** to hitchhike.

stopper *v.i.* to stop.

store *n.m.* blind, shade.

strangulation *n.f.* strangulation.

strapontin *n.m.* folding seat, flap-seat.

stratagème *n.m.* stratagem; *Fig.* artifice, trick, ruse.

stratège *n.m.* strategist.

stratégie *n.f.* strategy.

stratégique *adj.* strategic.

stress *n.m.* stress.

strict, e *adj.* strict, rigid, rigorous, severe, precise.

strictement *adv.* strictly, rigidly, rigorously.

strident, e *adj.* shrill, screeching, harsh.

strip-tease *n.m.* striptease.

stripteaseuse *n.f.* stripper.

structure *n.f.* structure; construction.

studieusement *adv.* studiously.

studieux, euse *adj.* studious.

studio *n.m.* studio, studio apartment.

stupéfaction *n.f.* stupefaction.

stupéfait, e *adj.* stupefied, astounded, astonished.

stupéfiant, e *adj.* stupefying; astounding. *n.m. Med.* drug, narcotic.

stupéfier *v.t.* to stupefy, to astound.

stupeur *n.f.* stupor; astonishment.

stupide *adj.* stupid; dull, foolish. *n.m.f.* stupid person.

stupidement *adv.* stupidly.

stupidité *n.f.* stupidity.

style *n.m.* style; pin or gnomon (of a dial); manner, tone, strain. **bon ~,** good style, language. **le ~ hardi des églises gothiques,** the bold style of Gothic churches. **vieux ~,** old style.

styler *v.t.* to train, to form, to bring up, to accustom.

styliste *n.m.f.* stylist, designer.

stylo *n.m.* pen.

suant, e *adj.* perspiring, sweaty, in a sweat.

suave *adj.* sweet; soft, agreeable, sweet-smelling.

suavement *adv.* sweetly, suavely.

subalterne *adj.* subordinate. *n.m.f.* subordinate, inferior.

subconscient, e *adj., n.m.* subconscious.

subir *v.t.* to undergo, to suffer, to bear, to sustain, to go through. **~ un interrogatoire,** to be cross-examined. **~ un examen,** to undergo, to pass an examination.

subit, e *adj.* sudden, unexpected.

subitement *adv.* suddenly, all of a sudden, unexpectedly.

subito, presto *adv. Infml.* suddenly.

subjectif, ive *adj.* subjective.

subjectivement *adv.* subjectively.

subjonctif *n.m.* subjunctive, subjunctive mood. *adj.* subjunctive.

subjuguer *v.t.* to subjugate; to subdue, to subject, to overpower.

sublime *adj.* sublime. *n.m.* sublime; sublimity, sublimeness.

submerger *v.t.* to submerge, to submerse; to drown.

submersion *n.f.* submersion.

subordination *n.f.* subordination.

subordonné, e *adj. n.m.f.* subordinate.

subordonner *v.t.* to subordinate. **se ~,** *v.refl.* to subordinate oneself.

suborner *v.t.* to suborn; to bribe, to corrupt; to tamper with. **~ des témoins,** to bribe witnesses.

subrepticement *adv.* surreptitiously.

subsidaire *adj.* subsidiary.

subsistance *n.f.* subsistence, maintenance, sustenance. **tirer sa ~ de son travail,** to make one's living by working.

subsister *v.i.* to subsist; to exist.

substance *n.f.* substance, matter; essence. **en ~,** in substance, in essence.

substituer *v.t.* to substitute. **se ~,** *v.refl.* (with à) to substitute oneself for.

substitut *n.m.* substitute, deputy.

substitution *n.f.* substitution.

subterfuge *n.m.* subterfuge; evasion, shift.

subtil, e *adj.* subtile; fine, delicate; acute, quick, sharp, nice. **un esprit ~,** a subtle mind.

subtiliser *v.t.* to steal, to pinch; to split hairs; to refine.

subtilité *n.f.* subtlety.

subvenir *v.i.* (with à) to relieve, to assist; to supply, to meet; to provide for. **~ aux besoins de quelqu'un,** to provide for a person.

subvention *n.f.* grant, subsidy.

subventionner *v.t.* to subsidize, to endow, to assist.

succéder *v.i.* to succeed; to take the place or office of; to inherit. **la nuit succède au jour,** night succeeds to day. **~ à un royaume,** to succeed to a kingdom. **se ~,** *v.refl.* to succeed, to follow each other.

succès *n.m.* success, hit, issue.

successeur *n.m.* successor.

succession *n.f.* succession; sequence; inheritance. **recueillir une ~,** to inherit a fortune, an estate.

successivement *adv.* successively.

succinct, e *adj.* succinct; short, brief, concise, summary.

succinctement *adv.* succinctly; briefly, concisely; *Infml.* lightly; meagerly, sparingly.

succion *n.f.* suction.

succomber *v.i.* to sink (beneath, under), to succumb; to sink, to yield, to fall; to die. **~ au sommeil,** to yield to sleep. **le malade a succombé,** the patient died.

succulent, e *adj.* succulent, juicy.

succursale *n.f.* branch; auxiliary.

sucer *v.t.* to suck, to suck up or in, to imbibe, to drain. **~ son pouce,** to suck one's thumb.

sucette *n.f.* lollipop.

suçon *n.m. Infml.* hicky, lovebite.

sucre *n.m.* sugar. **~ de canne,** sugarcane. **~ de betterave,** beet sugar. **~ raffiné,** refined sugar. **~ d'orge,** barley sugar. **il est tout ~ et tout miel,** he is all honey.

sucré, e *adj.* sugared, sugary, sweet.

sucrer *v.t.* to sugar; to sweeten.

sucrerie *n.f.* sugar refinery; *pl.* sweets, candy.

sucrier, ière *adj.* sugar, of sugar. *n.m.* sugar bowl.

sud *n.m.* south. *adj.* south; southern. **le pôle ~,** the south pole.

sudation *n.f.* sweating, sudation.

sud-est *n.m.* south east; south east wind. *adj.* south east.

sudiste *adj., n.m.* southern, southerner.

suer *v.i.* to sweat; to perspire; to toil, to labor, to druge. **~ à grosses gouttes,** to perspire profusely. **~ du sang,** to sweat drops of blood. **~ sang et eau,** to toil and moil.

sueur *n.f.* sweat; perspiration; *Fig.* labor, drudgery; pains. **à la ~ de son front,** by the sweat of one's brow.

suffire *v.i.* to suffice; to be sufficient, to be enough, to satisfy. **ça suffit!** enough. **se ~,** *v.refl.* to provide for oneself, to support oneself.

suffisamment *adv.* sufficiently, enough.

suffisant, e *adj.* sufficient; enough; adequate; conceited. *n.m.f.* conceited person.

suffocation *n.f.* suffocation; stifling; choking.

suffoquer *v.t.* to suffocate; to stifle, to choke, to be choked.

suffrage *n.m.* suffrage; vote.

suggérer *v.i.* to suggest; to offer.

suggestion *n.f.* suggestion; hint, intimation.

suicidaire *adj.* suicidal. *n.m.f.* person with suicidal tendencies.

suicide *n.m.* suicide.

suicider (se) *v.refl.* to commit suicide.

suie *n.f.* soot.

suinter *v.i.* to ooze, to ooze out, to sweat; to let out.

suite *n.f.* following, rest, suite, retinue, attendants, followers, train, sequel, continuation; succession; duration, series; order, perseverance; consequence. **il reprit la ~ de son histoire,** he went on with his story. **dans la ~,** in the sequel. **mourir des ~s d'une chute,** to die from the aftereffects of a fall. **avoir de la ~ dans les idées,** to be coherent in one's ideas. **à la ~, à la ~ de,** after. **de ~,** at once, right away. **tout de ~,** at once, immediately. **par ~ de,** in consequence of.

suivant *prep.* according to. **~ que,** depending on whether, according to whether.

suivant, e *adj.* following; next. **le jour ~,** the next day. *n.m.f.* next.

suivre *v.t.* to follow; to be next to, to attend; to pursue; to succeed in order of time; to come after; to result; to be the consequence of. **~ quelqu'un pas à pas,** to follow a person step by step. **le bateau suivait le courant,** the boat was going with the stream. **~ une règle,** to follow a rule. **~ son penchant, son inclination,** to follow one's inclination. **j'ai suivi ses progrès,** I watched his progress. **~ un cours,** to attend a class. **se ~,** *v.refl.* to follow each other, to follow in order. **ces pages se suivent,** these pages follow in order.

sujet, ette *adj.* subject; liable, amenable; prone. **~ à caution,** rather doubtful. **il est ~ à s'enivrer,** he is addicted to drink. *n.m.f.* subject.

sujet *n.m.* subject; cause, reason, motive, ground; person, individual. **nous avons ~ de nous plaindre,** we have reason to complain. **le ~ d'une comédie,** the subject of a comedy.

sujétion n.f. subjection.
super adj. great, super, terrific. n.m. premium gas.
superbe adj. superb, splendid, proud, haughty, arrogant, lofty, supercilious. n.m. proud, haughty person. n.f. pride, haughtiness, arrogance.
superbement adv. proudly, haughtily, arrogantly, superciliously; superbly, magnificently, splendidly.
supercherie n.f. cheat, deception.
superficie n.f. surface area.
superficiel, elle adj. superficial.
superficiellement adv. superficially.
superflu, e adj. superfluous, unnecessary, needless; idle; vain. n.m. superfluity, superfluousness, excess.
supérieur adj. superior, upper; higher. **les étages ~s,** the upper stories. n.m.f. superior.
supérieurement adv. superiorly.
supériorité n.f. superiority.
supermarché n.m. supermarket.
superposer v.t. to superimpose, to pile, to stack.
superposition n.f. superposition, superimposition.
superstitieux, euse adj. supersititious. n.m.f. superstitious person.
superstition n.f. superstition.
superviser v.t. to supervise.
suppléer v.t. to supply; to make good; to substitute.
supplément n.m. supplement; addition; extra; extra charge.
supplémentaire adj. supplementary, additional.
supplication n.f. supplication.
supplice n.m. punishment; torture, torment, anguish. **un fiim atroce,** a cruel punishment. **être au ~,** to be upon the rack.
supplicié, e n.m.f. victim of torture.
supplicier v.t. to torture.
supplier v.t. to supplicate, to beseech, to implore.
supplique n.f. petition.
support n.m. support; prop, rest, pillar; assistance, help; supporter.
supportable adj. bearable, supportable; endurable.
supporter v.t. to support, to bear; to sustain, to prop, to suffer, to endure, to stand. **~ la fatigue,** to bear fatigue. **se ~,** v.refl. to be supported, suffered, borne, endured; to bear with each other.
supposer v.t. to suppose; to imagine, to presume, to think; to imply, to infer.
supposition n.f. supposition; hypothesis; imagination, conjecture, surmise; assumption.
suppositoire n.m. suppository.
suppression n.f. suppression; abolition; concealment.
supprimer v.t. to suppress; to restrain from disclosure; to pass over in silence; to abolish; to repeal, to kill, to get rid of; to delete (computer). **~ un livre,** to suppress a book. **~ un emploi,** to abolish an office.

suppuration n.f. suppuration.
suppurer v.i. to suppurate.
supputation n.f. computation, reckoning, supputation, calculation.
supputer v.t. to compute, to reckon, to suppute, to calculate.
suprématie n.f. supremacy.
suprême adj. supreme; last. **le moment ~,** the last moment. **au ~ degré,** in the highest degree.
suprêmement adv. supremely.
sur, e adj. sour; tart.
sur prep. on, upon; over; above; at, near, by; about, to; regarding, concerning, touching; on account of. **s'asseoir ~ une chaise,** to sit on a chair. **graver ~ le cuivre,** to engrave on copper. **revenir ~ ses pas,** to retrace one's steps. **~ mon honneur,** on my honor. **prêter ~ gages,** to lend upon pledge. **avoir de l'argent ~ soi,** to have money on oneself. **ma fenêtre donne ~ la rue,** my window looks over the street. **dix pieds de long ~ cinq,** ten feet long by five. **il eut dix voix ~ quinze,** he had ten votes out of fifteen. **régner ~ un peuple,** to reign over a people. **~-le-champ,** immediately. **~ ces entrefaites,** in the meantime.
sûr, e adj. sure; certain; safe; secure. **je suis ~ de ce que je vous dis,** I am certain of what I'm telling you. **le plus ~ est de ne pas s'y fier,** the best way is not to trust it. **à coup ~,** surely, for certain.
surcharge n.f. overload, overcharge, additional burden; excess, surplus, surcharge.
surcharger v.i. to overcharge, to overload, to surcharge.
surchauffer v.t. to overheat.
surchoix n.m. first choice, finest quality.
surcroît n.m. addition, increase. **pour ~ de malheur,** to add to these misfortunes. **~ de biens,** increase of property. adv. in addition, to boot.
surdité n.f. deafness.
surdoué, e adj. gifted. n.m.f. gifted child.
surélever v.t. to raise higher, to increase.
sûrement adv. surely, certainly; safely, securely, in safety.
surenchère n.f. higher bid; outbidding.
surenchérir v.i. to outbid, to bid higher.
surestimation n.f. overvaluation, overestimate.
surestimer v.t. to overvalue, to overestimate.
sûreté n.f. safety, security; reliability, reliableness, trustworthiness; trust. **être en ~,** to be in safety.
surface n.f. surface, outside.
surgelé, e adj. deep-frozen.
surgeler v.t. to freeze, to deep-freeze.
surgir v.i. to appear suddenly, to spring up.
surhumain, e adj. superhuman.
surimposer v.t. to lay over, to place above; to overtax.
surlendemain n.m. the day after tomorrow, two days after tomorrow.

surmenage *n.m.* overwork.
surmener *v.t.* to overwork. **se ~,** to overwork oneself.
surmonter *v.t.* to surmount, to overcome; to surpass; to rise above; to overflow. **~ ses ennemis,** to overcome one's enemies. **~ les obstacles,** to overcome obstacles.
surnaturel, elle *adj.* supernatural. *n.m.* supernatural.
surnom *n.m.* nickname.
surnommer *v.t.* to nickname.
surpasser *v.t.* to surpass, to exceed; to rise above; to go beyond; to astonish. **cette dépense surpasse mes moyens,** that expense is beyond my means. **se ~,** *v.refl.* to surpass oneself, to outdo oneself.
surpeuplement *n.m.* overpopulation.
surplomber *v.i.* to overhang, to lean forward.
surplus *n.m.* surplus, excess. **au ~,** besides, after all.
surpopulation *n.f.* overpopulation.
surprenant, e *adj.* amazing, surprising, astonishing.
surprendre *v.t.* to surprise; to take by surprise; to overtake; to catch, to detect. **la pluie nous a surpris,** we were caught in the rain. **se ~,** *v.refl.* to surprise oneself, to surprise each other.
surprise *n.f.* surprise; astonishment, amazement. **faire une ~ à quelqu'un,** to surprise a person. **je ne reviens pas de ma ~,** I cannot get over my surprise.
sursaut *n.m.* start, jump. **en ~,** with a start. **se levant en ~,** starting up. **se réveiller en ~,** to awaken with a start.
sursauter *v.i.* to start, to jump.
sursis *n.m.* suspension; delay; respite; reprieve; deferment.
surtout *adv.* especially, above all.
surveillance *n.f.* supervision, inspection, overlooking; watch.
surveillant, e *adj.* vigilant; watchful. *n.m.f.* superintendent, inspector, overseer, surveyor; guardian; keeper.
surveiller *v.i.* to look after, to watch over, to inspect, to survey, to watch; to watch over, to look after; to see to. **~ quelqu'un,** to watch a person. **se ~,** *v.refl.* to watch over oneself, to watch each other.
survenir *v.i.* to supervene, to happen, to occur, to drop in by chance.
survêtement *n.m.* sweatsuit, tracksuit.
survivant, e *adj.* surviving. *n.m.f.* survivor.
survivre *v.i.* to survive; to outlast, to outlive. **~ à quelqu'un,** to survive a person. **~ à son malheur,** to outlive one's misfortune. **il a survécu à tous ses enfants,** he survived all his children. **se ~,** *v.refl.* to live on.
survoler *v.t.* to fly over.
susceptibilité *n.f.* susceptibility, sensitiveness, sensibility, susceptibleness; touchiness.
susceptible *adj.* susceptible, touchy, easily

offended. **il est extrêmement ~,** he is easily offended.
susciter *v.t.* to arouse; to raise up; to cause to excite.
susdit, e *adj.* aforesaid, above-mentioned.
suspect, e *adj.* suspicious; doubtful, suspected. **~ de trahison,** suspected of treason. **une affaire ~e,** a doubtful affair. *n.m.f.* suspect.
suspecter *v.t.* to suspect; to distrust.
suspendre *v.t.* to suspend; to hang, to hang up. **~ des travaux,** to suspend work. **il était suspendu à ses lèvres,** he was hanging on his/her words. **se ~,** *v.refl.* to suspend oneself, to hang; to be suspended, to be interrupted.
suspendu, e *p.p.* suspended; hung up; hanging.
suspens *adj.* suspended. **un prêtre ~,** a suspended priest. **en ~,** in suspense.
suspense *n.m.* suspense. **tenir une personne en ~,** to keep a person in suspense.
suspension *n.f.* suspension; suspending; suspense; deferment; adjournment.
suspicion *n.f.* suspicion.
susurrer *v.i.* to whisper, to buzz.
svelte *adj.* slender, slim, light.
syllabe *n.f.* syllable.
symbole *n.m.* symbol, emblem, sign.
symbolique *adj.* symbolic, symbolical; typical. *n.f.* symbolics.
symboliser *v.t.* to symbolize.
symétrie *n.f.* symmetry.
symétrique *adj.* symmetrical; proportionate, proportional.
symétriquement *adv.* symmetrically.
sympa *adj.* nice, friendly, cool. *Infml.* **c'est un mec très ~,** he's a cool guy.
sympathie *n.f.* liking, sympathy; friendship.
sympathique *adj.* nice, friendly, likeble; congenial; sympathetic (nerve).
sympathiser *v.i.* to hit it off.
symphonie *n.f.* symphony.
symptôme *n.m.* symptom; *Fig.* indication, token, sign, mark.
synagogue *n.f.* temple, synagogue.
synchronisation *n.f.* synchronization.
syncope *n.f.* blackout, fainting fit. **tomber en ~,** to pass out.
syndicat *n.m.* union, trade union, association. **~ d'initiative,** tourist information office.
syndiquer *v.t.* to join, to unite, to combine.
syndrome *n.m.* syndrome.
synonyme *adj.* synonymous. *n.m.* synonym.
synthèse *n.f.* synthesis, composition.
synthétique *adj.* synthetic.
syphilis *n.f.* syphilis.
systématique *adj.* systematic.
systématiquement *adv.* systematically.
systématiser *v.t.* to systematize.
système *n.m.* system.
systole *n.f.* systole.

T

T' contraction of **te** or **toi.**

Ta *adj. poss. fem.* your.

tabac *n.m.* tobacco. **passage à ~,** a beating up.

tabasser *v.t. Infml.* to beat up. **se faire ~,** to get beaten up.

table *n.f.* table, board; food, fare, index. **~ de cuisine,** kitchen table. **~ de jeu,** card table. **~ à ouvrage,** work table. **~ de nuit,** bedside table. **avoir la ~ et le logement chez quelqu'un,** to board and lodge at a person's house. **faire ~ rase,** to make a clean sweep. **~ des matières,** table of contents, index. **~ de multiplication,** multiplication table.

tableau *n.m.* picture; painting; scenery, scene; chalk board, bulletin board, list, catalog; roll; (of juries) panel. **~ vivant,** living picture.

tablée *n.f.* table; party of people.

tabler *v.i.* to rely, to keep a table.

tablette *n.f.* shelf (*pl.* shelves); tablet; a small table; notebook. **~ de chocolat,** chocolate bar.

tablier *n.m.* apron. **rendre son ~,** to resign.

tabou *adj., n.m.* taboo.

tabouret *n.m.* stool; footstool.

tac *n.m.* (noise) tap, click. **riposter du ~ au ~,** to give tit for tat.

tache *n.f.* spot; stain, blot. **~ d'huile,** oil stain. **~s de rousseur,** freckles.

tâche *n.f.* task; job. **remplir su ~,** to do one's task. **prendre à ~,** to make a point of doing a thing.

tacher *v.t.* to spot; to taint, to sully; to tarnish. **se ~,** *v.refl.* to spot, to stain one's clothes.

tâcher *v.i.* to endeavor, to try, to strive.

tacheté, e *adj.* spotted, with spots, speckled.

tacheter *v.t.* to speckle, to speck; to spot.

tacite *adj.* tacit; implied.

tacitement *adv.* tacitly; silently.

taciturne *adj.* taciturn; reserved.

tact *n.m.* tact, touch, feeling.

tactile *adj.* tactile.

tactique *n.f.* tactics. *adj.* tactic, tactical.

taie *n.f.* case. **~ d'oreiller,** pillowcase.

taille *n.f.* cutting, cut, pruning (of trees), dressing (of vines); *Engrav.* cut; edge; seam; waist, shape, tax; deal (at cards); *Mus.* tenor. **~ douce,** copper plate. **~ des pierres,** stonecutting. **petit de ~,** small in stature. **avoir la ~ fine,** to have a slender waist.

taillé, e *p.p.* cut; mended (pen); proportioned. **un homme bien ~,** a well-shaped man.

taille-crayon *n.m.* pencil sharpener.

tailler *v.t.* to cut; to prune, to clip; to dress; to hew; to carve; to engrave; to cut out. **~ la vigne,** to prune vines. **~ la barbe,** to cut the beard. **~ un diamant,** to cut a diamond. **~ des bavettes,** *Infml.* to chat, to gossip. **~ en pièces,** to cut to pieces.

tailleur *n.m.* tailor, cutter. **~ de pierre,** stonecutter; (at cards) dealer.

taillis *n.m.* coppice, copse, copsewood, underwood.

tain *n.m.* tinfoil. **miroir sans ~,** two-way mirror.

taire *v.t.* not to say, to suppress. **se ~,** *v.refl.* to be silent, to keep silent, to remain silent, to keep silence, to hold one's tongue. **elle promit de se ~,** she promised to be silent. **taisez-vous,** hold your tongue. **faire ~,** to silence. **faites le ~,** make him hold his tongue. **taisez-vous!** be quiet! shut up!

talc *n.m.* powder, talc.

talent *n.m.* talent; ability, gift, skill. **un homme de ~,** a talented man, a man of talent.

talon *n.m.* heel. *Print.* foot; *Naut.* sole (of an anchor); voucher, counterfoil, stub (of check books, etc.). **souliers à hauts ~s,** high-heeled shoes. **avoir l'estomac dans les ~s,** to be starving. **~ d'Achille,** weak spot.

talonner *v.t.* to be at the heels of, to pursue close; to spur; *Fig.* to press hard; to urge. *v.i.* to touch the ground; to strand.

talonnette *n.f.* heel piece (of a shoe).

talus *n.m.* slope, sloping, declivity; *Railw.* embankment.

tambour *n.m.* drum; drummer; tympanum, drum barrel, barrel. **battre le ~,** to beat the drum. **~ battant,** by beat of drums, with drums beating. **sans trompette ni ~,** without a fuss.

tambourin *n.m.* tambourine.

tambouriner *v.i.* to drum, to play on a drum. *Fig.* to cry up; to extol; to make known.

tamis *n.m.* sieve, sifter; strainer; to comb, to search.

tampon *n.m.* stopper, plug; pad; *Railw.* buffer; stamp, swab.

tamponner *v.t.* to plug, to stopper; *Railw.* to run against, to knock against. **se ~,** not to give a damn.

tandis *adv.* **~ que,** meanwhile, meantime, while; whereas.

tangible *adj.* tangible.

tanière *n.f.* den (for wild beasts), lair, hole, cave.

tank *n.m.* tank.

tanner *v.t.* to tan; to bore, to annoy, to tire, to wear.

tant *adv.* so much; *pl.* so many; such. **un escompte de ~ pour cent,** a discount of so much per cent. **il travaille ~,** he works so much. **~ bien que mal,** as well as possible. **~ que,** as long as. **~ que nous vivrons,** as long as we live. **~ mieux,** so much the better. **~ pis,** so much the worse, too bad. *Infml.* tough luck. **~ s'en faut que,** far from, so far from. **~ soit peu,** ever so little. **si ~ est que,** if that be so. **si ~ est que cela arrive,** supposing it happens. **cette femme ~ aimé,** this woman loved so much.

tante *n.f.* aunt.

tantinet *n.m.* a very little; very little bit. **un ~**, *adv.* rather, somewhat. **un ~ fâché**, rather angry.

tantôt *adv.* soon; shortly, by and by; just now; sometimes; now. **vous en verrez ~ la suite**, you will know the consequences soon. **je l'ai vu ~**, I saw him just now. **~ fort, ~ faible**, sometimes wrong, sometimes weak.

tapage *n.m.* uproar, noise, row, riot, racket; confusion; noise.

tapant, e *adj.* sharp, on the dot.

tape *n.f.* pat, slap.

taper *v.t.* to tap, to strike, to slap; to plug; to knock; to hit, to type. **~ du pied**, to stamp with one's foot. **se ~**, *v.refl.* to hit each other.

tapioca *n.m.* tapioca.

tapir (se) *v.refl.* to covert; to squat, to crouch.

tapis *n.m.* carpet, rug, mat. **mettre une affaire sur le ~**, to discuss a thing.

tapisser *v.t.* to carpet; to hang with tapestry, to hang; (with paper) to paper; to make tapestry.

tapisserie *n.f.* tapestry; needlework; upholstery.

taquiner *v.t.* to tease. **se ~**, *v.refl.* to tease each other.

tard *adv.* late. **se lever ~**, to get up late. **mieux vaut ~ que jamais**, better late than never. *adj.* late. *n.m.* late hour; late.

tarder *v.i.* to delay; to defer; to put off; to linger, to loiter; to long. **vous avez bien tardé à venir**, you were very long in coming. **il me tarde de vous voir**, I am longing to see you.

tardif, ive *adj.* tardy, late.

tare *n.f.* waste, loss, deficiency, defect, blemish, fault, vice.

taré, e *n.m.f.* degenerate, deteriorated, damaged. *adj. n.m.* disreputable.

tarif *n.m.* price list, tariff; rate; table, list.

tarir *v.t.* to dry up; to exhaust; to drain. **~ ses larmes**, to dry up one's tears. **se ~**, *v.refl.* to dry up; to be dried up.

tarte *n.f.* tart. **~ à la crème**, cream tart.

tartine *n.f.* slice of bread and butter. **en mettre une ~**, to make a long speech.

tartiner *v.t.* to spread on bread.

tas *n.m.* heap; pile, mass; *Agr.* shock, cock; crowd; set, lot. **un ~ de papiers**, a pile of papers. **un ~ de fumier**, a manure heap.

tasse *n.f.* cup. **~ à thé**, teacup.

tasser *v.t.* to pile up; to ram down. **se ~**, *v.refl.* to heap up; to settle.

tâter *v.t.* to feel; to try; to sound. **~ le pouls à quelqu'un**, to feel a person's pulse. **~ le terrain**, to feel one's way. **se ~**, *v.refl.* to feel oneself.

tâte-vin *n.m.* wine taster.

tâtonner *v.i.* to grope, to feel one's way; to fumble.

tâtons *adv.* gropingly, feeling one's way, by feeling about.

tatouer *v.t.* to tattoo.

taudis *n.m.* slum, dirty hole, wretched lodging.

taule *n.f.* clink.

taupe *n.f.* mole. **ne pas voir plus clair qu'une ~**, to be as blind as a bat.

taureau *n.m.* bull, Taurus the Bull.

taux *n.m.* rate; price, assessment. **~ d'intérêt**, interest rate. **~ de change**, exchange rate.

taxe *n.f.* price; rate; tax; assessment; toll.

taxer *v.t.* to fix the price of; to tax.

taxi *n.m.* cab, taxi.

te *pron. pers.* 2d. pers, you, to you. **écoute, il ~ parle!** listen, he is talking to you!

technicien, ne *n.m.f.* technician.

technique *adj.* technical. *n.f.* technology.

technologie *n.f.* technology.

technologique *adj.* technological.

teigne *n.f.* moth, ringworm.

teigneux, euse *adj.* scurvy. *n.m.f.* ringworm sufferer.

teindre *v.t.* to dye; to color. **se ~**, *v.refl.* to be dyed.

teint, e *n.m.* dye, color, hue, tint, complexion (of the face). **un beau ~**, a beautiful complexion.

teinter *v.t.* to tint, to color slightly.

teinture *n.f.* dye; color, dyeing.

teinturerie *n.f.* (dry) cleaners.

teinturier, ière *n.m.f.* (dry) cleaner.

tel, elle *adj.* such; similar, so, like. **elle est d'une ~ le gentillesse**, she is so nice. **~ quel**, such as it is. **de ~ le sorte que**, so that, in such a way that.

télé *n.f.* TV.

télécommande *n.f.* remote control.

télégramme *n.m.* wire, telegram.

télépathie *n.f.* telepathy.

téléphone *n.m.* telephone, phone.

téléphoner *v.t.* to telephone, to phone.

télescope *n.m.* telescope.

téléviser *v.t.* to televise.

téléviseur *n.m.* television.

télévision *n.f.* television, TV.

tellement *adv.* in such a manner; so much; so.

téméraire *adj.* daring.

témoignage *n.m.* testimony, witness, evidence; testimonial. **faux ~**, false testimony. **rendre ~ à la verité**, to bear witness to the truth.

témoigner *v.t.* to testify, to bear witness; to give evidence; to witness; to show. **~ de la juie**, to show pleasure.

témoin *n.m.* witness, eyewitness, testimony, evidence, proof. **prendre quelqu'un à ~**, to call, to take a person, to witness. **~ à charge**, witness for the prosecution. **~ à décharge**, witness for the defense.

tempe *n.f.* temple.

tempérament *n.m.* temperament; constitution; temper, disposition, nature, character.

température *n.f.* temperature.

tempéré, e *adj.* temperate; moderate.

tempête *n.f.* storm.

tempêteux, euse *adj.* stormy.

temple *n.m.* temple; church.

temporaire *adj.* temporary.

temporairement *adv.* temporarily.

temps *n.m.* time; period; while, season; weather; tense (of the verb). **le ~ passe vite,** time flies. **perdre son ~,** to waste time. **avec le ~,** in time. **je n'ai pas de ~ à perdre,** I have no time to lose. **les ~ son durs,** these are hard times. **cet habit a fait son ~,** this coat has had its day. **mesure à deux ~,** common measure. **le ~ est couvert,** the weather is cloudy. **gros ~, ~ orageux,** stormy weather. **~ pluvieux,** rainy weather. **~, in time. en même ~,** at the same time. **de ~ en ~, de ~ à autre,** from time to time, now and then. **de tout ~,** at all times. **en ~ et lieu,** in due time and place. **entre ~,** meanwhile, meantime.

tenable *adj.* bearable.

tenace *adj.* stubborn, tenacious; obstinate.

ténacité *n.f.* stubbornness, tenacity.

tenaille *n.f.* tongs, pliers.

tenailler *v.t.* to rack, to torture, to torment.

tendance *n.f.* tendency.

tendant, e *adj.* tending; directed to; aiming at.

tendon *n.m.* tendon; sinew; hamstring.

tendre *adj.* tender; soft; delicate; smooth; weak, feeble; loving. **avoir la peau ~,** to have a soft skin. **un coeur ~,** a kind heart. *n.m.* sensible part.

tendre *v.t.* to stretch; to stretch out, to bend (a bow); to spread; to hold out; to hang up (tapestry); to set, to lay (a snare). **~ une corde,** to stretch a rope. **~ des filets,** to spread nets. **~ l'autre joue,** turn the other cheek.

tendrement *adv.* tenderly; kindly; lovingly.

tendresse *n.f.* tenderness; fondness; *pl.* caresses, tender caresses.

tendu, e *p.p.* stretched; bent, laid, set. *adj.* tense, tight. **situation ~e,** a tense situation.

ténèbres *n.f.pl.* darkness, tenebrae.

ténébreux, euse *adj.* dark; obscure, gloomy, tenebrous, mysterious; dismal, sinister.

teneur *n.f.* contents, tenor; import, text.

tenir *v.t.* to hold; to have; to keep fast; to have hold of, to keep; to keep in; to contain. **~ un livre à la main,** to hold a book in one's hand. **tenez, voilà la clef,** here is the key. **~ quelqu'un par le bras,** to hold a person by the arm. **~ en bride,** to curb, to hold in check. **~ vaut mieux que courir,** it is better to have than to hope. **cette salle tient mille personnes,** that hall holds a thousand people. **~ sa langue,** to hold one's tongue. **votre fils tient cela de vous,** your son takes after you. **je le tiens pour honnête homme,** I believe him to be an honest man. **~ une maison,** to keep a house. **~ les yeux baissés,** to look down. **~ lieu de,** to replace, to serve instead of. **~ sa promesse,** to keep one's promise. **~ sa parole,** to keep one's word. **de qui tenez-vous la nouvelle?** whom did you get that news from?

~ la caisse, to be a cashier. **ne ~ aucun compte de,** to take no account of; not to mind. **faire ~,** to convey, to send, to forward, to transmit, to remit. *v.i.* to hold, to stick, to cleave; to hold on, to hold to; to last, not to give way. **tout cela tient bien ensemble,** all that holds together very well. **la vie ne tient qu'à un fil,** life is held by a thread. **qu'à cela ne tienne là,** so be it. **cet enfant tient de son père,** that child takes after his father. **le temps ne tiendra pas,** the weather will change. **~ bon, ~ ferme,** to hold, to hold on, to stand. **se ~,** *v.refl.* to be held; to hold (by), to cling (to); to stand (up), to remain. **se ~ à cheval,** to sit on horseback. **se ~ par la main,** to hold each other by the hand. **je veux savoir à quoi m'en ~,** I want to know what I am to expect. **il se tenait auprès de la porte,** he was standing by the door. **se ~ à sa place,** to keep one's place. **se ~ debout,** to keep standing. **il ne se tient pas pour battu,** he does not consider himself beaten. **le marché se tient le vendredi,** the market is held on Friday.

tennis *n.m.* tennis; sneakers (shoes).

tension *n.f.* tension; tenseness, strain; stiffness, hardness. **~ artérielle,** blood pressure.

tentation *n.f.* temptation.

tentative *n.f.* attempt, endeavor, trial.

tente *n.f.* tent, awning.

tenter *v.t.* to attempt, to try; to tempt.

tenue *n.f.* holding; attitude; discipline; deportment, bearing, behavior; outfit. **avoir une bonne ~,** to behave oneself. **être en grande ~,** to be in full dress, in uniform. **~ des livres,** bookkeeping.

tergiverser *v.i.* to beat around the bush.

terme *n.m.* term; limit; boundary; end; word, expression. **toucher au ~,** to be near one's end. **payer son ~,** to pay one's rent.

terminaison *n.f.* termination; ending.

terminal, e *adj.* terminal; twelfth grade, senior year.

terminer *v.t.* to limit, to end, to bring to a close, to put an end to, to terminate. **~ un ouvrage,** to finish a work. **se ~,** *v.refl.* to end, to close; to be finished, to finish.

terminologie *n.f.* terminology.

termite *n.m.* termite.

terne *adj.* dull; tarnished, dim. **style ~,** dull style. **des yeux ~s,** lustreless eyes.

ternir *v.t.* to tarnish; to dim, to dull, to sully, to blemish. **~ la réputation d'une personne,** to tarnish a person's reputation. **se ~,** *v.refl.* to tarnish; to lose lustre, to become dull; to be sullied.

terrain *n.m.* ground, piece of ground; soil. **gagner du ~,** to gain ground.

terre *n.f.* earth; ground, land; soil; mold. **~ calcaire,** calcareous earth. **~ glaise,** clay. **~ cuite,** terracotta; baked clay. **~ ferme,** firm land, dry land, terra firma; main land. **la ~ sainte,** the

Holy Land. **acheter une ~**, to buy an estate. **par
~**, on the ground.

terrestre *adj.* terrestrial, earthly; worldly.

terreur *n.f.* terror; dread, fright, dismay; awe.

terrible *adj.* terrible; dreadful; terrific, frightful.

terriblement *adv.* terribly; dreadfully; awfully;
enormously, excessively.

terrifier *v.t.* to terrify.

territoire *n.m.* territory.

territorial, e *adj.* territorial.

terroriser *v.t.* to terrify.

terrorisme *n.m.* terrorism.

terroriste *n.m.* terrorist.

tes *adj. poss. n.f. pl.* your.

test *n.m.* test.

testament *n.m.* testament; will. **l'Ancien ~**,
the Old Testament. **le Nouveau ~**, the New
Testament.

tester *v.i.* to test; to make one's will.

testicule *n.m.* testicle, testis.

têtard *n.m.* tadpole.

tête *n.f.* head; top; skull; face; brains, sense;
leader; beginning. **lever la ~**, to hold up one's
head. **perdre la ~**, to lose one's head. **tenir ~,
faire ~ à quelqu'un**, to resist, not to budge.
faire les choses à sa ~, to do as one likes, to do
something one's own way. **avoir la ~ chaude**, to
be hot-headed. **une forte ~**, a strong-minded
man. **faire un signe de ~**, to nod. **ne savoir
où donner de la ~**, not to know which way to
turn. **mettre la ~ de quelqu'un à prix**, to set a
price on a person's head. **être à la ~ d'une
entreprise**, to be at the head of a company. **~ à
~, adv.** face to face; in private. **en avoir par-
dessus la ~**, to be fed up.

téter *v.t.* to suck.

tétine *n.f.* teats (of female mammals); udder;
pacifier.

téton *n.m.* breast, teat.

têtu *adj.* stubborn, obstinate.

texte *n.m.* text; purview (of the law).

textile *adj.* textile.

texture *n.f.* texture.

thé *n.m.* tea plant; tea.

théâtral, e *adj.* theatrical.

théâtre *n.m.* theater, playhouse, stage; scene;
drama.

théière *n.f.* teapot.

thème *n.m.* theme; topic, subject; translation.

théologie *n.f.* theology.

théorie *n.f.* theory, speculation.

théorique *adj.* theoretical; speculative.

théoriquement *adv.* theoretically, speculatively.

thérapeute *n.m.f.* therapist.

thérapeutique *n.f.* therapeutics *pl.* therapy. *adj.*
therapeutic.

thermal, e *adj.* thermal. **station ~**, spa.

thermomètre *n.m.* thermometer.

thèse *n.f.* thesis; theme, subject, discussion.
soutenir sa ~, to support one's thesis.

thon *n.m.* tuna, tunafish.

thorax *n.m.* thorax.

thym *n.m.* thyme.

tibia *n.m.* tibia, shinbone.

tic *n.m.* twitch.

ticket *n.m.* ticket.

tic tac *n.m.* tick-tock; ticking.

tiède *adj.* lukewarm, tepid.

tiédeur *n.f.* lukewarmness, tepidity, tepidness.

tiédir *v.i.* to grow, to become tepid, lukewarm,
cool.

tien, tienne *adj.* yours. *pron. poss.* yours. **le ~ et
le mien**, yours and mine.

tiers, erce *adj.* third. **écrire à une tierce personne**, to write to a third person. *n.m.* third
part, third; third party, third person. **le ~
monde**, the Third World.

tige *n.f.* stem, stalk (of plants); stock, body, trunk
(of trees); shaft (of a column), leg (of a boot);
shank (of a key, of a nail); rod (of a piston, etc.).

tigre *n.m.* tiger.

tigré, e *adj.* spotted, speckled. **un chat ~**, a tab-
by cat.

tigresse *n.f.* tigress.

tilleul *n.m.* lime tree, linden tree.

timbrage *n.m.* stamping.

timbre *n.m.* bell; sound (of a bell); tone (of
voice); stamp; (postage) stamp. **cette lettre
porte le ~ de Londres**, that letter bears the
London postmark.

timbré, e *p.p.* stamped, marked. **papier ~**,
stamped paper; *Fig.* cracked. **il est un peu ~**,
he is nuts.

timbrer *v.t.* to stamp (paper, parchment, bills,
newspapers, letters, etc.); to postmark.

timide *adj.* timid, shy.

timidement *adv.* shyly; timidly.

timidité *n.f.* timidity; shyness.

tinter *v.t.* to ring (a bell); to toll; to ring for; to
tinkle; to jingle. **le oreilles lui tintent**, his ears
tingle.

tique *n.f.* tick.

tiquer *v.i.* to wince. **il n'a pas tiqué**, he didn't
raise an eyebrow.

tir *n.m.* shooting; firing. **chasse au ~**, shooting.
~ à la cible, practice.

tirade *n.f.* passage; tirade; declamation; strain;
long speech. **d'une ~, tout d'une ~**, in a
breath, at a stretch.

tirage *n.m.* drawing; towing (of boats); printing;
print; number printed, edition (of a book). **~ à
part**, offprint. **~ au sort**, drawing lots. **le ~
était de deux mille**, the number of copies
printed was two thousand.

tiraillement *n.m.* pulling; tug; pain, twitching;
twinge.

tiré, e *p.p.* drawn. **être ~ à quatre épingles**, to
be dressed to kill. **visage ~**, haggard, worn face.
~ par les cheveux, farfetched. *n.m.* drawee (of
a bill of exchange); shooting.

tire-bouchon *n.m.* corkscrew.

tire-d'aile *n.f.* rapid motion, *adv.* swiftly.

tirelire *n.f.* piggybank.

tirer *v.t.* to draw; to pull; to draw back; to draw (in, up, off, on, out, down), to drag; to haul, to tug; to extract, to take out, to take, to obtain; to get; to print. **~ quelqu'un**, to pull a person. **~ l'oreille, les oreilles à quelqu'un**, to pull a person's ears. **~ une affaire au clair**, to clear up a matter. **~ les rideaux**, to draw the curtains. **~ un coup de fusil**, to fire a gun, to shoot. **~ une lettre de change**, to draw a bill of exchange. **~ parti de**, to profit from. **~ les cartes**, to tell fortunes by the cards. **~ en l'air**, to fire in the air. **~ en longueur**, to delay, to put off, to spin out. **se ~**, *v.refl.* to get out, to extricate oneself, to save oneself, to get through; to be drawn; to be printed, struck off. **se ~ d'affaire**, to get away with something. **l'huile se tire des olives**, oil is extracted from olives.

tiret *n.m.* hyphen (-); dash (—).

tiroir *n.m.* drawer; slide, slide valve.

tisane *n.f.* herb(al) tea, tea, infusion (of herbs).

tisser *v.t.* to weave.

tissue, e *n.m.* fabric; material, cloth. **un ~ de mensonges**, a web of lies. *Med.* tissue. **le ~ urbain/social/industriel**; the urban/social/industrial fabric.

titiller *v.t.* to titillate; to tickle.

titre *n.m.* title; right; claim, deed; standard (of gold, silver, etc.). **le ~ d'un ouvrage**, the title of a work. **professeur en ~**, titulary professor. **à juste ~**, rightly, justly. **à ~ d'ami**, as a friend.

titré, e *adj.* titled.

titrer *v.t.* to title, to give a title to; to dose; to titrate (solution); to assay (ore). **se ~**, *v.refl.* to assume a title.

tituber *v.i.* to stagger, to stumble.

titulaire *adj.* titulary, titular. *n.m.f.* titular, titulary; incumbent; bearer, holder.

toast *n.m.* toast; **porter un ~**, to propose a toast.

toboggan *n.m.* toboggan; slide; overpass.

toc *n.m.* tap, rap; fake, custom jewelry.

toi *pron.pers.* you, yourself.

toile *n.f.* cloth; linen; canvas; curtain (of a theater). **~ d'araignée**, spiderweb.

toilettage *n.m.*, grooming.

toilette *n.f.* washing and dressing, dress, attire. **faire sa ~**, to dress.

toiser *v.t.* to eye up and down. **se ~**, *v.refl.* to eye, to observe each other.

toit *n.m.* roof. **crier sur les ~s**, to shout from the house tops.

toiture *n.f.* roofing, roof.

tôle *n.f.* sheet iron.

tolérable *adj.* toleable, bearable.

tolérance *n.f.* toleration; tolerance.

tolérant, e *adj.* tolerant.

tolérer *v.t.* to tolerate.

tomate *n.f.* tomato.

tombal, e *adj.* tomb(stone).

tombant, e *adj.* falling, drooping; flowing.

tombe *n.f.* tombstone, gravestone; tomb, grave.

tombeau *n.m.* tomb; tombstone.

tombée *n.f.* fall. **à la ~ de la nuit**, at nightfall.

tomber *v.i.* to fall; to fall down, to drop; to sink, to sink down, to tumble down; to droop. **~ des nues**, to fall from the clouds; to be astounded. **~ par terre**, to fall on the ground, to fall down. **~ de faiblesse, d'inanition**, to faint with weakness. **~ dans un piège**, to fall into a snare. **~ malade**, to fall ill. **~ amoureux de**, to fall in love with. **~ dans le ridicule**, to become ridiculous. **~ sans connaissance**, to pass out. **~ d'accord**, to agree. **~ en ruine**, to fall into ruins. **le jour commençait à ~**, it was growing dark. **la nuit tombe**, night is coming on. **laisser ~ la voix**, to lower one's voice. **~ en désuétude**, to grow obsolete. **le soupçon tomba sur lui**, suspicion fell upon him.

tome *n.m.* tome; volume.

ton *adv.poss. fem.* **ta** *pl.* **tes** your. **ton père et ta mère**, your father and your mother.

ton *n.m.* tone; tune; note, accent, strain; spirit; pitch. **~ de voix**, tone of voice. **hausser le ~**, to raise the voice. **le prendre sur un ~ bien haut**, to ride the high horse.

tonalité *n.f.* tonality; dial tone; mode.

tondeur, euse *n.f.* clipper, shears. **~ (à gazon)**, lawnmower.

tondre *v.t.* to shear; to clip, to trim, to crop (hair); to shave. **~ des brebis**, to shear sheep. **~ un chien**, to crop a dog.

tondu, e *p.p.* shorn, clipped, cropped, cut. *n.m.* a monk.

tonicité *n.f.* tonicity.

tonifier *v.t.* to tone up, to stimulate.

tonique *adj.* tonic. **accent ~**, tonic accent. *n.m.* tonic. *n.f.* tonic, keynote.

tonne *n.f.* ton; (large) cask.

tonneau *n.m.* barrel; cask.

tonner *v.i.* to thunder.

tonnerre *n.m.* thunder; lightning. *Fig.* **du ~**, wonderful.

topo *n.m.* article; lecture, summary.

topographe *n.m.* topographer.

topographie *n.f.* topography; map; plan.

top secret *adj.* top secret.

toque *n.f.* fur hat. **~ blanche**, chef's hat.

torche *n.f.* torch, torchlight, flashlight.

torcher *v.t.* to wipe, to wipe down.

torchon *n.m.* dish towel; (dish) cloth.

tordant, e *adj.* hilarious.

tordre *v.t.* to wring, to wrest; to writhe **~ du fil**, to twist thread. **se ~ les mains**, to wring one's hands. **se ~**, *v.refl.* to twist, to be twisted.

tordu, e *adj.* twisted; crooked; bent; distorted.

tornade *n.f.* tornado.

torpeur *n.f.* torpor.

torpille *n.f.* torpedo.

torpilleur *n.m.* torpedo boat.

torrent *n.m.* torrent, mountain stream; flood,

flow, **il pleut à ~s,** it's pouring. **un ~ de larmes,** a flood of tears.

torrentiel, elle *adj.* torrent; diluvian; drenching. **pluie ~le,** diluvian rain.

torrentueux, euse *adj.* torrent, torrential.

torride *adj.* torrid; burning.

torse *n.m.* torso, trunk, body.

torsion *n.f.* torsion.

tort *n.m.* wrong; injury, harm. **avoir ~,** to be in the wrong, to be wrong. **donner ~ à quelqu'un,** to lay the blame on someone. **réparer le ~ qu'on a fait,** to repair the injury one has done. **à ~,** wrongly; without reason. **à ~ et à travers,** at random.

torticolis *n.m.* stiff neck.

tortiller *v.t.* to twist; to wriggle; to twist about. **se ~,** *v.refl.* to wriggle.

tortionnaire *adj.* wrongful; of torture; *n.m.* torturer.

tortue *n.f.* tortoise. **~ de mer,** turtle.

tortueux, euse *adj.* tortuous; winding; crooked; crafty; unfair, indirect. **une rue étroite et ~se,** a narrow, winding street.

torture *n.f.* torture; torment, rack. **mettre à la ~,** to torture, to rack.

torturer *v.t.* to torture, to torment.

tôt *adv.* soon; early. **~ ou tard,** sooner or later. **au plus ~,** at the earliest. **plus ~ que,** sooner than.

total, e *adj.* total, entire, whole; complete; utter. *n.m.* total, whole; whole sum, sum total.

totalement *adv.* totally, wholly, entirely.

totalitaire *adj.* totalitarian.

totalitarisme *n.m.* totalitarianism.

totalité *n.f.* totality, whole, entirety.

toubib *n.m.* doctor, doc.

touchant, e *adj.* touching; affecting; moving, pathetic. **des paroles ~es,** touching words. **c'est un spectacle ~,** it is a touching sight. *n.m.* the pathetic. *prep.* touching; concerning, regarding, with respect to.

touche *n.f.* touch; manner (of painter); style (of writer); key (of piano, computer); shot (of drugs). **pierre de ~,** touchstone.

toucher *v.t.* to touch; to feel; to handle; to hit; to strike; to play on (the piano); to adjoin; to paint, to delineate; to offend; to move; to concern, to relate to; to play upon; to touch upon; to allude to; to concern; to receive (money). **~ de la main,** to touch with the hand. **ma maison touche la sienne,** my house adjoins his. **~ le but,** to get close to one's goal. **~ de l'argent,** to cash money. **regardez cela, mais n'y touchez pas,** look at it, but do not touch it. **~ à sa fin,** to be near one's end. **se ~,** *v.refl.* to touch each other; to touch, to join; to meet. **les extrêmes se touchent,** extremes meet. *n.m.* touch; feeling.

touffe *n.f.* tuft, bunch, cluster, clump. **~ d'arbres,** clump of trees **~ de cheveux,** tuft of hair.

touffu, e *adj.* thick, dense, bushy.

touiller *v.t. Infml.* to stir (up).

toujours *adj.* always, ever, forever, still, nevertheless. **je l'ai ~ dit,** I have always said so. **je demeure ~ à Paris,** I still live in Paris.

tour *n.f.* tower. **la ~ Eiffel,** Eiffel Tower.

tour *n.m.* turn, twist; reel; round circumference; excursion, tour, trip, feat, trick; sprain, strain. **~ de roue,** a turn of the wheel. **à ~ de bras,** with all one's might. **aller faire un ~,** to go take a walk. **jouer un ~ à quelqu'un,** to play a trick on someone. **c'est mon ~,** it is my turn. **à ~ de rôle,** by turns. **faire le ~ du monde,** to go round the world. **~ de force,** feat of strength. **des ~s de cartes,** card tricks. *n.f.* tower, castle (at chess). **~ carrée,** square tower.

tourbillon *n.m.* whirlwind, whirlpool. **des ~s de fumée,** clouds of smoke.

tourbillonnant, e *adj.* whirling; eddying.

tourbillonner *v.i.* to whirl, to swirl.

tourisme *n.m.* tourism.

touriste *n.m.f.* tourist.

tourment *n.m.* torment, pain, torture, anguish.

tourmente *n.f.* snowstorm; tempest, storm.

tourmenter *v.t.* to torment; to strain; to torture; to pain, to distress, to tease, to annoy. **se ~,** *v.refl.* to torment, to be uneasy, to fret; to be agitated, to be restless.

tourmenteur *n.m.* tormentor, torturer. *adj.* tormenting.

tournage *n.m.* shooting (film), turning.

tournant, e *adj.* turning; revolving. **pont ~,** revolving bridge, swing bridge.

tournée *n.f.* round; journey, tour, excursion; circuit; tour of inspection.

tournemain *n.m.* twinkling, instant.

tourner *v.t.* to turn; to express; to wind; to revolve; to wind; to go about, to move; to hesitate; to become dizzy; to result in; to become sour, to interpret; to change; to spoil, to taint. **~ la tête,** to turn one's head. **son affaire tourne bien,** he is doing good business. **~ en ridicule,** to turn into ridicule. **le vent a tourné,** the wind has turned. **tournez à droite,** turn to the right. **~ autour du pot,** to beat about the bush. **faire ~ la tête à quelqu'un,** to make someone dizzy. **le temps tourne au froid,** the weather is turning cold. **le lait a tourné,** the milk has turned; become sour. **se ~,** *v.refl.* to be turned; to turn; to turn over; to turn round, to turn about; to change, to be changed. **se ~ dans son lit,** to turn round in one's bed. **ne savoir de quel côté se ~,** not to know which way to turn.

tournesol *n.m.* sunflower.

tournevis *n.m.* screwdriver.

tournoi *n.m.* tournament.

tournure *n.f.* turn; cast; arrangement. **l'affaire prit une mauvaise ~,** the affair took a bad turn. **~ de phrase,** expression, construction of a sentence.

tourterelle *n.f.* turtledove, turtle.

tous V. TOUT.

tousser *v.i.* to cough; to hem.

toussoter *v.i.* to cough slightly.

tout, e *adj.* all; whole; the whole of; every, each. ~ **le monde,** everybody; all the world. ~e **la terre,** the entire earth. **tous les hommes,** all men. ~ **ceci,** all this. **nous avons tous une même origine,** we all have the same origin. **tous les jours,** every day. **tous les mois,** every month. ~ **es les deux heures,** every other hour. **à** ~**e bride,** (to run) full speed. ~ **homme qui,** any man that. ~ **autre que lui,** anybody but himself. *n.m.* whole; all; everything; anything. ~ **ou rien,** all or nothing. **ce n'est pas** ~, that is not all. **il sait un peu de** ~, he knows a little of everything. **après** ~, after all. **rien du** ~, nothing at all. **risquer, jouer le** ~ **pour le** ~, to stake all. *n.m.f.pl.* all, everyone, everybody. *adj.* quite, wholly, completely, entirely, all; fully. **je suis** ~ **à vous,** I am all yours. ~ **fait,** ready made. **ils sont** ~ **étonnés,** they are very surprised. **elle était** ~e **malade,** she was quite ill. ~ **haut,** very high. ~ **court,** very short. **parler** ~ **bas,** to speak very low. ~ **au moins,** at least. ~ **à fait,** quite, entirely. ~ **de suite,** directly, immediately.

toutefois *adv.* yet, however, nevertheless, still.

toux *n.f.* cough; coughing.

toxicomane *n.m.f.* drug addict.

toxicomanie *n.f.* drug addiction.

toxique *adj.* poisonous, toxic. *n.m.* poison.

trac *n.m.* stage fright, nervousness

tracas *n.m.* worry, bother.

tracasser *v.t.* to torment, to annoy, to worry. **se** ~, *v.refl.* to worry oneself.

trace *n.f.* trace; track; footprint; footstep; trail, remains, draft, sketch. **voilà la** ~ **de ses pas,** there are the traces of his footsteps.

tracé *n.m.* outline, sketch, line, direction (of a road, a canal, etc.). **faire le** ~ **de,** to lay out.

tracement *n.m.* laying out, marking, tracing.

tracer *v.t.* to trace, to draw, to chalk out. ~ **un plan,** to draw a plan.

trachée *n.f.* trachea; windpipe.

trachéotomie *n.f.* tracheotomy.

tract *n.m.* tract, pamphlet, leaflet.

tracteur *n.m.* tractor.

traction *n.f.* traction. ~ **avant,** front-wheel drive. **faire des** ~s, to do pull-ups/push-ups.

tradition *n.f.* tradition.

traditionnel, elle *adj.* traditional, usual.

traducteur *n.m.* translator.

traduction *n.f.* translation.

traduire *v.t.* to translate; to interpret, to remove, to transfer. ~ **un auteur,** to translate an author. ~ **devant, la cour d'assises,** to bring before the court. **se** ~, *v.refl.* to appear, to represent, to signify; to be translated.

traduisible *adj.* translatable.

trafic *n.m.* traffic; trade. ~ **des armes,** gunrunning; traffic in arms.

trafiquant *n.m.* trader, merchant, trafficker. ~ **de** or **en drogues,** drug trafficker.

tragédie *n.f.* tragedy.

tragédien, ienne *n.m.* tragedian.

tragi-comedie *n.f.* tragicomedy.

tragi-comique *adj.* tragicomic, tragicomical.

tragique *adj.* tragic. **un sort** ~, a tragic fate. *n.m.* tragedy, tragic poet, author, tragedian. **prendre les choses au** ~, to take things too seriously.

tragiquement *adv.* tragically.

trahir *v.t.* to betray, to be false to, to disclose, to mislead; to deceive. ~ **la confiance de quelqu'un,** to betray a person's confidence. **se** ~, *v.refl.* to betray oneself, to be false to each other.

trahison *n.f.* treachery, betrayal, treason.

train *n.m.* pace, rate; train. **aller à fond de** ~, to go at full speed. **aller grand** ~, to go fast. **au** ~ **dont il va,** at the rate he is going. **l'affaire va son** ~, the affair is getting on. **aller bon** ~, to get along smartly. **mettre une affaire en** ~, to set a thing going. **être en** ~ **de,** to be in the mood for, to be about to. **je ne suis pas en** ~ **de jouer,** I am not playing. **il est en** ~ **de se ruiner,** he is on the high road to ruin. ~ **de voyageurs,** passenger train. ~ **à grande vitesse,** fast train.

traîner *v.t.* to drag; to trail, to drag along; to protract. ~ **les pieds,** to drag one's feet. **ne laissez rien** ~, do not leave anything about. **cette affaire traîne,** this business is dragging. **se** ~, *v.refl.* to crawl, to crawl along, to drag oneself along.

trait *n.m.* trace, shaft, dart; bolt; ray (of light); stroke, hit; trait, mark; draft, drink; dash, feature (of the face). **boire à longs traits,** to gulp down. **des** ~**s d'esprit,** flashes of wit. **ruiner quelqu'un d'un** ~ **de plume,** to ruin a person by a stroke of the pen. ~ **d'union,** hyphen. **elle a de petits** ~**s,** she has small features. **avoir** ~ **à quelque chose,** to be connected to something.

traitable *adj.* tractable, manageable, docile; treatable.

traitant *adj.* medicated. **médecin** ~, medical practitioner.

traite *n.f.* trade; slave trade; speculation; draft; bill; milking; journey. **faire** ~ **sur,** to draw a bill on. **la** ~ **des blanches,** the white-slave trade.

traité *n.m.* treatise; tract. ~ **de paix,** peace treaty.

traitement *n.m.* treatment; salary, pay; treat; usage, manner of using. **bon** ~, good treatment.

traiter *v.t.* to treat, to attend; to handle, to manage; to discuss; to use, to negotiate; to traffic; to transact business. ~ **quelqu'un en ami,** to treat a person as a friend. ~ **quelqu'un de haut en bas,** to treat a person with contempt. ~ **une maladie,** to treat an illness. ~ **une question,** to deal with a question. **se** ~, *v.refl.* to treat oneself; to treat one another; to be treated.

traiteur *n.m.* caterer.

traître, tresse *adj.* traitorous, treacherous. *n.m.f.* treacherous person; traitor; traitress. **en ~,** treacherously, traitorously.

traîtreusement *adv.* treacherously, perfidiously.

traîtrise *n.f.* treachery, betrayal.

trajectoire *n.f.* trajectory.

trajet *n.m.* passage by water, voyage; journey (by land) distance; way; course (of artery, etc.).

tranchant *n.m.* edge.

tranchant, e *adj.* cutting, sharp, peremptory. **un instrument ~,** a sharp instrument.

tranche *n.f.* slice; cutlet.

tranchée *n.f.* drain, trench; ditch; cutting, excavation. *pl.* colic, gripes; pains.

trancer *v.t.* to cut, to cut off, to sever; to decide, to cut short, to solve, to decide, to determine; to dogmatize; (with **de**) to set up for. **~ la tête,** to cut off the head. **~ une question,** to settle a question. **le ~ net,** to speak plainly.

tranquille *adj.* quiet; tranquil, calm, still, easy; peaceful.

tranquillement *adv.* quietly, tranquilly.

tranquillisant, e *adj.* tranquilizing; *n.m.* tranquilizer.

tranquilliser *v.t.* to tranquilize, to quiet, to calm, to still. **se ~,** *v.refl.* to become tranquil.

tranquillité, n.f. tranquillity, tranquilness, quiet, quietness, stillness, calm, peace.

transaction *n.f.* compromise; transaction.

transalpin, e *adj.* transalpine.

transatlantique *adj.* transatlantic.

transcendance *n.f.* transcendency, transcendence.

transcendant, e *adj.* transcendent; *Math.* transcendental.

transcendantal, e *adj.* transcendental.

transe *n.f.* trance; fright, alarm, anxiety.

transférer *v.t.* to transfer; to transport, to remove; (of bishops), to translate.

transfert *n.m.* transfer.

transformation *n.f.* transformation, metamorphosis.

transformer *v.t.* to transform; to turn, to convert. **se ~,** *v.refl.* to transform oneself; to be transformed; to be converted.

transfusion *n.f.* transfusion. **~ du sang,** blood transfusion.

transgresser *v.i.* to transgress, to infringe; to break.

transgresseur *n.m.* transgressor, offender. *adj.* transgressional, transgressive, culpable.

transgression *n.f.* transgression; violation.

transi, e *adj.* chilled, benumbed; paralyzed.

transiger *v.i.* to make a compromise, to compound, to come to terms.

transir *v.t.* to chill, to freeze; to benumb; to overcome; to paralyse; to be chilled, benumbed; to tremble, to shiver; to be paralyzed. **le froid m'a transi,** I was chilled to the bone. **~ de froid,** to

chill to the bone. **~ de peur,** to be paralyzed with fear.

transit *n.m.* transit.

transition *n.f.* transition.

transitoire *adj.* transitory, transient; passing.

transmetteur *adj.* transmitting; signals. *n.m.* transmitter.

transmettre *v.t.* to transmit; to convey; to send on, to forward; to hand over to broadcast. **transmettez mon amitié à vos parents,** send my regards to your parents.

transmissible *adj.* transmissible; transferable. **sexuellement ~,** sexually transmitted.

transmission *n.f.* transmission; transfer; broadcasting. **~ direct** or **en direct,** live broadcast.

transmuable *adj.* transmutable.

transparaître *v.t.* to show through.

transparence *n.f.* transparency.

transparent, e *adj.* transparent; clear. *n.m.* transparency.

transpercer *v.t.* to transpierce, to transfix, to pierce; to go through.

transpiration *n.f.* transpiration; perspiration.

transpirer *v.i.* to transpire; to perspire; to exhale; to leak out.

transplantation *n.f.* transplantation

transplanter *v.t.* to transplant.

transport *n.m.* transport; conveyance; rapture, ecstasy, ravishment. **~ de marchandises,** carrying of goods. **~ de joie,** transport of joy. **frais de ~,** freight charges. **les ~s en commun,** public transportation.

transportable *adj.* transportable.

transporter *v.t.* to transport; to convey, to remove, to transfer; to enrapture, to ravish, to put into ecstasy. **la joie l'a transporté,** he is transported with joy. **se ~,** *v.refl.* to go, to repair, to proceed; to be transported.

transposer *v.t.* to transpose.

transposition *n.f.* transposition.

trappe *n.f.* trap (door); trap, pitfall, snare.

traquenard *n.m.* trap.

traquer *v.t.* to drive game; to track down, to hunt down; to enclose, to hunt out.

trauma *n.m.* trauma.

traumatique *adj.* traumatic.

traumatiser *v.t.* to traumatize.

travail *n.m. pl.* **travaux,** job, occupation, work; toil, labor, employment; industry, study, operation, workmanship. **le ~ de l'esprit,** intellectual work. **se mettre au ~,** to set to work. **suspendre les travaux,** to suspend work. **travaux forcés,** hard labor. **ce bijou est d'un beau ~,** the workmanship of this jewel is beautiful.

travailler *v.t.* to work, to labor, to toil; to fashion, to work up. **~ le marbre,** to work marble. **~ la terre,** to till, cultivate the ground. **~ son style,** to elaborate one's style. **~ trop,** to work too much. **le vin travaille,** wine ferments. **se ~,** *v.refl.* to be worked, to be wrought; to work oneself up, to torment oneself.

travailleur, euse *n.m.f.* worker; operative, mechanic. *adj.* working, hard-working, laborious, industrious, toiling, painstaking.

travelo *n.m.* transvestite, drag queen.

travers *n.m.* à ~, **au** ~ **de,** across, through. **à** ~ **champs,** through the fields. **de** ~, obliquely, crookedly; across. **regarder de** ~, to squint, to be cross-eyed. **regarder quelqu'un de** ~, to look askance at a person. **il prend tout de** ~, he takes everything wrong. **en** ~, across.

traverser *v.t.* to cross, to pass through, *Fig.* to thwart, to obstruct, to hinder, to balk. ~ **un pays,** to cross a country. ~ **la rue,** to cross the street. ~ **la rivière à la nage,** to swim across the river. **le couteau lui a traversé le bras,** the knife ran through his arm. **se** ~, *v.refl.* to be traversed; to thwart one another.

traversin *n.m.* bolster, crossbeam; stretchers.

travestir *v.t.* to disguise, to travesty. **se** ~, *v.refl.* to disguise oneself; to dress up as the opposite sex.

travestissement *n.m.* disguise; travesty; (of a work), parody.

traviole (de) *adv. Infml.* crooked.

trébucher *v.i.* to stumble, to trip, to fall.

trèfle *n.m.* trefoil; clover; (at cards) club.

treize *adj.* thirteen; thirteenth.

treizième *adj.* thirteenth.

tréma *n.m.* dieresis.

tremblement *n.m.* trembling; quaking; shaking, shuddering. ~ **de terre,** earthquake.

trembler *v.i.* to tremble; to quake, to shake, to shudder, to shiver; (of the voice) to quaver; to twinkle; (of a light) to flicker. ~ **de froid,** to shiver with cold.

tremblotant, e *adj.* trembling, tremulous, shivering, quivering; twinkling.

trembloter *v.i.* to tremble, to shiver, to quiver.

trempe *n.f.* steeping, soaking (in water); *Metall.* tempering, hardening; temper; caliber, character; beating. **la** ~ **de cet acier est excellente,** the temper of that steel is excellent.

tremper *v.t.* to soak; to steep; to wet thoroughly; *Print.* to wet; to temper (metals). ~ **son pain dans du vin,** to soak one's bread in wine. **du vin trempé,** diluted wine. ~ **dans un crime,** to be implicated in a crime. *v.refl.* to be soaked.

tremplin *n.m.* springboard, diving board; ski jump; stepping-stone.

trentaine *n.f.* thirty, about thirty.

trente *adj.* thirty; thirtieth *n.m.* thirty.

trentième *adj. n.m.* thirtieth.

trépas *n.m.* passage; narrow channel; death, decease.

trépasser *v.i.* to die, to pass away.

trépidation *n.f.* apprehension, trepidation.

trépied *n.m.* tripod; trivet.

trépigner *v.i.* to stamp, to patter. ~ **des pieds,** to stamp one's feet. ~ **d'impatience,** to stamp with impatience.

très *adj.* very, most, much, very much.

trésor *n.m.* treasure; treasury. **mon petit** ~, my little darling, my little precious.

trésorerie *n.f.* treasury.

trésorier, ière *n.m.f.* treasurer.

tressaillir *v.i.* to start (from surprise); to shudder (with fear); to thrill. ~ **de joie,** to thrill with joy.

tresse *n.f.* braid.

tresser *v.t.* to braid, to plait (hair).

trêve *n.f.* truce; quiet, rest.

tri *n.m.* sorting.

triage *n.m.* sorting, picking; choosing; selection; choice.

triangle *n.m.* triangle. *adj.* triangled, triangular.

triangulaire *adj.* triangular, triangled, three-angled.

tribu *n.f.* tribe.

tribulation *n.f.* tribulation.

tribunal *n.m.* tribunal, bench; court of justice.

triche *n.f. Infml.* cheating.

tricher *v.t.* to trick, to cheat, to deceive.

tricheur, euse *n.m.f.* cheater, cheat (at play); trickster, tricker.

tricolore *adj.* tricolored, three-colored.

tricot *n.m.* sweater; knitting.

tricoter *v.t. and v.i.* to knit.

trictrac *n.m.* backgammon; backgammon board.

trier *v.t.* to sort, (out); to pick, to choose.

trimbaler *v.t. Infml.* to drag about, to trail.

trimer *v.i. Infml.* to slave away, to work hard.

trimestre *n.m.* three months, quarter (of a year). **par** ~, quarterly.

trimestriel, elle *adj.* quarterly.

tringle *n.f.* rod; curtain rod; *Arch.* tringle.

trinquer *v.i.* to clink glasses; to drink, to have a drink, to booze; to suffer.

trio *n.m.* trio.

triomphal, e *adj.* triumphal.

triomphalement *adv.* triumphantly, in triumph.

triomphant, e *adj.* triumphant; victorious.

triomphe *n.m.* triumph. **c'est un beau** ~, it is a great success. **Arch de Triomphe,** Arch of Triumph.

triompher *v.i.* to triumph. ~ **de,** to triumph over.

tripe *n.f.* tripe.

triple *adj. and n.m.* triple, treble, threefold.

triplement *n.m.* tripling. *adv.* triply.

tripler *v.t.* to triple.

tripot *n.m. Infml.* dive, joint.

tripotage *n.m. Infml.* medley; mess; jumble; intrigue, underhanded dealing.

tripotée *n.f.* thrashing; horde, load, pile.

tripoter *v.i.* to jumble together, to intrigue, to meddle, to handle awkwardly.

triste *adj.* sad; sorrowful, melancholy, dispirited, dismal, gloomy; sorry, wretched. **des idées** ~**s,** gloomy, sad ideas. **une** ~ **nouvelle,** sad news. **le temps est** ~, the weather is

gray. **faire un ~ repas**, to make a poor meal.
tristement *adv.* sadly; sorrowfully, gloomily,
mournfully, deplorably.
tristesse *n.f.* sadness; sorrowfulness, melancholy, gloominess; dulness. **s'abandonner à la
~**, to give way to sadness.
troc *n.m.* exchange, barter, truck.
trogne *n.f. Infml.* face.
trognon *n.m.* core (of fruit); stump, stalk (of a
cabbage, etc.); *Infml.* cutie.
trois *adj.* three; third. **~ fois**, three times. *n.m.*
three; third (of the month).
troisième *adj.* third. *n.m.* third, third person;
third floor. *n.f.* third class.
troisièmement *adv.* thirdly.
trois-mâts *n.m.* three-masted ship.
trombe *n.f.* waterspout; **entrer/sortir en ~**, to
burst out.
trombone *n.m.* trombone; trombone player.
trompe *n.f.* trump; horn, hunting horn; trunk,
proboscis (of elephants) tube. **~ de fallope**, fallopian tube.
tromper *v.t.* to deceive; to cheat, to take in, to
dupe; to balk, to elude; to seduce. **se ~**, *v.refl.* to
mistake, to be mistaken, to make a mistake; to
deceive oneself. **se ~ de chemin**, to take the
wrong road. **vous vous trompez**, you are
mistaken.
trompette *n.f.* trumpet. **sonner de la ~**, to
sound the trumpet. **sans tambour ni ~**, in
silence, quietly. *n.m.* trumpeter; trumpet.
trompeur, euse *adj.* deceitful, deceptive. *n.m.*
Infml. deceiver, deluder, cheat, betrayer.
trompeusement *adv.* deceitfully, deceptively.
tronc *n.m.* trunk; stock; stem; poor box, alms box.
tronche *n.f. Infml.* face, mug.
trône *n.m.* throne.
trop *n.m.* too much; too great; excess. *adv.* too;
too much, too many, over. **il a ~ bu**, he has
drunk too much. **pas ~**, not too much, not too
many; not over, not very. **par ~**, too, excessive.
trophée *n.m.* trophy.
tropical, e *adj.* tropical.
tropique *n.m.* tropic. *adj.* tropic, tropical.
tropisme *n.m.* tropism.
trop-plein *n.m.* overflow; waste.
trot *n.m.* trot (of a horse).
trotte *n.f. Infml.* distance, way; walk.
trotter *v.i.* to trot; to run; to go about, to run
about.
trottoir *n.m.* sidewalk.
trou *n.m.* hole; opening; gap; orifice; hovel.
boucher un ~, to stop a hole, a gap. **le ~ de la
serrure, de la porte**, the keyhole.
trouble *n.m.* trouble; disorder, disturbance, confusion, troubles, disturbances. **susciter des ~s**,
to raise disturbances. *adj.* turbid; muddy; thick;
dull; cloudy, dim. **vin ~**, thick wine. **avoir la
vue ~**, to have blurred vision.
troubler *v.t.* to disturb; to trouble to upset; to
agiter, to perplex; to confuse; to annoy; to

interrupt; to blur, to dim (sight). **cela trouble
la digestion**, that is bad for the digestion.
~ l'eau, to disturb water. **se ~**, *v.refl.* to become
disturbed, agitated; to become confused; to
become unsettled; to get cloudy, overcast; to
grow dim; to get turbid, muddy, thick. **l'eau se
trouble**, the water is muddy. **il avait l'air troublé**, he looked troubled, he looked confused.
trouée, e *adj.* full of holes, with holes in.
trouer *v.t.* to make a hole in; to pierce. **se ~**,
v.refl. to get full of holes.
trouillard, e *n.m.f. Infml.* coward.
troupe *n.f.* troop, band; gang, crew; company
(of stage players); *pl.* troops; (of animals) flock;
(of birds) flight.
troupeau *n.m.* herd, drove, flock (of fowls or
small animals). **un ~ de boeufs**, a drove, a
herd of oxen. **~ de moutons**, flock of sheep.
trousse *n.f.* bundle; doctor's bag; pencil case.
être aux ~s de quelqu'un, to be at a person's
heels.
trousseau *n.m.* bunch (of keys); bundle (of
arrows); hope chest.
trouvaille *n.f.* find, thing found, finding.
trouver *v.t.* to find; find out; to discover, to come
across; to think. **~ un papier**, to find a paper.
~ la mort, to die. **~ le temps long**, to think
the time passes by slowly. **~ bon**, to think well
of, to like. **aller ~ quelqu'un**, to go look for a
person. **~ à redire**, to find fault with. **se ~**,
v.refl. to meet, to meet with; to be; to happen, to
feel, to be found; to exist; to happen to be. **se ~
bien**, to be well (in health). **se ~ mal**, to be
uncomfortable, to faint, to pass out.
truand, e *n.m. Infml.* crook.
truander *v.i. Infml.* to con. **il s'est fait ~**, he got
conned.
truc *n.m.* thing, thingy; trick; way. **hé ~!** hey,
you! **j'ai trouvé le ~**, I found the mechanism.
trucage *n.m. Cinema.* effect, special effect.
truffe *n.f.* truffle; (dog) nose, muzzle.
truie *n.f.* sow.
truite *n.f.* trout. **~ saumonnée**, salmon trout.
truquage *n.m.* V. TRUCAGE.
tu *pron. pers.* 2nd pers. *n.m.f.* you (familiar form
of address). V. VOUS.
tuant, e *adj.* killing, fatiguing, wearisome.
tube *n.m.* tube, pipe; hit (song); smash (movie).
tuberculose *n.f.* tuberculosis.
tué, e *p.p.* killed; slaughtered, murdered.
tuer *v.t.* to kill; to put to death; to slaughter; to
butcher; to bore; to destroy. **se faire ~**, to get
killed. **~ le temps**, to kill time. **se ~**, *v.refl.* to
kill oneself, to commit suicide, to make away
with oneself. **il s'est tué en tombant de
cheval**, he fell from his horse and was killed.
tue-tête (à) *adv.* **crier à ~**, to scream at the top
of one's lungs.
tuerie *n.f.* slaughter, massacre, butchery, carnage.
tueur, euse *n.m.f.* killer, murderer.
tuile *n.f.* tile; problem, bad luck.

tulipe *n.f.* tulip.

tumeur *n.f.* tumor, swelling.

tumulte *n.m.* commotion, turmoil, tumult; uproar, riot.

tumultueux, euse *adj.* tumultuous; riotous; noisy.

tunnel *n.m.* tunnel.

turbo- *prefix.* turbo-. **turbocompresseur** *n.m.* turbo-compressor.

turbot *n.m.* turbot (fish).

turbulence *n.f.* turbulence, agitation.

turbulent, e *adj.* turbulent; noisy; wild; tumultuous, disorderly, violent, riotous.

turf *n.m.* raceground, racecourse.

turpitude *n.f.* turpitude; vileness, depravity.

tutelle *n.f.* guardianship; supervision; tutelage; protection.

tuteur, trice *n.m.f.* guardian; tutor; protector, protectress.

tutoiement *n.m.* use of familiar **tu** and **toi.**

tutoyer *v.t.* to use the familiar **tu** and **toi** (as opposed to **vous**). **se ~,** *v.refl.* to use the informal **tu** and **toi** when speaking to each other.

tuyau *n.m.* pipe, tube; flue, shaft, funnel (of a chimney); nozzle (of bellows); stem (of tobacco pipes); stalk (of corn); tip. **~ à gaz,** gas pipe. **~ de dégagement,** waste pipe. **il m'a donné un bon ~,** he gave me a good tip.

type *n.m.* type; model, standard; *Print.* type letter; guy, fellow.

typique *adj.* typical.

tyran *n.m.* tyrant; despot, oppressor.

tyrannie *n.f.* tyranny.

tyrannique *adj.* tyrannical.

tyranniser *v.t.* to oppress; to tyrannize.

U

ulcère *n.m.* ulcer.

ulcéré, e *p.p.* ulcerated; exasperated; embittered.

ulcérer *v.t.* to ulcerate; to exasperate, to irritate, to embitter.

ultérieur, e *adj.* ulterior; further, posterior, subsequent.

ultérieurement *adv.* beyond; later, at a later period, subsequently.

ultimatum *n.m.* ultimatum.

ultime *adj.* last.

ultra *prefix.* ultra; beyond; extreme. *n.m.* ultra, ultraist.

un, une *adj.* one. **il est ~e heure,** it is one o'clock. *n.m.* (invariable) one; unit. **~ à ~,** one by one. *pron.* one. **l'~ et l'autre,** both. **les ~s et les autres,** everyone of them, everybody. **ni l'~ ni l'autre,** neither; neither the one nor the other. *n.m.f.* **l'~ ou l'autre,** either, either the one or the other. **les ~s ..., les autres ...,** some ..., others ... *indef. art.* a, an. **~ Français,** a Frenchman. **~ Anglais,** an Englishman.

unanime *adj.* unanimous.

unanimement *adv.* unanimously.

unanimité *n.f.* unanimity.

uni, e *adj.* united; joined; harmonious.

unification *n.f.* unification.

unifier *v.t.* to unify.

uniforme *adj.* uniform. *n.m.* uniform. **porter l'~,** to be a soldier.

uniformément *adv.* uniformly.

uniformiser *v.t.* to make uniform.

uniformité *n.f.* uniformity; resemblance.

union *n.f.* union; junction; conjunction, unity; concord, agreement, unity. **trait d'~,** hyphen. **~s ouvrières,** trade unions.

unique *adj.* only, sole, single; unique. **enfant ~,** only child.

uniquement *adv.* only, solely, alone.

unir *v.t.* to unite; to join; to combine; to level, to smooth; to plane. **s'~,** *v.refl.* to unite; to be united, to combine, to be allied.

unisexe *adj.* unisex (clothes, etc.).

unisson *n.m.* agreement, concord, harmony.

unité *n.f.* unit; unity, one.

univers *n.m.* universe.

universaliser *v.t.* to universalize.

universalité *n.f.* universality; whole, entirety.

universel, elle *adj.* universal; residuary. **légataire ~,** residuary legatee. *n.m.* universal.

universellement *adv.* universally.

universitaire *adj.* of the university. *n.m.* member of the university.

université *n.f.* college, university.

uranium *n.m.* uranium.

urbain, e *adj.* urban.

urbanisation *n.f.* urbanization.

urbaniser *v.t.* to urbanize, to build up.

urgence *n.f.* urgency. **déclarer ~,** to declare an emergency.

urgent, e *adj.* urgent, pressing.

urger *v.t.* to urge, to be urgent.

urinaire *adj.* urinary.

urine *n.f.* urine.

uriner *v.i.* to urinate.

urne *n.f.* urn, ballot box.

us *n.m.pl.* use, usage. **les ~ et coutumes,** the old customs.

usage *n.m.* use, practice, habit, usage, custom. **ce mot n'est plus en ~,** that word is obsolete. **c'est l'~,** it is the custom.

usagé, e *adj.* used, worn, secondhand.

usager, ère *n.m.f.* user.

usé, e *adj.* worn out; used up.

user *v.t.* to use, to exhaust, to wear out; to consume, to make use of; to exercise; to enjoy. **~ de son droit,** to exercise one's right. **en ~,** to act; to behave, to treat. **en ~ librement, familièrement avec quelqu'un,** to treat a person familiarly. **s'~,** *v.refl.* to wear out (as clothes);

to wear away; to be spent, to waste, to decay.

usine *n.f.* factory, manufactory; *pl.* works.

ustensile *n.m.* utensil; tool, implement, instrument.

usuel, elle *adj.* usual, customary, common, ordinary.

usuellement *adv.* usually, ordinarily.

usure *n.f.* usury, wear, wear and tear. **avec ~,** with interest.

usurier, ière *n.m.f.* usurer.

usurpateur, trice *n.m.f.* usurper. *adj.* usurping; encroaching.

usurper *v.t.* to usurp; to seize upon; to encroach upon. ~ **le bien d'autrui,** to usurp the property of others. ~ **un droit,** to usurp a right.

ut *n.m.* do, the first note in the musical scale; C.

utérin, e *adj.* uterine.

utérus *n.m.* uterus, womb.

utile *adj.* useful; of use, of utility. **en temps ~,** in due time, in good time. *n.m.* utility, useful, what is useful. **préférer l'~ à l'agréable,** to prefer the useful to the agreeable.

utilement *adv.* usefully.

utilisable *adj.* usable.

utilisation *n.f.* utilization.

utiliser *v.t.* to utilize; to make use of; to improve. ~ **son temps,** to make use of one's time. **s'~,** *v.refl.* to make oneself useful; (of things) to be made use of; to be utilized.

utilitaire *adj.* utilitarian.

utilité *n.f.* utility, usefulness; use, profit, avail; *pl. Theat.* **jouer les ~s,** to play small parts.

utopie *n.f.* utopia.

utopique *adj.* utopian.

uvée *n.f.* uvea.

uvulaire *adj.* uvular.

V

V., abbreviation of **voir.**

va *n.m.* go.

vacance *n.f.* vacancy; vacation. **prendre des ~s,** to take a vacation. **les grandes ~s,** summer vacation.

vacant, e *adj.* vacant; unoccupied; in abeyance.

vacarme *n.m.* tumult, uproar, noise, disturbance.

vacataire *n.m.f.* short term or temporary replacement.

vaccin *n.m.* vaccination, vaccine.

vaccination *n.f.* vaccination.

vacciner *v.t.* to vaccinate.

vache *n.f.* cow; cowhide. **traire les ~s,** to milk the cows. **manger de la ~ enragée,** *Fig.* to suffer great hardships. **oh, la ~!** *Infml.* (surprise, admiration), wow! (annoyance) hell! damn! **quelle ~!** what a jerk. **c'est ~ qu** and **même,** that's not (very) nice, that's not fair. **parler français comme une vache espagnole,** to torture the French language; *literally,* to speak French like a Spanish cow.

vachement *adv. Infml.* very; awfully. **bon/difficile,** very good/hard.

vacherie *n.f. Infml.* nastiness, dirty trick.

vacillation *n.f.* vacillation; staggering; flickering; unsteadiness. ~ **d'une lumière,** flickering of a light.

vaciller *v.i.* to vacillate; to stake, to totter; to stagger; to flicker, to waver. **la lumière,** the light flickers.

vacuité *n.f.* vacuity, emptiness.

vadrouille *n.f.* ramble, stroll, spree; mop, swab. **en vadrouille,** on the loose.

va-et-vient *n.m.* backward and forward motion, comings and goings.

vagabond, e *adj.* vagabond, vagrant; rambling; wandering, unsettled. *n.m.f.* vagabond, wanderer; vagrant, strolling beggar.

vagabondage *n.m.* vagrancy.

vagabonder *v.i.* to be a vagabond, to wander about; to ramble about, to rove about.

vagin *n.m.* vagina.

vaginal, e *adj.* vaginal; pertaining to the vagina.

vagir *v.i.* to cry (as an infant).

vague *n.f.* wave, billow, surge. *adj.* vacant, void, empty; waste; vague, uncertain, undefined; loose; roving, wandering. **terrain ~,** vacant plot. **des expressions ~s,** vague expressions. *n.m.* emptiness, vacuum, vacuity; empty space; waste land; vagueness; indefiniteness; looseness.

vaguement *adv.* vaguely.

vaillamment *adv.* valiantly, valorously, bravely, gallantly.

vain, e *adj.* waste, uncultivated; vain; empty; worthless; shadowy; fruitless, idle, unprofitable; conceited; puffed up. **de ~s, efforts,** vain efforts. **en ~,** vainly, in vain.

vaincre *v.t.* to defeat, to overcome, to overthrow; to overpower, to overcome, to subdue, to master. ~ **ses ennemis,** to conquer one's enemies.

vaincu, e *p.p. n.m.* defeated, beaten; vanquished.

vainement *adv.* wainly, in vain, to no purpose, fruitlessly.

vainqueur *n.m.* winner, victor; conqueror. *adj.* victorious, conquering; triumphant.

vaisseau *n.m.* vessel; ship; *Anat.* tube, canal; *Bot.* duct, tube. ~ **amiral,** admiral ship. ~ **de guerre,** warship. ~ **marchand,** merchant ship.

vaisselle *n.f.* dishes, plates; crockery; china. **faire la ~,** to wash up, to do the washing up. **lave-~,** *n.m.* dishwasher.

val *n.m.* valley, vale, dale.

valable *adj.* valid.

valablement *adv.* validly.

valdinguer *v.t. Infml.* to go flying. **il l'a envoyé ~,** he told him to clear off.

valet *n.m.* valet; servant; support rest, (of a mirror). ~ **de pied,** footman, lackey; jack (of cards).

valeur *n.f.* valor, bravery, gallantry; value; worth; import, meaning. ~ **nominale**, nominal value (of coin). ~ **reçue**, for value received. ~ **en espèces**, value in cash. **sans ~**, worthless. *pl. Bank.* bills, papers. **mettre des ~s en circulation**, to put bills in circulation.

valeureux, euse *adj.* valorous, valiant, brave, gallant.

validation *n.f.* validation, validating.

valide *adj.* valid. *n.m.* healthy person.

valider *v.t.* to render valid, to validate.

validité *n.f.* validity; validness.

valise *n.f.* suitcase, valise.

vallée *n.f.* valley, vale.

valoir *v.i.* to be worth; to procure, to obtain, to win (for). **ne faire rien qui vaille**, to do nothing good. **ne rien ~**, to be good for nothing, to be worthless. **combien vaut ce livre?** how much is this book? **faire ~ son droit**, to emphasize, to stress one's right. **faire ~ son argent**, to make the most of one's money. **à ~**, on account.

valorisation *n.f.* development; valorization, increase in the value of.

valoriser *v.t.* to increase in value; to develop.

valse *n.f.* waltz.

vampire *n.m.* vampire.

vandalisme *n.m.* vandalism.

vanille *n.f.* vanilla.

vanillé, e *adj.* flavored with vanilla.

vanité *n.f.* vanity; conceit.

vaniteux, euse *adj.* vain, conceited. *n.m.f.* vain, conceited person.

vanter *v.t.* to vaunt, to praise, to extol; to vaunt, to boast of. **se ~**, *v.refl.* to praise oneself; (with **de**) to boast of, to brag of; to vaunt in; to be proud of. **il n'y a pas de quoi se ~**, there is nothing to brag about.

vapeur *n.f.* steam, vapor; damp, mist; fume. **la ~ de l'eau**, steam. **bain de ~**, steambath. **aller à toute ~**, to go full speed. *n.m.* steamboat.

vaporeux, euse *adj.* steamy, vaporous. *Fig.* unreal.

vaporiser *v.t.* to spray, to vaporize.

vaquer *v.i.* to be vacant, unoccupied, empty; (of courts) not to sit. **la cour vaque cette semaine**, the court does not sit this week. ~ **à ses affaires**, to attend to one's business.

variable *adj.* variable. *n.m.* change.

variablement *adv.* variably.

variante *n.f.* different reading.

variation *n.f.* variation; change.

varicelle *n.f.* varicella, chickenpox.

varier *v.t.* to vary; to change, to alter; to be altered; to differ, to be different, to disagree.

variété *n.f.* variety; diversity. **spectacle de ~s**, variety show.

variole *n.f.* smallpox.

vasculaire *adj.* vascular. .

vase *n.m.* mud, mire, slime. *n.m.* vase.

vaseline *n.f.* petroleum jelly, Vaseline.

vaseux, euse *adj.* slimy, muddy, miry.

vaste *adj.* vast; wide, spacious; capacious.

vastement *adv.* vastly.

vaudevilliste *n.m.* vaudevilist, light comedy.

vaurien *n.m.* good-for-nothing.

vautour *n.m.* vulture; *Fig.* rapacious person.

vautrer *v.t.* to roll, to wallow. **se ~**, *v.refl.* to wallow; to roll (in mire); to plunge into.

veau *n.m.* calf; veal; *Fig.* calfskin, leather. ~ **gras**, fat calf. ~ **d'or**, golden calf. **manger du ~**, to eat veal.

vedette *n.f.* star. ~ **de cinéma**, movie star.

végétal, e *adj.* vegetable. *n.m.* vegetable.

végétarien *n.m.* vegetarian.

végétatif, ive *adj.* vegetative.

végétation *n.f.* vegetation.

végéter *v.i.* to vegetate.

véhémence *n.f.* vehemence, impetuosity.

véhément, e *adj.* vehement; violent, impetuous; passionate, ardent.

véhicule *n.m.* vehicle.

veille *n.f.* watch; wakefulness; watching, vigil, vigilance; sitting up; eve, the day before. **la ~ de Noël**, Christmas Eve. **dans une lettre écrite la ~ de sa mort**, in a letter written the day before he died.

veillée *n.f.* sitting up; watching. **les veillées sont longues dans cette saison**, the evenings are long at this season. **faire la ~**, to spend the evening at a person's house.

veiller *v.i.* to sit up, to stay up to watch; to be awake; to keep awake; to look to, to see to; to attend; to be on guard, to sit up with; to watch by; to nurse. ~ **de près sur quelqu'un**, to watch a person closely. ~ **un malade**, to watch over a sick person.

veilleuse *n.f.* watcher; night light.

veinard, e *n.m.f. n.m. Infml.* lucky person.

veine *n.f.* vein. *Geol.* lode; streak (in marble); *Infml.* luck. ~ **cave**, vena cava. **il a de la ~**, he is in luck. **je n'ai pas de ~**, I have no luck.

velléité *n.f.* slight desire, inkling, whim.

vélo *n.m.* bike, bicycle.

vélocité *n.f.* velocity, swiftness, rapidity. speed.

vélomoteur *n.m.* moped.

velours *n.m.* velvet. **faire patte de ~**, to be all smirks and smiles.

velouté, e *adj.* downy, velvet, velvety, smooth (of wine). *n.m.* velvet; softness. **le ~ d'une pêche**, the bloom of a peach.

velu, e *adj.* hairy, shaggy; *Bot.* villous. **tige ~e**, villous stem.

vendange *n.f.* harvest, vintage.

vendanger *v.t.* to harvest, to gather (grapes); to gather the grapes in.

vendeur, euse *n.m.f.* seller, vender (of), dealer (in).

vendre *v.t.* to sell; to sell for; to sell out; to betray. ~ **bon marché**, to sell cheap. **à ~**, for sale. ~ **ses complices**, to betray one's accomplices. **se ~**, *v.refl.* to sell, to be sold, to sell oneself.

vendredi *n.m.* Friday. **Vendredi ~ Saint,** Good Friday.

vendu, e *p.p.* sold; betrayed.

vénéneux, euse *adj.* poisonous.

vénérable *adj.* venerable; worshipful; reverend.

vénérablement *adv.* venerably.

vénération *n.f.* veneration.

vénérer *v.t.* to venerate.

vengeance *n.f.* vengeance, revenge. **assouvir sa ~,** to gratify one's vengeance. **par ~,** out of revenge. **demander ~,** to call for revenge.

venger *v.t.* to revenge; to avenge; to resent. **~ son honneur,** to vindicate one's honor. **se ~,** *v.refl.* to revenge; to take vengeance; to avenge oneself, to be revenged. **se ~ de ses ennemis,** to revenge oneself on one's enemies.

vengeur, eresse *n.m.f.* revenger, avenger. *adj.* revengeful, avenging.

venimeux, euse *adj.* venomous; poisonous; *Fig.* spiteful, malignant.

venin *n.m.* venom; poison; venomousness; spitefulness. **morte la bête, mort le ~,** dead men tell no tales. **le ~ de la petite vérole,** the virulency of smallpox. **jeter tout son ~,** to vent all one's spleen.

venir *v.t.* to come; to be coming; to come on, along; to proceed; to reach; to come up; to thrive; to occur, to proceed, to issue, to arise. **je viens pour vous dire,** I have come to tell you. **venez nous voir,** come and see us. **~ sur,** to come upon. **voir ~ quelqu'un,** to see a person coming. **à ~,** to come, future. **~ au monde,** to come into the world. **la voilà qui vient,** here she comes. **~ à bout de,** to succeed in. **il me vient une idée,** I just got an idea. **tout lui vient à souhait,** he succeeds in everything. **de quel pays venez-vous?** what country do you come from? **s'il venait à mourir,** if he were to die. **il vient de partir,** he has just left. **il vient de parler,** he has just spoken. **en ~ à,** to come to. **en ~ aux mains,** to come to blows. **mais il faut toujours en ~ là,** but it must always come to that. **où voulez-vous en ~?** what are you driving at? **c'est là que j'en voulais ~,** that was what I was driving at. **faire ~,** to send for. **faire ~ quelqu'un,** to send for a person. **faire ~ le médecin,** to call in a doctor. **faire ~ l'eau au moulin,** to bring grist to the mill. **faire ~ à la raison,** to bring to reason. **s'en ~,** *v.refl.* to come; to come away, to come back.

vent *n.m.* wind; breeze; scent; windage (of a cannon). **~ frais,** fresh breeze, fresh wind. **en plein ~,** in the open air. **avoir ~ de quelque chose,** *Infml.* to get wind of a thing. **instrument à ~,** wind instrument.

vente *n.f.* sale; place of public sale. **~ aux enchères,** auction sale. **mettre une chose en ~,** to put a thing up for sale. **~ par correspondance,** mail order.

ventilateur *n.m.* fan.

ventilation *n.f.* ventilation; airing; valuation (of property).

ventiler *v.t.* to ventilate; to fan; value (property).

ventre *n.m.* belly, stomach, womb. **~ à terre,** flat on the ground; *Infml.* **cã me ferait (bien) mal au ~,** that would make me sick. *Infml.* **n'avoir rien dans le ~,** to be gutless, to be chicken.

ventriloque *n.m.* ventriloquist.

venu, e *p.p.* come; received. **soyez le bien ~, la bien ~e,** welcome. *n.m.f.* corner. **un nouveau ~,** a newcomer. **le premier ~, la première ~s,** the first to arrive. *Fig.* any one. *n.f.* coming, arrival. **la ~ du Messie,** the coming of the Messiah. **allées et ~s,** goings and comings.

ver *n.m.* worm, larva (of insects); grub; maggot (in meat); moth; mite (in cheese). **~ de terre,** earthworm. **~ à soie,** silkworm. **tirer à quelqu'un les ~s du nez,** *Fig.* to pick someone's brain. **~ luisant,** glowworm.

véracité *n.f.* veracity; truthfulness.

véranda *n.f.* veranda.

verbal, e *adj.* verbal; spoken.

verbalement *adv.* verbally, by word of mouth.

verbe *n.m.* verb. voice, tone, tone of voice. **avoir le ~ haut,** to speak very loud.

verdâtre *adj.* greenish.

verdict *n.m.* verdit (of a jury).

verdoyant, e *adj.* verdant, green, fresh; (of colors) greenish.

verdoyer *v.i.* to grow, to turn, to become green; to be verdant.

verdure *n.f.* verdure; green, greenery; greenness; (green) vegetable. **couvert de ~,** covered with verdure; verdant. **la ~ des bois,** the greenness of the woods.

véreux, euse *adj.* worm-eaten, maggoty; rotten; doubtful; bad; unsafe. **une affaire ~ses,** an unsound, rotten deal.

verge *n.f.* rod, birch; switch; wand, stick; handle, rod (of a piston); penis.

verger *n.m.* orchard.

vergeture *n.f.* stretch mark.

verglas *n.m.* (black) ice; glaze.

vergogne *n.f.* shame. **sans ~,** shameless; shamelessly.

véridique *adj.* veracious, truthful.

vérifiable *adj.* verifiable.

vérification *n.f.* verification.

vérifier *v.t.* to check, to verify; to confirm. **se ~,** *v.refl.* to be checked; to be verified.

véritable *adj.* true; real; exact; genuine. **un ~ ami,** a true friend.

véritablement *adv.* truly; really; in reality, in truth.

vérité *n.f.* truth. **à la ~,** in truth, indeed. **en ~,** truly, really, in truth, indeed.

vermicelle *n.m.* vermicelli, noodles.

vermine *n.f.* vermin.

vernaculaire *adj.* vernacular.

vernir *v.t.* to polish, to varnish, to glaze.

vernis *n.m.* varnish; glazing; polish, gloss, ~ à ongles, nail polish.

vernissage *n.m.* glazing, varnishing; opening day of an exhibition.

verre *n.m.* glass; glassful, drink. ~ à vitres, sheet glass; window glass. ~ grossissant, magnifying glass. ~ taillé, cut glass. ~ à liqueur, liqueur glass. un ~ de vin, a glass of wine. un petit ~, a glass of brandy. ~pareballes, bulletproof glass. papier de ~, sand paper.

verrou *n.m.* bolt. fermer au ~, to bolt.

verrouiller *v.t.* to bolt. se ~, *v.refl.* to bolt oneself in.

verue *n.f.* wart.

vers *n.m.* verse, line (of poetry). faire des ~, to make verses. *prep.* toward; about; near to, nearly. nous partirons ~ midi, we'll leave around noon.

versant *n.m.* side (of a mountain), slope.

versatile *adj.* versatile; changeable, variable.

versatilité *n.f.* versatility, inconstancy.

verse *n.f.* à ~, *adv.* hard, fast. il pleut à ~, it is raining hard.

verseau *n.m.* Aquarius, waterbearer.

versement *n.m.* paying in, payment, deposit.

verser *v.t.* to pour, to pour out; to shed, to spill; to deposit (money); upset; to overturn, to upset, to break down. ~ des larmes, to shed tears. ~ du vin, to pour out wine. la voiture a versé dans le ravin, the car overturned in the ravine. se ~, *v.refl.* to be shed, spilt; to discharge itself.

verset *n.m.* verse (of a hymn, etc.).

version *n.f.* version; translation, (into mother tongue); account, relation, explanation, interpretation, translation.

verso *n.m.* reverse, back. voir au ~, see over (leaf).

vert, e *adj.* green; verdant, grassy; raw; unripe, immature; robust, lusty; tart (of wine). bois ~, green wood. des fruits ~s, unripe fruit. pois ~s, green peas. *n.m.* green; green color; grass; tartness (of wine). verte pomme, green apple. ~ foncé, dark green. j'en ai vu des ~ es et des pas mûrer, I have gone through hard times.

vert-de-gris *n.m.* verdigris.

vertébral, e *adj.* vertebral.

vertèbre *n.f.* vertebra.

vertébré, e *adj.* vertebrates.

vertical, e *adj.* vertical. *n.m.* vertical circle, vertical. premier ~, prime vertical.

verticalement *adv.* vertically.

vertige *n.m.* dizziness, giddiness; vertigo.

vertigineux, euse *adj.* giddy, dizzy, breathtaking.

vertu *n.f.* virtue; virtuousness; chastity; courage; property, efficacity. en ~ de, in, by virtue of.

vertueux, euse *adj.* virtuous.

verve *n.f.* whim, caprice, fancy; fervor, spirit, animation. ~ poétique, poetical spirit.

verveine *n.f.* vervain.

vésicule *n.f.* vesicle. ~ biliaire, gall bladder.

vessie *n.f.* bladder. faire prendre des ~s pour des lanternes, to pull the wool over someone's eyes.

veste *n.f.* vest; jacket.

vestiaire *n.m.* dressing room; cloakroom; locker room.

vestibule *n.m.* vestibule; entrance (hall), hall, lobby.

vestige *n.m.* remnant, remains, vestige; footstep; track; trace.

vêtement *n.m.* garment; dress, clothing, clothes.

vétéran *n.m.* veteran.

vétérinaire *adj.* veterinary *n.m.* veterinarian.

vétille *n.f.* trifle.

vêtir *v.t.* to clothe; to dress. se ~, *v.refl.* to dress oneself, to dress.

veto *n.m.* veto.

vêtu, e *p.p.* clothed, dressed.

veuf, veuve *n.m.f* and *adj.* widowed; widower *n.m.* widow *n.f.*

vexation *n.f.* vexation, annoyance.

vexatoire *adj.* vexatious.

vexer *v.t.* to vex, to torment, to harass; to molest. il l'a vexé, he hurt his feelings.

via *prep.* via, by way of.

viabilité *n.f.* viability.

viable *adj.* viable.

viaduc *n.m.* viaduct.

viager, ère *adj.* for life; life. *n.m.* life interest.

viande *n.f.* meat. ~ blanche, poultry, veal.

vibration *n.f.* vibration.

vibrer *v.i.* to vibrate.

vice *n.m.* vice. pauvreté n'est pas ~, poverty is no crime.

vice *prefix.* vice.

vice-chancelier *n.m.* vice-chancellor.

vice-consul *n.m.* vice-consul.

vice-présidence *n.f.* vice-presidency.

vice-président *n.m.* vice-president.

vice-versa *adv.* vice versa.

vicier *v.t.* to vitiate; to taint.

vicieusement *adv.* viciously.

vicieux, euse *adj.* depraved, corrupt, vicious.

vicissitude *n.f.* trials and tribulations, ups and downs, vicissitude.

victime *n.f.* victim.

victoire *n.f.* victory; triumph. remporter la ~, to win.

victorieusement *adv.* victoriously.

victorieux, euse *adg.* victorious. *n.m.* triumphant.

victuaille *n.f.* victuals, provisions.

vidange *n.f.* emptying; removing; cleaning; (auto) oil change.

vide *adj.* empty; vacant, unoccupied; open. avoir la tête ~, to be empty-headed. *n.m.* emptiness, vacuity; gap; blank (in a document). à ~, empty.

vide-ordures *n.m.* garbage disposal.

vidéo *adj.* video; *n.f.* video tape, videocassette.

vider *v.t.* to empty, to drain off (a pond); to

draw, to gut (as poultry, fish); to stone (fruit); to decide, to settle (a dispute); to clear out, to leave. ~ ses comptes, to settle one's accounts. ~ un différend, to settle a difference. ~ les lieux, to leave, to clear out. se ~, v.refl. to empty oneself, to be emptied; to be settled. la bouteille se vide, the bottle becomes empty.

videur n.m. bouncer (nightclub).

vie n.f. life, lifetime, living, livelihood; liveliness, spirit, animation, viviacity. ~ animale, animal life. prendre la ~, to lose one's life. demander la ~, to beg for life. j'y gagerais ma ~, I would bet my life on it. il y va de la ~, life is at stake. la ~ est courte, life is short. la ~ future, the life to come. mener joyeuse ~, to lead a happy life. gagner sa ~, to earn a living, a livelihood. la ~ est chère à Paris, living is expensive in Paris. à ~, for life. jamais de la ~, no way! not on your life! assurance ~, life insurance.

vieil or vieux, vieille adj. old; aged, advanced in years; ancient; venerable. un ~ homme, an old man. une vieille femme, an old woman. de vieilles gens, old people. un vieil ami, an old friend. une vieille ville, an old town. la vieille Angleterre, old England. n.f. old woman. n.m. old man.

vieillard n.m. old man.

vieillerie n.f. old things, old stuff; old clothes; old goods; rubbish, old lumber.

vieillesse n.f. old age, age, years.

vieillir v.i. to grow old, to get old, to become old, to make old; to make ... look old. se ~, v.refl. to make oneself look old.

vieillissant, e adj. growing old.

vieillissement n.m. aging.

vierge n.f. virgin, Virgo. adj. virgin; pure, chaste; virginal. terre ~, virgin soil. vigne ~, Virginian creeper.

vieux n.m. fam. mon ~, my old friend, pal.

vif, vive adj. alive, living, live; quick; lively, brisk, agile, alert; smart, ready, prompt, hasty, irascible; bare. eau vive, running water, spring water. chaux vive, quicklime. vous êtes trop ~, you are too hasty. un feu ~, a brisk fire. imagination vive, vivid imagination. un ~ laisir, a lively pleasure. air ~, keen air. un ~ désir, a great desire. des couleurs vives, bright colors. des yeux ~s, bright eyes. une vive lumière, a bright light. une vive prière, an earnest prayer. n.m. living person, quick, body, substance. piquer au ~, to sting to the quick. couper dans le ~, to cut to the quick. de vive voix, by word of mouth.

vigie n.f. lookout; watch.

vigilance n.f. vigilance, vigilancy, watchfulness.

vigilant, e adj. vigilant, watchful.

vigne n.f. vine, vineyard.

vigneron, onne n.m.f. vine grower.

vignette n.f. seal, stamp, label.

vignoble n.m. vineyard.

vigoureusement adv. vigorously.

vigoureux, euse adj. vigorous, lusty, stout, robust, energetic; bold, spirited.

vigueur n.f. vigor; strength, might; vigorousness; energy; power, spirit. agir avec ~, to act energetically. mettre en ~, to enforce.

vil, e adj. low; vile, base, mean.

vilain, e n.m.f. nasty person, villain. adj. ugly, vile, villanous, wicked, infamous; naughty (of a child); nasty, scurvy, dirty. ~ homme, bad man. une ~e action, a wicked action. voilà un ~ rhume, that is a bad cold. quel ~ temps! what bad weather.

villa n.f. villa, country house.

village n.m. village.

villageois, e n.m.f. villager; cottager. adj. rustic, village, country.

ville n.f. town; city. une petite ~ de province, a small country town. aller à la ~, to go to town. dîner en ~, to dine out.

vin n.m. wine. il faut savoir mettre de l'eau dans son ~, one must learn to compromise.

vinaigre n.m. vinegar. on prend plus de mouches avec du miel qu'avec du ~, more flies are caught with honey than with vinegar.

vinaigrette n.f. vinaigrette.

vinasse n.f. cheap wine, bad wine.

vindicatif, ive adj. vindictive, revengeful.

vindicte n.f. vengeance; prosecution (for crime).

vingt adj. num. twenty. vingt hommes, twenty men. vingt et un ans, twenty-one years. cent vingt, one hundred and twenty. vingt mille francs, twenty thousand francs. quatre-vingts francs, eighty francs. quatre-vingt-un, eighty-one. quatre-vingt-deux, eighty-two. ~ mille, twenty; twentieth day; twentieth. le ~ du mois, the twentieth of the month.

vingtaine n.f. twenty, about twenty.

vingtième adj. and n.m.f. twentieth.

vinicole adj. winegrowing.

viol n.m. rape.

violacé, e adj. purplish-blue. n.f.pl. Bot. violaceae.

violateur, trice n.m.f. violator; transgressor, infringer.

violation n.f. violation, transgression, non-observance.

violemment adv. violently.

violence n.f. violence; force.

violent, e adj. violent.

violenter v.t. to force, to comple, to do violence to. se ~, v.refl. to do violence to oneself.

violer v.t. to rape, to violate; to infringe. ~ la loi, to transgress the law. ~ une sépulture, to desecrate a tomb.

violet, ette adj. violet, violet-colored. n.m. violet.

violette n.f. Bot. violet. cueillir de la ~s, to gather violets. ~ de la Chandeleur, snowdrop.

violon n.m. violin, fiddle; violinist; lock up, the cells.

violoncelle n.m. cello; cellist.

violoncelliste n.m. cellist.

violoniste *n.m.* violinist.

vipère *n.f.* viper, asp, adder.

virage *n.m.* turn, curve. *Phot.* toning.

virée *n.f.* trip, ride.

virement *n.m.* turning; transfer (of credit). *Com. Fin.* transfer.

virer *v.i.* to turn about, to turn, to take a bend. **~ de bord,** to tack about.

virevolter *v.i.* to twirl around, to turn around.

virginité *n.f.* virginity; purity.

virgule *n.f.* comma. **point ~,** semicolon, point (decimal).

viril, e *adj.* virile; masculine; male; manly. **à ~,** manhood.

virilement *adv.* manly, in a manly way.

virilité *n.f.* virility, manhood.

virtualité *n.f.* virtuality; potentiality.

virtuel, elle *adj.* virtual; potential.

virtuellement *adv.* virtually, potentially.

virtuose *n.m.f.* virtuoso. *pl.* virtuosi.

virulence *n.f.* virulence.

virulent, e *adj.* virulent.

virus *n.m.* virus.

vis *n.f.* screw.

visa *n.m.* visa.

visage *n.m.* face. **avoir le ~ allongé,** to pull a long face. **changer de ~,** to change color. **à ~ découvert,** with an open face; openly.

vis-à-vis *prep.* opposite; facing. vis-à-vis.

viscéral, e *adj.* visceral.

viscosité *n.f.* viscosity, stickiness.

viser *v.t.* to aim at, to take aim at; to visa, to sign, to aim, to aspire.

visibilité *n.f.* visibility.

visible *adj.* visible; apparent, obvious, evident, manifest, conspicuous, clear, plain.

visiblement *adv.* visibly.

visière *n.f.* visor, peak (of a cap); shade (for the eyes).

vision *n.f.* vision; sight, apparition, specter.

visionnaire *adj.* *n.m.f.* visionary.

visitation *n.f.* visitation.

visite *n.f.* visit; visiting; inspection; examination. **faire ~,** to pay a visit. **faire une ~ à quelqu'un,** to pay a person a visit. **~ des lieux,** search, inspection of the premises.

visiter *v.t.* to visit; to inspect, to examine, to survey. **se ~,** *v.refl.* to visit each other.

visiteur, euse *n.m.f.* visitor; inspector.

vison *n.m.* mink.

visqueux, euse *adj.* viscous, sticky.

visser *v.t.* to screw, to screw down, to screw up, to screw on. **se ~,** *v.refl.* to be screwed.

visu (de) *adv.* with one's own eyes, for oneself.

visualisation *n.f.* visualization.

visualiser *v.t.* to visualize.

visuel, elle *adj.* visual.

vital, e *adj.* vital.

vitalité *n.f.* vitality.

vitamine *n.f.* vitamin.

vite *adj.* quick, swift, fast, rapid, hasty; prompt.

adv. quickly, quick, swiftly, speedily, rapidly; hastily, fast; expeditiously.

vitesse *n.f.* velocity; quickness, rapidity, swiftness; (auto) gear. **la ~ de la terre,** the velocity of the earth. **la ~ d'un oiseau,** the swiftness of a bird. **3ème vitesse,** 3rd gear.

viticole *adj.* vine-growing.

viticulteur *n.m.* wine grower.

viticulture *n.f.* wine growing, viticulture.

vitrail *n.m.* glass window, glazed window; stained-glass window.

vitre *n.f.* window, glass.

vitré, e *adj.* glass; vitreous.

vitrer *v.t.* to glaze.

vitreux, euse *adj.* vitreous, glassy.

vitrier *n.m.* glazier.

vitrifier *v.t.* to vitrify. **se ~,** *v.refl.* to vitrify.

vitrine *n.f.* window. **faire du lèche-~,** to go window-shopping.

vitriol *n.m.* vitriol.

vivable *adj.* livable. **il n'est pas ~,** he is impossible to live with.

vivace *adj.* long-lived; deep-rooted, inveterate, tenacious.

vivacité *n.f.* vivacity, liveliness; quickness; vehemence, vigor; animation, sprightliness; vividness; hastiness. **la ~ de la dispute,** the vehemence of the quarrel.

vivant, e *adj.* living; live, alive; *Script.* lasting, enduring; lively. **langue ~e,** modern language. **une scène ~e,** a lively scene. *n.m.* living person, living, person living, alive; *pl.* the living. **un bon ~,** a jolly fellow, a happy person. **du ~ de son père,** in his father's lifetime.

vivat *interj.* *Latin* long live, hurrah! *n.m.* hurrah; cheer.

vive *n.f.* weever fish, weever. **~ la reine,** long live the Queen.

vivement *adv.* briskly; quickly, eagerly, sharply; warmly; with animation; sprightly, vivaciously; keenly. **se lever ~,** to get up quickly. **il s'intéresse ~ à votre succès,** he takes a great interest in your success. **cette perte l'a ~ affligé,** he felt this loss very deeply.

vivier *n.m.* fishpond; fish tank.

vivifiant, e *adj.* envigorating, vivifying.

vivifier *v.t.* to vivify; to quicken, to enliven; to give vigor to; to animate. **se ~,** *v.refl.* to be revived, to be animated, to be enlivened.

vivoter *v.i.* to live hard, poorly.

vivre *v.i.* to live; to be living, to be alive, to subsist, to exist; to enjoy life. **les chênes vivent fort longtemps,** oaks live very long. **~ soixante ans,** to live sixty years. **~ bien,** to live well. **apprendre quelqu'un à ~,** to teach a person good manners. **~ de son travail,** to live by one's work. **avoir de quoi ~,** to have enough to live on. **~ au jour le jour,** to live from day to day. **vive le roi,** long live the king, God save the king! *n.m.* life; living; food; provisions. **couper les ~s,** to cut off supplies.

vocabulaire *n.m.* vocabulary.

vocation *n.f.* vocation; calling, call; talent. **suivre sa ~,** to follow one's calling.

vocifération *n.f.* vociferation, outcry, clamor, bawling.

vociférer *v.i.* to vociferate, to cry out, to bawl.

vœu *n.m.* vow; wish, desire. **faire un ~,** to make a wish. **prononcer ses ~x,** to take the vows.

vogue *n.f.* vogue; fashion.

voguer *v.i.* to sail, to drift. **~ à pleines voiles,** to go with full sail. **vogue la galère,** *Infml.* here goes!

voici *prep.* here, here is, here are; this is, these are. **me ~,** here I am. **~ de l'argent,** here is some money. **nous ~ arrivés,** here we are. **le ~ qui vient,** here he comes.

voie *n.f.* way; road; duct, canal; path; conduit; leak (in a ship, a cask, etc.). **la ~ lactée,** the Milky Way. **~ de garage,** siding. **aller par ~ de mer,** to go by sea. **être sur la bonne ~,** to be on the right track. **~s et moyens,** ways and means. **mettre quelqu'un sur la ~,** to set a person right. **~ferrée,** railroad.

voilà *prep.* there, there is, there are. **le ~,** there he is. **les ~,** there they are. **en ~ assez,** enough. **~ tout,** that's all.

voile *n.m.* veil; mask, cover. **un ~ épais,** a thick veil. **avoir un ~ devant les yeux,** *Fig.* to have a blur before one's eyes. *n.f.* sail; canvas; ship. **faire ~,** to sail, to set sail.

voiler *v.t.* to veil; to conceal, to hide; to cover, to disguise. **se ~,** *v.refl.* to wear a veil, to veil oneself, to put on a veil; to be veiled.

voilier *n.m.* sail boat. *adj.* sailing. **un fin ~,** a fast, a fine sailer.

voir *v.t.* to see; to view; to behold, to look upon; to notice; to visit; to examine, to see into, to look to, to see to, to observe; to attend; to judge, to think. **je l'ai vu de mes yeux,** I saw it with my own eyes. **aller ~ quelqu'un,** to go and see a person. **ça reste à ~,** it remains to be seen. **~ tout en rose,** to see the bright side of everything. **faire ~,** to show; to prove. **je vous ferai ~,** I'll show you. **laisser ~,** to let see; to allow to see. **je vais lui en faire ~,** he/she is going to be in trouble. **il en a vu de toutes les couleurs,** he has been through tough times. **ça n'a rien à ~ avec ce qu'il dit,** that has nothing to do with what he is saying. **~ clair,** to see clearly. **il voit juste,** he understands. **se ~,** *v.refl.* to see oneself; to see each other; to be seen.

voisin, e *adj.* neighboring; adjoining; adjacent; bordering (upon), next (to), near. *n.m.f.* neighbor.

voisinage *n.m.* neighborhood, vicinity, proximity.

voiture *n.f.* car; vehicle.

voix *n.f.* voice; vote. **une ~ faible,** a weak voice. **parler à ~ basse,** to whisper. **la ~ publique,** public opinion.

vol *n.m.* flight; flying, soaring; stretch (of a bird's wings), spread; cast (of hawks). **le ~ d'un oiseau,** the flight of a bird. **le ~ du temps,** the flight of time. **prendre un ~,** to take a flight. **à ~ d'oiseau,** in a straight line. *n.m.* theft; robbery. **~ avec effraction,** housebreaking; burglary, breaking and entering.

volaille *n.f.* poultry; fowl.

volant, e *adj.* flying; volatile; fly, loose (of paper). **poisson ~,** flying fish. *n.m.* steering wheel. **prendre le ~,** to take the wheel.

volatil, e *adj.* volatile.

volatile *n.m.* winged animal, bird, fowl.

volatiliser *v.t.* to volatilize. **se ~,** *v.refl.* to become volatile, to disappear, to vanish.

volcan *n.m.* volcano.

volcanique *adj.* volcanic.

volée *n.f.* flight; flock of birds flying together; bevy, covey, brood; volley (of blows, musketry), discharge; peal (of bells). **à la ~,** flying, in the air.

voler *v.i.* to fly; to fly about; to soar, to flee, to steal; to rob; to plunder. **le temps vole,** time flies. **~ de l'argent,** to steal money.

volet *n.m.* (window) shutter; flap. **être trié sur le ~,** to be screened, to be carefully selected.

voleur, euse *n.m.f.* thief.

volley-ball *n.m.* volleyball.

volontaire *adj.* voluntary, deliberate, intentional; headstrong, obstinate.

volontairement *adv.* voluntarily; willingly.

volonté *n.f.* will; determination; testament; *pl.* caprices, whims, fancies. **à ~,** at will, at pleasure.

volontiers *adv.* willingly, readily.

volt *n.m.* volt.

voltiger *v.i.* to flit; to fly; to flutter about.

volume *n.m.* volume; bulk, size, mass.

volumineux, euse *adj.* voluminous; large, bulky, considerable.

volupté *n.f.* (sensual) pleasure, delight.

voluptueux, euse *adj.* voluptuous. *n.m.f.* voluptuary, sensualist.

vomir *v.t.* to throw up, to vomit.

vomissement *n.m.* vomiting.

vorace *adj.* voracious.

voracité *n.f.* voracity, voraciousness.

vos *adj. poss. m.f.pl.* your.

vote *n.m.* vote.

voter *v.i.* to vote. **~ au scrutin secret,** to vote by ballot.

votre *adj. poss. m.f.* your.

vôtre *pr. poss.* yours. **le ~, la ~, les ~s,** yours. *n.m.* your own, yours; your property. **je suis des ~s,** I'm with you, on your side.

vouer *v.t.* to dedicate, to vow; to consecrate; to devote. **se ~,** *v.refl.* to devote oneself, to apply oneself. **ne savoir à quel saint se ~,** not to know which way to turn.

vouloir *v.t.* to want, to wish, to desire; to please, to choose; to like, to be willing; to be pleased. **je veux le faire,** I mean or I intend to do it. **je veux que vous le fassiez,** I want you to do it.

que voulez-vous? what do you want? what can you expect? nous voulons des fruits, we want fruit. je voudrais bien voir cela, I should like to see that. je voudrais apprendre le grec, I would like to learn Greek. cómbien en voulez-vous? how many do you want? ~ le bien de quelqu'un, to be anxious for a person's welfare. en ~ à, to have a grudge. il m'en veut, he is upset with me. à qui en veut-il? whom does he have a problem with. ~ dire, to mean. que veut dire ce mot, what does this word mean? n.m. will; intention.

voulu, e p.p. and adj. requisite; needful, necessary; indispensable; usual, due; received.

vous pers. pr. (formal singular, also plural) you. il ~ aime, he loves you. cette maison est à ~, that house is yours. ~-même(s), yourself, yourselves. V. TU, TOI.

voûte n.f. vault, arch.

voûter v.t. to vault, to arch. se ~, v.refl. to be bent; to arch; to stoop.

vouvoiement n.m. use of formal vous (for you).

vouvoyer v.i. to use the formal form vous (for you).

voyage n.m. trip, travel, traveling; journey; voyage. être en ~, to be traveling. ~ autour du monde, trip around the world. ~ de plaisir, tour, excursion, pleasure trip. ce bateau fait deux ~s par semaine, this boat runs twice a week.

voyager v.i. to travel; to journey; to voyage.

voyageur, euse n.m.f. traveler; voyager; passenger. ~ de commerce, traveling salesperson.

voyant, e adj. gaudy, glaring, showy. une couleur ~e, a gaudy, a showy color. n.m. seer, prophet.

voyelle n.f. vowel.

voyou n.m. hoodlum, hooligan.

vrac n.m. disorder, confusion. en ~, pell-mell; Naut. in bulk, loose.

vrai, e adj. true; real; truthful, genuine, right, regular; unique, only. il n'est pas ~ que ..., it is not true that ... un ~ diamant, a real diamond. n.m. truth; reality. être dans le ~, à dire ~, à ~ dire, to tell the truth. adv. truly, in truth, really, indeed.

vraiment adv. truly, in truth, really, in reality, indeed.

vraisemblable adj. likely, probable, plausible. n.m. likelihood, probability.

vraisemblablement adv. likely, probably, plausibly.

vraisemblance n.f. likelihood, probability.

vu, e prep. considering; seeing, on account of. ~ le prix, considering the price. ~ que, considering that, considering, seeing that. n.m. examination, inspection. ~ qu'il pleuvait, nous sommes rentrés, seeing that it was raining, we went back home.

vue n.f. view; sight; aspect, look, appearance, prospect; vision. cette chambre a une très belle ~, there is a very fine view from this room. ~ de Paris, view of Paris. mauvaise ~, bad sight. perdre une chose de ~, to lose sight of a thing. à première ~, at first sight. avoir quelqu'un en ~, to have a person in mind. point de ~, point of view; prospect. c'est là son point de ~, that is his opinion. à ~ de nez, roughly.

vulgaire adj. vulgar; low.

vulgariser v.t. to popularize.

vulgarité n.f. vulgarity; foul language.

vulnérable adj. vulnerable.

W

w n.m. letter not belonging to the French alphabet, and only used in foreign words.

wagon n.m. wagon, truck. ~ restaurant, dining car. ~ lit, sleeping car.

weekend n.m. weekend.

western n.m. western.

whisky n.m. whiskey.

wigwam n.m. wigwam.

wiski n.m. whiskey.

wolfram n.m. wolfram.

wombat n.m. wombat.

X

x n.m. rayon-x, x-ray.

xénophobe adj. xenophobic. n.m.f. xenophobe.

xénophobie n.f. xenophobia.

xérès n.m. sherry, wine of Xeres, Spain.

Y

y adv. there; (with motion) here. menez-les-y, take them there. il n'y est pas, he is not there. pron. in it, in them; in this, in that; in him, in her, in them; to it, to them; to this, to that. je n'y ai pas pensé, I did not think of it. vous n'y êtes pas, you do not understand. vous n'y gagnerez rien, you will get

nothing by it. ne vous y fiez pas, do not trust him.

yacht n.m. yacht.

yaourt n.m. yogurt.

yard n.m. yard.

yeux n.m.pl. eyes.

yoga n.m. yoga.

Z

zapper *v.t.* to zap (TV remote).
zappeur *n.m.* zapper (TV remote).
zèbre *n.m.* zebra.
zébré, e *adj.* zebra-striped.
zébrure *n.f.* stripe; stripes.
zébu *n.m.* zebu.
zèle *n.m.* zeal; ardor, fervency, enthusiasm.
zélé, e *adj.* zealous; ardent, eager, enthusiastic.
zéro *n.m.* zero. **le thermomètre est descendu à ~,** the thermometer is down to zero.
zest *interj. n.m.* zest; a piece of orange or lemon peel.
zézaiement *n.m.* lisping.
zézayer *v.t.* to lisp.
zigzag *n.m.* zigzag.

zinc *n.m.* zinc; counter, bar.
zizanie *n.f.* discord.
zodiacal, e *adj.* zodiacal.
zodiaque *n.m.* zodiac.
zombie *n.m.* zombie.
zone *n.f.* zone. **~ torride,** torrid zone. **~ tempérée,** temperate zone.
zoo *n.m.* zoo.
zoologie *n.f.* zoology.
zoologique *adj.* zoological
zoom *n.m.* zoom.
zou! *Excl.* shoo!
zouave *n.m.* fool. **faire le ~,** to play around, to fool around.
zozoter *v.i.* to lisp.
zut! *Excl.* oh man! darn!

A

a *art. indéf.* un, une. **twice a day,** deux fois par jour. *Mus.* la *m.*

aback *adv.* **to take ~,** masquer, déconcerter.

abacus *n.* abaque *m.*

abandon *v.t.* abandonner; délaisser, quitter. **to ~ oneself,** s'abandonner, se livrer à.

abandoned *adj.* abandonné.

abandonment *n.* abandon *m.,* délaissement *m.,* (of insured objects).

abase *v.t.* abaisser; avilir, rabattre.

abasement *n.* abaissement *m.,* humiliation *f.*

abash *v.t.* déconcerter, confondre; consterner, interdire.

abashment *n.* confusion *f.,* honte *f.*

abate *v.i.* s'abattre, s'affaiblir, s'apaiser, tomber.

abatement *n.* abattement *m.,* diminution *f.,* apaisement *m.,* affaiblissement *m.,* rabais *m.,* réduction *f.,* déduction *f.,* remise *f.* (of a tax). **no ~,** prix fixe *m.*

abbey *n.* abbaye *f.*

abbreviate *v.t.* abréger; raccourcir, resserrer.

abbreviated *adj.* abrégé, resserré.

abbreviation *n.* abréviation *f., Math.* réduction *f.; Mus.* crochet *m.*

ABC *m.* alphabet *m.* **it's as easy as ABC,** c'est simple comme bonjour.

abdicate *v.t.* abdiquer, renoncer à une charge, à une dignité; se démettre de.

abdication *n.* abdication *f.;* désaveu *m.*

abdomen *n.* abdomen *m.; bas-ventre *m.*

abduct *v.t.* enlever.

abduction *n.* abduction *f.* enlèvement *m.*

aberrant *adj.* aberrant.

aberration *n.* aberration *f.* erreur *f.* égarement *m.*

abet *v.t.* encourager, soutenir, provoquer, aider, appuyer.

abeyance *n.* abayance *f.,* suspension *f.; attente *f.*

abhor *v.t.* abhorrer, avoir en horreur.

abhorrence *n.* horreur *f.*

abhorrent *adj.* odieux, répugnant (to, à); exécrable.

abhorrently *adv.* avec horreur.

abide *v.i.* habiter, demeurer, rester. **to ~ by,** obéir, se soumettre, se conformer. **people have to ~ by the law,** les gens doivent obéir à la loi. *v.t.* souffrir; tolérer, supporter, subir.

abiding *adj.* permanent; obéissant, respectueux des lois.

ability *n.* pouvoir *m.* puissance *f.* habileté *f.,* talent *m.,* capacité *f.* **to the best of one's ~,** pour le mieux, de son mieux.

abject *adj.* abject; méprisable, misérable, déchu.

abjection *n.* abjection *f.; bassesse *f.,* lâcheté *f.*

abjectly *adv.* d'une manière abjecte.

abjure *v.t.* abjurer, renoncer à.

ablaze *adv.* en feu, en flammes.

able *adj.* capable, vigoureux. **to be ~ to,** être à même de.

able-bodied *adj.* fort, solide, bien constitué, bien portant.

ablution *n.* ablution *f.*

ably *adv.* habilement, avec habileté, avec talent.

abnegate *v.t.* renier; renoncer à.

abnegation *n.* abnegation *f.,* renonciation *f.*

abnormal *adj.* anormal.

aboard *adv.* à bord.

abode *n.* demeure *f.,* habitation *f.,* séjour *m.,* résidence *f.*

abolish *v.t.* abolir, annuler, détruire.

abolishment *n.* abolisment *m.,* abolition *f.*

abolition *n.* abolition *f.*

abominable *adj.* abominable, horrible.

abominate *v.t.* avoir en abomination, en horreur, abominer.

abomination *n.* abomination *f.,* horreur *f.*

aboriginal *adj.* aborigène.

aborigines *n.* aborigènes *m.pl.*

abort *v.i.* avorter; échouer.

abortion *n.* avortement *m.*

abortive *adj.* abortif; avorté.

abound *v.i.* abonder en, affluer en; avoir abondance de.

about *adv.* à la ronde, autour; presque, ça et là. **all ~,** partout. **somewhere ~,** quelque part. *prep.* autour de, environ, dans; vers, sur, touchant, à peu près, par, pour. **your brother has spoken to me ~ his wedding,** votre frère m'a entretenu de son mariage. **he is ~ twenty years of age,** il a environ vingt ans. **send him ~ his business,** envoyez-le promener. **it took ~ three hours to get there,** ça nous a pris environ trois heures.

above *adv.* au-dessus, par-dessus, en plus. **~ all,** surtout. *prep.* au-dessus de, plus haut que, pardessus, en sus de, plus de, plus que. **the sun is ~ the horizon,** le soleil est au-dessus de l'horizon. **fifteen degrees ~ zero,** quinze degrés audessus de zéro. **~ the market price,** au-dessus du cours. **~-mentioned,** sus-mentionné. **~ ground,** à la surface.

abrade *v.t.* user en frottant.

abrasion *n.* abrasion *f.*

abreast *adv.* de front, de côté, **~ of,** vis-à-vis de, à le hauteur de, côte-à-côte.

abridge *v.t.* abréger, raccourcir; réduire, restreindre.

abridgment *n.* abrégé *m.,* précis *m.*

abroad *adv.* dehors, au dehors, à l'étranger. **to go ~,** aller à l'étranger.

abrogate *v.t.* abroger.

abrogation *n.* abrogation *f.*

abrupt *adj.* abrupt; escarpé; brusque, précipité; heurté, décousu.

abruptly *adv.* soudainement, brusquement.

abscess *n.* abcès *m.*

abscond *v.i.* se cacher; fuir; se sauver.

absconding *n.* fuite *f.*, action de se cacher.

absence *n.* absence *f.*, distraction *f.*

absent *adj.* absent; distrait. *n.* absent *m.*, absente *f.*

absent *v.t.* **to ~ oneself**, s'absenter.

absentee *n.* absent, e *m.f.*

absenteeism *n.* absentéisme *m.*

absently *adv.* distraitement.

absolute *adj.* absolu, positif, parfait; fini.

absolutely *adv.* absolument; complètement, tout à fait.

absolution *n.* absolution *f.*

absolve *v.t.* absoudre, décharger de, affranchir de, relever de.

absorb *v.t.* absorber.

absorbent *adj.* absorbant. *n.* absorbant *m.*

absorption *n.* absorption *f.*, préoccupation *f.*

abstain *v.i.* **(from,** de) s'abstenir, se priver.

abstaining *n.* abstinence *f.*

abstemious *adj.* sobre, frugal.

abstention *n.* abstention *f.*; abstinence *f.*, privation *f.*

abstinence *n.* abstinence *f.* **day of ~,** jour maigre (d'abstinence).

abstinent *adj.* abstinent; sobre, tempérant.

abstract *v.t.* **(from,** de) détacher, extraire (a passage from a book, etc.), soustraire, dérober. *adj.* abstrait, distrait. **~ idea,** idée abstraite. *n.* résumé *m.*, analyse *f.*, précis *m.*, abrégé *m.* (of a book).

abstraction *n.* abstraction *f.*, extraction *f.*, distraction *f.*, soustraction *f.*

absurd *adj.* absurde.

absurdity *n.* absurdité *f.*

abundance *n.* abondance *f.*, suffisance *f.*, beaucoup.

abundant *adj.* abondant, plein, ample. **~ with or in,** abondant en.

abundantly *adv.* abondamment.

abuse *n.* abus *m.*, insulte *f.*, injure.

abuse *v.t.* abuser de, vider; user mal, tromper, pervertir; injurier. **to ~ privileges,** abuser des privilèges.

abuser *n.* ravisseur *m.* abuseur *m.*

abusive *adj.* abusif, insultant, injurieux, grossier.

abusively *adv.* abusivement.

abutment *n.* arc-butant *m.*, but *m.*, borne *f.*, limite *f.*

abyss *n.* abîme *m.*, gouffre *m.*

acacia *n.* acacia *m.*

academic *adj.* académique, universitaire. *n.* académicien *m.*

academically *adv.* académiquement.

academy *n.* académie *f.*, institution *f.* **~ of music,** conservatoire *m.*

accede *v.i.* **(to,** à) accéder à, consentir à, adhérer à, accepter, monter (to the throne).

accelerate *v.t.* accelerer, précipiter le mouvement, hâter.

acceleration *n.* accélération *f.*

accelerator *n.* accélérateur *m. Infml.* champignon *m.*

accent *n.* accent *m.*, **~ v.t.** accentuer, articuler, appuyer sur.

accentuate *v.t.* accentuer.

accentuation *n.* accentuation *f.*

accept *v.t.* accepter, agréer, accueilir, admettre.

acceptable *adj.* acceptable.

acceptance *n.* accueil *m.*, approbation *f.*, réception *f.* favorable, grace *f.*, faveur *f.*, acceptation *f.*; acception, sens (of a word).

access *n.* accès *m.*, abord *m.*, admission *f.*, entrée *f.*; crise *f.*, attaque *f.* (of an illness).

accessory *n.* complice *m.f.*, *adj.*

accessibility *n.* accessibilité *f.*

accessible *adj.* accessible, abordable, affable.

accession *n.* accès *m.* surcroît *m.*, augmentation *f.*, accroissement *m.*, avènement *m.* (to the throne etc.). **right of ~,** droit *m.* d'accession.

accident *n.* accident *m.*; hasard *m.*; malheur *m.*, sinistre *m.* **to meet someone by ~,** rencontrer quelqu'un par hasard.

accidental *adj.* accidentel, fortuit. *n.* accident *m.*

accidentally *adv.* accidentellement, par hasard, fortuitement.

acclaim *v.t.* acclamer, applaudir **~ n.** acclamation *f.*, applaudissement *m.*

acclamation *n.* acclamation *f.*

acclimate *v.t.* acclimater.

acclimation acclimatation *f.*

acclimatize *v.t.* acclimater. *v.i.* s'acclimater.

accolade *n.* accolade *f.*

accommodate *v.t.* accommoder; ajuster, disposer; obliger, approprier à; héberger, loger. **to ~ oneself to circumstances,** s'accommoder aux circonstances.

accommodating *adj.* accommodant; flexible, obligeant, serviable.

accommodation *n.* (followed by **to** or **with**) adaptation *f.*, **to come to an ~,** arriver à un compromis. facilités *f.pl.*; logement *m.*, hébergement *m.* **~s for the night,** logement à la nuit.

accompaniment *n.* accompagnement *m.*

accompany *v.t.* accompagner; suivre.

accomplice *n.* complice *m.f.*

accomplish *v.t.* accomplir, achever, finir, atteindre, venir à bout de.

accomplishment *n.* accomplissement *m.*; mérite *m.*, talent *m.*, perfection *f.*

accord *n.* accord *m.*; union *f.* bonne intelligence, proportion *f.* **with one ~,** d'un common accord. *v.t.* accorder, ajuster, concilier, accommoder. *v.i.* s'accorder, être d'accord.

accordance *n.* accord *m.*; convenance *f.*;

proportion, juste. **in ~ with,** conformément à.
accordant *adj.* d'accord (avec); conforme à.
according *pr.* harmonieux. **~ to,** selon, suivant,
conformément à.
accordingly *adv.* en conséquence.
accordion *n.* accordéon *m.*
accost *v.t.* accoster, aborder.
account *n.* compte *m.,* note *f.,* mémoire *m.,* facture *f.,* budget *m.* raison *f.;* cas *m.,* considération
f. **~ book,** livre *m.* de compte. **~ sales,** compte
m. de ventes. **to keep ~s by double entry,**
tenir des livres en partie double. **to settle an ~,**
régler un compte. **to open, to close an ~,**
ouvrir, fermer un compte. **to carry to ~,** porter
en compte. **to audit an ~,** vérifier un compte.
overdrawn ~, compte à découvert. **to call one
to ~,** demander des comptes. **by your ~,** à ce
que vous dites. **by all ~s,** au dire de tout le
monde. **on no ~,** par aucun motif. **on ~ of,** à
cause de. **on his ~,** à cause de lui. **to take no
~ of,** faire peu de cas de. *v.t.* estimer, juger,
compter pour, réputer, tenir ou regarder comme
ou pour. *v.i.* compter, rendre compte ou raison
de, expliquer; être responsable de.
accountability *n.* responsabilité *f.;*
comptabilité *f.*
accountable *adj.* responsable.
accountant *n.* comptable *m.f.* **certified public
accountant (CPA),** expert comptable.
accounting *m.* comptabilité *f.*
accredit *v.t.* accréditer, faire croire à.
accretion *n.* accroissement *m.*
accrue *v.i.* accroître à; provenir de, résulter de.
accumulate *v.t.* accumuler, entasser *v.i.* s'accumuler, s'entasser, s'amonceler, s'amasser; s'accroître *adj.* accumulé, amoncelé.
accumulation *n.* accumulation *f.,* tas *m.,* amas
m., monceau *m.,* entassement *m.,*
amoncellement *m.*
accumulative *adj.* accumulé; qui s'accumule.
accuracy *n.* exactitude *f.,* justesse *f.,* précision *f.,*
fidélité *f.*
accurate *adj.* exact, juste, correct, fidèle; précis.
accurately *adv.* exactement, correctement;
fidèlement.
accursed *adj.* maudit, exécrable, abominable.
accusable *adj.* accusable.
accusation *m.* accusation *f.;* acte *m.* d'accusation.
accusatory *adj.* accusatoire.
accuse *v.t.* accuser, dénoncer.
accused *adj.* accusé, prévenu.
accuser *n.* accusateur *m.,* accusatrice *f.*
accustom *v.t.* accouturrer, habituer. **to ~ oneself to,** s'accoutumer à, s'habituer à.
ace as *m.* atout *m.* **to have an ~ up one's
sleeve,** avoir un atout dans sa manche.
acerb *adj.* acerbe, aigre, amer, âcre.
acetate *n.* acétate *m.*
ache *n.* mal *m.* douleur *f.* **tooth~,** mal de dents.
v.i. souffrir; faire mal. **my head ~s,** j'ai mal à la
tête.

achievable *adj.* faisable, exécutable.
achieve *v.t.* atteindre à, réussir à, exécuter, mener
à fin, venir à bout de.
achievement *n.* exploit *m.;* oeuvre *f.;* accomplissement *m.*
achiever *n.* celui qui réussit, achève, exécute,
acquiert; auteur *m.* d'un exploit; vainqueur *m.*
aching *adj.* qui souffre, qui a mal; malade, affligé. *n.* douleur *f.,* souffrance *f.,* peine *f.,* chagrin *m.*
achy *adj.* pas bien, mal fichu.
acid *adj., n.m.* acide.
acidify *v.t.* acidifier.
acidulous *adj.* acidulé.
acknowledge *v.t.* reconnaître; admettre; avouer;
reconnaître pour; accuser (réception de).
acknowledgment *n.* reconnaissance *f.;* aveu *m.,*
remerciement *m.,* rémunération *f.;* reçu *m.,*
accusé *m.* de réception. **~s,** remerciements *m.pl.*
acme *n.* sommet *m.,* apogée *m.,* comble *m.,*
pinacle *m.,* point *m.,* culminant. **the ~ of
human greatness,** le pinacle de la grandeur
humaine.
acne *n.* acné *m.*
acorn *n.* gland *m.*
acoustic *adj.* acoustique.
acoustics *n.pl.* acoustique *f.*
acquaint *v.t.* faire connaître, rendre familier,
avertir de, faire part de, tenir au fait, au courant
de, communiquer. **to ~ oneself with,** se rendre
familier (avec). **to be ~ed with,** connaître.
acquaintance *n.* connaissance *f.* **she is an ~ of
mine,** c'est une de mes connaissances.
acquiesce *v.i.* acquiescer, se résigner; se
soumettre.
acquiescence *n.* acquiescement *m.,*
soumission *f.*
acquire *v.t.* acquérir; obtenir; apprendre.
acquirement *n.* acquisition *f.,* acquis *m.pl.*
acquirer *n.* acquéreur *m.*
acquisition *n.* acquisition *f.*
acquit *v.t.* acquitter; décharger, libérer;
absoudre, renvoyer. **to ~ oneself of a debt,**
s'acquitter d'une dette (la payer).
acquittal *n.* acquittement *m.*
acquittance *n.* acquittement *m.;* quittance *f.,*
reçu *m.;* acquit *m.*
acre *n.* acre *f.* arpent *m.;* champ *m.*
acrimony *n.* acrimonie *f.,* âcreté *f.,* aigreur *f.*
acrobat *n.* acrobate *m.f.,* funambule *m.f.*
across *adv.* de travers, en travers. *prep.* à travers,
au travers de. **to go ~ the fields,** passer par les
champs.
act *v.i., v.t.* agir, opérer; jouer une pièce, représenter un rôle; feindre. **it is time to ~,** il est
temps d'agir. **to ~ as a friend,** agir en ami. **to
~ the part of a judge,** remplir les fonctions de
juge. acte *m.,* action *f.;* fait *m.* **the ~ of walking,**
l'action de marcher. **an ~ of charity,** acte de
charité, action charitable. **that comedy is in
five ~s,** cette comédie est en cinq actes. **to act**

out, jouer, reproduire un fait; **to act up,** faire le bête, faire des siennes; **to act upon,** se conformer à.

acting *adj.* agissant, qui agit. **the ~ magistrate,** le magistrat en fonctions.

~ manager, gérant *m.* *n.* action *f.;* jeu *m.* (d'un acteur); comédie *f.*

action *n.* action *f.,* acte *m.;* motion *f.,* mouvement *m.;* combat *m.,* bataille *f.;* procès *m.* **mechanical ~,** action mécanique. **to bring into ~,** mettre en mouvement. **to take ~,** prendre des mesures.

activate *v.t.* activer, stimuler, accélérer.

active *adj.* actif; agissant, leste, vif, agile, alerte. **an ~ man,** un homme actif.

actively *adv.* activement, lestement, vivement; de fait.

activist *n.* activiste *m.f,* militant *m.f.*

activity *n.* activité *f.* occupation *f.*

actor *n.* acteur *m.;* comédien *m.*

actress *n.* actrice *f.;* comédienne. *f.*

actual *adj.* effectif, réel, véritable; présent, existant.

actuality *n.* réalité *f.,* actualité *f.*

actualize *v.t.* actualiser.

actually *adv.* en fait, à vrai dire, réellement, véritablement.

actuate *v.t.* mettre en activité, en action, en mouvement; effectuer, pousser; animer.

acumen *n.* pointe *f.* aigue; perspicacité *f.,* pénétration *f.* d'esprit.

acupuncture *n.* acuponcture *f.*

acute *adj.* aigu; pointu, terminé en pointe; anguleux; fin, subtil. **an ~ angle,** un angle aigu.

acutely *adv.* d'une manière aigue, finement, subtilement.

acuteness *n.* subtilité *f.,* finesse *f.,* pénétration *f.,* vivacité *f; Mus.* acuité *f.;* intensité *f.*

ad *n.* annonce *f.;* pub *n.f;* petite annonce.

adage *n.* adage.

adamant *adj.* inflexible.

adapt *v.t.* adapter; ajuster.

adaptability *n.* faculté d'être adapté *f.*

adaptable *adj.* qui s'adapte, qu'on peut adapter, applicable.

adaptation *n.* adaptation *f.*

adapter *n.* adaptateur *m.,* adaptatrice *f.,* fiche *f.* multiple, raccord *m.*

add *v.t.* ajouter, joindre, additionner. **to ~ in,** inclure, faire parti. **to ~ up,** additionner.

adder *n.* vipère *f.,* couleuvre *f.*

addict *v.t.* vouer livrer; donner, consacrer. *n.* toxicomane *m.f.* **to be ~ed to,** s'adonner à, s'abandonner à.

addiction *n.* **(to,** à, pour), dépendance *f.;* penchant *m.,* attachement *m.* (à).

addition *n.* addition *f.,* surcroît *m.*

additional *adj.* additionnel. *n.* addition *f.*

additionally *adv.* en sus, en outre, par addition.

addled *adj.* gâté, creux, vide (of the mind), stérile. **an ~ head,** tête écervelée.

address *v.t.* préparer, disposer, adresser, s'adresser; parler, aborder. **to ~ a letter,** adresser une lettre. *n.* adresse *f.,* prière *f.;* habileté *f.,* finesse *f.* **with ~,** avec finesse.

addressee *n.* destinataire *m.f.*

adduce *v.t.* amener, présenter, produire; fournir, apporter; alléguer, citer, avancer (un fait, un auteur, un passage).

adept *n.* adepte *m.f.* *adj.* habile, savant, versé.

adequacy *n.* juste proportion *f.,* rapport *m.* suffisance *f.*

adequate *adj.* égal, proportionné, suffisant.

adequately *adv.* suffisamment, proportionnément.

adhere *v.i.* adhérer, s'attacher à; s'en tenir à.

adherence *n.* adhérence *f.;* union *f.,* jonction *f.* étroite; attachement *m.* à une parti, une opinion.

adherent *adj.* adhérent, attaché, joint à quelque chose. *n.* adhérent *m.;* partisan *m.,* disciple *m.*

adhesion *n.* adhésion *f.;* adhérence *f.,* attachement *m.*

adhesive *adj.* adhésif.

adjacent *adj.* adjacent; contigu, voisin. *n.* proche *m.,* voisin *m.*

adjective *n., adj.* adjectif *m.*

adjoin *v.t.* **(to,** à) être contigue à, attenant à.

adjoining *adj.* contigu, attenant, voisin.

adjourn *v.t.* ajourner, remettre. *v.i.* s'ajourner; se retirer. **to ~ a meeting,** suspendre une séance.

adjournment *n.* ajournement *m.,* délai *m.*

adjudge *v.t.* adjuger, décerner, décider, juger, ordonner, décréter (que); condamner, estimer.

adjudicate *v.t.* adjuger, décerner. *v.i.* juger, prononcer, décider (in a trial).

adjudication *n.* adjudication *f.,* jugement *m.*

adjunct *n.* accessoire *m.,* adjoint *m.,* associé *m.,* collègue *m.-adj.* adjoint; accessoire à.

adjure *v.t.* adjurer, prier, demander avec insistance, implorer.

adjust *v.t.* ajuster, arranger, régler; concilier (people).

adjustable *adj.* réglable.

adjustment *n.* ajustement *m.;* mise *f.* au point, ajustage *m.*

ad lib *n.* improvisation. *v.t.* improviser. *adv.* improviser. spontané *adj.* à volonté, à discrétion. *adj.* improvisé.

advertising agent *n.* agent de pub(licité), publiciste *m.f.,* publicitaire *m.f.*

administer *v.t.* administrer; régir, dispenser (sacrements); donner, apporter, prêter, gérer, pourvoir à, subvenir à. **to ~ an oath,** faire prêter serment.

administration *n.* administration *f.;* gouvernement *m.*

administrative *adj.* administratif.

administrator *n.* administrateur, gérant.

admirable *adj.* admirable, merveilleux.

admirably *adv.* admirablement, à ravir.

admiration *n.* admiration *f.*

admire *v.t., v.i.* admirer.

admirer *n.* admirateur *m.,* admiratrice *f.*

admiring *adj.* admiratif.

admiringly *adv.* avec admiration.

admissibility *n.* acceptabilité *f.*

admissible *adj.* admissible, acceptable.

admission *n.* admission *f.,* acceptation *f.,* entrée *f.,* accès *m.* **free ~,** entrée libre.

admit *v.t.* admettre, recevoir, accepter, tolérer.

admittance *n.* accès *m.,* entrée *f.,* admission *f.*

admittedly *adv.* de l'aveu général.

admonish *v.t.* blâmer; avertir, prévenir; instruire.

admonition *n.* exhortation *f.,* remontrance *f.,* réprimande *f.*

ado *n.* peine *f.,* difficulté *f.,* embarras *m.,* bruit *m.,* vacarme *m.,* façons *m.pl.* **much ~ about nothing,** beaucoup de bruit pour rien. **without more ~,** sans plus de façons.

adobe *n.* adobe *m.*

adolescence *n.* adolescence *f.*

adolescent *n.* et *adj.* adolescent *m.,* adolescente *f.*

adopt *v.t.* adopter, choisir.

adopted *adj.* adopté, adoptif, d'adoption.

adoption *n.* adoption *f.*

adoptive *adj.* adoptif, d'adoption. *n.* adopté *m.,* adoptée *f.*

adorable *adj.* adorable.

adoration *n.* adoration *f.*

adore *v.t.* adorer.

adoringly *adv.* avec adoration.

adorn *v.t.* orner, parer, embellir.

adornment *n.* ornement *m.,* décoration *f.;* parure *f.,* embellissement *m.*

adrift *adv.* à la dérive, en dérive, à l'abandon.

adroit *adj.* adroit, habile.

adroitly *adv.* adroitement, habilement.

adroitness *n.* adresse *f.,* dextérité *f.,* habileté *f.*

adulate *v.t.* aduler.

adulation *n.* adulation *f.*

adulator *n.* adulateur *m.*

adult *adj.* adulte. *m.f.* adulte.

adulterate *v.t.* falsifier, frelater; adultérer.

adulteration *n.* falsification *f.,* frelatage *m.,* adultération *f.*

adulterer *m.f.* adultère.

adulterous *adj.* adultère.

adultery *n.* adultère *m.*

advance *v.t.* avancer; faire avancer, progresser, élever, hausser (a price). **I advanced him a month's salary,** je lui ai avancé un mois de son salaire. *v.i.* s'avancer. *n.* avance *f.;* progrès *m.,* avancement *m.* **to be on the ~,** être à la hausse. **in ~,** en avance.

advancement *n.* mouvement *m.* en avant, progrès *m.;* avancement *m.,* promotion *f.*

advantage *n.* avantage *m.,* profit *m.,* supériorité *f.;* intérêt *m.* **to take ~ of,** tirer avantage (or profit) de. *v.t.* avantager, favoriser.

advantageous *adj.* (followed by to or for) avantageux, profitable, utile.

advantageously *adv.* avantageusement, utilement.

advent *n.* venue *f.,* arrivée *f.;* Avent *m.;* avènement *m.*

adventure *n.* aventure *f.,* hasard *m.,* chance *f.,* risque *m.-v.t.* aventurer, risquer, exposer. *v.i.* se hasarder, courir la chance, s'exposer.

adventurer *n.* aventurier *m.,* aventurière *f.*

adventurous *adj.* aventureux, hasardeux, audacieux.

adverb *n.* adverbe *m.*

adversary *n.* adversaire *m.f.* ~ *adj.* adverse, opposé, contraire.

adverse *adj.* adverse; contraire, opposé; ennemi, hostile.

adversity *n.* adversité *f.*

advert *v.i.* se référer, se reporter à, faire allusion à.

advertise *v.t.* faire de la publicité; mettre une annonce.

advertisement *n.* publicité *f.,* réclame *f.,* spot, *m.* publicitaire; annonce *f.* (dans un journal).

advertising *n.* publicité *f.,* réclame *f.* **an ~ agent,** agent de publicité. *n.* action d'annoncer.

advice *n.* avis *m.,* conseil *m.* **to give a piece of ~,** donner un conseil, un avis.

advisable *adj.* convenable, à propos, sage, prudent.

advise *v.t.* conseiller, recommander, donner avis. **I cannot ~ you in that matter,** je ne saurais vous conseiller dans cette affaire.

advisedly *adv.* avec prudence, précaution, judicieusement; en connaissance de cause.

adviser *n.* conseiller *m.*

advisory *adj.* consultatif.

advocacy *n.* plaidoyer *m.;* profession *f.* d'avocat.

advocate *n.* avocat *m.,* défenseur *m.,* partisan *m.* ~ *v.t.* plaider; défendre, soutenir.

aerate *v.t.* aérer, oxygéner.

aerial *adj.* aérien.

aerobics *n.* aérobic *m.* **to do ~,** faire de l'aérobic.

aerodynamic *adj.* aérodynamique *f.*

aerodynamics *n.pl.* aérodynamique *f.*

aerogram *n.* aérogramme *m.*

aeronautic *adj.* aéronautique.

aeronautics *spl.* aéronautique.

aesthetic *adj.* esthétique.

aesthetics *n.* esthétique *f.*

afar *adv.* loin, au loin, de loin.

affability *n.* affabilité *f.*

affable *adj.* affable.

affableness *n.* affabilité *f.*

affably *adj.* d'une manière affable, avec affabilité.

affair *n.* affaire *f.,* entreprise *f.* liaison *f.* **that's my ~,** c'est mon affaire, **to have an ~ with a person,** avoir une liaison avec une personne.

affect *v.t.* affecter; toucher, émouvoir; attendrir; intéresser.

affectation *n.* affectation, fente *f.*

affectedly *adv.* d'une manière affectée, avec affectation.

affecting *adj.* touchant, pathétique, attendrissant.

affection *n.* affection *f.* inclination *f.,* penchant *m.*

affectionate *adj.* affectionné, tendre, aimant.

affectionately *adv.* affectueusement.

affective *adj.* affectif, touchant, pathétique, qui affecte.

affidavit *n.* déclaration *f.,* déposition *f.* sous serment.

affiliate *v.t.* affilier, s'affilier.

affiliation *n.* affiliation *f.;* détermination *f.* de paternité.

affinity *n.* affinité *f.;* attraction *f.*

affirm *v.t.* affirmer; confirmer, ratifier.

affirmation affirmation *f.* confirmation *f.;* déclaration *f.* solennelle.

affirmative *n.* affirmative *f.* ~ *adj.* affirmatif.

affirmatively *adv.* affirmativement, positivement.

affix *v.t.* ajouter, apposer, appliquer; rapporter, attacher, joindre, fixer.

afflict *v.t.* affliger.

affliction *n.* affliction *f.;* chagrin *m.*

affluence *n.* affluence *f.,* opulence *f.,* aise *f.*

affluent *adj.* affluent, abondant; opulent, riche. *n.* affluent *m.* (of a river).

afflux *n.* afflux *m.*

afford *v.t.* avoir les moyens de. **I cannot ~ to lose my time,** mes moyens ne me permettent pas de perdre mon temps. **I cannot ~ it,** je n'ai pas les moyens, je ne peux pas me le permettre.

afforest *v.t.* reboiser.

afforestation *n.* reboisement *m.*

affranchise *v.t.* affranchir.

affront *v.t.* affronter, braver, rencontrer face à face, offenser. *n.* affront *m.,* offense *m.*

afield *adv.* au loin, plus loin. **to search farther ~,** rechercher plus loin.

afire *adv.* en feu, embrasé.

aflame *adv.* en flammes; embrasé.

afloat *adv.* à flot.

afoot *adv.* à pied; sur pied.

aforementioned *adj.* sus- or ci-dessus mentionné, susdit.

aforenamed *adj.* nommé ci-dessus, sus-nommé.

aforesaid *adj.* sus-dit.

aforethought *adj.* prémédité.

afoul *adv.* **to run ~ of the law,** avoir des ennuis avec la police.

afraid *adj.* effrayé, qui a peur; regrettable. **I'm ~ I will not be able to attend,** je regrette de ne pouvoir être présent(e) à.

afresh *adv.* de nouveau, de plus belle, encore.

Africa *npr.* Afrique *f.*

African *adj.* Africain. *n.* Africain *m.,* Africaine *f.*

afro *adj.* afro (hair style); *pref.* afro-.

Afro-American *adj.* African-américain. *n.* African-américain, -aine *m.f.*

after *adv.* après; suivant; ensuite. **soon ~,** aus-

sitôt après. *prep.* après, après que, sur, selon, d'après. **the day ~ tomorrow,** après-demain. **~ all,** après tout. **I wrote letter ~ letter,** j'ai écrit lettre sur lettre. **~ the French fashion,** suivant la mode française, à la française. *adj.* postérieur, subséquent, qui vient après. **~life** *n.* vie *f.* future, l'autre vie. **~math,** *n.* suites *f.pl.,* résultat *m.,* séquelles *f.pl.,* après coup. **~taste,** *n.* arrière-goût *m.* **~thought,** *n.* réflexion *f.* tardive. **aftereffect** *n.* effect *m.* secondaire.

afternoon *n.* après-midi *f.*

afterward *adv.* après; ensuite, plus tard. **that happened long ~,** cela est arrivé longtemps après.

again *adv.* encore, de nouveau, à nouveau, de plus, d'ailleurs, d'un autre côté, et puis. **once ~,** encore une fois. **~ and ~,** encore et encore, à plusieurs reprises. **come ~ tomorrow,** revenez domain.

against *prep.* contre, près, auprès de. **~ the wall,** contre le mur.

agape *adv.* bouche bée.

age *n.* âge *m.* siècle *m.;* vieillesse *f.* **what is your ~,** quel âge avez-vous? **of middle ~,** entre deux âges. **he is of ~,** il est majeur. **the golden ~,** l'âge d'or. **it's been ~s since we last saw you,** ça fait des siècles qu'on ne vous a pas vu.

agency *n.* action *f.;* opération *f.,* agence *f.,* entremise *f.;* **employment ~,** agence de placement.

agenda *n.* agenda *m.,* ordre du jour *m.*

agent *n.* agent *m.,* représentant *m.* **secret ~,** agent secret.

Agent Orange *n.* agent orange *m.*

agglomeration *n.* agglomération *f.*

agglutinate *v.t.* agglutiner.

agglutination *n.* agglutination *f.*

aggravate *v.t.* aggraver; exagérer, amplifier; *Infml.* porter sur les nerfs, taper sur les nerfs.

aggravation *n.* aggravation *f.;* circonstance aggravante; exagération *f.,* charge *f.;* provocation *f.*

aggregate *v.t.* réunir, assembler des parties en un tout. *adj.* réuni, assemblé, collectif. **~ fruits,** fruits agrégés. *n.* agrégation *f.* assemblage *m.,* masse *f.,* total *m.,* agrégat *m.*

aggregation *n.* agrégation *f.;* assemblage *m.;* cohésion *f.*

aggression *n.* agression *f.*

aggressive *adj.* agressif.

aggressively *adv.* agressivement.

aggressiveness *n.* agressivité *f.*

aggressor *n.* agresseur *m.*

aggrieve *v.t.* vexer, chagriner, affliger; blesser.

aghast *adj.* atterré, frappé d'horreur, d'étonnement; effaré, pétrifié.

agile *adj.* agile, léger, leste, dispos.

agility *n.* agilité *f.,* légèreté *f.*

agitate *v.t.* agiter; troubler; discuter.

agitation *n.* agitation *f.;* trouble *m.,* de

l'esprit, etc.; discussion f., controverse f., examen m., débat m.

aglow *adj.* rougeoyant, embrasé, incandescent.

ago *adv.* passé. **long ~, a long while ~,** il y a longtemps. **ten minutes ~,** il y a dix minutes.

agog *adv.* être agité; en émoi. **to be all ~,** être agité.

agonize *v.t.* agoniser, être en angoisse, être à la torture, au supplice. *v.t.* torturer, tourmenter à l'extrême, martyriser.

agonizing *adj.* douloureux, cuisant, atroce, déchirant.

agonizingly *adv.* avec une angoisse extrême.

agony *n.* angoisse, douleur poignante, agonie f.

agree *v.i.* s'accorder, s'accommoder; convenir. **we never ~,** nous ne sommes jamais d'accord, nous ne nous entendons jamais. **to ~ on a thing,** être d'accord convenir d'une chose. **wine does not ~ with you,** le vin ne vous convient pas, vous fait mal.

agreeable *adj.* agréable, plaisant, aimable.

agreeably *adv.* (with to, with) conformément à, d'accord avec, conformément, agréablement.

agreed *adj.* accordé, d'accord; convenu. *adv.* d'accord, convenu, accepté.

agreement *n.* accord m., harmonie f., contrat m., arrangement m. **by mutual ~,** d'un commun accord.

agricultural *adj.* agricole, d'agriculture.

agriculture *n.* agriculture f.

agriculturist *n.* agriculteur m.

agronomy *n.* agronomie f.

aground *adv.* à terre, à la côte; échoué. **to run ~,** échouer, faire échouer; s'échouer.

ah *interj.* ah!

aha *interj.* ah! ah!

ahead *adv.* en avant, à l'avant, devant, debout, en tête. **to be ~,** être en avant. **to get ~ of,** prendre de l'avance, devancer. **go ~!** en avant ! avancez!

ahoy ho! là! **ship ~!** ohé du navire!

aid *v.t.* aider, assister, secourir. *n.* aide f., assistance f., secours m.; auxiliaire m.

AIDS *n.* SIDA m., sida m.

aide-de-camp aide de camp m.

ail *v.i.* avoir mal, être souffrant. **what ~s you?** qu'est-ce qui vous fait mal? qu'est-ce qui ne va pas?

ailing *adj.* indisposé, souffrant.

ailment *n.* mal m. maladie f., incommodité f., indisposition f.

aim *v.t., v.i.* viser, mirer, ajuster; aspirer, viser. **~ well,** ajustez bien. **he aimed the gun at him,** le revolver le visait. *n.* mire f., visée f., mise f. en joue d'un fusil, etc.; but m., point m. de mire. **to take ~ at,** coucher en joue, ajuster. **to miss one's ~,** manquer son but, son coup.

aimless *adj.* sans but.

ain't *Infml.* am not, is not, are not, has not, have not.

air *n.* air m., mine f., apparence f., maintien m. **pure ~,** air pur. **to build castles in the ~,**

bâtir des châteaux en Espagne. **to give oneself ~s,** se donner des airs, de grands airs. *v.t.* aérer, exposer à l'air; ventiler, éventer. **~ balloon,** *n.,* montgolfière f. **~-conditioned** *adj.* climatisé, air-conditionné. **~-conditioning** *n.* climatisation f. conditionnement m. de l'air. **~-cushion** *n.* coussin m. à air. **~-hole,** *n.* soupirail m. **~ mattress,** *n.* matelas m. pneumatique. **~ pump,** *n.* machine f. pneumatique.

aircraft *n.* appareil, avion.

airily *adv.* allègrement, légèrement, gaiement.

airiness *n.* exposition f., à l'air, situation f. aérée; légèreté f., vivacité f.

airing *n.* ventilation f.

airless *adj.* sans air, non aéré.

airline *n.* ligne aérienne.

airy *adj.* aérien, dans les airs; aéré; léger; chimérique, illusoire, léger, gai; rapide comme l'air.

airport *n.* aéroport m.

aisle *n.* aile f., bas-côté m.

ajar *adj.* entrebaillé, entr'ouvert.

akin *adj.* (people) (things) parent, apparenté; allié par nature.

alarm *n.* alarme f.; réveille-matin m. **~ clock,** réveille-matin m. *v.t.* alarmer, donner l'alarme; appeler aux armes.

alarming *adj.* alarmant.

alarmingly *adv.* d'une manière alarmante.

alas *interj.* hélas!

album *n.* album m.

albumen *n.* albumen m.; albumine f.

alcohol *n.* alcool m.

alcoholic *adj.* alcoolique. **~ drink,** boisson alcolisée n. alcoolique m.f.

alcove *n.* alcôve f.; cabinet m.

ale *n.* ale f., bière f.

alert *adj.* alerte, vigilant; leste, vif. **to be on the ~,** être sur le qui-vive.

alertness *n.* vigilance f., vivacité f.

alfalfa *n.* luzerne f.

algae *n.* algue f.

algebra *n.* algèbre f.

algebraic, algebraical *adj.* algébrique.

Algeria *npr.* Algérie.

alias *adv.* alias. *n.* nom d'emprunt m.

alibi *n.* alibi m.

alien *adj.* étranger; éloigné. *n.* étranger m., étrangère f.; extra-terrestre m.f.

alienate *v.t.* aliéner, éloigner, détourner.

alienation *n.* aliénation f., dérangement m., égarement m. de l'esprit. **~ of mind, mental ~,** aliénation mentale.

alight *v.i.* descendre (from car); s'abattre (bird).

align *v.t.* aligner.

alignment *n.* alignement m.

alike *adj.* semblable, égal, ressemblance; pareil, même. *adv.* pareillement, également, de même; à la fois.

aliment *n.* aliment m., nourriture f.

alimentary *adj.* alimentaire.

alimentation *n.* alimentation f.

alimony n. pension f. alimentaire.

alive adj. en vie, vivant, vif; animé, gai. **dead or ~**, mort ou vif. **no man ~**, aucun homme vivant, personne au monde.

alkali n. alcali m.

alkaline adj. alcalin.

alkaloid n. alcaloïde m. adj. alcaloïde.

all adj. tout m., toute f. (pl. tous, toutes) **~ day**, tout le jour, toute la journée. **~ men**, tous les hommes. **that's ~ I know**, c'est tout ce que je sais. **on ~ fours**, à quatre pattes. adv. tout, tout à fait, entièrement, complètement. **~ the same**, tout de même, tous/toutes la même chose, tous pareils, toutes pareilles. **~ at once**, tout à coup, tout d'un coup. n. tout m. **~ or nothing**, tout ou rien. **I tell you so once and for ~**, je vous le dis une fois pour toutes. **nothing at ~**, rien du tout. **nowhere at ~**, nulle part. **I'm ~ right**, ça va, je me sens bien, je vais bien. **~-absorbing**, qui absorbe tout. **~-binding**, qui lie tout. **~-efficient**, d'une parfaite efficacité, d'une efficacité sans limites. **~-powerful**, tout-puissant, toute-puissante.

allay v.t. apaiser, calmer, adoucir; modérer, tempérer; affaiblir, amortir. v.i. s'apaiser, se calmer, s'adoucir, se modérer, se tempérer.

allée n. allée f.

allegation n. allégation f.

allege v.t. alléguer; avancer, soutenir, affirmer.

alleged adj. prétendu, allégué; affirmé, avancé, déclaré.

allegedly adv. prétendument.

allegiance n. obéissance f., fidélité f.

allegoric, allegorical adj. allégorique.

allegorically adv. allégoriquement.

allegory n. allégorie f.

allelujah n. alleluia m.

allergic adj. allergique.

allergy n. allergie f.

alleviate v.t. alléger; diminuer, amoindrir, soulager.

alleviation n. allègement m.; atténuation f.; adoucissement m.; soulagement m.

alley n. f.; passage étroit; ruelle f.

alliance n. alliance f.; pacte m.

alligator n. alligator m.

alliteration n. allitération f.

allocate v.t. placer, mettre à part; distribuer.

allocation n. allocation f.

allocution n. allocution f.; adresse f. formelle.

allot v.t. lotir, diviser ou distribuer par lots, distribuer; accorder.

allotment n. partage m., lot m., part f.

allow v.t. permettre, accorder, donner, concéder; admettre, convenir, avouer, allouer. **~ me to tell you**, permettez-moi de vous dire.

allowable adj. admissible, permis, approuver.

allowance n. pension f. alimentaire, argent m. de poche; permission f. approbation f., sanction f., admission f.; allocation f., pension f.; portion f. assignée, diminution f., réduction f. **to make ~s**

for, tenir compte de, avoir de l'indulgence pour. **trade ~**, remise f. accordée au commerce. v.t. mettre à la ration.

alloy v.t. allier des métaux, altérer, diminuer. n. aloi m.; alliage m., mélange m.

allspice n. quatre épices m.

allude v.i. faire allusion.

allure v.t. attirer, séduire.

allurement n. appât m., séduction f.; charme m., attrait m.

alluring adj. séduisant, attrayant.

allusion n. allusion f.

allusive adj. allusif, figuré.

ally v.t. allier, unir. **to ~ oneself**, s'allier, n. allié m.

almanac n. almanach m.

almighty adj. tout-puissant n. le tout-puissant m. tout-puissant.

almond n. amande f. **butter ~s**, amandes amères. **sweet ~s**, amandes douces. **burnt ~s**, pralines f. **~ tree**, amandier m. **~-shaped**, en amande.

almost adv. presque, à peu près, quasi.

alms n. aumône f., aumônes f.pl. **to give ~**, faire l'aumône.

aloe n. aloès m.

aloft adv. haut, en haut, en l'air.

alone adj. seul; unique. **leave me ~**, laisse-moi tranquille. **let those books ~**, ne touche pas à ces livres.

along adv. au long, de son long. prep. le long de; en avant. **to go ~**, avancer. **to sail ~ the coast**, côtoyer le rivage. **all ~ the way**, tout le long du chemin.

alongside adv. and prep. le long de, à côté de, à bord de.

aloof adv. reservé.

aloofness n. réserve f., attitude f. distante.

aloud adv. haut, à haute voix.

alphabet n. alphabet m.

alphabetic, alphabetical adj. alphabétique.

alphabetically adv. alphabétiquement.

alphabetize v.t. classer par ordre alphabétique.

Alpinist n. alpiniste m.f.

already adv. déjà.

also adv. aussi, de plus, en outre.

altar n. autel m.

alter v.t. changer, alterer. v.i. se changer, se modifier.

alteration n. altération f.; changement m.; modification f., correction f. (of a text); retouche f. (of clothes).

altercation n. altercation f.

alternate adj. alternatif. n. alternative f. v.t. alterner. **the flood and ebb tides ~ with each other**, les hautes et basses marées se succèdent tour à tour.

alternately adv. alternativement, tour à tour.

alternation n. alternance f., alternation f., alternative f.; vicissitude f.

alternative adj. alternatif. n. alternative f., choix m.

alternatively adv. alternativement, tour à tour, en manière d'alternative.

although conj. quoique; bien que; quand même, quand bien même.

altimeter n. altimètre m.

altitude n. hauteur f. élévation; altitude f.

altogether adv. entièrement, tout à fait, complètement; somme toute, tout compte fait.

altruism n. altruisme m.

aluminium n. aluminium m.

alumnus (pl. **alumni**) n. ancien élève, ancien étudiant.

always adv. toujours.

amalgam n. amalgame m.

amalgamate v.t. amalgamer. v.i. s'amalgamer; se mêler, se confondre; fusionner, se fusionner.

amalgamation n. amalgamation f.

amass v.t. amasser, ramasser, empiler.

amateur n. amateur m., dilettant m.

amaze v.t. étonner, ahurir, stupéfier.

amazement n. étonnement m., surprise f., stupéfaction f.

amazing adj. étonnant.

amazingly adv. étonnamment.

Amazon n. Amazone f.

ambassador n. ambassadeur m., ambassadrice f.

amber n. ambre m. ~ adj. d'ambre.

ambiance n. ambiance f.

ambidextrous adj. ambidextre.

ambient adj. ambiant.

ambiguity n. ambiguïté f., équivoque.

ambiguous adj. ambigu, équivoque.

ambit n. tour m., contour m.; limites f.pl.

ambition n. ambition f.

ambitious adj. ambitieux.

ambitiously adv. ambitieusement.

ambivalence n. ambivalence f.

ambivalent adj. ambivalent.

amble n. amble m., pas m. d'amble. v.i. ambler; aller le pas; trottiner. **to ~ along,** aller son train.

ambulance ambulance f.

ambulatory adj. ambulatoire.

ambush n. embuscade f., embûche f. **to lie in ~,** se tenir en embuscade. v.t. embusquer. v.i. s'embusquer.

ameliorate v.t. améliorer, rendre meilleur. v.i. s'améliorer; devenir meilleur.

amelioration n. amélioration f.

amen n. amen.

amenable adj. soumis, docile; responsable, justiciable. **~ to the law,** responsable envers la justice.

amend v.t. amender, corriger; réformer. v.i. s'amender, se corriger.

amendment n. amendement m.; réformer f.

amends n. compensation f., dédommagement m.; réparation f. **to make ~ for,** dédommager.

amenity n. aménité f., amabilité f.; charme m., agrément m., politesses f.pl.

America npr. Amérique f. **North ~,** Amérique du nord. **South ~,** Amérique du sud. **Central ~,** Amérique centrale.

American adj. américain. n. américain m., américaine f.

Americanism n. américanisme m.

Americanize v.t. américaniser.

amethyst n. améthyste f.

amiability n. amabilité f.

amiable adj. aimable, affable.

amicable adj. amical; à l'amiable.

amicably adv. amicalement, à l'amiable; aimablement.

amid, amidst prep. au milieu de; parmi, entre.

amiss adv. mal, en mal, de travers. adj. mauvais; déplacé, inconvenant; indisposé.

amity n. bonne intelligence f.

ammonia n. ammoniaque f.

ammunition n. munitions f.pl.; approvisionnements m.pl. militaires.

amnesia n. amnésie f.

amnesty n. amnistie f.

among, amongst prep. parmi; entre, avec, chez. **~ honest folks,** parmi les honnêtes gens.

amoral adj. amoral.

amorous adj. concupiscent.

amorphous adj. amorphe.

amortization n. amortissement m.

amortize v.t. amortir.

amount n. montant m., total m., totalité f., résultat m., somme f. ~ v.i. monter à, s'élever à; revenir à, se réduire à. **what does his bill ~ to?** à combien s'élève sa note?

amphibious adj. amphibie.

amphitheater n. amphithéâtre m.

ample adj. ample, gros, grand, étendu; copieux, abondant; riche.

ampleness n. ampleur f., abondance f.

amplification n. amplification f.

amplifier n. amplificateur m.

amplify v.t. amplifier, exagérer, étendre.

amplitude n. amplitude f., étendue f., abondance f.

amply adv. amplement.

amputate v.t. amputer.

amputation n. amputation f.

amuck, amock adv. furieusement. **to run ~,** comme un fou furieux, se déchaîner (a crowd).

amulet n. amulette f.

amuse v.t. amuser, divertir.

amusement n. amusement m.

amusing adj. amusant; divertissant.

amusingly adv. d'une manière amusante.

an art. indef. un, une.

anachronism n. anachronisme m.

anagram n. anagramme f.

anal adj. anal.

analogy n. analogie f. **from ~,** par analogie.

analysis n. analyse f.

analytic, analytical *adj.* analytique.

analyze *v.t.* analyser, faire l'analyse de.

anarchic, anarchical *adj.* anarchique.

anarchist *n.* anarchiste *m.f.*

anarchy *n.* anarchie *f.*

anathema *n.* anathème *m.* ~ *adj.* anathème.

anatomical *adj.* anatomique.

anatomically *adv.* anatomiquement.

anatomy *n.* anatomie *f.*

ancestor *n.* ancêtre, aïeul *m.*, aïeule *f.*

ancestral *adj.* ancestral.

ancestry *n.* ancêtres, ascendance *f.*, lignée *f.*

anchor *n.* ancre *f.* **to ride at ~,** être à l'ancre. **to cast ~,** jeter l'ancre, mouiller. *v.t.* ancrer, mouiller. *v.i.* jeter l'ancre.

anchorage *n.* mouillage *m.*, ancrage *m.*, droit *m.* d'ancrage.

anchovy *n.* anchois *m.* ~ **paste,** beurre *m.* d'anchois.

ancient *adj.* ancien; vieux, vielle. **an ~ city,** une ville ancienne. *n.* ancien *m.* **that's ~ history!,** c'est de l'histoire ancienne, c'est une vieille histoire.

ancillary *adj.* ancillaire, subordonné; auxiliaire.

and *conj.* et. **his father ~ mother,** son père et sa mère. **two ~ two,** deux à deux. **less ~ less,** de moins en moins.

anecdote *n.* anecdote *f.*

anecdotal *adj.* anecdotique.

anemia *n.* anémie *f.*

anemone *n.* anémone *f.*

anesthesia *n.* anesthésie *f.*

anesthetic *adj., n.* anesthésique.

anesthetize *v.t.* anesthésier.

aneurism *n.* anévrisme *m.*

anew *adv.* de nouveau, à nouveau, encore; d'une manière nouvelle.

angel *n.* ange *m.* **guardian ~,** ange gardien. **fallen ~,** ange déchu. **~fish,** ange *m.* de mer. **~-winged,** aux ailes d'ange, ailé comme les anges. **be an ~ and give me that plate,** donne-moi cette assiette, tu seras un ange.

angelic, angelical *adj.* angélique.

angelus *n.* angélus *m.*

anger *n.* colère *f.*, emportement *m.*, courroux *m.* **a fit of ~,** un accès de colère. *v.t.* mettre en colère, irriter, courroucer, fâcher.

angina *n. Med.* angine *f.*

angle *n.* angle *m.*, aspect *m.* **a right, obtuse, acute ~,** angle droit, obtus, aigu. *v.i.* pêcher à la ligne. **to ~ for,** pêcher, séduire.

Anglican *adj.* anglican *n.* anglican *m.*

Anglicanism *n.* anglicanisme *m.*

Anglo- *adj.* anglo-, anglo-. **~-American,** *m.f.* Anglo-américain *m.* **~-américaine** *f.* **~-Saxon,** *m.f.* Anglo-Saxon *m.*, ~Saxonne *f.*

anglophile *n.* anglophile *m.f.*

anglophobe *n.* anglophobe.

angora *n.* chat *m.* **~ wool,** laine *f.* angora.

angrily *adv.* avec colère.

angry *adv.* en colère, irrité; provoqué,

furieux, fâché. **what are you ~ at (about or for),** pourquoi es-tu fâché/en colère? **the ~ waves,** les vagues irritées.

anguish *n.* angoisse *f.*, douleur *f.*, supplice *m.* **to be in ~,** être au supplice.

anguished *adj.* angoissé, tourmenté.

angular *adj.* angulaire; anguleux, angulé.

animal *n.* animal *m.* ~ *adj.* animal. **~ kingdom,** règne animal. **~ life,** vie animale. **~ spirits,** esprits animaux.

animate *v.t.* animer, vivifier; encourager; réjouir. *adj.* animé.

animated *adj.* animé, gai, vigoureux. **~ cartoon,** dessins animés.

animation *n.* animation *f.;* vivacité.

animator *n.* animateur *m.,* animatrice *f.*

animosity *n.* animosité *f.*

anise *n.* anis *m.*

ankle *n.* cheville *f.* **~-deep,** jusqu'à la cheville.

annalist *n.* annaliste *m.f.*

annals *spl.* annales *f.pl.* livre contenant des annales.

annex *v.t.* annexer, ajouter, attacher *v.i.* s'annexer, s'unir, se joindre. *n.* annexe *f.*

annexation *n.* annexion *f.*

annihilate *v.t.* annihiler, anéantir. *adj.* annihilé, anéanti.

annihilation *n.* annihilation *f.*

anniversary *n.* anniversaire *m.* **wedding ~,** anniversaire de mariage.

A(nno) D(omini) *Lat. Anno Domini (A.D.),* l'an du seigneur.

annotate *v.i.* annoter, faire des annotations.

annotation *n.* annotation *f.*

announce *v.t.* annoncer, prononcer.

announcement *n.* annonce *f.;* avisi *m.;* faire-part *m.*

announcer *n.* speaker *m.,* speakerine *f.,* présentateur *m.,* présentatrice *f.,* journaliste *m.f.*

annoy *v.t.* ennuyer; contrarier, gêner. **you ~ me,** vous m'ennuyez.

annoyance *n.* contrariété *f.,* inconvénient *m.,* ennui *m.* **to be an ~ to a person,** gêner, déranger quelqu'un.

annoying *adj.* agaçant, ennuyeux.

annual *adj.* annuel. *n.* plante *f.* annuelle.

annually *adv.* annuellement.

annuity *n.* annuité *f.,* pension *f.* **life ~,** rente viagère. **term ~,** rente remboursable à terme. **to buy up, to redeem an ~,** racheter une rente.

annul *v.t.* annuler, rendre nul.

annular *adj.* annulaire.

annulment *n.* annulation *f.,* abrogation *f.,* révocation *f.*

annunciate *v.t.* annoncer.

annunciation *n.* promulgation *f.;* annonce *f.,* avis *m.;* annonciation *f.*

anoint *v.t.* oindre, frotter; sacrer.

anomaly *n.* anomalie *f.*

anonymity *n.* anonymat *m.*

anonymous *adj.* anonyme.

anorexia *n.* anorexie *f.*

another *adj.* un autre, une autre; encore un. **I must have ~ pencil,** il me faut un autre crayon. *indef. pron.* un autre, une autre. **love one ~,** aimez-vous les uns les autres.

answer *v.i.* répondre, résoudre; satisfaire. **to ~ for a debt,** répondre d'une dette. *v.t.* répondre à, réfuter; remplir, satisfaire à; correspondre à. **to ~ a person, a question,** repondre à une personne, à une question. **the new machine ~s my needs admirably,** la nouvelle machine répond parfaitement à mes besoins. *n.* réponse *f.* **in ~ to your letter,** en réponse à votre lettre.

answerable *adj.* responsable; en rapport avec, conforme à, proportionné. **to be ~ for,** être responsable de.

ant *s.* fourmi *f.* tamanoir *m.* **~eater,** *n.* fourmilier *m.* **~hill,** *n.* fourmilière *f.*

antagonism *n.* antagonisme *m.*

antagonist *n.* antagoniste *m.f.*

antagonistic *adj.* d'antagoniste, opposant, contraire.

antagonize *v.i.* agir en opposition; contrarier.

antalgic *adj.* antalgique.

antarctic *adj.* antarctique.

ante *n.* (poker) mise *f.*

antecedence *n.* antécédence *f.*, antériorité *f.*

antecedent *adj.* antécédent. *n.* antécédent *m.*

antedate *n.* antidate *f.* **~** *v.t.* antidater; anticiper.

antediluvian *adj.* antédiluvien. *n.* être *m.* antédiluvien.

antelope *n.* antilope *f.*

antenna *pl.* **antennae** *n.* antenne *f.*

anterior *adj.* antérieur.

anteriority *n.* antériorité *f.*

anthem *n.* hymne *m.* national *Rel.* motet.

anthology *n.* anthologie *f.*

anthracite *n.* anthracite *m.*

anthrax *n.* (animal disease); charbon *m.* anthrax *m.*

anthropologist *n.* anthropologiste *m.f.*

anthropology *n.* anthropoligie *f.*

anthropomorphism *n.* anthropomorphisme *m.*

anthropomorphous *adj.* anthropomorphe.

anthropophagous *adj.* anthropophage.

anthropophagy *n.* anthropophagie *f.*

anti- *pref.* anti, contre.

antibiotic *n.* antibiotique *m.*

antibody *n.* anticorps *m.*

antic *n.* bouffon *m.;* geste *m.*, bouffonnerie *f.*, singerie *f.* **~** *adj.* grotesque, bizarre, fantasque. *v.t.* rendre bouffon, grotesque.

anticipate *v.t.* anticiper, prévenir, devancer; aller au devant de; s'attendre à.

anticipation *n.* anticipation *f.*; appréhension *f.*; attente *f.*

anticonstitutional *adj.* anticonstitutionnel.

antidote *n.* antidote *m.*

antifreeze *n.* antigel *f.*

antimilitarism *n.* antimilitarisme *m.*

antipathetic, antipathetical *adj.* antipathique.

antipathy *n.* antipathie *f.*

antiperspirant *adj. n.* déodorant *m.*

antipodes *pl. s.* antipode *m.*

antiquarian *adj.* d'antiquaire, relatif aux antiques.

antiquated devenu vieux, passé; vieilli, suranné.

antique *adj.* antique; ancien; suranné. *n.* antiquité *f.*

antiquity *n.* antiquité *f.*

antisemitism *n.* antisémitisme *m.*

antiseptic *adj.* antiseptique. *n.* antiseptique *m.*

antislavery *adj.* qui est opposé à l'esclavage.

antisocial *adj.* antisocial.

antitheft *adj.* antivol *m.*

anus *n.* anus *m.*

anvil *n.* enclume *f.*

anxiety anxiété *f.;* inquietude; appréhension *f.*

anxious *adj.* anxieux (**about, for,** de, sur); inquiet, désireux; angoissé.

anxiously *adv.* avec anxiété, d'un air inquiet.

any *adj. pron.* quelque, aucun, tout, quelconque; du, de la, des. **at ~ time, in ~ place,** à toute heure, en tout lieu. **~how,** de toute façon, n'importe comment. **~where,** partout, n'importe où. **~one, ~body,** quiconque, quelqu'un. n'importe qui, qui que ce soit, personne. **are there ~ here?** y-a-t-il quelqu'un ici? est-ce qu'il y a quelqu'un ici? **~ but him,** n'importe qui d'autre que lui. **~thing,** quelque chose, quoi que ce soit. **have you ~ money?** avez-vous de l'argent?

anyhow *adv.* n'importe comment; de toute façon. **(anyway)** *adv.*

aorta *n.* aorte *f.*

apace *adv.* rapidement, vite.

apart *adv.* à part; en dehors, à distance, à l'écart; séparément, en pièces.

apartheid *n.* apartheid *m.*

apartment *n.* appartement *m.*

apathetic *adj.* apathique.

apathy *n.* apathie *f.*

ape *n.* singe *m.* **~** *v.t.* singer, imiter.

aperitif *n.* apéritif *m.*

aperture *n.* ouverture *f.*, orifice *n.*, crevasse *f.*

apex *n.* sommet *f.*

aphasia *n.* aphasie *f.*

aphid *n.* aphis *m.*, puceron *m.*

aphonia aphonie *f.*

aphorism *n.* aphorisme *m.*

aphrodisiac *adj., n.* aphrodisiaque *m.*

apiary *n.* rucher *m.*

apiece *adv.* (things) pièce, la pièce, chacun; (people or animals) par tête, chacun.

aplomb *n.* assurance *f.*, aplomb *m.*

Apocalypse *n.* Apocalypse *f.*

apocalyptic *adj.* apocalyptique.

apogee *n.* apugée *m.*

apologetic *adj.* apologétique. **he was very ~ about,** il était confundu en excuses de ~er.

apologize *v.i.* s'excuser, faire des excuses.

apology *n.* apologie *f.*, excuse *f.*

apostle n. apôtre m.

apostrophe n. apostrophe f.

apotheosis n. apothéose f.

apotheosize v.t. déifier.

appall v.t. horrifier, épouvanter, consterner. v.i. être dans la consternation.

appalling adj. épouvantable, effrayant.

apparatus n. appareil inv. m; attirail m. **kitchen ~**, attirail de cuisine. **photographic ~**, appareil photographique.

apparel n. habillement m., habits m.pl., vêtement m. **wearing ~**, habits m.pl.

apparent adj. apparent; évident, manifeste. **heir ~**, héritier présomptif.

apparently adv. apparemment, vraisemblablement.

apparition n. apparition f.

appeal v.i. faire appel (à), lancer un appel (à), avoir recours à. n. appel m. **without ~**, sans appel. **to make an ~ to**, faire un appel à.

appealing adj. séduisant, attirant.

appear v.i. paraître; apparaître; comparaître (en justice); se présenter; sembler. **it ~s that**, il paraît que, il semble que. **to make ~**, faire voire, faire sembler, faire apparaître.

appearance n. apparition f.; apparence f.; aspect m., air m.; comparution f. (in court). **first ~**, début (of an artist). **to keep up ~s**, sauver les apparances. **to make one's ~**, faire son apparition.

appease v.t. apaiser; calmer, adoucir.

appeasement n. apaisement m.

appellation n. appellation f., n. désignation f., qualification f.

append v.t. ajouter, annexer, apposer (signature).

appendage n. dépendance f., accessoire m.; appendice m.

appendicitis n. appendicite f.

appendix pl. **appendices or appendixes** n. appendice m.; accessoire m.; dépendance f.

appertain v.i. appartenir.

appetite n. appétit m.; ardeur (pour), soif (de). **his ~ for revenge**, sa soif de vengeance.

appetizer n. apéritif m.; amuse-gueule m.

appetizing adj. appétissant.

applaud v.t. applaudir.

applause n. applaudissements m.pl. approbation f.

apple n. pomme f.; prunelle f. (of the eye). **Adam's ~**, pomme d'Adam. **~ core**, n. trognon m. de pomme. **~ fritter**, n. beignet m. de pomme. **~ peel**, pelure f. de pomme. **~ pie**, (without top crust), tourte f. aux pommes; (with top crust) tarte aux pommes. **~ tree**, pommier m. **~sauce**, compoto f. de pommes.

appliance n. appareil m., dispositif m. **household ~**, appareil ménager.

applicability n. possibilité d'appliquer.

applicable adj. applicable.

applicant n. postulant(e) m.f. candidat

m., demandeur(e) m.f. requérant(e) m.f.

application n. application f., emploi m., usage m., attention f. de l'esprit, étude f., demande f., sollication f. **the ~ of a process**, l'application d'un procédé. **by his ~ to studying**, par son application à l'étude. **a written ~**, une demands écrite. **~s to be made to**, s'adressera.

applicator in. applicateur n.

applied adj. appliqué (art, science).

apply v.t. appliquer, mettre, porter, adresser. v.i. **to ~ for a job**, poser sa candidature s'un poste. **~ to Mr. S.**, adressez-vous à M. S.

appoint v.t. désigner (a day, a place) arrêter, destiner, ordonner; prescrire, décider, nommer. **B. has been appointed first secretary**, B. a été nommé premier secrétaire.

appointment n. nomination f., charge f., office m., emploi m. place f.; arrangement m.; rendez-vous m.; ordre m.; décret m., commandement m. **before his ~ to that office**, avant sa nomination à cet emploi. **he made an ~ with me**, il m'a donné rendez-vous.

apportion v.t. répartir, assigner, proportionner.

apportionment n. répartition f., distribution f.

apposition n. apposition f.

appraisal n. estimation f., évaluation f.

appraise v.t. priser, estimer, évaluer.

appraiser n. estimateur m., commissaire-priseur m.

appreciable adj. appréciable.

appreciate v.t. apprécier. v.i. hausser de valeur, monter.

appreciation n. appréciation f., évaluation f., estimation f.; Fin. hausse f.

appreciative adj. reconnaissant.

apprehend v.t. appréhender; arrêter, saisir; craindre. **to ~ a criminal**, arrêter un criminel.

apprehension n. arrestation f., appréhension f.

apprehensive adj. qui soupçonne, appréhensif, inquiet, -ète m.f., craintif, -ive m.f.

apprehensively adv. avec intelligence, avec crainte.

apprentice n. apprenti(e) m.f. élève m.f. novice. v.t. placer, mettre en apprentissage.

apprenticeship n. apprentissage m.

approach v.i. approcher, s'approcher; se rapprocher. **the noise ~es**, le bruit approche. v.t. **to ~ a town**, s'approcher d'une ville. n. approche f.; accès; rapprochement m. (toward); proximité f. **at the ~ of winter**, aux approches de l'hiver.

approachable adj. accessible, abordable.

approaching adj. approchant, prochain.

approbation n. approbation f.

appropriate v.t. approprier, adapter, destiner; s'approprier. adj. approprié; propre, convenable. **~ language**, langage convenable.

appropriately adv. convenablement, pertinemment, d'une manière convenable.

appropriateness n. convenance f., propriété f. (word).

appropriation *n.* appropriation *f.;* crédit *m.* budgétaire.

approval *n.* approbation *f.*

approve *v.t.* approuver; agréer, consentir à; autoriser.

approving *adj.* approbatif, approbateur.

approvingly *adv.* avec approbation.

approximate *adj.* approximatif. *v.t.* approcher, rapprocher. *v.i.* approcher de, se rapprocher de.

approximately *adv.* approximativement.

approximation *f.* rapprochement *m.;* approximation *f.*

approximately *adv.* approximativement.

appurtenance *n.* appartenance *f.* dépendance *f.*

apricot *n.* abricot *m.* ~ **tree,** abricotier *m.*

April *n.* avril *m.* ~ **fool,** poisson *m.* d'avril. ~ **Fool's Day,** le premier avril.

apron *n.* tablier *m.; Théât.* avant-scène *f.*

apropos *adv.* à propos, opportunément; *adj.* opportun.

apt *adj.* apte; enclin, prompt à, propre à; capable.

aptitude *n.* aptitude *f.;* disposition *f.,* naturelle.

aptly *adv.* à propos, justement, convenablement, pertinemment.

aptness *n.* aptitude *f.;* tendance *f.*

aqualung *n.* équipement *m.,* de plongée sous-marine; *v.i.* faire de la plongée sous-marine.

aquafortis *n.* eau-forte *f.*

aquamarine *n.* eau *f.* de la mer; aigue-marine *f.*

aquanaut *n.* homme-grenouille *m.,* plongeur sous-marin *m.*

aquarium *n.* aquarium *m.*

Aquarius *n.* le Verseau *m.*

aquatic *adj.* aquatique.

aqueduct *n.* aqueduc *m.*

aqueous *adj.* aqueux.

aquiline *adj.* aquilin. **an** ~ **nose,** un nez aquilin.

Arabesque *adj.* arabesque. *n.* arabesques *f.pl.*

arable *adj.* arable, labourable.

arbiter *n.* arbitre *m.f.*

arbitrarily *adv.* arbitrairement.

arbitrary *adj.* arbitraire.

arbitrate *v.t.* arbitrer, décider, régler, décider de, prononcer sur.

arbitration *n.* arbitrage *m.*

arbitrator *n.* arbitre *m.f.,* médiateur *m.,* médiatrice *f.*

arboreous *adj.* d'arbre, arboré.

arbor *n.* berceau *m.,* bosquet *m.,* tonnelle *f.*

arc *n.* arc *m.*

arcade *n.* arcade *f.,* galerie *f.,* galerie marchande *f.*

arch *n.* arche *f.* arceau *m.,* voûte *f.,* arcade *f.,* arc *m.* ogive ~, arc gothique. *v.t.* voûter. cintrer; arquer, courber en arc. **to** ~ **over,** recouvrir en voûte, construire une voûte au-dessus de. **the ceiling is** ~**ed,** le plafond est voûté. *adj.* espiègle, malin, rusé. **an** ~ **look,** un regard malin.

archaic *adj.* archaïque.

archaism *n.* archaïsme *m.*

archangel *n.* archange *m.*

archbishop *n.* archevêque *m.*

archbishopric *n.* archevêché *m.*

arched *adj.* arqué.

archeologie, archeological *adj.* archéologique.

archeologist *n.* archéologue *m.*

archeology *n.* archéologie *f.*

archer *n.* archer *m.*

archery *n.* tir *m.* à l'arc.

architect *n.* architecte *m.f.*

architectural *adj.* architectural.

architecture *n.* architecture *f.*

archives *n.* archives *f.pl.*

archivist *n.* archiviste *m.f.*

Arctic *adj.* arctique.

ardent *adj.* passionné(e); fervent.

ardently *adv.* ardemment, passionnément, avec ferveur.

ardor *n.* ardeur *f.*

arduous *adj.* ardu; difficile, rude, pénible, laborieux.

arduously *adv.* péniblement, difficilement.

arduousness *n.* difficulté *f.*

are See BE.

area *n.* aire *f.;* enceinte *f.;* superficie *f.;* surface *f.;* étendue *f.;* cour *f.* **judicial** ~, du ressort de la justice. ~ **of knowledge,** domaine *m.* de connaissance.

arena *n.* arène *f.*

Argentina *n.* Argentine *f.*

Argentine *n.* **the** ~, l'Argentine, *adj.* argentine.

arguable *adj.* discutable, contestable.

arguably *adv.* sans doute, il se peut, il se pourrait.

argue *v.i.* se disputer, argumenter; discuter; soutenir. **to** ~ **with,** discuter avec. **it** ~**s well for him,** c'est un bon signe pour lui. *v.t.* débattre; prouver, démontrer. **they always** ~ **about the same thing,** ils se disputent sans cesse sur le même sujet.

argument *n.* argument *m.* discussion *f.,* dispute *f.,* débat *m.*

argumentation *n.* argumentation *f.*

argumentative *adj.* démonstratif, raisonné; encline à la discussion.

arid *adj.* aride.

aridity *n.* aridité *f.;* sécheresse *f.*

Aries *n.* le Bélier *m.*

aright *adv.* bien, avec justesse, correctement.

arise *v.i.* s'élever, monter; se lever (the sun, a person from a seat, etc.); se soulever; ressusciter; surgir. **when the sun arose,** lorsque le soleil se leva.

aristocracy *n.* aristocratie *f.*

aristocrat *n.* aristocrate *m.f.*

aristocratic *adj.* aristocratique.

arithmetic *n.* arithmétique *f.*

arithmetical *adj.* arithmétique.

ark arche *f.* Noah's ~, l'arche de Noé.

arm *n.* bras *m.,* arme *f.* accoudoir *m.* (of a chair). **at arm's length,** à la longueur du bras. **with** ~**s folded,** les bras croisés. **the secular** ~, le

bras séculier. **~chair,** fauteuil *m. v.t.* armer;
donner des armes à. *v.i.* s'armer, faire des préparatifs de guerre. **to ~ oneself with,** s'armer de,
se munir de.

armada *n.* armada *f.*

armament *n.* armement *m.;* matériel *m.* de
guerre.

armature *n.* armature *f.* (of a magnet), armure *f.*

armed *adj.* armé. **~ robbery,** *m.,* attaque *f.* à
main armée. **long ~, short ~,** qui a les bras
longs, les bras courts.

armful *n.* brassée *f.*

armistice *n.* armistice *m.*

armor *n.* armure *f.,* armature *f.*

armory *n.* salle *f.* d'armes, dépôt *m.* d'armes;
musée *m.* d'armes; armure *f.;* manufacture *f.*
d'armes.

armpit *n.* aisselle *f.*

army *n.* armée *f., Fig.* foule *f.,* nuée *f.,* grand
nombre *m.*

aroma *n.* arôme *m.*

aromatic *adj.* aromatique, odoriférant, parfumé.
n. aromate *m.*

around *prep.* autour de, tout autour de, à
l'entour de. *adv.* à l'entour, autour, à la ronde.
I saw him wandering ~, je l'ai vu qui errait
ça et là.

arouse *v.t.* éveiller, réveiller; exciter, stimuler.

arraign *v.t.* traduire devant un tribunal; mander; mettre en accusation, accuser. *n.* mise *f.* en
accusation.

arraignment *n.* mise *f.* en accusation, critique *f.*

arrange *v.t.* arranger; préparer, organiser, disposer, apprêter, ajuster.

arrangement *n.* arrangement; accommodement *m.*

arrant *adj.* insigne, franc, achevé.

array *n.* ordre *m.,* rang *m.;* **in battle ~,** en ordre
de bataille. *v.t.* disposer, mettre en ordre, ranger
(troops in battle); vêtir, revêtir; dresser la
liste de.

arrears *n.pl.* arriéré *m.* **rent in ~,** loyer arriéré.

arrest *v.t.* arrêter, saisir, appréhender; fixer
(attention); suspendre (judgment) *n.* arrestation
f. **under ~,** en état d'arrestation.

arrival *n.* arrivée *f.;* arrivage *m.* venue *f.* **upon ~,**
dès l'arrivée.

arrive *v.i.* (at, à; in, en, à) arriver; parvenir. **to ~
at a place,** arriver dans un endroit.

arrogance *n.* arrogance *f.*

arrogant *adj.* arrogant, insolent.

arrogate *v.t.* s'arroger.

arrow *n.* flèche *f.,* trait *m.* **to let fly, to shoot an
~,** décocher une flèche.

arsenal *n.* arsenal *m.*

arsenic *n.* arsenic *m.*

arson *n.* incendie *m.* volontaire.

art *n.* art *m.;* artifice *m.,* adresse *f.* **the fine ~s,**
les beaux-arts.

artefact *n.* objet fabriqué *Arch. n.m.*

arterial *adj.* artériel.

artery *n.* artère *f.;* route *f.*

artful *adj.* ingénieux, astucieux, insidieux.

artfully *adv.* avec art, astucieusement,
insidieusement.

artfulness *n.* habilité *f.,* adresse *f.;* astuce *f.*

arthritic *adj.* arthritique.

arthritis *n.* rhumatisme *m.* arthrite *f.*

artichoke *n.* artichaut *m.*

article *n.* article *m.,* clause *f.;* chapitre *f.,* rapport
m.; objet *m.;* marchandise *f.*

articulate *adj.* articulé; distinct. *v.i.* stipuler,
convenir de.

articulately *adv.* d'une manière articulée, dis-
tinctment; en détail.

articulation *n.* articulation *f.*

artifact *n.;* See ARTEFACT.

artifice *n.* artifice *m.;* ruse *f.*

artificial *adj.* artificiel, faux, synthétique.

artificiality *n.* nature *f.* artificielle; manque *m.*
de naturel.

artificially *adv.* artificiellement, avec art.

artillery *n.* artillerie *f.* **~man,** artilleur *m.*

artisan *n.* artisan *m.*

artist *n.* artiste *m.f.*

artistic *adj.* artistique.

artistically *adv.* artistiquement, artistement.

artless *adj.* dépourvu d'art, sans art, ingénu,
simple, naïf.

artlessly *adv.* sans art; simplement, naïvement,
ingénument.

artlessness *n.* simplicité *f.,* ingénuité *f.,* naïveté
f., candeur *f.*

arty *adj.* genre artiste, qui a des prétentions
artistiques.

art(s)y-craft(s)y *adj.* qui affiche un genre ou
bohème, artisanal (object).

as *conj.* comme; de même que, ainsi que; vu que,
puisque, suivant que; en tant que; à mesure
que; par exemple; en. **cold ~ ice,** froid commé
la glace. **we went to the party dressed ~
peasants,** nous sommes allés à la fête habillés
en paysans. **~ it were,** pour ainsi dire. **~ if he
did not see me,** comme s'il ne me voyait pas.
I find it easier ~ I advance, je le trouve plus
facile à mesure que j'avance. **~ good ~,** aussi
bon que. **~ to, ~ for,** quant à. **~ for me,** quant
à moi.

asbestos *n.* asbeste *m.* amiante *m.*

ascend *v.i.* monter s'élever, remonter. *v.t.* monter
à, sur; gravir (a mountain).

ascendancy *n.* ascendant *m.*

ascendant *n.* ascendant *m.* supériorité *f.* **~** *adj.*
supérieur, prédominant.

ascension *n.* ascension *f.;* Ascension *f.*

ascent *n.* ascension *f.;* montée *f.* **a steep ~,** montée escarpée.

ascertain *v.t.* établir, prédiser, déterminer;
constater, vérifier; s'assurer de, s'assurer que. **I
have ~ed,** je me suis assuré. **to ~ the origin
of a report,** s'assurer de découvrir l'origine
d'un bruit.

ascertainable *adj.* qu'on peut constater, déterminer.

ascertainment *n.* constatation *f.*, certitude *f.* établie.

ascetic *adj.* ascétique. *n.* ascète *m.f.*

ascribable *adj.* attribuable, imputable.

ascribe *v.t.* attribuer, imputer.

ascription *n.* attribution *f.*, imputation *f.*

asexual *adj.* asexué.

ash *n.* frêne *m.*; bois de frêne. *adj.* de frêne, en frêne. *n.* cendre *f.* ~ **color**, couleur de cendres. **~tray**, cendrier *m.* ~ **Wednesday**, le jour ou mercredi des Cendres.

ashamed *adj.* honteux, qui a honte. **to be ~**, avoir honte.

ashen *adj.* cendreux; cendré; (of ashwood) de frêne, en frêne.

ashore *adv.* à terre; **to go ~**, aller à terre, debarquer, venir à terre.

ashy *adj.* cendreux, cendeé.

Asian *adj.* asiatique, d'Asie.

aside *adv.* de côté, de travers; à l'écart; *Théât.* à part. *n. Théât.* aparté *m.*

asinine *adj.* d'âne, qui tient de l'âne, sot *m.*, sotte *f.*, stupide *m.f.*

ask *v.i.* demander. **to ~ for a person, a thing**, demander une personne, une chose. **to ~ about, after**, demander des nouvelles de, s'informer de, se renseigner sur. **to ~ a question**, poser une question. *v.t.* interroger, s'enquérir. **I asked him to dine with me**, je l'ai invité à diner avec moi.

askance *adv.* d'un regard désapprobateur, de travers, de côté, obliquement.

askew *adv.* de travers, obliquement, de côté.

asking *n.* demande *f.*; action *f.* de demander.

aslant *adv.* obliquement, de biais. *prep.* incliné sur.

asleep *adv.* endormi(e).

aslope *adv.* obliquement, en pente, en talus.

asp *n.* aspic *m.*

asparagus *n.* asperge *f.*

aspect *n.* aspect *m.*; mine *f.*, air *m.*, regard *m.*, vue *f.*, apparence *f.*

aspen *n.* tremble *m.* **to shake like an ~**, trembler comme une feuille.

asperity *n.* aspérité *f.*; sévérité *f.*

asperse *v.t.* diffamer, dénigrer.

aspersion *n.* aspersion *f.*; diffamation *f.*; déngrement *m.*, calomnie *f.*

aspersive *adj.* diffamatoire, scandaleux, calomniateur.

asphalt *n.* asphalte *m.*

asphyxiate *v.t.* asphyxier.

asphyxiation *n.* asphyxie *f.*

aspic *n.* aspic *m.*

aspirant *n.* aspirant *m.f.*; candidat *m.*

aspirate *v.t.* aspirer. *v.i.* s'aspirer. *n.* lettre *f.* aspirée. *adj.* aspiré.

aspiration *n.* aspiration *f.*

aspire *v.i.* (after, to, à) aspirer à; désirer avec ardeur; s'élever.

aspirin *n.* aspirine *f.*, comprimé *m.* d'aspirine.

aspiring *adj.* ambitieux.

asquint *adv.* du coin de l'oeil, obliquement, de travers, en louchant.

ass *n.* âne *m.*, ânesse *f.*; *Fig.* imbécile. **jack~**, *Infml.* crétin *m.*; *Vulg.* cul *m.*

assail *v.t.* assaillir; accabler.

assailant *n.* assaillant *m.*

assassin *n.* assassin *m.*

assassinate *v.t.* assassiner.

assassination *n.* assassinat *m.*

assault *n.* assaut *m.*; atteinte *f.*; agresion *f.*; menace *f.*; voie *f.pl.* de fait. ~ **and battery**, coups et blessures. **to** ~, donner l'assaut; attaquer, assaillir; menacer de voies de fait.

assay *n.* essai *m.*; vérification *f.*, épreuve *f.* ~ **furnace**, fourneau *m.* d'essayeur. *v.t.* essayer (metals). *v.i.* etenter, s'efforcer.

assemblage *n.* assemblage *m.*

assemble *v.t.* assembler; convoquer, appeler. *v.i.* s'assembler, se réunir.

assembly *n.* assemblée *f.*; réunion *f.* ~ **room**, salle *f.* des fêtes. ~ **line**, chaîne de montage.

assent *n.* assentiment *m.* consentement *m.*, sanction *f.* ~ *v.i.* donner son assentiment à.

assert *v.t.* affirmer, déclarer, proclamer; soutenir, défendre par des actes our des paroles, revendiquer.

assertion *n.* assertion *f.*; défense *f.* (of a cause), revendication *f.* (of a right).

assertive *adj.* assertif; péremptoire.

assess *v.t.* imposer; taxer, fixer, la valeur de, évaluer.

assessable *adj.* imposable; qui peut être évalué.

assessment *n.* répartition *f.* (of tax), cote *f.*, évaluation *f.*

assessor *n.* répartiteur *m.*, assesseur *m.*

assets *n.* biens *m.pl.*, capital *m.*, avoirs *m.pl.*; avantage *m.*, atout *m.*; actif *m.*

asseverate *v.t.* affirmer, déclarer solennellement.

asseveration *n.* affirmation *f.* positive.

assiduity *n.* assiduité *f.*

assiduous *adj.* assidu.

assiduously *adv.* assidûment, avec assiduité, d'une manière assidue.

assign *v.t.* assigner; désigner, fixer, déterminer; transférer, céder (a value, etc.) *n. Dr.* ayant-droit *m.*, ayant-cause *m.*

assignable *adj.* assignable; transférable, cessible.

assignation *n.* assignation *f.*; rendez-vous galant *m.*; transfert *m.*

assignee *n.* délégué *m.*, mandataire *m.*, fondé *m.* de pouvoirs, representant *m.*; syndic *m.*

assignment *n.* affectation *f.*; transport *m.*, cession *f.*; ajournement *m.* ~ **of a person to a post**, affectation d'une personne à un poste. **a school ~**, une tâche assignée.

assimilable *adj.* assimilable.

assimilate *v.t.* assimiler. *v.i.* s'assimiler.

assimilation *n.* assimilation *f.*

assist *v.t.* assister, prêter assistance, seconder, secourir, soutenir. *v.i.* aider.

assistance *n.* assistance *f.*, secours *m.*, aide *f.*; mainforte *f.*

assistant *n.* aide *m.f.* assistant *m.*, assistante *f.* *adj.* auxiliaire; qui vient en aide. ~ **judge**, juge-assesseur. ~**surgeon**, aide-chirurgien. ~ **manager**, sous-directeur *m.*, directeur adjoint.

assize *n.* asseses *f.pl.* cour *f.* d'assises.

associable *adj.* associable; uni.

associate *v.t.* associer; combiner, joindre, unir. *v.i.* s'associer, prendre part. *adj.* associé. *n.* associé, *m.*, associée *f.* adjoint *m.*, adjointe *f.*, collègue *m.f.*

association *n.* association *f.*; fréquentation *f.*; société *f.*, club *f.*

assonance *n.* assonance *f.*

assonant *adj.* assonant.

assort *v.t.* assortir. *v.i.* s'assortir; convenir. **to ~ with**, fréquenter, s'associer avec.

assorted *adj.* assorti; varié, divers.

assortment *n.* assortiment *m.*

assuage *v.t.* adoucir, apaiser, calmer, modérer, assouvir. *v.i.* s'apaiser, se calmer.

assuagement *n.* adoucissement *m.* apaisement *m.*

assume *v.t.* assumer, prendre sur soi, se charger de, revêtir, prendre l'apparence, le caractère de, s'approprier, s'arroger (a title, etc.); supposer. **he ~d a lofty air**, il prit un grand air. **it is ~d that**, un prétend que. *v.i.* être arrogant, trop présumer de soi-même.

assuming *adj.* arrogant. *n.* présomption *f.*

assumption *n.* l'action *f.* de prendre, de revêtir; assomption *f.*, supposition *f.*; Assomption *f.*

assurance *n.* assurance *f.*, certitude *f.*, conviction *f.*; confiance *f.* (en soi); audace *f.*

assure *v.t.* assurer; certifier, affirmer, garantir.

assured *adj.* certain, indubitable; assuré *m.* **be ~ that you are mistaken**, soyez sûr que vous vous trompez.

assuredly *adv.* assurément, certainement, indubitablement.

asterisk *n.* astérisque *m.*

astern *adv.* à l'arrière, en arrière, de l'arrière. **to go ~**, aller à l'arrière.

asteroid *n.* astéroïde *m.; adj.* en étoile.

asthma *n.* asthme *m.*

asthmatic *n.* asthmatique *m.f.*

astir *adj.* en mouvement; agité.

astonish *v.t.* étonner. **to be ~ed**, s'étonner de.

astonishing *adj.* étonant, surprenant.

astonishingly *adv.* étonnamment, d'une façon surprenante.

astonishment *n.* étonnement *m.*, admiration *f.*, surprise *f.*

astound *v.t.* étonner, frapper de surprise, consterner.

astounding *adj.* étonnant, étourdissant, foudroyant.

astral *adj.* astral.

astray *adv.* hors du droit chemin, égaré. **to go ~**, s'écarter, s'égarer.

astride *adv.* les jambes écartées; à cheval, à califourchon.

astringent *n.* astringent *m.*

astrologer *n.* astrologue *m.*

astrologic(al) *adj.* astrologique.

astrology *n.* astrologie *f.*

astronaut *n.* astronaute *m.f.*

astronomer *n.* astronome *m.f.*

astronomic(al) *adj.* astronomique.

astronomically *adv.* astronomiquement.

astronomy *n.* astronomie *f.*

astute *adj.* astucieux; fin.

astutely *adv.* astucieusement.

astuteness *n.* astuce *f.*

asunder *adv.* à part, séparément, en deux.

asylum *n.* asile *m.* **political ~**, asile politique.

asymmetric(al) *adj.* asymétrique.

asymmetry *n.* asymétrie *f.*

at *prép.* à, chez, en, dans; sur; contre; de; en train de; devant. ~ **church**, à l'église. ~ **home**, chez soi. ~ **the same time**, en même temps. ~ **peace**, en paix, ~ **rest**, en repos. ~ **your service**, à votre service. **take a good look ~ her**, regarde-la bien. **he is mad ~ me**, il est fâché contre moi. ~ **all**, du tout, en aucune manière. ~ **first**, d'abord. ~ **last**, enfin. ~ **once**, ensemble, de suite.

ate *pret* of EAT.

atheism *n.* athéisme *m.*

atheist *n.* athée *m.f.*

athirst *adj.* altéré.

athlete *n.* athlète *m.f.*

athletic *adj.* athlétique, d'athlète.

Atlantic *adj.* atlantique. **the ~ (ocean)**, l'Atlantique *m.*, l'océan Atlantique.

atlas *n.* Atlas *m.*

atmosphere *n.* atmosphère *f.*

atmospheric *adj.* atmosphérique.

atmospherics *n.* parasites *m.pl.* (radio).

atoll *m.* îlot de corail, atoll *m.*

atom *n.* atome *m.*

atomic *adj.* atomique. ~ **reactor**, réacteur *m.* nucléaire.

atomize *v.t.* réduire en atomes, pulvériser.

atomizer *n.* atomiseur *m.*, vaporisateur *m.*

atone *v.i.* faire réparation. *v.t.* faire accorder, réconcilier; expier, racheter.

atonement *n.* accord *m.*, reconciliation *f.*; expiation *f.*

atop *prep.* au sommet, au haut.

atrocious *adj.* atroce.

atrociously *adv.* atrocement.

atrocity *n.* atrocité *f.*

atrophy *n.* atrophie *f.*

attach *v.t.* attacher; joindre, unir, lier; mettre opposition à, saisir. **to be ~ed to**, s'attacher à, tenir à. **to ~ importance to**, attacher de l'importance à.

attaché *n.* attaché(e) *m.f.* ~**-case**, mallette *f.*

attachment *n.* attachement *m.* affection *f.* inclination *f.*, saisie *f.*

attack *v.t.* attaquer. *n.* attaque *f.; Méd.* accès, crise, attaque.

attacker *n.* aggresseur *m.* assaillant *m.*

attain *v.t.* atteindre, arriver à, parvenir à; gagner, acquérir. to ~ **one's goal,** atteindre son but, en arriver à ses fins.

attainable *adj.* qui peut être atteint, qui peut être acquis.

attainment *n.* réalisation *f.*, talent *m.*, acquisition *f.*, possession *f.*

attempt *v.t.* tente, s'efforcer, essayer, entreprendre; attaquer, tenter. to ~ **the impossible,** tenter l'impossible. *n.* tentative *f.*, effort *m.*, essai *m.*, entreprise *f.* **a first ~,** un coup d'essai.

attend *v.t.* accompagner, suivre, servir, assister; soigner (a sick person); se rendre auprès. to ~ to *v.i.* faire attention à, écouter, s'occuper de. to ~ **the sick,** soigner les malades. **he ~ed the meeting,** il était présent à la réunion. to ~ **public lectures,** suivre des cours publics. to ~ **to one's business,** s'occuper de ses affaires.

attendance *n.* **your ~ is necessary,** votre présence est nécessaire. **school ~,** fréquentation *f.* scolaire.

attendant *adj.* qui suit, qui recompagne. *n.* compagnon *m.*, surveillant *m.*, surveillante *f.*

attention. *n.* attention *f.* **to pay ~ to,** faire attention à.

attentive *adj.* attentif; plein d'égards; prévenant.

attentively *adv.* attentivement, avec soin.

attentiveness *n.* attention *f.*, soin *m.*, circonspection *f.*

attenuate *v.t.* atténuer; diminuer (the seriousness of a thing). *adj.* atténué. **attenuating circumstance,** circonstance *f.* atténuantes.

attenuation *n.* atténuation *f.*

attest *v.t.* attester; témoigner.

attestation *n.* attestation *f.*; témoignage *m.*

attic *n.* grenier *m.; mansarde *f.*

attire *n.* vêtements *m.pl.*

attitude *n.* attitude *f.*; pose *f.*

attorney *n.* procureur *m.*, avoué *m.*, fondé de pouvoires. **power of ~,** procuration *f.* **~-at-law,** avocat *m.*

attorney-general *n.* procureur général, avocat général.

attract *v.t.* attirer.

attraction *n.* attraction *f.*; attrait *m.*, charme *m.*

attractive *adj.* attractif; attrayant; attirant.

attractively *adj.* d'une manière attrayante.

attractiveness *n.* vertu *f.* attractive, propriété *f.* d'attirer.

attributable *adj.* attribuable.

attribute *v.t.* attribuer; imputer.

attribution *n.* attribution *f.*

attributive *adj.* attributif; *n.* attribut *m.*

attrition *n.* attrition *f.*; usure *f.* par frottement.

attune *v.t.* accorder, mettre d'accord; rendre harmonieux.

atypical *adj.* atypique.

auburn *adj.* châtain.

auction *n.* enchère *f.* **sale by ~,** vente aux enchères. **to put up for ~,** mettre aux enchères.

auctioneer *n.* commissaire-priseur *m.* ~ *v.t.* vendre à l'enchère, aux enchères.

audacious *adj.* audacieux, effronté, impudent.

audaciously *adv.* audacieusement.

audacity *n.* audace *f.*

audibility *n.* audibilité *f.*

audible *adj.* audible; perceptible.

audibly *adv.* de manière à être entendu.

audience *n.* spectateurs *m.pl.*, public *m.*, audience *f.*; auditoire *m.*

audio *pref.* audio.

audit *n.* audition *f.* de comptes, vérification *f.* de comptes. *v.t.* apurer (un compte).

audition *n.* audition *f.*; ~ *v.t.* auditionner.

auditor *n.* auditeur *m.*

auditorium *n.* salle *f.* (de théâtre).

auditory *n.* auditoire *m.; adj.* auditif.

augment *v.t.* augmenter, accroître, agrandir; *v.i.* s'augmenter. *n.* augmentation *f.*, accroissement *m.*, agrandissement *m.*

augmentation *n.* augmentation *f.*

augur *n.* augure *f.* ~ *v.i.* augurer.

august *adj.* auguste. *n.* **August,** août; vénérable, majestueux.

aunt *n.* tante *f.*

auntie *n. Infml.* tantine, tata, tatie.

au pair *adj.* au pair; *n.* (jeune fille) au pair.

auricle *n.* auricule *f.* (of the heart), pavillon de l'oreille.

aurora *n.pr.* Aurore *f.; aurore *f.*

auspice *n.* auspice *m.* auspices *m.pl.*, support *m.*

auspicious *adj.* propice, de bon augure.

auspiciously *adv.* sous de favorables auspices, favorablement.

austere *adj.* austère, rigide.

austerely *adv.* austèrement, sévèrement, rigidement.

austerity *n.* austérité *f.*

Australia *n.* Australie *f.*

Australian *adj.* australien. *n.* Australien *m.*

Austria *n.pr.* Autriche *f.*

Austrian *adj.* autrichien; Autrichien *m.*

authentic *adj.* authentique.

authenticate *v.t.* authentiquer; légaliser.

authentication *n.* action *f.* d'authentiquer.

authenticity *n.* authenticité *f.*

author *n.* auteur *m.; femme *f.* auteur.

authoritarian *adj.* autoritaire.

authoritative *adj.* autoritaire, imposant, péremptoire.

authoritatively *adv.* avec autorité, en maître.

authority *n.* autorité *f.* **I have it on good ~,** je le tiens de bonne source.

authorization *n.* autorisation *f.*

authorize *v.t.* autoriser, permettre.

autism *n.* autisme *m.*

autistic *adj.* autistique.

auto *pref.* auto.

autobiographer *n.* autobiographe *m.f.*

autobiographic, autobiographical *adj.* autobiographique.

autobiography *n.* autobiographie *f.*

autocracy *n.* autocratie *f.*

autocrat *n.* autocrate *m.*

autocratic(al) *adj.* autocratique.

autograph *n.* autographe *m.* ~ *v.t.* dédicacer, signer.

automate *v.t.* automatiser.

automated *adj.* automatisé.

automatic *adj.* automatique.

automatically *adj.* automatiquement.

automobile *n.* automobile *f.*

autonomy *n.* autonomie *f.*

autopsy *n.* autopsie *f.*

autumnal *adj.* automnal.

auxiliary *adj.* auxiliaire. *n.* auxiliaire *m.*

avail *v.t.* servir, profiter à. **to ~ oneself of**, profiter de. **I'll ~ myself of the earliest opportunity**, je profiterai de la première occasion. *v.i.* être utile, servir. **courage could not ~ against such fearful odds**, le courage no pouvait prévaloir contre une telle inégalité de forces. *n.* avantage *m.*, profit *m.*, utilité *f.*

availability *n.* disponibilité *f.*, validité *f.*

available *adj.* disponible, libre (person).

avalanche *n.* avalanche *f.*

avant-garde *adj.* avant-garde.

avarice *n.* avarice *f.*

avaricious *adj.* avare, avaricieux.

avariciously *adv.* avec avarice, avaricieusement.

avenge *v.t.* venger, faire justice à.

avenger *n.* vengeur *m.*, vengeresse *f.*

avenging *adj.* vengeur.

avenue *n.* avenue *f.*

aver *v.i.* affirmer; déclarer d'une manière positive.

average *n.* moyenne *f.* **on ~**, en moyenne. **general ~**, avaries grosses, communes. **to state the ~s**, régler les avaries. *adj.* moyen. **~ price, rate**, prix moyen, taux moyen. **the ~ loss is …**, la perte moyenne est de … *v.t.* réduire à une moyenne. *v.i.* donner une moyenne de. **they ~ ten francs apiece**, ils coûtent dix francs la pièce.

averse *adj.* qui a de l'aversion pour; opposé (à), contraire (à), ennemi (de).

aversion *n.* aversion *f.*, répugnance.

avert *v.t.* détourner, éloigner, conjurer, écarter.

aviary *n.* volière *f.*

aviation *n.* aviation *f.*

aviator *n.* aviateur *m.*, -trice *f.*

avid *adj.* avide, âpre, passionné, vorace.

avidity *n.* avidité *f.*

avidly *adv.* avec avidité; avidement.

avocado *n.* avocat *m.* **~ tree**, avocatier *m.*

avocation *n.* distraction *f.* violin d'Ingres.

avoid *v.t.* éviter, se tenir à distance de, chercher à éviter.

avoidable *adj.* évitable.

avoidance *n.* fuite *f.* écoulement.

avow *v.t.* avouer, déclarer ouvertement, confesser franchement.

avowable *adj.* avouable.

avowal *n.* aveu *m.*

avowed *adj.* avoué, déclare. **an ~ enemy**, ennemi avoué.

await *v.t.* attendre.

awake *v.t.* éveiller, réveiller; *Fig.* réveiller. *v.i.* s'éveiller, *adj.* éveillé, vigilant.

awaken *v.t., v.i.* éveiller, réveiller, s'éveiller, se réveiller.

award *v.t.* décerner (a prize); adjuger. *v.i.* rendre un arrêt, prononcer un jugement, décider. *n.* prix *m.*; récompense *f.*; jugement *m.*, arrêt *m.*

aware *adj.* conscient, instruit. **he is ~ of the problem**, il et au courant du problème, il est conscient du problème.

awash *adj.* à fleur d'eau; flottant; inondé.

away *adv.* à distance, loin, au loin, absent. **to go ~**, s'en aller. **to send ~**, envoyer loin; renvoyer. **to run ~**, s'échapper. **to drive ~**, chasser. *interj.* hors d'ici! arrière! partez!

awe *n.* crainte *f.*, terreur *f.*, effroi *m.*; respect *m.* **to strike with ~**, inspirer d'un respect mêlé de crainte. **to be ~struck**, être frappé d'admiration. *v.t.* imposer, tenir en respect.

awesome *adj.* terrifiant, impressionnant. *Infml.* super, géant. **it was ~!** c'était géant!

awful *adj.* *Infml.* affreux, atroce, terrible, redoutable.

awfully *adv.* terriblement, affreusement, très, vraiment. **I'm ~ sorry**, je suis terriblement désolé(e).

awhile *adv.* pendant; un instant, pour un temps.

awkward *adj.* gauche; maladroit, gênant. **an ~ question**, une question délicate. **an ~ situation**, une situation gênante.

awkwardly *adv.* gauchement, maladroitement; d'une manière gênante.

awkwardness *n.* gaucherie *f.*, maladresse *f.*

awl *n.* alêne *f.*

awning *n.* tente *f.*, pavillon *m.* banne *f.* (of a store).

awry *adj.* de travers.

ax *n.* hache *f.*

axial *adj.* de l'axe, apparténant à un axe.

axiom *n.* axiome *m.*

axiomatic *adj.* axiomatique.

axis *pl.* **axes** *n.* axe *m.*

axle *n.* essieu *m.*; axe *m.*

aye *adv.* oui (vote).

azalea *n.* azalée *f.*

azure *adj.* d'azur, azuré. *n.* azur *m.*

B

B *Mus.* si *m.*

B.A. or **A.B., bachelor of arts,** license ès-arts.

B.C. (before Christ) avant Jésus-Christ.

baa n. bê *m.,* bêlement *m.* ~ *v.i.* bêler, faire bê.

babble *v.i.* bredouiller, babiller; jaser; bavarder; murmurer. *v.t.* balbutier. **he babbles nonsense,** il dit des bêtises, il raconte n'importe quoi. ~ babil *m.,* caquetage *m.,* bavardage *m.*

babbler n. bavard *m.,* bavarde *f.*

babe n. enfant *m.* au berceau, bébé *m.; Infml.* nana *f.,* pépée *f.*

Babel *n.pr.* tour *f.* de Babel.

baboon n. babouin *m.*

baby n. bébé *m.* **the ~ of the family,** benjamin *m.* **~-boom,** baby-boom *m.* **~-buggy,** landau *m.* d'enfant. *v.t.* traiter en enfant; dorloter. ~ **boy/girl,** petit garçon, petite fille. **~-sitter,** babysitter; ~ **snatcher,** kidnappeur, ravisseur d'enfant, détournement de mineur, *Fig.* **he is a ~ snatcher,** il les prend au berceau.

babyish adj. enfantin, d'enfant.

baccalaureate n. baccalauréat *m.* (formal) license *f.*

bachelor n. célibataire *m.,* licencié *m.* **an old ~,** un vieux garçon. ~ **of arts,** licencié(e).

back n. dos *m.;* derrière *m.;* dossier *m.;* fonds *m.;* revers *m.;* reins *m.pl.* ~ **to ~,** dos à dos. **to turn one's ~,** tourner le dos, s'enfuir. **the ~ of a book,** le dos d'un livre. **the ~ of a chair,** le dos d'une chaise. **the ~ of the hand,** le revers de la main. **to have a pain in one's ~,** avoir mal aux reins. **the ~ of a house, of a mirror,** le derrière d'une maison, d'un miroir. **the ~ of a stage,** le fond d'un théâtre. *adj.* de derrière, arrière; écarté, éloigné. *adv.* arrière, en arrière; de retour. **some days ~,** il y a quelques jours. **to bring ~,** rapporter. **to call ~,** rappeler. **to come ~,** revenir. **to stand ~,** reculer. *interj.* ~ **to your seats,** retournez à vos places. *v.t.* reculer, faire reculer (a car, etc.); seconder, soutenir. **he was ~ed by all his friends,** il a été épaulé, aidé, soutenu par tous ses amis. *v.i.* reculer, aller à reculons. **to ~ out of,** sortir à reculons. **to ~ out of a promise,** retirer sa promesse. **~-ache** *m.,* mal *m.* de dos. **~-breaking,** fatigant, éreintant. **it ~fired on him,** ça s'est retourné contre lui. **~ wheel,** roue *f.* arrière. **~yard,** arrières cours *f.,* jardin *m.* **~pack** n. sac *m.* à dos *m.* **~side** n. derrière *m.* **~water** n. eau *f.* stagnante.

backbite *v.t.* parler en mal d'un absent, médire de.

backbiting n. médisance *f.,* méchants propos *m.pl.*

backbone n. épine *f.* dorsale. **to the ~,** jusqu'à la moelle des os.

backgammon n. trictac *m.*

background n. arrière plan; enfoncement *m.,* fond *m.* (of a painting).

backhanded adj. la main tournée en arrière. **a ~ blow,** un coup de revers. *adv.* avec le revers de la main.

backing n. soutien *m.,* appui *m.,* aide *f.;* recul *m.*

backstairs n. escalier *m.* de service, escalier *m.* dérobé.

backward adv. en arrière; à reculons; à rebours. **to walk ~ and forward,** aller et venir. *adj.* arriéré; en arrière; en retard, tardif; peu disposé à agir. ~ **movement,** mouvement rétrograde.

bacon n. lard *m.* **to save one's ~,** *Fig.* se tirer d'affaire.

bacteria *n.pl.* See BACTERIUM.

bacteriological adj. bactériologique.

bacterium n. bactérie *f.*

bad adj. mauvais, méchant. ~ **weather,** mauvais temps. **from ~ to worse,** de mal en pis. **to keep ~ hours,** rentrer tard, mener une vie désordonnée. **that's too ~,** c'est dommage, tant pis.

badge n. insigne *m.,* marque *f.,* plaque *f.,* médaille *f.*

badger n. blaireau *m.* ~ *v.t.* tourmenter, harceler.

badly adv. mal. ~ **made,** mal fait.

badness n. mauvaise qualité *f.;* mauvais état *m.* d'une chose; méchanceté *f.*

baffle *v.t.* tromper, déjouer, déconcerter; confondre; frustrer. **to ~ all description,** défier toute description.

bag n. sac *m.,* poche *f.* **traveling ~,** sac de voyage. **to pack up ~ and baggage,** plier bagages. *v.t.* ensacher; mettre dans un sac; tuer (game).

bagatelle n. bagatelle *f.*

baggage n. bagage *m.*

baggy adj. gonflé, bouffant.

bagpipe n. cornemuse *f.*

bail n. caution *f.,* cautionnement *m.* **to give ~,** fournir caution. **to be out on ~,** être en liberté provisoire (sous caution). *v.t.* élargir, sous caution; cautionner. **to ~ out, to ~ water,** faire mettre en liberté provisoire (sous caution).

bailiff n. huissier *m.*

bait n. amorce *f.,* appât *m.* **to take the ~,** mordre à l'hameçon, tomber dans le piège. *v.t.* amorcer, allécher.

bake *v.t.* cuire, faire cuire au four. **to ~ bread,** faire cuire du pain. **the ground ~s in a hot sun,** le sole se calcine sous les rayons d'un soleil brûlant.

baker n. boulanger *m.,* boulangère *f.*

bakery n. boulangerie *f.*

baking n. cuisson *f.;* fournée *f.*

balance n. balance *f.;* solde *m.* d'un compte. *Astron.* balance *f.;* équilibre *m.;* contre-poids *m.* **to turn the ~,** faire pencher la balance. **to strike a ~,** faire établir la balance. **the ~ of power,** l'équilibre politique. ~ **sheet,** bilan *m. v.t.* balancer; peser, contre-balancer. *v.i.* se balancer; se contre-balancer, hésiter.

balcony *n.* balcon *m.*

bald *adj.* chauve.

balderdash *n.* balivernes *f.pl.*, vain bavardage *m.*, ~ *v.t.* falsifier, frelater.

baldly *adv.* d'un style dépouillé.

baldness *n.* calvitie *f.*; *Fig.* maigreur *f.* (of style).

bale *n.* balle *f.*; ballot *m.* ~ *v.i.* emballer, mettre en ballot.

baleful *adj.* calamiteux; affligeant; sinistre, funeste.

balk *n.* poutre *f.*, traverse *f.* ~ *v.t.* contrarier; reculer; hésiter.

ball *n.* boule *f.*; globe *m.*; balle *f.*; pelote *f.*; peloton *m.*; boulet *m.* (of cannon); prunelle *f.*; bille *f.* (of billards); bal *m.*; boulette *f.* (of meat).
snow~, boule de neige. ~ **of cotton**, pelote de coton. **masked ~**, bal masqué. *v.i.* se peloter; se botter. *Infml.* **to have a ~**, se fendre la gueule, poire.

ballad *n.* ballade *f.*

ballast *n.* lest *m.* ballast *m.* ~ *v.t.* lester.

ballerina *n.* ballerine *f.*

ballet *n.* ballet *m.*

ballistic *adj.* balistique.

ballistics *n.* balistique *f.*

balloon *n.* ballon *m.*, montgolfière *f.*

ballot *n.* bulletin *m.* de vote, scrutin *m.*, ballottage *m.* ~ **box**, urne *f.* du scrutin; urne *f.*, électorale. *v.i.* voter au scrutin.

ballpoint *n.* ~ **pen**, stylo *m.* (à) bille.

ballroom *n.* salle *f.* de bal.

balm *n.* baume *m.*; mélisse *f.*

balmy *adj.* balsamique, odoriférant; calmant, adoucissant; embaumé, parfumé.

baloney *n.* *Fig.* foutaise *f.*, n'importe quoi.

balsamic *adj.* balsamique. *n.* remède *m.* balsamique.

baluster *n.* balustre *m.pl.* rampe *f.* d'escalier.

balustrade *n.* balustrade *f.*

bamboo *n.* bambou *m.*

bamboozle *v.t.* tromper, duper, mettre dedans.

ban *n.* ban *m.*; interdiction *f.*; ~ *v.t.* interdire; rejeter.

banal *adj.* banal.

banality *n.* banalité *f.*

banana *n.* banane *f.* ~**tree**, bananier *m.*

band *n.* bande *f.*; bandeau *m.*; cordon *m.*; rabat *m.*; ruban *m.*; orchestre *m.* **military ~**, musique *f.* militaire. *v.t.* unir en troupe, liguer. *v.i.* se liguer.

bandage *n.* bandeau *m.*; bandage *m.* ~ *v.t.* bander.

bandana *n.* bandana *f.*

bandit *n.* bandit *m.*, brigand *m.*

bandoleer *n.* bandolier *m.* bandoulière *f.*

bandy *n.* crosse *f.* ~ *v.t.* se renvoyer (words, jokes, etc.); *adj.* tordu.

bane *n.* poison *m.*; *Fig.* peste *f.*, ruine *f.*, destruction *f.* ~ *v.t.* empoisonner.

baneful *adj.* empoisonné, mortel, pernicieux, funeste, destructif.

bang *n.* coup *m.* ~ *v.t.* s'éclater, se claquer, se cogner, se frapper. **to** ~ **the door to,** ferme la porte à tout briser, *interj.* pan!; **bangs** *n.* frange *f.* (of hair).

banish *v.t.* bannir, déporer, exiler; éloigner, chasser.

banishment *n.* bannissement *m.*

baloney *n.* *Infml.* foutaise *f.*, baratin *m.*

banister *n.* rampe *f.* (d'escalier).

banjo *n.* banjo *m.*

bank *n.* banque *f.*, digue *f.*, terrasse *f.*; rive *f.*, bord *m.* banc *m.*; remblai *m.*, talus *m.* ~ *v.t.* endiguer. **the** ~ **of France**, la Banque de France. **savings** ~, caisse *f.* d'épargne. *v.t.* déposer des fonds dans une banque. **we** ~ **with S. and Co.**, S. et Cie sont nos banquiers. ~**book**, carnet *m.* de banque. ~ **note**, billet *m.* de banque. ~ **account**, compte *m.* en banque. ~ **statement**, relevé *m.* de compte.

bankable *adj.* recevable en banque, escomptable.

banker *n.* banquier *m.*

banking *n.* activité *f.* bancaire, occupations *f.pl.* de banquier.

bankrupt *n.* failli *m.* ~ *v.i.* faire faillite. *adj.* en faillite, insolvable; ruiné.

bankruptcy *n.* faillite *f.*

banner *n.* bannière *f.*

banns *n.* bans *m.pl.* (marriage).

banquet *n.* banquet *m.*, festin *m.*, fête *f.* ~ *v.t.* traiter, régaler, faire servir un grand repas. *v.i.* banqueter, festoyer, faire festin.

banter *v.t.* railler, plaisanter; *n.* raillerie *f.*, plaisanterie *f.*

baptism *n.* baptême *m.*

baptismal *adj.* baptismal.

Baptist *n.pr.* Baptiste *m.f.*

baptize *v.t.* baptiser.

bar *n.* bar *m.*; barre *f.*; barrière *f.*; barreau *m.*; banc *m.* (in a court), tribunal *m.*; *Mus.* mesure *f.*; comptoir *m.*, buvette *f.*; empêchement *m.*; lingot *m.* (de métal précieux); levier du gouvernail. **an iron ~**, un barre de fer. **to appear at the ~**, comparaître à la barre. *v.t.* barrer; intercepter; défendre, priver. **to ~ a way, a passage,** barrer un chemin, un passage.

Barbados *n.* Barbade *f.*

barbarian *adj.* barbare; grossier, non civilisé; cruel, inhumain. *n.* barbare *m.f.*

barbaric *adj.* barbare, des barbares.

barbarism *n.* barbarisme *m.*; barbarie *f.*

barbarity *n.* barbarie *f.*; cruauté *f.*, férocité *f.*; barbarisme *m.*

barbecue *n.* barbecue *m.* *v.t.* rôtir dehors.

barbed *adj.* bardé; complètement armé. ~ **wire**, fil *m.* de fer barbelé.

barber *n.* coiffeur *m.* pour hommes.

barbiturate *n.* barbiturique *m.*

bare *adj.* nu, dépouillé, découvert; simple. **to lay**

~, mettre à nu, à découvert. ~**back**, à poil. *v.t.*
mettre à nu; dénuder, dépouiller. **he killed him
with his ~ hands**, il l'a tué de ses propres
mains. ~**-headed**, nu-tête. ~**-footed**, nu-pieds,
les pieds nus.

barely *adv.* à peine; tout juste.

bareness *n.* nudité *f.*, dénûment *m.*

bargain *n.* marché *m.* affaire *f.* **a good ~**, une
bonne affaire. **to strike a ~**, conclure un marché. *v.i.* faire marché, marchander.

barge *n.* barque *f.*; allége *f.*, chaland *m.*; chaloupe
f. **to ~ in**, faire irruption, *Infml.* se rabouler.

bark *n.* aboiement *m.*; glapissement *m.* du
renard; hurlement *m.* du loup. *v.i.* aboyer.
écorce *f.* (of a tree). *v.t.* peler, décortiquer, enlever l'écorce.

barley *n.* orge *f.* **pearl ~**, orge *m.* perlé. ~**-meal**,
farine *f.* d'orge. **~ sugar**, sucre *m.* d'orge.

barmaid *n.* serveuse *f.*

barn *n.* grange *f.*, étable *f.*

barometer *n.* baromètre *m.*

barometric *adj.* barométrique.

baron *n.* baron.

barrack *n.* baraque *f.pl.*, caserne *f.*

barrage *n.* barrage *m.*

barrel *n.* tonneau *m.*

barren *adj.* stérile, aride; *Bot.* mâle. *n.* terrain *m.*,
terre *f.* stérile.

barrenly *adv.* stérilement, improductivement.

barrenness *n.* stérilité *f.*; aridité *f.*

barricade *n.* barricade *f.*; bastingage *m.* **~** *v.t.*
barricader; bastinguer.

barrier *n.* barrière *f.*; obstacle *m.*, empêchement *m.*

barring *prep.* sauf, à moins que, excepté.

bartender *n.* barman *m.*, serveur *m.*

barter *v.i.* faire un échange, un troc; trafiqguer.
v.t. échanger, troquer, trafiquer. *n.* échange *m.*,
troc *m.*

basal *adj.* basal, de la base, fondamental.

base *adj.* bas, abject. **a ~ fellow**, un homme
ignoble, abject. **a ~ action**, une action basse.
~**-minded**, ayant l'âme base; abject. *n.* base *f.*;
fondement *m.*; soubassement *m.*; *Mus.* basse *f.*;
barres *f.pl.* **~** *v.t.* baser. *Fig.* établir.

baseball *n.* base-ball *m.*

baseless *adj.* sans consistance; sans fondement.

basely *adv.* bassement, indignement.

basement *n.* sous-sol *m.*, cave *f.*

baseness *n.* bassesse *f.*; abjection *f.*, lâcheté *f.*

bash *v.i.* frapper, cogner; *n.* coup *m.*

bashful *adj.* timide, modeste.

bashfully *adv.* timidement.

bashfulness *n.* timidité *f.*, or modestie *f.*
extrême.

bashing *n.* dérouillée *f.*, raclée *f.*

bashless *adj.* sans honte, éhonté.

basic *adj.* *Chim.* basique; de base.

basically *adv.* en fait, quand même.

basil *n.* basilic *m.*

basilica *n.* basilique *f.*

basin *n.* bassin *m.*; cuvette *f.*; bol *m.*; jatte *f.*

basis *n.* **bases** *pl.* base *f.*; fondement *m.*

bask *v.t.* chauffer. *v.i.* se chauffer.

basket *n.* panier *m.*, corbeille *f.*

basketball *n.* basket-ball *m.*

bass *n.* basse *f.* perche *f.* **striped ~**, bar-rayé *f.*
~ viol, violoncelle. **double ~**, contrebasse *f.*
~ *adj. Mus.* bas, grave.

basset *n.* basset *m.*

bastard *n.* *Infml.* salaud *m.*, salope *f.*, salopard
m. bâtard *m.* *adv.* bâtard; faux. *v.t.* déclarer
bâtard.

bastardize *v.t.* corrompre; déclarer bâtard.

bastardly *adj.* dégénéré; corrompu; supposé.
adv. en bâtard.

bastardy *n.* bâtardise *f.*

baste *v.t.* bâtonner; arroser (a roast).

bat *n.* raquette *f.* (for ball-playing); chauve-souris *m.* **he is as blind as a ~**, il est aussi myope
qu'une taupe. **baseball ~**, batte de base-ball. *v.t.*
Infml. cligner, souriller. **she didn't ~ an eyelid**,
elle n'a pas sourcillé d'un poil.

batch *n.* fournée *f.*, tas *m.*

bath *n.* bain *m.* **cold ~**, bain froid. **foot ~**, bain
de pieds. ~**-room**, salle *f.* de bains. ~**robe**, peignoir *m.* ~**tub**, baignoire *f.*

bathe *v.t.* baigner. *v.i.* arroser, tremper. **to ~ a
child**, baigner un enfant. **to ~ one's face in
tears**, baigner son visage de larmes.

bathing *n.* bain *m.*; action *f.* de se baigner.
~ suite, maillet *m.* de bain.

baton *n.* matraque *f.*, bâton *m.*

batten *v.t.* voltiger; fermer. **~ down the
hatches**, se préparer à affronter la crise.

batter *v.t.* battre. *n.* pâte à frire. (baseball) celui
qui tient la batte.

battered *adj.* battu en brèche; battu.

batterer *n.* batteur *m.*

battering *n.* action *f.* de battre en brèche.

battery *n.* batterie *f.*; pile *f.* (car). **assault and ~**,
voies de fait. **floating ~**, batterie flottante.

battle *n.* bataille *f.* **to fight a ~**, livrer une
bataille. **the ~ of life**, la lutte de la vie. ~**field**,
champ *m.* de bataille. *v.i.* livrer bataille, combattre; bataille.

battlement *n.* créneau *m.*; muraille *f.* crénelée;
rempart *m.*

bawdy *adj.* obscène, impudique.

bawl *v.i.* *Infml.* brailler (shout), hurler.

bay *n.* baie *f.*, golfe *m.*; travée *f.*; laurier *m.pl.* lauriers (of a park); abois *m.pl.* **the ~ of Biscay**, le
golfe de Gascogne **the stag is at ~**, le cerf est
aux abois. **to be at ~**, être acculé. *adj.* bai. **a ~
horse**, **a ~ mare**, un cheval bai, une jument
baie. **~ window**, fenêtre en saillie. *v.i.* aboyer.
v.t. aboyer à, après, contre.

bayonet *n.* baïonnette *f.* **~** *v.t.* percer d'un coup
de baïonnette.

bazar or bazaar *n.* bazar *m.*

be *v.i.* être; exister; devoir; falloir; faire; se porter,
aller; avoir. **here he is**, le voici. **there she is**, la

voilà. **it is cold, fine, warm,** il fait froid, beau, chaud. **it is dark,** il fait sombre. **it was foggy,** il faisait du brouillard. **how is he?** comment se porte-t-il? **he is ill,** il se porte mal. **I am very cold,** j'ai très froid. **to ~ warm,** avoir chaud. **to ~ hungry,** avoir faim. **to ~ thirsty,** avoir soif. **she is not yet eighteen,** elle n'a pas encore dix-huit ans. **there was a quarrel,** il y avait une querelle. **there were many people,** il y avait beaucoup de monde. **we are to go to a concert,** nous devons aller à un concert.

beach *n.* plage *f.* – *v.t.* échouer (a ship).

beacon *n.* feu *m.;* phare *m.*

bead *n.* grain *m.* (of a necklace); *pl.* collier; chapelet *m.,* rosaire *m.;* perle *f.;* bulle *f.,* goutte *f.* **to thread ~s,** enfiler des perles.

beady *adj.* perçant. **~ eyes,** yeux perçants.

beak *n.* bec *m.,* corne *f.,* bigorne *f.*

beaker *n.* gobelet *m.,* coupe *f.;* vase *m.* à bec.

beam *n.* poutre *f.;* balancier *m.* (of a machine); fléau *m.* (car) feux *m.pl.* de croisement; rayon *m.* (of light). *v.t.* lancer, darder (light rays). *v.i.* rayonner; lancer des rayons.

beaming *ppr. adj.* rayonnant, dardant des rayons. *n.* rayonnement *m.*

bean *n.* haricot *m.,* fève *f.* **string ~,** haricot *m.* vert. **kidney ~,** haricot blanc, flageolet *m.* **to spill the ~s,** vendre la mèche, manger le merceau.

bear *n.* ours *m.,* ourse *f.* baissier *m.* – *v.t.* jouer à la baisse, spéculer à la baisse; faire baisser.

bear *v.t. pret.* porter, soutenir; supporter; produire. *v.i.* souffrir, endurer, y tenir; se comporter. **to ~ witness,** porter témoignage. **she cannot ~ the sea,** elle ne peut pas supporter la mer. **to ~ arms,** porter les armes. **to ~ up,** soutenir, se soutenir. **~ up as well as you can,** soutenez-vous de votre mieux. **to ~ up against,** résister à. **to ~ with,** tolérer, supporter quelque chose de déplaisant. **~ in mind that,** souvenez-vous que. **please, ~ with me,** soyez patient, s'il vous plait.

bearable *adj.* supportable, tolérable.

beard *n.* barbe *f.;* **a gray ~,** une barbe grise. **the ~ of a goat, of a cat, of an oyster** la barbe d'un bouc, d'un chat, d'une huître. *v.t.* braver.

bearded *adj.* barbu; barbelé.

bearer *n.* porteur *m.* porteuse *f.* arbre *m.* de rapport. **a draft payable to ~,** une traite, un mandat payable au porteur.

bearing *ppr.* portant, supportant, produisant. *n.* action *f.* de porter, de supporter de produire; port *m.,* conduite *f.,* maintien *m.,* air *m.;* aspect *m.; Arch.* support *m.;* situation *f.; Mécan.* coussinet *f.pl.* her modest ~, son air modeste. **the ~ is too long for the strength of the beam,** la portée est trop longue pour la force de la poutre.

bearish *adj.* comme un ours; (stock exchange) en baisse.

beast *n.* bête *f.,* brute *f.; Fig.* cochon *m.* **~ of burden,** bête de somme.

beastliness *n.* saloperie *f.,* saleté *f.;* bestialité *f.,* brutalité *f.*

beastly *adj.* bestial, brutal.

beat *v.t.* battre; frapper; vaincre; surpasser; piler, broyer. **to ~ to death,** battre, frapper (quelqu'un) à mort. **to ~ a carpet, a drum,** battre un tapis, un tambour. **to ~ the air,** battre l'air. **to ~ time,** battre la mesure. **to ~ down,** abattre (a wall); rabattre (the price); l'emporter sur. **to ~ in,** enfoncer, défoncer (a barrel). **to ~ off,** chasser. **to ~ out,** étouffer. **to ~ up,** surprendre (the enemy). *v.i.* battre; s'agiter, être agité. **his heart is ~ing fast,** son pouls est rapide. **the water ~s against the rocks,** l'eau se brise contre les rochers. **to ~ about the bush,** tourner autour du pot. **that ~s me,** je n'en ai aucune idée; je n'en sais rien. *n.* battement *m.* (heart); coup *m.;* batterie *f.* (drum); roulement *m.,* son *m.;* ronde *f.* (police).

beaten *adj.* battu; vaincu.

beatific *adj.* béatifique.

beating *n.* battement *m.f.*

beatitude *n.* béatitutde *f.*

beautician *n.* esthéticienne *f.*

beautiful *adj.* beau; belle; ravissant, admirable. *n.* le beau *m.*

beautifully *adv.* admirablement, d'une façon ravissante.

beautify *v.t.* rendre beau, embellir; décorer, orner. *v.i.* devenir beau, belle; s'embellir.

beauty *n.* beauté *f.;* charme *m.* **a young ~,** une jeune beauté. **the sleeping ~,** la belle au bois dormant. **the ~ of the thing,** le plaisant de la chose.

beauty spot *n.* mouche *f.* grain *m.* de beauté.

beaver *n.* castor *m.*

because *conj.* parce que. **~ of,** à cause de.

beck *n.* signe *m.* (of the head, hands). **to be at the ~ and call of,** être aux ordres de, dépendre de.

beckon *v.i.* faire signe. appeler (with a gesture).

becloud *v.t.* couvrir de nuages; obscurcir, assombrir.

become *v.i.* devenir. **to ~ of,** devenir. **what will ~ of me?** que deviendrai-je.

becoming *adj.* convenable, attirant.

becomingly *adv.* convenablement.

bed *n.* lit *m.,* assise *f.* couche *f.* gisement *m.;* planche *f.,* plate-bande *f.* **to take to one's ~,** s'aliter, se coucher. **~ linen,** linge *m.* delit, draps *m.pl.* de lit. **a ~ and breakfast,** chambre *f.* d'hôte.

bedazzle *v.t.* éblouir.

bedding *n.* drap *m.;* literie *f.*

bedeck *v.t.* orner, parer.

bedevil *v.t.* lutiner, faire endiabler.

bedroom *n.* chambre *f.* à coucher.

bedside *adj.* de chevet.

bedtime *n.* heure *f.* du coucher.

bee *n.* abeille *f.* **worker ~,** abeille ouvrière. **bumble ~,** bourdon *m.* **~ hive,** ruche *f.*

~keeper, apiculteur *m.* apicultrice *f.* **~'s wax**, cire *f.* d'abeilles.

beech *n.* hêtre *m.* **~ tree**, hêtre *m.*

beef *n.* bœuf *m.* **corned ~**, bœuf de conserve. **roast ~**, rôti *m.* (de bœuf); rosbif *m.* *Infml.* **what's your ~?** pourquoi tu râles?

beefy *adj. Infml.* costaud, bien en chair.

been *See* BE.

beep *n.* bip-bip *m.*, coup *m.* (car horn); *v.i.* faire bip.

beer *n.* bière *f.*

beet betterave *f.*

beetle *n.* gros maillet *m.*; hie *f.*, scarabée *m.*

beetroot *n.* betterave *f.*

befall *v.t.* arriver, survenir.

befit *v.t.* convenir à; être convenable.

before *prep.* (of time) avant; (of place) devant; avant de, avant que. *adv.* avant, auparavant. **the night ~**, la nuit d'avant, la veille.

beforehand *adv.* en avance, d'avance. **to give money ~**, donner de l'argent d'avance.

befriend *v.t.* se lier avec une personne; traiter en ami.

beg *v.t., v.i.* mendier, prier, solliciter, supplier. **I ~ your pardon**, je vous demande pardon. **to ~ for food**, mendier de la nourriture. **to ~ for mercy**, demander grâce/miséricorde.

beget *v.t.* engendrer, procréer; faire naître, enfanter.

beggar *n.* mendiant *m.*, mendiante *f.*

beggarly *adj.* gueux, abject, misérable. *adv.* d'une manière abjecte, méprisable.

beggary *n.*, mendicité *f.*

begin *v.t., v.i.* commencer; débuter, amorcer, entamer. **I'll ~ by informing you**, je commencerai par vous dire. **to ~ by doing a thing**, commencer par faire une chose.

beginner *n.* débutant *m.*, débutante *f.*

beginning *n.* commencement *m.*

begone *inter.* (*Arch., Lit.*) allez-vous en! sortez! retirez-vous! arrière!

begrudge *v.t.* envier à; se refuser.

beguile *v.t.* décevoir, tromper, abuser; charmer, faire oublier.

behalf *n.* faveur *f.*, avantage *m.*; défense *f.* **on his ~**, de sa part.

behave *v.t.* se conduire, se comporter.

behavior *n.* conduite *f.* (bonne ou mauvaise), comportement *m.* **he changed his ~**, il changea de conduite.

behead *v.t.* décapiter.

behest *n.* ordre *m.*, commandement *m.*

behind *prep.* derrière; après, en arrière. **look ~ you**, regardez derrière vous. **those ~ us**, ceux qui viendront après nous. *adv.* par derrière, en arrière. **to stay ~**, rester en arrière.

behold *v.t.* regarder avec attention; considérer.

beholden *adj.* obligé, redevable.

behoove *imper.* être propre à, être utile, avantageux. **it ~s**, il convient.

beige *n.* beige *m.*

being *ppr.* de be, étant. **such ~ the case**, la chose étant ainsi. *n.* être *m.*; existence *f.* **the supreme ~**, l'être suprême.

belated *adj.* attardé; tardif, en retard.

belch *v.i.* éructer, *n.* éructation *f.*

beleaguer *v.t.* cerner, assiéger.

belfry *n.* beffroi *m.*, clocher *m.*

Belgian *adj.* belge *n.* belge *m.*

Belgium *n.pr.* Belgique *f.*

belie *v.t.* montrer la fausseté de.

belief *n.* croyance *f.*, opinion *f.*; conviction *f.* **in the firm ~ that**, dans la ferme croyance, dans la conviction que.

believable *adj.* croyable.

believe *v.t.* croire. **I cannot ~ him**, je ne peux pas le croire. **to ~ in God**, croire en Dieu. **he believes in astrology**, il croit à l'astrologie.

believer *n.* croyant *m.*, croyante *f.*

belittle *v.t.* rabaisser, déprécier.

bell *n.* cloche *f.*; sonnette *f.*; grelot *m.*; clochette *f.*; pavillon *m.* **to ring the ~s**, sonner les cloches. **~tower**, clocher *m.*, beffroi *m.* **~boy**, groom.

belle *n.* beauty *f.*

bellicose *adj.* belliqueux, guerroyeur.

belligerent *adj.* belligérant *n.*

bellow *v.i.* mugir, beugler; brailler. *n.* beuglement *m.*, mugissement *m.*

bellows *n.* soufflet *m.*

belly *n. Infml.* estomac, ventre *m.* **~ache**, douleur *f.*, colique *f.* **~button**, nombril *m.*

bellyful *n.* ventre *m.*, plein, rempli, soûl *m.* **his ~**, tout son soûl.

belong *v.i.* appartenir à; être à.

belongings *n.pl.* affaires *f.pl.*, possessions *f.pl.*

beloved *adj.* aimé, chéri, bien-aimé.

below *prep.* au-dessous de, sous; en aval de (d'une rivière). **~ the horizon**, au-dessous de l'horizon. **the boat is moored ~ the bridge**, le bateau est amarré en aval du pont. *adv.* en bas, au-dessous. **here ~**, ici-bas, dans ce monde.

belt *n.* ceinture *f.*

beltway *n.* periphérique *f.*

bemoan *v.t.* gémir, pleurer, se lamenter.

bemuse *v.t.* confondre.

bench *n.* banc *m.*, banquette *f.*, siège *m.* cour *f.*, tribunal *m.* **a stone ~**, un banc de pierre.

bend *v.t.* courber, plier, fléchir, pencher, incliner. **to ~ the head**, s'incliner; pencher la tête. **to ~ the knee**, fléchir le genou. *v.i.* se courber, ployer; se pencher. **to ~ forward**, se pencher en avant. **the road there ~s to the right**, là, le chemin fait un détour à droite. *n.* pli *m.*, courbure *f.*; inclinaison *f.* **the ~ of the arm**, le pli du bras.

benchmark *n.* référence *f.*, repère *m.*

beneath *prep.* sous, dessous, au-dessous de. **~ his head**, sous sa tête. *adv.* dessous, au-dessous, en bas.

benediction *n.* bénédiction *f.*

benefaction *n.* bienfaisance *f.* bienfait *m.*

benefactor *n.* bienfaiteur *m.*, bienfaitrice *f.*

benefactress *n.* bienfaitrice *f.*

benefice *n.* bénéfice *m.*

beneficence *n.* bienfaisance *f.*

beneficent *adj.* bienfaisant.

beneficial *adj.* profitable, avantageux, utile. Fig. ~ to mankind, utile au genre humain.

beneficiary *adj.,n.* bénéficiaire *m.f.*

benefit *n.* bienfait *m.*, bien *m.*; bénéfice *m.*; avantage *m.* for the ~ of, au profit de. *v.t.* faire du bien à, avantager. to ~ trade, encourager, favoriser le commerce. *v.i.* bénéficier, profiter, tirer avantage. to ~ by good advice, profiter des bons conseils.

benevolence *n.* bienveillance *f.*; bonté *f.*, bienfaisance *f.*, générosité *f.*

benevolent *adj.* bienveillant, charitable.

benighted *adj.* anuité (of a traveler); dans les ténèbres de l'ignorance.

benign *adj.* bénin, bénigne; bon, doux; favorable.

bent *adj.* courbé, plié; incliné, penché; porté; décidé, résolu. *n.* courbure *f.*; pente *f.*, penchant *m.*; pli *m.*, habitude *f.* to follow one's own ~, suivre ses goûts, son penchant.

benumb *v.t.* engourdir.

bequeath *v.t.* léguer (to, à).

berate *v.t.* gronder vivement; réprimander.

bereave *v.t.* priver, dépouiller. he has been ~d, il est en deuil.

bereavement *n.* privation *f.*, porte *f.*, deuil *m.*

Bermudas *n.pr.* les Bermudes *f.pl.*

berry *n.* baie *f.*

berserk *adj.* fou furieux *m.* (folle furieuse *f.*). she went ~ when she saw him, elle est devenue complètement dingue quand elle l'a vu.

berth *n.* couchette *f.*

beseech *v.t.* prier instamment, supplier, implorer.

beset *v.t.* entourer, environner, cerner; assiéger, obséder, importuner; saillir, attaquer.

beside *prep.* à côté de, près de, auprès de; au delà de, outre, excepté; hors, hormis. to be ~ oneself, être hors de soi.

besides *adv.* en outre, d'ailleurs, de plus, bien plus, d'un autre côté.

besiege *v.t.* assiéger.

besmear *v.t.* barbouiller, salir.

besmirch *v.t.* gâter, salir, souiller.

besotted *adj.* hébété, abruti, stupide.

best *adj.* le meilleur, la meilleure. *n.* le mieux. all is for the ~, tout est pour le mieux. to do one's ~, faire de son mieux, faire son possible. at ~ *m.*, au mieux. to make the ~ of a bad situation, tirer tout ce qu'on peut d'une mauvaise affaire. to have the ~ of it, avoir le dessus. to ~ advantage, au mieux, le mieux, plus à propos. to like ~, aimer mieux. he thought it ~ not to speak, il jugea plus à propos de se taire.

bestial *adj.* bestial.

bestiality *n.* bestialité *f.*

bestir *v.t.* to ~ oneself, se démener, agir; se remuer, s'agiter vivement.

bestow *v.t.* mettre, placer, ranger; employer, consacrer, donner, accorder, conférer.

bestride *v.t.* enfourcher, être à califourchon; enjamber, franchir.

bet *n.* pari *m.* – *v.t.* parier; gager. *infml.* I ~ you can't do it, t'es pas chiche de le faire. I'll ~ my life on it, je peux parier jusqu'à ma dernière chemise.

betoken *v.t.* présager; dénoter.

betrayal *n.* trahison *f.*

better *adj.* meilleur; mieux. to be ~, être meilleur, valoir mieux, se porter mieux. to be ~ off, être mieux, être plus à son aise. to make ~, améliorer. *v.t.* améliorer, mettre en meilleur état. to ~ oneself, améliorer sa position, se dépasser. *n.* supérieur *m.*; l'avantage *m.*, le dessus. to get the ~ of, l'emporter sur, avoir l'avantage sur. *adv.* mieux. you cannot do ~, vous ne pouvez mieux faire. you had ~ follow my advice, tu ferais mieux de suivre mes conseils. he works ~ and ~, il travaille de mieux en mieux.

better *n.* parieur *m.*, parieuse *f.*

between *prep.* entre. ~ you and me, entre nous.

beverage *n.* boisson *f.*, breuvage *m.*

bevy *n.* volée *f.*, bande *f.*, compagnie *f.*; troupe *f.* a ~ of quails, une volée de cailles. a ~ of roebucks, une troupe de chevreuils. a ~ of fair ladies, une réunion de jolies femmes.

bewail *v.t.* déplorer, pleurer, lamenter. *v.i.* se lamenter, se désoler.

beware *v.i.* se méfier, prendre garde, se garder.

bewilder *v.t.* égarer, dépayser; troubler, déconcerter, embrouiller. to become bewildered, s'égarer, s'embrouiller.

bewilderment *n.* égarement *m.*, perplexité *f.*, confusion *f.*

bewitch *v.t.* ensorceler; fasciner, enchanter.

bewitching *adj.* fascinateur, enchanteur, charmant.

beyond *prep.* au delà de; outre; au-dessus de. ~ the seas, au delà des mers. he lives ~ his means, il dépense plus que son revenue. ~ all praise, au-dessus de tout éloge. *adv.* au loin, là-bas.

biannual *adj.* semestriel.

biannually *adv.* deux fois per an.

bias *n.* parti *m.* pris, biais *m.*, penchant *m.*, tendance *f.*; prévention *f.*; détours *m.* the ~ of his speech was, le but de son discours était. *v.t.* faire pencher d'un côté, donner; prévenir (contre). *adv.* de biais.

bib *n.* bavoir *m.*, bavette *f.* (of a child).

Bible *n.* Bible *f.*

biblical *adj.* biblique.

bibliographer *n.* bibliographe *m.f.*

bibliographic, bibliographical *adj.* bibliographique.

bibliography *n.* bibliographie *f.*

bibulous *adj.* qui aime trop boire, spongieux, poreux.

bicarbonate *n.* bicarbonate *m.*

biceps *n.* biceps *m.*

bicker *v.t.* se quereller, se disputer. *Infml.* se chamailler.

bicycle *n.* vélo *m.*, bicyclette *f.*

bid *v.t.* commander; offrir, faire une enchère; souhaiter. **~ him to stay,** priez-le de rester. **to ~ a fair price,** offrir un bon prix. *n.* enchère *f.*, offre *f.* **higher ~,** surenchère *f.*

bidder *n.* enchérisseur *m.*

bidding *p.p.n.* invitation *f.;* order *m.,* commandement *m.;* offre *f.,* enchère *f.*

bide *v.i.* demeurer, habiter, résider; rester.

bidet *n.* bidet *m.*

biennial *adj.* biennual, qui dure deux ans ou qui arrive tous les deux ans; *Bot.* bisannuel.

bier *n.* corbillard *m.*, civière *f.*, brancard *m.;* bière *f.,* cercueil *m.*

biff *n. Infml.* gnon.

bifurcate *v.i.* bifurquer.

bifurcation *n.* bifurcation *f.*

big *adj.* gros; grand, vaste. **a ~ woman,** une grosse femme. *Infml.* **~ shot,** grosse légume. **he has such a ~ mouth,** c'est une sacrée grande gueule. **a ~ heart,** un grand, bon coeur, généreux. **to earn ~ money,** gagner gros.

bigamist *n.* bigame *m.f.*

bigamy *n.* bigamie *f.*

bight *n.* crique *f.,* anse *f.*

bigot *n.* bigot *m.;* dévot *m.;* partisan *m.* fanatique.

bigotry *n.* bigoterie *f.,* fanatisme *m.*

bike *n.* vélo *m., Infml.* bécane *f.*

bikini *n.* bikini *m.,* maillot *m.* de bain (à) deux pièces, un deux pièces.

bilateral *adj.* bilateral.

bilberry *n.* airelle *f.,* myrtille *f.*

bilbo *n.* rapière *f.,* sabre *m.*

bile *n.* bile *f.*

bilge *n.* fond *m.* de cale; sentine *f.* **~ pump,** pompe *f.* du fond de cale. **~ water,** eau *f.* de cale. *v.i.* s'avarier; faire une voie d'eau par suite d'avarie à la quille.

bilingual *adj.* bilingue.

bilk *n.* fraude *f.* ~ *v.t.* tromper; *Infml.* flouer.

bill *n.* addition *f.* (restaurant); facture *f.;* billet *m.;* bec *m.;* pointe *f.* d'une ancre; serpe *f.;* hache *f.;* affiche *f.,* placard *m.;* note *f.,* mémoire *m.;* bill *m.,* projet *m.* de loi, requête *f.,* plainte *f.* **five dollar ~,** billet de cinq dollars. **~ of exchange,** lettre *f.* de change. **to pass a ~,** adopter, voter un projet de loi. *v.i.* se becqueter (birds); envoyer une facture; (theater) annoncer, afficher.

billiards *n.pl.* billiard *m.* **to play at ~,** jouer au billard. **~ ball,** bille *f.*

billion *n.* billion *m.*

billionaire *n.* millardaire *m.f.*

billow *n.* vague *f.,* lame *f.* ~ *v.i.* s'enfler, se soulever, s'agiter comme les vagues. *v.t.* soulever en vagues, en lames.

billowy *adj.* houleux *m.*

bin *n.* huche *f.,* coffre *m.*

binary *adj.* binaire.

bind *v.t.* lier; attacher, serrer; ceindre; relier; constiper; durcir; confirmer, obliger. **~ in sheaves,** lier en bottes, en gerbes. *v.i.* se resserrer, se contracter; se lier; lier.

binder *n.* classeur *m.,* relieur *m.;* lieur *m.;* lien *m.*

binding *adj.* qui resserre; obligatoire, qui lie; *Med.* constipant, reliure *f.* (d'un livre).

binge *n. Infml.* aller à l'excès. **she went on a food ~,** elle a mangé à s'en rendre malade.

bingo *n.* bingo *m.;* loto *m.*

binnacle *n.* habitacle *m.*

binoculars *n.pl.* jumelles *f.pl.*

biochemist *n.* biochimiste *m.f.*

biochemistry *n.* biochimie *f.*

biodegradable *adj.* biodégradable. *f.*

bioethics *n.* bioéthique *f.*

biographer *n.* biographe *m.*

biographic, biographical *adj.* biographique.

biography *n.* biographie *f.*

biological *adj.* biologique.

biology *n.* biologie *f.*

bionics *n.pl.* (usually with sing. verb) bionique *f.*

biophysics *n.pl.* (usually with sing. verb) biophysique *f.*

biopsy *n.* biopsie *f.*

biorhythm *n.* rythme *m.,* biologique, biorythme *m.*

biosphere *n.* biosphère *f.*

biotechnology, biotech *n.* biotechnologie *f.*

bipartisan *adj.* biparti, bipartite.

biped *n.* bipède *m.*

birch *n.* bouleau *m.,* verge *f.*

bird *n.* oiseau *m.* **~ of passage,** oiseau de passage. **~ of prey,** oiseau de proie. **song~,** oiseau chanteur. **~s of a feather,** gens de même espèce, de même farine. **to kill two ~s with one stone,** faire d'une pierre deux coups. **one ~ in the hand is worth two in the bush,** un tiens vaut mieux que deux tu l'auras. **jail~,** gigier de potence.

birdie *n. Infml.* petit oiseau.

birdcage *n.* cage *f.,* volière *f.*

birth *n.* naissance *f.,* accouchement *m.;* couches *f.pl.* enfantement *m.;* portée *f.* **to give ~ to,** accoucher, donner naissance à, faire naître.

birthday *n.* anniversaire *m.*

birthplace *n.* lieu *m.* de naissance.

birthright *n.* droit *m.* de naissance; droit d'aînesse; patrimoine *m.,* héritage *m.*

biscuit *n.* biscuit *m.*

bisexual *adj.* bisexué.

bishop *n.* évêque *m.;* (in chess) fou *m.*

bit *n.* petit morceau *m.,* brin *m.,* bout *m.;* mors *m.;* peu *adv.* **a ~ of bread,** un morceau de pain, un peu de pain. **not a ~,** pas le moins du monde. **a little ~,** un petit peu.

bitch *n.* chienne *f.,* louve *f.,* renarde *f. Infml.* salope *f.,* conasse *f.* ~ *adj.* garce. (person), vache (comment). *v.i.* rouspéter.

bite *v.t.* mordre; ronger, creuser; attraper, duper. **to ~ one's tongue,** se mordre la langue. **to ~ off,** emporter en mordant. *v.i.* piquer, pincer; mordre à l'hameçon; s'enfoncer. **the fish do not ~,** les poissons ne mordent pas. *n.* coup *m.* de dent; morsure (of a dog, etc.); piqûre *f.* (of an insect); bouchée *f.;* attrape *f.,* piège *m.;* **to ~ off,** arracher d'un coup de dents.

biting *adj.* mordant, piquant, âpre.

bitter *adj.* amer, mordant, piquant, railleur; *Fig.* pénible, poignant; cruel, rude. **as ~ as gall,** amer comme fiel. **~ tears,** des larmes amères. **~ words,** paroles cruelles. **~ enmity,** haine acharnée. **a ~ cold,** un froid piquant. *n.* amer *m.;* amertume *f.*

bitterly *adv.* amèrement, avec amertume; sévèrement, cruellement.

bitterness *n.* amertume *f.,* sévérité *f.,* dureté *f.* de caractère, inimitié *f.,* invétérée.

bivouac *n.* bivouac *m.* ~ *v.t.* bivouaquer.

biz *n. abbr.* of *business;* **show ~,** show business.

bizarre *adj.* bizarre.

blab *v.t.* révéler, divulguer (secrets). *v.i.* bavarder.

blabbermouth *n.* jaseur *m.,* jaseuse *f.;* bavard *m.,* bavarde *f.*

black *adj.* noir, obscurci, assombri; sombre. **~ eyes,** des yeux noirs; des yeux pochés. *n.* noir *m.;* deuil *m.* **jet ~,** noir de jais. **a ~ suit,** un costume noir, un vêtement de deuil. **~ magic,** magie *f.* noire. **~board,** tableau *m.* **~currant,** cassis *m.*

blackball *v.t.* blackbouler (a person).

blackberry *n.* mûre *f.* de ronce.

blackbird *n.* merle *m.*

blacken *v.t.* noircir; obscurcir, assombrir, couvrir de nuages; souiller, dénigrer, diffamer. *v.i.* se noircir, s'obscurcir, s'assombrir.

blacking *n.* cirage *m.* noir, noircissement *m.*

blackish *adj.* noirâtre.

blacklist *n.* liste *f.* noire. *v.t.* mettre (a person, an organization) sur la liste noire.

blackmail *n.* chantage. *v.t.* faire chanter.

blackmailer *n.* maître *m.* chanteur.

blackness *n.* noirceur *f.*

blackout *n.* black-out *m.;* panne *f.* d'électricité; évanouissement *m.* trou *m.* de mémoire.

blacksmith *n.* forgeron *m.*

blackthorn *n.* prunellier *m.* sauvage.

bladder *n.* vessie *f.,* vésicule *f.*

blade *n.* brin *m.* (of grass); lame *f.* (of knife, etc.); glaive *f.*

blah *n. Infml.* blablabla *m.,* baratin *m.*

blamable *adj.* blâmable.

blame *v.t.* blâmer. **you are to ~,** vous êtes à blâmer. *n.* blâme *m.*

blameful *adj.* blâmable, répréhensible.

blameless *adj.* sans reproche, irréprochable.

blamelessly *adv.* sans reproche.

blanch *v.t.* blanchir; peler; décortiquer (nuts); pâlir, faire pâlir. *Fig.* faiblir, biaiser.

bland *adj.* insipide, fade, mielleux, doucereux.

blandness *n.* insipidité *f.*

blank *adj.* blanc, pâle; sans rimes; confus. **a ~ page,** une page blanche. **to fire ~s,** tirer à blanc. *n.* blanc *m.;* vide *m.,* lacune *f.;* billet *m.* blanc. **point ~,** à bout portant. *v.t.* annuler; faire pâlir; déconcerter, confondre.

blanket *n.* couverture *f.* ~ *v.t.* envelopper d'une couverture.

blankly *adv.* avec pâleur, avec confusion.

blare *v.i.* beugler, rugir. *n.* rugissement *m.,* bruit *m.*

blaspheme *v.t.* blasphémer, injurier, outrager, calomnier.

blasphemer *n.* blasphémateur *m.,* blasphématrice *f.*

blasphemous *adj.* blasphématoire, impie.

blasphemy *n.* blasphème *m.*

blast *n.* coup *m.* de vent, rafale *f.,* bise *f.;* explosion *f.;* vent *m.* **the cold northern ~,** le vent froid du nord. **the ~ of a trumpet,** le son d'une trompette. **~ of steam,** jet *m.* de vapeur. **to turn the radio on full ~,** faire brailler la radio. **~ furnace,** haut fourneau *m.* ~ *v.t.* flétrir, sécher, brûler, détruire; fair sauter (mines). **to ~ one's hopes,** ruiner ses espérances.

blatant *adj.* sans honte, criant, voyant.

blather *v.i.* parler à tort et à travers, raconter des bêtises.

blaze *n.* flamme *f.,* jet *m.* de flamme; lumière *f.,* feu *m.;* éclat *m.* ~ *v.i.* flamber; flamboyer, briller d'un vif éclat. **pinewood ~s well,** le bois de sapin flambe bien. *v.t.* faire briller, faire connaître. **to ~ abroad,** publier au loin.

bleach *v.t.* blanchir; pâlir, faire pâlir; *n.* eau *f.* de javel.

bleak *n.* ablette *f.* ~ *adj.* hâve, pâle, blême; ouvert, exposé aux vents; froid, morne. **a ~ sky,** un ciel sombre et froid.

blear *adj.* chassieux. *v.t.* rendre les yeux troubles. **bleary eyes,** yeux troublés, voilés.

bleat *n.* bêlement *m.* ~ *v.i.* bêler.

bleed *v.i.* saigner; pleurer (vines). *Infml.* extorquer de l'argent.

bleeding *n.* saignée *f.;* saignement *m.*

blemish *v.t.* endommager; ternir, flétrir. *n.* défaut *m.,* tache *f.* (on the reputation); tare *f.*

blend *v.t.* mêler, mélanger; fondre, marier, allier. *v.i.* se fondre, se confondre avec; se mêler; s'allier, se marier.

blender *n.* mixer *m.*

bless *v.t.* bénir. **God ~ you!** que Dieu vous bénisse!

blessed *adj.* béni; saint, divin, bienheureux. **the ~ Virgin,** la sainte Vierge.

blessedness *n.* bonheur *m.,* félicité *f.,* sainteté *f.*

blessing *n.* bénédiction *f.,* bénédicité *m.;* bonheur *m.*

blight *n.* rouille (wheat) *f.,* nielle *f.,* brouissure *f.* *v.t.* rouiller, nieller, brouir; flétrir (wind).

blind *adj.* aveugle. **~ in one eye,** borgne. **~ alley,** impasse *f.* ~ *v.t.* aveugler, rendre aveugle, éblouir; voiler. n. voile m., masque m.; store m., persiennes f.pl. **Venetian ~s**, jalousies f.pl.

blindfold adj. ayant les yeux bandés, couverts. v.t. bander, couvrir les yeux, empêcher de voir.

blindly adv. aveuglément, en aveugle, à aveuglette.

blindness n. cécité f.; Fig. aveuglement m.

blink v.i. cligner les yeux, clignoter, lorgner. n. clignement m. d'oeil, clignotement m.; coup m. d'oeil m.

blinker n. clignotant. m.

bliss n. béatitude f., joies f.pl. célestes.

blissful adj. heureux, bienheureux.

blissfully adv. heureusement.

blister n. ampoule f., cloque f. ~ v.i. se couvrir d'ampoules et de cloques. v.t. couvrir d'ampoules.

blithe adj. gai, enjoué, vif.

blizzard n. blizzard m., tempête f. de neige.

bloat v.t. enfler, boursoufler, bouffir. v.i. enfler, gonfler, s'enfler, se gonfler.

bloated p.p. or adj. enflé, gonflé.

block n. bloc m.; pâté m. (de maisons); billot m.; poulie f. Print. encrier m.; obstacle m. **stumbling ~**, pierre f. d'achoppement. v.t. obstruer, barrer; bloquer. **~buster** n. bombe f. explosive; Fig. bombe f., dynamite f., superproduction f., faire un tabac m.; (film) film à grand succès; (book) roman à grand succès.

blockade n. blocus m. ~ v.t. bloquer.

blond(e) adj., n. blond(e) m.f.

blood n. sang m. **in cold ~**, de sang-froid. **to make one's ~ run cold**, glacer le sang. **~ vessel**, vaisseau m. sanguin; **~ bank** n. banque f. du sang. **~bath** n. bain m. de sang. **~ money** n. prix m. du sang. **~ pressure** n. tension f. artérielle, pression f. sanguine. **~shed** n. effusion f. de sang. **~sucker** n. sangsue f. ~ v.t. saigner.

bloodhound n. limier m.

bloodily adv. d'une manière sanglante, cruellement.

bloodiness n. état m. sanglant.

bloodless adj. privé de sang, pâle; exsangue.

bloodlessly adv. sans effusion de sang.

bloodstained adj. tâché de sang.

bloodthirsty adj. assoiffé de sang; sanguinaire.

bloody adj. sanglant, ensanglanté; sanguinaire. v.t. souiller de sang.

bloom n. fleur f. ~ v.i. fleurir, être en fleur.

blooming adj. en fleur dans sa fraîcheur, avec éclat.

blossom n. fleur f.; floraison f. ~ v.i. fleurir, éclore, s'épanouir; prospérer.

blot n. (of ink) pâté m., tache f.; flétrissure f., rature f. **to make a ~**, faire un pâté. v.t. tacher, salir, barbouiller. **~ out**, effacer, rayer, raturer. v.i. boire (the ink).

blotch n. pustule f. v.t. couvrir de pustules; éclabousser.

blotter n. registre m. (of arrests), ternisseur f.; ce qui efface (for ink), buvard m.

blouse n. chemisier m., blouse f.

blow n. coup m.; atteinte f. **unlucky ~**, mauvais coup. **to come to ~s**, en venir aux coups, aux mains. v.i. venter, épanouir, fleurir. **The wind ~s north**, le vent souffle du nord. **to ~ off**, être emporté par le vent. **to ~ out**, s'éteindre. **to ~ over**, passer, se dissiper. **to ~ up**, souffler; jouer; sonner, couvrir d'oeufs. **to ~ hot and cold**, souffler le chaud et le froid. **the wind blew his hat away**, le vent a emporté son chapeau. **to ~ down**, abattre, renverser. **~ out that candle**, soufflez, éteignez cette bougie. **to ~ up**, faire sauter (a thing). **the enemy attempted to ~ up a mine**, l'ennemi essaya de faire jouer une mine. **to ~-dry hair** v.t. sécher (avec un séchoir).

blowpipe n. chalumeau m.

blowzy adj. hâlé; rubicond, rougeaud.

blubber n. lard m. or graisse f. de baleine. v.i. pleurer comme un veau. v.t. gonfler les joues, défigurer les traits à force de pleurer.

bludgeon n. gourdin m. matraque f. v.t. matraquer.

blue n. bleu m., azur m. ~ adj. bleu, azuré. **~bell**, campanule f., clochette f. **once in a ~ moon**, en de rares occasions. **~ cheese**, fromage m. bleu. **to feel ~**, avoir le cafard. **~ film**, film m. porno. **the ~s**, Music. le blues.

blueprint n. plan (détaillé) du projet.

bluff n. cap m. à pic; falaise f., bluff m. adj. escarpé; fier, hautain, rude. v.t. bluffer.

bluish adj. bleuâtre.

blunder n. bévue f.; étourderie f. ~ v.i. se méprendre, se tromper; faire une bévue. v.t. brouiller, embrouiller.

blunderer n. gaffeur m., gaffeuse f. étourdi m., éfourdie f.

blunt adj. émoussé; obtus; brusque. **to get ~**, s'émousser. **~ truths**, de dures vérités. v.t. émousser, amortir.

bluntly adv. brusquement, grossièrement, sans délicatesse.

bluntness n. état de ce qui est émoussé; rudesse f., brusquerie f.

blur n. tache f. ~ v.t. tacher, souiller; ternir; brouiller, troubler, devenir flou, embuer.

blurt v.t. parler à tort et à travers, inconsidérément. **to ~ out**, lâcher, laisser échapper (a secret).

blush n. rougeur f.; rouge m., couleur f. rougeâtre. v.i. rougir. **she blushes at it**, elle en rougit.

blushing ppr. or adj. rougissant; vermeil.

bluster n. vacarme m., tumulte m.; fureur f., violence f. (of a storm). v.i. faire du vacarme, faire grand bruit, tempêter; mugir; gronder.

blustering adj. bruyant; tumultueux; orageux.

blusteringly adv. bruyamment, avec fracas.

blusterous adj. bruyant, tumultueux; orageux.

boa n. boa m.

boar n. verrat m. (male pig) **wild~**, sanglier m.

board n. planche f., ais m.; écriteau f.; tableau m. (in classroom); table f., pension f.; bureau m. **~ of directors,** conseil m. d'administration. **~ of trustees,** conseil de gestion. **chess~,** échiquier m. **draft ~,** damier m. **room and ~,** gîte f. et couvert. **to go on ~,** aller à bord, s'embarquer. v.t. nourrir, prendre en pension; mettre en pension; aborder (a boat), accoster. v.i. manger, être en pension.

boarder n. pensionnaire m.f.

boarding n. nourriture f., pension f.; abordage m. **~house,** pension. **~ school,** pensionnat m. **~ pass, card,** carte f. d'embarquement.

boast v.i. se vanter, se glorifier. v.t. vanter, exalter. n. vanterie f., jactance f.; gloire f. **to ~ of,** se vanter de.

boaster n. vantard m., vantarde f.

boastful adj. plein d'orgueil, vantard.

boastfully adv. avec vantardise f.

boasting n. vantardise f.

boat n. bateau m., barque f.; canot m. **fishing ~,** bateau pêcheur. **life ~,** canot de sauvetage. **~house,** hangar m. à bateaux. **~ neck** (on shirt, etc.) encolure f. bateau. **~ people,** boat people m.pl. v.t. transporter en bateau.

boating n. transport m. par eau; promenade f. en bateau; canotage m.

boatswain n. maître m. d'équipage.

bob n. petit coup m., petit ébranlement m.; gland m. **~** v.t. remuer, balloter, balancer; tromper, jouer. **to ~ one's head,** remuer, secouer la tête. v.i. osciller, pendiller, brandiller; pêcher à l'anguille avec un paquet de vers.

bobbin n. bobine f.

bobby pin n. pince f. à cheveux.

bode v.t. présager, pronostiquer, augurer. n. présage m., augure m.

bodiless adj. incorporel.

bodily adj. corporel. adv. corporellement; complètement.

boding n. présage m., pronostic m.

body n. corps m.; substance f., fond m.; corporation f.; personne f.; caisse f. (of a car). **a dead ~,** corps mort, cadavre. **a ~ of infantry,** un corps d'infanterie. **wine with a good ~,** vin qui a du corps. v.t. donner une forme, un corps à; corporifier. **~building** n., culturisme m., exercices m.pl. de musculation. **~guard** n., garde m. du corps.

bog n. marais m., marécage m. **~** v.t. embourber.

bogey(man) n. croquemitaine m., père m. fouettard, démon m.

boggle v.t. brouiller, embrouiller. **the mind ~s,** cela confond l'imagination.

boggy adj. marécageux.

bogus adj. faux, bidon, à la noix.

boil v.i. bouillir. **to ~ over,** se déborder. v.t. faire cuire à l'eau bouillante, faire bouillir. n. clou m., furoncle m.

boiler n. chaudière f.

boiling n. ébullition f., bouillonnement.

boisterous adj. bruyant, impétueux, violent, furieux.

boisterously adv. bruyamment; impétueusement, tumultueusement.

boisterousness n. violence f., impétuosité f.

bold adj. hardi, intrépide, téméraire, audacieux. **to be so ~ as to,** être assez hardi pour. **to make ~ to,** prendre la liberté de.

boldly adv. hardiment; effrontément.

boldness n. hardiesse f., audace f., courage m., assurance f., effronterie f.

bolster n. traversin m.; coussin m. **~ v.t. to ~ a person's confidence,** donner de la confiance à quelqu'un.

bolt n. flèche f., trait m., dard m., javelot m.; foudre f., verrou m.; boulon m., cheville f. pl. fers. v.t. verrouiller, boulonner, cheviller; dire hardiment; lâcher. v.i. se dérober; s'échapper.

bomb n. bombe f., fracas m. **~ proof,** à l'épreuve de la bombe. **~shell,** obus m. **~scare,** alerte f. à la bombe. v.i. éclater, résonner.

bombard v.t. bombarder.

bombardier n. bombardier m.

bombardment n. bombardement m.

bombast n. grandiloquence f. adj. pompeux boursouflé.

bombastic adj. boursouflé, enflé.

bomber n. bombardier m.

bona-fide adj. authentique, sérieux, de bonne foi.

bonanza n. Infml. mine f. d'or, filon m., aubaine f., veine f.

bond n. lien m., chaîne f., obligation f., engagement m., entrepôt m.; bon m.; valeur f., titre m. **matrimonial ~s,** lien conjugal. **~holder,** obligataire m.f. **~ v.t.** s'engager par écrit à payer, faire un billet; entreposer.

bondage n. esclavage m., captivité f., asservissement m.

bonded adj. par obligation écrite; entreposé (customs).

bone n. os m.; arête f. (of fish); Fig. restes m.pl. mortels. **he is nothing but skin and ~s,** il n'a que la peau et les os. **he made no ~s about it,** Infml. il a fait ni une ni deux. **~less,** sans os, sans arête. v.t. désosser (meat); ôter les arêtes (fish). **to pick a ~ with,** chercher des puces/poux à (quelqu'un). **old ~s,** vieux os. **~head** Infml. crâne m. d'oeuf.

boned adj. or **boneless** adj. désossé.

bonfire n. feu m.de joie.

bonus n. prime f.; gratification f., dividendes m.pl.

bony adj. osseux.

boo excl. houl; v.t. huer.

boob n. gaffe f; Infml. nichon m. (breast); Infml. idiot m., idiote f. (fool). **~ tube,** télé f.

booby n. niais m., nigaud m., sot m.

book n. livre m., cahier m., carnet m. **second-hand ~s,** livres d'occasion. **school ~s,** livres des classes. **cash ~,** livre de caisse. **~keeper,**

compatable *m.f.* ~**keeping**, compatabilité *f.*
~**maker**, parieur *m.* (of bets). **to go by the ~**,
suivre la règle. *v.t.* inscrire, enregistrer. **to ~
one's place**, retenir sa place.

bookbinder *n.* relieur *m.*, relieuse *f.*

bookcase *n.* bibliothèque *f.*

booking *n.* réservation *f.*, enregistrement *m.*
~ **office**, guichet *m.*

booklet *n.* livret *m.*, brochure *f.*

bookshelf *n.* étagère *f.* pour livres.

bookstore *n.* librairie *f.*

boom *n.* grondement *m.*, retentissement *m.*; en
plein essor, en expansion, en hausse. *v.i.* prospérer. *v.i.* gronder (comme le canon).

boon *n.* don *m.*, bienfait *m.* ~ *adj.* gai, joyeux,
jovial.

boondocks *n.pl. Infml.* bled *m.*, banlieue *f.*

boor *n.* rustre *m.*

boorish *adj.* rude, grossier.

boorishly *adv.* grossièrement, en rustre.

boorishness *n.* rudesse *f.*, manque d'éducation
m., grossièreté *f.*

boost *v.t.* soulever, faire remonter, propulser. **to
~ the economy**, développer, accroître
l'économie.

booster *n.* batterie *f.* de secours; piqûre *f.* de
rappel.

boot *n.* botte *f.*; bottine *f.* **to ~**, par-dessus le
marché. *v.t.* **to ~ a person out**, flanquer une
personne à la porte. **to ~ (a computer)**,
s'amorcer.

booth *n.* cabine *f.*, baraque *f.*, restaurant avec
une longue table au milieu de deux long sièges.

booty *n.* butin *m.*

booze *v.i. Infml.* pinard *m.*, gnôle *f.*

boozer *n.* poivrot *m.*, soulard *m.*

border *n.* bord *m.*, frontière *f.* (of a country);
bordure *f.*; cadre *m.* ~ *v.t.* border, limiter. *v.i.*
(with **on** or **upon**) confiner à, toucher à; friser.
France borders on Spain, la France touche à
l'Espagne.

bore *v.t.* percer, forer; sonder (land); assommer,
ennuyer. **to ~ a tunnel**, percer un tunnel. *v.i.*
percer; se frayer un chemin. **to ~ for coal**, sonder à la recherche du charbon de terre. *n.* trou
m. de sonde; ennui *m.*, corvée *f.*; ras *m.* de
marée. **what a ~!** quel raseur! *m.*

boredom *n.* ennui *m.*

born *ppa.* né. **to be ~**, naître. **new~**, nouveau-
né. **still~**, mort-né.

borough *n.* municipalité *f.*

borrow *v.t.* emprunter.

borrower *n.* emprunteur *m.*, emprunteuse *f.*

borrowing *n.* emprunt *m.*

Bosnia *n.pr.* Bosnie *f.*

Bosnian *adj.* bosnien; *n.* Bosnien.

bosom *n.* sein *m.*, le coeur, les affections. **the ~
of the sea**, le sein, les profondeurs de la mer.

boss *n.* patron *m.*, patronne *f.*, chef *m. v.t.* mener,
diriger. **I hate it when he ~es me around**, je
déteste qu'il me donne des ordres.

bossy *adj.* autoritaire.

botani(cal) *adj.* botanique, de botanique.

botanist *n.* botaniste *m.f.*

botany *n.* botanique *f.*

botch *n. Fig.* ouvrage *m.* mal fait. *v.t.* bousiller,
louper (a job). **to ~ up**, bousiller, massacrer.

both *adj.* deux, les deux; tous les deux, toutes les
deux, tous deux, toutes deux. ~ **his sons**, ses
deux fils. ~ **of them**, eux deux. ~ **of us**, nous
deux. *conj.* à la fois; tant. **he can ~ read and
write**, il sait et lire et écrire. ~ **by sea and
land**, par terre et par mer.

bother *v.t.* ennuyer, tracasser; embêter, casser la
tête. **stop ~ing me!** arrête de m'embêter! *n.*
ennui *m.*, tourment *m.*, tracas *m.*

bottle *n.* bouteille *f.*; botte *f.* **stone ~**, bouteille
de grès, cruchon *m.* **baby ~**, biberon *m.*
~**brush**, goupillon *m.* ~ **green**, vert-bouteille
m. ~ **rack**, porte-bouteilles. *v.t.* mettre en bouteilles; botteler (hay, etc.).

bottling *n.* mise *f.* en bouteilles.

bottom *n.* bas *m.*; fond *m.*; bout *m.*; fondement
m.; base *f.*; carène *f.* (of a boat). **from top to ~**,
de haut en bas. **to sink to the ~**, couler à fond.
the ~ of a chair, le fond d'une chaise. ~**s up!**
cul sec! *v.t.* fonder, asseoir, baser, établir.

bottomed *adj.* à fond. **flat-~ ship**, un vaisseau
à fond plat.

bottomless *adj.* sans fond, sans fin, *Fig.*
insondable.

bough *n.* branche *f.*, rameau *m.*

bought See **BUY.**

boulder *n.* (gros) bloc *m.* de pierre.

boulevard *n.* boulevard *m.*

bounce *v.i.* bondir, sauter, s'élancer; éclater. **to ~
against**, se jeter contre, heurter. *v.t.* faire bondir.
to ~ a ball, faire bondir une balle. ~**ed check**,
chèque *m.* sans provision.

bouncer *n.* videur *m.* (night club).

bound *n.* limite *f.*, borne *f.*; bond *m.*, saut *m.* **to
keep within ~s**, ne pas dépasser les bornes.
v.t. limiter, borner. *v.i.* bondir, sauter. *adj.* allant
à, en destination pour, chargé pour. ~ **for**, à destination de.

boundary *n.* borne *f.*; frontière *f.*, limite *f.*

boundless *adj.* sans limites, sans bornes,
illimité.

bounteous *adj.* charitable, bienfaisant,
généreux.

bountiful *adj.* généreux, libéral; bienveillant,
bon; fécond.

bountifully *adv.* généreusement, libéralement.

bountifulness *n.* bonté *f.*, générosité *f.*

bounty *n.* bonté *f.*, générosité *f.*, munificence *f.*;
prime *f.* d'engagement (in the army).

bouquet *n.* bouquet *m.*

bout *n.* coup *m.*, fois *f.*; partie *f.* **at one ~**, d'un
seul coup. **a drinking ~**, une orgie *f.*, une
débauche *f.*

boutique *n.* boutique *f.*, magasin *m.*

bovine *adj.* bovine *f.*

bow *v.t.* courber, plier; fléchir (knee); baisser, incliner (head). se courber, fléchir; saluer. **he ~ed his head**, il baissa la tête. *n.* salut *m.*, révérence *f.*, courbette *f.*; proue *f.*, avant (of a boat).

bow *n.* arc *m.*; archet *m.*; noeud *m.* (ribbon). **to have two strings to one's ~**, *Fig.* avoir plusieurs cordes à son arc. **~-leg**, jambe *f.* arquée, tordue. **~-saw**, scie *f.* à contourner. **~ window**, fenêtre *f.* en saillie.

bowel *n.* intestin *m.*, boyau *m.*; *pl.* entrailles *f.pl.*, intestins *m.pl.*, boyaux *m.pl.* **the ~s of the earth**, les entrailles de la terre.

bower *n.* retraite *f.* *v.t.* couvrir de branches d'arbres, arranger en berceau. *v.i.* habiter, éjourner.

bowl *n.* bol *m.*; coupe *f.*; jatte *f.*; fourneau *m.* (of a pipe); amphithéâtre *m.* (for concerts, sports); boule *f.*; *pl.* jeu *m.* de boules. *v.t.* rouler, faire rouler comme une boule.

bowling *n.* bowling *m.*

box *n.* buis *m.*, bois *m.* de buis; boîte *f.*; malle *f.*, caisse *f.*; tronc *m.*; coffre *m.*; loge *f.* (in a theater); soufflet *m.*. **dice-~**, cornet à dés. **mail~**, boîte à lettres. **P.O. ~**, boîte *f.* postale. *v.t.* enfermer dans une boîte, souffleter. *v.i.* boxer, se boxer.

boxer *n.* boxeur *m.*; (dog) boxer *m.*

boxing *n.* boxe *f.*

boy *n.* garçon *m.*

boycott *v.t.* boycotter; *n.* boycottage *m.*

boyhood *n.* enfance *f.*

boyish *adj.* d'enfant, enfantin, puéril.

bra *n.* soutien-gorge *m.*

brace *v.t.* lier, attacher; fortifier. *n.* attache *f.*, lien *m.*; bandage *m.*; brace(s), appareil *m.* dentaire, **braces**, bretelles *f.pl.* **ten ~ of partridges**, dix couples de perdrix.

bracelet *n.* bracelet *m.*

bracing *adj.* vif, fortifiant.

bracken *n.* fougère *f.*

bracket *n.* tasseau *m.*, console *f.*; *Typog.* crochet *m.*; chaise *f.*, corbeau *m.* **~** *v.t.* poser sur des tasseaux, des consoles.

brag *v.i.* se vanter. *n.* vanterie *f.*

braid *n.* tresse *f.* *v.t.* tresser, entrelacer.

Braille *n.* braille *m.*

brain *n.* cerveau *m.*, cervelle *f.*, *Fig.* intelligence, esprit, méninges *f.pl.* **his ~ is always at work**, son cerveau travaille toujours. **a calf's ~s**, une cervelle de veau. **~storm** *n.*, (brilliant idea), idée géniale *f.* **~wash** *n.*, lavage *m.* de cerveau. *v.t.* faire sauter la cervelle à.

brainless *adj.* sans cervelle, bête, stupide.

brainy *adj.* *Infml.* intelligent.

brake *n.* *Bot.* fougère *f.*; fougeraie *f.*; hallier *m.*; frein *m.* **~ fluid**, liquide *m.* de frein. **~light** *n.* feu *m.* de stop (on vehicle). *v.i.* freiner.

bramble *n.* ronce *f.*

bran *n.* son *m.*

branch *n.* branche *f.*; branchage *m.*; succursale *f.* (of a bank). **the ~es of a chandelier**, les branches d'un lustre. *v.t.* étendre des branches,

se ramifier. **to ~ off**, se ramifier; bifurquer. **to ~ out**, pousser des branches. *v.i.* diviser en branches.

brand *n.* marque *f.* (de fabrique), flétrissure *f.* **~ new**, tout neuf. *Fig.* stigmate *m.*; **~-new** *adj.* flambant neuf. *v.t.* marquer au fer rouge; flétrir.

brandish *v.t.* brandir.

brandy *n.* eau-de-vie *f.*

brash *adj.* effronté, impudent, exubérant.

brass *n.* cuivre *m.* jaune, laiton *m.* **~ band**, fanfare *f.* **~ instrument**, instrument *m.* à vent en cuivre.

brat *n.* gosse *m.f.*, marmot *m.*, bambin *m.*

brave *adj.* brave, courageux; **he is a ~ man**, c'est un homme courageux. *v.t.* braver, défier; narguer.

bravely *adv.* bravement.

bravery *n.* courage *m.*

bravo *n.* bravo *m.*; *interj.* bravo! très bien.

brawl *v.i.* se bagarrer. *n.* dispute *f.*, querelle *f.* bruyante; rixe *f.*, mêlée *f.*

brawn *n.* muscle *m.*; force *f.*, vigueur *f.* musculaire.

brawny *adj.* musculeux; musculeux, charnu, vigoureux, robuste.

bray *v.i.* braire; faire retentir. *n.* braiment *m.* (of a donkey); faire retentir. *n.* braiment *m.* (of a donkey), son *m.* rauque et désagréable.

braze *v.t.* travailler en cuivre; braser; souder.

brazen *adj.* impudent, effronté.

Brazil *n.pr.* le Brésil *m.* **~ nut**, noix *f.* du brésil.

Brazilian *adj.* brésilien. *n.* Brésilien *m.*, Brésilienne *f.*

breach *n.* brèche *f.*, rupture *f.*, violation *f.*, infraction *f.*; abus *m.* **~ of promise**, manque *m.* de parole. **~ of duty**, manquement *m.* au devoir. *v.t.* battrer en brèche, pratiquer une brèche.

bread *n.* pain *m.* **unleavened ~**, pain azyme, sans levain. **white ~**, pain blanc. **stale ~**, pain rassis. **his ~ is well buttered**, son avenir est assuré. **~crumbs** *n.* chapelure *f.* **~winner** *n.* gagne pain *m.*, soutien (familial) *m.*

break *v.t.* rompre, casser, briser, violer; enfreindre; dompter; ruiner. **to ~ a glass, a stick, a string**, casser un verre, un bâton, une corde. **to ~ silence**, rompre le silence. **to ~ the law**, violer la loi. **to ~ a bank**, faire sauter la banque (in gambling). **to ~ down**, abattre, renverser, éclater en sanglots, s'effondrer. **to ~ the heart**, briser le coeur. **to ~ in**, entrer par effraction, casser, rompre, former; dresser (an animal). **to ~ off**, casser. *Fig.* rompre, cesser. **I will ~ him of that habit**, je le corrigerai de cette habitude. **to ~ open**, enfoncer, ouvrir avec effraction. **to ~ through**, percer à travers, se frayer un passage à travers. **to ~ away**, forcer un passage, se frayer un chemin. *v.i.* rompre, se rompre; casser, se casser; briser, se briser; s'ouvrir, crever (a tumor); se gâter (time). **the rope broke**, la corde s'est rompue. **he begins to ~**, il commence à casser. **to ~ in**, pénétrer. **to ~ in**

upon, faire irruption dans. **to ~ loose,** se détacher, s'échapper de. **to ~ out,** éclater, échapper. **to ~ out in pimples,** se couvrir de boutons. **the meeting broke up,** l'assemblée se sépara. *n.* ouverture *f.;* percée *f.,* éclaircie *f.* (in a forest); cassure *f.,* défaut *m.;* lacune *f.;* pause *f.,* interruption *f.,* point *m.,* pointe *f.,* aube *f.* (of day); *Typog.* alinéa *m.,* nouvel alinéa; voiture *f.* de dressage. **there was a ~ in the conversation,** il y avait une pause dans la conversation. **I'm tired, I need a ~,** je suis fatigué(e), j'ai besoin de cinq minutes, j'ai besoin d'aller prendre l'air.

breakable *adj.* fragile, cassable.

breakage *n.* casse *f.*

breakdown *n.* panne *f.* (car); dépression *f.* nerveuse, effondrement *m.;* division *f.* par groupes analyse *f.*

breaker *n.* briseur *m.* briseuse *f.* *Fig.* violateur *m.* violatrice *f.* (of laws, etc.); brisant *m.* (wave).

breakfast *n.* petit déjeuner. *v.i.* prendre son petit déjeuner.

breaking *n.* fracture *f.,* bris *m.,* rupture *f.,* brisement *m.;* violation *f.,* infraction *f.,* éruption *n.f.* **~ point,** point *m.* de rupture.

breast *n.* poitrine *f.;* sein *m.,* mamelle *f.;* gorge *f.;* poitrail *m.* (of a horse). **~bone,** sternum *m.* **~feed** *v.t.* allaiter, donner le sein.

breath *n.* haleine *f.,* souffle *m.,* respiration *f.* **to gasp for ~,** haleter. **to be out of ~,** être hors d'haleine. **in one ~,** d'un trait. **last ~,** dernier soupir.

breathable *adj.* respirable.

breathe *v.t.* respirer; souffler, exhaler.

breathless *adj.* hors d'haleine, essoufflé; inanimé; mort.

breathlessness *n.* essoufflement *m.,* perte *f.* d'haleine.

breech (birth) *n.* accouchement *m.* par le siège. **(pair of) breeches,** culotte *f.* **~ action, ~ mechanism,** mécanisme *m.* de culasse. **~loader,** fusil *m.* se chargeant par la culasse. *v.t.* mettre une culasse à.

breed *v.t.* faire l'élevage *m.* de, engendrer; couver, faire éclore; élever, destiner à; produire. **well bred,** bien élevé. **to ~ birds,** élever des oiseaux. *v.t.* être enceinte; s'engendrer, s'accroître, se multiplier. *n.* race *f.,* lignée *f.;* espèce *f.,* engeance *f.,* portée *f.,* couvée *f.*

breeder *n.* éleveur *m.,* éleveuse *f.,* reproducteur *m.,* reproductrice *f.* **~ reactor,** surgénérateur *m.* **cattle ~,** éleveur de bestiaux.

breeding *n.* élevage *m.,* reproduction *f.* **good ~,** bonnes manières, savoir-vivre *m.*

breeze *n.* brise *f.;* vent *m.* frais.

brevity *n.* brièveté *f.;* concision *f.*

brew *v.t.* brasser; mêler, altérer, falsifier; couver, tramer, completer. *v.i.* se rassembler, fabriquer de la bière. **a storm is ~ing,** un orage se prépare. *n.* brassage *m.;* liqueur *f.* brassée.

brewer *n.* brasseur *m.* **~'s yeast,** levure *f.* de bière.

brewery *n.* brasserie *f.*

bribe *n.* pot-de-vin *m.,* appât *m.* *v.t.* séduire, corrompre, suborner.

bribery *n.* subornation *f.,* séduction *f.,* corruption *f.*

brick *n.* brique *f.* **~ yard,** briqueterie *f.* *v.t.* bâtir ou paver en briques, briqueter.

bridal *adj.* nuptial, de mariage, de noce.

bride *n.* jeune mariée *f.,* la mariée *f.*

bridegroom *n.* nouveau marié *m.,* le marié; fiancé *m.,* futur *m.*

bridesmaid *n.* demoiselle *f.* d'honneur.

bridge *n.* pont *m.;* chevalet *m.* (of string instruments); dos *m.* (of nose). **draw~,** pont-levis *m.* **foot~,** passerelle *f.* **suspension ~,** pont suspendu. *v.t.* construire un pont; jeter, établir un pont.

bridle *n.* bride *f.;* frein *m.* **~** *v.t.* brider, mettre une bride, un frein; *Fig.* contenir, maîtriser. *v.i.* porter la tête haute; se redresser, se rengorger.

brief *adj.* bref, brève, court. *n.* abrégé *m.,* épitomé *m.,* extrait *m.,* précis *m.;* dossier *m.* **~case** *n.* serviette *f.,* porte documents *m.*

briefing *n.* instructions *f.pl.,* briefing *m.*

briefly *adv.* brièvement.

briefs *n.pl.* slip *m.*

brier *n.* ronces *f.pl.,* broussailles *f.pl.*

bright *adj.* brillant, éclatant, clair, magnifique; vif, animé; intelligent *m.* **to make ~,** rendre luisant, polir. **~ color,** couleur vive. **~ eyes,** des yeux étincelants. **~ with joy,** rayonnant de joie.

brighten *v.t.* rendre brillant, éclatant; polir; arriver; éclaircir, dissiper. **to ~ up,** répandre un vif éclat sur; éclaircir. *v.i.* briller, devenir brillant; s'éclaircir; s'animer.

brightly *adv.* brillamment, avec éclat.

brightness *n.* éclat *m.,* vivacité *f.,* subtilité d'esprit.

brilliance *n.* splendeur *f.,* vif éclat *m.,* magnificence *f.*

brilliant *adj.* brillant, rayonnant; splendide, éclatant.

brilliantly *adv.* brillamment, magnifiquement, avec éclat.

brim *n.* bord *m.* **~** *v.t.,v.i.* remplir jusqu'au bord.

brimful *adj.* plein, rempli, jusqu'au bord.

brimstone *n.* soufre *m.*

brine *n.* saumure *f.* *v.t.* saler; mettre, tremper dans la saumure.

bring *v.t.* apporter; amener; mener; transporter; porter, occasionner, produire. **~ him with you,** amenez le avec vous. **~ your books,** apportez vos livres. **I could not ~ myself to do it,** je ne pouvais m'y résoudre. **to ~ to light,** mettre à jour. **to ~ to bed,** emmener (quelqu'un) se coucher. **to ~ about,** amener; accomplir. **to ~ away,** emmener, emporter. **to ~ back,** ramener, rapporter. **to ~ down,** descendre, abbatre; humilier; faire descendre. **to ~ forth,** faire sortir; mettre au monde; mettre bas; produire. **to ~ forward,** faire avancer; reporter (to the next page); mettre en avant (a proposition). **to ~ in,** introduire; produire. **to ~ off,** ramener, sauver, tirer d'affaire. **to ~ on,** amener, causer; occasionner. **to ~ out,** sortir; faire sortir; faire connaître, publier; faire paraître. **to ~ together,** mettre en rapport, réconcilier, raccomoder; rassembler. **to ~ under,** soumettre, assujettir. **to ~ up,** monter, faire monter; servir, introduire; élever (children) former. **~ him away,** emmenez-le. **to ~ forth fruit,** produire des fruits. **~ forward your witnesses,** produisez vos témoins. **how much did the estate ~ him in yearly?** combien cette propriété lui rapportait-elle par an? **~ the young man upstairs,** faites monter le jeune homme.

brink n. bord m., bordure f., extrémité f., marge f.

brisk adj. vif, alerte, éveillé, agile, piquant.

brisket n. poitrine f. (of an animal), poitrail m. (of a horse).

bristle n. soie f. (of pork). v.t. hérisser ses poils, ses plumes. v.i. se hérisser; se fâcher.

bristly adj. velu, épineux, rude.

brittle adj. fragile, cassant.

broach n. broche f. (roast). v.t. mettre à la broche, embrocher; Fig. **to ~ the subject,** aborder un sujet.

broad adj. large; vaste; prononcé. **in ~ daylight,** en plein jour, au grand jour.

broadcast v.t. diffuser, émettre. adj. diffusé, télévisé. n. diffusion f., émission f.

broadcasting n. (radio) diffusion f.

broaden v.t. élargir, étendre en largeur.

broadly adv. largement, d'une manière large; franchement.

broadside n. bordée f., bord m., flanc m.

broccoli n. brocoli m.

brochure n. prospectus m., brochure f.

broil v.t. griller, rôtir.

broiler n. gril m.

broke adj. Infml. fauché. **I'm ~,** je suis fauché(e), je n'ai pas un radis.

broken adj. cassé, brisé, rompu; courbé, abattu, entrecoupé, interrompu. **~ sleep,** sommeil interrompu. **to speak ~ English,** baragouiner l'anglais. **~-hearted,** au coeur brisé, désolé, désespéré.

broker n. agent (immobilier, finance) m., courtier m.

brokerage n. courtage m.

bronchitis n. bronchite f.

bronze n. bronze m. v.t. bronzer.

brooch n. broche f.

brood v.i. couver; se couver, se préparer en secret. **there is something ~ing,** il se couve quelque chose. v.t. couver; soigner, chérir; nourrir. n. couvée f., race f., progéniture f., lignée f.

brook n. ruisseau m. ~ v.t. mâcher, digérer; Fig. souffrir, endurer, tolérer.

broom n. genêt m. (shrub); balai m. (for sweeping).

broomstick n. manche m. à balai.

broth n. bouillon m.

brothel n. bordel m.

brother n. frère m.

brotherhood n. fraternité f.

brother-in-law n. beau-frère m.

brotherly adj. fraternel; affectueux. adv. fraternellement, en frère.

brought. See BRING.

brouhaha n. brouhaha m.

brow n. sourcil m.; front m..

browbeat v.t. intimider; imposer; déconcerter.

brown adj. brun; sobre, rembruni. n. brun m. v.t. brunir, Culin. rissoler.

brownie n. gâteau m. au chocolat et aux noix.

brownish adj. brunâtre.

browse n. brout m. ~ v.t., v.i. regarder sans but précis, bouquiner. **she always goes to ~ through the mall,** elle va toujours au centre commercial pour regarder.

bruise n. contusion f., meurtrissure f. v.t. contusionner, meurtrir, écraser.

brunch n. brunch m.

brunette n. brune f., brunette f.

brunt n. choc m.; coup m.; force f., violence f. d'un choc, attaque f. soudaine, assaut m.

brush n. brosse f.; pinceau m., balai m.; coup m. de balai, de pinceau; escarmouche f.; broussailles f.pl. **~wood,** taillis m., broussailles f.pl. ~ v.t. brosser; effleurer, raser. v.i. passer rapidement. **to ~ over,** effleurer, passer légèrement sur.

brusque adj. brusque.

brutal adj. brutal.

brutality n. brutalité f.

brutalize v.t. abrutir. v.i. s'abrutir.

brutally adv. brutalement, cruellement, grossièrement.

brute adj. insensible; inconscient, irrationnel; bestial; brutal; grossier. n. Fig. **you ~!** espèce d'animal!

bubble n. bulle f. Med. ampoule f., boursoufflement m. ~ v.i. bouillonner; murmurer (a stream).

bubbly adj. pétillant, écumant, bouillonnant.

buck n. daim m.; chevreuil m., Infml. dollar m. **that cost ten ~s!** ça a coûté dix dollars!

bucket n. sceau m.

buckle n. boucle f. ~ v.t. boucler. **to ~ up,** attacher (sa ceinture de sécurité); confiner. v.i. se boucler; s'incliner. **to ~ down to,** se mettre à, s'appliquer à. **to ~ under,** se résigner.

bud n. bourgeon m., bouton m., germe m.; Infml. pote m.t. écussonner, greffer à, en écusson. v.i. bourgeonner, s'épanouir, fleurir.

Buddha n.pr. Bouddha m.

buddhism n. bouddhisme m.

budding n. greffe f. en écusson. **~-knife,** ecussonnoir m.

buddy n. pote m.f., copain m., copine f.

budge v.i. bouger, remuer.

budget *n.* budget *m.*

buff *n.* buffle *m.;* peau *f.* de buffle; couleur chamois, jaune-clair. **he is a film ~,** c'est un cinéphile. *adj.* couleur de peau de buffle, chamois.

buffalo *n.* bison *m.*

buffet *n.* buffet *m.;* coup *m.* de poing; claque *f.* ~ *v.t.* battre; lutter contre.

buffoon *n.* bouffon *m.*

bug *n.* insecte *m.,* punaise *f.,* virus *m.;* défaut *m.;* micro *m.* clandestin; (computer) bogue *f.* ~ *v.t.* installer des micros en cachette dans, mettre sur table d'écoute; embêter, ennuyer, casser les pieds.

build *v.t.* bâtir, construire, édifier, élever, fonder. **he ~s castles in the air,** il fait des châteaux en Espagne.

builder *n.* constructeur *m.,* entrepreneur *m.*

building *n.* construction *f.;* bâtiment *m.,* édifice *m.;* art de construire.

bulb *n.* bulbe *m.,* oignon *m.* (of tulip, etc); ampoule *f.,* lampe *f. Bot.* bulbe *f.* ~ *v.i.* (with out) out) bomber, s'arrondir, être protubérant.

bulge *n.* bosse *f.,* protubérance *f.,* ventre *m.* ~ *v.i.* bomber.

bulimia *n.* boulimie *f.*

bulk *n.* volume *m.,* masse *f.;* grosseur *f.,* majorité *f.,* en gros *m.,* en vrac *m.*

bulkiness *n.* grosseur *f.,* volume *m.;* corpulence *f.*

bulky *adj.* volumineux, massif, gros.

bull *n.* taureau *m.;* (Stock Exchange) haussier *m.,* joueur à la hausse. **~dog,** bouledogue *m.,* dogue *m.* **~fight,** combat de taureaux. *Infml.* **he talks a lot of ~,** il raconte des conneries *f.pl.* **~'s-eye,** oeil-de-boeuf *m.;* centre *m.* d'une cible. **to hit the ~,** tirer dans le mille, faire mouche.

bulldozer *n.* bulldozer *m.*

bullet *n.* balle *f.* **~proof,** *n.* pareballe *inv.*

bulletin *n.* bulletin *m.,* communiqué *m.*

bullion *n.* argent *m.,* en lingots, en barres.

bullock *n.* boeuf *m.*

bully *n.* brute *f.,* tyran *m.* ~ *v.t.* intimider, être une brute.

bulrush *n.* jonc *m.*

bulwark *n.* boulevard *m.,* rempart *m.* ~ *v.t.* bastionner, entourer de remparts; protéger par des fortifications.

bum *n.* clochard *m.,* vagabond *m.,* bon à rien *m.;* derrière *m.* ~ *v.i.* faire du bruit, bourdonner.

bumblebee *n.* bourdon *m.*

bump *n.* bosse *f.,* enflure *f.,* protubérance *f.;* coup *m.,* violent. *v.t.* cogner. **I'll tell him if I ~ into him,** je le lui dirai si je le vois.

bumper *n.* pare-chocs *m.inv.*

bumpkin *n.* péquenot *m.,* rustre *m.*

bumptious *adj.* arrogant, dominant.

bun *n.* brioche *f.,* petit pain *m.;* chignon *m.*

bunch *n.* poignée *n.f.;* botte *f.* (of radishes, etc.); bouquet (of flowers); grappe *f.* (of grappes); trousseau *m.* (of keys). *v.t.* mettre, assembler, lier par botte, etc.

bundle *n.* paquet *m.,* botte *f.,* bouquet *m.,* poi-

gnée *f.;* liasse *f.* (of papers). *v.t.* lier, empaqueter; boteler. *v.i.* faire ses paquets. **to ~ up,** (s')emmitoufler.

bungalow *n.* bungalow *m.*

bungle *v.t.* gâter, massacrer (un ouvrage). *v.i.* bousiller, faire tout de travers.

bungler *n.* une personne maladroite.

bunion *n.* oignon *m.*

bunk *n.* couchette *f.,* logement *m.*

bunker *n.* grand coffre *m.,* soute *f.*

bunny *n.* Jeannot *m.* lapin.

buoy *n.* balise *f.* flottante; bouée *f.* **to ~ up,** flotter, surnager.

buoyancy *n.* flottabilité *f.,* vivacité *f.,* élan *m.,* ressort *m.*

buoyant *adj.* flottant, surnageant; élastique; léger sur l'eau.

burden *n.* charge *f.,* fardeau *m.,* contenance *f.,* capacité *f.,* tonnage *m.* **a beast of ~,** une bête de somme. *v.t.* charger, surcharger; fatiguer, accabler.

burdensome *adj.* onéreux; lourd, pesant, encombrant, fatigant; oppressif.

bureau *n.* bureau *m.;* commode *f.,* armoire *f.;* service *m.*

bureaucracy *n.* bureaucratie *f.*

bureaucratic *adj.* bureaucratique.

burgeon *v.t.* bourgeonner; *n.* bourgeon *m.*

burglar *n.* cambrioleur *m.*

burglary *n.* cambriolage *m.*

burial *n.* inhumation *f.,* enterrement *m.* **~ ground, ~ place,** lieu *m.* de sépulture, cimetière *m.* **~ service,** office *m.* des morts, service *m.* funèbre.

burlesque *adj., n.* burlesque *m.* ~ *v.t.* tourner en ridicule; travestir, rendre comique.

burly *adj.* grand de taille, robuste, bourru.

burn *v.t.* brûler; cuire, se consumer, flamber, cautériser. **to ~ down,** brûler de fond en comble. **to ~ up,** consumer entièrement. *v.i.* **to ~ with impatience,** brûler d'impatience. **to ~ out,** s'éteindre, *Fig.* saturer. *n.* brûlure *f.;* cuite *f.*

burner *n.* brûleur *m.;* incendiaire *m.;* bec *m.* (lamp).

burning *n.* brûlure *f.;* feu *m.,* flamme *f.;* embrasement *m.,* combustion *f.; Fig.* ardeur *f.* **there is a smell of ~ here,** ça sent le brûlé ici. **a ~ question,** question *f.* brûlante. *adj.* brûlant; en feu; ardent; très chaud.

burnish *v.t.* brunir, polir. *v.i.* se polir; devenir luisant. *n.* brunissure *f.,* éclat *m.,* lustre *m.*

burnt *adj.* brûlé, consumé.

burp *v.i.,v.t.* roter. *n.* rot *m.*

burrow *n.* clapier *m.,* terrier *m.* ~ *v.i.* creuser, pratiquer un trou en terre.

bursar *n.* boursier *m.,* économe *m.*

burst *n.* crever, éclater, se briser; rompre; ouvrir, s'ouvrir. **to ~ with laughing,** crever de rire. **to ~ asunder,** se fendre en deux. **to ~ into tears,** fondre en larmes. **to ~ forth,** s'élancer. **to ~**

through, percer, passer à travers. **to ~ open,** enfoncer. *n.* rupture *f.* soudaine; éclat *m.*, explosion *f.*

bury *v.t.* inhumer, enterrer.

bus *n.* bus *m.*, autobus *m.* **~boy** *n.*, aide-serveur *m.* **~ driver** *n.*, chauffeur *m.*, conducteur *m.* d'autobus. **~ load** *n.*, autobus plein. **~ station** *n.*, station *f.* d'autobus. **~ stop** *n.* arrêt *m.* de bus.

bush *n.* arbuste *m.*, arbrisseau *m.*; touffe *f.*, buisson *m.*; fourré *m.*, taillis *m.* **to beat about the ~,** tourner autour du pot.

bushed *adj. Infml.* claqué. **I'm ~,** je n'en peux plus.

bushy *adj.* broussailleux, épais et touffu, fourré.

busily *adv.* activement, d'une manière affairée.

business *n.* occupation *f.*; commerce *m.*, profession *f.*; affairs *f.pl.*; fonds *m.* de commerce. **he is a ~ man,** c'est un homme d'affaires. **this is none of your ~,** ça ne te regarde pas, ce ne sont pas tes affaires. **his line of ~,** sa partie, son genre d'affairs. **in ~,** dans les affaires. **on ~,** pour affairs. **to go into ~,** s'établir, entrer dans le commerce. **to retire from ~,** se retirer des affaires. **go about your ~,** allez vous promener, allez à vos affaires. **to mean ~,** ne pas plaisanter. **~ suit** *n.*, complet *m.* veston, tailleur (for women) *m.*

businesslike *adj.* propre aux affaires.

bust *n.* buste *m.* **~** *v.t.*,*v.i. Infml.* esquinter, casser, péter. *n.* raid *m. Infml.* **he got ~ed by the cops,** il s'est fait arrêter, prendre par les flics.

bustle *v.i.* se hâter, se presser. **to ~ through the crowd,** faire des efforts pour percer la foule. *n.* hâte *f.*, presse *f.*, tumulte *f.*

bustling *adj.* actif, affairé, remuant; animé, tumultueux. **what ~ people they are?** quelles gens affairés!

busty *adj.* à la poitrine généreuse.

busy *adj.* occupé, actif, remuant. **to be ~,** être occupé. *v.t.* occuper, employer, tenir actif.

but *conj.*, *adv.* mais; ne … que … ; seulement; excepté, si ce n'est, sinon; sans que. **I went to see him,** — **he was not at home,** je suis allé le voir, mais il n'était pas chez lui. **he does nothing ~ play,** il ne fait que jouer. **all this is nothing ~ gossip,** ce ne sont que des commérages. **who can it be ~ him?** qui sera-ce, sinon lui? **~ for his health,** sans sa santé, si ce n'était sa santé.

butane *n.* butane *m.*

butch *n. Infml.* gouine *f.* (lesbian). *adj.* (man and woman) très masculin.

butcher *n.* boucher *m.* **~ meat,** viande *f.* de

boucherie. ~'s shop, boucherie *f.* **~** *v.t.* égorger, massacrer.

butchery *n.* boucherie *f.*; *Fig.* carnage *m.*; massacre *m.*; tuerie *f.*

butler *n.* maître *m.* d'hôtel, majordome *m.*

butt *n.* fin *f.*; but *m.*; cible *f.*, butte *f.*; mégot *m.*, arrière-train *m.*, derrière *m. Infml.* **to ~ in,** *Infml.* s'incruster, mettre son grain de sel, se mêler de, coup *m.* de tête; tonneau *m.*, tête *f.* de bordage. **~ end,** gros bout, crosse *f.* (of rifle). *v.i.* cesser; frapper de la tête.

butter *n.* beurre *m.* **~cup,** bouton d'or *m.* **~ pot, ~ dish, ~ boat,** beurrier *m.* **~** *v.t.* beurrer; augmenter les enjeux. **~ bean** *n.*, haricot beurre. **~scotch** *n.*, caramel *m.* au beurre. **to ~ up someone,** passer de la pommade à quelqu'un.

butterfly *n.* papillon *m.*

buttock *n.* derrière *m.*, fesse *f.*; croupe (horse) cimier *m.*, culotte *f.* (beef).

button *n.* bouton *m.* **~~hole,** boutonnière *f.* **~** *v.t.* boutonner. **to ~ up,** boutonner.

buttress *n.* arc-boutant *m.* **~** *v.t.* soutenir, arc-bouter.

buxom *adj.* aux formes généreuses.

buy *v.t.* acheter. **to ~ cash,** acheter au comptant. **to ~ and sell,** acheter et vendre. **to ~ back,** racheter. **to ~ out,** racheter (rights). **to ~ off,** racheter. **to ~ up,** accaparer.

buyer *n.* acheteur *m.* acheteuse *f.*

buzz *n.* bourdonnement *m.* **~** *v.i.* bourdonner; chuchoter, murmurer. **to give a ~,** passer un coup de fil. *Infml.* **to ~ off,** se casser, se tailler, se barrer.

buzzard *n.* buse *f.*, busard *m.*

buzzer *n.* sonnerie *f.*

by *prep.* par; de; à; dans, en; près de, auprès de; devant; chez; à côté de; par. **~ luck,** par chance. **~ degrees,** petit à petit. **he is loved ~ everyone,** il est aimé de tout le monde. **~ far,** de beaucoup. **~pass** *n.*, déviation *m.*, contournement *m.* **~product** *n.*, produit dérivé de *m.* **to sell ~ the pound,** vendre à la livre. **they pay ~ the month,** ils payent au mois. **it is one ~ my watch,** il est une heure à ma montre. **one ~ one,** un à un. **~ no means,** en aucune manière. **close ~ here,** tout près d'ici. **he goes ~ that name,** il est connu sous ce nom. *adv.* près; à côté; en passant; en présence.

bye *n.* **~ the ~,** en passant, par parenthèse; à propos.

bye *excl.* salut!, au revoir! See GOODBYE.

bygone *adj.* passé, écoulé. chose *f.* passée, temps *m.* passé.

bystander *n.* spectateur *m.* spectatrice *f.*

C

C *n. Mus.* ut *m.*, do *m.*

cab *n.* taxi.

cabal *n.* cabale *f.*; intrigue *f.*

cabaret *n.* cabaret *m.*

cabbage *n.* chou *m.* **~ head,** pomme *f.* de chou.

cabby *n.* chauffeur *m.* de taxi.

cabin *n.* cabine *f.*; chaumière *f.*, hutte *f.* ~ **boy,** mousse *m.*

cabinet *n.* meuble *m.* à tiroirs, coffret *m.* filing ~, classeur *m.*, fichier *m.* **bathroom** ~, armoire *f.* à pharmacie. *Pol.* cabinet *m.*, ministère *m.* **to form a** ~, former un ministère, cabinet *m.* ~**maker,** ébéniste *m.* ~**making, ~work,** ébénisterie.

cable *n.* câble *m.*, encâblure *f.* ~ **car,** funiculaire *m.* ~ **television,** (télévision *f.* par) câble.

caboose *n.* fourgon *m.*

cache *n.* cache *f.*; cachette *f.*

cackle *v.i.* glousser, caqueter; ricaner. *n.* caquet *m.*

cacophony *n.* cacophonie *f.*

cactus *n.* cactus *m.*

cadaver *n.* cadavre *m.*

cadaverous *adj.* cadavéreux, cadavérique.

cadence *n.* cadence *f.*

cadet *n.* cadet *m.f.*; élève *m.*, officier *m.*, femme officier *f.*

cadge *v.t.* porter un fardeau. *v.i.* mendier, mener une vie vagabonde.

cadger *n.* mendiant *m.* mendiante *f.*

Caesarean *adj.* césarienne *f.*

café *n.* café *m.*, café-restaurant *m.*

caféteria *n.* cafétéria *f.*

caffein(e) *n.* caféine *f.* ~**free** *adj.* décaféiné.

cage *n.* cage *f.* *v.t.* mettre en cage; emprisonner.

cahoots *n.* *Infml.* complicité *f.*, de mèche (avec).

caiman *n.* caïman *m.*

cairn *n.* cairn *m.* (of stones).

cajole *v.t.* cajoler, enjôler, amadouer.

cajolery *n.* flatterie *f.*, cajolerie *f.*

cake *n.* gâteau *m.*; pâtisserie *f.* **that takes the** ~, ça, c'est le comble. *v.t.* former en gâteau; coaguler. *v.i.* se cailler, se coaguler; former une croûte.

calabash *n.* calebasse *f.*

calamary *n.* calmar *m.*

calamitous *adj.* calamiteux.

calamity *n.* calamité *f.*, malheur *m.*, désastre *m.*, ruine *f.*

calcareous *adj.* calcaire.

calcification *n.* calcification *f.*

calcify *n.a.* calcifier, *v.i.* se calcifier.

calcination *n.* calcination *f.*

calcine *v.i.* se calciner.

calcium *n.* calcium *m.*

calculable *adj.* calculable.

calculate *v.t.* calculer.

calculaton *n.* calcul *m.*; compte *m.*

calculator *n.* calculatrice *f.*

calculus *n.* calcul *m.*

calendar *n.* calendrier *m.*

calf *n. pl.* calves veau *m.* **golden** ~, veau d'or. mollet *m.*

caliber *n.* calibre *m.*

calibrate *v.t.* calibrer

caulking *n.* calque *m.*

call *v.t.* appeler, nommer; invoquer; faire venir; réunir I ~ed in the physician, j'ai fait venir le médecin. **to** ~ **one** names, dire des injures à quelqu'un. **to** ~ **again,** rappeler, faire revenir. **to** ~ **back,** révoquer, rétracter. **to** ~ **down,** faire descendre. **to** ~ **for,** appeler, demander, faire venir. **to** ~ **off,** annuler, stopper, arrêter. **to** ~ **on,** sommer, encourager; passer chez quelqu'un. **to** ~ **out,** faire sortir, faire venir. **to** ~ **together,** assembler, convoquer. **to** ~ **up,** appeler. *v.i.* passer. **to** ~ **after,** crier après. **to** ~ **for,** demander, réclamer. **to** ~ **on, in, upon,** passer chez quelqu'un. *n.* appel *m.*, invitation *f.*; demande *f.* **within** ~, à portée de la voix. ~ **girl** *n.*, call-girl *f.*

calligraphy *n.* calligraphie *f.*

calling *n.* appel *m.*, métier *m.*, profession *f.*, vocation *f.* ~ **card,** carte *f.* de téléphone.

callosity *n.* callosité *f.*, calus *m.*, durillon *m.*

callous *adj.* calleux, dur; endurci, insensible, opiniâtre.

callow *adj.* sans plumes, blanc-bec.

callus *n.* durillon *m.*, cal *m.*

calm *adj.* calme, tranquille. **to grow** ~, se calmer. *n.* calme *m.*, quiétude *f.* ~ *v.t.* calmer, apaiser, tranquilliser. ~ **down!** relax! calme-toi! **to** ~ **down,** s'apaiser, se calmer.

calming *ppr.* calmant, apaisant, tranquillisant.

calmly *adv.* tranquillement, avec calme.

calmness *n.* calme *m.*, repos *m.*, tranquillité *f.*

caloric *n.* calorique *m.*

calorie *n.* calorie *f.*

calorific *adj.* calorifique.

calumniate *v.t.* calomnier.

calumny *n.* calomnie *f.*

Calvary *n.* calvaire *m.*

Calvinism *n.* calvinisme *m.*

camber *n.* cambrure *f.*

camel *n.* chameau *m.* **she** ~, chamelle. ~**backed,** bossu; à dos de chameau. ~ **hair,** poil *m.* de chameau.

camellia *n.* camélia *m.*

cameo *n.* camée.

camera *n.* appareil-photo *m.* **in** ~, à huis clos.

camera-obscura *n.* chambre *f.* noire.

camomile *n.* camomille *f.*

camouflage *n.* camouflage *m.*; *v.t.* camoufler.

camp *n.* camp *m.* **to pitch a** ~, asseoir un camp. **to break up a** ~, lever un camp. ~**bed,** lit *m.* de camp. ~**stool,** pliant *m.* ~**fire,** feu *m.* de camp. **summer** ~ *n.*, colonie *f.* de vacances. ~**site,** *n.*, terrain *m.* de camping. **concentration** ~, camp de concentration. *v.i., v.t.* camper.

campaign *n.* campagne *f.* ~ *v.i.* faire campagne.

camper *n.* campeur *m.*, campeuse *f.*

camphor *n.* camphre *m.*

camping *n.* campement *m.*, camping *m.*

campus *n.* campus *m.*, ensemble *m.* universitaire.

can *v.i.* I can, je peux. **he** ~ **read and write,** il sait lire et écrire. **as soon as you** ~, aussitôt que vous pourrez. I ~**not help laughing,** je ne peux m'empêcher de rire. *v.t.* mettre, conserver (in cans). **~ned meat,** viande de conserve. *n.* bidon *m.;* boîte *f.* **oil~~,** burette *f.*

Canada *npr.* Canada *m.*

Canadian *adj.* canadien. *n.* Canadien *m.,* Canadienne *f.*

canal *n.* canal *m.*

canalization *n.* canalisation *f.*

canary canari *m.,* serin *m.* **~ seed,** millet *m.*

cancel *v.t.* annuler, décommander, effacer; résilier. *v.i.* devenir nul, s'effacer.

cancellation *n.* résiliation *f.,* annulation *f.*

cancer *n.* le Cancer *m.;* cancer *m.* **~ research,** cancérologie *f.*

cancerous *adj.* cancéreux.

candid *adj.* candide, ingénu; sincère.

candidacy *n.* candidature *f.*

candidate *n.* candidat *m.,* aspirant *m.*

candidly *adv.* candidement, franchement, ingénument, sans détours.

candidness *n.* candeur *f.,* ingénuité *f.,* franchise *f.;* loyauté *f.*

candle *n.* chandelle *f.,* bougie *f.* **~~light,** lumière *f.* d'une chandelle.

candlemass *n.* la chandeleur *f.*

candlestick *n.* chandelier *m.*

candor *n.* candeur *f.,* ingénuité *f.;* sincérité *f.,* franchise *f.*

candy *v.t.* faire candir, confire; cristalliser. *n.* bonbon *m.* **~ store** *n.,* confiserie *f.*

cane *n.* canne *f.,* jonc *m.* **sugar~** *n.* cane *f.* à sucre. *v.t.* donner des coups de canne, bâtonner; canner. **to ~ a chair,** canner une chaise.

canine *adj.* canin; *n.* canine *f.* (tooth).

caning *n.* volée *f.* de coups de canne, de trique *f.;* canage *m.* (of chairs).

canister *n.* boîte *f.* en fer-blanc.

canker *n.* chancre *m.;* ver *m.* rongeur. **~worm,** chenille *f.,* ver rongeur.

cankerous *adj.* chancreux.

cannabis *n.* chanvre *m.,* marijuana *f.,* hachisch *m.*

cannibal *n.* cannibale *m.,* anthropophage *m.* *adj.* de cannibale.

cannibalism *n.* cannibalisme *m.*

cannon *n.* canon *m.* **~ball,** boulet *m.* de canon. **~shot,** boulet *m.* de canon; portée *f.* de canon.

cannonade *n.* canonnade *f.* **~** *v.t.,v.i.* canonner.

cannot See CAN.

canny *adj.* avisé, prudent.

canoe *n.* pirogue *f.;* canoë *m.,* kayac *m.* **~** *v.i.* faire du canoë.

canon *n.* canon *m.;* règle *f.* (doctrine); chanoine *m.* **~ law,** droit *m.* canon.

canonical *adj.* canonique; canonial.

canopy *n.* baldaquin *m.;* voûte *f.*

cant *n.* hypocrisie *f.,* jargon *m.,* argot *m.* Mus. encan *m.,* enchère *f.* **~** *v.i.* psalmodier; parler avec hypocrisie. *v.t.* enchérir; incliner, obliquer; chavirer; lancer, pousser.

cantaloupe *n.* cantaloup *m.*

cantakerous *adj.* taquin, méchant, querelleur.

canteen *n.* bidon *m.;* cantine *f.*

canter *v.t.* aller au petit galop. *n.* petit galop *m.*

canticle *n.* cantique *m.*

cantor *n.* Rel. cantor *m.,* chantre *m.*

canvas *n.* canvas *m.;* toile *f.*

canvass *v.i., v.t.* faire une campagne *f.* électorale, solliciter (votes); faire du démarchage *m.;* examiner soigneusement, discuter, débattre.

canvasser *n.* soliciteur *m.,* sollituese *f.,* agent *m.* électoral.

canyon *n.* cañon *m.,* canyon *m.*

cap *n.* bonnet *m.,* toque *f.,* casquette *f.;* barrette *f.* (of a cardinal); capuchon *m.; Mil.* capsule *f.* **~** *v.t.* coiffer, couronner, surmonter; décoiffer.

capability *n.* capacité *f.*

capable *adj.* capable; susceptible de; habile, intelligent.

capableness *n.* capacité *f.*

capably *adv.* avec compétence.

capacious *adj.* spacieux, étendu, vaste.

capacity *n.* capacité *f.* **to have ~ to act,** avoir qualité *f.* pour agir. qualité *f.*

cape *n.* cap *m.*

caper *v.i.* bondir, sauter, cabrioler, gambader. *n.* saut *m.,* bond *m.,* cabriole *f.,* gambade *f.;* câpre *f.*

capillary *adj.* capillaire *n.* les capillaires *f.pl.*

capital *adj.* capital; grand; excellent. **~ punishment,** peine *f.* de mort. *n.* capitale *f.* (of city); essentiel *m.,* primordial *m.,* capital *m.,* fonds *f.* **in ~ letters,** en lettres majuscules *f.*

capitalist *n.* capitaliste *m.*

capitalize *v.t.* capitaliser; tirer profit de; imprimer en lettres capitales; tracer des lettres capitales, des majuscules.

capitulate *v.i.* capituler. *v.t.* rendre sous condition.

capitulation *n.* capitulation *f.*

caprice *n.* caprice *m.*

capricious *adj.* capricieux.

capriciously *adv.* capricieusement.

Capricorn *n.* Capricorne *m.*

capsicum *n.* piment *m.*

capsize *v.t.* chavirer, renverser.

capstan *n.* cabestan *m.*

capsule *n.* capsule *f.*

captain *n.* capitaine *m.*

captaincy *n.* grade *m.* de capitaine; capitainerie *f.*

caption *n.* sour-titre; prise *f.* de corps.

captious *adj.* captieux; insidieux; disposé à critiquer.

captivate *v.t.* captiver, séduire, charmer.

captivating *adj.* captivant.

captive *n.* captif *m.,* captive *f.* **~** *adj.* captif.

captivity *n.* captivité *f.;* servitude *f.*

capture *n.* capture *f.;* saisie *f.* butin *m.,* prise *f.* **~** *v.t.* capturer.

car *n.* voiture *f.;* wagon *m.* **~ pool** *n.,* entente entre plusieurs conducteurs d'utiliser leur voiture à tour de rôle pour aller au travail. **dining ~,**

wagon *m.* restaurant. **sleeping ~,** wagon-lit *m.*

carafe *n.* carafe *f.,* carafon *m.*

caramel *n.* caramel *m.*

carapace *n.* carapace *f.*

carat *n.* carat *m.*

caravan *n.* caravane *f.*

caraway *n.* cumin *m.*

carbon *n.* carbone *m.*

carbonate *n.* carbonate *m.*

carbonic *adj.* carbonique.

carbonize *v.t.* carboniser.

carcass *n.* carcasse *f.;* charpente *f.*

card *n.* carte *f.* **playing ~s,** cartes à jouer. **business ~,** carte de visite. **~ table,** table *f.* de jeu. *v.t.* carder.

cardboard *n.* carton *m.*

cardiac *adj.* cardiaque.

cardinal *adj.* cardinal.

cardiogram *n.* cardiogramme *m.*

cardiology *n.* cardiologie *f.*

care *n.* souci *m.,* sollicitude *f.,* anxiété *f.,* soins *m.pl.;* soin *m.* **take ~,** faites attention. **to take ~ of a thing,** prendre soin d'une chose. **~taker,** surveillant *m.;* gardien *m.,* gardienne *f.* ~ *v.i.* se soucier, s'inquiéter. **he ~s for me,** il s'inquiète pour moi, il tient à moi.

career *n.* course *f.;* carrière *f.,* profession *f.* ~ *v.i.* se mouvoir, courir rapidement.

careful *adj.* soucieux, inquiétant; soigneux, attentif. **be ~!** attention! sois sage!

carefully *adv.* attentivement; avec prudence.

carefulness *n.* prudence *f.*

careless *adj.* négligent, indifférent; inconsidéré.

carelessly *adv.* négligemment, sans soin, sans souci.

carelessness *n.* négligence *f.,* inattention *f.*

caress *v.t.* caresser. *n.* caresse *f.*

caressingly *adv.* d'une manière caressante.

cargo *n.* cargaison *f.;* chargement *m.*

caribou *n.* caribou *m.*

caricature *n.* caricature *f.* ~ *v.t.* caricaturer.

caricaturist *n.* caricaturiste *m.*

caries *n.* carie *f.*

carnage *n.* carnage *m.*

carnal *adj.* charnel, sensuel.

carnation *n.* incarnat *m.,* oeillet *m.*

carnival *n.* carnaval *m.*

carnivorous *adj.* carnivore.

carob, carob bean *n.* caroube *m.,* carouge *m.*

carol *n.* chant *m.;* cantique *m.;* gazouillement *m.* (birds). **Christmas ~,** chant de Noël *m.* ~ *v.i.* chanter, fredonner. *v.t.* célébrer en vers.

carotid *adj., n.* carotide.

carouse *v.i.* boire copieusement. *v.t.* boire avidement.

carousel *n.* manège *m.*

carp *v.i.* critiquer. **to ~ at,** critiquer. *n.* carpe *f.* **young ~,** carpeau *m.*

carpenter *n.* charpentier *m.,* menuisier *m.*

carpentry *n.* charpenterie *f.,* menuiserie *f.*

carpet *n.* tapis *m.* ~ *v.t.* tapisser.

carpeting *n.* moquette *f.*

carping *adj.* médisant, caustique.

carriage *n.* port *m.,* maintien *m.;* transport *m.* **baby ~,** poussette *f.*

carrier *n.* transporteur *m.,* transporteuse *f.,* messager *m.* **~ pigeon,** pigeon-voyageur.

carrion *n.* charogne *f.* ~ *adj.* de charogne.

carrot *n.* carotte *f.*

carry *v.t.* porter; transporter; emporter; conduire; entraîner; faire adopter; reporter. **to ~ a letter to the post office,** porter une lettre à la poste. **to ~ one's head high,** porter la tête haute. **to ~ forward,** reporter. **to ~ into practice,** mettre à exécution. **to ~ the day,** remporter la victoire. **to ~ one's point,** accomplir son dessein. **to ~ away,** enlever, emmener. **to ~ on,** continuer, exercer. **to ~ out,** réaliser, effectuer, accomplir. **to ~ through,** faire triompher, soutenir. **to be carried away with joy,** être transporté de joie.

carrying *n.* transport *m.* **~ trade,** industrie *f.* des transports.

cart *n.* charrette *f.;* tombereau *m.* **hand ~,** charrette à bras. **to put the ~ before the horse,** mettre la charrue devant les boeufs. *v.t.* transporter en charrette.

carte blanche *n.* carte *f.* blanche.

cartel *n.* cartel *m.*

carter *n.* charretier *m.*

cartilage *n.* cartilage *m.*

cartilaginous *adj.* cartilagineux.

cartographer *n.* cartographe *m.*

cartography *n.* cartographie *f.*

carton *n.* carton *m.* d'emballage.

cartoon *n.* dessin *m.* animé; dessin humoristique, bande *f.* dessinée, carton *m.*

cartoonist *n.* dessinateur *m.,* dessinatrice *f.,* caricaturiste *m.f.*

cartridge *n.* cartouche *f.;* gargousse *f.* **~ box,** giberne *f.*

carve *v.t.* découper (meat); sculpter (wood); ciseler. *v.i.* graver.

carver *n.* sculpteur *m.;* graveur *m.*

carving *n.* action *f.* de tailler, de couper; sculpture *f.* **fine oak ~s,** de belles sculptures en chêne. **~ knife,** couteau *m.* à découper.

cascade *n.* cascade *f.*

case *n.* étui *m.* (scissors, glasses, etc.); boîte *f.* (watch); caisse *f.* (packing); trousse *f.;* écrin *m.;* fourreau *m.;* procès *m.,* cause *f.;* cas *m.,* arguments *m.pl.;* Typ. casse *f.* **dressing ~,** nécessaire *m.* de toilette. **glass ~,** vitrine *f.* **book~,** bibliothèque *f.* **pillow~,** taie *f.* d'oreiller. **jewel ~,** boîte à bijoux. **in that ~,** dans ce cas. **the ~ in point,** le case dont il s'agit. **in ~ he should come,** au cas où il viendrait. **in that case,** dans ce cas. **she has built a strong ~ for the defense,** elle a préparé des arguments solides pour la défense. **suit~,** valise *f.* ~ *v.t.* mettre dans un étui; envelopper.

casement *n.* châssis *m.;* croisée *f.,* fenêtre *f.*

cash *n.* numéraire *m.,* espèces *f.pl.,* argent *m.* ~ **account,** compte *m.* de caisse. ~ **book,** livre *m.* de caisse. ~ **and carry** *n.,* paiement *m.* au comptant et (produit *m.*) à emporter. ~ **offer,** offre *m.* d'achat (avec paiement au comptant). *v.t.* toucher, en caisser, convertir en espèces; négocier, escompter un effet.

cashew *n.* anacardier *m.* ~ **nut,** noix *f.* d'acajou.

cashier *n.* caissier *m.,* caissière *f.* ~ *v.t.* casser; renvoyer, congédier.

cashmere *n.* cachemire *m.* ~ *adj.* de cachemire.

casing *n.* étui *m.,* enveloppe *f.*

casino *n.* casino *m.*

cask *n.* baril *m.,* barrique *f.,* tonneau *m.*

casket *n.* cercueil *m.*

cassava *n.* manioc *m.*

casserole *n.* cocotte *f.;* ragoût *m.* ~ *v.t.* faire cuire dans une cocotte.

cassette *n.* cassette *f.* ~ **player,** lecteur *m.* de cassette. ~ **recorder,** magnétophone *m.* à cassettes.

cast *v.t.* jeter; lancer; rejeter, répandre; dépouiller; perdre. **to** ~ **a stone,** jeter une pierre. **to** ~ **anchor,** jeter l'ancre. **to** ~ **lots,** jeter au sort. **to** ~ **a glance at,** jeter un coup d'oeil sur. **to** ~ **a bell,** fondre une cloche. **to** ~ **aside,** mettre de côté. **to** ~ **away,** bannir. **to** ~ **down,** jeter en bas; *Fig.* abattre. **to** ~ **out,** jeter, mettre dehors, chasser. *v.i.* projeter, concevoir; se déjeter. *n.* jet *m.,* coup *m.;* fonte *f.;* teinte *f.,* nuance *f.;* moule *m.,* empreinte *f.;* distribution (theater). ~ **iron,** fonte *f.* ~ **steel,** acier *m.* fondu.

castanet *n.* castagnette *f.*

caste *n.* caste *f.,* rang *m.,* classe *f.* sociale.

castigate *v.t.* châtier, corriger; critiquer sévèrement.

castigation *n.* châtiment *m.,* punition *f.,* correction *f.*

casting *n.* fonte *f.;* moulage *m.;* jet *m.* ~ **vote,** voix *f.* prépondérante. (theater) distribution *f.* (des rôles).

castle *n.* château *m.,* tour *f.* ~ *v.i.* roquer (chess).

castor *n.* castor.

castor oil *n.* huile *f.* de ricin.

castrate *v.t.* châtrer, castrer, emasculer.

castration *n.* castration *f.*

castrato *n.* castrat *m.*

casual *adj.* accidentel, fortuit, par hasard, désinvolte.

casually *adv.* par hasard, par accident, fortuitement; par à-coups, intermittence, irrégulièrement; avec désinvolture.

casualty *n.* accident *m.,* sinistre *m.,* pertes *f.pl.;* mort *f.* ou autre malheur.

cat *n.* chat *m.,* chatte *f.;* félin *m.* ~ **tom~,** matou *m.* **to rain** ~**s and dogs,** tomber des ballebardes. ~**'s eye,** oeil *m.* de chat.

cataclysm *n.* cataclysme *m.*

catacomb *n.* catacombe *f.*

catalog *n.* catalogue *m.* ~ *v.t.* cataloguer.

catamaran *n.* catimaron *m.*

catapult *n.* catapulte *f.*

cataract *n.* cataracte *f.*

catastrophe *n.* catastrophe *f.*

catastrophic *adj.* catastrophique

catch *v.t.* attraper, prendre, saisir, surprendre. **he was caught in the act,** il a été pris sur le fait. **to** ~ **a cold,** s'enrhumer. **to** ~ **hold of,** se saisir de, s'accrocher à. **to** ~ **up,** rattraper. *v.i.* se communiquer; se gagner. *n.* prise *f.,* capture *f.,* saisie *f.,* avantage *m.* **so what's the** ~? alors où est le problème?, quel est le truc? **I'm** ~**ing a cold,** je suis en train d'attraper un rhume. **a** ~**-22 situation,** quoiqu'on fasse, on perd.

catcher *n.* preneur *m.,* attrapeur *m.* (baseball).

catching *adj.* contagieux. *n.* action de saisir, d'attraper.

catchy *adj.* facile à retenir.

catechism *n.* catéchisme *m.*

categorical *adj.* catégorique.

categorically *adv.* catégoriquement.

categorise *v.t.* catégoriser.

category *n.* catégorie *f.;* ordre *m.,* classe *f.,* rang *m.*

cater *v.i.* fournir des aliments; pourvoir à.

caterer *n.* traiteur *m.*

caterwaul *v.i.* miauler (comme les chats).

catharsis *n.* catharsis *f.*

cathartic *adj.* cathartique.

cathedral *n.* cathédrale *f.* ~ *adj.* cathédral.

catholic *adj.* catholique. *n.* catholique *m.*

catholicism *n.* catholicisme *m.*

cattle *n.* bétail *m.,* bestiaux *m.pl.,* bovins *m.pl.* **to breed** ~, élever du bétail. ~ **show,** concours *m.,* exposition *f.* de bétail. ~ **trade,** commerce *m.* de bestiaux.

catty *adj. Infml.* méchant, vache.

Caucasian *adj.* caucasien; de groupe ethnique blanc; *n.,* caucasien *m.,* caucasienne *f.,* blanc *m.,* blanche *f.*

caucus *n.* comité *m.* électoral.

caudal *adj.* caudal.

caught See CATCH.

cauldron *n.* chaudron *m.*

cauliflower *n.* choufleur *m.*

causal *adj.* causal.

causality *n.* causalité *f.*

causation *n.* causation *f.*

causative *adj.* causatif; causant.

cause *n.* cause *f.;* raison *f.,* sujet *m.,* motif *m.* ~ *v.t.* causer; occasionner.

causeway *n.* chaussée *f.*

caustic *adj.* caustique; satirique, piquant. *n.* caustique *m.*

caustically *adv.* d'une manière caustique.

cauterize *v.t.* cautériser.

caution *n.* caution *f.,* garantie *f.;* prudence *f.;* précaution *f.;* avertissement *m.,* avis *m.*

~ *v.t.* précautionner, prémunir, avertir.

cautionary *adj.* d'avertissement, de précaution; remis à titre de garantie.

cautious *adj.* circonspect, prudent.

cautiously *adv.* avec circonspection, avec prudence.

cautiousness *n.* circonspection *f.*, prudence *f.*

cavalcade *n.* cavalcade *f.*

cavalier *n.* cavalier *m.* ~ *adj.* vaillant; cavalier, hautain.

cavalierly *adv.* cavalièrement, avec arrogance.

cavalry *n.* cavalerie *f.*

cave *n.* cave *f.*, grotte *f.*; souterrain *m.*; antre *m.*, caverne *f.*

caveat *n.* avertissement *m.*

cavern *n.* caverne *f.*

cavernous *adj.* caverneux.

caviar *n. Culin.* caviar *m.*

cavil *v.t.* chicaner, contester. *v.i.* ergoter, pointiller.

cavity *n.* cavité *f.*

cavort *v.i. Infml.* faire la rouba.

caw *v.i.* croasser.

cawing *n.* croassement *m.*

cayenne *n.* (poivre de) cayenne *m.*

cayman *n.* caïman *m.*

cease *v.i.* cesser, faire cesser, se désister. *v.t.* mettre fin à. *n.* without ~, sans cesse. ~fire *n.*, cesser le feu.

ceaseless *adj.* incessant, continuel.

cedar *n.* cèdre *m.*

cede *v.t.* céder; transférer, délivrer.

cedilla *n.* cédille *f.*

ceiling *n.* plafonnage *m.*; plafond *m.*

celebrate *v.t.* célébrer; fêter; commémorer.

celebrated *adj.* célèbre.

celebration *n.* festivités *f.pl.*, dîner *m.*, célébration *f.*

celebrity *n.* célébrité *f.*

celerity *n.* célérité *f.*

celery *n.* céleri *m.*

celibacy *n.* célibat *m.*

celibate *n.* celibataire *m.f.*

cell *n.* cellule *f.*; cachot *m.*

cellar *n.* cave *f.*, cellier *m.*

cellist *n.* violoncelliste *m.f.*

cello *n.* violoncelle *m.*

cellular *adj.* cellulaire.

cellulose *adj.* celluleux. *n.* cellulose *f.*

Celsius *adj.* Celsius.

cement *n.* ciment *m.*; mastic *m.* ~ *v.t.* cimenter, mastiquer; unir. *v.i.* se cimenter, adhérer; se réunir.

cementation *n.* cimentation *f.*

cemetery *n.* cimetière *m.*

censor *n.* censeur *m.* ~ *v.t.* censurer.

censorious *adj.* porté à censurer, à critiquer; caustique.

censorship *n.* censure *f.*

censurable *adj.* censurable, blâmable, répréhensible, digne de censure.

censure *n.* censure *f.* ~ *v.i.* censurer, blâmer, condamner.

census *n.* recensement *m.*

cent *n.* cent *m.* ten per ~, dix pour cent.

centenarian *n.* centenaire *m.f.*

centenary *n. adj.* centenaire.

centennial *adj.* centenaire; séculaire. *n.* centaire *m.f.*

center *n.* centre *m.*; milieu *m.*; foyer *m.* ~ of gravity, centre de gravité. *v.t.* centrer, placer au centre; concentrer, rassembler. *v.i.* être placé au centre; se concentrer.

centigrade *adj.* centigrade, à cent degrés.

centigram *n.* centigramme *m.*

centiliter *n.* centilitre *m.*

centimeter *n.* centimètre *m.*

centiped *n.* mille pattes *m.*

central *adj.* central.

centralization *n.* centralisation *f.*

centralize *v.t.* centraliser.

centrifugal *adj.* centrifuge.

century *n.* siècle *m.*

ceramic *adj.* céramique.

cereal *n.* céréale.

cerebellum *n.* cervelet *m.*

cerebral *adj.* cérébral.

cerebrum *n.* cerveau *m.*

ceremonial *adj.* cérémonial; cérémonieux, formaliste. *n.* cérémonial *m.*

ceremonious *adj.* cérémonial, de cérémonie; cérémonieux.

ceremoniously *adv.* cérémonieusement.

ceremony *n.* cérémonie *f.*; façons *f.pl.*

certain *adj.* certain, sur.

certainly *adv.* certainement; volontiers.

certainty *n.* certitude *f.*; assurance *f.*

certifiable *adj.* certifiable.

certificate *n.* certificat *m.*; diplôme *m.*; attestation *f.* par écrit; concordat *m.* birth ~, extrait *m.* de naissance.

certificated *adj.* diplômé.

certification *n.* certification *f.*; certificat *m.*

certified *adj.* certifié, diplômé.

certify *v.t.* certifier; attester par écrit; justifier.

certitude *n.* certitude *f.*

cervical *adj.* cervical.

cervix *n.* col de l'utérus *m.*

cesarean See CAESAREAN.

cessation *n.* cessation *f.*

cession *n.* action *f.* de céder, impulsion; cession *f.*

cesspool *n.* fosse *f.* d'aisances.

cetaceous *adj.* cétacé.

chafe *v.t.* chauffer, echauffer; *Fig.* irriter, froisser. *v.i.* s'irriter, se mettre en colère, s'emporter; s'user par le frottement.

chaff *n.* balle *f.*

chaffinch *n.* pinson *m.*

chagrin *n.* contrariété *f.*, déception *f.* ~ *v.t.* contrarier, decevoir.

chain *n.* chaine *f.*; enchaînement *m.* to shake off, to break one's ~, secouer, briser ses chaînes, ses fers. *v.t.* enchaîner. **to ~ up,** attacher avec une chaîne.

chair *n.* chaise *f.;* chaire *f.* (of a professor). **arm~,** fauteuil *m..* **wheel~,** chaise roulante. **electric ~,** chaise *f.* electrique. **folding ~,** chaise pliante. **to fill the ~,** présider. **to be in the ~,** occuper le fauteuil. **to put in the ~,** nommer à la présidence.

chairman *n.* président *m.,* présidente *f.*

chairmanship *n.* fonctions *f.pl.* de président d'une assemblée.

chalet *n.* chalet *m.;* bungalow *m.*

chalice *n.* chalice *m.;* coupe *f.*

chalk *n.* craie *f.* ~ *v.t.* blanchir; écrire, marquer.

chalky *adj.* crayeux.

challenge *v.t.* provoquer; défier; protester comtre; contester. *n.* défi *m.,* challenge *m.,* réclamation *f.;* recusation *f.* (of jurors).

challengeable *adj.* qui peut être provoqué; qu'on peut défier; récusable.

challenger *n.* provocateur *m.,* provocatrice *f.,* récusant *m.,* récusante *m.*

chamber *n.* chambre *f.,* salle *f.,* cabinet *m.* (of a lawyer); fosse *f.* (of nose); âme *f.,* chambre *f.* (of a gun). ~ **of commerce,** chambre de commerce. ~ **music,** musique *f.* de chambre.

chameleon *n.* caméléon *m.*

chamois *n.* chamois *m.;* peau *f.* de chamois.

chamomile *n.* camomille *f.*

champ *v.t.* ronger, mâcher. *n.* Infml. champion *m.*

champagne *n.* vin *m.* de Champagne, champagne *m..* **sparkling ~,** champagne grand mousseux.

champion *n.* champion *m.,* championne *f.* ~ *v.t.* défier au combat; défendre.

championship *n.* championnat *m.;* défense *f.*

chance *n.* hasard *m.;* chance *f.,* sort *m.* **to take a ~,** tenter fortune. **by mere ~,** par pur hasard. **there are ten ~s to one,** il y a dix à parier contre un. *v.i.* arriver par hasard; venir à; advenir. *adj.* fortuit, accidentel, de hasard.

chancel *n.* coeur *m.*

chancellery *n.* chancellerie *f.*

chancellor *n.* chancelier *m.,* ministre *m.f.*

chancellorship *n.* dignité *f.,* fonctions *f.pl.* de chancelier.

chandelier *n.* lustre *m.*

change *v.t.* changer; échanger, troquer *n.* changement *m.;* rechange *m.;* altération *f.;* permutation *f.;* change *m.,* monnaie *f.,* appoint *m.* **the ~s of life,** les vicissitudes *f.pl.* de la vie.

changeable *adj.* changeant, variable; versatile, volage.

changing *adj.* changeant, altérant. *n.* changement *m.*

channel *n.* canal *m.,* détroit *m.;* bras *m.* de mer; (TV) chaîne *f.;* direction *f.,* passe *f.;* voie *f.;* entremise *f.;* pas *m.* **switch ~s,** change de chaîne. **the English ~,** la Manche. **St. George's ~,** le canal de Saint-Georges. *v.t.* canaliser; sillonner, creuser.

chant *v.t.* chanter, célébrer en chant. *n.* chant *m.,* plain-chant *m.;* mélodie *f.*

chaos *n.* chaos *m.*

chaotic *adj.* chaotique.

chap *v.t.* gercer, crevasser, fendre. **my lips are chapped,** mes lèvres sont gercées. *v.i.* se gercer, se crevasser. *n.* gerçure *f.,* crevasse *f.*

chapel *n.* chapelle *f.;* temple *m.*

chaperon *n.* chaperon *m.,* chaperonne *f.* ~ *v.t.* chaperonner.

chaplain *n.* chapelain *m.;* aumônier *m.*

chaplet *n.* chapelet *m.;* guirlande *f.*

chaps *n.pl.* jambières *f.pl.* de cuir (of cowboys).

chapter *n.* chapitre *m.;* épisode *m.*

char *v.t.* carboniser, se carboniser.

character *n.* individu *m.* caractère *m.;* tempérament *m.,* réputation *f.;* rôle *m.;* personnage *m.;* certificate *m.* **to see a thing in its true ~,** voir une chose sous son véritable jour. **he is a ~, quite a ~,** c'est un original, un vrai original. **in the ~ of Othello,** dans le rôle d'Othello.

characteristic *adj., n.* caractéristique *f.*

characterization *n.* caractérisation.

characterize *v.t.* caractériser; graver, empreindre.

charade *n.* charade *f.*

charcoal *n.* charbon *m.*

charge *v.t.* charger; accuser; imposer; attaquer; faire payer, payer, mettre sur un compte; prendre; adjurer, sommer. **what functions is he ~d with?** de quelles fonctions est-il chargé? **who is in ~?** qui est le responsable? **to ~ a person with a crime,** accuser une personne d'un crime. **what do you ~ for this book?** combien demandez-vous pour ce livre? ~ **it on my credit card,** je vais payer avec ma carte de crédit, mettez-le/la sur ma carte de crédit. charger, faire la charge. *n.* charge *f.;* frais *m.pl.;* ordre *m.;* soin *m.;* garde *f.;* office *m.,* fonctions *f.pl.;* prix *m.;* dépôt *m.,* protégé *m.* **the diamonds were left in my ~,** les diamants m'ont été confiés en dépôt. **incidental ~s,** menus frais.

a reasonable ~, un prix raisonnable.

chargeable *adj.* à charge; imposable, inculpable.

charger *n. Tech.* chargeur *m.,* chargeuse *f.*

chariot *n.* coupé *m.;* char *m.,* chariot *m.*

charisma *n.* charisme *m.*

charismatic *adj.* charismatique.

charitable *adj.* charitable.

charitably *adv.* charitablement, par charité.

charity *n.* charité *f.;* aumône *f.* ~ **begins at home,** charité bien ordonnée commence par soi-même.

charlatan *n.* charlatan *m.*

charm *v.t.* charmer, enchanter. *n.* charme *m.*

charmer *n.* charmeur *m.,* charmeuse *f.;* enchanteur *m.,* enchanteresse *f.*

charming *adj.* charmant, ravissant.

charmingly *adv.* de manière charmante.

chart *n.* graphique *m.,* diagramme *m.,* carte *f.*

marine, carte f. hydrographique; hit-parade m.

charter n. charte f.; brevet m.; charter (plane) m. ~ v.t. affréter (a boat, a plane).

chary adj. prudent, circonspect; frugal, soigneux; circonspect.

chase v.t. chasser; poursuivre; ciseler (les métaux); enchâsser. n. chasse f.; poursuite f.; but m., objet m.

chasm n. fissure f., ravin m.; crevasse f., abîme m.; vide m.

chassis n. châssis m.; train m. d'atterrissage.

chaste adj. chaste, pur.

chastely adv. chastement, pudiquement.

chasten v.t. châtier; purifier; réprimer.

chastise v.t. châtier, corriger, contenir.

chastity n. chasteté f.

chat n. bavardage m., brin m. de causette. v.i. bavarder, papoter.

chattel n. bien m. meuble m., effet m., mobilier m.

chatter v.i. jaser; claquer; bavarder; papoter. n. bavardage m.

chauffeur n. chauffeur m.

chauvinism n. chauvinisme m.

chauvinist n. chauvin m., phallocrate m., machiste m.

cheap adj. à bon marché, à bas prix.

cheapen v.t. marchander; baisser, diminuer le prix.

cheaply adv. à bon marché, à bas prix.

cheat v.t. tricher; tromper, duper, jouer; Infml. flouer, tricher. n. tromperie f., ruse f., tricherie f., trompeur m.; tricheur m.

cheater n. tricheur m., tricheuse f.

check v.t. vérifier, contrôler; enregistrer (bagge); cocher (with a mark); réprimander; réprimer, mettre un frein, modérer; (in chess) faire échec à. n. chèque m.; échec m., empêchement m., frein m., contrôle m.; marque f.; chèque m., nok f., coche f. (mark). **to ~ a coat,** mettre au vestiaire. **to ~ luggage,** mettre à la consigne. **to ~ up on someone,** tenir quelqu'un en échec. **~book,** carnet m. de chèques.

checkers n.pl. jeu m. de dames.

checkmate n. échec et mat m.; Fig. défaite f. ~ v.t. donner, faire échec et mat.

cheek n. joue f.

cheekbone n. pommette f.

cheep v.i. azouiller, pépier. n. gazouilli, pépiment m.

cheer v.t. réjouir, encourager, animer; égayer, applaudir à. **to ~ up,** ranimer, s'égayer. v.i. se réjouir, s'égayer, applaudir. **come, ~ up!** allons, courage! n. hourra m. gaieté f.; chère f., régal m.; cri m. de joie, applaudissements m.pl., acclamations f.pl.

cheerful adj. joyeux, enjoué, gai.

cheerfully adv. joyeusement, de bon coeur, volontiers.

cheerfulness n. bonne humeur f., contentement m., allégresse f.

cheese n. fromage m. **cream ~,** petit suisse. **goat ~,** fromage de chèvre.

cheesy adj. Infml. moche.

cheetah n. guépard m.

chef n. chef m.

chemical adj. chimique.

chemically adv. chimiquement.

chemicals n.pl. produits m.pl. chimiques.

chemist n. chimiste m.

chemistry n. chimie f.

chemotherapy n. chimiothérapie f.

cherish v.t. chérir; favoriser.

cherry n. cerise f. **~ tree,** cerisier m.

cherub n. chérubin m.

chervil n. cerfeuil m.

chess n. échecs m.pl. **game of ~,** partie f. d'échecs. **~board,** échiquier m. **~man,** pion m.

chest n. coffre m., caisse f.; poitrine f. **a ~ of drawers,** commode f.

chestnut n. châtaigne f.; marron m. **~ tree,** châtaignier m. **horse ~, horse ~ tree,** marronnier. adj. châtain; alezan.

chew v.t. mâcher; ruminer. **to ~ tobacco,** mâcher du tabac, chiquer. n. chique f.

chewy adj. difficile à mâcher.

chiaroscuro n. clair-obscur m.

chic adj. chic inv.

chicanery n. chicanerie f.

chick n. poussin m. oisillon m.; Infml. (mon) poulet m; (ma) poulette f., pépée f.

chicken n. poulet m. trouillard m., froussard m. **~pox** n., varicelle f. **to ~ out,** se dégonfler.

chickpea n. pois m. chiche.

chicory n. chicorée f.

chide v.t. gronder, réprimander.

chief n. chef m.; commandant m. ~ adj. principal, en chef; premier. **the ~ rulers,** les principaux chefs. **~ executive officer,** directeur m. général.

chiefly adv. principalement, surtout.

chieftain n. chef m., commandant m., capitaine m.

chilblain n. engelure f. ~ v.t. couvrir d'engelures.

child n. children pl., enfant m. **to be with ~,** être enceinte. **a good ~,** un enfant sage. **~-bearing,** maternité f. **~birth,** accouchement m.

childhood n. enfance f.

childish adj. d'enfant, enfantin, puéril. **~ talk,** ~ **conduct,** enfantillage m.

childishness n. enfantillage m., frivolité f., puérilité f.

childless adj. sans enfant.

childlike adj. d'enfant, enfantin.

chill n. frisson m., froid m. **to take the ~ off,** faire dégourdir. adj. froid; réserve, glacial. v.t. glacer; refroidir; geler.

chilliness n. sensation f. de froid, frisson m.

chilling adj. refroidissant, faisant frissonner.

chilly *adj.* froid, un peu froid; frileux. *adv.* froidement.

chime *n.* concert *m.;* accord *m.* de sons; carillon *m.* (of bells). *v.i.* carillonner; convenir. **to ~ in with,** s'accorder avec. *v.t.* faire résonner en harmonie; carillonner.

chimera *n.* chimère *f.*

chimerical *adj.* chimérique, imaginaire.

chimney *n.* cheminée *f.*

chimpanzee *n.* chimpanzé *m.*

chin *n.* menton *m.*

china *n.pr.* Chine *f.;* porcelaine *f.,* vaisselle *f.* **~-ware,** porcelaines *f.pl.*

chinchilla *n.* chinchilla *m.*

Chinese *adj.* chinois. *n.sing.,pl.* Chinois *m.,* Chinoise *f.;* la langue chinoise.

chink *n.* fente *f.,* crevasse *f.,* fissure *f.;* tintement *m. ~ v.i.* se fendre, se crevasser.

chip *n.* petit morceau *m.,* fragment *m.;* copeau *m.,* éclat *m.,* écaille *f.,* écornure *f. ~ v.t.* couper, tailler en petits, fragments ou éclats; ébrécher. **to ~ off,** dégrossir, débruter. *v.i.* se briser, s'écailler, s'écorner.

chipmunk *n.* écureuil américain *m.*

chipping *n.* morceau *m.,* fragment *m.; brisure *f.,* éclat *m.;* écornure *f.*

chiropractic *n.* chiropraxie *f.,* chiropractie *f.*

chiropractor *n.* chiropracteur *m.*

chirp *v.i.* gazouiller. *n.* gazouillement *m.*

chirping *n.* gazouillement *m.*

chirrup *v.t.* See CHIRP.

chisel *n.* ciseau *m.* **cold ~,** ciseau à froid. *v.t.* sculpter, ciseler.

chit *n.* mot *m.,* note *f.*

chitchat *n.* bavardage *m.*

chitterlings *n.* tripes *f.pl;* andouilles *f.pl.*

chivalrous *adj.* chevaleresque.

chivalry *n.* chevalerie *f.*

chive *n.* ciboulette *f.*

chloride *n.* chlorure *m.*

chlorine *n.* chlore *m.*

chloroform *n.* chloroforme *m.*

chock *n.* cale *f.,* coin *m.;* cale *f.;* mèche *f.* **~full,** complètement rempli.

chocolate *n.* chocolat *m.*

choice *n.* choix *m.;* élection *f.;* assortiment *m.* **there's no ~,** il n'y a pas à choisir. *adj.* de choix, rare; exquis.

choiceless *adj.* qui n'a pas le choix.

choir *n.* choeur *m.*

choke *v.t.* étouffer; suffoquer. **to ~ up,** boucher, émouvoir. *v.i.* s'engorger; se formaliser. *n.* starter *m.,* buse *f.* (in car); étranglement *m.* (in voice).

choker *n.* collier *m.* de chien (necklace).

cholera *n.* cholera *m.*

choleric *adj.* colérique.

cholesterol *n.* cholestérol *m.*

choose *v.t.* choisir; élire; vouloir. **I don't ~ to do it,** cela ne me plaît pas de le faire. **many are called, but few are chosen,** il y a beaucoup d'appelés mais peu d'élus.

choosing *n.* choix *m.,* élection *f.*

chop *v.t.* couper, trancher, fendre; gercer; troquer, échanger. **to ~ off,** trancher. **to ~ finely,** hacher menu. **to ~ in,** s'abattre, tomber tout à coup sur. *n.* tranche *f.,* morceau *m.;* côtelette *f.;* gercure *f.;* crevasse *f.;* gueule *f.,* mâchoire *f.;* troc *m.,* échange *m.* **lamb~,** côtellette d'agneau.

chopper *n.* couperet *m.,* hachoir *m.;* hélicoptère *m.*

chopping *n.* coupe *f.* **~ block,** hachoir *m.* **~ knife,** hachoir *m.*

choppy *adj.* agité (sea).

chopsticks *n.pl.* baguettes (chinoises) *f.pl.*

chop suey *n.* fricassée *f.* (chinoise).

choral *adj.* choral; chanté en choeur.

chord *n.* corde *f.;* accord *m.;* Med. cordon *m.*

choreographic *adj.* chorégraphique.

choreography *n.* chorégraphie *f.*

chorus *n.* choeur *m.;* refrain *m.* **to sing in ~,** chanter en choeur; *Fig.* faire chorus.

chow *n.* chow-chow *m.; Infml.* bouffe *f.*

chowder *n.* bouillabaise américaine *f.*

Christ *n.* Christ *m.*

christen *v.t.* baptiser.

Christendom *n.* chrétienté *f.*

christening *n.* baptême *m.*

Christian *n.* and *adj.* chrétien *m.* **~ name,** nome de baptême.

Christianity *n.* christianisme *m.*

Christianize *v.t.* christianiser.

Christmas *n.* Noël *m.* adj. de noël **~ carol,** cantique *m.* de Noël **~ Eve,** veille *f.* de Noël. **~ log,** bûche *f.* de Noël. **~ tree,** arbre *m.* de Noël.

chrome *n.* chrome *m.*

chromosome *n.* chromosome *m.*

chronic *adj.* chronique.

chronicle *adj.* chronique *f.* **~ v.t.** chroniquer; raconter; mettre dans les annales.

chronicler *n.* chroniqueur *m.*

chronological *adj.* chronologique.

chronologically *adv.* chronogiquement.

chronology *n.* chronologie *f.*

chronometer *n.* chronomètre *m.*

chrysanthemum *n.* chrysanthème *m.*

chubby *adj.* potelé, joufflu.

chuck *v.t.* glousser. *v.t.* lacher; jeter, lancer. donner un petit coup à, une tape à. *n.* petite tape *f.* **~wagon,** charrette *f.* qui transporte la nourriture.

chuckle *v.t.* glousser. *n.* rire *m.* étouffé. *v.i.* ricaner, rire sous cape, *Infml.* rigoler.

chuckling *n.* rise *m.* étouffé.

chum *n.* copain *m.,* copine *f.,* pote *m.f.*

chump *n.* tronçon *m.,* gros morceau *m.* de bois; *Infml.* maboule *m.f.;* idiot *m.,* idiote *f.*

chunk *n.* morceau *m.,* quignon *m.* (bread).

chunky *adj.* trapu (person), gros (piece, sweater).

Chunnel *n.* le tunnel sous la Manche.

church *m.* église *f.;* temple *m.* **the Church of England,** l'Eglise anglicane. **you will be too**

late for ~, vous serez en retard pour l'office.

~ goer, pratiquant m., pratiquante f.

churn n. baratte f. ~ v.t. baratter.

chute n. glissière f.; Infml. parachute m.

cicada n. cigale f.

cider n. cidre m.

cigar n. cigare m. ~box, boîte à cigares. ~holder, porte-cigares m., fume-cigares m.

cigarette n. cigarette f. ~ lighter, briquet m.

cinch n. Infml. c'est du tout cuit.

cinder n. cendre f., escarbille f.

cinema n. cinéma m.

cinnamon n. cannelle f.

cipher n. zéro m.; chiffre m.

circle n. cercle m., verticille m., révolution f., orbite f. ~ v.t. entourer, environner. v.i. tourner, faire le tour.

circlet n. petit cercle m., anneau m., bandeau m.

circuit n. circuit m., rotation f., révolution f.; tour m.; tournée f. (of judges). ~ board, carte f. de circuits. ~ breaker, interrupteur m.

circuitous adj. détourné, indirect.

circuitously adv. d'une manière détournée.

circular adj. circulaire, rond. a ~ saw, scie f. circulaire. n. circulaire f. (letter).

circularly adv. circulairement.

circulate v.i. circuler. v.t. mettre en circulation; faire circuler.

circulation n. circulation f. to put into ~, mettre en circulation.

circulatory adj. circulaire; ambulant.

circumcise v.t. circoncire.

circumcision n. circoncision f.

circumference n. circonférence f.

circumflex n., adj. Gram. circonflexe m.

circumlocution n. circonlocution f., périphrase f.

circumnavigate v.t. naviguer autour.

circumnavigation n. circumnavigation f.

circumscribe v.t. circonscrire, limiter, restreindre.

circumscription n. circonscription f.

circumspect adj. circonspect.

circumspection n. circonspection f.

circumstance n. circonstance f., situation f. that depends on ~s, cela dépende des circonstances.

circumstantial adj. circonstanciel; de circonstance; accidentel, fortuit; circonstancié. ~ evidence, preuves indirectes.

circumstantiate v.t. circonstancier.

circumvent v.t. circonvenir.

circumvention n. circonvention f.

circus pl. cirque m.

cistern n. réservoir m.; chasse f. d'eau; cuvette f., cuve f.

citadel n. citadelle f.

citation n. citation f.

cite v.t. citer.

citizen n. citoyen m., citoyenne f. a fellow ~, concitoyen m., concitoyenne f.

citizenship n. nationalité f., citoyenneté f.

citrus adj. ~ fruit, agrume m.

city n. ville f. ~ hall, hôtel m. de ville, marie f.

civet n. civette f.

civic adj. civique.

civil adj. civil; civilisé; honnête, poli. ~ law, loi f. civile. ~ war, guerre f. civile. ~ engineer, ingénieur m. civil.

civilian n. civil m.

civilization n. civilisation f.

civilize v.t. civiliser.

civilly adv. civilement; honnêtement, poliment.

clack v.i. claquer; cliqueter; caqueter. n. claquet m.; clapet m.; caquetage m., caquet m.

clad adj. vêtu, habillé.

claim v.t. réclamer, revendiquer; prétendre à; proclamer. to ~ a privilege, prétendre à un privilège. n. réclamation f., revendication f., prétention f. à, prétention f. sur, droit m. à, droit m. sur, titre m. à. to lay, to make ~ to, prétendre à, avoir des droits à. to ~ responsibility for an attack, revendiquer un attentat. he ~s he was robbed, il déclare avoir été volé.

claimant n. prétendant m., réclamant m.; ayant droit m. ~ adj. réclamant; implorant.

clairvoyant adj., n. voyant m.; clairvoyant m.

clam n. praire f., palourde f. to ~ up, Infml. se la fermer.

clamber v.i. grimper.

clammy adj. moite.

clamor n. clameur f., tumulte m., bruit m. ~ v.t. crier, vociférer.

clamorous adj. braillard; bruyant.

clamorously adv. bruyamment, avec grand bruit.

clamp n. lien m.; crampon m.; emboîture f. v.t. cramponner, serrer, agrafer.

clan n. clan m.

clandestine adj. clandestin.

clang v.t. faire résonner. n. bruit/son métallique.

clank n. son m. retentissant, aigu; cliquetis m. v.i. rendre un son aigu. v.t. (faire) resonner.

clannish adj. étroitement uni.

clap v.t. applaudir, battre (wings); presser, serrer. n. coup m.; claquement m.; battement m. (de mains). Méd. he's got a dose of the ~, il a la chaude-pisse. a ~ of thunder, un coup de tonnerre.

clapper n. battant m.; clapet m.; clapier m.

clapping n. battement m., claquement m., applaudissement m.

clarification n. clarification f.

clarify v.t. clarifier; éclairer. v.i. se clarifier, s'éclaircir, s'épurer; devenir clair, brillant.

clarinet n. clarinette f.

clarion n. clairon m.

clarity n. clarté f.

clash v.i. se chequer, s'entrechoquer; se contrairer. their interests ~, leurs intérêtes sont opposés. n. choc m. violent, fracas m., cliquetis m.; conflit m., lutte f.

clasp *n.* agrafe *f.,* fermoir *m.;* étreinte *f.* ~ *v.t.* agrafer; serrer.

class *n.* classe *f.,* cours *m.;* catégorie *f.;* rang *m.* working ~, classe ouvrière. **evening** ~, cours du soir. ~**room,** *v.t.* classer. *f.* **the** ~ **of '99,** la promotion de '99.

classic, classical *adj.* classique. *n.* classique *m.*

classification *n.* classification *f.,* classement *m.*

classify *v.t.* classer, classifier.

classy *adj.* *Infml.* (super) chic; bon genre.

clatter *v.i.* faire du bruit, résonner. *n.* bruit *m.,* fracas *m.;* tapage *m.,* vacarme *m.,* brouhaha *m.*

clause *n.* clause *f.;* disposition *f.,* article *m.,* proposition *f.*

claustrophobia *n.* claustrophobie *f.*

claustrophobic *adj.* claustrophobe.

clavicle *n.* clavicule *f.*

claw *n.* griffe *f.;* ongle *m.* **the** ~**s of a cat,** les griffes d'un chat. ~ **hammer,** marteau *m.* à panne fendue. *v.t.* griffer; gratter; s'aggripper.

clay *n.* argile *f.,* glaise *f.,* terre *f.,* boue *f.,* limon *m.* baked ~, terre *f.* cuite. **fire** ~, argile réfractaire. **to play on a** ~ **court,** jouer sur la terre battue.

clayey *adj.* argileux.

clean *adj.* propre, net, clair. **a** ~ **glass,** un verre propre. ~ **water,** de l'eau claire. **a** ~ **heart,** une coeur pur. **he comes out with** ~ **hands,** il en sort les mains propres. *v.t.* nettoyer, laver, recurer, lessiver, décrotter.

cleaner *n.* appareil *m.* de nettoyage; teinturier *m.,* teinturière *f.*

cleaning *n.* nettoyage *m.,* curage *m.;* dégraissage *m.;* décapage (de métaux). ~ **lady,** femme de ménage *f.*

cleanliness *n.* propreté *f.*

cleanly *adj.* propre, net.

cleanness *n.* propeté *f.,* netteté *f.*

cleanse *v.t.* nettoyer; curer; purifier. **to** ~**, se** purifier.

cleanser *n.* démaquillant *m.,* detergent *m.,* détersif *m.*

cleansing *n.* nettoyage *m.;* purification *f.*

clear *adj.* clair net, aigu; innocent, pur; évident. ~ **weather,** un temps clair. **a** ~ **sky,** un ciel pur. **she has a** ~ **complexion,** elle a un teint clair. **to give a** ~ **account,** expliquer clairement. **the coast is** ~, la côte est libre, *Fig.* il n'y a pas de danger. **he is** ~ **of debt,** il n'a pas de dettes. **a** ~ **judgment,** un jugement impartial. **a** ~ **gain,** un profit clair et net. *adv.* clairement, évidemment, net. *v.t.* éclaircir (view, voice, doubt); dissiper (clouds); débrouiller (a matter), résoudre (a difficulty); nettoyer, débarrasser (la table); ouvrir (a passage); vider, évacuer (a prisoner); acquitter (debts). **to** ~ **customs,** acquitter les droits de douane. *v.i.* (weather) s'éclaircir; se remettre au beau; *Fig.* s'éclaircir. ~**-sighted,** qui a de bons yeux, qui voit clair. ~**-sightedness,** clairvoyance *f.,* perspicacité *f.*

clearance *n.* dégagement *m.,* évacuation *f.;* dédouanement *m.* ~ **sale,** soldes *f.pl.* liquidation *f.*

clearing *n.* défrichement *m.,* éclaircissement *m.;* clairière *f.,* compensation *f.* ~ **house,** chambre *f.* de compensation.

clearly *adv.* clairement, avec clarté; clair et net; evidemment

clearness *n.* pureté *f.;* netteté *f.;* clarté *f.*

cleavage *n.* action *f.* de fendre; clivage *m.,* décolleté *m.*

cleave *v.t.* fendre. **to** ~ **wood,** fendre du bois.

cleaver *n.* fendoir *m.*

clef *n.* clef *f.,* clé *f.*

cleft *n.* fente *f.,* ouverture *f.,* crevasse *f.;* éclat *m.*

clemency *n.* clémence *f.*

clement *adj.* clément, doux, compatissant.

clemently *adv.* d'une manière clémente, avec douceur.

clench *v.t.* serrer, empoigner, *v.i.* se serrer, s'empoigner.

clergy *n.* clergé *m.*

clergyman *n.* prêtre *m.,* ministre *m.,* ecclésiastique *m.*

clerical *adj.* clérical; d'employé, de bureau.

clerk *n.* clerc *m.,* ecclésiastique *m.;* commis *m.;* d'employé *m.;* employé *m.,* employée *f.;* vendeur *m.,* vendeuse *f.*

clever *adj.* intelligent; adroit, habile, ingénieux.

cleverly *adv.* habilement, adroitement.

cleverness *n.* habileté *f.,* adresse *f.*

cliché *n.* cliche *m.*

click *n.* faire tic-tac; loquet *m.* de porte; déclic *m.*

client *n.* client *m.,* cliente *f.*

clientele *n.* clientèle *f.;* habitués *m.pl.*

cliff *n.* falaise *f.;* précipice *m.*

climacteric *adj.* climatérique; de la ménopause; critique, crucial.

climate *n.* climat *m.*

climatic *adj.* climatique, de climat.

climatize *v.t.* acclimater.

climax *n.* apogée *m.,* point *m.* culminant; orgasme *m.;* gradation *f.* ~ *v.i.* porter au poit culminant, atteindre le point culminant.

climb *v.t.* grimper, escalader, faire l'ascension *f.,* monter. *v.i.* gravir, s'élever. **to** ~ **down,** descendre, effectuer la descente *n.* montée *f.,* côte *f.;* ascension *f.* ~ **down,** descente *f.*

climber *n.* alpiniste *m.f.,* plante *f.* grimpante; grimpeur *m.,* arriviste *m.f.*

climbing *n.* action de grimper, de gravir; escalade *f.*

clinch *v.t.* serrer dans la main; river; *Fig.* confirmer. *v.i.* être rivé. *n.* équivoque *f.,* répartie *f.* vive et spirituelle.

cling *v.i.* s'attacher, se coller; se cramponner.

clinging *adj.* adhérant fortement, se collant, enlaçant.

clinic *n.* clinique *m.,* dispensaire *m.*

clinical *adj.* clinique; médical.

clink *v.i.* tinter, résonner. *v.t.* faire tinter, faire résonner. *n.* *Infml.* taule; tintement *m.,* cliquetis *m.*

clip *v.t.* couper; rogner; tondre; attacher, pincer ensemble, agrafer *n.* tonte *f.;* coupe *f.;* pince *f.,* attache *f. m.* **video ~,** vidéo *f.*

clipboard *n.,* planchette *f.* porte-papiers.

clipper *n.* rogneur *m.;* tondeur *m.,* clipper *m.*

clipping *n.* rognure *f.;* coupure *f.* de presse.

clique *n.* clique *f.*

clitoris *n.* clitoris *m.*

cloak *n.* manteau *f.* **~** *v.t.* couvrir d'un manteau.

cloakroom *n.* vestiaire *m.*

clock *n.* horloge *f.,* pendule *f.* **to ~ in,** pointer (venue). **to ~ out,** pointer (sortie).

clockwise *adv., adj.* dans le sens des aiguilles d'une montre.

clockwork *n.* mouvement *m.* (d'horloge); ouvrage *m.* de précision. **like ~,** comme sur des roulettes, réglé comme du papier à musique.

clod *n.* motte *f.* de terre, masse *f.,* bloc *m.;* lourdaud *m.,* rustre *m.*

clog *v.t.* entraver, embarrasser; encombrer; charger, surcharger. *v.i.* s'attacher, se coller ensemble; s'embarrasser. *n.* entrave *f.;* empêchement *m.*

cloister *n.* cloître *m.* **~** *v.t.* cloîtrer.

close *v.t.* fermer; clore, terminer, finir; conclure; serrer. **to ~ a book,** fermer un livre. **to ~ a bargain, an account,** conclure un marché, clore un compte. **with ~d doors,** à huis clos. *v.i.* se fermer; se rejoindre; se serrer. **the day ~d gloomily,** le jour se termina tristement. **to ~ down,** fermer. *n.* conclusion *f.,* terminaison *f.,* fin *f.,* clôture *f.;* lutte *f.;* etreinte *f.;* clos *m.,* enclos *m.* **at the ~ of the day,** à la fin de la journée. *adj.* clos, bien fermé; serré, dense, près, proche; renfermé, discret. **in ~ confinement,** au secret. **a ~ fight,** un combat de corps à corps. **very ~ attention,** la plus scrupuleuse attention. *adv.* de près, tout près. **~ to the river,** tout près de la rivière. **to stick ~ by a person,** se tenir près d'une personne.

closed *adj.* fermé. **~ session,** huis clos.

closely *adv.* étroitement; de près; attentivement. **~ packed,** étroitement emballé. **we are ~ related,** nouse sommes proches parents. **a page ~ printed,** une page d'une impression compacte. **to examine ~,** examiner attentivement. **to question ~,** presser de questions.

closeness *n.* proximité *f.;* étroitesse *f.,* justesse *f.;* lourdeur *f.* (of the atmosphere); discrétion *f.,* silence *m.;* avarice *f.;* liaison *f.*

closet *n.* cabinet *m.,* armoire *f.,* placard *m.* **~** *v.t.* enfermer dans un cabinet.

closing *adj.* final, ce qui termine, ce qui conclut. *n.* fin *f.,* conclusion *f.*

closure *n.* clôture *f.,* fermeture *f.;* enclos *m.,* enceinte *f.,* conclusion *f.,* fin *f.*

clot *n.* grumeau *m.,* caillot *m.* (blood). *v.i.* se coaguler; se former en grumeaux ou caillots.

cloth *n.* toile *f.;* drap *m.* **cotton ~,** toile de coton. **linen ~,** toile de lin. **table~,** nappe *f.* **to lay the ~,** mettre la nappe. **man of the ~** *n.* clergé *m.*

clothe *v.t.* habiller, vêtir, revêtir; investir. **~d in**

glory, entouré de gloire. **to ~ with power,** investir d'un pouvoir.

clothes *n.* vêtements *m.pl.,* habits *m.pl.* **old ~,** vieux habits. **men's ~,** habits d'hommes. **~ brush,** brosse *f.* à habits. **~pin,** pince *f.* à linge.

clothing *n.* vêtements *m.pl.,* habillement *m.*

cloud *n.* nuage *m.,* nuée *f.,* nue *f., Fig.* obscurité *f.,* ténèbres *f.pl.* **to be in a ~,** être dans les nuages. **a ~ of arrows,** une nuée de flèches. *v.t.* couvrir d'un nuage; obscurcir; veiner, moirer. *v.i.* se couvrir de nuages, devenir nuageux, s'assombrir.

cloudily *adv.* obscurément, ténébreusement, avec des nuages.

cloudiness *n.* état *m.* nuageux; obscurité *f.,* ténèbres *f.pl.;* tristesse *f.*

cloudless *adj.* sans nuages; clair, lumineux.

cloudy *adj.* nuageux; obscure, sombre, ténébreux.

clout *n. Infml.* gifle *f.,* coup (de poing, de bâton *m.* **to have plenty of ~,** être puissant, avoir de l'influence.

clove *n.* clou *m.* de girofle; **garlic ~,** gousse *f.*

clover *n.* trèfle *m.* **to live in ~,** *Fig.* vivre comme un coq en pâte.

clown *n.* paysan *m.;* rustre *m.;* clown *m.*

clownish *adj.* de restre; rude, grossier.

cloy *v.t.* **cloying** *adj.* écourant, écoeurer.

club *n.* massue *f.* club *m.,* cercle *m.* **~foot,** pied *m.* bot. **~ sandwich** *n.,* sandwich *m.* à trois étages.

cluck *v.i.* glousser. *v.t.* appeler, faire venir en gloussant.

clue *n.* indice *f.; Infml.* **I don't have a ~,** je n'en ai aucune idée.

clump *n.* bloc *m.;* massif *m.;* bruit de pas pesant *m.* **~** *v.i.* marcher d'un pas lourd.

clumsily *adv.* gauchement, avec maladresse.

clumsiness *n.* maladresse *f.,* gaucherie *f.*

clumsy *adj.* gauche, maladroit.

cluster *n.* groupe *m.,* touffe *f.,* grappe *f.,* bouquet *m.;* amas *m.,* tas *m.* **a ~ of cherries,** un bouquet de cerises. **a ~ of islands,** un amas d'îles. *v.i.* eroître en grappe; s'amasser, (se) grouper, s'attrouper. *v.i.* amasser; réunir en grappe, en bouquet, mettre en tas.

clutch *v.t.* empoigner, tenir dans la main. *n. Auto.* embrayage; prise *f.; pl.* griffes *f.pl.* **to let in the ~,** embrayer. **to fall into the ~es of a criminal,** tomber sous les griffes d'un criminal.

clutter *n.* assemblage *m.,* confus, tas *m.;* encombrement *m.* **~** *v.t.* grouper en désordre; remplir de choses confuses.

Co. *abbr.* of **company,** compagnie *f.*

c/o *abbr.* **care of,** chez.

coach *n.* wagon *m.,* voiture (train) *f.,* autocar *m.;* entraîneur *m.* **stage~,** diligence. *v.t.* entraîner, préparer.

coachman *n.* cocher *m.*

coadjutor *n.* aide *m.,* adjoint *m.,* assistant *m.*

coagulate *v.t.* coaguler, figer, cailler. *v.i.* (se) coaguler.

coagulation *n.* coagulation *f.*

coal *n.* charbon *m.* to carry ~s to Newcastle, porter de l'eau à la rivière. ~-black, noir comme le charbon. ~field, bassin *m.* houiller, goudron *m.*

coalesce *v.i.* s'unir, se fondre (ensemble), se coaliser.

coalescence *n.* coalescence *f.*; réunion *f.*

coalition *n.* coalition *f.*

coarse *adj.* grossier, rude; gros, épais. ~ language, language *m.* grossier. this thread is too ~, ce fil est trop gros.

coarsely *adv.* grossièrement, rudement.

coarseness *n.* grossiéreté *f.*

coast *n.* côte *f.*; rivage *m.*; littoral *m.* the ~ is clear, la voie est libre. *v.i.* côter. *v.i.* approcher, accoster. to ~ down, descendre en roue libre.

coaster *n.* caboteur *m.*; cabotier *m.*; dessous de verre *m.*

coast guard *n.* la garde des côtes.

coat *n.* manteau *m.*, habit *m.*; jaquette *f.*; robe *f.* (of horse); couche *f.* (of paint). over~, pardessus *m.* ~ *v.t.* enduire, couvrir d'une couche.

coating *n.* revêtement *m.*, couche *f.*, enduit *m.*; dorure *f.*

coax *v.t.* amadouer, enjôler, flatter, cajoler.

cob *n.* épi *m.*

cobalt *n.* cobalt *m.*

cobble *n.* galet *m.* ~ *v.t.* rafistoler.

cobbler *n.* cordonnier *m.*

cobblestones *n.pl.*, cobbles *n.pl.*, pavés ronds *m.pl.*

cobra *n.* cobra *m.*

cobweb *n.* toile *f.* d'araignée.

cocaine *n.* cocaïne *f.*

coccyx *n.* coccyx *m.*

cock *n.* mâle *m.* (birds in general); coq *m.*; robinet *m.*; chien *m.* (of gun); meule *f.* (of hay). a ~ and bull story, histoire *f.* abracadabrante. ~-a-doodle-doo, cocorico. *m.* ~-fight, combat de coqs. ~-pit *n.*, poste de pilotage, cockpit *m.* ~ *v.t.* dresser (a gun); mettre en meules (hay, etc.).

cockatoo *n.* cacatoès *m.*

cocker (spaniel) *n.* cocker *m.* (dog).

cockerel *n.* jeune coq *m.*

cockle *n.* nielle *f.* des blés.

cockpit *n.* cockpit *m.*

cockroach *n.* cafard *m.*

cocktail *n.* cocktail *m.*

cocky *adj.* sûr de soi, arrogant.

cocoa *n.* cacao *m.*; cocotier *m.* ~ tree, cocotier *m.*

coconut *n.* noix *f.* de coco.

cocoon *n.* cocon *m.*

cod, codfish *n.* cabillaud *m.*, morue *f.* fraîche. ~ liver oil, huile *f.* de foie de morue.

coddle *v.t.* dorloter, faire bouillir légèrement.

code *n.* code *m.* ~ *v.t.* coder.

codification *n.* codification *f.*

codify *v.t.* codifier.

coeducation *n.* éducation *f.* mixte.

coefficient *n.* coefficient *m.*

coerce *v.t.* forcer, contraindre; restreindre, réprimer.

coercion *n.* coercition *f.*, contrainte *f.*

coercive *adj.* coercitif.

coercively *adv.* par coercition, par contrainte.

coexist *v.i.* coexister.

coexistence *n.* coexistence *f.*

coexistent *adj.* coexistant.

coffee *n.* café *m.* ~ bean, grain *m.* de café. ~ cup, tasse *f.* à café. ~ mill, moulin *m.* à café. ~ plantation, caféière *f.* ~pot, cafetière *f.* ~ tree, caféier *m.* ~ shop, café *m.* ~ table, table *f.* de salon.

coffer *n.* coffre *m.*, boîte *f.*; caisse *f.*; cassette *f.*

coffin *n.* cercueil *m.*, bière *f.*

cog *v.t.* fixer une dent de roue, denteler. *n.* dent *f.* ~wheel, roue *f.* dentée.

cogency *n.* puissance *f.*, force *f.* (of an argument).

cogent *adj.* fort, puissant.

cogently *adv.* avec une force irrésistible.

cogitate *v.i.* penser, méditer, réfléchir.

cogitation *n.* cogitation *f.*, pensée *f.*, méditation *f.*

cogitative *adj.* pensant, rêveur.

cognac *n.* cognac *m.*

cognate *adj.* mot *m.* de même origine; semblable, analogue. *n.* cognat *m.*

cognation *n.* cognation *f.*; consanguinité *f.*; analogie *f.*, rapport *m.*

cognition *n.* cognition *f.*

cognizance *n.* connaissance *f.*, compétence *f.*; reconnaissance *f.*, aveu *m.*; insigne *m.*

cognizant *adj.* ayant connaissance de.

cohabit *v.i.* cohabiter.

cohabitation *n.* cohabitation *f.*

coheir *n.* cohéritier *m.*

coheiress *n.* cohéritière *f.*

cohere *v.i.* adhérer, être attaché.

coherence *n.* cohérence *f.*; connexion *f.*, liaison *f.*

coherent *adj.* cohérent; uni, lié par quelque rapport de forme ou d'ordre; conséquent.

coherently *adv.* d'une manière, cohérente.

cohesion *n.* cohésion *f.*

cohesive *adj.* qui tend à adhérer.

cohort *n.* cohorte *f.*

coiffure *n.* coiffure *f.*

coil *v.t.* enrouler. *v.i.* se replier. *n.* replie *m.* (snake); rouleau *m.* (of ropes). the ~ or IUD, stérilet *m.*

coin *n.* monnaie *f.*, pièce *f.* de monnaie *v.t.* monnayer, frapper, fabriquer, inventer, forger.

coinage *n.* monnayage *m.*; frappe *f.*

coincide *v.i.* coïncider.

coincidence *n.* coïncidence *f.*

coitus *n.* coït *m.*

coke *n.* coke *m.*; cocaïne *f.*; coca-cola *m.*

colander *n.* passoire *f.*; filtre *m.*

cold *adj.* froid. **to be ~**, avoir froid; faire froid. **to get ~**, se refroidir. **a ~ reception**, une froide réception. **to give one the ~ shoulder**, battre froid à quelqu'un. **~-blooded**, à sang-froid; insensible. *n.* froid *m.*, rhume *m.* **to get a ~**, s'enrhumer.

coldish *adj.* frisquet, un peu froid.

coldly *adv.* froidement.

coldness *n.* froideur *f.*, indifférence *f.*; frigidité *f.*

coleslaw *n.* salade *f.* de chou cru.

colic *n.* colique *f.*

coliseum *n.* colisée *m.*

collaborate *v.i.* collaborer.

collaboration *n.* collaboration *f.*

collaborator *n.* collaborateur *m.*, collaboratrice *f.*

collage *n.* collage *m.*

collapse *n.* écroulement *m.*, affaiblissement *m.* *v.i.* tomber ensemble, s'écrouler; s'affaisser.

collapsible *adj.* pliant.

collar *n.* collier *m.*, col *m.*; collet *m.*; faux-col *m.* **a dog's ~**, un collier de chien. **~bone**, clavicule *f.* **to take by the ~**, prendre au collet. *v.t.* prendre, saisir au collet, mettre un collier à.

collate *v.t.* comparer, collationner, examiner, conférer. *v.i.* nommer.

collateral *adj.* collatéral, indirect, parallèle, subsidiaire. *n.* collatéral *m.*, parent *m.* collatéral.

collation *n.* collation *f.* (meal), comparaison *f.*, confrontation.

colleague *n.* collègue *m.f.*, confrère *m.*, consoeur *f.* ~ *v.t.* adjoindre.

collect *v.t.* recueillir, ramasser, collectionner, encaisser (funds), percevoir. *n.* collecte *f.*; quête *f.*, **~ call**, appel *m.* en PCV.

collection *n.* collection *f.*; recueil *m.*, amas *m.*; collecte *f.*, quête *f.*; encaissement *m.* (funds); levée *f.* (by the Post Office).

collective *adj.* collectif.

collectively *adv.* collectivement.

collectivity *n.* collectivité *f.*

collector *n.* collectionneur *m.*, collectionneuse *f.*

college *n.* université *f.*, établissement *m.* l'enseignement supérieur.

collide *v.i.* se heurter, se cogner, se frapper l'un contre l'autre.

collie *n.* colley *m.*

collision *n.* choc *m.*, collision *f.*

colloquial *adj.* familier, de conversation.

colloquialism *n.* expression *f.* familière.

colloquially *adv.* familièrement.

colloquy *n.* colloque *m.*, conversation *f.*, entretien *m.*, conférence *f.*, dialogue *m.*

collusion *n.* collusion *f.*

collusive *adj.* collusoire.

colon *n.* Anat. côlon *m.*; deux points [:].

colonel *n.* colonel *m.*

colonial *adj.* colonial.

colonist *n.* colon *m.*

colonization *n.* colonisation *f.*

colonize *v.t.* coloniser.

colonizer *n.* colonisateur *m.*

colonnade *n.* colonnade *f.*

colony *n.* colonie *f.*

coloration *n.* coloration *f.*; coloris.

colossal *adj.* colossal.

colosseum *n.* colisée *m.*

colossus *n.* colosse *m.*

color *n.* couleur *f.*; coloris *m.*; teint *m.*; rougeur *f.*; apparences *f.pl.*; drapeau *m.* **gaudy ~**, couleur voyante. **water~**, aquarelle *f.* **to lose one's ~**, perdre ses couleurs, devenir pâle. **she has a fresh ~**, elle a le teint frais. **~ blindness**, daltonisme *m.* **~ graphics**, graphisme *m.* en couleur. *v.t.* nuancer; colorier: teindre (hair). *v.i.* se colorer; rougir. **he ~ed up to the eyes**, il rougit jusqu'au blanc des yeux.

colorable *adj.* spécieux, plausible.

colored *adj.* coloré; de couleur; colorié; teint.

colorful *adj.* coloré, vif, éclatant, pittoresque, original.

coloring *n.* coloration *f.*

colorless *adj.* incolore; sans couleurs.

colt *n.* poulain *m.*, pouliche *f.*; pistolet *m.*

column *n.* colonne *f.* **~ spinal**, colonne vertébrale. (in newspaper) rubrique.

columnist *n.* journaliste *m.f.*, chroniqueur *m.*

colza *n.* colza *m.*

coma *n.* coma *m.*; chevelure *f.*

comatose *adj.* comateux.

comb *n.* peigne *m.*; crête *f.* (of a rooster); rayon *m.* (of honey). **fine-toothed ~**, peigne fin. *v.t.* peigner. **to ~ out**, démêler.

combat *v.i.* combattre. *v.t.* se battre. *n.* combat *m.*; duel. *m.* **single ~**, combat singulier.

combatant *adj.* qui combat. *n.* combattant *m.*

combativeness *n.* combativité *f.*

combination *n.* combinaison *f.*; association *f.*; coalition *f.*, complot *m.*; concours *m.*

combine *v.t.* lier; réunir. *v.i.* se combiner; s'unir, s'accorder; se coaliser; se liquer ensemble.

combustible *adj.* combustible *n.*

combustion *n.* combustion *f.*; ignition *f.*

come *v.i.* venir, arriver. **he will ~ today**, il viendra aujourd'hui. **here she comes**, la voici qui vient. **~ what may**, advienne que pourra. **how ~?** *Infml.* comment ça se fait?, pourquoi?, d'où vient que? **~, let's go!** allons, partons! **to ~ about**, parvenir à, arriver. **to ~ after**, venir après, succéder, suivre. **to ~ again**, revenir, retourner. **to ~ at**, atteindre, parvenir à. **to ~ by**, passer par; se procurer. **to ~ for**, venir chercher. **to ~ forward**, se présenter, se mettre en avant. **to ~ home**, rentrer chez soi. **to ~ in for**, entrer (pour chercher, prendre). **to ~ off**, sortir de; avoir lieu, se détacher, se retirer, s'en aller. **he came off well**, il s'en est bien tiré. **to ~ out with**, sortir avec; donner issue, laisser échapper, faire parade de. **to ~ short of**, échouer, manquer, ne pas atteindre. **to ~ to**, reprendre connaissance; venir à, parvenir à; en venir à,

être réduit à, revenir à. to ~ to pass, arriver,
advenir, s'effectuer. to ~ up to, s'approcher;
accoster, aborder, s'élever à; répondre à. to
~ upon, attaquer, saisir; surprendre. to ~
up with, atteindre, rejoindre; sortir; suggérer.
Infml. how do you ~ up with that stuff?,
d'où sors-tu des idées pareilles? ~ on! allons!,
allez!

comedian n. comique m.f.

comedienne n. comédienne f., actrice f.
comique.

comedy n. comédie f.

comeliness n. beauté f., bonne mine f.

comely adj. beau, bien fait, gracieux, avenant;
bienséant. adv. avec grâce, galamment; dans les
règles de la bienséance.

comer n. venant m., arrivant m.; venu m. to
all ~s, à tous venants. a new~, un nouveau
venu.

comet n. comète f.

comfort v.t. réconforter, encourager; consoler;
soulager. n. confort m.; bien-être m., aisance f.,
consolation f.; soulagement m.

comfortable adj. à son aise, confortable, commode; bon. a ~ life, une vie douce. to feel ~, se
sentir à son aise, bien.

comfortably adv. à son aise, confortablement;
agréablement.

comforter n. consolateur m., consolatrice f.;
édredon m.

comfortless adj. sans soutien; abandonné,
délaissé, incommode; désolé, inconsolable.

comfy adj. *Infml.* confortable.

comic adj., n. comique m.f.

comical adj. comique, drôle.

comically adv. comiquement, facétieusement.

coming adj. qui vient, prochain, à venir, futur.
this ~ winter, l'hiver prochain. n. venue f.,
approche f.; arrivée f., avenement m.

comma n. virgule f.

command v.t. commander, ordonner, posséder,
disposer de, avoir vue sur, dominer; inspirer. v.i.
gouverner. n. commandement m., ordre m.;
autorité f., pouvoir m.; empire m. he has a fair
~ both of French and English, il possède
assez bien les langues française et anglaise. to
have at one's ~, avoir à sa disposition.

commandant n. commandant m.

commander n. commandant m., chef m.; capitaine de frégate; commandeur m.

commandership n. commandement m.

commanding adj. commandant; dominant;
imposant.

commandement n. commandement m.

commando n. commando m.

commeasurable adj. commensurable.

commemorate v.t. commémorer.

commemoration n. commémoration f.; célébration f.; souvenir m.

commemorative adj. commémoratif.

commence v.i. commencer, débuter.

commencement n. commencement m.; remise
f. des diplômes.

commend v.t. recommander, louer; confier.

commendable adj. recommandable; méritoire,
louable.

commendably adv. louablement, d'une manière
digne d'être louée.

commendation n. recommandation louage f.;
décoration f.

commendatory adj. recommandatoire; élogieux, d'éloges, contenant un éloge.

commensurable adj. commensurable.

commensurate adj. ayant une mesure commune; proportionné. v.t. réduire à une mesure commune, aux mêmes proportions.

comment v.i. commenter, expliquer, interpréter,
gloser, annoter. n. commentaire m.; annotation
f., glose f.

commentary n. commentaire m.; mémoire m.

commentator n. commentateur m., commenta-
trice f.

commerce n. commerce m. foreign ~, commerce extérieur.

commercial adj. commercial; commerçant.

commercially adv. commercialement, dans un
dessein commercial.

commiserate v.t. avoir pitié de, avoir compassion de; plaindre, compatir.

commiseration n. commisération f., pitié f.,
compassion f.

commiserative adj. sensible, compatissant.

commissary n. commissaire m.; intendant m.
militaire; délégué m.; coopérative f.

commission n. commission f.; ordre m.; mandat
m., mission f.; emploi m.; perpétration f. (of a
crime). a ~ of ten percent, une commisssion
de dix pour cent. v.t. commissionner; autoriser;
charger.

commissioner n. commissionnaire m.

commit v.t. commettre, faire, perpétrer; livrer,
mettre; envoyer (to prison); confier. to ~
suicide, se suicider.

commitment n. emprisonnement m.; renvoi m.,
mandat m.; commission f. (of sin).

committal n. gage m., nantissement m.; envoi
m. (to prison).

committee n. comité m., bureau m.;
commission f.

commode n. commode f.

commodious adj. commode.

commodiously adv. commodément.

commodity n. commodité f., avantage m.; marchandise f., produit m.; denrée f.

commodore n. commodore m.; bâtiment m.
convoyeur.

common adj. commun, ordinaire, habituel; bas,
vulgaire; public. ~ friends, des amis communs.
~ sense, sense m. commun, bon sens. a ~
man, un homme du commun. ~ law, droit coutumier. n. biens m.pl. communaux, vaine pâture
f. in ~, en commun.

commoner n. homme m., femme f. du peuple; roturier m., roturière f.; qui a droit de vaine pâture.

commonly adv. communément, ordinairement.

commonness n. frequence f.

commonplace adj. commun, banal, trivial, vulgaire. n. lieu-commun m.

commonwealth n. chose f. publique; république f.

commotion n. agitation f.; commotion f.; emportement m.

communal adj. communal; communautaire.

commune v.i. converser, conférer, communier. n. commune f.; communauté f.

communicable adj. communicable; contagieux; communicatif.

communicant n. communiant m., communiante f.; informateur m.

communicate v.t. communiquer. v.i. communier.

communication n. communication f., commerce m., rapport m.

communicative adj. communicatif; expansif m.

communion n. commerce m., rapports m.pl.; communion f.

communiqué n. communiqué m.

communism n. communisme m.

community n. communauté; corps m. politique, la société f. ~ center, foyer m. socioculturel.

commutability n. permutabilité f.; qualité de pouvoir être communé.

commutation n. commutation f.; échange m.

commutative adj. commutatif.

commute v.t. échanger, changer; commuer; faire le trajet quotidien (maison-travaile et vice-versa).

commuter n. banlieusard m., banlieusarde f.

compact adj. compacte, condus, serré; uni. n. pacte m., convention f. ~ disc, CD, disque m. compact. v.t. rendre compacte, resserrer, unir, condenser, consolider.

compactly adv. d'une manière compacte, serrée, avec concision.

compactness n. compacité f., densité f.

companion n. compagnon m., compagne f., camarade m.f. lady's ~, dame de compagnie. a ~ in arms, un compagnon d'armes.

companionable adj. sociable.

companionship n. camaraderie f.; compagnie f.

company n. compagnie f., société f., assemblée f.; cercle m., troupe f., bande f.; équipage m. to have ~, avoir du monde. to keep ~, tenir compagnie. a trading ~, une société commerciale. a joint stock ~, une société par actions.

comparable adj. comparable.

comparative adj. relatif; comparatif, comparé. n. comparatif m.

comparatively adv. comparativement, par comparaison; relativement.

compare v.t. comparer. n. comparaison f. beyond ~, sans comparaison.

comparison n. comparaison f.

compartment n. compartiment m.; partie f., division f.

compass n. boussole f., étendue f., espace m.; circle m.; circuit m.; bornes f.pl., limites f.pl. ~ v.t. entourer; environner, atteindre, venir à bout de, accomplir; comploter.

compassion n. compassion f. out of ~ for, par compassion pour. v.t. prendre en pitié.

compassionate adj. compatissant. v.t. compatir à, prendre en pitié, avoir de la compassion pour, s'apitoyer sur.

compassionately adv. avec compassion, avec pitié.

compatibility n. compatibilité f.

compatible adj. compatible.

compatriot n. compatriote m.f.

compel v.t. contraindre, forcer, obliger.

compellation n. titre m.

compendium n. précis m., résumé m., sommaire m.

compensate v.t. compenser; dédommager, indemniser.

compensation n. compensation f.; dédommagement m.

compensatory adj. compensatoire.

compete v.i. être en compétition avec, faire concurrence à quelqu'un, rivaliser.

competence, competency n. compétence f., capacité f., aptitude f.; (Jur.) compétence f.

competent adj. compétent.

competently adv. avec compétence.

competition n. rivalité f., concurrence f. a poetry ~, un concours de poésie.

competitive adj. she's very ~, c'est une battante. ~ spirit, esprit de concurrence. ~ exam, concours. ~ prices, prix concurrentiels, compétitifs. a ~ examination, examen de concours.

competitor n. concurrent m., concurrente f., adversaire m.f., rival m.

compilation n. compilation f.

compile v.t. compiler; composer, écrire.

compiler n. compilateur m.

complacency n. contentement m. de soi; satisfaction f. ~ adj. complaisant, de complaisance.

complacently adv. d'un air suffisant.

complain v.i. se plaindre.

complaint n. plainte f., sujet m. de plainte; doléance f.; accusation f.; maladie f., mal m.

complaisance n. complaisance f.; courtoisie.

complaisant adj. complaisant; serviable, aimable.

complement n. complément m., comble m.; complet m. ~ v.t. compléter.

complementary adj. complémentaire.

complete adj. complet, achevé, accompli. v.t. compléter, achever, parfaire; réaliser.

completely adv. complètement, entièrement, parfaitement.

completeness n. état complet, perfection f.

completion *n.* accomplissement *m.*, achèvement *m.*

complex *adj.* complexe; compliqué, embrouillé. *n.* complexe *m.* (buildings). **shopping ~,** center *m.* commercial. **Oedipus ~,** complexe d'Oedipe.

complexion *n.* teint *m.*, couleur *f.*

complexity *n.* complexité *f.*

compliance *n.* conformité *f.*, obéissance *f.*; consentement *m.*, acquiescement *m.*; complaisance *f.*

compliant *adj.* condescendant, complaisant; flexible.

compliantly *adv.* avec complaisance.

complicate *v.t.* compliquer; confondre, mêler. *adj.* compliqué; complexe.

complication *n.* complication *f.*

complicity *n.* complicité *f.*

compliment *n.* compliment *m.* ~ *v.t.* complimenter, faire des compliments.

complimentary *adj.* gracieux, à titre gracieux.

comply *v.i.* s'accommoder, se soumettre, accorder; accomplir; satisfaire à.

component *adj.* constituant, composé. *n.* partie *f.* constitutive, pièces *f.pl.* détachées.

comport *v.i.* s'accorder, convenir à, se conduire, se comporter.

comportement *n.* comportement *m.*, conduite *f.*

compose *v.t.* composer; constituer; calmer, apaiser, arranger. **to ~ oneself,** remettre de l'ardre dans ses idées.

composed *adj.* calme, tranquille.

composer *n.* compositeur *m.*, compositrice *f.*

composition *n.* composition *f.*; arrangement *m.*, compromis *m.*

compositor *n.* compositeur *m.*

compost *n.* engrais *m.* ~ *v.t.* composter.

composure *n.* composition *f.*; maîtrise *f.* de soi; tranquillité *f.* d'esprit, calme *m.*, quiétude *f.*

compound *v.t.* composer; mêler; arranger. *v.i.* entrer en arrangement; s'arranger. *adj.* composé. *n.* composé *m.*; mélange *m.*; enclos *m.*, enceinte *f.*, terrain *m.*

comprehend *v.t.* comprendre, saisir.

comprehensible *adj.* compréhensible.

comprehension *n.* compréhension *f.*; intelligence *f.*

comprehensive *adj.* vaste, étendu; compréhensif.

compress *v.t.* comprimer; condenser, resserrer. *n.* compresse *f.*

compression *n.* compression *f.*

compressor *n.* compresseur *m.*

comprise *v.t.* comprendre, renfermer, inclure, contenir.

compromise *v.t.* arranger, accommoder; compromettre. *v.i.* transférer. *n.* compromis *m.*; arrangement *m.*, transaction *f.*

comptroller *n. Formal.* adminstrateur *m.*, administratrice *f.*; contrôleur *m.*, contrôleuse *f.*; auditeur *m.*, auditrice *f.* à la cour des comptes.

compulsion *n.* contrainte *f.*, coercition *f.*

compulsive *adj.* coercitif; compulsif.

compulsively *adv.* par contrainte, par force.

compulsory *adj.* coercitif, de contrainte, contraignant.

compunction *n.* componction *f.*; remords *m.*

computation *n.* calcul *m.*, estimation *f.*, évaluation *f.* **~ expert,** informaticien *m.*, informaticienne *f.* **~ science,** informatique *f.*

compute *v.t.* compter, calculer; estimer, évaluer. *n.* calcul *m.*, compte *m.*, évaluation *f.*

computer *n.* ordinateur *m.*

computerize *v.t.* informatiser.

comrade *n.* camarade *m.f.*

con *n.* contre *m.* **the pros and ~s,** les pour et les contre. *v.t.* escroquer. *n.* arnaque *f.*, escroquerie *f.* **~ man** *n.*, escroc *m.*

concatenation *n.* enchaînement *m.*, suite *f.*, série *f.*; concaténation *f.*

concave *adj.* concave.

conceal *v.t.* cacher; ôter, éloigner de la vue; recéler (a thief).

concealment *n.* secret *m.*; dissimulation *f.*; cachette *f.*, retraite *f.*; recèlement *m.*, recel *m.*

concede *v.t.* concéder. *v.i.* accorder, admettre.

conceit *n.* vanité *f.*, prétention *f.*, suffisance *f.*

conceited *adj.* prétentieux, vaniteux, suffisant.

conceitedly *adv.* d'une manière affectée; avec suffisance.

conceivable *adj.* concevable.

conceivably *adv.* d'une manière concevable.

conceive *v.t.* concevoir, comprendre; s'imaginer, penser. *v.i.* devenir enceinte; s'imaginer.

concentrate *v.t.* (se) concentrarer.

concentration *n.* concentration *f.*

concept *n.* concept *m.*

conception *n.* conception *f.*; idée *f.*, notion *f.*

conceptive *adj.* conceptif.

concern *v.t.* concerner; regarder; intéresser, toucher; inquiéter; appartenir à. **to ~ oneself about,** s'intéresser à. **why do you ~ yourself with it?** pourquoi vous en inquiétez?; pourquoi vous-y intéressez-vous? *n.* affaire *f.*; intérêt *m.*, importance *f.*; chagrin *m.*, souci *m.*; enterprise *f.* **to be sold as a going ~,** à vendre avec fonds. **that is no ~ of mine,** cela ne me regarde pas.

concerning *prep.* concernant, se rapportant à, regardant.

concert *v.i.* se concerter, se consulter, s'arranger pour. *n.* concert *m.*; accord *m.* **to act in ~ with,** agir de concert avec. **to go to a ~,** aller à un concert.

concerto *n.* concerto *m.*

concession *n.* concession *f.*

concessionary *adj.* par concession.

conch *n.* conque *f.*

conciliate *v.t.* concilier, réconcilier.

conciliation *n.* conciliation *f.*, réconciliation *f.*

conciliatory *adj.* conciliateur, conciliatoire.

concise *adj.* concis.

concisely *adv.* d'une manière concise, avec concision.

conciseness *n.* concision *f.*

conclude *v.t.* conclure; inférer, déduire. **what do you ~ from that?** qu'en concluez-vous? **to ~ a bargain,** conclure un marché. *v.i.* finir, se terminer.

concluding *adj.* final, dernier.

conclusion *n.* conclusion *f.*, fin *f.*; déduction *f.*, dénouement *m.*

conclusive *adj.* conclusif, concluant, décisif.

conclusively *adv.* d'une manière concluante, décisive.

concoct *v.t.* confectionner, composer; *Infml.* trafiquer, combiner, machiner.

concoction *n.* confection *f.*, mélange *m.*; *Infml.* combinaison *f.*; machination *f.*

concomitance *n.* concomitance *f.*

concomitant *adj.* concomitant. *n.* compagnon *m.*, compagne *f.*; suivant *m.*

concord *n.* concorde *f.*; accord *m.*; harmonie *f.*; *Gram.* concordance (of verbs). *v.i.* s'accorder, se mettre d'accord.

concordance *n.* concordance *f.*, accord *m.*

concordant *adj.* concordant, d'accord avec.

concordantly *adv.* de concert, conjointement.

concourse *n.* concours *m.*, foule *f.*, multitude *f.*, affluence *f.*

concrete *adj.* concret. *n. Log.* concret; béton *m.* *v.i.* se concréter. *v.t.* se solidifier.

concretely *adv.* d'une manière concrète.

concretion *n.* concrétion *f.*; calcul *m.*

concretize *v.t.* concrétiser.

concubine *n.* concubine *f.*

concupiscence *n.* concupiscence *f.*

concupiscent *adj.* concupiscent.

concur *v.i.* concourir; s'accorder, être d'accord.

concurrence *n.* concours *m.*; accord *m.*, consentement *m.*

concurrent *adj.* concurrent, concourant; coïncident.

concurrently *adv.* concurremment, avec union.

concuss *v.t.* commotionner.

concussion *n.* secousse *f.*; ébranlement *m.*, commotion *f.* cérébrale.

condemn *v.t.* condamner; déclarer, confisquer.

condemnable *adj.* condamnable; coupable, blâmable.

condemnation *n.* condamnation *f.*

condensation *n.* condensation *f.*

condense *v.i.* se condenser; s'épaissir, se resserrer.

condenser *n.* condensateur *m.*; condenseur *m.*

condescend *v.i.* condescendre; descendre, s'abaisser, daigner.

condescending *adj.* condescendant.

condescendingly *adv.* par condescendance.

condescension *n.* condescendance *f.*

condiment *n.* condiment *m.*

condisciple *n.* condisciple *m.*

condition *n.* condition *f.*; stipulation *f.*, état *m.*; rang *m.* **in good ~,** en bon état.

conditional *adj.* conditionnel. *n.* restriction

f., limitation *f.*, *Gram.* conditionnel *m.*

conditionally *adv.* conditionnellement.

condole *v.i.* partager la douleur; sympathiser.

condolence *n.* condoléances *f.pl.*

condom *n.* préservatif *m.*

condominium *n.* copropriété *f.*, condominium *m.*

condone *v.t.* pardonner.

condor *n.* condor *m.*

conducive *adj.* qui peut servir ou contribuer à.

conduct *n.* conduite *f.*; direction; *v.t.* diriger. **to ~ oneself,** se conduire, se comporter.

conductible *adj.* conductible.

conduction *n.* conduction *f.*

conductive *adj.* conduisant, dirigeant, administrant.

conductivity *n.* conductivité *f.*, conductibilité *f.*

conductor *n.* conducteur *m.*; guide *m.*; chef *m.* d'orchestre; chef *m.* de train. **lightning ~,** paratonnerre *m.*

conduit *n.* conduit *m.*, tuyau *m.*, canalisation *f.*

cone *n.* cone *m.*

confabulate *v.i.* bavarder, converser.

confabulation *n.* conciliabule *m.*

confederacy *n.* confédération *f.*; ligue *f.*; Etats *m.pl.* confédérés.

confederate *adj.* confédéré. *n.* confédéré *m.*, compère *m.*, complice *m.* ~ *v.i.* se confédérer, s'allier. *v.t.* former une ligue.

confederation *n.* confédération *f.*

confer *v.i.* conférer.

conference *n.* conférence *f.*, congrès *m.*; assemblée *f.*, réunion *f.*

conferment *n.* remise *f.*; action *f.* de conférer; octroi *m.*

confess *v.t.* avouer, reconnaître; se confesser.

confession *n.* confession *f.*, aveu *m.*

confetti *n.* confettis *m.pl.*

confidant *n.* confident *m.*, confidente *f.*

confide *v.i.* se confier (à), se fier. **you may ~ in me,** vous pouvez.

confidence *n.* confiance *f.*; assurance *f.*; confidence *f.*

confident *adj.* sûr, assuré, certain; positif; confiant. *n.* confident *m.*

confidential *adj.* de confiance; confidentiel.

confidentially *adv.* confidentiellement.

confidently *adv.* avec confiance, avec assurance.

confiding *adj.* plein de confiance.

configuration *n.* configuration *f.*

configure *v.t.* configurer.

confine *n.* confins *m.pl.*; limites *f.pl.* ~ *v.i.* confiner, borner, restreindre, contenir.

confinement *n.* emprisonnement *m.*, détention *f.*, couches *f.pl.*

confines *n.pl.* confins *m.pl.* (of a place).

confirm *v.t.* confirmer, assurer.

confirmation *n.* confirmation.

confirmative *adj.* confirmatif.

confiscate *v.t.* confisquer. *adj.* confisqué.

confiscation *n.* confiscation *f.*

conflagration *n.* conflagration *f.*, (grand) incendie *m.*

conflict *n.* conflit *m.*; lutte *f.* ~ *v.i.* **(with,** contre) se heurter, s'entre-choquer, lutter contre.

conflicting *adj.* opposé, contraire; contradictoire.

conflictive *adj.* tendant à un conflit, à une lutte.

confluence *n.* confluent *m.;* collection *f.*, réunion *f.*, assemblage *m.*

confluent *adj.* confluent.

conform *adj.* conforme. *v.t.* **(to,** à) rendre conforme, semblable. *v.i.* se conformer.

conformable *adj.* conforme.

conformation *n.* conformation *f.*

conformist *n.* conformiste *m.f.*

conformity *n.* conformité *f.*

confound *v.i.* confondre; embarrasser; déconcerter.

confront *v.t.* affronter, confronter; faire face à.

confrontation *n.* affrontement *m.*, confrontation *f.*

confuse *v.t.* embrouiller (a person). **to get confused,** s'embrouillir. **to ~ the issue,** compliquer les choses, confondre, embrouiller, obscurcir.

confusedly *adv.* confusément, avec confusion, en désordre, pêle-mêle, tumultueusement.

confusion *n.* confusion *f.*, bouleversement *m.*, désordre *m.*

congeal *v.t.* glacer. *v.i.* se congeler, se geler, se durcir.

congenial *adj.* agréble, sympathique.

congenital *adj.* congénital.

conger *n.* congre *m.*, anguille *f.* de mer.

congestion *n.* congestion *f.;* conbrement *m.*

congestive *adj.* congestif.

conglomerate *adj.* congloméré. *n.* conglomérat *m./f.* ~ *v.t.* conglomérer.

conglomeration *n.* conglomération *f.;* agglomération *f.*

congratulate *v.t.* féliciter.

congratulations *n.pl.* félicitations *f.pl.*

congregate *v.i.* se rassembler, se réunir.

congregation *n.* congrégation (d'eglise); assemblée *f.*

congress *n.* congrès *m.*

congressman, ~woman, *pl.* **~men, ~women** *n.* membre *m.* du congrès.

congruent *adj.* convenable, conforme, correspondant.

congruity *n.* convenance *f.;* justesse *f.;* à propos *m.;* conformité *f.*

congruous *adj.* convenable; conforme; congru.

conifer *n.* conifère *m.*

coniferous *adj.* conifère.

conjectural *adj.* conjectural.

conjecture *n.* conjecture *f.*, notion *f.* ~ *v.t.* conjecturer. v.i. se livre à des conjectures.

conjoin *v.i.* s'unir, s'adjoindre, s'associer, se liguer.

conjoint *adj.* conjoint; uni, allié.

conjointly *adv.* conjointement.

conjugal *adj.* conjugal.

conjugate *v.t.* conjuguer. *adj.* conjugué. *n.* conjugué *m.*

conjugation *n.* conjugaison *f.*

conjunct *adj.* conjoint, uni.

conjunction *n.* union *f.*, liaison *f.;* conjonction *f.*

conjure *v.t.* conjurer, prier, implorer. *v.t.* ensorceler. **to ~ up,** évoquer.

conjuring *n.* prestidigitation *f.*, illusionnisme *m.*, magie *f.*

connect *v.t.* joindre, unir; mettre en communication, embrayer. *v.i.* se lier, se rattacher.

connection *n.* connexion *f.;* enchaînement *m.;* liaison *f.*, rapport *m.*, relation *f.*

connivance *n.* connivence *f.*, complicité *f.*

connive *v.i.* être de connivence.

connoisseur *n.* connaisseur *m.*, expert *m.*, experte *f.*

connotation *n.* connotation *f.*, sens total *m.;* implication *f.*

connote *v.t.* signifier, impliquer.

connubial *adj.* conjugal.

conquer *v.t.* vaincre; dompter, surmonter; conquérir.

conqueror *n.* vainqueur *m.;* conquérant *m.*

conquest *n.* victoire *f.;* conquête.

consanguinity *n.* consanguinité *f.*

conscience *n.* conscience *f.* **to satisfy one's ~,** par acquit de conscience.

consienceless *adj.* qui n'a pas de conscience.

conscientious *adj.* consciencieux.

conscientiously *adv.* consciencieusement.

conscious *adj.* conscient. **to be ~ of,** avoir conscience de. **to be ~,** avoir connaissance.

consciously *adv.* consciemment, sciemment.

consciousness *n.* connaissance *f.*, conscience *f.*

conscript *n.* conscrit *m.*, appelé; *v.t.* enrôler, recruter.

conscription *n.* conscription *f.;* enrôlement *m.*

consecrate *v.t.* consacrer, dévouer à des usages sacrés; canoniser; sacrer (bishop, king). **to ~ a church,** consacrer une église.

consecration *n.* consécration *f.;* canonisation; sacre *m.* (bishop, king).

consecutive *adj.* consecutif; successif.

consecutively *adv.* consécutivement.

consensus *n.* consensus *m.*, unanimité *f.*

consent *n.* consentement *m.*, accord *m.* **silence gives ~,** qui ne dit mot consent. **with one ~,** d'un commun accord. *v.i.* consentir.

consequence *n.* conséquence *f.*, suite *f.*, effet *m.*, résultat *m.;* importance *f.* **a thing of no ~,** une chose sans importance.

consequent *adj.* consequent. *n.* conséquence *f.*

consequential *adj.* conséquent, consécutif, logique.

consequently *adv.* par conséquent, en conséquence.

conservation *n.* conservation *f.*, préservation *f.*

conservatism *n.* conservatisme *m.*

conservative adj. conservatif, préservatif; conservateur. n. conservateur m., conservatrice f.

conservatory n. conservatoire m.

conserve v.t. conserver; faire des conserves de; confire. n. conserve f.

consider v.t. considérer, estimer, faire cas de; réfléchir à; reconnaître.

considerable adj. considérable; très grand; (avec to) important.

considerably adv. considérablement, beaucoup.

considerate adj. prévenant, obligeant, circonspect; sense, réfléchi; attentif, modéré, raisonnable.

considerately adv. avec égards, prévenance.

consideration n. considération f.; importance; délibération f. **the affair is under ~,** l'affaire est en délibération.

considering p.pr. considérant; tenant compte de. prep. en raison de, en égard à.

consign adv. passer; confier, remettre; consigner. v.i. se soumettre, souscrire.

consist v.i. avoir de la consistance; subsister, se maintenir. **to ~ of,** se composer de, consister en. **to ~ in,** consister dans, à. **to ~ with,** être compatible, dépendre; s'accorder.

consistence, consistency n. consistancer f.; stabilité f.; suite f.

consistent adj. consistant, solide; conforme, conséquent; compatible. **this is ~ with reason,** cela est conforme à la raison.

consistently adv. conséquemment, d'une manière conséquente; conformément à, en confermité avec.

consolation n. consolation f.

consolatory adj. consolateur m.

console v.t. consoler. n. console f.

consolidate v.t. fortifier; affermir, réunir. v.i. se consolider. adj. consolidé.

consolidation n. consolidation f.

consonance n. consonance f.; accord m., conformité f., harmonie f., convenance f.

consonant adj. d'accord avec, consonnant, conforme. n. consonne f.

consort n. consort m., compagnon m., compagne f., époux m., épouse f. ~ v.i. (avec **with**) s'associer, fréquenter. v.t. unir, marier, accompagner.

conspicuous adj. visible, en vue, en évidence, apparent, manifeste. **to play a ~ part,** jouer un rôle marquant.

conspicuously adv. visiblement, manifestement.

conspicuousness n. visibilité f.; renommée f.; caractère m. remarquable.

conspiracy n. conspiration f., complot m.

conspirator n. conspirateur m., conspiratrice f., conjuré m., conjurée f.

conspire v.i. conspirer. v.t. comploter.

constancy n. stabilité f., constance f.

constant adj. constant, stable, fidèle.

constantly adv. constamment.

constellation n. constellation f.

consternation n. consternation f.

constipate v.t. constiper.

constipation n. constipation f.

constituency n. circonscription f. électorale, électeurs m.pl.

constituent adj. constituant. n. auteur m.; partie f. constituante; commettant m., mandataire m.

constitute v.t. constituer; instituer, établir; nommer.

constitution n. constitution f.; tempérament m.

constitutional adj. constitutionnel. n. (petite) promenade f.

constitutionally adv. constitutionellement.

constitutive adj. constitutif; constituant.

constrain v.t. contraindre, réprimer, renfermer; serrer, étreindre; enchaîner.

constraint n. contrainte f.; nécessité f., obligation f.; force f., violence f., gêne f.

constrict v.t. contracter, reserrer, rétrécir.

constuct v.t. construire, bâtir; interpréter, expliquer.

construction n. construction f., structure f.; interprétation f.

constructive adj. constructif, créateur.

constructively adv. de manière constructive.

constructor n. constructeur m.; ingénieur m., femme f. ingénieur.

construe v.t. construire; interpréter, expliquer.

consul n. consul m.

consular adj. consulaire.

consulate adj. consulat m.

consult v.i. se consulter. v.t. délibérer.

consultant n. conseiller m., conseillère f., spécialiste m.f.

consultation n. consultation f.; délibération f.

consume v.t. brûler; anéantir; gaspiller; consommer. v.i. se consumer, dépérir.

consumer n. consommateur m., consummatrice f., client m., cliente f.

consummate v.t. consommer; compléter, achever. adj. consommé; achevé.

consummation n. consommation f.; fin f., but m.

consumption n. consommation f.

contact n. contact m.; attachement m., rapport m. **~ lens,** verre m. ou lentille f. de contact v.t. contacter.

contagion n. contagion f.

contagious adj. contagieux.

contain v.t. contenir, renfermer; retenir, réprimer. **to ~ one's anger,** réprimer sa colère. **he couldn't ~ himself,** il n'a pas pu se contenir.

container n. recipient m.; conteneur m., container m.

contaminate v.t. contaminer, souiller. adj. souillé, pollué.

contamination n. contamination f.

contemplate v.t. contempler; méditer; songer à, considérer. v.i. rêver à.

contemplation n. contemplation f.; pensée f.
contemplative adj. contemplatif.
contemporaneous adj. contemporain.
contemporaneously adv. simultanément, à la même époque.
contemporary adj. n. contemporain m.
contempt n. mépris m., dédain m.; non-comparution f., outrage m. à la cour.
contemptible adj. méprisable, dédaigneux.
contemptuous adj. méprisant, dédaigneux, insolent.
contemptuously adv. d'un air de mépris, avec dédain.
contend v.t. contester. v.i. combattre, lutter; se disputer; prétendre, affirmer.
contender n. adversaire m.f., concurrent m., concurrente f., candidat m., candidate f.
contending adj. adverse, rival.
content adj. (with, de) content, tranquille, satis-fair. v.t. contenter, satisfaire, plaire. n. contente-ment m.
contented adj. content, satisfait.
contentedly adv. avec contentement.
contention n. contestation f., dispute f.
contentious adj. contentieux; querelleur.
contentment n. contentement m.
contents n.pl. contenu m.; contenance f. **the ~ of a book**, le contenu d'un livre. **table of ~**, table des matières. **the ~ of a barrel**, la capaci-té, le contenu d'un tonneau.
contest v.t. contester. v.i. se disputer, se débattre, rivaliser. n. lutte f., combat m., conflit m.; contes-tation f.
contestant n. adversaire m.f.; concurrent m., concurrente f.
contestation n. contestation f.; discussion f.
context n. contexte m.
contiguous adj. contigu.
continence n. continence f.
continent adj. continent, modéré; chaste. n. continent m.
continental adj. continental.
contingency n. contingence f., éventualité f.; cas m. imprévu.
contingent adj. conditionnel; contingent. n. cas m. fortuit, chance f.; contingent m.
continual adj. continuel.
continually adv. continuellement.
continuance n. continuation f.; furée f., remise f., ajournement m. (trial).
continuation n. continuation f., suite f.
continue v.i., v.t. continuer; poursuivre.
continuity n. continuité f.
continuous adj. continu.
continuously adv. en continuation, sans interruption.
contort v.t. tordre, contorsionner, contourner.
contortion n. contorsion f.; luxation f.
contortionist n. contorsionniste m.f.
contour n. contour m.
contra prep. contre.

contraband adj. de contrebande. n. contrebande f.
contraception n. contraception f.
contraceptive n. contraceptif m. ~ adj. contra-ceptif, anticonceptionnel.
contract v.t. abréger. **to ~ debts**, contracter, fai-re des dettes. v.i. se contracter, se resserrer. n. contrat m., adjudication f., pacte m., engagement m. **to draw up a ~**, rédiger un contract. **to sell by private ~**, vendre de gré à gré. **to do under ~**, faire par enterprise. **to ~ in**, s'engager. **to ~ out**, se libérer, sous-traiter.
contraction n. contraction f.; resserrement m., rétrécissement m.; crispation f. (nerves).
contractor n. contractant m., entrepreneur m., adjudicataire m., fournisseur m.
contradict v.t. contredire, démentir; s'opposer.
contradiction n. contradiction f.
contradictory adj. contradictoire; opposé, contraire, inconséquent. n. contradictoire f.
contradistinction n. contraste m.; à l'oppo-sé de.
contrarily adv. contrairement.
contrariness n. esprit m. de contradiction.
contrariwise adv. au contraire, d'autre part.
contrary adj. contraire; opposé. n. contraire m. **on the ~**, au contraire. **quite the ~**, tout au contraire
contrast v.t. faire contraster, mettre en con-traste. v.i. contraster; trancher. n. contraste m.
contravene v.t. enfreindre, violer, contrevenir.
contribute v.t. contribuer. v.i. (**to** or **toward**) contribuer, concourir à.
contribution n. contribution f.
contributor n. contribuataire m.f., collaborateur m., collaboratrice f.
contrite adj. contrit; pénitent.
contrition n. contrition f.
contrivance n. arrangement m., disposition f.; invention f., machination f.
contrive v.t. combiner, inventer; machiner, tra-mer. v.i. s'arranger pour, venir à bout de.
control n. contrôle m.; influence f., autorité f. v.t. contrôler, diriger, maîtriser, réprimer; régler, gouverner, surveiller. **remote ~**, télécommande f. **~ room**, poste de commande m.
controllable adj. contrôlable, domptable.
controller n. contrôleur m., contrôleuse f.
controversial adj. controversé.
controversy n. controverse f.; polémique f., dis-cussion f., contestation f.
controvert v.t. controverser; disputer, nier; réfuter.
contumacious adj. entêté, opiniâtre.
contumacy n. entêtement m., opiniâtreté f.
contusion n. contusion f., meurtrissure f.
conundrum n. devinette f., énigme m.
convalescence n. convalescence f.
convalescent adj. convalescent. n. convalescent m., convalescente f.
convection n. convection f.

convene v.i. se réunir, se rencontrer, s'assembler. v.t. convoquer.

convenience n. convenance f., commodité f., aise f., aisance f. **at your earliest ~**, dès que vous le pourrez, sans vous déranger. **~ store**, épicerie f. de voisinage.

convenient adj. pratique; convenable. **when will it be ~ for you to pay me?** quand vous conviendra-t-il de me payer? **will that be ~?** vous conviendra-t-il?

conveniently adv. convenablement; commodément. **~ located, situated,** bien situé.

convent n. couvent m.

convention n. union f., convention f.; accord m.

conventional adj. conventionnel.

conventionally adv. conventionnellement.

converge v.i. coverger.

convergence n. convergence f.

convergent adj. convergent.

conversant adj. intime, familier, au courant, entendu.

conversation n. conversation f., entretien m. **a private ~,** un tête-à-tête.

conversational adj. de conversation.

converse v.i. (**with**) converser, s'entretenir. adj. conraire, inverse; réciproque.

conversely adv. réciproquement, vice versa.

conversion n. conversion f.

convert v.t. changer. v.i. se convertir. n. converti m.

converter n. convertisseur m.; adaptateur m.

convertible adj. convertible. **~ car,** voiture f. décapotable.

convex adj. convexe.

convey v.t. porter, transporter; mener; communiquer; exprimer; transmettre. **that word does not ~ my meaning,** ce mot n'exprime pas mon idée.

conveyance n. transport m.; transmission f., transfer m.

conveyor n. transporteur m., convoyeur m.; transmetteur m. **~ belt,** tapis m. roulant.

convict v.t. trouver coupable; condamner. adj. prouvé coupable. n. détenu m., détenue f., forçat m.

conviction n. conviction f.; condamnation f.

convince v.t. convaincre; persuader.

convincing adj. convaincant, probant. **a ~ proof,** une preuve convaincante.

convincingly adv. d'une manière convaincante.

convivial adj. convivial, joyeux, jovial.

conviviality n. bonne jumeur f.; convivialité f., sociabilité f.

convocation n. convocation f.; assemblée f., réunion f.

convoke v.t. convoquer.

convolution n. circonvolution f.; enroulement m.; entrelacement m.

convolvulus n. volubilis m., belle-de-jour f.

convoy v.t. convoyer. n. convoi m.; escorte f.

convulse v.t. convulsionner; ébranler, agiter, bouleverser.

convulsion n. convulsion f., Fig. commotion, agitation f.

convulsive adj. convulsif.

coo v.i. roucouler.

cook v.t. faire cuire; falsifier, altérer. v.i. faire la cuisine, cuisiner. n. cuisinier m., cuisinière f., coq m. **~book,** livre m. de cuisine.

cooker n. cocotte f. **pressure ~,** cocotte minute.

cookery n. cuisine n.p.

cookie n. biscuit m.

cooking n. cuisine f.; cuisson f.

cool adj. frais; froid; indifférent; impudent, fort. **a ~ evening,** une soirée fraîche. **a ~ answer,** une réponse froide. n. fraîcheur f., frais m. **to enjoy the ~,** prendre le frais. v.t. Fig. calmer, apaiser, attiédir. **this will ~ you down,** ça va te calmer, t'apaiser. **keep ~,** relaxe, pas de panique. **~ it!** du calme! **I lost my ~,** j'ai perdu mon sang-froid. v.i. se refroidir, se rafraîchir, se modérer, se calmer.

cooler n. glacière f.; refraîchissant m., Infml. taule f. (prison).

coolish adj. un peu frais.

coolly adv. fraîchement; froidement.

coolness n. fraicheur f., frais m.

coop n. poulailler m. v.i. enfermer étroitement.

co-op n. coopérative f., coop f.

cooper n. tonnelier m.

cooperate v.i. coopérer; concourir à, contribuer à.

cooperation n. coopération f.

cooperative adj. coopératif; (apartement) en copropriété.

coordinate adj. coordonné. v.t. coordonner.

coordination n. coordination f.

cop n. flic m., poulet m. v.i. Infml. **to ~ out,** se défiler de ses responsabilités.

copartner n. coassocié m., coassociée f.

copartnership n. participation f.; coassociation f.

cope v.i. faire face, affronter, en venir à bout. **he can't ~ with it anymore,** il n'en peut plus.

copier n. photocopieur m.

copilot n. copilote m.f.

copious adj. copieux, abondant, ample, fort.

copiously adv. copieusement.

copper n. cuivre m., billon m., monnaie f. de cuivre. adj. de cuivre, en cuivre; cuivré. v.t. cuivrer. **~-bottomed, ~-plated,** doublé en cuivre. **~ coin,** monnaie f. de cuivre; billon m. **~ colored,** cuivré.

copulate adj. joint, uni. v.i. s'accoupler. v.t. joindre, unir, accoupler.

copulation n. copulation f.

copy n. copie f.; exemplaire m. (of a book); modèle m., manuscrit m. **a fair ~,** copie au net. **true ~,** copie conforme. **~ grosse** f., expédition f. **a rough copy,** brouillon m. **~ book,** cahier m. d'écriture. v.t. copier.

copycat n. Infml. copieur m., copieuse f.

copyedit *v.i.* corriger (les épreuves).

copy editor *n.* secretaire *m.f.* de rédaction.

copying *n.* transcription *f.;* (in school) copiage *m.*

copyist *n.* compiste *m.*

copyright *n.* droit *m.* d'auteur, droit *m.* de propriété littéraire.

coquetry *n.* coquetterie *f.*

coral *n.* corail *m.* *adj.* de corail, corallin.
~ **branch,** branche *f.* de corail. ~ **fishery,** ~ **fishing,** pêche *f.* du corail. ~ **reefs,** ~ **islands,** bancs *m.pl.* de corail.

cord *n.* corde *f.;* cordage *m.,* cordon *m.* **umbilical** ~, cordon *m.* ombilical. *v.t.* corder; lier avec une corde.

cordial *adj.* cordial. **a ~ welcome,** un accueil cordial. *n.* cordial *m.*

cordiality *n.* cordialité *f.*

cordially *adv.* cordialement.

cordon *n.* cordon *m.* ~ **bleu,** cordon *m.* bleu. **to ~ off,** interdire l'accès (police).

core *n.* coeur *m.;* trognon *m.* (of fruits). **the ~ of an apple,** trognon de pomme. **in the heart's ~,** au fond du coeur.

coriander *n.* coriandre *f.*

cork *n.* liège *m.,* chêne-liège *m.;* bouchon *m.* *v.t.* boucher avec un bouchon de liège. ~ **screw,** tire-bouchon *m.*

cormorant *n.* cormoran *m.*

corn *n.* maïs *m.;* cor *m.* (on toe). ~ **plaster,** coricide *m.* ~ **belt,** région *f.* du maïs. ~ **bread,** pain *m.* de farine de maïs. ~ **meal,** farine *f.* du maïs. ~ **oil,** huile *f.* de maïs. **that film was pure ~,** ce film n'était que banalités. ~ **field,** champ *m.* de maïs. ~ **flake,** céréales *f.pl.*

cornea *n.* cornée *f.*

corner *n.* coin *m.;* angle *m.,* encoignure *f.;* recoin *m.;* cachette *f.* ~ **house,** maison *f.* du coin. ~ **stone,** pierre *f.* angulaire. *v.t.* (with **up**) accaparer. **to cut ~s,** regarder aux dépenses, prendre des raccourcis.

cornice *n.* corniche *f.*

corny *adj.* *Infml.* bête, banal.

corolla *n.* corolle *f.*

corona *n.* couronne *f.;* larmier.

coronary *adj.* coronaire.

coronation *n.* couronnement *m.;* sacre *m.*

coroner *n.* coroner *m.*

corporal *n.* caporal *m.* ~ **punishment,** châtiment *m.* corporel.

corporate *adj.* corporatif de société. ~ **culture,** culture *f.* de société. ~ **law,** droit *m.* des sociétés. ~ **spirit,** esprit *m.* de corps.

corporation *n.* société *f.* enregistrée; compagnie *f.,* société *f.* légale.

corporeal *adj.* corporel, matériel.

corps *n.* corps *m.*

corpse *n.* corps *m.,* cadavre *m.,* restes *m.pl.*

corpulence *n.* corpulence *f.;* densité *f.*

corpulent *adj.* corpulent; replet.

corpus *n.* recueil *m.,* corpus *m.;* *Fin.* capital *m.*

Corpus Christi *n.* fête *f.* du Saint-Sacrement.

corpuscle *n.* corpuscule *m.*

correct *adj.* correct; juste, exact. *v.t.* corriger.

correction *n.* correction *f.*

correctional *adj.* correctionnel.

corrective *adj.* correctif. *n.* correctif *m.*

correctly *adv.* correctement.

correctness *adj.* justesse *f.;* exactitude *f.;* correction *f.*

correlate *v.i.* être corrélatif.

correlation *n.* corrélation *f.*

correspond *v.i.* correspondre, se correspondre, se rapporter; repondre à; s'accorder avec.

correspondence *adj.* correspondance *f.,* rapport *m.*

correspondent *adj.* correspondant, conforme, qui s'accorde avec. *n.* correspondant *m.,* correspondante *f.*

corridor *n.* corridor *m.*

corroborate *v.t.* corroborer, fortifier; confirmer.

corroboration *n.* corroboration *f.;* confirmation *f.*

corroborative *adj.* corroboratif. *n.* corroborant *m.*

corrode *v.t.* corroder, miner, ronger.

corrosion *n.* corrosion *f.*

corrosive *adj.* corrosif *m.*

corrosiveness *n.* corrosiveté *f.*

corrugate *v.t.* plisser, rider, froncer. *adj.* contracté, plissé, ridé, froncé.

corrugated *adj.* ridé, plissé. ~ **cardboard,** carton. *m.* ondulé.

corrupt *v.t.* altérer, falsifier, séduire, débaucher. **to ~ the morals,** corrompre les moeurs. **to ~ witnesses,** corrompre, suborner les témoins. *v.i.* se corrompre. *adj.* corrompu; dépravé.

corruption *n.* corruption *f.;* souillure *f.;* pus *m.*

corsage *n.* corsage *m.*

corsair *n.* corsaire *m.*

Corsica *n.pr.* Corse *f.*

Corsican *adj.* corse, de Corse. *n.* Corse *m.f.*

cortege *n.* cortège *m.*

corvette *n.* corvette *f.*

cosily *adv.* confortablement.

cosine *adj.* cosinus *m.*

cosmetic *adj.* cosmétique. *n.* cosmétique *m.*

cosmic *adj.* cosmique.

cosmopolitan *n.* cosmopolite *m.f.*

cosmos *n.* cosmos *m.*

cosset *v.t.* gàter, faire son favori de.

cost *n.* coût *m.;* prix *m.;* frais *m.pl.,* dépense *f.* **cost-effectiveness** *n.* rentabilité *f.* **cost-effective** *adj.* rentable. *v.t.* coûter.

costal *adj.* costal.

costar *n.* qui partage l'affiche. *v.i.* partager l'affiche.

costive *adj.* constipé.

costliness *n.* grande dépense *f.,* luxe *m.,* splendeur *f.*

costly *adj.* coûteux, somptueux, précieux.

costume *n.* costume *m.*

cosy adj. (place) douillet, (person) bien au chaud. **~ room**, pièce f. confortable.

cot n. cabane f.; doigtier m.; petit lit m. (for child); lit pliant; lit de camp.

cottage n. petite maison, chaumière f.

cotton n. coton m.; cotonnade f. ~ adj. de coton, composé de coton. **~ mill**, filature f. de coton. **~ tree, ~ plant**, cotonnier m. **~ print**, toile f. de coton imprimée en couleur. **~ spinning**, filature f. du coton. v.t. **to ~ to**, (take a liking to) se prendre d'amitié pour.

cottony adj. cotonneux.

couch v.i. formuler, rédiger. **their reply was ~ed in insulting language**, leur réponse était exprimée en termes injurieux. n. canapé m., divan m.

cougar n. couguar m.

cough n. toux f. **whooping ~**, coqueluche f. ~ v.i. tousser.

could pret. of verb CAN.

council n. conseil m., assemblée f. **city ~**, conseil municipal.

councillor n. conseiller m., conseillère f.

counsel n. consultation f., délibération f. **keep your own ~**, n'en parlez à personne. v.i. conseiller, aviser.

counselor n. conseiller m., conseil m. jurisconsulte m., avocat m., avocate f.

count v.t. compter; calculer, supputer, imputer, attribuer, tenir pour. **~ me in**, compte sur moi, j'en fais parti. **I ~ on you**, je compte sur vous. n. compte m., calcul m.; chef m. d'accusation. **a German ~**, un comte allemand.

countenance n. visage m., figure f., physionomie f., contenance f., maintien m., air m., mine f. **a cheerful ~**, un air gai. **to give ~ to**, seconder, appuyer. v.t. favoriser; aider.

counter n. comptoir m.; compteur m. adv. contrairement, à rebours, à l'encontre de.

counteract v.t. contrarier, contre-carrer; neutraliser; déjouer.

counteraction n. résistance f., empêchement m.

counterattack n. contre-attaque f. ~ v.t.,v.i. contre attaquer.

countercheck v.t. contrecarrer, tenir en échec; réprimander. n. force f. opposée, contre-échec m.; reproche m., réprimande f.

counterclockwise adv. dans le sens inverse des aiguilles d'une montre.

countercurrent n. contre-courant m. ~ adj. qui prend, qui suit une direction opposée.

counterespionage n. contre-espionnage m.

counterfeit v.t. contrefaire; imiter. **to ~ money**, faire de la fausse monnaie. v.i. dissimuler. adj. contrefait; faux; feint, simulé. **~ money**, fausse monnaie. n. contrefaçon f., imitation f.; imposteur m.

counterfoil n. talon m. (de souche).

counterintelligence n. contre-espionnage m.

countermand v.t. contremander; décommander. n. contre-ordre m.

counterpart n. homologue m.f., contrepartie f.; copie f.

countess n. comtesse f.

countless adj. sans nombre, innombrable.

countrified adj. rustique, rural, compagnard.

country n. campagne f.; province f.; contrée f.; paus m.; patrie f. mother ~, mère-patrie. **to love one's ~**, aimer son pays, sa patrie. adj. de la campagne, campagnard, champêtre, rural; provincial. **~ life**, la vie de campagne, la vie de province. **~ people**, campagnards, provinciaux.

countryman n. compatriote m.; campagnard m., provincial m. **my fellow ~men**, mes chers concitoyens m.

countrywoman, compatriote f., concitoyenne f.

county n. comté m.; département m. ~ adj. de comté. **~ court**, cour f., tribunal m. **~ seat**, chef-lieu m. de comté.

coup n. coup m., coup d'état.

couple n. couple f., moise f. **a ~ of eggs**, un couple d'oeufs. **an old ~**, un vieux couple, de vieux époux. v.t. coupler. v.i. s'unir, s'accoupler.

coupling n. accouplement m.; assemblage m.

coupon n. coupon m., bon m. de réduction.

courage n. courage m.

courageous adj. courageux.

courageously adv. courageusement.

courier n. courrier m., messager m.

course n. cours m.; course f., carrière f.; parcours m.; service m., entrée f. (of a meal); genre m., train m. (of life); courant m.; route f.; piste f., hippodrome m. **water ~**, cours d'eau. **the ~ of events**, le cours des événements. **in the ~ of the day**, pendant le cours de la journée. **~ of studies**, cours d'études. **the ~ of exchange**, le cours du change. **of ~**, évidemment, bien sûr, naturellement. **that is a matter of ~**, cela va sans dire. v.i. courir; circuler. v.t. donner la chasse à, faire courir.

court n. cour f.; tribunal m.; impasse f., court m. (sports). **front ~**, cour de devant. **the ~ has acquitted him**, la cour l'a acquitté. v.t. courtiser; faire la cour; solliciter, briguer.

courteous adj. affable, poli, courtois.

courteously adv. poliment, courtoisement.

courteousness n. politesse f., courtoisie f.

courtesy n. courtoisie f.

courtly adj. courtois, élégant, poli; flatteur. adv. poliment.

court-martial n. conseil m. de guerre.

courtship n. cour f.

courtyard n. cour f.

cousin n. cousin m., cousine f.

cove n. petite baie f., crique f., petite anse f.

covenant n. convention f., pacte m.

cover v.t. couvrir; cacher; vêtir, couver (birds). **the receipts have covered the expenses**, la recette a couvert les frais. **that horse can ~ thirty miles in two hours**, ce cheval peut faire trente milles en deux heures. n. couvercle m., couverture f. (bed); enveloppe f.; couvert m., pli *m.*, housse *f.* (furniture); abri *m.*, refuge *m.*, retraite *f.* under ~ of the night, à la faveur de la nuit. under ~ of friendship, sous le masque de l'amitié. under~, incognito, sous une fausse identité. ~ up, cacher, dissimuler. they tried to ~ up the murder, ils ont essayé de dissimuler le meurtre. to return to ~, revenir au gîte.

covering *n.* couverture *f.*; vêtement *m.*;

covert *adj.* couvert, caché; insidieux; protégé, à l'abri.

covertly *adv.* secrètement, insidieusement.

covet *v.t.* convoiter. *v.i.* éprouver en désir sérieux; aspirer.

covetous *adj.* avide; cupide; avare.

covey *n.* couvée *f.*; volée *f.*, vol *m.*

cow *n.* vache *f.* sacred ~, vache sacrée. *Infml.* when the cows come home, quand les poules auront des dents. *v.t.* intimider, décourager.

coward *n.* poltron *m.*, poltronne *f.*, lâche *m.f.*

cowardice *n.* lâcheté *f.*, poltronnerie *f.*

cowardliness *n.* poltronnerie *f.*, lâcheté *f.*

cowardly *adj.* poltron, lâche. *adv.* lâchement, en lâche, en poltron.

cower *v.i.* s'affaisser, se courber en fléchissant les genoux; s'abaisser; s'accroupir, se tapir.

cowhide *n.* peau *f.* de vache tannée.

cowl *n.* capuchon *m.*; chapeau *m.* de cheminée.

co-worker *n.* collègue *m.f.*

coy *adj.* réservé, timide, sauvage.

coyly *adv.* avec réserve, timidement.

coyness *n.* réserve *f.*, timidité *f.*

coyote *n.* coyote *m.*

crab *n.* crabe *m.*; *Astron.* cancer *m.*; ~ apple, pomme *f.* sauvage. ~ louse, morpion *m.*

crack *v.t.* casser; faire claquer (a whip). to ~ a glass, fêler un verre. to ~ a nut, casser une noisette. to ~ a bottle of wine with a friend, faire sauter le bouchon avec un ami. to ~ a joke, sortir une blague. to ~ up, éclater de rire. to ~ down, tomber sur. *v.i.* se fendre, se briser; se fêler, se gercer, se crevasser. the wood is cracking, le bois se fend. *n.* rupture *f.*, fente *f.*, fissure *f.*; craquement *m.*, éclat *m.*, détonation *f.* *adj.* fameux, de première force. a ~ regiment, un corps d'élite.

cracker *n.* craquelin *m.*, cracker *m.*, biscuit *m.* salé.

cracking *adj.* fendant; craquant, pétillant. Get cracking! au boulot!

crackle *v.i.* craqueter; pétiller; décrépiter.

cradle *n.* berceau *m.*; *v.t.* bercer.

craft *n.* art *m.*, habileté *f.*, métier *m.*, small ~, petits bâtiments de toutes espèces.

craftily *adv.* avec finesse; adroitement.

craftiness *n.* art *m.*, ruse *f.*, artifice *m.*

craftsman *n.* artisan *m.*, ouvrier *m.*

craftswoman *n.* artisane *f.*, ouvrière *f.*

crafty *adj.* fin, rusé, astucieux.

crag *n.* rocher *m.* escarpé, roc *m.* abrupte.

craggy *adj.* rocailleux.

cram *v.t.* remplir avec excès; entasser, bourrer; *Infml.* farcir; gorger (with food). *v.i.* se gorger de nourriture, se bourrer, *Infml.* bachoter (for an exam).

cramp *n.* crampe *f.* ~ *v.t.* donner, causer des crampes.

crampons *n.* crampon *m.*

cranberry *n.* canneberge *f.*, airelle *f.*

crane *n.* grue *f.* to work a ~, manoeuvrer une grue.

cranial *adj.* cranien.

cranium *n.* crâne *m.*, boîte *f.* crânienne.

crank *n.* manivelle *f.*; (person) maniaque *m.f.*

cranky *adj.* grinceux, de mauvaise humeur.

cranny *n.* fente *f.*, fissure *f.*, lézarde *f.*, crevasse *f.*

crap *n.* *Infml.* merde *f.*, conneries *f.pl.*

crape *n.* crêpe *m.*

crappy *adj.* *Infml.* merdique.

crash *v.t.* briser, fracasser. *v.i.* éclater avec fracas; entrer en collision; s'écraser. *n.* fracas *m.*; *Fin.* faillite, ruine *f.* totale, drap *m.*, écrasement *m.*, chute *f.*, catastrophe *f.*

crass *adj.* gros, épais, grossier.

crate *n.* caisse *f.* (à claire-voie); coucou (plane); bagnole (car).

crater *n.* cratère *m.*

crave *v.t.* désirer.

craven *n.* poltron *m.* ~ *adj.* lâche *m.*

craving *n.* désir *m.* ardent; supplication *f.*

crawfish, crayfish *n.* écrevisse *f.*

crawl *v.i.* marcher à quatre pattes, ramper; se traîner; crawler, faire le crawl. crawl *m.*

crayon *n.* crayon *m.* de pastel, pastel *m.*; dessin *m.* au pastel. *v.t.* dessiner au pastel; esquisser, faire un plan, ébaucher.

craze *v.t.* rendre fou, déranger. *n.* radotage *m.*; travers *m.*, manie *f.*

craziness *n.* folie *f.*, démence *f.*

crazy *adj.* insensé, fou.

creak *v.i.* grincer, crisser.

cream *n.* crème *f.* whipped ~, crème fouettée. ~ of tartar, crème de tartre. ~ cheese, fromage *m.* à la crème, petit suisse. ~-colored, couleur de crème. *v.t.* écrémer, *Fig.* battre.

creamy *adj.* crémeux; douceureux.

crease *n.* pli *m.*, faux-pli *m.*; raie *f.* creuse, rainure *f.*; étampe *f.* ~ *v.t.* faire des plis; chiffonner.

create *v.t.* créer; causer; produire. to ~ a sensation, produire une sensation.

creation *n.* création *f.*

creative *adj.* créateur.

creativity *n.* créavitité *f.*

creator *n.* créateur *m.*, créatrice *f.*

creature *n.* créature *f.*, un être vivant, une bête. our fellow ~s, nos semblables.

credence *n.* créance *f.*

credentials *n.pl.* références *f.pl.*, certificat *m.*, diplôme *m.*, lettres *f.pl.* de créance.

credibility *n.* crédibilité *f.*

credible *adj.* croyable.

credit *n.* crédit *m.*; croyance *f.*, créance *f.*, foi *f.*;

honneur *m.;* témoignage *m.* **I give him ~ for his work,** je rends justice à son travail. **he lost ~ within his party,** il a perdu tout crédit dans son parti. **to buy on ~,** acheter à crédit. **to give ~,** faire crédit. *v.t.* faire honneur à; créditer. **~ my account with this sum,** portez cette somme à mon avoir, créditez-moi de cette somme.

creditable *adv.* honorable, estimable, honnête.
creditor *n.* créancier *m.,* créancière *f.*
credulity *n.* crédulité *f.*
credulous *adj.* crédule.
creed *n.* symbole *m.,* profession *f.* de foi, credo *m.;* croyance *f.,* foi *f.*
creek *n.* courts *m.* d'eau, ruisseau *m.*
creep *v.i.* ramper; se trainer; se glisser, se faufiler. **to ~ along,** aller en rampant, se traîner. **to ~ in,** entrer en rampant. **to ~ out,** sortir en rampant; *Infml.* **he gave me the ~s,** il m'a foutu la frousse, il m'a fait froid dans le dos. *Infml.* **he is a ~,** c'est un vrai salaud.
creeper *n.* reptile *m.,* plante *f.* grimpante; crampons *m.pl.* à verglas.
creepy *adj.* qui donne la chair de poule.
cremate *v.t.* incinérer.
crematorium *n.* crématorium *m.*
creole *n.* créole *m.*
crêpe *n.* crêpe *f.*
crepitate *v.i.* crépiter, pétiller.
crepitation *n.* crépitation *f.,* pétillement *m.*
crepuscular *adj.* crépusculaire.
crescent *adj.* croissant. *n.* croissant *m.* demilune *f.*
cress *n.* cresson *m.*
crest *n.* cimier *m.;* crête *f.* (of cock); orgueil *m.* **~-fallen,** découragé, abattu.
crevasse *n.* fissure *f.*
crevice *n.* fente *f.,* fissure *f.*
crew *n.* équipage *m.*
crib *n.* lit *m.* d'enfant, mangeoire *f.,* étable *f.* à boeufs.
cricket *n.* cri-cri *m.,* grillon *m.; Sport.* cricket *m.*
crime *n.* crime *m.* **capital ~,** crime capital.
criminal *adj.* criminel. **~ law,** droit criminel. *n.* criminel *m.,* criminelle *f.*
criminality *n.* criminalité *f.*
crimonology *n.* criminologie *f.*
crimp *v.t.* friser, crêper (hair); gaufrer.
crimson *n.* cramoisi *m.,* rouge *m.,* incarnat *m.* *adj.* cramoisi. *v.i.* rougir.
cringe *v.i.* contracter. *v.i.* faire des courbettes.
crinkle *v.i.* froisser, froufrouter, plisser.
cripple *n.* estropié *m.,* estropiée *f.,* invalide *m.f.* **~** *adj.* impotent, estropié. *v.i.* estropier.
crisis or *pl.* **crises** *n.* crise *f.*
crisp *adj.* croustillant, croquant.
crispy *adj.* croustillant, croquant.
crisscross *adj.* entrecroisé; *v.i.* s'entrecroiser, *v.t.* entrecroiser.
criterion or *pl.* **criteria** *n.* critère *m.*
critic *n.* critique *m.* ~ *adj.* critique. *v.i.* critiquer.

critical *adj.* critique; *Med.* difficile, dangereux, décisif.
critically *adv.* d'une manière critique.
criticism *n.* critique *f.*
criticize *v.t.* critiquer; blâmer.
criticizer *n.* critique *m.*
critique *n.* critique *f.*
croak *v.i.* croasser (raven); coasser (frog); grogner, grommeler. *Infml.* die, crever. *n.* croassement *m.,* coassement *m.*
Croat *n.pr.* Croate *m.*
Croatia *n.pr.* Croatie *f.*
crock *n.* cruche *f.,* pot *m.* de terre; débris *m.pl.* tesson *m.*
crockery *n.* poterie *f.,* faïnce *f.*
crocodile *n.* crocodile *m.*
crocus *n.* crocus *m.,* safran *m.*
crony *n.* copain *m.,* copine *f.*
crook *n.* courbure *f.,* coude *m.;* houlette *f.;* ruse *f.,* detour *m.;* escroc *m.* **~** *v.t.* courber, recourber; pervertir.
crooked *adj.* courbe; courbé, recourbé, crochu.
crookedly *adv.* tortueusement.
crookedness *n.* courbure *f.,* détour *m.;* méchanceté *f.;* perversité *f.*
cron *v.i.,v.t.* fredonner, chantonner.
crooner *n.* chanteur *m.* de charme.
crop *adj.* jabot *m.* (bird); moisson *f.,* récolte *f.* *v.t.* tondre; moissonner, faucher; brouter; cueillir (fruits, flowers).
cropper *n.* chute *f.;* fiasco *m.* **to come a ~,** *Infml.* ramasser une pelle.
cross *n.* croix *f.;* revers *m.,* traverse *f.* **the holy ~,** la sainte croix. **the Latin ~,** la croix latine. **the Greek ~,** la croix grecque. *adj.* oblique; contraire, opposé; fâcheux; maussade, revêche; méchant; contrariant. **to look ~,** avoir l'air de mauvaise humeur. **to ~ purposes,** démêlés, brouilleries. *adv.* de travers, entravers, à rebours. *prep.* à travers, au travers de. *v.t.* croiser, traverser; rayer, biffer, raturer, faire une crois sur. **to ~ over,** traverser. *v.i.* se croiser, être en travers. **~-examination,** interrogatoire *m.* contradictoire. **~-legged,** ayant les jambes croisées. **~road,** carrefour *m.* **~ wind,** vent *m.* de travers, vent *m.* contraire. **~wise,** en travers, de travers; en croix, en forme de croix. **~word(s)** *n.,* mots *m.pl.* croisés.
crossing *n.* croisement *m.,* changement *m.* d voie; traversée *f.,* passage *m.;* carrefour *m.*
crotch *n.* fourche *f.;* entrejambe *m.*
crotchety *adj.* grognon.
crouch *v.i.* ramper, se tapir, se coucher; s'humilier.
croup *n.* croup *m.;* croupion *m.,* croupe *f.*
croupier *n.* croupier *m.*
crout *n.* choucroute *f.*
crow *n.* corneille *f.;* levier *m.,* pince *f.;* chant *m.* (cock). **~'s feet,** pattes *f.* d'oie. *v.i.* chanter (like a cock). **to ~ over,** chanter victoire.
crowd *n.* foule *f.,* multitude *f.* ~ *v.t.* presser,

pousser, fouler; remplir confusément; encombrer. **to ~ in, into**, faire entrer dans, fourrer dans. *v.i.* se presser en foule; pousser en avant; fourmiller.

crown *n.* couronne *f.*, sommet *m.*, comble *m.*, cime *f.*, tonsure *f.* ~ *v.t.* couronner; combler; damer (priest). **~ jewels**, joyaux *m.pl.* de la couronne.

crucial *adj.* crucial; décisif, définitif. **a ~ test**, une épreuve définitive.

crucifix *n.* crucifix *m.*

crucifixion *n.* crucifiement *m.*

cruciform *adj.* cruciforme.

crucify *v.t.* crucifier.

crude *adj.* cru, brut, apre, imparfait; grossier, rustre.

crudely *adv.* crûment.

crudeness *n.* crudité *f.*, état *m.* brut.

cruel *adj.* cruel.

cruelly *adv.* cruellement.

cruelty *n.* cruauté *f.*

cruet *n.* burette *f.* **~ stand**, huilier *m.*

cruise *v.i.* croiser, faire la course. **to cruise in a bar**, draguer. *n.* croisière *f.*; course *f.*

cruiser *n.* croiseur *m.*

cruller *n.* beignet *m.*

crumb *n.* miette *f.*; brin *m.* ~ *v.t.* émietter; paner (cutlets, etc.).

crumble *v.t.* *Fig.* diviser. *v.i.* s'émietter; s'écrouler, tomber en ruines.

crummy *adj.* *Infml.* minable.

crumple *v.t.* froisser, chiffonner. *v.i.* faire des plis, se rider.

crunch *v.t.* croquer, broyer. *n.* craquement *m.*

crunchy *adj.* croquant.

crusade *n.* croisade *f.*

crusader *n.* croisé *m.*

crush *v.t.* écraser, fracasser; anéantir, opprimer. *v.i.* se serrer. se presser. *n.* écrasement *m.*, foule *f.*

crust *n.* croûte *f.*, croûton *m.*; gratin *m.* **the ~ of bread**, la croûte du pain. *v.t.* couvrir d'une croûte; encroûter. *v.i.* se couvrir d'une croûte.

crustacea *n.* crustacés *m.pl.*

crusty *adj.* couvert d'une croûte, croustillant, (surly) bourru.

crutch *n.* béquille *f.*

cry *v.i.* pleurer, crier, s'écrier. **to ~ for joy**, pleurer de joie. **to ~ for help**, crier au secours. **to ~ for vengeance**, crier vengeance. **to ~ out**, pousser des cris; s'écrier. *n.* cri *m.*; clameur, hauts cris; meute *f.* (dogs).

crying *n.* pleur *m.*

cryogenics *n.* cryogénie *f.*

crypt *n.* crypte *f.*

cryptic(al) *adj.* secret, caché, occulte.

cryptography *n.* cryptographie *f.*

crystal *n.* cristal *m.*; verre *m.* de montre. **rock ~**, cristal de roche. *adj.* de cristal.

crystalline *adj.* cristallin.

crystallize *v.i.* se cristalliser.

cub *n.* le petit *m.* de certain animaux; lionceau

m.; louveteau *m.*; ourson *m.*; renardeau *m.*; baleincau *m.* ~ *v.i.* mettre bas, faire des petits.

cube *n.* cube *m.* **~ root**, racine *f.* cubique.

cubic *adj.* cubique; cube.

cubicle *n.* cabine *f.*, alcôve *f.*

cuckoo *n.* coucou *m.*

cucumber *n.* concombre *m.*

cuddle *v.i.* se blottir, câliner. *v.i.* caresser.

cue *adj.* queue *f.* (billard), bout *m.*; signe *m.*, avis *m.*, réplique *f.* **to give a person his ~**, fournir le mot à quelqu'un. *v.t.* donner la réplique.

cuff *n.* revers (of pants); manchette *f.*; poignet *m.* (of shirt), *Infml.* claque *f.*, taloche *f.*

cuisine *n.* cuisine, cooking.

culinary *adj.* culinaire.

cull *v.t.* arracher, cueillir; trier.

culminate *v.i.* culminer.

culmination *n.* culmination *f.*; sommet *m.*, cime *f.*, couronne *f.*, apogée *m.*

culpability *n.* culpabilité *f.*

culpable *adj.* coupable.

culprit *n.* accusé *m.*, prévenu *m.*; criminel *m.*; coupable *m.*

cult *n.* culte *m.*

cultivable *adj.* cultivable.

cultivate *v.t.* cultiver.

cultivation *n.* culture *f.*

cultivator *n.* cultivateur *m.*, fermier *m.*, laboureur *m.*, agriculteur *m.*

cultural *adj.* culturel.

culture *n.* culture *f.*

cumber *v.t.* encombrer, accabler.

cumbersome *adj.* encombrant, gênant.

cumin *n.* cumin *m.*

cumulate *v.t.* accumuler, entasser, amonceler.

cumulation *n.* accumulation *f.*

cumulative *adj.* cumulatif.

cumulus *n.* cumulus *m.*

cunning *adj.* rusé, fin, malin. *n.* fourberie *f.*, artifice *m.*, ruse *f.*, finesse *f.*

cunningly *adv.* astucieusement, avec ruse.

cunningness *n.* ruse *f.*, artifice *f.*, finesse *f.*

cup *n.* coupe *f.*, tasse *f.*, calice *m.* **that's not his ~ of tea**, ça ne lui plait pas; *Infml.* ça n'est pas son truc.

cupboard *n.* armoire *f.*, buffet *m.*

cupidity *n.* cupidité *f.*, convoitise *f.*

curable *adj.* curable, guérissable.

curb *n.* gourmette *f.*; frein *m.*, obstacle *m.*; bordure *f.* (of sidewalk). **~stone**, bordure *f.* de trottoir. **~ your dog**, nettoyez après votre chien.

curd *n.* lait *m.* caillé. *v.t.* cailler, coaguler, figer; faire cailler.

curdle *v.i.* se coaguler, se cailler, se figer, se congeler.

cure *n.* cure *f.*; guérison *f.*, remède *m.*; salaison *f.* ~ *v.t.* guérir; saler (fish, meat), fumer.

curfew *n.* couvre-feu *m.*

curiosity *n.* curiosité *f.*; recherche *f.* **out of ~**, par curiosité.

curious *adj.* curieux; bizarre; singulier.

curiously *adv.* curieusement; bizarrement.

curl *v.t.* courber, plier; friser, boucler; se tordre, se replier, s'enrouler. *v.i.* se crisper; onduler; se tordre. *n.* boucle *f.* (of hair); bouffée *f.* (of smoke).

curly *adj.* bouclé, frisé.

currant *n.* groseille *f.* **red** ~, groseille *f.* rouge. **black** ~, cassis *m.*

currency *n.* cours *m.* (of money); circulation *f.;* monnaie *f.;* devise *f.* **legal** ~, monnaie *f.* légale.

current *adj.* qui a cours, courant; admis, reçu. *n.* courant *m.* (of a river); cours *m;* marche *f.* (of time).

currently *adv.* actuellement, en ce moment.

curriculum *n.* program *m.* scolaire, d'etudes.

curry *n.* cari *m.,* curry *m.* — *v.t.* corroyer; étriller; frotter; caresser, flatter.

curse *v.t.* maudire. *v.i.* jurer, blasphémer. *n.* malédiction *f.,* juror.

cursed *adj.* maudit; afflicté de.

cursor *n.* curseur *m.* ~ **key,** touche *f.* de curseur.

cursory *adj.* précipité, fait à la hâte, superficiel.

curt *adj.* court; brusque, cassant.

curtail *v.t.* écourter; abréger, retrancher.

curtailment *n.* réduction *f.*

curtain *n.* rideau *m.;* toile *f.* **to drop the** ~, baisser le rideau. **behind the** ~, derrière le rideau, en secret, en cachette. **~-rod,** tringle *f.* de rideau. *v.t.* garnir de rideaux; voiler.

curtly *adj.* sèchement; brusquement.

curvature *n.* courbure *f.*

curve *adj.* courbe. *n.* courbe *f.* ~ *v.t.* courber, plier, infléchir; *Arch.* cintrer.

cushion *n.* coussin *m.;* matelas *m.* ~ *v.t.* asseoir, faire asseoir sur un coussin; garnir de coussins.

custard *n.* (pouring) crème *f.* anglaise; (set) crème *f.* renversée. ~ **tart,** flan *m.*

custodian *n.* conservateur *m.* of museum, gardien *m.,* gardienne *f.,* concierge *m.f.*

custody *n.* garde *f.,* emprisonnement *m.,* arrestation *f.* **to put in** ~, mettre en prison. **she has** ~ **of the children,** elle a la garde des enfants.

custom *n.* coutume *f.;* habitude *f.;* moeurs *f.pl.,* pratique *f.* ~ **duties,** droits *m.pl.* de douane. **~-house,** douane *f.,* *m.pl.* ~ **-made,** sur mesure.

customary *adj.* d'usage; habituel, ordinaire.

customer *n.* client *m.,* cliente *f.*

customize *v.t.* personnaliser, fabriquer sur commande.

cut *v.t.* couper, tailler; fendre; graver; trancher; découper. **to** ~ **in pieces,** couper en morceaux. **to** ~ **a pack of cards,** couper un jeu de cartes. **to** ~ **across,** couper en travers. **to** ~ **apart,** couper, trancher. **to** ~ **away,** enlever; élaguer, retrancher. **to** ~ **down,** couper; abattre. **to** ~ **off,** trancher; amputer; séparer, intercepter. **to** ~ **out,** couper; découper; retrancher. **to** ~ **short,** couper court, abréger. **the surgeon** ~ **to the quick,** le chirurgien trancha dans le vif. **to** ~ **up,** couper, arracher; *Infml.* faire le pître. *n.* coupure *f.,* balafre *f.,* affront *m.;* tranche *f.;* gravure *f.;* coupe *f.,* tournure *f.;* chemin *m.,* tranchee *f.* **a** ~ **on the finger,** une coupure au doigt. **a fashionable** ~, une coupe élégante. **it is the short** ~, c'est le chemin le plus court. **~throat,** coupe-jarret *m.,* assassin *m.* ~ **it out!** ça suffit! *Infml.* la ferme!

cutback *n.* réduction *f.*

cutaneous *adj.* cutané.

cute *adj.* mignon(ne), trognon.

cuticle *n.* épiderme *m.,* cuticule *f.;* épiderme *m.*

cuticular *adj.* de l'épiderme; de la nature de l'épiderme.

cutie *n.* jolie (fille) *f. Infml.* mignon(ne) *m.f.*

cutlass *n.* coutelas *m.*

cutlery *n.* coutellerie *f.*

cutlet *n.* côtelette *f.;* escalope *f.*

cutter *n.* coupeur *m.,* tailleur *m.;* découpoir.

cutting *n.* coupe *f.;* coupage *m.;* taille *f.;* coupure *f.* ~ *adj.* coupant; glacial, cinglant, mordant, blessant, caustique. **a** ~ **remark,** une remarque blessante.

cuttlefish, *n. f.* seiche.

cyanide *n. Chim.* evanure *m.*

cycle *n.* cycle *m.;* bicyclette *f.;* vélo *m.*

cyclic(al) *adj.* cyclique.

cycling *n.* cyclisme; *adj.* cycliste.

cyclist *n.* cycliste *m.f.*

cyclone *n.* cyclone *m.*

cygnet *n.* jeune cygne *m.*

cylinder *n.* cylindre *m.;* tambour *m.*

cymbal *n.* cymbale *f.*

cynic, cynical *adj.* ~ *n.* cynique *m.f.*

cynically *adv.* d'une manière cynique.

cypress *n.* cyprès *m.*

cyst *n.* kyste *m.*

cystic *adj.* cystique.

D

D-day, le jour J. **3-D,** en relief.

D.A. *Abbr.* District Attorney, procureur *m.* du gouvernement.

dab *v.t.* taper; tamponner; éponger; *n.* coup *m.* léger donné avec la main.

dabble *v.t.* arroser; éclabousser. *v.i.* barboter dans l'eau, patauger; s'ingérer (dans); se mêler de. **he ~s in politics,** il se mêle de politique.

dabbler *n.* barboteur *m.;* amateur *m.*

dactyl *n.* dactyle *m.*

dad, daddy *n. Infml.* papa *m.*

daffodil *n.* jonquelle *f.*

dagger *n.* dague *f.;* poignard *m.,* stylet *m.*

dahlia *n.* dahlia *m.*

daily *adj.* journalier; quotidien. *adv.* journellement, tous les jours, chaque jour.

daintily *adv.* délicatement.

daintiness *n.* délicatesse *f.*

dainty *adj.* friand, délicat. *n.* mets *m.* délicat, friandise *f.*

dairy *n.* laiterie *f.* crèmerie *f.* ~ *adj.* laitier.

dais *n.* estrade *f.*

daisy *n.* pâquerette *f.,* marguerite *f.*

dally *v.i.* tarder, différer.

dam *n.* mere *f.* (of some animals); digue *f.,* barrage *m.* *v.t.* endiguer; contenir. **to ~ in, to ~ up,** endiguer, contenir.

damage *n.* dommage *m.,* dégât *m.;* avaries *f.pl.* ~ *v.t.* endommager. *v.i.* (se) détériorer, s'avarier.

damageable *adj.* qui peut se détériorer.

dame *n.* dame *f.*

dammit *interj., Infml.* nom d'un chien! merde.

damn *v.t.* maudire, pester, jurer. *interj., Infml.* merde, bon sang. *Infml.* **I don't give a ~,** je n'en ai rien à faire!

damnable *adj.* damnable, odieux, détestable.

damnation *n.* damnation *f.;* condamnation *f.*

damned *adj.* damné, maudit, satané, abominable.

damp *adj.* humide, moite; *n.* humidité *f.;* vapeur *f.;* brouillard *m.* ~ *v.t.* humecter; rendre humide.

dampen *v.t.* humecter.

damper *n.* rabat-joie *m.,* évènement *m.* décourageant.

dampness *n.* humidité *f.*

dance *v.i.* danser. *n.* danse *f.*

dancer *n.* danseur *m.,* danseuse *f.*

dancing *adj.* dansant, *n.* danse *f.* **to lead the ~,** ouvrir le bal, mener la danse.

dandelion *n.* dent-de-lion *f.,* pissenlit *m.*

dandle *v.t.* faire sauter (sur ses genoux); bercer, caresser, dorloter.

dandruff *n.* pellicules *f.pl.*

danger *n.* danger *m.*

dangerous *adj.* dangereux, perilleux.

dangerously *adv.* dangereusement.

dangle *v.t.* pendiller, balancer, suspendre.

danish *adj.* danois. ~ **pastry,** *n.* feuilleté *m.*

dank *adj.* moite, humide. *n.* humidité *f.,* moiteur *f.*

dapper *adj.* vif, éveillé, leste.

dapple *adj.* tacheté. *v.t.* tacheter.

dare *v.i.* oser, se hasarder à. *v.t.* braver, affronter; défier, provoquer. *n.* défi *m.* provocation *f.*

daring *adj.* courageux, hardi; brave; audacieux, téméraire. *n.* audace *f.,* hardiesse *f.*

daringly *adv.* hardiment, audacieusement.

dark *adj.* sombre, obscur, foncé, ténébreux. ~ **weather,** un temps sombre. ~ **blue,** bleu foncé. ~ **night,** nuit obscure. **it grows ~,** il se fait nuit. ~ **ages,** l'âge des ténèbres. *n.* obscurité *f.;* ténèbres *f.pl.* ~**-eyed,** aux yeux noirs.

darken *v.t.* embrouiller; brunir, noircir; attrister. *v.i.* s'obscurcir, s'assombrir.

darkening *n.* noircissement *m.,* obscurcissement *m.*

darkness *n.* obscurité *f.* ténèbres *f.pl.*

darling *adj.* chéri, favori. *n.* chéri *m.,* chérie *f.,* bien-aimé *m.,* bien-aimée *f.*

darn *v.t.* raccommoder, *n.* reprise *f.,* raccommodage *m., Infml. interj.* flûte!, zut!

dart *n.* dard *m.;* trait *m.;* sarcasme *m.;* fléchette *f.* ~ *v.t.* darder; laucer; envoyer. *v.i.* s'élancer.

dash *v.t.* écraser; éclabousser; mêler; rayer, biffer; frustrer, ruiner. **to ~ to pieces,** briser en morceaux. **to ~ off,** faire à la hâte. **to ~ out,** barrer, raturer. *v.i.* (se) frapper, (se) heurter; (se) briser; jaillir; (se) précipiter, (se) jeter. *n.* choc *m.;* attaque *f.;* élan *m.,* coup *m.,* trait *m.,* tiret *m.;* teinte *f.,* doigt *m.,* goutte *f.,* larme *f.* **a ~ of vinegar,** un filet de vinaigre.

dashing *adj.* fougueux; brillant, élégant.

data *n.pl.* données *f.pl.*

date *n.* date *f.,* duree *f.;* millésime *m.* (of coins); datte *f.,* rendez-vous *m.* **out of ~,** démodé. *v.t.* dater; avoir un rendez-vous; sortir avec, sortir ensemble.

dateless *adj.* sans date, non daté.

daub *v.t.* barbouiller. *n.* barbouillage *m.,* croûte *f.*

daughter *n.* fille *f.* **~-in-law,** belle-fille *f.,* bru *f.*

daunt *v.t.* abattre (le courage), intimider, effrayer.

dauntless *adj.* intrépide.

dawdle *v.i.* musarder, lambiner, flâner.

dawdler *n.* flâneur *m.,* flâneuse *f.*

dawn *v.i.* poindre; faire jour, se montrer. **to ~ upon,** se faire jour. *n.* pointe *f.,* point *m.* du jour, aube *f.,* aurore *f.; Fig.* commencement *m.,* naissance *f.* **a ~ of hope,** une lueur d'espérance.

day *n.* jour *m.;* journée *f.,* lumière *f.;* victoire *f.* **in open ~,** en plein jour. **the ~ was beautiful,** la journée fut magnifique. **the next ~,** the **following ~,** le lendemain. **the ~ before yesterday,** avant-hier. **every other ~,** tous les deux jours. **from this ~ on,** dès aujourd'hui. **in my ~ s,** à mon époque. ~ **by ~,** jour après jour. **from ~ to ~,** de jour en jour. **have a good ~,** passez une bonne journée.

daybreak *n.* point *m.* or pointe *f.,* du jour, petite aube *f.*

daylight *n.* le jour *m.,* lumière *f.* du jour.

daytime *n.* jour *m.,* journée *f.*

daze *v.t.* éblouir, aveugler par une trop vive lumière, n. étourdissement *m.*

dazzle *v.t.* éblouir. *v.i.* être ébloui; *n.* éblouissement *m.*

dazzling *adj.* éblouissant, éclatant. *n.* éblouissement *m.*

dazzlingly *adv.* d'une manière éblouissante.

dead *adj.* mort; inanimé; insensible; lourd; terne, éventé. **a ~ tree,** un arbre mort. ~ **sound,** bruit sourd. **a ~ sleep,** un sommeil profond. ~ **cool,** charbon éteint. ~ **drunk,** ivre-mort. ~**lock,** serrure *f.* sans ressort. ~**-end,** impasse *f.* ~ **or alive,** mort ou vif. *Infml.* **over my ~ body,** il faudra qu'il/elle m'en passe sur le corps! *Infml.* ~**beat,** bon à rien. ~**-end** *n.,* cul-de-sac *m.,* impasse *f.* ~**-end job** *n.,* travail *m.* sans débouché. ~ **certainty,** certitude absolue.

n.pl. les morts *m.pl. n.* milieu *m.,* fond *m.,* coeur *m.* ~ **of the night,** silence de la nuit.

deaden *v.t.* amortir, émousser; assoupir; ternir.

deadly *adj.* mortel, fatal. *adv.* mortellement, à mort, impitoyablement.

deadness *n.* manque *m.* d'animation, engourdissement *m.*

deaf *adj.* sourd; insensible. **to turn a ~ ear,** faire la sourd oreille.

deafness *n.* surdité *f.*

deal *v.i.* trafiquer, commercer; agir, en user. **to ~ fairly,** faire son commerce loyalement. **to ~ in,** se mêler, s'occuper de. **to ~ in wine,** faire le commerce des vins. *v.t.* diviser, séparer, partager, distribuer; faire, donner les cartes. *n.* portion *f.,* partie *f.;* main *f.* (in cards). **a great ~ of trouble,** beaucoup de poine.

dealer *n.* marchand *m.,* marchande *f.* négociant *m.,* fournisseur, donneur *m.,* donneuse *f.* cards. **wholesale ~,** marchand en gros.

dean *n. Rel., Univ.* doyen *m.* doyenne *f.*

dear *adj.* cher; chéri, aimé. **my ~ friend,** mon cher ami. **to hold ~,** chérir. *n.* cher *m.,* chère *f.; interj.* **oh ~!** oh mon dieu!

dearly *adv.* chèrement, tendrement.

dearness *n.* tendresse *f.,* vive affection *f.*

dearth *n.* pénurie *f.,* manque *m.*

death *n.* mort *f.;* décès *m.,* trépas *m.* ~**bed,** lit *m.* de mort. ~**blow,** coup *m.* mortel. ~ **rattle,** râle *m.* de la mort.

deathless *adj.* immortel, impérissable.

deathly *adj.* fatal; mortel.

debar *v.t.* exclure; priver; interdire.

debase *v.t.* abaisser, avilir, ravaler; déprécier, altérer.

debasement *n.* abaissement *m.,* avilissement *m.,* dépréciation *f.*

debatable *adj.* discutable.

debate *n.* débat *m.;* discussion *f.;* querelle *f.,* conflit *m.* ~ *v.t.* débattre, discuter, agiter, examiner. **to ~ a question,** discuter une question.

debater *n.* orateur *m.*

debauch *v.t.* corrompre, pervertir; débaucher. *n.* débauche *f.,* excès *m.,* intempérance *f.*

debilitate *v.t.* débiliter.

debility *n.* débilité *f.,* faiblesse *f.*

debit *n.* débit *m.,* dû *m.* ~ *v.t.* débiter.

debrief *v.t.* faire un compte rendu après retour d'une mission, aller au rapport.

debris *n.* débris *m.pl.*

debt *n.* dette *f.,* créance *f.* **bad ~,** mauvaise créance. **to discharge a ~,** acquitter une dette. **deeply in ~,** accable de dettes.

debtor *n.* débiteur *m.,* débitrice *f.* débit *m.* (of an account).

debug *v.t.* (in computers) déboguer, mettre au point (a program); éliminer les micros clandestins.

debunk *v.t.* déboulonner (a person), démentir (a thing).

decade *n.* décennie *f.,* decade *f.*

decadence *n.* décadence *f.*

decaf *Abbr.* of **decaffeinate** *n.* décaféiné *m.* ~ *v.t.* décaféiner.

decal *n.* décalcomanie *f.,* vignette *f.*

decalcify *v.t.* déclacifier.

decameter *n.* décametre *m.*

decamp *v.i.* décamper.

decanter *n.* carafe *f.*

decapitate *v.t.* décapiter.

decapitation *n.* décapitation *f.*

decay *v.i.* décomposer. pourrir, *n.* pourrissement *m.;* décadence *f.,* déclin *m.*

decayed *adj.* tombé; gâté, détérioré. **a ~ branch,** une branche pourrie. ~ **teeth,** dents cariées.

decease *n.* décès *m.,* mort *f.,* trépas *m.* ~ *v.i.* décéder, mourir.

deceased *adj.* décédé, mort, défunt.

deceit *n.* supercherie *f.,* tromperie *f.,* déception *f.*

deceitful *adj.* décevant, faux, tempeur.

deceitfully *adv.* par tromperie, frauduleusement.

deceitfulness *n.* qualité *f.* trompeuse, tromperie *f.*

deceive *v.t.* tromper, abuser.

deceiver *n.* trompeur *m.,* trompeuse *f.*

decelerate *v.i.* ralentir.

December *n.* décembre *m.*

decency *n.* décence *f.,* bienséance *f.;* convenance *f.*

decent *adj.* décent; bienséant; passable; tolérable.

decently *adv.* décemment, modérément, passablement.

decentralize *v.t.* décentraliser.

deception *n.* duplicité *f.,* fraude *f.,* duperie *f.,* mauvaise foi *f.*

deceptive *adj.* déceptif, trompeur, mensonger, illusoire.

deceptively *adv.* d'une manière fallacieuse.

decide *v.t.* déterminer. *v.i.* (se) décider.

decided *adj.* décidé, résolu.

decidedly *adv.* incontestablement, décidément.

decider *n.* arbitre *m.f.*

deciduous *adj.* qui tombe; décidu.

decimal *adj.* décimal. *n.* décimale *f.,* fraction *f.,* décimale.

decimate *v.t.* décimer.

decimeter *n.* décimètre *m.*

decipher *v.t.* déchiffrer.

decision *n.* décision *f.;* jugement *m.;* fermeté *f.* **to come to a ~,** prendre un parti.

decisive *adj.* décisif.

decisively *adv.* décisivement, décidément, d'une façon concluante.

deck *v.t.* recouvrir; orner, parer, embellir; ponter. *n.* terrasse *f.* ~ **of cards,** jeu *m.* de cartes. **quarter ~,** gaillard d'arrière. **cassette ~,** platine *f.* à cassettes.

declaim *v.i.* déclamer.

declamation *n.* déclamation *f.*

declamatory *adj.* déclamatoire.

declaration n. déclation f.; proclamation f.

declare v.t. déclarer; proclamer; affirmer. to ~ one's opinions, proclamer ses opinions. v.i. se déclarer pour.

declared adj. déclaré; manifesté.

declassify v.t. ne plus considérer comme secret.

declination n. déclin m., refus m., déclinaison f.

decline v.i. pencher, baisser, dévier; décliner. he ~s to act, il refuse d'agir. v.t. abaisser. n. déclin m., décadence f.; baisse f., détérioration f.

declining adj. déclinant, baissant, tombant, refusant.

decode v.t. décoder.

decompose v.t. décomposer. v.i. (se) décomposer.

decomposition n. décomposition f.

decontaminate v.t. décontaminer.

decontamination n. décontamination f.

decor n. décor m.

decorate v.t. décorer; parer, embellir.

decoration n. décor m., décoration f.

decorative adj. décoratif.

decorous adj. décent, bienséant.

decorum n. décorum m.

decoy v.t. leurrer, attirer. n. leurre m., appât m., piège m.

decrease v.i. diminuer, v.t. amoindrir, (faire) décroître. n. amoindrissement m., diminution f., déclin m.

decreasingly adv. en diminuant.

decree n. décret m.; jugement m., arrêt m. ~ v.t. décréter; ordonner, arrêter.

decrepit adj. décrépit.

decrepitude n. décrépitude f.

decry v.t. décrier; dénigrer.

dedicate v.t. dédier, adreser un livre. adj. consacré.

dedication n. dédicace f.; dévouement m.

deduce v.t. (with from) tirer de, déduire, conclure.

deduct v.t. déduire, soustraire.

deductible adj. déductible.

deduction n. déduction f.; consequence f., remise f.

deed n. action f., fair m.; exploit m., haut fait m.; acte m. to draw up a ~, rédiger un acte.

deem v.t. juger, penser, estimer, supposer.

deep adj. profond, grand, extrême; foncé, grave. a river twenty feet ~, une rivière de vingt pieds de profondeur. a ~ thought, une pensée profonde. a ~ blue, un bleu foncé. n. the ~, mer f., ocean m.; abîme m. ~ adv. profondément.

deepen v.t. creuser; approfondir; rembrunir; rendre plus foncé (une couleur). to ~ a harbor, creuser un port. to ~ the gloom, augmenter l'obscurité. v.i. devenir plus profond.

deeply adv. profondément, complètement; à un haut degré; fortement; gravement.

deepness n. profondeur f.

deer n. daim m., cerf m., biche f.; chevreuil m.

deface v.t. défigurer; déteriorer; biffer, effacer; raturer, détruire.

defacement n. dégradation f.; détérioration f.

defamation n. diffamation f.

defamatory adj. diffamatoire, calomnieux.

defame v.t. diffamer.

default n. défaut m., faute f.; manque m. in ~ of payment, faute de payement. v.i. violer un engagement. v.t. donner défaut, ne pas comparaître.

defeat n. défaite f., déroute f. ~ v.t. défaire, mettre en déroute; faire échouer, renverser, déjouer. to ~ the law, éluder la loi.

defecate v.t. défequer.

defecation n. défécation f.

defect n. défant m., vice m.; défectuosité f., faute f., imperfection f.

defection n. défection f.

defective adj. défectueux; imparfait, incomplet; fautif.

defend v.t. défendre; protéger.

defendant adj. défensif, qui défend. n. défenseur m. défenderesse f., accusé m., accusée f.

defender n. défenseur m.

defense n. défense f., protection f.

defenceless adj. sans défense.

defensive adj. défensif n. défensive f. to be on the ~, se tenir sur la défensive.

defer v.t. différer, v.i. (avec to) s'en rapporter à.

deference n. déférence f.; soumission f.

deferential adj. de déference, respectueux.

deferment n. ajournement m.

defiance n. défi m.

defiant adj. provoquant, défiant.

deficiency n. manque m., défaut m.; déficit m.

deficient adj. défectueux, imparfait; insuffisant; déficient.

deficiently adv. imparfaitement, d'une manière défectueuse.

deficit n. déficit m.

defile v.t. souiller, sailir, violer, déshonorer. v.i. défiler.

define v.t. définir, limiter; v.i. (se) déterminer.

definite adj. défini; déterminé, précis, exact, clair. n. défini m.

definitely adv. absolument, sans aucun doute; c'est sûr; d'une manière définie, déterminée.

definition n. définition f.

definitive adj. définitif, déterminé, positif. n. article m., défini.

definitively adv. définitivement.

deflagration n. deflagration f.

deflate v.t. dégonfler; faire baisser (prices).

deflation n. dégonflement m.; Fin. déflation f.

deflect v.i. (faire) dévier. v.t. détourner.

defloration n. défloration f.

deflower v.t. défleurir.

defoliation n. défoliation f., défeuillaison f.

deforest v.t. déboiser.

deform v.t. déformer; défigurer. adj. difforme.

deformation n. défigurement m.; déformation f.

deformed adj. déformé; défigure; contrefait, difforme.

deformity n. difformité f.

defraud v.t. (with of) frauder.

defray v.t. couvrir (les frais).

defrost v.t.,v.i. dégivrer, décongeler.

defroster n. dégivreur m.

deft adj. adroit, habile, leste.

deftly adv. adroitement.

deftness n. adresse f., habileté f.

defunct adj. défunt, feu. n. défunt m., mort m.

defy v.t. défier; affronter, braver.

degenerate v.i. dégénérer. adj. dégénéré.

degeneration n. dégénération f.; dégénérescence f.

degradation n. dégradation f.; avilissement m.

degrade v.t. dégrader; avilir, déshonorer.

degrading adj. dégradant, déshonorant.

degree n. degré m., qualité f., condition f.; rang m., ordre m. **by ~s**, peu à peu. **of high ~**, d'un rang élevé.

dehumanize v.t. déshumaniser.

dehydrate v.t. déshydrater.

de-ice v.t. dégivrer.

de-icer n. dégivreur m.

deification n. déification f.

deify v.t. déifier, diviniser.

deign v.i. daigner. v.t. accorder, permettre.

deity n. divinité f.; déité f.

deject v.t. abattre; décourager, accabler, affliger. adj. abattu, affligé, triste.

dejected adj. abattu, décourage, afflige.

dejection n. abattement m., découragement m.; déjection f.

delay v.t. différer, retarder, remettre. v.i. tarder; s'arrêter. n. retard m., délai m.

delectable adj. délectable, délicieux.

delegate v.t. déléguer, députer. n. délégué m., déléguée f. ~ adj. délégué.

delegation n. délégation f.

delete v.t.,v.i. effacer, supprimer.

deletion n. effacement m., suppression f.

deliberate v.t. délibérer, considérer. adj. avise, prudent, circonspect; délibéré.

deliberately adv. prudemment; de propos délibéré.

deliberation n. délibération f.

deliberative adj. délibératif; délibérant.

delicacy n. délicatesse f., délicatesses f.pl., friandises f.pl.

delicate adj. délicat, tendre.

delicately adv. délicatement, avec délicatesse.

delicatessen n. charcuterie f., plats m.pl. cuisinés.

delicious adj. délicieux.

deliciously adv. délicieusement.

delight n. délice m., pl. délices f. ~ v.t. faire les délices de, ravir. (se) réjouir, se délecter. **to ~ in**, plaire à, faire ses délices.

delightful adj. délicieux, ravissant.

delightfully adv. délicieusement.

delimit v.t. délimiter.

delineate v.t. tracer, dessiner.

delineation n. délinéation f., ébauche f.

delinquency n. délinquance f.

delinquent adj. délinquant. n. délinquant m. délinquante f.

delirious adj. délirant.

delirium n. délire m.

deliver v.t. délivrer; remettre, livrer. ~ **(a baby)**, accoucher, mettre au monde. **to ~ goods**, livrer des marchandises. ~ **a message**, remettre un message.

deliverable adj. livrable.

deliverance n. délivrance f., libération f.

deliverer n. libérateur m., libératrice f.

delivery n. livraison f.; distribution f. **free ~**, livraison gratuite.

dell n. creux m.; vallon m.

delude v.t. tromper, jouer, décevoir. **to ~ oneself**, se faire des illusions.

deluge n. déluge m. ~ v.t. inonder, submerger.

delusion n. déception f.; erreur f.; illusion f.

deluxe adj. somptueux.

delve v.t. creuser, bêcher; sonder, pénétrer, approfondir.

demagogic adj. démagogique.

demagogue n. démagogue m.f.

demand v.t. réclamer, exiger. n. demande f., réclamation f., exigence f. **the book is in great ~**, le livre est fort demandé.

demarcation n. demarcation f.

demean v.t. s'abaisser, s'avilir.

demeanor n. conduite f., manière d'agir, de se comporter.

demented adj. fou, dément.

demerit n. démérite m., blâme m.

demi adj. demi; semi.

demilitarization n. démilitarisation n.

demilitarize v.t. démilitariser.

demobilization n. démobilisation f.

demobilize v.t.,v.i. démobiliser.

demise n. décès m.; mort f.; cession f.

demo n. démonstration f.; mani f.

democracy n. démocratie f.

democrat n. démocrate m.f.

democratic adj. démocratique, democrate.

democratically adv. démocratiquement.

demography n. démographie f.

demolish v.t. démolir.

demolition n. démolition f.

demon n. démon m.

demoniac adj. démoniaque; diabolique.

demonstrate v.t. démontrer, montrer.

demonstration n. démonstration; manifestations f.pl.

demonstrative adj. démonstratif.

demoralization n. démoralisation f.

demoralize v.t. démoraliser.

demote v.t. rétrograder.

demotion n. rétrogradation f.

demur v.i. hésiter, soulever des objections. **to ~**

at, ne pas faire raison à. n. temps m., d'arrêt, pause f.; hésitation f., doute m.

demure adj. modeste, réservé; d'une modestie affectée.

demystify v.t. démystifier.

den n. caverne f.; tanière f., antre m.; repaire m.

denationalize v.t. dénationaliser.

denial n. refus m.; désaveu m., reniement m., déni m. flat ~, dénégation absolue.

denigrate v.t. dénigrer.

denim n. jean m.

Denmark n.pr. Danemark.

denominate v.t. nommer, dénommer.

denomination n. dénomination f.; culte m., secte f., religieuse; confession f.

denominator n. dénominateur m.

denote v.t. dénoter; exprimer, indiquer, annoncer.

denounce v.t. dénoncer.

denouncement n. dénonciation f.

dense adj. dense, serré, compacte; épais.

densely adv. d'une façon très dense.

density n. densité f., épaisseur f.

dent n. brèche f., entaille f.; denture f. ~ v.t. denteler.

dental adj. dentaire; dental.

dented adj. bosselé, cabossé.

dentifrice n. dentifrice m.

dentist n. dentiste m.f.

dentistry n. profession f. de dentiste.

dentition n. dentition f.

dentures n.pl. dentier m.

denude v.t. dénuder.

denunciate v.t. dénoncer.

denunciation n. dénonciation f.

deny v.t. nier, dénier, démentir; renier; refuser. to ~ a request, refuser une demande. to ~ oneself, se refuser. he denied himself every pleasure, il se refusait tous les plaisirs.

deodorant adj., n. déodorant m., désodorisant m.

deodorize v.t. désodoriser.

depart v.i. partir, s'en aller; se returner; se départir. to ~ from one's principles, se départir de ses principes. v.t. séparer. n. départ m.

departed adj., n. défunt m., défunte f.

department n. département m.; division f., branche f.; rayon m., service m. ~ store, grand magasin m.

departure n. départ m.; Fig. mort f., trépas m.; désistement m. ~ time, heure f. du départ.

depend v.i. dépendre de; compter sur. that ~s on circumstances, cela dépend des circonstances. you can't ~ on him, on ne peut pas compter sur lui.

dependable adj. digne de confiance, fiable.

dependence, dependency n., dépendance f.

dependent adj. dépendant. to be ~ on, dépendre de. ~ n. (personne à) charge. how

many ~s does he have? combien a-t-il de personnes à charge?

depict v.t. peindre, dépeindre, décrire.

depilate v.t. épiler.

depilatory adj. dépilatoire. n. dépilatoire m.

depletion n. déplétion f.

deplorable adj. déplorable, lamentable, regrettable.

deplorably adv. déplorablement, pitoyablement.

deplore v.t. déplorer, plaindre.

deploy v.t. étendre. v.i. (se) déployer.

depopulation n. dépopulation f., dépeuplement m.

deport v.t. déporter, expulser. n. conduite f., tenue f., maintien m.

deportation n. déportation f., expulsion f.

deportment n. conduite f.

depose v.t.,v.i. déposer, attester.

deposit v.t. déposer, poser. n. dépôt m.; arrhes f.pl., a compte m., provision f.

deposition n. déposition f.; témoignage m.

depot n. dépôt m.; gare f.

depravation n. dépravation f.

deprave v.t. dépraver.

depraved adj. dépravé.

deprecate v.t. désapprouver.

depreciate v.t. déprécier. v.i. (se) déprécier, (se) dévaloriser.

depreciation n. dépréciation f.

depredation n. déprédation f.; ravage m.; destruction f.

depress v.t. baisser, déprimer, ralentir. to ~ trade, arrêter les affaires.

depressant adj., n. sédatif m.

depression n. dépression f., enfoncement m. d'une surface; affaissement m.; abattement m. the ~ of trade, la stagnation du commerce.

depressive adj. dépressif.

deprivation n. privation f.; délaissement m.; destitution f.

deprive v.t. priver, dépouiller, déposséder. to ~ one of his rights, priver une personne de ses droits.

depth n. profondeur f.; hauteur f., enfoncement m.; abîme m.; coeur m. (of the night). he is out of his ~, il n'a pas pied. ~ of water, profondeur f. des eaux.

deputation n. députation f.; délégation f.

deputy n. député m., représentant m., délégué m. ~ governor, lieutenant-gouverneur. ~ chairperson, vice-président. ~ paymaster, souspayer.

derail v.t.,v.i. dérailler.

derailment n. déraillement m.

derange v.t. déranger, troubler, dérégler. he is ~d, il a le cerveau dérangé.

derangement n. aliénation f., mentale, folie f., délire m.

deregulate v.t. déréglementer.

derelict n. (person) délaissé, délaissée, épave f., humaine.

deride v.t. railler, tourner en ridicule.

derision n. dérision f.; risée f.

derisive adj. dérisoire.

derivation n. dérivation f.

derivative adj., s. dérivé; dérivatif.

derive v.t. (faire) dériver; tenir, tirer; déduire, provenir (de), venir (de).

dermatology n. dermatologie f.

derogate v.t.,v.i. déroger (à), porter attente (à), amoindrir.

derogation n. dérogation f.; détriment m., préjudice m.

derogatory adj. dérigrant, dérogeant, péjoratif.

descend v.i.,v.t. descendre; s'abaisser; tomber.

descendant n. descendant m.; descendante f.

descendent adj. descendant, qui descend.

descent n. descente f.; pente f.; descendance f.; chute f.; postérité f.

describe v.t. décrire; dépeindre.

description n. description f.; signalement m.

descriptive adj. descriptif.

descry v.t. explorer; distinguer.

desecrate v.t. profaner.

desecration n. profanation f.

desegregate v.t. abolir la ségrégation raciale.

desegregation n. abolition f. de la ségrégation raciale.

desensitize v.t. désensibiliser.

desert n. désert m. ~ v.t. déserter, abandonner, délaisse m. mérite m. au pl. dû m.

deserter n. déserteur m.

desertion n. désertion f.; abandon m.

deserve v.t.,v.i. mériter. **he ~s to make it,** il mérite d'y arriver.

deservedly adv. justement, à juste titre.

deserving adj. méritant; méritoire.

design v.t. dessiner; projeter; avoir le dessein, l'intention, se proposer; destiner à. n. dessin m.; dessein m, projet, but m.

designate v.t. désigner; choisir.

designation n. désignation f.

designer n. créateur m.; créatrice f.; dessinateur m.; dessinatrice f.; décorateur m.; décoratrice f.

desirable adj. désirable, à souhaiter vivement; agréable; appétissant.

desire n. désir m.; envie f. ~ v.t. désirer; souhaiter; prier, demander.

desirous adj. désireux. **to be ~ of,** avoir envie de, désirer.

desist v.i. se désister, s'arrêter, cesser d'agir, discontinuer.

desk n. bureau m.; rédaction f.; chaire f., d'église. **~ clerk,** réceptionniste m.f.

desolate adj. désert; triste; solitaire; délaisse. v.t. dévaster, ruiner, saccager, désoler.

desolately adv. d'une manière désolée.

desolation n. désolation f.

despair n. désespoir m. ~ v.i. désespérer, (se) désespérer.

despairing adj. désespérant.

despairingly adv. d'une manière désespérée, désespérément.

desperado n. hors-la-loi m., casse-cou m.

desperate adj. désespéré; irrémédiable; furieux, acharné.

desperately adv. désespérément; extrêmement, furieusement.

desperation n. désespoir m., acharnement m., fureur f.

despicable adj. ignoble, abject, vil, bas, méprisable.

despicably adv. bassement, d'une manière méprisable.

despise v.t. mépriser; abhorrer, détester.

despite prep. en dépit de, malgré.

despoil v.t. dépouiller, priver.

despond v.i. désespérer; se décourager, se désoler, se laisser abattre. n. découragement m.

despondence, despondency n. désespoir m., découragement m., abattement m.

despondent adj. découragé, désespéré, abattu.

despondently adv. désespérément, sans espoir; dans l'abattement.

despot n. despote m., tyran m.

despotic adj. despotique.

dessert n. dessert m.

destination n. destination f.

destine v.t. destiner; vouer, consacrer.

destiny n. destinée f., destin m.; sort m.

destitute adj. dénué; dépourvu; délaissé, abandonné.

destitution n. dénûment m., indigence f., misère f.

destroy v.t. détruire, exterminer.

destroyable adj. destructible.

destroyer n. destructeur m.; destroyer m., contre-torpilleur m. (ship).

destruct v.t. détruire.

destructible adj. destructible.

destruction n. destruction f.; ruine f.

destructive adj. destructif, destructeur. n. destructeur m., démolisseur m.

desuetude n. désuetude f.

desultory adj. décousu, sans suite. **~ conversation,** entretien décousu.

detach v.t. détacher; séparer.

detachment n. détachement m.

detail v.t. détailler; spécifier. n. détail m.

detain v.t. retenir, détenir, arrêter.

detect v.t. découvrir, déceler.

detectable adj. perceptible, discernable.

detection n. découverte f., dénonciation f.

detective adj. révélateur. n. agent m. de la police judiciaire, détective m. (privé).

detention n. détention f., emprisonnement m.

deter v.t. détourner, retenir, arrêter, dissuader, empêcher.

detergent adj., n. détergent m.

deteriorate *v.t.* détériorer. *v.i.* (se) détériorer.

deterioration *n.* détérioration *f.*

determination *n.* détermination *f.;* décision *f.,* judiciaire; résolution *f.*

determine *v.t.* déterminer; (se) décider; terminer, achever. *v.i.* (se) déterminer, se résoudre, conclure.

determined *adj.* déterminé; résolu.

deterrent *adj.* force *f.* de dissuasion, préventif.

detest *v.t.* détester, abhorrer.

detestable *adj.* détestable, abominable.

detestably *adv.* détestablement.

detestation *n.* détestation *f.*

detonate *v.i.* détoner. *v.t.* (faire) détoner.

detonation *n.* détonation *f.*

detour *n.* detour *m.,* déviation *f.*

detoxification *Infml.* detox *n.* désintoxication *f.*

detract *v.t.* enlever, retirer de.

detraction *n. f.,* dénigrement.

detriment *n.* détriment *m.,* tort, préjudice, dommage, désavantage.

detrimental *adj.* nuisible, préjudiciable.

devaluate *v.t.* dévaluer.

devaluation *n.* dévaluation *f.*

devastate *v.t.* dévaster.

devestation *n.* dévastation *f.*

develop *v.t.* développer; exploiter (a region), réaliser (a plan); contracter (a fever, a habit).

development *n.* développement *m.;* dénouement *m.,* exploitation *f.,* réalisation *f.,* progrès *m.*

deviate *v.i.* dévier.

deviation *n.* déviation *f.,* écart, égarement *m.*

device *n.* appareil *m.,* gadget *m.,* engin *m., Infml.* machin *m.,* dessein *m.,* invention *f.,* stratagème *m.,* ruse *f.*

devil *n.* diable *m.,* démon *m.,* apprenti imprimeur. **a she-~,** une diablesse. **speaking of the ~,** quand on parle de loup, (on en voit la queue).

devilish *adj.* diabolique, infernal; satané; un diable de.

devilishly *adv.* en diable, diaboliquement; diablement.

devious *adj.* dévié, détourne.

deviously *adv.* de manière détournée.

deviousness *n.* écart *m.,* détour *m.*

devise *v.t.* inventer, découvrir, imaginer; tramer, projeter. *v.i.* méditer, dresser un plan. *n.* legs *m.*

devoid *adj.* dépourvu, dénué de; exempt de.

devolve *v.t.* transmettre; remettre. *v.i.* échoir; tomber; incomber; revenir.

devote *v.t.* vouer, dévouer, consacrer. **to ~ one's time to study,** consacrer son temps à l'étude. *adj.* voué; dévoué.

devotedness *n.* dévouement *m.,* zèle *m.*

devotee *n.* dévot *m.*

devotion *n.* dévotion *f.,* prière *f.;* empressement *m.;* dévouement *m.*

devotional *adj.* de dévotion, de prière. *n.* dévot *m.*

devour *v.t.* dévorer.

devout *adj.* dévot; pieux.

devoutness *n.* dévotion *f.,* piété *f.*

dew *n.* rosée *f.* ~ *v.t.* couvrir, humecter de rosée.

dewy *adj.* de rosée, humecté, mouillé par la rosée.

dexterity *n.* dextérité *f.;* adresse *f.,* habileté *f.,* tact *m.*

dexterous *adj.* habile, adroit.

dexterously *adv.* adroitement, avec dextérité.

diabetes *n.* diabète *m.*

diabetic *adj.* diabétique.

diabolical *adj.* diabolique.

diabolically *adv.* diaboliquement.

diadem *n.* diadème *m.*

diagnosis *n.* diagnostic *m.,* diagnose *f.*

diagnostic *adj., n.* diagnostic *m.*

diagonal *adj.* diagonal. *n.* diagonale *f.*

diagonally *adj.* diagonalement, en diagonale.

diagram *n.* diagramme *m.,* schéma *m.,* figure *f.*

dial *n.* cadran *m.,* tonalité *f.* **~-plate,** cadra *m.,* plaque *f.* de cadran solaire. *v.t.* composer. **~ the number and wait for the ~ tone,** composez le numéro et attendez la tonalité.

dialect *n.* dialecte *m.;* langage *m.;* patois *m.*

dialogue *n.* dialogue *m.*

diameter *n.* diamètre *m.*

diametrical *adj.* diamétral.

diametrically *adv.* diamétralement.

diamond *n.* diamant *m.;* (in cards) carreau *m.;* losange *m.* **cut ~,** diamant taillé. **rough ~,** diamant brut.

diapason *n.* diapason *m.;* prestant *m.*

diaper *n.* couche *f.*

diaphragm *n.* diaphragme *m.*

diarrhea *n.* diarrhée *f.*

diary *n.* journal *m.,* agenda *m.*

dice *n.pl.* de **die,** des *m.pl.*

dick *n. Infml.* queue *f.* (penis); stupide *m.f.,* idiot *m.*

dictate *v.t.* dicter, ordonner, commander, prescrire.

dictation *n.* dictée *f.;* précepte *m.,* prescription *f.*

dictator *n.* dictateur *m.*

dictatorial *adj.* dictatorial.

dictatorship *n.* dictature *f.*

diction *n.* diction *f.;* style *m.,* phraséologie *f.*

dictionary *n.* dictionaire *m.*

did See DO.

diddle *v.t.* tromper, duper.

die *v.i.* mourir; dépérir; s'éteindre. **to ~ off,** s'éteindre, se mourir. **the sound ~s away,** le son se meurt. *n. pl.* dice, des; hasard *m.,* chance *f.* **the ~ is cast,** le sort en est jeté.

diesel *adj.* diesel. **~ oil,** gazole *m.*

diet *n.* régime *m.,* nourriture *f.;* alimentation *f.* ~ *v.t., v.i.* suivre, observer un régime; s'alimenter.

dietary *adj.* diététique.

dietetic *adj.* diététique.

differ *v.i.* différer; avoir un différend.

difference *n.* difference *f.;* différend *m.,* dispute *f.* **that makes a great ~,** cela fait beaucoup. **we** have settled our ~, nous avons vidé notre différend.

different adj. différent, divers. **quite ~ from**, tout autre que.

differential adj. différentiel.

differentiate v.t. différencier, distinguer.

differently adv. différemment, d'une manière différente.

difficult adj. difficile, dur.

difficulty n. difficulté f., peine f., embarras.

diffidence n. manque m. de confiance, hésitation f.

diffident adj. défiant, modeste, réservé, timide.

diffidently adv. avec défiance, avec crainte, timidement.

diffuse v.t. verser, faire couler, s'étendre; propager, répandre.

diffuse adj. diffus; répandu.

diffusion n. diffusion f.; dispersion f.

dig v.t., v.i. creuser; fouiller; bêcher, piocher; faire des fouilles. **to ~ a ditch**, creuser un fossé. **to ~ up**, déraciner, déterrer. **to ~ out**, dénicher, déterrer.

digest n. digeste m., résumé m. ~ v.t. digérer.

digestion n. digestion f.

digit n. doigt; chiffre m. (number).

digital adj. digital, numérique. **~ clock**, horloge f. à affichage digital.

digitize v.t. convertir en numérique, numériser.

digitizer n. numériseur m.

dignified adj. digne.

dignify v.t. revêtir d'une dignité; honorer.

dignitary n. dignitaire m.f.

dignity n. dignité f.; rang m.

digress v.i. faire une digression, digresser, dévier, s'écarter.

digression n. digression f.

dike n. fossé m.; digue f. ~ v.i. diguer, endiguer.

dilapidated adj. délabré.

dilapidation n. délabrement m., dépérissement m.; dilapidation f.

dilate v.t. dilater. v.i. (se) dilater, s'étendre.

dilatory adj. lent, tardif; paresseux, dilatoire.

dilemma n. dilemme m.

dilettante n.pl. dilettante m.

diligence n. diligence f., assiduité f.

diligent adj. diligent.

diligently adv. diligemment; assidument.

dill n. aneth m.

dilute v.t. diluer.

diluvial adj. diluvien.

dim adj. faible; obscur, mystérieux; terne. **~ eyes**, les yeux faibles. **~-sighted**, qui a la vue faible. v.t. troubler; obscurcir, affaiblir; assombrir.

dime n. (coin) dix cents m.pl.

dimension n. dimension f.

diminish v.t. diminuer, amoindrir. v.i. (se) diminuer.

diminution n. diminution f., rabais m., amoindrissement m.

diminutive adj. diminutif, petit, chétif.

dimly adv. obscurement; d'une lueur faible, blafarde.

dimness n. obscurcissement m. de la vision, vue f., imparfaite; faiblesse f.

dimple n. fossette f., ride (water). v.i. former des fossettes; onduler, rider (water).

din n. bruit m.; tapage m., vacarme m., tintamarre m.

dine v.i. dîner. **to ~ out**, dîner dehors.

diner n. petit restaurant m.

ding v.t. résonner.

dinghy n. youyou m., canot m.

dinginess n. saleté f.

dingle n. vallon m.

dingy adj. terni, souillé, sale.

dining adj., n. dîner. **~ room**, salle f. à manger. **~ car**, wagon-restaurant m.

dinner n. dîner m. **~ service**, service m. de table. **~time**, heure f. du dîner.

dinosaur n. dinosaure m.

dint n. coup m.; force f.; **by ~ of**, à force de.

diocese n. diocèse m.

dip v.t. plonger; tremper; mouiller. v.i. s'enfoncer (in liquid). n. immersion f.; plongeon m. **a ~ in the water**, un plongeon dans l'eau.

diphtheria n. diphthérie f.

diploma n. diplôme m.

diplomacy n. diplomatie f.

diplomate v.t., n. diplomate m.f.

diplomatic adj. diplomatique.

dipper n. louche f.; benne f.; martin-pêcheur m.

dire adj. terrible, affreux, cruel.

direct adj. direct; droit, formel. v.t. diriger; conduire; gouverner; ordonner; renseigner; adresser (a letter).

direction n. direction f.; conduite f.; sens m.; côté m.; instruction f. **the ~ of affairs**, la direction des affaires.

directly adv. directement, immédiatement, à l'instant, tout de suite; positivement.

directness n. franchise f.

director n. directeur m.; directrise f.; chef m.; metteur m. en scène, réalisateur m., réalisatrice f.

directorial adj. directorial.

directory n. annuaire m.

dirt n. saleté f., boue f., crasse f.

dirtiness n. saleté f., malpropreté f., bassesse f.

dirty adj. sale, malpropre, crotté, impur, bas, vil. **a ~ action**, une sale action. v.t. salir, souiller.

disability n. incapacité f.; impuissance f.

disable v.t. rendre incapable, mettre hors d'état; désemparer (a ship).

disabled adj. privé de moyens; mis hors d'état, hors de service; désemparé; invalide.

disabuse v.t. détromper, désabuser.

disadvantage n. désavantage m. ~ v.t. préjudicier, désavantager.

disadvantageous adj. désavantageux.

disaffected *p.p., adj.* désaffectionné, aliéné, mécontente.

disaffection *n.* désaffection *f.*, mécontentement.

disagree *v.i.* ne pas être d'accord avec, être en désaccord avec; différer d'opinion.

disagreeable *adj.* désagréable.

disagreeableness *n.* contrariété *f.*; nature *f.*; déplaisante.

disagreement *n.* différence *f.*, dissemblance *f.*, contradiction *f.*; désaccord *m.*

disallow *v.t.* défendre, ne pas approuver, rejeter, condamner, repousser. *v.i.* refuser.

disappear *v.i.* disparaître.

disappearance *n.* disparition *f.*

disappoint *v.t.* décevoir, désappointer; tromper; faire échouer.

disappointment *n.* déception, contre-temps *m.*

disapprobation *n.* désapprobation *f.*

disapproval *n.* désapprobation *f.*, blâme *m.*

disapprove *v.t.* désapprouver.

disarm *v.t.* désarmer.

disarmament *n.* désarmement *m.*

disarming *n.* désarmement *m.*

disarrange *v.t.* déranger.

disarray *v.t.* mettre en désarroi, en déroute. *n.* désarroi *m.*, désordre *m.*, confusion *f.*

disassemble *v.t.* désassembler, démonter.

disassociate *v.t.* dissocier.

disassociation *n.* dissociation *f.*

disaster *n.* désastre *m.*, malheur *m.*

disastrous *adj.* désastreux.

disastrously *adv.* désastreusement.

disavow *v.i.* nier. *v.t.* désavouer.

disavowal *n.* désaveu *m.*, dénégation *f.*; rétractation *f.*

disband *v.t.* licencier, congédier; se séparer.

disbar *v.t.* exclure du barreau.

disbelief *n.* incrédulité *f.*, scepticisme *m.*

disbelieve *v.t.* ne pas croire.

disbeliever *n.* incrédule *m.f.*

disburse *v.t.* débourser, dépenser, payer.

disbursement *n.* déboursement *m.*; débours *m.pl.*

discard *v.t.* écarter; congédier; exclure; rejeter, repousser.

discern *v.t.* discerner, apercevoir; distinguer.

discernible *adj.* visible, perceptible, sensible.

discernibly *adv.* visiblement.

discerning *adj.* judicieux, pénétrant, clairvoyant. *n.* discernement *m.*

discernment *n.* discernement *m.*

discharge *v.t.* décharger; renvoyer; libérer, lancer; payer, acquitter; accomplir. **to ~ a fire alarm**, tirer, décharger une arme à feu. **he ~d his duties**, il s'est acquitté de ses devoirs. *n.* décharge *f.*, acquittement *m.*; mise *f.*, en liberté (of a prisoner); renvoi *m.* (from a job); quittance *f.*, acquit *m.*, reçu *m.* (from a debt); accomplissement *m.*, execution *f.* (of duties); *Med.* pertes *f.pl.* blanches, suppuration *f.*

disciple *n.* disciple *m.f.*

disciplinarian *adj.* disciplinaire.

disciplinary *adj.* disciplinaire.

discipline *n.* discipline *f.* ~ *v.t.* discipliner; former.

disclaim *v.t.* désavouer, renier; nier.

disclose *v.t.* divulguer, dévoiler, découvrir; mettre à jour; déclarer; réveler.

disclosure *n.* découverte *f.*; révélation *f.*, divulgation *f.*, déclaration *f.*, dénonciation *f.*; confidence *f.*

disco *n.* discothèque *f.* ~ **dancing**, disco *m.*

discolor *v.t.* décolorer; ternir. *v.i.* se décolorer.

discoloration *n.* décoloration *f.*

discomfit *v.t.* défaire; déconcerter, décontenancer; mettre en déroute. *n.* défaite *f.*, déroute *f.*, déconvenue *f.*

discomfort *n.* malaise *m.*, gêne *f.*; désagrément *m.* ~ *v.t.* gêner, incommoder.

discomposure *n.* trouble *m.*, agitation *f.*

disconcert *v.t.* déconcerter, troubler.

disconnect *v.t.* disjoindre, séparer, désunir; débrancher. **the line got ~ed**, la ligne (de téléphone) a été coupée.

disconnection *n.* disjonction *f.*, séparation *f.*

disconsolate *adj.* désolé, affligé, découragé, inconsolable.

discontent *n.* mécontentement *m.* ~ *v.t.* mécontenter.

discontented *adj.* mécontent.

discontinue *v.t.,v.i.* discontinuer; rompre; interrompre, se désabonner.

discontinuity *n.* discontinuité *f.*

discontinuous *adj.* discontinu, interrompu.

discord *n.* discorde *f.*; désaccord *m.*, discordance *f.*

discordance *n.* discordance *f.*

discordant *adj.* discordant.

discotheque *n.* discothèque *f.*

discount *n.* remise *f.*; escompte *m.* **with a ~**, sous escompte. *v.t.* décompter, escompter. *v.i.* faire l'escompte.

discountenance *v.t.* décontenancer, déconcerber.

discourage *v.t.* décourager; (with from) détourner, dégoûter; réprimer, empêcher, déjouer.

discouragement *n.* découragement *m.*

discouraging *adj.* décourageant.

discourse *n.* discours *m.*; conversation *f.*, entretien *m.* langage *m.* ~ *v.i.* discourir; raisonner. *v.t.* prononcer, traiter.

discourteous *adj.* discourtois, impoli.

discourtesy *n.* discourtoisie *f.*, impolitesse *f.*

discover *v.t.* découvri *f.*; montrer, faire preuve de.

discovery *n.* découverte *f.*, révélation *f.*, manifestation *f.*

discredit *v.t.* décréditer, discréditer, déshonorer, douter de.

discreditable *adj.* compromettant, déshonorant.

discreet *adj.* discret, prudent, circonspect, judicieux, avisé.

discreetly *adv.* discrètement, judicieusement.

discrepancy *n.* différence *f.*, désaccord *m.*, contradiction *f.*

discrete *adj.* discret, séparé, distinct.

discretion *n.* discrétion *f.*, prudence *f.*

discretionary *adj.* discrétionnaire.

discriminate *v.t.* distinguer; différencier; séparer.

discriminating *adj.* distinctif, particulier.

discrimination *n.* distinction *f.*, discrimination *f.*

discrimative *adj.* distinctif, caractéristique; judicieux.

discriminatory *adj.* discriminatoire.

discursive *adj.* décousu, sans suite; de raisonnement; discursif.

discuss *v.t.* discuter, débattre, raisonner sur.

discussion *n.* discussion *f.*

disdain *v.t.* dédaigner. *n.* dédain *m.*, mépris *m.*

disdainful *adj.* dédaigneux; méprisant, hautain, arrogant.

disdainfully *adv.* dédaigneusement.

disease *n.* maladie *f.*; mal *m.* ~ *v.t.* indisposer, rendre malade.

diseased *adj.* malade.

disembark *v.t.* débarquer.

disembarkation *n.* débarquement *m.*

disembodied *v.t.* désincarner.

disenchant *v.t.* désenchanter.

disenchantment *n.* désenchantement *m.*

disengage *v.t.* dégager, libérer, délivrer; détacher. *v.i.* (se) détacher, se débarrasser; se séparer.

adj. inocupé; dégagée; libre; débrayé.

disentangle *v.t.* débrouiller, démêler.

disentanglement *n.* débrouillement *m.*, démêlement *m.*

disfavor *n.* défaveur *f.*, disgrace *f.* ~ *v.t.* traiter avec défaveur; se prononcer contre, désapprouver.

disfigure *v.t.* défigurer, enlaidir, déformer.

disfigurement *n.* défigurement *m.*, enlaidissement *m.*

disfranchise *v.t.* priver des droits d'électeur, priver de franchises et d'immunités.

disgorge *v.t.* rendre, vomir, (se) dégorger.

disgrace *n.* disgrâce *f.*, défaveur *f.*; déshonneur *m.*, honte *f.* **to be in** ~, être mal vu de. **he is a** ~ **to his country**, il est l'oppobre de son pays. *v.t.* disgracier, noircir, déshonorer, avilir. **he** ~**s his name**, il déshonore le nom qu'il porte.

disgraceful *adj.* honteux, déshonorant, infâme.

disgracefully *adv.* honteusement, d'une manière déshonorante.

disgracefulness *n.* honte *f.*, opprobre *f.*, ignominie *f.*

disgruntled *adj.* maussade, de mauvaise humeur, mécontent.

disguise *v.t.* déguiser; défigurer; dissimuler. **to** ~ **one's feelings**, déguiser ses sentiments. *n.* déguisement *m.*, travestissement *m.*, masque *m.* **in** ~, déguisé.

disgust *n.* dégoût *m.*, aversion *f.* ~ *v.t.* dégoûter, offenser, blesser, déplaire, choquer.

disgusting *adj.* dégoûtant, repoussant.

disgustingly *adv.* d'une manière dégoûtante.

dish *n.* plat *m.*, mets *m.* **a silver** ~, un plat d'argent. ~**cloth**, torchon *m.* de cuisine. ~**rack**, *n.* égouttoir *m.* ~**washer**, lave-vaisselle *m.* **satellite** ~, antenne *f.* parabolique (TV, etc.). ~ **out**, *v.t.* mettre ou servir dans un plat; servir.

dishearten *v.t.* décourager, démoraliser.

disheveled *adj.* échevelé, ébouriffé.

dishonest *adj.* malhonnête; déloyal, de mauvaise foi.

dishonestly *adv.* malhonnêtement, de mauvaise foi.

dishonesty *n.* malhonnêté *f.*, mauvaise foi *f.*, fraude *f.*

dishonor *n.* déshonneur *m.*; non-payement *m.* d'un effet. *v.t.* déshonorer; avilir; refuser une traite.

dishonorable *adj.* déshonerant, honteux.

dishonorably *adv.* d'une manière déshonorante.

disillusion *n.* désillusionner, decevoir; *n.* désillusion *f.*

disinclination *n.* éloignement *m.*, aversion *f.*

disinfect *v.t.* désinfecter.

disinfectant *adj.*, *n.* désinfectant *m.*

disinfection *n.* désinfection *f.*

disingenuous *adj.* déloyal, de mauvaise foi.

disingenuously *adv.* déloyalement, sans sincérité.

disinherit *v.t.* déshériter.

disintegrate *v.t.* désintégrer, désagreger.

disintegration *n.* désagregation *f.*

disinter *v.t.* déterrer, exhumer.

disinterested *adj.* désinteresse, indifférent.

disinterestedness *n.* désintéressement *m.*

disinterment *n.* exhumation *f.*, déterrement *m.*

disjointed *adj.* décousu, sans suite (speech), incohérent.

disk *n.* disque *m.*; disquette *f.* (computer). ~ **operating system**, système *m.* d'exploitation de disques.

diskette *n.* disquette *f.*

dislike *n.* aversion *f.*, antipathie *f.* ~ *v.t.* désapprouver; ne pas aimer. **what do you** ~ **in her?** qu'est-ce qui vous déplait en elle?

dislocate *v.t.* déplacer; disloquer. *adj.* disloqué, démis, luxé.

dislocation *n.* déplacement *m.*; dislocation *f.*; luxation *f.*

dislodge *v.t.* déloger; déplacer, chasser.

disloyal *adj.* rebelle, déloyal; traitre.

disloyalty *n.* infidélité *f.*, déloyauté *f.*

dismal *adj.* lugubre, triste, sombre, sinistre, morne.

dismantle *v.t.* dépouiller, dévetir; démanteler; dégréer (a boat), désarmer.

dismay *v.t.* effrayer, terrifier; consterner. *n.* peur *f.*, effroi *m.*; terreur *f.*; épouvante *f.*; consternation *f.*

dismember *v.t.* démembrer.

dismemberment *n.* démembrement *m.*; mutilation *f.*

dismiss *v.t.* renvoyer; congédier; répudier; destituer.

dismissal *n.* congé *m.*, renvoi *m.*

dismount *v.i.* descendre (from a horse or bike), mettre pied à terre. *v.t.* démounter; désarçonner, faire descendre.

disobedience *n.* désobéissance *f.*; civil ~, résistance *f.* passive.

disobedient *adj.* désobéissant.

disobey *v.t.* désobéir (with à).

disobliging *adj.* désobligeant.

disorder *n.* désordre *m.*, dérèglement *m.*; maladie *f.*, trouble *m.*, dérangement *m.*

disorderly *adj.* confus, désordonne, déregle. **a ~ life,** une vie déréglée. *adv.* sans ordre, sans méthode; désordonnément.

disorganization *n.* désorganisation *f.*

disorganize *v.t.* désorganiser.

disorient *v.t.* désorienter.

disown *v.t.* désavouer, renier; nier.

disparage *v.t.* déprécier; avilir; dénigrer, décrier.

disparagement *n.* reproche *m.*, dénigrement *m.*, honte *f.*

disparaging *adj.* dénigrant, dépreciant, déshonorant.

disparagingly *adv.* désavantageusement; de manière à, déprécier, à dénigrer.

disparate *adj.* disparate, inégal. *n.pl.* disparates *m.pl.*

disparity *n.* disparité *f.*, inégalité *f.*

dispassion *n.* apathie *f.*, calme *m.*

dispassionate *adj.* calme, posé, de sang-froid; impartial.

dispatch *v.t.* dépêcher, envoyer, expédier *n.*, dépêche *f.*, envoi *m.*, expedition *f.*

dispel *v.t.* disperser, dissiper, chasser, éparpiller.

dispensable *adj.* dont on peut se passer.

dispensary *n.* dispensaire *m.*

dispense *v.t.* dispénser; distribuer; préparer; composer un médicament. **to ~ with,** dispenser de. **I would gladly have ~d with his services,** je me serais volontiers passé de ses services. *n.* dispense *f.*; dispensation *f.*

disperse *v.t.* (se) disperser, (se) dissiper, (se) séparer, éparpiller, distribuer. **to ~ a crowd,** disperser un attroupement.

dispersion *n.* dispersion *f.*; éparpillement *m.*

dispirit *v.t.* décourager, démoraliser, abattre.

displace *v.t.* déplacer, destituer.

displacement *n.* déplacement *m.*

display *v.t.* déployer, montrer, faire voir; manifester. **to ~ wisdom,** faire preuve de sagesse. **to ~ one's knowledge,** faire étalage de son savoir. *n.* déploiement *m.*, développement *m.*; spectacle *m.*, parade *f.*; étalage *m.* **a fine ~ of fireworks,** un beau feu d'artifice.

displease *v.t.* déplaire, mécontenter.

displeased *adj.* mécontent, fâché, contrarié.

displeasing *adj.* déplaisant, désagréable; mécontentant, offensant.

displeasure *n.* déplaisir *m.*; irritation *f.*

disposable *adj.* à jeter. ~ **napkins,** serviettes *f.pl.* en papier.

disposal *n.* disposition *f.*; arrangement *m.*; vente *f.* **the ~ of affairs,** la conduite, la direction des affaires. **at one's ~,** à sa disposition; rejet *m.*

dispose *v.t.* disposer, arranger.

disposition *n.* disposition *f.*; arrangement *m.*; distribution *f.*; tempérament *m.*

dispossess *v.t.* déposséder.

dispossession *n.* dépossession *f.*

disproof *n.* réfutation *f.*

disproportion *n.* disproportion *f.* ~ *v.t.* disproportionner

disproportionate *adj.* disproportionné.

disproportionately *adv.* disproportionnément.

disprove *v.t.* réfuter.

dispute *v.i.* disputer; *Infml.* se chamailler. *v.t.* contester, débattre, discuter, disputer. *n.* dispute *f.*; discussion *f.*, débat *m.*

disqualification *n.* incapacité *f.*; exclusion *f.*, disqualification *f.*

disqualify *v.t.* disqualifier. **to ~ for an office,** rendre incapable de remplir une fonction.

disquiet *n.* inquiétude *f.*, agitation *f.* ~ *v.t.* inquiéter.

disquisition *n.* dissertation *f.*

disregard *n.* dédain *m.*; indifférence *f.* ~ *v.t.* ne pas tenir compte de, ignorer, négliger; dédaigner; mépriser.

disrepair *n.* délabrement *m.*

disreputable *adj.* mal famé; méprisé; honteux, déshonorant.

disreputably *adv.* honteusement.

disrepute *n.* mauvaise réputation *f.*, décri *m.*, discrédit *m.*, déshonneur *m.*

disrespect *n.* manque *m.* de respect, irrévérence *f.* ~ *v.t.* manquer de respect (envers); mépriser.

disrespectful *adj.* irrespectueux; manquant d'égards pour.

disrespectfully *adv.* sans égard; irrespectueusement.

disrobe *v.t.* (se) déshabiller.

disroot *v.t.* déraciner.

disrupt *v.t.* interrompre; déranger.

disruption *n.* interruption *f.*, rupture *f.*

disruptive *adj.* perturbateur.

dissatisfaction *n.* mécontentement *m.*, déplaisir *m.*

dissatisfactory *adj.* peu satisfaisant, déplaisant.

dissatisfied *p.p.* mécontenté. *adj.* mécontent; offensé.

dissatisfy *v.t.* mécontenter.

dissect *v.t.* disséquer.

dissection *n.* dissection *f.*

dissemble *v.t.* dissimuler, déguiser. *v.i.* feindre.

disseminate *v.t.* disséminer; répandre.

dissemination n. dissémination f.

dissension n. dissension f.; discorde f.

dissent v.i. différer, d'opinion, de sentiment.

dissertation n. dissertation f.

dissident adj., n. dissident m.

dissimilar adj. dissemblable.

dissimulation n. dissimulation f.

dissipate v.t. dissiper, disperser. v.i. dissiper, (se) disperser, s'éparpiller, s'évanouir.

dissipation n. dissipation f.

dissociate v.t. dissocier.

dissociation n. dissociation f., séparation f., désunion f.

dissolute adj. dissolu; désordonné, dérégle.

dissolution n. dissolution f.

dissolvable adj. dissoluble.

dissolve v.i. (se) dissoudre; fondre. v.t. dissoudre; mourir. **to ~ a trading company**, dissoudre une société commerciale.

dissolvant n. dissolvant m.

dissonance n. dissonance f.; contrariété f.

dissonant adj. dissonant; opposé, contraire.

dissuade v.t. dissuader.

dissuasion n. dissuasion f.

dissuasive adj. dissuasif.

distance n. distance f.; éloignement m.; lointain m.; réserve f., respect m. **in the ~**, dans le lointain. **at a ~**, de loin. **to keep at a ~**, tenir à distance. v.t. éloigner, espacer; distancer.

distant adj. distant; éloigné, hautain, froid, réservé. **a ~ relative**, un parent éloigné.

distantly adv. à distance, de loin, avec réserve.

distaste n. dégoût m.; déplaisir.

distasteful adj. dégoûtant, nauséabond.

distemper n. maladie f., indisposition f.; maladie f. (of young animals).

distend v.t. distendre; élargir, dilater; enfler, gonfler, grossir.

distension n. distension f.; élargissement m.

distinct adj. distinct; clair, net; marqué.

distinction n. distinction f.; différence f.

distinctive adj. distinctif.

distinctly adv. distinctement.

distinguish v.t. distinguer (from, de). v.i. faire une différence.

distinguishable adj. qu'on peu distinguer.

distinguished adj. distingué; remarquable, célèbre.

distort v.t. tordre; distordre; contourner, déformer; fausser.

distorted adj. dénaturé, tordu, faussé, contourné, déformé.

distortion n. déformation f.; dénaturation f.; distorsion f.

distract v.t. distraire; troubler.

distracted adj. distrait; troublé.

distraction n. distraction f.; trouble m.

distraught adj. égaré.

distress n. saisie f.; détresse f.; désarroi m., misère f., adversité f. **a ship in ~**, un navire en détresse. v.t. affliger; désoler.

distressed adj. profondément affligé, accablé de malheurs; réduit à la misère.

distressful adj. malheureux, misérable; calamiteux.

distressing adj. douloureux, affligent.

distribute v.t. distribuer; répartir.

distributer n. distributeur m., distributrice f.

distribution n. distribution f.; répartition f.; administration f. (of justice).

district n. district m.; région f., secteur m.

~ attorney, procureur m. du gouvernement.

~ manager, directeur/directrice régional.

distrust v.t. se défier, se méfier. n. défiance f., méfiance f., doute m., soupçon m.

distrustful adj. défiant, méfiant, soupçonneux.

disturb v.t. troubler; déranger. **don't ~ yourself**, ne vous dérangez pas.

disturbance n. trouble m.; dérangement m.; confusion f., tumulte m.; désordre m.

disunion n. désunion f., séparation f.

disunite v.t. désunir, séparer. v.i. (se) désunir, (se) séparer.

disunity n. désunion f.

disuse n. désuétude f., non-usage m. **~** v.t. cesser de faire usage de; se déshabituer.

ditch n. fossé m. **~** v.t. faire, creuser un fossé. *Infml.* laisser tomber, plaquer. **she ~ed him**, elle l'a plaqué.

ditto adv. idem.

ditty n. chansonnette f.

diuretic adj. diurétique. n. diurétique m.

dive v.i. plonger; faire le plongeon; pénétrer; enforcer.

diver n. plongeur m.; plongeuse f.; scaphandrier m.; plongeon m. (bird).

diverge v.i. diverger.

divergence n. divergence f.

divergent adj. divergent.

divers adj. divers. **~ colored**, aux couleurs variées.

diverse adj. divers, différent.

diversify v.t. diversifier.

diversion n. diversion f.; amusement m., distraction f., divertissement m.

diversity n. diversité f., variété f.; différence f., dissemblance f.

divert v.t. (from, de) divertir; distraire; détourner (attention).

divest v.t. dépouiller, priver de.

divide v.t. (into) diviser, partager, séparer; distribuer. v.i. (se) diviser, (se) partager, se désunir.

dividend n. dividende m.

divider n. diviseur m.; séparation f.

divination n. divination f.

divine adj. divin. n. ecclésiastique m., prêtre m., théologien m., deviner; conjecturer, présager, prédire.

divinely adv. divinement.

diving adj. plongeant; pénétrant. **~ suit**, scaphandre m.

divisible adj. divisible.

division *n.* division *f.*; partage *m.*, distinction *f.*; discorde, scisson *f.*

divorce *n.* divorce *m.* ~ *v.t.* (**from**, de) divorcer; séparer.

divulge *v.t.* divulger.

dizziness *n.* étourdissement *m.*, vertige *m.*

dizzy *adj.* étourdi; vertigineux. *v.i.* donner le vertige; étourdir.

D.N.A. *n. Abbr.* **deoxyribonucleic acid,** acide désoxyribonucléique, A.D.N.

do *v.t., v.i.* faire, accomplir, exécuter; rendre; finir. **to ~ again,** refaire. **to ~ up,** arranger; raccommoder; emballer. *v.i.* faire; agir; se conduire; se porter; aller; convenir; finir. **to have to ~ with,** avoir affaire à. **to ~ without,** se passer de. **this beef is not ~ne enough,** ce boeuf n'est pas assez cuit. **I'm ~ne with him,** j'ai fini avec lui. **that will ~,** cela suffit; c'est bien.

do *n. Mus.* do *m.*

doc *n. Infml.* toubib *m.* (doctor).

docile *adj.* docile.

docility *n.* docilité *f.*

dock *v.t.* faire entrer dans un dock. *n.* dock *m.*, **floating wet ~,** bassin à flot. **dry ~,** bassin de radoub.

docket *n.* étiquette *f.*; rôle *m.* des causes. *v.t.* étiqueter; faire un extrait.

dockyard *n.* arsenal *m.*, deport, chantier *m.* naval.

doctor *n.* docteur *m.*; médecin *m.* ~ **in law,** docteur en droit. *v.t.* soigner.

doctorate *n.* doctorat *m.*

doctrine *n.* doctrine *f.*

document *n.* document *m.*, pièce *f.*, titre *m.* *v.t.* fournir des documents; enseigner, instruire.

documentary *adj.* documentaire *m.*

documentation *n.* documentation *f.*

dodder *v.i.* trembloter, dodeliner, chanceler.

dodge *n.* tour *m.*, ruse *f.*; évasion *f.* *v.i.* biaiser, tergiverser. *v.t.* esquiver, éviter.

dodger *n.* tire-au-flanc *m.*, roublard *m.* **draft~,** réfractaire.

doe *n.* daine *f.*

doer *n.* auteur *m.* d'une action; personne *f.* active, dynamique.

dog *n.* chien *m.*, chienne *f.* **a house ~,** chien de garde. *Infml.* **you, lucky ~!** veinard! *m.* ~ **briar,** églantier *m.* ~ **kennel,** chenil *m.* ~'**s-ear,** corne *f.*, oreille *f.* ~ *v.t.* suivre à la piste; harceler.

dogged *adj.* acharné, entêté.

doggedly *adv.* avec entêtement.

doggone *adj. Infml.* satané, sacré.

doggy *n. Infml.* toutou *m.*

doghouse *n.* niche *f.*

dogma *n.* dogme *m.*, doctrine *f.*

dogmatic *adj.* dogmatique; positif. *n.* dogmatiste *m.*

dogmatism *n.* arrogance *f.*; assurance *f.*, ton *m.*, tranchant.

doings *n.* choses *f.pl.*, faites, transactions *f.pl.*; exploits *m.pl.*

dole *n.* distribution *f.*; part *f.*, portion *f.*; aumône *f.* ~ *v.t.* distribuer. **to ~ out,** répartir.

doleful *adj.* douloureux, plaintif; triste, lugubre. **a ~ cry,** un cri lugubre.

dolefully *adv.* douloureusement, plaintivement, tristement.

doll *n.* poupée *f.*

dollar *n.* dollar *m.* ~ **bill,** billet *m.* d'un dollar.

dolly *n.* poupée *f.*; *Cine.* chariot *m.*, traveling *m.* ~ **in/out,** avancer/reculer (the camera).

dolphin *n.* dauphin *m.*

domain *n.* domaine *m.*

dome *n.* édifice *m.*; dôme *m.*

domestic *adj.* domestique; apprivoisé (of an animal), de famille. *n.* domestique *m.f.* serviteur *m.*

domesticate *v.t.* rendre casanier; rendre familier; domestiquer, apprivoiser.

domicile *n.* domicile *m.* ~ *v.t.* établir une résidence fixe.

dominant *adj.* dominant. *n. Mus.* dominante *f.*

dominate *v.t.* dominer.

domination *n.* domination *f.*

domineer *v.t.* dominer; tempêter. **to ~ over,** dominer avec insolence. *v.t.* gouverner.

domineering *adj.* dominateur, arrogant, impérieux.

dominion *n.* domination *f.*; empire *m.*, puissance *f.* **the Spanish ~s,** les possessions espagnoles.

domino *n.* domino *m.*

don *n.* professeur *m.*, Don *m.* ~ *v.t.* vêtir, revêtir.

donation *n.* donation *f.*; don *m.*; bienfait *m.*

done *p.p.* of do; *adj.* fait, cuit. **that's a ~ deal,** marché conclu.

donkey *n.* âne *m.*, anesse *f.*, baudet *m.*

donor *n.* donateur *m.*, donatrice *f.*; donneur *m.*; donneuse *f.* **organ ~,** donneur d'organe(s).

donut *n.* beignet *m.*

doodle *n.* griffannage *m.* ~ *v.t., v.i.* griffonner.

doom *v.t.* juger; condamner; destiner. *n.* jugement *m.*, sentence *f.*; arrêt *m.*, destinée *f.*, sort *m.*, lot *m.*

doomsday *n.* jour *m.*, du jugement dernier.

door *n.* porte *f.*; portière *f.* (of a car). **back ~,** porte de derrière. **folding ~s,** porte à deux battants. **half ~,** porte coupée. **sliding ~s,** porte à coulisse, qui glisse. ~**man,** portier *m.*, concierge *m.f.* ~**knob,** bouton *m.* de porte. ~**mat,** paillasson *m.* ~**way,** entrée *f.* de porte, porte *f.* cochère.

dope *n. Infml.* drogue *f.*, stupéfiant *m.* dopant *m.*; *Infml.* crétin *m.*; bête *m.* ~ *v.t.* droguer; doper; enduire.

dop(e)y *adj.* drogué; (stupid) crétin, (from sleep) abruti, endormi.

dorm *n. Infml.* dortoir *m.*

dormant *adj.* dormant; assoupi; caché, secret.

dormer, dormer window *n.* lucarne *f.*

dormitory *n.* dortoir *m.*

dormouse *n.* loir *m.*

dorsal *adj.* dorsal.

dose n. dose f.; potion f. ~ v.t. doser, médicamenter, droguer.

dot n. point m. ~ v.t. ponctuer; pointer, nuancer, pointiller. v.i. faire des points.

dotage n. radotage m.; seconde enfance.

dote v.i. radoter; (with **on, upon**) raffoler de.

double adj. double; faux; voûté; en deux. v.t. doubler, multiplier par deux; redoubler, répéter. **to ~ and twist**, retordre. v.i. biaiser, ruser. n. double m., ruse f., artifice m. adv. double, doublement, en double. ~ **barreled**, à deux coups, à deux canons. ~**-vested**, croisé. **to ~ cross**, v.t. duper. ~ **entry**, partie f. double. **to ~ lock**, fermer à double tour. ~ **meaning**, à double sens. ~**-talk**, paroles, phrases ambiguës.

doubling n. doublement m.

doubt v.i. bésiter; se douter; soupçonner. v.t. douter de; hésiter à croire. n. doute m.; soupçon m. **without ~**, sans aucun doute, indubitablement.

doubtful adj. douteux; indécis, méfiant, soupçonneux.

doubtfully adv. douteusement; avec doute, irrésolument; dans un état de crainte.

doubtfulness n. doute m., incertitude f., irrésolution f.; ambigüité f.

doubtless adv. indubitablement.

doubtlessly adv. indubitablement.

douche n. lavage m. interne, vaginal.

dough n. pâte f. Infml. fric m., pognon m., oseille f.

doughty adj. vaillant, courageux.

dour adj. austère; sévère.

douse v.t. plonger, larguer; mollir, amener, abaisser; éteindre.

dove n. colombe f. **ring ~**, pigeon m. ramier, ramier m. **turtle~**, tourterelle f. ~ **colored**, gorge-de-pigeon.

dowdy adj. mal habillé, mal fagoté.

down n. duvet m.; poil m.; coton m., dune f. adv. en bas, à bas; à terre; descendu. **to take ~**, décrocher, détacher. **the moon is ~**, la lune est au-dessous de l'horizon. **up and ~**, de haut en bas, de long en large. **upside ~**, sens dessus dessous. prep. en bas de, au bas de. **to be ~stairs**, être en bas, être descendu.

downcast adj. abattu.

downer n. Infml. sédatif m.; drogue f. sédative.

downfall n. chute f.; ruine f.; destruction f.

downhill adj. incliné, en pente. n. déclivité f., pente f., descente f., rampe f., inclinaison f.

downright adv. droit en bas, tout net, tout à fait. adj. allant droit au but; droit, simple, sans façon.

downstairs adj., adv. en bas.

downtrodden adj. foulé aux pieds, opprimé.

downtown adj., n. center ville m., quartier m. des affaires.

downward, downwards adv. en bas, par le bas.

downy adj. de duvet; duveté; doux.

doze v.i. s'assoupir, sommeiller. n. sommeil m., léger, assoupissement m., somme m.

dozen n. douzaine f.

dozy adj. adj. endormi, assoupi.

drab adj. terne, morne. n. gris m.

draft n. brouillon m. (of a letter); projet m. (of a law); trait m.; détachement m. (of soldiers); traite f., esquisse f., dessin m., tracé m. ~ v.t. dessiner; rédiger; appeler (soldiers); affecter; détacher (troops).

drafty adj. plein de courants d'air.

drag v.t. tirer avec force. **to ~ along**, traîner. **to ~ away**, entraîner. **to ~ down**, faire descendre de force. **to ~ out**, faire sortir de force, arracher. v.i. (se) traîner; draguer; avancer péniblement. **the affair ~s**, l'affaire traîne. n. tirage m., résistance f.; Infml. ennui m. **he was in ~**, il portait des vêtements de femme. **the main ~ (street)**, la rue principale.

dragon n. dragon m. ~**fly**, libellule f.

drain v.t. filtrer; faire égoutter; dessécher, tarir; drainer. v.i. s'écouler; égoutter. n. égout m., rigole f.; drain m., tranchée f.; fossé d'écoulement.

drainage n. égouttement m.; dessèchement m., épuisement m., drainage m.

drainer n. égouttoir m.

drake n. canard m., mâle, jars.

drama n. drama m.

dramatic adj. dramatique.

dramatist n. auteur m., dramatique, dramaturge m.

dramatize v.t. dramatiser.

drape v.t. draper; tendre n., rideaux m.pl.

drastic adj. drastique.

draw v.t. dessiner; tirer; traîner; entraîner; pomper; puiser; tracer, étirer. **to ~ wine from a cask**, tirer du vin d'un tonneau, soutirer du vin. **to ~ water from a well**, puiser de l'eau d'un puits. **to ~ lots**, tirer au sort. **to ~ a prize**, gagner un lot. **to ~ a line on paper**, tirer une ligne sur du papier. **to ~ from nature**, dessiner d'après nature. **to ~ a bill of exchange**, tirer une lettre de change. **to ~ again**, tirer de nouveau. **to ~ aside**, tirer à l'écart. **to ~ back**, tirer en arrière, reculer. **to ~ forth**, tirer en avant; sortir. **to ~ in**, retirer; attirer, entraîner; rentrer. **to ~ out**, tirer dehors; retirer; extraire; allonger; prolonger. v.i. se retirer, se contracter. **to ~ aside**, se mettre à l'écart, se ranger. **to ~ near**, approcher, s'avancer. **to ~ off**, se retirer; battre en retraite. **to ~ together**, se ranger, se rassembler, se réunir. **to ~ up**, se ranger, se mettre en ligne.

drawback n. drawback m.; décompte m., inconvénient m.

drawer n. tiroir m.; tireur m.; puiseur m., dessinateur m.

drawing n. dessin m., ébauche f., étirage m., laminage m.; tirage m. (of a lottery). **mechanical ~**, dessin linéaire. ~ **board**, planche f. à dessin. ~ **book**, cahier m. de dessin.

drawing room n. salon m.

drawl v.i. parler d'une voix traînante. n. débit m., traînant, voix f. lente.

drawn adj. nul, remis; indécis. a ~ game, une partie nulle.

dread n. terreur f.; effroi m., épouvante f. ~ adj. effroyable; terrible. v.t. redouter, craindre.

dreadful adj. affreux, terrible, épouvantable.

dreadfully adv. terriblement, d'une manière redoutable.

dreadfulness n. frayeur f., horreur f.

dream n. songe m., rêve m., rêverie f. ~ v.i. (with of) rêver; songer.

dreamer n. rêveur m., rêveuse f., visionnaire m.

dreamy adv. rêveur, songeur.

dreariness n. tristesse f., solitude f., lugubre.

dreary adj. triste, sombre, lugubre.

dredge n. drague f. v.t. draguer; enfariner, saupoudrer.

dregs n. lie f.; sédiment m.; rebut m.

drench v.t. tremper, mouiller. n. breuvage m.; Veter. purge f.

dress v.t. habiller, vêtir, parer. to ~ a lady's hair, coiffer une dame. to ~ up, bien s'habiller. v.i. s'habiller; faire sa toilette. n. robe f., habillement m., vêtement m., toilette f., mise f., tenue f. military ~, uniforme. high neck ~, robe montante. low neck ~, robe décolletée. full ~, grande toilette. ~ circle, fauteuils m.pl. de balcon.

dresser n. buffet m., toilette f., coiffeuse f.

dressing n. habillement m., vêtements m.pl., parure f.; pansement m. (of a wound); labor m.; fumure f., apprêt m., apprêtage m. ~ gown, peignoire m., robe f. de chambre.

dressmaker n. couturière f., couturier m.

dressy adj. habillé, élégant.

dribble v.i. égoutter; baver. v.t. verser goutte à goutte.

dried p.p. of dry adj. sec, sèche; déshydraté, en poudre.

drift n. force f. d'impulsion; but m.; tendance f., portée f.; averse f.; amas m.; dérive f. (meaning) sens m. général. ~s of dust, of snow, des tourbillons de poussière, de neige. v.i. pousser, chasser; flotter.

drifting n. action d'entraîner; action d'amonceler, d'entasser.

drill n. forer; percer; exercer, faire manoeuvrer; semer du grain par sillons. v.i. semer en lignes; faire faire l'exercice. n. foret m.; exercice m.; ruisseau m., semoir m.; coutil m.

drink v.i. boire. to ~ like a fish, boire comme un trou. to ~ in, absorber. n. boisson f., breuvage m. let's have a ~, allons prendre un verre. may I offer you a ~? puis-je vous offrir quelque chose à boire?

drinkable adj. potable; buvable.

drinker n. buveur m., buveuse f.

drinking adj. adonné à la boisson. n. action de boire; ivrognerie f.; boire m.

drip v.i. égoutter, dégoutter. v.t. laisser tomber goutte à goutte. n. goutte f.

dripping n. ruisselant; égouttement m.

drive v.t. entraîner, pousser; conduire, mener, obliger, forcer. to ~ to desperation, pousser au désespoir. to ~ mad, faire perdre la tête à. ~ that nail up to the head, enfoncez ce clou jusqu'à la tête. to ~ away, chasser. to ~ back, repousser; reconduire. to ~ on, pousser. v.i. s'avancer, être poussé, chassé; se faire conduire. you ~ too fast, vous allez trop vite. to ~ at, viser, prétendre à. what are you driving at? à quoi veux-tu en venir? to ~ back, revenir en voiture; reconduire. to ~ off, partir. to ~ on, continuer sa route. to ~ out, sortir en voiture. n. promenade f. (in a car); allée f.; course f.

drivel v.i. baver, radoter. n. bave f.

driver n. conducteur m., chauffeur m., chauffeuse f. ~'s license, permis m. de conduire.

driving adj. moteur, motrice; menant n. conduite f.

drizzle v.i. bruiner.

drizzly adj. de bruine.

droll adj. drôle, comique, amusant.

dromedary n. dromadaire m.

drone n. abeille f., mâle; bourdon m., frelon m.; fainéant m. ~ v.i. bourdonner; lire, parler d'une voix somnolente.

drool n. braver.

droop v.i. languir, dépérir, s'affaisser; se faner, se flétrir, (se) pencher; s'abaisser. v.t. pencher.

drooping adj. languissant, s'affaiblissant; se flétrissant.

drop n. goutte f.; pastille f. (candy). a ~ of wine, une goutte de vin. v.t. laisser tomber; laisser la, lâcher, quitter. let us ~ the subject, changeons de sujet. to ~ a letter in the post, mettre, déposer une lettre à la poste. ~ out, étudiant qui a abandonné ses études. I will ~ you off, je te raccompagnerai. v.i. tomber; distiller, tomber en petites gouttes; s'écouler en gouttes.

droplet n. gouttelette f.

dropping n. égouttement m. ~ adj. qui dégoutte. ~s, n.pl. fiente f., crotte f.

drought n. aridité f., sécheresse f.

drown v.t. (se) noyer; submerger, inonder; étouffer (sounds), couvrir. to be drowned, être noyé.

drowse v.i. s'assoupir, somnoler n. somnolence f. ~ v.t. assoupir.

drowsiness n. somnolence f.; assoupissement m.

drowsy adj. somnolent; assoupissant; léthargique.

drudge v.i. travailler rudement; trimer, peiner. n. homme (ou femme) de peine, souffre-douleur m.

drudgery n. corvée f.; travail m. fatigant.

drug n. drogue f., stupéfiant m., narcotique m.; médicament m. ~ addict, drogué m., droguée f. toxicomane m.f. ~ pusher, ravitailleur m. en drogue. ~ traffic, trafic m. des stupéfiants. v.i. droguer; empoisonner. v.t. droguer; administrer des drogues; endormir (au moyen d'un narcotique).

drum n. tambour m.; caisse f.; tympan m. (de

l'oreille). **big ~,** grosse caisse. **kettle~,** timbale *f.*
~ *v.i.* battre le tambour; tambouriner. **to ~ up,**
rassembler au son du tambour.

drummer *n.* tambour *m.*

drumstick *n.* baguette *f.* de tambour; cuisse
(fowl).

drunk *adj.* ivre, soûl, gris, enivré. **to get ~,**
s'enivrer.

drunkard *n.* ivrogne *m. Infml.* soulard *m.*

drunken *adj.* ivre, enivré, soûl, gris; ivrogne.

drunkenness *n.* ivresse *f.;* ivrognerie *f.*

dry *adj.* sec; aride, à sec; tari; altéré; caustique,
mordant. **~ weather,** temps sec. **~ goods,**
articles *m.pl.* de nouveauté. **to be ~,** avoir soif;
faire sec. **to ~ up,** mettre à sec, essuyer.
~ up your tears, essuyez vos larmes. **~ cleaning,** nettoyage *m.* à sec. *v.i.* (se) sécher, (se) dessécher.

dryer *n.* siccatif *m.,* sèche-linge *m.* **hair~,** sèche
cheveux *m.*

dryness *n.* sécheresse *f.* aridité *f.;* causticité *f.*

dual *adj.* à deux, double. **~ nationality,** double
nationalité *f.;* duel *m.*

dualism *n.* dualisme *m.*

dubbing *n.* doublage *m.,* synchronisation *f.*

dubious *adj.* douteux; incertain; ambigu.

dubiously *adv.* d'une manière douteuse,
incertaine.

dubiousness *n.* doute *m.,* incertitude *f.,* indécision *f.*

duck *n.* canard *m.,* cane *f.;* inclination *f.* (of the
head), courbette *f.;* plongeon *m.;* toile *f.* à voile.
v.t. plonger dans l'eau, incliner. *v.i.* (se) plonger
dans l'eau, enfoncer la tête dans l'eau; baisser la
tête subitement; éviter.

ducking *n.* plongeon *m.*

duckling *n.* caneton *m.* **ugly ~,** laideron *m.*
vilain petit canard *m.*

duct *n.* conduit *m.*

ductile *adj.* docile; souple, flexible.

dude *n. Infml.* type *m.,* gars *m.;* hôte *m.* d'un
ranch-hôtel. **~ ranch,** ranch-hôtel *m.*

dudgeon *n.* **in high ~,** en colère offensé.

due *adj.* dû; propre, juste, convenable. **two
months are now ~,** on doit maintenant deux
mois. **in ~ form,** en bonne et due forme. **in ~
time,** en temps voulu. *adv.* dûment, convenablement. *n.* dû *m.,* droit *m.* **~s,** cotisation *f.*

duel *n.* duel *m.* **~ *v.i.*** se battre en duel. *v.i.* attaquer en duel.

dug *n.* mamelle *f.* (of an animal).

duke *n.* duc *m.*

dukedom *n.* duché *m.*

dulcet *adj.* doucet, doucereux, doux; mélodieux,
harmonieux.

dull *adj.* lourd (weather), triste, sombre; terne;
languissant. **we had a ~ time,** nous nous
sommes bien ennuyés. **a ~ sound,** un bruit
sourd. **~ weather,** temps couvert. *v.t.*
émousser; assourdir. *v.i.* s'émousser; s'hébéter;
s'attrister.

duly *adv.* dûment, régulièrement; en temps
opportun.

dumb *adj.* muet; bête, idiot, sidéré.

dumbbells *n.* haltères *m.pl.*

dumbfound *v.t.* confondre, abasourdir.

dummy *n.* mannequin *m.,* marionette *f.;* figurant *m.*

dump *n.* tas *m.;* amas *m.;* décharge *f.* (publique),
dépotoir *m.; Infml.* trou *m.,* bled *m.* **~ *v.t.***
décharger; *Infml.* **she ~ed him,** elle l'a laissé
tomber.

dumpling *n. Culin.* boulette de pâte *f.* **apple ~,**
pomme *f.* enrobée de pâte.

dumpy *adj.* ramassé, trapu.

dun *adj.* brun-gris. *v.t.* réclamer; importuner,
relancer.

dunce *n.* cancre *m.*

dune *n.* dune *f.*

dung *n.* fumier *m.;* fiente *f.* **cow ~,** bouse *f.* de
vache.

dungaree *n.* bleus *m.pl.*

dunk *n.* tremper, tremper des mouillettes.

duo *n.* duo *m.*

dupe *n.* dupe *f.* **~ *v.t.*** duper.

duple *adj.* double.

duplex *n.* duplex *m.*

duplicate *adj.* double. *n.* double *m.;* duplicate *m.*
done in ~, fait en double. *v.t.* doubler, copier,
reproduire.

duplication *n.* reproduction *f.*

duplicity *n.* duplicité *f.*

durability *n.* durabilité *f.,* résistance *f.*

durable *adj.* durable, solide, résistant.

duration *n.* durée *f.;* permanence *f.*

duress *n.* contrainte *f.;* force *f.;* emprisonnement
m., détention *f.*

during *prep.* pendant, durant.

dusk *n.* crépuscule *m.*

duskiness *n.* commencement *m.*
d'obscurité.

dusky *adj.* obscur, sombre.

dust *n.* poussière *f.* **to bite the ~,** mordre la
poussière. **saw~,** sciure (de bois) *f. v.t.* épousseter; essuyer; saupoudrer.

duster *n.* essuie-meubles *m.*

dusty *adj.* poussiéreux, poudreux; couvert de
poussière.

Dutch *adj.* hollandais. *n.* Hollandais *m.,* la
Hollandaise; le hollandais (language). **to go ~,**
partager les frais.

dutiable *adj.* soumis aux droits de douane,
d'entrée.

dutiful *adj.* obéissant, soumis; respectueux.

dutifully *adv.* avec obéissance,
respectueusement.

duty *n.* devoir *m.;* devoirs *m.pl.,* respects *m.pl.;*
garde *f.,* fonction *f.,* droit *m.,* taxe *f.* **customs ~,**
droit de douane. **to be on ~,** être de service.
~-free, exempt de droit.

dwarf *n.* nain *m.,* naine *f.* **~** *adj.* nain. *v.t.* rapetisser.

dwell v.i. demeurer; habiter, rester. **to ~ on, upon,** s'étendre sur, s'appuyer, insister sur. **he always ~s on the past,** il revient sans cesse sur le passé.

dweller n. habitant m., habitante f.

dwelling n. habitation f., demeure f.

dwindle v.i. diminuer, décroitre. **to ~ away,** dépérir.

dye v.t. teindre, colorer. n. teinture f.; teint m., teinte f.

dyeing n. teinture f.

dying adj. mourant, agonisant, moribond; de mort. **these were his ~ words,** voici ses dernières paroles.

dyke n. digue f., levée f., Infml. gouine f.

dynamic adj. dynamique.

dynamite n. dynamite f.

dynasty n. dynastie f.

dysentry n. dysenterie f.

dyslexia n. dyslexie f.

dyspepsia n. dyspepsie f.

dyspeptic adj. dyspeptique.

dystrophy n. dystrophie f.

E

E n. E, e m. Abbr. of east, Géog. est. Mus. mi m.

each adj., pron. chaque, chacun, chacune. **~ of us had his apartment,** chacun de nous avait son appartement. **they hate ~ other,** ils/elles se détestent (l'un/l'autre, l'une/l'autre).

eager adj. ardent; vif, véhément; impatient de; avide. **to be ~ for,** être passionné pour.

eagerly adv. ardemment, vivement, passionnément.

eagerness n. ardeur f., empressement m., emportement m.

eagle n. aigle m.; aigle f. **bald ~,** aigle à tête blanche. **the Roman ~,** l'aigle romaine. **~-eyed,** aux yeux d'aigle.

ear n. oreille f.; épi m. (of corn); anse f., oreillette f. **to prick up one's ~s,** dresser les oreilles. **~ache,** mal m. d'oreille. **~lobe,** lobe m. de l'oreille. **~ring,** boucle f. d'oreille.

earl n. comte m.

early adj. matinal, premier, ancien; avancé; précoce, hâtif. **an ~ fruit,** un fruit précoce. adv. de bonne heure, de bon matin, tôt; bientôt. **~ in the morning,** de grand matin.

earn v.t., v.i. mériter; gagner; toucher, rapporter.

earnest adj. ardent, empressé, fervent; sérieux. **~ in one's duties,** appliqué à ses devoirs. n. sérieux m., sincérité f.; bonne foi f. **in ~,** tout de bon, sérieusement.

earnestly adv. ardemment; sérieusement.

earnestness n. ardeur f., zèle m., empressment m., diligence f.

earnings n.pl. gain m., salaire m., récompense f.

earphone n. écouteur m.

earpiece n. écouteur m.

earth n. terre f.; monde m.; sol m. v.t. enterrer, enfouir. v.i. se terrer. **~bound,** lié, attaché à la terre. **~worm,** ver m. de terre. **she is very down to ~,** elle a les pieds sur terre. **it's heaven on ~,** c'est paradis sur terre.

earthen adj. de terre, fait en terre.

earthenware n. vaisselle f. de terre, poterie f.; faïence f.

earthly adj. terrestre.

earthquake n. tremblement m. de terre.

earthy adj. terreux; terrestre; de terre.

ease n. aise f., aisance f., bienêtre m., repos m.; facilité f. **at ~,** à l'aise. **to take one's ~,** se mettre à l'aise. **they have a certain ~,** ils ont une certaine aisance. **to ~ off,** se détendre; soulager, faciliter; calmer. **to ~ off,** se détendre, devenir plus calme.

easel n. chevalet m.

easily adv. aisément, facilement.

easiness n. facilité f.; aisance f.

east n. est m.; l'orient m., le levant. adj. d'orient, de levant, oriental. **~ wind,** vent d'est. **~ Indies,** les Indes orientales.

eastbound adj. vers l'est, en direction de l'est.

Easter n. Pâques f. ~ day, jour m. de Pâques. **~ Monday,** le lundi de Pâques. **~ week,** semaine f. de Pâques.

easterly adj. d'est, d'orient, du levant. adv. à l'est, vers l'est.

eastern adj. oriental; à l'est, de l'est, au levant.

eastward adv. à l'est, vers l'est, vers l'orient.

easy adj. tranquille, paisible, aisé, à l'aise; facile, coulant, doux. **take it ~,** relax, ne vous en faites pas. **to be in ~ circumstances,** être dans l'aisance. **an ~ man,** un homme accommodant, facile à vivre.

eat v.t. manger; consumer, dévorer. **to ~ one's words,** retirer sa parole, se rétracter. **to ~ away,** manger, ronger. **to ~ up,** manger; consumer; ruiner. **to ~ into,** manger, ronger; mordre sur. **to ~ with appetite,** manger avec appétit. **to ~ into,** manger, ronger; mordre sur.

eatable adj. mangeable, comestible. n. nourriture f., vivres m.pl., comestible m., victuailles f.pl.

eater n. mangeur m., mangeuse f.

eating n. le manger m.

eaves n.pl. bords m.pl. du toit; larmier m.

eavesdrop v.i. espionner, écouter aux portes.

eavesdropping n. espionnage m.

ebb n. reflux m. jusant m.; Fig. déclin m. **at a low ~,** dans un bien triste état. v.i. refluer, descendre, déchoir; Fig. baisser, déchoir.

ebony n. ébénier m.; ébène f.

ebullience n. ébullition f.; effervescence f.

ebullient adj. bouillonnant.

ebullition n. ébullition f.; effervescence f.

eccentric adj. excentrique; original.

eccentricity n. excentricité f.

ecclesiastic adj. ecclésiastique.

ecclesiastic n. ecclésiastique m.

echo *n.* écho *m.* ~ *v.i.* faire écho, retentir, répercuter le son.

eclectic *adj., n.* éclectique *m.*

eclipse *n.* éclipse *f.* ~ *v.t.* éclipser; surpasser. *v.i.* s'éclipser, disparaître.

ecliptic *n.* écliptique *f. adj.*

eclosion *n.* éclosion *f.*

ecological *adj.* écologique.

ecologist *n.* écologiste *m.f.*

ecology *n.* écologie *f.*

economic *adj.* économique; économe.

economically *adv.* économiquement.

economics *n.* les sciences *f.pl.* economiques.

economist *n.* économiste *m.f.*

economize *v.i.* économiser, être économe.

economy *n.* économie *f.*; système *m.*, économique.

ecstasy *n.* extase *f.*, ravissement *m.*, transport *m.* ~ *v.t.* extasier.

ecstatic *adj.* extatique; ravissant.

ecstatically *adv.* d'une manière extatique.

eczema *n.* eczéma *m.*

eddy *n.* tourbillon *m.*; flot *m.*; remous *m.* ~ *v.i.* tourbillonner. *adj.* tourbillonnant.

Eden *n.* Eden *m.*

edge *n.* bord *m.*; marge *f.*; tranche *f.*; tranchant *m.*; lisière *f.*; arête. the ~ of a table, le bord d'une table. the ~ of a sword, le tranchant, le fil d'un épée. to take off the ~, émousser. to set the teeth on ~, agacer les dents. *v.t.* aiguiser, affiler, ébarber; border; inciter; exciter, piquer; aiguillonner. to ~ along, avancer peu à peu. *adj.* aiguisé, affilé. ~ tool, instrument *m.* tranchant.

edged *adj.* aigu, acéré, mordant, piquant.

edgewise *adv.* de champ; de côté, obliquement.

edging *n.* bordure *f.*; galon *m.*, passement *m.*, garniture *f.*

edgy *adj.* nervous, à cran, crispé.

edible *adj.* comestible, mangeable.

edict *n.* édit *m.*; décret *m.*, ordonannce *f.*

edification *n.* edification *f.*

edifice *n.* édifice *m.*

edify *v.t.* édifier.

edit *v.t.* éditer, publier.

edition *n.* édition *f.*, tirage *m.*

editor *n.* éditeur; rédacteur *m.* en chef.

editorial *adj.* d'éditeur, de rédacteur en chef, éditorial. *n.* article *m.* de tête, éditorial *m.*

editorialist *n.* éditorialiste *m.f.*

editorship *n.* métier *m.* d'éditeur; édition *f.*; fonctions *f.pl.* de rédacteur en chef.

educate *v.t.* élever; instruire.

education *n.* éducation *f.*, instruction *f.*

educational *adj.* éducateur, d'enseignement; scolaire.

educator *n.* éducateur *m.*, éducatrice *f.*

eel *n.* anguille *f.* electric ~, anguille électrique.

eerie *adj.* inquiétant, étrange.

efface *v.t.* effacer.

effect *n.* effet *m.*, action *f.*, résultat *m.*; objet *m.*

effets *m.pl.* to carry into ~, mettre à effet, executer. to produce an ~, faire de l'effet. *v.t.* effectuer, accomplir, réaliser, exécuter.

effective *adj.* effectif, efficace. an ~ speech, un discours énergique.

effectively *adv.* effectivement, avec effet; efficacement; réellement.

effectiveness *n.* efficacité *f.*

effectual *adj.* efficace. to prove ~, donner l'effet voulu.

effectually *adv.* efficacement, avec effet.

effectuate *v.t.* effectuer, accomplir.

effeminate *adj., n.* efféminé *m.* ~ *v.t.* efféminer. *v.i.* s'efféminer.

effervesce *v.i.* être en effervescence; mousser.

effervescence *n.* effervescence *f.*

effervescent *adj.* effervescent.

effete *adj.* stérile, émoussé, usé, épuisé par l'âge.

efficacious *adj.* efficace.

efficaciously *adv.* efficacement.

efficaciousness *n.* efficacité *f.*

efficacy *n.* efficacité *f.*

efficiency *n.* efficacité *f.*, compétence *f.*

efficient *adj.* efficient; compétent, de bon rendement.

efficiently *adv.* efficacement, avec compétence.

effigy *n.* effigie *f.*

effloresence *n.* efflorescence *f.*; épanouissement *m.*

efflorescent *adj.* efflorescent.

effluence *n.* effluence *f.*, émanation *f.*

effluvium *pl.* effluvia *n.* effluve *m.*, exhalaison *f.*, émanation *f.*

effort *n.* effort *m.*

effortless *adj.* facile, sans effort.

effrontery *n.* effronterie *f.*; audace *f.*

effusion *n.* effusion *f.*; épanchement *m.*; gaspillage *m.*

effusive *adj.* éxubérant, expansif.

effusively *adv.* avec effusion.

effusiveness *n.* effusion *f.*

eft *n.* salamandre *f.*

e.g. *Abbr.* exempli gratia par exemple, ex.

egalitarian *adj., n.* égalitaire *m.f.*

egg *n.* oeuf *m.*, ove *m.* a boiled ~, un oeuf à la coque. *v.t.* ~ on, exciter, pousser à. ~cup, coquetier *m.* ~plant, aubergine *f.* ~-shaped, oviforme.

eglantine *n.* églantine *f.*

ego *n.* moi, ego *m.*

egocentric *adj.* egocentric.

egoism *n.* égoïsme *m.*

egoist *n.* égoïste *m.f.*

egoistically *adv.* égoïstement.

egotism *n.* égoïsme *m.*

egotist *n.* égotiste *m.f.*

egotistical *adj.* egoiste.

egregious *adj.* insigne, énorme.

egress *n.* sortie *f.*

egret *n.* aigrette *f.*

Egypt *n.pr.* Egypte *f.*

Egyptian *adj.* égyptien. *n.* Egyptien *m.*

eh *interj.* eh! hein? quoi?

eight *adj.* huit.

eighteen *adj.* dix-huit.

eighteenth *adj.* dix-huitième.

eighth *adj.* huitième.

eightieth *adj.* quatre-vingtième.

eighty *adj.* quatre-vingts.

either *adj., pron.* l'un ou l'autre; l'un des deux; chaque; chacun; l'un et l'autre. **on ~ side,** de chaque côté. *conj.* soit, ou; soit que. *adv.* aussi; non plus.

ejaculate *v.t.* éjaculer, lancer; proférer, prononcer.

ejaculation *n.* éjaculation *f.;* émission *f.;* éjaculation *f.*

ejaculatory *adj.* éjaculatoire.

eject *v.t.* éjecter, chasser; jeter dehors, expulser; évacuer; évincer.

ejection *n.* expulsion *f.;* renvoi *m.,* rejet *m.,* évacuation *f.*

ejector *n.* ~ **seat,** siège *m.* éjectable.

eke *v.t.* augmenter; allonger; ajouter à. **to ~ out the time,** allonger le temps.

elaborate *v.t.* élaborer; travailler. *adj.* élaboré; étudié, préparé.

elaborately *adv.* laborieusement; d'une manière élaborée.

elaborateness *n.* élaboration *f.;* correction *f.*

elaboration *n.* élaboration *f.*

elapse *v.i.* passer, s'écouler, couler.

elastic *adj.* élastique, souple.

elasticity *n.* élasticité *f.*

elated *adj.* emporté; enivré; exalté. *v.t.* exalter, transporter.

elation *n.* exaltation *f.,* transport *m.*

elbow *n.* coude *m.;* bras *m.* (of a chair). ~ **room,** de la place; aisance des coudes; coudées franches. ~ **grease,** huile de coude. *v.t.* coudoyer; bousculer.

elder *adj.* plus âgé, aîné; plus ancien. *n.* doyen *m.,* ancient *m.,* aîné *m.,* ancêtre *m.;* aïeul *m.; Bot.* sureau.

elderly *adj.* un peu âgé; d'un certain âge.

eldest *adj.* aîné.

elect *v.t.* élire; choisir; nommer. *adj.* élu.

election *n.* élection *f.,* choix *m.*

electioneer *v.i.* faire une campagne électorale.

elective *adj.* électif; *Scol.* facultatif, à option. **the ~ franchise,** la franchise élective, le droit électoral.

elector *n.* électeur *m.,* électrice *f.*

electoral *adj.* électoral.

electorate *n.* électorat *m.*

electric, electrical *adj.* électrique.

electrically *adv.* par la voie de l'électricité.

electrician *n.* électricien *m.,* électricienne *f.*

electricity *n.* électricité *f.*

electrify *v.t.* électriser. *v.i.* s'électriser, devenir électrique.

electrocardiogram *n.* électrocardiogramme *m.*

electrochemical *adj.* électrochimique.

electrocute *v.t.* électrocuter.

electrocution *n.* électrocution *f.*

electrode *n.* électrode *f.*

electromagnetic *adj.* électromagnétique.

electron *n.* électron *m.*

electronic *adj.* électronique.

electronics *n.* électronique *f.*

electrostatics *n.* électrostatique *f.*

elegance *n.* élégance *f.*

elegant *adj.* élégant.

elegantly *adv.* élégamment, avec élégance.

elegiac *adj.* élégiaque.

elegy *n.* élégie *f.*

element *n.* élément *m.*

elemental *adj.* élémentaire.

elementary *adj.* élémentaire.

elephant *n.* éléphant *m.*

elevate *v.t.* élever, relever, hausser; exalter, enfler d'orgueil; égayer, réjouir.

elevated *adj.* élevé, enorgueilli; animé.

elevation *n.* élévation *f.;* exaltation *f.*

elevator *n.* ascenseur *m.* **grain ~,** élevateur *m.* à grains.

eleven *adj.* onze.

eleventh *adj.* onzième.

elf *n.* (*pl.* **elves**) elfe *m.,* esprit *m.,* follet, lutin *m.,* sylphe *m.*

elfin *adj.* des fées, des sylphes.

elicit *v.t.* faire sortir, mettre en lumière; faire jaillir. **to ~ the truth,** dévoiler la vérite.

eligibility *n.* éligibilité *f.*

eligible *adj.* éligible, désirable.

eliminate *v.t.* éliminer, faire disparaître, supprimer.

elimination *n.* élimination *f.*

elite *n.* élite *f.*

elixir *n.* élixir *m.*

elk *n.* élan *m.*

ellipse *n.* ellipse *f.*

ellipsis *pl.* **ellipses** *n.* ellipse *f.*

elliptical *adj.* elliptique.

elm *n.* orme *m.* ~ **grove,** ormaie *f.*

elocution *n.* élocution *f.;* déclamation *f.;* parole *f.,* faculté *f.* de parler.

elongate *v.t.* allonger, étendre; éloigner. *v.i.* s'éloigner de, s'écarter de.

elongation *n.* prolongement *m.;* distance *f.;* élongation *f.*

elope *v.i.* s'enfuir (pour se marier).

elopement *n.* fuite *f.* (amoureuse).

eloquence *n.* éloquence *f.*

eloquent *adj.* éloquent.

eloquently *adv.* éloquemment, avec éloquence.

else *adj.* autre; de plus. **who ~ is coming?** qui d'autre vient? **nobody ~,** personne d'autre. **nothing ~,** rien de plus. **nowhere ~,** nulle part. *adv.* autrement, ou; d'ailleurs, en outre, de plus; sinon. **come with me or ~!** viens avec moi sinon.

elsewhere *adv.* ailleurs, autre part.

elucidate *v.t.* élucider, éclaircir.

elucidation n. élucidation f., éclaircissement m.

elude v.t. éluder; tromper, échapper à.

elusive adj. qui élude, trompeur.

elusory adj. évasif, fallacieux, trompeur.

emaciate v.i. maigrir; s'étioler. v.t. amaigrir, étioler.

emaciation n. amaigrissement m.; étiolement m.; emaciation f.

e-mail n. courrier m. électronique.

emanate v.i. émaner.

emanation n. émanation f.

emanative adj. qui émane de, provenant de.

emancipate v.t. émanciper, affranchir.

emancipated adj. émancipé; affranchi.

emancipation n. émancipation f.; délivrance f., affranchissement m., libération f.

emasculate v.t. émasculer.

emasculation n. émasculation f.

embalm v.t. embaumer; parfumer.

embankment n. digue f., levée f.; remblai m.

embargo n. embargo m. **to lay an ~ on,** mettre l'embargo sur. v.t. mettre un embargo sur; interrompre.

embark v.t. embarquer. v.i. s'embarquer.

embarkation n. embarquement m.; cargaison f.

embarrass v.t. gêner.

embarrassing adj. gênant.

embarrassment n. gêne f.

embassy n. ambassade f.

embattle v.t. ranger en ordre de bataille; créneler. v.i. être rangé en bataille.

embed v.t. enfouir, emboîter, incrustor.

embellish v.t. embellir, orner.

embellishment n. embellissement m.; ornement m.

ember n. cendre f.; tison m. **~ days,** les Quatre-Temps m.pl. **~ week,** semaine des Quatre-Temps.

embezzle v.t. détourner, escroquer.

embezzlement n. détournement m. de fonds, abus m. de confiance, malversation.

embezzler n. escroc m.; auteur m. d'un détournement.

embitter v.t. rendre amer; empoisonner.

emblaze or emblazon v.t. blasonner; décorer; enflaminer.

emblem n. emblème m.

emblematic adj. emblématique.

embodiment n. incoporation f.; personnification f.; incarnation f.

embody v.t. incorporer; personnifier. v.i. s'incarner, s'incorporer.

embolden v.t. enhardir, animer, encourager.

embolism n. embolisme m.

embossment n. bosselure f.; bosse f., relief m.

embrace v.t. étreindre, embrasser (a belief, etc.). v.i. s'embrasser. n. étreinte f., embrassement m.

embrasure n. embrasure f.

embroider v.t. broder.

embroidery n. broderie f.

embroil v.t. brouiller, embrouiller; mêler; entre-mêler; engager. v.i. s'embrouiller.

embroilment n. embrouillement m., implication f., embarras m.

embryo n. embryon m.

emcee n. Infml. présentateur m., présentatrice f., animateur m., animatrice f.

emend v.t. corriger, améliorer.

emendation n. correction f.; émendation f.

emerald n. émeraude f.

emerge v.i. émerger; surgir, se dégager de; se montrer.

emergence n. émergence f.; apparition f.

emergency n. urgence f. **state of ~,** état m. d'urgence. **~ brake,** frein m. de secours.

emergent adj. émergent.

emery n. émeri m.

emigrant adj., n. émigrant m., émigrante f.

emigrate v.i. émigrer.

emigration n. émigration f.

émigré n. émigré(e) m.f.

eminence n. éminence f.; élévation f., distinction f.

eminent adj. éminent; élevé; distingué.

eminently adv. éminemment.

emir n. émir.

emissary n. émissaire m.

emission n. émission f.

emissive adj. émissif.

emit v.t. émettre; jeter, exhaler. **to ~ paper money,** émettre des billets de banque.

emitter n. émitteur m.

emolument n. émolument m., salaire m., appointements m.pl.; profit m.

emotion n. émotion f., trouble m.

emotional adj. émotif, impressionnable; plein d'émotion.

empanel n. nommer un jury; dresser la liste d'un jury.

emperor n. empereur m.

emphasis n. emphase f.; force f.; accent m.

emphasize v.t. appuyer sur; prononcer avec force.

emphatic adj. emphatique; expressif, énergique.

emphatically adv. emphatiquement, catégoriquement.

empire n. empire m.

empirical adj. empirique.

employ v.t. employer; occuper; se servir de. n. emploi m., occupation f.; service m.

employee n. employé(e) m. f.

employer n. employeur m., patron m., patronne f.

employment n. emploi m., travail m., occupation f.

empower v.t. autoriser; donner pouvoir à; mettre à même de; valoriser.

empress n. impératrice f.

emptiness n. vacuité f.; le vide m.; vanité f., inanité f.

empty adj. vide; vacant; dénué de, dépourvu de, vain. v.t. vider; évacuer; épuiser. v.i. (se) vider; se décharger. he came back ~-handed, il est revenu les mains vides.

emulate v.t. imiter, émuler.

emulation n. émulation f.

emulsion n. émulsion f.

enable v.t. mettre en état de; mettre à même de; permettre à.

enact v.t. décréter; faire passer en loi; effectuer; (act out) jouer, représenter.

enactment n. promulgation f.; acte m. législatif, ordonnance f., décret m., (of a play) représentation f.

enamel n. émail m. v.t. émailler.

enamored adj. amoureux, épris de.

encamp v.i. camper.

encampment n. campement m.

encase v.t. encaisser.

encaustic adj. encaustique.

enchain v.t. enchaîner.

enchainment n. enchainement m.

enchant v.t. enchanter.

enchanter n. enchanteur m.; sorcier m.

enchanting adj. enchanteur m., enchanteresse f.

enchantingly adv. par enchantement; ravissant; délicieusement.

enchantment n. enchantement m.

enchantress n. enchanteresse f.; sorcière f.

encircle v.t. ceindre, entourer; environner; embrasser.

enclose v.t. enclore, enfermer dans; renfermer, enfermer; entourer, environner, joindre, inclure.

enclosed adj. enclos, environné, entouré; renfermé; sous enveloppe, sous pli; inclus. the ~ letter, la lettre ci-jointe.

enclosure n. clôture f.; enclos m., pièce f. jointe.

encompass v.t. (with, de) entourer; enfermer.

encore adv. bis. v.t. redemander; crier bis; bisser.

encounter n. rencontre f.; lutte f., combat m., choc m.; incident m. ~ v.t. rencontrer; aborder; affronter. v.i. (se) rencontrer inopinément; s'attaquer; livrer bataille.

encourage v.t. encourager. to ~ trade, favoriser le commerce.

encouragement n. encouragement m.

encouraging adj. encourageant.

encroach v.i. (with on, upon) empiéter; usurper; abuser de.

encroachment n. empiètement m.

encrust v.t. incruster.

encumber v.t. embarrasser; encombrer; gêner; entraver. to ~ trade, entraver le commerce. an estate ~ed with mortgages, propriété grevée d'hypothèques.

encumbrance n. fardeau m., obstacle m., charge f.

encyclopedia n. encyclopédie f.

end n. fin f.; bout m.; terme m.; issue f.; but m.; intérêt m. to come to a bad ~, faire une mauvaise fin. to put an ~ to, mettre un terme à. v.t.

terminer, finir, conclure. v.i. cesser, prendre fin; expirer. the lease ~s in May, le bail expire en mai. to ~ in smoke, s'en aller en fumée. ~ up, finir, terminer. we ~ed up in a small restaurant, on a fini par se retrouver dans un petit restaurant.

endanger v.t. mettre en danger; hasarder, risquer.

endear v.t. rendre cher, faire chérir; rendre plus aimé; enchérir.

endearment n. charme m.; tendresse f.; attachement m.

endeavor n. effort m.; soin m.; tentative f. ~ v.i. s'efforcer; tâcher, essayer.

ending adj. finissant, terminant. n. fin f.; conclusion f.; terminaison f.

endive n. endive f., chicorée f., escarole f.

endless adj. infini, sans fin; perpétuel.

endlessly adv. sans fin; perpétuellement.

endlessness n. perpétuité f.; durée f., indéfinie.

endorse v.t. endosser, avaliser (bill); adhérer à (a candidacy).

endorsement n. endossement m.; appui m., adhésion f. à.

endow v.t. doter, fonder, enrichir.

endowment n. dotation f.; don m.; fondation f.

endue v.t. habiller, revêtir; douer de.

endurable adj. tolérable, supportable.

endurance n. endurance f., souffrance f., patience f., résignation f. beyond ~, insupportable.

endure v.i. durer, continuer. v.t. endurer, supporter, tolérer.

endways adv. bout à bout; debout.

enemy n. ennemi m., ennemie f., adversaire m.

energetic adj. énergique.

energetically adv. énergiquement.

energize v.t. donner de l'énergie à.

energy n. énergie f., force f.

enervate v.t. énerver.

enervation n. énervation f.; mollesse f.

enfeeble v.t. affaiblir, débiliter, énerver.

enfeeblement n. affaiblissement m.

enfold v.t. envelopper, enrouler; étreindre.

enforce v.t. fortifier, appuyer, donner de la force à; mettre en vigueur; obliger, forcer. to ~ obedience, faire obéir de force.

enforcement n. contrainte f., violence f.; sanction f.; exécution f., mise f. en vigueur. ~ of the law, application f. de la loi.

enfranchise v.t. affranchir; accorder le droit de vote.

enfranchisement n. affranchissement m.; admission f. au droit de vote.

engage v.t., v.i. s'engager, se lier, s'obliger; livrer combat; embaucher (employees).

engaged adj. engagé; fiancé, occupé; attaqué.

engagement n. engagement m.; occupation f.; fiançailles f.pl.; combat m. to meet one's ~s, faire honneur à ses engagements.

engaging adj. engageant, prévenant,

attrayant. ~ **manners**, manières engageantes.

engender v.t. engendrer. v.i. s'engendrer, se former, naître.

engine n. machine f., locomotive f.; instrument m. **jet** ~, moteur m. à réaction. **car** ~, moteur de voiture. **steam** ~, machine à vapeur.

engineer n. ingénieur m.; constructeur-mécanicien. **civil** ~, ingénieur m. civil, soldat du génie, officier du génie.

engineering n. génie m.

England n.pr. Angleterre f. **New** ~, Nouvelle-Angleterre.

English adj. anglais. n. Anglais m., Anglaise f. la langue anglaise.

engrave v.t. graver.

engraver n. graveur m.

engraving n. gravure f.; estampe f.

engross v.t. occuper, absorber, préoccuper; accaparer; grossoyer (a document). **to ~ the thoughts**, absorber les pensées. **to ~ the conversation**, faire les frais de la conversation.

engrossment n. accaparement m.; absorption f., rédaction f. de la grosse.

engulf v.t. engouffrer.

enhance v.t. hausser, mettre en valeur, enchérir, renchérir, rehausser.

enhancement n. hausse f., enchérissement m.; augmentation f.

enigma n. énigme f.

enigmatic adj. énigmatique.

enjoin v.t. enjoindre; interdire.

enjoy v.t. jouir de; goûter, savourer; prendre plaisir. **to ~ life**, jouir de la vie. **to ~ oneself**, s'amuser, se réjouir.

enjoyable adj. agréable.

enjoyment n. plaisir m., satisfaction f., jouissance f.

enlarge v.t. augmenter; dilater, élargir. v.i. s'agrandir, s'accroître, s'étendre, se dilater.

enlargement n. agrandissement m., augmentation f., développement m.

enlighten v.t. éclairer, instruire; ouvrir les yeux.

enlightenment n. éclaircissement m.; instruction f.; lumières f.pl.

enlist v.t. enrôler; engager. v.i. s'enrôler; s'engager.

enlistment n. enrôlement m., engagement m.

enliven v.t. vivifier, animer; égayer, réjouir.

enmesh v.t. prendre au filet.

enmity n. inimitié f., haine f., hostilité f.

enormity n. énormité f.

enormous adj. énorme; prodigieux; monstrueux.

enormously adv. énormément, excessivement.

enough adj., n. assez, suffisance f. ~ **money**, assez d'argent. **it was ~ for her to**, il lui suffisait de. adv. assez, suffisamment.

enounce v.t. énoncer, exprimer, déclarer.

enrage v.t. exaspérer; faire enrager, rendre furieux.

enrapture v.t. (**with**, de) ravir, transporter.

enrich v.t. enrichir; embellir.

enrichment n. enrichissement m.

enroll v.t. enrôler, inscrire, enregistrer.

enrollment n. enregistrement m.; enrôlement m.

ensconce v.t. se caler, se rencogner, se pelotonner.

ensemble n. ensemble m.

enshrine v.t. enchâsser; serrer, renfermer soigneusement.

enshroud v.t. couvrir, abriter.

ensign n. enseigne f.; drapeau m.; pavillon m. de poupe; insigne m.; enseigne m., porte-drapeau m. ~ **bearer**, porte-drapeau m.

enslave v.t. asservir, rendre esclave; vaincre.

enslavement n. asservissement m., servitude f.

ensnare v.t. prendre au piège, charmer.

ensue v.i. (**from**, de) s'ensuivre.

ensuing adj. découlant de, résultant de; suivant, prochain.

ensure v.t. assurer.

entail n. substitution f.; bien m. substitué. v.t. substituer; imposer; léguer.

entangle v.t. enchevêtrer, emmêler; embrouiller; empêtrer; engager; embarrasser. v.i. s'entortiller, s'embrouiller.

entanglement n. confusion f., complication f.; embarras m.

enter v.t. entrer dans, pénétrer; admettre; inscrire; faire enregistrer; initier. **to ~ a house**, entrer dans une maison. **to ~ a name in a book**, inscrire un nom sur un registre. **to ~ an action against one**, intenter une action contre quelqu'un. **to ~ into the details**, entrer dans les détails.

enteric adj. entérique.

enterprise n. entreprise f. v.t. entreprendre, tenter.

enterprising adj. entreprenant.

entertain v.t. amuser, divertir, recevoir, régaler, entretenir. **to ~ friendly sentiments**, entretenir des sentiments amicaux. **to ~ a proposal**, écouter une proposition.

entertainer n. artiste m. f., comique m. f.

entertaining adj. amusant, divertissant.

entertainment n. amusement m., divertissement m., passe-temps m.

enthral(l) v.t. captiver, passionner.

enthuse v.t., Infml. enthousiasmer.

enthusiasm n. enthousiasme m.

enthusiast n. enthousiaste m. f.

enthusiastic adj. enthousiaste.

enthusiastically adv. avec enthousiasme.

entice v.t. exciter; attirer, engager; séduire, entraîner.

enticement n. instigation f., suggestion f.; séduction f., entraînement m., attrait m.

entire adj. entier; complet.

entirely adv. entièrement, complètement.

entireness n. totalité f., plénitude f.; intégrité f., honnêteté f.

entirety n. tout m., ensemble m.; totalité f.

entitle v.t. intituler; conférer un titre; attribuer; donner droit à.

entity n. entité f.; individualité f.

entomb v.t. ensevelir, inhumer, mettre au tombeau.

entomological adj. entomologique.

entomologist n. entomologiste m. f.

entomology n. entomologie f.

entourage n. entourage m.

entrails pl. entrailles f.pl.

entrance n. entrée f.; commencement m., début m. ~ hall, vestibule m.

entrance v.t. transporter, ravir, extasier. to be entranced, être dans le ravissement.

entrap v.t. prendre au piège; attraper.

entreat v.t. supplier; implorer, prier.

entreaty n. instante prière f., vive sollicitation f., supplication f.

entrée n. droit m. d'entrée. Culin. plat m. principal.

entrench v.t. (se) retrancher.

entrepreneur n. entrepreneur m.

entropy n. entropie f.

entrust v.t. confier, charger. I ~ed him with the children, je lui ai confié la garde des enfants.

entry n. entrée f.; vestibule m., enregistrement m.; déclaration f.

entwine v.t. enlacer, entrelacer; enbortiller.

enumerate v.t. énumérer.

enumeration n. énumération f.

enunciate v.t. énoncer, déclarer, articuler.

enunciation n. énonciation f.; déclaration f., articulation f.

envelop v.i. envelopper; entourer; couvrir.

envelope n. enveloppe f.

envelopement n. enveloppement m.

envenom v.t. envenimer; rendre odieux.

enviable adj. enviable, digne d'envie.

envious adj. envieux; jaloux.

enviously adv. par envie, par jalousie.

enviousness n. envie f., jalousie f.

environment n. environnement m., milieu m., atmosphère f., ambiance f.

environmental adj. de l'environnement m., écologiste.

environmentalist n. écologiste m.f. ~ adj. écologique.

envisage v.t. envisager, prévoir.

envoy n. envoyé m.; messager m.

envy n. envier; porter envie à. n. envie f.; haine f., jalousie f.

ephemeral adj. éphémère.

epic adj. épique.

epicure n. épicurien m., épicurienne f., gourmet m., gastronome m.f.

epicurean adj. épicurien. n. épicurien m., épicurienne f.

epidemic adj. épidémique. n. épidémie f.

epidermis n. épiderme f.

epilepsy n. Med. épilepsie f.

epileptic adj., n. épileptique m.

epilogue n. épilogue m.

Epiphany n. épiphanie f., jour m. des Rois.

episcopal adj. épiscopal.

episode n. épisode m.

episodic adj. épisodique.

epistle n. épître f.

epitaph n. épitaphe f.

epithet n. épithète f.

epitome n. abrégé m., précis m.

epoch n. époque f.

Epsom n.pr. ~ salts, sel m. d'Epsom.

equable adj. égal.

equably adv. uniforme; uniformément.

equal adj. égal; proportionné; juste; propre; à la hauteur de. we are not ~ to such a task, nous ne sommes pas à la hauteur d'une tâche pareille. n. égal m., égale f.; pair m., pareil m. to be one's ~ in merit, égaler quelqu'un en mérite. v.t. égaler, égaliser.

equality n. égalité f.

equalisation n. égalisation f.

equalize v.t. égaliser.

equally adv. également, pareillement.

equanimity n. égalité f. d'âme; sérénité f., calme m. d'esprit.

equate v.t. égaler, égaliser; mettre en équation.

equation n. équation f.

equator n. équateur m.

equatorial adj., n. équatorial m.

equestrian adj. équestre; à cheval. n. cavalier m.

equilateral adj. équilatéral.

equilibrate v.t. équilibrer.

equilibration n. équilibre m.

equilibrium n. équilibre m.

equine adj. de cheval; chevaline.

equinoctial adj. équinoxial.

equinox n. équinoxe f.

equip v.t. équiper, fournir, doter. to ~ one with money, fournir de l'argent à quelqu'un.

equipage n. équipage m.

equipment n. équipement m.; outillage m.

equitable adj. équitable, honnête, impartial.

equitably adv. équitablement, impartialement.

equitation n. équitation f.

equity n. équité f.

equivalence n. équivalence f.

equivalent adj., n. équivalent m.

equivocal adj. équivoque. n. équivoque f.

equivocally adv. en termes équivoques, d'une manière équivoque.

equivocate v.i. équivoquer; tergiverser. v.t. rendre équivoque.

equivocation n. équivoque f.; subterfuge m.

era n. ère f., époque f.

eradicate v.t. déraciner, extirper.

eradication n. éradication f.; extirpation.

erase v.t. effacer, gommer.

eraser n. gomme f.

erasure n. rature f.

erect adj. droit, debout; élevé, haut, dressé. v.t. dresser; ériger; élever, bâtir, construire; établir.

erection n. érection f.; construction f.; établissement m., fondation f., dressage m.

ergonomic adj. ergonomique.

ergonomics n.pl. ergonomie f.

ermine n. hermine f.

erode v.t. éroder; corroder.

erosion n. érosion f.

erotic adj. érotique.

err v.i. errer; se tromper, s'égarer.

errand n. commission f.; course f. **to run ~s,** faire des commissions.

errant adj. errant.

erratic adj. erratique; errant, vagabond.

erroneous adj. inexact, faux; erroné.

erroneously adv. par erreur, à tort.

error n. erreur f.; faute f., bévue f.

eructate v.t. éructer.

eructation n. éructation f.; Infml. rot m.

erudite adj. érudit.

erudition n. érudition f.

erupt v.i. entre en éruption; exploser; éclater.

eruption n. éruption f.

escalate v.i. (s')intensifier; monter, grimper (price).

escalation n. intensification f.; montée f.

escalator n. escalier m. mécanique, escalator.

escapade n. escapade f.

escape v.t. échapper, à éviter. **to ~ notice,** échapper à l'attention. v.i. **(from,** de) s'échapper; s'enfuir, se soustraire. n. évasion f., fuite f.; délivrance. **we had a narrow ~,** nous l'avons échappé belle. **~ of gas,** fuite de gaz.

escapee n. échappé m., échappée f., évadé m., évadée f.

escapement n. échappement m.

escapism n. évasion f.

escarpment n. escarpement m.

eschew v.t. éviter, fuir.

escort n. escorte f.; cavalier m. **~** v.t. escorter, accompagner.

esophagus n. oesophage m., gosier m.

esoteric adj. ésoterique.

espalier n. espalier m.

esparto n. spart(e) m.

especial adj. spécial, particulier.

especially adv. surtout, spécialement, particulièrement.

espionage n. espionnage f.

esplanade n. esplanade f.

espouse v.t. épouser; fiancer.

esq(uire) n. Monsieur m.

essay v.t. essayer, tenter, tâcher; éprouver. n. essai m., traité m., épreuve f., experience f.

essayist n. essayiste m.f.

essence n. essence f.

essential adj., n. essentiel m.

essentially adv. essentiellement, en essence.

establish v.t. établir; affirmer; fonder; démontrer.

establishment n. établissement m.; maison f.; fondation f.; église f.

estate n. terre f., propriété f., rang m., condition f.; actif m. **real ~,** biens m.pl. immobiliers. **the deceased's ~,** la succession du défunt. **the third ~,** le tiers état.

esteem v.t. estimer, évaluer; regarder, considérer comme. n. estime f.

estimable adj. estimable.

estimate v.t. estimer; évaluer, apprécier, priser. n. estimation f., évaluation f.; détail m.; devis m.; jugement m., opinion f. **rough ~,** devis approximatif.

estimation n. estimation f.; évaluation f.; calcul m.; considération f., estime f.

estrange v.t. **(from,** de) éloigner; tenir à distance; aliéner, indisposer.

estrangement n. aliénation f.; éloignement m.; aversion f.

estuary n. estuaire m.

etc. adv. etc., et cetera.

etch v.t. graver à l'eau-forte, esquisser, dessiner.

etching n. gravure f. à l'eau-forte.

eternal adj. éternel. n. l'Eternel m.

eternally adv. éternellement, continuellement.

eternity n. éternité f.

eternize v.t. éterniser.

ether n. éther m.

ethereal adj. éthéré.

ethic n. morale f., éthique f.

ethical adj. éthique, moral.

ethically adv. conformément aux doctrines de la morale.

ethics n. éthique f.

ethnic adj. ethnique.

ethnographer n. ethnographe m.f.

ethnography n. ethnographie f.

ethnologic adj. ethnologique.

ethnology n. ethnologie f.

ethos n. génie (of people, culture).

etiolate v.i. s'étioler. v.t. étioler.

etiquette n. étiquette f., protocole m., cérémonial m.

etymological adj. étymologique.

etymology n. étymologie f.

eucalyptus n. eucalyptus m.

Eucharist n. Eucharistie f.

eulogize v.t. louer, faire l'éloge de; vanter, prôner.

eulogy n. éloge m.

eunuch n. eunuque m.

euphemism n. euphémisme m.

euphony n. euphonie f.

euphoria n. euphorie f.

euphoric adj. euphorique.

Europe n. Europe f.

European adj. européen. n. Européen m., Européenne f.

European Union (E.U.) n. Unione Européene (U.E.).

euthanasia n. euthanasie f.

evacuate v.t. évacuer.

evacuation n. évacuation f.

evade v.t. éviter, éluder; esquiver. v.i. s'évader, s'échapper, s'esquiver.

evaluate v.t. évaluer, mesurer.

evaluation n. évaluation f.

evanescence n. nature f. éphémère; instabilité f.

evanescent adj. évanescent; éphémère.

evangelic(al) adj. évangélique.

evangelism n. évangélisme.

evangelist n. évangéliste m. f.

evaporate v.i. s'évaporer. v.t. évaporer, faire évaporer. adj. évaporé.

evaporation n. évaporation f.

evasion n. évasion f.; fuite f.; subterfuge m., défaite f., prétexte m.

evasive adj. évasif.

evasively adv. évasivement.

eve n. soir m.; veille f., vigile f. **on the ~ of**, à l'approche de. **Christmas ~**, veille de Noël.

even adj. uni, plan, plat; uniforme; réglé; quitte, au niveau, à fleur; égal. **to make ~**, aplanir. **an ~ temper**, un caractère égal. **~ with the ground**, au niveau du sol. **an ~ number**, un nombre égal. **odd or ~**, pair ou impair. **to be ~ with one**, être quitte avec quelqu'un. **~-handed**, impartial, juste. **~ tempered**, placide. v.t. égaler, unir, aplanir, égaliser. **to ~ accounts**, regler, acquitter des comptes. adv. même; aussi bien; parfaitement. **~ now**, même maintenant, à présent. **~ so**, ainsi, de même, tout comme.

evening n. soir m., soirée f.; déclin m. **~ dress**, robe f., tenue f. de soirée. **~ star**, étoile f. du soir; Vénus f.

evenly adv. également, uniformément; de niveau; impartialement.

evenness n. égalité f., uniformité f., régularité f.; impartialité f.

event n. événement m.; issue f.; dénouement m. **in all ~s**, de toute manière; dans tous les cas.

eventful adj. plein d'événements.

eventual adj. final, définitif eventual.

eventuality n., éventualité f.

eventually adv. en fin de compte, finalement.

ever adv. jamais; toujours; à jamais. **hardly ~, scarcely ~**, presque jamais. **for ~ and ~**, pour toujours, à tout jamais. **~ so little**, quelque peu que ce soit.

everglade n. terres f.pl. marécageuses, everglade.

evergreen n. plante f. vivace; arbre vert.

everlasting adj. éternel, immortel; perpétuel. n. éternité f.; immortelle f.

everlastingly adv. éternellement, perpétuellement.

evermore adv. toujours, éternellement.

every adj. chaque; tout; tous les. **~ day**, tous les jours. **~ other day**, tous les deux jours. **~thing**, tout. **~where**, partout.

everybody pron. tout le monde, chacun, tous.

everyday adj. de tous les jours, ordinaire, habituel.

everyone pron. tout le monde, chacun, tous.

evict v.t. expulser.

eviction n. éviction f.

evidence n. évidence f.; preuve f.; témoignage m.; déposition f., témoin m. **to give ~**, témoigner de, porter témoignage de; déposer. **~ for the prosecution, state's ~**, témoin m. à charge. v.t. démontrer; témoigner, manifester.

evident adj. évident, clair, manifeste.

evidently adv. évidemment, manifestement.

evil adj. mauvais, méchant; pervers. adv. mal. n. mal m.pl. maux. **~doer**, méchant m.; malfaiteur m. **~ eye**, mauvais oeil m. **~ minded**, malintentionné; malveillant.

evince v.t. démontrer, prouver, témoigner de. **to ~ courage**, faire preuve de courage.

eviscerate v.t. éventrer; vider.

evocation n. évocation f.

evoke v.t. évoquer.

evolution n. évolution f.; développement m.; suite f.; marche f.; progrès m.; extraction f.

evolutionary adj. évolutionnaire.

evolve v.t. déployer, évolver, déplier; expulser; réjeter; dégager. v.i. (se) déployer, s'ouvrir; se découvrir; se dégager.

ewe n. brebis f.

ex prep. ex; ancien. **an ex-teacher**, un ancien professeur. **all her ex-boyfriends**, tous ses ex.

exacerbate v.t. exaspérer.

exacerbation n. irritation f.; exacerbation f.

exact adj. exact; strict; précis. v.t. exiger; extorquer. v.i. commettre des exactions.

exacting adj. exigeant.

exaction n. exaction f.

exactitude n. exactitude f.

exactly adv. exactement; juste; justement.

exactness n. exactitude f.; justesse f.

exaggerate v.t. exagérer.

exaggeration n. exagération f.

exalt v.t. élever; exalter.

exaltation n. élévation f.; exaltation f.; transport m., enivrement m.

exam n. Infml. exam(en) m.

examination n. examen m.; vérification f.; interrogatoire m.; audition f. **post-mortem ~**, autopsie f. **to take an ~**, passer, subir un examen. **under ~**, soumis à vérification.

examine v.t. examiner, vérifier; interroger. **to ~ a witness**, interroger un témoin.

examiner n. examinateur m., examinatrice f., juge m., instructeur m., instructrice f.

example n. exemple m.; modèle m. **to set an ~**, donner l'exemple.

exasperate v.t. exaspérer, irriter.

exasperation n. exaspération f.

excavate v.t. creuser; excaver; faire des fouilles.

excavation n. excavation f.; fouilles f.pl.; déblai m.

exceed *v.t.* (by, de; for, en) excéder, dépasser; exceller, surpasser. *v.i.* outrepasser.

exceedingly *adv.* excessivement; avec excès.

excel *v.t., v.i.* exceller; surpasser; l'emporter sur.

excellence *n.* excellence *f.;* perfection *f.;* supériorité *f.*

excellent *adj.* excellent; éminent; transcendant.

excellently *adv.* excellemment, d'une manière excellente.

except *v.t.* excepter. *v.i.* objecter; récuser, décliner. *prep.* excepté, hormis.

excepting *prep.* excepté, hormis.

exception *n.* exception *f.;* exclusion *f.; objection f.* without ~, sans exception. to make ~s to, élever des objections contre.

exceptional *adj.* exceptionnel.

exceptionally *adv.* exceptionnellement.

excerpt *n.* extrait *m.,* passage *m.* *v.t.* extraire, choisir, cueillir.

excess *n.* excès *m.;* excédent *m.* to commit ~es, commettre des excès.

excessive *adj.* excessif, exagéré, outré.

excessively *adv.* excessivement, à l'excès.

exchange *v.t.* changer; échanger. *n.* échange *m.,* change *m.* bourse *f.* to make an ~, faire un échange. bill of ~, lettre *f.* de change. in ~ for, en échange de. ~ business, commerce *m.* de change.

exchangeable *adj.* échangeable.

excisable *adj.* imposable, astreint, soumis au droit d'excise.

excitable *adj.* émotionnable, émotif, excitable.

excitant *n.* excitant *m.,* stimulant *m.*

excitation *n.* excitation *f.*

excite *v.t.* animer, stimuler, exciter.

excitement *n.* agitation *f.,* vive émotion, sur excitation *f.*

exclaim *v.i.* s'écrier.

exclamation *n.* exclamation *f.* ~ point, point *m.* d'exclamation.

exclamatory *adj.* exclamatif.

exclude *v.t.* exclure, rejeter; écarter.

excuse *v.t.* excuser, justifier, défendre, disculper, exempter, dispenser. to ~ oneself, s'excuser. *n.* excuse *f.;* prétexte *m.*

execrable *adj.* exécrable.

execrably *adv.* exécrablement.

execrate *v.t.* exécrer, avoir en exécration.

execration *n.* exécration *f.*

executable *adj.* exécutable.

execute *v.t.* exécuter; effectuer; remplir.

execution *n.* exécution *f.;* accomplissement *m.,* effet *m.;* saisie-exécution *f.*

executioner *n.* exécuteur *m.;* bourreau *m.*

executive *adj.* exécutif. *n.* pouvoir *m.* exécutif.

executor *n.* exécuteur *m.;* exécutrice *f.* testamentaire.

executory *adj.* exécutif; exécutoire.

executrix *n.* exécutrice *f.;* testamentaire.

exemplar *n.* exemple *m.,* modèle *m.*

exemplary *adj.* exemplaire.

exemplification *n.* démonstration *f.,* explication *f.* par des exemples; ampliation *f.*

exemplify *v.t.* montrer par l'exemple, donner des exemples de; transcrire.

exempt *v.t.* exempter, affranchir, dispenser. *adj.* exempt *m.*

exclusion *n.* exclusion *f.*

exclusive *adj.* exclusif fermé (club); choisi, select.

exclusively *adv.* exclusivement.

excommunicate *v.t.* excommunier. *n.* excommunié *m.;* excommuniée *f.*

excommunication *n.* excommunication *f.*

excoriate *v.t.* écorcher; excorier.

excoriation *n.* écorchure *f.; Chir.* excoriation *f.*

excrement *n.* excrément *m.*

excrescence *n.* excroissance *f.;* monstruosité *f.*

excrete *v.t.* excréter.

excretion *n.* excrétion *f.*

excruciating *adj.* atroce, extrêmement douloureux.

exculpate *v.t.* disculper.

exculpation *n.* disculpation *f.*

excursion *n.* excursion *f.;* tournée, *f.;* promenade *f.*

excusable *adj.* excusable.

exemption *n.* exemption *f.;* dispence *f.*

exercise *n.* exercice *m.;* thème *m.;* devoir *m.;* a Latin ~, un thème latin. ~ class, cours *m.* de gymnastique. *v.t.* exercer, dresser; s'exercer; prendre de l'exercice; inquiéter, embarrasser.

exert *v.t.* déployer, montrer, exercer; employer. to ~ caution, user de prudence.

exertion *n.* effort *m.,* exercice *m.,* usage *m.*

exfoliate *v.i.* s'exfolier. *v.t.* exfolier.

exhalation *n.* exhalation *f.,* exhalaison *f.*

exhale *v.t.* expirer, exhaler; émettre, dégager. *v.i.* s'exhaler.

exhaust *v.t.* épuiser, exténuer. to ~ a subject, épuiser un sujet. ~ pipe, tuyau *m.* d'échappement.

exhausted *adj.* épuisée, exténué, consumé, dissipé; anéanti.

exhausting *adj.* épuisant.

exhaustion *n.* épuisement *m.*

exhaustive *adj.* complet, exhaustif.

exhibit *v.t.* exhiber; produire; exposer; montrer. *n.* exposition *f.;* objet *m.* exposé; pièce *f.* à l'appui.

exhibition *n.* exposition *f.;* spectacle *m.;* exhibition *f.*

exhilarate *v.t.* vivifier, égayer; réjouir; récréer, divertir. *v.i.* s'égayer; se réjouir.

exhilarating *adj.* vivifiant, égayant, divertissant, exhilarant.

exhilaration *n.* joie *f.* de vivre, gaieté *f.*

exhort *v.t.* exhorter, inciter; conseiller, recommander.

exhortation *n.* exhortation *f.;* avis *m.,* conseil *m.*

exhumation *n.* exhumation *f.*

exhume *v.t.* exhumer, déterrer.

exigence, exigency *n.* exigence *f.;* besoin *m.;* nécessité *f.* pressante.

exigent adj. pressant, urgent.

exiguity n. exiguïté f.

exiguous adj. exigu.

exile n. exil m.; bannissement m., expulsion f.; exilé m. exilée f., banni m., bannie f. v.t. exiler. **to ~ oneself**, s'exiler, s'expatrier.

exist v.i. exister.

existence n. existence f.

existent adj. existant.

existentialism n. existentialisme m.

existing adj. existant.

exit n. sortie f.; issue f. ~ v.i. sortir.

exodus n. exode m.

exonerate v.t. soulager; décharger; disculper, justifier; exonérer.

exoneration n. exonération f., décharge f.; acquittement m.

exorbitance n. exorbitance f.; énormité f.; excès m., extravagance f.

exorbitant adj. exorbitant.

exorbitantly adv. énormément.

exorcism n. exorcisme m.

exorcist n. exorciste m.

exotic adj. exotique.

exoticism n. exotisme m.

expand v.t. étendre, développer; répandre; dilater. v.i. (se) développer; s'épanouir; se déployer; se répandre; se dilater.

expanse n. étendue f.

expansion n. expansion; étendue f.; développement; épanouissement m.

expansionism n. expansionnisme m.

expansive adj. expansif, démonstratif; communicatif.

expatiate v.i. discourir (longuement).

expatriate v.t. expatrier.

expatriation n. expatriation f.

expect v.t. attendre, s'attendre à; espérer; exiger; compter sur, attendre. **we ~ him for dinner**, nous l'espérons pour (le) dîner. **she's ~ing!** elle est enceinte!

expectancy n. attente f.; espoir m. **life ~**, espérance f. de vie.

expectant adj. expectant.

expectation n. attente f.; espoir m., espérance f. **to answer one's ~**, répondre à ses espérances. **he lives in ~**, il vit dans l'expectative.

expectorate v.t. expectorer.

expectoration n. expectoration f.

expedience, expediency n. convenance f., à-propos m.; opportunité f., utilité f.

expedient adj. expédient, à propos, convenable, utile, profitable, avantageux. n. expédient m., moyen m.

expedite v.t. expédier, hâter, accélérer; faciliter. adj. prompt, expéditif.

expedition n. diligence f.; expédition f.

expeditious adj. expéditif, prompt.

expel v.t. (with, **from, out of**). expulser, chasser, bannir; renvoyer.

expend v.t. dépenser; employer à; consommer.

expenditure n. dépense f.; consommation f. de munitions, etc.

expense n. dépense f., frais m.pl., dépens m. **to go to ~**, se mettre en dépense. **at any ~**, à tout prix. **living ~s**, frais de séjour.

expensive adj. coûteux, cher, onereux. dispendieux.

expensively adv. à grands frais, coûteusement.

experience n. expérience f. **by, from ~**, par expérience. v.t. éprouver, ressentir; faire l'expérience de, expérimenter, essayer.

experienced adj. habile, expérimenté.

experiment n. expérience f., essai m., épreuve f. **to make, to try an ~**, faire une expérience. v.t., v.i. expérimenter; faire des expériences.

experimental adj. expérimental.

experimentation n. expérimentation f.

expert adj. expert, habile; adroit, intelligent. n. expert m., spécialiste m.f.

expertly adv. habilement, adroitement.

expiate v.t. expier.

expiation n. expiation f.; réparation f.

expiatory adj. expiatoire.

expiration n. expiration f.

expire v.t. expirer; exhaler. v.i. expirer; mourir; s'éteindre.

expiry n. expiration f., fin f.

explain v.t. expliquer. v.i. s'expliquer, donner des explications.

explainable adj. explicable.

explanation n. explication f.

explanatory adj. explicatif.

explicable adj. explicable.

explicate v.t. déployer, développer; expliquer; éclaircir.

explication n. déploiement m.; explication f.

explicit adj. explicite, clair, formel, précis, catégorique.

explicitly adv. explicitement, en termes clairs.

explode v.i. éclater; exploser. **we all ~ed with laughter**, nous avons tous explosé de rire.

exploit n. exploite m., prouesse f. ~ v.t. exploiter, profiter de.

exploitation n. exploitation f.

exploratory adj. servant à explorer.

explore v.t. explorer; sonder.

explorer n. explorateur m., exploratrice f.

explosion n. explosion f.

explosive adj. explosif.

exponent n. interprète m.f.; exposant m.; représentant m.

export v.t. exporter. n. exportation f.; transport m. ~ **duty**, droit m. d'exportation. ~ **trade**, commerce m. d'exportation.

exportable adj. exportable.

exportation n. exportation f.

exporter n. exportateur m.; exportatrice f.

expose v.t. exposer. **to ~ oneself**, s'exposer, se rendre ridicule.

exposition n. exposition f.; explication f.; interprétation f.

expostulate *v.i.* faire des remontrances, des reproches; reprocher.

expostulation *n.* remontrance *f.*, réprimande *f.*

exposure *n.* exposition *f.*; éclat *m.*, scandale *m.*; découverte *f.*

expound *v.t.* exposer; expliquer, interpréter.

express *v.t.* exprimer; énoncer, décrire, désigner; représenter. **to ~ one's mind**, s'exprimer. *adj.* exprès, formel; explicite, clair. *n.* exprès *m.*; message *m.* **~ train**, l'express *m.*

expression *n.* expression *f.*

expressionless *adj.* inexpressif.

expressive *adj.* expressif.

expressively *adv.* avec expression.

expressly *adv.* expressément, explicitement.

expropriate *v.t.* exproprier.

expropriation *n.* abandon *m.*; expropriation *f.*

expulsion *n.* expulsion *f.*

expunge *v.t.* effacer, biffer, raturer.

expurgate *v.t.* expurger.

expurgation *n.* expurgation *f.*

exquisite *adj.* exquis, raffiné. **~ taste**, goût *m.*, exquis. **~ pleasure**, vif plaisir.

exquisitely *adv.* d'une manière exquise.

exquisiteness *n.* perfection *f.*; excellence *f.*; goût *m.*, exquis.

extant *adj.* existant, subsistant encore; actuel.

extemporaneous *adj.* improvisé.

extempore *adv.* à l'improviste; sur-le-champ. **to speak ~**, improviser.

extemporize *v.i.* improviser.

extend *v.t.* allonger, développer; tendre, prolonger. *v.i.* s'étendre; se continuer. **his power does not ~ so far**, son pouvoir ne s'étend pas si loin, ne va pas jusque-là.

extensible *adj.* extensible.

extension *n.* extension *f.*; étendue *f.*; rallonge *f.*; poste *m.* **he can be reached at 555-1234 ~ 21**, on peut le joindre au 555-1234 poste 21.

extensive *adj.* vaste, large, grand, spacieux.

extensively *adv.* largement, amplement.

extent *n.* étendue *f.*; degré *m.*, point *m.* **to a great ~**, à un haut degré, grandement. **to a certain ~**, jusqu'à un certain point.

extenuate *v.t.* diminuer; exténuer; amoindrir, pallier.

extenuation *n.* exténuation *f.*, atténuation *f.*

exterior *adj.* extérieur; externe, du dehors. *n.* extérieur *m.*, physique *m.*; apparence *f.*

exteriorize *v.t.* (s')extérioriser.

exteriorly *adv.* extérieurement.

exterminate *v.t.* exterminer; éliminer.

extermination *n.* extermination *f.*; élimination *f.*

exterminator *n.* exterminateur *m.*, exterminatrice *f.*

external *adj.* externe; extérieur. *n.pl.* formes *f.pl.* extérieures; extérieur *m.*; dehors *m.*

externally *adv.* extérieurement, en apparence, visiblement.

extinct *adj.* éteint, disparu, détruit; effacé; aboli.

extinction *n.* extinction *f.*

extinguish *v.t.* éteindre. **to ~ hopes**, mettre fin à des espérances.

extinguisher *n.* extincteur *m.*

extirpate *v.t.* extirper, exciser, enlever, complètement.

extirpation *n.* extirpation *f.*

extoll *v.t.* prôner, vanter, exalter, porter aux nues.

extort *v.t.* extorquer, soutirer; arracher.

extortion *n.* extorsion *f.*

extra *adj.* en sus, extraordinaire, supplémentaire; *Cine.* figurant *m.*; figurante *f.* **~ postage**, surtaxe *f.* **~ charge**, frais *m.pl.* additionnels. *n.* extra *m.*, supplément *m.*

extract *v.t.* extraire; tirer. *n.* extrait *m.*, passage *m.*

extraction *n.* extraction *f.*; extrait *m.*

extracurricular *adj.* hors-programme.

extradite *v.t.* extrader.

extradition *n.* extradition *f.*

extramarital *adj.* extra-conjugal.

extramural *adj.* extra-muros.

extraneous *adj.* étranger, extrinsèque.

extraordinarily *adv.* extraordinairement.

extraordinary *adj.* extraordinaire; spécial.

extrapolate *v.t.* extrapoler.

extraterrestrial *adj.* extraterrestre.

extraterritorial *adj.* d'exterritorialité.

extravagance *n.* extravagance *f.*; folie *f.*; dépense *f.* excessive.

extravagant *adj.* extravagant; exagéré.

extravagantly *adv.* d'une manière extravagante.

extravaganza *n.* oeuvre *f.* fantaisiste.

extreme *adj.* extrême; excessif. **an ~ heat**, une chaleur excessive. **~ unction**, extrême-onction. *n.* extrême *m.*; extrémité *f.*, fin *f.* **to carry to ~s**, pousser à l'extrême. **~s meet**, les extrêmes se touchent.

extremely *adv.* extrêmement; énormément.

extremist *adj.*, *n.* extrémiste *m.f.*

extremity *n.* extrémité *f.*; bout *m.*

extricate *v.t.* dégager, débarrasser, tirer d'embarras.

extrude *v.t.* pousser dehors, faire sortir, expulser.

extrusion *n.* expulsion *f.*

exuberance *n.* exuberance *f.*

exuberant *adj.* exubérant, surabondant, planureux.

exuberantly *adv.* exubéramment, avec profusion.

exude *v.t.* exsuder. *v.i.* exsuder; faire exsuder.

exult *v.i.* être transporté de joie, exulter; triompher.

exultation *n.* transport *m.* de joie, triomphe *m.*, ivresse *f.*

eye *n.* oeil *m.pl.* yeux, vue *f.*; regard *m.*; trou *m.* (needle); oeillet *m.* bourgeon *m.* **black ~**, oeil noir; oeil poché. **blind in one ~**, borgne. **with one's own ~s**, de ses propres yeux. **to keep a sharp ~ on**, surveiller de près. **to sail in**

the wind's ~, naviguer contre le vent. *v.t.* regarder; lorgner. **he ~d him from head to foot,** il l'a toisé de la tête aux pieds. **it was a real ~-opener for him,** ça lui a vraiment ouvert les yeux.

eyeball *n.* prunelle *f.* de l'oeil, globe *m.* de l'oeil.

eyebrow *n.* sourcil *m.*

eyed *adj.* aux yeux. **blue-~,** aux yeux bleus.

eyeful *n.* **to get an ~,** s'en mettre plein la vue, se

eyeglass, es *n.pl.* lunettes *f.pl.*

eyelash *n.* cil *m.*

eyelid *n.* paupière *f.*

eyesight *n.* sens *m.* de la vue; vue *f.,* observation *f.*

eyewitness *n.* témoin *m.* oculaire.

eyot *n.* îlot *m.,* petite île *f.*

eyry *n.* aire *f.* (of an eagle).

F

F *n. abbr.* **Fahrenheit. the F word,** le mot de Cambronne.

fa *n. Mus.* fa *m.*

fable *n.* fable *f.*

fabled *adj.* fabuleux, feint; de la fable.

fabric *n.* édifice *m.,* construction *f.;* fabrication *f.;* tissu *m.,* étoffe *f.* système *m.* **woolen ~s,** tissus de laine.

fabricate *v.t.* construire, bâtir; fabriquer; forger. **to ~ a story,** inventer une histoire.

fabrication *n.* construction *f.;* fabrication *f.;* fausseté *f.*

fabulous *adj.* fabuleux.

fabulously *adv.* fabuleusement.

façade *n.* façade *f.*

face *n.* face *f.;* figure *f.,* visage *m.;* facette *f.* (diamond); surface *f.;* façade *f.;* (watch) cadran *m.;* endroit *m.* (fabric); oeil *m.* (of a character). **a pretty ~,** une jolie figure. **he looked him in the ~,** il le regarda en face. **~ to ~,** face à face; nez à nez. **he put on a good ~,** il a fait bonne figure. **to put on a serious ~,** prendre un air sérieux. **to make ~s at,** faire des grimaces à. *v.t.* faire face à, braver; *Maçon.* revêtir, parer. *v.i.* **to about ~,** faire volte-face.

faceless *adj.* sans visage.

facet *n.* facette *f.*

facetious *adj.* facétieux.

facetiously *adv.* facétieusement.

facial *adj.* facial, soin du visage *m.*

facile *adj.* facile.

facilitate *v.t.* faciliter.

facility *n.* facilité *f.*

facing *n.* revêtement *m.,* parement *m.;* retroussis *m.*

facsimile *n.* fac-similé *m.,* télécopie *f.* **~ machine,** télécopieur *m.* **~** *v.t.* fac-similer.

fact *n.* fait *m.;* réalité *f.,* vérité *f.* **in ~,** en effet; en fait, au fait. **matter of ~,** un réalité, en fait.

faction *n.* faction *f.*

factious *adj.* factieux.

factitious *adj.* factice.

factitiously *adv.* artificiellement.

factor *n.* facteur *m.,* élément *m.*

factory *n.* manufacture *f.,* fabrique *f.,* usine *f.*

factual *adj.* factuel.

facultative *adj.* facultatif.

faculty *n.* faculté *f.;* corps *m.* professoral.

fad *n.* marotte *f.,* manie *f.;* lubie *f.*

fade *v.i.* se faner; se flétrir; se passer; disparaître, s'évanouir, s'effacer; dépérir, périr. *v.t.* faner, flétrir.

fading *adj.* passager, fugitif. *n.* perte *f.* de la couleur, de la fraîcheur; dépérissement *m.*

faery *adj.* féerique. *n.* féerie *f.*

fag *n. Pej.* pédé *m.;* pédale *f.*

fagot *n. Pej.* pédé *m.;* pédale *f.*

fail *v.i.* faillir. *v.t.* faire défaut à; défaillir, échouer. **his heart ~s,** le coeur, le courage lui manque. **his strength ~s,** sa vigueur diminue. **do not ~ to keep your promise,** ne manquez pas de tenir votre promesse. **I will not ~,** je n'y manquerai pas.

failing *adj.* défaillant; baissant. **his ~ powers,** ses forces défaillantes. *n.* défaillance *f.;* défaut *m.,* imperfection *f.*

failure *n.* échec *m.;* manque *m.,* défaut *m.;* manquement *m.;* faillite *f.* **heart ~,** syncope *f.* (mortelle).

fain *adj.* content, satisfait. *adv.* volontiers, avec plaisir.

faint *adj.* faible; abattu; timide, timoré. **in a ~ voice,** d'une voix faible. **a ~ resemblance,** une légère ressemblance. **to feel ~,** se sentir défaillir. *v.i.* s'évanouir. *n.* évanouissement *m.,* syncope *f.*

faint-hearted *adj.* pusillanime, timoré, timide.

fainting *n.* syncope *f.,* évanouissement *m.*

faintly *adv.* faiblement.

faintness *n.* faiblesse *f.;* défaillance *f.,* évanouissement *m.,* timidité *f.;* mollesse *f.*

fair *adj.* clair; blond; beau (weather); juste, impartial, loyal; passable. **of a ~ complexion,** au teint clair. **~ hair,** des cheveux blonds. **~ weather,** un beau temps. **the ~ sex,** le beau sexe. **to give a ~ trial,** donner, paser un jugement honnête. **~ play,** beau jeu, loyauté. **a ~ wind,** un vent favorable. **I shall be ~ with you,** je serai juste avec vous. **that is not ~,** cela n'est pas juste. **by ~ means or foul,** de gré ou de force. **~ dealings,** conduite loyale. **a ~ proposal,** une proposition acceptable. *adv.* bien; loyalement; avec succès; en bons termes. *n.* foire *f.* kermesse *f.*

fairly *adv.* bien; loyalement, de bonne foi; complètement, tout à fait. **to deal ~ with everybody,** agir de bonne foi avec tout le monde. **hence, one may ~ conclude,** de là, il est bien permis de conclure.

fairness n. impartialité f., intégrité f., équité f. honnêteté f. couleur f. blonde. **the ~ of his conduct**, l'honnêteté de sa conduite.

fairy n. fée f.; enchanteresse f.; Pej. tante, tapette f. ~ **tale**, n., conte de fée, histoire à dormir debout. adj. de fée, féerique.

faith n. foi f.; doctrine f., croyance f.; fidélité f.

faithful adj. fidèle; loyal.

faithfully adv. fidèlement, loyalement, sincèrement.

faithfulness n. fidélité f., loyauté f.

faithless adj. infidèle, sans foi; perfide; traître; déloyal.

faithlessness n. infidélité f.; perfidie f.; déloyauté f.

fake v.t. truquer, falsifier. adj. faux, truqué. n. faux m., article m. faux.

falcon n. faucon m.

fall v.i. tomber; succomber, périr; crouler; s'abattre; se calmer. **to ~ backward**, tomber à la renverse. **the wind ~s**, le vent s'apaise. **to ~ asleep**, s'endormir. **to ~ sick**, tomber malade. **to ~ in love**, tomber amoureux. **the barometer ~s**, le baromètre baisse. **to ~ back**, reculer, tomber en arrière, retomber. Mil. se replier. **ripe apples ~ off the tree**, les pommes mûres se détachent de l'arbre. **to ~ (up)on**, se jeter sur; attaquer; rencontrer; tomber sur. **to ~ out**, se quereller, rompre. **to ~ short**, manquer. **~ short of**, manquer de, se trouver à court de. n. chute f.; cascade f.; baisse f.; tombée f.; automne m. **the ~ of the curtain**, la tombée du rideau. **the ~ of the leaves**, la chute des feuilles.

fallacious adj. fallacieux; trompeur.

fallacy n. fausseté f.; tromperie f.; erreur f.; méprise f.; sophisme m.

fallibility n. faillibilité f.

fallible adj. faillible.

falling adj. tombant, en baisse. **a ~ star**, une étoile filante. n. chute f.; abandon m.; éboulement m.; écroulement m. **~ off**, baisse f.; abandon m., désertion f.

fallow adj. fauve; en friche, en jachère; inculte. **a ~ deer**, un daim. n. jachère f., sol m. en friche.

false adj. faux. **~ teeth**, fausses dents, dents artificielles. **~ imprisonment**, détention illégale. **~-bottomed**, à double fond.

falsehood n. mensonge m., fausseté f.; hypocrisie f.

falsely adv. faussement, de mauvaise foi.

falseness n. fausseté f., duplicité f., perfidie f.

falsification n. falsification f.

falsify v.t. falsifier, contrefaire, forger.

falsity n. fausseté f.

falter v.t. balbutier; bredouiller; chanceler, hésiter.

faltering n. bégayement m., bredouillement m.; hésitation f.; faiblesse f., défaillance f.

falteringly adv. en hésitant; en bredouillant; en tremblant.

fame n. renom m., célébrité f., renommée f., gloire f.

famed adj. renommé, en renom, famé. **ill-~**, mal famé.

familiar adj. familier; commun, ordinaire. **to be ~ with**, être familier avec. n. familier m.; intime m., ami m., demon familier.

familiarity n. familiarité f.

familiarize v.t. familiariser.

familiarly adv. familièrement.

family n. famille f. **~** adj. de famille. **~ man**, père m. de famille.

famine n. famine f.

famish v.t. affamer. v.i. être affamé, mourir de faim.

famous adj. fameux; célèbre; insigne.

famously adv. fameusement, prodigieusement.

fan n. éventail m., ventilateur m.; Infml. fana m.f.; mordu m. **~** v.i. éventer; vanner, attiser (passions, quarrels).

fanatic adj. fanatique n. fanatique m.f., enthousiaste m.f.; visionnaire m.f.

fanaticism n. fanatisme m.

fancier n. connaisseur m.; connaisseuse f.

fanciful adj. capricieux, fantasque; chimérique; fantastique.

fancy n. fantaisie f.; notion f.; idée f.; goût m., penchant m., caprice m. humeur f.; lubie f. **I took a ~ to her**, je l'ai prise en affection. v.i. s'imaginer, se figurer. v.t. imaginer; aimer; avoir du goût pour. **just ~ him in that situation!** imaginez-le dans cette situation! adj. beau, de fantaisie.

fang n. croc m. canine.

fanny n. Infml. fesses f.pl.

fantasia n. Mus. fantaisie f., caprice m.

fantasize v.i. fantasmer.

fantastic adj. fantastique, sensationnel; imaginaire, chimérique; fantasque; capricieux, bizarre.

fantastically adv. fantastiquement; singulièrement.

fantasy n. fantaisie f.; vision f.

far adj. éloigné; lointain; reculé. adv. loin, au loin; à une grande distance; de beaucoup, fort, très. **can you trace it so ~ back?** pouvez-vous le faire remonter si loin? **how ~**, combien, jusqu'où, jusqu'à quel point. **~ greater**, beaucoup plus grand. **~ too much**, beaucoup trop. **as ~ as I can guess**, autant que je puis conjecturer. **by ~**, de beaucoup. **how ~ is it to?** combien y a-t-il jusqu'à? **he is very ~ from being**, il est loin d'être, il s'en faut qu'il soit.

farce n. farce f.

farcical adj. bouffon, burlesque.

fare v.i. **to ~ well**, aller bien. n. prix m. des places; course f., passage m.; mets m.pl. **have you paid your ~?** avez-vous payé votre place?

farewell n. adieu m.; congé m.

farfetched adj. cherché au loin; cherché, forcé, tiré par les cheveux.

farm n. ferme f. métairie f. ~ v.t. exploiter, cultiver.

farmer n. fermier m., fermière f., cultivateur m.; cultivatrice f.; agriculteur m.; agricultrice f.

farming n. exploitation f. d'une terre; culture f., agriculture f.

fart n. Infml. pet m. ~ v.i. Infml. péter.

father adj. plus éloigné, plus lointain, ultérieur. adv. plus loin, au delà; en outre, puis.

farthest adj., adv. le plus éloigné, le plus lointain; au plus.

farthing n. farthing m., liard m.; le quart d'un penny. **not to be worth a ~,** ne pas valoire un rond.

fascicle n. faisceau m., bouquet m.; paquet m., botte f.

fascinate v.t. fasciner.

fascinating adj. fascinant.

fascination n. fascination f.

fascism n. fascisme m.

fascist n. fasciste m.f.

fashion n. vogue f., mode f., forme f.; façon f. coupe f. **the ~ of the day,** la mode du jour. **it is out of ~,** ce n'est plus de mode. v.t. façonner; former, modeler; arranger.

fashionable adj. à la mode, élégant, en vogue.

fashionably adv. à la mode, élégamment.

fast adj. rapide; ferme, solide; fixé; effronté, dissipé. ~-**food restaurant,** fast-food m., brasserie f. ~ **forward (button),** avance f. rapide. ~ **train,** un train rapide. **my watch is ~,** ma montre avance. n. jeûne m. ~ **day,** jour m. de jeûne. adv. vite, rapidement. **to hold ~,** tenir ferme. **to stick ~ to,** s'attacher fortement à, ne pas lâcher. **don't write so ~,** n'écrivez pas si vite. v.i. jeûner. n. jeûne m. ~ **day,** jour m. maigre.

fasten v.t. attacher, fixer; lier. v.i. s'attacher, se cramponner à.

fastener n. fermeture f., attache f.

fastening n. fermeture f., attache f., agrafe f.

fastidious adj. difficile, délicat.

fastidiously adv. avec dégoût.

fastidiousness n. dégoût m., gout m. difficile.

fat n. gras, matière f. grasse, graisse f. ~ v.t. engraisser. v.i. s'engraisser.

fatal adj. fatal, funeste, mortel.

fatalism n. fatalisme m.

fatalist n. fataliste m.f.

fatality n. fatalité f.

fatally adv. fatalement.

fate n. sort m., destin m.

fated adj. destiné (à), condamné (à).

fateful adj. fatidique.

father n. père m.; fontateur m. **to be a ~ to,** être comme un père pour. v.t. engendrer, inventer.

fatherhood n. paternité f.

father-in-law n. beau-père m.

fatherless adj. orphelin; sans père.

fatherly adj. de père; paternel. adv. paternellement, en père.

fathom n. Mar. brasse f.; portée f. ~ v.t. saisir, sonder; pénétrer, approfondir.

fathomless adj. sans fond; insondable, impénétrable.

fatigue n. fatigue f. **to endure ~,** endurer des fatigues. v.t. fatiguer.

fatness n. embonpoint m., corpulence f.; graisse f.; gras m.

fatten v.t. engraisser; enrichir. **to ~ on,** s'engraisser de.

fatty adj. graisseux; adipeux, huileux.

fatuity n. sottise f.

fatuous adj. imbécile; stupide.

faucet n. robinet m.

fault n. faute f.; défaut m.; erreur f. **at ~,** en défaut. **to find ~ with,** trouver à redire à.

faultily adv. defectueusement, d'une manière erronée, imparfaitement.

faultiness n. imperfection f., culpabilité f.

faultless adj. sans faute, sans défaut; parfait.

faultlessly adv. sans défaut; sans être coupable.

faulty adj. fautif; blâmable; défectueux.

faun n. faune m.

fauna n. faune f.

faux pas n. faux pas m., gaffe f., bévue f.

favor n. faveur f., service m.; bienveillance f.; grâce f.; pardon m.; couleurs f.pl.; rubans m.pl.; **could you do me a ~,** pourriez-vous me rendre un service? v.t. favoriser; gratifier; ménager.

favorable adj. favorable.

favorably adv. favorablement.

favored adj. favorisé, regardé avec bienveillance; flatté.

favorite n. favori m., favorite f. ~ adj. favori m., favorite f.

favoritism n. favoritisme m.

fawn v.i. faonner; faire le chien couchant; flatter, bassement, cajoler. n. faon m.; courbette f.; vile flatterie f.

fawning adj. qui flatte par ses bassesses. n. flatterie f.

fax n. ~ **machine;** télécopieur m., fax m. **to send a ~,** envoyer un fax.

fear n. peur f., crainte f., frayeur f., terreur f. **for ~ of falling,** de peur de tomber. **to be in ~ of,** avoire peur de. **there is nothing to ~,** il n'y a pas à craindre. v.t. craindre, redouter; avoir peur (de). **never ~,** ne craignez rien. **I ~ it is too late,** je crains qu'il ne soit trop tard.

fearful adj. craintif, timide; terrible, épouvantable. **to be ~ of,** craindre. **a ~ death,** une mort terrible.

fearfully adv. avec effroi, craintivement, timidement; terriblement.

fearfulness n. timidité f., crainte f.; effroi m., terreur f., alarme f.

fearless adj. courageux; sans peur; brave, intrépide, vaillant.

fearlessness n. intrépidité f., hardiesse f., courage m.

fearsome *adj.* effrayant.

feasibility *n.* faisabilité *f.*, praticabilité *f.*, possibilité *f.*

feasible *adj.* faisable; praticable, réalisable.

feasibly *adv.* d'une manière possible, praticable.

feast *n.* festin *m.*; régal *m.*; fête *f.* ~ *v.i.* faire bonne chère, être en festin. **to ~ on,** se régaler de. *v.t.* régaler, fêter.

feat *n.* haut fait *m.*, action *f.*, exploit *m.*; tour *m.* de force, tour d'adresse.

feather *n.* plume *f.*; aigrette *f.*; plumet *m.*; penne *f.*; down ~s, duvet *m.* **birds of a ~ flock together,** qui se ressemble s'assemble. **to be a ~ in one's cap,** donner de l'importance à quelqu'un. **to ~ one's nest,** amasser du bien. **he ~s his nest with it,** il en fait son profit. ~ **bed,** lit *m.* de plumes. ~ **duster,** plumeau *m.*

feathered *adj.* couvert, orné de plumes; empenné.

featherless *adj.* sans plumes; dépourvu de plumes.

feathery *adj.* couvert de plumes; emplumé; plumeux, penné, penniforme.

feature *n.* visage *m.*, figure *f.*; trait *m.*; physionomie *f.* caractéristique *f.*, long métrage. *v.t.*, mettre en vedette; faire figurer, jouer (in a film). **fine ~s,** une belle figure, un beau visage.

febrile *adj.* fébrile.

February *n.* février *m.*

feces *n.* fèces *f.pl.*, excrément *m.*, matière *f.* fécale.

feckless *adj.* incapable, inepte, irréfléchi.

fecund *adj.* fécond.

fecundate *v.t.* féconder.

fecundation *n.* fécondation *f.*

fecundity *n.* fécondité *f.*; fertilité *f.*

fed *pret.* of **feed,** *Infml.* **to be ~ up,** en avoir marre/ras-le-bol.

federal *adj.* fédéral.

federalist *n.* fédéraliste *m.*

federalism *n.* fédéralisme *m.*

federation *n.* fédération *f.*, ligue *f.*, confédération *f.*

fee *n.* salaire *m.*, honoraires *m.pl.*, gratification *f.*; fief *m.* **a lawyer's ~s,** les honoraires d'un avocat.

feeble *adj.* faible, débile, languissant. **to grow ~,** s'affaiblir. **~-minded,** faible d'esprit.

feebleness *n.* faiblesse *f.*

feebly *adv.* faiblement.

feed *v.t.* donner à manger à; élever; engraisser; alimenter (fire); paître, faire brouter. **to ~ the cattle,** faire paître le bétail. *v.i.* manger; se nourrir. **the bird ~s on fruits,** l'oiseau se nourrit de fruits. *n.* (animals) fourrage *m.*; pâture *f.*; pâturage *m.*

feedback *n.* réaction *f.*, rétroaction *f.*

feeder *n.* nourricier *m.*, alimenter *m.*, alimenteuse *f.*

feeding *n.* nourriture *f.*; alimentation *f.*; pâture *f.*

feel *v.t.* sentir; toucher; tâter, ressentir; éprouver;

souffrir. **how do you ~?** comment vous sentez-vous? **I ~ the cold,** je souffre du froid. **to ~ a patient's pulse,** tâter le pouls d'un malade. **to ~ one's way,** marcher en tâtonnant. *v.i.* sentir; se sentir. **to ~ soft, limp, cold,** être doux, souple, froid au toucher. **I ~ really stupid,** je me sens vraiment stupide. **to ~ sick,** se sentir malade. **I felt as if I'd seen him before,** j'avais l'impression de l'avoir déjà vu.

feeler *n.* antenne *f.*; tentacule *m.*

feeling *adj.* touchant, émouvant. *n.* toucher *m.*; tact *m.*; sentiment *m.*; sensation *f.* **good ~,** bon sentiment, bonne sensation *f.* **good ~s toward,** sentiment affectueux à l'égard de. **such is my ~,** telle est ma manière de voir. **to hurt one's ~s,** faire de la peine à; blesser, froisser. **to have no ~ for,** être sans pitié pour. **to speak with ~,** parler avec tendresse.

feelingly *adv.* avec sentiment; avec sensibilité.

feet *n.pl.* See FOOT.

feign *v.t.* feindre; faire semblant de. **to ~ a laugh,** faire semblant de rire.

feint *n.* feinte *f.*; déguisement *m.*; *adj.* feint, simulé.

felicitation *n.* félicitation *f.*; compliment *m.*

felicity *n.* félicité *f.*

feline *adj.* félin.

fell *n.* peau *f.* de bête, colline *f.* ~ *v.t.* abattre; terrasser, jeter à terre. **to ~ a tree,** abattre un arbre.

fellow *n.* compagnon *m.*, associé *m.*, camarade *m.*, égal *m.*, pareil *m.*, semblable *m.*, membre *m.*, agrégé *m.*; garçon *m.*, gaillard *m.*, individu *m.* **bed~,** camarade de lit. *Infml.* associé. **an honest ~,** un brave homme. **an old ~,** un vieux bonhomme. **a great big ~,** un grand gaillard. **~ citizen,** concitoyen *m.*, concitoyenne *f.* ~ **countryman,** compatriote *m.* **our ~ creatures,** nos semblables. **~ member,** confrère *m.*; collègue *m.* ~ **traveler,** compagnon *m.*, de voyage; *Infml.* communist. ~ **worker,** camarade *m.*, compagnon *m.* de travail.

fellowship *n.* société *f.*, association *f.*; agrégation *f.*; communion *f.*; compagnie *f.*; confraternité *f.*, camaraderie *f.*

felon *n.* criminel *m.* criminelle *f.*

felonious *adj.* méchant, cruel; criminel.

felony *n.* crime *m.*, délit *m.*

felt *n.* feutre *m.* ~ *v.t.* feutrer. **~-tip pen,** crayon *m.* feutre; *pret., p.p.* of **feel.**

female *n.* femelle *f.*; femme *f.* ~ *adj.* femelle; féminin, de femme.

feminine *adj.* féminin *f. m.f.*

femininity *n.* féminité *f.*

feminism feminisme *m.*

feminist *adj.*, *n.* féministe *m.f.*

femur *n.* fémur *m.*

fen *n.* marais *m.*, marécage *m.*

fence *n.* haie *f.*, palissade *f.*, clôture *f.*; barrière *f.*, défense *f.*; enceinte *f.*; escrime *f.* ~ *v.t.* enclore; entourer; défendre. *v.i.* faire des armes; se défendre.

fenceless *adj.* ouvert, sans clôture.

fencer *n.* escrimeur *m.*

fencing *n.* escrime *f.;* enceinte *f.,* clôture *f.*

fend *v.t.* to ~ for oneself, se débrouiller.

fender *n.* pare-chocs *m.inv.;* garde-feu *m.*

fennel *n.* fenouil *m.*

ferment *n.* ferment *m.;* effervescence *f.,* agitation *f.* ~ *v.t.* faire fermenter. *Fig.* exciter. *v.i.* fermenter, travailler.

fermentation *n.* fermentation *f.;* effervescence, agitation.

fern *n.* fougère *f.*

ferocious *adj.* féroce.

ferociously *adv.* d'une manière féroce.

ferociousness *n.* férocité *f.*

ferocity *n.* férocité *f.*

ferret *n.* furet *m.* ~ *v.t.* fureter. to ~ out, dénicher, dépister, traquer.

ferrule *n.* virole *f.*

ferry *v.t.* passer, traverser en bac. *n.* bac *m.* ~boat, bac *m.,* bateau *m.* de passeur.

fertile *adj.* fertile; fécond.

fertility *n.* fertilité *f.;* fécondité *f.,* richesse *f.*

fertilization *n.* fertilisation *f.;* fécondation *f.*

fertilize *v.t.* fertiliser.

fertilizer *n.* engrais *m.*

ferula *n.* férule *f.*

fervency *n.* ardeur *f.,* empressement *m.,* feu *m.;* ferveur *f.*

fervent *adj.* fervent, brûlant, très chaud; ardent, vif.

fervently *adv.* avec ferveur; ardemment.

fervid *adj.* très chaud, ardent, brûlant; empressé.

fervidly *adv.* avec ferveur.

fervor *n.* ferveur *f.;* chaleur *f.;* ardeur *f.,* zèle *m.*

fester *v.i.* se corrompre, s'ulcérer, s'envenimer.

festival *adj.* de fête; *n.* fête *f.,* festival *m.*

festive *adj.* de fête; gai, enjoué, joyeux.

festivity *n.* réjouissance *f.,* gaieté *f.;* fête *f.*

festoon *n.* feston *m.* ~ *v.t.* festonner.

fetch *v.t.* aller chercher. ~ me my hat, aller me chercher mon chapeau. (to dog) ~! va chercher!

fetid *adj.* fétide.

fetidness *n.* fétidité *f.*

fetlock *n.* fanon *m.;* boulet *m.*

fetter *n.* chaine *f.,* fers *m.pl.* entraves *f.pl.* ~ *v.t.* mettre dans les fers; enchaîner, entraver.

fettle *n.* forme *f.* condition *f.*

feud *n.* discorde *f.,* haine de famille; fief *m.*

feudal *adj.* féodal.

feudalism *n.* féodalité *f.*

fever *n.* fièvre *f.* scarlet ~, fièvre scarlatine.

feverish *adj.* fiévreux, fébrile, ardent, brûlant.

feverishly *adv.* fiévreusement.

few *adj.* peu, peu de, quelques; quelques-uns. in a ~ words, en peu de mots, brièvement. ~ people, peu de gens.

fey *adj.* lunatique.

fiancé *n.* fiancé *m.*

fiancée *n.* fiancée *f.*

fiasco *n.* fiasco *m.*

fiat *n.* ordonnance *f.* ~ *v.t.* autoriser.

fib *n.* mensonge *m.,* petit mensonge. *v.i.* raconter des petits mensonges.

fiber *n.* fibre *f.*

fiberglass *n.* fibre *f.* de verre.

fibrillation *n.* fibrillation *f.*

fibroid *adj.* fibroïde; *n.* fibrôme *m.*

fibroma *n.* fibrôme *m.*

fibrositis *n.* cellulite *f.*

fibrous *adj.* fibreux.

fibula *n.* péroné *m.*

fickle *adj.* volage, léger, inconstant, instable.

fickleness *n.* légèreté *f.;* irrésolution *f.,* incertitude *f.,* instabilité *f.*

fiction *n.* fiction *f.*

fictional *adj.* fictif, imaginaire.

fictitious *adj.* fictif; factice; faux; mensonger.

fictitiously *adv.* fictivement; faussement.

fiddle *n.* violon *m.;* crin-crin *m.* ~ *v.i.* jouer du violon, râcler du violon; baguenauder. a ~ with the accounts, truquer les comptes. ~-faddle, *n.* bagatelle *f.,* fadaise *f.,* niaiserie *f.,* sornette *f.* ~sticks! C'est ridicule.

fiddler *n.* joueur de violon.

fiddling *adj.* baguenaudant; niaisant. *n.* raclage *m.* (de violon); (fidgeting) trifouillage *m.* tripotage *m.*

fidelity *n.* fidélité *f.*

fidget *v.i.* se démener, s'agiter, se trémousser. *n.* agitation *f.* nerveuse.

fief *n.* fief *m.*

field *n.* champ *m.;* champ de bataille; combat *m.;* carrière *f.,* campagne *f.* across the ~, à travers champ. in the ~, en campagne. a ~ of ice, banc de glace. ~ hockey, *m.n.* hockey sur terrain. ~work, recherches *f.pl.* travail *m.* sur le terrain.

fiend *n.* démon *m.*

fiendish *adj.* hostile, diabolique, méchant.

fiendishness *n.* perversité *f.,* méchanceté *f.,* malice *f.*

fierce *adj.* féroce, cruel, farouche; violent; zélé. a ~ look, un regard farouche.

fiercely *adv.* férocement, cruellement; furieusement; excessivement.

fierceness *n.* férocité *f.,* fureur *f.;* acharnement *m.*

fieriness *n.* emportement *m.,* ardeur *f.,* fougue *f.*

fiery *adj.* de feu, ardent, fougueux, emporté. the ~ bush, le buisson ardent. ~ countenance, visage enflammé.

fiesta *n.* fiesta *f.*

fife *n.* fifre *m.*

fifteen *adj.* quinze.

fifteenth *adj.* quinzième. *n.* quinzième *m.*

fifth *adj.* cinquième. the emperor Charles the ~, l'empereur Charles-Quint. *n.* cinquième *m.; Mus.* quinte *f.*

fiftieth *adj.* cinquantième. *n.* cinquantième *m.*

fifty *adj.* cinquante.

fig *n.* figue *f.* ~ tree, figuier *m.*

fight *v.i.* se battre, combattre. *v.t.* combattre pour,

défendre. **to ~ a battle,** livrer bataille. *n.* combat *m.,* bataille *f.,* rixe *f.,* mêlée *f.* **~ back,** *v.t.* répendre; rendre la pareille, les coups.

fighter *n.* combattant *m.,* guerrier *m.,* soldat *m.;* chasseur (-bombardier) *m.;* boxeur *m.*

fighting *adj.* qui combat, militant. **a hundred thousand ~ men,** cent mille combattants. *n.* combat *m.,* bataille *f.*

figment *n.* invention *f.,* fiction *f.*

figuration *n.* configuration *f.;* figuration *f.;* forme *f.; Mus.* figure *f.*

figurative *adj.* figuratif; figuré. **in a ~ sense,** au figuré.

figuratively *adv.* au figuré.

figure *n.* forme *f.;* figure *f.;* image *f.,* silhouette *f.;* symbole *m.;* taille *f.,* tournure *f.;* chiffre *m.* ~ *v.t.* façonner, figurer. *v.i.* faire figure. **~ out,** comprendre, *Infml.* piger. **these ~s tell that,** ces chiffres nous disent que.

filament *n.* filament *m.;* filet *m.*

filch *v.t.* chiper; voler, dérober.

file *n.* lime *f.,* dossier *m.,* fiche *f.,* fichier *m.;* archives, liste *f.* **in Indian ~,** à la file. *v.t.* classer; enfiler; limer; déposer (for bankruptcy).

filet *n.* filet *m.,* tournedos *m.* ~ *v.t.* désosser.

filial *adj.* filial.

filiation *n.* filiation *f.*

filing *n.* limaille *f.;* classement *m.*

fill *v.t.* emplir, remplir; combler; remblayer. **to ~ up the time,** employer le temps. *v.i.* verser, donner (a'boire); se remplir. *n.* plénitude *f.,* suffisance *f.,* soûl *m.* **to take one's ~,** en prendre son soûl, s'en donner.

filler *n.* remplisseur *m.,* remplisseuse *f.* chargeur *m.;* remplissage *m.;* entonnoir *m.;* bouche-trou *m.*

filling *n.* remplisage *m.,* chargement *m.*

fillip *n.* chiquenaude *f.,* pichenette *f.*

filly *n.* pouliche *f.*

film *n.* film *m.* pellicule *f.;* membrane *f.;* voile *m.,* nuage *m.;* pellicule *f.* ~ *v.t.* filmer; couvrir d'une peau légère, d'une pellicule.

filmy *adj.* membraneux; mince, fragile, délié; voilé.

filter *n.* filtre *m.* ~ *v.t.* filtrer.

filth *n.* ordure *f.,* saleté *f.,* malpropreté *f.;* corruption *f.,* souillure *f.*

filthiness *n.* saleté *f.,* malpropreté; corruption *f.,* impureté *f.;* souillure *f.;* obscénité *f.*

filthy *adj.* sale, malpropre; impur; obscène, ordurier.

filtrate *v.t.* filtrer.

filtration *n.* filtration *f.*

fin *n.* nageoire *f.* aileron *m.;* fanon *m.* (of a whale).

final *adj.* final; dernier; définitif. **a ~ hope,** un dernier espoir. **a ~ judgment,** un jugement en dernier ressort.

finale *n.* finale *f.*

finalist *n.* finaliste *m.f.*

finality *n.* finalité *f.,* état *m.* final.

finalize *v.t.* rendre définitif, mettre au point.

finally *adv.* finalement, enfin, à la fin.

finance *n.* finances *f.pl.,* finance *f.* ~ *v.t.* financer.

financial *adj.* financier, de finances. **he is in a precarious ~ situation,** sa situation financière est très précaire.

financially *adv.* financièrement.

finch *n.* pinson *m.*

find *v.t.* trouver; rencontrer, estimer; apercevoir. **to ~ oneself,** se trouver; se porter, se sentir, être. **to ~ fault with,** trouver à dire, à redire. **to ~ out,** trouver; découvrir; démasquer. **to ~ out one's way,** trouver son chemin.

finding *n.* découverte *f.,* solution *f.;* déclaration *f.* d'un jury; verdict *m.*

fine *adj.* fin; beau; délicat; subtil; élégant, excellent. *n.* amende *f.;* donner une amende, contravention. **a heavy ~,** une forte amende. *v.t.* contravention *f.*

finely *adv.* finement; gentiment, délicatement, poliment.

fineness *n.* finesse *f.,* clarté *f.,* pureté *f.;* délicatesse *f.;* tranchant *f.*

finery *n.* éclat *m.,* brillant *m.,* splendeur *f.;* parure *f.,* affinerie *f.*

finesse *n.* finesse *f.* ~ *v.i.* finasser; user de subterfuges.

finger *n.* doigt *m.; Mus.* doigter *m.* **the ring ~,** l'annulaire. **the little ~,** l'auriculaire *m.,* le petit doigt. **~ tip,** bout du doigt. *v.t.* manier, exécuter avec les doigts; palper; jouer d'un instrument.

finicky *adj.* minutieux; difficile, pointilleux, allété.

finish *v.t.* finir, achever. *n.* fini *m.,* fin *f.*

finished *adj.* fini, terminé.

finite *adj.* fini, limité.

fir *n.* sapin *m.* **~ tree,** sapin *m.*

fire *n.* feu *m.;* incendie *m.;* fougue *f.* **to set ~ to,** **to set on ~,** mettre le feu à, mettre en feu, incendier. **by the ~,** auprès du feu. **slow ~,** petit feu. **to put out the ~,** éteindre le feu. **wild~,** feu grégeois *m.* ~ *v.t.* mettre le feu à, mettre en feu, allumer, tirer; enflammer; animer. **without firing a shot,** sans tirer un coup de feu. **to ~ off,** décharger. *v.t.* **to ~ an employee,** renvoyer, virer un employé. *v.i.* prendre feu; s'allumer, s'enflammer; *Mil.* tirer, faire feu. **to ~ at, upon,** tirer sur.

fire alarm *n.* avertisseur *m.* d'incendie.

firearm *n.* arme *f.* à feu.

firebrand *n.* tison *m.,* boute-feu *m.,* brandon *m.* de discorde.

fire engine *n.* pompe *f.* à incendie.

fire escape *n.* échelle *f.,* d'incendie, escalier *m.* de secours.

fire fighter *n.* pompier *m.* (volontaire).

firefly *n.* luciole *f.*

fireguard *n.* garde-feu *m.*

firelighter *n.* allume-feu *m.*

fireman *n.* pompier *m.*

fireplace *n.* âtre *m.,* cheminée *f.*

fireproof adj. incombustible.

firewood n. bois m. à brûler.

firework n. feu m. d'artifice.

firing n. décharge f.; fusillade f.; combustible m.; chauffage m.

firm adj. ferme, solide; dévoué. **the market is ~,** le marché est ferme. n. compagnie f.; raison f. sociale; maison f.

firmament n. firmament m.

firmly adv. fermement, solidement, ferme.

firmness n. fermeté f.

first adj. premier. **the twenty-~ of December,** le vingt et un décembre. adv. premièrement, auparavant; d'abord. **~ of all,** tout d'abord; pour commencer. **to go ~,** aller devant et. ~, d'abord. **~-born,** premier né, aîne. **~ class,** de premier ordre, excellent. **~-rate,** adj. du premier mérite, excellent.

firstly adv. premièrement.

fiscal adj. fiscal. n. fisc m.; receveur m. des taxes; fiscal m.

fish n. poisson m. **~ basket,** panier m. à poisson. **~ bone,** arrête f. **~hook,** hameçon m. **~ market,** marché m. aux poissons, poissonnerie f. **~pond,** étang m., vivier m. **to have other ~ to fry,** avoir d'autres chats à fouetter. v.i. pêcher; chercher. **to ~ for trout,** pêcher des truites. **to ~ for compliments,** chercher des compliments. **to ~ out secrets,** surprendre des secrets.

fisherman n. pêcheur m.

fishery n. pêche f.; pêcherie f.

fishing adj. de pêche. **~ boat,** barque de pêche. n. pêche f.; pêcherie f. **~ line,** ligne f. (à pêcher).

fishy adj. de poisson; poissonneux, Infml. douche. **a ~ story,** une histoire louche.

fission n. fission f.

fissure n. fissure f. **~** v.t. fendre, gercer.

fist n. poing m. **~** v.t. frapper avec le poing; empoigner.

fit n. accès m., attaque f.; convulsion f.; transport m.; caprice m., coupe f. (clothing). **that coat is a bad ~,** manteau va mal. **it is a tight ~,** c'est juste, c'est trop étroit. adj. propre, capable, apte; bon. **I am not ~ to go out,** je ne suis pas en état de sortir. **if you think ~,** si vous jugez à propos. v.t. ajuster, rendre propre à; disposer, rendre apte, rendre capable, mettre en état de; chausser, habiller. **your clothes ~ you well,** vos habits vous vont bien. **to ~ out,** équiper; fournir, les choses nécessaires, les moyens. v.i. être propre à, être f.; s'adapter; s'ajuster; joindre; aller.

fitness n. convenance f., à propos m., forme f.; capacité f.

fitter n. ajusteur m.

fitting adj. propre à; approprié, convenable. n. adaptation f. ajustement m., essayage m.

five adj. cinq m.

fix v.t. fixer; attacher; établir; arrêter. **~ your attention on,** fixez votre attention sur. **~ up,**

arranger. v.i. se fixer; s'établir. n. Infml. difficulté f.; embarras m.

fixation n. fixation f.

fixative n. fixateur m.

fixed adj. fixé, immobile.

fixings n.pl. Culin. garniture f.

fixity n. fixité f.

fixture n. appareil m. fixe.

fizz, fizzle n. pétillement m. **~** v.i. siffler; mousser.

flabby adj. mou m., molle f.; flasque.

flaccid adj. mou m., molle f.; flasque.

flaccidly adv. mollement, flasquement.

flaccidness, flaccidity n. flaccidité f.

flag v.i. pendre, flotter; être lâche, flasque; languir. v.t. laisser tomber, traîner; abattre. n. drapeau m.; pavillon m., dalle f.; dallage m. s. Bot. iris m. des marais, glaïeul m. **red ~,** pavillon rouge. **black ~,** pavillon noir. **to lower the ~,** amener le pavillon. **~ship,** vaisseau-amiral.

flagellate v.t. flageller.

flagellation n. flagellation f.

flagrant adj. flagrant, énorme.

flagrantly adv. d'une manière flagrante.

flair n. flair. **to have a ~ for,** avoir du nez pour.

flake n. flocon m.; écaille f.; flammèche f.; paillette f. **snow~s,** flocons de neige. **~s of copper,** écailles de cuivre. v.i. s'écailler; former en flocons.

flaky adj. floconneux; écailleux.

flamboyant adj. flamboyant.

flame n. flamme f.; feu m.; passion f. **~** v.i. flamber; briller, luire; flamboyer; enflammer.

flaming adj. flambant, flamboyant; magnifique.

flamingo n. flamant m.

flammable adj. inflammable.

flank n. flanc m.; côté m. aile f. **~** v.t. flanquer, prendre en flanc. v.i. aboutir à, toucher à; border; fortifier, défendre les flancs.

flannel n. flanelle f.

flap n. coup m., tape f.; battement (wing), pan m. (of clothing); revers m. (of clothing); rebord m. (of hat). v.t. frapper, battre; agiter, balancer. **to ~ wings,** battre des ailes.

flare v.i. flamboyer; flotter; briller, étinceler, éblouir; (sewing) (s') évaser, élargir. **to ~ up,** s'enflammer. n. lumière f. vacillante.

flaring adj. vacillant, brillant.

flash n. éclair m.; lueur f.; éclat m. passager; saillie f. **a ~ of lightning,** un éclair. **a ~ of wit,** un trait d'esprit. v.t. v.i. jaillir, éclater; avoir des saillies d'esprit; se donner des airs; en mettre plein la vue.

flasher n. exhibitionniste m.; dignotant m.

flashy adj. brillant, éclatant, tape à l'oeil.

flask n. bouteille f.; flacon m.

flat adj. plat, uni; positif, net, franc; calme, languissant. Mus. grave, bas, bémol. **the ~ country,** le pays plat. **to fall ~,** tomber à plat. **a ~ denial,** un refus net. n. plaine f., plateau m.; plat m.; Mus. bémol m. v.t. aplatir, aplanir, niveler;

affadir; affaiblir. v.i. (s')aplatir, (s')aplanir, (se) niveler, (s')affadir, (s')éventer.

flatly adv. à plat, de niveau; nettement, tout net, positivement.

flatness n. égalité f. (surface), niveau m.; platitude f. (style) fadeur f., insipidité f.; goût m. éventé.

flatten v.t. aplatir, aplanir; rendre plat. v.i. (s')aplatir, (s')aplanir; devenir plat; s'affadir.

flatter v.t. flatter. I ~ myself that, je me flatte que.

flatterer n. flatteur m., flatteuse f.; cajoleur m.; flagorneur m., flagorneuse f.

flattering adj. flatteur.

flatteringly adv. flatteusement.

flattery n. flatterie f.

flaunt v.i. s'étaler, se pavaner, flotter. n. grands airs m.pl., insolence f.; étalage m.

flautist n. flûtiste m.f.

flavor n. goût m., saveur f., fumet m. (of wine); bouquet m. (of wine). v.t. aromatiser; donner du fumet, de l'arôme, du parfum, du bouquet, de la saveur, etc.

flavorless adj. sans saveur, arôme, bouquet; insipide.

flaw n. fente f., imperfection f., fêlure f.; défaut m., paille f. (in precious stones). v.t. fendre, fendiller, fêler; endommager.

flawless adj. sans défaut, sans paille.

flax n. lin m.

flaxen adj. fait de lin; blond.

flay v.t. écorcher; battre.

flea n. puce f. ~ bite, morsure f., piqûre f. de puce. ~ market, marché m. aux puces.

fleck n. petite tache f.; particule f. ~ v.t. tacheter, moucheter, bigarrer.

fled. See FLEE.

fledge n. dru, emplumé. v.t. emplumer.

flee v.i.,v.t. fuir, s'enfuir, prendre la fuite.

fleece n. toison f. golden ~, toison d'or. v.t. tondre; Fig. dépouiller, plumer, écorcher.

fleecy adj. floconneux, laineux.

fleet n. flotte f., adj. rapide; léger, agile. ~footed, aux pieds légers, rapide.

fleeting adj. fugitif, passager, transitoire. the ~ hours, les heures fugitives.

flesh n. chair f. live ~, chair vive. ~-colored, couleur f. de chair. v.t. to ~ out, étoffer (a project).

fleshiness n. embonpoint m.

fleshy adj. charnu; gras; pulpeux.

flew See FLY.

flex n. souple. v.t. fléchir, ployer.

flexibility n. flexibilité f., souplesse f.

flexible adj. flexible; souple; docile.

flexion n. flexion f.

flexor n. fléchisseur m., muscle m. fléchisseur.

flick n. chiquenaude f., petit coup m. sec, film m.

flicker v.i. trémousser de l'aile; vaciller, trembler.

flickering adj. vacillant, tremblotant. ~ flame, flamme vacillante. n. trémoussement m., batte-

ment m. d'ailes; vacillation f.

flier n. prospectus m.

flight n. fuite f.; vol m., volée f., essor m.; essaim m.; transport m. to put to ~, mettre en fuite. at one ~, d'une volée. a ~ of arrows, une volée de flèches. a ~ of steps, perron m.; escalier m. ~ number, numéro m. de vol.

flightiness n. légèreté f., étourderie f.; inconstance f.

flighty adj. léger, étourdi; volage, inconstant.

flimsily adv. mollement.

flimsiness n. légèreté f., trivialité f.; insignifiance f.

flimsy adj. faible, léger; insignifiant; frivole; mollasse.

flinch v.i. reculer, hésiter, biaiser. to ~ from one's duty, manquer à son devoir.

fling v.t. lancer, jeter; darder. she flung her arms round his neck, elle se jeta à son cou. to ~ away, jeter, prodiguer. to ~ down, reverser, jeter par terre. v.i. s'agiter; se ruer; invectiver.

flint n. silex m., caillou m.; pierre f. à fusil. ~ hearted, insensible, au coeur de pierre. skin~, grippe-sou m.

flintiness n. qualité d'être siliceux; dureté f. excessive.

flinty adj. siliceux; très dur, cruel, impitoyable, inexorable.

flip n. chiquenaude f. ~ v.t. donner une chiquenaude; feuilleter. to ~ through the channels, changer constamment de chaînes.

flippancy n. désinvolture f.

flippant adj. désinvolte.

flippantly adv. avec désinvolture.

flipper n. nageoire f.; palmes f.pl.

flirt v.t. flirter. v.i. folâtrer; faire la coquette.

flirtation, flirting n. badinage m., flirt m.

flit v.i. voler, voltiger; s'agiter.

float v.i. flotter, planer; nager, faire la planche. to ~ away, être emporté par le courant. v.t. faire flotter, mettre à flot; renflouer. n. flot m. flux m., vague f., radeau m.; flotte f., flotteur m.

floatable adj. flottant.

floater n. flotteur m.

floating adj. flottant. ~ capital, capital m. flottant.

flocculent adj. floconneux.

flock n. troupeau m.; bande f.; volée f.; ouailles f.pl.; bourre f. de laine. v.i. s'assembler, accourir en foule. to ~ together, s'attrouper.

flog v.t. fouetter.

flogging n. fouet m.; fustigation f.

flood n. déluge m., inondation f.; torrent m., flux m. ~ v.t. inonder, submerger.

floodgate n. vanne f., écluse f.

flooding n. inondation f.

floor n. plancher m.; étage m.; aire f. ground ~, rez-de-chaussée m. ~ v.t. planchéier; terrasser.

floozy n. pouffiasse f.

flop v.t. trémousser de l'aile; agiter avec bruit. v.i. tomber lourdement; se flanquer.

floppy adj. mou; flottant. ~ disc, n. disque m.

souple.

flora n. flore f.

floral adj. floral.

florescence n. fleuraison f.

florid adj. fleuri.

floridity n. éclat m., fraîcheur f. de couleur, de teint.

florist n. fleuriste m.f.

flotilla n. flotille f.

flotsam n. épaves f.pl. de mer.

flounce v.i. s'agiter, se démener, se débattre; se mouvoir pesamment, bruyamment. v.t. garnir de volants. n. saccade f.; volant m.

flounder n. carrelet m. ~ v.i. se démener, se débattre, s'agiter; rouler, tomber, faire la culbute; patauger.

flour n. farine f. ~ v.t. moudre en farine; saupoudrer de farine, enfariner.

flourish v.i. fleurir; prospérer. v.i. fleurir; brandir (sword). n. éclat m, brandissement m. (sword), moulinet m., fioriture f., trait m. de plume.

flourishing adj. florissant, prospère.

flout v.t. railler, insulter, gouailler; braver. v.i. (se) railler, se gausser, se mequer. n. raillerie f., insulte f.

flow v.i. couler; s'écouler; fluer. **the water ~ed from the rock,** l'eau coulait du rocher. **how many ages have ~n away since that day!** que de siècles se sont écoulés depuis ce jour! **light ~s from the sun,** la lumière émane du soleil. v.t. inonder, submerger. n. flux m.; cours m. épanchement m., effusion f. **a ~ of words,** un flux de paroles.

flower n. fleur f. ~ v.i. fleurir; être en fleurs. v.t. orner de fleurs. **~ basket,** corbeille f. de fleurs. **~ garden,** parterre m., jardin m. à fleurs m. **~ leaf,** pétale m. **~ pot,** pot m. à fleur. **~ stalk,** pédoncule m. **~ stand,** jardinière f. **~ market,** marché m. aux fleurs.

flowered adj. garni de fleurs.

flowering adj. fleuri, en fleurs. n. floraison f.

flowery adj. fleuri.

flowing adj. coulant; flottant. n. écoulement m.; débordement m., inondation f.

flown See FLY.

flu n. grippe f.

fluctuate v.i. onduler, ondoyer; flotter; balancer, hésiter.

fluctuation n. fluctuation f.; incertitude f., irrésolution f. variation f.

flue n. tuyau m. de cheminée; duvet m. fin, poil m.

fluency n. fluidité f.; facilité f.; volubilité f. **to speak with ~,** parler couramment.

fluent adj. coulant; fluide; facile. **a ~ style,** un style coulant.

fluently adv. couramment. **she speaks English ~,** elle parle couramment anglais.

fluff n. duvet m. fin. v.t. faire bouffer.

fluffy adj. duveteux, bouffant, en peluche.

fluid adj. fluide; coulant. n. fluide m.

fluidity n. fluidité f.

fluke n. (coup de) chance f.; plie f., franche, carrelet m.

fluky adj. par chance; uncertain, capricieux.

flunk v.t. Infml. rater, louper. **he ~ed all his tests,** il a loupé tous ses examens.

flunky n. laquais m.

fluor n. fluer m.

fluorescent adj. fluorescent.

flurry n. bouflée f., bourrasque f., coup m. de vent soudain; précipitation f., commotion f., agitation f., trouble m. **what a ~ you are in!** dans quel état vous êtes! v.t. mettre en émoi, agiter.

flush v.i. se répandre soudainement; rougir, briller, rayonner. v.t. animer, exalter; réjouir, égayer; curer; tirer la chasse d'eau. adj. frais; plein de vigueur; de niveau, à fleurs, ras. n. rougeur f., rouge m.; fraîcheur f.; accès m.; prospérité f., abondance f.; (in cards) flush m. **the sudden ~ in his cheek,** le rouge qui tout à coup lui monta au visage.

fluster v.t. échauffer; troubler, agiter. n. emportement m., agitation f.

flute n. flûte f. **beaked ~,** flûte à bec, cannaluce f.; tuyau m.

flutter v.i. voltiger, voleter, se trémousser; onduler, flotter, balancer, hésiter. v.t. faire voltiger, faire voleter; troubler, déranger; agiter l'esprit. n. battement m. (of wings); trémoussement m., désordre m., tumulte m.; agitation f. de l'esprit. **to be all a ~,** être tout en émoi.

fluvial adj. fluvial.

flux n. courant m.; flux m. marée montante; fondant; courant m. ~ adj. changeant, variable. v.t. fondre; rendre fluide.

fluxion n. fluxion f.

fly v.i. s'envoler; fuir, s'enfuir, se sauver; voler. **the bird has flown away,** l'oiseau s'est envolé. **to ~ into a passion,** se mettre en colère, s'emporter. **to ~ out,** sortir brusquement; s'emporter. **to ~ to,** se réfugier; avoir recours à. **to let ~,** décharger, lancer. **to ~ one's country,** fuir, abandonner son pays. n. mouche f.; balancier m.; battant m. **~ catcher,** attrape-mouches m., gobe-mouches m. **~ fishing,** pêche à la mouche. **~ wheel,** volant m.

flyer n. prospectus m.

flying n. aviation f., pilotage m. **~ colors,** drapeaux m.pl. flottants. **~ fish,** poisson-volant m.

foal n. poulain m., pouliche f. ~ v.i. pouliner, mettre bas.

foam n. écume f., bouillon m. ~ v.i. écumer; moutonner; enrager.

foamy adj. écumeux, mousseux.

fob n. gousset m. ~ v.t. tromper; attraper, duper.

focal adj. focal; du foyer.

focus n. foyer m.; point m., de concentration. v.t. mettre à point; (se) fixer; (se) concenter.

fodder n. fourrage m.; pâture f. ~ v.t. affourager.

foe n. ennemi m.; adversaire.

foetal adj. foetal.

foetus n. foetus m.

fog n. brouillard m., brume f. ~ v.t., v.i. mystifier; embrumer, brouiller.

foggy adj. brumeux, nuageux; lourd, épais.

foible n. faible m., défaut m.; imperfection f.; infirmité f.

foil v.t. déjouer; découvrir. **to ~ an attempt**, rendre une tentative vaine. n. défaite f., échec m.; affaire manquée; fleuret m., feuille f. d'aluminium. Fig. repoussoir m., contraste m.

foist v.t. insérer, subrepticement; introduire, fourrer, glisser; mentir, forger. **to ~ a story upon one**, faire avaler une histoire à quelqu'un.

fold n. pli m., repli m. **the ~s of a snake**, les replis d'un serpent. **two~**, deux fois, double. v.t. plier, mettre en plis; croiser; serrer. **to ~ a letter**, plier une lettre. **to ~ the arms**, croiser les bras.

folder n. chemise f., dossier m., classeur m.

folding adj. pliant, rabattable. **~ doors**, porte à double battant. **~ chair**, chaise f. pliante. n. doublement m., pliage m.

foliage n. feuillage m., feuillée f.; bouquet m. de feuilles.

folio n. in-folio m., folio m., page f. ~ v.t. paginer.

folk n. gens f.pl. monde m.; personnes f.pl. **old ~s**, de vieilles gens. **~ songs** chanson f. folklorique.

folklore n. folklore m.

folksy adj. populaire, folklorique.

follicle n. follicule f.

follow v.t., v.i. suivre; poursuivre; succéder; imiter; s'ensuivre. **to ~ one's pleasures**, se livrer à ses plaisirs. **to ~ close upon**, suivre de près. **as ~s**, comme suit. **that does not ~**, cela ne s'ensuit pas.

follower n. partisan m. partisane f.; disiple m.f. subordonné m.

following adj. suivant, subséquent.

folly n. folie f.

foment v.t. fomenter.

fomentation n. fomentation f.

fond adj. fou, folle; extravagant; tendre, faible; passionné; chéri. **to be ~ of**, aimer à. **a ~ mother**, une tendre mère. **I'm ~ of you, but I don't love you**, je t'aime bien, mais c'est tout.

fondle v.t. caresser, choyer, dorloter.

fondling n. caresses f.pl., tendresses f.pl.

fondness n. tendresse f.; penchant m.; passion f.; goût m.

food n. nourriture f.; aliments m.pl. **~ chain**, chaîne f. alimentaire. **~ poisoning**, intoxication f. alimentaire.

fool n. fou m., folle f.; idiot m., idiote f. **I am not such a ~ as to believe it**, je ne suis pas assez bête pour le croire. **April ~**, poisson m. d'avril. **to play the ~**, faire l'imbécile, badiner. **~hardiness**, courage m. irréfléchi, témérité f. **~hardy**, téméraire, d'un courage insensé. v.i. faire le fou, faire des folies. v.t. duper, tromper, berner, attra-

per. **stop ~ing around!** arrête de faire l'idiot!, l'imbécile.

foolish adj. fou; insensé; sot, bête, imbécile. **he talks such ~ nonsense**, il tient des propos si sots, si bêtes.

foolishly adv. bêtement, follement.

foolishness n. sottise f., bêtise f.

foot n. pied m. patte f.; base f., bas m. **to go on ~**, aller à pied. **to walk bare~**, aller, marcher pieds nus. **the ~ of a pillar**, la base d'une colonne. **the ~ of a page**, le bas d'une page. **~ball**, ballon m. **~bridge**, passerelle f. **~path**, sentier m. **~ball**, football m., foot m. **to get cold feet**, avoir la trousse. v.i. marcher, aller à pied, v.t. fouler, marcher sur; mettre un pied à. **to ~ the bill**, payer la note.

footage n. métrage m.

footed adj. à pieds. **a four-~ animal**, quadrupède m. **bare ~**, nu-pieds.

footer n. bas m. de page. **the boat is a 10-~**, le bateau fait 10 pieds de long.

footing n. sol m. pour poser le pied; point m. d'appui; pied m.; situation f.; fondement m. **to get a ~**, prendre pied. **on a good ~**, sur un bon pied. **to get a ~ in a place**, s'ancrer quelque part.

footloose adj. Infml. libre comme l'air.

footman n. domestique m. en livrée.

footprint n. empreinte f. du pied.

footsie n. Infml. **to play ~ with**, faire du pied à. **those politicians have played ~ with each other**, ces politiciens ont fait de drôles de jeux ensemble.

footstep n. pas m.; signe m.; marque f.; trace f.; vestige m.; marche-pied m. **to follow in someone's ~**, emboîter le pas à quelqu'un, suivre le même chemin; suivre la même destinée que quelqu'un.

footstool n. tabouret m.

for prep. pour; à cause de; par; à; quant à, malgré; depuis, pendant. **~ God's sake**, pour l'amour de Dieu. **~ me**, pour moi. **I paid ten dollars ~ it**, je l'ai payé dix dollars. **they left him ~ dead**, on l'a laissé pour mort. **~ a week**, pendant une semaine. **~ever**, pour toujours, à jamais. **~ pity**, par pitié. **~ fear**, par crainte, de peur. **I cannot go ~ lack of money**, je ne peux pas y aller faute d'argent. **~ all I know**, autant que je sache. conj. car; parce que.

forage n. fourrage m., pâture f., provisions f.pl. ~ v.i. fourrager; rôder au loin; ravager.

foray n. incursion f.; ravage m.

forbear v.i., v.t. cesser, attendre; patienter; (s')abstenir; se garder de; se contenir.

forbearance n. abstention f.; patience f., tolérance f.; ménagement m.

forbid v.t. prohiber, défendre, interdire. **heaven ~**, le ciel m'en préserve!

forbidding adj. repoussant, rebutant, choquant. n. prohibition f., défense f., interdiction f.

force n. force f.; violence f.; contrainte f.; nécessité *f.pl.* troupes *f.pl.* by ~, de force. **the ~ of habit,** la force de l'habitude. **to raise ~s,** lever des troupes. **naval ~s,** forces navales. *v.t.* forcer; obliger; contraindre; violer; hâter. **to ~ nature,** forcer la nature. **to ~ a passage or a place,** forcer un passage, prendre une place par force. **to ~ back,** repousser. **to ~ out,** chasser, expulser.

forced *adj.* forcé; affecté; exagéré. ~ **style,** style forcé, affecté.

forceful *adj.* entraîné, poussé par la violence; poussé avec force; dur; impétueux.

forcefully *adv.* violemment, impétueusement.

forceps *n.* forceps *m.*

forcible *adj.* forcé; puissant; efficace; impétueux.

forcibly *adv.* violemment, par force; vigoureusement.

ford *n.* gué *m.* ~ *v.t.* passer à gué.

fore *adj.* antérieur, précédent, antécédent. **the ~ part,** le devant, la partie antérieure. *adv.* devant, auparavant. ~ **and aft,** de l'avant à l'arrière, de long en long.

foream *n.* avant-bras *m.* ~ *v.t.* armer, munir d'avance.

forebear *n.* ancêtre *m.*

forebode *v.t.* prédire; prévoir; presager.

foreboding *adj.* prophétique. *n.* pressentiment *m.*, présage *m.*, pronostic *m.*

forecast *v.t.* prévoir; projeter. *n.* prévision *f.* **weather ~,** la météo.

foreclose *v.t.* saisir, hypothéquer; fermer; arrêter, empêcher; exclure.

foreclosure *n.* saisie *f.*

foredoom *v.t.* prédestiner, destiner; condamner d'avance.

forefather *n.* ancêtre *m.*

forefinger *n.* index *m.*

forefoot *n.* pied *m.* patte *f.* de devant.

forefront *n.* devant *m.*, au premier rang; en première ligne.

forego *v.t.* se priver de; perdre; abandonner; céder.

foregoing *adj.* précédent, antérieur, antécédent.

foregone *adj.* prévu; réglé d'avance.

foreground *n.* premier plan *m.*

forehand *n.* avantmain *f.*

forehead *n.* front *m.*

foreign *adj.* étranger, extérieur; du dehors. ~ **products,** produits *m.pl.* exotiques. ~ **office,** ministère *m.* des affaires étrangères. **this is wholly ~ to our topic,** ceci est tout à fait étranger à notre sujet.

foreigner *n.* étranger *m.*, étrangère *f.*

foreknowledge *n.* prescience *f.;* prévision *f.*

foreland *n.* promontoire *m.*, cap *m.*

foreleg *n.* jambe *f.*, pied *m.*, patte *f.* de devant.

forelock *n.* mèche *f.*

foreman *n.* chef *m.;* contremaitre *m.;* (jury) président *m.*

foremost *adj.* le premier, le plus avancé, au premier rang.

forename *n.* prénom *m.*

forenoon *n.* matinée *f.*, matin *m.*

forensic *adj.* légal; judiciaire.

foreplay *n.* préliminaires *m.pl.* sexuels.

foresaid *adj.* susdit.

foresee *v.t.* prévoire.

foreshadow *v.t.* figurer, représenter, symboliser à l'avance.

foreshore *n.* plage *f.*

foreshorten *v.t.* raccourcir.

foresight *n.* prévision *f.;* prescience *f.;* prévoyance *f.,* prudence *f.*

foreskin *n.* prépuce *m.*

forest *n.* forêt *f.*

forestall *v.t.* prendre d'avance, anticiper; empêcher; accaparer.

forester *n.* forestier *m.*, arbre *m.* forestier.

foretaste *n.* avant-goût *m.*, anticipatien *f.* ~ *v.t.* goûter par avance, avoir un avant-goût de, anticiper.

foretell *v.t.* prédire; présager, pronostiquer.

forethought *n.* préméditation *f.;* prévoyance *f.,* prévision *f.*

forever *adv.* toujours, pour toujours, à jamais. **gone ~,** parti pour toujours.

forewarn *v.t.* prévenir, précautionner, prémunir.

forewoman *n.* premiere *f.;* (jury) présidente *f.;* contremaîtresse *f.*

foreword *n.* avant-propos *m.*

forfeit *v.t.* forfaire; être déchu de; perdre; manquer à. **to ~ one's estate,** perdre sa terre par confiscation. **to ~ one's credit,** perdre son crédit. *n.* déchéance *f.;* confiscation *f.;* amende *f.,* dédit *m.;* pénalité *f.;* gage *m.* **to pay the ~,** payer l'amende, le dédit. *adj.* perdu; déchu; confisqué.

forfeiture *n.* amende *f.;* dédit *m.;* confiscation *f.;* perte *f.*

forgather s'assembler, se réunir, se rencontrer.

forge *n.* forge *f.* ~ *v.t.* forger; inventer, fabriquer, falsifier. **to ~ coin,** faire de la fausse monnaie.

forger *n.* forgeur *m.,* faussaire *m.,* fabricateur *m.*

forgery *n.* falsification *f.;* contrefaçon *f.;* faux *m.*

forget *v.t.* oublier; perdre le souvenir de.

forgetful *adj.* distrait, négligent, inattentif.

forgetfulness *n.* oubli *m.;* négligence *f.;* insouciance *f.;* inattention *f.,* étourderie *f.*

forgivable *adj.* pardonnable.

forgive *v.t.* pardonner.

forgiveness *n.* pardon *m.;* grâce *f.;* clémence *f.;* remise *f.*

fork *n.* fourchette *f.,* fourche *f.;* zigzag *m.;* bifurcation *f.,* embranchement *m.* ~ *v.i.* (se) fourcher, se bifurquer.

forked *p.p. adj.* fourchu.

forlorn *adj.* délaissé, abandonné; désespéré; perdu.

form *n.* forme *f.;* modèle *m.;* formalité *f.;* ordre *m.;* formule *f.;* moule *m.;* gite *m.* (d'un lièvre). ~ **of worship,** cèrémonie du culte. *v.t.* former, façonner, construire, faire. *v.i.* (se) former.

formal *adj.* cérémonieux; formel; de forme. **a ~**

consent, un consentement formel.

formalism n. formalisme m.

formalist n. formaliste m.f.

formality n. formalité f.; cérémonie f., façons f.pl.; étiquette f.

formalize v.i. formaliser, être cérémonieux. v.t. donner une forme à, modeler, façonner.

formally adv. formellement; pour la forme; exactement.

formation n. formation f.

former adj. premier; précédent, passé, ancien. **in ~ times,** dans les anciens temps; jadis, autrefois. **the ~ president of the company,** l'ancien, l'ex-président de la compagnie.

formerly adv. autrefois, jadis, dans le temps.

formidable adj. terrifiant, effrayant, redoutable; formidable.

formidably adv. d'une manière redoutable; d'une manière formidable.

formless adj. informe, sans forme.

formula n., pl. **formulae** formule f.

formulate v.t. formuler; articuler, développer.

fornicate v.i. forniquer.

fornication n. fornication f.; impudicité f.

forsake v.t. délaisser, abandonner; se départir de.

forswear v.t.,v.i. abjurer, nier sous serment; renier. **to ~ oneself,** faire un faux serment, se parjurer.

fort n. fort m.; château fort.

forte n. point fort. **math is not his ~,** les maths ne sont pas son point fort. Mus. forte.

forth adv. en avant, en avance; devant. **from that day ~,** à partir de ce jour là. **and so ~,** et ainsi de suite. prep. hors de.

forthcoming adj. prêt à paraître, prochain.

forthright adv. droit, direct, franc.

forthwith adv. immédiatement, tout de suite.

fortieth adj. quarantième.

fortification n. fortification f., place f. fortifiée.

fortify v.i. fortifier.

fortitude n. force f. d'âme, courage m., résolution f., fermeté f.

fortress n. forteresse f.

fortuitous adj. fortuit.

fortuitously adv. fortuitement.

fortunate adj. fortuné, heureux, propice.

fortunately adv. heureusement.

fortune n. fortune f.; chance f.; avenir m., bonne aventure; biens m.pl. richesses f.pl. **to make one's ~,** faire sa fortune, s'enrichir. **to have one's ~ told,** se faire dire la bonne aventure. **to tell ~s by cards,** tirer les cartes. **~ hunter,** coureur m. de dots. **~teller,** diseur m., diseuse f. de bonne aventure. **~-telling,** cartomancie f.

forty adj. num. quarante. **about ~,** une quarantaine.

forum n. forum m.

forward adv. en avant, sur le devant; en évidence. adj. en avant, sur le devant; en tête, empressé; hâtif; présomptueux. **that man is too ~,** cet homme est trop avancé. v.t. avancer; hâter, acti-

ver; expédier, envoyer. **to ~ a letter,** faire parvenir une lettre. **goods ~ed,** marchandises f.pl. expédiées.

forwardness n. empressement m.; ardeur f.; assurance f., présomption f., progrès.

fossil adj. fossile.

fossilize v.t. convertir en fossile. v.i. se fossiliser.

foster v.t. élever; entretenir. **~ brother,** frère m. de lait. **~ child,** enfant en famille nourricière. **~ father,** père m. nourricier. **~ mother,** mère nourricière f.

foul adj. sale, infect, fétide, impur; obscène; vil; bas; honteux. **~ words,** paroles f.pl. obscènes. **~ language,** propos m.pl. orduriers. **~ air,** air m. infect, vicié. **~ breath,** mauvaise haleine. **~ weather,** vilain temps, mauvais temps. **~ winds,** vents m.pl. contraires. **a ~ deed,** une action abominable. **~ dealing, ~ play,** conduite f. déloyale, mauvaise foi.

foul-mouthed adj. grossier.

found v.t. établir, asseoir, fondre; (se) fonder. **to ~ a city,** bâtir une ville. See also FIND.

foundation n. fondation f.; fondement m.; base f.; création f. **~ stone,** première pierre.

founder n. fondateur m.; fondeur m. **~** v.t. Nav. sombrer, couler à fond.

foundling n. enfant m., abandonné, enfant trouvé.

foundry n. fonderie f.

fount n. fontaine f.; source f., origine f.

fountain n. source f.; jet m. d'eau vive; fontaine f.

four adj. quatre. **~ in quatre. the ~ of spades,** le quatre de pique. **on all ~s,** à quatre pattes. **~-footed,** quadrupède. **~-wheeled,** à quatre roues.

fourfold adj., n. quadruple m.

fourteen adj. quatorze.

fourteenth adj. quatorzième.

fourth adj. quatrième. n. quart m.; Mus. quarte f.

fourthly adv. quatrièmement, en quatrième lieu.

fowl n. oiseau m.; volaille f.; poule f. **~** v.i. chasser, tirer aux oiseaux sauvages.

fox n. renard m. **young ~,** renardeau m. **~ hound,** chien m. pour chasser le renard. **~ hunt,** chasse f. au renard.

foxy adj. rusé, malin, tenant du renard.

fracase n. fracas m.; tumulte m., vacarme m.

fraction n. fraction f.

fractional adj. fractionnaire.

fractious adj. hargneux, revêche; querelleur.

fracture n. fracture f. rupture. v.i. se fracturer, se casser, se briser.

fragile adj. fragile.

fragility n. fragilité f.; instabilité f.

fragment n. fragment m.; petite portion f.

fragmentation n. fragmentation f.

fragrance n. parfum m.

fragrant adj. parfumé, odoriférant, embaumé, aromatique.

frail adj. fragile, frêle.

frailness, frailty n. fragilité f., faiblesse f.

frame v.t. former, façonner; encadrer, arranger.

n. charpente *f.;* cadre *m.,* encadrement *m.;* châssis *m.* **he was in a strange ~ of mind,** il était d'une humeur *f.,* étrange.

framer *n.* encadreur *m.*

framework *n.* charpente *f.,* carcasse *f.,* cadre *m.*

franc *n.* franc *m.*

France *n.pr.* France *f.*

franchise *n.* franchise *f.;* concession *f.;* immunité *f.* ~ *v.t.* rendre libre; affranchir, exempter.

francophile *n.* francophile *m.f.*

francophobe *n.* francophobe *m.f.*

francophone *adj., n.* francophone *m.f.*

frank *adj.* franc, sincere. *n.* franc *m.f.*

frankfurter *n.* hot-dog *m.,* saucisse *f.* de Frankfort.

frankincense *n.* encens *m.*

frankly *adv.* franchement.

frankness *n.* franchise *f.;* sincérité *f.*

frantic *adj.* fou, forcené, éperdu; frénétique. ~ **with joy,** transporté de joie.

frantically *adv.* follement, éperdument, violemment.

fraternal *adj.* fraternel, de frère.

fraternally *adv.* fraternellement, en frère.

fraternity *n.* fraternité *f.;* confrérie *f.*

fraternization *n.* fraternisation *f.*

fraternize *v.i.* fraterniser.

fratricide *n.* fratricide *m.*

fraud *n.* fraude *f.;* supercherie *f.*

fraudulence *n.* fraude *f.,* tromperie *f.,* supercherie *f.*

fraudulent *adj.* frauduleux.

fraudulently *adv.* frauduleusement, par fraude.

fraught *adj.* (followed by **with**) chargé, frête; plein, rempli, gros de. *v.t.* charger, remplir, encombrer.

fray *v.t.* effilocher (clothing); *n.* mêlée *f.*

frazzle *n.* **to be worn to a ~,** être crevé, claqué, sur les rotules.

freak *n.* monstre *m.,* phénomène *m.* ~ *v.t.* barioler, bigarrar, tacheter.

freakish *adj.* monstrueux, phénoménal.

freckle *n.* tache *f.* de rousseur. *v.t.,v.i.* attraper des taches de rousseur.

freckled *adj.* plein de taches de rousseurs.

free *adj.* libre, volontaire, inoccupé; dégagé; ouvert; gratuit; exempt; familier. **I'll be ~ at six,** je serai libre à six heures. ~ **admission,** entrée *f.* libre. **he is too ~ in his manners,** il est trop familier, il est sans gêne. *v.t.* dégager, débarrasser; délivrer, exempter, affranchir; libérer; dispenser de. **of one's own ~ will,** de son propre gré. **the ~ world,** le monde libre. **is this table ~?** est-ce que cette table est libre? **as ~ as a bird,** libre comme l'air. ~ **enterprise,** libre entreprise.

freedom *n.* liberté *f.* ~ **of speech,** liberté *f.* de parole.

freely *adv.* librement; en liberté; voluntairement, spontanément, libéralement; gratuitement; complaisamment.

freemason *n.* franc-maçon *m.*

freeway *n.* autoroute *f.*

free will *n.* libre arbitre *m.*

freeze *v.i.* (se) geler; (se) congeler; (se) glacer; être glacé. *v.t.* geler, glacer.

freezer *n.* congélateur *m.,* freezer *m.*

freezing *n.* congélation *f.,* glace *f.*

freight *n.* fret *m.,* cargaison *f.; v.t.,v.i.* fréter, affréter, charger, transporter.

freighter *n.* fréteur *m.,* affréteur *m.*

French *adj.* français, à la française, (lesson, teacher) de français. *n.* Français *m.* ~ **bean,** haricot *m.* vert. *Infml.* **pardon my ~,** pardonner mon langage. **the French,** les Français.

frenchify *v.t.* franciser.

Frenchman *n. pl.* **Frenchmen** Français *m.*

Frenchwoman *n.* Française *f.*

frenetic *adj.* frénétique.

frenzy *n.* frénésie *f.,* folie *f.,* délire *m.*

frequency *n.* fréquence *f.*

frequent *adj.* fréquent, commun. *v.t.* fréquenter, hanter; courir.

frequently *adv.* fréquemment, souvent.

fresco *n.* fresque *f.*

fresh *adj.* frais; nouveau, récent; vigoureux, impertinent, culotté. **the air is ~,** l'air est frais vif. ~ **breeze,** brise fraîche. **don't you get ~ with me!** ne fais pas l'effronté(e)! ne joue pas à l'effronté(e) avec moi!

freshen *v.t.* rendre frais; rafraichir. *v.i.* se radoucir, franchir. ~ **up,** se refaire une beaute, faire un brin de toilette.

freshly *adv.* fraîchement, au frais; nouvellement.

freshman *n.* étudiant *m.* de première année; novice *m.*

freshness *n.* fraîcheur *f.;* vif éclat *m.;* nouveauté *f.,* état frais; vivacité *f.* du vent.

fret *v.t.* s'agiter, se tourmenter, s'inquiéter. *v.i.* s'excorier, s'affliger, se chagriner. **to ~ and fume,** se faire du mauvais sang. **do not ~,** ne vous tourmentez pas. *n.* agitation *f.;* irritation *f.;* touche *f.* (of guitar). *Arch.* grecque *f.,* frette *f.*

fretful *adj.* chagrin; de mauvaise humeur; irritable.

friability *n.* friabilité *f.*

friable *adj.* friable.

friar *n.* moine *m.*

fricassee *n.* fricassée *f. v.t.* fricasser.

friction *n.* friction *f.,* frottement *m.* ~ **wheel,** route *f.* à frottement.

Friday *n.* vendredi *m.* **Good ~,** Vendredi Saint.

fridge *n. Infml.* frigo *m.*

friend *n.* ami *m.,* amie *f.,* camarade *m.f.*

friendless *adj.* sans ami, abandonné.

friendliness *n.* amitié *f.,* bienveillance *f.*

friendly *adj.* amical; obligeant, serviable. **to be on ~ terms,** être en bons termes. **in a ~ way,** amicalement.

friendship *n.* amitié *f.*

frigging *adj. Infml.* **I almost fell on that ~**

step, j'ai failli tomber sur cette saloperie de
marche.
fright *n.* effroi *m.*, épouvante *f.*, épouvantail *m.*
to take ~ at, s'effrayer de. **what a ~ you gave
me!** tu m'as fait une de ces peurs!
frighten *v.t.* effrayer, épouvanter, terrifier; frapper d'effroi; faire peur à.
frightful *adj.* effroyable, effrayant; horrible,
affreux.
frightfully *adv.* effroyablement,
épouvantablement.
frightfulness *n.* horreur *f.*, frayeur *f.*
frigid *adj.* froid; glacial; frigide. **the ~ zone,** la
zone glaciale.
frigidity *n.* froideur *f.;* indifférence *f.;*
frigidité *f.*
frill *n.* jabot *m.;* fraise *f.,* orner de jabots, de
volants.
fringe *n.* frange *f.;* crépine *f.;* bord *m.,* extrémité
f.; lisière *f.* (of a forest). *v.t.* franger; garnir de
franges.
frisk *v.i.* se trémousser, sauter, frétiller; gambader, folâtrer, fouiller (a suspect). *n.* badinage *m.;*
saut *m.,* gambade *f.,* fouille (of a suspect).
friskiness *n.* gaieté *f.,* vivacité *f.*
frisky *adj.* gai, frétillant, sémillant.
fritter *n.* beignet *m.* **apple ~s,** beignets de
pommes. *v.t.* découper; morceler. **to ~ away,**
gaspiller.
frivolity *n.* frivolité *f.*
frivolous *adj.* frivole.
frivolously *adv.* d'une manière frivole.
frivolousness *n.* frivolité *f.*
frizz *v.t.* frizer.
frizzle *v.t.* grésiller, crépiter.
fro *adv.* en arrière. **to go to and ~,** aller et
venir.
frog *n.* grenouille *f.*
frolic *n.* gaieté *f.,* enjouement *m.,* badinage *m.;*
espièglerie *f.,* escapade *f.,* fredaine *f.* *v.i.* folâtrer,
faire le fou, gambader.
from *prep.* de; loin de, de par, de la part de;
d'après; dans; depuis, à partir de, dès. **~ time to
time,** de temps en temps. **~ above,** d'en haut.
~ afar, de loin. **~ behind,** de derrière. **~ hence, ~ here,** d'ici. **~ within,** de dedans. **~
without,** de dehors. **~ what I hear,** d'après ce
que j'apprends. **~ morning to night,** du matin
au soir.
frond *n.* fronde *f.;* feuillaison *f.*
front *n.* front *m.;* façade *f.;* devant *m.;* devanture *f.*
Mil. front *m.* **in ~ of,** devant. *adj.* du front, de face.
frontage *n.* façade *f.*
frontal *adj.* frontal. *n.* frontal *m.; Arch.* fronton *m.*
frontier *n.* frontière *f.* *adj.* frontière.
frost *n.* gelée *f.;* givre *m.* **white ~,** gelée blanche,
givre *m.* **~bitten,** gelé. *v.t.* givrer, glacer; blanchir (with sugar).
frosted *adj.* glacé.
frosty *adj.* de gelée; glacial; couvert de gelée, de
givre.

froth *n.* écume *f.,* mousse *f.* *v.t.* faire mousser;
écumer; bouillonner.
frothy *adj.* écumant, écumeux; mousseux; léger.
frown *v.i.* froncer le sourcil, se refrogner, se renfrogner, rechigner; (with on, **upon**) regarder
d'une manière menaçante. *n.* froncement *m.* de
sourcils.
frozen *adj.* gelé; glacé; glacial.
fructification *n.* fructification *f.*
fructify *v.t.,v.i.* rendre productif; fertiliser;
fructifier.
frugal *adj.* frugal; économe.
frugality *n.* frugalité *f.;* économie *f.*
frugally *adv.* frugalement.
fruit *n.* fruit *m.;* produit *m.;* profit *m.,* avantage
m. **~ basket,** cueilloir *m.,* panier *m.* à fruits.
~ bearer, arbre *m.* fruitier. **~ garden,** jardin *m.*
fruitier. **~ tree,** arbre *m.* fruitier.
fruitful *adj.* chargé de fruits; fructueux; fécond;
fertile.
fruitfully *adv.* fructueusement;
abondamment.
fruitfulness *n.* fécondité *f.,* fertilité *f.*
fruition *n.* jouissance *f.*
fruitless *adj.* sans fruit; sterile; infructueux,
inutile.
fruity *adj.* fruité.
frustrate *v.t.* frustrer, déjouer; déconcerter.
frustration *n.* déception *f.;* frustration *f.*
fry *v.t.* faire, faire frire.
frying pan *n.* poêle à frire.
fudge *n.* fondant *m.*
fuel *n.* combustible *m.;* carburant *m.;* chauffage
m. **to add ~ to the fire,** verser de l'huile sur le
feu. alimenter en combustible; alimenter.
fugitive *adj.* fugitif; *n.* fugitif *m.*
fulfill *v.t.* remplir; accomplir, exécuter; effectuer;
combler. **she has ~ed all her duties,** elle a
rempli tous ces devoirs.
fulfilling *adj.* satisfaisant.
fulfillment *n.* accomplissement *m.*
full *adj.* plein; rempli, replet, entier, complet; large, ample. **a house ~ of furniture,** une maison
pleine de meubles. **~ moon,** pleine lune *f.*
to run at ~ speed, courir à toute vitesse, à
brides abattues. **to work ~-time,** travailler à
plein temps. *n.* plein *m.;* comble *m.* **~** *adv.* tout à
fait, entièrement. **~ bloomed,** en pleine floraison, dans tout son éclat. **~-blown,** complètement épanouie. **~-bottomed,** à large fond.
~-faced, joufflu. **~-length,** de toute la
longueur.
fully *adv.* pleinement, completement.
fulminate *v.i.* fulminer; tonner. *v.t.* lancer. *n.* fulminate *m.*
fumble *v.i.v.t.* aller à tâtons, tâtonner; farfouiller;
jouer avec les doigts.
fume *n.* fumée *f.;* exhalaison *f.,* vapeur *f.;* rage *f.*
~ *v.i.,v.t.* fumer; parfumer; s'emporter; s'indigner; rager, se mettre en rage.
fun *n.* plaisanterie *f.;* amusement *m.* **they had ~**

at the party, ils/elles se sont bien amusé(e)s à la fête. **for ~,** pour rire.

funambulist n. funambule m.

function n. fonction f.; emploi m., charge f.

functional adj. fonctionnel.

fund n. fonds m.; capital m.; caisse f. **sinking ~,** fonds d'amortissement. **public ~s,** fonds publics. v.t. consolider (a debt); financer; pourvoir.

fundamental adj. fondamental; essentiel, necessaire. n. fondement m.

funeral n. funérailles f.pl., obsèques f.pl. **~ procession,** convoi m. **~** adj. funéraire. **~ march,** marche f. funèbre.

funereal adj. funèbre; sombre, triste; lugubre.

fungus n. champignon m.; fongus m.; excroissances f.pl.

funicular adj. funiculaire.

funky adj. cool, in. **it's a ~ place,** c'est un endroit cool.

funnel n. entonnoir m.; tuyau m. de cheminés.

funny adj. drôle; plaisant, comique. **~ bone,** le coude.

fur n. fourrure f.; pelage m. **~ trade,** pelleterie f. **~** v.t. gourrer; garnir d'une fourrure.

furbish v.t. fourbir.

furious adj. furieux.

furiously adv. furieusement, avec fureur.

furl v.t. ferler, serrer.

furlough n. congé m., permission f. **~** v.t. accorder une permission de s'absenter.

furnace n. fourneau m.; fournaise f.; four m.

furnish v.t. (with **with**) fournir, procurer, pourvoir; munir, approvisionner; garnir; meubler. **to ~ with goods,** fournir des marchandises. **to ~ a house,** meubler une maison.

furniture n. meubles m.pl., ustensiles m.pl. etc., ameublement m.; garniture f.; accessoires m.pl.

furor n. fureur f., rage f.

furred adj. fourré.

furrier n. fourreur m.

furrow n. sillon m.; rigole f., ride f., rainure f., trace. v.t. tracer, creuser des sillons; rider; rayer.

furry adj. fourré.

further adj. ultérieur; en sus; nouveau. **until ~ orders,** jusqu'à nouvel ordre. adv. plus loin, plus avant, au delà; de plus, encore, en outre. v.t. avancer; favoriser; seconder, aider.

furtherance n. appui m., aide f.; avancement m., progrès m. **for the ~ of,** pour l'avancement de.

furthermore adv. en outre, qui plus est, d'ailleurs.

furthermost adj. le plus éloigné.

furthest adj. adv. le plus éloigné.

furtive adj. dérobé; furtif.

furtively adv. furtivement.

fury n. furie f.; fureur f.; rage f., fougue f.

furze n. ajonc m.

fuse v.i. (se) fondre, se liquéfier. n. fusée f., fusible m., plomb m. **~ box,** boîte f. à fusibles.

fusillade n. fusillade f.

fusion n. fusion f.; fonte f.

fuss n. fracas m.; embarras m. **he made such a big ~ about it,** il en a fait tout un plat, il en a fait tout un tas d'histoires.

fussily adv. avec embarras.

fussy adj. difficile.

futile adj. futile; vain, inutile.

futility n. futilité f.

future adj. futur. n. futur m. **in the ~,** à l'avenir.

futuristic adj. futuriste.

fuze v.t. (se) fondre, (se) liquéfier.

fuzz n. duvet m., poil m., fin.

G

G Mus. sol m.; clef f. de sol. **~-string,** cache-sexe m.

gab n. bouche f. **he has the gift of ~,** il a la longue bien pendue; il a du bagou. v.i. bavarder.

gabardine n. gabardine f.

gabble v.i. babiller, bavarder, caqueter. n. caquetage m., babil m., bavardage m.

gad n. **to ~ about,** vagabonder.

gadabout n. coureur m.

gadfly n. taon m.

gadget n. gadget m., dispositif m., machin m., bidule m., truc m.

gaffe n. gaffe f., bêtise f., bévue f.

gag v.t. bâillonner; plaisanter. n. bâillon m., plaisanterie f., gag m.

gaga adj. gaga.

gage n. gage m.; gauge f. **~** v.t. mettre en gage; mesurer, jauger.

gaggle n. troupeau m.

gaiety n. gaieté f.; couleur f.; réjouissances f.pl.

gaily adv. gaiement.

gain v.t., v.i. gagner, remporter, acquérir, se procurer; se concilier. **to ~ one's end,** obtenir, parvenir à son but. **to ~ ground,** gagner du terrain. n. gain m., profit m.; avantage m.; bénéfice m; avance f.

gainful adj. profitable; lucratif.

gainings n. gains m.pl., profits m.pl.

gainsay v.t. contredire, nier.

gait n. port m.; démarche f; pas m.; allure f., maintien m.

gal n. fille f. **she's a nice ~,** c'est une fille sympa.

gala n. gala m.

galaxy n. galaxie f., voie f. **the Milky Way,** La Voie Lactée; Fig. constellation, réunion f. brillante.

gale n. vent m., frais; coup m. de vent, tempête f.

gall n. fiel m., bile f.; rancune, aigreur f.; Bot. galle f., noix f. de galle. **~bladder,** résicule biliaire f. **~** v.t. écorcher; excorier; piquer, froisser, vexer.

gallant adj. brave, vaillant; galant. **~ manners,**

des manières galantes. *n.* galant *m.; *cavalier *m.*
gallantly *adv.* galamment; bravement.
gallantry *n.* bravoure *f.,* courage *m.;* valeur *f.;* galanterie.
galleon *n.* galion *m.*
gallery *n.* galerie *f.;* corridor *m.,* tribune *f.;* balcon *m.*
galley *n.* galère *f.; Typ.* galée *f.;* cuisine *f.* (of boat).
gallic *adj.* gallique, gaulois; français.
galling *n.* écorchure *f. adj.* blessant; douloureux.
gallon *n.* gallon *m.* (3,785 litres).
gallop *v.i.* galoper, au galop. *n.* galop *m.* **full ~,** le grand galop.
galloping *adj.* galopant.
gallows *n.* gibet *m.,* potence *f.*
galore *adv.* en abondance.
galvanic *adj.* galvanique; crispé.
galvanize *v.t.* galvaniser.
gambit *n.* gambit *m.*
gamble *v.i.* jouer; miser sur. **he ~d away all his winnings,** il a perdu tout ce qu'il avait gagné aux jeux. *n.* jeu; affaire *f.* risquée.
game *n.* jeu *m.,* divertissement *m.;* gibier *m.;* chasse *f.* **to have a ~ of chess,** faire une partie d'échecs. **to give up the ~,** quitter la partie. **to eat ~,** manger du gibier. *v.i.* jouer; s'amuser, badiner.
gamekeeper *n.* gardechasse *m.*
gamut *n.* gamme *f.*
gander *n.* jars *m.; Infml.* **to take a ~,** jeter un coup d'oeil.
gang *n.* troupe *f.,* bande *f.,* tas *m.;* clique *f.;* équipe *f.* **a ~ of thieves,** une bande de voleurs. **~ up,** *v.i.* se mettre contre, se mettre à plusieurs sur.
gangling *adj.* dégingandé.
ganglion *n.* ganglion *m.*
gangrene *n.* gangrène *f.*
gangster *n.* ganster *m.,* bandit *m.*
gangway *n.* passage *m.,* couloir *m.*
gap *n.* trou *m.;* brèche *f.;* lacune *f.,* vide *m.* **to fill a ~,** boucher un trou.
gape *v.i.* bâiller, s'ouvrir, s'entr'ouvrir. **to stand gaping,** rester la bouche béante; bayer aux corneilles. *n.* bâillement *m.;* fente *f.*
garage *n.* garage *m.* **~ sale,** brocante *f.* chez un particulier.
garb *n.* costume *m.,* vêtement *m.;* apparence *f.*
garbage *n.* ordures *f.pl.,* déchets *m.pl.* **~ can,** poubelle *f.,* boîte *f.* à ordures. **~man,** éboueur *m.pl.* bêtises *f.pl.* **he's talking ~,** il dit n'importe quoi.
garble *v.t.* fausser; dénaturer; altérer.
garden *n.* jardin *m.* **kitchen ~,** jardin *m.* potage, potager *m.* **~** *v.i.* jardiner. *adj.* de jardin.
gardener *n.* jardinier *m.*
gardening *n.* jardinage *m.,* horticulture *f.*
gargle *v.t.* gargariser. *n.* gargarisme *m.*
gargoyle *n.* gargouille *f.*
garish *adj.* voyant, ébouissant.

garland *n.* garlande *f.;* couronne de fleurs.
garlic *n.* ail *m.* **clove of ~,** gousse *f.* d'ail.
garment *n.* vêtement *m.*
garner *v.t.* amasser, accumuler dans un grenier.
garnish *v.t.* garnir; parer, orner. *n.* garniture *f.;* ornement *m.,* décoration *f.*
garret *n.* mansarde *f.*
garrison *n.* garnison *f.* **~** *v.t.* mettre garnison; défendre.
garrote *n.* strangulation *f.* **~** *v.t.* étrangler.
garter *n.* jarretière *f.* **~** *v.t.* nouer avec une jarretière.
gas *n,* gaz *m.* **~ meter,** compteur à gaz. **~ station,** station *f.* service. **~ stove,** réchaud *m.* à gaz. **~ tank,** réservoir *m.* d'essence. *v.t.* gazer; asphyxier.
gaseous *adj.* gazeux.
gasket *n.* joint *m.* de culasse.
gasp *v.i.* haleter, suffoquer. **to ~ for breath,** respirer difficilement. **to ~ one's last,** rendre le denier soupir. *n.* respiration *f.;* soupir *m.*
gastric *adj.* gastrique.
gastritis *n.* gastrite *f.*
gastronome *n.* gastronome *m.*
gastronomic *adj.* gastronomique.
gastronomy *n.* gastronomie *f.*
gate *n.* porte *f.;* grille *f.;* grande porte; barrière *f.*
gateway *n.* porte *f.* cochère, porte *f.* d'entrée.
gather *v.t.* assembler, rassembler, réunir; cueiller; inférer; conclure. *v.i.* s'assembler, (se) rassembler; s'amonceler, s'amasser. **they ~ed together,** ils se rassemblèrent.
gathering *n.* rassemblement *m.;* assemblage *m.;* ramas *m.;* quête *f.*
gauche *adj.* gauche, maladroit. **gaudy** *adj.* voyant, criard.
gauge *v.t.* jauger. *n.* jauge *f.,* mesure *f.,* règle *f.,* étalon *m.* de mesure; capacité *f.;* éprouvette *f.*
gaunt *adj.* maigre, décharné, efflanqué.
gauze *n.* gaze *f.*
gavel *n.* marteau *m.*
gawk *v.i.* rester bouche bée.
gawky *adj.* maladroit, gauche; niais, sot.
gay *adj.* homosexuel, gai; joyeux; homosexuel(le) *m.f.* **as ~ as a lark,** gai comme un pinson.
gaze *v.i.* regarder fixement; contempler. *n.* regard *m.* fixe, attentif; contemplation *f.*
gazelle *n.* gazelle *f.*
gazette *n.* gazette *f.,* journal *m.*
gear *n.* appareil *m.;* accoutrement *m.;* attirail *m.;* engrenage *m.;* vitesse *f.* **to throw into ~,** embrayer.
gee *interj.* et ben dit donc!
gel *n.* gel *m.* **~** *v.i.* se coaguler.
gelatine *n.* gélatine *f.*
gelatinous *adj.* gélatineux.
geld *v.t.* châtrer, emasculer; hongrer.
gelding *n.* castration *f.;* mutilation *f.;* animal *m.* châtré.
gem *n. Joaill.* pierre *f.;* personne admirable. *f.* **~** *v.t.* orner de pierres précieuses; embellir, orner.

Gemini n. Ast. Gémeaux m.pl.

gender n. genre m.

gene n. gène m.

genealogical adj. généalogique.

genealogist n. généalogiste m.f.

genealogy n. généalogie f.

general adj. général, commun; public. the ~ welfare, le bien public. ~ officer, officier m. général. n. général m. lieutenant ~, lieutenant général.

generality n. généralité f.; masse f.; multitude f.; la plupart.

generalization n. généralisation f.

generalize v.t. généraliser.

generally adv. généralement, en général, communément.

generate v.t. engendrer; procréer; produire, causer.

generating adj. générateur, génératrice.

generation n. génération f.

generative adj. génératif, générateur; producteur.

generator n. génératrice f., dynamo m., générateur m.

generic adj. générique.

generosity n. générosité f.

generous adj. généreux.

generously adv. généreusement.

generousness n. générosité f.

genesis n. Genèse f.

genetic adj. génétique.

genetics n. génétique f.

genial adj. affable, de bonne humeur, doux, douce. ~ warmth, une chaleur bienfaisante.

geniality n. gaieté f., bonne humeur f., doceur f.

genii n. génie m., esprit m., démon m.

genital adj. génital.

genitals n. organes m.pl. génitaux.

genius n. pl. geniuses, génie m.; talent inné; pl.

genocide n. génocide m.

genteel adj. distingué, élégant; poli.

gentian n. gentiane f.

Gentile n. Ecclés. Gentil(e) m. (f.). adj. Ecclés. des Gentils.

gentle adj. doux, modéré; docile. a ~ horse, un cheval docile. she is such a ~ woman, c'est une femme tellement gentille, douce.

gentleman n. homme m. bien élevé, homme comme il faut; galant homme; monsieur. show the ~ to his room, conduisez monsieur à sa chambre.

gentlemanlike, gentlemanly adj. d'un homme honorable. ~ behavior, conduite noble.

gentlemanliness n. savoir-vivre m.; politesse f.; air m. distingué.

gentleness n. douceur f.

gently adv. doucement, poliment.

gentry n. petite noblesse; haute bourgeoisie; les gens comme il faut.

genuflection n. génuflexion f.

genuine adj. réel; naturel; sincère; authentique;

pur. ~ wine, vin naturel. a ~ text, un texte authentique.

genuinely adv. réellement; pated parement.

geographic, geographical adj. géographique.

geography n. géographie f.

geological adj. géologique.

geology n. géologie f.

geometric, geometrical adj. géométrique.

geometry n. géométrie f.

geophysics n. géophysique f.

geopolitics n.pl. géopolitique f.

geranium n. géranium m.

geriatric adj. gériatrique.

geriatrics n. gériatrie f.

germ n. germe m., microbe m.

German adj. germanique, allemand, d'Allemagne. n. Allemand m., Allemande f.

Germany n.pr. Geog. Germanie f.; Allemagne f.

germinate v.t. germer.

germination n. germination f.

gerrymander v.t. truquer, tricker (election).

gerund n. gerondif m.

gestation n. gestation f.

gesticulate v.i. gesticuler.

gesticulation n. gesticulation f.

gesture n. geste m., mouvement m. expressif. v.t.,v.i. faire des gestes, gesticuler; mimer.

get v.t.,v.i. gagner, obtenir, acquérir, trouver, procurer, (se) procurer, se faire, recevoir, tenir, avoir; devenir. to ~ money, gagner de l'argent. to ~ friends, se faire des amis. to ~ a name, se faire un nom. what will you ~ by all that? qu'est-ce que tout ça va t'apporter? I've got it, je l'ai. to ~ the better of, l'emporter sur. to ~ ready, (se) préparer. v.i. aller; arriver; devenir. to ~ home, retourner chez soi. to ~ better, s'améliorer; se porter mieux. to ~ clear of, se dégager de; s'échapper de. to ~ rid of, se débarrasser de. to ~ about, sortir, se déplacer. to ~ ahead of, devancer. to ~ at, atteindre. what are you ~ting at? à quoi veux-tu en venir? to ~ away, s'en aller; s'échapper. to ~ away from, échapper à, se soustraire à. to ~ back, reconvrer; retourner. to ~ down, descendre; faire descendre. to ~ forward, avancer. to ~ a hold of, saisir, prendre; obtenir. to ~ in, entrer; rentrer. to ~ into, faire entrer dans; pénétrer dans; mettre dans. to ~ off, descendre, ôter, enlever; s'en aller; se sauver. to ~ on, avancer; faire avancer; monter. to ~ along with, s'accorder avec quelqu'un; s'entendre avec. to ~ out, sortir; tirer de; ôter; se tirer de. to ~ over, passer; franchir; se remettre de; surmonter. don't worry, she'll ~ over him, ne t'inquiète pas, elle se remettra de lui. to ~ through, traverser, faire traverser; s'en tirer; venir à bout de. to ~ together, (se) réunir. to ~ under, soumettre, maitriser. to ~ up, se lever; monter; préparer. to ~ upon, monter sur.

ghastliness n. mine f. affreuse, aspect m. horrible; pâleur f., mortelle.

ghastly *adj.* semblable à un spectre; pâle, lugubre; affreux.

ghetto *n.* ghetto *m.*

ghost *n.* esprit *m.;* revenant *m.,* fantôme *m.*

ghostly *adj.* spectral.

G.I. *n.* soldat *m.* ~ *adj.* militaire.

giant *n.* géant *m.;* colosse *m.* ~ *adj.* de géant.

gibberish *n. Infml.* charabia *m.,* baragouinage *m.*

gibbet *n.* gibet *m.*

gibbon *n.* gibbon *m.*

gibe *v.i.* (with **at**) se moquer, railler; bafouer. *n.* raillerie *f.,* moquerie *f.*

giddily *adv.* vertigineusement; étourdiment.

giddiness *n.* vertige *m.;* étourdissement *m.;* étourderie *f.*

giddy *adj.* étourdi; vertigineux.

gift *n.* don *m.,* cadeau *m.,* donation *f.;* talent *m.* **a free ~,** un don gratuit. **he is ~ed,** il est doué.

gifted *adj.* doué.

gig *n.* yole *f.,* youyou *m.;* gig *m.* ~ *v.i.* jouer un concert.

gigantic *adj.* gigantesque.

giggle *n.* ricanement *m.* ~ *v.i.* glousser, rire nerveusement.

gigolo *n.* gigolo *m.*

gild *v.t.* dorer.

gill *n.* branchies *f.pl.,* ouïes *f.pl.;* jabot *m.,* abajoue *f.;* lierre *m.,* terrestre.

gilt *n.* dorure *f.*

gimmick *n.* astuce *f.,* truc *m.,* machin *m.*

gin *n.* genièvre *m.;* gin *m.* (drink); piège *m.* (trap). **cotton ~,** égreneuse *f.* de coton.

ginger *n.* gingembre *m.* ~ **ale,** limonade *f.* ~**bread,** pain *m.* d'épice.

gingerly *adv.* doucement, délicatement.

ginseng *n.* gingseng *m.*

giraffe *n.* girafe *f.*

gird *v.t.* lier, teindre, sangler, cerner; railler. **to ~ a horse,** sangler un cheval.

girder *n.* poutrelle *f.*

girdle *n.* ceinture *f.,* gaine *f.*

girl *n.* fille *f.*

girlfriend *n.* (petite) amie *f.*

girlish *adj.* de jeune fille.

girlishness *n.* manières de jeune fille; enfantillage *m.*

girth *v.t.* ceindre, entourer, sangler.

girth *n.* sangle *f.,* circonférence *f.;* tour *m.*

gist *n.* fond *m.,* substance *f.,* essence *f.,* point *m.,* capital.

give *v.a.,v.i.* donner; rendre; livrer; remettre. **to ~ notice,** avertir, donner congé. **to ~ praise,** louer. **to ~ thanks,** rendre grâces. **to ~ evidence,** témoigner. **to ~ pleasure,** faire plaisir, donner du plaisir à. **to ~ pain to,** faire de la peine à. **to ~ back,** rendre, restituer. **to ~ up,** renoncer à, abandonner. **to ~ way,** céder, reculer. **to ~ in,** céder.

given *adj.* donné, déterminé. **this project will have to be finished within the ~ time,** ce projet devra être terminé dans les temps donnés.

giver *n.* donneur *m.,* donneuse *f.;* donateur *m.;* donatrice *f.*

gizzard *n.* gésier *m.*

glacial *adj.* glacial.

glaciation *n.* congélation *f.;* glace *f.*

glacier *n.* glacier *m.;* amas *m.* de glace.

glad *adj.* content, heureux.

gladden *v.t.* réjouir, égayer. *v.i.* (se) réjouir, s'égayer.

glade *n.* clairiere *f.;* percée *f.;* allée *f.*

gladiator *n.* gladiateur *m.*

gladiolus *n.* glaïeul *m.*

gladly *adv.* avec plaisir, volontiers.

glamorous *adj.* séduisant.

glamour *n.* séduction *f.,* prestige *m.,* éclat *m.* ~ **boy,** *Infml.* beau mec. ~ **girl,** *Infml.* belle nana, pin-up.

glance *n.* coup d'oeil *m.,* aperçu *m.* **at the first ~,** au premier coup d'oeil. *v.i.* jeter un coup d'oeil. **to ~ at a book,** parcourir un livre des yeux.

gland *n. Anat.* glande *f.; Bot.* gland *m.*

glandular *adj.* glandulaire.

glare *n.* lumière *f.,* étincelante; regard *m.* enflammé. *v.i.* éblouir; jeter un regard furieux sur.

glaring *adj.* éblouissant, manifeste; (eyes) furieux; qui saute aux yeux, qui crève les yeux.

glass *n.* verre *m.;* glace *f.;* vitre *f.;* baromètre *m.* **cut ~,** cristal taillé. **to drink out of a ~,** boire dans un verre. **magnifying ~,** verre grossissant, loupe *f.* ~ *adj.* de verre. **a ~ bottle,** une bouteille de verre. ~ **door,** porte *f.* vitrée. ~**ware,** verrerie *f.;* verroterie *f.* ~**works,** verrerie *f.,* manufacture *f.* de verre. **wine ~,** verre à vin.

glasses *n.pl.* lunettes *f.pl.*

glassy *adj.* de verre; vitreux; vitré.

glaucoma *n.* glaucome *m.*

glaze *v.t.* vitrer; vernisser; glacer; lustrer.

glazier *n.* vitrier *m.*

gleam *n.* lueur *f.,* rayon *m.* **a ~ of hope,** une lueur d'espoir. *v.i.* luire, reluire, briller, rayonner; étinceler.

gleaming *n.* rayon *m.,* de lumière.

glean *v.t.,v.i.* glaner; recueillir.

glen *n.* vallon *m.,* vallée *f.*

glib *adj.* spécieux, glissant; coulant; délié (de la langue).

glibly *adv.* avec volubilité.

glibness *n.* spéciosité *f.,* faconde *f.*

glide *v.i.* couler (doucement), s'écouler; glisser; se glisser (with **through**). **to ~ through the waves,** fendre les eaux. *n.* glissade *f.,* glissement *m.*

glider *n.* planeur *m.;* hydroglisseur *m.*

gliding *adj.* glissant; s'écoulant doucement.

glimmer *v.i.* luire avec clarté douteuse. **the daylight begins to ~,** le jour commence à poindre. *n.* lueur *f.* faible.

glimmering *adj.* éclairant, brillant faiblement. **a ~ light,** une lueur vacillante. *n.* lueur *f.,* faible lueür f. a ~ of hope, une lueur d'espérance.

glimpse n. lumière f. faible, languissante; trait m., reflet m. de lumière, teinte f., apparence f. légère. v.i. se laisser entrevoir; jeter une lueur passagère.

glint v.i. briller, luire.

glisten v.i. briller, reluire.

glitter v.i. luire, reluire, briller, étineler. **all is not gold that ~s**, tout ce qui luit n'est pas or. n. brillant m., éclat m., splendeur f., lustre m; clinquant m.

glittering adj. scintillant, étincelant.

gloaming n. crépuscule m., mélancolie f.

gloat v.i. jubiler; regarder fixement; couver du regard, dévorer des yeux.

global adj. global.

globe n. globe m., sphère f.

globule n. globule m.

gloom, gloominess n. obscurité f.; ténèbres f.pl.; mélancolie f. ~ v.t., v.i. obscurcir; s'assombrir; attrister, rendre lugubre.

gloomily adv. obscurément, tristement.

gloomy adj. sombre, obscur; mélancolique, maussade, chagrin.

glorification n. glorification f.

glorify v.t. glorifier; célébrer, exalter, honorer.

glorious adj. glorieux; éclatant; radieux, resplendissant; magnifique.

gloriously adv. glorieusement.

glory n. gloire f., splendeur f.; vanité f.

gloss n. éclat m., lustre m.; vernis m.; commentaire m.; glossaire m.; paraphrase f. ~ v.t. lustrer; commenter; gloser; paraphraser.

glossary n. glossaire m.

glossy adj. poli, luisant.

glottis n. glotte f.

glove n. gant m. ~ **compartment**, boîte f. à gants. v.t. ganter.

glow v.i. briller; rougir; brûler; s'enflammer, s'animer. n. incandescence f.; flamme f., feu m.; éclat m.

glower v.i. lancer un méchant regard; n. regard noir.

glowing adj. éclatant; ardent, embrasé.

glucose n. glucose f.

glue n. colle f. ~ v.t. coller; attacher.

gluey adj. collant, visqueux.

glum adj. refrogné, maussade, morne.

glut v.t. avaler; gorger, rassasier; assouvir. n. excès m.; satiété f., engorgement m.

glutinous adj. glutineux.

glutton n. gourmand m.

gluttonous adj. glouton, goulu, gourmand.

gluttony n. gloutonnerie f.; gourmandise f.

glycerine n. glycérine f.

gnarled adj. noueux.

gnash v.t. grincer les dents.

gnat n. cousin m., moucheron m.

gnaw v.t. ronger; mordre.

gnome n. gnome m.

gnu n. gnou m.

go v.i. aller, marcher. to ~ **on foot**, aller à pied. to ~ **on horseback**, aller à cheval. to ~ **to England**, aller en Angleterre. to let ~, laisser aller; relâcher; lâcher prise. to ~ **about**, aller ça là, faire un détour. to ~ **abroad**, aller à l'étranger. to ~ **again**, retourner. to ~ **against**, aller contre. to ~ **along**, poursuivre son chemin. to ~ **along with**, accompagner. to ~ **astray**, s'égarer. to ~ **away**, s'en aller. to ~ **back**, se retirer, retourner. to ~ **backward**, reculer, marcher à reculons. to ~ **between**, s'interposer. to ~ **along with an explanation**, faire comme si on croit aux explications. to ~ **beyond**, aller au delà, excéder. to ~ **by**, passer; suivre, se régler sur. to ~ **down**, descendre. to ~ **for**, aller chercher, passer pour. to ~ **forward**, avancer. to ~ **in**, entrer. to ~ **in for**, concourir; s'appliquer à. to ~ **into**, entrer dans, aller entrer. to ~ **into mourning**, se mettre en deuil. to ~ **near**, approcher. to ~ **on**, avancer, continuer; se conduire. to ~ **out**, sortir; s'éteindre. to ~ **over** to, passer, traverser; déserter, parcourir; vérifier. to ~ **round**, faire le tour de; tourner. to ~ **through**, traverser; éprouver; accomplir, achever. to ~ **under**, passer sous. to ~ **up**, monter; se diriger. to ~ **upon**, monter sur; se fonder sur. to ~ **with**, accompagner. to ~ **without**, se passer de. it is no ~, cela ne prend pas.

goad n. aiguillon m. ~ v.t. aiguillonner, piquer, exciter, encourager.

goal n. but m., objectif m.; terme m.

goalie n. gardien m. de buts.

goat n. chèvre.

gobble v.t. avaler sans mâcher, engloutir.

go-between n. intermédiaire m.

goblin n. spectre m., fantome m.; lutin m.

God n. Dieu m. ~ **bless you**, Dieu vous bénisse. **thank ~**, Dieu merci, grâce à Dieu.

godchild n. filleul m., filleule f.

goddaughter n. filleule f.

goddess n. déesse f.

godfather n. parrain m.

godhead n. divinité f.

godless adj. impie.

godlike adj. divin.

godliness n. piété f.; dévotion f.

godly adj. de Dieu; pieux, dévot, religieux. adv. pieusement.

godmother n. marraine f.

godson n. filleul m.

goer n. allant m.; courer m., marcheur m.

goggle v.i. regarder de travers; faire les gros yeux. n. roulement m. d'yeux.

goggles n. lunettes f.pl. protectrices; oeillères f.pl. (for horses).

going n. action d'aller; départ m.; marche f.

gold n. or m. adj. d'or; en or. ~ **digger**, chercheur d'or. Fig. croqueuse f. de diamants. ~**fish**, poisson m. rouge, dorade f. **the ~ standard**, l'étalon-or m.

golden adj. d'or; doré, jaune.

goldsmith *n.* orfèvre *m.*

golf *n.* golf *m.*

golfer *n.* joueur *m.*, euse *f.* de golf, golfeur *m.*, euse *f.*

gone *p.p.* of go; *adj.* parti, disparu.

gong *n.* gong *m.*

gonna *v.i.* (contraction of going to) *Infml.* I'm ~ do it, j'vais le faire.

gonorrhea *n.* gonorrhée *f.*, blenmorragie *f.*

goo *n. Infml.* chose *f.* poisseuse, gluante; sentimentalité *f.*

good *adj.* bon; de bien; valide, valuable. ~ **wine**, bon vin. **to make** ~, réparer. **to be** ~ **at**, être connaisseur. ~ **for nothing**, *adj.* bon à rien. ~-**tempered**, *adj.* qui a bon caractère. ~ **Friday**, Vendredi *m.* Saint. ~**will**, bienveillance *f.*, bon vouloir *m.*

goodness *n.* bonté *f.*; obligeance *f.*; bienfait *m. Interj.* my ~! oh! mon Dieu!, bonté divine!

goods *n.pl.* marchandise.

goody *n. Excl.* chouette! ~**s**, friandises *f.pl.*

gooey *adj. Infml.* gluant.

goof *n. Infml.* gaffeur *m.*, *v.i. Infml.* faire une gaffe. **to** ~ **off**, tirer au flanc.

goofy *adj. Infml.* bêbête, niais.

goon *n. Infml.* idiot(e) *m.f.*, *Infml.* homme de main.

goose *n.pl.* geese oie *f. Fig.* personne stupide. ~ **bumps**, chair *f.* de poule.

gooseberry *n.* groseille *f.* à maquereau.

gore *n.* sang *m.*, sang caillé, coagulé; pointe *f.*; biais *m.* ~ *v.t.* encorner, transpercer; blesser de coups de cornes.

gorge *n.* gorge *f.* ~ *v.t.* gorger; assouvir; rassasier. *v.i.* (se) gorger, se bourrer.

gorgeous *adj.* magnifique; somptueux; superbe.

gorilla *n.* gorille *m.*

gorse *n. Bot.* ajoncs *m.pl.*

gory *adj.* sanglant, ensanglante.

gospel *n.* évangile *m.*

gossip *n.* (person) bavard *m.*, bavarde *f.*, commère *f.*; (talk) bavardage *m.*, commérage *m.* ~ *v.i.* bavarder, jacasser, jaser.

gossiper *n.* bavard *m.*, bavarde *f.*, commère *f.*

got See GET.

gothic *adj.* gothique. *n.* le gothique *m.*

gotta *v.t.* with *aux.* (contraction of got to) *Infml.* ~ **go**, j'dois partir.

gotten See GET.

gourd *n.* courge *f.*, calebasse *f.*, gourde *f.*

gourmet *n.* gourmet *m.*

govern *v.t.* gouverner; conduire, maîtriser.

governance *n.* gouvernement *m.*; gouverne *f.*

government *n.* gouvernement *m.*

governmental *adj.* gouvernemental.

governor *n.* gouverneur *m.*

gown *n.* robe *f.*; toge *f.* **night** ~, chemise *f.* de nuit.

grab *n.* prise *f.*, étreinte *f.* ~ **bag**, pochette surprise. *v.i.* empoigner, saisir.

grace *n.* grâce *f.*, favor *f.*; pardon *m.*; bénédicité *m.*; grâces *f.pl.* **day of** ~, temps de repentir. **days of** ~, jours de grâce. *v.t.* orner, honorer; favoriser.

graceful *adj.* gracieux, plein de grâce.

gracefully *adv.* gracieusement, avec grâce.

graces *n.* les grâces *f.pl.*

gracious *adj.* gracieux; bienveillant; miséricordieux, clément.

graciously *adv.* avec bienveillance; gracieusement.

graciousness *n.* gentillesse *f.*

grad *n.* (abbrev. of **graduate**), licencié, diplômé.

gradation *n.* gradation *f.*

grade *n.* grade *m.*, degré *m.*, rang *m.* ~ *v.t.* noter, calibrer, classer par rang, degré, catégorie.

gradient *n.* pente *f.*, rampe *f.*

gradual *adj.* progressif, graduel.

gradually *adv.* par degrés, petit à petit.

graduate *v.t.* obtenir un diplôme. *n.* diplômé *m.*, diplômée *f.*

graduation *n.* remise *f.* des diplômes, cérémonie de la remise des diplômes.

graffiti *n.pl.* graffiti *m.pl.*

graft *n.* greffe *f.* **skin** ~, greffe épidermique. (bribe) pots-de-vin *m.pl.* ~ *v.t.* greffer; obtenir par corruption.

grain *n.* grain *m.*; graine *f.*; blé *m.*, céréales *f.pl.*; fil *m.* **a** ~ **of sand**, un grain de sable. **against the** ~, contre le fil; à contre-coeur. *v.t.* grener; greneler.

gram *n.* gramme *m.*

grammar *n.* grammaire *f.* ~ **school**, école *f.* primaire.

grammarian *n.* grammairien *m.*, grammarienne *f.*

grammatical *adj.* grammatical; de grammaire.

gran *n. Infml.* grand-mère *f.*

grand *adj.* grand, sublime, grandiose. ~**child**, petit-enfant *m.* ~**daughter**, *n.* petite-fille *f.* ~**father**, *n.* grand-père *m.*, aïeul *m.* **great**~**father**, arrière grand-père, bisaïeul. ~**mother**, grand-mère *f.*, aïeule *f.* ~**son**, petit-fils *m. Infml.* mille dollars *m.pl.*, brique *f.*

grandeur *n.* grandeur *f.*, splendour *f.*, pompe *f.*, air *m.* imposant.

grandiloquence *n.* grandiloquence *f.*

grandiose *adj.* grandiose, pompeux.

granite *n.* granit *m.*

granny *n.* grand-maman *f.*, mamie *f.*

grant *v.t.* accorder, conférer; reconnaître; concéder; octroyer. **to take for granted**, prendre comme si c'est normal, présumer, regardez comme admis, accepté. *n.* subvention, bourse; concession *f.*; privilège *m.*, transmission *f.* par contrat.

granular *adj.* granuleux.

grape *n.* raisin *m.* **a bunch of** ~**s**, une grappe de raisin. ~**vine**, vigne *f.*

grapeshot *n.* mitraille *f.*

graphic *adj.* graphique; pittoresque.

graphite *n.* graphite *m.*

grapple *v.t.* saisir à bras le corps; accrocher. *v.i.* en venir aux mains. to ~ with, combattre.

grasp *v.t.* saisir, empoigner. *n.* poigne *f.*, étreinte *f.*, prise *f.*; compréhension *f.*

grasping *adj.* avaré; avide, cupide.

grass *n.* herbe *f.*, herbage *m.*; gazen *m.*; verdure *f.*, vert *m.* ~land, prairie *f.* ~ *v.t.* couvrir d'herbe. *v.i.* (se) couvrir d'herbe; herbu. the ~ is always greener on the other side (of the fence), c'est toujours mieux ailleurs.

grasshopper *n.* sauterelle *f.*, cigale *f.*

grass roots *adj.* de base. the grass-root feeling is . . . , le sentiment à la base est . . .

grassy *adj.* herbu; herbeux.

grate *n.* grille *f.*; grillage *m.*; foyer *m.* ~ *v.t.,v.i.* gratter, râper. to ~ the teeth, grincer les dents.

grateful *adj.* reconnaissant.

gratefully *adv.* avec reconnaissance.

gratefulness *n.* reconnaissance *f.*

grater *n.* râpe *f.*

gratification *n.* satisfaction *f.*, plaisir *m.*; agrément *m.*; gratification *f.*

gratify *v.t.* satisfaire, contenter; faire don à. to ~ one's pride, satisfaire son orgueil.

gratifying *adj.* agréable.

grating *adj.* rude, dur; discordant. *n.* son *m.* dur, criard; grincement *m.*; grille *f.*; grillage *m.*

gratis *adv.* gratis.

gratitude *n.* reconnaissance *f.*; gratitude *f.*

gratuitous *adj.* gratuit.

gratuitously *adv.* gratuitement.

gratuity *n.* gratification *f.*; pourboire *m.*

grave *n.* fosse *f.*; sépulcre *m.*, tombeau *m.*, tombe *f.* ~ *adj.* grave, sévère, sérieux. a ~ countenance, un air grave. ~digger, fossoyeur *m.* ~stone, pierre *f.* sépulcrale, tombe *f.* to make a ~ mistake, se tromper lourdement.

gravel *n.* gravier *m.* ~ pit, sablonnière *f.* ~ *v.t.* sabler; ensabler.

gravely *adv.* gravement.

graven *adj.* sculpté, gravé.

graving *f.* gravure *f.*; empreinte *f.*

gravitation *n.* gravitation *f.*

gravity *n.* gravité *f.*; pesanteur *f.*, poids *m.*

gravy *n.* jus *m.*; suc *m.*; sauce *f.*; jus *m.* de viande. ~ boat, saucière *f.*

gray *adj.* gris. ~ hair, cheveux gris. to turn ~, grisonner. ~-eyed, aux yeux gris. ~-haired, aux cheveux gris. *n.* gris *m.*

graze *v.t.* frôler, effleurer; raser; brouter (grass); paître; mettre au vert. *v.i.* être au vert, raser le sol.

grease *n.* graisse *f.*; crasse *f.* ~ *v.t.* graisser.

greasy *adj.* graisseux, gras; crasseux.

great *adj.* grand; important. she is a ~ artist, c'est une artiste fantastique. a ~ many, beaucoup, grand nombre.

Great Britain *n.pr.* la Grande-Bretagne.

greatly *adv.* grandement; fort, beaucoup.

greatness *n.* grandeur *f.* ~ of soul, grandeur *f.* d'ame.

Greece *n.pr.* la Grèce *f.*

greed *n.* avidité *f.*, cupidité *f.*, gloutonnerie *f.*

greedily *adv.* avidement.

greediness *n.* avidité *f.*; voracité *f.*; rapacité *f.*

greedy *adj.* avide; rapace; vorace.

Greek *adj.* grec, grecque. *n.* Grec *m.*, Grecque *f.*; le grec *m.*

green *adj.* vert; frais, récent; novice; tendre. ~-eyed, aux yeux verts. ~house, serre *f.* ~ room, foyer *m.* des acteurs. ~ pepper, poivron *m.* vert. to give the ~ light (to do a thing), donner le feu vert (pour faire une chose). ~back, billet *m.* vert. *n.* vert *m.*; pelouse *f.*; feuillage *m.*; verdure *f.* ~ *v.t.* verdir; rendre vert.

greenish *adj.* verdâtre.

Greenland *n.pr.* le Groenland *m.*

greenness *n.* verdure *f.* fraîcheur *f.*; vigueur *f.*; nouveauté *n.f.*, naïveté *f.*, inexpérience *f.*

greet *v.i.* saluer, complimenter; rencontrer.

greeting *n.* salut *m.*, salutations *f.pl.*

gregarious *adj.* grégaire.

grenade *n.* grenade *f.*

grenadier *n.* grenadier *m.*

grenadine *n.* grenadine *f.*

greyhound *n.* lévrier *m.*

grid *n.* grille *f.*, grillage *m.*

grief *n.* chagrin *m.*, tristesse *f.*, peine *f.*

grievance *n.* grief *m.*; injustice *f.*, dommage *m.*, tort *m.*, abus *m.*

grieve *v.t.* chagriner; affliger. *v.i.* (se) chagriner, s'affliger.

grievous *adj.* grave, accablant; affligeant, cruel.

grievously *adv.* avec douleur, grièvement. to be ~ sick, être grièvement malade.

griffin *n.* griffon *m.*

grille *n.* gril *n.*; griller.

grim *adj.* sinistre, macabre, menaçant, refrogné, rechigné.

grimace *n.* grimace *f.* ~ *v.i.* faire les grimaces.

grime *n.* barbouillage *m.*, saleté *f.*, crasse *f.*

grimness *n.* férocité *f.*, sévérité *f.*

grimy *adj.* sale; crasseux.

grin *v.t.* ricaner, grimacer. *v.i.* montrer les dents, grimacer. *n.* large, sourire *m.*, grimace *f.* qui découvre les dents.

grind *v.t.* moudre; broyer, écraser, aiguiser, meuler. to ~ one's teeth, grincer des dents. *n.* labeur *m.* monotone.

grinder *n.* broyeuse *f.*

grinding *n.* pulvérisation *f.*; broiement *m.*

grindstone *n.* meule *f.*

grinning *adj.* grinçant; montrant les dents. large sourire *m.*, grimace *n.*

grip *n.* étreinte *f.*, empoignement *m.*

gripe *n.* ronchonnerie *f.*, rouspétance *f.* gripes, colique *f.* ~ *v.i.* ronchonner, rouspéter.

grisly *adj.* farouche, terrifiant, effroyable.

grist *n.* blé *m.* à moudre. *Fig.* profit *m.*, gain *m.*

it's all ~ to the mill, cela fait venir l'eau au moulin.

gristle n. Anat. cartilage m.

grit n. sable m., gravier m. ~s, gruau m. de maïs.

groan v.i. gémir; Infml. geindre; grogner. n. gémissement m. soupir m.; grognement m.

grocer n. épicier m., épicière f.

grocery n. épicerie f.; pl. groceries, épicerie f. provisions, f.pl.

grog n. grog m.

groggy adj. chancelant, mal fichu.

groin n. aine f. Arch. arête f.

groom n. futur marié m. v.t. faire sa toilette.

groove n. rainure f., coulisse f. ~ v.t. entailler; canneler; sillonner.

grope v.i. tâter; aller à tâtons. to ~ about, aller à tâtons. to ~ one's way out, sortir à tâtons.

gross adj. gros; grossier; épais, lourd; rude; obscène. a ~ injustice, une grande injustice. the ~ sum, la somme totale. the ~ weight, le poids brut. ~ national product (G.N.P.), produit national brut.

grossly adv. grossièrement; lourdement.

grossness n. grosseur f.; énormité f.; grossièreté f.

grotesque adj. grotesque.

grotto n. grotte f.

grouch n. Infml. rouspéteur m., rouspéteuse f.

ground n. sol m., terrain m., terre f., fondement m.; sujet m.; raison f.; fond m. rising ~, bateur f., colline f. building ~, terrain m. à bâtir. to fall to the ~, tomber par terre. to gain ~, gagner du terrain. to lose ~, perdre du terrain, reculer. I cultivate my own ~, je cultive mes propres terres. it is not without ~s, ce n'est pas sans fondement, sans cause. to keep in the back~, tenir dans l'ombre. the back~ is too dark, le fond est trop noir. v.t. mettre à terre; asseoir; fonder, baser; punir. he was ~ed for a month, il a été puni pendant un mois. v.i. échouer, toucher le fond. adj. broyé, moulu; repassé; dépoli. ~ coffee, du café moulu. ~ floor, rez-de-chaussée m. ~work, fondement m., fondation f., base f.; principe m.

groundless adj. sans fondement; mal fondé, dénué de fondement.

grounds n.pl. dépôt m., sédiment m., lie f. coffee ~, mare de café.

group n. groupe m. v.t. grouper. to form into ~s, (se) grouper.

grouse n. coq m. de bruyère. v.i. rouspéter.

grout n. mortier m. liquide. v.t. couler (le ciment).

grove n. bosquet m., bocage m.

grovel v.i. se vautrer, ramper à terre.

grow v.i. croître, grandir; pousser, venir; s'accroître, s'augmenter. to ~ angry, se fâcher. to ~ better, s'améliorer, devenir meilleur. to ~ cold, se refroidir. it's ~ing late, il se fait tard. to ~ pale, pâlir. to ~ poor, devenir pauvre. to ~ again, repousser, reprendre racine; redevenir.

to ~ into a habit, devenir une habitude. to ~ up, croître, grandir. Agr. cultiver.

grower n. cultivateur m., cultivatrice f., producteur m., productrice f.

growing adj. croissant; grandissant.

growl v.i. gronder, grogner. v.t. exprimer en grondant, en grognant. n. grondement m.

grown adj. grandi, fait. a ~ man, un adulte m.

growth n. croissance f., pousse f., crue f., venue f., accroissement m., agrandissement m.

grub v.i. creuser, piocher; fouiller. to ~ on, végéter. n. puceron m.; ver m.; Infml. nourriture f.

grudge n. animosité f., rancune f., aversion f. he has a ~ against her, il lui en veut.

grudging adj. envieux; jaloux. n. envie f., jalousie f., malaise m.

grudgingly adv. à contrecœur, à regret, en murmurant.

gruel n. gruau m.

grueling adj. épuisant, éreintant.

gruesome adj. lugubre, terrifiant, macabre.

gruff adj. refrogné, rechigné, morose; bourru.

grumble v.i. grommeler; gronder, grogner; bougonner.

grumbling adj. grondant, bougonnant. n. grondement m., grognement m.

grumpy adj. grognon, morose.

grunt v.i. grogner. n. grognement m.

guarantee n. garantie f.; caution f.; garant m. to become ~ for, se porter caution pour. v.t. garantir.

guarantor n. garant(e) m.f.

guaranty n. garantie f., caution f.

guard v.t. garder; protéger; prémunir. v.i. se tenir sur ses gardes, se garder de. n. garde m.f., défense f.; sauvegarde f.; chef m. to be on ~, être de garde. to be on one's ~, être se tenir sur ses gardes.

guarded adj. protégé, circonspect, réservé.

guardedly adv. avec précaution; prudemment.

guardian n. gardien m., gardienne f., tuteur m., tutrice f. adj. tutélaire, gardien. ~ angel, ange m. gardien.

guardianship n. garde f.; tutelle f.; curatelle f.

guava n. goyave f., goyavier m.

gue(r)rilla n. guérillero m.

guess v.t.,v.i. conjecturer; deviner. n. conjecture f. ~work, simple conjecture. to make a ~ at, former une conjecture sur.

guest n. hôte m., invité m., invitée f., pensionnaire m.f., client m., cliente f.

guffaw n. gros rire m. ~ v.i. éclater de rire, pouffer aux éclats.

guidance n. direction f., conduite f. for your ~, pour votre gouverne.

guide v.t. guider; diriger; conduire. n. guide m. ~book, n. guide m. ~ dog, chien m. d'aveugle. ~post, ~lines, n.pl. indication f., instruction f., sommaire. n. poteau m. indicateur.

guild n. corporation f.; corps m. de métier.

guile *n.* ruse *f.*, artifice *m.*, tromperie *f.*, imposture *f.*, fraude *f.*

guileful *adj.* rusé, artificieux; insidieux, subtil, fourbe; perfide.

guileless *adj.* sincère; ingénu, naïf, sans artifice.

guillotine *n.* guillotine *f.* ~ *v.t.* guillotiner.

guilt *n.* culpabilité *f.*

guiltiness *n.* culpabilité *f.*, criminalité *f.*

guilty *adj.* coupable.

Guinea *n.pr.* Guinée *f.* ~ **fowl**, ~ **hen**, pintade *f.* ~ **pig**, cochon *m.* d'Inde, cobaye *m.*; *Fig.* cobaye *m.* **they used them as** ~ **pigs**, ils se sont servis d'eux comme cobayes.

guise *n.* guise *f.*, extérieur *m.*; apparence *f.*, prétexte *m.*

guitar *n.* guitare *f.*

guitarist *n.* guitariste *m.f.*

gulch *n.* ravin *m.*

gulf *n.* gulfe *m.*; gouffre *m.*, abîme *m.*

gull *v.t.* duper, tremper; flouer. *n.* mouette *f.*

gullet *n.* gosier *m.*, oesophage *m.*

gullibility *n.* crédulité *f.*

gullible *adj.* crédule.

gulp *v.t.* gober, avaler. *n.* gorgée *f.*, goulée *f.*

gum *n.* gencive *f.*, gomme *f.* ~ **tree**, acacia *m.*, gominier *m.* **chewing** ~, chewing gum. *v.t.* gommer.

gummy *adj.* gommeux; visqueux.

gun *n.* pistolet *m.*, revolver *m.*, arme *f.* à feu; fusil *m.*, carabine *f.*; *pl.* ~**s**, artillerie *f.* ~**powder**, poudre *f.* ~**shot**, portée *f.* de fusil, coup *m.* de feu. *v.t.* **to** ~ **down**, descendre, abattre, tuer. **he was held at** ~**point**, il était sous la menace du revolver. ~**man**, voleur *m.* à main armée.

gurgle *n.* glouglou *m.* ~ *v.i.* faire glouglou; *Infml.* glouglouter; murmurer.

gush *v.i.* jaillir; couler abondamment; ruisseler.

to ~ **out**, bouillonner. *n.* jaillissement *m.*, écoulement *m.* soudain; effusion *f.*; jet *m.*

gushing *n.* jaillissement *m.*; bouillonnement *m.*

gust *n.* rafale *f.*, coup *m.* de vent, bourrasque *f.*

gustation *n.* gustation *f.*

gusto *n.* enthousiasme *m.*

gusty *adj.* orageux, venteux.

gut *n.* intestin *m.*, boyau *m.*; *Infml.* estomac *m.*, ventre *m.* *Infml.* **he doesn't have the** ~**s to do it**, il n'a pas assez de cran pour le faire. *Infml.* **she hates his** ~**s**, elle ne peut pas le sentir, le blairer. *v.t.* éventrer; vider.

gutsy *adj.* *Infml.* qui a du cran, qui n'a pas froid aux yeux.

gutter *n.* gouttière *f.*; conduit *m.*, chenal *m.*; ruisseau *m.* (de rue). ~**spout**, gargouille *f.* ~ **tile**, tuile creuse. *v.t.* sillonner, canneler. *v.i.* être sillonné, creusé, cannelé.

guttural *adj. n.* gutturale *f.*

guy *n.* *Infml.* type *m.*; *Mar.* retenue *f.*, corde *f.* de retenue.

guzzle *v.i.* boire beaucoup; *Infml.* pomper, lamper.

gym *n.* gymnase *m.*; gym *f.*; gymnastique *f.*

gymnasium *n.* gymnase *m.*

gymnast *n.* gymnaste *m.f.*

gymnastic *adj.* gymnastique *f.*

gymnastics *n.* gymnastique *f.*

gynecological *adj.* gynécologique.

gynecologist *n.* gynécologue *m.f.*

gynecology *n.* gynécologie *f.*

gyp *v.t.* *Infml.* de faire avoir. **he** ~**ed me of ten bucks**, je me suis fait avoir de dix tunes.

gypsy *n.* gitan *m.*

gyrate *v.i.* tournoyer. *adj.* qui s'enroule, qui s'entortille, décrivant un cercle.

gyration *n.* giration *f.*

gyratory *adj.* giratoire.

H

H *n.* H, h *f.* ~**-bomb**, bombe H.

ha *interj.* ha!

habit *n.* habitude *f.*; coutume *f.*; moeurs *f.pl*, costume *m.*, habit *m.*

habitable *adj.* habitable.

habitat *n.* habitat *m.*

habitation *n.* habitation *f.*, demeure *f.*, domicile *m.*

habitual *adj.* habituel; ordinaire.

habitually *adv.* habituellement.

habitutate *v.t.* habituer. **to** ~ **oneself**, s'accoutumer.

habitude *n.* habitude *f.*; coutume *f.*, usage *m.*

hack *v.t.* hacher, mutiler, tuer, massacrer; écorcher (a language). *n.* entaille *f.*, coche *f.*, taxi *m.*, chauffeur *m.* de taxi.

hacking *adj.* **a** ~ **cough**, une toux sèche et pénible.

had See HAVE.

haddock *n.* églefin *m.*, haddock *m.*, merluche *f.*

hag *n.* vielle, sorcière *f.*; furie *f.*, mégère *f.*

haggard *adj.* hagard.

haggle *v.i.* chicaner, marchander.

hail *n.* grêle *f.*; salut *m.*; appel *m.* ~**stone**, grêlon *m.* ~**storm**, grêle *f.*, tempête *f.* de grêle. *v.t.* grêler. *v.t.* faire tomber dru comme grêle. *interj.* salut! bonjour!

hair *n.* cheveux *m.pl.*, poil *m.*, chevelure *f.*; soies *f.pl.*; crin *m.* **beautiful** ~, de beaux cheveux. **to split** ~**s**, fendre un cheveu en quatre. **to make one's** ~ **stand on end**, à faire dresser ses cheveux sur la tête. ~**brush**, brosse *f.* à cheveux. ~**dresser**, coiffeur *m.*, coiffeuse *f.* ~**pin**, épingle *f.* à cheveux.

hairy *adj.* velu, poilu.

hake *n.* merluche *f.*, colin *m.*

hale *adj.* sain; fort, robuste, vigoureux. ~ **and hearty**, vigoureux et bien portant. *v.t.* tirer, traîner, entraîner; hâler.

half *n.pl.* **halves** moitié *f.*, demi *m.*, demie *f.* **a pound and a** ~, une livre et demie. *adj.* demi. ~ **a dozen**, une demi-douzaine. *adv.* à demi, à moitié. **~ dead**, à moitié mort. **~ awake**, à moitié éveillé. **~ brother**, demi-frère *m.* **~ measure**, demi-mesure *f.* **~ moon**, demi-lune *f.* **~ sister**, demi-soeur *f.* **~way**, *adv.* à mi-chemin.

halibut *n.* flétan *m.*

halitosis *n.* mauvaise haleine *f.*

hall *n.* entrée *f.;* hall *m.;* vestibule *m.*, couloir *m.* **town ~**, hôtel *m.* de ville. **~mark**, poinçon *m.* **~way**, couloir *m.*, vestibule *m.*

hallelujah *n.* alléluia *m.*

Hallowe'en *n.* veille *f.* de la Toussaint, Halloween *f.*

hallucinate *v.t.* halluciner.

hallucination *n.* hallucination *f.*

halo *n.* halo *m.*, auréole *f.*

halogen *n.* halogène *m.*

halt *v.i.* s'arrêter; faire halte; hésiter; *n.* halte *f.*, repos *m.*

halve *v.t.* diviser en deux.

ham *n.* jambon *m.* **smoked ~**, jambon *m.* fumé.

hamburger *n.* steak *m.* hâché.

hamlet *n.* hameau *m.*

hammer *n.* marteau *m;* masse *f.* – *v.t.,v.i.* forger, marteler. **to ~ away at**, travailler d'arrache-pied à, piocher à.

hammering *n.* martelage *m.;* martèlement *m.*

hammock *n.* hamac *m.*

hamper *n.* manne *f.;* panier *m.;* coffre *m.* à linge. *v.t.* embarrasser, gêner; entraver.

hamster *n. Zool.* hamster *m.*

hand *n.* main *f.;* écriture *f.;* signature *f.;* jeu *m.* (of cards); aiguille *f.* (of watch, etc.); bras *m.* (workers). **the right ~**, la main droite; *Fig.* le bras droit. **to give a ~**, donner un coup de main; applaudir. **to lay ~s on**, mettre la main sur. **to shake ~s**, serrer la main. **to wash one's ~s of a thing**, s'en lever les mains. **to get the upper ~**, l'emporter, avoir l'avantage. **by ~**, à la main. **from ~ to mouth**, au jour le jour. **off~**, haut la main; couramment. **to be ~ and glove together**, être deux têtes sous un bonnet, être comme cul et chemise. **~bag**, sac *m.* à main. **~made**, fait main, fabriqué à la main. **~writing**, écriture *f.* **~ to ~**, corps à corps, de près. **in ~**, en main, en train. **short~**, stenographie *f.* **~** *v.t.* donner (avec la main); passer; transmettre. **to ~ down**, descendre; passer (de haut en bas). **to ~ out**, aider à sortir. **to ~ over**, remettre. **to ~ up**, monter; aider à monter. **~ed**, appartenant à, se rapportant à la main. **~basket**, panier *m.* à anse, manne *f.* **~book**, manuel *m.* **~rail**, garde-fou *m.;* rampe *m.*

handcuff *n.* menottes *f.pl.* **~** *v.t.* mettre les menottes à.

handed *adj.* palmé; aux mains. **right-~**, doitier. **left-~**, gaucher. **empty-~**, les mains vides.

handful *n.* poignée *f.;* brassée *f.;* petit nombre, peu.

handicap *n.* handicap *m.*

handicraft *n.* travail *m.* manuel, métier *m.*

handily *adv.* habilement; commodément.

handiness *n.* dextérité *f.*, adresse *f.;* commodité *f.*

handiwork *n.* ouvrage *m.* manuel; main-d'oeuvre *f.*

handkerchief *n.* mouchoir *m.*

handle *v.t.* manier, toucher; diriger; traiter, pratiquer. *n.* manche *m.;* poignée *f.;* anse *f.;* brimbale *f.;* manivelle *f.;* bras *m.;* queue *f.* **the ~ of a fork, of a knife, of a spoon**, le manche d'une fourchette, d'un couteau, d'une cuillère. **~bars**, guidon *m.* (of a bicycle).

handling *n.* maniement *m.*

handsome *adj.* beau, belle. **a ~ fortune**, une belle fortune. **he is a ~ man**, c'est un bel homme.

handsomely *adv.* gracieusement, élégamment; avec convenance; délicatement.

handy *adj.* de mains adroit, habile, sous la main; commode.

handyman *n.* bricoleur *m.*

hang *v.i.* pendre; suspendre; pencher; baisser; poser, tapisser, accrocher. **to ~ a picture**, accrocher un tableau. **to ~ down**, pencher, incliner. **to ~ out**, suspendre au dehors; déployer, traîner, fréquenter. *v.i.* être pendu; suspendu; pendiller, incliner. **to ~ about**, s'accrocher à, se tenir autour de; roder. **to ~ back**, rester en arrière; reculer. **to ~ loose**, pendiller. **to ~ over**, être suspendu à, menacer; surplomber. **to ~ together**, être étroitement unis; s'accorder. **~ out**, *n.* endroit *m.* où l'on traîne, un repère. *v.i.* traîner, se balader, aller de-ci de-là. **~ on!** ne quittez pas! *v.i.* s'accrocher en attente de.

hangar *n.* hangar *m.*

hanger *n.* portemanteau *m.*, cintre *m.* **pot ~**, crémaillère *f.*

hanging *n.* pendaison *f.;* tenture *f.*, tapisserie *f.*

hangover *n.* gueule *f.* de bois.

hanker *v.i.* (with **after**) désirer; soupirer après.

hankie, hanky *n. Infml.* mouchoir *m.*

happen *v.i.* arriver par hasard; se passer; rencontrer. **it sometimes ~s that**, il arrive quelquefois que. **he ~ed to come**, il est venu par hasard.

happening *n.* événement *m.*

happily *adv.* heureusement.

happiness *n.* bonheur *m.*

happy *adj.* heureux.

harangue *n.* harangue *f.* **~** *v.i., v.t.* haranguer.

harass *v.t.* harasser; harceler.

harassment *n.* tourment *m.;* harassement *m.*

harbor *n.* port *m.;* havre *m.*, port *m.* de mer; asile *m.*, abri *m.*, refuge *m.* – *v.t.,v.i.* abriter; accueillir; recéler; entretenir.

hard *adj.* dur; difficile, rude, cruel. **~ times**, des temps difficiles. **a ~ winter**, un rude hiver, un hiver rigoreux. *adv.* fort; avec force, ferme, durement. **strike ~**, frappez fort. **to be ~ on**, être dur pour. **to be ~ at it**, travailler ferme.

harden *v.t.* durcir; endurcir; affermir; tremper. *v.i.* (se) durcir, s'endurcir.

hardening *n.* durcissement *m.;* endurcissement *m.*

hardhearted *adj.* au coeur dur, impitoyable; insensible.

hardiness *n.* hardiesse *f.,* courage *m.,* résolution *f.;* vigueur *f.;* effronterie *f.*

hardly *adv.* à peine, presque pas; rigoureusement; durement.

hardness *n.* dureté *f.;* rigueur *f.;* difficulté *f.;* avarice *f.*

hardship *n.* épreuves *f.pl.,* peine *f.;* souffrance *f.;* malheur *m.*

hardware *n.* quincaillerie *f.* (computers) matériel *m.*

hardware store *n.* quincaillerie *f.* (magasin).

hardy *adj.* hardi, intrépide, téméraire; robuste.

hare *n.* lièvre *m.* **a young ~,** un levraut. **~lip,** bec *m.* de lièvre.

harebrained *adj.* écervelé.

harem *n.* harem *m.*

haricot *n.* haricot *m.*

hark *v.i.* écouter, prêter une oreille. *interj.* écoutez!

harm *n.* tort *m.,* dommage *m.,* préjudice *m.,* mal *m.* **to do ~,** faire du mal, nuire à. *v.t.* faire du mal à, faire tort à.

harmful *adj.* nuisible, malfaisant.

harmless *adj.* innocent; inoffensif.

harmonic *adj.* harmonique.

harmonica *n.* harmonica *m.*

harmonics *n.* harmonie *f.*

harmonious *adj.* harmonieux.

harmoniously *adv.* harmonieusement.

harmonize *v.i.* s'harmoniser; s'accorder. *v.t.* harmoniser.

harmony *n.* harmonie *f.;* consonnance *f.;* accord *m.* musical.

harness *n.* harnais *m.;* harnachement *m.* ~ *v.t.* harnacher, équiper.

harp *n.* harpe *f.* ~ *v.i.* jouer, pincer de la harpe; *Fig.* rabâcher; rebattre.

harpist *n.* harpiste *m.*

harpoon *n.* harpon *m.*

harpsichord *n.* clavecin *m.*

harpy *n.* harpie *f.*

harrier *n.* levrier *m.;* busard *m.,* soubuse *f.*

harrowing *n. adj.* torturant; déchirant.

harry *v.t.* harasser, harceler sans cesse.

harsh *adj.* dur, rude, âpre; bourru, revêche, morose; rigoureux, sévère. **a ~ word,** une parole blessante.

harshly *adv.* rudement, avec âpreté; durement.

harshness *n.* rudesse *f.,* âpreté *f.;* dureté *f.* de manières.

hart *n.* cerf *m.*

harvest *n.* moisson *f.,* récolte *f.* **to gather in, to get in the ~,** faire la récolte. *v.t.* moissonner; faire la moisson, la récolte.

has See HAVE.

hash *v.t.* hacher. *n.* hachis *m.,* émincé *m.;* *Fig.* gâchis *m. Infml.* hashish *m.*

hashish *n.* hashish *m.*

hassle *n. Infml.* emmerde *f.,* enquiquinement *m.;* *v.t.* casser les pieds, enquiquiner.

haste *n.* hâte *f.;* diligence *f.;* rapidité *f.*

haste, hasten *v.t.* hâter, presser. *v.i.* (se) hâter, (se) presser, s'empresser, (se) dépêcher.

hastily *adv.* en hâte, à la hâte; précipitamment.

hastiness *n.* hâte *f.;* précipitation *f.;* irritabilité *f.;* emportement *m.*

hasty *adj.* prompt, précipté; vif, emporté, hâtif.

hat *n.* chapeau *m.* **~s off!** chapeaux bas!

hatch *v.t.,v.i.* faire éclore; se préparer. *n.* éclosion *f.,* (of boat) ecoutille *f.;* porte coupée.

hatchet *n.* hatchette *f.;* cognet *m.*

hatchway *n.* écoutille *f.*

hate *v.t.* haïr; détester. *n.* haine *f.,* aversion *f.*

hateful *adj.* odieux; détestable; haineux.

hatefully *adv.* abominablement; détestablement.

hatred *n.* haine *f.,* aversion *f.*

haughtily *adv.* fièrement, avec arrogance.

haughtiness *n.* hauteur *f.,* arrogance *f.*

haughty *adj.* fier, hautain.

haul *v.t.* tirer, traîner; remorquer; haler. **to ~ down,** amener. *n.* traction *f.;* tiraillement *m.;* coup *m.* de filet.

haunt *v.t.* hanter; fréquenter, visiter, importuner. *v.i.* venir souvent, rôder autour de. *n.* lieu *m.* fréquenté, retraite *f.;* repaire *m.*

have *v.t.* avoir; posséder, tenir, saisir; être; recevoir; prendre; utiliser; tolérer, supporter. **~ your hair cut,** faites-vous couper les cheveux. **to ~ about one,** avoir sur soi. **to ~ visitors,** avoir des invités. **to ~ the flu,** avoir la grippe. **to ~ to do a thing,** avoir à faire, devoir faire une chose.

haven *n.* havre *m.,* port *m.;* abri *m.;* asile *m.*

haversack *n.* sac *m.* à dos, sac de camping.

having *n.* avoir *m.,* possession *f.;* biens *m.pl.* **it's worth the ~,** cela en vaut la peine.

havoc *n.* dégâts *m.pl.,* ravages *m.pl.,* pillage *m.* ~ *v.t.* ravager, piller, dévaster.

hawk *n.* faucon *m.,* épervier *m.* ~ *v.t.,v.i.* crier, offrir en vente (in the street); colporter.

hawthorn *n.* aubépine *f.*

hay *n.* foin *m.* **to make ~ when the sun shines,** battre le fer pendant qu'il est chaud. **~stack,** meule *f.* de foin. **~fever,** fièvre *f.* des foins. **~loft,** fenil *m.,* grenier *m.* à foin.

hazard *n.* hasard *m.,* risque *m.,* chance *f.* ~ *v.t.* hasarder; risquer. **to ~ one's life,** risquer sa vie. *v.i.* se risquer, s'aventurer.

hazardous *adj.* hasardeux.

haze *n.* brume *f.,* vapeur *f.* ~ *v.i.* embrumer.

hazel *n.* coudrier *m.,* noisetier *m.* ~ *adj.* brun-clair, de noisette, couleur *f.* noisette.

hazelnut *n.* noisette *f.*

haziness *n.* état *m.* brumeux; vague *m.*

hazy *adj.* brumeux.

he *pers. m.* il, lui; ce; le; celui, celui-la; mâle *m.* **~ is a lawyer,** ~ est avocat.

head *n.* tête *f.;* sujet *m.,* titre *m.,* rubrique *f.* **the**

two ~s of a cask, les deux fonds d'un tonneau. **they have set a price on his ~**, on a mis sa tête à prix. **at 3 francs a ~**, à 3 francs par tête. **he has a good ~**, il a une bonne tête. **you have hit the nail on the ~**, vous y êtes, vous avez deviné juste. **~ over heels**, par dessus la tête. **~s or tails**, à pile ou face. **to have neither ~ nor tail**, n'a voir ni queue ni tête. **~ache**, mal *m.* de tête. **~band**, bandeau *m.* **~ clerk**, premier commis *m;* chef *m.*, sous-chef. **~ cook**, chef *m.* **~dress**, coiffure *f.* **~master**, principal. **~ office**, bureau *m.* principal; direction *f.* **~quarters**, quartier *m.* général. **~stone**, pierre *f.* tombale. **~ waters**, sources *f.pl.* **~way**, sillage *m.* **~ work**, travail *m.* de tête. **~wind**, vent *m.* debout. *v.t.* diriger, conduire; venir de l'avant. *v.i.* prendre une tête.

headed *adj.* à tête. **clear-~**, qui voit clair. **thick-~**, à grosse tête, stupide.

heading *n.* titre *m.*, en-tête *m.;* fond *m.*

headless *adj.* sans tête.

headline *n.* gros titre *m.* **they made the ~s**, ils ont fait la une.

headlong *adj.* en précipice. *adv.* à corps perdu, étourdiment. **to run ~ into**, courir à sa perte.

headphone *n.* écouteur *m.*

headstrong *adj.* têtu, obstiné, opiniâtre; entêté.

heady *adj.* emporté, impétueux; capiteux (of wine, perfume, etc.).

heal *v.t.* guérir; faire cicatriser; concilier. *v.i.* (se) guérir, (se) cicatriser.

healer *n.* guérisseur *m.*, guérisseuse *f.*

healing *adj.* curatif, salutaire. *n.* guérison *f.*, cicatrisation *f.*

health *n.* santé *f.;* toast *m.* **public ~**, santé *f.* publique. **let's drink to his ~**, buvons à sa santé. **how is your ~?** comment va la santé? **~ food store**, magasin *m.* de produits diététique.

healthful *adj.* sain; salubre; salutaire.

healthily *adv.* de manière saine.

healthy *adj.* sain; en bonne santé; salutaire, salubre.

heap *n.* tas *m.*, amas *m.*, foule *f.* ~ *v.t.* entasser, amonceler; amasser. **to ~ up**, entasser.

hear *v.t.,v.i.* entendre; apprendre, écouter, exaucer. **my prayer was ~d**, ma prière a été exaucée. **I don't believe all you ~**, ne croyez pas tout ce que vous entendez dire. **I've ~d from him**, j'ai de ses nouvelles. **~ me out**, écoutez-moi. **I've ~d about her**, j'ai entendu parler d'elle. **he won't ~ of it**, il ne veut pas en entendre parler.

hearing *n.* ouïe *f.*, audition *f.;* audience *f.* **to be within ~**, être à portée de la voix.

hearsay *n.* ouï-dire *m.;* rumeur *f.* **~ evidence**, déposition *f.* sur la foi d'autrui.

hearse *n.* corbillard *m.*

heart *n.* coeur *m.;* courage *m.;* affection *f.;* milieu *m.*, center *m.* **to take ~**, prendre courage. **to take to ~**, prendre à coeur. **to learn by ~**,

apprendre par coeur. **~ache**, chagrin *m.* **~ attack**, crise *f.* cardiaque. **~break**, chagrin *m.* cuisant, crèvecoeur *m.* **~broken**, navré. **~burn**, brûlures *f.pl.* d'estomac. **~ disease**, maladie *f.* du coeur. **~rending**, déchirant, accablant de douleur. **~sick**, découragé, écoeuré.

heartbeat *n.* battement *m.* de coeur.

hearted *adj.* de coeur. **hard~**, au coeur dur. **light~**, au coeur léger.

heartfelt *adj.* profondément, senti.

hearth *n.* âtre *m.*, foyer *m.*

heartily *adv.* du coeur, de bon coeur, cordialement.

heartiness *n.* cordialité *f.*, empressement *m.*

heartless *adv.* sans coeur, sans pitié.

heartlessly *adj.* sans coeur, lâchement.

hearty *adj.* cordial, sincère; chaud; bien portant; vigoureux, fort (d'appetit). **~ welcome**, accueil *m.* cordial.

heat *n.* chaleur *f.;* ardeur *f.;* colère *f.;* fureur *f.;* épreuve *f.* (of horse races). **in the ~ of the fight**, au fort de la mêlée. *v.t.* chauffer, enflammer, animer. *v.i.* s'echauffer, devenir chaud.

heated *adj.* chaud, chauffé; animé, excité.

heater *n.* radiateur *m.;* appareil *m.* de chauffage.

heath *n.* bruyère *f.;* lande *f.*

heathen *n.* païen *m.*, païenne *f.*

heathenish *adj.* païen.

heathenism *n.* paganisme *m.;* grossièreté *f.*, barbarie *f.*, ignorance *f.*

heather *n.* bruyère *f.*

heating *adj.* échauffant; calorifique. **~ apparatus**, appareil *m.* de chauffage.

heave *v.t.* lever, élever, soulever; pousser; virer; hisser. **to ~ a sigh**, pousser un soupir. *v.i.* se gonfler, se dilater; haleter, palpiter. *n.* soulèvement *m.;* palpitation *f.*

heaven *n.* ciel *m.* (*pl.* cieux), paradis *m.*

heavenly *adj.* céleste; divin; bienheureux. *adv.* d'une manière céleste.

heavily *adv.* lourdement, pesamment; avec tristesse.

heaviness *n.* pesanteur *f.*, lourdeur *f.;* mélancolie *f.* découragement *m.*

heaving *n.* soulèvement *m.*, gonflement *m.;* palpitation *f.*

heavy *adj.* lourd, pesant, massif; abattu; grave; oppressif; gros.

heavyweight *n.* poids *m.* lourd.

hebraic *adj.* hébraïque, hébreu.

Hebrew *n.* Hebreu *m.* *adj.* hébraïque, israélite, juif.

hecatomb *n.* hécatombe *f.*

heck *interj.* flûte!, zut! **eh, what the ~!** hé, pourquoi pas, après tout!

heckle *v.t.* interrompre, harceler.

hectic *adj.* mouvementé, bousculé. **they went through quite a ~ time**, ils/elles sont passé(e)s par des temps assez mouvementés.

hector *v.t.* braver, malmener; tourmenter.

hedge *n.* haie *f.* ~ *v.t.* entourer (au moyen d'une

haie). *v.i.* se cacher, se mettre à l'abri s'esquiver. **~hog,** hérisson *m.*

heed *v.t.* faire attention à, observer, remarquer. ~ garde *f.,* attention *f.;* soin *m.* **take ~ of what you say,** faites attention à ce que vous dites.

heedful *adj.* attentif, prudent, circonspect.

heedless *adj.* inattentif, distrait, imprudent.

heedlessly *adv.* sans attention, inconsidérément.

heedlessness *n.* inattention *f.;* étourderie *f.*

heel *n.* talon *m.* **to take to one's ~,** *n.* prendre ses jambes à son cou. *v.i.* incliner, donner à la bande.

heft *n.* poids *m.* ~ *v.t.* soulever, peser.

hefty *adj. Infml.* costaud.

heifer *n.* génisse *f.*

height *n.* hauteur *f.,* élévation *f.,* haut *m.;* comble *m.,* faite *m.,* grandeur *f.,* taille. **the tower is one hundred feet in ~,** la tour a cent pieds de haut. **he is about my ~,** il est à peu près de ma taille. **the ~s of Meudon,** les hauteurs de Meudon.

heighten *v.t.* relever, rehausser; augmenter.

heightening *n.* rehaussement *m.;* augmentation *f.*

heinous *adj.* haïssable, détestable; odieux.

heinously *adv.* odieusement, atrocement.

heinousness *n.* atrocité *f.,* énormité *f.*

heir *n.* héritier *m.*

heiress *n.* héritière *f.*

heirloom *n.* objet *m.* précieux de famille.

held See HOLD.

helicopter *n.* hélicoptère *m.*

heliport *n.* héliport *m.*

hell *n.* enfer *m.* **~fire,** le feu *m.* de l'enfer. *Infml.* **get the ~ out of here!** fous-moi le camp! **what the ~ is going on here?** qu'est qui se passe ici? **the ~ with you,** va te faire voir.

hellish *adj.* infernal, diabolique, d'enfer.

hello *interj.* salut, bonjour.

helm *n.* gouvernail *m.,* barre *f.* du gouvernail.

helmet *n.* casque *m.*

help *v.t.* aider; assister, venir en aide; servir. **to ~ one another,** s'aider l'un l'autre, s'entr'aider. **I can't ~ it,** je n'y peux rien. **I can't ~ saying,** je ne peux m'empêcher de dire. *v.i.* contribuer. **every little bit ~s,** tout sert si peu que ce suit. *n.* aide *f.,* secours *m.,* remède *m.;* ressource *f.* **there is no ~ for it,** il n'y a rien à y faire.

helper *n.* aide *m.,* auxiliaire *m.*

helpful *adj.* utile; salutaire, salubre.

helping *adj.* secourable.

helpless *adj.* sans ressources, désemparé.

helplessly *adv.* sans ressource, irrémédiablement.

helplessness *n.* délaissement *m.,* abandon *m.;* manque *m.* de force; faiblesse *f.*

helter skelter *adv.* pêle-mêle; a la débandade.

hem *n.* bord *m.,* bordure *f.,* ourlet *m.* ~ *v.t.* bor-der; ourlir. **to ~ in,** enfermer, cerner, envelopper.

hemisphere *n.* hémisphère *m.*

hemoglobin *n.* hémoglobine *f.*

hemorrhage *n.* hémorragie *f.*

hemorrhoids *n.* hémorroïdes *f.pl.*

hemp *n.* chanvre *m.;* hashish *m.*

hen *n.* poule *f.* **~house,** poulailler *m.* **~-roost,** juchoir *m.*

hence *adv.* d'ici; hors d'ici. **ten years ~,** dans dix ans d'ici. **~ his anger,** de la sa colère.

henceforth *adv.* dorénavant, désormais.

hepatitis *n.* hépatite *f.*

her *pron.pers.* la, lui, à elle. *adj. fem. poss.* son, sa, ses, d'elle.

herald *n.* héraut *m.* avantcoureur *m.;* messager *m.* ~ *v.t.* annoncer, proclamer.

herb *n.* herbe *f.* **pot ~s,** herbes potagères.

herbaceous *adj.* herbacé.

herbage *n.* herbage *m.;* droit *m.;* d'herbage.

herbal *n.* herbier *m.* ~ *adj.* d'herbes, aux herbes.

herbalist *n.* botaniste *m.f.;* herboriste *m.f.*

herbivorous *adj.* herbivore.

herd *n.* troupeau *m.;* troupe *f.,* foule *f.;* cohue *f.;* pâtre *m.* ~ *v.i.* s'unir; vivre ensemble, garder, surveiller.

herdsman *n.* berger *m.,* pâtre *m.*

here *adv.* ici. **~ is, are,** voici. **~ I am,** me voici. **~ and there,** par ci, par la, ça et là. *interj.* présent! ici!.

hereabouts *adv.* par ici, près d'ici.

hereafter *adv.* désormais, dorénavant, à l'avenir.

hereby *adv.* par ceci; par ce moyen.

hereditary *adj.* héréditaire.

heredity *n.* hérédité *f.*

herein *adv.* en ceci, sur ce point.

hereof *adv.* de ceci, de cela.

heresy *n.* hérésie *f.*

heretic *n.* hérétique *m.*

hereupon *adv.* là-dessus, sur ces entrefaites.

herewith *adv.* avec cela, par cela.

heritage *n.* héritage *m.*

hermetic *adj.* hermétique.

hermetically *adv.* hermétiquement.

hermit *n.* ermite *m.*

hermitage *n.* ermitage *m.*

hernia *n.* hernie *f.*

hero *n.* héros *m.*

heroic *adj.* héroïque.

heroically *adv.* héroïquement.

heroin *n.* (drug) héroïne *f.*

heroine *n.* héroïne *f.*

heroism *n.* héroïsme *m.*

heron *n.* héron *m.*

herpes *n.* herpès *f.*

herring *n.* hareng *m.* **red ~s,** harengs saurs. **~ boat,** harenguier *m.*

hers *pers. pron.* à elle, d'elle; le sien, la sienne, les siens, les siennes. **the house is ~,** la maison est à elle.

herself *pers. pron.* elle-même, se, elle. **she will do it all by ~,** elle fera tout par elle-même, toute seule.

hesitate *v.i.* hésiter.

hesitating *adj.* hésitant.

hesitation *n.* hésitation *f.*

heterogeneous *adj.* hétérogène.

heterosexual *adj.*, *n.* hétérosexuel(le) *m.f.*

hew *v.t.* tailler, couper.

hexagon *n.* hexagone *m.*

hexagonal *adj.* hexagonal.

hey *interj.* eh bien!

heyday *n.m.* les beaux jours de la vie.

hi *interj.*, *Infml.* salut!

hiatus *n.* fente *f.*, breche *f. Gram.* hiatus *m.*, lacune *f.*

hibernate *v.i.* hiverner.

hibernation *n.* hibernation *f.*

hiccup *n.* hocquet *m. v.i.* avoir le hocquet.

hickory *n. Bot.* hickory *m.*, noyer *m.* d'Amerique.

hid See HIDE.

hide *v.t.* cacher, tenir secret. *v.i.* (se) cacher; se tenir caché. **~ and seek,** cache-cache *m. n.* cuir (leather) *m.*; peau *f.*

hideous *adj.* hideux; horrible, effrayant.

hideously *adv.* hideusement.

hideousness *n.* hideur *f.*; horreur *f.*

hiding *n.* cachotterie *f.* **~ place,** lieu *m.* de retraite, cachette *f.*

hierarchy *n.* hiérarchie *f.*

hieroglyphic, hieroglyphical *adj.* hiéroglyphique.

hi-fi *n.* chaîne *f.* hi-fi; haute fidélité *f.*

high *adj.* haut; élevé, grand; sublime; fier, arrogant; cher; prétentieux. **a ~ mountain,** une haute montagne. **~ price,** prix *m.* élevé. **a ~ wind,** un grand vent. **the ~ altar,** le maître-autel. **~way,** autoroute *f.* **~ living,** grand train de vie. **~ tide,** haute mer, pleine mer; marée haute. *adv.* haut, en haut. **to aim too ~,** viser trop haut. **to carry it ~,** le porter haut, être fier. **~-heeled shoes,** chaussures *f.pl.* à haut talons. **~light,** *v.t.* marquer, mettre en lumière, souligner. **~ seas,** la haute mer, l'ocean. **~ on cocaine,** défoncé à la cocaïne.

highly *adv.* grandement, hautement; très.

highmost *adj.* le plus élevé; suprême.

hijack *v.t.* détourner.

hijacker *n.* pirate *m.* de l'air.

hijacking *n.* détournement *m.*

hike *n.* randonnée *f.*, excursion *f.* **~** *v.i.* faire une excursion, randonnée.

hiker *n..* excursionniste *m.f.*

hilarious *adj.* hilare. *Infml.* tordant, marrant.

hill *n.* hauteur *f.*, colline *f.*, côte *f.*, coteau *m.* **over ~ and dale, up ~ and down dale,** par monte et par vaux.

hillock *n.* colline *f.*, hauteur *f.*, tertre *m.*, élévation *f.*

him *pron. pers. m. object* of **he,** le; lui, à lui; celui, celui-là.

himself *pron.* lui-même; se soi. **he thinks only of ~,** il ne pense qu'à lui. **by ~,** de lui-même; tout seul.

hind *n.* kiche *f. adj.* de derrière, postérieur, arrière.

hinder *v.t.* empêcher; retarder; détourner; gêner. **what ~s you from going?** qui vous empêche d'y aller?

hindrance *n.* empêchement *m.*; entrave *f.*

Hindu *n.* hindou *m.*

hindsight *n.* rétrospective *f.*, sagesse *f.* rétrospective.

hinge *n.* gond *m.*, charnière *f.*; pivot *m.* **to be off the ~s,** être hors des gonds. *v.t.* mettre des gonds à; plier, fléchir. *v.i.* dépendre de; tourner sur.

hint *v.t.* suggérer, insinuer, donner à entendre. *v.i.* (with at), faire entrevoir. *n.* allusion *f.*; insinuation *f.*, demi-mot *m.* **give me a ~,** donne-moi une indication. **he can't take a ~,** il n'y a rien à faire, il ne peut pas comprendre.

hip *n.* hanche *f.*; *adj.* coole.

hippie *adj.*, *n.* hippie *m.f.*

hippo *Infml.* hippopotame *m.*

hippodrome *n.* hippodrome *m.*

hippopotamus *n.* hippopotame *m.*

hire *v.t.* louer. **to ~ out,** louer; donner en location, embaucher, engager.

hirsute *adj.* velu, poilu; hérissé.

his *poss. pron.* de lui; à lui; le sien, la sienne, les siens, les siennes. *poss. adj.* son, sa, ses.

Hispanic *adj.* hispanique, latino.

hiss *v.i. v.t.* siffler. *n.* sifflement *m.*; sifflet *m.*

historian *n.* historien *m.*, historienne *f.*

historic, historical *adj.* historique.

historically *adv.* historiquement.

history *n.* histoire *f.*; historique *m.*

hit *v.t.*, *v.i.* frapper; heurter; taper; atteindre, toucher; tomber sur. **to ~ the mark,** atteindre le but, frapper juste. **to ~ home,** toucher juste, porter coup. **to ~ off,** saisir. **they really ~ it off,** ils sont comme de vieux amis. *n.* coup *m.*, heurt *m.*, choc *m.*; chance *f.*, hasard *m.* **~ record,** tube *m.* **~ movie,** spectacle *m.* à succès. **~ list,** liste *f.* de victimes à assassiner liste noire. **~man,** tuer, *m.* à gages.

hitch *v.t.* sautiller, se nouer, s'accrocher. *v.t.* lever, soulever; accrocher; amarrer. **to ~ a ride,** faire du stop. *n.* embarras *m.*, anicroche *f.*, arrêt *m.*; noeud *m.*

hitchhike *v.i.* faire du stop.

hi-tech *adj.* de haute technologie. *n.* technologie *f.* de pointe.

hive *n.* ruche *f.*; essaim *m.*

hoard *n.* amas *m.*; trésor *m.*, caché. *v.t.*, *v.i.* amasser, entasser. **to ~ money,** amasser de l'argent, faire un magot.

hoarse *adj.* enroué, rauque.

hoarsely *adv.* d'une voix enrouée, rauque.

hoarseness *n.* enrouement *m.*, raucité *f.*

hoary *adj.* blanc *m.*, blanche *f.*; blanchi par l'âge.

hoax *n.* canular *m.*, mystification *f.* **~** *v.t.* attraper, mystifier. **that was a ~,** *Infml.* c'était un attrape couillon, on s'est bien fait avoir.

hobble *v.i.* clocher, boîter, clopiner, aller clopin-clopant. *n.* clochement *m.;* embarras *m.*

hobby *n.* passe-temps *m.* hobby *m.*

hobo *n.* clochard *m.*

hockey *n.* hockey *m.*

hocus-pocus *n.* tour *m.* de passe-passe.

hog *n.* cochon *m.,* porc *m.,* pourceau *m.* ~ *v.t.* prendre plus que sa part de.

hoist *v.t.* lever, hausser; hisser, guinder; arborer. *n.* guindant *m.;* chèvre *f.,* grue *f.*

hold *v.t.* tenir, retenir, contenir; occuper; regarder comme; estimer; célébrer. **to ~ a job,** tenir un emploi. **to ~ in contempt,** avoir du mépris pour. **to ~ one's course,** poursuivre sa marche. **to ~ back,** retenir; se tenir en arrière. **to ~ fast,** tenir bon. **to ~ in,** retenir. **to ~ off,** éloigner. **to ~ on,** continuer, tenir bon. **to ~ out,** offrir; tenir ferme; continuer. *v.i.* persister, se maintenir, se soutenir; s'arrêter; s'empêcher. **~ it!** arrêtez. **to ~ against,** tenir contre, résister à. **to ~ back from,** se tenir écarté de, s'éloigner de. **to ~ on,** tenir bon; continuer. **~ on!** tiens ferme! **to ~ together,** tenir ensemble; être, rester unis. *n.* prise *f.;* soutien *m.;* appui *m.;* cale *f.* (de naivre). **to have ~ of,** avoir prise sur. **to lay ~ on,** mettre la main sur, saisir. **to keep ~ of,** tenir bon, ne pas lâcher prise.

holder *n.* titulaire *m.f.;* possesseur *m.;* détenteur *m.;* porteur *m.*

holdings *n. pl.; Fin.* portefeuille *m.,* capitaux *m.pl.*

hole *n.* trou *m.;* échappatoire *f.,* subterfuge *m.* **full of ~s,** tout troué. *v.t.* trouer.

holiday *n.* jour *m.* férié, jour de fête; jour de congé. *adj.* de fête.

holiness *n.* sainteté *f.*

Holland *n.pr.* la Hollande, Pays Bas.

hollow *adj.* creux, vide; sourd. *n.* creux *m.;* excavation *f.* ~ *v.t.* creuser; évider.

holly *n. Bot.* houx *m.*

holocaust *n.* holocauste *m.*

holy *adj.* saint; sacré, bénit. **~ Writ,** la Sainte Écriture.

hommage *n.* hommage *m.* **to pay ~,** rendre hommage.

home *n.* logis *m.,* maison *f.,* chez soi *m.,* intérieur *m.,* domicile *m.,* asile *m.,* retraite *f.* **at ~,** chez soi, à la maison. **to be quite at ~ with,** être à son aise; être dans son élément. **our last ~,** notre dernière demeure. *adj.* domestique, de chez soi; intérieur. *adv.* chez soi, en famille; dans son pays. **to come ~,** rentrez chez soi. **to strike ~,** frapper juste. **~made,** fait à la maison, fabrication maison. **~sick,** *adj.* qui a le mal du pays. **~sickness,** *n.* mal *m.* du pays, nostalgie *f.*

homeless *adj.* sans domicile, sans abri. *n.* **the ~,** les sans-logis *m.pl.,* les sans-abri *m.pl.*

homeopathic *adj.* homéopathique.

homeopathy *n.* homéopathie *f.*

homework *n.* devoirs *m.pl.*

homey *adj.* intime.

homicidal *adj.* homicide.

homicide *n.* homicide *m.*

homo *adj., n. Infml.* homo *m.,* pédé *m.*

homogeneous *adj.* homogène.

homologous *adj.* homologue.

homonym *n.* homonyme.

homosexual *adj., n.* homosexuel(le) *m.* (*f.*).

homosexuality *n.* homosexualité *f.*

hone *n.* pierre *f.* à rasoir. *v.t.* aiguiser sur une pierre à rasoir.

honest *adj.* honnête, probe, loyal; intègre. **~ dealings,** procédés *m.pl.* loyaux. **~ to God!** *Infml.* parole *f.* d'honneur, juré, craché.

honestly *adv.* honnêtement.

honesty *n.* honnêteté *f.,* intégrité *f.,* probité *f.,* loyauté *f.,* bonne foi *f.*

honey *n.* miel *m.* **~bee,** abeille *f.,* mouche *f.* à miel. **~comb,** rayon *m.,* gâteau *m.* de miel. **~dew,** manne *f.* **~moon,** lune *f.* de miel. *v.t.* édulcorer avec du miel; flatter.

honor *n.* honneur *m.,* estime *f.;* dignité *f.* ~ *v.t.* honorer; révérer, glorifier, faire honneur à.

honorable *adj.* honorable.

honorably *adv.* honorablement.

honorary *adj.* honoraire.

honorific *adj.* honorifique.

hood *n.* capuchon *m.;* capuche *f.;* gangster ~ *v.t.* encapuchonner.

hoodlum *n.* voyou *m.*

hooey *n. Infml.* foutaise *f.pl.,* salades *f.pl.*

hoof *n.* sabot *m.* ~ *v.t.* marcher.

hoo-ha *n. Infml.* boucan *m.,* raffut *m.*

hook *n.* croc *m.,* crochet *m.,* crampon *m.;* gaffe *f.;* agrafe *f.; v.t.* cramponner, agrafer.

hooker *n.* prostituée *f.*

hooligan *n.* voyou *m.*

hoop *n.* corceau *m.,* cercle *m.,* anneau *m.*

hooray *interj.* hourra!

hoot *v.i., v.t.* hululer; crier, hauer, siffler. *n.* huée *f.*

hop *v.i.* sauter sur un pied; à cloche-pied; sautiller. *n.* saut *m.,* sautillement *m.;* gambade *f.; Bot.* houblon *m.*

hope *n.* espoir *m.,* espérance *f.* ~ *v.i.* espérer. *v.t.* souhaiter.

hopeful *adj.* de grande espérance, qui promet beaucoup, plein d'espoir.

hopefully *adv.* avec le ferme espoir.

hopeless *adj.* sans espoir, désespéré.

hopelessly *adv.* sans espoir.

hopelessness *n.* désespoir *m.*

horde *n.* horde *f.*

horizon *n.* horizon *m.*

horizontal *adj.* horizontal.

horizontally *adv.* horizontalement.

hormone *n.* hormone *f.* **~ replacement therapy,** hormonothérapie *f.*

horn *n.* corne *f., Mus.* cor *m.,* cornet *m.;* bois *m.;* antenne *f.* (of an insect); tentacule *f.* **to draw in one's horns,** rentrer ses cornes, modérer ses pretentions.

hornet n. frelon m.; guêpe f.

horny adj. de corne; dor, calleux. *Infml.* (sex) excité, lasaif.

horoscope n. horoscope m.

horrendous adj. horrible, terrible, effroyable.

horrible adj. horrible.

horribly adv. horriblement.

horrid adj. horrible, affreux. **a ~ crime,** un crime atroce.

horridly adv. horriblement; affreusement.

horrific adj. horrible.

horrified adj. rendu horrible; frappé d'horreur.

horrify v.t. épouvanter.

horror n. horreur f. **~ stricken, ~ struck,** saisi, frappé d'horreur.

hors-d'oeuvre n. hors-d'oeuvre m. *inv.*

horse n. cheval m.; cavalerie f. **saddle ~,** cheval de selle. **chestnut ~,** cheval alezan. **~ race,** course f. aux chevaux. **~shoe,** fer m. à cheval. **~whip,** cravache f.

horseback n. à cheval. **to ride on ~,** monter à cheval.

horseman n. cavalier m.

horsemanship n. équitation f.

horsewoman n. écuyère f.

hortensia n. hortensia m.

horticulture n. horticulture f.

hose n. bas m.pl.; tuyau m.

hosiery n. bonneterie f.; bas m.pl.

hospitable adj. hospitalier.

hospitably adv. avec hospitalité.

hospital n. hôpital m.

hospitality n. hospitalité f.

host n. hôte m.; foule f., multitude f.; hostie f. **~** v.t.,v.i. recevoir, héberger; amuser.

hostage n. otage m.

hostel n. **youth ~,** auberge f. de jeunesse.

hostess n. hôtesse f.

hostile adj. hostile.

hostility n. hostilité f.

hot adj. chaud; brûlant; ardent, bouillant; épicé; violent. **how ~ it is!** comme il fait chaud! **to be ~,** avoir chaud. **he has some ~ (stolen) stuff,** *Infml.* il a eut des trucs volés.

hot-headed adj. qui a la tête chaude; emporté.

hotel n. hôtel m.

hothouse n. serre f. chaude.

hotly adv. avec chaleur, chaleureusement, chaudement.

hound n. chien m. courant, chien m. de chasse. **a pack of ~s,** une meute de chiens. v.t. chasser au chien courant, pousser.

hour n. heure f.; moment m.; temps m. **an ~ and a half,** une heure et demie. **half an ~,** une demi-heure. **within an ~,** en une heure. **~glass,** n. sablier m. **~ hand,** aiguille f. des heures.

hourly adj. fréquent, continuel. adv. à toute heure, à tout moment, fréquemment.

house n. maison f.; résidence f., demeure f.; famille f.; salle f. (de théâtre). **country ~,** maison de compagne. **~breaking,** vol m. avec

effraction. **~keeper, keeping,** femme f. de ménage.

~warming, pendaison f. de crémaillère. v.t. abriter, mettre à couvert; héberger; (faire) rentrer. v.i. se mettre à l'abri, (se) loger; demeurer.

household n. maison f., ménage m.; famille f. adj. de ménage, domestique. **~ furniture,** mobilier m., meubles m.pl.

housemaid n. servante f., femme de chambre.

housewife n. mère f. de famille, femme au foyer.

housing n. logement m.

hovel n. bicoque f., cabané f.; trou m.

hover v.i. voltiger; papillonner; rôder; planer sur.

how adv. comment; combien, comme; que; quel, quelle. **~ do you do?** comment allez-vous? **~ much is it?** ça coûte combien? **~ come?** pourquoi? **~ is it that?** comment se fait-il que? **~ old is he?** quel âge a-t-il? **~ well he looks!** comme il a bonne mine!

howdy interj. salut!

however adv. de quelque manière que, cependant, pourtant; quelque; **~ unhappy he might be,** quelque malheureux qu'il puisse être.

howl v.i. hurler; gémir; rugir. n. hurlement m.

howling adj. qui hurle, lugubre, morne. n. hurlement m.

hub n. moyeu m. (de roue); pivot m.

hubbub n. tumulte m.; vacarme m.

huckleberry n. myrtille f., airelle f.

huckster n. revendeur m., colporteur m.

huddle v.t. se blottir, se réunir, entasser. **to ~ together,** se presser, se serrer. n. foule f., tohubohu m.; confusion f., désordre m.

hue n. couleur f., teinte f., nuance f.; teinture f.; clameur f., cri m.

huff n. accès m. de colère; boutade f. **~** v.t. gonfler, souffler. v.i. s'enfler, (se) gonfler.

hug v.t. embrasser, serrer dans ses bras. **he ~ged me,** il m'a serré dans ses bras. **to ~ the land,** serrer la terre. n. étreinte f.

huge adj. énorme; immense, vaste.

hugely adv. énormément.

huh interj. eh! hein?

hulk n. corps m., carcasse f. (of a boat), mastodonte m., malabar m.

hull n. cosse f., gousse f., coque f., carcasse f. de naivre. v.t. écaler, écosser, éplucher.

hullabaloo n. vacarme m., tintamarre m.

hum v.i. fredonner; bourdonner; ronfler. v.t. chantonner, murmurer. n. bourdonnement m.; fredonnement m. interj. hem! hum!

human adj. humain; n. humain, être m. humain. **~kind,** genre m. humain.

humane adj. humain; plein d'humanite.

humanely adv. humainement.

humanist n. humaniste f.; philosophe m.

humanity n. humanité f.

humanize v.t. humaniser.

humanly adv. humainement.

humble adj. humble; modeste. v.t. humilier.

humblebee n. bourdon m.

humbleness n. humilité f., modestie f.

humbly adv. humblement.

humbug n. blague f., baliverne f.; blagueur m.

humdrum adj. monotone, banal; n., monotonie f., banalité f.

humerus humérus m.

humid adj. humide.

humidity n. humidité f.

humiliate v.t. humilier.

humiliating adj. humiliant.

humiliation n. humiliation f.

humility n. humilité f.

humming adj. bourdonnant. n. bourdonnement m., murmure m.

hummock n. tertre m., monticule m.

humor n. humeur f.; humour m.; gaieté f.; caprice m.; esprit m. she has such a good sense of ~, elle a un bon sens de l'humour. v.t. plaire à, complaire à; flatter; avoir de l'indulgence pour; gâter.

humorist n. humoriste m.

humoristic adj. en humoristie.

humorous adj. humoristique; plaisant.

humorously adv. plaisamment, comiquement; capricieusement.

humorousness n. humour m.; bizarrerie f., caprice m.

humorsome adj. maussade, chagrin; bizarre, humoristique.

hump n. bosse f.

humpback n. bossu m.

hunch n. bosse f., protubérance f.; gros morceau m. to have a ~, avoir un pressentiment. v.t. rendre bossu; coudoyer.

hunchback n. bossu m., bossue f.

hundred adj. cent. n. cent m.

hundredfold n. centuple m.

hundredth adj. centième.

Hungarian adj. hongrois. n. Hongrois m., Hongroise f.

Hungary n.pr. Hongrie f.

hunger n. faim f. ~ strike, grève f. de la faim. v.i. avoir faim.

hungrily adv. avidement, avec faim.

hungry adj. affamé, qui a faim.

hunky-dory adj. Infml. au poil. it's not all ~, tout ne va pas comme sur des roulettes.

hunt v.t. chasser, poursuivre, courir. to ~ down, forcer (une bête). to ~ out, dépister, découvrir. to ~ for, chercher; courir après. v.i. aller en chasse! n. chasse f.; poursuite f.; meute f.

hunter n. chasseur m.; cheval m. de chasse; montre f. de chasse.

hunting n. chasse f., poursuite f., recherche f. ~ lodge, pavillon m. ~ horn, cor m. de chasse. ~ dog, chien m. de chasse.

huntress n. chasseusse f.; chasseresse f.

huntsman n. chasseur m.; veneur m.

hurdle n. claie f., obstacle m.

hurl v.t., v.i. lancer, jeter avec force, précipiter.

hurly-burly n. brouhaha m., confusion f.

hurrah interj. hourra! bravo!

hurricane n. ouragan m.

hurried adj. précipité, pressé. a ~ note, un billet écrit à la hâte.

hurriedly adv. avec précipitation.

hurry v.t. hâter, presser; précipiter; faire dépêcher. to ~ away, faire partir à la hâte, bien vite. to ~ back, faire revenir en hâte. to ~ off, faire partir à la hâte. v.i. se hâter, se presser. n. précipitation f., hâte f.; désordre m.; tumulte m. in a great ~, en toute hâte. to be in a ~, être pressé, se presser. ~ up! dépêche-toi, dépêche-vous!

hurt v.t. blesser, faire mal, du mal à; offenser; nuire; léser. n. mal m.; blossure f.; tort m., douleur f.

hurtful adj. nuisible, pernicieux; malfaisant, douloureux.

hurtle v.i. se heurter, s'entrechoquer, se coudoyer. v.t. agiter violemment.

husband n. mari m., époux m. ~ v.t. ménager, épargner, économiser.

husbandry n. agriculture f., élevage (animal).

hush adj. silencieux, muet. v.t. faire taire; calmer, tranquiliser. to ~ up, étouffer, assoupir. v.i. se taire, garder le silence. interj. chut! silence!

husk n. gousse f., cosse f. ~ v.t. vanner; écosser; éplucher.

husky adj. sec, rauque; costaud; n. chien m. esquimau.

hussy n. coquine f., friponne f.

hustle v.t. pousser, bousculer. v.i. se pousser, se bousculer, arnaquer.

hustler n. Infml. débrouillard m.; arnaqueur m.

hut n. hutte f., cabane f., bicoque f.

hutch n. huche f., coffre m. à pain. rabbit ~, clapier m., cabane f.

hyacinth n. hyacinthe f., jacinthe f.

hybrid n. hybride n. ~ adj. hybride.

hydrant n. prise f. d'eau. fire ~, bouche f. d'incendie.

hydrate n. hydrate m. ~ v.t. hydrater.

hydraulic adj. hydraulique.

hydraulics n. hydraulique f.

hydrodynamic adj. hydrodynamique.

hydrodynamics n. hydrodynamique f.

hydrogen n, adj. ~-bomb, bombe f. à hydrogène, hydrogène m.

hydrogenate v.t. hydrogéner.

hydroplane n. hydroplane m., hydroglisseur m.; Aviat. hydroavion m.

hyena n. hyène f.

hygiene n. hygiène f.

hygienic adj. hygiénique.

hymen n. hymen m.

hymn n. hymne m., hymne f. ~ book, livre m. de cantiques.

hymnal n. livre m. de cantiques, des hymnes m.

hyperbola n. hyperbole f.

hyperbole n. hyperbole f.

hyperbolic adj. hyperblique.

hyperbolically adv. hyperboliquement.

hypercritical adj. qui exagère la critique; très exact.

hypertrophy *n.* hypertrophie *f.*
hyphen *n.* trait *m.* d'union.
hypnosis *n.* hypnose *f.*
hypnotic *adj., n.* hypnotique *m.*
hypnotist *n.* hypnotiseur *m.*
hypnotize *v.t.* hypnotiser.
hypochondria *n.* hypocondrie *f.*
hypochondriac *adj.* hypocondriaque.
hypochondriacal *adj.* hypocondriaque.
hypocrisy *n.* hypocrisie *f.*
hypocrite *n.* hypocrite *m.*
hypocritical *adj.* hypocrite.
hypocritically *adv.* hypocritement.

hypodermic *adj.* hypodermique.
hypotenuse *n.* hypoténuse *f.*
hypothermia *n.* hypothermie *f.*
hypothesis *n.* hypothèse *f.*
hypothetical *adj.* hypothétique.
hypothetically *adv.* hypothétiquement.
hysterectomy *n.* hystérectomie *f.*
hysteria *n.* hystérie *f.*
hysterical *adj.* hysterique. **he became ~,** il a
  eut une crise de nerfs.
hysterically *adv.* d'une manière
  hystérique.
hysterics *n.* hystérie *f.,* attaque *f.* de nerfs.

I

I *n.* I, i *m. pron.pers.* je, moi. **it is I,** c'est moi.
  ~ am going, je m'en vais.
ice *n.* glace *f.* **to break the ~,** rompre la glace.
  v.t. glacer, congeler. **~ cube,** glaçon. **~boat,**
  bateau *m.* briseglace. **~bound,** pris dans les
  glaces. **~ cream,** glace *f.* **~house,** glacière *f.*
iceberg *n.* banc *m.* de glace, banquise *f.*
iced *adj.* glacé; frappé.
Iceland *n.pr.* Islande *f.*
Icelander *n.* Islandais *m.*
Icelandic *adj.* islandais.
icicle *n.* glaçon *m.*
icing *n.* glaçage *m.,* givrage *m.*
iconoclast *n.* iconoclaste *m.f.*
iconography *n.* iconographie *f.*
icy *adj.* glacé, froid, glacial.
I.D. *n.,* **I.D. card,** (carte) d'identité *f.*
idea *n.* idée *f.* **to entertain an ~,** concevoir une
  idée.
ideal *adj., n.* idéal *m.*
idealism *n.* idéalisme *m.*
idealist *n.* idéaliste *m.f.*
idealize *v.t.* idéaliser.
ideally *adv.* idéalement.
identical *adj.* identique, le même.
identically *adv.* identiquement.
identification *n.* identification *f.*
identify *v.t.* identifier; reconnaître l'identité de;
  s'identifier avec, s'assimiler à.
identity *n.* identité *f.*
ideological *adj.* idéologique.
ideologist *n.* idéologue *m.f.*
ideology *n.* idéologie *f.*
idiocy *n.* idiotie *f.,* idiotisme *m.*
idiom *n.* locution *f.,* expression *f.* idiomatique.
idiomatic *adj.* idiomatique.
idiot *n.* idiot *m.,* idiote *f.*
idiotic *adj.* idiot, inepte.
idle *adj.* oisif, paresseux, désoeuvré; indolent,
  fainéant. **~ habits,** des habitudes *f.* de paresse.
  ~ hours, heures *f.* de loisir. **~ words,** des
  paroles *f.* en l'air. *v.i.* ne rien faire, fainéanter.
  to ~ away time, perdre son temps.
idleness *n.* oisiveté *f.,* désoeuvrement *m.;* paresse *f.,* fainéantise *f.;* inutilité *f.*

idler *n.* paresseux *m.,* paresseuse *f.*
idly *adv.* oisivement.
idol *n.* idole *f.*
idolater *n.* adorateur *m.,* adoratrice *f.*
idolatress *n.* adoratrice *f.*
idolatory *n.* idolâtrie *f.*
idolize *v.t.* idolâtrer.
idyl *n.* idylle *f.*
idyllic *adj.* idyllique.
if *conj.* si; pourvu que; supposé que. **~ not,**
  sinon; si ce n'est. **~ so,** si oui.
igloo *n.* igloo *m.*
ignite *v.t.* mettre en feu. *v.i.* prendre feu; s'enflammer.
ignition *n.* allumage *m.,* ignition *f.* **~ key,** clef *f.*
  de contact.
ignoble *adj.* ignoble.
ignobly *adv.* ignoblement.
ignominious *adj.* ignominieux.
ignominy *adj.* ignominie *f.;* infamie *f.*
ignoramus *n.* ignare *m.f.*
ignorance *n.* ignorance *f.* **out of ~,** par
  ignorance.
ignorant *adj.* ignorant.
ignorantly *adv.* avec ignorance.
ignore *v.t.* ignorer, mépriser.
iguana *n.* iguane *m.*
ill *adj.* malade; mauvais, méchant. *n.* mal *m.* *adv.*
  mal, peu, guère. **~ tempered,** de mauvais
  caractère; morose. **~ timed,** inopportun, intempestif; déplacé. **~ will,** mauvais vouloir *m.;* malveillance *f.*
illegal *adj.* illégal.
illegality *n.* illégalité *f.*
illegally *adv.* illégalement.
illegible *adj.* illisible.
illegibly *adv.* illisiblement.
illegitimacy *n.* illégitimité *f.*
illegitimate *adj.* illégitime; illégal.
illegitimately *adv.* illégitimement.
illicit *adj.* illicite.
illicitly *adv.* illicitement.
illimitable *adj.* illimitable.
illimitably *adv.* d'une manière illimitable; sans
  limites.

illimited *adj.* illimité.

illiteracy *n.* analphabétisme *m.*

illiterate *adj., n.* analphabète *m.f.,* illettré *m.,* illettrée *f.*

illness *n.* maladie *f.;* mal *m.;* indisposition *f.*

illogical *adj.* illogique.

illogically *adv.* illogiquement.

illuminate *v.t.* illuminer; éclairer. *n.* illuminé *m.*

illuminating *adj.* éclairant, lumineux.

illumination *n.* illumination *f.,* éclat *m.,* splendeur *f.*

illusion *n.* illusion *f.*

illusive *adj.* illusoire.

illusory *adj.* illusoire.

illustrate *v.t.* illustrer; démontrer, éclairer.

illustration *n.* illustration *f.;* image *f.,* comparaison *f.*

illustrative *adj.* qui explique, explicatif; qui rend illustre.

illustratively *adv.* par manière d'explication.

illustrious *adj.* illustre.

illustriously *adv.* d'une manière illustre.

I'm contraction of I am, je suis, j'ai. I'm cold, j'ai froid.

image *n.* image *f.,* ressemblance *f.* ~ *v.t.* figurer, représenter; s'imaginer.

imagery *n.* images *f.pl.;* imagination *f.,* apparence *f.;* chimère *f.*

imaginable *adj.* imaginable.

imaginary *adj.* imaginaire.

imagination *n.* imagination *f.;* pensée *f.;* invention *f.;* machination *f.*

imaginative *adj.* imaginatif.

imagine *v.t.,v.i.* imaginer; s'imaginer.

imbalance *n.* déséquilibre *m.*

imbecile *adj.* imbécile; impuissant. *n.* imbécile *m.f.*

imbecility *n.* débilité *f.;* imbécilité *f.*

imbed *v.t.* fixer, sceller, encastrer.

imbibe *v.t.* imbiber; absorber, boire.

imbroglio *n.* imbroglio *m.*

imbue *v.t.* inculquer.

imitable *adj.* imitable.

imitate *v.t.* imiter; contrefaire.

imitation *n.* imitation *f.;* pastiche *m.*

imitative *adj.* imitatif.

imitator *n.* imitateur *m.,* imitatrice *f.*

immaculate *adj.* immaculé.

immanent *adj.* immanent.

immaterial *adj.* immatériel; sans importance; indifferent.

immature *adj.* qui n'est pas mûr; précoce, qui manque de maturité.

immaturity *n.* immaturité *f.*

immeasurable *adj.* immesurable, incommensurable.

immeasurably *adv.* sans mesure.

immediate *adj.* immédiat; urgent.

immediately *adv.* immédiatement; tout de suite.

immemorable *adj.* immémorable.

immemorial *adj.* immémorial.

immense *adj.* immense.

immensely *adv.* immensément.

immensity *n.* immensité *f.*

immensurable *adj.* incommensurable

immerge *v.t.* inmerger. *v.i.* s'immerger.

immerse *v.t.* immerger; plonger; accabler.

immersible *adj.* capable d'être immergé.

immersion *n.* immersion *f.*

immigrant *n.* immigrant *m.,* immigrante *f.*

immigrate *v.t.* immigrer.

immigration *n.* immigration *f.*

imminence *n.* imminence *f.*

imminent *adj.* imminent.

imminently *adv.* imminemment.

immobile *adj.* immobile.

immobility *n.* immobilité *f.*

immoderate *adj.* immodéré.

immoderately *adv.* immodérément.

immoderation *n.* immodération *f.*

immodest *adj.* impudique.

immodestly *adv.* impudiquement.

immodesty *n.* immodestie *f.*

immolate *v.t.* immoler.

immolation *n.* immolation *f.;* sacrifice *m.*

immoral *adj.* immoral.

immorality *n.* immoralité *f.*

immorally *adv.* immoralement.

immortal *adj., n.* immortel *m.*

immorality *n.* immoralité *f.*

immortalize *v.t.* immortaliser. *v.i.* s'immortaliser.

immovable *adj.* immobile; immuable, inalterable.

immune *adj.* immunisé; vacciné.

immunity *n.* immunité *f.*

immunization *n.* immunisation *f.*

immure *v.t.* murer, emprisonner.

immutability *n.* immutabilité *f.*

immutable *adj.* immuable.

immutably *adv.* immuablement.

imp *n.* petit drôle *m.;* lutin *m.*

impact *n.* impact *m.,* contact *m.;* empreinte *f.;* choc *m.* ~ *v.t.* enfoncer, presser.

impair *v.t.* dégrader gâter, affaiblir, ruiner.

impairment *n.* dommage *m.,* détérioration *f.,* avarie *f.*

impalpable *adj.* impalpable.

impart *v.t.* accorder, conférer; commniquer.

impartial *adj.* impartial.

impartiality *n.* impartialité *f.*

impartially *adv.* impartialement.

impassable *adj.* impraticable.

impassible *adj.* impassible.

impassive *adj.* impassible, insensible.

impassivity *n.* impassibilité *f.* insensibilité *f.*

impatience *n.* impatience *f.*

impatient *adj.* impatient.

impatiently *adv.* impatiemment.

impeach *v.t.* mettre en accusation; accuser, attaquer.

impeachment n. mise f. en accusation; accusation f.

impeccable adj. impeccable.

impecuniosity n. manque m. d'argent.

impede v.t. empêcher, retarder.

impediment n. empêchement m., obstacle m.; embarras m.

impel v.t. pousser; forcer.

impending adj. imminent, menaçant.

impenetrability n. impénétrabilité f.

impenetrable adj. impénétrable.

impenitence n. impénitence f.

impenitent adj. impénitent. n. impénitent m., impénitente f.

imperative adj. impératif, impérieux, autoritaire.

imperatively adv. impérativement.

imperceptible adj. imperceptible.

imperceptibly adv. imperceptiblement.

imperfect adj. imparfait; incomplet.

imperfection n. imperfection f.

imperfectly adv. imparfaitement.

imperial adj. impérial. n. impériale f.

imperialism n. impérialisme m.

imperialist n. impérialiste m.f.

imperil v.t. mettre en péril.

imperious adj. impérieux; puissant.

imperiously adv. impérieusement.

imperiousness n. arrogance f., hauteur f.

imperishable adj. impérissable.

impermeability n. Phys. imperméabilité f.

impersonal adj. impersonnel.

impersonate v.t. personnifier.

impersonation n. personnification; imitation f.

impertinence n. impertinence f.; insolence f.

impertinent adj. impertinent, insolent. n. impertinent m., impertinente f.

impertinently adj. impertinemment.

imperturbable adj. imperturbable.

impervious adj. impénétrable, inaccessible.

impetuosity n. impetuosité f.

impetuous adj. impétueux.

impetuously adv. impétueusement.

impetus n. force f. d'impulsion; mouvement m. tuosité f.; impulsion f.

impiety n. impiété f.

impinge v.i. affecter; impieter sur.

impious adj. impie.

impish adj. espiègle.

implacable adj. implacable.

implant v.t. implanter; inculquer.

implantation n. implantation f.

implausibility n. invraisemblance f.

implausible adj. invraisemblance, peu plausible.

implement n. instrument m.; outil m., ustensile m. **agricultural ~s,** machines f.pl. agricoles.

implicate v.t. impliquer, compromettre; sous-entendre.

implication n. implication f.; insinuation f.

implicit adj. implicite; aveugle.

implicitly adv. implicitement.

implied adj. implicite, sous-entendu.

implore v.t. implorer. v.i. supplier.

implosion n. implosion f.

imply v.t. impliquer, sous-entendre, inférer, signifier; vouloir dire.

impolite adj. impoli.

impoliteness n. impolitesse f.

imponderable adj. impondérable.

import v.t. importer, signifier. n. article m. d'importation, importation f.

importance n. importance f.

important adj. important.

importation n. importation f.; transport m.

importer n. importateur m., importatrice f.

importunate adj. importun; urgent, pressant.

importunately adv. avec importunité.

importune v.t. importuner. adj. importun; inopportun.

importunity n. importunité f.

impose v.t. imposer; prescrire. **to ~ a fine,** imposer une amende. v.i. tromper; (with **on** or **upon**) en imposer à, abuser. **I have been ~d upon,** on m'a trompé.

imposing adj. imposant.

imposition n. imposition f.; injonction f.; tromperie f., imposture f.

impossibility n. impossibilité f.

impossible adj. impossible.

imposter n. imposteur m.

imposture n. imposture f.

impotence n. impuissance f.

impotent adj. impotent, impuissant.

impotently adv. faiblement; avec impuissance.

impound v.t. mettre en fourrière; enfermer, confisquer, saisir.

impoverish v.t. appauvrir.

impoverishment n. appauvrissement m.

impracticable adj. impracticable.

impracticably adv. d'une manière impracticable.

imprecation n. imprécation f.

imprecise adj. imprécis.

imprecision n. imprécision f., manque m. de précision.

impregnable adj. inexpugnable, imprenable, inattaquable.

impregnate v.t. féconder; impregner.

impregnation n. imprégnation f.; fécondation f.

impresario n. imprésario m.

impress v.t. imprimer; empreindre, frapper.

impression n. impression f.; empreinte f.; idée f.; édition f.

impressionable adj. impressionnable.

impressive adj. impressionnant, solennel, grave, touchant; sensible.

impressively adv. de manière impressionnante.

imprint v.t. imprimer, empreindre; fixer, graver. n. empreinte f., nom m. d'imprimeur.

imprison *n.* emprisonner.
imprisonment *n.* emprisonnement *m.;* détention *f.*
improbability *n.* improbabilité *f.*
improbable *adj.* improbable.
improbably *adv.* improbablement.
impromptu *adv.* en impromptu, tout de suite. *n., adj.* impromptu *m.*
improper *adj.* déplacé; peu convenable; inconvenant; incongru. ~ **manners,** des manières *f.pl.* inconvenantes. ~ **expressions,** des expressions *f.pl.* impropres, incongrues.
improperly *adv.* d'une manière qui ne convient pas; avec inconvenance; improprement.
impropriety *n.* impropriété *f.;* inconvenance *f.*
improve *v.t.* améliorer; perfectionner; bonifier (wine), embellir (a city, etc.); corriger, exploiter (a farm, a mine); faire valoir; tirer parti de. *v.i.* s'améliorer, se bonifier; se perfectionner; gagner. **to** ~ **oneself,** se perfectionner.
improvement *n.* amélioration *f.,* avancement *m.,* perfectionnement *m.,* progrès *m.;* culture *f.*
improvidence *n.* imprévoyance *f.*
improvident *adj.* imprévoyant.
improvisation *n.* improvisation *f.*
improvise *v.t.,v.i.* improviser.
imprudence *n.* imprudence *f.*
imprudent *adj.* imprudent.
imprudently *adv.* imprudemment.
impudence *n.* impudence *f.,* effronterie *f.,* insolence *f.*
impudent *adj.* impudent, effronté.
impudently *adv.* impudemment.
impugn *v.t.* impugner, contester.
impulse, impulsion *n.* impulsion *f.;* mouvement *m.,* inspiration *f.;* instigation *f.*
impulsive *adj.* impulsif.
impunity *n.* impunité *f.*
impure *adj.* impur.
impurity *n.* impureté *f.*
imputable *adj.* imputable.
imputation *n.* imputation *f.;* accusation *f.;* prévention *f.*
impute *v.t.* imputer, attribuer.
in *prep.* en, dans; à; dedans; y, par; pendant; pour; sur; sous; avec; chez; parmi, entre. ~ **an hour,** dans une heure. ~ **the country,** à la campagne. **to be** ~ **great trouble,** avoir de gros ennuis. **a book** ~ **the press,** un livre sous presse. ~ **the afternoon,** pendant l'après-midi. **the richest man** ~ **town,** l'homme le plus riche de la ville. *adv.* dedans, en, à la maison, chez soi. **is M. B.** ~? M. B. est-il chez lui?
~**born,** inné; congénital. ~**laws,** *m.pl.* belle famille *f.* ~**patient,** malade *m.f.* hospitalisé.
inability *n.* impuissance *f.;* incapacité *f.*
inaccessibility *n.* inaccessibilité *f.*
inaccessible *adj.* inaccessible.
inaccuracy *n.* inexactitude *f.;* erreur *f.*
inaccurate *adj.* inexact, incorrect.
inaction *n.* inaction *f.*

inactive *adj.* inactif, indolent; oisif, paresseux; inerte.
inactivity *n.* inactivité *f.;* fainéantise *f.,* oisiveté *f.*
inadequacy *n.* insuffisance *f.;* disproportion *f.;* imperfection *f.*
inadequate *adj.* insuffisant; disproportionné; inadéquat, inapproprié; inexact; incomplet.
inadmissable *adj.* inadmissible.
inadvertence *n.* inadvertence *f.*
inadvertent *adj.* inattentif; étourdi.
inadvertently *adv.* par inadvertence, par mégarde.
inalienable *adj.* inaliénable.
inalterable *adj.* inaltérable.
inane *adj.* vide, vain, stupide.
inanimate *adj.* inanimé.
inanition *n.* inanition *f.*
inanity *n.* inanité *f.*
inapplicable *adj.* inapplicable.
inappropriate *adj.* non approprié, peu approprié.
inappropriately *adv.* improprement, hors de propos.
inapt *adj.* inepte.
inaptitude *n.* incapacité *f.*
inarticulate *adj.* inarticulé.
inasmuch *adv.* (followed by **as**), attendu que, vu que, d'autant que.
inattention *n.* inattention *f.*
inattentive *adj.* inattentif.
inaudible *adj.* inaudible.
inaugural *adj.* inaugural.
inaugurate *v.t.* inaugurer.
inauguration *n.* inauguration *f.;* installation *f.*
inauspicious *adj.* peu propice, défavorable.
inborn *adj.* inné.
inbred *adj.* inné, naturel, consanguin.
incalculable *adj.* incalculable.
incalculably *adv.* incalculable.
incandescence *n.* incandescence *f.*
incandescent *adj.* incandescent.
incantation *n.* incantation *f.*
incapability *n.* incapacité *f.*
incapable *adj.* incapable.
incapacitate *v.t.* rendre incapable; mettre dans l'impossibilité de; frapper d'incapacité.
incapacity *n.* incapacité *f.;* inhabileté *f.*
incarcerate *v.t.* incarcérer.
incarceration *n.* incarcération *f.*
incarnate *v.t.* incarner. *adj.* incarné; incarnat.
incarnation *n.* incarnation *f.*
incautious *adj.* imprévoyant, imprudent, inconsidéré.
incautiously *adv.* sans précaution, imprudemment.
incendiary *n.* incendiaire *m.* ~ *adj.* incendiaire.
incense *n.* encens *m.* ~ *v.t.* exaspérer, irriter.
incentive *n.* motif *m.,* mobile *m.;* encouragement *m.*
inception *n.* commencement *m.*
incessant *adj.* incessant; continuel.
incessantly *adv.* sans cesse, incessamment.

incest n. inceste m.

incestuous adj. incestueux.

incestuously adv. incestueusement.

inch n. pouce m. **by ~s,** pouce par pouce, peu à peu. **give him an ~ and he'll take a mile,** donnez-lui-grand comme le doigt, et il en prendra long comme le bras. **within an ~ of,** à deux doigts de. v.t. évincer peu à peu.

inchoate adj. commencé, naissant.

incidence n. incidence f.

incident adj. accidentel, fortuit. n. incident m.; circonstance f.

incidental adj. fortuit; de circonstance, occasionnel. **~ expenses,** faux frais m.pl.; incident m.

incidentally adv. fortuitement, accidentellement.

incinerate v.t. incinérer.

incineration n. incinération f.

incipient adj. commençant, débutant, naissant.

incise v.t. inciser, couper, tailler dans; sculpter, graver.

incision n. coupure f.; découpure f.; incision f.

incisive adj. incisif.

incisor n. incisive f.

incitation n. incitation f.

incite v.t. inciter; stimuler; solliciter; suggérer; presser; provoquer.

incitement n. motif m., stimulant m., aiguillon m.

incivility n. incivilité f., impolitesse f.; grossièrete f.

inclemency n. inclémence f.

inclement adj. sévère dur; âpre, rude.

inclination n. inclinaison f., inclination f.

incline v.i.,v.t. incliner; pencher; s'incliner; se pencher. n. plan m. incliné; pente f., rampe f.

inclined adj. incliné; enclin, disposé.

include v.t. inclure, comprendre, comporter.

inclusion n. inclusion f.

inclusive adj. inclusif; inclus.

incognito adj., adv., n. incognito m.

incoherence n. incohérence f.

incoherent adj. incoherent.

incoherently adv. avec incohérence.

incombustible adj. incombustible.

income n. revenu m.; rentes f.pl. **~ tax,** impôt m. sur le revenu.

incoming adj. qui entre, qui arrive. n. revenu m. rentes f.pl., produit m.

incommensurable adj. incommensurable.

incommensurate adj. disproportionné, insuffisant.

incommode v.t. incommoder, gêner.

incommodious adj. incommode; embarrassant, importun, fâcheux.

incommunicable adj. incommunicable.

incomparable adj. incomparable.

incomparably adv. incomparablement.

incompatibility n. incompatibilité f.

incompatible adj. incompatible.

incompatibly adv. incompatiblement.

incompetence n. incapacité f.; impuissance f.; incompétence f.

incompetent adj. incompétent; insuffisant; inadmissible.

incomplete adj. incomplet.

incompletely adv. incomplétement.

incompleteness n. état m. incomplet.

incomprehensible adj. incompréhensible.

incomprehensibly adv. incompréhensiblement.

inconceivable adj. inconcevable.

inconclusive adj. inconcluant.

inconclusively adv. d'une manière peu concluante.

incongruent adj. incongru.

incongruity n. incongruité f.; inconvenance f.

inconsequence n. inconséquence f.

inconsequent adj. inconséquent.

inconsiderate adj. sans égards pour les autres.

inconsiderately adv. inconsidérément.

inconsistence n. inconséquence f., inconsistance f., contradiction f.; incompatibilité f.

inconsistent adj. inconséquent; incompatible.

inconsolable inconsolable.

inconspicuous adj. peu apparent, discret.

inconstancy n. inconstance f.

inconstant adj. inconstant.

inconstantly adv. inconstamment.

incontestable adj. incontestable.

incontestably adv. incontestablement.

incontinence n. incontinence f.

incontinent adj. incontinent.

incontrovertible adj. incontestable.

inconvenience n. inconvénient m., incommodité f.; embarras m., ennui m. **~** v.t. incommoder, déranger, gêner.

inconvenient adj. incommode; inopportun; gênant.

inconveniently adv. incommodément.

inconvertible adj. inconvertible.

incorporate v.t. incorporer. v.i. s'incorporer.

incorporation n. incorporation f.

incorporeal adj. incorporel.

incorrect adj. incorrect; inexact.

incorrectly adv. incorrectement, inexactement.

incorrigible adj. incorrigible.

incorrigibly adv. incorrigiblement.

incorruptible adj. incorruptible.

increase v.i. grandir, s'agrandir, croître; augmenter, s'accroître, s'augmenter; se multiplier, grossir. v.t. agrandir, augmenter, grossir, accroître. n. augmentation f.; accroissement; extension f., croissance f.; surcroît m.

increasingly adv. de plus en plus.

incredible adj. incroyable.

incredulity n. incrédulité f., scepticisme m.

incredulous adj. incrédule.

increment n. accroissement m.; quantité f. différentielle.

incriminate *v.t.* incriminer.
incrimination *n.* incrimination *f.*
incrust *v.t.* incruster; encroûter.
incrustation *n.* incrustation *f.*
incubate *v.i.* couver.
incubation *n.* incubation *f.*
incubator *n.* couveuse *f.* artificielle.
incubus *n.* incube *m.* cauchemar *m.*
inculcate *v.t.* inculquer.
inculcation *n.* inculcation *f.*
inculpate *v.t.* inculper.
inculpation *n.* inculpation *f.*
incumbent *adj.* incombant; penchant sur, urgent, indispensable. *n.* titulaire *m.* bénéficier *m.* ~ **president** (current) le président en exercice.
incur *v.t.* encourir, s'attirer. **to ~ expenses**, faire des frais.
incurability *n.* incurabilité *f.*
incurable *adj., n.* incurable *m.*
incurably *adv.* incurablement; irrémédiablement.
incursion *n.* incursion *f.*
indebted *adj.* endetté, redevable.
indebtedness *n.* dette(s) *f.pl.*
indecency *n.* indécence *f.*
indecent *adj.* indécent.
indecently *adv.* indécemment.
indecipherable *adj.* indéchiffrable.
indecision *n.* indécision *f.*
indecisive *adj.* indécisif, indécis; irrésolu.
indecisvely *adv.* d'une manière indécise, dans l'indécision.
indecisiveness *n.* indécision *f.*
indecorous *adj.* inconvenant, malséant; indécent.
indecorum *n.* indécence *f.*
indeed *adv.* en vérité, vraiment, en effet, à la vérité.
indefatigable *adj.* infatigable.
indefensible *adj.* insoutenable.
indefinable *adj.* indéfinissable.
indefinite *adj.* indéfini; indéterminé.
indefinitely *adv.* indéfiniment.
indelible *adj.* indélébile; ineffaçable.
indelicacy *n.* indélicatesse *f.*
indelicate *adj.* indélicat.
indemnification *n.* indemnisation *f.;* indemnité *f.*
indemnify *v.t.* indemniser; dédommager, réparer; assurer.
indemnity *n.* indemnité *f.*
indemonstrable *adj.* indémontrable.
indent *v.t.* denteler; ébrécher. *Typ.* renfoncer, rentrer; bossuer. *v.i.* s'échancrer, s'ebrécher, se déchiqueter. *n.* entaille *f.,* brèche *f.;* dentelure *f.;* empreinte *f.,* impression *f.*
indentation *n.* dentelure *f.;* échancrure *f.;* engrenage *m.*
indenture *n.* engagement *m.,* contrat lier par un contrat.

independence *n.* indépendance *f.*
independent *adj.* indépendant.
independently *adv.* indépendamment.
indescribable *adj.* indescriptible.
indestructable *adj.* indestructible.
indeterminable *adj.* indéterminable; interminable.
indeterminate *adj.* indéterminé.
index *n.* indice *m.;* indicateur *m.;* index *m.;* répertoire *m.;* table *f.* des matières; aiguille *f.;* exposant *m.* ~ *v.t.* mettre dans une table des matières.
India *n.pr.* Indie *f.,* Indes *f.pl.*
Indian *adj.* indien, des Indes. *n.* Indien *m.*
indicate *v.t.* indiquer.
indication *n.* indication *f.;* signe *m.,* indice *m.,* marque *f.*
indicator *n.* indicateur *m.*
indict *v.t.* accuser, poursuivre.
indictment *n.* accusation *f.;* acte *m.* d'accusation, mise *f.* en accusation.
Indies *n.pr.* **India. East ~,** les Indes orientales, les Grandes Indes. **West ~,** les Indes occidentales, les Antilles *f.pl.* les Caraïbes.
indifference *n.* indifférence *f.*
indifferent *adj.* indifférent; passable, médiocre.
indifferently *adv.* indifféremment.
indigence *n.* indigence *f.*
indigenous *adj.* indigène; natif.
indigent *adj.* indigent.
indigestion *n.* indigestion *f.*
indignant *adj.* indigné.
indignation *n.* indignation *f.;* courroux *m.,* colère *f.*
indignity *n.* indignité *f.,* outrage *m.,* affront *m.*
indigo *n.* indigo *m.* ~ **tree,** indigotier.
indirect *adj.* indirect; détourné.
indirectly *adv.* indirectement; obliquement.
indiscernible *adj.* indiscernable.
indiscipline *n.* indiscipline *f.*
indiscreet *adj.* indiscret.
indiscretion *n.* indiscrétion *f.;* imprudence *f.*
indiscriminate *adj.* ne distinguent pas; que rien ne fait distinguer, confus.
indiscriminately *adv.* sans distinction, confusément.
indispensable *adv.* indispensable.
indispensably *adv.* indispensablement.
indispose *v.t.* indisposer, détourner, éloigner, incommoder.
indisposed *adj.* indisposé, souffrant, incommodé.
indisposition *n.* indisposition *f.;* malaise *m.,* incommodité *f.*
indisputable *adj.* indisputable.
indisputably *adv.* indisputablement, incontestablement.
indissoluble *adj.* indissoluble.
indistinct *adj.* indistinct; vague, obscur, indéfini, ambigu, imparfait, confus, incertain.

indistinctly *adv.* indistinctement; vaguement.

indistinguishable *adj.* indistincte; d'une forme indéterminée.

individual *adj.* individuel, seul. *n.* individu *m.*, particulier *m.* **a private ~,** un simple particulier.

individualism *n.* individualisme *m.*

individualize *v.t.* individualiser.

individually *adv.* individuellement; isolément.

indivisible *adj., n.* indivisible.

indoctrinate *v.t.* endoctriner.

indoctrination *n.* endoctrinement *m.*

indolence *n.* indolence *f.*

indolent *adj.* indolent.

indolently *adv.* indolemment.

indomitable *adj.* indomptable.

indoor *adj.* qui est à l'intérieur; interne. **~ games,** jeux *m.* d'intérieur.

indoors *adv.* à l'intérieur, à la maison, à l'abri.

indorse *v.t.* endosser.

indorsement *n.* endossement *m.*

indubitable *adj.* indubitable.

indubitably *adv.* indubitablement.

induce *v.t.* engager, persuader, inciter, provoquer, induire.

inducement *n.* mobile *m.*, raison *f.*, motif *m.*, stimulant *m.*, incitation *f.*

inducible *adj.* qui peut être causé, occasionné.

induct *v.t.* installer, établir.

induction *n.* induction *f.*, entrée *f.*; préambule *m.*; installation *f.*

indulge *v.t.* permettre, tolérer, avoir de l'indulgence pour; souffrir; (se) permettre. *Infml.* se payer. **to ~ oneself,** prendre ses aises. **he ~d her with everything,** il lui accordait tout. *v.i.* en prendre à son aise, (se) permettre; complaire. **to ~ in expenses,** se permettre des dépenses.

indulgence *n.* facilité *f.*; plaisir *m.*; bonté *f.*, indulgence *f.*, faveur *f.*

indulgent *adj.* indulgent; favorable, facile, faible.

indulgently *adv.* sans contrainte; avec indulgence.

industrial *adj.* industriel.

industrially *adv.* industriellement.

industrious *adj.* laborieux, actif, travailleur; assidu, persévérant; zélé, ardent.

industriously *adv.* laborieusement.

industry *n.* travail *m.*; application *f.*, assiduité *f.*, persévérance *f.*, industrie *f.*

inebriate *n.* alcoolique *m.f.* *adj.* ivre. *v.i.* s'enivrer.

inedible *adj.* immangeable.

inedited *adj.* inédit.

ineffable *adj.* ineffable.

ineffective *adj.* ineffectif; inefficace.

ineffectual *adj.* inefficace, vain.

inefficiency *n.* inefficacité *f.*

inefficient *adj.* inefficace, incompétent, impuissant.

inefficiently *adv.* sans effet, sans résultat.

inelegance *n.* inélégance *f.*

inelegant *adj.* inélégant.

ineligible *adj.* inéligible; peu convenable.

ineluctable *adj.* inéluctable.

inept *adj.* inapte; inepte.

ineptitude *n.* inaptitude *f.*

inequality *n.* inégalité *f.*

inequitable *adj.* inéquitable; injuste.

inert *adj.* inerte.

inertia *n.* inertie *f.*

inestimable *adj.* inestimable; incalculable.

inevitable *adj.* inévitable.

inevitably *adv.* inévitablement.

inexact *adj.* inexact.

inexactness *n.* inexactitude *f.*

inexcusable *adj.* inexcusable.

inexhaustible *adj.* inépuisable.

inexorable *adj.* inexorable.

inexorably *adv.* inexorablement.

inexpensive *adj.* peu coûteux.

inexperience *n.* inexpérience *f.*

inexperienced *adj.* inexpérimenté.

inexpiable *adj.* inexpiable.

inexplicable *adj.* inexplicable.

inexplicably *adv.* inexplicablement.

inexpressible *adj.* inexprimable.

inexpressive *adj.* inexpressif.

inextricable *adj.* inextricable.

infallibility *n.* infaillibilité *f.*

infallible *adj.* infaillible.

infallibly *adv.* infailliblement, immanquablement.

infamous *adj.* infâme; mal famé.

infamously *adv.* d'une manière infâme; avec infamie.

infamy *n.* infamie *f.*

infancy *n.* enfance *f.*, bas âge *m.*

infant *n.* bébé *m.*, nourrisson *m.* *adj.* d'enfant, enfantin; en bas âge.

infanticide *n.* infanticide *m.*

infantile *adj.* d'enfant, enfantin.

infantry *n.* infanterie *f.*

infatuate *v.t.* attirer, *Infml.* embobiner, faire tourner la tête.

infatuation *n.* égarement *m.*; engouement *m.*

infect *v.t.* infecter; empester.

infection *n.* infection *f.*

infectious *adj.* infectieux; contagieux.

infelicity *n.* malheur *m.*, infortune *f.*

infer *v.t.* inférer; déduire; tirer; conclure.

inference *n.* déduction *f.*, conclusion *f.*, conséquence *f.*

inferior *adj., n.* inférieur *m.*

inferiority *n.* infériorité *f.*

infernal *adj.* infernal.

infertile *adj.* infertile; stérile.

infertility *n.* infertilité *f.*, infécondité *f.*, stérilité *f.*

infest *v.t.* infester.

infidel *adj., n.* infidèle *m.f.*; impie *m.f.*

infidelity *n.* infidélité *f.*

infiltrate *v.i.* s'infiltrer.

infiltration *n.* infiltration *f.*

infinite *adj.* infini; perpétuel.

infinitely *adv.* infinément.
infinitesimal *adj.* infinitésimal.
infinity *n.* infinité *f.*
infirm *adj.* infirme.
infirmary *n.* infirmerie *f.*
infirmity *n.* infirmité *f.;* faiblesse *f.*
inflame *v.t.* enflammer, exacerber, exciter. *v.i.* s'enflammer; embraser, s'envenimer.
inflammable *adj.* inflammable.
inflammation *n.* inflammation *f.*
inflammatory *adj.* inflammatoire; incendiaire.
inflate *v.t.* enfler, gonfler.
inflated *adj.* renflé; enflé, gonflé.
inflation *n.* enflure *f.,* orgueil *m.;* bouffissure *f.;* inflation; hausse *f.*
inflection See INFLEXION.
inflexibility *n.* inflexibilité *f.*
inflexible *adj.* inflexible.
inflict *v.t.* infliger; couvrir de.
infliction *n.* infliction *f.;* châtiment *m.,* peine *f.*
inflorescence *n.* inflorescence *f.*
inflow *n.* afflux *m.,* flot *m.*
influence *n.* (on, with) influence *f.* ~ *v.t.* influer sur; influencer; déterminer.
influential *adj.* influent.
influenza *n.* influenza *f.;* grippe *f.*
influx *n.* flux *m.;* écoulement *m.;* infusion *f.;* affluence *f.,* abondance *f.*
inform *v.t.* informer; prévenir; faire part de; avertir; aviser; (with **against**) accuser, dénoncer.
informal *adj.* officieux, simple, sans cérémonie, informel.
informality *n.* simplicité *f.,* absence *f.* de cérémonie.
informally *adv.* simplement, officieusement, irrégulièrement.
informant *n.* informateur *m.,* informatrice *f.*
information *n.* renseignement *m.,* information *f.,* nouvelle *f.,* avis *m.;* instruction *f.,* savoir *m.*
informative *adj.* éducatif, instructif.
informer *n.* dénonciateur *m.,* dénonciatrice *f.*
infraction *n.* infraction *f.*
infrequency *n.* rareté *f.*
infrequent *adj.* rare.
infringe *v.t.* enfreindre; violer, transgresser, contrevenir à.
infringement *n.* infraction *f.;* violation *f.;* contravention *f.;* empiètement sur.
infuriate *v.t.* rendre fou, furieux.
infuse *v.t.* infuser.
infusion *n.* infusion *f.*
ingenious *adj.* ingénieux.
ingeniousness *n.* ingéniosité *f.;* habileté *f.,* art *m.,* adresse *f.;* talent *m.*
ingenuity *n.* ingéniosité *f.*
ingenuous *adj.* ingénu; naïf, candide, sincère, honnête.
ingenuously *adv.* ingénument; franchement, naïvement.
ingenuousness *n.* ingénuité *f.;* franchise *f.,* naïveté *f.,* candeur *f.*

ingest *v.t.* ingérer.
ingestion *n.* ingestion *f.*
inglenook *n.* coin *m.* du feu.
inglorious *adj.* inglorieux; honteux, ignominieux.
ingot *n.* lingot *m.*
ingrain *v.t.* imprégner profondément.
ingratiate *v.t.* se concilier; insinuer dans les bonnes grâces. **to ~ oneself with,** se concilier la faveur de.
ingratitude *n.* ingratitude *f.*
ingredient *n.* ingrédient *m.;* élément *m.*
ingress *n.* entrée *f.,* droit *m.* d'entrée.
ingurgitate *v.i.* s'ingurgiter.
inhabit *v.i.* habiter, demeurer, vivre.
inhabitable *adj.* habitable.
inhabitant *n.* habitant *m.,* habitante *f.*
inhalation *n.* inhalation *f.*
inhale *v.t.* inhaler.
inhaler *n.* inhalateur *m.*
inharmonious *adj.* inharmonieux, discordant.
inherent *adj.* inhérent.
inherit *v.t.* hériter; recueillir. *v.i.* hériter, recueillir un héritage.
inheritance *n.* héritage *m.;* succession *f.;* hérédité *f.*
inhibit *v.t.* inhiber, défendre, prohiber, interdire.
inhibition *n.* inhibition *f.;* prohibition *f.;* embargo *m.;* interdiction *f.*
inhospitable *adj.* inhospitalier.
inhospitality *n.* inhospitalité *f.*
inhospitably *adv.* d'une manière inhospitablière.
inhuman *adj.* inhumain.
inhumanity *n.* inhumanité *f.*
inhumanly *adv.* inhumainement.
inhumation *n.* inhumation *f.*
inhume *v.t.* inhumer.
inimical *adj.* hostile; nuisible; contraire.
inimically *adv.* hostilement.
inimitable *adj.* inimitable.
inimitably *adv.* inimitablement.
iniquitous *adj.* inique; injuste.
iniquitously *adv.* iniquement, injustement.
iniquity *n.* iniquité *f.*
initial *adj.* initial; premier. *n.* initiale *f.*
initially *adv.* en commençant, pour commencer.
initiate *v.t.* initier; mettre au courant. *v.i.* prendre l'initiative.
initiation *n.* initiation *f.*
initiative *adj.* initiatif. *n.* initiative *f.*
inject *v.t.* injecter.
injection *n.* piqûre *f.,* injection *f.*
injudicious *adj.* injudicieux; imprudent, irréfléchi.
injudiciously *adv.* d'une manière injudicieuse, imprudemment.
injudiciousness *n.* manque *m.* de jugement.
injunction *n.* injonction *f.* commandement *m.*
injure *v.t.* blesser faire du tort; du mal à; léser; endommager; détériorer.

injured *adj.* blessé; accidenté; offensé; trompé. **the ~ party,** la partie blessée.

injurious *adj.* nuisible, préjudiciable; pernicieux; injurieux.

injury *n.* blessure *f.;* injustice *f.,* tort *m.;* mal *m.,* préjudice *m.,* dégât *m.;* avaries *f.pl.;* intempérie *f.,* injure *f.*

injustice *n.* injustice *f.*

ink *n.* encre *f.* ~ *v.t.* tâcher, couvrir, barbouiller d'encre.

inkling *n.* idée *f.,* avis *m.*

inlaid *adj.* incrusté.

inland *adj.* intérieur. **the ~ trade,** le commerce intérieur. *n.* intérieur *m.*

inlay *v.t.* incruster. **to ~ a floor,** parqueter un plancher. *n.* incrustation *f.*

inlet *n.* entrée *f.,* passage *m.;* voie *f.,* accès *m.;* anse *f.,* baie *f.*

inmate *n.* détenu *m.,* détenue *f.,* locataire *m.f.;* pensionnaire *m.f.*

inmost *adj.* le plus intérieur; le plus intime, le plus secret.

inn *n.* auberge *f.,* hôtellerie *f.*

innards *n.pl.* entrailles *f.pl.*

innate *adj.* inné.

inner *adj.* intérieur; intime.

innermost *adj.* le plus profond, intime.

inning *n.* (baseball) tour *m.* de batte.

innocence *n.* innocence *f.*

innocent *adj.* innocent. *n.* innocent *m.,* innocente *f.*

innocently *adv.* innocemment.

innocuous *adj.* innocent, inoffensif.

innovate *v.t., v.i.* innover.

innovation *n.* innovation *f.*

innovator *n.* innovateur *m.,* innovatrice *f.*

innuendo *n.* insinuation *f.,* allusion *f.* détournée.

innumerable *adj.* innombrable.

inobservant *adj.* inattentif; qui n'observe pas.

inobtrusive *adj.* inobstructif; discret.

inoculation *n.* inoculation *f.*

inoffensive *adj.* inoffensif.

inopportune *adj.* inopportun.

inopportunely *adv.* inopportunément, mal à propos.

inordinacy *n.* excès *m.;* dérèglement *m.;* désordre *m.*

inordinate *adj.* irrégulier; désordonné, excessif.

inorganic *adj.* inorganique.

input *n.* entrée *f.,* énergie *f.,* puissance *f.,* input *f.,* données *f.pl.*

inquest *n.* enquête *f.;* recherche *f.*

inquietude *n.* inquiétude *f.*

inquire *v.t.* s'enquérir, demander, s'informer; s'adresser. **to ~ after, into,** s'informer de. **~ within,** s'adresser ici. *v.t.* s'informer de.

inquiring *adj.* investigateur. **an ~ mind,** un esprit investigateur.

inquiry *n.* enquête *f.;* demande *f.,* interrogation *f.;* recherche *f.;* investigation *f.* **to make inqui-**

ries, prendre des renseignements. **on ~,** renseignement pris.

inquisition *n.* enquête *f.;* recherche *f.;* perquisition *f.;* inquisition *f.*

inquisitive *adj.* curieux, indiscret.

inquisitively *adv.* avec curiosité, indiscrètement.

inroad *n.* incursion *f.;* empiétement *m.,* usurpation *f.*

insalubrious *adj.* insalubre, malsain.

insalubrity *n.* insalubrité *f.*

insane *adj.* insensé; fou, folle, aliéné.

insanely *adv.* follement.

insanity *n.* insanité *f.*

insatiable *adj.* insatiable.

inscribe *v.t.* inscrire; graver sur; dédier.

inscription *n.* inscription *f.*

inscrutable *adj.* inscrutable; impénétrable.

insect *n.* insecte *m.*

insecticide *n.* insecticide *m.*

insecure *adj.* peu sûr; sans sécurité; en danger.

insecurely *adv.* sans sécurité.

insecurity *n.* insécurité *f.*

inseminate *v.t.* inséminer.

insemination *n.* insémination *f.*

insensate *adj.* insensé.

insensibility *n.* insensibilité *f.*

insensible *adj.* insensible.

insensibly *adv.* insensiblement; sans le savoir.

insensitive *adj.* insensible.

inseparable *adj.* inséparable; indivisible.

insert *v.t.* insérer; faire insérer.

insertion *n.* insertion *f.*

inset *v.t.* insérer, incruster, encarter; *m.,* schéma *m.,* carte *f.,* médaillon *m.*

inshore *adj.* côtier(ière); *adv.* près de la côte.

inside *n.* intérieur *m.,* le dedans *m.* **to turn ~ out,** mettre à l'envers. *adj.* en dedans, à l'intérieur.

insider *n.* initié *m.,* initiée *f.*

insidious *adj.* insidieux; perfide.

insidiously *adv.* insidieusement.

insight *n.* perspicacité *f.,* pénétration *f.,* éclaircissement *m.* **to give an ~ into,** donner une idée de.

insignia *n.* insignes *m.pl.*

insignificance *n.* insignifiance *f.*

insignificant *adj.* insignifiant.

insignificantly *adv.* sans signification.

insincere *adj.* feint; faux, de mauvaise foi, hypocrite.

insincerity *n.* manque *m.* de sincérité, dissimulation *f.,* hypocrisie *f.*

insinuate *v.t.* insinuer; glisser. *v.i.* s'insinuer; se glisser.

insinuation *n.* insinuation *f.*

insipid *adj.* insipide; fade.

insist *v.i.* insister; appuyer sur, exiger; persister.

insistence *n.* insistance *f.*

insistent *adj.* insistant, persistant; pressant.

insolation *n.* insolation *f.*

insolence *n.* insolence *f.*

insolent *adj.* insolent.

insolently *adv.* insolemment.

insoluble *adj.* insoluble.

insolvable *adj.* insoluble, insolvable.

insolvent *adj.* insolvable. *n.* débiteur *m.* insolvable. to become ~, déposer son bilan.

insomnia *n.* insomnie *f.*

insomuch *adv.* à tel point, si bien que, en tant que.

insouciance *n.* insouciance *f.*

inspect *v.t.* inspecter, surveiller; examiner.

inspection *n.* inspection *f.*

inspector *n.* inspecteur *m.*

inspiration *n.* inspiration *f.;* aspiration *f.*

inspire *v.i.* inspirer; aspirer. *v.t.* souffler dans.

instability *n.* instabilité *f.*

install *v.t.* installer.

installation *n.* installation *f.*

installment *n.* installation *f.;* à-compte *m.;* payement *m.* par à-comptes.

instance *n.* instance *f.;* sollicitation *f.;* demande *f.;* exemple *m.;* modèle *m.* in the first ~, dans le premier cas. for ~, par exemple. *v.i.* donner un exemple; offrir un cas. *v.t.* citer.

instant *adj.* instant; pressant, urgent; prompt; courant. *n.* instant *m.,* moment *m.*

instantaneous *adj.* instantané.

instantaneously *adv.* instantanément.

instantly *adv.* immédiatement, à l'instant même, instantanément.

instead *adv.* au lieu, à la place. ~ of, au lieu de.

instep *n.* cou-de-pied *m.;* tarse *m.*

instigate *v.t.* instiguer; exciter, pousser, inciter, encourager.

instigation *n.* instigation *f.*

instigator *n.* instigateur *m.,* instigatrice *f.*

instill *v.t.* instiller; inspirer, inculquer.

instinct *n.* instinct *m.*

instinctive *adj.* instinctif.

instinctively *adv.* instinctivement.

institute *v.t.* instituer; établir; commencer; créer. to ~ a society or college, fonder une société, un collège. *n.* institut *m.*

institution *n.* institution *f.,* établissement *m.*

instruct *v.t.* instruire, enseigner; donner des instructions.

instruction *n.* instruction *f.,* enseignement *m.;* leçon *f.*

instructive *adj.* instructif.

instructor *n.* instituteur *m.,* maître *m.,* professeur *m.* ~ *n.* moniteur *m.,* monitrice *f.*

instrument *n.* instrument *m.;* agent *m.* musical ~s, instruments de musique.

instrumental *adj.* instrumental, d'instrument. to be ~ in, être la cause de. ~ performer, exécutant *m.*

instrumentalist *n.* instrumentiste *m.f.*

insubordinate *adj.* insubordonné.

insubordination *n.* insubordination *f.*

insubstantial *adj.* immatériel, sans substance. ~ evidence, manque d'évidence *f.,* évidence insuffisante.

insufferable *adj.* insupportable, intolérable.

insufferably *adv.* d'une manière insupportable.

insufficiency *n.* insuffisance *f.,* incapacité *f.*

insufficient *adj.* insuffisant.

insular *adj.* and *n.* insulaire.

insulate *v.t.* isoler; insonoriser.

insulation *n.* isolement *m.;* insonorisation *f.*

insulator *n.* isolateur *m.,* isolant *m.*

insult *n.* insulte *f.,* affront *m.,* outrage *m.,* offense *f.,* injure *f.* ~ *v.t.* insulter.

insulting *adj.* insultant, outrageant.

insuperable *adj.* insurmontable.

insupportable *adj.* insupportable.

insupportably *adv.* insupportablement.

insurable *adj.* assurable.

insurance *n.* assurance *f.* life ~, assurance vie. fire ~, assurance contre l'incendie.

insure *v.t.* assurer. *v.i.* (s')assurer, se faire assurer.

insurer *n.* assureur *m.*

insurgency *n.* insurrection *f.*

insurgent *adj.* insurgé. *n.* insurgé *m.,* insurgée *f.*

insurmountable *adj.* insurmontable.

insurrection *n.* insurrection *f.*

intact *adj.* intact.

intake *n.* consommation *f.,* ration *f.* alimentaire; prise *f.;* admission *f.*

intangible *adj.* intangible.

integer *n.* intégralité *f.,* entier *m.;* entier *m.,* nombre *m.* entier.

integral *adj.* intégral; entier; intégrant. *n.* tout *m.,* totalité *f.;* intégralité *f.*

integrally *adv.* intégralement.

integrate *v.t.* rendre entier, compléter; *Math.* intégrer.

integration *n.* intégration *f.* racial ~, intégration raciale.

integrity *n.* intégrité *f.;* pureté *f.*

intellect *n.* intelligence *f.,* entendement *m.*

intellectual *adj.* intellectuel; mental, idéal. *n.* intellectuel *m.,* intellectuelle *f.*

intellectually *adv.* intellectuellement.

intelligence *n.* intelligence *f.;* esprit *m.;* avis *m.,* renseignement *m.*

intelligently *adv.* d'une manière intelligente.

intelligentsia *n.* l'élite *f.,* intellectuelle, l'intelligentsia *f.*

intelligibility *n.* intelligibilité *f.*

intelligible *adj.* intelligible, compréhensible; clair, net.

intelligibly *adv.* intelligiblement; clairement.

intemperance *n.* intempérance *f.*

intemperate *adj.* sans mesure; immodéré; démesuré; intempérant; excessif.

intend *v.t., v.i.* avoir l'intention de; pretendre; se proposer; se déployer.

intendant *n.* intendant *m.*

intended *adj.* destiné; voulu. *n.* prétendu *m.*

intense *adj.* intense; fort, vif, ardent; extrême.
~ **heat,** chaleur intense. ~ **sufferings,** de vives
souffrances.

intensely *adv.* avec intensité; excessivement;
attentivement, sérieusement.

intensity intensité *f.,* force *f.,* violence *f.,* opiniâtreté *f.;* ardeur *f.* **the ~ of the cold,** l'intensité
du froid. **the ~ of a fever,** la violence d'une
fièvre.

intensify *v.t.* intensifier.

intent *adj.* attentif, appliqué; profond. **to be ~
on,** être absorbé dans. *n.* intention *f.,* but *m.;*
dessein *m.* **with good ~,** à bonne intention.

intention *n.* intention *f.;* dessin *m.;* but *m.*

intentional *adj.* intentionnel; prémédite.

intentionally *adv.* intentionnellement; à dessein; exprès.

intently *adv.* attentivement; fixement.

inter *v.t.* enterrer, ensevelir, inhumer.

interact *v.i.* interagir (ré)agir réciproquement,
agir l'un sur l'autre.

interaction *n.* interaction *f.*

intercede *v.i.* intercéder.

intercept *v.t.* intercepter; empêcher;
inter-rompre.

interception *n.* interception *f.;* interruption *f.*

intercession *n.* intercession *f.;* médiation *f.*

interchange *v.t.* échanger; s'interchanger. *n.*
échange *m.;* réciprocité *f.;* alternative *f.*

interchangeable *adj.* échangeable; réciproque;
mutuel.

intercom *n.* interphone *m.*

intercommunicate *v.t.* communiquer
mutellement.

intercommunication *n.* intercommunication *f.*

intercontinental *adj.* intercontinental.

intercourse *n.* rapports *m.pl.;* commerce *m.*
sexual ~, rapports *m.pl.* sexuels.

interdict *v.t.* interdire; défendre. *n.* interdiction
f.; interdit *m.*

interdiction *n.* interdiction *f.;* défense *f.*

interest *v.t.* intéresser. **to take an ~ in something,** s'intéresser à quelque chose. **to ~ oneself in,** s'intéresser à. *n.* intérêt *m.;* credit *m.;*
protection *f.;* influence *f.* **compound ~,** intérêt
composé. **self-~,** intérêt particulier. **to pay
with ~,** payer avec usure. **at ~, upon ~,** à
intérêt.

interested *adj.* intéressé.

interesting *adj.* intéressant.

interface *n.* interface *f.* ~ *v.i.* avoir une interface.
v.t. mettre en interface.

interfere *v.i.* (**with**), s'interposer, intervenir; se
mêler de, s'ingérer. **to ~ in disputes,** s'immiscer dans des quérelles.

interference *n.* intervention *f.,* obstacle *m.,*
entrave *f.;* conflit *m.*

interim *n.* intérim *m.;* entre-faites *m.pl.* ~ *adj.*
provisoire, temporaire.

interior *adj.* and *n.* intérieur.

interiorly *adv.* intérieurement.

interject *v.t.* jeter entre; interposer; intercaler,
insérer. *v.i.* (se)jeter entre; (s')interposer;
(s')intercaler.

interjection *n.* interjection *f.*

interlace *v.t.* entrelacer, entremêler.

interline *v.t.* interligner.

interlinear *adj.* interlinéaire.

interlocutor *n.* interlocuteur *m.,* interlocutrice *f.*

interloper *n.* intrus *m.;* intruse *f.*

interlude *n.* intermède *m.*

intermarriage *n.* mariage *m.* consanguin.

intermediary *adj.* intermédiaire.

intermediate *adj.* intermédiaire.

interment *n.* enterrement *m.;* inhumation *f.*

interminable *adj.* interminable.

interminably *adv.* sans fin, sans limites.

intermingle *v.t.* mêler, mélanger. *v.i.* être mêlé,
mélangé.

intermission *n.* entracte *m.;* trêve *f.*

intermittent *adj.* intermittent. *s.* affection
intermittente.

intern *v.t.* interner; *n. Méd.* interne *m.f.*

internal *adj.* intérieur, interne; intime; intestin.

internally *adv.* intérieurement.

international *adj.* international.

internecine *adj.* d'extermination réciproque.

internee *n.* interné *m.,* internée *f.*

internment *n.* internement *m.*

interplanetary *adj.* interplanétaire.

interpolate *v.t.* interpoler; intercaler.

interpolation *n.* interpolation *f.*

interpose *v.t.* interposer; placer entre. *v.i.* s'interposer; intervenir.

interpret *v.t.* interpréter; traduire; expliquer.

interpretation *n.* interprétation *f.*

interpreter *n.* interprète *m.f.*

interracial *adj.* interethnique.

interrelate *v.t.,v.i.* mettre en corrélation.

interrelation *n.* corréllation *f.*

interrogate *v.t.* interroger; poser des questions.

interrogation *n.* interrogation *f.;*
interrogatoire *m.*

interrogative *adj.* interrogatif. *n.* interrogatif
m.; point *m.* d'interrogation.

interrogator *n.* interrogateur *m.,*
interrogatrice *f.*

interrogatory *adj.* interrogateur.

interrupt *v.t.* interrompre; (entre)couper.

interruption *n.* interruption *f.* **without ~,** sans
interruption.

intersect *v.t.* entrecouper; couper. *v.i.* (se)
couper.

intersection *n.* carrefour *m.;* intersection *f.*

intersperse *v.t.* entremêler; disperser, parsemer.

interstate *adj.* entre états.

interstellar *adj.* interstellaire.

interstice *n.* interstice *m.;* intervalle *m.*

intertwine *v.t.* entrelacer. *v.i.* s'entrelacer.

interval *n.* intervalle *m.*

intervene *v.i.* être, se trouver entre; être

situé entre; survenir, avoir lieu, intervenir,
(s')interposer.

intervention *n.* intervention *f.*, interposition *f.*

interview *n.* entrevue *f.*, interview *f.*

interweave *v.t.* tisser; tresser; entrelacer; entremêler.

intestate *adj.* intestat. **he died ~,** il est mort
sans tester. *n.* intestat *m.*

intestinal *adj.* intestinal.

intestine *n.* intestin *m.*

intimacy *n.* intimité *f.;* rapports *m.pl.* sexuels.

intimate *adj.* intime *m.* ~ *v.t.* donner à
entendre; insinuer, faire comprendre.

intimately *adv.* intimement.

intimation *n.* allusion *f.;* avis *m.* indirect.

intimidate *v.t.* intimider.

intimidation *n.* intimidation *f.*

into *prep.* en, dans; par. **to bring ~ the world,**
porter au monde, faire naître. **they broke ~ the
house,** ils sont entrés dans la maison par
effraction.

intolerable *adj.* intolérable.

intolerably *adv.* intolérablement.

intolerance *n.* intolérance *f.*

intolerant *adj.* intolerant *m.*

intonation *n.* intonation *f.*

intone *v.t.* entonner.

intoxicate *v.t.* enivrer; éblouir; rendre ivre.

intoxication *n.* intoxication *f.;* ivresse *f.*

intractable *adj.* intraitable; indocile.

intransigent *adj., n.* intransigeant.

intransitive *adj.* intransitif.

intrepid *adj.* intrépide.

intrepidity *n.* intrépidité *f.*

intricacy *n.* embrouillement *m.;* perplexité *f.;*
complication *f.*

intricate *adj.* embrouille, compliqué.

intrigue *n.* intrigue *f.* ~ *v.i.* intriguer; avoir des
intrigues.

intriguing *adj.* intrigant.

intrinsic *adj.* intrinsèque.

introduce *v.t.* introduire; faire entrer dans; présenter; faire connaître. **to ~ a friend to,** présenter un ami à.

introduction *n.* introduction *f.;* présentation *f.*
letter of ~, lettre *f.* d'introduction.

introductory *adj.* d'introduction; d'avant-
propos.

introspection *n.* introspection *f.*

introspective *adj.* introspectif.

introvert *n.* introverti *m.,* introvertie *f.*

intrude *v.i.* s'introduire; venir sans être invité.
am I intruding? est-ce que je vous dérange?
v.t. importuner; s'ingérer, s'immiscer.

intruder *n.* intrus *m.* intruse *f.*

intrusion *n.* intrusion *f.*, envahissement *m.*

intrusive *adj.* intrus; indiscret.

intuition *n.* intuition *f.*

intuitive *adj.* intuitif, d'intuition.

intuitively *adv.* intuitivement, par intuition.

inundate *v.t.* inonder.

inundation *n.* inondation *f.*

inure *v.t.* habituer à; endurcir à.

invade *v.t.* envahir; attaquer; usurper; empiéter
sur.

invader *n.* envahisseur *m.*

invading *adj.* envahissant, assaillant.

invalid *n.* invalide *m.f.* malade *m.f.* ~ *adj.* invalide, faible, infirme; non valide.

invalidate *v.t.* valider; annuler.

invalidation *n.* invalidation *f.*

invaluable *adj.* inestimable, inappréciable.

invariable *adj.* invariable.

invariably *adv.* invariablement.

invasion *n.* invasion *f.;* envahissement *m.,* violation *f.;* infraction *f.*

invasive *adj.* envahissant; d'invasion.

invective *n.* invective *f.*

inveigh *v.t.* (with **against**) invectiver;
déclaimer.

inveigle *v.t.* séduire, enjôler, amadouer.

inveigling *adj.* séduisant, amadouant.

invent *v.t.* inventer.

invention *n.* invention *f.*

inventor *n.* inventeur *m.,* inventrice *f.*

inventory *n.* inventaire *m.* ~ *v.t.* inventorier,
dresser un inventaire.

inverse *adj.* inverse.

inversely *adv.* inversement.

inversion *n.* inversion *f.;* renversement *m.*

invert *v.t.* renverser, intervertir, transposer.

invertebrate *adj., n.* invertébré *m.*

invest *v.t.* investir, placer (de l'argent). **to ~ in
real estate,** investir dans l'immobilier.

investigate *v.t.* rechercher, examiner avec soin;
faire des investigations.

investigation *n.* investigation *f.*

investigator *n.* investigateur *m.* investiga-
trice *f.*

investiture *n.* investiture *f.*

investment *n.* investissement *m.;* placement *m.*
d'argent.

investor *n.* actionnaire *m.f.*

inveteracy *n.* nature *f.* invétérée;
acharnement *m.*

inveterate *adj.* ancien; invétéré; acharné. **an ~
habit,** une habitude invétérée.

invidious *adj.* odieux, haissable.

invigorate *v.t.* fortifier, vivifier.

invigoration *n.* vigueur *f.,* force *f.*

invincible *adj.* invincible.

inviolable *adj.* inviolable.

invisibility *n.* invisibilité *f.*

invisible *adj.* invisible.

invitation *n.* invitation *f.*

invite *v.t.* inviter; engager; prier.

inviting *n.* invitation *f.* ~ *adj.* engageant,
attravant.

invocation *n.* invocation *f.* demande *f.*

invoice *n.* facture *f.* ~ *v.t.* facturer, faire une
facture.

invoke *v.t.* invoquer.

involuntarily *adv.* involontairement.

involuntary *adj.* involontaire.

involve *v.t.* envelopper, comprendre, impliquer, entraîner; brouiller. **he finally got ~d in the business,** il s'est finalement occupé du commerce. **don't get ~d in their business,** ne vous mêlez pas de leurs affaires.

involvement *n.* embarras *m.;* gêne *f.;* complication *f.;* participation *f.,* engagement *m.*

invulnerable *adj.* invulnérable.

inward *adj.* intérieur, interne, intime. *adv.* en dedans, intérieurement, à l'intérieur.

inwardly *adv.* intérieurement.

inwards *adv.* vers l'intérieur, en dedans.

iodine *n.* iode *m.*

ipso facto *adv.* ipso facto, de ce fait.

I.Q. *Abbrev. of* **intelligence quotient,** quotient *m.* intellectuel, Q.I.

Iran *npr.* Iran *m.*

irascible *adj.* irascible.

ire *n.* colère *f.,* courroux *m.*

Ireland *npr.* Irlande *f.*

iridescence *n.* iridescence *f.*

iridescent *adj.* iridescent.

iris *n.* iris *f.*

Irish *adj.* irlandais *n.* Irlandais *m.*

irk *v.t.* impers. contrarier.

irksome *adj.* fâcheux, ennuyeux.

iron *n.* fer *m.* **cast ~, pig ~,** fonte *f.* fer en saumon, en gueuse. **sheet ~,** tôle *f.* **wrought ~,** fer forgé. **~,** fer à repasser. *adj.* de fer. **an ~ bar,** une barre de fer. **the ~ age,** l'âge de fer. **~ware,** articles *m.pl.* en fer; ferronnerie *f.* **~work,** ferrure *f.,* grosse serrurerie *f.*

ironic(al) *adj.* ironique.

ironically *adv.* ironiquement.

irony *n.* ironie *f.*

irradiance *n.* rayonnement *m.;* éclat *m.,* lustre *m.,* splendeur *f.*

irradiant *adj.* étincelant; rayonnant.

irradiate *v.t.* rayonner (sur), illuminer.

irradiation *n.* irradiation *f.;* rayonnement *m.;* éclat *m.*

irrational *adj.* irrationnel; déraisonnable; insense.

irrationally *adv.* irrationnellement; sans raison.

irreconcilable *adj.* irréconciliable.·

irrecoverable *adj.* irrémédiable; irréparable; irrecouvrable.

irredeemable *adj.* irrémédiable.

irreducible *adj.* irréductible.

irrefutable *adj.* irréfutable.

irrefutably *adv.* d'une manière irréfutable.

irregular *adj.* irrégulier, déréglé.

irregularity *n.* irrégularité *f.;* désordre *m.;* conduite *f.* désordonnée.

irregularly *adv.* irrégulièrament.

irrelevant *adj.* non pertinent, inapplicable à; déplacé.

irreligious *adj.* irréligieux.

irremediable *adj.* irrémédiable, irréparable; incorrigible.

irremediably *adv.* irrémédiablement.

irreparable *adj.* irréparable.

irreplaceable *adj.* irremplaçable.

irrepressible *adj.* irrépressible.

irreproachable *adj.* irréprochable.

irreproachably *adv.* irréprochablement.

irresistible *adv.* irrésistible.

irresistibly *adv.* irrésistiblement.

irresolute *adj.* irrésolu, indécis.

irrespective *adj.* indépendant.

irresponsible *adj.* irresponsable.

irretrievable *adj.* irréparable, irrémédiable.

irreverence *n.* irrévérence *f.*

irreverent *adj.* irrévérent; irrévérencieux.

irreversible *adj.* irréversible; irrévocable.

irrevocable *adj.* irrévocable.

irrevocably *adv.* irrévocablement.

irrigate *v.t.* irriguer, arroser.

irrigation *n.* irrigation *f.*

irritable *adv.* irritable.

irritant *adj. n.* irritant *m.*

irritate *v.t.* irriter; exciter.

irritation *n.* irritation *f.*

irruption *n.* irruption *f.*

irruptive *adj.* qui fait irruption.

I.R.S. *Abbrev. of* **Internal Revenue Service,** services *m.pl.* fiscaux.

is See BE.

Islam *n.* islam *m.*.

Islamic *adj.* islamique.

island *n.* île *f.*.

islander *n.* insulaire *m.f.,* habitant, habitante d'une île.

isle *n.* île *f.*.

isolate *v.t.* isoler.

isolation *n.* isolation *f.;* isolement *m.*

Israel *n.* Israel *m.* **in ~,** en Israel.

Israeli *adj.* israélien; d'Israël *n.* Isráélien(ne) *m.f.*

issuable *adj.* émissible.

issue *n.* sujet *m.,* problème *m.;* numéro *m.,* fascicule *m.,* issue *f.;* sortie *f.;* émission *f.;* écoulement *m.;* produit *m.;* distribution *f.;* progéniture *f.* — *v.i.* couler, s'écouler, découler; sortir, émaner. *v.t.* émettre; mettre en circulation; délivrer. **to ~ banknotes,** mettre des billets de banque en circulation.

it *pron.* il, elle; le, la; lui; cela. **read the letter, ~ is interesting,** lisez la lettre, elle est intéressante. **~ is raining,** il pleut. **~ is I,** c'est moi. **what is ~?** qu'est-ce que c'est?

Italian *adj.* italien. *n.* Italien *m.,* Italienne *f.*

italic *adj.* italique.

italics *n.* italique *f.*

Italy *npr.* Italie *f.*

itch *n.* gale *f.;* démangeaison *f.* **~** *v.i.* démanger, avoir des démangeaisons.

itching *n.* démangeaison *f.;* désir *m.* ardent.

item *n.* article *m.*

itinerant *adj.* ambulant. *n.* personne ambulante.

itinerary *n.* itinéraire *m.*

its *poss. pron.* le sien, la sienne; les siens, les siennes. *poss. adj.* son, sa, ses.

itself *refl. pron.* lui-même, elle-même. **by ~,** isolé, tout seul, toute seule.

itsy-bitsy *adj. Infml.* tout petit, riquiqui, minuscule.

I.U.D. *n.* stérilet *m.*

ivory *n.* ivoire *m.* *adj.* d'ivoire. **~ worker,** ivoirier *m.*

ivy *n.* lierre *m.*

J

jab *v.t., v.i.* piquer, planter, enfoncer, perforer; (boxing) envoyer un droit; *n.* coup *m.*, coup *m.* droit.

jabber *v.i.* bafouiller; bredouiller; babiller, jacasser. *v.t.* baragouiner. *n.* bredouillement *m.*, baragouinage *m.*; jacasserie *f.*

jack *n.* jeannot *m.* valet *m.* (in cards); cric *m.* (for car). **~ass**, âne *m.*, crétin *m.* **~-in-the-box,** diable *m.*, à ressort. **~pot,** gros lot.

jackal *n.* chacal *m.*

jacket *n.* jaquette *f.*; veste *f.*, veston *m.*, camisole *f.*

jack-knife *n.* grand couteau *m.* de poche.

jade *n.* jade *m.*

jag *v.t.* ébrécher; déchiqueter. *n.* brèche *f.*; dent *f.* de scie.

jaguar *n.* jaguar *m.*

jail *n.* prison *f.* **~bird,** détenu *m.*, détenue *f.*, gibier *m.* de potence.

jam *n.* confiture *f.*; embouteillage *m.* **he got her out of a ~,** il l'a tirée du pétrin. *v.t.* serrer, presser; fouler, écraser; (se) bloquer, (se) coincer. **the door got ~med,** la porte s'est coincée.

jamb *n.* jambage *m.*; montant *m.*

jangle *v.t.* faire discorder. *v.i.* se chamailler; cliqueter. *n.* cliquetis *m.*

janitor *n.* concierge *m.f.*, gardien *m.*, gardienne *f.*

january *n.* janvier *m.*

Japan *npr.* Japon *m.*

Japanese *adj.* japonais. *n.* Japonais *m.*; japonais *m.*, langue *f.* japonaise.

jar *v.i.* résonner d'une manière discordante; détoner; choquer; s'entrechoquer, se heurter; se quereller, se disputer. *n.* vibration *f.*; secousse *f.*; choc *m.*, désaccord *m.*

jargon *n.* jargon *m.*

jasmine *n.* jasmin *m.*

jasper *n.* jaspe *m.*

jaundice *n.* jaunisse *f.*

jaunt *n.* excursion *f.*; tour *m.*, promenade *f.*; tournée *f.*

jauntiness *n.* gaîté *f.*; légèreté *f.*; vivacité *f.*

jaunty *adj.* pimpant, prétentieux.

javelin *n.* javeline *f.*, javelot *m.*

jaw *n.* mâchoire *f.*; *Fig.* bouche *f.*, gueule *f.*; gouffre *m.* **the ~s of death,** l'étreinte de la mort.

jay *n.* geai *m.* *v.i.* **to ~ walk,** traverser en dehors du passage pour piétons.

jazz *n.* jazz *m.*; entrain *m.* **to ~ up,** animer, mettre de l'ambiance.

jealous *adj.* jaloux; envieux.

jealousy *n.* jalousie *f.*

jean *n.* coutil *m.*; **~s,** jean *m.*

jeer *v.i.* railler; se moquer de. *n.* raillerie *f.*, moquerie *f.*

jejune *adj.* naïf, dépourvu d'intérêt.

jelly *n.* gelée *f.*

jellyfish *n.* méduse *f.*

jeopardize *v.t.* risquer, exposer, hasarder, mettre en péril.

jeopardy *n.* danger *m.*, péril *m.*

jerk *v.t.* lancer; secouer; saccader. *n.* secousse *f.*, saccadé *f.*, coup *m.* soudain. **he was ~ed out of the car,** il a été balancé hors de la voiture. *Infml.* crétin *m.*; crétine *f.*; abruti *m.*, abrutie *f.*

jersey *n.* chandail *m.*, tricot *m.* (de laine).

jest *n.* plaisanterie *f.*; mot *m.* pour rire, raillerie *f.* **~** *v.i.* plaisanter.

jet *n.* avion *m.* à réaction; jais *m.* jet *m.* (of water); coulée *f.* *v.i.* s'élancer, se projecter; faire saillie; se pavaner.

jetlag *m.* décalage *m.* horaire.

jetsam *n.* épaves *f.pl.* à la mer.

Jew *n.* Juif *m.*, Juive *f.* Israélite *m.f.* **~'s harp;** guimbarde *f.*

jewel *n.* bijou *m.*; joyau *m.*, pierre precieuse. **~ box, ~ case,** écrin *m.* **~** *v.t.* orner de bijoux; monter sur rubis.

jeweler *n.* joaillier *m.*, jouaillière *f.*, bijoutier *m.*, bijoutière *f.*

jewelry *n.* joyaux *m.pl.*, joaillierie *f.*, bijouterie *f.*

Jewish *adj.* juif.

jib *n.* foc *m.*; volée *f.*

jiffy *n.* moment *m.*, clin *m.* d'oeirl.

jig *n.* gigue *f.* (dance). *v.i.* danser une gigue; sautiller.

jiggle *v.i., v.t. Infml.* gigoter.

jigsaw *n.* puzzle *m.*, énigme *f.*

jilt *v.t.* laisser tomber, rompre (avec).

jingle *v.i.* cliqueter, sonner; s'entrechoquer; rimer. *v.t.* (faire) tinter, faire résonner. *n.* tintement *m.*; clochette *f.*; cliquetis *m.*

jinx *n.* poisse *f.* **~** *v.t.* donner la poisse, porter malheur.

jitters *n. Infml.* trouille *f.*, frousse *f.*

job *n.* travail *m.*; tâche *f.*, affaire *f.* **to do the ~,** faire l'affaire; *Infml.* boulot *m.*

jobless *adj.* sans emploi, sans travail, au chômage.

jock *n. Infml.* sportif *m.*, sportive *f.*

jockey *n.* jockey *m.* **~** *v.t.* duper.

jocular *adj.* plaisant, badin, burlesque.

jocund *adj.* joyeux, gai, jovial.

jog *v.t.* pousser; secouer; remuer; cahoter. **to**

go ~ing, faire du jogging. n. secousse f., poussée f.; coup m. de coude; cahot m. marche f.

joggle v.t. secouer légèrement, être secoué.

john n. le petit coin, les cabinets m.pl. long ~s, caleçon long.

join v.t. joindre; unir; allier, rejoindre; combiner. to ~ hands, joindre les mains. v.i. se toucher, (se) joindre.

joiner n. menuisier m.

joinery n. menuiserie f.

joining n. jonction f. assemblage m., union f.

joint n. joint m., jointure f., articulation f.; gros morceau de viande. elbow ~, coude f. out of ~, démis, disloqué, déboîté. ~ account, compte joint. v.t. couper dans les jointures.

jointed adj. articulé.

jointly adv. conjointement, de concert, d'accord.

joke n. plaisanterie f. bon mot m. to crack a ~, faire une plaisanterie, faire de l'esprit. a practical ~, une farce. v.i. plaisanter. v.t. railler, se moquer de.

joker n. farceur m., farceuse f.

jokingly adv. en riant, en plaisantant, pour rire.

jolly adj. gai, joyeux.

jolt v.i.,v.t. cahoter, secouer. n. cahot m., secousse f. soubresaut m.

jonquil n. jonquille f.

jostle v.i. bousculer, pousser, coudoyer.

jot n. iota m., point m. ~ v.t. noter, prendre note de, marquer.

journal n. journal m.; intime; compte-rendu m., revue f. ~ adj. journalier.

journalism n. journalisme m.

journalist n. journaliste m.f.

journey n. voyage m., excursion f., tour m., tournée f. ~ v.i. voyager.

journeyman n. ouvrier m.

jovial adj. jovial.

joviality n. jovialité f.

jovially adv. gaiement, joyeusement.

jovialness n. joie f. bruyante, gaieté f.

jowl n. joue f., bajoue f.

joyful adj. joyeux.

joyfully adv. joyeusement, avec joie.

joyous adj. joyeux, enjoué.

jubilant adj. qui déborde de joie, triomphant.

jubilation n. réjouissance f.

judaism n. judaïsme m.

judge n. juge m., connaisseur m. to be a good ~ of, se connaître en. v.i.,v.t. juger.

judgment n. jugement m.; décision; sentence f. condamnation f. to pass ~, rendre, prononcer un jugement.

judicature n. judicature f.

judicial adj. judiciaire.

judicious adj. judicieux; sage.

judiciously adv. judicieusement.

jug n. cruche f., pot m.

juggle v.i. faire des tours de passe-passe; jongler.

juggler n. jongleur m. jongleuse f.

jugular adj. jugulaire. n. jugulaire f.

juice n. jus m. suc m.

juicy adj. juteux; succulent.

jujube n. jujubier m.; jujube f.

jukebox n. juke-box m.

July n. juillet m.

jumble n. mélange m. confus, confusion f.; pêle-mêle m.; fatras m. ~ v.t. jeter pêle-mêle; embrouiller. v.i. se confondre, se mêler, s'embrouiller.

jumbling n. confusion f.

jumbo n. géant m.; avion m. géant. adj. énorme. ~ jet, avion m. géant, jumbo-jet m.

jump v.i. sauter, bondire. to ~ out of bed, sauter au bas du lit. to ~ up, se lever en sursaut. to ~ at an offer, s'empresser d'accepter une offre. v.t. franchir, passer. n. saut m.; bond m.

jumpy adj. nerveux, qui sursaute facilement. what are you so ~ about, qu'est-ce que tu as à sursauter tant?

junction n. jonction f.; combinaison f.; embranchement m.

juncture n. jonction f.; jointure f.; articulation f.; conjoncture f., moment m. critique.

June n. juin m.

jungle n. jungle f.

junior adj. jeune, cadet. ~ high, collège m.

juniper n. génévrier m.

junk n. camelote f., fouillis m. ~yard, dépotoir m. jonque f., vieux cordage m.

junket n. lait m. caillé; festin m., voyage m. d'agrément. to take a ~, faire un voyage d'agrément; banqueter, festover.

junkie n. drogué m., droguée f.

jurisdiction n. juridiction f.; compétence f.

jurisprudence n. jurisprudence f.

jurist n. juriste m.f.

juror n. juré m., jurée f.

jury n. jury m. ~ box, banc m. de jury.

just adj. juste, droit, équitable; exact, régulier. a ~ cause, une cause juste, une bonne cause. a ~ remark, une observation juste. adv. juste, tout juste, justement; un peu. ~ enough, juste assez. ~ by here, tout près d'ici. that's ~ like him, c'est bien lui. I was ~ saying, je disais à l'instant même.

justice n. justice f., juge m. to demand ~, demander justice. ~ of the peace, juge de paix.

justiceable adj. justiciable.

justifiable adj. justifiable; légitime, licite.

justification n. justification f.

justify v.t. justifier. v.i. (se) justifier.

justifying n. justification f.

justly adv. justement, à juste titre, juste, exactement.

justness n. justesse f., exactitude f., précision f., justice f.

jut v.i. faire saillie, avancer. to ~ out, bomber.

jute n. jute m. chanvre m. de l'Inde.

juvenile adj. juvénile, jeune, d'enfant.

juxtaposition n. juxtaposition f.

K

kabob n. See KEBAB.

kale n. chou m. frisé.

kaleidoscope n. kaleidoscope m.

kangaroo n. kangourou m.

kaput adj. Infml. foutu, fichu.

karma n. karma m.; destinée f.

kayak n. kayake m.

kebab n. brochette f.

keel n. quille f. ~ v.t. sillonner la mer, naviguer, montrer le fond.

keen aj. affilé, aigu, acéré, aiguisé; tranchant; vif, âpre, perçant, pénétrant, piquant, fin, subtil. to look ~, avoir l'air éveillé. a ~ appetite, un grand appétit. ~ wind, une bise âpre.

keenly adv. d'une maînière acérée, piquante, pénétrante; ardemment, douloureusement.

keenness n. ardeur f., véhémence f., âpreté f.; vivacité f.; subtilité f., finesse f., pénétration f.

keep v.t. garder, tenir, conserver, retenir, maintenir, observer, nourrir, élever. to ~ a store, tenir une boutique. to ~ one's word, tenir sa parole. to ~ accounts, tenir des comptes. to ~ silence, garder le silence. to ~ peace, garder la paix. to ~ in motion, entretenir en mouvement. to ~ a farm, cultiver, exploiter une ferme. to ~ company, rester avec quelqu'un. to ~ from danger, garantir du danger. I will not ~ you long, je ne vous retiendrai pas longtemps. to ~ away, tenir éloigné, éloigner. to ~ back, empêcher d'arriver; retarder, arrêter; cacher. to ~ by, garder, tenir en réserve. to ~ down, tenir en bas; baisser, contenir. to ~ from, tenir éloigné; garder, préserver; empêcher de. to ~ out, tenir dehors, éloigner. to ~ under, tenir dessous; empêcher de s'élever, contenir. to ~ up, tenir levé, tenir en l'air; maintenir, soutenir, empêcher de tomber, conserver, ne pas cesser de; prolonger. v.i. (se) tenir, (se) maintenir; (se) garder, (se) conserver; rester, continuer, durer. to ~ quiet, rester tranquille, se taire. to ~ along, suivre une route. to ~ aloof, se tenir à l'écart. to ~ away, se tenir à l'écart; s'absenter. to ~ back, se tenir à l'écart; se contenir. to ~ in, ne pas sortir; rester chez soi. to ~ off, se tenir à l'écart. to ~ off the grass, pelouse interdite. ~ up the good work, bonne continuation. to ~ on, continuer, ne pas cesser de. ~ on straight forward, marchez toujours droit devant vous. to ~ out of the way, se tenir à l'écart. to ~ to, rester auprès, ne pas quitter; s'en tenir à. to ~ it up, aller toujours, continuer. to ~ with, rester avec. n. garde f., soin m., nourriture f., entretien m.

keeper n. garde m., gardien m.; surveillant m. (d'une prison).

keeping n. garde f., conservation f.; harmonie f., unisson m., accord m.

keepsake n. souvenir m.

keg n. caque f., petit baril m.

ken n. within someone's ~; dans les connaissances de quelqu'un.

kennel n. chenil m.; loge f.; terrier m. (fox).

kept See KEEP.

kernel n. amande f.; grain m., graine f.; pépin m.; noyau m.

kerosene n. pétrole lampant; kérosène m.

kettle n. bouilloire f.; cocotte f., marmite f.

kettledrum n. timbale f.

key n. clef f.; clé f., touche f. (of piano); ton m., tonique f.; cale f., clavette f. master ~, passepartout m. ~board, clavier m. ~note, tonique f. ~stone, clef f. de voûte m. that's the ~, c'est la clef (de l'énigme), c'est la réponse (au problème). ~hole, trou m. de serrure.

khaki n. kaki m.

kick v.t. donner des coups de pied (à). to ~ out, chasser à coups de pied. to ~ the bucket, casser sa pipe. to ~ the habit, renoncer à une (mauvaise) habitude. n. coup m. de pied; ruade f.

kid n. Infml. gosse m.f., gamin m., gamine f., enfant m.f. chevreau m., cabir m. biquet m.

kidder n. Infml. blagueur m.

kidding n. Infml. blague f. you must be ~! vous vous moquez de moi? no ~! sans blague!

kiddy n. petit(e) gosse m.f.

kidnap v.t. enlever, kidnapper.

kidnapper n. kidnappeur m., kidnappeuse f.; ravisseur m., ravisseuse f.

kidnapping n. enlèvement m.

kidney n. rein m.; rognon m. ~ bean, haricot m.

kill v.t. tuer, faire mourir. to ~ by inches, faire mourir à petit feu. to ~ two birds with one stone, faire d'une pierre deux coups. n. mise à mort f.

killer n. tueur m. tueuse f., assassin m.

killing n. meurtre m., homicide m.; adj. this work is ~, c'est un travail tuant.

kiln n. fourneau m., four m.

kilogram n. kilogramme m.

kiloliter n. kilolitre m.

kilometer n. kilometre m.

kilt n. kilt m.

kin n. parenté f., affinité f., parent m., rapport m. next of ~, le plus proche parent. adj. similaire; allié.

kind n. genre m., espèce f., naturef., sorte f., façon f. the human ~, le genre humain. a different ~ of plant, une plante d'une espèce différente. to pay in ~, payer en nature. adj. (to, à, envers) bienveillant, bon, obligeant; affable, tendre. to be ~ to a person, être bon, être obligeant pour une personne. be so ~ as to, ayez la bonté, l'obligeance de. ~-hearted, doté d'un bon coeur.

kindle v.t. exciter, provoquer; éveiller, réveiller. (s')allumer, s'enflammer, prendre feu, s'éprendre, s'animer.

kindliness n. affection f., bienveillance f., bonté f.

kindly adj. doux, bienveillant adv. avec bonté; obligeamment.

kindness n. bienveillance f., bonté f., obligeance f.; bienfaisance f.; bienfait m., service m.

kindred n. parenté f., alliance f., parents m.pl.; rapport m., de la même espèce. adj. parent, allié, congénère.

king n. roi m.; dame f., dame-damée (in chess).

kingdom n. royaume m.; empire m. règne m. **the animal ~**, le règne animal.

kingfisher n. Ornith. martin-pêcheur m.

kingship n. royauté f.

kink n. coque f., noeud f.

kinky adj. qui a des goûts bizarres, excentrique.

kinsfolk n. parents m.pl., parenté f.

kinsman n. au pl. kinsmen, parent m.

kinswoman n. parente f.

kiosk n. kiosque m.

kipper n. hareng ouvert fumé. v.t. saler et fumer (fish).

kiss v.t. embrasser, faire une bise n. bise f., baiser m.

kit n. équipement m., matériel m. **first aid ~**, trousse d'urgence. trousse f. à outils.

kitchen n. cuisine f. **~ garden**, jardin m. potager.

kite n. cerf-volant m.

kith n. connaissance f., ami m. **~ and kin**, parents et amis m.pl.

kitten n. chaton m. v.i. mettre bas des petits chats.

kitty n. minet f., minou m.; cagnotte f.

kiwi n. kiwi m.

kleptomaniac n. kleptomane m.f.

knack n. talent m.; adresse f.; chic m.; tour m. d'adresse.

knapsack n. sac m., sac à dos m.

knead v.t. pétrir.

kneading n. pétrissage m.

knee n. genou m.pl. genoux. **to bend the ~**, fléchir le genou. **~cap**, rotule f. **~ deep**, jusqu'aux genoux. **~-length**, sui va jusqu'aux genoux.

kneel v.i. plier le genous; s'age-nouiller.

knick-knack n. babiole f., bibelot m.

knife n. couteau m. **carving ~**, couteau à découper. **kitchen ~**, couteau de cuisine. **chopping ~**, hachoir m. **paper ~**, coupe-papier m. ~ v.t. donner un coup de couteau à, poignarder.

knight n. chevalier m., champion m.; (in chess)

cavalier m. **~ errant**, chevalier-errant m. ~ v.t. créer chevalier.

knighthood n. chevalerie f.

knit v.t. tricoter, froncer (eyebrows); nouer, joindre, unir. **to ~ one's brow**, froncer le sourcil.

knitting n. tricoter. tricotage m.; tricot m.; union f. **~ needle**, aiguille.

knob n. protubérance f., bosse f.; pomme f., bouton m., poignée f. (door). **the ~ of a door**, bouton m. de porte.

knock v.i. frapper; cogner, heurter, se cogner, se heurter; se buter. **to ~ someone on the head**, frapper quelqu'un sur la tête. **to ~ down**, renverser, terrasser. **to ~ off**, faire tomber en frappant, cesser le travail. **~** n. choc m., heurt m., coup m. **to hear a ~**, entendre frapper à la porte.

knocking n. coup m., cognement m.

knoll n. monticule m., tertre m.

knot n. noeud m., difficulté f., intrigue f. **running ~, slip ~**, noeud coulant. **to tie a ~**, faire un noeud, nouer. **to go ten ~s an hour**, filer dix noeuds à l'heure. v.t. nouer, lier, faire un noeud; embrouiller. v.i. (se) nouer.

know v.t. savoir, connaître; discerner, distinguer (from, de); reconnaître. **to ~ by heart**, savoir par coeur. **to ~ by sight**, connaître de vue. **to ~ for certain**, être sûr de. **don't you ~ me ne me reconnaissez-vous pas?** **he ~s how to read and write**, il sait lire et écrire. **he ~s better.** il sait très bien ce qu'il doit faire. **she doesn't ~ how to do it**, elle ne sait pas comment (le) faire.

knowing adj. savant, instruit, bien informé, habile, fin, rusé. ~ n. savoir m. connaissance f.

knowingly adv. sciemment.

knowledge n. savoir m., connaissance f., science f., instruction f.; souvenir m. **without his ~**, à son insu. **to the best of my ~**, que je sache. **to have no ~ of**, n'avoir pas connaissance de, n'en rien savoir.

known p.p., adj. connu, appris, compris, reconnu. **thing ~**, chose sue. **a ~ fact**, un fait reconnu.

knuckle n. jointure f., articulation f. (of finger), doigt m. **~-duster**, coup de poing (américain). **~ of veal**, jarret m. de veau.

K.O. abbrev. of knock out, K.O.

Koran n. Coran m.

kosher adj. kasher.

L

L m. chiffre remain représentant 50, L., LB., (abbrev. of **Libra**) pound in weight, poids, livre.

la n. Mus. la m.

lab n. Infml. labo m.

label n. étiquette f., codicille m. ~ v.t. étiqueter.

labial adj., n. labiale f.

laboratory n. laboratoire m.

laborious adj. laborieux, pénible, difficile.

labor n. travail m.; peine f., labeur m., hard **~**, travaux forcés dans une prison. **~ pains**, douleurs f.pl. de l'accouchement. v.i. travailler, s'appliquer, s'attacher, Infml. bosser, piocher s'echiner, s'éreinter. **~-force**, main d'oeuvre ouvrière f. **Labour Party**, parti travailliste anglais m. **~ union**, syndicat m. **~** v.t. soigner, pousser, activer.

laborer n. travailleur m.

labyrinth *n.* labyrinthe *m.*

lace *n.* dentelle *f.,* point *m.;* lacet *m.;* cordon *m.,* galon *m.* **shoe~,** lacet *m.* ~ *v.t.* lacer, orner de dentelle.

lacerate *v.t.* lacérer.

laceration *n.* lacération *f.,* déchirement *m.;* déchirure *f.*

lachrymal *adj.* lacrymal.

lachrymose *adj.* pleurard, plaintif.

lack *v.t.* manquer de; ne pas posséder. **they ~ authority,** ils manquent d'autorité. *n.* besoin *m.;* manque *m.,* privation *f.* **for ~ of,** faute de.

lackadaisical *adj.* nonchalant.

laconic *adj.* laconique.

lacquer *n.* laque *f.* ~ *v.t.* laquer.

lactation *n.* lactation *f.,* allaitement *m.*

lacuna *n.* lacune *f.*

lad *n.* jeune homme *m.,* garçon *m.,* gars *m.;* gaillard *m.*

ladder *n.* échelle *f.* **social ~,** échelon *m.* social.

lading *n.* chargement *m.,* cargaison *f.* **bill of ~,** connaissement *m.*

ladle *n.* louche *f.* ~ *v.t.* servir à la louche.

lady *n.* dame *f.,* femme *f.* **young ~,** demoiselle, jeune personne. **~bug** *n.* coccinelle *f.* bête *f.* à bon Dieu. **~'s-slipper,** sabot *m.* de Vénus, soulier *m.* de la Vierge.

ladylike *adj.* bien élevée, douce; élégant; délicat.

lag *v.i.* marcher lentement; rester en arrière, traîner; lambiner. *v.t.* ralentir, affaiblir.

lagging *adj.* traînant, lambinant, lent.

lagoon *or* lagune *n.* lagune *f.*

laic *adj. n.* laïque *m.*

laid *ppa.* of **to lay** and **lay.** ~ **up,** forcé de garder le lit; hors de service.

lair *n.* repaire *m.* bauge *f.,* pâture *f.,* pâturage *m.*

laity *n.* les laïques *m.pl.;* le peuple *m.;* état *m.* séculier.

lake *n.* lac *m.*

lama *n.* lama *m.*

lamb *n.* agneau *m.* **~like,** d'agneau, doux. **~'s tongue lettuce,** doucette *f.,* mâche *f.* ~ **chop,** côte *f.* d'agneau. **~'s wool,** laine *f.* d'agneau.

lame *adj.* boiteux, estropié. *Fig.* imparfait, défectueux, mauvais. **a ~ comparison,** une comparaison défectueuse. **a ~ excuse,** une mauvaise excuse. *v.t.* estropier, rendre impotent.

lament *v.i.* (with **over**), se lamenter, déplorer. *v.t.* plaindre, déplorer, regretter, pleurer. *n.* lamentation *f.;* complainte *f.*

lamentable *adj.* lamentable; déplorable; pitoyable.

lamentably *adv.* lamentablement, déplorablement, pitoyablement.

lamentation *n.* lamentation *f.;* plainte *f.*

lamenting *n.* lamentation *f.,* plainte *f.*

laminate *v.t.* laminer, lamifier, stratifier.

lamp *n.* lampe *f.* **safety ~,** lampe de sûreté. **~post,** lampadaire *m.* ~ **shade,** abat-jour *m.* **~stand,** dessous *m.,* support *m.* de lampe.

lampoon *n.* satire *f.,* libelle *m.,* pamphlet *m. v.t.* outrager, écrire une satire contre.

lance *n.* lance *f.* ~ *v.t.* donner un coup de lance; percer ou couper, ouvrir avec une lancette.

land *n.* terre *f.,* pays *m.,* patrie *f.;* sol *m.* terrain *m.;* propriété *f.,* bien-fonds *m.* **native ~,** la terre natale. **main~,** terre ferme, continent *m.* **arable ~,** terre laborable. **pasture ~,** pâturage *m.* **to buy ~,** acheter des terres. *v.t.,v.i.* débarquer, mettre à terre, atterrir.

landed *adj.* foncier. ~ **property,** biens-fonds *m.pl.* ~ **security,** hypothèque *f.* foncière.

landfall *n.* atterrissage *m.,* succession *f.* inattendue de biens-fonds.

landing *n.* débarquement *m.;* débarcadère *m.;* palier *m.* d'escalier. ~ **card,** carte *f.* de débarquement.

landlady *n.* propriétaire *f.*

landlord *n.* propriétaire *m.*

landmark *n.* borne *f.;* point *m.* de reconnaissance.

landscape *n.* paysage *m.,* point *m.* de vue. ~ **gardener,** jardinier *m.f.* paysagiste *m.* ~ **painter,** paysagiste *m.*

landward *adv.* vers las terre, du côté de la terre.

land *n.* petit chemin *m.;* voie *f.*

language *n.* langage *m.;* langue *f.* **bad ~,** grossièretés *f.pl.* **the ~ of flowers,** le langage des fleurs. **the English ~,** la langue anglaise. **dead ~,** langue morte.

languid *adj.* languissant; faible. **to feel ~,** ne pas se sentir de force, être abattu.

languish *v.i.* languir, dépérir. *n.* langueur *f.*

languishing *n.* langueur *f.* ~ *adj.* langoureux, languissant.

lank *adj.* ~ **hair,** des cheveux plats.

lantern *n.* lanterne *f.;* fanal *m.;* feu *m.;* belvédère *f.* **dark ~,** lanterne sourde. **magic ~,** lanterne magique.

lap *n.* genoux *m.pl.;* giron *m.* tour *m.* **to be on the last ~,** être à la dernière étape. **on her ~,** sur ses genoux. *v.t.* ~ *v.i.* plier; enrouler, envelopper, entourer, retomber sur, se rabattre sur, croiser. *v.i.* laper. **the cat ~s milk,** le chat lape le lait.

lapdog *n.* petit chien *m.,* bichon *m.*

lapel *n.* revers *m.* d'habit.

lapidary *n.* lapidaire *f.*

lapse *n.* course *f.,* marche *f.;* chute *f.* ~ *v.i.* s'écouler; glisser, faillir par inattention, se taire, manquer à ses devoirs.

laptop *n.* portable *m.*

larceny *n.* larcin *m.,* vol *m.*

larch *n.* mélèze *m.*

lard *n.* saindoux, lard. *m. v.t.* larder; barder.

large *adj.* grand; gros; étendu, considérable, fort. **a ~ head,** une grosse tête. **a ~ sum,** une grosse somme. ~ **population,** population nombreuse. **at ~,** à l'aise; en liberté.

lark *n.* alouette *f.;* farce *f.*

larva *n.* larve *f.*

laryngitis *n.* laryngite *f.*

larynx *n.* larynx *m.*

laser *n.* laser *m.*

lash *n.* lanière *n.f,* courroie *n.f,* coup *m.* de fouet; fouet *m.;* cil *m.* ~ *v.t.* fouetter; flagaeller, cingler; **to ~ out**, envoyer un coup violent; *Infml.* envoyer des pardes cinglantes.

lashing *n.* flagellation *f.;* châtiment *m.*

lassitude *n.* lassitude *f.*

lasso *n.* lasso *m.* ~ *v.t.* attraper, prendre au lasso.

last *adj.* dernier. ~ **week,** la semaine dernière. **at ~,** enfin. *adv.* la dernière fois. dernièrement; finalement. *v.i.* durer; se conserver, se garder. *n.* forme *f.* de cordonnier.

lasting *adj.* durable, de longue durée.

lastingly *adv.* durablement.

latch *n.* loquet *m.* ~ *v.t.* attacher, fermer au loquet.

latchet *n.* cordon *m.* (shoe).

late *adj.* tardif, lent; dernier, ci-devant, récent; feu, décédé. **you are ~,** vous êtes en retard. **to keep ~ hours,** rentrer à des heures indues. **the ~ king,** le roi défunt, le feu roi. *adv.* tard récemment; dernièrement. **better ~ than never,** mieux vaut tard que jamais. **of ~,** depuis peu.

lately *adv.* récemment, dernièrement.

lateness *n.* retard *m.*

latent *adj.* latent, caché, secret.

later *adj.* plus tard, postérieur.

lateral *adj.* latéral, de côté.

laterally *adv.* latéralement, de côte.

lath *n.* latte *f.* **as thin as a ~,** sec, maigre comme une latte.

lathe *n.* tour *m.*

lather *v.i.* mousser, *v.t.* savonner, laver *n.* mousse *f.*

Latin *adj.* Latin. **the ~ language,** la langue latine. *n.* qui venait du pays ~.

latitude *n.* latitude *f.*

latrine *n.* latrines *f.pl.*

latter *adj.* postérieur; plus récent; dernier; celui-ci, etc. (opposed to celui-là). **the ~ part of the summer,** la fin de l'été.

latterly *adv.* dernièrement, récemment, depuis peu.

lattice *n.* treillis *m.* ~ **window,** fenêtre treillissée.

laud *n.* louange *f.,* éloge *m.;* *Eccles.* laudes *f.pl.* ~ *v.t.* chanter les louanges de, louer.

laudable *adj.* louable.

laudatory *adj.* élogieux, louangeur.

laugh *v.i.* rire. **to ~ at,** rire de. **to ~ aloud,** rire aux éclats. **to ~ heartily,** rire de bon coeur. **to ~ in one's sleeve,** rire dans sa barbe, rire sous cape. *n.* rire *m.;* ris *m.* **a loud ~,** un gros rire.

laughable *adj.* risible.

laughing *adj.* rieur, enjoué. ~ **eyes,** des yeux pleins de gaieté. *n.* rire *m.,* hilarité *f.* ~ **stock,** risée *f.*

laughingly *adv.* en riant; d'une manière enjouée.

laughter *n.* rire *m.,* ris *m.;* allégresse *f,* hilarité *f.;* risée *f.*

launch *v.t.* lancer **to ~ a ship,** lancer un navire. *v.i.* (se) lancer, s'élancer, se jeter. **to ~ out,** s'étendre sur un sujet. *n.* lancement *m.;* mise à l'eau d'un navire.

launching *n.* mise *f.* à l'eau, commencement *m.*

launder *v.t.* blanchir, laver.

laundry *n.* blanchisserie *f.* **to do the ~,** faire le linge, faire la lessive.

laureate *adj., n.* lauréat *m.,* lauréate *f.*

laurel *n.* laurier *m.* ~ **wreath,** couronne *f.* de laurier.

lava *n.* lave *f.*

lavatory *n.* toilettes *f.pl.,* cabinets *m.pl.* W.C. *m.pl.*

lavender *n.* lavande *f.*

lavish *adj.* prodique; extravagant, immodéré. ~ **of promises,** prodigue de promesses. *v.t.* prodiguer.

lavishly *adv.* avec prodigalité, avec profusion; en gaspillant.

lavishness *n.* prodigalité *f,* gaspillage *m.*

law *n.* loi *f.;* droit *m.;* jurisprudence. **civil ~,** le droit civil. **common ~,** le droit coutumier. ~**maker,** législateur *m.* ~ **student,** étudiant *m.* en droit.

lawful *adj.* légal; légitime; permis.

lawfully *adv.* légalement, légitimement.

lawn *n.* pelouse *f.* gazon *m.* ~ *adj.* de linon; fait en linon. ~ **mower,** tondeuse *f.* à gazon.

lawsuit *n.* procès *m.*

lawyer *n.* légiste *m.,* jurisconsulte *m.,* avocat *m.* avoué *m.*

lax *adj.* flasque, mou; lâche; relâché. ~ **morals,** une morale relâchée.

laxative *adj. n.* laxatif *m.*

laxity *n.* laxité *f.;* relâchement *m.*

lay *v.t.* mettre, poser, placer; coucher, renverser; calmer, apaiser; pondre (eggs). **to ~ bare,** mettre à nu. **to ~ waste,** dévaster, ravager. **to ~ a bet,** faire un pari. **to ~ the fault on someone else,** rejeter la faute sur quelqu'un d'autre. **to ~ aside,** mettre de côté. **to ~ before,** présenter, exposer. **to ~ down,** (s')allonger, déposer, mettre à terre; établir un fait; exposer. **to ~ on,** mettre dessus, enduire ~ **off, to ~ out,** disposer, déployer, tracer; dépenser, débourser.

layer *n.* couche *f,* lit *m.;* pondeuse *f.* (hen).

layette *n.* layette *f.*

laying *n.* mise *f,* pose *f,* ponte *f.*

laze *v.i.* paresser, fainéanter.

lazily *adv.* avec indolence, nonchalamment.

laziness *n.* paresse *f.*

lazy *adj.* paresseux; fainéant; languissant. ~**bones,** *Infml.* feignant(e) *m.f,* feignasse *f.*

lea *n.* pré *m.,* prairie *f,* pâturage *m.*

leach *v.t.* lessiver; filtrer.

lead *n.* plomb *m.* ~ **pencil,** crayon *n.m.* de mine de plomb.

lead *v.t.* mener, conduire, guider, emmener, pousser, induire, engager entraîner. **to ~ the dance,** mener la danse. **to ~ astray,** mener hors du droit chemin, égarer. **to ~ the way,** mener, marcher en tête. **to ~ to vice,** exciter au vice. **to ~ into error,** induire en erreur. **this led her to reflect,** cela la fit réfléchir. **to ~ away,** emmener, entraîner. **to ~ back,** ramener, reconduire. **to ~ on,** conduire en avant, attirer. **to ~ out,** conduire au dehors, faire sortir. **to ~ up,** faire monter, précéder. *v.i.* aller en avant, montrer le chemin, commander, diriger; débuter. *n.* conduite *f.* direction *f.;* commandement *m.,* influence *f.,* priorité *f.,* préséance *f.*

leaded *adj.* plombé.

leaden *adj.* de plomb, fait en plomb, lourd.

leader *n.* guide *m.,* conducteur *m.,* chef *m.,* commandant *m.,* meneur *m.*

leadership *n.* direction *f.*

leading *ppr.* plombant.

leading premier.

leaf *n.* feuille *f.;* feuillet *m.* (of a book), battant *m.* (of a door), rallonge *f.* **yellow leaves** feuilles jaunes. **gold ~,** feuille d'or. **I will make him turn over a new ~,** je lui ferai chanter une autre gamme, prendre un autre ton.

leafless *adj.* sans feuilles, effeuillé.

leafy *adj.* feuillu.

league *n.* ligue *f.* (association), lieue *f.* (measure). *v.i.* se liguer, s'allier.

leak *n.* fuite *f.,* filtration *f.* **to stop a ~,** boucher une voie d'eau. *v.i.* fuir, couler.

leakage *n.* fuite *f.;* voie *f.,* d'eau, perte *f.*

leaking *n.* perte *n.f,* fuite *f.*

lean *v.i.* incliner, s'appuyer. *v.t.* (faire) pencher, courber. **~ on me,** appuyez-vous sur moi, comptez sur moi. *adj.* maigre, pauvre, mesquin. **to grow ~,** maigrir, devenir maigre.

leaning *adj.* penchant *n.* tendance *f.,* inclination *f.*

leap *v.i.* sauter, s'élancer. **to ~ over,** sauter pardessus. **to ~ for joy,** sauter de joie. *v.t.* franchir. *n.* saut *m.,* bond *m.* **to take a ~,** faire un saut. **~frog,** saute-mouton *m.* **~ year,** année *f.* bissextile.

learn *v.t.* apprendre, s'instruire.

learned *adj.* instruit, érudit, savant. **a very ~ man,** un homme très instruit. **a ~ body,** un corps savant.

learner *n.* débutant *m.* débutante *f.* **she is a quick ~,** elle apprend très vite.

learning *n.* étude *f.,* savoir *m.,* instruction *f.,* érudition *f.*

lease *n.* bail *m.* **on a ~,** à bail. **to cancel a ~,** résilier un bail. *v.t.* louer.

leasehold *adj.* tenu à bail, possédé en vertu d'un bail. *n.* tenure *f.* par bail.

leaseholder *n.* locataire *m.f.* par bail.

leash *n.* laisse *f.* ~ *v.t.* attacher, tenir en laisse.

least *irreg. superl.* of **less,** le plus petit, le moindre. *adv.* le moins. **he who ~ deserves it,** celui qui le mérite le moins. **at ~,** au moins, du moins. **not in the ~,** pas le moins du monde, nullement.

leather *n.* cuir *m.,* peau *f.* **~ trade,** commerce *m.* de cuirs. ~ *v.t.* garnir de cuir.

leathery *adj.* ressemblant au cuir.

leave *n.* liberté *f.,* permission *f.;* congé *m.;* adieu *m.* **to take ~,** prendre congé dire adieu.

leave *v.t.* laisser; quitter; partir de; abandonner; léguer. **I ~ that to him,** je m'en rapporte à lui. **to ~ alone,** laisser, laisser tranquille. **to ~ behind,** laisser après soi. **to ~ off,** laissé de côté; ôter, quitter; discontinuer, renoncer à. **to ~ off a bad habit,** renoncer à une mauvaise habitude. **to ~ out,** laisser de côté; omettre, oublier. *v.i.* cesser.

leaved *adj.* garni de feuilles, feuillu; à feuilles.

leaven *n.* levain *m.,* levûre *f.* ~ *v.t.* fermenter, faire lever. **to ~ the dough,** faire lever la pâte.

leavening *n.* fermentation *f.*

leaving *n.* départ *m.*

lecher *n.* débauché *m.*

lecherous *adj.* lascif, impudique, lubrique.

lecture *n.* conférence *f.,* cours *m.;* sermon *m.;* semonce *f.* **to give ~s,** faire des conférences. *v.i.* faire une conférence, faire un cours, professer.

lecturer *n.* conférencier *m.,* conférencière *f.*

led See LEAD.

ledge *n.* bord *m.,* rebord *m.,* saillie *f.;* récif *m.;* chaîne de rochers, couche *f.,* strate *f.*

ledger *n.* grand-livre *m.;* registre *m.*

lee côté *m.* sous le vent. *adj.* sous le vent.

leech *n.* sangsue *f.*

leek *n.* poireau *m.*

leer *v.i.* regarder obliquement; lorgner. *n.* regard *m.* oblique; regard *m.* de travers; oeillade *f.*

lees *n.pl.* lie *n.f,* sédiment *m.*

leeward *adj.* sous le vent. *adv.* sous le vent.

leeway *n.* marge *f.*

left *adj.* gauche. **the ~ foot,** le pied gauche. *n.* gauche *f.* **to the ~,** à gauche. **~-handed,** gaucher.

leftovers *n.pl.* restes *m.pl.*

leg *n.* jambe *f.;* pied *m.* (of a table); cuisse *f.* (of poultry). **~ bone,** tibia *m.* **a ~ of mutton,** un gigot de mouton. **a ~ of pork,** run cuissot de porc. **a ~ of beef,** un trumeau de boeuf.

legacy *n.* legs *m.*

legal *adj.* légal; licite.

legality *n.* légalité *f.*

legalization *n.* légalisation *f.*

legalize *v.t.* légaliser; autoriser, légitimer; régulariser.

legally *adv.* légalement; juridiquement; licitement.

legation *n.* ambassade *f.,* députation *f.;* légation *f.*

legend *n.* légende *f.,* chronique *f.,* histoire *f.*

legendary *adj.* légendaire; fabuleux.

legging *n.* jambière *f.*

leggy *adj.* qui a les jambes longues.

legible *adj.* lisible.

legibly *adv.* lisiblement.

legion *n.* légion *f.*

legionary *adj.* légionnaire; de légion, de légions; nombreux.

legislate *v.i.* légiférer.

legislation *n.* législation *f.*

legislative *adj.* législatif.

legislator *n.* législateur *m.*, législature *f.*

legislature *n.* législature *f.*

legit *adj. Infml.* légal. **he is** ~, on peut lui faire confiance.

legitimate *adj.* légitime. *v.t.* légitimer.

legitimately *adv.* légitimement, légalement; purement, naturellement.

legitimation *n.* légitimation *f.*

legume *n.* légume *m.*

leguminous *adj.* légumineux.

leisure *n.* loisir *m.;* aise *f.* commodité *f.*

leisurely *adv.* à loisir, sans se hâter.

lemon *n.* citron *m.* ~ **tree,** citronnier *m.*

lemonade *n.* limonade *f.*

lend *v.t.* prêter. **to** ~ **a hand to,** donner un coup de main à, aider.

lender *n.* prêteur *m.* prêteuse *f.*

lending *n.* prêt *m.*

length *n.* longueur *f.;* étendue *f.;* point *m.*, degré *m.* **at full** ~, au long, tout au long. **the** ~ **of time,** la durée du temps.

lengthen *v.t.* allonger, rallonger; prolonger; étirer. *v.i.* s'allonger, s'étendre, se prolonger, croître, grandir. **the days** ~, les jours deviennent plus longs.

lengthening *n.* allongement *m.*, prolongement *m.*, prolongation *f.*

lengthwise *adv.* en longueur, dans le sens de sa longueur.

lengthy *adj.* long, plein de longueurs, prolixe.

leniency *n.* douceur *f.*, indulgence *f.*

lenient *adj.* indulgent.

lens *n.pl.* **lenses,** lentille *f.*

Lent *n.* carême *m.*

lentil *n.* lentille *f.*

leo *n. Astron.* le Lion *m.*

leopard *n.* léopard *m.*

leotard *n.* collant *m.* (dancer).

leper *n.* lépreux *m.*

leprechaun *n.* gnome *m.*, lutin *m.*

leprosy *n.* lepre *f.*

leprous *adj.* lépreux.

lesbian *adj.* lesbien; *n.* lesbienne *f.*

lesion *n.* lésion *f.*

less *adj.* plus petit, moindre. *adv.* moins. **much** ~, beaucoup moins. **the** ~ **he works the** ~ **he gains,** moins il travaille, moins il gagne. **so much the** ~, **all the** ~, d'autant moins que. *n.* inférieur *m.;* moins, pas tant de.

lessee *n.* preneur *m.*, locataire *m.*

lessen *v.t.* diminuer. *v.i.* s'amoindrir.

lesser *adj.* moindre, plus petit, inférieur.

lesson *n.* leçon *f.*, répétition *f.* **private** ~, leçon particulière. **singing** ~, leçon de chant.

lest *conj.* de peur que, pour que.

let *v.t.* laisser, permettre, souffrir faire, louer. **to**

~ **fall,** laisser tomber. **to** ~ **one know,** faire savoir à quelqu'un. ~ **me tell you,** permettez-moi de vous dire. **to** ~ **alone,** laisser là, laisser faire, laisser, quitter. **to** ~ **down,** faire descendre; descendre, baisser, lâcher. **to** ~ **in,** faire entrer, admettre. **to** ~ **loose,** lâcher, déchainer. **to** ~ **off,** laisser partir; faire grâce à, tirer, décharger (gun). **to** ~ **out,** laisser sortir; relâcher; élargir; laisser échapper; louer. **to** ~ **up,** cesser. *n.* délai *m.;* empêchement *m.*, obstacle *m.*

lethal *adj.* mortel, fatal.

lethargic *adj.* léthargique.

lethargy *n.* léthargie *f.*

letter *n.* lettre *f.* **capital** ~, majuscule *f.* **dead** ~, lettre refusée, lettre tombée en rebut. ~ **of attorney,** procuration *m.*, pouvoir *m. Typ.* casse *f.* ~ *v.t.* marquer avec des lettres, estampiller.

lettered *adj.* lettre.

lettering *n.* marque *f.*, inscription *f.*, estampillage *m.*

lettuce *n.* laitue *f.*

Levant *adj.* du Levant, de l'Orient, levantin. *n.* Levant *m.*

level *adj.* uniplan, de niveau avec. **to make** ~, rendre uni, aplanir, égaliser. *v.t.* niveler, unir, rendre uni, égaliser. *n.* niveau *m.*, égalité *f.*, portée *f.* **to set on a** ~ **with,** mettre de niveau avec. **dead** ~, niveau parfaitement établi. **plumb** ~, niveau à plomb. **spirit** ~, niveau à bulle d'air.

leveler *n.* niveleur *m.*

leveling *n.* nivellement *m.*

lever *n.* levier *m.*

leverage *n.* puissance *f.*, force *f.* d'un levier.

levitation *n.* lévitation *f.*

levity *n.* légèreté *f.*

levy *v.t.* lever, imposer. **to** ~ **taxes,** lever des impots. *n.* levée *f.*

lewd *adj.* dissolu, libertin, impudique; licencieux.

lewdly *adv.* en débauché, en libertin, impudiquement.

lewdness *n.* impudicité *f.*, dissolution *f.*, débauche *f.*, obscénité *f.*

lexicon *n.* lexique *m.*

liability *n.* responsabilité *f.*, risque *m.*, danger *m.*, au *pl.* **liabilities,** obligations *f.pl.*, engagements *m.pl.* **to incur** ~ **to,** se rendre responsable de.

liable *adj.* responsable, sujet à, exposé à, astreint à; *Dr.* passible de. ~ **for debts,** responsable de dettes. ~ **to mistake,** sujet à l'erreur.

liaison *n.* liaison *f.*

liar *n.* menteur *m.*

libel *n.* libelle *m.;* diffamation *f.* (par écrit). *v.t.* diffamer (par écrit); libeller, calomnier.

libeler *n.* diffamateur *m.*

libelous *adj.* diffammatoire.

liberal *adj.* n. libéral *m.*

liberalism *n.* libéralisme *m.*

liberalism *n.* libéralisme *m.*

liberate *v.t.* libérer (**from**, de) rendre libre; délivrer; mettre en liberté.

liberation *n.* mise *f.* en liberté; libération *f.*

liberator *n.* libérateur *m.*

liberty *n.* liberté *f.*; privilège *m.*; au *pl.* **liberties**, libertés, immunités, *f.* franchises *f.* **you are at ~ to**, libre à vous de. **to take liberties**, prendre des libertés.

libidinous *adj.* libidineux, sensuel, voluptueux.

Libra *n. Astron.* la Balance *f.*

librarian *n.* bibliothécaire *m.*

library *n.* bibliothèque *f.*

Libya *n.pr.* Libye *f.*

license *n.* licence *f.*; privilège *m.*; patente *f.* (de débiteur, etc.), autorisation *f.*, permission *f.* **a marriage ~**, une dispense des bans de mariage. *v.i.* permettre, autoriser; patenter, breveter; licencier.

licentiate *n.* licencié *m.*

licentious *adj.* licencieux.

lichen *n.* lichen *m.*

licit *adj.* licite.

licitly *adv.* licitement.

lick *v.t.* lécher. *Infml.* battre, rosser. **to ~ one's fingers**, se lécher les doigts. *n.* coup *m.* de langue; action de lécher; ce qui est lapé.

licorice *n.* réglisse *f.*

lid *n.* couvercle *m*; (de l'oeil) paupière *f.*

lie *n.* mensonge *m.*; *Infml.* menterie *f.* ~ *v.i.* mentir. ~ *v.i.* être couché, être étendu, (se) coucher; s'appuyer, être situé; gésir. **to ~ on the ground**, être couché, s'étendre par terre. **here ~s**, ci-gît, ici repose. **the book ~s on the table**, le livre est sur la table. **to ~ about**, mentir à propos de. **he ~d about us being together**, il a menti à propos de nous avoir été ensemble. **to ~ alongside**, *Naut.* être amarré bord à bord; être allongé l'un à côté de l'autre. **to ~ around**, traîner. **to ~ down**, (se) coucher, se reposer; être conché, être rabattu. **to ~ on, upon**, coucher sur, être sur, *Fig.* être du devoir de.

lien *n.* privilège *m.*

lieu *n.* lieu *m.*, place *f.*, motif *m.*, raison *f.* **in ~ of**, au lieu de, à la place de.

lieutenant *n.* lieutenant *m.*

life *n.pl.* **lives** vie *f.*; être *m.* animal ~, vie animale. **early ~**, jeunesse *f.* **for ~**, à vie, pour la vie. **larger than ~**, plus grand que nature. **from ~**, d'après nature. **still ~**, nature morte. **to give ~ to**, animer, faire vivre. ~ **annuity**, rente *f.* viagère. ~ **insurance**, assurance *f.* sur la vie. ~ **boat**, bateau *m.* de sauvetage. **~buoy**, bouée *f.* de sauvetage. **~guard**, maître nageur *m.* ~ **interest**, rente *f.* ou propriété *f.* viagère. ~ **jacket**, gilet *m.* de sauvetage. **~size**, grandeur naturelle. **~style**, mode *m.* de vie.

lifeless *adj.* sans vie, inanimé; *Fig.* froid.

lifelessness *n.* mort *f.*; absence *f.* d'énergie; inertie *f.*, absence *f.* de mouvement.

lifetime *n.* durée *f.* de la vie, vivant *m.* **in his ~**, de son vivant.

lift *v.t.* lever, élever, soulever, hausser; relever. *n.* action de lever, de soulever; monte-charge *m.* **to give a ~**, faire monter avec soi (dans sa voiture).

ligament *n.* ligament *m.*

ligation *n.* ligature *f.*, action de lier, lien *m.*; enchainement *m.*

light *n.* lumière *f.*; clarté *f.*, jour *m.*; clair *m.*; feu *m.* **in broad day~**, en plein jour. **moon~**, clair de lune. **it is ~**, il fait jour. **to expose to ~**, mettre en lumière, faire connaître. **to set a thing in the right ~**, mettre une chose dans son vrai jour. **give me a ~**, donnez-moi du feu. **a red ~**, un feu rouge. *adj.* (de couleur) clair, blond; léger, leste, agile; gai, frivole, insignifiant. **a ~ meal**, un repas léger. **a ~ task**, une tâche facile. ~ **hair**, des cheveux blonds.

~ **blue**, bleue clair. **~-colored**, clair. **~-complexioned**, au teint clair. **~-headed**, étourdi, volage. **~-hearted**, gai, sans souci, au coeur léger. *v.t.* allumer, mettre le feu à, enflammer. **to ~ a fire**, allumer du feu. **to ~ the way**, montrer le chemin. *v.i.* arriver, échoir, s'abattre.

lighten *v.i.* briller, luire, faire des éclairs. *v.t.* éclairer; illuminer; instruire; alléger; décharger; adoucir.

lighter *n.* briquet *m.*, allume-cigarette *m.*

lighthouse *n.* phare *m.*

lighting *n.* éclairage *m.*

lightly *adv.* légèrement, à la légère; facilement; gaiement, avec entrain; avec agilité.

lightness *n.* légèreté *f.*

lightning *n.* foudre *f.*; éclair *m.* **~-rod**, paratonnerre *m.* **a flash of ~**, un éclair. **~-proof**, à l'abri de la foudre.

lightweight *n.* dile.

likable *adj.* sympathique; plaisant.

like *adj.* semblable; pareil; ressemblant, tel; égal, probable, vraisemblable. ~ **father, ~ son**, tel père, tel fils. **nothing ~ that** experience in this world, il n'y a rien de tel que l'expérience en ce monde. **to look ~**, ressembler à, avoir l'air de. *n.* égal *m.*, semblable *m.*, pareil *m.*, pareille. **and the ~**, et autres chose pareilles. *adv.* comme, tel que, en. ~ **her**, comme elle. **that's just ~ him**, c'est bien lui. *v.t.,v.i.* aimer, approuver, trouver bon, trouver à son goût. **do you ~ that wine?** aimez-vous ce vin? **to ~ better**, aimer mieux, préférer. **I would ~ to see him**, j'aimerais (bien) le voir. **as you ~**, comme vous voudrez.

likelihood, likeliness *n.* probabilité *f.*, vraisemblance *f.*, possibilité *f.*

likely *adj.* probable, vraisemblable; (**with to**) de nature à, propre à. *adv.* probablement, vraisemblablement. **he is ~ to come**, il est bien probable qu'il vienne.

liken *v.t.* comparer; représenter comme ressemblant; assimiler; faire ressembler à.

likeness n. ressemblance f., air m., portrait m.

likewise adv. pareillement, ainsi que, de même, aussi.

liking n. goût m., affection f., penchant m.; gré m., plaisir m. **to take a ~ to**, prendre goût à quelque chose, prendre quelqu'un en affection.

lilac n. lilas m.

lilt n. rythme m., cadence f.

lily n. lis m. **~ of the valley**, muguet m. **water ~**, nénupharm m.

limb n. membre m. (body) gross branche f. (tree). v.t. demembrer; mettre en pièces.

limber adj. souple, flexible; Fig. faible, facile. n. **~ up**, rendre souple.

lime n. chaux f.; glu f.; tilleul m. (arbre); limette f.; limettier m. **quick~**, chaux vive. **~pit**, fosse f. à chaux. **~water**, eau f. de chaux. v.t. gluer, engluer, prendre au gluau; prendre au piege, attraper; cimenter, amender avec de la chaux.

limestone n. pierre f. calcaire, pierre f. à chaux.

limit n. limite f., borne f., terme m. ~ v.t. limiter; borner; restreindre.

limitation n. limitation f.; restriction f.; réserve f. Law. prescription f.

limited adj. étroit; circonscrit.

limitless adj. sans limites, illimité.

limousine n. limousine f.

limp v.t. boiter; clocher, clopiner. n. claudication f.; boitement m. ~ adj. mou, flasque.

limpet n. lépas m., patelle f.

limpid adj. limpide.

limpidity n. limpidité f., clarté f.

linden n. tilleul m.

line n. ligne f.; voie f. (de chemin de fer); vers m. (poetry); corde f.; tile f., alignement m.; trait m.; ride f.; branche f. (commerce), genre m. partie f. **main ~**, voie principale. **to get off the ~**, dérailler. **to wait in ~**, attendre en file, à la queue. **he stepped out of ~**, Infml. il a été trop loin, il a poussé un peu fort, il exagère. **she comes from a long ~ of intellectuals**, elle vient d'une longue lignée d'intellectuels. **to ~ up**, aligner, se mettre en rang.

line v.t. doubler, garnir, border, tracer. **to ~ with trees**, border d'arbres.

lineage n. lignée f.

lineal adj. en ligne directe.

linear adj. linéaire.

linen n. lin m., toile f. de lin, toile f.; linge m. **clean ~**, linge blanc. **baby ~**, layette f. **~ adj.** de toile, fait en toile; de linge.

liner n. vaisseau m. de ligne; paquebot.

ling n. bruyère f.

linger v.i., v.t. tarder, traîner en longueur, languir; hésiter; retarder; prolonger.

lingerie n. lingerie f., dessous m.pl.

lingering adj. tirant en longueur; qui traine, languissant. n. retard m.; lenteur f.; hésitation f.

lingo n. Vulg. langage m., jargon m.

lingual adj. lingual. n. linguale f.

linguist n. linguiste m.

linguistic adj. linguistique.

lining n. action de garnir; doublure f., garniture f.; Anat. paroi (intérieur) m., revêtement m.

link n. rapport m., lien m., relation f., anneau m., chaînon m., maille f.; attache f. **I can't see any ~ between these two murders**, je ne vois aucun lien/aucune relation entre ces deux meurtres. v.t. enchaîner, attacher, joindre.

linnet n. linette f.

linoleum n. lino(leum) m.

lint n. ouate (fabric).

lion n. lion m. **~-hearted**, de lion, coeur de lion.

lip n. lèvre f., bord m.; babine f.; Culin. bec.

lipstick n. rouge m. à lèvres.

liquefaction n. liquéfaction f.; fusion f.

liquefy v.t. liquéfier, fondre, dissoudre. v.i. se liquéfier.

liqueur n. liqueur f.

liquid adj. liquide, qui coule, en fusion. n. liquide m.

liquidate v.t. liquider.

liquidation n. liquidation f.

liquor n. liqueur f., spiritueux m.

Lisbon n.pr. Lisbonne f.

lisp v.i. bégayer, balbutier. n. zézayement m.

list n. lisière f., bande f. (d'une étoffe); liste f.; rôle m. **to draw up a ~**, dresser une liste. **to strike off the ~**, rayer de la liste. v.t. garnir de lisières, enregistrer. v.i. s'enrôler, s'engager.

listen v.t., v.i. écouter, prêter l'oreille (à).

listener n. auditeur m., écouteur m.

listless adj. inattentif, insouciant.

litany n. litanie f.

liter n. litre m.

literacy n. alphabétisation f. **the ~ rate**, le niveau/degré m. d'alphabétisation.

literal adj. littéral, de lettres.

literally adv. littéralement. **he took it ~**, il l'a pris au pied de la lettre/littéralement.

literary adj. littéraire, lettre. **~ man**, homme de lettres.

literate adj. qui sait lire et écrire.

literature n. littérature f.

lithe adj. souple, pliant, flexible.

Lithuania n.pr. Lituanie f.

litigant adj. plaidant; en litige. n. plaideur m.

litigate v.t. mettre en litige. v.i. plaidir, être en procès.

litigation n. procès m., litige m.

litigious adj. litigieux.

litter n. litière f.; civière f.; brancard m.; portée f. (baby animals); Fig. fouillis m., confusion f. **~ v.t.** faire la litière (horses, cattle); laisser traîner, salir; mettre en désordre.

little adj. petit; peu; faible, mesquin, exigu. **a ~ air**, un peu d'air. n. peu m., peu m. de chose. **wait a ~**, attendez un peu. adv. peu, un peu, guère. **not a ~**, pas mal, pas peu.

littleness n. petitosse f.

littoral adj. littoral.

liturgic, liturgical *adj.* liturgique.

liturgy *n.* liturgie *f.*

livable *adj.* supportable, habitable.

live *v.i.* vivre, demeurer, habiter, loger. **as long as I ~,** jusqu'à mon dernier jour. **to ~ well,** vivre bien. **to ~ from hand to mouth,** vivre au jour le jour. *v.t.* mener, passer. **to ~ a life of luxury,** vivre dans le luxe, luxurieusement.

live *adj.* en vie; vif; vivant. **~ fish,** poisson vivant. **~stock,** bétail *m.* **a ~ coal,** un charbon ardent.

livelihood *n.* moyens *m.pl.* d'existence, vie *f.,* gagne-pain *m.* **that's his ~,** c'est son gagne-pain.

liveliness *n.* vivacité *f.,* vigueur *f.;* gaieté *f.;* enjouement *m.*

lively *adj.* vif, animé, actif, vivant. *adv.* vivement, avec vivacité.

liver *n.* foie *m.*

livery *n.* livrée *f.*

livid *adj.* livide, pâle.

living *adj.* vivant, en vie; vif. **the ~ and the dead,** les vivants et les morts. *n.* moyens *m.pl.* d'existence; gagne-pain *m.* **to make/earn a ~,** gagner sa vie.

lizard *n.* lézard *m.*

llama *n.* lama.

load *n.* charge *f.;* fardeau *m.;* chargement *m.,* poids *m.* **a heavy ~,** un chargement *m.* lourd. *v.t.* charger, combler, accabler.

loaded *adj.* chargé; *Infml.* plein aux as, friqué, bourré de fric.

loaf *n.* pain *m.*

loafer *n.* fainéant *m.*

loam *n.* glaise *f.,* terre *f.* glaise. *v.t.* glaiser.

loan *n.* prêt *m.,* emprunt *m.* **~** *v.t.* prêter.

loath *adj.* à contre-coeur, ayant de la répugnance pour. **he was ~ to punish,** il lui répugnait de punir.

loathe *v.t.* détester, avoir en horreur, regarder avec aversion, avec degoût.

loathsome *adj.* dégoûtant, odieux, détestable; nauséabond, repoussant.

lob *v.t.* laisser tomber lourdement; (tennis) lober, faire un lob.

lobby *n.* vestibule *m.,* hall *m.,* salle d'attente *f.;* corridor *m.*

lobbyist *n.* membre *m.* d'un groupe de pression.

lobe *n.* lobe *m.*

lobster *n.* homard *m.*

local *adj.* local.

locale *n.* lieu *m.*

locality *n.* localité *f.;* position *f.,* situation *f.,* place *f.,* emplacement *m.*

localization *n.* localisation *f.*

localize *v.t.* localiser.

locally *adv.* localement.

locate *v.t.* établir, placer.

location *n.* action de placer; situation *f.,* location *f.*

lock *n.* serrure *f.;* cadenas *m.;* platine *f.* (gun);

mèche *f.,* boucle *f.* (hair); écluse *f.,* barrage *m.* (d'un canal). **to pick a ~,** crocheter une serrure. **~ of hair,** boucle de cheveux. **safety ~,** serrure de sûreté. *v.t.* fermer à clef, enfermer, renfermer, barrer. **~ the door,** fermez la porte à clef. *v.i.* se fermer, s'enfermer; se souder.

locker *n.* casier *m.* **~ room,** vestiaire *m.*

locket *n.* fermoir *m.;* médaillon *m.*

locksmith *n.* serrurier *m.*

locomotion *n.* locomotion *f.*

locust *n.* locuste *f.,* sauterelle *f.; Bot.* caroubier *m.*

locution *n.* locution *f.*

lode *n.* filon *m.*

lodge *v.t.* mettre, placer, déposer. *v.i.* se loger. *n.* maisonnette *f.,* loge *f.* (of a concierge); hutte *f.,* cabane *f.*

lodger *n.* locataire *m.;* habitant *m.*

lodging *n.* logement *m.,* ébergement *m.,* logis *m.,* appartement *m.* **furnished ~s,** appartement garni.

loft *n.* grenier *m.;* mansarde *f.*

loftily *adv.* de haut, en haut; *Fig.* fièrement; avec hauteur.

loftiness *n.* hauteur *f.,* grandeur *f.;* orgueil *m.,* fierté *f.;* sublimité *f.*

lofty *adj.* haut, élevé, orgueilleux, altier; sublime, digne.

log *n.* bûche *f.* (de bois); trone *m.* d'arbre. **~book,** livre/journal de bord *m.*

loge *n. Théât.* loge *f.*

logic *n.* logique *f.*

logical *adj.* logique.

logically *adv.* logiquement.

logician *n.* logicien *m.*

logistic, logistical *adj.* logistique.

logo *n.* marque *f.,* emblème *m.*

loin *n.* (meat) longe *f.; pl.* **loins,** reins *m.pl. Anat.* lombes *m.pl.*

loiter *v.i.* traîner, tarder, musarder, flâner, fainénter, s'amuser en chemin.

loiterer *n.* traînard *m.,* fainéant *m.,* flâneur *m.,* musard *m.*

loitering *adj.* s'amusant en route, flânant. *n.* lenteur *f.* de mouvements; fainéantise *f.*

loll *v.i.* se pencher, s'appuyer nonchalamment, s'étendre à son aise. *v.t.* tirer, faire ou laisser pendre la langue en dehors.

lollipop *n.* sucette *f.*

London *n.pr.* Londres.

lone *adj.* solitaire; isolé; seul.

loneliness *n.* solitude *f.,* retraite *f.*

lonely *adj.* solitaire, isolé.

loneness *n.* solitude *f.*

lonesome *adj.* solitaire, retiré.

lonesomeness *n.* solitude *f.*

long *adj.* long; allongé, lent. **in the ~ run,** à la longue. *adv.* longtemps, longuement. **~ after,** longtemps après. **~ since, ~ ago,** il y a long-temps. **have you known them ~?** vous les connaisez depuis longtemps? **as ~ as I live,**

jusqu'à mon dernier jour. **all night ~**, toute la nuit. *v.i.* désirer ardemment, soupirer après, avoir envie de. **I ~ to see him**, j'ai grande envie de la voir. **~ armed**, qui a les bras longs.

longevity *n.* longévité *f.*

longing *n.* désir *m.* ardent, envie *f.* impatiente, souhait *m.* vif.

longitude *n.* longitude *f.*

look *v.i.* regarder; paraître, avoir l'air. **to ~ ill**, avoir mauvaise mine, avoir l'air malade. **~ sharp**, dépêchez vous. **to ~ sharp, to ~ alive**, avoir l'air vif/éveillé, avoir l'air intelligent. **that ~s good on you**, ça vous va très bien. **the front ~s into the garden**, la façade donne sur le jardin. **to ~ after**, regarder après; avoir soin de; chercher; surveiller. **to ~ around**, regarder autour de soi; chercher du regard. **to ~ at**, regarder. **to ~ away**, détourner les yeux. **to ~ back**, regarder an arrière, *Fig.* faire un retour (sur), considérer, envisager; se reporter. **to ~ down**, regarder en bas; baisser les yeux; baisser; dompter (par les regards). **to ~ down on**, mépriser. **to ~ for**, chercher; attendre; s'attendre à. **to ~ into**, s'informer de, avoir vue sur; donner dans. **to ~ like**, ressembler à. **to ~ out**, être sur ses gardes. **to ~ over**, donner sur, regarder par dessus; examiner; revoir. **to ~ up**, lever les yeux; se relever; être à la hausse, chercher. **to ~ up**, avoir de la considération pour. *v.t.* chercher. **to ~ up a thing**, chercher une chose. *n.* air *m.*, mine *f.*; regard *m.*, coup *m.* d'oeil. **sweet ~**, regard doux. **angry ~s**, des regards irrités.

looker *n.* spectateur *m. Infml.* une très belle personne.

looking *adj.* à l'air de. **good-~, nice-~**, beau *m.* belle *f.* mignon(ne) *m.f.*

lookout *n.* guet *m.*; vue *f.*; *Naut.* découverte *f.*, vigie *f.*

loom *n.* métier *m.* à tisser. *v.i.* paraître; apparaître, se dessiner.

loon *n.* plongeon *m., Infml.* fou *m.*

loony *n.* dingue *m.f.*

loop *n.* boucle *f.*, croisé (skating) *m.*, stérilet *m.* (contraceptive). *v.t.* faire une boucle, boucler.

loophole *n.* meurtrière *f.*, échappatoire *m.*

loose *v.t.* détacher, délier, relâcher; délivrer, *v.i.* mettre en liberté; affranchir (d'une obligation). *adj.* lâche; délié, détaché; ample; *Fig.* décousu, sans suite; relâche, licencieux. **~ sleeves**, des manches larges. **~ morals**, morale relâchée. **to let ~, to set ~**, déchaîner, mettre en liberté.

loosely *adv.* lâchement, nonchalamment; licencieusement; librement; avec abandon.

loosen *v.t.,v.i.* délier, détacher; *Agr.* ameublir; dégager; relâcher.

looseness *n.* relâchement *m.*, irrégularité *f.*; déréglement *m.* des moeurs. *Méd.* dévoiement *m.*

loot *n.* butin *m.*, pillage *m.*

looting *n.* pillage *m.*, brigandage *m.*

lop *v.t.* ébrancher, émonder, élaguer.

lop-eared *adj.* aux oreilles pendantes.

loquacious *adj.* loquace.

loquacity *n.* loquacité *f.*

Lord *n.* seigneur *m.*, maître *m.* **land~**, propriétaire *m.* **the good Lord**, le bon Dieu *m.* **~** *v.i.* dominer; faire le maître, le seigneur.

lose *v.t.,v.i.* perdre, égarer; faire perdre; retarder (clock).

loser *n.* perdant *m.*

losing *adj.* faisant perdre, mauvais.

loss *n.* perte *f.*, préjudice *m.*, défaut *m.*

lost *adj.* perdu. **a ~ cause**, une cause perdue.

lot *n.* partie *f.*, sort *m.*, tirage au sort *m.*, lot *m.*, parcelle (land) *f.* ~ *adv.* beaucoup; souvent. quantité *f.*, hasard *m.*, fortune *f.* **a ~ of people**, beaucoup de monde. **they go there a ~**, ils y vont souvent, **to draw, to cast ~s**, tirer au sort. **to sell by or in lots**, vendre par lots. *v.t.* lotir; répartir.

lotion *n.* lotion *f.*

lottery *n.* loterie *f.*

loud *adj.* haut, fort, bruyant. **a ~ voice**, une voix forte. **a ~ laugh**, un rire bruyant, retentissant. *adv.* à haute voix, bruyamment.

loudly *adv.* fort, bruyamment.

loudness *n.* sou *m.* retentissant; retentissement *m.*

lounge *v.i.* flâner, badauder, s'étendre nonchalamment. *n.* chaise *f.* longue, petit salon.

louse *n.* pou *m.* **crab ~**, morpion *m.*

lousy *adj.* pouilleux., *Infml.* miteux. **what ~ weather!** quel temps pourri! *Infml.* **wait till I get hold of that ~ bastard!** attends que je lui mette la main dessus à cet enfant de salaud!

lout *n.* butor *m.*, lourdaud *m.*, rustre *m.*, maladroit *m.*

lovable *adj.* aimable.

love *v.t.* aimer, affectionner, chérir. *n.* amour *m.*; affection; amitié *f.* **to be in ~**, être amoureux. **self-~**, amour de soi-même; amour-propre. **to fall in ~ with**, tomber amoureux de. **to make ~ to**, faire l'amour à. **my ~ to all**, mes amitiés à tous.

loveless *adj.* sans amour.

loveliness *n.* beauté *f.*, grâce *f.*

lovely *adj.* aimable; beau, belle; charmant, ravissant.

lover *n.* amant *m.*, amoureux *m.*, amateur *m.*

loving *adj.* épris, amoureux, affectueux, tendre.

lovingly *adv.* avec amour, affectueusement.

low *adj.* bas, humble, petit, faible, commun, vulgaire; chétif, profond, grave. **~ water**, marée basse. **with a ~ voice**, à voix basse. *adv.* en bas, profondément; à bas prix, bas. **to bow ~**, faire un profond salut. **speak ~**, parlez bas. **~-priced**, à bas prix. *v.i.* beugler, meugler, mugir. *n.* beuglement *m.*, mugissement *m.*

lower *v.t.* baisser, diminuer, humilier, avilir. *v.i.* s'abaisser, tomber, s'affaiblir; *Naut.* affaler, caler. **~ the sails**, baisser les voiles. *adj.* bas; plus bas.

lower *v.i.* s'obscurcir, s'assombrir, se couvrir de nuages; *Fig.* se renfrogner.

lowering *n.* abaissement *m.;* humiliation *f.*

lowering *adj.* sombre, nuageux, menaçant.

lowliness *n.* humilité *f.;* modestie *f.*

lowly *adj.* humble, modeste. *adv.* humblement, modestement.

lowness *n.* humilité *f.,* médiocrité *f.* (de condition); modicité *f.* (de prix).

lox *n.* saumon fumé *m.*

loyal *adj.* loyal, fidèle.

loyally *adv.* fidèlement.

loyalty *n.* fidélité *f.*

lozenge *n.* losange *m.*

lubricant *n.* lubrifiant.

lubricate *v.t.* lubrifier.

lubrication *n.* lubrification *f.*

lubricity *n.* lubricité *f.*

lucid *adj.* lucide, limpide, brillant, lumineux; transparent.

lucidity *n.* clarté *f.,* éclat *m.;* limpidité *f.;* lucidité *f.*

lucidly *adv.* lucidement, clairement.

luck *n.* fortune *f.,* chance *f.,* hasard *m.* **good ~,** bonne chance.

luckily *adv.* heureusement, par bonheur.

luckiness *n.* bonheur *m.*

lucky *adj.* chanceux, heureux; propice, favorable.

lucrative *adj.* lucratif.

lucre *n.* lucre *m.*

ludicrous *adj.* grotesque, ridicule, absurde.

ludicrously *adv.* risiblement.

lug *v.t.* **to ~ away,** entraîner, enlever. **to ~ out,** tirer dehors. *v.i.* (se) traîner.

luggage *n.* bagages *m.pl.*

lugubrious *adj.* lugubre, triste.

lukewarm *adj.* tiède; froid, indifférent.

lull *v.t.* endormir. *v.i.* (se) calmer, s'apaiser, s'assoupir. *n.* ce qui calme, calmant *m.; Naut.* accalmie *f.*

lullaby *n.* berceuse *f.*

lumbago *n.* lumbago *m.*

lumbar *adj.* lombaire.

lumber *n.* bois de charpente *m.* ~ *v.i.* se traîner lourdement. **~jack,** bûcheron *m.*

lumbering *adj.* encombrant.

luminary *n.* corps *m.* lumineux; luminaire *m. Fig.* lumière *f.*

luminous *adj.* lumineux, clair, lucide; radieux. **a ~ idea,** une idée lumineuse.

luminosity *n.* luminosité *f.;* netteté *f.,* lucidité *f.,* clarté *f.*

lump *n.* morceau *m.,* grumeau *m.;* monceau *m.;* bloc *m.* **in a ~,** en masse, en bloc. *v.t.* entasser, mettre en tas; prendre en bloc.

lumpy *adj.* lourd; grumeleux.

lunacy *n.* état *m.,* lunatique; aliénation *f.* mentale; insanité *f.;* démence *f.*

lunar *adj.* lunaire.

lunatic *adj.* lunatique. *n.* lunatique *m.,* fou *m.*

lunch, luncheon *n.* déjeuner *m.* ~ *v.i.* déjeuner.

lung *n.* poumon *m.;* mou *m.* (du veau, etc.).

lurch embarras *m.* **to leave in the ~,** *Fig.* laisser dans l'embarras, planter là.

lure *n.* leurre *m.,* amorce *f.,* appât *m.* ~ *v.t.* leurrer.

lurid *adj.* blafard; livide; effrayant, triste, sombre, lugubre.

lurk *v.i.* être aux aguets; épier, se cacher. **to ~ about,** rôder autour de.

lurking *adj.* caché, secret, qui se cache. **~ rocks,** des rochers à fleur d'eau. **~ place,** embuscade *f.,* cachette *f.*

luscious *adj.* succulent, délicieux.

lush *adj.* luxuriant.

lust *n.* désir *m.* ardent; concupiscence *f.;* impudicité *f.,* luxure *f.* ~ *v.i.* désirer ardemment, convoiter.

luster *n.* lustre *m.,* éclat *m.,* splendeur *f.*

lustful *adj.* convoiteux, voluptueux; impudique, libidineux, lubrique, lascif.

lustfully *adv.* avec convoitise; impudiquement, lascivement.

lustfulness *n.* convoitise *f.;* appétits *m.pl.* charnels; impudicité *f.*

lustily *adv.* vigoureusement, avec vigueur, avec embonpoint.

lustiness *n.* vigueur *f.*

lustrous *adj.* luisant, brillant, lumineux.

lusty *adj.* fort, vigoureux, robuste; gros; corpulent.

Lutheran *adj.* luthérion. *n.* Luthérion *m.*

Lutheranism *n.* luthéranisme *m.*

luxuriance *n.* surabondance *f.;* exubérance *f.;* luxuriance *f.*

luxuriant *adj.* luxuriant, surabondant, exubérant; trop riche.

luxuriate *v.i.* croître avec exubérance; être trop abondant, vivre dans le luxe; *Fig.* s'étendre avec délices. **to ~ in,** se livrer avec abandon à.

luxurious *adj.* de luxe, somptueux; luxueux.

luxuriously *adv.* somptueusement, luxueusement; luxuriousement.

luxury *n.* luxe *m.;* somptuosité *f.;* volupté *f.;* luxure *f.*

lying *adj.* menteur (person), mensonger (thing).

lymph *n.* lymphe *f.*

lymphatic *adj.* lymphatique. *n.* vaisseau *m.* lymphatique.

lynch *v.t.* lyncher. **~ law,** loi *f.* de lynch.

lynx *n.* lynx *m.*

Lyons *n.pr.* Lyon.

lyric, lyrical *adj.* lyrique. *n.* poème *m.* lyrique; lyrique *m.*

M

M chiffre romain (représentant mille).

ma *n.* maman *f.*

M.A. *abbrev.* **Master of Arts,** maîtrise ès lettres.

ma'am *n. abbrev.* **madam,** madame *f.*

macabre *adj.* macabre.

macaroni *n.* macaroni *m.*

macerate v.t. macérer.

machete n. machette f.

machiavelism n. machiavélisme m.

machination n. machination f.

machine n. machine f.; mécanique f.; instrument m., engin m.

machinery n. machinerie f., mécanisme m.; les machines f.pl.; machine f.

machinist n. mécanicien m., machiniste m.

macho n. macho m.

mackerel n. maquereau m. adj. pommelé.

mad adj. fou, folle, insensé, aliéné, enragé, furieux. ~ **for, after,** fou de. **raving** ~, fou à lier. **to be** ~, être fou. **he is** ~ **at me,** il est furieux contre moi. ~**house,** maison f. de fous, hospice m. d'aliénés.

madam n. madame f.

madden v.t. rendre fou, faire perdre la tête. v.i. devenir fou; se démener.

made adj. fait, tout fait, confectionné. ~ **up,** confectionné; artificiel. **ready**~, confectionné, tout fait.

Madeira n.pr. Madère (island). n. madère m., vin m. de Madère.

madly adv. follement, comme un étourdi, avec fureur.

madman n. fou m., insensé m., aliéné m.

madness n. folie f., démence f.; en fou.

Madonna n. Madone f.

mafia n. mafia f.

mag n. Infml. magazine m.

magazine n. revue f., magasin m., arsenal m., soute f. aux poudres; revue f., magazine m.

maggot n. ver m., chenille f., larve f.

magi n.pl. Mages m.pl. les Trois Rois m.pl.

magic n. magie f.

magic, magical adj. magique.

magically adv. par magie.

magician n. magicien m.

magisterial adj. magistral, impérieux, arrogant, hautain, altier.

magistrate n. magistrat m.; juge m. de paix.

magnanimity n. magnanimité f. grandeur f. d'âme.

magnanimous adj. magnanime.

magnate n. magnat m.

magnesium n. magnésium m.

magnet n. aimant m.

magnetic adj. magnétique.

magnetism n. magnétisme m.

magnetize v.t. aimanter, magnétiser. v.i. s'aimanter.

magnific(al) adj. magnifique, éclatant, splendide.

magnificence n. magnificence f.

magnificent adj. magnifique.

magnifier n. loupe f.; personne qui grossit, panégyriste m.

magnify v.t. grandir, agrandir, magnifier; exalter, vanter.

magniloquence n. emphase f.; ampoulé.

magniloquent adj. emphatique, prétentieux.

magnitude n. grandeur f.; importance f.

magnolia n. magnolia m.

magnum n. magnum m.

magpie n. pie f.

mahogany n. acajou m.

maid n. fille f., jeune fille f.; vierge f., pucelle f.; servante, domestique f. ~ **of honor,** fille, dame d'honneur. **the** ~ **of Orleans,** la pucelle d'Orléans. **lady's** ~, femme de chambre. **kitchen** ~, fille de cuisine.

maiden n. fille f., jeune fille f., demoiselle f. adj. de fille, de jeune fille, (de) vierge. ~ **name,** nom de jeune fille.

mail n. courrier m.; dépêche f.; maille f., armure f. ~ v.t. envoyer par la poste; mettre une cotte de mailles, cuirasser.

mailbox n. boîte f. à lettres.

mailman n. mailman n.pl., facteur m.

maim v.t. estropier; mutiler.

main adj. principal; premier; grand, important, essentiel. ~ **building,** bâtiment principal. ~**mast,** grand mât. ~ **road,** route principale f. n. force f.; le gros m.; le total m., océan m., pleine mer; continent m.; conduit m., tuyau m. **in the** ~, au fond, absolument parlant. **with might and** ~, de toute sa force.

mainly adv. principalement, surtout.

maintain v.t. maintenir; soutenir; nourrir, alimenter. **to** ~ **a cause,** soutenir, défendre une cause.

maintenance n. entretien m., maintien m., moyens m.pl. de subsistance; appui m., soutien m., protection f.; Law. pension f. alimentaire.

maize n. maïs m.

majestic adj. majestueux.

majesty n. majesté f.

major adj. majeur; plus grand. **the** ~ **part,** la majeure partie. n. Milit. major m., chef m. de bataillon (infantry), chef d'escadron (cavalry); Law. majeur m.; Log. majeure f. ~ **general,** major général. v.t. **to** ~ **in science,** suivre le cours scientifique.

majority n. majorité f., le plupart. f. de major.

make v.t. faire; créer, produire, gagner (money); effectuer; causer; rendre; atteindre. **to** ~ **hats,** faire des chapeaux. **to** ~ **a speech,** faire un discours. **to** ~ **a bargain,** faire un marché. **to** ~ **a promise,** faire une promesse. **to** ~ **a mistake,** faire erreur, se tromper. **to** ~ **a bed,** faire un lit. **two and two** ~ **four,** deux et deux font quatre. **to** ~ **excuses,** faire des excuses. **to** ~ **a fortune,** faire fortune. **to** ~ **known,** faire connaître, faire savoir. ~ **him go,** faites-le aller. **that's enough to** ~ **me upset,** fa suffit pour me rendre en colère. **I will** ~ **it up to you,** je te compenserai (pour). **to** ~ **much of,** faire grand cas de. **to** ~ **sure of,** s'assurer de. **to** ~ **out,** se débrouiller, faire aller; comprendre, dresser, faire (list, check); discerner, distinguer, déchiffrer.

Infml. se faire des mamours se peloter. **I cannot ~ it out,** je n'y comprends rien. **to ~ a fool of,** se moquer de, se jouer de. **to ~ the best of,** tirer le meilleur parti possible de, mettre à profit. **to ~ over,** céder. **to ~ ready,** préparer. **to ~ it up,** inventer, raconter des histoires. **to ~ up one's mind,** se décider. *v.i.* aller à, tendre, s'avancer, se diriger; courir. **to ~ for,** aller, se diriger vers. **to ~ off,** s'en aller, s'enfuir, s'esquiver, décamper; *Vulg.* filer. **to ~ up for,** suppléer à, remplacer. **to ~ up to,** s'approcher de, s'avancer vers. *n.* façon, forme *f.,* coupe *f.* (clothing); fabrication *f.,* fabrique *f. n.* **~-believe,** trompe-l'oeil *m.* **~over,** transformation *f.* **~up,** maquillage *m.,* caractère *m.,* constitution *f.* **~up exam/test,** examen *m.* de rattrapage. **~up artist,** maquilleur(euse) *m.* (*f.*). **~up remover,** démaquillant *m.*

maker *n.* créateur *m.;* fabricant *m.,* faiseur *m.*

making *n.* création *f.,* travail *m.,* façon *f.;* composition *f.;* structure *f.* **that was the ~ of him,** c'est ce qui a fait sa fortune.

malady *n.* maladie *f.*

Malaysia *n.pr.* la Malaisie *f.*

malaria *n.* malaria *f.*

male *adj.* mâle, masculin. *n.* mâle *m.,* homme. **the differences between ~s and females are . . . ,** les différences *f.pl.* entre les hommes et les femmes sont . . . .

malediction *n.* malediction *f.*

malefice *n.* maléfice *m.,* enchantement *m.,* sortilège *m.*

malformation *n.* malformation *f.*

malfunction *n.* dérèglement *m.,* mauvaise fonction *f.* **~** *v.t.* se dérégler.

malice *n.* malice *f.;* méchanceté *f.,* malveillance *f.; Law.* intention *f.* criminelle. **with ~ aforethought,** avec préméditation.

malicious *adj.* malicieux, malveillant, méchant; *Law.* criminel.

maliciously *adv.* malicieusement; par méchanceté.

maliciousness *n.* malice *f.,* malveillance *f.,* méchanceté *f.*

malign *adj.* malin *m.,* maligne *f.* **~** *v.t.* nuire méchamment; calomnier, diffamer. *v.i.* avoir de la rancune.

malignant *adj.* malin *m.,* maligne *f.;* méchant, haineux; malfaisant. **a ~ tumor,** une tumeur maligne.

malingerer *n.* malingre *m.*

mall *n.* center commercial *m.*

malleable *adj.* malléable.

malnutrition *n.* malnutrition *f.*

malpractice *n.* néglicense *f.* professionnelle, malversation *f.*

malt *n.* malt *m.* **~ liquor,** bière *f.* **~ vinegar,** vinaigre *m.* de bière. *v.t.* faire du malt. *v.i.* se transformer en malt.

maltreat *v.t.* maltraiter.

maltreatment *n.* mauvais traitement *m.*

mama, mamma *n.* maman *f.*

mammal *n.* mammifère *m.*

mammary *adj.* mammaire.

mammoth *n.* mammouth *m.*

man *n.* (*pl.* **men**) homme *m.; Infml.* mon brave; personne *f.;* (chess) pièce *f.;* (checkers), dame *f.,* pion *m.* **the head ~,** le chef. **~hunt,** chasse à l'homme. **~-kind,** l'homme, le genre *m.* humain, la race *f.* humaine. **~made,** *adj.* artificiel. **~slaughter,** homicide *m.* involontaire. *v.t.* garnir d'hommes, équiper, armer, fortifier. **to ~ a fleet,** equipper une flotte. **to ~ the boat,** armer le canot. **~eater,** anthropophage *m.,* cannibale *m.*

manacle *n.* menottes *f.pl.* **~** *v.t.* mettre les menottes, garrotter.

manage *v.t.* conduire, gouverner, gérer, régir; ménager. **to ~ a business,** diriger un commerce. **to ~ a boat,** gouverne une barque. **don't worry, he'll ~,** ne t'en fais pas, il s'en sortira/il se débrouillera. **I will ~ it,** je le ménagerai. *v.i.* agir, s'arranger; trouver moyen de.

manageable *adj.* maniable; domptable; gouvernable; docile.

management *n.* maniement *m.,* conduite *f.,* gestion *f.,* direction *f.,* gouvernement *m.,* addresse *f.,* ménagement *m.*

manager *n.* directeur *m.,* administrateur *m.,* régisseur *m.,* gérant *m.;* économe *m.*

managing *adj.* gérant; qui dirige, qui conduit.

mandate *n.* mandat *m.* **~** *v.t.* mettre sous mandat.

mandatory *adj.* obligatoire; *n.* mandataire *m.f.*

mandible *n.* mandibule *f.*

mane *n.* crinière *f.*

manger *n.* mangeoire *f.,* crèche *f.*

mangle *n.* calandre *f.;* manglier *m.* **~** *v.t.* lacérer, mutiler; estropier.

mango *n.* mangue *f.* **~ tree,** manguier *m.*

mangy *adj.* galeux.

manhood *n.* virilité *f.,* âge *m.* viril.

mania *n.* manie *f.,* folie *f.*

maniac, maniacal *adj.* maniaque, frénétique, furieux, enragé, *Infml.* mordu (de). *n.* maniaque *m.*

manic *adj.* maniaque. **~-depressive,** *adj.* **~** *n.* maniaco-dépressif.

manicure *n.* manucure *m.*

manifest *adj.* manifeste, évident. *n.* manifeste *m.* **~** *v.t.* manifester, témoigner.

manifestation *n.* manifestation *f.*

manifesto *n.* manifeste *m.*

manifold *adj.* multiple, nombreux, de plusieurs manières.

manipulate *v.t.* manipuler.

manipulation *n.* maneuver *f.,* manipulation *f.*

mankind *n.* espèce humaine, genre *m.* humain, humanité *f.*

manlike *adj.* d'homme, viril, courageux.

manliness *n.* air *m.* mâle, dignité *f.;* courage *m.,* intrépidité *f.*

manly adj. mâle; en homme; viril, courageux. adv. en homme, bravement.

manna n. manne f.

mannequin n. mannequin m.

manner n. manière f.; sorte f., genre; façon f.; habitude f.; pl. manières f.pl., moeurs f.pl. **in this ~**, ainsi. **the ~ in which**, la manière dont. **in a ~**, en quelque sorte. **manners make the man**, on connaît un homme à ses manières.

mannerly adj. civil, poli, de bon ton, bien élevé. adv. poliment.

mannish adj. masculin.

manoeuver n. manoeuvre f. ~ v.i. maneuvrer. v.t. faire maneuvrer.

manor n. manoir m., domaine m. **~ house**, maison seigneuriale, château m.

manpower n. main-d'oeuvre f.; Mil. effectif m., potentiel m. humain.

mansion n. hôtel m., particulier; résidence f.

mantle n. manteau m., mante f. Fig. masque. **the ~ of night**, le manteau de la nuit. **~piece, ~ shelf**, cheminée f., manteau de cheminée. v.t. couvrir d'un manteau; voiler.

manual adj. n. manuel m.

manually adv. manuellement, à la main.

manufacture n. manufacture f.; fabrication f.; objet m. manufacturé. v.t. manufacturer; fabriquer.

manufacturer n. manufacturier m., fabricant m.

manure n. engrais m., fumier m., compost m.

manuscript n. adj. manuscrit m.

many adj. plusieurs, beaucoup, nombreux. **how ~**, combien. **so ~**, tant, autant. **as ~ as**, autant que. **too ~**, trop. n. multitude f., foule f., peuple m. **a great ~**, un grand nombre. **~-colored**, multi-colore.

map n. carte f. géographique; plan m. (city). **the ~ of the world**, la mappemonde. v.t. tracer ou dessiner une carte.

maple n. érable m.

mar v.t. gâter, endommager; abîmer; défigurer.

marathon n. marathon m.

marauding adj. maraudant. n. maraude f., maraudage m.

marble n. marbre m., bille f. (toy). adj. de marbre; dur, insensible. v.t. marbrer. **~ cutter**, marbrier m. **~-hearted**, au coeur de marbre; dur. **~ works**, marbrerie f.

marbled adj. marbré.

march v.i. marcher, se mettre en marche. **to ~ in**, entrer. **to ~ off**, se mettre en marche; décamper, plier bagage. **to ~ on**, avancer. **to ~ out**, sortir. **to ~ past**, défiler. v.t. faire marcher, mettre en marche, diriger une armée. **to ~ back**, faire revenir. n. marche f.; course f., progrès m.; mars (month).

mare n. jument f.

margarine n. margarine f.

margin n. bord m.; marge f.; lisière f.; Typ. blanc m. ~ v.t. border; marginer, mettre une marge.

marginal adj. marginal.

marigold n. souci m.

marijuana, marihuana n. marijuana f., marihuana f.

marina n. marina f., port de plaisance m.

marinate v.t. (faire) mariner.

marine adj. de mer; marin; naval. n. soldat de marine; marine f.

mariner n. marin m., matelot m.

marital adj. marital.

maritime adj. maritime.

marjoram n. marjolaine f., origan m.

mark n. marque f., preuve f., signe m.; point m.; note f. (school), distinction f.; but m., cible f.; ligne f. de départ (race). **trade~**, marque de fabrique, marque déposée. **~ of ignorance**, une preuve d'ignorance. **to hit the ~**, atteindre, toucher le but; frapper juste. **to miss one's ~**, manquer le but. **near the ~**, près de la réalité. **book~**, signet m. ~ v.t., v.i. marquer, remarquer, noter, observer.

marker n. marqueur m.

market n. marché m., halle f., vente f., débit m., débouché m. **to go to ~**, aller au marché. **corn ~**, halle au blé. **fish ~**, marché aux poissons. **flower ~**, marché aux fleurs. **~-place**, marché m., place f. du marché. v.i. vendre au marché; acheter au marché, faire son marché, faire ses provisions.

marketable adj. vendable; de bonne vente.

marketing n. commercialisation f., marketing m.

marmalade n. marmelade f.

marmoset n. ouistiti m.

marmot n. marmotte f.

maroon n. marron. adj. marron. v.t. abandonner sur une île déserte.

marriage n. mariage m. **~ contract**, contrat m. de mariage. **~ license**, dispense f. de bans.

married adj. marié, conjugal.

marrow n. moelle f. **~ bone**, os m. à moelle.

marry v.t. épouser. **to ~ one's daughter**, marier sa fille. v.i. (se) marier.

Mars n.pr. Mars m.

marsh n. marais m., marécage m. **salt ~**, marais salant. **~land**, sel m. marécageux ou fangeux. **~mallow**, guimauve f.

marshal n. maréchal m.; capitaine m. ~ v.t. ranger, régler, ordonner.

martial adj. martial, guerrier. **~ law**, état m. de siège; loi f. martiale.

martyr n. martyr m. ~ v.t. martyriser.

martyrdom n. martyre m.

martyrize v.t. martyriser.

marvel n. merveille f., prodige m. ~ v.i. être émerveillé; s'étonner.

marvelous adj. merveilleux. n. merveilleux m.

marvelously adv. merveilleusement, étonnant.

mascot n. mascotte f.

masculine adj. masculin, mâle; vigoureux. **the ~ gender**, le genre masculin.

mash n. mélange m.; pâte f., purée f.; (brewing) fardeau m. ~ v.t. mêler, melanger; écraser.

mask n. masque m. **to take off the ~,** lever le masque. v.t. déguiser. v.i. (se) masquer.

mason n. maçon m.; francmaçon m.

masonic adj. maçonnique.

masonry n. maçonnerie f. **free~,** franc-maçonnerie f.

masquerade n. mascarade f., bal masqué. v.t. se masquer; se déguiser.

mass n. masse f., amas m., gros m.; foule f.; messe f. (church). **to go to ~,** aller à la messe.

massacre n. massacre m. ~ v.t. massacrer.

massage n. massage m. ~ v.t. masser.

masseur n. masseur m.

masseuse n. masseuse f.

massif n. massif m.

massive adj. massif.

massively adv. massivement, en masse.

mast n. mât m. **fore~,** mât de misaine. **mizzen~,** mât d'artimon. **main~,** grand mât. **top~s,** mâts de hune. **before the ~,** sur le gaillard d'avant. v.t. mâter.

mastectomy n. mastectomie f.

master n. maître m.; possesseur m., chef m., maîtrise f. **she got her Master of Arts,** elle est titulaire d'une maîtrise ès lettres. **the ~ of the house,** le maître de la maison. **dancing ~,** maître de danse. **head~,** principal m., proviseur m., directeur. v.t. maîtriser, vaincre, soumettre; surmonter; posséder. adj. de maître, appartenant à un maître; chef, principal. **~ key,** passepartout m. **~ mason,** maître-maçon. **~mind,** esprit m. supérieur. **~piece,** chef-d'oeuvre m. **~stroke,** coup m. de maître. **~work,** grand oeuvre m.

masterly adj. de main de maître; parfait. adv. en maître, avec l'habileté d'un maître.

mastery n. empire m.; supériorité f.; victoire f.; possession f., maîtrise f.

masticate v.t. mâcher.

mastication n. mastication f.

mastiff n. mâtin m., dogue m.

masturbation n. masturbation f.

mat n. natte f. **door~,** un paillasson. v.t. couvrir de nattes ou de paillassons; natter, tresser.

match n. allumette f.; pareil m., égal m., parti m., mariage m., match Sports. **to meet one's ~,** trouver son maître. **she is a ~ for him,** elle est de taille à lui parler; elle l'arrangera. **the ~ lasted two hours,** le match dura deux heures. **~maker,** marieuse f. ~ v.t. égaler; tenir tête à, être de la force de, se mesurer avec; marier; assortir, appareiller. **to ~ colors,** assortir des couleurs. v.i. assortir à, s'assortir avec, aller avec.

matchless adj. qui n'a pas son pareil, incomparable.

mate n. compagnon m., compagne f.; camarade m.; époux m., épouse f.; mat (chess). v.t. marier; animal.

material adj. matériel; important; essentiel. n.

matériel m., étoffe f.; matière f.; matériaux m.pl. **raw ~,** matière première.

materialist n. matérialiste m.

materialistic adj. matérialiste.

materialize v.t. matérialiser.

materially adv. matériellement.

maternal adj. maternel.

maternity n. maternité f.

math n. abbrev. **mathematics,** math(s) f.(pl.).

mathematic(al) adj. mathématique.

mathematician n. mathématicien m.

mathematics n. mathématiques f.pl.

matinée n. Théât. matinée f.

mating n. accouplement m.

matriarch n. femme f. chef de groupe/de famille; matrone f.

matricide n. matricide m.

matriculate v.t. immatriculer. n. matriculaire m. adj. immatriculé.

matriculation n. immatriculation f.

matrimonial adj. matrimonial; conjugal, nuptial.

matrimony n. mariage m.

matte adj. mat.

matter n. matière f., corps m., sujet m., fond m., chose f., fait m., point m., importance f. **what's the ~?** qu'est-ce qu'il y a? **what is the ~ with you?** qu'avez-vous? **no ~,** n'importe. **for that ~,** quant à cela. **in ~s of religion,** dans les questions de religion. **a ~ of course,** une chose toute naturelle. **as a ~ of fact,** en réalité m. positif, réalité f. ~ v.i. importer. **it matters a lot,** il importe beaucoup. **that doesn't ~,** ça ne fait rien.

mattock n. pioche f.

mattress n. matelas m.

maturation n. maturation f.

mature adj. mûr. v.t. mûrir; faire mûrir. v.i. échoir.

maturely adv. mûrement.

maturity n. maturité f.

maudlin adj. gris, à moitié ivre; stupide, hébété.

maul n. maillet m. ~ v.t. (animal) tacérer, mutiler; (person) malmerer (sexually), brutaliser (sexually).

maunder Infml. bougonner.

maverick n. non-conformiste m.f., indépendant m.

mawkish adj. fade, insipide; dégoûtant.

maxillar, maxillary adj. maxillaire.

maxim n. maxime f.

maximise v.t. augmenter jusqu'au plus haut degré, porter au maximum.

maximum n. adj. maximum m.

may v. auxil. pouvoir. **it ~ be,** cela se peut, peut-être. **~ I use your phone?** puis-je me servir de votre téléphone? **she ~ leave tomorrow,** il se peut qu'elle s'en aille demain. n. mai m. (month); aubépine m. ~ v.i. cueillir des fleurs en mai. **~bug,** hanneton m. **~bush,** aubépine f. **~ day,** le premier jour m. de mai. **~flower,** fleur d'aubépine. **~pole,** mât m. de cocagne.

maybe *adv.* peut-être.

mayday *n.* signal *m.* de détresse, S.O.S. *m.*

mayo (mayonnaise) *n.* mayonnaise *f.*

mayor *n.* maire *m.* **Madam Mayor,** Madame le maire.

maze *n.* dédale *m.,* labyrinthe *m.,* embarras *m.*

me *pron.pers.* moi, me.

meadow *n.* pré *m.,* prairie *f.* **~grass,** herbe *f.* des prés, paturio *m.* **~land,** pâturages *m.pl.*

meadowy *adj.* de prairie, de pré.

meager *adj.* maigre, pauvre.

meagerly *adv.* maigrement.

meal *n.* repas *m.,* farine *f.* **hearty ~,** repas copieux.

mealy *adj.* farineux, farinacé, cotonneux (fruits). **~-mouthed,** qui a la parole doucereuse.

mean *adj.* bas, vil, abjet; médiocre, pauvre, mesquin; vulgaire, méprisable, sordide. **~-looking,** qui a l'air méchant. **that was ~,** c'était méchant, *Infml.* c'était pas sympa. **a ~ action,** une vile action. **in the ~time,** dans l'intervalle, sur ces entrefaites. *n.* (often *pl.*) manière *f.,* voie *f.,* revenu *m.,* fortune *f.,* milieu *m.,* moyen terme *m.,* médiocrité *f.* **by that means,** par ce moyen. **by fair means,** par des voies justes. **by all means,** faites donc, je vous en prie. **by no means,** d'aucune manière, nullement. **to live on one's means,** vivre de son revenu, de ses biens. *v.t.,v.i.* avoir en vue, vouloir, se proposer; signifier, entendre, vouloir dire. **what do you ~?** que veux-tu dire (par là)? **he did not ~ it,** il l'a fait sans le vouloir; il ne l'a pas fait exprès. **what does this word ~?** que veut dire ce mot? **I ~ exactly what I say,** j'entends précisément ce que je dis.

meander *n.* méandre *m.,* cours caricieux, sinuosités *f.pl.,* ondulations *f.pl.;* dédale *m.* **~** *v.t.* tourner, (faire) serpenter, rendre sinueux. *v.i.* être sinueux.

meandering *n.* détour *m.,* sinuosité *f.,* méandre *m.* **~** *adj.* sinueux.

meaning *adj.* intentionné, significatif. **a ~ look,** un regard significatif. *n.* intention *f.,* sens *m.,* signification *f.,* importance *f.,* dessein *m.,* pensée *f.* **double ~,** double sens.

meaningless *n.* insignifiant, vide de sens.

meanness *n.* méchanceté; bassesse *f.;* lâcheté *f.;* abjection *f.,* mesquinerie *f.*

meantime, meanwhile *adv.* dans l'intervalle; en attendant; entretemps.

measles *n.* rougeole *f.;* ladrerie *f.* (pigs).

measurable *adj.* mesurable; modéré.

measurably *adv.* modérément; avec mesure.

measure *n.* mesure *f.;* nombre *m.,* capacité *f.,* dimension *f.,* degré *m.;* *Typ.* justification *f.* **standard ~,** mésure type, étalon *m.* **square ~,** mesure de superficie. **to beat ~,** battre la mesure. **to take legal ~s,** avoir recours aux voies légales. **beyond ~,** outre mesure, avec excès. *v.i.* avoir (en dimensions). *v.t.* mesurer; toiser; arpenter.

measured *adj.* mesuré, assuré; limité, restreint.

measurement *n.* mesure *f.,* mensuration *f.,* arpentage *m.,* mesurage *m.*

meat *n.* viande *f.*

mechanic *n.* mécanicien *m.,* garagiste *Auto.*

mechanical *adj.* mécanique, machinal.

mechanics *n.* mécanique *f.*

mechanism *n.* mécanisme *f.*

medal *n.* médaille *f.*

medallion *n.* médaillon *m.*

medallist *n.* médalliste *m.;* médaillé *m.*

meddle *v.i.* (se) mêler (de), s'ingérer, s'immiscer, manier. **I won't let anybody ~ with my business,** je n'accepterai pas que qui que ce soit s'immisce dans mes affairs.

meddler *n.* touche-à-tout *m.,* qui fourre son nez partout.

meddlesome *adj.* intrigant; curieux, fouinard.

media *n.* (pl. of **medium**), la presse *f.,* les médias *m.pl.*

mediate *adj.* moyen; intermédiaire. *v.i.* s'interposter, être médiateur. *v.t.* procurer par la médiation.

mediation *n.* médiation *f.,* intervention *f.;* intercession *f.*

mediator *n.* médiateur *m.*

medic *n.* toubib *m.*

medical *adj.* médical, de médecin. **~ school,** école de médecine, faculté de médicin.

medicament *n.* médicament *m.*

medicate *v.t.* médicamenter; traiter.

medication *n.* médication *f.*

medicinal *adj.* médicinal; médical.

medicine *n.* médicine *f.,* médicament *m.* **~ chest,** petite pharmacie, droguier *m.* *v.t.* médicamenter, affecter comme médicine.

mediocre *adj.* médiocre.

mediocrity *n.* médiocrité *f.*

meditate *v.i.* méditer.

meditation *n.* méditation *f.*

meditative *adj.* méditatif.

Mediterranean *adj.* méditerranéen. **~ sea,** mer Méditeranée.

medium *n.* milieu *m.;* moyen *m.,* vehicule *m.,* voie *f.* **advertising ~,** moyen de publicité. **through the ~ of,** par l'intermédiaire de.

medlar *n.* nèfle *f.* **~ tree,** néflier *m.*

medley *n.* mixture *f.,* mélange *m.,* macédoine *f.,* pot-pourri *m.*

meek *adj.* doux, soumis; modeste. **~-eyed,** aux yeux doux. **~-spirited,** au caractère doux.

meet *v.t.* aller à la rencontre de; venir, aller audevant de; arriver; recevoir; faire la connaissance de; faire face à, faire honneur à. **~ me at 5 o'clock,** on se retrouve à 5 heures. **to ~ expenses,** faire face à des dépenses. *v.i.* (se) rencontrer, se trouver, se voir; s'assembler; se joindre; s'approcher et se rencontrer comme ennemis, se livrer bataille, se combattre, en venir aux mains. **till we ~ again,** à la prochaine fois. **the two armies met at,** les deux armées en vinrent aux mains à. **to make ends ~,** joindre les deux bouts. **to ~ with,** tomber sur; rencontrer. **to ~ with opposition,** rencontrer de l'opposition.

meeting *n.* rencontre *f.;* entrevue *f.;* rendez-vous *m.;* assemblée *f.,* séance *f.;* (religious) service *m.* **to call a ~,** convoquer une assemblée. **to close the ~,** clore la séance. **a ~ of shareholders,** une réunion d'actionnaires. **~ of rivers,** confluent de rivières. **~house,** *n.* maison *f.* de réunion *f.;* chapelle *f.,* temple *m.* (Quakers').

megaphone *n.* porte-voix *m.*

melancholic *adj.* mélancolique.

melancholy *n.* mélancolie *f.,* tristesse *f. adj.* mélancolique.

mellow *adj.* mou, mol; blet; fondant; mûr, tendre (fruits); melodieux, harmonieux; doux (wine). *v.t.* mûrir; faire mûrir. *v.i.* mûrir; s'adoucir, s'amollir.

mellowness *n.* maturité *f.,* douceur *f.;* velouté *m.,* moelleux *m.* (wine).

melodious *adj.* mélodieux.

melodiously *adv.* mélodieusement.

melodramatic *adj.* mélodramatique.

melodrama *n.* mélodrame *m.*

melody *n.* mélodie *f.*

melon *n.* melon *m.* **water~,** pasteque *f.,* melon *m.* d'eau.

melt *v.t.* liquéfier; réduire; attendrir, toucher. *v.i.* (se) fondre; s'adoucir, se dissoudre, s'attendrir. **to ~ away,** se fondre. **money melts away,** l'argent file, s'en va. **to ~ into tears,** fondre en larmes.

melting *adj.* qui fond, en fusion; attendrissant, touchant; étouffant. *n.* fusion *f.;* attendrissement *m.*

member *n.* membre *m.*

membership *n.* adhésion *f.,* abonnement *m.*

membrane *n.* membrane *f.*

memento *n.* memento *m.*

memo *n. Infml.* pense-bête *m.;* note *f.*

memoir *n.* mémoire *m.* (biography).

memorable *adj.* mémorable.

memorandum *n. pl.* **memoranda,** mémorandum *m.* **~ book,** mémorandum *m.,* agenda *m.,* calepin *m.,* carnet *m.*

memorial *adj.* mémorial; commémoratif. *n.* mémorial *m.;* souvenir *m.;* commémoration *f.;* note *f.,* mémoire *m.;* réclamation *f.,* pétition *f.,* requête *f.*

memorize *v.t.* rappeler, remettre en mémoire par écrit, apprendre par coeur.

memory *n.* mémoire *f.;* souvenir *m.* **within the ~ of man,** de mémoire d'homme. **in ~ of,** en mémoire, en souvenir de.

men *n.pl.* of **man.** See **MAN.**

menace *v.t.* menacer. *n.* menace *f.; Infml.* danger public.

menacing *adj.* menaçant.

ménage *n.* ménage *m.* **~ à trois,** ménage à trois.

menagerie *n.* ménagerie *f.*

mend *v.t.* raccommoder, réparer. **to ~ one's life,**

réformer sa conduite. **to ~ a watch,** réparer, faire raccommoder une montre. *v.i.* s'amender, s'améliorer; se corriger; se rétablir (en santé).

mendable *adj.* corrigible.

mendacious *adj.* menteur, faux, mensonger.

mendicant *adj.* de mendiant; mendiant. *n.* mendiant *m.*

mendicity *n.* mendicité *f.*

menopause *n.* ménopause *f.*

menses *n.* menstrues *f.pl.,* régles *f.pl.*

menstrual *adj.* menstruel.

menstruate *v.i.* avoir ses régles.

menstruation *n.* menstruation *f.*

mensurable *adj.* mensurable, mesurable.

mensuration *n.* mensuration *f.,* mesurage *m.*

mental *adj.* mental; intellectuel.

mentally *adv.* mentalement, intellectuellement.

mention *n.* mention *f.* ~ *v.t.* mentionner, faire mention de; citer; parler de. **above-mentioned,** ci-dessus nommé, mentionné. **don't ~ it,** il n'y a pas de quoi; je vous en prie.

mentor *n.* mentor *m.*

menu *n.* menu *m.,* carte *f.*

mercantile *adj.* mercantile, commerçant, marchand.

mercenary *adj.* mercenaire, vénal. **~ troops,** des troupes mercenaires. *n.* mercenaire *m.*

merchandise *n.* marchandise *f.* ~ *v.i.* commercer, trafiquer.

merchant *n.* marchand *m.,* négociant, commerçant *m.* ~ *adj.* marchand, commerçant. **~ service, ~ marine,** marine *f.* marchande.

merciful *adj.* miséricordieux, clément.

mercifully *adv.* miséricordieusement, avec clémence.

merciless *adj.* sans miséricorde; impitoyable.

mercurial *adj.* de mercure; actif, vif; mercuriel.

Mercury *n.pr. Myth.* Mercure *m.;* mercure *m.,* vif-argent *m.;* messager *m.; Fig.* vivacité *f.,* ardeur *f.*

mercy *n.* miséricorde *f.,* clémence *f.,* grâce *f.,* pardon *m.* **to show ~,** user de miséricorde. **for mercy's sake,** de grâce. **to cry ~,** demander grâce. **to be at the ~ of,** être à la merci, à la discrétion de.

mere *adj.* pur, simple, seul. **a ~ fiction,** une simple, une pure fiction. **the ~ truth,** la pure vérité. *n.* étang *m.,* lac *m.*

merely *adv.* simplement, purement. **~ a word,** rien qu'un mot.

merge *v.t.* immerger; éteindre; absorber. *v.i.* être englouti; se perdre, s'éteindre, s'incorporer.

merger *n.* fusion *f.,* incorporation *f.*

meridian *n.* méridien *m.;* midi *m. adj.* méridien; de midi.

meridional *adj.* méridional; du sud.

merit *n.* mérite *m.* ~ *v.t.* mériter.

meritorious *adj.* méritoire; méritant.

merlin *n.* émerillon *m.*

mermaid *n.* sirène *f.*

merrily *adv.* gaiement, joyeusement.

merriment n. joie f., réjouissance f., divertissements m.pl.

merry adj. gai, joyeux, plaisant, jovial. **~-go-round,** manège m., chevaux m.pl. de bois. **~-hearted,** d'humeur joyeuse.

mesh n. maille f. **~** v.t. prendre dans un filet.

mesmerize v.t. magnétiser.

mess n. Milit. pension f., mess m.; gachis m., désordre m., embarras m., saleté. **to make a ~,** faire du désordre. **to ~ up,** faire une bévue, Infml. cafouiller.

message n. message m.

messenger n. messager m., coursier m.

Messiah n. le Messie.

messy adj. sale, désordonné, en désordre.

met See MEET.

metal n. métal m.

metallic adj. métallique.

metallurgic adj. métallurgique.

metallurgy n. métallurgie f.

metamorphic adj. metamorphique.

metamorphose v.t. métamorphoser.

metamorphosis n. métamorphose f.

metaphor n. métaphore f.

metaphoric(al) adj. métaphorique.

metaphysics n. métaphysique f.

mete v.t. mesurer. **to ~ out,** infliger (punishment). n. mesure f., limite f.

meteor n. météore m.

meteoric adj. météorique.

meteorite n. météorite m.

meteorological adj. météorologique.

meteorology n. météorologie f.

meter n. mesureur m.; compteur m.; mètre m. **a gas ~,** un compteur à gaz.

method n. méthode f., ordre m.; règle, manière f.; moyen m.

methodic(al) adj. méthodique.

methodize v.t. classer, disposer dans un ordre requis; ranger.

meticulous adj. méticuleux.

metric(al) adj. métrique.

metronome n. métronome m.

metropolis n. métropole f.

metropolitan adj. métropolitain. n. mètropolitain m.

mettle n. courage m.; coeur m.; fougue f., feu m.

mettlesome adj. fougueux, ardent; fringant.

mettlesomeness n. ardeur f., feu m., fougue f.

mew n. mouette f.; mue f.; cage f. à oiseaux; miaulement m., enfermer, emprisonner dans une cage. v.i. miauler.

mewing n. miaulement m.

mewling n. vagissement m.

Mexican n. Mexicain m., Mexicaine f. adj. mexicain.

Mexico n.pr. le Mexique.

mezzanine n. mezzanine f.

mi n. Mus. mi m.

miaow n. miaulement m., miaulir.

mice See MOUSE.

mickey n. boisson f. droguée.

microbe n. microbe m.

microcosm n. microcosme m.

microphone n. microphone m.

microscope n. microscope m.

microscopic adj. microscopique.

microwave n. micro-ondes f.pl. **~ oven,** four à micro-ondes.

mid adj. du milieu, moyen. **~-air,** entre ciel et terre, en plein ceil. **~day,** midi m. **~way,** milieu de chemin. adv. à mi-chemin. **~winter,** coeur m., milieu de l'hiver; solstice m. d'hiver.

middle adj. du milieu, du center; moyen; intermédiaire, mitoyen. **~ Ages,** le moyen âge. **~-aged,** adj. d'âge moyen. **~ finger,** doigt m. du milieu. **~-sized,** adj. de grandeur moyenne. n. milieu m., center m. **the ~ of the body,** le milieu de corps, la ceinture.

middleman n. agent m. d'affaires, agent m., intermédiaire m.

middling adj. moyen, modéré, médiocre, passable; bon ordinaire.

midge n. cousin m., moucheron m.

midget n. nain m., miniature f.

midnight n. minuit m.

midst n. milieu m., center m.; fort m. **in the ~ of,** au milieu de, au plus fort de. adv. au milieu de, parmi.

midsummer n. milieu de l'été, solstice m. d'été.

midwife n. sage-femme f.

mien n. Forml. mine f., air m.

miff v.t. déplaire, offenser légèrement. n. Infml. mauvaise humeur f.

might pret. of may. n. force f.; puissance f.; pouvoir m. **with all one's ~,** Infml. à tour de bras.

mightily adv. puissamment; énergiquement; Infml. grandement, beaucoup.

mightiness n. puissance f., pouvoir m., grandeur f.

mighty adj. très-puissant; Infml. grand; très capable; très, beaucoup.

migraine n. migraine f.

migrant adj., n. migrant m.; migrateur m.

migrate v.i. émigrer; immigrer.

migration n. émigration f., migration f.

mike n. Abbr. of **microphone,** micro m.

mild adj. doux. **~ words,** de douces paroles. **to grow ~,** s'adoucir.

mildew n. moisissure f., mildiou m. (wine); nielle f., rouille f. des plantes; tache f. d'humidité. v.t. tacher de rouille; piquer.

mildly adv. doucement.

mildness n. douceur f.

mile n. mille m.

mileage n. kilométrage m.

milieu n. milieu m. (social).

militant adj., n. militant m.

military adj. militaire. n. militaire m., armée f.

militate v.i. militer, combattre.

militia n. milice f.

milk *n.* lait *m.* ~ *v.t.* traire.

milkiness *n.* nature *f.* laiteuse; *Fig.* douceur *f.*

milkwort *n.* euphorbe *f.*

milky *adj.* de lait, laiteux; lacté. **Milky Way,** voie lactée.

mill *n.* moulin *m.,* usine *f.,* fabrique *f.;* filature. **water** ~, moulin à eau. **wind**~, moulin à vent. **coffee** ~, moulin à café. **silk** ~, filature de soie. **cotton** ~, filature de coton. **saw**~, scierie *f.* ~ *v.t.* moudre; broyer; fouler. ~**stone,** pierre *f.* meulière.

millennial *adj.* millénaire.

millennium *n.* millénium *m.,* millénaire *m.*

miller *n.* meunier *m.;* minotier *m.*

millesimal *adj.* millième.

milligram(me) *n.* milligramme *m.*

milliliter *n.* millilitre *m.*

millimeter *n.* millimetre *m.*

million *n.* million *m. Infml.* **today I feel like a** ~ **bucks,** aujourd'hui je me sens en super forme.

millionaire *n.* millionaire *m.*

milt *n. Anat.* rate *f. Ichth.* laite *f.,* laitance *f.* des poissons. *v.t. Ichth.* féconder.

mime *n.* mime *m.* ~ *v.t.* mimer.

mimic *adj.* imitateur; imitatif, mimique. *n.* mime *m.,* imitateur *m.* ~ *v.t.* contrefaire; imiter, singer.

mimicking *n.* bouffonnerie *f.,* imitation *f.,* burlesque; farce *f.,* pantomime *f.*

mimosa *n.* mimosa *f.*

mince *v.t.* hacher; émincer; adoucir, atténuer. **to** ~ **meat,** hacher de la viande. **not to** ~ **matters,** parler net, ne pas y aller par quatre chemins. *v.i.* marcher à petits pas; minauder, faire le délicat. *adj.* haché.

mincing *adj.* affecté, minaudier. ~ **knife,** hachoir *m.*

mind *n.* esprit *m.,* intelligence *f.;* raison *f.;* intention *f.;* avis *m.;* envie *f.,* désir *m.;* résolution *f.;* souvenir *m.,* mémoire *f.* **I have made up my** ~, j'ai pris ma décision. **to call to** ~, rappeler en son esprit. **to be out of one's** ~, avoir perdu la raison, la tête. **to go out of one's** ~, perdre la raison, la tête. **to change one's** ~, se changer d'avis. **could you make up your** ~? vas-tu te décider à la fin? **is he out of his** ~? est-ce qu'il est devenu fou? **she has something on her** ~, elle est préoccupée, il y a quelque chose qui la préoccupe. **get her out of your** ~! oublie-la! **what do you have in** ~? à quoi penses-tu?, à quoi veux-tu en arriver? Quelle idée l'a traversé l'esprit? *v.t.* considérer, faire attention à, penser; prendre garde à, veiller à, prendre soin de; obleir à; avoir en vue. ~ **your health,** prenez soin de votre santé. ~ **your own business,** occupes-toi de tes affaires. **they do not** ~ **expense,** ils ne regardent pas à la dépense. **never** ~, ça ne fait rien, *Infml.* laisse tomber.

minded *adj.* disposé à; porté à. **right-**~, à l'esprit juste. **weak-**~, faible à l'esprit faible. **you**

are so narrow-~, vous avez vraiment l'esprit obtus.

mindedness *n.* disposition *f.,* inclination *f.* pour.

mindful *adj.* attentif.

mindless *adj.* inattentif; négligent; sans souci; oblieux.

mine *poss. pron.* le mien, la mienne, les miens, les miennes; à moi, etc. **this book is** ~, ce livre est á moi. *n.* mine *f.;* minerai *m.* **a gold** ~, une mine d'or. *v.i.* exploiter une mine; miner, creuser; *Fig.* saper. *v.t.* consumer, miner.

miner *n.* mineur *m.*

mineral *n., adj.* minéral *m.*

mineralization *n.* minéralisation *f.*

mineralize *v.t.* minéraliser.

mineralogy *n.* minéralogie *f.*

mingle *v.t.,v.i.* (se) mêler, (se) mélanger, se confondre. **they** ~**ed with the crowd,** ils se sont mêlés à la foule.

miniature *n.* ~ **painter,** miniaturiste, peintre en miniature. *adj.* en miniature; en petit; sur une petite échelle.

minimize *v.t.* minimiser.

minimum *n.pl.* minima, minimum *m.*

mining *adj.* de mine; de mineur. *n.* exploitation *f.* des mines.

minister *n.* ministre *m.;* pasteur *m.;* instrument *m.* officiating ~, desservant. *v.t.* administrer, donner, fournir. *v.i.* servir, soigner; contribuer; officier (à l'autel).

ministerial *adj.* ministeriel, de ministre, au service de; ecclésiastique.

ministry *n.* ministère *m.*

mink *n.* vison *m.* **a** ~ **coat,** un manteau de vison.

minor *adj.* mineur, moindre, plus petit; menu, mince, léger. **Asia Minor,** Asie mineure, mineur *m., Scol.* matière *f.* secondaire.

minority *n.* minorité *f.*

mint *n.* hôtel *m.* menthe. **pepper**~, menthe poivrée. ~ **condition,** comme neuf, en parfait état. *v.t.* monnayer, battre monnaie; forger, fabriquer.

minus *n.* moins.

minuscule *n.* minuscule *f.*

minute *adj.* menu, mince, très petit; minutieux.

minute *n.* minute *f.;* brouillon *m.;* note *f.* **to take** ~**s of,** prendre des notes de. *v.t.* minuter, prendre note de. **carnet.** ~ **hand,** grande aiguille *f.*

minutely *adv.* minutieusement, en détail.

miracle *n.* miracle *m.*

miraculous *adj.* miraculeux.

miraculously *adv.* miraculeusement, merveilleusement, d'une manière suprenante.

mirage *n.* mirage *m.*

mire *n.* fange *f.,* boue *f.,* vase *f.,* bourbier *m.* ~ *v.t.,v.i.* s'embourber; salir, barbouiller de boue; souiller.

mirror *n.* miroir *m.* ~ *v.t.* réfléchir (comme dans un miroir).

mirth *n.* joie *f.,* allégresse *f.,* gaieté *f.,* enjouement *m.*

misadventure *n.* mésaventure *f.*

misalliance *n.* mésalliance *f.*

misanthrope, misanthropist *n.* misantrope *m.*

misanthropy *n.* misanthropie *f.*

misapply *v.t.* mal appliquer.

misapprehend *v.t.* se méprendre sur; comprendre mal.

misapprehension *n.* mèprise *f.*, malentendu *m.*

misappropriate *v.t.* approprier à tort.

misappropriation *n.* appropriation *f.* erronée.

misbehave *v.i.* se conduire mal, se comporter mal.

misbehavior *n.* inconduite *f.*; impolitesse *f.*, grossièreté *f.*

misbelief *n.* mécréance *f.*, incrédulité *f.*

misc *abbrev.* miscellaneous. See MISCELLANEOUS.

miscalculate *v.t.* calculer mal, se tromper.

miscalculation *n.* calcul *m.*, erroné; faute *f.* de calcul, mécompte *m.*

miscarriage *n.* insuccès *m.*, échec *m.*; coup *m.* manqué; fausse couche *f.*

miscarry *v.i.* ne pas réussir, échouer; ne pas parvenir; faire une fausse couche, avorter.

miscellaneous *adj.* divers, varié.

mischief *n.* mal *m.*, tort *m.*, dommage *m.*; détriment *m.*; méfait *m.*, mauvais tour *m.* **to do ~,** faire du mal. **to make ~ between people,** brouiller les gens.

mischievous *adj.* funeste; porté au mal; méchant, nuisible, pernicieux; malin, espiègle.

misconceive *v.t.,v.i.* juger mal, concevoir mal, avoir une fausse conception de.

misconception *n.* fausse conception *f.*; méprise *f.*

misconduct *n.* inconduite *f.*, mauvaise conduite *f.*, mauvaise gestion *f.* **~** *v.t.* mal diriger.

misconstruction *n.* interprétation *f.*, fausse ou erronée; contre-sens *m.*

misconstrue *v.t.* interpréter mal; interpréter en mauvaise part, donner un mauvais sens.

miscount *v.t.* calculer mal. *v.i.* se mécompter.

misdeed *n.* méfait *m.*

misdemeanor *n.* mauvaise conduite *f.*; *Law.* infraction *f.*, délit *m.*

misdirect *v.t.* mal diriger; renseigner mal; donner une fausse indication; addresser mal.

miser *n.* avare *m.*

miserable *adj.* malheureux; triste; misérable.

miserably *adv.* pauvrement, pitoyablement.

misery *n.* souffrance *f.*, supplicé *m.*, misère *f.*

misfire *v.i.* avoir des râtes, rater, *Infml.* foirer, cafouiller.

misfortune *n.* malchance *f.*, infortune *f.*, malheur *m.*

misgiving *n.* crainte *f.*; pressentiment *m.*; défiance *f.*

misguide *v.t.* guider, mal; induire en erreur.

mishandle *v.t.* malmener.

mishap *n.* malheur *m.*, contretemps *m.*

mishear *v.t.* entendre mal.

misinform *v.t.* informer mal; renseigner mal.

misinformation *n.* information *f.* inexacte; faux avis *m.*

misinterpret *v.t.* mal interpréter; faire un contre-sens.

misinterpretation *n.* fausse, mauvaise interprétation *f.*; contre-sens *m.*

misjoin *v.t.* joindre mal.

misjudge *v.t.* juger mal, faire un mauvais jugement.

misjudgment *n.* jugement *m.* erroné; fausse idée *f.*

mislay *v.t.* placer mal; égarer.

mislead *v.t* égarer, fourvoyer, induire en erreur.

mismanage *v.t.* mal diriger, mal administrer, mal gérer.

mismanagement *n.* mauvaise direction *f.* gestion *f.*, mauvaise administration *f.*

misname *v.t.* mal nommer.

misogyny *n.* misogyme *f.*

misplace *v.t.* placer mal, déplacer; égarer, perdre.

misprint *v.i.* imprimer avec des fautes. *n.* faute *f.* d'impression, coquille *f.*

mispronounce *v.i.* prononcer incorrectement.

mispronunciation *n.* prononciation *f.* incorrecte.

misquote *v.t.* citer à faux.

misread *v.t.* mal lire.

misreport *v.t.* rendre un compte inexact de. *n.* rapport inexact.

misrepresent *v.t.* mal représenter; dénaturer.

misrepresentation *n.* faux rapport *m.*, exposé *m.* inexact.

misrule *n.* mauvaise administration.

miss *n.* demoiselle *f.*; mademoiselle *f.*; manque *m.*; perte *f.*, absence *f.*; meprise *f.*, erreur *f.* **~** *v.t.* manquer, se tromper; omettre, ne pas trouver, avoir besoin de. **to ~ the mark,** manquer son coup. **to ~ the train,** manquer le train. **he could not ~ the street,** il ne pouvait se tromper de rue. *v.i.* échouer; faillir, se méprendre. **one volume is missing,** il manque un volume.

missal *n.* missel *m.*

misshape *n.* forme *f.* mauvaise ou incorrecte. *v.t.* mal conformer; défigurer.

misshaped, misshapen *adj.* défiguré, difforme.

missile *adj.* de jet, de trait; lancé, envoyé. *n.* projectile *m.*; missile *m.*

missing *adj.* manquant, perdu, égaré. **to be ~,** manquer.

mission *n.* envoi *m.*; mission *f.*

missionary *n.* missionnaire *m.*

Mississippi *n.pr.* Mississippi *m.*

missive *adj.* jeté. *n.* missive *f.*

misspell *v.t.* épeler mal, orthographier mal.

misspelling *n.* orthographe *f.* incorrecte.

misstate *v.t.* exposer mal; faire un exposé erroné; dénaturer.

misstatement *n.* récit *m.* inexact, exposé *m.* erroné.

missy *n. Infml.* petite demoiselle.

mist *n.* brouillard *m.,* bruine *f.,* brume *f.* ~ *v.t.* couvrir de nuages, obscurcir, répandre un nuage sur.

mistake *v.t.* comprendre mal, (se) méprendre (sur); confondre; (se) tromper (sur). *v.i.* être dans l'erreur, faire une bévue. **to be mistaken**, se tromper, se méprendre *f.,* erreur *f.;* faute *f.*

mistaken *adj.* (of things) mal compris, mal entendu; (of persons) être dans l'erreur, se tromper. **I am ~**, je me trompe. **you are ~**, vous vous trompez.

mistakenly *adv.* par méprise, par erreur.

Mister *n.* monsieur *m.* (always in abbrev. form **Mr.**).

mistletoe *n.* gui *m.*

mistranslate *v.t.* traduire inexactement.

mistranslation *n.* traduction *f.,* version *f.* inexacte; contre-sens *m.*

mistress *n.* maîtresse *f.*

mistrial *n. Jur.* procès *m.* entaché de nullité.

mistrust *n.* méfiance *f.,* défiance *f.,* soupçon *m.* ~ *v.t.* suspecter, douter, soupçonner se méfier de.

mistrustful *adj.* méfiant, défiant.

misty *adj.* brumeux; nuageux; obscur, sombre.

misunderstand *v.t.* comprendre mal, se méprendre sur.

misunderstanding *n.* malentendu *m.,* désaccord *m.,* différend *m.*

misusage *n.* abus *m.;* mauvais traitements *m.pl.*

misuse *v.t.* abuser de; maltraiter. *n.* mauvais emploi *m.,* abus *m.;* mauvais traitements *m.pl.*

mite *n.* mite *f.;* petite pièce d'argent; obole *f.*

mitigate *v.t.* mitiger; calmer, apaiser, soulager, (s') adoucir, (s') atténuer.

mitigation *n.* adoucissement *m.,* soulagement *m.;* mitigation *f.*

mix *v.t. Pharm.* mixtionner. **he got completely ~ed up**, il s'est mis complètement embrouillé. *v.i.* (with, dans) (se) mélanger, (se) mêler.

mixture *n.* mélange *m.;* composition *f.;* mixtion *f.,* mixture *f.*

mnemonic *adj.* mnémonique.

mnemonics *n.* mnémonique *f.*

moan *v.t.* gémir (sur), (se) lamenter (sur). *v.i.* (se) plaindre. *n.* lamentation *f.,* plainte *f.,* gémissement *m.*

moat *n.* fossé *m.*

mob *n.* foule *f.,* cohue *f.;* populace *f.;* attroupement *m.,* rassemblement *m.* **the ~**, organisation *f.* criminelle.

mobility *n.* mobilité *f.*

mobilization *n.* mobilisation *f.*

mobilize *v.t.* mobiliser.

moccasin *n.* moccasin *m.*

mock *v.t.* contrefaire, singer; se moquer de, rire de, railler. *v.i.* se rire de, se jouer de. *n.* moquerie *f.,* raillerie *f.,* risée *f.,* dérision *f.,* ironie *f.* ~ *adj.* faux, fausse; contrefait; ironique.

mockery *n.* moquerie *f.;* raillerie *f.;* dérision *f.*

mocking *n.* moquerie *f.,* raillerie *f.* ~**-bird**, (oiseau) *m.* moqueur.

modality *n.* modalité *f.*

mode *n.* mode *f.;* manière *f.;* façon *f.,* fantaisie *f.*

model *n.* modèle *m.* exemple *m.;* image *f.,* représentation *f.* type *m.,* moule *m.;* (fashion) mannequin *m.* (person); *Naut.* gabarit *m.* **rough ~**, ébauche *f.,* maquette *f.* ~ *v.t.,v.i.* modeler, former. *adj.* modèle.

moderate *adj.* modéré, moyen, modique, raisonnable, passable. **a ~ price**, un prix modique. *v.t.* modérer; adoucir, tempérer, apaiser.

moderately *adv.* modérément; modiquement, médiocrement, passablement.

moderation *n.* modération *f.;* modicité *f.;* tempérance *f.,* sobriété *f.*

moderator *n.* modérateur *m.;* arbitre *m.;* président *m.;* régulateur *m.,* modérateur *m.*

modern *adj.* moderne; récent, nouveau. *n.* moderne.

modernize *v.t.* moderniser; *Arch.* moderner.

modest *adj.* modeste, pudique, modéré.

modestly *adv.* modestement, avec modestie.

modesty *n.* modestie *f.,* pudeur *f.;* modération *f.*

modification *n.* modification *f.*

modifier *n.* celui qui modifie; modificateur *m.*

modify *v.t.* modifier.

modulate *v.t.* moduler.

modulation *n.* modulation *f.;* melodie *f.*

module *n.* module *m.*

moist *adj.* moite; humide.

moisten *v.t.* rendre moite, humide, mouiller légèrement; humecter.

moisture *n.* humidité *f.,* moiteur *f.*

molar *adj.* molaire. *n.* dent *f.* molaire, molaire *f.*

molasses *n.* mélasse *f.*

mold *n.* moule *m.;* moisissure *f.;* terreau *m.;v.t.* mouler, faire fondre, façonner.

moldy *adj.* moisi, couvert de moisissure.

mole *n.* marque *f.;* grain *m.* de beauté; *Méd.* môle *f.; Zool.* taupe *f.* ~**-hill**, taupinière *f.*

molecular *adj.* moléculaire.

molecule *n.* molecule *f.*

molest *v.t.* molester; gêner; attenter à la pudeur.

molestation *n.* molestation *f.,* contrariété *f.,* inconvénient *m.;* attentat à la pudeur.

mollify *v.t.* mollifier; adoucir; attendrir; calmer.

mollusk *n.* mollusque(s) *m.*

mom *n.* maman *f.*

moment *n.* moment *m.;* instant *m.*

momentarily *adv.* à tout moment.

momentary *adj.* momentané.

momentous *adj.* important.

momentum *n.* moment *m.;* force *f.* d'impulsion, force *f.*

monarchy *n.* monarchie *f.*

monastery *n.* monastère *m.*

monastic *adj.* monastique.

Monday *n.* lundi *m.*

monetary *adj.* monétaire.

money *n.* argent *m.,* monnaie *f.* **bad ~**, fausse

monnaie. **ready ~**, argent comptant. **to get, to make ~**, faire de l'argent. **~lender**, prêteur m. d'argent; bailleur m. de fonds. **~ market**, la place f.; marché monétaire. **~ order**, mandat poste m. **do you think I'm made of ~?** qu'est-ce que tu crois, que je roule sur l'or? **put your ~ where your mouth is**, on le verra quand tu le feras.

moneyed adj. en fonds, riche.

mongrel adj. métis (m.).

monies pl. of money.

monitor n. moniteur m. ~ v.t. diriger, contrôler.

monk n. moine m.; religieux.

monkey n. singe m. ~ v.t. **~ around**, faire le singe, singer.

monogamy n. monogamie f.

monogram n. monogramme m.

monograph n. monographie f.

monologue n. monologue m.

monopolize v.i. accaparer; monopoliser.

monopoly n. monopole m.; accaparement m.

monosyllable n. monosyllabe m.

monotheism n. monothéisme m.

monotone n. monotonie f.

monotonous adj. monotone.

monotony n. monotonie f.

monsoon n. mousson f.

monster n. monstre m. ~ adj. monstre, monstrueux, énorme.

monstrosity n. monstruosité f.

monstrous adj. monstrueux; prodigieux; énorme; horrible.

montage n. montage m.

month n. mois m. **lunar ~**, mois lunaire. **calendar ~**, mois solaire.

monthly adj. mensuel, tous les mois. n. revue f. mensuel. adv. mensuellement, tous les mois.

monument n. monument m.

monumental adj. monumental.

moo n. meuglement m. ~ v.i. meugler.

mood n. humeur f., disposition f. **to be in a cheerful ~**, être de belle humeur.

moodiness n. humeur f. changeante.

moody adj. de mauvaise humeur.

moon n. lune f. **half-~**, demilune f. **full ~**, pleine lune. **~beam**, rayon m. lunaire. **~light** n. et adj. clair m. de lune. **by ~light**, au clair de lune.

moor n. lande f., bruyère f.; marécage m., marais m.; maure m. **~cock**, **~fowl**, coq m. de bruyère. **~hen**, Ornith. poule f. d'eau. v.t. Naut. amarrer. v.i. être amarré.

mooring n. amarrage m. ~ **ground**, mouillage m., ancrage m.

moose n. original m., élan m.

moot v.t. débattre, discuter, controverser. adj. discutable.

mop n. balai m. serpillière f. ~ v.t. layer, netoyer (avec un balai).

mope v.i. avoir le cafard, broyer du noir. n. cafardeux.

moped n. mobylette f. (trademark).

moral adj. moral; de moral. n. morale f.; moralité f.

morality n. morale f.; moralité f.

morally adv. moralement; vertueusement.

morals n. moeurs f.pl., moralité f.

morass n. marais m., marécage m.

morbid adj. morbide.

mordant adj. mordant. n. mordant m.

more adj. plus, plus de; encore, davantage. **give me some ~**, donnez-m'en encore. adv. plus, davantage. **much ~**, beaucoup plus. **no ~**, pas davantage. **the ~, the merrier**, plus on est de fous, plus on rit. **once ~**, encore une fois. n. plus autre chose. **we can do no ~**, nous ne pouvons rien faire de plus.

moreover adv. de plus, en outre, outre cela, d'ailleurs.

morgue n. morgue f.

Mormon n. mormon m.

morn n. Poet. matin m.; aurore f.

morning n. matin m.; matinée f.; Fig. matin m., aurore f. **tomorrow ~**, demain matin. **good ~**, bon jour. adv. matinal, du matin.

Morocco n. le Maroc.

moron n. crétin m., Vulg. con m.

morose adj. morose.

morphine n. morphine f.

morphology n. morphologie f.

morrow n. Lit. demain m.; lendemain m.

morse adj. ~ **code**, alphabet m. morse.

morsel n. morceau m.

mortal adj. mortel; fatal; meurtrier; humain. **a ~ sin**, un péché mortel. n. mortel m.

mortality n. mortalité f.

mortally adv. mortellement, à mort.

mortar n. mortier m.

mortgage n. hypothèque f. ~ v.t. hypothéquer, nantir.

mortification n. mortification f.

mortify v.i. (se) mortifier.

mortuary n. morgue f. ~ adj. mortuaire.

mosaic n. mosaïque f.

Moslem n. musulman m. ~ adj. islamique.

mosque n. mosquée f.

mosquito n. moustique m. ~ **net**, moustiquaire f.

moss n. mousse f. v.t. couvrir de mousse.

most adj. le plus; la plupart; le plus grand. **~ men**, la plupart des hommes. adv. le plus, très, fort, extrêmement. n. le plus, la plupart, le plus grande partie, le plus grand nombre. **at the ~**, au plus, tout au plus. **to make the ~ of**, tirer le meilleur parti de.

mostly adv. ordinairement, le plus souvent, la plupart du temps.

mote n. atome m. **to see the ~ in someone's eye**, voir la paille dans l'oeil de quelqu'un.

moth n. mite f.

mother n. mère f. **grand~**, grand'mère. **great-grand~**, bisaïeule. **~-in-law**, belle-mère.

step~, belle-mère. **to be a ~ to**, être une mère pour. *adj.* mère; maternel. **~ country,** mère patrie. **~ tongue,** langue maternelle. *v.t.* servir de mère à. **~-of-pearl,** nacre *f.* (de perle).

motherhood *n.* maternité *f.*

motherless *adj.* sans mère.

motherly *adj.* maternel.

motion *n.* mouvement *m.;* geste *m.;* motion *f.;* proposition *f.;* signe *m.* **to make a ~,** faire une proposition. **to carry a ~,** faire adopter une motion. **to put into ~,** mettre en mouvement. *v.t.* présenter une motion, faire une proposition.

motionless *adj.* immobile.

motive *adj.* moteur, motrice. **~ power,** force motrice. *n.* motif *m.,* cause *f.,* raison *f.,* mobile *m.*

motor *adj.* moteur, motrice. **~boat,** canot automobile. **~cycle,** motorcyclette *f.* moteur *m.*

motorcade *n.* défilé *m.* de voitures.

motorist *n.* automobiliste *m.f.*

motorize *v.t.* motoriser.

mottle *n.* madrure *f.* **~** *v.t.* madrer, moirer; marbrer.

motto *n.* devise *f.*

mound *n.* rempart *m.,* digue *f.;* jetée *f.;* remblai *m.* **~** *v.t.* fortifier par un rempart, par une digue.

mount *v.i.* monter; élever; monter sur. **to ~ a horse,** monter à cheval. *v.t.* **to ~ a hill,** gravir une montagne. *n.* mont *m.,* montagne *f.,* colline *f.;* monture (horse).

mountain *n.* montagne *f.;* monceau *m.;* masse *f.* **to make ~s of molehills,** *Fig.* faire d'une mouche un éléphant. *adj.* de montagne.

mountaineer *n.* montagnard *m.*

mountainous *adj.* montagneux.

mounting *n.* montée *f.,* ascension *f.;* montage *m.,* équipement *m.*

mourn *v.i.* porter le deuil, pleurer la mort de; pleurer, se lamenter, geindre. *v.i.* déplorer.

mourner *n.* personne *f.* qui fait parti d'un convoi funèbre.

mournful *adj.* triste, lugubre; affligé, éploré.

mourning *n.* funèbre, de deuil. *n.* gémissement *m.,* lamentation *f.;* affliction *f.,* deuil *m.* **to go into ~,** prendre le deuil.

mouse *n.* au *pl.* **mice,** souris *f.* **field~,** mulot. **~hole,** trou *m.* de souris. **~trap,** souricière *f.*

mouth *n.* bouche *f.;* gueule *f.* (animal); ouverture *f.,* orifice *m.;* entrée *f.;* bec *m.* (thing). **the ~ of a lion, a dog, a wolf,** la gueule d'un lion, d'un chien, a'un loup. **that makes one's ~ water,** cela fait venir l'eau à la bouche. **the ~ of a well, an oven,** la bouche d'un puits, d'un four. **the ~ of the Thames,** la bouche de la Tamise. **~ organ,** flûte *f.* de pan. **~piece,** embouchure (instrument musical); un qui parle pour un autre. *v.t.* déclamer, débiter avec emphase, outrager; mâcher. *v.i.* crier, tempêter, brailler, vociférer.

mouthed *adj.* **foul-~,** mal embouché.

mouthful *n.* bouchée *f.*

movable *adj.* mobile, meuble. *n.* meuble *m.,* mobilier *m.*

move *v.t.* bouger; déménager; (faire) mouvoir; exciter, irriter, émouvoir, toucher. **to ~ to laughter,** exciter à rire. **he was quite moved at it,** il en fut tout ému. *v.i.* se mouvoir; se remuer; s'agiter. **to ~ away,** s'en aller, s'éloigner déménager. **to ~ forward,** s'avancer. **to ~ in,** entrer, emménager. **to ~ out,** sortir, déménager. **to ~ up,** monter, passer devant. *n.* mouvement *m.;* coup *m.,* trait *m.* **the first ~ at chess,** le trait. **whose ~ is it?** à qui de jouer? **it is your ~,** c'est à vous à jouer.

movement *n.* mouvement *m.;* marche *f.,* excitation *f.,* agitation *f.; Mus.* mouvement *m.* (clock) mouvement *m.*

mover *n.* déménageur *m.*

moving *adj.* moteur, motrice, mobile; émouvant, touchant. **~ powers,** forces motrices. **~ sands,** sables mouvants. *n.* mouvement *m.;* impulsion *f.* **~ off,** départ *m.*

mow *v.t.* faucher, moissonner. **to ~ a field,** faucher un champ.

mower *n.* faucheur *m.* **lawn ~,** tondeuse *f.* à gazon.

mowing *n.* fauchage *m.;* fauche *f.* **~ machine,** faucheuse *f.* **~ time,** fauchaison *f.*

much *adj.* beaucoup de; grand. **~ money,** beaucoup d'argent. *adv.* beaucoup; de beaucoup; tant; très, fort. **~ more,** beaucoup plus. **so ~ the better,** taut mieux. **so ~ the worse,** tant pis. **how ~,** combien. **as ~ as,** autant que. **so ~,** tant. **too ~,** trop, trop de. **~ the same thing,** à peu pres la même chose. *n.* beaucoup de, une grande quantité de. **to make ~ of,** faire grand cas de. **to make ~ of one's time,** employer bien son temps.

muck *n.* fumier *m.;* boue *f.;* saleté *f.* **~** *v.t.* salir; amender avec fumier.

mucky *adj.* sale, malpropre.

mucous *adj.* muqueux.

mucus *n.* mucus *m.*

mud *n.* boue *f.,* vase *f.,* limon *m.,* bourbe *f.* **to stick in the ~,** s'embourber. *v.t.* enforcer dans la vase, dans la boue; couvrir de boue, salir. **his name is ~,** il est en disgrâce. **~ bank,** dépôt de vase. **~bath,** bain de boue. **~ wall,** mur *m.* de terre.

muddle *v.t.* salir, souiller; troubler (head), hébéter; griser. *v.i.* être dans un état trouble ou confus; être gris.

muddy *adj.* boueux, vaseux; trouble, bourbeux; couvert de boue. **~ street,** une rue boueuse. **~ boots,** des bottes crottées. *v.t.* couvrir de boue; crotter, salir.

muff *n.* manchon *m.*

muffin *n.* muffin *m.*

muffle *v.t.* couvrir, envelopper; assourdir (oars, bell); voiler (drum). *v.i.* marmotter.

muffler *n.* écharpe; *Auto.* silencieux *m.*

mug *n.* chope *f.* (beer). *Infml.* museau *m.;* bobine *f.,* tronche *f.* ~ *v.t.* agresser, attaquer.

mugger *n.* agresseur *m.*

mugging *n.* agression *f.,* attaque *f.*

muggy *adj.* moite, humide.

mulatto *n.* mulâtre *m.*

mulattress *n.* mulâtresse *f.*

mulberry *n.* mûre *f.* ~ **tree,** *n.* mûrier *m.*

mule *n.* mulet *m.,* mule *f.*

multicolored *adj.* multicolore.

multilingual *adj.* multilingue.

multiple *adj.* multiple. *n.* multiple *m.*

multiplication *n.* multiplication *f.*

multiplicator *n.* multiplicateur *m.*

multiplicity *n.* multiplicité *f.*

multiplier *n.* celui ou ce qui multiple; multiplicateur *m.*

multiply *v.i.* se multiplier.

multitude *n.* multitude *f.*

mum *adj.* silencieux, muet. **to keep** ~, avoir la bouche close, ne dire mot. *interj.* silence! chut! *n.* silence. **mum's the word,** c'est un secret.

mumble *v.i.,v.t.* murmurer, marmonner, marmotter; bredouiller.

mumbling *adj.* marmottant, bredouillant, machonnant.

mumbo-jumbo *n.* charabia *m.,* jargon *m.;* fétiche *m.*

mummification *n.* momification *f.*

mummify *v.t.* momifier.

mumming *n.* mascarade *f.* ~ *adj.* de mascarade.

mummy *n.* momie *f.*

mumps *m.pl.* oreillons *pl.*

munch *v.t.* croquer à belle dent.

mundane *adj.* mondain, du monde.

municipal *adj.* municipal.

municipality *n.* municipalité *f.*

munificence *n.* munificence *f.*

munition *n.* munitions *f.pl.*

mural *adj.* mural; *n.* peinture murale *f.*

murder *n.* meurtre *m.,* assassinat *m.;* *interj.* au meurtre! à l'assassin! *v.t.* assassiner, tuer; massacrer.

murderer *n.* meurtrier *m.,* assassin *m.*

murderous *adj.* homicide; sanguinaire, meurtrier.

murk *n.* obscurité *f.*

murky *adj.* sombre, obscur, triste.

murmur *n.* murmure *m.* ~ *v.i.* murmurer.

muscatel *n.* muscat *m.* (raisin et vin).

muscle *n.* muscle *m.*

muscular *adj.* musculaire, musclé.

muse *n.* muse *f.;* rêverie *f.,* méditation *f.* ~ *v.i.* méditer, contempler. *v.t.* penser à, réfléchir à, songer à.

museum *n.* musée *m.*

mush *n.* bouillie *f.;* sentimentalité *f.* à l'eau de rose.

mushroom *n.* champignon *m.* ~ **bed,** couche de champignons, champignonnière; *v.i.* pousser comme un champignon.

mushy *adj.* mou, spongieux. *Infml.* **you are so** ~, tu es une vrai guimauve.

music *n.* musique *f.* ~ **book,** cahier *m.* de musique. ~ **paper,** papier *m.* de musique. ~ **hall,** salle *f.* de concert. ~ **stand,** pupitre *m.* ~ **stool,** tabouret *m.* de piano. ~ **box,** boîte *f.* à musique.

musical *adj.* musical; harmonieux. ~ **instruments,** des instruments de musique.

musically *adv.* musicalement.

musician *n.* musicien *m.*

musk *n.* musc *m.*

musketeer *n.* mousquetaire *m.*

musky *adj.* musqué.

Muslim *adj., n.* musulman (e) *f.,* islamique.

muslin *n.* mousseline *f.* ~ *adj.* de mousseline.

muss *v.t.* décoiffer.

mussel *n.* moule *f.*

must *v.i. aux.* falloir, devoir. **I** ~ **go,** je dois partir, il faut que je parte. **you** ~ **be joking,** sans blague! **you** ~ **believe me,** vous devez me croire. *n.* moût *m.;* moisi *m.*

mustache *n.* moustache *f.*

mustard *n.* moutarde *f.* ~ **seed,** graine *f.* de moutarde.

muster *v.t.,v.i.* passer en revue; rassembler, réunir (troops). **to** ~ **up courage,** reprendre courage. *n.* rassemblement *m.,* réunion *f.;* appel *m.* (troops); revue *f.*

musty *adj.* moisi; passé, vieilli; qui sent le moisi, le renfermé.

mutable *adj.* muable; changeant, inconstant.

mutation *n.* mutation *f.*

mute *adj.* muet, silencieux. *n.* muet *m.;* *Mus.* sourdine *f.* ~ *Gram.* muette *f.*

muteness *n.* silence *m.,* mutisme *m.*

mutilate *v.t.* mutiler, tronquer, retrancher.

mutilation *n.* mutilation *f.*

mutineer *n.* mutin *m.*

mutinous *adj.* mutin, séditieux, rebelle.

mutiny *n.* mutinerie *f.* ~ *v.i.* se mutiner, se révolter.

mutt *n.* corniaud *m.*

mutter *v.i.,v.t.* marmonner, marmotter, murmerer. *n.* murmure *m.*

mutton *n.* mouton *n.n.,* viande *f.* de mouton. **leg of** ~, gigot *m.*

mutual *adj.* mutuel, réciproque.

mutually *adv.* mutuellement, réciproquement.

muzzle *n.* museau *m.;* (animals) bouche *f.,* gueule *f.,* bout *m.,* bec *m.;* muselière *f.* (to control a dog). **the** ~ **of a gun,** la bouche, la gueule d'un canon. **the** ~ **of an ox,** le mufle d'un boeuf. *v.t.* museler.

my *adj. poss.* mon, ma, mes, à moi.

myopia *n.* myopie *f.*

myriad *n.* myriade *f.*

myrrh *n.* myrrhe *f.*

myrtle n. myrte m.

myself pers.pron. moi-même, moi.

mysterious adj. mysterieux.

mysteriously adv. mystérieusement.

mystery n. mystère m. to make a ~ of, faire un mystère de.

mystic n. mystique m.

mystic, mystical adj. mystérieux, obscur, caché, secret; mystique.

mysticism n. mysticisme m.

mystification n. mystification f.

mystify v.t mystifier.

myth n. mythe m.

mythical adj. mythique.

N

N n. nord m.

nab v.t. Infml. choper, pincer. he got ~bed at the border, il s'est fait choper à la frontière.

nadir n. nadir m.; point le plus bas.

nag n. bidet m., jeune cheval m. Infml. enquiquineur n., Vulg. emmerdeur m. ~ v.t. narguer, enquiquiner, emtêter, Vulg. emmerder.

naiad n. naïade f.

nail n. clou m.; ongle m. (fingers, toes); griffe f. you hit the ~ on the head, vous avez mis le doigt dessus; vous y êtes. to drive in a ~, enfoncer un clou. ~ brush, brosse f. à ongles. ~ polish, vernis m. à ongles. ~ polish remover, dissolvant m. ~ v.t. clouer, clouter. to ~ down, clouer, fermer avec des clous. to ~ up, clouer; attacher avec des clous. the police ~ed him, il s'est fait pincer par la police.

naïve adj. naïf, naive.

naïvely adv. naïvement.

naïveté n. naïveté f.

naked adj. nu; à nu; dégarni; simple, pur. stark ~, tout nu, nu comme un ver. with the ~ eye, à l'oeil nu. the ~ truth, la simple vérité. n. nu m.

nakedly adv. à nu, à découvert; simplement.

nakedness n. nudité f.; dénûment m., misère f.

namby-pamby adj. gnangnan, maniéré, prétentieux, affecté.

name n. nom m.; renom m. nick~, surnom m. to call ~s, dire des injures. what is his ~? comment s'appelle-t-il? in the ~ of, au nom de. v.t. nommer, appeler choisir; intituler, qualifier.

named adj. qui a un nom; mentionné, désigné. above-~, ci-dessus mentionné.

nameless adj. sans nom; anonyme, inexprimable, qui n'a pas de nom.

namely adv. nommément, à savoir; c'est-à-dire.

namesake n. homonyme m.

nanny n. bonne f. d'enfant, nounou f. ~-goat n. chèvre f.

nap n. somme m., sieste f., poil m. (fabric), duvet m. (plants). to take a ~, faire un somme.

nape n. nuque f.

napkin n. serviette f. ~ ring, rond de serviette.

narcissus n.pr. narcisse m.

narcotic adj. narcotique; soporifique. n. narcotique m.

narrate v.t. narrer.

narration n. narration f.; récit m.

narrative adj. narratif. n. narration f., récit m.

narrator n. narrateur m.

narrow adj. étroit; petit borné, rétréci; minutieux; resserré, à l'étroit. a ~ passage, un passage étroit. ~ circumstances, gêne pécuniaire. a ~ mind, un esprit borné; obtus. a ~ search, une recherche minutieuse. to have a ~ escape, l'échapper belle, échapper de justesse. v.t. resserrer, borner. v.i. (se) rétrécir, devenir étroit.

narrowing n. rétrécissement m.

narrowly adv. étroitement; de près; minutieusement; mesquinement.

nasal adj. nasal. n. nasale f.

nascent adj. naissant.

nastily adv. salement, méchamment.

nastiness n. méchanceté f.

nasty adj. méchant.

natal adj. natal, de naissance.

nation n. nation f.; peuple m.; grand nombre m.; multitude f.

national adj. national.

nationality n. nationalité f.

nationally adv. nationalement.

native adj. natif, natal, naturel; indigène, du pays; originaire. ~ place, lieu natal. ~ language, langue maternelle. n. natif m., naturel m., indigène m.

nativity n. naissance f., nativité f.

natural adj. naturel; réel; naif. Mus. bécarre. ~ history, histoire naturelle. n. naturel m.; Mus. bécarre m.

naturalism n. naturalisme m.

naturalist n. naturaliste m.

naturalization n. naturalisation f.

naturalize v.t. naturaliser.

naturally adv. naturellement.

naturalness n. naturalisme m.; naïveté f.; simplicité f., grâce f. naturelle; naturel m.

nature n. nature f.; naturel m. good ~, bonne nature, bon naturel, bonté.

natured adj. de nature. good-~, bon, d'un bon naturel.

naughty adj. méchant, mauvais; pervers; indocile.

nausea n. nausée f.

nauseate v.i.,v.t. avoir, éprouver des nausées; se dégoûter; exciter le dégoût.

nauseous adj. nauséabond. she is feeling ~, elle a envie de vomir, elle ne se sent pas bien.

nautical adj. nautique; naval.

nautilus n. nautile m., argonaute m.

naval adj. naval; maritime; de mer. ~ officer, officier de la marine. ~ war, guerre maritime.

nave n. nef f. (church); moyeu m. (wheel).

navel n. nombril m.; Fig. center m., coeur m.

navigable *adj.* navigable.

navigate *v.i.* naviguer. *v.t.* diriger, gouverner un navire à la voile.

navigation *n.* navigation *f.*

navigator *n.* navigateur, marin *m.*

navy *n.* flotte *f.;* ~ **blue**, blue, marine *f.*

nay *adv. Lit.* non. *n.* refus *m.*, négation *f.*, démenti *m.; Parliam.* opposant *m.*

Nazi *adj., n.* nazi *m.*

near *adj.* proche, près de; près; rapproché; intime; cher, aimé. **a** ~ **relation**, un proche parent. *adv.* presque, à près; près, auprès. **quite** ~, tout près. **to draw** ~, s'approcher. *prep.* près de, auprès de. ~ **London**, près de Londres. *v.t.,v.i.* s'appro-cher de.

nearby *adj.* proche; *adv.* tout près.

nearly *adv.* de près, à peu de distance, non loin; étroitement; intimement. **they** ~ **had an acci-dent**, ils ont failli avoir un accident, ils étaient à deux doigts d'avoir un accident.

nearness *n.* proximité *f.;* parenté *f.*

nearsighted *adj.* myope.

neat *adj.* propre, net; rangé, soigné; pur (sans eau), simple. ~ **clothes**, des habits propres. **a** ~ **piece of work**, un travail propre, bien soigné. ~ **wine**, du vin pur.

neatly *adv.* proprement; avec soin; purenient, élégamment.

neatness *n.* propreté *f.;* netteté *f.;* pureté *f.;* élégance *f.*

nebulous *adj.* nébuleux.

necessary *adj.* nécessaire, obligé; inévitable. *n.* au *pl.* **necessaries**, nécessaire *m.*

necessitate *v.t.* nécessiter; contraindre.

necessity *n.* nécessité *f.;* indigence *f.*, besoin *m.* **you see the** ~ **of it**, vous en voyez la nécessité.

neck *n.* cou ou col *m.;* goulot *m.* (bottle); enco-lure *f.* (animals). ~ **of mutton**, collet *m.* de mouton. **stiff** ~, torticolis *m.* ~ **and shoul-ders**, encolure.

neckerchief *n.* foulard *m.*

necklace *n.* collier *m.*

necrology *n.* nécrologie *f.*

nectar *n.* nectar *m.*

nectarine *n.* brugnon *m.*

need *n.* besoin *m.;* nécessité *f.;* dénûment *m.*, pauvreté *f.* **to be in** ~ **of**, avoir besoin de. **to be in** ~, être dans le besoin. **a case of** ~, un cas de besoin. *v.t.* avoir besoin; manquer (de). *v.i.* fal-loir, être nécessaire.

needed *adj.* nécessaire.

needle *n.* aiguille *f.* **a knitting** ~, une aiguille à tricoter. **magnetic** ~, aiguille aimantée. ~**work**, travail *m.* à l'aiguille.

needless *adj.* inutile, superflu.

needy *adj.* nécessiteux, pauvre, indigent.

ne'er contraction of **never.**

nefarious *adj.* abominable, détestable; atroce; scélérat.

nigate *v.t.* nier.

negation *n.* négation *f.*

negative *adj.* négatif. *n.* négative *f.;* négation *f.*, *Law.* veto *m.*

negatively *adv.* négativement.

neglect *v.t.* négliger. *n.* négligence *f.;* oubli *m.*, omission *f.;* indifférence *f.*, désuétude *f.* **to fall into** ~, tomber dans l'oubli, tomber en désuétude.

neglectful *adj.* négligent.

neglectfully *adv.* avec négligence, négligémment.

négligée *n.* négligé *m.*

negligence *n.* négligence *f.*

negligent *adj.* négligent; nonchalant.

negotiable *adj.* négociable.

negotiate *v.i.* négocier.

negotiation *n.* négotiation *f.*

negotiator *n.* négociateur *m.*

Negro (African-American) spiritual *n.* negro-spiritual *m.*

neigh *v.i.* hennir. *n.* hennissement *m.*

neighbor *n.* voisin *m.*, voisine *f.; Bibl.* prochain *m.*, semblable *m.* **to love one's** ~, aimer son prochain. *v.t.* avoisiner; approcher. *adj.* voisin.

neighborhood *n.* voisinage *m.*, quartier *m.*, environs *m.pl.*, alentours *m.pl.*, proximité *f.* **a bad** ~, un mauvais quartier.

neighboring *adj.* voisin, avoisinant, d'alentour.

neighborly *adj.* en bon voisin. *adv.* en bon voisin.

neither *conj.* ni, non plus. ~ **this nor that**, ni ceci, ni cela. ~ **will I do it**, et je ne le ferai pas non plus. *pron.* ni l'un ni l'autre, ni l'une ni l'autre, ni les uns, ni les unes, ni les autres, aucun, pas un, pas une. ~ **of them was pres-ent**, aucun pas un d'eux n'était présent. *adj.* aucun. **to be on** ~ **side**, ne prendre parti ni pour l'un ni pour l'autre.

neologism *n.* néologie *f.*

neophyte *n.* néophyte *m.;* novice *m.* ~ *adj.* récemment entré dans une profession.

nephew *n.* neveu *m.*

nephrite *n.* néphrite *f.*

nepotism *n.* népotisme *m.*

neptune *n.pr.* neptune *m.*

nerve *n.* nerf *m.; Fig.* force, vigueur; *Anat., Bot.* nervure *f.* ~ *v.t.* donner du nerf, de la force; *Infml.* culot *m.* **he's got some** ~, il a du culot.

nervous *adj.* nerveux; énervé; *Bot.* nervé.

nervously *adv.* nerveusement.

nervousness *n.* nervosité *f.*, état nerveux.

nest *n.* nid *m.;* nichée *f., Fig.* repaire *m.* **to make a** ~, faire son nid, nicher. **a** ~ **of thieves**, un repaire de voleurs. **to feather one's** ~, faire son nid, faire ses orges. *v.i.,v.t.* nicher; faire son nid.

nestle *v.t.* se nicher, se loger, se remuer, s'agiter. *v.t.* nicher loger chérir, choyer. **to** ~ **in, to** ~ **close to**, se serrer contre.

nestling *n.* oisillon *m.*

net *n.* filet *m.*, réseau *m.*, rets *m.pl.;* tulle *m.* ~**work**, réseau *m.* ~ *v.t.* prendre au filet; rapporter un bénéfice net. *adj.* net de revient. ~ **gain**, pro-fit net. ~ **weight**, poids net.

nether *adj.* inférieur, plus bas.

Netherlands Pays-Bas *m.pl.*

nethermost *adj.* Lit. le plus lointain.

netting *n.* réseau *m.*

nettle *n.* ortie *f.* ~ *v.t.* fâcher, piquer, irriter, vexer, aigrir.

neuralgia *n.* névralgie *f.*

neurology *n.* névrologie *f.*

neurotic *adj.* nerveux, névrotique. **a ~ disease**, une maladie nerveuse. *n.* névrosé *f.*

neuter *adj.* neutre. *n.* neutre *m.* ~ *v.t.* châtrer.

neutral *adj., n.* neutre, indifferent.

neutrality *n.* neutralité *f.*

neutralization *n.* neutralisation *f.*

neutralize *v.t.* neutraliser.

never *adv.* jamais, ne . . . jamais; ne . . . aucunement; quelque . . . que ce soit. **he will ~ come**, il ne viendra jamais. ~ **mind**, tant pis. ~ **say ~**, ~ **in a million years**, je n'aurai jamais cru. ~ **again!** jamais plus!

nevertheless *adv.* néanmoins, cependant, pourtant, toutefois.

new *adj.* neuf; nouveau,, récent; frais, tendre. **a ~ coat**, un manteau neuf. **brand ~**, tout neuf. **a ~ book** (unused), un livre neuf; (newly published) un livre nouveau. **a ~ theory**, une nouvelle théorie. ~ **wine**, du vin nouveau. **the ~ Testament**, le Nouveau Testament. **the New Year**, le nouvel an. **the ~ moon**, la nouvelle lune. ~**born**, nouveau-né. ~**comer**, nouveau venu *m.*

newel *n.* noyau *m.*

Newfoundland *n.* Terre-Neuve *f.*

newly *adv.* nouvellement.

news *n.* nouvelle *f.*, nouvelles *f.pl.* **what is the ~?** quelles sont les nouvelles? qu'y a-t-il de nouveau? **no ~ is good ~**, pas de nouvelles, bonnes nouvelles. ~**room**, salle *f.* de rédaction.

newspaper *n.* journal *m.*, feuille *f.*, gazette *f.* **daily ~**, journal quotidien. **weekly ~**, journal hebdomadaire.

New Zealand *n.* Nouvelle-Zélande *f.*

next *adj.* prochain; le plus proche; voisin; suivant. **the ~ house**, la maison la plus proche. **the ~ heir**, l'héritier le plus proche; l'héritier présomptif. **the ~ day**, le jour suivant. **the ~ word**, le mot qui suit. *adv.* immédiatement; puis, ensuite, après. **he sat ~ to her**, il était assis près d'elle. **what's ~?** et après? ~ **to impossible**, presque impossible. ~ **to nothing**, presque rien.

nibble *v.t.* grignoter, ronger; ronger; ronger.

nice *adj.* sympa, gentil; bon, beau. **to be ~**, être gentil. ~ **flowers**, de belles fleurs. **a ~ child**, un gentil enfant. **a ~ man**, un homme aimable.

nicely *adv.* délicatement; finement; bien, agréablement; joliment; justement.

niche *n.* niche *f.*; un bon coin.

nick *n.* entaille *f.*; encoche *f.* **in the very ~ of time**, fort à propos, au moment propice. *v.t.* faire des entailles, des coches.

nickel *n.* nickel *m.*

nickname *n.* surnom *m.* ~ *v.t.* donner un surnom.

nicotine *n.* nicotine *f.*

niece *n.* nièce *f.*

nifty *adj.* Infml. chic; coquet; habile.

niggard *n.* avare *m.* ~ *adj.* avare, mesquin, chiche.

niggardly *adj.* mesquin, chiche. *adv.* en avare; avec lésinerie; chichement.

niggle *v.i.* être pointilleux, couper les cheveux en quatre.

nigh *adj.* Lit. See NEAR.

night *n.* nuit *f.*; soir *m.* **to ~**, ce soir. **last ~**, hier soir, la nuit dernière. **by ~**, de nuit ou la nuit. **Tuesday ~**, mardi soir. ~**cap**, bonnet *m.* de nuit; un dernier boisson. ~**club**, boîte *f.* de nuit. ~**fall**, tombée *f.* de la nuit. **good~**, bonne nuit. ~**light**, veilleuse *f.* ~**watch**, garde *m.* de nuit, guet *m.*, sentinelle *f.* de nuit; veille *f.* de nuit. ~ **work**, travail *m.* de nuit.

nightingale *n.* rossignol *m.*; philomèle *f.*

nightly *adj.* et *adv.* nocturne, de nuit, fait la nuit; toutes les nuits; nuitamment.

nightmare *n.* cauchemar *m.*

nil *adj.* nul.

Nile *n.pr.* Nil *m.*

nimble *adj.* agile; léger, prompt, vif, alerte. ~**witted**, à l'esprit vif.

nimbly *adv.* avec agilité, agilement, lestement.

nimbus *n.* nimbe *m.*; nimbus *m.*

nine *adj.* n. neuf *m.* Infml. **dressed to the ~s**, tiré à quatre épingles, sur son trente et un.

ninefold *adj.* répété neuf fois, multiplié par neuf.

nineteen *adj.,n.* dix-neuf *m.*

nineteenth *adj.* dix-neuvième.

ninetieth *adj.* quatre-vingt-dixième.

ninety *adj.,n.* quatre-vingt-dix.

ninny *n.* bécasse *f.*; bêbête *f.*; gourde *f.*

ninth *adj.* neuvième *m.*

nip *v.t.* pincer; grignoter; couper, tailler, tondre; détruire (par le froid); flétrir; brûler; enlever prématurément. **the frost has ~ped the wheat**, la gelée a brûle le blé. **to ~ in the bud**, fermer quelquechose au commencement. *n.* coup *m.* d'ongles, coup de dents; petite coupure *f.*, brûlure (buds, flowers); sarcasme *m.*

nipple *n.* mamelon *m.*, tétine *f.*; bout *m.* de sein.

nit *n.* lente *f.* (de pou).

nitrate *n.* nitrate *m.*

nitrogen *n.* nitrogène *m.*, azote *m.*

nitty-gritty *n.*, coeur *m.* du problème, détails pratiques *m.pl.* **let's get down to the ~**, venons-en aux choses sérieuses.

no *adv.* non, ne pas, pas, point. *adj.* aucun, nul. ~ **one**, personne. ~ **way!** aucunement, jamais! ~**where**, nulle part.

nobility *n.* noblesse *f.*

noble *adj.* grand, noble, illustre. *n.* noble *m.*

nobody *n.* personne *m.*; rien *m.* ~ **will know it**, personne ne le saura.

nocturnal *adj.* de nuit, nocturne.

nod *v.i.* incliner, pencher, courber la tête, s'incliner; s'assoupir. **to ~ to**, faire un signe de tête, saluer de la tête. *n.* signe *m.* de tête; mouvement *m.*, inclination *f.* de la tête; balancement *m.*

node *n.* noeud *m.*

Noel *n.* Noël *m.*

noise *n.* bruit *m.*; tapage *m.*, fracas *m.* **to make a ~**, faire du bruit. **what a ~! quel bruit!** *v.i.* faire du bruit. *v.i.* ébruiter, publier; troubler par du bruit.

noiseless *adj.* silencieux, sans bruit.

noisily *adv.* bruyamment.

noisome *adj.* insalubre, malsain, délétère; nuisible; infect.

noisy *adj.* bruyant, turbulent, tapageur.

nomad *adj., n.* nomade.

nom de plume *n.* pseudonyme *m.*

nomenclature *n.* nomenclature *f.*

nominal *adj.* nominal.

nominate *v.t.* nommer, designer, proposer comme candidat.

nomination *n.* nomination *f.*; présentation *f.*

nominee *n.* personne *f.* nominée, candidat *m.*

non préfixe négatif. **~acceptance**, non-acceptation *f.* **~aggression**, non-aggression *f.* **~flammable**, inflammable. **~commissioned**, sans brevet. **~conformist**, non-conformiste *m.* **~existence**, non être *m.*, néant *m.*, non-existence *f.*

nonchalant *adj.* nonchalant.

nondescript *adj.* non décrit, indéfinissable. *n.* chose qui n'a pas encore été décrite; chose *f.* indéfinissable.

none *pron. indéf.* aucun; pas un, pas une; nul; nulle; personne. **~ of that**, pas de ça. **he has ~**, il n'en a pas. **~theless**, néanmoins, toutefois, en dépit de, de toute manière.

nonentity *n.* personne *f.* insignifiante.

nonesuch *n.* sans pareil *m.*

nonpareil *n.* nonpareille *f.* **~** *adj.* nonpareil, incomparable.

nonplus *n.* embarras *m.* **~** *v.t.* embarrasser; mettre au pied du mur.

nonsense *n.* non-sens *m.*, absurdité *f.* **to talk ~**, dire des sottises. *interj.* balivernes! **~! allons donc! no ~**, droit et direct.

nonsensical *adj.* absurde, inepte.

non-smoker *n.* non-fumeur *m.*

noodle *n.* nouille *f.*

nook *n.* coin *m.*, recoin *m.*, enfoncement *m.*, réduit *m.*

noon *n.* midi *m.* **at ~**, à midi. *adj.* de midi.

noose *n.* noeud *m.* coulant; collet *m.*; piège *m.* *v.t.* nouer par un noeud coulant; attraper au filet.

nope *adv. Infml.* non.

nor *conj.* ni., ne, pas, non plus. **I will not clean this, ~ will you**, ni toi ni moi allons nettoyer ça.

norm *n.* norme *f.*

normal *adj.* normal.

normally *adv.* normalement, en temps normal.

north *n.* nord *m.*; *adj.* du nord, au nord. **~east**, *n.* nord-est *m.* **~eastern**, situé au nord-est ou dans la direction du nord-est. **~west**, nord-ouest *m.*

northern *adj.* au nord; vers le nord.

northward *adj.* et *adv.* vers le nord, au nord.

Norway *n.* Norvège *f.*

Norwegian *adj.* nervegien. *n.* Norvégien *m.*

nose *n.* nez *m.*; museau *m.* (certain animals); tuyau *m.* (bellows). **flat ~**, nez plat, écrasé. **to blow one's ~**, se moucher. **to pick one's ~**, se mettre le doigt dans le nez. **to have a good ~**, avoir bon nez. *v.t.* sentir; tenir tête à; fourrer le nez dans. **~ around**, fouiner, fureter, fouiller. **~ in**, s'immiscer. **~ at**, flairer.

nostalgia *n.* nostalgie *f.*

nostril *n.* narine *f.*, naseau *m.* (horse).

nosy *adj.* curieux, fouinard.

not *adv.* non, ne pas, ne point, pas, point. **why ~?** pourquoi pas? **~ at all**, pas du tout. **if ~**, sinon.

notable *adj.* notable, considerable. *n.* notable *m.*

notably *adv.* notablement, remarquablement; laborieusement, soigneusement.

notarial *adj.* notarial; notarié.

notarize *v.t.* authentifier.

notary *n.* notaire *m.*

notation *n.* notation *f.*; *Math.* numération *f.*

notch *n.* entaille *f.*, coche *f.*, cran *m.* **~** *v.t.* entailler, faire des coches.

note *n.* billet *m.*, note *f.*, marque *f.*, signe *m.*; remarque *f.*, observation *f.*, attention *f.*; *Mus.* note *f.*, ton *m.* **to take ~ of**, prendre note de. **bank~**, billet de banque. *v.t.* noter; remarquer; faire attention à.

noted *adj.* connu pour; fameux.

noteworthy *adj.* digne de remarque, d'attention.

nothing *n.* rien *m.*; néant *m.*; zéro *m.* **for ~**, pour rien, gratis. **less than ~**, moins que rien. **~ less**, rien de moins. **to come to ~**, ne mener à rien; se réduire à rien. *adv.* pas, aucunement, nullement.

nothingness *n.* néant *m.*; rien *m.*

notice *n.* observation *f.*; attention *f.*, remarque *f.*; connaissance *f.*, avis *m.*, avertissement *m.*; congé *m.* (leaving a job). **to take ~ of**, observer, faire attention à. **to give ~**, faire savoir, prévenir, donner congé, notifier. *v.t.* observer, remarquer, faire attention à, faire connaître; mentionner.

noticeable *adj.* digne d'attention; perceptible.

notification *n.* notification *f.*; avis *m.*, avertissement *m.*

notify *v.t* notifier; déclarer; avertir, prévenir.

notion *n.* notion *f.*, idée *f.*, pensée *f.* **he doesn't have any ~ of what is happening**, il n'a aucune idée de ce qui est en train de se passer.

notoriety *n.* notoriété *f.*

notorious *adj.* notoire; évident; (mauvais) reconnu, insigne, fieflé, fameux.

notoriously *adv.* notoirement.

notoriousness *n.* notoriété *f.*

notwithstanding *conj.* néanmoins, cependant, toutefois. *prep.* nonobstant, malgré.

noun *n.* nom *m.*; substantif *m.*

nourish *v.t.* nourrir; alimenter.

nourishing *adj.* nourrissant, nutritif.

nourishment *n.* nourriture *f.*

Nova Scotia *n.pr.* Nouvelle-Ecosse *f.*

novel *adj.* roman *m.*

novelist *n.* romancier *m.*

novelty *n.* nouveauté *f.*

November *n.* novembre *m.*

novice *n.* novice *m.f.* apprenti *m.*, débutant *m.*

now *adv.* maintenant, actuellement, à présent; tantôt; alors. **even ~,** à l'instant même. **till ~,** jusqu'à présent. **just ~,** tout à l'heure; à l'instant. **~ and then,** de temps en temps, de temps à autre. *conj.* maintenant que, à présent que. **~ that you have finished your homework,** maintenant que/puisque tu as fini tes devoirs.

nowadays *adv.* aujourd'hui, de nos jours.

nowhere *adv.* nulle part, en aucun lieu.

noxious *adj.* nuisible, pernicieux.

nozzle *n.* nez *m.*; bout *m.*, bec *m.*; tuyau *m.*

nuance *n.* nuance *f.*

nubile *adj.* nubile.

nuclear *adj.* nucléaire.

nucleus *n.* noyau *m.*; nucléus *m.*

nude *adj.* nu.

nudge *v.t.* toucher légèrement (pour avertir). *n.* léger coup *m.*

nudist *n.* nudiste *m.f.*

nudity *n.* nudité *f.*

nugget *n.* pépite *f.* (d'or).

nuisance *n.* dommage *m.*; ennui *m.*, inconvénient *m.*, abus *m.* **public ~,** plaie *f.* publique; honte *f.* **what a ~ you are!** tu me casses les pieds!

null *adj.* nul, nulle. **~ and void,** nul et non avenu.

nullify *v.t.* annuler.

nullity *n.* nullité *f.*

numb *adj.* engourdi; transi. *v.t.* engourdir, transir (de froid).

number *n.* nombre *m.*; numéro *m.* **an even or odd ~,** un nombre pair ou impair. **cardinal ~,** nombre cardinal. *v.t.* compter, nombrer, énumérer; numéroter.

numbering *n.* dénombrement *m.*; numérotage *m.*

numbness *n.* engourdissement *m.*, torpeur *f.*

numeral *adj.* numéral; numérique. *n.* lettre *f.* numérale; chiffre *m.*

numeration *n.* numération *f.*

numerator *n.* numérateur *m.*

numerical *adj.* numérique.

numerous *adj.* nombreux.

numerously *adv.* en grand nombre.

numerousness *n.* grand nombre *m.*

numismatic *adj.* numismatique.

numismatics *n.* numismatique *f.*

nun *n.* religieuse *f.*; *Infml.* nonne *f.*

nunnery *n.* couvent de femmes.

nuptial *adj.* nuptial, de noces; conjugal.

nuptials *n.* noces *f.pl.*

nurse *n.* infirmière *f.*, nourrice *f.*; bonne *f.* d'enfants; garde-malade *f.* **~** *v.t.* nourrir, allaiter, garder (un malade); alimenter, élever.

nursery *n.* crèche *f.*; *Gard.* pépinière *f.*

nursing *n.* allaitement *m.*; soins *m.pl.*

nursling *n.* nourrisson *m.*

nurture *n.* soins *m.pl.* *v.t.* prendre soin.

nut *n.* noix *f.*, écrou *m.* (hardware). **cashew ~,** noix d'acaiou. **hazel~,** noisette. **to crack ~s,** casser des noix. **a hard ~ to crack,** *Fig.* un person têtu, im. *v.t.* cueillir des noisettes. **~cracker,** casse-noix *m.*, casse-noisettes *m.* **~ oil,** huile *f.* de noix. **~shell,** coque *f.*, coquille *f.* de noix. **~ tree,** noisetier *m. Infml.* **he is a real ~ case,** il ne tourne vraiment pas rond.

nutmeg *n.* noix *f.* muscade, mascade *f.*

nutrient *adj.* nourrissant, nutritif. *n.* élément *m.* nutritif.

nutriment *n.* nourriture *f.*, aliment *m.*

nutrition *n.* nutrition *f.*; nourriture *f.*, aliment *m.*

nutritious *adj.* nourrissant, nutritif, alimentaire.

nutritive *adj.* nutritif.

nuts *adj. Infml.* fou. *Infml.* **are you ~?** ça va pas la tête!

nutting *n.* action de cueillir des noisettes.

nuzzle *v.i.* se cacher; fouiller avec le museau; aller la tête baissée. *v.t.* nicher.

nymph *n.* nymphe *f.*

nymphomania *n.* nymphomanie *f.*

O

oaf *n. Infml.* ballot *m.*; bêta *m.*

oafishness *n.* stupidité *f.*

oak *n.* chêne *m.*; bois *m.* de chêne. **~ tree,** chêne. **~ bark,** écorce *f.* de chêne.

oaken *adj.* de chêne.

oar *n.* rame *f.* aviron *m.* **~** *v.i.* ramer.

oasis *n.* oasis *f.*

oat *n.* avoine *f.* **~meal** *n.* flocons d'avoine *m.pl.*

oath *n.* serment *m.* **to take an ~,** prêter serment. **on, upon ~,** sous serment, sous la foi du serment. **to break one's ~,** manquer à son serment.

obduracy *n.* obstination *f.*, entêtement *m.*

obdurate *adj.* obstiné, inflexible, inexorable, opiniâtre.

obedience *n.* obéissance *f.*; soumission.

obedient *adj.* obéissant; soumis, respectueux.

obediently *adv.* avec obéissance.

obeisance *n.* hommage *m.*

obelisk *n.* obélisque *m.*

obese *adj.* obèse.

obesity *n.* obésité *f.*

obey *v.t.* obéir, obéir à.

obfuscate *v.t* assombrir, obscurcir; déconcerter.

obituary *n.* nécrologie *f.* ~ *adj.* obituaire.

object *n.* objet *m.;* sujet *m.;* matière *f.;* but *m.,* horreur *f.* (of pity); ~ **glass,** objectif *m.* ~ *v.t.* objecter. *v.i.* s'opposer (**to, against,** à).

objection *n.* objection *f.;* reproche *m.* **have you any ~?** vous opposez-vous à ce que …? **I have no ~,** je ne m'y oppose pas.

objectionable *adj.* blâmable, répréhensible, inacceptable.

objective *adj. et n.* objectif. ~ **case,** complément *m.,* régime *m.* direct.

objectively *adv.* objectivement; *Gram.* comme régime.

objectivity *n.* objectivité *f.*

objectless *adj.* sans objet, sans but.

objector *n.* qui fait, présente des objections.

obligate *v.t.* obliger.

obligation *n.* obligation *f.;* engagement *m.* **to be under ~,** avoir des obligations à.

obligatory *adj.* obligatoire.

oblige *v.t* obliger forcer; astreindre.

obliging *adj.* obligeant.

obligingly *adv.* obligeamment.

oblique *adj.* oblique; indirect.

obliterate *v.t.* oblitérer; effacer.

obliteration *n.* oblitération *f.,* rature *f.*

oblivion *n.* oubli *m.*

oblivious *adj.* oublieux; d'oubli. **to be ~ of,** oublier.

obliviousness *n.* oubli *m.*

oblong *adj.* oblong, oblongue. *n.* figure *f.* oblongue, rectangle *m.*

obloquy *n.* blâme *m.,* reproche *m.;* (honte) *f.*

obnoxious *adj.* dégoûtant, répugnant, infect.

oboe *n.* hautbois *m.*

obscene *adj.* obscène; indécent, impudique; sale, dégoûtant.

obscenity *n.* obscénité *f.*

obscure *adj.* obscur; de nuit; nocturne. *v.t.* obscurcir, cacher; éclipser.

obscurely *adv.* obscurément.

obscurity *n.* obscurité *f.*

obsequies *n.* obsèques *f.pl.*

obsequious *adj.* sonmis; obséquieux.

obsequiously *adv.* avec seumission; obséquieuseument.

observable *adj.* observable; remarquable.

observance *n.* obsèrvance *f.;* pratique *f.,* accomplissement *m.,* observance *f.;* devoir *m.*

observant *adj.* observateur *m.; Rel.* respectueux.

observation *n.* observation *f.,* attention *f.*

observatory *n.* observatoire *m.*

observe *v.t.,.v.i.* observer; faire observer, remarquer.

observer *n.* observateur *m.*

obsess *v.t.* obséder, hanter. **he is ~ed by,** il est hanté par.

obsession *n.* obsession *f.,* idée fixe *f.;* hantise *f.*

obsessive *adj.* absessif.

obsessively *adv.* d'une manière obsédante.

obsolescent *adj.* tombant en désuétude.

obsolete *adj.* suranné, vieux, antique.

obsoleteness *n.* désuétude *f.,* état de ce qui est suranné, de ce qui a vieilli.

obstacle *n.* obstacle *m.;* empêchement *m.*

obstetrics *n.* obstétrique *f.*

obstinacy *n.* obstination *f.;* opiniâtreté *f.,* entêtement *m.*

obstinate *adj.* obstiné; inflexible.

obstinately *adv.* obstinément.

obstinateness *n.* obstination *f.*

obstreperous *adj.* bruyant, turbulent, tapageur.

obstreperousness *n.* tapage *m.,* turbulence *f.*

obstruct *v.t.* obstruer; boucher, empêcher de passer.

obstruction *n.* obstruction *f.* obstacle *m.;* embarras.

obstructive *n.* obstruent *adj.* obstructif; mettant obstacle à; entravant.

obtain *v.t.* obtenir; se procurer, tenir.

obtainable *adj.* qui peut être obtenu, procuré.

obtainment *n.* obtention *f.*

obtrude *v.t.* imposer (**upon,** à). **to ~ oneself,** s'imposer. *v.i.* être importun.

obtrusion *n.* intrusion *f.*

obtrusive *adj.* importun, indiscret.

obtrusively *adv.* avec importunité; indiscrètement.

obtuse *adj.* obtus.

obtuseness *n.* lerdeur *f.* d'esprit, stupidité.

obverse *n.* revers; la face; *Typ.* recto *m.*

obviate *v.t.* obvier à; prévenir.

obvious *adj.* évident, clair, manifeste, visible.

obviously *adv.* évidemment, clairement, manifestement.

obviousness *n.* évidence *f.*

occasion *n.* occasion *f.;* rencontre *f.,* sujet *m.,* cause, circonstance *f.;* besoin *m.,* nécessité *f.* **on ~,** de temps à autre, à l'occasion. **on the first ~,** à la première occasion. **there is no ~ for,** il n'est pas nécessaire de. *v.t.* occasionner, causer, donner lieu au sujet.

occasional *adj.* par occasion; fortuit, casuel, accidental; occasionnel.

occasionally *adv.* quelquefois, par occasion.

occident *n.* occident *m.,* ouest *m.*

occidental *adj.* occidental.

occiput *n.* occiput *m.*

occult *adj.* occulte; caché, secret.

occupancy *n.* occupation *f.*

occupant *adj.* qui prend possession; possesseur *m.;* habitant *m.;* occupant *m.;* titulaire *m.f.*

occupation *n.* occupation *f.,* possession *f.;* emploi *m.;* profession *f.* **what is his ~?** qu'est ce qu'il fait?

occupy *v.t.* occuper; habiter. **to ~ oneself with,** s'occuper de.

occur *v.i.* se présenter (à l'esprit); rencontrer, frapper; arriver, survenir. **it occurred to us,** il nous est venu à l'idée que.

occurrence *n.* occurrence *f.,* événement *m.,* incident *m.*

ocean *n.* océan *m.; Fig.* immensité. the Atlantic ~, l'océan Atlantique. *adj.* de l'océan.

Oceania *n.pr.* Océanie.

oceanic *adj.* océanique *f.*

oceanography *n.* océanographie *f.*

ocelot *n.* ocelot *m.,* chattigre *m.* d'Amérique.

ocher *n.* ocre *f.*

o'clock *adv.* two ~, deux heures. it's five ~ on the dot, il est cinq heure pile.

octagon *n.* octogone *m.*

octagonal *adj.* octogonal.

octane *n.* octane *m.*

octave *n.* octave *f.*

October *n.* octobre *m.*

octogenarian *n.* octogénaire *m.*

octopus *n.* poulpe *m.,* pieuvre *f.*

octosyllabic *adj.* octosyllabe.

ocular *adj.* oculaire.

oculist *n.* oculiste *m.*

odd *adj.* impair (number); dépareillé; étrange, bizarre, drôle, de répit (moments); quelques. don't you think this is ~? ne pensez-vous pas que cela soit étrange?

oddity *n.* singularité *f.,* étrangeté *f.;* bizarrerie *f.*

oddly *adv.* étrangement, bizarrement.

oddness *n.* étrangeté *f.,* singularité *f.;* bizarrerie *f.;* irrégularité *f.*

odds *n. plur.* chances *f.pl.* the ~ are against us, les chances sont contre nous. the ~ were against me, la chance était contre moi. to set at ~, brouiller. to be at ~, être mal avec. ~ and ends, petits bouts *m.pl.*

ode *n.* ode *f.*

odious *adj.* odieux; détestable.

odiously *adv.* odieusement.

odiousness *n.* odieux *m.*

odium *n.* haine *f.;* odieux *m.*

odometer *n.* compteur kilométrique *m.*

odontology *n.* odontologie *f.*

odor *n.* odeur *f.,* senteur *f.;* parfum *m.*

odoriferous *adj.* odoriférant; odorant.

odorous *adj.* odorant.

odorless *adj.* inodore.

Odyssey *n.* odyssée *f.*

Oedipus complex *n.* complexe d'Oedipe *m.*

o'er See OVER.

o(e)strogen *n.* See ESTROGEN.

of *prep.* de, en, dans; par, à. ~ old, anciennement, jadis. ~ late, dernièrement. ~ course, évidemment, bien sûr, bien entendu. she is the best ~ all ~ them, c'est la meilleure de tous. ~ all the people who, de toutes les personnes qui. he did it out ~ necessity, il l'a fait parce qu'il fallait le faire. her ring was made ~ gold, son bague était en or.

off *adv.* loin, de distance; d'ici; de dessus. he is ~ to the country, il est parti à la campagne. the handle is ~, la poignée s'est détachée. hats ~! chapeaux bas! two percent ~, à déduire deux pour cent. ~ and on, tantôt, par intervalles. he is well ~, il est bien dans ses affaires; il est

riche *prep.* loin de, hors de; *Naut.* à la hauteur de. ~ the cape, à la hauteur du cap. *adj.* le plus éloigné; à droite. *interj.* hors d'ici! ~ with him! emmenez-le!

offend *v.t.* offenser; déplaire à, blesser, fâcher, scandaliser; insulter; transgresser. to ~ the law, transgresser la loi. *v.i.* pécher; violer (la loi).

offender *n.* offenseur *m.;* délinquant *m.,* contrevenant *m.,* coupable *m.,* criminel *m.;* nécheur *m.* old ~, récidiviste *m.*

offense *n.* offence *f.,* déplaisir *m.;* faute *f.;* délit *m.,* contravention *f.* there's no ~, il n'y a pas de mal. to take ~, se formaliser, s'offusquer.

offensive *adj.* offensant, blessant, insultant, choquant; offensif. *n.* offensive *f.*

offensively *adv.* injurieusement; par méchanceté; offensivement.

offer *v.t.* to ~ up, offrir (une prière, un sacrifice); sacrifier. *v.i.* s'offrir, se présenter, être sous la main. if the occasion offers, si l'occasion se présente. he offered to come, il s'est proposé à venir. *n.* offre *f.* to make an ~, faire une offre.

offering *n.* offrande *f.,* oblation *f.;* sacrifice *m.* thank ~s, actions de grâces.

offhand *adv.* haut la main; sur-le-champ; sans hésitation. *adj.* brusque, brutal.

office *n.* bureau *m.,* office *m.,* emploi *m.,* charge *f.;* service *m.;* pouvoir *m.;* cabinet *m.;* étude *f.* (de notaire, etc.). to be in ~, être au pouvoir. to be out of ~, n'être pas en fonctions. the government ~s, les bureaux de gouvernement; les ministères.

officer *n.* officier *m.;* fonctionnaire *m.;* huissier *m.* police ~, agent de police. staff ~, officier d'état-major. non-commissioned ~, sous-officier. naval ~, officier de la marine. *v.t.* donner pour officier; commander.

official *adj.* officiel; public. *n.* fonctionnaire *m.;* officier *m.;* official *m.* (de l'Eglise).

officially *adv.* officiellement.

officiate *v.i.* exercer; officier. to ~ for, remplacer. to ~ in, desservir (une église).

officious *adj.* officieux; trop obligeant; affairé, trop empressé.

officiously *adv.* officieusement; en officieux.

officiousness *n.* empressement *m.* officieux.

offing *n. Naut.* large *m.;* pleine mer *f.* in the ~, en perspective.

offset *n.* bourgeon *m.,* bouture *f.;* compensation *f.* ~ *v.t.* balancer, compenser. ~ printing, impression *f.* offset.

offshoot *n.* rejeton *m.*

offspring *n.* rejeton *m.,* enfant *m.;* descendant *m.,* descendants *m.pl.,* postérité *f.*

often *adv.* souvent, fréquemment. how often, combien de fois. too often, trop souvent.

ogive *n.* ogive *f.* ~ *adj.* (en) ogive.

ogle *n.* lorgner. *n.* coup *m.* d'oeil, oeillade *f.*

ogre *n.* ogre *m.*

ogress *n.* ogresse *f.*

oh *interj.* oh! ô! ha! ho! hélas!

oil *n.* huile *f.* **salad** ~, huile à manger. **castor** ~, huile de ricin. **cod-liver** ~, huile de foie de morue. **linseed** ~, huile de lin. **olive** ~, huile d'olives. ~**can**, burette *f.* ~**cloth**, ~**skin**, toile *f.* cirée. ~ **lamp**, lampe *f.* à huile. ~ **painting**, peinture *f.* à l'huile. ~ **seed**, graine *f.* oléagineuse. *v.t.* huiler.

oily *adj.* huileux; onctueux; oléagineux; gras, graisseux.

ointment *n.* onguent *m.*, pommade *f.*

O.K. *abbrev.* **okay** *excl.* d'accord, parfait, ça va. *n.* accord *m.*, approbation *f.* – *adj.* en règle, approuvé. *v.t.* approuver.

old *adj.* vieux ou vieil *m.*, vieille *f.* âgé; ancien, antique. **to grow** ~, vieillir, se faire vieux. ~ **age**, vieillesse *f.* **an** ~ **house**, une vieille maison. ~ **books**, de vieux livres. **how** ~ **are you?** quel âge avez-vous? **I am thirty years** ~, j'ai trente ans. **The** ~ **Testament**, l'Ancien Testament. **the** ~ **world**, l'ancien monde. **of** ~, anciennement. ~**fashioned**, à l'ancienne mode, démodé.

oldie *n. Infml.* vieux succès *m.*

oleaginous *adj.* oléagineux.

olfactory *adj.* olfactif.

oligarchy *n.* oligarchie *f.*

olive *n.* olive *f.*, olivier *m.* – *adj.* d'olive. ~ **tree**, olivier *m.*

Olympian *adj.* olympien.

Olympic *adj.* olympique.

omelet *n.* omelette *f.*

omen *n.* augure *m.* auspice *m.*, présage *m.*

ominous *adj.* de mauvais augure; sinistre.

ominously *adv.* de mauvais augure.

ominousness *n.* nature *f.* sinistre.

omission *n.* omission *f.*

omit *v.t.* omettre; négliger.

omnipotence *n.* omnipotence *f.*, toute-puissance *f.*

omnipotent *adj.* tout-puissant. *n.* tout-puissant *m.*

omnipotently *adv.* avec toute puissance, avec omnipotence.

omnipresence *n.* omniprésence *f.*, ubiquité *f.*

omnipresent *adj.* omniprésent.

omniscience *n.* omniscience *f.*

omniscient *adj.* omniscient.

omnivorous *adj.* omnivore.

on *prep.* sur; à, au, de; dessus; du, des, en, dans. **to live** ~ **vegetables**, vivre de légumes. ~ **board**, à bord. ~ **the right hand**, à droite, sur la droite. ~ **the contrary**, au contraire. ~ **foot**, à pied. ~ **horseback**, à cheval. ~ **average**, en moyenne. ~ **second thought**, après mûre réflexion. ~ **computer**, sur ordinateur. ~ **file**, sur fichier. ~ **stage**, sur scène. ~ **television**, à la télévision. *adv.* dessus, sur en avant; toujours. **he had a cap** ~, il portait une casquette. **move** ~, avancez. **to look** ~, regarder, considérer. **play** ~, continuez de jouer. **go** ~, continuez, allez toujours. **and so** ~, et ainsi de suite.

once *adv.* une fois. ~ **a year**, une fois par an. ~ **and for all**, une fois pour toutes. ~ **more**, encore une fois. ~ **upon a time**; il était une fois.

one *adj.* un, une; une seul, une seule; seul, unique. ~ **fine morning**, un beau matin. ~ **hundred and sixty**, cent soixante. *pron. indéf.* un, une; l'un, l'une; un seul; celui; on. ~ **by** ~, un par un. **he is the** ~ **who**, c'est lui qui. **ask any** ~, demandez à n'importe qui. **every** ~, chacun. **no** ~, personne. **some** ~, quelqu'un. ~**eyed**, borgne. ~**sided**. *adj.* qui penche d'un côté; partial. **the** ~ **and only**, le/la seul(e) et unique.

onerous *adj.* onéreux.

onerously *adv.* onéreusement.

one's *poss. pron.* son, sa, ses. **to have two strings to** ~ **bow**, avoir deux cordes à son arc.

oneself *réfl. pron.* se, soi, soi-même.

ongoing *adj.* en cours, en progrès.

onion *n.* oignon *m.* ~ **bed**, oignonière *f.*

only *adj.* seul, un seul, unique. *adv.* seulement, ne que, uniquement.

onomatopoeia *n.* onomatopée *f.*

onset *n.* attaque *f.*, assaut *m.*, charge *f.*; début *m.*, commencement *m.*

onslaught *n.* attaque *f.*, assaut *m.*

onto *prep.* sur, dans.

ontology *n.* ontologie *f.*

onus *n.* fardeau *m.*, poids *m.*

onward *adv.* en avant; progressivement. *adj.* avancé; progressif.

onyx *n.* onyx *m.*

oops *excl.* hop là; aïe aïe aïe.

ooze *v.i.* suinter filtrer. *n.* boue *f.*, vase *f.*, limon *m.*

opacity *n.* opacité *f.*; obscurité *f.*, ténèbres *f.pl.*

opal *n.* opale *f.*

opalescence *n.* opalescence *f.*

opalescent *adj.* opalin.

opaline *adj.* opalin.

opaque *adj.* opaque, sombre, ténébreux, obscur.

open *v.t.* déboucher (bottle); décacheter (letter); défaire (package); entamer, commencer; exposer; épancher (heart). *v.i.* (s')ouvrir; se diviser, s'entr'ouvrir. **my windows** ~ **on the road**, mes fenêtres donnent sur la route. **the flowers** ~, les fleurs s'épanouissent. *adj.* ouvert; découvert, nu, à nu; sincère, franc; vide. **wide** ~, tout grand ouvert; béant. **to pull** ~, ouvrir en tirant. ~ **country**, pays ouvert, découvert. **in the** ~ **fields**, en rase campagne. **in the** ~ **air**, en plein air. **to lay** ~, découvrir, mettre à nu. **an** ~ **question**, une question pendante. ~**handed**, libéral, généreux. ~**hearted**, candide, sincère.

opener *n.* **can** ~, ouvre-boîte.

opening *adj.* qui s'ouvre; commençant, naissant. *n.* ouverture *f.*, fente *f.*, commencement; entrée *f.*; début *m.*; débouché *m.*; occasion *f.*

openly *adv.* ouvertement.

openness n. situation f. découverte, clarté f., laiser-aller m., sincérité f., candeur f.

opera n. opéra m.

operate v.i. opérer, agir.

operation n. opération f., action f.; effet m.

operator n. agent m.; opérateur m.

ophidian adj. ophidien.

ophthalmology n. ophtalmologie f.

opiate n. opiat m.; narcotique m. ~ adj. narcotique.

opine v.i. opiner, être d'avis.

opinion n. opinion f.; avis m.; judgment m., sens m.; pensée f.

opinionated adj. opiniâtre, entêté, suffisant; présomptueux.

opium n. opium m.

opossum n. opossum m., sarigue f.

opponent adj. opposé en face; contraire. n. adversaire m.; antagoniste m.

opportune adj. opportun.

opportunely adv. en temps opportun, à propos.

opportunity n. opportunité f.; occasion f.

oppose v.t. opposer s'opposer à, résister à; mettre obstacle à; contrecarrer. v.i. s'opposer à; faire des objections.

opposite adj. opposé; contraire; hostile. n. opposant m., adversaire m., antagoniste m.; l'opposé m., le contraire m.

oppositely adv. vis-à-vis; en sens opposé.

opposition n. opposition f.; obstacle m.; résistance f.; concurrence f. in ~ to, en opposition à; par opposition à. to meet with ~, rencontrer de l'opposition.

oppress v.t. opprimer, oppresser.

oppression n. oppression f.; accablement m.; abattement m.

oppressive adj. oppressif; accablant, lourd.

oppressor n. oppresseur m.

opprobrious adj. méprisant, infamant; injurieux, scandaleux.

opt v.i. opter. v.t. choisir.

optical adj. optique.

optician n. opticien m.

optics optique f.

optimal adj. optimal, optimum.

optimism n. optimisme m.

optimist n. optimiste m.f.

optimistic adj. optimiste.

option n. option f.; choix m.

optional adj. facultatif.

opulence n. opulence f.

opulent adj. opulent, riche.

or conj. ou. either . . . or, ou . . . ou; soit . . . soit; ni . . . ni.

oracle n. oracle m.

oral adj.,n. oral m.

orally adv. oralement.

orange n. orange f. ~ tree, oranger m. ~ adj. orange, orangé, d'orange. ~ peel, écorce f. d'orange.

orangeade n. orangeade f.

orangery n. orangerie f.

orang-(o)utang n. orang-outan(g) m.

oration n. discours m. harangue f., oraison f. funèbre.

orator n. orateur m.

oratorical adj. oratoire, d'orateur.

oratory n. art m. oratoire; exercice m. d'éloquence; Eccl. oratoire m.

orbit n. orbito f.

orbital adj. orbitaire.

orchard n. verger m.

orchestra n. orchestre m.

orchestral adj. d'orchestre.

orchestrate v.t. orchestrer.

orchestration n. orchestration f.

orchid n. orchidée f.

ordain v.t. ordonner; prescrire; constituer. to ~ a priest, ordonner un prêtre.

ordeal n. épreuve f.

order n. ordre m.; portion. commande f.; mandat m., rang m., classe f. to put in ~, mettre en ordre. to be in ~, être en règle. to keep in ~, tenir en bon état. the ~ of the day, l'ordre du jour. an ~ of fries, une portion de frites. till further ~s, jusqu'à nouvel ordre. call to ~, rappel au règlement. to place an ~, passer une commande f. to take ~s, prendre les ordres. in ~ to please you, pour vous plaire. v.t. ordonner, disposer, régler; commander. well ordered, bien ordonné. to ~ a dinner, commander un dîner. to ~ in, faire entrer, faire apporter.

orderliness n. régularité f.; symétrie f.; ordre m., méthode f.

orderly adj. régulier, méthodique; en ordre, rangé; tranquille. adv. en bon ordre, régulièrement.

ordinance n. ordonnance f. règlement m.; décret m.

ordinarily adv. ordinairement.

ordinary adj. ordinaire; habituel. n. ordinaire m.

ordination n. ordination f.

ordnance n. artillerie f. heavy ~, grosse artillerie. ~ map, carte f. d'état-major. ~ survey, cadastre m.; levée f. des plans.

ore n. minerai m.; mine f.; métal m. iron ~, minerai de fer.

oregano n. origan m.

organ n. organe m.; orgue m., Mus. orgues f.pl. the ~ of speech, l'organe de la parole. barrel or street ~, orgue de Barbarie. sexual ~s, organes m.pl. génitaux. ~ loft, tribune f. d'orgue. ~ pipe, tuyau m. d'orgue. ~ stop, jeu m. d'orgue.

organic adj. organique.

organism n. organisme m.

organist n. organiste m.

organization n. organisation f.

organize v.t. organiser.

organizer n. organisateur m.

orgasm n. orgasme m.; Fig. paroxysme m.

orgy n. orgie f.

Orient n. Orient m., est m.

oriental adj. oriental, de l'Orient. n. Oriental m.

orientate v.t. orienter.

orientation n. orientation f.

orifice n. orifice m.

origin n. origine f.; source f.

original adj. original; primitif, vrai. ~ **sin**, péché originel. **an ~ picture**, un tableau original. n. original m.

originality n. originalité f.

originally adv. à l'origine, originellement; originairement; originellement.

originate v.t. (**from**, de) produire, faire naître. v.i. (avec **in**) naître de, provenir de, prendre naissance.

originator n. auteur m.; cause f. première.

ornament n. ornement m.; parure f. ~ v.t. orner, décorer.

ornamental adj. ornemental.

ornamentation n. ornementation f.

ornate adj. orné, décoré, paré, embelli.

ornithology n. ornithologie f.

orphan n. orphelin m., orpheline f. ~ adj. orphelin. v.t. réduire à l'état d'orphelin.

orphanage n. orphelinat m.

orthodontist n. orthodontiste m.f.

orthodox adj.,n. orthodoxe.

orthography n. orthographe f.

orthopedic adj. orthopédique.

orthopedics n. orthopédie f.

oscillate v.i. osciller.

oscillation n. oscillation f.

osculation n. osculation f.; Formal. embrassade f.

osier n. osier m.

osseous adj. osseux.

ossify v.t. ossifier. v.i. (s')ossifier.

ostensible adj. prétendu, visible.

ostensibly adv. ostensiblement, en apparence.

ostentation n. mine f., air m., apparence f.; ostentation f.; faste m.

ostentatious adj. plein d'ostentation; pompeux, fastueux.

osteopath n. ostéopathe m.f.

ostracism n. ostracisme m.

ostracize v.t. frapper d'ostracisme.

ostrich n. autruche f.

other adj. autre; différent. **the ~ day**, l'autre jour. **any ~**, tout autre. **each ~**, l'un l'autre. pron. autrui m.; autre m. **~s**, les autres, autrui. **no ~**, nul autre, aucun autre.

otherwise adv. autrement.

otter n. loutre f.

ouch interj. aïe!

ought adj. devoir, falloir. **you ~ to go**, vous devriez y aller.

ounce n. once f. (28.35 gr.).

our adj. notre; pl. nos; à nous.

ours pron. poss. le nôtre, la nôtre, les nôtres; à nous; de nous.

ourselves pron. réfl. nous-mêmes; nous.

oust v.t. enlever; évincer; chasser.

ouster n. éviction f.

out adv. hors, dehors, au dehors; sorti, absent, découvert; épuisé, éteint; publié, paru. **a way ~**, une issue, une sortie. **the fleet was ~**, la flotte était en mer. **the secret is ~**, le secret est découvert. **a book just ~**, un livre qui vient de paraître. **it is ~ of print**, il est épuisé. **the fire is ~**, le feu est éteint. **the wine was ~**, il n'y avait plus de vin. prép. (with **of**). **~ of fashion**, démodé. **~ of sight**, hors de la vue, perdu de vue. **~ of place**, déplacé. **he is ~ of pocket by it**, il y perd. **~ of tune**, discordant. **~ of kindness**, par amitié. **~ of laziness**, par paresse. **to drink ~ of a glass**, boire dans un verre. **one ~ of ten**, un sur dix. interj. ~! dehors!

outbreak n. explosion f.; éruption f.

outburst n. explosion f.

outcast adj. chassé, exilé m., proscrit m., banni m.

outcome n. conséquence f., résultat m.

outcry n. grand cri m., clameur f.; hauts cris m.pl.

outdated adj. démodé.

outdo v.t. exceller sur; surpasser; faire mieux ou plus que.

outdoor adj. au dehors; externe.

outdoors adj. au-dehors, en plein air, au grand air. **to sleep ~**, dormir à la belle étoile.

outer adj. situé dehors; extérieur, externe.

outermost adj. le plus extérieur; placé à l'extrême limite.

outfit n. tenue f.; équipement m.

outflow v.i. s'écouler. sortie f., émigration f.

outgoing adj. sortant; Fig. ouvert, Infml. sympa.

outgrow v.t. surpasser en croissance; dépasser.

outgrowth n. excroissance f.; Fig. résultat m.

outing n. sortie f., promenade f.

outlandish adj. étrange, bizarre.

outlast v.t. surpasser en durée; survivre à.

outlaw n. proscrit m.; hors la loi m., bandit m., brigand m. ~ v.t. proscrire; mettre hors la loi.

outlay n. frais m.pl., dépenses f.pl.

outlet n. issue f., sortie f.; débouché m.; gargouille f., rigole f. d'alimentation; magasin m.

outline n. contour m., esquisse f.; ébauche f. v.t. dessiner les contours.

outlive v.t. survivre à.

outlook n. vue f., horizon m.; perspective f.; conception f.

outmost adj. le plus lointain; extrême.

outnumber v.t. surpasser en nombre.

outpost n. garde f. avancée, poste m. avancé; avant-poste m.

outpour v.t. répandre à grands flots.

outpouring n. épanchement m.; effusion f.

output n. débit m. rendement m. extraction f. (mine).

outrage v.t. outrager. n. outrage m.; affront m.

outrageous adj. violent, furieux; outrageant; outrageux; outré, exagéré. ~ **crimes**, des crimes atroces. ~ **impudence**, effronterie f. incroyable.

outrageously *adv.* furieusement; tumultueusement; outrageusement; atrocement.

outright *adv.* sur-le-champ, tout de suite; entièrement; sans contrainte; carrément. **to laugh ~,** rire à gorge déployée. *adj.* total, catégorique.

outside *n.* dehors *m.;* extérieur *m.* **at the ~,** tout au plus. *adj.* en dehors; extérieur. *adv.* à l'extérieur, au dehors.

outsider *n.* étranger *m.;* outsider *m.*

outskirts *n.pl.* bord *m.;* lisière *f.* (woods); confins *m.pl.*

outsmart *v.t.* être plus malin/intelligent que.

outspoken *adj.* franc, ouvert.

outstanding *adj.* remarquable; *Comm.* courant; en suspens.

outstretch *v.t.* étendre, déployer.

outstretched *adj.* étendu, déployé.

outward *adj.* extérieur de dehors; externe. *n.* dehors *m.,* extérieur *m.* ~ *adv.* au dehors, à l'extérieur, extérieurement; à la sortie. ~ **bound,** en partance pour l'étranger.

outward *adv.* à l'extérieur.

outwardly *adv.* extérieurement, en apparence.

outweigh *v.t.* excéder en poids; l'emporter sur.

outwit *v.t.* attraper; surpasser en addresse, en finesse.

oval *adj., n.* ovale (*m.*).

ovary *n.* ovaire *m.*

ovation *n.* ovation *f.*

oven *n.* four *m.*

over *prép.* sur, au-dessus de; par-dessus; au delà de; de l'autre côté, à travers, au travers de; d'un côté à l'autre. **to cross ~ the river,** passer, traverser la rivière. **to watch ~ someone,** veiller sur quelqu'un. **head ~ heels,** par-dessus les oreilles. **he is ~ fifty,** il a plus de cinquante ans. *adv.* d'un côté à l'autre; au-dessus; au delà; plus de; trop; passé, fini. **to run ~,** écraser (with a car). **to jump ~,** sauter par-dessus. **~ and ~,** à plusieurs reprises, toujours; dans tous les sens. **the danger is ~,** le danger est passé.

overabound *v.i.* surabonder.

overact *v.t.* exagérer. *v.t.* outrer; charger.

overall *n.* salopette *f.*

overbearing *adj.* impérieux, dominateur, arrogant.

overbid *v.t.* offrir plus; enchérir; offrir trop pour.

overboard *adv.* pardessus le bord.

overcast *v.t.* assombrir, couvrir de nuages; s'exagérer. *adj.* obscurci, assombri; couvert.

overcharge *v.t.* surcharger; surfaire; faire payer trop cher. *n.* surcharge *f.,* prix *m.* excessif.

overcoat *n.* pardessus *m.*

overcook *v.t.* trop cuire.

overcome *v.t.* vaincre, maîtriser. *v.i.* l'emporter, avoir le dessus. *adj.* accablé.

overdo *v.t.* faire trop; outrer; exagérer.

overdose *n.* dose *f.* trop forte.

overdraw *v.t.* excéder, dépasser le montant de son crédit.

overdress *v.t.* habiller trop; surcharger de parure.

overdue *adj.* en retard; attendu. **his apology is long ~,** ça fait longtemps que son excuse est attendue.

overeager *adj.* trop ardent, trop empressé.

overestimate *v.t.* estimer, évaluer à un prix trop élevé.

overexcitement *n.* sur excitation *f.*

overflow *v.t.* déborder; inonder, submerger. *v.i.* se déborder; regorger. *n.* inondation *f.;* surabondance *f.*

overflowing *adj.* surabondant.

overgrown *adj.* reconvert de, tapissé de, rempli de; énorme, trop grand, qui a trop grandi. **a garden ~ with weeds,** un jardin rempli de mauvaises herbes.

overgrowth *n.* croissance *f.* excessive, démesurée.

overhang *v.t.* pencher (sur); être suspendu sur; *Fig.* menacer; surplomber. *n.* surplomb *m.*

overhanging *adj.* en surplomb; suspendu au-dessus.

overhaul *v.t* inspecter, réviser, examiner (de nouveau).

overhead *adv.* en haut; au ciel; au-dessus de la tête, en l'air. *n.* frais généraux *m.pl.*

overhear *v.t.* entendre par hasard; surprendre (une conversation).

overheat *v.t.* chauffer trop; échauffer.

overjoy *v.t.* combler de joie; ravir; enivrer.

overlap *v.t.* chevaucher, envelopper; recouvrir. *n.* chevauchement *m.,* recouvrement *m.*

overload *v.t.* surcharger; remplir trop.

overlook *v.t.* avoir vue sur; commander, dominer; surveiller, parcourir; ne pas voir, négliger. **the castle overlooks the town,** le château domine la ville.

overly *adv.* trop, excessivement.

overnight *adj.* la nuit, du jour au lendemain. **they'll stay here ~,** ils passeront la nuit ici.

overpay *v.t.* payer trop.

overpower *v.t.* dominer; subjuguer, maîtriser; accablen

overpowering *adj.* accablant, écrasant.

overreact *v.i.* réagir de trop.

override *v.t.* surmener; outrepasser, passer outre.

overripe *adj.* trop mûr.

overrule *v.t.* l'emporter sur; *Dr.* rejeter (des conclusions).

overrun *v.t.* couvrir, infester, envahir; ravager fouler, écraser; *Typ.* remanier. *v.i.* regorger, déborder.

overseas *adv.* outre-mer.

oversee *v.t.* surveiller.

oversensitive *adj.* hypersensible.

oversight *n.* omission *f.,* oubli *m.,* erreur *f.;* méprise *f.* **from ~,** par mégarde.

oversleep *v.t.* dormir trop longtemps, dépasser l'heure de réveil.

overstate v.t. exagérer.

overstep v.t. outre-passer, dépasser; aller au delà de.

overstretch v.t. forcer, étendre trop loin.

overt adj. patent, évident; public.

overtake v.t. atteindre, rejoindre; surprendre. **the storm overtook us,** la tempête nous surprit.

overtax v.t. surcharger de taxes.

overthrow v.t. renverser, bouleverser; abattre; détruire. n. renversement m.; ruine f.; destruction f.; défaite f., déroute f.

overtime n. heures f.pl., supplémentaires.

overtire v.t. excéder de fatigue.

overtly adv. ouvertement, publiquement.

overture n. Mus. ouverture f.; offre m.

overturn v.t. renverser; ruiner, détruire. n. renversement m.; bouleversement m.

overvalue v.t estimer, évaluer trop; faire trop grand cas de.

overweigh v.t. excéder en poids; surpasser.

overweight n. excédant m. de poids. **to be ~,** être trop gros, avoir un excès de poids.

overwhelm v.t. accabler, écraser combler.

overwhelming adj. accablant, écrasant.

overwork v.t. surmener; faire trop travailler; fatiguer; surcharger de travail. n. surmenage m.

overwrought excédé, trop travaillé.

overzealous adj. trop zélé.

ovine adj. ovine f.

ovulate v.i. ovuler.

ovulation n. ovulation f.

ovule n. ovule m.

owe v.t. devoir être redevable.

owing adj. dû.

owl n. hibou m. **barn ~,** chouette f. **screech ~,** chat-huant m.

own adj. propre. **the house is his ~,** la maison est à lui, lui appartient. v.t. posséder, être le propriétaire de; réclamer. **he owns this estate,** il possède cette terre. **to ~ up to,** avouer, confesser.

owner n. propriétaire m.

ownership n. propriété f.

ox n. pl. oxen, boeuf m.

oxidation n. oxydation f.

oxide n. oxyde m.

oxygen n. oxygène m.

oxygenate v.t. oxygéner.

oxygenation n. oxygénation f.

oyster n. huitre f. **~ bed,** bauc m. d'huîtres.

ozone n. ozone f.

P

pa n. papa m.

pace n. pas m., allure f.; marche f.; train m. **to keep ~ with,** se maintenir de front avec, marcher de pair avec. v.i. aller au pas; v.t. arpenter, marcher à pas mesurés; faire marcher.

paced adj. au pas. **slow-~,** qui a le pas lent; exercé, dressé.

pacemaker n. stimulateur m. cardiaque; Fig. chef m. de file.

pachyderme n. pachyderme m.

Pacific adj. pacifique; paisible. n.pr. Pacifique m.; océan m. Pacifique.

pacification n. pacification f.

pacifier n. pacificateur m.; tétine f., sucette f.

pacifist adj.,n. pacifiste (m.f.).

pacify v.t. pacifier; apaiser, calmer.

pack n. paquet m., ballot m., balle f.; jeu m. de cartes; meute f. (animals); tas m., bande f. **~horse,** cheval de bât. **~ saddle,** bât m. **~ v.t.** emballer, empaqueter; encaisser; faire sa malle, mettre en baril; encaquer (des harengs); serrer, charger (un cheval). **a ~ of lies,** un tissue m. de mensonges. **to ~ off,** expédier, faire partir. **to ~ up,** emballer, faire sa malle. v.i. plier bagage, décamper.

package n. paquet m., colis m.; emballage m. **~ tour,** voyage m. organisé.

pact n. pacte m.

pad n. tampon (ink); sous-main m.; bourrelet m.; coussinet m.; ouaté m. (suit); plastron m. (fencing). v.t. rembourrer, tamponner, ouater; garnir de coussins, de bourrelets; bourrer.

padding n. ouate f., bourre f., remplissage m.

paddle v.i. pagayer; ramer; barboter, clapoter jouer avec l'eau. v.t. sentir, tâter; jouer ou badiner avec. n. pagaie f.; aviron m.; palette f., aube f. (mill wheel). **~board,** palette f., palette f., aube f. de bois. **~wheel,** roue f. à aubes.

paddler n. rameur m.; personne qui barbotte dans l'eau.

paddock n. enclos m.; pâturage m., pré m.; champ m. de courses.

padlock n. cadenas m. **~ v.t.** cadenasser, mettre un cadenas; fermer.

pagan n. païen m. **~ adj.** païen, idolâtre.

paganism n. paganisme m.

page n. page m., messager m.; page f. **~ v.t.** faire appeler, appeler quelqu'un par l'intermédiaire d'un micro ou téléphone.

pageant n. parade f., spectacle m.; pompe f., apparat m.

pageantry n. pompe f., faste m., apparat m.

pagoda n. pagode f.

pail n. seau m.

pain n. mal m., douleur f., souffrance f.; souci m., peine f. **a ~ in the foot,** une douleur dans le pied. **to cry out with ~,** pousser des cris de douleur. **to take ~s,** être précis. **no ~, no gain,** on n'a rien san rien. **on ~ of death,** sous peine de mort. **he is such a ~ in the neck!** quel enquiquineur! adj. **~staking,** travailleur, laborieux; diligent. v.t. faire mal, faire souffrir; faire de la peine; affliger, chagriner, désoler.

painful adj. pénible, douloureux; affligeant, désolant; difficile; laborieux.

painfully adv. péniblement, douloureusement; laborieusement.

painless adj. sans douleur; sans peine.

painkiller n. calmant m., analgésique m.

paint v.t.,v.i. peindre; se farder; dépeindre, décrire. **she ~s,** elle peint. n. peinture f.

painter n. peintre m.

painting n. peinture f.; tableau m.; description f. **oil~,** peinture à l'huile.

pair n. paire f.; couple f. **a ~ of gloves,** une paire de gants. **a ~ of pigeons,** une couple de pigeons. v.i. s'apparier, s'accoupler; se marier, s'assortir. v.t. unir.

pairing n. accouplement m., pariade (birds). **~ off,** s'arranger par paire.

pajamas n.pl. pyjama m.

pal n. copain m., copine f., pote m.f.

palace n. palais m.

palatable adj. agréable au goût; appétissant.

palate n. palais m.

pale n. pieu m., clôture f.; enceinte f. **~** v.t.,v.i. enclore de palis, enfermer pâlir, devenir pâle. adj. pâle, blême, terne (color). **to grow ~,** pâlir. **~-faced,** au teint pâle. **a ~ blue,** un bleu pâle.

paleness n. pâleur f.

paleography n. paléographie f.

paleontology n. paléontologie f.

palette n. palette f.

paling n. palissade f.

palisade n. palissade f. **~** v.t. palissader.

pall n. manteau m. (ceremonial); pallium m.; Fig. manteau m., voile m.; drap m. mortuaire. v.t. couvrir d'un manteau; envelopper; affaiblir; affadir; rendre insipide. v.i. devenir fade, insipide; s'éventer; perdre de sa force.

palliate v.t. pallier; atténuer.

pallid adj. pâle.

pallidness n. pâleur f.

palm n. paume f. (hand); main f.; oreille f.; palmier (tree) m.; palme f. (branch). **to bear away the ~,** remporter la palme, la victoire. **~ oil,** huile f. de palme. **Palm Sunday,** dimanche m. des Rameaux. v.t. escamoter; tromper; manier; caresser avec la main. **to ~ off a thing,** Infml. faire accepter une chose, tromper.

palmist n. chiromancien m.

palmistry n. chiromancie f.

palmy adj. des palmiers; Fig. beau, glorieux, victorieux.

palpable adj. palpable; Fig. clair, évident.

palpably adv. evidemment.

palpation n. palpation f.

palpitate v.i. palpiter.

palpitation n. palpitation f.

palsy n. paralysie f.

paltry adj. méchant, piètre, mesquin, dérisoire, pitoyable; qui fait pitié.

pamper v.t. nourrir à l'excés; choyer; dorloter; caresser; flatter. **to ~ a child,** dorloter un enfant.

pamphlet n. brochure f.; pamphlet m.

pamphleteer n. écrivain de brochures; pamphlétaire m.

pan n. poêlon m.; terrine f.; casserole f. **stew** ou **sauce~,** casserole f. **frying ~,** poêle f. à frire. **a flash in the ~,** feu m. de paille. **to ~ out,** rendre, produire, réussir.

pancake n. crêpe f.

pancreas n. pancréas m.

panda n. panda m.

pander n. entremetteur m., complaisant m. v.t.,v.i. être l'entremetteur de se prêter à.

pane n. carreau m. (window); vitre f.

panegyric n. panégyrique m.

panegyrize v.t. faire le panégyrique, l'éloge de. v.i. se répandre en louanges.

panel n. panneau m.; liste (jurors). v.t. lambrisser, couvrir de panneaux.

pang n. pincement m. de coeur; souffrance f. extrême, douleur f. cuisante; transes f.pl.; affres f.pl.; agonie f.

panhandle v.i. mendier, Infml. faire la manche.

panic n. panique f. **~-stricken,** scisi de panique.

panic n. panique f.

panicky adj. qui s'affole facilement.

pannier n. panier m. d'osier; Arch. corbeille f.

panoply n. panoplie f.

panorama n. panorama m.

panoramic adj. panoramique.

pansy n. pensée f.

pant v.i. palpiter haleter. **to ~ for,** soupirer après. n. palpitation f.

pantheism n. panthéisme m.

pantheon n. panthéon m.

panther n. panthère f.

panties n.pl. Infml. culotte f.

pantihose n. collant m., bas-culotte m.

pantomime n. pantomime m.; pantomime f. (play).

pantry n. office f., gardemanger m.

pants n.pl. pantalon m.

papa n. papa m.

papacy n. papauté f.

papal adj. papal; du pape.

paper n. papier m.; pl. documents m.pl., effets m.pl. **drawing ~,** papier à dessin. **letter ~,** papier à lettres. **music ~,** papier à musique. **tissue ~,** papier de soie. **weekly ~,** journal hebdomadaire. v.t. tendre, tapisser de papier peint; envelopper dans du papier. adj. de papier, en papier, du papier. **~ factory,** papeterie f. fabrique de papier. **~ mill,** papeterie f., fabrique f. de papier. **~weight,** presse-papier m.

papier-mâché n. papier-mâché m.

par n. pair m. **to get on a ~ with,** s'élever au niveau de.

parable n. parabole f.

parabola n. parabole f.

parabolic, parabolical adj. parabolique.

parachute n. parachute m. ~ v.t. parachuter.
parade n. parade f., défilé m.; Mil. revue f.; procession f.; esplanade f. ~ v.t. passer en revue. v.i. parader; se donner en spectacle.
paradigm n. exemple m., modèle m.; Gram. paradigme m.
paradise n. paradis m.
paradisiac(al) adj. paradisiaque.
paradox n. paradoxe m.
paradoxical adj. paradoxal.
paraffin n. pétrole. ~ oil, huile de pétrole.
paragon n. paragon m.; modèle.
paragraph n. paragraphe m. ~ v.t. former ou écrire des paragraphes.
parakeet n. perruche f.
parallel adj. parallèle. n. parallèle f. (line); paralléle m.; comparaison f. without ~, sans comparaison. v.t. placer parallèlement; égaliser; égaler, être égal à; ressembler à; comparer.
parallelogram n. parallélogramme m.
paralysis n. paralysie f.
paralytic adj. paralytique. n. paralytique m.
paralyze v.t. paralyser.
paramount adj. souverain; suprême, très-haut. ~ to, supérieur à. ~ importance, de la plus haute importance. n. souverain m., chef m.
paranoia n. paranoia f.
paranoid adj. paranoiaque.
paranormal adj. paranormal, supernaturel.
parapet n. parapet m.
paraphrase n. paraphrase f. ~ v.t., v.i. paraphraser.
paraplegia n. paraplégie.
paraplegic adj., n. paraplégique m.f.
parasite n. parasite m.
parasol n. parasol m.
paratrooper n. parachutiste m.f.
parboil v.t. faire bouillir à demi ou légèrement.
parcel n. paquet m.; envoi (de marchandises); part f., portion f.; parcelle f. to be part and ~ of, faire partie intégrante de. v.t. morceler; diviser en parties; mettre en paquets. to ~ out, distribuer.
parch, to be parched with thirst, mourir de soif. v.i. se griller; se brûler; se dessécher.
parchment n. parchemin m.
pardon v.t. pardonner à; gracier, amnistier. ~ me, pardonnez-moi, excusez-moi. n. pardon m.; excuse f.
pardonable adj. pardonnable; excusable.
pare v.t. couper, rogner, ébarber.
parent n. père m. ou mère f. parents, père et mère, parents m.pl.
parentage n. extraction f., naissance f.
parental adj. de père, paternel; de mère, maternel.
parenthesis n.pl. parentheses, parenthèse f.
pariah n. paria m.
paring n. rognure f., épluchure f. pelure f.
parish n. paroisse f.; commune f. adj. paroissial, de la paroisse; communal. the ~ church, l'église paroissiale.

parishioner n. paroissien m.
Parisian n. Parisien m., Parisienne f.
parity n. parité f., égalité f.
park n. parc m. ~ guard, gardien m. de parc. v.t. (se) parquer, (se) garer, (se) stationner.
parking n. stationnement m. no ~, stationnement interdit. ~ ticket, n. contravention m. ~ lot, parc de stationnement.
parlance n. conversation f., langage m.
parliament n. parlement m.
parliamentary adj. parlementaire.
parlor n. parloir m.; petit salon m. beauty ~, salon m. de beauté.
parochial n. paroissial.
parody n. parodie f. ~ v.t. parodier.
parole n. Mil. parole f.; liberté f. conditionnelle. v.t. libérer sur parole.
paroxysm n. paroxysme m.
parricide n. parricide m.
parrot n. perroquet m.
parry v.t. parer; Fig. éluder. v.i. parer, se mettre en garde.
parsimonious adj. parcimonieux.
parsimoniously adv. avec parcimonie.
parsley n. persil m.
part n. part f., partie f.; portion; endroit m.; rôle m. (au théâtre); cause f., part m. the greatest ~ of mankind, la plus grande partie du genre humain, la plupart des hommes. for the most ~, pour la plupart. for my ~, pour ma part. in ~, en partie. to take ~, prendre part à, participer à. in foreign ~s, à l'étranger. to play a ~, jouer un rôle. v.t. diviser, séparer, diviser en parts. v.i. partager avoir une part; (from) se séparer de, abandonner, se quitter. we must ~, il faut nous quitter; (with) se défaire de, céder. I will not ~ with it at any price, je ne m'en déferai à aucun prix. she works part-time, elle travaille à temps m.
partial adj. partial (biased); partiel (in part). a ~ judge, un juge partial. ~ eclipse, éclipse partielle. to be ~ to, avoir du goût pour.
partiality n. partialité f.; prédilection f. préférence f.
partially adv. partialement; partiellement.
participant n. participant m.
participate v.i. (in) participer à.
participation n. participation f.
participle n. participe m.
particle n. particule f.; parcelle f.; grain m., atome m.
particular adj. particulier; exact; délicat, difficile, exigeant; singulier, propre; spécial. really you are too ~, vous êtes vraiment trop difficile. he has no ~ news, il n'a aucune nouvelle particulière. n. particularité f.; détail m.; renseignement m.

particularity *n.* particularité *f.;* fait *m.* particulier; détail *m.*

particularly *adv.* particulièrement; en particulier.

parting *adj.* d'adieu, de séparation; dernier. **a ~ glass,** un dernier verre. *n.* partage *m.;* division *f.;* séparation *f.;* adieu *m.*

partisan *n.* partisan *m.*

partition *n.* partage *m.;* division *f.,* séparation *f.;* cloison *f.* ~ **wall,** mur mitoyen. *v.t.* partager; séparer (par une cloison).

partly *adv.* en partie, partiellement.

partner *n.* associé *m.* Comm. compagnon *m.,* compagne *f.;* partenaire *m.* et *f.* (cards); danseur *m.,* danseuse *f.* **silent ~,** associé commanditaire *m.;* bailleur *m.* de fonds. **managing ~,** associé-gérant.

partnership *n.* société *f.,* association *f.*

partridge *n.* perdrix *f.*

party *n.* parti *m.;* partie *f.;* personne *f.,* individu *m.;* réunion *f.;* troupe *f.* **the concerned ~, the interested ~,** la partie intéressée. **a third ~,** un tiers. **to join the ~,** se mettre de la partie. **a hunting ~,** **a fishing ~,** une partie de chasse, de pêche. **an evening ~,** une soirée. **a dinner ~,** un grand dîner. **~ spirit,** esprit *m.* de parti.

pass *v.i.* passer par; se passer; arriver mourir, s'évanouir. **to ~ along,** passer. **to ~ away,** passer, se passer, se dissiper; mourir. **to ~ by,** passer par; passer à côté. **to ~ for,** passer pour, être regardé comme. **to ~ oneself off as,** se donner pour. **to ~ on,** passer son chemin; se passer. **to ~ over,** passer, se passer; s'écouler; mourir. *v.t.* faire passer; surpasser; filtrer; tamiser. **to ~ a river,** passer une rivière. **to ~ the bottle,** faire passer la bouteille. **to ~ remarks upon,** faire des observations sur. **to ~ a sentence,** prononcer un jugement. **to ~ away the time,** passer le temps. **to ~ by in silence,** passer sous silence. **to ~ out,** s'évanouir. *n.* passage *m.;* défilé; passe *f.;* permis *m.;* extrémité *f.,* état *m.* **~-key,** passe-partout *m.*

passable *adj.* passable; praticable.

passably *adv.* passablement, tolérablement.

passage *n.* passage *m.;* traversée *f.;* trajet *m.;* accès *m.;* corridor *m.,* vestibule *m.,* couloir *m.* **this ~ is obscure,** ce passage est obscur.

passenger *n.* voyageur *m.,* passager *m.*

passerby *n.* passant *m.*

passing *adj.* passager, éphémère; fugitif; excellent, eminent. *n.* passage *m.;* cours *m.,* mort *f.*

passion *n.* passion *f.,* colère *f.,* amour *m.;* ardeur *f.,* zele *m.*

passionate *adj.* irascible, emporté; passionné, ardent.

passionately *adv.* passionnément, avec passion, ardemment; avec colère, avec emportement.

passive *adj.* passif; inactif, inerte. ~ **obedience,** obéissance passive. ~ **verb,** verbe passif.

passively *adv.* passivement.

Passover *n.* pâque *f.* Juive.

passport *n.* passeport *m.*

password *n.* mot de passe.

past *adj.* passé, écoulé; dernier. **the ~ year,** l'année écoulée. *n.* passé *m.* *prep.* après. ~ **six o'clock,** après six heures.

pasta *n.* Culin. pâtes *f.pl.*

paste *n.* pâte *f.;* colle *f.,* stras (imitation gem) *m.* **anchovy ~,** beurre d'anchois. *v.t.* coller. **to ~ up,** afficher.

pasteboard *n.* carton *m.*

pastel *n.* pastel *m.*

pasteurization *n.* pasteurisation *f.*

pasteurize *v.t.* pasteuriser.

pastime *n.* passe-temps *m.*

pastor *n.* pasteur *m.*

pastoral *adj.* pastoral. *n.* pastorale *f.*

pastry *n.* pâtisserie *f.* ~ **cook,** patissier *m.*

pasturage *n.* élève *f.* du bétail; pâturage *m.;* pâture *f.*

pasture *n.* pâture *f.;* pâturage *m.* ~ *v.t.* faire paître.

pat *adj.* et *adv.* Infml. propre; à propos; à point; tout juste. *n.* tape *f.,* petit coup; coquille *f.* (butter). ~ **on the back,** une tape dans le dos. *v.t.* **to ~ on the back,** féliciter, complimenter. *v.t.* caresser (avec la main); taper; tapoter.

patch *n.* pièce *f.,* morceau *m.,* pièce *f.* de rapport. ~ **work,** rapiéctage *m.* ~ *v.t.* rapiécer; plâtrer, replâtrer; Infml. rafistoler. **to ~ a coat,** rapièce un habit. **to ~ up,** rafistoler.

pate *n.* tête *f.;* Infml. caboche *f.,* boule *f.*

pâté *n.* pâté *m.*

patent *adj.* patent, manifeste; brevete. *n.* patente *f.,* brevet *m.* ~ *v.t.* patenter, breveter.

paternal *adj.* paternel.

paternally *adv.* paternellement; en père.

paternity *n.* paternité *f.*

path *n.* sentier *m.,* chemin *m.,* allée *f.,* route *f.*

pathetic *adj.* pathétique; touchant.

pathological *adj.* pathologique.

pathology *n.* pathologie *f.*

pathos *n.* pathétique *m.*

patience *n.* patience *f.* **to lose ~, to be out of ~,** perdre patience.

patient *adj.* patient. *n.* malade *m.f.;* patient.

patiently *adv.* patiemment.

patriarch *n.* patriarche *m.*

patriarchal *adj.* patriarcal.

patricide *n.* patricide *m.* (act); patricide *m.f.* (person).

patrimonial *adj.* patrimonial.

patrimony *n.* patrimoine *f.*

patriot *n.* patriote *m.f.*

patriotic *adj.* patriotique.

patriotism *n.* patriotisme *m.*

patrol *n.* patrouille *f.* ~ **car,** voiture *f.* de police. *v.t.* faire la patrouille dans. *v.i.* patrouiller.

patron *n.* client *m.;* protecteur *m.*

patronage *n.* patronage *m.,* appui *m.;* clientèle *f.;* protection.

patronize *v.t.* patronner; traiter avec

condescendance; protéger; appuyer, favoriser.

patronymic *n.* nom *m.* patronymique, nom de famille. *adj.* patronymique.

patter *v.t.,v.i. n.* bagou *m.,* bavardage *m.,* baratin *m.;* marmotter. *v.i.* fouetter (as rain); piétiner, trépigner.

pattern *n.* exemple *m.,* modèle *m.;* spécimen *m.,* échantillon *m.;* patron *m.* ~ **book,** livre *m.* d'échantillons. *v.t.* copier; servir de modèle; imiter. ~ **oneself on,** prendre modèle sur.

patty *n.* petit pâté *m.*

paucity *n.* disette *f.,* pénurie *f.;* manque (de) *m.*

paunch *n.* panse *f.;* bedaine *f.,* ventre *m.*

pauper *n.* pauvre *m.,* indigent *m.*

pause *n.* pause *f.;* intervalle *m.;* temps *m.* d'arrêt; repos *m.;* doute *m.;* Mus. point *m.* d'orgue. *v.i.* s'arrêter; attendre; faire une pause. **to give ~,** faire réfléchir.

pave *v.t.* paver; *Fig.* préparer le chemin, frayer la voie.

pavement *n.* pavé *m.;* route pavée.

paw *n.* patte *f.* **keep your ~s off!** bar les pattes! trépigner. *v.t.* piaffer (horse).

pawn *n.* gage *m.;* pion *m.* (chess). ~**shop,** boutique du prêteur sur gages. *v.t.* mettre en gage, engager.

pawnbroker *n.* prêteur *m.* sur gage.

pay *v.t.* payer; acquitter, s'acquitter envers; solder (troops); rendre (homage); faire (attention, visit, compliment); témoigner (respect). **he ~s me with ingratitude,** il me paye d'ingratitude. ~ **him my respects,** présentez-lui mes respects. **you'll ~ for that,** je te rendrai la monnaie de la pièce, tu/vous vas/allez me le payer. **to ~ back,** rendre, restituer. **to ~ down,** payer argent comptant. **to ~ for,** payer; dédommager. **to ~ off,** congédier, donner son compte à; solder; acquitter. **to ~ through the nose,** se laisser écorcher; payer trop cher. **it does not ~,** ça n'en vaut pas la peine, cela ne rapporte rien. *n.* paye *f.;* salaire *m.;* gages *m.pl.;* traitement *m.;* solde *f.* (soldiers). **half-~,** demi-solde. ~**day,** jour *m.* de paie.

payable *adj.* payable.

payee *n.* bénéficiaire *m.f.*

payer *n.* payeur *m.*

payment *n.* payement/paiement *m.; Fig.* récompense *f.*

pea *n.* pois *m.,* pois *m.* **chick ~s,** pois chiches. **green ~s,** petits pois. **to shell ~s,** écosser des pois.

peace *n.* paix *f.;* tranquillité *f.* **at ~,** en paix. **to hold one's ~,** garder le silence, ne pas parler, se taire. **to keep the ~,** ne pas troubler la paix publique. ~**maker,** pacificateur *m.,* conciliateur *m.* ~ **offering,** sacrifice *m.* propitiatoire. ~ **officer,** officier *m.* de paix. ~ **talks,** pourparlers *m.pl.* de paix. ~ **treaty,** traité *m.* de paix. *interj.* paix! silence!

peaceable *adj.* paisible; pacifique.

peaceful *adj.* paisible; tranquille.

peacefully *adv.* paisiblement, pacifiquement.

peacefulness *n.* repos *m.,* calme *m.,* tranquillité *f.*

peach *n.* pêche *f.* ~ **blossom,** fleur *f.* de pêcher. ~**-colored,** couleur-pêche *f.* ~ **tree,** pêcher *m.*

peacock, peafowl *n.* paon *m.*

peahen *n.* paonne *f.*

peak *n.* pic *m.,* sommet *m.;* cime *f.;* pointe *f.* ~ *v.i.* plafonner.

peal *n.* carillon *m.* (bells); éclat *m.;* bruit *m.,* fracas *m.* ~ **of laughter,** éclat de rire. *v.i.* tonner. *v.t.* assourdir; ahurir; faire retentir, faire sonner; célébrer.

peanut *n.* cacah(o)uète *f.;* arachide *f.* (plant). ~ **butter,** beurre *m.* de cacah(o)uètes, beurre *m.* d'arachide.

pear *n.* poire *f.* ~ **tree,** poirier *m.*

pearl *n.* perle *f.* ~ **barley,** orge *m.* perlé. ~ **fishery,** ~ **fishing,** pêche *f.* des perles. ~ **oyster,** huître *f.* perlière. *v.t.* orner, garnir de perles, ressembler à une perle.

pearly *adj.* nacré, de perle.

peasant *n.* paysan *m.* ~ *adj.* de paysan; rural; rustique.

peasantry *n.* **the ~,** la paysannerie, les paysans *m.pl.,* les gens *m.pl.* des campagnes.

peat *n.* tourbe *f.* ~ **bog,** marais *m.* tourbeux; tourbière *f.* ~ **moss,** tourbe *f.*

pebble *n.* caillou *m.*

pecan *n.* noix *f.* pécan.

peccadillo *n.* peccadille *f.*

peck *n.* picotin *m.* (measure); coup de bec (bird). *v.t.* becqueter, donner des coups de bec, piquer; *Infml.* bécoter, faire une petite bise.

peculate *v.i.* détourner des fonds; voler.

peculation *n.* détournement de fonds, péculat *m.*

peculiar *adj.* particulier; singulier, spécial; propre. **something ~,** quelque chose de singulier.

peculiarity *n.* particularité *f.,* singularité *f.*

peculiarly *adv.* particulierement, en particulier singulièrement.

pecuniary *adj.* pécuniaire.

pedagogue *n.* pédagogue *m.*

pedagogy *n.* pédagogie *f.*

pedal *n.* pédale *f.* ~ *v.i.* pédaler.

pedant *n.* pédant *m.*

pedantic *adj.* pédantesque; pédant.

pedantry *n.* pédanterie *f.,* pédantisme *m.*

peddle *v.t.* colporter.

peddler *n.* colporteur *m.*

pederast *n.* pédéraste *m.*

pedestal *n.* piédestal *m.*

pedestrian *n.* à pied; pédestre. *n.* piéton *m.*

pediatrician *n.* pédiatre *m.f.*

pedicure *n.* pédicurie *f.,* podologie *f.;* pédicure *f.*

pedigree *n.* pedigree *m.,* généalogie *f.;* arbre *m.* généalogique.

peddler *n.* colporteur *m.*

pee *n. Infml.* pipi *m.* ~ *v.i.* faire pipi, pisser.

peek *n.* coup d'oeil *m.* ~ *v.i.* jeter un coup d'oeil.

peel v.t. décortiquer; écorcher; monder (barley). v.i. se peler, s'écailler. n. épluchure f.

peep v.i. poindre; percer éclore; regarder à la dérobée; jeter un oeil. **to ~ out**, regarder dehors avec précaution. n. pointe f., point m.; coup m. d'oeil, regard m. furtif, apparition. f. **~hole**, judas m. **~show**, séance f. (visuelle) pornographique.

peeping Tom n. voyeur m.

peer n. pareil m., compagnon m., camarade m. ~ v.i. poindre, apparaître; regarder à la dérobée; lorgner.

peerless adj. incomparable.

peevish adj. hargneux, bourru, maussade, morose, chagrin, revêche.

peevishly adv. d'un air chagrin; de mauvaise humeur.

peg n. cheville f.; patère f.; fausset m.; Fig. point m.; degré m., cran m. **to come down a ~**, baisser d'un cran. v.t. joindre avec des chevilles; cheviler.

pejorative adj., n. péjoratif m.

pelican n. pélican m.

pellucid adj. transparent.

pelt n. peau f., fourrure f. ~ v.t. jeter, lancer assaillir, lapider. **to ~ someone with snow-balls**, lancer des boules de neige à quelqu'un.

pelvic adj. pelvien.

pelvis n. bassin m.

pen n. stylo m.; poulailler m. (poultry); parc m. (sheep); Infml. faule f. (penitentiary). v.t. écrire; parquer. **to ~ up**, enfermer.

penal adj. pénal; passible d'une peine.

penalty n. peine f.; amende f.; pénalité f.

penance n. pénitence f. **to do ~ for**, faire pénitence de.

pencil n. crayon m.; faisceau m. (light rays). ~ **sharpener**, taille-crayon m., aiguisoir m. ~ v.t. dessiner; écrire au crayon.

pendant n. pendant m.; pendeloque f.; suspension f. (lampe).

pending adj. et prep. pendant, durant, en attendant.

penetrable adj. pénétrable.

penetrate v.i. pénétrer (dans).

penetrating adj. pénétrant.

penetration n. pénétration f.

penguin n. pinguoin m.

peninsula n. presqu'île f.

peninsular adj. péninsulaire.

penis n. pénis m.

penitence n. pénitence f.; repentir m.

penitent adj. pénitent; repentant n. pénitent m.

penitential adj. de pénitence; pénitentiel. n. pénitentiel m.

penitentiary adj. pénitentiaire. n. pénitent m.; pénitencier m.; maison de correction.

penitently adv. avec repentir, avec pénitence.

penniless adj. sans le sou; pauvre.

penny n. au pl. penny m. **a few pennies**, quelques sous.

pension n. pension f.; rente f.; retraite f. ~ v.t. pensionner. **to ~ off**, mettre à la retraite.

pensive adj. pensif, songeur.

pensively adv. d'un air pensif.

pentagon n. pentagone m. **the Pentagon**, le Pentagone.

pentateuch n. pentateuque m.

Pentecost n. Pentecôte f.

Pentecostal adj. de la Pentecôte; pentecostal (church).

penthouse n. appartement m. luxueux construit sur le toit d'un immeuble.

penultimate adj. pénultième.

penumbra n. pénombre f.

penurious adj. parcimonieux; pauvre, mesquin, peu abondant.

penury n. pénurie f.

peony n. pivoine f.

people n. peuple m.; nation gens m.pl.; personnes f.pl.; habitants m.pl.; monde m. **the English ~**, les Anglais. **country ~**, les gens des campagnes, les provinciaux. **~ of both sexes**, des personnes des deux sexes. **old ~**, les vieilles gens. **they are good ~**, ce sont de bonnes gens. **what will ~ say?** que dira-t-on? v.t. peupler.

pep n. entrain m. ~ v.t. ~ **up**, (s)animer, donner de l'entrain, de la vitalité; remonter le moral.

pepper n. poivre m. (spice), piment m. (vegetable). **~corn**, grain m. de poivre. **~tree**, poivrier m. ~ v.t. poivrer; cribler (de balles, de coups); Infml. rosser.

peppermint n. menthe poivrée.

per prep. par, pour; le, la, les. **5 ~cent**, 5 pour cent. **~ ton**, la tonne. **as ~ invoice**, suivant, d'après facture.

perceivable adj. perceptible, sensible.

perceive v.t. percevoir; apercevoir; remarquer, s'apercevoir de; sentir.

percentage n. pourcentage m.

perceptibility n. perceptibilité f.

perceptible adj. perceptible.

perceptibly adv. perceptiblement; sensiblement.

perception n. perception f., sensibilité f.; observation f.

perceptive adj. perceptif.

perch n. perche f. (fish); juchoir m., perchoir m. (birds). v.i. jucher; (se) percher. v.t. mettre sur une perche.

percolate v.t. filtrer.

percolation n. filtration f.

percussion n. percussion f.

percussive adj. qui frappe.

perdition n. perte f.; ruine f.; perdition f.

peregrination n. pérégrination f.; séjour m., demeure f. à l'étranger.

peremptory adj. péremptoire; absolu, définitif, réglé.

perennial adj. perpétuel; qui dure plusieurs années. n. plante f. vivace.

perennially adv. perpétuellement.

perfect *adj.* parfait; fini, achevé; complet. *v.t.* perfectionner; rendre parfait; finir.

perfection *n.* perfection *f.* **to ~**, à la, ou en perfection.

perfectly *adv.* parfaitement.

perfidious *adj.* perfide.

perfidy *n.* perfidie *f.;* déloyauté *f.*

perforate *v.t.* perforer.

perforation *n.* perforation *f.*

perform *v.t.* exécuter, accomplir, faire; s'acquitter de; jouer, représenter. **to ~ on the flute**, jouer de la flûte.

performance *n.* exécution *f.;* représentation *f.* (theater); ouvrage *m.;* exercice *m.;* jeu *m.* (of an actor). **no ~ tonight**, ce soir, relâche.

performer *n.* artiste *m.f.;* acteur *m.,* actrice *f.;* *Mus.* exécutant *m.*

perfume *n.* parfum *m.* ~ *v.t.* parfumer.

perfumer *n.* parfumeur *m.,* parfumeuse *f.*

perfumery *n.* parfumerie *f.*

perfunctorily *adv.* négligemment; par manière d'acquit.

perfunctory *adj.* négligent; fait pour la forme, par manière d'acquit.

perhaps *adv.* peut-être; il se pourrait que.

peril *n.* péril *m.;* danger *m.*

perilous *adj.* périlleux.

perilously *adv.* périlleusement.

perimeter *n.* périmètre *m.*

period *n.* période *f.,* espace *m.;* durée *f.;* époque *f.;* terme *m.;* fin *f.,* limite *f.;* point *m.* (punct); cours *m.;* règles *f.pl.,* menstrues *f.pl. Physiol.* you must finish your sentence with a ~, devez mettre un point à la fin de votre phrase. **a ~ of a thousand years,** l'espace de mille ans. **at an early ~ of history,** aux premiers temps de l'histoire.

periodic *adj.* périodique.

periodical *n.* revue *f.*

periodically *adv.* périodiquement.

peripatetic *adj.* péripatétique, péripatéticien. *n.* péripatéticien *m.*

peripheric *adj.* périphérique.

periphery *n.* périphérie *f.*

periphrase *n.* périphrase *f.* circonlocution *f.* ~ *v.t.,v.i.* périphraser.

periscope *n.* périscope *m.*

perish *v.i.* périr; dépérir, mourir.

perishable *adj.* périssable. *n.* ~**s,** denrées périssables *f.pl.*

perjure *v.t.* aire *ou* commettre un parjure. **to ~ oneself,** se parjurer. *n.* parjure *m.*

perjurer *n.* parjure *m.,* faux témoin *m.*

perjury *n.* parjure *m.,* faux serment *m.*

perk *n.* See PERQUISITE.

perk *v.i.* ~ **up,** se rengorger, lever la tête. *v.t.* parer, orner, décorer.

perky *adj.* éveillé, gai, enjoué; effronté.

perm *n.* permanente *f.,* indéfrisable *f.* ~ *v.t.* faire friser, faire une permanente.

permanence *n.* permanence *f.*

permanent *adj.* permanent.

permanently *adv.* en permanence.

permeability *n.* perméabilité *f.*

permeable *adj.* perméable, pénétrable.

permeate *v.t.* pénétrer.

permeation *n.* pénétration *f.*

permissible *adj.* qui peut être permis, admissible.

permission *n.* permission *f.;* permis *m.*

permissive *adj.* qui permet, qui tolère; toléré.

permit *v.t.* permettre permettre à. *n.* permis *m.,* autorisation *f.;* laisser-passer *m.;* passavant *m.;* congé *m.*

permutation *n.* permutation *f.*

permute *v.i.* (se) permuter.

pernicious *adj.* pernicieux, nuisible.

perniciously *adv.* pernicieusement.

perniciousness *n.* caractère *m.* pernicieux; nature *f.* nuisible, malfaisante.

peroration *n.* péroraison *f.*

peroxide *n.* peroxide *m.*

perpendicular *adj.* perpendiculaire. *n.* perpendiculaire *f.*

perpendicularly *adv.* perpendiculairement.

perpetrate *v.t.* perpétrer; faire exécuter.

perpetration *n.* perpétration *f.*

perpetrator *n.* coupable *m.,* auteur *m.* d'un crime.

perpetual *adj.* perpétuel.

perpetually *adv.* perpétuellement.

perpetuate *v.t.* perpétuer.

perpetuation *n.* perpétuation *f.*

perpetuity *n.* perpétuité *f.*

perplex *v.t.* embrouiller, brouiller; embarrasser tourmenter.

perplexed *adj.* embrouillé, brouillé; embarrassé; perplexe; tourmenté, inquiet.

perplexity *n.* embrouillement *m.,* confusion *f.;* embarras *m.;* perplexité *f.*

perquisite *n.* émolument *m.* casuel; *pl.* petits profits *m.pl.*

persecute *v.t.* persécuter.

persecution *n.* persécution *f.*

persecutor *n.* persécuteur *m.*

perseverance *n.* persévérance *f.*

persevere *v.i.* persévérer; persister.

Persia *n.pr.* Perse *f.*

Persian *adj.* de Perse, persan; *Arch. Geog.* persique. **the ~ Gulf,** le Golfe persique. *n.* Persan *m.,* Persane *f.;* lange *f.* persane.

persiflage *n.* persiflage *m.*

persist *v.i.* persister.

persistence *n.* persistance *f.,* insistance *f.;* obstination *f.*

persistent *adj.* persistant.

person *n.* personne *f.* personnage *m.,* caractère *m.; Gram.* **in the third ~,** à la troisième personne.

personable *adj.* de bonne mine, de bon air.

personage *n.* personnage *m.*

personal *adj.* personnel; *Law.* mobilier, meuble.

~ estate, biens *m.pl.* meubles. ~ **property,** propriété *f.* mobilière.
personality *n.* personalité *f.*
personally *adv.* personnellement.
personify *v.t.* personnifier.
perspective *n.* perspective *f.* in ~, en perspective. *adj.* perspectif.
perspicacious *adj.* clairvoyant; perspicace.
perspicacity *n.* perspicacité *f.*
perspiration *n.* transpiration *f.;* sueur *f.,* perspiration *f.*
perspire *v.i.* transpirer; suer.
persuade *v.t.* persuader; décider, engager.
persuasion *n.* persuasion *f.;* croyance *f.;* opinion religieuse.
persuasive *adj.* persuasif. *n.* incitation *f.;* exhortation *f.*
persuasively *adv.* de manière à persuader.
pert *adj.* vif, éveillé, harde, effronté, leste; impertinent.
pertain *v.i.* appartenir; se rapporter à.
pertinence *n.* convenance *f.,* justesse *f.,* à-propos *m.*
pertinent *adj.* pertinent, à propos, juste, propre.
pertinently *adv.* pertinemment.
pertly *adv.* avec impertinence.
pertness *n.* impertinence *f.*
perturb *v.t.* troubler, agiter.
perturbation *n.* trouble *m.,* agitation *f.;* perturbation *f.*
peruse *v.t.* lire; lire avec attention; examiner (un livre).
pervade *v.t.* pénétrer; se répandre dans; s'emparer de, saisir.
perverse *adj.* pervers, mauvais; contrariant.
perversely *adv.* avec perversité.
perversion perversion *f.;* déformation *f.,* dénaturation *f.;* travestissement *m.*
pervert *v.t.* pervertir; altérer, dénaturer, fausser corrompre; dépraver. to ~ **truth,** altérer la verité. to ~ **the meaning,** dénaturer le sens.
pessimist *n.* pessimiste *m.*
pessimistic *adj.* pessimiste.
pest *n.* insecte *m.* nuisible; *Fig. Infml.* casse-pied *m.*
pester *v.t.* troubler; ennuyer, importuner; assommer.
pesticide *n.* pesticide *m.*
pestilence *n.* peste *f.,* pestilence *f.*
pestilent *adj.* pestilentiel; pernicieux, malfaisant; importun.
pestilential *adj.* pestilentiel.
pestle *n.* pilon *m.*
pet *n.* animal *m.* familier; favori *m.,* chouchou *m.* he'd like to have a ~, il aimerait avoir un animal. *v.t.* caresser, câliner.
petal *n.* pétale *m.*
petard *n.* pétard *m.* hoist by one's own ~, pris à son propre piège.
peter *v.i.* ~ **out,** s'épuiser, se tarir.
petite *adj.* menue.

petition *n.* pétition *f.,* requête *f.,* demande *f.,* prière *f.* to **draw up a** ~, rédiger une pétition. *v.t* adresser une pétition, une requête; demander; solliciter.
petitioner *n.* pétitionnaire *m.;* solliciteur *m.*
petrify *v.t.,v.i.* (se) pétrifier.
petrifying *adj.* pétrifiant.
petroleum *n.* pétrole *m.*
pettiness *n.* petitesse *f.,* mesquinerie *f.*
pettish *adj.* bourru, revêche, de mauvaise humeur.
petty *adj.* petit, mesquin, inférieur, subalterne. **a** ~ **quarrel,** une querelle insignifiante.
petulence *n.* pétulance *f.*
petulant *adj.* pétulant, irritalde.
petulantly *adv.* avec petulance, avec vivacité.
pew *n.* banc *m.* d'église.
pewter *n.* étain.
phalanx *n.pl.* **phalanges** or **phalanxes,** phalange *f.*
phantom *n.* fantôme *m.;* fantasme *m.*
pharaoh *n.* pharaon *m.*
pharmaceutical *adj.* pharmaceutique.
pharmaceutics *n.* pharmaceutique *f.*
pharmacist *n.* pharmacien *m.*
pharmacology *n.* pharmacologie *f.*
pharmacy *n.* pharmacie *f.*
pharynx *n.* pharynx *m.*
phase phase *f.*
Ph.D. *abbrev.* **Doctor of Philosophy,** doctorat; docteur *m.,* femme docteur *f.*
pheasant *n.* faisan *m.*
phenomenal *adj.* phénoménal.
phenomenon *n.* au *pl.* **phenomena,** phénomène *m.*
phew *excl.* pouah!
Philadelphia *n.pr.* Philadelphie *f.*
philanthropic *adj.* philanthropique.
philanthropist *n.* philanthrope *m.*
philanthropy *n.* philanthropie *f.*
philately *n.* philatélie *f.*
philology *n.* philologie *f.*
philosopher *n.* philosophe *m.;* savant *m.* ~'s **stone,** pierre philosophale.
philosophic(al) *adj.* philosophique.
philosophize *v.i.* philosopher.
philosophy *n.* philosophie *f.*
phlebotomy *n.* phlébotomie *f.*
phlegm *n.* phlegme *ou* flegme *m.;* pituite *f.;* sangfroid *m.*
phlegmatic *adj.* flegmatique.
phobia *n.* phobie *f.*
phone *n.* téléphone *m.* ~**book,** annuaire *m.* ~ **call,** coup de fil. *v.t.* téléphoner, passer un coup de fil.
phonetic *adj.* phonétique.
phonetics *n.* phonétique *f.*
phonic *adj.* phonique.
phonics *n.* phonique *f.*
phonograph *n.* phonographe *m.*
phonology *n.* phonologie *f.*

phony *adj.* faux, simulé, *Infml.* bidon. *n.* fumiste *m.f.*, hypocrite *m.f.*

phosphate *n.* phosphate *m.*

phosphor *n.* phosphore *m.*

phosphorescence *n.* phosphorescence *f.*

phosphorescent *adj.* phosphorescent.

photo *n.* photo *f.* **~copier** *n.* photo copieur *m.* **~copy** *n.*, photo copie *f.*

photogenic *adj.* photogénique.

photograph *n.* photographie *f.*

photographic *adj.* photographique.

photographer *n.* photographe *m.*

photography *n.* photographie *f.*

phrase *n.* phrase *f.*; locution *f.*; style *m.* ~ *v.t.* exprimer; appeler, nommer. *v.i.* phraser.

physical *adj.* physique; médical. **~ strength**, force physique. **~ exam(ination)**, examen *m.* médical; check-up *m.*

physically *adv.* physiquement.

physician *n.* médecin *m.*

physics *n.* physique *f.*

physiologic(al) *adj.* physiologique.

physiology *n.* physiologie *f.*

physique *n.* physique *m.*

pianist *n.* pianiste *m.*

piano *n.* piano *m.* **upright ~**, piano droit. **grand ~**, piano à queue. **to play the ~**, jouer de piano.

pick *v.t.* cueillir (fruit, flowers, vegetables, etc.); ôter, enlever, ronger (a bone); curer (teeth); nettoyer (nose); éplucher (poultry); crocheter (lock). **to ~ the best**, prendre ce qu'il y a de mieux. **to ~ a quarrel with**, chercher querelle à. **to ~ pockets**, voler à la tire. **to ~ out**, choisir. **to ~ up**, ramasser; trouver; recueillir; reprendre. *n.* pic *m.*, pioche *f.* (tool); choix *m.* (choice); triage *m.* **I have to ~ her up at 3:00 p.m.**, je dois aller la chercher à 15h00.

pickaxe *n.* pic *m.*, pioche *f.*; pointerelle *f.*; houe *f.*

pickled *adj.* épluché; choisi, de choix, d'élite.

picket *n.* piquet *m.*; *Milit.* détachement *m.* **strike ~**, piquet *m.* de grève. *v.t.* entourer de piquets.

picking *n.* cueillage *m.*; nettoyage *m.* (bone); épluchage *m.* (poultry); triage *m.*; choix *m.*

pickle *n.* (gros) cornichon *m.*, saumure *f.* **to be in a fine ~**, être dans de beaux draps. *v.t.* saler (du poisson, de la viande); mariner, conserver dans la saumure; conserver au vinaigre.

pickled *adj.* salé; mariné.

pickpocket *n.* voleur *m.* à la tire.

picnic *n.* pique-nique *m.* ~ *v.i.* pique-niquer.

pictorial *adj.* de peintre.

picture *n.* image *f.*; gravure *f.*; tableau *m.*; peinture *f.*; portrait *m.*; description *f.* **he is the ~ of his father**, c'est le portrait de son père. **~ book**, livre *m.* d'images. **~ postcards**, cartes postales à vues. **~ frame**, cadre *m.* **~ gallery**, galerie *f.* de tableaux. *v.t.* faire le portrait de; dépeindre.

picturesque *adj.*

piddle *v.i.* faire pipi.

pie *n.* pâté *m.* (meat); tarte *f.*; tourte *f.* **apple ~**, tarte aux pommes. **to have a finger in the ~**, y être pour quelque chose, s'y mêler.

piece *n.* pièce *f.*, morceau *m.*; brin *m.*, bout *m.*; éclat *m.* **a ~ of furniture**, un meuble. **to fall to ~s**, tomber en pièces. **a ~ of music**, un morceau de musique. **a ~ of advice**, un conseil. *v.t.* **to ~ together**, recoller, assembler. *v.i.* se joindre.

piecemeal *adv.* en pièces, en morceaux; pièce; peu à peu. *adj.* particulier, séparé.

pied *adj.* bariolé; pie.

pier *n.* pile *f.* (bridge); jetée *f.*, quai *m.*, embarcadère *m.*

pierce *v.t.* percer; perforer, forer; mettre en perce. *v.i.* pénétrer dans:

piercing *adj.* perçant; pénétrant; aigu, perçant (sounds). *n.* percement *m.*

piercingly *adv.* d'une manière aiguë, perçante, pénétrante.

piety *n.* piété *f.*

pig *n.* cochen *m.*, porc *m.*, pourceau *m.*; *Metall.* lingot *m.*, saumon *m.* **sucking ~**, cochon de lait. **guinea ~**, cochon d'Inde. **to buy a ~ in a poke**, acheter chat en poche. **~-headed**, stupide, entêté. **~ iron**, fer *m.* en gueuse. **~sty**, porcherie *f.*

pigeon *n.* pigeon *m.*

piggish *adj.* de cochon.

pigment *n.* matière *f.* colorante; *Anat.* pigment *m.*

pigsty *n.* porcherie *f.*

pike *n.* pique *f.*; *Agr.* fourche *f.*; pointe *f.* de fer; *Ichth.* brochet *m.*

pile *n.* pile *f.*; tas *m.*; monceau *m.*, amas *m.*; pieu *m.*, pilotis *m.*; poil *m.* (fabric). **~ of papers**, tas de papiers. **a ~ of ruins**, un monceau de ruines. **to build upon ~s**, bâtir sur pilotis. **~-driver**, sonnette *f.* ~ *v.t.* empiler, entasser. **to ~ up**, accumuler; amonceler. *v.i.* enfoncer des pieux.

pilfer *v.i.*,*v.t.* chaparder, derober; chiper.

pilferer *n.* filou *m.*, fripon *m.*, petit voleur *m.*

pilgrim *n.* pélerin *m.*

pilgrimage *n.* pèlerinage *m.*

pill *n.* pilule *f.*

pillage *n.* pillage *m.* ~ *v.t.* piller; saccager.

pillar *n.* pilier *m.*, colonne *f.*; soutien *m.*

pillory *n.* pilori *m.* ~ *v.t.* condamner au pilori; mettre au pilori.

pillow *n.* oreiller *m.*; coussin *m.*; *Tech.* coussinet *m.* **~case**, taie *f.* d'oreiller. *v.t.* (s')appuyer, reposer, poser.

pilot *n.* pilote *m.*; *Infml.* guide *m.* **~ boat**, bateau-pilote *m.* **~** *v.t.* piloter; diriger; servir de pilote.

pimento *n.* piment *m.*

pimp *n.* souteneur *m.*, maquereau *m.* ~ *v.i.* faire le maquereau.

pimpernel *n.* mouron *m.*

pimple *n.* bouton *m.*

pin *n.* épingle *f.;* cheville *f.* (wood), clavette *f.;* broche *f.* hair~, épingle à cheveux. **rolling ~,** rouleau *m.* (de pâtissier). **~head,** tête *f.* d'épingle. *Fig.* petite tête *f.,* andouille *f.,* idiot *m.* *v.t.* épingler; attacher avec une épingle, clouer, attacher ensemble. **to ~ up,** relever avec des épingles. **~ down** *v.t.* attacher, fixer, tier. **~point** *v.t.* mettre le doigt sur, localiser, définir. **clothes~,** pince *f.* à linge.

pinafore *n.* tablier *m.*

pincers *n.* pince *f.*

pinch *v.t.* pincer serrer, (se) gêner, priver. **to ~ off a piece,** emporter une pièce. *v.i.* presser, se faire sentir; souffrir. *n.* pincement *m.,* pinçon *m.;* angoisse *f.,* pincée *f.,* prise *f.* **in a ~,** au besoin.

pine *n.* pin *m.,* bois *m.* de pin, de sapin. **pitch ~,** pin résineux. **~apple,** ananas *m.* **~cone,** pomme *f.* de pin. **~tree,** pin *m.* *v.i.* languir, s'affaiblir, dépérir. **to ~ away,** dépérir à vue d'oeil.

ping *n.* cliquetis *m.,* bruit *m.* métallique. *v.t.* cogner, tinter.

pinion *n.* aileron *m.* **~** *v.t.* *Fig.* lier; garrotter, enchaîner.

pink *n.* rose *m.* **~** *adj.* rose, de couleur rose. *v.t.* percer, découper.

pinkie *n.* *Infml,* petit doigt *m.*

pinkish *adj.* rosâtre, rosé.

pinnacle *n.* pinacle *m.;* *Fig.,* sommet *m.,* apogée *f.* **the ~ of glory,** le sommet de la gloire.

pint *n.* pirite *f.* (0.47 litres).

pioneer *n.* pionnier *m.* **~** *v.i.,v.t.* pionner; préparer les voies, être à l'avant-garde.

pious *adj.* pieux; pie. **a ~ woman,** une femme pieuse; **a ~ deed,** une oeuvre pie.

piously *adv.* pieusement.

pip *n.* pépin *m.* (fruits).

pipe *n.* tuyau *m.,* tube *m.;* pipe *f.* (tobacco); chalumeau *m.;* canal *m.;* flûte *f.,* pipeau *m.* (music). **branch ~,** tuyau d'embranchement. **discharging ~,** tuyau de décharge. **main ~,** tuyau principal. **waste ~,** tuyau de trop plein. **water ~,** conduite d'eau. **to light one's ~,** allumer sa pipe. **clay ~,** terre *f.* de pipe. **~line** *n.,* pipeline *m.,* (oil) oléoduc *m.* **~** *v.i.* jouer de la flûte; siffler. *v.t.* jouer (un air).

piquant *adj.* piquant; âcre; acide.

pique *n.* pique *f.,* brouille *f.,* brouillerie *f.;* point *m.* (d'honeaur). *v.t.* piquer. **to be in a ~,** s'offenser.

piracy *n.* piraterie *f.;* contrefaçon *f.*

pirate *n.* pirate *m.,* forban *m.,* corsaire *m.,* écumeur *m.* de mer; contrefacteur *m.* **~** *v.i.* pirater. *v.t.* contrefaire.

pirated *adj.* contrefait.

pirouette *n.* pirouette *f.* *v.i.* pirouetter.

Pisa *n.pr.* Pise *f.*

Pisces *n.* *Astron.* les Poissons *m.pl.*

piss *v.i.* uriner, pisser. *n.* urine *f.,* *Vulg.* he was so **~ed off,** il s'était tellement en colère.

pistachio *n.* pistache *f.*

pistil *n.* pistil *m.*

pistol *n.* pistolet *m.*

piston *n.* piston *m.*

pit *n.* fosse, trou *m.;* puits *m.* (de mine); creux *m.* (stomach). **coal ~,** houillère *f.,* mine *f.* de charbon. **sand ~,** sablière *f.* **bottomless ~,** abîme sans fond. *v.t.* creuser.

pitch *n.* poix *f.;* brai *m.* (tar); point *m.,* portée *f.;* *Mus.* ton *m.;* *Naut.* tangage *m.* jet (sport). **~ black,** noir comme du jais. **the highest ~,** le point le plus haut, le comble. **~fork,** fourche *f.* **~pipe,** diapason. *v.t.* brayer, enduire de poix; enfoncer, asseoir, fixer (tent), jeter, lancer, précipiter; *Mus.* donner le ton. *v.i.* descendre de; s'abattre; plonger; camper; se jeter; s'établir. **to ~ into,** se jeter dans.

pitcher *n.* cruche *f.,* pot *m.* de terre; (baseball) lanceur *m.*

piteous *adj.* malheureux; pitoyable; piteux.

piteously *adv.* avec pitié, tristement, piteusement; de manière à exciter la pitié; pitoyablement.

pitfall *n.* piège *m.* trappe *f.* **~** *v.t.* attirer dans un piège.

pith *n.* moelle *f.* (plant); force *f.;* énergie *f.,* importance *f.;* quintessence *f.* **~** *v.t.* ôter la moelle à.

pithy *adj.* moelleux; fort, plein de sève, approprié. **a ~ remark,** une remarque sagace.

pitiable *adj.* pitoyable.

pitiful *adj.* pitoyable; méprisable.

pitifully *adv.* pitoyablement.

pitiless *adj.* sans pitié, impitoyable.

pitilessly *adv.* impitoyablement, sans pitié.

pitilessness *n.* insensibilité *f.* (for others); nature *f.* impitoyable.

pittance *n.* pitance *f.*

pity *n.* pitié *f.;* compassion *f.;* dommage *m.* for **~'s sake,** par pitié. **it is a ~ that,** c'est dommage que. *v.t.* plaindre, avoir pitié de. **I ~ your misfortune,** je plains votre malheur. **he is to be pitied,** il est à plaindre. *v.i.* s'apitoyer sur, s'attendrir; *Bibl.* épargner.

pivot *n.* pivot *m.*

placard *n.* grande affiche *f.* *v.t.* placarder, afficher.

place *n.* place *f.,* endroit *m.,* lieu *m.;* localité *f.;* situation *f.;* séjour *m.,* demeure *f.;* emplacement *m.;* rang *m.* **keep a ~ for me near you,** gardez-moi une place près de vous. **to put one in his ~,** remettre quelqu'un à sa place. **in ~ of,** in the **~ of,** à la place de, au lieu de. **the ~ of his birth,** le lieu de sa naissance. **a ~ of refuge,** un lieu de refuge. **a good ~ for a house,** un bon emplacement pour une maison. **in no ~,** nulle part. **in the first ~,** en premier lieu, d'abord. **in the next ~,** ensuite. **to take ~,** avoir lieu. **quite out of ~,** tout à fait déplacé. **I took his ~ last Sunday,** je l'ai remplacé dimanche dernier. *v.t.* placer, mettre.

placement *n.* placement *m.,* investissement *m.;* stage *m.* (work intern).

placenta n. placenta m.

placid adj. placide, paisible; calme, tranquille, doux; serein.

placidly adv. placidement.

placidity n. placidité f.

plagiarism n. plagiat m.

plagiarize v.t. commettre un plagiat au détriment de.

plague n. peste f., fléau m.; plaie f. **the ten ~s of Egypt,** les dix plaies d'Egypte. v.t. empester, être un fléau pour; tourmenter, assommer; Infml. embêter.

plaid n. plaid m. manteau m. écossais. adj. écossais, à carreaux.

plain adj. uni, plat, égal; sincère, franc; évident; commun, ordinaire, simple; laid, laide; sans ornements. a ~ **man,** un homme sans façons. a ~ **story,** une simple histoire. **the ~ truth,** la pure vérité. ~**-spoken,** franc. **in ~ terms,** en termes clairs, formels. **in ~ English,** en bon anglais. ~ **food,** une nourriture simple. n. plaine f., pays plat. **in a ~,** en plaine. ~**-speaking,** le franc-parler m.

plainly adv. simplement; loyalement; franchement; nettement, distinctement; clairement; évidemment. **to speak ~ with someone,** parler franchement à quelqu'un.

plainness n. simplicité f.; franchise f., sincérité f.; clarté f., netteté f.

plaint n. Law. plainte f.

plaintiff n. Law. demandeur m., plaignant m.

plaintive adj. plaintif.

plan n. plan m.; projet m., dessein m. **to draw a ~,** lever un plan. v.i. tracer, faire le plan de; projeter, imaginer.

plane adj. Geom. plan; plat, de niveau. n. avion m., plan m.; surface plane; (tool), rabot m. ~ **tree,** platane m. ~ v.t. raboter; planer aplanir. **to ~ down,** raboter.

planet n. planète f.

planetarium n. planétarium m.

planetary adj. de planète; planétaire.

plangent adj. retentissant.

planisphere n. planisphère m.

plank n. uis m., planche f., madrier m. ~ v.t. planchéier; garnir de planches; Pol. article m., paragraphe m.

plankton n. planeton m.

planner n. personne qui forme un plan, un projet; planificateur m. (datebook).

plant n. Bot. plante f.; plant m.; matériel m.; usine (factory). **to plant a ~,** mettre une plante en terre. v.t. planter, semer; établir. **to ~ a colony,** fonder une colonie.

plantain n. plantain m., bananier m., plantanier m.

plantation n. plantation f., établissement m.

planter n. planteur m., colon m.

plaque n. plaque f.

plasma n. plasma m.

plaster n. plâtre m.; Pharm. emplâtre m. ~ **of Paris,** gypse m., plâtre. v.t. plâtrer; mettre un emplâtre à.

plasterer n. plâtrier m., maçon m.; mouleur m.

plastic adj.,n. plastique m.

plasticity n. plasticité f.

plate n. assiette f.; plaque f. (metal); vaisselle f. (gold, silver), gravure f., planche f. **dinner ~,** assiette de table. **silver ~,** argenterie f. ~**-glass,** glace f., verre m. à glaces. v.t. plaquer; laminer revêtir de plaques; argenter; étamèr (mirror).

plateau n. plateau m.

plateful n. assiettée f.

platform n. plate-forme f., estrade f.

plating n. placage m.; plaqué m.

platinum n. platine m.

platitude n. platitude f.

platonic adj. platonique, platonicien; de Platon.

platoon n. section f., peloton m.

platter n. plat m.

plaudit n. applaudissement m.

plausible adj. plausible.

plausibly adv. plausiblement.

play v.i. jouer; se divertir, s'amuser. **to ~ the violin,** jouer du violon. **to ~ cards,** jouer aux cartes. v.t. faire jouer; exécuter, représenter (theater). **to ~ a comedy,** jouer une comédie. **to ~ the fool,** faire la bête. **to ~ out the game,** jouer jusqu'au bout. **the game is played out.** Fig. le jeu est fini. n. jeu m., récréation f.; action f., mouvement m.; pièce f. de théâtre; spectacle m.; exécution f. **fair ~,** beau jeu, loyauté. **foul ~,** tricherie f., mauvais jeu. **at ~,** en jouant. **child's ~,** jeu d'enfant. **to bring into ~,** mettre en mouvement, en jeu. **to give full ~ to one's fancy,** donner l'essor à son imagination. ~**-bill,** programme m. de spectacle. ~**-mate,** camarade m., compagnon m. de jeu. ~**-ground,** cour f. de récréation. ~**-time,** heure f. de récréation. ~**-wright,** auteur m. dramatique, dramaturge m.

player n. joueur m., joueuse f.; acteur m., actrice f., artiste m.f.; joueur m. d'instruments de musique, exécutant m., artiste m.

playful adj. enjoué.

playfulness n. enjouement m.

plea n. appel m., supplication f.; defense f., procès m.; excuse f., prétexte m., justification f. **a plausible ~,** une excuse plausible.

plead v.i. plaider; (se) défendre; engager avec instance; alléguer, invoquer; Law. se déclarer. **to ~ guilty,** s'avouer coupable. v.t. faire valoir, citer en sa faveur; soutenir. **to ~ one's cause,** défendre sa cause.

pleading n. plaidoirie f.; argument m.

pleasant adj. agréable, aimable; riant; joyeux, plaisant.

pleasantly adv. agréablement, d'une manière charmante; joyeusement, gaiement.

pleasantness n. agrément m., charme m.; amabilité f.; gaieté f.

pleasantry n. plaisanterie f.

please v.t. plaire (à), faire plaisir à, contenter

charmer. **to ~ someone,** plaire à quelqu'un, lui faire plaisir. **how pleased I am to see you!** que je suis content de vous voir! *v.i.* vouloir; daigner. **as you ~,** comme il vous plaira, comme vous voudrez. **if you ~,** s'il vous plaît.

pleased *adj.* content, satisfait; heureux.

pleasing *adj.* agréable; charmant; aimable; gracieux; riant.

pleasingly *adv.* agréablement.

pleasurable *adj.* agréable, charmant; délectable.

pleasurably *adv.* avec plaisir.

pleasure *n.* plaisir *m.;* charme *m.,* agrément *m.;* volonté *f.,* gré *m.* **to feel, to take ~ in a thing,** prendre plaisir à une chose. **at his ~,** à son gré. **~ boat,** bateau *m.* de plaisance. **~ trip,** partie *f.* de plaisir. *v.t.* plaire, faire plaisir, complaire.

pledge *n.* promesse *f.* gage *m. f.,* garantie *f.,* garantir, se porter garant de, boire à (toast).

plenipotentiary *adj. n.,* plénipotentiaire *m.*

plenitude *n.* plénitude *f.*

plenteous *adj.* abondant, copieux, fécond; plein.

plenteously *adv.* en abondance, abondamment.

plentiful *adj.* abondant.

plentifully *adv.* abondamment, en abondance.

plentifulness *n.* abondance *f.;* fertilité *f.,* fécondité *f.*

plenty *n.* abondance *f.* **~ adj.** abondant, copieux.

plethoric *adj.* phléthorique.

plexus *n.* plexus *m.*

pliable *adj.* pliable, souple, flexible; docile.

pliancy *n.* flexibilité *f.,* souplesse *f.;* docilité *f.*

pliant *adj.* pliant, flexible, souple; pliable.

pliers *n.pl.* petites pinces *f.pl.,* tenailles *f.pl.*

plight *n.* état *m.,* difficile, condition *f.*

plod *v.i.* marcher lourdement; travailler avec peine; *Infml.* s'échiner. **to ~ on,** piocher.

plodding *adj.* laborieux, procheur, d'arrache-pied.

plot *n.* petit terrain *m.;* complot *m.,* trame *f.,* intrigue *f.* (book, play). *v.t.* faire un plan de; comploter, conspirer, intriguer, machiner.

plotter *n.* machinateur *m.;* conspirateur *m.,* conjuré *m.*

plotting *n.* complot *m.,* machination *f.,* trame *f.*

plow *n.* charrue *f.;* *Fig.* culture *f.,* labourage *m.;* agriculture *f.* **~ v.t.** labourer; creuser.

pluck *v.t.* tirer; arracher; plumer (poultry), cueillir (flowers).

plug *n.* cheville *f.,* tampon *m.,* bouchon *m.;* piston *m.* (sink) *v.t.* cheviller, tamponner, boucher.

plum *n.* prune *f.;* aubaine *f.,* morceau *m.* de choix; (job) *Infml.* boulot *m.* en or. **~ pudding,** plum-pudding *m.,* pouding *m.* aux raisins. **~ tree,** prunier *m.*

plumb *n.* plomb *m.,* fil *m.,* à plomb. *adj.* à plomb. **~ line,** fil à plomb. *adv.* d'aplomb, de niveau. *v.t.* mettre à plomb.

plumber *n.* plombier *m.*

plume *n.* plume *f.* (bird); plumet *m.;* panache *m.*

plummet *n.* sonde *f.;* fil *m.* à plomb. *v.i.* tomber à pic, plonger, tomber en chute libre.

plump *adj.* potelé, dodu, grassouillet.

plumpness *n.* embonpoint *m.;* rondeur *f.*

plunder *v.t.* piller; saccager. *n.* pillage *m.;* dépouille *f.,* butin *m.,* saccagement *m.*

plunderer *n.* pillard *m.*

plunge *v.i.* se plonger, se précipiter, se jeter, s'élancer dans. *n.* plongeon *m.,* embarras *m.;* abîme *m.*

plunger *n.* plongeur *m.;* ventouse *f.;* spéculateur *m.*

pluperfect *adj.* plus-que-parfait.

plural *adj.* de plus d'un, pluriel. *n.* pluriel *m.*

plurality *n.* pluralité *f.*

plus *adv.* plus.

plush *n.* peluche *f.* *adj.* luxieux.

ply *v.t.* s'attacher à; exercer; manier. *v.i.* plier, se courber.

p.m. *abbrev.* **post meridiem** après midi. **I'll see you at 7:00~,** je vous verrai à 19h00 (à sept heures du soir).

pneumatic *adj.* pneumatique. *n.* pneumatique *m.,* pneu *m.*

pneumonia *n.* pneumonie *f.*

poach *v.t.* pocher (eggs) voler (game) *v.i.* braconner; devenir humide, s'amoller (ground).

poacher *n.* braconnier *m.*

poaching *n.* braconnage *m.*

pock *n.* postule *f.* **~marked,** marqué de la petite vérole, grêlé.

pocket *n.* poche *f.;* blouse *f.,* (billiards). **out of one's ~,** de sa poche. **~book,** sac *m.* à main. **~ money,** argent *m.* de poche. *v.t.* empocher; prendre en cachette.

pod *n.* cosse *f.,* gousse *f.*

podiatrist *n.* pédicure *m.f.*

poem *n.* poeme *m.;* poésie *f.*

poet *n.* poète *m.*

poetic *adj.* poétique.

poetically *adv.* poétiquement.

poetics *n.* poétique *f.*

poetry *n.* poésie *f.*

poignancy *n.* piquant *m.,* pointe *f.;* nature poignante.

poignant *adj.* poignant, très pénible, cuisant.

poignantly *adv.* d'une manière poignante.

point *n.* pointe *f.,* burin *m.* (engraving); *Geog.* cap *m.;* trait *m.,* saille *f.;* (railway), aiguille *f.;* *Typ.* pointure *f.,* degré *m.;* object *m.;* dentelle *f.* **I was at the ~ of coming,** j'étais sur le point de venir. **freezing ~,** point de congélation. **cardinal ~s,** points cardinaux. **knotty ~,** question épineuse. **the main ~,** le point principal. **to come to the ~,** en arriver au fait. *v.t.* rendre pointu; aiguiser; montrer au doigt; viser; pointer; (masonry) pointoyer. **to ~ the finger at,** montrer du doigt. **to ~ out,** montrer, signaler. **to ~ a gun,** braquer, pointer un revolver. *v.i.* (avec to) se diriger.

point-blank *adj.* de but-en-blanc, à bout portant; catégorique, direct.

pointed adj. pointu; aigu, piquant; Fig. satirique, piquant, Arch. ogival, gothique.

pointedly adv. subtilement, explicitement; d'une manière significative.

pointer n. index m.; indicateur m.; chien m., d'arrêt.

pointless adj. vain, inutile, qui ne rime/sert à rien, dénué de sens.

poise n. balance f., équilibre m. ~ v.t. balancer; mettre en équilibre.

poison n. poison m. ~ v.t. empoisonner.

poisonous adj. empoisonné, vénéneux, venimeux (animals).

poke n. poche f., petit sac; poussée f. **to buy a pig in a** ~, acheter chat en poche. v.t. pousser, remuer; fouiller, farfouiller. **to** ~ **one's nose everywhere**, fourrer son nez partout. v.i. se mettre, se fourrer; tâtonner. **to go poking around**, fouiller, farfouiller partout.

poker n. tisonnier m.; (fireplace); poker (cards). ~ **face**, visage m. impassible.

Poland npr. Pologne f.

polar adj. polaire.

polarity n. polarité f.

polarization n. polarisation f.

polarize v.t. polariser.

pole n. poteau m.; perche f.; Astron. pôle m.; mât m., échalas m.; balancier m. **the North Pole,** le pôle nord. v.t. mettre des perches à; pousser avec une perche.

Pole n. Polonais m., Polonaise f.

polecat n. putois m.

polemic, polemical adj. polémique. polémique f.

polemics n. polémique f.

police n. police f. ~ **officer,** agent m. de police. ~ **station,** poste m. de police.

policed adj. policé.

policy n. politique f.; règle f., conduite f. Comm. police f. **insurance** ~, police d'assurances.

polis n. polio f.

Polish adj. polonais.

polish v.t. cirer, vernir. **to** ~ **glass, marble, metals,** polir le verre, le marbre, les métaux. **to** ~ **up a young man,** façonner, dégourdir un jeune homme. v.i. se polir; Fig. se façonner; se dégrossir. s vernis m., poli m.; Fig. grâce f., élégance f. de manières.

polished adj. poli; luisant; dégourdi.

polishing n. polissage m.; poli m.

polite adj. poli.

politely adv. poliment.

politeness n. politesse f.

politic adj. politique, fin, avisé.

political adj. politique. ~ **and civil rights,** droits politiques et civils.

politically adv. politiquement.

politician n. homme/femme, politique m.f.; politicien m.

politicly adv. politiquement.

politics n. politique f.

polity n. forme f. du gouvernement; politique f.

poll n. liste f. électorale, rôle m.; scrutin m.; élection f. **opinion** ~, sondage m. ~ **tax,** capitation, impôt par tête. v.t. inscrire sur une liste électorale; recueicillir (des votes); voter, donner son vote; sonder.

pollen n. pollen m.

polling n. action de voter, d'enregistrer les votes. ~ **booth,** isoloir m. ~ **place,** salle f. de vote.

pollute v.t. polluer, salir, souiller; flétrir; corrompre.

pollution n. pollution f.

poltergeist n. esprit m. frappeur.

polyandria n. polyandrie f.

polygamist n. polygame m.; polygamiste m.

polygamous adj. polygame.

polygamy n. polygamie f.

polyglot n. polyglotte n. polyglotte f.; polyglotte m.f. (person).

polygon n. polygone m.

Polynesia n.pr. Polynésie f.

polysyllabic adj. polysyllabe, polysyllabique.

polytechnic adj. polytechnique.

polytheism n. polythéisme m.

pomegranate n. grenade f. ~ **tree,** grenadier m.

pomp n. pompe f., faste m., magnificence f. éclat m.

pompous adj. pompeux.

pompously adv. pompeusement.

pompousness n. pompe f.; emphase f., enflure f. du style.

pond n. étang m.; bassin m.; vivier m. (for fish).

ponder v.t. peser (dans l'esprit); considérer, examiner. v.i. méditer, rêver.

ponderable adj. pondérable.

ponderous adj. pesant; important.

ponderously adv. d'un grand poids, pesamment.

ponderousness n. poids m., pesanteur f., gravité f.

pontiff n. pontife m.

pontifical adj. pontifical.

pontificate n. pontificat m. ~ v.i. pontifier; Infml. faire l'important.

pony n. au pl. **ponies,** poney m.

poodle n. caniche m.

pool n. étang m., mare f.; bassin m.; pool m., billiard m. (game); piscine f. (swimming).

poop n. Naut. dunette f., poupe f. n. Infml. caca m. ~ v.t. faire caca.

pooped adj. Infml. crevé, vanné, à plat.

poor adj. pauvre; indigent; chétif; mauvais. **a** ~ **man,** un (homme) pauvre. **as** ~ **as a church mouse,** gueux comme un rat d'église. **a** ~ **excuse,** une triste excuse. **the patient has had a** ~ **night,** le malade a passé une mauvaise nuit. **the** ~, les pauvres, les indigents. ~**box,** tronc m des pauvres.

poorly adv. pauvrement; médiocrement, chétivement; pitoyablement, tristement. adj. Infml. un peu malade, indisposé.

poorness n. pauvreté f., indigence f., médiocrité f.

pop n. petit son m. vif, soudain. v.i. survenir, arriver, partir brusquement. **to ~ down**, descendre tout à coup. **to ~ out**, sortir précipitamment. v.t. **he popped his head out of the water**, il sortit sa tête brusquement de l'eau. **to ~ the question**, demander en mariage. adv. soudain, tout à coup; interj. crac! patatras!

pop n. Infml. Pa; pop (music).

popcorn n. pop-corn m.

pope n. pape m.; pope m. (Eastern Orthodox church).

poplar n. peuplier.

poppy n. pavot m., coquelicot m., pavot sauvage.

poppycock n. Infml. sottise f., balivernes f.pl.

populace n. populace f.

popular adj. populaire.

popularity n. popularité f.

popularize v.t. populariser.

popularly adv. populairement.

populate v.t. peupler.

population n. population f.

populous adj. populeux.

porcelain n. porcelaine f.

porch n. porche m., portail m.; portique m.

porcine adj. porcine f. de porc.

porcupine n. proc-épic m.

pore n. pore m. v.i. (avec over) regarder avec beaucoup d'attention. **to ~ over a book**, être plongé/absorbé dans un livre.

pork n. porc m. **fresh ~**, porc frais. **~ butcher**, charcutier. **salt ~**, petit salé. **~ chop**, côtelette de porc.

porky adj. Infml. gros/gras comme un cochon.

pornography n. pornographie f.

porosity n. porosité f.

porous adj. poreux.

porpoise n. marsouin m.

port n. port m., havre m. Naut. bâbord m.; vin m. (de Porto). **sea~**, port de mer. **~ charges, ~ dues**, droits m.pl. de port. **~hole**, sabord m. **~** v.t. Naut. mettre à bâbord.

portable adj. portatif.

portage n. port m. (fees) transport m.

portal n. portail m.

portend v.t. présager.

portent n. préssage m. sinistre m. mauvais augure m.

portentous adj. de mauvais augure, sinistre; monstrueux, pompeux.

porter n. portier m., concierge m., porteur m.; commissionnaire m.; facteur (train).

portfolio n. serviette f.; portefeuille m.

portico n. portique m.

portion n. portion f., part f., partie f., dot f. **~** v.t. diviser; distribuer; assigner; doter.

portly adj. gros, corpulent.

portrait n. portrait m. **full-length ~**, portrait en pied. **to have one's ~ taken**, faire son portrait.

portray v.t. peindre; faire le portrait de; dépeindre.

pose n. pose f., attitude f.; Art. pose f.; affectation f. ~ v.t. poser, prendre la pose; se faire passer pour.

position n. position f., situation f.; attitude f.; posture f. **in a ~ to**, en état de.

positive adj. positif, formel, absolu, certain. **~ facts**, des faits positifs. **he is ~ about it**, il en est certain. n. positif m.

positively adv. positivement; sûrement, formellement; affirmativement.

posse n. bande f., force f., publique, foule f.

possess v.t. posséder, occuper; être en possession de, être maître de. **the devil ~es him**, il a le diable au corps.

possession n. possession f.; jouissance f. **to take ~**, entrer en possession de, prendre possession.

possessive adj. possessif.

possessor n. possesseur m.; maître m.

possibility n. possibilité f.; possible m.

possible adj. possible.

possibly adv. peut-être, par hasard; il est possible que.

post n. poteau m.; borne f.; poste m., emploi m.; poste f. courrier m. (mail). **to desert one's ~**, abandonner son poste. **~card**, carte postale. **~ paid**, franco de port. **~mark**, timbre m. (de la poste). **~master**, directeur des postes. **~ office**, bureau m. de poste, administration f. des postes. v.t. stationner, poster; afficher à un poteau; placarder; mettre à la poste; porter au grand-livre (accounting). **to ~**, afficher, poser (une affiche).

postage n. tarifs postaux m.pl., affranchissement m. **~ stamp**, timbre-poste m.

postal adj. postal.

postdate v.t. postdater.

poster n. affiche f.

posterior adj. postérieur; derrière m., postérieur m.

posterity n. postérité f.

postgraduate adj. (university) de troisième cycle; n., étudiant m. de troisième cycle.

posthumous adj. posthume.

postpone v.t. réserver, remettre, renvoyer, ajourner, différer.

postponement n. ajournement m.

postscript n. post-scriptum m.

postulant n. postulant m.

postulate n. postulat m. **~** v.t. postuler; s'arroger, s'attribuer.

posture n. attitude f., position f., état m.

pot n. pot m., vase m.; marmite f.; Infml. hasch m., herbe f. (drug). **flower~**, pot à fleurs. **to go to ~**, s'en aller au diable. **~-bellied**, ventru, pansu. **~luck**, la fortune f. du pot. v.t. mettre en pot; conserver en pot; empoter.

potable adj. potable, buvable. n. chose f. potable, qu'on peut boire.

potassium *n.* potassium *m.*

potato *n.* pomme *f.* de terre. **mashed ~es,** purée de pommes. **French-fried ~es** (pommes de terre) frites *f.pl.*

potency *n.* force *f.* morale, puissance *f.*

potent *adj.* fort.

potential *adj., n.* potentiel *m.*

potentiality *n.* potentialité *f.*

potentially *adv.* potentiellement, virtuellement.

potently *adv.* puissamment, efficacement.

potion *n.* potion *f.*

potpourri *n.* pot-pourri *m.*

pottery *n.* poterie *f.*

pouch *n.* poche *f.*, pochette *f.*, petit sac *m.*; **tobacco ~,** blague à tabac.

poultry *n.* volaille *f.* **~ yard,** basse cour *f.*

pounce *n.* attaque subite *f.* ~ *v.i.* (with **on**) foudre sur, s'abattre sur.

pound *n.* livre *f.* (weight), fourrière *f.* (animals). **half a ~,** une demi-livre. **by the ~,** à la livre. *v.t.* mettre en fourrière; plier; concasser, broyer, pulvériser.

pour *v.t.* verser, répandre. **to ~ out something to drink,** verser à boire. **to ~ forth,** exhaler, émettre. *v.i.* couler; fondre; se précipiter; pleuvoir à verse. **it's pouring,** il pleut à verse. **it never rains but it pours,** un malheur ne vient jamais seul. **pouring rain,** pluie battante.

pout *n.* moue *f.* ~ *v.i.* bouder, faire la moue.

poverty *n.* pauvreté *f.*; indigence *f.*

P.O.W. *abbrev.* **prisoner of war,** prisonier *m.* de guerre.

powder *n.* poudre *f.* **gunpowder,** poudre à canon. *v.t.* réduire en poudre; pulvériser, poudrer; saupoudrer. *v.i.* tomber en poussière, en poudre.

powdery *adj.* friable; poudreux.

power *n.* pouvoir *m.*; puissance *f.*; autorité *f.* **moving ~,** force motrice. **he has great natural ~s,** c'est un homme de beaucoup de talent, de grands moyens. **military ~,** autorité militaire. **the ~s of Europe,** les puissances européennes. **a ~ of attorney,** un pouvoir, une procuration. **~ line,** ligne *f.* à haute tension.

powerful *adj.* puissant, efficace.

powerless *adj.* impuissant; faible.

powwow *n.* assemblée *f.* (amérindiens). *v.i.* (s')assembler, (s')entretenir.

pox *n.* **chicken~,** varicelle *f.*

practicable *adj.* praticable.

practicably *adv.* d'une manière praticable, faisable.

practical *adj.* pratique. **~ joke,** *Infml.* farce.

practically *adv.* pratiquement, en pratique.

practicalness *n.* nature sens *m.f.* pratique.

practice *n.* pratique *f.*; habitude *f.*; usage *m.*; exercice *m.*; clientèle *f.* (professional). **to put in ~,** mettre en pratique. **to make it one's ~ to,** se faire une habitude de. **target ~,** exercice du tir à la cible. **~ makes perfect,** c'est en forgeant qu'on devient forgeron. *v.t.* pratiquer; exercer

(une profession); s'exercer à. *v.i.* étudier; tirer. **to ~ with a rifle,** s'exercer à la carabine. **to ~ what one preaches,** prêcher d'exemple.

practiced *adj.* pratique; habile; expérimenté. **a ~ speaker,** un orateur expérimenté.

practicing *adj.* en exercice. **~ lawyer,** avocat en exercice.

practitioner *n.* praticien *m.*; médecin *m.* praticien.

pragmatic *adj.* pragmatique.

prairie *n.* prairie *f.*

praise *n.* louange *f.*, éloge *m.* **worthy of ~,** louable. *v.t.* louer, faire l'éloge de; glorifier.

praiseworthy *adj.* louable.

prance *v.i.* se cabrer; se carrer.

prank *n.* fredaine *f.*, escapade *f.*, folie *f.*; niche *f.*, espièglerie *f.*, tour *m.* **to play ~s,** *Infml.* faire des siennes.

prattle *v.i.* bavarder, caqueter, *n.* babillage *m.*, babil *m.*, d'enfant, caquetage *m.*

prattler *n.* bavard *m.*

prawn *n.* crevette *f.* rose.

pray *v.i.* prier, faire ses prières. *v.t.* implorer, supplier.

prayer *n.* prière *f.*, supplication *f.*, demande *f.* **the Lord's ~,** l'oraison dominicale. **~ book,** livre de prières; rituel *m.*

preach *v.t.* prêcher. **to practice what one ~es,** prêcher par exemple.

preacher *n.* pasteur *m.*; prédicateur *m.*

preaching *n.* prédication *f.*; sermon *m.*

preamble *n.* préambule *m.*; avant-propos *m.*; exposé *m.* des motifs.

prearrange *v.t.* arranger au préambule/à l'avance.

precarious *adj.* précaire, incertain.

precariously *adv.* précairement.

precariousness *n.* état précaire; incertitude *f.*

precaution *n.* précaution *f.* **by ~,** par précaution. *v.t.* précautionner, prévenir, mettre en garde.

precautionary *adj.* de précaution. **~ measures,** moyens préventifs *m.pl.*

precede *v.t.* précéder.

precedence *n.* antériorité *f.*, priorité *f.* de temps; préséance *f.*, supériorité *f.* **to take ~ over,** prendre le pas sur; avoir le pas, la préséance sur.

precedent *adj.* précédent, antécédant. *n.* précédent *m.*; exemple.

preceding *adj.* précédent.

precept *n.* précepte *m.*; *Law.* mandat *m.*

precession *n.* précession *f.*

precinct *n.* circonscription *f.* électorale/administrative.

precious *adj.* précieux; **~ metals,** les métaux précieux.

preciously *adv.* précieusement.

preciousness *n.* nature *f.* précieuse, haute valeur *f.*

precipice *n.* précipice *m.*

precipitate *v.t.* hâter; accélérer. *v.i.* se précipiter, jeter; se hâter. *adj.* qui se précipite; précipité. *n.* précipité *m.*

precipitately *adv.* précipitamment.

precipitation *n.* precipitation *f.*

precipitous *adj.* très escarpé, à pic; rapide; précipité.

precipitously *adv.* à pic; en précipice; précipitamment, avec précipitation.

precise *adj.* précis, exact, scrupuleux; pointilleux. **at the ~ hour,** à l'heure précise.

precisely *adv.* précisément; scrupuleusement; d'une manière pointilleuse.

preciseness *n.* précision *f.;* régularité *f.;* scrupule *m.*

precision *n.* précision *f.*

preclude *v.t.* (from), exclure; empêcher, obéir à; prévenir. **to ~ the possibility of,** rendre impossible.

precocious *adj.* précoce.

precociously *adv.* avec précocité; prématurément.

precociousness, precocity *n.* précocité *f.*

precognition *n.* prénotion *f.,* connaissance antérieure.

preconceive *v.t.* préconcevoir.

preconceived *adj.* préconçu.

preconception *n.* préconception *f.*

precursor *n.* précurseur *m.*

predator *n.* prédateur *m.*

predatory *adj.* de proie, prédateur.

predecease *v.t.* prédécéder. *n.* prédécès *m.*

predecessor *n.* prédécesseur *m.*

predestination *n.* prédestination *f.*

predetermination *n.* dessein, arrêté d'avance; prédétermination *f.*

predetermine *v.t.* prédéterminer.

predicament *n.* prédicament *m.;* condition *f. Infml.* situation *f.* difficile.

predicate *v.t.* donner pour attribut; *v.i.* affirmer. *n.* prédicate *m.,* attribut *m.*

predication *n.* affirmation *f.*

predict *v.t.* prédire.

prediction *n.* prédiction *f.*

predilection *n.* predilection *f.*

predispose *v.t.* prédisposer.

predisposition *n.* disposition *f.* antérieure; *Med.* prédisposition *f.*

predominance *n.* prédominance *f.* influence *f.,* ascendant *m.*

predominant *adj.* prédominant.

predominate *v.i.* prédominer.

predomination *n.* prédominance *f.*

pre-eminence *n.* supériorité *f.;* prééminence *f.;* préséance *f.*

pre-eminent *adj.* prééminent; qui excelle, qui l'emporte; supérieur; (neg.) extraordinaire, remarquable.

pre-eminently *adv.* à un degré prééminent; par excellence.

pre-exist *v.i.* préexister.

pre-existence *n.* préexistence *f.*

pre-existent *adj.* préexistant.

prefabricate *v.t.* préfabriquer.

preface *n.* préface *f.* ~ *v.t.* faire une préface à; faire précéder de; préluder à. *v.i.* dire en manière de préface.

prefatory *adj.* préliminaire.

prefect *n.* préfet *m.*

prefecture *n.* préfecture *f.*

prefer *v.t.* préférer. **to ~ music to painting,** aimer mieux la musique que la peinture.

preferable *adj.* préférable.

preferably *adv.* préférablement, de préférence.

preference *n.* préférence *f.*

preferential *adj.* privilégié.

preferment *n.* avancement *m.* promotion *f.* fonction *f.* supérieure.

prefiguration *n.* préfiguration *f.*

prefigure *v.t.* préfigurer.

prefix *v.t.* mettre devant; faire précéder. *n.* préfixe *m.*

preform *v.t.* préformer.

pregnancy *n.* grossesse *f.; Fig.* fertilité *f.*

pregnant *adj.* enceinte; *Infml.* grosse; fécond, fertile; gros. **to be ~,** être enceinte.

prehensile *adj.* préhensile.

prehistoric *adj.* préhistorique.

prejudge *v.t.* préjuger; condamner d'avance.

prejudice *n.* préjugé *m.;* préjudice *m.;* détriment *m.* **without ~ to,** sans préjudice de. **to a person's ~,** au détriment de quelqu'un. *v.t.* (against, to) prévenir, porter préjudice à; faire du tort à; nuire à.

prejudicial *adj.* determiné par des préventions; préjudiciable; nuisible.

preliminary *adj.* préliminaire; préalable. *n.* préliminaire *m.*

prelude *n.* prélude *m.* ~ *v.t.* préluder (à).

premature *adj.* prématuré.

prematurely *adv.* prématurément.

prematurity *n.* prématurité *f.*

premeditate *v.t.* préméditer.

premeditated *adj.* prémédité; délibéré.

premeditation *n.* préméditation *f.*

premier *adj.* premier; chef; principal *n.* premier ministre *m.*

premises *n. pl. Log.* prêmisses *f.pl.;* établissement *m.;* local *m.,* lieux *m.pl.* on the ~, sur les lieux, dans l'établisssement.

premium *n.* prix *m.,* prime *f.;* récompense *f.* at a ~, prime.

premonition *n.* prémonition *f.*

premonitory *adj.* prémonitoire.

prenatal *adj.* prénatal.

prenuptial *adj.* prénuptial.

preoccupation *n.* préoccupation *f.; Law.* possession *f.* antérieure; anticipation *f.*

preoccupy *v.t.* prendre possession avant; préoccuper (mind).

prepaid *adj.* payé d'avance; affranchi.

preparation *n.* préparation *f.;* préparatif *m.,* apprêt *m.*

preparative *adj.* préparatoire. préparatif *m.*

preparatory *adj.* préparatoire; préalable; préliminaire.

prepare *v.t.* arranger, disposer; apprêter. **to ~ a dinner,** préparer un dîner. *v.i.* se préparer (à, pour); se disposer à; s'apprêter à.

prepay *v.t.* payer d'avance, affranchir (letter).

prepayment *n.* payement *m.* d'avance; affranchissement *m.*

preponderance *n.* prépondérance *f.*

preponderant *adj.* prépondérant.

preponderate *v.t.* surpasser; l'emporter sur. *v.i.* avoir la prépondérence sur.

preposition *n.* préposition *f.*

prepossess *v.t.* occuper avant un autre; préoccuper (mind), prévenir en faveur de.

prepossessing *adj.* prévenant, engageant.

prepossession *n.* occupation *f.* prélable; opinion *f.* préconçue.

preposterous *adj.* absurde, déraisonnable, ridicule, grotesque. **~ reasonings,** des raisonnements absurdes.

preposterously *adv.* absurdement.

preposterousness *n.* absurdité *f.*

preppy *n.* étudiant ou ancient étudiant d'écoles privées ou qui coûtent chères.

prerequisite *adj.* nécessaire au but qu'en se propose. *n.* condition *f.* préalable, cours préparatoire au cours supérieur.

prerogative *n.* prérogative *f.*

presage *n.* présage *m.* **~** *v.t.* présager. *v.i.* prédire.

presbytery *n.* presbytère *m.*

prescience *n.* prescience *f.*

prescient *adj.* prescient, doué de prescience.

prescribe *v.t.* prescrire, ordonner; faire une ordonnance. *v.i.* formuler.

prescription *n.* prescription *f.,* ordonnance *f.* (medicine).

presence *n.* présence *f.;* assistance *f.,* port *m.,* air *m.,* mine *f.;* personnage *m.* **~ of mind,** présence *f.* d'esprit.

present *adj.* présent; actuel; courant. **to be ~ at,** assister à. **the ~ month,** le mois courant. **~ tense,** temps présent. **in ~ present** *m.,* cadeau *m.* **at ~,** à présent, maintenant, actuellement. **by these ~s,** par ces présentes. **to make a ~,** faire un cadeau.

present *v.t.* présenter; offrir. **to ~ a petition,** présenter une pétition. **to ~ a person with a thing,** faire présent de quelque chose à quelqu'un.

presentable *adj.* présentable.

presentation *n.* présentation *f.;* représentation *f.*

presentiment *n.* pressentiment *m.*

presently *adv.* à présent, en ce moment.

preservation *n.* préservation *f.,* conservation *f.*

preservative *adj.* and *n.* préservatif *m.*

preserve *v.t.* (from) préserver; protéger; défendre; conserver. **to ~ health,** conserver la santé. *Cul.* **~d plums,** prunes en conserve. **to ~ appearances,** garder les

apparences. *n.* confiture *f.,* chasse *f.* réservée.

preside *v.i.* (over) présider.

presidency *n.* présidence *f.*

president *n.* président *m.* **vice ~,** vice-président.

presidential *adj.* présidentiel, de président.

presider *n.* personne *f.* qui préside.

press *v.t.* presser, pousser, serrer, pressurer; enrôler (de force); importuner; solliciter vivement. **she pressed me to accept,** elle m'a pressé d'accepter. **to ~ on, to ~ forward,** pousser en avant, faire avancer. **pressed for money,** pressé par le manque d'argent. **to ~ down,** presser, appuyer fortement sur; *Fig.* accabler, écraser. *v.i.* s'empresser, se présenter, accourir; pousser, poursuivre. **to ~ against the door,** pousser violemment la porte *n.* presse *f.,* pressoir *m.* (cider, etc.); foule *f.;* queue *f.,* empressement *m.,* enrôlement *m.* forcé. **printing ~,** presse typographique. **to go to ~,** mettre sous presse, imprimer.

pressing *adj.* urgent, pressant.

pressingly *adv.* d'une manière pressante, instamment.

pressure *n.* pression *f.,* contrainte *f.;* poussée *f.,* *Fig.* poids *m.,* oppression *f.;* urgence *f.* **high ~,** haute pression. **atmospheric ~,** pression atmosphérique. **the ~ of business,** le poids des affaires. **~ gauge,** manomètre *m.* **~ cooker,** cocotte minute.

prestidigitation *n.* prestidigitation *f.*

prestige *n.* prestige *m.*

prestigious *adj.* prestigieux.

presumably *adv.* probablement, vraisemblablement.

presume *v.t.* présumer, conjecturer, supposer; *v.i.* oser, se permettre, prendre la liberté. **he presumes too much on his merit,** il a trop bonne opinion de son mérite.

presuming *adj.* osant; prenant la liberté de; présomptueux.

presumption *n.* présomption *f.;* forte probabilité *f.* **the ~ is that,** il est à présumer que.

presumptive *adj.* présumé; présomptueux.

presumptuous *adj.* présomptueux.

presuppose *v.t.* présupposer.

pretend *v.t.* prétexter; alléguer, feindre; faire semblant, affecter. **he pretends to be ill,** il fait le malade; il fait semblant d'être malade.

pretense *n.* prétexte *m.;* faux semblant; excuse *f.,* défaite *f.;* feints *f.;* prétention *f.; Infml.* frime *f.* **on, upon, under ~ of,** sous prétexte de.

pretension *n.* prétention *f.,* prétexte *m.* **to lower one's ~s,** rabattre de ses prétentions, *Infml.* mettre de l'eau dans son vin.

pretentious *adj.* prétentieux.

preterit(e) *n.* prétérit *m.,* passé *m.* **~** *adj.* passé.

preternatural *adj.* contre nature.

pretext *n.* prétexte *m.;* feinte *f.*

pretty *adj.* joli, gentil, agréable, mignon, gracieux; plaisant, beau. **a ~ girl,** une jolie fille. *adv.* un peu, assez. **~ well,** assez bien. **a ~ penny.**

une jolie somme, une somme importante. **this house cost them a ~ penny**, cette maison leur a coûté une jolie somme.

pretzel n. bretzel m.

prevail v.i. prévaloir; l'emporter sur; gagner, dominer. **to ~ upon**, gagner. **to ~ over**, l'emporter sur. **to ~ with**, avoir l'empire sur.

prevailing adj. dominant, régnant; puissant.

prevalence n. influence f., empire m., efficacité f., ascendant m.

prevalent adj. dominant, puissant, efficace; qui prévaut.

prevaricate v.i. équivoquer, mentir, biaiser, tergiverser.

prevarication n. tergiversation f., équivoque f.; collusion f.; prévarication f.

prevent v.t. (from) prévenir, éviter, empêcher; devancer. **to ~ this misfortune**, pour prévenir ce malheur. **to ~ a person from doing a thing**, empêcher une personne de faire quelque chose.

preventable adj. qu'on peut empêcher.

prevention n. prévention f., empêchement m., obstacle m.

preventive adj. préventif; de précaution. **~ measures**, des mesures de précaution. n. ce qui empêche.

preview n. avant-première f.

previous adj. antérieur, précédent; **~ notice**, avis donné à l'avance.

previously adv. antérieurement; par avance.

prey f. proie f., butin m. **to be a ~ to**, être en proie à. v.i. (on) butiner; dévorer; faire sa proie de; Fig. miner, ronger (worry).

price n. prix m., récompense f. **average ~**, prix moyen. **fixed ~**, prix fixe. **full ~**, prix fort. **market ~**, cours, prix courant. **opening ~**, premier cours. **closing ~**, dernier cours. **at any ~**, à tout prix. **not at any ~**, pour rien au monde. v.t. mettre un prix à, évaluer.

priced adj. évalué.

priceless adj. sans prix; inappréciable.

prick v.t. dresser (ears); enfoncer, exciter. **to ~ with a needle**, piquer avec une aiguille. **to ~ up one's ears**, dresser les oreilles. v.i. se piquer; s'aigrir; s'ajuster; devenir piquant. n. pointe f.; piqûre f., vive douleur f., remords m.pl.

prickle n. épine f.; piquant m. v.t. picoter, piquer.

pride n. orgueil m., fierté f., vanité f., suffisance. v.t. enorgueillir. **to ~ oneself**, s'enorgueillir, tirer vanité de.

priest n. prêtre m. **high ~**, grand prêtre.

priestess n. prêtresse f.

priesthood n. prêtrise f.

prig n. Infml. petit saint, personne qui se prend pour supérieure aux autres.

prim adj. précis; affecté; tiré à quatre épingles.

primacy n. Eccles. primatie f.; suprématie f., primauté f.

primarily adv. principalement; primitivement, dans le principe.

primary adj. primitif; originel; principal; primaire, élémentaire. **the ~ colors**, les couleurs primitives.

primate n. primat m.

prime adj. premier; primitif; excellent, de première qualité, précoce; florissant; Arith. premier. **~ minister**, n. premier ministre m. aurore f., printemps m. (of life); force f., vigueur f.; élite f. **the ~ of life**, la force, la fleur de l'âge. **these trees are in their ~**, ces arbres sont dans toute leur beauté. v.t. amorcer (weapon); (paint) ébaucher; mettre la première couche.

prime rate n. prime rate.

prime time n. heure f. de grande écoute, prime time.

primeval adj. premier, primitif.

primitive adj. primitif.

primitively adv. primitivement.

primitiveness n. état primitif.

primogeniture n. primogéniture f.

primordial adj. primordial.

primrose n. primevère f.

prince n. prince m.

princedom n. principauté f.

princely adj. princier.

princess n. princesse f.

principal adj. principal. **the ~ thing**, la chose principale, l'essentiel. n. chef m., partie f. principale; patron m., principal m. associé m. principal; directeur m. (school); capital m. (money).

principality n. souveraineté f.; principauté f.

principally adv. principalement.

principle n. principe m. **on ~**, par principe. **a man of ~**, un homme de principes.

print v.t. imprimer; v.i. n. impression f.; imprimé m.; gravure f., estampe f.; empreinte f.; marque f., trace f. **the ~ of the nails**, l'empreinte des clous. **in ~**, imprimé. **out of ~**, épuisé.

printer n. imprimeur m. imprimante f. (computer).

printing n. imprimerie f., typographie f.; impression f. **~-house**, imprimerie f. **~ ink**, encre f. d'imprimerie. **~ press**, presse f. (à imprimer).

prior adj. antérieur, avant. **~ to**, antérieurement à. n. prieur m.

prioress n. prieure f.

priority n. priorité f.

prism n. prisme m.

prison n. prison f. **in ~**, en prison. **out of ~**, sorti de prison.

prisoner n. prisonnier m., détenu m.; prévenu m., accusé m.

privacy n. retraite f., solitude f., secret m., intimité f.

private adj. particulier, personnel, privé, intime; secret; à huis clos. **~ conversation**, entretien particulier. **~ lesson**, leçon particulière. **~ life**, vie privée. **a ~ place**, un endroit retiré. **a ~ staircase**, un escalier dérobé. **~ parts**, parties f.pl. genitales. **~ school**, école f. privée. **~ sector**, secteur m. privé.

privation n. privation f., manque m., besoin m.

privilege n. privilège m. v.t. privilégier.

prize n. prix m., bonne fortune, lot m. (lottery). **to win the ~,** remporter le prix. v.t. priser, estimer, evaluer; apprécier, faire grand cas de. **~ fighter,** boxeur m., **~-fighting,** lutte f., boxe f., pugilat m. **~ money,** part de prise.

pro prép. pour. **~ and con,** pour et contre. n. abbrev. **professional,** pro m.f., professionnel(le) m.f.

probability n. probabilité f.

probable adj. probable.

probably adv. probablement.

probate n. copie f., authentique d'un testament vérifié. **~ court,** cour chargée de la vérification des testaments.

probation n. preuve f.; épreuve f.; examen m.; probation f.; temps m. épreuve; liberté f. surveillée.

probe v.t. sonder; examiner à fond; scruter. n. sonde f.

probity n. probité f.

problem n. problème m.

problematic(al) adj. problématique.

proboscis n. proboscide f., trompe f.

procedure n. procédure f.; procédé m.; acte m.; operation f.

proceed v.i. procéder; avancer; se mettre à; aller; continuer; provenir de; en venir à. **they ~ed to London,** ils se rendirent à Londres. **to ~ with one's story,** poursuivre son récit. **to ~ cautiously,** s'y prendre avec précaution. **to ~ against,** intenter un procès à.

proceeding n. procédé m., conduite f., manière f., d'agir; acte m.; mesure f.; événement m., fait m.; au pl. procès-verbal m., poursuites f.pl. **cautious ~,** mesure de précaution. **the day's ~s,** les événements de la journée.

proceeds n. revenu m., produit m., rapport m. **net ~,** produit net.

process n. cours m., suite f.; marche f.; procédé m.; progrès m.; **chemical ~,** procédé - chimique.

procession n. procession f. **processional** adj. de procession m. processionnal m.

proclaim v.t. proclamer; déclarer, publier.

proclamation n. proclamation f.; ordonnance f.; édit m.

proclivity n. pente f., penchant m.; Fig. inclination f.; disposition f.

procrastinate v.t. remettre au lendemain, différer, remettre, temporiser, tirer en longueur. v.i. tarder, temporiser, user de délais.

procrastination n. remise f.; délai m., retardement m., temporisation f.

procrastinator n. celui qui remet au lendemain.

procreate v.t. procréer; produire.

procreation n. procréation f.

procreative adj. capable de procréer, de produire.

proctor n. avoué m., procureur m., surveillant m. ~ v.i. conduire, diriger.

procuration n. gestion f.; conduite f. (des affaires d'un autre); procuration f.

procurator n. procureur m., fondé m. de pouvoir; agent m. d'affaires, procurateur m.

procure v.t. faire avoir; obtenir; se procurer.

procurement n. obtention f.; acquisition f.

procurer n. proxénète m.f.

prod n. coup, poussée, secousse. v.t. donner un coup, pousser, secouer.

prodigal adj. prodigue. **the ~ son,** l'enfant prodigue. n. prodigue m.

prodigality n. prodigalité f.

prodigious adj. prodigieux.

prodigiously adv. prodigieusement.

prodigy n. prodige m.

produce v.t. produire; faire connaître.

producer n. celui qui produit; producteur m.

product n. produit m., production f., effet m.

production n. production f., fabrication f.

productive adj. productif; fertile.

productively adv. profitablement.

productivity n. productivité f.

prof n. abbrev. **professor,** prof m.f.

profanation n. profanation f.

profane adj. profane. v.t. profaner.

profanity n. langage m. profane; impiété f.

profaner n. profanateur m., profanatrice f.

profess v.t. professer; faire profession de; exercer. v.i. déclarer; faire des protestations.

professed adj. professé; déclaré.

profession n. profession f.; aveu m.; état m.

professional adj. professionnel.

professionally adv. par profession, en professionnel.

professor n. professeur m.

professorial adj. professoral, de professeur.

professorship n. professorat m.; chaire f. (de professeur).

proffer v.t. offrir; tenter, essayer. n. offre f., proposition f.

proficiency n. compétence f.

proficient adj. compétent, capable; expérimenté.

profile n. profil m., portrait m., esquisse f. **he is trying to keep a low ~ for a while,** il va essayer de passer inaperçu pendant quelques temps. v.t. profiler.

profit n. profit m., bénéfice m.; avantage m.; gain m. **gross ~,** bénéfice brut. **net ~,** bénéfice net. v.t. profiter (à); servir à; améliorer, perfectionner. v.i. gagner, bénéficier; servir, être utile. **to ~ by,** profiter de.

profitable adj. profitable; utile, avantageux.

profitably adv. profitablement, avec profit.

profligate adj. abandonné, dissolu, débauché, vicieux; corrompu, dépravé; scélérat. n. débauché m.; abandonné m.; scélérat m.

profound adj. profond. n. profondeur m.; abîme m.; océan m.

profoundly adv. profondément.

profoundness n. profondeur f.

profuse adj. prodigue, extravagant, excessif; abondant.

profusely adv. avec prodigalité; avec profusion.

profuseness n. prodigalité n.; profusion f.

profusion n. profusion f.

progenitor n. aïeul m.; ancêtre m.; Law. ascendant m. en ligne directe.

progeniture n. progéniture f.

progeny n. progéniture f.

prognosis n. pronostic m.

prognostic adj., n. prognostic m.

prognosticate v.t. pronostiquer; annoncer, présager, prédire.

prognostication n. présage m., signe m., prognostic m.

program n. programme m., émission f. ~ v.t. programmer.

progress n. progrès m.; marche f.; course f.; avancement m.; accroissement m. to make ~, faire des progrès. v.i. s'avancer; poursuivre son cours, progresser, faire des progrès.

progression n. progression f.; marche f., course f., voyage m., tournée f.; progrès m.

progressive adj.progressif.

progressively adv. progressivement.

prohibit v.t. interdire, défendre, empêcher; prohiber.

prohibition n. défense f., interdiction f., prohibition f.

prohibitive adj. prohibitif.

project v.t. jeter. v.i. s'avancer en saillie; se projeter. Arch. ressauter, faire ressaut.

project n. project m., programme m.

projectile adj. n. projectile m.

projecting adj. en saillie.

projection n. projection f.; saillie f.; Arch. ressaut m.

projector n. projecteur m., appareil m. de projection.

proletarian adj. prolétaire, de prolétaire; vulgaire, commun.

proletariat n. prolétariat m.

proliferation n. prolifération f.

prolific adj. prolifique; fecond, fertile.

prolificness n. fécondité f., fertilité f.

prolix adj. prolixe.

prologue n. prologue m. ~ v.t. faire précéder d'un prologue.

prolong v.t. prolonger; ajourner; différer.

prolongation n. prolongation f.

prom n. bal m. (de collégiens).

promenade n. promenade f. ~ v.i. se promener.

prominence n. éminence f.; Arch. saillie; distinction f.

prominent adj. celebre, éminent, saillant.

prominently adv. d'une manière, en saillie; éminemment; d'une manière marquée.

promiscuous adj. confus; mêlée; de moeurs légères, de conduite immorale.

promiscuously adv. immoralement; sans ordre.

promiscuousness n. promiscuité f.; confusion f.

promise n. promesse f.; espérances f.pl. to keep one's ~, tenir sa promesse. to break one's ~, manquer à sa promesse. v.t., v.i. promettre; faire des promesses.

promising adj. prometteur, qui promet; qui donne des espérances. a ~ youth, une jeune personne qui promet.

promissory adj. qui contient une promesse. ~ note, billet m. à ordre.

promontory n. promontoire m.

promote v.t. promouvoir, favoriser, encourager, protéger; élever.

promoter n. promoteur m.

promotion n. promotion f., agrandisement m.; encouragement m., avancement m.

prompt adj. prompt; vif; empressé. v.t. exciter, pousser, suggerer, dicter; Théât. souffler.

prompter n. personne qui pousse, qui excite à agir; Théât. souffleur m.

promptitude n. promptitude f.; facilité f.; bonne volonté; empressement m.

promptly adv. promptement.

promptness n. promptitude f.

promulgate v.t. promulguer, publier, proclamer.

promulgation n. promulgation f.; publication n.f.; déclaration f. officielle.

prone adj. penché en avant; incliné; couché (face down); enclin, porté, disposé, sujet à.

proneness n. état d'être couché la face contre terre; pente f., inclinaison f.; penchant m., disposition f.

prong n. fourchon m., dent f. (fork).

pronoun n. pronom m.

pronounce v.t. déclarer, affirmer. v.i. se prononcer.

pronounceable adj. prononçable.

pronouncement n. déclaration f.

pronunciation n. prononciation f.

proof n. preuve f.; épreuve n.f.; force f., degré m. (alcohol). ~ in writing, preuve par écrit. to be ~ against, être à l'épreuve de. to put to the ~, mettre à l'épreuve. ~ sheet, Typ. épreuve. water~, imperméable. m., adj. impénétrable.

prop n. appui m., soutien m., support m.; Carp. étai m., cale f.; Hort. tuteur m.; échalas m.; Théât. accessoire m.; Aviat. hélice f. ~ up, v.t. Carp. étayer, étançonner; Hort. mettre un tuteur à; Fig. soutenir, appuyer, étayer.

propaganda n. propagande f.

propagate v.t. répandre, étendre, faire croître. v.i. se propager.

propagation n. propagation f.; expansion f.; extension f.

propel v.t. propulser, faire mouvoir; mettre en mouvement; lancer.

propeller n. propulseur m.

propensity n. propension f.; tendance f.; penchant m.; goût m.

proper adj. propre; convenable; correct, juste; naturel; comme il faut. is it ~ to do so? est-ce correct de le faire? **to the ~ person,** à qui de droit.

properly *adv.* proprement; convenablement; exactement; naturellement; au propre; bien; à propos; comme il faut.

properness *n.* convenance *f.*

property *n.* biens *m.pl.,* propriété *f.,* qualité *f.;* propre *m.; Théât.* accessoires *m.pl.* literary ~, propriété littéraire. **real ~,** biens immeubles. **personal ~,** biens personnels.

prophecy *n.* prophétie *f.*

prophesy *v.t.* prophétiser.

prophet *n.* prophète *m.*

prophetic *adj.* prophétique.

prophylactic *adj.* prophylactique, préservatif. *n.* prophylactique *m.,* remède *m.* prophylactique.

propinquity *n.* proximité *f.;* parenté *f.*

propitiate *v.t.* rendre propice; apaiser. *v.i.* faire expiation.

propitiation *n.* propitiation *f.,* expiation *f.*

propitiatory *adj.* propitiatoire.

propitious *adj.* propice; favorable.

propitiously *adv.* d'une manière propice, favorablement.

proponent *n.* auteur *m.* d'une proposition.

proportion *n.* proportion *f.;* rapport *m.;* dimensions; raison *f.* **in ~,** en proportion, à proportion. **out of ~,** disproportionné. *v.t.* proportionner.

proportionally *adv.* proportionnellement, en proportion.

proportionate *adj.* proportionné. *v.t.* proportionner, rendre proportionnel.

proposal *n.* offre *f.,* proposition *f.*

propose *v.t.* offrir, présenter. *v.i.* se proposer.

proposition *n.* proposition *f.*

propound *v.t.* proposer; offrir; exposer.

proprietary *adj.* de propriétaire; privé, libre.

proprietor *n.* propriétaire *m.* et *f.*

proprietorship *n.* état d'être propriétaire.

propriety *n.* convenance *f.,* bienséance *f.,* propriété *f.*

propulsion *n.* propulsion *f.*

propulsive *adj.* propulseur.

prorogate *v.t.* proroger, différer, remettre.

prorogation *n.* prorogation *f.*

prosaic *adj.* prosaïque.

proscribe *v.t.* proscrire; interdire.

proscription *n.* proscription *f.*

prose *n.* prose *f.* ~ *v.t.* écrire en prose; raconter d'une manière fastidieuse. *adj.* de prose, en prose.

prosecute *v.t.* poursuivre, continuer, persévérer dans. *v.i.* attaquer en justice.

prosecution *n.* poursuite *f.;* procès *m.;* poursuites *f.pl.;* accusation *f.*

prosecutor *n.* procureur *m.;* plaignant *m.* **public ~,** ministère *m.* public.

proselyte *n.* prosélyte *m.f.* ~ *v.i.* convertir.

prospect *n.* vue *f.;* exposition *f.,* perspective *f.; Fig.* perspective *f.,* espoir *m.;* rattente *f.;* avenir

m. **he has fine ~s,** il a un bel avenir. **the ~ of future happiness,** l'attente d'un bonheur à venir. *v.t., v.i.* chercher, examiner; explorer des terrains.

prospective *adj.* en perspective, prévoyant, d'approche, de longue-vue.

prospectively *adv.* en perspective, pour l'avenir.

prospectus *n.* prospectus *m.*

prosper *v.t.* faire réussir. *v.i.* prospérer.

prosperity *n.* prospérité *f.*

prosperous *adj.* prospère; favorable; florissant, heureux.

prosperously *adv.* avec prospérité, avec bonheur, heureusement.

prostate *n.* prostate *f.*

prosthesis *n.* prothèse *f.*

prostitute *adj.* prostitué. *n.* prostitueé *f.* **male ~,** prostitué *m.* ~ *v.t.* prostituer.

prostitution *n.* prostitution *f.*

prostrate *adj.* couché, prosterné; abattu. *v.t.* coucher, étendre à plat; jeter par terre, abattre. **to ~ oneself,** se prosterner.

prostration *n.* action de coucher à plat; prosternation *f.;* prostration *f.;* découragement *m.; Méd.* anéantissement *m.*

prosy *adj.* ennuyeux, plat, peu animé; terre à terre.

protagonist *n.* protagoniste *m.f.*

protean *adj.* changeant.

protect *v.t.* protéger; défendre; sauvegarder; garantir; abriter; patronner, encourager, favoriser.

protection *n.* protection *f.,* défense *f.,* garantie *f.,* sûreté *f.,* sauvegarde *f.;* abri *m.;* privilège *m.*

protectionism *n.* protectionnisme *m.*

protectionist *n.* protectionniste *m.*

protective *adj.* protecteur.

protector *n.* protecteur *m.*

protectorate *n.* protectorat *m.*

protégé(e) *n.* protégé(e) *m.f.*

protein *n.* protéine *f.*

protest *v.i.* protester; assurer, certifier, attester. **to ~ against a resolution,** protester contre une résolution *v.t.* protester de; prendre à témoin.

protest *n.* protestation *f.* **to be under ~,** être protesté.

protestant *adj.* protestant *m.*

Protestantism *n.* Protestantisme *m.*

protestation *n.* protestation *f.*

protester *n.* protestataire *m.f.,* manifestant.

protocol *n.* protocole *m.*

prototype *n.* prototype *m.*

protract *v.t.* prolonger, tirer en longueur, faire traîner; allonger en durée.

protraction *n.* prolongation *f.;* remise *f.;* retard *m.*

protractor *n.* rapporteur *m.*

protrude *v.t.* pousser en avant; faire sortir. *v.i.* se pousser en avant; s'avancer, sortir.

protrusion *n.* action de pousser en avant, de faire sortir.

protrusive n. qui avance.

protuberance n. protubérance.

protuberant adj. protubérant, en saillie.

proud adj. fier, orgueilleux, arrogant, altier, présomptueux, hardi; pompeux; beau, noble.

proudly adv. fièrement, avec fierté; orgueilleusement.

prove v.t. prouver; établir; démontrer; éprouver; mettre à l'épreuve; homologuer, vérifier (a will). **to ~ the truth of,** démontrer la vérité de. **to ~ oneself able,** se montrer capable. v.i. faire une épreuve, essayer; se trouver; se trouver être, devenir, se montrer. **to ~ useful,** se trouver ou être reconnu utile. **to ~ incorrect,** se trouver inexact.

proven démontré.

provender n. fourrage m.; provende f.; provisions f.pl.

proverb n. proverbe m.

proverbial adj. proverbial.

provide v.t. pourvoir; fournir, procurer; préparer; approvisionner, donner. **they provide him with clothes,** on le pourvoit de vêtements. **he is provided with,** il a tout ce qu'il lui faut. **to ~ for someone,** pourvoir quelqu'un. **to ~ for the future,** prendre des précautions pour l'avenir. **to ~ against need,** se pourvoir contre le besoin.

provided conj. **~ that,** pourvu que.

providence n. providence f.

provident adj. prévoyant, prudent, sage.

providential adj. providentiel.

providently adv. avec prudence, avec prévoyance.

provider n. pourvoyeur m.

province n. province f., département m.; ressort m.; attributions f.pl., compétence f. **this is not within my ~,** cela ne fait pas partie de mes attributions.

provincial adj. provincial; de province. n. provincial m.

provision n. précaution f.; préparatifs m.pl.; provision f.; **~s pl.,** approvisionnements m.pl.; comestibles m.pl. **to make ~ for someone,** pourvoir aux besoins de quelqu'un. v.t. approvisionner.

provisional adj. provisionnel; provisoire.

proviso n. clause f. conditionnelle.

provocation n. provocation f.

provocative adj. provocateur, provocatrice; provocant; excitant.

provoke v.t. provoquer; exciter; inciter; fâcher, contrarier. **to ~ laughter,** provoquer le rire. **to ~ a smile,** faire sourire. **to ~ a person,** mettre une personne en colère.

provoking adj. provocant; contrariant, impatientant.

provokingly adv. d'une manière provocante.

prow n. proue n.f

prowess n. prouesse f., bravoure f., vaillance f.

prowl v.i. rôder. n. action de rôder.

prowler n. rôdeur m.

proximate adj. prochain, immédiat.

proximately adv. immédiatement.

proximity n. proximité f.

proxy n. procuration f.; fondé m. de pouvoir; délégué m. **to vote by ~,** voter par mandataire.

prude n. prude f.

prudence n. prudence f.

prudent adj. prudent.

prudential adj. de prudence; prudent.

prudentially adv. prudemment.

prudently adv. prudemment.

prudery adj. pruderie f.

prudish adj. prude, de prude.

prune n. pruneau m. v.t. tailler, élaguer, émonder; Fig. rogner, couper, arranger.

pruning n. taille f., élagage m., émondage m.

prurience n. lascivité f.

prurient adj. lascif.

pry v.i. scruter; chercher à pénétrer; fouiller; soulever avec un levie. **to ~ into,** Infml. mettre, fourrer le nez dans.

prying adj. cherchant indiscrètement à savoir; cherchant à pénétrer. n. curiosité f.; indiscrétion f.

psalm n. psaume m.

psalmody n. psalmodie f.

pseudo adj. pseudo, faux.

pseudonyme n. pseudonyme m.

pseudonymous adj. pseudonyme.

psyche n. psyché f.

psychedelic adj. psychédélique.

psychiatrist n. psychiatre m.f.

psychiatry n. psychiatrie f.

psychic n. médium m. **~** adj. psychique; télépathe.

psychological adj. psychologique.

psychologically adv. psychologiquement.

psychologist n. psychologue m.

psychology n. psychologie f.

psychopath n. psychopathe m.f.

puberty n. puberté f.

pubescence n. âge m. de puberté; pubescence f.

pubescent adj. pubère; pubescent.

pubic adj. pubien.

pubis n. pubis m.

public adj. public, publique. n. public m. **in ~,** en public. **~ enemy,** ennemi m. public. **~ figure,** personnalité f., personne f. connue. **~ relations,** relations publiques f.pl.

publication n. publication f.

publicist n. publiciste m.

publicity n. publicité f.; notoriété f.

publicly adv. publiquement.

publish v.t. publier.

publisher n. libraire-éditeur m.; éditeur m.

puce adj. puce.

puck n. palet (hockey).

pucker v.t. rider (skin); plisser, froncer (fabric). n. ride f., pli m., poche f., froncis m.

puddle n. flaque f. mare f.; bourbier m.

pudenda *n.* parties *f.pl.* génitales.

puerile *adj.* puéril.

puerility *n.* puérilité *f.*

puff *n.* souffle *m.* (de vent), bouffée *f.;* rafale *f.;* feuilleté *m.,* chausson *m.* (pastry), vol-au-vent *m.;* houppe *f.* **to give a ~,** souffler. **a ~ of smoke,** une bouffée de fumée. *v.i.* souffler; bouffer, gonfler (cheeks); haleter, boursoufler; faire l'article. **to ~ up,** bouffir; *v.t.* enfler; bouffir; vanter, prôner, faire mousser. **to ~ up,** enfler; bouffir.

puffiness *n.* boursouflure *f.,* gonflement *m.*

puffy *adj.* gonflé; enflé; bouffi; boursouflé, ampoulé, emphatique.

pug *n.* bichon *m.;* carlin *m.* **~ nose,** nez *m.* camus, épaté.

pugilism *n.* pugilat *m.*

pugilist *n.* boxeur *m.*

pugnacious *adj.* batailleur, querelleur.

pugnacity *n.* pugnacité *f.;* disposition batailleuse.

puke *Infml. n.,* vomit *m.* **~** *v.i. Infml.* vomir.

pulchritude *n.* beauté *f.,* grâce *f.;* beauté *f.* morale.

pull *v.t.* tirer; arracher; cueillir. **to ~ hard,** tirer fort. **to ~ around,** tirailler; traîner çà et là, de côté et d'autre. **to ~ along,** traîner avec soi. **to ~ apart,** arracher en deux, séparer. **to ~ away,** tirer, arracher, ôter avec force. **to ~ back,** tirer en arrière, retenir. **to ~ in,** tirer dedans; faire rentrer. **to ~ off,** tirer; ôter; défaire. **to ~ over,** s'arrêter sur le bas-côté. **to ~ out,** tirer; ôter; sortir, produire. **to ~ up,** tirer en haut; lever, hisser; monter; déraciner. *Auto.* avancer.

pullulate *v.i.* pulluler.

pulmonary *adj.* pulmonaire.

pulp *n.* pulpe *f.,* chair *f.,* moelle *f.;* pâte *f.* (paper).

pulpit *n.* chaire *f.;* tribune *f.*

pulpous *adj.* pulpeux.

pulsate *v.i.* battre; avoir des pulsations.

pulsation *n.* pulsation *f.*

pulse *n.* pouls *m.,* pulsation *f.* **weak ~,** pouls faible. **to feel someone's ~,** tâter le pouls à quelqu'un; *Fig.* sonder quelqu'un; tâter le terrain.

pulverization *n.* pulvérisation *f.*

pulverize *v.t.* pulvériser.

puma *n.* puma *m.*

pumice *n.* ponce *f.,* pierre *f.* ponce.

pump *n.* pompe *f.;* escarpin *m.* **air ~,** machine pneumatique. **hand ~,** pompe à bras. **~ handle,** brimbale *f.* de pompe. **to work a ~,** maneuvrer, faire jouer une pompe. *v.i.* pomper. *v.t.* tirer; *Fig.* sonder.

pumpkin *n.* potiron *m.,* citrouille *f.*

pun *n.* calembour *m.* **~** *v.i.* faire des calembours.

punch *n.* coup *m.* de poing; poinçon *m.,* emportepièce *m.* (tool); punch *m.* (drink); polichinelle *m.;* **~bowl,** bol à punch. *v.t.* donner un coup de poing, poinçonner, percer à l'emporte-pièce.

punchy *adj.* qui a du punch, dynamique; qui a la tête brouillé, qui a pris trop de coups de poing.

punctilio *n.* exactitude *f.* minutieuse; formalité *f.*

punctilious *adj.* pointilleux, vétilleux.

punctual *adj.* ponctuel, exact; juste, fidèle.

punctuality *n.* ponctualité *f.*

punctually *adv.* ponctuellement.

punctuate *v.t.* ponctuer.

punctuation *n.* ponctuation *f.*

puncture *n.* piqûre *f.* **~** *v.t.* piquer.

pungent *adj.* piquant, âcre, relevé; pénétrant; poignant.

pungently *adv.* d'une manière piquante.

punish *v.t.* punir.

punishable *adj.* punissable.

punishment *n.* punition *f.*

punitive *adj.* pénal.

punk *n. Infml.* merdeux *m.,* crétin *m.* **punk rock.**

puny *adj.* petit; chétif.

pup *n. v.* puppy.

pupa *n.* pupe *f.,* chrysalide *f.,* nymphe *f.*

pupil *n.* prunelle *f.* élève *m.,* écolier *m.* écolière *f.*

puppet *n.* marionnette *f.;* poupée *f.;* pantin *m.* **~ show,** spectacle *m.* de marionnettes.

puppy *n.* chiot *m.,* petit chien *m.* **~ love,** premier amour *m.*

purchase *v.t.* acheter, faire l'achat de; se procurer. **to ~ an estate,** acheter une terre, des biens immeubles. *n.* achat *m.,* acquisition *f.* **to make a ~,** faire un achat.

purchaser *n.* acquéreur *m.;* acheteur *m.*

pure *adj.* pur, franc; clair, de race.

purely *adv.* purement.

pureness *n.* pureté *f.*

purgative *adj. n.* purgatif *m.*

purgatory *n.* purgatoire *m.*

purge *v.t.* nettoyer; épurer, purifier. *v.i.* se purger. *n.* purge *f.,* purgation *f.*

purification *n.* purification *f.*

purify *v.i.* se purifier; s'épurer.

purist *n.* puriste *m.*

puritan *n.* puritain *m.,* puritaine *f. adj.* puritain.

purity *n.* pureté *f.*

purl *n.* maille *f.* à l'envers. *v.t.* faire une maille à l'envers.

purloin *v.t.* soustraire, dérober, voler; piller.

purple *adj.* pourpre; de pourpre; de pourpre *m.*

purport *n.* sens *m.,* portée *f.;* objet *m.,* dessein *m.,* but *m.;* teneur *f.* **~** *v.i.* tendre à montrer; signifier; vouloir dire; se donner (pour).

purpose *n.* dessein *m.,* intention *f.,* but *m.,* fin *f.,* intérêt *m.,* propos *m.* **on ~,** exprès. **it suits my ~,** cela fait mon affaire. **for what ~?** dans quel but, à quel effet? **to no ~,** en pure perte, en vain. **what ~ would that serve?** à quoi cela servirait-il? *v.i.,v.t.* avoir l'intention; se proposer.

purposeless *adj.* sans but, inutilement.

purposely *adv.* à dessein, exprès.

purr *n.* ronron *m.,* ronronnement *m.* **~** *v.i.* ronronner.

purse *n.* bourse *f.;* prix *m.;* sac *m.;* portefeuille *m.* **to ~ one's lips,** se pincer les lèvres.

pursuance *n.* poursuite *f.,* suite *f.,* conséquence *f.* **in ~ of,** par suite de, en vertu de.

pursuant *adj.* (to), par suite de; conforme à.

pursue *v.t.,v.i.* suivre; poursuivre; chercher. **to ~ an enemy,** poursuivre un ennemi.

pursuit *n.* poursuite *f.;* emploi *m.;* occupations *f.pl.;* travaux *m.pl.*

purulent *adj.* purulent.

purvey *v.t.* fournir, pourvoir, munir. *v.i.* faire des provisions; s'approvisionner.

purveyance *n.* approvisionnement *m.;* provisions *f.pl.*

purveyor *n.* pourvoyeur *m.* **~ to,** fournisseur *m.* de.

pus *n.* pus *m.*

push *v.t.* pousser, frapper, presser, gêner; bousculer. **to ~ away,** éloigner, repousser. **to ~ back,** repousser, faire reculer. **to ~ forward,** avancer. **to ~ in,** faire entrer. **to ~ off,** faire tomber; éloigner; partir. **to ~ on,** pousser; faire avancer. **to ~ out,** pousser dehors, expulser. **to ~ up,** lever, élever; faire monter. **to ~ back,** reculer. **to ~ by,** passer rapidement, brusquement. **to ~ down,** descendre rapidement. **to ~ forward,** se presser; se porter en avant. **to ~ into,** entrer brusquement. **to ~ off,** pousser au large. **to ~ on,** s'avancer. poussée *f.,* impulsion *f.* **a vigorous ~,** un assaut vigoureux. **when ~ comes to shove,** quand le moment critique viendra. **~-up.**

pusher *n.* (drugs) revendeur *m.,* ravitailleur *m.;* arriviste *m.f.*

pushing *adj.* entreprenant, fort, vigoureux.

push pin *n.* punaise *f.*

pushy *adj.* arriviste, arrogant.

pusillanimous *adj.* pusillanime.

pussy *n.* minet *m.,* minou *m.*

pustulate *v.t.* couvrir de pustules, d'ampoules.

pustule *n.* pustule *f.*

put *v.t.* mettre; placer, poser, établir. **to ~ into practice,** mettre en pratique. **to ~ to death,** mettre à mort. **to ~ aside,** mettre de côté. **~ away,** serrer, renvoyer; répudier. **~ that away,** mets ça de côté. **~ back the clock,** retardez l'horloge. **to ~ by,** mettre de côté, économiser. **to ~ down,** mettre à terre, poser; déposer; prendre note de; humilier; rabaisser. **to ~ forth,** avancer, produire; mettre en avant, proposer. **to ~ forward,** avancer. **to ~ in,** mettre dedans; mettre en; *Naut.* relâcher à. **to ~ off,** remettre, ajourner. **to ~ on,** mettre. **~ on your hat,** mettez votre chapeau. **to ~ on trial,** mettre en jugement. **to ~ out,** mettre dehors; renvoyer; éteindre. **to ~ to silence,** faire taire. **to ~ up,** mettre en haut; élever; loger. **to ~ up for sale,** mettre en vente. **to ~ up with,** supporter, tolérer. **to ~ up an umbrella,** ouvrir un parapluie. **to ~ upon,** mettre sur, imposer à. *adj., m.* put on, pretense.

putrefaction *n.* putréfaction *f.*

putrefy *v.i.* se putréfier.

putrid *adj.* putride.

putty *n.* mastic *m.* potée *f.* **~** *v.i.* mastiquer.

puzzle *n.* énigme *f.,* mystère. *v.t.* rendre perplexe. **this child really ~s me,** je n'arrive pas à comprendre cet enfant.

puzzling *adj.* énigmatique, perplexant, incompréhensible.

pyramid *n.* pyramide.

pyre *n.* bûcher *m.* funèbre.

Pyrenees *npr. pl.* Pyrénées *f.pl.*

pyromania *n.* pyromanie *f.*

python *n.* python *m.*

Q

quack *v.i.* caqueter; crier comme l'oie. *n.* charlatan *m.* *adj.* de charlatan. **a ~ medicine,** un remède de charlatan. **~ doctor,** charlatan *m.*

quackery *n.* charlatanisme *f.*

quadrangle *n.* quadrangle *m.*

quadrant *n.* quatrième partie *f.;* quart *m.* de cercle; octant *m.*

quadratic *adj.* quadratique *n.* équation *f.* du second dégré.

quadrennial *adj.* quatriennal.

quadrilaterial *adj.* quadrilatéral. *n.* quadrilatère *m.*

quadruped *adj.* quadrupède *m.*

quadruple *adj.* quadruple. *n.* quadruple. *v.t.* quadrupler.

quaff *v.t.* boire à longs traits; avaler; vider; s'abreuver de; savorer; *Infml.* lamper.

quagmire *n.* fondrière *f.* marécage *m.*

quail *v.i.* perdre courage; faiblir; trembler. *n.* caille *f.*

quaint *adj.* étrange, baroque, bizarre, original; affecté, prétentieux; recherché.

quaintly *adv.* étrangement, drôlement, bizarrement; d'une manière recherchée.

quaintness *n.* étrangeté *f.,* bizarrerie *f.,* originalité *f.,* singularité *f.*

quake *v.i.* trembler; s'agiter. **the earth ~s,** la terre tremble. *n.* tremblement *m.,* frémissement *m.*

Quaker *n.* quaker *m.,* quakeresse *f.*

qualification *n.* qualité *f.* requise, aptitude *f.,* compétence *f.;* capacité *f.;* titre *m.;* diminution *f.;* qualification *f.*

qualified *adj.* capable, apte, propre à; autorisé. **a man well ~ for,** un homme bien capable de.

qualify *v.t.* rendre apte, propre (à), capable (de); mettre en état, autoriser; qualifier. *v.i.* devenir, se rendre capable ou apte.

quality *n.* qualité *f.;* nature *n.f.;* propriété *f.;* disposition *f.;* rang *m.* (nobility). **his good qualities,** ses bonnes qualités. **his bad qualities,** ses défauts. **persons of ~,** personnes de qualité.

qualm *n.* mal *m.* de cœur, nausée *f.;* scrupule *m.*

quandary *n.* doute *m.,* incertitude *f.,* perplexité *f.*

quantitative *adj.* quantitatif.

quantity *n.* quantité *f.*

quarantine *n.* quarantaine *f.;* quarante jours *m.pl.* ~ *v.t.* mettre en quarantaine.

quarrel *n.* querelle *f.;* démêlé *f.;* dispute *f.; Infml.* noise *f.;* brouille *f.* **to pick a ~ with a person,** chercher querelle à quelqu'un, lui chercher des noises. *v.i.* se quereller; se disputer; se chamailler.

quarrelsome *adj.* querelleur.

quarry *n.* carrière *f.* (stone); proie *f.;* gibier *m. v.t.* extraire, tirer (d'une carrière).

quart *n.* quart *m.;* quarte *f.;* quatrième *f.* (in a game).

quarter *n.* quart *m.;* quartier *m.;* terme *m.,* trimestre *m.;* partie *f.,* région *f.* **a ~ of an hour,** un quart d'heure. **every ~,** tous les trimestres. **the four ~s,** les quatre parties. **from all ~s,** de tous côtés. **in high ~s,** en haut lieu. **head~s,** quartier général. **to give no ~,** ne pas faire de quartier. **~deck,** gaillard *m.* d'arrière. **~master,** fourrier *m.;* maréchal *m.* des logis; quartiermaître *m. ~ v.t.* partager, diviser en quarts; loger (soldiers). *v.i.* se loger; prendre ses quartiers.

quarterly *adj.* trimestriel. *n.* revue *f.* trimestrielle. *adv.* par quartier; par trimestre.

quartet *n. Mus.* quatuor *f.*

quarto *n.* in-quarto *m.*

quartz *n.* quartz *m.*

quash *v.t.* aplatir, écraser; anéantir; annuler.

quasi *adj.* quasi, presque.

quatrain *n.* quatrain *m.*

quaver *v.i.* faire un trémolo; trembler; vibrer. *n. Mus.* chevrotement *m.*

quay *n.* quai *m.*

queasiness *n.* mal *m.* au coeur, nausée *f.;* scrupules *m.pl.*

queasy *adj.* qui a mal au coeur, qui éprouve des nausées; nauséabond.

queen *n.* reine *f.;* dame (cards, chess, etc). **~ mother,** reine *f.* mère. *v.t.* faire la reine.

queer *adj.* étrange, singulier; baroque, original. **a ~ place,** une ville étrange.

queerness *n.* bizarrerie *f.,* singularité *f.*

quell *v.t.* réprimer; étouffer; dompter, calmer. *v.i.* s'apaiser, s'éteindre; mourir.

quench *v.t.* éteindre; apaiser; étancher (thirst); apaiser; modérer; étouffer. *v.i.* se refroidir; devenir froid.

quenchable *adj.* qui peut être éteint, apaisé.

querulous *adj.* toujours à se plaindre; chagrin, plaintif.

query *n.* question *f.* ~ *v.i.* demander, questionner. *v.t.* rechercher; s'informer, s'enquérir de; douter de.

quest *n.* recherche *f.,* enquête *f.,* examen *m.;* requête *f.* **in ~ of,** à la recherche de.

question *n.* question *f.,* demande *f.;* problème *m.;* sujet de discussion. **~ mark,** point *m.* d'in-

terrogation. **to ask someone a ~,** faire, poser une question. **to solve a ~,** résoudre un problème. **to put in ~,** mettre en question, révoquer en doute. **what is the ~?** de quoi s'agit-il? **to be out of the ~,** être hors de question. **without ~,** sans doute. *v.i.* questionner, interroger, s'informer. *v.t.* être incertain de; se défier de. **I ~ his prudence,** je me défie de sa prudence.

questionable *adj.* douteux; contestable, suspect.

questionably *adv.* avec doute.

questionnaire *n.* questionnaire *f.*

quibble *n.* argutie *f.,* chicane *f.,* quolibet *m.* ~ *v.i.* ergoter; chicaner, couper les cheveux en quatre.

quick *adj.* vif; vivant, prompt, pressé; agile; actif, rapide; intelligent. **the ~ and the dead,** les vivants et les morts. **a ~ eye,** un oeil vif. **~ step,** pas accéléré. *adv.* vite, vivement, promptement. *n.* vif *m.;* chair *f.* vive. **to cut, to touch to the ~,** piquer au vif. **~sand,** sable *m.* mouvant. **~witted,** à l'esprit vif.

quicken *v.t.* hâter, accélérer; stimuler. **to ~ one's steps,** accélérer ses pas.

quickly *adv.* rapidement, vivement, promptement, lestement, vite; tôt.

quickness *n.* hâte *f.,* vitesse *f.,* promptitude *f.,* rapidité *f.,* célérité *f.;* vivacité *f.* (intelligence); finesse *f.*

quicksilver *n.* vif-argent *m.,* mercure *m.*

quiescence *n.* repos *m.,* tranquillité *f.* (of mind), quiétude *f.*

quiescent *adj.* en repos; calme, tranquille.

quiet *adj.* tranquille; calme; paisible. **to be ~,** être ou rester tranquille. *n.* repos *m.;* tranquillité *f.,* calme *m.,* quiétude *f.;* paix *f.* ~ *v.t.* tranquilliser, calmer, apaiser; assoupir.

quietly *adv.* paisiblement, tranquillement.

quietness *n.* tranquillité *f.,* calme *m.,* paix *f.,* repos *m.*

quietude *n.* quiétude *f.* tranquillité *f.* calme *m.* repos *m.*

quill *n.* plume *f.* piquant *m.* (porcupine).

quilt *n.* édredon *m.;* courte-pointe *f.* couvre-pied *m.* piqué.

quince *n.* coing *m.* **~ tree,** cognassier *m.*

quintessence *n.* quintessence *f.*

quintuple *adj.* quintuple. *v.t.* quintupler.

quip *n.* raillerie *f.* ~ *v.t.* railler.

quirk *n.* détour *m.,* biais *m.,* finesse *f.,* fauxfuyant *m.,* argutie *f.,* chicane *f.,* sarcasme *m.*

quit *v.t.* quitter, abandonner, laisser, arrêter. **to give notice to ~,** donner congé. **to ~ a job,** se démettre d'un emploi.

quite *adv.* tout à fait, complètement. **~ recent,** très récent. **~ cold,** tout froid.

quits *adv.* quitte. **to call it ~,** cesser.

quittance *n.* quittance *f.;* acquit *m.;* récompense *f.;* retour *m.*

quitter *n.* celui qui quitte, qui abandonne; *Infml.* lâcheur *m.*

quiver *n.* carquois *m.* ~ *v.i.* trembler, frissonner.

quivering *n.* tremblement *m.;* frissonnement *m.*

quiz n. test m. ~ v.t. tester; poser des questions à.

quota n. quote-part f., quotité f.; contingent m., quota m.

quotation n. citation f.; Comm. cote f.; cours m.

quote v.t. citer; Comm. coter, marquer.

quotient n. quotient m.

R

Rabbi n. rabbin m.

rabbinical adj. rabbinique.

rabbit n. lapin m. tame ~, lapin domestique. wild ~, lapin de garenne.

rabble n. cohue f.; populace f., canaille f.

rabid adj. féroce, furieux, enragé (animal), forcené; dévorant.

rabies n. rage f.

raccoon n. raton laveur m.

race n. race f.; lignée f.; lignage m.; course f., marche f.; raz m. boat ~, régate f.; course aux canots. to win the ~, remporter la course. ~course, champ m. de course. ~horse, cheval m. de course. v.i. courir vite; lutter à la course.

racer n. coureur m., cheval m. de course.

racism n. racisme m.

racist n. raciste m.f.

rack n. roue f. (torture); chevalet m.; Fig. torture; dressoir m. (dishes) (clock) rochet m. bottle ~, porte-bouteilles m. hat~, porte-chapeaux m. ~ v.t. to ~ one's brain, se casser la tête. to ~ up, accumuler, gagner.

racket n. tapage m.; caquetage m.; raquette f., battoir m. what a ~ they made! quel vacarme ils ont fait!

racketeer n. racketteur m.

racketeering n. racket m.

racking adj. atroce, insoutenable.

racy adj. impropre; fort spiritueux; qui a du bouquet; vigoureux (language, style).

radar n. radar m.

radial adj. radial.

radiance n. éclat m., splendeur f.

radiant adj. radieux, resplendissant; brillant; rayonnant. n. point m. lumineux.

radiantly adv. en rayonnant; avec éclat.

radiate v.i. rayonner. v.t. éclairer, illuminer. adj. radié.

radiation n. rayonnement m., radiation f.

radiator n. Auto. radiateur m.; calorifère m. (heat). ~ cap, bouchon m. de radiateur.

radical adj. radical; fondamental. n. radical m.

radicalism n. radicalisme m.

radically adv. radicalement.

radio n. radio f. ~ v.t. télégraphier, envoyer un message par radio.

radiography n. radiographie f.

radiology n. radiologie f.

radish n. radis m., rave f. horse~, raifort m.

radium n. radium m.

radius n. (pl. radii) rayon m.; Anat. radius m.

raffle n. loterie f. ~ v.i. faire une loterie. v.t. mettre en loterie.

raft n. radeau m., train m. de bois. v.t. mener sur un radeau.

rag n. guenille f., loque f., haillon m., lambeau m.; au pl. drilles f., chiffons m.pl. to be all in ~s, être en loques, être déguenillé.

ragamuffin n. gueux m., maroufle m., voyou m.

rage n. fureur f., rage f., emportement m.; (of things) violence f., furie f.; passion f.; vogue f. to be in a ~, être en colère, en fureur. the ~ of a storm, la fureur d'une tempête. v.i. être furieux, s'emporter, tempêter; pester, sévir.

ragged adj. déchiré, déguenillé; en haillons, en loques; déchiqueté.

raging adj. furieux, en fureur, courroucé; enrageant, impétueux, violent. n. rage f., fureur f., courroux m.; violence f.

raid n. raid m., incursion f., irruption f., descente f.

rail n. barre f., barreau m., grille f., barrière f.; garde-fou m., barre f., d'appui (window); rampe f. (stairs). to run off the ~s, dérailler. to lay down the ~s, poser les rails. running off the ~s, déraillement m. by ~, en chemin de fer. v.t. enclore d'une grille, griller. v.i. injurier, invectiver. to ~ off, séparer avec une grille. to ~ at, outrager, déclamer contre.

railing adj. injurieux, outrageant. n. moquerie f., ricanement m., raillerie f.; paroles f.pl. outrageantes; clôture f.; palissade f.

raillery n. raillerie f., moquerie f.

railroad n. chemin de fer, voie f. ferrée. ~ station, station f., gare f. du chemin de fer.

rain v.i. pleuvoir. it's raining cats and dogs, il pleut des hallebardes. n. pluie f. pouring ~, averse f. ~drop, goutte f. de pluie.

rainbow n. arc-en-ciel m.

raincoat n. imperméable m.

rainy adj. pluvieux, de pluie; à la pluie.

raise v.t. lever, élever; soulever; relever; hausser; rehausser, ériger, bâtir; faire pousser (plants); se procurer (money); ressusciter (les morts). to ~ money, faire ou se procurer de l'argent. to ~ the price, augmenter le prix. to ~ expectations, faire concevoir des espérances.

raisin n. raisin m. sec.

raising n. action de lever, d'élever; élévation f.; soulèvement m., augmentation f., accroissement m.; élevage m. (cattle, plants, etc.); levée f. (troops, siege); perception f. (tax).

rake n. râteau m., ratissoire f.; mauvais sujet, libertin m., débauché m. ~ v.t. racler; Agr. râteler; Hort ratisser. to ~ off, enlever au râteau. to ~ up, ramasser; fouiller dans, chercher. to ~ together, ramasser. v.i. gratter.

rally v.t. railler, plaisanter. v.i. (se) rallier; (se) réunir; (se) rassembler; badiner, se moquer. n. ralliement m.; raillerie f., moquerie f.

ram n. bélier m.; *Astron.* le Bélier m., Aries; hie f. **battering ~,** bélier m. ~ v.t. enforcer, battre (à coups de hie), tasser, bourrer, rembourrer, farcir.

ramadan n. ramadan.

ramble v.i. courir çà et là, flâner; radoter; n. balade f., excursion f.

rambling adj. errant; eflânant. ~ **thoughts,** des pensées vagabondes. n. promenade f., flânerie f., divagations f.pl.

ramification n. ramification f.

ramp n. rampe f.; plain incliné m.

rampage n. déchaînement m. ~ v.t. saccager, se déchaîner.

rampant adj. surabondant, exubérant, effréné; rampant.

rampart n. rampart m.

ramshackle adj. délabré; qui menace ruine.

ranch n. ranch m. ~ **house,** maison f. rustique (one-story).

rancher n. propriétaire m.f. d'un ranch.

rancid adj. rance.

rancor n. rancune f.; haine f.

rancorous adj. rancunier.

rancorously adv. avec rancune; avec animosité.

random at ~, au hasard. adj. au hasard, fait au hasard; shot, coup perdu.

range v.t. ranger; aligner; arranger, mettre en ordre; classer; errer; parcourir; franchir, longer. **to ~ the forest,** parcourir la forêt. **to ~ the coast,** ranger la côte. v.i. **to ~ along,** se promener le long de. ~ rangée f.; file f., chaine f. (mountains); rang m., série f.; champ m., carrière f., étendue f.; grille f., fourneau m. (etc.); *Artill.* portée f. **a vast ~,** une vaste étendue. ~ **of observation,** cercle m. d'observation.

ranger n. garde m. forestier; chien m. courant; gendarmerie f. à cheval.

rank n. rang m., rangée f., grade m., classe f. **the ~ of captain,** le grade de capitaine. v.t. ranger, arranger. v.i. etre rangé, se ranger, prendre rang, figurer. **to ~ high,** occuper un haut rang. adj. rance. **a ~ poison,** un poison violent. **it is ~ idolatry,** c'est une idolâtrie grossière. ~ **butter,** du beurre rance.

rankle v.i. (s')ulcérer, (s')envenimer; s'irriter. v.t. aigrir, irriter.

rankness n. rancidité f.; rance m.

ransack v.t. saccager; piller, fouiller.

ransom n. rancon f., rachat m. ~ v.t. racheter; rançonner.

rant v.i. déclamer avec extravagance, extravaguer, tempêter. n. divagation f.

rap v.i. frapper; cogner, heurter. **to ~ at the door,** frapper à la porte. n. coup m. sec, tape f. **a ~ on the knuckles,** un coup sur les doigts. **he took the ~ for all of them,** il s'est fait punir pour eux tous.

rapacious adj. rapace.

rapaciously adv. avec rapacité.

rapacity n. rapacité f.

rape n. viol m. dévastation f. ~ **crisis center,** centre d'accueil pour les femmes violées. v.t. violer.

rapid adj. rapide m.

rapidity n. rapidité f.

rapidly adv. rapidement.

rapine n. rapine f.

rapist n. violeur m., auteur d'un viol m.

rapport n. rapport m. **they have established a good ~ with each other,** elles ont établi un bon rapport entre elles.

rapt adj. profond, intense; ravi, enchanté.

rapture n. ravissement m., transport m., extase f., enthousiasme m.

rare adj. rare, inusité; raréfié; *Culin.* saignant.

rarefaction n. raréfaction f.

rarefy v.i. (se) raréfier.

rarely adv. rarement, peu souvent.

rarity n. rareté f.; raréfaction f., ténuité f.

rascal n. coquin m., fripon m., canaille f.

rash adj. téméraire; irréfléchi, étourdi, inconsidéré. n. éruption f., rougeur f.

raspberry n. framboise f. ~ **bush,** framboisier m.

rat n. rat m. ~ **trap,** ratière f. **to smell a ~,** *Fig.* se douter de quelque piège.

rate n. prix m.; *Comm.* cours m.; degré m., rang m.; vitesse f.; taxe f., contribution f.; taux m.; proportion, raison f. **at a high ~,** à un taux élevé. **at any ~,** à quelque prix que ce soit. **a first-~ article,** un article de première qualité. **at a great ~,** à une grande vitesse. v.t. évaluer, imposer, taxer, tarifier; estimer; compter, calculer. v.i. faire une appréciation, une évaluation, une estimation. **to ~ as,** être classé comme, être estimé à.

rather adv. plutôt, un peu; de préference. **anything ~ than,** tout plutôt que. **I would ~,** j'aimerais mieux. **she is ~ pretty,** elle est assez jolie.

ratification n. ratification f.

ratify v.t. ratifier.

rating n. estimation f.; évaluation f.

ratio n. proportion f., rapport m.; *Math.* raison f. **in the ~ of,** dans le rapport de.

ration n. ration f.

rational adj. raisonnable; intelligent; raisonné; rationnel; judicieux.

rationale n. analyse f. raisonnée.

rationalism n. rationalisme m.

rationalist adj., n. rationaliste.

rationality n. rationalité f.; raison f., justesse f.

rationally adv. rationnellement; raisonnablement.

rattle v.i. faire du bruit; résonner. v.t. faire résonner, faire retentir; râler. **to ~ away,** aller toujours. n. bruit m., fracas m. cliquetis m., caquet m.; crécelle f., hochet m.; râle f. ~ **of chains,** cliquetis des chaînes. **death ~,** le râle de la mort. **~snake,** serpent m. à sonnettes.

rattling n. bruit m.; bruissement m. ~ adj. bruyant, étourdissant.

raucous *adj.* rauque.

ravage *n.* ravage *m.*, désolation *f.* ~ *v.t* ravager.

ravager *n.* ravageur *m.*, dévastateur *m.*

rave *v.i.* être en délire, avoir le délire, délirer; extravaguer. **she was raving about her work**, elle faisant l'éloge de son travail.

raven *n.* corbeau *m.*

ravenous *adj.* vorace.

ravenously *adv.* avec voracité.

ravine *n.* ravin *m.*, ravine *f.*

raving *adj.* en délire, extravagant; fou, furieux; frénétique. ~ **mad**, fou à lier. *n.* délire *m.*

ravish *v.t.* ravir, charmer; violer; enlever.

ravishing *adj.* ravissant, charmant.

ravishingly *adv.* à ravir.

ravishment *n.* ravissement *m.*

raw *adj.* cru, vif, écorché; brut; âpre (weather); froid; inexpérimenté; neuf. ~ **meat**, viande crue. ~ **flesh**, chair vive. ~ **material**, matière première.

ray *n.* rayon *m.*, éclat *m. Ichth.* raie *f.* ~ *v.t.* rayer, rayonner, darder.

raze *v.t.* raser.

razor *n.* rasoir *m.* ~ **blade**, lame *f.* de rasoir.

re *prep.* ~ **the memo**, concernant les notes.

reach *v.t.* tendre, atteindre, toucher, parvenir à, arriver à. to ~ **the ceiling**, toucher, atteindre le plafond. to ~ **home**, arriver chez soi. **the letter reached me at noon**, la lettre m'est parvenue à midi. to ~ **the ears of**, arriver aux oreilles de. *v.i.* s'etendre. to ~ **after**, s'efforcer, tâcher de parvenir à. to ~ **in, into**, pénétrer dans. *n.* extension *f.*; portée *f.*, capacité *f.* **out of** ~, hors d'atteinte.

react *v.i.* réagir.

reaction *n.* réaction. *f.*

reactionary *adj.* réactionnaire.

reactive *adj.* réactif.

reactor *n.* réacteur *m.*

read *v.t.,v.i.* lire. to ~ **aloud**, lire à haute voix. to ~ **over**, parcourir.

read *adj.* instruit, versé. **well ~**, savant, érudit. **he is well ~ in history**, il connaît bien l'histoire; il est fort en histoire.

readable *adj.* lisible; intéressant.

reader *n.* lecteur *m.*; **proof-~**, correcteur *m.*

readily *adv.* volontiers; aisément.

readiness *n.* promptitude *f.*, empressement *m.*, bonne volonté; facilité *f.*

reading *n.* lecture *f.*, interprétation *f.* ~ **room**, salon *m.* de lecture.

readjust *v.t.* rajuster.

readjustment *n.* rajustement *m.*

ready *adj.* prêt, disposé; prompt, vif, facile. **I'm ~**, je suis prêt(e). **she is ~ for him**, elle l'attend d'un pied ferme. *adv.* tout prêt, **~-made**, tout fait, confectionné. **~-to-wear clothes**, des vêtements de prêt à porter.

real *adj.* réel, vrai, véritable. ~ **estate**, biens immobiliers. *Infml.* **get ~!** arrête tes conneries!

realism *n.* réalisme *m.*

realist *n.* réaliste *m.*

realistic *adj.* réaliste.

reality *n.* réalité *f.*

realizable *adj.* réalisable.

realization *n.* réalisation *f.*

realize *v.t.* se rendre compte de; réaliser; considérer, admettre comme réel; sentir dans toute sa force; gagner. to ~ **a large profit**, faire de gros bénéfices.

really *adv.* réellement, en réalité; en effet.

realm *n.* royaume *m.*; domaine *m.*

realtor *n.* agent *m.* immobilier.

realty *n.* biens immeubles *m.pl.*

reanimate *v.t.* ranimer.

reap *v.t.* moissonner; couper; gagner, en tirer. *v.i.* faire la moisson.

reaper *n.* moissonneur *m.*

reaping *n.* moisson *f.*; récolte *f.* ~ **time**, moisson *f.*

reappear *v.i.* réapparaître.

reappearance *n.* réapparition *f.*

reappoint *v.t.* renommer; instituer, fixer de nouveau.

reappointment *n.* seconde nomination *f.*

rear *n.* arrière; le queue en arrière; le dernier. **~guard**, arrière-garde. *n.* derrière *m.*; dernier rang. *v.t.* élever; cultiver; faire l'éducation de; construire. to ~ **a large family**, élever une nombreuse famille. *v.i.* se cabrer.

rearmament *n.* réarmement *m.*

rearrange *v.t.* réarranger, remettre en order.

reason *n.* raison *f.*; cause *f.*, motif *m.* **it stands to ~**, il va sans dire. **for a good ~**, pour une bonne raison. **by ~ of**, à cause de. **you have ~ for alarm**, vous avez sujet d'être alarmé. *v.i.*, *v.t.* raisonner, discuter. to ~ **with**, raisonner. to ~ **out**, amener par le raisonnement.

reasonable *adj.* raisonnable.

reasonably *adv.* raisonnablement.

reasoning *n.* raisonnement *m.*; argumentation *f.*

reassemble *v.t.*, *v.i.* (se)rassembler.

reassert *v.t.* réaffirmer.

reassurance *n.* réassurance *f.*

reassure *v.t.* rassurer; réassurer.

rebate *v.t.* rabattre; diminuer. *n.* rabais *m.*, escompte *m.*; diminution *f.*

rebel *n.* rebelle *m.* ~ *v.i.* se révolter.

rebellion *n.* rébellion *f.*

rebellious *adj.* rebelle.

rebelliously *adv.* en rebelle.

rebirth *n.* renaissance *f.*; renouveau *m.*

reborn *adj.* né à nouveau; réincarné.

rebound *v.t.* (faire) rebondir, (faire) rejaillir; renvoyer. *n.* rebondissement *m.*; contre-coup *m.*, renvoi *m.*

rebroadcast *n.* retransmission *f.* ~ *v.t.* retransmettre.

rebuff *n.* échec *m.*; refus *m.*, rebuffade *f.* ~ *v.t.* rebuter, repousser.

rebuke *v.t.* gronder; réprimander; blâmer, reprocher, faire des reproches. *n.* réprimande *f.*; blâme *m.*, reproche *m.*

rebuild v.t. reconstruire.

rebus n. rébus m.

rebut v.t. repousser, rebuter; v.i. se retirer, reposter.

recalcitrant adj. récalcitrant.

recall v.t. rappeler, retracter, révoquer. n. rappel m.; révocation f.; rétraction f.

recant v.t. désavouer; revenir sur. v.i. (se) rétracter.

recantation n. rétractation f.; désaveu m.

recap n. abbr. **recapitulation**, récapitulation f.; v.i. récapituler; en résumé; réchapper.

recapitulate v.t. récapituler.

recapitulation n. récapitulation f.

recapture n. reprise f.; rescousse f. ~ v.t. reprendre.

recast v.t. refondre; mouler de nouveau; Théât. change les rôles/la distribution f. des rôles.

recede v.i. reculer; rétrograder; se retirer; se désister.

receipt n. reçu m., ticket m., de caisse. **give me a ~,** donnez-moi un reçu. **on ~ of,** au reçu de. **acknowledgment of ~,** accusé m. de réception. v.t. donner un reçu de.

receivable adj. recevable; admissible.

receive v.t. recevoir; accueillir; toucher (money); recéler (stolen goods).

receiver n. récepteur m.; celui qui reçoit; receveur m., consignataire m.; recéleur m. (stolen goods).

receiving n. réception f.; recel m.

recension n. révision f.; revue f.; examen m.; recensement m., énumération f.

recent adj. récent.

recently adv. récemment.

receptacle n. réceptacle m., récipient m.

reception n. réception f.; accueil m. **~ of a letter,** réception d'une lettre. **to give one a good ~,** faire bon accueil à quelqu'un.

receptionist n. réceptionniste m.f.

receptive adj. réceptif.

recess n., ajournement m.; récréation f. (school); Architect. renfoncement m., niche f.; vacances f.pl.

recession n. récession f.; régression f., recul m.

recidivist adj.n. récidiviste (m.f.).

recipe n. recette f.

recipient n.; m. destinataire m.f. (mail); bénéficiaire (money).

reciprocal adj. réciproque (f.).

reciprocally adv. réciproquement, mutuellement.

reciprocate v.i. rendre (la pareille); agir réciproquement. v.t. échanger, donner par réciprocité.

reciprocity n. réciprocité f.

recital n. récit m., narration f., répétition f.; exposé m.; énumération f. (details); Mus. récital m.

recitation n. récitation f.; répétition f.

recite v.t réciter; raconter.

reckless adj. téméraire, insouciant; indifférent.

recklessly adv. témérairement; hardiment.

recklessness n. insouciance f., témérité f., hardiesse f.

reckon v.t. compter, calculer, estimer, apprécier. Infml. supposer.

reckoning n. compte m., calcul m.; écot m., note f. à payer.

reclaim v.t. réclamer; revendiquer; corriger, réformer; dompter, dresser, amender. **to ~ marshland,** dessécher un marécage.

reclaimable adj. qui peut être réclamé; qui peut être amendé, corrigé.

reclamation n. réforme f., amendement m., correction f.; rentrée f. en possession.

recline v.t. (faire) pencher; appuyer d'un côte ou de côté. v.i. s'appuyer, reposer sur.

reclining adj. penché, incliné.

recluse adj.n. reclus (m.).

reclusive adj. de reclus; solitaire.

recognition n. reconnaissance f.

recognizable adj. reconnaissable.

recognize v.t. reconnaitre.

recoil v.i. reculer; lâcher pied; se retirer. **to ~ from,** se dédire; se révolter de. n. recul m.; reculade f.; contre-coup m. (gun).

recollect v.t. se rapeler, se souvenir de.

recollection n. souvenir m.; réminiscence f.; mémoire f. **to have some ~ of,** avoir quelque souvenir de.

recommence v.t. recommencer.

recommend v.t. recommander.

recommendation n. recommandation f.

recompense v.t. récompenser; dédommager; réparer. n. compensation f.; récompense f.; dédommagement m., réparation f.

recompose v.t. calmer, remettre; refaire, seressaisir.

reconcilable adj. conciliable; conciliable, compatible.

reconcile v.t. réconcilier, mettre d'accord, concilier, arranger. **to be reconciled with to,** être réconcilié avec.

reconciliation n. réconciliation f.; conciliation f.

recondite adj. secret; profond.

reconnaissance n. reconnaissance f.

reconnoiter v.t. reconnaître; faire la reconnaissance de.

reconsider v.t. considerer de nouveau; revenir sur.

reconsideration n. nouvel examen m., nouvelle réflexion f.

reconstitution n. reconstitution f.

reconstruct v.t. reconstruire.

reconstruction n. reconstruction f. (crime) reconstitution f.

record v.t. enregistrer; inscrire; rapporter, rappeler. n. registre m., copie f. authentique (document); procès-verbal m.; archives f.pl.; annales f.pl.; record m.; disque m. **on ~,** enregistré; rapporté par l'histoire. **he keeps the ~,** il tient le record. **the ~s, of past ages,** les annales des siècles passés. **~ office,** bureau des archives; greffe *m.*

recorder *n.* greffier *m.,* archiviste *m.;* juge *m.; Mus.* flageolet *m.;* enregistreur *m.,* magnétophone *m.*

recording *n.* enregistrement *m.;* recensement *m.* **~** *adj.* qui enregistre; qui fait un recensement. **~ studio,** studio *m.* d'enregistrement.

recount *v.t.* recompter; raconter.

recoup *v.t.* récupérer ses pertes, dédommager.

recourse *n.* recours *m.;* accès *m.* **to have ~ to,** avoir recours à, recourir à.

recover *v.t.* recouvrer, retrouver, reprendre; regagner retrouver. **to ~ one's health,** recouvrer la santé. **to ~ one's breath,** reprendre haleine. **to ~ a loss,** réparer une perte. *v.i.* relever de maladie, recouvrer la sante, se remettre, se rétablir, *Law.* obtenir gain de cause.

recovery *n.* recouvrement *m.,* rétablissement *m.,* guérison *f.;* reprise *f.* **past ~,** incurable; sans remède.

recreate *v.t.* délasser. *v.i.* (se) récréer, (se) divertir, se distraire.

recreate *v.t.* récréer, créer une seconde fois.

recreation *n.* récréation *f.,* passe-temps *m.*

recreative *adj.* récréatif.

recriminate *v.t.* récriminer (contre).

recrimination *n.* récrimination *f.*

recriminative, recriminatory *adj.* récriminatoire.

recruit *v.t.* recruter. *v.i.* faire des recrues. *n.* recrue *f.;* renfort *m.*

recruitment *n.* recrutement *m.*

rectangle *n.* rectangle *m.*

rectangular *adj.* rectangulaire.

rectifiable *adj.* rectifiable.

rectification *n.* rectification *f.*

rectify *v.t.* rectifier.

rectitude *n.* rectitude *f.*

recto *n.* recto *m.*

rector *n.* curé *m.;* recteur *m.* (university); supérieur *m.* (religious order).

rectory *n.* cure *f.* presbytère *m.*

rectum *n.* rectum *m.*

recumbent *adj.* couché, incliné; inactif.

recuperate *v.t.* recouvrer, récupérer.

recuperation *n.* récupération *f.*

recur *v.i.* revenir à la pensée; revenir, recourir.

recurrence *n.* retour *m.,* réapparation *f.,* rechute *f.;* recours *m.*

recurrent *adj.* qui revient de temps à autre; qui revient.

recycle *v.t.* recycler, récupérer.

red *adj.* rouge. **to turn ~,** devenir rouge, rougir. *n.* rouge *m.,* roux *m.* **a dark ~,** un rouge foncé. **~ hair,** cheveux roux. **~-hot,** rougi au feu. *f.* **~ tape,** la routine *f.* officielle.

redaction *n.* rédaction *f.,* édition *f.*

redden *v.t.* rougir.

reddish *adj.* rougeâtre.

redecorate *v.t.* repeindre, refaire à neuf.

redeem *v.t.* racheter, delivrer; dégager; retirer.

redeemable *adj.* rachetable.

Redeemer *n.* sauveur *m.,* libérateur *m.;* le Rédempteur *m.*

redeeming *adj.* qui rachète, réparateur.

redemption *n.* délivrance *f.;* rédemption *f.;* rachat *m.*

redeployment *n.* réorganisation *f.,* restructuration *f.*

redevelop *v.t.* remodeler; reconstruire.

red-handed *adj.* **he was caught ~,** il s'est fait prendre la main dans le sac.

redistribute *v.t.* redistribuer.

redistribution *n.* redistribution *f.*

redness *n.* rougeur *f.;* rouge *m.,* couleur *f.* rouge.

redolence *n.* senteur *f.,* odeur *f.* agréable, parfum *m.*

redolent *adj.* odorant, odoriféable, parfumé.

redouble *v.t.,v.i.* redoubler.

redoubtable *adj.* redoutable.

redound *v.i.* rejaillir, retomber, revenir.

redress *v.t.* mettre en ordre, redresser, rectifier, faire justice. **to ~ grievances,** réformer des abus. *n.* soulagement *m.;* redressement *m.,* réparation *f.* (of wrongs); justice *f.*

reduce *v.t.* réduire, diminuer, soumettre, dégrader, baisser. **to ~ to despair,** réduire au désespoir.

reduction *n.* réduction *f.;* diminution *f.,* amoindrissement *m.*

redundancy *n.* superfluité *f.,* surabondance *f.,* redondance *f.*

redundant *adj.* superflu, surabondant, excessif, exubérant; redondant.

reduplicate *v.t.* doubler. *adj.* double.

reduplication *n.* redoublement *m.*

reed *n. Bot.* roseau *m.,* pipeau *m.,* flèche *f.; Mus.* chalumeau *m.,* anche *f.*

re-educate *v.t.* rééduquer.

re-education *n.* rééducation *f.*

reef *n.* ris *m.*

reek *n.* fumée *f.,* puanteur *f.,* vapeur *f.,* exhalaison *f.* **~** *v.i.* fumer, exhaler une vapeur, pousser des exhalaisons.

reel *n.* dévidoir *m.,* bobine *f.* **~** *v.t.* dévider; *v.i.* chanceler, vaciller, trébucher.

re-elect *v.t.* réélire.

re-election *n.* réélection *f.*

re-enact *v.t.* ordonner de nouveau; reconstituer (crime).

re-enactment *n.* remise *f.* en vigueur, rétablissement *m.;* reconstitution *f.* (crime).

re-enter *v.t.* rentrer.

re-establish *v.t.* rétablir.

re-establishment *n.* rétablissement *m.;* restauration *f.*

re-examine *v.t.* revoir; examiner de nouveau.

ref *n.* (*abbr.* **referee**) arbitre *m.*

refectory *n.* réfectoire *m.*

refer *v.t.* renvoyer, rapporter, adresser. **to ~ the reader to a note,** renvoyer le lecteur à une note. *v.i.* (se) référer, se rapporter à; s'en référer, s'en rapporter.

referee *n.* arbitre *m.* ~ *v.t.* arbitrer.

reference *n.* rapport *m.*, allusion *f.*, renvoi *m.*; renseignements *m.pl.*; recommandations *f.pl.*; références *f.pl.* **to have good ~s**, avoir de bonnes recommandations, références. **by ~ to**, en s'adressant à, à l'égard de. **to have no ~ to**, ne pas se rapporter à. **he made ~ to**, il a fait allusion à.

referendum *n.* référendum.

refill *n.* cartouche *f.*; recharge *f.* ~ *v.t.* faire le plein, remplir.

refine *v.t.* clarifier. **to ~ sugar**, raffiner du sucre. *v.i.* (se)raffiner, (se)'épurer, (se)polir.

refined *adj.* raffiné; clarifié; affiné; poli, élégant.

refinement *n.* raffinement *m.*, poli *m.*, politesse *f.*; affinage *m.*, raffinage *m.*

refinery *n.* affinerie *f.* (metals), raffinerie *f.* (sugar, etc.).

refining *n.* épuration *f.*, raffinage *m.*, affinage *m.*; raffinement *m.*

refit *v.t., v.i.* réparer, préparer de nouveau; (ship); réparer des avaries; se radouber.

reflate *v.t.* relancer (economy).

reflect *v.t.* réfléchir, refléter, rejaillir, retomber sur. **I have ~ed on it**, j'y ai réfléchi. **to ~ on**, faire jaillir sur.

reflecting *adj.* réfléchissant, réfléchi.

reflection *n.* réflexion *f.*; reflet *m.* **upon ~**, en y réfléchissant.

reflective *adj.* réfléchissant; réflecteur.

reflector *n.* réflecteur *m.*

reflex *adj.* réflexe, par réflexion; *n.* réflexion *f.*

reforest *v.t.* reboiser.

reforestation *n.* reboisement *m.*

reform *v.t.* (se) réformer, se corriger. *n.* réforme *f.*

re-form *v.t.* reformer.

reformation *n.* réforme *f.*, réformation *f.*

reformatory *n.* pénitencier *m.*, maison *f.* de correction.

reformer *n.* réformateur *m.*

refract *v.t.* réfracter.

refraction *n.* réfraction *f.*

refractory *adj.* insoumis, indocile, rebelle, réfractaire.

refrain *v.i.* (se) refréner, (se) retenir, se contenir, s'empêcher de. **to ~ from tears**, retenir ses larmes. *n.* refrain *m.*

refresh *v.t.* rafraîchir; récréer, délasser, restaurer; refaire. **to ~ oneself**, se rafraîchir, se remettre.

refreshing *adj.* rafraîchissant. **~ sleep**, sommeil réparateur. **~ rain**, pluie agréable, qui répare.

refreshment *n.* rafraîchissement *m.*, repas *m.*, délassement *m.*

refrigerant *adj., n.* réfrigérant *m.*

refrigerate *v.t.* refroidir.

refrigeration *n.* refroidissement *m.*

refrigerator *n.* réfrigérateur *m.*, frigo *m.*; chambre frigorifique (room).

refuel *v.t.* se ravitailler, faire le plein d'essence.

refueling *n.* ravitaillement.

refuge *n.* refuge *m.*; protection *f.* **to take ~**, se réfugier. *v.t.* donner un refuge, un asile à.

refugee *n.* réfugié *m.*

refulgence *n.* brilliant *m.*, éclat *m.*, splendeur *f.*

refulgent *adj.* brilliant, éclatant, resplendissant.

refund *v.t.* rendre, restituer, rembourser (des fonds). *n.* remboursement *m.*

refurbish *v.t.* remettre à neuf.

refurnish *v.t.* remeubler.

refusal *n.* refus *m.*; première offre; choix *m.* **to meet with a ~**, essuyer un refus.

refuse *v.t., v.i.* refuser.

refuse *adj.* de rebut. *n.* rebut *m.*

refutable *adj.* réfutable.

refutation *n.* réfutation *f.*

refute *v.t.* réfuter.

regain *v.t.* regagner, reprendre; recouvrer; rattraper.

regal *adj.* royal, régalien.

regale *n.* banquet *m.* festin *m.* ~ *v.t.* réjouir; charmer. *v.i.* (se) régaler; être en festin.

regard *v.t.* regarder, considérer; avoir égard à, observer; avoir rapport à. *n.* regard *m.*; égard *m.*; égards *m.pl.*, considération *f.*, respect *m.*; rapport *m.* **without any ~ to**, sans avoir égard à. **out of ~ for you**, par égard pour vous. **in ~, with ~ to**, à l'égard de, quant à. **my ~s to**, mes amitiés à.

regarding *prep.* concernant, touchant, par rapport à, quant à.

regardless *adj.* insouciant, indifférent, peu soigneux. **~ of**, malgré.

regatta *n.* régate *f.*

regency *n.* régence *f.*

regenerate *v.t.* régénérer.

regenerating, regenerative *adj.* régénérateur.

regeneration *n.* régénération *f.*

regent *adj.* régnant; régent. *n.* gouverneur *m.*, régent *m.*, régente *f.*

regime *n.* régime *m.*

regiment *n.* régiment *m.* ~ *v.t.* enrégimenter.

region *n.* région *f.*

register *n.* registre *m.*, greffier *m.* **a church ~**, un registre de paroisse. *v.t.* enregistrer; inscrire; enrôler; immatriculer. **to ~ a letter**, recommander une lettre.

registrar *n.* officier *m.* d'état civil; teneur *m.* des registres, secrétaire-archiviste *m.* **~'s office**, secrétariat *m.* (university).

registration *n.* inscription *f.*, enregistrement *m.*

registry *n.* enregistrement *m.*

regress *v.i.* retourner revenir.

regression *n.* retour *m.*

regressive *adj.* régressif.

regret *n.* regret *m.* ~ *v.t.* regretter; se repentir.

regretful *adj.* plein de regrets.

regretfully *adv.* à/avec regret, à contre-coeur.

regrettable *adj.* regrettable.

regrettably adv. regrettablement, malheureusement.

regroup v.t. (se) regrouper.

regular adj. régulier, réglé, véritable. **a ~ life**, une vie réglée ou régulière. **as ~ as clockwork**, réglé comme une horloge, un papier de musique. un régulier m.

regularity n. régularité f.

regularly adv. régulièrement.

regulate v.t. régler; réglementer; ajuster; diriger.

regulation n. règlement m.

regulator n. régulateur m.

regurgitate v.t. rejeter, rendre; régurgiter. v.i. regorger.

regurgitation n. regorgement m.; régurgitation f.

rehabilitate v.t. réhabiliter.

rehabilitation n. réhabilitation f.

rehearsal répétition f.

rehearse v.t. répéter.

rehouse v.t. reloger.

reign v.i. régner. n. règne m., empire m. **in or during the ~ of**, sous le règne de.

reimburse v.t. rembourser.

reimbursement n. remboursement m.

rein n. rêne f., bride f., guide f., Fig. direction. **to take the ~s**, se saisir des rênes, prendre le pouvoir. **to keep, to hold a tight ~ over**, tenir la bride serrée à. v.t. diriger, conduire avec une bride; brider; contenir, réprimer, refréner.

reindeer n. renne m.

reinforce v.t. renforcer.

reinforcement n. renforcement m.; renforts m.pl.

reinsert v.t. insérer de nouveau.

reinstallment n. réinstallation f.

reinstate v.t. rétablir; réintégrer.

reinstatement n. rétablissement m.; réintégration f.

reinsurance n. reassurance f.

reinsure v.t. réassurer.

reintroduce v.t. réintroduire.

reinvest v.t. replacer.

reinvestigate v.t. rechercher de nouveau.

reinvestment n. replacement m.

reissue v.t. émettre une seconde fois. n. nouvelle émission f.

reiterate v.t. réitérer, répéter, répéter maintes fois.

reiteration n. réitération f.; répétition f.

reject v.t. rejeter.

rejection n. rejet m.

rejoice v.i. (se) réjouir. v.t. réjouir; égayer.

rejoicing n. réjouissance f.; allégresse f.; joie f.

rejoin v.t. rejoindre. v.i. repliquer, repartir.

rejuvenate v.t. rajeunir.

rejuvenation n. rajeunissement m.

rekindle v.t. rallumer; renflammer; réveiller.

relapse v.i. retomber, éprouver une rechute. n. rechute f.

relate v.t. relater, raconter; narrer. v.i. (with **to**) concerner se rapporter à; avoir trait à.

relating adj. concernant; qui a rapport à.

relation n. relation f., rapport m.; parent m., parente f. **in ~ to that**, par rapport à cela, à cet égard. **a distant ~**, un parent éloigné.

relationship n. parenté f.

relative adj. relatif. n. parent m., parente f.; Gram. relatif m.

relatively adv. relativement.

relativity n. relativité f.

relax v.t. relâcher, détendre, desserrer; mitiger; se relâcher de; céder. **to ~ one's mind**, donner du relâche à son esprit, se distraire. v.i. (se) relâcher, se ralentir; se délasser. **to ~ into**, se laisser aller.

relaxation n. relâchement m., relâche m.; délassement m.

relaxing adj. reposant, relaxant.

relay n. relais m. ~ v.t. replacer; retransmettre, relayer.

release v.t. relâcher, élargir; relaxer; dégager. **a new movie was just ~d**, un nouveau film vient de sortir. n. élargissement m.; délivrance f.; mise f. en liberté; abandon m.; remise f. (debt), décharge f.; soulagement m.

relegate v.t. bannir, exiler, reléguer.

relent v.i. se radoucir, s'attendrir, être attendri, se laisser toucher, fléchir.

relentless adj. impitoyable; implacable, inexorable.

relentlessly adv. impitoyablement.

relevance n. pertinence f., à-propos m., convenance f., rapport m., dépendance f.

relevant adj. approprié, applicable; pertinent, convenable.

reliable adj. digne de confiance.

reliance n. confiance f.

relic n. reste m., restes pl., dépouille f. mortelle.

relief n. soulagement m.; adoucissement m., secours m., délivrance f., réparation f.; Art. relief m. **to bring out in ~**, faire ressortir. **high ~**, haut relief.

relieve v.t. soulager, alléger, adoucir, secourir; relever des sentinelles; donner du relief à. **to ~ sufferings**, soulager des souffrances. **to ~ the poor**, secourir les pauvres.

religion n. religion f.

religious adj. religieux.

religiously adv. religieusement.

relinquish v.t. quitter, renoncer à; abandonner, se désister de, se dessaisir de.

relinquishment n. abandon m., reconciation n.f.

relish n. goût m.; saveur, condiment m.; charme m., parfum m. ~ v.t. donner du goût à; Fig. goûter, trouver bon.

relive v.i. revivre.

reload v.t. recharger.

reluctance n. répugnance f., antipathie f., aversion f.

reluctant adj. mal disposé; répugnant à; qui hesite; forcé.

reluctantly adv. avec répugnance, à contre-coeur.

rely v.i. compter sur, faire confiance, se reposer sur.

remain v.i. rester, demeurer. **he ~ed in town,** il resta en ville.

remainder n. reste m., restant m.

remains n. restes m.pl., debris m., dépouille f. mortelle, restes m.pl. mortels, cendres f.pl.

remake v.t. refaire; n. Cine. remake m.

remand v.t. rappeler, contremander; renvoyer à une autre audience.

remark n. remarque f. ~ v.t. remarquer; faire remarquer, faire observer.

remarkable adj. remarquable.

remarkably adv. remarquablement, extraordinairement.

remarry v.t. (se) remarier.

remediable adj. remediable.

remedial adj. réparateur, de rattrapage.

remedy n. remède m. v.t. remédier à; porter remède à.

remember v.t. se souvenir de; se ressouvenir de; se rappeler, rappeler au souvenir. **do you ~ him?** vous souvenez-vous de lui? **if I ~ correctly,** si je m'en souviens bien.

remembrance n. souvenir m.; mémoire f. **in ~ of,** en souvenir de, en mémoire de.

remind v.t. rappeler; remémorer, remettre en mémoire; faire souvenir. **I have to ~ him everyday,** je dois lui rappeler tous les jours.

reminder n. méments m., pense-bête m.; rappel m.

reminisce v.t. raconter ses souvenirs.

reminiscence n. réminiscence f.

reminiscent adj. qui rappelle, qui évoque.

remiss adj. négligent, nonchalant, inattentif; peu ardent.

remission n. remission f., relâchement m.; adoucissement m.; pardon m.

remit v.t. se relâcher de, diminuer, pardonner, Comm. envoyer, remettre, faire remise de. **to ~ money,** envoyer de l'argent. v.i. s'affaiblir, (s')adoucir, (se) calmer.

remittance n. remise f., envoi m.

remnant n. restant m.; coupon m. (fabric) vestige m.; débris m.; invendus m.pl.

remodel v.t. remodeler.

remonstrance n. remontrance f.; avertissement m., protestation f.; ostensoire m.

remonstrate v.i. remontrer.

remorse n. remords m.

remorseful adj. plein de remords, repentant.

remorseless adj. sans remords, impitoyable.

remote adj. éloigné, lointain, de loin, reculé, étranger. **~ country,** pays éloigné. **a ~ idea,** une faible idée. **~ control,** télécommande f., commande f. à distance.

remoteness n. éloignement m.; faible degré m., faiblesse f.

remount v.i. remonter. **to ~ a horse,** remonter à cheval.

removable adj. amovible; transportable.

removal n. éloignement m., renvoi m., destitution f.; levée f.; déplacement m.

remove v.t. éloigner; ôter de, déplacer, enlever, transporter; démettre, destituer (d'un emploi). **to ~ suspicion,** éloigner le soupçon. **~ that chair,** ôtez cette chaise. **to ~ the difficulties,** écarter, faire disparaître, aplanir les difficultés. **to ~ furniture,** emporter des meubles. v.i. changer de place, se déplacer, s'en aller. n. changement m. de place; coup m., degré (relatives).

remover n. dissolvant m. **nail polish ~,** dissolvant m.

remunerate v.t. rémunérer; rétribuer, payer.

remuneration n. rémunération f.

remunerative adj. rémunérateur.

renaissance n. renaissance f.

renal adj. rénal.

rename v.t. rebaptiser.

renard n. renard m.

renascent adj. renaissant.

rend v.t. déchirer, lacérer, fendre. **to ~ the heart,** déchirer, fendre le coeur. **to ~ asunder,** fendre, couper en deux.

render v.t. rendre, donner, remettre; traduire, exprimer. **to ~ a service,** rendre un service.

rendez-vous n. rendez-vous m. ~ v.i. se donner rendez-vous, aller à un rendez-vous; se réunir, donner rendez-vous à, rassembler, réunir.

rendition n. version f.; traduction f.; interprétation f.

renegade n. renégat m.

renege v.i. ne pas tenir (one's word, promise).

renew v.t. renouveler, renouer.

renewal n. renouvellement m.

renounce v.t.,v.i. renoncer à, renier à.

renouncement n. renonciation f.; renoncement m. (au monde).

renovate v.t. renouveler, rénover.

renovation n. rénovation f., renouvellement m.

renovator n. rénovateur m.

renown n. renommée f., renom m.

renowned adj. renommé; distingué, célèbre.

rent n. loyer m. (house), fermage m. (farm); déchirure f., accroc m., fente f., fissure f.; rupture f.; schisme m. ~ v.t. donner à loyer. v.i. (se) louer.

rentable adj. qui peut être loué.

rental n. montant m. de loyer, prix m. de location. adj. de location.

renter n. locataire n.m.

renunciation n. renonciation f.; renoncement m.

reopen v.t. rouvrir.

reorder v.t. passer une nouvelle commande; reclasser, réorganiser.

reorganization n. réorganisation f.

reorganize v.t. réorganiser.

rep n. abbr. **repertory,** repertoire m. abbr. **representative,** représentant.

repair v.t. réparer, raccommoder, rétablir; Naut.

radouber. **to ~ a house,** réparer une maison.
n. réparation *f.,* entretien *m.; Naut.* radoub *m.*
major ~s, grosses réparations. **to undergo ~,**
être en réparation. **to keep in ~,** entretenir. **in
~,** en bon état. **to be out of ~,** être en mauvais
état.

reparable *adj.* réparable.

reparation *n.* réparation *f.;* restauration *f.;*
satisfaction *f.*

repartee *n.* repartie *f.* **~** *v.i.* repartir; riposter.

repay *v.t.* rembourser rendre payer de retour,
récompenser, rendre la pareille.

repayment *n.* remboursement *m.,* payement *m.*

repeal *v.t.* révoquer, rapporter, rappeler, faire
revenir. *n.* abrogation *f.,* révocation *f.;* annulation *f.*

repealable *adj.* révocable.

repeat *v.t.* répéter, réciter; réitérer; redire. *n. Mus.*
reprise *f.,* répétition *f.*

repeatedly *adj.* à plusieurs reprises.

repeating *adj.* à répétition.

repel *v.t.* repousser.

repellent *adj.* répulsif. *n.* **water-~,** imperméable
m. **insect ~,** insecticide *m.*

repent *v.i.,v.t.* se repentir.

repentance *n.* repentir *m.*

repentant *adj.* repentant. *n.* pécheur *m.,* repentant, pénitent *m.*

repercussion *n.* répercussion *f.*

repertoire *n.* répertoire *m.*

repertory *n.* répertoire *m.*

repetition *n.* répétition *f.;* redite *f.; Mus.*
reprise *f.*

replace *v.t.* replacer, restituer; remplacer.

replacement *n.* remise *f.* en place; remplacement *m.*

replenish *v.t.* approvisionner. *v.i.* (se) remplir de
nouveau.

replenishment *n.* action de remplir, de garnir,
de fournir.

replete *adj.* plein, rempli; rassasié.

repletion *n.* satiété *f.,* plénitude *f.;* réplétion *f.*

replica *n.* réplique *f.,* copie *f.,* reproduction *f.*

replicate *adj.* replié. *n.* répétition *f.*

reply *v.t., v.i.* répliquer; répondre; répartir. *n.*
réplique *f.;* réponse *f.*

report *v.t.* rapporter, raconter, annoncer, dire, faire un compte rendu, faire un rapport (sur);
rendre compte de, signaler, dénoncer; se présen-
ters. **a crime was ~ed,** on a signalé un crime.
~ to the supervisor, présentez vous chez le
directeur. **it is reported that,** on dit que; le
bruit court que. *n.* rapport *m.,* compte *m.* rendu;
récit *m.;* reportage *m.;* bulletin *m.;* bruit *m.;*
détonation *f.;* procès-verbal *m.*

reportedly *adv.* aux dires de. **he ~ will not go
to jail,** il n'ira pas en prison selon ses dires.

reporter *n.* journaliste *m.f.,* **court~,** correspondant *m.*

repose *v.t.* mettre au repos; tranquilliser;
confier. *v.i.* (se) reposer. *n.* repos *m.*

repossess *v.t.* reposséder.

reprehensible *adj.* répréhensible.

reprehension *n.* répréhension *f.,* blâme *m.*

reprehensive *adj.* de reproches.

represent *v.t.* représenter.

representation *n.* représentation *f.*

representative *adv.* représentatif. *n.* représentant *m.;* représentation *f.*

repress *v.t.* réprimer.

repression *n.* répression *f.*

repressive *adj.* répressif.

reprieve *v.t.* surseoir à l'execution de; accorder
un sursis à. *n.* sursis *m.,* répit *m.;* délai *m.*

reprimand *v.t.* réprimander; blâmer. *n.* réprimande *f.*

reprint *v.t.* réimprimer. *n.* réimpression *f.*

reprisal *n.* représailles *f.pl.; n.* reprise *f.* **by way
of ~,** par représailles.

reproach *v.t.* reprocher; blâmer; accuser. **to ~
sharply, severely,** faire de vifs reproches à. *n.*
reproche *m.;* blâme *m.*

reproachful *adj.* plein de reproches,
réprobateur.

reproachfully *adv.* avec reproche.

reprobate *adj.* réprouvé. *n.* réprouvé *m.;*
méchant *m.;* vaurien *m.* **~** *v.t.* réprouver.

reproduce *v.t.* reproduire.

reproduction *n.* reproduction *f.*

reproductive *adv.* reproducteur.

reproof *n.* réprimande *f.,* reproche *m.,* répréhension *f.;* réimperméabiliser.

reprovable *adj.* blâmable, répréhensible.

reprove *v.t.* blâmer; réprimander.

reprovingly *adv.* en termes réprobateurs.

reptile *adj.* reptile. *n.* reptile *m.*

republic *n.* république *f.*

republican *adj.,n.* républicain (*m.*).

republish *v.t.* republier.

repudiate *v.t.* répudier.

repudiation *n.* répudiation *f.*

repugnance *n.* répugnance *f.*

repugnant *adj.* répugnant; antipathique. **to be
~ to,** répugner à.

repulse *n.* échec *m.;* refus *m.;* rebuffade *f.* **~** *v.t.*
repousser.

repulsion *n.* répulsion *f.;* action de repousser.

repulsive *adj.* repoussant; rebutant; froid; *Phys.*
répulsif.

repulsiveness *n.* caractere *m.* repoussant,
rebutant.

repurchase *v.t.* racheter. *n.* rachat *m.*

reputable *adj.* estimé; estimable; honorable,
considéré.

reputation *n.* réputation *f.,* renommée. **to gain
a ~,** se faire une réputation.

repute *v.t.* réputer, estimer comme. *n.* réputation
f., renom *m.* **in good ~,** en bonne réputation. **of
~,** renommé.

reputed *adj.* réputé; censé; supposé. **~ father,**
père putatif.

reputedly *adv.* suivant l'opinion commune. **she**

is ~ **wealthy,** elle est prétendument riche.
request *n.* requête *f.,* demande *f.;* prière *f.* **at the**
~ **of,** à la demande de. *v.t.* demander, solliciter;
prier implorer. **to ~ an answer,** demander une
réponse.
requiem *n.* requiem *m.*
require *v.t.* requérir, demander; exiger; réclamer.
this work ~s great attention, ce travail
demande, exige beaucoup d'attention. **two
receipts are ~d,** il faut deux reçus.
requirement *n.* demande *f.;* exigence *f.;* besoin
m., nécessité *f.*
requisite *adj.* indispensable; ce qu'il faut; essentiel. *n.* le nécessaire *m.;* l'indispensable *m.*
requisition *n.* réquisition *f.;* requête *f.*
requital *n.* représaille *f.;* retour *m.;* action *f.;*
réciproque.
rerun *n.* reprise *f.,* rediffusion *f.* ~ *v.i.* courir à
nouveau, rediffuser.
resale *n.* revente *f.*
rescind *v.t.* rescinder; abolir; abroger; annuler.
rescission *n.* rescision *f.;* abrogation *f.;* annulation *f.;* incision *f.*
rescue *v.t.* sauver; délivrer; arracher à. *n.* secours
m., delivrance *f.* (by force). **to the ~,** au secours,
à la rescousse.
rescuer *n.* sauveteur *m.* libérateur *m.;* secouriste
m.f.
research *n.* recherche *f.;* enquête *f.* ~ *v.t.*
rechercher.
researcher *n.* chercheur (euse) *m.f.*
resell *v.t.* revendre.
resemblance *n.* ressemblance *f.*
resemble *v.t.* ressembler à.
resent *v.t.* ressentir; se ressentir de; se venger. **to
~ an affront,** ressentir un affront. **I ~ him for
what he's done to her,** j'éprouve de la rancune
pour ce qu'il lui a fait.
resentful *adj.* plein de ressentiment; haineux;
rancunier.
resentfully *adv.* avec ressentiment.
resentment *n.* ressentiment *m.,* rancune *f.,* hostilité *n.f.*
reservation *n.* réservation *f.;* réserve *f.;* arrière-
pensée *f.;* restriction *f.*
reserve *v.t.* (se) réserver; garder; conserver. *n.*
réserve *f.;* retenue *f.,* réservation *f.;* restriction *f.*
without ~, sans réserve. **in ~,** en réserve.
reserved *adj.* réservé; discret, prudent; froid.
reservoir *n.* réservoir *m.*
reset *v.i.* remettre à l'heure/en place, remonter,
replacer.
resettle *v.t.* rétablir; rassurer.
resettlement *n.* rétablissement *m.;*
réinstallation *f.*
reshape *v.t.* reformer, remodeler.
reside *v.i.* résider; demeurer; habiter.
residence *n.* résidence *f.;* habitation *f.;*
domicile *m.*
resident *adj.* résidant. *n.* résident *m.;*
habitant *m.*

residential *adj.* résidentiel.
residual *adj.* de reste; qui reste, résiduel.
residue *n.* restant *m.,* reste *m.;* résidu *m.*
resign *v.t.* résigner; donner sa démission de;
soumettre, remettre; abdiquer.
resignation *n.* démission *f.* (job); résignation *f.;*
renonciation *f.;* abandon *m.;* soumission *f.,*
patience *f.* **hand in one's ~,** offrir sa
démission.
resigned *adj.* résigné.
resignedly *adv.* avec résignation.
resilience *n.* rejaillissement *m.;* rebondissement *m.*
resilient *adj.* rejaillissant; rebondissant. **she
was very ~ to all those obstacles,** elle a bien
surmonté tous ces obstacles.
resin *n.* résine *f.*
resinous *adj.* résineux.
resist *v.t.,v.i.* résister (à).
resistance *n.* résistance *f.;* opposition *f.;*
rébellion.
resolute *adj.* résolu; déterminé.
resolutely *adv.* résolument.
resoluteness *n.* résolution *f.;* fermeté *f.*
resolution *n.* résolution *f.;* solution *f.;* décision
f.; fermeté *f.* **move a ~,** faire une proposition.
resolve *v.t.* expliquer décider; instruire. **to ~ a
doubt,** éclaircir un doute. *v.i.* (se) résoudre; se
déterminer à; se décider à; se dissoudre; se
liquéfier. *n.* resolution *f.;* détermination arrêtée.
resolvedly *adv.* résolument.
resonance *n.* résonnance *f.*
resonant *adj.* résonnant.
resort *v.i.* avoir recours à; employer; recourir à;
se rendre, hanter. *n.* recours *m.;* ressource *f.;* lieu
fréquenté; refuge *m.,* rendezvous *m.;* station *f.*
estivale/balnéaire; lieu *m.* de sejour; ressort *m.*
last ~, dernier ressort; tribunal sans appel.
resound *v.i.* résonner, répéter. *v.t.* (faire) retentir;
renvoyer le son de.
resounding *adj.* résonnant; faisant écho.
resource *n.* ressource *f.*
resourceful *adj.* plein de resources;
débrouillard, ingénieux.
resourceless *adj.* sans ressource.
respect *v.t.* se rapporter à; respecter, honorer. *n.*
égard *m.,* rapport *m.;* respect *m.,* estime *f.,*
égards *m.pl.;* civilités *f.pl.;* hommages *m.pl.* **in
all ~s, in every ~,** à tous égards, sous tous les
rapports. **in some ~s,** à quelques égards, sous
quelques rapports. **to pay one's ~s,** présenter
ses respects. **to show ~ to someone,** témoigner du respect à quelqu'un. **to treat with ~,**
traiter respectueusement.
respectability *n.* respectabilité *f.;* considération
f.; extérieur *m.* décent.
respectable *adj.* respectable, honorable, notable;
estimable; comme il faut.
respectably *adv.* respectablement, de manière à
mériter l'estime; honorablement.
respectful *adj.* respecteux.

respectfully adv. respectueusement.

respecting prép. à l'égard de, par rapport à; relativement à; quant à.

respective adj. respectif; se rapportant à; relatif.

respectively adv. respectivement; particulièrement; relativement.

respiration n. respiration f.

respirator n. respirateur m.; masque m. à gaz.

respiratory adj. respiratoire.

respite n. répit m., relâche m.; Law. sursis m.; délai m. ~ v.t. accorder du répit, du relâche, du repos à; surseoir à.

resplendence n. resplendissement m.; vif éclat m.; splendeur f.

resplendent adj. resplendissant.

respond v.i. répondre à; convenir à.

respondent adj. qui répond à. n. Law. défendeur m., répondant m.

response n. réponse f., réaction f.

responsibility n. responsabilité f.

responsible adj. (for, de) responsable.

responsive adj. qui répond, qui fait une réplique; qui répond.

rest n. repos m.; paix f., appui m., support m.; Mus. pause f.; arrêt m.; reste m., restant m. **to have a good night's ~,** passer une bonne nuit; bien dormir. **to take a ~,** prendre du repos, se reposer. **give me the ~,** donnez-moi ce qui reste. **he and the ~,** lui et les autres. **~ room,** toilettes f.pl. publiques. v.i. (se) reposer, s'arrêter appuyer; dormir; demeurer; s'en tenir, rester. **~ a little longer,** reposez-vous encore un peu. **you may ~ assured that,** vous pouvez être certain que. **it ~s with him to decide,** il ne tient qu'à lui de décider. v.t. faire reposer; poser; calmer.

restful adj. paisible.

restitution n. restitution f.

restive adj. rétif.

restless adj. sans repos; inquiet, agité. **a ~ night,** une nuite agitée. **a ~ child,** un enfant remuant.

restlessly adv. sans repos; avec inquiétude, avec impatience.

restlessness n. inquiétude f.; turbulence f.; insomnie f.; mouvement m., agitation f.

restoration f. restauration f.; replacement m.; restitution f.; rétablissement m. (health).

restore v.t. restituer, rendre; rétablir; restaurer; réinstaller. **to ~ to health,** rendre à la santé. **to ~ to life,** rendre à la vie. **to ~ peace,** rétablir la paix.

restrain v.t. restreindre, borner, limiter retenir; réprimer. **to ~ from,** empêcher de, détourner de.

restraint n. contrainte f., gêne f., restriction f., frein m. **to be under ~,** être dans la contrainte, être gêné. **to put under ~,** interner.

[restr]ict v.t. borner, restreindre.

[restr]iction n. restriction f.

[restri]ctive adj. restrictif.

restructure v.t. restructurer.

result v.i. résulter; s'ensuivre; (**in**) finir, se terminer; avoir une issue. n. résultat m., conséquence f.; effet m.; décision m.

resultant adj. résultant.

resume v.t. reprendre; recommencer. **to ~ one's place,** reprendre sa place. **to ~ a journey,** se remettre en route.

résumé n. curriculum vitae m., c.v. abbr.

resumption n. reprise f.

resurface v.t. refaire surface; remonter à la surface.

resurgence n. réapparition f.

resurrection n. résurrection f.

resuscitate v.i. ressusciter; se réveiller. v.t. ranimer.

resuscitation n. résurrection f.

retail v.t. détailler; débiter, vendre au détail. n. détail m.

retailer n. détaillant m.

retain v.t. retenir; garder; conserver. **to ~ a sum of money,** garder, retenir une somme d'argent. **to ~ heat,** conserver la chaleur.

retainer n. acompte m.; honoraires m.pl. **~ fee for an attorney,** frais de provision pour un avocat

retake v.t. reprendre; Cine. reprendre à nouveau n. nouvelle prise f. de vues.

retaliate v.t.,v.i. rendre la pareille de, rendre; sa venger de.

retaliation n. représailles f.pl., pareille f.; revanche f.; talion m.

retaliatory adj. de représailles.

retard v.t. retarder, ralentir; remettre, différer.

retardation n. retardation f., retardement m.

retch v.i. vomir.

retell v.t. redire, répéter.

retention n. rétention f.; mémoire f.; conservation f.; action de retenir.

retentive adj. rétentif, fidèle (memory).

retentiveness n. faculté f., pouvoir m. de retenir; ténacité f.

reticence n. réticence f.

retina n. rétine f.

retinue n. cortège m., suite f.

retire v.i. (se) retirer, prendre sa retraite; s'en aller. **to ~ from business,** se retirer des affaires. v.t. faire retirer.

retired adj. retraité; retiré, isolé, caché; éloigné. **~ officer,** officier en retraite.

retirement n. retraite f.

retort v.i. renvoyer, rétorquer; répondre à. v.i. répliquer, riposter. n. réplique f., riposte f.

retouch v.t. retoucher. n. retouche f.

retrace v.t. retracer (drawing); revenir sur (steps), reprendre (route).

retract v.t. retirer. (se) rétracter, se dédire.

retractible adj. rétractile; qui peut être rétracté.

retractile adj. rétractile.

retraction n. rétraction f.; rétractation f.

retransmission n. retransmission f.

retransmit *v.t.* retransmettre.

retreat *n.* retraite *f.;* départ *m.* ~ *v.i.* se retirer, se réfugier; *Mil.* battre en retraite.

retrench *v.t.* (se) retrancher.

retrenchment *n.* retranchement *m.*

retrial *n.* nouveau procès *m.*

retribution *n.* châtiment *m.*, rétribution *f.*

retrievable *adj.* réparable, qui peut se réparer; recouvrable; récupérable.

retrieve *v.t.* restaurer, réparer regagner, retrouver; récupérer. **to ~ a loss**, réparer une perte.

retroactive *adj.* rétroactif.

retrograde *adj.* rétrograde. *v.i.* rétrograder. *v.t.* faire rétrograder, reculer.

retrogression *n.* rétrogradation *f.*

retrospect, retrospection *n.* regard *m.* jeté en arrière sur le passé; revue *f.;* nouvel examen *m.;* révision *f.*

retrospective *adj.* rétrospectif.

retroversion *n.* rétroversion *f.;* renversement *m.*

retry *v.t.* juger de nouveau.

return *v.i.* retourner, s'en retourner; revenir; être de retour; rentrer; répliquer, répondre; rendre, rapporter. **to ~ home**, s'en retourner, rentrer chez soi. **he was about to ~**, il était sur le point de s'en retourner. *v.t.* rendre, remettre; renvoyer. **to ~ a thing borrowed**, rendre une chose que l'on a empruntée. **to ~ a visit**, rendre une visite. **to ~ goods**, retourner des marchandises. *n.* retour *m.*, restitution *f.*, rentrée *f.;* renvoi *m.;* rapport *m.;* remboursement *m.;* profit *m.;* gain *m.* **on my ~ from**, à mon retour de. **in ~**, en retour, en échange. **the ~ of peace**, le retour de la paix. **election returns**, les résultats d'une élection.

reunion *n.* réunion *f.*

reunite *v.t.* réunir; raccommoder. *v.i.* (se) réunir, se rejoindre.

reveal *v.t.* révéler; découvrir; divulguer.

revealing *adj.* révélateur (trice *f.*).

reveille *n.* réveil *m.*

revel *v.i.* se réjouir; s'ébattre; festiner; banqueter faire ripaille. *n.* réjouissances *f.pl.,* ébats *m.pl.;* fête *f.;* divertissement *m.* bruyant; orgie *f.*

revelation *n.* révélation *f.*

reveler *n.* buveur *m.;* débauché *m.;* celui qui se réjouit bruyamment; joyeux convive; *Infml.* riboteur; bambocheur *m.*

revelry *n.* réjouissances *f.pl.* bruyantes, tumultuesus; orgie *f.;* fêtes *f.pl.,* ébats *m.pl.*

revenge *v.t.* venger; se venger de. *n.* revanche *f.;* vengeance *f.* **to be ~ed on**, se venger de.

revengeful *adj.* vindicatif; vengeur, vengeresse.

revengefully *adv.* par vengeance.

revengefulness *n.* esprit *m.* de vengeance.

revenger *n.* vengeur *m.*, vengeresse *f.*

revenue *n.* revenu *m.;* fisc *m.,* trésor.

reverberate *v.t.* renvoyer, réfléchir; répéter; renvoyer. *v.i.* retentir; résonner; se répercuter.

reverberation *n.* réverbération *f.;* répercussion *f.*

revere *v.t.* révérer, vénérer.

reverence *n.* révérence *f.;* vénération *f.;* salut *m.* ~ *v.t.* révérer.

reverend *adj.* vénérable; respectable; révérend.

reverent *adj.* révérencieux, respectueux.

reverently *adv.* avec respect, avec vénération.

reverie *n.* rêverie *f.*

reversal *n.* renversement *m.; Law.* annulation, cessation *f.*

reverse *v.t.* renverser; retourner; faire marche arrière; mettre sens dessus dessous; *Law.* infirmer. *n.* changement *m.;* vicissitude *f.;* revers *m.,* infortune *f.;* inverse *m.;* contraire *m.; Auto.* marche arrière.

reversible *adj.* réversible; annulable; révocable.

reversion *n.* retour *m.; Law* réversion *f.;* succession *f.*

revert *v.t.* changer; renverser. *v.i.* retourner; faire retour; revenir (to a subject).

review *v.t.* revoir; réviser; revenir sur; *Mil.* passer en revue. *n.* revue *f.* (publication); *Mil.* inspection de troupes; révision *f.;* examen *m.,* analyse critique; compte rendu *m.*

reviewer *n.* rédacteur *n.,* de revue; critique *m.*

revile *v.t.* injurier, outrager, bafouer.

revise *v.t.* reviser, revoir, modifier et corriger. *n.* révision *f.,* réexamen *m.*

revised *adj.* revisé.

revision *n.* révision *f.*

revitalize *v.t.* revivifier.

revival *n.* retour *m.* à la vie; recouvrement *m.* des forces; reprise *f.* (business); renaissance *f.* (learning); remise *f.* en vigueur (a law); réveil *m.* religieux.

revive *v.i.* revivre, revenir à la vie; reprendre ses sens; (se) ranimer. *v.t.* faire revivre, rappeler à la vie; ressusciter; rappeler. **to ~ the memory**, faire revivre la mémoire; rappeler à la mémoire.

revivification *n.* révivification *f.*

revivify *v.t.* révivifier.

revocable *adj.* révocable.

revocation *n.* révocation *f.;* rappel *m.;* annulation *f.* (a will, etc.).

revoke *v.t.* révoquer.

revolt *v.i.* (se) révolter. *v.t.* soulever contre. *n.* révolte *f.*

revolting *adj.* révoltant.

revolution *n.* révolution *f.* tour *m.* (wheel); *Phys.* rotation *f.,* mouvement *m.*

revolutionary *adj.* révolutionnaire.

revolutionize *v.t.* révolutionner.

revolve *v.i.* tourner, retourner; se mouvoir en rond.

revolver *n.* révolver *m.*

revolving *adj.* qui tourne; tournant.

revue *n.* revue *f.,* spectacle *m.*

revulsion *n.* révulsion *f.;* action de retenir, de tirer en arrière; séparation *f.* violente.

revulsive *adj.* révulsif.

reward v.t. récompenser; compenser. n. récompense f.; prix m.

rewarding adj. rémunérateur (trice f.), qui en vaut la peine.

rewind v.t. remonter (watch), rebobiner.

rewire v.t. refaire l'installation électrique.

rewrite v.t. récrire.

rhapsody n. rapsodie.

rhetoric n. rhétorique f.

rhetorical adj. de rhétorique; oratoire.

rheumatic adj. rhumatismal.

rheumatism n. rhumatisme m.

Rhine n.pr. le Rhin m.

rhino n. Infml. rhinocéros m.

rhinoceros n. rhinocéros m.

rhubarb n. rhubarbe f.

rhyme n. rime f.; vers m.pl. ~ v.i. rimer; rimailler; faire des vers.

rhythm n. rhythme m.

rhythmic(al) adj. rhythmique.

rib n. côte f.; Arch. nervure (vault); Bot. nervure (leaf); Carp. chevron m., cintre m.; support m.; baleine f. (umbrella). v.t. Infml. taquiner, mettre en boîte.

ribald n. ribaud m., débauché m., libertin m. adj. ribaud, impudique; paillard; ordurier, obscène, bas, grossier.

ribaldry n. paroles f.pl. obscènes, obscénités f.pl.; langage m. bas.

ribbed p.p., adj. pourvu, garni de côtes; à côtes. ~ **stockings**, bas à côtes.

ribbon n. ruban m.; Fig. lambeau m. ~ v.t. orner de rubans; enrubanner.

rice n. riz m. ~ **paddy**, rizière f.

rich adj. riche; abondant, fertile, excellent; succulent; beau, superbe; généreux. **a ~ soil**, un sol riche, fertile. **a ~ flavor**, une saveur exquise, délicieuse. ~ **colors**, des couleurs vives, éclatantes. **a ~ wine**, un vin généreux. **a ~ dish**, un mets de haut goût, relevé. **the ~ and the poor**, les riches et les pauvres.

riches n.pl. richesses f.pl., richesse f.

richly adv. richement, grandement, magnifiquement, amplement; bien.

richness n. richesse f., opulence, fortune; fécondité, fertilité f.; abondance, luxe m., nature f. succulente; haut goût m., fort assaisonnement m.; vigueur f.

rickets n. rachitis m., rachitisme m.

rickety adj. rachitique; faible.

ricochet n. ricochet m. ~ v.i. ricocher.

rid v.t. délivrer; débarrasser, défaire. **to get ~ of**, se débarrasser de, se défaire de.

riddle n. énigme f. ~ v.t. cribler. v.i. parler d'une manière énigmatique, équivoque.

ride v.i. aller à cheval, monter; aller, se promener (car); chevaucher; Naut. être à l'ancre, être mouillé; flotter. **to ~ along**, poursuivre sa route; voguer. v.t. conduire, être porté sur; flotter sur, fendre (waves), mener. **to ~ one's high horse**. Fig. monter sur ses grands chevaux. n. promenade f., excursion f. **to go for a ~**, aller faire une promenade. **to have a ~**, avoir un moyen de transport, prendre une transportation.

rider n. cavalier m.; écuyer m.; annexe f.; Law codicille m.

ridge n. crime f., crête f. (mountains); sommet m.; échine f., croupe f., arête f.; Agr. sillon m. v.t. sillonner, Agr. former des sillons.

ridicule n. ridicule m.; dérision f. **to turn into ~**, tourner en ridicule. v.t. ridiculiser; tourner en ridicule.

ridiculous adj. ridicule.

ridiculously adv. ridiculement.

riding adj. qui va à cheval; de promenade. n. promenade f.; équitation f. ~ **boots**, bottes f.pl. de cheval. **Little Red ~ Hood**, Petit Chaperon Rouge. ~ **master**, professeur m. d'équitation. ~ **school**, école f. d'équitation, manège m.

rife adj. qui règne, qui domine, qui court; commun.

rifle v.t. dérober, voler, piller; dévaliser. n. carabine f.

rift n. fente f., fissure f. ~ v.t. crever. v.i. (se) fendre, s'entr'ouvrir, se déchirer.

rig v.t. équiper, accoutrer. Naut. gréer, garnir. n. accoutrement m.; gréement m.

rigging n. gréement m.

right adj. droit, direct; juste, équitable; convenable; bien; bon, véritable, régulier. **the ~ way**, le droit chemin, ~ **angle**, angle droit. **that's ~**, c'est cela, c'est exact. **to set a thing ~**, Infml. mettre les points sur les i. ~ **hand**, main droite. **you are ~**, vous avez raison. adv. droit, tout droit, directement; avec raison, justement; bien. ~ **or wrong**, à tort ou à raison. **I am not quite ~**, je ne suis pas tout à fait bien. **the ~ reverend**, le très révérend. n. droit m.; justice f., équité f.; raison f.; intérêt m.; droite f. (right-hand side). **the ~s of citizens**, les droits des citoyens. **bill of ~s**, déclaration des droits. **by ~**, de plein droit, de droit. **on the ~, to the ~**, à droite. **to put to ~s**, mettre en ordre; rectifier. v.t. faire droit à, rendre justice à; Naut. dresser, redresser. v.i. (se) relever, (se) redresser.

~**-angled**, à angle droit. ~**-handed**, droitier.

~**-minded**, qui a l'esprit droit. ~**-mindedness**, droiture f., loyauté f.

righteous adj. droit; juste.

righteously adv. avec justice, avec équité.

righteousness n. droiture f.; justice f.; honnêteté f.

rightful adj. légitime; juste.

rightfully adv. légitimement, à bon droit.

rightly adv. justement; bien, comme il convient.

rigid adj. raide; rigide.

rigidity n. raideur f.; Fig. rigidité f.

rigor n. rigueur f., dureté f., raideur f.

rigorous adj. rigoureux; austère; dur. ~ **terms**, des conditions rigoureuses. **a ~ winter**, un hiver rigoureux.

rigorously adv. rigoureusement.

rile v.t. agacer porter sur les nerfs, crisper.

rim n. bord m., rebord m.; jante f. (wheel). v.t. mettre un bord, un rebord à.

rime n. Frml. givre m., gelée f. blanche; frimas m.pl.

rind n. pelure f., peau f., écorce f.

ring n. anneau m., bague f., rond m., cercle m.; cerne f. (tree, eyes); enceinte f. (horserace course); boucle f.; bruit m., retentissement de cloche; sonnerie f., carillon m. **a wedding ~**, une alliance. **a diamond ~**, une bague en diamant. **ear~s**, boucles d'oreilles. **~bolt**, cheville f. à boucle; piton m. **~ dove**, pigeon m. ramier. **~ finger**, doigt m. annulaire. **~worm**, herpès m. tonsurant. v.t. entourer, former un cercle autour de; sonner; faire sonner, faire retentir. to **~ the bells**, sonner les cloches. v.i. résonner, retentir, tinter. **the bell rings**, la cloche sonne. **to ~ a doorbell**, sonner.

ringing n. action de sonner, sonnerie f.; retentissement m., tintement m.

ringleader n. meneur m., chef m. de bande.

ringlet n. boucle f. de cheveux.

rinse n. rinçage m. v.t. rincer.

riot n. émeute f., révolte f.; sédition f., vacarme m. **to read someone the ~ act**, faire les trois sommations. v.i. faire dès excès; faire une orgie; Infml. riboter, faire une émeute; s'ameuter; tordant de rire (funny).

rioter n. Law émeutier m., séditieux m.

riotous adj. tumultueux, turbulent, bruyant, tapageur.

rip v.t. lacérer; découdre; arracher. **to ~ off**, enlever, arracher; voler. **to ~ open**, ouvrir, déchirer. **to ~ out**, arracher; lâcher. **to ~ up**, déchirer. v.i. (se) déchirer. n. déchirure f.; fente f., ouverture f.

ripe adj. mûr; parfait; propre à l'usage. **~ years**, âge mûr.

ripen v.i., v.t. mûrir, faire mûrir.

ripeness n. maturité f.; perfection f.; achèvement m.; opportunité f., à propos m.

ripple v.i. (se) rider. v.t. agiter (water). n. clapotage m., clapotis m.; rides f.pl.

rise v.i. (se) lever; se relever; s'élever, menter, naître, sortir; hausser (prices); augmenter. **to ~ from the table**, se lever de table. **the sun ~s**, le soleil se lève. **birds ~ in the air**, les oiseaux s'élèvent dans l'air. **the ground ~s**, le terrain monte, va en montant. **the tide is rising**, la marée monte. **to ~ in the world**, faire son chemin. **the dough is rising**, la pâte lève. **to ~ again**, se relever; ressusciter. **to ~ up**, se lever. **to ~ up in arms**, se soulever. n. lever m.; montée f., élévation f.; naissance f.; hausse f., augmentation f.; renchérissement m.; crue f. **sun ~**, lever du soleil. **the ~ of a river**, la crue d'une rivière. **to give ~ to**, donner naissance à. **the ~ of the stocks**, la hausse des fonds.

rising adj. se levant, levant, montant, croissant augmentant, naissant. **the ~ sun**, le soleil levant.

risk n. risque m., hasard m., péril m. **to run a ~**, courir un risque. v.t. risquer; hasarder.

risky adj. hasardeux.

risqué risqué, scabreux.

rite n. rite m.; cérémonie f.

ritual adj. rituel (m.).

rival n. rival m. **~** adj. rival. v.t. être le rival de, rivaliser avec.

rivalry n. rivalité f.

rive v.t.,v.i. (se) fendre, (s')entr'ouvrir, se crevasser.

river n. rivière f., fleuve m. **up the ~**, en amont m. **down the ~**, en aval. **~ course**, cours m. du fleuve. **~head**, source f. de la rivière.

rivet v.t. river, clouer, Fig. graver. n. rivet m.; clou rivé.

riveting n. rivetage m. **~** adj. fascinant.

Riviera n. Côte d'Azur (France). f.

rivulet n. petit ruisseau m., ruisselet m.; petit cours m. d'eau.

roach n. cafard m. mégot m. de joint (drug).

road n. route f., chemin m., voie f.; chaussée f. **cross~**, carrefour m. **rail~**, chemin m. de fer. **on the ~**, en route. **~side**, bord m. de la route.

roam v.i. errer. v.t. parcourir au hasard.

roaming adj. errant, rôdant vagabondant, divaguant.

roar v.i. rugir, mugir, beugler, gronder. **the sea ~s**, la mer gronde. n. grondement m., rugissement m., hurlement m., mugissemeut m., clameur f., cri m. **a ~ of laughter**, un éclat de rire.

roast v.t. rôtir, faire rôtir, griller, torréfier, bruler. **to ~ coffee**, brûler du café. v.i. se rôtir. n. rôti m. adj. rôti. **~ beef**, bœuf rôti, rosbif.

rob v.t. voler à main armée, dérober; piller. **I will not ~ you of that pleasure**, je ne veux pas vous priver de ce plaisir.

robber n. voleur m.; voleur à main armée.

robbery n. vol m.; vol à main armée.

robe n. peignoir m. sortie f. de bain; robe. v.t. revêtir d'une robe, vêtir, parer, orner.

robin n. rouge-gorge m.

robot n. robot m.

robust adj. robuste; vigoureux.

robustness f. force f. vigueur f.

rock n. roc m., roche f., rocher m. **~ crystal**, cristal m. de roche. **to hit ~ bottom**, tomber au plus bas. v.t. balancer; bercer, endormir, calmer. **to ~ a child**, bercer un enfant. v.i. osciller, chanceler; se balancer.

rocker n. bascule f. de berceau; bascule f.; berceuse f.; blouson m. noir, rocker (person); chaise à bascule (chair). **to be off one's ~**, être un peu cinglé.

rocket n. fusée f. **~** v.i. passer comme une flèche.

rocking adj. oscillant, vacillant, balançant; berçant. **~ chair**, siège m. à bascule. **~ horse**, cheval m. à bascule.

rocky adj. rocheux; de roche, très dur; pierreux; endurci; branlant; difficile.

rod n. baguette f., branche f., verge f.; tringle f.;

Mech. tige f. (piston, etc.); canne f. à pêche (fishing); perche f., bâton m.; **Fig.** sceptre m.; verge f. **curtain ~,** tringle de rideau.

rodent adj. rongeur. n. rongeur m.

roe n. chevreuil m.; biche f.; oeufs m.pl. de poisson.

rogue n. coquin m., fripon m., filou m., voleur m.

roguery n. friponnerie f., tromperie f.; malice f.

role n. rôle m.

roll v.t. tourner; entortiller. **to ~ a stone,** rouler une pierre; (se) rouler; (s')enrouler. **to ~ in money,** **Fig.** rouler sur l'or. **to ~ around,** rouler de tous côtés. **to ~ along,** s'écouler. **to ~ away,** s'éloigner en roulant. **to ~ back,** s'en retourner. **to ~ in,** entrer en roulant. **to ~ on,** continuer à rouler; s'écouler. **to ~ out,** sortir en roulant. **to ~ around,** se tourner. **to ~ up,** se rouler, s'enrouler. n. rouleau m.; roulement m. (drum); roulis m. (ship), petit pain; liste f.; rôle m.; registre m., tableau m.; archives f.pl. **to call the ~,** faire l'appel.

roller n. rouleau m.; cylindre m., roulette f. (furniture). **~-skate** v.i. faire du patin à roulettes. **~ skates** n.pl.; patins à roulettes. **~ blades** n.pl. patins à roues alignées.

rolling adj. tournant, roulant, qui roule. **~ eyes,** des yeux qui roulent dans la tête. **a ~ stone gathers no moss,** pierre qui roule n'amasse pas mousse. **~ pin,** rouleau m. de pâtissier.

romance n. romance f.; roman m. de chevalerie. adj. roman. **~ languages,** langues romanes. v.t. faire la cour à; enjoliver, broder.

romanesque adj. roman.

romantic adj. romanesque; romantique.

romantically adv. romanesquement; romantiquement.

romanticism n. romantisme m.

romanticist n. romantique m.

romp n. ébats m.pl., gambades f.pl. **~** v.i. gambader.

roof n. toit m., toiture f., voûte f. (mouth, palace). v.t. recouvrir d'un toit.

roofing n. toiture f.

rook n. corneille f.

rookie n. **Infml.** bleu m., néophyte m.

room n. chambre f., salle f., pièce f.; espace m., place f., lieu m. **bed~,** chambre à coucher. **dining ~,** salle à manger. **to make ~,** faire de la place. **to have ~,** avoir de la place. **~mate,** camarade de chambre; personne qui partage un appartement avec une ou plusieurs autres personnes. **~ service,** service m. des chambres (hotel). **~ temperature,** température f. ambiante.

roominess n. espace m.; grandeur f.

roomy adj. spacieux, vaste, grand.

roost n. juchoir m., perchoir m. **~** v.i. jucher, percher; **Infml.** se loger, se nicher.

rooster n. coq m.

root n. racine f., source f., **Mus.** base f. **to take ~,** prendre racine, s'enraciner. **square ~,** racine

carrée. **~bound,** enraciné. v.i. s'enraciner; prendre racine; fouiller. v.t. fixer en terre; graver profondément. **to ~ out, to ~ up,** déraciner, extirper; **~ for,** encourager.

rooted adj. enraciné; fixé; profond.

rope n. corde f., cordage m. **tight~,** corde tendue. **tight~ walker,** funambule m.f., danseur m. de corde. **~ ladder,** échelle f. de cordes. v.i. attacher avec une corde, lier.

rosary n. rosaire m.

rose n. rose f.; rosette f. (knot), rosace f. **no ~ without thorns,** pas de rose sans épines. **~bush, ~ tree,** rosier m. **~-colored,** couleur de rose. **~ diamond,** rose f., diamant m. à rosette. **~ water,** eau f. de rose. **~ window,** fenêtre f. à rosace.

rosé n. (wine) rosé m.

rosebud n. bouton m. de rose.

rosemary n. romarin m.

rosy adj. **Infml.** heureuse.

rot v.i. se pourrir, se gâter. v.t. putréfier. n. pourriture f. **dry ~,** pourriture sèche. **it's all ~,** **Infml.** balivernes que tout cela.

rotation n. rotation f.

rotator n. rotateur m., muscle m. rotateur.

rote n. machinalement, par coeur, routine f. **by ~,** par routine.

rotten adj. gâté, pourri, **Infml.** perfide, trompeur.

rottenness n. pourriture f.

rotund adj. rond.

rotunda n. rotonde f.

rouge n. rouge m.; fard m. **~** v.i.,v.t. se farder; se mettre du rouge.

rough adj. rude, raboteux; brut; grossier, brusque; dur, discordant; gros, houleux (sea); orageux. **a ~ draft,** un brouillon m. **a ~ sketch,** une ébauche f.; simple esquisse. **a ~ sea,** une mer houleuse, agitée. **a ~ voice,** une grosse voix. **his ~ manners,** ses manières grossières. **a dog with ~ hair,** un chien à poil hérissé. n. état brut m. **~** v.t. rendre rude; ébaucher. **to ~ it,** s'habituer à la dure. **to ~ cast,** ébaucher; mouler. **~ cast,** draft, ébauche f. **~ cut,** grossièrement coupé, taille. **~-grained,** grossièrement grenelé.

roughen v.t. rendre rude. v.t. devenir rude.

roughing n. crépi m., plâtrage m.

roughly adv. rudement, durement.

roughness n. inégalité f., aspérité f. (surface, etc.).

Romania n. Roumanie f.

roulette n. roulette f.

round adj. rond, circulaire; globuleux; net, positif. **to make ~,** arrondir. **a ~ number,** un nombre rond. n. rond m.; cercle m.; sphère f.; tour m., tournée f.; **Mus.** ronde f.; décharge f. (gun); rouelle f. (beef). **a ~ of applause,** une salve d'applaudissements. **~** v.t. arrondir; circulairement. **~about,** autour, à l'entour, tout autour. v.t. entourer. **to ~ off,** donner du fini a. **to ~ up,** rassembler, réunir, faire une rafle. v.i. s'arrondir, devenir rond. ~ **shouldered,** aux épaules rondes.

roundabout adj. detourné; indirect; étendu.

roundly adv. rondement, franchement.

roundness n. rondeur f.

rouse v.t. exciter; lancer, faire lever (game). v.i. s'éveiller, se réveiller; s'animer.

rousing adj. qui a le pouvoir d'éveiller, d'animer; émouvant.

rout n. déroute f. ~ v.t. mettre en déroute.

route n. route f., chemin m., itinéraire m.

routine n. routine f.

rove v.i. errer, aller à l'aventure; rôder; flâner; *Infml.* divaguer; battre la campagne.

rover n. rôdeur m., coureur m., vagabond m.; corsaire m., pirate m., écumeur de mer.

roving adj. errant, vagabond.

row n. vacarme m., tapage m., *Infml.* raffut m., boucan m.; querelle f.; mêlée f.

row n. rang m., rangée f., file f., ligne f.; promenade f. en bateau, partie de canot. **a ~ of trees,** une rangée d'arbres. **a ~ of figures,** une colonne de chiffres. ~ **boat,** bâteau m. à rames. v.t. faire aller, transporter à la rame; promener en bateau. v.i. ramer.

rowdiness n. chahut m., tapage m.

rowdy n. chahuteur m., bagarreur m., voyou m. adj. tapageur m.

rowing adj. faisant aller à la rame; ramant, maniant l'aviron. n. action de diriger, de faire aller à la rame; action de manier l'aviron, de ramer.

royal adj. royal, de roi; noble, magnanime.

royalism n. royalisme m.

royalist n. royaliste m.

royally adv. royalement, en roi.

royalty n. royauté f., dignité f. royale.

rub v.t. frictionner; contrarier. **to ~ oneself,** se frotter, se frictionner. **to ~ away,** enlever en frottant. **to ~ down,** nettoyer, bouchonner, étriller (horse). **to ~ off,** oter, enlever par le frottement. **to ~ out,** effacer. v.i. se frotter; s'érailler; s'irriter, se froisser. n. frottement m., friction f.; froissement m.; obstacle m.

rubber n. caoutchouc m.; *Infml.* condom m. ~ adj. en/de caoutchouc.

rubbish n. décombres m.pl., ordures f.pl.

rubble n. moellon m. brut, gravats m.pl.; décombres m.pl.

rubella n. rubède f.

rubric n. rubrique f.

ruby adj. rubis m., rouge m.; incarnat m. adj. vermeil. **her ~ lips,** ses lèvres vermeilles.

rucksack n. sac m. de camping, sac à dos m.

rudder n. gouvernail m.

ruddy adj. rouge, vermeil; frais, fraiche; fleuri; annonçant une bonne santé.

rude adj. rude, grossier, rigoureux; impoli, mal élevé; malhonnête; ignorant; barbare. **to be ~ to,** être impoli envers. **a ~ answer,** une réponse grossière. ~ **language,** des propos grossiers.

rudely adv. rudement; grossièrement.

rudeness n. rudesse f., grossièreté f., impolitesse f.

rudiment n. rudiment m.

rudimentary adj. rudimentaire.

rue v.t. se repentir, regretter. n. rue f.

rueful adj. déplorable, lamentable; triste.

ruffle v.t. froncer, plisser, chiffoner, froisser; déranger, agiter, irriter. v.i. s'agiter; se déchaîner; s'ébouriller; se chamailler. n. manchette f. en dentelle; commotion f., trouble m., agitation f.

rug n. tapis m. Oriental ~, tapis d'Orient; *Infml.* toupé.

rugby (football) n. rugby.

rugged adj. raboteux, âpre, rude; bourru, refrogné, ébouriffé. **a ~ look,** un air refrogné.

ruin n. ruine f., perte f. **to bring one to ~,** perdre ou ruiner quelqu'un. v.t. détruire. v.i. tomber en ruine; se ruiner.

ruinous adj. ruiné, de ruine; ruineux.

rule n. autorité f.; empire m.; domination f.; règle f.; réglement m. **to lay down a ~,** poser une règle. **to make it a ~ to,** se faire une loi, une règle de. v.t. régler, régir, gouverner; subjuguer; réprimer. **to ~ one's life,** régler sa vie. ~ **out,** v.t. exclure, excepter, écarter. v.i. régner; commander.

ruler n. chef m., souverain m.; gouveneur m.; gouvernant m.; règle f.

ruling adj. dominant, prédominant. n. jugement m., décision f.

rum n. rhum m.

rumble v.i. gronder (like thunder), rouler avec un bruit sourd (vehicle). n. bruit m., son m. sourd et prolongé; grondement m.; roulement m.

rumbling adj. qui produit un son sourd et prolongé; qui gronde; sourd. n. son m. sourd et prolongé; grondement m.; retentissement m.; roulement m.

ruminant adj. n. ruminant m.

ruminate v.i.a. ruminer. v.i. ruminer; méditer.

rumination n. rumination f.; rêverie f., méditation f.

rummage v.t. chercher. v.i. fouiller, remuer, farfouiller. n. vieilleries f.pl., objets divers. ~ **sale,** vente f. de charité.

rummy n. (cards) rami m.

rumor n. bruit m., rumeur f. v.t. **spread a ~,** faire courir un bruit.

rump n. croupse f.; culotte f. (beef). *Infml.* derrière (person).

rumple v.t. plisser, froisser, chiffonner, fripper; rider.

rumpus n. cahut m. ~ **room,** salle f. de jeu.

run v.i. courir; continuer, rouler; aller; passer; couler, couvrir (distance); tracer; fuir, (se) répandre, s'étendre. *Polit.* se présenter. **the note has sixty days to ~,** l'effet a encore soixante jours à courir. **to ~ around,** courir çà et là, courir partout; parcourir. **to ~ across,**

traverser en courant. **he ran across the street,** il traversa la rue en courant. **~ across a friend,** trouver une amie par hasard. **to ~ after,** courir après, s'efforcer de trouver. **to ~ against,** se heurter contre; choquer. **to ~ aground,** échouer, s'échouer. **to ~ ahead,** courir en avant. **to ~ along,** courir; parcourir. **to ~ at,** courir sur; attaquer. **to ~ away,** s'enfuir, fuir. **to ~ away with,** emporter; enlever. **to ~ back,** retourner vite. **to ~ down,** se faire écraser. **to ~ into money,** coûter de l'argent; découler; dégoutter. **to ~ for,** courir chercher. **~ for the doctor,** allez chercher le médecin. **~ for president. to ~ from,** s'enfuir de, se sauver de. **to ~ into,** entrer en courant dans; entrer dans; se livrer à; trouver par hasard. **to ~ off,** s'enfuir, se sauver. **to ~ on,** continuer, poursuivre; rouler sur. **to ~ out,** fuir; couler. **to ~ over,** parcourir; passer par-dessus. **to ~ through,** parcourir; passer par; dissiper. *v.t.* parcourir; fournir; suivre; poursuivre. **to ~ a race,** faire une course. **to ~ out,** épuiser; gaspiller. **his time is running out,** il n'a plus beaucoup de temps, son temps tire à sa fin. **to ~ over,** traverser; renverser, raconter à la hâte; repasser, revoir. **to ~ through,** dépenser; transpercer. **~ that by me again,** raconte-moi ça encore une fois. *n.* course *f.,* excursion *f.,* trajet *m.;* cours *m.,* vitesse *f.* **after a long ~,** après une longue course. **in the long ~,** à la longue, à la fin. **to have the ~ of a library,** avoir le libre accès d'une bibliothèque. **this play had a long ~,** cette pièce s'est jouée longtemps. **there was a ~ on the bank,** on s'est précipité sur la banque. **~-of-the-mill,** ordinaire.

runaway *adj. n.* fugitif *m.;* fuyard *m.,* déserteur *m.*
runner *n.* coureur *m.,* messager *m.,* courrier *m.;* tapis.
running *adj.* courant; qui court; de suite.

~ account, compte courant. **runny** *adj.* qui coule. **a ~ nose,** une nez qui coule.
runt *n.* animal *m.* chétif, avorton *m.*
runway *n.* piste *f.* (d'envoi), rampe *f.* de lancement.
rupture *n.* rupture *f.,* hernie *f.* ~ *v.t.* rompre, briser. **to ~ oneself,** se donner une hernie. *v.i.* se rompre, se briser.
rural *adj.* rural, rustique, champêtre.
ruse *n.* ruse *f.,* artifice *m.,* stratagème *m.*
rush *n. Bot.* jonc *m.;* course *f.* précipitée; secousse *f.;* attaque *f.;* foule *f.* de monde. **there was a ~ at the door,** on se pressait à la porte. *v.i.* se précipiter, fondre sur, courir à. **~ hours,** heures *f.pl.* d'affluence/de pointe. **to ~ at,** se jeter sur. **to ~ down,** descendre précipitamment, dévaler. **to ~ forward,** se précipiter, s'élancer en avant. **to ~ into,** se précipiter dans, faire sans réfléchir. **to ~ out,** sortir précipitamment de.
Russia *n.pr.* Russie *f.*
Russian *adj.* russe. *n.* Russe *m.f.*
rust *n.* rouille *f.,* moisissure *f.* ~ *v.i.* se rouiller.
rustic *adj.* rustique, champêtre. *n.* campagnard *m.,* paysan *m.* **a ~ dwelling,** une habitation rustique.
rustle *v.i.* bruire, frémir, frôler, faire frou-frou. *n.* bruissement *m.*
rustling *n.* bruissement *m.;* frémissement *m.;* frôlement *m.,* frou-frou *m. adj.* qui bruit; frémissant.
rusty *adj.* rouillé.
rut *n.* rut *m.;* ornière *f.* (roads). *v.i.* être, entrer en rut. *v.t.* s'encroûter.
rutabaga *n.* rutabaga *m.*
ruthless *adj.* cruel, impitoyable.
ruthlessly *adv.* impitoyablement.
ruthlessness *n.* cruauté *f.*
rye *n.* siegle *m.* **~ bread,** pain *m.* de siegle.

S

sabbath *n.* sabbat *m.;* dimanche *m.;* jour du repos.
sabbatical *adj.* sabatique.
saber *n.* sabre *m.;* glaive *m.*
sable *n.* zibeline *f.,* martre *f.; Fig.* vêtement *m.* noir, deuil *m.* ~ *adj.* noir, sombre. *v.t.* assombrir.
sabotage *n.* sabotage *m.* ~ *v.t.* saboter.
saboteur *n.* saboteur *m.*
sac *n.* bourse *f.*
saccharine *adj.* saccharin.
sachet *n.* sachet *m.*
sack *n.* sac *m.;* vin (des Canaries). **~cloth,** toile *f.* à sacs. *v.t.* mettre à sac; *Infml.* se faire virer. **~ out,** s'endormir.
sacrament *n.* sacrement *m.*
sacramental *adj.* sacremental.
sacred *adj.* sacré; saint.
sacrifice *v.t.,v.i.* sacrifier. *n.* sacrifice *m.*

sacrificial *adj.* de sacrifice; sacrificatoire.
sacrilege *n.* sacrilège *m.*
sacrum *n.* sacrum *m.*
sad *adj.* triste, mélancolique. **to grow ~,** s'attrister.
sadden *v.t.* affliger. *v.i.* s'attrister; devenir triste.
saddle *n.* selle *f.,* échine *f.* (mutton). **side~,** une selle de femme. *v.t.* seller. **to ~ with,** charger; mettre sur le dos à. **sacoche *f.* ~ horse,** cheval *m.* de selle.
sadism *η.* sadisme *m.*
sadist *n.* sadique *m.*
sadistic *adj.* sadique.
sadly *adv.* tristement, pitoyablement.
sadness *n.* tristesse *f.*
safe *adj.* sauf, sauve, sû; en sûreté, hors de danger, en sureté. **~ from,** à l'abri de. **~ and sound,** sain et sauf. **a ~ remedy,** un remède

sûr. **~conduct**, sauf-conduit *m.*. **~guard**, sauvegarde *f.*, garantie *f.*, protection *f.* **~** *v.t.* sauvegarder, protéger. **~ keeping**, bonne garde *f.*, sûreté *f.*; coffre-fort *m.*.

safely *adv.* sûrement, en sûreté.

safety *n.* sûreté *f.*, salut *m.* **~ belt**, ceinture *f.* de sauvetage. **~ measure**, *n.* mesure *f.* de précaution.

saffron *n.* safran *m.* *adj.* safrané.

sag *v.i.* fléchir, s'affaisser, chanceler; céder. *v.t.* faire pencher, faire plier.

saga *n.* saga *f.*

sagacious *adj.* sagace, subtil; pénétrant.

sagacity *n.* sagacité *f.*, perspicacité *f.*

sage *n. Bot.* sauge *f.*; sage *m.*, philosophe *m.* *adj.* sage; prudent.

sagging *n.* courbure *f.*, fléchissement *m.*

Sagittarius *n. Astron.* Sagittaire *m.*

said *adj.* dit, susdit.

sail *n.* voile *f.*, promenade *f.* à la voile; *Fig.* navire, vaisseau *m.* to set ~, mettre à la voile. **all ~s set, all ~s out**, toutes voiles dehors. **~cloth**, toile *f.* à voiles. *v.i.* mettre à la voile, appareiller; faire voile, cingler, flotter. **to ~ from**, partir de. **to ~ along the coast**, ranger à la côte, côtoyer. **to ~ into a port**, entrer, relâcher dans un port. *v.t.* naviguer sur; voguer sur; sillonner. **to ~ up, down a river**, monter, descendre un fleuve.

sailing *adj.* allant à la voile, naviguant; parcourant. *n.* mise *f.* à la voile, navigation *f.*

sailor *n.* marin *m.*, matelot *m.*, homme *m.* de mer.

saint *n.* saint *m.*, sainte *f.* **All Saints' Day**, la Toussaint. *v.t.* canoniser.

saintly *adj.* comme un saint; de saint.

sake *n.* cause *f.* finale; but *m.*, objet *m.*; amour *m.* **for God's ~**, pour l'amour de Dieu. **for pity's ~**, par pitié. **for your ~**, pour vous.

salacious *adj.* lascif, lubrique.

salad *n.* salade *f.* **~ bowl**, saladier *m.* **~ oil**, huile *f.* à manger.

salamander *n.* salamandre *f.*

salaried *adj.* salarié.

salary *n.* salaire *m.*, appointements *m.pl.*, traitement *m.*

sale *n.* vente *f.*, débit *m.* **~ by auction**, vente aux enchères.

salesman *n.* vendeur *m.*; représentant *m.*

salient *adj.* saillant.

saline *adj.* salin. *n.* source *f.* d'eau salée.

salivate *v.t.* (faire) saliver.

sallow *v.t.* saule *m.* **~ solution**. *adj.* blafard, blême.

salmon *n.* saumon *m.*

salon *n.* salon *m.* **beauty ~**, salon *m.* de beauté.

salt *n.* sel *m.* **rock ~**, sel gemme. **sea ~**, sel marin. **not to be worth one's ~**, ne pas valoir le pain que l'on mange. **Epsom ~s**, sel d'Epsom. *adj.* salé; salin, de sel; lubrique; amer. **~ marsh**, marais *m.* salant. *v.t.* saler, saupoudrer de sel.

salubrious *adj.* salubre.

salubrity *n.* salubrité *f.*

salutary *adj.* salutaire.

salutation *n.* salutation *f.*, salut *m.*

salute *v.t.* saluer; se présenter à; s'offrir aux regards. *n.* salut *m.*, salutation *f.*; *Mil.* salve *f.* (guns). **to return a ~**, rendre un salut. **to fire a ~**, tirer une salve.

salvage *n.* sauvetage *m.* **~** *v.t.* sauver, sauvegarder.

salvation *n.* salut *m.* **~ Army**, Armée *f.* du salut.

salve *n.* onguent *m.*, pommade *f.*; remède *m.*; *Fig.* baume *m.* **~** *v.t.* mettre un onguent; guérir; sauver.

salvo *n.* salve *f.*

same *adj.* même; égal. *n.* le même, la même chose. **~ as usual**, la même chose, comme d'habitude. **London isn't the ~ anymore**, London n'est plus comme avant/pareil. **we are in the ~ boat**, on est dans le même pétrin. **if it's all the ~ to you**, si cela vous est égal.

sameness *n.* identité *f.*; similitude *f.*, similarité *f.*, ressemblance *f.*; monotonie *f.*

sample *n.* spécimen *m.*; échantillon *m.*; modèle *m.* **~** *v.t.* échantillonner.

sanctification *n.* sanctification *f.*

sanctify *v.t.* sanctifier.

sanctimonious *adj.* dévot, béat.

sanction *n.* sanction *f.* **~** *v.t.* sanctionner.

sanctity *n.* sainteté *f.*

sanctuary *n.* sanctuaire *m.*, protection *f.*; refuge *m.*

sand *n.* sable *m.*; grève *f.* **fine ~**, sablon *m.*. **to be embedded in the ~**, être ensablé. **~bag**, sac *m.* de sable. **~bank**, banc *m.* de sable. **to run on to a ~bank**, échouer sur un banc de sable. **~paper**, papier *m.* de verre. **~piper**, bécasseau *m.* **~** *v.t.* sabler, ensabler.

sandal *n.* sandale *f.* **~wood**, bois *m.* de santal.

sandstone *n.* grès *m.*

sandwich *n.* sandwich *m.*

sandy *adj.* sablonneux; plein de sable; de la couleur du sable; roux, rousse; blond ardent. **~-haired**, qui a les cheveux roux.

sane *adj.* sain d'esprit.

sangfroid *n.* sang-froid *m.*

sanguine *adj.* sanguin, couleur de sang; confiant; téméraire.

sanitary *n.* sanitaire. **~ napkin**, serviette *f.* sanitaire.

sanitation *n.* installations *f.pl.* sanitaires; hygiène *f.* publique.

sanity *n.* bon sens *m.*, santé *f.* mentale; raison *f.* **he has to keep his ~**, il faut qu'il garde sa raison.

Santa, Santa Claus *n.* Père Noël *m.*

sap *n. Bot.* sève *f.*, *Fort.* sape *f.* **~** *v.t.* saper. **to ~ a wall**, saper une muraille. *v.i.* aller à la sape, s'avancer en minant.

sapphire *n.* saphir *m.*

sarcasm *n.* sarcasme *m.*

sarcastic *adj.* sarcastique.

sarcastically *adv.* d'une manière sarcastique, mordante.

sarcophagus *n.* sarcophage *m.*

sardine *n.* sardine *f.*

sardonic *adj.* sardonique.

sash *n.* ceinture *f.*; chassis *m.* (window). *v.t.* parer d'une ceinture, munir de châssis.

sassafras *n.* sassafras *m.*

Satan *n.pr.* Satan *m.*

satanic *adj.* satanique.

satanism *n.* esprit *m.* satanique, diabolique.

satchel *n.* cartable *m.*; sacoche *f.*

sate *v.t.* rassasier.

satellite *n.* satellite *m.*

satiate *v.t.* rassasier, assouvir. *adj.* rassasié.

satiation, satiety *n.* satiété *f.*

satin *n.* satin *m.* ~ *adj.* de satin, satiné. ~ **rib-bon**, ruban satiné.

satire *n.* satire *f.*

satirist *n.* satirique *m.*, auteur *m.* satirique.

satirize *v.t.* satiriser.

satisfaction *n.* satisfaction *f.*; contentement *m.*, plaisir *m.*; conviction *f.*; réparation *f.*

satisfactorily *adv.* d'une manière satisfaisante.

satisfactory *adj.* satisfaisant, suffisant.

satisfy *v.t.* satisfaire, contenter; persuader.

saturate *v.t.* saturer.

saturation *n.* saturation *f.*

Saturday *n.* samedi *m.*

Saturn *n.pr.* Saturne *m.*

satyr *n.* satyre *m.*

sauce *n.* sauce *f.* apple~, compote *f.* de pomme. ~**pan**, casserole *f.* ~ *v.t.* assaisonner.

saucer *n.* saucière *f.*; soucoupe *f.*

saucily *adv.* insolemment, d'une manière impertinente.

saucy *adj.* impudent, impertinent, insolent.

sauerkraut *n.* chou-croûte *f.*

sauna *n.* sauna *m.*

saunter *v.i.* flâner, musarder, badauder, battre le pavé. **to ~ down**, descendre nonchalamment. **to ~ about the streets**, courir les rues. *n.* flânerie *f.*; promenade *f.*

sausage *n.* saucisse *f.* dry ~, saucisson *m.*

savage *adj.* sauvage; farouche; féroce, barbare. *n.* sauvage *m.f.*

savagely *adv.* sauvagement.

savageness, savagery *n.* état *m.* sauvage; nature *f.* sauvage; sauvagerie *f.*; férocité *f.*

savanna(h) *n.* savane *f.*

save *v.t.* sauver; garder; épargner, économiser. **I saved your life**, je vous ai sauvé la vie. **to ~ money**, économiser de l'argent. **to ~ an expense**, éviter une dépense. *v.i.* faire des économies. *prep.* sauf, hors, hormis. *conj.* sinon, à moin que, si ce n'est que.

saving, ~ *n.* épargne *f.*, économie *f.*, réserve *f.* ~**s bank**, caisse *f.* d'épargne. *prep.* sauf, hormis, excepté.

Savior *n.* Sauveur *m.*

savor *n.* saveur *f.*; goût *m.*, odeur *f.*, senteur *f.*, parfum *m.* sweet ~, odeur suave. *v.t.* savorer, goûter, trouver à son goût.

savory *adj.* savoreux; suave.

saw *n.* scie *f.*; proverbe *m.*, dicton *m.* an old ~, un vieux dicton. *v.i.* se scier. *v.t.* découer avec une scie. ~ **blade**, lame *f.* de scie. ~**dust**, sciure *f.* ~ **mill**, scierie *f.*

sax, saxophone *n.* saxophone *m.*

say *v.t.* parler, déclarer; réciter; dire. **to ~ again**, redire. **to ~ one's prayers**, faire sa prière. **it's easier said than done**, c'est plus facile à dire qu'à faire. **enough said!** assez parlé! ~**s who?** qui l'a dit? *n.* mot *m.*, mot *m.* à dire; discours *m.* **to have one's ~**, dire son mot.

saying *n.* parole *f.*, mot *m.*; adage *m.*, dicton *m.* **as the ~ goes**, comme on dit.

scab *n.* croûte *f.*

scabrous *adj.* scabreux; raboteux.

scaffold *n.* échafaud *m.*; échafaudage *m.* **to erect a ~**, dresser un échafaud. *v.t.* échafauder.

scald *v.t.* échauder, faire bouillir.

scalding *adj.* brûlant, échaudant. ~ **water**, eau bouillante.

scale *n.* plateau *m.* (weighing); *Astron.* pl. la Balance *f.*; écaille *f.* (fish); échelle *f.*; escalade *f.*; *Mus.* gamme *f.* **on a large ~**, sur une grande échelle, en grand. **sliding ~**, échelle mobile. *v.t.* escalader; enlever par feuilles, comparer, mettre dans la balance; peser. *v.i.* s'écailler.

scallion *n.* oignon *m.* grelot.

scallop *n.* (fish) coquille *f.* Saint-Jacques; pétoncle *m.*; coquillage *m.*; coquille *f.*; dentelure *f.*, feston *m.*, découpure *f.* ~ *v.t.* denteler; festonner, cuire dans la coquille.

scalpel *n.* scalpel *m.*

scam *n.* piège *m.*, traquenard *m.*, attrape-couillon *m.*

scamp *n.* vaurien *m.*, chenapan *m.*, gredin *m.*

scan *v.t.* scruter, examiner avec soin; scander.

scandal *n.* scandale *m.*

scandalize *v.t.* scandaliser; diffamer; médire de.

scandalous *adj.* scandaleux; honteux; calomnieux; diffamatoire.

Scandinavia *n.pr.* Scandinavie *f.*

Scandinavian *n.* Scandinave *m.f.*

scanner *n.* scanner *m.*

scant or scanty *adj.* petit; mesquin, insuffisant, avare, ladre, chiche. ~ **meals**, maigres repas. ~ **clothing**, vêtements insuffisants.

scapegoat *n.* bouc *m.* émissaire.

scapula *n.* omoplate *m.*

scar *n.* cicatrice *f.*; balafre *f.* ~ *v.t.* cicatriser; balafrer, faire une balafre. *v.i.* se cicatriser.

scarab *n.* scarabée *m.*

scarce *adj.* rare. **money is ~**, l'argent est rare.

scarcely *adv.* à peine; presque pas. ~ **anything**, presque rien. ~ **ever**, presque jamais.

scarceness, scarcity *n.* disette *f.*, pénurie *f.*, besoin *m.*, rareté *f.*

scare *v.t.* épouvanter; effrayer; alarmer. **to ~**

away, faire fuir d'effroi; panique *f.,* frayer *f.* subite.

scarecrow *n.* épouvantail *m.*

scarf *n.* écharpe *f.;* foulard *m.*

scarlatina, scarlet fever *n.* scarlatine *f.,* fièvre *f.* scarlatine.

scarlet *n.* écarlate *f.* *adj.* écarlate; vermeil. **~ fever,** scarlatine *f.,* fièvre *f.* scarlatine.

scary *adj.* qui fait peur, effrayant.

scatter *v.t.* dissiper; répandre. **to ~ about,** disperser, dissiper; répandre. *v.i.* se disperser, s'éparpiller. **~-brained,** étourdi *m.*

scattered *adj.* dispersé, dissipé, écarté.

scavenger *n.* nécrophage *m.,* coprophage *m.;* éboueur.

scenario *n.* scénario *m.*

scene *n.* scène *f.;* théâtre *m.;* décoration *f.* **behind the ~s,** dans les coulisses. **he made such a ~,** il a fait toute une scène/histoire.

scenery *n.* scène *f.;* vue *f.,* paysage *m.;* décors *m.pl.*

scenic *adj.* scénique; théâtral.

scent *n.* odeur *f.;* parfum *m.,* senteur *f.;* piste *f.,* trace *f.;* flair *m.* (animals); nez *m.*(dog). **to be on the ~,** être sur la trace, sur la voie. **to throw off the ~,** mettre en défaut; dépister; donner le change. *v.t.* sentir; flairer; parfumer. *v.i.* suivre à la piste.

schedule *n.* calendrier *m.;* plan *m.;* horaire *m.;* programme *m.;* inventaire *m.;* *Comm.* bilan *m.* **according to the ~,** selon les prévisions. *v.t.* classer, inventorier; inscrire au programme, établir l'horaire.

scheme *n.* plan *m.,* projet *m.,* dessein *m.;* disposition *f.;* *Arch.* devis *m.;* combine *f.,* complot *m.,* machination *f.* **to form a ~,** former un projet. *v.t.* faire le plan de; projeter. *v.i.* former des projets, intriguer, comploter, conspirer.

schemer *n.* intrigant *m.;* comploteur *m.*

schism *n.* schisme *m.;* division *f.*

schizo *adj. n.* (*abbrev.* **schizophrenic**) schizophrène *m.f.*

schlepp *v.t.* *Infml.* porter, (se) trimbaler, (se) traîner.

schmuck *n.* *Infml.* crétin *m.,* idiot *m.,* con *m.*

scholar *n.* lettré *m.,* savant *m.,* érudit *m.*

scholarship *n.* savoir *m.,* érudition *f.,* science *f.;* bourse *f.* d'études.

scholastic *adj.* des écoles; scolastique. *n.* scolastique *m.*

school *n.* école *f.;* collège *m.;* banc (whales, etc.). **law ~,** école de droit. **high ~,** collège *m.,* lycée *m.,* école *f.* secondaire. **~ hours,** heures *f.pl.* de classe. *v.t.* instruire, enseigner.

schooling *n.* instruction *f.* (given in a school); enseignement *m.*

sciatica *n.* sciatique *f.*

science *n.* science *f.*

scientific *adj.* scientifique.

scientist *n.* savant *m.,* scientifique *m.f.*

scintillate *v.i.* scintiller, étinceler.

scissors *n.* ciseaux *m.pl.* **pair of ~,** paire *f.* de ciseaux.

scoff *v.i.* railler, plaisanter, se moquer, rire. *n.* raillerie *f.,* dérision *f.,* moquerie *f.*

scold *v.i.* crier, gronder. *v.i.* quereller; gourmander. *n.* femme *f.* querelleuse, criarde *f.;* mégère *f.;* criaillerie *f.*

scoop *n.* cuillerée *f.* **~** *v.t.* vider, retirer avec une écope; creuser (hole).

scoot *v.i.* *Infml.* filer, détaler.

scope *n.* espace *m.,* place *f.,* champ *m.;* étendue *f.* (of mind). **to have free ~,** avoir libre carrière, ses coudées franches.

scorch *v.t.,v.i.* roussir, *Fig.* rôtir, griller.

score *n.* marque *f.,* score *m.;* entaille *f.,* coche *f.,* trait *m.;* compte *m.,* dette *f.;* partition *f.* (music). **on that ~,** a ce compte-là. *v.t.* marquer, faire une cocire à, tailler, compter, énumérer; mettre sur le compte de; *Mus.* orchestrer.

scoring *n.* but *m.,* point *m.*

scorn *n.* mépris *m.;* objet *m.* de dédain. **to treat someone with ~,** traiter quelqu'un avec mépris. *v.t.* mépriser; dédaigner. *v.i.* railler, se rire de.

Scorpio *n.* *Astron.* Scorpion *m.*

scorpion *n.* scorpion *m.*

Scotland *n.pr.* Ecosse *f.*

Scottish *adj.* écossais.

scoundrel *n.* scélérat *m.,* coquin *m.,* gredin *m.,* misérable *m.*

scour *v.t.* nettoyer; frotter; laver; lessiver, décrasser, dégraisser, dessuinter; battre, parcourir. **to ~ the countryside,** battre la campagne. **to ~ the woods,** parcourir les bois. **to ~ the plain,** raser la plaine.

scourge *n.* fouet *m.,* punition *f.;* *Fig.* fléau *m.;* calamité *f.* **~** *v.t.* fouetter, flageller.

scout *n.* éclaireur *m.,* scout *m.* **~** *v.i.* aller en éclaireur; aller à la découverte.

scowl *v.i.* froncer les sourcils; se refrogner. *n.* froncement *m.* de sourcils; mine *f.* rechignée.

scramble *v.i.* marcher, avanser à l'aide des pieds et des mains; chercher à attraper; brouiller. **to ~ for,** s'efforcer de saisir; se battre pour; s'arracher. **to ~ up,** grimper; grimper sur (tree); gravir (mountain). **~d eggs,** oeufs *m.pl.* brouillés.

scrap *n.* brin *m.,* morceau *m.,* bout *m.,* fragment *m.,* bribe *f.;* bagarre *f.,* dispute *f.* **he sold his car for ~,** il a vendu sa voiture à la casse *f.* **~book,** album *m.,* recueil *m.* **~** *v.t.* envoyer à la ferraille, jeter; se bagarrer, se disputer.

scrape *v.t.* gratter, râcler. **to ~ together,** amasser péniblement ou petit à petit. **to ~ off,** ôter, enlever en grattant, en râclant. *n.* grattage *m.;* coup *m.* de grattoir; embarras *m.,* perplexité *f.* **to get someone into a ~,** mettre quelqu'un dans l'embarras. **to get out of a ~,** se tirer d'une mauvaise affaire.

scraper *n.* grattoir *m.;* racloir *m.;* ratissoire *f.*

scratch *v.t.* se gratter; égratigner. **to ~ out, off,** rayer, biffer. *v.i.* gratter, donner un coup de griffe. *n.* égratignure *f.,* coup *m.* d'ongle; coup *m.* de griffe; raie *f.,* marque *f.* **to start from** ~, partir de zéro.

scratchy *adj.* qui grince, qui gratte; rêche, rugueux; (writing) pattes de mouche.

scrawl *v.t.* barbouiller, griffonner. *v.i.* écrire mal. *n.* grillonnage *m.,* barbouillage *m.*

scrawny *adj.* décharné, famélique.

scream *v.i.* crier, pousser un cri perçant. *n.* cri *m.*

screaming *adj.* criant. *n.* cri *m.,* cris *m.pl.*

screech *v.i.* pousser des cris perçants; crier (like an owl). *n.* cri *m.* ~ **owl,** chat-huant *m.*

screen *n.* écran *m.;* paravent *m.,* Fig. abri *m.,* défense *f.;* crible *m.* ~ *v.t.* abriter, protéger, mettre à l'abri, cacher, cribler, passer au crible.

screening *n.* procédure *f.* de sélection.

screw *n.* vis *f.,* écrou *m.;* hélice *f.* **cork**~, tire-bouchon *m.* ~ **bolt,** boulon *m.* à vis. ~ **cap,** bouchon *m.* à vis. ~**driver,** tournevis *m.* ~ **nail,** clou *m.* à vis. ~ **nut,** écrou *m.* ~ **propeller,** propulseur *m.* à hélice; helice *f.* ~ *v.t.* visser, serrer, presser; Vulg. baiser. **to ~ down,** visser; fermer à vis. **to ~ in, to ~ into,** visser; faire entrer en vissant. **to ~ out,** défaire en tournant; dévisser, extorquer. **to ~ up,** Infml. bousiller.

screwball *adj., n.* Infml. détraqué *m.*

scribble *v.t.,v.i.* griffonner, barbouiller. *n.* griffonnage *m.;* mauvaise écriture.

scribbler *n.* gribouilleur *m.,* gratte-papier *m.*

scribbling *n.* griffonnage *m.,* barbouillage *m.*

script *n.* manuscrit *m.;* scénario *m.;* capie *f.;* document *m.* original.

Scripture *n.* Ecriture *f.* sainte.

scroll *n.* rouleau *m.,* parchemin *m.*

Scrooge *n.* avare *m.f.,* picsou *m.f.*

scrotum *n.* scrotum *m.*

scrub *v.t.* frotter, laver (avec une brosse dure); décrasser. *v.* nettoyage (avec une brosse dure) *f.*

scrum *n.* (rugby) mêlée *f.;* bousculade *f.*

scrumptious *adj.* Infml. super bon, délicieux.

scruple *n.* scrupule *m.;* doute *f.* ~ *v.i.* hésiter; se faire scrupule.

scrupulous *adj.* scrupuleux.

scrupulously *adv.* scrupuleusement.

scrutinize *v.t.* scruter, examiner.

scrutiny *n.* examen *m.* rigoureux, recherche *f.* minutieuse; scrutin *m.*

scuba *n.* scaphandre *m.* autonome. ~ **diving,** plongée *f.* en scaphandre autonome.

scuffle *n.* rixe *f.,* lutte *f.,* bagarre *f.* ~ *v.i.* se battre, avoir un démêle; lutter.

scull *n.* godille *f.;* aviron *m.* ~ *v.i.* ramer.

sculptor *n.* sculpteur *m.*

sculpture *n.* sculpture *f.,* ouvrage sculpté; ciselure *f.* ~ *v.t.* sculpter (stone); ciseler (metal).

scum *n.* écume *f.;* crasse *f.;* rebut *m.* **the ~ of society,** la lie du peuple. *v.t.* écumer.

scurrilous *adj.* grossier, insultant; indécent, déshonnête.

scuttle *n.* panier *m.;* seau *m.* **coal ~,** seau à charbon de terre.

scythe *n.* faux *f.* ~ *v.t.* faucher, coper avec une faux.

sea *n.* mer *f.* **at ~,** en mer. **by ~,** par mer. **open ~,** pleine mer. **on the high ~s,** sur la haute mer. ~ **anemone,** anémone *f.* de mer. ~ **breeze,** brise *f.* de mer. ~ **captain,** capitaine *m.* de vaisseau. ~**gull,** mouette *f.* ~**horse,** morse *m.* ~ **legs,** pied *m.* marin. ~**port,** port *m.* de mer. ~**shell,** coquille *f.* marine. ~**shore,** côte *f.,* bord *m.* de la mer; rivage *m.* ~**sick,** qui a le mal de mer. ~**sickness,** mal *m.* de mer. ~**weed,** algue, plante *f.* marine.

seal *n.* phoque *m.,* veau *m.* marin; sceau *m.,* cachet *m.;* Law. scellé *m.* ~ *v.t.* sceller; cacheter; Fig. fermer hermétiquement, clore; garder secret. **to ~ up,** sceller; mettre le sceau à; cacheter, fermer. **his fate is sealed,** son sort est décidé.

seam *n.* couture *f.;* cicatrice *f.,* couture *f.;* Anat. suture *f.,* Min. veine *f.,* filon *m.* ~ *v.t.* unir par une couture, cicatriser.

seamy *adj.* sordide. **the ~ side of life,** l'envers du décor.

séance *n.* séance *f.* de spiritisme.

sear *v.t.* brûler (la surface), cautériser; roussir; faner, dessécher.

search *v.t.* chercher, rechercher, fouiller, examiner; visiter, lire avec soin; sonder; approfondir. **to ~ a house,** faire une perquisition dans une maison. **to ~ out,** découvrir. *v.t.* faire des recherches. **to ~ for,** rechercher, essayer de découvrir. **to ~ into,** faire des recherches sur; approfondir. *n.* recherche *f.;* poursuite *f.;* étude *f.* **in ~ of,** à la recherche de. ~ **warrant,** Law. mandat *m.* de perquisition.

searching *adj.* pénétrant, perçant, scrutateur. **a ~ cold,** un froid pénétrant.

season *n.* saison *f.;* temps *m.* **in ~,** en temps opportun. *v.t.* assaisonner; relever; sécher (wood); accoutumer; tempérer. **to ~ a dish,** assaisonner un met. *v.i.* s'acclimater; se sécher.

seasonable *adj.* de saison; convenable; à propos, opportun.

seasonably *adv.* à propos, en temps opportun, de saison.

seasoning *n.* assaisonnement *m.;* condiment *m.*

seat *n.* siège *m.* (of a chair); place *f.;* fond *m.* (pants, chair, etc.); séjour *m.,* résidence *f.;* demeure *f.,* maison *f.* de campagne; site *m.,* situation *f.* **to keep one's ~,** rester assis. **a bishop's ~,** un siège épiscopal. ~ **in parliament,** un siège au parlement. **to take a ~,** prendre place. *v.t.* faire asseoir; placer; établir; mettre un fond à. **be seated,** veuillez vous asseoir.

seaward *adj.* dirigé, tourné vers la mer.

sec *n.* (abbrev. second) seconde *f.*

secede *v.i.* se retirer; faire scission.

secession *n.* sécession *f.,* scission *f.,* séparation *f.*

seclude *v.t.* écarter; renfermer, éloigner; retirer, s'enfermer.

secluded *adj.* feculé; de retraite.

seclusion *n.* retraite *f.*, solitude *f.*

second *adj.* second; deuxième. **~-rate**, de second rang; de deuxième qualité. **~ floor**, deuxième étage. **Charles the ~**, Charles II (Charles deux). **~-hand**, de seconde main, d'occasion. **in second** *m.*, témoin *m.*; *Mus.* seconde *f.* **~** *v.t.* seconder, appuyer. **to ~ a resolution**, appuyer une résolution.

secondary *adj.* secondaire; accessoire. *n.* délégue *m.*, député *m.*; subalterne *m.*

secondly *adv.* secondement; en second lieu.

secrecy *n.* secret *m.*, mystère; discrétion; solitude *f.*, retraite *f.* **in ~**, dans le secret.

secret *adj.* secret, secrète. **to keep ~**, tenir, garder secret. *n.* secret *m.*, confidence *f.* **in ~**, en secret. **to tell someone a ~**, confier un secret à quelqu'un.

secretary *n.* secrétaire *m.* **~ of State**, secrétaire d'Etat.

secrete *v.t.* cacher; tenir secret.

secretion *n.* sécrétion *f.*

secretly *adv.* secrètement *f.*

sect *n.* secte *f.*

section *n.* section *f.*; coupe *f.*; profil *m.* **~** *v.t.* sectionner.

sector *n.* secteur *m.*

secular *adj.* séculaire; séculier, temporel; profane (music); laïque. **~ education**, instruction laïque. *n.* séculier *m.*; laïque *m.*

secure *adj.* en sûreté, dans la sécurité; hors de danger; sauf; sû; assuré. **~ from**, à l'abri de. *v.t.* mettre à l'abri, en sûreté; défendre; protéger; s'assurer, s'emparer de, se rendre maître de; garantir le payment de. **~ your place**, retenez votre place.

security *n.* sûreté, sécurité *f.*, garantie *f.*; *Fin.* pl. valeurs *f.pl.*; cautionnement *m.*; caution *f.* **to give ~**, fournir caution.

sedan *n.* conduite *f.* intérieure.

sedate *adj.* tranquille, calme, posé, paisible, rassis. *v.t.* donner un sédatif.

sedately *adv.* posément, avec sang-froid.

sedative *n.* sédatif. *m.*

sedentary *adj.* sédentaire; inactif, immobile, engourdi, apathique.

sediment *n.* sédiment *m.*; lie *f.*, dépôt *m.*

sedimentary *adj.* sédimentaire.

sedition *n.* sédition *f.*; soulèvement *m.*; émeute *f.*

seditious *adj.* séditieux.

seduce *v.t.* séduire; corrompre, suborner, débaucher.

seduction *n.* séduction *f.*

seductive *adj.* séducteur; séduisant.

see *n.* siège *m.*; évêche *m.* **The Holy ~**, le Saint-Siège.

see *v.t.* voir; regarder, apercevoir. **I ~ nothing**, he ne vois rien. **to ~ the world**, voir le monde. **to ~ friends**, visiter des amis. **I will ~ you**

out, je vais vous conduire (à la porte). *v.i.* **let me ~**, laisse-moi voir. **I ~**, je vois, je comprends. **~ to it**, pensez-y, prenez soin de; assurez-vous que. **just ~ into that matter**, examinez un peu cette affaire là. **~ you!** salut! **~ you later**, à plus tard.

seed *n.* semence *f.*, graîne *f.*, pépin *m.*; sperme *m.* **~** *v.i.* monter en graine; grener. *v.t.* semer. **~ corn**, grain *m.* pour semis. **~ pod**, capsule *f.*

seedy *adj.* abondant en graines; parfumé, aromatisé; *Infml.* râpé, usé jusqu'à la corde.

seeing *conj.* **~ that**, vu que, puisque, attendu que.

seek *v.t.* chercher, demander. **to ~ out**, rechercher, tâcher de trouver. *v.i.* poursuivre, s'enquérir; solliciter.

seem *v.i.* paraître, sembler; avoir l'air de; faire semblant de. **it seems**, il semble. **without seeming to hear**, sans paraître entendre.

seeming *adj.* qui paraît, apparent; spécieux, plausible.

seemingly *adv.* apparemment, en apparence.

seemly *adj.* bienséant, décent. **it is not ~ to**, il ne sied pas de, il ne convient pas de. *adv.* avec décence, convenablement.

seep *v.t.* viltrer, (s')infiltrer.

seer *n.* prophète *m.*, voyant *m.*

seesaw *n.* bascule *f.* (game); va-et-vient *m.* **~** *v.i.* faire las bascule; se balancer à deux (sur une planche).

seethe *v.t.*,*v.i.* faire bouillir; faire cuire; bouillir; s'agiter, bouillenner, être en effervescence.

segment *n.* segment *m.*; portion *f.*, morceau *m.*

segregate *v.t.* séparer; mettre à part; isoler. *adj.* séparé; mis à part.

segregation *n.* séparation *f.*, mise *f.* à part; ségrégation *f.*

seize *v.t.* saisir; empoigner; se saisir de; s'emparer de; *Law.* faire une saisie; confisquer.

seizure *n.* saisie *f.*; prise *f.*, capture *f.*; *Law.* saisie *f.*, saisie-arrêt *f.*; chosie saisie; possession *f.*

seldom *adv.* rarement, peu souvent.

select *v.t.* choisir. *adj.* choisi, d'élite, préférable, de choix.

selected *adj.* choisi.

selection *n.* choix *m.*, sélection *f.*

self *pron.* pl. **selves** soi, soi-même; même. **my~**, moi-même. **your~**, **him~**, **her~**, **it~**, toi-même, vous-même, lui-même, elle-même. **our-selves, yourselves, themselves**, nous-mêmes, vous-mêmes, eux-mêmes, elles-mêmes. **one~**, soi-même. **they dress themselves**, ils, elles s'habillent. **to keep by one~**, rester tout seul. *n.*, *adj.* personne *f.*, individu *m.*; soi, soi-même; le moi. **my other ~**, un autre moi-même.

~-abased, humilié, abaissé par la conscience de sa honte. **~-abasement**, humiliation *f.*, abaissement *m.* **~-accusing**, qui s'accuse soi-même. **~-acting**, tout seul; automatique. **~-admiration**, admiration *f.* de soi-même, de sa personne. **~-command**, empire *m.* sur soi-même. **~-confidence**, assurance *f.*, confiance *f.* en soi-même. **~-confident**, confiant en soi-même. **~-conscious**, embarrassé, géné. **~-consciousness**, embarras *m.*, timidité *f.* gêne *f.* **~-control**, sang-froid *m.*, empire *m.* sur soi-même. **~-deceit**, illusion *f.* **~-deception**, illusion *f.* **~-delusion**, illusion *f.* **~-denial**, abnégation *f.*, oubli *m.* de soi-même. **~-destruction**, suicide *m.* **~-determination**, détermination *f.* **~-esteem**, estime *f.*, bonne opinion *f.* de soi-même. **~-evident**, évident par soi-même, évident. **~-examination**, examen *m.* de soi-même. **~-governed**, gouverné par soi-même. **~-government**, gouvernement *m.* d'un pays par lui-même. **~-healing**, qui se guérit soi-même. **~-indulgence**, indulgence *f.* pour soi-même. **~-inflicted**, infligé par soi-même. **~-interest**, intérêt *m.* personnel; égoïsme *m.* **~-made**, de sa propre création, fair par soi-même. **~-opinion**, haute opinion *f.* de soi. **~-possession**, possession *f.* de soi-même, sang-froid *m.*, calme. **~-praise**, éloge *m.* de soi-même. **~-preservation**, conservation *f.* de soi-même; défense *f.* personnelle. **~-regulating**, agissant de soi-même; automatique. **~-reliance**, confiance *f.* en soi-même, en ses propres forces. **~-reproach**, reproche *m.* de soi-même. **~-restrained**, contenu, retenu par soi-même. **~-restraint**, retenue *f.*, empire *m.* sur soi-même. **~-righteous**, qui se croit justifié, un juste. **~-satisfied**, satisfait, content de soi-même. **~-seeking**, *adj.* égoïste, intéressé. **~-styled**, soi-disant, prétendu. **~-sufficiency**, indépendence *f.*, vanité *f.* **~-sufficient**, indépendant. **~-sustaining**, soutenu par soi-même. **~-taught**, qui s'est instruit soi-même.

selfish *adj.* égoïste; intéressé; personnel.
selfishly *adv.* en égoïste; par égoïsme.
selfishness *n.* égoïsme *m.*
sell *v.t.* **to ~ for cash**, vendre au comptant. **to ~ retail, wholesale**, vendre au détail, en gros. **to ~ off**, liquider. **to ~ out**, vendre. *v.i.* se vendre.
seller *n.* vendeur *m.*, vendeuse *f.*
sellout *n.* **the movie was a ~**, les billets ont été vendus à guichet fermés; trahison *f.*
seltzer water *n.* eau *f.* de Seltz.
semblance *n.* resemblance *f.*; apparence *f.*; semblant *m.*
semen *n.* semence *f.*, sperme *m.*
semi *adj.* semi; à demi. **~-annual**, semi-annuel, semestrial. **~-circle**, semi-cercle *m.* **~-circular**, *adj.* demi-circulaire. **~-colon**, *n.* point virgule *m.* **~-official**, semi-officiel.
seminal *adj.* séminal.
seminar *n.* séminaire *m.*
semitic *adj.* sémite, sémitique.
semolina *n.* semoule *f.*
senate *n.* sénat *m.*
senator *n.* sénateur *m.*
senatorial *adj.* sénatorial.
send *v.t.* envoyer; faire partir; expédier; trans-

mettre. **to ~ a letter**, envoyer une lettre. **he was sent to China**, il a été envoyé en Chine. **to ~ one about his business**, envoyer quelqu'un promener. **to ~ away**, envoyer, faire partir; expédier; renvoyer, congédier. **to ~ back**, renvoyer, réexpédier. **to ~ for**, envoyer chercher. **to ~ forth**, jeter, lancer; publier, promulguer; exhaler. **to ~ in**, faire entrer, livrer. **to ~ off**, expédier, faire partir; congédier. **to ~ out**, envoyer dehors, exhaler, répandre. **to ~ up**, envoyer en haut; faire monter. *v.i.* faire venir, mander (quelqu'un).
sender *n.* envoyeur *m.*; expéditeur *m.*
senescence *n.* déclin *m.*
senile *adj.* sénile.
senility *n.* vieillesse *f.*, sénilité *f.*
senior *adj.* aîne, plus âge; père; supérieur; premier. **~ partner**, principal associé. *n.* aîné *m.*, ancien *m.*; vieillard *m.*
seniority *n.* priorité *f.*
sensation *n.* sensation *f.*; sentiment. **to create a ~**, faire sensation.
sensational *adj.* à sensation.
sense *n.* sens *m.*; perception *f.*, sentiment *m.*; raison *f.*; esprit *m.*; sensation *f.* **the five ~s**, les cinq sens. **common ~**, sens commun. **in a figurative ~**, au figuré. **I will bring him to his ~s**, je lui ferai entendre raison. **to come to one's ~s**, reprendre ses sens *or* connaissance.
senseless *adj.* insensible; sans connaissance, privé de sentiment; deraisonnable, insensé; absurde.
senselessly *adv.* d'une manière insensée.
senselessness *n.* manque *m.* de bon sens, sottise *f.*, absurdité *f.*, déraison *f.*
sensibility *n.* sensibilité *f.pl.* susceptibilité *f.*; sensiblerie *f.*
sensible *adj.* sensible; sensé, judicieux; convaincu; susceptible. **a ~ person**, une personne sensée.
sensibleness *n.* perceptibilité *f.*, bon sens; sensibilité *f.*; sagesse *f.*
sensibly *adv.* sensiblement; sagement, avec bon sens; judicieusement.
sensitive *adj.* sensitif; sensible; susceptible. **he is too ~**, il est trop susceptible.
sensitively *adv.* d'une manière sensitive.
sensitiveness *n.* sensibilité *f.*
sensory *adj.* sensorial.
sensual *adj.* sensuel.
sensuality *n.* sensualité *f.*
sensually *adv.* sensuellement.
sensuous *adv.* voluptueux, sensuel, tendre; passionné.
sensuously *adv.* tendrement, passionnément, voluptueusement.
sentence *n.* phrase *f.*, maxime *f.*, sentence *f.*; jugement *m.*, arrêt *m.* – *v.t.* rendre, prononcer un jugement contre; condamner.
sententious *adj.* sentencieux; énergique; laconique.

sententiously adv. sentencieusement; laconiquement.

sentient adj. sensible, sensitif.

sentiment n. sentiment m., avis m.; jugement m.; sens m.

sentimental adj. sentimental; sensible.

sentimentality n. sentimentalité f.

sentinel n. sentinelle f.

sentry n. factionnaire m., sentinelle f.; faction f.; garde f.

separable adj. séparable.

separate v.t. diviser; éloigner. v.i. se séparer; se disjoindre, se désunir. adj. séparé, détaché, distinct, different.

separated adj. séparé, disjoint; partagé.

separately adv. séparément.

separateness n. état m. de séparation.

separation n. séparation f.

separatist n. séparatiste f.; dissident.

sepia n. sepia f.

September n. septembre m.

septic adj. septique.

septuagenarian n. septuagénaire m.

sepulcher n. sépulcre m.

sepulchral adj. sépulcral.

sequel n. suite f.; consequence f.

sequence n. suite f.; effet m.; ordre m. de succession; série f., (cards) séquence f.

sequester v.t. séparer; Law. mettre en séquestre. v.i. s;éloigner, se séquestrer.

sequestered adj. sequestré; Law. en séquestre; ratire.

sequestrate v.t. séquestrer, mettre en séquestre.

sequestration n. séquestre m.; séquestration f.; retraite f.

seraph n. pl. **seraphs** or **seraphim** séraphin m.

serenade n. sérénade f. ~ v.t. donner une sérénade à.

serene adj. serein; sans nuages; calme; paisible. **a ~ look**, un regard, un front serein. **most ~**, sérénissime.

serenely adv. avec sénérité; avec sang-froid.

serenity n. sérénité f.

sergeant n. sergent (infantry); maréchal m. des logis (cavalry). **~ major**, sergent-major m., maréchal des logis chef. **~-at-arms**, sergent m., huissier m.

serial adj. de série. n. ouvrage m. qui paraît par séries, en livraisons. **~ killer**, auteur m. de meurtres multiples.

series n. pl. **series**, série f., suite f.

serious adj. sérieux, grave.

seriously adv. sérieusement. **to take ~**, prendre au sérieux.

seriousness n. sérieux m.

sermon n. sermon m.

sermonize v.i. prêcher; faire des sermons; sermonner.

serpent n. serpent m.

serpentine adj. de serpent; en serpent; serpentant. v.i. serpenter.

serrated adj. serré, serraté, en scie.

serum n. sérum f.

servant n. domestique m.f., serviteur m.; servante f.

serve v.t. servir; être au service (de); en user avec; servir à; Law. exécuter; ramettre; obliger; aider à. **to ~ one's country**, servir son pays. **to ~ dinner**, servir le dîner. **to ~ as an example**, servir d'example. **it ~d him right**, c'était bien fait pour lui. **to ~ up**, servir (le dîner). **to ~ at table**, servir à table.

server n. servant m.; serveur m.

service n. service m.; emploi m.; utilité f., usage m., hommage m. **to do a ~**, rendre un service. **military ~**, service militaire. **to enter the ~**, entrer au service. **to be of ~ to**, être utile à. **tea ~**, service à thé. **~ road**, route f. d'accès. **~ station**, station f. service v.t.

serviceable adj. utile, avantageux; profitable; Mil. propre au service.

servile adj. servile.

servilely adv. servilement.

servileness, servility n. servitude f., esclavage f.; condition servile; servilité f.

servitude n. servitude f., asservissement f.

sesame n. sésame m.

session n. session f., séance f.; Univ. trimestre m.

set v.t. mettre, poser, placer; planter; établir; monter; enchasser (gems); affiler, repasser; Typ. composer. **to ~ in order**, mettre en ordre, arranger. **to ~ free**, mettre en liberté. **to ~ a house on fire**, mettre le feu à une maison. **to ~ a price**, fixer un prix. **to ~ a stone in gold**, monter une pierre en or. **to ~ good examples**, donner de bons exemples. **to ~ sail**, mettre à la voile, partir. **to ~ about**, mettre à, appliquer; entreprendre. **to ~ against**, indisposer contre; opposer à. **to ~ oneself against a person**, s'opposer à quelqu'un. **to ~ apart**, mettre de côté; réserver. **to ~ aside**, laisser de côté; écarter; casser. **to ~ before**, placer devant; présenter. **to ~ down**, déposer (un object); inscrire; noter, prendre note de. **to ~ forth**, déployer, étaler; produire; publier; exposer, énoncer; se mettre en route, mettre en avant; partir; se mettre en marche. **to ~ forward**, avancer, favoriser. **to ~ off**, faire partir; parer; rehausser, faire ressortir. **to ~ upon**, poser sur; exciter; lâcher, tomber sur. **to ~ out**, avancer, tracer; étaler, montrer. **to ~ to music**, mettre en musique. **to ~ up**, dresser, ériger; abbrer; fonder; mettre sur ses pieds; établir. **his father ~ him up in business**, son père l'a établi dans le commerce. v.i. se mettre; s'appliquer; se coucher; se fixer, se figer (liquids). **to ~ to work**, se mettre à l'ouvrage. **the sun is ~ting**, le soleil se couche. **to ~ about**, se mettre à, commencer; s'y prendre. **to ~ in**, commencer. **cold weather has ~ in**, le froid a commencé. **to ~ off, to ~ out**, partir, se mettre en route. **to ~ up**, s'établir; se mettre dans les affaires. adj.

fixe, immobile; réglé, constant; régulier, établi; résolu. *n.* collection *f.;* assortiment *m.,* service *m.* (table); garniture *f.;* parure *f.* (diamonds); rang *m.,* rangée *f.;* bande *f.,* clique *f.;* jeu *m.;* poste (de télévision); couple *m.* (dancers). a ~ of books, une collection de livres. a ~ of studs, une garniture de boutons. a ~ of trees, une rangée d'arbres. a ~ of teeth, un râtelier, une denture. a ~ of men, une groupe d'hommes.

setting *n.* action de mettre, de poser *f.;* mise *f.;* plantation *f.;* mise *f.* en musique; montage *m.,* enchâssement *m.* (gem); monture *f.;* coucher *m.* (sun). *Fig.* déclin *m.*

settle *v.t.* tranquilliser; coloniser; ajuster, arranger; décider, régler; résoudre. that ~ the question, cela règle la question. *v.i.* s'établir; se fixer, se ranger, déposer; se tasser. they ~ed there, ils s'y sont établis. ~ down, installez-vous; calmez-vous. the dust ~s on everything, la poussière vient couvrir tout ici. let the wine ~, laisser reposer le vin. to ~ down, se fixer; s'ranger. to ~ on, s'abattre sur, descendre sur; se poser sur; s'arrêter à. to ~ upon, se décider à; s'attacher à. *n.* banc *m.,* siège *m.*

settlement *n.* établissement *m.,* fixation *f.;* colonie; constitution *f.* (of a pension, etc.); douaire *m.* (of a widow); contrat *m.;* ajustement *m.,* arrangement *m.,* liquidation *f.;* règlement *m.,* payment *m.;* décision *f.* (question). there's an old ~ by the river, une vieille colonie habite près de la rivière. here is $200 in ~ of my debt, voici $200 pour règlement de mon compte.

settler *n.* colon *m.*

seven *adj.* sept.

seventeen *adj.* dix-sept.

seventeenth *adj.* dix-septième.

seventh *adj.* septième. *n.* septième *m.*

seventieth *adj.* soixante-dixième.

seventy *adj.* soixante-dix.

sever *v.t.* séparer, couper; *Law.* disjoindre. *v.i.* faire une séparation, distinguer, se séparer.

several *adj.* plusieurs, divers, différent, distinct; respectif. ~ persons, plusieurs personnes.

severance *n. Law.* disjonction *f.,* séparation *f.,* division *f.* ~ pay, indemnité *f.* de licenciement.

severe *adj.* sévère, rigoureux, cruel; austere. a ~ winter, un hiver rigoureux. a ~ look, un regard sévère. a ~ cold, un gros rhume.

severely *adv.* sévèrement; rudement; rigueuresement, avec rigueur; cruellement.

severity *n.* sévérité *f.,* austérité; rigueur *f.* dureté. the ~ of the winter, la rigueur de l'hiver.

sew *v.t.* coudre. *v.i.* to ~ up, coudre, recoudre.

sewer *n.* égout *m.*

sewing *n.* couture *f.* ~ machine, machine à coudre.

sex *n.* sexe *m.* to have ~ with, coucher avec. ~ offender, délinquant *m.* sexuel.

sexagenarian *n.* sexagénaire *m.f.*

sextant *n.* sextant *m.*

sexton *n.* sacristain *m.;* fossoyeur *m.*

sexual *adj.* sexuel.

sexuality *n.* sexualité *f.*

sexually *adv.* d'une manière sexuelle.

sexy *adj.* sexy.

shabbily *adv.* avec des vêtements usés, râpés; pauvrement; mosquinement.

shabiness *n.* état *m.* usé, râpé (clothing), pauvreté *f.,* mesquinerie *f.*

shabby *adj.* usé, râpé, qui montre la corde, pauvre, mesquin, sordide. ~ clothes, des vêtements usés.

shack *n.* cabane *f.,* hutte *f.*

shackle *n.* chaînes *f.pl.;* fers *m.pl.; Fig.* entrave *f.* ~ *v.t.* enchaîner, charger de fers, mettre dans les fers, lier, garretter; *Fig.* géner, entraver.

shade *n.* ombre *f.,* ombrage *m.,* abat-jour *m.* (lamp); nuance *f.* (color). in the ~, à l'ombre. in the ~ of a tree, sous l'ombrage d'un arbre, à l'ombre d'une arbre. a cool ~, un ombrage frais. *v.t.* ombrager, couvrir; abriter, protéger, obscurcir; (painting) ombrer, nuancer.

shades *n.pl. Infml.* lunettes *f.pl.* de soleil. the ~ of night, les ombres de la nuit.

shadow *n.* ombre *f.,* silhouette *f.,* obscurité *f.;* ténèbres *f.pl.* the ~ of a tree, l'ombre d'un arbre. ~ of death, l'ombre de la mort. to pursue a ~, courir après une ombre. *v.t.* ombrager; arbiter, couvrir, obscurcir, suivre secrètement; (painting) ombrer; nuancer (colors).

shadowy *adj.* ombragé, couvert d'ombre, obscur, ténébreux, chimérique. a ~ affair, une affaire sans valeur. ~ shapes, formes chimériques.

shady *adj.* ombragé, ombreux, a l'ombre; sombre, obscure; *Infml.* louche.

shaft *n.* flèche *f.,* dard *m.,* trait *m. Fig.* trait *m.;* puits *m.* (mine); fût *m.* (column); timon *m.,* brancard *m.* (cart); souche *f.* (chimney); manche *m.* (weapon).

shaggy *adj.* velu, poilu; hérissé, aux poils hérissés; raboteux, inégal.

shake *v.t.* secouer, remuer; branler; faire trembler. to ~ a tree, secouer un arbre. to ~ hands with, serrer la main à, donner une poignée de main à. to ~ down, faire tomber (en secouant). to ~ off, faire tomber, secouer, se défaire de. to ~ out, secouer, faire sortir. he shook his fist at them, il leur montra le poing. to ~ up, remuer. *v.i.* s'agiter, s'ébranler; chanceler, trembler. his hand ~s, sa main tremble. to ~ all over, trembler de tous les membres. *n.* secousse *f.;* ébranlement *m.,* tremblement *m.;* poignée *f.* (de main). with a ~ of the head, en secouant la tête.

Shaker *n.pl.* trembleurs *m.pl.* (une secte).

shaking *n.* secouement *m.,* secousse *f.;* ébranlement *m.,* tremblement *m.*

shaky *adj.* branlant, tremblant, chevrotant; chancelant.

shall *v.i.,* défect, auxil. I ~ go, j'irai. thou shalt not steal, tu ne voleras point. ~ I shut the

window? voulez-vous que je, or faut-il que je ferme la fenêtre?

shallot n. échalote f.

shallow adj. peu profond, bas, Fig. léger, superficiel, faible (mind). **a ~ stream,** un courant peu profond. **~ water,** eau basse. **a ~ mind,** un esprit superficiel. n. haut-fond m., bas-fond m., écueil m.; banc m. de sable.

shallowness n. peu m. ou manque m. de profondeur, étroitesse f. d'ésprit, nature f. bornée.

sham n. imitation f., feinte f., simulacre m., farce f. ~ adj. faux, feint, simulé. **a ~ fight,** un combat simulé. v.t. feindre, simuler, tromper, duper, jouer, faire accrire. v.i. user de feinte, jouer la comédie.

shamble v.i. se traîner. **to ~ along,** marcher en se traînant.

shambles n.pl. boucherie f., abattoir m.; Infml. pagaille f., fouilli m.

shame n. honte f., ignominie f., déshonneur m., opprobre, pudeur f.; ce qui blesse ou peut blesser la décence. **what a ~!** quelle honte! quel dommage! **he has no ~,** il n'a aucune pudeur. v.t. faire honte à, faire rougir; déshonorer, couvrir de honte, se moquer de.

shamefaced adj. honteux.

shameful adj. honteux, déshonorant, déshonnête, indécent.

shamefully adv. honteusement; indignement, mal.

shameless adj. éhonté, impudent, effronté.

shamelessly adv. sans honte; effrontément.

shamelessness n. impudence f., effronterie f.

shampoo n. shampooing m. **~ v.t.** (se) shampooiner.

shamrock n. trèfle m.

Shangri-la n. paradis m. terrestre.

shank n. jambe f.; tibia m.

shanty n. cabane f.

shape v.t. former; donner une forme à, modeler; Fig. régler; diriger. v.i. convenir, s'accorder, cadrer. n. forme f.; figure; taille f., tournure f. **in the ~ of,** en forme de. **an elegant ~,** une taille élégante.

shapeless adj. sans forme; informe; difforme.

shapely adj. beau, bien fait, d'une forme gracieuse.

shard n. tesson m., têt m.

share n. part f., portion f., partage m.; Comm. action f. **~ v.t. to each his ~,** à chacun sa part. **~holder,** actionnaire m. **~ v.t.** distribuer; se partager. v.i. avoir part; participer. **to ~ alike,** partager également.

sharing n. partage m.

shark n. requin m.; Infml. escroc m. **~ v.t.** escroquer.

sharp adj. tranchant, affilé; aigu, acéré; pointu; vif, froid; piquant, amer, acerbe; prompt, sévère; fin, intelligent, alerte, vigilant; subtil, malin. **a ~ knife,** un couteau bien aiguisé. **a ~ tongue,** une langue bien affilée. **a ~ needle,** une aiguille

à pointe aiguisé. **~ features,** des traites saillants. **~ wind,** vent pénétrant. **~ cold,** froid perçant. **a ~ eye,** un oeil vif. **~ sight,** vue perçante. **to keep a ~ eye on,** surveiller de près, avoir l'oeil sur. **a ~ taste,** goût piquant, amer. **~ words,** des paroles mordants. **~ pain,** une vive douleur. **a ~ appetite,** un vig, un bon appétit. **~-edged,** à fil tranchant, bien affilé. n. son m. aigu; Mus. dièse m. ~ v.i. tricher.

sharpen v.t. aiguiser, affiler; affûter des outils; rendre pointu; exciter; aigrir; rendre subtil, fin.

sharply adv. avec le fil tranchant.

sharpness n. pointe f. acérée; qualité de ce qui est vif, piquant, pénétrant; intensité f., rigueur f. (of cold); âpreté f., vivacité f., pénétration f.; subtilité f.; finesse f.; sagacité f.; esprit m. vif, éveillé; acuité f. (sound); amertume f., aigreur f. (words); acidité f.; goût m. piquant; rigueur f.

shatter v.t. faire éclater, faire voler en éclats; Fig. déchirer; troubler, détraquer. v.i. se briser.

shave v.t. effleurer, se raser, couper ras; écorcher; plumer; tondre. **to ~ off,** rogner. **to ~ close,** raser de près. **to ~ oneself,** se raser. **to get ~ed,** se faire raser. v.i. se raser, se faire la barbe. n. plane f. (outil).

shaver n. rasoir m. **electric ~,** rasour m. électrique.

shaving n. action de raser, de faire la barbe. **~ cream,** crème f. à raser.

shawl n. châle m.

she p.p.f. elle f.; ce; la, celle, cella-là. **it is ~,** c'est elle. **here ~ comes,** la voici qui vient. femelle f. (animal).

sheaf n. or pl. **sheaves** gerbe f. (wheat); javelle f.; paquet m.; faisceau m. (arrows). **to bind in ~s,** mettre en gerbes. v.t. engerber, mettre en gerbes.

shear v.t. tondre; couper (wool); couper ras; Fig. dépouiller.

shearing n. tonte f.

shears n. pl. grands ciseaux m.pl.; cisailles f.pl.

sheath n. étui m.; enveloppe f.; fourreau m. (sword); gaîne f. (knife); condom m., préservatif m.

sheathe v.t. couvrir. **to ~ the sword,** remettre l'épée dans le fourreau.

shed v.t. verser, perdre (leaves); jeter; muer. **to ~ tears,** verser des larmes. **to ~ light,** répandre de la lumière. v.i. se répandre; se dépouiller. n. hangar m.; appentis m.; cabane f., baraque f., bicoque f.

sheen n. éclat m., splendeur f.

sheep n. pl. **sheep,** mouton m., brebis f.; Fig. ouailles f.pl. (flock of a clergyperson). **black ~,** brébis f. galeuse. **~ skin,** Fig. diplôme m. **~dog,** chien m. de berger.

sheepish adj. timide, bête, penaud; interdit.

sheepishly adv. timidement; d'un air penaud.

sheepishness n. timidité f. niaise, niaiserie f.

sheer adj. pur; sans mélange, véritable; translucide (fabric). **~ ignorance,** pure, complète ignorance. *adv.* net, tout d'un coup, d'un seul coup; tout, complètement. *v.i. Naut.* s'écarter; faire des embardées.

sheet *n.* drap *m.* (bed); feuille *f.* (paper); nappe *f.* (water), tôle *f.*

shelf *n. or pl.* shelves étagère *f.*; tablette *f.*, rayon *m.* (for books); *Min.* couche *f.*

shell *n.* coquille *f.*; coquillage *m.*; écaille *f.* (oyster); carapace *f.* (turtle); coque *f.*; écale *f.*; carcasse *f.* (house); *Artill.* bombe; obus *m.* ~**fish**, coquillage *m.*, mollusque *m.*; crustacé *m.* ~ *v.t.* ôter la coque; écaler (nuts); écosser; bombarder. *Infml.* payer.

shelter *n.* abri *m.*, couvert *m.*, refuge *m.*, asile *m.*; sécurité *f.*; protection *f.* **to take ~**, s'abriter, se réfugier. **under the ~ of**, à l'abri de. *v.t.* mettre à l'abri (de), abriter (contre); donner un asile à; protéger. *v.i.* s'abriter, se mettre à l'abri.

shelve *v.t.* poser sur un rayon, mettre de côté.

shepherd *n.* berger *m.*, pâtre *m.*; *Fig.* pastuer *m.*

shepherdess *n.* bergère *f.*

sherbet *n.* sorbet *m.*

sherry *n.* xérès *m.*, vin *m.* de Xérès.

shield *n.* bouclier *m.*; égide *f.*; défense *f.*; écu *m.*, écuason *f.* ~ *v.t.* couvrir d'un bouclier; protéger; abriter.

shift *v.i.* changer; varier; trouver des expédients, biaiser. *v.t.* remplacer, transporter. **to ~ around**, changer complètement de direction. *n.* changement *m.*; expédient *m.*, moyen *m.*; ruse *f.*; subterfuge *m.*, faux-fuyant *m.* **she works the night ~**, elle travaille l'équipe de nuit. *adj.* **make~**, expédient.

shiftless *adj.* sans initiative, empoté; flemmard.

shimmer *v.i.* luire faiblement, briller.

shin *n.* tibia *m.*, os *m.* de la jambe. ~**bone**, tibia *m.*

shine *v.i.* briller, luire, reluire. *n.* clarté *f.*

shingle *n.* bardeau *m.* (roof); galet *m.*, caillou *m.* (beach). *v.t.* couvrir de bardeaux.

shining *adj.* brillant, resplendissant, radieux.

shiny *adj.* luisant, brillant, splendide.

ship *n.* bâtiment *m.*, navire *m.*, vaisseau *m.* **war~**, vaisseau, bâtiment de guerre. **~ of the line**, vaisseau de ligne. **flag~**, vaisseau amiral. **merchant ~**, navire, bâtiment marchand. **to load a ~**, affréter un navire. *v.t.* embarquer, charger, transporter. ~**builder**, constructeur *m.* de navires. ~**load**, chargement *m.*, cargaison *f.* ~**shape**, *adv.* bien arrangé. ~**yard**, chantier *m.* de construction navale.

shipmate *n.* camarade *m.* (de bord).

shipment *n.* embarquement *m.*; chargement *m.*, cargaison *f.*

shipper *n.* chargeur *m.*, expéditeur *m.*

shipping *adj.* naval, maritime. **~ charges**, frais de chargement. *n.* vaisseau *m.pl.*, navires *m.pl.*; marine *f.*, embarquement *m.*

shipwreck *n.* naufrage *m.* ~ *v.t.* faire naufrage à, faire échouer, faire périr.

shipwrecked *adj.* naufragé.

shirk *v.t.* esquiver, ébiter; manquer à. *v.i.* se cacher, s'échapper.

shirt *n.* chemise *f.* d'homme, chemise *f.* **night ~**, chemise de nuit. **to sell the ~ off one's back**, vendre jusqu'à sa chemise. *v.t.* couvrir d'une chemise.

shit *n. Vulg.* merde *f.*; connerie *f.*

shiver *n.* frisson *m.*, frissonnement *m.*, tremblement *m.* ~ *v.i.* frissonner; grelotter de froid.

shoal *n.* banc *m.* (fish); haut-fond *m.*, banc *m.* de sable. *v.i.* diminuer de profondeur, baisser.

shock *n.* choc *m.*; rencontre *f.*, secousse *f.*, commotion *f.* (electric); *Fig.* coup *m.*, impression *f.* pénible. **the ~ of an earthquake**, la secousse d'un tremblement de terre. **a ~ of hair**, une chevelure épaisse. ~ **absorber**, amortisseur *m.* ~ **therapy**, électrochoc *m.* ~ *v.t.* secouer; soutenir le choc de; effrayer; terrifier; choquer, offenser. **to feel quite ~ed**, être vivement affligé. *v.i.* se choquer, se heurter.

shocker *n.* horreur *f.* **it's a real ~**, c'est une épouvante.

shocking *adj.* affreux, horrible; repoussant, chjoquant, offensant; qui choque, qui blesse (taste, conventions). **a ~ sight**, un affreux spectacle.

shockingly *adv.* affreusement, horriblement.

shoe *n.* chaussure *f.*; fer *m.* (horse). **to be in a person's ~s**, *Fig.* être à la place de quelqu'un. ~**lace**, lacet *m.*

shoemaker *n.* cordonnier *m.*

shoot *v.t.* lancer, darder, décocher, décharger, tirer, faire partir, fusiller. **to ~ an arrow**, lancer une flèche. **to ~ a soldier**, fusiller un soldat. **he was shot in the leg**, on lui a tiré dans la jambe. **to ~ forth**, lancer, darder, pousser, faire sortir, faire rejaillir. **to ~ off**, tirer, faire partir, décharger (weapon); emporter (by a gunshot). **to ~ out**, lancer, jeter, darder, pousser (dehors). **to ~ through**, traverser. *v.i.* pousser, croître; s'élancer, filer (stars). **he shoots well**, il tire bien. **to ~ ahead**, courir, se jeter en avant. **to ~ at**, tirer sur, contre. **to ~ forth**, s'élancer; jaillir, pousser (plant). **to ~ off**, partir, s'élancer comme un trait. **to ~ out**, s'élancer, s'avancer, pousser. **to ~ through**, passer rapidement à travers; traverser. **to ~ up**, croître, grandir; se shooter (drugs). *n.* rejeton *m.*, bourgeon *m.*, jeune branche *f.*

shooter *n.* tireur *m.*

shooting *adj.* de tir, de chasse, qui tire, qui lance; rapide, filant; lancinant, douloureux. ~ **gallery**, tir *m.* ~ **party**, partie *f.* de chasse. ~ **pain**, douleur lancinante. ~ **star**, étoile *f.* filante. *n.* chasse *f.* (au fusil).

shop *n.* boutique *f.*, magasin *m.*, atelier *m.* **to keep a ~**, tenir un magasin, une boutique. **to close up ~**, fermer la boutique; fermer boutique. ~**keeper**, marchand *m.*, boutiquier *m.* ~**lifter**, voleur *m.*, voleuse *f.* à l'étalage. *v.i.* courir les magasins, faire des emplettes.

shopping *n.* action de faire des emplettes. **to do the ~, to go ~,** courir les magasins, faire des emplettes.

shore *n.* côte *f.,* bord *m.,* rivage *m.* (sea); rive *f.,* bord *m.* (river, lake). **along the ~,** au bord de la mer. **off~,** au large. **on~,** à terre. *v.t.* étayer, étançonner; *Fig.* soutenir.

short *adj.* court; petit; bref, succinct; à court de; brusque, raide; tout court. **a ~ distance,** une courte, une petite distance. **in a ~ time,** dans un petit moment, bientôt. **a ~ answer,** une réponse brusque, sèche. **to be ~ of money,** être à court d'argent. **to cut ~,** couper court; couper la parole (of a person); faire cesser. **to fall ~ of,** être, rester au-dessus de la. **to shorten,** raccourcir; abréger. **to stop ~,** s'arrêter tout court. **he court in ~,** bref, en un mot. *adv.* court, tout court; peu. **~ circuit,** court-circuit *m.* **~coming,** insuffisance *f.,* manque *m.;* manquement *m.* (duty), omission *f.* **~hand,** sténographie *f.* **~sighted,** myope. **~sightedness,** myopie *f.; Fig.* imprévoyance *f.*

shortage *n.* manque *m.,* pénurie *f.,* insuffisance *f.* **a ~ of food,** un manque *m.* de nourriture.

shorten *v.i.* diminuer, se raccourcir, s'abréger, se resserrer.

shortening *n.* raccourcissement *m.,* ingrédient *m.* gross.

shortly *adv.* bientôt, sous peu; brièvement.

shortness *n.* petitesse *f.* (height); peu *m.* d'étendue; peu *m.,* brièveté *f.* (time), concision *f.,* faiblesse *f.,* manque *m.* **~ of breath,** manque d'haleine. **the ~ of life,** la brièveté de la vie.

shorts *n.pl.* short *m.*

shorty *n. Infml.* demi portion *m.,* minus *m.*

shot *n.* coup *m.* (gun), trait *m.,* flèche *f.,* balle *f.,* plomb *m.* (hunting gun); boulet *m.* (cannon); tireur *m.* **gun~,** coup de pistolet. **to fire a ~,** tirer un coup. **random ~,** coup perdu. **without firing a ~,** sans tirer un coup. **a good ~,** un bon tireur. **he went off like a ~,** il est parti comme une flèche.

should See SHALL. **I ~ go,** je devrais aller. **he ~n't have said such a thing,** il n'aurait jamais dû dire une chose pareille; une telle chose.

shoulder *n.* épaule *f.; Fig.* soutien *m.,* appui *m.* **to give the cold ~ to,** battre froid à. **~ blade,** os de l'épaule, omeplate *f.* **~ strap,** bretelle *f.* **~** *v.t.* pousser avec l'épaule, charger sur les épaules. *Mil.* porter. **~ arms!** portez armes! **round~ed,** *adj.* au dos rond.

shout *n.* acclamation *f.,* grand cri *m.,* cri *m.* de joie. **~** *v.i.* crier; jeter, pousser un cri. **to ~ out,** crier, s'écrier.

shouting *n.* cris *m.pl.;* cri *m.* de joie, d'allégresse; acclamation *f.*

shove *v.t.,v.i.* pousser. **to ~ along,** pousser en avant, faire avancer. **to ~ away,** pousser, éloigner. **to ~ back,** repousser, faire reculer. **to ~ down,** faire tomber (en poussant), renverser, descendre. **to ~ in,** faire entrer (en poussant),

pousser dedans. **to ~ off,** repousser, éloigner (en poussant). *n.* coup *m.,* secousse *f.;* poussée *f. Vulg.~ it!* ferme la! la ferme! ta gueule! **to voudrais bien te la ferme!**

shovel *n.* pelle *f.* **~** *v.t.* prendre, ramasser avec une peller, jeter avec une pelle.

show *v.t.* montrer; faire voir; faire connaître, démontrer; enseigner, expliquer, témoigner. **to ~ the way,** montrer le chemin. **to ~ kindness,** témoigner de la bienveillance. **~ the gentleman to his room,** conduisez monsieur à sa chambre. **to ~ publically,** exposer; montrer; publier, manifester. **to ~ in, into,** introduire, faire entrer. **~ him in,** faites-le entrer. **to ~ off,** faire montre de, mettre en relief; se faire remarquer. *Infml.* crâner. **to ~ out,** reconduire, faire sortir. **~ him over the bridge,** faites-lui traverser le pont. **to ~ up,** dévoiler, exposer; ressortir; s'amener. *n.* spectacle *m.;* représentation théâtrale; exposition *f.* flower **~,** exposition d'horticulture. **~case,** montre *f.,* vitrine *f.* **~room,** salle *f.* d'exposition.

shower *n.* douche *f.,* averse *f.,* ondée *f.* April **~s,** giboulées de mars. **a ~ of bullets,** une pluie de balles. *v.t.* inonder de pluie, arroser; faire pleuvoir, doucher. **to ~ down on,** faire pleuvoir sur.

showy *adj.* éclatant, brillant, voyant, somptueux, fastueux.

shred *v.t.* déchirer en lambeaux, hacher. *n.* bande *f.,* rognure *f.,* lambeau *m.*

shrew *n.* chipie *f.,* mégère *f.,* musaraigne *f.*

shrewd *adj.* sagace, clairvoyant, pénétrant, malin; rusé, adroit, fin. **a ~ man,** un homme fin, rusé. **a ~ question,** une question adroite.

shrewdly *adv.* subtilement, finement, avec sagacité, avec malice.

shrewdness *n.* sagacité *f.,* discernement *m.,* pénétration *f.,* finesse *f.,* ruse *f.,* malice *f.*

shrewish *adj.* acariâtre.

shriek *v.i.* crier, pousser un cri perçant. **to ~ out,** s'écrier. *n.* cri *m.* perçant.

shrill *adj.* aigu, perçant, clair. *v.i.* rendre un son aigu, perçant. *v.t.* faire rendre un son aigu; chanter d'une voix aiguë.

shrimp *n.* crevette *f.;* gringalet *m.* (person).

shrine *n.* lieu *m.* saint *f.,* reliquaire *m.;* autel *m.;* tombe *f.,* tombeau *m.; Fig.* temple *m.*

shrink *v.i.* se rétrécir; se rider; se ratatiner; diminuer; reculer; se refuser; frémir. **to ~ away,** se dérober, fuir. **to ~ back,** reculer. *n. Infml.* psychologue *m.f.*

shrinkage *n.* rétrécissement *m.,~* racourcissement *m.*

shrivel *v.i.* se rider, se ratatiner; se recroqueviller. *v.t.* faire des rides, grésiller, racornir; faire ratatiner.

shroud *n.* linceul *m.,* suaire *m.; Naut.* hauban *m.;* abri *m.,* couvert *m.* **~** *v.t.* abriter, mettre à couvert, protéger, couvrir; mettre dans un linceul, ensevelir, cacher. *v.i.* s'abriter.

Shrove Tuesday *n.* mardi *m.* gras.

shrub *n.* arbuste *m.*, arbrisseau *m.*

shrubbery *n.* lieu *m.* planté d'arbustes; bosquet *m.*

shrug *v.t.,v.i.* lever, hausser les épaules). *n.* haussement *m.* d'épaules.

shucks *interj.* zut!; mince!

shudder *v.i.* frémir, frissonner. *n.* frisson *m.*, frémissement *m.*; frissonnement *m.*

shuffle *v.t.* faire passer; agiter, remuer; mettre en désordre; mêler; battre (cards). to ~ along, traîner la jambe. *n.* action de battre les cartes; tour *m.*, tromperie *f.*, équivoque *f.*

shun *v.t.* fuir, éviter, se garder de.

shut *v.t.* fermer; clore. to ~ tight, fermer bien. to ~ the eyes, fermer les yeux. to ~ out from, exclure de. to ~ in, enfermer. to ~ off, intercepter, couper, éteindre. to ~ out, fermer la porte à; exclure. to ~ up, enfermer, renfermer; condamner (window, door). *Infml.* faire taire, se taire. to ~ up a house, fermer une maison.

shutter *n.* volet *m.*, contrevent *m.* (window); *Phot.* obturateur *m.*

shuttle *n.* navette *f.*

shuttlecock *n.* (badminton) volant *m.*

shy *adj.* timide. *v.i.* se jeter de côté, faire un écart.

shyly *adv.* timidement.

shyness *n.* timidité *f.*; réserve *f.*

shyster *n.* escroc *m.*; homme *m.* d'affaires véreux; avocat *m.* marron (lawyer).

Siamese *adj.* siamois. *n.* Siamois *m.*

Siberia *n.pr.* Sibérie *f.*

Siberian *adj.* sibérien, de Sibérie.

sibilant *adj.* sibilant, sifflant. *n.* sifflante *f.*, lettre *f.* sifflante.

siblings *n.* enfants *m.pl.* de mêmes parents.

sick *adj.* malade, qui a mal au coeur. a ~ man, un malade. to feel ~, avoir mal au coeur; avoir des nausées. to be sea~, avoir le mal de mer. to be home~, avoir le mal du pays. ~pay, indemnité *f.* patronale. ~bed, lit de douleur, de malade.

sicken *v.t.* rendre malade; faire mal au coeur à. *v.i.* tomber malade; être malade; languir, s'affaiblir; se dégoûter; se rassasier. it ~s me to see all that wasted, ça me rend malade/ça me dégoûte de voir tout ce gâchis.

sickening *adj.* qui rend malade; nauséabond, répugnant.

sickle *n.* faucille *f.*

sickle-cell anemia *n.* drépanocytose *f.*

sickly *adj.* maladif; languissant.

sickness *n.* maladie *f.*, mal *m.*; mal *m.* de coeur. sea~, mal de mer.

side *n.* côté *m.*, bord *m.*; pente *f.*, côte *f.* the right ~, le côté droit; bon côté. wrong ~, mauvais côté. the right ~ of a fabric, l'endroit. wrong ~, l'envers. ~ by ~, côte à côte. on that ~, de ce côté-là. on all ~s, de tous côtés, de toute part. the sea~, le bord de la mer. the ~ of the hill, le flanc de la colline. at the fire~, au coin du feu. to change ~s, changer de côté, de

parti. *adj.* latéral, de côté; oblique. *v.i.* pencher d'un côté; se ranger d'un côté; prendre parti. ~ door, porte *f.* latérale. ~saddle, selle *f.* de femme. ~ table, petite table (à part), buffet *m.*

sideboard *n.* buffet *m.*

sided *adj.* à côtés. one-~, à un côté, à une face; partial, injuste. two-~, à deux côtés.

sidelong *adj.* latéral, oblique, de côté. *adv.* latéralement, obliquement, de côté; sur le côté.

sideral *adj.* sidéral, astral.

sidewalk *n.* trottoir *m.*

sideways *adv.* de côté, obliquement, latéralement.

sidle *v.i.* aller, marcher de côté, obliquement, être sur le côté. to ~ up, s'avancer en marchant de côté.

siege *n.* siège *m.* to lay ~ to, assiéger, mettre le siège.

sieve *n.* sas *m.*, tamis *m.*; crible *m.*

sift *v.t.* tamiser, cribler, passer au crible; *Fig.* examiner; sonder. to ~ out, tâcher de découvrir; parvenir à connaître.

sifting *n.* tamisage *m.*; criblage *m.*; examen *m.*

sigh *n.* soupir *m.* deep ~, profond soupir. to heave a ~, pousser un soupir. *v.i.* soupirer. to ~ for, soupirer après. to ~ over, gémir sur; pleurer. *v.t.* exhaler (des soupirs); déplorer, lamenter; gémir sur.

sighing *adj.* soupirant.

sight *n.* vue *f.*; vision, spectacle *m.*; coup *m.* d'oeuil; regard *m.*; mire *f.* (gun). to have a ~ of, voir; jouir de la vue de. to lose ~ of, perdre de vue. in the ~ of, à la vue de, au vu de; en vue de; en présence de. within ~, en vue de. out of ~, hors de vue. at ~, à première vue; à livre ouvert. at first ~, à première vue. the ~s of Paris, les curiosités de Paris. to take a ~ing, viser, pointer, prendre son point de mire. ~seeing, *n.* visites *f.pl.* pour voir les curiosités, tourisme *m.* to go ~seeing, visiter; faire du tourisme. *v.t.* venir en vue de. *v.i.* viser.

sighted *adj.* à vue. near-~, qui a la vue basse; myope, *Fig.* pru clairvoyant.

sightless *adj.* aveugle, privé de la vue.

sign *n.* signe *m.*, marque *f.*; enseigne *f.* (shop, etc.); présage *m.*; symbole *m.*, miracle *m.* to give ~s of, donner signe de. ~ language, langage *m.* par signes, langue *f.* des signes. *v.t.* signer; montrer; faire voir, faire signe.

signal *n.* signal *m.*, signe *m.*, indice *m.* *adj.* signalé; insigne. *v.t.* communiquer par signaux.

signature *n.* signature *f.*, signe *m.*, marque *f.*

signet *n.* sceau *m.*

significance *n.* signification *f.*, sens *m.*; force *f.*, énergie *f.*; importance *f.*, poids *m.*, gravité *f.*, portée *f.*

significant *adj.* signifiant; significatif.

significantly *adv.* de manière significative.

signify *v.t.* signifier; dénoter; notifier.

silence *n.* silence *m.*

silent *adj.* silencieux; muet (letters, film); calme,

tranquille. **~ partner,** (associé) commanditaire *m.* be **~,** taisez-vous. **the ~ waters,** les flot silencieux. **a ~ letter,** une lettre muette.

silently *adv.* silencieusement; sous silence.

silhouette *n.* silhouette *f.* *v.t.* se profiler.

silk *n.* soie *f.;* soieries *f.pl.* **raw ~,** soie grège. *adj.* de soie. **a ~ gown,** une robe de soie. **~ goods,** soieries *f.pl.* **~worm,** ver *m.* à soie.

silken *adj.* de soie; soyeux, moelleux, doux, délicat, vêtu de soie.

silkiness *n.* nature *f.* soyeuse; douceur *f., Fig.* mollesse *f.*

silky *adj.* de soie, soyeux, doux, moelleux.

sill *n.* seuil *m.,* allège *f.,* appui *m.*

silliness *n.* niaiserie *f.,* sottise *f.*

silly *adj.* niais, sot, bête, étourdi, nigaud.

silt *n.* vase *f.,* limon *m.,* alluvion *f.* **~** *v.t.* ensabler, envaser.

silver *n.* argent *m.;* monnaie *f.* d'argent; vasselle *f.* d'argent, argenterie *f.* **~** *adj.* d'argent; en argent; argenté; argentin. **a ~ plate,** une assiette en argent. **~ foil,** feuille *f.* d'argent. **~-gray,** d'un gris argenté. **~ gilt,** vermeil *m.* **~-haired,** aux cheveux argentés. **~ ore,** minerai *m.* d'argent. **~-plated,** doublé d'argent. **~ware,** argenterie *f.* **~** *v.t.* argenter; étamer.

silversmith *n.* orfèvre *m.*

silvery *adj.* argenté, d'argent; argentin.

similar *adj.* semblable, pareil; similaire.

similarity *n.* similitude *f.,* ressemblance *f.;* similarité *f.*

similarly *adv.* d'une manière semblable; de la même manière.

similitude *n.* similitude *f.*

simmer *v.i.* bouillir doucement; mijoter.

simper *v.i.* sourire niaisement. *n.* sourire *m.* niais.

simple *adj.* simple. **~ manners,** des manières simples. **~-minded,** simple, candide, naïf.

simpleness *n.* simplicité *f.*

simplicity *n.* simplicité *f.*

simplification *n.* simplification *f.*

simplify *v.i.* simplifier.

simply *adv.* simplement.

simulate *v.t.* simuler, feindre.

simulation *n.* simulation *f.,* déguisement *m.,* feinte *f.*

simultaneity *n.* simultanéité *f.*

simultaneous *adj.* simultané.

simultaneously *adv.* simultanément.

sin *n.* péché *m.* **original ~,** péché originel. *v.i.* pécher.

since *conj.* puisque, vu que; depuis que. **~ there is nothing,** puisqu'il n'y a rien. **~ you saw him,** depuis que vous l'avez du. **~ the world began,** depuis que le monde existe. *adv.* depuis, il y a. **ever ~,** depuis lors. *prep.* depuis. **~ his death,** depuis sa mort.

sincere *adj.* sincère.

sincerely *adv.* sincèrement, avec sincérité.

sincerity *n.* sincérité *f.*

sinecure *n.* sinécure *f.*

sinew *n.* tendon *m.;* muscle *m.;* vigueur. *v.t.* lier, attacher (comme avec des tendons).

sinewed, sinewy *adj.* nerveux, musculeux; fort, vigoureux, robuste.

sinful *adj.* coupable de péché; pécheur; coupable.

sinfully *adv.* d'une manière coupable, dans le péché.

sing *v.i.* chanter. **to ~ out of tune,** chanter faux. *v.t.* célébrer. **to ~ a hymn,** chanter un hymne.

singe *v.t.* griller, brûler légèrement; roussir, flamber. **to ~ a fowl,** flamber une volaille.

singeing *n.* action de roussir, brûlure *f.* légère.

singer *n.* chanteur *m.,* chanteuse *f.*

singing *adj.* chanteur, mélodieux. *n.* chant *m.*

single *adj.* seul, unique, simple, particulier; chaque; célibataire. **he is ~,** il est célibataire. **a ~ word,** un seul mot. **~-handed,** seul, sans aide. *v.t.* choisir, distinguer; séparer; mettre à part. **to ~ out,** distinguer; faire ressortir.

singular *adj.* singulier, étrange, bizarre; seul, unique; simple. **a ~ woman,** une femme *f.* remarquable.

sinister *adj.* sinistre; méchant, pervers.

sink *v.i.* s'enfoncer; couler bas, couler à fond, sombrer; pénétrer; baisser, descendre; s'affaisser. **the ship began to ~,** le navire commença à couler. **the floor ~s,** le plancher s'affaisse. **to ~ to the ground,** tomber, se laisser tomber par terre. **to ~ into a deep sleep,** tomber dans un profond sommeil. *v.t.* immerger; couler. **to ~ a ship,** couler bas un navire. **to ~ a well,** creuser un puits. *Fin.* placer à fonds perdus; mettre en viager. *n.* évier *m.,* lavabo *m.*

sinking *n.* creusement *m.* (well). *Fin.* placement *m.* de viager; amortissement *m.* **~ fund,** fonds d'amortissement. **to get that ~ feeling,** se sentir accablé.

sinner *n.* pécheur *m.,* pécheresse *f.*

sinus *n.* sinus *m.*

sip *v.t.,v.i.* siroter; sucer, extraire. *n.* gorgée *f.*

siphon *n.* siphon *m.*

sir *n.* monsieur *m.* Sir *m.* (titre).

siren *n.* sirène *f.* *adj.* de sirène, enchanteur.

sirloin *n.* aloyau *m.*

sirup *n.* sirop *m.*

sirupy *adj.* sirupeux.

sis *n.* (*abbrev.* **sister**) frangine *f.*

sissy *n. Infml.* poule mouillée *f.;* (effeminate) efféminé *m. Infml.* tapette *f.*

sister *n.* soeur *f.;* religieuse *f.* **~-in-law,** belle-soeur. *adj.* soeur.

sisterhood *n.* société *f.,* communauté *f.* de femmes; les soeurs *f.pl.*

sisterly *adv.* de soeur; en soeur.

sit *v.i.* s'asseoir; être assis; être, rester; se tenir (horseback); percher, se poser; siéger; couver (eggs). *v.t.* asseoir; se tenir sur, monter. **to be sitting,** être assis. **to ~ at table,** être à table, se mettre à table. **to ~ on the ground,** s'asseoir par terre. **to ~ down,** s'asseoir, être assis;

mettre (à table); se reposer. **to ~ up,** se lever; se mettre sur son séant. **~ up straight,** tenez-vous droit.

sitcom *n.* (T.V.) (*abbrev.* situation comedy) comédie *f.* de situation.

site *n.* situation *f.,* emplacement *m.;* site *m.* (landscape).

sitter *n.* modèle *m.,* personne *f.* qui pose; gardienne *f.* d'enfants.

sitting *adj.* assis; en séance. *n.* session *f.;* audience *f.* (tribunal); séance *f.* **at one ~,** en une séance. **~ room,** salon.

situate *v.t.* situer.

situated *adj.* situé, placé.

situation *n.* situation *f.;* position *f.;* état *m.;* emploi *m.* **in a ~ to,** en position de.

six *adj. n.* six *m.*

sixteen *adj. n.* seize.

sixteenth *adj.* seizième.

sixth *adj.* sième. **the ~ of December,** le six décembre. *n.* sixième *m.; Mus.* sixte *f.*

sixtieth *adj.* soixantième.

sixty *adj. n.* soixante *m.*

sizable *adj.* d'une bonne grosseur.

size *n.* volume *m.,* grandeur *f.,* grosseur *f.;* taille *f.,* format *m.* (book, merchandise); *Comm.* numéro *m.;* pointure *f.* (shoes). **what ~ do you take?** quelle est votre pointure? (gloves) numéro. *v.t.* ajuster, proportionner.

sized *adj.* de grandeur, de taille, de grosseur. **large-~,** d'une grande dimension. **medium-~,** de moyenne grosseur.

sizzle *n.* grésillement. *v.t.* grésiller.

skate *n.* patin *m. v.i.* patiner. **in-line ~s,** patins *m.pl.* à roues alignées.

skateboard *n.* planche *f.* à roulettes.

skateboarding *v.i.* faire de la planche à roulettes.

skater *n.* patineur *m.,* patineuse *f.*

skating *adj.* patinant; qui patine. *n.* patinage *m.* **~ rink,** patinoir *m.*

skeleton *n.* squelette *m.,* carcasse *f.,* charpente *f.*

sketch *n.* esquisse *f.;* croquis, ébauche, aperçu *m.* **~book,** album *m.,* cahier *m.* d'esquisses. *v.t.* esquisser, ébaucher, croquer, tracer. **to ~ out,** esquisser, faire le croquis de.

sketchy *adj.* somaire; vague.

skew *adj.* oblique, de biais. *adv.* obliquement, en biais. *v.t.* tailler en biais; mettre en travers.

skewer *n.* brochette *f.* **~** *v.t.* mettre en brochettes.

ski *n.* ski *m.* **~** *v.i.* faire du ski.

skid *n.* dérapage. *v.i.* déraper.

skier *n.* skieur *m.*

skill *n.* habileté *f.,* adresse *f.,* dextérité *f.,* savoir-faire *m.,* talent *m.*

skilled *adj.* adroit, habile, expérimenté, versé.

skillet *n.* casserole *f.,* poêle *m.*

skillful *adj.* habile, adroit, expert, versé. **a ~ hand,** une main habile.

skillfully *adv.* habilement, adroitement.

skillfulness *n.* habileté *f.,* adresse *f.*

skim *n.* **~ milk,** lait écrémé. *v.t.* écumer, écrémer; effleurer, raser. *v.i.* passer légèrement, glisser. **to ~ over,** glisser sur, effleurer, raser.

skin *n.* peau *f.;* cuir *m.* **he is nothing but ~ and bones,** il n'a que la peau et les os. **~ deep,** léger, superficiel. *v.t.* écorcher; dépouiller, peler, (fruit), tondre.

skinflint *n.* avare *m.*

skinhead *m.* skin.

skinless *adj.* sans peau.

skinned *adj.* écorché, à peau.

skinny *adj.* maigre, décharné.

skip *v.i.* sauter; bondir. **to ~ for joy,** sauter de joie. **to ~ over,** sauter, omettre. **to ~ a chapter,** sauter un chapitre. *n.* saut *m.,* bond *m.*

skipper *m.* maître *m.,* patron *m.* de navire.

skirt *n.* jupe *f.,* bord *m.,* lisière *f.* (woods). **out~s,** extrémité *f.* **~** *v.t.* border, longer, cotoyer. *v.i.* être sur les bords.

skit *n.* raillerie *f.;* pièce *f.* satirique.

skittish *adj.* timide; ombrageux; folâtre, capricieux, volage.

skull *n.* crâne *m.*

skunk *n.* (animal); *Infml.* canaille *f.* (person), mouffette *f.*

sky *n.* ciel *m.;* **the skies,** les cieux. **blue ~,** ciel bleu, ciel azuré. **cloudy ~,** ciel chargé de nuages. **up to the skies,** jusqu'aux nues. **~lark,** alouette *f.* des champs, **~light,** châssis *m.* vitré, fenêtre *f.* en tabatière. **~rocket,** fusée *f.* volante. **~scraper,** gratte-ciel *m.*

skydiving *m.* parachutism.

skyward *adv.* vers le ciel.

slack *adj.* lâche, mou, faible, *Naut.* calme, stationnaire. **a ~ rope,** un cordage lâche. *adv.* imparfaitement; mollement. *n.* mou *m.* (rope). *v.i.* tarder à, diminuer; se ralentir; faiblir.

slacken *v.t.* relâcher, détendre. **to ~ one's pace,** ralentir sa marche.

slacks *n.pl.* pantalon *m.*

slackly *adv.* avec lenteur, d'une manière lâche; mollement; avec nonchalance.

slackness *n.* lenteur *f.;* relâchement *m.;* faiblesse *f.,* mollesse *f.,* nonchalance *f.*

slake *v.t.* étancher; assouvir.

slam *v.t.* fermer avec violence; claquer, faire une chelem, la vole (cards). **he ~med the door,** il a (fait) claqué la porte. *n.* action de fermer avec bruit, avec violence; vole *f.,* chelem *m.* (cards).

slander *n.* médisance *f.;* calomnie *f.;* diffamation *f.* **~** *v.t.* médire de, parler mal de, dénigrer; calomnier, diffamer.

slanderer *n.* médisant *m.;* calomniateur *m.,* diffamateur *m.*

slanderous *adj.* médisant; de médisance; calomnieux, diffamatoire.

slang *n.* jargon *m.;* argot *m.*

slant *v.t.* rendre oblique; faire biaiser; incliner; presenter avec parti pris (neus). *v.i.* être oblique;

être de biaio; pencher. n. plan m. incliné, pente f.; talus m.

slanting adj. oblique, de biais, de côté.

slap n. tape f., claque f. **~ in the face**, une claque au visage. v.t. taper, claquer.

slapdash adv. au hasard.

slash n. taillade f., coupure; balafre f. ~ v.t. taillader; balafrer (face).

slate n. ardoise f. ~ v.t. couvrir d'ardoises.

slaughter n. massacre m., tuerie f., boucherie f. **~house**, abattoir m. **~** v.t. tuer, abattre; massacrer, égorger (humans).

slave n. esclave m.f. **~ to fashion**, être esclave de la mode. **~ owner**, propriétaire m. d'esclaves. **~ ship**, négrier m., bâtiment m. qui fait la traite des noirs. **~ trade**, traite f. des noirs, traite f. **~** v.i. travailler comme un esclave.

slaver n. négrier m., bâtiment m. négrier.

slavery n. esclavage m.

slavish adj. d'esclave, servile.

slay v.t. tuer; égorger, massacrer, détruire.

sleazy adj. Infml. minable, miteux.

sledge n. traîneau m. **~** v.i. aller en traîneau.

sleek adj. lisse; luisant d'un beau poil; doux. ~ v.t. lisser, polir.

sleep v.i. dormir; coucher. **to ~ soundly**, dormir profondément. **to ~ in the open**, coucher à la belle étoile. **to ~ away (from home)**, découcher. v.i. passer (le temps) à dormir. **to ~ in**, faire la grasse matinée. **~ with**, coucher avev (faire l'amour). n. sommeil m., somme m. **deep, sound ~**, profond sommeil. **to go to ~**, s'endormir; aller dormir, aller se coucher. **to put to ~**, endormir. **to put a cat to ~**, faire piquer un chat. **~walker**, somnambule. **~walking**, somnambulisme.

sleeper n. dormeur m.; couchette f. (train).

sleepiness n. sommeil m.; assoupissement m.

sleeping adj. dormant, endormi; assoupi.

sleepless adj. sans sommeil, d'insomnie; éveillé.

sleeplessness n. insomnie f.

sleepy adj. endormi; assoupi, soporifique, langoreux, endormant. **~-looking**, qui a l'air endormi. **to be, to feel ~**, avoir sommeil. **~head**, endormi n.m.

sleet n. neige f. fondue, grésil m.; givre m., frimas m. **~** v.i. neiger et pleuvoir tout ensemble; grésiller. **it's ~ing**, il grésille.

sleeve n. manche f. **to laugh up one's ~**, rire sous cape, rire dans sa barbe.

sleigh n. traineau m.

slender adj. mince, menu, svelte; faible, léger; fragile, frêle, délicat. **a ~ waist**, une taille mince, svelte.

slenderness n. minceur f., sveltesse f.; faiblesse f.

slice n. tranche f., part f. **~ of life**, tranche f. de vie. v.t. couper par tranches, couper, diviser.

slick adj. habile, malin; glissant.

slide v.i. glisser, couler le long de, échapper; se glisser. **to ~ along**, se glisser, s'avancer. **to ~ down**, glisser en bas, descendre. **to ~ into**, se

glisser dans; tomber dans. **to ~ over**, glisser sur, effleurer. v.t. faire glisser, passer. n. toboggan m.; glissoire f., éboulement m.; coulant m.; coulisse f.

sliding adj. glissant, coulant; à coulisse; mobile; Fig. chancelant. **~ door**, m. porte f. à goulisse. **~ panel**, panneau m. mobile. **~ scale**, échelle f. mobile, échelle f. de proportion.

slight adj. léger; mince, faible, petit. **~ effort**, effort léger. **a ~ impression**, une impression légère. **a ~ scratch**, une petite égratignure. n. manque m. d'égards, de respect. v.t. manquer à (person); d'égards enverre, ignorez, blesser.

slightly adv. légèrement.

slim adj. mince, svelte. v.i. maigrir, faire maigrir. **to ~ down**, (s')amincir, perdre du poids.

slime n. matière f. visqueuse, gluante.

slimy adj. visqueux, gluant.

sling n. écharpe f. **he wears his arm in a ~**, il porte son bras en écharpe.

slink v.i. se glisser; s'esquiver; se dérober.

slip v.i. glisser; couler, manquer; échapper; se glisser; faire un faux pas. **to ~ away**, s'échapper, s'esquiver; (time) se passer, s'écouler. **to ~ in, into**, se glisser dans; se fourfiler dans. **to ~ off**, enlever. **to ~ on**, glisser sur. **to ~ out**, glisser dehors; sortir doucement. v.t. lâcher; laisser échapper, perdre. **I ~ped money into his hand**, je lui ai glissé de l'argent dans la main. n. glissade f., faux pas m.; Fig. faute f., méprise f., bévue f.; Hort. bouture f. **a ~ of the tongue**, un lapsus.

slipper n. chausson m., pantoufle f.; mule f.

slippery adj. glissant; incertain; scabreux.

slit v.i. fendre; séparer, trancher. n. fente f.

sliver v.t. fendre; couper en tranches; arracher. n. tranche f.

slob n. Infml. porc m., cochon m. **he is a fat ~**, c'est un gros porc.

slobber n. bave f., salive f., attendrissement m. v.i. saliver; s'attendrir de trop.

sloe n. prunelle f. **~ gin**, gin à la prunelle.

slogan n. slogan m.

slop v.t. renverser, repandre (liquid) faire du gâchis sur. n. gâchis m., saleté f. mauvaise boisson.

slope n. obliquité f., pente f.; penchant m., inclinaison f. (terrain); talus m. (ditch); rampe f. **~** v.t. incliner, pencher; aller en pente. v.i. être incliné.

sloping adj. incliné, de biais; en pente; en talus.

sloppiness n. gâchis m., saleté f.

sloppy adj. mal fait, fait à la hâte, bâclé, négligé.

slot n. entaille; fente f. **~ machine**, machien f. à sous; distributeur m. automatique.

sloth n. lenteur f.; paresse f., fainéantise f.; Zool. paresseux m.

slouch n. inclination f., démarche f. lourde, démarche f. de paysan; lourdaud m. **~** v.i. marcher en inclinant la tête, avoir une démarche lourde, s'avachir.

slough n. bourbier m.; fondrière f.; marécage m.; Fig. abime m.

slough n. dépouille f. (snake); peau f. ~ v.i. escarrifier, tomber.

sloven n. souillon f.; homme ou femme sale; malpropre.

slovenliness n. négligence f., malpropreté f.

slovenly adj. sans soin; mal mis; sale, malpropre. adv. salement, malproprement.

slow adj. lent; tardif, paresseux, indolent; (watch) en retard. a ~ poison, un poison lent. to be ~, être lent d'esprit. your watch is five minutes too ~, votre montre retarde de cinq minutes. ~-paced, qui va à pas lent.

slowly adv. lentement.

slowness n. lenteur f., retard m. (watches).

sludge n. boue f.

sludgy adj. boueux.

slug n. limace f.; Fig. paresseux m., fainéant.

sluggard adj. paresseux m., fainéant m. adj. paresseux, fainéant.

sluggishness n. paresse f., fainéantise f.; inertie f.

sluice n. écluse f. vanne f., ~ gate, vanne f.

slum n. taudis m., les bas-quartiers m.pl.; la zone f.

slumber v.i. sommeiller, dormir. v.t. assoupir, endormir. n. somme m., sommeil m., léger, assoupissement m.

slumbering adj. endormi, qui dort.

slump v.i. s'enfoncer; baisser subitement.

slur v.i.,v.t. tacher, ternir (la réputation); flétrir; dénigrer; Mus. lier, couler; articuler mal. n. flétrissure f.; blâme m.; ruse f.; Mus. liaison f., coulé m. a racial ~, insulte f. raciale.

slurp v.t. boire bruyamment.

slush n. neige f. fongue.

slut n. salope f.; chienne f.

sly adj. fin, rusé; sournois; malin. a ~ look, un regard en dessous. on the ~, en sourdine, en cachette, sournois.

slyly adv. en sournois; finement, avec ruse.

slyness n. ruse f., malice f., artifice m.

smack v.i. claquer, donner un baiser (noisily), Fig. se ressentir, sentir. v.t. faire claquer (lips, whip); claquer, donner une claque à. n. baiser m. retentissant; claquement m. (whip), claque f., gifle f., gout m., saveur f.; soupçon m.

small adj. petit, menu; médiocre, chétif. a ~ amount, une petite somme. a ~ group of people, un petit groupe de personnes, un groupe de gens peu nombreux. ~pox, variole f., petite vérole f. ~ talk, banalités f.pl. n. ~ of the back, chute f. des reins.

smallness n. petitesse f.; finesse f., ténuité f.; faiblesse f.; peu m. d'importance.

smart adj. intelligent, éveillé; habile, adroit; cuisant, douloureux; mordant, satirique; vif, vigoureux; fini; actif, alerte; élégant, coquet, chic. a ~ answer, une réponse mordante; une réponse intelligente. a ~ man, un homme intelligent. to

be ~, être intelligent. n. douleur f. cuisante, vive; peine f. ~ v.i. cuire; sentir, éprouver une cuisson; Infml. en cuire. my fingers ~, les doigts me cuisent.

smarten v.t. faire beau, rendre pimpant.

smartly adv. vivement; rudement; fort; d'une manière piquante; adroitement; lestement.

smartness n. vigueur f. (of a blow); mordant m., piquant m. (of a response); vivacité f.; activité f.; intelligence f.

smash v.t. mettre en pièces, briser en morceaux. to ~ in, enfoncer, défencer. to ~ up, démolir, Infml. bousiller. n. fracas m., faillite f.; déconfiture f. ~ hit, succès m. fou.

smashing adj. Infml. super, formidable.

smattering n. connaissance f. superficielle.

smear v.t. enduire; barbouiller, Fig. souiller, salir. n. tache f., barbouillage m.

smell v.i. sentir; flairer, Fig. se douter de. ~ this rose, sentez cette rose. to ~ a rat, Infml. soupçonner quelque chose. v.i. Fig. avoir l'apparence; (negative) sentir, sentir mauvais. to ~ nice, sentir bon. n. odorat m., flair m., nez m. (animals); odeur f., senteur f. to be offensive to the ~, blesser l'odorat. the ~ of a violet, l'odeur, le parfum d'une violette.

smelly adj. qui pue, puant; malodorant.

smelt n. Ichth. éperlan m. ~ v.t. fondre (ore).

smelting n. fonte f.

smile v.i.,v.t. sourir. to ~ at, sourire à. n. sourire m. with a ~, en souriant.

smiling adj. souriant, Fig. riant, charmant.

smirch v.t. noircir, barbouiller; souiller.

smirk v.i. sourire avec affectation; minauder. n. sourire m. affecté.

smirking adj. affecté, fourbe; de minauderie.

smite v.t. frapper; atteindre; captiver, charmer. to be smitten with, être épris, engoué de.

smith n. forgeron m. Fig. artisan m.

smock n. blouse f.

smoke n. fumée f.; vapeur f. to disappear in ~, s'en aller en fumée. where there's ~, there's fire, il n'y a pas de fumée sans feu. to ~ dry, fumer, sécher à la fumée. v.i. fumer. v.t. saurer (herring); enfumer.

smoker n. fumeur m.

smoking adj. fumant, qui fume; de fumeur. no ~, défense f. de fumer.

smoky adj. qui fume, plein de fumée, enfumé. a ~ chimney, cheminée qui fume.

smooth adj. uni; poli, lisse; facile, mielleux. a ~ surface, une surface unie. a ~ skin, une peau douce, une peau satinée. ~-cheeked, imberbe; à l'air doux. ~-tongued, aux paroles mielleuses. v.t. rendre uni, aplanir; niveler; lisser (hair); dérider (forehead); adoucir; rendre doux; aplanir (une difficulté); flatter. to ~ the way, aplanir un chemin. to ~ over, unir, adoucir; calmer; cajoler.

smoothing n. adoucissement m., aplanissement m.

smoothly *adv.* uniment; doucement, avec douceur; facilement, aisément. **to run ~,** couler doucement.

smoothness *n.* égalité *f.;* poli *m.;* douceur *f.;* calme *m.,* tranquillité *f.* **the ~ of a surface,** le poli d'une surface. **the ~ of the skin,** la douceur de la peau.

smother *v.t.* étouffer; suffoquer, asphyxier.

smudge *n.* tache *f. v.t.* tacher, barbouiller, salir.

smug *adj.* suffisant, content de sa personne.

smuggle *v.t.* passer en contrebande. **to ~ in,** faire la contrebande.

smuggled *adj.* de contrebande. **~ goods,** marchandises de contrebande.

smuggler *n.* contrebandier *m.,* fraudeur *m.*

smuggling *n.* fraude *f.,* contrebande *f.*

smut *n.* tache *f.,* noir *m.* (soot); nielle *f.* (grain), charbon *m.;* obscénité *f.*

snack *n.* goûter *m.,* casse-croûte *m.,* collation *f.* **~** *v.t.* prendre un casse-croûte, un goûter.

snafu *n. Infml.* salade *f.,* pagaille *f.*

snail *n.* escargot *m.*

snake *n.* serpent *m.* **rattle~,** serpent à sonnettes. **a ~ in the grass,** *Fig.* quelque anguille sous roche.

snap *v.t.* rompre, casser net; fermer avec un bruit sec; faire claquer (fingers, whip). **to ~ in two,** casser en deux. **to ~ off,** casser, enlever net. **to ~ up,** happer; gober, rudoyer, brusquer. **he ~ped at her,** il lui a parlé d'un ton brusque. *v.i.* se casser, rompre, craquer; tâcher de happer; gronder; brusquer. *n.* cassure *f.,* rupture *f.;* bruit *m.* sec, claquement *m.* (whip, fingers); fermoir *m.;* effort *m.* pour mordre. **to ~ at,** tâcher de happer. **~shot,** instantané *m.*

snare *n.* piège *m.,* lacet *m. v.t.* prendre au piège.

snarl *v.i.* (at) gronder, grogner; montrer les dents. *v.t.* emmêler, embrouiller. *n.* grognement *m.* **with a ~,** en grognant, en montrant les dents.

snatch *v.t.* saisir brusquement; se saisir de, prendre, *Infml.* gripper; arracher; ravir. **to ~ away,** arracher, enlever, emporter. **to ~ up,** empoigner, gripper. *v.i.* tâcher, de prendre, de saisir, d'attraper. *n.* prise *f.;* effort *m.* pour saisir; éclair *m.;* fragment *m.;* bribe *f.* **by ~es,** par fragments *m.pl,* par bribes *f.pl.*

sneak *v.i.* ramper, se glisser à la dérobée; s'avilir. **to ~ away, to ~ off,** s'en aller l'oreille basse, s'esquiver, s'enfuir; *Infml.* filer. *n.* pied *m.* plat; lâche *m.;* capon *m.;* cafard *m.* **~ preview,** avant-première *f.*

sneakers *n.pl.* chaussures *f.pl.* de tennis/de sport.

sneaking *adj.* qui se glisse furtivement; bas, servile, rampant.

sneaky *adj.* sournois, malin.

sneer *v.i.* ricaner; (at) se moquer, se railler de. *n.* ricanerie *f.,* moquerie *f.,* raillerie *f.*

sneeze *v.i.* éternuer. *n.* éternument *m.*

snicker *v.i.* rire en dessous, rire sous cape.

sniff *n.* reniflement *m. v.i.* renifler. *v.t.* aspirer en reniflant.

snigger See SNICKER.

snip *v.t.* couper avec des ciseaux. *n.* coup *m.* de ciseaux; morceau *m.* coupé.

sniper *n.* tireur *m.* embusqué.

snitch *v.t. Infml.* moucharder (inform); chaparder (steal).

snivel *n.* morve *f.;* goutte *f.* au nez. *v.i.* être morveux; pleurnicher (comme un enfant).

snob *n.* snob *m.f.*

snoop *v.i. Infml.* farfouiller, fouiner, se mêler de. *n.* inquisiteur *m.;* foureteur *m.*

snooze *v.i. Infml.* roupiller, sommeiller, dormir à demi. *n.* somme *m.,* roupillon *m.*

snore *v.i.* ronfler. *n.* ronflement *m.*

snorer *n.* ronfleur *m.*

snoring *n.* renflement *m.*

snort *v.i.* ronfler. *v.t.* renifler sur.

snout *n.* museau *m.;* mufle *m.;* groin *m.* (porc).

snow *n.* niege *f.* **~ball,** boule *f.* de niege. **~-capped,** couronné de neige. **~drift,** amas *m.,* monceau *m.* de neige. **~flake,** flocon *m.* de neige. **~shoe,** raquette *f.* de neige. **~storm,** tempête *f.* de neige. *v.i. imp.* neiger, tomber de la neige. **it's snowing,** il neige.

snowy *adj.* neigeux; de neige; blanc comme la neige.

snub *n.* réprimande *f.* **~ nose,** nez *m.* camus. *v.t.* rabrouer, rudoyer, brusquer; relever vivement; rebuffer.

snuff *v.t.* tabac à priser.

snuffle *v.i.* souffler par le nez; nasiller.

snug *adj.* serré, pressé; au chaud; tranquille, caché; commode, bien arrangé; agréable.

snuggle *v.i.* se tenir serré, chaudement, se pelotonner.

snugly *adv.* en se serrant; à l'aise, bien, commodément.

so *adv.* ainsi, de cette manière, de la sorte, comme cela; ainsi donc, par conséquent, tellement, tant aussi; soit. **is it ~?** est-ce ainsi? **if ~,** s'il en est ainsi. **~-called,** soi-disant, prétendu. **and ~ on,** et ainsi de suite. **will he be here in time? I hope ~,** sera-t-il ici à temps? je l'espère. **I think ~,** je le pense. **how ~?** comment cela? **Mr. ~-and-~,** monsieur un tel. **he doesn't have ~ much money,** il n'a pas tant d'argent. **~ that,** de sorte que, si bien que; pourvu que. *conj.* pourvu que.

soak *v.t.* tremper, mouiller. **to ~ bread,** tremper du pain. **to ~ in,** absorber, boire. *v.i.* tremper, s'imbiber; pénétrer. **water ~s into the earth,** l'eau pénètre dans la terre.

soaking *adj.* trempant; qui trempe. **a ~ rain,** une pluie battante, une pluie continuelle.

soap *n.* savon **~-dish,** porte-savon *m.* **~ opera,** mélo *m.* à épisodes, téléroman *m.* **~-opera star,** acteur/actrice de feuilleton mélo.

soapy *adj.* savonneux; savonné, *Fig.* doucereux.

soar *v.i.* s'élever, prendre son essor; planer.

soaring adj. élevé; qui s'élève. n. essor m., élan m.

sob v.i. sangloter; pousser des sanglots. n. sanglot m.

sober adj. sobre; calme, de sang-froid; raisonnable, grave, sérieux, sensé, qui n'est pas ivre. **to live a ~ life,** mener une vie sobre. **~-minded,** modéré; raisonnable, sage. **~-mindedness,** m. modération f.; sagesse f. ~ v.t. désenivrer, dégriser; rendre modéré; sobre, sensé; calmer. **to ~ up,** se désenivrer.

soberly adv. sobrement, modérément, de sang froid, avec calme; raisonnablement, sagement, sensément; sérieusement.

soberness, sobriety n. sobriété f.; tempérance, modération; absence f. d'ivresse; sang-froid m., calme m., bon sens m., raison f.; sérieux m., gravité f.

soccer n. football m. **to play ~,** jouer au football.

sociable adj. sociable, accueillant, bienveillant, affable.

sociably adv. d'une manière sociable; familièrement.

social adj. social, sociable, aimable.

socialism n. socialisme m.

socialist n. socialiste m.

socially adv. socialement; sociablement.

society n. société f.; monde m., le monde.

sociology n. sociologie f.

sock n. chaussette f.; Infml. gnon m., marron m., beigne f., coup m.; sox n.pl. chaussettes f.pl. ~ v.t. donner un coup, frapper. **to ~ away,** épargner (de l'argent).

socket n. emboîture f. (bone); orbite f. (eye).

sod n. gazon m.; motte f. de gazon. adj. de gazon, de motte de gaxon. v.t. gazonner.

soda n. soda m. **~ fountain,** buvette f.

sodium n. sodium m.

sodomy n. sodomie f.

sofa n. sofa m., canapé m.

soft adj. mon, mol m., molle f.; moelleux; tendre, doux, faible; niais, simple. **a ~ peach,** une pêche molle. **a ~ bed,** un lit moelleux. **~ wood,** du bois tendre. **~ skin,** une peau douce. **~-spoken,** à la voix douce, qui parle avec douceur. adv. doucement.

soften v.t. affaiblir; radoucir, calmer, fléchir. v.i. s'amollir, se rainollir; s'adoucir; s'attendrir, se calmer.

softening n. amollissement, ramollissement; adoucissement m.

softly adv. mollement, doucement, délicatement; tendrement.

softness n. mollesse f.; douceur f.; tendresse f.

soggy adj. mouillé, trempé.

software n. ~, logiciel m.

soil v.t. salir, tacher, beindre, couvrir de. **to ~ a garment,** salir un vêtement. n. salté f., tache f., souillure f., fumier m., engrais m.; sol m.; terroir m., terrain m.; patrie f., terre f. **sandy ~,**

un sol sablonneux. **on foreign ~,** sur une terre étrangère.

soirée n. soirée f.

sojourn v.i. séjourner. n. séjour m.

sol n. sol m.

solace v.t. consoler; soulager; égayer, réjouir. **to ~ oneself,** se consoler. n. consolation f.; adoucissement m., soulagement m.

solar adj. du soleil; solaire.

sold See SELL.

solder v.t. souder. n. soudure f.

soldier n. soldat m., militaire.

sole n. plante f. (foot), semelle f. (shoe); Ichth. sole f. ~ v.t. mettre une seinelle à. adj. seul, unique; Law. célibataire. **our ~ delight,** notre unique plaisir. **the ~ support,** l'unique soutien.

solecism n. solécisme m.

solely adv. seulement, uniquement.

solemn adj. solennel; pompeux, grave, imposant, sérieux. **a ~ silence,** un silence solennel.

solemnity n. solennité f., sérieux m., gravité f.

solemnize v.t. solenniser, célébrer avec cérémonie.

solemnly adv. solennellement, avec solennité; gravement.

solicit v.t. solliciter, demander; postuler, importuner, exiger; (prostitution) racoler. **to ~ a favor,** demander une faveur.

solicitation n. sollicitation f.

solicitous adj. désireux, jaloux de, (about, for) qui a de la sollicitude pour; qui s'intéresse à; inquiet de, soigneux de.

solid adj. solide; plein; massif, grave, sérieux. **to become ~,** se solidifier. **~ gold,** or massif. **a ~ reason,** une raison solide. n. solide m.

solidarity n. solidarité f.

solidify v.t. solidifier. v.i. se solidifier.

solidity n. solidité f.; état m. massif, Fig. solidité f.; sérieux m., gravité f., caractère m. posé.

solidly adv. solidement, avec solidité; sérieusement.

soliliquy n. soliloque m., monologue m.

solitaire n. solitaire m.

solitary adj. solitaire; seul; retiré; triste. **a ~ dwelling,** une demeure solitaire. **a ~ life,** une vie solitaire. n. solitaire m., hermite m.

solitude n. solitude f.

solo n. solo m.

solstice n. solstice m.

soluble adj. soluble.

solution n. solution f., dissolution f.

solve v.i. résoudre; éclaircir.

solvency n. solvabilité f.

solvent adj. dissolvant, solvable. n. dissolvant m.

somber adj. sombre; obscur.

somberly adv. sombrement.

some adj. quelque; un peu, certain, du, de la, des. **bring ~ water,** apportez de l'eau. **~ good books,** de bons livres. **~ people say,** certaines personnes disent. **in ~ way or other,** d'une manière ou d'une autre. pron. quelques-un *m.pl.*, quelques-unes *f.pl.*; les uns *m.pl.*, les unes *f.pl.*; en. ~ **are rich and** ~ **are poor,** les uns sont riches et les autres pauvres. **is there any fruit? there is** ~, y a-t-il du fruits? il y en a. **give me** ~, donnez-m'en. *Infml.* ~ **friends you've got!** t'en as de drôles d'amis! ça, ce sont des amis!

somebody *n.* quelqu'un *m.;* personnage *m.* **there's** ~ **outside,** il y a quelqu'un dehors. **he became** ~, il est devenu quelqu'un.

somehow *adv.* d'une manière ou d'une autre, de façon ou d'autre. **he succeeded** ~, il a réussi tant bien que mal.

someone See SOMEBODY.

somersault *n.* culbute *f.;* saut *m.* périlleux; gali-pette *f.* ~ *v.t.* faire la culbute.

something *n.* quelque chose *f.,* un peu. **fetch me** ~, apportez-moi quelque chose. ~ **strange,** quelque chose d'étrange.

sometime *adv.* autrefois, jadis, anciennement.

sometimes *adv.* quelquefois, parfois, tantôt.

somewhat *n.* un peu, tant soit peu, quelque peu. *adv.* un peu, quelque peu, tant soit peu. **I feel** ~ **tired,** je me sens quelque peu fatigué.

somewhere *adv.* quelque part, en quelque lieu.

somnambulist *n.* somnambule *m.f.*

somnolence *n.* somnolence *f.*

somnolent *adj.* accablé de sommeil; somnolent.

son *n.* fils *m.* ~**-in-law,** gendre *m.* **step**~, beau-fils *m. Vulg.* ~ **of a bitch!** merde! fils de pute! enfant de salaud! ~ **of a gun!** nom d'un petit bonhomme!

sonata *n.* sonate *f.*

song *n.* chanson *f.;* chant *m.,* poésie qui se chante; poéme *m.,* cantique *m..* ~**book,** chansonnier *m.* ~**writer,** chansonnier *m.* **for a** ~, pour rien, pour peu de chose.

sonorous *adj.* sonore.

soon *adv.* tôt, bientôt, vite; de bonne heure. **sonner,** plus tôt. **soonest,** le plus tôt. **I'll be back** ~, je reviendrai bientôt. so ~, si tôt. too ~, trop tôt. **how** ~, quand. **sooner or later,** tôt ou tard. **as** ~ **as,** aussitôt que, dès que.

soot *n.* suie *f.*

soothe *v.t.* calmer, flatter, caresser; charmer, satisfaire; apaiser, adoucir.

soothing *adj.* calmant, adoucissant; consolant; tendre, doux.

soothsayer *n.* devin *m.*

sophism *n.* sophisme *m.*

sophisticate *v.t.* sophistiquer. *n.* sophistiqué.

sophisticated *adj.* raffiné, sophistiqué, recher-ché; subtil.

sophistication *n.* sophistication *f.*

soporific *adj.* soporifique.

sopping *adj.* trempé.

soprano *n.* soprano *m.*

sorbet, sherbet *n.* sorbet *m.*

sorcerer *n.* sorcier *m.*

sorceress *n.* sorcière *f.*

sorcery *n.* sorcellerie *f.,* magie *f.,* sortilège *m.*

sordid *adj.* sale, malpropre; sordide, avare, vilain; vil, bas.

sordidly *adv.* sordidement, bassement, d'une manière vile.

sordidness *n.* saleté *f.;* avarice *f.;* sordidité *f.;* bassesse *f.*

sore *n.* plaie *f.;* mal *m.;* ulcère *m. adj.* sensible; *Fig.* susceptible, douloureux, irritable, rude. ~ **throat,** mal à la gorge. **to make** ~, rendre sensible, douloureux. *adv.* douloureusement; bien, fort, profondément; cruellement.

sorely *adv.* gravement, cruellement.

soreness *n.* mal *m.;* sensibilité *f.;* douleur *m.*

sorority *n.* club *m.* d'étudiantes (vivant généra-lement dans le même bâtiment).

sorrel *adj.* alezan. *n.* oseille.

sorrow *n.* tristesse *f.,* peine *f.,* douleur *f.,* chagrin *m.* in ~, dans la peine. **to my** ~, à mon grand regret. *v.i.* s'affliger; éprouver du chagrin.

sorrowful *adj.* chagrin, peiné, attristé; triste, mélancolique, affligeant, attristant, douloureux.

sorrowfulness *n.* tristesse *f.;* chagrin *m.*

sorry *adj.* peiné, affligé, chagrin; fâché, contra-rié, triste, mauvais, pitoyable. **I'm very** ~, je suis vraiment désolé. **a** ~ **sight,** un triste spectacle. **a** ~ **excuse,** une pauvre excuse.

sort *n.* sorte *f.;* espèce *f.,* genre *m.;* façon *f.,* manière *f.;* qualité *f.* **all** ~ **s of people,** per-sonnes de tous genres. **out of** ~**s,** de mauvaise humeur. **he is out of** ~**s,** il n'est pas dans son assiette. **of some** ~, en quelque sorte. *v.t.* ran-ger, classer; trier; assortir, réunir. **to** ~ **out,** trier.

so-so *adj. Infml.* comme-ci, comme-ça, bof, pas terrible.

soufflé *n., adj.* soufflé *m.*

sought See SEEK.

soul *n.* âme *f.,* être *m.;* vie. **with all my** ~, de toute mon âme, de tout mon coeur. **poor** ~, pauvre créature, pauvre âme *f.* **good** ~, bonne créature, bonne âme, bon coeur. **the** ~ **of elo-quence,** l'âme, l'essence de l'éloquence. ~ **brother/sister,** frère/soeur. ~**mate,** âme *f.* soeur. ~ **music,** soul music *f.* ~**searching,** introspection *f.,* examen m. de conscience.

sound *adj.* sain; valide; bien portant, en bon état; solide; pur, vrai; ortodoxe; sain d'esprit. ~ **health,** bonne santé. ~ **mind,** esprit sain. **a** ~ **body,** un corps sain. ~ **doctrine,** une doctri-ne orthodoxe. ~ **reasoning,** un raisonnement solide. ~ **sleep,** profond sommeil. *n.* son *m.,* bruit *m.,* timbre *f.* (bell). **shrill** ~, son perçant. **sharp** ~, son aigu. **harsh** ~, son rude. ~ **of the drum,** son du tambour. ~**board,** table *f.* d'har-monie (piano). ~**track** *m.* bande *f.* de film sono-re. *v.i.* sonder, tâter; essayer; sonner, résonner, retentir, paraître, avoir l'air, faire entendre; célé-brer, publier, proclamer. **to** ~ **good,** sonner bien. **to** ~ **strange,** sembler singulier, paraître étrange. ~ **his praise,** chantez sa louange.

sounding *n. Naut.* sonde *f.* See SOUND.

soundly *adv.* sainement; bien; solidement; com-

...anière; ferme, fort, ...ement; profondément.

...t *m.* sain; bonne condition *f.;* ...nne santé *f.;* force *f.,* vigueur *f.,* ...justesse *f.;* pureté *f.*

so... *n.* soupe *f.,* potage *m.;* bouillon *m.* ~ **kitchen** *n.* soupe *f.* populaire.

soupçon *n.* soupçon *m.,* pointe *f.*

sour *adj.* aigre, acide, *Fig.* revêche, morose. **to turn** ~, tourner; *Fig.* s'aigrir. ~ **cream**, crème *f.* sure. *v.t.* *Fig.* irriter; empoisonner. *v.i.* s'acidifier; surir; s'agrir, devenir aigre; tourner.

source *n.* source *f.,* origine *f.*

sourness *n.* aigreur *f.;* âpreté *f.*

south *n.* sud *m.,* midi *m. adj.* du sud, du midi, méridional, austral. **the South Pole**, le pôle sud. *adv.* vers le sud, au sud; du sud. ~**east**, sud-est *m.* ~**west**, sud-ouest *m.*

southerly *adj.* méridional, du sud, du midi; austral.

southern *adj.* du sud, du midi, méridional.

southerner *n.* habitant *m.* du sud; sudiste *m.f.*

souvenir *n.* souvenir *m.*

sovereign *adj.* souverain, suprême. *n.* souverain *m.;* monarque.

sow *n.* truie *f.*

sow *v.t.* semer, ensemencer. **to ~ one's wild oats**, jeter sa gourme. *v.i.* semer, faire les semailles.

soy(a) *n.* soy. ~ **sauce** *n.* sauce *f.* de soya. ~**bean**, germe *m.* de soya.

spa *n.pr.* station *f.* thermale.

space *n.* espace *m.;* étendue *f.* (time, distance); interligne *m.* ~**craft** *n.,* ~**ship** *n.* vaisseau *m.* spatial. ~ **shuttle** *n.* navette *f.* spatiale. *v.t.* espacer.

spacious *adj.* spacieux; vaste, immense.

spaciousness *n.* grandeur *f.,* grande dimension *f.;* vaste étendue *f.*

spade *n.* bêche *f.;* pique *m.* (cards). *v.t.* bêcher.

spaghetti *n.* spaghetti *m.pl.*

Spain *n.* Espagne *f.*

span *n.* moment *m.,* instant *m.; Arch.* ouverture *f.;* envergure *f.* ~ *v.t.* mesurer, embrasser; traverser.

spangle *n.* paillette *f.* ~ *v.i.* orner, parsemer de paillettes, *Fig.* émailler. **the Star-Spangled Banner**, le drapeau parsemé d'étoiles (des Etats-Unis).

Spaniard *n.* Espagnol *m.,* Espagnole *f.*

spaniel *n.* épagneul *m.*

Spanish *adj.* espagnol, d'Espagne. *n.* espagnol *m.* (language).

spank *v.t.* fesser, donner une fessée. *v.i.* filer.

spaning *n.* fessée *f.* ~ *adj.* fort, vigoureux, épatant.

spar *n. Naut.* espars *m.,* esparre *f.;* mâture *f.,* boxe *f.* à coups de poing. *v.i. Infml.* se disputer, se chamailler; boxer, se battre à coups de poing.

spare *v.t.* épargner, ménager, économiser; faire grâce à, réserver, disposer de; accorder, donner.

he doesn't ~ **himself**, il ne se ménage point. I **have some to** ~, j'en ai plus qu'il ne m'en faut. **we have to** ~ **him**, il faut le ménager. *adj.* frugal, sobre; maigre; de reste, disponible. ~ **clothes**, des vêtements de rechange. I **have no** ~ **time**, je n'ai pas un moment à moi.

sparing *adj.* sobre, frugal, économe, petit, faible, parcimonieux, avare. **he is** ~ **of his words**, il est avare de ses paroles.

spark *n.* étincelle *f., Fig.* petite lueur vive, bluette *f.*

sparkle *n.* étincelle *f.* ~ *v.i.* étinceler; pétiller, scintiller; mousser (beverages).

sparkling *adj.* étincelant, brilliant; pétillant.

sparrow *n.* moineau *m.* ~ **hawk**, épervier *m.*

sparse *adj.* épars; clairsemé.

sparsely *adv.* d'une manière éparse.

spasm *n.* spasme *m.*

spasmodic *adj.* spasmodique.

spatial *adj.* spatial.

spatter *v.t.* éclabousser; crotter; *Fig.* salir, nourcir; lancer. *n.* éclaboussure *f.*

spatula *n.* spatule *f.*

spawn *n.* frai *m.,* oeufs (fish); *Fig.* engeance *f.* ~ *v.t.* engendrer, donner naissance à. *v.i.* frayer, naître, sortir.

spay *v.t.* châtrer.

speak *v.i.* parler, prononcer; discourir, s'entretenir; dire. **to ~ loud**, parler à haute voix. **to ~ low**, parler à voix basse. **so to ~**, pour ainsi dire. **to ~ well of**, dire du bien de. **to ~ ill of**, parler mal de. **to ~ out**, parler haut. **to ~ up**, parler haut; élever la voix, parler hardiment, parler haut et fort. *v.t.* proférer; déclarer, proclamer, publier. **to ~ a language**, parler une langue. ~ **a word**, dire un mot. **to ~ the truth**, dire la vérité. **to ~ one's mind**, dire sa pensée.

speaker *n.* qui parle; orateur *m.;* président *m.* d'une assemblée; (haut-)parleur. **a good ~**, un bon orateur.

speaking *adj.* parlant, qui parle. **public ~**, art oratoire.

spear *n.* lance *f.,* harpon *m.* ~ *v.t.* percer avec une lance; harponner. ~**head**, pointe *f.* de lance.

spearmint *n.* menthe *f.* verte.

special *adj.* spécial; particulier; exprès; extraordinaire; ettitré. ~ **opportunities**, des occasions extraordinaires. ~ **agents**, représentants attitrés. **today's** ~, plat *m.* du jour.

specialist *n.* spécialiste *m.*

specialty *n.* spécialité *f.*

specially *adv.* spécialement, particulièrement.

specie *n. Fin.* espèces *f.pl.,* numéraire *m.*

species *n.* espèce *f.;* sorte *f.,* genre *m.,* espèces *f.pl.,* numéraire *m.* **the propagation of the ~**, la propagation de l'espèce.

specific *adj.* spécifique. *n.* propriété *f.* spécifique. **the ~s**, les détails *m.pl.*

specifically *adv.* spécifiquement.

specification *n.* spécification *f.;* chose *f.* spécifiée; description *f.* (of a patent), devis *m.* (of a job).

specify *v.t.* spécifier, déterminer.

specimen *n.* spécimen *m.*

specious *adj.* spécieux, trompeur.

speck *n.* petite tache *f.*, brin *m.*, marque *f.*, point *m.* ~ *v.t.* tacher, faire des taches à; tacheter; marquer.

speckle *n.* tache *f.*, moucheture *f.*, point *m.* ~ *v.t.* tacheter; moucheter.

spectacle *n.* spectacle *m.*, ~s lunettes *f.pl.*

spectator *n.* spectateur *m.*

spectral *adj.* spectral.

spectre *n.* spectre *m.*; vision *f.*

spectrum *n.* spectre *m.*

speculate *v.i.* spéculer.

speculation *n.* vue *f.*, vision *f.*; spéculation *f.*; méditation *f.*, réflexion *f.*; conjectures *f.pl.*

speculator *n.* spéculateur *m.*

speech *n.* parole *f.*, langage *m.*; idiome *m.*; discours *m.*, oraison *f.* **the parts of ~**, les parties du discours. **to make a ~**, prononcer un discours.

speechless *adj.* muet; interdit.

speed *v.i.* se presser, se dépêcher, accourir. *v.t.* expédier; dépêcher; faire partir à la hâte; hâter, accélérer. **to ~ up**, accélérer. *n.* vitesse *f.*, rapidité *f.*; célérité *f.*, promptitude *f.*, hâte *f.*; succès *m.* **full ~, at full ~**, à toutes jambes, à toute vitesse, à bride abattue, au grand galop, ventre à terre. **~-boat**, vedette *f.*, hors-bord *m.* **~ limit**, vitesse *f.* maximale.

speedily *adv.* rapidement, vite; promptement, à la hâte.

speedy *adj.* rapide; vite; prompt, expéditif.

spell *n.* charme *m.*, sort *m.*, sortilège; tour *m.* (of work); repos *m.*, arrêt *m.* **to break the ~**, rompre le charme. **~-bound**, charmé, sous le charme. **at a ~**, à la fois, d'un coup. *v.t.* épeler, écrire, orthographier; relever. **to ~ out**, spécifier, expliquer en détail.

spelling *n.* épellation *f.*; orthographe *f.*

spend *v.t.* dépenser; prodiguer, gaspiller; manger, perdre; passer (time); épuiser. **to ~ one's strength**, épuiser ses forces. **to ~ a day**, passer un jour. **they ~ their entire time playing**, ils/elles passent tout leur temps à jouer.

spendthrift *n.* dépensier *m.*, prodigue *m.*, dissipateur *m.*; *Infml.* panier *m.* percé.

spent *adj.* dépensé; passé, dissipé, épuisé, fatigué.

sperm *n.* sperme *m.* **~ whale** *n.* cachalot *m.*

spermatozoon *n.* **spermatozoa** *n.pl.* spermatozoïde *m.*

spermicide *n.* spermicide *m.*

spew *v.t.,v.i.* vomir, rendre.

sphere *n.* sphère *f.*, globe *m.* ~ *v.t.* arrondir, former en sphère.

spherical *adj.* sphérique.

sphincter *n.* sphincter *m.*

sphinx *n.* sphinx *m.*

spice *n.* épice *f.* ~ *v.t.* épicer; assaisonner; aromatiser.

spiciness *n.* goût *m.* épicé; bon goût.

spick-and-span *adj.* brillant, tout neuf. *adv.* tout neuf, tout battant, tout flambant, tout propre.

spicy *adj.* épicé.

spider *n.* araignée *f.* **~ web**, toile *f.* d'araignée.

spiel *n.* *Infml.* baratin *m.* *v.i.* baratiner.

spike *n.* clou *m.*; pointe *f.*; épi *m.* (wheat). *v.t.* clouer, conser (with alcohol).

spill *v.t.* répandre; renverser; verser; carguer. **to ~ milk**, répandre du lait. *v.i.* se répandre, se verser, gaspiller.

spin *v.t.* filer; faire tourner.

spinach *n.* épinards *m.pl.*

spinal *adj.* spinal; épinière *f.* **~ cord**, épine *f.* dorsale.

spindle *n.* fuseau *m.*; broche *f.*

spine *n.* épine *f.* dorsale, épine *f.*, colonne *f.*, vertébrale; *Bot.* épine *f.*

spinster *n.* vieille fille *f.* célibataire *f.*

spiny *adj.* épineux.

spiral *adj.* spirale; en hélice. *n.* spirale *f.* ~ *v.t.* s'élever en spirale.

spire *n.* flèche *f.*, clocher *m.*, sominet *m.*; brin *m.* (grass).

spirit *n.* esprit *m.*, souffle *m.*; âme *f.*; apparition *f.*, fantôme *m.*; coeur *m.*, courage *m.*; feu *m.*, ardeur *f.*; fougue *f.*; entrain *m.*, verve *f.*; sentiment *m.*, disposition *f.*; tendance *f.*; spiritueux *m.pl.* (liquor). **an evil ~**, un mauvais génie. **Holy Spirit**, Saint Esprit *m.* **a man of a generous ~**, un homme d'un caractère généreux. **party ~**, esprit de parti. **public ~**, esprit public. **with great ~**, avec beaucoup de courage. **to show ~**, montrer du coeur. **he acts with ~**, il agit avec vigueur. **high ~**, gaieté *f.*, entrain *m.* **full of ~s**, joyeux; plein d'ardeur. **in low ~s**, triste, abattu, découragé. **to keep up one's ~**, ne pas perdre courage. *v.t.* animer, vivifier; exciter, encourager. **to ~ away**, faire disparaître, escamoter.

spirited *adj.* animé; plein de vie, de force, vif, vigoureux, fougueux; plein de coeur, courageux; d'humeur; plein d'ardeur; chaleureux. **high-~**, de caractère; plein de coeur. **low-~**, sans coeur, pusillanime, abattu. **mean-~**, sans coeur, sans caractère.

spiritedly *adv.* courageusement, avec courage; chaleureusement, ardemment.

spiritual *adj.* spirituel, intellectuel; religieux; ecclésiastique.

spiritualism *n.* spiritisme *m.*, spiritualisme *m.*

spirituality *n.* spiritualité *f.*, spirituel *m.*

spiritually *adv.* spirituellement.

spirt *v.i.* jaillir, faire jaillir. *n.* jet *m.*, jaillissement *m.*

spit *n.* broche *f.*, coup *m.* de bêche, crachat *m.*; langue *f.* de terre. *v.t.* embrocher; mettre à la broche, bêcher, creuser. *v.i.* cracher.

spite *n.* dépit *m.*, haine *f.*; rancune *f.* **in ~ of**, en dépit de, malgré. **out of ~**, par dépit; par haine. *v.i.* en vouloir à; dépiter.

spiteful *adj.* plein de dépit; malicieux.

spitefully *adv.* par dépit, malicieusement.

spitefulness *n.* malice *f.*, méchanceté *f.*

splash *v.t.* éclabousser. *v.i.* patauger. *n.* éclaboussure *f.*, clapotage *m.*, clapotement *m.*, clapotis *m.*

splatter *v.i.* See SPLASH.

splay *v.t.* étendre, étaler; déployer. *n.* Arch. ébrasement *m.*, embrasure *f.* ~ *adj.* étalé, étendu, écarté. ~-footed, qui a les pieds tournés en dehors.

spleen *n.* Anat. rate *f.*; mauvaise humeur *f.*, bile *f.*, fiel *m.*, animosité *f.*, mélancolie *f.*, humeur *f.* noire.

splendid *adj.* splendide, éclatant, resplendissant, brillant, magnifique, somptueux.

splendidly *adv.* splendidement, fastueusement.

splendor *n.* splendeur *f.*; magnificence *f.*

splice *v.t.* joindre, unir. *n.* Naut. épissure *f.*

splint *n.* éclisse *f.*, attelle *f.* ~ *v.t.* éclisser.

splinter *n.* écharde *f.*; éclat *m.* de bois, éclat *m.*, esquille *f.* (bone). *v.t.* fendre, diviser; éclater, se briser en éclats.

split *v.t.* déchirer, Infml. se casser. to ~ a board, fendre une planche. to ~ in two, fendre en deux. to ~ one's sides with laughing, crever de rire. *v.i.* se fendre; se crever, se crevasser, se briser; éclater. *n.* fente *f.*; crevasse *f.* ~ *adj.* fendu, déchiré. ~ in two, fendu en deux.

splutter *n.* bafouillage *m.*; crachotement *m.* ~ *v.i.* bredouiller, bafouiller.

spoil *v.t.* spolier, piller. to ~ one's children, gâter ses enfants. *v.i.* voler, se corrompre, se gâter, s'abimer. *n.* butin *m.*; dépouille, proie *f.*, vol *m.*, pillage *m.*, ruine *f.*

spoiler *n.* spoliateur *m.*

spoke *n.* rais *m.*; bâton *m.*, rayon *m.* (wheel). *v.i.* See SPEAK.

spokesperson *n.* porte-paroles *m.*

sponge *n.* éponge *f.* ~ *v.t.*, *v.i.* éponger, passer l'éponge sur. to ~ on, écornifler. to ~ up, éponger.

sponger *n.* écornifleur, pique-assiette *m.*

spongy *adj.* spongieux; mouillé, trempé; plein d'eau.

sponsor *n.* garant *m.*, caution *f.*; parrain *m.*, marraine *f.*

spontaneity, spontaneousness *n.* spontanéité *f.*

spontaneous *adj.* spontané.

spontaneously *adv.* spontanément.

spook *n.* Infml. fantôme *m.*, revenant *m.* ~ *v.t.* hanter, effraye.

spooky *adj.* qui donne la chair de poule/le frisson/froid dans le dos.

spool *n.* bobine *f.* ~ *v.t.* bobiner.

spoon *n.* cuillère *f.* table~, cuillère à soupe. tea~, cuillère, cuillère à thé.

spoonful *n.* cuillerée *f.*

sporadic *adj.* sporadique.

sport *n.* sport *m.* she likes any type of ~, elle aime toutes sortes de sport. he always loses, but he is always a good ~ about it, il perd toujours mais il reste toujours un beau joueur.

he came in ~ing his new jacket, il est venu montrer sa nouvelle veste.

sportsman *n.* amateur *m.* du sport.

sporty *adj.* casual.

spot *n.* tache *f.*, moucheture *f.*; souillure *f.*; lieu *m.*, endroit *m.*; morceau *m.* (terrain). to take out a ~, ôter, enlever une tache. on the ~, sur-le-champ. *v.t.* tacher; souiller; moucheter, tacheter; repérer. she ~ted him out of the entire crowd, elle l'a repéré de toute la foule. ~light, *m.* feu de projecteur.

spotless *adj.* pur, sans tache.

spotted *adj.* tacché, souillé; moucheté, tacheté, truité.

spouse *n.* époux *m.*, épouse *f.*, mari *m.*, femme *f.*

spout *n.* tuau *m.*; gouttière *f.* (roof); bout *m.*, bec *m.* (vase); trombe *f.*; tourbillon d'eau *m.* *v.t.* lancer, faire jaillir; déclamer, débiter. *v.i.* jaillir. to ~ out, jaillir, sortir.

spouting *adj.*, *m.* jaillissement; déclamation *f.*

sprain *v.t.* se donner une entorse à, se fouler. *n.* entorse *f.*; foulure *f.*

sprawl *v.i.* s'étendre, s'étaler. to lie ~ing, être étendu tout de son long. *v.t.* (out) traîner. ~ing out his legs, trainant les jambes.

spray *n.* petite branche *f.* (tree), brindille *f.*, brin *m.*; Naut. poussière *f.* d'eau de mer, pomme *f.* (sprinkler); vaporisateur *m.* (perfume, etc.). ~ can, bombe *f.* aérosol.

spread *v.t.* répandre, étendre; déployer, couvrir, recouvrir, propager, publier; exhaler. *v.i.* s'étendre; se répandre; se disperser; s'exhaler; se propager. the trees their branches, les arbres étendent leurs branches. to ~ the word, mettre au courant, laisser savoir; avertir. to ~ a disease, répandre sa maladie. to ~ around, répandre au loin, propager. to ~ out, étendre, déployer, répandre. *n.* étendue *f.*, espace *m.*; expansion *f.*, développement *m.*; propagation; couverture *f.* (bed).

spreading *adj.* vaste, étendu, large; qui s'étend. ~ tree, un arbre touffu.

spree *n.* fête. she went on a shopping ~ with the $5,000 prize money, elle a fait des dépenses folles avec les $5000 qu'elle a gagné.

sprig *n.* brindille *f.*, brin *m.*, pousse *f.*; petit bouquet.

sprightly *adj.* vif, espiègle, éveillé, malin; joyeux, gaillard.

spring *v.i.* souter, jaillir, lancer, s'élancer; pousser, croitre, naître; avoir sa source, provenir; surgir, poindre; faire ressort, se détendre. to ~ again, repousser; renaître, reparaître. to ~ at, s'élancer sur. to ~ away, s'élancer d'un bond. to ~ back, s'élancer en arrière; reculer. to ~ forth, croître, pousser; jaillir. to ~ forward, sauter en avant. to ~ in, entrer (d'un bond). to ~ on, se jeter, s'élancer sur. to ~ out, sortir, s'élancer dehors. to ~ up, naître; pousser, croître; venir au jour; jaillir. *v.t.* faire lever, faire partir (from jail, etc.), produire; franchir, sauter; creuser. **to ~ a leak**, faire une voie d'eau. n. élan m.; bond m., saut m., ressort m.; élasticité; source f., origine f., cause f., printemps m. **the main~**, le grand ressort. **in the ~**, au printemps. **~board**, tremplin m. **~ tide**, haute marée f. **~time**, printemps m. **~ water**, eau f. de source.

springy adj. élastique; souple.

sprinkle v.t. répandre (en petites quantités); arroser; saupoudrer (sugar, etc.), semer, parsemer. **sprinkled with gold**, parsemé d'or. v.i. pleuvoir un peu. n. petite quantité f. répandue.

sprint n. course de vitesse sur petite distance.

sprinter n. coureur m. de vitesse, sprinter m.

sprite n. esprit m., revenant m.

sprout v.i. germer; bourgeonner; pousser. n. jet m., pousse f., bourgeon m., or pl. choux m.pl. verts. **Brussels ~s**, choux de Bruxelles.

spruce adj. propre, bien mis, beau, pimpant; élégant. v.t. **up**, parer, attifer. n. sapin m.

spry adj. vif, actif, plein d'entrain.

spud n. Infml. patate f.

spume n. écume f. ~ v.i. écumer.

spunk n. Infml. courage m.

spur n. éperon m., ergot m. (cock, grain); contrefort m. (mountains); arc-boutant m., pointe f., piquant m.; Fig. aiguillon m., stimulant m. **to set ~s to** donner de l'éperon. **on the ~ of the moment**, sur un coup de tête. v.t. éperonner; Fig. exciter, stimuler, pousser; orner d'éperons. v.i. jouer des éperons, exciter, stimuler. **to ~ on**, (se) presser.

spurious adj. faux; falsifié; sophistiqué; apocryphe. **~ books**, des livres apocryphes.

spurn v.t. dédaigner, repousser dédaigneusement, mépriser. v.i. traiter avec dédain, avec mépris; mépriser.

spurt n. jaillissement m.; regain m. d'énergie. v.i. jaillir.

sputter v.i. éclabousser; pétiller; siffler (while burning), bredouiller.

spy n. espion m. **~glass**, lunette f. d'approche. v.t. voir, apercevoir; épier, espionner. v.i. (into), examiner, scruter.

squabble v.i. se chamailler, se disputer. n. querelle f., dispute f.

squad n. escouade f.

squadron n. carré m., bataillon m. carré; escadron m.; flottille f.; escadre f.

squalid adj. sale, malpropre, crasseux.

squalidly adv. salement, malproprement.

squall v.i. brailler, crier. n. cri m., grand cri m.; grain m., rafale f., bourrasque f.

squander v.t. gaspiller, dissiper, dispenser.

squanderer n. prodigue m., dissipateur m., gaspilleur m.

square adj. carré; en équerre, honnête, juste, balancé. **a ~ table**, une table carrée. **~-shouldered**, aux épaules carrées. **~ number**, un nombre carré. **~ measure**, mesure de superficie. **~ root**, racine f. carrée. **the account**

is ~, le compte est juste. n. carré m., équerre f.; place f. publique; carreau m.; case f. (chessboard). **to form into a ~**, former en carré. v.t. rendre carré, ajuster, régler, balancer. **to ~ accounts**, régler les comptes. v.i. cadrer, aller, s'accorder, se quereller.

squarely adv. carrément; justement.

squash v.t. écraser, aplatir. n. courge f., gourde f.

squashy adj. mou; qui cède à la pression; humide, spongieux.

squat v.t. s'accroupir; squatter. adj. accroupi, n. accroupissement m.; posture f. accroupie.

squatter n. squatter m.

squeak v.i. crier, rendre un son aigu. n. cri m. aigu. **to give a ~**, crier, pousser un cri.

squeaky adj. glapissant; qui pousse un cri aigu. Infml. **~ clean**, super propre.

squeal v.i. pousser des cris aigus. Infml. dénoncer, vendre, donner. **he ~ed on his friends**, il a vendu/dénoncé ses amis.

squeamish adj. délicat; facile à dégoûter, sujet aux nausées, qui gait le dégoûte.

squeeze v.t. presser, étreindre; comprimer, pressurer. **to ~ an orange**, presser une orange. **to ~ in**, faire entrer en pressant. **to ~ out**, faire sortir. **to ~ through**, faire passer de force à travers. v.i. pousser; se frayer un passage à travers; traverser (crowd). n. compression f.; serrement m. (hands), pression f.; embrassade f., embrassement m.

squid n. cal(a)mar m., encornet m.

squint adj. louche; méfiant. **~-eyed**, louche, au regard louche. n. regard m. louche; strabisme m. **to have a ~**, loucher; regarder de côté. v.i. regarder en fronçant les sourcils/en clignant des yeux; loucher, être louche.

squire n. écuyer m.; chevalier m., cavalier m. (of a lady); monsieur m. **~ country ~**, propriétaire compagnard; hobereau m. ~ v.t. servir d'écuyer à; escorter.

squirm n. tortillement. v.i. se tortiller.

squirrel n. écureuil m.

squirt v.t. lancer; jaillir. n. seringue f.; jet m.

stab v.t.,v.i. percer, poignarder. n. coup m. d'épée, de poignard, couteau, etc.

stabbing n. aggression f. **back~**, coup bas. adj. lancinant (pain).

stability n. stabilité f., fermeté f.

stabilize v.t. stabiliser.

stable adj. stable, solide; durable; fixe, ferme, constant. n. étable f.; écurie f. ~ v.t. mettre à l'étable, loger.

stack n. meule f. (hay), pile f. (wood); souche f. (chimney). v.t. mettre en meule; empiler.

stadium n. stade m.

staff n. personnel m.; bâton m.; gourdin m., bois m. (lance), hampe f.; Mus. portée f.; état-major m., Fig. appui m., soutien m. **flag~**, mât de pavillon. **medical ~**, corps des médecins, personnel m. médical. **the teaching ~**, le corps enseignant, personnel enseignant.

stag n. cerf m.

stage n. scène f.; estrade f.; théâtre m.; relais m., étape; période f., phase f., degré m.; échafaud m. **to go on the ~**, entrer en scène. **to go off the ~**, quitter le théâtre/la scène. **in short ~s**, à petites étapes, à petites journées. **the last ~ of a disease**, la dernière période d'une maladie. **~ directions**, mise en scène.

stagger v.i. chanceler, tituber; faiblir. **to ~ along**, marcher en chancelant. v.t. faire chanceler, ébranler, faire fléchir, frapper de stupeur, étouner. **to ~ to one's feet**, se lever en chancelant. **to ~ back**, reculer en chancelant.

staggering adj. chancelant; saisissant, stupéfiant, étourdissant.

staging n. mise en scène; échaudage m.

stagnant adj. stagnant.

stagnate v.i. stagner, être stagnant, croupir; être dans un état de stagnation.

stagnation n. stagnation f.

staid adj. grave, posé, sérieux.

stain n. tache f., Fig. honte f. v.t. tacher; faire une tache, entacher.

stained adj. taché; souillé, teint; peint, imprimé; de couleur. **~ glass**, verre de couleur. **~-glass windows**, vitraux peints.

stairs n.pl. marche f.; escalier m. **down~s**, en bas. **up~s**, en haut. **back ~s**, escalier de service, escalier dérobé.

staircase n. escalier m.

stake n. pieu m., poteau m., enjeu m.; prix m. **to perish at the ~**, être brûlé sur le bûcher. **tied to the ~**, attaché au poteau. **to be at ~**, être en jeu. **his life is at ~**, il y va de sa vie. v.t. garnir de pieux; aiguiser en pieu; percer avec un pieu; mettre au jeu, jouer, hasarder.

stalactite n. stalactite f.

stalagmite n. stalagmite f.

stale adj. tassis; vieux, vieil; (liquids) éventé; suranné; usé. (horses).

stalemate n. pat m.

stalk n. tige f. (plants); queue (leaf); trognon m. (cabbage); tuyau m. (feather, pipe); démarcher f., pas m. raide, fière. v.i. aller d'un pas majestueux; chasser à l'affût. **to ~ around**, se parvaner. **to ~ over**, parcourir, arpenter.

stalker n. personne f. à l'affût.

stalking n. he was arrested for **~ her**, il s'est fait arrêter pour l'avoir suivie à l'affût.

stall v.t. caler. **the car ~ed**, la voiture a calé.

stallion n. étalon m.

stalwort adj. fort, robuste, vigoureux, vaillant.

stamen n. étamine f.

stamina n. vigueur f., résistance f.

stammer v.i., v.t. bégayer; balbutier. n. bégayement m.

stammerer n. bègue m.

stammering adj. bègue, de bégayement, qui balbutie. n. bégayement m.

stamp v.t. timbrer; frapper du pied, empreindre, mettre l'empreinte à; frapper (coin), monnayer,

contrôler (gold, silver); poinçonner; Fig. graver, fixer. **to ~ with initials**, marquer aux initiales. **to ~ out a disease**, enrayer une maladie. n. timbre m., sceau m., cachet m., estampe f.; trempe f. (engraving); coin m., marque f., empreinte f.; contrôle m.; estampille f., estampe f., gravure f.; coup m. frappé du pied. **postage ~**, timbre-poste. **to bear the ~ of**, porter le timbre, l'estampille de; porter le cachet, la marque de.

stampede n. panique; fuite f. précipitée (caussée par la terreur).

stamping n. trépignement m., piétinement m.; impression f.; timbrage m.

stance n. position f., posture f.

stanch v.t. étancher. v.i. s'arrêter, cesser de couler.

stand v.i. être debout, se tenir debout, se tenir, se soutenir; se dresser; être, se trouver; demeurer; durer, rester. v.t. mettre debout, placer, faire tenir debout, endurer, supporter, payer. **to be ~ing**, être debout. **~ there**, mettez-vous là. **as matters ~**, au point où en sont les choses. **~ still**, ne bougez pas, tenez-vous tranquille. **to let ~**, laisser reposer. **to ~ one's ground**, tenir bon. **to ~ around**, se tenir auprès; entourer. **to ~ against**, résister à, tenir contre. **to ~ alone**, être, se tenir seul. **to ~ aside**, se tenir à l'écart; se ranger. **to ~ back**, se tenir en arrière, reculer. **to ~ by**, être auprès, se tenir auprès; être présent, rester là, assister, soutenir, défendre. **I will ~ by you**, je vous soutiendrai. **the house ~s by itself**, la maison se trouve isolée. **to ~ for**, être pour, représenter; vouloir dire; concourir; soutenir, coinbattre pour. **to ~ away from**, s'écarter de, s'éloigner de. **to ~ in for someone**, remplacer quelqu'un. **to ~ in fear of**, avoir peur de. **to ~ in need of**, avoir besoin de. **to ~ in the way of**, gêner, être un obstacle à. **to ~ in defense of**, prendre la défense de, soutenir. **to ~ off**, se tenir à distance; reculer. **to ~ on**, se tenir sur; s'appuyer sur, se formaliser. **to ~ on ceremony**, faire des façons. **to ~ out**, avancer, ressortir, se détacher. **~ out of the way**, ôtez-vous du chemin, rangez-vous. **to ~ around**, se ranger en cercle; entourer. **it ~s to reason**, il est évident, il va sans dire. **to ~ together**, se tenir ensemble, s'accorder. **to ~ up**, se tenir debout; se lever. **to ~ up against**, s'élever contre, s'attaquer à, supporter. **to ~ up for**, se lever en faveur de, soutenir. **to ~ with**, être avec, se tenir avec; convenir, être d'accord avec. **I cannot ~ the cold**, je ne peux pas supporter le froid. **to ~ trial**, subir une épreuve; soutenir un examen, passer en justice. **I can't ~ it**, je ne peux pas le supporter/le souffrir. **to ~ one's ground**, défendre son terrain, se maintenir. n. place f.; poste m.; Fig. rang m., position f.; tribune f. (racetrack); halte f., pause f.; pied m., support m. **to take one's ~**, prendre sa place, se placer. **to make a ~**, prendre position. **a ~still**, arrêt m. **music ~**, pupitre m. à musique. **to**

come to a ~, s'arrêter. **to make a ~**, résister, faire une résistance.

standard *n.* étendard *m.*, bannière *f.*, drapeau *m.*; *Naut.* pavillon *m.*, étalon *m.*; (weights and measures), modèle *m.*, titre *m.* légal, régulateur *m.*, type *m.*; **~-bearer**, porte-étendard, porte-drapeau. **the ~ of taste**, le modèle du gout. *adj.* type, de type; régulateur; *Mon.* au titre. **~ prices**, des prix régulateurs.

standing *adj.* debout, sur pied; fixe, à demeure; stagnant; croupissant, constant; établi, invariable; solide, durable. **~ water**, eau stagnante. **~ rules**, règles *f.pl.* invariables. *n.* station *f.*; place *f.*; position *f.*, rang *m.*, état *m.*; durée *f.*; date *f.* **of long ~**, de longue date.

standpoint *n.* point *m.* de vue.

stanza *n.* stance *f.*

staple *n.* agrafe *f.*; denrée *f.* principale, produit *m.*, principal, *Fig.* sujet *m.*, objet *m.* principal, matière *f.* première; *adj.* d'entrepôt, de commerce; établi; marchand, principal. **~ goods**, marchandises principales. *v.t.* agrafer.

stapler *n.* agrafeuse *f.*

star *n.* étoile *f.*; astre *m.*; *Typ.* astérisque *m.* **pole ~**, étoile polaire. **~-spangled**, orné. **the Star-Spangled Banner**, la bannière étoilée. **~ fish**, étoiles *f.* de mer. **~gazer**, astronome *m.* **~gazing**, astronomie *f.*; astrologie *f.* **he was born under a lucky ~**, il est né sous une bonne étoile. **she is a big movie ~**, c'est une grande vedette de cinéma. *v.t.* étoiler; être la vedette.

starboard *n.* tribord *m.* *adj.* de tribord.

starch *n.* amidon *m.*, fécule *f.*; *Fig.* raideur *f.* *v.t.* amidonner.

starchy *adj.* d'amidon.

stardom *n.* célébrité.

stare *v.i.* fixer, regarder avec ébahissement; regarder; regarder avec effronterie; contempler. *v.i.* frapper du regard; regarder fixement. **to ~ a person in the face**, regarder quelqu'un en face; être évident, sauter aux yeux. *n.* regard *m.* fixe; regard *m.* étonné.

staring *adj.* fixe, grand ouvert; qui saute aux yeux, voyant.

stark *adj.* entier, vrai, véritable, pur, franc. **~ nonsense**, pure betise. *adv.* entièrement, complètement, tout à fait, tout. **~ raving mad**, complètement fou, fou à lier. **~ naked**, tout nu, entièrement nu.

starlight *n.* lumière *f.* des étoiles; *Astron.* lumière *f.* stellaire.

starling *n.* étourneau *m.*; sansonnet *m.*

starry *adj.* étoilé; étincelant, brillant.

start *v.i.* commencer; tressaillir; frémir, trembler; se lever soudainement; s'élancer; partir. **the movie ~s at two**, le film commence à deux heures. **to ~ in one's sleep**, tressaillir en dormant. **to ~ off**, partir précipitamment. **to ~ with**, débuter avec. *v.t.* faire tressaillir; alarmer; lever, faire lever (animal); faire naître; inventer. *n.* tressaillement *m.*; mouvement *m.* involuntai-

re; sursaut *m.*; saut *m.*, bond *m.*, élan *m.*, boutade *f.*; commencement *m.*, début *m.*; départ *m.* **he can't ~ the engine**, il n'arrive pas à faire démarrer la machine. **to give a ~**, donner un élan, une impulsion. **a good ~**, un bon début. **to get a head ~ on**, avoir l'avance sur, devancer. **~ing point**, point *m.* de départ.

starter *n.* starter *m.*

startle *v.i.* tressaillir, frémir, trembler (de peur). *v.t.* faire tressaillir, faire frémir; épouvanter, faire peur à; alarmer; saisir, détourner.

startling *adj.* saisissant; étonnant, renversant; atterrant.

starvation *n.* inanition *f.*; faim *f.*, besoin *m.*, dénûment *m.*

starve *v.i.* mourir de faim. *v.t.* faire mourir de faim, affamer; reduire par la faim. **what's for dinner? We are starving here!** qu'y-a-t-il à dîner? Nous mourons de faim ici!

state *n.* état *m.*, condition *f.* **the ~ of his health is good**, l'état de sa santé est satisfaisant. **in a ~ to**, en état de. **~ of mind**, état *m.* d'esprit. **Secretary of ~**, secrétaire d'État. **The United States of America**, les États-Unis d'Amérique. **affairs of ~**, affaires d'État. *v.t.* établir, poser (question), régler, fixer; exposer, énoncer, déclarer; expliquer. **to ~ the particulars**, faire connaître les détails.

stated *adj.* établi; réglé, fixe.

stately *adj.* majestueux, imposant, plein de dignité, noble, fastueux, orgueilleux. **a ~ edifice**, un superbe édifice. **~ manners**, des manières nobles, pleines de dignité. *adv.* majestueusement; avec dignité.

statement *n.* exposition *f.*; exposé *m.*, rapport *m.*, compte *m.*, rendu *m.*; récit *m.*; relevé *m.* *Comm.* situation *f.*, relevé *m.* (de compte).

statesman *n.* homme d'État.

static *adj.* statique.

station *n.* gare *f.*, station *f.*; place *f.*, position *f.*, condition *f.* **~ in life**, position sociale. *v.t.* mettre; *Milit.* poster; mettre dans un poste.

stationary *adj.* stationaire; fixe.

stationery *n.* papeterie *f.* **~** *adj.* de papetier.

statistical *adj.* statistique.

statistician *n.* statisticien *f.*

statistics *n.* *inv.* statistique *f.*

statuary *n.* statuaire *f.*

statue *n.* statue *f.*

stature *n.* stature *f.*; taille *f.*

statute *n.* statut *m.*, loi *f.*

statutory *adj.* statutaire; établi, fixé par la loi.

staunch *adj.* fort, solide; sûr, dévoué.

stay *v.i.* rester; séjourner; s'arrêter. **~ here**, restez ici. **to ~ a moment**, attendre un moment. **to ~ away**, rester éloigné; s'éloigner, s'absenter. **to ~ in**, rester chez soi. **to ~ out**, rester dehors, ne pas rentrer. *v.t.* arrêter, retenir, empêcher. *n.* séjour *m.*, délai *m.*, retard *m.*; obstacle *m.*, difficulté *f.*; étai *m.*, appui *m.* **to make a short ~**, faire un court séjour. **~sail**, *Naut.* voile *f.* d'étai.

steadfast adj. ferme; solide, stable, fixe, inébranlable; résolu, intrépide.

steadily adv. fermement; d'une manière rangée, posée; régulièrement.

steadiness n. fermeté f.; force f.; caractère ferme; assurance f.; persévérance f.; régularité f.

steady adj. ferme; solide, stable; constant; régulier, rangé, posé; Naut. fait. **to keep ~,** tenir ferme, maintenir. **to be ~,** être rangé, régulier. interj. Naut. comme ça! droit! v.t. raffermir, rendre ferme; assurer.

steak n. steak m., bifteck m.

steal v.t. dérober, voler, soustraire; séduire. **to ~ away,** (se) dérober; voler; détourner. v.i. glisser furtivement, à la dérobée. **to ~ along,** se glisser sans bruit, avancer à pas de loup; glisser le long de. n. bonne occasion f., bon prix m.

stealing n. vol m.

stealth n. vol m.; dérobée f.; cachette f. **by ~,** à la dérobée, en cachette, furtivement.

stealthy adj. furtif; fait à la dérobée.

steam n. vapeur f.; fumée f. **to work up ~,** chauffer. v.i. émettre de la vapeur; fumer; se dissiper, marcher à la vapeur. **to ~ away,** s'évaporer; s'éloigner à toute vapeur. v.t. faire évaporer; passer à la vapeur; cuire à la vapeur. **~boat,** bateau m. à vapeur. **~ boiler,** chaudière f. à vapeur. **~ engine,** machine f. à vapeur.
~ gauge, manomètre m.; éprouvette f. **to let off ~,** vider son sac.

steamer n. bateau m. à vapeur, cocotte f. minute.

steel n. acier m.; fer m. **cast ~,** acier fondu.
~works, aciérie f. adj. d'acier, en acier; de fer. v.t. acérer, garnir, armer d'acier; aiguiser; fortifier; endurcir, cuirasser. **to ~ the heart,** endurcir le coeur.

steep adj. escarpé, raide, à pic. **a ~ ascent,** une montée raide. **a ~ descent,** une pente rapide, escarpée. **a ~ mountain,** une montagne à pic. v.t. tremper dans un liquide; imbiber; macérer; (faire) infuser.

steeple n. clocher m.

steer n. bouvillon m. **~ v.t.** diriger, conduire, guider; Naut. gouverner. v.i. (se) gouverner, (se) diriger.

steering n. action de gouverner. **~ wheel,** volant m.; roue f. de gouvernail.

stem n. tige f.; tronc m.; queue f.; Fig. souche f.; Mus. queue f. **from ~ to stern,** de l'avant à l'arrière. v.t. arrêter.

stench n. puanteur f., mauvaise odeur f.

stenographer n. sténographe m.

stenography n. sténographie f.

step v.i. faire un pas; marcher (pas à pas); passer. **to ~ aside,** marcher, se tenir à l'écart; se retirer à l'écart. **to ~ back,** faire un pas en arrière, revenir sur ses pas, rebrousser chemin; retourner. **to ~ down,** descendre. **to ~ forward,** s'avancer; se mettre en avant. **to ~ in,** entrer; monter en voiture, dans une voiture. **to ~ out,** faire un pas dehors; sortir. **to ~ over,** passer, traverser; franchir, enjamber. **to ~ up,** monter d'un pas, aller, venir, s'avancer vers. v.t. poser, mettre (le pied); Naut. dresser (mast). n. pas m.; marche f. (stairs), degré m., gradin m.; échelon m. (ladder). **foot~,** trace f. **~ by ~,** pas à pas. **to take a ~,** faire un pas. **to retrace one's ~,** revenir sur ses pas, rebrousser chemin. **to take ~s,** faire des démarches. adj. beau, bel-le. **~brother,** beau-frère m. **~child,** beau-fils m.; belle-fille f. **~father,** beau-père m.
~mother, belle-mère f.

steppe n. steppe m.

stereo abbrev. **stereophonic** n., adj. stéréo m.

stereotype n. cliché m. adj. stéréotype; cliché. v.t. stéréotyper.

sterile adj. stérile.

sterility n. stérilité f.

sterilize v.t. stériliser.

sterling adj. sterling; pur, de bon aloi, vrai, véritable. **a pound ~,** une livre sterling. n. monnaie f. sterling; sterling m.

stern adj. sévère, austère; rigide; dur; rébarbatif. n. arrière m., poupe f.; derrière m.

sternly adv. sévèrement, durement.

sternness n. sévérité f., rudesse f.

sternum n. sternum m.

steroid n. steroïde m.

stethoscope n. stéthoscope m.

stew n. étuve f.; étuvée f., civet m., ragoût m.; compote f. (fruit). Fig. embarras m., confusion f. **to make a ~,** faire un ragoût, une compote. **to be in a ~,** être dans l'embarras. v.t. étuver; faire une compote de.

steward n. intendant m., régisseur m.; steward m.

stewardess n. stewardess f.; hôtesse f. de l'air.

stewardship n. intendance f.; fonction f. de régisseur; gestion f., administration f.

stick n. bâton m.; canne f.; baguette f.; brin m.
~ of licorice, bâton de réglisse. v.t. percer; piquer, trouer; larder; coller; fixer, afficher. **to ~ a nail in a wall,** enfoncer un clou dans un mur. **to ~ a pin,** piquer, enfoncer une épingle. **to ~ together,** coller ensemble, rester ensemble. **to ~ down,** attacher, clouer; coller. **to ~ on,** piquer; attacher; appliquer; coller. **to ~ out,** faire ressortir. **to ~ it out,** endurer, persister. **to ~ up,** afficher; se dresser; se redresser. **to ~ up for someone,** soutenir quelqu'un. v.i. s'attacher, (se) fixer; adhérer; (se) coller; s'arrêter; être embarrassé, se gêner; hésiter. **to ~ fast,** tenir ferme. **to ~ close,** s'attacher, adhérer fortement. **to ~ close to,** ne pas lâcher, ne pas quitter. **to ~ by,** s'attacher à; rester à; soutenir, rester fidèle à. **to ~ on,** s'attacher, adhérer, se coller. **to ~ to,** coller sur; s'attacher à, tenir à; demeurer à; se fixer à; persévérer dans; rester fidèle à; soutenir. **glue ~s to the fingers,** la colle s'attache aux doigts. **to what you've said,** soutenez ce que vous avez dit. **to ~ up,** se dresser, se redresser. Infml. **to be stuck up,** être suffisant, prétentieux. **to be stuck,** être coincé.

sticker *n.* auto-collant *m.*, étiquette *f.*, vignette *f.* adhésive.

stickiness *n.* viscosité *f.*; nature *f.* adhésive.

sticky *adj.* collant, visqueux, gluant.

stiff *adj.* raide, dur; inflexible; guindé; engourdi. **a limb ~ with cold**, un membre engourdi par le froid. **to grow ~**, raidir, s'engourdir. **~ neck**, torticolis *m.*

stiffen *v.t.* rendre ferme; durcir. *v.i.* (se) raidir; s'épaissir; s'engourdir; s'endurcir.

stiffener *n.* contrefort *m.*; col *m.*

stiffness *n.* raideur *f.*; engourdissement *m.*, torpeur *f.*; dureté *f.*

stifle *v.t.* étouffer, suffoquer. **to ~ with smoke**, étouffer par la fumée. **to ~ a noise**, étouffer un bruit.

stigma *n.* houte *f.pl.* **stigmata**, stigmate *m.*; flétrissure.

stigmatize *v.t.* stigmatiser.

still *v.t.* apaiser, calmer, tranquilliser, adoucir; distiller. *adj.* silencieux, calme, tranquille, immobile. **the air is ~**, l'air est calme. **~ water**, eau dormante. **to be ~**, rester tranquille. **~ life**, nature morte. **~born**, mort-né. *n.* alambic *m.*, silence *m.*; alambic *m.* ~ *adv.* encore, jusqu'à présent; toujours; toutefois. **~ more**, encore plus, encore davantage.

stillness *n.* calme *m.*, tranquillité *f.*, repos *m.*, silence *m.*

stilt *n.* échasse *f.*; pilotis *m.*, pieu *m.* (bridge). **~ bird**, échassier *m.*

stilted *adj.* formel, guindé.

stimulant *adj.*, *n.* stimulant *m.*

stimulate *v.t.* stimuler.

stimulation *n.* stimulation *f.*; excitation *f.*, incitation *f.*

stimulus *n.* stimulant *m.*, aiguillon *m.*; stimulus *m.*

sting *v.t.* piquer, percer. *n.* aiguillon *m.*, dard *m.*; piqûre *f.*; *Fig.* remords *m.*; morsure *f.*

stinginess *n.* avarice *f.*, ladrerie *f.*; mesquinerie *f.*

stingy *adj.* avare, ladre, mesquin.

stink *v.i.* puer; sentir mauvais. *n.* puanteur *f.*, mauvaise odeur *f.*

stinking *adj.* puant, empesté.

stint *v.t.* restreindre, borner, limiter; retrancher, rogner. *n.* borne *f.*, limite *f.*, restriction *f.*; ration *f.*, besogne *f.*, boulot *m.*

stipend *n.* salaire *m.*, traitement *m.* ~ *v.t.* salarier, stipendier.

stipulate *v.i.* stipuler (que), convenir (de), s'engager (à).

stipulation *n.* stipulation *f.*

stir *v.t.* émouvoir; exciter, animer. **to ~ around**, remuer, tourner en remuant. **to ~ up**, remuer, mettre en mouvement, exciter; faire du bruit/du désordre. **~ him up**, animez-le, encouragez-le. *v.i.* (se) remuer; bouger, s'agiter. **to be ~ing**, se remuer, se donner du mouvement. *n.* remuement *m.*, mouvement *m.*, remue-ménage *m.*;

stirring *adj.* actif, remuant.

stirrup *n.* étrier *m.* **~ cup**, coup *m.* de l'étrier.

stitch *v.t.* coudre, piquer, brocher. **to ~ up**, faire un point à. *n.* point *m.* de couture, point *m.*; maille *f.*; point *m.* de côte; point *m.* de suture.

stock *n.* soucha *f.*, race *f.*, famille *f.*; bois *m.* (gun), bétail *m.*; fonds *m.* (commerce), provision *f.*; capital *m.*, fonds *m.pl.*; *Comm.* stock *m.* **to take ~**, faire son inventaire. **~ in hand**, stock, marchandises en magasin. **~ in trade**, marchandises disponibles. **live~**, bétail *m.*, bestiaux *m.pl.* **government ~**, fonds *m.pl.* publics, fonds *m.pl.* **railroad ~**, action de chemin de fer. **a laughing~**, une risée, objet de moquerie. **~broker**, agent *m.* de change. **~ exchange**, Bourse *f.*; compagnie *f.* des agents de change. **~holder**, actionnaire *m.* **~ market**, Bourse *f.* ~ *v.t.* fournir, approvisionner, monter; peupler; empoissonner, pourvoir de bétail.

stockade *n.* palissade *f.* ~ *v.t.* palissader.

stocking *n.* bas *m.*, collant *m.*

stocky *adj.* trapu.

stoic *n.* stoïcien, stoïque *n.f.*, *adj.* stoïque.

stoicism *n.* stoïcisme *m.*

stoke *v.t.* attiser (le feu).

stolid *adj.* lourd, impassible.

stomach *n.* estomac *m.*; appétit *m.*; goût *m.*; coeur *m.*, courage *m.* **to turn the ~**, soulever le coeur. **~ache**, mal *m.* d'estomac. *v.t.* digérer, endurer.

stomp *v.i.* marcher d'un pas lourd et bruyant.

stone *n.* pierre *f.*; noyau *m.* (fruit). *Med.* calcul *m.* **building ~**, pierre à bâtir. **sand~**, grès *m.* **mill~**, meule *f.* (de moulin). **lode~**, aimant *m.*, pierre d'aimant. **pumice ~**, pierre ponce. **flint~**, pierre à fusil. **precious ~**, pierre précieuse. **philosopher's ~**, pierre philosophale. **to hew a ~**, tailler une pierre. **to leave no ~ unturned**, n'épargner aucun effort, mettre tout en oeuvre, remuer ciel et terre. *adj.* de pierre, en pierre; de grès, en grès. **~ cold**, froid, du marbre. **~cutter**, tailleur *m.* de pierres. **~ dead**, raide mort. **~-hearted**, au coeur de pierre. **~ quarry**, carrière *f.* de pierre. **~ware**, poterie *f.* de grès. **~work**, maçonnerie *f.*, ouvrage *m.* de maçonnerie. *v.t.* lapider; ôter le noyant, les pépins de; maçonner.

stony *adj.* de pierre, pierreux; pétrifiant; *Fig.* dur, insensible.

stooge *n.* *Théât.* comparse *m.f.*

stool *n.* tabouret *m.*, escabeau *m.*, *Med.* selle *f.*

stoop *v.i.* se baisser, (se) pencher, se tenir courbé; courber la tête; s'abaisser; fondre (to one's prey). **to ~ down**, se baisser. **to ~ in walking**, marcher courbé. *v.i.* incliner; soumettre. *n.* inclination *f.*; action de se baisser; *Fig.* abaissement *m.* **to have a ~**, se tenir courbé.

stop *v.t.* arrêter; fermer; faire cesser, empecher;

ponctuer. **to ~ payment,** suspendre ses paye-ments. **to ~ a leak,** boucher une voie d'eau. *v.i.* s'arrêter, rester, finir; stopper. **to ~ short,** s'arrê-ter court. **my watch has stopped,** ma montre s'est arrêtée. *n.* halte *f.,* pause *f.;* repos *m.;* arrêt *m.;* point *m.* d'arrêt; obstacle *m.,* empêchement *m.;* ponctuation *f.;* *Mus.* trou *m.* (de flûte); registre *m.* (d'orgue). **to make a ~,** s'arrêter; faire une pause/un arrêt. **to put a ~ to,** arrêter; mettre un terme à, faire cesser. **~watch,** montre *f.* à arrêt.

stoppage *n.* action de boucher, arrêter; temps *m.* d'arrêt, repos *m.;* halte *f.;* interruption *f.;* chô-mage *m.;* obstruction *f.,* embarras *m.* (dans une rue); retenue *f.* (de payements).

stopper *n.* bouchon *m.* (carafe, etc.); tampon *v.t.* boucher.

storage *n.* emmagasinage *m.;* magasinage *m.,* droit *m.* d'emmagasinage; entreposage *m.*

store *n.* provision *f.;* réserve *f.;* masse *f.,* fonds *m.;* dépôt *m.;* magasin *m.;* *Milit.* vivres *m.pl.;* munitions *f.pl.,* matériel *m.* **to lie in ~,** être en réserve. **to set great ~ by,** attacher du prix à. **~house,** magasin *m.;* entrepôt *m.* **~keeper,** garde-magasin *m.,* magasinier *m.;* entreposeur *m.* **~room,** magasin *m.;* réserve *f.* **~ ~** *v.t.* pour-voir, fournir, munir; approvisionner; amasser, accumuler; mettre en réserve; emmagasiner. **to ~ up,** amasser.

storied *adj.* historié; rapporté par l'histoire; à étages.

stork *n.* cigogne *f.*

storm *n.* orage *m.;* tempête *f.;* tourmente *f.;* *Milit.* assaut *m.* **to raise a ~,** soulever une tempête, soulever une tollée générale. *v.t.* donner l'assaut à. *v.i.* faire de l'orage, faire une tempête; tempê-ter, s'emporter; fulminer.

stormy *adj.* orageux; *Fig.* emporté, violent.

story *n.* histoire *f.;* nouvelle *f.;* conte *m.;* menson-ge *m.* **to tell a ~,** raconter une histoire; *Fig.* mentir. **~teller,** conteur *m.* d'histoires; menteur *m.* **~telling,** débit *m.* d'histoires; mensonges *m.pl.* **~book,** livre *m.* de contes; étage *m.* **a ten-~ building,** un immeuble *m.* de dix étages. *v.t.* raconter, rapporter.

stout *adj.* fort; vigoureux; gros, corpulent; vaillant; courageux, résolu. **~-hearted,** coura-geux, au coeur intrépide. *n.* bière *f.* brune.

stove *n.* cuisinière *f.,* réchaud *m.;* four *m.;* poêle *f.*

stow *v.t.* serrer; mettre; fourrer; entasser; cacher, renfermer; *Naut.* arrimer. *n.* **~away,** passager *m.* clandestin.

stowage *n.* mise *f.* en place; *Naut.* arrimage *m.;* chargement *m.;* droit *m.* de magasinage.

straddle *v.i.* enfourcher; chevaucher; enjamber; écarter les jambes; marcher les jambes écartées. *v.t.* enfourcher, se mettre à califourchon (sur). *n.* écartement *m.,* enjambement *m.,* chevauche-ment *m.*

straggle *v.t.* pousser au hasard; être dispersé; l'épars/disséminé.

straggling *adj.* écarté, séparé; isolé; éparpillé; égaré; perdu; qui rôde; de rôdeurs.

straight *adj.* droit, vertical; *Fig.* juste, équitable; direct, tout droit. **to make ~,** rendre droit; arranger. *adv.* droit, tout droit, directement; sur-le-champ, tout de suite, immédiatement; hétéro-sexuel *m.*

straighten *v.t.* rendre droit, dresser; redresser; raidir, bander; rétrécir, resserrer; gêner, embar-rasser. **she'll ~ him up,** elle va lui apprendre les bonnes manières.

straightforward *adj.* droit, direct; franc, juste.

straightforwardly *adv.* en ligne droite; avec franchise.

strain *v.t.* tendre; tendre trop; se fouler; filtrer, passer, forcer, contraindre; fatiguer; exagérer. **to ~ one's neck,** tendre, allonger le cou. **to ~ oneself,** se forcer; s'efforcer; se donner un effort. **to ~ one's eyes,** se fatiguer la vue. *v.i.* s'efforcer; (se) forcer; (se) filtrer. *n.* tension *f.;* extension *f.* (muscles, nerves); effort; entorse *f.;* foulure *f.;* élan *m.;* style *m.,* ton *m.;* chant *m.;* accords *m.pl.;* race *f.,* lignée *f.* **a great ~ on the nerves,** une grande tension de nerfs.

strainer *n.* filtre *m.,* passoire *f.*

strait *adj.* gorge *f.,* au *pl.* détroit *m.* **to be in dire ~s,** être gêné; avoir un grand besoin d'argent.

straitened *adj.* **in ~ circumstances,** gêné dans ses affaires, gêné, dans la gêne.

straitjacket *n.* camisole *f.* de force.

strand *n.* rivage *m.,* plage *f.,* grève *f.;* rive *f.* (lake, river); brin *m.;* cordon *m.* (rope, thread). *v.t.* échouer, jeter à la côte; rompre un toron (d'une corde). *v.i.* échouer.

strange *adj.* étrange; surprenant; bizarre. **it is ~ that,** il est étrange que. **~ to say!** chose étrange!

strangely *adv.* étrangement.

strangeness *n.* étrangeté *f.*

stranger *n.* étranger *m.;* étrangère *f.*

strangle *v.t.* étrangler.

strangler *n.* étrangleur *m.*

strangulated *adj.* étranglé.

strangulation *n.* étranglement *m.*

strap *n.* lanière *f.,* courroie *f.* **~** *v.t.* donner des coups de courroie à; donner des étrivières à; lier, attacher avec des courroies.

stratagem *n.* stratagème *m.*

strategic *adj.* stratégique.

strategy *n.* stratégie *f.*

stratification *n.* stratification *f.*

stratify *v.t.* stratifier.

stratum *n.,* *pl.* **strata,** strate *f.,* couche *f.,* assise *f.*

straw *n.* paille *f.,* litière *f.* **~ hat,** chapeau de paille. **~-colored,** paille, de couleur paille. **~ mat,** paillasson *m.* **~ poll,** sondage *m.* d'opinion.

strawberry *n.* fraise *f.* **~ bed,** fraisière *f.*

stray *v.i.* errer, vaguer, *Infml.* flâner, s'écarter, s'éloigner; s'égarer, se perdre. *adj.* égaré, perdu, fortuit. *n.* animal *m.* égaré, perdu.

streak *n.* raie *f.,* bande *f.,* bigarrure *f.,* panachure *f.*; trainée *f.* (light). *v.t.* rayer, barioler, bigarrer; sillonner.

stream *n.* courant *m.*; cours *m.* d'eau, ruisseau *m.*; jet *m.*; *Fig.* flots *m.pl.* **down the ~,** d'aval, en aval. **with the ~,** avec le courant. **up the ~,** d'amont, en amont. **against the ~,** contre le courant. *v.i.* couler, ruisseler, jaillir; flotter. **to ~ with blood,** ruisseler de sang.

streamer *n.* bannière *f.*, drapeau *m.*; *Naut.* flamme *f.*, banderole *f.*

street *n.* rue *f.* **~-walker,** prostituée *f.*

strength *n.* force *f.*; vigueur *f.*; pouvoir; énergie *f.* **beyond one's ~,** audessus de ses forces. **~ of character,** force de caractère.

strengthen *v.t.* fortifier; renforcer; raffermir. *v.i.* (se) fortifier; (se) renforcer; (se) raffermir.

strenuous *adj.* exténuant, ardent; zélé, énergique; intrépide.

strenuously *adv.* ardemment, avec ardeur; énergiquement, intrépidement.

stress *n.* stress; force *f.*, poids *m.*, importance *f.*; emphase *f.*, accent *m.*, tonique; effort *m.*, tension *f.* **to lay great ~ upon,** insister, appuyer fortement sur, stresser, appuyer (sur). **he is extremely ~ed out,** il est très stressé.

stressful *adj.* plein de stress.

stressot *n.* agent *m.* de stress.

stretch *v.t.* tendre; raidir; forcer. **to ~ the wings,** déployer, étendre les ailes. **to ~ forth,** étendre, déployer. **to ~ out,** étendre, allonger, déployer; prolonger. **to ~ oneself out,** s'étendre, s'étirer. *v.i.* s'étendre; s'étirer; s'élargir, s'efforcer, tâcher; exagérer. **to ~ as far as,** pousser, aller jusqu'à. **to ~ over,** s'étendre sur. *n.* déploiement *m.* extension *f.*; effort *m.*, tension *f.*, force *f.*, portée *f.*, étendue *f.* **a ~ of imagination,** un effort de l'imagination. **at a ~,** d'un coup, d'un trait. **~-mark,** vergéture *f.*

strew *v.t.* répandre, semer, joncher. **to ~ with flowers,** joncher de fleurs.

stricken *adj.* frappé, atteint, blessé; affligé; avancé (en âge).

strict *adj.* strict, sévère, exact, étroit, rigoureux, serré, tendu. **~ laws,** des lois sévères.

strictly *adv.* étroitement, strictement.

strictness *n.* étroitesse *f.*; précision *f.*; exactitude *f.* stricte; rigueur *f.*; sévérité *f.*

stride *n.* grand pas *m.*; enjambée *f.* **~** *v.i.* marcher à grands pas; être à, se tenir à califourchon. **to ~ over,** enjamber.

strident *adj.* strident, perçant.

strife *n.* lutte *f.*; opposition *f.*, contraste *m.*, antipathie *f.*

strike *v.t.* frapper, battre; taper, frapper de; impressionner; affecter; affliger, sonner (hour); amener (pavilion); lever (camp); conclure (bargain). **without striking a blow,** sans frapper un coup, sans coup férir. **to ~ the ear,** frapper l'oreille. **to ~ the fancy,** frapper l'imagination. **to ~ dumb,** rendre muet, frapper de mutisme. **to ~ to the ground,** assommer, jeter par terre.

to ~ a match, allumer une allumette. **to ~ down,** abattre, renverser. *v.i.* faire grève, se mettre en grève. **to ~ out across,** prendre à travers (fields). **to ~,** at frapper; s'attaquer à. **to ~ out,** s'éloigner; se lancer; se jeter, se précipiter; se mettre en route; faire un retrait sur trois prises (baseball). *n.* **to be on ~,** être en grève.

striker *n.* gréviste *m.f* celui ou ce qui frappe.

striking *adj.* frappant; remarquable; à sonnerie.

strikingly *adv.* d'une manière frappante; remarquablement.

string *n.* ficelle *f.*, cordon *m.*, corde *f.*, fil *m.*; *Bot.* fiber *f.* **to have two ~s to one's bow,** *Fig.* avoir deux cordes à son arc. **a ~ of beads,** un fil de perles; un chapelet. **~ of onions,** chapelet, glane *f.* d'oignons. *v.t.* mettre de la ficelle à; munir, garnir de cordes, enfiler; accorder (stringed instrument); enlever les fibres de; ôter les filandres de.

stringed *adj.* à cordes; de cordes.

stringent *adj.* qui serre; strict, rigoureux.

stringy *adj.* fibreux, filamenteux; filandreux.

strip *v.t.* dépouiller; déshabiller, ôter enlever; piller, dévaliser, écorcer (tree). **to ~ naked,** déshabiller entièrement; mettre à nu. **to ~ from,** dépouiller de. **to ~ off,** arracher. **to ~ oneself,** se dépouiller; se déshabiller, retirer ses vêtements. *v.i.* (se) déshabiller; enlever ses vêtements. *n.* lambeau *m.*; bande *f.*

stripe *n.* raie *f.*; rayure *f.*, zébrure *f.*; barre *f.*; bande *f.*; galon *m.* (officer, etc.). *v.t.* rayer.

striped *adj.* à raies, rayé.

strive *v.i.* s'efforcer, tâcher, faire des efforts, rivaliser. **to ~ against,** lutter contre, rivaliser.

stroke *n.* coup *m.*, attaque *f.*; affliction, calamité *f.*; trait *m.* (pen). *Fig.* touche *f.*; trait *m.*, mouvement *m.*, effort *m.*; brassée *f.* (swimming). **finishing ~,** coup de grace. *v.t.* passer la main sur; flatter, caresser.

stroll *v.i.* errer, vaguer, flâner. **to ~ around, to ~ up and down,** errer çà et là. *n.* promenade *f.*, flânerie *f.* **to take a ~,** faire une promenade, faire un tour.

stroller *nn.* flâneur *m.*; poussette *f.* (for children).

strong *adj.* fort; vigoureux, robuste; ardent, véhément, énergique. **~ liquors,** des liqueurs fortes. **~-box,** coffre-fort *m.* **~-minded,** résolu; décidé.

strongly *adv.* fortement, avec force; énergiquement.

strop *n.* cuir *m.* à repasser (razor). *v.t.* repasser sur le cuir.

strophe *n.* strophe *f.*

structural *adj.* de structure.

structure *n.* structure *f.*; construction *f.*; édifice *m.*

struggle *v.i.* lutter; disputer; faire de grands efforts; se débattre, s'agiter. *n.* effort *m.*, lutte *f.*; combat *m.*, dispute *f.*

strum *v.i.* taper, tapoter.

strut *v.i.* se pavaner; carrer. *n.* démarche *f.* fière; pose *f.*; *Carp.* contrefiche *f.*

strychnine *n.* strychnine *f.*

stub *n.* souche *f.;* chicot *m., Fig.* bûche *f.* ~ *v.t.* bouter (toe).

stubble *n.* chaume *m.,* paille *f.*

stubborn *adj.* entêté, têtu; soutenu; raide; dur, inflexible. **a** ~ **child,** un enfant entêté.

stubbornness *n.* entêtement *m.,* obstination *f.,* raideur *f.*

stud *n.* étalon *m.* (horse); *Arch.* montant *m.,* poteau *m.;* clou *m.* à grosse tête; clou *m.* d'ornement; bouton *m.* de chemise; homme *m.* à femmes. *v.t.* clouter; garnir de clous; parsemer. **studded with gems,** orné de pierreries.

student *n.* étudiant *m.*

studied *adj.* étudié; affecté, recherché.

studio *n.* atelier *m.,* studio *m.*

studious *adj.* studieux; qui s'applique, qui travaille à; appliqué; empressé; soigneux, attentif; étudié; fait avec soin.

study *n.* étude *f.;* cabinet *m.* de travail; salle *f.* (d'étude). *v.i.* étudier; travailler; s'appliquer à l'étude. *v.t.* considérer attentivement, examiner avec soin; s'étudier à, s'appliquer à.

stuff *n.* matière *f.;* chose, substance; meubles *m.pl.,* mobilier *m.;* materiaux *m.pl.;* effets *m.pl.* **what's all this** ~? qu'est-ce que c'est que tout ça? **silly** ~, des sottises, des sornettes. *v.t.* remplir, bourrer; *Culin.* farcir; rembourrer; empailler, entasser; serrer; grossir; enfler; boucher. **to** ~ **a chair,** rembourrer une chaise. **to** ~ **in,** bourrer; se bourrer de. **to** ~ **up a hole,** boucher un trou.

stuffing *n.* bourre *f., Culin.* farce *f.,* hachis *m.*

stuffy *adj.* lourd (air), sans air, mal aéré.

stultify *v.i.* abrutir, hébéter.

stumble *v.i.* faire un faux pas, trébucher; faillir; ~ **on, upon,** tomber sur.

stump *n.* souche *f.* (tree); trognon *m.* (cabbage); tronçon *m.,* moignon *m. v.t.* laisser perplexe; faire un tour électorale.

stun *v.t.* étourdir; abasourdir.

stunning *adj.* étourdissant; stupéfiant, épatant.

stunt *v.t.* empêcher de grandir, arrêter dans sa croissance; *n.* acrobatie *f.,* haute voltige *f.* ~**man,** ~**woman,** cascadeur *m.,* cascadeuse *f.*

stupefy *v.t.* hébéter; stupéfier.

stupendous *adj.* étonnant, stupéfiant, prodigieux.

stupid *adj.* stupide.

stupidity *n.* stupidité *f.,* bêtise *f.,* sottise *f.*

stupidly *adv.* stupidement, bêtement.

stupor *n.* stupeur *f.*

sturdiness *n.* résolution *f.,* fermeté *f.;* hardiesse *f.;* vigueur *f.*

sturdy *adj.* hardi, ferme, résolu; vigoureux, fort.

sturgeon *n.* esturgeon *m.*

stutter *v.i.* bégayer; balbutier.

stutterer *n.* bègue *m.*

stuttering *n.* bégayement *m.*

sty *n.* étable *f.* à cochons, taudis *m.,* bouge *m.;* *Med.* orgelet *m.,* compère-loriot *m.*

style *n.* style *m.;* genre *m.,* manière *f.;* goût *m.* **a flowing** ~, un style coulant. **in good** ~, d'un bon style, de bon genre. **to live in** ~, avoir un train de maison. *v.t.* **to** ~ **oneself,** se faire appeler. **self-**~**d,** soi-disant.

stylish *adj.* élégant, distingué; à la mode.

styrofoam *n.* polystyrene *m.*

suave *adj.* suave, doucereux.

subcommittee *n.* souscomité *m.*

subconscious *adj., n.* subconscient *m.*

subcontractor *n.* sous-traitant *m.*

subculture *n.* subculture *f.*

subcutaneous *adj.* sous-cutané.

subdivide *v.t.* subdiviser. *v.i.* (se) subdiviser.

subdivision *n.* subdivision *f.*

subdue *v.t.* subjuguer, soumettre, assujettir, asservir, dompter, maîtriser, arrêter.

subdued *adj.* subjugué, soumis, dompté; adouci.

subhuman *adj.* indigne de l'homme.

subject *adj.* inférieur, soumis, assujetti; sujet. *n.* sujet *m.* ~ **matter,** sujet *m.,* matière *f.* ~ *v.t.* mettre, placer sous; soumettre, asservir; subjuguer.

subjection *n.* subjugation *f.,* soumission *f.,* assujettissement *m.*

subjective *adj.* subjectif.

subjectively *adv.* subjectivement.

subjectiveness, subjectivity *n.* subjectivité *f.*

subjugate *v.t.* subjuguer; soumettre; asservir.

subjugation *n.* subjugation *f.*

subjunctive *adj., n.* subjonctif *m.*

sublease *n.* sous-bail *m.;* sous-location *f.* ~ *v.t.* sous-louer.

sublet *v.t.* sous-louer. *n.* sous-location *f.*

sublimate *v.t.* sublimer; élever au sublime; élever; exalter. *adj., n.* sublimé *m.*

sublimation *n.* sublimation *f.;* élévation *f.;* raffinement *m.,* perfection *f.;* quintessence *f.*

sublime *adj.* sublime, élevé, haut; majestueux, imposant. *n.* sublime *m.* ~ *v.t.* élever, exalter. *v.i.* (se) sublimer; être sublime.

submarine *adj., n.* sous-marin *m.*

submerge *v.i.* plonger, (se) submerger.

submersion *n.* submersion *f.*

submission *n.* soumission *f.,* déférence *f.,* respect *m.*

submissive *adj.* soumis; résigné; de soumission, humble.

submissively *adv.* avec soumission, humblement.

submissiveness *n.* soumission *f.,* humilité *f.;* repentir *m.*

submit *v.t.* abaisser. **to** ~ **oneself,** se soumettre. *v.i.* (se) soumettre, se résigner, être soumis.

subnormal *n.* sousnormale *f.*

subordinate *adj.* subordonné; inférieur. *n.* subordonné *m.,* inférieur *m.* ~ *v.t.* subordonner *m.*

subordination *n.* subordination *f.,* soumission *f.*

suborn *v.t.* suborner.

subornation *n.* subornation *f.;* séduction *f.,* corruption *f.*

subpoena *n.* citation *f.,* assignation *f.* sous peine d'amende. *v.t.* citer, assigner.

subscribe *v.i.* s'abonner; être abonné (newspaper, etc.).

subscriber *n.* abonné *m.* (newspaper, etc.).

subscription *n.* abonnement *m.* (newspaper, etc.); adhésion *f.*

subsection *n.* subdivision *f.*

subsequent *adj.* subséquent, suivant.

subsequently *adv.* postérieurement; par la suite.

subservient *adj.* subordonné; qui sert.

subside *v.i.* tomber au fond; baisser, s'abaisser, se calmer; tasser.

subsidence *n.* dépôt *m.;* affaissement *m. Fig.* apaisement *m.*

subsidiary *adj.* subsidiaire, auxiliaire. *n.* aide *m.,* auxiliaire *m.* et *f.*

subsidize *v.t.* subventionner.

subsidy *n.* subvention *f.*

subsist *v.i.* être, exister; demeurer, rester; (of things) subsister.

subsistence *n.* existence *f.;* substance *f.;* subsistance *f.*

subsoil *n.* sous-sol *m.;* tréfonds *m.*

substance *n.* substance *f.;* bien *m.,* avoir *m.* **the ~ of a book,** la substance d'un livre. **in ~,** en substance, au fond.

substantial *adj.* substantiel; essentiel; réel, vrai, solide; matériel, corporel; aisé, qui a du bien. **~ happiness,** bonheur réel, véritable. **~ doors,** de solides portes. **~ food,** nourriture substantielle.

substantially *adv.* substantiellement; réellement; solidement.

substantiate *v.t.* faire exister; prouver, établir.

substantive *adj.* indépendant; substantif. *n. Gram.* substantif; nom *m.*

substitute *v.t.* substituer. **to ~ for,** substituer à. *n.* substitut *m.,* remplaçant *m.;* représentant *m.*

substitution *n.* substitution *f.*

substructure *n.* infrastructure *f.*

subterfuge *n.* subterfuge *m.,* échappatoire *f.,* faux-fuyant *m.,* défaite *f.*

subterranean *adj.* souterrain.

subtitle *n.* sous-titre *m.* **~** *v.t.* sous-titrer.

subtle *adj.* subtil; rusé, artificieux; fin, ingénieux; trop raffiné.

subtlety *n.* subtilité *f.;* ruse *f.,* adresse *f.;* finesse *f.;* distinction subtile.

subtly *adv.* subtilement, avec finesse.

subtract *v.t.* soustraire; ôter, retrancher.

suburb *n.* banlieue *f.*

suburban *adj.* suburbain, de banlieue.

suburbanite *n. Infml.* banlieusard *m.*

subvention *n.* subvention *f.*

subversion *n.* subversion *f.*

subversive *adj.* subversif.

subvert *v.t.* subvertir; corrompre, pervertir.

subway *n.* métro *m.*

succeed *v.i., v.t.* succéder, remplacer; réussir; (se) succéder. **you ~ in everything you do,** vous réussissez à tout ce que vous entreprenez. **he ~ed his father,** il succéda à son père.

succeeding *adj.* suivant; à venir, futur, successif.

success *n.* succès *m.,* réussite *f.* **to have ~,** réussir, avoir du succès. **I wish you ~,** je vous souhaite de réussir.

successful *adj.* heureux, qui a du succès, qui réussit.

successfully *adv.* heureusement; avec succès.

succession *n.* succession *f.;* suite *f.;* droit *m.* de succession; avènement *m.* (to throne), postérité *f.* **in ~,** successivement.

successive *adj.* successif, héréditaire.

successor *n.* successeur *m.*

succinct *adj.* succinct, concis.

succinctly *adv.* succinctement.

succor *v.t.* secourir; aider, assister. *n.* secours *m.;* aide, assistance.

succulent *adj.* succulent.

succumb *v.i.* succomber; céder; se soumettre.

such *adj. et pron.* tel; pareil, semblable; certain, ceux, celles. **~ men,** de tels hommes. **he made ~ a noise that,** il a fait un tel bruit que. **~ and ~,** un tel, une telle. **~ an honest man,** un homme si honnête.

suck *v.t.* sucer; téter; aspirer, humer; *Fig.* attirer. **to ~ in,** sucer; aspirer; humer. **to ~ out,** aspirer; pomper; vider. **to ~ up,** sucer; aspirer; pomper; absorber.

sucker *n.* suceur *m.;* piston *m.* (pump); tuyau *m.* d'aspiration; suçoir *m., Bot.* drageon *m.; Infml.* gobeur *m.,* poire *f.*

suckle *v.t.* allaiter, donner à téter; donner le sein.

suckling *n.* allaitement *m.;* nourrisson *m.;* animal *m.* qui tette encore.

suction *n.* succion *f.;* aspiration *f.;* sucement *m.* **~ pump,** pompe *f.* aspirante.

sudden *adj.* soudain; subit, inopiné, imprévu; emporté. **a ~ death,** une mort subite. **all of a ~,** soudain, soudainement, subitement.

suddenly *adv.* soudain; soudainement, subitement; tout à coup.

suddenness *n.* soudaineté *f.*

suds *n.pl.* eau *f.* de savon, lessive *f.* **soap~,** eau de savon.

sue *v.t.* poursuivre. *v.i.* attaquer (en justice). **to ~ for damages,** poursuivre en dommages-intérêts.

suede *n.* daim *m.* **~ shoes,** chaussures *f.pl.* en daim.

suet *n.* graisse *f.*

suffer *v.t.* souffrir; endurer; supporter; tolérer; subir. **to ~ wrong,** supporter l'injustice. **to ~ loss,** souffrir, subir une perte. **to ~ for,** souffrir de, pâtir de, porter la peine de.

sufferance *n.* souffrance *f.;* modération *f.;* tolérance *f.*

sufferer *n.* personne *f.* qui souffre; malade *m.;*

patient *m.;* victime *f.* **migraine ~**, qui souffre de migraines.

suffering *adj.* souffrant, qui souffre. *n.* souffrance *f.;* peine *f.;* tolérance *f.,* permission *f.*

suffice *v.i.* suffire. *v.t.* suffire à, être suffisant (pour); contenter.

sufficiency *n.* suffisance *f.;* aptitude *f.,* talent *m.*

sufficient *adj.* suffisant, assez. **to have ~**, avoir assez, suffisamment.

sufficiently *adv.* suffisamment, assez.

suffix *n.* suffixe *m.* **~** *v.t.* ajouter (une lettre, une syllabe) à la fin d'un mot.

suffocate *v.t.* suffoquer, étouffer; asphyxier.

suffocating *adj.* suffocant, étouffant.

suffocation *n.* suffocation *f.,* étouffement *m.;* asphyxie *f.*

suffrage *n.* suffrage *m.*

suffuse *v.t.* couvrir (with a color), se répandre sur; baigner.

sugar *n.* sucre *m.* **cane ~**, sucre de canne. **~cane**, canne *f.* à sucre. **brown ~**, cassonade *f.* **lump ~**, sucre en morceaux. **~ bowl**, sucrier *m.* **~ candy**, sucre *m.* candi. **~ tongs**, tongs, pince *f.* à sucre. *v.t.* sucrer, adoucir.

sugary *adj.* sucré; saccharin; mielleux.

suggest *v.t.* suggérer; inspirer à.

suggestion *n.* inspiration *f.,* suggestion *f.;* instigation; insinuation *f.*

suggestive *adj.* qui inspire; qui suggère.

suicidal *adj.* de suicide; du suicide.

suicide *n.* suicide *m.*

suit *n.* costume *m.,* habillement *m.;* couleur *f.* (cards); pétition *f.,* demande *f.* (marriage); poursuite *f.* (court), procès *m.* **a suit**, un complet *m.,* un tailleur *m.,* un costume *m.* **to follow ~**, jouer de la même couleur, fournir. **to bring ~ against**, intenter un procès à. *v.t.* adapter; approprier, accommoder, arranger; convenir à, aller à. **that suits you very well**, cela vous va parfaitement. *v.i.* s'accorder avec; être approprié.

suitable *adj.* adapté, approprié; convenable, propre.

suitably *adv.* convenablement; conformément.

suite *n.* suite *f.;* appartement *m.* **bedroom ~**, une chambre à coucher.

suitor *n.* prétendant *m.,* amant *m.;* Law. plaideur *m.*

sulfate *n.* sulfate *m.*

suflur *n.* soufre.

sulk *v.i.* bouder.

sulkily *adv.* en boudant; d'un air boudeur.

sulkiness *n.* bouderie *f.;* maussaderie *f.*

sulks *n.pl.* mauvaise humeur *f.*

sulky *adj.* boudeur; maussade; morose. **to be ~**, bouder, être boudeur.

sullen *adj.* maussade; morose, chagrin; revêche, sombre; triste. **a ~ look**, un air chagrin.

sully *v.t.* souiller, noircir. *v.i.* (se) ternir, devenir terne.

sultan *n.* sultan *m.*

sultry *adj.* étouffant, suffocant; lourd.

sum *n.* somme *f.,* total *m.;* Fig. comble *m.,* substance *f.* **a ~ of money**, une somme d'argent. *v.t.* additionner, faire l'addition de. **to ~ up**, résumer, récapituler.

sumac *n.* sumac *m.*

summarize *v.t.* résumer, récapituler.

summary *adj.* sommaire. *n.* sommaire *m.,* résumé *m.,* abrégé *m.,* extrait *m.,* précis *m.*

summer *n.* été *m.* **~ house**, pavillon *m.* d'été, maison *f.* de campagne. **in ~time**, en été, pendant l'été. *adj.* d'été, estival. **~ season**, saison *f.* d'été.

summit *n.* sommet *m.,* faîte *m.,* Fig. point, degré le plus élevé.

summon *v.t.* appeler; mander; convoquer (assembly, jury). Law. citer; sommer. **to ~ up**, convoquer; rappeler (courage).

summons *n.* appel *m.;* convocation *f.* Law. citation *f.,* assignation *f.,* mandat *m.* de comparution; sommation *f.*

sumptuous *adj.* somptueux.

sumptuously *adv.* somptueusement.

sumptuousness *n.* somptuosité *f.*

sun *n.* soleil *m.* **~ rising ~**, soleil levant. **setting ~**, soleil couchant. **the ~ rises**, le soleil se lève. **the ~ sets**, le soleil se couche. **~-bath**, bain *m.* de soleil. **~beam**, rayon *m.* de soleil. **~burnt**, brûlé par le soleil, hâlé, basané. **~dial**, cadran *m.* solaire. **~-dried**, séché au soleil. **~flower**, tournesol *m.* **~-glasses**, lunettes *f.pl.* de soleil. **~light**, lumière *f.* du soleil. **~-roof**, toit *m.* ouvrant. **~-tanned**, bronzé. **~-shade**, parasol *m.* **~stroke**, coup *m.* de soleil, insolation *f.* **~** *v.t.* exposer au soleil, chauffer au soleil, sécher au soleil. **to ~ oneself**, se chauffer au soleil.

sunburn *v.t.* hâler. *n.* hâle *m.,* coup de soleil *m.*

sundae *n.* glace *f.* au sirop.

Sunday *n.* dimanche *m.* **on ~**, dimanche, le dimanche.

sunder *v.t.* séparer, diviser, couper en deux, rompre, briser.

sundries *n.pl.* diverses choses *f.pl.,* le reste *m.,* faux frais *m.pl.;* (accounting) divers *m.pl.*

sundry *adj.* divers, différent.

sunken *adj.* enfoncé, profond, creux; amaigri. **~ eyes**, les yeux caves, enfoncés. **~ cheeks**, les joues creuses.

sunny *adj.* brillant, radieux; Fig. riant, gai, du soleil, ensoleillé. **a ~ morning**, un matin ensoleillé.

sunrise *n.* lever *m.* du soleil, soleil *m.* levant.

sunset *n.* coucher *m.* du soleil, soleil *m.* couchant; occident *m.,* couchant *m.*

sunshine *n.* clarté *f.* du soleil, soleil *m.,* Fig. éclat *m.,* splendeur *f.* **in the ~**, au soleil.

sup *v.i.* souper.

super *n.* gardien *m.* (d'un immeuble), concierge *m.* **~** *adj.* super, formidable.

superabundant *adj.* surabondant.

superb *adj.* superbe.

superbly *adv.* superbement.

supercilious adj. hautain, fier; arrogant; dédaigneux.

superciliously adv. arrogamment; orgueilleusement; avec dédain, dédaigneusement.

superficial adj. superficiel; de superficie. **a ~ knowledge**, une connaissance superficielle.

superficially adv. superficiellement.

superfluous adj. superflu.

superhuman adj. surhumain.

superimpose v.t. superposer.

superintend v.t. surveiller; diriger.

superintendence n. surveillance f.; contrôle m.; direction f.

superintendent n. surveillant m.; inspecteur m.; surintendant m.; administrateur m.

superior adj. supérieur. n. supérieur m., supérieure f.

superiority n. supériorité f.

superlative adj., n. suprême; superlatif m.

supernatural adj. surnaturel.

superpose v.t. superposer.

superposition n. superposition f.

supersede v.t. supprimer, faire abandonner; remplacer; prendre la place de; suspendre; annuler.

superstition n. superstition f.

superstitious adj. superstitieux.

superstitiously adv. superstitieusement.

supervise v.t. surveiller, inspecter.

supervisor n. surveillant m., inspecteur m.; reviseur m.

supine adj. couché sur le dos, indolent, nonchalant, incline.

supper n. souper m.

supplant v.t. supplanter.

supple adj. souple, flexible; Fig. docile, soumis. v.t. assouplir; rendre souple. v.i. s'assouplir.

supplement n. supplément m. ~ v.t. ajouter.

supplemental, supplementary adj. supplémentaire.

suppleness n. souplesse f.

suppliant adj. suppliant. n. suppliant m.; requérant m.; pétitionnaire m.

supplicant adj., n. suppliant.

supplicate v.t. supplier. v.i. faire des supplications.

supplication n. supplication f.; supplique f.

supplier n. fournisseur m., pourvoyeur m.

supply v.t. suppléer; fournir, pourvoir de; alimenter; approvisionner. **to be supplied with**, être pourvu de. **to ~ our daily needs**, pour subvenir à nos besoins quotidiens. **to lay in a ~ of**, s'approvisionner de, faire une provision de. **we ~ them**, nous sommes leur fournisseur. n. approvisionnement m.; provision f.; fourniture f.; renfort m.; pl. fonds m.pl.; offre f.; subsides m.pl. **a fresh ~**, une nouvelle provision. **a ~ of food**, des aliments. **~ and demand**, l'offre et la demande.

support v.t. supporter; porter, soutenir; appuyer; endurer; subir; fournir (funds). **to ~ a friend**,

soutenir un ami. **to ~ life**, soutenir la vie. **to ~ a family**, soutenir une famille. **to ~ oneself**, soutenir, s'entretenir. n. soutien m.; support m., appui m.; nourriture f., subsistance f., entretien m.; assistance f.; (masonry) soutènement m. **fixed ~**, support fixe. **for the ~ of**, pour soutenir; pour appuyer, pour le soutien de, pour l'entretien de. **in ~ of**, en faveur de, à l'appui de.

supporter n. soutien m.; support m., appui m.; protecteur m., défenseur m., partisan m.; Sport. supporter m.

suppose v.t. supposer; présumer.

supposition n. supposition f.

suppress v.t. réprimer; supprimer; faire cesser; étouffer; détruire, tenir secret, cacher. **to ~ a rebellion**, réprimer une révolte. **to ~ a smile**, réprimer un sourire.

suppression n. répression f.; suppression f.

suppurate v.i. suppurer. v.t. faire suppurer.

suppuration n. suppuration f., pus m.

supremacy n. suprématie f.

supremacist n. personne f. qui croit en la supériorité des blancs m.

supreme adj. suprême.

supremely adv. suprêmement.

surcharge v.t. surcharger. n. surcharge f.

sure adj. sûr; certain, assuré, stable. **to be ~**, sûrement, certainement, assurément, à coup sûr. **to make ~ of**, s'assurer de. adv. sûrement, certainement.

surely adv. sûrement; certainement.

sureness n. certitude f.

surety n. certitude f., assurance f.; sûreté f.; garantie f.; Law. caution f., garant m.

surf n. brisants m.pl.; ressac m. **~board**, planche f. v.i. surfer.

surface n. surface f. ~ v.i. resurger, apparaître. **he ~d again**, il a réapparut, il a resurgit.

surfeit v.t. rassasier, gorger. v.i. être rassasié. n. rassasiement m.; satiété f.; excès m.pl. (de table).

surge nn. houle f.; lame f., vague f., flot m. v.i. s'élever, s'enfler, se grossir (as waves); déferler.

surgeon n. chirugien m.

surgery n. chirurgie f. **plastic ~**, chirurgie f. esthétique.

surgical adj. chirurgical.

surly adj. morose; bizarre; hargneux, revêche; sombre.

surmise v.t. conjecturer, soupçonner, de souter de; concevoir. v.i. insinuer, donner à entendre. n. conjecture f.; soupçon m., supposition f.

surmount v.t. surmonter; dépasser, surpasser.

surmountable adj. surmontable.

surname n. nom m. de famille, nom m.

surpass v.t. surpasser; l'emporter sur.

surplus n. surplus m.; excédant.

surprise n. surprise f. **~ attack**, attaque soudaine. **to take by ~**, prendre par surprise. v.t. surprendre; étonner; déconcerter; faire une surprise.

surprising adj. surprenant; étonnant.

surprisingly adv. d'une manière surprenante.

surrender *v.t.* rendre, livrer; abandonner. **to ~ oneself,** se rendre; se constituer prisonnier. **to ~ an office,** résigner un emploi. *v.i.* (se) rendre; se soumettre. *n.* reddition *f.*; abandon *m.*; soumission *f.*; renonciation *f.*, désistement *m.*; *Law.* cession *f.* de biens, cession *f.* **the ~ of a town,** la reddition d'une ville.

surreptitious *adj.* subreptice.

surreptitiously *adv.* subrepticement.

surrogate *n.* délégué *m.*, substitut *m.* **~ mother,** mère *f.* substitute.

surround *v.t.* entourer; environner; *Milit.* cerner (town).

surroundings *n.* entourage *m.*; alentours *m.pl.*

survey *v.t.* contempler; regarder, considérer; examiner; inspecter; arpenter, mesurer; visiter; lever le plan de. **to ~ a building,** examiner un bâtiment. *n.* examen *m.*, inspection *f.*; expertise *f.*, estimation *f.*; arpentage *m.*; cadastre *m.*; études *f.pl.*, topographiques. **to make, to take a ~ of,** faire l'examen de, examiner; faire l'expertise de; sondage *m.* (opinion).

surveyor *n.* inspecteur *m.*; surveillant *m.*; inspecteur *m.* des travaux publics; arpenteur *m.*, géomètre *m.*; conducteur *m.* (bridges, roads).

survival *n.* survivance *f.*; *Law.* survie *f.*

survive *v.t.* survivre (à).

survivor *n.* survivant *m.*

susceptibility *n.* susceptibilité *f.*; sensibilité *f.*

susceptible *adj.* susceptible; sensible.

susceptibly *adv.* d'une manière susceptible.

suspect *adj.*, *n.* suspect *m.* **~** *v.t.* suspecter; soupçonner; se douter de, se méfier de.

suspend *v.t.* suspendre; arrêter, cesser. **to ~ an officer,** suspendre un fonctionnaire. **to ~ payment,** suspendre ses payements.

suspenders *n.pl.* bretelles *f.pl.*

suspense *n.* incertitude *f.*, doute *m.*; suspension *f.* **in ~,** en suspens.

suspension *n.* suspension *f.* **~ bridge,** pont *m.* suspendu.

suspicion *n.* soupçon *m.* *Law.* suspicion *f.*

suspicious *adj.* soupçonneux; suspect.

suspiciously *adv.* avec méfiance; d'une manière suspecte.

sustain *v.t.* soutenir; supporter; entretenir, nourrir; endurer, souffrir; résister à; défendre; favoriser. **to ~ an attack,** soutenir une attaque.

sustenance *n.* subsistence *f.*, aliments *m.pl.*, nourriture *f.*, vivres *m.pl.*, soutien *m.*, entretien *m.*

suture *n.* suture *f.* **~** *v.t.* suturer.

svelte *adj.* svelte.

swab *n.* coton tige *m.*, serpillière *f.* **~** *v.t.* laver, nettoyer.

swaddle *v.t.* emmailloter.

swag *n.* butin *m.*

swagger *v.i.* faire le fier, crâner; se donner des airs. *n.* crânerie *f.*; air *m.* important.

swallow *n.* *Ornith.* hirondelle *f.*, gorgée *f.*, *Carp.* **~tail,** queue *f.* d'aronde. *v.t.* avaler; *Fig.* ravaler;

engloutir; accaparer. **to ~ down,** avaler; engloutir. **to ~ up,** avaler avidement; absorber; accaparer. **he had to ~ his pride,** il a dû ravaler sa fierté.

swamp *n.* marais *m.*, marécage *m.* **~** *v.t.* enfoncer dans un marécage; submerger; *Fig.* ruiner; enfoncer, couler.

swampy *adj.* marécageux.

swan *n.* cygne *m.*

swap *v.i.*, *v.t.* troquer, échanger. *n.* échange *m.*, troc *m.*

swarm *n.* essaim *m.*; *Fig.* foule *f.*; fourmilière *f.* **~ of bees,** essaim d'abeilles. *v.i.* s'attrouper, accourir en foule; fourmiller. **to ~ with,** fourmiller de.

swarthy *adj.* noir, basané; an teint hâlé, bruni.

swat *v.t.* taper, écraser. **she ~ted the spider,** elle écrasa l'araignée.

sway *v.t.* man ier, faire pencher, balancer, ballotter; influer sur; influencer. **to ~ the world,** gouverner régir le monde. **don't be ~ed by him,** ne vous laissez pas gagner par lui. *v.i.* pencher, incliner; se pencher, influer; gouverner. **to ~ with the wind,** balancer avec le vent. *n.* supériorité *m.*; empire *m.*; influence *f.* **the sovereign ~,** l'autorité souveraine. **to hold ~,** être au pouvoir.

swear *v.i.* jurer; prêter serment, faire serment. **to ~ to,** jurer de. **to ~ like a trooper,** jurer comme un charretier. *v.t.* prêter (an oath); déposer (under oath); attester; faire jurer à. **to ~ under oath,** preter serment, faire serment, jurer. **to ~ in,** faire prêter serment à, assermenter. **~ word,** gros mot *m.*

sweat *n.* sueur *f.* **to be in a ~,** être en sueur, *Infml.* être en nage. **by the ~ of,** à la sueur de. **~shop,** usine *f.* dont les employés sont exploités. *v.i.* suer; transpirer; *Fig.* s'exténuer, se fatiguer. *v.t.* faire suer, faire transpirer.

sweater *n.* sweater *m.*, pull *m.*, chandail *m.*

sweaty *adj.* en sueur, de sueur; *Fig.* pénible, fatigant.

Swede *n.* Suédois *m.*, Suédoise *f.*

Sweden *n.pr.* Suède *f.*

Swedish *adj.* suédois.

sweep balayer; ramoner (chimney); *Fig.* chasser; emporter; *Naut.* draguer; parcourir rapidement; effleurer. **to ~ a floor,** balayer un plancher. **to ~ a chimney,** ramoner une cheminée. **to ~ away,** balayer; enlever, emporter. **to ~ up,** balayer; balayer en tas; remasser. *v.i.* passer rapidement; voler; passer majestueusement, avec pompe; s'étendre. **to ~ along,** balayer; passer sur; raser. *n.* balayage *m.*; coup *m.* de balai; ramonage *m.* (chimney); ramoneur *m.* (chimney); ravage *m.*, portée *f.*, étendue *f.*, course *f.*, cours *m.*; *Fig.* essor *m.*; longue courbe. **a long ~,** un grand coup. **she was swept off her feet,** elle a eu le coup de foudre. **it was swept under the rug,** c'était gardé sous silence.

sweeping *adj.* qui balaye; impétueux; qui

emporte tout; vaste, étendu; général. *n.* balayage *m.*; ramonage *m.*

sweepstakes *n.* sweepstake *m.*

sweet *adj.* doux, sucré, suave, odoriférant; embaumé, mélodieux; frais; beau, joli; agréable. **~ as honey,** doux comme le miel. **a ~ smell,** une odeur douce, suave. **to smell ~,** sentir bon. **~ music,** une musique douce, mélodieuse. **a ~ girl,** une gentille fille. **a ~ smile,** un doux sourire. *n.* chose *f.* douce, au *pl.* douceurs *f.pl.,* sucreries *f.pl.,* friandises *f.pl.;* chère *f.,* chéri *m.,* chérie *f.* **~bread,** *Anat.* pancréas *m.;* *Culin.* ris *m.* de veau. **~ pea,** pois *m.* de senteur. **~ potato,** patate douce. **~ smelling,** odoriférant. **~-talker,** orateur *m.,* beau parleur. **~-toothed,** qui aime les choses sucrées. **~ tooth,** bec *m.* sucré.

sweeten *v.t.* sucrer; édulcorer; adoucir; apaiser, calmer; embaumer, purifier, désinfecter. **to ~ tea,** sucrer du thé. **to ~ life,** adoucir l'existence.

sweetener *n.* personne *f.* qui adoucit; chose qui adoucit; adoucissement *m.,* charme *m.*

sweetheart *n.* mon (petit) coeur. **high-school ~,** amoureux depuis le collège. **don't cry, ~,** ne pleure pas mon petit coeur.

sweetie *n. Infml.* puce *f.,* coco *m.,* cocotte *f.,* coeur *m.* **come here, ~,** viens ici, ma puce.

sweetness *n.* douceur *f.,* saveur douce; goût sucré; charme *m.,* mélodie *f.;* suavité *f.,* parfum *m.*

swell *v.i.* s'enfler; se gonfler, (se) grossir; (se) bouffir. **to ~ out,** bouffer; bomber. **rains ~ the rivers,** les pluies grossissent les rivières. **to ~ one's chest with pride,** se gonfler, se bouffer d'orgueil. *n.* enflure *f.,* gonflement *m.;* renflement *m.;* élévation *f.;* tertre *m.;* ondulation *f.,* houle *f.,* grosse lame *f.,* grosse vague *f.;* *Mus.* voix *f.,* son *m.* grave (organ). *adj.*

swelling *adj.* qui enfle. **~ sea,** mer houleuse. *n.* enflure *f.;* grossissement *m.;* gonflement *m.;* renflement *m.;* bosse *f.;* grosseur *f.*

swelter *v.i.* étouffer de chaleur, être accablé de chaleur.

swerve *v.i.* errer; s'égarer, s'écarter, se détourner, dévier, s'éloigner. **to ~ from,** dévier de.

swift *adj.* rapide; vite; vif; prompt.

swiftly *adv.* rapidement, vite.

swig *v.i., v.t.* boire à longs traits. *n.* bon coup *m.;* grand trait *m.* (liquid).

swill *v.t.* boire avec avidité, arroser, laver, mouiller, enivrer. *v.i.* s'enivrer, se griser. *n.* bon coup *m.,* long trait *m.* (of a drink); eaux *f.pl.* de vaisselle.

swim *v.i.* nager; naviguer, glisser; être inondé. **to ~ across,** traverser à la nage. *v.t.* passer, traverser à la nage; fendre (a current). *n.* action de nager. **to take a ~,** nager.

swimmer *n.* nageur *m.*

swimming *n.* natation *f.* **to be fond of ~,** aimer à nager, aimer la natation. **~ pool,** piscine *f.*

swindle *v.t.* escroquer. *n.* escroquerie *f.*

swindler *n.* escroc *m.*

swine *n. inv.* porc *m.,* cochon *m.,* pourceau *m.* **a herd of ~,** un troupeau de porcs.

swing *v.i.* (se) balancer; osciller. *v.t.* balancer, faire osciller; agiter, remuer; brandir (weapon). *n.* oscillation *f.;* vibration *f.;* balancement *m.;* balançoire *f.* (playground), d'impulsion; portée *f.;* penchant *m.,* élan *m.* **in full ~,** en pleine marche, en pleine activité.

swinging *adj.* oscillant; brandissant. *n.* oscillation *f.;* balancement *m.*

swinish *adj.* de cochon; malpropre; grossier.

swipe *n.* coup violent *m.* **~** *v.t.* frapper à tout volée; chiper.

swirl *n.* tourbillon *m.* **~** *v.i.* tourbilloner, tournoyer.

Swiss *adj.*suisse, de Suisse. *n.* Suisse *m.,* Suissesse *f.*

switch *n.* interrupteur *m.;* échange *m.,* baguette *f.,* badine *f.,* houssine *f.* **~** *v.t.* **~ on,** allumer. **~ off,** éteindre, changer, alterner.

Switzerland *n.pr.* Suisse *f.*

swivel *n.* pivot *m.* **~** *v.i.* tourner sur un pivot, pivoter.

swoon *v.i.* s'évanouir, se trouver mal; se pâmer. *n.* évanouissement *m.;* défaillance *f.,* pâmoison *f.,* syncope *f.*

swoop *v.t.* fondre sur, s'abattre sur (prey); s'emparer de. *n.* action de fondre, de s'abattre (on prey); attaque *f.;* coup *m.* **at one fell ~,** d'un seul coup.

sword *n.* épée *f.;* sabre *m.;* glaive *m.;* fer *m.* **~ in hand,** l'épée à la main. **to draw the ~,** tirer l'épée, dégainer. **to put to the ~,** passer au fil de l'épée. **the ~ of justice,** le glaive de la justice. **~fish,** *Ichth.* espadon *m.*

sworn *adj.* juré; dévoué; *Law.* juré; assermenté.

sybaritic *adj.* sybarite; de sybarite.

sycamore *n.* sycamore *m.*

sycophancy *n.* flatterie *f.,* flagornerie *f.*

sycophant *n.* sycophante *m.,* adulateur *m.,* flagorneur *m.*

syllabic *adj.* syllabique.

syllable *n.* syllabe *f.*

syllabus *n.* programme *m.,* sommaire *m.*

symbol *n.* symbole *m.;* emblème *m.;* signe *m.,* attribut *m.*

symbolic *adj.* symbolique.

symbolize *v.i.* symboliser. *v.t.* symboliser; regarder comme un symbole.

symmetrical *adj.* symétrique.

symmetry *n.* symétrie *f.*

sympathetic *adj.* compatissant, bienveillant. **a ~ look,** un regard bienveillant.

sympathize *v.i.* compatir à, avoir de la compassion pour.

sympathy *n.* compassion *f.*

symphony *n.* symphonie *f.*

symptom *n.* symptome *m.*

synagogue *n.* synagogue *f.*

synchronize *v.i.* synchroniser.

syncopate v.t. syncoper.

syncopation n. syncope f.

syndicate n. syndicat m. ~ v.t. syndiquer.

synonym n. synonyme m.

synonymous adj. synonyme.

synopsis n. au pl. **synopses**, synopsis f.; tableau m. synoptique, sommaire m., résumé m.

syntax n. syntaxe f.

synthesis n. synthèse f.

synthetic adj. synthétique.

syphilis n. syphilis f.

Syria n.pr. Syrie f.

syringe n. seringue f. ~ v.t. seringuer.

syrup n. sirop m.

system n. système m. **the solar ~**, le système solaire.

systematic adj. systématique.

systematically adv. systématiquement.

T

T-shirt n. tee-shirt m.

tab n. note f., addition f., facture f.; étiquette f.; languette f. **to keep ~s on**, tenir à vue, garder l'œil (sur).

tabernacle n. tabernacle m.; sanctuaire m.

table n. table f.; tablette f.; tableau m.; liste f. **round ~**, table ronde. **dining ~**, table à manger. **to set the ~**, mettre, dresser la table. **to clear the ~**, débarrasser la table, desservir. **a ~ of contents**, une table des matières. **multiplication ~**, table de multiplication. **to turn the ~s**, faire tourner la chance. **the ~s are turned**, les chances ont tourné. **~cloth**, nappe f. **~ napkin**, serviette f. de table. **~spoon**, cuiller f. à bouche, à soupe.

tablet n. tablette f.; plaque f., comprimé m., pastille f.

tabloid n. torchon m., tabloïd m.

taboo n. tabou m. ~ v.t. rendre taboo, interdire.

tabulate v.t. disposer en tables, en tableaux synoptiques; cataloguer; aplanir.

tabulation n. mise f., arrangement m. en tableaux.

tacit adj. tacito.

taciturn adj. taciturne.

tack v.t. attacher; bâtir, faufiler, coudre. **to ~ about**, virer de bord. n. petit clou m. à tête; broquette f. Naut. amure f. (sail); bordée f., bord m.

tackle n. fishing ~, articles de pêche. v.t. fournir, garnir; équiper, armer; harnacher; attaquer, empoigner; plaquer (football); attaquer (work, etc.).

tacky adj. minable.

tact n. tact m.

tactical adj. tactique.

tactics n.pl. tactique f.

tactile adj. tactile, tangible.

tag n. étiquette f.; refrain m., dicton m. ~ v.t. ~ along, suivre.

tail n. queue f.; bout m., fin f., extrémité f.; revers m. (coin), pile f.; Law. substitution f. **to turn ~**, tourner le dos les talons. **head or ~**, pile ou face. v.t. tirer par la queue; suivre de près, filer. **to ~ in**, Arch. engager. **to ~gate**, coller trop près, coller au pare-chocs.

tailor n. tailleur m. ~ v.i. façonner, habiller.

tailoring n. ouvrage m. de tailleur.

taint v.t. gâter (de viande); infecter, salir, entacher, ternir, flétrir; violer. v.i. s'altérer, (se) gâter,

(se) corrompre; se souiller. n. tache f., souillure f., flétrissure f.; corruption f.; infection f.

take v.t. pret. prendre; saisir; s'emparer de, capturer, se rendre maître de; enlever, ôter; prélever; soustraire; tirer; accepter; admettre; comprendre, interpréter, regarder, envisager; supposer, admettre; louer; mener, conduire, manger, boire. **to ~ a person by the hand**, prendre quelqu'un par la main. **he was ~n prisoner**, il a été fait prisonnier. **to ~ hold of**, prendre, saisir, s'emparer de. **I ~ the liberty of saying**, je prends la liberté de dire. **he took it from me**, il me l'a pris. **to ~ apart**, demonter. Fig. démolir. **~ my word for it**, croyez-m'en sur ma parole. **to ~ advantage of**, mettre à profit, prendre, profiter de. **to ~ unfair advantage of**, abuser de. **to ~ things as they come**, prendre les choses comme elles viennent. **to ~ part**, prendre part. **to ~ pains**, se donner de la peine, du mal. **to ~ care of**, prendre soin de; surveiller. **to ~ courage**, prendre courage. **to ~ to heart**, prendre à cœur. **to ~ a breath**, reprendre haleine. **to ~ notice**, observer, remarquer, faire attention. **to ~ something seriously**, prendre quelque chose au sérieux. **to ~ a thing for granted**, prendre quelque chose pour compte. **to ~ root**, prendre racine. **to ~ aim**, viser. **to ~ effect**, porter coup; réussir, entrer en effet. **to ~ place**, avoir lieu, survenir. **to ~ leave**, prendre congé. **to ~ one's own course**, suivre son cours. **to ~ the advice of**, suivre le conseil de. **~s two hours to go there**, il a fallu deux heures pour y aller. **to ~ an oath**, faire, prêter serment, jurer. **to ~ a nap**, faire un somme. **to ~ a walk**, faire une promenade. **to ~ revenge**, tirer vengeance, se venger. **to ~ along**, prendre avec soi, emmener, emporter. **to ~ away**, emmener (person); enlever, ôter. **to ~ back**, reprendre; remmener, reconduire. **to ~ down**, descendre; faire descendre; abaisser; humilier; démonter; prendre par écrit, prendre note de. **to ~ down a book from a shelf**, descendre un livre d'un rayon. **to ~ down a speech**, prendre un discours par écrit. **to ~ from**, prendre à; ôter à; diminuer de. **to ~ in**, rentrer; faire rentrer; admettre; accueillir, recueillir; donner asile à; comprendre, renfermer; Infml. tromper, attraper, mettre dedans. **you have been ~n in**, on vous a trompé. **to ~**

in hand, prendre en main, se charger de. **to ~ into**, faire entrer dans; prendre en (considéra-tion); se mettre dans. **he took it into his head to stay**, il s'est mis dans la tête de rester. **to ~ off**, ôter, enlever; emporter; partir; décoller *Aviat.;* couper, supprimer, vider, tirer. **they took off**, ils ont filé; va-t-en! **to ~ out**, faire sortir; sortir; emmener; ôter, enlever; arracher, extrai-re; séparer. **to ~ out a spot**, enlever une tache. **to ~ out a tooth**, arracher une dent. **to ~ out a patent**, prendre un brevet. **to ~ up**, prendre; lever, élever, monter; faire monter, s'emparer de; appréhender au corps; empoigner; acquérir; percevoir; commencer, entamer; reprendre, rele-ver; absorber, accaparer; puiser; prendre en main, se charger de. **to ~ up the whole space**, occuper tout l'espace. **to ~ up the time**, prendre le temps. *v.i.* aller, prendre; se refugier, plaire; réussir; s'adonner à, avoir de goût pour. **to ~ after**, tenir de; imiter, copier. **the boy ~s after his father**, le garçon ressemble à son père. **to ~ up with**, s'attacher à. **to ~ off**, s'enle-ver, s'ôter. **to ~ over**, prendre le pouvoir/la relè-ve/le relai/la place.

takeoff *n.* imitation *f.*, charge *f.*, *Aviat.* décollage *m.*

takeover *n.* prise *f.* de pouvoir.

talc *n.* talc *m.*

tale *n.* histoire *f.*, récit *m.*, conte *m.*, fable *f.*, légende *f.;* mensonge *m.* **to tell ~s**, raconter des histoires; dire des mensonges.

talent *n.* talent *m.*

talented *adj.* de talent, qui a du talent, habile, doué.

talisman *n.* talisman *m.*

talk *v.i.* converser, parler, s'entretenir, bavarder. **to ~ of**, parler à. *v.t.* **to ~ to**, parler à. **to ~ away**, passer (le temps) à parler, à causer, à bavarder. **to ~ into**, persuader; faire faire. **she ~ed him into buying a boat**, elle lui a fait acheter un bateau. **to ~ out of**, dissuader de; soutirer. **to ~ over**, discuter. *n.* conversation *f.*, entretien *m.;* propos *m.;* rumeur *f.;* bavardage *m.* **to have a ~ with**, avoir une discussion/un entretien avec. **to be the ~ of**, être le sujet des conversations de. **~ show**, tête à tête *m.* télévisé.

talkative *adj.* bavard; bavard.

talker *n.* parleur *m.;* bavard *m.;* hâbleur *m.*, van-tard *m.*

tall *adj.* grand; haut, élevé. **a ~ man**, un homme grand. **to grow ~**, grandir.

tally *n.* taille *f.;* entaille *f.;* coche *f.* ~ *v.t.* marquer, faire des coches sur la taille. *v.i.* **(with)** s'accor-der avec, correspondre à.

Talmud *n.* Talmud *m.*

talmudic *adj.* talmudique.

talon *n.* serre *f.;* griffe *f.*

tamarind *n.* tamarin *m.*, tamar *m.* **Indian ~**, tamar indien. **~ tree**, tamarinier *m.*

tambourine *n.* tambour *m.* de basque.

tame *adj.* apprivoisé; dompte, domestique; sou-mis, lâche; plat; docile; doux; terne; fade. *v.t.* dompter; apprivoiser; soumettre.

tamely *adv.* sans résistance, docilement.

tamper *v.i.* se mêler, s'occuper (de), tremper (dans); **(with)** altérer, pratiquer, chercher à cor-rompre, suborner (witnesses).

tampon *n.* tampon *m.* hygiénique.

tan *n.* tan *m.* hâle *m.*, bronzage *m.* ~ *v.t.* tanner; hâler, bronzer.

tandem *n.* tandem *m.*

tang *n.* arrière-goût *m.*, goût *m.* fort.

tangent *n.* tangente *f.* ~ *adj.* tangent.

tangerine *n.* mandarine *f.*

tangible *adj.* tangible; palpable.

tangle *v.t.* mêler, emmêler, entremêler, enchevê-trer, embrouiller. *v.i.* s'emmêler; s'embrouiller. *n.* noeud *m.;* confusion *f.*

tangled *adj.* emmêlé; entrelacé; enchevêtré.

tank *n.* citerne *f.*, réservoir *m.;* bassin *m.*

tanker *n.* bateau-citerne *m.*, pétrolier *m.;* tanker *m.;* wagon-citerne *m.*

tanner *n.* tanneur *m.*

tannery *n.* tannerie *f.*

tantalize *v.t.* tantaliser, tourmenter, faire souffrir.

tantamount *adj.* équivalent, qui équivaut; égal.

tantrum *n.* accès *m.* de colère, crise *f.* **to throw a ~**, faire une crise.

tap *v.t.* mettre en perce (barrel); tirer; percer; taper, frapper; mettre sur écoute (phone). *n.* buvette *f.*, tape *f.*, petit coup *m.* **~-dance**, cla-quettes *f.pl.*

tape *n.* ruban *m.*, bande *f.* (d'enregistrement), cassette. **~ recorder**, magnétophone *m.* **red ~**, bureaucratie *f.*, routine *f.* ~ *v.t.* enregistrer.

tapered *adj.* conique, terminé en pointe, pointu; effilé. *v.i.*, *v.t.* se terminer en pointe; s'effiler; effiler.

tapestry *n.* tapisserie *f.* ~ *v.t.* tapisser.

tapioca *n.* tapioca *m.*

tapir *n.* tapir *m.*

tar *n.* goudron *m.* ~ *v.t.* goudronner.

tarantula *n.* tarentule *f.*

tardiness *n.* lenteur *f.;* retard *m.*

tardy *adj.* lent; tardif; en retard.

target *n.* cible *f.*, but *m.* ~ *v.t.*, *v.i.* viser (à). **the government is ~ing minorities for . . .**, le gouvernement vise les minorités pour . . . .

tariff *n.* tarif *m.* ~ *v.t.* tarifer.

tarnish *v.t.* ternir. *v.i.* (se) ternir, être terni.

tarot *n.*, *adj.* tarot *m.*

tarragon *n.* estragon *m.*

tarry *v.i.* s'arrêter, séjourner, rester en arrière; s'attarder; tarder. *adj.* de goudron; couvert de goudron.

tart *adj.* aigre; acerbe, piquant, mordant. *n.* tarte *f.*

Tartar *n.* tartre *m.;* Tartar *m.* **steak ~(e)**, steak *m.* tartare. **~ sauce**, sauce *f.* tartare.

task *n.* tâche *f.;* devoir *m.* **to set a ~**, donner, assigner une tâche. **to take to ~**, réprimander;

prendre à partie. **harsh ~master,** maître sévère, oppresseur *m.*

tassel *n.* gland *m.*; pompom *m.*

taste *v.t.* déguster (drink); éprouver; savourer; goûter (de), subir; sentir. **to ~ wine,** goûter, déguster du vin. *v.i.* **to ~ bitter,** avoir un goût amer. *n.* goût *m.*; saveur *f.*; petit peu *m.*, soupçon *m.*, idée *f.* **a bitter ~,** un goût amer. **to have a ~ for,** avoir du goût pour. **a matter of ~,** une question de goût. **he got a ~ of jail,** il a eu un aperçu/un échantillon de la prison. **~bud,** papille *f.* gustative.

tasteful *adj.* de bon goût.

tasteless *adj.* insipide, sans goût, fade.

taster *n.* personne *f.* qui goûte; dégustateur *m.*

tasty *adj.* de bon goût; savoureux.

tatter *n.* haillon *m.*, lambeau *m.*, guenille *f.*

tattle *v.i.* bavarder, caqueter. *n.* bavardage *m.*, babil *m.*, babillage *m.*; cancan *m.*

tattoo *n.* tatouage *m.*; *Mil.* retraite *f.* *v.t.* tatouer.

taunt *v.t.* railler, bafouer, (se) moquer; **taunting,** *n.* raillerie *f.*, moquerie *f.*, sarcasme *m.*

Taurus *n.* *Astron.* le Taureau.

taut *adj.* raide, tendu; enflée (sail).

tautology *n.* tautologie *f.*

tavern *n.* taverne *f.*; auberge. **~keeper,** aubergiste *m.*; tavernier *m.*

tawdry *adj.* voyant, criard, de mauvais goût. **~ colors,** des couleurs criardes.

tawny *adj.* tanné, basané, hâlé, (animals) fauve.

tax *n.* taxe *f.*; impôt *m.*, contribution *f.* **~ collector,** percepteur *m.* des contributions. **~payer,** contribuable *m.* **~ evasion,** fraude *f.* fiscale. **~free,** exonéré, exempt d'impôts. **~ haven,** refuge *m.* fiscal. *v.t.* taxer; imposer, frapper d'un impôt.

taxable *adj.* imposable; sujet à la taxe.

taxation *n.* imposition *f.* de taxes; assiette *f.*, des impôts.

taxi(cab) *n.* taxi *m.*

taxidermy *n.* taxidermie *f.*

tea *n.* thé *m.*; tisane *f.*, infusion *f.* **~cup,** tasse *f.* à thé. **~kettle,** bouilloire *f.* à thé. **~pot,** théière *f.* **~ service,** service *m.* à thé. **~spoon,** cuillère à thé *f.*

teach *v.t.*, *v.i.* enseigner, instruire; apprendre.

teacher *n.* professeur *m.*, enseignant(e) *m.f.*, instituteur (trice) *m.f.*, maître *m.*; maîtresse *f.*

teaching *n.* enseignement *m.*; instruction *f.*

team *n.* équipe *f.* **~work,** collaboration *f.*, travail d'équipe *m.*, travail de groupe *m.* *v.i.* **~ up,** faire équipe, s'associer.

tear *n.* larme *f.*; pleurs *m.pl.* **to shed ~s,** verser des larmes. **in ~s,** tout en larmes, tout éploré. **to dissolve in ~s,** fondre en larmes. **~ gas,** gaz *m.*, lacrymogène. **~jerker,** mélo *m.*

tear *v.t.* déchirer, lacérer; arracher. **to ~ to pieces,** mettre en pièces. **to ~ oneself from,** s'arracher de, s'arracher à. **to ~ one's hair,** s'arracher les cheveux. **to ~ away,** arracher; séparer. **to ~ off,** enlever (en tirant). **to ~ out,**

arracher, enlever. **to ~ up,** mettre en pièces; déraciner; détruire. *v.i.* courir précipitamment. *n.* déchirure *f.*, accroc *m.* **wear and ~,** avaries *f.pl.;* usage *m.*

tearful *adj.* plein de larmes, en pleurs.

tease *v.t.* tourmenter, ennuyer, taquiner. *n.* *Infml.* allumeuse *f.*

teat *n.* mamelon *m.*; bout *m.* de sein; mamelle *f.*; téton *m.*

technical *adj.* technique.

technicality *n.* caractère *m.* technique; vice *m.* de forme.

technician *n.* technicien(ne) *m.f.*

technology *n.* technologie *f.*

teddybear *n.* ours *m.* en peluche, nounours *m.*, ourson *m.*

tedious *adj.* ennuyeux, fastidieux; fatigant.

tedium *n.* ennui *m.*, fatigue *f.*

teem *v.i.* fourmiller. **to ~ with,** regorger de.

teenage *adj.* d'adolescent.

teen(ager) *n.* ado(lescente(e)) *m.f.*

teens *n. pl.* âge *m.* de l'adolescence (treize à dix-neuf ans).

teeny(-weeny) *adj.* *Infml.* riquiqui, rikiki, tout petit.

tee-shirt *n.* T-shirt *m.*

teeth *n.* See TOOTH.

teethe *v.i.* faire ses dents.

teetotaler *n.* personne *f.* qui ne boit jamais d'alcoöl, buveur *m.* d'eau.

telecommunication *n.* télécommunication *f.*

telegram *n.* télégramme *m.*, dépêche *f.* télégraphique.

telegraph *n.* télégraphe *m.* **~** *v.t.* télégraphier.

telepathy *n.* télépathie *f.*

telephone *n.* téléphone *m.* **~** *v.i.* téléphoner.

telescope *n.* télescope *m.*; lunette *f.* d'approche; longue vue *f.*

television *n.* télévision *f.*

tell *v.t.* dire; énoncer; raconter; faire savoir, expliquer; confesser; dévoiler, divulguer; publier; énumérer, compter; distinguer, discerner. **~ it to him,** dites-le lui. **I have been told that,** j'ai appris que, on m'a dit que. **to ~ truth,** dire la vérité.

teller *n.* diseur *m.*, conteur *m.*, narrateur *m.*; caissier *m.*; agent *m.* comptable; receveur *m.* des finances. **fortune~,** diseur de bonne aventure.

telltale *n.* rapporteur *m.*, bavard *m.*; *Infml.* cafard *m.*; compteur *m.* **~** *adj.* rapporteur; indiscret; qui parle.

temerity *n.* témérité *f.*

temp *n.* (*abr.* **temporary**) intérimaire *m.f.*

temper *v.t.* tempérer, modérer, adoucir; tremper (steel); mêler; mélanger, façonner; détremper (colors); accommoder. *n.* caractère *m.*, naturel *m.*; tempérament *m.*, colère *f.*; mélange *m.*, calme *m.*, sang-froid *m.*, trempe *f.* **even ~,** caractère égal. **sweet ~,** caractère charmant. **to get out of ~,** se fâcher, s'emporter. **to keep one's ~,** garder son sang-froid. **to lose one's ~,**

se fâcher. **he has a bad ~**, il a un mauvais caractère.

temperament *n.* tempérament *m.*

temperance *n.* tempérance *f.;* modération; sobriété *f.;* patience. **~ society**, société *f.* de tempérance.

temperate *adj.* tempéré; modéré; tempérant; sobre; modéré. **a ~ climate**, un climat tempéré.

temperature *n.* température *f.*

tempered *adj.* trempé. **a good-~ man**, un homme d'un bon caractère.

tempest *n.* tempête *f.;* orage *m.*

tempestuous *adj.* tempêtueux; orageux; impétueux.

temple *n.* temple *m.*

temporal *adj.* temporel; séculier; temporal.

temporarily *adv.* temporairement.

temporary *adj.* temporaire; provisoire.

temporize *v.i.* temporiser; se plier; se rendre, consentir.

tempt *v.t.* tenter; éprouver; attirer; exciter; provoquer.

temptation *n.* tentation *f.*

tempting *adj.* tentant, séduisant, attrayant; entraînant.

temptingly *adv.* d'une manière tentante, entraînant.

ten *adj.* dix. **it's a ~ to one shot,** il y a dix contre un à parier que. *n.* dix *m.;* dizaine *f.*

tenable *adj. Milit.* tenable; soutenable.

tenacious *adj.* tenace.

tenaciously *adv.* avec ténacité.

tenant *n.* locataire *m.*

tend *v.t.* garder, veiller (sur); soigner, avoir soin de. *v.i.* avoir tendance à, se diriger; tendre; aboutir; contribuer. **to ~ toward,** se diriger vers; **(to)** faire attention à.

tendency *n.* tendance *f.*

tender *n.* serviteur *m.;* (railroad) tender *m.;* offre *f.;* Law offre de payement; monnaie *f.* soumission *f.* **to make a ~ offer,** faire une offre. **legal ~,** monnaie légale. **bar-~,** barman (maid) *m.f.* — *v.t.* offrir, proposer; offrir en payement, soumissionner. *adj.* tendre; délicat; jeune; sensible; doux, cher. **he has a ~ heart,** il a le coeur tendre. **a ~ subject,** un sujet scabreux, délicat. **~-hearted,** au coeur tendre; sensible, compatissant.

tenderness *n.* tendresse *f.;* délicatesse *f.;* sensibilité *f.;* douceur *f.;* faiblesse *f.;* sollicitude *f.* **with ~,** avec tendresse, avec douceur.

tendon *n.* tendon *m.*

tenebrous *adj.* ténébreux; obscur.

tenement *n.* habitation *f.* délabrée.

tenet *n.* dogme *m.,* principe *m.,* doctrine *f.;* opinion *f.,* croyance *f.*

tennis *n.* tennis *m.* **~ court,** terrain *m./court m.* de tennis. **~ elbow,** synovite *f.* du coude.

tenor *n.* cours *m.;* caractère *m.,* genre *m.;* teneur *f.;* sens *m.,* esprit *m.;* portée *f.;* Mus. ténor *m.;* alto *m.* (instrument).

tense *adj.* tendu, raide. *n.* temps *m.*

tensely *adv.* avec tension.

tension *n.* tension *f.*

tent *n.* tente *f.*

tentacle *n.* tentacule *m.*

tentative *adj.* expérimental, d'assai, d'épreuve.

tenth *adj.* dixième; **on the ~ of April,** le dix avril. *n.* dixième *m.;* dîme *f.; Mus.* dixième *f.*

tenuous *adj.* ténu, mince.

tenure *n.* tenure *f.;* mouvance *f.;* redevance *f.;* droit *m.*

tepid *adj.* tiède.

term *n.* limite *f.;* terme *m.,* borne *f.;* expression *f.,* mot *m.;* temps *m.,* durée *f.;* Law session *f.;* période *f.* scolaire. pl. conditions *f.pl.* (of payment). **scientific ~s,** termes de science. **to be on good ~s with,** être en de bons termes avec, être bien avec. **what are your ~s?** quelles sont vos conditions? **to come to ~s,** s'arranger, tomber d'accord. **on familiar ~s,** sur un pied de familiarité. *v.t.* appeler, nommer; désigner.

terminal *adj.* extrême, terminal.

terminate *v.t.* terminer. *v.i.* (se)terminer.

termination *n.* limitation *f.;* extrémité *f.,* limite *f.;* terminaison *f.;* cessation *f.;* fin *f.;* terme *m.*

terminology *n.* terminologie *f.*

terminus *n.* terminus *m.*

termite *n.* termite *m.*

tern *n.* sterne *f.,* hirondelle *f.* de mer.

terrace *n.* terrasse *f.* **~** *v.t.* former, disposer en terrasse; ouvrir au jour.

terrestrial *adj.* terrestre. *n.* habitant *m.* de la terre.

terrible *adj.* terrible, affreux; formidable; excessif; extraordinaire.

terribly *adv.* terriblement.

terrier *n.* terrier *m.*

terrific *adj.* formidable, merveilleux.

terrify *v.t.* terrifier, épouvanter.

territorial *adj.* territorial.

territory *n.* territoire *m.*

terror *n.* terreur *f.;* épouvante *f.;* effroi *m.* **he is the ~ of the country,** il est la terreur du pays. **~-stricken,** frappé de terreur.

terrorism *n.* terrorisme *m.*

terrorist *n.* terroriste *m.f.*

terrorize *v.t.* terroriser.

terse *adj.* élégant, poli, pur; abrupt.

tertiary *adj.* tertiaire.

test *n.* examen *m.f.;* réactif *m.;* épreuve *f.,* expérience *f.,* critérium *m.;* type *m.,* modèle *m.;* preuve *f.* **to put to the ~,** mettre à l'épreuve. **~ tube,** éprouvette *f. v.t.* éprouver, essayer, faire l'épreuve de, l'essai de.

testament *n.* testament *m.*

testamentary *adj.* testamentaire.

testate *adj.* qui a fait un testament.

testator *n.* testateur *m.*

testatrix *n.* testatrice *f.*

testicle *n.* testicule *m.*

testify *v.i.* témoigner; déposer, attester; déclarer.

to ~ to, rendre témoignage à; attester; témoigner de.

testimony *n.* témoignage *m.; Law.* déposition *f.;* attestation *f.;* preuve *f.,* confirmation *f.* **in ~ whereof,** en foi de quoi.

testing *n.* essai *m.,* épreuve *f.*

testis *n.* (*pl.* **testes**) testicule *m.*

testy *adj.* maussade; de mauvaise humeur; susceptible.

tetanus *n.* tétanos *m.*

tête-à-tête *n., adv.* tête à tête *m.*

tether *n.* longe *f.,* attaché *f.; Fig.* lien *m.,* bride *f.,* chaîne *f.* **~** *v.t.* attacher, mettre à l'attache.

text *n.* texte *m.;* écriture *f.* **~book,** livre *m.,* manuel *m.*

textile *adj.* textile, tissue *m.* matière *f.* textile.

texture *n.* tissage *m.;* tissu *m.;* texture *f.*

than *conj.* que; (after a comparative) de. **better ~ that,** mieux que cela, **rather ~,** plutôt que. **more ~ a hundred men,** plus de cent hommes. **less ~ thirty,** moins de trente.

thank *v.t.* remercier; rendre grâces. **I ~ you kindly,** je vous remercie bien. **~ God,** Dieu merci. *n.pl.* remerciement *m.* **~s to you,** grâce à vous. **to return ~s,** faire ses remerciements. **~ offering,** sacrifice *m.* d'actions de grâces. **~sgiving,** remerciements *m.pl.,* actions *f.pl.* de grâces; jour de l'Action de Grâce.

thankful *adj.* reconnaissant.

thankfully *adv.* avec reconnaissance.

thankless *adj.* ingrat; oublié, méconnu.

that *démonst.adj.* those, *pl.* ce or cet *m.,* cette *f.;* ce ... là. **~ woman,** cette femme. *démonst.pron.* celui-là *m.,* celle-là *f.;* celui *m.,* celle *f.;* cela, ce, ça; le. **~ which,** celui que; ce qui, ce que. **~belongs to me,** cela m'appartient. **~ is,** cela est; c'est-à-dire. *rel. pron.* qui, que, lequel, laquelle. **the friend ~ I speak of,** l'ami dont je parle. *conj.* que; afin que, pour que. **you know ~ I must go,** vous savez que je dois partir. **supposing ~,** en supposant. **so ~,** pour que, afin que; de façon que. **he came so ~ he might see her,** il est venu afin de la voir.

thatch *n.* chaume *m.* **~** *v.t.* couvrir de chaume.

thatched *adj.* couvert de chaume; de chaume.

thaw *v.i.* dégeler. *v.t.* faire fondre. *n.* dégel *m.*

the *def. art.* le *m.,* la *f.;* l' *m.f.,* les *m.f.pl.*

theater *n.* théâtre *m.,* spectacle *m.;* salle *f.* de spectacle; amphithéâtre *m.* (for lectures).

theatrical *adj.* théâtral.

thee *pers. pron.* te, toi.

theft *n.* vol *m.*

their *poss. adj.* leur *m.f.* leurs *m.f.pl.*

theirs *poss. pron.* le leur, la leur, les leurs; à eux, à elles.

theism *n.* théisme *m.*

them *pers. pron.* eux *m.pl.* elles *f.pl.,* les *m.f.pl.;* eux, elles, leur. **of ~,** d'eux, d'elles; en. **to ~,** à eux, à elles, leur; y. **in ~,** en eux, en elles; y.

theme *n.* thème *m.;* sujet de discours; texte *m.,* matière *f.;* thèse *f.*

themselves *refl. pron.* eux-mêmes *m.pl.,* elles-mêmes *f.pl.* se.

then *adv.* alors; puis; ensuite; après; en conséquence, donc. **till ~,** jusqu'alors. **now and ~,** de temps en temps. *adj.* alors, à cette époque.

thence *adv.* de là, en; dès lors; depuis lors; de là, par là.

thenceforth *adv.* dès lors, dès ce moment-là.

theocracy *n.* théocratie *f.*

theologian *n.* théologien *m.*

theological *adj.* théologique.

theologically *adv.* théologiquement.

theology *n.* théologie *f.*

theorem *n.* théorème *m.*

theoretical *adj.* théorique.

theoretically *adv.* théoriquement.

theorist *n.* théoricien *m.*

theorize *v.i.* théoriser.

theory *n.* théorie *f.*

therapeutic *adj.* thérapeutique.

therapeutics *n. pl.* thérapeutique *f.*

therapist *n.* thérapeute *m.f.*

therapy *n.* thérapie *f.*

there *adv.* là, y. **down ~,** là-bas. **up ~,** là-haut. **in ~,** là-dedans. **here and ~,** çà et là. **~ he is,** le voilà. **~ is, ~ are,** il y a; voilà. **~ was, ~ were,** il y avait. **~ you are wrong,** là, tu as tort. **~abouts,** par-là; là-dessus; aux environs; à peu près. **~after,** là-dessus, après cela; en conséquence. **~by,** par là, par ce moyen; par là. **~fore,** c'est pourquoi, pour cela; aussi; donc. **~in,** là dedans, en cela; y. **~of,** de cela, en. **~upon,** là-dessus, sur cela.

thermal *adj.* thermal.

thermometer *n.* thermomètre *m.*

these *demonst. pl. adj.* ces *m.f.pl.;* ces ... ci. *démonst.pron.* ceux-ci *m.pl.,* celles-ci *f.pl.*

thesis *n. pl.* theses, thèse *f.*

they *pers.pron. pl.* ils, eux *m.pl.* elles *f.pl.;* ceux *m.pl.,* celles *f.pl.*

thick *adj.* épais, gros, fort; dense; dru; grossier; pesant; gras; trouble. **~headed,** qui a la tête dure. **a ~ fog,** un brouillard épais. **~ crowd,** foule compacte. **they are as ~ as thieves,** ils s'entendent comme larrons en foire. *n.* partie *f.* épaisse; le plus épais *m.,* milieu *m.;* fort *m.;* mêlée *f.;* fourré *m.,* taillis *m.* **in the ~ of the fight,** au plus fort du combat. **through ~ and thin,** à travers tous les obstacles. *adv.* épais; profondément; dru, en foule; vite, rapidement; péniblement. **~-coated,** à peau épaisse.

thicken *v.t.* épaissir; serrer, grossir. **to ~ soup,** épaissir la soupe. *v.i.* (s')épaissir; s'obscurcir; (se) serrerm (se) resserer (se) grossir; s'échauffer.

thickening *n.* épaississement *m., Culin.* liaison *f.*

thicket *n.* fourré *m.* d'arbres, bosquet *m.;* ballier *m.*

thickness *n.* épaisseur *f.;* densité *f.;* consistance *f.;* lourdeur.

thief *n., pl.* thieves, voleur *m.*

thieve *v.i.* voler, dérober.

thigh *n.* cuisse *f.* ~ **bone**, fémur *m.*

thimble *n.* dé *m.* à coudre.

thin *adj.* mince; maigre, efflanqué; clairsemé; léger, faible. **thinner**, plus mince. **to become, to get ~**, s'amincir. ~ **coat of paint**, mince couche de peinture. *adv.* mince, menu; clair; ténu. *v.t.* amincir; amaigrir; éclaircir; diminuer, réduire; raréfier (air).

thine *poss. pron.* le tien; la tienne, les tiens, les tiennes; à toi.

thing *n.* chose *f.;* substance; objet; affaire; créature *f.* ~**s**, choses *f.pl.;* affaires *f.pl.;* effets *m.pl.;* habits *m.pl,* vêtements *m.pl.; Infml.* truc *m.,* machin *m.* **put your ~s away**, range tes affaires. **any~**, n'importe quoi. **no such ~**, pas du tout. **it was a bad ~ for him**, ce n'était pas bien pour lui. **every living ~**, toute créature vivante. **the poor ~!** le/la pauvre!

think *v.i.* penser; songer; croire; s'imaginer; trouver. **to ~ of**, penser à. **to ~ well of**, penser du bien de, avoir une bonne opinion de. **I ~ so**, je crois bien, je la pense, je crois que ouï. **what are you thinking about?** à quoi pensez-vous? *v.t.* juger; estimer; regarder comme.

thinker *n.* penseur *m.* **free~**, libre-penseur *m.*

thinking *adj.* pensant. *n.* pensée *f.;* réflexion *f.;* opinion *f.;* sens *m.;* jugement *m.* **to my ~**, à mon sens, dans mon opinion; selon moi.

thinness *n.* minceur *f.;* maigreur *f.;* ténuité *f.;* fluidité *f.* rareté *f.*

third *adj.* troisième; trois; tiers, tierce. ~ **floor**, troisième étage. **the ~ of April**, le trois avril. **a ~ party**, une tierce personne. *n.* tiers *m.* ~ **world**, tiers monde; *Mus.* tierce *f.*

thirst *n.* soif *f.;* (of, for, after) grande envie. **to be dying of ~**, mourir de soif. ~ **for revenge**, soif de vengeance. *v.i.* avoir soif, être altéré.

thirsty *adj.* altéré, qui a soif. **to be ~**, avoir soif.

thirteen *adj.* treize.

thirteenth *adj., n.* treizième, treize; *Mus.* treizième *f.*

thirtieth *adj.* trentième.

thirty *adj.* trente.

this *démonst. adj.* **these**, *pl.* ce, cet *m.,* cette *f.;* ce ...-ci, cet ...-ci, cette ...-ci; ceci. ~ **woman**, cette femme. ~ **way**, par ici. **by ~ time**, maintenant; à l'heure qu'il est. *démonst. pron.* celui-ci *m.,* celle-ci *f.,* ceci, ce *m.;* voici. ~ **or that**, ceci ou cela; celui-ci ou celui-là. ~ **is the way**, voici le chemin.

thistle *n.* chardon *m.*

thong *n.* courroie *f.,* lanière *f.*

thoracic *adj.* thoracique.

thorax *n.* thorax *m.*

thorn *n.* épine *f.,* piquant *m.;* aiguillon *m.*

thorny *adj.* épineux.

thorough *adj.* entier, complet; achevé, accompli, consommé, parfait; (neg.) franc, fieffé. *n.f.* ~**bred**, pur sang; *adj.* de pur sang. ~**going**, déterminé, à outrance.

thoroughfare *n.* passage *m.,* voie *f.* de communication; rue *f.* passante. **no ~**, on ne passe pas; rue barrée.

thoroughly *adj.* entièrement, tout à fait, à fond, parfaitement.

those *pron., adj., pl.* ces; ces ...-là; ceux-là, celles-là; ceux, celles.

thou *pers.pron.* tu, toi.

though *conj.* quoique, bien que. **even ~**, quand même, quand bien même. **as ~**, comme si.

thought *n.* pensée *f.;* conception *f.;* sentiment *m.;* inquiétude *f.;* mélancolie *f.;* idée *f.;* soupçon *m.* **to read a person's ~s**, lire dans la pensée de quelqu'un.

thoughtful *adj.* (of) attentif (à), attentionné, prévenant. **to be ~ of**, penser à, ne pas oublier, ne pas négliger.

thoughtfulness *n.* rêverie *f.* profonde, méditation *f.;* recueillement *m.;* prévenance *f.;* sollicitude *f.,* anxiété *f.*

thoughtfully *adv.* d'un air pensif, tout pensif; avec prévenance; avec sollicitude.

thoughtless *adj.* irréfléchi, étourdi, insouciant.

thoughtlessly *adv.* étourdiment; avec insouciance.

thoughtlessness *n.* irréflexion *f.;* étourderie *f.;* insouciance *f.*

thousand *adj.* mille; mil. **two ~**, deux mille. **the year one ~, nine hundred and ninety-four**, l'an mil neuf cent quatre-vingt-quatorze. *n.* mille *m.,* millier *m.* **by the ~s**, par milliers.

thousandth *adj.* millième *m.*

thrash *v.t.* battre, étriller; rosser.

thread *n.* fil *m.;* filament *m.* **to hang by a ~**, tenir à un fil. *v.t.* enfiler; traverser, passer par.

threadbare *adj.* usé jusqu'à la corde, râpé; usé; épuisé.

threat *n.* menace *f.*

threaten *v.t.* menacer.

threatening *adj.* menaçant.

three *adj. n.* trois *m.* ~**-D**, tridimensionnel. ~**-legged**, à trois pieds. ~**-sided**, à trois côtés.

threefold *adj.* triple.

threshold *n.* seuil *m.*

thrift *n.* frugalité *f.,* économie *f.;* épargne *f.*

thrifty *adj.* frugal; florissant, économe, ménager; soigneux.

thrill *v.t.* faire tressaillir. *v.i.* frémir. *m.* tressaillement *m.;* frémissement *m.* **what a ~ to go there**, quelle joie d'y aller.

thrilling *adj.* émouvant, palpitant; frémissant. **she has a ~ job**, elle a un emploi du tonnerre.

thrive *v.i.* réussir, prospérer, s'enrichir, faire son chemin.

thriving *adj.* qui prospère, qui réussit; prospère; qui profite.

throat *n.* gorge *f.;* gosier. **a sore ~**, un mal de gorge. **to seize by the ~**, prendre à la gorge.

throb *v.i.* palpiter, battre. *n.* palpitation *f.,* battement *m.;* pulsation *f.;* élancement *m.* (pain).

throbbing *adj.* palpitant; lancinant. **a ~ pain,**

une douleur lancinante. *n.* battement *m.*; palpitation *f.* (heart).

throes *n.pl.* angoisse *f.*, torture *f.*; douleurs *f.pl.* (of childbirth); agonie *f.* (of death).

throne *n.* trône *m.* **to ascend the ~**, monter sur le trône.

throng *n.* foule *f.*, multitude *f.*, presse *f.* **~** *v.i.* (se) presser, accourir en foule; s'attrouper. *v.t.* presser; encombrer, obstruer.

throttle *n.* papillon *m.* **~** *v.t.* étouffer, suffoquer, étrangler.

through *prep.* au travers de; à travers; par. **to pass ~ a gate**, passer par une porte. **~ the window**, par la fenêtre. **~ the nose**, par le nez. *adv.* de part en part, d'outre en outre, d'un bout à l'autre; entièrement; à bonne fin. **to read a book ~**, lire une livre d'un bout à l'autre. **to carry ~**, mener à bonne fin.

throughout *prép., adv.* à travers; durant, pendant; d'un bout à l'autre de, partout, dans tout. **~ the year**, toute l'année, pendant l'année. **~ England**, dans toute l'Angleterre, à travers l'Angleterre.

throw *v.t.* jeter; lancer, renverser. **to ~ stones**, jeter des pierres; **to ~ into prison**, jeter en prison; **to ~ around**, jeter de côté et d'autre; **to ~ aside**, jeter, mettre de côté; **to ~ away**, jeter, réjeter, gaspiller, dissiper; **he ~s his money away**, il gaspille son argent; **to ~ away one's life**, gâcher sa vie; **to ~ down**, jeter en bas; renverser, jeter à terre; terrasser; détruire; **to ~ in**, jeter dedans; introduire dans, rajouter; **to ~ off**, jeter; ôter, dépouiller; rompre avec; **to ~ out**, jeter dehors; chasser; faire entendre; **the bill was ~n out**, le projet de loi a été rejeté; **to ~ up**, jeter en l'air; vomir, rendre. *n.* jet *m.*; coup *m.*; élan *m.*; couverture *f.*

thru *adv.* See THROUGH.

thrust *v.t.* pousser, faire entrer, introduire; fourrer; presser, serrer. **to ~ aside**, pousser de côté. **to ~ away**, repousser; écarter. **to ~ back**, repousser. **to ~ down**, pousser en bas; enfoncer. **to ~ in**, pousser dedans; enfoncer, fourrer. **to ~ into**, pousser dans; fourrer dans; contraindre à. **to ~ out**, pousser dehors; jeter dehors; éloigner. *v.i.* (at) (se) jeter, (s')introduire; (se)fourrer; s'immiscer (dans); se mêler (de). *n.* coup *m.*; poussée *f.*; attaque; assaut *m.*; Arch. poussée *f.* **to make a ~ at**, allonger un coup à, porter une botte à.

thud *n.* bruit *m.* sourd. *v.i.* faire un bruit sourd.

thumb *n.* pouce *m.* **to go ~s up**, tirer son chapeau (à).

thump *n.* coup *m.* de poing. *v.t.* frapper lourdement, cogner.

thunder *n.* tonnerre *m.*; foudre *f.* **~bolt**, foudre *f.* **~storm**, orage *m.* accompagné de tonnerre. *v.i.* tonner; gronder; retentir, résonner.

thunderstruck *adj.* foudroyé; anéanti; stupéfait.

Thursday *n.* jeudi *m.*

thus *adv.* ainsi, si, tant. **~ far**, jusqu'ici, jusque-là.

thwart *adj.* transversal, oblique, en travers, de travers; pervers, contrariant. *v.t.* traverser; croiser; Fig. contrarier, contrecarrer.

thy (Archaic) *poss. adj.* ton *m.*, ta *f.*, tes *m.f.pl.*

thyme *n.* thym *m.* **wild ~**, serpolet *m.*

thyself *réfl. pron.* toi-même, te, toi.

tibia *n.* tibia *m.*

tick *n.* Entom. tique *f.*, tic tac *m. v.i.* faire tic tac.

ticket *n.* billet *m.*; ticket *m.*, bon *m.*; Com. étiquette *f.*, marque *f.* **round-trip ~**, billet d'aller et retour. **season ~**, billet de saison, d'abonnement. *v.t.* marquer, étiqueter, numéroter (merchandise).

tickle *v.t.* chatouiller; titiller, flatter; plaire à, sourire à.

tickling *n.* chatouillement *m.*

ticklish *adj.* chatouilleux; susceptible; délicat; scabreux.

tidal *adj.* de marée; périodique.

tide *n.* temps *m.*, saison *f.*; marée *f.*; cours *m.*, courant *m.*, torrent *m.* **ebb ~**, èbe *m.*, reflux *m.*, marée *f.* descendante. **high ~**, haute marée. **low ~**, basse marée. **to go with the ~**, suivre le courant.

tidiness *n.* propreté *f.*, netteté *f.*; bonne tenue *f.*

tidings *n. pl.* nouvelles *f.pl.*

tidy *adj.* propre; net; proprement mis; en ordre. *v.t.* ranger, mettre en ordre.

tie *v.t.* lier; attacher, nouer; unir, enchaîner; engager, astreindre, obliger, assujettir. **to ~ a knot**, faire un noeud. **to ~ the knot**, se marier. **to ~ tight**, serrer fort. **to ~ down**, lier (en bas), assujettir, contraindre. **to ~ on**, attacher; assujettir. **to ~ up**, attacher, lier. **~ that dog up**, attachez ce chien. *n.* lien *m.*; attache *f.*; engagement *m.* noeud *m.* cravate *f.* **the ties of friendship**, les liens de l'amitié.

tier *n.* rangée *f.*, rang *m.*

tiger *n.* tigre *m.*, tigress *f.*

tight *adj.* tendu, serré; juste; étroit; collant (pants); clos, fermé; dur, sévère; raide, guindé. **the string is too ~**, la ficelle est trop tendue. **air~**, imperméable à l'air. *adv.* fort, fortement; bien; bon. **to hold ~**, tenir bien.

tighten *v.t.* tendre, serrer, raidir, resserrer.

tightly *adv.* d'une manière tendue, serrée, raide; étroitement; bien, ferme; fort.

tightness *n.* tension *f.*, raideur *f.*; dureté *f.*; parcimonie *f.*, avarice *f.*; imperméabilité *f.*; Naut. état *m.* étanche.

tights *n. pl.* bas *m.* collant.

tile *n.* tuile *f.*; carreau *m.* **~** *v.t.* couvrir de tuiles.

till *n.* caisse *f.*, tiroir *m.* à argent. *prép.* jusque, jusqu'à. **~ now**, jusqu'à présent. **~ then**, jusqu'alors. *conj.* jusqu'à ce que; que . . . ne; que, avant que; avant de. **wait ~ you get it**, attendez jusqu'à ce que vous l'ayez. *v.t.* labourer, cultiver.

tiller *n.* barre *f.* du gouvernail, barre *f.*

tilt *n.* coup *m.*; inclinaison *f.*, pente *f.*

timber *n.* bois *m.* de construction, bois *m.* de charpente; arbres *m.pl.* Naut. membres *m.pl.*

timbre n. timbre m.

time n. temps m.; fois f.; moment m., époque f.; terme m., délai m., Mus. mesure f. ~ **is money**, le temps c'est de l'argent. **in course of** ~, avec le temps. **at the same** ~, en même temps, au même moment. **at no** ~, à aucun moment; jamais. **from ~ to ~**, de temps en temps. **a long ~ ago**, il y a longtemps. **in the mean** ~, dans l'intervalle, en attendant. **to appoint a** ~, fixer, désigner un moment. **to kill** ~, tuer le temps. **in the day** ~, de jour. **at any** ~, à quelque moment que ce soit, à tout moment. **in** ~, à temps; en son temps. **in due** ~, en temps opportun. **in good** ~, à temps, à propos, en temps voulu. **in the nick of** ~, au bon moment. **at the present** ~, aujourd'hui, maintenant. **to beat** ~, battre la mesure. **to keep** ~, Mus. aller en mesure. **what ~ is it?** quelle heure est-il? **the first** ~, la première fois. **every** ~, toutes les fois, chaque fois. **three ~s**, trois fois. **many a** ~, mainte fois, plus d'une fois. **four at a** ~, quatre à la fois. **at ~s**, parfois. **come another** ~, venez une autre fois. v.t. calculer sur une montre, chronométrer; choisir le moment de faire, calculer; regler; Mus. donner la mesure à. ~**table**, indicateur m. horaire m. ~**worn**, usé par le temps. **well-~d**, opportun, à propos.

timeliness n. opportunité f., à propos m.

timely adj. opportun, à propos; en temps opportun. adv. à propos; en temps opportun, à temps.

timid adj. timide.

timidity n. timidité f.

timing n. action de faire à propos.

timorous adj. timide; timoré.

tin n. étain m.; fer-blanc m. ~ v.t. étamer. ~ **foil**, papier m. aluminium; boite.

tincture n. essence f.; Pharm. teinture f.; extrait m.; teinte; nuance f.; goût m. ~ v.t. teindre; imprégner.

tinge v.t. teindre; donner une teinte à; imprégner. n. teinte f.; nuance f.

tingle v.i. tinter; fourmiller, picoter; démanger; tressaillir.

tingling n. tintement m.; picotement m.

tinsel n. clinquant m., faux éclat; guirlandes f.pl. de Noël. adj. de clinquant, faux. v.t. orner de clinquant, donner un faux éclat à.

tint n. teinte f. ~ v.t. teinter.

tiny adj. tout petit; minuscule, mince.

tip n. bout m., pointe f., extrémité f.; pourboire m., renseignement m., tuyau m. **the ~ of the tongue**, le bout de la langue. v.t. garnir le bout; ferrer. **to ~ over**, renverser; verser. **to ~ off**, informer, avertir. v.i. incliner; tomber.

tipsy adj. ivre, gris.

tiptoe n. pointe f. du pied. **on ~**, sur la pointe des pieds.

tire n. pneu m. ~ v.t. fatiguer, lasser; ennuyer, importuner. **to ~ out**, harasser, épuiser; accabler, assommer, ennuyer à mourir. **to be ~d of**,

être fatigué de. v.i. (se) fatiguer, (se) lasser; se dégoûter.

tiredness n. lassitude f.; fatigue f.

tiresome adj. fatigant; ennuyeux, fastidieux.

tissue n. tissu m. ~ **paper**, papier m. de soie. **cellular** ~, tissu cellulaire; mouchoir m. en papier, Kleenex m. (trademark).

tit n. néné m. Ornith. mésange f. ~ **for tat**, un prêté rendu; à bon chat bon rat.

tithe n. dixième m.; dîme f. ~ v.t. lever la dîme sur. v.i. payer la dîme.

titillate v.i. chatouiller, titiller.

title n. titre m.; nom m.; épithète f. **the ~ of a book**, le titre d'un livre. ~ **deed**, titre m., document n.m. ~ v.t. intituler; qualifier de.

titter v.i. ricaner. n. ricanement m., rire m. moqueur.

tittle n. point m., iota m., rien m.

titular adj. n. titulaire m.

to prép. à; en, vers; sur; jusqu'à; envers; pour; auprès de. **to go** ~ **New York**, aller à New York. **to go** ~ **the U.S.**, aller aux Etats Unis. **I spoke ~ her**, je lui ai parlé. **from day** ~ **day**, de jour en jour. ~ **the last penny**, jusqu'au dernier sou. ~ **his face**, à sa face, en face. **the way** ~ **the station**, le chemin de la gare. **in that case, come** ~ **see me**, en pareil cas venez me trouver.

toad n. crapaud m. ~ **stool**, champignon m.

toady n. flatteur m. ~ v.i. aduler, ramper auprès de.

toast v.t. faire rôtir, griller, toaster, porter la santé de. n. rôtie f.; pain grillé; toast m., santé f.

toaster n. grille-pain m.

tobacco n. tabac m.

toboggan n. toboggan m. ~ v.i. faire du toboggan.

tocsin n. tocsin m.

today n., adv. aujourd'hui m.

toddle v.i. chanceler, aller à petits pas, trottiner.

toddler n. bébé qui commence à marcher.

toe n. orteil m.; doigt du pied.

toffy n. caramel m. (nougat). (fait de mélasse).

together adv. ensemble; en même temps; de suite. ~ **with**, avec; ainsi que.

toil v.i. travailler beaucoup, peiner; Infml. s'échiner. n. travail m. pénible; peine f., fatigue f.

toilet n. toilettes f.pl. ~ **paper**, papier m. hygiénique.

token n. signe m., marque f.; témoignage m.; gage m., souvenir m. **as a ~ of**, en signe de.

Toledo n. Tolède.

tolerable adj. tolérable, supportable; passable.

tolerance n. patience f.; force f. d'âme; tolérance f.

tolerant adj. tolérant.

tolerate v.t. tolérer.

toll n. droit m.; péage m., tintement m. de cloche, glas m. ~**free call**, appel m. gratuit. v.i., v.t. tinter, sonner. **to ~ the (funeral) knell**, sonner le glas. **to ~ the bell**, sonner la cloche.

tomahawk n. tomahawk m. ~ v.t. frapper, tuer d'un coup de tomahawk.

tomato n. tomate f.

tomb n. tombe f.; tombeau m.; sépulcre m.

tomboy n. garçon m. manqué.

tombstone n. tombe f., pierre f. tombale.

tomcat n. matou m., chat m.

tome n. tome m., volume m.

tomorrow n., adv. demain.

ton n. tonne f.

tone n. ton m., accent; timbre m. (voice); Paint. teinte. **low ~,** ton bas, voix basse.

tongs n.pl. pincettes f.pl., tenailles f.pl., pinces f.pl.

tongue n. langue f.; langage m.; parole f.; faconde f.; idiome m. **the English ~,** la langue anglaise. **~-tied,** qui a le filet; qui a la langue liée; muet. **mother ~,** langue f. maternelle.

tonic adj. tonique f.

tonight n., adv. cette nuit f.; ce soir m.

tonnage n. tonnage m.

tonsil n. amygdale f.

too adv. trop; aussi, en outre, par trop. **~ much, ~ many,** trop, trop de. **and you ~,** et vous aussi.

tool n. outil m., instrument m. **~chest,** coffre m. à outils.

toot v.t., v.i. sonner.

tooth s. **teeth** pl. dent f. **decayed ~,** dent cariée, gâtée. **to grind one's teeth,** grincer des dents. **to show one's teeth,** montrer les dents; menacer. **to have a sweet ~,** aimer les douceurs, avoir le bec sucré. **~ and nail,** à belles dents, de toute sa force. **~ache,** mal m. de dents. **~brush,** brosse f. à dents. **~paste,** dentifrice m. **~pick,** cure-dents m. **~** v.t. garnir de dents; denteler; s'engrener.

toothless adj. édenté, sans dents.

top n. haut m., sommet m.; cime f. (mountain, tree); faîte m. (building); Fig comble m., tête f. premier rang m.; dessus m.; toupie f. (toy). **from ~ to bottom,** du haut en bas. **at the ~ of his lungs,** à tue-tête. adj. d'en haut; de dessus; premier, principal. v.t. dominer, exceller; surpasser les autres. v.t. couvrir; s'élever au-dessus de, dépasser; Fig. surpasser; Hort. étêter (tree).

topaz n. topaze f.

topic n. sujet m. thème m., matière f.; Méd. topique m. **~ of conversation,** sujet de conversation.

topical adj. général, commun; local; topique.

topically adv. d'une manière locale.

topless adj. aux seins nus, sans haut. **~ bathing suit,** monokini m.

topmost adj. le plus haut, le plus élevé; supérieur.

topography n. topographie f.

topping n. glaçage m. **do you want a ~ on your ice cream?** voulez-vous du sirop sur votre glace?

topple v.i. tomber en avant. **to ~ over,** dégringoler. v.t. faire tomber, jeter.

topsy-turvy adv. sens dessus dessous.

torch n. torche f.; flambeau m. **~light,** lumière f. de torche.

torment v.t. tourmenter.

torment n. tourment m.; supplice m., torture f.

tornado n. tornade f.

torpedo n. torpille f. **~ boat,** torpilleur m.

torpid adj. engourdi, torpide, inerte.

torpor n. torpeur f., engourdissement m.; apathie f.

torrent n. torrent m. **~** adj. torrentueux, impétueux.

torrid adj. brûlant; brûlé, torride.

torsion n. torsion f.

torso n. terse m.

tort n. tort m., dommage m.

tortoise n. tortue f. **~shell,** s'écaille f. de tortue.

tortuous adj. tordu, tortueux; sinueux.

torture n. torture f.; tourment m.; supplice m. **~** v.t. tourmenter, torturer.

torturer n. bourreau m.

toss v.t. lancer (into the air); secouer, ballotter; Fig. agiter. **to ~ about,** jeter, ballotter. **to ~ back,** rejeter, renvoyer. **to ~ up,** jeter en l'air; relever. v.i. (se) jeter; être ballotté; rouler; s'agiter, se démener, n. jet m.; secousse f., hochement m. (of head).

tot n. tout petit m., bambin m.

total adj. total m.

totality n. totalité f.

totally adv. totalement, entièrement.

tote v.t. porter.

totter v.i. branler, chanceler (walking); menacer ruine.

touch v.t. toucher (à); léser; affecter, émouvoir; regarder, intéresser; atteindre; esquisser. **to ~ one another,** se toucher. **to ~ off,** esquisser, ébaucher. **to ~ up,** retoucher; rehausser. n. toucher m., tact m., contact m., essai m.; preuves f.pl.; teinte f., teinture f., allusion f. **by the ~,** au toucher. **to be in ~ with,** être en rapport avec. **~ down,** but m., score m.

touché interj. touché! dans le mille!

touched adj. touché; timbré, toqué.

touching adj. touchant, émouvant, pathétique. prép. touchant, concernant.

touchy adj. irritable, susceptible.

tough adj. dur, tenace, visqueux; coriace; fort, solide; flexible, résistant. **a ~ skin,** peau f. dure. **~ meat,** viande f. coriace. **as ~ as leather,** dur comme le cuir.

toughen v.i. durcir; raidir.

toughness n. solidité f., force f.; raideur f.; dureté f., nature f. coriace; ténacité f.; viscosité f.; opiniâtreté f.

toupee n. toupet m.

tour n. tour m.; voyage m.; excursion.

tourism n. tourisme m.

tourist n. touriste m.

tournament n. tournoi m.

tousle v.t. chiffonner; houspiller.

tout v.i. racoler, solliciter.

tow v.t. remorquer. n. remorque f. **in ~**, à la remorque.

toward, towards prép. vers, du côté de; envers, pour. **he came ~ me**, il vint vers moi. **~ midnight**, vers minuit.

towel n. serviette f. **paper ~**, essuie-tout m. inv.

tower n. tour f.; clocher m.; citadelle f; forteresse f.; hauteur f. **~** v.i. s'élever; dominer.

town n. ville f. **to go to ~**, aller en ville. **~ council**, conseil m. municipal. **~ hall**, hôtel m. de ville.

township n. commune f.; corps m. municipal, municipalité f.

toxic adj. toxique.

toxin n. toxine f.

toxicology n. toxicologie f.

toy n. jouet m., joujou m. **~** v.i. jouer, badiner, folâtrer.

trace n. trace f., vestige m.; piste, trait m., harnais m. **~** v.t. tracer, calquer; suivre la trace de, suivre à la trace; copier, imiter; remonter, parcourir. **to ~ back**, faire remonter, reporter. **to ~ out**, tracer; faire le tracé de; découvrir.

trachea n. trachée f.

track n. trace f., voie f., piste f., route f., cours m., ornière f. (tire); marque f.; vestige m. **to be on the ~**, être sur la trace. v.t. suivre à la trace, à la piste.

tract n. espace m., étendue f., région f., contrée f.; durée f.; traite m., brochure f. (religious subject).

traction n. traction f.; tension f.; attraction f.

tractor n. tracteur m.

trade n. commerce m., négoce m., métier m. **domestic ~**, commerce intérieur. **foreign ~**, commerce extérieur. **~mark**, marque f. de fabrique, marque f. déposée. **it is his ~**, c'est son métier. **~ winds**, vents m.pl. alizés. v.i. commercer, négocier. **to ~ in silk**, faire le commerce des soieries. **to ~ with**, faire des affaires avec.

trader n. commerçant m., négociant m., marchand m.

trading adj. commercial; marchand, commerçant, de commerce. n. commerce m., négoce m.

tradition n. tradition f.

traditional adj. traditionnel.

traduce v.t. blâmer, censurer; décrier, dénigrer, médire de; calomnier.

traffic n. trafic m., négoce m.; transport m.; circulation f. **~** v.i. trafiquer; commercer. v.t. négocier; vendre.

tragedy n. tragédie f.

tragic adj. tragique.

tragically adv. tragiquement.

tragicomedy n. tragi-comédie f.

tragicomic adj. tragi-comique.

trail v.t. suivre à la piste; traîner. v.i. passer lentement. n. trace f., piste f. (animal); chemin m., route f.; traînée f. **~ of light**, traînée lumineuse. **a ~ of smoke**, une traînée de fumée.

trailer n. remorque f.; caravane f.

train v.t. traîner; entraîner, dresser (horse), former, discipliner; tailler. **to ~ soldiers**, discipliner des soldats, instruire des recrues. n. train m. (sur voie ferrée); traînée f. queue f. (robe); suite f., cortège m.; enchaînement m., marche f.; procession f. **a ~ of ideas**, une suite d'idées. **fast ~**, train de grande vitesse.

trainer n. dresseur m., instructeur, entraîneur m. (horses).

training n. instruction f.; exercice m.; instruction f. militaire, entraînement m.

trait n. trait m.

traitor n. traître m.

traitorous adj. traître, perfide.

trajectory n. trajectoire f.

trammel n. entraves f.pl.; obstacle m. **~** v.t. entraver, embarrasser; empêtrer.

tramp v.t. fouler aux pieds, faire à pied. v.i. voyager à pied; rôder, vagabonder. n. marche f. pesante; piétinement m.; voyage m. à pied; vagabond m., rôdeur m., Infml. traînée f., coureuse (loose woman).

trample v.t. fouler aux pieds; marcher sur; dédaigner. v.i. piétiner.

trance n. transe f., extase f.; catalepsie f.

tranquil adj. tranquille.

tranquilize v.t. calmer, tranquilliser.

tranquillity n. tranquillité f., quiétude f.

transact v.t. faire, exécuter; conclure, expédier; négocier, traiter. **to ~ business with**, faire des affaires avec.

transaction n. gestion f. affaire f., Comm. opération f.; transaction f.

transatlantic adj., s. transatlantique.

transcend v.t. dépasser; excéder; surpasser.

transcendent adj. transcendant.

transcribe v.t. transcrire, copier.

transcript n. copie f.; transcription f.

transcription n. transcription f., copie f.

transept n. transept m.

transfer v.t. transférer; transporter; Law. céder.

transferable adj. transférable; négociable.

transfigure v.t. (se) transfigurer.

transfix v.t. transpercer.

transform v.t. convertir; transsubstantier. v.i. (se) transformer.

transformation n. transformation f.

transfuse v.t. transvaser, transfuser.

transfusion n. transfusion f.

transgress v.t. transgresser, enfreindre. v.i. pécher.

transgression n. transgression f.; faute f., péché m.

transgressor n. transgresseur m.; violateur m.

transient adj. passager; transitoire, éphémère.

transit n. transit m. **~** v.t. Astron. passer sur.

transition n. transition f.

transitory adj. transitoire, passager; fugitif.

translate v.t. traduire. **to ~ word for word**, traduire mot à mot. **to ~ into French**, traduire en français.

translation n. traduction f.

translator n. traducteur m.

translucent adj. translucide; transparent, diaphane.

transmigration n. transmigration f., métempsycose f.; transformation f.

transmission n. transmission f.

transmit v.t. transmettre; faire parvenir, conduire.

transmitter n. celui qui transmet; transmetteur m.

transmutation n. transmutation f.

transmute v.t. transmuer; transformer.

transom n. traverse f. (window), meneau m.; linteau m. (door).

transparency n. transparence f.; diaphanéité f.

transparent adj. transparent, diaphane; clair.

transpire v.i. transpirer; (s)'exhaler; arriver; se passer, avoir lieu. v.t. exhaler; transpirer.

transplant v.t. transplanter, transporter, déplacer. n. transplantation f.; déplacement m.

transport v.t. transporter, déporter, ravir. **to ~ goods**, transporter des marchandises. n. transport m.; Naut. bâtiment de transport; Fig. ravissement m., accès m. (joy, anger, etc.).

transportation n. transport m.; déportation f.; transmission f.

transpose v.t. transposer.

transposition n. transposition f.

transverse adj. transversal; transverse; oblique.

trap n. trappe f., traquenard m., trébuchet m.; piège m., panneau m., embûche f. **mouse~**, souricière f. **rat ~**, ratière f. **~door**, trappe f. ~ v.t. prendre au piège, attraper; prendre par ruse. v.i. tendre un piège.

trapeze n. trapèze m.

trash n. ordures f.pl.; poubelle f.; Infml. merde f.; cochonnerie f. ~ v.t. salir, mettre à sac.

trashy adj. sans valeur.

trauma n. trauma m.; traumatisme m.

traumatic adj. traumatique.

travel v.i. voyager; faire route; aller. **to ~ on**, avancer; poursuivre sa route. **to ~ over**, voyager dans, parcourir. v.t. voyager dans, parcourir. n. voyage. **~s in Turkey**, voyages en Turquie.

traveler n. voyageur m.

traveling adj. de voyage; voyageur. **a ~ companion**, un compagnon de voyage. **~ expenses**, frais de voyage.

traverse v.t. traverser; parcourir; croiser.

travesty n. parodie f. ~ v.t. travestir; parodier.

trawler n. chalutier m.

tray n. plateau m.

treacherous adj. traître; perfide, déloyal.

treachery n. trahison f.; perfidie f.

tread v.t. poser le pied; appuyer le pied. **to ~ on**, fouler aux pieds; écraser. v.i. aller, marcher (sur); fouler; écraser. n. pas m. **~mill**, trépigneuse f.

treason n. trahison f. **high ~**, haute trahison; lèse-majesté.

treasure n. trésor m. ~ v.t. trésauriser; garder précieusement.

treasurer n. trésorier m.

treasury n. trésor m.; trésorerie f.

treat v.t. traiter; agir envers; soigner; régaler; payer; négocier; disserter sur. **to ~ a subject**, traiter un sujet. v.i. parler de. n. régal m.; festin m.; fête f.

treatise n. traité m.

treatment n. traitement m.

treaty n. négociation f.; traité m.; pacte m., convention f.

treble adj. triple; Mus. de dessus. n. triple m.; Mus. dessus m., soprano m. ~ v.t., v.i. tripler.

tree n. arbre m., bois m. **fruit ~**, arbre fruitier.

trefoil n. trèfle m.

trek v.i. cheminer, avancer avec peine. n., randonnée f., cheminement m.

trellis n. treillis m.

tremble v.i. trembler; chevroter (voice).

trembling n. tremblement m.

tremendous adj. terrible; épouvantable, prodigieux; énorme; imposant.

tremendously adv. terriblement; affreusement.

tremor n. tremblement m.

tremulous adj. tremblant, tremblotant.

trench v.t. creuser; sillonner; faire des tranchées dans; Milit. retrancher. v.t. empiéter. n. tranchée f., fosse f., retranchement m.

trend v.i. courir, se diriger, tendre. n. mode f., direction f., tendance f. **fashion ~**, tendance de la mode.

trendy adj. à la dernière mode, du dernier cri.

trepidation n. tremblement m., crainte f.

trespass v.i. empiéter; violer la propriété; faillir; enfreindre. **to ~ against**, enfreindre, violer (a law); offenser. **to ~ upon**, empiéter sur. n. Law. violation f. de propriété.

trespasser n. violateur m. de propriétés; vagabond m.; qui est en contravention.

tress n. tresse f.

trestle n. tréteau m.; support m. (of boards, etc.).

triad n. triade f.

trial n. effort m., essai m., expérience f.; épreuve f.; malheur m., affliction f.; Law. jugement m. **a severe ~**, une cruelle épreuve. **~ by jury**, jugement par jury. **the ~ lasted a month**, le procès a duré un mois. **to bring to ~**, mettre en jugement. **on ~**, à l'essai.

triangle n. triangle m.

triangular adj. triangulaire.

tribe n. tribu f.; peuplade f.

tribulation n. tribulation f.

tribunal n. tribunal m.

tributary adj. tributaire; sujet; subordonné. n. tributaire m.; vassal m.; affluent m. (river).

tribute n. tribut m.

trick n. tour m., ruse f., artifice m.; finesse f., duperie f.; coup m.; espièglerie f. (of a child); tour d'adresse. **to play a ~ on a person**, jouer un tour à quelqu'un. v.t. tromper, duper; mettre dedans.

trickery n. ruse f., fourberie f., tricherie f.

trickle *v.i.* couler goutte à goutte; ruisseler, s'infiltrer.

trickling *n.* écoulement *m.;* murmure *m.* de l'eau qui coule.

tricycle *n.* tricycle *m.*

triennial *adj.* triennal.

triennially *adv.* tous les trois ans.

trifle *n.* peu de chose; bagatelle *f.,* babiole *f.,* vétille *f.* ~ *v.i.* s'amuser à des riens, baguenauder; badiner, vétiller. **to ~ with,** rire de; se jouer de; plaisanter avec.

trifling *adj.* léger, de rien, insignifiant, petit; frivole, futile, oiseux.

trigger *n.* détente *f.* **to pull the ~,** presser la détente. **~-happy,** à la gâchette facile.

trigonometry *n.* trigonométrie *f.*

trilingual *adj.* trilingue.

trill *n.* trille *m.;* cadence *f.* ~ *v.t.* triller; faire résonner.

trillion *n.* billion *m.*

trim *adj.* soigné, bien tenu; bien fait, beau; gentil, coquet, bien ajusté. *n.* parure *f.,* ornement *m.;* toilette *f.;* attirail *m.;* état *m. Naut.* assiette *f.;* orientement *m.* (sails); allure *f.* ~ *v.t.* arranger, mettre en ordre; adapter, orner, parer, habiller; garnir (clothes); couper, tailler (hair, beard), faire (beard); tailler (trees), émonder, ébrancher; *Carp.* dégrossir; *Naut.* orienter (sails).

trimester *n.* trimestre *f.*

trimming *n.* garniture *f.*

trinity *n.* trinité *f.*

trinket *n.* petit bijou *m.;* breloque *f.;* brimborion *m.,* colifichet *m.;* babiole *f.*

trio *n.* trio *m.*

trip *v.t.* faire tomber. *v.i.* trébucher, faire un faux pas; aller avec légèreté; faire un voyage. **take a ~, up,** désarçonner. *n.* faux pas *m.;* excursion *f.,* voyage *m.;* trajet *m.*

tripe *n.* tripe *f.* gras double *m.; Infml.* ventre *m.,* panse *f.;* bedaine *f.*

triple *adj.* triple *v.t.* tripler.

triplet *n.* trio *m.;* triplet *m.*

tripod *n.* trépied *m.*

trite *adj.* usé, rebattu, banal commun.

triumph *n.* triomphe *m.;* allégresse *f.* ~ *v.i.* triompher, prospérer, fleurir; ~ **over,** vaincre, l'emporter sur; surmonter, maîtriser.

triumphal *adj.* triomphal, de triomphe.

triumphant *adj.* triomphal, de triomphe, triomphant.

trivial *adj.* trivial; insignifiant, vulgaire.

triviality *n.* trivialité *f.;* insignifiance *f.*

troll *v.i.* pêcher au brochet à la ligne. *n.* troll *m.,* gnome *m.*

trombone *n.* trombone *n.*

troop *n.* troupe *f.;* compagnie *f.,* bande *f.;* foule *f.;* troupes *f.pl.* ~ *v.i.* s'attrouper, venir, aller en foule, marcher en corps.

trooper *n.* cavalier *m.,* soldat *m.* de cavalerie.

trophy *n.* trophée *m.*

tropic *n.* tropique *m.* **in the ~s,** sous les tropiques.

tropical *adj.* des tropiques, tropical.

trot *v.i.* trotter; aller au trot; courir. **to ~ along,** trotter. *n.* trot *m.*

troubadour *n.* troubadour *m.*

trouble *v.t.* troubler, agiter; déranger, importuner; inquiéter, affliger; ennuyer. **to ~ someone for something,** demander quelque chose à quelqu'un, prier quelqu'un de faire quelque chose. **to ~ oneself about,** s'inquiéter de. **it troubles me to see that,** ça m'embête de voir que. **don't ~ yourself,** ne vous dérangez pas. **may I ~ you to send me the book?** puis-je vous prier de m'envoyer le livre? *n.* peine *f.;* douleur *f.;* chagrin *m.,* affliction *f.,* mal *m.;* perplexité *f.;* souci, tourment *m.;* ennui *m.,* importunité *f.;* trouble *m.,* perturbation *f.* **to be in ~,** être dans la peine; avoir du chagrin. être dans l'inquiétude; être en peine. **to give ~,** donner de la peine à. **to take the ~ to,** prendre se donner la peine de. **it is not worth the ~,** cela n'en vaut pas la peine.

troubled *adj.* inquiet, tourmenté; peiné, chagriné, affligé; trouble. **~ waters,** eau trouble.

troublemaker *n. Infml.* mauvaise *f.* tête; provocateur *m.*

troublesome *adj.* ennuyeux; gênant, embarrassant; importun, fâcheux; à charge; fatigant, pénible, tracassier. **how ~!** que c'est ennuyeux! **~ visitors,** des importuns.

trough *n.* auge *f.;* auget *m.,* baquet *m.* **horse ~,** abreuvoir (pour chevaux).

trounce *v.t.* battre, rosser, étriller.

trousers *n. pl.* pantalon *m.* **a pair of ~,** un pantalon.

trout *n.* truite *f.*

trowel *n.* truelle *f.;* (garden) déplantoir *m.*

truant *adj.* fainéant, paresseux, flâneur. *n.* fainéant *m.,* paresseux *m.,* flâneur *m.;* vagabond *m.,* vaurien *m.;* truand *m.* **to play ~,** faire l'école buissonnière.

truce *n.* trève *f.;* relâche *f.*

truck *v.i., v.t.* transporter; *n.* camion *m.;* troc *m.,* échange *m.;* payement en marchandises. **~ driver,** routier *m.,* camionneur *m.;* **~-load,** plein camion *m.*

truculent *adj.* féroce, barbare; bagarreur *m.*

trudge *v.i.* cheminer, faire route à pied; marcher péniblement.

true *adj.* vrai; véritable; réel, fidèle, exact; sincère, loyal, véridique. **a ~ story,** une histoire vraie. **the ~ motive,** le vrai, le véritable motif. **a ~ witness,** un témoin véridique. **a ~ friend,** un ami loyal. **~ to one's word,** fidèle à sa parole. **a ~ copy,** une copie exacte, une copie conforme. **~ love,** bien-aimé *m.*

truffle *n.* truffe *f.*

truism *n.* axiome *m.,* vérité *f.* évidente; truisme *m.*

truly *adv.* vraiment, réellement; fidèlement; en vérité.

trump *n.* atout *m.;* triomphe *f.* **~ card,** retourne *f.;* atout *m.* **to play** ~s, jouer atout. *v.t.* couper avec l'atout, couper; tromper; imposer. **to** ~ **up,** inventer, forger. *v.i.* jouer atout.

trumpet *n.* trompette *f.* (instrument, porte-voix *m.;* trompette *m.* ~ *v.t.* trompeter; publier, proclamer.

trumpeter *n.* trompette *m.; Ornith.* trompette *f.*

truncate *v.t.* tronquer, mutiler.

trundle *n.* ~ **bed,** lit *m.* à roulettes. *v.i., v.t.* rouler.

trunk *n.* tronc *m.;* tige *f.;* buste (human body); *Paint. Sculpt.* torse *m.;* trompe *f.* (elephant); coffre *m.;* malle *f.* (luggage). **bathing** ~s, maillet *m.* de bain.

truss *n.* trousse *f.,* bandage *m.* herniaire, brayer *m.* ~ *v.t.* serrer, empaqueter; trousser, lier. **to** ~ **up,** lier, serrer, resserrer.

trust *n.* confiance *f.;* espérance *f.,* attente *f.;* charge *f.,* devoir *m.;* confidence *f.;* crédit *m.;* garde *f.; Law.* fidéicommis *m.;* trust *m.* **on** ~, de confiance; à crédit. **to hold in** ~, tenir, garder en dépôt. **to have in** ~, avoir sous sa garde. **to sell on** ~, vendre à crédit. *v.t.* se fier à, se confier à, avoir confiance; espérer faire crédit à. **he is not to be trusted,** on ne peut pas lui faire confiance. **to** ~ **in, on, to,** se fier à, se confier à, avoir confiance en; se reposer sur, compter.

trustee *n.* gardien *m.,* dépositaire *m.; Law.* fidéicommissaire *m.;* commissaire *m.;* administrateur *m.*

trustingly *adv.* avec confiance.

trusty *adj.* fidèle, loyal; digne de confiance.

truth *n.* vérité *f.;* vrai *m.;* véracité *f.;* loyauté *f.,* probité *f.,* honnêteté *f.;* fidélité *f.;* exactitude *f.* **to speak the** ~, dire la vérité. **to tell the** ~, à dire vrai.

truthful *adj.* véridique, vrai; plein de vérité.

try *v.i.* essayer, tâcher. *v.t.* faire l'épreuve de; expérimenter; tenter, mettre à l'épreuve; tâter, sonder; vérifier, affiner, purifier (metals); fatiguer; mettre en jugement. **to** ~ **on,** essayer. *n.* épreuve *f.;* essai *m.,* expérience *f.*

trying *adj.* d'épreuve; pénible, critique; fatigant; contrariant.

tub *n.* baignoire *f.;* baquet *m.,* cuve *f.;* tonneau *m.,* baril *m.*

tube *n.* tuyau *m.;* tube *m.; Anat.* conduit *m.,* canal *m.* **capillary** ~, tube capillaire. **Fallopian** ~s, trompes *f.pl.* de Fallope.

tuberculosis, T.B. *n.* tuberculose *f.*

tuck *n.* pli *m.,* rempli *m.* (in clothing). *v.t.* relever, retrousser, trousser. **to** ~ **in,** rentrer, border; couvrir.

Tuesday *n.* mardi *m.*

tuft *n.* touffe *f.;* aigrette *f.,* houppe *f.* ~ *v.t.* former en touffes; orner de touffes.

tug *v.t., v.i.* tirer avec effort; tirailler; arracher; lutter, se donner du mal. *n.* effort *m.* en tirant; tiraillement *m.* ~ **boat,** bateau *m.* remorqueur. **to give a** ~, tirer fort.

tuition *n.* frais d'inscription *m.pl.*

tulip *n.* tulipe *f.*

tumble *v.i.* se rouler; se tourner, retomber, descendre en roulant; s'écrouler, s'ébouler; sauter. **to** ~ **down,** dégringoler, s'écrouler. **to** ~ **into bed,** se jeter dans son lit. *v.t.* jeter (violemment), faire tomber; précipiter; déranger, bouleverser; bousculer. *n.* chute *f.;* dégringolade *f.* culbute *f.* **to take a** ~, faire une chute, tomber. ~**down,** *adj.* délabré, en ruine.

tumor *n.* tumeur *f.*

tumult *n.* tumulte *m.*

tumultuous *adj.* tumultueux.

tuna *n.* thon *m.*

tune *n.* air *m.;* ton *m.;* accord *m.;* harmonie *f.;* son *m.;* humeur *f.;* veine *f.* **to be in** ~, être d'accord. **to be out of** ~, être faux. **to sing in** ~, chanter juste. **to change one's** ~, changer de ton. **to the** ~ **of a hundred dollars,** pour la somme de cent dollars. *v.t.* accorder, mettre d'accord. **to** ~ **up an engine,** mettre un moteur au point. **to** ~ **in to a station,** accrocher un poste.

tuner *n.* accordeur *m.;* tuner *m.*

tune up *n.* mise au point.

tungsten *n.* tungstène *m.*

tunic *n.* tunique *f.*

tuning *n.* action d'accorder (instruments). ~ **fork,** diapason *m.*

tunnel *n.* tunnel *m.;* souterrain *m.* ~ *v.t.* percer; construire un tunnel.

turban *n.* turban *m.*

turbid *adj.* trouble, bourbeux, vaseux.

turbine *n.* turbine *f.*

turbo *pref.* ~**jet** *n.* turboréacteur *m.*

turbot *n.* turbot *m.*

turbulence *n.* turbulence *f.;* trouble *m.,* désordre *m.*

turbulent *adj.* turbulent; agité, en tumulte, tumultueux.

turf *n.* gazon *m.;* pelouse *f.;* turf *m.* (races), hippodrome *m.*

turgid *adj.* gonflé, turgide, turgescent, *Fig.* enflé, ampoulé.

Turk *n.* Turc *m.,* Turque *f.*

Turkey *npr.* Turquie *f.* ~ *Ornith.* dindon *m.*

Turkish *adj.* turc, turque, de Turquie, des Turcs.

turmoil *n.* confusion *n.f;* trouble *m.,* vacarme *m.,* peine *f.*

turn *v.t.* tourner, faire tourner; retourner; former; façonner; disposer; diriger vers, faire pencher, convertir, troubler; agiter. **to** ~ **a wheel,** tourner une roue. **to** ~ **one's back to,** tourner le dos à. **to** ~ **one's mind to,** diriger son esprit vers, s'occuper de. **to** ~ **to good account,** mettre à profit. **to** ~ **into gold,** changer en or. **to** ~ **around,** tourner, retourner; détourner. **to** ~ **aside,** détourner, éloigner, écarter. **to** ~ **away,** écarter; renvoyer. **to** ~ **back,** tourner en arrière; faire retourner; renvoyer. **to** ~ **down,** repousser, refuser, rejeter; retourner; défaire (bed); rabattre (collar). **to** ~ **from,** détourner de. **to** ~ **in,** tourner en dedans;

rendre. *Infml.* se coucher. **to ~ off**, éteindre, fermer. **to ~ on**, ouvrir, lâcher; allumer. **to ~ out**, renvoyer; mettre à la porte; s'avérer, se révéler. **to ~ over**, retourner, tourner, renverser; transférer; peser, réfléchir à. **to ~ over a new leaf.** *Fig.* changer de conduite. **to ~ over and over again**, tourner et retourner. **to ~ around**, tourner, retourner. **to ~ up**, tourner en haut; retourner; faire lever; relever (collar); retrousser; soulever (earth); apparaître. **to ~ up a card**, retourner une carte. **to ~ up one's nose at**, dédaigner. **to ~ on**, allumer; excite. **to ~ upside down**, bouleverser, mettre sens dessus dessous. *v.i.* se diriger vers, se gâter, se cailler, devenir sur; avoir recours à, s'adresser; se détourner, dévier; (se) changer, se faire, devenir. **to ~ in one's bed**, se retourner dans son lit. **to ~ red**, rougir, devenir rouge. **to ~ pale**, pâlir, devenir pâle. **to ~ around**, se tourner, se retourner. **to ~ aside**, s'écarter, s'éloigner. **to ~ away**, se détourner; s'éloigner. **to ~ back**, s'en retourner; revenir. **to ~ in**, entrer, rentrer, se coucher. **to ~ into**, entrer dans; se changer en. **to ~ off**, changer de route, tourner, faire un détour. **to ~ out**, éteindre; tourner en dehors; dévier, se trouver, être; devenir; finir par être. **to ~ out right**, finir bien; réussir. **to ~ over**, se tourner, se retourner; se renverser; verser (car accident); démarrer (engine). **to ~ around**, se retourner. **to ~ to**, tourner à; se diriger vers; se changer en; recourir à; s'y mettre. **to ~ up**, tourner en haut; se relever; se retrousser, être retroussé; (cards) retourner; devenir; arriver. **to ~ upon**, rouler sur; tendre à, rejaillir sur. *n.* tour *m.*, révolution *f.*; promenade *f.*; vicissitude *f.*; détour *m.*, coude *m.*; tournure (of phrase); service *m.*, office *m.*; occasion *f.* **by ~s, in ~s**, à tour à tour, à tour de rôle. **at every ~**, en toute occasion, à tout moment. **~coat**, renégat *m.* **~over**, chausson *m.* (pastry).

turning *n.* tour *m.*; mouvement *m.* (pour se retourner); coude *m.* (road, etc.); sinuosité *f.*; changement *m.* **~ of the tide**, changement de la marée. **~ point**, moment *m.* critique, point *m.* décisif.

turnip *n.* navet *m.*; rave *f.*

turnpike *n.* autoroute *f.*, route à péage.

turpentine *n.* térébenthine *f.*

turpitude *n.* turpitude *f.*

turret *n.* tourelle *f.*

turtle *n.* tortue *f.* **~dove**, tourterelle *f.*

tush, tushy *n.* derrière *m.*

tusk *n.* croc *m.* (animal); défense *f.* (éléphant, boar).

tussle *n.* lutte *f.*, bataille *f.*, bagarre *f.*

tutor *n.* précepteur *m.* **~** *v.t.* instruire, enseigner à.

tuxedo *n.* smoking *m.*

T.V. *n.* télé *f.*

twaddle *n.* caquetage *m.*; babillage *m.*; babil *m.*; sottises *f.pl.*, bêtises *f.pl.* **~** *v.i.* babiller, caqueter.

twang *v.i.*, *v.t.* faire vibrer *n.* son *m.* aigu, strident; accent *m.* nasillard.

tweak *v.t.* pincer, serrer entre les doigts; tirer.

tweezers *n.pl.* petites pinces *f.pl.*, pince *f.* à épiler.

twelfth *adj.* douzième; douze. **on the ~ of August**, le douze août. **~ Night**, l'Epiphanie *f.*, le jour *m.* des Rois, les Rois *m.pl.*

twelve adj. douze. *n.* douze *m.*; douzaine *f.*

twentieth *adj.* vingtième.

twenty adj. vingt.

twice *adv.* deux fois.

twiddle *n.* tortillement. *v.t.* tortiller.

twig *n.* petite branche *f.* brindille *f.*

twilight *n.* crépuscule *m.*, demi-jour *m.* **~** *adj.* sombre, imparfaitement éclairé.

twin *n.* jumeau *m.*, jumelle *f.*, *Astron.* Gémeaux *m.pl.* **~** *adj.* jumeau, jumelle, *Bot.* double, géminé. **~ brother**, frère jumeau. **~ sister**, soeur jumelle.

twine *v.t.* tordre; retordre, lisser. *v.i.* tourner; (s')enlacer, s'entrelacer, (s')enrouler, (s')unir, (se) lier. *n.* ficelle *f.*, fil *m.* retors; *Naut.* fil *m.* à voile.

twinge *v.t.* occasionner une douleur cuisante à, serrer, pincer, tirer. *v.i.* élancer, cuire. *n.* douleur *f.* aigue; *Fig.* remords *m.*

twinkle *v.i.* scintiller, étinceler; cligner.

twinkling *n.* scintillement *m.*, scintillation *f.*; clin *m.* d'oeil, clignotement *m.* **in the ~ of an eye**, en un clin d'oeil.

twirl *v.t.* (faire) tourner. *v.i.* tournoyer; pirouetter. *n.* rotation *f.*, révolution *f.*; tournoiement *m.*; pirouette *f.*; enroulement *m.*; tortillement *m.*

twist *v.t.* tordre; retordre, tourner de travers; tortiller; torturer, défigurer; filer, enlacer, entrelacer. **to ~ thread**, retordre du fil. **to ~ the neck of**, tordre le cou à. *v.i.* (s')entrelacer; s'enrouler, s'entortiller, (se) tordre. *n.* corde *f.*; cordon *m.*; cordonnet *m.*; torsion *f.*; torn *m.* ironique. **~ of lemon**, zeste *m.* de citron *f.*

twisted *adj.* tordu; tors.

twister *n.* tornade *f.*

twitch *v.t.* tirer brusquement; saisir, arracher. *v.i.* se contracter (from pain). *n.* tiraillement *m.*, élancement *m.*

twitter *n.* gazouillement *m.* **~** *v.i.* gazouiller.

two adj. deux. **~ by ~**, deux à deux, deux par deux. **~ to one**, deux contre un. *n.* deux *m.* **~-faced**, à deux faces, faux. **~-legged**, à deux jambes, à deux pieds, bipède.

twofold *adj.* double *adv.* doublement, deux fois.

tycoon *n.* magnat *m.*

type *n.* genre *m.*, sorte *f.*; signe *m.*, cachet *m.*, caractère *m.*, type *m.*, empreinte, modèle. **~writer**, machine *i.f.* à écrire, *v.i.* écrire à la machine, taper.

typhoid *adj.* typhoïde *f.*

typhoon *n.* typhon *m.*

typhus *n.* typhus *m.*

typically *adv.* d'une manière typique.

typify *v.t.* symboliser.

typographer n. imprimeur m. typographe.
typographical adj. typographique, typique, emblématique.
typography n. typographie.
tyrannical adj. tyrannique.

tyrannize v.i. faire le tyran. **to ~ over,** tyranniser.
tyranny n. tyrannie f.
tyrant n. tyran m.
tzar n. tzar m., czar m.

U

U n. U, u m. **U-turn,** demi-tour m.
udder n. mamelle f.; pis m.
U.F.O. (Unidentified Flying Object), ovni, objet m. volant non-identifié.
ugliness n. laideur f.
ugly adj. laid; vilain.
ulcer n. ulcère m.
ulcerate v.i. (s')ulcérer v.t. Méd. ulcérer.
ulceration n. ulcération f.
ulna n. cubitus m.
ulterior adj. ultérieur; postérieur, subséquent.
ultimate adj. dernier, extrême, final, définitif.
ultimately adv. à la fin, finalement.
ultimatum n. ultimatum m.
ultra adj. ultra n. ultra m. **~sound,** ultra-son m. **~violet, U.V.,** ultra-violet, U.V.
umber n. ombre f., terre f. d'ombre.
umbilical adj. ombilical.
umbilicus n. ombilic m.
umbrage n. ombrage m. **to take ~,** prendre ombrage.
umbrella n. parapluie m. **~ stand,** porte-parapluie m.
umpire n. arbitre m.; Law. tiers-arbitre m.
un prefix (neg.) non, peu.
U.N. abbr. **United Nations,** O.N.U., Organisation f. des Nations Unies.
unabashed adj. qui n'est pas confus; sans se déconcerter.
unabated adj. qui n'est pas abattu, non affaibli.
unabbreviated adj. non abrégé.
unable adj. incapable, impuissant.
unabridged adj. non abrégé.
unaccented adj. non accentué.
unacceptable adj. inacceptable.
unaccepted adj. inaccepté, non accepté.
unaccommodating adj. peu accomodant, désobligeant.
unaccompanied adj. seul, non-accompagné.
unaccomplished adj. incomplet; inachevé; sans talents.
unaccountable adj. inexplicable.
unaccustomed adj. inaccoutumé; peu habitué.
unacknowledged adj. non reconnu; inavoué, sans réponse (letter); non accrédité.
unacquainted adj. peu familiarisé avec; peu versé dans; peu familier avec.
unadapted adj. inadapté.
unadorned adj. sans ornements, sans parure.
unadulterated adj. non falsifié; pur, naturel.
unadventurous adj. timide; qui n'est pas aventureux.

unaffected adj. sans affectation; sincère, impassible.
unaffectionate adj. inaffectueux.
unaided adj. sans aide, sans secours.
unalterable adj. inaltérable, invariable.
unalterably adv. invariablement.
unaltered adj. sans altération; qui n'est pas changé.
unambiguous adj. clair, net.
unambitious adj. qui n'est pas ambitieux; sans prétention.
unanimity n. unanimité f.
unanimous adj. unanime.
unanimously adv. unanimement, à l'unanimité.
unannounced adj. sans être annoncé.
unanswerable adj. irréfutable; incontestable.
unanswered adj. sans réponse; incontesté.
unappreciated adj. qui n'est pas apprécié.
unapproachable adj. inabordable, inaccessible.
unarmed adj. désarmé, sans armes.
unasked adj. non demandé, non sollicité.
unassailable adj. inattaquable, hors d'atteinte.
unassisted adj. sans aide, sans secours, seul.
unassuming adj. modeste, sans prétention.
unattached adj. non attaché; Mil. en disponibilité.
unattackable adj. inattaquable.
unattainable adj. hors d'atteinte; inaccessible.
unattended adj. sans surveillance, qui n'est pas accompagné; négligé.
unattested adj. atteste, sans attestation.
unattractive adj. peu attrayant.
unauthenticated adj. qui n'est pas reconnu authentique; Law. non légalisé.
unauthorized adj. sans autorisation.
unavailable adj. indisponible.
unavoidable adj. inévitable.
unaware adj. ignorant, qui ignore, qui n'est pas au courant.
unawares adv. à l'improviste, inopinément; par mégarde. **to take ~,** prendre au dépourvu, à l'improviste.
unbalanced adj. sans contre-poids; Comm. qui n'est pas balancé.
unbearable adj. insupportable, intolérable.
unbeaten adj. qui n'est pas battu, non battu.
unbecoming adj. inconvenant; malséant, déplacé.
unbecomingly adv. déplacé; avec inconvenance.
unbefitting adj. qui ne convient pas, qui ne sied pas.

unbelief *n.* incrédulité *f.;* scepticisme.

unbeliever *n.* incrédule *m.;* incroyant *m.*

unbelieving *adj.* incrédule.

unbend *v.t.* débander (bow for shooting), détendre (rope); *Fig.* délasser, détendre (mind). *v.i.* se détendre; se redresser, se délasser.

unbending *adj.* qui ne fléchit pas; raide, inflexible.

unbiased *adj.* sans prévention; impartial.

unbidden *adj.* sans être sollicité; spontané; sans être invité.

unbind *v.t.* délier, desserrer, détacher.

unblemished *adj.* sans tache, sans souillure.

unbolt *v.t.* ouvrir, tirer le verrou de.

unborn *adj.* qui n'est pas encore né; à venir.

unbosom *v.t.* révéler, confier; découvrir.

unbound *adj.* délié, détaché; libre, non relié.

unbounded *adj.* illimité, sans bornes; effréné, sans mesure.

unbroken *adj.* non brisé, rompu; intact; non interrompu; indompté, non dressé (of horse); ferme, inflexible.

unbuckle *v.t.* déboucler.

unburden *v.t.* décharger, alléger.

unburied *adj.* sans sépulture, non enterré.

unburnt *adj.* non brûlé, non consumé.

unbutton *v.t.* déboutonner.

uncalled-for *adj.* injustifié, déplacé.

uncared-for *adj.* négligé, abandonne.

unceasing *adj.* incessant; sans relâche.

unceasingly *adv.* sans cesse, incessamment.

unceremonious *adj.* sans cérémonie, sans façon; sans gêne.

unceremoniously *adv.* sans cérémonie, sans façon.

uncertain *adj.* incertain.

uncertainty *n.* incertitude *f.;* éventualité *f.*

uncertified *adj.* non certifié.

unchain *v.t.* déchaîner, affranchir, delivrer.

unchallenged *adj.* sans être provoqué.

unchangeable *adj.* invariable; immuable.

unchanged *adj.* qui n'est pas changé; invariable.

unchanging *adj.* invariable; inaltérable.

uncharitable *adj.* qui n'est pas charitable.

unchecked *adj.* non réprimé, sans frein, effréné; qui n'est pas vérifié, collationné.

uncircumscribed *adj.* non circonscrit.

uncivil *adj.* impoli, malhonnête.

uncivilized *adj.* non civilisé, incivilisé.

unclad *adj.* nu, non vêtu.

unclaimed *adj.* non réclamé.

unclasp *v.t.* dégrafer; ouvrir le fermoir de, détacher; desserrer.

uncle *n.* oncle *m.*

unclean *adj.* sale, malpropre; impur, immonde.

unclouded *adj.* clair, sans nuages.

uncoil *v.t.* dérouler; détortiller.

uncombed *adj.* non peigné; mal peigné.

uncomfortable *adj.* mal à son aise, gêné; gênant, incommode; inquiet; désolé; malheureux.

uncomfortably *adv.* mal à l'aise; sans aisance; incommmodément; fâcheusement; tristement; avec inquiétude.

uncommitted *adj.* non commis; non compromis.

uncommon *adj.* non commun; peu ordinaire; extraordinaire.

uncommonly *adv.* peu communément; extraordinairement.

uncommunicated *adj.* non communiqué.

uncommunicative *adj.* peu communicatif.

uncompensated *adj.* sans compensation.

uncomplaining *adj.* qui ne se plaindre.

uncomplimentary *adj.* peu flatteur.

uncompromising *adj.* peu disposé à transiger; inflexible, intraitable, ferme.

unconcealed *adj.* non caché.

unconcern *n.* indifférence *f.,* insouciance *f.*

unconcerned *adj.* indifférent, désintéressé.

unconditional *adj.* sans condition; sans réserve.

unconditionally *adv.* sans condition, absolument.

unconfirmed *adj.* non confirmé; qui ne se confirme pas.

uncongenial *adj.* peu sympathique.

unconnected *adj.* sans liaison, non joint; sans rapport, décousu.

unconquerable *adj.* invincible, insurmontable.

unconscionable *adj.* déraisonnable, démesuré; sans conscience.

unconscionably *adv.* déraisonnablement; sans conscience.

unconscious *adj.* inconscient; **(of)** ignorant de, ne se doutant pas; sans connaissance; innocent.

unconsciously *adv.* conscience; sans le savoir, involontairement.

unconsciousness *n.* inconscience *f.;* ignorance *f.;* insensibilité *f.*

unconsidered *adj.* non consideré; sans examen, inconsidéré; inaperçu.

unconstitutional *adj.* inconstitutionnel.

unconstitutionally *adv.* inconstitutionnellement.

unconstrained *adj.* sans contrainte; volontaire; spontane.

uncontaminated *adj.* sans souillure.

uncontested *adj.* incontesté.

uncontrollable *adj.* indomptable; irrésistible.

uncontrollably *adv.* irrésistiblement.

uncontrolled *adj.* sans contrôle; sans frein.

unconvinced *adj.* non convaincu, non persuadé.

unconvincing *adj.* qui n'est pas convaincant.

uncork *v.t.* déboucher.

uncorrected *adj.* qui n'est pas corrigé.

uncorrupted *adj.* qui n'est pas corrompu.

uncouth *adj.* lourd, bourru, grossier.

uncover *v.t.* découvrir; déshabiller; (se) découvrir.

uncrowded *adj.* qui n'est pas pressé (par la foule); libre.

unction *n.* onction *f.;* baume *m.*

unctuous *adj.* onctueux, huileux.

uncultivated *adj.* inculte; *Fig.* ignorant, grossier.

uncurl *v.t.* dérouler; déboucler, défriser. *v.i.* se défaire; flotter, se dérouler.

uncut *adj.* non coupé, non taillé.

undamaged *adj.* en bon état; *Comm.* non avarié.

undated *adj.* sans date.

undaunted *adj.* intrépide, déterminé.

undecayed *adj.* non pourri, non corrompu; sain, intact.

undeceive *v.t.* détromper, désabuser.

undecided *adj.* indécis; incertain, irrésolu.

undecipherable *adj.* indéchiffrable.

undefended *adj.* sans défense; qui n'est pas défendu.

undefiled *adj.* pur, sans tache, sans souillure.

undefined *adj.* non défini.

undelivered *adj.* non délivré.

undeniable *adj.* indéniable, incontestable.

undeniably *adv.* incontestablement, sans contredit.

under *prep.* sous, dessous; au-dessous, soumis à; au-dessous de; inférieur à. ~ **the table,** sous la table. ~ **lock and key,** sous clef. **to bring ~,** soumettre, assujettir. ~ **fifteen,** au-dessous de quinze ans. ~ **consideration,** en considération. *adv.* dessous, au-dessous; à moins. *adj.* de dessous, inférieur, subalterne; sous; subordonné; bas. **an ~garment,** un sous-vêtement. ~**bid,** *n.* mineur *m.* ~**bid,** *v.t.* offrir moins qu'un autre. ~**brush,** *n.* broussailles. ~**clothes,** *n.pl.* sous-vêtements *m.pl.* ~**current,** *n.* courant *m.* sous-marin. ~**done,** *adj.* pas assez cuit; saignant. ~**dressed,** *adj.* pas assez bien mis. ~**foot,** *adv.* sous pied. ~**graduate,** *n.* étudiant *m.* ~**ground,** *adj.* souterrain. ~**handed,** *adj.*, *adv.* clandestin; secret; caché; sous main, clandestinement. ~**line,** *v.t.* souligner. ~**paid,** *adj.* sous-payé, mal payé.

undergo *v.t.* subir; souffrir, endurer, supporter; être sous le coup de. **to ~ fatigue,** supporter la fatigue. **to ~ an operation,** subir une opération.

underling *n.* subalterne *m.,* inférieur *m.*

underlying *adj.* sous-jacent.

undermine *v.t.* détruire peu à peu.

underneath *adv.* dessous, au-dessous, en dessous, par-dessous; ci-dessous, là-dessous. *prep.* sous, au-dessous de, par-dessous.

underpants *n.pl.* caleçon *m.,* slip *m.* (men's); culotte *f.* (women's).

underrate *v.t.* estimer au-dessous de la valeur; déprécier, rabaisser.

undersell *v.t.* vendre a plus bas prix que, vendre meilleur marché que.

undersigned *adj.* soussigné. *n.* soussigné *m.*

understand *v.t.* comprendre, entendre; apprendre, connaître; être informe. **do you ~?** comprenez-vous? **to ~ one another,** se comprendre, s'entendre. *v.i.* concevoir; être instruit

de; savoir. **I ~ that,** j'apprends que, on me dit que.

understanding *n.* intelligence *f.;* entendement *m.;* compréhension *f.;* accord *m.;* entente *f.* **there is a good ~ between them,** ils sont on bonne intelligence, ils s'entendent bien. **to come to an ~ with,** s'entendre avec, en venir à un arrangement/accord avec.

understate *v.t.* ne pas assez dire, atténuer, diminuer, donner un chiffre trop bas.

undertake *v.t.* s'engager à faire. *v.i.* entreprendre (de), (se) charger (de), prendre sur soi, assumer.

undertaker *n.* entrepreneur *m.* de pompes funèbres.

undertaking *n.* entreprise *f.*

undervalue *v.t.* estimer trop bas, évaluer au-dessous, de la valeur réelle, déprécier.

underwrite *v.t.* souscrire; assurer. *v.i.* faire des assurances.

underwriter *n.* assureur *m.*

undeserved *adj.* immérité; injuste.

undeservedly *adv.* à tort, injustement.

undeserving *adj.* indigne (de); sans mérite.

undesirable *adj.* peu désirable.

undesired *adj.* qu'on ne désire pas.

undetected *adj.* non découvert; inaperçu.

undetermined *adj.* indéterminé; indécis; irrésolu.

undeterred *adj.* qui n'est pas effrayé/arrêté.

undeveloped *adj.* qui n'est pas développé.

undigested *adj.* non digéré, indigeste.

undignified *adj.* sans dignité; vulgaire.

undiluted *adj.* non délayé; sans eau.

undiminished *adj.* qui n'est pas diminué.

undiplomatic *adj.* qui n'est pas diplomatique.

undirected *adj.* sans direction.

undiscerning *adj.* peu judicieux; sans discernement.

undisciplined *adj.* indiscipliné; sans discipline.

undisclosed *adj.* non découvert; non révélé.

undiscouraged *adj.* non découragé.

undiscovered *adj.* non découvert; inconnu.

undisguised *adj.* non déguisé, sans déguisement.

undismayed *adj.* sans peur, non effrayé.

undisputed *adj.* incontesté; sans conteste.

undissolved *adj.* non dissous, non fondu.

undistinguished *adj.* sans distinction.

undisturbed *adj.* non troublé, impassible.

undivided *adj.* entier, indivisé.

undo *v.t.* défaire, détacher, délier, ouvrir; perdre, ruiner. **to ~ a knot,** défaire un noeud. **to leave undone,** ne pas faire.

undoing *n.* ruine *f.,* perte *f.*

undoubted *adj.* indubitable; hors de doute.

undoubtedly *adv.* indubitablement.

undress *v.t.* déshabiller. **to ~ oneself,** se déshabiller.

undressed *adj.* négligé, en déshabillé; écru, non appêté.

undrinkable *adj.* non potable, non buvable.

undue *adj.* irrégulier; indu; exagéré.

undulate *v.i.* endoyer. *v.t.* faire onduler; moduler (sounds).

undulation *n.* ondulation *f.*

unduly *adv.* indûment; trop, à l'excès.

undutiful *adj.* désobéissant, indocile; irrespectueux.

undying *adj.* impérissable, immortel.

unearned *adj.* immérité; non gâgné.

unearth *v.t.* déterrer.

unearthly *adj.* qui n'est pas terrestre; surnaturel.

uneasily *adv.* difficilement; mal à l'aise; avec gêne.

uneasiness *n.* inquiétude *f.*; peine *f.*, difficulté *f.*, malaise *m.*

uneasy *adj.* inquiet; mal à son aise; incommode; désagréable.

uneducated *adj.* sans éducation; sans instruction.

unembarrassed *adj.* sans embarras; non gêné; à l'aise.

unemployed *adj.* non employé; sans emploi; dormant (du capital).

unencumbered *adj.* non encombré; non grevé.

unending *adj.* sans fin.

unendurable *adj.* intolérable.

unenlightened *adj.* non éclairé; peu éclairé, ignorant.

unenviable *adj.* peu enviable.

unequal *adj.* inégal; inférieur; au-dessous de, insuffisant; disproportionné.

unequaled *adj.* sans égal; qui n'a pas son pareil.

unequally *adj.* inégalement.

unequivocal *adj.* non équivoque.

unequivocally *adv.* sans équivoque.

unerring *adj.* infaillible.

unerringly *adv.* infailliblement.

uneven *adj.* inégal; variable, irrégulier.

unevenly *adv.* inégalement.

uneventful *adj.* peu fecond en événements; monotone, peu accidenté.

unexaggerated *adj.* qui n'est pas exageré.

unexampled *adj.* sans exemple.

unexcelled *adj.* qui n'est pas surpassé.

unexceptionable *adj.* irréprochable; irrécusable.

unexceptionably *adv.* irréprochablement.

unexpected *adj.* inattendu; imprévu.

unexpectedly *adv.* d'une manière inattendu; à l'improviste.

unexpired *adj.* non expiré.

unexplainable *adj.* inexplicable.

unexplained *adj.* non expliqué; inexpliqué.

unexplored *adj.* inexploré.

unexposed *adj.* qui n'a pas été exposé.

unexpressed *adj.* inexprimé; sous-entendu.

unfaded *adj.* non fané, non flétri.

unfailing *adj.* inépuisable; infaillible, immanquable.

unfair *adj.* injuste, sans probité.

unfairly *adv.* injustement.

unfairness *n.* injustice *f.*

unfaithful *adj.* infidèle; déloyal.

unfaithfully *adv.* infidèlement; déloyalement.

unfaithfulness *n.* infidélité *f.*, déloyauté *f.*

unfaltering *adj.* qui n'hésite pas.

unfamiliar *adj.* peu familier.

unfashionable *adj.* démodé; qui ne suit pas la mode.

unfasten *v.t.* défaire, détacher; desserrer.

unfathomable *adj.* insondable.

unfavorable *adj.* defavorable.

unfavorably *adv.* défavorablement.

unfed *adj.* sans nourriture; non nourri.

unfeeling *adj.* insensible; impitoyable, sans pitié.

unfeelingly *adv.* cruellement, sans pitié; froidement.

unfeigned *adj.* sincère, qui n'est pas feint.

unfeignedly *adv.* sincèrement, sans feinte.

unfinished *adj.* inachevé.

unfit *adj.* inapte (**for**) peu propre à; pas fait pour; incapable de; (**to**) peu fait pour; peu convenable. *v.t.* rendre incapable (de), rendre peu propre (à).

unfitness *n.* incapacité *f.*; inaptitude *f.*; inconvenance *f.*; manque *m.* d'à-propos.

unfitting *adj.* inconvenant.

unfold *v.t.* ouvrir; déplier; déployer; développer; dévoiler; exposer; expliquer. ~ **your arms,** ouvrez vos bras. **to ~ a napkin,** déplier une serviette.

unforced *adj.* sans être forcé; naturel, simple; facile.

unforeseen *adj.* imprévu.

unforgiving *adj.* qui ne pardonne pas; implacable.

unforgotten *adj.* non oublié.

unfortunate *adj.* infortuné; malheureux.

unfortunately *adv.* malheureusement.

unfounded *adj.* sans fondement, sans preuve.

unfrequented *adj.* peu fréquenté.

unfriendly *adj.* peu amical; hostile.

unfruitful *adj.* infertile; infructueux, stérile.

unfruitfulness *n.* infertilité *f.*; stérilité *f.*; infécondité *f.*

unfulfilled *adj.* non accompli; inexécuté.

unfunded *adj.* Fin. non consolidé.

unfurl *v.t.* déployer; Naut. déferler.

unfurnished *adj.* non meublé.

ungainly *adj.* gauche, maladroit; sans grâce.

ungenerous *adj.* peu généreux; mesquin.

ungenerously *adv.* peu généreux.

ungentlemanly *adj.* qui n'est pas d'un homme comme il faut; peu distingué; qui ne sait pas vivre.

unglue *v.t.* décoller.

ungodly *adj.* impie, irréligieux.

ungovernable *adj.* ingouvernable, indomptable; désordonné.

ungraceful *adj.* disgracieux, sans grâce.

ungracious *adj.* disgracieux, déplaisant; peu aimable.

ungraciously *adv.* d'une manière peu gracieuse; disgracieusement; mal.

ungrammatical *adj.* incorrect, contraire aux régles grammaticales.

ungrammatically *adv.* contre la grammaire.

ungrateful *adj.* ingrat; désagréable, qui n'est pas reconnaissant.

ungratefully *adv.* avec ingratitude, sans reconnaissance.

ungrounded *adj.* sans fondements, mal fondé.

ungrudging *adj.* qui donne de bon coeur.

ungrudgingly *ad.* de bon coeur.

unguarded *adj.* non gardé; sans défense; imprudent; inconsidéré; irréfléchi.

unhang *v.t.* décrocher, détacher; démonter.

unhappily *adv.* malheureusement.

unhappiness *n.* malheur *m.*

unhappy *adj.* malheureux.

unharmed *adj.* sain et sauf, non blessé.

unhealthy *adj.* maladif; malsain, insalubre.

unheard *adj.* sans être entendu; inconnu, ignoré. ~ **of**, inouï, sans précédent.

unheeded *adj.* négligé, inaperçu.

unheeding *adj.* inattentif, distrait.

unhelpful *adj.* qui n'aide pas; inutile; vain, stérile.

unhesitating *adj.* qui n'hésité pas; résolu; prompt.

unhesitatingly *adv.* sans hésiter.

unhinge *v.t.* ôter des gonds; démonter; *Fig.* mettre en colère; bouleverser, déranger.

unholy *adj.* profane; impie; impur.

unhook *v.t.* décrocher.

unhurt *adj.* sans blessure, intact; sain et sauf.

unicorn *n.* licorne *f.*

unification *n.* unification *f.*

uniform *adj., n.* uniforme *m.*

uniformity *n.* uniformité *f.*

uniformly *n.* uniformément.

unify *v.t.* unifier.

unimaginable *adj.* inimaginable.

unimpaired *adj.* entier; non détérioré; en bon état.

unimpeachable *adj.* irréprochable; inattaquable.

unimpeded *adj.* sans obstacle.

unimportance *n.* peu *m.* d'importance.

unimportant *adj.* peu important.

unimposing *adj.* peu imposant.

unimpressed *adj.* non gravé; sans être touché.

unimpressive *adj.* peu impressif, peu touchant.

unimproved *adj.* non amélioré, non perfectionné; qui n'a pas fait de progrès; dont on ne tire pas parti, sans culture; non exploité.

uninfluenced *adj.* non influencé; sans prévention.

uninfluential *adj.* sans influence, peu influent.

uninformed *adj.* ignorant, non instruit; sans instruction.

uninhabitable *adj.* inhabitable.

uninhabited *adj.* inhabité; sans habitants.

uninitiated *adj.* non initié.

uninjured *adj.* non endommagé; intact; sans blessure; sain et sauf.

uninspired *adj.* non inspiré, sans inspiration.

uninsured *adj.* pas assuré.

unintelligent *adj.* inintelligent.

unintelligible *adj.* inintelligible.

unintended, unintentional *adj.* pas intentionnel; non prémédité; involontaire.

unintentionally *adv.* sans intention.

uninterested *adj.* désintéressé.

uninteresting *adj.* peu intéressant.

uninterrupted *adj.* ininterrompu, sans interruption.

uninterruptedly *adv.* sans interruption.

uninvited *adj.* qui n'est pas invité, sans invitation.

union *n.* union *f.;* réunion *f.;* accord *m.,* harmonie *f.* **trade ~**, association *f.* des ouvriers, syndicat *m.*

European Union (E.U.), Union Européen (U.E.).

unique *adj.* unique.

uniquely *adv.* d'une manière unique.

unison *n.* unisson *m.*

unit *n.* unité *f.*

Unitarian *n.* unitaire *m.* *adj.* unitaire.

Unitarianism *n.* unitarianisme, unitarisme *m.*

unite *v.t.* unir; réunir; joindre, attacher. *v.i.* s'unir; (se) joindre; s'allier, s'associer; (se) réunir.

united *adj.* uni; réuni; joint; attaché. **the United Kingdom,** le Royaume-Uni. **the United States,** les Etats-Unis.

unity *n.* unité *f.,* union *f.,* concorde *f.*

universal *adj.* universel.

universally *adv.* universellement.

universe *n.* univers *m.*

university *n.* université *f.*

unjust *adj., n.* injuste.

unjustifiable *adj.* injustifiable; inexcusable.

unjustifiaby *adv.* d'une manière injustifiable.

unjustified *adj.* non justifié.

unjustly *adv.* injustement.

unkind *adj.* peu aimable; désobligeant; cruel.

unkindly *adj.* malveillant; malfaisant. *adv.* sans bienveillance; froidement; durement; cruellement.

unkindness *n.* malveillance *f.;* manque *m.* d'amabilité; méchanceté *f.*

unknowing *adj.* ignorant.

unknowingly *adv.* non sciemment, sans le savoir; par ignorance.

unknown *adj.* inconnu; ignoré. ~ **to**, inconnu de; sans qu'on le sache; à l'insu de. ~ **to me,** à mon insu.

unladylike *adj.* vulgaire.

unlamented *adj.* non pleuré, non regretté.

unlatch *v.t.* ouvrir, lever le loquet de.

unlawful *adj.* illégal; illicite; illégitime.

unlawfully *adv.* illégalement.

unlearn *v.t.* désapprendre.

unlearned *adj.* ignorant, illettré; non appris (des choses).

unleavened *adj.* sans levain; azyme.

unless *conj.* à moins que; excepté, si ce n'est. ~ **they come,** à moins qu'ils ne viennent.

unlettered *adj.* illettré, sans instruction.

unlicensed *adj.* non autorisé; sans authorisation; illicite; sans patente, non patenté.

unlike *adj.* dissemblable, différent, invraisemblable. *prep.* contrairement à, à la difference de.

unlikely *adj.* invraisemblable; peu probable. **it is very ~,** c'est fort peu probable. *adv.* invraisemblablement.

unlimited *adj.* sans limites; indéterminé.

unload *v.t.* décharger, alléger.

unlock *v.t.* ouvrir (une porte fermée à clef).

unloved *adj.* qui n'est pas aimé.

unloving *adj.* peu aimant, froid.

unluckily *adv.* malheureusement, par malheur.

unlucky *adj.* malheureux; infortuné; malencontreux.

unmanageable *adj.* ingouvernable, indocile; difficile à gouverner; intraitable, indomptable.

unmannerly *adj.* mal élevé, grossier, mal appris. *adv.* grossièrement, malhonnêtement; avec mauvais goût.

unmarked non marqué; sans marque.

unmarketable *adj.* invendable.

unmarriageable *adj.* non mariable.

unmarried *adj.* non marié; celibataire.

unmask *v.t.* démasquer; dévoiler, découvrir. *v.i.* (se) démasquer, lever le masque.

unmatched *adj.* sans égal; unique, incomparable.

unmentionable *adj.* dont il ne peut être fait mention.

unmentioned *adj.* non désigné, ignoré, inconnu.

unmerciful *adj.* sans miséricorde, cruel; impitoyable.

unmercifully *adv.* sans miséricorde, sans pitié.

unmerited *adj.* non mérité; immérité.

unmistakable *adj.* sur quoi on ne peut se méprendre; évident.

unmixed *adj.* sans mélange.

unmotherly *adj.* indigne d'une mère.

unmoved *adj.* immobile, inébranlable; impassible, froid.

unnamed *adj.* non nommé.

unnatural *adj.* contraire à la nature, contre nature, dénaturé.

unnaturally *adj.* contre nature.

unnavigable *adj.* non navigable.

necessarily *adv.* sans nécessité, inutilement.

unnecessary *adj.* inutile.

unnerve *v.t.* énerver; affaiblir.

unnoticed *adj.* inaperçu, sans être remarqué.

unnumbered *adj.* non numéroté, innombrable.

unobjectionable *adj.* irréprochable, irrécusable.

unobserved *adj.* inaperçu.

unobservant *adj.* qui n'observe pas, inattentif.

unobstructed *adj.* non obstrué.

unobtainable *adj.* qui ne peut pas être obtenu.

unobtrusive *adj.* discret, modeste, réservé.

unoccupied *adj.* non occupé; inoccupé; disponible.

unofficial *adj.* non officiel.

unopened *adj.* fermé, non ouvert; (lettre) cachetée.

unopposed *adj.* sans opposition.

unorganized *adj.* non organizé.

unorthodox *adj.* hétérodoxe, peu orthodoxe.

unpack *v.t.* déballer, dépaqueter.

unpaid *adj.* non payé.

unpainted *adj.* qui n'est pas peint.

unpalatable *adj.* désagréable au goût.

unparalleled *adj.* sans pareil, sans égal, incomparable.

unpardonnable *adj.* impardonnable.

unpleasant *adj.* déplaisant, désagréable.

unpleasantly *adv.* d'une manière désagréable.

unpleasantness *n.* désagrément *m.*

unpolished *adj.* non pli; dépoli; mat, grossier, rude.

unpolluted *adj.* non profané; sans souillure, pur.

unpopular *adj.* impopulaire.

unprecedented *adj.* sans précédent.

unprejudiced *adj.* sans préjugés; sans préventions.

unpremeditated *adj.* sans préméditation; improvisé.

unprepared *adj.* sans être préparé; sans préparation.

unprepossessing *adj.* peu engageant; qui n'est pas prévenant.

unpresentable *adj.* peu présentable.

unprincipled *adj.* sans principes; sans mœurs, immoral.

unproductive improductif.

unprofessional *adj.* non professionnel.

unprofitable *adj.* peu profitable; sans profit; inutile.

unprofitableness *n.* inutilité *f.;* nature peu profitable.

unprofitably *adv.* sans profit.

unpromising *adj.* qui donne peu d'espoir; qui s'annonce mal; ingrat.

unpronouncable *adj.* imprononçable.

unpropitious *adj.* peu propice, contraire.

unprotected *adj.* non protégé; sans protection.

unprovoked *adj.* non provoqué; sans provocation.

unpublished *adj.* non publié; inédit.

unpunished *adj.* impuni.

unqualified *adj.* **(for).** peu propre à, incapable de; non autorisé, qui n'a pas l'autorisation nécessaire; entier; sans restriction; formel.

unquenchable *adj.* insatiable.

unquestionable *adj.* incontestable; indubitable.

unquestionably *adv.* incontestablement, sans contredit.

unquestioned *adj.* incontesté, hors de doute; sans être questionné.

unquiet *adj.* inquiet; agité; turbulent.

unquietly *adv.* avec inquietude.

unravel *v.t.* démêler, débrouiller; dénouer. *v.i.* (se) démêler; (se) dénouer; *Fig.* se débrouiller.

unraveling *n.* dénouement *m.;* éclaircissement *m.*

unreadable *adj.* illisible; ennuyeux à lire.

unready *adj.* qui n'est pas prêt, non préparé; sans empressement; peu vif, lent; maladroit.

unreal *adj.* non réel; faux; vain, chimérique.

unreasonable *adj.* déraisonnable; extravagent; immodéré, excessif.

unreasonableness *n.* absurdité *f.;* extravagence *f.*

unreasonably *adv.* sans raison; déraisonablement; avec extravagence.

unrefined *adj.* non raffiné, non purifié; non épuré; brut, grossier, peu raffiné.

unregulated *adj.* non réglé, non ordonné.

unrehearsed *adj.* non répété.

unrelated *adj.* (to) sans parenté avec, sans rapport.

unrelenting *adj.* implacable, sans pitié, impitoyable; inexorable.

unreliable *adj.* indigne de confiance.

unrelieved *adj.* non soulagé, adouci; sans secours.

unremarkable *adj.* peu remarquable.

unremarked *adj.* inaperçu.

unremitting *adj.* sans relâche, incessant; infatigable.

unremittingly *adv.* sans relâche, sans cesse.

unrepentant *adj.* impénitent, sans repentir.

unrequited *adj.* non payé de retour; méconnu.

unreserved *adj.* sans réserve; expansif.

unreservedly *adv.* sans réserve; ouvertement.

unresisted *adj.* sans résistance.

unresisting *adj.* qui ne résiste pas.

unresolved *adj.* irrésolu; sans solution.

unrest *n.* inquiétude *f.;* agitation *f.*

unrestored *adj.* non rendu; non restauré; non rétabli, non guéri.

unrestrained *adj.* non contenu; sans contrainte, sans frein, effréné.

unrestricted *adj.* sans restriction.

unrewarded *adj.* non récompensé; sans récompense.

unrighteous *adj.* injuste, inique.

unrighteousness *n.* injustice *f.;* iniquité *f.*

unripe *adj.* vert; qui n'est pas mûr; précoce, prématuré.

unrivaled *adj.* sans rival; sans pareil, incomparable.

unroll *v.t.* dérouler; déployer, ouvrir.

unromantic *adj.* peu romanesque; peu romantique.

unruliness *n.* déreglement *m.,* indiscipline *f.*

unruly *adj.* turbulent, ingouvernable; indisciplinable; désordonné; fougueux.

unsafe *adj.* dangereux, peu sûr; hasardeux, périlleux.

unsaid *adj.* non dit. **to leave ~,** ne pas dire, taire.

unsalted *adj.* non salé, frais.

unsanctioned *adj.* non sanctionné.

unsatisfactorily *adv.* d'une manière peu satisfaisante.

unsatisfactory *adj.* peu satisfaisant.

unsatisfied *adj.* non satisfait; non rassasié; inassouvi.

unsatisfying *adj.* peu satisfaisant; insuffisant.

unsavory *adj.* fade, insipide, sans saveur; désagréable, déplaisant.

unscarred *adj.* sans cicatrices.

unscathed *adj.* intact; sain et sauf.

unscientific *adj.* peu scientifique.

unscratched *adj.* non gratté; non égratiné.

unscrew *v.t.* devisser.

unscrupulous *adj.* peu scrupuleux.

unscrupulously *adv.* sans scrupules.

unscrupulousness *n.* manque *m.* de scrupules.

unsearchable *adj.* unscrutable; impénétrable.

unseasonable *adj.* hors de saison; mal à propos, inopportun, intempestif, indu.

unseemliness *n.* inconvenance *f.;* indécence *f.*

unseemly *adj.* inconvenant, indécent.

unseen *adj.* inaperçu; invisible.

unselfish *adj.* désintéressé; peu égoiste.

unsettle *v.t.* déranger, ébranler, troubler, agiter, bouleverser. *v.i.* (se) déranger; s'embranler.

unsettled *adj.* instable, non fixé; dérangé; troublé; irrésolu; bouleversé; variable (weather).

unshaken *adj.* ferme, inébranlable.

unshod *adj.* déchaussé; (foot) nu, (horse) déferré.

unsightliness *n.* laideur *f.,* difformité *f.*

unsightly *adj.* laid, difforme.

unskilled *adj.* inhabile, maladroit; peu versé.

unsociable *adj.* insociable; pen communicatif.

unsociably *adv.* insociablement; en sauvage.

unsocial *adj.* insocial.

unsold *adj.* non vendu; invendu.

unsolicited *adj.* non sollicité.

unsolved *adj.* non résolu, sans solution.

unsophisticated *adj.* simple.

unsought *adj.* qu'on n'a pas cherché; spontané.

unsound *adj.* peu sain; défectueux, en mauvais état; malsain; maladif; faux, erroné, non orthodoxe, peu solide.

unsoundness *n.* mauvais état, état malsain; fausseté *f.;* erreur *f.;* vice *m.;* défaut *m.* de solidité; faiblesse *f.*

unsparing *adj.* prodigue, généreux; impitoyable, sans pitié.

unsparingly *adv.* avec profusion.

unspeakable *adj.* inexprimable, indicible; ineffable; *Bibl.* inénarrable.

unspeakably adv. d'une manière inexprimable, indicible.

unspecified adj. non spécifié.

unspent adj. non dépensé; non épuisé.

unspoiled adj. non dépouillé; non gâté; intact; non ruiné.

unspotted adj. pur, sans tache.

unstable adj. instable, mobile; changeant; irrésolu, indécis.

unstained adj. sans tache, non souillé; non teint.

unsteadily adv. sans fermeté; sans assurance; irrésolument; avec légèreté; irrégulierement.

unsteadiness n. manque m. de fermeté; faiblesse f.; instabilité f.; peu m. d'assurance; irrésolution f., mobilité f.; irrégularité f.

unsteady adj. peu solide, chancelant, vacillant; peu sûr; changeant, variable; irrégulier.

unstring v.t. délier; ôter les cordes de; désenfiler (pearls).

unsuccessful adj. malheureux; qui ne réussit pas; sans succès.

unsuccessfully adv. sans réussir.

unsuitable adj. mal adapté, non approprié; peu propre; peu sortable; déplacé, inconvenant.

unsuitableness n. incompatibilité f.; inconvenance f.; incongruité f.

unsuitably adv. peu approprié; avec inconvenance.

unsuited adj. mal approprié; peu convenable; mal assorti.

unsullied adj. sans tache; non terni; pur, sans souillure.

unsupported adj. sans support, sans soutien; non soutenu.

unsure adj. peu sûr, incertain.

unsurpassed adj. non surpassé.

unsuspected adj. non soupçonné; non suspect.

unsuspecting adj. qui ne soupçonne pas; sans soupçons.

unsuspectingly adv. sans soupçon.

unsuspicious adj. sans soupçons; qui ne soupçonne pas; confiant.

unswerving adj. ferme, inébranlable.

unsympathetic adj. sans sympathie.

unsystematic adj. sans système.

untamed adj. non apprivoisé; indompté, insoumis.

untarnished adj. non terni; sans tache, sans souillure.

unteachable adj. indocile; qui ne peut rien apprendre.

untenable adj. intenable; insoutenable.

untended adj. non gardé; non soigné.

untested adj. non éprouvé.

unthinkable adj. impensable, inimaginable.

unthinking adj. irréfléchi, inconsidéré; étourdi.

unthinkingly adv. inconsidérément, sans réfléchir.

untidily adv. sans soin, sans ordre.

untidiness n. malpropreté f.; désordre m.

untidy adj. malpropre, sans soin.

untie v.t. dénouer; délier, détacher; démêler.

until prep. jusqu'à, jusque, avant. ~ **now**, jusqu'ici. ~ **tomorrow**, jusqu'à demain. conj. jusqu'à ce que, en attendant que; que; avant que. ~ **they come,** en attendant qu'ils viennent.

untimely adj. prématuré; inopportun, mal à propos. adv. prématurément; avant le temps; mal à propos.

untiring adj. infatigable.

unto prep. See TO.

untold adj. qu'on ne dit pas; non raconté; non compté. **to leave ~,** ne pas dire, ne pas raconter.

untouched adj. non touché; non ému, insensible.

untrained adj. exercé, inexpérimenté; non dressé.

untrammelled adj. sans entraves.

untranslatable adj. intraduisible.

untried adj. non essayé; non éprouvé; non tenté; non vérifié; non contrôlé; *Law.* qui n'a pas été jugé.

untrimmed adj. non fini; non arrangé; non ajusté; sans parure; (clothes) non garni; (hair, beard) négligé, non taillé. *Hort.* non taillé, non élagué.

untrod, untrodden adj. qui n'est pas foulé; non frayé, non battu.

untroubled adj. calme, sans inquiétude, clair, limpide.

untrue adj. faux; qui n'est pas vrai; inexact; infidèle.

untrustworthy adj. indigne de confiance.

untruth n. fausseté f.; mensonge m.

untruthful adj. faux, mensonger.

unused adj. inusité; peu usité; neuf, inaccoutumé.

unusual adj. peu commun, inaccoutumé, extraordinaire.

unusually adv. rarement; d'une manière insolite.

unutterable adj. indicible, inexprimable, ineffable.

unvanquished adj. invaincu.

unvaried adj. non varié; invariable; monotone.

unvarnished adj. non verni, vernissé; sans vernis.

unvarying adj. invariable.

unveil v.t. dévoiler, découvrir.

unventilated adj. non ventilé; non aéré.

unwarily adv. imprudement, sans précaution.

unwariness n. imprévoyance f., étourderie f.; imprudence f.

unwarranted adj. non autorisé; injustifiable; sans motifs; *Comm.* non garanti.

unwary adj. imprudent; imprévoyant; inconsidéré.

unwashed adj. non lavé; sale.

unwavering adj. resolu, décidé, déterminé.

unwed adj. non marié.

unwelcome adj. mal accueilli; qui n'est pas

bienvenu; (things) fâcheux, déplaisant; qui déplaît; peu désiré. **~ news**, des nouvelles désagréables.

unwell *adj.* indisposé, souffrant.

unwept *adj.* non pleuré, non regretté.

unwholesome *adj.* malsain, insalubre; nuisible, mauvais.

unwholesomeness *n.* insalubrité *f.*

unwieldy *adj.* lourd, pesant; enorme.

unwilling *adj.* qui ne veut pas, de mauvaise volonté; mal disposé. **he was ~ to go out**, il n'avait pas envie de sortir. **willing or ~**, bon gré mal gré.

unwillingly *adv.* de mauvaise volonté, à contre-coeur.

unwillingness *n.* mauvais vouloir *m.;* répugnance *f.;* aversion *f.*

unwind *v.t.* dévider; dérouler, démêler, débrouiller. *v.i.* (se) dérouler.

unwise *adj.* peu sage, imprudent; mal avisé.

unwisely *adv.* peu sagement; imprudemment.

unwittingly *adv.* sans le savoir, à son insu.

unwomanly *adj.* indigne d'une femme.

unwonted *adj.* inaccoutumé, peu commun.

unwordly *adj.* étranger au monde; peu mondain.

unworn *adj.* non porté; neuf.

unworthily *adv.* indignement; sans le mériter.

unworthiness *n.* indignité *f.;* défaut *m.* de mérite.

unworthy *adj.* indigne, sans mérite.

unwrap *v.t.* defaire; ôter l'enveloppe de.

unwrinkled *adj.* sans rides, non ridé.

unwritten *adj.* non écrit; verbal; en blanc.

unyielding *adj.* inflexible, ferme.

up *adv.* en haut; haut, en l'air; debout, levé, sur pied. **~ there**, là-haut. **~ and down**, en haut et en bas; çà et là; en long et en large. **to go ~**, monter. **the sun is ~**, le soleil est levé. **to raise ~**, soulever. **hard ~ for money**, *Infml.* très gêné, dans l'embarras, sans argent. **the hour is ~**, l'heure est expirée. *prep.* au haut de; en haut de; sur; en montant; à; dans l'intérieur de. **~stairs**, en haut. **~ the river**, en remontant le fleuve; en amont. **~ to**, jusqu'à, à; capable de; au courant de, au fait de. **to be ~ to it**, se sentir capable de. **to be ~ on it**, être bien informé. **where does he come ~ with those crazy ideas?** (d')où trouve-t-il toutes ces idées folles? *n.* haut *m.* **the ~s and downs**, les hauts et les bas *m.pl.;* les vicissitudes.

upbraid *v.t.* faire des reproches à; réprimander.

update *n.* mise *f.* à jour. *v.t.* mettre à jour.

upheaval *n.* soulèvement *m.*

uphill *adj.* qui monte; difficile; pénible, rude, fatigant. *adv.* en côte, en montant. *n.* montée *f.,* côte *f.*

uphold *v.t.* élever; soutenir; encourager.

upholsterer *n.* tapissier *m.;* marchand *m.* de meubles.

upholstery *n.* tapisserie *f.* d'ameublement.

upland *n.* terrain *m.* élevé; plateau *m.,* hauteur *f.* **~** *adj.* élevé, montagneux; des hautes terres; des montagnes.

uplift *v.t.* lever, élever.

upon *prep.* sur, à; en; dans; par. See on. **~ my word**, sur ma parole. **there~**, là-dessus.

upper *adj.* plus haut, supérieur; au-dessus; haut. **~ case**, majuscule *m.* **~ deck**, *Naut.* le plus haut pont *m.* **~ hand**, avantage *m.,* dessus *m.*

uppermost *adj.* le plus haut, le plus élevé; supérieur; au-dessus.

upright *adj.* droit, d'aplomb; debout; honnête, intègre. *n.* Arch. élévation *f.; Const.* montant *m.*

uprightly *adv.* verticalement, droit, debout; d'aplomb; *Fig.* honnêtement, avec droiture.

uprightness *n.* aplomb *m.; Fig.* droiture *f.;* intégrité *f.;* loyauté *f.*

uprising *n.* lever *m.*

uproar *n.* vacarme *m.,* tapage *m.;* désordre *m.*

uproarious *adj.* bruyant, tumultueux.

uproariously *adv.* bruyamment; avec vacarme.

uproot *v.t.* déraciner; extirper.

upset *v.t.* renverser, verser; faire chavirer (boat); rendre malade; contrarier; mettre en colère; bouleverser.

upset *n.* renversement *m.;* bouleversement *m.*

upshot *n.* fin *f.,* conclusion *f.,* issue *f.* **the ~ of it is,** le fin mot de l'affaire, c'est que.

upside *n.* dessus *m.* **to turn ~ down**, mettre sens dessus dessous; mettre à l'envers.

upstairs *adv.* en haut.

upstart *n.* parvenu *m.;* nouvel enrichi *m.* **~** *adj.* parvenu; subit, soudain.

upward, upwards *adv.* en haut; en remontant; vers le ciel. **~ and downward**, en haut et en bas. *adj.* tourné, dirigé en haut; levé (au ciel); qui s'élève; mouvement ascensionnel.

uranium *n.* uranium *m.*

Uranus *n.pr. Astron.* Uranus *m.*

urban *adj.* urbain.

urbane *adj.* poli, courtois.

urbanity *n.* urbanité *f.;* manières polies.

urchin *n.* hérisson *m.;* bambin *m.,* marmot *m.,* moutard *m.*

ureter *n.* uretère *m.*

urethra *n.* urèthre *m.*

urge *v.t.* pousser, faire avancer; accélérer; inciter; engager; alléguer, prétendre; soutenir; insister sur. **to ~ on**, hâter, pousser, presser. *v.i.* (se) hâter, (se) presser.

urgency *n.* urgence *f.;* nécessité *f.* urgente; besoin *m.* pressant; instances *f.pl.*

urgent *adj.* urgent; pressant.

urgently *adv.* avec urgence, d'une manière urgente; instamment.

urinal *n.* urinal *m.*

urinary *adj.* urinaire.

urinate *v.i.* uriner.

urine *n.* urine *f.*

urn *n.* urne *f.*

us *pron.* nous.

usage *n.* traitement *m.*; usage *m.*; procédé *m.*

use *n.* usage *m.*; emploi *m.*; utilité *f.*; exercice *m.*; habitude *m.*; us *m.pl.*; profit *m.*, avantage *m.*; besoin *m.*, intérêt *m.* **what is the ~?** à quoi bon? **it is no ~ going,** ça ne sert à rien d'y aller. **to be of no ~,** ne pas servir, n'être d'aucune utilité, être inutile. **to make ~ of,** faire usage de; se servir de; utiliser. **to put to good ~,** se servir à bon escient.

use *v.t.* faire usage de, se servir de, user, consommer; traiter, en user avec; agir envers. **to ~ up,** user, consommer, épuiser. *v.i.* **to be ~d to,** être accoutumé à avoir coutume, avoir l'habitude; être habitué.

useful *adj.* utile, profitable; qui sert.

usefully *adv.* utilement, avec utilité; avantageusement.

usefulness *n.* utilité *f.*

useless *adj.* inutile.

uselessly *adv.* inutilement.

uselessness inutilité *f.*

usher *v.t.* introduire; annoncer. **to ~ in,** introduire; précéder. **to ~ out,** reconduire.

usual *adj.* usuel, ordinaire; habituel. **as ~,** comme d'habitude, comme d'ordinaire.

usually *adv.* usuellement; ordinairement; habituellement.

usurious *adj.* usuraire; exorbitant.

usurp *v.t.* usurper; s'emparer de.

usurper *n.* usurpateur *m.*, usurpatrice *f.*

usury *n.* intérêt *m.*, usure *f.*

utensil *n.* ustensile *m.*

uterine *adj.* utérine.

uterus *n.* utérus *m.*

utilitarian *adj.* utilitaire.

utility *n.* utilité *f.*

utilize *v.t.* utiliser.

utmost *adj.* extrême, dernier; le plus reculé; le plus extrême. *n.* plus haut degré *m.*; le plus *m.*; le plus possible *m.*; tout son possible *m.* **to do one's ~,** faire tout son possible, faire de son mieux. **at the ~,** tout au plus.

utopia *n.* utopie *f.*

utopian *adj.* utopiste.

utopianism *n.* utopisme *m.*

utter *adj.* extérieur; extrême, le plus grand; entier; total; absolu; complètement. **~ darkness,** l'obscurité complète. **~ destruction,** destruction complète. *v.t.* prononcer; proférer; pousser (a cry); publier. **he uttered these last words,** il prononça ces derniers mots.

utterance *n.* émission *f.* (spoken); prononciation *f.* articulation *f.*; parole *f.*

utterly *adv.* complètement, entièrement, tout à fait.

uttermost *adj.* See UTMOST.

uvula *n.* luette *f.*

uxorious *adj.* esclave de sa femme.

V

V chiffre romain représentant 5.

vacancy *n.* disponibilité *f.*; vide *m.*; lacune *f.*; loisir *m.*

vacant *adj.* vide; vacant; inoccupé, libre, distrait; sans expression (look); indifférent. **a ~ look,** un regard distrait.

vacate *v.t.* annuler; laisser vacant; vider; quitter.

vacation *n.* vacances *f.pl.*

vaccinate *v.t.* vacciner.

vaccination *n.* vaccination *f.*

vaccine *n.* vaccin *m.*

vacillate *v.i.* vaciller.

vacillation *n.* vacillation *f.*

vacuity *n.* vacuité *f.*; vide *m.*, espace *m.* vide; lacune *f.*

vacuum *n.* vide *m.*, vacuum *m.* **~ cleaner,** aspirateur *m.*

vagabond *adj.* vagabond, errant; flottant. *n.* vagabond *m.*

vagary *n.* fantaisie *f.*, caprice *m.*, boutade *f.*; rêverie *f.*; chimère *f.*

vagina *n.* vagin *m.*

vaginal *adj.* vaginal.

vagrancy *n.* vagabondage *m.*

vagrant *adj.* vagabond, errant. *n.* vagabond *m.*, mendiant *m.*

vague *adj.* vague, flou.

vaguely *adv.* vaguement.

vain *adj.* vain; inutile, infructueux; vaniteux, orgueilleux. **~ attempts,** de vains efforts. **~ persons,** des personnes vaines, vaineuses. **in ~,** en vain, vainement; en pure perte.

valentine *n.* valentin *m.*; valentine *f.*; billet *m.* doux, déclaration *f.* de la Saint-Valentin. **~'s day,** la Saint-Valentin.

valet *n.* valet *m.*

valiant *adj.* fort, vigoureux; vaillant, valeureux.

valid *adj.* valide; fort, puissant.

validity *n.* validité *f.*

valley *n.* vallée *f.*; val *m.*; *Arch.* chenal *m.*, chéneau *m.*

valor *n.* valeur *f.*; bravoure *f.*; vaillance *f.*

valorous *adj.* valeureux, vaillant.

valuable *adj.* de prix, de valeur; précieux; estimable.

valuables *n.pl.* objets *m.pl.* de valeur.

valuation *n.* évaluation *f.*; valeur *f.*; prix *m.*

value *n.* valeur *f.*; prix; importance *f.*, signification. *v.t.* évaluer; estimer; priser; apprécier; faire cas de.

valve *n.* *Mec.* soupape *f.*; *Bot.*, *Anat.* valve *f.*, valvule *f.*; battant *m.* **safety ~,** soupape de sûreté.

vampire *n.* vampire *m.*

van *n.* avant-garde *f.*; front *m.*; fourgon *m.*; camionnette *f.* **~-guard,** avant-garde *f.*

vandal *n.* vandale *m.*

vandalism *n.* vandalisme *m.*

vane *n.* girouette *f.*; barbe *f.* (feather).

vanilla n. vanille f.

vanish v.i. s'évanouir, disparaître. **to ~ away,** s'évanouir, disparaître; passer. **to ~ from,** s'en aller de; s'échapper de.

vanity n. vanité f.; vain désir m., futilité f.

vanquish v.t. vaincre.

vantage n. gain m.; avantage m.; supériorité f.; dessus m.; occasion f. favorable. **~ point,** position f. avantageuse, terrain m. avantageux.

vapid adj. insipide; fade; (liquid) éventé, plat.

vapor n. vapeur f.; fumée f.; flatuosité f.; brouillard m., brume f.

vaporize v.t. vaporiser. v.i. (se) vaporiser.

variable adj. variable, changeant; variant; inconstant, versatile. n. variable f.

variably adv. variablement, d'une manière variable.

variance n. variation f.; Law. modification f.; désaccord m., différend m.; brouille f. **to be at ~,** être en désaccord, brouille.

variant adj. variant. n. variante f.

variation n. variation f.; changement m.; Astron. déclinaison f. (of needle).

varicella n. Med. varicelle f.

varicocele n. varicocèle f.

varicose adj. variqueux.

varied adj. qui varie; varié; mélangé.

variegate v.t. varier; diaprer, barioler, bigarrer; nuancer.

variegation n. diversité f. (of colours); variété f.

variety n. variété f.; diversité f.

various adj. divers, différent; plusieurs; varié, diversifié.

variously adv. diversement, différemment; avec variété.

varnish n. vernis m. **~ maker,** vernisseur m. v.t. vernir; vernisser (pottery); farder.

vary v.t. varier; diversifier. v.i. changer; différer d'opinions; dévier, s'écarter.

varying adj. variant; changeant.

vascular adj. vasculaire.

vase n. vase m.

vassal n. vassal m. (pl. vassaux); serviteur m.; serf m.

vast adj. vaste, étendu; immense; énorme; puissant.

vastly adv. immensément, énormément.

vastness n. immensité f.; grandeur f.; importance f., gravité f.

vat n. cuve f.; fosse f. (tanner); réservoir m.

vaudeville n. vaudeville m.

vault n. coffre-fort m.; chambre f. forte; voûte f.; caveau m. (church); cave f., cellier m.; saut m.; Sport. voltige f. **the ~ of heaven,** la voûte des cieux. v.t. voûter; cintrer. v.i. sauter; bondir; Sport. voltiger.

vaulted adj. en voûte.

vaunt v.i. se vanter, se glorifier. v.t. vanter; faire parade de.

VCR abbr. **videocassette recorder** n. magnétoscope m.

veal n. veau m.

vector n. rayon m.; vecteur m.

veer v.i. tourner; Naut. virer. **to ~ about,** virer; virer de bord.

vegetable n. légume m. adj. végétal; végétatif f.

vegetal adj. végétal.

vegetarian n., adj. végétarien m.

vegetarianism n. végétarisme m.

vegetate v.i. végéter.

vegetation n. végétation f.

vegetative adj. végétatif.

vehemence n. véhémence f.; force f.

vehement adj. véhément; qui entraîne; violent; ardent.

vehemently adv. avec véhémence; fortement.

vehicle n. véhicule m., voiture f.

vehicular adj. de transport.

veil n. voile m.; rideau m. **~ v.t. voiler; revêtir, couvrir.**

vein n. veine f.; Min. filon m.; Bot. nervure f. (leaf).

velocity n. vitesse f., rapidité f., vélocité f.

velour(s) n. velours m.

velvet n. velours m. adj. de velours; velouté f. Fig. doux, mielleux.

velveteen n. velours m. de coton.

velvety adj. velouté.

venal adj. vénal.

vend v.t. vendre, débiter.

vender n. vendeur m., débitant m.

vending n. vinte f. **~ machine,** distributeur m. automatique.

vendor n. vendeur m.

veneer n. feuille f. de placage, feuille f. (cabinetry); vernie. v.t. plaquer.

venerable adj. vénérable; respectable; sacré. n. vénérable m.

venerate v.t. vénérer; avoir en vénération; révérer.

veneration n. vénération f.

venereal adj. vénérien; syphilitique.

Venetian n. Vénitien m. **~ blind,** store m.; vénitien m.

vengeance n. vengeance f. **with a ~,** Infml. furieusement, terriblement.

vengeful adj. vindicatif; vengeur, vengeresse.

venial adj. véniel; pardonnable, excusable. **~ sin,** péché véniel.

Venice n.pr. Venise f.

venison n. venaison f.

venom n. venin m.

venomous adj. venimeux; vénéneux.

venous adj. veineux.

vent n. ouverture f.; passage m.; issue f.; cours m.; divulgation f.; soupirail m. **to give ~ to,** donner de l'air; donner libre cours à. v.t. donner issue, donner passage à; donner un libre cours à; exhaler, faire éclater; dire, débiter; divulguer.

ventilate v.t. ventiler; Fig. discuter, agiter.

ventilation n. ventilation f., aération f.

ventilator n. ventilateur m.

ventricle *n.* ventricule *m.*
ventricular *adj.* ventriculaire.
ventriloquism *n.* ventriloquie *f.*
ventriloquist *n.* ventriloque *m.*
venture *n.* aventure *f.;* risque *m.;* hasard *m.;* Comm. pacotille *f.;* spéculation *f.* ~ *v.i.* oser; (se) hasarder, s'aventurer. **to ~ on, upon,** se risquer sur; entreprendre. **to ~ out,** oser sortir; se risquer dehors. *v.t.* aventurer, risquer.
nothing ~d, nothing gained, qui ne risque rien n'a rien.
venturesome *adj.* aventureux; hardi, entreprenant.
venue *n.* voisinage *m.*
Venus *n.* Vénus *f.*
veracious *adj.* véridique; vrai, véritable.
veracity *n.* véracité *f.*
veranda *n.* veranda *f.*
verb *n.* verbe *m.*
verbal *adj.* verbal.
verbally *adv.* verbalement.
verbatim *adv.* mot pour mot, à la lettre.
verbiage *n.* verbiage *m.*
verbose *adj.* verbeux; diffus.
verboseness *n.* verbosité *f.;* prolixité *f.*
verdant *adj.* verdoyant; fleurissant; en fleurs.
verdict *n.* verdict *m.;* jugement *m.;* décision *f.;* avis *m.*
verge *n.* bord *m.;* extrémité *f.;* limite *f.;* confins *m.pl.;* lisière *f.* (forest). **on the ~ of,** au bord de; sur le point de. *v.i.* pencher, incliner; approcher de, toucher à. **to ~ on,** approcher, friser.
verification *n.* vérification *f.*
verify *v.t.* vérifier; confirmer; prouver.
verisimilitude *n.* vraisemblance *f.*
veritable *adj.* véritable.
vermicelli *n.* vermicelle *m.*
vermin *n. inv.* vermine *f.*
vernacular *n.* vernaculaire *m.* **~ language,** langue courrante.
vernal *adj.* printanier; du printemps. **~ equinox,** équinoxe du printemps.
versatile *adj.* mobile; versatile.
versatility *n.* mobilité *f.;* versatilité *f.;* souplesse *f.;* flexibilité *f.*
verse *n.* vers *m.;* vers *m.pl.,* poésie *f.;* couplet *m.;* verset *m.*
versed *adj.* versé; familier avec.
version *n.* traduction *f.;* version *f.*
versus, vs *prep.* contre.
vertebra *n. pl.* vertebrae, vertèbre *f.*
vertebral *adj.* vertébral.
vertebrate *adj.,n.* vertébré *m.*
vertex *n. pl.* vertices, sommet *m.;* zénith *m.*
vertical *adj.* vertical. *n.* verticale *f.*
vertically *adv.* verticalement.
vertigo *n.pl.* vertigines, vertige *m.*
verve *n.* verve *f.;* nerf *m.*
very *adj.* vrai, véritable, réel; même; parfait. **to the ~ end,** jusqu'au bout. *adv.* très, fort, très bien; tout à fait; justement. **~ much,** beaucoup.

it is the ~ same thing, c'est tout à fait la même chose.
vespers *n.* vêpres *f.pl.*
vessel *n.* vase *m.;* vaisseau *m.,* navire *m.*
vest *n.* veste *f.;* gilet *m.* *v.t. Law.* mettre en possession. **to ~ with,** vêtir, investir de. **to be ~ed in,** être assigné à. **~ed interests,** les intérêts *m.pl.,* les droits acquis *m.pl.*
vestibule *n.* vestibule *m.*
vestige *n.* vestige *m.*
vestment *n.* vêtement *m.*
vestry *n.* sacristie *f.;* vestiaire *m.;* assemblée *f.* paroissiale.
vet *n. Abbr.* **veterinarian, veteran,** vétérinaire *m.f.;* vétéran *m.,* ancient combattant.
veteran *n.* vétéran *m.* ancient combattant. *adj.* expérimenté, aguerri, éprouvé.
veterinarian *n.* vétérinaire *m.f.*
veterinary *adj.* vétérinaire.
veto *n.* veto *m.* ~ *v.t.* mettre son veto à; s'opposer à.
vex *v.t.* fâcher; vexer; tourmenter, affliger; contrarier; taquiner. *v.i.* s'irriter, (se) fâcher; (se) vexer.
vexation *n.* vexation *f.;* contrariété *f.;* taquinerie *f.;* chagrin *m.,* affliction *f.*
vexed *adj.* contrarié, vexé; fâché; agité.
vexing *adj.* contrariant, ennuyeux; vexant.
via *n., adv.* par la voie de, par.
viability *n.* viabilité *f.*
viable *adj.* viable.
viaduct *n.* viaduc *m.*
vibes *n.pl. Infml.* **she could feel the bad ~ in the room,** elle pouvait ressentir l'atmosphère tendue dans la pièce.
vibrate *v.i.* vibrer; osciller; retentir; vaciller. *v.t.* faire vibrer; faire osciller; agiter.
vibration *n.* vibration *f.;* oscillation *f.*
vicar *n.* vicaire *m.;* curé *m.;* ministre *m.* protestant.
vicarious *adj.* délégué; substitué.
vice *n.* vice *m.;* défaut *m.* *adj.* vice; sous. **~-admiral,** vice-amiral *m.* **~-admiralty,** vice-amirauté *f.* **~-chancellor,** vice-chancelier *m.* **~-consul,** vice-consul *m.* **~ president,** vice-président *m.*
vice versa *adv.* vice versa.
vicinity *n.* voisinage *m.,* environs *m.pl.;* parages *m.pl.*
vicious *adj.* vicieux, haineux, pervers.
viciously *adv.* méchamment, vicieusement.
viciousness *n.* méchanceté *f.;* nature *f.* vicieuse.
vicissitude *n.* vicissitude *f.*
victim *n.* victime *f.*
victimize *v.t.* prendre pour victim; exercer des représailles sur.
victor *n.* vainqueur *m.*
victorious *adj.* victorieux; de victoire.
victoriously *adv.* victorieusement.
victory *n.* victoire *f.* **to achieve a ~,** remporter une victoire.
victuals *n.pl.* vivres *m.pl.,* provisions *f.pl.*

video *n.* vidéo *f.*

vie *v.i.* rivaliser, disputer; lutter. **to ~ with**, rivaliser avec.

Vienna *n.pr.* Vienne *f.*

view *v.t.* regarder, considérer; contempler; voir; apercevoir; examiner; envisager. *n.* vue *f.;* regard; coup d'oeil *m.;* perspective *f.* aspect *m.;* exposition *f.,* point *m.* de vue; aperçu *m.;* examen *m.;* exposé *m.;* opinion *f.,* avis *m.* **at first ~**, à première vue; au premier abord. **to take a ~ of**, voir, apercevoir; regarder, examiner. **in this ~**, à ce point de vue; sous ce rapport. **with a ~ to**, en vue de, dans le but de. **on ~**, exposé.

viewer *n.* téléspectateur(trice) *m.f.*

vigil *n.* veille *f.;* vigile *f.*

vigilance *n.* veille *f.;* vigilance *f.;* garde *f.,* surveillance *f.*

vigilant *adj.* vigilant.

vigilantly *adv.* avec vigilance.

vigor *n.* vigueur *f.*

vigorous *adj.* vigoureux.

vigorously *adv.* vigoureusement.

vile *adj.* corrompu; souillé.

vilely *adv.* vilement; bassement; honteusement; lâchement.

vileness *n.* bassesse *f.,* nature *f.* vile; avilissement *m.,* dégradation *f.*

vilify *v.t.* avilir; diffamer, décrier.

villa *n.* villa *f.,* maison *f.* de campagne.

village *n.* village *m.*

villager *n.* villageois *m.*

villain *n.* vilain *m.;* scélérat *m.,* misérable *m.,* gredin *m.*

villainous *adj.* vil, infâme; méprisable; scélérat; de scélérat.

vinaigrette *n.* vinaigrette *f.*

vindicate *v.t.* défendre, justifier; affirmer; soutenir; venger.

vindication *n.* défense *f.,* justification *f.* **in ~ of**, en défense de, pour la justification de.

vindictive *adj.* vindicatif.

vindictiveness *n.* caractère *m.* vindicatif; rancune *f.*

vine *n.* vigne *f.;* tige *f.* **grape~**, vigne *f.*

vinegar *n.* vinaigre *m.*

vineyard *n.* vigne *f.;* vignoble *m.*

vintage *n.* vin *m.* de cru. *adj.* classique.

vintner *n.* marchand *m.* de vin.

violate *v.t.* violer; troubler, interrompre; outrager; offenser.

violation *n.* violation.

violence *n.* violence *f.;* infraction *f.* **to do ~ to**, violenter.

violent *adj.* violent; fort, extrême. **a ~ wind**, un vent violent. **~ death**, mort violente.

violently *adv.* violemment, avec violence.

violet *n.* violette *f.* **~** *adj.* violet.

violin *n.* violon *m.*

violinist *n.* violoniste *m.*

violist *n.* violiste *m.*

violoncello *n.* violoncelle *m.*

viper *n.* vipère *f.*

virgin *n.* vierge *f.* **~** *adj.* vierge; chaste.

virginal *adj.* virginal. *n.* virginal *m.*

virginity *n.* virginité *f.*

Virgo *n.* Astron. Vierge *f.*

virile *adj.* viril; mâle.

virility *n.* virilité *f.*

virtual *adj.* virtuel. **~ reality**, réalité virtual.

virtually *adv.* virtuellement.

virtue *n.* vertu *f.;* chasteté *f.;* valeur *f.;* excellence *f.* **in** or **by ~ of**, en vertu de.

virtuoso *n.* virtuose *m.*

virtuous *adj.* vertueux.

virulence *n.* virulence *f.;* force *f.,* violence *f.*

virulent *adj.* virulent.

virus *n.* virus *m.*

visa *n.* visa *m.*

vis-à-vis *n.* vis-à-vis *m.*

viscera *n.pl.* viscères *m.pl.*

visceral *adj.* viscéral.

viscosity *n.* viscosité *f.*

viscous *adj.* visqueux; gluant.

vise *n.* étau *m.*

visibility *n.* visibilité *f.*

visible *adj.* visible; évident, manifeste; sensible.

visibly *adv.* visiblement; manifestement.

vision *n.* vision *f.;* vue *f.;* apparition *f.,* fantôme *m.*

visionary *adj.* visionnaire; chimérique, imaginaire. *n.* visionnaire *m.f.*

visit *v.t.* visiter; faire une visite; inspecter; examiner; rendre visite à. *v.i.* faire des visites, aller en visite. **to go visiting**, aller en visite. *n.* visite *f.;* examen *m.* **to pay a ~**, faire une visite. **on a ~**, en visite.

visitor *n.* personne *f.* qui fait des visites; visiteur *m.,* visiteuse *f.;* inspecteur *m.*

visor *n.* visière *f.* (cap, helmet).

vista *n.* vue *f.;* panorama *m.;* échappée *f.* de vue, percée *f.,* éclaircie *f.;* perspective *f.;* avenue *f.*

visual *adj.* visuel.

visualize *v.t.* visualiser; envisager; s'imaginer; prévoir.

vital *adj.* de vie, de la vie, de l'existence; vital.

vitality *n.* vitalité *f.*

vitamin *n.* vitamine *f.*

vitiate *v.t.* gâter, corrompre, vicier.

viticulture *n.* viticulture *f.*

vitreous *adj.* vitreux; de verre.

vitriol *n.* vitriol *m.*

vituperation *n.* blâme *m.,* reproche *m.*

vituperative *adj.* de blâme, de reproche.

vivacious *adj.* vivace; plein de vie; vif, animé; vivace.

vivaciously *adv.* avec vivacité.

vivaciousness, vivacity *n.* vivacité *f.*

vivid *adj.* vif; éclatant, animé.

vividly *adv.* vivement; avec force; avec éclat.

vividness *n.* vivacité *f.;* force *f.;* éclat *m.*

vivisection *n.* vivisection *f.*

vixen *n.* renarde *f.;* mégère *f.*

vocabulary n. vocabulaire m.
vocal adj. vocal; de la voix.
vocalist n. chanteur m., chanteuse f.
vocalization n. vocalisation f.
vocalize v.t. vocaliser.
vocally adv. par la voix; de vive voix.
vocation n. vocation f.; profession f.; métier m., état m.
vociferate v.i. vociferer. v.t. crier, hurler.
vociferation n. vociférations f.pl.; clameur f.
vociferous adj. bruyant, hurlant.
vociferously adv. en vociférant.
vogue n. vogue f.
voice n. voix f.; parole f.; langage m.; vote m., opinion f.; accent m. **to raise one's ~,** élever la voix. **active ~,** voix active. **passive ~,** voix passive. v.t. exprimer; publier, proclamer; voter.
voiceless adj. sans voix, sans vote.
void adj. vide; vacant. Law. nul; de nul effet; exempt, libre; dénué, dépourvu; vain, imaginaire. n. vide m., espace m. vide. ~ v.t. évacuer, expulser, chasser; laisser vacant; Law. annuler. v.i. (se) vider.
volatile adj. volant, volatil.
volatility n. volatilité f.; légèreté f.; nature f. volage.
volcanic adj. volcanique.
volcano n. volcan m.
volition n. volition f.; volonté f.
volley n. volée f.; décharge f., salve f.; grêle f. (blows); torrent m. (insults); déluge m. (words). **~ball,** n. volley(-ball) m. ~ v.t. renvoyer (la balle) de volée.
volt n. volte f.
voltage n. voltage m., tension f.
volubility n. volubilité f.
voluble adj. (of tongue) déliée; bien pendue; (words) facile; (speech) coulant; abondant.
volume n. volume m., tome m.; masse f.; étendue de la voix.
voluminous adj. enroulé; replié; volumineux.
voluntarily adv. volontairement.
voluntary adj. libre; volontaire; spontané; à dessein. n. Mus. improvisation f.
volunteer n. bénévole m.f.; Mil. volontaire. adj.

volontaire. v.t. s'offrir volontairement. v.i. s'engager comme volontaire.
voluptuous adj. voluptueux.
voluptuousness n. volupté f.
vomit v.i.,v.t. vomir; rendre. n. vomissement m.
vomiting n. vomissement m.
voodoo n. vaudou m.
voracious adj. vorace.
voraciously adv. avec voracité.
voraciousness n. voracité f.
vortex n.pl. **vortices, vortexes,** tourbillon m.
vote n. vote m., suffrage m., voix f.; bulletin m. (ballot); resolution f. **to put to the ~,** mettre aux voix. v.i. voter, opiner. v.t. élire.
voter n. votant m.; électeur m., electrice f.
voting n. vote m.; scrutin m.
votive adj. votif; commémoratif. **~ offering,** offrande f. votive, ex-voto m.
vouch v.t. attester; certifier; garantir; soutenir. v.i. porter témoignage, (for) témoigner de; répondre de; garantir, certifier.
voucher n. témoin m.; garant m.; répundant m.; garantie f., titre m., pièce justificative; Law. mande f. en garantie.
vouchsafe v.t. permettre; accorder, octroyer, donner. v.i. daigner, condescendre.
vow n. voeu m., serment m. **to take a ~,** prononcer ses voeux. v.t. vouer; faire voeu (de); jurer. v.i. promettre; protester.
vowel n. voyelle f. ~ adj. vocal, de voyelle.
voyage n. voyage m. par mer; traversée f. ~ v.i. voyager par mer; faire un voyage par mer.
voyager n. navigateur m.; passager m.; voyageur m.
voyeur n. voyeur m.
vs abbrev. **versus** conj. contre.
vulgar adj. vulgaire; du peuple; commun. **~ manners,** manières communes. **~ people,** des gens vulgaires, communs.
vulgarity n. nature f. vulgaire; bassesse f.; manières f.pl. communes, vulgaires.
vulgarize v.t. vulgariser.
vulnerability n. nature f. vulnérable.
vulnerable adj. vulnérable.
vulture n. vautour m.

W

wacky adj. Infml. cinglé; timbré.
wad n. ouate f., tampon m., botte f. (straw, hay); touffe f. ~ v.t. bourrer.
wadding n. fourre f.; ouate f.
waddle v.i. se balancer, se dandiner; marcher en se dandinant.
waddling n. dandinement m.
wade v.i. marcher. **to ~ across,** traverser à gué. **to ~ through water,** marcher dans l'eau. v.t. passer, traverser à gué.
wader n. Ornith. échassier m. ~**s,** wissardes f.pl. (boots).
wafer n. gaufrette f.; (church) hostie f.

waffle n. gaufre f. ~ v.i. tergiverser.
waft v.t. porter, transporter (on water or air); faire flotter. v.i. flotter, voguer.
wag v.t. braler (head); remuer, secouer. v.i. se mouvoir, se remuer; aller, marcher. **the dog ~s its tail,** le chien remue sa queue. n. plaisant m.; farceur m.; loustic m.; hochement m. (head).
wage v.t. entreprendre; soutenir. **to ~ war,** faire la guerre. n. gage m.
wager n. pari m., gageure f., gage m.; pari m. **to place a ~,** faire un pari, parier. v.i.,v.t. parier, gager.

wages n.pl. salaire m.; gages m.pl. (working person); solde f. (soldier); prix m., récompense f.

waggish adj. plaisant; drôle; malin, espiègle.

waggle v.i. se dandiner; se remuer légèrement. v.t. remuer doucement.

wagon n. chariot m.; wagon m., (train) fourgon m.

waif n. enfant m. égaré.

wail v.i. (se) lamenter. n. plainte f., lamentation f.

wailing n. plainte f., lamentation f., gémissement m. **the Wailing Wall**, le mur des Lamentations.

wainscot n. boiserie f., lambris m. ~ v.t. lambrisser; Fig. revêtir.

wainscotting n. lambrissage m. boiserie f.

waist n. ceinture f., taille f.; mi-corps m.

waistband n. ceinture f.

waistline n. taille f.

wait v.i. attendre; être dans l'attente; servir. **I'll ~ till he comes**, j'attendrai qu'il vienne. **to keep waiting**, faire attendre. **to ~ on tables**, servir à table. **to ~ for**, attendre. n. attente f., arrêt m. **to lie in ~**, être aux aguets; se tenir en embuscade.

waiter n. serviteur m.; garçon m. (café, etc.).

waiting adj. qui attend; qui sert. n. attente f. **~ room**, salle f. d'attente.

waitress n. serveuse f.

waive v.t. abandonner; renoncer à; se desister de; laisser.

wake v.i. veiller, être éveillé; (se) réveiller; s'éveiller. **to ~ up**, s'éveiller, se réveiller. v.t. ranimer. **to ~ up**, réveiller, réveiller. n. veille f.; veillée f. (by a corpse). Naut. sillage m.

wakeful adj. éveillé; vigilant, attentif.

waken v.i. veiller. See WAKE.

waking adj. éveillé. **~ hours**, heures de veille.

Wales n.pr. Pays m. de Galles. **New South ~**, la Nouvelle Galles du Sud.

walk v.i. marcher, aller à pied; se promener. **to ~ home**, rentrer à pied. **to ~ by oneself**, se promener seul. **to ~ around**, se promener. **to ~ along**, s'avancer, marcher. **to ~ away**, s'en aller, partir. **to ~ back**, retourner sur ses pas. **to ~ down**, descendre. **to ~ in**, entrer. **to ~ off**, partir, s'en aller. **to ~ on**, continuer de marcher. **to ~ out**, sortir. **to ~ up**, monter. **to ~ up and down**, se promener de long en large. v.t. parcourir, marcher dans, arpenter, traverser; faire; promener; mettre au pas, faire aller au pas (horse). n. marche f.; promenade f., tour m.; démarche f., port m., tournure f.; avenue f., allée f. **to go for a ~**, aller se promener. **shady ~**, allée ombragée, couverte. **in various ~s of life**, dans différents milieux.

walker n. marcheur m., marcheuse f.; pieton m.; promeneur m., promeneuse f. **sleep~**, somnambule m. et f.

wall n. mur m., muraille f.; rempart m.; Anat. paroi f. **within the ~s**, dans l'enceinte des murs, intra-muros. **~paper**, papier m. peint. v.t. entourer de murs; clore; fortifier, murer, boucher. **to ~ in, to ~ up**, murer.

wallet porte-monnaie m. (women); portefeuille m. (men).

wallop v.i. rosser, battre.

wallow v.i. (se) rouler, se vautrer; coupir. v.t. rouler. n. boue f., bourbe f.; trou m. bourbeux.

walnut n. noix f. **~ tree**, noyer. **~ shell**, coquille f. de noix, brou m. de noix.

walrus n. morse m., cheval m. marin.

waltz n. valse f. ~ v.i. valser.

wan adj. pâle, blême, terne, blafard.

wand n. baguette f. (magic).

wander v.i. errer; s'égarer; avoir le délire, battre la campagne. **to ~ around**, errer, vaguer. **to ~ from**, quitter, s'éloigner de; dévier de, transgresser. **to ~ up and down**, errer çà et là. v.t. parcourir.

wanderer n. personne f. qui erre; vagabond m.

wandering adj. errant; vagabond; égaré, absent, distrait. **~ mind**, esprit distrait. n. course f. vagabonde; excursion f.; égarement m., écart m., erreur f.; distraction f.; étourderie f.; divagation f.; égarement d'esprit.

wane v.i. décroître, diminuer; (moon) décroître; (day, night) s'écouler; baisser, décliner. n. déclin m.; décroissance f., décours m. de la lune, décadence f. **to be on the ~**, être sur son déclin; baisser.

wangle v.t. se débrouiller; Infml. goupiller.

wanna v.t. contraction of want to/a. See WANT.

want n. besoin m.; manque m., absence f.; dénûment m.; misère f.; pénurie f.; désir m. **to be in ~**, être dans le besoin. **to be in ~ of**, avoir besoin de. **for ~ of**, faute de. v.t. vouloir; manquer (de); falloir; avoir besoin de; demander; chercher. **I ~ a watch**, je veux une montre. **he ~s to go**, il veut partir.

wanting adj. voulant; manquant, qui manque; absent.

wanton adj. folâtre, enjoué, léger; fait de gaieté de coeur; par méchanceté; licencieux; capricieux. libertin m., débauché m.; personne f. personne f. frivole.

wantonly adv. capricieusement, en folâtrant, gaiement; lascivement; par malice.

wantonness n. libertinage m.; lasciveté f.

war n. guerre f. **civil ~**, guerre civile. **at ~**, en guerre. **to wage ~ against**, faire la guerre. **~ crime**, crime m. de guerre. v.i. (against) faire la guerre à, combattre; (with) lutter contre.

warble v.t. moduler, gazouiller; chanter. v.i. ramager.

warbler n. fauvette f.

ward v.t. garder; défendre; parer (blow). **to ~ off**, parer, détourner. n. Law. tutelle f.; Law. pupille m.f.; arrondissement m. (city); salle f. (hospital). **~robe**, garderobe f. **~room**, Naut. carré m. des officiers.

warden n. garde m.; gardien m.; gouverneur m.; directeur m. (prison).

warehouse n. entrepôt m., dépôt m.

wares n.pl. marchandises f.pl.

warfare n. guerre f. art militaire.

warily adv. prudemment, avec circonspection, avec précaution.

wariness n. prudence f., circonspection f.; précaution f.

warlike adj. belliqueux, guerrier; militaire; de guerre.

warm adj. chaud; chaleureux, ardent; zélé; passionné; vif. **to be ~**, avoir chaud; faire chaud. **to make ~**, chauffer, échauffer; réchauffer. **to get ~**, s'échauffer, commencer à faire chaud. **~-blooded**, à sang chaud. v.t. chauffer, échauffer; réchauffer; ranimer. **to ~ a room**, chauffer une chambre. **to ~ up**, réchauffer (food). **to ~ oneself**, se réchauffer. v.i. (se) chauffer, (se) réchauffer; s'échauffer, s'animer.

warmer n. plate ~, réchaud m.

warmly adv. chaudement; chaleureusement, avec chaleur; vivement.

warmth n. chaleur f. douce, chaleur f.; Fig. ardeur f., vivacité f.

warn v.t. vertir; prévenir, informer; notifier. **to ~ against**, avertir contre.

warning n. avertissement m., avis m.; notification f.

warp n., v.i. se déjeter, travailler; s'éloigner; Filat. se touer. v.t. faire gauchir; courber; cambrer (wood); détourner; fausser, pervertir.

warrant v.t. garantir, répondre de; assurer; certifier; justifier. n. autorisation f., autorité f.; raison f.; brevet m.; mandat m. (arrest), sûreté f.; garant m. **to issue a ~**, lancer un mandat d'arrêt. **death ~**, ordre d'exécution. **search ~**, mandat de perquisition.

warranty n. garantie f.; autorisation f.; pourvoir m.

warren n. garenne f.; pare m.

warrior n. guerrier m.

Warsaw n.pr. Varsovie f.

wart n. verrue f.

wary adj. prudent; discret, réservé; sur ses gardes.

wash v.t. laver; baigner, arroser (riverbanks); savonner; recouvrir (metal). **to ~ away**, off, enlever en levant; nettoyer; emporter, effacer (en levant). **to ~ out**, laver; effacer, se laver. **to ~ over**, submerger, inonder. Paint. laver. **to ~ up**, laver. v.i. (se) laver; faire ses ablutions; se baigner; laver, faire la lessive. n. lavage m., blanchissage m.; savonnage m.; lessive f.; Paint. lavis m.; enduit m.; couche f. (metal).

washer n. lave-linge m., laveuse f. **dish~**, lave vaisselle m.

washing n. lavage m.; blanchissage m.; lessive f. **~ machine**, machine f. à laver, lave-linge m., laveuse f.

wasp n. guêpe f.

WASP, Wasp, abbrev. of **White Anglo-Saxon Protestant**, blanc protestant d'origine anglo-saxonne.

waspish adj. irritable, irascible; bourru, maussade.

waste v.t. user; affaiblir; consumer; gaspiller, prodiguer, perdre (time); dévaster. **to ~ time**, perdre son temps. v.i. s'user, (se) consumer; dépérir; se perdre, se dissiper. **to ~ away**, dépérir; se dissiper. adj. dévasté, ravagé; (terrain) vague; (land) en friche; perdu, de rebut. **to lay ~**, dévaster. **~paper**, perte de rebut. n. gaspillage m.; perte f.; déchet m.; dépense f. inutile; terrain m. vague; terre f. inculte; désert m., solitude f.; désolation f.; ravage m.; restes m.pl.; (table, etc.); débris m.pl. **a mere ~ of time**, une pure perte de temps.

wasteful adj. prodigue; destructeur; ruineux; en pure perte.

watch n. veille f., veillée f.; vigilance f.; surveillance f.; guet m.; aguets m.pl.; Mil. garde f.; Naut. vigie f.; quart m.; poste m.; montre f. **to keep good ~**, faire bonne garde. **to be on the ~**, être sur ses gardes, avoir l'œil au guet; Naut. être de quart. **night~**, quart de nuit. **by my ~**, à ma montre. **~dog**, chien m. de garde. **~maker**, horloger m. **~making**, horlogerie f., fabrication f. de montres. **~tower**, tour f. d'observation. v.i. veiller; faire attention; prendre garde; faire sentinelle; epier, guetter. **to ~ for**, attendre, guetter, épier. **to ~ over**, veiller sur, surveiller. v.t. veiller, garder; veiller sur, surveiller; prendre garde à.

watchful adj. vigilant, attentif; en garde, en éveil.

watchman n. gardien m. de nuit; veilleur m.; Naut. vigie f.

water n. eau f. fresh ~, soft ~, eau fraîche, eau douce. **hard ~**, eau crue, dure. **salt ~**, eau salée, eau de mer. **spring~**, eau de source. **rain~**, eau de pluie, eau de ciel. **mineral ~**, eaux minérales. **high ~**, haute mer f.; pleine mer. **low ~**, mer f. basse, marée f. basse. **to be in hot ~**, Fig. être sur le gril. v.t. arroser; mouiller; abreuver (animal); moirer (fabric). v.i. pleurer; puiser de l'eau. **his mouth ~s**, l'eau lui vient à la bouche. **~color**, aquarelle f. **~cooler**, distribuer d'eau fraîche. **~cress**, cresson m. d'eau, cresson m. **~ level**, niveau m. de l'eau; niveau m. d'eau. **~ lily**, nénuphar m. **~logged**, engagé, à moitié plein d'eau. **~mark**, niveau m. des eaux; Pap. filigrane m. **~melon**, pastèque f., melon m. d'eau. **~ mill**, moulin m. à eau. **~ pipe**, tuyau m. d'eau. **~ plant**, plante f. aquatique. **~ power**, force f. motrice de l'eau. **~ pressure**, pression f. de l'eau. **~proof**, adj. imperméable à l'eau, waterproof. **~ supply**, approvisionnement m. d'eau. **~ tank**, réservoir m., citerne f. **~tight**, imperméable à l'eau, imperméable.

watercress n. cresson m.

watered adj. mouillé; arrosé; moire (fabric).

waterfall n. chute f. d'eau; cascade f.

watery adj. aqueux; liquide; de l'eau; humide; humecté.

wave n. vague f. flot m.; onde f.; ondulation f.; moire f. (fabric). v.i. ondoyer, onduler; s'agiter; vaciller. v.t. faire flotter; agiter (hand, flag, etc.).

waver v.i. vaciller, balancer, hésiter.

waving *adj.* agité, onduleux, ondoyant.

wavy *adj.* onduleux, ondulé, ondoyant.

wax *n.* cire *f.* of ~, de cire. ~ **candle**, bougie *f.* de cire. *v.t.* cirer. *v.i.* croître, s'accroître, grandir; devenir, se faire.

waxen *adj.* de cire.

waxy *adj.* semblable à de la cire; mou; visqueux.

way *n.* voie *f.*, chemin *m.*, route *f.*, sentier *m.*; passage *m.*; côté *m.*, direction *f.*, sens *m.*; distance *f.*; manière *f.*, méthode *f.*, façon *f.* **high~**, autoroute *f.* Milky Way, Voie Lactée. **all the ~**, tout le chemin, jusqu'au bout. **by ~ of**, par la voie de, en passant par. **by the ~**, en passant, soit dit en passant, à propos. **out of the ~**, hors du chemin; caché. **to be in the ~**, être dans le chemin; gêner, embarrasser. **to lose one's ~**, s'égarer. **to get out of the ~**, éloigner; écarter; se ranger; se sauver; se cacher. **to give or make ~**, faire place; céder; s'abandonner. **to lead the ~**, marcher devant, marcher en tête; conduire. **to make one's ~**, s'ouvrir un passage; faire son chemin; réussir. **to show the ~**, montrer le chemin; donner l'exemple. **to get under~**, se mettre en route. **one ~ or another**, d'une manière/façon ou d'une autre. **that ~**, de ce côté, par là. **this ~**, de ce côté, par ici. **which ~?** par où? de quel côté? **the right ~**, le bon chemin, la bonne voie. **the wrong ~**, le mauvais chemin, la mauvaise voie. **the best ~ is**, le meilleur moyen est. **his ~ of speaking**, sa façon de parler. **in no ~**, en aucune façon, nullement. **by ~ of**, en guise de; en passant par. **let him have his own ~**, laissez le faire, qu'il fasse à sa manière, à sa guise.

wayfarer *n.* voyageur *m.*

wayfaring *adj.* qui voyage; voyageur.

waylay *v.t.* tendre des embûches à; guetter au passage.

wayward *adj.* obstiné, entêté; volontaire; bourru; pervers.

we *pers.pron.* nous.

weak *adj.* faible; débile; affaibli. **a ~ mind**, un esprit faible. **to get, to grow ~**, s'affaiblir. **~-eyed**, qui a les yeux faibles, la vue faible. **~-minded**, faible d'esprit, simple.

weaken *v.i.* s'affaiblir.

weakening *adj.* affaiblissant; débilitant.

weakling *n.* être *m.* faible, chétif.

weakly *adv.* faiblement, timidement.

weakness *n.* faiblesse *f.*; faible *m.*

wealth *n.* richesse *f.*; biens *m.pl.*, richesses *f.pl.*; fortune *f.*

wealthy *adj.* riche, opulent.

wean *v.t.* sevrer; détacher (from an affection). **to ~ a child**, sevrer un enfant.

weapon *n.* arme *f.*; défense *f.*

wear *v.t.* porter (clothing), avoir; montrer; user, effacer, consumer; harasser; fatiguer. **he wears glasses**, il porte des lunettes. **worn to a thread**, usé jusqu'à la corde. **to ~ away**, user, consumer; détruire, effacer, passer. **to ~ off**, effacer, détruire peu à peu. **to ~ out**, user, épuiser; harasser, fatiguer. **worn-out clothes**, vieux habits. **to ~ well**, faire bon usage. **to ~ away**, s'user, se consumer; s'effacer; se passer. **to ~ off**, s'user; s'effacer; se passer, se dissiper. **to ~ out**, s'user, se consumer; vieillir. *n.* user *m.*; usage *m.*; usure *f.*; dépérissement par l'usage. **~ and tear**, usure *f.*; fatigue *f.*, détérioration *f.*

wearily *adv.* avec lassitude; ennuyeusement.

weariness *n.* lassitude *f.*; ennui *m.*; dégoût *m.*

wearisome *adj.* fatigant; ennuyeux; fastidieux; *Infml.* assommant.

weary *adj.* las, fatigué; ennuyé; fatigant; fastidieux, ennuyeux. *v.t.* lasser, fatiguer; ennuyer.

weasel *n.* belette *f.*; *Infml.* fouine *f.*

weather *n.* temps *m.* **cloudy ~**, temps couvert. **foggy ~**, temps brumeux, temps de brouillard. **rainy ~**, temps pluvieux. **stormy ~**, temps d'orage; *Naut.* gros temps. **how is the ~ today?** quel temps fait-il aujourd'hui? *v.t.* exposer à l'air; résister à, supporter; *Naut.* passer au vent de; doubler (a cape). **to ~ the storm**, résister à la tempête. *adj.* au vent, du côté du vent.

weave *n.* tissage *m.* ~. *v.t.* tisser; tresser, enlacer, entrelacer; entremêler. *v.i.* tisser, travailler au métier.

weaver *n.* tisserand *m.* **~bird**, tisserin *m.*

web *n.* toile *f.*; palmure *f.* (ducks, etc.). **spider ~**, toile d'araignée. **~-footed**, palmipède, aux pieds palmés.

wed *v.t.* épouser. *Fig.* enchaîner, adopter. **to be wedded to**, être attaché à. *v.i.* se marier.

wedded *adj.* marié, épousé; légitime; conjugal.

wedding *n.* mariage *m.* ~ **presents**, corbeille *f.*, cadeaux *m.pl.* de noces. ~ **ring**, alliance *f.*, anneau *m.* nuptial.

wedge *n.* coin *m.*; cale *f.*; lingot *m.* (metal). *v.t.* serrer (avec des coins); caler, fixer. **to ~ in**, pousser; enfoncer; serrer; enclaver.

wedlock *n.* mariage *m.* **mothers out of ~**, mères *f.pl.* célibataires.

Wednesday *n.* mercredi *m.*

wee *adj.* tout petit, minuscule.

wee-wee (child) pipi *m.*

weed *n.* herbe *f.*, mauvaise herbe *f.* ~ *v.t.* sarcler; arracher les mauvaises herbes; *Fig.* extirper, déraciner; débarrasser, purifier. **to ~ out**, extirper, arracher.

weedy *adj.* d'herbes, de plantes; plein de mauvaises herbes.

week *n.* semaine *f.*; huitaine *f.* **by the ~**, à la semaine. ~ **in ~ out**, d'une semaine à l'autre. **~day**, jour ouvrable. **last ~**, la semaine dernière. **~-end**, fin *f.* de semaine, week-end *m.*

weekly *adj.* hebdomadaire. ~ **paper**, journal hebdomadaire. *adv.* toutes les semaines, hebdomadairement. *n.* journal *m.* or revue *f.* hebdomadaire.

weeny *adj.* tout petit. **teeny ~**, riquiqui.

weep *v.i.* pleurer; gémir; se plaindre. **to ~ for joy**, pleurer de joie.

weeping adj. qui pleure, en larmes; Bot. pleureur. **~ willow**, saule m. pleureur. n. pleurs m.pl.; larmes f.pl.; lamentations f.pl.

weigh v.t. peser; examiner, considérer; balancer; lever (anchor). **to ~ oneself**, se peser. **to ~ down**, affaisser, accabler, abattre. **to ~ out**, peser (en petites quantités). **to ~ upon**, peser sur, accabler. **to ~ down**, pencher (par son propre poids); s'affaisser. n. poids m.; pesée f.

weight n. poids m.; pesanteur f.; Fig. charge f., embarras m. **gross ~**, poids brut. **net ~**, poids net. **standard ~**, poids légal. **by ~**, au poids. **to be worth its ~ in gold**, valoir son pesant d'or. **his remarks carried great ~**, ses observations étaient d'un grand poids; avaient une grand valeur. **~lifting**, haltérophilie f.

weightless adj. sans poids, léger.

weighty adj. lourd, pesant; de poids; sérieux, important; grave.

weird adj. bizarre, singulier, curieux; étrange.

weirdo n. Infml. dérangé m., pas net m., un gars bizarre.

welcome adj. bienvenu; agréable, heureux; bein reçu; qui vient à propos. **you are ~**, vous êtes le bienvenu; il n'y a pas de quoi. interj. soyez le bienvenu! bienvenue f.; bon accueil m., salut m. de bienvenue. **a hearty ~**, une réception cordiale. v.t. souhaiter la bienvenue à; saluer; faire bon acceuil à.

welcoming adj. de bienvenue.

weld n. soudure f. **~** v.t. souder.

welder n. soudeur m.; celui qui soude.

welding n. soudure f. **~** adj. de soudure.

welfare n. bien-être m., bien m., bonheur m.; prospérité f. (of a state); assistance f. publique.

well n. source f.; puits m.; réservoir m. d'eau; citerne f. **to sink a ~**, creuser un puits. v.i. sourdre, jaillir, couler.

well adj. bien, bien portant, en bonné santé; bon, heureux; utile, avantageux, profitable. **to be ~ off**, être dans l'aisance, être dans une bonne position. **to be ~ to do**, être à son aise. **all's ~ that ends ~**, tout est bien qui finit bien. interj. eh bien! soit. adv. bien; adroitement, comme il faut; amplement; très, fort; beaucoup; heureusement; parfaitement. **~ done**, bien fait. **very ~**, très bien. **as ~ as**, aussi bien que. **~ behaved**, qui se conduit bien; poli, courtois. **~-being**, bien-être m.; bonheur m.; prospérité f. **~-bred**, bien élevé. **~-disposed**, bien disposé. **~ done**, interj. très bien! **~-educated**, qui a reçu une bonne éducation. **~-informed**, bien informé. **~-intentioned**, bien intentionné. **~-known**, bien connu; notoire. **~-spoken**, qui parle bien; aux belles paroles; bien dit. **~-timed**, opportun; fait à propos. **~-wisher**, ami m., protecteur m., qui veut du bien, celui qui perte intérêt à quelqu'un.

Welsh adj. gallois, du pays de Galles (language). n. Gallois m., Galloise f.

welter n. confusion f., pêle-mêle m.

wend v.i. aller; tourner. v.t. diriger, poursuivre; passer. **to ~ one's way**, se diriger, diriger ses pas.

were plur. pret. to be. See BE.

werewolf n. loup-garou m.

west n. ouest m., occident m., couchant m. adj. occidental, d'occident, de l'ouest, d'ouest, ouest. **West Indies**, Antilles f.pl. adv. à l'ouest, au couchant.

western adj. occidental, d'occident, de l'ouest, ouest; couchant; à l'ouest, vers l'ouest. n. Cine. western m.

westward(s) adv. à l'ouest, vers l'ouest, vers l'occident. adj. à l'ouest, vers l'ouest. n. ouest m.

wet adj. humide, mouillé, humecté, arrosé; pluvieux. **~ nurse**, nourrice f. **to be soaking ~**, être trempé, être mouillé jusqu'aux os. n. humidité f.; eau f.; pluie f. **~** v.t. mouiller, tremper; humecter.

whack v.t. battre, rosser, étriller. n. coup m.

whale n. baleine f. **~bone**, baleine f.

whaler n. baleinier m.

wham excl. vlan! v.t. frapper, cogner.

wharf n.pl. **wharfs** or **wharves**, quai m.; môle m.

what rel. pron. que, quoi; ce que; (subject) ce qui; ce que c'est; quoi que ce soit; ceci; combien. **do ~ you want**, fais ce que tu veux. **I'll tell you ~**, je vais te dire. **to know what's ~**, savoir de qui il s'agit/il est question. **~ is that?** qu'est-ce que c'est (que ça?). **~ if**, et si, quand même. **and ~ if I did it?** et si je le faisais? **~ then?** et puis, ensuite, après? adj. quel; que de. **~ money we had was taken away**, on nous á prit tout l'argent que nous avions. **~ book is this?** quel est ce livre? **~ presence of mind!** quelle présence d'esprit!

whatever, whatsoever rel. pron. tout ce qui; tout ce que; quoi que, quel que; quoi que ce soit. **~ you do**, quoi que vous fassiez. **~ he may say**, quoi qu'il dise. adj. tout ... qui; quelconque; aucun; quelque ... que; quel que soit; quel que. **~ way you take**, quelque chemin que vous reniez.

wheat n. blé m., froment m.

wheedle v.t. enjuler v.t. flatter; cajoler.

wheel n. roue f.; disque m.; rond m., tour m.; révolution f.; rotation f., tour m. **big ~**, person important. **cog~**, roue dentée, roue d'engrenage. **~chair**, fauteuil m. roulant. **water~**, roue hydraulique. **~-barrow**, brouette f. **~** v.t. rouler; tourner; faire tourner; brouetter. v.i. avancer en roulant; (se) tourner, retourner.

wheeled adj. à roues. **a two-~ vehicle**, une voiture à deux roues.

wheeze v.i. siffler, souffler.

wheezing adj. asthmatique. n. sifflement m., respiration f. bruyante.

when conj. ~ adv. quand, lorsque; où; alors que. **~ I call you**, quand je vous appelle. **since ~?** depuis quand?

whence adv. d'où; de là. conj. c'est pourquoi, par conséquent; donc, ainsi.

whenever *adv.* n'importe quand; à chaque fois; toutes les fois que, quand, lorsque.

where *adv.* où. **any~**, n'importe où, partout. **no~**, nulle part. **every~**, partout.

whereabout(s) *adv.* où, à peu près où, de quel côté. **the police want to know of his ~s**, la police veut savoir où il se trouve.

whereas *conj.* tandis que; mais au contraire.

whereby *adv.* par quoi, par où; par lequel.

wherefore *adv.* pourquoi. *conj.* c'est pourquoi, donc, aussi.

whereof *adv.* dont, duquel; de quoi?

whereupon *adv.* où, sur quoi, sur lequel; là-dessus.

wherever *adv.* partout où, n'importe où.

wherewithal *m.* de quoi. **to have the ~ to**, avoir de quoi.

whet *v.t.* aiguiser; affiler, affûter; *Fig.* exciter, stimuler; animer. **to ~ a knife**, aiguiser, repasser un couteau. **to ~ the appetite**, aiguiser l'appétit.

whether *conj., pron.* si; soit; soit que. **I do not know ~**, je ne sais si. **~ he succeeds or not**, qu'il réussisse ou non.

whetstone *n.* pierre *f.* à aiguiser, pierre *f.* à repasser.

whey *n.* petit-lait *m.*

which *rel. pron.* qui, que; *n.* lequel *m.*, laquelle *f.*, lesquels *m.pl*, lesquelles *f.pl*. *adj.* lequel *m.*, laquelle *f.*; lesquels *m.pl*, lesquelles *f.pl.*, quelle *f.*, quels *m.pl.*, quelles *f.pl*.

whichever *indef. pron., indef. adj.* quel que soit; l'un ou l'autre; celui qui, celui que.

whiff *n.* bouffée *f.*, souffle *f.*

while *n.* temps *m.*; espace de temps; moment *m.*, instant *m.*; durée *f.*; fois *f.* **a long ~**, longtemps. **a long ~ ago**, il y a longtemps. **a little ~**, un peu de temps, un moment. **in the mean~**, pendant ce temps-là, sur ces entrefaites. **all the ~**, pendant tout le temps. **it is not worth~**, ça n'en vaut pas la peine, ce n'est pas la peine. *conj.* pendant que, tandis que; tant que. *v.i.* passer lentement; laminer. *v.t.* passer, faire passer (time).

whim *n.* caprice *m.*, fantaisie *f.*, lubie *f.*

whimper *v.i.* avoir le coeur gros; se plaindre; pleurnicher. *v.t.* dire en sanglotant.

whimsical *adj.* capricieux, fantasque.

whine *v.i.* se plaindre, se lamenter; geindre; pleurnicher. *n.* plainte *f.*; gémissement *m.*; pleurnicherie *f.*

whining *adj.* plaintif, dolent. *n.* pleurnicherie *f.*

whinny *v.i.* hennir.

whip *v.t.* fouetter; frapper; flageller, fustiger; *Fig.* critiquer; battre (eggs, cream, etc.). **to ~ up**, confectionner rapidement. **to crack a ~**, faire claquer un fouet. **horse~**, cavache *f.* **~lash**, coup de fouet.

whipping *n.* flagellation *f.*; coups *m.pl.* de fouet; fouet *m.*

whir *v.i.* tournoyer (avec bruit); bruire.

whirl *v.t.* tourner rapidement; (faire) tourner; agiter, bouleverser. **to ~ around**, tourner rapidement; agiter rapidement. *n.* tournoiement *m.*; tour *m.*; tourbillon *m.*; tourbillonnement *m.*; pirouette *f.* (toy).

whirlpool *n.* tourbillon *m.* (d'eau).

whirlwind *n.* tourbillon *m.*, trombe *f.*

whisk *n.* plumedu *m.* **~** *v.t.* brosser, vergeter; épousser; battre (eggs), fouetter (cream). **to ~ away**, enlever vivement, expédier. *v.i.* passer rapidement. **to ~ off**, s'en aller vite.

whisker *n.* favori *m.*; moustache *f.* (cat).

whiskey *n.* whisky *m.*

whisper *v.i.* chuchoter; parler tout bas; soupirer. *v.t.* dire tout bas, dire à l'oreille; souffler; prévenir. *n.* chuchotement *m.*, murmure *m.*; rumeur *f.* **in a ~**, tout bas, à voix basse.

whistle *v.i.,v.t.* siffler. **the winds ~**, les vents sifflent. *n.* sifflet *m.*; coup *m.* de sifflet; sifflement *m.* **to wet one's ~**, s'humecter le gosie.

white *adj.* blanc *m.*, blanche *f.*, pâle; blême; sans tache; pur. **~ as a sheet**, blanc comme un linge. **to turn ~**, blanchir. **to turn ~**, pâlir, devenir pâle. *n.* blanc *m.* **to dress in ~**, s'habiller de blanc.

whiten *v.t.* blanchir. *v.i.* (se) blanchir, devenir blanc.

whiteness *n.* blancheur *f.*, pâleur.

whitewash *n.* lait *m.* de chaux; badigeon *m.* **~** *v.t.* blanchir; badigeonner (walls); disculper.

whitewater *n.* rapid *m.*

whittle *v.i.* taillader.

who *rel. pron.* qui.

whoever *indef. pron.* qui que ce soit, quiconque, qui.

whole *adj.* tout, entier; total, complet; intact; sain. **the ~ world**, le monde entier. **the ~ sum**, toute la somme. *n.* tout *m.*, totalité *f.*; ensemble *m.*, somme *f.*, total *m.*, montant *m.* **on, upon the ~**, en somme, à tout prendre.

wholesale *n.* commerce *m.* de gros, gros *m.*, masse *f.* **by ~**, en gros, gros. *adj.* en gros; de gros.

wholesome *adj.* sain; salutaire, bienfaisant, utile.

wholly *adv.* entièrement; tout à fait, totalement.

whom *rel. pron.* que; lequel *m.*, laquelle *f.*, lesquels *m.pl*, lesquelles *f.pl* **~ have you seen?** qui avez-vous vu? **~ was it from?** de qui était-ce?

whoop *n.* cri *m.*; huée *f.*; cri *m.* de guerre. *v.i., v.t.* crier, huer.

whooping *n.* **~ cough**, coqueluche *f.*

whopping *adj.* *Infml.* grand, fameux, épatant.

whore *n.* *Infml.* pute *f.* **~house**, bordel *m.* **~** *v.t.* débaucher; fréquenter les femmes de mauvaise vie.

whose *rel. pron.* dont, de qui, duquel *m.*, de laquelle *f.*, desquels *m.pl*, desquelles *f.pl.*; quel; (interrogatively) à qui. **he ~ name**, celui dont le nom. **~ book is this?** à qui est ce livre?

why *adv.* pourquoi.

wick *n.* mèche *f.*

wicked *adj.* méchant, mauvais, pervers; nuisible, pernicieux.

wickedly *adv.* méchamment, avec méchanceté.

wickedness *n.* perversité *f.;* mal *m.,* vice *m.;* immoralité *f.;* impiété *f.,* méchanceté *f.*

wicker *n.* osier *m.* **~work,** vannerie *f.;* treillis *m.* ~ *adj.* d'osier en osier. ~ **basket,** panier d'osier. ~ **bottle,** bouteille *f.* clissée.

wide *adj.* large; vaste, spacieux, ample. **three centimeters** ~, trois centimètres de large. **the** ~ **world,** le vaste monde. *adv.* loin, au loin; largement; tout à fait. ~ **open,** grand ouvert. ~**-awake,** *adj.* bien éveillé, sur ses gardes. *n.* ~**spread,** qui s'étend au loin; immense, vaste.

widely *adv.* loin, au loin, bien loin; largement; grandement.

widen *v.t.* élargir; dilater (les marines). *v.i.* s'élargir; s'étendre, s'agrandir.

wideness *n.* largeur *f.;* étendue *f.,* grandeur *f.*

widow *n.* veuve *f.* ~ *v.t.* rendre veuve.

widowed *adj.* veuf, veuve; abandonné, solitaire.

widower *n.* veuf *m.*

widowhood *n.* veuvage *m.;* douaire *m.*

width *n.* largeur *f.;* ampleur *f.,* étendue *f.*

wield *v.t.* manier; diriger; tenir, porter.

wife *n. pl.* **wives,** femme *f.,* épouse *f.*

wig *n.* perruque *f.*

wiggle *v.i.* gigoter, remuer, se tortiller.

wild *adj.* sauvage; inculte; naturel, désert; barbare, féroce, farouche; violent, fou, extravagant, effaré, fantasque; capricieux. **a** ~ **ox,** un boeuf sauvage. ~ **beasts,** des bêtes féroces. ~**flowers,** fleurs de champs. ~ **passions,** des passions violentes. **to run** ~, se déchaîner; être inculte (plants, garden, etc.). **a** ~ **look,** un regard effaré. ~ **boar,** sanglier *m.* ~**fire,** feu *m.* grégeois. ~**life,** vie *f.* animale, faune *f.*

wilderness *n.pl.* régions *f.pl.* sauvages, désert *m.;* forêt *f.;* solitude *f.,* désordre *m.*

wildness *n.* nature *f.* sauvage (animals); état *m.* sauvage, état *m.* inculte (place); férocité *f.;* violence *f.,* fureur *f.,* tumulte *m.;* dérèglement *m.,* désordre *m.;* égarement *m.* (mind); folie *f.;* bizarrerie *f.*

wile *n.* artifice *m.,* ruse *f.;* tour *m.*

will *n.* volonté *f.;* vouloir *m.;* intention *f.;* gré *m.,* bon plaisir *m.;* désir *m.;* voeu *m.;* testament *m.* **free** ~, libre arbitre *m.* **where there's a** ~, **there's a way,** vouloir c'est pouvoir. **at** ~, à volonté. **good**~, bonne volonté *f.,* bon vouloir *m.* **ill**~, mauvaise volonté *f.,* mauvais vouloir *m.* **to make one's** ~, faire son testament. *v.t.* vouloir; ordonner; léguer (by testament).

willful *adj.* volontaire, entêté, obstiné, opiniâtre; têtu; fait à dessein; prémédité.

willing *adj.* de bonne volonté; bien disposé (à); désireux; prêt (à). ~ **or unwilling,** bon gré mal gré.

willingly *adv.* volontiers; de bon coeur; de bonne volonté.

willingness *n.* bonne volonté *f.,* bon vouloir *m.;* empressement *m.;* complaisance *f.*

willow *n.* saule *m.* **weeping** ~, saule pleureur. ~ **tree,** saule *m.*

willowy *adj.* élancé, svelte, mince.

willpower *n.* volonté *f.,* vouloir *m.*

wilt *v.i.* se faner, se flétrir.

wily *adj.* rusé, artificieux, astucieux.

wimp *n. Infml.* froussard *m.,* faiblard *m.,* poule *f.* mouillée.

win *v.t.* gagner; remporter, obtenir; séduire. **to** ~ **over,** séduire gagner. *v.i.* triompher, l'emporter.

wince *v.i.* reculer, frémir; sourciller.

winch *n.* manivelle *f.;* treuil *m.*

wind *f.* vent *m.;* souffle *m.;* respiration *f.;* haleine *f.* **high** ~, vent fort. ~ **instrument,** instrument *m.* à vent. ~**mill,** moulin *m.* à vent. *v.t.* éventer; exposer au vent.

wind *v.t.* donner, sonner (horn); tourner; faire tourner; retourner; entourer; enlacer; tourner, rouler, enrouler, dévider; remonter (watch, etc.); arranger; régler; terminer. *v.i.* se rouler, s'enrouler, s'entortiller; tourner; changer, serpenter; circuler. **to** ~ **around,** s'enrouler autour de; tourner autour de. **to** ~ **up,** (clocks) se remonter; monter en tournant; conclure, régler.

windfall *n.* fruit *m.* tombé (par le vent); bonne aubaine *f.*

winding *adj.* sinueux, tortueux; en limaçon; qui s'entortille. ~ **staircase,** escalier *m.* tournant, en limaçon.

window *n.* fenêtre *f.,* croisée *f.;* baie *f.,* ouverture *f.,* jour *m.;* châssis portant les vitres; vitre *f.;* carreau *m.;* treillis *m.;* étalage *m.,* montre *f.;* devanture *f.* **to look out of the** ~, regarder par la fenêtre. **bay** ~, fenêtre cintrée. ~ **frame,** chassis *m.* de fenêtre. ~ **shutter,** volet *m.;* contrevent *m.*

windpipe *n.* trachée artère *f.*

windshield *n.* pare-brise *m.*

windward *adv.* au vent. *adj.* au vent; qui porte au vent; du vent. *n.* vent *m.;* côté *m.* du vent.

windy *adj.* venteux; orageux; de vent; *Fig.* vain, creux. **it's** ~, il fait du vent, il vente.

wine *n.* vin *m.;* boisson *f.* ~ **bottle,** bouteille *f.* de vin. ~ **cask,** fût *m.,* tonneau *m.* à vin. ~ **cellar,** cave *f.* à vin. ~ **press,** pressoir *m.*

wing *n.* aile *f.; Fig.* vol *m.,* essor *m.;* course *f.;* parti. *Pol.* **left/right** ~, la gauche *f.,* la droite *f.* ~ *v.t.* donner des ailes à, porter, transporter sur ses ailes; parcourir (en volant); *Mil.* flanquer, protéger; blesser à l'aile. *v.i.* voler, s'envoler.

wink *v.i.* fermer les yeux; cligner de l'oeil; sourciller. **to** ~ **at,** fermer les yeux sur, tolérer; regarder du coin de l'oeil. *n.* clin *m.* d'oeil; oeillade *f.*

winner *n.* vainqueur *m.;* gagnant *m.*

winning *adj.* gagnant, qui gagne; séduisant, attrayant. *n.* ~**s,** gains *m.pl.*

winnow *v.t.* vanner; sasser; trier; séparer.

winter *n.* hiver *m.* ~ *adj.* d'hiver. ~ **season,** saison d'hiver. *v.i.* hiverner, passer l'hiver. *v.t.* nourrir pendant l'hiver; conserver pendant l'hiver. **~ garden,** jardin *m.* d'hiver.

wintry *adj.* d'hiver, hivernal, froid.

wipe *v.t.* essuyer, nettoyer (en frottant); effacer. **to ~ off,** essuyer, effacer. **to ~ out,** essuyer, effacer, faire disparaître. *n.* nettoyage *m.*

wiper *n.* essuie glace *m.*

wire *n.* fil *m.* métallique; fil de fer *m.;* télégramme *m.; Mus.* corde *f.;* tringle *f.* **brass ~,** fil de laiton. **copper ~,** fil de cuivre. *v.t.* lier avec un fil métallique; griller; télégraphier. **~ fence,** clôture *f.* en fils de fer.

wireless *adj.* sans fil. *n.* message *m.* sans fil; appareil *m.* de télégraphie sans fil.

wisdom *n.* sagesse *f.*

wise *adj.* sage; judicieux; sagace; prudent, circonspect; grave, capable. **a ~ person,** une personne raisonnable.

wisecrack *n. Infml.* vanne *f.*

wisely *adv.* sagement.

wish *v.i.,v.t.* souhaiter, désirer, vouloir, demander; prier. **to ~ for,** souhaiter, désirer, demander. **to ~ well to,** vouloir du bien à. *n.* souhait *m.,* désir *m.,* voeu *m.;* demande *f.* **to have one's ~,** avoir ce que l'on désire. **to make a ~,** faire un voeu.

wistful *adj.* attentif, sérieux; soucieux, de désir; de regret.

wistfully *adv.* d'un air d'envie.

wit *n.* intelligence *f.,* entendement *m.;* esprit *m.;* finesse *f.;* habileté *f.;* homme ou femme d'esprit; bel esprit. **ready ~,** esprit vif. **to be at one's wits' end,** être au bout de son latin; ne savoir plus à quel saint se vouer. **to be out of one's ~s,** avoir perdu la tête. **to have one's ~s about one,** avoir toute sa présence d'esprit.

witch *n.* sorcière *f.*

witchcraft *n.* sorcellerie *f.,* magie *f.;* sortilège *m.;* charme *m.*

with *prep.* avec; de; à; par contre; chez; parmi; auprès de; envers, à l'égard de, pour. **~ all my heart,** de tout mon coeur. **filled ~,** rempli de. **infatuated ~,** infatué de. **taken ~,** charmé de. **a girl ~ blue eyes,** une jeune fille aux yeux bleus. **angry ~,** fâché contre.

withdraw *v.t.* retirer, rapeler; éloigner, détourner. **to ~ a charge,** retirer une accusation. *v.i.* se retirer; s'en aller.

withdrawal *n.* retraite *f.,* retrait *m.* (bank account, etc.).

wither *v.i.* se dessécher; se faner, dépérir, languir. *v.t.* faner; flétrir; faire dépérir; faire languir.

withhold *v.t.* retenir, empêcher; contenir; refuser; écarter.

within *prep.* dans; en dedans de, en; dans l'espace de; en; dans les limites de, en deçà de. **~ the walls,** dans l'intérieur des murs. **~ a short distance,** à peu de distance, pas loin, tout pres. **~ an hour,** dans l'heure. *adv.* dedans, en dedans; chez soi, intérieurement, en dedans.

without *prep.* sans. *conj.* à moins que, sans que, si ce n'est que, si.

withstand *v.t.* résister à; s'opposer à.

witless *adj.* sans esprit, sans intelligence, sot, imbécile.

witness *n.* témoin *m.;* témoignage *m.* **eye ~,** témoin oculaire. **false ~,** faux témoignage. **~ stand,** banc *m.* des témoins, barre *f.* **to bear ~,** porter témoignage. *v.t.* être témoin de, assister à, voir; témoigner (de), attester. *v.i.* rendre témoignage.

witted *adj.* **quick-~,** à l'esprit vif.

witticism *n.* trait *m.* d'esprit, mot *m.* spirituel; saillie *f.*

wittiness *n.* esprit *m.,* sel *m.*

wittingly *adv.* sciemment, avec connaissance de cause; à dessein.

witty *adj.* spirituel, d'esprit, ingénieux; piquant, mordant.

wizard *n.* sorcier *m.,* magicien *m.*

wobble *v.i.* remuer irrégulièrement.

woe *n.* douleur *f.,* peine *f.;* affliction *f.;* malheur *m.,* calamité *f.* **~begone,** triste, désolé.

woeful *adj.* triste, malheureux, désolé, éploré; douloureux; déplorable; piteux.

wok *n.* poêle *f.* profonde chinoise.

wolf *n.pl.* **wolves,** loup *m.* **she-~,** louve *f.*

wolverine *n.* glouton *m.*

woman *n.pl.* **women** *n.* femme *f.*

womanhood *n.* qualité *f.;* état *m.* de femme.

womanish *adj.* de femme, féminin; efféminé, mou; pusillanime.

womanizer *n.* coureur de jupons *m.,* Don Juan *m.*

womanly *adj.* de femme, féminin, gracieux; efféminé. *adv.* en femme, comme une femme.

womb *n.* utérus *m.,* matrice *f.; Fig.* sein *m.,* entrailles *f.pl.,* flancs *m.pl.*

wonder *n.* étonnement *m.,* surprise *f.;* ébahissement *m.;* merveille *f.,* miracle *m.* **to do ~s,** faire des merveilles. **no ~!** ce n'est pas étonnant! **~struck,** émerveillé, frappé d'étonnement, ébahi. **~ worker,** faiseur *m.* de prodiges, de miracles. *v.i.* s'étonner, être étonné; s'extasier, s'émerveiller, *Infml.* s'ébahir; se demander, être curieux de savoir. **to ~ at,** s'étonner de. **I ~ whether,** je me demande si.

wonderful *adj.* étonnant, merveilleux, prodigieux, miraculeux; surprenant.

wonderfully *adv.* étonnamment, merveilleusement, prodigieusement.

wondering *adj.* étonné; ébahi.

wondrous *adj.* merveilleux, prodigieux; admirable.

wont *n.* habitude *f.,* coutume *f.*

wonted *adj.* habitué, accoutumé; ordinaire.

woo *v.t.* courtiser, faire la cour à; rechercher en mariage, supplier, implorer; demander, appeler; désirer. *v.i.* faire la cour; se courtiser.

wood *n.* bois *m.;* forêt *f.* **green ~,** bois vif, bois vert. **~cut,** gravure *f.* sur bois. **~ cutter,** bûcheron *m.* **~land,** pays *m.* boisé. **~pecker,** pivert *m.* **~work,** boiserie *f.*

wooded *adj.* boisé, couvert de bois.

wooden *adj.* de bois, en bois. **~-headed**, qui a la tête dure.

woody *adj.* couvert de bois, boisé, de bois; des bois; ombragé.

wool *n.* laine *f.*, poil *m.*, duvet *m.*; lainage *m.* **all ~**, pure laine, tout en laine. **lamb's ~**, laine d'agneau, laine agneline. **~-gathering**, *Infml.* distraction *f.*, absence *f.* d'esprit.

woolen *adj.* de laine, en laine; de lainages. **~ cloth**, drap *m.*

woolly *adj.* de laine, en laine; laineux; floconneux; (hair) crépu, frisé.

woozy *adj. Infml.* pompette; vaseux, dans les vapes.

word *n.* mot *m.*; parole *f.*; langage *m.*; promesse *f.*; discussion *f.* **good ~**, bonne parole. **by ~ of mouth**, verbalement, de vive voix. **~ for ~**, mot à mot, mot pour mot. **to have ~s**, avoir une dispute, se disputer. **to give one's ~**, donner sa parole. **to keep one's ~**, tenir sa parole. **take my ~ for it**, croyez-moi, vous pouvez m'en croire sur parole. **to bring ~ that**, apporter la nouvelle que. **to send ~**, donner avis, faire dire. *v.t.* exprimer, énoncer, rendre; rédiger.

wordiness *n.* verbosité *f.*, prolixité *f.*

wording *n.* expression *f.*, énonciation *f.*, rédaction *f.*; termes *m.pl.* (of a letter).

wordless *adj.* sans paroles, silencieux.

wordy *adj.* verbeux; de mots; prolixe, long.

work *v.i.* travailler; avoir de l'occupation; fermenter; fonctionner; marcher, aller; s'agiter. **to ~ hard**, travailler durement. **the machine works well**, la machine fonctionne bien. **to ~ at**, travailler à, s'occuper de. **to ~ in**, entrer (peu à peu). **to ~ into**, entrer dans, pénétrer dans; s'insinuer dans. **to ~ on**, travailler à; agir sur; exciter; émouvoir; exploiter. **to ~ out**, faire du sport/de la gym; résoudre. **to ~ through**, traverser à force de travail. **to ~ up**, s'exciter. *v.t.* travailler; façonner; ouvrer, fabriquer; exploiter (mine); tailler (gems); broder (fabric). **to ~ iron**, travailler le fer. *n.* ouvrage *m.*; travail *m.*; tâche *f.*, besogne *f.*; oeuvre *f.*; production *f.*; broderie *f.*; mécanisme *m.*; *pl.* **works**, usine *f.*, fabrique *f.*; mouvement *m.* (clock); *Miner.* exploitation *f.* **at ~**, à l'ouvrage, au travail. **hard ~**, travail pénible. **piece of ~**, ouvrage *m.*, oeuvre *f.*, travail *m.* **good ~s**, bonnes oeuvres. **~-room**, **~-shop**, atelier *m.*

worker *n.* personne *f.* qui travaille; ouvrier *m.*; travailleur *m.*

working *adj.* qui travaille; laborieux; de travail; en mouvement. **~ classes**, la classe ouvrière. *n.* travail, ouvrage *m.*; labeur *m.*; exploitation *f.*; fermentation *f.* (liquid); fonctionnement *m.*, jeu *m.* (machines); *Fig.* opération *f.* **~ day**, *n.* jour *m.* ouvrable.

workman *n.* ouvrier *m.*, artisan *m.*

workmanlike *adj.* habile, adroit; d'ouvrier; bien fait.

workmanship *n.* oeuvre *f.*, ouvrage *m.*, travail *m.*; main-d'oeuvre *f.*

world *n.* monde *m.*, vie *f.*; grand nombre; quantité *f.*; multitude *f.*; foule *f.* **in this ~**, dans ce monde, ici-bas. **the old ~**, l'ancien monde. **the new ~**, le nouveau monde. **the next ~**, l'autre monde.

worldliness *n.* mondanité *f.*; frivolité *f.*; nature *f.* positive.

worldly *adj.* du monde; mondain, de ce monde; positif. **~ pleasures**, les plaisirs du monde. *adv.* mondainement. **~-minded**, mondain, d'un caractère mondain. **~-mindedness**, mondanité *f.*

worldwide *adj.* mondial, universel.

worm *n.* ver *m.*, vermisseau *m.*; larve *f.*; chenille *f.* **earth~**, ver de terre. **silk~**, ver à soie. **~-eaten**, mangé, piqué aux vers; (wood) vermoulu. *v.i.* ramper; se glisser; *Fig.* s'insinuer. *v.t.* miner, saper sourdement.

worn See WEAR.

worried *adj.* inquiet, ète *m.f.* **~ to death**, fou *m.*/folle *f.* d'inquiétude.

worry *v.t.* tracasser, tourmenter; taquiner; ennuyer; agacer. *v.i.* (se) tourmenter, (se) tracasser. *n.* tourment *m.*, ennui *m.*; tracasserie *f.*

worse *adj.* plus mauvais, pire. **~ and ~**, de mal en pis; de plus en plus mauvais. **for the ~**, en mal, au plus mal. *adv.* pis, plus mal. **so much the ~**, tant pis. **to be ~ off**, être plus mal.

worship *n.* adoration *f.*, culte *m.* *v.t.* adorer; révérer; honorer.

worshiper *n.* adorateur *m.*, adoratrice *f.*

worst *adj.* (le) plus mauvais; (le) pire. *adv.* (le) pis, (le) plus mal. *n.* pis *m.*, plus mal *m.*; pis aller *m.*; dessous *m.* **at the ~**, au pire, au pis aller; au plus mal.

worth *n.* valeur *f.*; prix *m.*; mérite *m.* **a man of ~**, un homme de mérite. *adj.* qui vaut; égal à; qui est digne de. **to be ~**, valoir; posséder, avoir, être riche de. **he is ~ millions**, il possède des millions. **it is ~while**, ça en vaut la peine.

worthiness *n.* mérite *m.*, valeur *f.*; excellence *f.*

worthless *adj.* sans valeur; indigne; méprisable, vil.

worthlessness *n.* manque *m.* de valeur.

worthy *adj.* (of) digne de; honorable, respectable. *n.* homme *m.* illustre; héros *m.*

would *pret.* will vouloir.

would-be *adj.* soi-disant, prétendu.

wound *n.* blessure *f.*; plaie *f.* *v.t.* blesser; offenser.

wow *interj.* super! terrible!

wraith *n.* apparition *f.*, fantôme *m.*

wrangle *v.i.* discuter; se disputer, se quereller, se chamailler. *n.* dispute *f.*, altercation *f.*

wrap *v.t.* rouler, enrouler; envelopper. **to ~ up**, envelopper; renfermer.

wrapper *n.* enveloppe *f.*, couverture *f.*, toile *f.*, papier *m.* (packing); chemise *f.* (for papers); bande *f.* (for newspapers).

wrapping n. enveloppe f., couverture f.; toile f. etc. (for packing).

wrath n. colère f., courroux m., rage f.

wreak v.t. exécuter; infliger; assouvir; venger.

wreath n. tresse f.; guirlande f.; couronne f.; feston m.; nuage m., tourbillon m.

wreathe v.t. enrouler; entortiller; tresser; entrelacer; entourer; ceindre, couronner. v.i. s'entrelacer; s'enrouler.

wreck n. naufrage m.; vaisseau naufragé; débris m.; Law. épave f.; Fig. perte f., ruine f., destruction f. ~ v.i. faire naufrage; échouer; se perdre. v.t. perdre, ruiner, détruire.

wreckage n. naufrage m., destruction f.

wren n. roitelet m.

wrench v.t. arracher (en tordant); tordre, se fouler. n. torsion f.; effort m. violent; arrachement m.; clef f.

wrest v.t. arracher (en tordant), enlever; fausser. n. torsion f.; tordage m.; action f. d'arracher (en tordant); clef f. (for tuning).

wrestle v.i. lutter, combattre.

wrestling n. catch m., lutte f.

wrestler n. catcheur m.; lutteur m.

wretch n. misérable m., malheureux m., infortuné m.; pauvre diable m.; scélérat m.

wretched adj. malheureux, infortuné, pauvre; triste, pitoyable; misérable, vil. to look ~, faire peine à voir.

wretchedness n. misère f., infortune f.; souffrance f.; pauvreté f.; nature f. misérable; nature f. méprisable; pitoyable, mesquin.

wriggle v.i. (se) remuer, (se) tortiller, frétiller. to ~ into, s'insinuer dans. to ~ out of, s'échapper de, sortir de. v.t. remuer, tortiller.

wring v.t. tordre, arracher, serrer; torturer; tourmenter. to ~ one's hands, se tordre les mains. to ~ off, arracher, enlever (en tordant). to ~ out, faire sortir (en tordant, en pressant); tordre. v.i. (se) tordre, (se) débattre. n. torsion f.

wrinkle n. ride f. (face), pli m. (fabric). v.t. rider, plisser, froncer (brow); faire un faux pli à

(fabric); chiffonner, froisser. v.i. (se) rider.

wrist n. poignet m., carpe m. ~band, poignet m.

writ n., Law. ordonnance f.; mandat m., assignation f. holy ~, Écriture sainte. to serve a ~ upon, signifier un acte judiciaire, une assignation.

write v.t. écrire, composer, faire, imprimer. to ~ a few words, écrire quelques mots. to ~ down, écrire, mettre par écrit. to ~ out, copier, transcrire; rédiger. v.i. to ~ away for, mander, faire venir (par lettre); commander par lettre.

writer n. écrivain m.; auteur.

writhe v.t. tordre. v.i. (se) tordre, souffrir.

writing n. écriture f., main f.; écrit m.; ouvrage m., oeuvre f.; Law. acte m., document m. ~s, écrits m.pl. in ~, par écrit.

wrong adj. mauvais, injuste, mal; faux, erroné, impropre, inexact, incorrect. the ~ side, le mauvais côté; l'envers. that is ~ of you, c'est mal de votre part. to be ~, avoir tort. ~ ideas, des idées fausses. a ~ statement, un rapport inexact. n. mal m.; tort m., injustice f.; dommage m., préjudice m.; erreur f.; injure f., atteinte f. to do ~, mal agir, faire du tort, porter préjudice. to be in the ~, avoir tort, être dans l'erreur. ~doer, auteur m. d'un tort; méchant m.; pervers m. ~doing, mal m., injustice f. adv. mal, à tort, injustement; inexactement; de travers. right or ~, bien ou mal, à tort ou à raison. v.t. faire du tort à, nuire à, léser; être injuste pour.

wrongful adj. injuste, inique; nuisible, préjudiciable.

wrongfully adv. injustement, iniquement; à tort, faussement.

wrongly adv. injustement; à tort.

wrongness n. mal m.; injustice f.; fausseté f.; erreur f., inexactitude f.

wrought adj. travaillé, façonné; (fabric) oeuvré; (iron) forgé.

wry adj. tordu, de travers; tors, oblique, faux, faussé. ~ face, grimace f.

X

X n.m., chiffre romain qui équivaut à 10.

xenophobia n. xénophobie f.

xerox n. (trademark) photocopieuse f., photocopie f. ~ v.t. photocopier.

Xmas n. abbrev. **Christmas**, Noël.

x-ray n. rays m. X, radio(graphie) f. ~ v.t. faire une radio(graphie); radiographier.

xylophone n. xylophone m.

Y

yacht n. yacht m. **pleasure** ~, bateau m. de plaisance.

yachting n. voyage m. en yacht; excursion f. en yacht. adj. de yacht.

yack v.i. Infml. caqueter, jacasser.

yam n. patate f. douce.

yank n. coup sec m., saccade f. ~ v.t. tirer brusquement, arracher.

yankee n. yankee m.

yap n. Infml. gueule f.; japper; jacasser.

yard n. yard m.; cour f., préau m.; chantier m.

yarn n. fil m.; laine f. filée; Infml. histoire f., conte m. to spin a ~, raconter une longue histoire, histoire à dormir debout.

yawl n. Naut. yole f.

yawn v.i. bailler. n. baillement m.

yawning *adj.* qui baille; endormi, assoupi.

yea *n.* oui *m.*; vote affirmatif.

yeah *adv. Infml.* ouais.

year *n.* année *f.*, an *m.* **leap ~**, année bissextile. **the new ~**, le nouvel an. **New Year's Day**, jour *m.* de l'an. **~book**, annuaire *m.* d'université.

yearly *adj.* annuel; d'un an. *adv.* annuellement, tous les ans.

yearn *v.i.* s'affliger, souffrir; s'émouvoir. **to ~ after, for**, soupirer après, désirer vivement.

yearning *n.* aspiration *f.*; désir *m.* ardent; élan *m.* de tendresse, d'affection.

yeast *n.* levure *f.*

yell *v.i.,v.t.* hurler, pousser des hurlements; dire en hurlant, hurler. *n.* hurlement *m.*; cri *m.* de terreur.

yelling *adj.* hurlant; qui hurle. *n.* action *f.* de hurler; hurlements *m.pl.*

yellow *adj.* jaune; doré; blond, d'or. **to turn, to make, to become ~**, jaunir. **Yellow Pages**, pages jaunes *f.pl.* (phone book). *v.t.* jaunir. ~ jaune *m.*, couleur *f.* jaune. **~ fever**, fièvre *f.* jaune.

yellowish *adj.* jaunâtre.

yelp *v.i.* abover; glapir.

yes *adv.* oui. *n.* oui *m.*

yesterday *n.* hier *m.* *adv.* hier. **~ morning**, hier matin. **~ evening**, hier soir.

yet *conj.* cependant, pourtant, toutefois. *adv.* encore. **not ~**, pas encore. **as ~**, jusqu'à présent, jusqu'ici.

yield *v.t.* produire, rapporter, rendre; émettre (odor); céder, livrer. **to ~ six percent**, rapporter six pour cent. **to ~ assistance**, prêter du secours. **to ~ up**, rendre, livrer. *v.i.* céder; se soumettre; se rendre; consentir. **to ~ to**, se rendre à; consentir à. *n.* produit *m.*; Agr. récolte *f.*; rendement *m.*

yielding *adv.* souple, facile, accommodant; complaisant.

yoga *n.* yoga *m.*

yog(h)(o)urt *n.* yaourt *m.*, yogourt *m.*

yoke *n.* joug *m.*; paire *f.*; couple *m.*; attelage *m.* (oxen); servitude *f.*; (sewing) empiècement *m.* **~** *v.t.* mettre au joug, atteler; **(with)** accoupler avec.

yolk *n.* jaune *m.* d'oeuf.

yon, yonder *adj.* ce … là-bas, qui est là-bas, que voila, la-haut, au loin. *adv.* là-bas, dans le lointain.

you *pers.pron.* vous; tu, te, toi.

young *adj.* jeune; neuf, novice, inexpérimenté. **~ one**, petit (animal). **~ people, ~ folks**, les jeunes gens *m.pl.*, la jeunesse *f.pl.* jeunes gens *m.pl.*, jeunesse *f.*, (animals) petits *m.pl.* **with ~**, pleine.

younger *compar.adj.* plus jeune; cadet.

youngest *superl.adj.* (le) plus jeune; (le) cadet; dernier.

youngster *n.* jeune personne *f.*, enfant *m.*

your *poss. adj.* votre, vos, à vous, ton, ta, tes, à toi.

yours *poss. pron.* le vôtre, la vôtre, les votres, à vous, le tien, la tienne, les tiens, les tiennes, à toi. **~ truly**, bien à vous.

yourself *refl. pron.*, *pl.* **yourselves** vous-même; vous; toi-même, te, toi. **dress yourself**, habillez-vous, habille-toi. **dress yourselves**, habillez-vous.

youth *n.* jeunesse *f.*, adolescence *f.*; les jeunes gens *m.pl*

youthful *adj.* jeune; de la jeunesse, *Fig.* vif, vigoureux.

yucca *n.* yucca *m.*

yule *n.* Noël *m.*, fête *f.* de Noël. **~ log**, bûche *f.* de Noël.

yummy *adj. Infml.* vachement bon. *excl.* miam, miam!

Z

zany *adj.* fou.

zap *v.t.* effacer (computer). éliminee (video game).

zeal *n.* zèle m., enthousiasme *m.*

Zealand *n.pr.* New **~**, la Nouvelle-Zélande.

zealot *n.* zélateur *m.*; zélatrice *f.*; fanatique *m.*, partisan *m.* aveugle.

zealous *adj.* zélé; plein de zèle.

zealously *adv.* avec zèle.

zebra *n.* zèbre *m.*

zenith *n.* zénith *m.*

zero *n.* zéro *m.*

zest *n.* zeste *m.*; *Fig.* goût *m.*, saveur *f.* **~** *v.t.* donner du goût à, relever le goût de.

zigzag *n.* zigzag *m.* *adj.* en zigzag. *v.t.,v.i.* former en zigzags; faire des zigzags.

zillion *n. Infml.* million *m.*, milliard *m.*

zinc *n.* zinc *m.*

zip *n.* sifflement *m.* **~ code**, code postal *m.* **~ yui** *v.i.* siffler; passer vite. **~ up**, fermer à glissière.

zipper *n. Infml.* fermeture *f.* Eclair (trademark), fermeture à glissière.

zippy *adj. Infml.* plein d'entrain/d'énergie.

zit *n.* bouton (d'acné) *m.*

zither *n.* cithare *f.*

zodiac *n.* zodiaque *m.*

zombie *n.* zombe *m.*

zone *n.* zone *f.*; secteur *m.* **torrid ~**, zone torride. **frigid ~**, zone glaciale.

zoo *n.* zoo *m.*

zoologist *n.* zoologiste *m.*, zoologue *m.*

zoology *n.* zoologie *f.*

zoom *n.* vrombissement; *Photo.* (lens) zoom. *v.i.* passer en trombe, vrombir.

zucchini *n.* courgette *f.*

Numerals

Cardinal

one	1	un, une	thirty-one	31	trente et un
two	2	deux	thirty-two	32	trente-deux
three	3	trois	forty	40	quarante
four	4	quatre	fifty	50	cinquante
five	5	cinq	sixty	60	soixante
six	6	six	seventy	70	soixante-dix
seven	7	sept	seventy-one	71	soixante et onze
eight	8	huit	seventy-one	72	soixante-douze
nine	9	neuf	seventy-one	73	soixante-trieze
ten	10	dix	seventy-one	74	soixante-quatorze
eleven	11	onze	seventy-one	75	soixante-quinze
twelve	12	douze	seventy-one	76	soixante-seize
thirteen	13	treize	seventy-one	77	soixante-dix-sept
fourteen	14	quatorze	seventy-one	78	soixante-dix-huit
fifteen	15	quinze	seventy-one	79	soixante-dix-neuf
sixteen	16	seize	eighty	80	quatre-vingts
seventeen	17	dix-sept	eighty-one	81	quatre-vingt-un
eighteen	18	dix-huit	eighty-two	82	quatre-vingt-deux
nineteen	19	dix-neuf	ninety	90	quatre-vingt-dix
twenty	20	vingt	ninety-one	91	quatre-vingt-onze
twenty-one	21	vingt et un	ninety-two	92	quatre-vingt-douze
twenty-two	22	vingt-deux	one hundred	100	cent
twenty-three	23	vingt-trois	one hundred one	101	cent un
twenty-four	24	vingt-quatre	one hundred two	102	cent deux
twenty-five	25	vingt-cinq	two hundred	200	deux cents
twenty-six	26	vingt-six	three hundred	300	trois cents
twenty-seven	27	vingt-sept	three hundred one	301	trois cent un
twenty-eight	28	vingt-huit	one thousand	1,000	mille
twenty-nine	29	vingt-neuf	five thousand	5,000	cinq mille
thirty	30	trente	one million	1,000,000	un million

Ordinal

first	1st	premier, première
second	2nd	deuxième, second
third	3rd	troisième
fourth	4th	quatrième
fifth	5th	cinquième
sixth	6th	sixième
seventh	7th	septième
eighth	8th	huitième
ninth	9th	neuvième
tenth	10th	dixième
eleventh	11th	onzième
twelfth	12th	douzième
thirteenth	13th	treizième
fourteenth	14th	quatorzième

fifteenth	15th	quinzième
sixteenth	16th	seizième
seventeenth	17th	dix-septième
eighteenth	18th	dix-huitième
nineteenth	19th	dix-neuvième
twentieth	20th	vingtième
twenty-first	21st	vingt-et-unième
twenty-second	22nd	vingt-deuxième
thirtieth	30th	trentième
fortieth	40th	quarantième
fiftieth	50th	cinquantième
sixtieth	60th	soixantième
seventieth	70th	soixante-dixième
eightieth	80th	quatre-vingtième
ninetieth	90th	quatre-vingt-dixième
hundredth	100th	centième
hundred-and-first	101st	cent-unième
hundred-and-second	102nd	cent-deuxième
hundred-and-third	103rd	cent-troisième
three-hundredth	300th	trois-centième
thousandth	1,000th	millième
millionth	1,000,000th	millionième

Weights and Measures

The French use the *Metric System* of weights and measures, a decimal system in which multiples are shown by the prefixes **déci-** (one-tenth); **centi-** (one hundredth); **milli-** (one thousandth); **hecto-** (hundred); and **kilo-** (thousand).

1 centimètre	=	.3937 inch	1 tonne	=	2.204 pounds
1 mètre	=	39.37 inches	1 centilitre	=	.338 ounce
1 kilomètre	=	.621 mile	1 litre	=	1.0567 quart
1 centigramme	=	.1543 grain			(liquid);
1 gramme	=	15.432 grains		=	.908 quart
100 grammes	=	3.527 ounces			(dry)
1 kilogramme	=	2.2046 pounds	1 kilolitre	=	264.18 gallons

Signs

Caution	Attention	Go Slow	Ralentir
Danger	Danger	No smoking	Défense de fumer
Exit	Sortie	No admittance	Défense d'entrer
Entrance	Entrée	Women	Dames
Stop	Halte, Arrêtez	Men	Hommes
Closed	Fermé	Lavatory	Lavabos,
Open	Ouvert		Toilettes

Useful Words and Phrases

Hello. Bonjour.

Good day. Bonjour.

Good afternoon. Bonjour.

Good evening. Bonsoir.

Good night. Bonne nuit.

Good-bye. Au revoir.

How are you? Comment allez-vous?

Fine, thank you. Très bien, merci.

Glad to meet you. Enchanté de faire votre connaissance.

Thank you very much. Merci beaucoup.

You're welcome. Pas de quoi.

Please. S'il vous plaît.

Excuse me. Excusez-moi.

Good luck Bonne chance.

To your health. A votre santé.

I am lost. Je me suis perdu(e).

Please help me. Aidez-moi, s'il vous plaît.

Do you understand? Comprenez-vous?

I don't understand. Je ne comprends pas.

Speak slowly, please. Parlez lentement, s'il vous plaît.

Please repeat. Répétez, s'il vous plaît.

I don't speak French. Je ne parle pas français.

Do you speak English? Parlez-vous anglais?

Does anyone here speak English? Y a-t-il quelqu'un qui parle anglais?

How do you say ... in French? Comment dit-on ... en français?

What do you call this? Comment appelle-ton ceci?

What is you name? Comment vous appelez-vous?

My name is ... Je m'appelle ...

I am an American. Je suis américain.

May I introduce ... Permettez-moi de vous présenter ...

How is the weather? Quel temps fait-il?

What time is it? Quelle heure est-il?

What is it? Qu'est-ce que c'est?

I would like ... Je voudrais ...

Please give me ... S'il vous plaît, donnez-moi ...

Please bring me ... S'il vous plaît, apportez-moi ...

How much does this cost? Combien est ceci?

It is too expensive. C'est trop cher.

May I see something cheaper? Pourrais-je voir quelque chose à meilleur marché?

May I see some thing better? Pourrais-je voir quelque chose de meilleur?

It is not exactly what I want. Ce n'est pais exactement ce que je cherche.

I want to buy ... Je voudrais acheter ...

Do you accept traveler's checks? Acceptez-vous les chèques de voyage?

I want to eat. Je voudrais manger.

Can you recommend a restaurant? Pouvez-vous recommander un restraurant?

I am hungry. J'ai faim.

I am thirsty. J'ai soif.

May I see the menu? Pourrais-je voir le menu?

Check, please. L'addition, s'il vous plaît.

Is service included in the bill? Le service est-il compris?

Where can I get a taxi? Où pourrais-je trouver un taxi?

What is the fare to ... Quel est le tarif jusqu'à ...?

Please take me to this address. Veuillez me conduire à cette adresse.

I have a reservation. J'ai une réservation.

Where is the nearest drugstore? Où est la pharmacie la plus proche?

Is there a hotel here? Y a-t-il un hôtel ici?

Where is ...? Où est ...?

Where is the men's (women's) room? Où est la toilette pour messieurs (dames)?

What is the way to ...? Quelle est la route de ...?

Take me to ... Conduisez-moi à ...

I need ... J'ai besoin de ...

I am ill. Je suis malade.

Please call a doctor. Appelez un docteur, s'il vous plaît.

Please call the police. Appelez la police, s'il vous plaît.

I want to send a telegram. Je voudrais envoyer un télégramme.

Where can I change money? Où puis-je changer de l'argent?

Where is the nearest bank? Où est la banque la plus proche?

Will you accept checks? Acceptez-vous des chèques?

Is there any mail for me? Y a-t-il du courrier pour moi?

Where can I mail this letter? Où est-ce que je peux mettre cette lettre à la poste?

What is the postage? Quel est l'affranchissement?

Please help me with my baggage S'il vous plaît, adiez-moi avec mes bagages.

Right away. Tout de suite.

Help! Au secours!

Who is it? Qui est-ce que c'est?

Come in. Entrez.

Stop. Arrêtez.

Hurry. Dépêchez-vous.

Go on. Continuez.

Right. A droite.

Left. A gauche.

Straight ahead. Tout droit.

Hello! (on telephone) Allô!

As soon as possible. Aussitôt que possible.

Pardon me. Pardon or Pardonnez-moi or Je m'excuse.

Look out! Attention! or Faites attention!

Just a minute! Un instant!

Days of the Week

Sunday	dimanche
Monday	lundi
Tuesday	mardi
Wednesday	mercredi
Thursday	jeudi
Friday	vendredi
Saturday	samedi

Months

January	janvier
February	février
March	mars
April	avril
May	mai
June	juin
July	juillet
August	août
September	septembre
October	octobre
November	novembre
December	décembre